CASES AND MATERIALS

CONSTITUTIONAL LAW

TWELFTH EDITION

by

WILLIAM COHEN
C. Wendell and Edith M. Carlsmith
Professor Emeritus, Stanford Law School

JONATHAN D. VARAT
Professor of Law
University of California, Los Angeles

VIKRAM AMAR
Professor of Law
University of California, Hastings College of the Law

FOUNDATION PRESS
NEW YORK, NEW YORK
2005

THOMSON

WEST

© 1959, 1963, 1968, 1973, 1977, 1981, 1985, 1989, 1993, 1997, 2001 FOUNDATION PRESS
© 2005 By FOUNDATION PRESS
   395 Hudson Street
   New York, NY 10014
   Phone Toll Free 1–877–888–1330
   Fax (212) 367–6799
   fdpress.com
Printed in the United States of America

ISBN 1–58778–881–0

 TEXT IS PRINTED ON 10% POST CONSUMER RECYCLED PAPER

For Nancy, Barbara, Becky, and Margaret
WC

For Barbara, Adam, Diana, and Jennifer
JDV

For Dipanwita, who helps me more than she knows
VA

*

PREFACE

There has been both remarkable stability as well as notable change since the last edition of this casebook was published. As for stability, the membership of the Supreme Court remains precisely as it was four years ago. The Justices who sit on the high Court have been together since 1994, making this the longest-serving nine-person Court in the nation's history, and the second longest-serving Court overall, behind only the seven Justices who sat on the Marshall Court from 1811–1823.

Like the composition of the Court, the structure of the book is essentially similar to the way it was in 2001. The authors thought and talked seriously—and solicited input from many teachers who use the book—about reorganizing the chapters to place the Fourteenth Amendment materials before those dealing with federalism and federal separation of powers. But in the end, the strong if not perfectly complete consensus was that well enough should be left alone, and that most of the goals of a reorganization could be accomplished within the existing framework by including additional notes, transitional passages and internal outlining that make more overt some of the connections between the materials on federal-state relations and those focusing on the Reconstruction and individual rights, taken up later in the book.

As for change, the last four Supreme Court Terms have seen important doctrinal development in a number of areas: the Court's cases interpreting Section 5 of the Fourteenth Amendment have taken complicated and somewhat surprising turns; the First Amendment's Free Speech and Establishment Clauses continue to generate a large number of complex and vexing questions the Court feels obliged to address; and the so-called "War on Terror" in the wake of the attacks of September 11, 2001 has given rise to important disputes that made their way to the high Court for the first time this past year. Incorporation of new principal cases in these three indispensable areas accounts almost entirely for the increase in overall pages in this new edition. There are also significant new cases included in this edition dealing with Takings and Substantive Due Process.

In keeping with past practice, we used the occasion of a new edition to look for places where the presentation of older cases could be tightened and refined and sometimes summarized to better serve students and teachers. Users might want to pay particular attention in Chapter 10 to the insertion of a long explanatory note on the background of affirmative action that leads up to the most recent principal affirmative action rulings culminating in the *Grutter v. Bollinger* case, which in this edition has replaced *Regents of the Univ. of Calif. v. Bakke*. The note materials on desegregation remedies in that same chapter have been reorganized and reduced in a way that we hope is clearer and more effective. Chapter 6—dealing largely with Dormant Commerce Clause doctrine—also makes more extensive use of explanatory notes and summaries to reduce the number of pages taken to introduce cases that many might deem to be of secondary importance but still worthy of examination. And the passage of four years also has allowed us to reflect a bit more on the 1998 impeachment of President William Clinton and the still controversial 2000 *Bush v. Gore* decision; the constitutional significance and potential doctrinal implications of these episodes are noted at relevant points in this edition much more so than in 2001.

Finally, a new co-editor has been added. He shares the basic vision of the book, which we have described in the past as using as much as possible "the raw materials—cases, constitutional provisions, statutes [and historical documents]—allowing teachers maximum freedom to pursue their own teaching strategies and requiring students to create their own generalizations from the materials." This basic approach is not, of course, incompatible with our citation to relevant and current legal scholarship, our posing of basic questions throughout the book, and our explicit identification of linkages between different sets of materials. But it remains our abiding hope that our selection, organization and editing of the cases and materials that we provide will "maximize the ability of users to structure their own courses in their own ways."[1]

Consistent with our past practice, we have included in this publication cases decided by the Supreme Court during the October 2003 Term; a 2005 softbound supplement will cover cases that are handed down between now and this coming fall.

Notes on style: As we have done in earlier editions, we have indicated our restatement of the facts in principal cases by placing square brackets around our factual descriptions; we have omitted footnotes of the Court without specifically indicating that fact; footnotes that we have kept retain their original numbering; footnotes that we have added to cases are indicated by letters.

WILLIAM COHEN

JONATHAN D. VARAT

VIKRAM D. AMAR

Stanford, California
Los Angeles, California
San Francisco, California
January 2005

---

[1] Because we view the selection, sequencing and editing of cases and other source documents as a primary service we provide in the book, we have in some instances included cases and historical materials that pre-date 2001 even though they were absent from the Eleventh and prior editions, and in other places we have restored portions of opinions and other materials that we now conclude had perhaps been edited too severely in earlier editions.

SUMMARY OF CONTENTS

PART IV.   CONSTITUTIONAL PROTECTION OF EXPRESSION AND CONSCIENCE

TABLE OF CONTENTS

**PART II. Allocation of Governmental Powers: The Nation
and the States; The President, The Congress, and The Courts**

PART IV. Constitutional Protection of Expression and Conscience

CHAPTER 13. Governmental Control of the Content of Expression 1250

CHAPTER 15. Protection of Penumbral First Amendment Rights --- 1566

TABLE OF CASES

Principal cases are in bold type. Non-principal cases are in roman type. References are to Pages.

CONSTITUTIONAL LAW

*

PART I

THE CONSTITUTION AND THE COURTS: THE JUDICIAL FUNCTION IN CONSTITUTIONAL CASES

CHAPTER 1

THE CONSTITUTION

SECTION 1. THE CONSTITUTION OF THE UNITED STATES OF AMERICA

We the People of the United States, in Order to form a more perfect Union, establish Justice, insure domestic Tranquility, provide for the common defence, promote the general Welfare, and secure the Blessings of Liberty to ourselves and our Posterity, do ordain and establish this Constitution for the United States of America.

ARTICLE I

Section 1. All legislative Powers herein granted shall be vested in a Congress of the United States, which shall consist of a Senate and House of Representatives.

Section 2. [1] The House of Representatives shall be composed of Members chosen every second Year by the People of the several States, and the Electors in each State shall have the Qualifications requisite for Electors of the most numerous Branch of the State Legislature.

[2] No Person shall be a Representative who shall not have attained to the Age of twenty five Years, and been seven Years a Citizen of the United States, and who shall not, when elected, be an Inhabitant of that State in which he shall be chosen.

[3] Representatives and direct Taxes shall be apportioned among the several States which may be included within this Union, according to their respective Numbers, which shall be determined by adding to the whole Number of free Persons, including those bound to Service for a Term of Years, and excluding Indians not taxed, three fifths of all other Persons. The actual Enumeration shall be made within three Years after the first Meeting of the Congress of the United States, and within every subsequent Term of ten Years, in such Manner as they shall by Law direct. The Number of Representatives shall not exceed one for every thirty Thousand, but each State shall have at Least one Representative; and until such enumeration shall be made, the State of New Hampshire shall be entitled to chuse three, Massachusetts eight, Rhode Island and Providence Plantations one, Connecticut five, New York six, New Jersey four, Pennsylvania eight, Delaware one, Maryland six, Virginia ten, North Carolina five, South Carolina five, and Georgia three.

[4] When vacancies happen in the Representation from any State, the Executive Authority thereof shall issue Writs of Election to fill such Vacancies.

[5] The House of Representatives shall chuse their Speaker and other Officers; and shall have the sole Power of Impeachment.

Section 3. [1] The Senate of the United States shall be composed of two Senators from each State, chosen by the Legislature thereof, for six Years; and each Senator shall have one Vote.

[2]   Immediately after they shall be assembled in Consequence of the first Election, they shall be divided as equally as may be into three Classes. The Seats of the Senators of the first Class shall be vacated at the Expiration of the Second Year, of the second Class at the Expiration of the fourth Year, and of the third Class at the Expiration of the sixth Year, so that one third may be chosen every second Year; and if Vacancies happen by Resignation, or otherwise, during the Recess of the Legislature of any State, the Executive thereof may make temporary Appointments until the next Meeting of the Legislature, which shall then fill such Vacancies.

[3]   No Person shall be a Senator who shall not have attained to the Age of thirty Years, and been nine Years a Citizen of the United States, and who shall not, when elected, be an Inhabitant of that State for which he shall be chosen.

[4]   The Vice President of the United States shall be President of the Senate, but shall have no Vote, unless they be equally divided.

[5]   The Senate shall chuse their other Officers, and also a President pro tempore, in the Absence of the Vice President, or when he shall exercise the Office of President of the United States.

[6]   The Senate shall have the sole Power to try all Impeachments. When sitting for that Purpose, they shall be on Oath or Affirmation. When the President of the United States is tried, the Chief Justice shall preside: And no Person shall be convicted without the Concurrence of two thirds of the Members present.

[7]   Judgment in Cases of Impeachment shall not extend further than to removal from Office, and disqualification to hold and enjoy any Office of honor, Trust, or Profit under the United States: but the Party convicted shall nevertheless be liable and subject to Indictment, Trial, Judgment, and Punishment, according to Law.

Section 4.   [1] The Times, Places and Manner of holding Elections for Senators and Representatives, shall be prescribed in each State by the Legislature thereof; but the Congress may at any time by Law make or alter such Regulations, except as to the Places of chusing Senators.

[2]   The Congress shall assemble at least once in every Year, and such Meeting shall be on the first Monday in December, unless they shall by Law appoint a different Day.

Section 5.   [1] Each House shall be the Judge of the Elections, Returns, and Qualifications of its own Members, and a Majority of each shall constitute a Quorum to do Business; but a smaller Number may adjourn from day to day, and may be authorized to compel the Attendance of absent Members, in such Manner, and under such Penalties as each House may provide.

[2]   Each House may determine the Rules of its Proceedings, punish its Members for disorderly Behavior, and, with the Concurrence of two thirds, expel a Member.

[3]   Each House shall keep a Journal of its Proceedings, and from time to time publish the same, excepting such Parts as may in their Judgment require Secrecy; and the Yeas and Nays of the Members of either House on any question shall, at the Desire of one fifth of those Present, be entered on the Journal.

[4]   Neither House, during the Session of Congress, shall, without the Consent of the other, adjourn for more than three days, nor to any other Place than that in which the two Houses shall be sitting.

Section 6. [1] The Senators and Representatives shall receive a Compensation for their Services, to be ascertained by Law, and paid out of the Treasury of the United States. They shall in all Cases, except Treason, Felony and Breach of the Peace, be privileged from Arrest during their Attendance at the Session of their respective Houses, and in going to and returning from the same; and for any Speech or Debate in either House, they shall not be questioned in any other Place.

[2] No Senator or Representative shall, during the Time for which he was elected, be appointed to any civil Office under the Authority of the United States, which shall have been created, or the Emoluments whereof shall have been increased during such time; and no Person holding any Office under the United States, shall be a Member of either House during his Continuance in Office.

Section 7. [1] All Bills for raising Revenue shall originate in the House of Representatives; but the Senate may propose or concur with Amendments as on other Bills.

[2] Every Bill which shall have passed the House of Representatives and the Senate, shall, before it become a Law, be presented to the President of the United States; If he approve he shall sign it, but if not he shall return it, with his Objections to the House in which it shall have originated, who shall enter the Objections at large on their Journal, and proceed to reconsider it. If after such Reconsideration two thirds of that House shall agree to pass the Bill, it shall be sent together with the Objections, to the other House, by which it shall likewise be reconsidered, and if approved by two thirds of that House, it shall become a Law. But in all such Cases the Votes of both Houses shall be determined by yeas and Nays, and the Names of the Persons voting for and against the Bill shall be entered on the Journal of each House respectively. If any Bill shall not be returned by the President within ten Days (Sundays excepted) after it shall have been presented to him, the Same shall be a Law, in like Manner as if he had signed it, unless the Congress by their Adjournment prevent its Return in which Case it shall not be a Law.

[3] Every Order, Resolution, or Vote, to Which the Concurrence of the Senate and House of Representatives may be necessary (except on a question of Adjournment) shall be presented to the President of the United States; and before the Same shall take Effect, shall be approved by him, or being disapproved by him, shall be repassed by two thirds of the Senate and House of Representatives, according to the Rules and Limitations prescribed in the Case of a Bill.

Section 8. [1] The Congress shall have Power To lay and collect Taxes, Duties, Imposts and Excises, to pay the Debts and provide for the common Defence and general Welfare of the United States; but all Duties, Imposts and Excises shall be uniform throughout the United States;

[2] To borrow money on the credit of the United States;

[3] To regulate Commerce with foreign Nations, and among the several States, and with the Indian Tribes;

[4] To establish an uniform Rule of Naturalization, and uniform Laws on the subject of Bankruptcies throughout the United States;

[5] To coin Money, regulate the Value thereof, and of foreign Coin, and fix the Standard of Weights and Measures;

[6] To provide for the Punishment of counterfeiting the Securities and current Coin of the United States;

[7]   To Establish Post Offices and Post Roads;

[8]   To promote the Progress of Science and useful Arts, by securing for limited Times to Authors and Inventors the exclusive Right to their respective Writings and Discoveries;

[9]   To constitute Tribunals inferior to the supreme Court;

what congress has the power to do.

[10]   To define and punish Piracies and Felonies committed on the high Seas, and Offenses against the Law of Nations;

[11]   To declare War, grant Letters of Marque and Reprisal, and make Rules concerning Captures on Land and Water;

[12]   To raise and support Armies, but no Appropriation of Money to that Use shall be for a longer Term than two Years;

[13]   To provide and maintain a Navy;

[14]   To make Rules for the Government and Regulation of the land and naval Forces;

[15]   To provide for calling forth the Militia to execute the Laws of the Union, suppress Insurrections and repel Invasions;

[16]   To provide for organizing, arming, and disciplining, the Militia, and for governing such Part of them as may be employed in the Service of the United States, reserving to the States respectively, the Appointment of the Officers, and the Authority of training the Militia according to the discipline prescribed by Congress;

[17]   To exercise exclusive Legislation in all Cases whatsoever, over such District (not exceeding ten Miles square) as may, by Cession of particular States, and the Acceptance of Congress, become the Seat of the Government of the United States, and to exercise like Authority over all Places purchased by the Consent of the Legislature of the State in which the Same shall be, for the Erection of Forts, Magazines, Arsenals, dock-Yards, and other needful Buildings;—And

[18]   To make all Laws which shall be necessary and proper for carrying into Execution the foregoing Powers, and all other Powers vested by this Constitution in the Government of the United States, or in any Department or Officer thereof.

Section 9.   [1] The Migration or Importation of Such Persons as any of the States now existing shall think proper to admit, shall not be prohibited by the Congress prior to the Year one thousand eight hundred and eight, but a Tax or duty may be imposed on such Importation, not exceeding ten dollars for each Person.

Limitations on the powers given above.

[2]   The privilege of the Writ of Habeas Corpus shall not be suspended, unless when in Cases of Rebellion or Invasion the public Safety may require it.

[3]   No Bill of Attainder or ex post facto Law shall be passed.

[4]   No Capitation, or other direct, Tax shall be laid, unless in Proportion to the Census or Enumeration herein before directed to be taken.

[5]   No Tax or Duty shall be laid on Articles exported from any State.

[6]   No Preference shall be given by any Regulation of Commerce or Revenue to the Ports of one State over those of another: nor shall Vessels bound to, or from, one State be obliged to enter, clear, or pay Duties in another.

[7]   No money shall be drawn from the Treasury, but in Consequence of Appropriations made by Law; and a regular Statement and Account of the

Receipts and Expenditures of all public Money shall be published from time to time.

[8]   No Title of Nobility shall be granted by the United States: And no Person holding any Office of Profit or Trust under them, shall, without the Consent of the Congress, accept of any present, Emolument, Office or Title, of any kind whatever, from any King, Prince, or foreign State.

Section 10.   [1] No State shall enter into any Treaty, Alliance, or Confederation; grant Letters of Marque and Reprisal; coin Money; emit Bills of Credit; make any Thing but gold and silver Coin a Tender in Payment of Debts; pass any Bill of Attainder, ex post facto Law, or Law impairing the Obligation of Contracts, or grant any Title of Nobility.

[2]   No State shall, without the Consent of the Congress, lay any Imposts or Duties on Imports or Exports, except what may be absolutely necessary for executing its inspection Laws: and the net Produce of all Duties and Imposts, laid by any State on Imports or Exports, shall be for the Use of the Treasury of the United States; and all such Laws shall be subject to the Revision and Controul of the Congress.

[3]   No State shall, without the Consent of Congress, lay any Duty of Tonnage, keep Troops, or Ships of War in time of Peace, enter into any Agreement or Compact with another State, or with a foreign Power, or engage in War, unless actually invaded, or in such imminent Danger as will not admit of delay.

ARTICLE II

Section 1.   [1] The executive Power shall be vested in a President of the United States of America. He shall hold his Office during the Term of four Years, and, together with the Vice President, chosen for the same Term, be elected, as follows:

[2]   Each State shall appoint, in such Manner as the Legislature thereof may direct, a Number of Electors, equal to the whole Number of Senators and Representatives to which the State may be entitled in the Congress; but no Senator or Representative, or Person holding an Office of Trust or Profit under the United States, shall be appointed an Elector.

[3]   The Electors shall meet in their respective States, and vote by Ballot for two Persons, of whom one at least shall not be an Inhabitant of the same State with themselves. And they shall make a List of all the Persons voted for, and of the Number of Votes for each; which List they shall sign and certify, and transmit sealed to the Seat of the Government of the United States, directed to the President of the Senate. The President of the Senate shall, in the Presence of the Senate and House of Representatives, open all the Certificates, and the Votes shall then be counted. The Person having the greatest Number of Votes shall be the President, if such Number be a Majority of the whole Number of Electors appointed; and if there be more than one who have such Majority, and have an equal Number of Votes, then the House of Representatives shall immediately chuse by Ballot one of them for President; and if no Person have a Majority, then from the five highest on the List the said House shall in like Manner chuse the President. But in chusing the President, the Votes shall be taken by States, the Representation from each State having one Vote; A quorum for this Purpose shall consist of a Member or Members from two thirds of the States, and a Majority of all the States shall be necessary to a Choice. In every Case, after the Choice of the President, the Person having the greater Number of Votes of the Electors shall be the Vice President. But if there should

remain two or more who have equal Votes, the Senate shall chuse from them by Ballot the Vice President.

[4]   The Congress may determine the Time of chusing the Electors, and the Day on which they shall give their Votes; which Day shall be the same throughout the United States.

[5]   No person except a natural born Citizen, or a Citizen of the United States, at the time of the Adoption of this Constitution, shall be eligible to the Office of President; neither shall any Person be eligible to that Office who shall not have attained to the Age of thirty five Years, and been fourteen Years a Resident within the United States.

[6]   In case of the removal of the President from Office, or of his Death, Resignation or Inability to discharge the Powers and Duties of the said Office, the Same shall devolve on the Vice President, and the Congress may by Law provide for the Case of Removal, Death, Resignation or Inability, both of the President and Vice President, declaring what Officer shall then act as President, and such Officer shall act accordingly, until the Disability be removed, or a President shall be elected.

[7]   The President shall, at stated Times, receive for his Services, a Compensation, which shall neither be increased nor diminished during the Period for which he shall have been elected, and he shall not receive within that Period any other Emolument from the United States, or any of them.

[8]   Before he enter on the Execution of his Office, he shall take the following Oath or Affirmation: "I do solemnly swear (or affirm) that I will faithfully execute the Office of President of the United States, and will to the best of my Ability, preserve, protect and defend the Constitution of the United States."

Section 2.   [1] The President shall be Commander in Chief of the Army and Navy of the United States, and of the militia of the several States, when called into the actual Service of the United States; he may require the Opinion, in writing, of the principal Officer in each of the executive Departments, upon any Subject relating to the Duties of their respective Offices, and he shall have Power to grant Reprieves and Pardons for Offenses against the United States, except in Cases of Impeachment.

[2]   He shall have Power, by and with the Advice and Consent of the Senate, to make Treaties, provided two thirds of the Senators present concur; and he shall nominate, and by and with the Advice and Consent of the Senate, shall appoint Ambassadors, other public Ministers and Consuls, Judges of the supreme Court, and all other Officers of the United States, whose Appointments are not herein otherwise provided for, and which shall be established by Law; but the Congress may by Law vest the Appointment of such inferior Officers, as they think proper, in the President alone, in the Courts of Law, or in the Heads of Departments.

[3]   The President shall have Power to fill up all Vacancies that may happen during the Recess of the Senate, by granting Commissions which shall expire at the End of their next Session.

Section 3.   He shall from time to time give to the Congress Information of the State of the Union, and recommend to their Consideration such Measures as he shall judge necessary and expedient; he may, on extraordinary Occasions, convene both Houses, or either of them, and in Case of Disagreement between them, with Respect to the Time of Adjournment, he may adjourn them to such Time as he shall think proper; he shall receive Ambassadors and other public

Ministers; he shall take Care that the Laws be faithfully executed, and shall Commission all the Officers of the United States.

Section 4.   The President, Vice President and all civil Officers of the United States, shall be removed from Office on Impeachment for, and Conviction of, Treason, Bribery, or other high Crimes and Misdemeanors.

ARTICLE III

Section 1.   The judicial Power of the United States, shall be vested in one supreme Court, and in such inferior Courts as the Congress may from time to time ordain and establish. The Judges, both of the supreme and inferior Courts, shall hold their Offices during good Behaviour, and shall, at stated Times, receive for their Services a Compensation, which shall not be diminished during their Continuance in Office.

Section 2.   [1] The judicial Power shall extend to all Cases, in Law and Equity, arising under this Constitution, the Laws of the United States, and Treaties made, or which shall be made, under their Authority;—to all Cases affecting Ambassadors, other public Ministers and Consuls;—to all Cases of admiralty and maritime Jurisdiction,—to Controversies to which the United States shall be a Party;—to Controversies between two or more States;—between a State and Citizens of another State;—between Citizens of different States;—between Citizens of the same State claiming Lands under the Grants of different States, and between a State, or the Citizens thereof, and foreign States, Citizens or Subjects.

[2]   In all Cases affecting Ambassadors, other public Ministers and Consuls, and those in which a State shall be a Party, the supreme Court shall have original Jurisdiction. In all the other Cases before mentioned, the supreme Court shall have appellate Jurisdiction, both as to Law and Fact, with such Exceptions, and under such Regulations as the Congress shall make.

[3]   The trial of all Crimes, except in Cases of Impeachment, shall be by Jury; and such Trial shall be held in the State where the said Crimes shall have been committed; but when not committed within any State, the Trial shall be at such Place or Places as the Congress may by Law have directed.

Section 3.   [1] Treason against the United States, shall consist only in levying War against them, or, in adhering to their Enemies, giving them Aid and Comfort. No Person shall be convicted of Treason unless on the Testimony of two Witnesses to the same overt Act, or on Confession in open Court.

[2]   The Congress shall have Power to declare the Punishment of Treason, but no Attainder of Treason shall work Corruption of Blood, or Forfeiture except during the Life of the Person attainted.

ARTICLE IV

Section 1.   Full Faith and Credit shall be given in each State to the public Acts, Records, and judicial Proceedings of every other State. And the Congress may by general Laws prescribe the Manner in which such Acts, Records and Proceedings shall be proved, and the Effect thereof.

Section 2.   [1] The Citizens of each State shall be entitled to all Privileges and Immunities of Citizens in the several States.

[2]   A Person charged in any State with Treason, Felony, or other Crime, who shall flee from Justice, and be found in another State, shall on demand of the executive Authority of the State from which he fled, be delivered up, to be removed to the State having Jurisdiction of the Crime.

[3]   No Person held to Service or Labour in one State, under the Laws thereof, escaping into another, shall, in Consequence of any Law or Regulation therein, be discharged from such Service or Labour, but shall be delivered up on Claim of the Party to whom such Service or Labour may be due.

Section 3.   [1] New States may be admitted by the Congress into this Union; but no new State shall be formed or erected within the Jurisdiction of any other State; nor any State be formed by the Junction of two or more States, or Parts of States, without the Consent of the Legislatures of the States concerned as well as of the Congress.

[2]   The Congress shall have Power to dispose of and make all needful Rules and Regulations respecting the Territory or other Property belonging to the United States; and nothing in this Constitution shall be so construed as to Prejudice any Claims of the United States, or of any particular State.

Section 4.   The United States shall guarantee to every State in this Union a Republican Form of Government, and shall protect each of them against Invasion; and on Application of the Legislature, or of the Executive (when the Legislature cannot be convened) against domestic Violence.

ARTICLE V

The Congress, whenever two thirds of both Houses shall deem it necessary, shall propose Amendments to this Constitution, or, on the Application of the Legislatures of two thirds of the several States, shall call a Convention for proposing Amendments, which, in either Case, shall be valid to all Intents and Purposes, as part of this Constitution, when ratified by the Legislatures of three fourths of the several States, or by Conventions in three fourths thereof, as the one or the other Mode of Ratification may be proposed by the Congress; Provided that no Amendment which may be made prior to the Year One thousand eight hundred and eight shall in any Manner affect the first and fourth Clauses in the Ninth Section of the first Article; and that no State, without its Consent, shall be deprived of its equal Suffrage in the Senate.

ARTICLE VI

[1]   All Debts contracted and Engagements entered into, before the Adoption of this Constitution shall be as valid against the United States under this Constitution, as under the Confederation.

[2]   This Constitution, and the Laws of the United States which shall be made in Pursuance thereof; and all Treaties made, or which shall be made, under the Authority of the United States, shall be the supreme Law of the Land; and the Judges in every State shall be bound thereby, any Thing in the Constitution or Laws of any State to the Contrary notwithstanding.

[3]   The Senators and Representatives before mentioned, and the Members of the several State Legislatures, and all executive and judicial Officers, both of the United States and of the several States, shall be bound by Oath or Affirmation, to support this Constitution; but no religious Test shall ever be required as a Qualification to any Office or public Trust under the United States.

ARTICLE VII

The Ratification of the Conventions of nine States shall be sufficient for the Establishment of this Constitution between the States so ratifying the Same.

Done in Convention by the Unanimous Consent of the States present the Seventeenth Day of September in the Year of our Lord one thousand seven hundred and Eighty seven and of the Independence of the United States of America the Twelfth.

ARTICLES IN ADDITION TO, AND AMENDMENT OF, THE CONSTITUTION OF THE UNITED STATES OF AMERICA, PROPOSED BY CONGRESS, AND RATIFIED BY THE LEGISLATURES OF THE SEVERAL STATES PURSUANT TO THE FIFTH ARTICLE OF THE ORIGINAL CONSTITUTION.

AMENDMENT I [1791]

Congress shall make no law respecting an establishment of religion, or prohibiting the free exercise thereof; or abridging the freedom of speech, or of the press; or the right of the people peaceably to assemble, and to petition the Government for a redress of grievances.

AMENDMENT II [1791]

A well regulated Militia, being necessary to the security of a free State, the right of the people to keep and bear Arms, shall not be infringed.

AMENDMENT III [1791]

No Soldier shall, in time of peace be quartered in any house, without the consent of the Owner, nor in time of war, but in a manner to be prescribed by law.

AMENDMENT IV [1791]

The right of the people to be secure in their persons, houses, papers, and effects, against unreasonable searches and seizures, shall not be violated, and no Warrants shall issue, but upon probable cause, supported by Oath or affirmation, and particularly describing the place to be searched, and the persons or things to be seized.

AMENDMENT V [1791]

No person shall be held to answer for a capital, or otherwise infamous crime, unless on a presentment or indictment of a Grand Jury, except in cases arising in the land or naval forces, or in the Militia, when in actual service in time of War or public danger; nor shall any person be subject for the same offense to be twice put in jeopardy of life or limb; nor shall be compelled in any criminal case to be a witness against himself, nor be deprived of life, liberty, or property, without due process of law; nor shall private property be taken for public use, without just compensation.

AMENDMENT VI [1791]

In all criminal prosecutions, the accused shall enjoy the right to a speedy and public trial, by an impartial jury of the State and district wherein the crime shall have been committed, which district shall have been previously ascertained by law, and to be informed of the nature and cause of the accusation; to be confronted with the witnesses against him; to have compulsory process for obtaining witnesses in his favor, and to have the Assistance of Counsel for his defence.

AMENDMENT VII [1791]

In Suits at common law, where the value in controversy shall exceed twenty dollars, the right of trial by jury shall be preserved, and no fact tried by jury, shall be otherwise re-examined in any Court of the United States, than according to the rules of the common law.

AMENDMENT VIII [1791]

Excessive bail shall not be required, nor excessive fines imposed, nor cruel and unusual punishments inflicted.

AMENDMENT IX [1791]

The enumeration in the Constitution, of certain rights, shall not be construed to deny or disparage others retained by the people.

AMENDMENT X [1791]

The powers not delegated to the United States by the Constitution, nor prohibited by it to the States, are reserved to the States respectively, or to the people.

States power

AMENDMENT XI [1798]

The Judicial power of the United States shall not be construed to extend to any suit in law or equity, commenced or prosecuted against one of the United States by Citizens of another State, or by Citizens or Subjects of any Foreign State.

sovereign Immunity

AMENDMENT XII [1804]

The Electors shall meet in their respective states and vote by ballot for President and Vice–President, one of whom, at least, shall not be an inhabitant of the same state with themselves; they shall name in their ballots the person voted for as President, and in distinct ballots the person voted for as Vice–President, and they shall make distinct lists of all persons voted for as President, and of all persons voted for as Vice–President, and of the number of votes for each, which lists they shall sign and certify, and transmit sealed to the seat of the government of the United States, directed to the President of the Senate;—The President of the Senate shall, in the presence of the Senate and House of Representatives, open all the certificates and the votes shall then be counted;—The person having the greatest number of votes for President, shall be the President, if such number be a majority of the whole number of Electors appointed; and if no person have such majority, then from the persons having the highest numbers not exceeding three on the list of those voted for as President, the House of Representatives shall choose immediately, by ballot, the President. But in choosing the President, the votes shall be taken by states, the representation from each state having one vote; a quorum for this purpose shall consist of a member or members from two-thirds of the states, and a majority of all the states shall be necessary to a choice. And if the House of Representatives shall not choose a President whenever the right of choice shall devolve upon them before the fourth day of March next following, then the Vice–President shall act as President, as in the case of the death or other constitutional disability of the President.—The person having the greatest number of votes as Vice–President, shall be the Vice–President, if such number be a majority of the whole number of Electors appointed, and if no person have a majority, then from the two highest numbers on the list, the Senate shall choose the Vice–President; a quorum for the purpose shall consist of two-thirds of the whole number of Senators, and a majority of the whole number shall be necessary to a choice. But no person constitutionally ineligible to the office of President shall be eligible to that of Vice–President of the United States.

AMENDMENT XIII [1865]

Section 1.   Neither slavery nor involuntary servitude, except as a punishment for crime whereof the party shall have been duly convicted, shall exist within the United States, or any place subject to their jurisdiction.

Section 2.   Congress shall have power to enforce this article by appropriate legislation.

AMENDMENT XIV [1868]

Section 1.   All persons born or naturalized in the United States, and subject to the jurisdiction thereof, are citizens of the United States and of the State wherein they reside. No State shall make or enforce any law which shall abridge the privileges or immunities of citizens of the United States; nor shall any State deprive any person of life, liberty, or property, without due process of law; nor deny to any person within its jurisdiction the equal protection of the laws.

Section 2.   Representatives shall be apportioned among the several States according to their respective numbers, counting the whole number of persons in each State, excluding Indians not taxed. But when the right to vote at any election for the choice of electors for President and Vice President of the United States, Representatives in Congress, the Executive and Judicial officers of a State, or the members of the Legislature thereof, is denied to any of the male inhabitants of such State, being twenty-one years of age, and citizens of the United States, or in any way abridged, except for participation in rebellion, or other crime, the basis of representation therein shall be reduced in the proportion which the number of such male citizens shall bear to the whole number of male citizens twenty-one years of age in such State.

Section 3.   No person shall be a Senator or Representative in Congress, or elector of President and Vice President, or hold any office, civil or military, under the United States, or under any State, who having previously taken an oath, as a member of Congress, or as an officer of the United States, or as a member of any State legislature, or as an executive or judicial officer of any State, to support the Constitution of the United States, shall have engaged in insurrection or rebellion against the same, or given aid or comfort to the enemies thereof. But Congress may by a vote of two-thirds of each House, remove such disability.

Section 4.   The validity of the public debt of the United States, authorized by law, including debts incurred for payment of pensions and bounties for services in suppressing insurrection or rebellion, shall not be questioned. But neither the United States nor any State shall assume or pay any debt or obligation incurred in aid of insurrection or rebellion against the United States, or any claim for the loss or emancipation of any slave; but all such debts, obligations and claims shall be held illegal and void.

Section 5.   The Congress shall have power to enforce, by appropriate legislation, the provisions of this article.

AMENDMENT XV [1870]

Section 1.   The right of citizens of the United States to vote shall not be denied or abridged by the United States or by any State on account of race, color, or previous condition of servitude.

Section 2.   The Congress shall have power to enforce this article by appropriate legislation.

AMENDMENT XVI [1913]

The Congress shall have power to lay and collect taxes on incomes, from whatever source derived, without apportionment among the several States, and without regard to any census or enumeration.

AMENDMENT XVII [1913]

[1]   The Senate of the United States shall be composed of two Senators from each State, elected by the people thereof, for six years; and each Senator shall have one vote. The electors in each State shall have the qualifications requisite for electors of the most numerous branch of the State legislatures.

[2]   When vacancies happen in the representation of any State in the Senate, the executive authority of such State shall issue writs of election to fill such vacancies: *Provided,* That the legislature of any State may empower the executive thereof to make temporary appointments until the people fill the vacancies by election as the legislature may direct.

[3]   This amendment shall not be so construed as to affect the election or term of any Senator chosen before it becomes valid as part of the Constitution.

AMENDMENT XVIII [1919]

Section 1.   After one year from the ratification of this article the manufacture, sale, or transportation of intoxicating liquors within, the importation thereof into, or the exportation thereof from the United States and all territory subject to the jurisdiction thereof for beverage purposes is hereby prohibited.

Section 2.   The Congress and the several States shall have concurrent power to enforce this article by appropriate legislation.

Section 3.   This article shall be inoperative unless it shall have been ratified as an amendment to the Constitution by the legislatures of the several States, as provided in the Constitution, within seven years from the date of the submission hereof to the States by the Congress.

AMENDMENT XIX [1920]

[1]   The right of citizens of the United States to vote shall not be denied or abridged by the United States or by any State on account of sex.

[2]   Congress shall have power to enforce this article by appropriate legislation.

AMENDMENT XX [1933]

Section 1.   The terms of the President and Vice President shall end at noon on the 20th day of January, and the terms of Senators and Representatives at noon on the 3d day of January, of the years in which such terms would have ended if this article had not been ratified; and the terms of their successors shall then begin.

Section 2.   The Congress shall assemble at least once in every year, and such meeting shall begin at noon on the 3d day of January, unless they shall by law appoint a different day.

Section 3.   If, at the time fixed for the beginning of the term of the President, the President elect shall have died, the Vice President elect shall become President. If the President shall not have been chosen before the time fixed for the beginning of his term, or if the President elect shall have failed to qualify, then the Vice President elect shall act as President until a President shall have qualified; and the Congress may by law provide for the case wherein neither a President elect nor a Vice President elect shall have qualified, declaring who shall then act as President, or the manner in which one who is to act shall be selected, and such person shall act accordingly until a President or Vice President shall have qualified.

Section 4. The Congress may by law provide for the case of the death of any of the persons from whom the House of Representatives may choose a President whenever the right of choice shall have devolved upon them, and for the case of the death of any of the persons from whom the Senate may choose a Vice President whenever the right of choice shall have devolved upon them.

Section 5. Sections 1 and 2 shall take effect on the 15th day of October following the ratification of this article.

Section 6. This article shall be inoperative unless it shall have been ratified as an amendment to the Constitution by the legislatures of three-fourths of the several States within seven years from the date of its submission.

AMENDMENT XXI [1933]

Section 1. The eighteenth article of amendment to the Constitution of the United States is hereby repealed.

Section 2. The transportation or importation into any State, Territory, or possession of the United States for delivery or use therein of intoxicating liquors, in violation of the laws thereof, is hereby prohibited.

Section 3. This article shall be inoperative unless it shall have been ratified as an amendment to the Constitution by conventions in the several States, as provided in the Constitution, within seven years from the date of the submission hereof to the States by the Congress.

AMENDMENT XXII [1951]

Section 1. No person shall be elected to the office of the President more than twice, and no person who has held the office of President, or acted as President, for more than two years of a term to which some other person was elected President shall be elected to the office of President more than once. But this Article shall not apply to any person holding the office of President when this Article was proposed by the Congress, and shall not prevent any person who may be holding the office of President, or acting as President, during the term within which this Article becomes operative from holding the office of President or acting as President during the remainder of such term.

Section 2. This article shall be inoperative unless it shall have been ratified as an amendment to the Constitution by the legislatures of three-fourths of the several States within seven years from the date of its submission to the States by the Congress.

AMENDMENT XXIII [1961]

Section 1. The District constituting the seat of Government of the United States shall appoint in such manner as the Congress may direct:

A number of electors of President and Vice President equal to the whole number of Senators and Representatives in Congress to which the District would be entitled if it were a State, but in no event more than the least populous state; they shall be in addition to those appointed by the states, but they shall be considered, for the purposes of the election of President and Vice President, to be electors appointed by a state; and they shall meet in the District and perform such duties as provided by the twelfth article of amendment.

Section 2.   The Congress shall have power to enforce this article by appropriate legislation.

AMENDMENT XXIV [1964]

Section 1.   The right of citizens of the United States to vote in any primary or other election for President or Vice President, for electors for President or Vice President, or for Senator or Representative in Congress, shall not be denied or abridged by the United States or any State by reason of failure to pay any poll tax or other tax.

Section 2.   The Congress shall have power to enforce this article by appropriate legislation.

AMENDMENT XXV [1967]

Section 1.   In case of the removal of the President from office or of his death or resignation, the Vice President shall become President.

Section 2.   Whenever there is a vacancy in the office of the Vice President, the President shall nominate a Vice President who shall take office upon confirmation by a majority vote of both Houses of Congress.

Section 3.   Whenever the President transmits to the President pro tempore of the Senate and the Speaker of the House of Representatives his written declaration that he is unable to discharge the powers and duties of his office, and until he transmits to them a written declaration to the contrary, such powers and duties shall be discharged by the Vice President as Acting President.

Section 4.   Whenever the Vice President and a majority of either the principal officers of the executive departments or of such other body as Congress may by law provide, transmit to the President pro tempore of the Senate and the Speaker of the House of Representatives their written declaration that the President is unable to discharge the powers and duties of his office, the Vice President shall immediately assume the powers and duties of the office as Acting President.

Thereafter, when the President transmits to the President pro tempore of the Senate and the Speaker of the House of Representatives his written declaration that no inability exists, he shall resume the powers and duties of his office unless the Vice President and a majority of either the principal officers of the executive departments or of such other body as Congress may by law provide, transmit within four days to the President pro tempore of the Senate and the Speaker of the House of Representatives their written declaration that the President is unable to discharge the powers and duties of his office. Thereupon Congress shall decide the issue, assembling within forty-eight hours for that purpose if not in session. If the Congress, within twenty-one days after receipt of the latter written declaration, or, if Congress is not in session, within twenty-one days after Congress is required to assemble, determines by two-thirds vote of both Houses that the President is unable to discharge the powers and duties of his office, the Vice President shall continue to discharge the same as Acting President; otherwise, the President shall resume the powers and duties of his office.

AMENDMENT XXVI [1971]

Section 1. The right of citizens of the United States, who are eighteen years of age or older, to vote shall not be denied or abridged by the United States or by any State on account of age.

Section 2. The Congress shall have power to enforce this article by appropriate legislation.

AMENDMENT XXVII [1992][1]

No law, varying the compensation for the services of Senators and Representatives, shall take effect, until an election for Representatives shall have intervened.

SECTION 2. HISTORY OF THE ADOPTION OF THE CONSTITUTION AND ITS MOST SIGNIFICANT AMENDMENTS

A. THE ARTICLES OF CONFEDERATION AND THE ORIGINAL CONSTITUTION

The Constitutional Convention, which met in Philadelphia in May, 1787, resulted from a growing belief that the federal government set up by the Articles of Confederation was inadequate. Under the Confederation, the United States were governed by Congress, a unicameral body in which each state had one vote. Nine votes were required for any significant action, and, more restrictively, "alteration" of the Articles required unanimity.[2] There was no national executive, and no significant federal judiciary. Congress lacked the power to tax and, since states were often delinquent in responding to Congress' requisitions, Congress was perpetually hampered by lack of funds. Congress lacked the power to regulate interstate commerce, leading to commercial wars between the states.[3]

1. The twenty seventh amendment was one of twelve amendments proposed by Congress in 1789. Ten of those twelve amendments were ratified by 1791 and became the first ten amendments to the Constitution. After more than two centuries, interest in the amendment was revived and the 38th State ratified it in 1992. In the intervening years it had never been resubmitted for ratification by Congress. For discussion of the controversy concerning whether the twenty seventh amendment is part of the Constitution, see note, infra p. 123.

2. This mandate of unanimity for alterations has led some to question the "legality" of the Constitution itself, insofar as Article VII of the Constitution states that it would take effect upon the ratification of 9–not all– the states. For opposing views on this "legality" question, see Ackerman, *The Storrs Lectures: Discovering the Constitution*, 93 Yale L.J. 1013 (1987) and Akhil Amar, *Popular Sovereignty and Constitutional Amendment*, in *Responding to Imperfection: The Theory and Practice of Constitutional Amendment* 92–95 (Levenson ed. 1995).

In addition to requiring unanimous consent for all amendments in Article XIII, the Articles of Confederation, in Article II, stated that "[e]ach state retains its sovereignty, freedom and independence, and every power, jurisdiction, and right, which is not by this Confederation expressly delegated to the United States, in Congress assembled." When you read Marbury v. Madison, 5 U.S. (1 Cranch) 137 (1803) in Chapter 2 and McCulloch v. Maryland, 17 U.S. (4 Wheat.) 316 (1819) in Chapter 4, compare Chief Justice Marshall's descriptions of the essence of the United States Constitution to the character of Articles of Confederation that emerges from the sovereignty language of Article II.

3. While a number of the features of the Constitution that emerged from the Convention can be traced to perceived inadequacies in the Articles of Confederation, other provisions reflect provisions contained in the Articles. Under the Articles, Congress controlled war, peace and foreign policy; a number of lesser powers described in Art. I, § 8,

Agreement at the Constitutional Convention that a new federal govern-ment should be established, with power to act directly on individuals and not just upon the member states, masked considerable disagreement as to the extent of the powers of that new government. It took four months of debate and compromise before the final draft of the Constitution was approved on September 17, 1787. To protect free debate, the Convention adopted a secrecy rule, and no contemporary accounts were available of the debates and decisions at the Convention. A sketchy journal was kept by William Jackson, secretary of the Convention. The journal remained in the archives of the Department of State until published in 1818 under the editorship of John Quincy Adams. More comprehensive information about the Convention's deliberations is contained in James Madison's account. Madison's notes, however, were not published until 1840, four years after his death, and more than half a century after ratification.

Ratification of the Constitution by the necessary nine states was completed in 1788. The ratification controversy was intense. The Federalist Papers, produced in the debate over ratification, are an important source of information as to contemporary views of the meaning of the Constitution. They are a series of 85 letters published in the New York papers from October, 1787 to April, 1788, under the pseudonym "Publius." The Federalist Papers were, in fact, written by Alexander Hamilton, James Madison and John Jay. One should keep in mind that the Federalist Papers, despite their high quality and the promi-nence of their authors, were intended as partisan debate on the side of ratification and not as dispassionate analysis of the meaning of the Constitu-tion. Historical treatments of the Confederation period and of the drafting and ratification of the Constitution include: G. Bancroft, *History of the Formation of the Constitution of the United States of America* (1893); J. Fiske, *The Critical Period of American History* (1888); M. Jensen, *The Articles of Confederation: An Interpretation of the Social–Constitutional History of the American Revolu-tion, 1774–1781* (1940); A. McLaughlin, *The Confederation and the Constitu-tion: 1783–1789* (1905); J. Rakove, *Original Meanings: Politics and Ideas in the Making of the Constitution* (1996); C. Rossiter, *1787: The Grand Convention* (1966); C. Van Doren, *The Great Rehearsal: The Story of the Making and Ratification of the Constitution of the United States* (1948); C. Warren, *The Making of the Constitution* (1928); B. Wright, *Consensus and Continuity, 1776–1787* (1958). The Federalist is available in a number of editions. Documentary collections include: H. Commager (ed.), *Documents of American History* (9th ed. 1973); J. Elliott (ed.), *The Debates of the Several State Conventions on the Adoption of the Federal Constitution* (1836); M. Farrand (ed.), *The Records of the Federal Convention of 1787* (1911, 1937); P. Kurland and R. Lerner (ed.), *The Founders' Constitution* (1987).

B. THE BILL OF RIGHTS

PROTECTION OF FREEDOM IN THE CONSTITUTION OF 1787

The emphasis that must be placed upon the Bill of Rights and other amendments to the Constitution, Professor Chafee reminds us, should not lead one to ignore the protections for individual liberty which were built into the original document; perhaps the most important of these is the limitation on suspension by the national government of the writ of *habeas corpus*.[1] Professor Chafee adds:

of the Constitution appeared in the Articles; the concepts of privileges and immunities of state citizens, extradition of fugitives, and full faith and credit were contained in Article IV of the Articles of Confederation.

1. Art. I, § 9. Chafee, *How Human Rights Got Into the Constitution* (1952) 51.

"Among the affirmative rights in Article I are the immunity of debates in Congress; the Interstate Commerce Clause which, without expressly mentioning any human right, has in fact been invoked to protect freedom of movement across state lines; ... and the prohibition of bills of attainder and *ex post facto* laws in the nation or the states. ... Article III on the judiciary obliges criminal cases to be tried by a jury of the neighborhood. It also contains the definition of treason.... Finally, the miscellaneous provisions found in Article IV entitle citizens of one state to enjoy in another state 'all the Privileges and Immunities' of its own citizens, and empower the United States to preserve in every state a 'Republican Form of Government' and to protect the right to life 'against domestic violence.' "[2]

Professor Chafee's brief summary does not purport to be complete. For example, the protection of economic (and even intellectual) liberty was possible under the prohibition in Article I, Section 10, against state laws impairing the obligation of contracts. But in spite of the importance of these and other guaranties established by the original document, federal constitutional protection for individual liberty must be derived, for the most part, from two groups of amendments separated in time by almost eighty years: the Bill of Rights and the three post-Civil War amendments. The objectives of these two groups of amendments and the relationship between them raise questions that are as important as they are difficult.

THE BILL OF RIGHTS

The importance of a written declaration of the rights of the individual loomed large in the minds of early Americans. This tradition had grown out of struggles against royal prerogative, and was reflected in written guaranties of Magna Carta (1215),[3] the Petition of Right (1628)[4] and the Bill of Rights (1689).[5]

This tradition was carried to the New World. Many of the early Colonial Charters offered important assurances to the settlers of "all Liberties and Immunities of free and natural Subjects."[6] But the most direct antecedents of

---

2. Id. at 5–6 (Footnotes omitted.) See also: *The Federalist No. 84* (Hamilton); Story, *Commentaries on the Constitution of the United States* (4th ed. 1873) § 1859.

3. Magna Carta exacted from King John numerous limitations on his prerogative. Chapter 39 read: "No freeman shall be seized or imprisoned or disseised or outlawed or in any way destroyed nor will we go against him or send against him except by the lawful judgment of his peers, or by the law of the land."

4. The Petition of Right directed to Charles I contained the prayer that further military commissions for proceedings by martial law should not issue "lest by colour of them any of your majesty's subjects be destroyed or put to death, contrary to the laws and franchise of the land...."

5. The Bill of Rights was designed to limit the power of William of Orange. It proclaimed "... that it is the right of the subjects to petition the king and all commit-

ments and prosecutions for such petitioning are illegal ... that the subjects which are Protestants may have arms for their defense suitable for their conditions and as allowed by law; that election of members of parliament ought to be free; that the freedom of speech and debates or proceedings in parliament ought not to be impeached or questioned in any court or place out of parliament; that excessive bail ought not to be required, nor excessive fines imposed, nor cruel and unusual punishment inflicted; that jurors ought to be duly impanelled and returned, and jurors which pass upon men in trials for high treason ought to be freeholders...."

6. Charter of Connecticut, 1662, in 1 Thorpe, *American Charters, Constitutions and Organic Laws,* 529, 533 (1909). Similar provisions occur in other colonial charters. See Chafee, *How Human Rights Got into the Constitution* 36 (1952). Several of the charters also had guarantees of religious freedom. Id. at 40–42. Cf. Rutland, *The Birth of the Bill of Rights* (1955).

modern guarantees of individual rights appeared in the constitutions that the colonists framed for themselves at the outbreak of the Revolution. In eight state constitutions, these guarantees were gathered into separate provisions called a Bill of Rights or Declaration of Rights; three states wove them into the fabric of the document.[7] Probably the most influential of these early bills of rights was that of Virginia.

Since the Articles of Confederation (1777) did not grant significant legislative power to the central government, the absence of a bill of rights is understandable. It is more surprising that proposals for a Bill of Rights made in the Constitutional Convention of 1787 were rejected. No single explanation is compelling. There is some evidence of concern lest prohibiting Congress from intruding into enumerated areas of individual rights might suggest that Congress possessed power to invade other rights not specifically protected. Another deterrent appears to have been the fear that disagreement over the definition of individual rights might jeopardize the Convention's completion of the Constitution and the launching of the new government.[8] Finally, there is evidence that the delegates were persuaded to avoid the problem by the supposition that the limited powers of Congress made a Bill of Rights unnecessary.[9]

One of the few records of the debates on this question in the constitutional convention is as follows:[10]

"Mr. Pinkney & Mr. Gerry, moved to insert a declaration 'that the liberty of the Press should be inviolably observed—'

"Mr. Sherman—It is unnecessary—The power of Congress does not extend to the Press. On the question, (it passed in the negative)."

The reasons that impelled the Constitutional Convention to omit a federal bill of rights proved unsatisfactory in crucial state ratification conventions. After relatively smooth sailing in Delaware, Pennsylvania, New Jersey, Georgia and Connecticut, the storm broke in Massachusetts. Opposition was quieted in part by the proposal that ratification be coupled with suggestions for amendments to the Constitution that would protect individual liberty; the Federalists tendered a gentleman's agreement to give them favorable consideration. Many of the subsequent state conventions suggested amendments[11] that included proposals for a bill of rights.[12]

---

7. Connecticut and Rhode Island retained their colonial charters. Chafee, op. cit. supra, pp. 18–19.

8. On September 12 a motion for a committee to prepare a bill of rights was defeated by a vote of 10–0; the only recorded objection to the motion was in connection with a proposed guaranty of jury trial in civil cases. "Mr. Gorham. It is not possible to discriminate equity cases from those in which juries are proper. The Representatives of the people may be safely trusted in this matter," 2 Farrand, *Records of the Federal Convention* (1911) 587, 588.

Speaking in the South Carolina House of Representatives, C.C. Pinckney summarized the reasons listed above and added the further point that bills of rights "generally begin with declaring that all men are by nature born free. Now, we should make that declara-

tion with a very bad grace, when a large part of our property consists in men who are actually born slaves." 3 Id. at 256.

9. This and other arguments against the adoption of a Bill of Rights were reviewed and answered at length by Madison in his proposals to the House of Representatives. 1 *Annals of Congress* 438–439 (1834).

10. 2 Farrand, op. cit. supra 617–618 (Madison's notes for September 14).

11. Bloom, *History of the Formation of the Union under the Constitution* (1941) 24–27, 280 et seq.; Hart, *Formation of the Union* (1892) 130–31; 1 Nichols & Nichols, *The Republic of the United States* (1942) 262.

12. Madison believed that the chief basis of popular opposition to ratification of the Constitution to be its omission of such guarantees, 1 *Annals of Congress* 433 (1834).

To keep faith with these states, James Madison compiled a set of proposed amendments based on the state bills of rights and the amendments proposed by the state conventions. His conception of the role of a bill of rights is summarized in a letter to Jefferson dated October 17, 1788:[13]

"My own opinion has always been in favor of a bill of rights; providing it be so framed as not to imply powers not meant to be included in the enumeration. At the same time I have never thought the omission a material defect, nor been anxious to supply it even by *subsequent* amendment, for any other reason than that it is anxiously desired by others. I favored it because I have supposed it might be of use, and if properly executed could not be of disservice. I have not viewed it in an important light 1. because I conceive that in a certain degree, though not in the extent argued by Mr. Wilson, the rights in question are reserved by the manner in which the federal powers are granted, 2. because there is great reason to fear that a positive declaration of some of the most essential rights could not be obtained in the requisite latitude ... 3. because the limited powers of the federal Government and the jealousy of the subordinate Governments, afford a security which has not existed in the case of the State Governments, and exists in no other, 4. because experience proves the inefficacy of a bill of rights on those occasions when its control is most needed.... What use then it may be asked can a bill of rights serve in popular Governments? ... 1. The political truths declared in that solemn manner acquire by degrees the character of fundamental maxims of free Government, and as they become incorporated with the national sentiment, counteract the impulses of interest and passion. 2. Altho[ugh] it be generally true ... that the danger of oppression lies in the interested majorities of the people rather than in usurped acts of the Government, yet there may be occasions on which the evil may spring from the latter source; and on such, a bill of rights will be a good ground for an appeal to the sense of the community ... *absolute* restrictions in cases that are doubtful, or where emergencies may overrule them, ought to be avoided."

In the First Congress, Madison proposed detailed amendments to the text of the Constitution which, after material modification, led to the Bill of Rights.[14]

The original Constitution contained relatively few express limitations on state power. (The most important of these are in Section 10 of Article I, and Sections 1 and 2 of Article IV.) The addition of the Bill of Rights left state power unchanged. Forty-two years after their ratification, Chief Justice Marshall confirmed that the provisions of the Bill of Rights were limitations only on the power of the federal government. Barron v. Baltimore, 32 U.S. (7 Pet.) 243

13. *Writings of James Madison* 269, 271–274 (Hunt ed. 1904); see further 1 *Annals of Congress* 436–44 (1834). For Jefferson's prodding of Madison see Bowers, *Jefferson and the Bill of Rights,* 41 Va.L.Rev. 709, 712–714 (1955).

14. Madison's initial proposals called for amendments that were to be worked into the body of the Constitution, rather than supplements added to the original text. Thus, Madison's proposals included ten new provisions to be added to Article I, Section 9. 1 *Annals of Congress* 434–35 (1834). These correspond, for the most part, to the first ten amendments which finally received approval.

Madison's proposals also included the following addition to Article I, Section 10: "No state shall violate the equal rights of conscience, or the freedom of the press, or the trial by jury in criminal cases." 1 Id. at 435. He further proposed to rewrite Article III, Section 2 to require, inter alia, that "in all crimes punishable with loss of life or member, presentment or indictment by a grand jury shall be an essential preliminary ..." and that "In suits at common law, between man and man, the trial by jury, as one of the best securities to the rights of the people, ought to remain inviolate" Ibid.

(1833). Until after the Civil War, state constitutions—interpreted by state courts—were the source of most constitutional limitations on state government.

C.   THE ADOPTION OF THE CIVIL WAR AMENDMENTS

Appomattox marked the end of the struggle over the constitutional issue of secession but it precipitated the country's most serious social problem: the future status of the four million individuals who had been held in slavery. This transition to freedom posed an acute problem of assimilation reflected in grave problems of constitutional law.

Slavery and the Thirteenth Amendment. By language only thinly veiled, the Constitution of 1787 recognized and sanctioned slavery.[1] Thus, although Lincoln's Emancipation Proclamation[2] declared an end to slavery in the Confederacy, firm legal support for the eradication of slavery required constitutional change. This support was provided in 1865 by the Thirteenth Amendment.[3] The original proposition for the Amendment was introduced in Congress in December, 1863, achieving final passage in January, 1865. It was declared ratified and in force on December 18, 1865.

The 1866 Civil Rights Acts and the Fourteenth and Fifteenth Amendments. The Civil Rights Act of 1866 was before Congress at the same time as the Fourteenth Amendment. In large part, the Amendment was designed to assure the constitutionality of the Act.

The Act was Congress's response to the so-called "Black Codes" enacted in several states. Mississippi enactments of 1865, for example, provided:

"... Every civil officer shall, and every person may, arrest and carry back to his or her legal employer any freedman, free negro, or mulatto who shall have quit the service of his or her employer before the expiration of his or her term of service without good cause....

"... If any freedman, free negro or mulatto, convicted of any of the misdemeanors provided against in this act, shall fail or refuse for the space of five days after conviction, to pay the fine and costs imposed, such person shall be hired out by the sheriff or other officer, at the public outcry, to any white person who will pay said fine and all costs, and take the convict for the shortest time."[4]

Other provisions of some of the Black Codes barred Blacks from any business except "husbandry" without obtaining a special license, or forbade them from renting or leasing land except in towns and cities.[5]

The Civil Rights Act,[6] which was introduced in January 1866, passed in March, vetoed by President Johnson, and passed over his veto in early April, was designed to put an end to these laws. The two opening sections provided:

"Sec. 1. ... all persons born in the United States and not subject to any foreign power, excluding Indians not taxed, are hereby declared to be citizens of

---

1.   Art. I, § 2, ¶ 3; Art. I, § 9, ¶ 1; Art. IV, § 2, ¶ 3.

2.   12 Stat. 1268 (1863).

3.   See tenBroek, *Thirteenth Amendment to the Constitution of the United States—Consummation to Abolition and Key to the Fourteenth Amendment,* 39 Cal.L.Rev. 171 (1951).

4.   Laws of Mississippi, 1865, 82, 84, 166–167. See also Laws of Mississippi, 1865,

86–96; Acts of the General Assembly of Louisiana Regulating Labor. Extra Session, 1865, 3 et seq.; 2 Commager, *Documents of American History,* 2–7 (5th ed. 1949).

5.   Stephenson, *Race Distinctions in American Law* 41–43 (1910); Maslow and Robison, *Civil Rights Legislation and the Fight for Equality,* 20 U.Chi.L.Rev. 363, 367 (1953).

6.   Act of April 9, 1866, 14 Stat. 27.

the United States; and such citizens, of every race and color, without regard to any previous condition of slavery or involuntary servitude, except as a punishment for crime whereof the party shall have been duly convicted, shall have the same right, in every State and Territory in the United States, to make and enforce contracts, to sue, be parties, and give evidence, to inherit, purchase, lease, sell, hold, and convey real and personal property, and to full and equal benefit of all laws and proceedings for the security of person and property, as is enjoyed by white citizens, and shall be subject to like punishment, pains, and penalties, and to none other, any law, statute, ordinance, regulation, or custom, to the contrary notwithstanding.

"Sec. 2. *And be it further enacted,* That any person who, under color of any law, statute, ordinance, regulation, or custom, shall subject, or cause to be subjected, any inhabitant of any State or Territory to the deprivation of any right secured or protected by this act, or to different punishment, pains, or penalties on account of such person having at any time been held in a condition of slavery or involuntary servitude, except as a punishment for crime whereof the party shall have been duly convicted, or by reason of his color or race, than is prescribed for the punishment of white persons, shall be deemed guilty of a misdemeanor, and, on conviction, shall be punished by fine not exceeding one thousand dollars, or imprisonment not exceeding one year, or both, in the discretion of the court."

The question arose: was there constitutional support for this Act? Did the racial discrimination in question reach the level of "involuntary servitude" encompassed by the Thirteenth Amendment? If not, where else could constitutional support be found? This difficulty was one of President Johnson's grounds for vetoing the bill. He said:[7]

"Hitherto every subject embraced in the enumeration of rights contained in this bill has been considered as exclusively belonging to the States. They all relate to the internal police and economy of the States. They are matters which in each State concern the domestic condition of its people, varying in each according to its own peculiar circumstances, and the safety and well-being of its own citizens. I do not mean to say that upon all these subjects there are not Federal restraints, as for instance, in the State power of legislation over contracts, there is a Federal limitation that no State shall pass a law impairing the obligations of contracts; and, as to crimes, that no State shall pass an *ex post facto* law; and, as to money that no State shall make anything but gold and silver a legal tender. But where can we find a Federal prohibition against the power of any state to discriminate, as do most of them, between aliens and citizens, between artificial persons called corporations, and natural persons, in the right to hold real estate?

"If it be granted that Congress can repeal all State laws discriminating between whites and blacks in the subjects covered by this bill, why, it may be asked, may not Congress repeal in the same way all State laws discriminating between the two races on the subjects of suffrage and office? If Congress can declare by law who shall hold lands, who shall testify, who shall have capacity to make a contract in a State, then Congress can by law also declare who, without regard to color or race, shall have the right to sit as a juror or as a judge, to hold any office, and, finally, to vote 'in every State and Territory of the United States.' "

Concurrently with the early debates on the Civil Rights Bill Congress was also considering drafts of a constitutional amendment. The Joint Committee on

---

7. Cong.Globe, 39th Cong., 1st Sess., 1680 (1866).

Reconstruction referred to Congress on February 10, 1866 a draft of an amendment designed to grant Congress general power to legislate for the protection of civil rights.[8] The draft was promptly tabled in the Senate. On February 26–28 it was debated in the House but action was postponed and it was never taken up.

Although Congress had overridden the President's veto of the Civil Rights Act, the challenge to the constitutionality was not resolved. So in April the Joint Committee on Reconstruction returned to the problem of constitutional amendment, reporting a new version to Congress on April 28. This version was debated in May and June and finally adopted with amendments on June 13. By March, 1867, the Amendment had been ratified by 20 states and rejected by 11. Also in March Congress passed over the President's veto a bill setting the conditions under which the Rebel States would be entitled to representation in Congress. One of those conditions for readmission was that the state should have ratified the Fourteenth Amendment and that the Amendment should have become part of the Constitution. By July, 1868, 9 more states had ratified, including 7 of the southern states seeking readmission pursuant to the 1867 statute, and the Amendment was declared adopted on July 28.

One of the conditions imposed for the readmission of the Rebel States was that their constitutions guarantee the continuance of the suffrage provisions adopted during the period of federal control through the Reconstruction Acts. These constitutions guaranteed Negro suffrage and disenfranchised large elements of the white population. Texas, Mississippi, and Virginia were delayed in readmission because of opposition to the franchise provisions. In 1869 a bargain was struck under which these states were not required to accept the rigor of the original franchise provisions but were required to ratify a constitutional amendment then being proposed to guarantee the franchise to Negroes. The three states complied, were readmitted in early 1870, and the Fifteenth Amendment was finally ratified in March, 1870.[9]

---

8. Unlike Section 1 of the final draft, these earlier versions of the Fourteenth Amendment were, in form, grants to Congress of a general power to legislate for the protection of civil rights. The first draft reported by the committee considering the amendment read: "Congress shall have power to make all laws necessary and proper to secure to all citizens of the United States, in every State, the same political rights and privileges; and to all persons in every State equal protection in the enjoyment of life, liberty and property." See Fairman, *Does the Fourteenth Amendment Incorporate the Bill of Rights: The Original Understanding*, 2 Stan.L.Rev. 5, 20–21 (1949); Flack, *The Adoption of the Fourteenth Amendment* (1908); Akhil Amar, *The Bill of Rights* (1999)

9. For background on and analysis of the Reconstruction Amendments, particularly the Fifteenth, see Vikram Amar, *Jury Service as Political Participation Akin to Voting*, 80 Cornell L.Rev. 203 (1995).

CHAPTER 2

JUDICIAL REVIEW

SECTION 1. THE LEGITIMACY OF JUDICIAL REVIEW

THE CONSTITUTIONAL CONVENTION

In the Constitutional Convention of 1787 the Virginia Plan proposed to the Convention by Mr. Randolph (Va.) on May 29 served as the basis for the ensuing discussion and action of the delegates.

The sixth resolution in the Virginia Plan contained the provision that the national legislature be empowered "to negative all laws passed by the several States, contravening in the opinion of the National Legislature the articles of Union...." This provision was ultimately rejected, in part because of the adoption of the Supremacy Clause, Art. VI, cl. 2.

The eighth resolution provided "that the Executive and a convenient number of the National Judiciary, ought to compose a council of revision with authority to examine every act of the National Legislature before it shall operate, & every act of a particular Legislature before a Negative thereon shall be final; and that the dissent of the said Council shall amount to a rejection, unless the Act of the National Legislature be again passed, or that of a particular Legislature be again negatived by _____a of the members of each branch." The Convention ultimately rejected the participation of the judiciary in the veto process and adopted the executive veto. Art. I, § 7, cl. 2.

The following excerpts from the debate on the eighth resolution will give a little of the flavor of the discussion that led to its rejection. They are taken from Madison's Notes of the proceedings on July 21, 1787, 2 Farrand, *The Records of the Federal Convention of 1787* (1911) 74, 76, 78:

"Mr. [Madison]—considered the object of the motion as of great importance to the meditated Constitution. It would be useful to the Judiciary departmt. by giving it an additional opportunity of defending itself agst: Legislative encroachments; It would be useful to the Executive, by inspiring additional confidence & firmness in exerting the revisionary power: It would be useful to the Legislature by the valuable assistance it would give in preserving a consistency, conciseness, perspicuity & technical propriety in the laws, qualities peculiarly necessary; & yet shamefully wanting in our republican Codes. It would moreover be useful to the Community at large as an additional check agst. a pursuit of those unwise & unjust measures which constituted so great a portion of our calamities. If any solid objection could be urged agst. the motion, it must be on the supposition that it tended to give too much strength either to the Executive or Judiciary. He did not think there was the least ground for this apprehension. It was much more to be apprehended that notwithstanding this cooperation of the two departments, the Legislature would still be an overmatch for them. Experience in all the States had evinced a powerful tendency in the Legislature to absorb all power into its vortex. This

a. Blank left in original.

24

was the real source of danger to the American Constitutions; & suggested the necessity of giving every defensive authority to the other departments that was consistent with republican principles. . . .

"Mr. L. Martin. considered the association of the Judges with the Executive as a dangerous innovation; as well as one which, could not produce the particular advantage expected from it. A knowledge of mankind, and of Legislative affairs cannot be presumed to belong in a higher degree to the Judges than to the Legislature. And as to the Constitutionality of laws, that point will come before the Judges in their proper official character. In this character they have a negative on the laws. Join them with the Executive in the Revision and they will have a double negative. It is necessary that the Supreme Judiciary should have the confidence of the people. This will soon be lost, if they are employed in the task of remonstrating agst. popular measures of the Legislature. Besides in what mode & proportion are they to vote in the Council of Revision? . . .

"Col Mason Observed that the defence of the Executive was not the sole object of the Revisionary power. He expected even greater advantages from it. Notwithstanding the precautions taken in the Constitution of the Legislature, it would so much resemble that of the individual States, that it must be expected frequently to pass unjust and pernicious laws. This restraining power was therefore essentially necessary. It would have the effect not only of hindering the final passage of such laws; but would discourage demagogues from attempting to get them passed. It had been said (by Mr. L. Martin) that if the Judges were joined in this check on the laws, they would have a double negative, since in their expository capacity of Judges they would have one negative. He would reply that in this capacity they could impede in one case only, the operation of laws. They could declare an unconstitutional law void. But with regard to every law however unjust oppressive or pernicious, which did not come plainly under this description, they would be under the necessity as Judges to give it a free course. He wished the further use to be made of the Judges, of giving aid in preventing every improper law. Their aid will be the more valuable as they are in the habit and practice of considering laws in their true principles, and in all their consequences."

Marbury v. Madison

5 U.S. (1 Cranch) 137, 2 L.Ed. 60 (1803).

[John Marshall was Secretary of State in the Adams administration when he took office as Chief Justice on January 31, 1801. He continued as Acting Secretary of State until the last day of the Adams administration, March 3, 1801. William Marbury was one of a number of persons who were appointed justices of the peace in the District of Columbia and who were confirmed by the Senate on March 3. His commission remained in Marshall's office undelivered when the new administration took over. President Jefferson directed his Secretary of State, James Madison, to withhold several commissions, including that of Marbury. Marbury then brought this suit against Madison, taking the unusual step of starting the action in the Supreme Court, invoking its original jurisdiction.[a]]

a. For accounts of the background of the case, see Burton, *The Cornerstone of Constitutional Law: The Extraordinary Case of Marbury v. Madison*, 36 A.B.A.J. 805 (1950); Van Alstyne, *A Critical Guide to Marbury v.* *Madison,* 1969 Duke L.J. 1. Two good symposia collection of essays commemorating the bicentennial anniversary of *Marbury* can be found in Volume 101 of the Michigan Law

Mr. Chief Justice Marshall delivered the opinion of the Court.

At the last term on the affidavits then read and filed with the clerk, a rule was granted in this case, requiring the secretary of state to shew cause why a mandamus should not issue, directing him to deliver to William Marbury his commission as a justice of the peace for the county of Washington, in the district of Columbia.

No cause has been shewn, and the present motion is for a mandamus. The peculiar delicacy of this case, the novelty of some of its circumstances, and the real difficulty attending the points which occur in it, require a complete exposition of the principles, on which the opinion to be given by the court, is founded.

These principles have been, on the side of the applicant, very ably argued at the bar. In rendering the opinion of the court, there will be some departure in form, though not in substance, from the points stated in that argument.

In the order in which the court has viewed this subject, the following questions have been considered and decided.

1st. Has the applicant a right to the commission he demands?

2dly. If he has a right, and that right has been violated, do the laws of his country afford him a remedy?

3dly. If they do afford him a remedy, is it a *mandamus* issuing from this court?

The first object of enquiry is,

1st. Has the applicant a right to the commission he demands?

His right originates in an act of congress passed in February 1801, concerning the district of Columbia.

After dividing the district into two counties, the 11th section of this law enacts, "that there shall be appointed in and for each of the said counties, such number of discreet persons to be justices of the peace as the president of the United States shall, from time to time, think expedient, to continue in office for five years."

It appears, from the affidavits, that in compliance with this law, a commission for William Marbury as a justice of peace for the county of Washington, was signed by John Adams, then president of the United States; after which the seal of the United States was affixed to it; but the commission has never reached the person for whom it was made out.

In order to determine whether he is entitled to this commission, it becomes necessary to enquire whether he has been appointed to the office. For if he has been appointed, the law continues him in office for five years, and he is entitled to the possession of those evidences of office, which, being completed, became his property.

The 2d section of the 2d article of the constitution, declares, that, "the president shall nominate, and, by and with the advice and consent of the senate, shall appoint ambassadors, other public ministers and consuls, and all other officers of the United States, whose appointments are not otherwise provided for."

Review (2003), and Volume 20 of Constitutional Commentary (2003).

For an interesting discussion of the last minute appointment of judges by President Adams, see Turner, *The Midnight Judges,* 109 U.Pa.L.Rev. 494 (1961).

The third section declares, that "he shall commission all the officers of the United States." . . .

It is therefore decidedly the opinion of the court, that when a commission has been signed by the President, the appointment is made; and that the commission is complete, when the seal of the United States has been affixed to it by the secretary of state. . . .

To withhold his commission, therefore, is an act deemed by the court not warranted by law, but violative of a vested legal right.

This brings us to the second enquiry; which is,

2dly. If he has a right, and that right has been violated, do the laws of his country afford him a remedy?

The very essence of civil liberty certainly consists in the right of every individual to claim the protection of the laws, whenever he receives an injury. One of the first duties of government is to afford that protection. In Great Britain the king himself is sued in the respectful form of a petition, and he never fails to comply with the judgment of his court. . . .

The government of the United States has been emphatically termed a government of laws, and not of men. It will certainly cease to deserve this high appellation, if the laws furnish no remedy for the violation of a vested legal right.

If this obloquy is to be cast on the jurisprudence of our country, it must arise from the peculiar character of the case. . . .

It follows then that the question, whether the legality of an act of the head of a department be examinable in a court of justice or not, must always depend on the nature of that act. . . .

By the constitution of the United States, the President is invested with certain important political powers, in the exercise of which he is to use his own discretion, and is accountable only to his country in his political character, and to his own conscience. To aid him in the performance of these duties, he is authorized to appoint certain officers, who act by his authority and in conformity with his orders.

In such cases, their acts are his acts; and whatever opinion may be entertained of the manner in which executive discretion may be used, still there exists, and can exist, no power to control that discretion. The subjects are political. They respect the nation, not individual rights, and being entrusted to the executive, the decision of the executive is conclusive. The application of this remark will be perceived by adverting to the act of congress for establishing the department of foreign affairs. This officer, as his duties were prescribed by that act, is to conform precisely to the will of the President. He is the mere organ by whom that will is communicated. The acts of such an officer, as an officer, can never be examinable by the courts.

But when the legislature proceeds to impose on that officer other duties; when he is directed peremptorily to perform certain acts; when the rights of individuals are dependent on the performance of those acts; he is so far the officer of the law; is amenable to the laws for his conduct; and cannot at his discretion sport away the vested rights of others.

The conclusion from this reasoning is, that where the heads of departments are the political or confidential agents of the executive, merely to execute the will of the President, or rather to act in cases in which the executive possesses a constitutional or legal discretion nothing can be more perfectly clear than that their acts are only politically examinable. But where a specific duty is assigned by law, and individual rights depend upon the performance of that duty, it seems equally clear that the individual who considers himself injured, has a right to resort to the laws of his country for a remedy. . . .

It remains to be enquired whether,

3dly. He is entitled to the remedy for which he applies. This depends on,

1st. The nature of the writ applied for, and,

2dly. The power of this court.

1st. The nature of the writ. . . .

This writ, if awarded, would be directed to an officer of government, and its mandate to him would be, to use the words of Blackstone, "to do a particular thing therein specified, which appertains to his office and duty and which the court has previously determined, or at least supposes, to be consonant to right and justice." Or, in the words of Lord Mansfield, the applicant, in this case, has a right to execute an office of public concern, and is kept out of possession of that right.

These circumstances certainly concur in this case.

Still, to render the mandamus a proper remedy, the officer to whom it is to be directed, must be one to whom, on legal principles, such writ may be directed; and the person applying for it must be without any other specific and legal remedy.

1st. With respect to the officer to whom it would be directed. The intimate political relation, subsisting between the president of the United States and the heads of departments, necessarily renders any legal investigation of the acts of one of those high officers peculiarly irksome, as well as delicate; and excites some hesitation with respect to the propriety of entering into such investigation. Impressions are often received without much reflection or examination, and it is not wonderful that in such a case as this, the assertion, by an individual, of his legal claims in a court of justice, to which claims it is the duty of that court to attend; should at first view be considered by some, as an attempt to intrude into the cabinet, and to intermeddle with the prerogatives of the executive.

It is scarcely necessary for the court to disclaim all pretensions to such a jurisdiction. An extravagance, so absurd and excessive, could not have been entertained for a moment. The province of the court is, solely, to decide on the rights of individuals, not to enquire how the executive, or executive officers, perform duties in which they have a discretion. Questions, in their nature political, or which are, by the constitution and laws, submitted to the executive, can never be made in this court.

But, if this be not such a question; if so far from being an intrusion into the secrets of the cabinet, it respects a paper, which according to law, is upon record, and to a copy of which the law gives a right, on the payment of ten cents; if it be no intermeddling with a subject, over which the executive can be considered as having exercised any control; what is there in the exalted station of the officer, which shall bar a citizen from asserting, in a court of justice, his legal rights, or shall forbid a court to listen to the claim; or to issue a mandamus, directing the performance of a duty, not depending on executive discretion, but on particular acts of congress and the general principles of law? . . .

This, then, is a plain case for a mandamus, either to deliver the commission, or a copy of it from the record; and it only remains to be enquired,

Whether it can issue from this court.

The act to establish the judicial courts of the United States authorizes the supreme court "to issue writs of mandamus, in cases warranted by the principles and usages of law, to any courts appointed, or persons holding office, under the authority of the United States."[b]

The secretary of the state, being a person holding an office under the authority of the United States, is precisely within the letter of the description; and if this court is not authorized to issue a writ of mandamus to such an officer, it must be because the law is unconstitutional, and therefore absolutely incapable of conferring the authority, and assigning the duties which its words purport to confer and assign.

The constitution vests the whole judicial power of the United States in one supreme court, and such inferior courts as congress shall, from time to time, ordain and establish. This power is expressly extended to all cases arising under the laws of the United States; and consequently, in some form, may be exercised over the present case; because the right claimed is given by a law of the United States.

In the distribution of this power it is declared that "the supreme court shall have original jurisdiction in all cases affecting ambassadors, other public ministers and consuls, and those in which a state shall be a party. In all other cases, the supreme court shall have appellate jurisdiction."

It has been insisted, at the bar, that as the original grant of jurisdiction to the supreme and inferior courts, is general, and the clause, assigning original jurisdiction to the supreme court, contains no negative or restrictive words; the power remains to the legislature, to assign original jurisdiction to that court in other cases than those specified in the article which has been recited; provided those cases belong to the judicial power of the United States.

If it had been intended to leave it in the discretion of the legislature to apportion the judicial power between the supreme and inferior courts according to the will of that body, it would certainly have been useless to have proceeded further than to have defined the judicial power, and the tribunals in which it should be vested. The subsequent part of the section is mere surplusage, is entirely without meaning, if such is to be the construction. If congress remains at liberty to give this court appellate jurisdiction, where the constitution has declared their jurisdiction shall be original; and original jurisdiction where the constitution has declared it shall be appellate; the distribution of jurisdiction, made in the constitution, is form without substance.

Affirmative words are often, in their operation, negative of other objects than those affirmed; and in this case a negative or exclusive sense must be given to them or they have no operation at all.

It cannot be presumed that any clause in the constitution is intended to be without effect; and therefore such a construction is inadmissible, unless the words require it.

b. The full sentence, a part of Section 13 of the Judiciary Act of 1789, read: "The Supreme Court shall also have appellate jurisdiction from the circuit courts and courts of the several states, in the cases herein after specially provided for; and shall have power to issue writs of prohibition to the district courts, when proceeding as courts of admiralty and maritime jurisdiction, and writs of mandamus, in cases warranted by the principles and usages of law, to any courts appointed, or persons holding office, under the authority of the United States."

If the solicitude of the convention, respecting our peace with foreign powers, induced a provision that the supreme court should take original jurisdiction in cases which might be supposed to affect them; yet the clause would have proceeded no further than to provide for such cases, if no further restriction on the powers of congress had been intended. That they should have appellate jurisdiction in all other cases, with such exceptions as congress might make, is no restriction; unless the words be deemed exclusive of original jurisdiction. . . .

To enable this court then to issue a mandamus, it must be shewn to be an exercise of appellate jurisdiction, or to be necessary to enable them to exercise appellate jurisdiction.

It has been stated at the bar that the appellate jurisdiction may be exercised in a variety of forms, and that if it be the will of the legislature that a mandamus, should be used for that purpose, that will must be obeyed. This is true, yet the jurisdiction must be appellate, not original.

It is the essential criterion of appellate jurisdiction, that it revises and corrects the proceedings in a cause already instituted, and does not create that cause. Although, therefore, a mandamus may be directed to courts, yet to issue such a writ to an officer for the delivery of a paper, is in effect the same as to sustain an original action for that paper, and therefore seems not to belong to appellate, but to original jurisdiction. Neither is it necessary in such a case as this, to enable the court to exercise its appellate jurisdiction.

The authority, therefore, given to the supreme court by the act establishing the judicial courts of the United States, to issue writs of mandamus to public officers, appears not to be warranted by the constitution; and it becomes necessary to enquire whether a jurisdiction, so conferred, can be exercised.

The question, whether an act, repugnant to the constitution, can become the law of the land, is a question deeply interesting to the United States; but, happily, not of an intricacy proportioned to its interest. It seems only necessary to recognize certain principles, supposed to have been long and well established, to decide it.

That the people have an original right to establish, for their future government, such principles as, in their opinion, shall most conduce to their own happiness, is the basis, on which the whole American fabric has been erected. The exercise of this original right is a very great exertion; nor can it, nor ought it to be frequently repeated. The principles, therefore, so established, are deemed fundamental. And as the authority, from which they proceed, is supreme, and can seldom act, they are designed to be permanent.

This original and supreme will organizes the government, and assigns, to different departments, their respective powers. It may either stop here; or establish certain limits not to be transcended by those departments.

The government of the United States is of the latter description. The powers of the legislature are defined, and limited; and that those limits may not be mistaken, or forgotten, the constitution is written. To what purpose are powers limited, and to what purpose is that limitation committed to writing, if these limits may, at any time, be passed by those intended to be restrained? The distinction, between a government with limited and unlimited powers, is abolished, if those limits do not confine the persons on whom they are imposed, and if acts prohibited and acts allowed, are of equal obligation. It is a proposition too plain to be contested, that the constitution controls any legislative act repugnant to it; or, that the legislature may alter the constitution by an ordinary act.

Between these alternatives there is no middle ground. The constitution is either a superior, paramount law, unchangeable by ordinary means, or it is on a level with ordinary legislative acts, and like other acts, is alterable when the legislature shall please to alter it.

If the former part of the alternative be true, then a legislative act contrary to the constitution is not law: if the latter part be true, then written constitutions are absurd attempts, on the part of the people, to limit a power, in its own nature illimitable.

Certainly all those who have framed written constitutions contemplate them as forming the fundamental and paramount law of the nation, and consequently the theory of every such government must be, that an act of the legislature, repugnant to the constitution, is void.

This theory is essentially attached to a written constitution, and is consequently to be considered, by this court, as one of the fundamental principles of our society. It is not therefore to be lost sight of in the further consideration of this subject.

If an act of the legislature, repugnant to the constitution, is void, does it, notwithstanding its invalidity, bind the courts, and oblige them to give it effect? Or, in other words, though it be not law, does it constitute a rule as operative as if it was a law? This would be to overthrow in fact what was established in theory; and would seem, at first view, an absurdity too gross to be insisted on. It shall, however, receive a more attentive consideration.

It is emphatically the province and duty of the judicial department to say what the law is. Those who apply the rule to particular cases, must of necessity expound and interpret that rule. If two laws conflict with each other, the courts must decide on the operation of each.

So if a law be in opposition to the constitution; if both the law and the constitution apply to a particular case, so that the court must either decide that case conformably to the law disregarding the constitution, or conformably to the constitution disregarding the law; the court must determine which of these conflicting rules governs the case. This is of the very essence of judicial duty.

If then the courts are to regard the constitution, and the constitution is superior to any ordinary act of the legislature, the constitution, and not such ordinary act, must govern the case to which they both apply.

Those then who controvert the principle that the constitution is to be considered, in court, as a paramount law, are reduced to the necessity of maintaining that courts must close their eyes on the constitution, and see only the law.

This doctrine would subvert the very foundation of all written constitutions. It would declare that an act, which, according to the principles and theory of our government, is entirely void, is yet, in practice, completely obligatory. It would declare, that if the legislature shall do what is expressly forbidden, such act, notwithstanding the express prohibition, is in reality effectual. It would be giving to the legislature a practical and real omnipotence, with the same breath which professes to restrict their powers within narrow limits. It is prescribing limits, and declaring that those limits may be passed at pleasure.

That it thus reduces to nothing what we have deemed the greatest improvement on political institutions—a written constitution—would of itself be sufficient, in America, where written constitutions have been viewed with so much reverence, for rejecting the construction. But the peculiar expressions of the constitution of the United States furnish additional arguments in favour of its rejection.

The judicial power of the United States is extended to all cases arising under the constitution.

Could it be the intention of those who gave this power, to say that, in using it, the constitution should not be looked into? That a case arising under the constitution should be decided without examining the instrument under which it arises?

This is too extravagant to be maintained.

In some cases then, the constitution must be looked into by the judges. And if they can open it at all, what part of it are they forbidden to read, or to obey?

There are many other parts of the constitution which serve to illustrate this subject.

It is declared that "no tax or duty shall be laid on articles exported from any state." Suppose a duty on the export of cotton, of tobacco or of flour; and a suit instituted to recover it. Ought judgment to be rendered in such a case? ought the judges to close their eyes on the constitution, and only see the law?

The constitution declares that "no bill of attainder or *ex post facto* law shall be passed."

If, however such a bill should be passed and a person should be prosecuted under it; must the court condemn to death those victims whom the constitution endeavours to preserve?

"No person," says the constitution, "shall be convicted of treason unless on the testimony of two witnesses to the same overt act, or on confession in open court."

Here the language of the constitution is addressed especially to the courts. It prescribes, directly for them, a rule of evidence not to be departed from. If the legislature should change that rule, and declare one witness, or a confession out of court, sufficient for conviction, must the constitutional principle yield to the legislative act?

From these, and many other selections which might be made, it is apparent, that the framers of the constitution contemplated that instrument, as a rule for the government of courts, as well as of the legislature.

Why otherwise does it direct the judges to take an oath to support it? This oath certainly applies, in an especial manner, to their conduct in their official character. How immoral to impose it on them, if they were to be used as the instruments, and the knowing instruments, for violating what they swear to support.

The oath of office, too, imposed by the legislature, is completely demonstrative of the legislative opinion on this subject. It is in these words, "I do solemnly swear, that I will administer justice without respect to persons, and do equal right to the poor and to the rich; and that I will faithfully and impartially discharge all the duties incumbent on me as _____ according to the best of my abilities and understanding, agreeably to the constitution, and laws of the United States."

Why does a judge swear to discharge his duties agreeably to the constitution of the United States, if that constitution forms no rule for his government? if it is closed upon him, and cannot be inspected by him?

If such be the real state of things, this is worse than solemn mockery. To prescribe, or to take this oath, becomes equally a crime.

It is also not entirely unworthy of observation, that in declaring what shall be the supreme law of the land, the constitution itself is first mentioned; and not the laws of the United States generally, but those only which shall be made in pursuance of the constitution, have that rank.

Thus, the particular phraseology of the constitution of the United States confirms and strengthens the principle, supposed to be essential to all written constitutions, that a law repugnant to the constitution is void; and that courts, as well as other departments, are bound by that instrument.

The rule must be discharged.[c]

LEGITIMACY OF JUDICIAL REVIEW: SOME COMMENTS

(1) Gibson, J., dissenting, in Eakin v. Raub, 12 S. & R. 330, 344–358 (Pa.1825) considered the question of the legitimacy of judicial review of the constitutionality of legislation. The following excerpts will illustrate the course of his argument:

"The constitution and the *right* of the legislature to pass the act, may be in collision; but is that a legitimate subject for judicial determination? If it be, the judiciary must be a peculiar organ, to revise the proceedings of the legislature, and to correct its mistakes; and in what part of the constitution are we to look for this proud preeminence? Viewing the matter in the opposite direction, what would be thought of an act of assembly in which it should be declared that the supreme court had in a particular case, put a wrong construction on the constitution of the *United States,* and that the judgment should therefore be reversed? It would, doubtless, be thought a usurpation of judicial power. But it is by no means clear, that to declare a law void, which has been enacted according to the forms prescribed in the constitution, is not a usurpation of legislative power. It is an act of sovereignty; and sovereignty and legislative power are said by Sir William *Blackstone* to be convertible terms. It is the business of the judiciary, to interpret the laws, not scan the authority of the lawgiver; and without the latter, it cannot take cognisance of a collision between a law and the constitution. So that, to affirm that the judiciary has a right to judge of the existence of such collision, is to take for granted the very thing to be proved; and that a very cogent argument may be made in this way, I

---

c. During the tenure of Marshall as Chief Justice, the only other case holding an Act of Congress unconstitutional was the obscure decision in Hodgson v. Bowerbank, 9 U.S. (5 Cranch) 303 (1809). In a brief opinion, Marshall held a provision of the Judiciary Act of 1789 unconstitutional in conferring jurisdiction on federal courts to try suits between aliens. (For a strong argument that Marshall interpreted the statute and did not declare it to be unconstitutional, see Mahoney, *A Historical Note on Hodgson v. Bowerbank,* 49 U.Chi.L.Rev. 725 (1982)). The next Act of Congress to be declared unconstitutional was the Missouri Compromise in Dred Scott v. Sandford, 60 U.S. (19 How.) 393 (1857), overruled by the Civil War. The first Act of Congress of general applicability to be declared unconstitutional was the Legal Ten-

der Act in Hepburn v. Griswold, 75 U.S. (8 Wall.) 603 (1870). This decision was promptly overruled by the Court itself in Knox v. Lee, 79 U.S. (12 Wall.) 457 (1871).

The modern Court, because the modern Congress has enacted a much larger volume of legislation and for other reasons as well, has been much more active in striking down federal statutes. During the years 1995 to 2000, for instance, the Court invalidated at least twenty-four congressional enactments. See Akhil Amar, *The Document and the Doctrine,* 114 Harv.L.Rev. 26, 84 n.194 (2000); Vikram Amar, How Much Protection Do Injunctions Against Enforcement of Allegedly Unconstitutional Statutes Provide?, 31 Ford. Urb.L.J. 657, 660 n.17 (2004).

am not disposed to deny; for no conclusions are so strong as those that are drawn from the *petitio principii*....

"But the judges are sworn to support the constitution, and are they not bound by it as the law of the land? In some respects they are. In the very few cases in which the judiciary, and not the legislature, is the immediate organ to execute its provisions, they are bound by it, in preference to any act of assembly to the contrary; in such cases, the constitution is a rule to the courts. But what I have in view in this inquiry, is, the supposed right of the judiciary, to interfere, in cases where the constitution is to be carried into effect through the instrumentality of the legislature, and where that organ must necessarily first decide on the constitutionality of its own act. The oath to support the constitution is not peculiar to the judges, but is taken indiscriminately by every officer of the government, and is designed rather as a test of the political principles of the man, than to bind the officer in the discharge of his duty: otherwise, it were difficult to determine, what operation it is to have in the case of a recorder of deeds, for instance, who in the execution of his office, has nothing to do with the constitution. But granting it to relate to the official conduct of the judge, as well as every other officer, and not to his political principles, still, it must be understood in reference to supporting the constitution, *only as far as that may be involved in his official duty;* and consequently, if his official duty does not comprehend an inquiry into the authority of the legislature, neither does his oath.

"It is worthy of remark here, that the foundation of every argument in favor of the right of the judiciary, is found, at last, to be an assumption of the whole ground in dispute. Granting that the object of the oath is to secure a support of the constitution in the discharge of official duty, its terms may be satisfied by restraining it to official duty in the exercise of the *ordinary* judicial powers. Thus, the constitution may furnish a rule of construction, where a particular interpretation of a law would conflict with some constitutional principle; and such interpretation, where it may, is always to be avoided. But the oath was more probably designed to secure the powers of each of the different branches from being usurped by any of the rest; for instance, to prevent the house of representatives from erecting itself into a court of judicature, or the supreme court from attempting to control the legislature; and in this view, the oath furnishes an argument equally plausible *against* the right of the judiciary. But if it require a support of the constitution in anything beside official duty, it is, in fact, an oath of allegiance to a particular form of government; and considered as such, it is not easy to see, why it should not be taken by the citizens at large, as well as by the officers of the government. It has never been thought, that an officer is under greater restraint as to measures which have for their avowed end a total change of the constitution, than a citizen who has taken no oath at all. The official oath, then, relates only to the official conduct of the officer, and does not prove that he ought to stray from the path of his ordinary business, to search for violations of duty in the business of others; nor does it, as supposed, define the powers of the officer.

"But do not the judges do a *positive* act in violation of the constitution, when they give effect to an unconstitutional law? Not if the law has been passed according to the forms established in the constitution. The fallacy of the question is, in supposing that the judiciary adopts the acts of the legislature as its own; whereas, the enactment of a law and the interpretation of it are not concurrent acts, and as the judiciary is not required to concur in the enactment, neither is it in the breach of the constitution which may be the consequence of the enactment; the fault is imputable to the legislature, and on it the responsibility exclusively rests...."

(2) Abraham Lincoln, First Inaugural Address, March 4, 1861, in 4 Basler, *The Collected Works of Abraham Lincoln* 262, 268 (1953): "I do not forget the position assumed by some, that constitutional questions are to be decided by the Supreme Court; nor do I deny that such decisions must be binding in any case, upon the parties to a suit, as to the object of that suit, while they are also entitled to very high respect and consideration, in all parallel cases by all other departments of the government. And while it is obviously possible that such decision may be erroneous in any given case, still the evil effect following it, being limited to that particular case, with the chance that it may be overruled and never become a precedent for other cases, can better be borne than could the evils of a different practice. At the same time the candid citizen must confess that if the policy of the government upon vital questions affecting the whole people, is to be irrevocably fixed by decisions of the Supreme Court, the instant they are made, in ordinary litigation between parties in personal actions, the people will have ceased, to be their own rulers, having, to that extent, practically resigned their government, into the hands of that eminent tribunal. Nor is there, in this view, any assault upon the court, or the judges. It is a duty, from which they may not shrink, to decide cases properly brought before them; and it is no fault of theirs if others seek to turn their decisions to political purposes."

Consider also the words of President Andrew Jackson in 1832, when he vetoed a bill to continue the Bank of the United States, an institution whose constitutionality was upheld by the Court 13 years earlier in McCulloch v. Maryland, 17 U.S. (4 Wheat.) 316 (1819): "It is maintained by the advocates of the bank that its constitutionality in all its features ought to be considered as settled by precedent and by the decision of the Supreme Court. To this conclusion I can not assent. Mere precedent is a dangerous source of authority, and should not be regarded as deciding questions of constitutional power except where the acquiescence of the people and the States can be considered as well settled.... [Even] [i]f the opinion of the Supreme Court covered the whole ground of this act, it ought not to control the coordinate authorities of this Government. The Congress, the Executive, and the Court must each for itself be guided by its own opinion of the Constitution. Each public officer who takes an oath to support the Constitution swears that he will support it as he understands it, and not as it is understood by others. It is as much the duty of the House of Representatives, of the Senate, and of the President to decide upon the constitutionality of any bill or resolution which may be presented to them for passage or approval as it is of the supreme judges when it may be brought before them for judicial decision...."

(3) In Cooper v. Aaron, 358 U.S. 1, 17 (1958) the Court made the following statements in answer to an argument that the Governor and the Legislature of Arkansas were not bound by the holding of the Court in the case of Brown v. Board of Educ., 347 U.S. 483 (1954):

"It is necessary only to recall some basic constitutional propositions which are settled doctrine.

"Article VI of the Constitution makes the Constitution the 'supreme Law of the Land'. In 1803, Chief Justice Marshall, speaking for a unanimous Court, referring to the Constitution as 'the fundamental and paramount law of the nation,' declared in the notable case of Marbury v. Madison, 1 Cranch 137, 177, that 'It is emphatically the province and duty of the judicial department to say what the law is.' This decision declared the basic principle that the federal judiciary is supreme in the exposition of the law of the Constitution, and that principle has ever since been respected by this Court and the Country as a permanent and indispensable feature of our constitutional system. It follows that the interpretation of the Fourteenth Amendment enunciated by this Court in the *Brown* case is the supreme law of the land, and Art. VI of the Constitution makes it of binding effect on the States 'any Thing in the Constitution or Laws of any State to the Contrary notwithstanding.' "

(4) For more than a century after *Marbury v. Madison,* judicial review of legislation was largely an American phenomenon. The Twentieth Century, particularly the years following World War II, has seen an explosion of the concept both on the national and international levels. A comparison of judicial review in the United States and in Western Europe is particularly instructive. Austria, Italy and Germany have specialized constitutional courts to determine the constitutional validity of legislation. Ordinary courts cannot decide whether laws are constitutional or not, although they can refer those questions for decision to the constitutional courts. This system of "centralized" judicial review is often contrasted with the "decentralized" system represented by *Marbury v. Madison.* Nearly all of the decisions in this volume are by the Supreme Court of the United States, and most attention centers on the function of judicial review as performed by that court. The theory of *Marbury,* however, requires every court, even the most inferior, to decide whether laws are constitutional. Does it also require that executive officials determine whether their official actions are consistent with the Constitution? Compare the view of President Lincoln, in note 2 above, with that of the Court in *Cooper v. Aaron,* note 3. For an analysis and description of judicial review systems outside the United States, see Cappelletti and Cohen, *Comparative Constitutional Law: Cases and Materials* 1–196 (1979).

(5) In 1994, Walter Dellinger, then-Assistant Attorney General heading up the Office of Legal Counsel, authored a memorandum entitled "Presidential Authority to Decline to Execute Unconstitutional Statutes." In it he said that there is "significant judicial approval of [the] proposition" that "there are circumstances in which the President may appropriately decline to enforce a statute that he views as unconstitutional." He also noted, however, that the "Supreme Court plays a special role in resolving disputes about the constitutionality of enactments. As a general matter, if the President believes that the Court would sustain a particular provision as constitutional, the President should execute the statute, notwithstanding his own beliefs about the constitutional issue." Is this blending of the views of Presidents Lincoln and Jackson on the one hand, and of the Court itself in Cooper v. Aaron on the other hand, coherent?

(6) The dispute over the legitimacy of judicial review of legislation has long raged among legal scholars. However, Bator, Meltzer, Mishkin and Shapiro, *Hart and Wechsler's The Federal Courts and the Federal System* 9 (3d ed. 1988) [hereinafter cited as Hart and Wechsler, *Federal Courts* (3d ed. 1988)], after a modern reappraisal of the dispute conclude: "The grant of judicial power was to include the power, where necessary in the decision of cases, to disregard state or federal statutes found to be unconstitutional. Despite the curiously persisting myth of usurpation, the Convention's understanding on this point emerged from its records with singular clarity." See also Wechsler, *Principles, Politics, and Fundamental Law* 4 (1961): "Let me begin by saying that I have not the slightest doubt respecting the legitimacy of judicial review, whether the action called in question in a case which otherwise is proper for adjudication is legislative or executive, federal or state."

(7) One particularly influential observer, Alexander Bickel, identified the crux of the problem as the "counter-majoritarian" quality of judicial review. In

his famous work *The Least Dangerous Branch-The Supreme Court at the Bar of Politics* 16–18 (1962), Bickel observed: "The root difficulty is that judicial review is a counter-majoritarian force in our society. There are various ways of sliding over this ineluctable reality.... Most assuredly, no democracy operates by taking continuous nose counts on the broad range of daily government activities.... Nevertheless, although democracy does not mean constant reconsideration of decisions once made, it does mean that a representative majority has the power to accomplish a reversal [of policy]. This power is of the essence, and no less so because it is often merely held in reserve.... [There is] nothing in the further complexities and perplexities of the system [that] can alter the essential reality that judicial review is a deviant institution in the American democracy." Are there easy answers to the difficulty Bickel identifies? For more discussions of judicial review and the role of the Supreme Court, consult Bickel, *The Supreme Court and the Idea of Progress* (1970); Gunther, *The Subtle Vices of the "Passive Virtues"—A Comment on Principle and Expediency in Judicial Review,* 64 Colum.L.Rev. 1 (1964); Tribe, *American Constitutional Law, Volume 1* (3d ed. 2000); Ely, *Democracy and Distrust: A Theory of Judicial Review* (1980).

Students interested in the general historical background of judicial review should examine, in addition to the works cited above, 1 *Selected Essays on Constitutional Law* 1–173 (1938), hereinafter cited as *Selected Essays* (1938).

SECTION 2.   CONGRESSIONAL CONTROL OF JUDICIAL REVIEW BY THE FEDERAL COURTS

THE SCOPE OF CONGRESSIONAL POWER OVER THE JURISDICTION OF LOWER FEDERAL COURTS

While Article III of the Constitution created the Supreme Court, it deliberately gave Congress the option to create "such inferior Courts as the Congress may from time to time ordain and establish." Since inferior federal courts, in theory, exist at the pleasure of Congress, it has always been clear that Article III does not require that any single lower federal court exercise all, or any particular part, of the judicial power described by that Article. Indeed, the current general jurisdiction of the inferior federal courts in civil cases arising under federal law was not conferred until after the Civil War. What has been an issue, however, is whether all of the judicial power must be lodged somewhere in the federal judicial system—either originally in a lower federal court, or on appeal of state court decisions to the Supreme Court.

Justice Story, in dicta in Martin v. Hunter's Lessee, 14 U.S. (1 Wheat.) 304 (1816), stressed the mandatory language of Article III ("The judicial power of the United States shall be vested...." "The judicial power shall extend....") He concluded that Congress had an obligation to vest the entire judicial power somewhere within the federal judicial system. Later, in his writings, he argued that any contrary conclusion would mean that "the judiciary, as a co-ordinate department of the government, may, at the will of Congress, be annihilated, or stripped of all its important jurisdiction." 2 *Commentaries on the Constitution of the United States* 395 (4th ed. 1873). Story's position was authoritatively rejected in Sheldon v. Sill, 49 U.S. (8 How.) 441 (1850). In upholding a restriction on the diversity jurisdiction, the Court concluded that since Congress had the option to create inferior federal courts it also had the power to create them as courts of limited jurisdiction. "[H]aving a right to prescribe, Congress may withhold from any court of its creation jurisdiction of any of the enumerated controversies. Courts created by statute can have no jurisdiction but such as the statute confers." Id. at 449. Notice that the Supreme Court, which was created by the Constitution, has never had power to review state court decisions on the basis that the parties are of diverse citizenship. The result in Sheldon v. Sill was thus to deny all federal courts a portion of the judicial power. If Congress must create a supreme court, must Congress vest in that Court the judicial power not lodged somewhere else in the federal judicial system?

Ex Parte McCardle

74 U.S. (7 Wall.) 506, 19 L.Ed. 264 (1868).

Appeal from the Circuit Court for the Southern District of Mississippi.

The case was this:

The Constitution of the United States ordains as follows:

"§ 1. The judicial power of the United States shall be vested *in one Supreme Court,* and in such inferior courts as the Congress may from time to time ordain and establish."

"§ 2. The judicial power shall extend to all cases in law or equity arising *under this Constitution, the laws of the United States,*" & c.

And in these last cases the Constitution ordains that,

"The Supreme Court shall have appellate jurisdiction, both as to law and fact, *with such exceptions, and under such regulations, as the Congress shall make.*"

With these constitutional provisions in existence, Congress, on the 5th February, 1867, by "An act to amend an act to establish the judicial courts of the United States, approved September 24, 1789," provided that the several courts of the United States, and the several justices and judges of such courts, within their respective jurisdiction, in addition to the authority already conferred by law, should have power to grant writs of *habeas corpus* in all cases where any person may be restrained of his or her liberty in violation of the Constitution, or of any treaty or law of the United States. And that, from the final decision of any judge, justice, or court inferior to the Circuit Court, appeal might be taken to the Circuit Court of the United States for the district in which the cause was heard, and *from the judgment of the said Circuit Court to the Supreme Court of the United States.*

This statute being in force, one McCardle, alleging unlawful restraint by military force, preferred a petition in the court below, for the writ of *habeas corpus.*

The writ was issued, and a return was made by the military commander, admitting the restraint, but denying that it was unlawful.

It appeared that the petitioner was not in the military service of the United States, but was held in custody by military authority for trial before a military commission, upon charges founded upon the publication of articles alleged to be incendiary and libellous, in a newspaper of which he was editor. The custody was alleged to be under the authority of certain acts of Congress.

Upon the hearing, the petitioner was remanded to the military custody; but, upon his prayer, an appeal was allowed him to this court, and upon filing the usual appeal-bond, for costs, he was admitted to bail upon recognizance, with sureties, conditioned for his future appearance in the Circuit Court, to abide by and perform the final judgment of this court. The appeal was taken under the above-mentioned act of February 5, 1867.

A motion to dismiss this appeal was made at the last term, and, after argument, was denied.

Subsequently, on the 2d, 3d, 4th, and 9th March, the case was argued very thoroughly and ably upon the merits, and was taken under advisement. While it was thus held, and before conference in regard to the decision proper to be made, an act was passed by Congress, returned with objections by the President, and, on the 27th March, repassed by the constitutional majority, the second section of which was as follows:

"*And be it further enacted,* That so much of the act approved February 5, 1867, entitled 'An act to amend an act to establish the judicial courts of the United States, approved September 24, 1789', as authorized an appeal from the judgment of the Circuit Court to the Supreme Court of the United States, or the exercise of any such jurisdiction by said Supreme Court, on appeals which have been, or may hereafter be taken, be, and the same is hereby repealed."

The attention of the court was directed to this statute at the last term, but counsel having expressed a desire to be heard in argument upon its effect, and the Chief Justice being detained from his place here, by his duties in the Court of Impeachment, the cause was continued under advisement. Argument was now heard upon the effect of the repealing act. . . .

The Chief Justice delivered the opinion of the Court.

The first question necessarily is that of jurisdiction; for, if the act of March, 1868, takes away the jurisdiction defined by the act of February, 1867, it is useless, if not improper, to enter into any discussion of other questions.

It is quite true, as was argued by the counsel for the petitioner, that the appellate jurisdiction of this court is not derived from acts of Congress. It is strictly speaking, conferred by the Constitution. But it is conferred "with such exceptions and under such regulations as Congress shall make."

It is unnecessary to consider whether, if Congress had made no exceptions and no regulations, this court might not have exercised general appellate jurisdiction under rules prescribed by itself. For among the earliest acts of the first Congress, at its first session, was the act of September 24th, 1789, to establish the judicial courts of the United States. That act provided for the organization of this court, and prescribed regulations for the exercise of its jurisdiction.

The source of that jurisdiction, and the limitations of it by the Constitution and by statute, have been on several occasions subjects of consideration here. In the case of Durousseau v. The United States [6 Cranch 307 (1810)], particularly, the whole matter was carefully examined, and the court held, that while "the appellate powers of this court are not given by the judicial act, but are given by the Constitution," they are, nevertheless, "limited and regulated by that act, and by such other acts as have been passed on the subject." The court said, further, that the judicial act was an exercise of the power given by the Constitution to Congress "of making exceptions to the appellate jurisdiction of the Supreme Court." "They have described affirmatively," said the court, "its jurisdiction, and this affirmative description has been understood to imply a negation of the exercise of such appellate power as is not comprehended within it."

The principle that the affirmation of appellate jurisdiction implies the negation of all such jurisdiction not affirmed having been thus established, it was an almost necessary consequence that acts of Congress, providing for the exercise of jurisdiction, should come to be spoken of as acts granting jurisdiction, and not as acts making exceptions to the constitutional grant of it.

The exception to appellate jurisdiction in the case before us, however, is not an inference from the affirmation of other appellate jurisdiction. It is made in terms. The provision of the act of 1867, affirming the appellate jurisdiction of this court in cases of *habeas corpus* is expressly repealed. It is hardly possible to imagine a plainer instance of positive exception.

We are not at liberty to inquire into the motives of the legislature. We can only examine into its power under the Constitution; and the power to make exceptions to the appellate jurisdiction of this court is given by express words.

What, then, is the effect of the repealing act upon the case before us? We cannot doubt as to this. Without jurisdiction the court cannot proceed at all in any cause. Jurisdiction is power to declare the law, and when it ceases to exist, the only function remaining to the court is that of announcing the fact and dismissing the cause. And this is not less clear upon authority than upon principle.

. . .

It is quite clear, therefore, that this court cannot proceed to pronounce judgment in this case, for it has no longer jurisdiction of the appeal; and judicial duty is not less fitly performed by declining ungranted jurisdiction than in exercising firmly that which the Constitution and the laws confer.

Counsel seem to have supposed, if effect be given to the repealing act in question, that the whole appellate power of the court, in cases of *habeas corpus,* is denied. But this is an error. The act of 1868 does not except from that jurisdiction any cases but appeals from Circuit Courts under the act of 1867. It does not affect the jurisdiction which was previously exercised.

The appeal of the petitioner in this case must be dismissed for want of jurisdiction.

United States v. Klein, 80 U.S. (13 WALL.) 128 (1871). An 1863 Statute provided for seizure and sale of captured or abandoned property in areas of rebellion, and for payment of the proceeds into the united states treasury. The statute further provided that loyal owners, upon proof that they had not given aid or comfort to the rebellion, could recover those proceeds by suit in the court of claims. In United States v. Padelford, 76 U.S. (9 Wall.) 531 (1870), the statute was construed to permit recovery by a claimant who had not been loyal in fact, but who had been given a presidential pardon. Radical Republicans in Congress were outraged with the Court's decision and promptly passed a statute providing that a Presidential pardon was not proof of loyalty, but was proof that the claimant had given aid to the rebellion. The 1870 statute provided further that, upon proof of a pardon, either in the court of claims or the Supreme Court, "the court shall forthwith dismiss the suit of such claimant." Klein's case was similar to Padelford's. At the time the 1870 Act was passed, the court of claims had given judgment for the claimant, and the government's appeal was pending in the Supreme Court. The government moved in the Supreme Court that Klein's suit be dismissed as required by the act. the court denied the motion, and affirmed the judgment of the court of claims.

Chief Justice Chase's opinion concluded that the 1870 statute was unconstitutional in two respects—in prescribing how a court should decide an issue of fact, and in denying effect to a Presidential pardon. Since the law was unconstitutional, the Court could not constitutionally be required to dismiss Klein's case. "We must think that Congress has inadvertently passed the limit which separates the legislative from the judicial power.... Congress has already provided that the Supreme Court shall have jurisdiction of the judgments of the Court of Claims on appeal. Can it prescribe a rule in conformity with which the court must deny to itself its jurisdiction thus conferred, because and only because the decision, in accordance with settled law, must be adverse to the government and favorable to the suitor?"

THE SCOPE OF CONGRESSIONAL POWER OVER SUPREME COURT JURISDICTION UNDER THE EXCEPTIONS CLAUSE

(1) For full accounts of the background of the *McCardle* case see Fairman, 433–514, and 2 Warren, *Supreme Court in United States History* 464–484 (Rev. ed. 1926).

(2) In his plurality opinion in Glidden v. Zdanok, 370 U.S. 530, 567–568 (1962), Justice Harlan suggested this distinction between the *McCardle* and *Klein* cases: *McCardle* sustained Congressional power to withdraw jurisdiction to proceed with a case then *sub judice; Klein* was an unconstitutional restriction of judicial power because it prescribed an unconstitutional rule of decision in a pending case. (In dissent, Justice Douglas implied that the two cases were inconsistent, and doubted whether the principle of *McCardle* could command a modern majority. Id. at 605, n. 11.) Is it significant that McCardle had lost his case below and Congress directed dismissing his *appeal,* while Klein had won in the court below and Congress directed dismissing his suit? (The Congressional direction to the Supreme Court to dismiss claimants' suits, rather than simply dismiss appeals, was not "inadvertent." Sponsors of the legislation wanted to overturn the results in the cases of claimants who had obtained judgment in the court of claims where the government's appeal was pending in the Supreme Court.)

(3) The *McCardle* case is the only example of a result-oriented restriction on the Supreme Court's appellate jurisdiction sustained by the Supreme Court. Is it significant that it *was* sustained, even as applied to a case which had been argued and submitted for decision? Less than a year after *McCardle,* another newspaper editor in military custody, who had been denied habeas corpus by a lower federal court, successfully invoked the Supreme Court's jurisdiction to issue an "original" writ of habeas corpus under Section 14 of the Judiciary Act of 1789. Ex parte Yerger, 75 U.S. (8 Wall.) 85 (1868). (The government avoided a constitutional test of the powers of military reconstruction governments by releasing Yerger from military custody, mooting the case.) Can the *McCardle* case then be explained as a narrow decision that one route of Supreme Court review can always be closed so long as another remains open? See Van Alstyne, *A Critical Guide to Ex Parte McCardle,* 15 Ariz.L.Rev. 229, 244–254 (1973).

(4) Some proposals to restrict the jurisdiction of inferior federal courts in constitutional cases would leave undisturbed the appellate jurisdiction of the Supreme Court. Does that kind of legislation present lesser constitutional problems than legislation that closes the door to the Supreme Court? Consider, for example, the "Human Life Statute," introduced in 1981 in both the Senate and House of Representatives.[1] Section 2[2] provided:

---

1. 97th Cong., 1st Sess., H.R. 900 (Hyde and Mazzoli) and S. 158 (Helms and D'Amato).

2. Section 1 of the Human Life Statute was a substantive provision attempting to change the result in the Supreme Court's abortion decisions by ordinary legislation.

"Notwithstanding any other provision of law, no inferior Federal court ordained and established by Congress under article III of the Constitution of the United States shall have jurisdiction to issue any restraining order, temporary or permanent injunction, or declaratory judgment in any case involving or arising from any State law or municipal ordinance that (1) protects the rights of human persons between conception and birth, or (2) prohibits, limits, or regulates (a) the performance of abortions, or (b) the provision at public expense of funds, facilities, personnel, or other assistance for the performance of abortions."

Notice that the proposed statute would leave intact the authority of the Supreme Court to review state court decisions, including both abortion convictions and state court actions for injunctions and declaratory judgments. Also undisturbed would be the lower courts' jurisdiction in habeas corpus to review state abortion convictions.

Most troublesome of all are proposals that both deny the lower federal courts' jurisdiction to entertain actions, and the Supreme Court's jurisdiction to review state court decisions, concerning particular constitutional issues. Consider the examples in the next three notes.

(5) The Omnibus Crime Control and Safe Streets Act of 1968 as it was reported to the Senate by the Senate Judiciary Committee contained the following provision which was eliminated on the floor prior to final passage of the bill: "Neither the Supreme Court nor any inferior court ordained and established by Congress under article III of the Constitution of the United States shall have jurisdiction to review or to reverse, vacate, modify, or disturb in any way, a ruling of any trial court of any State in any criminal prosecution admitting in evidence as voluntarily made an admission or confession of an accused if such ruling has been affirmed or otherwise upheld by the highest court of the State having appellate jurisdiction of the cause." See U.S.Code Cong. and Adm.News, 90th Cong.Sec.Sess.1968, p. 2138. This provision was designed to "revise" the holding in Miranda v. Arizona, 384 U.S. 436 (1966). Would it have been constitutional?

(6) In 1962 and 1963, the Court held that prayers and Bible readings in public schools were unconstitutional, whether or not objecting pupils were excused. Engel v. Vitale, 370 U.S. 421 (1962); Abington School Dist. v. Schempp and Murray v. Curlett, 374 U.S. 203 (1963). Public furor created by the decisions led to proposals for constitutional amendments, on which the House Judiciary Committee held hearings in 1964.

On April 9, 1979, the Senate passed, as a rider to a bill on Supreme Court jurisdiction, an amendment originally proposed by Senator Jesse Helms, which would have added the following two new sections to 28 U.S.C.:

§ 1259. Notwithstanding the provisions of sections 1253, 1254 and 1257 of this chapter the Supreme Court shall not have jurisdiction to review, by appeal, writ or certiorari, or otherwise, any case arising out of any State statute ... which relates to voluntary prayers in public school and public buildings.

§ 1364. Notwithstanding any other provision of law, the district courts shall not have jurisdiction of any case or question which the Supreme Court does not have jurisdiction to review under Section 1259....

If the Helms Amendment were to be enacted, and were to be sustained by the federal courts, what would be the impact of the Supreme Court's earlier decisions concerning school prayers when cases were litigated in state courts?

of Appeals, presided over by Judge Spencer Roane,[1] refused to comply with the decision.]

See Warren, *Legislative and Judicial Attacks on the Supreme Court of the United States—A History of the Twenty–Fifth Section of the Judiciary Act,* 47 Am.L.Rev. 1, 3 (1913).

Story, J., delivered the opinion of the court:

This is a writ of error from the Court of Appeals of Virginia, founded upon the refusal of that court to obey the mandate of this court, requiring the judgment rendered in this very cause, at February term, 1813, to be carried into due execution. . . .

The government . . . can claim no powers which are not granted to it by the constitution, and the powers actually granted, must be such as are expressly given, or given by necessary implication. On the other hand, this instrument, like every other grant, is to have a reasonable construction, according to the import of its terms; and where a power is expressly given in general terms, it is not to be restrained to particular cases, unless that construction grow out of the context expressly, or by necessary implication. The words are to be taken in their natural and obvious sense, and not in a sense unreasonably restricted or enlarged. . . .

But, even admitting that the language of the constitution is not mandatory, and that Congress may constitutionally omit to vest the judicial power in courts of the United States, it cannot be denied that when it is vested it may be exercised to the utmost constitutional extent.

This leads us to the consideration of the great question as to the nature and extent of the appellate jurisdiction of the United States. We have already seen that appellate jurisdiction is given by the constitution to the Supreme Court in all cases, where it has not original jurisdiction; subject, however, to such exceptions and regulations as Congress may prescribe. It is, therefore, capable of embracing every case enumerated in the constitution, which is not exclusively to be decided by way of original jurisdiction. But the exercise of appellate jurisdiction is far from being limited by the terms of the constitution to the Supreme Court. There can be no doubt that Congress may create a succession of inferior tribunals, in each of which it may vest appellate as well as original jurisdiction. The judicial power is delegated by the constitution in the most general terms, and may, therefore, be exercised by Congress under every variety of form, of appellate or original jurisdiction. And as there is nothing in the constitution which restrains or limits this power, it must, therefore, in all other cases, subsist in the utmost latitude of which, in its own nature, it is susceptible. . . .

It must, therefore, be conceded that the constitution not only contemplated, but meant to provide for cases within the scope of the judicial power of the United States, which might yet depend before state tribunals. It was foreseen that in the exercise of their ordinary jurisdiction, state courts would incidentally take cognizance of cases arising under the constitution, the laws and treaties of the United States. Yet to all these cases the judicial power, by the very terms of the constitution, is to extend. It cannot extend by original jurisdiction if that was already rightfully and exclusively attached in the state courts, which (as has been already shown) may occur; it must, therefore, extend by appellate

(7) In 2004, the House of Representatives passed two bills that would have stripped all federal courts of jurisdiction over certain federal questions. The first, the so-called Marriage Protection Act, purported to build upon the Defense of Marriage Act (DOMA), 28 U.S.C.§ 1738C, which was passed by Congress and signed into law in 1996. The DOMA attempts to permit each state to refuse to recognize same-sex marriages entered into in other states, notwithstanding the requirement in Article IV of the Constitution that each state give "full faith and credit" to the judgments of other states. The Marriage Protection bill passed by the House was seemingly the result of a fear that federal courts might strike down the DOMA as unconstitutional. The bill provided that: "No court created by Act of Congress shall have any jurisdiction, and the Supreme Court shall have no appellate jurisdiction, to hear or decide any question pertaining to the interpretation of, or the validity under the Constitution of, section 1738C [that is, DOMA] or this section."

The second jurisdiction-stripping bill passed by the House, about two months later, concerned the Pledge of Allegiance. Apparently worried that the federal courts, including the Supreme Court, might invalidate the inclusion of the words "one nation under God" in the Pledge as it is recited in public schools and other public institutions—a question raised, but not decided by the Court, in Elk Grove Unified School Dist. v. Newdow, 124 S.Ct. 2301 (2004)— the House passed a measure that would have deprived all federal courts of any "jurisdiction[] to hear or decide any question pertaining to the interpretation of, or the validity under the Constitution of, the Pledge of Allegiance . . . or its recitation."

(8) For discussion of the limits of Congressional power to control jurisdiction of the lower federal courts, and a summary of the enormous literature on that question, see Gunther, *Congressional Power to Curtail Federal Court Jurisdiction: An Opinionated Guide to an Ongoing Debate,* 36 Stan.L.Rev. 895 (1984); Akhil Amar, *A Neo–Federalist View of Article III: Separating the Two Tiers of Federal Jurisdiction,* 65 B.U.L.Rev. 205 (1985).

---

1. Judge Roane was the chief judicial opponent of Chief Justice Marshall's federalist views. It is commonly thought that if the Office of Chief Justice had been vacant when Thomas Jefferson became President, he would have nominated Roane for the position.

CHAPTER 3

THE JURISDICTION OF FEDERAL COURTS IN CONSTITUTIONAL CASES

Introduction. Judicial review can be understood only in the context of constitutional litigation. Minimum familiarity with jurisdictional boundaries and the special rules devised for constitutional cases is necessary to understanding the substantive doctrines. This chapter is designed to present a brief introduction to a very complicated set of doctrines.

The first two sections deal with the complexities introduced into constitutional litigation by the existence of independent state and federal court systems, each with ultimate responsibility for final interpretation of the law originating in its own level of government and with concurrent jurisdiction to adjudicate disputes in which constitutional questions arise. Section 1 covers Supreme Court jurisdiction to review decisions of state courts. Section 2 deals with constitutional litigation originating in the federal courts. Section 3 considers a variety of related doctrines that govern both Supreme Court review and the conduct of the lower federal courts. Those doctrines concern the definition of "cases" and "controversies" and the extent to which issues of constitutional interpretation are justiciable.

SECTION 1. SUPREME COURT REVIEW OF STATE COURT DECISIONS

A. HISTORY AND STRUCTURE

ARTICLE III OF THE CONSTITUTION AND SECTION 25 OF THE JUDICIARY ACT OF 1789

At the Constitutional Convention, there was general agreement that one major weakness of the central government under the Articles of Confederation was the absence of a central court system. Accordingly, there was little discussion of the question whether there should be a federal judicial system with power to act directly on individuals and member states. Article III extends the federal judicial power to cases, among others, "arising under this Constitution, the Laws of the United States, and Treaties made, or which shall be made, under their Authority."

The major dispute at the Convention concerned the nature of the tribunals that would exercise the federal judicial power. Nationalist proposals provided for mandatory establishment of both a supreme court and inferior trial courts. Competing plans provided only for a supreme court. Notice that both sides of the debate conceded the propriety of appellate review over state court decisions, and that a supreme court should be established by the Constitution itself. The controversy concerned whether appeal of state court decisions to a national supreme court was a sufficient mechanism for insuring national authority and

the uniformity of application of federal laws. The resulting compromise gave Congress the option to provide for lower federal courts.

The First Congress, in 1789, exercised its option to create lower federal courts. Those courts were given exclusive jurisdiction to try federal crimes and concurrent jurisdiction with the state courts in cases in which the United States was the plaintiff. The lower federal courts were not given general jurisdiction in civil cases arising under federal law. (The most important civil jurisdiction of the lower federal courts was in diversity of citizenship and admiralty cases.) For the most part, enforcement of private federal law rights (then quite few) was entrusted to the state courts, which were required to apply federal law over inconsistent state law by the Supremacy Clause of Article VI of the Constitution.

Appellate review of state court decisions was the primary method for enforcing the Supremacy Clause. Section 25 of the Judiciary Act of 1789 provided that "a final judgment or decree in any suit, in the highest court of law or equity of a State in which a decision in the suit could be had" could be "re-examined and reversed or affirmed in the Supreme Court of the United States upon a writ of error," in three classes of cases: (1) "where is drawn in question the validity of a treaty or statute of, or an authority exercised under the United States, and the decision is against their validity"; (2) "where is drawn in question the validity of a statute of, or an authority exercised under any State, on the ground of their being repugnant to the constitution, treaties or laws of the United States, and the decision is in favour of such of their validity"; (3) "where is drawn in question the construction of any clause of the constitution, or of a treaty, or statute of, or commission held under the United States, and the decision is against the title, right, privilege or exemption ... claimed by either party, under such clause of the said Constitution, treaty, statute or commission." Notice that all three provisions limited review to those cases where state courts had rejected claims made under the federal Constitution and laws. State court decisions sustaining those claims were not reviewable. (That remained true until 1914. See p. 51, infra.)

For an extensive review of the history of Article III and the Judiciary Act of 1789, and citation to other authority, see Hart and Wechsler, Federal Courts 1–33 (4th ed. 1996).

Martin v. Hunter's Lessee

14 U.S. (1 Wheat.) 304, 4 L.Ed. 97 (1816).

[In 1816 the jurisdiction of the Supreme Court under Section 25 of the Judiciary Act of 1789 was denied by the highest court of Virginia. The Virginia estates of Lord Fairfax (who died in England in 1781) had descended to a relative, Thomas Martin. Virginia claimed to have acquired the estates in 1777 under state legislation confiscating the property of loyalist British subjects and in 1789 had made a conveyance to David Hunter. Hunter's lessee, claiming under this conveyance, brought an action of ejectment. The Fairfax heirs contended that their rights were supported by the treaties of 1783 and 1794 giving protection to British owned property. After years of negotiation and litigation, the Virginia Court of Appeals sustained Hunter's claim. The Supreme Court of the United States reversed and remanded the case, holding that the treaty of 1794 confirmed the title remaining in the Fairfax heirs. Fairfax's Devisee v. Hunter's Lessee, 11 U.S. (7 Cranch) 603 (1813). The Virginia Court jurisdiction, or not at all. It would seem to follow that the appellate power of the United States must, in such cases, extend to state tribunals; and if in such cases, there is no reason why it should not equally attach upon all others within the purview of the constitution.

It has been argued that such an appellate jurisdiction over state courts is inconsistent with the genius of our governments, and the spirit of the constitution. That the latter was never designed to act upon state sovereignties, but only upon the people, and that if the power exists, it will materially impair the sovereignty of the states, and the independence of their courts. We cannot yield to the force of this reasoning; it assumes principles which we cannot admit, and draws conclusions to which we do not yield our assent.

It is a mistake that the constitution was not designed to operate upon states, in their corporate capacities. It is crowded with provisions which restrain or annul the sovereignty of the states in some of the highest branches of their prerogatives. The tenth section of the first article contains a long list of disabilities and prohibitions imposed upon the states. Surely, when such essential portions of state sovereignty are taken away, or prohibited to be exercised, it cannot be correctly asserted that the constitution does not act upon the states. The language of the constitution is also imperative upon the states as to the performance of many duties. It is imperative upon the state legislatures to make laws prescribing the time, places, and manner of holding elections for senators and representatives, and for electors of President and Vice–President. And in these, as well as some other cases, Congress have a right to revise, amend, or supersede the laws which may be passed by state legislatures. When, therefore, the states are stripped of some of the highest attributes of sovereignty, and the same are given to the United States; when the legislatures of the states are, in some respects, under the control of Congress, and in every case are, under the constitution, bound by the paramount authority of the United States; it is certainly difficult to support the argument that the appellate power over the decisions of state courts is contrary to the genius of our institutions. The courts of the United States can, without question, revise the proceedings of the executive and legislative authorities of the states, and if they are found to be contrary to the constitution, may declare them to be of no legal validity. Surely the exercise of the same right over judicial tribunals is not a higher or more dangerous act of sovereign power.

Nor can such a right be deemed to impair the independence of state judges. . . .

The argument urged from the possibility of the abuse of the revising power is equally unsatisfactory. It is always a doubtful course to argue against the use or existence of a power, from the possibility of its abuse. It is still more difficult, by such an argument, to ingraft upon a general power a restriction which is not to be found in the terms in which it is given. From the very nature of things, the absolute right of decision, in the last resort, must rest somewhere—wherever it may be vested it is susceptible of abuse. In all questions of jurisdiction the inferior, or appellate court, must pronounce the final judgment; and common sense, as well as legal reasoning, has conferred it upon the latter. . . .

This is not all. A motive of another kind, perfectly compatible with the most sincere respect for state tribunals, might induce the grant of appellate power over their decisions. That motive is the importance, and even necessity of uniformity of decisions throughout the whole United States, upon all subjects within the purview of the constitution. Judges of equal learning and integrity, in different states, might differently interpret a statute, or a treaty of the United States, or even the constitution itself. If there were no revising authority to control these jarring and discordant judgments, and harmonize them into uniformity, the laws, the treaties and the constitution of the United States would be different in different states, and might, perhaps, never have precisely the same construction, obligation, or efficacy, in any two states. The public mischiefs that would attend such a state of things would be truly deplorable; and it cannot be believed that they could have escaped the enlightened convention which formed the constitution. What, indeed, might then have been only prophecy, has now become fact; and the appellate jurisdiction must continue to be the only adequate remedy for such evils. . . .

On the whole, the court are of opinion that the appellate power of the United States does extend to cases pending in the state courts; and that the 25th section of the judiciary act, which authorizes the exercise of this jurisdiction in the specified cases, by a writ of error, is supported by the letter and spirit of the constitution. We find no clause in that instrument which limits this power; and we dare not interpose a limitation where the people have not been disposed to create one. . . .

We have thus gone over all the principal questions in the cause, and we deliver our judgment with entire confidence, that it is consistent with the constitution and laws of the land.

We have not thought it incumbent on us to give any opinion upon the question, whether this court have authority to issue a writ of mandamus to the Court of Appeals to enforce the former judgments, as we do not think it necessarily involved in the decision of this cause.

It is the opinion of the whole court that the judgment of the Court of Appeals of Virginia, rendered on the mandate in this cause, be reversed, and the judgment of the District Court, held at Winchester, be, and the same is hereby affirmed.

Johnson, J. It will be observed in this case, that the court disavows all intention to decide on the right to issue compulsory process to the state courts; thus leaving us, in my opinion, where the constitution and laws place us— supreme over persons and cases as far as our judicial powers extend, but not asserting any compulsory control over the state tribunals.

In this view, I acquiesce in their opinion, but not altogether in the reasoning, or opinion, of my brother who delivered it. Few minds are accustomed to the same habit of thinking, and our conclusions are most satisfactory to ourselves when arrived at in our own way. . . .

STATE COURT RESISTANCE TO SUPREME COURT ORDERS

Since Martin v. Hunter's Lessee there have been many instances of state court resistance to Supreme Court orders. For a discussion of some of the episodes and of the varying techniques used to attempt to compel compliance, see Murphy, *Lower Court Checks on Supreme Court Power,* 53 Am.Pol.Sci.Rev. 1017 (1959); Note, *State Court Evasion of United States Supreme Court Mandates,* 56 Yale L.J. 574 (1947); Note, Evasion of Supreme Court Mandates in Cases Remanded to State Courts Since 1941, 67 *Harv.L.Rev. 1251 (1954); Beatty,* State Court Evasion of United States Supreme Court Mandates During the Last Decade of the Warren Court, 6 *Valparaiso L.Rev. 260 (1972).*

THE CURRENT JURISDICTION OF THE SUPREME COURT TO REVIEW STATE COURT DECISIONS

In 1916 and 1925, Congress had provided that the Supreme Court would have discretion, on writ of certiorari, whether or not to review the majority of state cases deciding federal questions. (The practice of the Supreme Court, disclosed to Congress when the 1925 statute was enacted, is that granting certiorari—scheduling a case for oral argument prior to decision on the merits—requires only the vote of four Justices.)

Between 1925 and 1988, (when most of the cases in this book were decided), two categories of state court decisions were subject to obligatory review on appeal—if a state statute was held constitutional, or if a federal statute or treaty was held unconstitutional. In 1988, Congress eliminated these appeals, as well as most appeals from decisions of lower federal courts. The current statute, 28 U.S.C. § 1257, provides in substance for discretionary Supreme Court review of all state court decisions turning on issues of federal law:

> "Final judgments or decrees rendered by the highest court of a State in which a decision could be had may be reviewed by the Supreme Court by writ of certiorari where the validity of a treaty or statute of the United States is drawn in question or where the validity of a statute of any State is drawn in question on the ground of its being repugnant to the Constitution, treaties or laws of the United States, or where any title, right, privilege, or immunity is specially set up or claimed under the Constitution or the treaties or statutes of, or any commission held or authority exercised under, the United States."

The requirement that the state court's decision be "final" has been carried forward from the Judiciary Act of 1789. The Court's current flexible definition of that requirement is discussed in Cox Broadcasting Corp. v. Cohn, 420 U.S. 469, 476–487 (1975). The requirement that the decision be of the highest state court "in which a decision could be had" also stems from the 1789 Judiciary Act. This provision can permit review of the decision of inferior state courts, if further appeals within the state system are not possible. For example, Thompson v. Louisville, 362 U.S. 199 (1960), reviewed the decision of a police court.

B.   ISSUES OF STATE LAW IN THE SUPREME COURT: THE ADEQUATE AND INDEPENDENT STATE GROUND

REVIEW OF ISSUES OF STATE LAW IN CASES INVOLVING FEDERAL QUESTIONS: THE ADEQUATE AND INDEPENDENT STATE GROUND

The Judiciary Act of 1789 contained a proviso expressly limiting Supreme Court review of state court decisions to the federal questions that provided the basis for its jurisdiction. That proviso was repealed in 1867, and does not now appear in 28 U.S.C. § 1257. In a landmark case, the Supreme Court held that repeal of the proviso did not change the basic principle that state court decisions on issues of state law cannot be reviewed by the Supreme Court. Murdock v. Memphis, 87 U.S. (20 Wall.) 590 (1874). State courts are thus the final expositors of the meaning of state law.

Corollary to the finality of state court interpretations of state law is the principle that issues of federal law resolved by state courts will not be reviewed by the Supreme Court if the state court's judgment rests upon an "adequate and independent" state ground. Thus, if a state court rules against a party on two alternative grounds, one federal and one state, the Supreme Court lacks jurisdiction to inquire into the correctness of the federal law ruling. The rationale of the adequate and independent state ground rule has been explained as follows. "Our only power over state judgments is to correct them to the

[handwritten margin note:] state cts are final authority on state decisions

extent that they incorrectly adjudge federal rights. And our power is to correct wrong judgments, not to revise opinions. We are not permitted to render an advisory opinion, and if the same judgment would be rendered by the state court after we corrected its views of Federal laws, our review could amount to nothing more than an advisory opinion." Jackson, J., for the Court in Herb v. Pitcairn, 324 U.S. 117, 125–26 (1945).

The adequate and independent state ground rule has two branches. The first is procedural. It arises when the state court has refused or simply failed to rule on the merits of the federal issues because they were not presented to the state court in the manner required by state procedure. On the one hand, the procedure for raising issues in the state courts—even issues of federal law—is governed by state rules of practice and not by federal law standards. On the other hand, from the beginning the state courts have been important fora for vindication of federal rights and defenses. Complete deference to state court rulings refusing to honor federal claims because of state procedure creates possibilities that federal claims will be difficult to enforce, or that state courts will evade the supremacy of federal law. Justice Holmes said, in a famous dictum: "Whatever springes the State may set for those who are endeavoring to assert rights that the State confers, the assertion of Federal rights, when plainly and reasonably made, is not to be defeated in the name of local practice." Davis v. Wechsler, 263 U.S. 22, 24 (1923).

It is clear that a state court's failure or refusal to decide on federal law issues will not block Supreme Court review if the procedural decision is not "adequate." What is less than clear is the standard for judging the "adequacy" of state procedural grounds. Suppose, for example, that the defendant has been convicted for violating a state criminal statute claimed to violate the United States Constitution. The highest state court has affirmed the conviction, but has refused to decide whether or not the state statute is constitutional because that issue was not raised at the trial, because it was raised too late, because it was raised in improper form, or the like. Can the Supreme Court now review the question whether the statute is constitutional? The Supreme Court's last full-scale discussion of the problem was in Henry v. Mississippi, 379 U.S. 443 (1965). The Court stated that "in every case" it was necessary to inquire whether "enforcement of a procedural forfeiture" served "a legitimate state interest." The *Henry* opinion, however, failed to clarify the standard for judging the adequacy of state procedures. For different assessments of the law prior to *Henry,* and the impact of that decision, see Sandalow, *Henry v. Mississippi and the Adequate State Ground: Proposals for a Revised Doctrine,* 1965 Sup.Ct.Rev. 187 and Hill, *The Inadequate State Ground,* 65 Colum.L.Rev. 943 (1965); Matasar & Bruch, *Procedural Common Law, Federal Jurisdiction Policy, and Abandonment of the Adequate and Independent State Ground Doctrine,* 86 Colum.L.Rev. 1291 (1986). A novel and technical ruling on an issue of state procedure may still be judged inadequate either because it is suspected that the state court is evading decision of the federal issue, or because the rule throws unreasonable obstacles in the way of enforcement of federal rights. Williams v. Georgia, 349 U.S. 375, 399 (1955) (Clark, J., dissenting).

There is more certainty, and more deference to state court decisions, in the second branch of the doctrine—where the state ground is substantive. A common situation is one where the state court has held a state statute to be invalid under both the United States and state constitutions. If the state court is one of stature, its disposition of the federal question may have considerable impact in other courts. The application of the independent and adequate state ground rule in that situation is, nevertheless, clear. There is no realistic inquiry into the adequacy of the state ground. The sole issue is whether the state substantive ground is independent—that is, whether, no matter how the federal issue is resolved, the state ground will be dispositive.[1] Thus a state court decision invalidating a state law on both state and federal constitutional grounds cannot be reviewed by the Supreme Court, even if the bulk of the state court's discussion concerned the United States Constitution.

SUPREME COURT REVIEW OF STATE COURT DECISIONS UPHOLDING CLAIMS OF FEDERAL CONSTITUTIONAL RIGHT

Until 1914, the Supreme Court's authority to review state court decisions was limited to cases that denied claims of federal right. Thus, a state court decision that erroneously decided that a state law violated the United States Constitution could not be reviewed in the United States Supreme Court. The 1914 amendment permitting review of state decisions that sustained federal claims and defenses can be traced to a single case. The New York Court of Appeals held that New York's pioneer workers' compensation law was unconstitutional under the fourteenth amendment, on the ground that the employer's liability without fault was a taking of property without due process of law. *Ives v. South Buffalo Ry. Co.*, 201 N.Y. 271, 94 N.E. 431 (1911). The decision could not be reviewed by the United States Supreme Court, because the state court had upheld the claim of federal constitutional right asserted. The decision, which has been described as "the most famous and most bitterly attacked holding of any American court regarding workmen's compensation," (Dodd, *Administration of Workmen's Compensation* 30 [1936]), led to the enactment of a provision permitting Supreme Court review of state court decisions upholding claims of federal right.

[handwritten margin note: 1914 amendment changed what fed. cts. could review]

It is both ironic and instructive to note that the 1914 amendment would not, in fact, have permitted the United States Supreme Court to review the *Ives* decision. The New York Court of Appeals had also struck down the workers' compensation law as a violation of the New York Constitution—an independent state ground. New York could—and did—amend its State Constitution to authorize enactment of a workers' compensation law. The New York law was sustained by the Supreme Court in New York Central R. Co. v. White, 243 U.S. 188 (1917). For five years, however, proponents of workers' compensation laws throughout the country were confronted with a decision of the most prestigious state court that the basic principle of those laws violated the United States Constitution.

[handwritten margin note: Supreme cts. review of state decisions that hold state laws invalid under the U.S. const.]

Recent years have seen an increase in the number of state court decisions that have relied on parallel state constitutional provisions, precluding Supreme Court review of decisions that state laws violate the United States Constitution. Falk, *The State Constitution: A More Than "Adequate" Non-federal Ground,* 61 Cal.L.Rev. 273 (1973); Howard, *State Courts and Constitutional Rights in the Day of the Burger Court,* 62 Va.L.Rev. 873 (1976). See also Brennan, *State Constitutions and the Protection of Individual Rights,* 90 Harv.L.Rev. 489 (1977). Where state courts have not relied on state grounds, there has been a significant increase in the number of cases reviewed, and reversed, by the Supreme Court because state courts have read the United States Constitution too expansively. Sager, *Fair Measure: The Legal Status of Underenforced Constitutional Norms,* 91 Harv.L.Rev. 1212, 1243–1247 (1978).

---

1. Reliance on the state constitution will not preclude Supreme Court review, for example, if the state's constitution has been construed to adopt the United States Supreme Court's construction of the United States Constitution. In that case, if the state court strikes down the state law, the result is compelled by the state court's interpretation of federal law. See Delaware v. Prouse, 440 U.S. 648 (1979).

Should the Supreme Court be able to review state decisions holding state laws invalid under the United States Constitution, even when the decision is also based on the state constitution? For an argument that an interest in uniformity of interpretation of the Constitution should permit that review in appropriate cases, see Sandalow, *Henry v. Mississippi and the Adequate State Ground: Proposals for a Revised Doctrine,* 1965 Sup.Ct.Rev. 187, 199–203. On the other hand, should the Supreme Court refuse to review state court decisions holding state laws invalid under the United States Constitution, even when the decision is based entirely on the federal ground? For arguments that the state courts should have some leeway to interpret the United States Constitution more expansively than does the Supreme Court, and that review of those decisions is inappropriate or unwise, see Sager, supra, at 1247–1263, and Tribe, *American Constitutional Law,* 31–33 (1978). For a rebuttal to those arguments, see Tribe, *American Constitutional Law, Volume One* 263–264 (3d ed. 2000).

Michigan v. Long

463 U.S. 1032, 103 S.Ct. 3469, 77 L.Ed.2d 1201 (1983).

Justice O'Connor delivered the opinion of the Court.

In Terry v. Ohio, 392 U.S. 1 (1968), we upheld the validity of a protective search for weapons in the absence of probable cause to arrest because it is unreasonable to deny a police officer the right "to neutralize the threat of physical harm," id., at 24, when he possesses an articulable suspicion that an individual is armed and dangerous. We did not, however, expressly address whether such a protective search for weapons could extend to an area beyond the person in the absence of probable cause to arrest. In the present case, respondent David Long was convicted for possession of marijuana found by police in the passenger compartment and trunk of the automobile that he was driving. The police searched the passenger compartment because they had reason to believe that the vehicle contained weapons potentially dangerous to the officers. We hold that the protective search of the passenger compartment was reasonable under the principles articulated in *Terry* and other decisions of this Court. We also examine Long's argument that the decision below rests upon an adequate and independent state ground, and we decide in favor of our jurisdiction.

I

The Barry County Circuit Court denied Long's motion to suppress the marijuana taken from both the interior of the car and its trunk. He was subsequently convicted of possession of marijuana.... The Michigan Supreme Court reversed. The court held that "the sole justification of the *Terry* search, protection of the police officers and others nearby, cannot justify the search in this case." 413 Mich., at 472, 320 N.W.2d, at 869. The marijuana found in Long's trunk was considered by the court below to be the "fruit" of the illegal search of the interior, and was also suppressed.

. . .

II

Before reaching the merits, we must consider Long's argument that we are without jurisdiction to decide this case because the decision below rests on an adequate and independent state ground. The court below referred twice to the

[handwritten margin note: decision rests upon an adequate & independant state ground.]

(7) In 2004, the House of Representatives passed two bills that would have stripped all federal courts of jurisdiction over certain federal questions. The first, the so-called Marriage Protection Act, purported to build upon the Defense of Marriage Act (DOMA), 28 U.S.C.§ 1738C, which was passed by Congress and signed into law in 1996. The DOMA attempts to permit each state to refuse to recognize same-sex marriages entered into in other states, notwithstanding the requirement in Article IV of the Constitution that each state give "full faith and credit" to the judgments of other states. The Marriage Protection bill passed by the House was seemingly the result of a fear that federal courts might strike down the DOMA as unconstitutional. The bill provided that: "No court created by Act of Congress shall have any jurisdiction, and the Supreme Court shall have no appellate jurisdiction, to hear or decide any question pertaining to the interpretation of, or the validity under the Constitution of, section 1738C [that is, DOMA] or this section."

The second jurisdiction-stripping bill passed by the House, about two months later, concerned the Pledge of Allegiance. Apparently worried that the federal courts, including the Supreme Court, might invalidate the inclusion of the words "one nation under God" in the Pledge as it is recited in public schools and other public institutions—a question raised, but not decided by the Court, in Elk Grove Unified School Dist. v. Newdow, 124 S.Ct. 2301 (2004)— the House passed a measure that would have deprived all federal courts of any "jurisdiction[] to hear or decide any question pertaining to the interpretation of, or the validity under the Constitution of, the Pledge of Allegiance . . . or its recitation."

(8) For discussion of the limits of Congressional power to control jurisdiction of the lower federal courts, and a summary of the enormous literature on that question, see Gunther, *Congressional Power to Curtail Federal Court Jurisdiction: An Opinionated Guide to an Ongoing Debate,* 36 Stan.L.Rev. 895 (1984); Akhil Amar, *A Neo–Federalist View of Article III: Separating the Two Tiers of Federal Jurisdiction*, 65 B.U.L.Rev. 205 (1985).

THE JURISDICTION OF FEDERAL COURTS IN CONSTITUTIONAL CASES

Introduction. Judicial review can be understood only in the context of constitutional litigation. Minimum familiarity with jurisdictional boundaries and the special rules devised for constitutional cases is necessary to understanding the substantive doctrines. This chapter is designed to present a brief introduction to a very complicated set of doctrines.

The first two sections deal with the complexities introduced into constitutional litigation by the existence of independent state and federal court systems, each with ultimate responsibility for final interpretation of the law originating in its own level of government and with concurrent jurisdiction to adjudicate disputes in which constitutional questions arise. Section 1 covers Supreme Court jurisdiction to review decisions of state courts. Section 2 deals with constitutional litigation originating in the federal courts. Section 3 considers a variety of related doctrines that govern both Supreme Court review and the conduct of the lower federal courts. Those doctrines concern the definition of "cases" and "controversies" and the extent to which issues of constitutional interpretation are justiciable.

SECTION 1. SUPREME COURT REVIEW OF STATE COURT DECISIONS

A. HISTORY AND STRUCTURE

ARTICLE III OF THE CONSTITUTION AND SECTION 25 OF THE JUDICIARY ACT OF 1789

At the Constitutional Convention, there was general agreement that one major weakness of the central government under the Articles of Confederation was the absence of a central court system. Accordingly, there was little discussion of the question whether there should be a federal judicial system with power to act directly on individuals and member states. Article III extends the federal judicial power to cases, among others, "arising under this Constitution, the Laws of the United States, and Treaties made, or which shall be made, under their Authority."

The major dispute at the Convention concerned the nature of the tribunals that would exercise the federal judicial power. Nationalist proposals provided for mandatory establishment of both a supreme court and inferior trial courts. Competing plans provided only for a supreme court. Notice that both sides of the debate conceded the propriety of appellate review over state court decisions, and that a supreme court should be established by the Constitution itself. The controversy concerned whether appeal of state court decisions to a national supreme court was a sufficient mechanism for insuring national authority and the uniformity of application of federal laws. The resulting compromise gave Congress the option to provide for lower federal courts.

The First Congress, in 1789, exercised its option to create lower federal courts. Those courts were given exclusive jurisdiction to try federal crimes and concurrent jurisdiction with the state courts in cases in which the United States was the plaintiff. The lower federal courts were not given general jurisdiction in civil cases arising under federal law. (The most important civil jurisdiction of the lower federal courts was in diversity of citizenship and admiralty cases.) For the most part, enforcement of private federal law rights (then quite few) was entrusted to the state courts, which were required to apply federal law over inconsistent state law by the Supremacy Clause of Article VI of the Constitution.

Appellate review of state court decisions was the primary method for enforcing the Supremacy Clause. Section 25 of the Judiciary Act of 1789 provided that "a final judgment or decree in any suit, in the highest court of law or equity of a State in which a decision in the suit could be had" could be "re-examined and reversed or affirmed in the Supreme Court of the United States upon a writ of error," in three classes of cases: (1) "where is drawn in question the validity of a treaty or statute of, or an authority exercised under the United States, and the decision is against their validity"; (2) "where is drawn in question the validity of a statute of, or an authority exercised under any State, on the ground of their being repugnant to the constitution, treaties or laws of the United States, and the decision is in favour of such of their validity"; (3) "where is drawn in question the construction of any clause of the constitution, or of a treaty, or statute of, or commission held under the United States, and the decision is against the title, right, privilege or exemption ... claimed by either party, under such clause of the said Constitution, treaty, statute or commission." Notice that all three provisions limited review to those cases where state courts had rejected claims made under the federal Constitution and laws. State court decisions sustaining those claims were not reviewable. (That remained true until 1914. See p. 51, infra.)

For an extensive review of the history of Article III and the Judiciary Act of 1789, and citation to other authority, see Hart and Wechsler, Federal Courts 1–33 (4th ed. 1996).

Martin v. Hunter's Lessee

14 U.S. (1 Wheat.) 304, 4 L.Ed. 97 (1816).

[In 1816 the jurisdiction of the Supreme Court under Section 25 of the Judiciary Act of 1789 was denied by the highest court of Virginia. The Virginia estates of Lord Fairfax (who died in England in 1781) had descended to a relative, Thomas Martin. Virginia claimed to have acquired the estates in 1777 under state legislation confiscating the property of loyalist British subjects and in 1789 had made a conveyance to David Hunter. Hunter's lessee, claiming under this conveyance, brought an action of ejectment. The Fairfax heirs contended that their rights were supported by the treaties of 1783 and 1794 giving protection to British owned property. After years of negotiation and litigation, the Virginia Court of Appeals sustained Hunter's claim. The Supreme Court of the United States reversed and remanded the case, holding that the treaty of 1794 confirmed the title remaining in the Fairfax heirs. Fairfax's Devisee v. Hunter's Lessee, 11 U.S. (7 Cranch) 603 (1813). The Virginia Court of Appeals, presided over by Judge Spencer Roane,[1] refused to comply with the decision.]

See Warren, *Legislative and Judicial Attacks on the Supreme Court of the United States—A History of the Twenty–Fifth Section of the Judiciary Act*, 47 Am.L.Rev. 1, 3 (1913).

Story, J., delivered the opinion of the court:

This is a writ of error from the Court of Appeals of Virginia, founded upon the refusal of that court to obey the mandate of this court, requiring the judgment rendered in this very cause, at February term, 1813, to be carried into due execution. . . .

The government . . . can claim no powers which are not granted to it by the constitution, and the powers actually granted, must be such as are expressly given, or given by necessary implication. On the other hand, this instrument, like every other grant, is to have a reasonable construction, according to the import of its terms; and where a power is expressly given in general terms, it is not to be restrained to particular cases, unless that construction grow out of the context expressly, or by necessary implication. The words are to be taken in their natural and obvious sense, and not in a sense unreasonably restricted or enlarged. . . .

But, even admitting that the language of the constitution is not mandatory, and that Congress may constitutionally omit to vest the judicial power in courts of the United States, it cannot be denied that when it is vested it may be exercised to the utmost constitutional extent.

This leads us to the consideration of the great question as to the nature and extent of the appellate jurisdiction of the United States. We have already seen that appellate jurisdiction is given by the constitution to the Supreme Court in all cases, where it has not original jurisdiction; subject, however, to such exceptions and regulations as Congress may prescribe. It is, therefore, capable of embracing every case enumerated in the constitution, which is not exclusively to be decided by way of original jurisdiction. But the exercise of appellate jurisdiction is far from being limited by the terms of the constitution to the Supreme Court. There can be no doubt that Congress may create a succession of inferior tribunals, in each of which it may vest appellate as well as original jurisdiction. The judicial power is delegated by the constitution in the most general terms, and may, therefore, be exercised by Congress under every variety of form, of appellate or original jurisdiction. And as there is nothing in the constitution which restrains or limits this power, it must, therefore, in all other cases, subsist in the utmost latitude of which, in its own nature, it is susceptible. . . .

It must, therefore, be conceded that the constitution not only contemplated, but meant to provide for cases within the scope of the judicial power of the United States, which might yet depend before state tribunals. It was foreseen that in the exercise of their ordinary jurisdiction, state courts would incidentally take cognizance of cases arising under the constitution, the laws and treaties of the United States. Yet to all these cases the judicial power, by the very terms of the constitution, is to extend. It cannot extend by original jurisdiction if that was already rightfully and exclusively attached in the state courts, which (as has been already shown) may occur; it must, therefore, extend by appellate

---

1. Judge Roane was the chief judicial opponent of Chief Justice Marshall's federalist views. It is commonly thought that if the Office of Chief Justice had been vacant when Thomas Jefferson became President, he would have nominated Roane for the position.

state constitution in its opinion, but otherwise relied exclusively on federal law. Long argues that the Michigan courts have provided greater protection from searches and seizures under the state constitution than is afforded under the Fourth Amendment, and the references to the state constitution therefore establish an adequate and independent ground for the decision below.

It is, of course, "incumbent upon this Court ... to ascertain for itself ... whether the asserted non-federal ground independently and adequately supports the judgment." Abie State Bank v. Bryan, 282 U.S. 765, 773 (1931). Although we have announced a number of principles in order to help us determine whether various forms of references to state law constitute adequate and independent state grounds,[4] we openly admit that we have thus far not developed a satisfying and consistent approach for resolving this vexing issue. In some instances, we have taken the strict view that if the ground of decision was at all unclear, we would dismiss the case.... In other instances, we have vacated, ..., or continued a case, ..., in order to obtain clarification about the nature of a state court decision.... In more recent cases, we have ourselves examined state law to determine whether state courts have used federal law to guide their application of state law or to provide the actual basis for the decision that was reached....

This *ad hoc* method of dealing with cases that involve possible adequate and independent state grounds is antithetical to the doctrinal consistency that is required when sensitive issues of federal-state relations are involved. Moreover, none of the various methods of disposition that we have employed thus far recommends itself as the preferred method that we should apply to the exclusion of others, and we therefore determine that it is appropriate to reexamine our treatment of this jurisdictional issue in order to achieve the consistency that is necessary.

The process of examining state law is unsatisfactory because it requires us to interpret state laws with which we are generally unfamiliar, and which often, as in this case, have not been discussed at length by the parties. Vacation and continuance for clarification have also been unsatisfactory both because of the delay and decrease in efficiency of judicial administration, ... and, more important, because these methods of disposition place significant burdens on state courts to demonstrate the presence or absence of our jurisdiction.... Finally, outright dismissal of cases is clearly not a panacea because it cannot be doubted that there is an important need for uniformity in federal law, and that this need goes unsatisfied when we fail to review an opinion that rests primarily upon federal grounds and where the *independence* of an alleged state ground is not apparent from the four corners of the opinion....

---

4. For example, we have long recognized that "where the judgment of a state court rests upon two grounds one of which is federal and the other non-federal in character, our jurisdiction fails if the non-federal ground is independent of the federal ground and adequate to support the judgment." Fox Film Corp. v. Muller, 296 U.S. 207, 210 (1935). We may review a state case decided on a federal ground even if it is clear that there was an available state ground for decision on which the state court could properly have relied. Beecher v. Alabama, 389 U.S. 35, 37, n. 3 (1967). Also, if, in our view, the state court "felt compelled by what it understood to be federal constitutional considerations to construe ... its own law in the manner that it did," then we will not treat a normally adequate state ground as independent, and there will be no question about our jurisdiction. Delaware v. Prouse, 440 U.S. 648, 653 (1979) (quoting Zacchini v. Scripps–Howard Broadcasting Co., 433 U.S. 562, 568 (1977)). See also South Dakota v. Neville, 459 U.S. 553, 556, n. 5 (1983). Finally, "where the non-federal ground is so interwoven with the [federal ground] as not to be an independent matter, or is not of sufficient breadth to sustain the judgment without any decision of the other, our jurisdiction is plain." Enterprise Irrigation District v. Farmers' Mutual Canal Company, 243 U.S. 157, 164 (1917).

Respect for the independence of state courts, as well as avoidance of rendering advisory opinions, have been the cornerstones of this Court's refusal to decide cases where there is an adequate and independent state ground. It is precisely because of this respect for state courts, and this desire to avoid advisory opinions, that we do not wish to continue to decide issues of state law that go beyond the opinion that we review, or to require state courts to reconsider cases to clarify the grounds of their decisions. Accordingly, when, as in this case, a state court decision fairly appears to rest primarily on federal law, or to be interwoven with the federal law, and when the adequacy and independence of any possible state law ground is not clear from the face of the opinion, we will accept as the most reasonable explanation that the state court decided the case the way it did because it believed that federal law required it to do so. If a state court chooses merely to rely on federal precedents as it would on the precedents of all other jurisdictions, then it need only make clear by a plain statement in its judgment or opinion that the federal cases are being used only for the purpose of guidance, and do not themselves compel the result that the court has reached. In this way, both justice and judicial administration will be greatly improved. If the state court decision indicates clearly and expressly that it is alternatively based on bona fide separate, adequate, and independent grounds, we of course, will not undertake to review the decision.

This approach obviates in most instances the need to examine state law in order to decide the nature of the state court decision, and will at the same time avoid the danger of our rendering advisory opinions. It also avoids the unsatisfactory and intrusive practice of requiring state courts to clarify their decisions to the satisfaction of this Court. We believe that such an approach will provide state judges with a clearer opportunity to develop state jurisprudence unimpeded by federal interference, and yet will preserve the integrity of federal law. . . .

The principle that we will not review judgments of state courts that rest on adequate and independent state grounds is based, in part, on "the limitations of our own jurisdiction." Herb v. Pitcairn, 324 U.S. 117, 125 (1945). The jurisdictional concern is that we not "render an advisory opinion, and if the same judgment would be rendered by the state court after we corrected its views of federal laws, our review could amount to nothing more than an advisory opinion." Id., at 126. Our requirement of a "plain statement" that a decision rests upon adequate and independent state grounds does not in any way authorize the rendering of advisory opinions. Rather, in determining, as we must, whether we have jurisdiction to review a case that is alleged to rest on adequate and independent state grounds, . . . we merely assume that there are no such grounds when it is not clear from the opinion itself that the state court relied upon an adequate and independent state ground and when it fairly appears that the state court rested its decision primarily on federal law.[8]

---

8. . . .

In dissent, Justice Stevens proposes the novel view that this Court should never review a state court decision unless the Court wishes to vindicate a federal right that has been endangered. The rationale of the dissent is not restricted to cases where the decision is arguably supported by adequate and independent state grounds. Rather, Justice Stevens appears to believe that even if the decision below rests exclusively on federal grounds, this Court should not review the decision as long as there is no federal right that is endangered.

The state courts handle the vast bulk of all criminal litigation in this country. . . . The state courts are required to apply federal constitutional standards, and they necessarily create a considerable body of "federal law" in the process. It is not surprising that this Court has become more interested in the application and development of federal law by state courts in the light of the recent significant expansion of federally created standards that we have imposed on the States.

[handwritten margin note:] state cts should just state in opinions that its decision is based on adequate & independant state grounds

Our review of the decision below under this framework leaves us uncon-vinced that it rests upon an independent state ground. Apart from its two citations to the state constitution, the court below relied *exclusively* on its understanding of *Terry* and other federal cases. Not a single state case was cited to support the state court's holding that the search of the passenger compartment was unconstitutional. . . .

[handwritten margin note: no plain statement - not adequate? independant.]

Rather than dismissing the case, or requiring that the state court reconsid-er its decision on our behalf solely because of a mere possibility that an adequate and independent ground supports the judgment, we find that we have jurisdiction in the absence of a plain statement that the decision below rested on an adequate and independent state ground. . . .

IV

. . .

V

The decision of the Michigan Supreme Court is reversed, and the case is remanded for further proceedings not inconsistent with this opinion.

It is so ordered.

Justice Blackmun, concurring in part and concurring in the judgment.

Justice Stevens, dissenting.

The jurisprudential questions presented in this case are far more impor-tant than the question whether the Michigan police officer's search of respon-dent's car violated the Fourth Amendment. The case raises profoundly signifi-cant questions concerning the relationship between two sovereigns—the State of Michigan and the United States of America.

. . .

The nature of the case before us hardly compels a departure from tradition. These are not cases in which an American citizen has been deprived of a right secured by the United States Constitution or a federal statute. Rather, they are cases in which a state court has upheld a citizen's assertion of a right, finding the citizen to be protected under both federal and state law. The complaining party is an officer of the state itself, who asks us to rule that the state court interpreted federal rights too broadly and "overprotected" the citizen.

[handwritten margin note: Dissent compares it to another cauntry]

Such cases should not be of inherent concern to this Court. The reason may be illuminated by assuming that the events underlying this case had arisen in another country, perhaps the Republic of Finland. If the Finnish police had arrested a Finnish citizen for possession of marijuana, and the Finnish courts had turned him loose, no American would have standing to object. If instead they had arrested an American citizen and acquitted him, we might have been concerned about the arrest but we surely could not have complained about the acquittal, even if the Finnish Court had based its decision on its understanding of the United States Constitution. That would be true even if we had a treaty with Finland requiring it to respect the rights of American citizens under the United States Constitution. We would only be motivated to intervene if an American citizen were unfairly arrested, tried, and convicted by the foreign tribunal.

In this case the State of Michigan has arrested one of its citizens and the Michigan Supreme Court has decided to turn him loose. The respondent is a United States citizen as well as a Michigan citizen, but since there is no claim that he has been mistreated by the State of Michigan, the final outcome of the state processes offended no federal interest whatever. Michigan simply provided greater protection to one of its citizens than some other State might provide or, indeed, than this Court might require throughout the country.

I believe that in reviewing the decisions of state courts, the primary role of this Court is to make sure that persons who seek to *vindicate* federal rights have been fairly heard. . . .

Until recently we had virtually no interest in cases of this type. Thirty years ago, this Court reviewed only one. Nevada v. Stacher, 346 U.S. 906 (1953). Indeed, that appears to have been the only case during the entire 1952 Term in which a state even sought review of a decision by its own judiciary. Fifteen years ago, we did not review any such cases, although the total number of requests had mounted to three. Some time during the past decade, perhaps about the time of the 5-to-4 decision in Zacchini v. Scripps–Howard Broadcasting Co., 433 U.S. 562 (1977), our priorities shifted. The result is a docket swollen with requests by states to reverse judgments that their courts have rendered in favor of their citizens. I am confident that a future Court will recognize the error of this allocation of resources. When that day comes, I think it likely that the Court will also reconsider the propriety of today's expansion of our jurisdiction.

The Court offers only one reason for asserting authority over cases such as the one presented today: "an important need for uniformity in federal law [that] goes unsatisfied when we fail to review an opinion that rests primarily upon federal grounds and where the independence of an alleged state ground is not apparent from the four corners of the opinion." Of course, the supposed need to "review an opinion" clashes directly with our oft-repeated reminder that "our power is to correct wrong judgments, not to revise opinions." Herb v. Pitcairn, 324 U.S. 117, 126 (1945). The clash is not merely one of form: the "need for uniformity in federal law" is truly an ungovernable engine. That same need is no less present when it is perfectly clear that a state ground is both independent and adequate. In fact, it is equally present if a state prosecutor announces that he believes a certain policy of nonenforcement is commanded by federal law. Yet we have never claimed jurisdiction to correct such errors, no matter how egregious they may be, and no matter how much they may thwart the desires of the state electorate. We do not sit to expound our understanding of the Constitution to interested listeners in the legal community; we sit to resolve disputes. If it is not apparent that our views would affect the outcome of a particular case, we cannot presume to interfere.

. . .

I respectfully dissent.
. . .[a]

SECTION 2. CONSTITUTIONAL LITIGATION INITIATED IN THE FEDERAL COURTS

Introduction. Justice Black for the Court in Atlantic Coast Line R. Co. v. Brotherhood of Locomotive Engineers, 398 U.S. 281, 285 (1970):

". . . When this Nation was established by the Constitution, each State surrendered only a part of its sovereign power to the national government. But

a. A dissent by Justices Brennan and Marshall was not addressed to the adequate and independent state ground issue.

those powers that were not surrendered were retained by the States and unless a State was restrained by 'the supreme Law of the Land' as expressed in the Constitution, laws, or treaties of the United States, it was free to exercise those retained powers as it saw fit. One of the reserved powers was the maintenance of state judicial systems for the decision of legal controversies. Many of the Framers of the Constitution felt that separate federal courts were unnecessary and that the state courts could be entrusted to protect both state and federal rights. Others felt that a complete system of federal courts to take care of federal legal problems should be provided for in the Constitution itself. This dispute resulted in compromise. One 'supreme Court' was created by the Constitution, and Congress was given the power to create other federal courts. In the first Congress this power was exercised and a system of federal trial and appellate courts with limited jurisdiction was created by the Judiciary Act of 1789, 1 Stat. 73.

Judiciary Act of 1789 – created system of Fed. Cts.

"While the lower federal courts were given certain powers in the 1789 Act, they were not given any power to review directly cases from state courts, and they have not been given such powers since that time. Only the Supreme Court was authorized to review on direct appeal the decisions of state courts. Thus from the beginning we have had in this country two essentially separate legal systems. Each system proceeds independently of the other with ultimate review in this Court of the federal questions raised in either system. Understandably this dual court system was bound to lead to conflicts and frictions. Litigants who foresaw the possibility of more favorable treatment in one or the other system would predictably hasten to invoke the powers of whichever court it was believed would present the best chance of success. Obviously this dual system could not function if state and federal courts were free to fight each other for control of a particular case. Thus, in order to make the dual system work and 'to prevent needless friction between state and federal courts,' ... it was necessary to work out lines of demarcation between the two systems. Some of these limits were spelled out in the 1789 Act. Others have been added by later statutes as well as judicial decisions."

JURISDICTION OF LOWER FEDERAL COURTS TO ENFORCE FEDERAL RIGHTS

Until after the end of the Civil War, state courts, subject to review by the Supreme Court, were entrusted with litigation to enforce the limited number of private federal rights. The immediate post-Civil War period saw not only an explosion in the creation of federal rights against state governments, but a Congressional decision to use the lower federal courts as the primary mechanism for enforcing those rights.

Section 1 of the Civil Rights Act of 1866 created rights for freed slaves, while Section 2 made it a federal crime for persons to deny those rights under color of state law. After ratification of the Fourteenth Amendment, the Civil Rights Acts of 1870 and 1871 created private rights of action for those who were denied federal rights, and provided for jurisdiction in the lower federal courts to enforce those rights. Section 1 of the 1871 Act is the source of two provisions which are central to modern constitutional litigation. Section 1983 of 42 U.S.C. provides a cause of action for deprivations of federal rights:

cause of action for deprivation of federal rights

Every person who, under color of any statute, ordinance, regulation, custom, or usage, of any State or Territory or the District of Columbia, subjects, or causes to be subjected, any citizen of the United States or other person within the jurisdiction thereof to the deprivation of any rights, privileges, or immunities secured by the Constitution and laws, shall be liable to the party injured in an action at law, suit in equity, or other proper proceeding for redress.

The corresponding jurisdictional provision is 28 U.S.C. § 1343(a)(3):

The district courts shall have original jurisdiction of any civil action authorized by law to be commenced by any person:....

(3) to redress the deprivation, under color of any State law, statute, ordinance, regulation, custom or usage, of any right, privilege or immunity secured by the Constitution of the United States or by any Act of Congress providing for equal rights of citizens or of all persons within the jurisdiction of the United States;....

A common form of litigation concerning the constitutionality of state laws is a suit to enjoin the enforcement of those laws, or to obtain a declaratory judgment of their invalidity. Those suits are premised on 42 U.S.C. § 1983. The federal district courts are given jurisdiction over those suits, concurrent with the state courts, by 28 U.S.C. § 1343(3).[1]

No statutory provision, equivalent to 42 U.S.C. § 1983, exists to create an explicit cause of action for denial of constitutional rights by federal officers. The Court has held, however, that the Constitution itself creates a limited cause of action against federal officers. Bivens v. Six Unknown Named Agents of the Fed. Bureau of Narcotics, 403 U.S. 388 (1971).[2] The jurisdictional basis for those suits is 28 U.S.C. § 1331, the general federal question statute, which provides jurisdiction in all cases "arising under the Constitution or laws of the United States." The predecessor of that statute was not enacted until 1875.[3]

Questions of constitutional dimension can, of course, also arise in the course of other cases within the district courts' jurisdiction, such as federal criminal cases and civil cases within the diversity of citizenship jurisdiction, or in the course of review by the courts of appeals of formal orders of federal regulatory agencies. The full complexities surrounding the jurisdiction of feder-

[handwritten margin note: 28 U.S.C § 1343 – gives district cts original jdx on any civil action authorized by law.]

[handwritten margin note: 28 U.S.C § 1331 – jdx in all cases arising under the constitution or laws of the U.S.]

---

1. In 1910, Congress required that a special three–judge court be convened in cases seeking to enjoin the enforcement of state laws on federal constitutional grounds. Direct, and nondiscretionary, review of the decision of those courts was by the Supreme Court. Because of the heavy burdens imposed on the lower federal judiciary, and upon the Supreme Court, the three-judge court requirement was substantially repealed in 1975. (Three-judge courts are still required in cases involving apportionment of congressional districts or state legislatures. 28 U.S.C. § 2284.) Prior to its repeal, the three-judge court was a primary source of United States Supreme Court cases concerning the constitutional validity of state laws. A significant number of the cases in this book reached the Court through that route.

2. In light of the limitations and criticisms of so-called *Bivens* causes of action, might there be an argument for the creation of a statutory right of action against federal officials who violate the Constitution? And might even states enact such statutes, creat-

ing "converse–1983" claims? See Akhil Amar, *"Using State Law to Protect Federal Constitutional Rights: Some Questions and Answers About Converse–1983,"* 64 Colo.L.Rev. 159 (1993); Vikram Amar, *Converse § 1983 Suits in Which States Police Federal Agents: An Idea Whose Time Has Arrived,* 69 Brook. L.Rev. 1369 (2004).

3. A variety of provisions of the Judicial Code (Title 28 of the United States Code) provide for jurisdiction in other cases arising under federal law. Among the more important are, those involving: actions under federal laws regulating commerce (§ 1337); admiralty and maritime cases (§ 1333); bankruptcy cases (§ 1334); internal revenue (§ 1340); patents, copyrights, and trademarks (§ 1338); and actions in which the United States is a party (§§ 1345, 1346). Numerous substantive federal statutes contain their own provisions for federal court jurisdiction. Unlike § 1331, the jurisdiction of the federal district court is exclusive under some of these provisions, and not concurrent with the state courts.

al courts are, of course, beyond the competence of a general course in constitutional law. Students interested in particular federal jurisdictional issues should consult, among other sources, Wright, *Federal Courts* (4th ed. 1983); Hart and Wechsler, *Federal Courts* (4th ed. 1996).

Review of decisions of the federal district courts is by the United States Court of Appeals. 18 U.S.C. § 3731; 28 U.S.C. §§ 1291–1292. Appeals to the courts of appeals are a matter of right. Decisions of the courts of appeals are reviewable in the Supreme Court by certiorari. 28 U.S.C. § 1254(1). The Supreme Court is empowered to review cases filed "in" a court of appeals prior to that court's judgment, and in rare important cases has done so in the interest of expedition. E.g., Youngstown Sheet & Tube Co. v. Sawyer, 343 U.S. 579 (1952), infra p. 393; United States v. Nixon, 418 U.S. 683 (1974), infra p. 453.

SECTION 3. CASES AND CONTROVERSIES AND JUSTICIABILITY

A. IN GENERAL

Introduction. The limitations explored below arose initially from the Court's early rejection of an advisory opinion role for the federal courts and from the theory of *Marbury v. Madison* that judicial review is simply a function of deciding ordinary litigation between adverse parties in which it becomes necessary to determine the constitutional validity of legislation to resolve the disputes.

The doctrines involved in this section are characteristically "soft" in the sense that it is difficult to define the rules with precision and in the sense that they do not appear to be consistent in their application. The imprecision and inconsistency result in part from the fact that these doctrines are used by the Court to regulate the extent of its impact An "activist" Court seeking to expand the application of certain constitutional doctrines is more likely to construe justiciability limitations narrowly in order to reach the merits of cases; a Court interested in "retrenchment and consolidation" is more likely to construe justiciability limitations broadly in order to avoid reaching the merits of cases.

ADVISORY OPINIONS

In 1793 President Washington over the objection of Hamilton, who thought the matter was not within the province of the judiciary, submitted to the Justices 29 questions relating to international law, neutrality, and the construction of the French and British treaties. Secretary of State Jefferson wrote as follows to Chief Justice Jay:

"The war which has taken place among the powers of Europe produces frequent transactions within our ports and limits, on which questions arise of considerable difficulty, and of greater importance to the peace of the United States. These questions depend for their solution on the construction of our treaties, on the laws of nature and nations, and on the law of the land, and are often presented under circumstances which do not give a cognizance of them to the tribunals of the country. Yet their decision is so little analogous to the ordinary functions of the Executive as to occasion much embarrassment and difficulty to them. The President would, therefore, be much relieved if he found himself free to refer questions of this description to the opinions of the Judges of the Supreme Court of the United States, whose knowledge of the subject would secure us as against errors dangerous to the peace of the United States, and their authority ensure the respect of all parties. He has therefore asked the attendance of such of the Judges as could be collected in time for the occasion, to know, in the first place, their opinion, whether the public may, with propriety, be availed of their advice on these questions. And if they may, to present, for their advice, the abstract questions which have already occurred, or may soon occur, from which they will themselves strike out such as any circumstances might, in their opinion, forbid them to pronounce on."

After considering the matter for a few weeks the Justices replied as follows:

"We have considered the previous question stated in a letter written by your direction to us by the Secretary of State, on the 18th of last month regarding the lines of separation, drawn by the Constitution between the three departments of the government. These being in certain respects checks upon each other, and our being Judges of a Court in the last resort, are considerations which afford strong arguments against the propriety of our extra-judicially deciding the questions alluded to, especially as the power given by the Constitution to the President, of calling on the heads of departments for opinions, seems to have been *purposely* as well as expressly united to the *Executive* departments. We exceedingly regret every event that may cause embarrassment to your Administration, but we derive consolation from the reflection that your judgment will discern what is right, and that your usual prudence, decision and firmness will surmount every obstacle to the preservation of the rights, peace, and dignity of the United States."

The Flast v. Cohen Summary

Warren, C.J., for the Court in Flast v. Cohen, 392 U.S. 83, 94–97 (1968):

"The jurisdiction of federal courts is defined and limited by Article III of the Constitution. In terms relevant to the question for decision in this case, the judicial power of federal courts is constitutionally restricted to 'cases' and 'controversies.' As is so often the situation in constitutional adjudication, those two words have an iceberg quality, containing beneath their surface simplicity submerged complexities which go to the very heart of our constitutional form of government. Embodied in the words 'cases' and 'controversies' are two complementary but somewhat different limitations. In part those words limit the business of federal courts to questions presented in an adversary context and in a form historically viewed as capable of resolution through the judicial process. And in part those words define the role assigned to the judiciary in a tripartite allocation of power to assure that the federal courts will not intrude into areas committed to the other branches of government. Justiciability is the term of art employed to give expression to this dual limitation placed upon federal courts by the case and controversy doctrine.

"Justiciability is itself a concept of uncertain meaning and scope. Its reach is illustrated by the various grounds upon which questions sought to be adjudicated in federal courts have been held not to be justiciable. Thus, no justiciable controversy is presented when the parties seek adjudication of only a political question, when the parties are asking for an advisory opinion, when the question sought to be adjudicated has been mooted by subsequent developments, and when there is no standing to maintain the action. Yet it remains true that '[j]usticiability is . . . not a legal concept with a fixed content of susceptible or scientific verification. Its utilization is the resultant of many subtle pressures. . . .' Poe v. Ullman, 367 U.S. 497, 508 (1961).

"Part of the difficulty in giving precise meaning and form to the concept of justiciability stems from the uncertain historical antecedents of the case and controversy doctrine. . . . [I]t is quite clear that 'the oldest and most consistent thread in the federal law of justiciability is that federal courts will not give advisory opinions.' Wright, Federal Courts 34 (1963). Thus, the implicit policies embodied in Article III, and not history alone, impose the rule against advisory opinions on federal courts. When the federal judicial power is invoked to pass upon the validity of actions by the Legislative and Executive Branches of the Government, the rule against advisory opinions implements the separation of powers prescribed by the Constitution and confines federal courts to the role assigned them by Article III. . . . However, the rule against advisory opinions also recognizes that such suits often 'are not pressed before the Court with that clear concreteness provided when a question emerges precisely framed and necessary for decision from a clash of adversary argument exploring every aspect of a multifaced situation embracing conflicting and demanding interests.' United States v. Fruehauf, 365 U.S. 146, 157 (1961). Consequently, the Article III prohibition against advisory opinions reflects the complementary constitutional considerations expressed by the justiciability doctrine: Federal judicial power is limited to those disputes which confine federal courts to a role consistent with a system of separated powers and which are traditionally thought to be capable of resolution through the judicial process.

"Additional uncertainty exists in the doctrine of justiciability because that doctrine has become a blend of constitutional requirements and policy considerations. And a policy limitation is 'not always clearly distinguished from the constitutional limitation.' Barrows v. Jackson, 346 U.S. 249, 255 (1953). For example, in his concurring opinion in Ashwander v. Tennessee Valley Authority, 297 U.S. 288, 345–348 (1936), Mr. Justice Brandeis listed seven rules developed by this Court 'for its own governance' to avoid passing prematurely on constitutional questions. Because the rules operate in 'cases confessedly within [the Court's] jurisdiction,' id., at 346, they find their source in policy, rather than purely constitutional, considerations. However, several of the cases cited by Mr. Justice Brandeis in illustrating the rules of self-governance articulated purely constitutional grounds for decision. See, e.g., Massachusetts v. Mellon, 262 U.S. 447 (1923); Fairchild v. Hughes, 258 U.S. 126 (1922); Chicago & Grand Trunk R. Co. v. Wellman, 143 U.S. 339 (1892). The 'many subtle pressures' which cause policy considerations to blend into the constitutional limitations of Article III make the justiciability doctrine one of uncertain and shifting contours."

JUSTICIABILITY AND THE FORM OF THE LITIGATION— RAISING CONSTITUTIONAL ISSUES

(1) **Raising Constitutional Issues.** How do persons go about getting an adjudication concerning the constitutionality of statutes (or other governmental actions) which affect them? In any individual case one or more of the following methods may be available:

> (1) If the statute is made the basis of claim or defense in a suit between private individuals, the constitutional issue can be litigated. For an important constitutional law case which arose in this manner, see Gibbons v. Ogden, 22 U.S. (9 Wheat.) 1 (1824), set out infra p. 148.

[handwritten margin note: ways to raise constitutional issues:]

(2) If the government (federal or state) brings a civil suit based on the statute, the claim of unconstitutionality can be raised in defense. For a leading constitutional case which arose in this matter, see McCulloch v. Maryland, 17 U.S. (4 Wheat.) 316 (1819), set out infra p. 134.

(3) If the government institutes criminal proceedings based on the statute, unconstitutionality of the statute is a defense. For cases in which important issues of state and federal taxing power were raised in this fashion, see Brown v. Maryland, 25 U.S. (12 Wheat.) 419 (1827); United States v. Kahriger, 345 U.S. 22 (1953).

(4) One damaged by governmental action claimed to be unconstitutional may be able to raise the issue in a suit for damages. For a case where a plaintiff succeeded in such a suit see United States v. Causby, 328 U.S. 256 (1946).

(5) Persons held in official custody may challenge the constitutionality of their detention by writ of habeas corpus (or a statutory substitute for the writ such as 28 U.S.C. § 2255). See, e.g., Fay v. Noia, 372 U.S. 391 (1963).

(6) One may bring a suit seeking an injunction or a declaratory judgment as to the constitutionality of a statute. Frequently such an action is brought in order to challenge constitutionality without taking the risk of civil or criminal liability involved in acting in disregard of the statute. A large portion of constitutional litigation takes this form.

(2) **Relevance of Form of Litigation to Justiciability.** Few issues of justiciability arise where constitutional issues are determined in suits taking the first five forms described above. The litigation involves adverse parties in traditional forms. The constitutional issue is posed in a way quite compatible with the theory of Marbury v. Madison. However, when suits are brought seeking to enjoin the enforcement of statutes on the ground of unconstitutionality or seeking judgments declaring statutes unconstitutional, problems of case and controversy and justiciability frequently arise. The student will notice that most of the cases in this section involve such suits.

B.   Standing

1.   "CONVENTIONAL" STANDING

Warth v. Seldin

422 U.S. 490, 95 S.Ct. 2197, 45 L.Ed.2d 343 (1975).

Mr. Justice Powell delivered the opinion of the Court.

Petitioners, various organizations and individuals resident in the Rochester, New York, metropolitan area, brought this action in the District Court for the Western District of New York against the Town of Penfield, an incorporated municipality adjacent to Rochester, and against members of Penfield's Zoning, Planning, and Town Boards. Petitioners claimed that the town's zoning ordinance, by its terms and as enforced by the defendant board members, respondents here, effectively excluded persons of low and moderate income from living in the town, in contravention of petitioners' First, Ninth, and Fourteenth Amendment rights and in violation of 42 U.S.C. §§ 1981, 1982, and 1983. The District Court dismissed the complaint and denied a motion by petitioner Rochester Home Builders Association, Inc., for leave to intervene as party-plaintiff. The Court of Appeals for the Second Circuit affirmed, holding that none of the plaintiffs, nor Home Builders Association, had standing to prosecute the action. . . .

. . . .

II

We address first the principles of standing relevant to the claims asserted by the several categories of petitioners in this case. In essence the question of standing is whether the litigant is entitled to have the court decide the merits of the dispute or of particular issues. This inquiry involves both constitutional limitations on federal court jurisdiction and prudential limitations on its exercise. . . . In both dimensions it is founded in concern about the proper—and properly limited—role of the courts in a democratic society. . . .

In its constitutional dimension, standing imports justiciability: whether the plaintiff has made out a "case or controversy" between himself and the defendant within the meaning of Art. III. This is the threshold question in every federal case, determining the power of the court to entertain the suit. As an aspect of justiciability, the standing question is whether the plaintiff has "alleged such a personal stake in the outcome of the controversy" as to warrant *his* invocation of federal-court jurisdiction and to justify exercise of the court's remedial powers on his behalf. . . . The Art. III judicial power exists only to redress or otherwise to protect against injury to the complaining party, even though the court's judgment may benefit others collaterally. A federal court's jurisdiction therefore can be invoked only when the plaintiff himself has suffered "some threatened or actual injury resulting from the putatively illegal action. . . ." . . .

Apart from this minimum constitutional mandate, this Court has recognized other limits on the class of persons who may invoke the courts' decisional and remedial powers. First, the Court has held that when the asserted harm is a "generalized grievance" shared in substantially equal measure by all or a large class of citizens, that harm alone normally does not warrant exercise of jurisdiction. . . . Second, even when the plaintiff has alleged injury sufficient to meet the "case or controversy" requirement, this Court has held that the plaintiff generally must assert his own legal rights and interests, and cannot rest his claim to relief on the legal rights or interests of third parties. . . . Without such limitations—closely related to Art. III concerns but essentially matters of judicial self-governance—the courts would be called upon to decide abstract questions of wide public significance even though other governmental institutions may be more competent to address the questions and even though judicial intervention may be unnecessary to protect individual rights. . . .

Although standing in no way depends on the merits of the plaintiff's contention that particular conduct is illegal, . . . it often turns on the nature and source of the claim asserted. The actual or threatened injury required by Art. III may exist solely by virtue of "statutes creating legal rights, the invasion of which creates standing. . . ." . . . Moreover, the source of the plaintiff's claim to relief assumes critical importance with respect to the prudential rules of standing that, apart from Art. III's minimum requirements, serve to limit the role of the courts in resolving public disputes. Essentially, the standing question in such cases is whether the constitutional or statutory provision on which the claim rests properly can be understood as granting persons in the plaintiff's position a right to judicial relief. In some circumstances, countervailing considerations may outweigh the concerns underlying the usual reluctance to exert judicial power when the plaintiff's claim to relief rests on the legal rights of third parties.... In such instances, the Court has found, in effect, that the constitutional or statutory provision in question implies a right of action in the plaintiff.... See generally Part IV, *infra*. Moreover, Congress may grant an express right of action to persons who otherwise would be barred by prudential standing rules. Of course, Art. III's requirement remains: the plaintiff still must allege a distinct and palpable injury to himself, even if it is an injury shared by a large class of other possible litigants.... But so long as this requirement is satisfied, persons to whom Congress has granted a right of action, either expressly or by clear implication, may have standing to seek relief on the basis of the legal rights and interests of others, and, indeed, may invoke the general public interest in support of their claim....

One further preliminary matter requires discussion. For purposes of ruling on a motion to dismiss for want of standing, both the trial and reviewing courts must accept as true all material allegations of the complaint, and must construe the complaint in favor of the complaining party.... At the same time, it is within the trial court's power to allow or to require the plaintiff to supply, by amendment to the complaint or by affidavits, further particularized allegations of fact deemed supportive of plaintiff's standing. If, after this opportunity, the plaintiff's standing does not adequately appear from all materials of record, the complaint must be dismissed.

Dismissed if case has no standing.

III

With these general considerations in mind, we turn first to the claims of petitioners Ortiz, Reyes, Sinkler, and Broadnax, each of whom asserts standing as a person of low or moderate income and, coincidentally, as a member of a minority racial or ethnic group. We must assume, taking the allegations of the complaint as true, that Penfield's zoning ordinance and the pattern of enforcement by respondent officials have had the purpose and effect of excluding persons of low and moderate income, many of whom are members of racial or ethnic minority groups. We also assume, for purposes here, that such intentional exclusionary practices, if proved in a proper case, would be adjudged violative of the constitutional and statutory rights of the persons excluded.

But the fact that these petitioners share attributes common to persons who may have been excluded from residence in the town is an insufficient predicate for the conclusion that petitioners themselves have been excluded, or that the respondents' assertedly illegal actions have violated their rights. Petitioners must allege and show that they personally have been injured, not that injury has been suffered by other, unidentified members of the class to which they belong and which they purport to represent. Unless these petitioners can thus demonstrate the requisite case or controversy between themselves personally and respondents, "none may seek relief on behalf of himself or any other member of the class."

can't bring suit unless they can prove that they personally have been harmed

In their complaint, petitioners Ortiz, Reyes, Sinkler, and Broadnax alleged in conclusory terms that they are among the persons excluded by respondents' actions. None of them has ever resided in Penfield; each claims at least implicitly that he desires, or has desired, to do so. Each asserts, moreover, that he made some effort, at some time, to locate housing in Penfield that was at once within his means and adequate for his family's needs. Each claims that his efforts proved fruitless. We may assume, as petitioners allege, that respondents' actions have contributed, perhaps substantially, to the cost of housing in Penfield. But there remains the question whether petitioners' inability to locate suitable housing in Penfield reasonably can be said to have resulted, in any concretely demonstrable way, from respondents' alleged constitutional and statutory infractions. Petitioners must allege facts from which it reasonably could be inferred that, absent the respondents' restrictive zoning practices, there is a substantial probability that they would have been able to purchase or lease in Penfield and that, if the court affords the relief requested, the asserted inability of petitioners will be removed. . . .

We find the record devoid of the necessary allegations. As the Court of Appeals noted, none of these petitioners has a present interest in any Penfield property; none is himself subject to the ordinance's strictures; and none has ever been denied a variance or permit by respondent officials. Instead, petitioners claim that respondents' enforcement of the ordinance against third parties—developers, builders, and the like—has had the consequence of precluding the construction of housing suitable to their needs at prices they might be able to afford. The fact that the harm to petitioners may have resulted indirectly does not in itself preclude standing. When a governmental prohibition or restriction imposed on one party causes specific harm to a third party, harm that a constitutional provision or statute was intended to prevent, the indirectness of the injury does not necessarily deprive the person harmed of standing to vindicate his rights. E.g., Roe v. Wade, 410 U.S. 113, 124, 147 (1973). But it may make it substantially more difficult to meet the minimum requirement of Art. III: to establish that, in fact, the asserted injury was the consequence of the defendants' actions, or that prospective relief will remove the harm.

Here, by their own admission, realization of petitioners' desire to live in Penfield always has depended on the efforts and willingness of third parties to build low-and moderate-cost housing. The record specifically refers to only two such efforts: that of Penfield Better Homes Corp., in late 1969, to obtain the rezoning of certain land in Penfield to allow the construction of subsidized cooperative townhouses that could be purchased by persons of moderate income; and a similar effort by O'Brien Homes, Inc., in late 1971. But the record is devoid of any indication that these projects, or other like projects, would have satisfied petitioners' needs at prices they could afford, or that, were the court to remove the obstructions attributable to respondents, such relief would benefit petitioners. Indeed, petitioners' descriptions of their individual financial situations and housing needs suggest precisely the contrary—that their inability to reside in Penfield is the consequence of the economics of the area housing market, rather than of respondents' assertedly illegal acts. In short, the facts alleged fail to support an actionable causal relationship between Penfield's zoning practices and petitioners' asserted injury.

In support of their position, petitioners refer to several decisions in the District Courts and Courts of Appeals, acknowledging standing in low-income, minority-group plaintiffs to challenge exclusionary zoning practices. In those cases, however, the plaintiffs challenged zoning restrictions as applied to particular projects that would supply housing within their means, and of which they were intended residents. The plaintiffs thus were able to demonstrate that unless relief from assertedly illegal actions was forthcoming, their immediate and personal interests would be harmed. Petitioners here assert no like circumstances. Instead, they rely on little more than the remote possibility, unsubstantiated by allegations of fact, that their situation might have been better had respondents acted otherwise, and might improve were the court to afford relief.

We hold only that a plaintiff who seeks to challenge exclusionary zoning practices must allege specific, concrete facts demonstrating that the challenged practices harm *him,* and that he personally would benefit in a tangible way from the court's intervention. . . .

IV

Tax-payer Petitioners

The petitioners who assert standing on the basis of their status as taxpayers of the city of Rochester present a different set of problems. These "taxpayer-petitioners" claim that they are suffering economic injury consequent to Penfield's allegedly discriminatory and exclusionary zoning practices. Their argument, in brief, is that Penfield's persistent refusal to allow or to facilitate construction of low-and moderate-cost housing forces the city of Rochester to provide more such housing than it otherwise would do; that to provide such housing, Rochester must allow certain tax abatements; and that as the amount of tax-abated property increases, Rochester taxpayers are forced to assume an increased tax burden in order to finance essential public services.

. . .

. . . In short the claim of these petitioners falls squarely within the prudential standing rule that normally bars litigants from asserting the rights or legal interests of others in order to obtain relief from injury to themselves. As we have observed above, this rule of judicial self-governance is subject to exceptions, the most prominent of which is that Congress may remove it by statute. Here, however, no statute expressly or by clear implication grants a right of action, and thus standing to seek relief, to persons in petitioners' position. In several cases, this Court has allowed standing to litigate the rights of third parties when enforcement of the challenged restriction against the litigant would result indirectly in the violation of third parties' rights. . . . But the taxpayer-petitioners are not themselves subject to Penfield's zoning practices. Nor do they allege that the challenged zoning ordinance and practices preclude or otherwise adversely affect a relationship existing between them and the persons whose rights assertedly are violated. . . . No relationship, other than an incidental congruity of interest, is alleged to exist between the Rochester taxpayers and persons who have been precluded from living in Penfield. Nor do the taxpayer-petitioners show that their prosecution of the suit is necessary to insure protection of the rights asserted, as there is no indication that persons who in fact have been excluded from Penfield are disabled from asserting their own right in a proper case. In sum, we discern no justification for recognizing in the Rochester taxpayers a right of action on the asserted claim.

V

Associations representing members

We turn next to the standing problems presented by the petitioner associations—Metro–Act of Rochester, Inc., one of the original plaintiffs; Housing Council in the Monroe County Area, Inc., which the original plaintiffs sought to join as a party-plaintiff; and Rochester Home Builders Association, Inc., which moved in the District Court for leave to intervene as plaintiff. There is no question that an association may have standing in its own right to seek judicial relief from injury to itself and to vindicate whatever rights and immunities the association itself may enjoy. Moreover, in attempting to secure relief from injury to itself the association may assert the rights of its members, at least so long as the challenged infractions adversely affect its members' associational ties. . . . With the limited exception of Metro–Act, however, none of the associational petitioners here has asserted injury to itself.

Even in the absence of injury to itself, an association may have standing solely as the representative of its members. . . . The possibility of such representational standing, however, does not eliminate or attenuate the constitutional requirement of a case or controversy. . . . The association must allege that its members, or any one of them, are suffering immediate or threatened injury as a result of the challenged action of the sort that would make out a justiciable case had the members themselves brought suit. . . . So long as this can be established, and so long as the nature of the claim and of the relief sought does not make the individual participation of each injured party indispensable to proper resolution of the cause, the association may be an appropriate representative of its members, entitled to invoke the court's jurisdiction.

A

Petitioner Metro–Act's claims to standing on its own behalf as a Rochester taxpayer, and on behalf of its members who are Rochester taxpayers or persons of low or moderate income, are precluded by our holdings in Parts III and IV, supra, as to the individual petitioners, and require no further discussion. Metro–Act . . . alleges . . . that 9% of its membership is composed of present residents of Penfield. It claims that, as a result of the persistent pattern of exclusionary zoning practiced by respondents and the consequent exclusion of persons of low and moderate income, those of its members who are Penfield residents are deprived of the benefits of living in a racially and ethnically integrated community. Referring to our decision in Trafficante v. Metropolitan Life Ins. Co., 409 U.S. 205 (1972), Metro–Act argues that such deprivation is a sufficiently palpable injury to satisfy the Art. III case-or-controversy requirement, and that it has standing as the representative of its members to seek redress.

Metro-Act Petitioner

We agree with the Court of Appeals that *Trafficante* is not controlling here. In that case, two residents of an apartment complex alleged that the owner had discriminated against rental applicants on the basis of race, in violation of § 804 of the Civil Rights Act of 1968 . . . In light of the clear congressional purpose in enacting the 1968 Act, and the broad definition of "person aggrieved" in § 810(a), . . . we held that petitioners, as "person[s] who claim[ed] to have been injured by a discriminatory housing practice," had standing to litigate violations of the Act. We concluded that Congress had given residents of housing facilities covered by the statute an actionable right to be free from the adverse consequences to them of racially discriminatory practices directed at and immediately harmful to others. . . .

Metro–Act does not assert on behalf of its members any right of action under the 1968 Civil Rights Act, nor can the complaint fairly be read to make out any such claim. In this, we think, lies the critical distinction between *Trafficante* and the situation here. As we have observed above, Congress may create a statutory right or entitlement the alleged deprivation of which can confer standing to sue even where the plaintiff would have suffered no judicially cognizable injury in the absence of statute. . . .

. . . [T]heir complaint is that they have been harmed indirectly by the exclusion of others. This is an attempt to raise putative rights of third parties, and none of the exceptions that allow such claims is present here. In these circumstances, we conclude that it is inappropriate to allow Metro–Act to invoke the judicial process.

B

Petitioner Home Builders, in its intervenor-complaint, asserted standing to represent its member firms engaged in the development and construction of residential housing in the Rochester area, including Penfield. . . .

Petitioner Home- Builders

. . .

Home Builders' prayer for prospective relief fails. . . . It can have standing as the representative of its members only if it has alleged facts sufficient to make out a case or controversy had the members themselves brought suit. No such allegations were made. The complaint refers to no specific project of any of its members that is currently precluded either by the ordinance or by respondents' action in enforcing it. There is no averment that any member has applied to respondents for a building permit or a variance with respect to any current project. Indeed, there is no indication that respondents have delayed or thwarted any project currently proposed by Home Builders' members, or that any of its members has taken advantage of the remedial processes available under the ordinance. In short, insofar as the complaint seeks prospective relief, Home Builders has failed to show the existence of any injury to its members of sufficient immediacy and ripeness to warrant judicial intervention.

A like problem is presented with respect to petitioner Housing Council. The affidavit accompanying the motion to join it as plaintiff states that the Council includes in its membership "at least seventeen" groups that have been, are, or will be involved in the development of low and moderate-cost housing. But, with one exception, the complaint does not suggest that any of these groups has focused its efforts on Penfield or has any specific plan to do so. . . . The exception is the Penfield Better Homes Corp. . . . It is . . . possible that in 1969, or within a reasonable time thereafter, Better Homes itself and possibly Housing Council as its representative would have had standing to seek review of respondents' action. The complaint, however, does not allege that the . . . project remained viable in 1972 when this complaint was filed, or that respondents' actions continued to block a then-current construction project. In short, neither the complaint nor the record supplies any basis from which to infer that the controversy between respondents and Better Homes, however vigorous it may once have been, remained a live, concrete dispute when this complaint was filed.

VI

The rules of standing, whether as aspects of the Art. III case-or-controversy requirement or as reflections of prudential considerations defining and limiting the role of the courts, are threshold determinants of the propriety of judicial intervention. It is the responsibility of the complainant clearly to allege facts demonstrating that he is a proper party to invoke judicial resolution of the dispute and the exercise of the court's remedial powers. We agree with the District Court and the Court of Appeals that none of the petitioners here has met this threshold requirement. Accordingly, the judgment of the Court of Appeals is

Affirmed.

Mr. Justice Douglas, dissenting.

. . .

Standing has become a barrier to access to the federal courts, just as "the political question" was in earlier decades. The mounting caseload of federal courts is well known. But cases such as this one reflect festering sores in our society; and the American dream teaches that if one reaches high enough and persists there is a forum where justice is dispensed. I would lower the technical barriers and let the courts serve that ancient need. . . .

. . .

... I would let the case go to trial and have all the facts brought out. Indeed, it would be better practice to decide the question of standing only when the merits have been developed.

I would reverse the Court of Appeals.

Mr. Justice Brennan, with whom Mr. Justice White and Mr. Justice Marshall join, dissenting.

In this case, a wide range of plaintiffs, alleging various kinds of injuries, claimed to have been affected by the Penfield zoning ordinance, on its face and as applied, and by other practices of the defendant officials of Penfield. Alleging that as a result of these laws and practices low-and moderate-income and minority people have been excluded from Penfield, and that this exclusion is unconstitutional, plaintiffs sought injunctive, declaratory, and monetary relief. The Court today, in an opinion that purports to be a "standing" opinion but that actually, I believe, has overtones of outmoded notions of pleading and of justiciability, refuses to find that any of the variously situated plaintiffs can clear numerous hurdles, some constructed here for the first time, necessary to establish "standing." While the Court gives lip service to the principle, oft repeated in recent years, that "standing in no way depends on the merits of the plaintiff's contention that particular conduct is illegal," in fact the opinion, which tosses out of court almost every conceivable kind of plaintiff who could be injured by the activity claimed to be unconstitutional, can be explained only by an indefensible hostility to the claim on the merits. I can appreciate the Court's reluctance to adjudicate the complex and difficult legal questions involved in determining the constitutionality of practices which assertedly limit residence in a particular municipality to those who are white and relatively well off, and I also understand that the merits of this case could involve grave sociological and political ramifications. But courts cannot refuse to hear a case on the merits merely because they would prefer not to, and it is quite clear, when the record is viewed with dispassion, that at least three of the groups of plaintiffs have made allegations, and supported them with affidavits and documentary evidence, sufficient to survive a motion to dismiss for lack of standing.

. . .

II

Low–Income and Minority Plaintiffs

. . .

... [T]he Court's real holding is not that these petitioners have not *alleged* an injury resulting from respondents' action, but that they are not to be allowed to prove one, because "realization of petitioners' desire to live in Penfield always has depended on the efforts and willingness of third parties to build low and moderate-cost housing," and "the record is devoid of any indication that ... [any] projects, would have satisfied petitioners' needs at prices they could afford."

Certainly, this is not the sort of demonstration that can or should be required of petitioners at this preliminary stage. . . .

Here, the very fact that, as the Court stresses, these petitioners' claim rests in part upon proving the intentions and capabilities of third parties to build in Penfield suitable housing which they can afford, coupled with the exclusionary character of the claim on the merits, makes it particularly inappropriate to assume that these petitioners' lack of specificity reflects a fatal weakness in their theory of causation. Obviously they cannot be expected, prior to discovery and trial, to know the future plans of building companies, the precise details of the housing market in Penfield, or everything which has transpired in 15 years of application of the Penfield zoning ordinance, including every housing plan suggested and refused. To require them to allege such facts is to require them to prove their case on paper in order to get into court at all. . .

III

Associations Including Building Concerns

. . .

Again, the Court ignores the thrust of the complaints and asks petitioners to allege the impossible. According to the allegations, the building concerns' experience in the past with Penfield officials has shown any plans for low-and moderate-income housing to be futile for, again according to the allegations, the respondents are engaged in a purposeful, conscious scheme to exclude such housing. Particularly with regard to a low-or moderate-income project, the cost of litigating, with respect to any particular project, the legality of a refusal to approve it may well be prohibitive. And the merits of the exclusion of this or that project is not at the heart of the complaint; the claim is that respondents will not approve *any* project which will provide residences for low and moderate-income people.

When this sort of pattern-and-practice claim is at the heart of the controversy, allegations of past injury, which members of both of these organizations have clearly made, and of a future intent, if the barriers are cleared, again to develop suitable housing for Penfield, should be more than sufficient. The past experiences, if proved at trial, will give credibility and substance to the claim of interest in future building activity in Penfield. These parties, if their allegations are proved, certainly have the requisite personal stake in the outcome of *this* controversy, and the Court's conclusion otherwise is only a conclusion that *this* controversy may not be litigated in a federal court.

I would reverse the judgment of the Court of Appeals.

VILLAGE OF ARLINGTON HEIGHTS v. METROPOLITAN HOUSING DEVELOPMENT CORP., 429 U.S. 252 (1977). Metropolitan Housing Development Corporation (MHDC), a builder of low and moderate income housing in the Chicago area, contracted to purchase a 15–acre site in the Village of Arlington Heights. The contract was contingent upon MHDC securing zoning clearances from the Village and Federal approval to build a 190–unit project with subsidies under § 236 of the National Housing Act. MHDC submitted detailed plans for the project to the Village which refused to rezone the property to permit construction of multiple–family housing. MHDC and three individuals brought suit in the federal district court seeking an injunction and declaratory relief, alleging that the denial was racially discriminatory. The Supreme Court, in an opinion by Justice Powell, held that the plaintiffs had standing, saying in part:

"Clearly MHDC has met the constitutional requirements and it therefore has standing to assert its own rights. Foremost among them is MHDC's right to be free of arbitrary or irrational zoning actions.... [T]he heart of this litigation ... has been the claim that the Village's refusal to rezone discriminates against racial minorities in violation of the Fourteenth Amendment. As a corporation, MHDC has no racial identity and cannot be the direct target of the petitioners' alleged discrimination. In the ordinary case, a party is denied standing to assert the rights of third persons. Warth v. Seldin, 422 U.S., at 499. But we need not decide whether the circumstances of this case would justify departure from that prudential limitation and permit MHDC to assert the constitutional rights of its prospective minority tenants.... For we have at least one individual plaintiff who has demonstrated standing to assert these rights as his own.

"Respondent Ransom, a Negro, works at the Honeywell factory in Arlington Heights and lives approximately 20 miles away in Evanston in a 5–room house with his mother and his son. The complaint alleged that he seeks and would qualify for the housing MHDC wants to build in Arlington Heights. Ransom testified at trial that if Lincoln Green were built he would probably move there, since it is closer to his job.

"The injury Ransom asserts is that his quest for housing nearer his employment has been thwarted by official action that is racially discriminatory. If a court grants the relief he seeks, there is at least a 'substantial probability,' that the Lincoln Green project will materialize, affording Ransom the housing opportunity he desires in Arlington Heights. His is not a generalized grievance. Instead, ... it focuses on a particular project and is not dependent on speculation about the possible actions of third parties not before the court. ... Unlike the individual plaintiffs in *Warth,* Ransom has adequately averred an 'actionable causal relationship' between Arlington Heights' zoning practices and his asserted injury. ... We therefore proceed to the merits."[a]

contrasts standing with Warth

STANDING AND THE REQUIREMENT OF "INJURY IN FACT"

Dicta in Flast v. Cohen, 392 U.S. 83, 102 (1968), stated that to establish standing, plaintiffs must demonstrate not only that they were injured by the challenged legislation but must also show a nexus between that injury and the constitutional violation claimed. The supposed requirement of "nexus" was at issue in Duke Power Co. v. Carolina Environmental Study Group, 438 U.S. 59 (1978). People living near a nuclear power plant under construction brought suit for a declaratory judgment that the Price–Anderson Act was unconstitutional in limiting liability for nuclear accidents in federally licensed private nuclear power plants. The federal district court reached the merits, and held the statute unconstitutional as a violation of the due process clause of the fifth amendment. On direct appeal, the Supreme Court reversed, on the merits.

Duke Power v. CESG

The Court raised on its own motion, and rejected, the argument that plaintiffs lacked standing to challenge the limitation of liability. The "injury in fact" relied upon by the Court to establish standing, however, was not the possibility that the plaintiffs would be denied adequate compensation in the event of a future nuclear accident. Instead, the relevant injury stemmed from the environmental and esthetic harm that would occur to the plaintiffs by the building of the plant. The statute "caused" the injury only because, without the limitation-of-liability provision, nuclear plants would not be built.

The Court concluded that it was not necessary, to establish standing, that plaintiffs' injuries be caused directly by the alleged unconstitutional feature of the statute—the denial of full compensation in the event of nuclear accident. It was enough to show that without the limitation-of-liability provision the proposed plant would not be built and the environmental injury would not occur. The requirement of nexus was limited to standing in taxpayers' suits.[1] In conventional lawsuits, a plaintiff need only demonstrate "injury in fact and a

Requirement of nexus was limited to taxpayer suits other suits just show injury in fact....

---

a. For the decision on the merits, see infra p. 71.

1. The problem of standing in taxpayers' suits is examined below in subsection 3.

substantial likelihood that the judicial relief requested will prevent or redress the claimed injury" in order to establish standing.[2] Plaintiffs had met that standard.[3]

Consider the following cases dealing with the issue whether plaintiffs had shown the requisite injury in fact to establish standing. Are they consistent?[4]

Linda R.S. v. Richard D., 410 U.S. 614 (1973). The mother of a child born out of wedlock brought suit to compel a state prosecutor to prosecute the child's father for non-support. Plaintiff challenged the constitutionality of a state statute making failure to support children a crime because the state courts had construed it to apply only to the parents of children born in marriage. The Supreme Court concluded plaintiff had no standing. Plaintiff had shown injury from the father's failure to pay support, but it was speculative that the relief requested—jailing the father—would remedy the injury by providing support payments from him.

Sierra Club v. Morton, 405 U.S. 727 (1972). The Court held that an environmental group lacked standing to challenge the construction of a recreation area in a national forest. The fact that the Sierra Club—which did not allege that any of its members were affected by the proposed development—had an interest in the problem of maintaining the environment did not confer standing.

United States v. SCRAP, 412 U.S. 669 (1973). An environmental group had standing to challenge a railroad rate structure of the Interstate Commerce Commission claimed to discourage the shipment, and use, of recycled materials and promote the use of raw materials. Plaintiff alleged that its members (five law students): were caused to pay more for finished products; used the forests, rivers, mountains and other natural resources in the vicinity of Washington, D.C. and those recreational uses had been affected by increased littering; breathed the air in the Washington metropolitan area, which had suffered increased air pollution. All of these effects were alleged to be caused by the ICC rate structure which caused the increased use of raw materials and decreased recycling. (In *Sierra Club* the plaintiff had alleged only a "public interest" and not the injury to its members.)

SCRAP, like *Sierra Club,* was an action based on a provision of the Administrative Procedure Act, conferring standing to sue on persons "adversely affected" or "aggrieved" by an agency's decision. The Court concluded that standing, under that provision, was neither confined to those who suffer economic harm nor denied to many people who suffer the same injury. Otherwise, the most injurious and widespread government actions could be questioned by nobody. (On the merits, the Court reversed the lower court's decision enjoining the Commission's rate structure.)

Lujan v. National Wildlife Federation, 497 U.S. 871 (1990). Members of an environmental group were not "adversely affected" or "aggrieved" by Bureau of Land Management policy decisions concerning mining on public lands. Affidavits alleged only that they used unspecified lands "in the vicinity

---

2. As in *Warth v. Seldin,* the Court stated that even when the requisite injury in fact was established, other limits stemming from prudential concerns might apply.

3. For an argument that *Duke Power* was a departure from traditional standards of standing and ripeness, see Varat, *Variable*

Justiciability and the Duke Power Case, 58 Tex.L.Rev. 273 (1980).

4. For an argument that they are not, unless many other factors beyond the issue of "injury in fact" are considered, see Nichol, *Rethinking Standing,* 72 Cal.L.Rev. 68 (1984).

of'' large tracts, on some undetermined portions of which mining might occur because of the challenged actions.

Simon v. Eastern Kentucky Welfare Rights Organization, 426 U.S. 26 (1976). Indigent persons lacked standing to challenge Internal Revenue Service rulings granting favorable tax treatment to nonprofit hospitals providing inadequate hospital services to indigents. Allegations that the rulings "encouraged" hospitals to deny services were speculative. It was just as plausible that the relevant hospitals would forego favorable tax treatment rather than expend substantial funds for increased hospital services to indigents. Thus, plaintiffs' complaint did not demonstrate a substantial likelihood that declaring the rulings invalid would result in their receiving the hospital services they desire.

Allen v. Wright, 468 U.S. 737 (1984). Parents of black children attending public schools did not have standing to challenge IRS practices concerning denial of tax exemptions to racially discriminatory private schools. Plaintiffs' allegations that the IRS practices inhibited the process of desegregation in their children's public schools did not show injury traceable to the challenged government policy. It was speculative whether denial of tax exemption to any private school would induce it to change its policies and whether children would be transferred to public schools if their private schools were threatened with loss of tax exemption.

3rd party causation problem

Lujan v. Defenders of Wildlife, 504 U.S. 555 (1992). The Endangered Species Act of 1973 requires the Secretary of Interior to promulgate a list of endangered species, and requires all federal agencies to insure that any action by them is not likely to threaten their continued existence. The Interior Department issued a regulation interpreting the Act to be inapplicable to projects undertaken outside the United States. Two scientists claimed they would be affected by overseas projects: one had observed in the past, and intended to observe in the future, crocodiles that would be endangered by rehabilitation of the Aswan Dam in Egypt; another had observed in the past, and intended to observe in the future, elephants and leopards endangered by a project in Sri Lanka. Plaintiffs lacked standing because their injury was speculative, since they alleged only that they intended to return to the overseas sites "some day," without specifying a definite date.

Associated General Contractors v. City of Jacksonville, 508 U.S. 656 (1993). Non-minority contractors who alleged that they would have bid on construction work set aside for minority contractors had standing to challenge the requirement that 10% of city contracts be awarded to minority-owned businesses. It was not necessary that plaintiffs allege or prove that they would have been awarded contracts but for the challenged program. In equal protection cases, the injury in fact is not the denial of the benefit itself but the denial of equal treatment imposed by a barrier to obtaining a benefit—here the inability to compete on an equal footing in the bidding process.

United States v. Hays, 515 U.S. 737 (1995). Voters attacking an alleged racial gerrymander lack standing unless they show that they, personally, have been subject to racial discrimination. White voters who neither resided in the challenged predominantly-Black district, nor were excluded from that district because they were White, had only a "generalized grievance" and had not suffered "individualized harm."

Texas v. Lesage, 528 U.S. 18 (1999). An applicant for admission to a graduate program in a state university who challenges an ongoing race-conscious program and seeks forward-looking relief need not establish that he or she would have been admitted to the program if race were not considered.

The relevant injury is "the inability to compete on an equal footing." The rejected applicant's claim for damages, however, is defeated by the university's demonstration that it would have made the same decision absent the alleged discrimination. If the government would have made the same decision regardless, there is no cognizable injury justifying the award of damages.

2.   STANDING TO ASSERT THE RIGHTS OF THIRD PARTIES

Craig v. Boren

429 U.S. 190, 97 S.Ct. 451, 50 L.Ed.2d 397 (1976).

Mr. Justice Brennan delivered the opinion of the Court.

This action was brought in the District Court for the Western District of Oklahoma on December 20, 1972, by appellant Craig, a male then between 18 and 21 years of age, and by appellant Whitener, a licensed vendor of 3.2% beer. The complaint sought declaratory and injunctive relief against enforcement of [statutes prohibiting the sale of 3.2% beer to males under age 21 and females under age 18] on the ground that it constituted invidious discrimination against males 18–20 years of age. A three-judge court convened under 28 U.S.C. § 2281 sustained the constitutionality of the statutory differential and dismissed the action.... We reverse.

I

only vendor has standing

We first address a preliminary question of standing. Appellant Craig attained the age of 21 after we noted probable jurisdiction. Therefore, since only declaratory and injunctive relief against enforcement of the gender-based differential is sought, the controversy has been rendered moot as to Craig. ... The question thus arises whether appellant Whitener, the licensed vendor of 3.2% beer, who has a live controversy against enforcement of the statute, may rely upon the equal protection objections of males 18–20 years of age to establish her claim of unconstitutionality of the age-sex differential. We conclude that she may.

Initially, it should be noted that, despite having had the opportunity to do so, appellees never raised before the District Court any objection to Whitener's reliance upon the claimed unequal treatment of 18–20–year–old males as the premise of her equal protection challenge to Oklahoma's 3.2% beer law. Indeed, at oral argument Oklahoma acknowledged that appellees always "presumed" that the vendor, subject to sanctions and loss of license for violation of the statute, was a proper party in interest to object to the enforcement of the sex-based regulatory provision. While such a concession certainly would not be controlling upon the reach of this Court's constitutional authority to exercise jurisdiction under Art. III, ... our decisions have settled that limitations on a litigant's assertion of *jus tertii* are not constitutionally mandated, but rather stem from a salutary "rule of self-restraint" designed to minimize unwarranted intervention into controversies where the applicable constitutional questions are ill-defined and speculative.... These prudential objectives, thought to be enhanced by restrictions on third-party standing, cannot be furthered here, where the lower court already has entertained the relevant constitutional challenge and the parties have sought—or at least have never resisted—an authoritative constitutional determination. In such circumstances, a decision by us to forgo consideration of the constitutional merits in order to await the initiation of a new challenge to the statute by injured third parties would be impermissibly to foster repetitive and time-consuming litigation under the guise of caution and prudence. Moreover, insofar as the applicable constitutional questions have been and continue to be presented vigorously and "cogently," . . . the denial of *jus tertii* standing in deference to a direct class suit can serve no functional purpose. . . .

In any event, we conclude that appellant Whitener has established independently her claim to assert *jus tertii* standing. The operation of §§ 241 and 245 plainly has inflicted "injury in fact" upon appellant sufficient to guarantee her "concrete adverseness," . . . and to satisfy the constitutionally based standing requirements imposed by Art. III. The legal duties created by the statutory sections under challenge are addressed directly to vendors such as appellant. She is obliged either to heed the statutory discrimination, thereby incurring a direct economic injury through the constriction of her buyers' market, or to disobey the statutory command and suffer, in the words of Oklahoma's Assistant Attorney General, "sanctions and perhaps loss of license." . . .

As a vendor with standing to challenge the lawfulness of §§ 241 and 245, appellant Whitener is entitled to assert those concomitant rights of third parties that would be "diluted or adversely affected" should her constitutional challenge fail and the statutes remain in force. . . . Otherwise, the threatened imposition of governmental sanctions might deter appellant Whitener and other similarly situated vendors from selling 3.2% beer to young males, thereby ensuring that "enforcement of the challenged restriction against the [vendor] would result indirectly in the violation of third parties' rights.". . . . Accordingly, vendors and those in like positions have been uniformly permitted to resist efforts at restricting their operations by acting as advocates of the rights of third parties who seek access to their market or function.

We therefore hold that Whitener has standing to raise relevant equal protection challenges to Oklahoma's gender-based law. We now consider those arguments.

. . .

Mr. Chief Justice Burger, dissenting.

. . .

At the outset I cannot agree that appellant Whitener has standing arising from her status as a saloonkeeper to assert the constitutional rights of her customers. In this Court, "a litigant may only assert his own constitutional rights or immunities." . . . There are a few, but strictly limited exceptions to that rule; despite the most creative efforts, this case fits within none of them.

In sum, permitting a vendor to assert the constitutional rights of vendees whenever those rights are arguably infringed introduces a new concept of constitutional standing to which I cannot subscribe.[a]

. . .

3.   TAXPAYER AND CITIZEN STANDING

TAXPAYER STANDING

In Frothingham v. Mellon, 262 U.S. 447 (1923), a federal taxpayer brought suit challenging the constitutionality of the Maternity Act of 1921, which provided federal funding to states for maternal and infant health care. The

---

a. For the opinions on the merits, see page 759, infra.

Court held that federal taxpayers lacked standing to challenge unconstitutional federal expenditures, because any injury was "remote, fluctuating and uncertain." In Flast v. Cohen, 392 U.S. 83 (1968), the Court upheld taxpayer standing to challenge the expenditure of federal funds in violation of the establishment clause, which was a "specific constitutional limitation" on the taxing and spending powers.

The Court has reaffirmed the principle that federal taxpayers have standing to challenge federal statutes authorizing expenditures alleged to violate the establishment clause. Bowen v. Kendrick, 487 U.S. 589 (1988). However, the Court has consistently denied federal taxpayers standing to raise other constitutional challenges to federal expenditures. In United States v. Richardson, 418 U.S. 166 (1974), taxpayers lacked standing to challenge the statute appropriating funds for the Central Intelligence Agency on the ground that it violated Art. I, § 9, cl. 7 of the Constitution, which requires "a regular statement and account of the receipts and expenditures of all public money." Schlesinger v. Reservists Committee to Stop the War, 418 U.S. 208 (1974), held that taxpayers had no standing to challenge membership of Members of Congress in the military reserve, which was claimed to violate the prohibition of Art. I, § 6, cl. 2, prohibiting Members of Congress to hold "any office under the United States."

The holding in *Flast v. Cohen* was narrowed further in Valley Forge Christian College v. Americans United for Separation of Church and State, Inc., 454 U.S. 464 (1982). Federal taxpayers challenged the constitutionality of a grant of federal land to a religious college, claiming a violation of the establishment clause. The Court noted "the rigor with which the *Flast* exception to the *Frothingham* principle ought to be applied." It held that there was no taxpayer standing, because the legislation authorizing the donation was not an exercise of the taxing and spending power, but of the power under Art. IV, § 3, cl. 2, to make "rules and regulations respecting the ... property belonging to the United States."

Lujan v. Defenders of Wildlife

504 U.S. 555, 112 S.Ct. 2130, 119 L.Ed.2d 351 (1992).

Justice Scalia delivered the opinion of the Court with respect to Parts I, II, III–A, and IV, and an opinion with respect to Part III–B in which The Chief Justice, Justice White, and Justice Thomas join.

This case involves a challenge to a rule promulgated by the Secretary of the Interior interpreting § 7 of the Endangered Species Act of 1973 (ESA), 87 Stat. 892, as amended, 16 U.S.C. § 1536, in such fashion as to render it applicable only to actions within the United States or on the high seas. The preliminary issue, and the only one we reach, is whether the respondents here, plaintiffs below, have standing to seek judicial review of the rule.

I

The ESA ... seeks to protect species of animals against threats to their continuing existence caused by man.... The ESA instructs the Secretary of the Interior to promulgate by regulation a list of those species which are either endangered or threatened under enumerated criteria, and to define the critical habitat of these species.... Section 7(a)(2) of the Act then provides, in pertinent part: "Each Federal agency shall, in consultation with and with the assistance of the Secretary [of the Interior], insure that any action authorized, funded, or carried out by such agency ... is not likely to jeopardize the continued existence of any endangered species or threatened species or result in the destruction or adverse modification of habitat of such species which is determined by the Secretary, after consultation as appropriate with affected States, to be critical." ...

In 1978, the Fish and Wildlife Service (FWS) and the National Marine Fisheries Service (NMFS), on behalf of the Secretary of the Interior and the Secretary of Commerce respectively, promulgated a joint regulation stating that the obligations imposed by § 7(a)(2) extend to actions taken in foreign nations.... The next year, however, the Interior Department began to reexamine its position.... A revised joint regulation, reinterpreting § 7(a)(2) to require consultation only for actions taken in the United States or on the high seas, was proposed in 1983....

Shortly thereafter, respondents, organizations dedicated to wildlife conservation and other environmental causes, filed this action against the Secretary of the Interior, seeking a declaratory judgment that the new regulation is in error as to the geographic scope of § 7(a)(2), and an injunction requiring the Secretary to promulgate a new regulation restoring the initial interpretation.... [T]he Secretary moved for summary judgment on the standing issue, and respondents moved for summary judgment on the merits. The District Court denied the Secretary's motion, ... and ordered the Secretary to publish a revised regulation. The Eighth Circuit affirmed....

. . .

[The court held that two members of the organization who alleged that they intended to observe animals endangered by specific projects had not suffered an "injury in fact."]

IV

The Court of Appeals found that respondents had standing for an additional reason: because they had suffered a "procedural injury." The so-called "citizen-suit" provision of the ESA provides, in pertinent part, that "any person may commence a civil suit on his own behalf (A) to enjoin any person, including the United States and any other governmental instrumentality or agency ... who is alleged to be in violation of any provision of this chapter." 16 U.S.C. § 1540(g). The court held that, because § 7(a)(2) requires interagency consultation, the citizen-suit provision creates a "procedural righ[t]" to consultation in all "persons"—so that anyone can file suit in federal court to challenge the Secretary's (or presumably any other official's) failure to follow the assertedly correct consultative procedure, notwithstanding their inability to allege any discrete injury flowing from that failure. To understand the remarkable nature of this holding one must be clear about what it does not rest upon: This is not a case where plaintiffs are seeking to enforce a procedural requirement the disregard of which could impair a separate concrete interest of theirs (e.g., the procedural requirement for a hearing prior to denial of their license application, or the procedural requirement for an environmental impact statement before a federal facility is constructed next door to them). Nor is it simply a case where concrete injury has been suffered by many persons, as in mass fraud or mass tort situations. Nor, finally, is it the unusual case in which Congress has created a concrete private interest in the outcome of a suit against a private party for the government's benefit, by providing a cash bounty for the victorious plaintiff. Rather, the court held that the injury-in-fact requirement had been satisfied by congressional conferral upon all persons of an abstract, self-contained, noninstrumental "right" to have the Executive observe the procedures required by law. We reject this view.

We have consistently held that a plaintiff raising only a generally available grievance about government—claiming only harm to his and every citizen's interest in proper application of the Constitution and laws, and seeking relief that no more directly and tangibly benefits him than it does the public at large—does not state an Article III case or controversy....

     . . .

     ... In United States v. Richardson, 418 U.S. 166 (1974), we dismissed for lack of standing a taxpayer suit challenging the Government's failure to disclose the expenditures of the Central Intelligence Agency, in alleged violation of the constitutional requirement, Art. I, § 9, cl. 7, that "a regular Statement and Account of the Receipts and Expenditures of all public Money shall be published from time to time." We held that such a suit rested upon an impermissible "generalized grievance," and was inconsistent with "the framework of Article III" because "the impact on [plaintiff] is plainly undifferentiated and common to all members of the public." ... And in Schlesinger v. Reservists Committee to Stop the War, 418 U.S. 208 (1974), we dismissed for the same reasons a citizen-taxpayer suit contending that it was a violation of the Incompatibility Clause, Art. I, § 6, cl. 2, for Members of Congress to hold commissions in the military Reserves. We said that the challenged action, "standing alone, would adversely affect only the generalized interest of all citizens in constitutional governance...." ... Since Schlesinger we have on two occasions held that an injury amounting only to the alleged violation of a right to have the Government act in accordance with law was not judicially cognizable because "assertion of a right to a particular kind of Government conduct, which the Government has violated by acting differently, cannot alone satisfy the requirements of Art. III without draining those requirements of meaning." Allen, 468 U.S., at 754; Valley Forge Christian College v. Americans United for Separation of Church and State, Inc., 454 U.S. 464, 483 (1982). And only two Terms ago, we rejected the notion that Article III permits a citizen-suit to prevent a condemned criminal's execution on the basis of "the ... Eighth Amendment;" once again, "[t]his allegation raise[d] only the generalized interest of all citizens in constitutional governance ... and [was] an inadequate basis on which to grant ... standing." Whitmore, 495 U.S., at 160.

To be sure, our generalized-grievance cases have typically involved Government violation of procedures assertedly ordained by the Constitution rather than the Congress. But there is absolutely no basis for making the Article III inquiry turn on the source of the asserted right. Whether the courts were to act on their own, or at the invitation of Congress, in ignoring the concrete injury requirement described in our cases, they would be discarding a principle fundamental to the separate and distinct constitutional role of the Third Branch—one of the essential elements that identifies those "Cases" and "Controversies" that are the business of the courts rather than of the political branches. "The province of the court," as Chief Justice Marshall said in Marbury v. Madison, 1 Cranch 137, 170 (1803) "is, solely, to decide on the rights of individuals." Vindicating the public interest (including the public interest in government observance of the Constitution and laws) is the function of Congress and the Chief Executive. The question presented here is whether the public interest in proper administration of the laws (specifically, in agencies' observance of a particular, statutorily prescribed procedure) can be converted into an individual right by a statute that denominates it as such, and that permits all citizens (or, for that matter, a subclass of citizens who suffer no distinctive concrete harm) to sue. If the concrete injury requirement has the separation-of-powers significance we have always said, the answer must be obvious: To permit Congress to convert the undifferentiated public interest in executive officers' compliance with the law into an "individual right" vindicable in the courts is to permit Congress to transfer from the President to the courts the Chief Executive's most important constitutional duty, to "take Care that the Laws be faithfully executed," Art. II, § 3. It would enable the courts, with the permission of Congress, "to assume a position of authority over the governmental acts of another and co-equal department," Frothingham v. Mellon, 262 U.S., at 489 ... We have always rejected that vision of our role....

Nothing in this contradicts the principle that "[t]he ... injury required by Art. III may exist solely by virtue of 'statutes creating legal rights, the invasion of which creates standing.' " ... Both of the cases used by *Linda R.S.* as an illustration of that principle involved Congress's elevating to the status of legally cognizable injuries concrete, de facto injuries that were previously inadequate in law (namely, injury to an individual's personal interest in living in a racially integrated community, see Trafficante v. Metropolitan Life Ins. Co., 409 U.S. 205, 208–212 (1972), and injury to a company's interest in marketing its product free from competition, see Hardin v. Kentucky Utilities Co., 390 U.S. 1, 6 (1968)). As we said in *Sierra Club,* "[Statutory] broadening" [of] the categories of injury that may be alleged in support of standing is a different matter from abandoning the requirement that the party seeking review must himself have suffered an injury.... Whether or not the principle set forth in *Warth* can be extended beyond that distinction, it is clear that in suits against the government, at least, the concrete injury requirement must remain.

. . .

We hold that respondents lack standing to bring this action and that the Court of Appeals erred in denying the summary judgment motion filed by the United States. The opinion of the Court of Appeals is hereby reversed, and the cause remanded for proceedings consistent with this opinion.

It is so ordered.[a]

Justice Kennedy, with whom Justice Souter joins, concurring in part and concurring in the judgment.

. . .

I ... join Part IV of the Court's opinion with the following observations. As government programs and policies become more complex and far-reaching, we must be sensitive to the articulation of new rights of action that do not have clear analogs in our common-law tradition. Modern litigation has progressed far from the paradigm of Marbury suing Madison to get his commission, Marbury v. Madison, 1 Cranch 137 (1803), or Ogden seeking an injunction to halt Gibbons' steamboat operations. Gibbons v. Ogden, 9 Wheat. 1 (1824). In my view, Congress has the power to define injuries and articulate chains of causation that will give rise to a case or controversy where none existed before, and I do not read the Court's opinion to suggest a contrary view.... In exercising this power, however, Congress must at the very least identify the injury it seeks to vindicate and relate the injury to the class of persons entitled

a. Justice Scalia's position in *Lujan* was originally propounded in Scalia, *The Doctrine of Standing as an Essential Element of the Separation of Powers*, 17 SUFFOLK U. L. REV. 831 (1983). For a critique, see Sunstein, *What's Standing After Lujan? Of Citizen Suits, "Injuries," and Article III*, 91 MICH. L. REV. 163 (1992).

to bring suit. The citizen-suit provision of the Endangered Species Act does not meet these minimal requirements, because while the statute purports to confer a right on "any person . . . to enjoin . . . the United States and any other governmental instrumentality or agency . . . who is alleged to be in violation of any provision of this chapter," it does not of its own force establish that there is an injury in "any person" by virtue of any "violation." 16 U.S.C. § 1540(g)(1)(A).

The Court's holding that there is an outer limit to the power of Congress to confer rights of action is a direct and necessary consequence of the case and controversy limitations found in Article III. I agree that it would exceed those limitations if, at the behest of Congress and in the absence of any showing of concrete injury, we were to entertain citizen-suits to vindicate the public's nonconcrete interest in the proper administration of the laws. While it does not matter how many persons have been injured by the challenged action, the party bringing suit must show that the action injures him in a concrete and personal way. This requirement is not just an empty formality. It preserves the vitality of the adversarial process by assuring both that the parties before the court have an actual, as opposed to professed, stake in the outcome, and that "the legal questions presented . . . will be resolved, not in the rarefied atmosphere of a debating society, but in a concrete factual context conducive to a realistic appreciation of the consequences of judicial action." . . . In addition, the requirement of concrete injury confines the Judicial Branch to its proper, limited role in the constitutional framework of government.

An independent judiciary is held to account through its open proceedings and its reasoned judgments. In this process it is essential for the public to know what persons or groups are invoking the judicial power, the reasons that they have brought suit, and whether their claims are vindicated or denied. The concrete injury requirement helps assure that there can be an answer to these questions; and, as the Court's opinion is careful to show, that is part of the constitutional design.

. . .

Justice Stevens, concurring in the judgment.

Because I am not persuaded that Congress intended the consultation requirement in § 7(a)(2) of the Endangered Species Act . . . to apply to activities in foreign countries, I concur in the judgment of reversal. I do not, however, agree with the Court's conclusion that respondents lack standing because the threatened injury to their interest in protecting the environment and studying endangered species is not "imminent." . . .

. . .

Justice Blackmun, with whom Justice O'Connor joins, dissenting.

. . . I question the Court's breadth of language in rejecting standing for "procedural" injuries. I fear the Court seeks to impose fresh limitations on the constitutional authority of Congress to allow citizen-suits in the federal courts for injuries deemed "procedural" in nature. I dissent.

. . .

II

The Court concludes that any "procedural injury" suffered by respondents is insufficient to confer standing. It rejects the view that the "injury-in-fact requirement . . . [is] satisfied by congressional conferral upon all persons of an abstract, self-contained, noninstrumental 'right' to have the Executive observe the procedures required by law." ...

Congress legislates in procedural shades of gray not to aggrandize its own power but to allow maximum Executive discretion in the attainment of Congress' legislative goals. Congress could simply impose a substantive prohibition on executive conduct; it could say that no agency action shall result in the loss of more than 5% of any listed species. Instead, Congress sets forth substantive guidelines and allows the Executive, within certain procedural constraints, to decide how best to effectuate the ultimate goal.... The Court never has questioned Congress' authority to impose such procedural constraints on executive power. Just as Congress does not violate separation of powers by structuring the procedural manner in which the Executive shall carry out the laws, surely the federal courts do not violate separation of powers when, at the very instruction and command of Congress, they enforce these procedures.

To prevent Congress from conferring standing for "procedural injuries" is another way of saying that Congress may not delegate to the courts authority deemed "executive" in nature. Here Congress seeks not to delegate "executive" power but only to strengthen the procedures it has legislatively mandated....

Ironically, this Court has previously justified a relaxed review of congressional delegation to the Executive on grounds that Congress, in turn, has subjected the exercise of that power to judicial review.... The Court's intimation today that procedural injuries are not constitutionally cognizable threatens this understanding upon which Congress has undoubtedly relied. In no sense is the Court's suggestion compelled by our "common understanding of what activities are appropriate to legislatures, to executives, and to courts." In my view, it reflects an unseemly solicitude for an expansion of power of the Executive Branch.

. . .

Raines v. Byrd

521 U.S. 811, 117 S.Ct. 2312, 138 L.Ed.2d 849 (1997).

Chief Justice Rehnquist delivered the opinion of the Court.**

The District Court for the District of Columbia declared the Line Item Veto Act unconstitutional. On this direct appeal, we hold that appellees lack standing to bring this suit, and therefore direct that the judgment of the District Court be vacated and the complaint dismissed.

I

The appellees are six Members of Congress, four of whom served as Senators and two of whom served as Congressmen in the 104th Congress (1995–1996). On March 27, 1996, the Senate passed a bill entitled the Line Item Veto Act by a vote of 69–31. All four appellee Senators voted "nay." ... The next day, the House of Representatives passed the identical bill by a vote of 232–177. Both appellee Congressmen voted "nay." ... On April 4, 1996, the President signed the Line Item Veto Act (Act) into law. ... The Act went into effect on January 1, 1997.... The next day, appellees filed a complaint in the District Court for the District of Columbia against the two appellants, the Secretary of the Treasury and the Director of the Office of Management and Budget, alleging that the Act was unconstitutional.

** Justice Ginsburg joins this opinion.

The provisions of the Line Item Veto Act do not use the term "veto." Instead, the President is given the authority to "cancel" certain spending and tax benefit measures after he has signed them into law. ... The President's "cancellation" under the Act takes effect when the "special message" notifying Congress of the cancellation is received in the House and Senate. ... With respect to "new direct spending" items or "limited tax benefit[s]," a cancellation means that the relevant legal provision, legal obligation, or budget authority is "prevent[ed] ... from having legal force or effect." ...

The Act establishes expedited procedures in both Houses for the consideration of "disapproval bills," ... bills or joint resolutions which, if enacted into law by the familiar procedures set out in Article I, § 7 of the Constitution, would render the President's cancellation "null and void,".…

The Act provides that "[a]ny Member of Congress or any individual adversely affected by [this Act] may bring an action, in the United States District Court for the District of Columbia, for declaratory judgment and injunctive relief on the ground that any provision of this part violates the Constitution." ... Appellees brought suit under this provision, claiming that "[t]he Act violates Article I" of the Constitution. Specifically, they alleged that the Act "unconstitutionally expands the President's power," and "violates the requirements of bicameral passage and presentment by granting to the President, acting alone, the authority to 'cancel' and thus repeal provisions of federal law." They alleged that the Act injured them "directly and concretely ... in their official capacities" in three ways: "The Act ... (a) alter[s] the legal and practical effect of all votes they may cast on bills containing such separately vetoable items, (b) divest[s] the [appellees] of their constitutional role in the repeal of legislation, and (c) alter[s] the constitutional balance of powers between the Legislative and Executive Branches, both with respect to measures containing separately vetoable items and with respect to other matters coming before Congress."

... [T]he District Court denied appellants' motion to dismiss, holding that appellees had standing to bring this suit....

. . .

... On the merits, the court held that the Act violated the Presentment Clause, Art. I, § 7, cl. 2, and constituted an unconstitutional delegation of legislative power to the President.

The Act provides for a direct, expedited appeal to this Court. ... We now hold that appellees have no standing to bring this suit, and therefore direct that the judgment of the District Court be vacated and the complaint dismissed.

II

. . .

We have always insisted on strict compliance with this jurisdictional standing requirement.... And our standing inquiry has been especially rigorous when reaching the merits of the dispute would force us to decide whether an action taken by one of the other two branches of the Federal Government was unconstitutional.... In the light of this overriding and time-honored concern about keeping the Judiciary's power within its proper constitutional sphere, we must put aside the natural urge to proceed directly to the merits of this important dispute and to "settle" it for the sake of convenience and efficiency. Instead, we must carefully inquire as to whether appellees have met their burden of establishing that their claimed injury is personal, particularized, concrete, and otherwise judicially cognizable.

III

We have never had occasion to rule on the question of legislative standing presented here. In Powell v. McCormack, 395 U.S. 486, 496, 512–514 (1969), we held that a Member of Congress' constitutional challenge to his exclusion from the House of Representatives (and his consequent loss of salary) presented an Article III case or controversy. But *Powell* does not help appellees. First, appellees have not been singled out for specially unfavorable treatment as opposed to other Members of their respective bodies. Their claim is that the Act causes a type of institutional injury (the diminution of legislative power), which necessarily damages all Members of Congress and both Houses of Congress equally.... Second, appellees do not claim that they have been deprived of something to which they personally are entitled—such as their seats as Members of Congress after their constituents had elected them. Rather, appellees' claim of standing is based on a loss of political power, not loss of any private right, which would make the injury more concrete. Unlike the injury claimed by Congressman Adam Clayton Powell, the injury claimed by the Members of Congress here is not claimed in any private capacity but solely because they are Members of Congress. If one of the Members were to retire tomorrow, he would no longer have a claim; the claim would be possessed by his successor instead. The claimed injury thus runs (in a sense) with the Member's seat, a seat which the Member holds (it may quite arguably be said) as trustee for his constituents, not as a prerogative of personal power....

The one case in which we have upheld standing for legislators (albeit state legislators) claiming an institutional injury is Coleman v. Miller, 307 U.S. 433 (1939). Appellees, relying heavily on this case, claim that they, like the state legislators in *Coleman*, "have a plain, direct and adequate interest in maintaining the effectiveness of their votes," ... sufficient to establish standing. In *Coleman*, 20 of Kansas' 40 State Senators voted not to ratify the proposed "Child Labor Amendment" to the Federal Constitution. With the vote deadlocked 20–20, the amendment ordinarily would not have been ratified. However, the State's Lieutenant Governor, the presiding officer of the State Senate, cast a deciding vote in favor of the amendment, and it was deemed ratified (after the State House of Representatives voted to ratify it). The 20 State Senators who had voted against the amendment, joined by a 21st State Senator and three State House Members, filed an action in the Kansas Supreme Court seeking a writ of mandamus that would compel the appropriate state officials to recognize that the legislature had not in fact ratified the amendment. That court held that the members of the legislature had standing to bring their mandamus action, but ruled against them on the merits....

This Court affirmed. By a vote of 5–4, we held that the members of the legislature had standing. In explaining our holding, we repeatedly emphasized that if these legislators (who were suing as a bloc) were correct on the merits, then their votes not to ratify the amendment were deprived of all validity.... It is obvious, then, that our holding in *Coleman* stands (at most) for the proposition that legislators whose votes would have been sufficient to defeat (or enact) a specific legislative act have standing to sue if that legislative action goes into effect (or does not go into effect), on the ground that their votes have been completely nullified.

It should be equally obvious that appellees' claim does not fall within our holding in *Coleman*, as thus understood. They have not alleged that they voted

[margin handwritten note: govt officials are subject to standing as well.]

[margin handwritten note: Powell v. McCormack]

for a specific bill, that there were sufficient votes to pass the bill, and that the bill was nonetheless deemed defeated. In the vote on the Line Item Veto Act, their votes were given full effect. They simply lost that vote. Nor can they allege that the Act will nullify their votes in the future in the same way that the votes of the *Coleman* legislators had been nullified. In the future, a majority of Senators and Congressman can pass or reject appropriations bills; the Act has no effect on this process. In addition, a majority of Senators and Congressman can vote to repeal the Act, or to exempt a given appropriations bill (or a given provision in an appropriations bill) from the Act; again, the Act has no effect on this process. *Coleman* thus provides little meaningful precedent for appellees' argument.

Nevertheless, appellees rely heavily on our statement in *Coleman* that the Kansas senators had "a plain, direct, and adequate interest in maintaining the effectiveness of their votes." Appellees claim that this statement applies to them because their votes on future appropriations bills (assuming a majority of Congress does not decide to exempt those bills from the Act) will be less "effective" than before, and that the "meaning" and "integrity" of their vote has changed....

[T]heir argument pulls *Coleman* too far from its moorings.... There is a vast difference between the level of vote nullification at issue in *Coleman* and the abstract dilution of institutional legislative power that is alleged here. To uphold standing here would require a drastic extension of *Coleman*. We are unwilling to take that step.

Not only do appellees lack support from precedent, but historical practice appears to cut against them as well. It is evident from several episodes in our history that in analogous confrontations between one or both Houses of Congress and the Executive Branch, no suit was brought on the basis of claimed injury to official authority or power. The Tenure of Office Act, passed by Congress over the veto of President Andrew Johnson in 1867, was a thorn in the side of succeeding Presidents until it was finally repealed at the behest of President Grover Cleveland in 1887.... It provided that an official whose appointment to an Executive Branch office required confirmation by the Senate could not be removed without the consent of the Senate.... In 1868, Johnson removed his Secretary of War, Edwin M. Stanton. Within a week, the House of Representatives impeached Johnson.... One of the principal charges against him was that his removal of Stanton violated the Tenure of Office Act.... At the conclusion of his trial before the Senate, Johnson was acquitted by one vote.... Surely Johnson had a stronger claim of diminution of his official power as a result of the Tenure of Office Act than do the appellees in the present case. Indeed, if their claim were sustained, it would appear that President Johnson would have had standing to challenge the Tenure of Office Act before he ever thought about firing a cabinet member, simply on the grounds that it altered the calculus by which he would nominate someone to his cabinet. Yet if the federal courts had entertained an action to adjudicate the constitutionality of the Tenure of Office Act immediately after its passage in 1867, they would have been improperly and unnecessarily plunged into the bitter political battle being waged between the President and Congress.

... A sort of mini-Tenure of Office Act covering only the Post Office Department had been enacted in 1872, ... and it remained on the books after the Tenure of Office Act's repeal in 1887. In the last days of the Woodrow Wilson administration, Albert Burleson, Wilson's Postmaster General, came to believe that Frank Myers, the Postmaster in Portland, Oregon, had committed fraud in the course of his official duties. When Myers refused to resign,

Burleson, acting at the direction of the President, removed him. Myers sued in the Court of Claims to recover lost salary. In Myers v. United States, 272 U.S. 52 (1926), more than half a century after Johnson's impeachment, this Court held that Congress could not require senatorial consent to the removal of a Postmaster who had been appointed by the President with the consent of the Senate. . . . In the course of its opinion, the Court expressed the view that the original Tenure of Office Act was unconstitutional. . . .

If the appellees in the present case have standing, presumably President Wilson . . . would . . . have had standing, and could have challenged the law preventing the removal of a presidential appointee without the consent of Congress. Similarly, in INS v. Chadha, 462 U.S. 919 (1983), the Attorney General would have had standing to challenge the one-House veto provision because it rendered his authority provisional rather than final. By parity of reasoning, President Gerald Ford could have sued to challenge the appointment provisions of the Federal Election Campaign Act which were struck down in Buckley v. Valeo, 424 U.S. 1 (1976), and a Member of Congress could have challenged the validity of President Coolidge's pocket veto that was sustained in The Pocket Veto Case, 279 U.S. 655 (1929).

There would be nothing irrational about a system which granted standing in these cases; some European constitutional courts operate under one or another variant of such a regime. . . . But it is obviously not the regime that has obtained under our Constitution to date. Our regime contemplates a more restricted role for Article III courts. . . .

IV

In sum, appellees have alleged no injury to themselves as individuals (contra *Powell*), the institutional injury they allege is wholly abstract and widely dispersed (contra *Coleman*), and their attempt to litigate this dispute at this time and in this form is contrary to historical experience. We attach some importance to the fact that appellees have not been authorized to represent their respective Houses of Congress in this action, and indeed both Houses actively oppose their suit. We also note that our conclusion neither deprives Members of Congress of an adequate remedy (since they may repeal the Act or exempt appropriations bills from its reach), nor forecloses the Act from constitutional challenge (by someone who suffers judicially cognizable injury as a result of the Act). Whether the case would be different if any of these circumstances were different we need not now decide.

We therefore hold that these individual members of Congress do not have a sufficient "personal stake" in this dispute and have not alleged a sufficiently concrete injury to have established Article III standing. The judgment of the District Court is vacated, and the case is remanded with instructions to dismiss the complaint for lack of jurisdiction.

It is so ordered.

Justice Souter, concurring in the judgment, with whom Justice Ginsburg joins, concurring.

. . .

Because it is fairly debatable whether appellees' injury is sufficiently personal and concrete to give them standing, it behooves us to resolve the question under more general separation-of-powers principles underlying our standing requirements. . . . [R]espect for the separation of powers requires the Judicial Branch to exercise restraint in deciding constitutional issues by resolving those implicating the powers of the three branches of Government as a "last resort,".... The counsel of restraint in this case begins with the fact that a dispute involving only officials, and the official interests of those, who serve in the branches of the National Government lies far from the model of the traditional common-law cause of action at the conceptual core of the case-or-controversy requirement....

While it is true that a suit challenging the constitutionality of this Act brought by a party from outside the Federal Government would also involve the Court in resolving the dispute over the allocation of power between the political branches, it would expose the Judicial Branch to a lesser risk. Deciding a suit to vindicate an interest outside the Government raises no specter of judicial readiness to enlist on one side of a political tug-of-war, since "the propriety of such action by a federal court has been recognized since Marbury v. Madison...." And just as the presence of a party beyond the Government places the Judiciary at some remove from the political forces, the need to await injury to such a plaintiff allows the courts some greater separation in the time between the political resolution and the judicial review....

The virtue of waiting for a private suit is only confirmed by the certainty that another suit can come to us.... While the Court has declined to lower standing requirements simply because no one would otherwise be able to litigate a claim, ... the certainty of a plaintiff who obviously would have standing to bring a suit to court after the politics had at least subsided from a full boil is a good reason to resolve doubts about standing against the plaintiff invoking an official interest....

I therefore conclude that appellees' alleged injuries are insufficiently personal and concrete to satisfy Article III standing requirements of personal and concrete harm. Since this would be so in any suit under the conditions here, I accordingly find no cognizable injury to appellees.

Justice Stevens, dissenting.

The Line Item Veto Act purports to establish a procedure for the creation of laws that are truncated versions of bills that have been passed by the Congress and presented to the President for signature. If the procedure were valid, it would deny every Senator and every Representative any opportunity to vote for or against the truncated measure that survives the exercise of the President's cancellation authority. Because the opportunity to cast such votes is a right guaranteed by the text of the Constitution, I think it clear that the persons who are deprived of that right by the Act have standing to challenge its constitutionality. Moreover, because the impairment of that constitutional right has an immediate impact on their official powers, in my judgment they need not wait until after the President has exercised his cancellation authority to bring suit. Finally, the same reason that the respondents have standing provides a sufficient basis for concluding that the statute is unconstitutional.

. . .

Justice Breyer, dissenting.

. . .

I concede that there would be no case or controversy here were the dispute before us not truly adversary, or were it not concrete and focused. But the interests that the parties assert are genuine and opposing, and the parties are therefore truly adverse....

Nonetheless, there remains a serious constitutional difficulty due to the fact that this dispute about lawmaking procedures arises between government officials and is brought by legislators. The critical question is whether or not this dispute, for that reason, is so different in form from those "matters that were the traditional concern of the courts at Westminster" that it falls outside the scope of Article III's judicial power.... Justice Frankfurter explained this argument in his dissent in *Coleman*, saying that courts traditionally "leave intra-parliamentary controversies to parliaments and outside the scrutiny of law courts...." Justice Frankfurter dissented because, in his view, the "political" nature of the case, which involved legislators, placed the dispute outside the scope of Article III's "case" or "controversy" requirement. Nonetheless, the *Coleman* court rejected his argument.

Although the majority today attempts to distinguish *Coleman*, I do not believe that Justice Frankfurter's argument or variations on its theme can carry the day here. First, as previously mentioned, the jurisdictional statute before us eliminates all but constitutional considerations, and the circumstances mentioned above remove all but the "political" or "intragovernmental" aspect of the constitutional issue.

Second, the Constitution does not draw an absolute line between disputes involving a "personal" harm and those involving an "official" harm.... *Coleman* itself involved injuries in the plaintiff legislators' official capacity. And the majority in this case, suggesting that legislators might have standing to complain of rules that "denied" them "their vote ... in a discriminatory manner," concedes at least the possibility that any constitutional rule distinguishing "official" from "personal" injury is not absolute.

Third, Justice Frankfurter's views were dissenting views, and the dispute before us, when compared to *Coleman*, presents a much stronger claim, not a weaker claim, for constitutional justiciability. The lawmakers in *Coleman* complained of a lawmaking procedure that, at worst, improperly counted Kansas as having ratified one proposed constitutional amendment, which had been ratified by only 5 other States, and rejected by 26, making it unlikely that it would ever become law.... The lawmakers in this case complain of a lawmaking procedure that threatens the validity of many laws (for example, all appropriations laws) that Congress regularly and frequently enacts. The systematic nature of the harm immediately affects the legislators' ability to do their jobs. The harms here are more serious, more pervasive, and more immediate than the harm at issue in *Coleman*....

.   .   .

In sum, I do not believe that the Court can find this case nonjusticiable without overruling *Coleman*. Since it does not do so, I need not decide whether the systematic nature, seriousness, and immediacy of the harm would make this dispute constitutionally justiciable even in *Coleman*'s absence. Rather, I can and would find this case justiciable on *Coleman*'s authority. I add that because the majority has decided that this dispute is not now justiciable and has expressed no view on the merits of the appeal, I shall not discuss the merits either, but reserve them for future argument.

FEDERAL ELECTION COMMISSION v. AKINS, 524 U.S. 11 (1998). A group of voters brought an administrative complaint before the Commission, alleging that an organization was a "political committee" required by the Federal Election Campaign Act to register and make certain information public. The Commission dismissed the complaint and the voters sought judicial review in the federal courts. The Court held that the voters had standing to challenge the Commission's dismissal of the complaint under the Act, which authorized "any party aggrieved" by an FEC order dismissing a complaint to seek judicial review. Congress had the constitutional power to authorize federal courts to adjudicate the lawsuit. The voters suffered injury in fact from their inability to obtain information that would help them evaluate candidates for public office. That harm was fairly traceable to the Commission's decision, and could be redressed by judicial decision. Justice Breyer's opinion for the court rejected the argument that there was no standing because the lawsuit involved only a "generalized grievance shared in substantially equal measure by all or a large class of citizens."

"Whether styled as a constitutional or prudential limit on standing, the Court has sometimes determined that where large numbers of Americans suffer alike, the political process, rather than the judicial process, may provide the more appropriate remedy for a widely shared grievance....

"The kind of judicial language ... invariably appears in cases where the harm at issue is not only widely shared, but is also of an abstract and indefinite nature—for example, harm to the 'common concern for obedience to law.' ... The abstract nature of the harm—for example, injury to the interest in seeing that the law is obeyed—deprives the case of the concrete specificity that characterized those controversies which were 'the traditional concern of the courts at Westminster,' ...

"Often the fact that an interest is abstract and the fact that it is widely shared go hand in hand. But their association is not invariable, and where a harm is concrete, though widely shared, the Court has found 'injury in fact.' ... Thus the fact that a political forum may be more readily available where an injury is widely shared (while counseling against, say, interpreting a statute as conferring standing) does not, by itself, automatically disqualify an interest for Article III purposes. Such an interest, where sufficiently concrete, may count as an 'injury in fact.' This conclusion seems particularly obvious where (to use a hypothetical example) large numbers of individuals suffer the same common-law injury (say, a widespread mass tort), or where large numbers of voters suffer interference with voting rights conferred by law. ... We conclude that similarly, the informational injury at issue here, directly related to voting, the most basic of political rights, is sufficiently concrete and specific such that the fact that it is widely shared does not deprive Congress of constitutional power to authorize its vindication in the federal courts."

Justice Scalia, joined by Justices O'Connor and Thomas, dissented. On the constitutional issue, he said, in part:

"The Constitution's line of demarcation between the Executive power and the judicial power presupposes a common understanding of the type of interest needed to sustain a 'case or controversy' against the Executive in the courts. A system in which the citizenry at large could sue to compel Executive compliance with the law would be a system in which the courts, rather than of the President, are given the primary responsibility to 'take Care that the Laws be faithfully executed,' Art. II, § 3.... When the Executive can be directed by the courts, at the instance of any voter, to remedy a deprivation which affects the entire electorate in precisely the same way—and particularly when that deprivation (here, the unavailability of information) is one inseverable part of a larger enforcement scheme— there has occurred a shift of political responsibility to a branch designed not to protect the public at large but to protect individual rights. ... If today's decision is correct, it is within the power of Congress to authorize any interested person to manage (through the courts) the Executive's enforcement of any law that includes a requirement for the filing and public availability of a piece of paper."

Clinton v. City of New York

524 U.S. 417, 118 S.Ct. 2091, 141 L.Ed.2d 393 (1998).

(The report in this case appears, infra page 424.)

C. MOOTNESS

"The usual rule in federal cases is that an actual controversy must exist at stages of appellate or certiorari review, and not simply at the date the action is initiated." Roe v. Wade, 410 U.S. 113, 125 (1973).

DeFunis v. Odegaard

416 U.S. 312, 94 S.Ct. 1704, 40 L.Ed.2d 164 (1974).

Per Curiam.

In 1971 the petitioner, Marco DeFunis, Jr., applied for admission as a first-year student at the University of Washington Law School ... DeFunis was eventually notified that he had been denied admission. He thereupon commenced this suit in a Washington trial court, contending that the procedures and criteria employed by the Law School Admissions Committee invidiously discriminated against him on account of his race in violation of the Equal Protection Clause of the Fourteenth Amendment to the United States Constitution.

DeFunis brought the suit on behalf of himself alone, and not as the representative of any class, against the various respondents, who are officers, faculty members, and members of the Board of Regents of the University of Washington. He asked the trial court to issue a mandatory injunction commanding the respondents to admit him as a member of the first-year class entering in September of 1971, on the ground that the Law School admissions policy had resulted in the unconstitutional denial of his application for admission. The trial court agreed with his claim and granted the requested relief. DeFunis was, accordingly, admitted to the Law School and began his legal studies there in the fall of 1971. On appeal, the Washington Supreme Court reversed the judgment of the trial court and held that the Law School admissions policy did not violate the Constitution. By this time DeFunis was in his second year at the Law School.

He then petitioned this Court for a writ of certiorari, and Mr. Justice Douglas, as Circuit Justice, stayed the judgment of the Washington Supreme Court pending the "final disposition of the case by this Court." By virtue of this stay, DeFunis has remained in law school, and was in the first term of his third and final year when this Court first considered his certiorari petition in the fall of 1973....

We granted the petition for certiorari on November 19, 1973, 414 U.S. 1038. The case was in due course orally argued on February 26, 1974.

In response to questions raised from the bench during the oral argument, counsel for the petitioner has informed the Court that DeFunis has now registered "for his final quarter in law school." Counsel for the respondents have made clear that the Law School will not in any way seek to abrogate this registration. In light of DeFunis' recent registration for the last quarter of his final law school year, and the Law School's assurance that his registration is fully effective, the insistent question again arises whether this case is not moot, and to that question we now turn.

... The inability of the federal judiciary "to review moot cases derives from the requirement of Article III of the Constitution under which the exercise of judicial power depends upon the existence of a case or controversy." ... Although as a matter of Washington state law it appears that this case would be saved from mootness by "the great public interest in the continuing issues raised by this appeal," ... the fact remains that under Art. III "[e]ven in cases arising in the state courts, the question of mootness is a federal one which a federal court must resolve before it assumes jurisdiction." ...

... [A]ll parties agree that DeFunis is now entitled to complete his legal studies at the University of Washington and to receive his degree from that institution. A determination by this Court of the legal issues tendered by the parties is no longer necessary to compel that result, and could not serve to prevent it. DeFunis did not cast his suit as a class action, and the only remedy he requested was an injunction commanding his admission to the Law School. He was not only accorded that remedy, but he now has also been irrevocably admitted to the final term of the final year of the law school course. The controversy between the parties has thus clearly ceased to be "definite and concrete" and no longer "touch[es] the legal relations of parties having adverse legal interests." ...

> *He no longer needs admission or to be given his relief*

. . .

It might also be suggested that this case presents a question that is "capable of repetition, yet evading review," ... and is thus amenable to federal adjudication even though it might otherwise be considered moot. But DeFunis will never again be required to run the gauntlet of the Law School's admission process, and so the question is certainly not "capable of repetition" so far as he is concerned. Moreover, just because this particular case did not reach the Court until the eve of the petitioner's graduation from law school, it hardly follows that the issue he raises will in future evade review. If the admissions procedures of the Law School remain unchanged, there is no reason to suppose that a subsequent case attacking those procedures will not come with relative speed to this Court, now that the Supreme Court of Washington has spoken. . . .

... [T]he judgment of the Supreme Court of Washington is vacated, and the cause is remanded for such proceedings as by that Court may be deemed appropriate.

It is so ordered.

Mr. Justice Brennan, with whom Mr. Justice Douglas, Mr. Justice White, and Mr. Justice Marshall concur, dissenting.

. . .

... [I]n endeavoring to dispose of this case as moot, the Court clearly disserves the public interest. The constitutional issues which are avoided today concern vast numbers of people, organizations and colleges and universities, as evidenced by the filing of twenty-six *amici curiae* briefs. Few constitutional questions in recent history have stirred as much debate, and they will not disappear. They must inevitably return to the federal courts and ultimately again to this Court. ... Because avoidance of repetitious litigation serves the public interest, that inevitability counsels against mootness determinations, as here, not compelled by the record.... Although the Court should, of course, avoid unnecessary decisions of constitutional questions, we should not transform principles of avoidance of constitutional decisions into devices for sidestepping resolution of difficult cases....

On what appears in this case, I would find that there is an extant controversy and decide the merits of the very important constitutional questions presented.

CAPABLE OF REPETITION YET EVADING REVIEW

An exception to the requirement that there be a live controversy at the time of decision exists for those controversies "capable of repetition yet evading review." In its *DeFunis* opinion, the Court concludes that the exception is inapplicable because DeFunis would not be affected by the challenged admission policy in the future and other challengers to the admission procedures could litigate the issues before their claims became moot.[1]

The simplest cases involving the exception are those where the litigated issue will always be mooted by the passage of time in litigation, and the plaintiff will be subject to the challenged action in the future. That was the situation in United States v. New York Tel. Co., 434 U.S. 159 (1977), where a telephone company challenged a federal district court order requiring it to install and use "pen registers" and furnish the Federal Bureau of Investigation with information concerning the use of two telephones. Such orders were issued only for brief periods, and even if an order was stayed pending judicial review, the showing of probable cause that supported the order would become stale before review was completed. Given the telephone company's policy of refusing to comply voluntarily with such orders, it was clear that it would be subjected to similar orders in the future.

More complex are those cases where the plaintiff will not face the litigated issue in the future, but others similarly situated will. That was the situation in Dunn v. Blumstein, 405 U.S. 330 (1972), where plaintiff challenged a state requirement that voters live in the state for one year and the county for three months prior to an election. Plaintiff became eligible to vote long before termination of the litigation. Other new residents would, however, be subject to the durational residency requirement. That was also the situation in Roe v. Wade, 410 U.S. 113 (1973), where a pregnant woman challenged a state abortion statute, asserting her inability to obtain a legal abortion in the state. Plaintiff's 1970 pregnancy had obviously terminated prior to the Court's 1973 decision, and she did not allege that she was affected by the abortion statute with reference to future pregnancies. In both cases, the Court determined that the controversy was capable of repetition, yet evading review. In *Roe*, the Court said:

> "[W]hen ... pregnancy is a significant fact in the litigation, the normal 266–day gestation period is so short that the pregnancy will come to term before the usual appellate procedure is complete. If that termination makes a case moot, pregnancy litigation seldom will survive much beyond the trial stage, and appellate review will be effectively denied. Our law should not be that rigid."

---

1. The issue mooted in *DeFunis* was decided by the Court four years later in Regents of the University of California v. Bakke, 438 U.S. 265 (1978), infra p. 836. Bakke had been denied admission to medical school, and was not attending the school when his case reached the Supreme Court. The Court revisited the merits of *Bakke*, and essentially embraced Justice Powell's writing in it, in Grutter v. Bollinger, 539 U.S. 306 (2003), infra p. 876.

Both *Dunn* and *Roe* were class actions. Where litigation is not capable of repetition as to the named plaintiff, later cases have combined concerns about whether the plaintiff's claim is "capable of repetition yet evading review" with questions whether the action to enjoin enforcement of the challenged law has been certified as a class action. In Sosna v. Iowa, 419 U.S. 393 (1975), plaintiffs challenged a state law imposing a durational residency requirement for obtaining a divorce. Sosna had satisfied the residency requirement before the completion of litigation. The Court explained that the case had not become moot because: (1) the case had been certified as a class action, with a class whose members were still subject to the durational residency requirement, *and;* (2) the problem was one capable of repetition yet evading review as to the class.[2] Since *Sosna,* complications have arisen when the claims of the named plaintiff have become moot prior to class certification.[3]

[handwritten margin note: Sosna was not declared moot]

D. RIPENESS

Criminal prosecutions and suits for damages in tort or contract relate to past conduct. If it is necessary to decide a constitutional issue in order to determine the legal consequences of that conduct, no issues of ripeness or concreteness arise. Such cases present the question of judicial review in the classic *Marbury v. Madison* form.

Suits for injunctions and declaratory judgments, however, present different problems. Characteristically, they relate to the future. It may not be clear what either the plaintiff or the defendant actually will do. It may not be certain that the conduct alleged to give rise to the constitutional issue will ever take place. The declaratory judgment action, in particular, takes a form suspiciously like that of an advisory opinion. It is in such cases that the Court articulates the doctrines relating to the concreteness of the factual situation and the ripeness of the controversy.

The cases set out below constitute a sample of the Court's approach to the problem. Because of the amorphous nature of the rules being applied, the cases do not fit neatly into rational categories.

For discussions of the problems in this section from differing points of view see Bickel, *The Least Dangerous Branch* 71, 111–98 (1962); Scharpf, *Judicial Review and the Political Question: A Functional Analysis,* 75 Yale L.J. 517, 528–533 (1966).

UNITED PUBLIC WORKERS v. MITCHELL, 330 U.S. 75 (1947). The Hatch Act forbade certain classes of federal government employees from taking "any active part in political management or in political campaigns." A group of employees sought an injunction forbidding the Civil Service Commission from enforcing this aspect of the Act. One group of plaintiffs alleged that they desired to engage in specified acts of political management and political campaigning. One plaintiff (Poole) alleged that he had engaged in forbidden

---

2. Greenstein, *Bridging the Mootness Gap in Federal Court Class Actions,* 35 Stan. L.Rev. 897, 903 (1983), points out that the combination of two reasons is confusing. "If certification conferred legal status upon the claims of the class and if there were always class members with *current* claims, what did it matter ... that the claims were 'capable of repetition?' And in what sense were they 'evading review'?"

3. See Deposit Guar. Nat'l Bank v. Roper, 445 U.S. 326 (1980), and United States Parole Commission v. Geraghty, 445 U.S. 388 (1980). In both cases, the trial court had denied class certification, and the individual plaintiff's claim became moot while the case was on appeal. The Court held that a justiciable controversy remained concerning whether the class should have been certified. For discussion of these cases, see Greenstein, supra note 2.

political activity and that proceedings to discharge him were under way. The court held that the first group of plaintiffs could not proceed in a federal court but that Poole could do so. The Court said, in part:

"As is well known the federal courts established pursuant to Article III of the Constitution do not render advisory opinions. For adjudication of constitutional issues, 'concrete legal issues, presented in actual cases, not abstractions,' are requisite. This is as true of declaratory judgments as any other field. These appellants seem clearly to seek advisory opinions upon broad claims of rights protected by the First, Fifth, Ninth and Tenth Amendments to the Constitution. ... Appellants want to engage in 'political management and political campaigns,' to persuade others to follow appellants' views by discussion, speeches, articles and other acts reasonably designed to secure the selection of appellants' political choices. Such generality of objection is really an attack on the political expediency of the Hatch Act, not the presentation of legal issues. It is beyond the competence of courts to render such a decision. ...

"The power of courts, and ultimately of this Court to pass upon the constitutionality of acts of Congress arises only when the interests of litigants require the use of this judicial authority for their protection against actual interference. A hypothetical threat is not enough. We can only speculate as to the kinds of political activity the appellants desire to engage in or as to the contents of their proposed public statements or the circumstances of their publication. ...

"... No threat of interference by the Commission with rights of these appellants appears beyond that implied by the existence of the law and the regulations. ... We should not take judicial cognizance of the situation presented on the part of the appellants considered in this subdivision of the opinion. These reasons lead us to conclude that the determination of the trial court, that the individual appellants, other than Poole, could maintain this action, was erroneous."

ADLER v. BOARD OF EDUCATION, 342 U.S. 485 (1952). Plaintiffs brought suit in the New York courts seeking a judgment declaring unconstitutional the Feinberg law, which required that teachers who belonged to allegedly subversive groups be discharged. The Supreme Court decided the case on the merits without considering issues of ripeness or concreteness. Justice Frankfurter, dissenting, said:

"The allegations in the present action fall short of these found insufficient in the *Mitchell* Case. These teachers do not allege that they have engaged in proscribed conduct or ... that they have been, or are, deterred from supporting causes or from joining organizations for fear of the Feinberg Law's interdict, except to say generally that the system complained of will have this effect on teachers as a group. ... Since we rightly refused in the *Mitchell* Case to hear government employees whose conduct was much more intimately affected by the law there attacked than are the claims of the plaintiffs here, this suit is wanting in the necessary basis for our review."

NOTES ON MITCHELL AND ADLER

1. *Mitchell* and *Adler* suggest that the degree of concreteness required may vary with the nature of the constitutional issue presented. By moving for a judgment on the pleadings the plaintiffs in *Adler* presented the question whether there could be any constitutional applications of the statute—a ques-

[handwritten margin note: unlike Mitchell: If ct. refused to hear in Mitchell when det. had more of a connection, they have to refuse here too.]

tion that could be decided without reference to the particular conduct of the plaintiffs. See Scharpf, *Judicial Review and the Political Question: A Functional Analysis,* 75 Yale L.J. 517, 531–533 (1966). In United States Civil Service Comm'n. v. Letter Carriers, 413 U.S. 548 (1973) the Court upheld the Hatch Act a second time in a suit brought by plaintiffs who did no more than allege their desire to engage in various political activities—allegations essentially similar to those held inadequate in *Mitchell.* The Court did not discuss the ripeness and concreteness issues. However, this time the Court was considering contentions that the Act was unconstitutional on its face as vague and over-broad—constitutional contentions that do not depend upon the facts of the particular case for resolution.

2.   Are *Adler* and *Mitchell* distinguishable on another basis? *Mitchell* arose in a federal court action, and the ripeness issue concerned the standards for granting federal declaratory judgments. In *Adler,* the Court was reviewing a state court decision holding that the challenged statute did not violate the United States Constitution, and the issue of ripeness concerned the appropriate standard for reviewing a state court decision. Contrast Poe v. Ullman, which follows, another case seeking review of a state court declaratory judgment.

POE v. ULLMAN, 367 U.S. 497 (1961). A doctor and his patients brought declaratory judgment actions in the Connecticut courts seeking a determination that a Connecticut statute making it a crime to use birth control devices was unconstitutional. The state courts upheld the validity of the statute. The Supreme Court dismissed the appeals on the ground that there was no real controversy since the Connecticut statute was not enforced and hence there was no real fear of personal. In discussing the declaratory judgment problem in the plurality opinion, Justice Frankfurter said: "For just as the declaratory judgment device does not 'purport to alter the character of the controversies which are the subject of the judicial power under the Constitution,' ... it does not permit litigants to invoke the power of this court to obtain constitutional rulings in advance of necessity. ... The court has been on the alert against use of the declaratory judgment device for avoiding the rigorous insistence on exigent adversity as a condition for evoking court adjudication. This is as true of state court suits for declaratory judgments. ..."

YOUNGER v. HARRIS, 401 U.S. 37 (1971). A suit was brought in federal district court to enjoin the district attorney of Los Angeles County from prosecuting the plaintiffs under the California Criminal Syndicalism Act. On the question of the concreteness of the controversy the Court said:

"Appellee Harris has been indicted, and was actually being prosecuted by California for a violation of its Criminal Syndicalism Act at the time this suit was filed. He thus has an acute, live controversy with the State and its prosecutor. But none of the other parties plaintiff in the District Court, Dan, Hirsch, or Broslawsky, has such a controversy. None has been indicted, arrested, or even threatened by the prosecutor. About these three the three-judge court said:

'Plaintiffs Dan and Hirsch allege that they are members of the Progressive Labor Party, which advocates change in industrial ownership and political change, and that they feel inhibited in advocating the program of their political party through peaceful, nonviolent means, because of the presence of the Act "on the books", and because of the pending criminal prosecution against Harris. Plaintiff Broslawsky is a history instructor, and he alleges that he is uncertain as to whether his normal practice of teaching his students about the doctrines of Karl Marx and reading from the Communist Manifesto and other revolutionary works may subject him to prosecution for violation of the Act.'

"... If these three had alleged that they would be prosecuted for the conduct they planned to engage in, and if the District Court had found this allegation to be true ... then a genuine controversy might be said to exist. But here appellees ... do not claim that they have ever been threatened with prosecution, that a prosecution is likely, or even that a prosecution is remotely possible. They claim the right to bring this suit solely because, in the language of their complaint, they 'feel inhibited.' We do not think this allegation even if true, is sufficient to bring the equitable jurisdiction of the federal courts into play to enjoin a pending state prosecution. A federal lawsuit to stop a prosecution in a state court is a serious matter. And persons having no fears of state prosecution except those that are imaginary or speculative, are not to be accepted as appropriate plaintiffs in such cases ... Since Harris is actually being prosecuted under the challenged laws, however, we proceed with him as a proper party."

cannot bring suit for fear of being prosecuted under an Act in the future

City of Los Angeles v. Lyons

461 U.S. 95, 103 S.Ct. 1660, 75 L.Ed.2d 675 (1983).

Justice White delivered the opinion of the Court.

The issue here is whether respondent Lyons satisfied the prerequisites for seeking injunctive relief in the federal district court.

I

This case began on February 7, 1977, when respondent, Adolph Lyons, filed a complaint for damages, injunction, and declaratory relief in the United States District Court for the Central District of California. The defendants were the City of Los Angeles and four of its police officers. The complaint alleged that on October 6, 1976, at 2 a.m., Lyons was stopped by the defendant officers for a traffic or vehicle code violation and that although Lyons offered no resistance or threat whatsoever, the officers, without provocation or justification, seized Lyons and applied a "chokehold"—either the "bar arm control" hold or the "carotid-artery control" hold or both—rendering him unconscious and causing damage to his larynx. Counts I through IV of the complaint sought damages against the officers and the City. Count V, with which we are principally concerned here, sought a preliminary and permanent injunction against the City barring the use of the control holds. That count alleged that the city's police officers, "pursuant to the authorization, instruction and encouragement of defendant City of Los Angeles, regularly and routinely apply these choke holds in innumerable situations where they are not threatened by the use of any deadly force whatsoever," that numerous persons have been injured as the result of the application of the chokeholds, that Lyons and others similarly situated are threatened with irreparable injury in the form of bodily injury and loss of life, and that Lyons "justifiably fears that any contact he has with Los Angeles police officers may result in his being choked and strangled to death without provocation, justification or other legal excuse." Lyons alleged the threatened impairment of rights protected by the First, Fourth, Eighth and Fourteenth Amendments. Injunctive relief was sought against the use of the control holds "except in situations where the proposed victim of said control reasonably appears to be threatening the immediate use of deadly force." Count

VI sought declaratory relief against the City, i.e., a judgment that use of the chokeholds absent the threat of immediate use of deadly force is a *per se* violation of various constitutional rights.

The District Court, by order, granted the City's motion for partial judgment on the pleadings and entered judgment for the City on Count V and VI. The Court of Appeals reversed the judgment for the City on Count V and VI, holding over the City's objection that despite our decisions in O'Shea v. Littleton, 414 U.S. 488 (1974), and Rizzo v. Goode, 423 U.S. 362 (1976), Lyons had standing to seek relief against the application of the chokeholds. 615 F.2d 1243. The Court of Appeals held that there was a sufficient likelihood that Lyons would again be stopped and subjected to the unlawful use of force to constitute a case or controversy and to warrant the issuance of an injunction, if the injunction was otherwise authorized. We denied certiorari. 449 U.S. 934.

On remand . . . [a] preliminary injunction was entered enjoining "the use of both the carotid-artery and bar arm holds under circumstances which do not threaten death or serious bodily injury." An improved training program and regular reporting and record keeping were also ordered.[3] The Court of Appeals affirmed in a brief *per curiam* opinion. . . . We . . . reverse.

. . .

III

It goes without saying that those who seek to invoke the jurisdiction of the federal courts must satisfy the threshold requirement imposed by Article III of the Constitution by alleging an actual case or controversy. . . .

In O'Shea v. Littleton, 414 U.S. 488 (1974), we dealt with a case brought by a class of plaintiffs claiming that they had been subjected to discriminatory enforcement of the criminal law. Among other things, a county magistrate and judge were accused of discriminatory conduct in various respects, such as sentencing members of plaintiff's class more harshly than other defendants. The Court of Appeals reversed the dismissal of the suit by the District Court, ruling that if the allegations were proved, an appropriate injunction could be entered.

We reversed for failure of the complaint to allege a case or controversy. . . . Although it was claimed in that case that particular members of the plaintiff class had actually suffered from the alleged unconstitutional practices, we observed that "[p]ast exposure to illegal conduct does not in itself show a present case or controversy regarding injunctive relief . . . if unaccompanied by any continuing, present adverse effects." . . . Past wrongs were evidence bearing on "whether there is a real and immediate threat of repeated injury." . . . But the prospect of future injury rested "on the likelihood that [plaintiffs] will again be arrested for and charged with violations of the criminal law and will again be subjected to bond proceedings, trial, or sentencing before petitioners." . . . The most that could be said for plaintiffs' standing was "that *if* [plaintiffs] proceed to violate an unchallenged law and *if* they are charged, held to answer, and tried in any proceedings before petitioners, they will be subjected to the discriminatory practices that petitioners are alleged to have followed." . . . We could not find a case or controversy in those circumstances:

---

3. By its terms, the injunction was to continue in force until the court approved the training program to be presented to it. It is fair to assume that such approval would not be given if the program did not confine the use of the strangleholds to those situations in which their use, in the view of the District Court, would be constitutional. Because of successive stays entered by the Court of Appeals and by this court, the injunction has not gone into effect.

the threat to the plaintiffs was not "sufficiently real and immediate to show an existing controversy simply because they anticipate violating lawful criminal statutes and being tried for their offenses...." ... It was to be assumed "that [plaintiffs] will conduct their activities within the law and so avoid prosecution and conviction as well as exposure to the challenged course of conduct said to be followed by petitioners." ...

We ... went on to hold that even if the complaint presented an existing case or controversy, an adequate basis for equitable relief against petitioners had not been demonstrated:

> "[Plaintiffs] have failed, moreover, to establish the basic requisites of the issuance of equitable relief in these circumstances—the likelihood of substantial and immediate irreparable injury, and the inadequacy of remedies at law. We have already canvassed the necessarily conjectural nature of the threatened injury to which [plaintiffs] are allegedly subjected.... [I]f any of the [plaintiffs] are ever prosecuted and face trial, or if they are illegally sentenced, there are available state and federal procedures which could provide relief from the wrongful conduct alleged." ...

Another relevant decision for present purposes is Rizzo v. Goode, 423 U.S. 362 (1976), a case in which plaintiffs alleged widespread illegal and unconstitutional police conduct aimed at minority citizens and against City residents in general.... The claim of injury rested upon "what one or a small, unnamed minority of policemen might do to them in the future because of that unknown policeman's perception" of departmental procedures.... This hypothesis was "even more attenuated than those allegations of future injury found insufficient in O'Shea to warrant [the] invocation of federal jurisdiction." ... The Court also held that plaintiffs' showing at trial of a relatively few instances of violations by individual police officers, without any showing of a deliberate policy on behalf of the named defendants, did not provide a basis for equitable relief.

Golden v. Zwickler, 394 U.S. 103 (1969), a case arising in an analogous situation, is directly apposite. Congressman Zwickler sought a declaratory judgment that a New York statute prohibiting anonymous handbills directly pertaining to election campaigns was unconstitutional. Although Zwickler had once been convicted under the statute, he was no longer a Congressman apt to run for reelection. A unanimous Court held that because it was "most unlikely" that Zwickler would again be subject to the statute, no case or controversy of "sufficient immediacy and reality" was present to allow a declaratory judgment....

. . .

IV

No extension of *O'Shea* and *Rizzo* is necessary to hold that respondent Lyons has failed to demonstrate a case or controversy with the City that would justify the equitable relief sought. Lyons' standing to seek the injunction requested depended on whether he was likely to suffer future injury from the use of the chokeholds by police officers. Count V of the complaint alleged the traffic stop and choking incident five months before. That Lyons may have been illegally choked by the police on October 6, 1976, while presumably affording Lyons standing to claim damages against the individual officers and perhaps against the City, does nothing to establish a real and immediate threat that he would again be stopped for a traffic violation, or for any other offense, by an officer or officers who would illegally choke him into unconsciousness without any provocation or resistance on his part. The additional allegation in the complaint that the police in Los Angeles routinely apply chokeholds in situations where they are not threatened by the use of deadly force falls far short of the allegations that would be necessary to establish a case or controversy between these parties.

In order to establish an actual controversy in this case, Lyons would have had not only to allege that he would have another encounter with the police but also to make the incredible assertion either, (1) that *all* police officers in Los Angeles *always* choke any citizen with whom they happen to have an encounter, whether for the purpose of arrest, issuing a citation or for questioning or, (2) that the City ordered or authorized police officers to act in such manner. Although Count V alleged that the City authorized the use of the control holds in situations where deadly force was not threatened, it did not indicate why Lyons might be realistically threatened by police officers who acted within the strictures of the City's policy. If, for example, chokeholds were authorized to be used only to counter resistance to an arrest by a suspect, or to thwart an effort to escape, any future threat to Lyons from the City's policy or from the conduct of police officers would be no more real than the possibility that he would again have an encounter with the police and that either he would illegally resist arrest or detention or the officers would disobey their instructions and again render him unconscious without any provocation.[7]

Under *O'Shea* and *Rizzo,* these allegations were an insufficient basis to provide a federal court with jurisdiction to entertain Count V of the complaint.... For several reasons—each of them infirm, in our view—the Court of Appeals thought reliance on *O'Shea* and *Rizzo* was misplaced and reversed the District Court.

First, the Court of Appeals thought that Lyons was more immediately threatened than the plaintiffs in those cases since, according to the Court of Appeals, Lyons need only be stopped for a minor traffic violation to be subject to the strangleholds. But even assuming that Lyons would again be stopped for a traffic or other violation in the reasonably near future, it is untenable to assert, and the complaint made no such allegation, that strangleholds are applied by the Los Angeles police to every citizen who is stopped or arrested regardless of the conduct of the person stopped. We cannot agree that the "odds" that Lyons would not only again be stopped for a traffic violation but would also be subjected to a chokehold without any provocation whatsoever are sufficient to make out a federal case for equitable relief....

7. The centerpiece of Justice Marshall's dissent is that Lyons had standing to challenge the City's policy because to recover damages he would have to prove that what allegedly occurred on October 6, 1976, was pursuant to City authorization. We agree completely that for Lyons to succeed in his damages action, it would be necessary to prove that what happened to him—that is, as alleged, he was choked without any provocation or legal excuse whatsoever—was pursuant to a City policy....

... [E]ven if the complaint must be read as containing an allegation that officers are authorized to apply the chokeholds where there is no resistance or other provocation, it does not follow that Lyons has standing to seek an injunction against the application of the restraint holds in situations that he has not experienced, as for example, where the suspect resists arrest or tries to escape but does not threaten the use of deadly force. Yet that is precisely the scope of the injunction that Lyons prayed for in Count B.

... [I]n any event, to have a case or controversy with the City that could sustain Count V, Lyons would have to credibly allege that he faced a realistic threat from the future application of the City's policy. Justice Marshall nowhere confronts this requirement—the necessity that Lyons demonstrate that he, himself, will not only again be stopped by the police but will be choked without any provocation or legal excuse. Justice Marshall plainly does not agree with that requirement, and he was in dissent in O'Shea v. Littleton. We are at issue in that respect.

... [I]t is surely no more than speculation to assert either that Lyons himself will again be involved in one of those unfortunate instances, or that he will be arrested in the future and provoke the use of a chokehold by resisting arrest, attempting to escape, or threatening deadly force or serious bodily injury.

Second, the Court of Appeals viewed *O'Shea* and *Rizzo* as cases in which the plaintiffs sought "massive structural" relief against the local law enforcement systems and therefore that the holdings in those cases were inapposite to cases such as this where the plaintiff, according to the Court of Appeals, seeks to enjoin only an "established," "sanctioned" police practice assertedly violative of constitutional rights. *O'Shea* and *Rizzo,* however, cannot be so easily confined to their facts. If Lyons has made no showing that he is realistically threatened by a repetition of his experience of October, 1976, then he has not met the requirements for seeking an injunction in a federal court, whether the injunction contemplates intrusive structural relief or the cessation of a discrete practice.

The Court of Appeals also asserted that Lyons "had a live and active claim" against the City "if only for a period of a few seconds" while the stranglehold was being applied to him and that for two reasons the claim had not become moot so as to disentitle Lyons to injunctive relief: First, because under normal rules of equity, a case does not become moot merely because the complained of conduct has ceased; and second, because Lyons' claim is "capable of repetition but evading review" and therefore should be heard. We agree that Lyons had a live controversy with the City. Indeed, he still has a claim for damages against the City that appears to meet all Article III requirements. Nevertheless, the issue here is not whether that claim has become moot but whether Lyons meets the preconditions for asserting an injunctive claim in a federal forum. The equitable doctrine that cessation of the challenged conduct does not bar an injunction is of little help in this respect, for Lyons' lack of standing does not rest on the termination of the police practice but on the speculative nature of his claim that he will again experience injury as the result of that practice even if continued.

. . .

V

Lyons fares no better if it be assumed that his pending damages suit affords him Article III standing to seek an injunction as a remedy for the claim arising out of the October 1976 events. . . .

. . .

Absent a sufficient likelihood that he will again be wronged in a similar way, Lyons is no more entitled to an injunction than any other citizen of Los Angeles; and a federal court may not entertain a claim by any or all citizens who no more than assert that certain practices of law enforcement officers are unconstitutional. . . .

We decline the invitation to slight the preconditions for equitable relief; for as we have held, recognition of the need for a proper balance between state and federal authority counsels restraint in the issuance of injunctions against state officers engaged in the administration of the states' criminal laws in the absence of irreparable injury which is both great and immediate. . . .

. . .

. . . [T]he state courts need not impose the same standing or remedial requirements that govern federal court proceedings. The individual states may permit their courts to use injunctions to oversee the conduct of law enforcement authorities on a continuing basis. But this is not the role of a federal court absent far more justification than Lyons has proffered in this case.

The judgment of the Court of Appeals is accordingly

Reversed.

Justice Marshall, with whom Justice Brennan, Justice Blackmun and Justice Stevens join, dissenting.

The District Court found that the City of Los Angeles authorizes its police officers to apply life-threatening chokeholds to citizens who pose no threat of violence, and that respondent, Adolph Lyons, was subjected to such a chokehold. The Court today holds that a federal court is without power to enjoin the enforcement of the City's policy, no matter how flagrantly unconstitutional it may be. Since no one can show that he will be choked in the future, no one—not even a person who, like Lyons, has almost been choked to death—has standing to challenge the continuation of the policy. The City is free to continue the policy indefinitely as long as it is willing to pay damages for the injuries and deaths that result. I dissent from this unprecedented and unwarranted approach to standing.

II

At the outset it is important to emphasize that Lyons' entitlement to injunctive relief and his entitlement to an award of damages both depend upon whether he can show that the City's chokehold policy violates the Constitution. . . .

III

Since Lyons' claim for damages plainly gives him standing, and since the success of that claim depends upon a demonstration that the City's chokehold policy is unconstitutional, it is beyond dispute that Lyons has properly invoked the District Court's authority to adjudicate the constitutionality of the City's chokehold policy. The dispute concerning the constitutionality of that policy plainly presents a "case or controversy" under Article III. The Court nevertheless holds that a federal court has no power under Article III to adjudicate Lyons' request, in the same lawsuit, for injunctive relief with respect to that very policy. . . .

A

It is simply disingenuous for the Court to assert that its decision requires "[n]o extension" of O'Shea v. Littleton, 414 U.S. 488 (1974), and Rizzo v. Goode, 423 U.S. 362 (1976). In contrast to this case O'Shea and Rizzo involved disputes focusing solely on the threat of future injury which the plaintiffs did not allege past injury and did not seek compensatory relief. In Rizzo, the plaintiffs sought only declaratory and injunctive relief and alleged past instances of police misconduct only in an attempt to establish the substantiality of the threat of future injury . . . was similarly no claim for damages based on past injuries in Ashcroft v. Mattis, 431 U.S. 171 (1977), or Golden v. Zwickler, 394 U.S. 103 (1969), on which the Court also relies.

. . . As the Court recognized in O'Shea, standing under Article III is established by an allegation of "threatened or actual injury." Id., 414 U.S., at 493, quoting Linda R.S. v. Richard D., 410 U.S. 614, 617 (1973) (emphasis added). See also 414 U.S., at 493, n. 2. Because the plaintiffs in *O'Shea, Rizzo, Mattis,* and *Zwickler* did not seek to redress past injury, their standing to sue depended entirely on the risk of future injury they faced. Apart from the desire to eliminate the possibility of future injury, the plaintiffs in those cases had no other personal stake in the outcome of the controversies.

By contrast, Lyons' request for prospective relief is coupled with his claim for damages. . . . In addition to the risk that he will be subjected to a chokehold in the future, Lyons has suffered past injury. Because he has a live claim for damages, he need not rely solely on the threat of future injury to establish his personal stake in the outcome of the controversy. In the cases relied on by the majority, the Court simply had no occasion to decide whether a plaintiff who has standing to litigate a dispute must clear a separate standing hurdle with respect to each form of relief sought.

. . .

C

By fragmenting the standing inquiry and imposing a separate standing hurdle with respect to each form of relief sought, the decision today departs significantly from this Court's traditional conception of the standing requirement and of the remedial powers of the federal courts. We have never required more than that a plaintiff have standing to litigate a claim. Whether he will be entitled to obtain particular forms of relief should he prevail has never been understood to be an issue of standing.

. . .

IV

Apart from the question of standing, the only remaining question presented in the petition for certiorari is whether the preliminary injunction issued by the District Court must be set aside because it "constitute[s] a substantial interference in the operation of a municipal police department." In my view it does not.

. . .

The principles of federalism simply do not preclude the limited preliminary injunction issued in this case. Unlike the permanent injunction at issue in *Rizzo,* the preliminary injunction involved here entails no federal supervision of the LAPD's activities. The preliminary injunction merely forbids the use of chokeholds absent the threat of deadly force, permitting their continued use where such a threat does exist. This limited ban takes the form of a preventive injunction, which has traditionally been regarded as the least intrusive form of equitable relief. Moreover, the City can remove the ban by obtaining approval of a training plan. Although the preliminary injunction also requires the City to provide records of the uses of chokeholds to respondent and to allow the court access to such records, this requirement is hardly onerous, since the LAPD already maintains records concerning the use of chokeholds.

V

Apparently because it is unwilling to rely solely on its unprecedented rule of standing, the Court goes on to conclude that, even if Lyons has standing, "[t]he equitable remedy is unavailable." . . .

. . .

The District Court concluded, on the basis of the facts before it, that Lyons was choked without provocation pursuant to an unconstitutional City policy. Given the necessarily preliminary nature of its inquiry, there was no way for the District Court to know the precise contours of the City's policy or to ascertain the risk that Lyons, who had alleged that the policy was being applied in a discriminatory manner, might again be subjected to a chokehold. But in view of the Court's conclusion that the unprovoked choking of Lyons was pursuant to a City policy, Lyons has satisfied "the usual basis for injunctive relief, 'that there exists some cognizable danger of recurrent violation' " . . . The risk of serious injuries and deaths to other citizens also supported the decision to grant a preliminary injunction. Courts of equity have much greater latitude in granting injunctive relief "in furtherance of the public interest . . . than when only private interests are involved." . . . In this case we know that the District Court would have been amply justified in considering the risk to the public, for after the preliminary injunction was stayed, five additional deaths occurred prior to the adoption of a moratorium. Under these circumstances, I do not believe that the District Court abused its discretion.

VI

The Court's decision removes an entire class of constitutional violations from the equitable powers of a federal court. It immunizes from prospective equitable relief any policy that authorizes persistent deprivations of constitutional rights as long as no individual can establish with substantial certainty that he will be injured, or injured again, in the future. . . . Under the view expressed by the majority today, if the police adopt a policy of "shoot to kill," or a policy of shooting one out of ten suspects, the federal courts will be powerless to enjoin its continuation. . . . The federal judicial power is now limited to levying a toll for such a systematic constitutional violation.

E.   POLITICAL QUESTIONS

BAKER v. CARR, 369 U.S. 186 (1962). The court held that a suit by voters seeking reapportionment because the apportionment of a state legislature denied them equal protection of the laws did not involve a nonjusticiable political question. Justice Brennan's opinion for the court contained this summary of political question doctrine.

"We have said that 'in determining whether a question falls within [the political question] category, the appropriateness under our system of government of attributing finality to the action of the political departments and also the lack of satisfactory criteria for a judicial determination are dominant considerations.' . . . The nonjusticiability of a political question is primarily a function of the separation of powers. Much confusion results from the capacity of the 'political question' label to obscure the need for case-by-case inquiry. Deciding whether a matter has in any measure been committed by the Constitution to another branch of government, or whether the action of that branch exceeds whatever authority has been committed, is itself a delicate exercise in constitutional interpretation, and is a responsibility of this Court as ultimate interpreter of the Constitution. To demonstrate this requires no less than to analyze representative cases and to infer from them analytical threads that make up the political question doctrine. We shall then show that none of those threads catches this case.

"*Foreign Relations.* There are sweeping statements to the effect that all questions touching foreign relations are political questions. Not only does resolution of such issues frequently turn on standards that defy judicial application, or involve the exercise of a discretion demonstrably committed to the executive or legislature; but many such questions uniquely demand single-voiced statement of the Government's views. Yet it is error to suppose that every case or controversy which touches foreign relations lies beyond judicial cognizance. Our cases in this field seem invariably to show a discriminating analysis of the particular question posed, in terms of the history of its management by the political branches, of its susceptibility to judicial handling in the light of its nature and posture in the specific case, and of the possible consequences of judicial action. For example, though a court will not ordinarily inquire whether a treaty has been terminated, since on that question 'governmental action . . . must be regarded as of controlling importance,' if there has been no conclusive 'governmental action' then a court can construe a treaty and may find it provides the answer. Compare Terlinden v. Ames, 184 U.S. 270, 285, with Society for the Propagation of the Gospel in Foreign Parts v. New Haven, 8 Wheat. 464, 492–495. Though a court will not undertake to construe a treaty in a manner inconsistent with a subsequent federal statute, no similar hesitancy obtains if the asserted clash is with state law. Compare Whitney v. Robertson, 124 U.S. 190, with Kolovrat v. Oregon, 366 U.S. 187. . . .

"*Dates of Duration of Hostilities.* Though it has been stated broadly that 'the power which declared the necessity is the power to declare its cessation, and what the cessation requires,' Commercial Trust Co. v. Miller, 262 U.S. 51, 57, here too analysis reveals isolable reasons for the presence of political questions, underlying this Court's refusal to review the political departments' determination of when or whether a war has ended. Dominant is the need for finality in the political determination, for emergency's nature demands 'a prompt and unhesitating obedience,' Martin v. Mott, 12 Wheat. 19, 30 (calling up of militia). . . .

"*Validity of Enactments.* In *Coleman v. Miller,* supra, this Court held that the questions of how long a proposed amendment to the Federal Constitution remained open to ratification and what effect a prior rejection had on a subsequent ratification, were committed to congressional resolution and involved criteria of decision that necessarily escaped the judicial grasp. Similar considerations apply to the enacting process: 'the respect due to coequal and independent departments,' and the need for finality and certainty about the status of a statute contribute to judicial reluctance to inquire whether, as passed, it complied with all requisite formalities. Field v. Clark, 143 U.S. 649, 672, 676–677; see Leser v. Garnett, 258 U.S. 130, 137. But it is not true that courts will never delve into a legislature's records upon such a quest: If the enrolled statute lacks an effective date, a court will not hesitate to seek it in the legislative journals in order to preserve the enactment. Gardner v. Collector, 6 Wall. 499. The political question doctrine, a tool for maintenance of governmental order, will not be so applied as to promote only disorder. . . .

"It is apparent that several formulations which vary slightly according to the settings in which the questions arise may describe a political question, although each has one or more elements which identifies it as essentially a function of the separation of powers. Prominent on the surface of any case held to involve a political question is found a textually demonstrable constitutional commitment of the issue to a coordinate political department; or a lack of judicially discoverable and manageable standards for resolving it; or the impossibility of deciding without an initial policy determination of a kind clearly for nonjudicial discretion; or the impossibility of a court's undertaking independent resolution without expressing lack of the respect due coordinate branches of government; or an unusual need for unquestioning adherence to a political decision already made; or the potentiality of embarrassment from multifarious pronouncements by various departments on one question.

"Unless one of these formulations is inextricable from the case at bar, there should be no dismissal for non-justiciability on the ground of a political question's presence. The doctrine of which we treat is one of 'political questions,' not one of 'political cases.' The courts cannot reject as 'no law suit' a bona fide controversy as to whether some action denominated 'political' exceeds constitutional authority. The cases we have reviewed show the necessity for discriminating inquiry into the precise facts and posture of the particular case, and the impossibility of resolution by any semantic cataloguing.

"But it is argued that this case shares the characteristics of decisions that constitute a category not yet considered, cases concerning the Constitution's guaranty, in Art. IV, § 4, of a republican form of government. A conclusion as to whether the case at bar does present a political question cannot be confidently reached until we have considered those cases with special care. We shall discover that Guaranty Clause claims involve those elements which define a 'political question,' and for that reason and no other, they are nonjusticiable. In particular, we shall discover that the nonjusticiability of such claims has nothing to do with their touching upon matters of state governmental organization.

"*Republican Form of Government.* Luther v. Borden, 7 How. 1, 48 U.S. 1, though in form simply an action for damages for trespass was, as Daniel Webster said in opening the argument for the defense, 'an unusual case.' The defendants, admitting an otherwise tortious breaking and entering, sought to justify their action on the ground that they were agents of the established lawful government of Rhode Island, which State was then under martial law to defend itself from active insurrection; that the plaintiff was engaged in that insurrection; and that they entered under orders to arrest the plaintiff. The case arose 'out of the unfortunate political differences which agitated the people of Rhode Island in 1841 and 1842,' 7 How. at 34, which had resulted in a situation wherein two groups laid competing claims to recognition as the lawful government. The plaintiff's right to recover depended upon which of the two groups was entitled to such recognition; but the lower court's refusal to receive evidence or hear argument on that issue, its charge to the jury that the earlier established or 'charter' government was lawful, and the verdict for the defendants, were affirmed upon appeal to this Court. . . .

"Clearly, several factors were thought by the Court in Luther to make the question there 'political': the commitment to the other branches of the decision as to which is the lawful state government; the unambiguous action by the President, in recognizing the charter government as the lawful authority; the need for finality in the executive's decision; and the lack of criteria by which a court could determine which form of government was republican."

Luther v. Borden [margin note]

Powell v. McCormack

395 U.S. 486, 89 S.Ct. 1944, 23 L.Ed.2d 491 (1969).

Mr. Chief Justice Warren delivered the opinion of the Court.

In November 1966, Petitioner Adam Clayton Powell, Jr., was duly elected from the 18th Congressional District of New York to serve in the United States House of Representatives for the 90th Congress. However, pursuant to a House resolution, he was not permitted to take his seat. Powell (and some of the voters of his district) then filed suit in Federal District Court claiming that the

House could exclude him only if it found he failed to meet the standing requirements of age, citizenship, and residence contained in Art. I, § 2, of the Constitution—requirements the House specifically found Powell met—and thus had excluded him unconstitutionally. The District Court dismissed petitioners' complaint "for want of jurisdiction of the subject matter." The Court of Appeals affirmed the dismissal, although on somewhat different grounds, each judge filing a separate opinion. We have determined that it was error to dismiss the complaint and that Petitioner Powell is entitled to a declaratory judgment that he was unlawfully excluded from the 90th Congress.

. . .

[At the organization of the 90th Congress in January, 1967, Powell was asked to step aside while the oath was administered to the other members. A Select Committee was then appointed which reported that Powell met the standing qualifications but that he had asserted an unwarranted privilege and immunity from the processes of the courts of New York; that he had wrongfully diverted House funds for the use of others and himself; and that he had made false reports on expenditures of foreign currency to a House committee. After a ruling by the Speaker that only a majority vote would be needed to exclude Powell and declare the seat vacant, the House adopted such a resolution of exclusion. By the time the case got to the Supreme Court Powell had been elected again and was seated in the 91st Congress. The Court held that the case was not moot because Powell had asked for damages. The Court also held that the vote by the House could not be treated as a vote to expel even though the actual vote exceeded a two-thirds majority. The Court's discussion of the political question objection to ruling on the validity of the action of the House follows.]

. . .

F. POLITICAL QUESTION DOCTRINE

1. Textually demonstrable constitutional commitment

Respondents maintain that even if this case is otherwise justiciable, it presents only a political question. . . .

Respondents' first contention is that this case presents a political question because under Art. I, § 5, there has been a "textually demonstrable constitutional commitment" to the House of the "adjudicatory power" to determine Powell's qualifications. Thus it is argued that the House, and the House alone, has power to determine who is qualified to be a member.

In order to determine whether there has been a textual commitment to a co-ordinate department of the Government, we must interpret the Constitution. In other words, we must first determine what power the Constitution confers upon the House through Art. I, § 5, before we can determine to what extent, if any, the exercise of that power is subject to judicial review. Respondents maintain that the House has broad power under § 5, and, they argue, the House may determine which are the qualifications necessary for membership. On the other hand, petitioners allege that the Constitution provides that an elected representative may be denied his seat only if the House finds he does not meet one of the standing qualifications expressly prescribed by the Constitution.

If examination of § 5 disclosed that the Constitution gives the House judicially unreviewable power to set qualifications for membership and to judge whether prospective members meet those qualifications, further review of the

House determination might well be barred by the political question doctrine. On the other hand, if the Constitution gives the House power to judge only whether elected members possess the three standing qualifications set forth in the Constitution; further consideration would be necessary to determine whether any of the other formulations of the political question doctrine are "inextricable from the case at bar."[42] Baker v. Carr, supra, at 217.

. . .

In order to determine the scope of any "textual commitment" under Art. I, § 5, we necessarily must determine the meaning of the phrase "be the judge of the qualifications of its own members." . . . Our examination of the relevant historical materials leads us to the conclusion that petitioners are correct and that the Constitution leaves the House without authority to *exclude* any person, duly elected by his constituents, who meets all the requirements for membership expressly prescribed in the Constitution.

[A long review of the historical precedents is omitted.]

Had the intent of the Framers emerged from these materials with less clarity, we would nevertheless have been compelled to resolve any ambiguity in favor of a narrow construction of the scope of Congress' power to exclude members-elect. A fundamental principle of our representative democracy is, in Hamilton's words, "that the people should choose whom they please to govern them." 2 Elliot's Debates 257. . . . Moreover, it would effectively nullify the Convention's decision to require a two-third vote for expulsion. Unquestionably, Congress has an interest in preserving its institutional integrity, but in most cases that interest can be sufficiently safeguarded by the exercise of its power to punish its members for disorderly behavior and, in extreme cases, to expel a member with the concurrence of two-thirds. In short, both the intention of the Framers, to the extent it can be determined, and an examination of the basic principles of our democratic system persuade us that the Constitution does not vest in the Congress a discretionary power to deny membership by a majority vote.

For these reasons, we have concluded that Art. I, § 5, is at most a "textually demonstrable commitment" to Congress to judge only the qualifications expressly set forth in the Constitution. Therefore, the "textual commitment" formulation of the political question doctrine does not bar federal courts from adjudicating petitioners' claims.

2. *Other considerations*

Respondents' alternate contention is that the case presents a political question because judicial resolution of petitioners' claim would produce a "potentially embarrassing confrontation between coordinate branches" of the Federal Government. But, as our interpretation of Art. I, § 5, discloses, a determination of Petitioner Powell's right to sit would require no more than an interpretation of the Constitution. Such a determination falls within the traditional role accorded courts to interpret the law, and does not involve a "lack of respect due [a] coordinate [branch] of government," nor does it involve an "initial policy determination of a kind clearly for nonjudicial discretion." Baker v. Carr, supra, at 217. Our system of government requires that federal courts on occasion interpret the Constitution in a manner at variance with the

---

42. Consistent with this interpretation, federal courts might still be barred by the political question doctrine from reviewing the House's factual determination that a member did not meet one of the standing qualifications. This is an issue not presented in this case and we express no view as to its resolution.

construction given the document by another branch. The alleged conflict that such an adjudication may cause cannot justify the courts' avoiding their constitutional responsibility. . . .

Nor are any of the other formulations of a political question "inextricable from the case at bar." Baker v. Carr, supra, at 217. Petitioners seek a determination that the House was without power to exclude Powell from the 90th Congress, which, we have seen, requires an interpretation of the Constitution—a determination for which clearly there are "judicially . . . manageable standards." Finally, a judicial resolution of petitioners' claim will not result in "multifarious pronouncements by various departments on one question." For, as we noted in Baker v. Carr, supra, at 211, it is the responsibility of this Court to act as the ultimate interpreter of the Constitution. Marbury v. Madison, 5 U.S. (1 Cranch) 137 (1803). Thus, we conclude that petitioners' claim is not barred by the political question doctrine, and having determined that the claim is otherwise generally justiciable, we hold that the case is justiciable.

. . .

Nixon v. United States

506 U.S. 224, 113 S.Ct. 732, 122 L.Ed.2d 1 (1993).

Chief Justice Rehnquist delivered the opinion of the Court.

Petitioner Walter L. Nixon, Jr., asks this court to decide whether Senate Rule XI, which allows a committee of Senators to hear evidence against an individual who has been impeached and to report that evidence to the full Senate, violates the Impeachment Trial Clause, Art. I, § 3, cl. 6. That Clause provides that the "Senate shall have the sole Power to try all Impeachments." But before we reach the merits of such a claim, we must decide whether it is "justiciable," that is, whether it is a claim that may be resolved by the courts. We conclude that it is not.

Nixon, a former Chief Judge of the United States District Court for the Southern District of Mississippi, was convicted by a jury of two counts of making false statements before a federal grand jury and sentenced to prison. . . .

On May 10, 1989, the House of Representatives adopted three articles of impeachment for high crimes and misdemeanors. . . .

After the House presented the articles to the Senate, the Senate voted to invoke its own Impeachment Rule XI, under which the presiding officer appoints a committee of Senators to "receive evidence and take testimony." . . . The Senate committee held four days of hearings. . . . Pursuant to Rule XI, the committee presented the full Senate with a complete transcript of the proceeding and a report stating the uncontested facts and summarizing the evidence on the contested facts. Nixon and the House impeachment managers submitted extensive final briefs to the full Senate and delivered arguments from the Senate floor during the three hours set aside for oral argument in front of that body. Nixon himself gave a personal appeal, and several Senators posed questions directly to both parties. . . . The Senate voted by more than the constitutionally required two-thirds majority to convict Nixon on the first two articles. . . . The presiding officer then entered judgment removing Nixon from his office as United States District Judge.

Nixon thereafter commenced the present suit, arguing that Senate Rule XI violates the constitutional grant of authority to the Senate to "try" all impeachments because it prohibits the whole Senate from taking part in the evidentiary hearings.... The District Court held that his claim was nonjusticiable, and the Court of Appeals for the District of Columbia Circuit agreed.

A controversy is nonjusticiable—i.e., involves a political question—where there is "a textually demonstrable constitutional commitment of the issue to a coordinate political department; or a lack of judicially discoverable and manageable standards for resolving it...." Baker v. Carr, 369 U.S. 186, 217 (1962). But the courts must, in the first instance, interpret the text in question and determine whether and to what extent the issue is textually committed. ... As the discussion that follows makes clear, the concept of a textual commitment to a coordinate political department is not completely separate from the concept of a lack of judicially discoverable and manageable standards for resolving it; the lack of judicially manageable standards may strengthen the conclusion that there is a textually demonstrable commitment to a coordinate branch.

In this case, we must examine Art. I, § 3, cl. 6, to determine the scope of authority conferred upon the Senate by the Framers regarding impeachment. It provides:

> "The Senate shall have the sole Power to try all Impeachments. When sitting for that Purpose, they shall be on Oath or Affirmation. When the President of the United States is tried, the Chief Justice shall preside: And no Person shall be convicted without the Concurrence of two thirds of the Members present."

The language and structure of this Clause are revealing. The first sentence is a grant of authority to the Senate, and the word "sole" indicates that this authority is reposed in the Senate and nowhere else. The next two sentences specify requirements to which the Senate proceedings shall conform: the Senate shall be on oath or affirmation, a two-thirds vote is required to convict, and when the President is tried the Chief Justice shall preside.

Petitioner argues that the word "try" in the first sentence imposes by implication an additional requirement on the Senate in that the proceedings must be in the nature of a judicial trial. From there petitioner goes on to argue that this limitation precludes the Senate from delegating to a select committee the task of hearing the testimony of witnesses, as was done pursuant to Senate Rule XI....

There are several difficulties with this position which lead us ultimately to reject it. The word "try," both in 1787 and later, has considerably broader meanings than those to which petitioner would limit it. ... [W]e cannot say that the Framers used the word "try" as an implied limitation on the method by which the Senate might proceed in trying impeachments. "As a rule the Constitution speaks in general terms, leaving Congress to deal with subsidiary matters of detail as the public interests and changing conditions may require...." Dillon v. Gloss, 256 U.S. 368, 376 (1921).

The conclusion that the use of the word "try" in the first sentence of the Impeachment Trial Clause lacks sufficient precision to afford any judicially manageable standard of review of the Senate's actions is fortified by the existence of the three very specific requirements that the Constitution does impose on the Senate when trying impeachments: the members must be under oath, a two-thirds vote is required to convict, and the Chief Justice presides when the President is tried. These limitations are quite precise, and their nature suggests that the Framers did not intend to impose additional limitations on the form of the Senate proceedings by the use of the word "try" in the first sentence.

... [The first sentence of Clause 6] provides that "[t]he Senate shall have the sole Power to try all Impeachments." We think that the word "sole" is of considerable significance. Indeed, the word "sole" appears only one other time in the Constitution—with respect to the House of Representatives' "*sole* Power of Impeachment." Art. I, § 2, cl. 5 (emphasis added). The common sense meaning of the word "sole" is that the Senate alone shall have authority to determine whether an individual should be acquitted or convicted. . . .

. . . .

Petitioner . . . argues that even if significance be attributed to the word "sole" in the first sentence of the clause, the authority granted is to the Senate, and this means that "the Senate—not the courts, not a lay jury, not a Senate Committee—shall try impeachments." It would be possible to read the first sentence of the Clause this way, but it is not a natural reading. Petitioner's interpretation would bring into judicial purview not merely the sort of claim made by petitioner, but other similar claims based on the conclusion that the word "Senate" has imposed by implication limitations on procedures which the Senate might adopt. Such limitations would be inconsistent with the construction of the Clause as a whole, which, as we have noted, sets out three express limitations in separate sentences.

The history and contemporary understanding of the impeachment provisions support our reading of the constitutional language. The parties do not offer evidence of a single word in the history of the Constitutional Convention or in contemporary commentary that even alludes to the possibility of judicial review in the context of the impeachment powers. R. Berger, Impeachment: The Constitutional Problems 116 (1973). This silence is quite meaningful in light of the several explicit references to the availability of judicial review as a check on the Legislature's power with respect to bills of attainder, ex post facto laws, and statutes. . . .

The Framers labored over the question of where the impeachment power should lie. Significantly, in at least two considered scenarios the power was placed with the Federal Judiciary. See 1 Farrand 21–22 (Virginia Plan); id., at 244 (New Jersey Plan). Indeed, Madison and the Committee of Detail proposed that the Supreme Court should have the power to determine impeachments. See 2 id., at 551 (Madison); id., at 178–179, 186 (Committee of Detail). Despite these proposals, the Convention ultimately decided that the Senate would have "the sole Power to Try all Impeachments." Art. I, § 3, cl. 6. According to Alexander Hamilton, the Senate was the "most fit depositary of this important trust" because its members are representatives of the people. See The Federalist No. 65, p. 440 (J. Cooke ed. 1961). The Supreme Court was not the proper body because the Framers "doubted whether the members of that tribunal would, at all times, be endowed with so eminent a portion of fortitude as would be called for in the execution of so difficult a task" or whether the Court "would possess the degree of credit and authority" to carry out its judgment if it conflicted with the accusation brought by the Legislature—the people's representative. See id., at 441. In addition, the Framers believed the Court was too small in number: "The awful discretion, which a court of impeachments must necessarily have, to doom to honor or to infamy the most confidential and the most distinguished characters of the community, forbids the commitment of the trust to a small number of persons." Id., at 441–442.

There are two additional reasons why the Judiciary, and the Supreme Court in particular, were not chosen to have any role in impeachments. First, the Framers recognized that most likely there would be two sets of proceedings for individuals who commit impeachable offenses—the impeachment trial and a separate criminal trial. In fact, the Constitution explicitly provides for two separate proceedings. See Art. I, § 3, cl. 7. The Framers deliberately separated the two forums to avoid raising the specter of bias and to ensure independent judgments . . . Certainly judicial review of the Senate's "trial" would introduce the same risk of bias as would participation in the trial itself.

Second, judicial review would be inconsistent with the Framers' insistence that our system be one of checks and balances. In our constitutional system, impeachment was designed to be the only check on the Judicial Branch by the Legislature. . . . Judicial involvement in impeachment proceedings, even if only for purposes of judicial review, is counterintuitive because it would eviscerate the "important constitutional check" placed on the Judiciary by the Framers. . . . Nixon's argument would place final reviewing authority with respect to impeachments in the hands of the same body that the impeachment process is meant to regulate.

Nevertheless, Nixon argues that judicial review is necessary in order to place a check on the Legislature. Nixon fears that if the Senate is given unreviewable authority to interpret the Impeachment Trial Clause, there is a grave risk that the Senate will usurp judicial power. The Framers anticipated this objection and created two constitutional safeguards to keep the Senate in check. The first safeguard is that the whole of the impeachment power is divided between the two legislative bodies, with the House given the right to accuse and the Senate given the right to judge. . . . This split of authority "avoids the inconvenience of making the same persons both accusers and judges; and guards against the danger of persecution from the prevalency of a factious spirit in either of those branches." The second safeguard is the two-thirds supermajority vote requirement. . . .

In addition to the textual commitment argument, we are persuaded that the lack of finality and the difficulty of fashioning relief counsel against justiciability. See Baker v. Carr, 369 U.S., at 210. . . . This lack of finality would manifest itself most dramatically if the President were impeached. The legitimacy of any successor, and hence his effectiveness, would be impaired severely, not merely while the judicial process was running its course, but during any retrial that a differently constituted Senate might conduct if its first judgment of conviction were invalidated. Equally uncertain is the question of what relief a court may give other than simply setting aside the judgment of conviction. Could it order the reinstatement of a convicted federal judge, or order Congress to create an additional judgeship if the seat had been filled in the interim?

Petitioner finally contends that a holding of nonjusticiability cannot be reconciled with our opinion in Powell v. McCormack, 395 U.S. 486 (1969). . . .

Our conclusion in *Powell* was based on the fixed meaning of "[q]ualifications" set forth in Art. I, § 2. . . . The decision as to whether a member satisfied these qualifications was placed with the House, but the decision as to what these qualifications consisted of was not.

In the case before us, there is no separate provision of the Constitution which could be defeated by allowing the Senate final authority to determine the meaning of the word "try" in the Impeachment Trial Clause. We agree with Nixon that courts possess power to review either legislative or executive action that transgresses identifiable textual limits. . . . But we conclude . . . that the word "try" in the Impeachment Clause does not provide an identifiable textual limit on the authority which is committed to the Senate.

For the foregoing reasons, the judgment of the Court of Appeals is

Affirmed.

Justice Stevens, concurring.

For me, the debate about the strength of the inferences to be drawn from the use of the words "sole" and "try" is far less significant than the central fact that the Framers decided to assign the impeachment power to the Legislative Branch.... Respect for a coordinate Branch of the Government forecloses any assumption that improbable hypotheticals like those mentioned by Justice ... Souter will ever occur....

Justice White, with whom Justice Blackmun joins, concurring in the judgment.

Petitioner contends that the method by which the Senate convicted him on two articles of impeachment violates Art. I, § 3, cl. 6 of the Constitution.... The Court is of the view that the Constitution forbids us even to consider his contention. I find no such prohibition and would therefore reach the merits of the claim. I concur in the judgment because the Senate fulfilled its constitutional obligation to "try" petitioner.

I

It should be said at the outset that, as a practical matter, it will likely make little difference whether the Court's or my view controls this case. This is so because the Senate has very wide discretion in specifying impeachment trial procedures and because it is extremely unlikely that the Senate would abuse its discretion and insist on a procedure that could not be deemed a trial by reasonable judges. Even taking a wholly practical approach, I would prefer not to announce an unreviewable discretion in the Senate to ignore completely the constitutional direction to "try" impeachment cases....

II

. . .

Of course the issue in the political question doctrine is not whether the Constitutional text commits exclusive responsibility for a particular governmental function to one of the political branches. There are numerous instances of this sort of textual commitment, e.g., Art. I, § 8, and it is not thought that disputes implicating these provisions are nonjusticiable. Rather, the issue is whether the Constitution has given one of the political branches final responsibility for interpreting the scope and nature of such a power.

. . .

The historical evidence reveals above all else that the Framers were deeply concerned about placing in any branch the "awful discretion, which a court of impeachments must necessarily have." ... Viewed against this history, the discord between the majority's position and the basic principles of checks and balances underlying the Constitution's separation of powers is clear. In essence, the majority suggests that the Framers' conferred upon Congress a potential tool of legislative dominance yet at the same time rendered Congress' exercise of that power one of the very few areas of legislative authority immune from any judicial review.... In a truly balanced system, impeachments tried by the Senate would serve as a means of controlling the largely unaccountable judiciary, even as judicial review would ensure that the Senate adhered to a minimal set of procedural standards in conducting impeachment trials.

. . .

III

. . .

In short, textual and historical evidence reveals that the Impeachment Trial Clause was not meant to bind the hands of the Senate beyond establishing a set of minimal procedures. Without identifying the exact contours of these procedures, it is sufficient to say that the Senate's use of a factfinding committee under Rule XI is entirely compatible with the Constitution's command that the Senate "try all impeachments." Petitioner's challenge to his conviction must therefore fail.

. . .

Justice Souter, concurring in the judgment.

I agree with the Court that this case presents a nonjusticiable political question. Because my analysis differs somewhat from the Court's, however, I concur in its judgment by this separate opinion.

. . .

Whatever considerations feature most prominently in a particular case, the political question doctrine is "essentially a function of the separation of powers," . . . existing to restrain courts "from inappropriate interference in the business of the other branches of Government," United States v. Munoz–Flores, 495 U.S. 385, 394 (1990), and deriving in large part from prudential concerns about the respect we owe the political departments. . . . Not all interference is inappropriate or disrespectful, however, and application of the doctrine ultimately turns, as Learned Hand put it, on "how importunately the occasion demands an answer." L. Hand, The Bill of Rights 15 (1958).

This occasion does not demand an answer. It seems fair to conclude that the [Impeachment Trial] Clause contemplates that the Senate may determine, within broad boundaries, such subsidiary issues as the procedures for receipt and consideration of evidence necessary to satisfy its duty to "try" impeachments. Other significant considerations confirm a conclusion that this case presents a nonjusticiable political question. . . . As the Court observes, judicial review of an impeachment trial would under the best of circumstances entail significant disruption of government.

One can, nevertheless, envision different and unusual circumstances that might justify a more searching review of impeachment proceedings. If the Senate were to act in a manner seriously threatening the integrity of its results, convicting, say, upon a coin-toss, or upon a summary determination that an officer of the United States was simply "a bad guy," . . . judicial interference might well be appropriate. In such circumstances, the Senate's action might be so far beyond the scope of its constitutional authority, and the consequent impact on the Republic so great, as to merit a judicial response despite the prudential concerns that would ordinarily counsel silence. . . .

Goldwater v. Carter

444 U.S. 996, 100 S.Ct. 533, 62 L.Ed.2d 428 (1979).

ORDER

The petition for a writ of certiorari is granted. The judgment of the Court of Appeals is vacated and the case is remanded to the District Court with directions to dismiss the complaint.

Mr. Justice Marshall concurs in the result.

Mr. Justice Powell concurs in the judgment and has filed a statement.

Mr. Justice Rehnquist concurs in the judgment and has filed a statement in which Mr. Chief Justice Burger, Mr. Justice Stewart, and Mr. Justice Stevens join.

Mr. Justice White and Mr. Justice Blackmun join in the grant of the petition for a writ of certiorari but would set the case for argument and give it plenary consideration. Mr. Justice Blackmun has filed a statement in which Mr. Justice White joins.

Mr. Justice Brennan would grant the petition for certiorari and affirm the judgment of the Court of Appeals and has filed a statement.

Mr. Justice Powell, concurring.

Although I agree with the result reached by the Court, I would dismiss the complaint as not ripe for judicial review.

I.

This Court has recognized that an issue should not be decided if it is not ripe for judicial review. Buckley v. Valeo, 424 U.S. 1, 113–114 (1976) (per curiam). Prudential considerations persuade me that a dispute between Congress and the President is not ready for judicial review unless and until each branch has taken action asserting its constitutional authority. Differences between the President and the Congress are commonplace under our system. The differences should, and almost invariably do, turn on political rather than legal considerations. The Judicial Branch should not decide issues affecting the allocation of power between the President and Congress until the political branches reach a constitutional impasse. Otherwise, we would encourage small groups or even individual Members of Congress to seek judicial resolution of issues before the normal political process has the opportunity to resolve the conflict.

In this case, a few Members of Congress claim that the President's action in terminating the treaty with Taiwan has deprived them of their constitutional role with respect to a change in the supreme law of the land. Congress has taken no official action. In the present posture of this case, we do not know whether there ever will be an actual confrontation between the Legislative and Executive Branches. Although the Senate has considered a resolution declaring that Senate approval is necessary for the termination of any mutual defense treaty, no final vote has been taken on the resolution. Moreover, it is unclear whether the resolution would have retroactive effect. It cannot be said that either the Senate or the House has rejected the President's claim. If the Congress chooses not to confront the President, it is not our task to do so. I therefore concur in the dismissal of this case.

II.

Mr. Justice Rehnquist suggests, however, that the issue presented by this case is a nonjusticiable political question which can never be considered by this Court. I cannot agree. In my view, reliance upon the political-question doctrine is inconsistent with our precedents. As set forth in the seminal case of Baker v. Carr, 369 U.S. 186, 217 (1962), the doctrine incorporates three inquiries: (i) Does the issue involve resolution of questions committed by the text of the Constitution to a coordinate branch of government? (ii) Would resolution of the question demand that a court move beyond areas of judicial expertise? (iii) Do prudential considerations counsel against judicial intervention? In my opinion the answer to each of these inquiries would require us to decide this case if it were ready for review.

First, the existence of "a textually demonstrable constitutional commitment of the issue to a coordinate political branch," ibid., turns on an examination of the constitutional provisions governing the exercise of the power in question. Powell v. McCormack, 395 U.S. 486, 519 (1969). No constitutional provision explicitly confers upon the President the power to terminate treaties. Further, Art. II, § 2 of the Constitution authorizes the President to make treaties with the advice and consent of the Senate. Article VI provides that treaties shall be a part of the supreme law of the land. These provisions add support to the view that the text of the Constitution does not unquestionably commit the power to terminate treaties to the President alone. . . .

Second, there is no "lack of judicially discoverable and manageable standards for resolving" this case; nor is a decision impossible "without an initial policy determination of a kind clearly for nonjudicial discretion." Baker v. Carr, 369 U.S., at 217. We are asked to decide whether the President may terminate a treaty under the Constitution without congressional approval. Resolution of the question may not be easy, but it only requires us to apply normal principles of interpretation to the constitutional provisions at issue. See Powell v. McCormack, 395 U.S., at 548–549. The present case involves neither review of the President's activities as Commander-in-Chief nor impermissible interference in the field of foreign affairs. Such a case would arise if we were asked to decide, for example, whether a treaty required the President to order troops into a foreign country. But "it is error to suppose that every case or controversy which touches foreign relations lies beyond judicial cognizance." Baker v. Carr, supra, 369 U.S., at 211. This case "touches" foreign relations, but the question presented to us concerns only the constitutional division of power between Congress and the President.

A simple hypothetical demonstrates the confusion that I find inherent in Mr. Justice Rehnquist's concurring opinion. Assume that the President signed a mutual defense treaty with a foreign country and announced that it would go into effect despite its rejection by the Senate. Under Mr. Justice Rehnquist's analysis that situation would present a political question even though Art. II, § 2, clearly would resolve the dispute. Although the answer to the hypothetical case seems self-evident because it demands textual rather than interstitial analysis, the nature of the legal issue presented is no different from the issue presented in the case before us. In both cases, the Court would interpret the Constitution to decide whether congressional approval is necessary to give a Presidential decision on the validity of a treaty the force of law. Such an inquiry demands no special competence or information beyond the reach of the judiciary.

Finally, the political-question doctrine rests in part on prudential concerns calling for mutual respect among the three branches of government. Thus, the Judicial Branch should avoid "the potentiality of embarrassment [that would result] from multifarious pronouncements by various departments on one question." Similarly, the doctrine restrains judicial action where there is an "unusual need for unquestioning adherence to a political decision already made." Baker v. Carr, supra, 369 U.S., at 217.

If this case were ripe for judicial review, see Part I supra, none of these prudential considerations would be present. Interpretation of the Constitution does not imply lack of respect for a coordinate branch. Powell v. McCormack, 395 U.S., at 548. If the President and the Congress had reached irreconcilable positions, final disposition of the question presented by this case would eliminate, rather than create, multiple constitutional interpretations. The spectre of the Federal Government brought to a halt because of the mutual intransigence of the President and the Congress would require this Court to provide a resolution pursuant to our duty "to say what the law is." United States v. Nixon, 418 U.S. 683, 703, quoting Marbury v. Madison, 1 Cranch 137, 177 (1803).

III.

In my view, the suggestion that this case presents a political question is incompatible with this Court's willingness on previous occasions to decide whether one branch of our government has impinged upon the power of another. See Buckley v. Valeo, 424 U.S. 1, 138 (1976); United States v. Nixon, 418 U.S. 683, 707 (1974); The Pocket Veto Case, 279 U.S. 655, 676–678 (1929); Myers v. United States, 272 U.S. 52 (1926).[2] Under the criteria enunciated in Baker v. Carr, we have the responsibility to decide whether both the Executive and Legislative Branches have constitutional roles to play in termination of a treaty. If the Congress, by appropriate formal action, had challenged the President's authority to terminate the treaty with Taiwan, the resulting uncertainty could have serious consequences for our country. In that situation, it would be the duty of this Court to resolve the issue.

Mr. Justice Rehnquist, with whom The Chief Justice, Mr. Justice Stewart, and Mr. Justice Stevens join, concurring.

I am of the view that the basic question presented by the petitioners in this case is "political" and therefore nonjusticiable because it involves the authority of the President in the conduct of our country's foreign relations and the extent to which the Senate or the Congress is authorized to negate the action of the President. In Coleman v. Miller, 307 U.S. 433 (1939), a case in which members of the Kansas Legislature brought an action attacking a vote of the State Senate in favor of the ratification of the Child Labor Amendment, Mr. Chief Justice Hughes wrote in what is referred to as the "Opinion of the Court":

> "We think that . . . the question of the efficacy of ratifications by state legislatures, in the light of previous rejection or attempted withdrawal, should be regarded as a political question pertaining to the political departments, with the ultimate authority in the Congress in the exercise of its control over the promulgation of the adoption of the Amendment. . . . The precise question as now raised is whether, when the legislature of the State, as we have found, has actually ratified the proposed Amendment, the Court should restrain the State officers from certifying the ratification to the Secretary of State, because of an earlier rejection, and thus prevent

---

2. Coleman v. Miller, 307 U.S. 433 (1939), is not relevant here. In that case, the Court was asked to review the legitimacy of a State's ratification of a constitutional amendment. Four Members of the Court stated that Congress has exclusive power over the ratification process. Id., at 456–460 (Black, J., concurring, with whom Roberts, Frankfurter, and Douglas, JJ., joined). Three Members of the Court concluded more narrowly that the Court could not pass upon the efficacy of state ratification. They also found no standards by which the Court could fix a reasonable time for the ratification of a proposed amendment. Id., at 452–454.

The proposed constitutional amendment at issue in *Coleman* would have overruled decisions of this Court. . . . Thus, judicial review of the legitimacy of a State's ratification would have compelled this Court to oversee the very constitutional process used to reverse Supreme Court decisions. In such circumstances it may be entirely appropriate for the Judicial Branch of government to step aside. See Scharpf, Judicial Review and The Political Question: A Functional Analysis, 75 Yale L.J. 517, 589 (1966). The present case involves no similar principle of judicial nonintervention.

the question from coming before the political departments. We find no basis in either Constitution or statute for such judicial action. Article V, speaking solely of ratification, contains no provision as to rejection...." Id., at 450.

Thus, Mr. Chief Justice Hughes' opinion concluded that "Congress in controlling the promulgation of the adoption of a constitutional amendment has the final determination of the question whether by lapse of time its proposal of the amendment had lost its vitality prior to the required ratifications." Id., at 456.

I believe it follows *a fortiori* from *Coleman* that the controversy in the instant case is a nonjusticiable political dispute that should be left for resolution by the Executive and Legislative Branches of the Government. Here, while the Constitution is express as to the manner in which the Senate shall participate in the ratification of a Treaty, it is silent as to that body's participation in the abrogation of a Treaty. In this respect the case is directly analogous to *Coleman,* supra. As stated in Dyer v. Blair, 390 F.Supp. 1291, 1302 (N.D.Ill.1975) (three-judge court):

> "A question that might be answered in different ways for different amendments must surely be controlled by political standards rather than standards easily characterized as judicially manageable."

In light of the absence of any constitutional provision governing the termination of a Treaty, and the fact that different termination procedures may be appropriate for different treaties, the instant case in my view also "must surely be controlled by political standards."

I think that the justifications for concluding that the question here is political in nature are even more compelling than in *Coleman* because it involves foreign relations—specifically a treaty commitment to use military force in the defense of a foreign government if attacked....

The present case differs in several important respects from Youngstown Sheet & Tube Co. v. Sawyer, 343 U.S. 579 (1952), cited by petitioners as authority both for reaching the merits of this dispute and for reversing the Court of Appeals. In *Youngstown* private litigants brought a suit contesting the President's authority under his war powers to seize the Nation's steel industry, an action of profound and demonstrable domestic impact. Here, by contrast, we are asked to settle a dispute between coequal branches of our government, each of which has resources available to protect and assert its interests, resources not available to private litigants outside the judicial forum.[1] Moreover, as in *Curtiss–Wright,* the effect of this action, as far as we can tell, is "entirely external to the United States, and [falls] within the category of foreign affairs."

---

1. As observed by Judge Wright in his concurring opinion below:

"Congress has initiated the termination of treaties by directing or requiring the President to give notice of termination, without any prior presidential request. Congress has annulled treaties without any presidential notice. It has conferred on the President the power to terminate a particular treaty, and it has enacted statutes practically nullifying the domestic effects of a treaty and thus caused the President to carry out termination.... Moreover, Congress has a variety of powerful tools for influencing foreign policy decisions that bear on treaty matters. Under Article I, Section 8 of the Constitution, it can regulate commerce with foreign nations, raise and support armies, and declare war. It has power over the appointment of ambassadors and the funding of embassies and consulates. Congress thus retains a strong influence over the President's conduct in treaty matters. As our political history demonstrates, treaty creation and termination are complex phenomena rooted in the dynamic relationship between the two political branches of our government. We thus should decline the invitation to set in concrete a particular constitutionally acceptable arrangement by which the President and Congress are to share treaty termination."

Finally, as already noted, the situation presented here is closely akin to that presented in *Coleman,* where the Constitution spoke only to the procedure for ratification of an amendment, not to its rejection.

Having decided that the question presented in this action is nonjusticiable, I believe that the appropriate disposition is for this Court to vacate the decision of the Court of Appeals and remand with instructions for the District Court to dismiss the complaint. . . .

Mr. Justice Blackmun, with whom Mr. Justice White joins, dissenting in part.

In my view, the time factor and its importance are illusory; if the President does not have the power to terminate the Treaty (a substantial issue that we should address only after briefing and oral argument), the notice of intention to terminate surely has no legal effect. It is also indefensible, without further study, to pass on the issue of justiciability or on the issues of standing or ripeness. While I therefore join in the grant of the petition for certiorari, I would set the case for oral argument and give it the plenary consideration it so obviously deserves.

Mr. Justice Brennan, dissenting.

I respectfully dissent from the order directing the District Court to dismiss this case, and would affirm the judgment of the Court of Appeals insofar as it rests upon the President's well-established authority to recognize, and withdraw recognition from, foreign governments.

In stating that this case presents a non-justiciable "political question," the plurality, in my view, profoundly misapprehends the political question principle as it applies to matters of foreign relations. Properly understood, the political question doctrine restrains courts from reviewing an exercise of foreign policy judgment by the coordinate political branch to which authority to make that judgment has been "constitutional[ly] commit[ted]." Baker v. Carr, 369 U.S. 186, 211–213, 217 (1962). But the doctrine does not pertain when a court is faced with the *antecedent* question whether a particular branch has been constitutionally designated as the repository of political decisionmaking power. Cf. Powell v. McCormack, 395 U.S. 486, 519–521 (1969). The issue of decisionmaking authority must be resolved as a matter of constitutional law, not political discretion; accordingly, it falls within the competence of the courts.

The constitutional question raised here is prudently answered in narrow terms. Abrogation of the defense treaty with Taiwan was a necessary incident to Executive recognition of the Peking government, because the defense treaty was predicated upon the now-abandoned view that the Taiwan government was the only legitimate political authority in China. Our cases firmly establish that the Constitution commits to the President alone the power to recognize, and withdraw recognition from, foreign regimes. . . . That mandate being clear, our judicial inquiry into the treaty rupture can go no further. . . .

POLITICAL QUESTIONS

(1) That aspect of the political question doctrine relying on "a textually demonstrable commitment of the issue to a coordinate political department" is, as the Court noted in Baker v. Carr, "primarily a function of the separation of powers." The issue will be raised again in Chapter 7—see especially United States v. Nixon, infra p. 454. One question concerning "textually demonstrable commitments" is alluded to by Justice White's concurrence in the case involving Judge Nixon, see supra p. 111: What is distinctive about some text in the Constitution that creates a "commitment" of an issue to a branch other than

the courts? For example, the Constitution in Article I empowers Congress to pass laws that are "necessary and proper" but does not exclude the judiciary from visiting the question whether specific congressional enactments are "necessary and proper." Is there something particular about certain language in the Constitution, e.g., the impeachment provisions or the provisions enabling each house to judge qualifications and discipline itself, that reflects a distinct kind of textual commitment?

(2) In Baker v. Carr, the Court noted that a case might be held to involve a political question because of "a lack of judicially discoverable and manageable standards for resolving it." The Court held that reapportionment cases did not require "the Court to enter upon policy determinations for which judicially manageable standards are lacking. Judicial standards under the Equal Protection Clause are well developed and familiar, and it has been open to courts since the enactment of the Fourteenth Amendment to determine, if on the particular facts they must, that a discrimination reflects *no* policy, but simply arbitrary and capricious action." When studying the subsequent reapportionment cases, including those involving the use of race by those who draw district lines, infra Chapter 10, the student should ask whether the Court's prediction as to the manageability of the standards proved to be true.

The Supreme Court found a lack of judicially manageable standards for resolving a claim that Pennsylvania's legislature had violated the Constitution by taking partisan considerations into account too much in the drawing of district lines. Rejecting the analogy to the racial redistricting cases, where the Court has held that race may not "predominate" over other districting criteria, the Justices held, 5–4, in Vieth v. Jubelirer, 541 U.S. 267 (2004), reported in full at p. 980 infra, that claims in that case that one political party had used districting unfairly to ensure that party's success in too many legislative districts were not amenable to federal adjudication. Importantly, Justice Kennedy, who provided the fifth vote and concurred in the judgment only, wrote separately to emphasize the possibility that manageable standards not present today may be developed over time.

(3) Consider the suggestion in footnote 2 of Justice Powell's concurrence in Goldwater v. Carter, supra p. 115, that when adjudication would "compel[] this Court to oversee the very constitutional process used to reverse Supreme Court decisions" judicial discretion is particularly important. While Justice Powell was referring to cases involving the validity of constitutional amendments, which are discussed below, are there other constitutional processes "used to reverse Supreme Court decisions" in which the Court should tread lightly? In this regard, consider the Court's controversial decision to enter into the 2000 Presidential election dispute in Florida and the Bush v. Gore, 531 U.S. 98 (2000), decision described at pp. 1003 and 147 infra.

(4) Professor Henkin suggests that there is no separate political question doctrine:

"The thesis I offer for discussion is that there may be no doctrine requiring abstention from judicial review of 'political questions.' The cases which are supposed to have established the political question doctrine required no such extra-ordinary abstention from judicial review; they called only for the ordinary respect by the courts for the political domain. Having reviewed, the Court refused to invalidate the challenged actions because they were within the constitutional authority of President or Congress. In no case did the Court have to use the phrase 'political question'...."

Henkin, *Is There a "Political Question" Doctrine?*, 85 Yale L.J. 597, 600 (1976).

In connection with Professor Henkin's thesis, consider U.S. Department of Commerce v. Montana, 503 U.S. 442 (1992). Following the apportionment method dictated by a 1941 federal statute, Congressional reapportionment pursuant to the 1990 census reduced Montana's delegation from two representatives to one. Montana claimed that the federal statute was unconstitutional insofar as it caused Montana to be represented by a single district 231,189 persons larger than an average district. The Court rejected the argument that Congressional selection of an apportionment method was a political question not subject to judicial review. Article I, § 2, places substantive limitations on Congress' apportionment power, including a requirement that representatives be apportioned to the states "according to their respective numbers." Violation of that limitation would present a justiciable controversy. The Court concluded, however, that the apportionment method mandated by the 1941 statute was not unconstitutional. Since Congressional districts cannot cross State lines, it is impossible for all districts to be the same size.

> "The constitutional framework ... must ... delegate to Congress a measure of discretion that is broader than that accorded to the States in the much easier task of determining district sizes within State borders.... Its apparently good-faith choice of a method of apportionment of Representatives among the several States 'according to their respective numbers' commands far more deference than a state districting decision that is capable of being reviewed under a relatively rigid mathematical standard."

THE AMENDMENT PROCESS—A DIGRESSION

The amendment process as set out in Article V has given rise to a number of questions. Since the Court has indicated that some of these questions are non-justiciable political questions, a general look at the problems relating to Article V seems appropriate at this point.

Proposal of Amendments

Amendments may be proposed either by a two-thirds majority in both Houses of Congress or by a convention called by Congress upon the application of the legislatures of two-thirds of the states. Every proposal made thus far has come from Congress. The process has been generally uncontroversial.

While Article V's alternative mode of proposing amendments by convention has yet to be exercised, it is by no means a dead letter. Well over 300 applications calling for conventions have been sent to Congress by state legislatures to date. Every state has submitted at least one such petition. The applications have ranged from those calling for a general constitutional convention to those calling for conventions to consider such specific topics as slavery, anti-polygamy, and integration of public schools. During the 1960's, in the aftermath of the Supreme Court's decision mandating reapportionment of state legislatures to conform with population distribution, nearly two-thirds of the states submitted applications calling for a convention on the subject of apportionment. Most recently, more than thirty states have requested a convention on the issue of a balanced federal budget.

It is generally agreed that the framers made provision for the proposal of amendments by convention at least in part because they feared that the excesses of the federal government could be most difficult to curtail through amendment if only Congress could initiate constitutional change. While resort to the convention process has not been required to subdue an oppressive Congress, its prospect has operated to prod a reluctant one to action. The raft of applications for a convention to propose popular election of U.S. Senators inspired Congress to propose the Seventeenth Amendment, post haste. Recent applications, such as those addressed to reapportionment and bussing, suggest that the device may be used to apprise Congress of serious dissatisfaction with decisions of the Supreme Court and possibly to directly institute curative amendments.

The treatment in Article V of the convention method of proposing amendments is cryptic indeed, and uncertainty regarding it is the rule rather than the exception. Issues as to the meaning of Article V were widely debated in the aftermath of calls for a convention on apportionment issues in the 1960's,[1] and most recently in the context of calls for a convention on the issue of a balanced budget and other issues such as federal legislative term limits.[2] Among the more important questions are these:

1.   What constitutes a valid application which Congress must count? Is an application valid if it calls for an unlimited convention? If it calls for a convention applicable to a particular subject? If it calls for a convention to vote up or down the text of a particular amendment?

2.   How is it to be determined whether two-thirds of the states have applied for a convention? What is the length of time for which applications will be counted? Should applications be counted if they differ with reference to the subject of the proposed convention?

3.   If it is decided that there are valid calls for a convention from two-thirds of the states, what are the powers of Congress in calling such a convention? Does Congress have discretion not to call the convention? Can Congress specify the manner of selection of delegates and their numbers? Can Congress specify the procedures to be followed by the Convention? Can Congress limit the subject matter to be considered by the convention?

4.   If a convention is called, are Congressional limitations on procedure and subject matter binding on the convention?

5.   What is the power of Congress concerning the product of a convention? Can Congress refuse to submit proposed amendments to the states for ratification if the convention ignores Congressional directions on voting requirements or limitations on subject matter?

6.   What role may the people of each state play in triggering a convention? What devices may the people of each state use to put pressure on their state legislatures to call for a convention?

The lack of answers to most of the preceding questions has raised the spectre of a "runaway convention," called for a limited purpose but proposing far-reaching amendments to the Constitution and the Bill of Rights.

---

1. E.g., American Bar Association Special Constitutional Convention Study Committee, Amendment of the Constitution by the Convention Method under Article V (1974); Bonfield, *The Dirksen Amendment and the Article V Convention Process,* 66 Mich.L.Rev. 949 (1968); Ervin, *Proposed Legislation to Implement the Convention Method of Amending the Constitution,* 66 Mich.L.Rev. 875 (1968); Black, *Amending The Constitution: A Letter to a Congressman,* 82 Yale L.J. 189 (1972).

2. E.g., Bator et al., *A Constitutional Convention: How Well Would it Work?* (American Enterprise Institute 1979); Dellinger, *The Recurring Question of the "Limit-* ed" Constitutional Convention, 88 Yale L.J. 1623 (1979); Gunther, *The Convention Method of Amending the United States Constitution,* 14 Ga.L.Rev. 1 (1979); Van Alstyne, *Does Article V Restrict the States to Calling Unlimited Conventions Only?—A Letter to a Colleague,* 1978 Duke L.J. 1295 (1979); Akhil Amar, *The Consent of the Governed: Constitutional Amendment Outside Article V,* 94 Colum.L.Rev. 457 (1994) Vikram Amar, *The People Made Me Do It: Can the People of the States Instruct and Coerce Their State Legislatures in the Article V Constitutional Amendment Process?,* 41 Wm. & Mary L.Rev. 1037 (2000).

Ratification of Amendments

Just as Article V offers two methods for proposal of amendments, it also sets forth alternative modes of ratification: "by the Legislatures of three fourths of the several states, or by Conventions in three fourths thereof, as one or the other Mode of Ratification may be proposed by the Congress...." Congress has generally preferred ratification by the state legislatures, invoking the state convention device in only one instance—the Twenty–First Amendment's repeal of national prohibition.

Since amendments to the Constitution have been ratified on eighteen occasions, questions concerning the ratification process are fewer than the untested questions concerning amendments proposed by a constitutional convention. There are questions whose answers are not obvious, however. These concern, among others, the time during which ratification may take place, the extent to which state law controls ratification by state legislatures, and the legal effect of ratification by states that previously, or subsequently, reject an amendment. Two questions that arose in the context of the unsuccessful attempt to ratify the Equal Rights Amendment are instructive.

One question concerns the time limit for ratification. The Eighteenth, Twentieth, Twenty-first and Twenty-second Amendments contain seven year time limits for ratification in their texts. (No time limit for ratification was set in connection with the Nineteenth Amendment.) Time limits for ratification of subsequent amendments were not placed in the amendment text, but in the proposing clause of the resolution submitting the amendment for ratification. The change in practice, designed to avoid "cluttering up" the text of the Constitution with obsolete provisions concerning time limits for ratification, created no legal issues prior to the proposed Equal Rights Amendment, since ratifications occurred well within the seven year limit. The requisite number of states had not ratified the ERA when the time limitation expired on March 22, 1979. In October 1978, Congress extended the time limit to June, 1982. Among the questions raised were whether it was necessary to resubmit the ERA anew, whether the extension measure required a two-thirds vote (it received substantial majorities in both houses, but less than two-thirds), and whether the President's signature was necessary (the President in fact signed the extension measure).[3]

Extension of the time for ratification of ERA exacerbated a second issue. A number of states that had originally ratified acted to rescind their ratifications, and rescission campaigns were pending in other states. One view is that ratification is a final act that can not be withdrawn. The contrary view is that the requisite number of states must agree on ratification at the same time.[4] In

---

3. On the issue of time for ratification of the ERA see: *Equal Rights Amendment Extension: Hearings on H.J. Res. 638 Before the Subcomm. on Civil and Constitutional Rights of the House Comm. on the Judiciary,* 95th Cong., 1st and 2d Sess. (1977–78); *Equal Rights Amendment Extension: Hearings on S.J.Res. 134 Before the Subcomm. on the Constitution of the Senate Comm. on the Judiciary,* 95th Cong., 2d Sess. (1978); Ginsburg, *Ratification of the Equal Rights Amendment: A Question of Time,* 57 Tex. L.Rev. 919 (1979).

The proposed District of Columbia Representation in Congress Amendment, submitted by Congress for ratification on August 22, 1978, returns to the earlier pattern. The seven year time limit for ratification is contained in the amendment text.

4. Considerable law review commentary discusses the issue of rescission. E.g., Heckman, *Ratification of a Constitutional Amendment: Can a State Change Its Mind?* 6 Conn. L.Rev. 28 (1973); Elder, *Article V, Justiciability and the Equal Rights Amendment,* 31 Okla.L.Rev. 63 (1978); Ginsburg, supra note 3; Comment, *The Equal Rights Amendment and Article V: A Framework for Analysis of the Extension and Recission Issues,* 127 U.Pa. L.Rev. 494 (1978); Note, *Reversals in the Federal Constitutional Amendment Process: Efficacy of State Ratifications of the Equal* approving extension of the time for ratification, Congress did not resolve this issue.

Congressional Resolution of Constitutional Issues Concerning the Amendment Process

Congress can attempt to determine whether a particular amendment has been ratified by the requisite number of states. In July of 1868, Congress passed a joint resolution declaring that the Fourteenth Amendment had been ratified by the requisite number of states—resolving the question whether states that had previously rejected the Amendment, and states that had rescinded their ratification, should be counted. The Secretary of State's proclamation that the Amendment had been ratified accordingly included both states which had earlier rejected the Amendment, and those that had purported to withdraw their ratifications.[5]

Congress can also attempt to resolve legal issues concerning the amendment process by a general statute not applicable to any particular amendment. Senator Ervin introduced legislation in 1971 and 1973 concerning proposal of amendments by constitutional conventions.[6] An identical "Federal Constitutional Procedures Act" was introduced in 1979 by Senator Helms.[7] Its controversial provisions include requiring state calls for a convention to state the nature of the amendments proposed, requiring a Congressional call for a convention to specify the subject, and authorizing Congress to block submission of amendments on other subjects.

Justiciability

In the absence of a Congressional decision, can any of the questions previously put be answered in litigation? If Congress resolves any of these questions, either in the context of a particular amendment or by general legislation, would those answers be binding on a court? Issues of justiciability are nearly as uncertain as the substantive answers to the constitutional questions.[8]

Prior to 1939, the Supreme Court adjudicated a number of issues concerning the ratification process. (Notice that none of the decisions rejected a contrary resolution of an issue by Congress.) In United States v. Sprague, 282 U.S. 716 (1931), the Supreme Court held that the choice between modes of ratification lies in the sole discretion of Congress. In an earlier Eighteenth Amendment case, Dillon v. Gloss, 256 U.S. 368 (1921), the Court held that Article V implicitly required that ratification be completed within some reasonable time after the proposal of an amendment, and that Congress could fix a definite period for the ratification. Hawke v. Smith, No. 1, 253 U.S. 221 (1920), held that the efficacy of a resolution of Ohio's legislature ratifying the Eighteenth Amendment could not be made subject by the state's constitution to the requirement of approval in a popular referendum. Leser v. Garnett, 258 U.S. 130 (1922), rejected a claim that by virtue of state constitutional constraints,

Rights Amendment, 49 Ind.L.J. 147 (1973); Paulsen, *A General Theory of Article V: The Constitutional Lessons of the Twenty–Seventh Amendment,* 103 Yale L.J. 677 (1993).

5. The history of the ratification of the Fourteenth Amendment is contained in Coleman v. Miller, 307 U.S. 433, 448–449 (1939).

6. S. 215, 92d Cong., 1st Sess., 117 Cong.Rec. 36804–38806 (1971); S. 1272, 93d Cong., 1st Sess., 119 Cong.Rec. 22731–37 (1973).

7. S. 520, 96th Cong., 1st Sess., 125 Cong.Rec.S. 1935 (1979).

8. Much of the commentary cited in the previous footnotes discusses issues of justiciability. See also, Orfield, *The Amending of the Federal Constitution* (1942).

certain state legislatures were without power to ratify the Nineteenth Amendment. The Court stated that the federal ratification function "transcends any limitations sought to be imposed by the people of a State." (258 U.S. at 137)[9]

Questions have been raised whether the 27th Amendment, proposed in 1789 and ratified by a thirty eighth state in 1992, has become part of the Constitution. Michigan ratified the Amendment on May 7, 1992. The Congressional leadership, responding to election-year political concerns about appearing to question a limitation on the power to raise their own salaries, announced that Congress would accept the Amendment. On May 21, 1992, Congress by joint resolution declared the 27th Amendment to be "valid ... as part of the Constitution of the United States." In the unlikely event that Congress should enact a Congressional pay raise or pay cut taking effect before an intervening election, could a Court decide whether ratification of the Amendment was effective?

As indicated, in Dillon v. Gloss, 256 U.S. 368 (1921), the Court stated that effective ratification must occur within a reasonable time after an amendment is proposed. The Court explained that the requirement insures that approval reflects "the will of the people in all sections at relatively the same period, which of course ratification scattered through a long series of years would not do." It is hard to escape the conclusion that ratification votes scattered between 1789 and 1992 do not satisfy the "reasonable time" requirements of the *Dillon* dictum. Has the 27th Amendment, nevertheless, become part of the Constitution because Congress, without holding hearings, has acquiesced?

In Coleman v. Miller, 307 U.S. 433 (1939), the Court held two questions concerning ratification to be political. Most interesting, in light of the contemporary controversy concerning the 27th Amendment, the Court concluded that the issue whether the child labor amendment was open to ratification thirteen years after it was proposed was not justiciable. The Court emphasized the absence of judicial criteria to determine the length of time that was reasonable. If Congress sets a time limit for ratification of a proposed amendment, as it has almost always done in the last 75 years, it is obvious that the Court will accept that Congressional decision. Was it so obvious that the judicial process was incapable of resolving the issue whether thirteen years was a reasonable time for ratifying the proposed child labor amendment when Congress set no time limit? If *Dillon*'s "reasonable time" requirement is implicit in Article V, is the question whether 203 years is unreasonable beyond judicial capacity?

Is there a larger issue here beyond the question whether there are manageable judicial criteria for resolving the reasonable time question? Significantly, four concurring Justices in Coleman v. Miller (Black, Roberts, Frankfurter and Douglas) rejected prior decisions of the Court adjudicating issues concerning the amending process, including *Dillon,* and argued that all such issues were political. Was it inappropriate for the Court in *Dillon* to adjudicate the issue whether Article V implicitly requires ratification within a reasonable time?

---

9. See also the National Prohibition Cases, 253 U.S. 350 (1920) (two-thirds vote requirement for proposing amendment means two-thirds of a quorum present and voting); Hollingsworth v. Virginia, 3 U.S. (3 Dall.) 378 (1798) (Presidential participation not required in proposing an amendment).

*

PART II

ALLOCATION OF GOVERNMENTAL POWERS: THE NATION AND THE STATES; THE PRESIDENT, THE CONGRESS, AND THE COURTS

A principal concern in the Constitutional Convention was the allocation of governmental powers. Two major issues were addressed: (1) The distribution of power among the three branches of the national government—the separation of powers. The aim here was to see that no particular branch was able to achieve an undue concentration of power. (2) The division of powers between the nation and the states. The great objective of the federal system that dominated the thinking of the Framers was a national government with adequate power to handle matters of national interest while the states retained autonomy over local affairs.

One aspect of separation of powers has been introduced in Part I in connection with the discussion of the scope of the judicial power. Other separation of powers issues will appear from time to time in this part of the book, but major discussion, particularly of the relationships between the President and Congress, will be deferred until Chapter 7 at the end of this part.

The bulk of Part II will be devoted to studying the division of powers between the nation and the states. The aim is to give the student a working sense of the principal issues of federalism and the manner in which the Supreme Court addresses them.

Fortunately for our constitutional development, the Convention did not attempt any such detailed specification of national and state powers as is contained in some modern federal constitutions.[1] The Framers were content to give us a rather general enumeration of national powers (principally in Art. I, § 8) plus the principle (made explicit in the Tenth Amendment) that all power not delegated to the national government remains with the states.[2] Thus, provisions delegating power to the national government may be construed in two different contexts: (1) as fixing the scope of national power; and (2) as determining the retained powers of the states. This interrelation of national and state power is explored in Chapters 4, 5, and 6.

Whatever the particular nature of the federalism issue raised, consider the following excerpt from Gregory v. Ashcroft, 501 U.S. 452, 457–458 (1991), describing the intended design and expected benefits of dividing power between the Nation and the States:

"The Constitution created a Federal Government of limited powers.... The States thus retain substantial sovereign authority under our constitutional system. As James Madison put it:

'The powers delegated by the proposed Constitution to the federal government are few and defined. Those which are to remain in the State governments are numerous and indefinite.... The powers reserved to the several States will extend to all the objects which, in the ordinary course of affairs, concern the lives, liberties, and properties of the people, and the internal order, improvement, and prosperity of the State.' The Federalist No. 45, pp. 292–293 (C. Rossiter ed. 1961) (J. Madison).

"This federalist structure of joint sovereigns preserves to the people numerous advantages. It assures a decentralized government that will be more sensitive to the diverse needs of a heterogenous society; it increases opportunity for citizen involvement in democratic processes; it allows for more innovation and experimentation in government; and it makes government more responsive by putting the States in competition for a mobile citizenry....

"Perhaps the principal benefit of the federalist system is a check on abuses of government power.... Just as the separation and independence of the coordinate Branches of the Federal Government serves to prevent the accumulation of excessive power in any one Branch, a healthy balance of power between the States and the Federal Government will reduce the risk of tyranny and abuse from either front...."

1. See, for example, the 1949 Constitution of India where the division of powers is accomplished by three detailed lists annexed to the Constitution. List I (the "Union List") itemizes the exclusive powers of the central government. List II (the "State List") itemizes the powers given exclusively to the states. List III (the concurrent list) specifies the subjects with which the states may deal in the absence of inconsistent legislation by the Parliament of India. For a general treatise, see Basu, Constitutional Law of India (6th ed. 1991).

2. The Constitution as originally adopted contains a few explicit limitations on the powers of the states. See Art. I, § 10.

CHAPTER 4

THE SCOPE OF NATIONAL POWER

SECTION 1. THE CONSTITUTIONAL CONVENTION AND THE ESTABLISHMENT OF A NATIONAL GOVERNMENT

Introduction. The following excerpts from the records of the Constitutional Convention of 1787 are designed to afford an intimate glimpse into the process of deliberation and compromise that produced the Constitution and also to provide a sample of the materials available for an examination of the historical setting and meaning of provisions of the Constitution.

A thorough examination of the historical setting and "legislative history" of constitutional provisions requires the weighing of voluminous material; there is room here for only a small sample. But the excerpts that follow can provide a basis for hypotheses, to be checked against the full record, concerning: (1) The weaknesses of the Articles of Confederation that the framers sought to avoid in their new constitution; (2) The choice (or compromise) between conflicting views concerning the power to be given the national government; (3) The nature and scope of the national power over commerce contemplated by the draftsmen.

Proceedings in the Federal Convention: May 29, 1787

Madison's Notes; I Farrand, Records of the Federal Convention of 1787 (1911) 18–19 (Hereafter Cited as "Farrand").[1]

Mr. Randolph [Va.] opened the main business. He expressed his regret, that it should fall to him, rather than those, who were of longer standing in life and political experience, to open the great subject of their mission. But, as the convention had originated from Virginia, and his colleagues supposed, that some proposition was expected from them, they had imposed this task on him.

He then commented on the difficulty of the crisis, and the necessity of preventing the fulfillment of the prophecies of the American downfall.

He observed that in revising the federal system we ought to inquire (1) into the properties, which such a government ought to possess, (2) the defects of the confederation, (3) the danger of our situation and (4) the remedy.

1. The character of such a governme[nt] ought to secure (1) against foreign invasion: (2) against dissentions between members of the Union, or seditions in particular states: (3) to p[ro]cure to the several states various blessings, of which an isolated situation was i[n]capable: (4) to be able to defend itself against encroachment: and (5) to be paramount to the state constitutions.

2. In speaking of the defects of the confederation he professed a high respect for its authors, and considered them as having done all that patriots

---

1. This and the following excerpts are copied by permission of the Yale University Press. [Bracketed references to the states from which the delegates came have been added by the editors.]

could do, in the then infancy of the science, of constitutions, and of confedera-cies,—when the inefficiency of requisitions was unknown—no commercial dis-cord had arisen among any states—no rebellion had appeared as in Massachu-setts—foreign debts had not become urgent—the havoc of paper money had not been foreseen—treaties had not been violated—and perhaps nothing better could be obtained from the jealousy of the states with regard to their sovereign-ty.

He then proceeded to enumerate the defects:[2] (1) that the confederation produced no security agai[nst] foreign invasion; congress not being permitted to prevent a war nor to support it by th[eir] own authority—of this he cited many examples; most of whi[ch] tended to show that they could not cause infractions of treaties or of the law of nations, to be punished; that particular states might by their conduct provoke war without control; and that neither militia nor draughts being fit for defense on such occasions, enlistments only could be successful, and these could not be executed without money.

(2) that the federal government could not check the quarrels between states, nor a rebellion in any not having constitutional power Nor means to interpose according to the exigency:

(3) That there were many advantages, which the U.S. might acquire, which were not attainable under the confederation—such as a productive impost—counteraction of the commercial regulations of other nations—pushing of commerce ad libitum— & c & c.

(4) that the federal government could not defend itself against the in-croachments from the states:

(5) that it was not even paramount to the state constitutions, ratified as it was in [many] of the states.

3. He next reviewed the danger of our situation appealed to the sense of the best friends of the U.S.—the prospect of anarchy from the laxity of government everywhere; and to other considerations.

4. He then proceeded to the remedy; the basis of which he said, must be the republican principle.

He proposed as conformable to his ideas the following resolutions, which he explained one by one.

Note. The "resolutions" to which Randolph referred at the close of this excerpt constituted the "Virginia Plan"—probably developed by James Madi-son. See Warren, *The Making of the Constitution* 139–141 (1928). These resolutions formed the basis for discussion and action by the Convention in the days that followed. Thus the proposition debated in the following excerpt from the proceedings of May 31 was the second part of the sixth "resolution" which Randolph proposed.

Proceedings in the Federal Convention: May 31, 1787

Madison's Notes; I Farrand 53.

On the proposition for giving "Legislative power in all cases to which the State Legislatures were individually incompetent".

2. Reasons for the failure of the Arti-cles of Confederation and the need for a stronger national union were eloquently ex-pounded by Alexander Hamilton in The Fed-eralist, Nos. 15 and 22. See also Kelly & Harbison, *The American Constitution* 108– 110 (1970). On the influence of Hamilton, *see:* Morris, *Alexander Hamilton and the Founding of the Nation* (1957); Dietze, *Ham-ilton's Federalist, Treatise for Free Govern-ment,* 42 Corn.L.Q. 307, 501 (1957).

Defects of the Articles 1-5

Mr. Pinkney [S.Car.] & Mr. Rutledge [S.Car.] objected to the vagueness of the term *incompetent*, and said they could not well decide how to vote until they should see an exact enumeration of the powers comprehended by this definition.

Mr. Butler [S.Car.] repeated his fears that we were running into an extreme in taking away the powers of the States, and called on Mr. Randolph for the extent of his meaning.

Proposed giving Fed gov't power in all cases where states were "incompetent"

Mr. Randolph [Va.] disclaimed any intention to give indefinite powers to the national Legislature, declaring that he was entirely opposed to such an inroad of the State jurisdictions, and that he did not think any considerations whatever could ever change his determination. His opinion was fixed on this point.

Mr. Madison [Va.] said that he had brought with him into the Convention a strong bias in favor of an enumeration and definition of the powers necessary to be exercised by the national Legislature; but had also brought doubts concerning its practicability. His wishes remained unaltered; but his doubts had become stronger. What his opinion might ultimately be he could not yet tell. But he should shrink from nothing which should be found essential to such a form of Govt. as would provide for the safety, liberty and happiness of the Community. This being the end of all our deliberations, all the necessary means for attaining it must, however reluctantly be submitted to.

On the question for giving powers, in cases to which the States are not competent,

Massts. ay. Cont. divd. (Sherman no Ellsworth ay) N.Y. ay. N.J. ay. Pa. ay. Del. ay. Va. ay. N.C. ay. S.Carolina ay. Georgia. ay. [Ayes—9; noes—0; divided—1].

Proceedings in the Federal Convention: July 17, 1787

(a) Journal; II Farrand 21.

It was moved and seconded to postpone the consid[eration] of the second clause of the Sixth resolution[3] reported from the Committee of the whole House in order to take up the following:

> "To make laws binding on the People of the United States in all cases which may concern the common interests of the Union: but not to interfere with the government of the individual States in any matters of internal police, which respect the government of such States only, and wherein the general welfare of the United States is not concerned."

clause was altered & then was accepted

which passed in the negative [Ayes–2; noes–8.]

It was moved and seconded to alter the second clause of the 6th resolution so as to read as follows, namely

> "and moreover to legislate in all cases for the general interests of the Union, and also in those to which the States are separately incompetent, or

---

3. The Sixth Resolution, based on Randolph's propositions, as adopted by the Committee of the Whole House on May 31, 1787 (see the excerpt from Madison's notes quoted supra), provided in part: "That the national legislature ought to be empowered to enjoy the legislative rights vested in Congress by the Confederation; and moreover To legislate in all cases, to which the separate States are incompetent or in which the harmony of the United States may be interrupted by the exercise of individual legislation." See 1 Farrand 47 (Journal, May 31, 1787).

} 6th resolution

in which the harmony of the United States may be interrupted by the exercise of individual legislation."

which passed in the affirmative [Ayes–6; noes–4.]

[To agree to the second clause of the 6. resolution as amended. Ayes–8; noes–2.]

(b) The same proceedings are reported more fully in Madison's Notes;

II FARRAND 25–27

The 6th Resoln. in the Report of the Comm. of the whole relating to the powers, which had been postponed in order to consider the 7 & 8th, relating to the Constitution of the Natl. Legislature, was now resumed—

Mr. Sherman [Conn.] observed that it would be difficult to draw the line between the powers of the Genl. Legislatures, and those to be left with the States; that he did not like the definition contained in the Resolution, and proposed in place of the words "of individual legislation" line 4 inclusive, to insert "to make laws binding on the people of the (United) States in all cases (which may concern the common interests of the Union); but not to interfere with (the Government of the individual States in any matters of internal police which respect the Govt. of such States only, and wherein the General) welfare of the U. States is not concerned."

Mr. Wilson [Pa.] 2ded. the amendment as better expressing the general principle.

Mr. Govr. Morris [Pa.] opposed it. The internal police, as it would be called & understood by the States ought to be infringed in many cases, as in the case of paper money & other tricks by which Citizens of other states may be affected.

Mr. Sherman, in explanation of his ideas read an enumeration of powers, including the power of levying taxes on trade, but not the power of *direct taxation*.

Mr. Govr. Morris remarked the omission, and inferred that for the deficiencies of taxes on consumption, it must have been the meaning of Mr. Sherman, that the Genl. Govt. should recur to quotas & requisitions, which are subversive of the idea of Govt.

Mr. Sherman acknowledged that his enumeration did not include direct taxation. Some provision he supposed must be made for supplying the deficiency of other taxation, but he had not formed any.

On Question on Mr. Sherman's motion, (it passed in the negative)

Mas. no. Cont. ay. N.J. no. Pa. no. Del. no. Md. ay. Va. no. N.C. no. S.C. no. Geo. no. [Ayes–2; noes–8].

Mr. Bedford [Del.] moved that the (2d. number of Resolution 6.) be so altered as to read "(and moreover) to legislate in all cases for the general interests of the Union, and also in those to which the States are 'separately incompetent,' (or in which the harmony of the U. States may be interrupted by the exercise of individual Legislation".)

Mr. Govr. Morris 2ds. (the motion.)

Mr. Randolph. This is a formidable idea indeed. It involves the power of violating all the laws and constitutions of the States, and of intermeddling with their police. The last member of the sentence is (also) superfluous, being included in the first.

Mr. Bedford. It is not more extensive or formidable than the clause as it stands: *no State* being *separately* competent to legislate for the *general interest* of the Union.

On question for agreeing to Mr. Bedford's motion (it passed in the affirmative).

Mas. ay. Cont. no. N.J. ay. Pa. ay. Del. ay. Md. ay. Va. no. N.C. ay. S.C. no. Geo. no. [Ayes–6; noes–4].

On the sentence as amended (it passed in the affirmative).

Mas. ay. Cont. ay. N.J. ay. Pa. ay. Del. ay. Md. ay. Va. ay. N.C. ay. S.C. no. Geo. no. [Ayes–8; noes–2].

Report of the Committee of Detail: August 6, 1787

II Farrand 181–182.

[On July 24, 1787, the Convention appointed a Committee of Detail[4] "to report a Constitution conformable to the Resolutions passed by the Convention" (II Farrand 106). The Report of the Committee on August 6, 1787 defined as follows the powers of the National Government:]

Art. VII, [erroneously numbered as VI by printer's error].

Sect. I. The Legislature of the United States shall have the power to lay and collect taxes, duties, imposts and excises;

To regulate commerce with foreign nations, and among the several States;

To establish an uniform rule of naturalization throughout the United States;

To coin money;

To regulate the value of foreign coin;

To fix the standard of weights and measures;

To establish Post-offices;

To borrow money, and emit bills on the credit of the United States;

To appoint a Treasurer by ballot;

To constitute tribunals inferior to the Supreme Court;

To make rules concerning captures on land and water;

To declare the law and punishment of piracies and felonies committed on the high seas, and the punishment of counterfeiting the coin of the United States, and of offences against the law of nations;

To subdue a rebellion in any State, on the application of its legislature;

To make war;

To raise armies;

To build and equip fleets;

To call forth the aid of the militia, in order to execute the laws of the Union, enforce treaties, suppress insurrections, and repel invasions;

4. The members of the Committee of Detail were John Rutledge (So.Car.), Edmund Randolph (Va.), Nathaniel Gorham (Mass.), Oliver Ellsworth (Conn.), and James Wilson (Pa.).

And to make all laws that shall be necessary and proper for carrying into execution the foregoing powers, and all other powers vested, by this Constitution, in the government of the United States, or in any department or officer thereof.

NOTE

It is evident from the foregoing excerpts that questions of large import are presented by the shift from a general and loosely-phrased grant of power to the national government, which the Convention initially approved on May 31 and July 17, to the itemized list of national powers embodied in the August 6 report of the Committee of Detail. Consideration should be given to two conflicting interpretations: (a) The enumeration by the Committee of Detail, which the Convention employed as a basis for final action, should be construed to reach towards the same generalized grant of power to the national government which the Convention had earlier approved; (b) The decision to enumerate the powers of Congress reflects a decision sharply to circumscribe national power.[1]

With respect to the commerce clause in particular, the proposal submitted on August 6 by the Committee of Detail was unanimously approved on August 16, 1787. (II Farrand 308). After this vote, however, strong Southern opposition to this commercial power developed out of fear that commercial regulations in the interest of Northern shipping might restrict free access for Southern staples to foreign shipping and foreign markets. This opposition was in part placated by an agreement by Northern delegates to prohibit the taxation of exports (Art. I, Sec. 9, cl. 1). See II Farrand 305–308 (Aug. 16), 359–363 (Aug. 21), 414–417 (Aug. 25); Warren, *The Making of the Constitution* 567–589 (1928); 2 Curtis, *History of the United States Constitution* 279–308 (1858).

On August 29, 1787, Charles Pinckney of South Carolina proposed requiring a ⅔ vote of each House for federal regulation of commerce. The deliberation preceding the Convention's rejection of this proposal (II Farrand 449–53) included these remarks of James Madison:

"Mr. Madison [Va.] went into a pretty full view of the subject. He observed that the disadvantage to the S. States from a navigation act, lay chiefly in a temporary rise of freight, attended however with an increase of Southn. as well as Northern Shipping—with the emigration of Northern seamen & merchants to the Southern States— & with a removal of the existing & injurious retaliations among the States (on each other). The power of foreign nations to obstruct our retaliating measures on them by a corrupt influence would also be less if a majority shd be made competent than if ⅔ of each House shd. be required to legislative acts in this case. An abuse of the power would be qualified with all these good effects. But he thought an abuse was rendered improbable by the provision of 2 branches—by the independence of the Senate, by the negative of the Executive, by the interest of Connecticut & N. Jersey which were agricultural, not commercial States; by the interior interest which was also agricultural in the most commercial States—by the accession of Western States which wd. be altogether agricultural. He added that the Southern States would derive an essential advantage in the general security afforded by the increase of our maritime strength. He stated the vulnerable situation of them all, and

---

1. See Abel, *The Commerce Clause in the Constitutional Convention and in Contemporary Comment,* 25 Minn.L.Rev. 432 (1941). For general studies, see Warren, *The Making* of the Constitution* (1928); Farrand, *The Framing of the Constitution of the United States* (1913). Cf. Brown, *Charles Beard and the Constitution* (1956).

of Virginia in particular. The increase of the Coasting trade, and of seamen, would also be favorable to the S. States, by increasing, the consumption of their produce. If the Wealth of the Eastern should in a still greater proportion be augmented, that wealth wd. contribute the more to the public wants, and be otherwise a national benefit.''

SECTION 2.   SOURCES OF NATIONAL POWER: EARLY DEVELOPMENTS

A.   THE MARSHALL COURT'S VIEW

Introduction. The allocation of powers between the nation and the states in the Constitution has given rise to a number of major sets of issues, which arose early after the Constitution's adoption and which remain with us today:

(1) What is the scope of the power of the federal government to regulate the private realm? Are the specifically-granted powers to be construed narrowly or broadly? What is the significance of the clause conferring on Congress the power to make all laws which shall be "necessary and proper" for executing the powers granted to it and the other federal branches?

(2) What are the limits imposed on the powers of the states to regulate and to tax the private realm? When does the mere grant of a power to the federal government imply the exclusion of the states from exercising the same power? When does the exercise of a granted power by the federal government imply the exclusion of the states from exercising the same power?

(3) Does the Constitution impose any special limitations when the regulations or taxes of the national government impinge on the state governments? To what extent may the states impose regulations or collect taxes from the federal government or its instrumentalities? In short, what intergovernmental immunities are created by the Constitution?

(4) What immunities do states and their subdivisions enjoy from lawsuits brought against them designed to enforce national or federal norms? Where does any sovereign immunity states enjoy come from?

The first three of these issues came before the Court in a set of great cases between 1819 and 1851. The major cases—*McCulloch v. Maryland, Gibbons v. Ogden,* and *Cooley v. Board of Port Wardens*—are set out in this section. They provide a useful introduction to the various doctrinal threads pursued in this chapter and in Chapters 5, 6 and 12, which also take up the fourth question, that of state sovereign immunity. The early decisions are also relevant to modern concerns since they are often discussed and applied in current Supreme Court cases. When you read each of these Nineteenth century cases, try to discern the theory or theories of federalism–the relationship between the federal and state governments–on which the Court appears to be acting. What values does the division of power between the national and state governments promote?

For modern collections of good introductory essays on the meaning of federalism historically and today, readers may wish to consult various law review symposia published on the general subject, including *Federalism's Future*, 47 Vand. L.Rev. 1205 (1994) and *Major Issues in Federalism*, 38 Az. L.Rev. 793 (1996).

THE BANK OF THE UNITED STATES

The Bank of the United States moved into the legal arena only after a quarter-century of political controversy. The plan for the Bank was developed by Alexander Hamilton promptly upon the establishment of the new government and led to a bill enacted by Congress in 1791. This First Bank, like the Second Bank involved in *McCulloch*, was operated primarily on the basis of privately invested capital and through private control. The national government subscribed to seven millions of the Second Bank's total capitalization of thirty-five millions; the President appointed five of the twenty-five directors. The Act that established the Bank, however, imposed upon it certain public obligations such as providing for free transfer of government deposits and making frequent statements to the Secretary of the Treasury.

Disputes in President Washington's cabinet over the constitutionality of the First Bank shed some light on the issues at stake in *McCulloch*. When in 1791 the bill to establish the bank reached the President, he called upon three members of his cabinet for their opinions. Attorney General Edmund Randolph submitted two opinions, one negative and the other noncommittal. Secretary of the Treasury Alexander Hamilton prepared an opinion that Daniel Webster closely followed in his argument for the bank and which in turn was reflected in Marshall's opinion. The opinion of the Secretary of State, Thomas Jefferson, presented a sharply narrower view of the basic powers of the national government.

Washington followed the advice of Hamilton rather than of Jefferson, and signed the bill. During the next twenty years the Bank became unpopular; attempts in 1811 to renew the charter failed. However, the disorganization of the nation's business and fiscal structure during and following the War of 1812 led to support, even among Jefferson's Republican party which then was in power, for a central banking institution to stabilize the economy; in 1816 Congress adopted a plan for a second Bank of the United States that President Madison approved. This new Bank soon encountered hostility from those who believed that its policies were contributing to the financial distress of the state banks. Several states passed legislation to curb the Bank;[1] one of these laws led to the following case.

McCulloch v. Maryland

17 U.S. (4 Wheat.) 316, 4 L.Ed. 579 (1819).

[The State of Maryland brought an action for debt against McCulloch, cashier of the Baltimore branch of the Bank of the United States. It was admitted that the Bank had issued bank notes which were not on stamped paper as required by the following statute:

"An act to impose a tax on all banks or branches thereof in the state of Maryland, not chartered by the legislature.

---

1. See Warren, *The Supreme Court in United States History* (Rev. ed. 1932) 505–06. The Constitutions of Indiana and Illinois prohibited establishment of banks chartered outside the state. Five states, other than Maryland, resorted to taxation to accomplish the same result; Tennessee and Ohio, $50,000 per branch, North Carolina, $5,000 per branch, and Kentucky, $60,000 per branch. Georgia laid a tax of 31¼% on bank stock employed within the state which on its face appeared nondiscriminatory; the following year the legislature declared that the intent was to tax the Bank of the United States only.

"Be it enacted by the General Assembly of Maryland. That if any bank has established, or shall without authority from the State first had and obtained, establish any branch, office of discount and deposit, or office of pay and receipt, in any part of this state, it shall not be lawful for the said branch, office of discount and deposit, or office of pay and receipt, to issue notes in any manner, of any other denomination than five, ten, twenty, fifty, one hundred, five hundred and one thousand dollars, and no note shall be issued except upon stamped paper of the following denominations; that is to say, every five dollar note shall be upon a stamp of ten cents; every ten dollar note upon a stamp of twenty cents; every twenty dollar note, upon a stamp of thirty cents; every fifty dollar note, upon a stamp of fifty cents; every one hundred dollar note, upon a stamp of one dollar; every five hundred dollar note, upon a stamp of ten dollars; and every thousand dollar note, upon a stamp of twenty dollars; which paper shall be furnished by the Treasurer of the Western Shore, under the direction of the Governor and Council, to be paid for upon delivery. Provided always, That any institution of the above description may relieve itself from the operation of the provisions aforesaid, by paying annually, in advance, to the Treasurer of the Western Shore, for the use of the State, the sum of fifteen thousand dollars.

"And be it enacted, That the President, Cashier, each of the Directors and officers of every institution established, or to be established as aforesaid, offending against the provisions aforesaid, shall forfeit a sum of five hundred dollars for each and every offence . . ."

The Court of Appeals of the State of Maryland affirmed a judgment for the plaintiff.]

Mr. Chief Justice Marshall delivered the opinion of the Court:

In the case now to be determined, the defendant [in error], a sovereign state, denies the obligation of a law enacted by the legislature of the Union, and the plaintiff [in error], on his part, contests the validity of an act which has been passed by the legislature of that state. The constitution of our country, in its most interesting and vital parts, is to be considered; the conflicting powers of the government of the Union and of its members, as marked in that constitution, are to be discussed; and an opinion given, which may essentially influence the great operations of the government. No tribunal can approach such a question without a deep sense of its importance, and of the awful responsibility involved in its decision. But it must be decided peacefully, or remain a source of hostile legislation, perhaps of hostility of a still more serious nature; and if it is to be so decided, by this tribunal alone can the decision be made. On the Supreme Court of the United States has the constitution of our country devolved this important duty.

The first question made in the cause is, has Congress power to incorporate a bank?[a]

. . .

The power now contested was exercised by the first Congress elected under the present constitution. The bill for incorporating the bank of the United States did not steal upon an unsuspecting legislature, and pass unobserved. Its principle was completely understood, and was opposed with equal zeal and ability. After being resisted, first in the fair and open field of debate, and afterwards in the executive cabinet, with as much persevering talent as any

a. What is the relationship between the constitutionality of the act of Congress creat- ing the bank and the constitutionality of the Maryland tax?

Bank was ok after much debate + argument.

measure has ever experienced, and being supported by arguments which convinced minds as pure and as intelligent as this country can boast, it became a law. The original act was permitted to expire; but a short experience of the embarrassments to which the refusal to revive it exposed the government, convinced those who were most prejudiced against the measure of its necessity and induced the passage of the present law. It would require no ordinary share of intrepidity to assert that a measure adopted under these circumstances was a bold and plain usurpation, to which the constitution gave no countenance.

These observations belong to the cause; but they are not made under the impression that, were the question entirely new, the law would be found irreconcilable with the constitution.

In discussing this question, the counsel for the state of Maryland have deemed it of some importance, in the construction of the constitution, to consider that instrument not as emanating from the people, but as the act of sovereign and independent states. The powers of the general government, it has been said, are delegated by the states, who alone are truly sovereign; and must be exercised in subordination to the states who alone possess supreme dominion....

The government of the Union, ... (whatever may be the influence of this fact on the case), is, emphatically, and truly, a government of the people. In form and in substance it emanates from them. Its powers are granted by them, and are to be exercised directly on them, and for their benefit.

This government is acknowledged by all to be one of enumerated powers. The principle, that it can exercise only the powers granted to it, would seem too apparent to have required to be enforced by all those arguments which its enlightened friends, while it was depending before the people, found it necessary to urge. That principle is now universally admitted. But the question respecting the extent of the powers actually granted, is perpetually arising, and will probably continue to arise, as long as our system shall exist.

In discussing these questions, the conflicting powers of the general and state governments must be brought into view, and the supremacy of their respective laws, when they are in opposition, must be settled.

If any one proposition could command the universal assent of mankind, we might expect it would be this—that the government of the Union, though limited in its powers, is supreme within its sphere of action. This would seem to result necessarily from its nature. It is the government of all; its powers are delegated by all; it represents all, and acts for all. Though any one state may be willing to control its operations, no state is willing to allow others to control them. The nation, on those subjects on which it can act, must necessarily bind its component parts. But this question is not left to mere reason; the people have, in express terms, decided it by saying, "this constitution, and the laws of the United States, which shall be made in pursuance thereof," "shall be the supreme law of the land," and by requiring that the members of the state legislatures, and the officers of the executive and judicial departments of the states shall take the oath of fidelity to it.

The government of the United States, then, though limited in its powers, is supreme; and its laws, when made in pursuance of the constitution, form the supreme law of the land, "anything in the constitution or laws of any state to the contrary notwithstanding."

Among the enumerated powers, we do not find that of establishing a bank or creating a corporation. But there is no phrase in the instrument which, like the articles of confederation, excludes incidental or implied powers,[b] and which requires that everything granted shall be expressly and minutely described. Even the 10th amendment, which was framed for the purpose of quieting the excessive jealousies which had been excited, omits the word "expressly," and declares only that the powers "not delegated to the United States, nor prohibited to the states, are reserved to the states or to the people;" thus leaving the question, whether the particular power which may become the subject of contest has been delegated to the one government, or prohibited to the other, to depend on a fair construction of the whole instrument. The men who drew and adopted this amendment had experienced the embarrassments resulting from the insertion of this word in the articles of confederation, and probably omitted it to avoid those embarrassments. A constitution, to contain an accurate detail of all the subdivisions of which its great powers will admit, and of all the means by which they may be carried into execution, would partake of a prolixity of a legal code, and could scarcely be embraced by the human mind. It would probably never be understood by the public. Its nature, therefore, requires, that only its great outlines should be marked, its important objects designated, and the minor ingredients which compose those objects be deduced from the nature of the objects themselves. That this idea was entertained by the framers of the American constitution, is not only to be inferred from the nature of the instrument but from the language. Why else were some of the limitations, found in the ninth section of the 1st article, introduced? It is also, in some degree, warranted by their having omitted to use any restrictive term which might prevent its receiving a fair and just interpretation. In considering this question, then, we must never forget that it is a constitution we are expounding.

Although, among the enumerated powers of government, we do not find the word "bank" or "incorporation," we find the great powers to lay and collect taxes; to borrow money; to regulate commerce; to declare and conduct a war; and to raise and support armies and navies. The sword and the purse, all the external relations, and no inconsiderable portion of the industry of the nation, are entrusted to its government. It can never be pretended that these vast powers draw after them others of inferior importance, merely because they are inferior. Such an idea can never be advanced. But it may with great reason be contended, that a government, entrusted with such ample powers, on the due execution of which the happiness and prosperity of the nation so vitally depends, must also be entrusted with ample means for their execution. The power being given, it is the interest of the nation to facilitate its execution. It can never be their interest, and cannot be presumed to have been their intention, to clog and embarrass its execution by withholding the most appropriate means. Throughout this vast republic, from the St. Croix to the Gulf of Mexico, from the Atlantic to the Pacific, revenue is to be collected and expended, armies are to be marched and supported. The exigencies of the nation may require that the treasure raised in the north should be transported to the south, that raised in the east conveyed to the west, or that this order should be reversed. Is that construction of the constitution to be preferred which would render these operations difficult, hazardous, and expensive? Can we adopt that construction (unless the words, imperiously require it) which would impute to the framers of that instrument, when granting these powers for the public good, the intention of impeding their exercise by withholding a

---

b. The Articles of Confederation (1777) provided in Article II: "Each State retains its sovereignty, freedom and independence, and every power, jurisdiction and right, which is not by this confederation expressly delegated to the United States, in Congress assembled."

choice of means? If, indeed, such be the mandate of the constitution, we have only to obey; but that instrument does not profess to enumerate the means by which the powers it confers may be executed; nor does it prohibit the creation of a corporation, if the existence of such a being be essential to the beneficial exercise of those powers. It is, then, the subject of fair inquiry, how far such means may be employed. . . .

But the constitution of the United States has not left the right of Congress to employ the necessary means for the execution of the powers conferred on the government to general reasoning. To its enumeration of powers is added that of making "all laws which shall be necessary and proper, for carrying into execution the foregoing powers, and all other powers vested by this constitution, in the government of the United States, or in any department thereof."

The counsel for the State of Maryland have urged various arguments, to prove that this clause, though in terms a grant of power, is not so in effect; but is really restrictive of the general right, which might otherwise be implied, of selecting means for executing the enumerated powers.

In support of this proposition, they have found it necessary to contend, that this clause was inserted for the purpose of conferring upon Congress the power of making laws. That, without it, doubts might be entertained, whether Congress could exercise its powers in the form of legislation. . . .

But the argument on which most reliance is placed, is drawn from the peculiar language of this clause. Congress is not empowered by it to make all laws, which may have relation to the powers conferred on the government, but such only as may be "necessary and proper" for carrying them into execution. The word "necessary" is considered as controlling the whole sentence, and as limiting the right to pass laws for the execution of the granted powers, to such as are indispensable, and without which the power would be nugatory. That it excludes the choice of means, and leaves to Congress, in each case, that only which is most direct and simple.

"necessary" shows that you can't just make the laws they want to make

Is it true that this is the sense in which the word "necessary" is always used? Does it always import an absolute physical necessity, so strong that one thing, to which another may be termed necessary, cannot exist without that other? We think it does not. If reference be had to its use, in the common affairs of the world, or in approved authors, we find that it frequently imports no more than that one thing is convenient, or useful, or essential to another. To employ the means necessary to an end, is generally understood as employing any means calculated to produce the end, and not as being confined to those single means, without which the end would be entirely unattainable. Such is the character of human language, that no word conveys to the mind, in all situations, one single definite idea; . . . The word "necessary" is of this description. It has not a fixed character peculiar to itself. It admits of all degrees of comparison; and is often connected with other words. . . . A thing may be necessary, very necessary, absolutely or indispensably necessary. . . . This comment on the word is well illustrated, by the passage cited at the bar, from the 10th section of the 1st article of the constitution. It is, we think, impossible to compare the sentence which prohibits a State from laying "imposts, or duties on imports or exports, except what my be *absolutely* necessary for executing its inspection laws," with that which authorizes Congress "to make all laws which shall be necessary and proper for carrying into execution" the powers of the general government, without feeling a conviction that the convention understood itself to change materially the meaning of the word "necessary," by prefixing the word "absolutely." This word, then, like

compares to Art I §10, which uses Absolutely necessary

others, is used in various senses; and, in its construction, the subject, the context, the intention of the person using them, are all to be taken into view.

Let this be done in the case under consideration. The subject is the execution of those great powers on which the welfare of a nation essentially depends. It must have been the intention of those who gave these powers, to insure, as far as human prudence could insure, their beneficial execution. This could not be done by confining the choice of means to such narrow limits as not to leave it in the power of Congress to adopt any which might be appropriate, and which were conducive to the end. This provision is made in a constitution intended to endure for ages to come, and, consequently, to be adapted to the various crises of human affairs. To have prescribed the means by which government should, in all future time, execute its powers, would have been to change, entirely, the character of the instrument, and give it the properties of a legal code....

. . .

In ascertaining the sense in which the word "necessary" is used in this clause of the constitution, we may derive some aid from that with which it is associated. ... This clause, as construed by the State of Maryland, would abridge, and almost annihilate this useful and necessary right of the legislature to select its means. ... [T]his could not be intended ... for the following reasons.

1st. The clause is placed among the powers of Congress, not among the limitation on those powers.

2nd. Its terms purport to enlarge, not to diminish the powers vested in the government. ... No reason has been, or can be assigned for thus concealing an intention to narrow the discretion of the national legislature under words which purport to enlarge it. The framers of the constitution wished its adoption, and well knew that it would be endangered by its strength, not its weakness. ... If, then, their intention had been, by this clause, to restrain the free use of means which might otherwise have been implied, that intention would have been inserted in another place, and would have been expressed in terms resembling these. "In carrying into execution the foregoing powers, and all others, & c. 'no laws shall be passed but such as are necessary and proper.'" Had the intention been to make this clause restrictive, it would unquestionably have been so in form as well as effect.

The result of the most careful and attentive consideration bestowed upon this clause is, that if it does not enlarge, it cannot be construed to restrain the powers of Congress, or to impair the right of the legislature to exercise its best judgment in the selection of measures to carry into execution the constitutional powers of the government. If no other motive for its insertion can be suggested, a sufficient one is found in the desire to remove all doubts respecting the right to legislate on that vast mass of incidental powers which must be involved in the constitution, if that instrument be not a splendid bauble.

We admit, as all must admit, that the powers of the government are limited, and that its limits are not to be transcended. But we think the sound construction of the constitution must allow to the national legislature that discretion, with respect to the means by which the powers it confers are to be carried into execution, which will enable that body to perform the high duties assigned to it, in the manner most beneficial to the people. Let the end be legitimate, let it be within the scope of the constitution, and all means which are appropriate, which are plainly adapted to that end, which are not prohibited, but consist with the letter and spirit of the constitution, are constitutional. . . .

If a corporation may be employed indiscriminately with other means to carry into execution the powers of the government, no particular reason can be assigned for excluding the use of a bank, if required for its fiscal operations. . . .

But, were its necessity less apparent, none can deny its being an appropriate measure; and if it is, the degree of its necessity, as has been very justly observed, is to be discussed in another place. Should Congress, in the execution of its powers, adopt measures which are prohibited by the constitution; or should Congress, under the pretext of executing its powers, pass laws for the accomplishment of objects not entrusted to the government, it would become the painful duty of this tribunal, should a case requiring such a decision come before it, to say that such an act was not the law of the land. But where the law is not prohibited, and is really calculated to effect any of the objects entrusted to the government, to undertake here to inquire into the degree of its necessity, would be to pass the line which circumscribes the judicial department, and to tread on legislative ground. This court disclaims all pretensions to such a power. . . .

After the most deliberate consideration, it is the unanimous and decided opinion of this court that the act to incorporate the bank of the United States is a law made in pursuance of the constitution, and is a part of the supreme law of the land. . . .

Holding → for Q1

It being the opinion of the court that the act incorporating the bank is constitutional, and that the power of establishing a branch in the state of Maryland might be properly exercised by the bank itself, we proceed to inquire:

2nd question:

2. Whether the state of Maryland may, without violating the constitution, tax that branch?

That the power of taxation is one of vital importance; that it is retained by the states; that it is not abridged by the grant of a similar power to the government of the Union; that it is to be concurrently exercised by the two governments: are truths which have never been denied. But, such is the paramount character of the constitution that its capacity to withdraw any subject from the action of even this power, is admitted. The states are expressly forbidden to lay any duties on imports or exports, except what may be absolutely necessary for executing their inspection laws. If the obligation of this prohibition must be conceded—if it may restrain a state from the exercise of its taxing power on imports and exports—the same paramount character would seem to restrain, as it certainly may restrain, a state from such other exercise of this power, as is in its nature incompatible with, and repugnant to, the constitutional laws of the Union. A law, absolutely repugnant to another, as entirely repeals that other as if express terms of repeal were used.

On this ground the counsel for the bank place its claim to be exempted from the power of a state to tax its operations. There is no express provision for the case, but the claim has been sustained on a principle which so entirely pervades the constitution, is so intermixed with the materials which compose it, so interwoven with its web, so blended with its texture, as to be incapable of being separated from it without rending it into shreds.

This great principle is, that the constitution and the laws made in pursuance thereof are supreme; that they control the constitution and laws of the respective states, and cannot be controlled by them. . . .

. . .

That the power to tax involves the power to destroy; that the power to destroy may defeat and render useless the power to create; that there is a plain repugnance, in conferring on one government a power to control the constitutional measures of another, which other, with respect to those very measures, is declared to be supreme over that which exerts the control, are propositions not to be denied. But all inconsistencies are to be reconciled by the magic of the word CONFIDENCE. Taxation, it is said, does not necessarily and unavoidably destroy. To carry it to the excess of destruction would be an abuse, to presume which, would banish that confidence which is essential to all government.

Taxes can destroy & no one state would trust another with that power.

But is this a case of confidence? Would the people of any one state trust those of another with a power to control the most insignificant operations of their state government? We know they would not. Why, then, should we suppose that the people of any one state should be willing to trust those of another with a power to control the operations of a government to which they have confided the most important and most valuable interests? In the legislature of the Union alone, are all represented. The legislature of the Union alone, therefore, can be trusted by the people with the power of controlling measures which concern all, in the confidence that it will not be abused. This, then, is not a case of confidence, and we must consider it as it really is....

If the states may tax one instrument, employed by the government in the execution of its powers, they may tax any and every other instrument. They may tax the mail; they may tax the mint; they may tax patent-rights; they may tax the papers of the custom-house; they may tax judicial process; they may tax all the means employed by the government, to an excess which would defeat all the ends of government. This was not intended by the American people. They did not design to make their government dependent on the states....

It has also been insisted, that, as the power of taxation in the general and state governments is acknowledged to be concurrent, every argument which would sustain the right of the general government to tax banks chartered by the states, will equally sustain the right of the states to tax banks chartered by the general government.

But the two cases are not on the same reason. The people of all the states have created the general government, and have conferred upon it the general power of taxation. The people of all the states, and the states themselves, are represented in Congress, and, by their representatives, exercise this power. When they tax the chartered institutions of the states, they tax their constituents; and these taxes must be uniform. But, when a state taxes the operations of the government of the United States, it acts upon institutions created, not by their own constituents, but by people over whom they claim no control. It acts upon the measures of a government created by others as well as themselves, for the benefit of others in common with themselves. The difference is that which always exists, and always must exist, between the action of the whole on a part, and the action of a part on the whole—between the laws of a government declared to be supreme, and those of a government which, when in opposition to those laws, is not supreme.

But if the full application of this argument could be admitted, it might bring into question the right of Congress to tax the state banks, and could not prove the right of the states to tax the Bank of the United States.

The court has bestowed on this subject its most deliberate consideration. The result is a conviction that the states have no power, by taxation or otherwise, to retard, impede, burden, or in any manner control the operations of the constitutional laws enacted by Congress to carry into execution the

Holding of Q2

powers vested in the general government. This is, we think, the unavoidable consequence of that supremacy which the constitution has declared.

Holding of case

We are unanimously of opinion that the law passed by the legislature of Maryland, imposing a tax on the Bank of the United States, is unconstitutional and void.

This opinion does not deprive the states of any resources which they originally possessed. It does not extend to a tax paid by the real property of the bank, in common with the other real property within the state, nor to a tax imposed on the interest which the citizens of Maryland may hold in this institution, in common with other property of the same description throughout the state. But this is a tax on the operations of the bank, and is, consequently, a tax on the operation of an instrument employed by the government of the Union to carry its powers into execution. Such a tax must be unconstitutional.

. . . It is, therefore, adjudged and ordered, that the said judgment of the said Court of Appeals of the state of Maryland in this case, be, and the same hereby is, reversed and annulled. And this court, proceeding to render such judgment as the said Court of Appeals should have rendered; it is further adjudged and ordered, that the judgment of the said Baltimore County Court be reversed and annulled, and that judgment be entered in the said Baltimore County Court for the said James W. M'Culloch.

MCCULLOCH AND THE SCOPE OF FEDERAL POWER

(1) Marshall rejected the argument that the powers of the federal government were delegated to it by the sovereign states. The government of the Union, he said, is a government of the people, it "emanates from them. Its powers are granted by them, and are to be exercised directly on them, and for their benefit." What is the significance of this reasoning by Marshall? If powers were granted by the states, could the states insist upon their own interpretation of the powers granted? Could a state legally secede from the Union? These questions assumed importance from the beginning of the country. Examples include the Kentucky–Virginia Resolutions of 1798, the New England resistance to the War of 1812, Calhoun's doctrine of nullification as reflected in the South Carolina Exposition of 1828 and the Statute of Nullification of 1832. The ultimate test took place in the Civil War where the right of secession was rejected on the battlefield. For an account of these early episodes and others, see Reference Note, *Interposition vs. Judicial Power,* 1 Race Rel.L.Rep. 465 (1956). The issue recurred in the middle 1950s when state legislatures passed resolutions seeking to nullify the enforcement of Brown v. Board of Educ., 347 U.S. 483 (1954). The Alabama Resolution, e.g., commenced as follows:

"WHEREAS the Constitution of the United States was formed by the sanction of the several states, given by each in its sovereign capacity; and

"WHEREAS the States, being the parties to the constitutional compact, it follows of necessity that there can be no tribunal above their authority to decide, in the last resort, whether the compact made by them be violated; and, consequently, they must decide themselves, in the last resort, such questions as may be of sufficient magnitude to require their interposition; . . ." Act No. 42, Spec.Sess., 1956, Feb. 2, 1956, set out 1 Race Rel.L.Rptr. 437 (1956). Other resolutions of the time are set out id. 438–447.

The Supreme Court gave its answer to these latter-day nullifiers in Cooper v. Aaron, 358 U.S. 1 (1958).

(2) The Constitution did not contain an express power to create banks. Did Marshall rely primarily upon the "necessary and proper" clause as the basis for inferring such a power from other powers expressly granted? Or is Professor Black correct in suggesting that Marshall "does not place principal reliance on this clause as a ground of decision; that before he reaches it he has already decided, on the basis of far more general implications ...; that he addresses himself to the ... clause only in response to counsel's arguing its *restrictive* force; and that he never really commits himself to the proposition that the necessary and proper clause enlarges governmental power...." Black, *Structure and Relationship in Constitutional Law* 14 (1969). For an elaborate exegesis of the necessary and proper clause, see Engdahl, *Constitutional Federalism* 16–73 (2d ed. 1987).

(3) Near the end of the Constitutional Convention, Benjamin Franklin moved that Congress be given "a power to provide for cutting canals where deemed necessary." Madison then suggested enlarging Franklin's motion to add the power "to grant charters of incorporation where the interest of the U.S. might require & the legislative provisions of individual States may be incompetent." The Convention rejected these proposals. II Farrand, 615–616. Consider the possible relevance of that rejection to the preceding question of federal power to charter the Bank of the United States and the following question of federal power to build roads and canals.

FEDERAL POWER TO BUILD ROADS AND CANALS

The second great issue on the scope of national legislative power grew out of proposals for the building of national roads and canals. A bill appropriating funds for such "internal improvements" was passed in 1817, but was vetoed by President Madison as not "among the enumerated powers; or ..., by any just interpretation, within the power to make laws necessary and proper for carrying into execution those or other powers vested by the Constitution in the Government of the United States." II Messages and Papers of the Presidents 569, 570 (1897). The commerce power did not reach that far "without a latitude of construction departing from the ordinary import of the terms," and to construe the power "to provide for the common defence and general welfare" to do so "would be contrary to the established and consistent rules of interpretation, as rendering the special and careful enumeration of powers, which follow the clause, nugatory and improper. Such a view of the Constitution would have the effect of giving to Congress a general power of legislation, instead of the defined and limited one hitherto understood to belong to them...." Id.

On similar strict construction grounds, President Monroe vetoed "with great regret" an appropriation passed in 1822 for the preservation and repair of the Cumberland Road. He suggested that Congress propose a constitutional amendment authorizing the necessary federal power.

MCCULLOCH AND STATE POWER TO CONTROL THE SELECTION OF MEMBERS OF CONGRESS

McCulloch concluded "that the states have no power, by taxation or otherwise, to retard, impede, burden, or in any manner control the operations of the constitutional laws enacted by Congress...." Powell v. McCormack, 395 U.S. 486 (1969), held that Congress could not alter the qualifications set forth in the Constitution for election to Congress. Where Congress lacks power to act and the Constitution is silent regarding state power, does *McCulloch* bear on state power to control who may be elected to Congress to exercise federal power?

states, like congress lack the power to make changes to qualifications for congress.

Not a reserve power given to states by 10th amend.

Qualification clauses intended to prevent states from having that power.

In U.S. Term Limits, Inc. v. Thornton, 514 U.S. 779 (1995), the Court concluded that the States, like Congress, lack the power to add to the "exclusive qualifications" of age, citizenship and residency the Constitution prescribes for members of Congress. It invalidated a voter-adopted Arkansas constitutional amendment that prohibited the name of an otherwise-eligible candidate for Congress from appearing on the general election ballot if that candidate had already served three terms in the House or two terms in the Senate.

Justice Stevens' opinion for the Court relied on *McCulloch* in two respects to reject the argument that the State's voters had "reserved power" to impose term limit qualifications on candidates for Congress from their State. First, "the power to add qualifications is not within the 'original power' of the States, and thus is not reserved to the States by the Tenth Amendment." *McCulloch* "rejected the argument that the Constitution's silence on the subject of state power to tax corporations chartered by Congress implies that the States have 'reserved' power to tax such federal instrumentalities." Just as in *McCulloch* "an 'original right to tax' . . . federal entities 'never existed, and the question whether it has been surrendered, cannot arise[,]' . . . electing representatives to the National Legislature was a new right, arising from the Constitution itself[,] . . . [and] any state power to set the qualifications for membership in Congress must derive not from the reserved powers of state sovereignty, but rather from the delegated powers of national sovereignty."

Second, even if the States' original power embraced some control over congressional qualifications, "the Qualifications Clauses were intended to preclude the States from exercising any such power." Recognizing state power to add qualifications would violate the "fundamental principle of our representative democracy" that "the people should choose whom they please to govern them." That right "belongs not to the States, but to the people"—a proposition supported by *McCulloch*:

> "Permitting individual States to formulate diverse qualifications for their representatives would result in a patchwork of state qualifications, undermining the uniformity and the national character that the Framers envisioned and sought to ensure. Cf. McCulloch v. Maryland, 4 Wheat., at 428–429 (1819) ('Those means are not given by the people of a particular State, not given by the constituents of the legislature, . . . but by the people of all the States. They are given by all, for the benefit of all—and upon theory should be subjected to that government only which belongs to all'). Such a patchwork would also sever the direct link that the Framers found so critical between the National Government and the people of the United States."

Concurring separately, Justice Kennedy also emphasized *McCulloch* in support of his view that "the National Government . . . owes its existence to the act of the whole people who created it" and that there "can be no doubt, if we are to respect the republican origins of the Nation and preserve its federal character, that there exists a federal right of citizenship, a relationship between the people of the Nation and their National Government, with which the States may not interfere." Insisting "that the people of the United States . . . have a political identity . . . independent of, though consistent with, their identity as citizens of the State of their residence[,]" Justice Kennedy stated:

> "It might be objected that because the States ratified the Constitution, the people can delegate power only through the States or by acting in their capacities as citizens of particular States. But in *McCulloch v. Maryland*, the Court set forth its authoritative rejection of this idea: 'The . . . constitution . . . was submitted to the people. . . . It is true, they . . . act in their States. But the

measures they adopt do not, on that account, cease to be the measures of the people themselves, or become the measures of the State governments.' ...

"The political identity of the entire people of the Union is reinforced by the proposition ... that, though limited as to its objects, the National Government is and must be controlled by the people without collateral interference by the States. *McCulloch* affirmed this proposition as well, when the Court rejected the suggestion that States could interfere with federal powers.... The States have no power, reserved or otherwise, over the exercise of federal authority within its proper sphere...."

Justice Thomas, joined by Chief Justice Rehnquist and Justices O'Connor and Scalia, dissented. Stressing that the "ultimate source of the Constitution's authority is the consent of the people of each individual State, not the consent of the undifferentiated people of the Nation as a whole[,]" he found nothing in *McCulloch* that denied "*the people* of the States" a reserved power under the Tenth Amendment to prescribe eligibility requirements for the candidates who seek to represent them in Congress, given the Constitution's silence on the question. The majority misunderstood *McCulloch*, he argued:

"... *McCulloch* did make clear that a power need not be 'expressly' delegated to the United States or prohibited to the States in order to fall outside the Tenth Amendment's reservation; delegations and prohibitions can also arise by necessary implication. [But] *McCulloch* indicated that all powers as to which the Constitution does not speak (whether expressly or by necessary implication) are 'reserved' to the state level ... [without] turn[ing] on whether the States had enjoyed the power before the framing.... *McCulloch* seemed to assume that the people had 'conferred on the general government the power contained in the constitution, and on the States the whole residuum of power.' ..."

"The structure of *McCulloch*'s analysis also refutes the majority's position....

"For the past 175 years, *McCulloch* has been understood to rest on the proposition that the Constitution affirmatively barred Maryland from imposing its tax on the Bank's operations.... For the majority, however, *McCulloch* apparently turned on the fact that before the Constitution was adopted, the States had possessed no power to tax the instrumentalities of the governmental institutions that the Constitution created. This understanding of *McCulloch* makes most of Chief Justice Marshall's opinion irrelevant; according to the majority, there was no need to inquire into whether federal law deprived Maryland of the power in question, because the power could not fall into the category of 'reserved' powers anyway."

Justice Thomas also found "perfectly consistent with my position" *McCulloch*'s argument "that the people of a single State may not tax the instrumentalities employed by the people of all the States through the National Government, because such taxation would effectively subject the people of the several States to the taxing power of a single State":

"This sort of argument proves that the people of a single State may not prescribe qualifications for the President of the United States; the selection of the President, like the operation of the Bank of the United States, is not up to the people of any single State.... It does not follow, however, that the people of a single State may not prescribe qualifications for their own representatives in Congress."

Following similar reasoning, the Court later invalidated another state attempt to influence congressional elections in favor of candidates who sup-

[handwritten margin note: states can't regulate the rights of the people.]

Another case about congressional term limits & state power

ported congressional term limits. Cook v. Gralike, 531 U.S. 510 (2001). A state constitutional amendment adopted by Missouri voters attempted to "instruct" the members of Missouri's congressional delegation, and nonincumbent congressional candidates who might win election, to support a particular form of Congressional Term Limits Amendment to the United States Constitution. Incumbents who did not comply were to have "DISREGARDED VOTERS' INSTRUCTION ON TERM LIMITS" placed next to their names on all primary and general ballots; nonincumbents who refused to pledge support were to have "DECLINED TO PLEDGE TO SUPPORT TERM LIMITS" placed next to their names on all such ballots.

Justice Stevens' majority opinion first found insufficient evidence "that either the people or the States had a right to give legally binding, *i.e.*, nonadvisory, instructions to their representatives that the Tenth Amendment reserved, much less that such a right would apply to federal representatives." Moreover, "even assuming the existence of the reserved right . . ., the question remains whether the State may use ballots for congressional elections as a means of giving its instructions binding force." As to that question, he wrote:

"The federal offices at stake 'aris[e] from the Constitution itself.' U.S. Term Limits, Inc. v. Thornton. . . . Because any state authority to regulate election to those offices could not precede their very creation by the Constitution, such power 'had to be delegated to, rather than reserved by, the States.' Id., . . . Through the Elections Clause, the Constitution delegated to the States the power to regulate the 'Times, Places and Manner of holding Elections for Senators and Representatives,' subject to a grant of authority to Congress to 'make or alter such Regulations.' Art. I, § 4, cl. 1. . . . No other constitutional provision gives the States authority over congressional elections, and no such authority could be reserved under the Tenth Amendment. By process of elimination, the States may regulate the incidents of such elections, including balloting, only within the exclusive delegation of power under the Elections Clause."

states may only regulate according to the election clause

Because the adverse ballot designations were intended to "handicap candidates for the United States Congress" just at the crucial time when votes were cast, they constituted attempts to "dictate electoral outcomes" rather than regulations of "the procedural mechanisms of elections," however, and thus the state law did not fall within the power delegated to the State by the Elections Clause.

In a concurring opinion, Justice Kennedy wrote:

"A State is not permitted to interpose itself between the people and their National Government as it seeks to do here. Whether a State's concern is with the proposed enactment of a constitutional amendment or an ordinary federal statute it simply lacks the power to impose any conditions on the election of Senators and Representatives, save neutral provisions as to the time, place, and manner of elections pursuant to Article I, § 4. . . .

"The dispositive principle in this case is fundamental to the Constitution, to the idea of federalism, and to the theory of representative government. The principle is that Senators and Representatives in the National Government are responsible to the people who elect them, not to the States in which they reside. The Constitution was ratified by Conventions in the several States, not by the States themselves, U.S. Const., Art. VII, a historical fact and a constitutional imperative which underscore the proposition that the Constitution was ordained and established by the people of the United States. U.S. Const., preamble. The idea of federalism is that a

National Legislature enacts laws which bind the people as individuals, not as citizens of a State; and, it follows, freedom is most secure if the people themselves, not the States as intermediaries, hold their federal legislators to account for the conduct of their office. If state enactments were allowed to condition or control certain actions of federal legislators, accountability would be blurred, with the legislators having the excuse of saying that they did not act in the exercise of their best judgment but simply in conformance with a state mandate.... Neither the design of the Constitution nor sound principles of representative government are consistent with the right or power of a State to interfere with the direct line of accountability between the National Legislature and the people who elect it...."

Justice Thomas continued to "disagree with the Court's premise, derived from *U.S. Term Limits*, that the States have no authority to regulate congressional elections except for the authority that the Constitution expressly delegates to them[,]" but he concurred because the parties had conceded its validity. Chief Justice Rehnquist, joined by Justice O'Connor, concurred in the judgment on the ground that the State had violated the First Amendment by "discriminat[ing] on the basis of viewpoint because only those candidates who fail to conform to the State's position receive derogatory labels."

It bears noting that neither *Thornton* nor *Gralike* involved the power of a state people to exert control and/or pressure on state, as opposed to federal, legislators in the drive for federal term limits. On the power of a state people to control their own state legislators in the federal term limits context, see Vikram Amar, *The People Made Me Do It: Can the People of the State Instruct and Coerce Their State Legislatures in the Article V Constitutional Amendment Process?*, 41 Wm. & Mary L.Rev. 1037 (2000).

STATE POWER TO ADMINISTER PRESIDENTIAL ELECTIONS

Even though *Thornton* and *Gralike* make clear that states may not impose qualifications for members of Congress (and presumably the President), other cases make note of the ways in which the Constitution, especially before the Seventeenth Amendment, involves states in the process of constituting federal offices. For example, writing for the Court in Garcia v. San Antonio Metropolitan Transit Authority, 469 U.S. 528, 551 (1985), Justice Blackmun observed that:

"The Framers ... gave the States a role in the selection both of the Executive and the Legislative Branches of the Federal Government. The States were vested with indirect influence over the House of Representatives and the Presidency by their control of electoral qualifications and their role in presidential elections. U.S. Const., Art. I, § 2, and Art. II, § 1. They were given more direct influence in the Senate, where each State received equal representation and each Senator was to be selected by the legislature of his State. Art. I, § 3."

The role of the states, and in particular the interplay between state legislatures and state courts, in Presidential selection prompted Chief Justice Rehnquist, joined by Justices Scalia and Thomas, to write a concurring opinion in Bush v. Gore, 531 U.S. 98, 112 (2000), in which he remarked:

"In most cases, comity and respect for federalism compel us to defer to the decisions of state courts on issues of state law. That practice reflects our understanding that the decisions of state courts are definitive pronouncements of the will of the States as sovereigns. ... But there are a few exceptional cases in which the Constitution imposes a duty or confers a power on a particular branch of a State's government. This is one of them. Article II, § 1. cl. 2, provides that '[e]ach State shall appoint, in such Manner as the Legislature thereof may direct,' electors for President and Vice President. Thus, the text of the election law itself, and not just its interpretation by the courts of the States, takes on independent significance.

In McPherson v. Blacker, 146 U.S. 1 (1892), we explained that Article II, § 1, cl. 2, 'convey[s] the broadest power of determination' and 'leaves it to the legislature exclusively to define the method' of appointment.'"[a]

In essence, the concurring opinion in Bush v. Gore argues that the phrase "legislature []of" "each State" in Article II essentially insulates state legislative decisions in the Presidential selection realm from state judicial revision, even if state law principles might otherwise justify state judicial involvement. The phrase "legislature of each state," or something very similar to it, appears in the Constitution outside of Article II as well, for example in Article V's amendment provisions, in Article I's congressional election provisions, and Article IV's provisions concerning the creation of new states. For a discussion of the meaning of these terms, and one that differs from the concurring opinion in Bush v. Gore, see Vikram Amar and Alan Brownstein, Bush v. Gore *and Article II: Pressured Judgment Makes Dubious Law,* 48 Fed. Lawyer 27 (2001).

[Handwritten margin note: Bush v. Gore, keeps state judicial branch from being involved in state ~~executi~~ legislative branch's presidential selection]

Gibbons v. Ogden

22 U.S. (9 Wheat.) 1, 6 L.Ed. 23 (1824).

[Ogden obtained an injunction from the Court of Chancery of New York ordering Gibbons to stop operating his ferry-boats in the waters of the State of New York. In 1803 the New York legislature had granted to Robert Livingston and Robert Fulton the exclusive right for twenty years to operate ships powered by fire or steam in New York waters; in 1808, on proof that Livingston and Fulton had built a steamboat that could operate at more than four miles per hour, the grant was extended until 1838. Ogden alleged that he held an assignment from these grantees of the exclusive right to run a steamboat between Elizabethtown, New Jersey, and New York City, and that the defendant, Gibbons, was running two boats between these points. Gibbons alleged that his boats, the *Stoudinger* and *Bellana,* had been duly enrolled and licensed under the laws of the United States for carrying on the coasting trade.

Chancellor Kent sustained the injunction prohibiting the operation of Gibbons' boats. 4 Johns. Ch. 150 (1819). The Chancellor rejected the defendant's contention that plaintiff's monopoly was inconsistent with the United States coasting license; Chancellor Kent concluded that the coasting license was designed merely to relieve American ships of the burdens imposed upon foreign shipping. In an earlier case involving the steamboat monopoly the Chancellor had further rejected the contention that this state law, in regulating interstate commerce, fell within an area exclusively reserved to Congress. On the contrary, Chancellor Kent held that the states could regulate interstate commerce unless Congress had enacted inconsistent legislation. Livingston v. Van Ingen, 9 Johns. 507 (1812).

The New York Court for the Correction of Errors affirmed the order sustaining Ogden's injunction. 17 Johns. 488 (1820).]

a. Factual background on Bush v. Gore, and the reliance by the majority opinion in that case on federal equal protection principles, is discussed infra, at p. 1003.

Mr. Chief Justice Marshall delivered the opinion of the Court, ...

The appellant contends that this decree is erroneous, because the laws which purport to give the exclusive privilege it sustains, are repugnant to the constitution and laws of the United States.

They are said to be repugnant:

1st. To that clause in the constitution which authorizes Congress to regulate commerce....

The words are: "Congress shall have power to regulate commerce with foreign nations, and among the several states, and with the Indian tribes."

The subject to be regulated is commerce; and our constitution being, as was aptly said at the bar, one of enumeration, and not of definition, to ascertain the extent of the power it becomes necessary to settle the meaning of the word. The counsel for the appellee would limit it to traffic, to buying and selling, or the interchange of commodities, and do not admit that it comprehends navigation. This would restrict a general term, applicable to many objects, to one of its significations. Commerce, undoubtedly is traffic, but it is something more; it is intercourse. It describes the commercial intercourse between nations, and parts of nations, in all its branches, and is regulated by prescribing rules for carrying on that intercourse. The mind can scarcely conceive a system for regulating commerce between nations, which shall exclude all laws concerning navigation, which shall be silent on the admission of the vessels of the one nation into the ports of the other, and be confined to prescribing rules for the conduct of individuals, in the actual employment of buying and selling, or of barter.

If commerce does not include navigation, the government of the Union has no direct power over that subject, and can make no law prescribing what shall constitute American vessels, or requiring that they shall be navigated by American seamen. Yet this power has been exercised from the commencement of the government, has been exercised with the consent of all, and has been understood by all to be a commercial regulation. All America understands, and has uniformly understood, the word "commerce" to comprehend navigation. It was so understood, and must have been so understood, when the constitution was framed. The power over commerce, including navigation, was one of the primary objects for which the people of America adopted their government, and must have been contemplated in forming it. The convention must have used the word in that sense; because all have understood it in that sense, and the attempt to restrict it comes too late....

The word used in the constitution, then, comprehends, and has been always understood to comprehend, navigation within its meaning; and a power to regulate navigation is as expressly granted as if that term had been added to the word "commerce."

To what commerce does this power extend? The constitution informs us, to commerce "with foreign nations, and among the several states, and with the Indian tribes."

It has, we believe, been universally admitted that these words comprehend every species of commercial intercourse between the United States and foreign nations. No sort of trade can be carried on between this country and any other, to which this power does not extend. It has been truly said, that commerce, as the word is used in the constitution, is a unit, every part of which is indicated by the term.

If this be the admitted meaning of the word, in its application to foreign nations, it must carry the same meaning throughout the sentence, and remain a unit, unless there be some plain intelligible cause which alters it.

The subject to which the power is next applied, is to commerce "among the several states." The word "among" means intermingled with. A thing which is among others, is intermingled with them. Commerce among the states cannot stop at the external boundary line of each state, but may be introduced into the interior.

It is not intended to say that these words comprehend that commerce which is completely internal, which is carried on between man and man in a state, or between different parts of the same state, and which does not extend to or affect other states. Such a power would be inconvenient, and is certainly unnecessary.

Comprehensive as the word "among" is, it may very properly be restricted to that commerce which concerns more states than one. The phrase is not one which would probably have been selected to indicate the completely interior traffic of a state, because it is not an apt phrase for that purpose; and the enumeration of the particular classes of commerce to which the power was to be extended, would not have been made had the intention been to extend the power to every description. The enumeration presupposes something not enumerated; and that something, if we regard the language or the subject of the sentence, must be the exclusively internal commerce of a state. The genius and character of the whole government seem to be, that its action is to be applied to all the external concerns of the nation, and to those internal concerns which affect the states generally; but not to those which are completely within a particular state, which do not affect other states, and with which it is not necessary to interfere, for the purpose of executing some of the general powers of the government. The completely internal commerce of a state, then, may be considered as reserved for the state itself.

But, in regulating commerce with foreign nations, the power of Congress does not stop at the jurisdictional lines of the several states. It would be a very useless power if it could not pass those lines. The commerce of the United States with foreign nations, is that of the whole United States. Every district has a right to participate in it. The deep streams which penetrate our country in every direction, pass through the interior of almost every state in the Union, and furnish the means of exercising this right. If Congress has the power to regulate it, that power must be exercised whenever the subject exists. If it exists within the states, if a foreign voyage may commence or terminate at a port within a state, then the power of Congress may be exercised within a state.

This principle is, if possible, still more clear, when applied to commerce "among the several states." They either join each other, in which case they are separated by a mathematical line, or they are remote from each other, in which case other states lie between them. What is commerce "among" them; and how is it to be conducted? Can a trading expedition between two adjoining states commence and terminate outside of each? And if the trading intercourse be between two states remote from each other, must it not commence in one, terminate in the other, and probably pass through a third? Commerce among the states must, of necessity, be commerce with the states. In the regulation of trade with the Indian tribes, the action of the law, especially when the constitution was made, was chiefly within a state. The power of Congress, then, whatever it may be, must be exercised within the territorial jurisdiction of the several states. The sense of the nation, on this subject, is unequivocally manifested by the provisions made in the laws for transporting goods, by land, between Baltimore and Providence, between New York and Philadelphia, and between Philadelphia and Baltimore.

We are now arrived at the inquiry, What is this power?

It is the power to regulate; that is, to prescribe the rule by which commerce is to be governed. This power, like all others vested in Congress, is complete in itself, may be exercised to its utmost extent, and acknowledges no limitations, other than are prescribed in the constitution. These are expressed in plain terms, and do not affect the questions which arise in this case, or which have been discussed at the bar. If, as has always been understood, the sovereignty of Congress, though limited to specified objects, is plenary as to those objects, the power over commerce with foreign nations, and among the several States, is vested in Congress as absolutely as it would be in a single government, having in its constitution the same restrictions on the exercise of the power as are found in the constitution of the United States. The wisdom and the discretion of Congress, their identity with the people, and the influence which their constituents possess at elections, are, in this, as in many other instances, as that, for example, of declaring war, the sole restraints on which they have relied, to secure them from its abuse. They are the restraints on which the people must often rely solely, in all representative governments. . . .

But it has been urged, with great earnestness, that although the power of Congress to regulate commerce with foreign nations, and among the several states, be co-extensive with the subject itself, and have no other limits than are prescribed in the constitution, yet the states may severally exercise the same power within their respective jurisdictions. In support of this argument, it is said that they possessed it as an inseparable attribute of sovereignty, before the formation of the constitution, and still retain it, except so far as they have surrendered it by that instrument; that this principle results from the nature of the government, and is secured by the tenth amendment; that an affirmative grant of power is not exclusive, unless in its own nature it be such that the continued exercise of it by the former possessor is inconsistent with the grant, and that this is not of that description.

The appellant, conceding these postulates, except the last, contends that full power to regulate a particular subject, implies the whole power, and leaves no residuum; that a grant of the whole is incompatible with the existence of a right in another to any part of it.

Both parties have appealed to the constitution, to legislative acts, and judicial decisions; and have drawn arguments from all these sources to support and illustrate the propositions they respectively maintain.

The grant of the power to lay and collect taxes is, like the power to regulate commerce, made in general terms, and has never been understood to interfere with the exercise of the same power by the states; and hence has been drawn an argument which has been applied to the question under consideration. But the two grants are not, it is conceived, similar in their terms or their nature. Although many of the powers formerly exercised by the states, are transferred to the government of the Union, yet the state governments remain, and constitute a most important part of our system. The power of taxation is indispensable to their existence, and is a power which, in its own nature, is capable of residing in, and being exercised by, different authorities at the same time. We are accustomed to see it placed, for different purposes, in different hands. Taxation is the simple operation of taking small portions from a perpetually accumulating mass, susceptible of almost infinite division; and a power in one to take what is necessary for certain purposes, is not, in its nature, incompatible with a power in another to take what is necessary for other purposes. Congress is authorized to lay and collect taxes, & c., to pay the debts, and provide for the common defence and general welfare of the United States. This does not interfere with the power of the States to tax for the support of their own governments; nor is the exercise of that power by the States, an exercise of any portion of the power that is granted to the United States. In imposing taxes for State purposes, they are not doing what Congress is empowered to do. Congress is not empowered to tax for those purposes which are within the exclusive province of the States. When, then, each government exercises the power of taxation, neither is exercising the power of the other. But, when a State proceeds to regulate commerce with foreign nations, or among the several States, it is exercising the very power that is granted to Congress, and is doing the very thing which Congress is authorized to do. There is no analogy, then, between the power of taxation and the power of regulating commerce....

But, the inspection laws are said to be regulations of commerce, and are certainly recognized in the constitution, as being passed in the exercise of a power remaining with the States.

That inspection laws may have a remote and considerable influence on commerce, will not be denied; but that a power to regulate commerce is the source from which the right to pass them is derived, cannot be admitted. The object of inspection laws, is to improve the quality of articles produced by the labour of a country; to fit them for exportation; or, it may be, for domestic use. They act upon the subject before it becomes an article of foreign commerce, or of commerce among the States, and prepare it for that purpose. They form a portion of that immense mass of legislation, which embraces everything within the territory of a State, not surrendered to the general government: all which can be most advantageously exercised by the States themselves. Inspection laws, quarantine laws, health laws of every description, as well as laws for regulating the internal commerce of a State, and those which respect turnpike roads, ferries, & c., are component parts of this mass.

No direct general power over these objects is granted to Congress; and, consequently, they remain subject to State legislation. If the legislative power of the Union can reach them, it must be for national purposes; it must be where the power is expressly given for a special purpose, or is clearly incidental to some power which is expressly given. It is obvious, that the government of the Union, in the exercise of its express powers, that, for example, of regulating commerce with foreign nations and among the States, may use means that may also be employed by a State, in the exercise of its acknowledged powers; that, for example, of regulating commerce within the State. If Congress license vessels to sail from one port to another, in the same State, the act is supposed to be, necessarily, incidental to the power expressly granted to Congress, and implies no claim of a direct power to regulate the purely internal commerce of a State, or to act directly on its system of police. So, if a State, in passing laws on subjects acknowledged to be within its control, and with a view to those subjects, shall adopt a measure of the same character with one which Congress may adopt, it does not derive its authority from the particular power which has been granted, but from some other, which remains with the State, and may be executed by the same means. All experience shows, that the same measures, or measures scarcely distinguishable from each other, may flow from distinct powers; but this does not prove that the powers themselves are identical. Although the means used in their execution may sometimes approach each other so nearly as to be confounded, there are other situations in which they are sufficiently distinct to establish their individuality....

It has been contended by the counsel for the appellant, that, as the word "to regulate" implies in its nature full power over the thing to be regulated, it excludes, necessarily, the action of all others that would perform the same operation on the same thing. That regulation is designed for the entire result, applying to those parts which remain as they were, as well as to those which are altered. It produces a uniform whole, which is as much disturbed and deranged by changing what the regulating power designs to leave untouched, as that on which it has operated.

There is great force in this argument, and the Court is not satisfied that it has been refuted.

Since, however, in exercising the power or regulating their own purely internal affairs, whether of trading or police, the States may sometimes enact laws, the validity of which depends on their interfering with, and being contrary to, an act of Congress passed in pursuance of the constitution, the Court will enter upon the inquiry, whether the laws of New York, as expounded by the highest tribunal of that State, have, in their application to this case, come into collision with an act of Congress, and deprived a citizen of a right to which that act entitles him. Should this collision exist, it will be immaterial whether those laws were passed in virtue of a concurrent power "to regulate commerce with foreign nations and among the several States," or in virtue of a power to regulate their domestic trade and police. In one case and the other, the acts of New York must yield to the law of Congress; and the decision sustaining the privilege they confer, against a right given by a law of the Union, must be erroneous. . . .

But we will proceed briefly to notice those sections which bear more directly on the subject.

The first section declares, that vessels enrolled by virtue of a previous law, and certain other vessels, enrolled as described in that act, and having a license in force, as is by the act required, "and no others, shall be deemed ships or vessels of the United States, entitled to the privileges of ships or vessels employed in the coasting trade."

This section seems to the Court to contain a positive enactment, that the vessels it describes shall be entitled to the privileges of ships or vessels employed in the coasting trade. These privileges cannot be separated from the trade, and cannot be enjoyed, unless the trade may be prosecuted. The grant of the privilege is an idle, empty form, conveying nothing, unless it convey the right to which the privilege is attached, and in the exercise of which its whole value consists. To construe these words otherwise than as entitling the ships or vessels described, to carry on the coasting trade, would be, we think to disregard the apparent intent of the act.

. . .

But if the license be a permit to carry on the coasting trade, the respondent denies that these boats were engaged in that trade, or that the decree under consideration has restrained them from prosecuting it. The boats of the appellant were, we are told, employed in the transportation of passengers; and this is no part of that commerce which Congress may regulate.

If, as our whole course of legislation on this subject shows, the power of Congress has been universally understood in America, to comprehend navigation, it is a very persuasive, if not a conclusive argument, to prove that the construction is correct; and, if it be correct, no clear distinction is perceived between the power to regulate vessels employed in transporting men for hire, and property for hire. . . .

Powerful and ingenious minds, taking, as postulates, that the powers expressly granted to the government of the Union, are to be contracted by construction, into the narrowest possible compass, and that the original powers of the States are retained, if any possible construction will retain them, may, by a course of well digested, but refined and metaphysical reasoning, founded on these premises, explain away the constitution of our country, and leave it, a magnificent structure, indeed, to look at, but totally unfit for use. They may so entangle and perplex the understanding, as to obscure principles, which were before thought quite plain, and induce doubts where, if the mind were to pursue its own course, none would be perceived. In such a case, it is peculiarly necessary to recur to safe and fundamental principles to sustain those principles, and, when sustained, to make them the tests of the arguments to be examined.

Mr. Justice Johnson.[a] The judgment entered by the Court in this cause, has my entire approbation; but having adopted my conclusions on views of the subject materially different from those of my brethren, I feel it incumbent on me to exhibit those views. I have, also, another inducement: in questions of great importance and great delicacy, I feel my duty to the public best discharged, by an effort to maintain my opinions in my own way.

In attempts to construe the constitution, I have never found much benefit resulting from the inquiry, whether the whole, or any part of it, is to be construed strictly, or liberally. The simple, classical, precise, yet comprehensive language, in which it is couched, leaves, at most, but very little latitude for construction; and when its intent and meaning is discovered, nothing remains but to execute the will of those who made it, in the best manner to effect the purposes intended....

. . .

The power of a sovereign state over commerce, ... amounts to nothing more than a power to limit and restrain it at pleasure. And since the power to prescribe the limits to its freedom, necessarily implies the power to determine what shall remain unrestrained, it follows, that the power must be exclusive; it can reside but in one potentate; hence, the grant of this power carries with it the whole subject, leaving nothing for the State to act upon....

Commerce, in its simplest signification, means an exchange of goods; but in the advancement of society, labour, transportation, intelligence, care, and various mediums of exchange, become commodities, and enter into commerce; the subject, the vehicle, the agent, and their various operations, become the objects of commercial regulation. Ship building, the carrying trade, and propagation of seamen, are such vital agents of commercial prosperity, that the nation which could not legislate over these subjects, would not possess power to regulate commerce.

That such was the understanding of the framers of the constitution is conspicuous from provisions contained in that instrument....

It is impossible, with the views which I entertain of the principle on which the commercial privileges of the people of the United States, among themselves, rests, to concur in the view which this Court takes of the effect of the coasting license in this cause. I do not regard it as the foundation of the right set up in behalf of the appellant. If there was any one object riding over every other in

a. Justice William Johnson, of South Carolina, was appointed to the Supreme Court in 1804 by Jefferson with the hope that the new justice would provide an antidote to Marshall and his Federalism. See Morgan, Justice William Johnson, The First Dissenter (1954). Was this hope realized in the *Gibbons* case?

the adoption of the constitution, it was to keep the commercial intercourse among the States free from all invidious and partial restraints. And I cannot overcome the conviction, that if the licensing act was repealed to-morrow, the rights of the appellant to a reversal of the decision complained of, would be as strong as it is under this license. One half the doubts in life arise from the defects of language, and if this instrument had been called an exemption instead of a license, it would have given a better idea of its character....

Decree.... [T]his Court is of opinion, that the several licenses to the steam boats, the Stoudinger and the Bellona, to carry on the coasting trade ... which were granted under an act of congress, passed in pursuance of the constitution of the United States, gave full authority to those vessels to navigate the waters of the United States, by steam or otherwise, for the purpose of carrying on the coasting trade, any law of the State of New York to the contrary notwithstanding; and that so much of the several laws of the State of New York, as prohibits vessels, licensed according to the laws of the United States, from navigating the waters of the State of New York, by means of fire or steam, is repugnant to the said constitution, and void [Reversed.][b]

NOTE

The Chief Justice regarded "inspection laws, quarantine laws, health laws of every description, as well as laws for regulating the internal commerce of a State, and those which respect turnpike roads, ferries, etc." as component parts of "that immense mass of legislation, which embraces everything within the territory of a State, not surrendered to the general government." According to Justice Story, such laws "are not so much regulations of commerce as of police" and the powers exercised in their enactment "are entirely distinct in their nature from that to regulate commerce". Story on the Constitution (1833), § 1066. In what sense these powers, when applied to interstate or foreign commerce, are entirely distinct from the power to regulate such commerce was not made clear, but doctrinal foundations were thus laid which could enable the Court to sustain certain state laws affecting commerce while asserting that the power to regulate such commerce was vested exclusively in the national government. Marshall actually applied the "police power" view in only one case, which follows.

WILLSON v. BLACK–BIRD CREEK MARSH CO., 27 U.S. (2 Pet.) 245 (1829). The legislature of Delaware authorized a company owning marshy lands along Black Bird Creek to dam and bank the creek with a view to improving their lands. The creek, which was navigable, flowed into the Delaware, but was described by counsel for the company as "one of those sluggish, reptile streams, that do not run but creep, and which wherever it passes, spreads its venom, and destroys the health of all those who inhabit its marshes." the owners of a sloop, licensed and enrolled under the navigation laws of the United States,

b. The arguments to the Court drove home the fact that the *Gibbons* case involved more than the run between Elizabethtown and New York. In the preceding decade, navigation by steam had developed at a rapid pace. Monopolies for the development of this modern means of travel, similar to that conferred on Fulton by New York, had been granted by New Jersey, Connecticut, Ohio, Massachusetts, New Hampshire, Vermont and Georgia; a particularly significant monopoly by Louisiana covered the mouth of the Mississippi. The legislation of New Jersey and Connecticut was designed to retaliate against New York. William Wirt's peroration enlarged on the theme that these "three states are almost on the verge of war". 9 Wheat. 184. For popular response to the *Gibbons* decision see: 1 Warren, *The Supreme Court in United States History* 615.

broke the dam in order to secure passage for their vessel. The company sued for the resulting damage and defendants claimed that since the dam obstructed navigation, the state law authorizing it was in violation of the commerce clause.

Chief Justice Marshall wrote a brief unanimous opinion for the Court containing the following observations: "The act of assembly by which the plaintiffs were authorized to construct their dam, shows plainly that this is one of those many creeks, passing through a deep, level marsh adjoining the Delaware, up which the tide flows for some distance. The value of the property on its banks must be enhanced by excluding the water from the marsh, and the health of the inhabitants probably improved. Measures calculated to produce these objects, provided they do not come into collision with the powers of the general government, are undoubtedly within those which are reserved to the States.... If congress had passed any act which bore upon the case; any act in execution of the power to regulate commerce, the object of which was to control State legislation over those small navigable creeks into which the tide flows, and which abound throughout the lower country of the middle and southern States; we should feel not much difficulty in saying that a state law coming in conflict with such act would be void. But congress has passed no such act. The repugnancy of the law of Delaware to the Constitution is placed entirely on its repugnancy to the power to regulate commerce with foreign nations and among the several States; a power which has not been so exercised as to affect the question. We do not think that the act [authorizing the dam] can, under all the circumstances of the case, be considered as repugnant to the power to regulate commerce in its dormant state, or as being in conflict with any law passed on the subject."

B.   POWER OF CONGRESS TO REGULATE INTERSTATE COMMERCE— EXCLUSIVE OR CONCURRENT

For more than half a century after *Gibbons v. Ogden,* nearly all of the litigation under the commerce clause was concerned with the constitutionality of state rather than national laws. Crucial to the decision of challenges to state legislation was resolution of the issue that Marshall raised but did not decide in *Gibbons:* Was the grant of power to Congress exclusive? If so, a sharp line had to be drawn between the commerce Congress could regulate and that the states could regulate, because a determination that one had the power was also a determination that the other did not.

In order to understand the dispute over this issue—that had a substantial impact on early determinations by the Court with respect to the scope of national power—it is necessary at this point to examine some early cases involving the scope of state power to regulate and to tax—subjects that will be pursued in detail in Chapter 6.

THE LICENSE CASES, 46 U.S. (5 How.) 504 (1847). Roger Taney, appointed Chief Justice by President Jackson in 1836, attacked the view Marshall appeared to support, that the grant of power to Congress was exclusive. These cases sharply posed the issue. State laws requiring licenses to sell intoxicating liquor were challenged by sellers who brought liquor from outside the state. A unanimous Court sustained these laws but produced six opinions (covering sixty pages) giving differing reasons for the result. Chief Justice Taney summarized his view as follows:

"It is well known that upon this subject a difference of opinion has existed, and still exists, among the members of this court. But with every respect for the opinion of my brethren with whom I do not agree, it appears to me to be very clear, that the mere grant of power to the general government cannot, upon any just principles of construction, be construed to be an absolute prohibition to exercise of any power over the same subject by the States. The controlling and supreme power over commerce with foreign nations and the several States is undoubtedly conferred upon Congress. Yet, in my judgment, the State may nevertheless, for the safety or convenience of trade, or for the protection of the health of its citizens, make regulations of commerce for its own ports and harbours, and for its own territory; and such regulations are valid unless they come in conflict with a law of Congress."

Taney's opinion was vigorously seconded by Mr. Justice Catron, who wrote:

"... So minute and complicated are the wants of commerce when it reaches its port of destination, that even the State legislatures have been incapable of providing suitable means for its regulation between ship and shore, and therefore charters, granted by the State legislatures, have conferred the power on city corporations. Owing to situation and climate, every port and place where commerce enters a State must have peculiarity in its regulations; and these it would be exceedingly difficult for Congress to make; nor could it depute the power to corporations, as the States do. The difficulties standing in the way of Congress are fast increasing with the increase of commerce and the places where it is carried on. And where it enters States through their inland borders, by land and water, the complication is not less, and especially on the large rivers. There, too, Congress has the undisputed power to regulate commerce coming from State to State; but as every village would require special legislation, and constant additions as it grew and its commerce increased, to deal with the subject on the part of Congress would be next to impossible in practice. I admit that this condition of things does not settle the question of contested power; but it satisfactorily shows that Congress cannot do what the States have done, are doing, and must continue to do, from a controlling necessity, even should the exclusive power in Congress be maintained by our decision. And this state of things was too prominently manifest for the convention to overlook it.

"... Congress has stood by for nearly sixty years, and seen the States regulate the commerce of the whole country, more or less, at the ports of entry and at their borders, without objection, and for this court now to decide that the power did not exist in the States, and that all they had done in this respect was void from the beginning, would overthrow and annul entire codes of State legislation on the particular subject. We would by our decision expunge more State laws and city corporate regulations than Congress is likely to make in a century on the same subject, and on no better assumption than that Congress and the State legislatures had been altogether mistaken as to their respective powers for fifty years and more. If long usage, general acquiescence, and the absence of complaint can settle the interpretation of the clause in question, then it should be deemed as settled in conformity to the usage by the courts."

Mr. Justice McLean apparently felt that he avoided any question of collision with the national commercial power by concluding: "The license acts ... do not purport to be a regulation of commerce. They are essentially police laws." Mr. Justice Grier similarly disposed of the problem: "I do not consider the question of the exclusiveness of the power of Congress to regulate commerce as necessarily connected with the decision of this point;" and quoted with approval the view that "the powers which relate to merely municipal regulations, or what may more properly be called internal police, are not surrendered by the States...."

The divisions of the Court revealed in the License Cases were continued in the Passenger Cases, 48 U.S. (7 How.) 283 (1849). These cases (*Smith v. Turner, Health Commissioner of the Port of New York* and *Norris v. The City of Boston*) involved New York and Massachusetts laws imposing taxes on alien passengers arriving from foreign countries, the proceeds to be used to support a marine hospital (New York) and alien paupers (Massachusetts). It was argued that the laws were police power measures passed for protection against disease and pauperism from abroad. The Court held (5 to 4) that the laws were unconstitutional regulations of foreign commerce, but again there was no opinion subscribed to by a majority of the Justices. Of the dissenters, Taney, C.J., Daniel, J. and Nelson, J., reasserted the general view that the national commerce power is not exclusive. The fourth dissenter, Woodbury, J., argued that the commerce power was partly exclusive and partly concurrent but he based his vote largely on the ground of state police power.

Cooley v. Board of Wardens of the Port of Philadelphia

53 U.S. (12 How.) 299, 13 L.Ed. 996 (1851).

[A Pennsylvania statute of 1803 required vessels coming into or leaving the Port of Philadelphia to accept local pilots for pilotage through the Delaware River and upon failure to do so the master, owner or consignee of the vessel was made liable to pay half the pilotage fees as a penalty. Cooley was sued as the consignee of two vessels that sailed from Philadelphia without taking on a local pilot as required by the statute. The court below sustained judgment against Cooley.]

Mr. Justice Curtis[a] delivered the opinion of the court: ...

That the power to regulate commerce includes the regulation of navigation, we consider settled. And when we look to the nature of the service performed by pilots, to the relations which that service and its compensations bear to navigation between the several States, and between the ports of the United States and foreign countries, we are brought to the conclusion, that the regulation of the qualifications of pilots, of the modes and times of offering and rendering their services, of the responsibilities which shall rest upon them, of the powers they shall possess, of the compensation they may demand, and of the penalties by which their rights and duties may be enforced, do constitute regulations of navigation, and consequently of commerce, within the just meaning of this clause of the Constitution.

The power to regulate navigation is the power to prescribe rules in conformity with which navigation must be carried on. It extends to the persons who conduct it, as well as to the instruments used. Accordingly, the first Congress assembled under the Constitution passed laws, requiring the masters of ships and vessels of the United States to be citizens of the United States, and established many rules for the government and regulation of officers and seamen. 1 Stat. at Large, 55, 131. These have been from time to time added to and changed, and we are not aware that their validity has been questioned. . . .

The act of 1789, (1 Stat. at Large, 54,) already referred to, contains a clear legislative exposition of the Constitution by the first Congress, to the effect that the power to regulate pilots was conferred on Congress by the Constitution; . . . . And a majority of the court are of opinion, that a regulation of pilots is a regulation of commerce, within the grant to Congress of the commercial

a. Justice Curtis had just been appointed to the Court by President Fillmore; he succeeded Justice Woodbury, who died in 1851.

power, contained in the third clause of the eighth section of the first article of the Constitution.

It becomes necessary, therefore, to consider whether this law of Pennsylvania, being a regulation of commerce, is valid.

The act of Congress of the 7th of August, 1789, sect. 4, is as follows:

"That all pilots in the bays, inlets, rivers, harbors, and ports of the United States shall continue to be regulated in conformity with the existing laws of the States, respectively, wherein such pilots may be, or with such laws as the States may respectively hereafter enact for the purpose, until further legislative provision shall be made by Congress."

If the law of Pennsylvania, now in question, had been in existence at the date of this act of Congress, we might hold it to have been adopted by Congress, and thus made a law of the United States, and so valid. Because this act does, in effect, give the force of an act of Congress, to the then existing State laws on this subject, so long as they should continue unrepealed by the State which enacted them.

But the law on which these actions are founded was not enacted till 1803. What effect then can be attributed to so much of the act of 1789, as declares, that pilots shall continue to be regulated in conformity, "with such laws as the States may respectively hereafter enact for the purpose, until further legislative provision shall be made by Congress"?

If the States were divested of the power to legislate on this subject by the grant of the commercial power to Congress, it is plain this act could not confer upon them power thus to legislate. If the Constitution excluded the States from making any law regulating commerce, certainly Congress cannot regrant, or in any manner reconvey to the States that power. And yet this act of 1789 gives its sanction only to laws enacted by the States. This necessarily implies a constitutional power to legislate; for only a rule created by the sovereign power of a State acting in its legislative capacity, can be deemed a law, enacted by a State; and if the State has so limited its sovereign power that it no longer extends to a particular subject, manifestly it cannot, in any proper sense, be said to enact laws thereon. Entertaining these views we are brought directly and unavoidably to the consideration of the question, whether the grant of the commercial power to Congress, did per se deprive the States of all power to regulate pilots. This question has never been decided by this court, nor, in our judgment, has any case depending upon all the considerations which must govern this one, come before this court. The grant of commercial power to Congress does not contain any terms which expressly exclude the States from exercising an authority over its subject-matter. If they are excluded it must be because the nature of the power, thus granted to Congress, requires that a similar authority should not exist in the States. If it were conceded on the one side, that the nature of this power, like that to legislate for the District of Columbia, is absolutely and totally repugnant to the existence of similar power in the States, probably no one would deny that the grant of the power to Congress, as effectually and perfectly excludes the States from all future legislation on the subject, as if express words had been used to exclude them. And on the other hand, if it were admitted that the existence of this power in Congress, like the power of taxation, is compatible with the existence of a similar power in the States, then it would be in conformity with the contemporary exposition of the Constitution, (Federalist, No. 32,) and with the judicial construction, given from time to time by this court, after the most deliberate consideration, to hold that the mere grant of such a power to Congress, did not imply a prohibition on the States to exercise the same power; that it is not the mere existence of such a power, but its exercise by Congress, which may be incompatible with the exercise of the same power by the States, and that the States may legislate in the absence of congressional regulations. Sturges v. Crowninshield, 4 Wheat. 122; Houston v. Moore, 5 Wheat. 1; Willson v. Black–Bird Creek Marsh Co., 2 Peters 245.

The diversities of opinion, therefore, which have existed on this subject, have arisen from the different views taken of the nature of this power. But when the nature of a power like this is spoken of, when it is said that the nature of the power requires that it should be exercised exclusively by Congress, it must be intended to refer to the subjects of that power, and to say they are of such a nature as to require exclusive legislation by Congress. Now the power to regulate commerce embraces a vast field, containing not only many, but exceedingly various subjects, quite unlike in their nature; some imperatively demanding a single uniform rule, operating equally on the commerce of the United States in every port; and some, like the subject now in question, as imperatively demanding that diversity, which alone can meet the local necessities of navigation.

Either absolutely to affirm, or deny that the nature of this power requires exclusive legislation by Congress, is to lose sight of the nature of the subjects of this power, and to assert concerning all of them, what is really applicable but to a part. Whatever subjects of this power are in their nature national, or admit only of one uniform system, or plan of regulation, may justly be said to be of such a nature as to require exclusive legislation by Congress. That this cannot be affirmed of laws for the regulation of pilots and pilotage is plain. The act of 1789 contains a clear and authoritative declaration by the first Congress, that the nature of this subject is such, that until Congress should find it necessary to exert its power, it should be left to the legislation of the States; that it is local and not national; that it is likely to be the best provided for, not by one system, or plan of regulations, but by as many as the legislative discretion of the several States should deem applicable to the local peculiarities of the ports within their limits.

Viewed in this light, so much of this act of 1789 as declares that pilots shall continue to be regulated "by such laws as the States may respectively hereafter enact for that purpose," instead of being held to be inoperative, as an attempt to confer on the States a power to legislate, of which the Constitution had deprived them, is allowed an appropriate and important signification. It manifests the understanding of Congress, at the outset of the government, that the nature of this subject is not such as to require its exclusive legislation. The practice of the States, and of the national government, has been in conformity with this declaration, from the origin of the national government to this time; and the nature of the subject when examined is such as to leave no doubt of the superior fitness and propriety, not to say the absolute necessity, of different systems of regulation, drawn from local knowledge and experience, and conformed to local wants. How then can we say, that by the mere grant of power to regulate commerce, the States are deprived of all the power to legislate on this subject, because from the nature of the power the legislation of Congress must be exclusive. This would be to affirm that the nature of the power is in any case, something different from the nature of the subject to which, in such case, the power extends, and that the nature of the power necessarily demands, in all cases, exclusive legislation by Congress, while the nature of one of the subjects of that power, not only does not require such exclusive legislation, but may be best provided for by many different systems enacted by the States, in conformity with the circumstances of the ports within their limits. In construing an instrument designed for the formation of a government, and in determining the extent of one of its important grants of power to legislate, we can make no such distinction between the nature of the power and the nature of the subject on which that power was intended practically to operate, nor consider the grant more extensive by affirming of the power, what is not true of its subject now in question.

It is the opinion of a majority of the court that the mere grant to Congress of the power to regulate commerce, did not deprive the States of power to regulate pilots, and that although Congress had legislated on this subject, its legislation manifests an intention, with a single exception, not to regulate this subject, but to leave its regulation to the several States. To these precise questions, which are all we are called on to decide, this opinion must be understood to be confined. It does not extend to the question what other subjects, under the commercial power, are within the exclusive control of Congress, or may be regulated by the States in the absence of all congressional legislation; nor to the general question how far any regulation of a subject by Congress may be deemed to operate as an exclusion of all legislation by the States upon the same subject. We decide the precise questions before us, upon what we deem sound principles, applicable to this particular subject in the state in which the legislation of Congress has left it. We go no further. . . .

Judgment affirmed.

[McLean and Wayne, JJ., dissented; Daniel, J., concurred for other reasons.]

QUESTIONS

(1) The *Cooley* "rule" has become famous in constitutional law; we shall meet it repeatedly in subsequent cases. What solution did it offer to the controversy over whether or not the commerce power was exclusive?

(2) The majority of the Court concluded that the pilot regulations did not deal with one of those "*subjects*" of the commerce power which "*are in their nature national, or admit only of one uniform system, or plan of regulation.*" Do you see any reason for this conclusion other than the fact that Congress had expressly left the matter to the states? Would the result apparently have been different if Congress had said nothing on the subject?

(3) For an excellent discussion of early commerce clause theory, see Ribble, *State and National Power Over Commerce* (1937).

POWER OF CONGRESS TO CONSENT TO STATE REGULATION OF INTERSTATE COMMERCE

In *Cooley,* it will be remembered, the Court said: "If the Constitution excluded the States from making any law regulating commerce, certainly Congress cannot regrant, or in any manner reconvey to the States that power." By the 1890s, however, the Court had hit upon a theory that would permit Congress to redefine the distribution of power as marked out by the courts. In Leisy v. Hardin, 135 U.S. 100 (1890), the Court in holding that the state could not forbid the sale of liquor brought from another state while in the original package, said:

"Whenever . . . a particular power of the general government is one which must necessarily be exercised by it, and Congress remains silent, this is not only not a concession that the powers reserved by the States may be exerted as if the specific power had not been elsewhere reposed, but, on the contrary, the only legitimate conclusion is that the general government intended that power should not be affirmatively exercised, and the action of the States cannot be permitted to effect that which would be incompatible with such intention. Hence, inasmuch as interstate commerce, consisting in the transportation, purchase, sale and exchange of commodities, is national in its character, and must be governed by a uniform system, so long as Congress does not pass any law to regulate it, or allowing the States so to do, it thereby indicates its will that such commerce shall be free and untrammelled. ... Brown v. Houston, 114 U.S. 622, 631; Wabash, St. Louis & c. Railway v. Illinois, 118 U.S. 557. ..."

Congress took the hint and enacted the Wilson Act (26 Stat. 313) of 1890, providing that all intoxicating liquors transported into any state or remaining therein for use, sale or storage, should "upon arrival in such state" be subject to the state's laws "enacted in the exercise of its police powers," to the same extent as though such liquor had been produced in the state and should "not be exempt therefrom by reason of being introduced therein in original packages or otherwise." The constitutionality of this statute was sustained in Wilkerson v. Rahrer, 140 U.S. 545 (1891), over the objection that as applied to liquor imported and remaining in the original packages it attempted an invalid delegation of the national commerce power to the states. The Court (per Fuller, C.J.) said: "Congress can neither delegate its own powers nor enlarge those of a state," but "Congress has not attempted to delegate the power to regulate commerce, or to exercise any power reserved to the states, or to grant a power not possessed by the states, or to adopt state laws. It has taken its own course and made its own regulation, applying to these subjects of interstate commerce one common rule, whose uniformity is not affected by variations in state laws in dealing with such property." Since the Wilson Act did not authorize state prohibition of importation, but only prohibition of sales after importation, Congress passed the Webb–Kenyon Act (37 Stat. 699) of 1913 forbidding the transportation in interstate commerce of liquor intended to be used contrary to any law of the state of destination. This Act was sustained in James Clark Distilling Co. v. Western Maryland R. Co., 242 U.S. 311 (1917).

See W. Cohen, *Congressional Power to Validate Unconstitutional State Laws: A Forgotten Solution to an Old Enigma*, 35 Stan.L.Rev. 387 (1983); Vikram Amar, *Indirect Effects of Direct Election: A Structural Examination of the Seventeenth Amendment*, 49 Vand.L.Rev. 1347 (1996); Bikle, *The Silence of Congress,* 41 Harv.L.Rev. 200 (1927).

SECTION 3.   THE SCOPE OF NATIONAL POWER TODAY

A.   THE COMMERCE POWER

Introduction. An evil genius choosing a time for a new constitution that would tax its capacity for adaptability could hardly have selected a more trying time than 1789. Though some foresaw that the coastal settlements might expand across the continent, the framers had no inkling of the impact of the industrial revolution. The power of steam was soon harnessed for steamships and for railroads, which by 1869 spanned the continent. This new source of power also led to undreamed expansion of industrial production. The new Constitution thus was established on the eve of the great transition from an economy based on agriculture and handicraft to an economy based on power, machines and factories. The new forms of production were accompanied by the

[margin note: New const. was made on the eve of the industrial revolution]

development of legal devices to organize and concentrate wealth: the business corporation and their combination through "trusts."

Correlated with this account, Congress did not often exercise its commerce power during most of the nineteenth century, but began to do so in significant ways starting with railroad regulation in the 1887 Interstate Commerce Act, followed closely by the Sherman Antitrust Act in 1890. The quantity of congressional commerce regulation jumped sharply beginning with Franklin Roosevelt's New Deal responses to the Great Depression and has continued at high levels. In response, the Supreme Court's commerce clause decisions after Gibbons v. Ogden, supra p. 148, have fallen into three roughly 50–year periods. Until the late 1800's the Court primarily addressed, not Congress' power to legislate, but state power to regulate where Congress might have. Then, from the beginning of significant congressional regulation of the incidents of nation-wide transportation systems and industrial production until 1936, the Court adopted a variety of approaches simultaneously to limit perceived excesses of the commerce power and approve perceived needful uses. Finally, from 1937 until at least the 1995 decision in United States v. Lopez, the Court largely abandoned the attempt to restrain congressional power to regulate the economy.

In lieu of more extensive treatment of these developments, the following summary tracing the Court's precedents is drawn from a portion of Justice Kennedy's concurring opinion in United States v. Lopez, 514 U.S. 549, 568–73 (1995), augmented with footnote annotations by the editors:

"Chief Justice Marshall announced that the national authority reaches 'that commerce which concerns more States than one' and that the commerce power 'is complete in itself, may be exercised to its utmost extent, and acknowledges no limitations, other than are prescribed in the constitution.' Gibbons v. Ogden, 22 U.S. (9 Wheat.) 1, 194, 196, 6 L.Ed. 23 (1824). His statements can be understood now as an early and authoritative recognition that the Commerce Clause grants Congress extensive power and ample discretion to determine its appropriate exercise. The progression of our Commerce Clause cases from Gibbons to the present was not marked, however, by a coherent or consistent course of interpretation; for neither the course of technological advance nor the foundational principles for the jurisprudence itself were self-evident to the courts that sought to resolve contemporary disputes by enduring principles.

"Furthermore, for almost a century after the adoption of the Constitution, the Court's Commerce Clause decisions did not concern the authority of Congress to legislate. Rather, the Court faced the related but quite distinct question of the authority of the States to regulate matters that would be within the commerce power had Congress chosen to act. The simple fact was that in the early years of the Republic, Congress seldom perceived the necessity to exercise its power in circumstances where its authority would be called into question....

. . .

"One approach the Court used to inquire into the lawfulness of state authority was to draw content-based or subject-matter distinctions, thus defining by semantic or formalistic categories those activities that were commerce and those that were not. For instance, in deciding that a State could prohibit the in-state manufacture of liquor intended for out-of-state shipment, it distinguished between manufacture and commerce.... Kidd v. Pearson, 128 U.S. 1, 20 (1888). Though that approach likely would not have survived even if

[Handwritten margin notes:]
prior to this congress rarely exercised their commerce power

until 1800's – state power to regulate
until 1936 – variety of approaches
1937-1995 – congressional power

unlimited congressional power for interstate

confined to the question of a State's authority to enact legislation, it was not at all propitious when applied to the quite different question of what subjects were within the reach of the national power when Congress chose to exercise it.

"This became evident when the Court began to confront federal economic regulation enacted in response to the rapid industrial development in the late 19th century. Thus, it relied upon the manufacture-commerce dichotomy in United States v. E.C. Knight Co., 156 U.S. 1 (1895), where a manufacturers' combination controlling some 98% of the Nation's domestic sugar refining capacity was held to be outside the reach of the Sherman Act. Conspiracies to control manufacture, agriculture, mining, production, wages, or prices, the Court explained, had too 'indirect' an effect on interstate commerce.[a] Id., at 16. And in Adair v. United States, 208 U.S. 161 (1908), the Court rejected the view that the commerce power might extend to activities that, although local in the sense of having originated within a single state, nevertheless had a practical effect on interstate commercial activity. The Court concluded that there was not a 'legal or logical connection ... between an employee's membership in a labor organization and the carrying on of interstate commerce,' id., at 178, and struck down a federal statute forbidding the discharge of an employee because of his membership in a labor organization....

"Even before the Court committed itself to sustaining federal legislation on broad principles of economic practicality, it found it necessary to depart from these decisions. The Court disavowed *E.C. Knight*'s reliance on the manufacturing-commerce distinction in Standard Oil Co. of New Jersey v. United States, 221 U.S. 1 (1911), declaring that approach 'unsound.' The Court likewise rejected the rationale of *Adair* when it decided, in Texas & New Orleans R. Co. v. Railway Clerks, 281 U.S. 548, 570–571 (1930), that Congress had the power to regulate matters pertaining to the organization of railroad workers.

"In another line of cases, the Court addressed Congress' efforts to impede local activities it considered undesirable by prohibiting the interstate movement of some essential element. In the Lottery Case, 188 U.S. 321 (1903), the Court rejected the argument that Congress lacked power to prohibit the interstate movement of lottery tickets because it had power only to regulate, not to prohibit. See also Hipolite Egg Co. v. United States, 220 U.S. 45 (1911); Hoke v. United States, 227 U.S. 308 (1913). In Hammer v. Dagenhart, 247 U.S. 251 (1918), however, the Court insisted that the power to regulate commerce 'is directly the contrary of the assumed right to forbid commerce from moving,' id., at 269–270, and struck down a prohibition on the interstate transportation of goods manufactured in violation of child labor laws.[b]

a. The Court worried "that, if the national power extends to all contracts and combinations in manufacture, agriculture, mining, and other productive industries, whose ultimate result may affect external commerce, comparatively little of business operations and affairs would be left for state control." In Addyston Pipe & Steel Co. v. United States, 175 U.S. 211 (1899), however, the Court held that the Sherman Act could apply to a conspiracy among companies engaged in the manufacture, sale, and transportation of iron pipe to divide sales territory and arrange for noncompetitive bidding, because, unlike *Knight,* the agreement directly restrained not only the manufacture but also the purchase, sale or exchange of the manufactured commodity among the states. And in Northern Securities Co. v. United States, 193 U.S. 197 (1904), the Court held that the Act could be applied to break up joint control of competing railroads by a holding company, because this directly embraced interstate commerce.

b. The Court distinguished the cases involving interstate transport of lottery tickets, impure food and drugs (*Hipolite Egg*), women for purposes of prostitution and debauchery (*Hoke*), and liquor (Clark Distilling Co. v. Western Maryland R. Co., 242 U.S. 311 (1917)), as "instances ... of interstate transportation ... necessary to the accomplish-

"Even while it was experiencing difficulties in finding satisfactory principles in these cases, the Court was pursuing a more sustainable and practical approach in other lines of decisions, particularly those involving the regulation of railroad rates. In the Minnesota Rate Cases, 230 U.S. 352 (1913), the Court upheld a state rate order, but observed that Congress might be empowered to regulate in this area if 'by reason of the interblending of the interstate and intrastate operations of interstate carriers' the regulation of interstate rates could not be maintained without restrictions on 'intrastate rates which substantially affect the former.' Id., at 432–433. And in the Shreveport Rate Cases, 234 U.S. 342 (1914), the Court upheld an ICC order fixing railroad rates with the explanation that congressional authority, 'extending to these interstate carriers as instruments of interstate commerce, necessarily embraces the right to control their operations in all matters having such a close and substantial relation to interstate traffic that the control is essential or appropriate to the security of that traffic, to the efficiency of the interstate service, and to the maintenance of conditions under which interstate commerce may be conducted upon fair terms and without molestation or hindrance.' "[c] Id., at 351.

R.R. cases, were allowed to be regulated rates by congress

ment of harmful results[,]" whereas in *Hammer* "[t]he act in its effect does not regulate transportation among the states, but aims to standardize the ages at which children may be employed in mining and manufacturing within the states. The goods shipped are of themselves harmless...." The Court also rejected the argument that the act was a valid attempt to protect business in states with high labor standards from unfair interstate competition resulting from production in those states permitting child labor conditions:

"The commerce clause was not intended to give to Congress a general authority to equalize such conditions. In some of the states laws have been passed fixing minimum wages for women, in others the local law regulates the hours of labor of women in various employments. Business done in such states may be at an economic disadvantage when compared with states which have no such regulations; surely this fact does not give Congress the power to deny transportation in interstate commerce to those who carry on business where the hours of labor and the rate of compensation for women have not been fixed by a standard in use in other states and approved by Congress...."

The act was held unconstitutional as invading the reserved powers of the states.

Justice Holmes (with McKenna, Brandeis and Clarke, JJ.) dissented, saying:

"The notion that prohibition is any less prohibition when applied to things now thought evil I do not understand. But if there is any matter upon which civilized countries have agreed—far more unanimously than they have with reference to intoxicants ... — it is the evil of premature and excessive child labor....

"But I had thought that the propriety of the exercise of a power admitted to exist in

some cases was for the consideration of Congress alone and that this Court always had disavowed the right to intrude its judgment upon questions of policy or morals. It is not for this Court to pronounce when prohibition is necessary to regulation if it ever may be necessary—to say that it is permissible as against strong drink but not as against the product of ruined lives.

"The Act does not meddle with anything belonging to the States. They may regulate their internal affairs and their domestic commerce as they like. But when they seek to send their products across the State line they are no longer within their rights. If there were no Constitution and no Congress their power to cross the line would depend upon their neighbors. Under the Constitution such commerce belongs not to the States but to Congress to regulate. It may carry out its views of public policy whatever indirect effect they may have upon the activities of the States...."

After *Hammer*, Congress imposed a 10% tax on net profits of factories employing child labor, which the Court invalidated as being palpably prohibitory and regulatory in a manner indistinguishable from *Hammer*, rather than being a valid tax. The Child Labor Tax Case, 259 U.S. 20 (1922).

c. In order to end rate discrimination, the ICC order effectively required railroads engaged in both interstate and intrastate traffic to raise rates on intrastate hauls because proportionately higher rates it had approved were in effect for interstate hauls. The Court also said: "Wherever the interstate and intrastate transactions of carriers are so related that the government of the one involves the control of the other, it is Congress, and not the state, that is entitled to prescribe the final and dominant rule, for

[Handwritten margin note: Didn't look technically at def. of commerce, but practically ↓ determined that is does affect commerce.]

"Even the most confined interpretation of 'commerce' would embrace transportation between the States, so the rate cases posed much less difficulty for the Court than cases involving manufacture or production. Nevertheless, the Court's recognition of the importance of a practical conception of the commerce power was not altogether confined to the rate cases. In Swift & Co. v. United States, 196 U.S. 375 (1905), the Court upheld the application of federal antitrust law to a combination of meat dealers that occurred in one State but that restrained trade in cattle 'sent for sale from a place in one State, with the expectation that they will end their transit . . . in another.' Id., at 398. The Court explained that 'commerce among the States is not a technical legal conception, but a practical one, drawn from the course of business.' Id., at 398. Chief Justice Taft followed the same approach in upholding federal regulation of stockyards in Stafford v. Wallace, 258 U.S. 495 (1922). Speaking for the Court, he rejected a 'nice and technical inquiry,' id., at 519, when the local transactions at issue could not 'be separated from the movement to which they contribute,' id., at 516.

"Reluctance of the Court to adopt that approach in all of its cases caused inconsistencies in doctrine to persist, however. In addressing New Deal legislation the Court resuscitated the abandoned abstract distinction between direct and indirect effects on interstate commerce. See Carter v. Carter Coal Co., 298 U.S. 238, 309 (1936) (Act regulating price of coal and wages and hours for miners held to have only 'secondary and indirect' effect on interstate commerce);[d] Railroad Retirement Bd. v. Alton R. Co., 295 U.S. 330 (1935) (compulsory retirement and pension plan for railroad carrier employees too 'remote from any regulation of commerce as such'); A.L.A. Schechter Poultry Corp. v.

[Handwritten margin note: Carter V. Carter Coal Co. cant regulate wages ↓ hours of miners]

otherwise Congress would be denied the exercise of its constitutional authority, and the state, and not the nation, would be supreme within the national field."

d. The *Carter* case arose in the middle of the Depression at the end of the Court's most active period of assault on congressional control of the economy. It held unconstitutional the Guffey Coal Act, which sought to regulate minimum coal prices and minimum wages and maximum hours for mine workers, and in which Congress declared "that the production and distribution by producers of such coal bear upon and directly affect interstate commerce, and render regulation of production and distribution imperative for the protection of such commerce . . . ." Justice Sutherland, for the majority, said in part:

"The proposition, often advanced and as often discredited, that the power of the federal government inherently extends to purposes affecting the nation as a whole with which the states severally cannot deal or cannot adequately deal, and the related notion that Congress, entirely apart from those powers delegated by the Constitution, may enact laws to promote the general welfare, have never been accepted but always definitely rejected by this court. . . .

. . .

"A consideration of [many cases, including *Knight*] renders inescapable the conclu-

sion that the effect of the labor provisions of the act, including those in respect of minimum wages, wage agreements, collective bargaining, and the Labor Board and its powers, primarily falls upon production and not upon commerce; and confirms the further resulting conclusion that production is a purely local activity. It follows that none of these essential antecedents of production constitutes a transaction in or forms any part of interstate commerce. . . .

. . .

"Whether the effect of a given activity or condition is direct or indirect is not always easy to determine. . . . And the extent of the effect bears no logical relation to its character. The distinction between a direct and an indirect effect turns, not upon the magnitude of either the cause or the effect, but entirely upon the manner in which the effect has been brought about. . . . It is quite true that rules of law are sometimes qualified by considerations of degree, as the government argues. But the matter of degree has no bearing upon the question here, since that question is not—What is the *extent* of the local activity or condition, or the *extent* of the effect produced upon interstate commerce? but—What is the *relation* between the activity or condition and the effect? . . ."

United States, 295 U.S. 495 (1935) (wage and hour law provision of National Industrial Recovery Act had 'no direct relation to interstate commerce')[e].

"The case that seems to mark the Court's definitive commitment to the practical conception of the commerce power is NLRB v. Jones & Laughlin Steel Corp., 301 U.S. 1 (1937), where the Court sustained labor laws that applied to manufacturing facilities, making no real attempt to distinguish *Carter* ... and *Schechter*.... 301 U.S., at 40–41.[f] The deference given to Congress has since

[handwritten margin note: NLRB v. Jones & laughlin Steel — Ct. sustained labor laws applying to manufacturing facilities]

e. The NIRA was perhaps the most widely heralded New Deal measure designed to stimulate recovery from the Great Depression. Schechter Poultry, a Brooklyn business that bought poultry at markets or railroad terminals within New York City and slaughtered and distributed poultry wholesale to New York dealers who resold to New York consumers, was convicted of code violations "in any transaction in or affecting foreign or interstate commerce." The evidence indicated that ninety-six per cent of the live poultry marketed in New York came from other states. The Supreme Court reversed the conviction, first, because the act had attempted an unconstitutional delegation of power to the President, and second, because as applied it exceeded the commerce power. For a unanimous Court, Chief Justice Hughes concluded that the poultry transactions involved were not "in" interstate commerce: "The poultry had come to a permanent rest within the State. It was not held, used, or sold by defendants in relation to any further transactions in interstate commerce and was not destined for transportation to other states. Hence, decisions which deal with a stream of interstate commerce—where goods come to rest within a state temporarily and are later to go forward in interstate commerce—and with the regulations of transactions involved in that practical continuity of movement, are not applicable here. See Swift & Co. v. United States, 196 U.S. 375, 387, 388; ... Stafford v. Wallace, 258 U.S. 495, 519...." Defendant's transactions did not "directly 'affect' interstate commerce so as to be subject to federal regulation.... In determining how far the federal government may go in controlling intrastate transactions upon the ground that they 'affect' interstate commerce, there is a necessary and well-established distinction between direct and indirect effects. The precise line can be drawn only as individual cases arise, but the distinction is clear in principle.... If the commerce clause were construed to reach all enterprises and transactions which could be said to have an indirect effect upon interstate commerce, the federal authority would embrace practically all the activities of the people and the authority of the state over its domestic concerns would exist only by sufferance of the federal government...." Concurring, Justice Cardozo stated: "The law is not indifferent to considerations of degree. Activities local in their immediacy do not become interstate

and national because of distant repercussions. What is near and what is distant may at times be uncertain.... There is no penumbra of uncertainty obscuring judgment here. To find immediacy or directness here is to find it almost everywhere. If centrifugal forces are to be isolated to the exclusion of the forces that oppose and counteract them, there will be an end to our federal system."

f. Under the National Labor Relations Act, enacted in 1935, the newly created National Labor Relations Board ordered Jones & Laughlin to cease and desist from interfering with the right of its employees at a steel and iron manufacturing plant to organize and bargain collectively. The Court upheld the NLRB's order under the commerce power, relying in part on the notion of the Shreveport Rate Case, supra, that "intrastate activities, by reason of close and intimate relation to interstate commerce, may fall within federal control...." The Court now said that the "question is necessarily one of degree" and "the fact that the employees here concerned were engaged in production is not determinative. The question remains as to the effect upon interstate commerce of the labor practice involved." As to that, the Court said:

"[T]he stoppage of [respondent's manufacturing] operations by industrial strife would have a most serious effect upon interstate commerce. In view of respondent's far-flung activities, it is idle to say that the effect would be indirect or remote. It is obvious that it would be immediate and might be catastrophic. We are asked to shut our eyes to the plainest facts of our national life and to deal with the question of direct and indirect effects in an intellectual vacuum. Because there may be but indirect and remote effects upon interstate commerce in connection with a host of local enterprises throughout the country, it does not follow that other industrial activities do not have such a close and intimate relation to interstate commerce as to make the presence of industrial strife a matter of the most urgent national concern. When industries organize themselves on a national scale making their relation to interstate commerce the dominant factor in their activities, how can it be maintained that their industrial labor relations constitute a forbidden field into which Congress may not enter when it is necessary to protect interstate been confirmed. United States v. Darby, 312 U.S. 100, 116–117 (1941), overruled Hammer v. Dagenhart, supra. And in Wickard v. Filburn, 317 U.S. 111 (1942), the Court disapproved *E.C. Knight* and the entire line of direct-indirect and manufacture-production cases, explaining that 'broader interpretations of the Commerce Clause [were] destined to supersede the earlier ones,' id., at 122, and 'whatever terminology is used, the criterion is necessarily one of degree and must be so defined . . .', id., at 123, n. 24. . . ."

THE ROOSEVELT COURT PLAN

The initial New Deal program had been shattered by the series of major judicial defeats suffered in the Supreme Court. Stricken down in succession were the Railroad Retirement Act of 1934, the National Industrial Recovery Act of 1933, the Agricultural Adjustment Act of 1933, and the Bituminous Coal Conservation Act of 1935. By the time of the *Carter Coal* decision of May 18, 1936, a feeling was growing within the administration that something had to be done about the Supreme Court. Actual steps awaited the election of November 1936, which returned Roosevelt to the presidency by an overwhelming majority. On February 7, 1937, the President sent to Congress a message calling for legislation to "reorganize the judicial branch"—a proposal commonly known as the court-packing plan. After dealing at some length with other less controversial problems of judicial organization, the message turned to "the question of aged or infirm judges—a subject of delicacy and yet one which requires frank discussion." The message stressed the difficulty for older men to keep up with the work of the courts, and also stated: "A lowered mental or physical vigor leads men to avoid an examination of complicated and changed conditions. Little by little, new facts become blurred through old glasses fitted, as it were, for the needs of another generation; older men, assuming that the scene is the same as it was in the past, cease to explore or inquire into the present or the future." The message then recommended that legislation provide for "the appointment of additional judges, in all Federal Courts, without exception, where there are incumbent judges of retirement age who do not choose to retire or resign." At that time six members of the Supreme Court had passed the voluntary retirement age of 70: Hughes (75), Sutherland (75), Butler (71), Brandeis (81), McReynolds (75), and Van Devanter (78).

The proposal produced a hurricane of controversy which lasted for months.[a] Opposition mounted as it became increasingly clear that the Presi-

commerce from the paralyzing consequences of industrial war?"

After *Jones & Laughlin* the Court sustained the application of the NLRA to a variety of smaller industrial enterprises. In National Labor Relations Board v. Fainblatt, 306 U.S. 601 (1939), involving a manufacturer who processed materials into about a thousand dozen garments a month shipped in interstate commerce, the Court said that it was not important "that the volume of the commerce here involved though substantial, was relatively small as compared with that in the cases arising under the National Labor Relations Act which have hitherto engaged our attention. The power of Congress to regulate interstate commerce is plenary and extends to all such commerce be it great or small." The Court went on to note that the garment industry was one in which relatively small units contributed in the aggregate to a vast volume of commerce and that strikes in the industry would have a substantial effect on interstate commerce.

a. For subsequent developments, and especially the generalship of Chief Justice Hughes in meeting this challenge, see Pusey, *Charles Evans Hughes* (1951). Cf. Robert H. Jackson, *The Struggle for Judicial Supremacy,* 176 et seq. (1941); Leuchtenburg, *The Origins of Franklin D. Roosevelt's "Court-Packing" Plan,* 1966 Supreme Court Review 347 (1966). In answer to the charge that this proposal produced a "switch in time that saved nine", Justice Roberts left a paper with Justice Frankfurter for posthumous publication, which shows that Justice Roberts's vote to sustain state minimum wage legislation in West Coast Hotel Co. v. Parrish, 300 U.S. 379 (1937), although announced on March 29, dent's object was to change the judicial philosophy of the Supreme Court; on June 14, 1937, the Senate Judiciary Committee recommended rejection of the proposed legislation "as a needless, futile, and utterly dangerous abandonment of constitutional principle," Report No. 711, 75th Cong., 1st Sess. (1937). On July 22, the bill was killed by recommitment to the Judiciary Committee. During this interval, there were before the Supreme Court cases involving the constitutionality of the National Labor Relations Act and the Social Security Act, which had been enacted along with the Bituminous Coal Act in the summer of 1935; National Labor Relations Board v. Jones & Laughlin Steel Corp., supra, was argued February 10, 11, 1937, and decided April 12; Charles C. Steward Machine Co. v. Davis, 301 U.S. 548, was argued April 8, 9, 1937, and decided May 24.

Legislation held valid while debate continues

In both cases the legislation was held valid by votes of 5 to 4.

President Roosevelt lost the battle but won the war. Within four years he was given the opportunity to replace seven members of the Court. In 1937 Justice Van Devanter retired and was succeeded by Senator Hugo Black. The following year Justice Sutherland retired, to be succeeded by Solicitor General Stanley Reed. In 1939, Justice Cardozo was succeeded by Professor Felix Frankfurter, Justice Brandeis by William O. Douglas, Chairman of the Securities and Exchange Commission, and Justice Butler by Attorney General Frank Murphy. In 1941, Justice McReynolds resigned and was succeeded by Senator James Byrnes. Later in 1941, Chief Justice Hughes resigned, Justice Stone was made Chief Justice, and Attorney General Robert H. Jackson was added to the Court.

Roosevelt's plan passed.

By 1942 the Court had dramatically reversed itself, sustaining in their broadest applications the National Labor Relations Act, the Fair Labor Standards Act, and the Agricultural Adjustment Act. As we will see in later chapters, the Court also changed its interpretation of the due process and equal protection clauses so as to increase substantially governmental regulatory powers over economic matters.

Act were also reversed.

THE POST–DEPRESSION COMMERCE POWER

As Justice Kennedy hints in his survey, United States v. Darby, 312 U.S. 100 (1941), and Wickard v. Filburn, 317 U.S. 111 (1942), confirmed a sweepingly deferential approach to Congress' exercise of its commerce power. The way these twin pillars of modern commerce clause doctrine did so is noteworthy.

Wickard v. Filburn

Darby sustained application of the Fair Labor Standards Act of 1938, first, in § 15(a)(1), to prohibit the shipment in interstate commerce of lumber manufactured by employees whose wages were less than a prescribed minimum or whose weekly hours of labor at that wage were greater than a prescribed maximum, and, second, in § 15(a)(2), to prohibit employment in the production of goods "for interstate commerce" at other than the prescribed wages and hours. As to § 15(a)(1), the Court rejected the contention "that while the prohibition is nominally a regulation of [interstate] commerce its motive or purpose is regulation of wages and hours of persons engaged in manufacture, the control of which has been reserved to the states"—that "under the guise of a regulation of interstate commerce, it undertakes to regulate wages and hours

U.S v. Darby Fair Labor Standards Act - congress can regulate

1937, reflected a vote taken in conference on December 19, 1936. See Frankfurter, Mr. Justice Roberts, 104 U.Pa.L.Rev. 311, 314, 315 (1955). This memorandum does not deal with the relationship between the *Carter* case, supra, and the *Jones & Laughlin* case, supra.

within the state contrary to the policy of the state which has elected to leave them unregulated." Justice Stone's opinion for the Court responded:

> "The motive and purpose of the present regulation are plainly to make effective the Congressional conception of public policy that interstate commerce should not be made the instrument of competition in the distribution of goods produced under substandard labor conditions, which competition is injurious to the commerce and to the states from and to which the commerce flows. The motive and purpose of a regulation of interstate commerce are matters for the legislative judgment upon the exercise of which the Constitution places no restriction and over which the courts are given no control. McCray v. United States, 195 U.S. 27; Sonzinsky v. United States, 300 U.S. 506, 513, and cases cited...."

Dagenhart is overruled by Darby

Since the "reasoning and conclusion of the Court's opinion [in Hammer v. Dagenhart] cannot be reconciled with the conclusion which we have reached, that the power of Congress under the Commerce Clause is plenary to exclude any article from interstate commerce subject only to the specific prohibitions of the Constitution[,] ... it should be and now is overruled."

15(a)(2) if labor standards of employers falls under commerce. yes →

As to § 15(a)(2), "the validity of the prohibition turns on ... whether the employment, under other than the prescribed labor standards, of employees engaged in the production of goods for interstate commerce is so related to the commerce and so affects it as to be within the reach of the power of Congress to regulate it." Justice Stone gave two answers. First, "Congress, having by the present Act adopted the policy of excluding from interstate commerce all goods produced for the commerce which do not conform to the specified labor standards, it may choose the means reasonably adapted to the attainment of the permitted end, even though they involve control of intrastate activities." Second,

"... § 15(a)(2) ... is sustainable independently of § 15(a)(1).... [T]he evils aimed at by the Act are the spread of substandard labor conditions through the use of the facilities of interstate commerce for competition by the goods so produced with those produced under the prescribed or better labor conditions; and the consequent dislocation of the commerce itself caused by the impairment or destruction of local businesses by competition made effective through interstate commerce. The Act is thus directed at the suppression of a method or kind of competition in interstate commerce which it has in effect condemned as 'unfair'....

does fall under commerce

"The means adopted by § 15(a)(2) ... is so related to the commerce and so affects it as to be within the reach of the commerce power.... Congress ... has made no distinction as to the volume or amount of shipments in the commerce or of production for commerce by any particular shipper or producer. It recognized that in present day industry, competition by a small part may affect the whole and that the total effect of the competition of many small producers may be great. See H.Rept. No. 2182, 75th Cong. 1st Sess., p. 7. The legislation aimed at a whole embraces all its parts....

. . . .

Tenth Amendment

"Our conclusion is unaffected by the Tenth Amendment which provides: 'The powers not delegated to the United States by the Constitution, nor prohibited by it to the States, are reserved to the States respectively, or to the people'. The amendment states but a truism that all is retained which has not been surrendered...."

The decision in Wickard v. Filburn, a suit to enjoin the marketing penalty imposed by the Agricultural Adjustment Act of 1938 upon that part of Filburn's

1941 wheat crop that was available for marketing in excess of the marketing quota established for his farm, went further. As Justice Jackson's opinion for the Court said, the commerce power challenge raised "would merit little consideration since our decision in United States v. Darby, 312 U.S. 100, sustaining the federal power to regulate production of goods for commerce except for the fact that this Act extends federal regulation to production not intended in any part for commerce but wholly for consumption on the farm." The opinion contained these observations:

"The Court's recognition of the relevance of the economic effects in the application of the Commerce Clause ... has made the mechanical application of legal formulas no longer feasible. Once an economic measure of the reach of the power granted to Congress in the Commerce Clause is accepted, questions of federal power cannot be decided simply by finding the activity in question to be 'production' nor can consideration of its economic effects be foreclosed by calling them 'indirect.' ...

"... [E]ven if appellee's activity be local and though it may not be regarded as commerce, it may still, whatever its nature, be reached by Congress if it exerts a substantial economic effect on interstate commerce and this irrespective of whether such effect is what might at some earlier time have been defined as 'direct' or 'indirect.'"

The Court noted that "[c]ommerce among the states in wheat is large and important[,]" that the "wheat industry has been a problem industry for some years[,]" and that "[t]he effect of consumption of homegrown wheat on interstate commerce is due to the fact that it constitutes the most variable factor in the disappearance of the wheat crop." The Court continued:

"... The effect of the statute before us is to restrict the amount which may be produced for market and the extent as well to which one may forestall resort to the market by producing to meet his own needs. That appellee's own contribution to the demand for wheat may be trivial by itself is not enough to remove him from the scope of federal regulation where, as here, his contribution, taken together with that of many others similarly situated, is far from trivial. ...

"... One of the primary purposes of the Act ... was to increase the market price of wheat and to that end to limit the volume thereof that could affect the market. It can hardly be denied that a factor of such volume and variability as home-consumed wheat would have a substantial influence on price and market conditions. This may arise because being in marketable condition such wheat overhangs the market and if induced by rising prices tends to flow into the market and check price increases. But if we assume that it is never marketed, it supplies a need of the man who grew it which would otherwise be reflected by purchases in the open market. Home-grown wheat in this sense competes with wheat in commerce. The stimulation of commerce is a use of the regulatory function quite as definitely as prohibitions or restrictions thereon. This record leaves us in no doubt that Congress may properly have considered that wheat consumed on the farm where grown if wholly outside the scheme of regulation would have a substantial effect in defeating and obstructing its purpose to stimulate trade therein at increased prices."[a]

a. United States v. South–Eastern Underwriters Ass'n, 322 U.S. 533 (1944), sustained the applicability of the Sherman Anti–Trust Act to the insurance business, overturning a district court decision based on Paul v. Virginia, 75 U.S. 168 (1868), that "a policy of insurance is not a transaction of commerce" and insurance contracts "are not interstate transactions, although the parties are domiciled in different states". The opin-

Heart of Atlanta Motel, Inc. v. United States

379 U.S. 241, 85 S.Ct. 348, 13 L.Ed.2d 258 (1964).

constitutionality of Title II of the Civil Rights Act of 1964.

[The owner of the Motel brought a declaratory judgment action, attacking the constitutionality of Title II of the Civil Rights Act of 1964. A three-judge court sustained the Act and enjoined its further violation by the Motel. An appeal was taken to the Supreme Court.]

Mr. Justice Clark delivered the opinion of the Court.

. . .

1.   THE FACTUAL BACKGROUND AND CONTENTIONS OF THE PARTIES

. . . Appellant owns and operates the Heart of Atlanta Motel which has 216 rooms available to transient guests. The motel is located on Courtland Street, two blocks from downtown Peachtree Street. It is readily accessible to interstate highways 75 and 85 and state highways 23 and 41. Appellant solicits patronage from outside the State of Georgia through various national advertising media, including magazines of national circulation; it maintains over 50 billboards and highway signs within the State, soliciting patronage for the motel; it accepts convention trade from outside Georgia and approximately 75% of its registered guests are from out of State. Prior to passage of the Act the motel had followed a practice of refusing to rent rooms to Negroes, and it alleged that it intended to continue to do so. In an effort to perpetuate that policy this suit was filed.

. . .

Since Title II is the only portion under attack here, we confine our consideration to those public accommodation provisions.

3.   TITLE II OF THE ACT

This Title is divided into seven sections beginning with § 201(a) which provides that:

Title II of Act

"All persons shall be entitled to the full and equal enjoyment of the goods, services, facilities, privileges, advantages, and accommodations of any place of public accommodation, as defined in this section, without discrimination or segregation on the ground of race, color, religion, or national origin."

There are listed in § 201(b) four classes of business establishments, each of which "serves the public" and "is a place of public accommodation" within the meaning of § 201(a) "if its operations affect commerce, or if discrimination or segregation by it is supported by State action." The covered establishments are:

"(1) any inn, hotel, motel, or other establishment which provides lodging to transient guests, other than an establishment located within a

ion, by Justice Black, emphasized the size of the insurance business and the extent to which companies located in one part of the country write insurance contracts for persons in other states. The opinion also stated:

"We may grant that a contract of insurance, considered as a thing apart from negotiation and execution, does not itself constitute interstate commerce. . . . But . . . a nationwide business is not deprived of its interstate character merely because it is built upon

sales contracts which are local in nature. Were the rule otherwise, few businesses could be said to be engaged in interstate commerce. . . .

"The power granted Congress . . . is the power to legislate concerning transactions which, reaching across state boundaries, affect the people of more states than one;—to govern affairs which the individual states, with their limited territorial jurisdictions, are not fully capable of governing."

building which contains not more than five rooms for rent or hire and which is actually occupied by the proprietor of such establishment as his residence; . . ."

Section 201(c) defines the phrase "affect commerce" as applied to the above establishments. It first declares that "any inn, hotel, motel, or other establishment which provides lodging to transient guests" affects commerce *per se. . . .*

4.   APPLICATION OF TITLE II TO HEART OF ATLANTA MOTEL

It is admitted that the operation of the motel brings it within the provisions of § 201(a) of the Act and that appellant refused to provide lodging for transient Negroes because of their race or color and that it intends to continue that policy unless restrained.

The sole question posed is, therefore, the constitutionality of the Civil Rights Act of 1964 as applied to these facts. The legislative history of the Act indicates that Congress based the Act on § 5 and the Equal Protection Clause of the Fourteenth Amendment as well as its power to regulate interstate commerce. . . .

[handwritten margin note: ISSUE Based on §5, 14th & regulation of commerce]

The Senate Commerce Committee made it quite clear that the fundamental object of Title II was to vindicate "the deprivation of personal dignity that surely accompanies denials of equal access to public establishments." At the same time, however, it noted that such an objective has been and could be readily achieved "by congressional action based on the commerce power of the Constitution." S.Rep. No. 872, supra, at 16–17. Our study of the legislative record, made in the light of prior cases, has brought us to the conclusion that Congress possessed ample power in this regard, and we have therefore not considered the other grounds relied upon. . . .

. . .

6.   THE BASIS OF CONGRESSIONAL ACTION

While the Act as adopted carried no congressional findings the record of its passage through each house is replete with evidence of the burdens that discrimination by race or color places upon interstate commerce. . . . This testimony included the fact that our people have become increasingly mobile with millions of people of all races traveling from State to State; that Negroes in particular have been the subject of discrimination in transient accommodations, having to travel great distances to secure the same; that often they have been unable to obtain accommodations and have had to call upon friends to put them up overnight, . . .; and that these conditions had become so acute as to require the listing of available lodging for Negroes in a special guidebook which was itself "dramatic testimony to the difficulties" Negroes encounter in travel. . . . We shall not burden this opinion with further details since the voluminous testimony presents overwhelming evidence that discrimination by hotels and motels impedes interstate travel.

[handwritten margin note: such discrim. greatly impedes travel for minorities]

7.   THE POWER OF CONGRESS OVER INTERSTATE TRAVEL

. . .

[T]he determinative test of the exercise of power by the Congress under the Commerce Clause is simply whether the activity sought to be regulated is "commerce which concerns more States than one" and has a real and substantial relation to the national interest. Let us now turn to this facet of the problem.

[handwritten margin note: Determinative Test]

That the "intercourse" of which the Chief Justice [Marshall] spoke [in Gibbons v. Ogden] included the movement of persons through more States than one was settled as early as 1849.... Nor does it make any difference whether the transportation is commercial in character....

The same interest in protecting interstate commerce which led Congress to deal with segregation in interstate carriers and the white-slave traffic has prompted it to extend the exercise of its power to gambling, Lottery Case, 188 U.S. 321 (1903) ... and to racial discrimination by owners and managers of terminal restaurants, Boynton v. Virginia, 364 U.S. 454 (1960).

That Congress was legislating against moral wrongs in many of these areas rendered its enactments no less valid. In framing Title II of this Act Congress was also dealing with what it considered a moral problem. But that fact does not detract from the overwhelming evidence of the disruptive effect that racial discrimination has had on commercial intercourse. It was this burden which empowered Congress to enact appropriate legislation, and, given this basis for the exercise of its power, Congress was not restricted by the fact that the particular obstruction to interstate commerce with which it was dealing was also deemed a moral and social wrong.

It is said that the operation of the motel here is of a purely local character. But, assuming this to be true, "[i]f it is interstate commerce that feels the pinch, it does not matter how local the operation which applies the squeeze." United States v. Women's Sportswear Mfrs. Assn., 336 U.S. 460, 464 (1949)....

. . .

We, therefore, conclude that the action of the Congress in the adoption of the Act as applied here to a motel which concededly serves interstate travelers is within the power granted it by the Commerce Clause of the Constitution, as interpreted by this Court for 140 years. . . .

Affirmed.

[Justice Douglas's opinion stated that although he agreed with the Court's opinion, he was reluctant to rest solely on the commerce clause because of his belief that the right of people to be free of state action that discriminates against them because of race "occupies a more protected position in our constitutional system than does the movement of cattle, fruit, steel and coal across state lines." Black and Goldberg, JJ., filed concurring opinions. All of these opinions also applied to the following case.]

Katzenbach v. McClung

379 U.S. 294, 85 S.Ct. 377, 13 L.Ed.2d 290 (1964).

[This case was argued and decided with Heart of Atlanta Motel v. United States. McClung, as an owner of Ollie's Barbecue restaurant, sued to contest the constitutionality of Title II of the Civil Rights Act of 1964. A three-judge court enjoined Attorney General Katzenbach from enforcing the Act against the restaurant and an appeal was taken.]

Mr. Justice Clark delivered the opinion of the Court.

. . .

2.   THE FACTS

Ollie's Barbecue is a family-owned restaurant in Birmingham, Alabama, specializing in barbecued meats and homemade pies, with a seating capacity of

220 customers. It is located on a state highway 11 blocks from an interstate one and a somewhat greater distance from railroad and bus stations. The restaurant caters to a family and white-collar trade with a take-out service for Negroes. It employs 36 persons, two-thirds of whom are Negroes.

In the 12 months preceding the passage of the Act, the restaurant purchased locally approximately $150,000 worth of food, $69,783 or 46% of which was meat that it bought from a local supplier who had procured it from outside the State. The District Court expressly found that a substantial portion of the food served in the restaurant had moved in interstate commerce. The restaurant has refused to serve Negroes in its dining accommodations since its original opening in 1927, and since July 2, 1964, it has been operating in violation of the Act. The court below concluded that if it were required to serve Negroes it would lose a substantial amount of business.

. . .

3. THE ACT AS APPLIED

. . . Sections 201(b)(2) and (c) place any "restaurant . . . principally engaged in selling food for consumption on the premises" under the Act "if . . . it serves or offers to serve interstate travelers or a substantial portion of the food which it serves . . . has moved in commerce."

Ollie's Barbecue admits that it is covered by these provisions of the Act. The Government makes no contention that the discrimination at the restaurant was supported by the State of Alabama. There is no claim that interstate travelers frequented the restaurant. The sole question, therefore, narrows down to whether Title II, as applied to a restaurant receiving about $70,000 worth of food which has moved in commerce, is a valid exercise of the power of Congress. The Government has contended that Congress had ample basis upon which to find that racial discrimination at restaurants which receive from out of state a substantial portion of the food served does, in fact, impose commercial burdens of national magnitude upon interstate commerce. The appellees' major argument is directed to this premise. They urge that no such basis existed. It is to that question that we now turn.

4. THE CONGRESSIONAL HEARINGS

As we noted in *Heart of Atlanta Motel* both Houses of Congress conducted prolonged hearings on the Act. . . . The record is replete with testimony of the burdens placed on interstate commerce by racial discrimination in restaurants. . . .

Moreover there was an impressive array of testimony that discrimination in restaurants had a direct and highly restrictive effect upon interstate travel by Negroes. . . .

We believe that this testimony afforded ample basis for the conclusion that established restaurants in such areas sold less interstate goods because of the discrimination, that interstate travel was obstructed directly by it, that business in general suffered and that many new businesses refrained from establishing there as a result of it. Hence the District Court was in error in concluding that there was no connection between discrimination and the movement of interstate commerce. The court's conclusion that such a connection is outside "common experience" flies in the face of stubborn fact.

It goes without saying that, viewed in isolation, the volume of food purchased by Ollie's Barbecue from sources supplied from out of state was insignificant when compared with the total foodstuffs moving in commerce.

Rule like Wickard: one person is trivial but many make a great impact

But, as our late Brother Jackson said for the Court in Wickard v. Filburn, 317 U.S. 111 (1942): "That appellee's own contribution to the demand for wheat may be trivial by itself is not enough to remove him from the scope of federal regulation where, as here, his contribution, taken together with that of many others similarly situated, is far from trivial." . . .

. . .

With this situation spreading as the record shows, Congress was not required to await the total dislocation of commerce. . . .

5.   THE POWER OF CONGRESS TO REGULATE LOCAL ACTIVITIES

. . . Much is said about a restaurant business being local but "even if appellee's activity be local and though it may not be regarded as commerce, it may still, whatever its nature, be reached by Congress if it exerts a substantial economic effect on interstate commerce. . . ." . . .

This Court has held time and again that this power extends to activities of retail establishments, including restaurants, which directly or indirectly burden or obstruct interstate commerce. . . .

Nor are the cases holding that interstate commerce ends when goods come to rest in the state of destination apposite here. That line of cases has been applied with reference to state taxation or regulation but not in the field of federal regulation.

The appellees contend that Congress has arbitrarily created a conclusive presumption that all restaurants meeting the criteria set out in the Act "affect commerce." Stated another way, they object to the omission of a provision for a case-by-case determination—judicial or administrative—that racial discrimination in a particular restaurant affects commerce.

But Congress' action in framing this Act was not unprecedented. In United States v. Darby, 312 U.S. 100 (1941), this Court held constitutional the Fair Labor Standards Act. . . .

Here, as there, Congress has determined for itself that refusals of service to Negroes have imposed burdens both upon the interstate flow of food and upon the movement of products generally. Of course, the mere fact that Congress has said when particular activity shall be deemed to affect commerce does not preclude further examination by this Court. But where we find that the legislators, in light of the facts and testimony before them, have a rational basis for finding a chosen regulatory scheme necessary to the protection of commerce, our investigation is at an end. The only remaining question—one answered in the affirmative by the court below—is whether the particular restaurant either serves or offers to serve interstate travelers or serves food a substantial portion of which has moved in interstate commerce.

. . .

Confronted as we are with the facts laid before Congress, we must conclude that it had a rational basis for finding that racial discrimination in restaurants had a direct and adverse effect on the free flow of interstate commerce. . . . We think in so doing that Congress acted well within its power to protect and foster commerce in extending the coverage of Title II only to those restaurants offering to serve interstate travelers or serving food, a substantial portion of which has moved in interstate commerce.

The absence of direct evidence connecting discriminatory restaurant service with the flow of interstate food, a factor on which the appellees place much reliance, is not, given the evidence as to the effect of such practices on other aspects of commerce, a crucial matter.

... The Civil Rights Act of 1964, as here applied, we find to be plainly appropriate in the resolution of what the Congress found to be a national commercial problem of the first magnitude. We find it in no violation of any express limitations of the Constitution and we therefore declare it valid.

No violation of any limitations

The judgment is therefore reversed.

Reversed.

[Justices Black, Douglas, and Goldberg concurred.]

THE "NEW" FEDERALISM

Beginning in the late 1980s/early 1990s, the Supreme Court has revisited, and to some extent revised, its thinking on the four sets of questions discussed at the beginning of this chapter, supra p. 133. The Court has redefined the scope of federal powers and state immunities in a number of decisions: cases involving Congress' power to regulate the private sector under the Commerce Clause (discussed in this chapter below); cases involving Congress' power to regulate state entities in order to implement federal legislative goals (discussed in Chapter 5); cases addressing the question when states can be subject to suit by private citizens in federal court (also discussed in Chapter 5 and Chapter 12); and cases involving the limits on Congress' authority to regulate private and public sectors under Section 5 of the Fourteenth Amendment (discussed in Chapter 12). While each of these groups of cases is complex and distinct, they are all also related. As you read the recently-decided decisions in the balance of this chapter, as well as those presented in Chapters 5, 6 and 12, consider what the animating spirit or theory of the Court's current attitude toward the division of power between the federal and state governments appears to be. Are decisions to rule in favor of state power grounded primarily in the benefits of state public policy experimentation and diversity? Are states worthy of protection from federal overreaching so that they can act as counterbalances to the federal government, and if so, why are counterbalances needed and precisely how can states perform this function? Are states simply entitled to respect as a matter of constitutional etiquette? Consider also how the particular doctrinal devices the Court has employed in each of these lines of cases–the requirements and limits various cases have imposed on the federal government—correlate with any particular explanation for why federalism remains a vital idea. Finally, consider what other kinds of cases the Court might address in the intermediate future if the "new" federalism is to be meaningful.

The recent federalism decisions have given rise to a host of scholarly works. For additional background discussion and analysis, students may want to consult Todd Pettys, *Competing for the People's Affection: Federalism's Forgotten Marketplace*, 56 Vand. L.Rev. 329 (2003); Vikram Amar, *The New 'New Federalism,'* 6 Green Bag 2d 349 (2003); Vikram Amar and Samuel Estreicher, *Conduct Unbecoming a Coordinate Branch*, 4 Green Bag 2d 351 (2001); Akhil Amar, *Of Sovereignty and Federalism*, 96 Yale L.J. 1425 (1987).

United States v. Morrison

529 U.S. 598, 120 S.Ct. 1740, 146 L.Ed.2d 658 (2000).

Chief Justice Rehnquist delivered the opinion of the Court.

... 42 U.S.C. § 13981 ... provides a federal civil remedy for the victims of gender-motivated violence. The ... Fourth Circuit, sitting en banc, struck down § 13981 because it concluded that Congress lacked constitutional authority to enact the section's civil remedy. . . . [W]e affirm.

I

[Petitioner Christy Brzonkala alleged that shortly after she enrolled at Virginia Tech in 1994 two members of the varsity football team, Morrison and Crawford, assaulted and repeatedly raped her, and that both then and later Morrison made shockingly vulgar remarks about women. She left the university and brought an action alleging that their attack violated § 13981.]

The District Court . . . held that Brzonkala's complaint stated a claim against Morrison and Crawford under § 13981, but . . . that Congress lacked authority to enact the section under either the Commerce Clause or § 5 of the Fourteenth Amendment. . . .

[The en banc Court of Appeals affirmed both] the District Court's conclusion that Brzonkala stated a claim under § 13981 . . . [and,] by a divided vote . . . that Congress lacked constitutional authority to enact § 13981's civil remedy. . . .

Section 13981 was part of the Violence Against Women Act of 1994 . . . It states that "[a]ll persons within the United States shall have the right to be free from crimes of violence motivated by gender." 42 U.S.C. § 13981(b). To enforce that right, subsection (c) declares:

§ 13981

"A person (including a person who acts under color of any statute, ordinance, regulation, custom, or usage of any State) who commits a crime of violence motivated by gender and thus deprives another of the right declared in subsection (b) of this section shall be liable to the party injured, in an action for the recovery of compensatory and punitive damages, injunctive and declaratory relief, and such other relief as a court may deem appropriate."

Section 13981 defines a "crim[e] of violence motivated by gender" as "a crime of violence committed because of gender or on the basis of gender, and due, at least in part, to an animus based on the victim's gender." § 13981(d)(1). It also provides that the term "crime of violence" includes any

Definition of a "crime of violence"

"(A) . . . act or series of acts that would constitute a felony against the person or that would constitute a felony against property if the conduct presents a serious risk of physical injury to another, and that would come within the meaning of State or Federal offenses described in section 16 of Title 18, whether or not those acts have actually resulted in criminal charges, prosecution, or conviction and whether or not those acts were committed in the special maritime, territorial, or prison jurisdiction of the United States;" and

"(B) includes an act or series of acts that would constitute a felony described in subparagraph (A) but for the relationship between the person who takes such action and the individual against whom such action is taken." § 13981(d)(2).

Further clarifying the broad scope of § 13981's civil remedy, subsection (e)(2) states that "[n]othing in this section requires a prior criminal complaint, prosecution, or conviction to establish the elements of a cause of action under subsection (c) of this section."

Although the foregoing language of § 13981 covers a wide swath of criminal conduct, Congress placed some limitations on the section's federal civil remedy. Subsection (e)(1) states that "[n]othing in this section entitles a person to a cause of action under subsection (c) of this section for random acts of violence unrelated to gender or for acts that cannot be demonstrated, by a preponderance of the evidence, to be motivated by gender." Subsection (e)(4) further states that § 13981 shall not be construed "to confer on the courts of the United States jurisdiction over any State law claim seeking the establishment of a divorce, alimony, equitable distribution of marital property, or child custody decree."

. . . Congress explicitly identified the sources of federal authority on which it relied in enacting § 13981. It said that a "federal civil rights cause of action" is established "[p]ursuant to the affirmative power of Congress . . . under section 5 of the Fourteenth Amendment to the Constitution,[a] as well as under section 8 of Article I of the Constitution." 42 U.S.C. § 13981(a). . . .

II

Due respect for the decisions of a coordinate branch of Government demands that we invalidate a congressional enactment only upon a plain showing that Congress has exceeded its constitutional bounds. See United States v. Lopez, 514 U.S., at 568, 577–578 (Kennedy, J., concurring). . . .

As we discussed at length in *Lopez*, our interpretation of the Commerce Clause has changed as our Nation has developed. . . . We need not repeat that detailed review of the Commerce Clause's history here; it suffices to say that, in the years since NLRB v. Jones & Laughlin Steel Corp., 301 U.S. 1 (1937), Congress has had considerably greater latitude in regulating conduct and transactions under the Commerce Clause than our previous case law permitted. . . .

Lopez emphasized, however, that even under our modern, expansive interpretation of the Commerce Clause, Congress' regulatory authority is not without effective bounds. Id., at 557.

"[E]ven [our] modern-era precedents which have expanded congressional power under the Commerce Clause confirm that this power is subject to outer limits. *In Jones & Laughlin Steel*, the Court warned that the scope of the interstate commerce power 'must be considered in the light of our dual system of government and may not be extended so as to embrace effects upon interstate commerce so indirect and remote that to embrace them, in view of our complex society, would effectually obliterate the distinction between what is national and what is local and create a completely centralized government.' " Id., at 556–557 (quoting *Jones & Laughlin Steel, supra*, at 37).

As we observed in *Lopez*, modern Commerce Clause jurisprudence has "identified three broad categories of activity that Congress may regulate under its commerce power." 514 U.S., at 558. . . . "First, Congress may regulate the use of the channels of interstate commerce." 514 U.S., at 558 (citing Heart of Atlanta Motel, Inc. v. United States, 379 U.S. 241, 256 (1964)); United States v. Darby, 312 U.S. 100, 114 (1941)). "Second, Congress is empowered to regulate and protect the instrumentalities of interstate commerce, or persons or things in interstate commerce, even though the threat may come only from intrastate activities." 514 U.S., at 558 (citing Shreveport Rate Cases, 234 U.S. 342

[handwritten margin note: Lopez → 3 categories congress may regulate under commerce clause]

---

a. That portion of the opinion concluding that § 13981 was invalid under § 5 of the fourteenth amendment appears infra, page 1196.

(1914)); Southern R. Co. v. United States, 222 U.S. 20 (1911).... "Finally, Congress' commerce authority includes the power to regulate those activities having a substantial relation to interstate commerce, ... i.e., those activities that substantially affect interstate commerce." 514 U.S., at 558–559 (citing *Jones & Laughlin Steel, supra,* at 37).

Petitioners do not contend that these cases fall within either of the first two of these categories of Commerce Clause regulation. They seek to sustain § 13981 as a regulation of activity that substantially affects interstate commerce. Given § 13981's focus on gender-motivated violence wherever it occurs (rather than violence directed at the instrumentalities of interstate commerce, interstate markets, or things or persons in interstate commerce), we agree that this is the proper inquiry.

This case falls under the 3rd. category

Since *Lopez* most recently canvassed and clarified our case law governing this third category of Commerce Clause regulation, it provides the proper framework for conducting the required analysis of § 13981. In *Lopez,* we held that the Gun–Free School Zones Act of 1990, 18 U.S.C. § 922(q)(1)(A), which made it a federal crime to knowingly possess a firearm in a school zone, exceeded Congress' authority under the Commerce Clause.... Several significant considerations contributed to our decision.

using Lopez which said Act exceeded congress' authority

First, we observed that § 922(q) was "a criminal statute that by its terms has nothing to do with 'commerce' or any sort of economic enterprise, however broadly one might define those terms." ... Reviewing our case law, we noted that "we have upheld a wide variety of congressional Acts regulating intrastate economic activity where we have concluded that the activity substantially affected interstate commerce." ... Although we cited only a few examples, including Wickard v. Filburn, 317 U.S. 111 (1942); Hodel, supra; Perez, supra; Katzenbach v. McClung, 379 U.S. 294 (1964); and Heart of Atlanta Motel, supra, we stated that the pattern of analysis is clear.... "Where economic activity substantially affects interstate commerce, legislation regulating that activity will be sustained." ...

Both petitioners and Justice Souter's dissent downplay the role that the economic nature of the regulated activity plays in our Commerce Clause analysis. But a fair reading of *Lopez* shows that the noneconomic, criminal nature of the conduct at issue was central to our decision in that case. See, e.g., id., at 551 ("The Act [does not] regulat[e] a commercial activity"), 560 ("Even *Wickard,* which is perhaps the most far reaching example of Commerce Clause authority over intrastate activity, involved economic activity in a way that the possession of a gun in a school zone does not").... *Lopez*'s review of Commerce Clause case law demonstrates that in those cases where we have sustained federal regulation of intrastate activity based upon the activity's substantial effects on interstate commerce, the activity in question has been some sort of economic endeavor....[4]

[S]econd[,] ... the statute contained "no express jurisdictional element which might limit its reach to a discrete set of firearm possessions that additionally have an explicit connection with or effect on interstate commerce." Id., at 562. Such a jurisdictional element may establish that the enactment is in pursuance of Congress' regulation of interstate commerce.

Third, we noted that neither § 922(q) " 'nor its legislative history contain[s] express congressional findings regarding the effects upon interstate

---

4. Justice Souter's dissent ... cannot persuasively contradict *Lopez*'s conclusion that, in every case where we have sustained federal regulation under *Wickard*'s aggregation principle, the regulated activity was of an apparent commercial character....

commerce of gun possession in a school zone.'" ... While "Congress normally is not required to make formal findings as to the substantial burdens that an activity has on interstate commerce," 514 U.S., at 562 ... the existence of such findings may "enable us to evaluate the legislative judgment that the activity in question substantially affect[s] interstate commerce, even though no such substantial effect [is] visible to the naked eye." ...

Finally, our decision in *Lopez* rested in part on the fact that the link between gun possession and a substantial effect on interstate commerce was attenuated.... The United States argued that the possession of guns may lead to violent crime, and that violent crime "can be expected to affect the functioning of the national economy in two ways. First, the costs of violent crime are substantial, and, through the mechanism of insurance, those costs are spread throughout the population. Second, violent crime reduces the willingness of individuals to travel to areas within the country that are perceived to be unsafe." ... The Government also argued that the presence of guns at schools poses a threat to the educational process, which in turn threatens to produce a less efficient and productive workforce, which will negatively affect national productivity and thus interstate commerce....

[margin note: How in Lopez gun control is linked to commerce]

We rejected these "costs of crime" and "national productivity" arguments because they would permit Congress to "regulate not only all violent crime, but all activities that might lead to violent crime, regardless of how tenuously they relate to interstate commerce." ... We noted that, under this but-for reasoning:

[margin note: why ct. rejected these arguments in Lopez]

> "Congress could regulate any activity that it found was related to the economic productivity of individual citizens: family law (including marriage, divorce, and child custody), for example. Under the[se] theories ..., it is difficult to perceive any limitation on federal power, even in areas such as criminal law enforcement or education where States historically have been sovereign. Thus, if we were to accept the Government's arguments, we are hard pressed to posit any activity by an individual that Congress is without power to regulate." ...

With these principles underlying our Commerce Clause jurisprudence as reference points, the proper resolution of the present cases is clear. Gender-motivated crimes of violence are not, in any sense of the phrase, economic activity. While we need not adopt a categorical rule against aggregating the effects of any noneconomic activity in order to decide these cases, thus far in our Nation's history our cases have upheld Commerce Clause regulation of intrastate activity only where that activity is economic in nature....

Like the Gun–Free School Zones Act at issue in *Lopez*, § 13981 contains no jurisdictional element establishing that the federal cause of action is in pursuance of Congress' power to regulate interstate commerce. Although *Lopez* makes clear that such a jurisdictional element would lend support to the argument that § 13981 is sufficiently tied to interstate commerce, Congress elected to cast § 13981's remedy over a wider, and more purely intrastate, body of violent crime.[5]

[margin note: Lopez]

---

5. ... § 13981 is not the sole provision of the Violence Against Women Act of 1994 to provide a federal remedy for gender-motivated crime. Section 40221(a) of the Act creates a federal criminal remedy to punish "interstate crimes of abuse including crimes committed against spouses or intimate partners during interstate travel and crimes commit-ted by spouses or intimate partners who cross State lines to continue the abuse." S.Rep. No. 103–138, p. 43 (1993). That criminal provision has been codified at 18 U.S.C. § 2261(a)(1), which states:

> "A person who travels across a State line or enters or leaves Indian country with the intent to injure, harass, or intimidate

In contrast with the lack of congressional findings that we faced in *Lopez*, § 13981 is supported by numerous findings regarding the serious impact that gender-motivated violence has on victims and their families.... But the existence of congressional findings is not sufficient, by itself, to sustain the constitutionality of Commerce Clause legislation. As we stated in *Lopez*, " '[S]imply because Congress may conclude that a particular activity substantially affects interstate commerce does not necessarily make it so.' " ... Rather, " '[w]hether particular operations affect interstate commerce sufficiently to come under the constitutional power of Congress to regulate them is ultimately a judicial rather than a legislative question, and can be settled finally only by this Court.' " ...

In these cases, Congress' findings are substantially weakened by the fact that they rely so heavily on a method of reasoning that we have already rejected as unworkable if we are to maintain the Constitution's enumeration of powers. Congress found that gender-motivated violence affects interstate commerce

congress' argument as to how gender violence affects commerce

"by deterring potential victims from traveling interstate, from engaging in employment in interstate business, and from transacting with business, and in places involved in interstate commerce; ... by diminishing national productivity, increasing medical and other costs, and decreasing the supply of and the demand for interstate products." H.R. Conf. Rep. No. 103–711, at 385, U.S.Code Cong. & Admin.News 1994, pp. 1803, 1853.

Accord, S.Rep. No. 103–138, at 54. Given these findings and petitioners' arguments, the concern that we expressed in *Lopez* that Congress might use the Commerce Clause to completely obliterate the Constitution's distinction between national and local authority seems well founded.... The reasoning that petitioners advance seeks to follow the but-for causal chain from the initial occurrence of violent crime (the suppression of which has always been the prime object of the States' police power) to every attenuated effect upon interstate commerce. If accepted, petitioners' reasoning would allow Congress to regulate any crime as long as the nationwide, aggregated impact of that crime has substantial effects on employment, production, transit, or consumption. Indeed, if Congress may regulate gender-motivated violence, it would be able to regulate murder or any other type of violence since gender-motivated violence, as a subset of all violent crime, is certain to have lesser economic impacts than the larger class of which it is a part.

snowballing reasons, policy to reject congress' arg.

Petitioners' reasoning, moreover, will not limit Congress to regulating violence but may, as we suggested in *Lopez*, be applied equally as well to family law and other areas of traditional state regulation since the aggregate effect of marriage, divorce, and childrearing on the national economy is undoubtedly significant. Congress may have recognized this specter when it expressly precluded § 13981 from being used in the family law context. See 42 U.S.C.

that person's spouse or intimate partner, and who, in the course of or as a result of such travel, intentionally commits a crime of violence and thereby causes bodily injury to such spouse or intimate partner, shall be punished as provided in subsection (b)."

The Courts of Appeals have uniformly upheld this criminal sanction as an appropriate exercise of Congress' Commerce Clause authority, reasoning that "[t]he provision properly falls within the first of *Lopez*'s categories as it regulates the use of channels of interstate commerce—i.e., the use of the interstate transportation routes through which persons and goods move." United States v. Lankford, 196 F.3d 563, 571–572 (C.A.5 1999) (collecting cases) (internal quotation marks omitted).

§ 13981(e)(4). Under our written Constitution, however, the limitation of congressional authority is not solely a matter of legislative grace.[7] ...

We accordingly reject the argument that Congress may regulate noneconomic, violent criminal conduct based solely on that conduct's aggregate effect on interstate commerce. The Constitution requires a distinction between what is truly national and what is truly local.... In recognizing this fact we preserve one of the few principles that has been consistent since the Clause was adopted. The regulation and punishment of intrastate violence that is not directed at the instrumentalities, channels, or goods involved in interstate commerce has always been the province of the States. See, e.g., Cohens v. Virginia, 6 Wheat. 264, 426, 428 (1821) (Marshall, C.J.) (stating that Congress "has no general right to punish murder committed within any of the States," and that it is "clear ... that congress cannot punish felonies generally"). Indeed, we can think of no better example of the police power, which the Founders denied the National Government and reposed in the States, than the suppression of violent crime and vindication of its victims....

. . .

IV

... If the allegations [of Brzonkala's complaint] are true, no civilized system of justice could fail to provide her a remedy for the conduct of respondent Morrison. But under our federal system that remedy must be provided by the Commonwealth of Virginia, and not by the United States. The judgment of the Court of Appeals is

Affirmed.

Justice Thomas, concurring.

The majority opinion correctly applies our decision in United States v. Lopez, 514 U.S. 549 (1995), and I join it in full. I write separately only to express my view that the very notion of a "substantial effects" test under the Commerce Clause is inconsistent with the original understanding of Congress' powers and with this Court's early Commerce Clause cases. By continuing to apply this rootless and malleable standard, however circumscribed, the Court has encouraged the Federal Government to persist in its view that the Commerce Clause has virtually no limits. Until this Court replaces its existing Commerce Clause jurisprudence with a standard more consistent with the original understanding, we will continue to see Congress appropriating state police powers under the guise of regulating commerce.

7. Justice Souter's dissent theory that Gibbons v. Ogden, 9 Wheat. 1 (1824), Garcia v. San Antonio Metropolitan Transit Authority, 469 U.S. 528 (1985), and the Seventeenth Amendment provide the answer to these cases is remarkable because it undermines this central principle of our constitutional system. As we have repeatedly noted, the Framers crafted the federal system of government so that the people's rights would be secured by the division of power....

No doubt the political branches have a role in interpreting and applying the Constitution, but ever since Marbury this Court has remained the ultimate expositor of the constitutional text.... Contrary to Justice Souter's suggestion, Gibbons did not exempt the commerce power from this cardinal rule of constitutional law. His assertion that, from Gibbons on, public opinion has been the only restraint on the congressional exercise of the commerce power is true only insofar as it contends that political accountability is and has been the only limit on Congress' exercise of the commerce power within that power's outer bounds. As the language surrounding that relied upon by Justice Souter makes clear, Gibbons did not remove from this Court the authority to define that boundary....

Justice Souter, with whom Justice Stevens, Justice Ginsburg, and Justice Breyer join, dissenting.

. . .

I

Our cases, which remain at least nominally undisturbed, stand for the following propositions. Congress has the power to legislate with regard to activity that, in the aggregate, has a substantial effect on interstate commerce. See Wickard v. Filburn, 317 U.S. 111, 124–128 (1942); Hodel v. Virginia Surface Mining & Reclamation Assn., 452 U.S. 264, 277 (1981). The fact of such a substantial effect is not an issue for the courts in the first instance, ibid., but for the Congress, whose institutional capacity for gathering evidence and taking testimony far exceeds ours. By passing legislation, Congress indicates its conclusion, whether explicitly or not, that facts support its exercise of the commerce power. The business of the courts is to review the congressional assessment, not for soundness but simply for the rationality of concluding that a jurisdictional basis exists in fact. . . . Any explicit findings that Congress chooses to make, though not dispositive of the question of rationality, may advance judicial review by identifying factual authority on which Congress relied. Applying those propositions in these cases can lead to only one conclusion.

One obvious difference from United States v. Lopez, 514 U.S. 549 (1995), is the mountain of data assembled by Congress, here showing the effects of violence against women on interstate commerce. Passage of the Act in 1994 was preceded by four years of hearings, . . . and we have the benefit of specific factual findings in the eight separate Reports issued by Congress and its committees over the long course leading to enactment. . . .

[Citing evidence received by Congress concerning the extensive nature, scope and effects of domestic violence and rape, Justice Souter noted that b]ased on the data thus partially summarized, Congress found that

> "crimes of violence motivated by gender have a substantial adverse effect on interstate commerce, by deterring potential victims from traveling interstate, from engaging in employment in interstate business, and from transacting with business, and in places involved, in interstate commerce . . . [,] by diminishing national productivity, increasing medical and other costs, and decreasing the supply of and the demand for interstate products. . . ." H.R. Conf. Rep. No. 103–711, p. 385 (1994), U.S.Code Cong. & Admin.News 1994, pp. 1803, 1853.

Congress thereby explicitly stated the predicate for the exercise of its Commerce Clause power. Is its conclusion irrational in view of the data amassed? . . . [T]he sufficiency of the evidence before Congress to provide a rational basis for the finding cannot seriously be questioned. . . .

Indeed, the legislative record here is far more voluminous than the record compiled by Congress and found sufficient in two prior cases upholding Title II of the Civil Rights Act of 1964 against Commerce Clause challenges. In Heart of Atlanta Motel, Inc. v. United States, 379 U.S. 241 (1964), and Katzenbach v. McClung, 379 U.S. 294 (1964), the Court referred to evidence showing the consequences of racial discrimination by motels and restaurants on interstate commerce. Congress had relied on compelling anecdotal reports that individual instances of segregation cost thousands to millions of dollars . . . Congress also had evidence that the average black family spent substantially less than the average white family in the same income range on public accommodations, and that discrimination accounted for much of the difference. . . .

While Congress did not, to my knowledge, calculate aggregate dollar values for the nationwide effects of racial discrimination in 1964, in 1994 it did rely on evidence of the harms caused by domestic violence and sexual assault, citing annual costs of $3 billion in 1990, see S. Rep. 101–545, and $5 to $10 billion in 1993, see S.Rep. No. 103–138, at 41. Equally important, though, gender-based violence in the 1990's was shown to operate in a manner similar to racial discrimination in the 1960's in reducing the mobility of employees and their production and consumption of goods shipped in interstate commerce. Like racial discrimination, "[g]ender-based violence bars its most likely targets— women—from full partic[ipation] in the national economy." Id., at 54.

If the analogy to the Civil Rights Act of 1964 is not plain enough, one can always look back a bit further. In *Wickard*, we upheld the application of the Agricultural Adjustment Act to the planting and consumption of homegrown wheat. The effect on interstate commerce in that case followed from the possibility that wheat grown at home for personal consumption could either be drawn into the market by rising prices, or relieve its grower of any need to purchase wheat in the market. . . . The Commerce Clause predicate was simply the effect of the production of wheat for home consumption on supply and demand in interstate commerce. Supply and demand for goods in interstate commerce will also be affected by the deaths of 2,000 to 4,000 women annually at the hands of domestic abusers, see S.Rep. No. 101–545, at 36, and by the reduction in the work force by the 100,000 or more rape victims who lose their jobs each year or are forced to quit, see id., at 56, H.R.Rep. No. 103–395, at 25– 26. Violence against women may be found to affect interstate commerce and affect it substantially.[10]

II

The Act would have passed muster at any time between *Wickard* in 1942 and *Lopez* in 1995, a period in which the law enjoyed a stable understanding that congressional power under the Commerce Clause, complemented by the authority of the Necessary and Proper Clause, Art. I. § 8 cl. 18, extended to all activity that, when aggregated, has a substantial effect on interstate commerce. . . . [A]t the passage of the Civil Rights Act of 1964, . . . the Court not only reaffirmed the cumulative effects and rational basis features of the substantial effects test, . . . but declined to limit the commerce power through a formal distinction between legislation focused on "commerce" and statutes addressing "moral and social wrong[s]," Heart of Atlanta, supra, at 257.

. . .

. . . [T]he majority is . . . moving toward [a] new system of congressional deference subject to selective discounts . . . on the basis of characteristics other than their commercial effects. Such exclusions come into sight when the activity regulated is not itself commercial or when the States have traditionally addressed it in the exercise of the general police power. . . .

---

10. It should go without saying that my view of the limit of the congressional commerce power carries no implication about the wisdom of exercising it to the limit. I and other Members of this Court appearing before Congress have repeatedly argued against the federalization of traditional state crimes and the extension of federal remedies to problems for which the States have historically taken responsibility and may deal with today if they have the will to do so. . . .

... From the fact that Art. I, § 8, cl. 3 grants an authority limited to regulating commerce, it follows only that Congress may claim no authority under that section to address any subject that does not affect commerce. It does not at all follow that an activity affecting commerce nonetheless falls outside the commerce power, depending on the specific character of the activity, or the authority of a State to regulate it along with Congress. My disagreement with the majority is not, however, confined to logic, for history has shown that categorical exclusions have proven as unworkable in practice as they are unsupportable in theory.

A

. . .

... [The] revival of a distinction between commercial and noncommercial conduct is at odds with *Wickard*, which repudiated that analysis, and the enquiry into commercial purpose, first intimated by the *Lopez* concurrence, see *Lopez*, supra, at 580 (opinion of Kennedy, J.), is cousin to the intent-based analysis employed in *Hammer*, ... but rejected for Commerce Clause purposes in *Heart of Atlanta* ... and *Darby*....

Why is the majority tempted to reject the lesson so painfully learned in 1937? ... It was obvious in *Wickard* that growing wheat for consumption right on the farm was not "commerce" in the common vocabulary,[13] but that did not matter constitutionally so long as the aggregated activity of domestic wheat growing affected commerce substantially. Just a few years before *Wickard*, however, it had certainly been no less obvious that "mining" practices could substantially affect commerce, even though *Carter Coal Co., supra*, had held mining regulation beyond the national commerce power. [T]he two cases ... did not go in different directions because the *Carter Coal* Court could not understand a causal connection that the *Wickard* Court could grasp; the difference, rather, turned on the fact that the Court in *Carter Coal* had a reason for trying to maintain its categorical, formalistic distinction.... The Court in *Carter Coal* was still trying to create a laissez-faire world out of the 20th-century economy, and formalistic commercial distinctions were thought to be useful instruments in achieving that object. The Court in *Wickard* knew it could not do any such thing and in the aftermath of the New Deal had long since stopped attempting the impossible. Without the animating economic theory, there was no point in contriving formalisms in a war with Chief Justice Marshall's conception of the commerce power.

If we now ask why the formalistic economic/noneconomic distinction might matter today, after its rejection in *Wickard*, the answer is not that the majority fails to see causal connections in an integrated economic world. The answer is that in the minds of the majority there is a new animating theory that makes

---

13. Contrary to the Court's suggestion, *Wickard* applied the substantial effects test to domestic agricultural production for domestic consumption, an activity that cannot fairly be described as commercial, despite its commercial consequences in affecting or being affected by the demand for agricultural products in the commercial market. The *Wickard* Court admitted that Filburn's activity "may not be regarded as commerce" but insisted that "it may still, whatever its nature, be reached by Congress if it exerts a substantial economic effect on interstate commerce...." 317 U.S., at 125. The characterization of home wheat production as "commerce" or not is, however, ultimately beside the point. For if substantial effects on commerce are proper subjects of concern under the Commerce Clause, what difference should it make whether the causes of those effects are themselves commercial? ... The Court's answer is that it makes a difference to federalism, and the legitimacy of the Court's new judicially derived federalism is the crux of our disagreement.

categorical formalism seem useful again. Just as the old formalism had value in the service of an economic conception, the new one is useful in serving a conception of federalism. It is the instrument by which assertions of national power are to be limited in favor of preserving a supposedly discernible, proper sphere of state autonomy to legislate or refrain from legislating as the individual States see fit. . . .

B

. . . [T]he theory of traditional state concern as grounding a limiting principle has been rejected previously, and more than once. . . .

The objection to reviving traditional state spheres of action as a consideration in commerce analysis . . . is compounded by . . . the majority's rejection of the Founders' considered judgment that politics, not judicial review, should mediate between state and national interests as the strength and legislative jurisdiction of the National Government inevitably increased through the expected growth of the national economy. . . .

. . . Madison . . . took care . . . to hedge his argument for limited power by explaining the importance of national politics in protecting the States' interests. The National Government "will partake sufficiently of the spirit [of the States], to be disinclined to invade the rights of the individual States, or the prerogatives of their governments." The Federalist No. 46, at 319. . . . In any case, this Court recognized the political component of federalism in the seminal *Gibbons* opinion. . . .

Politics as the moderator of the congressional employment of the commerce power was the theme many years later in *Wickard*, for after the Court acknowledged the breadth of the *Gibbons* formulation it invoked Chief Justice Marshall yet again in adding that "[h]e made emphatic the embracing and penetrating nature of this power by warning that effective restraints on its exercise must proceed from political rather than judicial processes." . . . Hence, "conflicts of economic interest . . . are wisely left under our system to resolution by Congress under its more flexible and responsible legislative process. Such conflicts rarely lend themselves to judicial determination. And with the wisdom, workability, or fairness, of the plan of regulation we have nothing to do." . . .

As with "conflicts of economic interest," so with supposed conflicts of sovereign political interests implicated by the Commerce Clause: the Constitution remits them to politics. . . . [In Garcia v. San Antonio Metropolitan Transit Authority, 469 U.S. 528, 552, the Court] concluded that

> "the Framers chose to rely on a federal system in which special restraints on federal power over the States inhered principally in the workings of the National Government itself, rather than in discrete limitations on the objects of federal authority. State sovereign interests, then, are more properly protected by procedural safeguards inherent in the structure of the federal system than by judicially created limitations on federal power."
>
> . . .

The *Garcia* Court's rejection of "judicially created limitations" in favor of the intended reliance on national politics was all the more powerful owing to the Court's explicit recognition that in the centuries since the framing the relative powers of the two sovereign systems have markedly changed. Nationwide economic integration is the norm, the national political power has been augmented by its vast revenues, and the power of the States has been drawn down by the Seventeenth Amendment, eliminating selection of senators by state legislature in favor of direct election.

. . . The significance for state political power of ending state legislative selection of senators was no secret in 1913, and the amendment was approved despite public comment on that very issue. . . .

Amendments that alter the balance of power between the National and State Governments, like the Fourteenth, or that change the way the States are represented within the Federal Government, like the Seventeenth, are not rips in the fabric of the Framers' Constitution, inviting judicial repairs. The Seventeenth Amendment may indeed have lessened the enthusiasm of the Senate to represent the States as discrete sovereignties, but the Amendment did not convert the judiciary into an alternate shield against the commerce power.

C

. . . Today's majority . . . finds no significance whatever in the state support for the Act based upon the States' acknowledged failure to deal adequately with gender-based violence in state courts, and the belief of their own law enforcement agencies that national action is essential.

The National Association of Attorneys General supported the Act unanimously, . . . and Attorneys General from 38 States urged Congress to enact the Civil Rights Remedy, representing that "the current system for dealing with violence against women is inadequate," . . . .

The collective opinion of state officials that the Act was needed continues virtually unchanged, and when the Civil Rights Remedy was challenged in court, the States came to its defense. Thirty-six of them and the Commonwealth of Puerto Rico have filed an amicus brief in support of petitioners in these cases, and only one State has taken respondents' side. It is, then, not the least irony of these cases that the States will be forced to enjoy the new federalism whether they want it or not. . . .

III

All of this convinces me that today's ebb of the commerce power rests on error, and at the same time leads me to doubt that the majority's view will prove to be enduring law. There is yet one more reason for doubt. Although we sense the presence of *Carter Coal*, *Schechter*, and *Usery* once again, the majority embraces them only at arm's-length. Where such decisions once stood for rules, today's opinion points to considerations by which substantial effects are discounted. Cases standing for the sufficiency of substantial effects are not overruled; cases overruled since 1937 are not quite revived. . . . [T]he practice of such ad hoc review cannot preserve the distinction between the judicial and the legislative, and this Court, in any event, lacks the institutional capacity to maintain such a regime for very long. This one will end when the majority realizes that the conception of the commerce power for which it entertains hopes would inevitably fail the test expressed in Justice Holmes's statement that "[t]he first call of a theory of law is that it should fit the facts." O. Holmes, The Common Law 167 (Howe ed.1963). The facts that cannot be ignored today are the facts of integrated national commerce and a political relationship between States and Nation much affected by their respective treasuries and constitutional modifications adopted by the people. The federalism of some earlier time is no more adequate to account for those facts today than the theory of laissez-faire was able to govern the national economy 70 years ago.

Justice Breyer, with whom Justice Stevens joins, and with whom Justice Souter and Justice Ginsburg join as to Part I–A, dissenting.

No one denies the importance of the Constitution's federalist principles.... The question is how the judiciary can best implement that original federalist understanding where the Commerce Clause is at issue.

I

... [T]he majority's holding illustrates the difficulty of finding a workable judicial Commerce Clause touchstone—a set of comprehensible interpretive rules that courts might use to impose some meaningful limit, but not too great a limit, upon the scope of the legislative authority that the Commerce Clause delegates to Congress.

A

Consider the problems. The "economic/noneconomic" distinction is not easy to apply. Does the local street corner mugger engage in "economic" activity or "noneconomic" activity when he mugs for money? See Perez v. United States, 402 U.S. 146 (1971) (aggregating local "loan sharking" instances); United States v. Lopez, 514 U.S. 549, 559 (1995) (loan sharking is economic because it consists of "intrastate extortionate credit transactions"). Would evidence that desire for economic domination underlies many brutal crimes against women save the present statute? ...

The line becomes yet harder to draw given the need for exceptions. The Court itself would permit Congress to aggregate, hence regulate, "noneconomic" activity taking place at economic establishments. See Heart of Atlanta Motel, Inc. v. United States, 379 U.S. 241 (1964) (upholding civil rights laws forbidding discrimination at local motels); Katzenbach v. McClung, 379 U.S. 294 (1964) (same for restaurants); *Lopez*, supra, at 559 (recognizing congressional power to aggregate, hence forbid, noneconomically motivated discrimination at public accommodations). And it would permit Congress to regulate where that regulation is "an essential part of a larger regulation of economic activity, in which the regulatory scheme could be undercut unless the intrastate activity were regulated." *Lopez*, supra, at 561; cf. Controlled Substances Act, 21 U.S.C. § 801 et seq. (regulating drugs produced for home consumption). Given the former exception, can Congress simply rewrite the present law and limit its application to restaurants, hotels, perhaps universities, and other places of public accommodation? Given the latter exception, can Congress save the present law by including it, or much of it, in a broader "Safe Transport" or "Workplace Safety" act?

More important, why should we give critical constitutional importance to the economic, or noneconomic, nature of an interstate-commerce-affecting cause? If chemical emanations through indirect environmental change cause identical, severe commercial harm outside a State, why should it matter whether local factories or home fireplaces release them? The Constitution itself refers only to Congress' power to "regulate Commerce ... among the several States," and to make laws "necessary and proper" to implement that power. Art. I, § 8, cls. 3, 18. The language says nothing about either the local nature, or the economic nature, of an interstate-commerce-affecting cause.

... Nothing in the Constitution's language, or that of earlier cases prior to *Lopez*, explains why the Court should ignore one highly relevant characteristic of an interstate-commerce-affecting cause (how "local" it is), while placing critical constitutional weight upon a different, less obviously relevant, feature (how "economic" it is).

Most important, the Court's complex rules seem unlikely to help secure the very object that they seek, namely, the protection of "areas of traditional state regulation" from federal intrusion. The Court's rules, even if broadly interpreted, are underinclusive. The local pickpocket is no less a traditional subject of state regulation than is the local gender-motivated assault. Regardless, the Court reaffirms, as it should, Congress' well-established and frequently exercised power to enact laws that satisfy a commerce-related jurisdictional prerequuisite—for example, that some item relevant to the federally regulated activity has at some time crossed a state line. . . .

And in a world where most everyday products or their component parts cross interstate boundaries, Congress will frequently find it possible to redraft a statute using language that ties the regulation to the interstate movement of some relevant object, thereby regulating local criminal activity or, for that matter, family affairs. See, e.g., Child Support Recovery Act of 1992, 18 U.S.C. § 228. Although this possibility does not give the Federal Government the power to regulate everything, it means that any substantive limitation will apply randomly in terms of the interests the majority seeks to protect. How much would be gained, for example, were Congress to reenact the present law in the form of "An Act Forbidding Violence Against Women Perpetrated at Public Accommodations or by Those Who Have Moved in, or through the Use of Items that Have Moved in, Interstate Commerce"? Complex Commerce Clause rules creating fine distinctions that achieve only random results do little to further the important federalist interests that called them into being. That is why modern (pre-*Lopez*) case law rejected them. . . .

The majority, aware of these difficulties, is nonetheless concerned with what it sees as an important contrary consideration. To determine the lawfulness of statutes simply by asking whether Congress could reasonably have found that aggregated local instances significantly affect interstate commerce will allow Congress to regulate almost anything. Virtually all local activity, when instances are aggregated, can have "substantial effects on employment, production, transit, or consumption." . . .

This consideration, however, while serious, does not reflect a jurisprudential defect, so much as it reflects a practical reality. We live in a Nation knit together by two centuries of scientific, technological, commercial, and environmental change. Those changes, taken together, mean that virtually every kind of activity, no matter how local, genuinely can affect commerce, or its conditions, outside the State—at least when considered in the aggregate. . . . And that fact makes it close to impossible for courts to develop meaningful subject-matter categories that would exclude some kinds of local activities from ordinary Commerce Clause "aggregation" rules without, at the same time, depriving Congress of the power to regulate activities that have a genuine and important effect upon interstate commerce.

Since judges cannot change the world, the "defect" means that, within the bounds of the rational, Congress, not the courts, must remain primarily responsible for striking the appropriate state/federal balance. . . . Moreover, Congress often can better reflect state concerns for autonomy in the details of sophisticated statutory schemes than can the judiciary, which cannot easily gather the relevant facts and which must apply more general legal rules and categories. See, e.g., 42 U.S.C. § 7543(b) (Clean Air Act); 33 U.S.C. § 1251 et seq. (Clean Water Act); see also New York v. United States, 505 U.S. 144, 167–168 (1992) (collecting other examples of "cooperative federalism"). Not surprisingly, the bulk of American law is still state law, and overwhelmingly so.

B

I would also note that Congress, when it enacted the statute, followed procedures that help to protect the federalism values at stake. It provided adequate notice to the States of its intent to legislate in an "are[a] of traditional state regulation." And in response, attorneys general in the overwhelming majority of States (38) supported congressional legislation, telling Congress that "[o]ur experience as Attorneys General strengthens our belief that the problem of violence against women is a national one, requiring federal attention, federal leadership, and federal funds." . . .

. . . Congress compiled a "mountain of data" explicitly documenting the interstate commercial effects of gender-motivated crimes of violence[,] . . . focused the federal law upon documented deficiencies in state legal systems[,a]nd . . . tailored the law to prevent its use in certain areas of traditional state concern, such as divorce, alimony, or child custody. 42 U.S.C. § 13981(e)(4). . . .

. . .

. . . [A]ny judicial insistence that Congress follow particular procedures might itself intrude upon congressional prerogatives and embody difficult definitional problems. But the intrusion, problems, and consequences all would seem less serious than those embodied in the majority's approach.

I continue to agree with Justice Souter that the Court's traditional "rational basis" approach is sufficient. . . . But I recognize that the law in this area is unstable and that time and experience may demonstrate both the unworkability of the majority's rules and the superiority of Congress' own procedural approach—in which case the law may evolve towards a rule that, in certain difficult Commerce Clause cases, takes account of the thoroughness with which Congress has considered the federalism issue.

For these reasons, as well as those set forth by Justice Souter, this statute falls well within Congress's Commerce Clause authority, and I dissent from the Court's contrary conclusion.[a]

. . .

NOTE ON THE LEVEL OF GENERALITY AT WHICH CHALLENGES TO CONGRESSIONAL POWER ARE FRAMED

In *Morrison* and *Lopez*, the Court evaluated each of the two federal statutes in question on its face—without regard to whether the defendants' particular conduct was the kind that Congress could reach. In Sabri v. United States, 541 U.S. 600, (2004), excerpts of which appear infra 201, a defendant indicted under a federal statute that makes it a crime to bribe an official of a state or local governmental entity that receives at least $10,000 in federal funds challenged the statute on its face as beyond Congress' regulatory powers because the statute does not require the government to prove in each case that the bribery involved any of the programs for which federal funds were received. After pointing out that the defendant's alleged acts of bribery did involve federally-funded programs, and after holding that Congress can, under its Spending Clause powers, prohibit bribery of officials who receive federal funding whether or not the bribery involves federally-funded programs, the Court in

a. For earlier commentary on the issues raised by *Lopez*, see the contributions to Symposium, *Reflections on United States v.* *Lopez*, 94 Michigan Law Review 533–831 (1995).

an opinion by Justice Souter had this to say about facial attacks against Congressional laws challenging Congress' enumerated authority to regulate:

"Although passing on the validity of a law wholesale may be efficient in the abstract, any gain is often offset by losing the lessons taught by the particular, to which common law method normally looks. Facial adjudication carries too much promise of [decisionmaking] on the basis of factually bare-bones records.... [It is] obvious that the acts charged against Sabri himself were well within the limits of legitimate congressional concern.... [T]he most he could say was that the statute could not be enforced against him, because it could not be enforced against someone else whose behavior would be outside the scope of Congress's Article I authority to legislate. Facial challenges of this sort are especially to be discouraged.... We have recognized the validity of facial attacks alleging overbreadth (though not necessarily using that term) in relatively few settings.... Outside of these limited settings, and absent a good reason, we do not extend an invitation to bring overbreadth claims."

This discussion prompted Justice Kennedy, with whom Justice Scalia concurred, to write separately to say that the Court's overbreadth observations "do[] not specifically question the practice we have followed in cases such as United States v. Lopez ... and United States v. Morrison ..., [where] the Court did resolve the basic question whether Congress, in enacting the statutes challenged there, had exceeded its legislative power under the Constitution." A similar facial/as-applied issue arose in the context of a challenge to Congress' power under Section 5 of the Fourteenth Amendment in Tennessee v. Lane, 541 U.S. 509 (2004), which appears infra on p. 1230.

PIERCE COUNTY v. GUILLEN, 537 U.S. 129 (2003). To receive funding to improve dangerous public road conditions under the federal Hazard Elimination Program, states and localities must identify hazardous locations, 23 U.S.C. § 152. To overcome state fears that doing so without the protection of confidentiality would subject them to increased liability risks at hazardous locations before improvements could be made, Congress provided state and local agencies with a federal privilege to decline to disclose information compiled or collected for purposes of the Program only, 23 U.S.C. § 409. In a suit to extract such information brought under a state public disclosure law, the Court unanimously rejected a challenge to the commerce power of Congress to provide the federal privilege, saying: " ... Congress could reasonably believe that adopting a measure eliminating an unforeseen side effect of the information-gathering requirement of § 152 would result in more diligent efforts to collect the relevant information, more candid discussions of hazardous locations, better informed decisionmaking, and, ultimately, greater safety on our Nation's roads. Consequently, [§ 409 and its 1995 amendment] can be viewed as legislation aimed at improving safety in the channels of commerce and increasing protection for the instrumentalities of interstate commerce. As such, they fall within Congress' Commerce Clause power."

RENO v. CONDON, 528 U.S. 141 (2000). The Driver's Privacy Protection Act of 1994 (DPPA) limits both disclosure by state motor vehicle departments of drivers' personal information without their consent and disclosure by private persons who have obtained drivers' personal information from a state DMV. The Court's unanimous rejection of South Carolina's contention that the DPPA violates principles of federalism (see infra p. 256) first ruled that the Act fell within Congress' commerce power based "on the fact that the personal, identifying information that the DPPA regulates is a 'thin[g]' in interstate commerce,' and that the sale or release of that information in interstate commerce is therefore a proper subject of congressional regulation. United States v. Lopez, 514 U.S. 549, 558–559 (1995).... The motor vehicle information which the states have historically sold is used by insurers, manufacturers, direct marketers, and others engaged in interstate commerce to contact drivers with customized solicitations. The information is also used in the stream of interstate commerce by various public and private entities for matters related to interstate motoring. Because drivers' information is, in this context, an article of commerce, its sale or release into the interstate stream of business is sufficient to support congressional regulation. We therefore need not address the Government's alternative argument that the states' individual, intrastate activities in gathering, maintaining, and distributing drivers' personal information has a sufficiently substantial impact on interstate commerce to create a constitutional base for federal legislation."

B. THE TAXING POWER

Sonzinsky v. United States

300 U.S. 506, 57 S.Ct. 554, 81 L.Ed. 772 (1937).

Mr. Justice Stone delivered the opinion of the Court.

The question for decision is whether § 2 of the National Firearms Act of June 26, 1934, c. 757, 48 Stat. 1236, 26 U.S.C. §§ 1132–1132q, which imposes a $200 annual license tax on dealers in firearms, is a constitutional exercise of the legislative power of Congress. [*Issue*]

Petitioner was convicted ... [of] violati[ng] § 2, by dealing in firearms without payment of the tax....

Section 2 of the National Firearms Act requires every dealer in firearms to register with the Collector of Internal Revenue in the district where he carries on business, and to pay a special excise tax of $200 a year. Importers or manufacturers are taxed $500 a year. Section 3 imposes a tax of $200 on each transfer of a firearm, payable by the transferor, and § 4 prescribes regulations for the identification of purchasers. The term "firearm" is defined by § 1 as meaning a shotgun or a rifle having a barrel less than eighteen inches in length, or any other weapon, except a pistol or revolver, from which a shot is discharged by an explosive, if capable of being concealed on the person, or a machine gun, and includes a muffler or silencer for any firearm.... Petitioner [*Def of firearm §1*] does not deny that Congress may tax his business as a dealer in firearms. He insists that the present levy is not a true tax, but a penalty imposed for the purpose of suppressing traffic in a certain noxious type of firearms, the local regulation of which is reserved to the states because not granted to the national government. To establish its penal and prohibitive character, he relies on the amounts of the tax imposed by § 2 on dealers, manufacturers and importers, and of the tax imposed by § 3 on each transfer of a "firearm," payable by the transferor. The cumulative effect on the distribution of a limited class of firearms, of relatively small value, by the successive imposition of different taxes, one on the business of the importer or manufacturer, another on that of the dealer, and a third on the transfer to a buyer, is said to be prohibitive in effect and to disclose unmistakably the legislative purpose to regulate rather than to tax. [*claiming their purpose is not to tax but to prohibit*]

The case is not one where the statute contains regulatory provisions related to a purported tax in such a way as has enabled this Court to say in other cases that the latter is a penalty resorted to as a means of enforcing the regulations. See Child Labor Tax Case, 259 U.S. 20, 35; Hill v. Wallace, 259 U.S. 44; Carter v. Carter Coal Co., 298 U.S. 238. Nor is the subject of the tax described or treated as criminal by the taxing statute. Compare United States v. Constantine,[a] 296 U.S. 287. Here § 2 contains no regulation other than the mere registration provisions, which are obviously supportable as in aid of a revenue purpose. On its face it is only a taxing measure, and we are asked to say that the tax, by virtue of its deterrent effect on the activities taxed, operates as a regulation which is beyond the congressional power.

Every tax is in some measure regulatory. To some extent it interposes an economic impediment to the activity taxed as compared with others not taxed. But a tax is not any the less a tax because it has a regulatory effect, . . .; and it has long been established that an Act of Congress which on its face purports to be an exercise of the taxing power is not any the less so because the tax is burdensome or tends to restrict or suppress the thing taxed. Veazie Bank v. Fenno, 8 Wall. 533, 548; McCray v. United States, 195 U.S. 27, 60–61. . . .

Inquiry into the hidden motives which may move Congress to exercise a power constitutionally conferred upon it is beyond the competency of courts. Veazie Bank v. Fenno, supra; McCray v. United States, supra, 56–59; United States v. Doremus, supra, 93–94. They will not undertake, by collateral inquiry as to the measure of the regulatory effect of a tax, to ascribe to Congress an attempt, under the guise of taxation, to exercise another power denied by the Federal Constitution. McCray v. United States, supra; cf. Magnano Co. v. Hamilton, supra, 45.

Here the annual tax of $200 is productive of some revenue.[1] We are not free to speculate as to the motives which moved Congress to impose it, or as to the extent to which it may operate to restrict the activities taxed. As it is not attended by an offensive regulation, and since it operates as a tax, it is within the national taxing power. . . .

Affirmed.[a]

a. In the *Constantine* case (1935) the Court held invalid a federal excise tax of $1000 on liquor dealers "carrying on business . . . contrary to the laws of a State . . . or municipality". The tax was 10 to 50 times greater than the federal tax on dealers operating legally. The Court concluded: "The condition of the imposition is the commission of a crime. This, together with the amount of the tax, is . . . significant of penal and prohibitory intent rather than the gathering of revenue." Cardozo, J., (joined by Brandeis and Stone, JJ.) dissented, saying: "Congress may reasonably have believed in view of the attendant risks, a business carried on illegally and furtively is likely to yield larger profits than one transacted openly by law-abiding men. Not repression, but payment commensurate with the gains is thus the animating motive. . . . Congress may also have believed that the furtive character of the business would increase the difficulty and expense of the process of tax collection."

1. The $200 tax was paid by 27 dealers in 1934, and by 22 dealers in 1935. Annual Report of the Commissioner of Internal Revenue, Fiscal Year Ended June 30, 1935, pp. 129–131; id., Fiscal Year Ended June 30, 1936, pp. 139–141.

a. The *McCray–Doremus–Sonzinsky* line of cases was followed in United States v. Sanchez, 340 U.S. 42 (1950), sustaining a federal tax on persons importing or dealing in marijuana.

United States v. Kahriger, 345 U.S. 22 (1953), presented the following situation: As a result of the widely publicized investigations by the Kefauver Crime Committee of the Senate, Congress included in the 1951 Revenue Act provisions requiring persons engaged in the business of accepting wagers to pay an annual tax of $50 plus 10% of the wagers placed. Each person liable for the tax was also required to file a registration statement with the Internal Revenue Service giving his name, residence, place of business and the name and address of each person accepting wagers for him. The lower court held the tax unconstitutional under United States v. Constantine, 296 U.S. 287 (1935). The Supreme Court reversed, pointing out: "The wagering tax with which we are here concerned applies to all persons engaged in the

UNITED STATES v. PTASYNSKI, 462 U.S. 74 (1983). The Crude Oil Windfall Profit Tax of 1980 imposed a federal tax on oil produced, but contained an exception for "exempt Alaskan oil." The exemption covered about 20% of current Alaskan oil and some oil from offshore northern waters outside of state boundaries. A suit was brought challenging the exemption as a violation of the uniformity clause, which provides that federal taxes "shall be uniform throughout the United States." The Court, in an opinion by Justice Powell, unanimously upheld the validity of the exemption, saying:

[handwritten margin note: suit brought saying the Act was a violation of the uniformity clause]

"We do not think that the language of the Clause or this Court's decisions prohibit all geographically defined classifications.... [T]he Uniformity Clause requires that an excise tax apply, at the same rate, in all portions of the United States where the subject of the tax is found. Where Congress defines the subject of a tax in nongeographic terms, the Uniformity Clause is satisfied.... We cannot say that when Congress uses geographic terms to identify the same subject, the classification is invalidated. The Uniformity Clause gives Congress wide latitude in deciding what to tax and does not prohibit it from considering geographically isolated problems.... But where Congress does choose to frame a tax in geographic terms, we will examine the classification closely to see if there is actual geographic discrimination.

"In this case, we hold that the classification is constitutional. As discussed above, Congress considered the windfall profit tax a necessary component of its program to encourage the exploration and production of oil. It perceived that the decontrol legislation would result—in certain circumstances—in profits essentially unrelated to the objective of the program, and concluded that these profits should be taxed. Accordingly, Congress divided oil into various classes and gave more favorable treatment to those classes that would be responsive to increased prices.

[handwritten margin note: Hold that geographical classification is const.]

"Congress clearly viewed 'exempt Alaskan oil' as a unique class of oil that, consistent with the scheme of the Act, merited favorable treatment. It had before it ample evidence of the disproportionate costs and difficulties—the fragile ecology, the harsh environment, and the remote location—associated with extracting oil from this region. We cannot fault its determination, based on neutral factors, that this oil required separate treatment. Nor is there any

business of receiving wagers regardless of whether such activity violates state law.... Appellee would have us say that because there is legislative history indicating a Congressional motive to suppress wagering, this tax is not a proper exercise of such taxing power.... It is conceded that a federal excise tax does not cease to be valid merely because it discourages or deters the activities taxed. Nor is the tax invalid because the revenue obtained is negligible.... Unless there are provisions extraneous to any tax need, courts are without authority to limit the exercise of the taxing power. All the provisions of this excise are adapted to the collection of a valid tax." Frankfurter, J. (joined by Douglas, J.) dissented, saying: "[W]hen oblique use is made of the taxing power as to matters which substantively are not within the powers delegated to Congress, the Court cannot shut its eyes to what is obviously, because designedly, an attempt to control conduct which the Constitution left to the responsibility of the States, merely because Congress wrapped the legislation in the verbal cellophane of a revenue measure." He believed that "the context of the circumstances which brought forth this enactment—sensationally exploited disclosures regarding gambling in big cities and small, the relation of this gambling to corrupt politics, the impatient public response to these disclosures, the feeling of ineptitude or paralysis on the part of local law-enforcing agencies—emphatically supports ... that what was formally a means of raising revenue ... was essentially an effort to check if not to stamp out professional gambling." Black and Douglas, JJ., also dissented on the ground that the reporting provisions of the act required taxpayers to incriminate themselves in violation of the Fifth Amendment. This position was later sustained in Marchetti v. United States, 390 U.S. 39 (1968), which overruled Kahriger on the self-incrimination point. For comment on the *Kahriger* case, see: 67 Harv.L.Rev. 164–7 (1953); 52 Mich. L.Rev. 150 (1953); 101 U.Pa.L.Rev. 877 (1953).

indication that Congress sought to benefit Alaska for reasons that would offend the purpose of the Clause. Nothing in the Act's legislative history suggests that Congress intended to grant Alaska an undue preference at the expense of other oil-producing States. This is especially clear because the windfall profit tax itself falls heavily on the State of Alaska.''

C. THE SPENDING POWER

UNITED STATES v. BUTLER, 297 U.S. 1 (1936). One of the major measures of the "new deal", in combating the great depression, was the Agriculture Adjustment Act of 1933. It was designed to raise farm prices and reduce the farm surplus of certain crops through curtailment of production and a tax upon the first processing of these crops. The Secretary of Agriculture was authorized to enter into agreements with individual farmers to reduce acreage in exchange for benefit payments computed on the basis of the reduction. Funds for the payments were derived from a tax levied upon the processor of the commodity involved, the total revenue from the tax being devoted to crop control and no part of it available for general governmental use. The secretary entered into agreements for the reduction of acreage devoted to cotton (as well as certain other crops) and a processing tax was imposed upon the processors, including Hoosac Mills for which Butler was receiver. Suit was brought to recover the tax on the ground that it was invalid as an integral part of an unconstitutional program to control agricultural production.

The act did not purport to be a regulation of interstate or foreign commerce and the government did not attempt to uphold it on the basis of the commerce clause. The court of appeals held the tax unconstitutional and the Supreme Court affirmed.

Justice Roberts, speaking for the Court, said:

"The clause thought to authorize the legislation ... confers upon the Congress power 'to lay and collect taxes, duties, imposts and excises to pay the debts and provide for the common defence and general welfare of the United States'. ... It is not contended that this provision grants power to regulate agricultural production upon the theory that such legislation would promote the general welfare. ... The true construction undoubtedly is that the only thing granted is the power to tax for the purpose of providing funds for payment of the nation's debts and making provision for the general welfare. ...

"Since the foundation of the nation, sharp differences of opinion have persisted as to the true interpretation of the phrase [to provide for the general welfare]. Madison asserted it amounted to no more than a reference to the other powers enumerated in the subsequent clauses of the same section; that, as the United States is a government of limited and enumerated powers, the grant of power to tax and spend for the general national welfare must be confined to the enumerated legislative fields committed to the Congress. In this view the phrase is mere tautology, for taxation and appropriation are or may be necessary incidents of the exercise of any of the enumerated legislative powers. Hamilton, on the other hand, maintained the clause confers a power separate and distinct from those later enumerated, is not restricted in meaning by the grant of them, and Congress consequently has a substantive power to tax and to appropriate, limited only by the requirement that it shall be exercised to provide for the general welfare of the United States. Each contention has had the support of those whose views are entitled to weight. This court has noticed the question, but has never found it necessary to decide which is the true construction. Mr. Justice Story, in his Commentaries, espouses the Hamiltonian position. We shall not review the writings of public men and commentators or discuss the legislative practice. Study of all these leads us to conclude that the reading advocated by Mr. Justice Story is the correct one. While, therefore, the power to tax is not unlimited, its confines are set in the clause which confers it, and not in those of section 8 which bestow and define the legislative powers of the Congress. It results that the power of Congress to authorize expenditure of public moneys for public purposes is not limited by the direct grants of legislative power found in the Constitution.

"But the adoption of the broader construction leaves the power to spend subject to limitations. . . .

"We are not now required to ascertain the scope of the phrase 'general welfare of the United States' or to determine whether an appropriation in aid of agriculture falls within it. Wholly apart from that question, another principle embedded in our Constitution prohibits the enforcement of the Agricultural Adjustment Act. The act invades the reserved rights of the states. It is a statutory plan to regulate and control agricultural production, a matter beyond the powers delegated to the federal government. The tax, the appropriation of the funds raised, and the direction for their disbursement, are but parts of the plan. They are but means to an unconstitutional end.

"From the accepted doctrine that the United States is a government of delegated powers, it follows that those not expressly granted, or reasonably to be implied from such as are conferred, are reserved to the states or to the people. To forestall any suggestion to the contrary, the Tenth Amendment was adopted. The same proposition, otherwise stated, is that powers not granted are prohibited. None to regulate agricultural production is given, and therefore legislation by Congress for that purpose is forbidden.

"It is an established principle that the attainment of a prohibited end may not be accomplished under the pretext of the exertion of powers which are granted. . . .

"The power of taxation, which is expressly granted, may, of course, be adopted as a means to carry into operation another power also expressly granted. But resort to the taxing power to effectuate an end which is not legitimate, not within the scope of the Constitution, is obviously inadmissible. . . .

"In the Child Labor Tax Case, 259 U.S. 20, and in Hill v. Wallace, 259 U.S. 44, this court had before it statutes which purported to be taxing measures. But their purpose was found to be to regulate the conduct of manufacturing and trading, not in interstate commerce, but in the states—matters not within any power conferred upon Congress by the Constitution—and the levy of the tax a means to force compliance. The court held this was not a constitutional use, but an unconstitutional abuse of the power to tax. . . . These decisions demonstrate that Congress could not, under the pretext of raising revenue, lay a tax on processors who refuse to pay a certain price for cotton, and exempt those who agree so to do, with the purpose of benefiting producers.

"If the taxing power may not be used as the instrument to enforce a regulation of matters of state concern with respect to which the Congress has no authority to interfere, may it, as in the present case, be employed to raise the money necessary to purchase a compliance which the Congress is powerless to command? The government asserts that whatever might be said against the validity of the plan if compulsory, it is constitutionally sound because the end is accomplished by voluntary co-operation. There are two sufficient answers to the contention. The regulation is not in fact voluntary. The farmer, of course, may refuse to comply, but the price of such refusal is the loss of benefits. The amount offered is intended to be sufficient to exert pressure on him to agree to the proposed regulation. The power to confer or withhold unlimited benefits is the power to coerce or destroy. . . .

"But if the plan were one for purely voluntary co-operation it would stand no better so far as federal power is concerned. At best, it is a scheme for purchasing with federal funds submission to federal regulation of a subject reserved to the states. . . .

"We are not here concerned with a conditional appropriation of money, nor with a provision that if certain conditions are not complied with the appropriation shall no longer be available. . . . There is an obvious difference between a statute stating the conditions upon which moneys shall be expended and one effective only upon assumption of a contractual obligation to submit to a regulation which otherwise could not be enforced. . . .

"Congress has no power to enforce its commands on the farmer to the ends sought by the Agricultural Adjustment Act. It must follow that it may not indirectly accomplish those ends by taxing and spending to purchase compliance. . . ."

Stone, J. (joined by Brandeis and Cardozo, JJ.) dissented, stating in part:

"The Constitution requires that public funds shall be spent for a defined purpose, the promotion of the general welfare. Their expenditure usually involves payment on terms which will insure use by the selected recipients within the limits of the constitutional purpose. Expenditures would fail of their purpose and thus lose their constitutional sanction if the terms of payment were not such that by their influence on the action of the recipients the permitted end would be attained. The power of Congress to spend is inseparable from persuasion to action over which Congress has no legislative control. Congress may not command that the science of agriculture be taught in state universities. But if it would aid the teaching of that science by grants to state institutions, it is appropriate, if not necessary, that the grant be on the condition, incorporated in the Morrill Act [July 2, 1862], 12 Stat. at L. 503, chap. 130, U.S.C. title 7, § 301, August 30, 1890, 26 Stat. at L. 417, chap. 841, U.S.C. title 7, § 322, that it be used for the intended purpose. Similarly it would seem to be compliance with the Constitution, not violation of it, for the government to take and the university to give a contract that the grant would be so used. It makes no difference that there is a promise to do an act which the condition is calculated to induce. Condition and promise are alike valid since both are in furtherance of the national purpose for which the money is appropriated."

He added: "It is a contradiction in terms to say that there is power to spend for the national welfare, while rejecting the power to impose conditions reasonably adapted to the attainment of the end which alone would justify the expenditure."

CHAS. C. STEWARD MACHINE CO. v. DAVIS, 301 U.S. 548 (1937), presented a challenge to Title IX of the Social Security Act of 1935 relating to unemployment compensation. A tax was imposed on employers of eight or more persons; the proceeds were not earmarked, but went into the general funds of the treasury. If the taxpayer made contributions to a state unemployment compensation fund created by state law certified by the Social Security Board as meeting certain minimum standards, he was entitled to credit such contributions against his federal tax up to 90% of the tax. In order to assure proper administration of the state compensation system, it was required that contributions to the state fund be paid over to the Secretary of the Treasury to the credit of the Unemployment Trust Fund, the Secretary then being required to pay back to the authorized state agency the sums requisitioned by it. Federal machinery for the administration of the Social Security Act was quickly provided and most states immediately enacted legislation making possible their participation in the program. Steward Machine Company sued Davis, a Collector of Internal Revenue, to recover payroll taxes paid, claiming that the law, particularly the 90% credit provisions, resulted in "coercion of the states" in violation of the Tenth Amendment or of restrictions implicit in our federal system.

In a 5–4 decision the Court sustained the statute. In rejecting the coercion argument, the Court referred to the widespread unemployment during the Great Depression and continued:

"... The fact developed quickly that the states were unable to give the requisite relief. The problem had become national in area and dimensions. There was need of help from the nation if the people were not to starve. It is too late today for the argument to be heard with tolerance that in a crisis so extreme the use of the moneys of the nation to relieve the unemployed and their dependents is a use for any purpose narrower than the promotion of the general welfare. Cf. United States v. Butler, 297 U.S. 1, 65, 66.... The Social Security Act is an attempt to find a method by which all these public agencies may work together to a common end. Every dollar of the new taxes will continue in all likelihood to be used and needed by the nation as long as states are unwilling, whether through timidity or for other motives, to do what can be done at home. At least the inference is permissible that Congress so believed, though retaining undiminished freedom to spend the money as it pleased. On the other hand, fulfillment of the home duty will be lightened and encouraged by crediting the taxpayer upon his account with the Treasury of the nation to the extent that his contributions under the laws of the locality have simplified or diminished the problem of relief and the probable demand upon the resources of the fisc.... The difficulty with the petitioner's contention is that it confuses motive with coercion. 'Every tax is in some measure regulatory. To some extent it interposes an economic impediment to the activity taxed as compared with others not taxed.' Sonzinsky v. United States, 300 U.S. 506. In like manner every rebate from a tax when conditioned upon conduct is in some measure a temptation. But to hold that motive or temptation is equivalent to coercion is to plunge the law in endless difficulties....

"In ruling as we do, we leave many questions open. We do not say that a tax is valid, when imposed by act of Congress, if it is laid upon the condition that a state may escape its operation through the adoption of a statute unrelated in subject-matter to activities fairly within the scope of national policy and power. No such question is before us. In the tender of this credit Congress does not intrude upon fields foreign to its function. The purpose of its intervention, as we have shown, is to safeguard its own treasury and as an incident to that protection to place the states upon a footing of equal opportunity. Drains upon its own resources are to be checked; obstructions to the freedom of the states are to be leveled. It is one thing to impose a tax dependent upon the conduct of the taxpayers, or of the state in which they live, where the conduct to be stimulated or discouraged is unrelated to the fiscal need subserved by the tax in its normal operation, or to any other end legitimately national. The Child Labor Tax Case, 259 U.S. 20, and Hill v. Wallace, 259 U.S. 44, were decided in the belief that the statutes there condemned were exposed to that reproach. Cf. United States v. Constantine,

296 U.S. 287. It is quite another thing to say that a tax will be abated upon the doing of an act that will satisfy the fiscal need, the tax and the alternative being approximate equivalents. In such circumstances, if in no others, inducement or persuasion does not go beyond the bounds of power. We do not fix the outermost line. Enough for present purposes that wherever the line may be, this statute is within it. Definition more precise must abide the wisdom of the future. . . .

"United States v. Butler, supra, is cited by petitioner as a decision to the contrary. . . . The decision was by a divided court, a minority taking the view that the objections were untenable. None of them is applicable to the situation here developed.

"(a) The proceeds of the tax in controversy are not earmarked for a special group.

"(b) The unemployment compensation law which is a condition of the credit has had the approval of the state and could not be a law without it.

"(c) The condition is not linked to an irrevocable agreement, for the state at its pleasure may repeal its unemployment law, § 903(a)(6), terminate the credit, and place itself where it was before the credit was accepted.

"(d) The condition is not directed to the attainment of an unlawful end, but to an end, the relief of unemployment, for which nation and state may lawfully cooperate. . . ."

The Court also concluded that the statute did not call "for a surrender by the states of powers essential to their quasi-sovereign existence."

". . . A credit to taxpayers for payments made to a state under a state unemployment law will be manifestly futile in the absence of some assurance that the law leading to the credit is in truth what it professes to be. An unemployment law framed in such a way that the unemployed who look to it will be deprived of reasonable protection is one in name and nothing more. What is basic and essential may be assured by suitable conditions. The terms embodied in these sections are directed to that end. A wide range of judgment is given to the several states as to the particular type of statute to be spread upon their books. . . . What they may not do if they would earn the credit, is to depart from those standards which in the judgment of Congress are to be ranked as fundamental. Even if opinion may differ as to the fundamental quality of one or more of the conditions, the difference will not avail to vitiate the statute. In determining essentials, Congress must have the benefit of a fair margin of discretion. . . ."

Justices McReynolds, Sutherland, Van Devanter and Butler dissented.

HELVERING v. DAVIS, 301 U.S. 619 (1937). This case involved the old age benefit provisions (Titles II and VIII) of the Social Security Act. In meeting the contention that the program for paying old age benefits was not authorized by the general welfare clause, the Court reviewed evidence of the widespread economic plight of the aged and added:

"The problem is plainly national in area and dimensions. Moreover, laws of the separate states cannot deal with it effectively. Congress, at least, had a basis for that belief. States and local governments are often lacking in the resources that are necessary to finance an adequate program of security for the aged. This is brought out with a wealth of illustration in recent studies of the problem. Apart from the failure of resources, states and local governments are at times reluctant to increase so heavily the burden of taxation to be borne by their residents for fear of placing themselves in a position of economic disadvantage as compared with neighbors or competitors.

"We have seen this in our study of the problem of unemployment compensation. Steward Machine Co. v. Davis, supra. A system of old age pensions has special dangers of its own, if put in force in one state and rejected in another. The existence of such a system is a bait to the needy and dependent elsewhere, encouraging them to migrate and seek a haven of repose. Only a power that is national can serve the interests of all.

"Whether wisdom or unwisdom resides in the scheme of benefits set forth in Title II, it is not for us to say. The answer to such inquiries must come from Congress, not the courts. Our concern here, as often, is with power, not with wisdom. Counsel for respondent has recalled to us the virtues of self-reliance and frugality. There is a possibility, he says, that aid from a paternal government may sap those sturdy virtues and breed a race of weaklings. If Massachusetts so believes and shapes her laws in that conviction, must her breed of sons be changed, he asks, because some other philosophy of government finds favor in the halls of Congress? But the answer is not doubtful. One might ask with equal reason whether the system of protective tariffs is to be set aside at will in one state or another whenever local policy prefers the rule of laissez faire. The issue is a closed one. It was fought out long ago. When money is spent to promote the general welfare, the concept of welfare or the opposite is shaped by Congress, not the states. So the concept be not arbitrary, the locality must yield. Constitution, Art. VI, Par. 2...."

SABRI v. UNITED STATES, 541 U.S. 600, (2004). The Court upheld under Congress' Spending Clause powers 18 U.S.C. § 666(a)(2), which criminally proscribes bribery of state or local officials of entities that receive at least $10,000 in federal funds. Defendant, who was accused of offering three separate bribes to a Minneapolis councilman, "raises what he calls a facial challenge to § 666(a)(2): the law can never be applied constitutionally because it fails to require proof of any connection between a bribe or kickback and some federal money. It is fatal, as he sees it, that the statute does not make the link an element of the crime.... We can readily dispose of this position that, to qualify as a valid exercise of Article I power, the statute must require proof of connection with federal money as an element of the offense.... Congress has authority under the Spending Clause to appropriate federal monies to promote the general welfare, Art. I. § 8, cl. 1, and it has corresponding authority under the Necessary and Proper Clause, Art. I, § 8, cl. 18, to see to it that taxpayer dollars appropriated under that power are in fact spent for the general welfare, and not frittered away in graft or on projects undermined when funds are siphoned off or corrupt public officers are derelict about demanding value for dollars.... Congress does not have to sit by and accept the risk of operations thwarted by local and state improbity.... Section 666(a)(2) addresses the problem at the sources of bribes, by rational means, to safeguard the integrity of the state [and] local recipients of federal dollars. It is true, as Sabri says, that not every bribe or kickback offered or paid to agents of governments covered by § 666(b) will be traceably skimmed from specific federal payments.... But ... corruption does not have to be that limited to affect the federal interest. Money is fungible, bribed officials are untrustworthy stewards of federal funds, and corrupt contractors do not deliver dollar-for-dollar value.... It is certainly enough that the statutes condition the offense on a threshold amount of federal dollars defining the federal interest, such as that provided here, and on a bribe that goes well beyond liquor and cigars."

THE IMPACT OF FEDERAL GRANTS TO THE STATES

Federal grants to the states and local governments have increased rapidly in recent years. Total federal grants-in-aid and shared revenue increased from just under 11 billion dollars in 1965 to an estimated total of 228 billion in 1995. *Statistical Abstract* 1995, p. 302. The percentage of state and local government budgets received from the federal government was 23% in 1994, id.

BUCKLEY v. VALEO, 424 U.S. 1 (1976). Subtitle H of the Federal Election Campaign Act, as amended in 1974, establishes a Presidential Election Campaign Fund, financed from general revenues in the aggregate amount designated by individual taxpayers who on their income tax returns may authorize payment to the fund of one dollar of their tax liability in case of an individual return or two dollars in case of a joint return. The Fund consists of separate accounts to finance party nominating conventions, general election campaigns, and primary campaigns. To the contention that Subtitle H is invalid as contrary to the general welfare clause of Article I, § 8, The Court responded as follows:

"Appellants' 'general welfare' contention erroneously treats the General Welfare Clause as a limitation upon congressional power. It is rather a grant of power, the scope of which is quite expansive, particularly in view of the enlargement of power by the Necessary and Proper Clause. McCulloch v. Maryland, 4 Wheat. 316, 420 (1819). Congress has power to regulate Presidential elections and primaries, United States v. Classic, 313 U.S. 299 (1941); Burroughs v. United States, 290 U.S. 534 (1934); and public financing of Presidential elections as a means to reform the electoral process was clearly a choice within the granted power. It is for Congress to decide which expenditures will promote the general welfare: '[T]he power of Congress to authorize expenditure of public moneys for public purposes is not limited by the direct grants of legislative power found in the Constitution.' United States v. Butler, 297 U.S. 1, 66 (1936). See Helvering v. Davis, 301 U.S. 619, 640–641 (1937). Any limitations upon the exercise of that granted power must be found elsewhere in the Constitution. In this case, Congress was legislating for the 'general welfare'—to reduce the deleterious influence of large contributions on our political process, to facilitate communication by candidates with the electorate, and to free candidates from the rigors of fundraising. See S.Rep. No. 93–689, pp. 1–10 (1974). Whether the chosen means appear 'bad,' 'unwise,' or 'unworkable' to us is irrelevant; Congress has concluded that the means are 'necessary and proper' to promote the general welfare and we thus decline to find this legislation without the grant of power in Art. I, § 8.

"Appellants' challenge to the dollar check-off provision (§ 6096) fails for the same reason. They maintain that Congress is required to permit taxpayers to designate particular candidates or parties as recipients of their money. But the appropriation to the Fund in § 9006 is like any other appropriation from the general revenue except that its amount is determined by reference to the aggregate of the one-and two-dollar authorization on taxpayers' income tax returns. This detail does not constitute the appropriation any less an appropriation by Congress. The fallacy of appellants' argument is therefore apparent; every appropriation made by Congress uses public money in a manner to which some taxpayers object."[a]

***

a. For further discussion of conditional spending issues, see New York v. United States, infra p. 231. See generally Rosenthal, *Conditional Federal Spending and the Constitution*, 39 Stanford Law Review 1103 (1987).

SOUTH DAKOTA v. DOLE, 483 U.S. 203 (1987). South Dakota challenged a federal statute that instructed the Secretary of Transportation to withhold a percentage of federal highway funds to which a state would otherwise be entitled if the state permitted anyone under the age of 21 to purchase or possess in public alcohol. Writing for himself and six other Justices, Chief Justice Rehnquist upheld the condition on the receipt of federal funds. Even assuming the Constitution, in particular the Twenty–First Amendment, prohibited Congress from directly enacting a national minimum drinking age, Congress could legislate under its spending power to encourage uniformity in the States' drinking ages. The Court laid out a four-part test to judge Congress' exercises of spending clause authority. First, "the exercise of the spending power must be in pursuit of 'the general welfare,' "—a question on which Congress is entitled to considerable deference. Second, Congress' conditions on the receipt of federal funds must be imposed "unambiguously" so that the States are able to " 'exercise their choice knowingly, cognizant of the consequences of their participation.' " Third, the condition on federal funding must be related to " 'the federal interest in particular national projects or programs.' " Last, other constitutional provisions may provide "an independent bar" to the conditions imposed. Applying this test, the Court upheld the highway funding statute. In particular, the Court found that Congress' goal of safe highways was one that explained the existence of federal funding in the first place, and that explained the drinking age limitation. Justice O'Connor dissented, complaining that the Court's "application of the requirement that the condition imposed be reasonably related to the purpose for which the funds are expended, is cursory and unconvincing." She objected to the Court's "attenuated" linkage between the goals for which spending was provided, and the conditions imposed on states. Under such a relaxed inquiry, she said, Congress could "regulate almost any area of a State's social, political or economic life. . . ."

[handwritten margin note: Test for limitations to spending]

D. WAR AND TREATY POWERS

THE SOURCES OF NATIONAL POWER

Since the primary purpose of the Founding Fathers was "to form a more perfect Union" with a stronger national government, one might suppose that the national powers over foreign affairs would have been quite fully and explicitly stated. But such was not the case. The constitutional provisions dealing expressly with foreign relations, or matters particularly related thereto, are rather sparse and uncorrelated. Most of them appear in the enumeration of executive powers: the President is made "Commander-in-Chief" of the armed forces; he is given the power, with the approval of two-thirds of the Senate, "to make Treaties"; and, with the "advice and consent" of the Senate, he "shall appoint Ambassadors, other public Ministers and Consuls," i.e., our representatives abroad (Art. II, § 2). Also, "he shall receive Ambassadors and other public Ministers" (Art. II, § 3). There are two additional provisions (not referring particularly to foreign affairs) under which the President has extensive undefined power. They provide "the executive power shall be vested in" him (Art. II, § 1) and "he shall take care that the Laws be faithfully executed" (Art. II, § 3).

Aside from Senate participation in the making of treaties, the powers of Congress explicitly relating to foreign affairs or national defense are: the power to regulate commerce with foreign nations; to establish "a uniform rule of naturalization"; to define and punish piracies and felonies committed on the high seas and offenses against the law of nations; to declare war; to maintain an army and navy; and to make rules for the regulation of the armed forces (Art. I, § 8).

To make clear that some of these powers are exclusively national, a few explicit limitations are imposed on the states: no State shall enter into any treaty, alliance, or confederation; nor, without the consent of Congress, lay any imposts or duties on imports or exports, except what may be necessary for executing state inspection laws; nor, without the consent of Congress, keep "troops or ships of war" in time of peace, or engage in war unless actually invaded or in imminent danger thereof (Art. I, § 10).

UNITED STATES v. CURTISS–WRIGHT EXPORT CORP., 299 U.S. 304 (1936). By a Joint Resolution of May 28, 1934, Congress purported to authorize the President to embargo the sale of arms to countries engaged in armed conflict in the Chaco. (Bolivia and Paraguay were so engaged.) The President, by proclamation, immediately imposed an embargo in accordance with the Joint Resolution. Curtiss–Wright contested the validity of the embargo on the ground that the Joint Resolution attempted an unconstitutional delegation of legislative power to the executive. In rejecting this contention, the Court (per Sutherland, J.) expressed the view that there are fundamental differences between "the powers of the federal government in respect of foreign or external affairs and those in respect of domestic or internal affairs." The opinion continued:

"The two classes of powers are different, both in respect of their origin and their nature. The broad statement that the federal government can exercise no powers except those specifically enumerated in the Constitution, and such implied powers as are necessary and proper to carry into effect the enumerated powers, is categorically true only in respect of our internal affairs. In that field, the primary purpose of the Constitution was to carve from the general mass of legislative powers *then possessed by the states* such portions as it was thought desirable to vest in the federal government, leaving those not included in the enumeration still in the states. Carter v. Carter Coal Co., 298 U.S. 238, 294. That this doctrine applies only to powers which the states had, is self evident. And since the states severally never possessed international powers, such powers could not have been carved from the mass of state powers but obviously were transmitted to the United States from some other source. . . .

"It results that the investment of the federal government with the powers of external sovereignty did not depend upon the affirmative grants of the Constitution. The powers to declare and wage war, to conclude peace, to make treaties, to maintain diplomatic relations with other sovereignties, if they had never been mentioned in the Constitution, would have vested in the federal government as necessary concomitants of nationality. . . . As a member of the family of nations, the right and power of the United States in that field are equal to the right and power of the other members of the international family. Otherwise, the United States is not completely sovereign. The power to acquire territory by discovery and occupation (Jones v. United States, 137 U.S. 202, 212), the power to expel undesirable aliens (Fong Yue Ting v. United States, 149 U.S. 698, 705 et seq.), the power to make such international agreements as do not constitute treaties in the constitutional sense (Altman & Co. v. United States, 224 U.S. 583, 600–601; Crandall, Treaties, Their Making and Enforcement, 2d ed., p. 102 and note 1), none of which is expressly affirmed by the Constitution, nevertheless exist as inherently inseparable from the conception of nationality. This the court recognized, and in each of the cases cited found the warrant for its conclusions not in the provisions of the Constitution, but in the law of nations."[1]

Woods v. Cloyd W. Miller Co.

333 U.S. 138, 68 S.Ct. 421, 92 L.Ed. 596 (1948).

Mr. Justice Douglas delivered the opinion of the Court.

The case is here on a direct appeal from a judgment of the District Court holding unconstitutional Title II of the Housing and Rent Act of 1947. 61 Stat. 193, 196.

The Act became effective on July 1, 1947, and the following day the appellee demanded of its tenants increases of 40% and 60% for rental accommodations in the Cleveland Defense–Rental Area, an admitted violation of the Act and regulations adopted pursuant thereto. Appellant thereupon instituted this proceeding under § 206(b) of the Act to enjoin the violations. A preliminary injunction issued. After a hearing it was dissolved and a permanent injunction denied.

The District Court was of the view that the authority of Congress to regulate rents by virtue of the war power (see Bowles v. Willingham, 321 U.S. 503) ended with the Presidential Proclamation terminating hostilities on December 31, 1946, since that proclamation inaugurated "peace-in-fact" though it did not mark termination of the war. . . .

We conclude, in the first place, that the war power sustains this legislation. The Court said in Hamilton v. Kentucky Distilleries Co., 251 U.S. 146, 161, that the war power includes the power "to remedy the evils which have arisen from its rise and progress" and continues for the duration of that emergency. Whatever may be the consequences when war is officially terminated, the war power does not necessarily end with the cessation of hostilities. We recently held that it is adequate to support the preservation of rights created by wartime legislation, Fleming v. Mohawk Wrecking & Lumber Co., 331 U.S. 111. But it has a broader sweep. In *Hamilton v. Kentucky Distilleries Co.,* supra, and Ruppert v. Caffey, 251 U.S. 264, prohibition laws which were enacted after the Armistice in World War I were sustained as exercises of the war power because they conserved manpower and increased efficiency of production in the critical days during the period of demobilization, and helped to husband the supply of grains and cereals depleted by the war effort. Those cases followed the reasoning of Stewart v. Kahn, 11 Wall. 493, which held that Congress had the power to toll the statute of limitations of the States during the period when the process of their courts was not available to litigants due to the conditions obtaining in the Civil War.

[handwritten margin note: power continues as long as war conditions exist.]

[handwritten margin note: Broader application to prohibition laws]

The constitutional validity of the present legislation follows *a fortiori* from those cases. The legislative history of the present Act makes abundantly clear that there has not yet been eliminated the deficit in housing which in consider-

---

1. Justice Sutherland's theory of extra-constitutional powers over foreign affairs has been frequently discussed but never resolved. See Henkin, *Foreign Affairs and the United States Constitution* (2d ed. 1996), Ch. I; Dodd, *Implied Powers and Implied Limitations in Constitutional Law,* 29 Yale L.J. 137 (1919), 1 Selected Essays (1938) 330; Riesenfeld, *The Power of Congress and the President in Inter-* *national Relations,* 25 Calif.L.Rev. 643 (1937). See also Henkin, *The Treaty Makers and the Law Makers,* 107 U.Pa.L.Rev. 903, 922–936 (1959); Perez v. Brownell, 356 U.S. 44, 57 (1958). *Perez* was overruled in Afroyim v. Rusk, 387 U.S. 253 (1967), but not the statement about the extra-constitutional foundations of the power over foreign relations.

able measure was caused by the heavy demobilization of veterans and by the cessation or reduction in residential construction during the period of hostilities due to the allocation of building materials to military projects. Since the war effort contributed heavily to that deficit, Congress has the power even after the cessation of hostilities to act to control the forces that a short supply of the needed article created. If that were not true, the Necessary and Proper Clause, Art. I, § 8, cl. 18, would be drastically limited in its application to the several war powers. The Court has declined to follow that course in the past. Hamilton v. Kentucky Distilleries Co., supra, pp. 155, 156; Ruppert v. Caffey, supra, pp. 299, 300. We decline to take it today. The result would be paralyzing. It would render Congress powerless to remedy conditions the creation of which necessarily followed from the mobilization of men and materials for successful prosecution of the war. So to read the Constitution would be to make it self-defeating.

We recognize the force of the argument that the effects of war under modern conditions may be felt in the economy for years and years, and that if the war power can be used in days of peace to treat all the wounds which war inflicts on our society, it may not only swallow up all other powers of Congress but largely obliterate the Ninth and the Tenth Amendments as well. There are no such implications in today's decision. We deal here with the consequences of a housing deficit greatly intensified during the period of hostilities by the war effort. Any power, of course, can be abused. But we cannot assume that Congress is not alert to its constitutional responsibilities. And the question whether the war power has been properly employed in cases such as this is open to judicial inquiry. Hamilton v. Kentucky Distilleries Co., supra; Ruppert v. Caffey, supra. . . .

Reversed.

Mr. Justice Frankfurter concurs in this opinion because it decides no more than was decided in Hamilton v. Kentucky Distilleries Co., 251 U.S. 146, and Jacob Ruppert v. Caffey, 251 U.S. 264, and merely applies those decisions to the situation now before the Court.

Mr. Justice Jackson, concurring.

I agree with the result in this case, but the arguments that have been addressed to us lead me to utter more explicit misgivings about war powers than the Court has done. The Government asserts no constitutional basis for this legislation other than this vague, undefined and undefinable "war power."

No one will question that this power is the most dangerous one to free government in the whole catalogue of powers. It usually is invoked in haste and excitement when calm legislative consideration of constitutional limitation is difficult. It is executed in a time of patriotic fervor that makes moderation unpopular. And, worst of all, it is interpreted by judges under the influence of the same passions and pressures. Always, as in this case, the Government urges hasty decision to forestall some emergency or serve some purpose and pleads that paralysis will result if its claims to power are denied or their confirmation delayed.

Particularly when the war power is invoked to do things to the liberties of people, or to their property or economy that only indirectly affect conduct of the war and do not relate to the management of the war itself, the constitutional basis should be scrutinized with care.

I think we can hardly deny that the war power is as valid a ground for federal rent control now as it has been at any time. We still are technically in a state of war. I would not be willing to hold that war powers may be indefinitely prolonged merely by keeping legally alive a state of war that had in fact ended.

I cannot accept the argument that war powers last as long as the effects and consequences of war, for if so they are permanent—as permanent as the war debts. But I find no reason to conclude that we could find fairly that the present state of war is merely technical. We have armies abroad exercising our war power and have made no peace terms with our allies, not to mention our principal enemies. I think the conclusion that the war power has been applicable during the lifetime of this legislation is unavoidable.

INTERNATIONAL AGREEMENTS

To what extent may the national government provide the law governing local affairs through entering into international agreements in areas where it is otherwise incompetent to act? This question poses the central issue to be pursued at this point in the materials. The division of authority between the President and Congress with respect to the making of international agreements will be discussed briefly in Chapter 7, Separation of Powers. The international aspects of treaties and executive agreements—the way in which they regulate relationships with other countries and international organizations—is a separate subject reserved for courses in international law and international transactions. For a general study of the problems of federal states in the field of international agreements, see Hendry, *Treaties and Federal Constitutions* (1955). For a penetrating discussion of all of the issues involved here see Henkin, *Foreign Affairs and the United States Constitution* (2d ed. 1996).

HAUENSTEIN v. LYNHAM, 100 U.S. 483 (1880). Hauenstein died intestate a resident of Richmond, Virginia, where he owned considerable real estate. The proceeds from the sale of this property were claimed by his heirs who were citizens of Switzerland. Their claim was resisted on the ground that the property had escheated to the state because Virginia law provided that aliens were not qualified to inherit property in the state. An 1850 treaty between the United States and Switzerland provided that in this situation the alien–heirs should be permitted to sell the property and withdraw the proceeds. The Virginia courts decided against the heirs.

The Supreme Court reversed and remanded the case, saying:

"That the laws of the State, irrespective of the treaty, would put the fund into her coffers, is no objection to the right or the remedy claimed by the plaintiffs in error. The efficacy of the treaty is declared and guaranteed by the Constitution of the United States.... If doubts could exist before the adoption of the present national government, they must be entirely removed by the sixth article of the Constitution, which provides that 'all treaties made or which shall be made under the authority of the United States, shall be *the supreme law of the land,* and the judges in every State shall be bound thereby, any thing in the Constitution or laws of any State to the contrary notwithstanding.' ... A treaty cannot be *the supreme law of the land,* that is, of all the United States, if any act of a State legislature can stand in its way.... It must always be borne in mind that the Constitution, laws, and treaties of the United States are as much a part of the law of every State as its own local laws and Constitution. This is a fundamental principle in our system of complex national policy.... We have no doubt that this treaty is within the treaty-making power conferred by the Constitution. And it is our duty to give it full effect. We forbear to pursue the topic further...."

CONGRESSIONAL LEGISLATION INCONSISTENT WITH A TREATY

A treaty that manifests an intention to become effective as domestic law of the United States supersedes inconsistent provisions of earlier acts of Congress as well as inconsistent state laws, ALI, *Restatement, Third, (The Foreign Relations Law of the United States)* §§ 111, 115 (1987).[17] However, subsequent Congressional legislation will be given effect even though inconsistent with a prior treaty. See the Chinese Exclusion Cases, 130 U.S. 581 (1889), which sustained legislation excluding the entry of Chinese even though such exclusion was in violation of a treaty with China. The Court said: "The last expression of sovereign will must control." In such a situation, enforcement of the international obligation, if any, must be found in diplomatic negotiations or an international tribunal.

Missouri v. Holland

252 U.S. 416, 40 S.Ct. 382, 64 L.Ed. 641 (1920).

Mr. Justice Holmes delivered the opinion of the Court.

This is a bill in equity brought by the State of Missouri to prevent a game warden of the United States from attempting to enforce the Migratory Bird Treaty Act of July 3, 1918, c. 128, 40 Stat. 755, and the regulations made by the Secretary of Agriculture in pursuance of the same. The ground of the bill is that the statute is an unconstitutional interference with the rights reserved to the States by the Tenth Amendment, and that the acts of the defendant done and threatened under that authority invade the sovereign right of the State and contravene its will manifested in statutes. The State also alleges a pecuniary interest, as owner of the wild birds within its borders and otherwise, admitted by the Government to be sufficient, but it is enough that the bill is a reasonable and proper means to assert the alleged quasi sovereign rights of a State. Kansas v. Colorado, 185 U.S. 125, 142 ... A motion to dismiss was sustained by the District Court on the ground that the Act of Congress is constitutional.... The State appeals.

On December 8, 1916, a treaty between the United States and Great Britain was proclaimed by the President. It recited that many species of birds in their annual migrations traversed many parts of the United States and of Canada, that they were of great value as a source of food and in destroying insects injurious to vegetation, but were in danger of extermination through lack of adequate protection. It therefore provided for specified closed seasons and protection in other forms, and agreed that the two powers would take or propose to their lawmaking bodies the necessary measures for carrying the treaty out. 39 Stat. 1702. The above mentioned act of July 3, 1918, ... prohibited the killing, capturing or selling any of the migratory birds included in the terms of the treaty except as permitted by regulations compatible with those terms to be made by the Secretary of Agriculture.... It is unnecessary to go into any details, because, as we have said, the question raised is the general one whether the treaty and statute are void as an interference with the rights reserved to the States.

To answer this question it is not enough to refer to the Tenth Amendment, reserving the powers not delegated to the United States, because by Article 2, Section 2, the power to make treaties is delegated expressly, and by Article 6 treaties made under the authority of the United States, along with the Constitution and laws of the United States made in pursuance thereof, are declared the supreme law of the land. If the treaty is valid there can be no

17. There is a distinction between "self-executing" and "non-self-executing" treaties. In general, a non-self-executing trea-ty is one that, by its terms, requires implementation by legislative or executive action in order to be effective.

dispute about the validity of the statute under Article 1, Section 8, as a necessary and proper means to execute the powers of the Government. The language of the Constitution as to the supremacy of treaties being general, the question before us is narrowed to an inquiry into the ground upon which the present supposed exception is placed.

It is said that a treaty cannot be valid if it infringes the Constitution, that there are limits, therefore, to the treaty-making power, and that one such limit is that what an act of Congress could not do unaided, in derogation of the powers reserved to the States, a treaty cannot do. An earlier act of Congress that attempted by itself and not in pursuance of a treaty to regulate the killing of migratory birds within the States had been held bad in the District Court. United States v. Shauver, 214 Fed. 154. United States v. McCullagh, 221 Fed. 288. Those decisions were supported by arguments that migratory birds were owned by the States in their sovereign capacity for the benefit of their people, and that under cases like Geer v. Connecticut, 161 U.S. 519, this control was one that Congress had no power to displace. The same argument is supposed to apply now with equal force.

Whether the two cases cited were decided rightly or not they cannot be accepted as a test of the treaty power. Acts of Congress are the supreme law of the land only when made in pursuance of the Constitution, while treaties are declared to be so when made under the authority of the United States. It is open to question whether the authority of the United States means more than the formal acts prescribed to make the convention. We do not mean to imply that there are no qualifications to the treaty-making power; but they must be ascertained in a different way. It is obvious that there may be matters of the sharpest exigency for the national well being that an act of Congress could not deal with but that a treaty followed by such an act could, and it is not lightly to be assumed that, in matters requiring national action, "a power which must belong to and somewhere reside in every civilized government" is not to be found.... We are not yet discussing the particular case before us but only are considering the validity of the test proposed. With regard to that we may add that when we are dealing with words that also are a constituent act, like the Constitution of the United States, we must realize that they have called into life a being the development of which could not have been foreseen completely by the most gifted of its begetters. It was enough for them to realize or to hope that they had created an organism; it has taken a century and has cost their successors much sweat and blood to prove that they created a nation. The case before us must be considered in the light of our whole experience and not merely in that of what was said a hundred years ago. The treaty in question does not contravene any prohibitory words to be found in the Constitution. The only question is whether it is forbidden by some invisible radiation from the general terms of the Tenth Amendment. We must consider what this country has become in deciding what that amendment has reserved.

The State as we have intimated founds its claim of exclusive authority upon an assertion of title to migratory birds, an assertion that is embodied in statute. No doubt it is true that as between a State and its inhabitants the State may regulate the killing and sale of such birds, but it does not follow that its authority is exclusive of paramount powers. To put the claim of the State upon title is to lean upon a slender reed. Wild birds are not in the possession of anyone; and possession is the beginning of ownership. The whole foundation of the State's rights is the presence within their jurisdiction of birds that yesterday had not arrived, tomorrow may be in another State and in a week a thousand miles away. If we are to be accurate we cannot put the case of the State upon higher ground than that the treaty deals with creatures that for the moment are within the state borders, that it must be carried out by officers of the United States within the same territory, and that but for the treaty the State would be free to regulate this subject itself.

As most of the laws of the United States are carried out within the States and as many of them deal with matters which in the silence of such laws the State might regulate, such general grounds are not enough to support Missouri's claim. Valid treaties of course "are as binding within the territorial limits of the States as they are elsewhere throughout the dominion of the United States." Baldwin v. Franks, 120 U.S. 678, 683. No doubt the great body of private relations usually fall within the control of the State, but a treaty may override its power....

Here a national interest of very nearly the first magnitude is involved. It can be protected only by national action in concert with that of another power. The subject matter is only transitorily within the State and has no permanent habitat therein. But for the treaty and the statute there soon might be no birds for any powers to deal with. We see nothing in the Constitution that compels the Government to sit by while a food supply is cut off and the protectors of our forests and our crops are destroyed. It is not sufficient to rely upon the States. The reliance is vain, and were it otherwise, the question is whether the United States is forbidden to act. We are of opinion that the treaty and statute must be upheld.

Decree affirmed.

Mr. Justice Van Devanter and Mr. Justice Pitney dissent.

UNITED STATES v. BELMONT, 301 U.S. 324 (1937). On November 16, 1933 President Roosevelt and Maxim Litvinov executed an agreement whereby the United States first gave recognition to the U.S.S.R. In addition, by this agreement the U.S.S.R. Assigned to the United States its claims against Americans who held funds of Russian companies whose assets were confiscated by the Soviets after the revolution.

The United States brought an action based on this agreement to recover money which the Petrograd Metal Works, a Russian corporation, had deposited with the New York banker, August Belmont. The lower federal courts dismissed this action on the ground that recovery of these claims would be contrary to the policy and law of the State of New York which denied effect to decrees of foreign governments purporting to confiscate property in the state. The United States Supreme Court reversed. The opinion by Justice Sutherland included the following:

"We do not pause to inquire whether in fact there was any policy of the State of New York to be infringed, since we are of opinion that no state policy can prevail against the international compact here involved....

"A treaty signifies 'a compact made between two or more independent nations with a view to the public welfare.' Altman & Co. v. United States, 224 U.S. 583, 600. But an international compact, as this was, is not always a treaty which requires the participation of the Senate. There are many such compacts, of which a protocol, a *modus vivendi*, a postal convention, and agreements like that now under consideration are illustrations. See 5 Moore, *Int.Law Digest,* 210–221....

"Plainly, the external powers of the United States are to be exercised without regard to state laws or policies. The supremacy of a treaty in this respect has been recognized from the beginning.... And while this rule in respect of treaties is established by the express language of cl. 2, Art. VI, of the Constitution, the same rule would result in the case of all international compacts and agreements from the very fact that complete power over international affairs is in the national government and is not and cannot be subject to any curtailment or interference on the part of the several states. Compare United States v. Curtiss–Wright Export Corp., 299 U.S. 304, 316, et seq."

UNITED STATES v. PINK, 315 U.S. 203 (1942). The United States brought a further action on the Roosevelt–Litvinov agreement to recover the funds of the New York branch of a Russian Insurance Company. The New York court dismissed the action because of its rule, mentioned above, barring effect to foreign expropriation decrees. The Supreme Court again reversed. The opinion by Justice Douglas relied upon the above language of the Belmont case, and added:

"A treaty is a 'Law of the Land' under the supremacy clause (Art. 6, Cl. 2) of the Constitution. Such international compacts and agreements as the Litvinov Assignment have a similar dignity. . . .

". . . the action of New York tends to restore some of the precise irritants which had long affected the relations between these two great nations and which the policy of recognition was designed to eliminate.

". . . If state action could defeat or alter our foreign policy, serious consequences might ensue. The nation as a whole would be held to answer if a State created difficulties with a foreign power . . . Certainly, the conditions for 'enduring friendship' between the nations, which the policy of recognition in this instance was designed to effectuate, are not likely to flourish where, contrary to national policy, a lingering atmosphere of hostility is created by state action."

REID v. COVERT, 354 U.S. 1 (1957). Mrs. Covert, a civilian, killed her husband, a sergeant at a U.S. air base in England where she was residing with him. Her conviction by court–martial was challenged on the ground that it violated the guaranties of indictment and trial by jury as provided by Article III and the Fifth Amendment. A companion case involved a similar conviction of Mrs. Smith for the murder of her husband in Japan. The convictions were reversed and an opinion by Black, J. (joined by Warren, C.J., Douglas and Brennan, JJ.) Contained the following discussion regarding the constitutional status of international agreements:

"At the time of Mrs. Covert's alleged offense, an executive agreement was in effect between the United States and Great Britain which permitted United States' military courts to exercise exclusive jurisdiction over offenses committed in Great Britain by American servicemen or their dependents. For its part, the United States agreed that these military courts would be willing and able to try and to punish all offenses against the laws of Great Britain by such persons. In all material respects, the same situation existed in Japan when Mrs. Smith killed her husband. Even though a court-martial does not give an accused trial by jury and other Bill of Rights protections, the Government contends that Art. 2(11) of the UCMJ, insofar as it provides for the military trial of dependents accompanying the armed forces in Great Britain and Japan, can be sustained as legislation which is necessary and proper to carry out the United States' obligations under the international agreements made with those countries. The obvious and decisive answer to this, of course, is that no agreement with a foreign nation can confer power on the Congress, or on any other branch of Government, which is free from the restraints of the Constitution.

"Article VI, the Supremacy Clause of the Constitution, declares:

" 'This Constitution, and the Laws of the United States which shall be made in Pursuance thereof; and all Treaties made, or which shall be made,

[handwritten note in right margin:] quoted case in class

under the Authority of the United States, shall be the supreme Law of the Land;....'

"There is nothing in this language which intimates that treaties and laws enacted pursuant to them do not have to comply with the provisions of the Constitution. Nor is there anything in the debates which accompanied the drafting and ratification of the Constitution which even suggests such a result. These debates as well as the history that surrounds the adoption of the treaty provision in Article VI make it clear that the reason treaties were not limited to those made in 'pursuance' of the Constitution was so that the agreements made by the United States under the Articles of Confederation, including the important peace treaties which concluded the Revolutionary War, would remain in effect. It would be manifestly contrary to the objectives of those who created the Constitution, as well as those who were responsible for the Bill of Rights— let alone alien to our entire constitutional history and tradition—to construe Article VI as permitting the United States to exercise power under an international agreement without observing constitutional prohibitions. In effect, such construction would permit amendment of that document in a manner not sanctioned by Article V. The prohibitions of the Constitution were designed to apply to all branches of the National Government and they cannot be nullified by the Executive or by the Executive and the Senate combined....

"There is nothing in Missouri v. Holland, 252 U.S. 416, which is contrary to the position taken here. There the Court carefully noted that the treaty involved was not inconsistent with any specific provision of the Constitution. The Court was concerned with the Tenth Amendment which reserves to the States or the people all power not delegated to the National Government. To the extent that the United States can validly make treaties, the people and the States have delegated their power to the National Government and the Tenth Amendment is no barrier...."

Missouri v. Holland

THE UNITED NATIONS AND THE TREATY POWER

The UN Charter, Art. 55, states that "The United Nations shall promote ... universal respect for, and observance of, human rights and fundamental freedoms for all without distinction as to race, sex, language, or religion." By Article 56, all members "pledge themselves to take joint and separate action in cooperation with the Organization for the achievement of the purposes set forth in Article 55." In Fujii v. State, 217 P.2d 481 (Cal.App.1950), an intermediate court of appeal in California held the state's discriminatory land law invalid on the ground that the UN Charter was self-executing. The California Supreme Court affirmed the judgment, but on the ground that the state law violated the Fourteenth Amendment, 38 Cal.2d 718, 242 P.2d 617 (1952).

Work in the United Nations toward the drafting of a Covenant on Human Rights[a] and Genocide Convention, and some of the implications of the *Belmont* and *Pink* cases, generated alarm in some quarters over the scope of the power to make treaties and other international agreements. As a result, various proposals were made to amend the Constitution. On March 5, 1956, the Senate

a. Chafee, *Federal and State Powers and the U.N. Covenant on Human Rights,* 1951 Wis.L.Rev. 389, 623 (1951); Schwelb, *International Conventions on Human Rights,* 9 Int. & Comp.L.Q. 654 (1960). A striking example of the impact on internal law of the European Convention on Human Rights is reported in Golsong, *The European Convention in a German Court,* 33 Brit.Yearb. of Int.L. 317 (1957) (deportation of person convicted of crime (homosexuality) who had recently married would violate his right under the Convention "to respect for his private and family life").

Judiciary Committee favorably reported the following proposed constitutional amendment:

> "Sec. 1. A provision of a treaty or other international agreement which conflicts with any provision of this Constitution shall not be of any force or effect.

> "Sec. 2. On the question of advising and consenting to the ratification of a treaty, the vote shall be determined by yeas and nays, and the names of the persons voting for and against shall be entered on the journal of the Senate."

The next year Senator Bricker proposed a more detailed amendment which included a provision that, "A treaty or other international agreement shall have legislative effect within the United States as a law thereof only through legislation, except to the extent that the Senate shall provide affirmatively, in its resolution advising and consenting to a treaty, that a treaty shall have legislative effect."

None of the proposed amendments received the requisite two-thirds majority vote.[b]

Does the language in *Reid v. Covert,* supra, show that no amendment was necessary?

E. THE PROPERTY POWER

Kleppe v. New Mexico

426 U.S. 529, 96 S.Ct. 2285, 49 L.Ed.2d 34 (1976).

Mr. Justice Marshall delivered the opinion of the Court.

At issue in this case is whether Congress exceeded its powers under the Constitution in enacting the Wild Free–Roaming Horses and Burros Act.

I.

The Wild Free–Roaming Horses and Burros Act (the Act), 85 Stat. 649–651, 16 U.S.C. (Supp. IV) §§ 1331–1340, was enacted in 1971 to protect "all unbranded and unclaimed horses and burros on public lands of the United States," § 2(b) of the Act, 16 U.S.C. § 1332(b), from "capture, branding, harassment, or death." § 1 of the Act, 16 U.S.C. § 1331. The Act provides that all such horses and burros on the public lands administered by the Secretary of the Interior through the Bureau of Land Management (BLM) or by the Secretary of Agriculture through the Forest Service are committed to the jurisdiction of the respective Secretaries, who are "directed to protect and manage [the animals] as components of the public lands . . . in a manner that is

---

b. The debate over the proper scope of the treaty power produced voluminous and heated discussion. See e.g. Holman, *Treaty Law–Making; A Blank Check for Writing a New Constitution,* 36 A.B.A.J. 707 (1950). Finch, *The Treaty Clause Amendment: The Case for the Association,* 38 A.B.A.J. 467 (1952); Hatch, *The Treaty Power and the Constitution; The Case for Amendment,* 40 A.B.A.J. 207 (1954); Chafee, *Amending the Constitution to Cripple Treaties,* 12 La.L.Rev. 345 (1952); Sutherland, *Restricting the Trea-ty Power,* 65 Harv.L.Rev. 1305 (1952); Dean, *Amending the Treaty Power,* 6 Stanford L.Rev. 589 (1954); Nelson, *Subject–Matter Limitation upon the Treaty–Making Power,* 11 J.Pub.L. 122 (1962); Henkin, *Treaty Makers and the Law Makers: The Law of the Land and Foreign Relations,* 107 U. of Pa. L.Rev. 903 (1959); McLaughlin, *Scope of the Treaty Power in the United States,* 43 Minn. L.Rev. 651 (1959). See also Henkin, *Foreign Affairs and the United States Constitution* (2d ed. 1996) 185–214.

designed to achieve and maintain a thriving natural ecological balance on the public lands." § 3(a) of the Act, 16 U.S.C. § 1333(a). If protected horses or burros "stray from public lands onto privately owned land, the owners of such land may inform the nearest federal marshall or agent of the Secretary, who shall arrange to have the animals removed." § 4 of the Act, 16 U.S.C. § 1334. . . .

The differences between the [New Mexico] Livestock Board and the Secretaries came to a head in February 1974. On February 1, 1974, a New Mexico rancher, Kelley Stephenson, was informed by BLM that several unbranded burros had been seen near Taylor Well, where Stephenson watered his cattle. Taylor Well is on federal property, and Stephenson had access to it and some 8,000 surrounding acres only through a grazing permit issued pursuant to the Taylor Grazing Act, 48 Stat. 1270, as amended, 43 U.S.C. § 315b. After BLM made it clear to Stephenson that it would not remove the burros and after he personally inspected the Taylor Well area, Stephenson complained to the Livestock Board that the burros were interfering with his livestock operation by molesting his cattle and eating their feed.

Thereupon the Board rounded up and removed 19 unbranded and unclaimed burros pursuant to the New Mexico Estray Law. Each burro was seized on the public lands of the United States and, as the director of the Board conceded, each burro fit the definition of a wild free-roaming burro under § 2(b) of the Act. App. 43. On February 18, 1974, the Livestock Board, pursuant to its usual practice, sold the burros at a public auction. After the sale, BLM asserted jurisdiction under the Act and demanded that the Board recover the animals and return them to the public lands.

On March 4, 1974, appellees filed a complaint in the United States District Court for the District of New Mexico seeking a declaratory judgment that the Wild Free–Roaming Horses and Burros Act is unconstitutional and an injunction against its enforcement. A three-judge court was convened pursuant to 28 U.S.C. § 2282.

Following an evidentiary hearing, the District Court held the Act unconstitutional and permanently enjoined the Secretary of the Interior (the Secretary) from enforcing its provisions. . . . We . . . now reverse.

II.

The Property Clause of the Constitution provides that "Congress shall have Power to dispose of and make all needful Rules and Regulations respecting the Territory or other Property belonging to the United States." U.S. Const., Art. IV, § 3, cl. 2. . . .

For these reasons, Congress determined to preserve and protect the wild free-roaming horses and burros on the public lands of the United States. The question under the Property Clause is whether this determination can be sustained as a "needful" regulation "respecting" the public lands. In answering this question, we must remain mindful that, while courts must eventually pass upon them, determinations under the Property Clause are entrusted primarily to the judgment of Congress.

Appellees argue that the Act cannot be supported by the Property Clause. They contend that the Clause grants Congress essentially two kinds of power: (1) the power to dispose of and make incidental rules regarding the use of federal property; and (2) the power to protect federal property. According to appellees, the first power is not broad enough to support legislation protecting wild animals that live on federal property; and the second power is not implicated since the Act is designed to protect the animals, which are not themselves federal property, and not the public lands. As an initial matter, it is far from clear that the Act was not passed in part to protect the public lands of the United States or that Congress cannot assert a property interest in the regulated horses and burros superior to that of the State. But we need not consider whether the Act can be upheld on either of these grounds, for we reject appellees' narrow reading of the Property Clause....

In brief, beyond the dicta [in two cases], appellees have presented no support for their position that the Clause grants Congress only the power to dispose of, to make incidental rules regarding the use of, and to protect federal property. This failure is hardly surprising, for the Clause, in broad terms, gives Congress the power to determine what are "needful" rules "respecting" the public lands. And while the furthest reaches of the power granted by the Property Clause have not yet been definitively resolved, we have repeatedly observed that "[t]he power over the public lands thus entrusted to Congress is without limitations."

The decided cases have supported this expansive reading. It is the Property Clause, for instance, that provides the basis for governing the territories of the United States. Hooven & Allison Co. v. Evatt, 324 U.S. 652, 673–674 (1945). And even over public land within the States, "[t]he general Government doubtless has a power over its own property analogous to the police power of the several States, and the extent to which it may go in the exercise of such power is measured by the exigencies of the particular case." Camfield v. United States, 167 U.S. 518, 525 (1897). We have noted, for example, that the Property Clause gives Congress the power over the public lands "to control their occupancy and use, to protect them from trespass and injury and to prescribe the conditions upon which others may obtain rights in them.... "Utah Power & Light Co. v. United States, 243 U.S. 389, 405 (1917). And we have approved legislation respecting the public lands "[i]f it be found necessary for the protection of the public, or of intending settlers [on the public lands]." Camfield v. United States, 167 U.S., at 525. In short, Congress exercises the powers both of a proprietor and of a legislature over the public domain. Alabama v. Texas, 347 U.S., at 273; Sinclair v. United States, 279 U.S. 263, 297 (1929); United States v. Midwest Oil Co., 236 U.S. 459, 474 (1915). Although the Property Clause does not authorize "an exercise of a general control over public policy in a State," it does permit "an exercise of the complete power which Congress has over particular public property entrusted to it." United States v. San Francisco, 310 U.S., at 30 (footnote omitted). In our view, the "complete power" that Congress has over public lands necessarily includes the power to regulate and protect the wildlife living there....

F. OTHER FEDERAL POWERS

1. FISCAL POWERS

NORMAN v. BALTIMORE & OHIO RAILROAD CO., 294 U.S. 240 (1935). By the Joint Resolution of June 5, 1933, Congress attempted to nullify the effect of "gold clauses"[a] in contracts for the payment of money. The Resolution (one of a series of measures relating to the currency) provided that such contracts "shall be discharged, dollar for dollar, in any coin or currency

---

a. A "gold clause" is a provision in a contract entitling the creditor to payment in currency of equivalent value, in terms of gold, to the currency in circulation at the time the contract was made. The purpose is to protect the creditor against devaluation of the currency.

which at the time of payment is legal tender for public and private debts''. The Court sustained this measure as applied to contracts previously entered into between private parties. On the question of the power of Congress to establish a monetary system, the Court observed:

"... It is unnecessary to review the historic controversy as to the extent of this power, or again to go over the ground traversed by the Court in reaching the conclusion that the Congress may make treasury notes legal tender in payment of debts previously contracted, as well as of those subsequently contracted, whether that authority be exercised in course of war or in time of peace.[b] Knox v. Lee, 12 Wall. 457; Juilliard v. Greenman, 110 U.S. 421. We need only consider certain postulates upon which that conclusion rested.

"The Constitution grants to the Congress power 'To coin money, regulate the value thereof, and of foreign coin.' Art. I, § 8, par. 5. But the Court in the legal tender cases did not derive from that express grant alone the full authority of the Congress in relation to the currency. The Court found the source of that authority in all the related powers conferred upon the Congress and appropriate to achieve 'the great objects for which the government was framed,'—'a national government, with sovereign powers.' McCulloch v. Maryland, 4 Wheat. 316, 404–407; Knox v. Lee, supra, pp. 532, 536; Julliard v. Greenman, supra, p. 438. The broad and comprehensive national authority over the subjects of revenue, finance and currency is derived from the aggregate of the powers granted to the Congress, embracing the powers to lay and collect taxes, to borrow money, to regulate commerce with foreign nations and among the several States, to coin money, regulate the value thereof, and of foreign coin, and fix the standards of weights and measures, and the added express power 'to make all laws which shall be necessary and proper for carrying into execution' the other enumerated powers. Juilliard v. Greenman, supra, pp. 439, 440.

"The Constitution 'was designed to provide the same currency, having a uniform legal value in all the States.' It was for that reason that the power to regulate the value of money was conferred upon the Federal government, while the same power, as well as the power to emit bills of credit, was withdrawn from the States. The States cannot declare what shall be money, or regulate its value. Whatever power there is over the currency is vested in the Congress. Knox v. Lee, supra, p. 545. Another postulate of the decision in that case is that the Congress has power 'to enact that the government's promises to pay money shall be, for the time being, equivalent in value to the representative of value determined by the coinage acts, or to multiples thereof.' Id., p. 553. Or, as was stated in the *Juilliard* case, supra, p. 447, the Congress is empowered 'to issue the obligations of the United States in such form, and to impress upon them such qualities as currency for the purchase of merchandise and the payment of debts, as accord with the usage of sovereign governments.' The authority to impose requirements of uniformity and parity is an essential feature of this control of the currency. The Congress is authorized to provide 'a sound and

b. The Legal Tender Acts, passed during the Civil War, made United States notes (greenbacks) legal tender for debts, with certain exceptions. The acts were held invalid as applied to antecedent debts in Hepburn v. Griswold, 8 Wall. 603 (1869). The Court (then composed of eight justices) rendered the decision by a 5 to 3 vote. The Hepburn decision was overruled (5 to 4) in Legal Tender Cases, 12 Wall. 457 (1871), President Grant having appointed two new members of the Court, one of whom (Strong, J.) wrote the opinion. The struggles in the Court over the legal tender issue are described in Fairman, *Mr. Justice Miller and the Supreme Court,* Chap. 7 (1939) and the same author's Reconstruction and Reunion 1864–88, Part I, 677–775 (1971). See also Ratner, *Was the Supreme Court Packed by President Grant?,* 50 Pol. Sci.Q. 343 (1935).

uniform currency for the country,' and to 'secure the benefit of it to the people by appropriate legislation.' Veazie Bank v. Fenno, 8 Wall. 533, 549. . . .

"Dealing with the specific question as to the effect of the legal tender acts upon contracts made before their passage, that is, those for the payment of money generally, the Court, in the legal tender cases, recognized the possible consequences of such enactments in frustrating the expected performance of contracts,—in rendering them 'fruitless or partially fruitless.' The Court pointed out that the exercise of the powers of Congress may affect 'apparent obligations' of contracts in many ways. The Congress may pass bankruptcy acts. The Congress may declare war, or, even in peace, pass non-intercourse acts, or direct an embargo, which may operate seriously upon existing contracts. And the Court reasoned that if the legal tender acts 'were justly chargeable with impairing contract obligations, they would not, for that reason, be forbidden, unless a different rule is to be applied to them from that which has hitherto prevailed in the construction of other powers granted by the fundamental law.' The conclusion was that contracts must be understood as having been made in reference to the possible exercise of the rightful authority of the Government, and that no obligation of a contract 'can extend to the defeat' of that authority. Knox v. Lee, supra, pp. 549–551. . . ."

2. NATURALIZATION

Article I, § 8, Clause 4, provides that Congress shall have power to "establish a uniform Rule of Naturalization." From the beginning the Court said that the power of Naturalization is vested exclusively in Congress to the exclusion of the states. Chirac v. Chirac's Lessee, 15 U.S. (2 Wheat.) 259, 269 (1817). The Court has also said that "Naturalization is a privilege, to be given, qualified or withheld as Congress may determine, and which the alien may claim as of right only upon compliance with the terms which Congress imposes." United States v. Mcintosh, 283 U.S. 605, 615 (1931).

The problems of defining citizenship and of expatriation and denaturalization will be considered in Chapter 8, infra.

3. REGULATION OF ALIENS

KLEINDIENST v. MANDEL, 408 U.S. 753 (1972). The Court upheld the Attorney General's refusal to waive a statutory provision excluding aliens who advocate world communism and grant a visa to a person invited to speak to an academic meeting in the United States. The Court noted that "Mandel personally, as an unadmitted and nonresident alien, had no constitutional right of entry to this country as a nonimmigrant or otherwise." In response to the argument that the first amendment rights of persons in this country who wished to hear Mandel were involved, the court said, in part:

"Recognition that First Amendment rights are implicated, however, is not dispositive of our inquiry here. In accord with ancient principles of the international law of nation-states, the Court in The Chinese Exclusion Case, 130 U.S. 581, 609 (1889), and in Fong Yue Ting v. United States, 149 U.S. 698 (1893), held broadly ... that the power to exclude aliens is 'inherent in sovereignty, necessary for maintaining normal international relations and defending the country against foreign encroachments and dangers—a power to be exercised exclusively by the political branches of government. . . .' Since that time, the Court's general reaffirmations of this principle have been legion. The Court without exception has sustained Congress' 'plenary power to make rules for the admission of aliens and to exclude those who possess those characteristics which Congress has forbidden.' Boutilier v. Immigration and Naturalization Service, 387 U.S. 118, 123 (1967). '[O]ver no conceivable subject is the legislative power of Congress more complete than it is over' the admission of aliens. Oceanic Navigation Co. v. Stranahan, 214 U.S. 320, 339 (1909). In Lem Moon Sing v. United States, 158 U.S. 538, 547 (1895), the first Mr. Justice Harlan said: 'The power of Congress to exclude aliens altogether from the United States, or to prescribe the terms and conditions upon which they may come to this country, and to have its declared policy in that regard enforced exclusively through executive officers, without judicial intervention, is settled by our previous adjudications.' Mr. Justice Frankfurter ably articulated this history in Galvan v. Press, 347 U.S. 522 (1954), a deportation case, and we can do no better. After suggesting, that 'much could be said for the view' that due process places some limitations on congressional power in this area 'were we writing on a clean slate,' he continued:

" 'But the slate is not clean. As to the extent of the power of Congress under review, there is not merely 'a page of history' . . . but a whole volume. Policies pertaining to the entry of aliens and their right to remain here are peculiarly concerned with the political conduct of government. In the enforcement of these policies, the Executive Branch of the Government must respect the procedural safeguards of due process. . . . But that the formulation of these policies is entrusted exclusively to Congress has become about as firmly embedded in the legislative and judicial tissues of our body politic as any aspect of our government. . . .'

" 'We are not prepared to deem ourselves wiser or more sensitive to human rights than our predecessors, especially those who have been most zealous in protecting civil liberties under the Constitution, and must therefore under our constitutional system recognize congressional power in dealing with aliens. . . .'

"We are not inclined in the present context to reconsider this line of cases. . . ."[a]

4. THE ADMIRALTY POWER

Article III, § 2 provides that "the judicial power shall extend . . . to all cases of admiralty and maritime jurisdiction. . . ." Although in form only a grant of jurisdiction to the courts, the admiralty clause early became recognized as a basis for national legislation. "The framers of the Constitution did not contemplate that the maritime law should remain unalterable. The purpose was to place the entire subject, including its substantive as well as its procedural features, under national control. From the beginning the grant was regarded as implicitly investing legislative power for that purpose in the United States. When the Constitution was adopted, the existing maritime law became the law of the United States subject to power in Congress to modify or supplement it as experience or changing conditions might require. But in amending and revising the maritime law, the Congress necessarily acts within a sphere restricted by the concept of the admiralty and maritime jurisdiction." Detroit Trust Co. v. Barlum S.S. Co. (The Thomas Barlum), 293 U.S. 21, 43–44 (1934).

This interpretation of the admiralty clause sustained the power of Congress to legislate with respect to events or transactions occurring on navigable waters of the United States (defined as including only those capable in fact of being used for interstate or foreign commerce) whether or not the particular

---

a. The constitutional limitations upon the power of Congress to classify aliens who have been admitted to the country and im- pose special burdens on them is considered in Chapter 10, infra.

event or transaction occurred in interstate commerce. Thus in In re Garnett, 141 U.S. 1, 12 (1891), the Court upheld the Limited Liability Act as applied to all vessels on inland waters, saying:

> "It is unnecessary to invoke the power given to Congress to regulate commerce with foreign nations, and among the several States, in order to find authority to pass the law in question. The Act of Congress which limits the liability of ship owners was passed in amendment of the maritime law of the country, and the power to make such amendments is co-extensive with that law. It is not confined to the boundaries or class of subjects which limit and characterize the power to regulate commerce; but, in maritime matters, it extends to all matters and places to which the maritime law extends."

For a discussion of the early development, see Note, *From Judicial Grant to Legislative Power: The Admiralty Clause in the Nineteenth Century,* 67 Harv. L.Rev. 1214 (1954).

It may be that this is all ancient history of minimal modern relevance to federal power. It has been suggested that "the conception of the commerce power that now prevails would probably suffice, without reference to any inference from the admiralty judicial power, to validate every statutory enactment in question." Gilmore & Black, *The Law of Admiralty* 47 (2d ed. 1975). This suggestion is reinforced by Kaiser Aetna v. United States, 444 U.S. 164, 170–174 (1979), in which the Court said: "Reference to the navigability of a waterway adds little if anything to the breadth of Congress' regulatory power over interstate commerce. It has long been settled that Congress has extensive authority over this Nation's waters under the Commerce Clause." The Court added: "[A] wide spectrum of economic activities 'affect' interstate commerce and thus are susceptible of congressional regulation under the Commerce Clause irrespective of whether navigation, or, indeed, water, is involved. The cases that discuss Congress' paramount authority to regulate waters used in interstate commerce are consequently best understood when viewed in terms of more traditional Commerce Clause analysis than by reference to whether the stream in fact is capable of supporting navigation or may be characterized as 'navigable water of the United States.' "[1]

5. THE COPYRIGHT AND PATENT POWERS

ELDRED v. ASHCROFT, 537 U.S. 186 (2003). Under the 1998 Copyright Term Extension Act (CTEA), Congress increased by 20 years the general duration of copyright protection—for both existing and future copyrights—over that contained in the 1976 Copyright Act, from a term measured from the work's creation until 50 years after the author's death to a term measured from the work's creation until 70 years after the author's death. The Court upheld the CTEA over the objection that Congress, by extending the duration of *existing* copyrights, had exceeded its power under Art. I, § 8, cl. 8, to bestow copyright protection only "for limited Times."[a] Justice Ginsburg's majority opinion said, in part:

"Petitioners' argument essentially reads into the text of the Copyright Clause the command that a time prescription, once set, becomes forever 'fixed'

---

1. Congress also has extensive power over American Indians based on its power to regulate commerce "with the Indian Tribes." No attempt is made to look at the work of the Supreme Court in this area. See generally F. Cohen, *Handbook of Federal Indian Law* (1982 ed.).

a. The Court also rejected a First Amendment challenge to the CTEA, which is discussed infra, p. 359.

or 'inalterable.' The word 'limited,' however, does not convey a meaning so constricted. At the time of the Framing, that word meant what it means today: 'confine[d] within certain bounds,' 'restrain[ed],' or 'circumscribe[d].'

"... History reveals an unbroken congressional practice of granting to authors of works with existing copyrights the benefit of term extensions so that all under copyright protection will be governed evenhandedly under the same regime. [T]he First Congress accorded the protections of the Nation's first federal copyright statute to existing and future works alike. 1790 Act § 1. Since then, Congress has regularly applied duration extensions to both existing and future copyrights. 1831 Act ...; 1909 Act ...; 1976 Act ...[6]

"Because the Clause empowering Congress to confer copyrights also authorizes patents, congressional practice with respect to patents informs our inquiry. We count it significant that early Congresses extended the duration of numerous individual patents as well as copyrights.... The courts saw no 'limited Times' impediment to such extensions; renewed or extended terms were upheld in the early days, for example, by Chief Justice Marshall and Justice Story sitting as circuit justices....

"Further, although prior to the instant case this Court did not have occasion to decide whether extending the duration of existing copyrights complies with the 'limited Times' prescription, the Court has found no constitutional barrier to the legislative expansion of existing patents. *McClurg v. Kingsland*, 1 How. 202 (1843)....

"... Guided by text, history, and precedent, we cannot agree with petitioners' submission that extending the duration of existing copyrights is categorically beyond Congress' authority under the Copyright Clause.

"Satisfied that the CTEA complies with the 'limited Times' prescription, we turn now to whether it is a rational exercise of the legislative authority conferred by the Copyright Clause. On that point, we defer substantially to Congress....

"The CTEA reflects judgments of a kind Congress typically makes, judgments we cannot dismiss as outside the Legislature's domain.... [A] key factor in the CTEA's passage was a 1993 European Union (EU) directive instructing EU members to establish a copyright term of life plus 70 years.... Consistent with the Berne Convention, the EU directed its members to deny this longer term to the works of any non-EU country whose laws did not secure the same extended term.... By extending the baseline United States copyright term to life plus 70 years, Congress sought to ensure that American authors would receive the same copyright protection in Europe as their European counterparts. The CTEA may also provide greater incentive for American and other authors to create and disseminate their work in the United States....

"In addition to international concerns, Congress passed the CTEA in light of demographic, economic, and technological changes ... and rationally credited projections that longer terms would encourage copyright holders to invest in the restoration and public distribution of their works...."

6. Moreover, the precise duration of a federal copyright has never been fixed at the time of the initial grant....

CHAPTER 5

State Sovereignty and Federal Regulation

SECTION 1. State Immunity From Federal Regulation

STATE REGULATORY IMMUNITY, 1936–1985

United States v. California, 297 U.S. 175 (1936), sustained a penalty imposed on a state-owned railroad for violation of the Federal Safety Appliance Act. It was not necessary to address California's argument that the non-profit operation of the railroad was performance of "a public function in its sovereign capacity." It was irrelevant whether operation of the railroad was in a sovereign or private capacity. "The sovereign power of the states is necessarily diminished to the extent of the grants of power to the federal government in the Constitution." Chief Justice Stone's opinion for the Court also rejected any analogy to a state's constitutional immunity from federal taxation. "[W]e look to the activities in which the states have traditionally engaged as marking the boundary of the restriction upon the federal taxing power. But there is no such limitation upon the plenary power to regulate commerce. The state can no more deny the power if its exercise has been authorized by Congress than can an individual."

Until 1976, constitutional attacks on application of federal regulatory statutes to state activities were uniformly rejected. Case v. Bowles, 327 U.S. 92 (1946), upheld application of a maximum price under the Emergency Price Control Act as applied to a timber sale by the State of Washington. State of California v. Taylor, 353 U.S. 553 (1957), rejected a challenge to application of the Railway Labor Act to a state owned railroad. (The Act made wages and working conditions subject to a collective bargaining agreement rather than state civil service laws.) Parden v. Terminal Ry. of Alabama State Docks Dept., 377 U.S. 184 (1964), held that a state owned railroad was subject to liability to an injured employee under the Federal Employers' Liability Act. Maryland v. Wirtz, 392 U.S. 183 (1968), sustained application of the wage and hour provisions of the Fair Labor Standards Act to employees of public schools and hospitals. Fry v. United States, 421 U.S. 542 (1975) sustained application of the Economic Stabilization Act to limit wage increases of public employees.

Significantly, however, Justices Douglas and Stewart dissented in Maryland v. Wirtz, arguing that the commerce power could not be exercised in a way that unreasonably interfered with a state's sovereign power. Justice Rehnquist's dissent in Fry v. United States argued that Maryland v. Wirtz should be overruled. Finally, a footnote to Justice Marshall's opinion for the Court in *Fry* contained this statement: "While the Tenth Amendment has been characterized as 'a truism,' ... United States v. Darby, 312 U.S. 100, 124 (1941), it is not without significance. The Amendment expressly declares the constitutional policy that Congress may not exercise power in a fashion that impairs the

National League of Cities v. Usery

States' integrity or their ability to function effectively in a federal system...."
427 U.S. at 547, n. 7.

Maryland v. Wirtz was overruled in the five to four decision of the Court in National League of Cities v. Usery, 426 U.S. 833 (1976). 1974 amendments to the Fair Labor Standards Act extended the Act's maximum hour and minimum wage provisions to employees of the states and their political subdivisions. The Court held that the Act could not constitutionally be applied to state employees performing traditional governmental functions. Justice Rehnquist's opinion for the Court relied on the statement in the footnote to the *Fry* opinion that Congress could not "exercise power in a fashion that impairs the States' integrity or their ability to function effectively in a federal system." Applying the Fair Labor Standards Act to state employees would impose costs and limit flexibility. The Court concluded that "insofar as the challenged amendments operate to directly displace the States' freedom to structure integral operations in areas of traditional government functions, they are not within the authority granted Congress by" the Commerce Clause. Justice Blackmun joined the Court's opinion, but admitted in a concurrence that he was "not untroubled by certain possible implications of the Court's opinion." He explained that he joined the Court's opinion because he read it to adopt "a balancing approach" that permitted federal regulation "where the federal interest is demonstrably greater and where state ... compliance with imposed federal standards would be essential." Justice Brennan's dissent, joined by Justices White and Marshall, argued that "restraints upon exercise by Congress of its plenary commerce power lies in the political process and not in the judicial process.... [T]he political branches of our Government are structured to protect the interests of the States, as well as the Nation as a whole, and ... the States are fully able to protect their own interests...." Justice Stevens' dissent emphasized the absence of standards distinguishing invalid federal regulation and "federal regulation of state activities that I consider unquestionably permissible."

In Hodel v. Virginia Surface Mining and Reclamation Association, Inc., 452 U.S. 264 (1981), the Court summarized three requirements that *National League of Cities* challenges to federal legislation must meet in order to succeed. "First, there must be a showing that the challenged statute regulates the 'states as states.' ... Second, the federal regulation must address matters that are indisputably 'attribute[s] of state sovereignty.' ... And, third, it must be apparent that the States' compliance with the federal law would directly impair their ability 'to structure integral operations in areas of traditional governmental functions.'" (The Court also mentioned in a footnote the possibility that a challenged federal law would be valid, even if all three requirements were satisfied, under the balancing test suggested by Justice Blackmun's concurrence in *National League of Cities*.)

In United Transportation Union v. Long Island Railroad Co., 455 U.S. 678 (1982), the Court was unanimous, concluding that a state-owned railroad was not immune from application of the labor provisions of the Railway Labor Act, because operation of a railroad was not a "traditional" state function. In Equal Employment Opportunity Commission v. Wyoming, 460 U.S. 226 (1983), however, the Court divided five to four with Justice Blackmun joining the four *National League of Cities* dissenters to form the majority. The Court upheld a 1974 amendment to the Age Discrimination in Employment Act extending the Act to state employees. The case arose out of the involuntary retirement of a state game warden at age 55, which violated provisions of the Act forbidding involuntary retirement prior to age 70. Justice Brennan's opinion for the Court concluded that state compliance with the Act would be less costly than, and would not impair flexibility to the same degree as, the minimum wage and maximum hour provisions at issue in *National League of Cities.* The prohibitions of the Age Discrimination Act thus involved federal intrusion that was "sufficiently less serious" and did not impair states' ability to structure their integral operations—a question that "must depend . . . on considerations of degree."

Garcia v. San Antonio Metropolitan Transit Authority

469 U.S. 528, 105 S.Ct. 1005, 83 L.Ed.2d 1016 (1985).

Justice Blackmun DELIVERED THE OPINION OF THE COURT.

We revisit in these cases an issue raised in National League of Cities v. Usery, 426 U.S. 833 (1976). In that litigation, this Court, by a sharply divided vote, ruled that the Commerce Clause does not empower Congress to enforce the minimum-wage and overtime provisions of the Fair Labor Standards Act (FLSA) against the States "in areas of traditional governmental functions." Id., at 852. Although *National League of Cities* supplied some examples of "traditional governmental functions," it did not offer a general explanation of how a "traditional" function is to be distinguished from a "nontraditional" one. Since then, federal and state courts have struggled with the task, thus imposed, of identifying a traditional function for purposes of state immunity under the Commerce Clause.

In the present cases, a Federal District Court concluded that municipal ownership and operation of a mass-transit system is a traditional governmental function and thus, under *National League of Cities,* is exempt from the obligations imposed by the FLSA. Faced with the identical question, three Federal Courts of Appeals and one state appellate court have reached the opposite conclusion.

Our examination of this "function" standard applied in these and other cases over the last eight years now persuades us that the attempt to draw the boundaries of state regulatory immunity in terms of "traditional governmental function" is not only unworkable but is inconsistent with established principles of federalism and, indeed, with those very federalism principles on which *National League of Cities* purported to rest. That case, accordingly, is overruled.

I

. . .

The FLSA obligations of public mass-transit systems like SATS were expanded in 1974 when Congress provided for the progressive repeal of the surviving overtime exemption for mass-transit employees. Fair Labor Standards Amendments of 1974, § 21(b), 88 Stat. 68. Congress simultaneously brought the States and their subdivisions further within the ambit of the FLSA by extending FLSA coverage to virtually all state and local-government employees. §§ 6(a)(1) and (6), 88 Stat. 58, 60, 29 U.S.C. §§ 203(d) and (x). SATS complied with the FLSA's overtime requirements until 1976, when this Court, in *National League of Cities,* supra, overruled *Maryland v. Wirtz,* and held that the FLSA could not be applied constitutionally to the "traditional governmental functions" of state and local governments. Four months after *National League of Cities* was handed down, SATS informed its employees that the decision relieved SATS of its overtime obligations under the FLSA.

. . .

... After initial argument, the cases were restored to our calendar for reargument, and the parties were requested to brief and argue the following additional question:

"Whether or not the principles of the Tenth Amendment as set forth in National League of Cities v. Usery, 426 U.S. 833 (1976), should be reconsidered?" ...

II

The controversy in the present cases has focused on the third *Hodel* requirement—that the challenged federal statute trench on "traditional governmental functions." ...

Thus far, this Court itself has made little headway in defining the scope of the governmental functions deemed *protected* under *National League of Cities*. In that case the Court set forth examples of protected and unprotected functions, ... but provided no explanation of how those examples were identified. The only other case in which the Court has had occasion to address the problem is *Long Island*. We there observed: "The determination of whether a federal law impairs a state's authority with respect to 'areas of traditional [state] functions' may at times be a difficult one." ... The accuracy of that statement is demonstrated by this Court's own difficulties in *Long Island* in developing a workable standard for "traditional governmental functions." We relied in large part there on "the *historical reality* that the operation of railroads is not among the functions *traditionally* performed by state and local governments," but we simultaneously disavowed "a static historical view of state functions generally immune from federal regulation." ... Finally, having disclaimed a rigid reliance on the historical pedigree of state involvement in a particular area, we nonetheless found it appropriate to emphasize the extended historical record of federal involvement in the field of rail transportation.

Many constitutional standards involve "undoubte[d] ... gray areas," ... and, despite the difficulties that this Court and other courts have encountered so far, it normally might be fair to venture the assumption that case-by-case development would lead to a workable standard for determining whether a particular governmental function should be immune from federal regulation under the Commerce Clause....

. . .

The distinction the Court discarded as unworkable in the field of tax immunity has proved no more fruitful in the field of regulatory immunity under the Commerce Clause. Neither do any of the alternative standards that might be employed to distinguish between protected and unprotected governmental functions appear manageable. We rejected the possibility of making immunity turn on a purely historical standard of "tradition" in *Long Island,* and properly so. The most obvious defect of a historical approach to state immunity is that it prevents a court from accommodating changes in the historical functions of States, changes that have resulted in a number of once-private functions like education being assumed by the States and their subdivisions. At the same time, the only apparent virtue of a rigorous historical standard, namely, its promise of a reasonably objective measure for state immunity, is illusory. Reliance on history as an organizing principle results in linedrawing of the most arbitrary sort; the genesis of state governmental functions stretches over a historical continuum from before the Revolution to the present, and courts would have to decide by fiat precisely how longstanding a pattern of state involvement had to be for federal regulatory authority to be defeated.

A nonhistorical standard for selecting immune governmental functions is likely to be just as unworkable as is a historical standard. . . .

We believe, however, that there is a more fundamental problem at work here, a problem that explains why the Court was never able to provide a basis for the governmental-proprietary distinction in the inter-governmental tax immunity cases and why an attempt to draw similar distinctions with respect to federal regulatory authority under *National League of Cities* is unlikely to succeed regardless of how the distinctions are phrased. The problem is that neither the governmental-proprietary distinction nor any other that purports to separate out important governmental functions can be faithful to the role of federalism in a democratic society. The essence of our federal system is that within the realm of authority left open to them under the Constitution, the States must be equally free to engage in any activity that their citizens choose for the common weal, no matter how unorthodox or unnecessary anyone else— including the judiciary—deems state involvement to be. Any rule of state immunity that looks to the "traditional," "integral," or "necessary" nature of governmental functions inevitably invites an unelected federal judiciary to make decisions about which state policies it favors and which ones it dislikes. . . .

We therefore now reject, as unsound in principle and unworkable in practice, a rule of state immunity from federal regulation that turns on a judicial appraisal of whether a particular governmental function is "integral" or "traditional." Any such rule leads to inconsistent results at the same time that it disserves principles of democratic self-governance, and it breeds inconsistency precisely because it is divorced from those principles. If there are to be limits on the Federal Government's power to interfere with state functions—as undoubtedly there are—we must look elsewhere to find them. We accordingly return to the underlying issue that confronted this Court in *National League of Cities*—the manner in which the Constitution insulates States from the reach of Congress' power under the Commerce Clause.

III

The central theme of *National League of Cities* was that the States occupy a special position in our constitutional system and that the scope of Congress' authority under the Commerce Clause must reflect that position. Of course, the Commerce Clause by its specific language does not provide any special limitation on Congress' actions with respect to the States. . . . It is equally true, however, that the text of the Constitution provides the beginning rather than the final answer to every inquiry into questions of federalism. . . .

What has proved problematic is not the perception that the Constitution's federal structure imposes limitations on the Commerce Clause, but rather the nature and content of those limitations. . . . In *National League of Cities* itself, for example, the Court concluded that decisions by a State concerning the wages and hours of its employees are an "undoubted attribute of state sovereignty." . . . The opinion did not explain what aspects of such decisions made them such an "undoubted attribute," and the Court since then has remarked on the uncertain scope of the concept. . . .

We doubt that courts ultimately can identify principled constitutional limitations on the scope of Congress' Commerce Clause powers over the States merely by relying on *a priori* definitions of state sovereignty. In part, this is because of the elusiveness of objective criteria for "fundamental" elements of state sovereignty, a problem we have witnessed in the search for "traditional governmental functions." There is, however, a more fundamental reason: the sovereignty of the States is limited by the Constitution itself. A variety of sovereign powers, for example, are withdrawn from the States by Article I, § 10. Section 8 of the same Article works an equally sharp contraction of state sovereignty by authorizing Congress to exercise a wide range of legislative powers and (in conjunction with the Supremacy Clause of Article VI) to displace contrary state legislation. . . .

The States unquestionably do "retai[n] a significant measure of sovereign authority." . . . They do so, however, only to the extent that the Constitution has not divested them of their original powers and transferred those powers to the Federal Government. . . .

. . .

When we look for the States' "residuary and inviolable sovereignty," The Federalist No. 39, p. 285 (B. Wright ed. 1961) (J. Madison), in the shape of the constitutional scheme rather than in predetermined notions of sovereign power, a different measure of state sovereignty emerges. Apart from the limitation on federal authority inherent in the delegated nature of Congress' Article I powers, the principal means chosen by the Framers to ensure the role of the States in the federal system lies in the structure of the Federal Government itself. It is no novelty to observe that the composition of the Federal Government was designed in large part to protect the States from overreaching by Congress.[11] The Framers thus gave the States a role in the selection both of the Executive and the Legislative Branches of the Federal Government. The States were vested with indirect influence over the House of Representatives and the Presidency by their control of electoral qualifications and their role in presidential elections. U.S. Const., Art. I, § 2, and Art. II, § 1. They were given more direct influence in the Senate, where each State received equal representation and each Senator was to be selected by the legislature of his State. Art. I, § 3. The significance attached to the States' equal representation in the Senate is underscored by the prohibition of any constitutional amendment divesting a State of equal representation without the State's consent. Art. V.

The extent to which the structure of the Federal Government itself was relied on to insulate the interests of the States is evident in the views of the Framers. . . . In short, the Framers chose to rely on a federal system in which special restraints on federal power over the States inhered principally in the workings of the National Government itself, rather than in discrete limitations on the objects of federal authority. State sovereign interests, then, are more properly protected by procedural safeguards inherent in the structure of the federal system than by judicially created limitations on federal power.

The effectiveness of the federal political process in preserving the States' interests is apparent even today in the course of federal legislation. On the one hand, the States have been able to direct a substantial proportion of federal revenues into their own treasuries in the form of general and program-specific grants in aid. The federal role in assisting state and local governments is a longstanding one; Congress provided federal land grants to finance state governments from the beginning of the Republic, and direct cash grants were

---

11. See, e.g., J. Choper, Judicial Review and the National Political Process 175–184 (1980); Wechsler, The Political Safeguards of Federalism: The Role of the States in the Composition and Selection of the National Government, 54 Colum.L.Rev. 543 (1954); La Pierre, The Political Safeguards of Federalism Redux: Intergovernmental Immunity and the States as Agents of the Nation, 60 Wash. U.L.Q. 779 (1982).

awarded as early as 1887 under the Hatch Act. In the past quarter-century alone, federal grants to States and localities have grown from $7 billion to $96 billion. As a result, federal grants now account for about one-fifth of state and local government expenditures. The States have obtained federal funding for such services as police and fire protection, education, public health and hospitals, parks and recreation, and sanitation. Moreover, at the same time that the States have exercised their influence to obtain federal support, they have been able to exempt themselves from a wide variety of obligations imposed by Congress under the Commerce Clause. For example, the Federal Power Act, the National Labor Relations Act, the Labor–Management Reporting and Disclosure Act, the Occupational Safety and Health Act, the Employee Retirement Insurance Security Act, and the Sherman Act all contain express or implied exemptions for States and their subdivisions. The fact that some federal statutes such as the FLSA extend general obligations to the States cannot obscure the extent to which the political position of the States in the federal system has served to minimize the burdens that the States bear under the Commerce Clause.

We realize that changes in the structure of the Federal Government have taken place since 1789, not the least of which has been the substitution of popular election of Senators by the adoption of the Seventeenth Amendment in 1913, and that these changes may work to alter the influence of the States in the federal political process. Nonetheless, against this background, we are convinced that the fundamental limitation that the constitutional scheme imposes on the Commerce Clause to protect the "States as States" is one of process rather than one of result. Any substantive restraint on the exercise of Commerce Clause powers must find its justification in the procedural nature of this basic limitation, and it must be tailored to compensate for possible failings in the national political process rather than to dictate a "sacred province of state autonomy." EEOC v. Wyoming, 460 U.S., at 236.

Insofar as the present cases are concerned, then, we need go no further than to state that we perceive nothing in the overtime and minimum-wage requirements of the FLSA, as applied to SAMTA, that is destructive of state sovereignty or violative of any constitutional provision. SAMTA faces nothing more than the same minimum-wage and overtime obligations that hundreds of thousands of other employers, public as well as private, have to meet.

. . .

IV

This analysis makes clear that Congress' action in affording SAMTA employees the protections of the wage and hour provisions of the FLSA contravened no affirmative limit on Congress' power under the Commerce Clause. The judgment of the District Court therefore must be reversed.

These cases do not require us to identify or define what affirmative limits the constitutional structure might impose on federal action affecting the States under the Commerce Clause. . . .

We do not lightly overrule recent precedent. We have not hesitated, however, when it has become apparent that a prior decision has departed from a proper understanding of congressional power under the Commerce Clause. . . . Due respect for the reach of congressional power within the federal system mandates that we do so now.

National League of Cities v. Usery, 426 U.S. 833 (1976), is overruled. The judgment of the District Court is reversed, and these cases are remanded to that court for further proceedings consistent with this opinion.

It is so ordered.

Justice Powell, with whom The Chief Justice, Justice Rehnquist, and Justice O'Connor join, dissenting.

The Court today, in its 5–4 decision, overrules National League of Cities v. Usery, 426 U.S. 833 (1976), a case in which we held that Congress lacked authority to impose the requirements of the Fair Labor Standards Act on state and local governments. Because I believe this decision substantially alters the federal system embodied in the Constitution, I dissent.

I

There are, of course, numerous examples over the history of this Court in which prior decisions have been reconsidered and overruled. There have been few cases, however, in which the principle of *stare decisis* and the rationale of recent decisions were ignored as abruptly as we now witness. . . .

. . .

Whatever effect the Court's decision may have in weakening the application of *stare decisis,* it is likely to be less important than what the Court has done to the Constitution itself. A unique feature of the United States is the *federal* system of government guaranteed by the Constitution and implicit in the very name of our country. Despite some genuflecting in Court's opinion to the concept of federalism, today's decision effectively reduces the Tenth Amendment to meaningless rhetoric when Congress acts pursuant to the Commerce Clause. . . .

II

. . .

B

Today's opinion does not explain how the States' role in the electoral process guarantees that particular exercises of the Commerce Clause power will not infringe on residual State sovereignty. Members of Congress are elected from the various States, but once in office they are members of the federal government. Although the States participate in the Electoral College, this is hardly a reason to view the President as a representative of the States' interest against federal encroachment. We noted recently "the hydraulic pressure inherent within each of the separate Branches to exceed the outer limits of its power. . . ." Immigration and Naturalization Service v. Chadha, 462 U.S. 919, 951 (1983). The Court offers no reason to think that this pressure will not operate when Congress seeks to invoke its powers under the Commerce Clause, notwithstanding the electoral role of the States.[9]

9. At one time in our history, the view that the structure of the federal government sufficed to protect the States might have had a somewhat more practical, although not a more logical, basis. Professor Wechsler, whose seminal article in 1954 proposed the view adopted by the Court today, predicated his argument on assumptions that simply do not accord with current reality. Professor Wechsler wrote: "National action has . . . always been regarded as exceptional in our polity, an intrusion to be justified by some necessity, the special rather than the ordinary case." Wechsler, The Political Safeguards of Federalism: The Role of the States in the Composition and Selection of the National Government, 54 Colum.L.Rev. 543, 544 (1954). Not only is the premise of this

... The fact that Congress generally does not transgress constitutional limits on its power to reach State activities does not make judicial review any less necessary to rectify the cases in which it does do so. The States' role in our system of government is a matter of constitutional law, not of legislative grace. "The powers not delegated to the United States by the Constitution, nor prohibited by it to the States, are reserved to the States, respectively, or to the people." U.S. Const., Amend. 10.

More troubling than the logical infirmities in the Court's reasoning is the result of its holding, i.e., that federal political officials, invoking the Commerce Clause, are the sole judges of the limits of their own power. This result is inconsistent with the fundamental principles of our constitutional system. ... At least since *Marbury v. Madison* it has been the settled province of the federal judiciary "to say what the law is" with respect to the constitutionality of acts of Congress.... In rejecting the role of the judiciary in protecting the States from federal overreaching, the Court's opinion offers no explanation for ignoring the teaching of the most famous case in our history.

III

A

. . .

... Far from being "unsound in principle," judicial enforcement of the Tenth Amendment is essential to maintaining the federal system so carefully designed by the Framers and adopted in the Constitution.

B

. . .

The Framers believed that the separate sphere of sovereignty reserved to the States would ensure that the States would serve as an effective "counterpoise" to the power of the federal government. The States would serve this essential role because they would attract and retain the loyalty of their citizens. The roots of such loyalty, the Founders thought, were found in the objects peculiar to state government. ...

Thus, the harm to the States that results from federal overreaching under the Commerce Clause is not simply a matter of dollars and cents. ... Nor is it a matter of the wisdom or folly of certain policy choices. Rather, by usurping functions traditionally performed by the States, federal overreaching under the Commerce Clause undermines the constitutionally mandated balance of power

view clearly at odds with the proliferation of national legislation over the past 30 years, but "a variety of structural and political changes in this century have combined to make Congress particularly *insensitive* to state and local values." Advisory Comm'n on Intergovernmental Relations [ACIR], Regulatory Federalism: Policy, Process, Impact and Reform 50 (1984). The adoption of the Seventeenth Amendment (providing for direct election of senators), the weakening of political parties on the local level, and the rise of national media, among other things, have made Congress increasingly less representative of State and local interests, and more

likely to be responsive to the demands of various national constituencies. Id., at 50–51. As one observer explained, "As Senators and members of the House develop independent constituencies among groups such as farmers, businessmen, laborers, environmentalists, and the poor, each of which generally supports certain national initiatives, their tendency to identify with state interests and the positions of state officials is reduced." Kaden, "Federalism in the Courts: Agenda for the 1980s," in ACIR, The Future of Federalism in the '80s, at 97 (1981).

. . .

between the States and the federal government, a balance designed to protect our fundamental liberties.

. . .

IV

The question presented in this case is whether the extension of the FLSA to the wages and hours of employees of a city-owned transit system unconstitutionally impinges on fundamental state sovereignty. . . .

I return now to the balancing test approved in *National League of Cities* and accepted in *Hodel, Long Island R. Co.,* and FERC v. Mississippi. The Court does not find in this case that the "federal interest is demonstrably greater." 426 U.S., at 856 (Blackmun, J., concurring). No such finding could have been made, for the state interest is compelling. The financial impact on States and localities of displacing their control over wages, hours, overtime regulations, pensions, and labor relations with their employees could have serious, as well as unanticipated, effects on state and local planning, budgeting, and the levying of taxes. As we said in *National League of Cities,* federal control of the terms and conditions of employment of State employees also inevitably "displaces state policies regarding the manner in which [States] will structure delivery of those governmental services that citizens require." . . .

The Court emphasizes that municipal operation of an intracity mass transit system is relatively new in the life of our country. It nevertheless is a classic example of the type of service traditionally provided by local government. It is *local* by definition. It is indistinguishable in principle from the traditional services of providing and maintaining streets, public lighting, traffic control, water, and sewerage systems. . . .

V

. . .

As I view the Court's decision today as rejecting the basic precepts of our federal system and limiting the constitutional role of judicial review, I dissent.

Justice Rehnquist, dissenting.

I join both Justice Powell's and Justice O'Connor's thoughtful dissents. Justice Powell's reference to the "balancing test" approved in *National League of Cities* is not identical with the language in that case, which recognized that Congress could not act under its commerce power to infringe on certain fundamental aspects of state sovereignty that are essential to "the States' separate and independent existence." Nor is either test, or Justice O'Connor's suggested approach, precisely congruent with Justice Blackmun's views in 1976, when he spoke of a balancing approach which did not outlaw federal power in areas "where the federal interest is demonstrably greater." But under any one of these approaches the judgment in this case should be affirmed, and I do not think it incumbent on those of us in dissent to spell out further the fine points of a principle that will, I am confident, in time again command the support of a majority of this Court.

Justice O'Connor, with whom Justice Powell and Justice Rehnquist join, dissenting.

The Court today surveys the battle scene of federalism and sounds a retreat. Like Justice Powell, I would prefer to hold the field and, at the very least, render a little aid to the wounded. I join Justice Powell's opinion. I also write separately to note my fundamental disagreement with the majority's views of federalism and the duty of this Court.

. . .

. . . [S]tate autonomy is a relevant factor in assessing the means by which Congress exercises its powers.

This principle requires the Court to enforce affirmative limits on federal regulation of the States to complement the judicially crafted expansion of the interstate commerce power. . . . The Court today rejects *National League of Cities* and washes its hands of all efforts to protect the States. In the process, the Court opines that unwarranted federal encroachments on state authority are and will remain " 'horrible possibilities that never happen in the real world.' " There is ample reason to believe to the contrary.

. . .

The problems of federalism in an integrated national economy are capable of more responsible resolution than holding that the States as States retain no status apart from that which Congress chooses to let them retain. The proper resolution, I suggest, lies in weighing state autonomy as a factor in the balance when interpreting the means by which Congress can exercise its authority on the States as States. It is insufficient, in assessing the validity of congressional regulation of a State pursuant to the commerce power, to ask only whether the same regulation would be valid if enforced against a private party. That reasoning, embodied in the majority opinion, is inconsistent with the spirit of our Constitution. . . .

It has been difficult for this Court to craft bright lines defining the scope of the state autonomy protected by *National League of Cities*. Such difficulty is to be expected whenever constitutional concerns as important as federalism and the effectiveness of the commerce power come into conflict. Regardless of the difficulty, it is and will remain the duty of this Court to reconcile these concerns in the final instance. . . . I share Justice Rehnquist's belief that this Court will in time again assume its constitutional responsibility.

I respectfully dissent.

. . .

New York v. United States

505 U.S. 144, 112 S.Ct. 2408, 120 L.Ed.2d 120 (1992).

Justice O'Connor delivered the opinion of the Court.

This case implicates one of our Nation's newest problems of public policy and perhaps our oldest question of constitutional law. The public policy issue involves the disposal of radioactive waste: In this case, we address the constitutionality of three provisions of the Low–Level Radioactive Waste Policy Amendments Act of 1985, Pub.L. 99–240, 99 Stat. 1842, 42 U.S.C. § 2021b et seq. The constitutional question is as old as the Constitution: It consists of discerning the proper division of authority between the Federal Government and the States. We conclude that while Congress has substantial power under the Constitution to encourage the States to provide for the disposal of the radioactive waste generated within their borders, the Constitution does not confer upon Congress the ability simply to compel the States to do so. We therefore find that only two of the Act's three provisions at issue are consistent with the Constitution's allocation of power to the Federal Government.

I

We live in a world full of low level radioactive waste. Radioactive material is present in luminous watch dials, smoke alarms, measurement devices, medical fluids, research materials, and the protective gear and construction materials used by workers at nuclear power plants. Low level radioactive waste is generated by the Government, by hospitals, by research institutions, and by various industries. The waste must be isolated from humans for long periods of time, often for hundreds of years. Millions of cubic feet of low level radioactive waste must be disposed of each year. . . .

. . . [S]ince 1979 only three disposal sites—those in Nevada, Washington, and South Carolina—have been in operation. Waste generated in the rest of the country must be shipped to one of these three sites for disposal. . . . In 1979, both the Washington and Nevada sites were forced to shut down temporarily, leaving South Carolina to shoulder the responsibility of storing low level radioactive waste produced in every part of the country. The Governor of South Carolina, understandably perturbed, ordered a 50% reduction in the quantity of waste accepted at the Barnwell site. The Governors of Washington and Nevada announced plans to shut their sites permanently.

Faced with the possibility that the Nation would be left with no disposal sites for low level radioactive waste, Congress responded by enacting the Low–Level Radioactive Waste Policy Act, . . . Relying largely on a report submitted by the National Governors' Association, Congress declared a federal policy of holding each State "responsible for providing for the availability of capacity either within or outside the State for the disposal of low-level radioactive waste generated within its borders," and found that such waste could be disposed of "most safely and efficiently . . . on a regional basis." § 4(a)(1) . . . The 1980 Act authorized States to enter into regional compacts that, once ratified by Congress, would have the authority beginning in 1986 to restrict the use of their disposal facilities to waste generated within member States. § 4(a)(2)(B) . . . The 1980 Act included no penalties for States that failed to participate in this plan.

By 1985, only three approved regional compacts had operational disposal facilities; not surprisingly, these were the compacts formed around South Carolina, Nevada, and Washington, the three sited States. The following year, the 1980 Act would have given these three compacts the ability to exclude waste from nonmembers, and the remaining 31 States would have had no assured outlet for their low level radioactive waste. With this prospect looming, Congress once again took up the issue of waste disposal. The result was the legislation challenged here, the Low–Level Radioactive Waste Policy Amendments Act of 1985.

The 1985 Act was again based largely on a proposal submitted by the National Governors' Association. In broad outline, the Act embodies a compromise among the sited and unsited States. The sited States agreed to extend for seven years the period in which they would accept low level radioactive waste from other States. In exchange, the unsited States agreed to end their reliance on the sited States by 1992.

The mechanics of this compromise are intricate. The Act directs: "Each State shall be responsible for providing, either by itself or in cooperation with other States, for the disposal of . . . low-level radioactive waste generated within the State," . . ., with the exception of certain waste generated by the Federal Government . . . The Act authorizes States to "enter into such [interstate] compacts as may be necessary to provide for the establishment and operation of regional disposal facilities for low-level radioactive waste." . . . For an additional seven years beyond the period contemplated by the 1980 Act, from the beginning of 1986 through the end of 1992, the three existing disposal sites "shall make disposal capacity available for low-level radioactive waste generated by any source," with certain exceptions not relevant here. . . . But the three States in which the disposal sites are located are permitted to exact a graduated surcharge for waste arriving from outside the regional compact. . . . After the seven-year transition period expires, approved regional compacts may exclude radioactive waste generated outside the region. . . . The Act provides three types of incentives to encourage the States to comply with their statutory obligation to provide for the disposal of waste generated within their borders.

1. Monetary incentives. One quarter of the surcharges collected by the sited States must be transferred to an escrow account held by the Secretary of Energy. . . . The Secretary then makes payments from this account to each State that has complied with a series of deadlines. By July 1, 1986, each State was to have ratified legislation either joining a regional compact or indicating an intent to develop a disposal facility within the State. . . . By January 1, 1988, each unsited compact was to have identified the State in which its facility would be located, and each compact or stand-alone State was to have developed a siting plan and taken other identified steps. . . . By January 1, 1990, each State or compact was to have filed a complete application for a license to operate a disposal facility, or the Governor of any State that had not filed an application was to have certified that the State would be capable of disposing of all waste generated in the State after 1992. . . . The rest of the account is to be paid out to those States or compacts able to dispose of all low level radioactive waste generated within their borders by January 1, 1993. . . . Each State that has not met the 1993 deadline must either take title to the waste generated within its borders or forfeit to the waste generators the incentive payments it has received. . . .

2. Access incentives. The second type of incentive involves the denial of access to disposal sites. States that fail to meet the July 1986 deadline may be charged twice the ordinary surcharge for the remainder of 1986 and may be denied access to disposal facilities thereafter. . . . States that fail to meet the 1988 deadline may be charged double surcharges for the first half of 1988 and quadruple surcharges for the second half of 1988, and may be denied access thereafter. . . . States that fail to meet the 1990 deadline may be denied access. . . . Finally, States that have not filed complete applications by January 1, 1992, for a license to operate a disposal facility, or States belonging to compacts that have not filed such applications, may be charged triple surcharges. . . .

3. The take title provision. The third type of incentive is the most severe. The Act provides: "If a State (or, where applicable, a compact region) in which low-level radioactive waste is generated is unable to provide for the disposal of all such waste generated within such State or compact region by January 1, 1996, each State in which such waste is generated, upon the request of the generator or owner of the waste, shall take title to the waste, be obligated to take possession of the waste, and shall be liable for all damages directly or indirectly incurred by such generator or owner as a consequence of the failure of the State to take possession of the waste as soon after January 1, 1996, as the generator or owner notifies the State that the waste is available for shipment." . . . These three incentives are the focus of petitioners' constitutional challenge.

In the seven years since the Act took effect, Congress has approved nine regional compacts, encompassing 42 of the States. All six unsited compacts and four of the unaffiliated States have met the first three statutory milestones.

New York, a State whose residents generate a relatively large share of the Nation's low level radioactive waste, did not join a regional compact. Instead, the State complied with the Act's requirements by enacting legislation providing for the siting and financing of a disposal facility in New York. The State has identified five potential sites, three in Allegany County and two in Cortland County. Residents of the two counties oppose the State's choice of location.

Petitioners—the State of New York and the two counties—filed this suit against the United States in 1990. They sought a declaratory judgment that the Act is inconsistent with the Tenth ... Amendment to the Constitution, ... and with the Guarantee Clause of Article IV of the Constitution. The States of Washington, Nevada, and South Carolina intervened as defendants. The District Court dismissed the complaint. The Court of Appeals affirmed....

II

A

These questions can be viewed in either of two ways. In some cases the Court has inquired whether an Act of Congress is authorized by one of the powers delegated to Congress in Article I of the Constitution.... In other cases the Court has sought to determine whether an Act of Congress invades the province of state sovereignty reserved by the Tenth Amendment.... In a case like this one, involving the division of authority between federal and state governments, the two inquiries are mirror images of each other. If a power is delegated to Congress in the Constitution, the Tenth Amendment expressly disclaims any reservation of that power to the States; if a power is an attribute of state sovereignty reserved by the Tenth Amendment, it is necessarily a power the Constitution has not conferred on Congress....

It is in this sense that the Tenth Amendment "states but a truism that all is retained which has not been surrendered." United States v. Darby, 312 U.S. 100, 124 (1941). ... This has been the Court's consistent understanding: "The States unquestionably do retai[n] a significant measure of sovereign authority ... to the extent that the Constitution has not divested them of their original powers and transferred those powers to the Federal Government." Garcia v. San Antonio Metropolitan Transit Authority, supra, at 549 ...

... The Tenth Amendment ... restrains the power of Congress, but this limit is not derived from the text of the Tenth Amendment itself, which, as we have discussed, is essentially a tautology. Instead, the Tenth Amendment confirms that the power of the Federal Government is subject to limits that may, in a given instance, reserve power to the States. The Tenth Amendment thus directs us to determine, as in this case, whether an incident of state sovereignty is protected by a limitation on an Article I power.

. . .

This framework has been sufficiently flexible over the past two centuries to allow for enormous changes in the nature of government. The Federal Government undertakes activities today that would have been unimaginable to the Framers ... Yet the powers conferred upon the Federal Government by the Constitution were phrased in language broad enough to allow for the expansion of the Federal Government's role. Among the provisions of the Constitution that have been particularly important in this regard, three concern us here.

First, the Constitution allocates to Congress the power "[t]o regulate Commerce ... among the several States." ... As interstate commerce has become ubiquitous, activities once considered purely local have come to have effects on the national economy, and have accordingly come within the scope of Congress' commerce power. . . .

Second, the Constitution authorizes Congress "to pay the Debts and provide for the . . . general Welfare of the United States." . . . While the spending power is "subject to several general restrictions articulated in our cases," . . . these restrictions have not been so severe as to prevent the regulatory authority of Congress from generally keeping up with the growth of the federal budget.

. . .

Finally, the Constitution provides that "the Laws of the United States . . . shall be the supreme Law of the Land . . . any Thing in the Constitution or Laws of any State to the Contrary notwithstanding." . . . As the Federal Government's willingness to exercise power within the confines of the Constitution has grown, the authority of the States has correspondingly diminished to the extent that federal and state policies have conflicted. . . .

. . .

B

Petitioners do not contend that Congress lacks the power to regulate the disposal of low level radioactive waste. . . . Petitioners likewise do not dispute that under the Supremacy Clause Congress could, if it wished, pre-empt state radioactive waste regulation. Petitioners contend only that the Tenth Amendment limits the power of Congress to regulate in the way it has chosen. Rather than addressing the problem of waste disposal by directly regulating the generators and disposers of waste, petitioners argue, Congress has impermissibly directed the States to regulate in this field.

Most of our recent cases interpreting the Tenth Amendment have concerned the authority of Congress to subject state governments to generally applicable laws. The Court's jurisprudence in this area has traveled an unsteady path. See . . . San Antonio Metropolitan Transit Authority . . . (overruling *National League of Cities*) . . . This case presents no occasion to apply or revisit the holdings of any of these cases, as this is not a case in which Congress has subjected a State to the same legislation applicable to private parties. . . .

This case instead concerns the circumstances under which Congress may use the States as implements of regulation; that is, whether Congress may direct or otherwise motivate the States to regulate in a particular field or a particular way. Our cases have established a few principles that guide our resolution of the issue.

1

As an initial matter, Congress may not simply "commandee[r] the legislative processes of the States by directly compelling them to enact and enforce a federal regulatory program." Hodel v. Virginia Surface Mining & Reclamation Assn., Inc., 452 U.S. 264, 288 (1981). In *Hodel,* the Court upheld the Surface Mining Control and Reclamation Act of 1977 precisely because it did not "commandeer" the States into regulating mining. The Court found that "the States are not compelled to enforce the steep-slope standards, to expend any state funds, or to participate in the federal regulatory program in any manner whatsoever. If a State does not wish to submit a proposed permanent program that complies with the Act and implementing regulations, the full regulatory burden will be borne by the Federal Government." ...

    . . .

... While Congress has substantial powers to govern the Nation directly, including in areas of intimate concern to the States, the Constitution has never been understood to confer upon Congress the ability to require the States to govern according to Congress' instructions....

Indeed, the question whether the Constitution should permit Congress to employ state governments as regulatory agencies was a topic of lively debate among the Framers. Under the Articles of Confederation, Congress lacked the authority in most respects to govern the people directly. In practice, Congress "could not directly tax or legislate upon individuals; it had no explicit 'legislative' or 'governmental' power to make binding 'law' enforceable as such." Amar, Of Sovereignty and Federalism, 96 Yale L.J. 1425, 1447 (1987).

The inadequacy of this governmental structure was responsible in part for the Constitutional Convention. ...

The Convention generated a great number of proposals for the structure of the new Government, but two quickly took center stage. Under the Virginia Plan, as first introduced by Edmund Randolph, Congress would exercise legislative authority directly upon individuals, without employing the States as intermediaries.... Under the New Jersey Plan, as first introduced by William Paterson, Congress would continue to require the approval of the States before legislating, as it has under the Articles of Confederation. ...

    . . .

In the end, the Convention opted for a Constitution in which Congress would exercise its legislative authority directly over individuals rather than over States; for a variety of reasons, it rejected the New Jersey Plan in favor of the Virginia Plan. ...

In providing for a stronger central government, therefore, the Framers explicitly chose a Constitution that confers upon Congress the power to regulate individuals, not States. As we have seen, the Court has consistently respected this choice. We have always understood that even where Congress has the authority under the Constitution to pass laws requiring or prohibiting certain acts, it lacks the power directly to compel the States to require or prohibit those acts. ... The allocation of power contained in the Commerce Clause, for example, authorizes Congress to regulate interstate commerce directly; it does not authorize Congress to regulate state governments' regulation of interstate commerce.

2

This is not to say that Congress lacks the ability to encourage a State to regulate in a particular way, or that Congress may not hold out incentives to the States as a method of influencing a State's policy choices. Our cases have identified a variety of methods, short of outright coercion, by which Congress may urge a State to adopt a legislative program consistent with federal interests. Two of these methods are of particular relevance here.

First, under Congress' spending power, "Congress may attach conditions on the receipt of federal funds." South Dakota v. Dole, 483 U.S., at 206. Such conditions must (among other requirements) bear some relationship to the purpose of the federal spending, ...; otherwise, of course, the spending power could render academic the Constitution's other grants and limits of federal authority. Where the recipient of federal funds is a State, as is not unusual today, the conditions attached to the funds by Congress may influence a State's legislative choices.... *Dole* was one such case: The Court found no constitutional flaw in a federal statute directing the Secretary of Transportation to withhold federal highway funds from States failing to adopt Congress' choice of a minimum drinking age....

Second, where Congress has the authority to regulate private activity under the Commerce Clause, we have recognized Congress' power to offer States the choice of regulating that activity according to federal standards or having state law pre-empted by federal regulation. Hodel v. Virginia Surface Mining & Reclamation Assn., Inc., supra, at 288. See also FERC v. Mississippi, supra, at 764–765. This arrangement, which has been termed "a program of cooperative federalism," *Hodel,* supra, at 289, is replicated in numerous federal statutory schemes. These include the Clean Water Act, ...; the Occupational Safety and Health Act of 1970, ... the Resource Conservation and Recovery Act of 1976, ...; and the Alaska National Interest Lands Conservation Act, ...

By either of these two methods, as by any other permissible method of encouraging a State to conform to federal policy choices, the residents of the State retain the ultimate decision as to whether or not the State will comply. If a State's citizens view federal policy as sufficiently contrary to local interests, they may elect to decline a federal grant. If state residents would prefer their government to devote its attention and resources to problems other than those deemed important by Congress, they may choose to have the Federal Government rather than the State bear the expense of a federally mandated regulatory program, and they may continue to supplement that program to the extent state law is not pre-empted. Where Congress encourages state regulation rather than compelling it, state governments remain responsive to the local electorate's preferences; state officials remain accountable to the people.

By contrast, where the Federal Government compels States to regulate, the accountability of both state and federal officials is diminished. If the citizens of New York, for example, do not consider that making provision for the disposal of radioactive waste is in their best interest, they may elect state officials who share their view. That view can always be pre-empted under the Supremacy Clause if it is contrary to the national view, but in such a case it is the Federal Government that makes the decision in full view of the public, and it will be federal officials that suffer the consequences if the decision turns out to be detrimental or unpopular. But where the Federal Government directs the States to regulate, it may be state officials who will bear the brunt of public disapproval, while the federal officials who devised the regulatory program may remain insulated from the electoral ramifications of their decision. Accountability is thus diminished when, due to federal coercion, elected state officials cannot regulate in accordance with the views of the local electorate in matters not pre-empted by federal regulation....

With these principles in mind, we turn to the three challenged provisions of the Low–Level Radioactive Waste Policy Amendments Act of 1985.

III

The parties in this case advance two quite different views of the Act. As petitioners see it, the Act imposes a requirement directly upon the States that they regulate in the field of radioactive waste disposal in order to meet Congress' mandate that "[e]ach State shall be responsible for providing ... for the disposal of ... low-level radioactive waste." ... Petitioners understand this provision as a direct command from Congress, enforceable independent of the three sets of incentives provided by the Act. Respondents, on the other hand, read this provision together with the incentives, and see the Act as affording the States three sets of choices. According to respondents, the Act permits a State to choose first between regulating pursuant to federal standards and losing the right to a share of the Secretary of Energy's escrow account; to choose second between regulating pursuant to federal standards and progressively losing access to disposal sites in other States; and to choose third between regulating pursuant to federal standards and taking title to the waste generated within the State. . . .

The Act could plausibly be understood either as a mandate to regulate or as a series of incentives. Under petitioners' view, however, . . . the Act would clearly "commandee[r] the legislative processes of the States by directly compelling them to enact and enforce a federal regulatory program." . . . We must reject this interpretation of the provision for two reasons. First, such an outcome would, to say the least, "upset the usual constitutional balance of federal and state powers." . . . Second, "where an otherwise acceptable construction of a statute would raise serious constitutional problems, the Court will construe the statute to avoid such problems unless such construction is plainly contrary to the intent of Congress." . . .

We therefore decline petitioners' invitation to construe § 2021c(a)(1)(A), alone and in isolation, as a command to the States independent of the remainder of the Act. Construed as a whole, the Act comprises three sets of "incentives" for the States to provide for the disposal of low level radioactive waste generated within their borders. We consider each in turn.

A

The first set of incentives works in three steps. First, Congress has authorized States with disposal sites to impose a surcharge on radioactive waste received from other States. Second, the Secretary of Energy collects a portion of this surcharge and places the money in an escrow account. Third, States achieving a series of milestones receive portions of this fund.

The first of these steps is an unexceptionable exercise of Congress' power to authorize the States to burden interstate commerce. . . . Whether or not the States would be permitted to burden the interstate transport of low level radioactive waste in the absence of Congress' approval, the States can clearly do so with Congress' approval, which is what the Act gives them.

The second step, the Secretary's collection of a percentage of the surcharge, is no more than a federal tax on interstate commerce, which petitioners do not claim to be an invalid exercise of either Congress' commerce or taxing power. . . .

The third step is a conditional exercise of Congress' authority under the Spending Clause: Congress has placed conditions—the achievement of the milestones—on the receipt of federal funds. Petitioners do not contend that Congress has exceeded its authority in any of the four respects our cases have identified. . . . The expenditure is for the general welfare . . .; the States are required to use the money they receive for the purpose of assuring the safe disposal of radioactive waste. . . . The conditions imposed are unambiguous . . .; the Act informs the States exactly what they must do and by when they must do it in order to obtain a share of the escrow account. The conditions imposed are reasonably related to the purpose of the expenditure, . . .; both the conditions and the payments embody Congress' efforts to address the pressing problem of radioactive waste disposal. Finally, petitioners do not claim that the conditions imposed by the Act violate any independent constitutional prohibition. . . .

The Act's first set of incentives, in which Congress has conditioned grants to the States upon the States' attainment of a series of milestones, is thus well within the authority of Congress under the Commerce and Spending Clauses. Because the first set of incentives is supported by affirmative constitutional grants of power to Congress, it is not inconsistent with the Tenth Amendment.

B

In the second set of incentives, Congress has authorized States and regional compacts with disposal sites gradually to increase the cost of access to the sites, and then to deny access altogether, to radioactive waste generated in States that do not meet federal deadlines. As a simple regulation, this provision would be within the power of Congress to authorize the States to discriminate against interstate commerce. . . . Where federal regulation of private activity is within the scope of the Commerce Clause, we have recognized the ability of Congress to offer states the choice of regulating that activity according to federal standards or having state law pre-empted by federal regulation. . . .

This is the choice presented to nonsited States by the Act's second set of incentives: States may either regulate the disposal of radioactive waste according to federal standards by attaining local or regional self-sufficiency, or their residents who produce radioactive waste will be subject to federal regulation authorizing sited States and regions to deny access to their disposal sites. The affected States are not compelled by Congress to regulate, because any burden caused by a State's refusal to regulate will fall on those who generate waste and find no outlet for its disposal, rather than on the State as a sovereign. A State whose citizens do not wish it to attain the Act's milestones may devote its attention and its resources to issues its citizens deem more worthy; the choice remains at all times with the residents of the State, not with Congress. The State need not expend any funds, or participate in any federal program, if local residents do not view such expenditures or participation as worthwhile. . . . Nor must the State abandon the field if it does not accede to federal direction; the State may continue to regulate the generation and disposal of radioactive waste in any manner its citizens see fit.

The Act's second set of incentives thus represents a conditional exercise of Congress' commerce power, along the lines of those we have held to be within Congress' authority. As a result, the second set of incentives does not intrude on the sovereignty reserved to the States by the Tenth Amendment.

C

The take title provision is of a different character. This third so-called "incentive" offers States, as an alternative to regulating pursuant to Congress' direction, the option of taking title to and possession of the low level radioactive waste generated within their borders and becoming liable for all damages waste generators suffer as a result of the States' failure to do so promptly. In this provision, Congress has crossed the line distinguishing encouragement from coercion.

The take title provision offers state governments a "choice" of either accepting ownership of waste or regulating according to the instructions of Congress. Respondents do not claim that the Constitution would authorize Congress to impose either option as a freestanding requirement. On one hand, the Constitution would not permit Congress simply to transfer radioactive waste from generators to state governments. Such a forced transfer, standing alone, would in principle be no different than a congressionally compelled subsidy from state governments to radioactive waste producers. The same is true of the provision requiring the States to become liable for the generators' damages. Standing alone, this provision would be indistinguishable from an Act of Congress directing the States to assume the liabilities of certain state residents. Either type of federal action would "commandeer" state governments into the service of federal regulatory purposes, and would for this reason be inconsistent with the Constitution's division of authority between federal and state governments. On the other hand, the second alternative held out to state governments—regulating pursuant to Congress' direction—would, standing alone, present a simple command to state governments to implement legislation enacted by Congress. As we have seen, the Constitution does not empower Congress to subject state governments to this type of instruction.

Because an instruction to state governments to take title to waste, standing alone, would be beyond the authority of Congress, and because a direct order to regulate, standing alone, would also be beyond the authority of Congress, it follows that Congress lacks the power to offer the States a choice between the two. Unlike the first two sets of incentives, the take title incentive does not represent the conditional exercise of any congressional power enumerated in the Constitution. In this provision, Congress has not held out the threat of exercising its spending power or its commerce power; it has instead held out the threat, should the States not regulate according to one federal instruction, of simply forcing the States to submit to another federal instruction. A choice between two unconstitutionally coercive regulatory techniques is no choice at all. . . .

The take title provision appears to be unique. No other federal statute has been cited which offers a state government no option other than that of implementing legislation enacted by Congress.

. . .

IV

Respondents raise a number of objections to this understanding of the limits of Congress' power.

A

The United States proposes three alternative views of the constitutional line separating state and federal authority. While each view concedes that Congress generally may not compel state governments to regulate pursuant to federal direction, each purports to find a limited domain in which such coercion is permitted by the Constitution.

First, the United States argues that the Constitution's prohibition of congressional directives to state governments can be overcome where the federal interest is sufficiently important to justify state submission. This argument contains a kernel of truth: In determining whether the Tenth Amendment limits the ability of Congress to subject state governments to generally applicable laws, the Court has in some cases stated that it will evaluate the strength of federal interests in light of the degree to which such laws would prevent the State from functioning as a sovereign; that is, the extent to which such generally applicable laws would impede a state government's responsibility to represent and be accountable to the citizens of the State. . . . The Court has more recently departed from this approach. See, e.g., . . . Garcia v. San Antonio Metropolitan Transit Authority. . . . But whether or not a particularly strong federal interest enables Congress to bring state governments within the orbit of generally applicable federal regulation, no Member of the Court has ever suggested that such a federal interest would enable Congress to command a state government to enact state regulation. No matter how powerful the federal interest involved, the Constitution simply does not give Congress the authority to require the States to regulate. The Constitution instead gives Congress the authority to regulate matters directly and to pre-empt contrary state regulation. Where a federal interest is sufficiently strong to cause Congress to legislate, it must do so directly; it may not conscript state governments as its agents.

Second, the United States argues that the Constitution does, in some circumstances, permit federal directives to state governments. Various cases are cited for this proposition, but none support it. Some of these cases discuss the well established power of Congress to pass laws enforceable in state courts. See Testa v. Katt, 330 U.S. 386 (1947).... Federal statutes enforceable in state courts do, in a sense, direct state judges to enforce them, but this sort of federal "direction" of state judges is mandated by the text of the Supremacy Clause. No comparable constitutional provision authorizes Congress to command state legislatures to legislate.

Additional cases cited by the United States discuss the power of federal courts to order state officials to comply with federal law.... Again, however, the text of the Constitution plainly confers this authority on the federal courts, the "judicial Power" of which "shall extend to all Cases, in Law and Equity, arising under this Constitution, [and] the Laws of the United States ...; [and] to Controversies between two or more States; [and] between a State and Citizens of another State." U.S. Const., Art. III, § 2. The Constitution contains no analogous grant of authority to Congress. Moreover, the Supremacy Clause makes federal law paramount over the contrary positions of state officials; the power of federal courts to enforce federal law thus presupposes some authority to order state officials to comply. ...

In sum, the cases relied upon by the United States hold only that federal law is enforceable in state courts and that federal courts may in proper circumstances order state officials to comply with federal law, propositions that by no means imply any authority on the part of Congress to mandate state regulation.

.   .   .

B

The sited State respondents focus their attention on the process by which the Act was formulated. They correctly observe that public officials representing the State of New York lent their support to the Act's enactment.... Respondents note that the Act embodies a bargain among the sited and unsited States, a compromise to which New York was a willing participant and from which New York has reaped much benefit. Respondents then pose what appears at first to be a troubling question: How can a federal statute be found an unconstitutional infringement of State sovereignty when state officials consented to the statute's enactment?

.   .   .

Where Congress exceeds its authority relative to the States ... the departure from the constitutional plan cannot be ratified by the "consent" of state officials. An analogy to the separation of powers among the Branches of the Federal Government clarifies this point. The Constitution's division of power among the three Branches is violated where one Branch invades the territory of another, whether or not the encroached-upon Branch approves the encroach-ment.... The constitutional authority of Congress cannot be expanded by the "consent" of the governmental unit whose domain is thereby narrowed, whether that unit is the Executive Branch or the States.

State officials thus cannot consent to the enlargement of the powers of Congress beyond those enumerated in the Constitution. Indeed, the facts of this case raise the possibility that powerful incentives might lead both federal and state officials to view departures from the federal structure to be in their personal interests. Most citizens recognize the need for radioactive waste disposal sites, but few want sites near their homes. As a result, while it would be well within the authority of either federal or state officials to choose where the disposal sites will be, it is likely to be in the political interest of each individual official to avoid being held accountable to the voters for the choice of location. If a federal official is faced with the alternatives of choosing a location or directing the States to do it, the official may well prefer the latter, as a means of shifting responsibility for the eventual decision. If a state official is faced with the same set of alternatives—choosing a location or having Congress direct the choice of a location—the state official may also prefer the latter, as it may permit the avoidance of personal responsibility. The interests of public officials thus may not coincide with the Constitution's intergovernmental allocation of authority. Where state officials purport to submit to the direction of Congress in this manner, federalism is hardly being advanced.

Nor does the State's prior support for the Act estop it from asserting the Act's unconstitutionality. While New York has received the benefit of the Act in the form of a few more years of access to disposal sites in other States, New York has never joined a regional radioactive waste compact. Any estoppel implications that might flow from membership in a compact, ... thus do not concern us here. The fact that the Act, like much federal legislation, embodies a compromise among the States does not elevate the Act ... to the status of an interstate agreement requiring Congress' approval under the Compact Clause.... That a party collaborated with others in seeking legislation has never been understood to estop the party from challenging that legislation in subsequent litigation.

V

Petitioners also contend that the Act is inconsistent with the Constitution's Guarantee Clause, which directs the United States to "guarantee to every State in this Union a Republican Form of Government." Because we have found the take title provision of the Act irreconcilable with the powers delegated to Congress by the Constitution and hence with the Tenth Amendment's reservation to the States of those powers not delegated to the Federal Government, we need only address the applicability of the Guarantee Clause to the Act's other two challenged provisions.

We approach the issue with some trepidation, because the Guarantee Clause has been an infrequent basis for litigation throughout our history. In most of the cases in which the Court has been asked to apply the Clause, the Court has found the claims presented to be nonjusticiable under the "political question" doctrine. See, e.g., ... Pacific States Tel. & Tel. Co. v. Oregon, 223 U.S. 118, 140–151 (1912) (challenge to initiative and referendum provisions of state constitution).

The view that the Guarantee Clause implicates only nonjusticiable political questions has its origin in Luther v. Borden, 7 How. 1 (1849), in which the Court was asked to decide, in the wake of Dorr's Rebellion, which of two rival governments was the legitimate government of Rhode Island. The Court held that "it rests with Congress," not the judiciary, "to decide what government is the established one in a State." ... Over the following century, this limited holding metamorphosed into the sweeping assertion that "[v]iolation of the great guaranty of a republican form of government in States cannot be challenged in the courts." Colegrove v. Green, 328 U.S. 549, 556 (1946) (plurality opinion).

. . .

More recently, the Court has suggested that perhaps not all claims under the Guarantee Clause present nonjusticiable political questions. See Reynolds v. Sims, 377 U.S. 533, 582 (1964) ("some questions raised under the Guarantee Clause are nonjusticiable"). . . .

We need not resolve this difficult question today. Even if we assume that petitioners' claim is justiciable, neither the monetary incentives provided by the Act nor the possibility that a State's waste producers may find themselves excluded from the disposal sites of another State can reasonably be said to deny any State a republican form of government. ... The twin threats imposed by the first two challenged provisions of the Act—that New York may miss out on a share of federal spending or that those generating radioactive waste within New York may lose out-of-state disposal outlets—do not pose any realistic risk of altering the form or the method of functioning of New York's government. Thus even indulging the assumption that the Guarantee Clause provides a basis upon which a State or its subdivisions may sue to enjoin the enforcement of a federal statute, petitioners have not made out such a claim in this case.

VI

Having determined that the take title provision exceeds the powers of Congress, we must consider whether it is severable from the rest of the Act.

. . .

... [T]he take title provision may be severed without doing violence to the rest of the Act. The Act is still operative and it still serves Congress' objective of encouraging the States to attain local or regional self-sufficiency in the disposal of low level radioactive waste. ...

VII

. . .

States are not mere political subdivisions of the United States. ...

... The Federal Government may not compel the States to enact or administer a federal regulatory program. ... The Constitution enables the Federal Government to pre-empt state regulation contrary to federal interests, and it permits the Federal Government to hold out incentives to the States as a means of encouraging them to adopt suggested regulatory schemes. It does not, however, authorize Congress simply to direct the States to provide for the disposal of the radioactive waste generated within their borders. While there may be many constitutional methods of achieving regional self-sufficiency in radioactive waste disposal, the method Congress has chosen is not one of them. The judgment of the Court of Appeals is accordingly

Affirmed in part and reversed in part.

Justice White, with whom Justice Blackmun and Justice Stevens join, concurring in part and dissenting in part.

. . .

I

My disagreement with the Court's analysis begins at the basic descriptive level of how the legislation at issue in this case came to be enacted. . . . The Low–Level Radioactive Waste Policy Act of 1980 . . ., and its amendatory Act of 1985, resulted from the efforts of state leaders to achieve a state-based set of remedies to the waste problem. They sought not federal pre-emption or intervention, but rather congressional sanction of interstate compromises they had reached.

. . .

. . . Unlike legislation that directs action from the Federal Government to the States, the 1980 and 1985 Acts reflected hard-fought agreements among States as refereed by Congress. The distinction is key, and the Court's failure properly to characterize this legislation ultimately affects its analysis of the take title provision's constitutionality.

II

. . .

. . . I am unmoved by the Court's vehemence in taking away Congress' authority to sanction a recalcitrant unsited State now that New York has reaped the benefits of the sited States' concessions.

A

In my view, New York's actions subsequent to enactment of the 1980 and 1985 Acts fairly indicate its approval of the interstate agreement process embodied in those laws within the meaning of Art. I, § 10, cl. 3. . . .

. . .

The State should be estopped from asserting the unconstitutionality of a provision that seeks merely to ensure that, after deriving substantial advantages from the 1985 Act, New York in fact must live up to its bargain by establishing an in-state low-level radioactive waste facility or assuming liability for its failure to act. . . .

. . .

III

The Court announces that it has no occasion to revisit such decisions as . . . Garcia v. San Antonio Metropolitan Transit Authority, 469 U.S. 528 (1985) . . . Although this statement sends the welcome signal that the Court does not intend to cut a wide swath through our recent Tenth Amendment precedents, it nevertheless is unpersuasive. I have several difficulties with the Court's analysis in this respect: it builds its rule around an insupportable and illogical distinction in the types of alleged incursions on state sovereignty; it derives its rule from cases that do not support its analysis; it fails to apply the appropriate tests from the cases on which it purports to base its rule; and it omits any discussion of the most recent and pertinent test for determining the take title provision's constitutionality.

The Court's distinction between a federal statute's regulation of States and private parties for general purposes, as opposed to a regulation solely on the activities of States, is unsupported by our recent Tenth Amendment cases. In no case has the Court rested its holding on such a distinction.... An incursion on state sovereignty hardly seems more constitutionally acceptable if the federal statute that "commands" specific action also applies to private parties. The alleged diminution in state authority over its own affairs is not any less because the federal mandate restricts the activities of private parties.

. . .

... In *Garcia*, we stated the proper inquiry.... [T]he Court tacitly concedes that a failing of the political process cannot be shown in this case because it refuses to rebut the unassailable arguments that the States were well able to look after themselves in the legislative process that culminated in the 1985 Act's passage.

Ultimately, I suppose, the entire structure of our federal constitutional government can be traced to an interest in establishing checks and balances to prevent the exercise of tyranny against individuals. But these fears seem extremely far distant to me in a situation such as this. ... Congress has acceded to the wishes of the States by permitting local decisionmaking rather than imposing a solution from Washington. New York itself participated and supported passage of this legislation at both the gubernatorial and federal representative levels, and then enacted state laws specifically to comply with the deadlines and timetables agreed upon by the States in the 1985 Act. For me, the Court's civics lecture has a decidedly hollow ring at a time when action, rather than rhetoric, is needed to solve a national problem.

IV

Though I disagree with the Court's conclusion that the take title provision is unconstitutional, I do not read its opinion to preclude Congress from adopting a similar measure through its powers under the Spending or Commerce Clauses.... Congress could ... condition the payment of funds on the State's willingness to take title if it has not already provided a waste disposal facility.... Similarly, should a State fail to establish a waste disposal facility by the appointed deadline ..., Congress has the power pursuant to the Commerce Clause to regulate directly the producers of the waste. Thus, ... Congress could amend the statute to say that if a State fails to meet the January 1, 1996 deadline for achieving a means of waste disposal, and has not taken title to the waste, no low-level radioactive waste may be shipped out of the State of New York.... [T]he threat of federal pre-emption may suffice to induce States to accept responsibility for failing to meet critical time deadlines for solving their low-level radioactive waste disposal problems, especially if that federal intervention also would strip state and local authorities of any input in locating sites for low-level radioactive waste disposal facilities. And of course, should Congress amend the statute to meet the Court's objection and a State refuse to act, the National Legislature will have ensured at least a federal solution to the waste management problem.

Finally, our precedents leave open the possibility that Congress may create federal rights of action in the generators of low-level radioactive waste against persons acting under color of state law for their failure to meet certain functions designated in federal-state programs.... In addition to compensating injured parties for the State's failure to act, the exposure to liability established by such suits also potentially serves as an inducement to compliance with the program mandate.

V

The ultimate irony of the decision today is that in its formalistically rigid obeisance to "federalism," the Court gives Congress fewer incentives to defer to the wishes of state officials in achieving local solutions to local problems. This legislation was a classic example of Congress acting as arbiter among the States in their attempts to accept responsibility for managing a problem of grave import.... By invalidating the measure designed to ensure compliance for recalcitrant States, such as New York, the Court upsets the delicate compromise achieved among the States and forces Congress to erect several additional formalistic hurdles to clear before achieving exactly the same objective. Because the Court's justifications for undertaking this step are unpersuasive to me, I respectfully dissent.

Justice Stevens, concurring in part and dissenting in part.

Under the Articles of Confederation, the Federal Government had the power to issue commands to the States.... Because that indirect exercise of federal power proved ineffective, the Framers of the Constitution empowered the Federal Government to exercise legislative authority directly over individuals within the States, even though that direct authority constituted a greater intrusion on State sovereignty. Nothing in that history suggests that the Federal Government may not also impose its will upon the several States as it did under the Articles. The Constitution enhanced, rather than diminished, the power of the Federal Government.

The notion that Congress does not have the power to issue "a simple command to state governments to implement legislation enacted by Congress," is incorrect and unsound. There is no such limitation in the Constitution. The Tenth Amendment surely does not impose any limit on Congress' exercise of the powers delegated to it by Article I. Nor does the structure of the constitutional order or the values of federalism mandate such a formal rule. To the contrary, the Federal Government directs state governments in many realms. The Government regulates state-operated railroads, state school systems, state prisons, state elections, and a host of other state functions. Similarly, there can be no doubt that, in time of war, Congress could either draft soldiers itself or command the States to supply their quotas of troops. I see no reason why Congress may not also command the States to enforce federal water and air quality standards or federal standards for the disposition of low-level radioactive wastes.

. . .

Printz v. United States

521 U.S. 898, 117 S.Ct. 2365, 138 L.Ed.2d 914 (1997).

Justice Scalia delivered the opinion of the Court.

The question presented in these cases is whether certain interim provisions of the Brady Handgun Violence Prevention Act, Pub.L. 103–159, 107 Stat. 1536, commanding state and local law enforcement officers to conduct background checks on prospective handgun purchasers and to perform certain related tasks, violate the Constitution.

I

The Gun Control Act of 1968 (GCA), 18 U.S.C. § 921 et seq., establishes a detailed federal scheme governing the distribution of firearms....

In 1993, Congress amended the GCA by enacting the Brady Act. The Act requires the Attorney General to establish a national instant background check system by November 30, 1998, ... and immediately puts in place certain interim provisions until that system becomes operative. Under the interim provisions, a firearms dealer who proposes to transfer a handgun must first: (1) receive from the transferee a statement (the Brady Form) ... containing the name, address and date of birth of the proposed transferee along with a sworn statement that the transferee is not among any of the classes of prohibited purchasers, ... verify the identity of the transferee by examining an identification document, ... and (3) provide the "chief law enforcement officer" (CLEO) of the transferee's residence with notice of the contents (and a copy) of the Brady Form ... With some exceptions, the dealer must then wait five business days before consummating the sale, unless the CLEO earlier notifies the dealer that he has no reason to believe the transfer would be illegal. ...

The Brady Act creates two significant alternatives to the foregoing scheme. A dealer may sell a handgun immediately if the purchaser possesses a state handgun permit issued after a background check, ... or if state law provides for an instant background check ... In States that have not rendered one of these alternatives applicable to all gun purchasers, CLEOs are required to perform certain duties. When a CLEO receives the required notice of a proposed transfer from the firearms dealer, the CLEO must "make a reasonable effort to ascertain within 5 business days whether receipt or possession would be in violation of the law, including research in whatever State and local recordkeeping systems are available and in a national system designated by the Attorney General." ... The Act does not require the CLEO to take any particular action if he determines that a pending transaction would be unlawful; he may notify the firearms dealer to that effect, but is not required to do so. If, however, the CLEO notifies a gun dealer that a prospective purchaser is ineligible to receive a handgun, he must, upon request, provide the would-be purchaser with a written statement of the reasons for that determination. ... Moreover, if the CLEO does not discover any basis for objecting to the sale, he must destroy any records in his possession relating to the transfer, including his copy of the Brady Form. ...

[T]he CLEOs for Ravalli County, Montana, and Graham County, Arizona ... filed separate actions challenging the constitutionality of the Brady Act's interim provisions. In each case, the District Court held that the provision requiring CLEOs to perform background checks was unconstitutional, but concluded that that provision was severable from the remainder of the Act, effectively leaving a voluntary background-check system in place. ... A divided panel of the Court of Appeals for the Ninth Circuit reversed, finding none of the Brady Act's interim provisions to be unconstitutional. ...

II

[T]he Brady Act purports to direct state law enforcement officers to participate, albeit only temporarily, in the administration of a federally enacted regulatory scheme. Regulated firearms dealers are required to forward Brady Forms not to a federal officer or employee, but to the CLEOs, whose obligation to accept those forms is implicit in the duty imposed upon them to make "reasonable efforts" within five days to determine whether the sales reflected in the forms are lawful. While the CLEOs are subjected to no federal requirement that they prevent the sales determined to be unlawful (it is perhaps assumed that their state-law duties will require prevention or apprehension), they are empowered to grant, in effect, waivers of the federally prescribed 5–

day waiting period for handgun purchases by notifying the gun dealers that they have no reason to believe the transactions would be illegal.

The petitioners here object to being pressed into federal service, and contend that congressional action compelling state officers to execute federal laws is unconstitutional. Because there is no constitutional text speaking to this precise question, the answer to the CLEOs' challenge must be sought in historical understanding and practice, in the structure of the Constitution, and in the jurisprudence of this Court. . . .

Petitioners contend that compelled enlistment of state executive officers for the administration of federal programs is, until very recent years at least, unprecedented. The Government contends, to the contrary, that "the earliest Congresses enacted statutes that required the participation of state officials in the implementation of federal laws." The Government's contention demands our careful consideration, since early congressional enactments "provid[e] 'contemporaneous and weighty evidence' of the Constitution's meaning," . . . Conversely if, as petitioners contend, earlier Congresses avoided use of this highly attractive power, we would have reason to believe that the power was thought not to exist.

The Government observes that statutes enacted by the first Congresses required state courts to [perform a variety of enforcement functions.] . . .

These early laws establish, at most, that the Constitution was originally understood to permit imposition of an obligation on state *judges* to enforce federal prescriptions, insofar as those prescriptions related to matters appropriate for the judicial power. That assumption was perhaps implicit in one of the provisions of the Constitution, and was explicit in another. In accord with the so-called Madisonian Compromise, Article III, § 1, established only a Supreme Court, and made the creation of lower federal courts optional with the Congress—even though it was obvious that the Supreme Court alone could not hear all federal cases throughout the United States. . . . And the Supremacy Clause, Art. VI, cl. 2, announced that "the Laws of the United States . . . shall be the supreme Law of the Land; and the Judges in every State shall be bound thereby." It is understandable why courts should have been viewed distinctively in this regard; unlike legislatures and executives, they applied the law of other sovereigns all the time. . . . The Constitution itself, in the Full Faith and Credit Clause, Art. IV, § 1, generally required such enforcement with respect to obligations arising in other States. . . .

For these reasons, we do not think the early statutes imposing obligations on state courts imply a power of Congress to impress the state executive into its service. Indeed, it can be argued that the numerousness of these statutes, contrasted with the utter lack of statutes imposing obligations on the States' executive (notwithstanding the attractiveness of that course to Congress), suggests an assumed absence of such power. The only early federal law the Government has brought to our attention that imposed duties on state executive officers is the Extradition Act of 1793, which required the "executive authority" of a State to cause the arrest and delivery of a fugitive from justice upon the request of the executive authority of the State from which the fugitive had fled. . . . That was in direct implementation, however, of the Extradition Clause of the Constitution itself, see Art. IV, § 2.

. . .

To complete the historical record, we must note that there is not only an absence of executive-commandeering statutes in the early Congresses, but there is an absence of them in our later history as well, at least until very recent years....

. . .

The Government points to a number of federal statutes enacted within the past few decades that require the participation of state or local officials in implementing federal regulatory schemes.... Even assuming they represent assertion of the very same congressional power challenged here, they are of such recent vintage that they are no more probative than the statute before us of a constitutional tradition that lends meaning to the text. Their persuasive force is far outweighed by almost two centuries of apparent congressional avoidance of the practice....

III

The constitutional practice we have examined above tends to negate the existence of the congressional power asserted here, but is not conclusive. We turn next to consideration of the structure of the Constitution....

A

It is incontestible that the Constitution established a system of "dual sovereignty." ... This is reflected throughout the Constitution's text, ... including (to mention only a few examples) the prohibition on any involuntary reduction or combination of a State's territory, Art. IV, § 3; the Judicial Power Clause, Art. III, § 2, and the Privileges and Immunities Clause, Art. IV, § 2, which speak of the "Citizens" of the States; the amendment provision, Article V, which requires the votes of three-fourths of the States to amend the Constitution; and the Guarantee Clause, Art. IV, § 4, which "presupposes the continued existence of the states and ... those means and instrumentalities which are the creation of their sovereign and reserved rights," ... Residual state sovereignty was also implicit, of course, in the Constitution's conferral upon Congress of not all governmental powers, but only discrete, enumerated ones, Art. I, § 8, which implication was rendered express by the Tenth Amendment ...

The Framers' experience under the Articles of Confederation had persuaded them that using the States as the instruments of federal governance was both ineffectual and provocative of federal-state conflict. ... [T]he Framers rejected the concept of a central government that would act upon and through the States, and instead designed a system in which the state and federal governments would exercise concurrent authority over the people....

This separation of the two spheres is one of the Constitution's structural protections of liberty.... The power of the Federal Government would be augmented immeasurably if it were able to impress into its service—and at no cost to itself—the police officers of the 50 States.

B

We have thus far discussed the effect that federal control of state officers would have upon ... the division of power between State and Federal Governments. It would also have an effect upon ... the separation and equilibration of powers between the three branches of the Federal Government itself. The Constitution does not leave to speculation who is to administer the laws enacted by Congress; the President, it says, "shall take Care that the Laws be faithfully executed," Art. II, § 3, personally and through officers whom he appoints ... The Brady Act effectively transfers this responsibility to thousands of CLEOs in the 50 States, who are left to implement the program without meaningful Presidential control (if indeed meaningful Presidential control is possible without the power to appoint and remove). The insistence of the Framers upon unity in the Federal Executive—to insure both vigor and accountability—is well known. See The Federalist No. 70 (A.Hamilton).... That unity would be shattered, and the power of the President would be subject to reduction, if Congress could act as effectively without the President as with him, by simply requiring state officers to execute its laws.[12]

. . .

IV

. . .

... [I]n New York v. United States, ... [we held:] "The Federal Government," ... "may not compel the States to enact or administer a federal regulatory program." ...

. . .

The Government ... maintains that requiring state officers to perform discrete, ministerial tasks specified by Congress does not violate the principle of *New York* because it does not diminish the accountability of state or federal officials. This argument fails even on its own terms. By forcing state governments to absorb the financial burden of implementing a federal regulatory program, Members of Congress can take credit for "solving" problems without having to ask their constituents to pay for the solutions with higher federal taxes. And even when the States are not forced to absorb the costs of implementing a federal program, they are still put in the position of taking the blame for its burdensomeness and for its defects.... Under the present law, for example, it will be the CLEO and not some federal official who stands between the gun purchaser and immediate possession of his gun. And it will likely be the CLEO, not some federal official, who will be blamed for any error (even one in the designated federal database) that causes a purchaser to be mistakenly rejected.

. . .

Finally, the Government puts forward a cluster of arguments that can be grouped under the heading: "The Brady Act serves very important purposes, is most efficiently administered by CLEOs during the interim period, and places a minimal and only temporary burden upon state officers." ... Assuming *all* ... were true, [it] might be relevant if we were evaluating whether the incidental application to the States of a federal law of general applicability excessively interfered with the functioning of state governments. See, e.g., ... National League of Cities v. Usery ... (overruled by Garcia v. San Antonio Metropolitan Transit Authority ...) ... But where, as here, it is the whole *object* of the law to direct the functioning of the state executive, and hence to compromise the structural framework of dual sovereignty, such a "balancing" analysis is inappropriate. It is the very *principle* of separate state sovereignty that such a law offends, and no comparative assessment of the various interests can overcome that fundamental defect....

12. ... The dissent is correct ... that control by the unitary Federal Executive is also sacrificed when States voluntarily administer federal programs, but the condition of voluntary state participation significantly reduces the ability of Congress to use this device as a means of reducing the power of the Presidency.

We ... conclude categorically, as we concluded categorically in *New York*: "The Federal Government may not compel the States to enact or administer a federal regulatory program." The mandatory obligation imposed on CLEOs to perform background checks on prospective handgun purchasers plainly runs afoul of that rule.

. . .

We held in *New York* that Congress cannot compel the States to enact or enforce a federal regulatory program. Today we hold that Congress cannot circumvent that prohibition by conscripting the State's officers directly. The Federal Government may neither issue directives requiring the States to address particular problems, nor command the States' officers, or those of their political subdivisions, to administer or enforce a federal regulatory program. It matters not whether policymaking is involved, and no case-by-case weighing of the burdens or benefits is necessary; such commands are fundamentally incompatible with our constitutional system of dual sovereignty. . . .

Justice O'Connor, concurring.

Our precedent and our Nation's historical practices support the Court's holding today. . . .

[T]he Court appropriately refrains from deciding whether other purely ministerial reporting requirements imposed by Congress on state and local authorities pursuant to its Commerce Clause powers are similarly invalid. See, e.g., 42 U.S.C. § 5779(a) (requiring state and local law enforcement agencies to report cases of missing children to the Department of Justice). The provisions invalidated here, however, which directly compel state officials to administer a federal regulatory program, utterly fail to adhere to the design and structure of our constitutional scheme.

Justice Thomas, concurring.

. . .

In my "revisionist" view, the Federal Government's authority under the Commerce Clause does not extend to the regulation of wholly *intra*state, point-of-sale transactions. See United States v. Lopez, 514 U.S. 549, 584 (1995) (concurring opinion). Absent the underlying authority to regulate the intrastate transfer of firearms, Congress surely lacks the corollary power to impress state law enforcement officers into administering and enforcing such regulations. . . .

Even if we construe Congress' authority to regulate interstate commerce to encompass those intrastate transactions that "substantially affect" interstate commerce, I question whether Congress can regulate the particular transactions at issue here. . . . If ... the Second Amendment is read to confer a *personal* right to "keep and bear arms," a colorable argument exists that the Federal Government's regulatory scheme, at least as it pertains to the purely intrastate sale or possession of firearms, runs afoul of that Amendment's protections. As the parties did not raise this argument, however, we need not consider it here. . . . In the meantime, I join the Court's opinion striking down the challenged provisions of the Brady Act as inconsistent with the Tenth Amendment.

Justice Stevens, with whom Justice Souter, Justice Ginsburg, and Justice Breyer join, dissenting.

When Congress exercises the powers delegated to it by the Constitution, it may impose affirmative obligations on executive and judicial officers of state and local governments as well as ordinary citizens. This conclusion is firmly supported by the text of the Constitution, the early history of the Nation, decisions of this Court, and a correct understanding of the basic structure of the Federal Government.

These cases do not implicate the more difficult questions associated with congressional coercion of state legislatures addressed in New York v. United States, 505 U.S. 144 (1992). . . . The question is whether Congress, acting on behalf of the people of the entire Nation, may require local law enforcement officers to perform certain duties during the interim needed for the development of a federal gun control program. It is remarkably similar to the question, heavily debated by the Framers of the Constitution, whether the Congress could require state agents to collect federal taxes. Or the question whether Congress could impress state judges into federal service to entertain and decide cases that they would prefer to ignore.

. . . Matters such as the enlistment of air raid wardens, the administration of a military draft, the mass inoculation of children to forestall an epidemic, or perhaps the threat of an international terrorist, may require a national response before federal personnel can be made available to respond. If the Constitution empowers Congress and the President to make an appropriate response, is there anything in the Tenth Amendment, "in historical understanding and practice, in the structure of the Constitution, [or] in the jurisprudence of this Court" that forbids the enlistment of state officers to make that response effective? More narrowly, what basis is there in any of those sources for concluding that it is the Members of this Court, rather than the elected representatives of the people, who should determine whether the Constitution contains the unwritten rule that the Court announces today?

. . .

The Brady Act was passed in response to what Congress described as an "epidemic of gun violence." . . . [T]he congressional decision surely warrants more respect than it is accorded in today's unprecedented decision.

I

The text of the Constitution provides a sufficient basis for a correct disposition of this case . . .

Congress['s] power to regulate commerce among the States . . . adequately supports the regulation of commerce in handguns effected by the Brady Act. Moreover, the additional grant of authority . . . "[t]o make all Laws which shall be necessary and proper for carrying into Execution the foregoing Powers" is surely adequate to support the temporary enlistment of local police officers in the process of identifying persons who should not be entrusted with the possession of handguns. . . .

Unlike the First Amendment, which prohibits the enactment of a category of laws that would otherwise be authorized by Article I, the Tenth Amendment imposes no restriction on the exercise of delegated powers. . . . Thus, the Amendment provides no support for a rule that immunizes local officials from obligations that might be imposed on ordinary citizens. Indeed, it would be more reasonable to infer that federal law may impose greater duties on state officials than on private citizens because another provision of the Constitution requires that "all executive and judicial Officers, both of the United States and of the several States, shall be bound by Oath or Affirmation, to support this Constitution." . . .

. . .

There is not a clause, sentence, or paragraph in the entire text of the Constitution of the United States that supports the proposition that a local police officer can ignore a command contained in a statute enacted by Congress pursuant to an express delegation of power enumerated in Article I.

II

Under the Articles of Confederation the National Government had the power to issue commands to the several sovereign states, but it had no authority to govern individuals directly. Thus, it raised an army and financed its operations by issuing requisitions to the constituent members of the Confederacy, rather than by creating federal agencies to draft soldiers or to impose taxes.

That method of governing proved to be unacceptable, not because it demeaned the sovereign character of the several States, but rather because it was cumbersome and inefficient. Indeed, a confederation that allows each of its members to determine the ways and means of complying with an overriding requisition is obviously more deferential to state sovereignty concerns than a national government that uses its own agents to impose its will directly on the citizenry. The basic change in the character of the government that the Framers conceived was designed to enhance the power of the national government, not to provide some new, unmentioned immunity for state officers....

Indeed, the historical materials strongly suggest that the Founders intended to enhance the capacity of the federal government by empowering it—as a part of the new authority to make demands directly on individual citizens—to act through local officials....

More specifically, during the debates concerning the ratification of the Constitution, it was assumed that state agents would act as tax collectors for the federal government....

. . .

Bereft of support in the history of the founding, the Court rests its conclusion on the claim that there is little evidence the National Government actually exercised such a power in the early years of the Republic.... [W]e have never suggested that the failure of the early Congresses to address the scope of federal power in a particular area or to exercise a particular authority was an argument against its existence....

. . .

... [T]he majority's opinion consists almost entirely of arguments *against* the substantial evidence weighing in opposition to its view; the Court's ruling is strikingly lacking in affirmative support. Absent even a modicum of textual foundation for its judicially crafted constitutional rule, there should be a presumption that if the Framers had actually intended such a rule, at least one of them would have mentioned it.

III

The Court's "structural" arguments are not sufficient to rebut that presumption....

... Given the fact that the Members of Congress are elected by the people of the several States, with each State receiving an equivalent number of Senators in order to ensure that even the smallest States have a powerful voice in the legislature, it is quite unrealistic to assume that they will ignore the sovereignty concerns of their constituents. It is far more reasonable to presume that their decisions to impose modest burdens on state officials from time to time reflect a considered judgment that the people in each of the States will benefit therefrom.

Indeed, the presumption of validity that supports all congressional enactments has added force with respect to policy judgments concerning the impact of a federal statute upon the respective States. . . .

. . . The majority expresses special concern that were its rule not adopted the Federal Government would be able to avail itself of the services of state government officials "at no cost to itself." . . . But this specific problem of federal actions that have the effect of imposing so-called "unfunded mandates" on the States has been identified and meaningfully addressed by Congress in recent legislation.[18] See Unfunded Mandates Reform Act of 1995, Pub.L. 104–4, 109 Stat. 48.

. . . Whatever the ultimate impact of the new legislation, its passage demonstrates that unelected judges are better off leaving the protection of federalism to the political process in all but the most extraordinary circumstances.

Perversely, the majority's rule seems more likely to damage than to preserve the safeguards against tyranny provided by the existence of vital state governments. By limiting the ability of the Federal Government to enlist state officials in the implementation of its programs, the Court creates incentives for the National Government to aggrandize itself. In the name of State's rights, the majority would have the Federal Government create vast national bureaucracies to implement its policies. . . .

[T]he Court suggests that the unity in the Executive Branch of the Federal Government "would be shattered, and the power of the President would be subject to reduction, if Congress could . . . require . . . state officers to execute its laws." Putting to one side the obvious tension between the majority's claim that impressing state police officers will unduly tip the balance of power in favor of the federal sovereign and this suggestion that it will emasculate the Presidency, the Court's reasoning contradicts New York v. United States.

That decision squarely approved of cooperative federalism programs, designed at the national level but implemented principally by state governments. . . . Congress may require the States to implement its programs as a condition of federal spending, in order to avoid the threat of unilateral federal action in the area, or as a part of a program that affects States and private parties alike. . . .

Nor is there force to the assumption undergirding the Court's entire opinion that if this trivial burden on state sovereignty is permissible, the entire structure of federalism will soon collapse. . . . [T]his case, unlike any precedent

---

18. The majority also makes the more general claim that requiring state officials to carry out federal policy causes states to "tak[e] the blame" for failed programs. . . . This concern is vastly overstated.

. . . .

The problem is of little real consequence in any event, because to the extent that a particular action proves politically unpopular, we may be confident that elected officials charged with implementing it will be quite clear to their constituents where the source of the misfortune lies. These cases demonstrate the point. Sheriffs Printz and Mack have made public statements, including their decisions to serve as plaintiffs in these actions, denouncing the Brady Act. . . . Moreover, we can be sure that CLEOs will inform disgruntled constituents who have been denied permission to purchase a handgun about the origins of the Brady Act requirements. . . .

in which the Court has held that Congress exceeded its powers, merely involves the imposition of modest duties on individual officers. . . .

Far more important than the concerns that the Court musters in support of its new rule is the fact that the Framers entrusted Congress with the task of creating a working structure of intergovernmental relationships around the framework that the Constitution authorized. . . . As a general matter, Congress has followed the sound policy of authorizing federal agencies and federal agents to administer federal programs. That general practice, however, does not negate the existence of power to rely on state officials in occasional situations in which such reliance is in the national interest. . . .

IV

. . .

The provision of the Brady Act that crosses the Court's newly defined constitutional threshold is more comparable to a statute requiring local police officers to report the identity of missing children to the Crime Control Center of the Department of Justice than to an offensive federal command to a sovereign state. If Congress believes that such a statute will benefit the people of the Nation, and serve the interests of cooperative federalism better than an enlarged federal bureaucracy, we should respect both its policy judgment and its appraisal of its constitutional power.

Accordingly, I respectfully dissent.

Justice Souter, dissenting.

I join Justice Stevens's dissenting opinion, but subject to the following qualifications. . . . I do not find anything dispositive in the paucity of early examples of federal employment of state officers for executive purposes. . . .

[I]t is The Federalist that finally determines my position. . . .

. . .

. . . I do not read any of The Federalist material as requiring the conclusion that Congress could require administrative support without an obligation to pay fair value for it. . . . If, therefore, my views were prevailing in these cases, I would remand for development and consideration of petitioners' points, that they have no budget provision for work required under the Act and are liable for unauthorized expenditures. . . .

Justice Breyer, with whom Justice Stevens joins, dissenting.

. . . The federal systems of Switzerland, Germany, and the European Union . . . provide that constituent states, not federal bureaucracies, will themselves implement many of the laws, rules, regulations, or decrees enacted by the central "federal" body. . . . They do so in part because they believe that such a system interferes less, not more, with the independent authority of the "state," member nation, or other subsidiary government, and helps to safeguard individual liberty as well. . . .

Of course, we are interpreting our own Constitution, not those of other nations, and there may be relevant political and structural differences between their systems and our own. . . . But their experience may nonetheless cast an empirical light on the consequences of different solutions to a common legal problem—in this case the problem of reconciling central authority with the need to preserve the liberty-enhancing autonomy of a smaller constituent governmental entity. . . . And that experience here offers empirical confirmation of the implied answer to a question Justice Stevens asks: Why, or how, would what the majority sees as a constitutional alternative—the creation of a new federal gun-law bureaucracy, or the expansion of an existing federal bureaucracy—better promote either state sovereignty or individual liberty?

. . .

. . . [T]hat direct federal assignment of duties to state officers is not common . . . likely reflects, not a widely shared belief that any such assignment is incompatible with basic principles of federalism, but rather a widely shared practice of assigning such duties in other ways. . . . [T]here is neither need nor reason to find in the Constitution an absolute principle, the inflexibility of which poses a surprising and technical obstacle to the enactment of a law that Congress believed necessary to solve an important national problem.

. . .

RENO v. CONDON, 528 U.S. 141 (2000). The Driver's Privacy Protection Act of 1994 (DPPA) restricts the ability of state motor vehicle departments to disclose drivers' personal information without consent. (The Act also regulates disclosure by private persons who have obtained drivers' personal information from a state DMV.) South Carolina claimed that the DPPA violated the federalism principles of New York v. United States. A unanimous Court rejected that argument. DPPA did not require states to enact any laws or regulations, as did the statute in *New York*, nor require State officials to assist in the enforcement of federal statutes regulating private individuals, as did the law in *Printz*. DPPA regulated State activities, rather than controlling State regulation of private parties. It was not necessary to address South Carolina's argument that Congress may only regulate States by "generally applicable" laws that apply to individuals as well as States. DPPA is "generally applicable". It "regulates the universe of entities that participate as suppliers to the market for motor vehicle information—the States as initial suppliers of the information in interstate commerce and private resellers or redisclosers of that information in commerce."

SECTION 2. ENFORCEMENT OF FEDERAL RIGHTS IN SUITS AGAINST STATE OFFICERS: THE ELEVENTH AMENDMENT

Pennhurst State School & Hospital v. Halderman

465 U.S. 89, 104 S.Ct. 900, 79 L.Ed.2d 67 (1984).

Justice Powell delivered the opinion of the Court.

This case presents the question whether a federal court may award injunctive relief against state officials on the basis of state law.

I

This litigation, here for the second time, concerns the conditions of care at petitioner Pennhurst State School and Hospital, a Pennsylvania institution for the care of the mentally retarded. . . .

. . . Respondents' amended complaint charged that conditions at Pennhurst violated the class members' rights under the Eighth and Fourteenth Amendments; § 504 of the Rehabilitation Act of 1973, 87 Stat. 394, as amended, 29 U.S.C. § 794 (1976 ed. and Supp. V); the Developmentally Disabled Assistance and Bill of Rights Act, 42 U.S.C. §§ 6001–6081 (1976 ed. and Supp. V); and the

Pennsylvania Mental Health and Mental Retardation Act of 1966 (the "MH–MR Act"), Pa.Stat.Ann., Tit. 50, §§ 4101–4704 (Purdon 1969 and Supp.1982). Both damages and injunctive relief were sought.

. . .

The Court of Appeals for the Third Circuit [decided] that respondents had a right to habilitation in the least restrictive environment, but it grounded this right solely on the "bill of rights" provision in the Developmentally Disabled Assistance and Bill of Rights Act. . . .

This Court reversed the judgment of the Court of Appeals, finding that 42 U.S.C. § 6010 did not create any substantive rights. . . . We remanded the case to the Court of Appeals to determine if the remedial order could be supported on the basis of state law, the Constitution, or § 504 of the Rehabilitation Act. . . .

On remand the Court of Appeals . . . concluded that [the] state statute fully supported its prior judgment, and therefore did not reach the remaining issues of federal law. It also rejected petitioners' argument that the Eleventh Amendment barred a federal court from considering this pendent state-law claim. . . .

We . . . reverse and remand.

II

Petitioners [contend that] the Eleventh Amendment prohibited the District Court from ordering state officials to conform their conduct to state law. . . . We . . . find the Eleventh Amendment challenge dispositive.

A

Article III, § 2 of the Constitution provides that the federal judicial power extends, *inter alia,* to controversies "between a State and Citizens of another State." Relying on this language, this Court in 1793 assumed original jurisdiction over a suit brought by a citizen of South Carolina against the State of Georgia. *Chisholm v. Georgia,* 2 Dall. 419 (1793). The decision "created such a shock of surprise that the Eleventh Amendment was at once proposed and adopted." *Monaco v. Mississippi,* 292 U.S. 313, 325 (1934). The Amendment provides:

> "The Judicial power of the United States shall not be construed to extend to any suit in law or equity, commenced or prosecuted against one of the United States by Citizens of another State, or by Citizens or Subjects of any Foreign State."

The Amendment's language overruled the particular result in *Chisholm,* but this Court has recognized that its greater significance lies in its affirmation that the fundamental principle of sovereign immunity limits the grant of judicial authority in Art. III. Thus, in *Hans v. Louisiana,* 134 U.S. 1 (1890), the Court held that, despite the limited terms of the Eleventh Amendment, a federal court could not entertain a suit brought by a citizen against his own State. After reviewing the constitutional debates concerning the scope of Art. III, the Court determined that federal jurisdiction over suits against unconsenting States "was not contemplated by the Constitution when establishing the judicial power of the United States." Id., at 15. See *Monaco v. Mississippi, supra,* 292 U.S., at 322–323 (1934). In short, the principle of sovereign immunity is a constitutional limitation on the federal judicial power established in Art. III:

. . .

B

This Court's decisions thus establish that "an unconsenting State is immune from suits brought in federal courts by her own citizens as well as by citizens of another state." *Employees,* supra, 411 U.S., at 280. There may be a question, however, whether a particular suit in fact is a suit against a State. It is clear, of course, that in the absence of consent a suit in which the State or one of its agencies or departments is named as the defendant is proscribed by the Eleventh Amendment.... This jurisdictional bar applies regardless of the nature of the relief sought. . . .

When the suit is brought only against state officials, a question arises as to whether that suit is a suit against the State itself. Although prior decisions of this Court have not been entirely consistent on this issue, certain principles are well established. The Eleventh Amendment bars a suit against state officials when "the state is the real, substantial party in interest." . . . And, as when the State itself is named as the defendant, a suit against state officials that is in fact a suit against a State is barred regardless of whether it seeks damages or injunctive relief. . . .

The Court has recognized an important exception to this general rule: a suit challenging the constitutionality of a state official's action is not one against the State. This was the holding in Ex parte Young, 209 U.S. 123 (1908), in which a federal court enjoined the Attorney General of the State of Minnesota from bringing suit to enforce a state statute that allegedly violated the Fourteenth Amendment. This Court held that the Eleventh Amendment did not prohibit issuance of this injunction. The theory of the case was that an unconstitutional enactment is "void" and therefore does not "impart to [the officer] any immunity from responsibility to the supreme authority of the United States." . . . Since the State could not authorize the action, the officer was "stripped of his official or representative character and [was] subjected to the consequences of his official conduct." . . .

While the rule permitting suits alleging conduct contrary to "the supreme authority of the United States" has survived, the theory of *Young* has not been provided an expansive interpretation. Thus, in Edelman v. Jordan, 415 U.S. 651 (1974), the Court emphasized that the Eleventh Amendment bars some forms of injunctive relief against state officials for violation of federal law. . . . In particular, *Edelman* held that when a plaintiff sues a state official alleging a violation of federal law, the federal court may award an injunction that governs the official's future conduct, but not one that awards retroactive monetary relief. Under the theory of *Young,* such a suit would not be one against the State since the federal-law allegation would strip the state officer of his official authority. Nevertheless, retroactive relief was barred by the Eleventh Amendment.

III

With these principles in mind, we now turn to the question whether the claim that petitioners violated *state law* in carrying out their official duties at Pennhurst is one against the State and therefore barred by the Eleventh Amendment. Respondents advance two principal arguments in support of the judgment below. [T]hey contend that under the doctrine of Edelman v. Jordan, supra, the suit is not against the State because the courts below ordered only prospective injunctive relief. . . .

[margin note: Cts. ordered prospective injunctive relief.]

A

. . . The Court of Appeals held that if the judgment below rested on federal law, it could be entered against petitioner state officials under the doctrine established in *Edelman* and *Young* even though the prospective financial burden was substantial and ongoing. The court assumed, and respondents assert, that this reasoning applies as well when the official acts in violation of state law. This argument misconstrues the basis of the doctrine established in *Young* and *Edelman*.

As discussed above, the injunction in *Young* was justified, notwithstanding the obvious impact on the State itself, on the view that sovereign immunity does not apply because an official who acts unconstitutionally is "stripped of his official or representative character,". . . . This rationale, of course, created the "well-recognized irony" that an official's unconstitutional conduct constitutes state action under the Fourteenth Amendment but not the Eleventh Amendment. . . . Nonetheless, the *Young* doctrine has been accepted as necessary to permit the federal courts to vindicate federal rights. . . .

The Court also has recognized, however, that the need to promote the supremacy of federal law must be accommodated to the constitutional immunity of the States. This is the significance of Edelman v. Jordan . . . [W]e declined to extend the fiction of *Young* to encompass retroactive relief, for to do so would effectively eliminate the constitutional immunity of the States. Accordingly, we concluded that . . . an award of retroactive relief necessarily "fall[s] afoul of the Eleventh Amendment if that basic constitutional provision is to be conceived of as having any present force." . . . In sum *Edelman's* distinction between prospective and retroactive relief fulfills the underlying purpose of Ex parte Young while at the same time preserving to an important degree the constitutional immunity of the States.

This need to reconcile competing interests is wholly absent, however, when a plaintiff alleges that a state official has violated *state* law. In such a case the entire basis for the doctrine of *Young* and *Edelman* disappears. A federal court's grant of relief against state officials on the basis of state law, whether prospective or retroactive, does not vindicate the supreme authority of federal law. On the contrary, it is difficult to think of a greater intrusion on state sovereignty than when a federal court instructs state officials on how to conform their conduct to state law. Such a result conflicts directly with the principles of federalism that underlie the Eleventh Amendment. We conclude that *Young* and *Edelman* are inapplicable in a suit against state officials on the basis of state law.

[margin note: Because they cant enforce state law! violates state sovereignity]

[margin note: why? what is the difference?]

B

The contrary view of Justice Stevens' dissent rests on fiction, is wrong on the law, and, most important, would emasculate the Eleventh Amendment. . . .

. . . To the extent there was a violation of state law in this case, it is a case of the State itself not fulfilling its legislative promises.

. . . .

. . . Under the dissent's view of the *ultra vires* doctrine, the Eleventh Amendment would have force only in the rare case in which a plaintiff foolishly attempts to sue the State in its own name, or where he cannot produce some state statute that has been violated to his asserted injury. Thus, the *ultra vires* doctrine, a narrow and questionable exception, would swallow the general rule that a suit is against the State if the relief will run against it. . . .

. . .

D

Respondents urge that application of the Eleventh Amendment to pendent state-law claims will have a disruptive effect on litigation against state officials. . . .

It may be that applying the Eleventh Amendment to pendent claims results in federal claims being brought in state court, or in bifurcation of claims. That is not uncommon in this area. Under Edelman v. Jordan, supra, a suit against state officials for retroactive monetary relief, whether based on federal or state law, must be brought in state court. Challenges to the validity of state tax systems under 42 U.S.C. § 1983 also must be brought in state court. . . . Under the abstention doctrine, unclear issues of state law commonly are split off and referred to the state courts.

In any case, the answer to respondents' assertions is that such considerations of policy cannot override the constitutional limitation on the authority of the federal judiciary to adjudicate suits against a State. . . .

. . .

V

Fed ct. lacked jdx

. . . We hold that these federal courts lacked jurisdiction to enjoin petitioner state institutions and state officials on the basis of this state law. The District Court also rested its decision on the Eighth and Fourteenth Amendments and § 504 of the Rehabilitation Act of 1973. On remand the Court of Appeals may consider to what extent, if any, the judgment may be sustained on these bases. The court also may consider whether relief may be granted to respondents under the Developmentally Disabled Assistance and Bill of Rights Act, 42 U.S.C. §§ 6011, 6063. The judgment of the Court of Appeals is reversed, and the case remanded for further proceedings consistent with this opinion.

It is so ordered.

Justice Brennan, dissenting.

Dont understand this!

I fully agree with Justice Stevens' dissent. Nevertheless, I write separately to explain that in view of my continued belief that the Eleventh Amendment "bars federal court suits against States only by citizens of other States," . . . I would hold that petitioners are not entitled to invoke the protections of that Amendment in this federal court suit by citizens of Pennsylvania. . . . To the extent that such nonconstitutional sovereign immunity may apply to petitioners, I agree with Justice Stevens that since petitioners' conduct was prohibited by state law, the protections of sovereign immunity do not extend to them.

Justice Stevens, with whom Justice Brennan, Justice Marshall, and Justice Blackmun join, dissenting.

. . . In a completely unprecedented holding, today the Court concludes that Pennsylvania's sovereign immunity prevents a federal court from enjoining the conduct that Pennsylvania itself has prohibited. No rational view of the sovereign immunity of the States supports this result. To the contrary, the question whether a federal court may award injunctive relief on the basis of state law has been answered affirmatively by this Court many times in the past. Yet the Court repudiates at least 28 cases, spanning well over a century of this Court's jurisprudence, proclaiming instead that federal courts have no power to enforce the will of the States by enjoining conduct because it violates state law. This new pronouncement will require the federal courts to decide federal constitutional questions despite the availability of state-law grounds for decision, a result inimical to sound principles of judicial restraint. Nothing in the Eleventh Amendment, the conception of state sovereignty it embodies, or the history of this institution, requires or justifies such a perverse result.

. . .

II

The majority proceeds as if this Court has not had previous occasion to consider the Eleventh Amendment argument made by petitioners, and contends that Ex parte Young, 209 U.S. 123 (1908) has no application to a suit seeking injunctive relief on the basis of state law. That is simply not the case. . . .

. . .

. . . Until today the rule has been simple: conduct that exceeds the scope of an official's lawful discretion is not conduct the sovereign has authorized and hence is subject to injunction. Whether that conduct also gives rise to damage liability is an entirely separate question.

III

. . .

The pivotal consideration in *Young* was that it was not conduct of the sovereign that was at issue. The rule that unlawful acts of an officer should not be attributed to the sovereign has deep roots in the history of sovereign immunity and makes *Young* reconcilable with the principles of sovereign immunity found in the Eleventh Amendment, rather than merely an unprincipled accommodation between federal and state interests that ignores the principles contained in the Eleventh Amendment.

. . .

It follows that the basis for the *Young* rule is present when the officer sued has violated the law of the sovereign; in all such cases the conduct is of a type that would not be permitted by the sovereign and hence is not attributable to the sovereign under traditional sovereign immunity principles. . . .

young rule

[T]he majority's rule has nothing to do with the basic reason the Eleventh Amendment was added to the Constitution. There is general agreement that the Amendment was passed because the States were fearful that federal courts would force them to pay their Revolutionary War debts, leading to their financial ruin. Entertaining a suit for injunctive relief based on state law implicates none of the concerns of the Framers. . . .

IV

. . .

[T]he rule the majority creates today serves none of the interests of the State. The majority prevents federal courts from implementing State policies through equitable enforcement of State law. Instead, federal courts are required to resolve cases on federal grounds that no State authority can undo. Leaving violations of state law unredressed and ensuring that the decisions of federal courts may never be reexamined by the States hardly comports with the respect for States as sovereign entities commanded by the Eleventh Amend-ment.

. . .

APPLICATION OF THE ELEVENTH AMENDMENT IN SUITS FOR "RETROACTIVE RELIEF"

Given prior law that the Eleventh Amendment applied to suits by a state's own citizens, and that it applied although only state officers were named parties if the state was the real party in interest, the "stripping doctrine" of Ex parte Young was crucial in permitting private federal court litigation to compel state compliance with the Constitution and federal laws.[1]

The stripping doctrine is not broad enough, however, to permit actions for "retroactive relief" that must be paid from public funds. While a judgment for damages that must be paid only from the state official's personal assets presents no Eleventh Amendment problem, Scheuer v. Rhodes, 416 U.S. 232 (1974), the Eleventh Amendment is still a serious obstacle if a private plaintiff's suit seeks the payment of state funds for past violations of federal law. That was the situation in Edelman v. Jordan, 415 U.S. 651 (1974), where welfare recipients were seeking reimbursement for past welfare payments withheld by state officials in violation of federal law. The Court held that, while the principle of Ex Parte Young supported the lower federal courts' judgment ordering state welfare officials to pay future benefits, the Eleventh Amendment barred any retroactive relief for benefits withheld in the past.

A second fiction—of state "consent" or "waiver" of sovereign immunity—had been applied to permit federal court damage actions against states for violation of federal statutes. Edelman v. Jordan, however, considerably limited that theory—concluding that a state could not be sued in federal court for retroactive relief unless Congress, "by the most express language or by such overwhelming implications from the text," demonstrated its intent to abrogate the state's immunity under the Eleventh Amendment.

In Atascadero State Hospital v. Scanlon, 473 U.S. 234 (1985), Justice Brennan's lengthy dissent reiterated his position that the Eleventh Amendment does not establish a constitutional rule of sovereign immunity. For the first time, that position gained the endorsement of three other Justices (Marshall, Blackmun and Stevens), who joined the dissent. The majority in *Scanlon* disagreed, concluding that the Eleventh Amendment creates a constitutional rule of sovereign immunity. The precise basis of the decision, however, was that

Atascadero v. Scanlon [margin note]

---

1. The Eleventh Amendment is inapplicable to suits by the federal government against states. United States v. Texas, 143 U.S. 621 (1892). Local political subdivisions, such as cities and counties are not "states" within the meaning of the Eleventh Amendment, and are fully subject to private party suits in the federal courts. Mt. Healthy City Sch. Dist. v. Doyle, 429 U.S. 274 (1977).

While the Eleventh Amendment has no application to suits against the United States, Indian tribes, or foreign countries, independent conceptions of sovereign immunity do apply. In private actions against federal officials, the stripping doctrine has been applied to determine the extent of federal sovereign immunity. Larson v. Domestic & Foreign Commerce Corp., 337 U.S. 682 (1949); Dugan v. Rank, 372 U.S. 609 (1963); Note, *The Sovereign Immunity Doctrine and Judicial Review of Federal Administrative Action,* 2 U.C.L.A.L.Rev. 382 (1955). In 1976, Public Law 94–574, § 1, 90 Stat. 2721, amended the Administrative Procedure Act (5 U.S.C. §§ 702, 703) to eliminate the defense of sovereign immunity in private suits seeking relief other than money damages against the United States. (Congress had long before consented to suit for money damages for tort and contract claims against the United States.) On the immunity of Indian tribes, see Santa Clara Pueblo v. Martinez, 436 U.S. 49, 58 (1978).

Congress had not "unequivocally" expressed its intention to abrogate state sovereign immunity. When that intention has been "unequivocally" expressed, are there limits to Congress' power to permit federal court suits against unconsenting states? The following case deals with that question.

Seminole Tribe of Florida v. Florida

517 U.S. 44, 116 S.Ct. 1114, 134 L.Ed.2d 252 (1996).

Chief Justice Rehnquist delivered the opinion of the Court.

The Indian Gaming Regulatory Act provides that an Indian tribe may conduct certain gaming activities only in conformance with a valid compact between the tribe and the State in which the gaming activities are located. . . . 25 U.S.C. § 2710(d)(1)(C). The Act, passed by Congress under the Indian Commerce Clause, U.S. Const., Art. I, § 10, cl. 3, imposes upon the States a duty to negotiate in good faith with an Indian tribe toward the formation of a compact, § 2710(d)(3)(A), and authorizes a tribe to bring suit in federal court against a State in order to compel performance of that duty, § 2710(d)(7). We hold that notwithstanding Congress' clear intent to abrogate the States' sovereign immunity, the Indian Commerce Clause does not grant Congress that power, and therefore § 2710(d)(7) cannot grant jurisdiction over a State that does not consent to be sued. We further hold that the doctrine of Ex parte Young, 209 U.S. 123 (1908), may not be used to enforce § 2710(d)(3) against a state official.

I

. . .

In September 1991, the Seminole Tribe of Indians, petitioner, sued the State of Florida and its Governor, Lawton Chiles, respondents. Invoking jurisdiction under 25 U.S.C. § 2710(d)(7)(A), as well as 28 U.S.C. §§ 1331 and 1362, petitioner alleged that respondents had "refused to enter into any negotiation for inclusion of [certain gaming activities] in a tribal-state compact," thereby violating the "requirement of good faith negotiation" contained in § 2710(d)(3). Respondents moved to dismiss the complaint, arguing that the suit violated the State's sovereign immunity from suit in federal court. The District Court denied respondents' motion. . . .

The Court of Appeals for the Eleventh Circuit reversed the decision of the District Court, holding that the Eleventh Amendment barred petitioner's suit against respondents. . . .

. . . [W]e granted certiorari . . . in order to consider two questions: (1) Does the Eleventh Amendment prevent Congress from authorizing suits by Indian tribes against States for prospective injunctive relief to enforce legislation enacted pursuant to the Indian Commerce Clause?; and (2) Does the doctrine of Ex parte Young permit suits against a State's governor for prospective injunctive relief to enforce the good faith bargaining requirement of the Act? We answer the first question in the affirmative, the second in the negative, and we therefore affirm the Eleventh Circuit's dismissal of petitioner's suit.

. . .

Here, petitioner has sued the State of Florida and it is undisputed that Florida has not consented to the suit. . . . Petitioner nevertheless contends that its suit is not barred by state sovereign immunity. First, it argues that Congress through the Act abrogated the States' sovereign immunity. Alterna-

 # 2

tively, petitioner maintains that its suit against the Governor may go forward under Ex parte Young, supra. We consider each of those arguments in turn.

II

questions to answer #1

... In order to determine whether Congress has abrogated the States' sovereign immunity, we ask two questions: first, whether Congress has "unequivocally expresse[d] its intent to abrogate the immunity," ... and second, whether Congress has acted "pursuant to a valid exercise of power." ...

A

1A.)

Congress' intent to abrogate the States' immunity from suit must be obvious from "a clear legislative statement." ... This rule arises from a recognition of the important role played by the Eleventh Amendment and the broader principles that it reflects. ... "[G]eneral authorization for suit in federal court is not the kind of unequivocal statutory language sufficient to abrogate the Eleventh Amendment." ...

Here, ... Congress has in § 2710(d)(7) provided an "unmistakably clear" statement of its intent to abrogate. ... [T]he numerous references to the "State" in the text ... make it indubitable that Congress intended through the Act to abrogate the States' sovereign immunity from suit.

B

1B)

... [W]e turn now to consider whether the Act was passed "pursuant to a valid exercise of power." ...

. . .

[O]ur inquiry into whether Congress has the power to abrogate unilaterally the States' immunity from suit is narrowly focused on one question: Was the Act in question passed pursuant to a constitutional provision granting Congress the power to abrogate? See, e.g., Fitzpatrick v. Bitzer, 427 U.S. 445, 452–456 (1976). Previously, in conducting that inquiry, we have found authority to abrogate under only two provisions of the Constitution. In *Fitzpatrick*, we recognized that the Fourteenth Amendment, by expanding federal power at the expense of state autonomy, had fundamentally altered the balance of state and federal power struck by the Constitution. ... We noted that § 1 of the Fourteenth Amendment contained prohibitions expressly directed at the States and that § 5 of the Amendment expressly provided that "The Congress shall have the power to enforce, by appropriate legislation, the provisions of this article." ... We held that through the Fourteenth Amendment, federal power extended to intrude upon the province of the Eleventh Amendment and therefore that § 5 of the Fourteenth Amendment allowed Congress to abrogate the immunity from suit guaranteed by that Amendment.

In only one other case has congressional abrogation of the States' Eleventh Amendment immunity been upheld. In Pennsylvania v. Union Gas Co., 491 U.S. 1 (1989), a plurality of the Court found that the Interstate Commerce Clause, Art. I, § 8, cl. 3, granted Congress the power to abrogate state sovereign immunity, stating that the power to regulate interstate commerce would be "incomplete without the authority to render States liable in damages." ... Justice White added the fifth vote necessary to the result in that case, but wrote separately in order to express that he "[did] not agree with much of [the plurality's] reasoning." ...

. . .

... [T]he plurality opinion in *Union Gas* allows no principled distinction in favor of the States to be drawn between the Indian Commerce Clause and the Interstate Commerce Clause.

... Generally, the principle of stare decisis, and the interests that it serves, ... counsel strongly against reconsideration of our precedent. Nevertheless, we always have treated stare decisis as a "principle of policy," ... and not as an "inexorable command," ... "[W]hen governing decisions are unworkable or are badly reasoned, 'this Court has never felt constrained to follow precedent.'" ... Our willingness to reconsider our earlier decisions has been "particularly true in constitutional cases, because in such cases 'correction through legislative action is practically impossible.'" ...

The Court in *Union Gas* reached a result without an expressed rationale agreed upon by a majority of the Court. ...

The plurality's rationale also deviated sharply from our established federalism jurisprudence and essentially eviscerated our decision in *Hans.* ... It was well established in 1989 when *Union Gas* was decided that the Eleventh Amendment stood for the constitutional principle that state sovereign immunity limited the federal courts' jurisdiction under Article III. ...

Never before the decision in *Union Gas* had we suggested that the bounds of Article III could be expanded by Congress operating pursuant to any constitutional provision other than the Fourteenth Amendment. Indeed, it had seemed fundamental that Congress could not expand the jurisdiction of the federal courts beyond the bounds of Article III. Marbury v. Madison, 1 Cranch 137 (1803). ...

The plurality's extended reliance upon our decision in Fitzpatrick v. Bitzer ... that Congress could under the Fourteenth Amendment abrogate the States' sovereign immunity was also, we believe, misplaced. *Fitzpatrick* was based upon a rationale wholly inapplicable to the Interstate Commerce Clause, viz., that the Fourteenth Amendment, adopted well after the adoption of the Eleventh Amendment and the ratification of the Constitution, operated to alter the preexisting balance between state and federal power achieved by Article III and the Eleventh Amendment. ... *Fitzpatrick* cannot be read to justify "limitation of the principle embodied in the Eleventh Amendment through appeal to antecedent provisions of the Constitution." ...

... Reconsidering the decision in *Union Gas*, we conclude that none of the policies underlying stare decisis require our continuing adherence to its holding. ... The case involved the interpretation of the Constitution and therefore may be altered only by constitutional amendment or revision by this Court. ...

. . .

In overruling *Union Gas* today, we reconfirm that the background principle of state sovereign immunity embodied in the Eleventh Amendment is not so ephemeral as to dissipate when the subject of the suit is an area, like the regulation of Indian commerce, that is under the exclusive control of the Federal Government. Even when the Constitution vests in Congress complete law-making authority over a particular area, the Eleventh Amendment prevents congressional authorization of suits by private parties against unconsenting States. The Eleventh Amendment restricts the judicial power under Article III, and Article I cannot be used to circumvent the constitutional limitations placed upon federal jurisdiction. Petitioner 's suit against the State of Florida must be dismissed for a lack of jurisdiction.

III

Petitioner argues that we may exercise jurisdiction over its suit to enforce § 2710(d)(3) against the Governor notwithstanding the jurisdictional bar of the Eleventh Amendment. Petitioner notes that since our decision in Ex parte Young, 209 U.S. 123 (1908), we often have found federal jurisdiction over a suit against a state official when that suit seeks only prospective injunctive relief in order to "end a continuing violation of federal law." . . . The situation presented here, however, is sufficiently different from that giving rise to the traditional Ex parte Young action so as to preclude the availability of that doctrine.

Here, the "continuing violation of federal law" alleged by petitioner is the Governor's failure to bring the State into compliance with § 2710(d)(3). But the duty to negotiate imposed upon the State by that statutory provision does not stand alone. Rather, . . . Congress passed § 2710(d)(3) in conjunction with the carefully crafted and intricate remedial scheme set forth in § 2710(d)(7).

Where Congress has created a remedial scheme for the enforcement of a particular federal right, we have, in suits against federal officers, refused to supplement that scheme with one created by the judiciary. . . .

Here, Congress intended § 2710(d)(3) to be enforced against the State in an action brought under § 2710(d)(7); the intricate procedures set forth in that provision show that Congress intended therein not only to define, but also significantly to limit, the duty imposed by § 2710(d)(3). . . .

Here, of course, we have found that Congress does not have authority under the Constitution to make the State suable in federal court under § 2710(d)(7). Nevertheless, the fact that Congress chose to impose upon the State a liability which is significantly more limited than would be the liability imposed upon the state officer under Ex parte Young strongly indicates that Congress had no wish to create the latter under § 2710(d)(3). Nor are we free to rewrite the statutory scheme in order to approximate what we think Congress might have wanted had it known that § 2710(d)(7) was beyond its authority. . . .

IV

p's claim is dismissed.

The Eleventh Amendment prohibits Congress from making the State of Florida capable of being sued in federal court. The narrow exception to the Eleventh Amendment provided by the Ex parte Young doctrine cannot be used to enforce § 2710(d)(3) because Congress enacted a remedial scheme, § 2710(d)(7), specifically designed for the enforcement of that right. The Eleventh Circuit's dismissal of petitioner's suit is hereby affirmed.

It is so ordered.

Justice Stevens, dissenting.

This case is about power—the power of the Congress of the United States to create a private federal cause of action against a State, or its Governor, for the violation of a federal right. . . . [I]n a sharp break with the past, today the Court holds that with the narrow and illogical exception of statutes enacted pursuant to the Enforcement Clause of the Fourteenth Amendment, Congress has no such power.

The importance of the majority's decision to overrule the Court's holding in Pennsylvania v. Union Gas Co. cannot be overstated. The majority's opinion does not simply preclude Congress from establishing the rather curious statutory scheme under which Indian tribes may seek the aid of a federal court to secure a State's good faith negotiations over gaming regulations. Rather, it prevents Congress from providing a federal forum for a broad range of actions against States, from those sounding in copyright and patent law, to those concerning bankruptcy, environmental law, and the regulation of our vast national economy.

There may be room for debate over whether, in light of the Eleventh Amendment, Congress has the power to ensure that such a cause of action may be enforced in federal court by a citizen of another State or a foreign citizen. There can be no serious debate, however, over whether Congress has the power to ensure that such a cause of action may be brought by a citizen of the State being sued. Congress' authority in that regard is clear.

. . .

For these reasons, as well as those set forth in Justice Souter's opinion, I respectfully dissent.

Justice Souter, with whom Justice Ginsburg and Justice Breyer join, dissenting.

. . .

The fault I find with the majority today is not in its decision to reexamine *Union Gas*, for the Court in that case produced no majority for a single rationale supporting congressional authority. Instead, I part company from the Court because I am convinced that its decision is fundamentally mistaken, and for that reason I respectfully dissent.

. . .

It is useful to separate three questions: (1) whether the States enjoyed sovereign immunity if sued in their own courts in the period prior to ratification of the National Constitution; (2) if so, whether after ratification the States were entitled to claim some such immunity when sued in a federal court exercising jurisdiction either because the suit was between a State and a non-state litigant who was not its citizen, or because the issue in the case raised a federal question; and (3) whether any state sovereign immunity recognized in federal court may be abrogated by Congress.

The answer to the first question is not clear, although some of the Framers assumed that States did enjoy immunity in their own courts. The second question was not debated at the time of ratification, except as to citizen-state diversity jurisdiction; there was no unanimity, but in due course the Court in Chisholm v. Georgia, 2 Dall. 419 (1793), answered that a state defendant enjoyed no such immunity. As to federal question jurisdiction, state sovereign immunity seems not to have been debated prior to ratification, the silence probably showing a general understanding at the time that the States would have no immunity in such cases.

The adoption of the Eleventh Amendment soon changed the result in *Chisholm*, not by mentioning sovereign immunity, but by eliminating citizen-state diversity jurisdiction over cases with state defendants. . . . The *Hans* Court erroneously assumed that a State could plead sovereign immunity against a noncitizen suing under federal question jurisdiction, and for that reason held that a State must enjoy the same protection in a suit by one of its citizens. . . .

The Court's answer today to the third question is likewise at odds with the Founders' view that common law, when it was received into the new American legal systems, was always subject to legislative amendment. . . .

. . .

The *Hans* doctrine was erroneous, but it has not previously proven to be unworkable.... I would therefore treat *Hans* as it has always been treated in fact until today, as a doctrine of federal common law. For, as so understood, it has formed one of the strands of the federal relationship for over a century now, and the stability of that relationship is itself a value that stare decisis aims to respect.

.   .   .

[T]he political safeguards of federalism are working, ... a plain statement rule is an adequate check on congressional overreaching, and ... today's abandonment of that approach is wholly unwarranted.

.   .   .

CONGRESSIONAL POWER TO AUTHORIZE SUITS AGAINST STATES IN FEDERAL COURT

Relying on *Seminole Tribe*, the Court held that Congress could not subject States to federal court jurisdiction in damage actions for infringement of trademarks and patents. College Savings Bank v. Florida Prepaid Postsecondary Education Expense Board, 527 U.S. 666 (1999); Florida Prepaid Postsecondary Education Expense Board v. College Savings Bank, 527 U.S. 627 (1999). In Kimel v. Florida Board of Regents, 528 U.S. 62 (2000), the Court held that damage actions against state agencies under the Age Discrimination in Employment Act of 1967 were barred by the Eleventh Amendment. Board of Trustees of the University of Alabama v. Garrett, 531 U.S. 356, 121 S.Ct. 955, 148 L.Ed.2d 866 (2001), held that Congress could not authorize damage suits against State agencies for failure to comply with the provisions of Title I of the Americans with Disabilities Act of 1990.

In each case, the Court rejected an argument that the abrogation of State sovereign immunity was justified by Section Five of the Fourteenth Amendment. The Court's analysis in *Kimel* of the scope of Congressional power to enforce the Fourteenth Amendment, appears infra page 1215. The Court's analysis of the Section 5 question *in Garrett* appears infra page 1215. Nevada Department of Human Resources v. Hibbs, 538 U.S. 721 (2003), however, upheld a damage action against the State under the 1993 Federal Family and Medical Leave Act. The year after *Hibbs*, in Tennessee v. Lane, 541 U.S. 509, 124 S.Ct. 1978 (2004), the Court again upheld a damage action against a State, this one brought under Title II of the Americans With Disabilities Act by persons who sought access to courts. The decision in *Hibbs* appears infra p. 1223. The decision in *Lane* appears infra p. 1230.

STATE SOVEREIGN IMMUNITY IN STATE COURT SUITS

Alden v. Maine

In Alden v. Maine, 527 U.S. 706 (1999), the Court held that States could assert sovereign immunity when sued in State court, that Congress lacked power to abrogate that immunity, and that States do not waive immunity by permitting suit in similar cases involving state law claims. Affirming a State court decision dismissing an overtime pay claim under the Fair Labor Standards Act, the Court said:

"the sovereign immunity of the States neither derives from nor is limited by the terms of the Eleventh Amendment. Rather, as the Constitution's structure, and its history, and the authoritative interpretations by this Court make clear, the States' immunity from suit is a fundamental aspect of the sovereignty which the States enjoyed before the ratification of the

Constitution, and which they retain today . . . except as altered by the plan of the Convention or certain constitutional Amendments.''

STATE SOVEREIGN IMMUNITY FROM FEDERAL ADMINISTRATIVE PROCEEDINGS

In Federal Maritime Commission v. South Carolina State Ports Authority, 535 U.S. 743 (2002), the Court held that a federal administrative proceeding which bore a "remarkably strong resemblance to civil litigation in federal courts" implicated the Eleventh Amendment immunity enjoyed by states. The Court rejected the arguments by the United States that a federal administrative proceeding should be treated differently than a judicial proceeding because the administrative agency's orders are not self-executing in the way that a court's orders are. The Court also found unavailing the federal government's suggestion that private actions brought against states before federal administrative bodies do not present the same threat that judicial litigation does to the financial integrity of states. The Court observed that sovereign immunity is designed to protect states not only from monetary liability, but also from the affront to their dignity that arises from suit itself.

FMC v. S. Carolina ports Authority

Fed. administrative proceeding should be treated the same as judicial proceedings/litigation.

CHAPTER 6

THE SCOPE OF STATE POWER

SECTION 1. INTRODUCTION

A. REGULATION

In Chapter 4 we explored the early Nineteenth Century dispute in the Supreme Court between those who read the commerce clause as granting to Congress exclusive power to regulate interstate commerce and those who contended that the grant was merely concurrent, leaving full power in the states to regulate in the absence of conflicting federal regulation. In Cooley v. Board of Wardens, 53 U.S. (12 How.) 299 (1851), set out supra p. 158, the Court reached a compromise position under which the commerce clause would permit some state regulations of interstate commerce but forbid others even in the absence of federal regulation. Ever since *Cooley* the Court has been struggling to find a formula to determine when state regulations of commerce are permissible.

In *Cooley* the Court attempted to resolve the problem by looking at the subjects being regulated. "Whatever subjects of this power are in their nature national, or admit only of one uniform system, or plan of regulation may justly be said to be of such a nature as to require exclusive legislation by Congress." Other subjects (such as harbor pilots, in that case) are of such a nature "as to leave no doubt of the superior fitness and propriety, not to say the absolute necessity, of different systems of regulation, drawn from local knowledge and experience, and conformed to local wants."

Later cases were more likely to speak in terms of "direct" burdens on commerce being forbidden, "indirect" burdens permitted. Thus in Erb v. Morasch, 177 U.S. 584 (1900) the Court said that a city ordinance regulating the speed of trains was "even as to interstate trains, one only indirectly affecting interstate commerce, and is within the power of the state until at least Congress shall take action in the matter." On the other hand, in Shafer v. Farmers' Grain Co. of Embden, 268 U.S. 189 (1925), the Court held invalid a state regulation of the purchase of wheat for interstate shipment because it constituted a "direct burden" on interstate commerce.

More recently the Court has addressed the problem in substantive rather than formal terms. In Brown–Forman Distillers Corporation v. New York State Liquor Authority, 476 U.S. 573, 578 (1986), for example, the Court said:

"This Court has adopted what amounts to a two-tiered approach to analyzing state economic regulation under the Commerce Clause. When a state statute directly regulates or discriminates against interstate commerce, or when its effect is to favor in-state economic interests over out-of-state interests, we have generally struck down the statute without further inquiry.... When, however, a statute has only indirect effects on interstate commerce and regulates evenhandedly, we have examined whether the State's interest is legitimate and whether the burden on interstate commerce clearly exceeds the local benefits. Pike v. Bruce Church, Inc., 397

270

U.S. 137, 142 (1970). We have also recognized that there is no clear line separating the category of state regulation that is virtually *per se* invalid under the Commerce Clause, and the category subject to the Pike v. Bruce Church balancing approach. In either situation the critical consideration is the overall effect of the statute on both local and interstate activity."

B.   TAXATION

Ever since its first case dealing with state taxation of commerce—Brown v. Maryland, 25 U.S. (12 Wheat.) 419, decided in 1827—the Court has struggled with whether the Constitution intended that property moving in interstate and foreign commerce or businesses engaged in such commerce should be to some extent, at least, immune from state taxation. With respect to interstate commerce the question arises under the general grant of power to Congress to regulate commerce among the states. With respect to foreign commerce the question arises under the general power of Congress to regulate commerce with foreign nations and under the provision in Art. I, § 10: "No State shall, without the Consent of the Congress, lay any Imposts or Duties on Imports or Exports, except what may be absolutely necessary for executing its inspection Laws...."

[margin note: Art I § 10]

The cases have been clear from the earliest times that taxes that formally discriminate against interstate or foreign commerce are forbidden. The import-export clause obviously was intended at least to preclude states from erecting tariff barriers on goods from abroad. In Welton v. Missouri, 91 U.S. 275 (1875), the Court firmly stated the rule against discrimination, invalidating a statute that imposed a special license tax on peddlers who sold goods "which are not the growth, produce, or manufacture of the state."

But the enormously difficult question is whether there is an immunity beyond that against discrimination. Are the states precluded from imposing nondiscriminatory taxes on goods or instrumentalities of commerce physically present within their borders merely because they are moving in interstate commerce? Are the states precluded from imposing nondiscriminatory taxes on either the net or the gross proceeds from interstate commerce activity that takes place within their borders?

In the major nineteenth century cases the Court, reflecting the early suggestions in the state regulation cases that the power given to Congress by the commerce clause was exclusive, tended to find a wide scope of immunity against any state taxes that could be said to bear directly upon interstate or foreign commerce.

[margin note: Limit when states can benefit & make revenue from interstate commerce instead of not allowing it at all]

The Court did not go so far as to hold that states never could secure revenue from interstate business, however. A broad immunity would have placed the states in the position of being required to provide governmental services to property and business within their borders without being able to secure any contribution from such property and business to the cost of government. Hence, the states sought to devise means to secure such revenues, and the Court began to draw lines between permissible and impermissible taxes on commerce. Originally, the lines drawn were largely formal. A state could impose a tax on the net proceeds from interstate activity within its borders but not on gross proceeds because the former bore only indirectly upon commerce while the latter bore directly. United States Glue Co. v. Town of Oak Creek, 247 U.S. 321 (1918). A state could impose a tax on the privilege of doing business and measure it by net income, including net income from interstate commerce attributable to the state, if the company did some local business but

[margin note: Tax - net proceeds Not gross proceeds]

not if all of its activity within the state was interstate commerce. Spector Motor Service v. O'Connor, 340 U.S. 602 (1951).

In Western Live Stock v. Bureau of Revenue, 303 U.S. 250, 254, 255 (1938), the Court began the search for a less formalistic basis upon which to decide the cases. It enunciated what has become known as the "multiple burdens" doctrine. First, the Court said "it was not the purpose of the commerce clause to relieve those engaged in interstate commerce from their just share of state tax burden even though it increases the cost of doing the business." Second, the Court indicated that the commerce clause should be construed to protect commerce against the multiple burdens which would result if more states than one could tax the same property or activity. In essence, the Court was simply restating the rule against discrimination when it attempted to rationalize prior cases: "The vice characteristic of those which have been held invalid is that they have placed on the commerce burdens of such a nature as to be capable in point of substance, of being imposed ... with equal right by every state which the commerce touches, merely because interstate commerce is being done, so that without the protection of the commerce clause it would bear cumulative burdens not imposed on local commerce."

The decision in *Western Live Stock* did not, however, mark an end to the older idea that interstate commerce itself could not be directly taxed. As recently as 1946 in Freeman v. Hewit, 329 U.S. 249, 256, the Court would say: "Nor is there any warrant in the constitutional principles heretofore applied by this Court to support the notion that a State may be allowed one single tax-worth of direct interference with the free flow of commerce. An exaction by a State from interstate commerce falls not because of a proven increase in the cost of the product. What makes the tax invalid is the fact that there is interference by a State with the freedom of interstate commerce.... Trade being a sensitive plant, a direct tax upon it to some extent at least deters trade even if its effect is not precisely calculable." For more than three decades after *Western Live Stock* the cases continued to reflect first one and then the other of these conflicting approaches.

Finally, in 1977, in Complete Auto Transit, Inc. v. Brady, 430 U.S. 274, 277, the Court rejected the formalistic approaches. Mississippi imposed a tax on the privilege of transporting for compensation persons or property between points within the state. In upholding the tax, the Court began by saying:

"Appellant ... did *not* allege that its activity which Mississippi taxes does not have a sufficient nexus with the State; or that the tax discriminates against interstate commerce; or that the tax is unfairly apportioned; or that it is unrelated to services provided by the State. No such claims were made before the Mississippi Supreme Court, and although appellant argues here that a tax on 'the privilege of doing interstate commerce' creates an unacceptable risk of discrimination and undue burdens, it does not claim that discrimination or undue burdens exist in fact.

"Appellant's attack is based solely on decisions of this Court holding that a tax on the 'privilege' of engaging in an activity in the State may not be applied to an activity that is part of interstate commerce. See, e.g., Spector Motor Service v. O'Connor, 340 U.S. 602 (1951); Freeman v. Hewit, 329 U.S. 249 (1946). This rule looks only to the fact that the incidence of the tax is the 'privilege of doing business'; it deems irrelevant any consideration of the practical effect of the tax. The rule reflects an underlying philosophy that interstate commerce should enjoy a sort of 'free trade' immunity from state taxation.

"Appellee, in its turn, relies on decisions of this Court stating that '[i]t was not the purpose of the commerce clause to relieve those engaged in interstate commerce from their just share of state tax burden even though it increases the cost of doing the business,' Western Live Stock v. Bureau of Revenue, 303 U.S. 250, 254 (1938). These decisions have considered not the formal language of the tax statute, but rather its practical effect, and have sustained a tax against Commerce Clause challenge when the tax is applied to an activity with a substantial nexus with the taxing state, is fairly apportioned, does not discriminate against interstate commerce, and is fairly related to the services provided by the State.

"Over the years, the Court has applied this practical analysis in approving many types of tax that avoided running afoul of the prohibition against taxing the 'privilege of doing business,' but in each instance it has refused to overrule the prohibition. Under the present state of the law, the *Spector* rule, as it has come to be known, has no relationship to economic realities. Rather it stands only as a trap for the unwary draftsman."[a]

Despite *Complete Auto*, the Court later reaffirmed that portion of its 1967 ruling in National Bellas Hess, Inc. v. Department of Revenue of Ill., 386 U.S. 753, that states requiring out-of-state mail-order businesses with no in-state physical presence to collect and remit taxes on purchases for intrastate use thereby "created an unconstitutional burden on interstate commerce." Quill Corporation v. North Dakota, 504 U.S. 298 (1992). Although *Bellas Hess* was "decided ... in the middle of this latest rally between formalism and pragmatism" bounded by *Spector Motor* and *Complete Auto*, and "[w]hile contemporary Commerce Clause jurisprudence might not dictate the same result were the issue to arise for the first time today, *Bellas Hess* is not inconsistent with *Complete Auto* and our recent cases." Rather, said the majority opinion by Justice Stevens, "*Bellas Hess* concerns the first of [*Complete Auto's*] tests and stands for the proposition that a vendor whose only contacts with the taxing State are by mail or common carrier lacks the 'substantial nexus' required by the Commerce Clause." Moreover, even though *Quill* did overrule that part of *Bellas Hess* holding that the Due Process Clause prohibited application of the use tax against a business lacking in-state physical presence, satisfaction of "the due process 'minimum contacts' test" did not meet "the Commerce Clause 'substantial nexus' test." Justice Stevens elaborated:

"... The second and third parts of [*Complete Auto's*] analysis, which require fair apportionment and non-discrimination,[b] prohibit taxes that pass an

a. The Court refined the four-part analytical approach of *Complete Auto Transit* in two decisions upholding state taxes against commerce clause challenges. Both were especially instructive with respect to the requirement that a state tax not discriminate against interstate commerce.

In Goldberg v. Sweet, 488 U.S. 252 (1989), the taxpayers urged that a 5% Illinois tax on interstate phone calls charged to an Illinois service address discriminated against interstate commerce, despite a similar 5% tax on intrastate calls, because a larger share of the overall tax burden fell on interstate calls. In rejecting this contention the Court noted that in contrast to taxes burdening out-of-state taxpayers "who would have difficulty effecting legislative change, the economic burden of the Illinois telecommunications tax falls on the Illinois telecommunications consumer, the insider who presumably is able to complain about and change the tax through the Illinois political process." The Court then said: "It is not a purpose of the Commerce Clause to protect state residents from their own taxes." This statement provoked disagreement and separate concurrences from Justices Stevens and O'Connor, who took the position that "a state may not discriminate among its own residents by placing a heavier tax on those who engage in interstate commerce than those who merely engage in local commerce."

b. Use taxes imposed on out-of-state sellers would be unconstitutionally discriminatory were there no corresponding sales tax imposed on in-state sellers (as there was in *Quill*). Under the "compensatory tax doc-unfair share of the tax burden onto interstate commerce. The first and fourth prongs, which require a substantial nexus and a relationship between the tax and State-provided services, limit the reach of State taxing authority so as to ensure that State taxation does not unduly burden interstate commerce.[6] Thus, the 'substantial-nexus' requirement is not, like due process' 'minimum-contacts' requirement, a proxy for notice, but rather a means for limiting state burdens on interstate commerce. Accordingly, . . . a corporation may have the 'minimum contacts' with a taxing State as required by the Due Process Clause, and yet lack the 'substantial nexus' with that State as required by the Commerce Clause.

. . .

" . . . [N]ot all formalism is alike. . . . [T]he bright-line rule of *Bellas Hess* furthers the ends of the dormant Commerce Clause. Undue burdens on interstate commerce may be avoided not only by a case-by-case evaluation of the actual burdens imposed by particular regulations or taxes, but also, in some situations, by the demarcation of a discrete realm of commercial activity that is free from interstate taxation. *Bellas Hess* followed the latter approach and created a safe harbor for vendors 'whose only connection with customers in the [taxing] State is by common carrier or the United States mail.' . . ."

The artificiality "at its edges" of the bright-line rule of *Bellas Hess* was "more than offset by the benefits of a clear rule[,]" encouraged "settled expectations and . . . foster[ed] investment by businesses and individuals. Indeed, it is not unlikely that the mail-order industry's dramatic growth over the last quarter-century is due in part to the bright-line exemption from state taxation created in *Bellas Hess*." Finally, now that the due process impediment had been cleared away, Congress was "free to decide whether, when, and to what extent the States may burden interstate mail-order concerns with a duty to collect use taxes."

Dissenting from the Court's commerce clause ruling, Justice White objected that "[w]hat we disavowed in *Complete Auto* was not just the 'formal distinction between "direct" and "indirect" taxes on interstate commerce,' but

---

trine," an otherwise facially discriminatory tax imposed on interstate commerce does not violate the negative commerce clause if it is only "the equivalent of an 'identifiable and substantially similar tax on intrastate commerce . . .'" Associated Industries of Missouri v. Lohman, 511 U.S. 641, 648 (1994). The doctrine, "designed simply to make interstate commerce bear a burden already borne by intrastate commerce[,]" is carefully circumscribed, however. Thus, in *Lohman*, the Court allowed Missouri to compensate for local sales taxes by imposing a uniform, statewide use tax on all goods purchased out-of-state but used in-state—but only in those local jurisdictions with sales tax rates equal to or greater than the use tax rate. That the sum of local sales taxes might exceed the total statewide use tax did not justify applying the use tax in locales with lower sales tax rates, for "strict parity is demanded by the compensatory tax doctrine."

More generally, Fulton Corp. v. Faulkner, 516 U.S. 325, 332–34 (1996), "distilled" from earlier cases "three conditions necessary for a valid compensatory tax"—state identification of the intrastate tax burden prompting a compensatory tax, a showing that the tax on interstate commerce does not exceed that on intrastate commerce, and proof that the compensating taxes fall on "substantially equivalent events." Even if a state theoretically might prove that the actual incidence of any two taxes would allow "a finding of combined neutrality on interstate competition[,]" doubts are to be resolved against the state and "courts will ordinarily be unable to evaluate the economic equivalence of allegedly compensatory tax schemes that go beyond traditional sales/use taxes."

6. North Dakota's use tax illustrates well how a state tax might unduly burden interstate commerce. On its face, North Dakota law imposes a collection duty on every vendor who advertises in the State three times in a single year. . . . What is more significant, similar obligations might be imposed by the Nation's 6,000—plus taxing jurisdictions. . . .

also the whole notion underlying the *Bellas Hess* physical presence rule—that 'interstate commerce is immune from state taxation.' " He found:

> "no relationship between the physical presence-nexus rule the Court retains and Commerce Clause considerations that allegedly justify it. Perhaps long ago a seller's 'physical presence' was a sufficient part of a trade to condition imposition of a tax on such presence. But in today's economy, physical presence frequently has very little to do with a transaction a State might seek to tax. Wire transfers of money involving billions of dollars occur every day; purchasers place orders with sellers by fax, phone, and computer linkup; sellers ship goods by air, road, and sea through sundry delivery services without leaving their place of business.... [A]n out-of-state direct marketer derives numerous commercial benefits from the State in which it does business[,] includ[ing] laws establishing sound local banking institutions to support credit transactions; courts to insure collection of the purchase price from the seller's customers; means of waste disposal from garbage generated by mail order solicitations; and creation and enforcement of consumer protection laws.... To create, for the first time, a nexus requirement under the Commerce Clause independent of that established for due process purposes is one thing; to attempt to justify an anachronistic notion of physical presence in economic terms is quite another."

The taxation cases have run an elaborate course independently of the regulation cases. In part the difference results from the fact that balancing cannot be done in the same fashion in taxation cases as in regulation cases. In the former the state interest is the same in every case—the receipt of revenue to meet the costs of government. Therefore the issues have been primarily those of examining the burdens on commerce rather than those of comparing burdens with benefits. In Department of Revenue of Washington v. Association of Washington Stevedoring Companies, 435 U.S. 734, 748 (1978), the Court noted this difference:

> "Although the balancing of safety interests naturally differs from the balancing of state financial needs, [we have] recognized that a State has a significant interest in exacting from interstate commerce its fair share of the cost of state government. All tax burdens do not impermissibly impede interstate commerce. The Commerce Clause balance tips against the tax only when it unfairly burdens commerce by exacting more than a just share from the interstate activity."

It is no longer possible in a basic constitutional law book to trace the intricate doctrines involved in the hundreds of taxation cases. Those materials must be left to specialized courses in state and local taxation. Here, an occasional tax case will be used where it helps illuminate issues involved in the regulation cases.

SECTION 2. DISCRIMINATION AGAINST INTERSTATE COMMERCE

New Energy Co. of Indiana v. Limbach
486 U.S. 269, 108 S.Ct. 1803, 100 L.Ed.2d 302 (1988).

Justice Scalia delivered the opinion of the Court.

Appellant New Energy Company of Indiana has challenged the constitutionality of Ohio Rev.Code Ann. § 5735.145(B) (1986), a provision that awards *challenged on constitutionality*

a tax credit against the Ohio motor vehicle fuel sales tax for each gallon of ethanol sold (as a component of gasohol) by fuel dealers, but only if the ethanol is produced in Ohio or in a State that grants similar tax advantages to ethanol produced in Ohio. The question presented is whether § 5735.145(B) discriminates against interstate commerce in violation of the Commerce Clause, U.S. Const., Art. I, § 8, cl. 3.

I

Ethanol, or ethyl alcohol, is usually made from corn. In the last decade it has come into widespread use as an automotive fuel, mixed with gasoline in a ratio of 1:9 to produce what is called gasohol. The interest in ethanol emerged in reaction to the petroleum market dislocations of the early 1970's. The product was originally promoted as a means of achieving energy independence while providing a market for surplus corn; more recently, emphasis has shifted to its environmental advantages as a replacement for lead in enhancing fuel octane.... Ethanol was, however (and continues to be), more expensive than gasoline, and the emergence of ethanol production on a commercial scale dates from enactment of the first federal subsidy, in the form of an exemption from federal motor fuel excise taxes, in 1978.... Since then, many States, particularly those in the grain-producing areas of the country, have enacted their own ethanol subsidies.... Ohio first passed such a measure in 1981, providing Ohio gasohol dealers a credit of so many cents per gallon of ethanol used in their product against the Ohio motor vehicle fuel sales tax payable on both ethanol and gasoline. This credit was originally available without regard to the source of the ethanol.... In 1984, however, Ohio enacted § 5735.145(B), which denies the credit to ethanol coming from States that do not grant a tax credit, exemption, or refund to ethanol from Ohio, or, if a State grants a smaller tax advantage than Ohio's, granting only an equivalent credit....

Appellant ... manufactures ethanol in South Bend, Indiana, for sale in several States, including Ohio. Indiana repealed its tax exemption for ethanol, effective July 1, 1985, ... at which time it also passed legislation providing a direct subsidy to Indiana ethanol producers (the sole one of which was appellant) ... Thus, by reason of Ohio's reciprocity provision, appellant's ethanol sold in Ohio became ineligible for the Ohio tax credit. Appellant sought declaratory and injunctive relief in [an Ohio state court,] alleging that § 5735.145(B) violated the Commerce Clause by discriminating against out-of-state ethanol producers to the advantage of in-state industry. The court denied relief, and the Ohio Court of Appeals affirmed. A divided Ohio Supreme Court initially reversed, finding that § 5735.145(B) discriminated without adequate justification against products of out-of-state origin, and shielded Ohio producers from out-of-state competition. [On] rehearing [it] reversed itself, a majority of the court finding that the provision was not protectionist or unreasonably burdensome....

II

commerce clause limits power of states to discriminate against interstate commerce

It has long been accepted that the Commerce Clause not only grants Congress the authority to regulate commerce among the States, but also directly limits the power of the States to discriminate against interstate commerce. See, e.g., Hughes v. Oklahoma, 441 U.S. 322, 326 (1979); H.P. Hood & Sons, Inc. v. Du Mond, 336 U.S. 525, 534–535 (1949); Welton v. Missouri, 91 U.S. 275 (1876). This "negative" aspect of the Commerce Clause prohibits economic protectionism—that is, regulatory measures designed to benefit in-state economic interests by burdening out-of-state competitors. See, e.g., Bacchus Imports, Ltd. v. Dias, 468 U.S. 263, 270–273 (1984); *H.P. Hood & Sons,* supra, at 532–533; Guy v. Baltimore, 100 U.S. 434, 443 (1880). Thus, state statutes that clearly discriminate against interstate commerce are routinely struck down, see, e.g., Sporhase v. Nebraska ex rel. Douglas, 458 U.S. 941 (1982); Lewis v. BT Investment Managers, Inc., 447 U.S. 27 (1980); Dean Milk Co. v. Madison, 340 U.S. 349 (1951), unless the discrimination is demonstrably justified by a valid factor unrelated to economic protectionism, see, e.g., Maine v. Taylor, 477 U.S. 131 (1986).

The Ohio provision at issue here explicitly deprives certain products of generally available beneficial tax treatment because they are made in certain other States, and thus on its face appears to violate the cardinal requirement of nondiscrimination. Appellees argue, however, that the availability of the tax credit to some out-of-state manufacturers (those in States that give tax advantages to Ohio-produced ethanol) shows that the Ohio provision, far from discriminating against interstate commerce, is likely to promote it, by encouraging other States to enact similar tax advantages that will spur the interstate sale of ethanol. We rejected a similar contention in an earlier "reciprocity" case, Great Atlantic & Pacific Tea Co. v. Cottrell, 424 U.S. 366 (1976). The regulation at issue there permitted milk from out of State to be sold in Mississippi only if the State of origin accepted Mississippi milk on a reciprocal basis. Mississippi put forward, among other arguments, the assertion that "the reciprocity requirement is in effect a free-trade provision, advancing the identical national interest that is served by the Commerce Clause." Id., at 378. In response, we said that "Mississippi may not use the threat of economic isolation as a weapon to force sister States to enter into even a desirable reciprocity agreement." Id., at 379. More recently, we characterized a Nebraska reciprocity requirement for the export of ground water from the State as "facially discriminatory legislation" which merited " 'strictest scrutiny.' " Sporhase v. Nebraska ex rel. Douglas, supra, at 958, quoting Hughes v. Oklahoma, supra, at 337.

It is true that in *Cottrell* and *Sporhase* the effect of a State's refusal to accept the offered reciprocity was total elimination of all transport of the subject product into or out of the offering State; whereas in the present case the only effect of refusal is that the out-of-state product is placed at a substantial commercial disadvantage through discriminatory tax treatment. That makes no difference for purposes of Commerce Clause analysis. In the leading case of Baldwin v. G.A.F. Seelig, Inc., 294 U.S. 511 (1935), the New York law excluding out-of-state milk did not impose an absolute ban, but rather allowed importation and sale so long as the initial purchase from the dairy farmer was made at or above the New York State-mandated price. In other words, just as the appellant here, in order to sell its product in Ohio, only has to cut its profits by reducing its sales price below the market price sufficiently to compensate the Ohio purchaser-retailer for the forgone tax credit, so also the milk wholesaler-distributor in *Baldwin,* in order to sell its product in New York, only had to cut its profits by increasing its purchase price above the market price sufficiently to meet the New York-prescribed minimum. We viewed the New York law as "an economic barrier against competition" that was "equivalent to a rampart of customs duties." Id., at 527. Similarly, in Hunt v. Washington Apple Advertising Comm'n, 432 U.S. 333, 349–351 (1977), we found invalid under the Commerce Clause a North Carolina statute that did not exclude apples from other States, but merely imposed additional costs upon Washington sellers and deprived them of the commercial advantage of their distinctive grading system. The present law likewise imposes an economic

This disc. is not justified

disadvantage upon out-of-state sellers; and the promise to remove that if reciprocity is accepted no more justifies disparity of treatment than it would justify categorical exclusion. We have indicated that reciprocity requirements are not *per se* unlawful. See *Cottrell,* supra, at 378. But the case we cited for that proposition, Kane v. New Jersey, 242 U.S. 160, 167–168 (1916), discussed a context in which, if a State offered the reciprocity did not accept it, the consequence was, to be sure, *less favored* treatment for its citizens, but nonetheless treatment that complied with the minimum requirements of the Commerce Clause. Here, quite to the contrary, the threat used to induce Indiana's acceptance is, in effect, taxing a product made by its manufacturers at a rate higher than the same product made by Ohio manufacturers, without (as we shall see) justification for the disparity.

Appelles argue that law application is limited to few people ct says irrelevant.

Appellees argue that § 5735.145(B) should not be considered discrimination against interstate commerce because its practical scope is so limited. Apparently only one Ohio ethanol manufacturer exists (appellee South Point Ethanol) and only one out-of-state manufacturer (appellant) is clearly disadvantaged by the provision. Our cases, however, indicate that where discrimination is patent, as it is here, neither a widespread advantage to in-state interests nor a widespread disadvantage to out-of-state competitors need be shown. For example, in *Bacchus Imports, Ltd. v. Dias,* supra, we held unconstitutional under the Commerce Clause a special exemption from Hawaii's liquor tax for certain locally produced alcoholic beverages (okolehao and fruit wine), even though other locally produced alcoholic beverages were subject to the tax. 468 U.S., at 265, 271. And in *Lewis v. BT Investment Managers, Inc.,* supra, we held unconstitutional a Florida statute that excluded from certain business activities in Florida not all out-of-state entities, but only out-of-state bank holding companies, banks, or trust companies. In neither of these cases did we consider the size or number of the in-state businesses favored or the out-of-state businesses disfavored relevant to our determination. Varying the strength of the bar against economic protectionism according to the size and number of in-state and out-of-state firms affected would serve no purpose except the creation of new uncertainties in an already complex field.

. . .

It has not escaped our notice that the appellant here, which is eligible to receive a cash subsidy under Indiana's program for in-state ethanol producers, is the potential beneficiary of a scheme no less discriminatory than the one that it attacks, and no less effective in conferring a commercial advantage over out-of-state competitors. To believe the Indiana scheme is valid, however, is not to believe that the Ohio scheme must be valid as well. The Commerce Clause does not prohibit all state action designed to give its residents an advantage in the marketplace, but only action of that description *in connection with the State's regulation of interstate commerce.* Direct subsidization of domestic industry does not ordinarily run afoul of that prohibition; discriminatory taxation of out-of-state manufactures does. Of course, even if the Indiana subsidy were invalid, retaliatory violation of the Commerce Clause by Ohio would not be acceptable. See *Cottrell,* 424 U.S., at 379–380.

III

state can validate disc. if it cant be adequately done otherwise

Our cases leave open the possibility that a State may validate a statute that discriminates against interstate commerce by showing that it advances a legitimate local purpose that cannot be adequately served by reasonable nondiscriminatory alternatives. See, e.g., Maine v. Taylor, 477 U.S., at 138, 151; Sporhase v. Nebraska ex rel. Douglas, 458 U.S., at 958; Hughes v. Oklahoma,

441 U.S., at 336–337; Dean Milk Co. v. Madison, 340 U.S., at 354. This is perhaps just another way of saying that what may appear to be a "discriminatory" provision in the constitutionally prohibited sense—that is, a protectionist enactment—may on closer analysis not be so. However it be put, the standards for such justification are high. Cf. Philadelphia v. New Jersey, 437 U.S. 617, 624 (1978) ("[W]here simple economic protectionism is effected by state legislation, a virtually *per se* rule of invalidity has been erected"); Hughes v. Oklahoma, 441 U.S., at 337 ("[F]acial discrimination by itself may be a fatal defect" and "[a]t a minimum . . . invokes the strictest scrutiny").

Appellees advance two justifications for the clear discrimination in the present case: health and commerce. As to the first, they argue that the provision encourages use of ethanol (in replacement of lead as a gasoline octane-enhancer) to reduce harmful exhaust emissions, both in Ohio itself and in surrounding States whose polluted atmosphere may reach Ohio. Certainly the protection of health is a legitimate state goal, and we assume for purposes of this argument that use of ethanol generally furthers it. But § 5735.145(B) obviously does not, except perhaps by accident. As far as ethanol use in Ohio itself is concerned, there is no reason to suppose that ethanol produced in a State that does not offer tax advantages to ethanol produced in Ohio is less healthy, and thus should have its importation into Ohio suppressed by denial of the otherwise standard tax credit. And as far as ethanol use outside Ohio is concerned, surely that is just as effectively fostered by other States' subsidizing ethanol production or sale in some fashion other than giving a tax credit to Ohio-produced ethanol; but these helpful expedients do not qualify for the tax credit. It could not be clearer that health is not the purpose of the provision, but is merely an occasional and accidental effect of achieving what is its purpose, favorable tax treatment for Ohio-produced ethanol. Essentially the same reasoning also responds to appellees' second (and related) justification for the discrimination, that the reciprocity requirement is designed to increase commerce in ethanol by encouraging other States to enact ethanol subsidies. What is encouraged is not ethanol subsidies in general, but only favorable treatment for Ohio-produced ethanol. In sum, appellees' health and commerce justifications amount to no more than implausible speculation, which does not suffice to validate this plain discrimination against products of out-of-state manufacture.

. . .

Reversed.

NOTE

New Energy presents the one doctrine on which all justices appear to agree—state statutes discriminating against interstate commerce will normally be found unconstitutional. Beyond this proposition there are wide areas of disagreement. Some commentators have argued that courts generally should not invalidate non-discriminatory state regulations on the basis that the burden on interstate commerce outweighs local benefits. For one example, see Regan, *The Supreme Court and State Protectionism: Making Sense of the Dormant Commerce Clause,* 84 Mich.L.Rev. 1091 (1986). For an article citing the attacks on the Court's use of the commerce clause and largely defending the Court, see Collins, *Economic Union as a Constitutional Value,* 63 New York U.L.Rev. 43 (1988). Justice Scalia rejects the balancing approach to negative commerce clause cases and says: "In my view, a state statute is invalid under the Commerce Clause if, and only if, it accords discriminatory treatment to interstate commerce in a respect not required to achieve a lawful state purpose. When such a validating purpose exists, it is for Congress and not us to determine it is not significant enough to justify the burden on commerce." Bendix Autolite Corp. v. Midwesco Enterprises, Inc., 486 U.S. 888, 898 (1988)(opinion concurring in judgment).

SECTION 3.   IMPLIED RESTRICTIONS OF THE COMMERCE CLAUSE—TRANSPORTATION

STATE ECONOMIC REGULATION OF TRANSPORTATION BUSINESSES

The Supreme Court early took the position that since the right to carry on interstate commerce was conferred by the Constitution, the states had no power to require licenses as conditions of carrying on such commerce. Thus in Crutcher v. Kentucky, 141 U.S. 47 (1891), the Court held invalid a state statute requiring agents of foreign express companies to secure a license that could be secured on payment of a nominal fee and on showing a minimum level of assets. The state argued that the statute was necessary to protect citizens against unreliable and insolvent businesses. The Court responded: "To carry on interstate commerce is not a franchise or a privilege granted by the State; it is a right which every citizen of the United States is entitled to exercise under the Constitution and laws of the United States. ... We have repeatedly decided that a state law is unconstitutional which requires a party to take out a license for carrying on interstate commerce. ..." The principal application of that rule was in the following case:

BUCK v. KUYKENDALL, 267 U.S. 307 (1925), invalidated a statute of the state of Washington requiring all common carriers for hire using highways in the state to obtain certificates of convenience and necessity. The state denied a certificate to a motor carrier operating between Seattle, Washington, and Portland, Oregon on the ground that the route was already adequately served. (No federal regulation of motor carriers existed at the time.) The Supreme Court, in an opinion by Justice Brandeis, held the state had no power to require such a license from an interstate carrier:

"It may be assumed that section 4 of the state statute is consistent with the Fourteenth Amendment; and also, that appropriate state regulations adopted primarily to promote safety upon the highways and conservation in their use are not obnoxious to the commerce clause, where the indirect burden imposed upon interstate commerce is not unreasonable. ... The provision here in question is of a different character. Its primary purpose is not regulation with a view to safety or to conservation of the highways, but the prohibition of competition. It determines, not the manner of use, but the persons by whom the highways may be used. It prohibits such use to some persons, while permitting it to others for the same purpose and in the same manner. Moreover, it determines whether the prohibition shall be applied by resort, through state officials, to a test which is peculiarly within the province of the federal action—the existence of adequate facilities for conducting interstate commerce. ..."

However, the Court has upheld license requirements in cases where the state has not been asserting the authority to prevent the movement of traffic interstate. In California v. Thompson, 313 U.S. 109 (1941), the Court held valid a California statute requiring agents engaged in selling transportation on the public highways of the state to obtain a license and post a bond. Criminal prosecution was brought against an unlicensed agent who sold interstate transportation in cars not operated as regular carriers; federal regulation of motor carriers which began in 1935 did not apply to such persons. The Court said that the state statute "is not shown to be other than what on its face it appears to be, a measure to safeguard the members of the public desiring to secure transportation by motor vehicle, who are peculiarly unable to protect themselves from fraud and overreaching of those engaged in a business notoriously subject to those abuses. . . . Fraudulent or unconscionable conduct of those so engaged which is injurious to their patrons, is peculiarly a subject of local concern and the appropriate subject of local regulation".

The Court disclaimed any intent to overrule *Crutcher v. Kentucky,* supra, saying: "The present case is not one of prohibiting interstate commerce or licensing it on conditions which restrict or obstruct it. Cf. Crutcher v. Kentucky, 141 U.S. 47; Dahnke–Walker Co. v. Bondurant, 257 U.S. 282. For here the regulation is applied to one who is not himself engaged in the transportation but who acts only as broker or intermediary in negotiating a transportation contract between the passengers and the carrier. The license required of those engaged in such business is not conditioned upon any control or restriction of the movement of the traffic interstate but only on the good character and responsibility of those engaged locally as transportation brokers."

The federal government now imposes economic regulations on all forms of interstate transportation and communication. Problems such as those involved in *Buck* no longer arise. Thus in 1935 Congress enacted the Federal Motor Carrier Act, which became Part II of the Interstate Commerce Act and gave the Interstate Commerce Commission wide power to regulate common carriers and contract carriers engaged in interstate transportation by motor vehicle. 49 U.S.C. §§ 301–327. It is now the I.C.C. which determines whether licenses to carry on such transportation shall be issued.

STATE SAFETY REGULATIONS AND INTERSTATE TRANSPORTATION

A much more enduring problem has been that of determining the circumstances under which states may impose regulations on interstate carriers in the interests of safety. Congress was slow to move into the field of safety regulation and hence for a long time the obvious public interest in safety was served only by state regulation. In recent years federal safety regulations have become far more extensive, but the federal government has not purported to assert exclusive authority. As a result there is a continuing docket of litigation involving state safety regulations and the question whether the commerce clause of its own force prohibits them.

Originally, the Court upheld most state safety regulations, but it had difficulty in articulating coherent doctrinal reasons. A common reason given in the early cases for upholding the state regulation was that it only "indirectly" affected interstate commerce. In Erb v. Morasch, 177 U.S. 584 (1900), e.g., the Court held that a city ordinance regulating the speed of trains could be applied to interstate trains because it only "indirectly" affected commerce. The Court was not able, however, to explain why some regulations were direct and others indirect and it soon became apparent that other factors were at work. A principal example of the problem arose in litigation challenging a Georgia statute requiring all trains to check their speed at grade crossings so that they might stop if necessary to avoid hitting persons or vehicles crossing the tracks. Persons injured at grade crossings sued the railroads, seeking to base liability on the failure of the railroad to comply with the statute. In Southern Ry. Co. v. King, 217 U.S. 524 (1910), the Court upheld the sustaining of a demurrer to an answer by the railroad which merely alleged that the statute was in violation of the commerce clause and imposed a direct burden on interstate traffic. The Court said the averments were mere conclusions. "They set forth no facts which would make the operation of the statute unconstitutional. They do not show the number or location of the crossings at which the railway company would be required to check the speed of its trains, so as to interfere with their successful operation. For aught that appears as allegations of fact in this answer, the crossing at which this injury happened may have been so located and of such dangerous character as to make the slackening of trains at that point necessary to the safety of those using the public highway, and a statute making such requirement only a reasonable police regulation, and not an unlawful attempt to regulate or hinder interstate commerce." In a later case of the same type, Seaboard Air Line Ry. Co. v. Blackwell, 244 U.S. 310 (1917), the railroad's answer alleged that the train involved was running in interstate commerce from Atlanta, Georgia, to other points in Georgia and South Carolina; that in the 123–mile run from Atlanta to the state line there were 124 crossings at which the statute required each train to check its speed; that three minutes would be consumed at each crossing, or about six hours in all, thus increasing the running time between Atlanta and the state line from the scheduled 4 ½ to a total of 10 ½ hours. The Court stated that the facts alleged "compel the conclusion that the statute is a direct burden upon interstate commerce, and, being such, is unlawful". Judgment for the plaintiff was reversed.

The Court was even willing to sustain state licensing regulations, at least when they did not totally exclude carriers from interstate commerce, if reasonably necessary to promote safety. The following case, which should be contrasted with *Buck v. Kuykendall,* supra, is illustrative.

BRADLEY v. PUBLIC UTILITIES COMMISSION, 289 U.S. 92 (1933). The Ohio Public Utilities Commission denied Bradley's application for a certificate of public convenience and necessity to operate a motor carrier service over state Route No. 20 from Cleveland to Flint, Michigan. After a hearing, the Commission determined that Route 20 was so badly congested that adding Bradley's service "would create and maintain an excessive and undue hazard to the safety and security of the traveling public." The Supreme Court unanimously upheld the denial of the certificate. First, the Court noted that the order did not exclude Bradley from operating in interstate commerce. He had failed to apply for an alternate route and had not shown that a feasible route with less congestion was not available.

Second, the Court said:

"It is contended that an order denying to a common carrier by motor a certificate to engage in interstate transportation necessarily violates the Commerce Clause. The argument is that under the rule declared in Buck v. Kuykendall, 267 U.S. 307, . . . an interstate carrier is entitled to a certificate as of right; and that hence the reason for the commission's refusal and its purpose are immaterial. In those cases, safety was doubtless promoted when the certificate was denied, because intensification of traffic was thereby prevented. . . . But there promotion of safety was merely an incident of the denial. Its purpose was to prevent competition deemed undesirable. The test employed was the adequacy of existing transportation facilities; and since the transportation in question was interstate, denial of the certificate invaded the province of Congress. In the case at bar, the purpose of the denial was to promote safety;

and the test employed was congestion of the highway. The effect of the denial upon interstate commerce was merely an incident.

"Protection against accidents, as against crime, presents ordinarily a local problem. Regulation to ensure safety is an exercise of the police power. It is primarily a state function, whether the locus be private property or the public highways. Congress has not dealt with the subject. Hence, even where the motorcars are used exclusively in interstate commerce, a state may freely exact registration of the vehicle and an operator's license, Hendrick v. Maryland, 235 U.S. 610, 622.... The state may exclude from the public highways vehicles engaged exclusively in interstate commerce, if of a size deemed dangerous to the public safety, Morris v. Duby, 274 U.S. 135, 144; Sproles v. Binford, 286 U.S. 374, 389–390. Safety may require that no additional vehicle be admitted to the highway. The Commerce Clause is not violated by denial of the certificate to the appellant, if upon adequate evidence denial is deemed necessary to promote the public safety."[a]

The balance of this section will present cases from 1938 to the present involving state safety regulations as applied to interstate transportation. The student should consider whether there is a coherent doctrine which explains the results in these cases.

SOUTH CAROLINA STATE HIGHWAY DEPARTMENT v. BARN-WELL BROTHERS, 303 U.S. 177 (1938). A South Carolina statute forbade the use on state highways of motor trucks whose width exceeded 90 inches and whose weight including load exceeded 20,000 pounds. A Federal district court weighed conflicting evidence and determined that the width and weight limitations were more restrictive than needed to protect the highways of the state and the users of such highways. It also determined that the limitations imposed substantial burdens on interstate commerce since 85 to 90 percent of the trucks used in interstate commerce were 96 inches wide and of a gross weight when loaded in excess of 20,000 pounds.

The Supreme Court reversed in an opinion by Justice Stone, stating:

"While the constitutional grant to Congress of power to regulate interstate commerce has been held to operate of its own force to curtail state power in some measure,[2] it did not forestall all state action affecting interstate commerce....

"The commerce clause by its own force, prohibits discrimination against interstate commerce, whatever its form or method, and the decisions of this Court have recognized that there is scope for its like operation when state legislation nominally of local concern is in point of fact aimed at interstate commerce, or by its necessary operation is a means of gaining a local benefit by throwing the attendant burdens on those without the state.... The commerce

---

a. For an excellent discussion of the *Buck* and *Bradley* cases as well as state motor carrier regulation prior to the adoption of the Federal Motor Carrier Act in 1935, see Kauper, *State Regulation of Interstate Motor Carriers*, 31 Mich.L.Rev. 920, 1097 (1933). A later brief discussion will be found in Swerer, *State Regulation of Interstate Transportation by Motor Carriers*, 16 Rocky Mt.L.Rev. 1 (1943).

2. State regulations affecting interstate commerce, whose purpose or effect is to gain for those within the state an advantage at the expense of those without, or to burden those

out of the state without any corresponding advantage to those within, have been thought to impinge upon the constitutional prohibition even though Congress has not acted....

Underlying the stated rule has been the thought, often expressed in judicial opinion, that when the regulation is of such a character that its burden falls principally upon those without the state, legislative action is not likely to be subjected to those political restraints which are normally exerted on legislation where it affects adversely some interests within the state....

clause has also been thought to set its own limitation upon state control of interstate rail carriers so as to preclude the subordination of the efficiency and convenience of interstate traffic to local service requirements.

"But the present case affords no occasion for saying that the bare possession of power by Congress to regulate the interstate traffic forces the states to conform to standards which Congress might, but has not adopted, or curtails their power to take measures to insure the safety and conservation of their highways which may be applied to like traffic moving intrastate. Few subjects of state regulation are so peculiarly of local concern as is the use of state highways. There are few, local regulation of which is so inseparable from a substantial effect on interstate commerce. Unlike the railroads, local highways are built, owned, and maintained by the state or its municipal subdivisions. The state has a primary and immediate concern in their safe and economical administration. The present regulations, or any others of like purpose, if they are to accomplish their end, must be applied alike to interstate and intrastate traffic both moving in large volume over the highways. The fact that they affect alike shippers in interstate and intrastate commerce in large number within as well as without the state is a safeguard against their abuse.

. . .

"Congress, in the exercise of its plenary power to regulate interstate commerce, may determine whether the burdens imposed on it by state regulation, otherwise permissible, are too great, and may, by legislation designed to secure uniformity or in other respects to protect the national interest in the commerce, curtail to some extent the state's regulatory power. But that is a legislative, not a judicial, function, to be performed in the light of the congressional judgment of what is appropriate regulation of interstate commerce, and the extent to which, in that field, state power and local interests should be required to yield to the national authority and interest. In the absence of such legislation the judicial function, under the commerce clause, as well as the Fourteenth Amendment, stops with the inquiry whether the state Legislature in adopting regulations such as the present has acted within its province, and whether the means of regulation chosen are reasonably adapted to the end sought. . . .

"Here the first inquiry has already been resolved by our decisions that a state may impose nondiscriminatory restrictions with respect to the character of motor vehicles moving in interstate commerce as a safety measure and as a means of securing the economical use of its highways. In resolving the second, courts do not sit as Legislatures, either state or national. . . . When the action of a Legislature is within the scope of its power, fairly debatable questions as to its reasonableness, wisdom, and propriety are not for the determination of courts, but for the legislative body, on which rests the duty and responsibility of decision. . . . It is not any the less a legislative power committed to the states because it affects interstate commerce, and courts are not any the more entitled, because interstate commerce is affected, to substitute their own for the legislative judgment. . . .

"Since the adoption of one weight or width regulation, rather than another, is a legislative, not a judicial, choice, its constitutionality is not to be determined by weighing in the judicial scales the merits of the legislative choice and rejecting it if the weight of evidence presented in court appears to favor a different standard. . . . Being a legislative judgment it is presumed to be supported by facts known to the Legislature unless facts judicially known or proved preclude that possibility. Hence, in reviewing the present determination, we examine the record, not to see whether the findings of the court below are supported by evidence, but to ascertain upon the whole record whether it is possible to say that the legislative choice is without rational basis. . . . Not only does the record fail to exclude that possibility but it shows affirmatively that there is adequate support for the legislative judgment. . . ."

SOUTHERN PACIFIC CO. v. ARIZONA, 325 U.S. 761 (1945). An Arizona law forbade the operation of railroad trains of more than fourteen passenger or seventy freight cars and authorized the state to recover a monetary penalty for each violation. In 1940 the state brought suit against the railroad in an Arizona state court seeking to recover the statutory penalties for violation of the act. An extended trial was had after which the trial court made detailed findings of fact as to the extent to which the statute burdened commerce and the extent to which it benefited state interests and concluded that the statute was unconstitutional. The Arizona Supreme Court reversed, directing entry of judgment for the state. The Supreme Court in an opinion by Chief Justice Stone, reversed, stating in part:

TC - statute was unconstitutional

AC - reversed

". . . [E]ver since Gibbons v. Ogden, 9 Wheat. 1, the states have not been deemed to have authority to impede substantially the free flow of commerce from state to state, or to regulate those phases of the national commerce which, because of the need of national uniformity, demand that their regulation, if any, be prescribed by a single authority.[2] *Cooley v. Board of Wardens,* supra. . . . Whether or not this long recognized distribution of power between the national and the state governments is predicated upon the implications of the commerce clause itself, Minnesota Rate Cases, supra, 399, 400; South Carolina Highway Dept. v. Barnwell Bros., supra, 185 . . . or upon the presumed intention of Congress, where Congress has not spoken, . . . the result is the same.

"In the application of these principles some enactments may be found to be plainly within and others plainly without state power. But between these extremes lies the infinite variety of cases in which regulation of local matters may also operate as a regulation of commerce, in which reconciliation of the conflicting claims of state and national power is to be attained only by some appraisal and accommodation of the competing demands of the state and national interests involved. . . .

. . .

"Congress has undoubted power to redefine the distribution of power over interstate commerce. It may either permit the states to regulate the commerce in a manner which would otherwise not be permissible, In re Rahrer, supra, 140 U.S. 561, 562, . . . or exclude state regulation even of matters of peculiarly local concern which nevertheless affect interstate commerce. . . .

"But in general Congress has left it to the courts to formulate the rules thus interpreting the commerce clause in its application, doubtless because it has appreciated the destructive consequences to the commerce of the nation if their protection were withdrawn, Gwin, etc., Inc. v. Henneford, supra, 305 U.S. 441, and has been aware that in their application state laws will not be invalidated without the support of relevant factual material which will 'afford a sure basis' for an informed judgment. . . .

2. In applying this rule the Court has often recognized that to the extent that the burden of state regulation falls on interests outside the state, it is unlikely to be alleviated by the operation of those political restraints normally exerted when interests within the state are affected. . . .

"Hence the matters for ultimate determination here are the nature and extent of the burden which the state regulation of interstate trains, adopted as a safety measure, imposes on interstate commerce, and whether the relative weights of the state and national interests involved are such as to make inapplicable the rule, generally observed, that the free flow of interstate commerce and its freedom from local restraints in matters requiring uniformity of regulation are interests safeguarded by the commerce clause from state interference.

"While this Court is not bound by the findings of the state court, and may determine for itself the facts of a case upon which an asserted federal right depends, the facts found by the state trial court showing the nature of the interstate commerce involved, and the effect upon it of the train limit law, are not seriously questioned. Its findings with respect to the need for and effect of the statute as a safety measure, although challenged in some particulars which we do not regard as material to our decision, are likewise supported by evidence. Taken together the findings supply an adequate basis for decision of the constitutional issue.

. . .

"The unchallenged findings leave no doubt that the Arizona Train Limit Law imposes a serious burden on the interstate commerce conducted by appellant. It materially impedes the movement of appellant's interstate trains through that state and interposes a substantial obstruction to the national policy proclaimed by Congress, to promote adequate, economical and efficient railway transportation service. . . . Enforcement of the law in Arizona, while train lengths remain unregulated or are regulated by varying standards in other states, must inevitably result in an impairment of uniformity of efficient railroad operation because the railroads are subjected to regulation which is not uniform in its application. Compliance with a state statute limiting train lengths requires interstate trains of a length lawful in other states to be broken up and reconstituted as they enter each state according as it may impose varying limitations upon train lengths. The alternative is for the carrier to conform to the lowest train limit restriction of any of the states through which its trains pass, whose laws thus control the carriers' operations both within and without the regulating state.

. . .

"The trial court found that the Arizona law had no reasonable relation to safety, and made train operation more dangerous. Examination of the evidence and the detailed findings makes it clear that this conclusion was rested on facts found which indicate that such increased danger of accident and personal injury as may result from the greater length of trains is more than offset by the increase in the number of accidents resulting from the larger number of trains when train lengths are reduced. In considering the effect of the statute as a safety measure, therefore, the factor of controlling significance for present purposes is not whether there is basis for the conclusion of the Arizona Supreme Court that the increase in length of trains beyond the statutory maximum has an adverse effect upon safety of operation. The decisive question is whether in the circumstances the total effect of the law as a safety measure in reducing accidents and casualties is so slight or problematical as not to outweigh the national interest in keeping interstate commerce free from interferences which seriously impede it and subject it to local regulation which does not have a uniform effect on the interstate train journey which it interrupts.

. . .

"Here we conclude that the state does go too far. Its regulation of train lengths, admittedly obstructive to interstate train operation, and having a seriously adverse effect on transportation efficiency and economy, passes beyond what is plainly essential for safety since it does not appear that it will lessen rather than increase the danger of accident. Its attempted regulation of the operation of interstate trains cannot establish nation-wide control such as is essential to the maintenance of an efficient transportation system, which Congress alone can prescribe. The state interest cannot be preserved at the expense of the national interest by an enactment which regulates interstate train lengths without securing such control, which is a matter of national concern. To this the interest of the state here asserted is subordinate.

. . .

"*South Carolina State Highway Dept. v. Barnwell Bros.*, supra, was concerned with the power of the state to regulate the weight and width of motor cars passing interstate over its highways, a legislative field over which the state has a far more extensive control than over interstate railroads. In that case, . . . we were at pains to point out that there are few subjects of state regulation affecting interstate commerce which are so peculiarly of local concern as is the use of the state's highways. . . ."

Justices Black and Douglas dissented. Justice Black stated that the ruling of the Court "makes it necessary for a judge to hear all the evidence offered as to why a legislature passed a law and to make findings of fact as to the validity of those reasons. If under today's ruling a court does make findings, as to a danger contrary to the findings of the legislature, and the evidence heard 'lends support' to those findings, a court can then invalidate the law. In this respect, the Arizona County Court acted, and this Court today is acting, as a 'super-legislature.'"

Justice Douglas said: "My view has been that the courts should intervene only where the state legislation discriminated against interstate commerce or was out of harmony with laws which Congress had enacted."

BIBB v. NAVAJO FREIGHT LINES, INC., 359 U.S. 520 (1959). An Illinois statute required the use of a certain type of rear fender mudguard on trucks and trailers operating on highways in the state. The statute made illegal the use of straight mudflaps which were legal in at least 45 states and required in the state of Arkansas. A Federal district court held the statute invalid as placing an undue burden on interstate commerce. The Supreme Court affirmed in an opinion by Justice Douglas.

Justice Douglas commenced his opinion by citing *Barnwell* for the proposition that regulation of highways is peculiarly local and that policy decisions are for the state legislature. "Unless we can conclude on the whole record that the 'total effect of the law as a safety measure in reducing accidents and casualties is so slight or problematic as not to outweigh the national interest in keeping interstate commerce free from interferences which seriously impede it' (*Southern Pacific v. Arizona* . . .) we must uphold the statute."

Justice Douglas then reviewed the evidence as to the cost of equipping all interstate vehicles with contour mudguards and as to the relative safety of such mudguards and conventional mudflaps. He concluded that review by saying: "If we had here only a question whether the cost of adjusting an interstate operation to these new local safety regulations prescribed by Illinois unduly burdened interstate commerce, we would have to sustain the law.... The same result would obtain if we had to resolve the much discussed issues of safety presented in this case."

"This case," he said, "presents a different issue." The equipment here could not pass muster in every state; instead the question is whether one state can prescribe standards which will require shifting cargo to differently designed vehicles at the state border. Because of the practice of "interlining"—transferring loaded trailers between an originating carrier and another carrier—the statute would require carriers who do only a minor amount of their business in Illinois to equip all of their trailers with the contour mudguards.

He then rejected the argument that *Barnwell* stood for the proposition that despite "the rather massive showing of burden on interstate commerce", it was for the state legislature, not the courts, to weigh the relative merits of contour mudguards against any other kind. "The various exercises by the States of their police power stand ... on an equal footing. All are entitled to the same presumption of validity when challenged under the Due Process Clause.... Similarly the various state regulatory statutes are of equal dignity when measured against the Commerce Clause, ... Local regulation which would pass muster under the Due Process Clause might nonetheless fail to survive other challenges to constitutionality that bring the Supremacy Clause into play. Like any local law that conflicts with federal regulatory measure ..., state regulations that run afoul of the policy of free trade reflected in the Commerce Clause must also bow.

"This is one of those cases—few in number—where local safety measures that are nondiscriminatory place an unconstitutional burden on interstate commerce.... A State which insists on a design out of line with the requirements of almost all the other States may sometimes place a great burden of delay and inconvenience on those interstate motor carriers entering or crossing its territory. Such a new safety device—out of line with the requirements of the other States—may be so compelling that the innovating State need not be the one to give way. The present showing—balanced against the clear burden on commerce—is far too inconclusive to make this mudguard meet that test."

Kassel v. Consolidated Freightways Corporation

450 U.S. 662, 101 S.Ct. 1309, 67 L.Ed.2d 580 (1981).

Justice Powell announced the judgment of the Court and delivered an opinion in which Justice White, Justice Blackmun, and Justice Stevens joined.

The question is whether an Iowa statute that prohibits the use of certain large trucks within the State unconstitutionally burdens interstate commerce.

I

Respondent Consolidated Freightways Corporation of Delaware (Consolidated) is one of the largest common carriers in the country. It offers service in 48 States under a certificate of public convenience and necessity issued by the Interstate Commerce Commission. Among other routes, Consolidated carries commodities through Iowa on Interstate 80, the principal east-west route linking New York, Chicago, and the west coast, and on Interstate 35, a major north-south route.

[handwritten margin note: Too big of a burden on interstate commerce in the face of safety. regulation not valid.]

[handwritten margin note: Issue:]

Consolidated mainly uses two kinds of trucks. One consists of a three-axle tractor pulling a 40–foot two-axle trailer. This unit, commonly called a single, or "semi," is 55 feet in length overall. Such trucks have long been used on the Nation's highways. Consolidated also uses a two-axle tractor pulling a single-axle trailer which, in turn, pulls a single-axle dolly and a second single-axle trailer. This combination, known as a double, or twin, is 65 feet long overall. Many trucking companies, including Consolidated, increasingly prefer to use doubles to ship certain kinds of commodities. Doubles have larger capacities, and the trailers can be detached and routed separately if necessary. Consolidated would like to use 65–foot doubles on many of its trips through Iowa.

The State of Iowa, however, by statute restricts the length of vehicles that may use its highways. Unlike all other States in the West and Midwest, Iowa generally prohibits the use of 65–foot doubles within its borders. Instead, most truck combinations are restricted to 55 feet in length. Doubles, mobile homes, trucks carrying vehicles such as tractors and other farm equipment, and singles hauling livestock, are permitted to be as long as 60 feet. Notwithstanding these restrictions, Iowa's statute permits cities abutting the state line by local ordinance to adopt the length limitations of the adjoining State. Iowa Code § 321.457(7) (1979). Where a city has exercised this option, otherwise oversized trucks are permitted within the city limits and in nearby commercial zones. Ibid.

Exception to statute

Iowa also provides for two other relevant exemptions. An Iowa truck manufacturer may obtain a permit to ship trucks that are as large as 70 feet. Iowa Code § 321E.10 (1979). Permits also are available to move oversized mobile homes, provided that the unit is to be moved from a point within Iowa or delivered for an Iowa resident. Id., § 321E.28(5).[7]

Exceptions

Because of Iowa's statutory scheme, Consolidated cannot use its 65–foot doubles to move commodities through the State. Instead, the company must do one of four things: (i) use 55–foot singles; (ii) use 60–foot doubles; (iii) detach the trailers of a 65–foot double and shuttle each through the State separately; or (iv) divert 65–foot doubles around Iowa.

Dissatisfied with these options, Consolidated filed this suit in the District Court averring that Iowa's statutory scheme unconstitutionally burdens interstate commerce. Iowa defended the law as a reasonable safety measure enacted pursuant to its police power. The State asserted that 65–foot doubles are more dangerous than 55–foot singles and, in any event, that the law promotes safety and reduces road wear within the State by diverting much truck traffic to other States.

State's reasons that it is done for safety

In a 14–day trial, both sides adduced evidence on safety, and on the burden on interstate commerce imposed by Iowa's law. [T]he District Court found that the "evidence clearly establishes that the twin is as safe as the semi." ... For that reason,

"there is no valid safety reason for barring twins from Iowa's highways because of their configuration."

} District ct. holding

. . .

---

7. The parochial restrictions in the mobile home provision were enacted after Governor Ray vetoed a bill that would have permitted the interstate shipment of all mobile homes through Iowa. Governor Ray commented, in his veto message:

"This bill ... would make Iowa a bridge state as these oversized units are moved into Iowa after being manufactured in another state and sold in a third. None of this activity would be of particular economic benefit to Iowa."

TC- burdened interstate comm.
AC - affirms

In light of [its] findings, the District Court applied the standard we enunciated in Raymond Motor Transportation, Inc. v. Rice, 434 U.S. 429 (1978), and concluded that the state law impermissibly burdened interstate commerce. . . .

The . . . Eighth Circuit affirmed. . . .

. . . We now affirm.

II

. . .

. . . [A] State's power to regulate commerce is never greater than in matters traditionally of local concern. . . . For example, regulations that touch upon safety—especially highway safety—are those that "the Court has been most reluctant to invalidate." *Raymond,* supra, at 443; . . . Indeed, "if safety justifications are not illusory, the court will not second-guess legislative judgment about their importance in comparison with related burdens on interstate commerce." *Raymond,* supra, at 449 (Blackmun, J., concurring). Those who would challenge such bona fide safety regulations must overcome a "strong presumption of validity." Bibb v. Navajo Freight Lines, Inc., 359 U.S. 520, 524 (1959).

But the incantation of a purpose to promote the public health or safety does not insulate a state law from Commerce Clause attack. Regulations designed for that salutary purpose nevertheless may further the purpose so marginally, and interfere with commerce so substantially, as to be invalid under the Commerce Clause. . . .

III

Applying these general principles, we conclude that the Iowa truck-length limitations unconstitutionally burden interstate commerce.

No concrete evidence that it promotes safety

In Raymond Motor Transportation, Inc. v. Rice, [434 U.S. 429 (1978),] the Court held that a Wisconsin statute that precluded the use of 65–foot doubles violated the Commerce Clause. This case is *Raymond* revisited. Here, as in *Raymond,* the State failed to present any persuasive evidence that 65–foot doubles are less safe than 55–foot singles. Moreover, Iowa's law is now out of step with the laws of all other Midwestern and Western States. Iowa thus substantially burdens the interstate flow of goods by truck. In the absence of congressional action to set uniform standards, some burdens associated with state safety regulations must be tolerated. But where, as here, the State's safety interest has been found to be illusory, and its regulations impair significantly the federal interest in efficient and safe interstate transportation, the state law cannot be harmonized with the Commerce Clause.

Law cannot be harmonized, it causes interstate burden

A

. . . As noted above, the District Court found that the "evidence clearly establishes that the twin is as safe as the semi." The record supports this finding.

. . .

. . . [T]he State points to only three ways in which the 55–foot single is even arguably superior: singles take less time to be passed and to clear intersections; they may back up for longer distances; and they are somewhat less likely to jackknife.

The first two of these characteristics are of limited relevance on modern interstate highways. As the District Court found, the negligible difference in the time required to pass, and to cross intersections, is insignificant on 4–lane divided highways because passing does not require crossing into oncoming traffic lanes, *Raymond*, 434 U.S., at 444, and interstates have few, if any, intersections. The concern over backing capability also is insignificant because it seldom is necessary to back up on an interstate. In any event, no evidence suggested any difference in backing capability between the 60–foot doubles that Iowa permits and the 65–foot doubles that it bans. Similarly, although doubles tend to jackknife somewhat more than singles, 65–foot doubles actually are less likely to jackknife than 60–foot doubles.

Statistical studies supported the view that 65–foot doubles are at least as safe overall as 55–foot singles and 60–foot doubles. ... Iowa concedes that it can produce no study that establishes a statistically significant difference in safety between the 65–foot double and the kinds of vehicles the State permits. Nor ... did Iowa present a single witness who testified that 65–foot doubles were more dangerous overall than the vehicles permitted under Iowa law....

B

Consolidated, meanwhile, demonstrated that Iowa's law substantially burdens interstate commerce. Trucking companies that wish to continue to use 65–foot doubles must route them around Iowa or detach the trailers of the doubles and ship them through separately. Alternatively, trucking companies must use the smaller 55–foot singles or 60–foot doubles permitted under Iowa law. Each of these options engenders inefficiency and added expense. The record shows that Iowa's law added about $12.6 million each year to the costs of trucking companies. Consolidated alone incurred about $2 million per year in increased costs.

In addition to increasing the costs of the trucking companies (and, indirectly, of the service to consumers), Iowa's law may aggravate, rather than ameliorate, the problem of highway accidents. ...

IV

Perhaps recognizing the weakness of the evidence supporting its safety argument, and the substantial burden on commerce that its regulations create, Iowa urges the Court simply to "defer" to the safety judgment of the State. It argues that the length of trucks is generally, although perhaps imprecisely, related to safety. The task of drawing a line is one that Iowa contends should be left to its legislature.

The Court normally does accord "special deference" to state highway safety regulations. *Raymond*, 434 U.S., at 444, n. 18. This traditional deference "derives in part from the assumption that where such regulations do not discriminate on their face against interstate commerce, their burden usually falls on local economic interests as well as other States' economic interests, thus insuring that a State's own political processes will serve as a check against unduly burdensome regulations." Ibid. Less deference to the legislative judgment is due, however, where the local regulation bears disproportionately on out-of-state residents and businesses. Such a disproportionate burden is apparent here. Iowa's scheme, although generally banning large doubles from the State, nevertheless has several exemptions that secure to Iowans many of the benefits of large trucks while shunting to neighboring States many of the costs associated with their use.

Exemptions indicate that it wasnt to ban larger trucks but to discourage interstate traffic

At the time of trial there were two particularly significant exemptions. First, singles hauling livestock or farm vehicles were permitted to be as long as 60 feet. Iowa Code §§ 321.457(5), 321.457(3) (1979). As the Court of Appeals noted, this provision undoubtedly was helpful to local interests. Cf. *Raymond,* supra, at 434 (exemption in Wisconsin for milk shippers). Second, cities abutting other States were permitted to enact local ordinances adopting the larger length limitation of the neighboring State. Iowa Code § 321.457(7) (1979). This exemption offered the benefits of longer trucks to individuals and businesses in important border cities without burdening Iowa's highways with interstate through traffic. Cf. *Raymond,* supra, at 446–447, and n. 24 (exemption in Wisconsin for shipments from local plants).

The origin of the "border cities exemption" also suggests that Iowa's statute may not have been designed to ban dangerous trucks, but rather to discourage interstate truck traffic. In 1974, the legislature passed a bill that would have permitted 65–foot doubles in the State. Governor Ray vetoed the bill. He said:

> "I find sympathy with those who are doing business in our state and whose enterprises could gain from increased cargo carrying ability by trucks. However, with this bill, the Legislature has pursued a course that would benefit only a few Iowa-based companies while providing a great advantage for out-of-state trucking firms and competitors at the expense of our Iowa citizens."

After the veto, the "border cities exemption" was immediately enacted and signed by the Governor.

. . .

V

. . .

Because Iowa has imposed this burden without any significant countervailing safety interest, its statute violates the Commerce Clause. The judgment of the Court of Appeals is affirmed.

It is so ordered.

Justice Brennan, with whom Justice Marshall joins, concurring in the judgment.

. . .

For me, analysis of Commerce Clause challenges to state regulations must take into account three principles: (1) The courts are not empowered to second-guess the empirical judgments of lawmakers concerning the utility of legislation. (2) The burdens imposed on commerce must be balanced against the local benefits actually sought to be achieved by the State's lawmakers, and not against those suggested after the fact by counsel. (3) Protectionist legislation is unconstitutional under the Commerce Clause, even if the burdens and benefits are related to safety rather than economics.

I

Both the opinion of my Brother Powell and the opinion of my Brother Rehnquist are predicated upon the supposition that the constitutionality of a state regulation is determined by the factual record created by the State's lawyers in trial court. But that supposition cannot be correct, for it would make the constitutionality of state laws and regulations depend on the vagaries of litigation rather than on the judgments made by the State's lawmakers.

In considering a Commerce Clause challenge to a state regulation, the judicial task is to balance the burden imposed on commerce against the local benefits sought to be achieved by the State's *lawmakers*. See Pike v. Bruce Church, Inc., 397 U.S. 137, 142 (1970). In determining those benefits, a court should focus ultimately on the regulatory purposes identified by the lawmakers and on the evidence before or available to them that might have supported their judgment. . . . Since the court must confine its analysis to the purposes the lawmakers had for maintaining the regulation, the only relevant evidence concerns whether the lawmakers could rationally have believed that the challenged regulation would foster those purposes. . . . It is not the function of the court to decide whether *in fact* the regulation promotes its intended purpose, so long as an examination of the evidence before or available to the lawmaker indicates that the regulation is not wholly irrational in light of its purposes.

II

My Brothers Powell and Rehnquist make the mistake of disregarding the intention of Iowa's lawmakers and assuming that resolution of the case must hinge upon the argument offered by Iowa's attorneys: that 65–foot doubles are more dangerous than shorter trucks. . . . Iowa sought to discourage interstate truck traffic on Iowa's highways. Thus, the safety advantages and disadvantages of the types and lengths of trucks involved in this case are irrelevant to the decision.[3]

My Brother Powell concedes that "[i]t is . . . far from clear that Iowa was motivated primarily by a judgment that 65–foot doubles are less safe than 55–foot singles. Rather, Iowa seems to have hoped to limit the use of its highways by deflecting some through traffic." This conclusion is more than amply supported by the record and the legislative history of the Iowa regulation. . . .

. . .

Although the Court has stated that "[i]n no field has . . . deference to state regulation been greater than that of highway safety," Raymond Motor Transportation, Inc. v. Rice, supra, 434 U.S., at 443, it has declined to go so far as to presume that size restrictions are inherently tied to public safety. The Court has emphasized that the "strong presumption of validity" of size restrictions "cannot justify a court in closing its eyes to uncontroverted evidence of record,"—here the obvious fact that the safety characteristics of 65–foot doubles did not provide the motivation for either legislators or Governor in maintaining the regulation.

3. My Brother Rehnquist claims that the "argument" that a Court should defer to the actual purposes of the lawmakers rather than to the *post hoc* justifications of counsel "has been consistently rejected by the Court in other contexts." . . .

. . .

If, as here, the only purpose ever articulated by the State's lawmakers for maintaining a regulation is illegitimate, I consider it contrary to precedent as well as to sound principles of constitutional adjudication for the courts to base their analysis on purposes never conceived by the lawmakers. This is especially true where, as the dissent's strained analysis of the relative safety of 65–foot doubles to shorter trucks amply demonstrates, the *post hoc* justifications are implausible as well as imaginary. I would emphasize that, although my Brother Powell's plurality opinion does not give as much weight to the illegitimacy of Iowa's actual purpose as I do, see Part III, infra, both that opinion and this concurrence have found the actual motivation of the Iowa lawmakers in maintaining the truck-length regulation highly relevant to, if not dispositive of, the case.

III

Though my Brother Powell recognizes that the State's actual purpose in maintaining the truck-length regulation was "to limit the use of its highways by deflecting some through traffic," he fails to recognize that this purpose, being *protectionist* in nature, is *impermissible* under the Commerce Clause. The Governor admitted that he blocked legislative efforts to raise the length of trucks because the change "would benefit only a few Iowa-based companies while providing a great advantage for out-of-state trucking firms and competitors at the expense of our Iowa citizens." Appellant Raymond Kassel, Director of the Iowa Department of Transportation, while admitting that the greater 65–foot length standard would be *safer* overall, defended the more restrictive regulations because of their benefits *within Iowa* . . .

Iowa may not shunt off its fair share of the burden of maintaining interstate truck routes, nor may it create increased hazards on the highways of neighboring States in order to decrease the hazards on Iowa highways. . . .

This Court's heightened deference to the judgments of state lawmakers in the field of safety is largely attributable to a judicial disinclination to weigh the interests of safety against other societal interests, such as the economic interest in the free flow of commerce. Thus, "if safety justifications are not illusory, the Court will not second-guess legislative judgment about their importance *in comparison with related burdens on interstate commerce.*" Raymond Motor Transportation, Inc. v. Rice, supra, at 449 (Blackmun, J., concurring) (emphasis added). Here, the decision of Iowa's lawmakers to promote *Iowa's* safety and other interests at the direct expense of the safety and other interests of neighboring States merits no such deference. . . .

I therefore concur in the judgment.

Justice Rehnquist, with whom The Chief Justice and Justice Stewart join, dissenting.

. . . Although the plurality and concurring opinions strike down Iowa's law by different routes, I believe the analysis in both opinions oversteps our "limited authority to review state legislation under the commerce clause," Brotherhood of Locomotive Firemen v. Chicago, R.I. & P.R. Co., 393 U.S. 129, 136 (1968), and seriously intrudes upon the fundamental right of the States to pass laws to secure the safety of their citizens. . . .

. . . .

II

. . . .

A determination that a state law is a rational safety measure does not end the Commerce Clause inquiry. A "sensitive consideration" of the safety purpose in relation to the burden on commerce is required. *Raymond,* supra, at 441. When engaging in such a consideration the Court does not directly compare safety benefits to commerce costs and strike down the legislation if the latter can be said in some vague sense to "outweigh" the former. Such an approach would make an empty gesture of the strong presumption of validity accorded state safety measures, particularly those governing highways. It would also arrogate to this Court functions of forming public policy, functions which, in the absence of congressional action, were left by the Framers of the Constitution to state legislatures. . . .

The purpose of the "sensitive consideration" referred to above is rather to determine if the asserted safety justification, although rational, is merely a pretext for discrimination against interstate commerce. We will conclude that it is if the safety benefits from the regulation are demonstrably trivial while the burden on commerce is great. Thus the Court in *Bibb* stated that the "strong presumption of validity" accorded highway safety measures could be overcome only when the safety benefits were "slight or problematical," 359 U.S., at 524. . . .

III

. . . There can be no doubt that the challenged statute is a valid highway safety regulation and thus entitled to the strongest presumption of validity against Commerce Clause challenges. . . . There can also be no question that the particular limit chosen by Iowa—60 feet—is rationally related to Iowa's safety objective. Most truck limits are between 55 and 65 feet, and Iowa's choice is thus well within the widely accepted range.

Iowa adduced evidence supporting the relation between vehicle length and highway safety. . . .

. . . In sum, there was sufficient evidence presented at trial to support the legislative determination that length is related to safety, and nothing in Consolidated's evidence undermines this conclusion.

. . .

My Brother Brennan argues that the Court should consider only *the purpose the Iowa legislators actually sought to achieve by the length limit*, and not the purposes advanced by Iowa's lawyers in defense of the statute. . . . The argument has been consistently rejected by the Court in other contexts, compare, e.g., United States Railroad Retirement Board v. Fritz, 449 U.S. 166, 187–188 (1980) with id., at 187–188 (Brennan, J., dissenting) and Michael M. v. Superior Court of Sonoma County, [450 U.S.] at 469–470, (1981) (plurality opinion) with id., at 494–496 (Brennan, J., dissenting), and Justice Brennan can cite no authority for the proposition that possible legislative purposes suggested by a State's lawyers should not be considered in Commerce Clause cases. The problems with [such] a view . . . are apparent. To name just a few, it assumes that individual legislators are motivated by one discernible "actual" purpose, and ignores the fact that different legislators may vote for a single piece of legislation for widely different reasons. . . . How, for example, would a court . . . approach a statute, the legislative history of which indicated that 10 votes were based on safety considerations, 10 votes were based on protectionism, and the statute passed by a vote of 40–20? What would the *actual* purpose of the *legislature* have been in that case? This Court has wisely "never insisted that a legislative body articulate its reasons for enacting a statute." *Fritz,* supra, at 177.

Both the plurality and concurring opinions attach great significance to the Governor's veto of a bill passed by the Iowa Legislature permitting 65–foot doubles. Whatever views one may have about the significance of legislative motives, it must be emphasized that the law which the Court strikes down today was not passed to achieve the protectionist goals the plurality and the concurrence ascribe to the Governor. Iowa's 60–foot length limit was established in 1963, at a time when very few States permitted 65–foot doubles. Striking down legislation on the basis of asserted legislative motives is dubious enough, but the plurality and concurrence strike down the legislation involved in this case because of asserted impermissible motives for *not* enacting *other* legislation, motives which could not possibly have been present when the legislation under challenge here was considered and passed. Such action is, so far as I am aware, unprecedented in this Court's history.

Furthermore, the effort in both the plurality and concurring opinions to portray the legislation involved here as protectionist is in error. Whenever a State enacts more stringent safety measures than its neighbors, in an area which affects commerce, the safety law will have the incidental effect of deflecting interstate commerce to the neighboring States. . . .

. . . The true problem with today's decision is that it gives no guidance whatsoever to these States as to whether their laws are valid or how to defend them. For that matter, the decision gives no guidance to Consolidated or other trucking firms either. Perhaps, after all is said and done, the Court today neither says nor does very much at all. We know only that Iowa's law is invalid and that the jurisprudence of the "negative side" of the Commerce Clause remains hopelessly confused.

FEDERAL REGULATION OF TRUCK SIZES

In 1983 Congress provided that states must allow twin trailer combinations with each trailer 28 feet long (approximate total length 65 feet) and 102 inches wide to use the interstate highway system and federal aided primary highways designated by the Secretary of Transportation. 49 U.S.C. §§ 2311, 2316. On April 6, 1983, the Federal Highway Administration designated about 140,000 miles of federally aided highways in addition to 42,000 miles of interstate highways upon which the larger trucks must be allowed to operate. 48 Fed.Reg. 14844 (1983). In 1984 the statute was amended to provide that the Federal Highway Administration could designate highways other than interstate highways only with the consent of the governor of the state. It also provided that the governor of a state may make findings that parts of the interstate system in the state are not safe for trucks as wide as 102 inches and request the Federal Highway Administration to make an exception from the normal rules for those parts of the system.

SECTION 4. IMPLIED RESTRICTIONS OF THE COMMERCE CLAUSE—PRODUCTION AND TRADE

A. RESTRICTING IMPORTATION AND INSULATING IN-STATE BUSINESS FROM OUT-OF-STATE COMPETITION

STATE QUARANTINE AND INSPECTION LAWS

From the days of Chief Justice Marshall, the Court repeatedly has asserted that the Commerce Clause, absent action by Congress, does not prevent the states from constitutionally enacting quarantine or inspection laws that affect interstate and foreign commerce, although the result has been rationalized in different ways at different times. In Hannibal & St. Joseph R. Co. v. Husen, 95 U.S. 465 (1877), the question was the validity of a Missouri statute providing that no Texas, Mexican, or Indian cattle should be driven or transported into, or remain in, the state between March 1 and November 1 of each year. The Court said: "While we unhesitatingly admit that a State may pass sanitary laws, and laws for the protection of life, liberty, health, or property within its borders; while it may prevent persons and animals suffering under contagious or infectious diseases, or convicts, etc., from entering the State; while for the purpose of self-protection it may establish quarantine, and reasonable inspection laws, it may not interfere with transportation into or through the State, beyond what is absolutely necessary for its self-protection. It may not, under the cover of exerting its police powers, substantially prohibit or burden either foreign or interstate commerce." The Court, not finding the statute to be a legitimate quarantine or inspection law because of the unconditional character of the prohibition on bringing cattle into the state during the specified months of the year, held it invalid.

Found quarantine law to be invalid.

In Kimmish v. Ball, 129 U.S. 217 (1889), however, the Court upheld an Iowa statute making liable in damages any person having possession of "Texas cattle" that had not wintered north of the southern boundary of Missouri or Kansas. Justice Field's opinion said: "the case is, therefore, reduced to this, whether the State may not provide that whoever permits diseased cattle in his possession to run at large within its limits shall be liable for any damages caused by the spread of the disease occasioned thereby; and upon that question we do not entertain the slightest doubt."

MINTZ v. BALDWIN, 289 U.S. 346 (1933). A New York regulation designed to guard against Bang's disease required cattle imported into New York for dairy and breeding purposes and the herds from which they came to be certified free from the disease by the chief sanitary official of the state of origin. A Wisconsin cattle breeder shipped 20 head of cattle from Wisconsin to a purchaser in New York. They were accompanied by a certificate that they were free of Bang's disease but there was nothing to show that the herd from which they came was free of the disease. The New York Commissioner of agriculture issued an order that denied the shipper permission to deliver the cattle. The shipper brought suit in a federal district court seeking an injunction against enforcement of the order. The court dismissed the suit. It made special findings to the effect that Bang's disease prevails throughout the United States, causing limitations on reproduction and milk yield and creating the risk of undulant fever in humans drinking raw milk. It also found that there was a body of expert opinion that cattle should be admitted to a state only when certified to have come from a clean herd because tests on individual cattle might not disclose the disease in its incubative stage.

The Supreme Court affirmed, stating: "The order is an inspection measure. Undoubtedly it was promulgated in good faith and is appropriate for the prevention of further spread of the disease among dairy cattle and to safeguard public health. It cannot be maintained therefore that the order so unnecessarily burdens interstate transportation as to contravene the commerce clause."

BALDWIN v. G.A.F. SEELIG, INC., 294 U.S. 511 (1935). The great depression of the 1930s had a particularly disastrous impact on dairy farmers. Prices paid to producers for milk in the New York area fell by some 61 percent and the milk supply was threatened as farmers slaughtered cattle rather than remain in a losing business. New York enacted the Milk Control Act of 1933 in an attempt to remedy the situation. A Milk Control Board was empowered to fix both the retail price of milk and the price paid to producers. The statute made it unlawful to sell milk purchased from out–of–state producers at prices less than those required to be paid to farmers within the state.

Seelig was engaged in business as a milk dealer in New York City, buying milk in Vermont and transporting it to New York. Seelig purchased the milk in Vermont at prices lower than the minimum payable to New York producers under the New York law. The State Commissioner of Farms and Markets refused to grant Seelig a milk dealer's license to sell milk purchased from producers at prices below the minimum required by the law. Seelig brought suit to restrain the enforcement of the Milk Control Act. The Supreme Court held that an injunction should issue.

Justice Cardozo, speaking for a unanimous Court, said: "Such a power, if exerted, will set a barrier to traffic between one state and another as effective as if customs duties, equal to the price differential, had been laid upon the thing transported.... Nice distinctions have been made at times between direct and indirect burdens [on commerce]. They are irrelevant when the avowed purpose of the obstruction, as well as its necessary tendency, is to suppress or mitigate the consequences of competition between the states.... If New York in order to promote the economic welfare of her farmers, may guard them against competition with the cheaper prices of Vermont, the door has been opened to rivalries and reprisals that were meant to be averted by subjecting commerce between the states to the power of the nation."

The state argued that a major objective of the Milk Control Act was the maintenance of a regular and adequate supply of pure and wholesome milk. The Court replied: "This would be to eat up the rule under the guise of an exception. Economic welfare is always related to health, for there can be no health if men are starving. Let such an exception be admitted, and all that a state will have to do in times of stress and strain is to say that its farmers and merchants and workmen must be protected against competition from without, lest they go upon the poor relief lists or perish altogether. To give entrance to that excuse would be to invite a speedy end of our national solidarity. The Constitution was framed under the dominion of a political philosophy less parochial in range. It was framed upon the theory that the peoples of the several states must sink or swim together, and that in the long run prosperity and salvation are in union and not division.... The line of division between direct and indirect restraints of commerce involves in its marking a reference to considerations of degree. Even so, the borderland is wide between the restraints upheld as incidental and those attempted here.... None of these statutes [upheld by the Court]—inspection laws, game laws, laws intended to curb fraud or exterminate disease—approaches in drastic quality the statute here in controversy which would neutralize the economic consequences of free trade among the states."

Dean Milk Co. v. City of Madison, Wis.

340 U.S. 349, 71 S.Ct. 295, 95 L.Ed. 329 (1951).

Mr. Justice Clark delivered the opinion of the Court.

This appeal challenges the constitutional validity of two sections of an ordinance of the City of Madison, Wisconsin, regulating the sale of milk and milk products within the municipality's jurisdiction. One section in issue makes it unlawful to sell any milk as pasteurized unless it has been processed and bottled at an approved pasteurization plant within a radius of five miles from the central square of Madison. Another section, which prohibits the sale of milk, or the importation, receipt or storage of milk for sale, in Madison unless from a source of supply possessing a permit issued after inspection by Madison officials, is attacked insofar as it expressly relieves municipal authorities from any duty to inspect farms located beyond twenty-five miles from the center of the city.

Appellant is an Illinois corporation engaged in distributing milk and milk products in Illinois and Wisconsin. It contended below, as it does here, that both the five-mile limit on pasteurization plants and the twenty-five-mile limit on sources of milk violate the Commerce Clause and the Fourteenth Amendment to the Federal Constitution. The Supreme Court of Wisconsin upheld the five-mile limit on pasteurization. As to the twenty-five-mile limitation the court ordered the complaint dismissed for want of a justiciable controversy. This appeal [contests] both rulings. . . .

The City of Madison is the county seat of Dane County. Within the county are some 5,600 dairy farms with the total raw milk production . . . more than ten times the requirements of Madison. Aside from the milk supplied to Madison, fluid milk produced in the county moves in large quantities to Chicago and more distant consuming areas, and the remainder is used in making cheese, butter and other products. At the time of trial the Madison milkshed was not of "Grade A" quality by the standards recommended by the United States Public Health Service, and no milk labeled "Grade A" was distributed in Madison.

The area defined by the ordinance with respect to milk sources encompasses practically all of Dane County and includes some 500 farms which supply milk for Madison. Within the five-mile area for pasteurization are plants of five processors, only three of which are engaged in the general wholesale and retail trade in Madison. Inspection of these farms and plants is scheduled once every thirty days and is performed by two municipal inspectors, one of whom is full-time. The courts below found that the ordinance in question promotes convenient, economical and efficient plant inspection.

Appellant purchases and gathers milk from approximately 950 farms in northern Illinois and southern Wisconsin, none being within twenty-five miles of Madison. Its pasteurization plants are located at Chemung and Huntley, Illinois, about 65 and 85 miles respectively from Madison. Appellant was denied a license to sell its products within Madison solely because its pasteurization plants were more than five miles away.

It is conceded that the milk which appellant seeks to sell in Madison is supplied from farms and processed in plants licensed and inspected by public health authorities of Chicago, and is labeled "Grade A" under the Chicago ordinance which adopts the rating standards recommended by the United States Public Health Service. Both the Chicago and Madison ordinances, though not the sections of the latter here in issue, are largely patterned after the Model Milk Ordinance of the Public Health Service. However, Madison contends and we assume that in some particulars its ordinance is more rigorous than that of Chicago.

Upon these facts we find it necessary to determine only the issue raised under the Commerce Clause, for we agree with appellant that the ordinance imposes an undue burden on interstate commerce.

This is not an instance in which an enactment falls because of federal legislation which, as a proper exercise of paramount national power over commerce, excludes measures which might otherwise be within the police power of the states. There is no pertinent national regulation by the Congress. . . .

Nor can there be objection to the avowed purpose of this enactment. We assume that difficulties in sanitary regulation of milk and milk products originating in remote areas may present a situation in which "upon a consideration of all the relevant facts and circumstances it appears that the matter is one which may appropriately be regulated in the interest of the safety, health and well-being of local communities. . . ." . . . We also assume that since Congress has not spoken to the contrary, the subject matter of the ordinance

Even though it is a legit state regulation it is not valid if it hurts interstate commerce

ISSUE: can the discr. action be justified by local interest.

There are alternative ways to enforce their health standards

judgment sustaining ordinance must be reversed

lies within the sphere of state regulation even though interstate commerce may be affected. . . .

But this regulation, . . . in practical effect excludes from distribution in Madison wholesome milk produced and pasteurized in Illinois. . . . In thus erecting an economic barrier protecting a major local industry against competition from without the State, Madison plainly discriminates against interstate commerce.[4] This it cannot do, even in the exercise of its unquestioned power to protect the health and safety of its people, if reasonable nondiscriminatory alternatives, adequate to conserve legitimate local interest, are available. . . . A different view, that the ordinance is valid simply because it professes to be a health measure, would mean that the Commerce Clause of itself imposes no limitations on state action other than those laid down by the Due Process Clause, save for the rare instance where a state artlessly discloses an avowed purpose to discriminate against interstate goods. Our issue then is whether the discrimination inherent in the Madison ordinance can be justified in view of the character of the local interests and the available methods of protecting them. . . .

It appears that reasonable and adequate alternatives are available. If the City of Madison prefers to rely upon its own officials for inspection of distant milk sources, such inspection is readily open to it without hardship for it could charge the actual and reasonable cost of such inspection to the importing producers and processors. . . . Moreover, appellee Health Commissioner of Madison testified that as proponent of the local milk ordinance he had submitted the provisions here in controversy and an alternative proposal based on § 11 of the Model Milk Ordinance recommended by the United States Public Health Service. The model provision imposes no geographical limitation on location of milk sources and processing plants but excludes from the municipality milk not produced and pasteurized conformably to standards as high as those enforced by the receiving city. In implementing such an ordinance, the importing city obtains milk ratings based on uniform standards and established by health authorities in the jurisdiction where production and processing occur. The receiving city may determine the extent of enforcement of sanitary standards in the exporting area by verifying the accuracy of safety ratings of specific plants or of the milkshed in the distant jurisdiction through the United States Public Health Service, which routinely and on request spot checks the local ratings. The Commissioner testified that Madison consumers "would be safeguarded adequately" under either proposal and that he had expressed no preference. The milk sanitarium of the Wisconsin State Board of Health testified that the State Health Department recommends the adoption of a provision based on the Model Ordinance. Both officials agreed that a local health officer would be justified in relying upon the evaluation by the Public Health Service of enforcement conditions in remote producing areas.

To permit Madison to adopt a regulation not essential for the protection of local health interests and placing a discriminatory burden on interstate commerce would invite a multiplication of preferential trade areas destructive of the very purpose of the Commerce Clause. Under the circumstances here presented, the regulation must yield to the principle that "one state in its dealings with another may not place itself in a position of economic isolation."

For these reasons we conclude that the judgment below sustaining the five-mile provision as to pasteurization must be reversed.

4. It is immaterial that Wisconsin milk from outside the Madison area is subjected to the same proscription as that moving in interstate commerce. . . .

The Supreme Court of Wisconsin thought it unnecessary to pass upon the validity of the twenty-five-mile limitation, apparently in part for the reason that this issue was made academic by its decision upholding the five-mile section. In view of our conclusion as to the latter provision, a determination of appellant's contention as to the other section is now necessary. As to this issue, therefore, we vacate the judgment below and remand for further proceedings not inconsistent with the principles announced in this opinion. . . .

Judgment vacated and cause remanded.

Mr. Justice Black, with whom Mr. Justice Douglas and Mr. Justice Minton concur, dissenting.

Today's holding invalidates § 7.21 of the Madison, Wisconsin, ordinance on the following reasoning: (1) the section excludes wholesome milk coming from Illinois; (2) this imposes a discriminatory burden on interstate commerce; (3) such a burden cannot be imposed where, as here, there are reasonable, nondiscriminatory and adequate alternatives available. I disagree with the Court's premises, reasoning, and judgment.

(1) This ordinance does not exclude wholesome milk coming from Illinois or anywhere else. It does require that all milk sold in Madison must be pasteurized within five miles of the center of the city. But there was no finding in the state courts, nor evidence to justify a finding there or here, that appellant, Dean Milk Company, is unable to have its milk pasteurized within the defined geographical area. As a practical matter, so far as the record shows, Dean can easily comply with the ordinance whenever it wants to. Therefore, Dean's personal preference to pasteurize in Illinois, not the ordinance, keeps Dean's milk out of Madison.

[handwritten margin note: personal pref. keeps from following ordinance]

(2) Characterization of § 7.21 as a "discriminatory burden" on interstate commerce is merely a statement of the Court's result, which I think incorrect. The section does prohibit the sale of milk in Madison by interstate and intrastate producers who prefer to pasteurize over five miles distant from the city. But both state courts below found that § 7.21 represents a good-faith attempt to safeguard public health by making adequate sanitation inspection possible. While we are not bound by these findings, I do not understand the Court to overturn them. Therefore, the fact that § 7.21, like all health regulations, imposes some burden on trade, does not mean that it "discriminates" against commerce.

[handwritten margin note: Burden on trade does not mean it disc. against commerce]

(3) This health regulation should not be invalidated merely because the Court believes that alternative milk-inspection methods might insure the cleanliness and healthfulness of Dean's Illinois milk. . . . Since the days of Chief Justice Marshall, federal courts have left states and municipalities free to pass bona fide health regulations subject only "to the paramount authority of Congress if it decides to assume control. . . ." . . . No case is cited, and I have found none, in which a bona fide health law was struck down on the ground that some other method of safeguarding health would be as good as, or better than, the one the Court was called on to review. In my view, to use this ground now elevates the right to traffic in commerce for profit above the power of the people to guard the purity of their daily diet of milk.

If, however, the principle announced today is to be followed, the Court should not strike down local health regulations unless satisfied beyond a reasonable doubt that the substitutes it proposes would not lower health standards. I do not think that the Court can so satisfy itself on the basis of its judicial knowledge. And the evidence in the record leads me to the conclusion that the substitute health measures suggested by the Court do not insure milk as safe as the Madison ordinance requires. . . .

From what this record shows, and from what it fails to show, I do not think that either of the alternatives suggested by the Court would assure the people of Madison as pure a supply of milk as they receive under their own ordinance. On this record I would uphold the Madison law. At the very least, however, I would not invalidate it without giving the parties a chance to present evidence and get findings on the ultimate issues the Court thinks crucial—namely, the relative merits of the Madison ordinance and the alternatives suggested by the Court today.

MINNESOTA v. CLOVER LEAF CREAMERY CO., 449 U.S. 456 (1981). Under a Minnesota law, the retail sale of milk in plastic nonreturnable, nonrefillable containers was prohibited, but the sale of milk in nonreturnable, nonrefillable containers made of things other than plastic—such as paperboard cartons—was allowed. A Minnesota dairy that owns equipment for making nonreturnable plastic jugs and others challenged the statute as a violation of the Equal Protection and Commerce Clauses. In an opinion by Justice Brennan, the Court rejected both challenges. The Court concluded that the law survived "rational basis" review under equal protection principles because it bore a rational relationship to the legitimate goals of resource conservation and the easing of solid waste problems. As for the Commerce Clause claim, the Court applied the balancing test in Pike v. Bruce Church, Inc., 397 U.S. 137, 142 (1970), see p. 310 infra, because the law regulated "evenhandedly" without regard to the state of origin of the milk, the containers or the sellers. The Court then concluded that the "incidental" burden on interstate commerce was not "clearly excessive" relative to the "putative local benefits" because: (1) the burden on out-of-state interests was minor; (2) the state's environmental and conservation interests were substantial; and (3) other alternatives would either be more burdensome on commerce, or less effective in accomplishing the state's goals.

[handwritten margin note: statute was upheld - benefit was greater than burden]

West Lynn Creamery v. Healy

512 U.S. 186, 114 S.Ct. 2205, 129 L.Ed.2d 157 (1994).

Justice Stevens delivered the opinion of the Court.

A Massachusetts pricing order imposes an assessment on all fluid milk sold by dealers to Massachusetts retailers. About two-thirds of that milk is produced out of State. The entire assessment, however, is distributed to Massachusetts dairy farmers. The question presented is whether the pricing order unconstitutionally discriminates against interstate commerce. We hold that it does.

I

Petitioner . . . is a milk dealer licensed to do business in Massachusetts. It purchases raw milk, which it processes, packages, and sells to wholesalers, retailers, and other milk dealers. About 97% of the raw milk it purchases is produced by out-of-state farmers. . . .

. . . In the 1980's and early 1990's, Massachusetts dairy farmers began to lose market share to lower cost producers in neighboring States. In response, the Governor of Massachusetts appointed a Special Commission to study the dairy industry. The Commission found that many producers had sold their dairy farms during the past decade and that if prices paid to farmers for their milk were not significantly increased, a majority of the remaining farmers in

Massachusetts would be "forced out of business within the year." App. 13. [R]elying on the Commission's Report, the Commissioner of the Massachusetts Department of Food and Agriculture (respondent) declared a State of Emergency . . . [and promptly] issued the [challenged]pricing order.

The order requires every "dealer" in Massachusetts to make a monthly "premium payment" [based on the amount of its fluid milk product sales] into the "Massachusetts Dairy Equalization Fund." . . . Each month the fund is distributed to Massachusetts producers[;i.e, dairy farmers]. Each Massachusetts producer receives a share of the total fund equal to his proportionate contribution to the State's total production of raw milk.

Petitioners . . . [sued unsuccessfully] in state court. . . .

. . . We . . . reverse.

II

. . .

. . . Massachusetts' pricing order is clearly unconstitutional. Its avowed purpose and its undisputed effect are to enable higher cost Massachusetts dairy farmers to compete with lower cost dairy farmers in other States. The "premium payments" are effectively a tax which makes milk produced out of State more expensive. Although the tax also applies to milk produced in Massachusetts, its effect on Massachusetts producers is entirely (indeed more than) offset by the subsidy provided exclusively to Massachusetts dairy farmers. Like an ordinary tariff, the tax is thus effectively imposed only on out-of-state products. The pricing order thus allows Massachusetts dairy farmers who produce at higher cost to sell at or below the price charged by lower cost out-of-state producers.[10] If there were no federal minimum prices for milk, out-of-state producers might still be able to retain their market share by lowering their prices. Nevertheless, out-of-staters' ability to remain competitive by lowering their prices would not immunize a discriminatory measure. New Energy Co. of Indiana v. Limbach, 486 U.S., at 275. In this case, because the Federal Government sets minimum prices, out-of-state producers may not even have the option of reducing prices in order to retain market share. The Massachusetts pricing order thus will almost certainly "cause local goods to constitute a larger share, and goods with an out-of-state source to constitute a smaller share, of the total sales in the market." Exxon Corp. v. Governor of Maryland, 437 U.S. 117, 126, n. 16 (1978). In fact, this effect was the motive behind the promulgation of the pricing order. This effect renders the program unconstitutional, because it, like a tariff, "neutralize[s] advantages belonging to the place of origin." Baldwin, 294 U.S., at 527.

In some ways, the Massachusetts pricing order is most similar to the law at issue in Bacchus Imports, Ltd. v. Dias, 468 U.S. 263 (1984). Both involve a broad-based tax on a single kind of good and special provisions for in-state producers. *Bacchus* involved a 20% excise tax on all liquor sales, coupled with an exemption for fruit wine manufactured in Hawaii and for okolehao, a brandy distilled from the root of a shrub indigenous to Hawaii. The Court held that Hawaii's law was unconstitutional because it "had both the purpose and effect of discriminating in favor of local products." . . . By granting a tax exemption for local products, Hawaii in effect created a protective tariff. Goods produced out of State were taxed, but those produced in State were subject to no net tax.

---

10. . . . The net effect of the tax and subsidy, like that of a tariff, is to raise the   after-tax price paid by the dealers. . . .

It is obvious that the result in *Bacchus* would have been the same if instead of exempting certain Hawaiian liquors from tax, Hawaii had rebated the amount of tax collected from the sale of those liquors. See New Energy Co. of Indiana v. Limbach, 486 U.S. 269 (1988) (discriminatory tax credit). And if a discriminatory tax rebate is unconstitutional, Massachusetts' pricing order is surely invalid; for Massachusetts not only rebates to domestic milk producers the tax paid on the sale of Massachusetts milk, but also the tax paid on the sale of milk produced elsewhere. The additional rebate of the tax paid on the sale of milk produced elsewhere in no way reduces the danger to the national market posed by tariff-like barriers, but instead exacerbates the danger by giving domestic producers an additional tool with which to shore up their competitive position.[14]

III

Respondent advances four arguments against the conclusion that its pricing order imposes an unconstitutional burden on interstate commerce: (A) Because each component of the program—a local subsidy and a non-discriminatory tax—is valid, the combination of the two is equally valid; (B) The dealers who pay the order premiums (the tax) are not competitors of the farmers who receive disbursements from the Dairy Equalization Fund, so the pricing order is not discriminatory; (C) The pricing order is not protectionist, because the costs of the program are borne only by Massachusetts dealers and consumers, and the benefits are distributed exclusively to Massachusetts farmers; and (D) the order's incidental burden on commerce is justified by the local benefit of saving the dairy industry from collapse....

A

Respondent's principal argument is that ... if the State may impose a valid tax on dealers, it is free to use the proceeds of the tax as it chooses; and if it may independently subsidize its farmers, it is free to finance the subsidy by means of any legitimate tax.

Even granting respondent's assertion that both components of the pricing order would be constitutional standing alone,[15] the pricing order nevertheless must fall. A pure subsidy funded out of general revenue ordinarily imposes no burden on interstate commerce, but merely assists local business. The pricing order in this case, however, is funded principally from taxes on the sale of milk

---

14. One might attempt to distinguish *Bacchus* by noting that the rebate in this case goes not to the entity which pays the tax (milk dealers) but to the dairy farmers themselves. Rebating the taxes directly to producers rather than to the dealers, however, merely reinforces the conclusion that the pricing order will favor local producers. If the taxes were refunded only to the dealers, there might be no impact on interstate commerce, because the dealers might not use the funds to increase the price or quantity of milk purchased from Massachusetts dairy farmers. The refund to the dealers might, therefore, result in no advantage to in-state producers. On the other hand, by refunding monies directly to the dairy farmers, the pricing order ensures that Massachusetts producers will benefit.

15. We have never squarely confronted the constitutionality of subsidies, and we need not do so now. We have, however, noted that "[d]irect subsidization of domestic industry does not ordinarily run afoul" of the negative Commerce Clause. New Energy Co. of Indiana v. Limbach, 486 U.S., at 278; see also Hughes v. Alexandria Scrap Corp., 426 U.S. 794, 815 (1976) (Stevens, J., concurring). In addition, it is undisputed that States may try to attract business by creating an environment conducive to economic activity, as by maintaining good roads, sound public education, or low taxes. Zobel v. Williams, 457 U.S. 55, 67 (1982) (Brennan, J., concurring); Bacchus Imports, Ltd. v. Dias, 468 U.S., at 271; Metropolitan Life Ins. Co. v. Ward, 470 U.S. 869, 876–878 (1985).

produced in other States.[16] By so funding the subsidy, respondent not only assists local farmers, but burdens interstate commerce. The pricing order thus violates the cardinal principle that a State may not "benefit in-state economic interests by burdening out-of-state competitors." New Energy Co. of Indiana v. Limbach, 486 U.S., at 273–274. . . .

More fundamentally, respondent errs in assuming that the constitutionality of the pricing order follows logically from the constitutionality of its component parts. By conjoining a tax and a subsidy, Massachusetts has created a program more dangerous to interstate commerce than either part alone. Nondiscriminatory measures, like the evenhanded tax at issue here, are generally upheld, in spite of any adverse effects on interstate commerce, in part because "[t]he existence of major in-state interests adversely affected . . . is a powerful safeguard against legislative abuse." Minnesota v. Clover Leaf Creamery Co., 449 U.S. 456, 473, n. 17 (1981). . . . However, when a nondiscriminatory tax is coupled with a subsidy to one of the groups hurt by the tax, a state's political processes can no longer be relied upon to prevent legislative abuse, because one of the in-state interests which would otherwise lobby against the tax has been mollified by the subsidy. So, in this case, one would ordinarily have expected at least three groups to lobby against the order premium, which, as a tax, raises the price (and hence lowers demand) for milk: dairy farmers, milk dealers, and consumers. But because the tax was coupled with a subsidy, one of the most powerful of these groups, Massachusetts dairy farmers, instead of exerting their influence against the tax, were in fact its primary supporters.[18]

. . . [W]e cannot divorce the premium payments from the use to which the payments are put. [T]he entire program . . . simultaneously burdens interstate commerce and discriminates in favor of local producers. The choice of constitutional means—nondiscriminatory tax and local subsidy—cannot guarantee the constitutionality of the program as a whole. New York's minimum price order also used constitutional means—a State's power to regulate prices—but was held unconstitutional because of its deleterious effects. Baldwin v. G. A. F. Seelig, Inc., 294 U.S. 511 (1935). Similarly, the law held unconstitutional in *Bacchus* . . . involved the exercise of Hawaii's undisputed power to tax and to grant tax exemptions.

. . .

B

Respondent['s argument] that since the Massachusetts milk dealers who pay the order premiums are not competitors of the Massachusetts farmers, the pricing order imposes no discriminatory burden on commerce . . . cannot withstand scrutiny. Is it possible to doubt that if Massachusetts imposed a higher sales tax on milk produced in Maine than milk produced in Massachusetts that the tax would be struck down, in spite of the fact that the sales tax was imposed on consumers, and consumers do not compete with dairy farmers?

---

16. . . . [M]ost of the tax collected comes from taxes on milk from other States. In addition, the tax on in-state milk, unlike that imposed on out-of-state milk, does not impose any burden on in-state producers, because in-state dairy farmers can be confident that the taxes paid on their milk will be returned to them via the Dairy Stabilization Fund.

18. As the Governor's Special Commission . . . realized, consumers would be unlike-

ly to organize effectively to oppose the pricing order. The Commission's report remarked, "the estimated two cent increase per quart of milk would not be noticed by the consuming public," App. 18, because the price of milk varies so often and for so many reasons that consumers would be unlikely to feel the price increases or to attribute them to the pricing order.

For over 150 years, our cases have rightly concluded that the imposition of a differential burden on any part of the stream of commerce—from wholesaler to retailer to consumer—is invalid, because a burden placed at any point will result in a disadvantage to the out-of-state producer....

C

Respondent also argues that "the operation of the Order disproves any claim of protectionism," because "only in-state consumers feel the effect of any retail price increase ... [and] [t]he dealers themselves ... have a substantial in-state presence." ... This argument, if accepted, would undermine almost every discriminatory tax case. State taxes are ordinarily paid by in-state businesses and consumers, yet if they discriminate against out-of-state products, they are unconstitutional.... The cost of a tariff is also borne primarily by local consumers, yet a tariff is the paradigmatic Commerce Clause violation.

More fundamentally, ... the purpose and effect of the pricing order are to divert market share to Massachusetts dairy farmers. This diversion necessarily injures the dairy farmers in neighboring States.... The obvious impact of the order on out-of-state production demonstrates that it is simply wrong to assume that the pricing order burdens only Massachusetts consumers and dealers.

D

Finally, respondent argues that any incidental burden on interstate commerce "is outweighed by the 'local benefits' of preserving the Massachusetts dairy industry." ... In a closely related argument, respondent urges that "the purpose of the order, to save an industry from collapse, is not protectionist." ... If we were to accept these arguments, we would make a virtue of the vice that the rule against discrimination condemns. Preservation of local industry by protecting it from the rigors of interstate competition is the hallmark of the economic protectionism that the Commerce Clause prohibits....

The judgment ... is reversed.

Justice Scalia, with whom Justice Thomas joins, concurring in the judgment.

. . .

I

... [W]e have never held, that every state law which obstructs a national market violates the Commerce Clause. Yet that is what the Court says today. It seems to have canvassed the entire corpus of negative-Commerce–Clause opinions, culled out every free-market snippet of reasoning, and melded them into the sweeping principle that the Constitution is violated by any state law or regulation that "artificially encourag[es] in-state production even when the same goods could be produced at lower cost in other States." ...

As the Court seems to appreciate by its eagerness expressly to reserve the question of the constitutionality of subsidies for in-state industry, this expansive view of the Commerce Clause calls into question a wide variety of state laws that have hitherto been thought permissible. It seems to me that a State subsidy would clearly be invalid under any formulation of the Court's guiding principle identified above.... [E]ven where the funding does not come in any part from taxes on out-of-state goods, "merely assist[ing]" in-state businesses unquestionably neutralizes advantages possessed by out-of-state enterprises. Such subsidies ... are often admitted to have as their purpose—indeed, are nationally advertised as having as their purpose—making it more profitable to conduct business in-state than elsewhere, i.e., distorting normal market incentives.

The Court's guiding principle also appears to call into question many garden-variety state laws heretofore permissible under the negative Commerce Clause. A state law, for example, which requires, contrary to the industry practice, the use of recyclable packaging materials, favors local non-exporting producers, who do not have to establish an additional, separate packaging operation for in-state sales....

II

... I will, on *stare decisis* grounds, enforce a self-executing "negative" Commerce Clause in two situations: (1) against a state law that facially discriminates against interstate commerce, and (2) against a state law ... indistinguishable from a type of law previously held unconstitutional by this Court....

[A]t least four possible devices ... would enable a State to produce the economic effect that Massachusetts has produced here: (1) a discriminatory tax upon the industry, imposing a higher liability on out-of-state members than on their in-state competitors; (2) a tax upon the industry that is nondiscriminatory in its assessment, but that has an "exemption" or "credit" for in-state members; (3) a nondiscriminatory tax upon the industry, the revenues from which are placed into a segregated fund, which fund is disbursed as "rebates" or "subsidies" to in-state members of the industry (the situation at issue in this case); and (4) with or without nondiscriminatory taxation of the industry, a subsidy for the in-state members of the industry, funded from the State's general revenues. It is long settled that the first of these methodologies is unconstitutional under the negative Commerce Clause.... The second ... is no different in principle from the first, and has likewise been held invalid.... The fourth methodology, application of a state subsidy from general revenues, is so far removed from what we have hitherto held to be unconstitutional, that prohibiting it must be regarded as an extension of our negative-Commerce–Clause jurisprudence and therefore, to me, unacceptable. See New Energy Co. of Indiana v. Limbach, 486 U.S. 269, 278 (1988). Indeed, in my view our negative-Commerce–Clause cases have already approved the use of such subsidies. See Hughes v. Alexandria Scrap Corp., 426 U.S. 794, 809–810 (1976).

The issue before us in the present case is whether the third of these methodologies must fall. Although the question is close, I conclude it would not be a principled point at which to disembark from the negative-Commerce–Clause train. The only difference between methodology (2) (discriminatory "exemption" from nondiscriminatory tax) and methodology (3) (discriminatory refund of nondiscriminatory tax) is that the money is taken and returned rather than simply left with the favored in-state taxpayer in the first place. The difference between (3) and (4), on the other hand, is the difference between assisting in-state industry through discriminatory taxation, and assisting in-state industry by other means. I would therefore allow a State to subsidize its domestic industry so long as it does so from nondiscriminatory taxes that go into the State's general revenue fund. Perhaps, as some commentators contend, that line comports with an important economic reality: a State is less likely to maintain a subsidy when its citizens perceive that the money (in the general fund) is available for any number of competing, non-protectionist, purposes.... That is not, however, the basis for my position, for as The Chief Justice explains, "[a]nalysis of interest group participation in the political process may serve many useful purposes, but serving as a basis for interpreting the dormant Commerce Clause is not one of them." Instead, I draw the line where I do because it is a clear, rational line at the limits of our extant negative-Commerce–Clause jurisprudence.

Chief Justice Rehnquist, with whom Justice Blackmun joins, dissenting.

. . .

Massachusetts has . . . provid[ed] a subsidy to aid its beleaguered dairy farmers. In case after case, we have approved the validity under the Commerce Clause of such enactments. . . . "Direct subsidization of domestic industry does not ordinarily run afoul of the [dormant Commerce Clause]; discriminatory taxation of out-of-state manufacturers does." New Energy Co. of Indiana v. Limbach, 486 U.S. 269, 278 (1988). But today the Court relegates these well-established principles to a footnote and . . . gratuitously casts doubt on the validity of state subsidies, observing that "[w]e have never squarely confronted" their constitutionality. . . .

. . . The State has not acted to strong-arm sister States as in *Limbach*; rather, its motives are purely local. . . .

. . . The Court [objects] that the method of imposing the tax and subsidy distorts the State's political process. . . . But as the Court itself points out, there are still at least two strong interest groups opposed to the milk order—consumers and milk dealers. More importantly, nothing in the dormant Commerce Clause suggests that the fate of state regulation should turn upon the particular lawful manner in which the state subsidy is enacted or promulgated. Analysis of interest group participation in the political process may serve many useful purposes, but serving as a basis for interpreting the dormant Commerce Clause is not one of them.

. . . [B]oth *Baldwin* and *Bacchus* are a far cry from this case.

. . . [Unlike the adverse effect on out-of-state milk producers from the minimum price regulation in *Baldwin*, here m]ilk dealers have the same incentives to purchase lower priced milk from out-of-state farmers; dealers of all milk are taxed equally. . . .

. . . [And] the milk order does not produce the same effect on interstate commerce as the tax exemption in *Bacchus*. I agree with the Court's statement that *Bacchus* can be distinguished "by noting that the rebate in this case goes not to the entity which pays the tax (milk dealers) but to the dairy farmers themselves." This is not only a distinction, but a significant difference. No decided case supports the Court's conclusion that the negative Commerce Clause prohibits the State from using money that it has lawfully obtained through a neutral tax on milk dealers and distributing it as a subsidy to dairy farmers. . . .

. . . The wisdom of a messianic insistence on a grim sink-or-swim policy of laissez-faire economics would be debatable had Congress chosen to enact it; but Congress has done nothing of the kind. It is the Court which has imposed the policy under the dormant Commerce Clause, a policy which bodes ill for the values of federalism which have long animated our constitutional jurisprudence.

PHARMACEUTICAL RESEARCH AND MANUFACTURERS OF AMERICA v. WALSH, 538 U.S. 644 (2003). In part on dormant commerce clause grounds, an association of nonresident drug manufacturers challenged a Maine law, establishing the "Maine Rx Program," that required drug manufacturers selling prescription drugs in the state through any publicly supported financial assistance program to agree to provide rebates on those sales. The rebates were to go to a state-administered fund for distribution to participating pharmacies from which needy residents could purchase the prescription drugs at discounted prices. The Court rejected the contention "that the rebate requirement constitutes impermissible extraterritorial regulation," because the law " 'does not regulate the price of any out-of-state transaction, either by its express terms or by its inevitable effect.' " The Court also rejected the argument that the law "discriminates against interstate commerce in order to subsidize in-state retail sales[,]" saying:

> "Petitioner argues that Maine's Rx fund is similar [to the Massachusetts milk pricing order invalidated in West Lynn Creamery, Inc. v. Healy, *supra*,] because it would be created entirely from rebates paid by out-of-state manufacturers and would be used to subsidize sales by local pharmacists to local consumers. Unlike the situation in *West Lynn,* however, the Maine Rx Program will not impose a disparate burden on any competitors. A manufacturer could not avoid its rebate obligation by opening production facilities in Maine and would receive no benefit from the rebates even if it did so; the payments to the local pharmacists provide no special benefit to competitors of rebate-paying manufacturers. The rule that was applied in *West Lynn* is thus not applicable to this case."

B.   REQUIRING BUSINESS OPERATIONS TO BE PERFORMED IN THE HOME STATE

MINNESOTA v. BARBER, 136 U.S. 313 (1890). A Minnesota statute prohibited the sale for human food of fresh meat not taken from animals inspected in Minnesota within 24 hours before slaughter. The case involved the sale in Minnesota of fresh beef slaughtered in Illinois but not inspected in Minnesota as the statute required. Supporters of the legislation argued that inspection on the hoof, within a very short time before animals are slaughtered, was necessary to ascertain their condition with certainty.

The Court stated: "[I]f, as alleged, the inspection of fresh beef, veal, mutton, lamb or pork will not necessarily show whether the animal from which it was taken was diseased when slaughtered, it would not follow that a statute like the one before us is within the constitutional power of the State to enact. On the contrary, the enactment of a similar statute by each one of the States composing the Union would result in the destruction of commerce among the several States, so far as such commerce is involved in the transportation from one part of the country to another of animal meats designed for human food, and entirely free from disease. A careful examination of the Minnesota Act will place this construction of it beyond question.... As the inspection must take place within the twenty-four hours immediately before the slaughtering, the act, by its necessary operation, excludes from the Minnesota market practically all fresh beef, veal, mutton, lamb or pork—in whatever form, and although entirely sound, healthy and fit for human food—taken from animals slaughtered in other States; and directly tends to restrict the slaughtering of animals, whose meat is to be sold in Minnesota for human food, to those engaged in such business in that State.... It will not do to say—certainly no judicial tribunal can, with propriety, assume—that the people of Minnesota may not, with due regard to their health, rely upon inspections in other States of animals there slaughtered for purposes of human food.... [A] law providing for the inspection of animals whose meats are designed for human food cannot be regarded as a rightful exertion of the police powers of the State, if the inspection

[margin note: statute was held invalid]

prescribed is of such a character, or is burdened with such conditions, as will prevent altogether the introduction into the State of sound meats, the product of animals slaughtered in other States."

The statute was held invalid as applied in the case.

FOSTER–FOUNTAIN PACKING CO. v. HAYDEL, 278 U.S. 1 (1928). A Louisiana statute declared all shrimp in Louisiana waters to be the property of the state but authorized the taking of shrimp on certain conditions. Among these conditions was the provision that no shipment out of state could be made of shrimp from which the heads and hulls had not been removed or of the raw heads and hulls "as they are required to be manufactured into fertilizer or used for an element in chicken feed." No restriction was placed on the shipment out of the state of fertilizer or chicken feed. The court held the statute invalid, saying:

"As the representative of its people, the state might have retained the shrimp for consumption and use therein. But, in direct opposition to conservation for intrastate use, this enactment permits all parts of the shrimp to be shipped and sold outside the state. The purpose is not to retain the shrimp for the use of the people of Louisiana; it is to favor the canning of the meat and the manufacture of bran in Louisiana by withholding raw or unshelled shrimp from the Biloxi [Mississippi] plants. But by permitting its shrimp to be taken and all the products thereof to be shipped and sold in interstate commerce, the state necessarily releases its hold. . . . And those taking the shrimp . . . become entitled to the rights of private ownership and the protection of the commerce clause."

[margin note: statute held invalid]

PIKE v. BRUCE CHURCH, INC., 397 U.S. 137 (1970). Appellee grows cantaloupes of superior quality in Parker, Arizona. Since the company lacked packing sheds in Parker, it transported the cantaloupes to nearby facilities in California where they were packed under regulations similar to those of Arizona, but shipped in containers bearing the name of the California packer. Pike, a state official acting under the Arizona Fruit and Vegetable Standardization Act, which was designed to prevent deceptive packaging, entered an order prohibiting the company from shipping its cantaloupes outside the state unless they were packed in containers approved by him. He contended that his order was necessary to ensure that the cantaloupes be identified as of Arizona origin. The company sought injunctive relief, claiming that the order would require it to build packing facilities in or near Parker at a cost of about $200,000 and this would constitute an unconstitutional burden on interstate commerce. A three-judge court granted relief. The court unanimously affirmed, saying:

[margin note: Pike Test]

". . . Although the criteria for determining the validity of state statutes affecting interstate commerce have been variously stated, the general rule that emerges can be phrased as follows: Where the statute regulates even-handedly to effectuate a legitimate local public interest, and its effects on interstate commerce are only incidental, it will be upheld unless the burden imposed on such commerce is clearly excessive in relation to the putative local benefits. Huron Cement Co. v. Detroit, 362 U.S. 440, 443. If a legitimate local purpose is found, then the question becomes one of degree. And the extent of the burden that will be tolerated will of course depend on the nature of the local interest involved, and on whether it could be promoted as well with a lesser impact on interstate activities. Occasionally the Court has candidly undertaken a balancing approach in resolving these issues, Southern Pacific Co. v. Arizona, 325 U.S. 761, but more frequently it has spoken in terms of 'direct' and 'indirect' effects and burdens. . . ."

Referring to the stipulation of the State that the primary purpose of the Arizona law was to protect the reputation of Arizona growers by prohibiting deceptive packaging, the Court continued: "We are not, then, dealing here with 'state legislation in the field of safety where the propriety of local regulation has long been recognized,' or with an Act designed to protect consumers in Arizona from contaminated or unfit goods. Its purpose and design are simply to protect and enhance the reputation of growers within the State. These are surely legitimate state interests. Sligh v. Kirkwood, 237 U.S. 52, 61. We have upheld a State's power to require that produce packaged in the State be packaged in a particular kind of receptacle, Pacific States Box & Basket Co. v. White, 296 U.S. 176. And we have recognized the legitimate interest of a State in maximizing the financial return to an industry within it. Parker v. Brown, 317 U.S. 341. . . .

"But application of the Act through the appellant's order to the appellee company has a far different impact, and quite a different purpose. . . . The appellant . . . is not complaining because the company is putting the good name of Arizona on an inferior or deceptively packaged product, but because it is not putting that name on a product that is superior and well packaged. . . . [T]he State's tenuous interest in having the company's cantaloupes identified as originating in Arizona cannot constitutionally justify the requirement that the company build and operate an unneeded $200,000 packing plant in the State. The nature of that burden is, constitutionally, more significant than its extent. For the Court has viewed with particular suspicion state statutes requiring business operations to be performed in the home State that could more efficiently be performed elsewhere. Even where the State is pursuing a clearly legitimate local interes, this particular burden on commerce has been declared to be virtually *per se* illegal. Foster–Fountain Packing Co. v. Haydel, 278 U.S. 1. . . ."

C & A CARBONE v. TOWN OF CLARKSTOWN 511 U.S. 383(1994). The Town of Clarkstown passed a law requiring that all nonhazardous solid waste in the town be processed at a designated "transfer station," located in town, before it left the municipality. Although the law was facially neutral, in that it applied equally to in-state and out-of-state companies, the Court nonetheless struck it down because of its effect on interstate commerce. In particular, another competing processing center in Clarkstown, the Carbone facility, received and processed waste from places outside of Clarkstown and outside of the State. Because the ordinance required Carbone to send nonrecyclable waste that it had already processed to the designated transfer station—and pay an $81/ton "tipping fee" for use of the transfer station—before the waste could leave Clarkstown, the ordinance drove up the cost for out-of-state interests to dispose of their solid waste. As Justice Kennedy wrote for the majority: "While the immediate effect of the ordinance is to direct local transport of solid waste to a designated site within the local jurisdiction, its economic effects are interstate in reach. . . . [E]ven as to waste originant in Clarkstown, the ordinance prevents everyone except the favored local operator from performing the initial processing step. The ordinance thus deprives out-of-state businesses of access to a local market. . . . [Because] . . . the ordinance discriminates against interstate commerce, we need not resort to the *Pike* [balancing] test. . . . [T]he flow control ordinance discriminates, for it allows only the favored operator to process waste that is within the limits of the town. The ordinance is no less discriminatory because in-state or in-town processors are also covered by the prohibition." Justice O'Connor concurred in the judgment, arguing that the law was invalid not because of "facial or effective discrimination" but rather because it burdened interstate commerce excessively under the *Pike* balancing approach. Justice Souter, joined by Chief Justice Rehnquist and Justice Blackmun, dissented.

C.   PRESERVING RESOURCES FOR IN-STATE CONSUMPTION

PENNSYLVANIA v. WEST VIRGINIA, 262 U.S. 553 (1923). In the early twentieth century West Virginia was the major producing state for natural gas. production exceeded local needs and the state permitted pipeline corporations to purchase natural gas and transport it to customers in Pennsylvania and Ohio. Large numbers of residential and industrial consumers in those states became dependent on the supply of gas from West Virginia. Eventually, demand for the gas exceeded the supply and the only way more gas could be provided in one of the states was to reduce the amount supplied in the others.

West Virginia passed a statute requiring every pipeline company transporting gas produced in West Virginia to satisfy the needs, domestic or industrial, of all West Virginia customers, old or new, willing to pay for the gas and use it within the state. The states of Pennsylvania and Ohio brought suit to enjoin West Virginia from enforcing this statute. The Court held the statute invalid.

Justice Van Devanter, writing for the Court, said in part:

"Natural gas is a lawful article of commerce, and its transmission from one state to another for sale and consumption in the latter is interstate commerce. A state law, whether of the state where the gas is produced or that where it is to be sold, which by its necessary operation prevents, obstructs or burdens such transmission is a regulation of interstate commerce—a prohibited interference. . . .

"But it is urged that there are special considerations which take the act out of the general rule and sustain its validity, even though there be an interference. . . .

"[One such consideration] is that the gas is a natural product of the state and has become a necessity therein, that the supply is waning and no longer sufficient to satisfy local needs and be used abroad, and that the act is therefore a legitimate measure of conservation in the interest of the people of the state. If the situation be as stated, it affords no ground for the assumption by the state of power to regulate interstate commerce, which is what the act attempts to do. That power is lodged elsewhere."

In a dissenting opinion Justice Holmes said: "I see nothing in the commerce clause to prevent a State from giving a preference to its inhabitants in the enjoyment of its natural advantages."

H.P. Hood & Sons v. Du Mond

336 U.S. 525, 69 S.Ct. 657, 93 L.Ed. 865 (1949).

[Hood & Sons distributed milk and milk products to the Boston area, which obtained about 90% of its milk from states other than Massachusetts. Hood had obtained milk in New York State for shipment to Boston and for this purpose had operated three receiving depots in the state. It proposed to open a fourth at Greenwich, New York, in an area developed by Hood and a competitor as part of the Boston Milkshed. Greenwich is ten miles from Salem and twelve miles from Eagle Bridge, where two of Hood's existing New York depots were located. Hood applied for a license to open the new depot, as required by the

New York law providing that, before issuing the license, the Commission of Agriculture and Markets should be satisfied "that the issuance of a license will not tend to a destructive competition in a market already adequately served, and that the issuance of the license is in the public interest." Pursuant to this provision, the Commissioner refused to issue the license, although Hood met all the other statutory requirements.]

Mr. Justice Jackson delivered the opinion of the Court. . . .

The Commissioner found that Hood, if licensed at Greenwich, would permit its present suppliers, at their option, to deliver at the new plant rather than the old ones and for a substantial number this would mean shorter hauls and savings in delivery costs. The new plant also would attract twenty to thirty producers, some of whose milk Hood anticipates will or may be diverted from other buyers. Other large milk distributors have plants within the general area and dealers serving Troy obtain milk in the locality. He found that Troy was inadequately supplied during the preceding short season.

. . . .

Pennsylvania enacted a law including provisions to protect producers which were very similar to those of this New York Act. A concern which operated a receiving plant in Pennsylvania from which it shipped milk to the New York City market challenged the Act upon grounds thus defined by this Court: "The respondent contends that the act, if construed to require it to obtain a license, to file a bond for the protection of producers, and to pay the farmers the prices prescribed by the Board, unconstitutionally regulates and burdens interstate commerce." Milk Control Bd. v. Eisenberg Co., 306 U.S. 346, 350. This Court, specifically limiting its judgment to the Act's provisions with respect to license, bond and regulation of prices to be paid to producers, id. at 306 U.S. at 352, considered their effect on interstate commerce "incidental and not forbidden by the Constitution, in the absence of regulation by Congress." Id. at 306 U.S. at 353.

The present controversy begins where the *Eisenberg* decision left off. New York's regulations, designed to assure producers a fair price and a responsible purchaser, and consumers a sanitary and modernly equipped handler, are not challenged here but have been complied with. It is only additional restrictions, imposed for the avowed purpose and with the practical effect of curtailing the volume of interstate commerce to aid local economic interests, that are in question here, and no such measures were attempted or such ends sought to be served in the Act before the Court in the *Eisenberg* case.

Our decision in a milk litigation most relevant to the present controversy deals with the converse of the present situation. Baldwin v. G.A.F. Seelig, Inc., 294 U.S. 511, . . . is an explicit, impressive, recent and unanimous condemnation by this Court of economic restraints on interstate commerce for local economic advantage, but it does not stand alone. This Court consistently has rebuffed attempts of states to advance their own commercial interests by curtailing the movement of articles of commerce, either into or out of the state, while generally supporting their right to impose even burdensome regulations in the interests of local health and safety. As most states serve their own interests best by sending their produce to market, the cases in which this Court has been obligated to deal with prohibitions or limitations by states upon exports of articles of commerce are not numerous. . . .

[The] principle that our economic unit is the Nation, which alone has the gamut of powers necessary to control of the economy, including the vital power of erecting customs barriers against foreign competition, has as its corollary that the states are not separable economic units. As the Court said in Baldwin v. G.A.F. Seelig, Inc., 294 U.S. 511, 527, "What is ultimate is the principle that one state in its dealings with another may not place itself in a position of economic isolation." In so speaking it but followed the principle that the state may not use its admitted powers to protect the health and safety of its people as a basis for suppressing competition. In Buck v. Kuykendall, 267 U.S. 307, the Court struck down a state act because, in the language of Mr. Justice Brandeis, "Its primary purpose is not regulation with a view to safety or to conservation of the highways, but the prohibition of competition." The same argument here advanced, that limitation of competition would itself contribute to safety and conservation, and therefore indirectly serve an end permissible to the state, was there declared "not sound." 267 U.S. 307, 315. It is no better here. . . .

The material success that has come to inhabitants of the states which make up this federal free trade unit has been the most impressive in the history of commerce, but the established interdependence of the states only emphasizes the necessity of protecting interstate movement of goods against local burdens and repressions. . . .

Our system, fostered by the Commerce Clause, is that every farmer and every craftsman shall be encouraged to produce by the certainty that he will have free access to every market in the Nation, that no home embargoes will withhold his export, and no foreign state will by customs duties or regulations exclude them. Likewise, every consumer may look to the free competition from every producing area in the Nation to protect him from exploitation by any. Such was the vision of the Founders; such has been the doctrine of this Court which has given it reality. . . .

Since the statute as applied violates the Commerce Clause and is not authorized by federal legislation pursuant to that Clause, it cannot stand. The judgment is reversed and the cause remanded for proceedings not inconsistent with this opinion. It is so ordered.

Reversed and remanded.

Mr. Justice Frankfurter, with whom Mr. Justice Rutledge joins, dissenting.

. . .

Mr. Justice Black, dissenting.

In this case the Court sets up a new constitutional formula for invalidation of state laws regulating local phases of interstate commerce. I believe the New York law is invulnerable to constitutional attack under constitutional rules which the majority of this Court have long accepted. The new formula subjects state regulations of local business activities to greater constitutional hazards than they have ever had to meet before. The consequences of the new formula, as I understand it, will not merely leave a large area of local business activities free from state regulation. All local activities that fall within the scope of this new formula will be free from any regulatory control whatever. For it is inconceivable that Congress could pass uniform national legislation capable of adjustment and application to all the local phases of interstate activities that take place in the 48 states. It is equally inconceivable that Congress would attempt to control such diverse local activities through a "swarm of statutes only locally applicable, and utterly inconsistent." Kidd v. Pearson, 128 U.S. 1, 21. . . .

. . .

The language of this state Act is not discriminatory, the legislative history shows it was not so intended, and the commissioner has not administered it with a hostile eye. . . .

The basic question here is not the greatness of the commerce clause concept, but whether all local phases of interstate business are to be judicially immunized from state laws against destructive competitive business practices such as those prohibited by New York's law. Of course, there remains the bare possibility Congress might attempt to federalize all such local business activities in the forty-eight states. While I have doubt about the wisdom of this New York law, I do not conceive it to be the function of this Court to revise that state's economic judgments. Any doubt I may have concerning the wisdom of New York's law is far less, however, than is my skepticism concerning the ability of the Federal Government to reach out and effectively regulate all the local business activities in the forty-eight states.

I would leave New York's law alone.

Mr. Justice Murphy joins in this opinion.

Philadelphia v. New Jersey

437 U.S. 617, 98 S.Ct. 2531, 57 L.Ed.2d 475 (1978).

Mr. Justice Stewart delivered the opinion of the Court.

A New Jersey law prohibits the importation of most "solid or liquid waste which originated or was collected outside the territorial limits of the State. . . ." In this case we are required to decide whether this statutory prohibition violates the Commerce Clause of the United States Constitution.

. . .

[Operators of private landfills in New Jersey and several cities in other states that had agreements with these operators for waste disposal brought suit against New Jersey in state court challenging the validity of the statute and regulations issued under it. The New Jersey Supreme Court upheld the legislation. The plaintiffs appealed to the United States Supreme Court.]

III.

A.

. . .

The opinions of the Court through the years have reflected an alertness to the evils of "economic isolation" and protectionism, while at the same time recognizing that incidental burdens on interstate commerce may be unavoidable when a State legislates to safeguard the health and safety of its people. Thus, where simple economic protectionism is effected by state legislation, a virtually per se rule of invalidity has been erected. See, e.g., *Hood & Sons v. Du Mond,* supra; Toomer v. Witsell, 334 U.S. 385, 403–406; *Baldwin v. G.A.F. Seelig,* supra; Buck v. Kuykendall, 267 U.S. 307, 315–316. The clearest example of such legislation is a law that overtly blocks the flow of interstate commerce at a State's borders. Cf. Welton v. Missouri, 91 U.S. 275. But where other legislative objectives are credibly advanced and there is no patent discrimination against interstate trade, the Court has adopted a much more flexible approach, the general contours of which were outlined in Pike v. Bruce Church, Inc., 397 U.S. 137, 142:

... The crucial inquiry, therefore, must be directed to determining whether ch. 363 is basically a protectionist measure, or whether it can fairly be viewed as a law directed to legitimate local concerns, with effects upon interstate commerce that are only incidental.

B.

The purpose of ch. 363 is set out in the statute itself as follows:

"The Legislature finds and determines that ... the volume of solid and liquid waste continues to rapidly increase, that the treatment and disposal of these wastes continues to pose an even greater threat to the quality of the environment of New Jersey, that the available and appropriate land fill sites within the State are being diminished, that the environment continues to be threatened by the treatment and disposal of waste which originated or was collected outside the State and that the public health, safety and welfare require that the treatment and disposal within this State of all wastes generated outside of the State be prohibited."

The New Jersey Supreme Court accepted this statement of the state legislature's purpose. The state court additionally found that New Jersey's existing landfill sites will be exhausted within a few years; that to go on using these sites or to develop new ones will take a heavy environmental toll, both from pollution and from loss of scarce open lands; that new techniques to divert waste from landfills to other methods of disposal and resource recovery processes are under development, but that these changes will require time; and finally, that "the extension of the lifespan of existing landfills, resulting from the exclusion of out-of-state waste, may be of crucial importance in preventing further virgin wetlands or other undeveloped lands from being devoted to landfill purposes." 68 N.J., at 460–465, 348 A.2d, at 509–512. Based on these findings, the court concluded that ch. 363 was designed to protect not the State's economy, but its environment, and that its substantial benefits outweigh its "slight" burden on interstate commerce. Id., at 471–478, 348 A.2d, at 515–519.

The appellants strenuously contend that ch. 363, "while outwardly cloaked 'in the currently fashionable garb of environmental protection,' ... is actually no more than a legislative effort to suppress competition and stabilize the cost of solid waste disposal for New Jersey residents. ...."

. . .

The appellees, on the other hand, deny that ch. 363 was motivated by financial concerns or economic protectionism....

This dispute about ultimate legislative purpose need not be resolved, because its resolution would not be relevant to the constitutional issue to be decided in this case. Contrary to the evident assumption of the state court and the parties, the evil of protectionism can reside in legislative means as well as legislative ends. Thus, it does not matter whether the ultimate aim of ch. 363 is to reduce the waste disposal costs of New Jersey residents or to save remaining open lands from pollution, for we assume New Jersey has every right to protect its residents' pocketbooks as well as their environment. And it may be assumed as well that New Jersey may pursue those ends by slowing the flow of all waste into the State's remaining landfills, even though interstate commerce may incidentally be affected. But whatever New Jersey's ultimate purpose, it may not be accomplished by discriminating against articles of commerce coming from outside the State unless there is some reason, apart from their origin, to treat them differently. Both on its face and in its plain effect, ch. 363 violates this principle of nondiscrimination.

The Court has consistently found parochial legislation of this kind to be constitutionally invalid, whether the ultimate aim of the legislation was to assure a steady supply of milk by erecting barriers to allegedly ruinous outside competition, Baldwin v. G.A.F. Seelig, supra, at 522–524; or to create jobs by keeping industry within the State, Foster Packing Co. v. Haydel, 278 U.S. 1, 10; Johnson v. Haydel, 278 U.S. 16; Toomer v. Witsell, supra, at 403–404; or to preserve the State's financial resources from depletion by fencing out indigent immigrants, Edwards v. California, 314 U.S. 160, 173–174. In each of these cases, a presumably legitimate goal was sought to be achieved by the illegitimate means of isolating the State from the national economy.

Also relevant here are the Court's decisions holding that a State may not accord its own inhabitants a preferred right of access over consumers in other States to natural resources located within its borders. West v. Kansas Natural Gas Co., 221 U.S. 229; Pennsylvania v. West Virginia, 262 U.S. 553. These cases stand for the basic principle that a "State is without power to prevent privately owned articles of trade from being shipped and sold in interstate commerce on the ground that they are required to satisfy local demands or because they are needed by the people of the State." Foster Packing Co. v. Haydel, supra, at 10.

The New Jersey law at issue in this case falls squarely within the area that the Commerce Clause puts off-limits to state regulation. On its face, it imposes on out-of-state commercial interests the full burden of conserving the State's remaining landfill space. It is true that in our previous cases the scarce natural resource was itself the article of commerce, whereas here the scarce resource and the article of commerce are distinct. But that difference is without consequence. In both instances, the State has overtly moved to slow or freeze the flow of commerce for protectionist reasons. It does not matter that the State has shut the article of commerce inside the State in one case and outside the State in the other. What is crucial is the attempt by one State to isolate itself from a problem common to many by erecting a barrier against the movement of interstate trade.

The appellees argue that not all laws which facially discriminate against out-of-state commerce are forbidden protectionist regulations. In particular, they point to quarantine laws, which this Court has repeatedly upheld even though they appear to single out interstate commerce for special treatment. See Baldwin v. G.A.F. Seelig, supra, at 525; Bowman v. Chicago & Northwestern R. Co., supra, at 489. In the appellees' view, ch. 363 is analogous to such health-protective measures, since it reduces the exposure of New Jersey residents to the allegedly harmful effects of landfill sites.

It is true that certain quarantine laws have not been considered forbidden protectionist measures, even though they were directed against out-of-state commerce.... But those quarantine laws banned the importation of articles such as diseased livestock that required destruction as soon as possible because their very movement risked contagion and other evils. Those laws thus did not discriminate against interstate commerce as such, but simply prevented traffic in noxious articles, whatever their origin.

The New Jersey statute is not such a quarantine law. There has been no claim here that the very movement of waste into or through New Jersey endangers health, or that waste must be disposed of as soon and as close to its point of generation as possible. The harms caused by waste are said to arise after its disposal in landfill sites, and at that point, as New Jersey concedes, there is no basis to distinguish out-of-state waste from domestic waste. If one is inherently harmful, so is the other. Yet New Jersey has banned the former while leaving its landfill sites open to the latter. The New Jersey law blocks the importation of waste in an obvious effort to saddle those outside the State with the entire burden of slowing the flow of refuse into New Jersey's remaining landfill sites. That legislative effort is clearly impermissible under the Commerce Clause of the Constitution.

Today, cities in Pennsylvania and New York find it expedient or necessary to send their waste to New Jersey for disposal, and New Jersey claims the right to close its borders to such traffic. Tomorrow, cities in New Jersey may find it expedient or necessary to send their waste into Pennsylvania or New York for disposal, and those States might then claim the right to close their borders. The Commerce Clause will protect New Jersey in the future, just as it protects her neighbors now, from efforts by one State to isolate itself in the stream of interstate commerce from a problem shared by all.

The judgment is reversed.

Mr. Justice Rehnquist, with whom The Chief Justice joins, dissenting.

. . .

[T]he Court implies that the challenged laws must be invalidated because New Jersey has left its landfills open to domestic waste. But, as the Court notes . . . this Court has repeatedly upheld quarantine laws "even though they appear to single out interstate commerce for special treatment." The fact that New Jersey has left its landfill sites open for domestic waste does not, of course, mean that solid waste is not innately harmful. Nor does it mean that New Jersey prohibits importation of solid waste for reasons other than the health and safety of its population. New Jersey must out of sheer necessity treat and dispose of its solid waste in some fashion, just as it must treat New Jersey cattle suffering from hoof-and-mouth disease. It does not follow that New Jersey must, under the Commerce Clause, accept solid waste or diseased cattle from outside its borders and thereby exacerbate its problems.

The Supreme Court of New Jersey expressly found that ch. 363 was passed "to preserve the health of New Jersey residents by keeping their exposure to solid waste and landfill areas to a minimum." . . . The Court points to absolutely no evidence that would contradict this finding by the New Jersey Supreme Court. Because I find no basis for distinguishing the laws under challenge here from our past cases upholding state laws that prohibit the importation of items that could endanger the population of the State, I dissent.

NOTE

The Court reaffirmed and applied *Philadelphia v. New Jersey* in two 1992 companion cases. In Chemical Waste Management, Inc. v. Hunt, 504 U.S. 334 (1992), the Court struck down an Alabama statute imposing an additional fee for disposal of hazardous wastes generated outside the State at commercial facilities in Alabama. Alabama's legitimate health, safety, and environmental interests had to be served through less discriminatory alternatives, such as "a generally applicable per-ton additional fee on *all* hazardous waste disposed of within Alabama, . . . or a per-mile tax on *all* vehicles transporting hazardous waste across Alabama roads, . . . or an evenhanded cap on the total tonnage landfilled . . . , which would curtail volume from all sources." Moreover, because "every concern related to quarantine applies perforce to local hazardous waste, which pays no additional fee[,]" the discrimination against interstate commerce was unjustified.

The other decision, Fort Gratiot Sanitary Landfill, Inc. v. Michigan Department of Natural Resources, 504 U.S. 353 (1992), declared invalid under the Commerce Clause a state law prohibiting private landfill operators from accepting solid waste that originated outside the *county* encompassing the landfill facilities, unless the county authorized the importation. The Court rejected an argument that the Michigan Waste Import Restrictions did not discriminate against interstate commerce "because they treat waste from other Michigan counties no differently than waste from other States." The Court said that "prior cases teach that a State (or one of its political subdivisions) may not avoid the strictures of the Commerce Clause by curtailing the movement of articles of commerce through subdivisions of the State, rather than through the State itself." Furthermore, "the fact that several Michigan counties accept out-of-state waste" may have "reduced the scope of the discrimination[,]" but it did not "qualify" the statute's "discriminatory character." *Philadelphia v. New Jersey* thus applied with full force.

In dissent, Chief Justice Rehnquist, joined by Justice Blackmun, argued in part that "this facially neutral restriction (i.e., it applies equally to both interstate and intrastate waste)" should be understood as part of a comprehensive solid waste disposal scheme that legitimately "required counties within the State to be responsible for the waste created within the county." He noted that the regulation was likely to increase disposal costs for Michigan consumers and "require some Michigan counties—those that until now have been exporting their waste to other locations in the State—to confront environmental and other risks that they previously have avoided." He then continued:

"Commerce Clause concerns are at their nadir when a state act works in this fashion—raising prices for all the State's consumers, and working to the substantial disadvantage of other segments of the State's population—because in these circumstances 'a State's own political processes will serve as a check against unduly burdensome regulations.' ... In sum, the law simply incorporates the commonsense notion that those responsible for a problem should be responsible for its solution *to the degree they are responsible for the problem but not further.*"

Hughes v. Oklahoma

441 U.S. 322, 99 S.Ct. 1727, 60 L.Ed.2d 250 (1979).

Mr. Justice Brennan delivered the opinion of the Court.

The question presented for decision is whether Okla.Stat., Tit. 29, § 4–115(B) (Supp.1978) violates the Commerce Clause, Art. I, § 8, cl. 3, of the United States Constitution, insofar as it provides that "No person may transport or ship minnows for sale outside the state which were seined or procured within the waters of this state...."[1]

Appellant William Hughes holds a Texas license to operate a commercial minnow business near Wichita Falls, Tex. An Oklahoma Game Ranger arrested him on a charge of violating § 4–115(B) by transporting from Oklahoma to Wichita Falls a load of natural minnows purchased from a minnow dealer licensed to do business in Oklahoma. Hughes' defense that § 4–115(B) was

---

1. ... The prohibition against transportation out of State for sale thus does not apply to hatchery-bred minnows, but only to "natural" minnows seined or procured from waters within the State.

unconstitutional because it was repugnant to the Commerce Clause was rejected, and he was convicted and fined. The Oklahoma Court of Criminal Appeals
affirmed.... We reverse. Geer v. Connecticut, [161 U.S. 519 (1896),] on which
the Court of Criminal Appeals relied, is overruled. In that circumstance, § 4–
115(B) cannot survive appellant's Commerce Clause attack.

I.

... The cases defining the scope of permissible state regulation in areas of
congressional silence reflect an often controversial evolution of rules to accommodate federal and state interests. *Geer v. Connecticut* was decided relatively
early in that evolutionary process. We hold that time has revealed the error of
the early resolution reached in that case, and accordingly *Geer* is today
overruled.

A.

Geer sustained against a Commerce Clause challenge a statute forbidding
the transportation beyond the State of game birds that had been lawfully killed
within the State. The decision rested on the holding that no interstate commerce was involved. This conclusion followed in turn from the view that the
State had the power, as representative for its citizens, who "owned" in
common all wild animals within the State, to control not only the *taking* of
game but the *ownership* of game that had been lawfully reduced to possession.
By virtue of this power, Connecticut could qualify the ownership of wild game
taken within the State by, for example, prohibiting its removal from the State:
"The common ownership imports the right to keep the property, if the
sovereign so chooses, always within its jurisdiction for every purpose." Accordingly, the State's power to qualify ownership raised serious doubts whether the
sale or exchange of wild game constituted "commerce" at all; in any event the
Court held that the qualification imposed by the challenged statute removed
any transactions involving wild game killed in Connecticut from *interstate*
commerce.

Mr. Justice Field and the first Mr. Justice Harlan dissented, rejecting as
artificial and formalistic the Court's analysis of "ownership" and "commerce"
in wild game. They would have affirmed the State's power to provide for the
protection of wild game, but only "so far as such protection ... does not
contravene the power of Congress in the regulation of interstate commerce."
Their view was that "[w]hen an animal ... is lawfully killed for the purposes of
food or other uses of man, it becomes an article of commerce, and its use cannot
be limited to the citizens of one state to the exclusion of citizens of another
state."

B.

The view of the *Geer* dissenters increasingly prevailed in subsequent cases.
Indeed, not only has the *Geer* analysis been rejected when natural resources
other than wild game were involved, but even state regulations of wild game
have been held subject to the strictures of the Commerce Clause under the
pretext of distinctions from *Geer*.

. . .

C.

The case before us is the first in modern times to present facts essentially
on all fours with *Geer*. We now conclude that challenges under the Commerce
Clause to state regulations of wild animals should be considered according to

the same general rule applied to state regulations of other natural resources, and therefore expressly overrule *Geer*. We thus bring our analytical framework into conformity with practical realities. Overruling *Geer* also eliminates the anomaly, created by the decisions distinguishing *Geer*, that statutes imposing the most extreme burdens on interstate commerce (essentially total embargoes) were the most immune from challenge. At the same time, the general rule we adopt in this case makes ample allowance for preserving, in ways not inconsistent with the Commerce Clause, the legitimate state concerns for conservation and protection of wild animals underlying the 19th century legal fiction of state ownership.

II.

We turn then to the question whether the burden imposed on interstate commerce in wild game by § 4–115(B) is permissible under the general rule articulated in our precedents governing other types of commerce. See, e.g., Pike v. Bruce Church, supra, 397 U.S., at 142. . . .

Section 4–115(B) on its face discriminates against interstate commerce. It forbids the transportation of natural minnows out of the State for purposes of sale, and thus "overtly blocks the flow of interstate commerce at [the] State's border." Philadelphia v. New Jersey, supra, 437 U.S., at 624. Such facial discrimination by itself may be a fatal defect, regardless of the State's purpose, because "the evil of protectionism can reside in legislative means as well as legislative ends." Id., at 626. At a minimum such facial discrimination invokes the strictest scrutiny of any purported legitimate local purpose and of the absence of nondiscriminatory alternatives.

Oklahoma argues that § 4–115(B) serves a legitimate local purpose in that it is "readily apparent as a conservation measure." The State's interest in maintaining the ecological balance in state waters by avoiding the removal of inordinate numbers of minnows may well qualify as a legitimate local purpose. . . . But the scope of legitimate state interests in "conservation" is narrower under this analysis than it was under *Geer*. A State may no longer "keep the property, if the sovereign so chooses, always within its jurisdiction for every purpose." Geer v. Connecticut, supra, 161 U.S., at 530. The fiction of state ownership may no longer be used to force those outside the State to bear the full costs of "conserving" the wild animals within its borders when equally effective nondiscriminatory conservation measures are available.

Far from choosing the least discriminatory alternative, Oklahoma has chosen to "conserve" its minnows in the way that most overtly discriminates against interstate commerce. The State places no limits on the numbers of minnows that can be taken by licensed minnow dealers; nor does it limit in any way how these minnows may be disposed of within the State. Yet it forbids the transportation of any commercially significant number of natural minnows out of the State for sale. Section 4–115(B) is certainly not a "last ditch" attempt at conservation after nondiscriminatory alternatives have proven unfeasible. It is rather a choice of the most discriminatory means even though nondiscriminatory alternatives would seem likely to fulfill the State's purported legitimate local purpose more effectively.

We therefore hold that § 4–115(B) is repugnant to the Commerce Clause.

III.

The overruling of *Geer* does not leave the States powerless to protect and conserve wild animal life within their borders. Today's decision makes clear, however, that States may promote this legitimate purpose only in ways consistent with the basic principle that "our economic unit is the Nation," H.P. Hood & Sons, Inc. v. Du Mond, supra, 336 U.S., at 537, and that when a wild animal "becomes an article of commerce . . . its use cannot be limited to the citizens of one State to the exclusion of citizens of another State." Geer v. Connecticut, supra, 161 U.S., at 538 (Field, J., dissenting).

Reversed.[a]

Mr. Justice Rehnquist, with whom The Chief Justice joins, dissenting . . . .

Contrary to the view of the Court, I do not think that Oklahoma's regulation of the commercial exploitation of natural minnows either discriminates against out-of-state enterprises in favor of local businesses or that it burdens the interstate commerce in minnows. At least, no such showing has been made on the record before us. . . . This is not a case where a State's regulation permits residents to export naturally seined minnows but prohibits nonresidents from so doing. No person is allowed to export natural minnows for sale outside of Oklahoma; the statute is evenhanded in its application. See Okla.Stat., Tit. 29, § 4–115(B). The State has not used its power to protect its own citizens from outside competition. . . . Nor is this a case where a State requires a nonresident business, as a condition to exporting minnows, to move a significant portion of its operations to the State or to use certain State resources in pursuit of its business for the benefit of the local economy. . . . And, notwithstanding the Court's protestations to the contrary, Oklahoma has not blocked the flow of interstate commerce in minnows at the State's borders. . . . Petitioner, or anyone else, may freely export as many minnows as he wishes, so long as the minnows so transported are hatchery minnows and not naturally seined minnows. On this record, I simply fail to see how interstate commerce in minnows, the commodity at issue here, is impeded in the least by Oklahoma's regulatory scheme.

Oklahoma does regulate the manner in which both residents and nonresidents procure minnows to be sold outside the State. But there is no showing in this record that requiring petitioner to purchase his minnows from hatcheries instead of from persons licensed to seine minnows from the State's waters in any way increases petitioner's costs of doing business. There also is nothing in the record to indicate that naturally seined minnows are any more desirable as items of commerce than hatchery minnows. So far as the record before us indicates, hatchery minnows and naturally seined minnows are fungible. Accordingly, any minimal burden that may result from requiring petitioner to purchase minnows destined for sale out of state from hatcheries instead of from those licensed to seine minnows is, in my view, more than outweighed by Oklahoma's substantial interest in conserving and regulating exploitation of its natural minnow population. I therefore would affirm the judgment of the Oklahoma Court of Criminal Appeals.

SPORHASE v. NEBRASKA, 458 U.S. 941 (1982). Appellants jointly own contiguous tracts of land in Nebraska and Colorado. A well physically located on the Nebraska tract pumps ground water used for irrigation in both the Nebraska and Colorado tracts. Appellants did not seek a permit pursuant to a

---

a. Apparently Oklahoma did not argue nor did the Court consider the relevance of 16 U.S.C. § 852 making it unlawful for any person knowingly "to transport . . . in interstate or foreign commerce, any black bass and other fish, if such . . . transportation is contrary to the law of the State . . . from which such black bass is transported." See Hellerstein, Hughes v. Oklahoma: The Court, The Commerce Clause, and State Control of Natural Resources, 1979 Sup.Ct.Rev. 51, 54. For an application of that Act to enforce a state ban on the export of fish, see United States v. Howard, 352 U.S. 212 (1957).

Nebraska statute which requires a permit to transport ground water taken in the state for use in another state and specifies that the permit should be granted only if the withdrawal of ground water "is reasonable, is not contrary to the conservation and use of ground water, and is not otherwise detrimental to the public welfare" and if the state in which the water is used grants reciprocal rights to withdraw water for use in Nebraska. Nebraska brought suit in the state court to enjoin appellants from transferring the water across the border without a permit. The Nebraska trial court granted the injunction and the Nebraska Supreme Court affirmed.

The Supreme Court invalidated the statutory reciprocity requirement. In the first part of Justice Stevens' opinion, the Court concluded that ground water is an article of commerce and that "[g]round water overdraft is a national problem and Congress has the power to deal with it on that scale." In a third part of the opinion the Court held that Congress had not affirmatively authorized the state to impose otherwise impermissible burdens on interstate commerce in ground water.

In the opinion's middle section the Court appeared to say that only the reciprocity requirement was invalid and the remainder would survive if the state court found the invalid provision separable. Opening its discussion with the standard quotation from *Pike v. Bruce Church, Inc.,* the Court then said:

"The only purpose that appellee advances ... is to conserve and preserve diminishing sources of ground water. The purpose is unquestionably legitimate and highly important, and the other aspects of Nebraska's ground water regulation demonstrate that it is genuine.... [S]pecial rules and regulations governing ground water withdrawal and use [apply in] 'critical' ... townships, [and] appellants' Nebraska tract is located within a critical township.... They ... strictly limit the intrastate transfer of ground water: transfers are only permitted between lands controlled by the same ground water user, and all transfers must be approved by the district board of directors.

"The State's interest in conservation and preservation of ground water is advanced by the first three conditions ... for the withdrawal of water for an interstate transfer.... Although Commerce Clause concerns are implicated by the fact that [the statute] applies to interstate transfers but not to intrastate transfers, there are legitimate reasons for the special treatment accorded requests to transport ground water across state lines. Obviously, a State that imposes severe withdrawal and use restrictions on its own citizens is not discriminating against interstate commerce when it seeks to prevent the uncontrolled transfer of water out of the State. An exemption for interstate transfers would be inconsistent with the ideal of evenhandedness in regulation. At least in the area in which appellants' Nebraska tract is located, the first three standards ... may well be no more strict in application than the limitations upon intrastate transfers....

"Moreover, in the absence of a contrary view expressed by Congress, we are reluctant to condemn as unreasonable measures taken by a State to conserve and preserve for its own citizens this vital resource in times of severe shortage. Our reluctance stems from the 'confluence of [several] realities.' Hicklin v. Orbeck, 437 U.S. 518, 534 (1978). First, a State's power to regulate the use of water in times and places of shortage for the purpose of protecting the health of its citizens—and not simply the health of its economy—is at the core of its police power. For Commerce Clause purposes, we have long recognized a difference between economic protectionism, on the one hand, and health and safety regulation, on the other. See H.P. Hood & Sons v. Du Mond, 336 U.S. 525, 533 (1949). Second, the legal expectation that under certain circumstances each State may restrict water within its borders has been fostered over the years not only by our equitable apportionment decrees, see, e.g., Wyoming v. Colorado, 353 U.S. 953 (1957), but also by the negotiation and enforcement of interstate compacts. Our law therefore has recognized the relevance of state boundaries in the allocation of scarce water resources. Third, although appellee's claim to public ownership of Nebraska ground water cannot justify a total denial of federal regulatory power, it may support a limited preference for its own citizens in the utilization of the resource. See Hicklin v. Orbeck, supra, at 533–534. In this regard, it is relevant that appellee's claim is logically more substantial than claims to public ownership of other natural resources. Finally, given appellee's conservation efforts, the continuing availability of ground water in Nebraska is not simply happenstance; the natural resource has some indicia of a good publicly produced and owned in which a State may favor its own citizens in times of shortage. See Reeves, Inc. v. Stake, 447 U.S. 429 (1980).... A facial examination of the [statute's] first three conditions ... does not, therefore, indicate that they impermissibly burden interstate commerce. Appellants, indeed, seem to concede their reasonableness.

"Appellants, however, do challenge the [reciprocity] requirement.... Because Colorado forbids the exportation of its ground water, the reciprocity provision operates as an explicit barrier to commerce between the two States. The State therefore bears the initial burden of demonstrating a close fit between the reciprocity requirement and its asserted local purpose.

"The reciprocity requirement fails to clear this initial hurdle. For there is no evidence that this restriction is narrowly tailored to the conservation and preservation rationale. Even though the supply of water in a particular well may be abundant, or perhaps even excessive, and even though the most beneficial use of that water might be in another State, such water may not be shipped into a neighboring State that does not permit its water to be used in Nebraska. If it could be shown that the State as a whole suffers a water shortage, that the intrastate transportation of water from areas of abundance to areas of shortage is feasible regardless of distance, and that the importation of water from adjoining States would roughly compensate for any exportation to those States, then the conservation and preservation purpose might be credibly advanced for the reciprocity provision. A demonstrably arid state conceivably might be able to marshal evidence to establish a close means-end relationship between even a total ban on the exportation of water and a purpose to conserve and preserve water. Appellee, however, does not claim that such evidence exists. We therefore are not persuaded that the reciprocity requirement—when superimposed on the first three restrictions in the statute—significantly advances the State's legitimate conservation and preservation interest; it surely is not narrowly tailored to serve that purpose. The reciprocity requirement does not survive the 'strictest scrutiny' reserved for facially discriminatory legislation."

Justices Rehnquist and O'Connor dissented.

MAINE v. TAYLOR, 477 U.S. 131 (1986). The Supreme Court sustained the constitutionality of a Maine statute prohibiting the importation of live baitfish, despite insisting that the ban "is constitutional only if it satisfies the requirements ordinarily applied under *Hughes v. Oklahoma* to local regulation that discriminates against interstate trade: the statute must serve a legitimate local purpose, and the purpose must be one that cannot be served as well by available nondiscriminatory means." For the Court, Justice Blackmun said in part:

III

"The District Court found after an evidentiary hearing that both parts of the *Hughes* test were satisfied, but the Court of Appeals disagreed. We conclude that the Court of Appeals erred in setting aside the findings of the District Court. . . .

A

"The evidentiary hearing on which the District Court based its conclusions was one before a magistrate. . . .

" . . .

"Weighing all the testimony, the magistrate concluded that both prongs of the *Hughes* test were satisfied. . . . [T]he District Court, after an independent review of the evidence, reached the same conclusions. First, the court found that Maine 'clearly has a legitimate and substantial purpose in prohibiting the importation of live bait fish,' because 'substantial uncertainties' surrounded the effects that baitfish parasites would have on the State's unique population of wild fish, and the consequences of introducing non-native species were similarly unpredictable. . . . Second, the court concluded that less discriminatory means of protecting against these threats were currently unavailable, and that, in particular, testing procedures for baitfish parasites had not yet been devised. . . .

" . . .

"[T]he Court of Appeals . . . conclud[ed] that Maine had not demonstrated that any legitimate local purpose served by the ban could not be promoted equally well without discriminating so heavily against interstate commerce. . . .

" . . .

B

"Although the proffered justification for any local discrimination against interstate commerce must be subjected to 'the strictest scrutiny,' Hughes v. Oklahoma, 441 U.S., at 337, the empirical component of that scrutiny, like any other form of factfinding, 'is the basic responsibility of district courts, rather than appellate courts,' Pullman–Standard v. Swint, 456 U.S. 273, 291 (1982). . . . [A]ppellate courts are not to decide factual questions *de novo,* reversing any findings they would have made differently. . . .

" . . . [W]hether scientifically accepted techniques exist for the sampling and inspection of live baitfish is one of fact, and the District Court's finding that such techniques have not been devised cannot be characterized as clearly erroneous. Indeed, the record probably could not support a contrary finding. . . .

" . . .

"More importantly, we agree with the District Court that the 'abstract possibility,' of developing acceptable testing procedures, particularly when there is no assurance as to their effectiveness, does not make those procedures an '[a]vailable . . . nondiscriminatory alternativ[e],' *Hunt,* 432 U.S., at 353, for purposes of the Commerce Clause. A State must make reasonable efforts to avoid restraining the free flow of commerce across its borders, but it is not required to develop new and unproven means of protection at an uncertain cost. Appellee . . . is free to . . . develop scientifically acceptable sampling and inspection procedures for golden shiners; if and when such procedures are developed, Maine no longer may be able to justify its import ban. The State need not join in those efforts, however, and it need not pretend they already have succeeded.

C

"... After reviewing the expert testimony presented to the magistrate, ... we cannot say that the District Court clearly erred in finding that substantial scientific uncertainty surrounds the effect that baitfish parasites and non-native species could have on Maine's fisheries. Moreover, we agree with the District Court that Maine has a legitimate interest in guarding against imperfectly understood environmental risks, despite the possibility that they may ultimately prove to be negligible....

"Nor do we think that much doubt is cast on the legitimacy of Maine's purposes by what the Court of Appeals took to be signs of protectionist intent....[19]

"The ... evidence of protectionism identified by the Court of Appeals is no[t] persuasive....

IV

"The Commerce Clause ... does not elevate free trade above all other values.... The evidence in this case amply supports the District Court's findings that Maine's ban on the importation of live baitfish serves legitimate local purposes that could not adequately be served by available nondiscriminatory alternatives."

In dissent, Justice Stevens said:

"There is something fishy about this case. Maine is the only State in the Union that blatantly discriminates against out-of-state baitfish by flatly prohibiting their importation. Although golden shiners are already present and thriving in Maine (and, perhaps not coincidentally, the subject of a flourishing domestic industry), Maine excludes golden shiners grown and harvested (and, perhaps not coincidentally, sold) in other States. This kind of stark discrimination against out-of-state articles of commerce requires rigorous justification by the discriminating State....

"... Since the State engages in obvious discrimination against out-of-state commerce, it should be put to its proof. Ambiguity about dangers and alternatives should actually defeat, rather than sustain, the discriminatory measure.

"This is not to derogate the State's interest in ecological purity. But the invocation of environmental protection or public health has never been thought to confer some kind of special dispensation from the general principle of nondiscrimination in interstate commerce.... If Maine wishes to rely on its interest in ecological preservation, it must show that interest, and the infeasibility of other alternatives, with far greater specificity. Otherwise, it must further that asserted interest in a manner far less offensive to the notions of comity and cooperation that underlie the Commerce Clause.

"... [T]he State has not carried its substantial burden of proving why it cannot meet its environmental concerns in the same manner as other States with the same interest in the health of their fish and ecology...."

---

19. ... [E]ven overt discrimination against interstate trade may be justified where, as in this case, out-of-state goods or services are particularly likely for some reason to threaten the health and safety of a State's citizens or the integrity of its natural resources, and where "outright prohibition of entry, rather than some intermediate form of regulation, is the only effective method of protecti[on]." Lewis v. BT Investment Managers, Inc., 447 U.S. 27, 43 (1980).

CAMPS NEWFOUND/OWATONNA, INC. v. TOWN OF HARRISON,
520 U.S. 564 (1997). A Maine statute generally exempts charitable institutions
from state property taxes, but it withheld the exemption from those charitable
organizations "in fact conducted or operated principally for the benefit of
persons who are not residents of Maine." A nonprofit Maine corporation
operating a summer camp in Maine for children, about 95% of whom were not
Maine residents, sued for tax relief from the denial of the exemption. The
Supreme Court, 5–4, held invalid under the Commerce Clause the "disparate
real estate tax treatment of a nonprofit service provider based on the residence
of the consumers it serves."

Concluding that interstate commerce was implicated by the nonprofit
camp's interstate purchases and the interstate movement of campers, and that
real estate taxes, "like any other tax, may impermissibly burden interstate
commerce[,]" Justice Stevens' majority opinion first determined that "were
this statute targeted at profit-making entities, it would violate the dormant
Commerce Clause[,]" because its text expressly discriminates against interstate
commerce by "singling out camps that serve mostly in-staters for beneficial tax
treatment, and penalizing those camps that do a principally interstate business.
As a practical matter, the statute encourages affected entities to limit their out-
of-state clientele, and penalizes the principally nonresident customers of businesses catering to a primarily interstate market." The opinion continued:

"If such a policy were implemented by a statutory prohibition against
providing camp services to nonresidents, the statute would almost certainly be
invalid. We have 'consistently . . . held that the Commerce Clause . . . precludes
a state from mandating that its residents be given a preferred right of access,
over out-of-state consumers, to natural resources located within its borders or
to the products derived therefrom.' New England Power Co. v. New Hampshire,
455 U.S. 331, 338 (1982). . . . Petitioner's 'product' is in part the natural beauty
of Maine itself, and in addition the special services that the camp provides. In
this way, the Maine statute is like a law that burdens out-of-state access to
domestically generated hydroelectric power, *New England Power*, or to local
landfills, Philadelphia v. New Jersey, 437 U.S. 617 (1978). In those cases, as in
this case, the burden fell on out-of-state access both to a natural resource, and
to related services provided by state residents.

". . . By encouraging economic isolationism, prohibitions on out-of-state
access to in-state resources serve the very evil that the dormant Commerce
Clause was designed to prevent.

"Of course, this case does not involve a total prohibition. Rather, the
statute provides a strong incentive for affected entities not to do business with
nonresidents if they are able to so avoid the discriminatory tax. . . .

"To the extent that affected Maine organizations are not deterred by the
statute from doing a principally interstate business, it is clear that discriminatory burdens on interstate commerce imposed by regulation or taxation may
also violate the Commerce Clause. We have held that special fees assessed on
nonresidents directly by the State when they attempt to use local services
impose an impermissible burden on interstate commerce. See, e.g., *Chemical
Waste*, 504 U.S., at 342 (discriminatory tax imposed on disposal of out-of-state
hazardous waste). That the tax discrimination comes in the form of a deprivation of a generally available tax benefit, rather than a specific penalty on the
activity itself, is of no moment . . . New Energy Co. of Ind. v. Limbach, 486 U.S.
269, 274 (1988). . . . Given the fact that the burden of Maine's facially discriminatory tax scheme falls by design in a predictably disproportionate way on out-

of-staters, the pernicious effect on interstate commerce is the same as in our cases involving taxes targeting out-of-staters alone.

. . .

". . . [T]he Maine statute . . . functionally serves as an export tariff that targets out-of-state consumers by taxing the businesses that principally serve them. [T]his sort of discrimination is at the very core of activities forbidden by the dormant commerce clause. . . .

. . .

. . . .[16]

V

"The unresolved question . . . is whether a different rule should apply to tax exemptions for charitable and benevolent institutions. . . .

. . .

"We see no reason why the nonprofit character of an enterprise should exclude it from the coverage of either the affirmative or the negative aspect of the Commerce Clause. . . . There are a number of lines of commerce in which both for-profit and nonprofit entities participate. Some educational institutions, some hospitals, some child-care facilities, some research organizations, and some museums generate significant earnings; and some are operated by not-for-profit corporations. . . .

". . . Nothing intrinsic to the nature of nonprofit entities prevents them from engaging in interstate commerce. Summer camps may be operated as for-profit or nonprofit entities; nonprofits may depend—as here—in substantial part on fees charged for their services. . . . Whether operated on a for-profit or nonprofit basis, they purchase goods and services in competitive markets, offer their facilities to a variety of patrons, and derive revenues from a variety of sources, some of which are local and some out of State.

. . .

". . . Protectionism, whether targeted at for-profit entities or serving, as here, to encourage nonprofits to keep their efforts close to home, is forbidden under the dormant Commerce Clause. If there is need for a special exception for nonprofits, Congress not only has the power to create it, but also is in a far better position than we to determine its dimensions.

VI

"Rather than urging us to create a categorical exception for nonprofit entities, the Town argues that Maine's exemption statute should be viewed as an expenditure of government money designed to lessen its social service burden and to foster the societal benefits provided by charitable organizations.

---

16. . . .

. . . Maine has ample alternatives short of a facially discriminatory property tax exemption to achieve its apparent goal of subsidizing the attendance of the State's children at summer camp. Maine could, for example, achieve this end by offering direct financial support to parents of resident children. . . . Though we have not had the occasion to address the issue, it might also be permissible for the State to subsidize Maine camps directly to the extent that they serve residents. See West Lynn Creamery, Inc. v. Healy, 512 U.S., at 199, n. 15; New Energy Co. of Ind. v. Limbach, 486 U.S. 269, 278 (1988) (noting that "[d]irect subsidization of domestic industry does not ordinarily run afoul" of the Commerce Clause). . . .

. . .

So characterized, the Town submits that its tax exemption scheme is either a legitimate discriminatory subsidy of only those charities that choose to focus their activities on local concerns, or alternatively a governmental 'purchase' of charitable services falling within the narrow exception to the dormant Commerce Clause for States in their role as 'market participants,' see, e.g., Hughes v. Alexandria Scrap Corp., 426 U.S. 794 (1976); Reeves, Inc. v. Stake, 447 U.S. 429 (1980). We find these arguments unpersuasive. . . .

". . . We have 'never squarely confronted the constitutionality of subsidies,' and we need not . . . today. Assuming, *arguendo*, that . . . a direct subsidy benefitting only those nonprofits serving principally Maine residents would be permissible, our cases do not sanction a tax exemption serving similar ends.

. . .

"[Nor can] Maine's tax exemption statute . . . be characterized as a proprietary activity falling within the market-participant exception. . . . A tax exemption is not the sort of direct state involvement in the market that falls within the market-participation doctrine.

"Even if we were prepared to expand the exception . . . , the Maine tax statute at issue here would be a poor candidate. . . . [T]he exemption that has been denied to petitioner is available to a broad category of charitable and benevolent institutions. For that reason, nothing short of a dramatic expansion of the 'market participant' exception would support its application to this case. *Alexandria Scrap* involved Maryland's entry into the market for automobile hulks, a discrete activity focused on a single industry. Similarly, South Dakota's participation in the market for cement was—in part because of its narrow scope—readily conceived as a proprietary action of the State. In contrast, Maine's tax exemption—which sweeps to cover broad swathes of the nonprofit sector—must be viewed as action taken in the State's sovereign capacity rather than a proprietary decision to make an entry into all of the markets in which the exempted charities function. . . . The Town's version of the 'market participant' exception would swallow the rule against discriminatory tax schemes. [T]he notion that whenever a State provides a discriminatory tax abatement it is 'purchasing' some service in its proprietary capacity is not readily confined to the charitable context. . . .

VII

". . . The history of our Commerce Clause jurisprudence has shown that even the smallest scale discrimination can interfere with the project of our federal Union. [T]o countenance discrimination of the sort that Maine's statute represents would invite significant inroads on our 'national solidarity'. . . ."

Justice Scalia authored a dissent that Chief Justice Rehnquist and Justices Thomas and Ginsburg joined. Characterizing the challenged statutory provision as "a narrow tax exemption, designed merely to compensate or subsidize those organizations that contribute to the public fisc by dispensing public benefits the State might otherwise provide" to its residents, the dissent found the state's interest "deserving of exemption from negative-commerce-clause invalidation"—an exemption that "will not place the 'national market' in any peril." Justice Scalia questioned whether the statute facially discriminated against interstate commerce, because "for purposes of entitlement to a tax subsidy from the State, it is certainly reasonable to think that property gratuitously devoted to relieving the State of some of its welfare burden is not similarly situated to property used 'principally for the benefit of persons who are not residents of [the State],' § 652(1)(A)." Moreover, the dissent continued:

"[T]his is one of those cases in which the 'virtually *per se* rule of invalidity' does not apply. Facially discriminatory or not, the exemption is no more an artifice of economic protectionism than any state law which dispenses public assistance only to the State's residents.[3] Our cases have always recognized the legitimacy of limiting state provided welfare benefits to bona fide residents....

"... [T]he Court today relies not on any discrimination against out-of-state nonprofits, but on the supposed discrimination against nonresident would-be *recipients* of charity (the nonprofits' 'customers'); surely those individuals are similarly discriminated against in the direct distribution of state benefits. The problem ... [includes] municipal employment[,] free public schooling, ... libraries, orphanages, homeless shelters and refuges for battered women. One could hardly explain the constitutionality of a State's limiting its provision of these to its own residents on the theory that the State is a 'market participant.' These are traditional governmental functions, far removed from commercial activity and utterly unconnected to any genuine private market.

"If, however, a State that provides social services directly *may* limit its largesse to its own residents, I see no reason why a State that chooses to provide some of its social services indirectly—by compensating or subsidizing private charitable providers—cannot be similarly restrictive....

"... [T]he 'subsidy' and 'market participant' exceptions do not exhaust the realm of state actions that we should abstain from scrutinizing under the Commerce Clause. In my view, the provision by a State of free public schooling, public assistance, and other forms of social welfare to only (or principally) its own residents—whether it be accomplished directly or by providing tax exemptions, cash or other property to private organizations that perform the work for the State—implicates none of the concerns underlying our negative-commerce-clause jurisprudence...."

In a separate dissent, Justice Thomas first argued (joined by Chief Justice Rehnquist and Justice Scalia) that the "negative Commerce Clause has no basis in the text of the Constitution, makes little sense, and has proved virtually unworkable in application." He then urged (joined only by Justice Scalia) that the problem of discriminatory state taxation of interstate commerce that the Court had long acted to correct via the dormant Commerce Clause instead should be addressed under the Import–Export Clause, Article I, § 10, cl. 2, which the Court—wrongly in Justice Thomas' view—had held in Woodruff v. Parham, 8 Wall. 123 (1869), applied only to restrict state "duties" and "imposts" on foreign, but not interstate, trade.

With respect to his first argument, Justice Thomas contended that "neither of the Court's [historically] proffered theoretical justifications—exclusivity or preemption-by-silence—currently supports our negative Commerce Clause jurisprudence, if either ever did." The rationale "that the Commerce Clause itself constituted an exclusive grant of power to Congress ... was likely wrong from the outset, ... seriously questioned even in early cases[,] ... long since 'repudiated' [by the Court, and] ..., as this Court's definition of the scope of congressional authority under the positive Commerce Clause has expanded, the exclusivity rationale has moved from untenable to absurd." The theory "that Congress, by its silence, pre-empts state legislation" by virtue of the presump-

---

3. [T]he Court ... concludes that ... "Maine has ample alternatives short of a facially discriminatory property tax exemption," such as offering direct cash subsidies to parents of resident children or to camps that serve residents. These are *nonregulatory* alternatives (and hence immune from negative-commerce-clause attack), but they are not *nondiscriminatory* alternatives, which is what the exception to the "virtually *per se* rule of invalidity" requires....

tion "that congressional 'inaction' [is] 'equivalent to a declaration that inter-State commerce shall be free and untrammelled[,]' Welton v. Missouri, 91 U.S. 275, 282 (1876)[, also] has long since been rejected by this Court in virtually every analogous area of the law" and "virtually amounts to legislation by default, in apparent violation of the constitutional requirements of bi-cameralism and presentment."

Justice Thomas continued with these observations:

"Moreover, our negative Commerce Clause jurisprudence has taken us well beyond the invalidation of obviously discriminatory taxes on interstate commerce. We have used the Clause to make policy-laden judgments that we are ill-equipped and arguably unauthorized to make.... In so doing, we have developed multifactor tests in order to assess the perceived 'effect' any particular state tax or regulation has on interstate commerce.... And in an unabashedly legislative manner, we have balanced that 'effect' against the perceived interests of the taxing or regulating State, as the very description of our 'general rule' [in *Pike v. Bruce Church*] indicates....

"Any test that requires us to assess (1) whether a particular statute serves a 'legitimate' local public interest; (2) whether the effects of the statute on interstate commerce are merely 'incidental' or 'clearly excessive in relation to the putative benefits'; (3) the 'nature' of the local interest; and (4) whether there are alternative means of furthering the local interest that have a 'lesser impact' on interstate commerce, and even then makes the question 'one of degree,' surely invites us, if not compels us, to function more as legislators than as judges...."

D. PRESERVING STATE-OWNED RESOURCES FOR IN-STATE USE

Reeves, Inc. v. Stake

447 U.S. 429, 100 S.Ct. 2271, 65 L.Ed.2d 244 (1980).

Mr. Justice Blackmun delivered the opinion of the Court.

The issue in this case is whether, consistent with the Commerce Clause, U.S. Const., Art. I, § 8, ch. 3, the State of South Dakota, in a time of shortage, may confine the sale of the cement it produces solely to its residents.

> *Issue*

I.

In 1919, South Dakota undertook plans to build a cement plant. The project, a product of the State's then prevailing Progressive political movement, was initiated in response to recent regional cement shortages that "interfered with and delayed both public and private enterprises," and that were "threatening the people of this state." Eakin v. South Dakota State Cement Comm'n, 44 S.D. 268, 272, 183 N.W. 651, 652 (1921). In 1920, the South Dakota Cement Commission anticipated "[t]hat there would be a ready market for the entire output of the plant within the state." Report of State Cement Commission 9 (1920). The plant, however, located at Rapid City, soon produced more cement than South Dakotans could use. Over the years, buyers in no less than nine nearby States purchased cement from the State's plant. Between 1970 and 1977, some 40% of the plant's output went outside the State.

The plant's list of out-of-state cement buyers included petitioner Reeves, Inc. Reeves is a ready-mix concrete distributor organized under Wyoming law and with facilities in Buffalo, Gillette, and Sheridan, Wyo. From the beginning of its operations in 1958, and until 1978, Reeves purchased about 95% of its cement from the South Dakota plant. In 1977, its purchases were $1,172,000. In turn, Reeves has supplied three northwestern Wyoming counties with more than half their ready-mix concrete needs. For 20 years the relationship between Reeves and the South Dakota cement plant was amicable, uninterrupted, and mutually profitable.

As the 1978 construction season approached, difficulties at the plant slowed production. Meanwhile, a booming construction industry spurred demand for cement both regionally and nationally. The plant found itself unable to meet all orders. Faced with the same type of "serious cement shortage" that inspired the plant's construction, the Commission "reaffirmed its policy of supplying all South Dakota customers first and to honor all contract commitments, with the remaining volume allocated on a first come, first served basis."

Reeves, which had no pre-existing long-term supply contract, was hit hard and quickly by this development. On June 30, 1978, the plant informed Reeves that it could not continue to fill Reeves' orders, and on July 5, it turned away a Reeves truck. Unable to find another supplier, Reeves was forced to cut production by 76% in mid-July.

On July 19, Reeves [sued] the Commission, challenging the plant's policy of preferring South Dakota buyers.... After ... a hearing ..., the District Court found no substantial issue of material fact and permanently enjoined the Commission's practice. The court reasoned that South Dakota's "hoarding" was inimical to the national free market envisioned by the Commerce Clause.

The ... Eighth Circuit reversed. ... We granted ... certiorari to consider once again the impact of the Commerce Clause on state proprietary activity. 444 U.S. 1031 (1980).

II.

A.

Hughes v. Alexandria Scrap.

[*Hughes v.*] *Alexandria Scrap* [*Corp.*, 426 U.S. 794 (1976)] concerned a Maryland program designed to remove abandoned automobiles from the State's roadways and junkyards. To encourage recycling, a "bounty" was offered for every Maryland-titled junk car converted into scrap. Processors located both in and outside Maryland were eligible to collect these subsidies. The legislation, as initially enacted in 1969, required a processor seeking a bounty to present documentation evidencing ownership of the wrecked car. This requirement however, did not apply to "hulks," inoperable automobiles over eight years old. In 1974, the statute was amended to extend documentation requirements to hulks, which comprised a large majority of the junk cars being processed. Departing from prior practice, the new law imposed more exacting documentation requirements on out-of-state than in-state processors. By making it less remunerative for suppliers to transfer vehicles outside Maryland, the reform triggered a "precipitate decline in the number of bounty-eligible hulks supplied to appellee's [Virginia] plant from Maryland sources." ... Indeed, "[t]he practical effect was substantially the same as if Maryland had withdrawn altogether the availability of bounties on hulks delivered by unlicensed suppliers to licensed non-Maryland processors." ...

. . .

... In th[is] Court's view, ... *Alexandria Scrap* did not involve "the kind of action with which the Commerce Clause is concerned." 426 U.S., at 805. Unlike prior cases voiding state laws inhibiting interstate trade, "Maryland has not sought to prohibit the flow of hulks, or to regulate the conditions under which it may occur. Instead, it has entered into the market itself to bid up their price," id., at 806, "as a purchaser, in effect, of a potential article of interstate commerce," and has restricted "its trade to its own citizens or businesses within the State." Id., at 808.

Having characterized Maryland as a market participant, rather than as a market regulator, the Court found no reason to "believe the Commerce Clause was intended to require independent justification for [the State's] action." Id., at 809. The Court couched its holding in unmistakably broad terms. "Nothing in the purposes animating the Commerce Clause prohibits a State, in the absence of congressional action, from participating in the market and exercising the right to favor its own citizens over others." Id., at 810 (footnote omitted).

B.

The basic distinction drawn in *Alexandria Scrap* between States as market participants and States as market regulators makes good sense and sound law. As that case explains, the Commerce Clause responds principally to state taxes and regulatory measures impeding free private trade in the national marketplace. 426 U.S., at 807–808, citing H.P. Hood & Sons v. Du Mond, 336 U.S. 525, 539 (1949) (referring to "home embargoes," "customs duties," and "regulations" excluding imports). There is no indication of a constitutional plan to limit the ability of the States themselves to operate freely in the free market. See L. Tribe, American Constitutional Law 336 (1978) ("the commerce clause was directed, as an historical matter, only at regulatory and taxing actions taken by states in their sovereign capacity"). The precedents comport with this distinction.

Restraint in this area is also counseled by considerations of state sovereignty,[10] the role of each State " 'as guardian and trustee for its people,' " Heim v. McCall, 239 U.S. 175, 191 (1915), quoting Atkin v. Kansas, 191 U.S. 207, 222–223 (1903), and "the long recognized right of trader or manufacturer, engaged in an entirely private business, freely to exercise his own independent discretion as to parties with whom he will deal." United States v. Colgate & Co., 250 U.S. 300, 307 (1919). Moreover, state proprietary activities may be, and often are, burdened with the same restrictions imposed on private market participants. Evenhandedness suggests that, when acting as proprietors, States should similarly share existing freedoms from federal constraints, including the inherent limits of the Commerce Clause.... Finally, as this case illustrates, the competing considerations in cases involving state proprietary action often will be subtle, complex, politically charged, and difficult to assess under traditional Commerce Clause analysis. Given these factors, *Alexandria Scrap* wisely recognizes that, as a rule, the adjustment of interests in this context is a task better suited for Congress than this Court.

III.

South Dakota, as a seller of cement, unquestionably fits the "market participant" label more comfortably than a State acting to subsidize local scrap

---

10. ... Considerations of sovereignty independently dictate that marketplace actions involving "integral operations in areas of traditional governmental functions"—such as the employment of certain state workers—may not be subject even to congressional regulation pursuant to the commerce power. National League of Cities v. Usery, 426 U.S. 833, 852 (1976). It follows easily that the intrinsic limits of the Commerce Clause do not prohibit state marketplace conduct that falls within this sphere. Even where "integral operations" are not implicated, States may fairly claim some measure of a sovereign interest in retaining freedom to decide how, with whom, and for whose benefit to deal. The Supreme Court, 1975 Term, 90 Harv. L.Rev. 56, 63 (1976).

processors. Thus, the general rule of *Alexandria Scrap* plainly applies here. Petitioner argues, however, that the exemption for marketplace participation necessarily admits of exceptions. While conceding that possibility, we perceive in this case no sufficient reason to depart from the general rule.

A.

In finding a Commerce Clause violation, the District Court emphasized "that the Commission ... made an election to become part of the interstate commerce system." The gist of this reasoning, repeated by petitioner here, is that one good turn deserves another. Having long exploited the interstate market, South Dakota should not be permitted to withdraw from it when a shortage arises. This argument is not persuasive. It is somewhat self-serving to say that South Dakota has "exploited" the interstate market. An equally fair characterization is that neighboring States long have benefited from South Dakota's foresight and industry. Viewed in this light, it is not surprising that *Alexandria Scrap* rejected an argument that the 1974 Maryland legislation challenged there was invalid because cars abandoned in Maryland had been processed in neighboring States for five years. As in *Alexandria Scrap,* we must conclude that "this chronology does not distinguish the case, for Commerce Clause purposes, from one in which a State offered [cement] only to domestic [buyers] from the start." 426 U.S., at 809.

Our rejection of petitioner's market-exploitation theory fundamentally refocuses analysis. It means that to reverse we would have to void a South Dakota "residents only" policy even if it had been enforced from the plant's very first days. Such a holding, however, would interfere significantly with a State's ability to structure relations exclusively with its own citizens. It would also threaten the future fashioning of effective and creative programs for solving local problems and distributing government largesse. A healthy regard for federalism and good government renders us reluctant to risk these results. . . .

B.

[P]etitioner advances four more arguments for reversal:

First, petitioner protests that South Dakota's preference for its residents responds solely to the "non-governmental objective[ ]"of protectionism. Therefore, petitioner argues, the policy is *per se* invalid. See Philadelphia v. New Jersey, 437 U.S. 617, 624 (1978).

We find the label "protectionism" of little help in this context. The State's refusal to sell to buyers other than South Dakotans is "protectionist" only in the sense that it limits benefits generated by a state program to those who fund the state treasury and whom the State was created to serve. Petitioner's argument apparently also would characterize as "protectionist" rules restricting to state residents the enjoyment of state educational institutions, energy generated by a state-run plant, police and fire protection, and agricultural improvement and business development programs. Such policies, while perhaps "protectionist" in a loose sense, reflect the essential and patently unobjectionable purpose of state government—to serve the citizens of the State.

Second, petitioner echoes the District Court's warning:

"If a state in this union, were allowed to hoard its commodities or resources for the use of their own residents only, a drastic situation might evolve. For example, Pennsylvania or Wyoming might keep their coal, the northwest its timber, and the mining states their minerals. The result being that embargo may be retaliated by embargo and commerce would be halted at state lines."

See, e.g., Baldwin v. Montana Fish & Game Comm'n, 436 U.S. 371, 385–386 (1978). This argument, although rooted in the core purpose of the Commerce Clause, does not fit the present facts. Cement is not a natural resource, like coal, timber, wild game, or minerals. Cf. Hughes v. Oklahoma, 441 U.S. 322 (1979) (minnows); Philadelphia v. New Jersey, supra (landfill sites); Pennsylvania v. West Virginia, 262 U.S. 553 (1923) (natural gas); West v. Kansas Natural Gas Co., 221 U.S. 229 (1911) (same).... It is the end-product of a complex process whereby a costly physical plant and human labor act on raw materials. South Dakota has not sought to limit access to the State's limestone or other materials used to make cement. Nor has it restricted the ability of private firms or sister States to set up plants within its borders. Moreover, petitioner has not suggested that South Dakota possesses unique access to the materials needed to produce cement. Whatever limits might exist on a State's ability to invoke the *Alexandria Scrap* exemption to hoard resources which by happenstance are found there, those limits do not apply here.

Third, it is suggested that the South Dakota program is infirm because it places South Dakota suppliers of ready-mix concrete at a competitive advantage in the out-of-state market; Wyoming suppliers, such as petitioner, have little chance against South Dakota suppliers who can purchase cement from the State's plant and freely sell beyond South Dakota's borders.

The force of this argument is seriously diminished, if not eliminated, by several considerations. The argument necessarily implies that the South Dakota scheme would be unobjectionable if sales in other States were totally barred. It therefore proves too much, for it would tolerate even a greater measure of protectionism and stifling of interstate commerce than the challenged system allows.... Nor is it to be forgotten that *Alexandria Scrap* approved a state program that "not only ... effectively protect[ed] scrap processors with existing plants in Maryland from the pressures of competitors with nearby out-of-state plants, but [that] implicitly offer[ed] to extend similar protection to any competitor ... willing to erect a scrap processing facility within Maryland's boundaries." 391 F.Supp., at 63. Finally, the competitive plight of out-of-state ready-mix suppliers cannot be laid solely at the feet of South Dakota. It is attributable as well to their own States' not providing or attracting alternative sources of supply and to the suppliers' own failure to guard against shortages by executing long-term supply contracts with the South Dakota plant.

In its last argument, petitioner urges that, had South Dakota not acted, free market forces would have generated an appropriate level of supply at free market prices for all buyers in the region. Having replaced free market forces, South Dakota should be forced to replicate how the free market would have operated under prevailing conditions.

This argument appears to us to be simplistic and speculative. The very reason South Dakota built its plant was because the free market had failed adequately to supply the region with cement. There is no indication, and no way to know, that private industry would have moved into petitioner's market area, and would have ensured a supply of cement to petitioner either prior to or during the 1978 construction season. Indeed, it is quite possible that petitioner would never have existed—far less operated successfully for 20 years—had it not been for South Dakota cement.

C.

We conclude, then, that the arguments for invalidating South Dakota's resident-preference program are weak at best. Whatever residual force inheres in them is more than offset by countervailing considerations of policy and fairness. Reversal would discourage similar state projects, even though this project demonstrably has served the needs of state residents and has helped the entire region for more than a half century. Reversal also would rob South Dakota of the intended benefit of its foresight, risk, and industry. Under these circumstances, there is no reason to depart from the general rule of *Alexandria Scrap.*

The judgment of the United States Court of Appeals is affirmed.

It is so ordered.

Mr. Justice Powell, with whom Mr. Justice Brennan, Mr. Justice White, and Mr. Justice Stevens join, dissenting.

... I cannot agree that South Dakota may withhold its cement from interstate commerce in order to benefit private citizens and businesses within the State.

. . .

I share the Court's desire to preserve state sovereignty. But the Commerce Clause long has been recognized as a limitation on that sovereignty, consciously designed to maintain a national market and defeat economic provincialism. The Court today approves protectionist state policies. In the absence of contrary congressional action, those policies now can be implemented as long as the State itself directly participates in the market.

By enforcing the Commerce Clause in this case, the Court would work no unfairness on the people of South Dakota. They still could reserve cement for public projects and share in whatever return the plant generated. They could not, however, use the power of the State to furnish themselves with cement forbidden to the people of neighboring States.

The creation of a free national economy was a major goal of the States when they resolved to unite under the Federal Constitution. The decision today cannot be reconciled with that purpose.

White v. Massachusetts Council of Construction Employers, Inc.

460 U.S. 204, 103 S.Ct. 1042, 75 L.Ed.2d 1 (1983).

Justice Rehnquist delivered the opinion of the Court.

In 1979 the mayor of Boston, Massachusetts, issued an executive order which required that all construction projects funded in whole or in part by city funds, or funds which the city had the authority to administer, should be performed by a work force consisting of at least half *bona fide* residents of Boston. The Supreme Judicial Court of Massachusetts decided that the order was unconstitutional, observing that the Commerce Clause "presents a clear obstacle to the city's order." 384 Mass. 466, 425 N.E.2d 346 (1981). We granted certiorari to decide whether the Commerce Clause of the United States Constitution, Art. I, § 8, cl. 3, prevents the city from giving effect to the mayor's order.... We now conclude that it does not and reverse.

I

. . .

Alexandria Scrap and *Reeves* . . . stand for the proposition that when a state or local government enters the market as a participant it is not subject to the restraints of the Commerce Clause. As we said in *Reeves,* in this kind of case there is "a single inquiry: whether the challenged 'program constituted direct state participation in the market.' " Id., at 436, n. 7. We reaffirm that principle now.

The Supreme Judicial Court of Massachusetts concluded that the City of Boston is not participating in the market in the sense described in *Alexandria Scrap Corp.* and *Reeves* because the order applies where the city is acting in a nonproprietary capacity, has a significant impact on interstate commerce, is more sweeping than necessary to achieve its objectives, and applies to funds the city receives from federal grants. . . . For the same reasons the court found that the city is not a market participant, it concluded that the executive order violated the substantive restraints of the Commerce Clause. Ibid.

II

. . . The only issues before us . . . are the propriety of applying the mayor's executive order to projects funded wholly with city funds and projects funded in part with federal funds. We address first the application of the order to city funded projects.

The Supreme Judicial Court of Massachusetts expressed reservations as to the application of the "market participation" principle to the city here, reasoning that "the implementation of the mayor's order will have a significant impact on those firms which engage in specialized areas of construction and employ permanent works crews composed of out-of-State residents." . . . Even if this conclusion is factually correct it is not relevant to . . . whether the city is participating in the marketplace when it provides city funds for building construction. If the city is a market participant, then the Commerce Clause establishes no barrier to conditions such as these which the city demands for its participation. Impact on out-of-state residents figures in the equation only after it is decided that the city is regulating the market rather than participating in it, for only in the former case need it be determined whether any burden on interstate commerce is permitted by the Commerce Clause.

. . .

The Supreme Judicial Court of Massachusetts also observed that "a significant percentage of the funds affected by the order are received from Federal sources." . . . The record does indicate that of approximately $54 million expended on projects affected by the mayor's executive order, some $34 million represented projects being funded in part through Urban Development Action Grants (UDAGs). While the record assigns specific dollar amounts only for UDAGs, the parties also have stipulated that the executive order applies to Community Development Block Grants (CDBGs) and Economic Development Administration Grants (EDAGs).

But all of this proves too much. The Commerce Clause is a grant of authority to Congress, and not a restriction on the authority of that body. See American Power & Light Co. v. SEC, 329 U.S. 90 (1946); Gibbons v. Ogden, 9 Wheat. 1 (1824). Congress, unlike a state legislature authorizing similar expenditures, is not limited by any negative implications of the Commerce Clause in the exercise of its spending power. Where state or local government action is specifically authorized by Congress, it is not subject to the Commerce Clause even if it interferes with interstate commerce. Southern Pacific Co. v. Arizona, 325 U.S. 761, 769 (1945). Thus, if the restrictions imposed by the city on construction projects financed in part by federal funds are directed by Congress then no dormant Commerce Clause issue is presented.

An examination of the applicable statutes reveals that these federal programs were intended to encourage economic revitalization, including improved opportunities for the poor, minorities, and unemployed. Examination of the regulations . . . indicates that the mayor's executive order sounds a harmonious note; the federal regulations for each program affirmatively permit the type of parochial favoritism expressed in the order.

III

We hold that on the record before us the application of the mayor's executive order to the contracts in question did not violate the Commerce Clause of the United States Constitution.[12] Insofar as the city expended only its own funds in entering into construction contracts for public projects, it was a market participant and entitled to be treated as such under the rule of *Hughes v. Alexandria Scrap Corp.,* supra. Insofar as the mayor's executive order was applied to projects funded in part with funds obtained from the federal programs described above, the order was affirmatively sanctioned by the pertinent regulations of those programs. The judgment of the Supreme Judicial Court of Massachusetts is therefore reversed, and the case is remanded to that court for proceedings not inconsistent with this opinion.

It is so ordered.

Justice Blackmun, with whom Justice White joins, concurring in part and dissenting in part.

. . .

SOUTH–CENTRAL TIMBER DEVELOPMENT v. WUNNICKE, 467 U.S. 82 (1984). Alaska announced that it would sell a large amount of timber owned by the state. A special provision in all of its contracts of sale required the purchaser partially to process the timber (primarily by slabbing the logs on at least one side) before shipping it outside the state. South–Central Timber, a company that purchased logs and shipped them outside the state without any processing, brought this action alleging, inter alia, that the processing requirement violated the commerce clause. The state argued that its restrictions on export of unprocessed timber from state–owned lands were exempt from the commerce clause under the market participation doctrine.

A plurality of the Court (Justices White, Brennan, Blackmun, and Stevens) held that the market-participation doctrine did not apply here, saying, in part:

"The limit of the market-participant doctrine must be that it allows a State to impose burdens on commerce within the market in which it is a participant, but allows it to go no further. The State may not impose conditions, whether by statute, regulation, or contract, that have a substantial regulatory effect outside

---

12. Respondents ask us to decide whether the executive order offends the Privileges and Immunities Clause of Art. IV, § 2, cl. 1, which provides: "The Citizens of each State shall be entitled to all Privileges and Immunities of Citizens in several States." . . .

This question has not been, to any great extent, briefed or argued in this Court. We did not grant certiorari on the issue and remand without passing on its merits. . . . [On the Privileges and Immunities issue, see United Building and Construction Trades Council v. City of Camden, infra p. 356].

of that particular market.[10] Unless the 'market' is relatively narrowly defined, the doctrine has the potential of swallowing up the rule that States may not impose substantial burdens on interstate commerce even if they act with the permissible state purpose of fostering local industry.

"At the heart of the dispute in this case is disagreement over the definition of the market. Alaska contends that it is participating in the processed timber market, although it acknowledges that it participates in no way in the actual processing. South–Central argues, on the other hand, that although the State may be a participant in the timber market, it is using its leverage in that market to exert a regulatory effect in the processing market, in which it is not a participant. We agree with the latter position.

"There are sound reasons for distinguishing between a State's preferring its own residents in the initial disposition of goods when it is a market participant and a State's attachment of restrictions on dispositions subsequent to the goods coming to rest in private hands. First, simply as a matter of intuition a State market participant has a greater interest as a 'private trader' in the immediate transaction than it has in what its purchaser does with the goods after the State no longer has an interest in them. The common law recognized such a notion in the doctrine of restraints on alienation. . . . Similarly, the antitrust laws place limits on vertical restraints. It is no defense in an action charging vertical trade restraints that the same end could be achieved through vertical integration; if it were, there would be virtually no antitrust scrutiny of vertical arrangements. We reject the contention that a State's action as a market regulator may be upheld against Commerce Clause challenge on the ground that the State could achieve the same end as a market participant. We therefore find it unimportant for present purposes that the State could support its processing industry by selling only to Alaska processors, by vertical integration, or by direct subsidy.

"Second, downstream restrictions have a greater regulatory effect than do limitations on the immediate transaction. Instead of merely choosing its own trading partners, the State is attempting to govern the private, separate economic relationships of its trading partners; that is, it restricts the post-purchase activity of the purchaser, rather than merely the purchasing activity. In contrast to the situation in *White,* this restriction on private economic activity takes place after the completion of the parties' direct commercial obligations, rather than during the course of an ongoing commercial relationship in which the city retained a continuing proprietary interest in the subject of the contract. In sum, the State may not avail itself of the market-participant doctrine to immunize its downstream regulation of the timber-processing market in which it is not a participant."

Three justices did not reach this issue. Justice Rehnquist joined by Justice O'Connor dissented, saying:

"The contractual term at issue here no more transforms Alaska's sale of timber into 'regulation' of the processing industry than the resident-hiring

---

10. The view of the market-participant doctrine expressed by Justice Rehnquist would validate under the Commerce Clause any contractual condition that the State had the economic power to impose, without regard to the relationship of the subject matter of the contract and the condition imposed. If that were the law, it would have been irrelevant that the employees in White v. Massa-chusetts Council of Construction Employers, Inc., 460 U.S. 204 (1983), were in effect "working for the city." If the only question were whether the condition is imposed by contract, a residency requirement could have been imposed with respect to the work force on all projects of any employer doing business with the city.

preference imposed by the city of Boston in White v. Massachusetts Council of Const. Employers, 460 U.S. 204 (1983), constituted regulation of the construction industry. Alaska is merely paying the buyer of the timber indirectly, by means of a reduced price, to hire Alaska residents to process the timber. Under existing precedent, the State could accomplish that same result in any number of ways. For example, the State could choose to sell its timber only to those companies that maintain active primary-processing plants in Alaska. Reeves, Inc. v. Stake, 447 U.S. 429 (1980). Or the State could directly subsidize the primary-processing industry within the State. Hughes v. Alexandria Scrap Corp., 426 U.S. 794 (1976). The State could even pay to have the logs processed and then enter the market only to sell processed logs. It seems to me unduly formalistic to conclude that the one path chosen by the State as best suited to promote its concerns is the path forbidden it by the Commerce Clause."

NEW ENERGY CO. OF INDIANA v. LIMBACH, 486 U.S. 269 (1988). An Ohio taxing statute awarded a tax credit against the Ohio motor vehicle fuel sales tax for each gallon of ethanol sold (as a component of gasohol) by fuel dealers, but only if the ethanol was produced in Ohio or in a state that granted similar tax advantages to ethanol produced in Ohio. New energy produced ethanol in Indiana, a state which gave a direct subsidy to local ethanol producers but no tax exemption. New energy challenged the constitutionality of Ohio imposing a tax on the ethanol it sold in Ohio on grounds that the Ohio tax scheme discriminated against interstate commerce, a contention upheld by the Court. Ohio contended that in any event its tax scheme was valid under the market participant doctrine. the court responded as follows:

"Appellees contend that even if § 5735.145(B) is discriminatory, the discrimination is not covered by the Commerce Clause because of the so-called market participant doctrine. That doctrine differentiates between a State's acting in its distinctive governmental capacity, and a State's acting in the more general capacity of a market participant; only the former is subject to the limitations of the negative Commerce Clause. See Hughes v. Alexandria Scrap Corp., 426 U.S. 794, 806–810 (1976). Thus, for example, when a State chooses to manufacture and sell cement, its business methods, including those that favor its residents, are of no greater constitutional concern than those of a private business. See Reeves, Inc. v. Stake, 447 U.S. 429, 438–439 (1980).

"The market participant doctrine has no application here. The Ohio action ultimately at issue is neither its purchase nor its sale of ethanol, but its assessment and computation of taxes—a primeval governmental activity. To be sure, the tax credit scheme has the purpose and effect of subsidizing a particular industry, as do many dispositions of the tax laws. That does not transform it into a form of state participation in the free market. Our opinion in *Alexandria Scrap,* supra, a case on which appellees place great reliance, does not remotely establish such a proposition. There we examined, and upheld against Commerce Clause attack on the basis of the market-participant doctrine, a Maryland cash subsidy program that discriminated in favor of in-state auto-hulk processors. The purpose of the program was to achieve the removal of unsightly abandoned autos from the State, 426 U.S., at 796–797, and the Court characterized it as proprietary rather than regulatory activity, based on the analogy of the State to a private purchaser of the auto hulks, id., at 808–810. We have subsequently observed that subsidy programs unlike that of *Alexandria Scrap* might not be characterized as proprietary. See *Reeves, Inc.,* supra, at 440, n. 14. We think it clear that Ohio's assessment and computation of its fuel sales tax, regardless of whether it produces a subsidy, cannot plausibly be analogized to the activity of a private purchaser."

CAMPS NEWFOUND/OWATONNA, INC. v. TOWN OF HARRISON, 520 U.S. 564 (1997). The Supreme Court found impermissibly discriminatory against interstate commerce a state statutory provision that withheld a property tax exemption generally available to charitable institutions from those charitable organizations "in fact conducted or operated principally for the benefit of persons who are not residents of Maine." The Court found "unpersuasive" the claim that the exemption scheme constituted "a governmental 'purchase' of charitable services falling within the narrow exception to the dormant commerce clause for states in their role as 'market participants,' see, E.G., Hughes v. Alexandria Scrap Corp., 426 U.S. 794 (1976); Reeves, Inc. v. Stake, 447 U.S. 429 (1980)." It said:

"... A tax exemption is not the sort of direct state involvement in the market that falls within the market-participation doctrine.

"Even if we were prepared to expand the exception ..., the Maine tax statute at issue here would be a poor candidate.... [T]he exemption ... denied to petitioner is available to a broad category of charitable and benevolent institutions. For that reason, nothing short of a dramatic expansion of the 'market participant' exception would support its application to this case. *Alexandria Scrap* involved Maryland's entry into the market for automobile hulks, a discrete activity focused on a single industry. Similarly, South Dakota's participation in the market for cement was—in part because of its narrow scope—readily conceived as a proprietary action of the State. In contrast, Maine's tax exemption—which sweeps to cover broad swathes of the nonprofit sector—must be viewed as action taken in the State's sovereign capacity rather than a proprietary decision to make an entry into all of the markets in which the exempted charities function.... The Town's version of the 'market participant' exception would swallow the rule against discriminatory tax schemes. [T]he notion that whenever a State provides a discriminatory tax abatement it is 'purchasing' some service in its proprietary capacity is not readily confined to the charitable context. A special tax concession for liquors indigenous to Hawaii, for example, might be conceived as a 'purchase' of the jobs produced by local industry, or an investment in the unique local cultural value provided by these beverages. Cf. Bacchus, 468 U.S., at 270–271. Discriminatory schemes favoring local farmers might be seen as the 'purchase' of agricultural services in order to ensure that the State's citizens will have a steady local supply of the product...."

E.   LIMITS ON BUSINESS ENTRY

Lewis v. BT Investment Managers, Inc.

447 U.S. 27, 100 S.Ct. 2009, 64 L.Ed.2d 702 (1980).

Mr. Justice Blackmun delivered the opinion of the Court.

. . .

I.

Appellee Bankers Trust New York Corporation (Bankers Trust) is a corporation organized under the laws of the State of New York. It maintains its principal place of business in that State. It is a bank holding company within the meaning of § 2(a) of the Bank Holding Company Act of 1956, 70 Stat. 133, as amended, 12 U.S.C. § 1841(a) (1976 ed. and Supp. II) (the Act). Accordingly, it is subject to federal restrictions on the kinds of subsidiaries it may own or control. . . .

In 1972, the management of Bankers Trust decided to seek the Board [of Governors of the Federal Reserve System's] approval for an investment management subsidiary to operate in Florida. On October 3 of that year, Bankers Trust filed a formal proposal for such a subsidiary, which it planned to operate from offices in Palm Beach. Appellee BT Investment Managers, Inc. (BTIM), was Bankers Trust's intended vehicle for entry into the Florida market. It was incorporated under the laws of the State of Delaware as a wholly owned subsidiary on November 24, 1972. Three days later it qualified to do business in Florida. The application to the Board proposed that BTIM would provide "portfolio investment advice," as well as "general economic information and advice, general economic statistical forecasting services and industry studies" to persons other than banks. . . .

When Bankers Trust filed its application with the Board, certain Florida statutes restricted the ability of out-of-state bank holding companies to compete in the State's financial market. At that time Fla.Stat. § 659.141(1), added by 1972 Fla.Laws, ch. 72–96, § 1, and effective March 28, 1972, prohibited Bankers Trust from owning or controlling a bank or trust company located within the State; the same statute also prohibited it from owning businesses furnishing investment advisory services to local banks or trust companies. In addition, Fla.Stat. § 660.10 prohibited any corporation, other than a state-chartered bank and trust company or a national banking association located in Florida, from performing certain trust and fiduciary functions. Neither statute, however, directly prohibited an out-of-state bank holding company from owning or controlling a business furnishing investment advisory services to the general public. Thus, at the time Bankers Trust filed its application with the Board, it appeared that ownership of BTIM would not violate Florida law, although BTIM would be restricted in the types of financial services it could perform and the customers it could serve.

The reaction of the Florida financial community to Bankers Trust's proposed investment subsidiary was decidedly negative. The State Comptroller, the Florida Bankers Association, and the Palm Beach County Bankers Association, Inc., all filed comments with the Board objecting to the Bankers Trust proposal. More importantly for present purposes, the state legislature was persuaded to take action. On November 30, 1972, shortly after BTIM had qualified to do business in the State, a special session of the legislature amended Fla.Stat. § 659.141(1). That statute, which had been on the books only since March 28 of that year, was expanded to prohibit an out-of-state bank holding company from owning or controlling a business within the State that sells investment advisory services to any customer, rather than just to "trust companies or banks" in Florida, as the statute theretofore had read. This amendment took effect, without the Governor's approval, on December 21, 1972. There is evidence that the amendment was a direct response to Bankers Trust's pending application, and that it had the strong backing of the local financial community.

On April 26, 1973, the Board rejected Bankers Trust's proposal on the ground that it would conflict with state law. 59 Fed.Res.Bull. 364. The Board observed that the proposal contemplated *de novo* entry into the Florida investment management market rather than acquisition of an existing concern, and it noted that *de novo* entry ordinarily has a desirable procompetitive impact. Absent evidence of a contrary effect in this case, the Board intimated that it would have been favorably inclined toward the proposal. But it found that the December amendment to Fla.Stat. § 659.141(1) "was intended to, and does, prohibit the performance of investment advisory services in Florida by non-Florida bank holding companies." 59 Fed.Res.Bull. 365. In view of its obligation to respect the dictates of state law, the Board found itself constrained to reject the proposal. . . .

Within six months of the Board's decision, the two appellees [sued] seeking declaratory and injunctive relief. Count I of their complaint alleged that Fla.Stat. § 659.141(1) "is not designed to promote lawful regulatory objectives, but is intended to shelter those organizations presently conducting an investment advisory business in Florida from competition by [BTIM]." The complaint alleged violations of the due process and equal protection guarantees of the Fourteenth Amendment, as well as violation of the Commerce Clause. Count II alleged similar constitutional defects as the result of the joint operation of §§ 659.141(1), and 660.10. Appellees alleged that "[b]ut for the existence of the challenged statutes," Bankers Trust would seek authority from the Board to establish "a subsidiary trust company having a national bank charter or a Florida state charter" that would engage exclusively in one or more of the functions regulated by § 660.10. . . .

[T]he [three-judge] District Court held [on summary judgment] that the challenged portions of the two statutes violate the Commerce Clause. . . .

. . . .

III.

[W]e first turn to § 659.141(1). . . . The statute prohibits ownership of local investment or trust businesses by firms possessing two characteristics: a certain kind of business organization and purpose, whether it be as a bank, trust company, or a bank holding company; and location of principal operations outside Florida.

Appellant and the *amici* supporting his position argue that the District Court's analysis of § 659.141(1) is flawed in three respects: First, the statute assertedly affects only matters of local character that have insufficient interstate attributes to bring federal constitutional limitations into play. Second, the District Court erroneously labeled the statute protectionist legislation and thus incorrectly relied upon the *"per se* rule of invalidity" identified in Philadelphia v. New Jersey, 437 U.S., at 624. Appellant argues that the statute should be treated as neutral legislation subject to the less stringent standards of Pike v. Bruce Church, Inc., supra, and he argues that it meets this test. Third, the District Court failed to accord proper significance, in appellant's view, to the Bank Holding Company Act of 1956. Appellant argues that the Act grants authority to the States to prohibit out-of-state bank holding companies from owning local subsidiaries that provide bank-related services.

A.

The first of these arguments needs only brief mention. We readily accept the submission that, both as a matter of history and as a matter of present commercial reality, banking and related financial activities are of profound local concern. . . . Thus, it is not surprising that ever since the early days of our Republic, the States have chartered banks and have actively regulated their activities.

Nonetheless, it does not follow that these same activities lack important interstate attributes. . . .

B.

The contentions that the District Court erred by applying too stringent a standard in defining the limits of Florida's regulatory authority, and that § 659.141(1) is evenhanded local regulation, are more substantial. We nonetheless agree with the District Court's conclusion that this statute is "parochial" in the sense that it overtly prevents foreign enterprises from competing in local markets.

The statute makes the out-of-state location of a bank holding company's principal operations an explicit barrier to the presence of an investment subsidiary within the State. As Bankers Trust's application before the Board itself indicates, it thus prevents competition in local markets by out-of-state firms with the kinds of resources and business interests that make them likely to attempt *de novo* entry. Appellant virtually concedes this effect, and the circumstances of enactment suggest that it was the legislature's principal objective.

Appellant argues, however, that the statute ought not to be declared *per se* invalid because it does not prevent all out-of-state investment enterprises from entering local markets. Investment enterprises that are *not* bank holding companies, banks, or trust companies either may own investment subsidiaries in Florida or may enter the state investment market directly by obtaining a license to do business. Furthermore, locally incorporated bank holding companies are subject to the same restrictions as their foreign counterparts if they maintain their principal operations elsewhere. Appellant thus analogizes § 659.141(1) to the Maryland statute prohibiting local retail operations by vertically integrated petroleum companies that the Court upheld in Exxon Corp. v. Governor of Maryland, 437 U.S. 117 (1978). The statute, it is said, discriminates against a particular kind of corporate organizational structure more than it does against the origin or citizenship of a particular business enterprise.

The statute involved in *Exxon* flatly prohibited producers and refiners of petroleum products from opening or operating retail services within Maryland under a variety of corporate or contractual arrangements. It was enacted in response to perceived inequities in the allocation of petroleum products to retail outlets during the fuel shortage of 1973. Various oil companies, all of which engaged in production and refining as well as in sale of petroleum products, ... claimed that the statute violated the Commerce Clause because it discriminated against producers and refiners, all of which were interstate concerns, in favor of independent retailers, most of which were local businesses.

The Court rejected this contention. After holding that the statute served the legitimate state purpose of "controlling the gasoline retail market," the Court separately analyzed its effect on interstate commerce in the producing-refining and retailing ends of the petroleum industry. The Court concluded that the statute could not discriminate against interstate petroleum producers and refiners in favor of locally based competitors because, as a matter of fact, there were no such local producers or refiners to be favored. For the same reason, it concluded that the flow of petroleum products in interstate commerce would not be reduced. It also rejected a claim of discrimination at the retail level because the statute placed "no barriers whatsoever" on competition in local markets by "interstate independent dealers" that did not own production or refining facilities. Despite the fact that the number of stations operated by independent dealers was small relative to the number operated by producer-refiners, the Court concluded that neither the placing of a disparate burden on some interstate competitors nor the shifting of business from one part of the interstate market to another was enough, under the circumstances, to establish a Commerce Clause violation.

There are some points of similarity between *Exxon* and the present case. In the former, the statute in issue discriminated against vertical organization in the petroleum industry. Section 659.141(1) similarly discriminates against a particular kind of conglomerate organization in the investment and financial industries. And the Maryland statute permitted some kinds of interstate competitors free entry into the local market, as does the Florida statute at issue here.

We disagree, however, with the suggestion that *Exxon* should be treated as controlling precedent for this case. Section 659.141(1) engages in an additional form of discrimination that is highly significant for purposes of Commerce Clause analysis. Under the Florida statute, discrimination against affected business organizations is *not* evenhanded because only banks, bank holding companies, and trust companies with principal operations *outside* Florida are prohibited from operating investment subsidiaries or giving investment advice within the State. It follows that § 659.141(1) discriminates *among* affected business entities according to the extent of their contacts with the local economy. The absence of a similar discrimination between interstate and local producer-refiners was a most critical factor in *Exxon*. Both on its face and in actual effect, § 659.141(1) thus displays a local favoritism or protectionism that significantly alters its Commerce Clause status. See Philadelphia v. New Jersey, 437 U.S., at 626–627; Baldwin v. G.A.F. Seelig, Inc., 294 U.S., at 527.

We need not decide whether this difference is sufficient to render the Florida legislation *per se* invalid, for we are convinced that the disparate treatment of out-of-state bank holding companies cannot be justified as an incidental burden necessitated by legitimate local concerns. In the District Court and to some extent on this appeal, appellant and supporting *amici* have argued that the Florida legislation advances several important state policies. Among those that have been specifically identified are an interest in discouraging undue economic concentration in the arena of high finance; an interest in regulating financial practices, presumably to protect local residents from fraud; and an interest in maximizing local control over locally based financial activities. We think that these alleged purposes fail to justify the extent of the burden placed upon out-of-state bank holding companies.

Discouraging economic concentration and protecting the citizenry against fraud are undoubtedly legitimate state interests. But we are not persuaded that these interests justify the heavily disproportionate burden this statute places on bank holding companies that operate principally outside the State. Appellant has demonstrated no basis for an inference that all out-of-state bank holding companies are likely to possess the evils of monopoly power, that they are more likely to do so than their home-grown counterparts, or that they are any more inclined to engage in sharp practices than bank holding companies that are locally based. Nor is there any reason to conclude that outright prohibition of entry, rather than some intermediate form of regulation, is the only effective method of protecting against the presumed evils, particularly when other out-of-state businesses that may be just as large or far-flung are permitted to compete in the local market. We conclude that these asserted state interests simply do not suffice to eliminate § 659.141(1)'s apparent constitutional defect. . . .

With regard to the asserted interest in promoting local control over financial institutions, we doubt that the interest itself is entirely clear of any tinge of local parochialism. In almost any Commerce Clause case it would be possible for a State to argue that it has an interest in bolstering local ownership, or wealth, or control of business enterprise. Yet these arguments are at odds with the general principle that the Commerce Clause prohibits a State from using its regulatory power to protect its own citizens from outside competition. See H.P. Hood & Sons, Inc. v. Du Mond, 336 U.S., at 538; Buck v. Kuykendall, 267 U.S. 307, 315–316 (1925); cf. Toomer v. Witsell, 334 U.S. 385, 403–404 (1948). In any event, the interest is not well-served by the present legislation. The statute, for example, does not restrict out-of-state ownership of local bank holding companies. Nor, as appellant concedes does it prevent entry by out-of-state entities other than those having the prohibited organizational forms. There is thus no reason to believe that the State's interest in local control, to the extent it legitimately exists, has been significantly or evenhandedly advanced by the statutory means that have been employed.

For these reasons, we conclude that the District Court did not err in holding that § 659.141(1) directly burdens interstate commerce in a manner that contravenes the Commerce Clause's implicit limitation on state power.

. . .

V.

In summary, we affirm the judgment of the District Court insofar as it declares unconstitutional the challenged portions of § 659.141(1) and enjoins their enforcement. . . .

It is so ordered.

EDGAR v. MITE CORP., 457 U.S. 624 (1982). The Illinois Business Takeover Act requires takeover offers for acquisition of shares in Illinois–affiliated target companies[1] to be registered with the Illinois Secretary of State twenty days before the offer becomes effective. during the twenty–day period, the offeror may not communicate with shareholders, but the target company is free to disseminate information to its shareholders. The Secretary can refuse registration, after hearing, if the offer is not accompanied by full and fair disclosure, or the offer is inequitable or fraudulent. the court held that the Illinois statute imposed an unconstitutional burden on interstate commerce.

Justice White's opinion offered two distinct rationales, only one of which commanded the votes of five Justices.[2] Those five joined Part V.B. of the opinion, which rested squarely on the "balancing approach" articulated in Pike v. Bruce Church (p. 310, supra). On this point, Justice White's opinion said in part:

1. The Act applies where Illinois residents own 10% of the securities subject to the offer. It also applies where two of three conditions are met: (1) the target company's principal executive office is in Illinois; (2) the target company is organized under Illinois law; (3) 10% of the target company's stated capital and surplus is represented within Illinois.

2. Part V.A. of Justice White's opinion concluded that the Illinois statute placed an impermissible burden on interstate commerce because of its extraterritorial effect, regulating transactions across state lines with out-of-state shareholders. Justice Powell, one of the five Justices to join part V.B. of the opinion, did not join part V.A., which thus received the votes of only four Justices. Justice Powell explained that he joined part V.B. (and not V.A.) because its rationale "leaves some room for state regulation of tender offers." Justice White's opinion also took the position that the Illinois Act was preempted by the Williams Act, a 1968 amendment to the Federal Securities and Exchange Act. Only Chief Justice Burger and Justice Blackmun concurred in this portion of the opinion. Justice Blackmun took no position on the commerce clause issue. Justices Brennan, Marshall and Rehnquist argued that the case was moot and did not express a position on the merits of either the commerce clause or preemption issues.

"The effects of allowing the Illinois Secretary of State to block a nation-wide tender offer are substantial. Shareholders are deprived of the opportunity to sell their shares at a premium. The reallocation of economic resources to their highest-valued use, a process which can improve efficiency and competition, is hindered. The incentive the tender offer mechanism provides incumbent management to perform well so that stock prices remain high is reduced.

"Appellant claims the Illinois Act ... seeks to protect resident security holders.... We agree with the Court of Appeals that [this interest is] insufficient to outweigh the burdens Illinois imposes on interstate commerce.

"While protecting local investors is plainly a legitimate state objective, the state has no legitimate interest in protecting non-resident shareholders. Insofar as the Illinois law burdens out-of-state transactions, there is nothing to be weighed in the balance to sustain the law. We note, furthermore, that the Act completely exempts from coverage a corporation's acquisition of its own shares.... Thus Chicago Rivet was able to make a competing tender offer for its own stock without complying with the Illinois Act, leaving Chicago Rivet's shareholders to depend only on the protections afforded them by federal securities law, protections which Illinois views as inadequate to protect investors in other contexts. This distinction is at variance with Illinois' asserted legislative purpose, and tends to undermine appellant's justification for the burdens the statute imposes on interstate commerce.

"We are also unconvinced that the Illinois Act substantially enhances the shareholders' position. The Illinois Act seeks to protect shareholders of a company subject to a tender offer by requiring disclosures regarding the offer, assuring that shareholders have adequate time to decide whether to tender their shares, and according shareholders withdrawal, proration and equal consideration rights.... As the Court of Appeals noted, the disclosures required by the Illinois Act which go beyond those mandated by the Williams Act and the regulations pursuant to it may not substantially enhance the shareholders' ability to make informed decisions. It also was of the view that the possible benefits of the potential delays required by the Act may be outweighed by the increased risk that the tender offer will fail due to defensive tactics employed by incumbent management. We are unprepared to disagree with the Court of Appeals in these respects, and conclude that the protections the Illinois Act affords resident security holders are, for the most part, speculative."

CTS Corp. v. Dynamics Corp. of America

481 U.S. 69, 107 S.Ct. 1637, 95 L.Ed.2d 67 (1987).

Justice Powell delivered the opinion of the Court.

This case presents the questions whether the Control Share Acquisitions Chapter of the Indiana Business Corporation Law, Ind.Code § 23–1–42–1 et seq. (Supp.1986), is preempted by the Williams Act, 82 Stat. 454, as amended, 15 U.S.C. §§ 78m(d)–(e) and 78n(d)–(f) (1982 ed. and Supp. III), or violates the Commerce Clause of the Federal Constitution, Art. I, § 8, cl. 3.

I

[The Control Share Acquisitions Chapter applies only to an Indiana "issuing public corporation,"] defined as:

"a corporation that has:

"(1) one hundred (100) or more shareholders;

"(2) its principal place of business, its principal office, or substantial assets within Indiana; and

"(3) either:

"(A) more than ten percent (10%) of its shareholders resident in Indiana;

"(B) more than ten percent (10%) of its shares owned by Indiana residents; or

"(C) ten thousand (10,000) shareholders resident in Indiana." § 23–1–42–4(a).

The Act focuses on the acquisition of "control shares" in an issuing public corporation. Under the Act, an entity acquires "control shares" whenever it acquires shares that, but for the operation of the Act, would bring its voting power in the corporation to or above any of three thresholds: 20%, 33 ⅓%, or 50%. § 23–1–42–1. An entity that acquires control shares does not necessarily acquire voting rights. Rather, it gains those rights only "to the extent granted by resolution approved by the shareholders of the issuing public corporation." § 23–1–42–9(a). Section 9 requires a majority vote of all disinterested shareholders holding each class of stock for passage of such a resolution. § 23–1–42–9(b). The practical effect of this requirement is to condition acquisition of control of a corporation on approval of a majority of the pre-existing disinterested shareholders.

. . .

[Dynamics, after announcing a tender offer for a million shares in CTS, an Indiana Corporation, sought declaratory and injunctive relief in federal court against CTS's use of the Act. The District Court first held that the Williams Act pre-empted the Indiana Act and later held that it violated the Commerce Clause. The Seventh Circuit affirmed, but the Supreme Court reversed.]

II

. . .

[T]hat the Indiana Act will delay some tender offers is insufficient to require a conclusion that the Williams Act pre-empts the Act. The longstanding prevalence of state regulation in this area suggests that, if Congress had intended to pre-empt all state laws that delay the acquisition of voting control following a tender offer, it would have said so explicitly. The regulatory conditions that the Act places on tender offers are consistent with the text and the purposes of the Williams Act. Accordingly, we hold that the Williams Act does not pre-empt the Indiana Act.

III

As an alternative basis for its decision, the Court of Appeals held that the Act violates the Commerce Clause of the Federal Constitution. . . .

A

The principal objects of dormant Commerce Clause scrutiny are statutes that discriminate against interstate commerce. See, e.g., Lewis v. BT Investment Managers, Inc., 447 U.S. 27, 36–37 (1980); Philadelphia v. New Jersey, 437 U.S. 617, 624 (1978). See generally Regan, The Supreme Court and State Protectionism: Making Sense of the Dormant Commerce Clause, 84 Mich.

L.Rev. 1091 (1986). The Indiana Act is not such a statute. It has the same effects on tender offers whether or not the offeror is a domiciliary or resident of Indiana. Thus, it "visits its effects equally upon both interstate and local business," Lewis v. BT Investment Managers, Inc., supra, at 36.

Dynamics nevertheless contends that the statute is discriminatory because it will apply most often to out-of-state entities. This argument rests on the contention that, as a practical matter, most hostile tender offers are launched by offerors outside Indiana. But this argument avails Dynamics little. "The fact that the burden of a state regulation falls on some interstate companies does not, by itself, establish a claim of discrimination against interstate commerce." Exxon Corp. v. Governor of Maryland, 437 U.S. 117, 126 (1978). See Minnesota v. Clover Leaf Creamery Co., 449 U.S. 456, 471–472 (1981) (rejecting a claim of discrimination because the challenged statute "regulate[d] evenhandedly ... without regard to whether the [commerce came] from outside the State"); Commonwealth Edison Co. v. Montana, 453 U.S. 609, 619 (1981) (rejecting a claim of discrimination because the "tax burden [was] borne according to the amount ... consumed and not according to any distinction between in-state and out-of-state consumers"). Because nothing in the Indiana Act imposes a greater burden on out-of-state offerors than it does on similarly situated Indiana offerors, we reject the contention that the Act discriminates against interstate commerce.

B

This Court's recent Commerce Clause cases also have invalidated statutes that adversely may affect interstate commerce by subjecting activities to inconsistent regulations. E.g., Brown–Forman Distillers Corp. v. New York State Liquor Authority, 476 U.S. 573, 583 (1986); Edgar v. MITE Corp., 457 U.S., at 642 (plurality opinion of White, J.); Kassel v. Consolidated Freightways Corp., 450 U.S. 662, 671 (1981) (plurality opinion of Powell, J.). See Southern Pacific Co. v. Arizona, 325 U.S. 761, 774 (1945) (noting the "confusion and difficulty" that would attend the "unsatisfied need for uniformity" in setting maximum limits on train lengths); Cooley v. Board of Wardens, supra, at * 319 (stating that the Commerce Clause prohibits States from regulating subjects that "are in their nature national, or admit only of one uniform system, or plan of regulation"). The Indiana Act poses no such problem. So long as each State regulates voting rights only in the corporations it has created, each corporation will be subject to the law of only one State. No principle of corporation law and practice is more firmly established than a State's authority to regulate domestic corporations, including the authority to define the voting rights of shareholders. See Restatement (Second) of Conflict of Laws § 304 (1971) (concluding that the law of the incorporating State generally should "determine the right of a shareholder to participate in the administration of the affairs of the corporation"). Accordingly, we conclude that the Indiana Act does not create an impermissible risk of inconsistent regulation by different States.

C

The Court of Appeals did not find the Act unconstitutional for either of these threshold reasons. Rather, its decision rested on its view of the Act's potential to hinder tender offers. We think the Court of Appeals failed to appreciate the significance for Commerce Clause analysis of the fact that state regulation of corporate governance is regulation of entities whose very existence and attributes are a product of state law.... Every State in this country has enacted laws regulating corporate governance. By prohibiting certain transactions, and regulating others, such laws necessarily affect certain aspects of interstate commerce. This necessarily is true with respect to corporations with shareholders in States other than the State of incorporation. Large corporations that are listed on national exchanges, or even regional exchanges, will have shareholders in many States and shares that are traded frequently. The markets that facilitate this national and international participation in ownership of corporations are essential for providing capital not only for new enterprises but also for established companies that need to expand their businesses. This beneficial free market system depends at its core upon the fact that a corporation—except in the rarest situations—is organized under, and governed by, the law of a single jurisdiction, traditionally the corporate law of the State of its incorporation.

These regulatory laws may affect directly a variety of corporate transactions. Mergers are a typical example. In view of the substantial effect that a merger may have on the shareholder's interests in a corporation, many States require supermajority votes to approve mergers.... By requiring a greater vote for mergers than is required for other transactions, these laws make it more difficult for corporations to merge. State laws also may provide for "dissenters' rights" under which minority shareholders who disagree with corporate decisions to take particular actions are entitled to sell their shares to the corporation at fair market value.... By requiring the corporation to purchase the shares of dissenting shareholders, these laws may inhibit a corporation from engaging in the specified transactions.

It thus is an accepted part of the business landscape in this country for States to create corporations, to prescribe their powers, and to define the rights that are acquired by purchasing their shares. A State has an interest in promoting stable relationships among parties involved in the corporations it charters, as well as in ensuring that investors in such corporations have an effective voice in corporate affairs.

[T]he Act reflects these concerns. The primary purpose of the Act is to protect the shareholders of Indiana corporations. It does this by affording shareholders, when a takeover offer is made, an opportunity to decide collectively whether the resulting change in voting control of the corporation, as they perceive it, would be desirable. A change of management may have important effects on the shareholders' interests; it is well within the State's role as overseer of corporate governance to offer this opportunity. The autonomy provided by allowing shareholders collectively to determine whether the takeover is advantageous to their interests may be especially beneficial where a hostile tender offer may coerce shareholders into tendering their shares.

Appellee Dynamics responds to this concern by arguing that the prospect of coercive tender offers is illusory, and that tender offers generally should be favored because they reallocate corporate assets into the hands of management who can use them most effectively.... As indicated, Indiana's concern with tender offers is not groundless. Indeed, the potentially coercive aspects of tender offers have been recognized by the Securities and Exchange Commission, see SEC Release No. 21079, p. 86,916, and by a number of scholarly commentators.... The Constitution does not require the States to subscribe to any particular economic theory. We are not inclined "to second-guess the empirical judgments of lawmakers concerning the utility of legislation," Kassel v. Consolidated Freightways Corp., 450 U.S., at 679 (Brennan, J., concurring in judgment). In our view, the possibility of coercion in some takeover bids offers additional justification for Indiana's decision to promote the autonomy of independent shareholders.

Dynamics argues in any event that the State has "no legitimate interest in protecting the nonresident shareholders." ... Dynamics relies heavily on the statement by the *MITE* Court that "[i]nsofar as the ... law burdens out-of-state transactions, there is nothing to be weighed in the balance to sustain the law." 457 U.S., at 644. But that comment was made in reference to an Illinois law that applied as well to out-of-state corporations as to in-state corporations. We agree that Indiana has no interest in protecting nonresident shareholders *of nonresident corporations.* But this Act applies only to corporations incorporated in Indiana. We reject the contention that Indiana has no interest in providing for the shareholders of its corporations the voting autonomy granted by the Act. Indiana has a substantial interest in preventing the corporate form from becoming a shield for unfair business dealing. Moreover, unlike the Illinois statute invalidated in *MITE,* the Indiana Act applies only to corporations that have a substantial number of shareholders in Indiana.... Thus, every application of the Indiana Act will affect a substantial number of Indiana residents, whom Indiana indisputably has an interest in protecting.

"...

IV

On its face, the Indiana Control Share Acquisitions Chapter even-handedly determines the voting rights of shares of Indiana corporations. The Act does not conflict with the provisions or purposes of the Williams Act. To the limited extent that the Act affects interstate commerce, this is justified by the State's interest in defining the attributes of shares in its corporations and in protecting shareholders. Congress has never questioned the need for state regulation of these matters. Nor do we think such regulation offends the Constitution. Accordingly, we reverse the judgment of the Court of Appeals.

It is so ordered.

Justice Scalia, concurring in part and concurring in the judgment.

I join Parts I, III–A, and III–B of the Court's opinion. However, having found, as those Parts do, that the Indiana Control Share Acquisitions Chapter neither "discriminates against interstate commerce," nor "create[s] an impermissible risk of inconsistent regulation by different States," I would conclude without further analysis that it is not invalid under the dormant Commerce Clause. While it has become standard practice at least since Pike v. Bruce Church, Inc., 397 U.S. 137 (1970), to consider, in addition to these factors, whether the burden on commerce imposed by a state statute "is clearly excessive in relation to the putative local benefits," id., at 142, such an inquiry is ill suited to the judicial function and should be undertaken rarely if at all.... Whether the control shares statute "protects shareholders of Indiana corporations," or protects incumbent management seems to me a highly debatable question, but it is extraordinary to think that the constitutionality of the Act should depend on the answer. Nothing in the Constitution says that the protection of entrenched management is any less important a "putative local benefit" than the protection of entrenched shareholders, and I do not know what qualifies us to make that judgment—or the related judgment as to how effective the present statute is in achieving one or the other objective—or the ultimate (and most ineffable) judgment as to whether, given importance-level x, and effectiveness-level y, the worth of the statute is "outweighed" by impact-on-commerce z.

One commentator has suggested that, at least much of the time, we do not in fact mean what we say when we declare that statutes which neither discriminate against commerce nor present a threat of multiple and inconsistent burdens might nonetheless be unconstitutional under a "balancing" test. See Regan, The Supreme Court and State Protectionism: Making Sense of the Dormant Commerce Clause, 84 Mich.L.Rev. 1091 (1986). If he is not correct, he ought to be. . . .

I also agree . . . that the Indiana Control Shares Act is not pre-empted by the Williams Act. . . .

. . .

Justice White, with whom Justice Blackmun and Justice Stevens join as to Part II, dissenting.

The majority today upholds . . . a statute which will predictably foreclose completely some tender offers for stock in Indiana corporations. I disagree . . . that the Chapter is neither pre-empted by the Williams Act nor in conflict with the Commerce Clause. The Chapter undermines the policy of the Williams Act by effectively preventing minority shareholders, in some circumstances, from acting in their own best interests by selling their stock. In addition, the Chapter will substantially burden the interstate market in corporate ownership, particularly if other States follow Indiana's lead as many already have done. The Chapter, therefore, directly inhibits interstate commerce, the very economic consequences the Commerce Clause was intended to prevent. . . .

. . .

The State of Indiana . . . admits that at least one of the Chapter's goals is to protect Indiana Corporations. . . . A state law which permits a majority of an Indiana corporation's stockholders to prevent individual investors, including out-of-state stockholders, from selling their stock to an out-of-state tender offeror and thereby frustrate any transfer of corporate control, is the archetype of the kind of state law that the Commerce Clause forbids.

Unlike state blue sky laws, Indiana's Control Share Acquisitions Chapter regulates the purchase and sale of stock of Indiana corporations in interstate commerce. Indeed, . . . the Chapter will inevitably be used to block interstate transactions in such stock. Because the Commerce Clause protects the "interstate market" in such securities, Exxon Corp. v. Governor of Maryland, 437 U.S. 117, 127 (1978), and because the Control Share Chapter substantially interferes with this interstate market, the Chapter clearly conflicts with the Commerce Clause.

. . .

BENDIX AUTOLITE CORP. v. MIDWESCO ENTERPRISES, INC., 486 U.S. 888 (1988). Under Ohio law, an otherwise available statute of limitations defense was tolled, and hence made unavailable, with respect to foreign corporations that did not appoint an agent for service of process, a step that operated as consent to the general jurisdiction of the Ohio courts. The Supreme Court held the tolling provision invalid under the commerce clause. Although observing that the "Ohio statute before us might have been held to be a discrimination that invalidates without extended inquiry[,]" the court rested its conclusion on a "find[ing] that the burden imposed on interstate commerce by the tolling statute exceeds any local interest that the State might advance." Justice Kennedy's opinion for the majority said in part:

"The burden the tolling statute places on interstate commerce is significant. Midwesco has no corporate office in Ohio, is not registered to do business there, and has not appointed an agent for service of process in the State. To gain the protection of the limitations period, Midwesco would have had to appoint a resident agent for service of process in Ohio and subject itself to the general jurisdiction of the Ohio courts. This jurisdiction would extend to any suit against Midwesco, whether or not the transaction in question had any connection with Ohio. The designation of an agent subjects the foreign corporation to the general jurisdiction of the Ohio courts in matters to which Ohio's tenuous relation would not otherwise extend.... The Ohio statutory scheme thus forces a foreign corporation to choose between exposure to the general jurisdiction of Ohio courts or forfeiture of the limitations defense, remaining subject to suit in Ohio in perpetuity. Requiring a foreign corporation to appoint an agent for service in all cases and to defend itself with reference to all transactions, including those in which it did not have the minimum contacts necessary for supporting personal jurisdiction, is a significant burden....

"... Where a State denies ordinary legal defenses or like privileges to out-of-state persons or corporations engaged in commerce, the State law will be reviewed under the Commerce Clause to determine whether the denial is discriminatory on its face or an impermissible burden on commerce....

"...

"... Ohio cannot justify its statute as a means of protecting its residents from corporations who become liable for acts done within the State but later withdraw from the jurisdiction, for it is conceded by all parties that the Ohio long arm statute would have permitted service on Midwesco throughout the period of limitations. The Ohio statute of limitations is tolled only for those foreign corporations that do not subject themselves to the general jurisdiction of Ohio courts. In this manner the Ohio statute imposes a greater burden on out-of-state companies than it does on Ohio companies, subjecting the activities of foreign and domestic corporations to inconsistent regulations. CTS Corp. v. Dynamics Corp. of America, 481 U.S. 69, 87–89 (1987)."

"... [S]ubject[ing] Midwesco to the general jurisdiction of Ohio courts over transactions in which Ohio had no interest ... is an unreasonable burden on commerce."

In an opinion concurring in the judgment, Justice Scalia objected to the Court's balancing of the challenged provision's burdens on interstate commerce against its local benefits: "Weighing the governmental interests of a State against the needs of interstate commerce is ... a task squarely within the responsibility of Congress, see U.S. Const., Art. I, § 8, cl. 3, and 'ill suited to the judicial function.' CTS Corp. v. Dynamics Corp. of America, 481 U.S. 69, 95 (1987) (Scalia, J., concurring in part and concurring in judgment)." He urged abandonment of "the 'balancing' approach to these negative commerce clause cases" and explained his concurrence as follows:

"In my view, a state statute is invalid under the Commerce Clause if, and only if, it accords discriminatory treatment to interstate commerce in a respect not required to achieve a lawful state purpose. When such a validating purpose exists, it is for Congress and not us to determine it is not significant enough to justify the burden on commerce. The Ohio tolling statute, Ohio Rev.Code Ann. § 2305.15 (Supp.1987), is on its face discriminatory because it applies only to out-of-state corporations. That facial discrimination cannot be justified on the basis that 'it advances a legitimate local purpose that cannot be adequately served by reasonable nondiscriminatory alternatives,' New Energy Co. of Indiana v. Limbach, 486 U.S. 269, 278 (1988). A tolling statute that operated only against persons beyond the reach of Ohio's long-arm statute, or against all persons that could not be found for mail service, would be narrowly tailored to advance the legitimate purpose of preserving claims; but the present statute extends the time for suit even against corporations which (like appellee) are fully suable within Ohio, and readily reachable through the mails.''

F.   INTERSTATE MOBILITY OF PERSONS

Shortly after the Civil War the Court was called upon to consider the constitutional freedom of persons to move from state to state. Nevada had enacted a statute levying a capitation tax of one dollar upon every person leaving the state by railroad, stage coach or other vehicle employed in the business of transporting persons for hire. The carrier was required to report the persons so transported and pay the tax. In Crandall v. Nevada, 73 U.S. (6 Wall.) 35 (1867), the Court held this act invalid. The majority of the Court did not place the decision on the commerce clause, but stated:

"The people of these United States constitute one nation. They have a government in which all of them are deeply interested. This government has necessarily a capital established by law, where its principal operations are conducted. Here sits its legislature, composed of senators and representatives, from the States and from the people of the States. Here resides the President directing through thousands of agents, the execution of the laws over all this vast country. Here is the seat of the supreme judicial power of the nation, to which all its citizens have a right to resort to claim justice at its hands. Here are the great executive departments, administering the offices of the mails, or the public lands, of the collection and distribution of the public revenues, and of our foreign relations. These are all established and conducted under the admitted powers of the Federal government. That government has a right to call to this point any or all of its citizens to aid in its service, as members of the Congress, of the courts, of the executive departments, and to fill all its other offices; and this right cannot be made to depend upon the pleasure of a State over whose territory they must pass to reach the point where these services must be rendered. The government, also, has its offices of secondary importance in all other parts of the country. On the sea-coasts and on the rivers it has its ports of entry. In the interior it has its land offices, its revenue offices, and its sub-treasuries. In all these it demands the services of its citizens, and is entitled to bring them to those points from all quarters of the nation, and no power can exist in a State to obstruct this right that would not enable it to defeat the purposes for which the government was established. . . .

"But if the government has these rights on her own account, the citizen also has correlative rights. He has the right to come to the seat of government to assert any claim he may have upon that government, or to transact any business he may have with it. To seek its protection, to share its offices, to engage in administering its functions. He has a right to free access to its seaports, through which all the operations of foreign trade and commerce are conducted, to the sub-treasuries, the land offices, the revenue offices, and the courts of justice in the several States, and this right is in its nature independent of the will of any State over whose soil he must pass in the exercise of it. . . .''

The question of interstate mobility arose again in Edwards v. California, 314 U.S. 160 (1941), where the Court struck down a law making it a misdemeanor to bring into California "any indigent person who is not a resident of the State, knowing him to be an indigent person." Resting the decision on the commerce clause the majority of the Court quoted the *Baldwin v. Seelig* statement that the Constitution "was framed upon the theory that the peoples of the several states must sink or swim together." Referring to the language in *New York v. Miln* regarding the "moral pestilence of paupers," the Court said:

"Whatever may have been the notion then prevailing, we do not think that it will now be seriously contended that because a person is without employment and without funds he constitutes a 'moral pestilence'."

But four of the Justices (Douglas, Black, Murphy and Jackson) were not willing to place their concurrence on the commerce clause. They believed that the right of persons "to move freely from state to state is an incident of national citizenship protected by the privileges and immunities clause of the Fourteenth Amendment" and added Justice Jackson: "[T]he migrations of a human being do not fit easily into my notions as to what is commerce. To hold that the measure of his rights is the commerce clause is likely to result eventually in distorting the commercial law or in denaturing human rights."

The constitutional freedom of interstate migration will be met again later. See Chapter 10.

SECTION 5.   EFFECT OF OTHER CONSTITUTIONAL PROVISIONS ON STATE REGULATORY POWER

A.   THE PRIVILEGES AND IMMUNITIES CLAUSE OF ARTICLE IV, SECTION 2

Article IV, Section 2 provides: "The Citizens of each State shall be entitled to all Privileges and Immunities of Citizens in the several States." The progenitor of this provision was the Fourth of the Articles of Confederation which read as follows:

"The better to secure and perpetuate mutual friendship and intercourse among the people of the different States in this Union, the free inhabitants of each of these states, paupers, vagabonds and fugitives from justice excepted, shall be entitled to all privileges and immunities of free citizens in the several States; and the people of each State shall have free ingress and regress to and from any other State, and shall enjoy therein all the privileges of trade and commerce, subject to the same duties, impositions and restrictions as the inhabitants thereof respectively . . . .".

These provisions were prompted by a fundamental problem of the federal system of government—how to reconcile the advantages of a common citizenship with a dispersed sovereignty in a number of independent, or largely independent, states. The basic character of the problem is illustrated by the fact that the Constitution of Australia contains a similar provision (Sec. 117) which reads: "A subject of the Queen, resident in any State, shall not be subject in any other State, to any disability or discrimination which would not be equally applicable to him if he were a subject of the Queen resident in such other State."

The first opinion on Article IV, Section 2, was given in Corfield v. Coryell, 4 Wash.C.C. 371, 6 Fed.Cas. 546 (E.D.Pa.1823), by Justice Washington of the Supreme Court when on circuit. A New Jersey statute of 1820 made it unlawful for any person who was not "an actual inhabitant and resident" of the state to rake or gather clams, oysters, or shells in any of the rivers, bays, or waters of the state. The question was the validity of this statute as applied to a Pennsylvania citizen who was gathering oysters in New Jersey waters. Justice Washington declared that the phrase "privileges and immunities of citizens in the several states" should be confined to "those privileges and immunities which are, in their nature, *fundamental*" and "which belong, of right, to the

[handwritten: Corfield v. Coryell]

citizens of all free governments." Among these, he said, were the "right of a citizen of one State to pass through, or to reside in any other State, for the purposes of trade, agriculture, professional pursuits, or otherwise;" the right "to take, hold and dispose of property, either real or personal; and an exemption from higher taxes or impositions than are paid by the other citizens of the State."

"But," he continued, "We cannot accede to the proposition which was insisted on by the counsel, that, under this provision of the Constitution, the citizens of the several States are permitted to participate in all *the rights* which belong exclusively to the citizens of any other particular State, merely upon the ground that they are enjoyed by those citizens; much less, that in regulating the use of the common property of the citizens of such State, the legislature is bound to extend to the citizens of all the other States the same advantages as are secured to their own citizens." The right to fish in the waters of the state for running fish or stationary shell fish, when not ceded by the state, he regarded as the common property of all the citizens of the state. "[I]t would, in our opinion, be going quite too far to construe the grant of privileges and immunities of citizens, as amounting to a grant of a co-tenancy in the common property of the State, to the citizens of all the other states."

The statute was sustained.

Justice Washington's reasoning was followed in McCready v. Virginia, 94 U.S. 391 (1877), which upheld the power of a state to limit to its own citizens the right to plant oysters in public waters.

The statute challenged in the *Corfield* case drew the line on the basis of "residence" rather than citizenship, but no point was made of this in the opinion. After the adoption of the Fourteenth Amendment it became even more difficult to distinguish between residence and state citizenship, for that Amendment provides that "All persons born or naturalized in the United States, and subject to the jurisdiction thereof, are citizens of the United States *and of the State wherein they reside.*" (Emphasis added.)

It was early held that the clause protected only individuals who are citizens and that a corporation could not claim the protection of the clause even though all of its incorporators were citizens of the state of incorporation. Bank of Augusta v. Earle, 38 U.S. (13 Pet.) 519 (1839).

United Building and Construction Trades Council of Camden County and Vicinity v. Mayor and Council of the City of Camden

465 U.S. 208, 104 S.Ct. 1020, 79 L.Ed.2d 249 (1984).

Justice Rehnquist delivered the opinion of the Court.

A municipal ordinance of the city of Camden, New Jersey requires that at least 40% of the employees of contractors and subcontractors working on city construction projects be Camden residents. Appellant, the United Building and Construction Trades Council of Camden and Vicinity (the Council), challenges that ordinance as a violation of the Privileges and Immunities Clause, Article IV, § 2, of the United States Constitution. The Supreme Court of New Jersey rejected appellant's privileges and immunities attack on the ground that the ordinance discriminates on the basis of *municipal,* not state, residency. The court "decline[d] to apply the Privileges and Immunities Clause in the context of a municipal ordinance that has identical effects upon out-of-state citizens and New Jersey citizens not residing in the locality." ... We conclude that the challenged ordinance is properly subject to the strictures of the Clause. We therefore reverse the judgment of the Supreme Court of New Jersey and remand the case for a determination of the validity of the ordinance under the appropriate constitutional standard.

On August 28, 1980, the Camden City Council, acting pursuant to a state-wide affirmative action program, adopted an ordinance setting minority hiring "goals" on all public works contracts. The ordinance also created a hiring preference for Camden residents.... As subsequently amended, the ordinance requires that on all construction projects funded by the city:

> "The developer-contractor, in hiring for jobs, shall make every effort to employ persons residing within the City of Camden but, in no event, shall less than forty percent (40%) of the entire labor force be residents of the City of Camden."

The contractor is also obliged to ensure that any subcontractors working on such projects adhere to the same requirement.

. . .

... We first address the argument, accepted by the Supreme Court of New Jersey, that the Clause does not even apply to a *municipal* ordinance such as this. Two separate contentions are advanced in support of this position: first, that the Clause only applies to laws passed by a *State* and, second, that the Clause only applies to laws that discriminate on the basis of *state* citizenship.

The first argument can be quickly rejected. The fact that the ordinance in question is a municipal, rather than a state, law does not somehow place it outside the scope of the Privileges and Immunities Clause. First of all, one cannot easily distinguish municipal from state action in this case: the municipal ordinance would not have gone into effect without express approval by the State Treasurer.... The constitutional challenge to the resident hiring preference, therefore, must also "be interpreted as a challenge to the State Treasurer's general power" to adopt such a preference....

More fundamentally, a municipality is merely a political subdivision of the State from which its authority derives. City of Trenton v. New Jersey, 262 U.S. 182, 187 (1923). It is as true of the Privileges and Immunities Clause as of the Equal Protection Clause that what would be unconstitutional if done directly by the State can no more readily be accomplished by a city deriving its authority from the State.... Thus, even if the ordinance had been adopted solely by Camden, and not pursuant to a state program or with state approval, the hiring preference would still have to comport with the Privileges and Immunities Clause.

The second argument merits more consideration. The New Jersey Supreme Court concluded that the Privileges and Immunities Clause does not apply to an ordinance that discriminates solely on the basis of *municipal* residency. The Clause is phrased in terms of *state* citizenship and was designed "to place the citizens of each State upon the same footing with citizens of other States, so far as the advantages resulting from citizenship in those States are concerned." Paul v. Virginia, 8 Wall. 168, 180 (1869)....

> "The primary purpose of this clause, like the clauses between which it is located—those relating to full faith and credit and to interstate extradition of fugitives from justice—was to help fuse into one Nation a collection of independent, sovereign States. It was designed to insure to a citizen of State A who ventures into State B the same privileges which the citizens of

State B enjoy. For protection of such equality the citizen of State A was not to be restricted to the uncertain remedies afforded by diplomatic processes and official retaliation." Toomer v. Witsell, 334 U.S. 385, 395 (1948).

Municipal residency classifications, it is argued, simply do not give rise to the same concerns.

We cannot accept this argument. We have never read the Clause so literally as to apply it only to distinctions based on state citizenship. For example, in Mullaney v. Anderson, 342 U.S. 415, 419–420 (1952), the Court held that the Alaska Territory had no more freedom to discriminate against those not residing in the Territory than did any State to favor its own citizens. And despite some initial uncertainty, ..., it is now established that the terms "citizen" and "resident" are "essentially interchangeable," Austin v. New Hampshire, 420 U.S. 656, 662, n. 8 (1975), for purposes of analysis of most cases under the Privileges and Immunities Clause. See Hicklin v. Orbeck, 437 U.S. 518, 524, n. 8 (1978); Toomer v. Witsell, 334 U.S. 385, 397 (1948). A person who is not residing in a given State is *ipso facto* not residing in a city within that State. Thus, whether the exercise of a privilege is conditioned on state residency or on municipal residency he will just as surely be excluded.

Given the Camden ordinance, an out-of-state citizen who ventures into New Jersey will not enjoy the same privileges as the New Jersey citizen residing in Camden. It is true that New Jersey citizens not residing in Camden will be affected by the ordinance as well as out-of-state citizens. And it is true that the disadvantaged New Jersey residents have no claim under the Privileges and Immunities Clause. The Slaughter–House Cases, 16 Wall. 36, 77 (1872). But New Jersey residents at least have a chance to remedy at the polls any discrimination against them. Out-of-state citizens have no similar opportunity, Austin v. New Hampshire, 420 U.S. 656, 662 (1975), and they must "not be restricted to the uncertain remedies afforded by diplomatic processes and official retaliation." Toomer v. Witsell, 334 U.S. 385, 395 (1948).[9] We conclude that Camden's ordinance is not immune from constitutional review at the behest of out-of-state residents merely because some in-state residents are similarly disadvantaged.

Application of the Privileges and Immunities Clause to a particular instance of discrimination against out-of-state residents entails a two-step inquiry. As an initial matter, the court must decide whether the ordinance burdens one of those privileges and immunities protected by the Clause. Baldwin v. Montana Fish and Game Comm'n, 436 U.S. 371, 383 (1978). Not all forms of discrimination against citizens of other States are constitutionally suspect.

"Some distinctions between residents and nonresidents merely reflect the fact that this is a Nation composed of individual States, and are permitted; other distinctions are prohibited because they hinder the formation, the purpose, or the development of a single Union of those States. Only with respect to those 'privileges' and 'immunities' bearing upon the vitality of

---

9. The dissent suggests that New Jersey citizens not residing in Camden will adequately protect the interests of out-of-state residents and that the scope of the Privileges and Immunities Clause should be measured in light of this political reality.... What the dissent fails to appreciate is that the Camden ordinance at issue in this case was adopted pursuant to a comprehensive, state-wide program applicable in all New Jersey cities. The Camden resident-preference ordinance has already received state sanction and approval, and every New Jersey city is free to adopt a similar protectionist measure. Some have already done so. Thus, it is hard to see how New Jersey residents living outside Camden will protect the interests of out-of-state citizens.

. . .

the Nation as a single entity must the State treat all citizens, resident and nonresident, equally."

As a threshold matter, then, we must determine whether an out-of-state resident's interest in employment on public works contracts in another State is sufficiently "fundamental" to the promotion of interstate harmony so as to "fall within the purview of the Privileges and Immunities Clause." Id., at 388. . . .

Certainly, the pursuit of a common calling is one of the most fundamental of those privileges protected by the Clause. Baldwin v. Montana Fish and Game Comm'n, 436 U.S. 371, 387 (1978). Many, if not most, of our cases expounding the Privileges and Immunities Clause have dealt with this basic and essential activity. See, e.g., Hicklin v. Orbeck, 437 U.S. 518 (1978); Austin v. New Hampshire, 420 U.S. 656 (1975); Mullaney v. Anderson, 342 U.S. 415 (1952); Toomer v. Witsell, 334 U.S. 385 (1948); Ward v. Maryland, 79 U.S. 418 (1871). Public employment, however, is qualitatively different from employment in the private sector; it is a subspecies of the broader opportunity to pursue a common calling. We have held that there is no fundamental right to government employment for purposes of the Equal Protection Clause. Massachusetts v. Murgia, 427 U.S. 307, 313 (1976) (per curiam). Cf. McCarthy v. Philadelphia Civil Service Comm'n, 424 U.S. 645 (1976) (per curiam) (rejecting equal protection challenge to municipal residency requirement for municipal workers). And in White, 103 S.Ct., at 1046, n. 7, we held that for purposes of the Commerce Clause everyone employed on a city public works project is, "in a substantial if informal sense, 'working for the city.' "

It can certainly be argued that for purposes of the Privileges and Immunities Clause everyone affected by the Camden ordinance is also "working for the city" and, therefore, has no grounds for complaint when the city favors its own residents. But we decline to transfer mechanically into this context an analysis fashioned to fit the Commerce Clause. Our decision in White turned on a distinction between the city acting as a market participant and the city acting as a market regulator. The question whether employees of contractors and subcontractors on public works projects were or were not, in some sense, working for the city was crucial to that analysis. The question had to be answered in order to chart the boundaries of the distinction. But the distinction between market participant and market regulator relied upon in White to dispose of the Commerce Clause challenge is not dispositive in this context. The two Clauses have different aims and set different standards for state conduct.

The Commerce Clause acts as an implied restraint upon state regulatory powers. Such powers must give way before the superior authority of Congress to legislate on (or leave unregulated) matters involving interstate commerce. When the State acts solely as a market participant, no conflict between state *regulation* and federal regulatory authority can arise. White, 103 S.Ct., at 1044; Reeves, Inc. v. Stake, 447 U.S. 429, 436–437 (1980); Hughes v. Alexandria Scrap Corp., 426 U.S. 794, 810 (1976). The Privileges and Immunities Clause, on the other hand, imposes a direct restraint on state action in the interests of interstate harmony. Hicklin v. Orbeck, 437 U.S. 518, 523–524 (1978); Ward v. Maryland, 79 U.S. 418, 430 (1871); Paul v. Virginia, 8 Wall. 168, 180 (1869). This concern with comity cuts across the market regulator-market participant distinction that is crucial under the Commerce Clause. It is discrimination against out-of-state residents on matters of fundamental concern which triggers the Clause, not regulation affecting interstate commerce. Thus, the fact that Camden is merely setting conditions on its expenditures for goods and services in the marketplace does not preclude the possibility that those conditions violate the Privileges and Immunities Clause.

In Hicklin v. Orbeck, 437 U.S. 518 (1978), we struck down as a violation of the Privileges and Immunities Clause an "Alaska Hire" statute containing a resident hiring preference for all employment related to the development of the State's oil and gas resources. Alaska argued in that case "that because the oil and gas that are the subject of Alaska Hire are *owned* by the State, this ownership, of itself, is sufficient justification for the Act's discrimination against nonresidents, and takes the Act totally without the scope of the Privileges and Immunities Clause." We concluded, however, that the State's interest in controlling those things it claims to own is not absolute. "Rather than placing a statute completely beyond the Clause, a State's ownership of the property with which the statute is concerned is a factor—although often the crucial factor—to be considered in evaluating whether the statute's discrimination against noncitizens violates the Clause." ... Much the same analysis, we think, is appropriate to a city's efforts to bias private employment decisions in favor of its residents on construction projects funded with public monies. The fact that Camden is expending its own funds or funds it administers in accordance with the terms of a grant is certainly a factor—perhaps the crucial factor—to be considered in evaluating whether the statute's discrimination violates the Privileges and Immunities Clause. But it does not remove the Camden ordinance completely from the purview of the Clause.

In sum, Camden may, without fear of violating the Commerce Clause, pressure private employers engaged in public works projects funded in whole or in part by the city to hire city residents. But that same exercise of power to bias the employment decisions of private contractors and subcontractors against out-of-state residents may be called to account under the Privileges and Immunities Clause. A determination of whether a privilege is "fundamental" for purposes of that Clause does not depend on whether the employees of private contractors and subcontractors engaged in public works projects can or cannot be said to be "working for the city." The opportunity to seek employment with such private employers is "sufficiently basic to the livelihood of the Nation," Baldwin v. Montana Fish and Game Comm'n, 436 U.S. 371, 388 (1978), as to fall within the purview of the Privileges and Immunities Clause even though the contractors and subcontractors are themselves engaged in projects funded in whole or part by the city.

The conclusion that Camden's ordinance discriminates against a protected privilege does not, of course, end the inquiry. We have stressed in prior cases that "[l]ike many other constitutional provisions, the privileges and immunities clause is not an absolute." Toomer v. Witsell, 334 U.S. 385, 396 (1948). It does not preclude discrimination against citizens of other States where there is a "substantial reason" for the difference in treatment. "[T]he inquiry in each case must be concerned with whether such reasons do exist and whether the degree of discrimination bears a close relation to them." As part of any justification offered for the discriminatory law, nonresidents must somehow be shown to "constitute a peculiar source of the evil at which the statute is aimed."

The city of Camden contends that its ordinance is necessary to counteract grave economic and social ills. Spiralling unemployment, a sharp decline in population, and a dramatic reduction in the number of businesses located in the city have eroded property values and depleted the city's tax base. The resident hiring preference is designed, the city contends, to increase the number of employed persons living in Camden and to arrest the "middle class flight" currently plaguing the city. The city also argues that all nonCamden residents employed on city public works projects, whether they reside in New Jersey or Pennsylvania, constitute a "source of the evil at which the statute is aimed." That is, they "live off" Camden without "living in" Camden. Camden contends that the scope of the discrimination practiced in the ordinance, with its municipal residency requirement, is carefully tailored to alleviate this evil without unreasonably harming nonresidents, who still have access to 60% of the available positions.

Every inquiry under the Privileges and Immunities Clause "must ... be conducted with due regard for the principle that the states should have considerable leeway in analyzing local evils and in prescribing appropriate cures." Toomer v. Witsell, 334 U.S. 385, 396 (1948). This caution is particularly appropriate when a government body is merely setting conditions on the expenditure of funds it controls. The Alaska Hire statute at issue in Hicklin v. Orbeck, 437 U.S. 518 (1978), swept within its strictures not only contractors and subcontractors dealing directly with the State's oil and gas; it also covered suppliers who provided goods and services to those contractors and subcontractors. We invalidated the Act as "an attempt to force virtually all businesses that benefit in some way from the economic ripple effect of Alaska's decision to develop its oil and gas resources to bias their employment practices in favor of the State's residents." No similar "ripple effect" appears to infect the Camden ordinance. It is limited in scope to employees working directly on city public works projects.

Nonetheless, we find it impossible to evaluate Camden's justification on the record as it now stands. No trial has ever been held in the case. No findings of fact have been made. The Supreme Court of New Jersey certified the case for direct appeal after the brief administrative proceedings that led to approval of the ordinance by the State Treasurer. It would not be appropriate for this Court either to make factual determinations as an initial matter or to take judicial notice of Camden's decay. We, therefore, deem it wise to remand the case to the New Jersey Supreme Court. That court may decide, consistent with state procedures, on the best method for making the necessary findings.

The judgment of the Supreme Court of New Jersey is reversed, and the case is remanded for proceedings not inconsistent with this opinion.

Reversed and Remanded.

Justice Blackmun, dissenting.

For over a century the underlying meaning of the Privileges and Immunities Clause of the Constitution's Article IV has been regarded as settled: at least absent some substantial, noninvidious justification, a State may not discriminate between its own residents and residents of other States on the basis of state citizenship ...

Today, however, the Court casually extends the scope of the Clause by holding that it applies to laws that discriminate *among* state residents on the basis of *municipal* residence, simply because discrimination on the basis of municipal residence disadvantages citizens of other States *"ipso facto."* This novel interpretation arrives accompanied by little practical justification and no historical or textual support whatsoever. Because I believe that the Privileges and Immunities Clause was not intended to apply to the kind of municipal discrimination presented by this case, I would affirm the judgment of the Supreme Court of New Jersey.

. . .

Contrary to the Court's tacit assumption, discrimination on the basis of municipal residence is substantially different in this regard from discrimination on the basis of state citizenship. The distinction is simple but fundamental: discrimination on the basis of municipal residence penalizes persons within the State's political community as well as those without. The Court itself points out that while New Jersey citizens who reside outside Camden are not protected by the Privileges and Immunities Clause, they may resort to the State's political processes to protect themselves. What the Court fails to appreciate is that this avenue of relief for New Jersey residents works to protect residents of other States as well; disadvantaged state residents who turn to the state legislature to displace ordinances like Camden's further the interests of nonresidents as well as their own. Nor is this mechanism for relief merely a theoretical one; in the past decade several States, including California and Georgia, have repealed or forbidden protectionist ordinances like the one at issue here. In short, discrimination on the basis of municipal residence simply does not consign residents of other States, in the words of *Toomer,* supra, to "the uncertain remedies afforded by diplomatic processes and official retaliation." The Court thus has applied the Privileges and Immunities Clause without regard for the political ills that it was designed to cure.

.   .   .

Supreme Court of Virginia v. Friedman

487 U.S. 59, 108 S.Ct. 2260, 101 L.Ed.2d 56 (1988).

Justice Kennedy delivered the opinion of the Court.

Qualified lawyers admitted to practice in other States may be admitted to the Virginia bar "on motion," that is, without taking the bar examination which Virginia otherwise requires. The State conditions such admission on a showing, among other matters, that the applicant is a permanent resident of Virginia. The question for decision is whether this residency requirement violates the Privileges and Immunities Clause of the United States Constitution, Art. IV, § 2. We hold that it does.

I

Myrna E. Friedman was admitted to the Illinois bar by examination in 1977 and to the District of Columbia bar by reciprocity in 1980. From 1977 to 1981, she was employed by the Department of the Navy in Arlington, Virginia, as a civilian attorney, and from 1982 until 1986, she was an attorney in private practice in Washington, D.C. In January 1986, she became associate general counsel for ERC International, Inc., a Delaware corporation. Friedman practices and maintains her offices at the company's principal place of business in Vienna, Virginia. Her duties at ERC International include drafting contracts and advising her employer and its subsidiaries on matters of Virginia law.

From 1977 to early 1986, Friedman lived in Virginia. In February 1986, however, she married and moved to her husband's home in Cheverly, Maryland. In June 1986, Friedman applied for admission to the Virginia bar on motion.

The applicable rule, promulgated by the Supreme Court of Virginia pursuant to statute, is Rule 1A:1. The Rule permits admission on motion of attorneys who are licensed to practice in another jurisdiction, provided the other jurisdiction admits Virginia attorneys without examination. The applicant must have been licensed for at least five years and the Virginia Supreme Court must determine that the applicant:

"(a) Is a proper person to practice law.

"(b) Has made such progress in the practice of law that it would be unreasonable to require him to take an examination.

"(c) Has become a permanent resident of the Commonwealth.

"(d) Intends to practice full time as a member of the Virginia bar."

In a letter accompanying her application, Friedman alerted the Clerk of the Virginia Supreme Court to her change of residence, but argued that her application should nevertheless be granted. Friedman gave assurance that she would be engaged full-time in the practice of law in Virginia, that she would be available for service of process and court appearances, and that she would keep informed of local rules. She also asserted "that there appears to be no reason to discriminate against my petition as a nonresident for admission to the Bar on motion," that her circumstances fit within the purview of this Court's decision in Supreme Court of New Hampshire v. Piper, 470 U.S. 274 (1985), and that accordingly she was entitled to admission under the Privileges and Immunities Clause of the Constitution Art. IV, § 2.

[handwritten margin note: New Hampshire v. Piper]

The Clerk wrote Friedman that her request had been denied. He explained that because Friedman was no longer a permanent resident of the Commonwealth of Virginia, she was not eligible for admission to the Virginia bar pursuant to Rule 1A:1. He added that the court had concluded that our decision in *Piper,* which invalidated a residency requirement imposed on lawyers who had passed a State's bar examination, was "not applicable" to the "discretionary requirement in Rule 1A:1 of residence as a condition of admission by reciprocity."

Friedman then commenced this action, against the Supreme Court of Virginia and its Clerk, in the United States District Court for the Eastern District of Virginia. She alleged that the residency requirement of Rule 1A:1 violated the Privileges and Immunities Clause. The District Court entered summary judgment in Friedman's favor, holding that the requirement of residency for admission without examination violates the Clause.*

The Court of Appeals for the Fourth Circuit unanimously affirmed....

... We ... affirm.

II

Article IV, § 2, of the Constitution provides that the "Citizens of each State shall be entitled to all Privileges and Immunities of Citizens in the several States." The provision was designed "to place the citizens of each State upon the same footing with citizens of other States, so far as the advantages resulting from citizenship in those States are concerned." Paul v. Virginia, 8 Wall. 168, 180 (1869). See also Toomer v. Witsell, 334 U.S. 385, 395 (1948) (the Privileges and Immunities Clause "was designed to insure to a citizen of State A who ventures into State B the same privileges which the citizens of State B enjoy"). The Clause "thus establishes a norm of comity without specifying the particular subjects as to which citizens of one State coming within the jurisdic-

---

* The District Court did not address Friedman's claims that the residency requirement of Rule 1A:1 also violates the Commerce Clause and the Equal Protection Clause of the Fourteenth Amendment. The Court of Appeals did not pass on these contentions either, and our resolution of Friedman's claim that the residency requirement violates the Privileges and Immunities Clause makes it unnecessary for us to reach them.

tion of another are guaranteed equality of treatment." Austin v. New Hampshire, 420 U.S. 656, 660 (1975).

While the Privileges and Immunities Clause cites the term "Citizens," for analytic purposes citizenship and residency are essentially interchangeable. See United Building & Construction Trades Council v. Mayor of Camden, 465 U.S. 208, 216 (1984). When examining claims that a citizenship or residency classification offends privileges and immunities protections, we undertake a two-step inquiry. First, the activity in question must be "sufficiently basic to the livelihood of the 'Nation' . . . as to fall within the purview of the Privileges and Immunities Clause. . . ." Id., at 221–222, quoting Baldwin v. Montana Fish & Game Comm'n, 436 U.S. 371, 388 (1978). For it is "[o]nly with respect to those 'privileges' and 'immunities bearing on the vitality of the Nation as a single entity' that a State must accord residents and nonresidents equal treatment." Supreme Court of New Hampshire v. Piper, 470 U.S., at 279, quoting *Baldwin,* supra, at 383. Second, if the challenged restriction deprives nonresidents of a protected privilege, we will invalidate it only if we conclude that the restriction is not closely related to the advancement of a substantial State interest. *Piper,* supra, at 284. Appellants assert that the residency requirement offends neither part of this test. We disagree.

A

Appellants concede, as they must, that our decision in *Piper* establishes that a nonresident who takes and passes an examination prescribed by the State, and who otherwise is qualified for the practice of law, has an interest in practicing law that is protected by the Privileges and Immunities Clause. Appellants contend, however, that the discretionary admission provided for by Rule 1A:1 is not a privilege protected by the Clause for two reasons. First, appellants argue that the bar examination "serves as an adequate, alternative means of gaining admission to the bar." In appellants' view, "[s]o long as any applicant may gain admission to a State's bar, without regard to residence, by passing the bar examination," the State cannot be said to have discriminated against nonresidents "as a matter of fundamental concern." Second, appellants argue that the right to admission on motion is not within the purview of the Clause because, without offense to the Constitution, the State could require all bar applicants to pass an examination. Neither argument is persuasive.

We cannot accept appellants' first theory because it is quite inconsistent with our precedents. We reaffirmed in *Piper* the well-settled principle that "one of the privileges which the Clause guarantees to citizens of State A is that of doing business in State B on terms of substantial equality with the citizens of that State." *Piper,* supra, at 280, quoting Toomer v. Witsell, supra, at 396. See also *United Building & Construction Trades Council,* supra, at 219 ("Certainly, the pursuit of a common calling is one of the most fundamental of those privileges protected by the Clause"). After reviewing our precedents, we explicitly held that the practice of law, like other occupations considered in those cases, is sufficiently basic to the national economy to be deemed a privilege protected by the Clause. See *Piper,* supra, at 280–281. The clear import of *Piper* is that the Clause is implicated whenever, as is the case here, a State does not permit qualified nonresidents to practice law within its borders on terms of substantial equality with its own residents.

Nothing in our precedents, moreover, supports the contention that the Privileges and Immunities Clause does not reach a State's discrimination against nonresidents when such discrimination does not result in their total exclusion from the State. In Ward v. Maryland, 12 Wall. 418 (1871), for example, the Court invalidated a statute under which residents paid an annual fee of $12 to $150 for a license to trade foreign goods, while nonresidents were required to pay $300. Similarly, in *Toomer,* supra, the Court held that nonresident fishermen could not be required to pay a license fee one hundred times the fee charged to residents. In Hicklin v. Orbeck, 437 U.S. 518 (1978), the Court invalidated a statute requiring that residents be hired in preference to nonresidents for all positions related to the development of the State's oil and gas resources. Indeed, as the Court of Appeals correctly noted, the New Hampshire rule struck down in *Piper* did not result in the total exclusion of nonresidents from the practice of law in that State. . . .

Further, we find appellants' second theory—that Virginia could constitutionally require that all applicants to its bar take and pass an examination—quite irrelevant to the question whether the Clause is applicable in the circumstances of this case. A State's abstract authority to require from resident and nonresident alike that which it has chosen to demand from the nonresident alone has never been held to shield the discriminatory distinction from the reach of the Privileges and Immunities Clause. Thus, the applicability of the Clause to the present case no more turns on the legality *vel non* of an examination requirement than it turned on the inherent reasonableness of the fees charged to nonresidents in *Toomer* and *Ward.* The issue instead is whether the State has burdened the right to practice law, a privilege protected by the Privileges and Immunities Clause, by discriminating among otherwise equally qualified applicants solely on the basis of citizenship or residency. We conclude it has.

B

. . . The Clause does not preclude disparity in treatment where substantial reasons exist for the discrimination and the degree of discrimination bears a close relation to such reasons. . . . In deciding whether the degree of discrimination bears a sufficiently close relation to the reasons proffered by the State, the Court has considered whether, within the full panoply of legislative choices otherwise available to the State, there exist alternative means of furthering the State's purpose without implicating constitutional concerns. See *Piper,* 470 U.S., at 284.

Appellants offer two principal justifications for the Rule's requirement that applicants seeking admission on motion reside within the Commonwealth of Virginia. First, they contend that the residence requirement assures, in tandem with the full-time practice requirement, that attorneys admitted on motion will have the same commitment to service and familiarity with Virginia law that is possessed by applicants securing admission upon examination. Attorneys admitted on motion, appellants argue, have "no personal investment" in the jurisdiction; consequently, they "are entitled to no presumption that they will willingly and actively participate in bar activities and obligations, or fulfill their public service responsibilities to the State's client community." Second, appellants argue that the residency requirement facilitates enforcement of the full-time practice requirement of Rule 1A:1. We find each of these justifications insufficient to meet the State's burden of showing that the discrimination is warranted by a substantial State objective and closely drawn to its achievement.

We acknowledge that a bar examination is one method of assuring that the admitted attorney has a stake in her professional licensure and a concomitant interest in the integrity and standards of the bar. A bar examination, as we know judicially and from our own experience, is not a casual or lighthearted exercise. The question, however, is whether lawyers who are admitted in other

States and seek admission in Virginia are less likely to respect the bar and further its interests solely because they are nonresidents. We cannot say this is the case. While *Piper* relied on an examination requirement as an indicium of the nonresident's commitment to the bar and to the State's legal profession, see *Piper,* supra, at 285, it does not follow that when the State waives the examination it may make a distinction between residents and nonresidents.

Friedman's case proves the point. She earns her living working as an attorney in Virginia, and it is of scant relevance that her residence is located in the neighboring State of Maryland. It is indisputable that she has a substantial stake in the practice of law in Virginia. Indeed, despite appellants' suggestion at oral argument that Friedman's case is "atypical," the same will likely be true of all nonresident attorneys who are admitted on motion to the Virginia bar, in light of the State's requirement that attorneys so admitted show their intention to maintain an office and a regular practice in the State.... This requirement goes a long way toward ensuring that such attorneys will have an interest in the practice of law in Virginia that is at least comparable to the interest we ascribed in *Piper* to applicants admitted upon examination. Accordingly, we see no reason to assume that nonresident attorneys who, like Friedman, seek admission to the Virginia bar on motion will lack adequate incentives to remain abreast of changes in the law or to fulfill their civic duties.

Further, to the extent that the State is justifiably concerned with ensuring that its attorneys keep abreast of legal developments, it can protect these interests through other equally or more effective means that do not themselves infringe constitutional protections.... The Supreme Court of Virginia could, for example, require mandatory attendance at periodic continuing legal education courses.... The same is true with respect to the State's interest that the nonresident bar member does her share of volunteer and *pro bono* work. A "nonresident bar member, like the resident member, could be required to represent indigents and perhaps to participate in formal legal-aid work." *Piper,* supra, at 287 (footnote omitted).

We also reject appellants' attempt to justify the residency restriction as a necessary aid to the enforcement of the full-time practice requirement of Rule 1A:1. Virginia already requires ... that attorneys admitted on motion maintain an office for the practice of law in Virginia. As the Court of Appeals noted, the requirement that applicants maintain an office in Virginia facilitates compliance with the full-time practice requirement in nearly the identical manner that the residency restriction does, rendering the latter restriction largely redundant.... The office requirement furnishes an alternative to the residency requirement that is not only less restrictive, but also is fully adequate to protect whatever interest the State might have in the full-time practice restriction.

III

We hold that Virginia's residency requirement for admission to the State's bar without examination violates the Privileges and Immunities Clause. The nonresident's interest in practicing law on terms of substantial equality with those enjoyed by residents is a privilege protected by the Clause. A State may not discriminate against nonresidents unless it shows that such discrimination bears a close relation to the achievement of substantial State objectives. Virginia has failed to make this showing. Accordingly, the judgment of the Court of Appeals is affirmed.

It is so ordered.

Chief Justice Rehnquist, with whom Justice Scalia joins, dissenting.

Three Terms ago the Court invalidated a New Hampshire Bar rule which denied admission to an applicant who had passed the state bar examination because she was not, and would not become, a resident of the State. Supreme Court of New Hampshire v. Piper, 470 U.S. 274 (1985). In the present case the Court extends the reasoning of *Piper* to invalidate a Virginia Bar rule allowing admission on motion without examination to qualified applicants, but restricting the privilege to those applicants who have become residents of the State.

For the reasons stated in my dissent in *Piper,* I also disagree with the Court's decision in this case. I continue to believe that the Privileges and Immunities Clause of Article IV, § 2, does not require States to ignore residency when admitting lawyers to practice in the way that they must ignore residency when licensing traders in foreign goods, Ward v. Maryland, 12 Wall. 418 (1871), or when licensing commercial shrimp fishermen, Toomer v. Witsell, 334 U.S. 385 (1948).

I think the effect of today's decision is unfortunate even apart from what I believe is its mistaken view of the Privileges and Immunities Clause. Virginia's rule allowing admission on motion is an ameliorative provision, recognizing the fact that previous practice in another State may qualify a new resident of Virginia to practice there without the necessity of taking another bar examination. The Court's ruling penalizes Virginia, which has at least gone part way towards accommodating the present mobility of our population, but of course leaves untouched the rules of those States which allow no reciprocal admission on motion. Virginia may of course retain the privilege of admission on motion without enforcing a residency requirement even after today's decision, but it might also decide to eliminate admission on motion altogether.[a]

BARNARD v. THORSTENN, 489 U.S. 546 (1989). Two attorneys practicing law in New York City sought admission to practice law in the Virgin Islands without becoming residents. They challenged a rule requiring that a bar applicant demonstrate residence in the Virgin Islands for at least one year before admission and intent to continue to reside and practice law there. By statute Congress has made the Privileges and Immunities clause of Article IV applicable to the territory of the Virgin Islands. Relying on Supreme Court of New Hampshire v. Piper, 470 U.S. 274 (1985), and Supreme Court of Virginia v. Friedman, 487 U.S. 59 (1988), the Court invalidated the rule's residency requirements. Despite the distance and geographic isolation of the Virgin Islands, the Court held that associating local counsel was an adequate alternative to serve the "interest in assuring that counsel will be available on short notice for unscheduled proceedings" and the interest in managing congested court dockets without having to accommodate delays due to attorney travel. Nor was excluding nonresidents as a class justified to solve the problems of conflicting court appearances, keeping attorneys current in their knowledge of local law, or supervising the ethics of a nationwide bar membership. Finally, with respect to the requirement that active members of the bar be available to accept appointments to appear on behalf of indigent criminal defendants, the court found that nonresident attorneys could be required to share this burden but that making arrangements for substitute counsel when necessary, as an alternative to personal appearances, undercut the need for a "blanket exclusion of nonresidents." The Court concluded by saying:

a. See, generally, Varat, *State "Citizenship" and Interstate Equality,* 48 U.Chi. L.Rev. 487 (1981).

"When the Privileges and Immunities Clause was made part of our Constitution, commercial and legal exchange between the distant States of the Union was at least as unsophisticated as that which exists today between the Virgin Islands and the mainland United States. Nevertheless, our Founders, in their wisdom, thought it important to our sense of nationhood that each State be required to make a genuine effort to treat nonresidents on an equal basis with residents. By extending the Privileges and Immunities Clause to the Virgin Islands, Congress has made the same decision with respect to that Territory."

Chief Justice Rehnquist, joined by Justices White and O'Connor, dissented, in the belief that "the unique circumstances of legal practice in the Virgin Islands, as compared to the mainland States, could justify upholding [the] simple residency requirement even under [*Piper*'s view of the Privileges and Immunities Clause]."

B. THE TWENTY–FIRST AMENDMENT

Introduction. The relation of the Twenty–First Amendment to the commerce clause is quite different from that of Article IV, Section 2. Does the Amendment nullify the commerce clause as applied to the liquor trade?

Bacchus Imports, Ltd. v. Dias

468 U.S. 263, 104 S.Ct. 3049, 82 L.Ed.2d 200 (1984).

Justice White delivered the opinion of the Court.

Appellants challenge the constitutionality of the Hawaii Liquor Tax, which is a 20% excise tax imposed on sales of liquor at wholesale. Specifically at issue are exemptions from the tax for certain locally produced alcoholic beverages. The Supreme Court of Hawaii upheld the tax against challenges based upon the Equal Protection Clause, the Import–Export Clause, and the Commerce Clause. . . . We . . . reverse.

I

The Hawaii Liquor Tax was originally enacted in 1939 to defray the costs of police and other governmental services that the Hawaii legislature concluded had been increased due to the consumption of liquor. At its inception the statute contained no exemptions. However, because the legislature sought to encourage development of the Hawaiian liquor industry, it enacted an exemption for *okolehao* from May 17, 1971, until June 20, 1981, and an exemption for fruit wine from May 17, 1976, until June 30, 1981. . . .

Appellants . . . are liquor wholesalers who sell to licensed retailers. They sell the liquor at their wholesale price plus the 20% excise tax imposed by § 244–4, plus a one-half percent tax imposed by Hawaii Rev.Stat. § 237–13. . . . [T]he wholesalers . . . sought refunds of all taxes paid. Their complaint alleged that the Hawaii liquor tax was unconstitutional because it violates both the Import–Export Clause and the Commerce Clause of the United States Constitution. . . .

The Tax Appeal Court rejected both constitutional claims. On appeal, the Supreme Court of Hawaii affirmed the decision of the Tax Appeal Court and rejected an equal protection challenge as well. . . .

. . .

III

A cardinal rule of Commerce Clause jurisprudence is that "[n]o State, consistent with the Commerce Clause, may 'impose a tax which discriminates against interstate commerce ... by providing a direct commercial advantage to local business.' " Boston Stock Exchange v. State Tax Commission, 429 U.S. 318, 329 (1977) (quoting Northwestern States Portland Cement Co. v. Minnesota, 358 U.S. 450, 457 (1959). Despite the fact that the tax exemption here at issue seems clearly to discriminate on its face against interstate commerce by bestowing a commercial advantage on okolehao and pineapple wine, the State argues—and the Hawaii Supreme Court held—that there is no improper discrimination.

A

Much of the State's argument centers on its contention that okolehao and pineapple wine do not compete with the other products sold by the wholesalers....

... On the stipulated facts in this case, we are unwilling to conclude that no competition exists between the exempted and the nonexempted liquors.

B

. . .

... [W]e need not guess at the legislature's motivation, for it is undisputed that the purpose of the exemption was to aid Hawaiian industry. Likewise, the effect of the exemption is clearly discriminatory, in that it applies only to locally produced beverages, even though it does not apply to all such products. Consequently, as long as there is some competition between the locally produced exempt products and nonexempt products from outside the State, there is a discriminatory effect.

. . .

We therefore conclude that the Hawaii Liquor Tax exemption for okolehao and pineapple wine violated the Commerce Clause because it had both the purpose and effect of discriminating in favor of local products.

IV

The State argues in this Court that even if the tax exemption violates ordinary Commerce Clause principles, it is saved by the Twenty-first Amendment to the Constitution....

Despite broad language in some of the opinions of this Court written shortly after enactment of the Amendment,[13] more recently we have recognized the obscurity of the legislative history of § 2. See California Retail Liquor

---

13. For example, in State Board of Equalization v. Young's Market Co., 299 U.S. 59, 62 (1936), the Court stated:

"The plaintiffs ask us to limit this broad command. They request us to construe the Amendment as saying, in effect: The State may prohibit the importation of intoxicating liquors provided it prohibits the manufacture and sale within its borders; but if it permits such manufacture and sale, it must let imported liquors compete with the domestic on equal terms. To say that, would involve not a

construction of the Amendment, but a rewriting of it."

The Court went on to observe, however, that a high license fee for importation may "serve as an aid in policing the liquor traffic." Id., at 63.

See also Mahoney v. Joseph Triner Corp., 304 U.S. 401, 403 (1938) ("since the adoption of the Twenty-first Amendment, the equal protection clause is not applicable to imported intoxicating liquor"). Cf. Craig v. Boren, 429 U.S. 190 (1976).

Dealers Assn. v. Midcal Aluminum, Inc., 445 U.S. 97, 107 n. 10 (1980). No clear consensus concerning the meaning of the provision is apparent. Indeed, Senator Blaine, the Senate sponsor of the Amendment resolution, appears to have espoused varying interpretations. In reporting the view of the Senate Judiciary Committee, he said that the purpose of § 2 was "to restore to the States ... absolute control over interstate commerce affecting intoxicating liquors...." 76 Cong.Rec. 4143 (1933). On the other hand, he also expressed a narrower view: "So to assure the so-called dry States against the importation of intoxicating liquor into those States, it is proposed to write permanently into the Constitution a prohibition along that line." Id., at 4141.

It is by now clear that the Amendment did not entirely remove state regulation of alcoholic beverages from the ambit of the Commerce Clause. . . .

Approaching the case in this light, we are convinced that Hawaii's discriminatory tax cannot stand. Doubts about the scope of the Amendment's authorization notwithstanding, one thing is certain: The central purpose of the provision was not to empower States to favor local liquor industries by erecting barriers to competition. It is also beyond doubt that the Commerce Clause itself furthers strong federal interests in preventing economic Balkanization. . . . State laws that constitute mere economic protectionism are therefore not entitled to the same deference as laws enacted to combat the perceived evils of an unrestricted traffic in liquor. Here, the State does not seek to justify its tax on the ground that it was designed to promote temperance or to carry out any other purpose of the Twenty-first Amendment, but instead acknowledges that the purpose was "to promote a local industry." Consequently, because the tax violates a central tenet of the Commerce Clause but is not supported by any clear concern of the Twenty-first Amendment, we reject the State's belated claim based on the Amendment.

V

. . .

These refund issues, which are essentially issues of remedy for the imposition of a tax that unconstitutionally discriminated against interstate commerce, were not addressed by the state courts. Also, the Federal constitutional issues involved may well be intertwined with, or their consideration obviated by, issues of state law. Also, resolution of those issues, if required at all, may necessitate more of a record than so far has been made in this case. We are reluctant, therefore, to address them in the first instance. Accordingly, we reverse the judgment of the Supreme Court of Hawaii and remand for further proceedings not inconsistent with this opinion.

So ordered.

Justice Brennan took no part in the consideration or decision of this case.

Justice Stevens, with whom Justice Rehnquist and Justice O'Connor join, dissenting.

. . . I would affirm the judgment of the Supreme Court of Hawaii because the wholesalers' Commerce Clause claim is squarely foreclosed by the Twenty-first Amendment to the United States Constitution.

. . .

III

Today the Court, in essence, holds that the Hawaii tax is unconstitutional because it places a burden on intoxicating liquors that have been imported into Hawaii for use therein that is not imposed on liquors that are produced locally. As I read the text of the Amendment, it expressly authorizes this sort of burden. Moreover, as I read Justice Brandeis' opinion for the Court in the seminal case of State Board of Equalization v. Young's Market Co., 299 U.S. 59 (1936), the Court has squarely so decided.

In *Young's Market,* the Court upheld a California statute that imposed a license fee on the privilege of importing beer to any place in California. After noting that the statute would have been obviously unconstitutional prior to the Twenty-first Amendment, the Court explained that the Amendment enables a State to establish a local monopoly and to prevent or discourage competition from imported liquors. . . .

. . . .

As a matter of pure constitutional power, Hawaii may surely prohibit the importation of all intoxicating liquors. It seems clear to me that it may do so without prohibiting the local sale of liquors that are produced within the State. In other words, even though it seems unlikely that the okolehao lobby could persuade it to do so, the Hawaii Legislature surely has the power to create a local monopoly by prohibiting the sale of any other alcoholic beverage. If the State has the constitutional power to create a total local monopoly—thereby imposing the most severe form of discrimination on competing products originating elsewhere—I believe it may also engage in a less extreme form of discrimination that merely provides a special benefit, perhaps in the form of a subsidy or a tax exemption, for locally produced alcoholic beverages.

The Court's contrary conclusion is based on the "obscurity of the legislative history" of § 2. What the Court ignores is that it was argued in *Young's Market* that a "limitation of the broad language" of § 2 was "sanctioned by its history," but the Court, observing that the language of the Amendment was "clear," determined that it was unnecessary to consider the history, 299 U.S., at 63–64—the history which the Court today considers unclear. But now, according to the Court, the force of the Twenty-first Amendment contention in this case is diminished because the "central purpose of the provision was not to empower States to favor local liquor industries by erecting barriers to competition." It follows, according to the Court, that "state laws that constitute mere economic protectionism are not entitled to the same deference as laws enacted to combat the perceived evils of an unrestricted traffic in liquor." This is a totally novel approach to the Twenty-first Amendment. The question is not one of "deference," nor one of "central purposes;" the question is whether the provision in this case is an exercise of a power expressly conferred upon the States by the Constitution. It plainly is.

Accordingly, I respectfully dissent.

BROWN–FORMAN DISTILLERS CORP. v. NEW YORK STATE LIQUOR AUTHORITY, 476 U.S. 573 (1986). This case involved an attack on a New York law requiring liquor distillers to sell liquor in the state at a price no higher than the lowest price charged for similar sales in other states. The Court first held the law in violation of the Commerce Clause and then rejected New York's twenty–first amendment defense, saying:

"New York finally contends that the Twenty-first Amendment, which bans the importation or possession of intoxicating liquors into a State 'in violation of the laws thereof,' saves the ABC Law from invalidation under the Commerce

Clause. That Amendment gives the States wide latitude to regulate the importation and distribution of liquor within their territories, California Liquor Dealers Assn. v. Midcal Aluminum, Inc., 445 U.S. 97, 107 (1980). Therefore, New York argues, its ABC Law, which regulates the sale of alcoholic beverages within the State, is a valid exercise of the State's authority.

"It is well settled that the Twenty-first Amendment did not entirely remove state regulation of alcohol from the reach of the Commerce Clause. See Bacchus Imports, Ltd. v. Dias, 468 U.S. 263 (1984). Rather, the Twenty-first Amendment and the Commerce Clause 'each must be considered in light of the other and in the context of the issues and interests at stake in any concrete case.' Hostetter v. Idlewild Bon Voyage Liquor Corp., 377 U.S. 324, 332 (1964). Our task, then, is to reconcile the interests protected by the two constitutional provisions.

"New York has a valid constitutional interest in regulating sales of liquor within the territory of New York. Section 2 of the Twenty-first Amendment, however, speaks only to state regulation of the 'transportation or importation into any State ... for delivery or use therein' of alcoholic beverages. That Amendment, therefore, gives New York only the authority to control sales of liquor in New York, and confers no authority to control sales in other states. The Commerce Clause operates with full force whenever one State attempts to regulate the transportation and sale of alcoholic beverages destined for distribution and consumption in a foreign country, *Idlewild Bon Voyage Liquor Corp.,* supra, or another State. Our conclusion that New York has attempted to regulate sales in other States of liquor that will be consumed in other States therefore disposes of the Twenty-first Amendment issue.

"Moreover, New York's affirmation law may interfere with the ability of other States to exercise their own authority under the Twenty-first Amendment. Once a distiller has posted prices in New York, it is not free to lower them in another State, even in response to a regulatory directive by that State, without risking forfeiture of its license in New York. New York law, therefore, may force other States either to abandon regulatory goals or to deprive their citizens of the opportunity to purchase brands of liquor that are sold in New York. New York's reliance on the Twenty-first Amendment is therefore misplaced...."

Capital Cities Cable, Inc. v. Crisp

467 U.S. 691, 104 S.Ct. 2694, 81 L.Ed.2d 580 (1984).

Justice Brennan delivered the opinion of the Court.

The question presented in this case is whether Oklahoma may require cable television operators in that State to delete all advertisements for alcoholic beverages contained in the out-of-state signals that they retransmit by cable to their subscribers. Petitioners contend that Oklahoma's requirement abridges their rights under the First and Fourteenth Amendments and is pre-empted by federal law. Because we conclude that this state regulation is pre-empted, we reverse the judgment of the Court of Appeals for the Tenth Circuit and do not reach the First Amendment question.

. . . .

II

Petitioners and the FCC contend that the federal regulatory scheme for cable television systems administered by the Commission is intended to pre-empt any state regulation of the signals carried by cable system operators. Respondent apparently concedes that enforcement of the Oklahoma statute in this case conflicts with federal law, but argues that because the State's advertising ban was adopted pursuant to the broad powers to regulate the transportation and importation of intoxicating liquor reserved to the States by the Twenty-first Amendment, the statute should prevail notwithstanding the conflict with federal law. As in California Retail Liquor Dealers Assn. v. Midcal Aluminum, Inc., 445 U.S. 97 (1980), where we held that a California wine pricing program violated the Sherman Act notwithstanding the State's reliance upon the Twenty-first Amendment in establishing that system, we turn first before assessing the impact of the Twenty-first Amendment to consider whether the Oklahoma statute does in fact conflict with federal law.

. . .

III

Respondent contends that even if the Oklahoma advertising ban is invalid under normal pre-emption analysis, the fact that the ban was adopted pursuant to the Twenty-first Amendment rescues the statute from pre-emption. A similar claim was advanced in California Retail Liquor Dealers Assn. v. Midcal Aluminum, Inc., 445 U.S. 97 (1980). In that case, after finding that a California wine pricing program violated the Sherman Act, we considered whether § 2 of the Twenty-first Amendment, which reserves to the States certain power to regulate traffic in liquor, "permits California to countermand the congressional policy—adopted under the commerce power—in favor of competition." 445 U.S., at 106. Here, we must likewise consider whether § 2 permits Oklahoma to override the federal policy, as expressed in FCC rulings and regulations, in favor of promoting the widespread development of cable communication.

The States enjoy broad power under § 2 of the Twenty-first Amendment to regulate the importation and use of intoxicating liquor within their borders. Ziffrin, Inc. v. Reeves, 308 U.S. 132 (1939). At the same time, our prior cases have made clear that the Amendment does not license the States to ignore their obligations under other provisions of the Constitution. See, e.g., Larkin v. Grendel's Den, 459 U.S. 116, 122 n. 5 (1982); California v. LaRue, 409 U.S. 109, 115 (1972); Wisconsin v. Constantineau, 400 U.S. 433, 436 (1971); Department of Revenue v. James B. Beam Distilling Co., 377 U.S. 341, 345–346 (1964). Indeed, "[t]his Court's decisions . . . have confirmed that the Amendment primarily created an exception to the normal operation of the Commerce Clause." Craig v. Boren, 429 U.S. 190, 206 (1976). Thus, as the Court explained in Hostetter v. Idlewild Bon Voyage Liquor Corp., 377 U.S. 324 (1964), § 2 reserves to the States power to impose burdens on interstate commerce in intoxicating liquor that, absent the Amendment, would clearly be invalid under the Commerce Clause. Id., at 330; State Board of Equalization v. Young's Market Co., 299 U.S. 59, 62–63 (1936). We have cautioned, however, that "[t]o draw a conclusion . . . that the Twenty-first Amendment has somehow operated to 'repeal' the Commerce Clause wherever regulation of intoxicating liquors is concerned would . . . be an absurd oversimplification." Hostetter, supra, at 331–332. Notwithstanding the Amendment's broad grant of power to the States, therefore, the Federal Government plainly retains authority under the Commerce Clause to regulate even interstate commerce in liquor. . . .

In rejecting the claim that the Twenty-first Amendment ousted the Federal Government of all jurisdiction over interstate traffic in liquor, we have held that when a State has not attempted directly to regulate the sale or use of liquor within its borders—the core § 2 power—a conflicting exercise of federal authority may prevail. In *Hostetter,* for example, the Court found that in-state sales of intoxicating liquor intended to be used only in foreign countries could be made under the supervision of the federal Bureau of Customs, despite contrary state law, because the state regulation was not aimed at preventing unlawful use of alcoholic beverages within the state, but rather was designed "totally to prevent transactions carried on under the aegis of a law passed by Congress in the exercise of its explicit power under the Constitution to regulate commerce with foreign nations." Similarly, in *Midcal Aluminum,* supra, we found that "the Twenty-first Amendment provides no shelter for the violation of the Sherman Act caused by the State's wine pricing program," because the State's interest in promoting temperance through the program was not substantial and was therefore clearly outweighed by the important federal objectives of the Sherman Act.

Of course, our decisions in *Hostetter* and *Midcal Aluminum* were concerned only with conflicting state and federal efforts to regulate transactions involving liquor. In this case, by contrast, we must resolve a clash between an express federal decision to pre-empt all state regulation of cable signal carriage and a state effort to apply its ban on alcoholic beverage advertisements to wine commercials contained in out-of-state signals carried by cable systems. Nonetheless, the central question presented in those cases is essentially the same as the one before us here: whether the interests implicated by a state regulation are so closely related to the powers reserved by the Twenty-first Amendment that the regulation may prevail, notwithstanding that its requirements directly conflict with express federal policies. As in *Hostetter* and *Midcal Aluminum,* resolution of this question requires a "pragmatic effort to harmonize state and federal powers" within the context of the issues and interests at stake in each case. 445 U.S., at 109.

There can be little doubt that the comprehensive regulations developed over the past twenty years by the FCC to govern signal carriage by cable television systems reflect an important and substantial federal interest....

On the other hand, application of Oklahoma's advertising ban to out-of-state signals carried by cable operators in that State is designed principally to further the State's interest in discouraging consumption of intoxicating liquor. Although the District Court found that "consumption of alcoholic beverages in Oklahoma has increased substantially in the last 20 years despite the ban on advertising of such beverages," we may nevertheless accept Oklahoma's judgment that restrictions on liquor advertising represent at least a reasonable, albeit limited, means of furthering the goal of promoting temperance in the State. The modest nature of Oklahoma's interests may be further illustrated by noting that Oklahoma has chosen not to press its campaign against alcoholic beverage advertising on all fronts. For example, the State permits both print and broadcast commercials for beer, as well as advertisements for all alcoholic beverages contained in newspapers, magazines and other publications printed outside of the State. The ban at issue in this case is directed only at wine commercials that occasionally appear on out-of-state signals carried by cable operators. By their own terms, therefore, the State's regulatory aims in this area are narrow. Although a state regulatory scheme obviously need not amount to a comprehensive attack on the problems of alcohol consumption in order to constitute a valid exercise of state power under the Twenty-first Amendment, the selective approach Oklahoma has taken toward liquor advertising suggests limits on the substantiality of the interests it asserts here. In contrast to state regulations governing the conditions under which liquor may be imported or sold within the state, therefore, the application of Oklahoma's advertising ban to the importation of distant signals by cable television operators engages only indirectly the central power reserved by § 2 of the Twenty-first Amendment—that of exercising "control over whether to permit importation or sale of liquor and how to structure the liquor distribution system." *Midcal Aluminum,* 445 U.S., at 110.

When this limited interest is measured against the significant interference with the federal objective of ensuring widespread availability of diverse cable services throughout the United States—an objective that will unquestionably be frustrated by strict enforcement of the Oklahoma statute—it is clear that the state's interest is not of the same stature as the goals identified in the FCC's rulings and regulations. As in *Midcal Aluminum,* therefore, we hold that when, as here, a state regulation squarely conflicts with the accomplishment and execution of the full purposes of federal law, and the state's central power under the Twenty-first Amendment of regulating the times, places, and manner under which liquor may be imported and sold is not directly implicated, the balance between state and federal power tips decisively in favor of the federal law, and enforcement of the state statute is barred by the Supremacy Clause.[16]

IV

We conclude that the application of Oklahoma's alcoholic beverage advertising ban to out-of-state signals carried by cable operators in that State is pre-empted by federal law and that the Twenty-first Amendment does not save the regulation from pre-emption. The judgment of the Court of Appeals is

Reversed.

324 LIQUOR CORP. v. DUFFY, 479 U.S. 335 (1987). The Court held that a New York statute requiring retailers to charge at least 112 percent of the posted wholesale price for liquor, but permitting wholesalers to sell to retailers at less than the posted price, violated the Sherman Act. It then addressed the question whether the twenty–first amendment immunized the state law from the Sherman Act, saying:

"The States' Twenty-first Amendment powers, though broad, are circumscribed by other provisions of the Constitution. See Larkin v. Grendel's Den, Inc., 459 U.S. 116, 122, n. 5 (1982) (Establishment Clause); Craig v. Boren, 429 U.S. 190, 204–209 (1976) (Equal Protection Clause); Wisconsin v. Constantineau, 400 U.S. 433, 436 (1971) (procedural due process); Department of Revenue v. James Beam Co., 377 U.S. 341, 345–346 (1964) (Export–Import Clause). Although § 2 directly qualifies the federal commerce power, the Court has rejected the view that 'the Twenty-first Amendment has somehow operated to "repeal" the Commerce Clause wherever regulation of intoxicating liquors is concerned.' Hostetter v. Idlewild Liquor Corp., 377 U.S. 324 331–332 (1964). Instead the Court has engaged in a 'pragmatic effort to harmonize state and federal powers.' *Midcal,* supra, 445 U.S., at 109. The question in each case is whether the interests implicated by a state regulation are so closely related to the powers reserved by the Twenty-first Amendment that the regulation may prevail, notwithstanding that its requirements directly conflict with express federal policies. Capital Cities Cable, Inc. v. Crisp, 467 U.S. 691, 714 (1984)."

---

16. Because we have resolved the pre-emption and Twenty-first Amendment issues in petitioners' favor, we need not consider the additional question whether Oklahoma's advertising ban constitutes an invalid restriction on protected commercial speech, and we therefore express no view on that issue.

The Court then went on to find that there were no adequate state interests protected here to override the federal statute. Two justices dissented.

NORTH DAKOTA v. UNITED STATES, 495 U.S. 423 (1990). North Dakota requires all persons bringing liquor into the state to report all shipments and returns. It allows out–of–state distillers, who normally may sell only to licensed North Dakota wholesalers but not retailers, to sell liquor directly to federal enclaves within the state. When they do so, however, the distillers must label each item, indicating that the liquor is for domestic consumption only within the federal enclave. With no majority opinion, the court upheld both the reporting and the labeling regulations over the objections of the United States that, as applied to sales of liquor destined for federal enclaves—in this case military bases over which the United States and North Dakota exercise concurrent jurisdiction—the regulations violate the federal government's constitutional immunity from state regulation and in any event are preempted by a 1986 federal procurement statute directing that liquor be obtained from the most competitive source.

Justice Stevens, for a plurality of four, acknowledged that prior cases involving state power to pass liquor control regulations burdening the Federal Government had "concluded that [a] State had no authority to regulate in an area or over a transaction that fell outside of its jurisdiction." Still, other cases "made clear that the States have the power to control shipments of liquor during their passage through their territory and to take appropriate steps to prevent the unlawful diversion of liquor into its regulated intrastate market."

"The two North Dakota regulations fall within the core of the State's power under the Twenty-first Amendment. In the interest of promoting temperance, ensuring orderly market conditions, and raising revenue, the State has established a comprehensive system for the distribution of liquor within its borders. That system is unquestionably legitimate. . . . [The reporting and labeling requirements] are necessary components of the regulatory regime. . . . The risk of diversion into the retail market and disruption of the liquor distribution system is . . . both substantial and real. . . . Given the special protection afforded to state liquor control policies by the Twenty-first Amendment, [the regulations] are supported by a strong presumption of validity and should not be set aside lightly."

Armed with that presumption, Justice Stevens found no intergovernmental immunity violation, because neither regulation regulated the United States directly or discriminated against it or those with whom it deals. As for the pre-emption claim, although "Congress has the power to confer immunity from state regulation on government suppliers beyond that conferred by the Constitution alone, . . . even when the state regulation is enacted pursuant to the State's powers under the Twenty-first Amendment[,] when the Court is asked to set aside a regulation at the core of [those] powers . . . it must proceed with particular care." He then concluded that "Congress has not here spoken with sufficient clarity to pre-empt North Dakota's attempt to protect its liquor distribution system."

Justice Scalia concurred in the judgment, taking the position that the Twenty–First Amendment abolished the Federal Government's immunity from state liquor import regulation. Hence the State could have required that *all* liquor sold in-state be purchased from a licensed in-state wholesaler, and the fact that North Dakota gave the "Federal Government a choice between purchasing label-free bottles from in-state wholesalers or purchasing labelled bottles from out-of-state distillers, . . . an option that no other retailer in the

State enjoys[,]" negated any viable claim of discrimination against the Federal Government.

Four Justices agreed that the nondiscriminatory reporting requirement was lawful but would have held the labelling regulation invalid because it "substantially obstructs federal operations, and it discriminates against the Federal Government and its chosen business partners." These four also disagreed with Justice Scalia, arguing that the Twenty–First Amendment did not empower the States to regulate liquor shipments to military bases over which the Federal Government and a State share concurrent jurisdiction.

SECTION 6. PREEMPTION OF STATE LEGISLATION BY FEDERAL LEGISLATION—THE IMPACT OF THE SUPREMACY CLAUSE

Introduction. We first met the preemption problem in Gibbons v. Ogden, supra p. 148, where the Court held the New York grant of a monopoly on a steamboat route to be inconsistent with the grant of a federal license to another steamboat to operate on the route. Marshall stated the ultimate principle— should there be a "collision" between an Act of Congress passed pursuant to the Constitution and a state statute, the state law "must yield to the law of Congress."

While simple to state, the principle is difficult to apply. The Supreme Court has applied a variety of verbal formulas over the years in seeking to determine when there is such a "collision" that the state law must fall. In many early cases it took a broad view of the subject, suggesting that merely by regulating in an area Congress should be taken as having "occupied the field" and determined that the states should not regulate in that field. See, e.g., Napier v. Atlantic Coast Line R. Co., 272 U.S. 605 (1926), in which the Court held that by granting power to the Interstate Commerce Commission to prescribe rules governing the safety of locomotives, Congress "intended to occupy the field" and state statutes requiring cab curtains and particular types of firebox doors were invalid even though the Commission had not issued any rules relating to cab curtains and firebox doors.

More recently the Court has been less likely to imply Congressional intent to supersede state laws in the absence of fairly direct conflict. In Rice v. Santa Fe Elevator Corp., 331 U.S. 218, 230 (1947), e.g., the Court said that when Congress has legislated "in a field which the States have traditionally occupied," we "start with the assumption that the historic police powers of the States were not to be superseded by the Federal Act unless that was the clear and manifest purpose of Congress. . . . Such a purpose may be evidenced in several ways. The scheme of federal regulation may be so pervasive as to make reasonable the inference that Congress left no room for the States to supplement it. . . . Or the Act of Congress may touch a field in which the federal interest is so dominant that the federal system will be assumed to preclude enforcement of state laws on the same subject. Likewise, the object sought to be obtained by the federal law and the character of obligations imposed by it may reveal the same purpose. . . . Or the state policy may produce a result inconsistent with the objective of the federal statute. . . . It is often a perplexing question whether Congress has precluded state action or by the choice of selective regulatory measures has left the police power of the States undisturbed except as the state and federal regulations collide."

A useful law review note—*Pre-emption as a Preferential Ground: A New Canon of Construction,* 12 Stan.L.Rev. 308 (1959), Selected Essays on Constitutional Law, 1938–1962 (1963), 310—contains the following paragraph:

> "[T]he Court has adopted the same weighing of interests approach in pre-emption cases that it uses to determine whether a state law unjustifiably burdens interstate commerce. In a number of situations the Court has invalidated statutes on the pre-emption ground when it appeared that the state laws sought to favor local economic interests at the expense of the interstate market. On the other hand, when the Court has been satisfied that valid local interests, such as those in safety or in the reputable operation of local business, outweigh the restrictive effect on interstate commerce, the Court has rejected the pre-emption argument and allowed state regulation to stand...."

The case that follows illustrates the Court's approach to pre-emption cases. It is relevant to note that federal regulation may present pre-emption problems whether or not state law regulates interstate commerce. See, e.g., DeCanas v. Bica, 424 U.S. 351 (1976), involving an alleged conflict between a California statute regulating employment of illegal aliens and the federal immigration laws.

Gade v. National Solid Wastes Management Association

505 U.S. 88, 112 S.Ct. 2374, 120 L.Ed.2d 73 (1992).

Justice O'Connor announced the judgment of the Court and delivered an opinion, Parts I, III, and IV of which represent the views of the Court, and Part II of which is joined by The Chief Justice, Justice White, and Justice Scalia.

In 1988, the Illinois General Assembly enacted the Hazardous Waste Crane and Hoisting Equipment Operators Licensing Act ... and the Hazardous Waste Laborers Licensing Act.... The stated purpose of the acts is both "to promote job safety" and "to protect life, limb and property." ... [W]e consider whether these "dual impact" statutes, which protect both workers and the general public, are pre-empted by the federal Occupational Safety and Health Act of 1970 ... (OSH Act), and the standards promulgated ... by the Occupational Safety and Health Administration (OSHA).

I

. . .

... OSHA ... promulgated regulations on "Hazardous Waste Operations and Emergency Response," including detailed regulations on worker training requirements.... The OSHA regulations require ... that workers engaged in an activity that may expose them to hazardous wastes receive a minimum of 40 hours of instruction off the site, and a minimum of three days actual field experience under the supervision of a trained supervisor.... On-site managers and supervisors directly responsible for hazardous waste operations must receive the same initial training as general employees, plus at least eight additional hours of specialized training on various health and safety programs.... Employees and supervisors are required to receive eight hours of refresher training annually....

In 1988 ... Illinois enacted the licensing acts at issue here. The laws are designated as acts "in relation to environmental protection," and their stated

aim is to protect both employees and the general public by licensing hazardous waste equipment operators and laborers working at certain facilities. Both acts require a license applicant to provide a certified record of at least 40 hours of training under an approved program conducted within Illinois, to pass a written examination, and to complete an annual refresher course of at least eight hours of instruction.... In addition, applicants for a hazardous waste crane operator's license must submit "a certified record showing operation of equipment used in hazardous waste handling for a minimum of 4,000 hours."
. . .

. . .

. . . [T]he Association [sued] . . . to enjoin . . . enforc[ement of] the Illinois licensing acts, claiming [they] were pre-empted by the OSH Act and OSHA regulations and that they violated the Commerce Clause of the United States Constitution.... [T]he District Court held [the state] acts . . . not pre-empted because each protected public safety in addition to promoting job safety.... [It] invalidated the requirement that applicants for a hazardous waste license be trained "within Illinois" on the ground that the provision did not contribute to Illinois's stated purpose of protecting public safety [and] declined to consider the Association's Commerce Clause challenge for lack of ripeness....

. . . [The] Court of Appeals . . . affirmed in part and reversed in part....

II

Before addressing the scope of the OSH Act's pre-emption of dual impact state regulations, we consider petitioner's threshold argument . . . that the Act does not pre-empt nonconflicting state regulations at all. "[T]he question whether a certain state action is pre-empted by federal law is one of congressional intent. 'The purpose of Congress is the ultimate touchstone.' " . . . "To discern Congress' intent we examine the explicit statutory language and the structure and purpose of the statute." . . .

In the OSH Act, Congress endeavored "to assure so far as possible every working man and woman in the Nation safe and healthful working conditions." . . . To that end, Congress authorized . . . mandatory occupational safety and health standards applicable to all businesses affecting interstate commerce, . . . and thereby brought the Federal Government into a field that traditionally had been occupied by the States. Federal regulation of the workplace was not intended to be all-encompassing, however. First, Congress expressly saved two areas from federal pre-emption. [One is state worker compensation laws. In addition,] Section 18(a) provides that the Act does not "prevent any State agency or court from asserting jurisdiction under State law over any occupational safety or health issue with respect to which no [federal] standard is in effect." . . .

Congress . . . also, in § 18(b) of the Act, gave the States the option of preempting federal regulation entirely. That section provides: . . .

"Any State which, at any time, desires to assume responsibility for development and enforcement therein of occupational safety and health standards relating to any occupational safety or health issue with respect to which a Federal standard has been promulgated [by the Secretary under the OSH Act] shall submit a State plan for the development of such standards and their enforcement." . . .

About half the States have received the Secretary's approval for their own state plans as described in this provision.... Illinois is not among them.

[We agree with] the Court of Appeals . . . that § 18(b) "unquestionably" pre-empts any state law or regulation that establishes an occupational health and safety standard on an issue for which OSHA has already promulgated a standard, unless the State has obtained the Secretary's approval for its own plan. . . .

Pre-emption may be either expressed or implied, and "is compelled whether Congress' command is explicitly stated in the statute's language or implicitly contained in its structure and purpose." Jones v. Rath Packing Co., 430 U.S. 519, 525 . . . (1977); . . . . Absent explicit pre-emptive language, we have recognized at least two types of implied pre-emption: field pre-emption, where the scheme of federal regulation is "so pervasive as to make reasonable the inference that Congress left no room for the States to supplement it," . . . (quoting Rice v. Santa Fe Elevator Corp., 331 U.S. 218, 230 . . . (1947)), and conflict pre-emption, where "compliance with both federal and state regulations is a physical impossibility," Florida Lime & Avocado Growers, Inc. v. Paul, 373 U.S. 132, 142–143 . . . (1963), or where state law "stands as an obstacle to the accomplishment and execution of the full purposes and objectives of Congress." Hines v. Davidowitz, 312 U.S. 52, 67 . . . (1941); . . . .

Our ultimate task in any pre-emption case is to determine whether state regulation is consistent with the structure and purpose of the statute as a whole. Looking to "the provisions of the whole law, and to its object and policy," . . . we hold that nonapproved state regulation of occupational safety and health issues for which a federal standard is in effect is impliedly pre-empted as in conflict with the full purposes and objectives of the OSH Act. *Hines v. Davidowitz,* supra. The design of the statute persuades us that Congress intended to subject employers and employees to only one set of regulations, be it federal or state, and that the only way a State may regulate an OSHA-regulated occupational safety and health issue is pursuant to an approved state plan that displaces the federal standards.

The principal indication that Congress intended to pre-empt state law is § 18(b)'s statement that a State "shall" submit a plan if it wishes to "assume responsibility" for "development and enforcement . . . of occupational safety and health standards relating to any occupational safety or health issue with respect to which a Federal standard has been promulgated." The unavoidable implication of this provision is that a State may not enforce its own occupational safety and health standards without obtaining the Secretary's approval, and petitioner concedes that § 18(b) would require an approved plan if Illinois wanted to "assume responsibility" for the regulation of occupational safety and health within the State. Petitioner contends, however, that an approved plan is necessary only if the State wishes completely to replace the federal regulations, not merely to supplement them. . . .

Petitioner's interpretation . . . is not tenable in light of the OSH Act's surrounding provisions. . . . The OSH Act as a whole evidences Congress' intent to avoid subjecting workers and employers to duplicative regulation; a State may develop an occupational safety and health program tailored to its own needs, but only if it is willing completely to displace the applicable federal regulations.

Cutting against petitioner's interpretation of § 18(b) is the language of § 18(a), which saves from pre-emption any state law regulating an occupational safety and health issue with respect to which no federal standard is in effect. . . . [P]reservation of state authority in the absence of a federal standard presupposes a background pre-emption of all state occupational safety and health standards whenever a federal standard governing the same issue is in effect.

Our understanding of the implications of § 18(b) is likewise bolstered by § 18(c) of the Act, ... which sets forth the conditions that must be satisfied before the Secretary can approve a plan submitted by a State under subsection (b). State standards that affect interstate commerce will be approved only if they "are required by compelling local conditions" and "do not unduly burden interstate commerce." ... If a State could supplement federal regulations without undergoing the § 18(b) approval process, then the protections that § 18(c) offers to interstate commerce would easily be undercut. It would make little sense to impose such a condition on state programs intended to supplant federal regulation and not those that merely supplement it: the burden on interstate commerce remains the same.

Section 18(f) also confirms our view. . . . That provision gives the Secretary the authority to withdraw her approval of a state plan. . . . Once approval is withdrawn, the plan "cease[s] to be in effect". . . . Under petitioner's reading of § 18(b), § 18(f) should permit the continued exercise of state jurisdiction over purely "supplemental" and nonconflicting standards. Instead, § 18(f) assumes that the State loses the power to enforce all of its occupational safety and health standards once approval is withdrawn.

The same assumption of exclusive federal jurisdiction in the absence of an approved state plan is apparent in the transitional provisions contained in § 18(h) of the Act. . . . Section 18(h) authorized the Secretary of Labor, during the first two years after passage of the Act, to enter into an agreement with a State by which the State would be permitted to continue to enforce its own occupational health and safety standards for two years or until final action was taken by the Secretary pursuant to § 18(b), whichever was earlier. Significantly, § 18(h) does not say that such an agreement is only necessary when the State wishes fully to supplant federal standards. Indeed, the original Senate version of the provision would have allowed a State to enter into such an agreement only when it wished to enforce standards "not in conflict with Federal occupational health and safety standards," a category which included "any State occupational health and safety standard which provides for more stringent health and safety regulations than do the Federal standards." ... Although that provision was eliminated from the final draft of the bill, thereby allowing agreements for the temporary enforcement of less stringent state standards, it is indicative of the congressional understanding that a State was required to enter into a transitional agreement even when its standards were stricter than federal standards. The Secretary's contemporaneous interpretation of § 18(h) also expresses that understanding. . . .

... Our review of the Act persuades us that Congress sought to promote occupational safety and health while at the same time avoiding duplicative, and possibly counterproductive, regulation. It thus established a system of uniform federal occupational health and safety standards, but gave States the option of pre-empting federal regulations by developing their own occupational safety and health programs. In addition, Congress offered the States substantial federal grant monies to assist them in developing their own programs. . . . To allow a State selectively to "supplement" certain federal regulations with ostensibly nonconflicting standards would be inconsistent with this federal scheme of establishing uniform federal standards, on the one hand, and encouraging States to assume full responsibility for development and enforcement of their own OSH programs, on the other.

We cannot accept petitioner's argument that the OSH Act does not pre-empt nonconflicting state laws because those laws, like the Act, are designed to promote worker safety. In determining whether state law "stands as an obstacle" to the full implementation of a federal law, ... "it is not enough to say that the ultimate goal of both federal and state law" is the same.... "A state law also is pre-empted if it interferes with the methods by which the federal statute was designed to reach th[at] goal." ... The OSH Act does not foreclose a State from enacting its own laws to advance the goal of worker safety, but it does restrict the ways in which it can do so. If a State wishes to regulate an issue of worker safety for which a federal standard is in effect, its only option is to obtain the prior approval of the Secretary of Labor, as described in § 18 of the Act.[2]

III

... We now consider whether a dual impact law can be an "occupational safety and health standard" subject to pre-emption under the Act.

... [P]etitioner asserts that if the state legislature articulates a purpose other than (or in addition to) workplace health and safety, then the OSH Act loses its pre-emptive force. We disagree.

Although "part of the pre-empted field is defined by reference to the purpose of the state law in question, ... another part of the field is defined by the state law's actual effect." ... In assessing the impact of a state law on the federal scheme, we have refused to rely solely on the legislature's professed purpose and have looked as well to the effects of the law. As we explained over two decades ago:

"We can no longer adhere to the aberrational doctrine ... that state law may frustrate the operation of federal law as long as the state legislature in passing its law had some purpose in mind other than one of frustration. Apart from the fact that it is at odds with the approach taken in nearly all our Supremacy Clause cases, such a doctrine would enable state legislatures to nullify nearly all unwanted federal legislation by simply publishing a legislative committee report articulating some state interest or policy—other than frustration of the federal objective—that would be tangentially furthered by the proposed state law.... [A]ny state legislation which frustrates the full effectiveness of federal law is rendered invalid by the Supremacy Clause." Perez v. Campbell, 402 U.S., at 651–652....

---

2. Justice Kennedy, while agreeing on the pre-emptive scope of the OSH Act, finds that its pre-emption is express rather than implied.... In the end, even Justice Kennedy finds express pre-emption by relying on the negative "inference" of § 18(b), which governs when *state* law will pre-empt *federal* law. We cannot agree that the negative implications of the text, although ultimately dispositive to our own analysis, *expressly* address the issue of federal pre-emption of state law. We therefore prefer to place this case in the category of implied pre-emption. Although we have chosen to use the term "conflict" pre-emption, we could as easily have stated that the promulgation of a federal safety and health standard "pre-empts the field" for any nonapproved state law regulating the same safety and health issue.... ("[F]ield pre-emption may be understood as a species of conflict pre-emption: A state law that falls within a pre-empted field conflicts with Congress' intent (either express or plainly implied) to exclude state regulation").... Frequently, the pre-emptive "label" we choose will carry with it substantive implications for the scope of pre-emption. In this case, however, it does not. Our disagreement with Justice Kennedy as to whether the OSH Act's pre-emptive effect is labelled "express" or "implied" is less important than our agreement that the implications of the text of the statute evince a congressional intent to pre-empt nonapproved state regulations when a federal standard is in effect.

[A] dual impact state regulation cannot avoid OSH Act pre-emption simply because the regulation serves several objectives rather than one.... The key question is thus at what point the state regulation sufficiently interferes with federal regulation that it should be deemed pre-empted under the Act.

... [T]he Court of Appeals ... [held] that, in the absence of the approval of the Secretary, the OSH Act pre-empts all state law that "constitutes, in a direct, clear and substantial way, regulation of worker health and safety." ... We agree that this is the appropriate standard.... On the other hand, state laws of general applicability (such as laws regarding traffic safety or fire safety) that do not conflict with OSHA standards and that regulate the conduct of workers and non-workers alike would generally not be pre-empted. Although some laws of general applicability may have a "direct and substantial" effect on worker safety, they cannot fairly be characterized as "occupational" standards, because they regulate workers simply as members of the general public.... [Here,] a law directed at workplace safety is not saved from pre-emption simply because the State can demonstrate some additional effect outside of the workplace.

In sum, a state law requirement that directly, substantially, and specifically regulates occupational safety and health is an occupational safety and health standard within the meaning of the Act. That such a law may also have a nonoccupational impact does not render it any less of an occupational standard for purposes of pre-emption analysis....

IV

We recognize that "the States have a compelling interest in the practice of professions within their boundaries, and that as part of their power to protect the public health, safety, and other valid interests they have broad power to establish standards for licensing practitioners and regulating the practice of professions." ... But under the Supremacy Clause ... "any state law, however clearly within a State's acknowledged power, which interferes with or is contrary to federal law, must yield." ... We therefore reject petitioner's argument that the State's interest in licensing various occupations can save from OSH Act pre-emption those provisions that directly and substantially affect workplace safety.

... Because neither of the OSH Act's saving provisions are implicated, and because Illinois does not have an approved state plan under § 18(b), the state licensing acts are pre-empted by the OSH Act to the extent they establish occupational safety and health standards for training those who work with hazardous wastes....

Justice Kennedy, concurring in part and concurring in the judgment.

Though I concur in the Court's judgment and with the ultimate conclusion that the state law is pre-empted, I would find express pre-emption from the terms of the federal statute. I cannot agree that we should denominate this case as one of implied pre-emption. The contrary view of the plurality is based on an undue expansion of our implied pre-emption jurisprudence....

. . .

Our decisions establish that a high threshold must be met if a state law is to be pre-empted for conflicting with the purposes of a federal Act.... In my view, this type of pre-emption should be limited to state laws which impose prohibitions or obligations which are in direct contradiction to Congress' primary objectives, as conveyed with clarity in the federal legislation.

... Any potential tension between a scheme of federal regulation of the workplace and a concurrent, supplementary state scheme would not ... rise to the level of "actual conflict" described in our pre-emption cases. Absent the express provisions of § 18 ..., I would not say that state supplementary regulation conflicts with the purposes of the OSH Act, or that it "interferes with the methods by which the federal statute was designed to reach [its] goal."

The plurality's broad view of actual conflict pre-emption is contrary to two basic principles of our pre-emption jurisprudence. First, we begin "with the assumption that the historic police powers of the States [are] not to be superseded ... unless that was the clear and manifest purpose of Congress," Rice v. Santa Fe Elevator Corp., ... (1947). Second, "the purpose of Congress is the ultimate touchstone" in all pre-emption cases.... A free-wheeling judicial inquiry into whether a state statute is in tension with federal objectives would undercut the principle that it is Congress rather than the courts that pre-empts state law.

Nonetheless, I agree with the Court ... [, because its] result is mandated by the express terms of § 18(b) of the OSH Act. It follows ... that the pre-emptive scope of the Act is also limited to the language of the statute. When the existence of pre-emption is evident from the statutory text, our inquiry must begin and end with the statutory framework itself.

... Though most statutes creating express pre-emption contain an explicit statement to that effect, a statement admittedly lacking in § 18(b), we have never required any particular magic words in our express pre-emption cases. Our task in all pre-emption cases is to enforce the "clear and manifest purpose of Congress." ... We have held, in express pre-emption cases, that Congress' intent must be divined from the language, structure, and purposes of the statute as a whole.... The language of the OSH statute sets forth a scheme in light of which the provisions of § 18 must be interpreted, and from which the express pre-emption that displaces state law follows.

As the plurality's analysis amply demonstrates, Congress has addressed the issue of pre-emption in the OSH Act.... The most reasonable inference from th[e] language [of § 18(b)]is that when a State does not submit and secure approval of a state plan, it may not enforce occupational safety and health standards in that area. Any doubt that this is what Congress intended disappears when subsection (b) is considered in conjunction with subsections (a), (c), and (f).... Unartful though the language of § 18(b) may be, the structure and language of § 18 leave little doubt that ... Congress intended to pre-empt supplementary state regulation of an occupational safety and health issue with respect to which a federal standard exists.

... The dissent would give the States, rather than the Federal Government, the power to decide whether as to any particular occupational safety and health issue there will exist a single or dual regulatory scheme. Under this theory the State may choose exclusive federal jurisdiction by not regulating; or exclusive state jurisdiction by submitting a state plan; or dual regulation by adopting supplementary rules, as Illinois did here. That position undermines the authority of OSHA in many respects. For example, § 18(c)(2) of the OSH Act allows OSHA to disapprove state plans which "unduly burden interstate commerce." The dissent would eviscerate this important administrative mechanism by allowing the States to sidestep OSHA's authority through the mechanism of supplementary regulation. Furthermore, concurrent state and federal jurisdiction might interfere with the enforcement of the federal regulations without creating a situation where compliance with both schemes is a physical impossibility, which the dissent would require for pre-emption. I would not attribute to Congress the intent to create such a hodge-podge scheme of authority. My views in this regard are confirmed by the fact that OSHA has [consistently] ... viewed § 18 as providing it with exclusive jurisdiction in areas where it issues a standard.... [W]hile the dissent may be correct that as a theoretical matter the separate provisions of § 18 may be reconciled with allowing concurrent jurisdiction, it is neither a natural nor a sound reading of the statutory scheme.

The necessary implication of finding express pre-emption in this case is that the pre-emptive scope of the OSH Act is defined by the language of § 18(b). Because this provision requires federal approval of state occupational safety and health standards alone, only state laws fitting within the description are pre-empted. For that reason I agree with the Court that state laws of general applicability are not pre-empted. I also agree that "a state law requirement that directly, substantially, and specifically regulates occupational safety and health is an occupational safety and health standard within the meaning of the Act," and therefore falls within the scope of pre-emption. So-called "dual impact" state regulations which meet this standard are pre-empted by the OSH Act, regardless of any additional purpose the law may serve, or effect the law may have, outside the workplace. As a final matter, I agree that the Illinois Acts are not saved because they operate through a licensing mechanism rather than through direct regulation of the workplace. I therefore join all but Part II of the Court's opinion, and concur in the judgment of the Court.

Justice Souter, with whom Justice Blackmun, Justice Stevens, and Justice Thomas join, dissenting.

... In light of our rule that federal pre-emption of state law is only to be found in a clear congressional purpose to supplant exercises of the States' traditional police powers, the text of the Act fails to support the Court's conclusion.

I

. . .

... [W]hether the pre-emption at issue is described as occupation of each narrow field in which a federal standard has been promulgated, as pre-emption of those regulations that conflict with the federal objective of single regulation, or, as Justice Kennedy describes it, as express pre-emption, the key is congressional intent, and I find the language of the statute insufficient to demonstrate an intent to pre-empt state law in this way.

II

Analysis begins with the presumption that "Congress did not intend to displace state law." Maryland v. Louisiana, 451 U.S. 725, 746 ... (1981)....
"... This assumption provides assurance that the 'federal-state balance,' ... will not be disturbed unintentionally by Congress or unnecessarily by the courts...." *Jones, ...* If the statute's terms can be read sensibly not to have a pre-emptive effect, the presumption controls and no pre-emption may be inferred.

III

At first blush, respondent's strongest argument might seem to rest on § 18(a) of the Act....

. . . The plurality reasons that there must be pre-emption . . . when there is a federal standard in effect, else § 18(a) would be rendered superfluous because "there is no possibility of conflict where there is no federal regulation."

. . . The plurality ignores the possibility that the provision simply rules out field pre-emption and is otherwise entirely compatible with the possibility that pre-emption will occur only when actual conflict between a federal regulation and a state rule renders compliance with both impossible. . . . Unlike the case where field pre-emption occurs, the provision tells us, absence of a federal standard leaves a State free to do as it will on the issue. . . . [T]he provision is perfectly consistent with the conclusion that as long as compliance with both a federal standard and a state regulation is not physically impossible, . . . each standard shall be enforceable. If, indeed, the presumption against pre-emption means anything, § 18(a) must be read in just this way.

Respondent also relies on § 18(b). . . .

. . . [I]n actually providing a mechanism for a State to "assume responsibility" for an issue with respect to which a federal standard has been promulgated (that is, to pre-empt federal law), § 18(b) is far from pre-emptive of anything adopted by the States. Its heading . . . speaks expressly of the "development and enforcement of State standards to preempt applicable Federal standards." The provision does not in any way provide that absent such state pre-emption of federal rules, the State may not even supplement the federal standards with consistent regulations of its own. . . . The provision . . . makes perfect sense on the assumption that a dual regulatory scheme is permissible but subject to state pre-emption if the State wishes to shoulder enough of the federal mandate to gain approval of a plan.

Nor does the provision setting out conditions for the Secretary's approval of a plan indicate that a state regulation on an issue federally addressed is never enforceable unless incorporated in a plan so approved. . . . Respondent argues, and the plurality concludes, that if state regulations were not preempted, . . . States acting independently could enforce regulations that did burden interstate commerce unduly. . . . But this simply does not follow. The subsection puts a limit on the Secretary's authority to approve a plan that burdens interstate commerce, thus capping the discretion that might otherwise have been read into the congressional delegation of authority to the Secretary to approve state plans. From this restriction applying only to the Secretary's federal authority it is clearly a non sequitur to conclude that pre-emption must have been intended to avoid the equally objectionable undue burden that independent state regulation might otherwise impose. Quite the contrary; the dormant Commerce Clause can take care of that, without any need to assume pre-emption.

The final provision that arguably suggests pre-emption merely by promulgation of a federal standard is § 18(h). . . .

. . . All it necessarily means is that the Secretary could agree to permit the State for a limited time to enforce whatever State regulations would otherwise have been pre-empted, as would have been true when they actually so conflicted with the federal standard that an employer could not comply with them and still comply with federal law as well. Thus, in the case of a State wishing to submit a plan, the provision as I read it would have allowed for the possibility of just one transition, from the pre-Act state law to the post-Act state plan. Read as the Court reads it, however, employers and employees in such a State would have been subjected first to state law on a given issue; then, after promulgation of a federal standard, to that standard; and then, after approval of the plan, to a new state regime. One enforced readjustment would have been better than two, and the statute is better read accordingly.[1]

IV

... The Act does not, in so many words, pre-empt all state regulation of issues on which federal standards have been promulgated, and respondent's contention at oral argument that reading subsections (a), (b), and (h) could leave no other "logical" conclusion but one of pre-emption is wrong. Each provision can be read consistently with the others without any implication of pre-emptive intent.... They are in fact just as consistent with a purpose and objective to permit overlapping state and federal regulation as with one to guarantee that employers and employees would be subjected to only one regulatory regime.... I can only conclude that, as long as compliance with federally promulgated standards does not render obedience to Illinois' regulations impossible, the enforcement of the state law is not prohibited by the Supremacy Clause....

PREEMPTION ILLUSTRATIONS

Three decisions issued in the year 2000, each in a different context, held state law preempted by federal. Taken together, the cases illustrate modern variations on the preemption theme. In United States v. Locke, 529 U.S. 89 (2000), the Court unanimously held some Washington state oil spill regulations preempted by the federal Ports and Waterways Safety Act of 1972 (PWSA) and remanded the case to determine if others were also. Deeming it unnecessary to decide whether "a significant and intricate complex of international treaties and maritime agreements bearing upon the licensing and operation of vessels" had "binding, pre-emptive force[,]" the Court relied on the federal statutory structure instead. Justice Kennedy's opinion noted that the " 'assumption' of nonpreemption" articulated in *Rice*—"that the historic police powers of the States were not to be superseded by the Federal Act unless that was the clear and manifest purpose of Congress"—"is not triggered when the State regulates in an area where there has been a history of significant federal presence." State laws "bearing upon national and international maritime commerce" address such an area.

Absent the assumption of non-preemption, the Court reaffirmed an earlier decision (Ray v. Atlantic Richfield Co., 435 U.S. 151 (1978), that "[w]hile ... Congress, in Title I of the PWSA, preserved state authority to regulate the peculiarities of local waters if there was no conflict with federal regulatory determinations, ... Congress, in Title II of the PWSA, mandated federal rules on the subjects or matters there specified, demanding uniformity[,]" and "require[d] the Coast Guard to impose national regulations governing the general seaworthiness of tankers and their crews[,]" so that "only the Federal Government may regulate the 'design, construction, alteration, repair, maintenance, operation, equipping, personnel qualification, and manning' of tanker vessels." In defining "the scope of ... field pre-emption" under Title II, the Court adverted to "whether the [state] rule is justified by conditions unique to a particular port or waterway" and said more generally: "Local rules not preempted under Title II ... pose a minimal risk of noncompliance, do not affect

---

1. The plurality also relies on § 18(f), ... which deals with withdrawal of approval of a state plan.... At most [that subsection] assumes that the State loses its capacity to enforce the plan.... It says nothing about state law that may remain on the books exclusive of the plan's authority, or about new law enacted after withdrawal of the Secretary's approval.

vessel operations outside the jurisdiction, do not require adjustment of systemic aspects of the vessel, and do not impose a substantial burden on the vessel's operation within the local jurisdiction itself." Using this approach, state tanker crew training and English language proficiency requirements, as well as navigation watch requirements, were invalidated as inconsistent with Title II's field pre-emption.

By contrast, the Court treated the state's requirement to report marine casualty incidents wherever in the world they occurred as an issue of conflict pre-emption, finding the state regulation in conflict with Title I's provision that the Coast Guard "prescribe regulations on the marine casualties to be reported and the manner of reporting." The Court explained that it "is not always a sufficient answer to a claim of pre-emption to say that state rules supplement, or even mirror, federal requirements." Rather, in light of its assessment that the "State's reporting requirement is a significant burden in terms of cost and the risk of innocent noncompliance" and "affects a vessel operator's out-of-state obligations and conduct, where a State's jurisdiction and authority are most in doubt[,]" the Court concluded "that Congress intended that the Coast Guard regulations be the sole source of a vessel's reporting obligations. . . ." Finally, in the face of state arguments that "certain of its regulations, such as its watch requirement in times of restricted visibility, are of limited extraterritorial effect and necessary to address the peculiarities of Puget Sound[,]" the Court remanded the remaining regulations for further determination of possible "Title I conflict pre-emption or Title II field pre-emption" or pre-emption "under any other federal law or international agreement. . . ."

In a second unanimous decision, the Court invalidated a Massachusetts law severely limiting the power of state agencies to buy goods or services from companies doing business with Burma. Crosby v. National Foreign Trade Council, 530 U.S. 363 (2000). Under Hines v. Davidowitz, 312 U.S. 52, 67 (1941), the state law presented "an obstacle to the accomplishment and execution of the full purposes and objectives of Congress" by "undermin[ing] at least three provisions" of a subsequently enacted federal statute imposing mandatory and conditional sanctions on Burma—"its delegation of effective discretion to the President to control economic sanctions against Burma, its limitation of sanctions solely to United States persons and new investment, and its directive to the President to proceed diplomatically in developing a comprehensive, multilateral strategy towards Burma." A footnote at this point in Justice Souter's opinion for the Court left "for another day a consideration in this context of a presumption against preemption[,]" because even if such a presumption were appropriate, the state Act "presents a sufficient obstacle . . . to find it preempted." For the same reason, it was unnecessary to address "field preemption as a separate issue" or "the foreign affairs power or the dormant commerce clause."[a] The preceding footnote made a different point,

---

a. Three years later, in American Insurance Association v. Garamendi, 539 U.S. 396 (2003), the Court invoked *Crosby* to invalidate a California statute that required each insurance company doing business in the state to disclose information about all policies sold in Europe between 1920 and 1945 by the company itself or any of its "related" entities. California sought the information to facilitate resolution of claims by Holocaust victims against insurance companies that wrongfully failed to honor policies in existence before and during World War II.

The Court in *Garamendi* ruled that California's law conflicted with the spirit and goals of a series of executive agreements entered into between the President and various foreign entities; the agreements were intended to induce voluntary compensation instead of litigation or other coercive sanctions. The Court by a 5–4 vote held that although the executive agreements contained no preemption clauses, California had nonetheless, as Massachusetts had in *Crosby*, interfered with national foreign policy. As the majority put it, "California seeks to use an iron fist where noting that the Court had "already rejected the argument that a State's 'statutory scheme ... escapes preemption because it is an exercise of the State's spending power rather than its regulatory power.' Wisconsin Dept. of Industry v. Gould Inc., 475 U.S. 282, 287 (1986)."

In the course of his textual analysis, Justice Souter, citing *Gade*, remarked: "The fact of a common end hardly neutralizes conflicting means, ... and the fact that some companies may be able to comply with both sets of sanctions does not mean that the state Act is not at odds with achievement of the federal decision about the right degree of pressure to employ.... [T]he inconsistency of sanctions here undermines the congressional calibration of force." Without deferring "unquestioningly ... to the legal judgments expressed in Executive Branch statements when determining a federal Act's preemptive character," moreover, Justice Souter wrote that "repeated representations by the Executive Branch [that the State Act has complicated its dealing with foreign sovereigns and proven an impediment to accomplishing objectives assigned it by Congress,] supported by formal diplomatic protests and concrete [international] disputes[,] are more than sufficient to demonstrate that the state Act stands in the way of Congress's diplomatic objectives." Finally, the Court rejected the State's argument "that Congress's continuing failure to enact express preemption implies approval, particularly in light of occasional instances of express preemption of state sanctions in the past":

> "... A failure to provide for preemption expressly may reflect nothing more than the settled character of implied preemption doctrine that courts will dependably apply, and in any event, the existence of conflict cognizable under the Supremacy Clause does not depend on express congressional recognition that federal and state law may conflict.... [T]he silence of Congress is ambiguous. Since we never ruled on whether state and local sanctions against South Africa in the 1980s were preempted or otherwise invalid, arguable parallels between the two sets of federal and state Acts do not tell us much about the validity of the latter."

In the third decision, the Court divided 5–4, with the majority holding that a state common-law tort action, based on an auto manufacturer's failure to provide airbags, was preempted by the 1984 version of a Federal Motor Vehicle Safety Standard (FMVSS 208) promulgated by the Department of Transportation pursuant to the national Traffic and Motor Vehicle Safety Act of 1966—a Standard with which the manufacturer had complied. Geier v. American Honda Motor Co., Inc., 529 U.S. 861 (2000). Justice Breyer's majority opinion first concluded, with respect to the Act's express pre-emption provision, that there was "no convincing indication that Congress wanted to pre-empt, not only state statutes and regulations, but also common-law tort actions...." On the other hand, he determined that the Act's "saving" clause—which provides that "[c]ompliance with" a federal safety standard "does not exempt any person from any liability under common law"—did not reflect "an intent to save state-law tort actions that conflict with federal regulations." He found it "difficult to understand why Congress would have insisted on a compliance-with-federal-regulation precondition to the provision's applicability had it wished the Act to 'save' all state-law tort actions, regardless of their potential threat to the objectives of federal safety standards promulgated under that Act." Finally, the majority held the tort action pre-empted because of actual conflict with the

the President has consistently chosen kid gloves." The dissenters took issue with the "considerable weight" the majority placed on *Crosby*, pointing out that Crosby's statutory preemption analysis should not carry over to executive agreements that are not ratified by statutes.

"means-related federal objective" of FMVSS 208, in that the Standard "deliberately sought variety ... allowing manufacturers to choose among different passive restraint mechanisms, such as airbags, automatic belts, or other passive restraint technologies" and "also deliberately sought a *gradual* phase-in of passive restraints[,]" whereas the tort action depended on a claim that manufacturers had no choice, but a duty, to install airbags, and to do so in 1987, with no leeway for phase-in, which also "could have made less likely the adoption of a state mandatory buckle-up law."

In response to the dissent, Justice Breyer also said in part:

"Neither do we believe that the pre-emption provision, the saving provision, or both together, create some kind of 'special burden' beyond that inherent in ordinary pre-emption principles—which ... would specially disfavor pre-emption here. The two provisions, read together, reflect a neutral policy, not a specially favorable or unfavorable policy, towards the application of ordinary conflict pre-emption principles....

"Why ... would Congress not have wanted ordinary pre-emption principles to apply where an actual conflict with a federal objective is at stake? ... Insofar as petitioners' argument would permit common-law actions that 'actually conflict' with federal regulations, it would take from those who would enforce a federal law the very ability to achieve the law's congressionally mandated objectives that the Constitution, through the operation of ordinary pre-emption principles, seeks to protect.

" . . .

"A 'special burden' would also promise practical difficulty by further complicating well-established pre-emption principles that already are difficult to apply. The dissent does not contend that this 'special burden' would apply in a case in which state law penalizes what federal law requires—i.e., a case of impossibility. But if it would not apply in such a case, then how, or when, would it apply? ... The Court has not previously driven a legal wedge—only a terminological one—between 'conflicts' that prevent or frustrate the accomplishment of a federal objective and 'conflicts' that make it 'impossible' for private parties to comply with both state and federal law. Rather, it has said that both forms of conflicting state law are 'nullified' by the Supremacy Clause, ... and it has assumed that Congress would not want either kind of conflict. The Court has thus refused to read general 'saving' provisions to tolerate actual conflict both in cases involving impossibility ... and in 'frustration-of-purpose' cases.... [T]he dissent's willingness to impose a 'special burden' here stems ultimately from its view that 'frustration-of-purpos[e]' conflict pre-emption is a freewheeling, 'inadequately considered' doctrine that might well be 'eliminate[d].' ...

" 'One final point: We place some weight upon DOT's interpretation of FMVSS 208's objectives and its conclusion ... that a tort suit such as this one would ' "stan[d] as an obstacle to the accomplishment and execution" ' ' of those objectives.... Congress has delegated to DOT authority to implement the statute; the subject matter is technical; and the relevant history and background are complex and extensive. The agency is likely to have a thorough understanding of its own regulation and its objectives and is 'uniquely qualified' to comprehend the likely impact of state requirements....

" . . .

"The dissent would require a formal agency statement of pre-emptive intent as a prerequisite to concluding that a conflict exists.... [T]hough the Court has looked for a specific statement of pre-emptive intent where it is claimed that the mere 'volume and complexity' of agency regulations demonstrate an implicit intent to displace all state law in a particular area . . .—so-called 'field pre-emption'—the Court has never before required a specific, formal agency statement identifying conflict in order to conclude that such a conflict in fact exists. . . . To insist on a specific expression of agency intent to pre-empt, made after notice-and-comment rulemaking, would be in certain cases to tolerate conflicts that an agency, and therefore Congress, is most unlikely to have intended. The dissent . . . apparently welcomes that result, at least where 'frustration-of-purpos[e]' pre-emption by agency regulation is at issue. . . . We do not."

Justice Stevens, joined by Justices Souter, Thomas and Ginsburg, dissented at length, "especially from the Court's unprecedented extension of the doctrine of pre-emption." In light of the presumption against pre-emption of "state laws—particularly those, such as the provision of tort remedies to compensate for personal injuries, that are within the scope of the States' historic police powers[,]" and in light of the Act's "saving" clause, which "was obviously intended to limit the pre-emptive effect of the Secretary's safety standards," the dissent found it "quite wrong for the Court to assume that a possible implicit conflict with the purposes to be achieved by such a standard should have the same pre-emptive effect 'as an obstacle to the accomplishment and execution of the full purposes and objectives of Congress.' Properly construed, the Safety Act imposes a special burden on a party relying on an arguable implicit conflict with a temporary regulatory policy—rather than a conflict with congressional policy or with the text of any regulation—to demonstrate that a common-law claim has been pre-empted." In this case, for various reasons, including "the important fact that by definition all of the standards established under the Safety Act impose minimum, rather than fixed or maximum, requirements" and the dissent's belief that "gradualism" and "variety" were "not . . . of independent importance to the Secretary[,]" the dissent found that "Honda has not crossed the high threshold established by our decisions regarding pre-emption of state laws that allegedly frustrate federal purposes: it has not demonstrated that allowing a common-law no-airbag claim to go forward would impose an obligation on manufacturers that directly and irreconcilably contradicts any primary objective that the Secretary set forth with clarity in Standard 208." More generally, the dissent thought "the presumption against pre-emption should control":

" . . . The signal virtues of this presumption are its placement of the power of pre-emption squarely in the hands of Congress, which is far more suited than the Judiciary to strike the appropriate state/federal balance (particularly in areas of traditional state regulation), and its requirement that Congress speak clearly when exercising that power. In this way, the structural safeguards inherent in the normal operation of the legislative process operate to defend state interests from undue infringement. Garcia v. San Antonio Metropolitan Transit Authority, 469 U.S. 528, 552 (1985). . . . In addition, the presumption serves as a limiting principle that prevents federal judges from running amok with our potentially boundless (and perhaps inadequately considered) doctrine of implied conflict pre-emption based on frustration of purposes—i.e., that state law is pre-empted if it 'stands as an obstacle to the accomplishment and execution of the full purposes and objectives of Congress.' Hines v. Davidowitz, 312 U.S., at 67. . . .

"While the presumption is important in assessing the pre-emptive reach of federal statutes, it becomes crucial when the pre-emptive effect of an administrative regulation is at issue. Unlike Congress, administrative agencies are clearly not designed to represent the interests of States, yet with relative ease they can promulgate comprehensive and detailed regulations that have broad pre-emption ramifications for state law. . . . [W]e generally 'expect an administrative regulation to declare any intention to pre-empt state law with some specificity.' . . . This expectation . . . serves to ensure that States will be able to have a dialog with agencies regarding pre-emption decisions *ex ante* through the normal notice-and-comment procedures of the Administrative Procedure Act (APA), 5 U.S.C. § 553.''

CHAPTER 7

SEPARATION OF POWERS

This chapter focuses on issues of division of power between the President and Congress. The coverage is, of necessity, both introductory and very selective, since the topic could easily be the sole concern of many volumes. Section 1 raises the question of the extent to which the President has the power to determine national policies. Section 2 deals with the other side of the coin, examining some instances where it is claimed that Congress has interfered with recognized Presidential powers. Section 3 is concerned with Presidential immunity from Congressional and judicial process.

SECTION 1.   THE PRESIDENT'S POWER TO DETERMINE NATIONAL POLICY

A.   IN GENERAL

Introduction. A simplistic description of the division of powers between the legislature and the executive is that a nation's policies are set by the legislature in the laws, and carried into force by the executive. Even the casual student of American history knows that the reality of the division of authority between the President and Congress has been much more complex.

Youngstown Sheet & Tube Co. v. Sawyer (The Steel Seizure Case)

343 U.S. 579, 72 S.Ct. 863, 96 L.Ed. 1153 (1952).

[This important decision emerged from a tangled background of labor legislation, price and wage negotiation in the steel industry, unhappiness between Congress and President Truman and the frustrating inability of the government to find an end for the war in Korea, then in its third year.[a]

[Part of the setting was disagreement between Congress and President Truman over the means of resolving major labor disputes. In 1947 Congress, over President Truman's veto, had passed the Taft–Hartley Act subjecting union practices to national control; one part of the Act provided that if a strike would endanger national health and safety the President was authorized to seek an injunction against the strike during a cooling-off period of eighty days during which a secret ballot of the workers could be held. These various provisions were bitterly resisted by labor. While this law was under consideration in Congress an amendment was offered for government seizure of

---

a. The fullest account of the case is Westin, The Anatomy of a Constitutional Law Case (1958). Other accounts on which this discussion draws are Kauper, The Steel Seizure Case, 51 Mich.L.Rev. 141 (1952), Se- lected Essays, 129 (1963); Freund, Foreword: The Year of the Steel Case, 66 Harv.L.Rev. 89 (1952); McConnell, The Steel Seizure of 1952 (1958); The Steel Seizure Case, 82d Cong., 2d Sess., H.Doc.No. 534.

industries to avoid serious shut-downs; Congress rejected the proposal. In his hard-hitting and astonishingly successful 1948 campaign for reelection, Truman slashed at the "do-nothing" record of this session of Congress, and called for repeal of the "oppressive" Taft–Hartley Act.

[Another dimension to the problem was the Administration's controversy with the steel industry. Wage negotiations between the United Steel Workers and the industry had been opened in November 1951, five months before the final crisis. The negotiations were deadlocked, and in December the President referred this controversy to the Wage Stabilization Board—which was part of the program of controls over wages and prices that had been established during the Korean War. The Board did not have authority to dictate a settlement; its chief sanction was to decide the extent to which labor cost increases could be taken into account by the Office of Price Stabilization in acting on requests for increases in ceiling prices. The Wage Stabilization Board recommended certain wage increases; the steel industry rejected this recommendation unless it received a $12 per ton increase in the ceiling price. The stabilization officials refused to approve this increase on the ground that high earnings of the steel industry permitted the absorption of at least a part of the increase in labor costs.

[On April 3, Philip Murray, President of the United Steelworkers, called a general steel strike for 12:01 a.m., April 9. On the night of April 8, following a radio address to the nation, President Truman issued Executive Order 10340 directing the Secretary of Commerce "to take possession" and "to operate or arrange for the operation" of the production facilities of the steel industry. The Order outlined the vital part of steel in the war effort, and concluded that "a work stoppage would immediately jeopardize and imperil our national defense." The Secretary of Commerce was instructed to leave control, insofar as possible, in the hands of the present management, but the Order included a pointed authorization to "determine and prescribe terms and conditions of employment." The next morning, President Truman sent Congress a message reporting on this action and stating that if Congress preferred a different course of action, "That is a matter for the Congress to determine."

[Just before midnight on April 8, within an hour after the President's Order, attorneys for the steel companies arrived at the home of a United States District Judge with a motion for immediate relief. A hearing was set for 11:30 the next morning. The relief initially requested by the companies was the prevention of a change in wage rates during government management—a move designed to block the government's plan to force a settlement by establishing a new wage level that, as a practical matter, would be irreversible; but the case quickly reached larger dimensions and on April 29 District Judge David Pine held the seizure illegal and enjoined government officials from remaining in control of the industry. The case was rapidly carried to the Supreme Court.]

Mr. Justice Black delivered the opinion of the Court.

We are asked to decide whether the President was acting within his constitutional power when he issued an order directing the Secretary of Commerce to take possession of and operate most of the Nation's steel mills. The mill owners argue that the President's order amounts to lawmaking, a legislative function which the Constitution has expressly confided to the Congress and not to the President. The Government's position is that the order was made on findings of the President that his action was necessary to avert a national catastrophe which would inevitably result from a stoppage of steel production, and that in meeting this grave emergency the President was acting within the aggregate of his constitutional powers as the Nation's Chief Execu-

tive and the Commander–in–Chief of the Armed Forces of the United States.
. . .

. . .

The President's power, if any, to issue the order must stem either from an act of Congress or from the Constitution itself. There is no statute that expressly authorizes the President to take possession of property as he did here. Nor is there any act of Congress to which our attention has been directed from which such a power can fairly be implied. . . .'

Moreover, the use of the seizure technique to solve labor disputes in order to prevent work stoppages was not only unauthorized by any congressional enactment; prior to this controversy, Congress had refused to adopt that method of settling labor disputes. When the Taft–Hartley Act was under consideration in 1947, Congress rejected an amendment which would have authorized such governmental seizures in cases of emergency. . . . Instead, the plan sought to bring about settlements by use of the customary devices of mediation, conciliation, investigation by boards of inquiry, and public reports. In some instances temporary injunctions were authorized to provide cooling-off periods. All this failing, unions were left free to strike after a secret vote by employees as to whether they wished to accept their employers' final settlement offer.

It is clear that if the President had authority to issue the order he did, it must be found in some provision of the Constitution. And it is not claimed that express constitutional language grants this power to the President. The contention is that presidential power should be implied from the aggregate of his powers under the Constitution. Particular reliance is placed on provisions in Article II which say that "the executive Power shall be vested in a President . . ."; that "he shall take Care that the Laws be faithfully executed"; and that he "shall be Commander in Chief of the Army and Navy of the United States."

The order cannot properly be sustained as an exercise of the President's military power as Commander in Chief of the Armed Forces. The Government attempts to do so by citing a number of cases upholding broad powers in military commanders engaged in day-to-day fighting in a theater of war. Such cases need not concern us here. Even though "theater of war" be an expanding concept, we cannot with faithfulness to our constitutional system hold that the Commander in Chief of the Armed Forces has the ultimate power as such to take possession of private property in order to keep labor disputes from stopping production. This is a job for the Nation's lawmakers, not for its military authorities.

Nor can the seizure order be sustained because of the several constitutional provisions that grant executive power to the President. In the framework of our Constitution, the President's power to see that the laws are faithfully executed refutes the idea that he is to be a lawmaker. The Constitution limits his functions in the lawmaking process to the recommending of laws he thinks wise and the vetoing of laws he thinks bad. And the Constitution is neither silent nor equivocal about who shall make laws which the President is to execute. The first section of the first article says that "All legislative Powers herein granted shall be vested in a Congress of the United States. . . ."After granting many powers to the Congress, Article I goes on to provide that Congress may "make all Laws which shall be necessary and proper for carrying into Execution the foregoing Powers and all other Powers vested by this Constitution in the Government of the United States, or in any Department or Officer thereof."

The President's order does not direct that a congressional policy be executed in a manner prescribed by Congress—it directs that a presidential policy be executed in a manner prescribed by the President. The preamble of the order itself, like that of many statutes, sets out reasons why the President believes certain policies should be adopted, proclaims these policies as rules of conduct to be followed, and again, like a statute, authorizes a government official to promulgate additional rules and regulations consistent with the policy proclaimed and needed to carry that policy into execution. The power of Congress to adopt such public policies as those proclaimed by the order is beyond question. It can authorize the taking of private property for public use. It can make laws regulating the relationships between employers and employees, prescribing rules designed to settle labor disputes, and fixing wages and working conditions in certain fields of our economy. The Constitution does not subject this lawmaking power of Congress to presidential or military supervision or control.

It is said that other Presidents without congressional authority have taken possession of private business enterprises in order to settle labor disputes. But even if this be true, Congress has not thereby lost its exclusive constitutional authority to make laws necessary and proper to carry out the powers vested by the Constitution "in the Government of the United States, or in any Department or Officer thereof."

The Founders of this Nation entrusted the lawmaking power to the Congress alone in both good and bad times. It would do no good to recall the historical events, the fears of power and the hopes for freedom that lay behind their choice. Such a review would but confirm our holding that this seizure order cannot stand.

The judgment of the District Court is affirmed.

Affirmed.

[All of the Justices who joined Justice Black's opinion for the Court also wrote individual concurring opinions. Justice Frankfurter stated that questions concerning the extent of Presidential power in the absence of legislation were not before the Court. The Labor Management Relations Act of 1947 was equivalent to an explicit Congressional negation of the authority asserted by the seizure. For Justice Burton the "controlling fact" was that Congress had prescribed specific procedures, not including seizure, for the present type of emergency. Justice Douglas argued that Congress, as the only branch with power to appropriate money to compensate for seizures, was the only branch with power to authorize or ratify them. A few often-quoted passages from Justice Jackson's lengthy concurring opinion follow.]

Mr. Justice Jackson, concurring in the judgment and opinion of the Court.

. . .

The actual art of governing under our Constitution does not and cannot conform to judicial definitions of the power of any of its branches based on isolated clauses or even single Articles torn from context. While the Constitution diffuses power the better to secure liberty, it also contemplates that practice will integrate the dispersed powers into a workable government. It enjoins upon its branches separateness but interdependence, autonomy but reciprocity. Presidential powers are not fixed but fluctuate, depending upon their disjunction or conjunction with those of Congress. We may well begin by a somewhat over-simplified grouping of practical situations in which a President may doubt, or others may challenge, his powers, and by distinguishing roughly the legal consequences of this factor of relativity.

1.   When the President acts pursuant to an express or implied authorization of Congress, his authority is at its maximum, for it includes all that he possesses in his own right plus all that Congress can delegate. In these circumstances, and in these only, may he be said (for what it may be worth), to personify the federal sovereignty. If his act is held unconstitutional under these circumstances, it usually means that the Federal Government as an undivided whole lacks power. A seizure executed by the President pursuant to an Act of Congress would be supported by the strongest of presumptions and the widest latitude of judicial interpretation, and the burden of persuasion would rest heavily upon any who might attack it.

2.   When the President acts in absence of either a congressional grant or denial of authority, he can only rely upon his own independent powers, but there is a zone of twilight in which he and Congress may have concurrent authority, or in which its distribution is uncertain. Therefore, congressional inertia, indifference or quiescence may sometimes, at least as a practical matter, enable, if not invite, measures on independent presidential responsibility. In this area, any actual test of power is likely to depend on the imperatives of events and contemporary imponderables rather than on abstract theories of law.

3.   When the President takes measures incompatible with the expressed or implied will of Congress, his power is at its lowest ebb, for then he can rely only upon his own constitutional powers minus any constitutional powers of Congress over the matter. Courts can sustain exclusive Presidential control in such a case only by disabling the Congress from acting upon the subject. Presidential claim to a power at once so conclusive and preclusive must be scrutinized with caution, for what is at stake is the equilibrium established by our constitutional system.

. . .

. . . [T]he current seizure [can] be justified only by the severe tests under the third grouping, where it can be supported only by any remainder of executive power after subtraction of such powers as Congress may have over the subject. In short, we can sustain the President only by holding that seizure of such strike-bound industries is within his domain and beyond control by Congress. Thus, this Court's first review of such seizures occurs under circumstances which leave Presidential power most vulnerable to attack and in the least favorable of possible constitutional postures.

. . .

But I have no illusion that any decision by this Court can keep power in the hands of Congress if it is not wise and timely in meeting its problems. A crisis that challenges the President equally, or perhaps primarily, challenges Congress. If not good law, there was worldly wisdom in the maxim attributed to Napoleon that "The tools belong to the man who can use them." We may say that power to legislate for emergencies belongs in the hands of Congress, but only Congress itself can prevent power from slipping through its fingers.

. . .

Mr. Justice Clark, concurring in the judgment of the Court . . .

I conclude that where Congress has laid down specific procedures to deal with the type of crisis confronting the President, he must follow those procedures ...

Mr. Chief Justice Vinson, with whom Mr. Justice Reed and Mr. Justice Minton join, dissenting. ...

. . .

One is not here called upon even to consider the possibility of executive seizure of a farm, a corner grocery store or even a single industrial plant. Such considerations arise only when one ignores the central fact of this case—that the Nation's entire basic steel production would have shut down completely if there had been no Government seizure....'

. . .

A review of executive action demonstrates that our Presidents have on many occasions exhibited the leadership contemplated by the Framers when they made the President Commander in Chief, and imposed upon him the trust to "take Care that the Laws be faithfully executed." With or without explicit statutory authorization, Presidents have at such times dealt with national emergencies by acting promptly and resolutely to enforce legislative programs, at least to save those programs until Congress could act. Congress and the courts have responded to such executive initiative with consistent approval....'

. . .

Focusing now on the situation confronting the President on the night of April 8, 1952, we cannot but conclude that the President was performing his duty under the Constitution to "take Care that the Laws be faithfully executed"—a duty described by President Benjamin Harrison as "the central idea of the office." ...

. . .

B.   INTERNATIONAL RELATIONS

Introduction. Most of the constitutional grants of power to the federal government relating to foreign affairs appear in the enumeration of executive powers: the President is made "Commander-in-Chief" of the armed forces; he is given the power, with the approval of two-thirds of the Senate, "to make Treaties"; and, with the "advice and consent" of the Senate, he "shall appoint Ambassadors, other public Ministers and Consuls," i.e., our representatives abroad (Art. II, § 2). Also, "he shall receive Ambassadors and other public Ministers" (Art. II, § 3). Those spare provisions, however, hardly begin to capture the scope of "the executive power" to conduct the nation's foreign affairs.

United States v. Curtiss–Wright Export Corp., 299 U.S. 304, 320 (1936), concerned the validity of a delegation of power from Congress to the President. In the course of upholding the delegation the Court noted that the legislative power was combined with "the very delicate, plenary and exclusive power of the President as the sole organ of the Federal government in the field of international relations—a power which does not require as a basis for its exercise an act of Congress, but which, of course, like every other governmental power, must be exercised in subordination to the applicable provisions of the Constitution. It is quite apparent that if, in the maintenance of our international relations, embarrassment—perhaps serious embarrassment—is to be avoided and success for our aims achieved, congressional legislation which is to be made effective through negotiation and inquiry within the international field must often accord to the President a degree of discretion and freedom from statutory restriction which would not be admissible were domestic affairs alone involved. Moreover, he, not Congress, has the better opportunity of knowing the conditions which prevail in foreign countries, and especially is this true in time of war. He has his confidential sources of information. He has his agents in the form of diplomatic, consular and other officials. Secrecy in respect of information gathered by them may be highly necessary, and the premature disclosure of it productive of harmful results. Indeed, so clearly is this true that the first President refused to accede to a request to lay before the House of Representatives the instructions, correspondence and documents relating to the negotiation of the Jay Treaty—a refusal the wisdom of which was recognized by the House itself and has never since been doubted."

INTERNATIONAL AGREEMENTS

The scope of national power to override state law and policy through the use of international agreements was discussed in Chapter 4. In that connection, United States v. Belmont, supra p. 210, and United States v. Pink, supra p. 211, relate to the power of the President to consummate international agreements without going through the process of having formal treaties ratified by the Senate and the effect of such agreements on state law.

Belmont and *Pink* raised a separate issue that has proved highly controversial—whether executive agreements can be employed to circumvent the role of the Senate embodied in Article 2 of the Constitution. Some commentators were critical. Borchard, *Shall the Executive Agreement Replace the Treaty?*, 53 Yale L.J. 664 (1944), 54 Yale L.J. 616 (1945). Others supported the use of executive agreements (buttressed in some cases by joint action by the two houses of Congress) as a well-established means to provide flexibility in dealing with international relations. McDougal & Lans, *Treaties and Congressional–Executive or Presidential Agreements: Interchangeable Instruments of National Policy*, 54 Yale L.J. 181, 534 (1945). This dispute does not concern the propriety of the bulk of agreements made between the heads of governments in their day-to-day handling of routine arrangements (like an agreement for the exchange of visits by naval vessels) or military arrangements like the line in conquered territory where allied armies will meet. Some such arrangements may fall within the independent power of the President as "commander-in-chief", others within "the executive power" of the President to conduct the day-to-day business of foreign relations. But one of the questions stirred by the *Belmont* and *Pink* cases is whether the President might use executive agreements for basic long-range commitments of the nation when it might be impossible to obtain the two-thirds vote of the Senate for treaty ratification.

DAMES & MOORE v. REGAN, 453 U.S. 654 (1981). On January 20, 1981, Iran released hostages captured in the seizure of the American Embassy, in Teheran, pursuant to an agreement with the United States. One provision of the agreement provided for termination of litigation in American courts against Iran, with the arbitration of those claims before an International Claims Tribunal. On January 19, 1981, President Carter issued executive orders providing for transfer of blocked Iranian funds in the United States, and nullifying attachments issued against those funds. On February 24, 1981, President Reagan ratified the Executive Orders, and suspended all claims filed in United States courts that could be presented to the claims tribunal.

Petitioner was a company that had procured a judgment against Iran in a federal trial court for breach of its contract to conduct studies for a proposed nuclear plant in Iran. It brought this action against the Secretary of the Treasury to prevent enforcement of the Executive Orders. Reserving questions whether the Executive Orders' suspension of claims constituted an uncompensated taking of property, the Court held that the Executive Orders did not exceed Presidential powers.

The provisions of the Executive Orders suspending attachments against persons holding blocked Iranian funds, and directing the transfer of those funds to Iran, were held to be authorized by provisions of the International Emergency Economic Powers Act (IEEPA). The Court concluded, however, that neither IEEPA, nor the Hostage Act of 1868, specifically authorized the President to suspend claims pending in United States Courts. In upholding the validity of this aspect of the Executive Orders, Justice Rehnquist's opinion for the Court said, in part:

"Concluding that neither the IEEPA nor the Hostage Act constitutes specific authorization of the President's action suspending claims, however, is not to say that these statutory provisions are entirely irrelevant to the question of the validity of the President's action. We think both statutes highly relevant in the looser sense of indicating congressional acceptance of a broad scope for executive action in circumstances such as those presented in this case. . . . '

"Although we have declined to conclude that the IEEPA or the Hostage Act directly authorizes the President's suspension of claims . . ., we cannot ignore the general tenor of Congress' legislation in this area in trying to determine whether the President is acting alone or at least with the acceptance of Congress. . . . Congress cannot anticipate and legislate with regard to every possible action the President may find it necessary to take or every possible situation in which he might act. Such failure of Congress specifically to delegate authority does not, 'especially . . . in the areas of foreign policy and national security,' imply 'congressional disapproval' of action taken by the Executive. . . . On the contrary, the enactment of legislation closely related to the question of the President's authority in a particular case which evinces legislative intent to accord the President broad discretion may be considered to 'invite' 'measures on independent presidential responsibility.' *Youngstown,* . . . (Jackson, J., concurring). At least this is so where there is no contrary indication of legislative intent and when, as here, there is a history of congressional acquiescence in conduct of the sort engaged in by the President. . . ."

C.   WAR AND NATIONAL DEFENSE

Introduction. The Constitution is not silent about Congressional participation in one aspect of foreign affairs. Article I, Section 8, Clause 11, of the Constitution specifies that it is a Congressional prerogative "to declare war."

The Prize Cases

67 U.S. (2 Black) 635, 17 L.Ed. 459 (1863).

[In April, 1861, President Lincoln declared a blockade of southern ports. Pursuant to this blockade, in May and July, 1861, Union ships seized merchant vessels and cargoes of foreign neutrals and residents of the southern states. The ships were condemned by federal court order. The owners of the ships and cargo appealed. The Supreme Court regarded the first question to be: "Had the

President authority to institute a blockade of southern ports which neutrals were bound to respect?'' The following excerpts are addressed to that question.]

Mr. Justice Grier

. . .

By the Constitution, Congress alone has the power to declare a national or foreign war. It cannot declare war against a State or any number of States, by virtue of any clause in the Constitution. The Constitution confers on the President the whole executive power. He is bound to take care that the laws be faithfully executed. He is Commander-in-Chief of the Army and Navy of the United States, and of the militia of the several States when called into the actual service of the United States. He has no power to initiate or declare a war either against a foreign nation or a domestic State. But by the Acts of Congress of Feb. 28th, 1795 and 3d of March, 1807, he is authorized to call out the militia and use the military and naval forces of the United States in case of invasion by foreign nations, and to suppress insurrection against the government of a State or of the United States.

If a war be made by invasion of a foreign nation, the President is not only authorized but bound to resist force, by force. He does not initiate the war, but is bound to accept the challenge without waiting for any special legislative authority. And whether the hostile party be a foreign invader, or States organized in rebellion, it is none the less a war, although the declaration of it be *"unilateral."* . . .

. . .

This greatest of civil wars was not gradually developed by popular commotion, tumultuous assemblies, or local unorganized insurrections. However long may have been its previous conception, it nevertheless sprung forth suddenly from the parent brain, a Minerva in the full panoply of war. The President was bound to meet it in the shape it presented itself, without waiting for Congress to baptize it with a name; and no name given to it by him or them could change the fact. . . .'

Whether the President in fulfilling his duties, as Commander-in-Chief, in suppressing an insurrection, has met with such armed hostile resistance, and a civil war of such alarming proportions as will compel him to accord to them the character of belligerents, is a question to be decided by him, and this court must be governed by the decisions and acts of the Political Department of the government to which this power was intrusted. "He must determine what degree of force the crisis demands." The proclamation of blockade is, itself, official and conclusive evidence to the court that a state of war existed which demanded and authorized a recourse to such a measure, under the circumstances peculiar to the case.

. . .

If it were necessary to the technical existence of a war, that it should have a legislative sanction, we find it in almost every Act passed at the extraordinary session of the Legislature of 1861, which was wholly employed in enacting laws to enable the government to prosecute the war with vigor and efficiency. And finally, in 1861, we find Congress *"ex majore cautela"* and in anticipation of such astute objections, passing an Act "approving, legalizing and making valid all the acts, proclamations, and orders of the President, & c., as if they had been issued and done under the previous express authority and direction of the Congress of the United States."

Without admitting that such an Act was necessary under the circumstances, it is plain that if the President had in any manner assumed powers which it was necessary should have the authority or sanction of Congress, that ... this ratification has operated to perfectly cure the defect....'

[The decrees of condemnation were affirmed except for certain cargoes which were bought and paid for in the South before the war broke out and which were being removed shortly thereafter.]

Mr. Justice Nelson [joined by Chief Justice Taney and Justices Catron and Clifford, dissenting]. ...

The Acts of 1795 and 1807 did not, and could not, under the Constitution, confer on the President the power of declaring war against a State of this Union, or of deciding that war existed, and upon that ground authorize the capture and confiscation of the property of every citizen of the State whenever it was found on the waters. The laws of war, whether the war be civil or *inter gentes,* as we have seen, convert every citizen of the hostile State into a public enemy, and treat him accordingly, whatever may have been his previous conduct. This great power over the business and property of the citizen is reserved to the Legislative Department by the express words of the Constitution. It cannot be delegated or surrendered to the Executive. Congress alone can determine whether war exists or should be declared, and until they have acted, no citizen of the State can be punished in his person or property, unless he has committed some offense against a law of Congress passed before the act was committed, which made it a crime, and defined the punishment. The penalty of confiscation for the acts of others with which he had no concern cannot lawfully be inflicted....'

[This dissenting opinion also came to the conclusion that congressional ratification of the seizures was ... invalid.]

Mora v. McNamara

389 U.S. 934, 88 S.Ct. 282, 19 L.Ed.2d 287 (1967).

Petition for writ of certiorari to the United States Court of Appeals for the District of Columbia Circuit.

Nov. 6, 1967. Denied.

Mr. Justice Marshall took no part in the consideration or decision of this petition.

Mr. Justice Stewart, with whom Mr. Justice Douglas joins, dissenting.

The petitioners were drafted into the United States Army in late 1965, and six months later were ordered to a West Coast replacement station for shipment to Vietnam. They brought this suit to prevent the Secretary of Defense and the Secretary of the Army from carrying out those orders, and requested a declaratory judgment that the present United States military activity in Vietnam is "illegal." The District Court dismissed the suit, and the Court of Appeals affirmed.

There exist in this case questions of great magnitude. ...

I. Is the present United States military activity in Vietnam a "war" within the meaning of Article I, Section 8, Clause 11 of the Constitution?

II. If so, may the Executive constitutionally order the petitioners to participate in that military activity, when no war has been declared by the Congress?

III. Of what relevance to Question II are the present treaty obligations of the United States?

IV. Of what relevance to Question II is the Joint Congressional ("Tonkin Gulf") Resolution of August 10, 1964?[a] ...

These are large and deeply troubling questions. Whether the Court would ultimately reach them depends, of course, upon the resolution of serious preliminary issues of justiciability. We cannot make these problems go away simply by refusing to hear the case of three obscure Army privates. I intimate not even tentative views upon any of these matters, but I think the Court should squarely face them by granting certiorari and setting this case for oral argument.

Mr. Justice Douglas, with whom Mr. Justice Stewart concurs, dissenting.

The questions posed by Mr. Justice Stewart cover the wide range of problems which the Senate Committee on Foreign Relations recently explored, in connection with the SEATO treaty of February 19, 1955, and the Tonkin Gulf Resolution.

Mr. Katzenbach, representing the Administration, testified that he did not regard the Tonkin Gulf Resolution to be "a declaration of war" ... He added:

"The use of the phrase 'to declare war' as it was used in the Constitution of the United States had a particular meaning in terms of the events and the practices which existed at the time it was adopted...."

"[I]t was recognized by the Founding Fathers that the President might have to take emergency action to protect the security of the United States, but that if there was going to be another use of the armed forces of the United States, that was a decision which Congress should check the Executive on, which Congress should support. It was for that reason that the phrase was inserted in the Constitution.

" ...

"A declaration of war would not, I think, correctly reflect the very limited objectives of the United States with respect to Vietnam. It would not correctly reflect our efforts there, what we are trying to do, the reasons why we are there, to use an outmoded phraseology, to declare war."

The view that Congress was intended to play a more active role in the initiation and conduct of war than the above statements might suggest has been espoused by Senator Fulbright ..., quoting Thomas Jefferson who said:

"We have already given in example one effectual check to the Dog of war by transferring the power of letting him loose from the Executive to the Legislative body, from those who are to spend to those who are to pay."

These opposed views are reflected in the Prize Cases, ...

a. The Tonkin Gulf Resolution was enacted at the request of President Johnson as a result of specific naval incidents in the Gulf of Tonkin. It stated that "Congress approves and supports the determination of the President, as Commander-in-Chief, to take all necessary measures to repel any armed attack against the forces of the United States and to prevent further aggression." H.R.J.Res. 1145, 88th Cong., 2d Sess., 78 Stat. 384 (1964). It was repealed December 31, 1970. Did the repeal have any effect on the President's powers to continue operations in Vietnam?

THE COURT AND THE VIETNAM CONTROVERSY

After the *Mora* decision, efforts to obtain a Supreme Court ruling on whether or not American military operations in Vietnam amounted to an "unconstitutional" war continued, but without success. The lower courts generally ruled that the issue was not justiciable.

Professor Henkin argues that the "courts, despite sometimes-misguided efforts to compel them to do so (as on Vietnam), are not likely to step into intense confrontations between President and Congress, or inhibit either when the other does not object. Whether from the sense that the boundary between Congress and President . . . , cannot be defined by law, whether from realization of the inherent limitations of judicial power or from prudence, whether under a doctrine of 'political questions' or by other judicial devices and formulae for abstention, courts will not make certain what was left uncertain, will not curtail the power of the political branches, will not arbitrate their differences. Then, in time, the issues will recede, stirring neither controversy nor case." *Foreign Affairs and the Constitution*, 274–275 (1972).

See, generally, John Hart Ely, *War and Responsibility* (1993).

Hamdi v. Rumsfeld

___ U.S. ___, 124 S.Ct. 2633, 159 L.Ed.2d 578 (2004).

Justice O'Connor announced the judgment of the Court and delivered an opinion, in which The Chief Justice, Justice Kennedy, and Justice Breyer join.

[W]e are called upon to consider the legality of the Government's detention of a United States citizen on United States soil as an "enemy combatant" and to address the process that is constitutionally owed to one who seeks to challenge his classification as such. The United States Court of Appeals for the Fourth Circuit held that petitioner's detention was legally authorized and that he was entitled to no further opportunity to challenge his enemy-combatant label. We now vacate and remand. We hold that although Congress authorized the detention of combatants in the narrow circumstances alleged here, due process demands that a citizen held in the United States as an enemy combatant be given a meaningful opportunity to contest the factual basis for that detention before a neutral decisionmaker.

I

On September 11, 2001, the al Qaeda terrorist network used hijacked commercial airliners to attack prominent targets in the United States[, killing a]pproximately 3,000 people. . . . One week later . . . Congress passed a resolution authorizing the President to "use all necessary and appropriate force against those nations, organizations, or persons he determines planned, authorized, committed, or aided the terrorist attacks" or "harbored such organizations or persons, in order to prevent any future acts of international terrorism against the United States by such nations, organizations or persons." Authorization for Use of Military Force ("the AUMF"). . . . Soon thereafter, the President ordered United States Armed Forces to Afghanistan, with a mission to subdue al Qaeda and quell the Taliban regime that was known to support it.

This case arises out of the detention of [Yaser Esam Hamdi, born an American citizen but residing in Afghanistan by 2001,] whom the Government alleges took up arms with the Taliban during this conflict. . . . [S]eized by members of the Northern Alliance, a coalition of military groups opposed to the Taliban government, [he] was turned over to the United States military[, which] transferred him to a naval brig in Norfolk, Virginia [after learning of his American citizenship.] The Government contends that Hamdi is an "enemy combatant," and that this status justifies holding him in the United States indefinitely—without formal charges or proceedings—unless and until it makes the determination that access to counsel or further process is warranted.

... Hamdi's father [sought] a writ of habeas corpus ... argu[ing] that ... Hamdi's detention in the United States without charges, access to an impartial tribunal, or assistance of counsel "violated and continue[s] to violate the Fifth and Fourteenth Amendments to the United States Constitution." ... Hamdi's father has asserted ... that his son went to Afghanistan to do "relief work," ... was traveling on his own for the first time ..., and "[b]ecause of his lack of experience, he was trapped in Afghanistan once that military campaign began." ...

The District Court ... appointed ... counsel ... and ordered that counsel be given access to Hamdi.... The ... Fourth Circuit reversed ..., holding that the District Court had failed to extend appropriate deference to the Government's security and intelligence interests[, and] ... direct[ing] the District Court to consider "the most cautious procedures first[.]" ...

On remand, the Government [moved] to dismiss [and] attached ... a declaration from one Michael Mobbs ..., who identified himself as Special Advisor to the Under Secretary of Defense for Policy[, involved with] the detention of enemy combatants in the current war [and familiar with the facts and circumstances related to the capture of Hamdi and his detention by U.S. military forces, who] set forth what remains the sole evidentiary support that the Government has provided to the courts for Hamdi's detention. The declaration states that Hamdi "traveled to Afghanistan" in July or August 2001, and that he thereafter "affiliated with a Taliban military unit and received weapons training." ... It asserts that Hamdi "remained with his Taliban unit following the attacks of September 11" and that, during the time when Northern Alliance forces were "engaged in battle with the Taliban," "Hamdi's Taliban unit surrendered" to those forces, after which he "surrender[ed] his Kalishnikov assault rifle" to them.... The Mobbs Declaration also states that, because al Qaeda and the Taliban "were and are hostile forces engaged in armed conflict with the armed forces of the United States," "individuals associated with" those groups "were and continue to be enemy combatants." ... Mobbs states that Hamdi was labeled an enemy combatant "[b]ased upon his interviews and in light of his association with the Taliban." ... According to the declaration, a series of "U.S. military screening team[s]" determined that Hamdi met "the criteria for enemy combatants," and "a subsequent interview of Hamdi has confirmed that he surrendered and gave his firearm to Northern Alliance forces, which supports his classification as an enemy combatant." ...

... The District Court found that the Mobbs Declaration fell "far short" of supporting Hamdi's detention [and] ordered the Government to turn over numerous materials for *in camera* review ... [to enable] "meaningful judicial review" of whether Hamdi's detention was legally authorized and whether Hamdi had received sufficient process to satisfy the Due Process Clause of the Constitution and relevant treaties or military regulations....'

[On a certified appeal, t]he Fourth Circuit reversed, ... [c]oncluding that the factual averments in the Mobbs Declaration, "if accurate," provided a sufficient basis upon which to conclude that the President had constitutionally detained Hamdi pursuant to the President's war powers, [and] it ordered the habeas petition dismissed....'

. . .

... We now vacate the judgment below and remand.

II

The threshold question before us is whether the Executive has the authority to detain citizens who qualify as "enemy combatants." ... [F]or purposes of this case, the "enemy combatant" [the Government] is seeking to detain is an individual who, it alleges, was "part of or supporting forces hostile to the United States or coalition partners" in Afghanistan and who "engaged in an armed conflict against the United States" there.... We therefore answer only the narrow question before us: whether the detention of citizens falling within that definition is authorized.

The Government maintains that no explicit congressional authorization is required, because the Executive possesses plenary authority to detain pursuant to Article II of the Constitution. We do not reach the question whether Article II provides such authority, however, because we agree with the Government's alternative position, that Congress has in fact authorized Hamdi's detention, through the AUMF.

... [Hamdi argues] that his detention is forbidden by 18 U.S.C. § 4001(a)[, which] states that "[n]o citizen shall be imprisoned or otherwise detained by the United States except pursuant to an Act of Congress." Congress passed § 4001(a) in 1971 as part of a bill to repeal the Emergency Detention Act of 1950, ... which provided procedures for executive detention, during times of emergency, of individuals deemed likely to engage in espionage or sabotage. Congress was particularly concerned about the possibility that the Act could be used to reprise the Japanese internment camps of World War II.... The Government ... argues [first] that § 4001(a) ... applies only to "the control of civilian prisons and related detentions," not to military detentions.... Second, it maintains that § 4001(a) is satisfied, because Hamdi is being detained "pursuant to an Act of Congress"—the AUMF.... [W]e conclude that the AUMF is explicit congressional authorization for the detention of individuals in the narrow category we describe (assuming, without deciding, that such authorization is required), and that the AUMF satisfied § 4001(a)'s requirement that a detention be "pursuant to an Act of Congress" (assuming, without deciding, that § 4001(a) applies to military detentions).

... [D]etention of individuals falling into the limited category we are considering, for the duration of the particular conflict in which they were captured, is so fundamental and accepted an incident to war as to be an exercise of the "necessary and appropriate force" Congress has authorized the President to use.

... The purpose of detention is to prevent captured individuals from returning to the field of battle and taking up arms once again....

There is no bar to this Nation's holding one of its own citizens as an enemy combatant. ... A citizen, no less than an alien, ... if released, would pose the same threat of returning to the front during the ongoing conflict.

In light of these principles, it is of no moment that the AUMF does not use specific language of detention. Because detention to prevent a combatant's return to the battlefield is a fundamental incident of waging war, in permitting the use of "necessary and appropriate force," Congress has clearly and unmistakably authorized detention in the narrow circumstances considered here.

Hamdi objects, nevertheless, that Congress has not authorized the *indefinite* detention to which he is now subject.... The prospect Hamdi raises is ... not far-fetched. If the Government does not consider this unconventional war [on terror] won for two generations, and if it maintains during that time that Hamdi might, if released, rejoin forces fighting against the United States, then the position it has taken throughout the litigation of this case suggests that Hamdi's detention could last for the rest of his life.

It is a clearly established principle of the law of war that detention may last no longer than active hostilities. See Article 118 of the Geneva Convention (III) Relative to the Treatment of Prisoners of War, Aug. 12, 1949....'

... Certainly, we agree that indefinite detention for the purpose of interrogation is not authorized. Further, we understand Congress' grant of authority ... to include the authority to detain for the duration of the relevant conflict, and our understanding is based on longstanding law-of-war principles. If the practical circumstances of a given conflict are entirely unlike those of the conflicts that informed the development of the law of war, that understanding may unravel. But that is not the situation we face as of this date. Active combat operations against Taliban fighters apparently are ongoing in Afghanistan.... The United States may detain, for the duration of these hostilities, individuals legitimately determined to be Taliban combatants who "engaged in an armed conflict against the United States." If the record establishes that United States troops are still involved in active combat in Afghanistan, those detentions are part of the exercise of "necessary and appropriate force," and therefore are authorized by the AUMF.

Ex parte Milligan, 4 Wall. 2, 125 (1866), does not undermine our holding.... In that case, the Court made repeated reference to the fact that its inquiry into whether the military tribunal had jurisdiction to try and punish Milligan turned in large part on the fact that Milligan was not a prisoner of war, but a resident of Indiana arrested while at home there.... The Court's repeated explanations that Milligan was not a prisoner of war suggest that had these different circumstances been present he could have been detained under military authority for the duration of the conflict, whether or not he was a citizen.

Moreover, as Justice Scalia acknowledges, the Court in [its unanimous opinion in] *Ex parte Quirin,* 317 U.S. 1 (1942), dismissed the language of *Milligan* that the petitioners had suggested prevented them from being subject to military process....'

. . .

... To be clear, our opinion only finds legislative authority to detain under the AUMF once it is sufficiently clear that the individual is, in fact, an enemy combatant....'

... Justice Scalia largely ignores the context of this case: a United States citizen captured in a *foreign* combat zone....

... Justice Scalia can point to no case or other authority for the proposition that those captured on a foreign battlefield (whether detained there or in U.S. territory) cannot be detained outside the criminal process.

Moreover, Justice Scalia presumably would come to a different result if Hamdi had been kept in Afghanistan or even Guantanamo Bay. This creates a perverse incentive. Military authorities faced with the stark choice of submitting to the full-blown criminal process or releasing a suspected enemy combat-ant captured on the battlefield will simply keep citizen-detainees abroad. Indeed, the Government transferred Hamdi from Guantanamo Bay to the United States naval brig only after it learned that he might be an American citizen. It is not at all clear why that should make a determinative constitution-al difference.

III

Even in cases in which the detention of enemy combatants is legally authorized, there remains the question of what process is constitutionally due to a citizen who disputes his enemy-combatant status. . . .'

A

Though they reach radically different conclusions on the process that ought to attend the present proceeding, the parties begin on common ground. All agree that, absent suspension, the writ of habeas corpus remains available to every individual detained within the United States. U.S. Const., Art. I, § 9, cl. 2 ("The Privilege of the Writ of Habeas Corpus shall not be suspended, unless when in Cases of Rebellion or Invasion the public Safety may require it"). Only in the rarest of circumstances has Congress seen fit to suspend the writ. See, *e.g.*, Act of Mar. 3, 1863 . . . ; Act of April 20, 1871. . . . At all other times, it has remained a critical check on the Executive, ensuring that it does not detain individuals except in accordance with law. . . . All agree suspension of the writ has not occurred here. Thus, it is undisputed that Hamdi was properly before an Article III court to challenge his detention under 28 U.S.C. § 2241. . . .'

The simple outline of § 2241 makes clear both that Congress envisioned that habeas petitioners would have some opportunity to present and rebut facts and that courts in cases like this retain some ability to vary the ways in which they do so as mandated by due process. The Government recognizes the basic procedural protections required by the habeas statute, . . . but asks us to hold that, given both the flexibility of the habeas mechanism and the circumstances presented in this case, the presentation of the Mobbs Declaration to the habeas court completed the required factual development. It suggests two separate reasons for its position that no further process is due.

B

First, the Government urges . . . that because it is "undisputed" that Hamdi's seizure took place in a combat zone, the habeas determination can be made purely as a matter of law, with no further hearing or factfinding necessary. This argument is easily rejected. . . . [T]he circumstances . . . cannot in any way be characterized as "undisputed," . . . ". . . because Hamdi has not been permitted to speak for himself or even through counsel as to those circumstances." . . . The habeas petition states only that "[w]hen seized by the United States Government, Mr. Hamdi resided in Afghanistan." . . . An asser-tion that one *resided* in a country in which combat operations are taking place is not a concession that one was "*captured* in a zone of active combat operations in a foreign theater of war," . . . and certainly is not a concession that one was "part of or supporting forces hostile to the United States or coalition partners" and "engaged in an armed conflict against the United States." Accordingly, we reject any argument that Hamdi has made concessions that eliminate any right to further process.

C

The Government's second argument [is] that further factual exploration is unwarranted and inappropriate in light of the extraordinary constitutional interests at stake. Under the Government's most extreme rendition of this argument, "[r]espect for separation of powers and the limited institutional capabilities of courts in matters of military decision-making in connection with an ongoing conflict" ought to eliminate entirely any individual process, restricting the courts to investigating only whether legal authorization exists for the broader detention scheme.... At most, the Government argues, courts should review its determination that a citizen is an enemy combatant under a very deferential "some evidence" standard. ("Under the some evidence standard, the focus is exclusively on the factual basis supplied by the Executive to support its own determination" ...). Under this review, a court would assume the accuracy of the Government's articulated basis for Hamdi's detention, as set forth in the Mobbs Declaration, and assess only whether that articulated basis was a legitimate one....'

In response, Hamdi emphasizes that this Court consistently has recognized that an individual challenging his detention may not be held at the will of the Executive without recourse to some proceeding before a neutral tribunal to determine whether the Executive's asserted justifications for that detention have basis in fact and warrant in law. ...

Both of these positions highlight legitimate concerns. And both emphasize the tension that often exists between the autonomy that the Government asserts is necessary in order to pursue effectively a particular goal and the process that a citizen contends he is due before he is deprived of a constitutional right. The ordinary mechanism that we use for balancing such serious competing interests, and for determining the procedures that are necessary to ensure that a citizen is not "deprived of life, liberty, or property, without due process of law," U.S. Const., Amdt. 5, is the test that we articulated in *Mathews v. Eldridge,* 424 U.S. 319 (1976).... *Mathews* dictates that the process due in any given instance is determined by weighing "the private interest that will be affected by the official action" against the Government's asserted interest, "including the function involved" and the burdens the Government would face in providing greater process. ... The *Mathews* calculus then contemplates a judicious balancing of these concerns, through an analysis of "the risk of an erroneous deprivation" of the private interest if the process were reduced and the "probable value, if any, of additional or substitute safeguards." ...

1

. . .

... [T]he risk of erroneous deprivation of a citizen's liberty in the absence of sufficient process here is very real.... Moreover, as critical as the Government's interest may be in detaining those who actually pose an immediate threat to the national security of the United States during ongoing international conflict, history and common sense teach us that an unchecked system of detention carries the potential to become a means for oppression and abuse of others who do not present that sort of threat.... We reaffirm today the fundamental nature of a citizen's right to be free from involuntary confinement by his own government without due process of law, and we weigh the opposing governmental interests against the curtailment of liberty that such confinement entails.

2

On the other side of the scale are the weighty and sensitive governmental interests in ensuring that those who have in fact fought with the enemy during a war do not return to battle against the United States.... Without doubt, our Constitution recognizes that core strategic matters of warmaking belong in the hands of those who are best positioned and most politically accountable for making them....'

The Government also argues ... that its interests in reducing the process available to alleged enemy combatants are heightened by the practical difficulties that would accompany a system of trial-like process. In its view, military officers who are engaged in the serious work of waging battle would be unnecessarily and dangerously distracted by litigation half a world away, and discovery into military operations would both intrude on the sensitive secrets of national defense and result in a futile search for evidence buried under the rubble of war.... To the extent that these burdens are triggered by heightened procedures, they are properly taken into account in our due process analysis.

3

... It is during our most challenging and uncertain moments that our Nation's commitment to due process is most severely tested; and it is in those times that we must preserve our commitment at home to the principles for which we fight abroad....

. . .

We ... hold that a citizen-detainee seeking to challenge his classification as an enemy combatant must receive notice of the factual basis for his classification, and a fair opportunity to rebut the Government's factual assertions before a neutral decisionmaker.... These essential constitutional promises may not be eroded.

At the same time, the exigencies of the circumstances may demand that, aside from these core elements, enemy combatant proceedings may be tailored to alleviate their uncommon potential to burden the Executive at a time of ongoing military conflict. Hearsay, for example, may need to be accepted as the most reliable available evidence from the Government in such a proceeding. Likewise, the Constitution would not be offended by a presumption in favor of the Government's evidence, so long as that presumption remained a rebuttable one and fair opportunity for rebuttal were provided. Thus, once the Government puts forth credible evidence that the habeas petitioner meets the enemy-combatant criteria, the onus could shift to the petitioner to rebut that evidence with more persuasive evidence that he falls outside the criteria. A burden-shifting scheme of this sort would meet the goal of ensuring that the errant tourist, embedded journalist, or local aid worker has a chance to prove military error while giving due regard to the Executive once it has put forth meaningful support for its conclusion that the detainee is in fact an enemy combatant....'

... The parties agree that initial captures on the battlefield need not receive the process we have discussed here; that process is due only when the determination is made to *continue* to hold those who have been seized. The Government has made clear ... that documentation regarding battlefield detainees already is kept in the ordinary course of military affairs.... Any factfinding imposition created by requiring a knowledgeable affiant to summarize these records to an independent tribunal is a minimal one. Likewise, arguments that military officers ought not have to wage war under the threat of litigation lose much of their steam when factual disputes at enemy-combatant hearings are limited to the alleged combatant's acts. This focus meddles little, if at all, in the strategy or conduct of war, inquiring only into the appropriateness of continuing to detain an individual claimed to have taken up arms against the United States. While we accord the greatest respect and consideration to the judgments of military authorities in matters relating to the actual prosecution of a war, and recognize that the scope of that discretion necessarily is wide, it does not infringe on the core role of the military for the courts to exercise their own time-honored and constitutionally mandated roles of reviewing and resolving claims like those presented here. . . .'

In sum, while the full protections that accompany challenges to detentions in other settings may prove unworkable and inappropriate in the enemy-combatant setting, the threats to military operations posed by a basic system of independent review are not so weighty as to trump a citizen's core rights to challenge meaningfully the Government's case and to be heard by an impartial adjudicator.

D

In so holding, we necessarily reject the Government's assertion that separation of powers principles mandate a heavily circumscribed role for the courts in such circumstances. Indeed, the position that the courts must forgo any examination of the individual case and focus exclusively on the legality of the broader detention scheme cannot be mandated by any reasonable view of separation of powers, as this approach serves only to *condense* power into a single branch of government. We have long since made clear that a state of war is not a blank check for the President when it comes to the rights of the Nation's citizens. *Youngstown Sheet & Tube,* 343 U.S., at 587. Whatever power the United States Constitution envisions for the Executive in its exchanges with other nations or with enemy organizations in times of conflict, it most assuredly envisions a role for all three branches when individual liberties are at stake. *Mistretta v. United States,* 488 U.S. 361, 380 (1989) (it was "the central judgment of the Framers of the Constitution that, within our political scheme, the separation of governmental powers into three coordinate Branches is essential to the preservation of liberty"); *Home Building & Loan Assn. v. Blaisdell,* 290 U.S. 398, 426 (1934) (The war power "is a power to wage war successfully, and thus it permits the harnessing of the entire energies of the people in a supreme cooperative effort to preserve the nation. But even the war power does not remove constitutional limitations safeguarding essential liber-ties"). Likewise, we have made clear that, unless Congress acts to suspend it, the Great Writ of habeas corpus allows the Judicial Branch to play a necessary role in maintaining this delicate balance of governance, serving as an important judicial check on the Executive's discretion in the realm of detentions. See *St. Cyr,* 533 U.S., at 301 ("At its historical core, the writ of habeas corpus has served as a means of reviewing the legality of Executive detention, and it is in that context that its protections have been strongest"). Thus, while we do not question that our due process assessment must pay keen attention to the particular burdens faced by the Executive in the context of military action, it would turn our system of checks and balances on its head to suggest that a citizen could not make his way to court with a challenge to the factual basis for his detention by his government, simply because the Executive opposes making available such a challenge. Absent suspension of the writ by Congress, a citizen detained as an enemy combatant is entitled to this process.

. . .

... Aside from unspecified "screening" processes ... and military interrogations in which the Government suggests Hamdi could have contested his classification, ... Hamdi has received no process. An interrogation by one's captor, however effective an intelligence-gathering tool, hardly constitutes a constitutionally adequate factfinding before a neutral decisionmaker. ... Plainly, the "process" Hamdi has received is not that to which he is entitled under the Due Process Clause.

There remains the possibility that the standards we have articulated could be met by an appropriately authorized and properly constituted military tribunal. ... In the absence of such process, however, a court that receives a petition for a writ of habeas corpus from an alleged enemy combatant must itself ensure that the minimum requirements of due process are achieved. ... We have no reason to doubt that courts faced with these sensitive matters will pay proper heed both to the matters of national security that might arise in an individual case and to the constitutional limitations safeguarding essential liberties that remain vibrant even in times of security concerns.

IV

... Since our grant of certiorari in this case, Hamdi has been appointed counsel, ... with whom he is now being granted unmonitored meetings. He unquestionably has the right to access to counsel in connection with the proceedings on remand. No further consideration of this issue is necessary at this stage of the case.

* * *

The judgment ... is vacated, and the case is remanded for further proceedings.

Justice Souter, with whom Justice Ginsburg joins, concurring in part, dissenting in part, and concurring in the judgment.

... It is undisputed that the Government has not charged [Hamdi] with espionage, treason, or any other crime under domestic law. It is likewise undisputed that for one year and nine months, on the basis of an Executive designation of Hamdi as an "enemy combatant," the Government denied him the right to send or receive any communication beyond the prison where he was held and, in particular, denied him access to counsel to represent him.[1] The Government asserts a right to hold Hamdi under these conditions indefinitely, that is, until the Government determines that the United States is no longer threatened by the terrorism exemplified in the attacks of September 11, 2001.

. . .

... The Government has failed to demonstrate that the Force Resolution authorizes the detention complained of here even on the facts the Government claims. If the Government raises nothing further than the record now shows, the Non–Detention Act entitles Hamdi to be released.

. . .

... Should the severity of the [Non–Detention] Act be relieved when the Government's stated factual justification for incommunicado detention is a war on terrorism, so that the Government may be said to act "pursuant" to congressional terms that fall short of explicit authority to imprison individuals?

---

1. The Government has since February 2004 permitted Hamdi to consult with counsel as a matter of policy, but does not concede that it has an obligation to allow this. ...'

With one possible though important qualification, ... the answer has to be no....'

. . .

... [T]hat Congress intended to guard against a repetition of the World War II internments when it repealed the 1950 statute and gave us § 4001(a) provides a powerful reason to think that § 4001(a) was meant to require clear congressional authorization before any citizen can be placed in a cell.... [T]he internments of the 1940's were accomplished by Executive action.... When, therefore, Congress repealed the 1950 Act and adopted § 4001(a) for the purpose of avoiding another *Korematsu*, it intended to preclude reliance on vague congressional authority (for example, providing "accommodations" for those subject to removal) as authority for detention or imprisonment at the discretion of the Executive (maintaining detention camps of American citizens, for example). In requiring that any Executive detention be "pursuant to an Act of Congress," then, Congress necessarily meant to require a congressional enactment that clearly authorized detention or imprisonment.

Second, when Congress passed § 4001(a) it was acting in light of an interpretive regime that subjected enactments limiting liberty in wartime to the requirement of a clear statement and it presumably intended § 4001(a) to be read accordingly....'

Finally, ... [i]n a government of separated powers, deciding finally on what is a reasonable degree of guaranteed liberty whether in peace or war (or some condition in between) is not well entrusted to the Executive Branch of Government, whose particular responsibility is to maintain security. For reasons of inescapable human nature, the branch of the Government asked to counter a serious threat is not the branch on which to rest the Nation's entire reliance in striking the balance between the will to win and the cost in liberty on the way to victory; the responsibility for security will naturally amplify the claim that security legitimately raises. A reasonable balance is more likely to be reached on the judgment of a different branch, just as Madison said in remarking that "the constant aim is to divide and arrange the several offices in such a manner as that each may be a check on the other—that the private interest of every individual may be a sentinel over the public rights." The Federalist No. 51, p. 349 (J. Cooke ed. 1961). Hence the need for an assessment by Congress before citizens are subject to lockup, and likewise the need for a clearly expressed congressional resolution of the competing claims.

... [N]one of the Government's arguments suffices to justify Hamdi's detention.

... Th[e] legislative history indicates that Congress was aware that § 4001(a) would limit the Executive's power to detain citizens in wartime to protect national security, and it is fair to say that the prohibition was thus intended to extend not only to the exercise of power to vindicate the interests underlying domestic criminal law, but to statutorily unauthorized detention by the Executive for reasons of security in wartime, just as Hamdi claims.

... [T]he Force Resolution ... is fairly read to authorize the use of armies and weapons, whether against other armies or individual terrorists. But ... it never so much as uses the word detention, and there is no reason to think Congress might have perceived any need to augment Executive power to deal with dangerous citizens within the United States, given the well-stocked statutory arsenal of defined criminal offenses covering the gamut of actions that a citizen sympathetic to terrorists might commit....'

. . .

... [T]he Government here repeatedly argues that Hamdi's detention amounts to nothing more than customary detention of a captive taken on the field of battle: if the usages of war are fairly authorized by the Force Resolution, Hamdi's detention is authorized for purposes of § 4001(a).

There is no need, however, to address the merits of such an argument in all possible circumstances. For now it is enough to recognize that the Government's stated legal position in its campaign against the Taliban (among whom Hamdi was allegedly captured) is apparently at odds with its claim here to be acting in accordance with customary law of war and hence to be within the terms of the Force Resolution in its detention of Hamdi. [T]he Government says that "the Geneva Convention applies to the Taliban detainees." ... Hamdi presumably is such a detainee ... according to the Government's own account [and] would therefore seem to qualify for treatment as a prisoner of war under the Third Geneva Convention, to which the United States is a party....'

By holding him incommunicado, however, the Government obviously has not been treating him as a prisoner of war, and in fact the Government claims that no Taliban detainee is entitled to prisoner of war status....'

Whether, or to what degree, the Government is in fact violating the Geneva Convention and is thus acting outside the customary usages of war are not matters I can resolve at this point. What I can say, though, is that the Government has not made out its claim that in detaining Hamdi in the manner described, it is acting in accord with the laws of war authorized to be applied against citizens by the Force Resolution. I conclude accordingly that the Government has failed to support the position that the Force Resolution authorizes the described detention of Hamdi for purposes of § 4001(a).

It is worth adding a further reason for requiring the Government to bear the burden of clearly justifying its claim to be exercising recognized war powers before declaring § 4001(a) satisfied. Thirty-eight days after adopting the Force Resolution, Congress passed the ... USA PATRIOT ACT ... authoriz[ing] the detention of alien terrorists for no more than seven days in the absence of criminal charges or deportation proceedings.... It is very difficult to believe that the same Congress that carefully circumscribed Executive power over alien terrorists on home soil would not have meant to require the Government to justify clearly its detention of an American citizen held on home soil incommunicado.

... [T]he Government hints of a constitutional challenge to the statute, but it presents none here. I will, however, stray across the line between statutory and constitutional territory just far enough to note the weakness of the Government's mixed claim of inherent, extrastatutory authority under a combination of Article II of the Constitution and the usages of war.... [I]t is instructive to recall Justice Jackson's observation that the President is not Commander in Chief of the country, only of the military. *Youngstown Sheet & Tube Co. v. Sawyer,* 343 U.S. 579, 643–644 (1952) (concurring opinion)....'

There may be room for one qualification to Justice Jackson's statement, however: in a moment of genuine emergency, when the Government must act with no time for deliberation, the Executive may be able to detain a citizen if there is reason to fear he is an imminent threat to the safety of the Nation and its people (though I doubt there is any want of statutory authority). This case, however, does not present that question, because an emergency power of necessity must at least be limited by the emergency; Hamdi has been locked up for over two years....'

Whether insisting on the careful scrutiny of emergency claims or on a vigorous reading of § 4001(a), we are heirs to a tradition given voice 800 years ago by Magna Carta, which, on the barons' insistence, confined executive power by "the law of the land."

Because I find Hamdi's detention forbidden by § 4001(a) and unauthorized by the Force Resolution, I would not reach any questions of what process he may be due in litigating disputed issues in a proceeding under the habeas statute or prior to the habeas enquiry itself. For me, it suffices that the Government has failed to justify holding him in the absence of a further Act of Congress, criminal charges, a showing that the detention conforms to the laws of war, or a demonstration that § 4001(a) is unconstitutional. I would therefore vacate the judgment of the Court of Appeals and remand for proceedings consistent with this view.

Since this disposition does not command a majority of the Court, however, the need to give practical effect to the conclusions of eight members of the Court rejecting the Government's position calls for me to join with the plurality in ordering remand on terms closest to those I would impose.... Although I think litigation of Hamdi's status as an enemy combatant is unnecessary, the terms of the plurality's remand will allow Hamdi to offer evidence that he is not an enemy combatant, and he should at the least have the benefit of that opportunity.

[I]n joining with the plurality to produce a judgment, I do not adopt the plurality's resolution of constitutional issues that I would not reach. It is not that I could disagree ... that someone in Hamdi's position is entitled at a minimum to notice of the Government's claimed factual basis for holding him, and to a fair chance to rebut it before a neutral decision maker; nor, of course, could I disagree with the plurality's affirmation of Hamdi's right to counsel. On the other hand, I do not mean to imply agreement that the Government could claim an evidentiary presumption casting the burden of rebuttal on Hamdi, or that an opportunity to litigate before a military tribunal might obviate or truncate enquiry by a court on habeas.

Subject to these qualifications, I join with the plurality in a judgment of the Court vacating ... and remanding the case.

Justice Scalia, with whom Justice Stevens joins, dissenting.

. . .

Where the Government accuses a citizen of waging war against it, our constitutional tradition has been to prosecute him in federal court for treason or some other crime. Where the exigencies of war prevent that, the Constitution's Suspension Clause, Art. I, § 9, cl. 2, allows Congress to relax the usual protections temporarily. Absent suspension, however, the Executive's assertion of military exigency has not been thought sufficient to permit detention without charge. No one contends that the congressional Authorization for Use of Military Force ... is an implementation of the Suspension Clause. Accordingly, I would reverse....'

I

The very core of liberty secured by our Anglo–Saxon system of separated powers has been freedom from indefinite imprisonment at the will of the Executive....'

. . .

The gist of the Due Process Clause, as understood at the founding and since, was to force the Government to follow those common-law procedures traditionally deemed necessary before depriving a person of life, liberty, or property....'

. . .

These due process rights have historically been vindicated by the writ of habeas corpus. In England before the founding, the writ developed into a tool for challenging executive confinement....'

. . .

The writ of habeas corpus was preserved in the Constitution—the only common-law writ to be explicitly mentioned. See Art. I, § 9, cl. 2.... Hamilton lauded "the establishment of the writ of *habeas corpus*" in his Federalist defense as a means to protect against "the practice of arbitrary imprisonments ... in all ages, [one of] the favourite and most formidable instruments of tyranny." The Federalist No. 84....'

II

... The relevant question ... is whether there is a different, special procedure for imprisonment of a citizen accused of wrongdoing *by aiding the enemy in wartime.*

A

Justice O'Connor, writing for a plurality of this Court, asserts that captured enemy combatants (other than those suspected of war crimes) have traditionally been detained until the cessation of hostilities and then released. That is probably an accurate description of wartime practice with respect to enemy *aliens*. The tradition with respect to American citizens, however, has been quite different. Citizens aiding the enemy have been treated as traitors subject to the criminal process.

. . .

... The Founders inherited the understanding that a citizen's levying war against the Government was to be punished criminally. The Constitution provides: "Treason against the United States, shall consist only in levying War against them, or in adhering to their Enemies, giving them Aid and Comfort"; and establishes a heightened proof requirement (two witnesses) in order to "convic[t]" of that offense. Art. III, § 3, cl. 1.

In more recent times, too, citizens have been charged and tried in Article III courts for acts of war against the United States, even when their noncitizen co-conspirators were not....'

The modern treason statute ... basically tracks the language of the constitutional provision. Other provisions of Title 18 criminalize various acts of warmaking and adherence to the enemy.... The only citizen other than Hamdi known to be imprisoned in connection with military hostilities in Afghanistan against the United States *was* subjected to criminal process and convicted upon a guilty plea. See *United States v. Lindh*....

B

The Suspension Clause was by design a safety valve, the Constitution's only "express provision for exercise of extraordinary authority because of a crisis," *Youngstown Sheet & Tube Co. v. Sawyer*, 343 U.S. 579, 650 (1952)

(Jackson, J., concurring). Very early in the Nation's history, President Jefferson unsuccessfully sought a suspension of habeas corpus to deal with Aaron Burr's conspiracy to overthrow the Government. See 16 Annals of Congress 402–425 (1807). During the Civil War, Congress passed its first Act authorizing Executive suspension of the writ of habeas corpus, see Act of Mar. 3, 1863, 12 Stat. 755, to the relief of those many who thought President Lincoln's unauthorized proclamations of suspension (*e.g.*, Proclamation No. 1, 13 Stat. 730 (1862)) unconstitutional. . . .'

. . .

III

. . . Even if suspension of the writ on the one hand, and committal for criminal charges on the other hand, have been the only *traditional* means of dealing with citizens who levied war against their own country, it is theoretically possible that the Constitution does not *require* a choice between these alternatives.

I believe, however, that substantial evidence does refute that possibility. First, the text of the 1679 Habeas Corpus Act makes clear that indefinite imprisonment on reasonable suspicion is not an available option of treatment for those accused of aiding the enemy, absent a suspension of the writ. . . .'

Writings from the founding generation also suggest that, without exception, the only constitutional alternatives are to charge the crime or suspend the writ. . . .'

The absence of military authority to imprison citizens indefinitely in wartime—whether or not a probability of treason had been established by means less than jury trial—was confirmed by [caselaw from the eras of the War of 1812 and the Civil War, including *Ex parte Milligan, supra*, where] the Court issued the writ to an American citizen who had been tried by military commission for offenses that included conspiring to overthrow the Government, seize munitions, and liberate prisoners of war. . . . The Court rejected . . . the Government's assertion that military jurisdiction was proper "under the 'laws and usages of war,' " . . . :

". . . [T]hose laws and usages . . . can never be applied to citizens in states which have upheld the authority of the government, and where the courts are open and their process unobstructed."

. . . [T]he reasoning and conclusion of *Milligan* logically cover the present case. The Government justifies imprisonment of Hamdi on principles of the law of war and admits that, absent the war, it would have no such authority. But if the law of war cannot be applied to citizens where courts are open, then Hamdi's imprisonment without criminal trial is no less unlawful than Milligan's trial by military tribunal.

. . .

[C]riminal process was viewed as the primary means—and the only means absent congressional action suspending the writ—not only to punish traitors, but to incapacitate them.

The proposition that the Executive lacks indefinite wartime detention authority over citizens is consistent with the Founders' general mistrust of military power permanently at the Executive's disposal. . . . No fewer than 10 issues of the Federalist were devoted in whole or part to allaying fears of oppression from the proposed Constitution's authorization of standing armies in peacetime. Many safeguards in the Constitution reflect these concerns.

Congress's authority "[t]o raise and support Armies" was hedged with the proviso that "no Appropriation of Money to that Use shall be for a longer Term than two Years." U.S. Const., Art. 1, § 8, cl. 12. Except for the actual command of military forces, all authorization for their maintenance and all explicit authorization for their use is placed in the control of Congress under Article I, rather than the President under Article II. . . .'

A view of the Constitution that gives the Executive authority to use military force rather than the force of law against citizens on American soil flies in the face of the mistrust that engendered these provisions.

IV

. . . *Ex parte Quirin,* 317 U.S. 1 (1942), a World War II case upholding the trial by military commission of eight German saboteurs, one of whom, Hans Haupt, was a U.S. citizen . . . was not this Court's finest hour. The Court upheld the commission and denied relief in a brief *per curiam* issued the day after oral argument concluded . . .; a week later the Government carried out the commission's death sentence upon six saboteurs, including Haupt. The Court eventually explained its reasoning in a written opinion issued several months later [that "revised" rather than "described" *Milligan.*]

. . .

But even if *Quirin* gave a correct description of *Milligan,* or made an irrevocable revision of it, *Quirin* would still not justify denial of the writ here. In *Quirin* it was uncontested that the petitioners were members of enemy forces. . . . But where . . . the petitioner insists that he is *not* a belligerent . . . *Quirin* left the pre-existing law in place: Absent suspension of the writ, a citizen held where the courts are open is entitled either to criminal trial or to a judicial decree requiring his release.

V

It follows from what I have said that Hamdi is entitled to a habeas decree requiring his release unless (1) criminal proceedings are promptly brought, or (2) Congress has suspended the writ of habeas corpus. . . .'

. . .

[The Authorization for Use of Military Force] is not remotely a congressional suspension of the writ, and no one claims that it is. Contrary to the plurality's view, I do not think this statute even authorizes detention of a citizen with the clarity necessary to satisfy the interpretive canon that statutes should be construed so as to avoid grave constitutional concerns; or with the clarity necessary to overcome the statutory prescription that "[n]o citizen shall be imprisoned or otherwise detained by the United States except pursuant to an Act of Congress." 18 U.S.C. § 4001(a). But even if it did, I would not permit it to overcome Hamdi's entitlement to habeas corpus relief. The Suspension Clause of the Constitution, which carefully circumscribes the conditions under which the writ can be withheld, would be a sham if it could be evaded by congressional prescription of requirements *other than the common-law requirement of committal for criminal prosecution* that render the writ, though available, unavailing. If the Suspension Clause does not guarantee the citizen that he will either be tried or released, unless the conditions for suspending the writ exist and the grave action of suspending the writ has been taken; if it merely guarantees the citizen that he will not be detained unless Congress by ordinary legislation says he can be detained; it guarantees him very little indeed.

It should not be thought, however, that the plurality's evisceration of the Suspension Clause augments, principally, the power of Congress. As usual, the major effect of its constitutional improvisation is to increase the power of the Court. Having found a congressional authorization for detention of citizens where none clearly exists; and having discarded the categorical procedural protection of the Suspension Clause; the plurality then proceeds, under the guise of the Due Process Clause, to prescribe what procedural protections *it* thinks appropriate. It "weigh[s] the private interest ... against the Government's asserted interest," and—just as though writing a new Constitution—comes up with an unheard-of system in which the citizen rather than the Government bears the burden of proof, testimony is by hearsay rather than live witnesses, and the presiding officer may well be a "neutral" military officer rather than judge and jury. It claims authority ... from *Mathews v. Eldridge,* 424 U.S. 319 (1976), a case involving ... *the withdrawal of disability benefits!* ... [*Mathews*] has no place where the Constitution and the common law already supply an answer.

Having distorted the Suspension Clause, the plurality finishes up by transmogrifying the Great Writ—disposing of the present habeas petition by remanding for the District Court to "engag[e] in a factfinding process that is both prudent and incremental." ... This judicial remediation of executive default is unheard of. The role of habeas corpus is to determine the legality of executive detention, not to supply the omitted process necessary to make it legal.... It is not the habeas court's function to make illegal detention legal by supplying a process that the Government could have provided, but chose not to. If Hamdi is being imprisoned in violation of the Constitution (because without due process of law), then his habeas petition should be granted; the Executive may then hand him over to the criminal authorities, whose detention for the purpose of prosecution will be lawful, or else must release him.

There is a certain harmony of approach in the plurality's making up for Congress's failure to invoke the Suspension Clause and its making up for the Executive's failure to apply what it says are needed procedures.... The problem with this approach is not only that it steps out of the courts' modest and limited role in a democratic society; but that by repeatedly doing what it thinks the political branches ought to do it encourages their lassitude and saps the vitality of government by the people.

VI

Several limitations give my views in this matter a relatively narrow compass. They apply only to citizens, accused of being enemy combatants, who are detained within the territorial jurisdiction of a federal court. This is not likely to be a numerous group; currently we know of only two, Hamdi and Jose Padilla. Where the citizen is captured outside and held outside the United States, the constitutional requirements may be different....'

... If the situation demands it, the Executive can ask Congress to authorize suspension of the writ—which can be made subject to whatever conditions Congress deems appropriate, including even the procedural novelties invented by the plurality today.... If civil rights are to be curtailed during wartime, it must be done openly and democratically, as the Constitution requires, rather than by silent erosion through an opinion of this Court.

. . .

Justice Thomas, dissenting.

... [Hamdi's] detention falls squarely within the Federal Government's war powers, and we lack the expertise and capacity to second-guess that decision. As such, petitioners' habeas challenge should fail, and there is no reason to remand the case...."

. . .

The Founders intended that the President have primary responsibility—along with the necessary power—to protect the national security and to conduct the Nation's foreign relations. They did so principally because the structural advantages of a unitary Executive are essential in these domains...."

... "Of all the cares or concerns of government, the direction of war most peculiarly demands those qualities which distinguish the exercise of power by a single hand." The Federalist No. 74, p. 500 (A. Hamilton).... To this end, the Constitution vests in the President "[t]he executive Power," Art. II, § 1, provides that he "shall be Commander in Chief of the" armed forces, § 2, and places in him the power to recognize foreign governments, § 3.

This Court has long recognized these features and has accordingly held that the President has *constitutional* authority to protect the national security and that this authority carries with it broad discretion...."

The Court has acknowledged that the President has the authority to "employ [the Nation's Armed Forces] in the manner he may deem most effectual to harass and conquer and subdue the enemy." *Fleming v. Page,* 9 How. 603, 615 (1850). With respect to foreign affairs as well, the Court has recognized the President's independent authority and need to be free from interference. See, *e.g., United States v. Curtiss–Wright Export Corp.,* 299 U.S. 304, 320 (1936)...."

Congress, to be sure, has a substantial and essential role in both foreign affairs and national security. But it is crucial to recognize that *judicial* interference in these domains destroys the purpose of vesting primary responsibility in a unitary Executive...."

Several points ... are worth emphasizing. First, with respect to certain decisions relating to national security and foreign affairs, the courts simply lack the relevant information and expertise to second-guess determinations made by the President based on information properly withheld. Second, even if the courts could compel the Executive to produce the necessary information, such decisions are simply not amenable to judicial determination because "[t]hey are delicate, complex, and involve large elements of prophecy." ... Third, the Court ... has correctly recognized the primacy of the political branches in the foreign-affairs and national-security contexts.

... [T]hat Congress has provided the President with broad authorities does not imply—and the Judicial Branch should not infer—that Congress intended to deprive him of particular powers not specifically enumerated...."

... [T]he Court has explained, in a case analogous to this one, that "the detention[,] ordered by the President in the declared exercise of his powers as Commander in Chief of the Army in time of war and of grave public danger[, is] not to be set aside by the courts without the clear conviction that [it is] in conflict with the Constitution or laws of Congress constitutionally enacted." *Ex parte Quirin,* 317 U.S. 1, 25 (1942).... This deference extends to the President's determination of all the factual predicates necessary to conclude that a given action is appropriate...."

. . .

I acknowledge that ... whether Hamdi's executive detention is lawful is a question properly resolved by the Judicial Branch, though the question comes to the Court with the strongest presumptions in favor of the Government. The plurality agrees that Hamdi's detention is lawful if he is an enemy combatant. But the question whether Hamdi is actually an enemy combatant is "of a kind for which the Judiciary has neither aptitude, facilities nor responsibility and which has long been held to belong in the domain of political power not subject to judicial intrusion or inquiry." ... That is, although it is appropriate for the Court to determine the judicial question whether the President has the asserted authority, ... we lack the information and expertise to question whether Hamdi is actually an enemy combatant, a question the resolution of which is committed to other branches....'

II

"The war power of the national government is 'the power to wage war successfully.'" *Lichter v. United States,* 334 U.S. 742, 767, n. 9 (1948).... It ... quite obviously includes the ability to detain those (even United States citizens) who fight against our troops or those of our allies, see, *e.g., Quirin....*'

Although the President very well may have inherent authority to detain those arrayed against our troops, I agree with the plurality that we need not decide that question because Congress has authorized the President to do so [by t]he Authorization for Use of Military Force....'

The plurality, however, qualifies its recognition of the President's authority to detain enemy combatants in the war on terrorism in ways that are at odds with our precedent.... It ... appears to limit the President's authority to detain by requiring that the record establis[h] that United States troops are still involved in active combat in Afghanistan because, in that case, detention would be "part of the exercise of 'necessary and appropriate force.'" But I do not believe that we may diminish the Federal Government's war powers by reference to a treaty and certainly not to a treaty that does not apply. Further, we are bound by the political branches' determination that the United States is at war.... And, in any case, the power to detain does not end with the cessation of formal hostilities. See, *e.g., Madsen v. Kinsella,* 343 U.S. 341, 360 (1952); *Johnson v. Eisentrager,* 339 U.S. 763, 786 (1950)....'

. . .

III

I agree with the plurality that the Federal Government has power to detain those that the Executive Branch determines to be enemy combatants. But I do not think that the plurality has adequately explained the breadth of the President's authority to detain enemy combatants, an authority that includes making virtually conclusive factual findings. In my view, the structural considerations discussed above, as recognized in our precedent, demonstrate that we lack the capacity and responsibility to second-guess this determination.

. . .

In this context, due process requires nothing more than a good-faith executive determination. To be clear: The Court has held that an executive, acting pursuant to statutory and constitutional authority may, consistent with the Due Process Clause, unilaterally decide to detain an individual if the executive deems this necessary for the public safety *even if he is mistaken.*

. . .

The Government's asserted authority to detain an individual that the President has determined to be an enemy combatant, at least while hostilities continue, comports with the Due Process Clause. [T]he Executive's decision that a detention is necessary to protect the public need not and should not be subjected to judicial second-guessing. Indeed, at least in the context of enemy-combatant determinations, this would defeat the unity, secrecy, and dispatch that the Founders believed to be so important to the warmaking function. . . .'

I therefore cannot agree with Justice Scalia's conclusion that the Government must choose between using standard criminal processes and suspending the writ. . . .'

. . .

. . . By detaining Hamdi, the President, in the prosecution of a war and authorized by Congress, has acted well within his authority. Hamdi thereby received all the process to which he was due under the circumstances. I therefore believe that this is no occasion to balance the competing interests, as the plurality unconvincingly attempts to do.

IV

. . . [Also,] the plurality misapplies its chosen framework, one that if applied correctly would probably lead to the result I have reached. . . . [A]s the Government explains, detention can serve to gather critical intelligence regarding the intentions and capabilities of our adversaries, a function that the Government avers has become all the more important in the war on terrorism. . . .'

Additional process, the Government explains, will destroy the intelligence gathering function. . . . It also does seem quite likely that, under the process envisioned by the plurality, various military officials will have to take time to litigate this matter. And though the plurality does not say so, a meaningful ability to challenge the Government's factual allegations will probably require the Government to divulge highly classified information to the purported enemy combatant, who might then upon release return to the fight armed with our most closely held secrets.

. . .

. . . [I]n the war context, we know neither the strength of the Government's interests nor the costs of imposing additional process.

. . .

Undeniably, Hamdi has been deprived of a serious interest, one actually protected by the Due Process Clause. Against this, however, is the Government's overriding interest in protecting the Nation. [A] deprivation of liberty can be justified by the need to protect . . . the Nation. . . .'

. . .[a]

a. The same day that *Hamdi* was decided, the Court issued two other decisions involving challenges to prolonged Executive detention of alleged "enemy combatants." One, Rumsfeld v. Padilla, 124 S.Ct. 2711 (2004), involved a habeas petition filed in New York on behalf of a United States citizen first held in criminal custody in New York as a material witness in connection with a federal grand jury investigation of the September 11th terrorist attacks and then transferred to a Naval Brig in South Carolina for indefinite detention pursuant to Presidential directive. A 5–4 majority remanded, holding that the habeas petition had to be brought in South Carolina where Padilla was confined by the time the petition had been filed. Justice Stevens' dissent, joined by Justices Souter, Ginsburg and

D. THE LINE ITEM VETO

DELEGATION OF LEGISLATIVE POWER TO THE EXECUTIVE

Many disputes about executive power implicate concerns that are sometimes collectively referred to as the non-delegation doctrine—the idea that Congress may not delegate its legislative powers to the executive. Although the Court has not invoked the doctrine as a formal basis for invalidating a Congressional law since the New Deal, for at least 150 years the Court's decisions have been sprinkled with categorical statements that Congress may not relinquish any of its powers to enact legislation through grants to federal administrators. The following excerpt from Justice O'Connor's opinion for the Court in Touby v. United States, 500 U.S. 160, 163–65 (1991), is illustrative:

"The Constitution provides that '[a]ll legislative Powers herein granted shall be vested in a Congress of the United States.' U.S. Const., Art. I, § 1. From this language the Court has derived the nondelegation doctrine: that Congress may not constitutionally delegate its legislative power to another Branch of government. . . .'

". . . [T]he nondelegation doctrine does not prevent Congress from seeking assistance, within proper limits, from its coordinate Branches. . . . Thus, Congress does not violate the Constitution merely because it legislates in broad terms, leaving a certain degree of discretion to executive or judicial actors. So long as Congress 'lay[s] down by legislative act an intelligible principle to which the person or body authorized to [act] is directed to conform, such legislative action is not a forbidden delegation of legislative power.' . . .

". . . [The Court has] upheld as providing sufficient guidance statutes authorizing the War Department to recover 'excessive profits' earned on military contracts, see Lichter v. United States, 334 U.S. 742, 778–786 (1948); authorizing the Price Administrator to fix 'fair and equitable' commodities prices, see Yakus v. United States, 321 U.S. 414, 426–427 (1944); and authorizing the Federal Communications Commission to regulate broadcast licensing in

Breyer (who had joined the plurality opinion in *Hamdi*), said in a footnote: "I believe that the Non–Detention Act . . . prohibits—and the Authorization for Use of Military Force Joint Resolution . . . does not authorize—the protracted, incommunicado detention of American citizens arrested in the United States." The dissent concluded as follows:

"At stake in this case is nothing less than the essence of a free society. Even more important than the method of selecting the people's rulers and their successors is the character of the constraints imposed on the Executive by the rule of law. Unconstrained Executive detention for the purpose of investigating and preventing subversive activity is the hallmark of the Star Chamber. Access to counsel for the purpose of protecting the citizen from official mistakes and mistreatment is the hallmark of due process.

"Executive detention of subversive citizens, like detention of enemy soldiers to keep them off the battlefield, may sometimes be justified to prevent persons from launching or becoming missiles of destruction. It may not, however, be justified by the naked interest in using unlawful procedures to extract information. Incommunicado detention for months on end is such a procedure. Whether the information so procured is more or less reliable than that acquired by more extreme forms of torture is of no consequence. For if this Nation is to remain true to the ideals symbolized by its flag, it must not wield the tools of tyrants even to resist an assault by the forces of tyranny."

The other decision involved aliens captured in Afghanistan during the military campaign against al Qaeda and the Taliban. The Court held that the habeas corpus jurisdiction of United States courts extends to judicial review of the legality of Executive detention of foreign nationals at the United States Naval Base in Guantanamo Bay, Cuba, over which the United States—by virtue of a lease agreement with Cuba—exercises plenary and exclusive jurisdiction, but not "ultimate sovereignty." Rasul v. Bush, 124 S.Ct. 2686 (2004).

the 'public interest,' see National Broadcasting Co. v. United States, 319 U.S. 190, 225–226 (1943)."

The non-delegation idea is said to have both textual and theoretical underpinnings. As a matter of text, Article I, Section 1 of the Constitution provides that "All legislative Powers herein granted shall be vested in a Congress of the United States, which shall consist of a Senate and House of Representatives." As a matter of theory, the non-delegation doctrine reflects the basic idea that all decisions by government ought to be traceable to the governmental body to which the people have conferred permission to make those particular decisions.

Of course, things are not so simple. To begin with, it is not clear that "vested" means "nondelegable." After all, Article II "vests" executive power in a President alone, and yet he permissibly delegates what would have to be conceded to be executive authority to his underlings in the executive branch. And if their exercise of authority on his behalf is allowed because it can be traced back to him, why not the same for the President's exercise of power on behalf of Congress?

Some might respond that the President is free to reclaim power from his underlings, and that Congress might have difficulty retrieving power given to the President. This refinement of the non-delegation idea—that power ought not to be delegated in a way that it cannot be reclaimed—might explain some cases, but it might call into question the results of others. It might also suggest that Congressional delegation to the President might be different than delegation by Congress to other bodies, like states. In the following case, as well as the *Chadha* decision in the next section, consider whether and how non-delegation principles bear on the Court's analyses.

Clinton v. City of New York

524 U.S. 417, 118 S.Ct. 2091, 141 L.Ed.2d 393 (1998).

Justice Stevens delivered the opinion of the Court.

The Line Item Veto Act (Act) ... was enacted in April 1996 and became effective on January 1, 1997. The following day, six Members of Congress who had voted against the Act brought suit in the District Court for the District of Columbia challenging its constitutionality. ... We determined, however, that the Members of Congress did not have standing to sue because they had not "alleged a sufficiently concrete injury to have established Article III standing," Raines v. Byrd, 521 U.S. 811 (1997). ...'

Less than two months after our decision in that case, the President exercised his authority to cancel one provision in the Balanced Budget Act of 1997, ... and two provisions in the Taxpayer Relief Act of 1997 ... Appellees, claiming that they had been injured by two of those cancellations, filed these cases in the District Court. That Court again held the statute invalid, ... and we again expedited our review.... We now hold that these appellees have standing to challenge the constitutionality of the Act and, reaching the merits, we agree that the cancellation procedures set forth in the Act violate the Presentment Clause, Art. I, § 7, cl. 2, of the Constitution.

[handwritten margin note: suit brought by 6 members of congress – claiming Line Veto Act to be unconstitutional But didn't have standing.]

I

We begin by reviewing the canceled items that are at issue in these cases.

Title XIX of the Social Security Act, ... authorizes the Federal Government to transfer huge sums of money to the States to help finance medical care for the indigent. ... In 1991, Congress directed that those federal subsidies be reduced by the amount of certain taxes levied by the States on health care providers. In 1994, the Department of Health and Human Services (HHS) notified the State of New York that 15 of its taxes were covered by the 1991 Act, and that as of June 30, 1994, the statute therefore required New York to return $955 million to the United States. The notice advised the State that it could apply for a waiver on certain statutory grounds. New York did request a waiver for those tax programs, as well as for a number of others, but HHS has not formally acted on any of those waiver requests. New York has estimated that the amount at issue for the period from October 1992 through March 1997 is as high as $2.6 billion.

Because HHS had not taken any action on the waiver requests, New York turned to Congress for relief. ... Section 4722(c) of the Balanced Budget Act of 1997 identifies the disputed taxes and provides that they "are deemed to be permissible health care related taxes and in compliance with the requirements" of the relevant provisions of the 1991 statute.

On August 11, 1997, the President sent identical notices to the Senate and to the House of Representatives canceling "one item of new direct spending," specifying § 4722(c) as that item ...

A person who realizes a profit from the sale of securities is generally subject to a capital gains tax. Under existing law, however, an ordinary business corporation can acquire a corporation, including a food processing or refining company, in a merger or stock-for-stock transaction in which no gain is recognized to the seller ...; the seller's tax payment, therefore, is deferred. If, however, the purchaser is a farmers' cooperative, the parties cannot structure such a transaction because the stock of the cooperative may be held only by its members, ...; thus, a seller dealing with a farmers' cooperative cannot obtain the benefits of tax deferral.

In § 968 of the Taxpayer Relief Act of 1997, Congress amended § 1042 of the Internal Revenue Code to permit owners of certain food refiners and processors to defer the recognition of gain if they sell their stock to eligible farmers' cooperatives. The purpose of the amendment, as repeatedly explained by its sponsors, was "to facilitate the transfer of refiners and processors to farmers' cooperatives." The amendment to § 1042 was one of the 79 "limited tax benefits" authorized by the Taxpayer Relief Act of 1997 and specifically identified in Title XVII of that Act as "subject to [the] line item veto."

On the same date that he canceled the "item of new direct spending" involving New York's health care programs, the President also canceled this limited tax benefit. ...

II

Appellees filed two separate actions against the President and other federal officials challenging these two cancellations. The plaintiffs in the first case are the City of New York, two hospital associations, one hospital, and two unions representing health care employees. The plaintiffs in the second are a farmers' cooperative consisting of about 30 potato growers in Idaho and an individual farmer who is a member and officer of the cooperative. The District Court consolidated the two cases and determined that at least one of the plaintiffs in each had standing under Article III of the Constitution.

On the merits, the District Court held that the cancellations did not conform to the constitutionally mandated procedures for the enactment or repeal of laws . . .

III

As in the prior challenge to the Line Item Veto Act, we initially confront jurisdictional questions. The appellees invoked the jurisdiction of the District Court under the section of the Act entitled "Expedited Review." That section . . . expressly authorizes "[a]ny Member of Congress or any individual adversely affected" by the Act to bring an action for declaratory judgment or injunctive relief on the ground that any provision of the Act is unconstitutional. . . .

. . . .

. . . [T]hese cases differ from *Raines*, not only because the President's exercise of his cancellation authority has removed any concern about the ripeness of the dispute, but more importantly because the parties have alleged a "personal stake" in having an actual injury redressed rather than an "institutional injury" that is "abstract and widely dispersed." . . .

. . . [W]e are satisfied that both of these actions are Article III "Cases" that we have a duty to decide.

IV

The Line Item Veto Act gives the President the power to "cancel in whole" three types of provisions that have been signed into law: "(1) any dollar amount of discretionary budget authority; (2) any item of new direct spending; or (3) any limited tax benefit." . . . It is undisputed that the New York case involves an "item of new direct spending" and that the Snake River case involves a "limited tax benefit" as those terms are defined in the Act. It is also undisputed that each of those provisions had been signed into law pursuant to Article I, § 7, of the Constitution before it was canceled.

The Act requires the President to adhere to precise procedures whenever he exercises his cancellation authority. . . . He must determine, with respect to each cancellation, that it will "(i) reduce the Federal budget deficit; (ii) not impair any essential Government functions; and (iii) not harm the national interest." . . . Moreover, he must transmit a special message to Congress notifying it of each cancellation within five calendar days . . . after the enactment of the canceled provision. . . . It is undisputed that the President meticulously followed these procedures in these cases.

A cancellation takes effect upon receipt by Congress of the special message from the President. . . . If, however, a "disapproval bill" pertaining to a special message is enacted into law, the cancellations set forth in that message become "null and void." . . . [N]o such bill was passed for either of the cancellations involved in these cases. A majority vote of both Houses is sufficient to enact a disapproval bill. The Act does not grant the President the authority to cancel a disapproval bill, . . . but he does, of course, retain his constitutional authority to veto such a bill.

. . . With respect to both an item of new direct spending and a limited tax benefit, the cancellation prevents the item "from having legal force or effect." . . . Thus, under the plain text of the statute, the two actions of the President that are challenged in these cases prevented one section of the Balanced Budget Act of 1997 and one section of the Taxpayer Relief Act of 1997 "from having legal force or effect." The remaining provisions of those statutes, with the exception of the second canceled item in the latter, continue to have the same force and effect as they had when signed into law.

In both legal and practical effect, the President has amended two Acts of Congress by repealing a portion of each. ... There is no provision in the Constitution that authorizes the President to enact, to amend, or to repeal statutes. ...

There are important differences between the President's "return" of a bill pursuant to Article I, § 7, and the exercise of the President's cancellation authority pursuant to the Line Item Veto Act. The constitutional return takes place before the bill becomes law; the statutory cancellation occurs after the bill becomes law. The constitutional return is of the entire bill; the statutory cancellation is of only a part. Although the Constitution expressly authorizes the President to play a role in the process of enacting statutes, it is silent on the subject of unilateral Presidential action that either repeals or amends parts of duly enacted statutes.

There are powerful reasons for construing constitutional silence on this profoundly important issue as equivalent to an express prohibition. The procedures governing the enactment of statutes set forth in the text of Article I were the product of the great debates and compromises that produced the Constitution itself. ... Our first President understood the text of the Presentment Clause as requiring that he either "approve all the parts of a Bill, or reject it in toto." What has emerged in these cases from the President's exercise of his statutory cancellation powers, however, are truncated versions of two bills that passed both Houses of Congress. They are not the product of the "finely wrought" procedure that the Framers designed.

. . .

V

The Government advances two related arguments to support its position that despite the unambiguous provisions of the Act, cancellations do not amend or repeal properly enacted statutes in violation of the Presentment Clause. First, relying primarily on Field v. Clark, 143 U.S. 649 (1892), the Government contends that the cancellations were merely exercises of discretionary authority granted to the President by the Balanced Budget Act and the Taxpayer Relief Act read in light of the previously enacted Line Item Veto Act. Second, the Government submits that the substance of the authority to cancel tax and spending items "is, in practical effect, no more and no less than the power to 'decline to spend' specified sums of money, or to 'decline to implement' specified tax measures."

In Field v. Clark, the Court upheld the constitutionality of the Tariff Act of 1890. ... That statute contained a "free list" of almost 300 specific articles that were exempted from import duties "unless otherwise specially provided for in this act." ... Section 3 was a special provision that directed the President to suspend that exemption for sugar, molasses, coffee, tea, and hides "whenever, and so often" as he should be satisfied that any country producing and exporting those products imposed duties on the agricultural products of the United States that he deemed to be "reciprocally unequal and unreasonable...." ... The section then specified the duties to be imposed on those products during any such suspension. The Court [concluded that] § 3 had not delegated legislative power to the President ...

[There are] three critical differences between the power to suspend the exemption from import duties and the power to cancel portions of a duly enacted statute. First, the exercise of the suspension power was contingent upon a condition that did not exist when the Tariff Act was passed: the imposition of "reciprocally unequal and unreasonable" import duties by other countries. In contrast, the exercise of the cancellation power within five days after the enactment of the Balanced Budget and Tax Reform Acts necessarily was based on the same conditions that Congress evaluated when it passed those statutes. Second, under the Tariff Act, when the President determined that the contingency had arisen, he had a duty to suspend; in contrast, while it is true that the President was required by the Act to make three determinations before he canceled a provision, ..., those determinations did not qualify his discretion to cancel or not to cancel. Finally, whenever the President suspended an exemption under the Tariff Act, he was executing the policy that Congress had embodied in the statute. In contrast, whenever the President cancels an item of new direct spending or a limited tax benefit he is rejecting the policy judgment made by Congress and relying on his own policy judgment. Thus, the conclusion in Field v. Clark that the suspensions mandated by the Tariff Act were not exercises of legislative power does not undermine our opinion that cancellations pursuant to the Line Item Veto Act are the functional equivalent of partial repeals of Acts of Congress that fail to satisfy Article I, § 7.

The Government's reliance upon other tariff and import statutes ... is unavailing for the same reasons. ...

The cited statutes all relate to foreign trade, and this Court has recognized that in the foreign affairs arena, the President has "a degree of discretion and freedom from statutory restriction which would not be admissible were domestic affairs alone involved." United States v. Curtiss–Wright Export Corp., 299 U.S. 304, 320 (1936). ... More important, when enacting the statutes discussed in Field, Congress itself made the decision to suspend or repeal the particular provisions at issue upon the occurrence of particular events subsequent to enactment, and it left only the determination of whether such events occurred up to the President. ...

Neither are we persuaded by the Government's contention that the President's authority to cancel new direct spending and tax benefit items is no greater than his traditional authority to decline to spend appropriated funds. The Government has reviewed in some detail the series of statutes in which Congress has given the Executive broad discretion over the expenditure of appropriated funds. ... It is argued that the Line Item Veto Act merely confers comparable discretionary authority over the expenditure of appropriated funds. The critical difference between this statute and all of its predecessors, however, is that unlike any of them, this Act gives the President the unilateral power to change the text of duly enacted statutes. None of the Act's predecessors could even arguably have been construed to authorize such a change.

VI

. . .

If there is to be a new procedure in which the President will play a different role in determining the final text of what may "become a law," such change must come not by legislation but through the amendment procedures set forth in Article V of the Constitution. ...

The judgment of the District Court is affirmed.

It is so ordered.

Justice Kennedy, concurring.

. . .

I write to respond to my colleague Justice Breyer, who observes that the statute does not threaten the liberties of individual citizens, a point on which I disagree. . . . Liberty is always at stake when one or more of the branches seek to transgress the separation of powers.

Separation of powers was designed to implement a fundamental insight: concentration of power in the hands of a single branch is a threat to liberty. . . .'

In recent years, perhaps, we have come to think of liberty as defined by that word in the Fifth and Fourteenth Amendments and as illuminated by the other provisions of the Bill of Rights. The conception of liberty embraced by the Framers was not so confined. They used the principles of separation of powers and federalism to secure liberty in the fundamental political sense of the term, quite in addition to the idea of freedom from intrusive governmental acts. The idea and the promise were that when the people delegate some degree of control to a remote central authority, one branch of government ought not possess the power to shape their destiny without a sufficient check from the other two. In this vision, liberty demands limits on the ability of any one branch to influence basic political decisions. . . .

. . .

The principal object of the statute, it is true, was not to enhance the President's power to reward one group and punish another, to help one set of taxpayers and hurt another, to favor one State and ignore another. Yet these are its undeniable effects. The law establishes a new mechanism which gives the President the sole ability to hurt a group that is a visible target, in order to disfavor the group or to extract further concessions from Congress. The law is the functional equivalent of a line item veto and enhances the President's powers beyond what the Framers would have endorsed.

. . .

. . . With these observations, I join the opinion of the Court.

Justice Breyer, with whom Justice O'Connor and Justice Scalia join as to Part III, dissenting.

I

. . . In my view the Line Item Veto Act does not violate any specific textual constitutional command, nor does it violate any implicit Separation of Powers principle. Consequently, I believe that the Act is constitutional.

II

I approach the constitutional question before us with three general considerations in mind. First, the Act represents a legislative effort to provide the President with the power to give effect to some, but not to all, of the expenditure and revenue-diminishing provisions contained in a single massive appropriations bill. And this objective is constitutionally proper.

When our Nation was founded, Congress could easily have provided the President with this kind of power. . . . At that time, a Congress, wishing to give a President the power to select among appropriations, could simply have embodied each appropriation in a separate bill, each bill subject to a separate Presidential veto.

Today, however, ... Congress cannot divide such a bill into thousands, or tens of thousands, of separate appropriations bills, each one of which the President would have to sign, or to veto, separately. Thus, the question is whether the Constitution permits Congress to choose a particular novel means to achieve this same, constitutionally legitimate, end.

Second, the case in part requires us to focus upon the Constitution's generally phrased structural provisions, provisions that delegate all "legislative" power to Congress and vest all "executive" power in the President. The Court, when applying these provisions, has interpreted them generously in terms of the institutional arrangements that they permit. ...

Indeed, Chief Justice Marshall, in a well-known passage, explained,

"To have prescribed the means by which government should, in all future time, execute its powers, would have been to change, entirely, the character of the instrument, and give it the properties of a legal code. It would have been an unwise attempt to provide, by immutable rules, for exigencies which, if foreseen at all, must have been seen dimly, and which can be best provided for as they occur." McCulloch v. Maryland...'

This passage ... calls attention to the genius of the Framers' pragmatic vision, which ... find[s] constitutional room for necessary institutional innovation.

Third, we need not here referee a dispute among the other two branches. ...

These three background circumstances mean that, when one measures the literal words of the Act against the Constitution's literal commands, the fact that the Act may closely resemble a different, literally unconstitutional, arrangement is beside the point. ...

. . .

III

The Court believes that the Act violates the literal text of the Constitution. A simple syllogism captures its basic reasoning:

Major Premise: The Constitution sets forth an exclusive method for enacting, repealing, or amending laws.

Minor Premise: The Act authorizes the President to "repea[l] or amen[d]" laws in a different way, namely by announcing a cancellation of a portion of a previously enacted law.

Conclusion: The Act is inconsistent with the Constitution.

I find this syllogism unconvincing, however, because its Minor Premise is faulty. When the President "canceled" the two appropriation measures now before us, he did not repeal any law nor did he amend any law. He simply followed the law, leaving the statutes, as they are literally written, intact.

. . .

... Literally speaking, the President has not "repealed" or "amended" anything. He has simply executed a power conferred upon him by Congress, which power is contained in laws that were enacted in compliance with the exclusive method set forth in the Constitution. See Field v. Clark, ...

. . .

IV

Because I disagree with the Court's holding of literal violation, I must consider whether the Act nonetheless violates Separation of Powers principles ... There are three relevant Separation of Powers questions here: (1) Has Congress given the President the wrong kind of power, i.e., "non-Executive" power? (2) Has Congress given the President the power to "encroach" upon Congress' own constitutionally reserved territory? (3) Has Congress given the President too much power, violating the doctrine of "nondelegation?" ... [W]ith respect to this Act, the answer to all these questions is "no."

A

Viewed conceptually, the power the Act conveys is the right kind of power. It is "executive." ... Conceptually speaking, it closely resembles the kind of delegated authority—to spend or not to spend appropriations, to change or not to change tariff rates—that Congress has frequently granted the President, any differences being differences in degree, not kind.

... This Court has frequently found that the exercise of a particular power, such as the power to make rules of broad applicability, ... can fall within the constitutional purview of more than one branch of Government. ...

The Court has upheld congressional delegation of rulemaking power and adjudicatory power to federal agencies, ... and prosecutor-appointment power to judges ... It is far easier conceptually to reconcile the power at issue here with the relevant constitutional description ("executive") than in many of these cases....'

If there is a Separation of Powers violation, then, it must rest, not upon purely conceptual grounds, but upon some important conflict between the Act and a significant Separation of Powers objective.

B

The Act does not undermine what this Court has often described as the principal function of the Separation of Powers, which is to maintain the tripartite structure of the Federal Government—and thereby protect individual liberty ...

... [O]ne cannot say that the Act "encroaches" upon Congress' power, when Congress retained the power to insert, by simple majority, into any future appropriations bill, into any section of any such bill, or into any phrase of any section, a provision that says the Act will not apply. ...Thus this Act is not the sort of delegation "without ... sufficient check" that concerns Justice Kennedy ...

Nor can one say that the Act's basic substantive objective is constitutionally improper, for the earliest Congresses could have, and often did, confer on the President this sort of discretionary authority over spending, ... Where the burden of overcoming legislative inertia lies is within the power of Congress to determine by rule. Where is the encroachment?

Nor can one say the Act's grant of power "aggrandizes" the Presidential office. The grant is limited to the context of the budget. It is limited to the power to spend, or not to spend, particular appropriated items, and the power to permit, or not to permit, specific limited exemptions from generally applicable tax law from taking effect. ... The delegation of those powers to the President may strengthen the Presidency, but any such change in Executive Branch authority seems minute when compared with the changes worked by

delegations of other kinds of authority that the Court in the past has upheld.
. . .

C

The "nondelegation" doctrine represents an added constitutional check
upon Congress' authority to delegate power to the Executive Branch. . . .

        . . .

. . . The President must determine that, to "prevent" the item or amount
"from having legal force or effect" will "reduce the Federal budget deficit; . . .
not impair any essential Government functions; and . . . not harm the national
interest." . . .

The resulting standards are broad. But this Court has upheld standards
that are equally broad, or broader. . . .

        . . .

. . . I believe that the power the Act grants the President to prevent
spending items from taking effect does not violate the "nondelegation" doctrine.

        . . .

. . . [T]he "limited tax benefit" provisions do not differ enough from the
"spending" provisions to warrant a different "nondelegation" result.

V

In sum, I recognize that the Act before us is novel. In a sense, it skirts a
constitutional edge. But that edge has to do with means, not ends. The means
chosen do not amount literally to the enactment, repeal, or amendment of a
law. Nor, for that matter, do they amount literally to the "line item veto" that
the Act's title announces. Those means do not violate any basic Separation of
Powers principle. They do not improperly shift the constitutionally foreseen
balance of power from Congress to the President. Nor, since they comply with
Separation of Powers principles, do they threaten the liberties of individual
citizens. They represent an experiment that may, or may not, help representative government work better. The Constitution, in my view, authorizes Congress and the President to try novel methods in this way. Consequently, with
respect, I dissent.

**Justice Scalia, with whom Justice O'Connor joins, and with whom
Justice Breyer joins as to Part III, concurring in part and dissenting
in part.**

. . . In my view, the Snake River appellees lack standing to challenge the
President's cancellation of the "limited tax benefit," and the constitutionality
of that action should not be addressed. I think the New York appellees have
standing to challenge the President's cancellation of an "item of new direct
spending" . . . [U]nlike the Court I find the President's cancellation of spending
items to be entirely in accord with the Constitution.

        . . .

III

I agree with the Court that the New York appellees have standing to
challenge the President's cancellation of § 4722(c). . . . Unlike the Court, how-

ever, I do not believe that Executive cancellation of this item of direct spending violates the Presentment Clause.

... [T]he Court's problem with the Act is not that it authorizes the President to veto parts of a bill and sign others into law, but rather that it authorizes him to "cancel"—prevent from "having legal force or effect"—certain parts of duly enacted statutes.

Article I, § 7 of the Constitution obviously prevents the President from canceling a law that Congress has not authorized him to cancel. ... It was certainly arguable, as an original matter, that Art. I, § 7 also prevents the President from canceling a law which itself authorizes the President to cancel it. But as the Court acknowledges, that argument has long since been made and rejected. ...

... There are, to be sure, limits ... Those limits are established, however, not by some categorical prohibition of Art. I, § 7, which our cases conclusively disprove, but by what has come to be known as the doctrine of unconstitutional delegation of legislative authority ...

It is this doctrine, and not the Presentment Clause, ... that is the issue presented by the statute before us here. ...

. . .

... [T]here is not a dime's worth of difference between Congress's authorizing the President to cancel a spending item, and Congress's authorizing money to be spent on a particular item at the President's discretion. And the latter has been done since the Founding of the Nation. ...

. . .

The short of the matter is this: Had the Line Item Veto Act authorized the President to "decline to spend" any item of spending contained in the Balanced Budget Act of 1997, there is not the slightest doubt that authorization would have been constitutional. What the Line Item Veto Act does instead—authorizing the President to "cancel" an item of spending—is technically different. But the technical difference does not relate to the technicalities of the Presentment Clause, which have been fully complied with; and the doctrine of unconstitutional delegation, which is at issue here, is preeminently not a doctrine of technicalities. The title of the Line Item Veto Act, which was perhaps designed to simplify for public comprehension, or perhaps merely to comply with the terms of a campaign pledge, has succeeded in faking out the Supreme Court. The President's action it authorizes in fact is not a line-item veto and thus does not offend Art. I, § 7; and insofar as the substance of that action is concerned, it is no different from what Congress has permitted the President to do since the formation of the Union.

. . .

SECTION 2.   CONGRESSIONAL INTERFERENCE WITH PRESIDENTIAL PREROGATIVES

A.   THE LEGISLATIVE VETO

Immigration and Naturalization Service v. Chadha

462 U.S. 919, 103 S.Ct. 2764, 77 L.Ed.2d 317 (1983).

Chief Justice Burger delivered the opinion of the Court.

... [These cases present] a challenge to the constitutionality of the provision in § 244(c)(2) of the Immigration and Nationality Act ... authorizing one House of Congress, by resolution, to invalidate the decision of the Executive Branch, pursuant to authority delegated by Congress to the Attorney General of the United States, to allow a particular deportable alien to remain in the United States.

I

Chadha ... was lawfully admitted to the United States in 1966 on a nonimmigrant student visa. His visa expired on June 30, 1972. On October 11, 1973, the District Director of the Immigration and Naturalization Service ordered Chadha to show cause why he should not be deported for having "remained in the United States for a longer time than permitted." ... [A] deportation hearing was held before an immigration judge on January 11, 1974. Chadha conceded that he was deportable for overstaying his visa and the hearing was adjourned to enable him to file an application for suspension of deportation under § 244(a)(1) of the Act, [which authorizes suspension in the case of] "a person whose deportation would, in the opinion of the Attorney General, result in extreme hardship to the alien or to his spouse, parent, or child, who is a citizen of the United States or an alien lawfully admitted for permanent residence."

... [T]he immigration judge ... ordered that Chadha's deportation be suspended. The immigration judge found that Chadha met the requirements of § 244(a)(1): he had resided continuously in the United States for over seven years, was of good moral character, and would suffer "extreme hardship" if deported.

Pursuant to (§ 244(c)(1) of the Act), ... the immigration judge suspended Chadha's deportation and a report of the suspension was transmitted to Congress. Section 244(c)(1) provides:

"Upon application by any alien who is found by the Attorney General to meet the requirements of subsection (a) of this section the Attorney General may in his discretion suspend deportation of such alien. If the deportation of any alien is suspended under the provisions of this subsection, a complete and detailed statement of the facts and pertinent provisions of law in the case shall be reported to the Congress with the reasons for such suspension. Such reports shall be submitted on the first day of each calendar month in which Congress is in session."

Once the Attorney General's recommendation for suspension of Chadha's deportation was conveyed to Congress, Congress had the power under § 244(c)(2) of the Act ... to veto the Attorney General's determination that Chadha should not be deported. Section 244(c)(2) provides:

"(2) ... if during the session of the Congress at which a case is reported, or prior to the close of the session of the Congress next following the session at which a case is reported, either the Senate or the House of Representatives passes a resolution stating in substance that it does not favor the suspension of such deportation, the Attorney General shall thereupon deport such alien or authorize the alien's voluntary departure at his own expense under the order of deportation in the manner provided by law. If, within the time above specified, neither the Senate nor the House of Representatives shall pass such a resolution, the Attorney General shall cancel deportation proceedings."

The June 25, 1974 order of the immigration judge suspending Chadha's deportation remained outstanding as a valid order for a year and a half. For reasons not disclosed by the record, Congress did not exercise the veto authority reserved to it under § 244(c)(2) until the first session of the 94th Congress. This was the final session in which Congress, pursuant to § 244(c)(2), could act to veto the Attorney General's determination that Chadha should not be deported....'

On December 12, 1975, Representative Eilberg, Chairman of the Judiciary Subcommittee on Immigration, Citizenship, and International Law, introduced a resolution opposing "the granting of permanent residence in the United States to [six] aliens", including Chadha. ... On December 16, 1975, the resolution was discharged from further consideration by the House Committee on the Judiciary and submitted to the House of Representatives for a vote. ... The resolution had not been printed and was not made available to other Members of the House prior to or at the time it was voted on. Ibid. ... House consideration of the resolution was based on Representative Eilberg's statement from the floor that

> "[i]t was the feeling of the committee, after reviewing 340 cases, that the aliens contained in the resolution [Chadha and five others] did not meet these statutory requirements, particularly as it relates to hardship; and it is the opinion of the committee that their deportation should not be suspended."....'

The resolution was passed without debate or recorded vote. Since the House action was pursuant to § 244(c)(2), the resolution was not treated as an Article I legislative act; it was not submitted to the Senate or presented to the President for his action.

After the House veto ..., the immigration judge reopened the deportation proceedings ... Chadha was ordered deported pursuant to the House action.

. . .

Pursuant to § 106(a) of the Act, ... Chadha filed a petition for review of the deportation order in the United States Court of Appeals for the Ninth Circuit. The Immigration and Naturalization Service agreed with Chadha's position before the Court of Appeals and joined him in arguing that § 244(c)(2) is unconstitutional. In light of the importance of the question, the Court of Appeals invited both the Senate and the House of Representatives to file briefs *amici curiae*.

... [T]he Court of Appeals held that the House was without constitutional authority to order Chadha's deportation ...

... [W]e ... affirm.

II

. . .

F

Case or Controversy

It is also contended that this is not a genuine controversy but "a friendly, non-adversary, proceeding," Ashwander v. Tennessee Valley Authority, supra, 297 U.S., at 346 (Brandeis, J., concurring), upon which the Court should not pass. This argument rests on the fact that Chadha and the INS take the same position on the constitutionality of the one-House veto. But it would be a curious result if, in the administration of justice, a person could be denied access to the courts because the Attorney General of the United States agreed with the legal arguments asserted by the individual.

III

A

We turn now to the question whether action of one House of Congress under § 244(c)(2) violates strictures of the Constitution. We begin, of course, with the presumption that the challenged statute is valid. . . .

By the same token, the fact that a given law or procedure is efficient, convenient, and useful in facilitating functions of government, standing alone, will not save it if it is contrary to the Constitution. Convenience and efficiency are not the primary objectives—or the hallmarks—of democratic government and our inquiry is sharpened rather than blunted by the fact that Congressional veto provisions are appearing with increasing frequency in statutes which delegate authority to executive and independent agencies:

> "Since 1932, when the first veto provision was enacted into law, 295 congressional veto-type procedures have been inserted in 196 different statutes as follows: from 1932 to 1939, five statutes were affected; from 1940–49, nineteen statutes; between 1950–59, thirty-four statutes; and from 1960–69, forty-nine. From the year 1970 through 1975, at least one hundred sixty-three such provisions were included in eighty-nine laws." *Abourezk, The Congressional Veto: A Contemporary Response to Executive Encroachment on Legislative Prerogatives,* 52 Ind.L.Rev. 323, 324 (1977).

Justice White undertakes to make a case for the proposition that the one-House veto is a useful "political invention," and we need not challenge that assertion. We can even concede this utilitarian argument although the long range political wisdom of this "invention" is arguable. It has been vigorously debated and it is instructive to compare the views of the protagonists. See, e.g., *Javits & Klein, Congressional Oversight and the Legislative Veto: A Constitutional Analysis,* 52 N.Y.U.L.Rev. 455 (1977), and *Martin, The Legislative Veto and the Responsible Exercise of Congressional Power,* 68 Va.L.Rev. 253 (1982). But policy arguments supporting even useful "political inventions" are subject to the demands of the Constitution which defines powers and, with respect to this subject, sets out just how those powers are to be exercised.

Explicit and unambiguous provisions of the Constitution prescribe and define the respective functions of the Congress and of the Executive in the legislative process. . . .

. . . [T]he purposes underlying the Presentment Clauses, Art. I, § 7, cls. 2, 3, and the bicameral requirement of Art. I, § 1 and § 7, cl. 2, guide our resolution of the important question presented in this case. . . .

B

The Presentment Clauses

The records of the Constitutional Convention reveal that the requirement that all legislation be presented to the President before becoming law was uniformly accepted by the Framers. Presentment to the President and the Presidential veto were considered so imperative that the draftsmen took special pains to assure that these requirements could not be circumvented. . . .

The decision to provide the President with a limited and qualified power to nullify proposed legislation by veto was based on the profound conviction of the Framers that the powers conferred on Congress were the powers to be most carefully circumscribed. It is beyond doubt that lawmaking was a power to be shared by both Houses and the President. . . .

The President's role in the lawmaking process also reflects the Framers' careful efforts to check whatever propensity a particular Congress might have to enact oppressive, improvident, or ill-considered measures. . . . Presentment Clauses serve the important purpose of assuring that a "national" perspective is grafted on the legislative process. . . .

C

Bicameralism

The bicameral requirement of Art. I, §§ 1, 7 was of scarcely less concern to the Framers than was the Presidential veto and indeed the two concepts are interdependent. By providing that no law could take effect without the concurrence of the prescribed majority of the Members of both Houses, the Framers reemphasized their belief, already remarked upon in connection with the Presentment Clauses, that legislation should not be enacted unless it has been carefully and fully considered by the Nation's elected officials. . . .

. . .

We see therefore that the Framers were acutely conscious that the bicameral requirement and the Presentment Clauses would serve essential constitutional functions. The President's participation in the legislative process was to protect the Executive Branch from Congress and to protect the whole people from improvident laws. The division of the Congress into two distinctive bodies assures that the legislative power would be exercised only after opportunity for full study and debate in separate settings. The President's unilateral veto power, in turn, was limited by the power of two thirds of both Houses of Congress to overrule a veto thereby precluding final arbitrary action of one person. See 1 M. Farrand, supra, at 99–104. It emerges clearly that the prescription for legislative action in Art. I, §§ 1, 7 represents the Framers' decision that the legislative power of the Federal government be exercised in accord with a single, finely wrought and exhaustively considered, procedure.

IV

. . . [W]e must . . . establish that the challenged action under § 244(c)(2) is of the kind to which the procedural requirements of Art. I, § 7 apply. Not every action taken by either House is subject to the bicameralism and presentment requirements of Art. I. Whether actions taken by either House are, in law and fact, an exercise of legislative power depends not on their form but upon "whether they contain matter which is properly to be regarded as legislative in its character and effect." . . .

Examination of the action taken here by one House pursuant to § 244(c)(2) reveals that it was essentially legislative in purpose and effect. In purporting to exercise power defined in Art. I, § 8, cl. 4 to "establish an uniform Rule of Naturalization," the House took action that had the purpose and effect of altering the legal rights, duties and relations of persons, including the Attorney General, Executive Branch officials and Chadha, all outside the legislative branch. . . .

. . .

Since it is clear that the action by the House under § 244(c)(2) was not within any of the express constitutional exceptions authorizing one House to act alone, and equally clear that it was an exercise of legislative power, that action was subject to the standards prescribed in Article I.[21] ...

The veto authorized by § 244(c)(2) doubtless has been in many respects a convenient shortcut; the "sharing" with the Executive by Congress of its authority over aliens in this manner is, on its face, an appealing compromise. In purely practical terms, it is obviously easier for action to be taken by one House without submission to the President; but it is crystal clear from the records of the Convention, contemporaneous writings and debates, that the Framers ranked other values higher than efficiency. The records of the Convention and debates in the States preceding ratification underscore the common desire to define and limit the exercise of the newly created federal powers affecting the states and the people. There is unmistakable expression of a determination that legislation by the national Congress be a step-by-step, deliberate and deliberative process.

. . .

V

We hold that the Congressional veto provision in § 244(c)(2) is ... unconstitutional. Accordingly, the judgment of the Court of Appeals is

Affirmed.

Justice Powell, concurring in the judgment.

... [O]ur holding should be no more extensive than necessary to decide this case. In my view, the case may be decided on a narrower ground. When Congress finds that a particular person does not satisfy the statutory criteria for permanent residence in this country it has assumed a judicial function in violation of the principle of separation of powers. Accordingly, I concur in the judgment.

. . .

II

. . .

On its face, the House's action appears clearly adjudicatory. The House did not enact a general rule; rather it made its own determination that six specific persons did not comply with certain statutory criteria. It thus undertook the type of decision that traditionally has been left to other branches. Even if the House did not make a *de novo* determination, but simply reviewed the Immigration and Naturalization Service's findings, it still assumed a function ordinarily entrusted to the federal courts. ...

Justice White, dissenting.

Today the Court not only invalidates § 244(c)(2) of the Immigration and Nationality Act, but also sounds the death knell for nearly 200 other statutory provisions in which Congress has reserved a "legislative veto." ...

---

21. Justice Powell's position is that the one-House veto in this case is a *judicial* act and therefore unconstitutional as beyond the authority vested in Congress by the Constitution. We agree that there is a sense in which one-House action pursuant to § 244(c)(2) has a judicial cast, since it purports to "review" Executive action.... But the attempted anal- ogy between judicial action and the one-House veto is less than perfect. ... [N]o justiciable case or controversy was presented by the Attorney General's decision to allow Chadha to remain in this country. [N]o party to such action has either the motivation or the right to appeal from it. ...

The prominence of the legislative veto mechanism in our contemporary political system and its importance to Congress can hardly be overstated. It has become a central means by which Congress secures the accountability of executive and independent agencies. Without the legislative veto, Congress is faced with a Hobson's choice: either to refrain from delegating the necessary authority, leaving itself with a hopeless task of writing laws with the requisite specificity to cover endless special circumstances across the entire policy landscape, or in the alternative, to abdicate its lawmaking function to the executive branch and independent agencies. To choose the former leaves major national problems unresolved; to opt for the latter risks unaccountable policymaking by those not elected to fill that role. Accordingly, over the past five decades, the legislative veto has been placed in nearly 200 statutes. The device is known in every field of governmental concern: reorganization, budgets, foreign affairs, war powers, and regulation of trade, safety, energy, the environment and the economy.

I

. . .

During the 1970's the legislative veto was important in resolving a series of major constitutional disputes between the President and Congress over claims of the President to broad impoundment, war, and national emergency powers. The key provision of the War Powers Resolution, 50 U.S.C. § 1544(c), authorizes the termination by concurrent resolution of the use of armed forces in hostilities. A similar measure resolved the problem posed by Presidential claims of inherent power to impound appropriations. Congressional Budget and Impoundment Control Act of 1974, 31 U.S.C. § 1403. In conference, a compromise was achieved under which permanent impoundments, termed "rescissions," would require approval through enactment of legislation. In contrast, temporary impoundments, or "deferrals," would become effective unless disapproved by one House. This compromise provided the President with flexibility, while preserving ultimate Congressional control over the budget. Although the War Powers Resolution was enacted over President Nixon's veto, the Impoundment Control Act was enacted with the President's approval. . . .'

. . .

. . . [T]he legislative veto is more than "efficient, convenient, and useful." It is an important if not indispensable political invention that allows the President and Congress to resolve major constitutional and policy differences, assures the accountability of independent regulatory agencies, and preserves Congress' control over lawmaking. Perhaps there are other means of accommodation and accountability, but the increasing reliance of Congress upon the legislative veto suggests that the alternatives to which Congress must now turn are not entirely satisfactory.

The history of the legislative veto also makes clear that it has not been a sword with which Congress has struck out to aggrandize itself at the expense of the other branches—the concerns of Madison and Hamilton. Rather, the veto has been a means of defense, a reservation of ultimate authority necessary if Congress is to fulfill its designated role under Article I as the nation's lawmaker. While the President has often objected to particular legislative vetoes, generally those left in the hands of congressional committees, the Executive has more often agreed to legislative review as the price for a broad delegation of authority. To be sure, the President may have preferred unrestricted power, but that could be precisely why Congress thought it essential to retain a check on the exercise of delegated authority.

II

For all these reasons, the apparent sweep of the Court's decision today is regrettable. The Court's Article I analysis appears to invalidate all legislative vetoes irrespective of form or subject. Because the legislative veto is commonly found as a check upon rulemaking by administrative agencies and upon broad-based policy decisions of the Executive Branch, it is particularly unfortunate that the Court reaches its decision in a case involving the exercise of a veto over deportation decisions regarding particular individuals. ... Unfortunately, today's holding is not so limited.

. . .

III

. . .

... The Court's holding today that all legislative-type action must be enacted through the lawmaking process ignores that legislative authority is routinely delegated to the Executive branch, to the independent regulatory agencies, and to private individuals and groups. ...

This Court's decisions sanctioning such delegations make clear that Article I does not require all action with the effect of legislation to be passed as a law.

The wisdom and the constitutionality of these broad delegations are matters that still have not been put to rest. ... There is no question but that agency rulemaking is lawmaking in any functional or realistic sense of the term. ...

If Congress may delegate lawmaking power to independent and executive agencies, it is most difficult to understand Article I as forbidding Congress from also reserving a check on legislative power for itself. Absent the veto, the agencies receiving delegations of legislative or quasi-legislative power may issue regulations having the force of law without bicameral approval and without the President's signature. It is thus not apparent why the reservation of a veto over the exercise of that legislative power must be subject to a more exacting test. In both cases, it is enough that the initial statutory authorizations comply with the Article I requirements.

. . .

... If the effective functioning of a complex modern government requires the delegation of vast authority which, by virtue of its breadth, is legislative or "quasi-legislative" in character, I cannot accept that Article I—which is, after all, the source of the non-delegation doctrine—should forbid Congress from qualifying that grant with a legislative veto.

. . .

IV

. . .

I do not suggest that all legislative vetoes are necessarily consistent with separation of powers principles. A legislative check on an inherently executive function, for example that of initiating prosecutions, poses an entirely different question. But the legislative veto device here—and in many other settings—is far from an instance of legislative tyranny over the Executive. It is a necessary check on the unavoidably expanding power of the agencies, both executive and independent, as they engage in exercising authority delegated by Congress.

. . .

Justice Rehnquist, with whom Justice White joins, dissenting.

. . .

By severing [the legislative veto in] § 244(c)(2) [and leaving, the rest of the statute in place,] the Court permits suspension of deportation in a class of cases where Congress never stated that suspension was appropriate. I do not believe we should expand the statute in this way without some clear indication that Congress intended such an expansion. . . .

. . .

MISTRETTA v. UNITED STATES, 488 U.S. 361 (1989). The Sentencing Reform Act of 1984 created the United States Sentencing Commission, consisting of seven voting members appointed by the President with the advice and consent of the Senate. At least three of its members must be federal judges, selected after consideration of a list of six judges recommended by the Judicial Conference of the United States. The commission, established "as an independent commission in the judicial branch of the United States," promulgates binding sentencing guidelines for federal crimes. The Court upheld the commission's sentencing guidelines against a claim that the Act violated the principle of separation of powers. The Court stressed that a "concern of encroachment and aggrandizement . . . has animated our separation of powers jurisprudence."

> "Accordingly, we have not hesitated to strike down provisions of law that either accrete to a single branch powers more appropriately diffused among separate branches or that undermine the authority and independence of one or another coordinate branch. . . . By the same token, we have upheld statutory provisions that to some degree commingle the functions of the Branches, but that pose no danger of either aggrandizement or encroachment."

Locating the Commission within the judicial branch did not violate the provisions of Article III, limiting the judicial power to resolution of "cases" and "controversies." Analogous to the provisions for judicial rulemaking, "Congress may delegate to the Judicial Branch nonadjudicatory functions that do not trench upon the prerogatives of another Branch and that are appropriate to the central mission of the Judiciary." Although the Commission wields rulemaking authority, it has not aggrandized the authority of the judicial branch, since judges had, as an aggregate, determined appropriate criminal sentences prior to passage of the Act.

Although the Commission does not wield "judicial power," Article III does not prohibit Article III judges from undertaking extrajudicial duties "in their individual capacities." In each case, the issue is "whether a particular extrajudicial assignment undermines the integrity of the Judicial Branch." Service on the Commission is voluntary, and participation in promulgation of the sentencing guidelines would not affect member-judges' ability to adjudicate sentencing issues.

> "Judicial contribution to the enterprise of creating rules to limit the discretion of sentencing judges does not enlist the resources or reputation of the Judicial Branch in either the legislative business of determining what conduct should be criminalized or the executive business of enforcing the law. Rather, judicial participation on the Commission ensures that

judicial experience and expertise will inform the promulgation of rules for the exercise of the Judicial Branch's own business—that of passing sentence on every criminal defendant.''

Justice Scalia dissented, saying:

"Today's decision follows the regrettable tendency of our recent separation-of-powers jurisprudence ... to treat the Constitution as though it were no more than a generalized prescription that the functions of the Branches should not be commingled too much—how much is too much to be determined, case-by-case, by this Court. The Constitution is not that. Rather, as its name suggests, it is a prescribed structure, a framework, for the conduct of government.... Consideration of the degree of commingling that a particular disposition produces may be appropriate at the margins, where the outline of the framework itself is not clear; but it seems to me far from a marginal question whether our constitutional structure allows for a body which is not the Congress, and yet exercises no governmental powers except the making of rules that have the effect of laws.

"... [T]here are many desirable dispositions that do not accord with the constitutional structure we live under. And in the long run the improvisation of a constitutional structure on the basis of currently perceived utility will be disastrous.''

B.   APPOINTMENT, DISCHARGE, AND SUPERVISION OF "OFFICERS OF THE UNITED STATES"

Morrison v. Olson

487 U.S. 654, 108 S.Ct. 2597, 101 L.Ed.2d 569 (1988).

Chief Justice Rehnquist delivered the opinion of the Court.

This case presents us with a challenge to the independent counsel provisions of the Ethics in Government Act of 1978 ... We hold today that these provisions of the Act do not violate the Appointments Clause of the Constitution, Art. II, § 2, cl. 2, or the limitations of Article III, nor do they impermissibly interfere with the President's authority under Article II in violation of the constitutional principle of separation of powers.

I

Briefly stated, Title VI of the Ethics in Government Act (Title VI or the Act) ... allows for the appointment of an "independent counsel" to investigate and, if appropriate, prosecute certain high ranking government officials for violations of federal criminal laws. The Act requires the Attorney General, upon receipt of information that he determines is "sufficient to constitute grounds to investigate whether any person [covered by the Act] may have violated any Federal criminal law," to conduct a preliminary investigation of the matter. When the Attorney General has completed this investigation, or 90 days has elapsed, he is required to report to a special court (the Special Division) created by the Act "for the purpose of appointing independent counsels." ... If ... the Attorney General has determined that there are "reasonable grounds to believe that further investigation or prosecution is warranted," then he "shall apply to the division of the court for the appointment of an independent counsel." ... Upon receiving this application, the Special Division "shall appoint an appropriate independent counsel and shall define that independent counsel's prosecutorial jurisdiction." . . .

With respect to all matters within the independent counsel's jurisdiction, the Act grants the counsel "full power and independent authority to exercise all investigative and prosecutorial functions and powers of the Department of Justice, the Attorney General, and any other officer or employee of the Department of Justice." . . . Two statutory provisions govern the length of an independent counsel's tenure in office. The first defines the procedure for removing an independent counsel. Section 596(a)(1) provides:

> "An independent counsel appointed under this chapter may be removed from office, other than by impeachment and conviction, only by the personal action of the Attorney General and only for good cause, physical disability, mental incapacity, or any other condition that substantially impairs the performance of such independent counsel's duties."

. . . [A]n independent counsel can obtain judicial review of the Attorney General's action by filing a civil action in the United States District Court for the District of Columbia. . . . The reviewing court is authorized to grant reinstatement or "other appropriate relief.".

The other provision governing the tenure of the independent counsel defines the procedures for "terminating" the counsel's office. . . . [T]he office of an independent counsel terminates when he notifies the Attorney General that he has completed or substantially completed any investigations or prosecutions undertaken pursuant to the Act. In addition, the Special Division, acting either on its own or on the suggestion of the Attorney General, may terminate the office of an independent counsel at any time if it finds that "the investigation of all matters within the prosecutorial jurisdiction of such independent counsel . . . have been completed or so substantially completed that it would be appropriate for the Department of Justice to complete such investigations and prosecutions." . . .

Finally, the Act provides for Congressional oversight of the activities of independent counsels. An independent counsel may from time to time send Congress statements or reports on his activities. § 595(a)(2). The "appropriate committees of the Congress" are given oversight jurisdiction in regard to the official conduct of an independent counsel, and the counsel is required by the Act to cooperate with Congress in the exercise of this jurisdiction. . . .

. . .

. . . In 1985, the majority members of the [House] Judiciary Committee published a lengthy report [which] suggested that appellee Olson had given false and misleading testimony to the subcommittee . . . The Chairman of the Judiciary Committee forwarded a copy of the report to the Attorney General with a request, pursuant to 28 U.S.C. § 592(c), that he seek the appointment of an independent counsel . . .

. . . The Attorney General accordingly requested appointment of an independent counsel to investigate whether Olson's March 10, 1983, testimony ". . . violated 18 U.S.C. § 1505, § 1001, or any other provision of federal criminal law." . . . The Attorney General also requested that the independent counsel have authority to investigate "any other matter related to that allegation."

On April 23, 1986, the Special Division appointed James C. McKay as independent counsel. . . .

McKay later resigned as independent counsel, and on May 29, 1986, the Division appointed appellant Morrison as his replacement. . . .

. . .

. . . [I]n May and June 1987, appellant caused a grand jury to issue and serve subpoenas ad testificandum and duces tecum on appellees. All three appellees moved to quash the subpoenas, claiming, among other things, that the independent counsel provisions of the Act were unconstitutional and that appellant accordingly had no authority to proceed. On July 20, 1987, the District Court upheld the constitutionality of the Act and denied the motions to quash. . . .'

A divided Court of Appeals reversed. . . . We now reverse.

II

. . .

III

. . .

The parties do not dispute that "[t]he Constitution for purposes of appointment . . . divides all its officers into two classes." . . . As we stated in Buckley v. Valeo, 424 U.S. 1, 132 (1976), "[p]rincipal officers are selected by the President with the advice and consent of the Senate. Inferior officers Congress may allow to be appointed by the President alone, by the heads of departments, or by the Judiciary." The initial question is, accordingly, whether appellant is an "inferior" or a "principal" officer. If she is the latter, as the Court of Appeals concluded, then the Act is in violation of the Appointments Clause.

The line between "inferior" and "principal" officers is one that is far from clear, and the Framers provided little guidance into where it should be drawn. . . . We need not attempt here to decide exactly where the line falls between the two types of officers, because in our view appellant clearly falls on the "inferior officer" side of that line. Several factors lead to this conclusion.

First, appellant is subject to removal by a higher Executive Branch official. Although appellant may not be "subordinate" to the Attorney General (and the President) insofar as she possesses a degree of independent discretion to exercise the powers delegated to her under the Act, the fact that she can be removed by the Attorney General indicates that she is to some degree "inferior" in rank and authority. Second, appellant is empowered by the Act to perform only certain, limited duties. An independent counsel's role is restricted primarily to investigation and, if appropriate, prosecution for certain federal crimes. Admittedly, the Act delegates to appellant "full power and independent authority to exercise all investigative and prosecutorial functions and powers of the Department of Justice," . . . but this grant of authority does not include any authority to formulate policy for the Government or the Executive Branch, nor does it give appellant any administrative duties outside of those necessary to operate her office. The Act specifically provides that in policy matters appellant is to comply to the extent possible with the policies of the Department. . . .

Third, appellant's office is limited in jurisdiction. Not only is the Act itself restricted in applicability to certain federal officials suspected of certain serious federal crimes, but an independent counsel can only act within the scope of the jurisdiction that has been granted by the Special Division pursuant to a request by the Attorney General. Finally, appellant's office is limited in tenure. There is concededly no time limit on the appointment of a particular counsel. Nonetheless, the office of independent counsel is "temporary" in the sense that an independent counsel is appointed essentially to accomplish a single task, and when that task is over the office is terminated, either by the counsel herself or by action of the Special Division. Unlike other prosecutors, appellant has no ongoing responsibilities that extend beyond the accomplishment of the mission that she was appointed for and authorized by the Special Division to undertake. In our view, these factors relating to the "ideas of tenure, duration ... and duties" of the independent counsel, ... are sufficient to establish that appellant is an "inferior" officer in the constitutional sense.

.   .   .

This does not, however, end our inquiry under the Appointments Clause. Appellees argue that even if appellant is an "inferior" officer, the Clause does not empower Congress to place the power to appoint such an officer outside the Executive Branch. They contend that the Clause does not contemplate congressional authorization of "interbranch appointments," in which an officer of one branch is appointed by officers of another branch. The relevant language of the Appointments Clause is worth repeating. It reads: "... but the Congress may by Law vest the Appointment of such inferior Officers, as they think proper, in the President alone, in the courts of Law, or in the Heads of Departments." On its face, the language of this "excepting clause" admits of no limitation on interbranch appointments. Indeed, the inclusion of "as they think proper" seems clearly to give Congress significant discretion to determine whether it is "proper" to vest the appointment of, for example, executive officials in the "courts of Law." We recognized as much in one of our few decisions in this area, *Ex parte Siebold,* supra, where we stated:

> "It is no doubt usual and proper to vest the appointment of inferior officers in that department of the government, executive or judicial, or in that particular executive department to which the duties of such officers appertain. But there is no absolute requirement to this effect in the Constitution; and, if there were, it would be difficult in many cases to determine to which department an office properly belonged...'

"..." 100 U.S., at 397–398.

.   .   .

We also note that the history of the Clause provides no support for appellees' position.... [T]here was little or no debate on the question of whether the Clause empowers Congress to provide for interbranch appointments, and there is nothing to suggest that the Framers intended to prevent Congress from having that power.

We do not mean to say that Congress' power to provide for interbranch appointments of "inferior officers" is unlimited. In addition to separation of powers concerns, which would arise if such provisions for appointment had the potential to impair the constitutional functions assigned to one of the branches, *Siebold* itself suggested that Congress' decision to vest the appointment power in the courts would be improper if there was some "incongruity" between the functions normally performed by the courts and the performance of their duty to appoint. ... In this case, however, we do not think it impermissible for Congress to vest the power to appoint independent counsels in a specially created federal court.... We have recognized that courts may appoint private attorneys to act as prosecutor for judicial contempt judgments. ... In *Siebold,* as well, we indicated that judicial appointment of federal marshals, who are "executive officer[s]," would not be inappropriate. ... Congress of course was concerned when it created the office of independent counsel with the conflicts of interest that could arise in situations when the Executive Branch is called upon to investigate its own high-ranking officers. If it were to remove the appointing authority from the Executive Branch, the most logical place to put it was in the Judicial Branch. ... [W]e do not think that appointment of the independent counsels by the court runs afoul of the constitutional limitation on "incongruous" interbranch appointments.

IV

Appellees next contend that the powers vested in the Special Division by the Act conflict with Article III of the Constitution. We have long recognized that by the express provision of Article III, the judicial power of the United States is limited to "Cases" and "Controversies." .... As a general rule, we have broadly stated that "executive or administrative duties of a nonjudicial nature may not be imposed on judges holding office under Art. III of the Constitution." ... The purpose of this limitation is to help ensure the independence of the Judicial Branch and to prevent the judiciary from encroaching into areas reserved for the other branches. ... With this in mind, we address in turn the various duties given to the Special Division by the Act.

Most importantly, the Act vests in the Special Division the power to choose who will serve as independent counsel and the power to define his or her jurisdiction.... Clearly, once it is accepted that the Appointments Clause gives Congress the power to vest the appointment of officials such as the independent counsel in the "courts of Law," there can be no Article III objection to the Special Division's exercise of that power, as the power itself derives from the Appointments Clause, a source of authority for judicial action that is independent of Article III. Appellees contend, however, that the Division's Appointments Clause powers do not encompass the power to define the independent counsel's jurisdiction. We disagree. In our view, Congress' power under the Clause to vest the "Appointment" of inferior officers in the courts may, in certain circumstances, allow Congress to give the courts some discretion in defining the nature and scope of the appointed official's authority. Particularly when, as here, Congress creates a temporary "office" the nature and duties of which will by necessity vary with the factual circumstances giving rise to the need for an appointment in the first place, it may vest the power to define the scope of the office in the court as an incident to the appointment of the officer pursuant to the Appointments Clause. This said, we do not think that Congress may give the Division *unlimited* discretion to determine the independent counsel's jurisdiction. In order for the Division's definition of the counsel's jurisdiction to be truly "incidental" to its power to appoint, the jurisdiction that the court decides upon must be demonstrably related to the factual circumstances that gave rise to the Attorney General's investigation and request for the appointment of the independent counsel in the particular case.

The Act also vests in the Special Division various powers and duties in relation to the independent counsel that, because they do not involve appointing the counsel or defining her jurisdiction, cannot be said to derive from the Division's Appointments Clause authority. These duties include granting extensions for the Attorney General's preliminary investigation, ... receiving the report of the Attorney General at the conclusion of his preliminary investigation, ... referring matters to the counsel upon request, ... receiving reports from the counsel regarding expenses incurred, ... receiving a report from the Attorney General following the removal of an independent counsel, ... granting attorney's fees upon request to individuals who were investigated but not indicted by an independent counsel, ... receiving a final report from the counsel, . . . deciding whether to release the counsel's final report to Congress or the public and determining whether any protective orders should be issued, . . . and terminating an independent counsel when his task is completed. . . .

Leaving aside for the moment the Division's power to terminate an independent counsel, we do not think that Article III absolutely prevents Congress from vesting these other miscellaneous powers in the Special Division pursuant to the Act. . . . [T]he powers granted by these provisions are themselves essentially ministerial. . . . And, the functions that the Special Division is empowered to perform are not inherently "executive"; indeed, they are directly analogous to functions that federal judges perform in other contexts. . . .

We are more doubtful about the Special Division's power to terminate the office of the independent counsel . . . As appellees suggest, the power to terminate, especially when exercised by the Division on its own motion, is "administrative" to the extent that it requires the Special Division to monitor the progress of proceedings of the independent counsel and come to a decision as to whether the counsel's job is "completed." . . . It also is not a power that could be considered typically "judicial," as it has few analogues among the court's more traditional powers. Nonetheless, we do not, as did the Court of Appeals, view this provision as a significant judicial encroachment upon executive power or upon the prosecutorial discretion of the independent counsel.

. . . [I]t is the duty of federal courts to construe a statute in order to save it from constitutional infirmities, . . . and to that end we think a narrow construction is appropriate here. The termination provisions of the Act do not give the Special Division anything approaching the power to remove the counsel while an investigation or court proceeding is still underway—this power is vested solely in the Attorney General. As we see it, "termination" may occur only when the duties of the counsel are truly "completed" or "so substantially completed" that there remains no need for any continuing action by the independent counsel. It is basically a device for removing from the public payroll an independent counsel who has served her purpose, but is unwilling to acknowledge the fact. So construed, the Special Division's power to terminate does not pose a sufficient threat of judicial intrusion into matters that are more properly within the Executive's authority to require that the Act be invalidated as inconsistent with Article III.

. . .

We emphasize . . . that the Special Division has no authority to take any action or undertake any duties that are not specifically authorized by the Act. The gradual expansion of the authority of the Special Division might in another context be a bureaucratic success story, but it would be one that would have serious constitutional ramifications. The record in other cases involving independent counsels indicate that the Special Division has at times given advisory opinions or issued orders that are not directly authorized by the Act. . . . The propriety of the Special Division's actions in these instances is not before us as such, but we nonetheless think it appropriate to point out not only that there is no authorization for such actions in the Act itself, but that the division's exercise of unauthorized powers risks the transgression of the constitutional limitations of Article III that we have just discussed.

V

We now turn to consider whether the Act is invalid under the constitutional principle of separation of powers. Two related issues must be addressed: The first is whether the provision of the Act restricting the Attorney General's power to remove the independent counsel to only those instances in which he can show "good cause," taken by itself, impermissibly interferes with the President's exercise of his constitutionally appointed functions. The second is whether, taken as a whole, the Act violates the separation of powers by reducing the President's ability to control the prosecutorial powers wielded by the independent counsel.

A

Two Terms ago we had occasion to consider whether it was consistent with the separation of powers for Congress to pass a statute that authorized a government official who is removable only by Congress to participate in what we found to be "executive powers." Bowsher v. Synar, 478 U.S. 714, 730 (1986). We held in *Bowsher* that "Congress cannot reserve for itself the power of removal of an officer charged with the execution of the laws except by impeachment." ... A primary antecedent for this ruling was our 1925 decision in Myers v. United States, 272 U.S. 52 (1926). *Myers* had considered the propriety of a federal statute by which certain postmasters of the United States could be removed by the President only "by and with the advice and consent of the Senate." There too, Congress' attempt to involve itself in the removal of an executive official was found to be sufficient grounds to render the statute invalid. ...'

Unlike both *Bowsher* and *Myers,* this case does not involve an attempt by Congress itself to gain a role in the removal of executive officials other than its established powers of impeachment and conviction. The Act instead puts the removal power squarely in the hands of the Executive Branch; an independent counsel may be removed from office, "only by the personal action of the Attorney General, and only for good cause." ... There is no requirement of congressional approval of the Attorney General's removal decision, though the decision is subject to judicial review. ... In our view, the removal provisions of the Act make this case more analogous to Humphrey's Executor v. United States, 295 U.S. 602 (1935), and Wiener v. United States, 357 U.S. 349 (1958), than to *Myers* or *Bowsher.*

In *Humphrey's Executor,* the issue was whether a statute restricting the President's power to remove the commissioners of the Federal Trade Commission only for "inefficiency, neglect of duty, or malfeasance in office" was consistent with the Constitution. 295 U.S., at 619. We stated that whether Congress can "condition the [President's power of removal] by fixing a definite term and precluding a removal except for cause, will depend upon the character of the office." ... Contrary to the implication of some dicta in *Myers,*[24] the President's power to remove government officials simply was not "all-inclusive in respect of civil officers with the exception of the judiciary provided for by the Constitution." ... At least in regard to "quasi-legislative" and "quasi-judicial" agencies such as the FTC, "[t]he authority of Congress, in creating [such] agencies, to require them to act in discharge of their duties independently of executive control ... includes, as an appropriate incident, power to fix the period during which they shall continue in office, and to forbid their removal except for cause in the meantime." ... In *Humphrey's Executor,* we found it "plain" that the Constitution did not give the President "illimitable power of removal" over the officers of independent agencies. ... Were the President to

---

24. The Court expressly disapproved of any statements in *Myers* that "are out of harmony" with the views expressed in *Humphrey's Executor.* 295 U.S., at 626. We recognized that the only issue actually decided in *Myers* was that "the President had power to remove a postmaster of the first class, without the advice and consent of the Senate as required by act of Congress." ...

have the power to remove FTC commissioners at will, the "coercive influence" of the removal power would "threate[n] the independence of [the] commission." ...

Similarly, in *Wiener* we considered whether the President had unfettered discretion to remove a member of the War Claims Commission, which had been established by Congress in the War Claims Act of 1948 ... The Commission's function was to receive and adjudicate certain claims for compensation from those who had suffered personal injury or property damage at the hands of the enemy during World War II. Commissioners were appointed by the President, with the advice and consent of the Senate, but the statute made no provision for the removal of officers, perhaps because the Commission itself was to have a limited existence. As in *Humphrey's Executor,* however, the Commissioners were entrusted by Congress with adjudicatory powers that were to be exercised free from executive control. In this context, "Congress did not wish to have hang over the Commission the Damocles' sword of removal by the President for no reason other than that he preferred to have on that Commission men of his own choosing." ... Accordingly, we rejected the President's attempt to remove a Commissioner "merely because he wanted his own appointees on [the] Commission," stating that "no such power is given to the President directly by the Constitution, and none is impliedly conferred upon him by statute." ...

Appellees contend that *Humphrey's Executor* and *Wiener* are distinguishable from this case because they did not involve officials who performed a "core executive function." They argue that our decision in *Humphrey's Executor* rests on a distinction between "purely executive" officials and officials who exercise "quasi-legislative" and "quasi-judicial" powers. In their view, when a "purely executive" official is involved, the governing precedent is *Myers,* not *Humphrey's Executor.* ... And, under *Myers,* the President must have absolute discretion to discharge "purely" executive officials at will. See *Myers,* 272 U.S., at 132–134.

We undoubtedly did rely on the terms "quasi-legislative" and "quasi-judicial" to distinguish the officials involved in *Humphrey's Executor* and *Wiener* from those in *Myers,* but our present considered view is that the determination of whether the Constitution allows Congress to impose a "good cause"-type restriction on the President's power to remove an official cannot be made to turn on whether or not that official is classified as "purely executive." The analysis contained in our removal cases is designed not to define rigid categories of those officials who may or may not be removed at will by the President, but to ensure that Congress does not interfere with the President's exercise of the "executive power" and his constitutionally appointed duty to "take care that the laws be faithfully executed" under Article II. *Myers* was undoubtedly correct in its holding, and in its broader suggestion that there are some "purely executive" officials who must be removable by the President at will if he is to be able to accomplish his constitutional role. ... But as the Court noted in *Wiener,*

> "The assumption was short-lived that the *Myers* case recognized the President's inherent constitutional power to remove officials no matter what the relation of the executive to the discharge of their duties and no matter what restrictions Congress may have imposed regarding the nature of their tenure." 357 U.S., at 352.

At the other end of the spectrum from *Myers,* the characterization of the agencies in *Humphrey's Executor* and *Wiener* as "quasi-legislative" or "quasi-judicial" in large part reflected our judgment that it was not essential to the President's proper execution of his Article II powers that these agencies be headed up by individuals who were removable at will. We do not mean to suggest that an analysis of the functions served by the officials at issue is irrelevant. But the real question is whether the removal restrictions are of such a nature that they impede the President's ability to perform his constitutional duty, and the functions of the officials in question must be analyzed in that light.

Considering for the moment the "good cause" removal provision in isolation from the other parts of the Act at issue in this case, we cannot say that the imposition of a "good cause" standard for removal by itself unduly trammels on executive authority. . . . Although the counsel exercises no small amount of discretion and judgment in deciding how to carry out her duties under the Act, we simply do not see how the President's need to control the exercise of that discretion is so central to the functioning of the Executive Branch as to require as a matter of constitutional law that the counsel be terminable at will by the President.

Nor do we think that the "good cause" removal provision at issue here impermissibly burdens the President's power to control or supervise the independent counsel, as an executive official, in the execution of her duties under the Act. This is not a case in which the power to remove an executive official has been completely stripped from the President, thus providing no means for the President to ensure the "faithful execution" of the laws. Rather, because the independent counsel may be terminated for "good cause," the Executive, through the Attorney General, retains ample authority to assure that the counsel is competently performing her statutory responsibilities in a manner that comports with the provisions of the Act. . . . Here, as with the provision of the Act conferring the appointment authority of the independent counsel on the special court, the congressional determination to limit the removal power of the Attorney General was essential, in the view of Congress, to establish the necessary independence of the office. We do not think that this limitation as it presently stands sufficiently deprives the President of control over the independent counsel to interfere impermissibly with his constitutional obligation to ensure the faithful execution of the laws.

B

The final question to be addressed is whether the Act, taken as a whole, violates the principle of separation of powers by unduly interfering with the role of the Executive Branch. Time and again we have reaffirmed the importance in our constitutional scheme of the separation of governmental powers into the three coordinate branches. . . . We have not hesitated to invalidate provisions of law which violate this principle. . . . On the other hand, we have never held that the Constitution requires that the three Branches of Government "operate with absolute independence." . . . In the often-quoted words of Justice Jackson,

> "While the Constitution diffuses power the better to secure liberty, it also contemplates that practice will integrate the dispersed powers into a workable government. It enjoins upon its branches separateness but interdependence, autonomy but reciprocity." Youngstown Sheet & Tube Co. v. Sawyer . . . (concurring opinion).

We observe first that this case does not involve an attempt by Congress to increase its own powers at the expense of the Executive Branch. . . . Indeed, with the exception of the power of impeachment—which applies to all officers of the United States—Congress retained for itself no powers of control or supervision over an independent counsel. . . .

Similarly, we do not think that the Act works any *judicial* usurpation of properly executive functions.... The Act does give a federal court the power to review the Attorney General's decision to remove an independent counsel, but in our view this is a function that is well within the traditional power of the judiciary.

Finally, we do not think that the Act "impermissibly undermine[s]" the powers of the Executive Branch, ... or "disrupts the proper balance between the coordinate branches [by] prevent[ing] the Executive Branch from accomplishing its constitutionally assigned functions," ... It is undeniable that the Act reduces the amount of control or supervision that the Attorney General and, through him, the President exercises over the investigation and prosecution of a certain class of alleged criminal activity.... Nonetheless, the Act does give the Attorney General several means of supervising or controlling the prosecutorial powers that may be wielded by an independent counsel.... Notwithstanding the fact that the counsel is to some degree "independent" and free from Executive supervision to a greater extent than other federal prosecutors, in our view these features of the Act give the Executive Branch sufficient control over the independent counsel to ensure that the President is able to perform his constitutionally assigned duties.

VI

In sum, we conclude today that it does not violate the Appointments Clause for Congress to vest the appointment of independent counsels in the Special Division; that the powers exercised by the Special Division under the Act do not violate Article III; and that the Act does not violate the separation of powers principle by impermissibly interfering with the functions of the Executive Branch. The decision of the Court of Appeals is therefore

Reversed.

Justice Kennedy took no part in the consideration or decision of this case.

Justice Scalia, dissenting.

. . .

II

. . .

... It seems to me ... that the decision of the Court of Appeals invalidating the present statute must be upheld on fundamental separation-of-powers principles if the following two questions are answered affirmatively: (1) Is the conduct of a criminal prosecution (and of an investigation to decide whether to prosecute) the exercise of purely executive power? (2) Does the statute deprive the President of the United States of exclusive control over the exercise of that power? Surprising to say, the Court appears to concede an affirmative answer to both questions, but seeks to avoid the inevitable conclusion that since the statute vests some purely executive power in a person who is not the President of the United States it is void.

. . .

... [I]t is ultimately irrelevant *how much* the statute reduces presidential control. The case is over when the Court acknowledges, as it must, that "[i]t is undeniable that the Act reduces the amount of control or supervision that the

Attorney General and, through him, the President exercises over the investigation and prosecution of a certain class of alleged criminal activity." ...

. . .

Is it unthinkable that the President should have such exclusive power, even when alleged crimes by him or his close associates are at issue? No more so than that Congress should have the exclusive power of legislation, even when what is at issue is its own exemption from the burdens of certain laws.... No more so than that this Court should have the exclusive power to pronounce the final decision on justiciable cases and controversies, even those pertaining to the constitutionality of a statute reducing the salaries of the Justices.... A system of separate and coordinate powers necessarily involves an acceptance of exclusive power that can theoretically be abused.... While the separation of powers may prevent us from righting every wrong, it does so in order to ensure that we do not lose liberty. The checks against any Branch's abuse of its exclusive powers are twofold: First, retaliation by one of the other Branch's use of *its* exclusive powers: Congress, for example, can impeach the Executive who willfully fails to enforce the laws; the Executive can decline to prosecute under unconstitutional statutes ...; and the courts can dismiss malicious prosecutions: Second, and ultimately, there is the political check that the people will replace those in the political branches ... who are guilty of abuse. Political pressures produced special prosecutors—for Teapot Dome and for Watergate, for example—long before this statute created the independent counsel....'

. . .

III

Because appellant (who all parties and the Court agree is an officer of the United States) was not appointed by the President with the advice and consent of the Senate, but rather by the Special Division of the United States Court of Appeals, her appointment is constitutional only if (1) she is an "inferior" officer within the meaning of the above clause, and (2) Congress may vest her appointment in a court of law.

. . .

... [I]t is not clear from the Court's opinion why the factors it discusses— [putting aside the question whether they are] applied correctly to the facts of this case—are determinative of the question of inferior status. ... I think it [is] preferable to look to the text of the Constitution and the division of power that it establishes. These demonstrate, I think, that the independent counsel is not an inferior officer because she is not *subordinate* to any officer in the Executive Branch (indeed, not even to the President). Dictionaries in use at the time of the Constitutional Convention gave the word "inferiour" two meanings which it still bears today: (1) "lower in place" ... and (2) "subordinate." ... At the only other point in the Constitution at which the word "inferior" appears, it plainly connotes a relationship of subordination. Article III vests the judicial power of the United States in "one supreme Court, and in such inferior Courts as the Congress may from time to time ordain and establish." ...

That "inferior" means "subordinate" is ... consistent with what little we know about the evolution of the Appointments Clause....'

. . .

Because appellant is not subordinate to another officer, she is not an "inferior" officer and her appointment other than by the President with the advice and consent of the Senate is unconstitutional.

IV

... [T]he restrictions upon the removal of the independent counsel also violate our established precedent dealing with that specific subject....'

. . .

Since our 1935 decision in Humphrey's Executor v. United States, 295 U.S. 602—which was considered by many at the time the product of an activist, anti-New Deal court bent on reducing the power of President Franklin Roosevelt—it has been established that the line of permissible restriction upon removal of principal officers lies at the point at which the powers exercised by those officers are no longer purely executive....'

One can hardly grieve for the shoddy treatment given today to *Humphrey's Executor,* which, after all, accorded the same indignity (with much less justification) to Chief Justice Taft's opinion 10 years earlier in Myers v. United States, supra—gutting, in six quick pages devoid of textual or historical precedent for the novel principle it set forth ... *Humphrey's Executor* at least had the decency formally to observe the constitutional principle that the President had to be the repository of *all* executive power, ... which, as *Myers* carefully explained, necessarily means that he must be able to discharge those who do not perform executive functions according to his liking....'

V

Under our system of government, the primary check against prosecutorial abuse is a political one. The prosecutors who exercise this awesome discretion are selected and can be removed by a President, whom the people have trusted enough to elect. Moreover, when crimes are not investigated and prosecuted fairly, nonselectively, with a reasonable sense of proportion, the President pays the cost in political damage to his administration....'

. . .

... [The Court] extends into the very heart of our most significant constitutional function the "totality of the circumstances" mode of analysis that this Court has in recent years become fond of. Taking all things into account, we conclude that the power taken away from the President here is not really *too* much....'

The ad hoc approach to constitutional adjudication has real attraction, even apart from its work-saving potential. It is guaranteed to produce a result, in every case, that will make a majority of the Court happy with the law. The law is, by definition, precisely what the majority thinks, taking all things into account, it *ought* to be. I prefer to rely upon the judgment of the wise men who constructed our system, and of the people who approved it, and of two centuries of history that have shown it to be sound. Like it or not, that judgment says, quite plainly, that "[t]he executive Power shall be vested in a President of the United States."

SECTION 3.   PRESIDENTIAL IMMUNITIES

United States v. Nixon

418 U.S. 683, 94 S.Ct. 3090, 41 L.Ed.2d 1039 (1974).

Mr. Chief Justice Burger delivered the opinion of the Court.

This litigation presents for review the denial of a motion, filed on behalf of the President of the United States, in the case of United States v. Mitchell et al.

... to quash a third-party subpoena *duces tecum* issued by the United States District Court for the District of Columbia ... The subpoena directed the President to produce certain tape recordings and documents relating to his conversations with aides and advisers. The court rejected the President's claims of absolute executive privilege ... The President appealed to the Court of Appeals. We granted the United States' petition for certiorari before judgment, ...

On March 1, 1974, a grand jury of the United States District Court for the District of Columbia returned an indictment charging seven named individuals[3] with various offenses, including conspiracy to defraud the United States and to obstruct justice. Although he was not designated as such in the indictment, the grand jury named the President, among others, as an unindicted coconspirator. On April 18, 1974, upon motion of the Special Prosecutor, a subpoena *duces tecum* was issued ... to the President by the United States District Court and made returnable on May 2, 1974. This subpoena required the production, in advance of the September 9 trial date, of certain tapes, memoranda, papers, transcripts, or other writings relating to certain precisely identified meetings between the President and others.... On May 1, 1974, the President's counsel, filed a "special appearance" and a motion to quash the subpoena ...

On May 20, 1974, the District Court denied the motion to quash ...

. . .

II.   Justiciability

In the District Court the President's counsel argued that the court lacked jurisdiction to issue the subpoena because the matter was an intra-branch dispute between a subordinate and superior officer of the Executive Branch and hence not subject to judicial resolution. ... Since the Executive Branch has exclusive authority and absolute discretion to decide whether to prosecute a case, ..., it is contended that a President's decision is final in determining what evidence is to be used in a given criminal case. ...

Our starting point is the nature of the proceeding for which the evidence is sought—here a pending criminal prosecution. ... [The regulation under which the Special Prosecutor is acting] gives the Special Prosecutor explicit power to contest the invocation of executive privilege....

So long as this regulation is extant it has the force of law....

[Although] it is theoretically possible for the Attorney General to amend or revoke the regulation defining the Special Prosecutor's authority ... he has not done so. So long as the regulation remains in force the Executive Branch is bound by it....

. . .

IV.   The Claim of Privilege

A.

... [W]e turn to the claim that the subpoena should be quashed because it demands "confidential conversations between a President and his close advis-

---

3. The seven defendants were John N. Mitchell, H.R. Haldeman, John D. Ehrlichman, Charles W. Colson, Robert C. Mardian, Kenneth W. Parkinson, and Gordon Strachan. Each had occupied either a position of responsibility on the White House staff or the Committee for the Re-election of the President. Colson entered a guilty plea on another charge and is no longer a defendant.

ors that it would be inconsistent with the public interest to produce." The first contention is a broad claim that the separation of powers doctrine precludes judicial review of a President's claim of privilege. The second contention is that if he does not prevail on the claim of absolute privilege, the court should hold as a matter of constitutional law that the privilege prevails over the subpoena *duces tecum.*

In the performance of assigned constitutional duties each branch of the Government must initially interpret the Constitution, and the interpretation of its powers by any branch is due great respect from the others. The President's counsel, as we have noted, reads the Constitution as providing an absolute privilege of confidentiality for all presidential communications. Many decisions of this Court, however, have unequivocally reaffirmed the holding of Marbury v. Madison, . . . that "it is emphatically the province and duty of the judicial department to say what the law is." . . .

. . .

B.

In support of his claim of absolute privilege the President's counsel urges two grounds one of which is common to all governments and one of which is peculiar to our system of separation of powers. The first ground is the valid need for protection of communications between high Government officials and those who advise and assist them in the performance of their manifold duties; the importance of this confidentiality is too plain to require further discussion. Human experience teaches that those who expect public dissemination of their remarks may well temper candor with a concern for appearances and for their own interests to the detriment of the decisionmaking process. Whatever the nature of the privilege of confidentiality of presidential communications in the exercise of Art. II powers, the privilege can be said to derive from the supremacy of each branch within its own assigned area of constitutional duties. Certain powers and privileges flow from the nature of enumerated powers; the protection of the confidentiality of Presidential communications has similar constitutional underpinnings.

The second ground asserted by the President's counsel in support of the claim of absolute privilege rests on the doctrine of separation of powers. Here it is argued that the independence of the Executive Branch within its own sphere insulates a president from a judicial subpoena in an ongoing criminal prosecution, and thereby protects confidential Presidential communications.

However, neither the doctrine of separation of powers, nor the need for confidentiality of high level communications without more, can sustain an absolute, unqualified Presidential privilege of immunity from judicial process under all circumstances. The President's need for complete candor and objectivity from advisers calls for great deference from the courts. However, when the privilege depends solely on the broad, undifferentiated claim of public interest in the confidentiality of such conversations, a confrontation with other values arises. Absent a claim of need to protect military, diplomatic or sensitive national security secrets, we find it difficult to accept the argument that even the very important interest in confidentiality of Presidential communications is significantly diminished by production of such material for *in camera* inspection with all the protection that a district court will be obliged to provide.

The impediment that an absolute, unqualified privilege would place in the way of the primary constitutional duty of the Judicial Branch to do justice in criminal prosecutions would plainly conflict with the function of the courts under Art. III. In designing the structure of our Government and dividing and allocating the sovereign power among three coequal branches, the Framers of the Constitution sought to provide a comprehensive system, but the separate powers were not intended to operate with absolute independence.... To read the Art. II powers of the President as providing an absolute privilege as against a subpoena essential to enforcement of criminal statutes on no more than a generalized claim of the public interest in confidentiality of nonmilitary and nondiplomatic discussions would upset the constitutional balance of "a workable government" and gravely impair the role of the courts under Art. III.

C.

Since we conclude that the legitimate needs of the judicial process may outweigh Presidential privilege, it is necessary to resolve those competing interests in a manner that preserves the essential functions of each branch. The right and indeed the duty to resolve that question does not free the Judiciary from according high respect to the representations made on behalf of the President. United States v. Burr, 25 F. Cas. 187, 190, 191–192 (No. 14,694) (CC Va. 1807).

... The privilege is fundamental to the operation of Government and inextricably rooted in the separation of powers under the Constitution. ...

But this presumptive privilege must be considered in light of our historic commitment to the rule of law.... The very integrity of the judicial system and public confidence in the system depend on full disclosure of all the facts, within the framework of the rules of evidence. To ensure that justice is done, it is imperative to the function of courts that compulsory process be available for the production of evidence needed either by the prosecution or by the defense.

Only recently the Court restated the ancient proposition of law, albeit in the context of a grand jury inquiry rather than a trial, "that 'the public ... has a right to every man's evidence,' except for those persons protected by a constitutional, common-law or statutory privilege." ...

. . .

The right to the production of all evidence at a criminal trial ... has constitutional dimensions. The Sixth Amendment explicitly confers upon every defendant in a criminal trial the right "to be confronted with the witnesses against him" and "to have compulsory process for obtaining witnesses in his favor." Moreover, the Fifth Amendment also guarantees that no person shall be deprived of liberty without due process of law. It is the manifest duty of the courts to vindicate those guarantees, and to accomplish that it is essential that all relevant and admissible evidence be produced.

In this case we must weigh the importance of the general privilege of confidentiality of Presidential communications in performance of the President's responsibilities against the inroads of such a privilege on the fair administration of criminal justice. The interest in preserving confidentiality is weighty indeed and entitled to great respect. However we cannot conclude that advisers will be moved to temper the candor of their remarks by the infrequent occasions of disclosure because of the possibility that such conversations will be called for in the context of a criminal prosecution.

On the other hand, the allowance of the privilege to withhold evidence that is demonstrably relevant in a criminal trial would cut deeply into the guarantee of due process of law and gravely impair the basic function of the courts. ...

We conclude that [the] generalized assertion of privilege must yield to the demonstrated, specific need for evidence in a pending criminal trial.

. . .

Affirmed.

Mr. Justice Rehnquist took no part in the consideration or decision of these cases.

Clinton v. Jones

520 U.S. 681, 117 S.Ct. 1636, 137 L.Ed.2d 945 (1997).

Justice Stevens delivered the opinion of the Court.

This case raises a constitutional and a prudential question concerning the Office of the President of the United States. Respondent, a private citizen, seeks to recover damages from the current occupant of that office based on actions allegedly taken before his term began. The President submits that in all but the most exceptional cases the Constitution requires federal courts to defer such litigation until his term ends and that, in any event, respect for the office warrants such a stay. Despite the force of the arguments supporting the President's submissions, we conclude that they must be rejected.

I

... In 1991 [President Clinton] was the Governor of the State of Arkansas. Respondent, Paula Corbin Jones ... lived in Arkansas [in 1991], and was an employee of the Arkansas Industrial Development Commission.

On May 6, 1994, she commenced this action in the United States District Court ...

Th[e] allegations [in the complaint] principally describe events that are said to have occurred on the afternoon of May 8, 1991, during an official conference held at the Excelsior Hotel in Little Rock, Arkansas. The Governor delivered a speech at the conference; respondent—working as a state employee—staffed the registration desk. She alleges that ... the Governor ... made "abhorrent" sexual advances that she vehemently rejected. She further claims that her superiors at work subsequently dealt with her in a hostile and rude manner, and changed her duties to punish her for rejecting those advances. ...

... Her complaint contains four counts. The first charges that petitioner, acting under color of state law, deprived her of rights protected by the Constitution, in violation of ... 42 U.S.C. § 1983. ... [T]he alleged misconduct of petitioner was unrelated to any of his official duties as President of the United States and, indeed, occurred before he was elected to that office.

II

. . .

The District Judge denied the motion to dismiss on immunity grounds and ruled that discovery in the case could go forward, but ordered any trial stayed until the end of petitioner's Presidency. . . .'

Both parties appealed. A divided panel of the Court of Appeals affirmed the denial of the motion to dismiss, but because it regarded the order postponing the trial until the President leaves office as the "functional equivalent" of a grant of temporary immunity, it reversed that order. . . .'

. . .

III

. . .

. . . [There are] two important constitutional issues not encompassed within the questions presented by the petition for certiorari that we need not address today.

First, because the claim of immunity is asserted in a federal court and relies heavily on the doctrine of separation of powers . . ., it is not necessary to consider or decide whether a comparable claim might succeed in a state tribunal. If this case were being heard in a state forum, instead of advancing a separation of powers argument, petitioner would presumably rely on federalism and comity concerns[13] as well as the interest in protecting federal officials from possible local prejudice that underlies the authority to remove certain cases brought against federal officers from a state to a federal court . . .

Second, our decision rejecting the immunity claim and allowing the case to proceed does not require us to confront the question whether a court may compel the attendance of the President at any specific time or place. We assume that the testimony of the President, both for discovery and for use at trial, may be taken at the White House at a time that will accommodate his busy schedule, and that, if a trial is held, there would be no necessity for the President to attend in person, though he could elect to do so.[14]

IV

Petitioner's principal submission—that "in all but the most exceptional cases," the Constitution affords the President temporary immunity from civil damages litigation arising out of events that occurred before he took office—cannot be sustained on the basis of precedent.

Only three sitting Presidents have been defendants in civil litigation involving their actions prior to taking office. Complaints against Theodore Roosevelt and Harry Truman had been dismissed before they took office; the dismissals were affirmed after their respective inaugurations. Two companion cases arising out of an automobile accident were filed against John F. Kennedy in 1960 during the Presidential campaign. After taking office, he unsuccessfully argued that his status as Commander in Chief gave him a right to a stay under the Soldiers' and Sailors' Civil Relief Act of 1940. . . . The motion for a stay was denied by the District Court, and the matter was settled out of court. Thus, none of those cases sheds any light on the constitutional issue before us.

The principal rationale for affording certain public servants immunity from suits for money damages arising out of their official acts is inapplicable to unofficial conduct. . . . That rationale provided the principal basis for our holding that a former President of the United States was "entitled to absolute

---

13. Because the Supremacy Clause makes federal law "the supreme Law of the Land," Art. VI, cl. 2, any direct control by a state court over the President, who has principal responsibility to ensure that those laws are "faithfully executed," Art. II, § 3, may implicate concerns that are quite different from the interbranch separation of powers questions addressed here. . . .

14. Although Presidents have responded to written interrogatories, given depositions, and provided videotaped trial testimony, no sitting President has ever testified, or been ordered to testify, in open court.

immunity from damages liability predicated on his official acts," [Nixon v.] *Fitzgerald*, 457 U.S. [731 (1982)] . . . Our central concern was to avoid rendering the President "unduly cautious in the discharge of his official duties." . . .

This reasoning provides no support for an immunity for *unofficial* conduct. As we explained in *Fitzgerald*, "the sphere of protected action must be related closely to the immunity's justifying purposes." . . . Because of the President's broad responsibilities, we recognized in that case an immunity from damages claims arising out of official acts extending to the "outer perimeter of his authority." . . . But we have never suggested that the President, or any other official, has an immunity that extends beyond the scope of any action taken in an official capacity. . . .'

Moreover, when defining the scope of an immunity for acts clearly taken *within* an official capacity, we have applied a functional approach. "Frequently our decisions have held that an official's absolute immunity should extend only to acts in performance of particular functions of his office." . . . As our opinions have made clear, immunities are grounded in "the nature of the function performed, not the identity of the actor who performed it." . . .

Petitioner's effort to construct an immunity from suit for unofficial acts grounded purely in the identity of his office is unsupported by precedent.

V

We are also unpersuaded by the evidence from the historical record to which petitioner has called our attention. He points to a comment by Thomas Jefferson protesting the subpoena *duces tecum* Chief Justice Marshall directed to him in the Burr trial . . .

Respondent, in turn, has called our attention to conflicting historical evidence. . . .

In the end, as applied to the particular question before us, we reach the same conclusion about these historical materials that Justice Jackson described when confronted with an issue concerning the dimensions of the President's power. "Just what our forefathers did envision, or would have envisioned had they foreseen modern conditions, must be divined from materials almost as enigmatic as the dreams Joseph was called upon to interpret for Pharoah. A century and a half of partisan debate and scholarly speculation yields no net result but only supplies more or less apt quotations from respected sources on each side. . . . They largely cancel each other." Youngstown Sheet & Tube Co. v. Sawyer . . . (concurring opinion).

VI

Petitioner's strongest argument supporting his immunity claim is based on the text and structure of the Constitution. He does not contend that the occupant of the Office of the President is "above the law," in the sense that his conduct is entirely immune from judicial scrutiny. The President argues merely for a postponement of the judicial proceedings that will determine whether he violated any law. His argument is grounded in the character of the office that was created by Article II of the Constitution, and relies on separation of powers principles that have structured our constitutional arrangement since the founding.

As a starting premise, petitioner contends that he occupies a unique office with powers and responsibilities so vast and important that the public interest demands that he devote his undivided time and attention to his public duties. He submits that—given the nature of the office—the doctrine of separation of powers places limits on the authority of the Federal Judiciary to interfere with the Executive Branch that would be transgressed by allowing this action to proceed.

We have no dispute with the initial premise of the argument. Former presidents, from George Washington to George Bush, have consistently endorsed petitioner's characterization of the office. ... Thus, while we suspect that even in our modern era there remains some truth to Chief Justice Marshall's suggestion that the duties of the Presidency are not entirely "unremitting," United States v. Burr, 25 F. Cas. 30, 34 (C.C.Va.1807), we accept the initial premise of the Executive's argument.

It does not follow, however, that separation of powers principles would be violated by allowing this action to proceed. ...

... [I]n this case there is no suggestion that the Federal Judiciary is being asked to perform any function that might in some way be described as "executive." Respondent is merely asking the courts to exercise their core Article III jurisdiction to decide cases and controversies. Whatever the outcome of this case, there is no possibility that the decision will curtail the scope of the official powers of the Executive Branch. The litigation of questions that relate entirely to the unofficial conduct of the individual who happens to be the President poses no perceptible risk of misallocation of either judicial power or executive power.

... [P]etitioner contends that this particular case—as well as the potential additional litigation that an affirmance of the Court of Appeals judgment might spawn—may impose an unacceptable burden on the President's time and energy, and thereby impair the effective performance of his office.

Petitioner's predictive judgment finds little support in either history or the relatively narrow compass of the issues raised in this particular case. As we have already noted, in the more than 200–year history of the Republic, only three sitting Presidents have been subjected to suits for their private actions. If the past is any indicator, it seems unlikely that a deluge of such litigation will ever engulf the Presidency. As for the case at hand, if properly managed by the District Court, it appears to us highly unlikely to occupy any substantial amount of petitioner's time.

Of greater significance, petitioner errs by presuming that interactions between the Judicial Branch and the Executive, even quite burdensome interactions, necessarily rise to the level of constitutionally forbidden impairment of the Executive's ability to perform its constitutionally mandated functions.... The fact that a federal court's exercise of its traditional Article III jurisdiction may significantly burden the time and attention of the Chief Executive is not sufficient to establish a violation of the Constitution. Two long-settled propositions, first announced by Chief Justice Marshall, support that conclusion.

First, we have long held that when the President takes official action, the Court has the authority to determine whether he has acted within the law. Perhaps the most dramatic example of such a case is our holding that President Truman exceeded his constitutional authority when he issued an order directing the Secretary of Commerce to take possession of and operate most of the Nation's steel mills ... Youngstown Sheet & Tube Co. v. Sawyer ... Our holding was an application of the principle established in Marbury v. Madison ... that "[i]t is emphatically the province and duty of the judicial department to say what the law is." ...

Second, it is also settled that the President is subject to judicial process in appropriate circumstances. Although Thomas Jefferson apparently thought otherwise, Chief Justice Marshall, when presiding in the treason trial of Aaron Burr, ruled that a subpoena *duces tecum* could be directed to the President. United States v. Burr, 25 F. Cas. 30 (No. 14,692D) (CC Va. 1807). We unequivocally and emphatically endorsed Marshall's position when we held that President Nixon was obligated to comply with a subpoena commanding him to produce certain tape recordings of his conversations with his aides. . . .

Sitting Presidents have responded to court orders to provide testimony and other information with sufficient frequency that such interactions between the Judicial and Executive Branches can scarcely be thought a novelty . . . Moreover, sitting Presidents have also voluntarily complied with judicial requests for testimony. . . .

. . . If the Judiciary may severely burden the Executive Branch by reviewing the legality of the President's official conduct, and if it may direct appropriate process to the President himself, it must follow that the federal courts have power to determine the legality of his unofficial conduct. The burden on the President's time and energy that is a mere by-product of such review surely cannot be considered as onerous as the direct burden imposed by judicial review and the occasional invalidation of his official actions. We therefore hold that the doctrine of separation of powers does not require federal courts to stay all private actions against the President until he leaves office.

The reasons for rejecting such a categorical rule apply as well to a rule that would require a stay "in all but the most exceptional cases." . . . In all events, the question whether a specific case should receive exceptional treatment is more appropriately the subject of the exercise of judicial discretion than an interpretation of the Constitution. Accordingly, we turn to the question whether the District Court's decision to stay the trial until after petitioner leaves office was an abuse of discretion.

VII

The Court of Appeals described the District Court's discretionary decision to stay the trial as the "functional equivalent" of a grant of temporary immunity. . . . Although we ultimately conclude that the stay should not have been granted, we think the issue is more difficult than the opinion of the Court of Appeals suggests.

Strictly speaking the stay was not the functional equivalent of the constitutional immunity that petitioner claimed, because the District Court ordered discovery to proceed. Moreover, a stay of either the trial or discovery might be justified by considerations that do not require the recognition of any constitutional immunity. The District Court has broad discretion to stay proceedings as an incident to its power to control its own docket. . . . The high respect that is owed to the office of the Chief Executive, though not justifying a rule of categorical immunity, is a matter that should inform the conduct of the entire proceeding, including the timing and scope of discovery.

Nevertheless, we are persuaded that it was an abuse of discretion for the District Court to defer the trial until after the President leaves office. Such a lengthy and categorical stay takes no account whatever of the respondent's interest in bringing the case to trial. . . .

The decision to postpone the trial was, furthermore, premature. The proponent of a stay bears the burden of establishing its need. . . . In this case, at the stage at which the District Court made its ruling, there was no way to assess whether a stay of trial after the completion of discovery would be warranted. Other than the fact that a trial may consume some of the President's time and attention, there is nothing in the record to enable a judge to assess the potential harm that may ensue from scheduling the trial promptly after discovery is concluded....'

VIII

We add a final comment on two matters that are discussed at length in the briefs: the risk that our decision will generate a large volume of politically motivated harassing and frivolous litigation, and the danger that national security concerns might prevent the President from explaining a legitimate need for a continuance.

We are not persuaded that either of these risks is serious. Most frivolous and vexatious litigation is terminated at the pleading stage or on summary judgment, with little if any personal involvement by the defendant. ... Moreover, the availability of sanctions provides a significant deterrent to litigation directed at the President in his unofficial capacity for purposes of political gain or harassment. History indicates that the likelihood that a significant number of such cases will be filed is remote. ...

If Congress deems it appropriate to afford the President stronger protection, it may respond with appropriate legislation.... If the Constitution embodied the rule that the President advocates, Congress, of course, could not repeal it. But our holding today raises no barrier to a statutory response to these concerns.

The Federal District Court has jurisdiction to decide this case. Like every other citizen who properly invokes that jurisdiction, respondent has a right to an orderly disposition of her claims. Accordingly, the judgment of the Court of Appeals is affirmed.

It is so ordered.

Justice Breyer, concurring in the judgment.

I agree with the majority that the Constitution does not automatically grant the President an immunity from civil lawsuits based upon his private conduct....'

In my view, however, once the President sets forth and explains a conflict between judicial proceeding and public duties, the matter changes. At that point, the Constitution permits a judge to schedule a trial in an ordinary civil damages action (where postponement normally is possible without overwhelming damage to a plaintiff) only within the constraints of a constitutional principle—a principle that forbids a federal judge in such a case to interfere with the President's discharge of his public duties. I have no doubt that the Constitution contains such a principle applicable to civil suits, based upon Article II's vesting of the entire "executive Power" in a single individual, implemented through the Constitution's structural separation of powers, and revealed both by history and case precedent.

I recognize that this case does not require us now to apply the principle specifically, thereby delineating its contours.... Yet I fear that to disregard it now may appear to deny it. ... Further, if the majority is wrong in predicting the future infrequency of private civil litigation against sitting Presidents, acknowledgment and future delineation of the constitutional principle will prove a practically necessary institutional safeguard....'

. . .

I agree with the majority that [historical] precedents reject any absolute Presidential immunity from all court process. But they do not cast doubt upon Justice Story's basic conclusion that "in civil cases," a sitting President "possess[es] an official inviolability" as necessary to permit him to "perform" the duties of his office without "obstruction or impediment."

. . .

. . . [A] lawsuit that significantly distracts an official from his public duties can distort the content of a public decision just as can a threat of potential future liability. If the latter concern can justify an "absolute" immunity in the case of a President no longer in office, where distraction is no longer a consideration, so can the former justify, not immunity, but a postponement, in the case of a sitting President.

. . .

. . . [T]his Court has now made clear that such lawsuits may proceed against a sitting President. The consequence, as the Court warned in *Fitzgerald*, is that a sitting President, given "the visibility of his office," could well become "an easily identifiable target for suits for civil damages,". . . . The threat of sanctions could well discourage much unneeded litigation, but some lawsuits (including highly intricate and complicated ones) could resist ready evaluation and disposition; and individual district court procedural rulings could pose a significant threat to the President's official functions.

I concede the possibility that district courts . . . might prove able to manage private civil damage actions against sitting Presidents without significantly interfering with the discharge of Presidential duties—at least if they manage those actions with the constitutional problem in mind. Nonetheless, predicting the future is difficult, and I am skeptical. . . . I believe that ordinary case-management principles are unlikely to prove sufficient to deal with private civil lawsuits for damages unless supplemented with a constitutionally based requirement that district courts schedule proceedings so as to avoid significant interference with the President's ongoing discharge of his official responsibilities.

. . .

NOTE ON THE APPLICABILITY OF EXECUTIVE PRIVILEGE TO THE VICE PRESIDENCY

In *Cheney v. United States District Court for the District of Columbia*, ___ U.S. ___, 124 S.Ct. 2576 (2004), the Supreme Court was asked to apply Executive Privilege considerations to a case seeking information from, among others, Vice President Richard Cheney. The *Cheney* litigation began when various public interest groups sued the Vice President and the National Energy Policy Development Group (NEPDG) that President Bush directed him to head. The plaintiffs, relying on the Federal Advisory Committee Act (FACA), sought to obtain records of the group's meetings. The defendants responded by arguing, among other things, that applying FACA to the Vice–President in a case like this would be problematic under separation-of-powers/executive privilege-type doctrines. After having its arguments largely rejected in the district court and the Court of Appeals, the Vice President sought relief in the Supreme Court.

Although the Court did not direct an outcome in the case, but rather remanded it for more consideration, the Court did send signals that the lower courts should be respectful of the Executive Branch's need to be free from outside interference: "All courts should be mindful of the burdens imposed on the Executive Branch in any future proceedings. Special considerations applicable to the President and the Vice–President suggest that the courts should be sensitive to requests by the Government for [immediate] appeals to reexamine, for example, whether the [FACA really does apply in these circumstances]."

The Court distinguished U.S. v. Nixon on the ground that it had involved a criminal proceeding in which the necessity for relevant evidence was stronger. By contrast, civil cases—like those under the FACA—do not implicate such a compelling need for "every man's evidence."

Consider the implications of the following additional language in *Cheney* for two of the other major separation of powers cases presented earlier in this chapter—Morrison v. Olson and Clinton v. Jones:

"The observation in *Nixon* that production of confidential information would not disrupt the functioning of the Executive Branch cannot be applied in a mechanistic fashion to civil litigation. In the criminal justice system, there are various constraints, albeit imperfect, to filter out insubstantial legal claims. The decision to prosecute a criminal case, for example, is made by a publicly accountable prosecutor subject to budgetary considerations. . . . In contrast, there are no analogous checks in the civil discovery process here. Although under Federal Rule of Civil Procedure 11, sanctions are available, and private attorneys owe an obligation of candor to the judicial tribunal, those safeguards have proved insufficient to discourage filing of meritless claims against the executive Branch. 'In view of the visibility of' the Offices of the President and the Vice–President and the 'effect of their actions on countless people,' they are 'easily identifiable target[s] for suits for civil damages.' "

The *Cheney* Court did not discuss whether, why and how Executive Privilege claims by Vice Presidents might be different than those by the President or Cabinet members, in light of the fact that the Vice President performs some legislative duties (e.g., presiding over and casting tie-breaking votes in the Senate), is not removable by the President the way cabinet members are, and is not required by the Constitution to be elected on a Presidential ticket. For discussion of these issues, and the *Cheney* case more generally, see Vikram Amar, *The Cheney Decision—A Missed Chance to Straighten Out Some Muddled Issues*, 2004 Cato Sup. Ct. Review 185 (2004).

NOTE ON THE IMPEACHMENT OF PRESIDENT WILLIAM CLINTON

The Congressional Act upheld in the *Morrison* case, combined with information unearthed in the *Clinton v. Jones* litigation, helped set the stage for the impeachment of President William Jefferson Clinton by the House of Representatives in December 1998. President Clinton was ultimately acquitted by the Senate in Feburary 1999, and served out the remainder of his second term. The Clinton impeachment experience raised a host of constitutional questions, including the following: What precisely does the Article II's "high crimes and misdemeanors" standard mean?; Can this standard be satisfied by "private" misdeeds that do not implicate misuse of federal resources?; How do the impeachment standards for Presidents relate to those for other officals, like federal judges?; Is Congress under any constitutional duty to impeach where "high crimes and misdemeanors" may be present?; What role should the views of the public play in Congressional impeachment proceedings?; and What alternatives does Congress have to impeachment in dealing with alleged Presidential misdeeds? These and other profound constitutional questions never made their way into a court, but had to be dealt with by conscientious legislators as well as the rest of the country. For an introduction to some of the most vexing issues, see Klarman, *Constitutional Fetishism and the Clinton Impeachment Debate*, 85 Va. L.Rev. 631 (1999) and Vikram Amar, *The Truth, the Whole Truth and Nothing But the Truth About 'High Crimes and Misdemeanors' and the Constitution's Impeachment Process*," 16 Const. Comm. 403 (1999).

PART III

GOVERNMENT AND THE INDIVIDUAL: THE PROTECTION OF LIBERTY AND PROPERTY UNDER THE DUE PROCESS AND EQUAL PROTECTION CLAUSES

In this Part, the emphasis shifts from exploring the constitutional relationships among different parts of the governmental structure to the protection of individual rights from interference by all levels and branches of government.

The central question is definition of the proper judicial role in giving content to the vague language of the due process clauses of the fifth and fourteenth amendments, and of the equal protection clause of the fourteenth amendment.

Chapter 8 concerns the interrelationship between the bill of rights and the Civil War amendments to the Constitution. Chapter 9 deals with the application of the due process clause. Chapter 10 discusses the equal protection clause. Chapter 11 completes the analysis with an examination of constitutional norms of fair procedure. (The discrete problems of constitutional protection of speech and conscience under the first amendment are reserved for Part IV.)

Chapter 12 returns to an issue of division of national and state power. After examining the application of the Civil War amendments to private conduct, the bulk of this chapter concerns the extent of Congressional power to enforce the amendments.

CHAPTER 8

THE BILL OF RIGHTS, THE CIVIL WAR AMENDMENTS AND THEIR INTER-RELATIONSHIP

Introduction. In Chapter 1 it was noted that the original constitution included only a few limitations upon government power to regulate life, liberty and property. The principal restraints on state regulation were those forbidding the impairment of the obligation of contracts (Art. I, 10), banning bills of attainder and ex post facto laws (Art. I, § 10), and guaranteeing citizens of one state the right to enjoy in another state "all the Privileges and Immunities" of its own citizens (Art. IV, § 2).

The Bill of Rights (Amendments 1–10) adopted in 1791 imposed a substantial series of protections for the individual against government. Almost 80 years later the Civil War Amendments (13, 14, and 15) specifically imposed restraints on the power of states to regulate the personal and property interests of their citizens.

The primary purpose of this Chapter is to give a brief historical introduction to the Court's application of these three sets of restraints on the power of government to regulate liberty and property. A major focus will be the dispute over the interrelationship between the Bill of Rights and the Civil War Amendments.

Early interpretations of the individual rights provisions contained in the text of the original Constitution, the Bill of Rights, and the Civil War Amendments should be augmented, however, by a preliminary reference to the possibility of nontextual constitutional restraints stemming from principles of natural justice invoked and elaborated by courts. This possibility was raised early in Calder v. Bull, 3 U.S. (3 Dall.) 386 (1798), where two Justices sharply disagreed, in an historically important exchange of *dicta*, over the propriety of basing a determination of unconstitutionality on principles not specified in the Constitution. Justice Chase upheld the challenged state law, but wrote:

> "I cannot subscribe to the omnipotence of a state Legislature, or that it is absolute and without control; although its authority should not be expressly restrained by the constitution, or fundamental law, of the state. The people of the United States erected their constitutions or forms of government, to establish justice, to promote the general welfare, to secure the blessings of liberty, and to protect their persons and property from violence. The purposes for which men enter into society will determine the nature and terms of the social compact; and as they are the foundation of the legislative power, they will decide what are the proper objects of it: The nature, and ends of legislative power will limit the exercise of it. This fundamental principle flows from the very nature of our free Republican governments, that no man should be compelled to do what the laws do not require; nor to refrain from acts which the laws permit. There are acts

which the federal, or state, Legislature cannot do, without exceeding their authority. There are certain vital principles in our free Republican governments, which will determine and overrule an apparent and flagrant abuse of legislative power; as to authorize manifest injustice by positive law; or to take away that security for personal liberty, or private property, for the protection whereof the government was established. An act of the Legislature (for I cannot call it a law) contrary to the great first principles of the social compact, cannot be considered a rightful exercise of legislative authority.... A few instances will suffice to explain what I mean. A law that punished a citizen for an innocent action, or, in other words, for an act, which, when done, was in violation of no existing law; a law that destroys, or impairs, the lawful private contracts of citizens; a law that makes a man a judge in his own cause; or a law that takes property from A. and gives it to B. It is against all reason and justice, for a people to entrust a Legislature with such powers; and, therefore, it cannot be presumed that they have done it. The genius, the nature, and the spirit, of our state governments, amount to a prohibition of such acts of legislation; and the general principles of law and reason forbid them.... To maintain that our federal, or state, Legislature possesses such powers, if they had not been expressly restrained, would, in my opinion, be a political heresy, altogether inadmissible in our free republican governments."

Justice Iredell responded:

"[S]ome speculative jurists have held, that a legislative act against natural justice must, in itself, be void; but I cannot think that, under such a government, any court of justice would possess a power to declare it so....

"[I]t has been the policy of all the American States, which have, individually, framed their state constitutions since the revolution, and of the people of the United States, when they framed the federal constitution, to define with precision the objects of the legislative power, and to restrain its exercise within marked and settled boundaries. If any act of Congress, or of the legislature of a state, violates those constitutional provisions, it is unquestionably void.... If on the other hand, the legislature of the union, or the legislature of any member of the union, shall pass a law, within the general scope of their constitutional power, the court cannot pronounce it to be void, merely because it is, in their judgment, contrary to the principles of natural justice. The ideas of natural justice are regulated by no fixed standard; the ablest and the purest men have differed upon the subject; and all that the court could properly say, in such an event, would be, that the legislature (possessed of an equal right of opinion) had passed an act which, in the opinion of the judges, was inconsistent with the abstract principles of natural justice."

The substance of this debate has been a continuing theme in constitutional law, whether framed as a debate about an expansive interpretation of an open-ended text or about a "noninterpretive" principle of fundamental right. For discussion of the contemporary dimensions of the debate, compare Grey, *Do We Have an Unwritten Constitution?*, 27 Stan.L.Rev. 703 (1975); Perry, *The Constitution, The Courts, and Human Rights* (1982); and Sedler, *The Legitimacy Debate in Constitutional Adjudication*, 44 Ohio St.L.J. 10 (1983); with Ely, *Foreword: On Discovering Fundamental Values*, 92 Harv.L.Rev. 5 (1978); and Linde, *Judges, Critics, and the Realist Tradition*, 82 Yale L.J. 227 (1972).

SECTION 1.   THE PRE–CIVIL WAR BACKGROUND

A.   THE CONTRACT CLAUSE AND THE PRIVILEGES AND IMMUNITIES CLAUSE OF ARTICLE IV—EARLY INTERPRETATIONS

THE CONTRACT CLAUSE

The first case in which the Supreme Court held a state statute to be in conflict with the constitution involved the contract clause. In Fletcher v. Peck, 10 U.S. (6 Cranch.) 87 (1810), the Court held invalid an act of the Georgia legislature rescinding a sale of land it had previously approved. Marshall writing for the Court held that the contract clause applied to public contracts and that a grant of land constituted a contract not to reassert rights over the land granted. In invalidating the law he relied both on the contract clause and on the more general notion that "the nature of society and of government [ ]prescribe some limits to the legislative power."

The Court went on to decide a large number of cases under the contract clause.

> "During the nineteenth century no constitutional clause was so frequently the basis of decision by the Supreme Court of the United States as that forbidding the states to pass laws impairing the obligation of contracts. If we exclude the commerce clause as being primarily a grant of power to the national government, although it is significant because of its treatment as a restriction on state powers, the contract clause was the constitutional justification for more cases involving the validity of state laws than all of the other clauses of the Constitution together."

Wright, *The Contract Clause of the Constitution* xi (1938).

No attempt is made here to review the early cases. Much of the historical material is discussed in two modern cases, Allied Structural Steel Co. v. Spannaus, 438 U.S. 234 (1978), and United States Trust Co. of New York v. New Jersey, 431 U.S. 1 (1977), both set out, infra, Chapter 9.

THE PRIVILEGES AND IMMUNITIES CLAUSE OF ARTICLE IV

CORFIELD v. CORYELL, 4 Wash.C.C. 371, 6 Fed.Cas. 546 (1823). A New Jersey statute of 1820 made it unlawful for any person who was not "an actual inhabitant and resident" of the state to rake or gather clams, oysters, or shells in any of the rivers, bays, or waters of the state. The statute was challenged by a Pennsylvania citizen gathering oysters in New Jersey waters. In disposing of the claim made under Article IV, section 2, Supreme Court Justice Washington, sitting on circuit, said:

"The next question is, whether this act infringes that section of the constitution which declares that 'the citizens of each state shall be entitled to all the privileges and immunities of citizens in the several states?' The inquiry is, what are the privileges and immunities of citizens in the several states? We feel no hesitation in confining these expressions to those privileges and immunities which are, in their nature, fundamental; which belong, of right, to the citizens of all free governments; and which have, at all times, been enjoyed by the citizens of the several states which compose this Union, from the time of their becoming free, independent, and sovereign. What these fundamental principles are, it would perhaps be more tedious than difficult to enumerate. They may, however, be all comprehended under the following general heads: Protection by the government; the enjoyment of life and liberty, with the right to acquire and possess property of every kind, and to pursue and obtain happiness and safety; subject nevertheless to such restraints as the government may justly prescribe for the general good of the whole. The right of a citizen of one state to pass through, or to reside in any other state, for purposes of trade, agriculture, professional pursuits, or otherwise; to claim the benefit of the writ of habeas corpus; to institute and maintain actions of any kind in the courts of the state; to take hold and dispose of property, either real or personal; and an exemption from higher taxes or impositions than are paid by the other citizens of the state; may be mentioned as some of the particular privileges and immunities of citizens, which are clearly embraced by the general description of privileges deemed to be fundamental: to which may be added, the elective franchise, as regulated and established by the laws or constitution of the state in which it is to be exercised. These, and many others which might be mentioned, are, strictly speaking, privileges and immunities, and the enjoyment of them by the citizens of each state, in every other state, was manifestly calculated (to use the expressions of the preamble of the corresponding provision in the old articles of confederation) 'the better to secure and perpetuate mutual friendship and intercourse among the people of the different states of the Union.' But we cannot accede to the proposition which was insisted on by the counsel, that, under this provision of the constitution, the citizens of the several states are permitted to participate in all the rights which belong exclusively to the citizens of any other particular state, merely upon the ground that they are enjoyed by those citizens; much less, that in regulating the use of the common property of the citizens of such state, the legislature is bound to extend to the citizens of all the other states the same advantages as are secured to their own citizens. A several fishery, either as the right to it respects running fish, or such as are stationary, such as oysters, clams, and the like, is as much the property of the individual to whom it belongs, as dry land, or land covered by water; and is equally protected by the laws of the state against the aggressions of others, whether citizens or strangers. Where those private rights do not exist to the exclusion of the common right, that of fishing belongs to all the citizens or subjects of the state. It is the property of all; to be enjoyed by them in subordination to the laws which regulate its use. They may be considered as tenants in common of this property; and they are so exclusively entitled to the use of it, that it cannot be enjoyed by others without the tacit consent, or the express permission of the sovereign who has the power to regulate its use."

PAUL v. VIRGINIA, 75 U.S. (8 Wall.) 168, 180 (1868). The Court upheld a state law imposing special burdens on insurance companies incorporated in other states as a condition of doing business on the ground that a corporation is not a citizen protected by the privileges and immunities clause of Article IV. In construing the clause the Court said:

"It was undoubtedly the object of the clause in question to place the citizens of each State upon the same footing with citizens of other States, so far as the advantages resulting from citizenship in those States are concerned. It relieves them from the disabilities of alienage in other States; it inhibits discriminating legislation against them by other States; it gives them the right of free ingress into other States, and egress from them; it insures to them in other States the same freedom possessed by the citizens of those States in the acquisition and enjoyment of property and in the pursuit of happiness; and it secures to them in other States the equal protection of their laws. It has been justly said that no provision in the Constitution has tended so strongly to constitute the citizens of the United States one people as this. Lemmon v. People, 20 N.Y. 607.

"Indeed, without some provision of the kind removing from the citizens of each State the disabilities of alienage in the other States, and giving them equality of privilege with citizens of those States, the Republic would have constituted little more than a league of States; it would not have constituted the Union which now exists.

"But the privileges and immunities secured to citizens of each State in the several States, by the provision in question, are those privileges and immunities which are common to the citizens in the latter States under their Constitution and laws by virtue of their being citizens. Special privileges enjoyed by citizens in their own States are not secured in other States by this provision. It was not intended by the provision to give to the laws of one State any operation in other States. They can have no such operation, except by the permission, express or implied, of those States. The special privileges which they confer must, therefore, be enjoyed at home, unless the assent of other States to their enjoyment therein be given."

B. THE BILL OF RIGHTS

Barron v. Mayor and City Council of Baltimore

32 U.S. (7 Pet.) 243, 8 L.Ed. 672 (1833).

[Barron brought an action on the case against the City of Baltimore. He presented evidence that municipal street construction diverted the flow of streams so that they deposited silt in front of his wharf, making the water so shallow that vessels could no longer reach the wharf. In the County Court Barron obtained a verdict for $45,000 that was reversed on appeal by the Maryland Circuit Court. By writ of error in the United States Supreme Court Barron contended that the state court had failed to grant his property the protection guaranteed it by the Fifth Amendment to the United States Constitution.]

Marshall, Ch. J., delivered the opinion of the court.

The judgment brought up by this writ of error having been rendered by the court of a state, this tribunal can exercise no jurisdiction over it, unless it be shown to come within the provisions of the 25th section of the judicial act. The plaintiff in error contends that it comes within that clause in the fifth amendment to the constitution, which inhibits the taking of private property for public use, without just compensation. He insists that this amendment, being in favor of the liberty of the citizen, ought to be so construed as to restrain the legislative power of a state, as well as that of the United States. If this proposition be untrue, the court can take no jurisdiction of the cause.

The question thus presented is, we think, of great importance, but not of much difficulty. The constitution was ordained and established by the people of the United States for themselves, for their own government, and not for the government of the individual states. Each state established a constitution for itself, and in that constitution, provided such limitations and restrictions on the powers of its particular government, as its judgment dictated. The people of the United States framed such a government for the United States as they supposed best adapted to their situation and best calculated to promote their interests. The powers they conferred on this government were to be exercised by itself; and the limitations on power, if expressed in general terms, are naturally, and, we think, necessarily, applicable to the government created by the instrument. They are limitations of power granted in the instrument itself; not of distinct governments, framed by different persons and for different purposes.

If these propositions be correct, the fifth amendment must be understood as restraining the power of the general government, not as applicable to the states. In their several constitutions, they have imposed such restrictions on their respective governments, as their own wisdom suggested; such as they deemed most proper for themselves. It is a subject on which they judge exclusively, and with which others interfere no further than they are supposed to have a common interest.

. . .

Had the people of the several states, or any of them, required changes in their constitutions; had they required additional safe-guards to liberty from the apprehended encroachments of their particular governments; the remedy was in their own hands, and could have been applied by themselves. A convention could have been assembled by the discontented state, and the required improve-ments could have been made by itself. The unwieldy and cumbrous machinery of procuring a recommendation from two-thirds of congress, and the assent of three-fourths of their sister states, could never have occurred to any human being, as a mode of doing that which might be effected by the state itself. Had the framers of these amendments intended them to be limitations on the powers of the state governments, they would have imitated the framers of the original constitution, and have expressed that intention. Had congress engaged in the extraordinary occupation of improving the constitutions of the several states, by affording the people additional protection from the exercise of power by their own governments, in matters which concerned themselves alone, they would have declared this purpose in plain and intelligible language.

But it is universally understood, it is a part of the history of the day, that the great revolution which established the constitution of the United States, was not effected without immense opposition. Serious fears were extensively entertained, that those powers which the patriot statesmen, who then watched over the interests of our country, deemed essential to union, and to the attainment of those invaluable objects for which union was sought, might be exercised in a manner dangerous to liberty. In almost every convention by which the constitution was adopted, amendments to guard against the abuse of power were recommended. These amendments demanded security against the apprehended encroachments of the general government—not against those of the local governments. In compliance with a sentiment thus generally ex-pressed, to quiet fears thus extensively entertained, amendments were pro-posed by the required majority in congress, and adopted by the states. These amendments contain no expression indicating an intention to apply them to the state governments. This court cannot so apply them.

We are of opinion, that the provision in the fifth amendment to the constitution, declaring that private property shall not be taken for public use, without just compensation, is intended solely as a limitation on the exercise of power by the government of the United States, and is not applicable to the legislation of the states. We are, therefore, of opinion, that there is no repugnancy between the several acts of the general assembly of Maryland, given in evidence by the defendants at the trial of this cause, in the court of that state, and the constitution of the United States. This court, therefore, has no jurisdiction of the cause, and it is dismissed.

PRE–CIVIL WAR INTERPRETATIONS OF THE BILL OF RIGHTS

The decision in Barron v. Baltimore that the Bill of Rights was not designed to restrict actions of the states has been repeatedly affirmed by the Supreme Court. More striking is the fact that in the three-quarters of a century prior to the Civil War there were only a small handful of cases in which the Bill of Rights was invoked to challenge actions of the national government. See Wright, *The Growth of American Constitutional Law,* 77–78 (1942).

On two occasions, however, the Court did attempt to define the scope of the words "due process of law" in the fifth amendment. In Murray's Lessee v. Hoboken Land & Improvement Co., 59 U.S. (18 How.) 272 (1856), a fifth amendment challenge was made to a summary procedure used by the United States treasury to fix a lien on the property of a customs collector whose accounts were found to be short by over a million dollars. In upholding the procedure the Court said:

"The words, 'due process of law,' were undoubtedly intended to convey the same meaning as the words, 'by the law of the land,' in *Magna Charta.* Lord Coke, in his commentary on those words, (2 Inst. 50,) says they mean due process of law. The constitutions which had been adopted by the several States before the formation of the federal constitution, following the language of the great charter more closely, generally contained the words, 'but by the judgment of his peers, or the law of the land.' The ordinance of congress of July 13, 1787, for the government of the territory of the United States northwest of the River Ohio, used the same words.

"The constitution of the United States, as adopted, contained the provision, that 'the trial of all crimes, except in cases of impeachment, shall be by jury.' When the fifth article of amendment containing the words now in question was made, the trial by jury in criminal cases had thus already been provided for. By the sixth and seventh articles of amendment, further special provisions were separately made for that mode of trial in civil and criminal cases. To have followed, as in the state constitutions, and in the ordinance of 1787, the words of *Magna Charta,* and declared that no person shall be deprived of his life, liberty, or property but by the judgment of his peers or the law of the land, would have been in part superfluous and inappropriate. To have taken the clause, 'law of the land' without its immediate context, might possibly have given rise to doubts, which would be effectually dispelled by using those words which the great commentator on *Magna Charta* had declared to be the true meaning of the phrase, 'law of the land,' in that instrument, and which were undoubtedly then received as their true meaning.

"That the warrant now in question is legal process, is not denied. It was issued in conformity with an act of Congress. But is it 'due process of law?' The constitution contains no description of those processes which it was intended to allow or forbid. It does not even declare what principles are to be applied to ascertain whether it be due process. It is manifest that it was not left to the legislative power to enact any process which might be devised. The article is a restraint on the legislative as well as on the executive and judicial powers of the government, and cannot be so construed as to leave congress free to make any process 'due process of law,' by its mere will. To what principles, then, are we to resort to ascertain whether this process, enacted by congress, is due process? To this the answer must be twofold. We must examine the constitution itself, to see whether this process be in conflict with any of its provisions. If not found to be so, we must look to those settled usages and modes of proceeding existing in the common and statute law of England, before the emigration of our ancestors, and which are shown not to have been unsuited to their civil and political condition by having been acted on by them after the settlement of this country. . . .

"Tested by the common and statute law of England prior to the emigration of our ancestors, and by the laws of many of the States at the time of the adoption of this amendment, the proceedings authorized by the act of 1820 cannot be denied to be due process of law, when applied to the ascertainment and recovery of balances due to the government from a collector of customs, unless there exists in the constitution some other provision which restrains congress from authorizing such proceedings. For, though 'due process of law' generally implies and includes *actor, reus, judex,* regular allegations, opportunity to answer, and a trial according to some settled course of judicial proceedings, . . . yet, this is not universally true. There may be, and we have seen that there are cases, under the law of England after *Magna Charta,* and as it was brought to this country and acted on here, in which process, in its nature final, issues against the body, lands, and goods of certain public debtors without any such trial; and this brings us to the question, whether those provisions of the constitution which relate to the judicial power are incompatible with these proceedings?"[a]

In Dred Scott v. Sandford, 60 U.S. (19 How.) 393 (1857), the Court had before it a challenge to the validity of the Act of Congress known as the Missouri Compromise which excluded slavery from specified northern portions of the United States territory. The opinion of the Court, by Chief Justice Taney, after referring to the free speech and other guaranties of the Bill of Rights, continued:

"These powers, and others in relation to rights of person, which it is not necessary here to enumerate, are, in express and positive terms, denied to the general government; and the rights of private property have been guarded with equal care. Thus the rights of property are united with the rights of person, and placed on the same ground by the fifth amendment to the Constitution, which provides that no person shall be deprived of life, liberty and property, without due process of law. And an Act of Congress which deprives a citizen of the United States of his liberty or property, merely because he came himself or brought his property into a particular Territory of the United States, and who had committed no offense against the laws, could hardly be dignified with the name of due process of law."

SECTION 2. THE INITIAL INTERPRETATION OF THE CIVIL WAR AMENDMENTS

Slaughter–House Cases

83 U.S. (16 Wall.) 36, 21 L.Ed. 394 (1872).

[The Louisiana legislature chartered a corporation and granted to it, for twenty-five years, an exclusive right to operate facilities in New Orleans for the

---

a. During this period there were a few state court opinions applying state constitutional phrases such as "due process of law" and "the law of the land" not only to require fair procedure but also to invalidate special or "class" legislation and retroactive impairment of "vested rights". See, e.g., Wynehamer v. The People, 13 N.Y. 378, 393–395 (1856), quoting comparable approaches by the courts of Pennsylvania and North Carolina. For general discussion see: Corwin, Liberty against Government 75–82, 91–110 (1948); Mott, Due Process of Law 241–274 (1926); Howe, The Meaning of "Due Process of Law" Prior to the Adoption of the Fourteenth Amendment, 18 Calif.L.Rev. 583, 596–610 (1930).

landing, keeping, and slaughter of livestock. All competing plants were required to cease operation, and independent butchers were given a right to slaughter at the corporation's plant on paying maximum charges that were fixed by statute.

New Orleans butchers sued in the state courts to have the act declared invalid as a violation of both the Thirteenth and Fourteenth Amendments. The statute was upheld by the Louisiana Supreme Court.]

Mr. Justice Miller delivered the opinion of the court....

This statute is denounced not only as creating a monopoly and conferring odious and exclusive privileges upon a small number of persons at the expense of the great body of the community of New Orleans, but it is asserted that it deprives a large and meritorious class of citizens—the whole of the butchers of the city—of the right to exercise their trade, the business to which they have been trained and on which they depend for the support of themselves and their families; and that the unrestricted exercise of the business of butchering is necessary to the daily subsistence of the population of the city.

But a critical examination of the act hardly justifies these assertions....

The power here exercised by the legislature of Louisiana is, in its essential nature, one which has been, up to the present period in the constitutional history of this country, always conceded to belong to the States, however it may *now* be questioned in some of its details.... This is called the police power; and it is declared by Chief Justice Shaw that it is much easier to perceive and realize the existence and sources of it than to mark its boundaries, or prescribe limits to its exercise.

This power is, and must be from its very nature, incapable of any very exact definition or limitation. Upon it depends the security of social order, the life and health of the citizen, the comfort of an existence in a thickly populated community, the enjoyment of private and social life, and the beneficial use of property....

It may, therefore, be considered as established, that the authority of the legislature of Louisiana to pass the present statute is ample, unless some restraint in the exercise of that power be found in the constitution of that State or in the amendments to the Constitution of the United States, adopted since the date of the decisions we have already cited....

The plaintiffs in error accepting this issue, allege that the statute is a violation of the Constitution of the United States in these several particulars:

That it creates an involuntary servitude forbidden by the thirteenth article of amendment;

That it abridges the privileges and immunities of citizens of the United States;

That it denies to the plaintiffs the equal protection of the laws; and,

That it deprives them of their property without due process of law; contrary to the provisions of the first section of the fourteenth article of amendment.

This court is thus called upon for the first time to give construction to these articles.

We do not conceal from ourselves the great responsibility which this duty devolves upon us. No questions so far-reaching and pervading in their consequences, so profoundly interesting to the people of this country, and so important in their bearing upon the relations of the United States, and of the several States to each other and to the citizens of the States and of the United

States, have been before this court during the official life of any of its present members. . . .

Twelve articles of amendment were added to the Federal Constitution soon after the original organization of the government under it in 1789. Of these all but the last were adopted so soon afterwards as to justify the statement that they were practically contemporaneous with the adoption of the original; and the twelfth, adopted in eighteen hundred and three, was so nearly so as to have become, like all the others, historical and of another age. But within the last eight years three other articles of amendment of vast importance have been added by the voice of the people to that now venerable instrument.

The most cursory glance at these articles discloses a unity of purpose, when taken in connection with the history of the times, which cannot fail to have an important bearing on any question of doubt concerning their true meaning. Nor can such doubts, when any reasonably exist, be safely and rationally solved without a reference to that history; for in it is found the occasion and the necessity for recurring again to the great source of power in this country, the people of the States, for additional guarantees of human rights; additional powers to the Federal government; additional restraints upon those of the States. Fortunately that history is fresh within the memory of us all, and its leading features, as they bear upon the matter before us, free from doubt.

The institution of African slavery, as it existed in about half the States of the Union, and the contests pervading the public mind for many years, between those who desired its curtailment and ultimate extinction and those who desired additional safeguards for its security and perpetuation, culminated in the effort, on the part of most of the States in which slavery existed, to separate from the Federal government, and to resist its authority. This constituted the war of the rebellion, and whatever auxiliary causes may have contributed to bring about this war, undoubtedly the overshadowing and efficient cause was African slavery.

In that struggle slavery, as a legalized social relation, perished. It perished as a necessity of the bitterness and force of the conflict. When the armies of freedom found themselves upon the soil of slavery they could do nothing less than free the poor victims whose enforced servitude was the foundation of the quarrel. And when hard pressed in the contest these men (for they proved themselves men in that terrible crisis) offered their services and were accepted by thousands to aid in suppressing the unlawful rebellion, slavery was at an end wherever the Federal government succeeded in that purpose. The proclamation of President Lincoln expressed an accomplished fact as to a large portion of the insurrectionary districts, when he declared slavery abolished in them all. But the war being over, those who had succeeded in re-establishing the authority of the Federal government were not content to permit this great act of emancipation to rest on the actual results of the contest or the proclamation of the Executive, both of which might have been questioned in after times, and they determined to place this main and most valuable result in the Constitution of the restored Union as one of its fundamental articles. Hence the thirteenth article of amendment of that instrument. Its two short sections seem hardly to admit of construction, so vigorous is their expression and so appropriate to the purpose we have indicated.

. . .

To withdraw the mind from the contemplation of this grand yet simple declaration of the personal freedom of all the human race within the jurisdiction of this government—a declaration designed to establish the freedom of four millions of slaves—and with a microscopic search endeavor to find in it a reference to servitudes, which may have been attached to property in certain localities, requires an effort, to say the least of it.

That a personal servitude was meant is proved by the use of the word "involuntary," which can only apply to human beings. The exception of servitude as a punishment for crime gives an idea of the class of servitude that is meant. The word servitude is of larger meaning than slavery, as the latter is popularly understood in this country, and the obvious purpose was to forbid all shades and conditions of African slavery. It was very well understood that in the form of apprenticeship for long terms, as it had been practiced in the West India Islands, on the abolition of slavery by the English government, or by reducing the slaves to the condition of serfs attached to the plantation, the purpose of the article might have been evaded, if only the word slavery had been used. The case of the apprentice slave, held under a law of Maryland, liberated by Chief Justice Chase, on a writ of habeas corpus under this article, illustrates this course of observation. And it is all that we deem necessary to say on the application of that article to the statute of Louisiana, now under consideration.

The process of restoring to their proper relations with the Federal government and with the other States those which had sided with the rebellion, undertaken under the proclamation of President Johnson in 1865, and before the assembling of Congress, developed the fact that, notwithstanding the formal recognition by those States of the abolition of slavery, the condition of the slave race would, without further protection of the Federal government, be almost as bad as it was before. Among the first acts of legislation adopted by several of the States in the legislative bodies which claimed to be in their normal relations with the Federal government, were laws which imposed upon the colored race onerous disabilities and burdens, and curtailed their rights in the pursuit of life, liberty, and property to such an extent that their freedom was of little value, while they had lost the protection which they had received from their former owners from motives both of interest and humanity.

They were in some States forbidden to appear in the towns in any other character than menial servants. They were required to reside on and cultivate the soil without the right to purchase or own it. They were excluded from many occupations of gain, and were not permitted to give testimony in the courts in any case where a white man was a party. It was said that their lives were at the mercy of bad men, either because the laws for their protection were insufficient or were not enforced.

These circumstances, whatever of falsehood or misconception may have been mingled with their presentation, forced upon the statesmen who had conducted the Federal government in safety through the crisis of the rebellion, and who supposed that by the thirteenth article of amendment they had secured the result of their labors, the conviction that something more was necessary in the way of constitutional protection to the unfortunate race who had suffered so much. They accordingly passed through Congress the proposition for the fourteenth amendment, and they declined to treat as restored to their full participation in the government of the Union the States which had been in insurrection, until they ratified that article by a formal vote of their legislative bodies.

Before we proceed to examine more critically the provisions of this amendment, on which the plaintiffs in error rely, let us complete and dismiss the history of the recent amendments, as that history relates to the general purpose which pervades them all. A few years' experience satisfied the thoughtful men who had been the authors of the other two amendments that, notwithstanding the restraints of those articles on the States, and the laws passed under the additional powers granted to Congress, these were inadequate for the protection of life, liberty, and property, without which freedom to the slave was no boon. They were in all those States denied the right of suffrage. The laws were administered by the white man alone. It was urged that a race of men distinctively marked as was the negro, living in the midst of another and dominant race, could never be fully secured in their person and their property without the right of suffrage.

15th amd.

Hence the fifteenth amendment, which declares that "the right of a citizen of the United States to vote shall not be denied or abridged by any State on account of race, color, or previous condition of servitude." The negro having, by the fourteenth amendment, been declared to be a citizen of the United States, is thus made a voter in every State of the Union.

We repeat, then, in the light of this recapitulation of events, almost too recent to be called history, but which are familiar to us all; and on the most casual examination of the language of these amendments, no one can fail to be impressed with the one pervading purpose found in them all, lying at the foundation of each, and without which none of them would have been even suggested; we mean the freedom of the slave race, the security and firm establishment of that freedom, and the protection of the newly-made freeman and citizen from the oppressions of those who had formerly exercised unlimited dominion over him. It is true that only the fifteenth amendment, in terms, mentions the negro by speaking of his color and his slavery. But it is just as true that each of the other articles was addressed to the grievances of that race, and designed to remedy them as the fifteenth.

We do not say that no one else but the negro can share in this protection. Both the language and spirit of these articles are to have their fair and just weight in any question of construction. Undoubtedly while negro slavery alone was in the mind of the Congress which proposed the thirteenth article, it forbids any other kind of slavery, now or hereafter. If Mexican peonage or the Chinese coolie labor system shall develop slavery of the Mexican or Chinese race within our territory, this amendment may safely be trusted to make it void. And so if other rights are assailed by the States which properly and necessarily fall within the protection of these articles, that protection will apply, though the party interested may not be of African descent. But what we do say, and what we wish to be understood is, that in any fair and just construction of any section or phrase of these amendments, it is necessary to look to the purpose which we have said was the pervading spirit of them all, the evil which they were designed to remedy, and the process of continued addition to the Constitution, until that purpose was supposed to be accomplished, as far as constitutional law can accomplish it.

First section of the 14th article

The first section of the fourteenth article, to which our attention is more specially invited, opens with a definition of citizenship—not only citizenship of the United States, but citizenship of the States. No such definition was previously found in the Constitution, nor had any attempt been made to define it by act of Congress. It had been the occasion of much discussion in the courts, by the executive departments, and in the public journals. It had been said by eminent judges that no man was a citizen of the United States, except as he was a citizen of one of the States composing the Union. Those, therefore, who had been born and resided always in the District of Columbia or in the Territories, though within the United States, were not citizens. Whether this proposition was sound or not had never been judicially decided. But it had been held by this court, in the celebrated Dred Scott case, only a few years before the outbreak of the civil war, that a man of African descent, whether a slave or not, was not and could not be a citizen of a State or of the United States. This decision, while it met the condemnation of some of the ablest statesmen and constitutional lawyers of the country, had never been overruled; and if it was to be accepted as a constitutional limitation of the right of citizenship, then all the negro race who had recently been made freemen, were still, not only not citizens, but were incapable of becoming so by anything short of an amendment to the Constitution.

To remove this difficulty primarily, and to establish a clear and comprehensive definition of citizenship which should declare what should constitute citizenship of the United States, and also citizenship of a State, the first clause of the first section was framed.

[margin note: 1st clause of the 1st section]

"All persons born or naturalized in the United States, and subject to the jurisdiction thereof, are citizens of the United States and of the State wherein they reside."

The first observation we have to make on this clause is, that it puts at rest both the questions which we stated to have been the subject of differences of opinion. It declares that persons may be citizens of the United States without regard to their citizenship, of a particular State, and it overturns the Dred Scott decision by making *all persons* born within the United States and subject to its jurisdiction citizens of the United States. That its main purpose was to establish the citizenship of the negro can admit of no doubt. The phrase, "subject to its jurisdiction" was intended to exclude from its operation children of ministers, consuls, and citizens or subjects of foreign States born within the United States.

The next observation is more important in view of the arguments of counsel in the present case. It is, that the distinction between citizenship of the United States and citizenship of a State is clearly recognized and established. Not only may a man be a citizen of the United States without being a citizen of a State, but an important element is necessary to convert the former into the latter. He must reside within the State to make him a citizen of it, but it is only necessary that he should be born or naturalized in the United States to be a citizen of the Union.

It is quite clear, then, that there is a citizenship of the United States, and a citizenship of a State, which are distinct from each other, and which depend upon different characteristics or circumstances in the individual.

We think this distinction and its explicit recognition in this amendment of great weight in this argument, because the next paragraph of this same section, which is the one mainly relied on by the plaintiffs in error, speaks only of privileges and immunities of citizens of the United States, and does not speak of those of citizens of the several States. The argument, however, in favor of the plaintiffs rests wholly on the assumption that the citizenship is the same, and the privileges and immunities guaranteed by the clause are the same.

[margin note: says no state shall enforce against p & i of citizens of U.S. Not against citizens of a state from legislation of that state]

The language is, "No State shall make or enforce any law which shall abridge the privileges or immunities of citizens of *the United States.*" It is a little remarkable, if this clause was intended as a protection to the citizen of a State against the legislative power of his own State, that the word citizen of the State should be left out when it is so carefully used, and used in contradistinction to citizens of the United States, in the very sentence which precedes it. It is too clear for argument that the change in phraseology was adopted understandingly and with a purpose.

Of the privileges and immunities of the citizen of the United States, and of the privileges and immunities of the citizen of the State, and what they respectively are, we will presently consider; but we wish to state here that it is only the former which are placed by this clause under the protection of the Federal Constitution, and that the latter, whatever they may be, are not intended to have any additional protection by this paragraph of the amendment.

If, then, there is a difference between the privileges and immunities belonging to a citizen of the United States as such, and those belonging to the citizen of the State as such, the latter must rest for their security and protection where they have heretofore rested; for they are not embraced by this paragraph of the amendment.

The first occurrence of the words "privileges and immunities" in our constitutional history, is to be found in the fourth of the articles of the old Confederation.

It declares "that the better to secure and perpetuate mutual friendship and intercourse among the people of the different States in this Union, the free inhabitants of each of these States, paupers, vagabonds, and fugitives from justice excepted, shall be entitled to all the privileges and immunities of free citizens in the several States; and the people of each State shall have free ingress and regress to and from any other State, and shall enjoy therein all the privileges of trade and commerce, subject to the same duties, impositions, and restrictions as the inhabitants thereof respectively."

In the Constitution of the United States, which superseded the Articles of Confederation, the corresponding provision is found in section two of the fourth article, in the following words: "The citizens of each State shall be entitled to all the privileges and immunities of citizens of the several States."

There can be but little question that the purpose of both these provisions is the same, and that the privileges and immunities intended are the same in each. In the article of the Confederation we have some of these specifically mentioned, and enough perhaps to give some general idea of the class of civil rights meant by the phrase.

Fortunately we are not without judicial construction of this clause of the Constitution. The first and the leading case on the subject is that of *Corfield v. Coryell*, decided by Mr. Justice Washington in the Circuit Court for the District of Pennsylvania in 1823.

"The inquiry," he says, "is, what are the privileges and immunities of citizens of the several States? We feel no hesitation in confining these expressions to those privileges and immunities which are *fundamental;* which belong of right to the citizens of all free governments, and which have at all times been enjoyed by citizens of the several States which compose this Union, from the time of their becoming free, independent, and sovereign. What these fundamental principles are, it would be more tedious than difficult to enumerate. They may all, however, be comprehended under the following general heads: protection by the government, with the right to acquire and possess property of every kind, and to pursue and obtain happiness and safety, subject, nevertheless, to such restraints as the government may prescribe for the general good of the whole."

... The description, when taken to include others not named, but which are of the same general character, embraces nearly every civil right for the establishment and protection of which organized government is instituted. They are, in the language of Judge Washington, those rights which are fundamental. Throughout his opinion, they are spoken of as rights belonging to the individual as a citizen of a State. They are so spoken of in the constitutional provision which he was construing. And they have always been held to be the class of rights which the State governments were created to establish and secure.

. . . [Article IV] did not create those rights, which it called privileges and immunities of citizens of the States. It threw around them in that clause no security for the citizen of the State in which they were claimed or exercised. Nor did it profess to control the power of the State governments over the rights of its own citizens.

Its sole purpose was to declare to the several States, that whatever those rights, as you grant or establish them to your own citizens, or as you limit or qualify, or impose restrictions on their exercise, the same, neither more nor less, shall be the measure of the rights of citizens of other States within your jurisdiction.

It would be the vainest show of learning to attempt to prove by citations of authority, that up to the adoption of the recent amendments, no claim or pretence was set up that those rights depended on the Federal government for their existence or protection, beyond the very few express limitations which the Federal Constitution imposed upon the States—such, for instance, as the prohibition against ex post facto laws, bills of attainder, and laws impairing the obligation of contracts. But with the exception of these and a few other restrictions, the entire domain of the privileges and immunities of citizens of the States, as above defined, lay within the constitutional and legislative power of the States, and without that of the Federal government. Was it the purpose of the fourteenth amendment, by the simple declaration that no State should make or enforce any law which shall abridge the privileges and immunities of *citizens of the United States,* to transfer the security and protection of all the civil rights which we have mentioned, from the States to the Federal government? And where it is declared that Congress shall have the power to enforce that article, was it intended to bring within the power of Congress the entire domain of civil rights heretofore belonging exclusively to the States?

All this and more must follow, if the proposition of the plaintiffs in error be sound. For not only are these rights subject to the control of Congress whenever in its discretion any of them are supposed to be abridged by State legislation, but that body may also pass laws in advance, limiting and restricting the exercise of legislative power by the States, in their most ordinary and usual functions, as in its judgment it may think proper on all such subjects. And still further, such a construction followed by the reversal of the judgments of the Supreme Court of Louisiana in these cases, would constitute this court a perpetual censor upon all legislation of the States, on the civil rights of their own citizens, with authority to nullify such as it did not approve as consistent with those rights, as they existed at the time of the adoption of this amendment. The argument we admit is not always the most conclusive which is drawn from the consequences urged against the adoption of a particular construction of an instrument. But when, as in the case before us, these consequences are so serious, so far-reaching and pervading, so great a departure from the structure and spirit of our institutions; when the effect is to fetter and degrade the State governments by subjecting them to the control of Congress, in the exercise of powers heretofore universally conceded to them of the most ordinary and fundamental character; when in fact it radically changes the whole theory of the relations of the State and Federal governments to each other and of both these governments to the people; the argument has a force that is irresistible, in the absence of language which expresses such a purpose too clearly to admit of doubt.

We are convinced that no such results were intended by the Congress which proposed these amendments, nor by the legislatures of the States which ratified them.

Having shown that the privileges and immunities relied on in the argument are those which belong to citizens of the States as such, and that they are left to the State governments for security and protection, and not by this article placed under the special care of the Federal government, we may hold ourselves excused from defining the privileges and immunities of citizens of the United States which no State can abridge, until some case involving those privileges may make it necessary to do so.

But lest it should be said that no such privileges and immunities are to be found if those we have been considering are excluded, we venture to suggest some which owe their existence to the Federal government, its National character, its Constitution, or its laws.

One of these is well described in the case of *Crandall v. Nevada.* It is said to be the right of the citizen of this great country, protected by implied guarantees of its Constitution, "to come to the seat of government to assert any claim he may have upon that government, to transact any business he may have with it, to seek its protection, to share its offices, to engage in administering its functions. He has the right of free access to its seaports, through which all operations of foreign commerce are conducted, to the sub-treasuries, land offices, and courts of justice in the several States." And quoting from the language of Chief Justice Taney in another case, it is said "that *for all the great purposes for which the Federal government* was established, we are one people, with one common country, *we are all citizens of the United States;*" and it is, as such citizens, that their rights are supported in this court in Crandall v. Nevada.

Another privilege of a citizen of the United States, is to demand the care and protection of the Federal government over his life, liberty, and property when on the high seas or within the jurisdiction of a foreign government. Of this there can be no doubt, nor that the right depends upon his character as a citizen of the United States. The right to peaceably assemble and petition for redress of grievances, the privilege of the writ of *habeas corpus,* are rights of the citizen guaranteed by the Federal Constitution. The right to use the navigable waters of the United States, however they may penetrate the territory of the several States, all rights secured to our citizens by treaties with foreign nations, are dependent upon citizenship of the United States, and not citizenship of a State. One of these privileges is conferred by the very article under consideration. It is that a citizen of the United States can, of his own volition, become a citizen of any State of the Union by a *bona fide* residence therein, with the same rights as other citizens of that State. To these may be added the rights secured by the thirteenth and fifteenth articles of amendment, and by the other clause of the fourteenth, next to be considered.

But it is useless to pursue this branch of the inquiry, since we are of opinion that the rights claimed by these plaintiffs in error, if they have any existence, are not privileges and immunities of citizens of the United States within the meaning of the clause of the fourteenth amendment under consideration. . . .

The argument has not been much pressed in these cases that the defendant's charter deprives the plaintiffs of their property without due process of law, or that it denies to them the equal protection of the law. The first of these paragraphs has been in the Constitution since the adoption of the fifth amendment, as a restraint upon the Federal power. It is also to be found in some form of expression in the constitutions of nearly all the States, as a restraint upon the power of the States. This law then, has practically been the same as it now is during the existence of the government, except so far as the present amendment may place the restraining power over the States in this matter in the hands of the Federal government.

We are not without judicial interpretation, therefore, both State and National, of the meaning of this clause. And it is sufficient to say that under no construction of that provision that we have ever seen, or any that we deem admissible, can the restraint imposed by the State of Louisiana upon the exercise of their trade by the butchers of New Orleans be held to be a deprivation of property within the meaning of that provision.

"Nor shall any State deny to any person within its jurisdiction the equal protection of the laws."

In the light of the history of these amendments, and the pervading purpose of them, which we have already discussed, it is not difficult to give a meaning to this clause. The existence of laws in the States where the newly emancipated negroes resided, which discriminated with gross injustice and hardship against them as a class, was the evil to be remedied by this clause, and by it such laws are forbidden.

If, however, the States did not conform their laws to its requirements, then by the fifth section of the article of amendment Congress was authorized to enforce it by suitable legislation. We doubt very much whether any action of a State not directed by way of discrimination against the negroes as a class, or on account of their race, will ever be held to come within the purview of this provision. It is so clearly a provision for that race and that emergency, that a strong case would be necessary for its application to any other. But as it is a State that is to be dealt with, and not alone the validity of its laws, we may safely leave that matter until Congress shall have exercised its power, or some case of State oppression, by denial of equal justice in its courts, shall have claimed a decision at our hands. We find no such case in the one before us, and do not deem it necessary to go over the argument again, as it may have relation to this particular clause of the amendment.

In the early history of the organization of the government, its statesmen seem to have divided on the line which should separate the powers of the National government from those of the State governments, and though this line has never been very well defined in public opinion, such a division has continued from that day to this.

The adoption of the first eleven amendments to the Constitution so soon after the original instrument was accepted, shows a prevailing sense of danger at that time from the Federal power. And it cannot be denied that such a jealousy continued to exist with many patriotic men until the breaking out of the late civil war. It was then discovered that the true danger to the perpetuity of the Union was in the capacity of the State organizations to combine and concentrate all the powers of the State, and of contiguous States, for a determined resistance to the General Government.

Unquestionably this has given great force to the argument, and added largely to the number of those who believe in the necessity of a strong National government.

But, however pervading this sentiment, and however it may have contributed to the adoption of the amendments we have been considering, we do not see in those amendments any purpose to destroy the main features of the general system. Under the pressure of all the excited feeling growing out of the war, our statesmen have still believed that the existence of the States with powers for domestic and local government, including the regulation of civil rights—the rights of person and of property—was essential to the perfect working of our complex form of government, though they have thought proper to impose additional limitations on the States, and to confer additional power on that of the Nation.

But whatever fluctuations may be seen in the history of public opinion on this subject during the period of our national existence, we think it will be found that this court, so far as its functions required, has always held with a steady and an even hand the balance between State and Federal power, and we trust that such may continue to be the history of its relation to that subject so long as it shall have duties to perform which demand of it a construction of the Constitution, or of any of its parts.

The judgments of the Supreme Court of Louisiana in these cases are

uphold statute

Affirmed.

Mr. Justice Field, dissenting:

. . .

The act of Louisiana presents the naked case, unaccompanied by any public considerations, where a right to pursue a lawful and necessary calling, previously enjoyed by every citizen, and in connection with which a thousand persons were daily employed, is taken away and vested exclusively for twenty-five years, for an extensive district and a large population, in a single corporation, or its exercise is for that period restricted to the establishments of the corporation, and there allowed only upon onerous conditions. . . .

Issue:

The question presented is, therefore, one of the gravest importance, not merely to the parties here, but to the whole country. It is nothing less than the question whether the recent amendments to the Federal Constitution protect the citizens of the United States against the deprivation of their common rights by State legislation. In my judgment the fourteenth amendment does afford such protection, and was so intended by the Congress which framed and the States which adopted it. . . .

The amendment does not attempt to confer any new privileges or immunities upon citizens, or to enumerate or define those already existing. It assumes that there are such privileges and immunities which belong of right to citizens as such, and ordains that they shall not be abridged by State legislation. If this inhibition has no reference to privileges and immunities of this character, but only refers, as held by the majority of the court in their opinion, to such privileges and immunities as were before its adoption specially designated in the Constitution or necessarily implied as belonging to citizens of the United States, it was a vain and idle enactment, which accomplished nothing, and most unnecessarily excited Congress and the people on its passage. With privileges and immunities thus designated or implied no State could ever have interfered by its laws, and no new constitutional provision was required to inhibit such interference. The supremacy of the Constitution and the laws of the United States always controlled any State legislation of that character. But if the amendment refers to the natural and inalienable rights which belong to all citizens, the inhibition has a profound significance and consequence.

What, then, are the privileges and immunities which are secured against abridgment by State legislation?

In the first section of the Civil Rights Act Congress has given its interpretation to these terms, or at least has stated some of the rights which, in its judgment, these terms include; it has there declared that they include the right "to make and enforce contracts, to sue, be parties and give evidence, to inherit, purchase, lease, sell, hold, and convey real and personal property, and to full and equal benefit of all laws and proceedings for the security of person and property." . . .

The common law of England . . . condemned all monopolies in any known trade or manufacture, and declared void all grants of special privileges whereby others could be deprived of any liberty which they previously had, or be hindered in their lawful trade. The statute of James I, to which I have referred, only embodied the law as it had been previously declared by the courts of England, although frequently disregarded by the sovereigns of that country.

The common law of England is the basis of the jurisprudence of the United States. . . . And when the Colonies separated from the mother country no privilege was more fully recognized or more completely incorporated into the fundamental law of the country than that every free subject in the British empire was entitled to pursue his happiness by following any of the known established trades and occupations of the country, subject only to such restraints as equally affected all others. . . .

[The dissenting opinion discussed state court decisions in Illinois, Connecticut and New York striking down monopolies and exclusive privileges.]

. . .

This equality of right, with exemption from all disparaging and partial enactments, in the lawful pursuits of life, throughout the whole country, is the distinguishing privilege of citizens of the United States. To them, everywhere, all pursuits, all professions, all avocations are open without other restrictions than such as are imposed equally upon all others of the same age, sex, and condition. The State may prescribe such regulations for every pursuit and calling of life as will promote the public health, secure the good order and advance the general prosperity of society, but when once prescribed the pursuit or calling must be free to be followed by every citizen who is within the conditions designated, and will conform to the regulations. This is the fundamental idea upon which our institutions rest, and unless adhered to in the legislation of the country our government will be a republic only in name. The fourteenth amendment, in my judgment, makes it essential to the validity of the legislation of every State that this equality of right should be respected. How widely this equality has been departed from, how entirely rejected and trampled upon by the act of Louisiana, I have already shown. And it is to me a matter of profound regret that its validity is recognized by a majority of this court, for by it the right of free labor, one of the most sacred and imprescriptible rights of man, is violated. As stated by the Supreme Court of Connecticut, in the case cited, grants of exclusive privileges, such as is made by the act in question, are opposed to the whole theory of free government, and it requires no aid from any bill of rights to render them void. That only is a free government, in the American sense of the term, under which the inalienable right of every citizen to pursue his happiness is unrestrained, except by just, equal, and impartial laws.

I am authorized by the Chief Justice [Chase], Mr. Justice Swayne, and Mr. Justice Bradley, to state that they concur with me in this dissenting opinion.

[Justices Bradley and Swayne also filed dissenting opinions.]

THE PRIVILEGES AND IMMUNITIES CLAUSE OF THE FOURTEENTH AMENDMENT

Does the 14th amendment privileges and immunities clause have any independent significance as interpreted by the Court in the Slaughterhouse Cases? Would any case be decided differently because of the presence of that clause? How does it differ from the privileges and immunities clause in Art. IV?

The conventional interpretations of the Art. IV clause would render unconstitutional an attempt by a state to impose higher taxes on nonresidents doing business in the state than upon residents. See, e.g., Austin v. New Hampshire, 420 U.S. 656 (1975). In Madden v. Kentucky, 309 U.S. 83 (1940), overruling Colgate v. Harvey, 296 U.S. 404 (1935), the Court had before it a challenge to a state tax which required residents of that state to pay a higher tax on deposits in banks outside the state than in local banks. The argument was made that the privileges and immunities clause of the 14th amendment protected a resident of a state against this discrimination against property and activities outside the state. The Court rejected this argument: "[T]he privileges and immunities clause protects all citizens against abridgment by states of rights of national citizenship as distinct from the fundamental or natural rights inherent in state citizenship.... We think it quite clear that the right to carry out an incident to a trade, business or calling such as the deposit of money in banks is not a privilege of national citizenship."

The Court's opinion in Saenz v. Roe, 526 U.S. 489 (1999), reported fully *infra* at page 1035, again highlighted the question whether, after the Slaughterhouse Cases, the Fourteenth Amendment Privileges and Immunities Clause does any independent constitutional work. Justice Stevens' majority opinion, holding unconstitutional a California law limiting welfare benefits for families residing in the State less than a year to the amounts they would have received in their States of previous residence, found "the right of the newly arrived citizen to the same privileges and immunities enjoyed by other citizens of the same State ... protected not only by the new arrival's status as a state citizen, but also by her status as a citizen of the United States.... Despite fundamentally differing views concerning the coverage of the Privileges or Immunities Clause of the Fourteenth Amendment, most notably expressed in the majority and dissenting opinions in the Slaughter–House Cases, 16 Wall. 36 (1872), it has always been common ground that this Clause protects [that right]." Later in the opinion, Justice Stevens wrote that "the protection afforded to the citizen by the Citizenship Clause of that Amendment is a limitation on the powers of the National Government as well as the States[,]" and at the end of the opinion he wrote: "Citizens of the United States, whether rich or poor, have the right to choose to be citizens 'of the State wherein they reside.' U.S. Const., Amdt. 14, § 1. The States, however, do not have any right to select their citizens." Does Justice Stevens' reasoning and conclusion depend on the Privileges and Immunities Clause itself?

In dissent, Chief Justice Rehnquist, joined by Justice Thomas, objected to the Court's "breath[ing] new life into the previously dormant Privileges or Immunities Clause of the Fourteenth Amendment...." In another dissent, Justice Thomas, joined by the Chief Justice, expressed the view that "the majority attributes a meaning to the Privileges or Immunities Clause that likely was unintended when the Fourteenth Amendment was enacted and ratified." Is Justice Stevens' opinion really a departure from the Court's interpretation of the Fourteenth Amendment Privileges and Immunities Clause in the Slaughterhouse Cases?

DUE PROCESS AND JURISDICTION

Even before the adoption of the fourteenth amendment the Court restricted the jurisdiction of state legislatures and state courts without any clear constitutional basis for the restrictions. The Court held, e.g., in Baldwin v. Hale, 68 U.S. (1 Wall.) 223, 234 (1864), that "[i]nsolvent laws of one State cannot discharge the contracts of citizens of other States, because they have no extraterritorial operation, and consequently the tribunal sitting under them, unless in cases where a citizen of such other State voluntarily becomes a party to the proceedings, has no jurisdiction in the case. Legal notice cannot be given and, consequently, there can be no obligation to appear, and of course, there can be no legal default." The requirement of personal service of process within the jurisdiction or voluntary appearance as a basis for securing a valid judgment in personam was early brought under the due process rubric in Pennoyer v. Neff, 95 U.S. 714, 732 (1877).

Not until the turn of the century, however, did the Court apply the due process clause to limit the jurisdiction of the states to tax tangible property located outside the state. As an example, in Louisville & Jeffersonville Ferry Co. v. Kentucky, 188 U.S. 385, 396, 397 (1903), the Court, in holding that Kentucky could not tax a franchise granted a ferry by Indiana to convey passengers from Indiana to Kentucky, said that the taxing power of the states "is limited by a principle inhering in the very nature of constitutional government, namely, that the taxation imposed must have relation to a subject within the jurisdiction of the taxing government."

DUE PROCESS AND FAIR PROCEDURE

In 1856 in *Murray's Lessee,* supra p. 473, the Court started to mark out the limits imposed by the due process clause of the fifth amendment on procedures devised by Congress. But in 1864 the Court was still finding limits on state power to establish procedures for civil cases without any definite constitutional basis. Thus in Baldwin v. Hale, 68 U.S. (1 Wall.) 223, 233 (1864), the Court said: "Parties whose rights are to be affected are entitled to be heard; and in order that they may enjoy that right they must first be notified. Common justice requires that no man shall be condemned in his person or property without notice and an opportunity to make his defense."

After the fourteenth amendment was adopted, however, the Court quickly placed the guarantee of fair procedures in the states firmly on the due process clause of that amendment. In Hagar v. Reclamation District, 111 U.S. 701, 708 (1884), the Court said: "Undoubtedly, where life and liberty are involved, due process requires that there be a regular course of judicial proceedings, which imply that the party to be affected shall have notice and an opportunity to be heard; so, also, where title or possession of property is involved." And in Hurtado v. California, 110 U.S. 516, 534 (1884), the Court, in holding that a state could substitute a preliminary hearing for indictment by grand jury in criminal cases, said that the due process clause in the fourteenth amendment meant the same as it did in the fifth amendment and that any state proceeding constituted due process of law if it was "exerted within the limits of those fundamental principles of liberty and justice which lie at the base of all our civil and political institutions. . . ."

THE FOURTEENTH AMENDMENT AND CITIZENSHIP

The distinction between alienage and citizenship is fundamental, and vitally important issues turn on it. A citizen may not be deported nor excluded from the United States. United States v. Wong Kim Ark, 169 U.S. 649 (1898), held, for example, that a person born in the United States and therefore a citizen could not be excluded from the country when he attempted to enter even though his foreign-born parents were not eligible for naturalization. An alien, on the other hand, may be deported for any of a substantial list of reasons. 8 U.S.C. § 1251. In Harisiades v. Shaughnessy, 342 U.S. 580 (1952), it was held that an alien (resident of the United States for thirty years) could be deported because of Communist Party membership even though this membership had terminated before enactment of the deportation statute. Aliens may also be excluded from the United States for an even longer list of reasons. 8 U.S.C. § 1182. An alien seeking entry into the United States has no constitutional right to a hearing, and the exercise of power by the Attorney General to deny admission without a hearing has been upheld. United States ex rel. Knauff v. Shaughnessy, 338 U.S. 537 (1950). However, an administrative hearing is provided by statute for most exclusion cases. 8 U.S.C. § 1226.

In Landon v. Plasencia, 459 U.S. 21 (1982), the Court held that a permanent resident alien returning from a brief trip abroad was not entitled to a deportation hearing but did have a due process right to a fair exclusion hearing. The Court said:

"This Court has long held that an alien seeking initial admission to the United States requests a privilege and has no constitutional rights regarding his application, for the power to admit or exclude aliens is a sovereign prerogative.... As we explained in Johnson v. Eisentrager, 339 U.S. 763, 770 (1950), however, once an alien gains admission to our country and begins to develop the ties that go with permanent residence his constitutional status changes accordingly. Our cases have frequently suggested that a continuously present resident alien is entitled to a fair hearing when threatened with deportation...."

The Court then cited cases which it described as holding that a permanent resident alien returning from a temporary trip abroad would be treated like an alien continuously residing and physically present in the United States, with the result that the former would be entitled as a matter of due process to a hearing on the charges underlying any attempt to exclude him.

In view of the importance of citizenship it is surprising that the constitution originally did not define it. However, the desire to assure citizenship to former slaves (who had been held not to be citizens in Dred Scott v. Sandford, 60 U.S. (19 How.) 393 (1857)) led to the definition contained in the opening sentence of the fourteenth amendment: "All persons born or naturalized in the United States, and subject to the jurisdiction thereof, are citizens of the United States and of the State wherein they reside." In United States v. Wong Kim Ark, 169 U.S. 649 (1898), it was stated that the phrase, "and subject to the jurisdiction thereof" excluded "by the fewest and fittest words (besides children of members of the Indian tribes, standing in a peculiar relation to the National Government, unknown to the common law) ... two classes of cases—children born of alien enemies in hostile occupation, and children of diplomatic representatives of a foreign state...."

By statute Congress has added three principal categories to the constitutional definition of citizenship: (1) persons born in the United States to members of Indian, Eskimo, Aleutian, or other aboriginal tribes; (2) persons born outside the United States of parents both of whom are citizens and one of whom has had a residence in the United States prior to birth of such person; and (3) persons born outside the United States where only one parent is a citizen and that parent has resided in the United States for a prescribed period. See generally 8 U.S.C. § 1401.

Congress has long recognized the right of citizens to renounce their United States citizenship. 8 U.S.C. § 1481(a)(6), (7). Major problems have arisen, however, as a result of statutory provisions providing for loss of nationality upon the doing of certain acts—e.g. obtaining naturalization in a foreign state, taking an oath of allegiance to a foreign state, entering and serving in the armed forces of a foreign state without official consent. 8 U.S.C. § 1481. In Vance v. Terrazas, 444 U.S. 252 (1980), the court addressed the subtle question whether Congress may presume an intent to renounce citizenship from performance of certain acts, e.g., taking an oath of allegiance to a foreign state. It first referred to the earlier case of Afroyim v. Rusk, 387 U.S. 253 (1967), in which it had rejected the idea that "Congress has any general power, express or implied, to take away an American citizen's citizenship without his assent" and stated that § 1 of the fourteenth amendment is "most reasonably . . . read as defining a citizenship which a citizen keeps unless he voluntarily relinquishes it." The Court then held that in addition to proving that the plaintiff, a dual citizen of the United States and Mexico from birth, had taken an oath of allegiance to Mexico voluntarily, the government also had to prove that he did so intending to relinquish his citizenship. The Court also held, however, that it was constitutional for Congress to provide that the government's burden to establish intent to renounce could be a preponderance of the evidence.

SECTION 3. APPLICATION OF THE BILL OF RIGHTS TO THE STATES

Introduction. Early in the process of giving content to the due process clause of the fourteenth amendment the question arose as to the relationship between the Bill of Rights and the fourteenth amendment. An early example of the Court's approach was Twining v. New Jersey, 211 U.S. 78 (1908). The question posed was whether the provision in the fifth amendment that no person "shall be compelled in any criminal case to be a witness against himself" applied to restrain the states. Twining argued first that the "privileges and immunities of citizens of the United States" protected against state action by the fourteenth amendment included those fundamental personal rights which were protected against national action by the first eight Amendments; that this was the intention of the framers of the fourteenth amendment. The Court rejected this argument, relying on the interpretation of the privileges and immunities clause in the Slaughterhouse Cases. Second, Twining argued that a denial of the privilege against self-incrimination constituted a denial of due process of law. The Court rejected this argument, holding that the privilege against self-incrimination was not "an immutable principle of justice which is the inalienable possession of every citizen of a free government" and hence to deny it was not to deny due process.

Whether the first eight amendments could be utilized to make more specific the meaning of "due process of law" was not settled by *Twining*. The subsequent cases involved primarily criminal procedure, and detailed consideration of those cases is left to criminal procedure courses. Presented here are

Twining v. New Jersey

just a few of the principal cases illustrating the dispute over the incorporation problem and the nature of judicial review itself.

One aspect of the incorporation doctrine has become the foundation for most of the modern developments concerning freedom of speech, press, and religion. Almost casually, the Court in 1925 asserted in Gitlow v. New York, 268 U.S. 652, 666: "For present purposes we may and do assume that freedom of speech and of the press—which are protected by the 1st Amendment from abridgment by Congress—are among the fundamental personal rights and 'liberties' protected by the due process clause of the 14th Amendment from impairment by the states."

THE INCORPORATION DOCTRINE

In Chapter 9 we will see how the Court gave an early expansive meaning to such fourteenth amendment terms as "liberty", "property", and "due process of law" in the context of judicial review of the substance of economic regulations. We will also see the Court's withdrawal from that expansive interpretation in recent decades.

In the field of procedure (primarily procedure in criminal cases), a similar development had a different twist. In the early years the Court found in the fourteenth amendment restrictions upon state procedures that denied "immutable principles of justice" that are "the inalienable possession of every citizen of a free government" or that deprived the accused of "sufficient notice of the accusation" and "an adequate opportunity to defend himself". These expansive terms, and others, tended to limit rather than to expand (as was the case with respect to the substance of economic regulations) the scope of Court review of state procedures. More recently, through the idea that the fourteenth amendment applies to the states the more specific procedural guaranties in the Bill of Rights, the Court has expanded the scope of review of state court procedures while making somewhat more specific the applicable standards.

This section is designed to show the development of the incorporation doctrine and to underline the dispute within the Court as to the wisdom of seeking to restrain judicial review by confining it to the areas covered by the Bill of Rights. In reading the cases the student should consider how successful the Court has been in achieving more specific standards.

Palko v. Connecticut

302 U.S. 319, 58 S.Ct. 149, 82 L.Ed. 288 (1937).

Mr. Justice Cardozo delivered the opinion of the Court.

A statute of Connecticut permitting appeals in criminal cases to be taken by the state is challenged by appellant as an infringement of the Fourteenth Amendment of the Constitution of the United States. . . .

Appellant was indicted in Fairfield County, Conn., for the crime of murder in the first degree. A jury found him guilty of murder in the second degree, and he was sentenced to confinement in the state prison for life. Thereafter the State of Connecticut, with the permission of the judge presiding at the trial, gave notice of appeal to the Supreme Court of Errors. This it did pursuant to an act adopted in 1886. . . . Upon such appeal, the Supreme Court of Errors reversed the judgment and ordered a new trial. . . .

Pursuant to the mandate of the Supreme Court of Errors, defendant was brought to trial again. Before a jury was impaneled, and also at later stages of the case, he made the objection that the effect of the new trial was to place him twice in jeopardy for the same offense, and in so doing to violate the Fourteenth Amendment of the Constitution of the United States. Upon the overruling of the objection the trial proceeded. The jury returned a verdict of murder in the first degree, and the court sentenced the defendant to ... death. The Supreme Court of Errors affirmed the judgment of conviction....

1. The execution of the sentence will not deprive appellant of his life without the process of law assured to him by the Fourteenth Amendment of the Federal Constitution.

The argument for appellant is that whatever is forbidden by the Fifth Amendment is forbidden by the Fourteenth also. The Fifth Amendment, which is not directed to the States, but solely to the federal government, creates immunity from double jeopardy. No person shall be "subject for the same offense to be twice put in jeopardy of life or limb." The Fourteenth Amendment ordains, "nor shall any State deprive any person of life, liberty, or property, without due process of law." To retry a defendant, though under one indictment and only one, subjects him, it is said, to double jeopardy in violation of the Fifth Amendment, if the prosecution is one on behalf of the United States. From this the consequence is said to follow that there is a denial of life or liberty without due process of law, if the prosecution is one on behalf of the people of a state....

We have said that in appellant's view the Fourteenth Amendment is to be taken as embodying the prohibitions of the Fifth. His thesis is even broader. Whatever would be a violation of the original bill of rights (Amendments 1 to 8) if done by the federal government is now equally unlawful by force of the Fourteenth Amendment if done by a state. There is no such general rule.

The Fifth Amendment provides, among other things, that no person shall be held to answer for a capital or otherwise infamous crime unless on presentment or indictment of a grand jury. This court has held that, in prosecutions by a state, presentment or indictment by a grand jury may give way to informations at the instance of a public officer. Hurtado v. California, 110 U.S. 516.... The Fifth Amendment provides also that no person shall be compelled in any criminal case to be a witness against himself. This court has said that, in prosecutions by a state, the exemption will fail if the state elects to end it. Twining v. New Jersey, 211 U.S. 78, 106, 111, 112.... The Sixth Amendment calls for a jury trial in criminal cases and the Seventh for a jury trial in civil cases at common law where the value in controversy shall exceed $20. This court has ruled that consistently with those amendments trial by jury may be modified by a state or abolished altogether. Walker v. Sauvinet, 92 U.S. 90; Maxwell v. Dow, 176 U.S. 581....

On the other hand, the due process clause of the Fourteenth Amendment may make it unlawful for a state to abridge by its statutes the freedom of speech which the First Amendment safeguards against encroachment by the Congress ... or the like freedom of the press, ... or the free exercise of religion, ... or the right of peaceable assembly, without which speech would be unduly trammeled, ... or the right of one accused of crime to the benefit of counsel (Powell v. Alabama, 287 U.S. 45). In these and other situations immunities that are valid as against the federal government by force of the specific pledges of particular amendments have been found to be implicit in the concept of ordered liberty, and thus, through the Fourteenth Amendment, become valid as against the states.

The line of division may seem to be wavering and broken if there is a hasty catalogue of the cases on the one side and the other. Reflection and analysis will induce a different view. There emerges the perception of a rationalizing principle which gives to discrete instances a proper order and coherence. The right to trial by jury and the immunity from prosecution except as the result of an indictment may have value and importance. Even so, they are not of the very essence of a scheme of ordered liberty. To abolish them is not to violate a "principle of justice so rooted in the traditions and conscience of our people as to be ranked as fundamental." Snyder v. Massachusetts, supra, 291 U.S. 97, at page 105; Brown v. Mississippi, 297 U.S. 278, at page 285; Hebert v. Louisiana, 272 U.S. 312, 316. Few would be so narrow or provincial as to maintain that a fair and enlightened system of justice would be impossible without them. What is true of jury trials and indictments is true also, as the cases show, of the immunity from compulsory self-incrimination. *Twining v. New Jersey,* supra. This too might be lost, and justice still be done. Indeed, today as in the past there are students of our penal system who look upon the immunity as a mischief rather than a benefit, and who would limit its scope, or destroy it altogether.[3] No doubt there would remain the need to give protection against torture, physical or mental. *Brown v. Mississippi,* supra. Justice, however, would not perish if the accused were subject to a duty to respond to orderly inquiry. The exclusion of these immunities and privileges from the privileges and immunities protected against the action of the States has not been arbitrary or casual. It has been dictated by a study and appreciation of the meaning, the essential implications, of liberty itself.

We reach a different plane of social and moral values when we pass to the privileges and immunities that have been taken over from the earlier articles of the Federal Bill of Rights and brought within the Fourteenth Amendment by a process of absorption. These in their origin were effective against the federal government alone. If the Fourteenth Amendment has absorbed them, the process of absorption has had its source in the belief that neither liberty nor justice would exist if they were sacrificed. . . . This is true, for illustration, of freedom of thought and speech. Of that freedom one may say that it is the matrix, the indispensable condition, of nearly every other form of freedom. With rare aberrations a pervasive recognition of that truth can be traced in our history, political and legal. So it has come about that the domain of liberty, withdrawn by the Fourteenth Amendment from encroachment by the states, has been enlarged by latter-day judgments to include liberty of the mind as well as liberty of action. The extension became, indeed, a logical imperative when once it was recognized, as long ago it was, that liberty is something more than exemption from physical restraint, and that even in the field of substantive rights and duties the legislative judgment, if oppressive and arbitrary, may be overridden by the courts. . . . Fundamental too in the concept of due process and so in that of liberty, is the thought that condemnation shall be rendered only after trial. . . . The hearing, moreover, must be a real one, not a sham, or a pretense. Moore v. Dempsey, 261 U.S. 86; Mooney v. Holohan, 294 U.S. 103. For that reason, ignorant defendants in a capital case were held to have been condemned unlawfully when in truth, though not in form, they were refused the aid of counsel. Powell v. Alabama, supra, 287 U.S. 45, at pages 67, 68. The decision did not turn upon the fact that the benefit of counsel would have been

---

3. See, e.g., Bentham, Rationale of Judicial Evidence, Book IX, Pt. 4, c. III; Glueck, Crime and Justice, p. 94. Cf. Wigmore, Evidence, vol. 4, § 2251.

Compulsory self-incrimination is part of the established procedure in the law of Continental Europe. Wigmore, supra, p. 824; Gar-ner, Criminal Procedure in France, 25 Yale L.J. 255, 260; Sherman, Roman Law in the Modern World, vol. 2, pp. 493, 494; Stumberg, Guide to the Law and Legal Literature of France, p. 184. Double jeopardy too is not everywhere forbidden. Radin, Anglo American Legal History, p. 228.

guaranteed to the defendants by the provisions of the Sixth Amendment if they had been prosecuted in a federal court. The decision turned upon the fact that in the particular situation laid before us in the evidence the benefit of counsel was essential to the substance of a hearing.

Our survey of the cases serves, we think, to justify the statement that the dividing line between them, if not unfaltering throughout its course, has been true for the most part to a unifying principle. On which side of the line the case made out by the appellant has appropriate location must be the next inquiry and the final one. Is that kind of double jeopardy to which the statute has subjected him a hardship so acute and shocking that our policy will not endure it? Does it violate those "fundamental principles of liberty and justice which lie at the base of all our civil and political institutions"? . . . The answer surely must be "no." What the answer would have to be if the state were permitted after a trial free from error to try the accused over again or to bring another case against him, we have no occasion to consider. We deal with the statute before us and no other. The state is not attempting to wear the accused out by a multitude of cases with accumulated trials. It asks no more than this, that the case against him shall go on until there shall be a trial free from the corrosion of substantial legal error. . . . This is not cruelty at all, nor even vexation in any immoderate degree. If the trial had been infected with error adverse to the accused, there might have been review at his instance, and as often as necessary to purge the vicious taint. A reciprocal privilege, subject at all times to the discretion of the presiding judge . . . has now been granted to the state. There is here no seismic innovation. The edifice of justice stands, its symmetry, to many, greater than before.

2. The conviction of appellant is not in derogation of any privileges or immunities that belong to him as a citizen of the United States.

There is argument in his behalf that the privileges and immunities clause of the Fourteenth Amendment as well as the due process clause has been flouted by the judgment.

Maxwell v. Dow, supra, 176 U.S. 581, at page 584, gives all the answer that is necessary.

The judgment is affirmed.

Mr. Justice Butler dissents.

ADAMSON v. CALIFORNIA, 332 U.S. 46 (1947). Defendant was convicted of murder in the first degree. As permitted by California law the judge and the prosecutor commented on the failure of the defendant to explain or deny evidence against him. Under California law the jury could have been made aware on cross-examination of prior convictions of the defendant if he had taken the stand. In the Supreme Court the defendant argued both that his conviction under this procedure was a denial of the fifth amendment privilege against self-incrimination and that it denied him a fair trial in contravention of the due process clause of the Fourteenth Amendment. The Court affirmed the conviction. Speaking for the Court, Justice Reed stated the holding as follows:

(1) The privilege against self-incrimination is not a privilege of national citizenship protected by the Fourteenth Amendment. "The Slaughter–House Cases decided . . . that these rights, as privileges and immunities of state citizenship, remained under the sole protection of the state governments. . . . This construction has become embedded in our federal system as a functioning element in preserving the balance between national and state power."

(2) The privilege against self-incrimination does not to its full scope inhere in the right to a fair trial protected by the due process clause of the Fourteenth

[handwritten margin note: ct. affirmed conviction]

Amendment. "Nothing has been called to our attention that either the framers of the Fourteenth Amendment or the states that adopted intended its due process clause to draw within its scope the earlier amendments to the Constitution."

(3) The particular state procedure involved here did not violate "the protection against state action that the due process clause does grant to an accused. The due process clause forbids compulsion to testify by fear of hurt, torture or exhaustion. It forbids any other type of coercion that falls within the scope of due process."

Justice Frankfurter, concurring, said, in part:

"The short answer to the suggestion that the provision of the Fourteenth Amendment, which ordains 'nor shall any State deprive any person of life, liberty, or property, without due process of law,' was a way of saying that every State must thereafter initiate prosecutions through indictment by a grand jury, must have a trial by a jury of 12 in criminal cases, and must have trial by such a jury in common law suits where the amount in controversy exceeds $20, is that it is a strange way of saying it. It would be extraordinarily strange for a Constitution to convey such specific commands in such a roundabout and inexplicit way. After all, an amendment to the Constitution should be read in a ' "sense most obvious to the common understanding at the time of its adoption." ... For it was for public adoption that it was proposed.' ... Those reading the English language with the meaning which it ordinarily conveys, those conversant with the political and legal history of the concept of due process, those sensitive to the relations of the States to the central government as well as the relation of some of the provisions of the Bill of Rights to the process of justice, would hardly recognize the Fourteenth Amendment as a cover for the various explicit provisions of the first eight Amendments. Some of these are enduring reflections of experience with human nature, while some express the restricted views of Eighteenth–Century England regarding the best methods for the ascertainment of facts. The notion that the Fourteenth Amendment was a covert way of imposing upon the States all the rules which it seemed important to Eighteenth Century statesmen to write into the Federal Amendments, was rejected by judges who were themselves witnesses of the process by which the Fourteenth Amendment became part of the Constitution. Arguments that may now be adduced to prove that the first eight Amendments were concealed within the historic phrasing of the Fourteenth Amendment were not unknown at the time of its adoption. A surer estimate of their bearing was possible for judges at the time than distorting distance is likely to vouchsafe. Any evidence of design or purpose not contemporaneously known could hardly have influenced those who ratified the Amendment. Remarks of a particular proponent of the Amendment, no matter how influential, are not to be deemed part of the Amendment. What was submitted for ratification was his proposal, not his speech. Thus, at the time of the ratification of the Fourteenth Amendment the constitutions of nearly half of the ratifying States did not have the rigorous requirements of the Fifth Amendment for instituting criminal proceedings through a grand jury. It could hardly have occurred to these States that by ratifying the Amendment they uprooted their established methods for prosecuting crime and fastened upon themselves a new prosecutorial system.

"Indeed, the suggestion that the Fourteenth Amendment incorporates the first eight Amendments as such is not unambiguously urged. Even the boldest innovator would shrink from suggesting to more than half the States that they may no longer initiate prosecutions without indictment by grand jury, or that thereafter all the States of the Union must furnish a jury of 12 for every case involving a claim above $20. There is suggested merely a selective incorporation of the first eight Amendments into the Fourteenth Amendment. Some are in and some are out, but we are left in the dark as to which are in and which are out. Nor are we given the calculus for determining which go in and which stay out. If the basis of selection is merely that those provisions of the first eight Amendments are incorporated which commend themselves to individual justices as indispensable to the dignity and happiness of a free man, we are thrown back to a merely subjective test. The protection against unreasonable search and seizure might have primacy for one judge, while trial by a jury of 12 for every claim above $20 might appear to another as an ultimate need in a free society. In the history of thought 'natural law' has a much longer and much better founded meaning and justification than such subjective selection of the first eight Amendments for incorporation into the Fourteenth. If all that is meant is that due process contains within itself certain minimal standards which are 'of the very essence of a scheme of ordered liberty,' Palko v. Connecticut, 302 U.S. 319, 325, putting upon this Court the duty of applying these standards from time to time, then we have merely arrived at the insight which our predecessors long ago expressed. We are called upon to apply to the difficult issues of our own day the wisdom afforded by the great opinions in this field. . . . This guidance bids us to be duly mindful of the heritage of the past, with its great lessons of how liberties are won and how they are lost. As judges charged with the delicate task of subjecting the government of a continent to the Rule of Law, we must be particularly mindful that it is 'a *constitution* we are expounding,' so that it should not be imprisoned in what are merely legal forms even though they have the sanction of the Eighteenth Century. . . .

"And so, when, as in a case like the present, a conviction in a State court is here for review under a claim that a right protected by the Due Process Clause of the Fourteenth Amendment has been denied, the issue is not whether an infraction of one of the specific provisions of the first eight Amendments is disclosed by the record. The relevant question is whether the criminal proceedings which resulted in conviction deprived the accused of the due process of law to which the United States Constitution entitled him. Judicial review of that guaranty of the Fourteenth Amendment inescapably imposes upon this Court an exercise of judgment upon the whole course of the proceedings in order to ascertain whether they offend those canons of decency and fairness which express the notions of justice of English-speaking peoples even toward those charged with the most heinous offenses. These standards of justice are not authoritatively formulated anywhere as though they were prescriptions in a pharmacopoeia. But neither does the application of the Due Process Clause imply that judges are wholly at large. The judicial judgment in applying the Due Process Clause must move within the limits of accepted notions of justice and is not to be based upon the idiosyncrasies of a merely personal judgment. The fact that judges among themselves may differ whether in a particular case a trial offends accepted notions of justice is not disproof that general rather than idiosyncratic standards are applied. An important safeguard against such merely individual judgment is an alert deference to the judgment of the State court under review."

Justices Murphy and Rutledge, dissenting, noted:

"While in substantial agreement with the views of Mr. Justice Black, I have one reservation and one addition to make.

"I agree that the specific guarantees of the Bill of Rights should be carried over intact into the first section of the Fourteenth Amendment. But I am not prepared to say that the latter is entirely and necessarily limited by the Bill of

Rights. Occasions may arise where a proceeding falls so far short of conforming to fundamental standards of procedure as to warrant constitutional condemnation in terms of a lack of due process despite the absence of a specific provision in the Bill of Rights." . . .

Justice Black joined by Justice Douglas delivered a long dissenting opinion. The following paragraphs illustrate his thesis:

"This decision reasserts a constitutional theory spelled out in Twining v. New Jersey, 211 U.S. 78, that this Court is endowed by the Constitution with boundless power under 'natural law' periodically to expand and contract constitutional standards to conform to the Court's conception of what at a particular time constitutes 'civilized decency' and 'fundamental principles of liberty and justice.' Invoking this Twining rule, the Court concludes that although comment upon testimony in a federal court would violate the Fifth Amendment, identical comment in a state court does not violate today's fashion in civilized decency and fundamentals and is therefore not prohibited by the Federal Constitution as amended.

"The Twining case was the first, as it is the only decision of this Court, which has squarely held that states were free, notwithstanding the Fifth and Fourteenth Amendments, to extort evidence from one accused of crime. I agree that if Twining be reaffirmed, the result reached might appropriately follow. But I would not reaffirm the Twining decision. I think that decision and the 'natural law' theory of the Constitution upon which it relies, degrade the constitutional safeguards of the Bill of Rights and simultaneously appropriate for this Court a broad power which we are not authorized by the Constitution to exercise. . . . My reasons for believing that the Twining decision should not be revitalized can best be understood by reference to the constitutional, judicial, and general history that preceded and followed the case. . . .

"My study of the historical events that culminated in the Fourteenth Amendment, and the expressions of those who sponsored and favored, as well as those who opposed its submission and passage, persuades me that one of the chief objects that the provisions of the Amendment's first section, separately, and as a whole, were intended to accomplish was to make the Bill of Rights applicable to the states. With full knowledge of the import of the Barron decision, the framers and backers of the Fourteenth Amendment proclaimed its purpose to be to overturn the constitutional rule that case had announced. This historical purpose has never received full consideration or exposition in any opinion of this Court interpreting the Amendment. . . .

"For this reason, I am attaching to this dissent, an appendix which contains a résumé, by no means complete, of the Amendment's history. In my judgment that history conclusively demonstrates that the language of the first section of the Fourteenth Amendment, taken as a whole, was thought by those responsible for its submission to the people, and by those who opposed its submission, sufficiently explicit to guarantee that thereafter no state could deprive its citizens of the privileges and protections of the Bill of Rights. Whether this Court ever will, or whether it now should, in the light of past decisions, give full effect to what the Amendment was intended to accomplish is not necessarily essential to a decision here. However that may be, our prior decisions, including Twining, do not prevent our carrying out that purpose, at least to the extent of making applicable to the states, not a mere part, as the Court has, but the full protection of the Fifth Amendment's provision against compelling evidence from an accused to convict him of crime. And I further contend that the 'natural law' formula which the Court uses to reach its conclusion in this case should be abandoned as an incongruous excrescence on our Constitution. I believe that formula to be itself a violation of our Constitution, in that it subtly conveys to courts, at the expense of legislatures, ultimate power over public policies in fields where no specific provision of the Constitution limits legislative power....

"I cannot consider the Bill of Rights to be an outworn 18th Century 'strait jacket' as the Twining opinion did. Its provisions may be thought outdated abstractions by some. And it is true that they were designed to meet ancient evils. But they are the same kind of human evils that have emerged from century to century wherever excessive power is sought by the few at the expense of the many. In my judgment the people of no nation can lose their liberty so long as a Bill of Rights like ours survives and its basic purposes are conscientiously interpreted, enforced and respected so as to afford continuous protection against old, as well as new, devices and practices which might thwart those purposes. I fear to see the consequences of the Court's practice of substituting its own concepts of decency and fundamental justice for the language of the Bill of Rights as its point of departure in interpreting and enforcing that Bill of Rights. If the choice must be between the selective process of the Palko decision applying some of the Bill of Rights to the States, or the Twining rule applying none of them, I would choose the Palko selective process. But rather than accept either of these choices, I would follow what I believe was the original purpose of the Fourteenth Amendment—to extend to all the people of the nation the complete protection of the Bill of Rights. To hold that this Court can determine what, if any, provisions of the Bill of Rights will be enforced, and if so to what degree, is to frustrate the great design of a written Constitution....

"It is an illusory apprehension that literal application of some or all of the provisions of the Bill of Rights to the States would unwisely increase the sum total of the powers of this Court to invalidate state legislation. The Federal Government has not been harmfully burdened by the requirement that enforcement of federal laws affecting civil liberty conform literally to the Bill of Rights. Who would advocate its repeal? It must be conceded, of course, that the natural-law-due-process formula, which the Court today reaffirms, has been interpreted to limit substantially this Court's power to prevent state violations of the individual civil liberties guaranteed by the Bill of Rights. But this formula also has been used in the past and can be used in the future, to license this Court, in considering regulatory legislation, to roam at large in the broad expanses of policy and morals and to trespass, all too freely, on the legislative domain of the States as well as the Federal Government.

"Since Marbury v. Madison, 1 Cranch 137, was decided, the practice has been firmly established for better or worse, that courts can strike down legislative enactments which violate the Constitution. This process, of course, involves interpretation, and since words can have many meanings, interpretation obviously may result in contraction or extension of the original purpose of a constitutional provision thereby affecting policy. But to pass upon the constitutionality of statutes by looking to the particular standards enumerated in the Bill of Rights and other parts of the Constitution is one thing; to invalidate statutes because of application of 'natural law' deemed to be above and undefined by the Constitution is another. 'In the one instance, courts proceeding within clearly marked constitutional boundaries seek to execute policies written into the Constitution; in the other they roam at will in the limitless area of their own beliefs as to reasonableness and actually select policies, a responsibility which the Constitution entrusts to the legislative representatives of the people.' Federal Power Commission v. Natural Gas Pipeline Co., 315 U.S. 575, 599, 601, n. 4.''

THE HISTORICAL DEBATE

Justice Black's historical thesis is more fully set out in an Appendix in *Adamson* found at 332 U.S. at 92. See also the discussion in the opinions of Justices Black and Harlan in Duncan v. Louisiana, set out *infra*. Scholars attempting to discover the true intent of the framers of the fourteenth amendment have consulted many sources, including: The pre-Civil War literature and party platforms of abolitionist groups. Judicial and legislative pronouncements in the foreground when the amendment was drafted: Barron v. Mayor and City Council Baltimore, 32 U.S. (7 Pet.) 243 (1833), Murray's Lessee v. Hoboken Land & Improvement Co., 59 U.S. (18 How.) 272 (1855), and Dred Scott v. Sandford, 60 U.S. (19 How.) 393 (1857), and the provisions of the Freedman's Bureau bill and the Civil Rights Act. Debates in the Congress and the state ratification bodies. Newspaper and magazine comment of the time. Post-ratification statements purporting to explain the meaning of the amendment by two of the draftsmen, John A. Bingham and Roscoe Conkling.

Out of this vast body of material, diverse conclusions have been drawn as to the import of almost every clause of the amendment. On the specific issue of the amendment's incorporation of the first eight amendments to the federal constitution, historical support can be mustered both for the majority and the dissenting opinions in *Adamson*. The argument for incorporation rests on the known aversion of some of the framers to Barron v. Baltimore, and focuses on the 1871 speech of Bingham stating this as the meaning of the privileges and immunities clause. This position is documented in the works of Guthrie, *The Fourteenth Article of Amendment to the Constitution of the United States* (1898); Flack, *The Adoption of the Fourteenth Amendment* (1908); 2 Crosskey, *Politics and the Constitution* chs. XXXI, XXXII (1953); Boudin, *Truth and Fiction about the Fourteenth Amendment,* 16 N.Y.U.L.Q.Rev. 19 (1938) (with additional support from the due process clause). Equally assiduous work by other researchers has led them to conclude that no such specific content was contemplated for the fourteenth amendment. The writers who argue from abolitionist history point to a greater concern for substantive protection of rights vaguely categorized as principles of natural law than to any particular set of rules for the conduct of trials. Ten Broek, *The Antislavery Origins of the Fourteenth Amendment* (1951); Graham, *The "Conspiracy Theory" of the Fourteenth Amendment,* 47 Yale L.J. 371 (1938) and Graham, *The Early Antislavery Background of the Fourteenth Amendment,* 1950 Wis.L.Rev. 479, 610. Other authors have pointed to the lack of specific debate on this point as indicative of absence of intent to achieve incorporation. They maintain that such a revolutionary change of state procedures, already then divergent from the federal model, would certainly not have been accepted *sub silentio* by the state conventions, if they had so understood the amendment. Fairman and Morrison, *Does the Fourteenth Amendment Incorporate the Bill of Rights?,* 2 Stan.L.Rev. 5, 140 (1949); and see Meyer, *The Blaine Amendment and the Bill of Rights,* 64 Harv.L.Rev. 939 (1951).

For a recent debate of the historical materials, see Curtis, *The Bill of Rights as a Limitation on State Authority: A Reply to Professor Berger,* 16 Wake Forest L.Rev. 45 (1980); Berger, *Incorporation of the Bill of Rights in the Fourteenth Amendment: A Nine–Lived Cat,* 42 Ohio St.L.J. 435 (1981); Curtis, *Further Adventures of the Nine Lived Cat: A Response to Mr. Berger on Incorporation of the Bill of Rights,* 43 Ohio St.L.J. 89 (1982); Berger, *Incorporation of the Bill of Rights: A Reply to Michael Curtis' Response,* 44 Ohio St.L.J. 1 (1983).

In appraising these historical analyses of the fourteenth amendment, you should ask yourself what the utility and relevance of conclusions derived from ambiguous historical records are for present day constitutional law. How can we validly infer the intent of Congress and the ratifying states from the speeches of individual supporters and opponents of the amendment? How can the enactment of the first section of the amendment be separated from the furor and passion accompanying the other sections, then perhaps deemed more important, and now dead letters?

Duncan v. Louisiana

391 U.S. 145, 88 S.Ct. 1444, 20 L.Ed.2d 491 (1968).

Mr. Justice White delivered the opinion of the Court.

Appellant, Gary Duncan, was convicted of simple battery[,] a misdemeanor, punishable by two years' imprisonment and a $300 fine. Appellant sought trial by jury, but because the Louisiana Constitution grants jury trials only in cases in which capital punishment or imprisonment at hard labor may be imposed, the trial judge denied the request. Appellant was convicted and sentenced to serve 60 days in the parish prison and pay a fine of $150. Appellant sought review in the Supreme Court of Louisiana, asserting that the denial of jury trial violated rights guaranteed to him by the United States Constitution. The Supreme Court, finding "no error of law in the ruling complained of," denied appellant a writ of certiorari. [A]ppellant sought review in this Court, alleging that the Sixth and Fourteenth Amendments to the United States Constitution secure the right to jury trial in state criminal prosecutions where a sentence as long as two years may be imposed. . . .

I.

The Fourteenth Amendment denies the States the power to "deprive any person of life, liberty, or property, without due process of law." In resolving conflicting claims concerning the meaning of this spacious language, the Court has looked increasingly to the Bill of Rights for guidance; many of the rights guaranteed by the first eight Amendments to the Constitution have been held to be protected against state action by the Due Process Clause of the Fourteenth Amendment. That clause now protects the right to compensation for property taken by the State; the rights of speech, press, and religion covered by the First Amendment; the Fourth Amendment rights to be free from unreasonable searches and seizures and to have excluded from criminal trials any evidence illegally seized; the right guaranteed by the Fifth Amendment to be free of compelled self-incrimination; and the Sixth Amendment rights to counsel, to a speedy and public trial, to confrontation of opposing witnesses, and to compulsory process for obtaining witnesses.

The test for determining whether a right extended by the Fifth and Sixth Amendments with respect to federal criminal proceedings is also protected against state action by the Fourteenth Amendment has been phrased in a variety of ways in the opinions of this Court. The question has been asked whether a right is among those "fundamental principles of liberty and justice which lie at the base of all our civil and political institutions," Powell v. Alabama, 287 U.S. 45, 67 (1932); whether it is "basic in our system of jurisprudence," In re Oliver, 333 U.S. 257, 273 (1948); and whether it is "a fundamental right, essential to a fair trial," Gideon v. Wainwright, 372 U.S. 335, 343–344 (1963); Malloy v. Hogan, 378 U.S. 1, 6 (1964); Pointer v. Texas, 380 U.S. 400, 403 (1965). The claim before us is that the right to trial by jury guaranteed by the Sixth Amendment meets these tests. The position of Louisiana, on the other hand, is that the Constitution imposes upon the States no duty to give a jury trial in any criminal case, regardless of the seriousness of the crime or the size of the punishment which may be imposed. Because we believe that trial by jury in criminal cases is fundamental to the American scheme of justice, we hold that the Fourteenth Amendment guarantees a right of jury trial in all criminal cases which—were they to be tried in a federal court—would come within the Sixth Amendment's guarantee.[14] Since we consider the appeal before us to be such a case, we hold that the Constitution was violated when appellant's demand for jury trial was refused.

The history of trial by jury in criminal cases has been frequently told....

. . .

Even such skeletal history is impressive support for considering the right to jury trial in criminal cases to be fundamental to our system of justice, an importance frequently recognized in the opinions of this Court....

Jury trial continues to receive strong support. The laws of every State guarantee a right to jury trial in serious criminal cases; no State has dispensed with it; nor are there significant movements underway to do so....

14. In one sense recent cases applying provisions of the first eight amendments to the States represent a new approach to the "incorporation" debate. Earlier the Court can be seen as having asked, when inquiring into whether some particular procedural safeguard was required of a State, if a civilized system could be imagined that would not accord the particular protection. For example, Palko v. Connecticut, 302 U.S. 319, 325 (1937), stated: "The right to trial by jury and the immunity from prosecution except as the result of an indictment may have value and importance. Even so, they are not of the very essence of a scheme of ordered liberty.... Few would be so narrow or provincial as to maintain that a fair and enlightened system of justice would be impossible without them." The recent cases, on the other hand, have proceeded upon the valid assumption that state criminal processes are not imaginary and theoretical schemes but actual systems bearing virtually every characteristic of the common-law system that has been developing contemporaneously in England and in this country. The question thus is whether given this kind of system a particular procedure is fundamental—whether, that is, a procedure is necessary to an Anglo–American regime of ordered liberty. It is this sort of inquiry that can justify the conclusions that state courts must exclude evidence seized in violation of the Fourth Amendment, Mapp v. Ohio, 367 U.S. 643 (1961); that state prosecutors may not comment on a defendant's failure to testify, Griffin v. California, 380 U.S. 609 (1965); and that criminal punishment may not be imposed for the status of narcotics addiction, Robinson v. California, 370 U.S. 660 (1962). Of immediate relevance for this case are the Court's holdings that the States must comply with certain provisions of the Sixth Amendment, specifically that the States may not refuse a speedy trial, confrontation of witnesses, and the assistance, at state expense if necessary, of counsel.... Of each of these determinations that a constitutional provision originally written to bind the Federal Government should bind the States as well it might be said that the limitation in question is not necessarily fundamental to fairness in every criminal system that might be imagined but is fundamental in the context of the criminal processes maintained by the American States.

When the inquiry is approached in this way the question whether the States can impose criminal punishment without granting a jury trial appears quite different from the way it appeared in the older cases opining that States might abolish jury trial. See, e.g., Maxwell v. Dow, 176 U.S. 581 (1900). A criminal process which was fair and equitable but used no juries is easy to imagine. It would make use of alternative guarantees and protections which would serve the purposes that the jury serves in the English and American systems. Yet no American State has undertaken to construct such a system. Instead, every American State, including Louisiana, uses the jury extensively, and imposes very serious punishments only after a trial at which the defendant has a right to a jury's verdict. In every State, including Louisiana, the structure and style of the criminal process—the supporting framework and the subsidiary procedures—are of the sort that naturally complement jury trial, and have developed in connection with and in reliance upon jury trial.

We are aware of prior cases in this Court in which the prevailing opinion contains statements contrary to our holding today that the right to jury trial in serious criminal cases is a fundamental right and hence must be recognized by the States as part of their obligation to extend due process of law to all persons within their jurisdiction.... None of these cases, however, dealt with a State which had purported to dispense entirely with a jury trial in serious criminal cases.... Respectfully, we reject the prior dicta regarding jury trial in criminal cases.

The guarantees of jury trial in the Federal and State Constitutions reflect a profound judgment about the way in which law should be enforced and justice administered. A right to jury trial is granted to criminal defendants in order to prevent oppression by the Government.... The deep commitment of the Nation to the right of jury trial in serious criminal cases as a defense against arbitrary law enforcement qualifies for protection under the Due Process Clause of the Fourteenth Amendment, and must therefore be respected by the States.

Of course jury trial has "its weaknesses and the potential for misuse," Singer v. United States, 380 U.S. 24, 35 (1965). We are aware of the long debate, especially in this century, among those who write about the administration of justice, as to the wisdom of permitting untrained laymen to determine the facts in civil and criminal proceedings. Although the debate has been intense, with powerful voices on either side, most of the controversy has centered on the jury in civil cases. Indeed, some of the severest critics of civil juries acknowledge that the arguments for criminal juries are much stronger....

The State of Louisiana urges that holding that the Fourteenth Amendment assures a right to jury trial will cast doubt on the integrity of every trial conducted without a jury. Plainly, this is not the import of our holding. Our conclusion is that in the American States, as in the federal judicial system, a general grant of jury trial for serious offenses is a fundamental right, essential for preventing miscarriages of justice and for assuring that fair trials are provided for all defendants. We would not assert, however, that every criminal trial—or any particular trial—held before a judge alone is unfair or that a defendant may never be as fairly treated by a judge as he would be by a jury. Thus we hold no constitutional doubts about the practices, common in both federal and state courts, of accepting waivers of jury trial and prosecuting petty crimes without extending a right to jury trial. However, the fact is that in most places more trials for serious crimes are to juries than to a court alone; a great many defendants prefer the judgment of a jury to that of a court. Even where defendants are satisfied with bench trials, the right to a jury trial very likely serves its intended purpose of making judicial or prosecutorial unfairness less likely.[30]

---

30. Louisiana also asserts that if due process is deemed to include the right to jury trial, States will be obligated to comply with all past interpretations of the Sixth Amendment, an amendment which in its inception was designed to control only the federal courts and which throughout its history has operated in this limited environment where uniformity is a more obvious and immediate consideration. In particular, Louisiana objects to application of the decisions of this Court interpreting the Sixth Amendment as guaranteeing a 12-man jury in serious criminal cases, Thompson v. Utah, 170 U.S. 343 (1898); as requiring a unanimous verdict before guilt can be found, Maxwell v. Dow, 176 U.S. 581, 586 (1900); and as barring procedures by which crimes subject to the Sixth Amendment jury trial provision are tried in the first instance without a jury but at the first appellate stage by *de novo* trial with a jury, Callan v. Wilson, 127 U.S. 540, 557 (1888). It seems very unlikely to us that our decision today will require widespread changes in state criminal processes. First, our

II.

Louisiana's final contention is that even if it must grant jury trials in serious criminal cases, the conviction before us is valid and constitutional because here the petitioner was tried for simple battery and was sentenced to only 60 days in the parish prison. We are not persuaded. It is doubtless true that there is a category of petty crimes or offenses which is not subject to the Sixth Amendment jury trial provision and should not be subject to the Fourteenth Amendment jury trial requirement here applied to the States. Crimes carrying possible penalties up to six months do not require a jury trial if they otherwise qualify as petty offenses, Cheff v. Schnackenberg, 384 U.S. 373 (1966). But the penalty authorized for a particular crime is of major relevance in determining whether it is serious or not and may in itself, if severe enough, subject the trial to the mandates of the Sixth Amendment. District of Columbia v. Clawans, 300 U.S. 617 (1937). The penalty authorized by the law of the locality may be taken "as a gauge of its social and ethical judgments," 300 U.S., at 628 of the crime in question. In *Clawans* the defendant was jailed for 60 days, but it was the 90-day authorized punishment on which the Court focused in determining that the offense was not one for which the Constitution assured trial by jury. In the case before us the Legislature of Louisiana has made simple battery a criminal offense punishable by imprisonment for two years and a fine. The question, then is whether a crime carrying such a penalty is an offense which Louisiana may insist on trying without a jury.

We think not....

. . .

The judgment below is reversed and the case is remanded for proceedings not inconsistent with this opinion.

Mr. Justice Black, with whom Mr. Justice Douglas joins, concurring.

... The dissent in this case ... makes a spirited and forceful defense of [the] now discredited [*Twining*]doctrine. I do not believe that it is necessary for me to repeat the historical and logical reasons for my challenge to the *Twining* holding contained in my *Adamson* dissent and Appendix to it. My Brother Harlan's objections to my *Adamson* dissent history, like that of most of the objectors, relies most heavily on a criticism written by Professor Charles Fairman[,] ... 2 Stan.L.Rev. 5 (1949) ... [, which] in my view ... has completely failed to refute the inferences and arguments that I suggested in my *Adamson* dissent. Professor Fairman's "history" relies very heavily on what was *not* said in the state legislatures that passed on the Fourteenth Amendment. Instead of relying on this kind of negative pregnant, my legislative experience has convinced me that it is far wiser to rely on what *was* said, and most importantly, said by the men who actually sponsored the Amendment in the Congress.... [B]oth its sponsors and those who opposed it believed the Fourteenth Amendment made the first eight Amendments of the Constitution (The Bill of Rights) applicable to the States.

decisions interpreting the Sixth Amendment are always subject to reconsideration, a fact amply demonstrated by the instant decision. In addition, most of the States have provisions for jury trials equal in breadth to the Sixth Amendment, if that amendment is construed, as it has been, to permit the trial of petty crimes and offenses without a jury. Indeed, there appear to be only four States in which juries of fewer than 12 can be used without the defendant's consent for offenses carrying a maximum penalty of greater than one year. Only in Oregon and Louisiana can a less-than-unanimous jury convict for an offense with a maximum penalty greater than one year....

. . . [Contrary to the dissent's view,] the words "No State shall make or enforce any law which shall abridge the privileges or immunities of citizens of the United States" seem to me an eminently reasonable way of expressing the idea that henceforth the Bill of Rights shall apply to the States.[1] What more precious "privilege" of American citizenship could there be than that privilege to claim the protections of our great Bill of Rights? I suggest that any reading of "privileges or immunities of citizens of the United States" which excludes the Bill of Rights' safeguards renders the words of this section of the Fourteenth Amendment meaningless. . . .

. . . Brother Harlan's . . . view, as was indeed the view of *Twining,* is that "due process is an evolving concept" and therefore that it entails a "gradual process of judicial inclusion and exclusion" to ascertain those "immutable principles of free government which no member of the Union may disregard." Thus the Due Process Clause is treated as prescribing no specific and clearly ascertainable constitutional command that judges must obey in interpreting the Constitution, but rather as leaving judges free to decide at any particular time whether a particular rule or judicial formulation embodies an "immutable principl[e] of free government" or "is implicit in the concept of ordered liberty," or whether certain conduct "shocks the judge's conscience" or runs counter to some other similar, undefined and undefinable standard. Thus due process, according to my Brother Harlan, is to be a word with no permanent meaning, but one which is found to shift from time to time in accordance with judges' predilections and understandings of what is best for the country. If due process means this, the Fourteenth Amendment, in my opinion, might as well have been written that "no person shall be deprived of life, liberty or property except by laws that the judges of the United States Supreme Court shall find to be consistent with the immutable principles of free government." It is impossible for me to believe that such unconfined power is given to judges in our Constitution that is a written one in order to limit governmental power.

. . . [Moreover,] the "fundamental fairness" test is one on a par with that of shocking the conscience of the Court. Each . . . depends entirely on the particular judge's idea of ethics and morals instead of requiring him to depend on the boundaries fixed by the written words of the Constitution. Nothing in the history of the phrase "due process of law" suggests that constitutional controls are to depend on any particular judge's sense of values. . . .

Finally . . . I am not bothered by the argument that applying the Bill of Rights to the States, "according to the same standards that protect those rights against federal encroachment," interferes with our concept of federalism in that it may prevent States from trying novel social and economic experiments. I have never believed that under the guise of federalism the States should be able to experiment with the protections afforded our citizens through the Bill of Rights. . . . It seems to me totally inconsistent to advocate on the one hand, the power of this Court to strike down any state law or practice which it finds "unreasonable" or "unfair," and on the other hand urge that the States be given maximum power to develop their own laws and procedures. Yet the due process approach of my Brothers Harlan and Fortas . . . does just that since in effect it restricts the States to practices which a majority of this Court is willing to approve on a case-by-case basis. No one is more concerned than I that the States be allowed to use the full scope of their powers as their citizens see fit. And that is why I have continually fought against the expansion of this Court's

---

1. My view has been and is that the Fourteenth Amendment, *as a whole,* makes the Bill of Rights applicable to the States. This would certainly include the language of the Privileges and Immunities Clause, as well as the Due Process Clause.

authority over the States through the use of a broad, general interpretation of due process that permits judges to strike down state laws they do not like.

. . . I believe as strongly as ever that the Fourteenth Amendment was intended to make the Bill of Rights applicable to the States. I have been willing to support the selective incorporation doctrine, however, as an alternative, although perhaps less historically supportable than complete incorporation. The selective incorporation process, if used properly, does limit the Supreme Court in the Fourteenth Amendment field to specific Bill of Rights' protections only and keeps judges from roaming at will in their own notions of what policies outside the Bill of Rights are desirable and what are not. And, most importantly for me, the selective incorporation process has the virtue of having already worked to make most of the Bill of Rights' protections applicable to the States.

Mr. Justice Fortas, concurring.

I join the judgments and opinions of the Court in these cases because I agree that the Due Process Clause of the Fourteenth Amendment requires that the States accord the right to jury trial in prosecutions for offenses that are not petty. . . .

. . .

Mr. Justice Harlan, whom Mr. Justice Stewart joins, dissenting.

Every American jurisdiction provides for trial by jury in criminal cases. The question before us is not whether jury trial is an ancient institution, which it is; nor whether it plays a significant role in the administration of criminal justice, which it does; nor whether it will endure, which it shall. The question in this case is whether the State of Louisiana, which provides trial by jury for all felonies, is prohibited by the Constitution from trying charges of simple battery to the court alone. In my view, the answer to that question, mandated alike by our constitutional history and by the longer history of trial by jury, is clearly "no."

. . .

I.

I believe I am correct in saying that every member of the Court for at least the last 135 years has agreed that our Founders did not consider the requirements of the Bill of Rights so fundamental that they should operate directly against the States. They were wont to believe rather that the security of liberty in America rested primarily upon the dispersion of governmental power across a federal system. . . .

. . .

A few members of the Court have taken the position that the intention of those who drafted the first section of the Fourteenth Amendment was simply, and exclusively, to make the provisions of the first eight amendments applicable to state action. This view has never been accepted by this Court. In my view, . . . the first section of the Fourteenth Amendment was meant neither to incorporate, nor to be limited to, the specific guarantees of the first eight amendments. The overwhelming historical evidence marshalled by Professor Fairman demonstrates, to me conclusively, that the Congressmen and state legislators who wrote, debated, and ratified the Fourteenth Amendment did not think they were "incorporating" the Bill of Rights[9] and the very breadth and

9. Fairman, Does the Fourteenth Amendment Incorporate the Bill of Rights? The Original Understanding, 2 Stan.L.Rev. 5 (1949). Professor Fairman was not content to generality of the Amendment's provisions suggests that its authors did not suppose that the Nation would always be limited to mid–19th century conceptions of "liberty" and "due process of law" ... [N]either history, nor sense, supports using the Fourteenth Amendment to put the States in a constitutional straitjacket with respect to their own development in the administration of criminal or civil law.

Although I therefore fundamentally disagree with the total incorporation view of the Fourteenth Amendment, it seems to me that such a position does at least have the virtue, lacking in the Court's selective incorporation approach, of internal consistency: we look to the Bill of Rights, word for word, clause for clause, precedent for precedent because, it is said, the men who wrote the Amendment wanted it that way. . . .

Apart from the ... absolute incorporationists, I can see only one method of analysis that has any internal logic. That is to start with the words "liberty" and "due process of law" and attempt to define them in a way that accords with American traditions and our system of government. This approach, involving a much more discriminating process of adjudication than does "incorporation," is, albeit difficult, the one that was followed throughout the Nineteenth and most of the present century. It entails a "gradual process of judicial inclusion and exclusion," seeking, with due recognition of constitutional tolerance for state experimentation and disparity, to ascertain those "immutable principles of free government which no member of the Union may disregard." . . .

. . .

Today's Court still remains unwilling to accept the total incorporationists' view. . . . The Court is also, apparently, unwilling to face the task of determining whether denial of trial by jury in the situation before us, or in other situations, is fundamentally unfair. Consequently, the Court has compromised on the ease of the incorporationist position, without its internal logic. It has simply assumed that the question before us is whether the Jury Trial Clause of the Sixth Amendment should be incorporated into the Fourteenth, jot-for-jot

rest upon the overwhelming fact that the great words of the four clauses of the first section of the Fourteenth Amendment would have been an exceedingly peculiar way to say that "The rights heretofore guaranteed against federal intrusion by the first eight Amendments are henceforth guaranteed against state intrusion as well." He therefore sifted the mountain of material comprising the debates and committee reports relating to the Amendment in both Houses of Congress and in the state legislatures that passed upon it. He found that in the immense corpus of comments on the purpose and effects of the proposed amendment, and on its virtues and defects, there is almost no evidence whatever for "incorporation." The first eight amendments are so much as mentioned by only two members of Congress, one of whom effectively demonstrated (a) that he did not understand Barron v. Baltimore, 7 Pet. 243, and therefore did not understand the question of incorporation, and (b) that he was not himself understood by his colleagues. One state legislative committee report, rejected by the legislature as a whole, found § I of the Fourteenth Amendment superfluous because it duplicated the Bill of Rights: the committee obviously did not understand Barron v. Baltimore either. That is all Professor Fairman could find, in hundreds of pages of legislative discussion prior to passage of the Amendment, that even suggests incorporation.

To this negative evidence the judicial history of the Amendment could be added. For example, it proved possible for a court whose members had lived through Reconstruction to reiterate the doctrine of *Barron v. Baltimore*, that the Bill of Rights did not apply to the States, without so much as questioning whether the Fourteenth Amendment had any effect on the continued validity of that principle. E.g., Walker v. Sauvinet, 92 U.S. 90; see generally Morrison, Does the Fourteenth Amendment Incorporate the Bill of Rights? The Judicial Interpretation, 2 Stan.L.Rev. 140 (1949).

and case-for-case, or ignored. Then the Court merely declares that the clause in question is "in" rather than "out."

. . .

The Court has justified neither its starting place nor its conclusion. . . .

II.

. . . When a criminal defendant contends that his state conviction lacked "due process of law," the question before this Court, in my view, is whether he was denied any element of fundamental procedural fairness. Believing, as I do, that due process is an evolving concept and that old principles are subject to reevaluation in light of later experience, I think it appropriate to deal on its merits with the question whether Louisiana denied appellant due process of law when it tried him for simple assault without a jury. . . .

In sum, there is a wide range of views on the desirability of trial by jury, and on the ways to make it most effective when it is used; there is also considerable variation from State to State in local conditions such as the size of the criminal caseload, the ease or difficulty of summoning jurors, and other trial conditions bearing on fairness. . . . [This situation should invoke] the celebrated dictum of Mr. Justice Brandeis [that it is]

"one of the happy incidents of the federal system that a single courageous State may, if its citizens choose, serve as a laboratory. . . ." New State Ice Co. v. Liebmann, 285 U.S. 262, 280, 311 (dissenting opinion).

This Court, other courts, and the political process are available to correct any experiments in criminal procedure that prove fundamentally unfair to defendants. . . . [I]nstead, and quite without reason, the Court has chosen to impose upon every State one means of trying criminal cases; it is a good means, but it is not the only fair means, and it is not demonstrably better than the alternatives States might devise.

I would affirm the judgment of the Supreme Court of Louisiana.

INCORPORATION AND THE JURY TRIAL CASES

Prior to *Duncan* it had been assumed that the jury trial guaranteed in the sixth and seventh amendments was the traditional unanimous jury of twelve. Footnote 30 in *Duncan* opened the door to reconsideration of that assumption. The results are worth reporting.

In Williams v. Florida, 399 U.S. 78 (1970), the Court upheld as consistent with the sixth amendment, as made applicable to the states through the fourteenth, a state law permitting conviction by a unanimous jury of six in all non-capital criminal cases. Justice Harlan, concurring, accused the Court of diluting "a federal guarantee in order to reconcile the logic of 'incorporation,' the 'jot-for-jot and case-for-case' application of the federal right to the States, with the reality of federalism. Can one doubt that had Congress tried to undermine the common law right to trial by jury before *Duncan* came on the books the history today recited would have barred such action? Can we expect repeat performances when this Court is called upon to give definition and meaning to other federal guarantees that have been 'incorporated'?" Justice Black, concurring, responded: "Today's decision is in no way attributable to any desire to dilute the Sixth Amendment in order more easily to apply it to the States, but follows solely as a necessary consequence of our duty to re-examine prior decisions to reach the correct constitutional meaning in each case." In Colgrove v. Battin, 413 U.S. 149 (1973), the Court applied the logic of *Williams* in holding that a jury of six persons in a civil case in the federal courts was not in violation of the seventh amendment. However, in Ballew v. Georgia, 435 U.S. 223 (1978), the Court held that the constitutional minimum size for a jury in non-petty criminal offenses was six, invalidating a state statute providing for conviction by unanimous vote of a jury of five.

In Apodaca v. Oregon, 406 U.S. 404 (1972), the Court upheld an Oregon statute providing for conviction in criminal cases by a vote of 10 persons out of a jury of twelve. Justice Powell repeated Justice Harlan's objection in *Williams* that the Court was diluting the scope of sixth amendment rights in the federal courts in order to avoid imposing "unnecessarily rigid" requirements on the states. Most recently in Burch v. Louisiana, 441 U.S. 130 (1979), the Court held invalid a statute providing for trial "before a jury of six persons, five of whom must concur to render a verdict." The Court recognized that "having already departed from the strictly historical requirements of jury trial, it is inevitable that lines must be drawn somewhere if the substance of jury trial right is to be preserved." The Court left open the question whether it would be consistent with the sixth amendment to provide for a nonunanimous vote by any jury of less than twelve but more than six.

DUE PROCESS AS A LIMITATION ON PROCEDURES NOT FORBIDDEN BY THE BILL OF RIGHTS

Justice Black substantially won his argument that the fourteenth amendment should be construed to make the Bill of Rights applicable to the states. As the following case indicates, however, he lost his battle to confine Court review of state procedures to the "specific" provisions of the Bill of Rights.

IN RE WINSHIP, 397 U.S. 358 (1970). In a case addressing what process must be accorded in juvenile proceedings, the Court examined the requirement that proof of criminal charges be beyond a reasonable doubt, concluding that it "plays a vital role in the American scheme of criminal procedure" and that its use "is indispensable to command the respect and confidence of the community in applications of the criminal law." based on such judgments as to the importance of the standard, the Court said:

"Lest there remain any doubt about the constitutional stature of the reasonable-doubt standard, we explicitly hold that the Due Process Clause protects the accused against conviction except upon proof beyond a reasonable doubt of every fact necessary to constitute the crime with which he is charged."

Justice Harlan concurred in the opinion and judgment. Justice Black dissented at length, opening his opinion with the following:

"... The Court has never clearly held ... that proof beyond a reasonable doubt is either expressly or impliedly commanded by any provision of the Constitution. The Bill of Rights, which in my view is made fully applicable to the States by the Fourteenth Amendment, see Adamson v. California, 332 U.S. 46, 71–75 (1947) (dissenting opinion), does by express language provide for, among other things, a right to counsel in criminal trials, a right to indictment, and the right of a defendant to be informed of the nature of the charges against him. And in two places the Constitution provides for trial by jury, but nowhere in that document is there any statement that conviction of crime requires proof of guilt beyond a reasonable doubt. The Constitution thus goes into some detail to spell out what kind of trial a defendant charged with crime should have, and I believe the Court has no power to add to or subtract from the procedures set forth by the Founders. I realize that it is far easier to substitute individual judges' ideas of 'fairness' for the fairness prescribed by the Constitution, but I shall not at any time surrender my belief that that document itself should be our guide, not our own concept of what is fair, decent, and right. That this old 'shock-the-conscience' test is what the Court is relying on, rather than the words of the Constitution, is clearly enough revealed by the reference of the majority to 'fair treatment' and to the statement by the dissenting judges in the New York Court of Appeals that failure to require proof beyond a reasonable doubt amounts to a 'lack of fundamental fairness.' As I have said time and time again, I prefer to put my faith in the words of the written Constitution itself rather than to rely on the shifting, day-to-day standards of fairness of individual judges."[a]

More recently, Court holdings that fourteenth amendment due process limits state procedures not forbidden by the Bill of Rights have provoked disagreement within the Court about what methodology the Court should employ in defining the additional prohibitions. For example, having previously held in Browning–Ferris Industries v. Kelco Disposal, Inc., 492 U.S. 257 (1989), that the Eighth Amendment ban on excessive fines does not apply to punitive damage awards in cases between private parties, the Court decided that the Due Process Clause does circumscribe state procedures for awarding punitive damages. Pacific Mutual Life Insurance Co. v. Haslip, 499 U.S. 1 (1991).

Justice Blackmun's majority opinion upheld Alabama's traditional common-law method of assessing punitive damages, under which the decisions of court-instructed juries were subject to trial and appellate review, but only after inquiring whether that method was "inherently unfair." Furthermore, even though "well established before the Fourteenth Amendment was enacted" and with "[n]othing in that Amendment's text or history indicat[ing] an intention on the part of its drafters to overturn the prevailing method[,]" "general concerns of reasonableness and adequate guidance from the court when the case is tried to a jury properly enter into the constitutional calculus."

Justice Scalia's concurrence objected to the Court's "fairness" or "reasonableness" inquiry. In his view, "jury-assessed punitive damages" are "categorically" valid, because no Bill of Rights provision is implicated and the Due Process Clause itself is not violated so long as a particular procedure is "a traditional one." Asserting that "it is not for the Members of this Court to decide from time to time whether a process approved by the legal traditions of our people is 'due process' . . . ," he concluded that "traditional practice (unless contrary to the Bill of Rights) is conclusive of 'fundamental fairness.' "

Justice Kennedy concurred separately, agreeing "that the judgment of history should govern the outcome" in this case, but disagreeing with Justice Scalia "that widespread adherence to a historical practice always forecloses further inquiry when a party challenges an ancient institution or procedure as violative of due process." Justice O'Connor's even more emphatic dissent said that "[i]t does not matter that the system has been around for a long time, or

---

a. In Apprendi v. New Jersey, 530 U.S. 466 (2000), the Court, invoking *Winship*, held, 5–4, that the Due Process Clause of the Fourteenth Amendment requires that "[o]ther than the fact of a prior conviction, any fact that increases the penalty for a crime beyond the prescribed statutory maximum must be submitted to a jury, and proved beyond a reasonable doubt." Accordingly, a state statute that permitted a trial judge, at sentencing, to extend the prison term of a defendant convicted of a crime carrying a maximum 10-year sentence beyond 10 years on a finding, by only a preponderance of the evidence, that the defendant had acted with a purpose to intimidate because of bias, was unconstitutional for not allowing a jury determination of the finding and for not requiring proof of the hate crime purpose "beyond a reasonable doubt." See also Blakely v. Washington, ___ U.S. ___ (2004); United States v. Booker, ___ U.S. ___ (2005).

that the result in this particular case may not seem glaringly unfair." She responded to Justice Scalia as follows:

> "Circumstances are different than they were 200 years ago, and nothing in the Fourteenth Amendment requires us to blind ourselves to this fact.... Just the opposite is true. Due process demands that we possess some degree of confidence that the procedures employed to deprive persons of life, liberty, and property are capable of producing fair and reasonable results. When we lose that confidence, a change must be made."[b]

The separate opinions in Medina v. California, 505 U.S. 437 (1992), reflect a similar divergence of viewpoints. There the Court rejected a criminal defendant's due process claim that the State could not require him to carry the burden of proving his incompetence by a preponderance of evidence. Justice Kennedy's majority opinion said in part:

> "In the field of criminal law, we 'have defined the category of infractions that violate "fundamental fairness" very narrowly' based on the recognition that, '[b]eyond the specific guarantees enumerated in the Bill of Rights, the Due Process Clause has limited operation.' Dowling v. United States, 493 U.S. 342 ... (1990);.... The Bill of Rights speaks in explicit terms to many aspects of criminal procedure, and the expansion of those constitutional guarantees under the open-ended rubric of the Due Process Clause invites undue interference with both considered legislative judgments and the careful balance that the Constitution strikes between liberty and order...."

> . . .

> "... [B]ecause the States have considerable expertise in matters of criminal procedure and the criminal process is grounded in centuries of common-law tradition, it is appropriate to exercise substantial deference to legislative judgments in this area....

> "Based on our review of the historical treatment of the burden of proof in competency proceedings, the operation of the challenged rule, and our precedents, we cannot say that the allocation of the burden of proof to a criminal defendant to prove incompetence 'offends some principle of justice so rooted in the traditions and conscience of our people as to be ranked as fundamental.' "

In particular, that review examined "[h]istorical practice"—deemed "probative of whether a procedural rule can be characterized as fundamental";

---

b. Compare with *Haslip* the Court's subsequent decision in Honda Motor Co. v. Oberg, 512 U.S. 415 (1994), invalidating under due process Oregon's denial of judicial review of the size of punitive damage awards. Noting that "[o]ur recent cases have recognized a substantive limit on the size of punitive damage awards" and that judicial review as a safeguard against excessive verdicts was a well-established common law tradition from which Oregon alone had deviated (and had done so without providing a substitute procedure), Justice Stevens observed for the majority in pertinent part:

"Oregon's abrogation of a well-established common law protection against arbitrary deprivations of property raises a presumption that its procedures violate the Due Process Clause.... [T]raditional practice provides a touchstone for constitutional analysis.... Because the basic procedural protections of the common law have been regarded as so fundamental, very few cases have arisen in which a party has complained of their denial. In fact, most of our Due Process decisions involve arguments that traditional protections provide too little protection and that additional safeguards are necessary to ensure compliance with the Constitution.... Pacific Mut. Life Ins. v. Haslip...."

For a discussion of the substantive due process limitations the Court has applied to the review of punitive damages awards, see Note, "Due Process Limitations on State Punitive Damages Awards," infra p. 534.

"[c]ontemporary practice"—regarded as "of limited relevance to the due process inquiry"; and "whether the rule transgresses any recognized principle of 'fundamental fairness' in operation."

Justice O'Connor concurred, joined by Justice Souter, rejecting any "intimation that the balancing of equities is inappropriate in evaluating whether state criminal procedures amount to due process." Though she "agree[d] with the Court that historical pedigree can give a procedural practice a presumption of constitutionality," she thought "the presumption must surely be rebuttable." She also said:

"... Against the historical status quo, I read the Court's opinion to allow some weight to be given countervailing considerations of fairness in operation.... Any less charitable reading of the Court's opinion would put it at odds with many of our criminal due process cases, in which we have required States to institute procedures that were neither required at common law nor explicitly commanded by the text of the Constitution...."

Justice Blackmun's dissent, joined by Justice Stevens, also "read" the majority "to acknowledge that ... the Court [is not relieved] from evaluating the underlying fairness of imposing the burden of proof of incompetency upon the defendant." In his view, "[b]ecause the *Due* Process Clause is not the *Some* Process Clause, ... it requires careful balancing of the individual and governmental interests at stake to determine what process is due."

"INCORPORATION"—ITS CURRENT SCOPE

Which portions of the Bill of Rights have been "incorporated" by the fourteenth amendment so as to be applicable against the states? The current situation is outlined below.

(1) **The First Amendment.** The Court has long applied to the states under the fourteenth amendment the same restrictions upon regulations relating to speech, religion, and association as it applies to the federal government under the first amendment. See, e.g., West Virginia State Board of Education v. Barnette, 319 U.S. 624 (1943); Everson v. Board of Education, 330 U.S. 1 (1947); Edwards v. South Carolina, 372 U.S. 229 (1963). For a case in which there was a dissent from the application of identical standards to the states as to the federal government, see Roth v. United States, 354 U.S. 476 (1957).

(2) **The Fourth Amendment.** *Arrest and Search.* That the fourth amendment applies to the states with the same coverage as it has with respect to the federal government was decided in Mapp v. Ohio, 367 U.S. 643 (1961), and Ker v. California, 374 U.S. 23 (1963).

(3) **The Fifth Amendment**

Indictment. The Court held in Hurtado v. California, 110 U.S. 516 (1884), that states could permit prosecutions on the basis of information filed by district attorneys rather than indictments by grand juries. In Alexander v. Louisiana, 405 U.S. 625 (1972), the Court in refusing to permit a male defendant to challenge an exemption of women from the grand jury, said: "Although the Due Process Clause guarantees petitioner a fair trial, it does not require the States to observe the Fifth Amendment's provision for presentment or indictment by a grand jury.... the Court has never held that federal concepts of a 'grand jury', binding on the federal courts under the Fifth Amendment, are obligatory for the States. Hurtado v. California...."

Double Jeopardy. In Benton v. Maryland, 395 U.S. 784 (1969), the Court held that charges of double jeopardy in state proceedings "must be judged not by the watered-down standard enunciated in Palko, but under this Court's interpretations of the Fifth Amendment double jeopardy provision." In Ashe v. Swenson, 397 U.S. 436 (1970), the Court held that the doctrine of collateral estoppel is included in the fifth amendment guaranty and made applicable to the states.

Privilege Against Self-incrimination. "[T]he Fifth Amendment's exception from compulsory self-incrimination is also protected by the Fourteenth Amendment against abridgment by the States." Malloy v. Hogan, 378 U.S. 1 (1964). See also Griffin v. California, 380 U.S. 609 (1965); Williams v. Florida, 399 U.S. 78 (1970); California v. Byers, 402 U.S. 424 (1971).

Taking of Property Without Just Compensation. The "taking" clause has long been held applicable to the states. In Penn Central Transportation Co. v. New York City, 438 U.S. 104 (1978), the Court said that "of course" the taking clause "is made applicable to the States through the Fourteenth Amendment," citing Chicago, B. & Q.R. Co. v. Chicago, 166 U.S. 226 (1897).

(4) The Sixth Amendment

Speedy Trial. Klopfer v. North Carolina, 386 U.S. 213, 223 (1967): "We hold here that the right to a speedy trial is as fundamental as any of the rights secured by the Sixth Amendment." The Court reversed an order under a state procedure which permitted the prosecutor to bring a case to trial at any time on his own motion.

Public Trial. The Court first held that the fourteenth amendment guaranteed to defendants a public trial in In re Oliver, 333 U.S. 257 (1948). In Estes v. Texas, 381 U.S. 532, 538 (1965), dealing with a state prosecution the Court said: "We start with the proposition that it is a 'public trial' that the Sixth Amendment guarantees to the 'accused.'"

Jury Trial. See Duncan v. Louisiana, 391 U.S. 145 (1968), supra.

Notice of Charge. "No principle of procedural due process is more clearly established than that notice of the specific charge, and a chance to be heard in a trial of the issues raised by that charge, if desired, are among the constitutional rights of every accused in a criminal proceeding in all courts, state or federal." Cole v. Arkansas, 333 U.S. 196, 201 (1948). See also In re Oliver, 333 U.S. 257 (1948); In re Gault, 387 U.S. 1, 31 (1967).

Confrontation of Witnesses. In Pointer v. Texas, 380 U.S. 400 (1965) the Court reversed a conviction where the transcript of the testimony of a witness whom the defendant had not had a fair opportunity to cross-examine was used at the trial. "We hold today that the Sixth Amendment's right of an accused to confront the witnesses against him is likewise a fundamental right and is made obligatory on the States by the Fourteenth Amendment." See also Parker v. Gladden, 385 U.S. 363 (1966).

Compulsory Process for Obtaining Witnesses. In Washington v. Texas, 388 U.S. 14 (1967), the Court reversed a conviction where the application of a state statute forbidding persons charged as principals, accomplices, or accessories in the same crime to be witnesses for each other deprived defendant of the testimony of the only other witness to the crime. "The right of an accused to have compulsory process for obtaining witnesses in his favor stands on no lesser footing than the other Sixth Amendment rights that we have previously held applicable to the States."

Right to Counsel. The Court first held that the sixth amendment guaranty of the right to counsel applied as such to the states through the Fourteenth Amendment in Gideon v. Wainwright, 372 U.S. 335 (1963).

(5) **The Seventh Amendment.** The Court held in Walker v. Sauvinet, 92 U.S. 90 (1875), that the fourteenth amendment did not require the states to provide a jury in civil cases. In Palko v. Connecticut, 302 U.S. 319, 324 (1937), the Court said that trial by jury in civil cases can be abolished altogether. This interpretation has not been modified and the states have been left free to construct their own systems for providing jury trial in civil cases.

(6) **The Eighth Amendment**

Bail. The Court has not decided whether the states are under federal constitutional constraints with reference to bail, but in Schilb v. Kuebel, 404 U.S. 357 (1971), it noted that "the Eighth Amendment's proscription of excessive bail has been assumed to have application to the states through the Fourteenth Amendment."

Excessive Fines. In Browning–Ferris Industries v. Kelco Disposal, Inc., 492 U.S. 257, 276 n. 22 (1989), the Court expressly declined to "decide whether the Eighth Amendment's prohibition on excessive fines applies to the several States through the Fourteenth Amendment. . . ."

Cruel and Unusual Punishment. In Robinson v. California, 370 U.S. 660, 667 (1962), the Court held that "a state law which imprisons a person (afflicted with the illness of narcotic addiction) as a criminal, even though he has never touched any narcotic drug within the State or been guilty of any irregular behavior there, inflicts a cruel and unusual punishment in violation of the Fourteenth Amendment." In Furman v. Georgia, 408 U.S. 238 (1972), the court held "that the imposition and carrying out of the death penalty in these cases constitutes cruel and unusual punishment in violation of the Eighth and Fourteenth Amendments."

CHAPTER 9

THE DUE PROCESS, CONTRACT, AND JUST COMPENSATION CLAUSES AND THE REVIEW OF THE REASONABLENESS OF LEGISLATION

SECTION 1.   ECONOMIC REGULATORY LEGISLATION

A.   THE RISE AND FALL OF DUE PROCESS

DUE PROCESS AS A RESTRAINT ON THE SUBSTANCE OF LEGISLATION

The due process clauses of the Fifth and Fourteenth Amendments presented two major initial problems of interpretation: (1) Were the clauses, like Magna Carta, intended only as a restraint upon the executive? Did they operate only to provide that the executive branch of the government shall operate in accordance with the common or statutory law in force? Or were they intended in the context of the United States to function as limitations upon the powers of Congress and of the state legislatures? (2) If they were intended to limit the legislatures, did they serve to restrain only the enactment of procedures which are not "due" or "fair"? Or did they serve to impose restraints on the substance of legislation?

In two cases arising under the fifth amendment prior to the Civil War the Court almost casually gave answers to these questions. In 1856 in Murray's Lessee v. Hoboken Land & Improvement Co., 59 U.S. (18 How.) 272, 276 (1855), the Court answered the first question: "It is manifest that it was not left to the legislative power to enact any process which might be devised. The article is a restraint on the legislative as well as on the executive and judicial powers of government, and cannot be so constructed as to leave congress free to make any process 'due process of law' by its mere will." In 1857 in Dred Scott v. Sandford, 60 U.S. (19 How.) 393, 450 (1856), the Court with equal casualness gave a substantive content to the clause: "And an Act of Congress which deprives a citizen of the United States of his liberty or property, merely because he came himself or brought his property into a particular Territory of the United States, and who had committed no offense against the laws, could hardly be dignified with the name of due process of law."

In the *Slaughter–House Cases* in 1872, set out supra p. 474, the Court summarily rejected a challenge to a law granting a monopoly based on due process, in the face of a dissent by Justice Bradley arguing that "a law which prohibits a large class of citizens from adopting a lawful employment, or from following a lawful employment previously adopted, does deprive them of liberty as well as property, without due process of law. Their right of choice is a portion of their liberty; their occupation is their property."

murray's Lessee

The Court addressed the issues again in 1878 in Davidson v. New Orleans, 96 U.S. 97. The Court upheld an application of a Louisiana statute providing for a special assessment against property for drainage purposes. In discussing the meaning of the due process clause the Court said: "It is easy to see that when the great Barons of England wrung from King John, at the point of the sword, the concession that neither their lives nor their property should be disposed of by the Crown, except as provided by the law of the land, they meant by 'law of the land' the ancient and customary laws of the English people, or laws enacted by the Parliament of which those Barons were a controlling element. It was not in their minds, therefore, to protect themselves against the enactment of laws by the Parliament of England. But when, in the year of grace 1866, there is placed in the Constitution of the United States a declaration that 'No State shall deprive any person of life, liberty, or property without due process of law,' can a State make anything due process of law which, by its own legislation, it chooses to declare such? To affirm this is to hold that the prohibition to the States is of no avail, or has no application where the invasion of private rights is affected under the forms of state legislation. It seems to us that a statute which declared in terms, and without more, that the full and exclusive title of a described piece of land, which is now in A, shall be and is hereby vested in B, would, if effectual, deprive A of his property without due process of law, within the meaning of the constitutional provision. . . ."

THE FLOWERING OF ECONOMIC DUE PROCESS

In the first few economic regulation cases to come before it under the fourteenth amendment the Court indicated a very limited scope for due process review. A challenge to a statutory monopoly was rejected in the *Slaughter-House Cases,* supra. In Munn v. Illinois, 94 U.S. 113 (1876), the Court upheld an Illinois statute fixing maximum charges for the storage of grain in warehouses. The Court concluded that such warehouses were sufficiently related to the public interest that they would be governed by the common law rule requiring charges to be reasonable. Hence, whatever might be the case with respect to merely private contracts this type could be regulated and the determination as to reasonableness of the price could be made legislatively rather than judicially. "Rights of property which have been created by the common law cannot be taken away without due process; but the law itself, as a rule of conduct, may be changed at the will, or even at the whim, of the legislature, unless prevented by constitutional limitations. Indeed, the great office of statutes is to remedy defects in the common law as they are developed, and to adapt it to the changes of time and circumstances. . . . We know that this is a power which may be abused; but that is no argument against its existence. For protection against abuses by Legislatures the people must resort to the polls, not the courts." Justices Field and Strong dissented.

Between 1877 and 1900, the Court gradually broadened its interpretation of the meaning of the due process clause with reference to economic regulations. During this period the membership of the Court changed completely—by 1898 not a single judge remained who had sat at the time of *Munn v. Illinois.* The expressed opinions of the leaders of the bar helped create a favorable climate for this broadened interpretation. See Twiss, *Lawyers and the Constitution* (1942).

A major step was the decision that corporations were "persons" within the meaning of the fourteenth amendment and hence able to claim under the due process and equal protection clauses. The point was first argued to the Court, but not decided, in San Mateo County v. Southern Pacific R. Co., 116 U.S. 138

(1885). It was decided without argument or opinion in Santa Clara County v. Southern Pacific R. Co., 118 U.S. 394 (1886) when Chief Justice Waite announced: "The Court does not wish to hear argument on the question whether the provision in the Fourteenth Amendment to the Constitution, which forbids a State to deny to any person within its jurisdiction the equal protection of the laws, applies to these Corporations. We are all of the opinion that it does." For the story behind this decision, see Graham, *The "Conspiracy Theory" of the Fourteenth Amendment,* 47 Yale L.J. 371 (1938), 48 id. 171 (1938).

The Court's more expansive view was signaled in Mugler v. Kansas, 123 U.S. 623 (1887). While it upheld a state law prohibiting the manufacture and sale of alcoholic beverages, it stated that not every regulatory statute "is to be accepted as a legitimate exertion of the police powers of the State. There are, of necessity, limits beyond which legislation cannot rightfully go.... The courts are not bound by mere forms, nor are they to be misled by mere pretenses. They are at liberty—indeed, are under a solemn duty—to look at the substance of things, whenever they enter upon the inquiry whether the Legislature has transcended the limits of its authority. If therefore, a statute purporting to have been enacted to protect the public health, the public morals, or the public safety, has no real or substantial relations to those objects, or is a palpable invasion of rights secured by the fundamental law, it is the duty of the courts to so adjudge, and thereby give effect to the Constitution."

The first major use of the due process clause to invalidate state economic regulations arose in the context of state regulation of railroad rates. In Chicago, M. & St. P.R. Co. v. Minnesota, 134 U.S. 418 (1890), the Court held unconstitutional a Minnesota statute authorizing a state commission to fix rates to be charged by railroads and forbidding any judicial review of the rates set. The Court said that under the due process clause the railroad companies were entitled to a judicial hearing on the question whether the rates set were reasonable. "The question of the reasonableness of a rate of charge for transportation by a railroad company, involving as it does the element of reasonableness both as regards the company and as regards the public, is eminently a question for judicial investigation, requiring due process of law for its determination. If the company is deprived of the power of charging reasonable rates for the use of its property, and such deprivation takes place in the absence of an investigation by judicial machinery, it is deprived of the lawful use of its property, and thus, in substance and effect, of the property itself, without due process of law and in violation of the Constitution of the United States...."

In Smyth v. Ames, 169 U.S. 466, 546 (1898) the Court established a constitutional standard to be applied in reviewing rate regulations: "We hold ... that the basis of all calculations as to the reasonableness of rates to be charged by a corporation maintaining a highway under legislative sanction must be the fair value of the property being used by it for the convenience of the public."[a]

ALLGEYER v. LOUISIANA, 165 U.S. 578 (1897). The Court held that under the due process clause Louisiana could not make it a misdemeanor for a resident to use the mails to enter into a contract in New York with an insurance company not licensed to do business in Louisiana to insure goods

---

a. The long and complicated history of the attempt by the courts to apply this doctrine is summarized in Cook, *History of Rate–Determination Under Due Process Clauses,* 11 U.Chi.L.Rev. 297 (1944); Jourolmon, *The Life and Death of Smyth v. Ames,* 18 Tenn.L.Rev. 347, 663, 756 (1944–45); Dakin, *The Changing Nature of Public Utility Rate Regulation: Just Compensation, Due Process, and Equal Protection,* 36 Tulane L.Rev. 401, 711 (1962).

shipped from Louisiana to Europe. The court said: "The Supreme Court of Louisiana says that the act of writing within that State the letter of notification, was an act therein done to effect an insurance on property then in the State, in a marine insurance company which had not complied with its laws, and such act was, therefore, prohibited by the statute. As so construed we think the statute is a violation of the Fourteenth Amendment of the Federal Constitution, in that it deprives the defendants of their liberty without due process of law. The statute which forbids such act does not become due process of law, because it is inconsistent with the provisions of the Constitution of the Union. The liberty mentioned in that amendment means not only the right of the citizen to be free from the mere physical restraint of his person, as by incarceration, but the term is deemed to embrace the right of the citizen to be free in the enjoyment of all his faculties; to be free to use them in all lawful ways; to live and work where he will; to earn his livelihood by any lawful calling; to pursue any livelihood or avocation, and for that purpose to enter into all contracts which may be proper, necessary and essential to his carrying out to a successful conclusion the purposes above mentioned."

Lochner v. New York

198 U.S. 45, 25 S.Ct. 539, 49 L.Ed. 937 (1905).

Mr. Justice Peckham ... **delivered the opinion of the Court**:

The indictment, it will be seen, charges that the plaintiff in error violated the 110th section of article 8, chapter 415, of the Laws of 1897, known as the labor law of the state of New York, in that he wrongfully and unlawfully required and permitted an employee working for him to work more than sixty hours in one week....

It is not an act merely fixing the number of hours which shall constitute a legal day's work, but an absolute prohibition upon the employer permitting, under any circumstances, more than ten hours' work to be done in his establishment. The employee may desire to earn the extra money which would arise from his working more than the prescribed time, but this statute forbids the employer from permitting the employee to earn it.

The statute necessarily interferes with the right of contract between the employer and employees, concerning the number of hours in which the latter may labor in the bakery of the employer. The general right to make a contract in relation to his business is part of the liberty of the individual protected by the 14th Amendment of the Federal Constitution. Allgeyer v. Louisiana, 165 U.S. 578. Under that provision no state can deprive any person of life, liberty, or property without due process of law. The right to purchase or to sell labor is part of the liberty protected by this amendment, unless there are circumstances which exclude the right. There are, however, certain powers, existing in the sovereignty of each state in the Union, somewhat vaguely termed police powers, the exact description and limitation of which have not been attempted by the courts. Those powers, broadly stated, and without, at present, any attempt at a more specific limitation, relate to the safety, health, morals, and general welfare of the public. Both property and liberty are held on such reasonable conditions as may be imposed by the governing power of the state in the exercise of those powers, and with such conditions the 14th Amendment was not designed to interfere. Mugler v. Kansas, 123 U.S. 623....

Therefore, when the state, by its legislature, in the assumed exercise of its police powers, has passed an act which seriously limits the right to labor or the right of contract in regard to their means of livelihood between persons who are *sui juris* (both employer and employee), it becomes of great importance to determine which shall prevail,—the right of the individual to labor for such time as he may choose, or the right of the state to prevent the individual from laboring, or from entering into any contract to labor, beyond a certain time prescribed by the state.

This court has recognized the existence and upheld the exercise of the police powers of the states in many cases which might fairly be considered as border ones, and it has, in the course of its determination of questions regarding the asserted invalidity of such statutes, on the ground of their violation of the rights secured by the Federal Constitution, been guided by rules of a very liberal nature, the application of which has resulted, in numerous instances, in upholding the validity of state statutes thus assailed. Among the later cases where the state law has been upheld by this court is that of Holden v. Hardy, 169 U.S. 366. A provision in the act of the legislature of Utah was there under consideration, the act limiting the employment of workmen in all underground mines or workings, to eight hours per day, "except in cases of emergency, where life or property is in imminent danger." It also limited the hours of labor in smelting and other institutions for the reduction or refining of ores or metals to eight hours per day, except in like cases of emergency. The act was held to be a valid exercise of the police powers of the state....

It must, of course, be conceded that there is a limit to the valid exercise of the police power by the state.... In every case that comes before this court, therefore, where legislation of this character is concerned, and where the protection of the Federal Constitution is sought, the question necessarily arises: Is this a fair, reasonable, and appropriate exercise of the police power of the state, or is it an unreasonable, unnecessary, and arbitrary interference with the right of the individual to his personal liberty, or to enter into those contracts in relation to labor which may seem to him appropriate or necessary for the support of himself and his family? Of course the liberty of contract relating to labor includes both parties to it. The one has as much right to purchase as the other to sell labor.

This is not a question of substituting the judgment of the court for that of the legislature. If the act be within the power of the state it is valid, although the judgment of the court might be totally opposed to the enactment of such a law. But the question would still remain: Is it within the police power of the state? and that question must be answered by the court.

The question whether this act is valid as a labor law, pure and simple, may be dismissed in a few words. There is no reasonable ground for interfering with the liberty of persons or the right of free contract, by determining the hours of labor, in the occupation of a baker.... Viewed in the light of a purely labor law with no reference whatever to the question of health, we think that a law like the one before us involves neither the safety, the morals, nor the welfare of the public, and that the interest of the public is not in the slightest degree affected by such an act. The law must be upheld, if at all, as a law pertaining to the health of the individual engaged in the occupation of a baker....

We think the limit of the police power has been reached and passed in this case. There is, in our judgment, no reasonable foundation for holding this to be necessary or appropriate as a health law to safeguard the public health, or the health of the individuals who are following the trade of a baker....

It is also urged, pursuing the same line of argument, that it is to the interest of the state that its population should be strong and robust, and therefore any legislation which may be said to tend to make people healthy must be valid as health laws, enacted under the police power. If this be a valid argument and a justification for this kind of legislation, it follows that the protection of the Federal Constitution from undue interference with liberty of person and freedom of contract is visionary, wherever the law is sought to be justified as a valid exercise of the police power. Scarcely any law but might find shelter under such assumptions, and conduct, properly so called, as well as contract, would come under the restrictive sway of the legislature. Not only the hours of employees, but the hours of employers, could be regulated, and doctors, lawyers, scientists, all professional men, as well as athletes and artisans, could be forbidden to fatigue their brains and bodies by prolonged hours of exercise, lest the fighting strength of the state be impaired. We mention these extreme cases because the contention is extreme. We do not believe in the soundness of the views which uphold this law.... Statutes of the nature of that under review, limiting the hours in which grown and intelligent men may labor to earn their living, are mere meddlesome interferences with the rights of the individual, and they are not saved from condemnation by the claim that they are passed in the exercise of the police power and upon the subject of the health of the individual whose rights are interfered with, unless there be some fair ground, reasonable in and of itself, to say that there is material danger to the public health, or to the health of the employees, if the hours of labor are not curtailed....

It is impossible for us to shut our eyes to the fact that many of the laws of this character, while passed under what is claimed to be the police power for the purpose of protecting the public health or welfare, are, in reality, passed from other motives. We are justified in saying so when, from the character of the law and the subject upon which it legislates, it is apparent that the public health or welfare bears but the most remote relation to the law. The purpose of a statute must be determined from the natural and legal effect of the language employed; and whether it is or is not repugnant to the Constitution of the United States must be determined from the natural effect of such statutes when put into operation, and not from their proclaimed purpose....

It is manifest to us that the limitation of the hours of labor as provided for in this section of the statute under which the indictment was found, and the plaintiff in error convicted, has no such direct relation to, and no such substantial effect upon, the health of the employee, as to justify us in regarding the section as really a health law. It seems to us that the real object and purpose were simply to regulate the hours of labor between the master and his employees (all being men, *sui juris*), in a private business, not dangerous in any degree to morals, or in any real and substantial degree to the health of the employees. Under such circumstances the freedom of master and employee to contract with each other in relation to their employment, and in defining the same, cannot be prohibited or interfered with, without violating the Federal Constitution.

The judgment of the Court of Appeals of New York, as well as that of the Supreme Court and of the County Court of Oneida County, must be reversed and the case remanded to the County Court for further proceedings not inconsistent with this opinion.

Reversed.

Mr. Justice Harlan (with whom Mr. Justice White and Mr. Justice Day concurred) dissenting:

. . . .

I take it to be firmly established that what is called the liberty of contract may, within certain limits, be subjected to regulations designed and calculated to promote the general welfare, or to guard the public health, the public morals, or the public safety. "The liberty secured by the Constitution of the United States to every person within its jurisdiction does not import," this court has recently said, "an absolute right in each person to be at all times and in all circumstances wholly freed from restraint. There are manifold restraints to which every person is necessarily subject for the common good." . . .

Restraints to personal liberty

Granting, then, that there is a liberty of contract which cannot be violated even under the sanction of direct legislative enactment, but assuming, as according to settled law we may assume, that such liberty of contract is subject to such regulations as the state may reasonably prescribe for the common good and the well-being of society, what are the conditions under which the judiciary may declare such regulations to be in excess of legislative authority and void? Upon this point there is no room for dispute; for the rule is universal that a legislative enactment, Federal or state, is never to be disregarded or held invalid unless it be, beyond question, plainly and palpably in excess of legislative power. . . . If there be doubt as to the validity of the statute, that doubt must therefore be resolved in favor of its validity and the courts must keep their hands off leaving the legislature to meet the responsibility for unwise legislation. If the end which the legislature seeks to accomplish be one to which its power extends, and if the means employed to that end, although not the wisest or best, are yet not plainly and palpably unauthorized by law, then the court cannot interfere. In other words, when the validity of a statute is questioned, the burden of proof, so to speak, is upon those who assert it to be unconstitutional. McCulloch v. Maryland, 4 Wheat. 316, 421.

Let these principles be applied to the present case. By the statute in question it is provided that "no employee shall be required, or permitted, to work in a biscuit, bread, or cake bakery, or confectionery establishment, more than sixty hours in any one week, or more than ten hours in any one day, unless for the purpose of making a shorter work day on the last day of the week; nor more hours in any one week than will make an average of ten hours per day for the number of days during such week in which such employee shall work."

It is plain that this statute was enacted in order to protect the physical well-being of those who work in bakery and confectionery establishments. It may be that the statute had its origin, in part, in the belief that employers and employees in such establishments were not upon an equal footing, and that the necessities of the latter often compelled them to submit to such exactions as unduly taxed their strength. Be this as it may, the statute must be taken as expressing the belief of the people of New York that, as a general rule, and in the case of the average man, labor in excess of sixty hours during a week in such establishments may endanger the health of those who thus labor. Whether or not this be wise legislation it is not the province of the court to inquire. Under our systems of government the courts are not concerned with the wisdom or policy of legislation. So that, in determining the question of power to interfere with liberty of contract, the court may inquire whether the means devised by the state are germane to an end which may be lawfully accomplished and have a real or substantial relation to the protection of health, as involved in the daily work of the persons, male and female, engaged in bakery and confectionery establishments. But when this inquiry is entered upon I find it impossible, in view of common experience, to say that there is here no real or substantial relation between the means employed by the state and the end sought to be accomplished by its legislation. Mugler v. Kansas, 123 U.S. 623,

Is for health of laborer

661. Nor can I say that the statute has no appropriate or direct connection with that protection to health which each state owes to her citizens ... or that it is not promotive of the health of the employees in question ... or that the regulation prescribed by the state is utterly unreasonable and extravagant or wholly arbitrary.... Still less can I say that the statute, is, beyond question, a plain, palpable invasion of rights, secured by the fundamental law.... Therefore I submit that this court will transcend its functions if it assumes to annul the statute of New York. It must be remembered that this statute does not apply to all kinds of business. It applies only to work in bakery and confectionery establishments, in which, as all know, the air constantly breathed by workmen is not as pure and healthful as that to be found in some other establishments or out of doors.

. . .

Mr. Justice Holmes dissenting:

I regret sincerely that I am unable to agree with the judgment in this case, and that I think it my duty to express my dissent.

This case is decided upon an economic theory which a large part of the country does not entertain. If it were a question whether I agreed with that theory, I should desire to study it further and long before making up my mind. But I do not conceive that to be my duty, because I strongly believe that my agreement or disagreement has nothing to do with the right of a majority to embody their opinions in law. It is settled by various decisions of this court that state constitutions and state laws may regulate life in many ways which we as legislators might think as injudicious, or if you like as tyrannical, as this, and which, equally with this, interfere with the liberty to contract. Sunday laws and usury laws are ancient examples. A more modern one is the prohibition of lotteries. The liberty of the citizen to do as he likes so long as he does not interfere with the liberty of others to do the same, which has been a shibboleth for some well-known writers, is interfered with by school laws, by the Postoffice, by every state or municipal institution which takes his money for purposes thought desirable, whether he likes it or not. The 14th Amendment does not enact Mr. Herbert Spencer's Social Statics. The other day we sustained the Massachusetts vaccination law. Jacobson v. Massachusetts, 197 U.S. 11. United States and state statutes and decisions cutting down the liberty to contract by way of combination are familiar to this court. Northern Securities Co. v. United States, 193 U.S. 197. Two years ago we upheld the prohibition of sales of stock on margins, or for future delivery, in the Constitution of California. Otis v. Parker, 187 U.S. 606. The decision sustaining an eight-hour law for miners is still recent. Holden v. Hardy, 169 U.S. 366. Some of these laws embody convictions or prejudices which judges are likely to share. Some may not. But a Constitution is not intended to embody a particular economic theory, whether of paternalism and the organic relation of the citizen to the state or of *laissez faire*. It is made for people of fundamentally differing views, and the accident of our finding certain opinions natural and familiar, or novel, and even shocking, ought not to conclude our judgment upon the question whether statutes embodying them conflict with the Constitution of the United States.

General propositions do not decide concrete cases. The decision will depend on a judgment or intuition more subtle than any articulate major premise. But I think that the proposition just stated, if it is accepted, will carry us far toward the end. Every opinion tends to become a law. I think that the word "liberty," in the 14th Amendment, is perverted when it is held to prevent the natural outcome of a dominant opinion, unless it can be said that a rational and fair man necessarily would admit that the statute proposed would infringe fundamental principles as they have been understood by the traditions of our people and our law. It does not need research to show that no such sweeping condemnation can be passed upon the statute before us. A reasonable man might think it a proper measure on the score of health. Men whom I certainly could not pronounce unreasonable would uphold it as a first instalment of a general regulation of the hours of work. Whether in the latter aspect it would be open to the charge of inequality I think it unnecessary to discuss.

THE POST–LOCHNER DEVELOPMENTS

(1) Liberty of Contract and Labor Legislation.

Maximum hours. In Muller v. Oregon, 208 U.S. 412 (1908), the Court upheld the validity of a statute forbidding the employment of women in factories or laundries more than 10 hours per day as applied to a laundry. The Court distinguished *Lochner* on the ground that the state had a stronger interest in regulating the hours of work of women than of men. The physical differences between women and men were emphasized and the Court said that "history discloses the fact that woman has always been dependent upon man." The Court, in taking judicial notice of the general belief that "woman's physical structure, and the functions she performs in consequence thereof, justify special legislation restricting or qualifying the conditions under which she should be permitted to toil," relied on a brief filed in the Court by Mr. Louis D. (later Justice) Brandeis that included a large collection of opinions from non-judicial sources.[a] It then said: "Constitutional questions . . . are not settled by even a consensus of present public opinion, for it is the peculiar value of a written constitution that it places in unchanging form limitations upon legislative action, and thus gives a permanence and stability to popular government which otherwise would be lacking. At the same time, when a question of fact is debated and debatable, and the extent to which a special constitutional limitation goes is affected by the truth in respect to that fact, a widespread and long continued belief concerning it is worthy of consideration." Several years later, without mentioning *Lochner,* the Court upheld a law providing a maximum 10–hour day for factory workers of both sexes that also permitted up to three hours a day overtime at time-and-a-half rate. Bunting v. Oregon, 243 U.S. 426 (1917).

"Yellow–Dog" Contracts. In Adair v. United States, 208 U.S. 161 (1908) and Coppage v. Kansas, 236 U.S. 1 (1915), the Court held invalid federal and state legislation forbidding employers to require employees to agree not to become or remain members of any labor organizations during the period of their employment. In *Coppage* the Court said: "An interference with this liberty [to make contracts] so serious as that now under consideration, and so disturbing of equality of right, must be deemed to be arbitrary, unless it be supportable as a reasonable exercise of the police power of the State." The Court went on to reject the argument of the state that such legislation was necessary to protect the interests of employees who were not financially as able to be independent in making contracts as employers, saying: "[S]ince it is self-evident that, unless all things are held in common, some persons must have more property than others, it is from the nature of things impossible to uphold

---

a. The famous "Brandeis Brief" has been lauded as introducing the Court "to a new technique in the weighing of constitutional issues. This occurred when Mr. Louis D. Brandeis handed the Court . . . his famous brief, three pages of which were devoted to a statement of the constitutional principles involved and 113 pages of which were devoted to the presentation of facts and statistics, backed by scientific authorities, to show the evil effects of too long hours on women, 'the mothers of the race'." Johnson, *Social Planning Under the Constitution,* 2 Selected Essays (1938) 131, 145.

freedom of contract and the right of private property without at the same time recognizing as legitimate those inequalities of fortune that are the necessary result of the exercise of those rights."

Minimum Wages. Adkins v. Children's Hosp., 261 U.S. 525 (1923), involved an Act of Congress prescribing minimum wages for women and children in the District of Columbia. The Court held the statute invalid when challenged by a hospital that employed women at lower than the minimum rate and by a woman elevator operator who was discharged by her employer to avoid the penalties of the act. The Court prefaced its discussion by saying: "There is, of course, no such thing as absolute freedom of contract. It is subject to a great variety of restraints. But freedom of contract is, nevertheless, the general rule and restraint the exception; and the exercise of legislative authority to abridge it can be justified only by the existence of exceptional circumstances." In distinguishing Muller v. Oregon, the Court said:

"But the ancient inequality of the sexes, otherwise than physical, as suggested in the *Muller* case, has continued 'with diminishing intensity.' In view of the great—not to say revolutionary—changes which have taken place since that utterance, in the contractual, political and civil status of women, culminating in the Nineteenth Amendment, it is not unreasonable to say that these differences have now come almost, if not quite, to the vanishing point. In this aspect of the matter, while the physical differences must be recognized in appropriate cases, and legislation fixing hours or conditions of work may properly take them into account, we cannot accept the doctrine that women of mature age, sui juris, require or may be subjected to restrictions upon their liberty of contract which could not lawfully be imposed in the case of men under similar circumstances."

It then went on to say that the statute could not be justified as safeguarding the morals of women because it "cannot be shown that well paid women safeguard their morals more carefully than those who are poorly paid." It concluded that the real flaw in the statute was that "it exacts from the employer an arbitrary payment for a purpose and upon a basis having no causal connection with his business or the contract or the work the employee engages to do." This, the Court said, "is so clearly the product of a naked, arbitrary exercise of power that it cannot be allowed to stand under the Constitution of the United States."

Justice Holmes in dissent said: "It will need more than the Nineteenth Amendment to convince me that there are no differences between men and women, or that legislation cannot take those differences into account. I should not hesitate to take them into account if I thought it necessary to sustain this act.... But after Bunting v. Oregon, 243 U.S. 426, I had supposed that it was not necessary, and that Lochner v. New York, 198 U.S. 45, would be allowed a deserved repose."

(2) Liberty of Contract and Business Regulations Relating to Prices and Other Economic Issues.

Price Fixing. In Tyson & Bro.–United Theatre Ticket Offices v. Banton, 273 U.S. 418 (1927), the court held invalid a statute regulating the prices of theater tickets. The Court said "that the right of the owner to fix a price at which his property shall be sold or used is an inherent attribute of the property itself." Hence, the power to fix prices "does not exist in respect of merely private property or business ... but exists only where the business or the property involved has become 'affected with a public interest.'" A long line of cases developed marking out the distinction between ordinary businesses and those "affected with a public interest" and so subject to price regulations. See, e.g., Williams v. Standard Oil Co., 278 U.S. 235 (1929), holding invalid a state statute regulating the price of gasoline. For later modifications of this doctrine, see Nebbia v. New York, 291 U.S. 502 (1934), set out below.

Restrictions on Business Entry. The Court applied an approach similar to that in the price fixing cases with regard to legislation restricting entry into particular businesses. In New State Ice Co. v. Liebmann, 285 U.S. 262 (1932), it held invalid a statute requiring any person desiring to engage in the ice business to obtain a certificate of public convenience and necessity. It said that the question was "whether the business is so charged with a public use as to justify" the restriction. It also said: "Plainly, a regulation which has the effect of denying or unreasonably curtailing the common right to engage in a lawful private business, such as that under review, cannot be upheld consistent with the 14th Amendment."

(3) Regulations of Business Designed to Protect Public Health and Safety. Most business regulations that came before the court were upheld where the legislative objective was to protect public health and safety rather than to interfere with the free market. However, in some cases the Court held regulations invalid because they were not sufficiently related to the legislative objectives. In Weaver v. Palmer Bros. Co., 270 U.S. 402 (1926), e.g., the Court held invalid a statute completely forbidding the use of shoddy (cut up fabrics) in the manufacture of bedding and providing for the use of other second-hand materials and feathers only if sterilized. The parties conceded that shoddy could be made harmless by disinfection or sterilization and there was no evidence to show that sickness or disease had been caused by the use of shoddy. The Court recognized that state regulations designed to protect public health and to protect the public from deception were generally valid but held that this statute did not sufficiently serve those ends. The measure could not be sustained as a measure to protect health because sterilization would eliminate the danger. Nor could it be sustained as a measure to protect deception because the regulation provided for adequate notice to the public of the contents of the bedding. It then concluded: "The constitutional guarantees may not be made to yield to mere convenience ... The business here involved is legitimate and useful; and, while it is subject to all reasonable regulation, the absolute prohibition of the use of shoddy in the manufacture of comfortables is purely arbitrary and violates the due process clause of the Fourteenth Amendment."

Nebbia v. New York

291 U.S. 502, 54 S.Ct. 505, 78 L.Ed. 940 (1934).

Mr. Justice Roberts delivered the opinion of the Court.

. . .

[A New York statute provided for the fixing of maximum and minimum prices for the sale of milk. The legislature, after extensive hearings, had determined that economic conditions and destructive trade practices jeopardized an adequate milk supply at reasonable prices to consumers and producers and that price controls would help. Nebbia, owner of a grocery store, was convicted for selling milk at a price below the minimum fixed. He contended, inter alia, that the statute deprived him of due process of law. The Court upheld the law by a vote of 5 to 4. Excerpts from Justice Roberts' long opinion follow.]

[handwritten margin notes: selling milk below min price / & upheld statute]

The reports of our decisions abound with cases in which the citizen, individual or corporate, has vainly invoked the Fourteenth Amendment in resistance to necessary and appropriate exertion of the police power.

. . . .

But we are told that because the law essays to control prices it denies due process. . . . The argument runs that the public control of rates or prices is per se unreasonable and unconstitutional save as applied to businesses affected with a public interest; that a business so affected is one in which property is devoted to an enterprise of a sort which the public itself might appropriately undertake, or one whose owner relies on a public grant or franchise for the right to conduct the business, or in which he is bound to serve all who apply; in short, such as is commonly called a public utility; or a business in its nature a monopoly. The milk industry, it is said, possesses none of these characteristics, and therefore, not being affected with a public interest, its charges may not be controlled by the state. . . .

We may as well say at once that the dairy industry is not, in the accepted sense of the phrase, a public utility. We think the appellant is also right in asserting that there is in this case no suggestion of any monopoly or monopolistic practice. It goes without saying that those engaged in the business are in no way dependent upon public grants or franchises for the privilege of conducting their activities. But if, as must be conceded, the industry is subject to regulation in the public interest, what constitutional principle bars the state from correcting existing maladjustments by legislation touching prices? We think there is no such principle. The due process clause makes no mention of sales or of prices any more than it speaks of business or contracts or buildings or other incidents of property. The thought seems nevertheless to have persisted that there is something peculiarly sacrosanct about the price one may charge for what he makes or sells, and that, however able to regulate other elements of manufacture or trade, with incidental effect upon price, the state is incapable of directly controlling the price itself. This view was negatived many years ago. Munn v. Illinois, 94 U.S. 113. . . .

It is clear that there is no closed class or category of businesses affected with a public interest, and the function of courts in the application of the Fifth and Fourteenth Amendments is to determine in each case whether circumstances vindicate the challenged regulation as a reasonable exertion of governmental authority or condemn it as arbitrary or discriminatory. . . . The phrase "affected with a public interest" can, in the nature of things, mean no more than that an industry, for adequate reason, is subject to control for the public good. In several of the decisions of this court wherein the expressions "affected with a public interest," and "clothed with a public use," have been brought forward as the criteria of the validity of price control, it has been admitted that they are not susceptible of definition and form an unsatisfactory test of the constitutionality of legislation directed at business practices or prices. These decisions must rest, finally, upon the basis that the requirements of due process were not met because the laws were found arbitrary, in their operation and effect. But there can be no doubt that upon proper occasion and by appropriate measures the state may regulate a business in any of its aspects, including the prices to be charged for the products or commodities it sells.

So far as the requirement of due process is concerned, and in the absence of other constitutional restriction, a state is free to adopt whatever economic policy may reasonably be deemed to promote public welfare, and to enforce that policy by legislation adapted to its purpose. The courts are without authority either to declare such policy, or, when it is declared by the legislature, to override it. If the laws passed are seen to have a reasonable relation to a proper legislative purpose, and are neither arbitrary nor discriminatory, the requirements of due process are satisfied, and judicial determination to that effect renders a court functus officio.... With the wisdom of the policy adopted, with the adequacy or practicability of the law enacted to forward it, the courts are both incompetent and unauthorized to deal. The course of decision in this court exhibits a firm adherence to these principles. Times without number we have said that the Legislature is primarily the judge of the necessity of such an enactment, that every possible presumption is in favor of its validity, and that though the court may hold views inconsistent with the wisdom of the law, it may not be annulled unless palpably in excess of legislative power.... Price control, like any other form of regulation, is unconstitutional only if arbitrary, discriminatory, or demonstrably irrelevant to the policy the Legislature is free to adopt, and hence an unnecessary and unwarranted interference with individual liberty.

State legislation is only unconstitutional if it is —arbitrary, —discriminatory —or demonstrably irrelevant to the policy leg. is free to adopt

THE OVERTURNING OF ADKINS v. CHILDREN'S HOSPITAL

In Morehead v. New York ex rel. Tipaldo, 298 U.S. 587 (1936), Justice Roberts, author of the opinion in *Nebbia,* joined with the *Nebbia* dissenters in applying *Adkins* to hold invalid a New York law providing for minimum wages for women workers. The Court noted that the petitioner had not asked the Court to reconsider the constitutional question decided in *Adkins.* Finding no sufficient basis for distinction, the Court held the statute invalid.

morehead v. NY

The next year, however, the Court, by a vote of 5 to 4 with Justice Roberts joining the majority, specifically overruled Adkins v. Children's Hospital. West Coast Hotel Co. v. Parrish, 300 U.S. 379 (1937). The Court responded to the argument based on freedom of contract by saying:

overruled Adkins by coast hotel co v. parish

"What is freedom? The Constitution does not speak of freedom of contract. It speaks of liberty and prohibits the deprivation of liberty without due process of law.... But the liberty safeguarded is liberty in a social organization which requires the protection of law against the evils which menace the health, safety, morals and welfare of the people. Liberty under the constitution is thus necessarily subject to the restraints of due process, and regulation which is reasonable in relation to its subject and is adopted in the interests of the community is due process. This essential limitation of liberty in general governs freedom of contract in particular.

"What can be closer to the public interest than the health of women and their protection from unscrupulous and overreaching employers? And if the protection of women is a legitimate end of the exercise of state power, how can it be said that the requirement of the payment of a minimum wage fairly fixed in order to meet the very necessities of existence is not an admissible means to that end? The legislature of the State was clearly entitled to consider the situation of women in employment, the fact that they are in the class receiving the least pay, that their bargaining power is relatively weak, and that they are the ready victims of those who would take advantage of their necessitous circumstances. The legislature was entitled to adopt measures to reduce the evils of the 'sweating system,' the exploiting of workers at wages so low as to be insufficient to meet the bare cost of living, thus making their very helplessness the occasion of a most injurious competition.... The adoption of similar requirements by many States evidences a deep-seated conviction both as to the presence of the evil and as to the means adapted to check it. Legislative response to that conviction cannot be regarded as arbitrary or capricious, and that is all we have to decide. Even if the wisdom of the policy be regarded as

public interest to protect women from discrimination and unfair employment practices debatable and its effects uncertain, still the legislature is entitled to its judgment."

It should be noted that the decision in *West Coast Hotel* was announced while President Roosevelt's "Court packing" proposal was pending in Congress. For a reference to the question whether this decision was intended to have an impact on that proposal, see n. a, supra p. 168.

United States v. Carolene Products Co.

304 U.S. 144, 58 S.Ct. 778, 82 L.Ed. 1234 (1938).

Mr. Justice Stone delivered the opinion of the Court.

The question for decision is whether the "Filled Milk Act" of Congress of March 4, 1923 ..., which prohibits the shipment in interstate commerce of skimmed milk compounded with any fat or oil other than milk fat, so as to resemble milk or cream, transcends the power of Congress to regulate interstate commerce or infringes the Fifth Amendment....

[On review of an indictment for shipping in interstate commerce packages of "Milnut," a compound of condensed skimmed milk and coconut oil made in imitation or semblance of condensed milk or cream, the Supreme Court first upheld the statute as being within the power of Congress to regulate commerce and then addressed the due process issue.]

... [W]e might rest decision wholly on the presumption of constitutionality. But affirmative evidence also sustains the statute. In twenty years evidence has steadily accumulated of the danger to the public health from the general consumption of foods which have been stripped of elements essential to the maintenance of health. The Filled Milk Act was adopted by Congress after committee hearings, in the course of which eminent scientists and health experts testified. An extensive investigation was made of the commerce in milk compounds in which vegetable oils have been substituted for natural milk fat, and of the effect upon the public health of the use of such compounds as a food substitute for milk. The conclusions drawn from evidence presented at the hearings were embodied in reports of the House Committee on Agriculture ... and the Senate Committee on Agriculture and Forestry.... Both committees concluded, as the statute itself declares, that the use of filled milk as a substitute for pure milk is generally injurious to health and facilitates fraud on the public.

There is nothing in the Constitution which compels a Legislature, either national or state, to ignore such evidence, nor need it disregard the other evidence which amply supports the conclusions of the Congressional committees that the danger is greatly enhanced where an inferior product, like appellee's, is indistinguishable from a valuable food of almost universal use, thus making fraudulent distribution easy and protection of the consumer difficult.

. . .

Third. We may assume for present purposes that no pronouncement of a Legislature can forestall attack upon the constitutionality of the prohibition which it enacts by applying opprobrious epithets to the prohibited act, and that a statute would deny due process which precluded the disproof in judicial proceedings of all facts which would show or tend to show that a statute depriving the suitor of life, liberty, or property had a rational basis.

But such we think is not the purpose or construction of the statutory characterization of filled milk as injurious to health and as a fraud upon the public. There is no need to consider it here as more than a declaration of the legislative findings deemed to support and justify the action taken as a constitutional exertion of the legislative power, aiding informed judicial review, as do the reports of legislative committees, by revealing the rationale of the legislation. Even in the absence of such aids, the existence of facts supporting the legislative judgment is to be presumed, for regulatory legislation affecting ordinary commercial transactions is not to be pronounced unconstitutional unless in the light of the facts made known or generally assumed it is of such a character as to preclude the assumption that it rests upon some rational basis within the knowledge and experience of the legislators.[4] . . .

Rational Basis Test

Where the existence of a rational basis for legislation whose constitutionality is attacked depends upon facts beyond the sphere of judicial notice, such facts may properly be made the subject of judicial inquiry, . . . and the constitutionality of a statute predicated upon the existence of a particular state of facts may be challenged by showing to the court that those facts have ceased to exist. . . . Similarly we recognize that the constitutionality of a statute, valid on its face, may be assailed by proof of facts tending to show that the statute as applied to a particular article is without support in reason because the article, although within the prohibited class, is so different from others of the class as to be without the reason for the prohibition. . . . But by their very nature such inquiries, where the legislative judgment is drawn in question, must be restricted to the issue whether any state of facts either known or which could reasonably be assumed affords support for it. Here the demurrer challenges the validity of the statute on its face and it is evident from all the considerations presented to Congress, and those of which we may take judicial notice, that the question is at least debatable whether commerce in filled milk should be left unregulated, or in some measure restricted, or wholly prohibited. As that decision was for Congress, neither the finding of a court arrived at by weighing the evidence, nor the verdict of a jury can be substituted for it.[a]

. . .

4. There may be narrower scope for operation of the presumption of constitutionality when legislation appears on its face to be within a specific prohibition of the Constitution, such as those of the first ten Amendments, which are deemed equally specific when held to be embraced within the Fourteenth. See Stromberg v. California, 283 U.S. 359, 369, 370; Lovell v. Griffin, 303 U.S. 444.

It is unnecessary to consider now whether legislation which restricts those political processes which can ordinarily be expected to bring about repeal of undesirable legislation, is to be subjected to more exacting judicial scrutiny under the general prohibitions of the Fourteenth Amendment than are most other types of legislation. On restrictions upon the right to vote, see Nixon v. Herndon, 273 U.S. 536; Nixon v. Condon, 286 U.S. 73; on restraints upon the dissemination of information, see Near v. Minnesota, 283 U.S. 697, 713–714, 718–720, 722; Grosjean v. American Press Co., 297 U.S. 233; Lovell v. Griffin, supra; on interferences with political organizations, see Stromberg v. California, supra, 283 U.S. 359, 369; Fiske v. Kansas, 274 U.S. 380; Whitney v. California, 274 U.S. 357,

373–378; Herndon v. Lowry, 301 U.S. 242, and see Holmes, J., in Gitlow v. New York, 268 U.S. 652, 673; as to prohibition of peaceable assembly, see De Jonge v. Oregon, 299 U.S. 353, 365.

Nor need we enquire whether similar considerations enter into the review of statutes directed at particular religious, Pierce v. Society of Sisters, 268 U.S. 510, or national, Meyer v. Nebraska, 262 U.S. 390; Bartels v. Iowa, 262 U.S. 404; Farrington v. Tokushige, 273 U.S. 284, or racial minorities. *Nixon v. Herndon,* supra; *Nixon v. Condon,* supra: whether prejudice against discrete and insular minorities may be a special condition, which tends seriously to curtail the operation of those political processes ordinarily to be relied upon to protect minorities, and which may call for a correspondingly more searching judicial inquiry. Compare McCulloch v. Maryland, 4 Wheat. 316, 428; South Carolina State Highway Department v. Barnwell Bros., 303 U.S. 177, and cases cited.

a. Thirty-four years later, after the appearance on the market of imitation milk and

Reversed.

Mr. Justice Black concurs in the result and in all of the opinion except the part marked "Third."

Mr. Justice McReynolds thinks that the judgment should be affirmed.

Mr. Justice Cardozo and Mr. Justice Reed took no part in the consideration or decision of this case.

Mr. Justice Butler.

I concur in the result....

THE DEMISE OF LIBERTY OF CONTRACT

During the 1940s the Supreme Court (which received seven new members between 1937 and 1941) overturned the old precedents and rejected all challenges to legislation based on assertions of a constitutional preference for a free economic market place.

In United States v. Darby, 312 U.S. 100 (1941), the Court upheld the provisions of the Fair Labor Standards Act fixing maximum hours and minimum wages for all covered employees. The Court said that "it is no longer open to question" that it is within the legislative power to fix wages and hours for men as well as women.

In Phelps Dodge Corp. v. National Labor Relations Bd., 313 U.S. 177 (1941), the Court upheld the provision of the N.L.R.A. making it an unfair labor practice for an employer to encourage or discourage membership in any labor union, saying that "[t]he course of decisions in this Court since *Adair v. United States* ... and *Coppage v. Kansas* ... have completely sapped those cases of their authority."

In Olsen v. Nebraska, 313 U.S. 236 (1941), the Court upheld a state statute fixing the fees chargeable by a private employment agency and in Lincoln Fed. Labor Union v. Northwestern Iron & Metal Co., 335 U.S. 525 (1949), upheld a state law providing that no person should be denied an opportunity to obtain employment because he was or was not a member of a labor union. In the latter case it rejected a claim by a labor union that the "open shop" law was invalid by saying: "Just as we have held that the due process clause erects no obstacle

[handwritten margin note:] U.S v. Darby fix max & min wages for all employees

Phelps Dodge Corp v. NLRB unfair to disc. or encourage membership in any union

non-dairy creamer products that did not fall within the prohibition against interstate shipment of "filled milk," the successor company to Carolene Products Co. successfully attacked the constitutionality of this Act as applied on the ground that its enforcement against only filled milk substitutes denied equal protection—an element of the Fifth Amendment due process limitation on federal power discussed infra p. 694. Milnot Co. v. Richardson, 350 F.Supp. 221 (N.D.Ill.1972). The unappealed district court decision said that "the constitutionality of a statute predicated upon the existence of a particular state of facts may be challenged by showing to the court that those facts have ceased to exist. Chastleton Corp. v. Sinclair, 264 U.S. 543 (1924)." The Court found that "[f]rom the undisputed facts in the record here, it appears crystal clear that certain imitation milk and dairy products are so similar to Milnot in composition, appearance, and use that different treatment as to interstate shipment ... violates ... due process...." It reasoned that the "possibility of confusion, or passing off, in the marketplace, which justified the statute in 1944, can no longer be used rationally as a constitutional prop to prevent interstate shipment of Milnot" because "[t]here is at least as much danger in this regard with imitation milk as with filled milk, and actually no longer any such real danger with either." The decision was limited "to the conclusion, as a matter of law, that the Filled Milk Act, as applied to prohibit interstate shipment of Milnot, deprives the plaintiff of due process and provides no rational means for the achievement of any announced objective of the Act."

to block legislative protection of union members, we now hold that legislative protection can be afforded non-union members."

In Daniel v. Family Sec. Life Ins. Co., 336 U.S. 220 (1949), the Court upheld a statute which prohibited life insurance companies and their agents from engaging in the undertaking business and undertakers from acting as life insurance agents. The statute was challenged by an undertaker selling "funeral insurance." His claim that the statute resulted from the activities of the "insurance lobby" was rejected by the Court: "[A] judiciary must judge by results, not by the varied factors which may have determined legislators' votes. We cannot undertake a search for motive in testing constitutionality." In rejecting the claim that the statute was arbitrary and unreasonable, the Court said: "Looking through the form of this plea to its essential basis, we cannot fail to recognize it as an argument for invalidity because this Court disagrees with the desirability of the legislation. We rehearse the obvious when we say that our function is thus misconceived. We are not equipped to decide desirability; and a court cannot eliminate measures which do not happen to suit its tastes if it seeks to maintain a democratic system. The forum for the correction of ill-considered legislation is a responsive legislature.

"We cannot say that South Carolina is not entitled to call the funeral insurance business an evil. Nor can we say that the statute has no relation to the elimination of those evils. There our inquiry must stop."

[handwritten margin note: Daniel v. Family Sec. Life]

Williamson v. Lee Optical of Oklahoma, Inc.

348 U.S. 483, 75 S.Ct. 461, 99 L.Ed. 563 (1955).

Mr. Justice Douglas delivered the opinion of the Court.

This suit was instituted in the District Court to have an Oklahoma law ... declared unconstitutional and to enjoin state officials from enforcing it, ... for the reason that it allegedly violated various provisions of the Federal Constitution.

The District Court held unconstitutional portions of three sections of the Act. First, it held invalid under the Due Process Clause of the Fourteenth Amendment the portions of § 2 which make it unlawful for any person not a licensed optometrist or ophthalmologist to fit lenses to a face or to duplicate or replace into frames lenses or other optical appliances, except upon written prescriptive authority of an Oklahoma licensed ophthalmologist or optometrist.

An ophthalmologist is a duly licensed physician who specializes in the care of the eyes. An optometrist examines eyes for refractive error, recognizes (but does not treat) diseases of the eye, and fills prescriptions for eyeglasses. The optician is an artisan qualified to grind lenses, fill prescriptions, and fit frames.

The effect of § 2 is to forbid the optician from fitting or duplicating lenses without a prescription from an ophthalmologist or optometrist. In practical effect, it means that no optician can fit old glasses into new frames or supply a lens, whether it be a new lens or one to duplicate a lost or broken lens, without a prescription. The District Court conceded that it was in the competence of the police power of a State to regulate the examination of the eyes. But it rebelled at the notion that a State could require a prescription from an optometrist or ophthalmologist "to take old lenses and place them in new frames and then fit the completed spectacles to the *face* of the eyeglass wearer." ... It held that such a requirement was not "reasonably and rationally related to the health and welfare of the people." ... The court found that through mechanical devices and ordinary skills the optician could take a broken lens or a fragment

[handwritten margin note: To have OK law declared unconstitutional & to enjoin state officials from enforcing it.]

[handwritten margin note: DC → within police power to regulate But to require prescription was not]

thereof, measure its power, and reduce it to prescriptive terms. The court held that "Although on this precise issue of duplication, the legislature in the instant regulation was dealing with a matter of public interest, the particular means chosen are neither reasonably necessary nor reasonably related to the end sought to be achieved." . . . It was, accordingly, the opinion of the court that this provision of the law violated the Due Process Clause by arbitrarily interfering with the optician's right to do business.

. . .

The Oklahoma law may exact a needless, wasteful requirement in many cases. But it is for the legislature, not the courts, to balance the advantages and disadvantages of the new requirement. It appears that in many cases the optician can easily supply the new frames or new lenses without reference to the old written prescription. It also appears that many written prescriptions contain no directive data in regard to fitting spectacles to the face. But in some cases the directions contained in the prescription are essential, if the glasses are to be fitted so as to correct the particular defects of vision or alleviate the eye condition. The legislature might have concluded that the frequency of occasions when a prescription is necessary was sufficient to justify this regulation of the fitting of eyeglasses. Likewise, when it is necessary to duplicate a lens, a written prescription may or may not be necessary. But the legislature might have concluded that one was needed often enough to require one in every case. Or the legislature may have concluded that eye examinations were so critical, not only for correction of vision but also for detection of latent ailments or diseases, that every change in frames and every duplication of a lens should be accompanied by a prescription from a medical expert. To be sure, the present law does not require a new examination of the eyes every time the frames are changed or the lenses duplicated. For if the old prescription is on file with the optician, he can go ahead and make the new fitting or duplicate the lenses. But the law need not be in every respect logically consistent with its aims to be constitutional. It is enough that there is an evil at hand for correction, and that it might be thought that the particular legislative measure was a rational way to correct it.

The day is gone when this Court uses the Due Process Clause of the Fourteenth Amendment to strike down state laws, regulatory of business and industrial conditions, because they may be unwise, improvident, or out of harmony with a particular school of thought. . . .

We emphasize again what Chief Justice Waite said in Munn v. State of Illinois, 94 U.S. 113, 134, "For protection against abuses by legislatures the people must resort to the polls, not to the courts."

. . .

Third, the District Court held unconstitutional, as violative of the Due Process Clause of the Fourteenth Amendment, that portion of § 3 which makes it unlawful "to solicit the sale of . . . frames, mountings . . . or any other optical appliances." The court conceded that state regulation of advertising relating to eye examinations was a matter "rationally related to the public health and welfare", 120 F.Supp. at 140, and therefore subject to regulation. . . . But regulation of the advertising of eyeglass frames was said to intrude "into a mercantile field only casually related to the visual care of the public" and restrict "an activity which in no way can detrimentally affect the people."

An eyeglass frame, considered in isolation, is only a piece of merchandise. But an eyeglass frame is not used in isolation, as Judge Murrah said in dissent below; it is used with lenses; and lenses, pertaining as they do to the human

[handwritten margin note: Regulate selling & advertising of glasses was not related to health? safety]

[handwritten margin note: # 3]

eye, enter the field of health. Therefore, the legislature might conclude that to regulate one effectively it would have to regulate the other. Or it might conclude that both the sellers of frames and the sellers of lenses were in a business where advertising should be limited or even abolished in the public interest.... The advertiser of frames may be using his ads to bring in customers who will buy lenses. If the advertisement of lenses is to be abolished or controlled, the advertising of frames must come under the same restraints; or so the legislature might think. We see no constitutional reason why a State may not treat all who deal with the human eye as members of a profession who should use no merchandising methods for obtaining customers.

If regulate lenses, must also regulate glasses

Fourth, the District Court held unconstitutional, as violative of the Due Process Clause of the Fourteenth Amendment, the provision of § 4 of the Oklahoma Act which reads as follows:

4th criticism

> "No person, firm, or corporation engaged in the business of retailing merchandise to the general public shall rent space, sublease departments, or otherwise permit any person purporting to do eye examination or visual care to occupy space in such retail store."

It seems to us that this regulation is on the same constitutional footing as the denial to corporations of the right to practice dentistry. Semler v. Oregon State Board of Dental Examiners, supra, 294 U.S. at 611. It is an attempt to free the profession, to as great an extent as possible, from all taints of commercialism. It certainly might be easy for an optometrist with space in a retail store to be merely a front for the retail establishment. In any case, the opportunity for that nexus may be too great for safety, if the eye doctor is allowed inside the retail store. Moreover, it may be deemed important to effective regulation that the eye doctor be restricted to geographical locations that reduce the temptations of commercialism. Geographical location may be an important consideration in a legislative program which aims to raise the treatment of the human eye to a strictly professional level. We cannot say that the regulation has no rational relation to that objective and therefore is beyond constitutional bounds.

What we have said is sufficient to dispose of the appeal in No. 185 from the conclusion of the District Court that that portion of § 3 which makes it unlawful to solicit the sale of spectacles, eyeglasses, lenses, and prisms by the use of advertising media is constitutional.

Dispose of element #3 declared it constitutional?

. . .

Mr. Justice Harlan took no part in the consideration or decision of this case.

Ferguson v. Skrupa

372 U.S. 726, 83 S.Ct. 1028, 10 L.Ed.2d 93 (1963).

Mr. Justice Black delivered the opinion of the Court.

In this case, ... we are asked to review the judgment of a three-judge District Court enjoining, as being in violation of the Due Process Clause of the Fourteenth Amendment, a Kansas statute making it a misdemeanor for any person to engage "in the business of debt adjusting" except as an incident to "the lawful practice of law in this state." The statute defines "debt adjusting" as "the making of a contract, express, or implied with a particular debtor whereby the debtor agrees to pay a certain amount of money periodically to the person engaged in the debt adjusting business who shall for a consideration distribute the same among certain specified creditors in accordance with a plan agreed upon."

The complaint, filed by appellee Skrupa doing business as "Credit Advisors," alleged that Skrupa was engaged in the business of "debt adjusting" as defined by the statute, that his business was a "useful and desirable" one, that his business activities were not "inherently immoral or dangerous" or in any way contrary to the public welfare, and that therefore the business could not be "absolutely prohibited" by Kansas. The three-judge court heard evidence by Skrupa tending to show the usefulness and desirability of his business and evidence by the state officials tending to show that "debt adjusting" lends itself to grave abuses against distressed debtors, particularly in the lower income brackets, and that these abuses are of such gravity that a number of States have strictly regulated "debt adjusting" or prohibited it altogether. The court found that Skrupa's business did fall within the Act's proscription and concluded, one judge dissenting, that the Act was prohibitory, not regulatory, but that even if construed in part as regulatory it was an unreasonable regulation of a "lawful business," which the court held amounted to a violation of the Due Process Clause of the Fourteenth Amendment. The court accordingly enjoined enforcement of the statute.

The only case discussed by the court below as support for its invalidation of the statute was Commonwealth v. Stone, 191 Pa.Super. 117, 155 A.2d 453 (1959), in which the Superior Court of Pennsylvania struck down a statute almost identical to the Kansas act involved here.... In doing so, the Pennsylvania court relied heavily on Adams v. Tanner, 244 U.S. 590 (1917), which held that the Due Process Clause forbids a State to prohibit a business which is "useful" and not "inherently immoral or dangerous to public welfare."

Both the District Court in the present case and the Pennsylvania court in Stone adopted the philosophy of *Adams v. Tanner,* and cases like it, that it is the province of courts to draw on their own views as to the morality, legitimacy, and usefulness of a particular business in order to decide whether a statute bears too heavily upon that business and by so doing violates due process. Under the system of government created by our Constitution, it is up to legislatures, not courts, to decide on the wisdom and utility of legislation. There was a time when the Due Process Clause was used by this Court to strike down laws which were thought unreasonable, that is, unwise or incompatible with some particular economic or social philosophy. In this manner the Due Process Clause was used by this Court to strike down laws which were thought unreasonable, that is, unwise or incompatible with some particular economic or social philosophy. In this manner the Due Process Clause was used, for example, to nullify laws prescribing maximum hours for work in bakeries, Lochner v. New York, 198 U.S. 45 (1905), outlawing "yellow dog" contracts, Coppage v. Kansas, 236 U.S. 1 (1915), setting minimum wages for women, Adkins v. Children's Hospital, 261 U.S. 525 (1923), and fixing the weight of loaves of bread, Jay Burns Baking Co. v. Bryan, 264 U.S. 504 (1924). This intrusion by the judiciary into the realm of legislative value judgments was strongly objected to at the time, particularly by Mr. Justice Holmes and Mr. Justice Brandeis....

The doctrine that prevailed in *Lochner, Coppage, Adkins, Burns,* and like cases—that due process authorizes courts to hold laws unconstitutional when they believe the legislature has acted unwisely—has long since been discarded. We have returned to the original constitutional proposition that courts do not substitute their social and economic beliefs for the judgment of legislative bodies, who are elected to pass laws....

In the face of our abandonment of the use of the "vague contours" of the Due Process Clause to nullify laws which a majority of the Court believed to be economically unwise, reliance on *Adams v. Tanner* is as mistaken as would be adherence to *Adkins v. Children's Hospital,* overruled by West Coast Hotel Co. v. Parrish, 300 U.S. 379 (1937).... We conclude that the Kansas Legislature was free to decide for itself that legislation was needed to deal with the business of debt adjusting. Unquestionably, there are arguments showing that the business of debt adjusting has social utility, but such arguments are properly addressed to the legislature, not to us. We refuse to sit as a "superlegislature to weigh the wisdom of legislation," and we emphatically refuse to go back to the time when courts used the Due Process Clause "to strike down state laws, regulatory of business and industrial conditions, because they may be unwise, improvident, or out of harmony with a particular school of thought." Nor are we able or willing to draw lines by calling a law "prohibitory" or "regulatory." Whether the legislature takes for its textbook Adam Smith, Herbert Spencer, Lord Keynes, or some other is no concern of ours. The Kansas debt adjusting statute may be wise or unwise. But relief, if any be needed, lies not with us but with the body constituted to pass laws for the State of Kansas.

Reversed & found to be constitutional? up to legislation, not cts?

. . .

Reversed.

Mr. Justice Harlan concurs in the judgment on the ground that this state measure bears a rational relation to a constitutionally permissible objective. See Williamson v. Lee Optical Inc., 348 U.S. 483, 491.

DOES THE DUE PROCESS CLAUSE TODAY IMPOSE ANY LIMITATIONS ON THE SUBSTANCE OF ECONOMIC REGULATORY LEGISLATION?

Does the decision in *Ferguson v. Skrupa* constitute a complete abandonment by the Court of the use of due process to impose a minimum standard of rationality on legislation? Does Justice Harlan's concurring opinion indicate that he thought the Court was no longer going to insist that legislation "bear a rational relationship to a constitutionally permissible objective"?

If one looks only at the outcome of cases challenging economic regulatory legislation under due process, the answer would appear to be that no effective review is undertaken by the Court. No economic regulatory statute has been held invalid under due process since 1937. Only in cases where the Court has been able to find a "taking" of property without just compensation in violation of the taking clause of the fifth amendment or an impairment of contract within the meaning of the contract clause has it invalidated legislation in the economic area.

However, the Court continues to write opinions in which it states that it is applying a due process standard that requires legislation to bear a rational relationship to a legitimate state objective. In Exxon Corp. v. Governor of Maryland, 437 U.S. 117, 125 (1978), the Court, in upholding a statute prohibiting producers or refiners of petroleum products from operating retail service stations in the state, rejected a due process objection stating: "[W]e have no hesitancy in concluding that it bears a reasonable relation to the State's legitimate purpose in controlling the gasoline retail market." And in PruneYard Shopping Center v. Robins, 447 U.S. 74 (1980), the Court rejected a due process challenge to a state court judgment ordering a private property owner to permit use of a portion of that property by persons soliciting signatures on petitions. It quoted from Nebbia v. New York, set out supra p. 523: "The guaranty of due process … demands only that the law shall not be unreasonable, arbitrary or capricious, and that the means selected shall have a real and substantial relation to the objective sought to be [obtained]." The Court then added: "Appellants have failed to provide sufficient justification for concluding that this test is not satisfied by the State's asserted interest in promoting more expansive rights of free speech and petition than conferred by the Federal Constitution."

STATE COURTS AND BUSINESS REGULATIONS

Many state courts have refused to go as far as the United States Supreme Court in abandoning judicial control of economic legislation. For example, the Supreme Court in Day–Brite Lighting v. Missouri, 342 U.S. 421 (1952), held valid a Missouri statute providing that an employee could absent himself from his employment without loss of pay for up to four hours on election day for the purpose of voting. In Heimgaertner v. Benjamin Elec. Mfg. Co., 6 Ill.2d 152, 128 N.E.2d 691 (1955), however, the Supreme Court of Illinois refused to follow the Day–Brite decision and held a similar law invalid under the due process clause of the state constitution. The court rejected the Day–Brite decision with the following statement:

"Although the decision eliminates the Federal aspects of the problems surrounding such regulations, it serves to reaffirm that it is for each State to determine if its legislature is empowered to enact such a statute and to determine if the means selected to further the public welfare bear a real and substantial relation to the objects sought to be obtained. It is the duty of each State to pass upon the validity of its own legislation and, if no Federal question is involved, the United States Supreme Court will adopt and follow the decision of the State court."

For a comprehensive review of the cases, see Hetherington, *State Economic Regulation and Substantive Due Process of Law,* 53 Northwest U.L.Rev. 13, 226 (1958); Kirby, *Expansive Judicial Review of Economic Regulation Under State Constitutions,* 48 Tenn.L.Rev. 241 (1981); *Developments in the Law—The Interpretation of State Constitutional Rights,* 95 Harv.L.Rev. 1324, 1463–1493 (1982). See also Carpenter, *Our Constitutional Heritage: Economic Due Process and the State Courts,* 45 A.B.A.J. 1027 (1959); Linde, *Constitutional Law—1959 Oregon Survey,* 39 Ore.L.Rev. 138, 143–160 (1960); Paulsen, *The Persistence of Substantive Due Process in the States,* 34 Minn.L.Rev. 91 (1950); Note, 53 Col.L.Rev. 827 (1953); Note, 18 Ohio St.L.J. 384 (1957). For a discussion of state cases which advocates greater review of economic regulations by the United States Supreme Court see Struve, *The Less–Restrictive–Alternative Principle and Economic Due Process,* 80 Harv.L.Rev. 1463 (1967).

DUE PROCESS LIMITATIONS ON STATE PUNITIVE DAMAGES AWARDS

In contrast to its highly deferential approach to due process review of the reasonableness of economic *legislation*, the Court in the 1990's began to define substantive due process limits to assure the reasonableness of punitive damages awards imposed in civil trials, based on the perception that "[p]unitive damages pose an acute danger of arbitrary deprivation of property[,]" Honda Motor Co. v. Oberg, 512 U.S. 415, 432 (1994). In State Farm Mutual Automobile Insurance Co. v. Campbell, 538 U.S. 408 (2003), the Court affirmed that the "Due Process Clause of the Fourteenth Amendment prohibits the imposition of grossly excessive or arbitrary punishments on a tortfeasor" and overturned as "neither reasonable nor proportionate to the wrong committed, and ... an irrational deprivation of the property of the defendant" a punitive damages award of $145 million, where full compensatory damages were $1 million. Justice Kennedy's majority opinion applied "three guideposts" the Court had adopted in BMW of North America, Inc. v. Gore, 517 U.S. 559 (1996), as instructions for courts reviewing punitive damages to consider: "(1) the degree of reprehensibility of the defendant's misconduct; (2) the disparity between the actual or potential harm suffered by the plaintiff and the punitive damages award; and (3) the difference between the punitive damages awarded by the jury and the civil penalties authorized or imposed in comparable cases." The majority also declared more generally:

"We decline ... to impose a bright-line ratio which a punitive damages award cannot exceed. Our jurisprudence and the principles it has now established demonstrate, however, that, in practice, few awards exceeding a single-digit ratio between punitive and compensatory damages, to a significant degree, will satisfy due process. In [Pacific Mutual Life Insurance Co. v. Haslip, 499 U.S. 1, 23–24 (1991)], in upholding a punitive damages award, we concluded that an award of more than four times the amount of compensatory damages might be close to the line of constitutional impropriety.... We cited that 4–to–1 ratio again in *Gore*.... The Court further referenced a long legislative history, dating back over 700 years and going forward to today, providing for sanctions of double, treble, or quadruple damages to deter and punish.... While these ratios are not binding, they are instructive. They demonstrate what should be obvious: Single-digit multipliers are more likely to comport with due process, while still achieving the State's goals of deterrence and retribution, than awards with ratios in range of 500 to 1, or, in this case, of 145 to 1.

"Nonetheless, because there are no rigid benchmarks that a punitive damages award may not surpass, ratios greater than those we have previously upheld may comport with due process where 'a particularly egregious act has resulted in only a small amount of economic damages.' ... The converse is also true, however. When compensatory damages are substantial, then a lesser ratio, perhaps only equal to compensatory damages, can reach the outermost limit of the due process guarantee. The precise award in any case, of course, must be based upon the facts and circumstances of the defendant's conduct and the harm to the plaintiff.

"In sum, courts must ensure that the measure of punishment is both reasonable and proportionate to the amount of harm to the plaintiff and to the general damages recovered."

Three Justices dissented. Justice Scalia "adhere[d] to the view expressed in my dissenting opinion in ... *Gore* ... that the Due Process Clause provides no substantive protections against 'excessive' or 'unreasonable' awards of punitive damages." He added "that the punitive damages jurisprudence which has sprung forth from *BMW v. Gore* is insusceptible of principled application...." Justice Thomas " 'continue[d] to believe that the Constitution does not constrain the size of punitive damages awards.' *Cooper Industries, Inc. v. Leatherman Tool Group, Inc.*, 532 U.S. 424, 443 (2001)." Finally, Justice Ginsburg opined that although "[t]he large size of the award upheld by the Utah Supreme Court in this case indicates why damage-capping legislation may be altogether fitting and proper[, n]either the amount of the award nor the trial record ... justifies this Court's substitution of its judgment for that of Utah's competent decisionmakers." She also wrote: "In a legislative scheme or a state high court's design to cap punitive damages, the handiwork in setting single-digit and 1-to-1 benchmarks could hardly be questioned; in a judicial decree imposed on the States by this Court under the banner of substantive due process, the numerical controls today's decision installs seem to me boldly out of order." She concluded her opinion as follows: "I remain of the view that this Court has no warrant to reform state law governing awards of punitive damages. *Gore,* 517 U.S., at 607 (Ginsburg, J., dissenting). Even if I were prepared to accept the flexible guides prescribed in *Gore,* I would not join the Court's swift conversion of those guides into instructions that begin to resemble marching orders."

B.   THE CONTRACT CLAUSE—WHAT DOES IT ADD TO THE DUE PROCESS LIMITATION?

United States Trust Co of New York v. New Jersey
431 U.S. 1, 97 S.Ct. 1505, 52 L.Ed.2d 92 (1977).

[The New York and New Jersey Port Authority was formed by compact of the two States in 1921, as a financially independent agency. The Authority's income from bridge and tunnel tolls was pledged to the retirement of bonds it issued. In 1960, the Authority's proposed takeover of a financially troubled, privately owned commuter train led to concern that use of tolls to finance the railroad's deficits would conflict with rights of holders of the Authority's bonds. The response was the 1962 "Statutory Covenant," enacted into law in both States, which provided, as part of the legislation authorizing the takeover, that "the 2 States covenant and agree with each other and with the holders of any affected bonds" not to finance deficits of other future mass transit facilities with revenue pledged to pay bonds, except as permitted by exceptions in the 1962 statutes. In 1974, New York and New Jersey retroactively repealed the 1962 covenant, in order to permit greater use of bridge and tunnel tolls to subsidize mass transit. Appellant, trustee and holder of Authority bonds, brought suit in a New Jersey State court for a declaratory judgment that New Jersey's repeal of the 1962 covenant was prohibited by the Contract Clause. The trial court's decision, that the repeal was a reasonable exercise of New Jersey's police power and not in violation of the Contract Clause, was affirmed by the Supreme Court of New Jersey.]

Mr. Justice Blackmun delivered the opinion of the court.

. . .

II.

At the time the Constitution was adopted, and for nearly a century thereafter, the Contract Clause was one of the few express limitations on state power. The many decisions of this Court involving the Contract Clause are evidence of its important place in our constitutional jurisprudence. Over the last century, however, the Fourteenth Amendment has assumed a far larger place in constitutional adjudication concerning the States. We feel that the present role of the Contract Clause is largely illuminated by two of this Court's decisions. In each, legislation was sustained despite a claim that it had impaired the obligations of contracts.

Home Building & Loan Assn. v. Blaisdell, 290 U.S. 398 (1934), is regarded as the leading case in the modern era of Contract Clause interpretation. At issue was the Minnesota Mortgage Moratorium Law, enacted in 1933, during the depth of the Depression and when that state was under severe economic stress, and appeared to have no effective alternative. The statute was a temporary measure that allowed judicial extension of the time for redemption; a mortgagor who remained in possession during the extension period was required to pay a reasonable income or rental value to the mortgagee. A closely divided Court, in an opinion by Mr. Chief Justice Hughes, observed that "emergency may furnish the occasion for the exercise of power" and that the "constitutional question presented in the light of an emergency is whether the power possessed embraces the particular exercise of it in response to particular conditions." It noted that the debates in the Constitutional Convention were of little aid in the construction of the Contract Clause, but that the general purpose of the Clause was clear: to encourage trade and credit by promoting confidence in the stability of contractual obligations. Nevertheless, a State "continues to possess authority to safeguard the vital interests of its people. . . . This principle of harmonizing the constitutional prohibition with the necessary residuum of state power has had progressive recognition in the decisions of this Court." The great clauses of the Constitution are to be considered in the light of our whole experience, and not merely as they would be interpreted by its Framers in the conditions and with the outlook of their time.

This Court's most recent Contract Clause decision is El Paso v. Simmons, 379 U.S. 497 (1965). That case concerned a 1941 Texas statute that limited to a 5-year period the reinstatement rights of an interest-defaulting purchaser of land from the State. For many years prior to the enactment of that statute, such a defaulting purchaser, under Texas law, could have reinstated his claim to the land upon written request and payment of delinquent interest, unless rights of third parties had intervened. This Court held that "it is not every modification of a contractual promise that impairs the obligation of contract under federal law." It observed that the State "has the 'sovereign right . . . to protect the . . . general welfare of the people' " and "we must respect the 'wide discretion on the part of the legislature in determining what is and what is not necessary,' " quoting East New York Savings Bank v. Hahn, 326 U.S. 230, 232–233 (1945). The Court recognized that "the power of a State to modify or affect the obligation of contract is not without limit," but held that "the objects of the Texas statute make abundantly clear that it impairs no protected right under the Contract Clause."

Both of these cases eschewed a rigid application of the Contract Clause to invalidate state legislation. Yet neither indicated that the Contract Clause was without meaning in modern constitutional jurisprudence, or that its limitation on state power was illusory. Whether or not the protection of contract rights comports with current views of wise public policy, the Contract Clause remains a part of our written Constitution. We therefore must attempt to apply that constitutional provision to the instant case with due respect for its purpose and the prior decisions of this Court.

III.

We first examine appellant's general claim that repeal of the 1962 covenant impaired the obligation of the States' contract with the bondholders. It long has been established that the Contract Clause limits the power of the States to modify their own contracts as well as to regulate those between private parties. Fletcher v. Peck, 6 Cranch 87, 137–139 (1810); Dartmouth College v. Woodward, 4 Wheat. 518 (1819). Yet the Contract Clause does not prohibit the States from repealing or amending statutes generally, or from enacting legislation with retroactive effects.[13] Thus, as a preliminary matter, appellant's claim

---

13. The Contract Clause is in the phrase of the Constitution which contains the prohibition against any State's enacting a bill of attainder or *ex post facto* law. Notwithrequires a determination that the repeal has the effect of impairing a contractual obligation.

In this case the obligation was itself created by a statute, the 1962 legislative covenant. It is unnecessary, however, to dwell on the criteria for determining whether state legislation gives rise to a contractual obligation. The trial court found, ... and appellees do not deny, that the 1962 covenant constituted a contract between the two States and the holders of the Consolidated Bonds issued between 1962 and the 1973 prospective repeal....

The trial court recognized that there was an impairment in this case: "To the extent that the repeal of the covenant authorizes the Authority to assume greater deficits for such purposes, it permits a diminution of the pledged revenues and reserves and may be said to constitute an impairment of the states' contract with the bondholders." ...

Having thus established that the repeal impaired a contractual obligation of the States, we turn to the question whether that impairment violated the Contract Clause.

IV.

Although the Contract Clause appears literally to proscribe "any" impairment, this Court observed in *Blaisdell* that "the prohibition is not an absolute one and is not to be read with literal exactness like a mathematical formula." Thus, a finding that there has been a technical impairment is merely a preliminary step in resolving the more difficult question whether that impairment is permitted under the Constitution. In the instant case, as in *Blaisdell*, we must attempt to reconcile the strictures of the Contract Clause with the "essential attributes of sovereign power," necessarily reserved by the States to safeguard the welfare of their citizens.

The trial court concluded that repeal of the 1962 covenant was a valid exercise of New Jersey's police power because repeal served important public interests in mass transportation, energy conservation, and environmental protection. Yet the Contract Clause limits otherwise legitimate exercises of state legislative authority, and the existence of an important public interest is not always sufficient to overcome that limitation. "Undoubtedly, whatever is reserved of state power must be consistent with the fair intent of the constitutional limitation of that power." *Blaisdell,* 290 U.S., at 439. Moreover, the scope of the State's reserved power depends on the nature of the contractual relationship with which the challenged law conflicts.

The States must possess broad power to adopt general regulatory measures without being concerned that private contracts will be impaired, or even destroyed, as a result. Otherwise, one would be able to obtain immunity from the state regulation by making private contractual arrangements. This principle is summarized in Mr. Justice Holmes' well-known dictum: "One whose rights, such as they are, are subject to state restriction, cannot remove them from the power of the State by making a contract about them." Hudson Water Co. v. McCarter, 209 U.S. 349, 357.

standing Mr. Chief Justice Marshall's reference to these two other forbidden categories in Fletcher v. Peck, 6 Cranch, at 138–139, it is clear that they limit the powers of the States only with regard to the imposition of punishment. Cummings v. Missouri, 4 Wall. 277, 322–326, 18 L.Ed. 356 (1867); Calder v. Bull, 3 Dall. 386, 390–391, 1 L.Ed. 648 (1798). The Due Process Clause of the Fourteenth Amendment generally does not prohibit retrospective civil legislation, unless the consequences are particularly "harsh and oppressive." Welch v. Henry, 305 U.S. 134, 147 (1938). See Usery v. Turner Elkhorn Mining Co., 428 U.S. 1, 14–20 (1976).

Yet private contracts are not subject to unlimited modification under the police power. The Court in *Blaisdell* recognized that laws intended to regulate existing contractual relationships must serve a legitimate public purpose. A State could not "adopt as its policy the repudiation of debts or the destruction of contracts or the denial of means to enforce them." Legislation adjusting the rights and responsibilities of contracting parties must be upon reasonable conditions and of a character appropriate to the public purpose justifying its adoption. As is customary in reviewing economic and social regulation, however, courts properly defer to legislative judgment as to the necessity and reasonableness of a particular measure.

. . .

When a State impairs the obligation of its own contract, the reserved-powers doctrine has a different basis. The initial inquiry concerns the ability of the State to enter into an agreement that limits its power to act in the future. As early as Fletcher v. Peck, the Court considered the argument that "one legislature cannot abridge the powers of a succeeding legislature." 6 Cranch, at 135. It is often stated that "the legislature cannot bargain away the police power of a State." Stone v. Mississippi, 101 U.S. 814, 817 (1880).[20] This doctrine requires a determination of the State's power to create irrevocable contract rights in the first place, rather than an inquiry into the purpose or reasonableness of the subsequent impairment. In short, the Contract Clause does not require a State to adhere to a contract that surrenders an essential attribute of its sovereignty.

In deciding whether a State's contract was invalid *ab initio* under the reserved powers doctrine, earlier decisions relied on distinctions among the various powers of the State. Thus, the police power and the power of eminent domain were among those that could not be "contracted away," but the State could bind itself in the future exercise of the taxing and spending powers.[21] Such formalistic distinctions perhaps cannot be dispositive, but they contain an important element of truth. Whatever the propriety of a State's binding itself to a future course of conduct in other contexts, the power to enter into effective financial contracts cannot be questioned. Any financial obligation could be regarded in theory as a relinquishment of the State's spending power, since money spent to repay debts is not available for other purposes. Similarly, the taxing power may have to be exercised if debts are to be repaid. Notwithstanding these effects, the Court has regularly held that the States are bound by their debt contracts.

The instant case involves a financial obligation and thus as a threshold matter may not be said automatically to fall within the reserved powers that cannot be contracted away.... [The] promise [here] is purely financial and thus not necessarily a compromise of the State's reserved powers.

20. Stone v. Mississippi sustained the State's revocation of a 25–year charter to operate a lottery. Other cases similarly have held that a State is without power to enter into binding contracts not to exercise its police power in the future....

21. In New Jersey v. Wilson, 7 Cranch 164 (1812), the Court held that a State could properly grant a permanent tax exemption and that the Contract Clause prohibited any impairment of such an agreement. This holding has never been repudiated, although tax exemption contracts generally have not re-ceived a sympathetic construction. See B. Wright, The Contract Clause of the Constitution 179–194 (1938).

By contrast, the doctrine that a State cannot contract away the power of eminent domain has been established since West River Bridge Co. v. Dix, 6 How. 507 (1848). See Contributors to Pennsylvania Hospital v. Philadelphia, 245 U.S., at 23–24. The doctrine that a State cannot be bound to a contract forbidding the exercise of its police power is almost as old. See n. 20, supra.

Of course, to say that the financial restrictions of the 1962 covenant were valid when adopted does not finally resolve this case. The Contract Clause is not an absolute bar to subsequent modification of a State's own financial obligations. As with laws impairing the obligations of private contracts, an impairment may be constitutional if it is reasonable and necessary to serve an important public purpose. In applying this standard, however, complete deference to a legislative assessment of reasonableness and necessity is not appropriate because the State's self-interest is at stake. A governmental entity can always find a use for extra money, especially when taxes do not have to be raised. If a State could reduce its financial obligations whenever it wanted to spend the money for what it regarded as an important public purpose, the Contract Clause would provide no protection at all.

The trial court recognized to an extent the special status of a State's financial obligations when it held that *total* repudiation, presumably for even a worthwhile public purpose, would be unconstitutional. But the trial court regarded the protection of the Contract Clause as available only in such an extreme case: "The states' inherent power to protect the public welfare may be validly exercised under the Contract Clause even if it impairs a contractual obligation so long as it does not destroy it."

The trial court's "total destruction" test is based on what we think is a misreading of W.B. Worthen Co. v. Kavanaugh, 295 U.S. 56 (1935).... The extent of impairment is certainly a relevant factor in determining its reasonableness. But we cannot sustain the repeal of the 1962 covenant simply because the bondholders' rights were not totally destroyed.

. . .

V.

Mass transportation, energy conservation, and environmental protection are goals that are important and of legitimate public concern. Appellees contend that these goals are so important that any harm to bondholders from repeal of the 1962 covenant is greatly outweighed by the public benefit. We do not accept this invitation to engage in a utilitarian comparison of public benefit and private loss. Contrary to Mr. Justice Black's fear expressed on sole dissent in El Paso v. Simmons, 379 U.S., at 517, the Court has not "balanced away" the limitation on state action imposed by the Contract Clause. Thus a State cannot refuse to meet its legitimate financial obligations simply because it would prefer to spend the money to promote the public good rather than the private welfare of its creditors. We can only sustain the repeal of the 1962 covenant if that impairment was both reasonable and necessary to serve the admittedly important purposes claimed by the State.[27]

The more specific justification offered for the repeal of the 1962 covenant was the States' plan for encouraging users of private automobiles to shift to public transportation. The States intended to discourage private automobile use by raising bridge and tunnel tolls and to use the extra revenue from those tolls to subsidize improved commuter railroad service. Appellees contend that repeal of the 1962 covenant was necessary to implement this plan because the new mass transit facilities could not possibly be self-supporting and the covenant's "permitted deficits" level had already been exceeded. We reject this justifica-

---

27. The dissent suggests that such careful scrutiny is unwarranted in this case because the harm to bondholders is relatively small. For the same reason, however, contractual obligations of this magnitude need not impose barriers to changes in public policy. The States remain free to exercise their powers of eminent domain to abrogate such contractual rights, upon payment of just compensation.

tion because the repeal was neither necessary to achievement of the plan nor reasonable in light of the circumstances.

The determination of necessity can be considered on two levels. First, it cannot be said that total repeal of the covenant was essential; a less drastic modification would have permitted the contemplated plan without entirely removing the covenant's limitations on the use of Port Authority revenues and reserves to subsidize commuter railroads.[28] Second, without modifying the covenant at all, the States could have adopted alternative means of achieving their twin goals of discouraging automobile use and improving mass transit. Appellees contend, however, that choosing among these alternatives is a matter for legislative discretion. But a State is not completely free to consider impairing the obligations of its own contracts on a par with other policy alternatives. Similarly, a State is not free to impose a drastic impairment when an evident and more moderate course would serve its purposes equally well. In *El Paso v. Simmons,* supra, the . . . Court held that adoption of a statute of limitation was a reasonable means to "restrict a party to those gains reasonably to be expected from the contract" when it was adopted.

By contrast, in the instant case the need for mass transportation in the New York metropolitan area was not a new development, and the likelihood that publicly owned commuter railroads would produce substantial deficits was well known. As early as 1922, over a half century ago, there were pressures to involve the Port Authority in mass transit. It was with full knowledge of these concerns that the 1962 covenant was adopted. Indeed, the covenant was specifically intended to protect the pledged revenues and reserves against the possibility that such concerns would lead the Port Authority into greater involvement in deficit mass transit.

During the 12–year period between adoption of the covenant and its repeal, public perception of the importance of mass transit undoubtedly grew because of increased general concern with environmental protection and energy conservation. But these concerns were not unknown in 1962, and the subsequent changes were of degree and not of kind. We cannot say that these changes caused the covenant to have a substantially different impact in 1974 than when it was adopted in 1962. And we cannot conclude that the repeal was reasonable in the light of changed circumstances.

We therefore hold that the Contract Clause of the United States Constitution prohibits the retroactive repeal of the 1962 covenant. The judgment of the Supreme Court of New Jersey is reversed.

. . .

Mr. Justice Stewart took no part in the decision of this case.

Mr. Justice Powell took no part in the consideration or decision of this case.

Mr. Chief Justice Burger, concurring.

. . .

For emphasis, I note that the Court pointedly does not hold that, on the facts of this case, any particular "less drastic modification" would pass constitutional muster, n. 28.

---

28. Of course, we express no opinion as to whether any of these lesser impairments would be constitutional.

Mr. Justice Brennan, with whom Mr. Justice White and Mr. Justice Marshall join, dissenting.

Decisions of this Court for at least a century have construed the Contract Clause largely to be powerless in binding a State to contracts limiting the authority of successor legislatures to enact laws in furtherance of the health, safety, and similar collective interests of the polity. In short, those decisions established the principle that lawful exercises of a State's police powers stand paramount to private rights held under contract. Today's decision ... rejects this previous understanding and remolds the Contract Clause into a potent instrument for overseeing important policy determinations of the state legislature. At the same time, by creating a constitutional safe haven for property rights embodied in a contract, the decision substantially distorts modern constitutional jurisprudence governing regulation of private economic interests. I might understand, though I could not accept this revival of the Contract Clause were it in accordance with some coherent and constructive view of public policy. But elevation of the clause to the status of regulator of the municipal bond market at the heavy price of frustration of sound legislative policymaking is as demonstrably unwise as it is unnecessary. . . .

. . .

... Given that this is the first case in some 40 years in which this Court has seen fit to invalidate purely economic and social legislation on the strength of the Contract Clause, one may only hope that it will prove a rare phenomenon, turning on the Court's particularized appraisal of the facts before it. But there also is reason for broader concern. It is worth remembering that there is nothing sacrosanct about a contract. All property rights, no less than a contract, are rooted in certain "expectations" about the sanctity of one's right of ownership. . . . And other constitutional doctrines are akin to the Contract Clause in directing their protections to the property interests of private parties. Hence the command of the Fifth Amendment that "private property [shall not] be taken for public use, without just compensation" also "remains a part of our written Constitution." And during the heyday of economic due process associated with Lochner v. New York, 198 U.S. 45 (1905), and similar cases long since discarded, ... this Court treated "the liberty of contract" under the Due Process Clause as virtually indistinguishable from the Contract Clause. . . . In more recent times, however, the Court wisely has come to embrace a coherent, unified interpretation of all such constitutional provisions, and has granted wide latitude to "a valid exercise of [the States'] police powers," Goldblatt v. Hempstead, 369 U.S. 590, 592 (1962), even if it results in severe violations of property rights. . . . If today's case signals a return to substantive constitutional review of States' policies, and a new resolve to protect property owners whose interest or circumstances may happen to appeal to Members of this Court, then more than the citizens of New Jersey and New York will be the losers.

I would not want to be read as suggesting that the States should blithely proceed down the path of repudiating their obligations, financial or otherwise. Their credibility in the credit market obviously is highly dependent on exercising their vast lawmaking powers with self-restraint and discipline, and I, for one, have little doubt that few, if any, jurisdictions would choose to use their authority "so foolish[ly] as to kill a goose that lays golden eggs for them." But in the final analysis, there is no reason to doubt that appellant's financial welfare is being adequately policed by the political processes and the bond marketplace itself. The role to be played by the Constitution is at most a limited one. For this Court should have learned long ago that the Constitution—be it through the Contract or Due Process Clause—can actively intrude into such economic and policy matters only if my Brethren are prepared to bear enormous institutional and social costs. Because I consider the potential dangers of such judicial interference to be intolerable, I dissent.

Allied Structural Steel Co. v. Spannaus

438 U.S. 234, 98 S.Ct. 2716, 57 L.Ed.2d 727 (1978).

Mr. Justice Stewart delivered the opinion of the Court.

[Allied had its principal place of business in Illinois, but maintained an office with 30 employees in Minnesota. In 1963 it adopted a pension plan providing a vested pension, payable at 65, for employees who worked until the age of 65, employees who reached 60 and had worked for 15 years, employees who reached 55 and whose age plus work years equalled 75, and employees under 55 whose age plus work years equalled 80.]

The company not only retained a virtually unrestricted right to amend the plan in whole or in part, but was also free to terminate the plan and distribute the trust assets at any time and for any reason.... The plan also specifically advised employees that neither its existence nor any of its terms were to be understood as implying any assurance that employees could not be dismissed from their employment with the company at any time.

In sum, an employee who did not die, did not quit, and was not discharged before meeting one of the requirements of the plan would receive a fixed pension at age 65 if the company remained in business and elected to continue the pension plan in essentially its existing form.

[In 1974 Minnesota enacted the Private Pension Benefits Protection Act, which subjected a private employer who provided pension benefits] to a "pension funding charge" if he either terminated the plan or closed a Minnesota office. The charge was assessed if the pension funds were not sufficient to cover full pensions for all employees who had worked at least 10 years. The Act required the employer to satisfy the deficiency by purchasing deferred annuities, payable to the employees at their normal retirement age. A separate provision specified that periods of employment prior to the effective date of the Act were to be included in the 10-year employment criterion.

During the summer of 1974 the company began closing its Minnesota office. On July 31, it discharged 11 of its 30 Minnesota employees, and the following month it notified the Minnesota Commissioner of Labor and Industry, as required by the Act, that it was terminating an office in the State. At least nine of the discharged employees did not have any vested pension rights under the company's plan, but had worked for the company for 10 years or more and thus qualified as pension obligees of the company under the law that Minnesota had enacted a few months earlier. On August 18, the State notified the company that it owed a pension funding charge of approximately $185,000 under the provisions of the Private Pension Benefits Protection Act.

The company ... claimed that the Act unconstitutionally impaired its contractual obligations to its employees under its pension agreement....

II.

A.

There can be no question of the impact of the Minnesota Private Pension Benefits Protection Act upon the company's contractual relationships with its employees. The Act substantially altered those relationships by superimposing pension obligations upon the company conspicuously beyond those that it had voluntarily agreed to undertake. But it does not inexorably follow that the Act, as applied to the company, violates the Contract Clause of the Constitution.

The language of the Contract Clause appears unambiguously absolute: "No State shall ... pass any ... Law impairing the Obligation of Contracts." U.S. Const. Art. 1, § 10. The Clause is not, however, the draconian provision that its words might seem to imply. As the Court has recognized, "literalism in the construction of the contract clause ... would make it destructive of the public interest by depriving the State of its prerogative of self-protection." W.B. Worthen Co. v. Thomas, 292 U.S. 426, 433.

Although it was perhaps the strongest single constitutional check on state legislation during our early years as a Nation, the Contract Clause receded into comparative desuetude with the adoption of the Fourteenth Amendment, and particularly with the development of the large body of jurisprudence under the Due Process Clause of that Amendment in modern constitutional history. Nonetheless, the Contract Clause remains part of the Constitution. It is not a dead letter....

First of all, ... the Contract Clause does not operate to obliterate the police power of the States. "It is the settled law of this court that the interdiction of statutes impairing the obligation of contracts does not prevent the State from exercising such powers as are vested in it for the promotion of the common weal, or are necessary for the general good of the public, though contracts previously entered into between individuals may thereby be affected. This power, which in its various ramifications is known as the police power, is an exercise of the sovereign right of the Government to protect the lives, health, morals, comfort and general welfare of the people, and is paramount to any rights under contracts between individuals." Manigault v. Springs, 199 U.S. 473, 480. As Mr. Justice Holmes succinctly put the matter in his opinion for the Court in Hudson Water Co. v. McCarter, 209 U.S. 349, 357: "One whose rights, such as they are, are subject to state restriction, cannot remove them from the power of the State by making a contract about them. The contract will carry with it the infirmity of the subject matter."

B.

If the Contract Clause is to retain any meaning at all, however, it must be understood to impose some limits upon the power of a State to abridge existing contractual relationships, even in the exercise of its otherwise legitimate police power. The existence and nature of those limits were clearly indicated in a series of cases in this Court arising from the efforts of the States to deal with the unprecedented emergencies brought on by the severe economic depression of the early 1930's.

In Home Building & Loan Assn. v. Blaisdell, 290 U.S. 398, the Court upheld against a Contract Clause attack a mortgage moratorium law that Minnesota had enacted to provide relief for homeowners threatened with foreclosure. Although the legislation conflicted directly with lenders' contractual foreclosure rights, the Court there acknowledged that, despite the Contract Clause, the States retain residual authority to enact laws "to safeguard the vital interests of [their] people." ... In upholding the state mortgage moratorium law, the Court found five factors significant. First, the state legislature had declared in the Act itself that an emergency need for the protection of homeowners existed.... Second, the state law was enacted to protect a basic societal interest, not a favored group.... Third, the relief was appropriately tailored to the emergency that it was designed to meet.... Fourth, the imposed conditions were reasonable.... And, finally, the legislation was limited to the duration of the emergency....

The *Blaisdell* opinion thus clearly implied that if the Minnesota moratorium legislation had not possessed the characteristics attributed to it by the Court, it would have been invalid under the Contract Clause of the Constitution. These implications were given concrete force in three cases that followed closely in *Blaisdell's* wake.

In W.B. Worthen Co. v. Thomas, 292 U.S. 426, the Court dealt with an Arkansas law that exempted the proceeds of a life insurance policy from collection by the beneficiary's judgment creditors. Stressing the retroactive effect of the state law, the Court held that it was invalid under the Contract Clause, since it was not precisely and reasonably designed to meet a grave temporary emergency in the interest of the general welfare. In W.B. Worthen Co. v. Kavanaugh, 295 U.S. 56, the Court was confronted with another Arkansas law that diluted the rights and remedies of mortgage bondholders. The Court held the law invalid under the Contract Clause. "Even when the public welfare is invoked as an excuse," Mr. Justice Cardozo wrote for the Court, the security of a mortgage cannot be cut down "without moderation or reason or in a spirit of oppression." ... And finally, in Treigle v. Acme Homestead Assn., 297 U.S. 189, the Court held invalid under the Contract Clause a Louisiana law that modified the existing withdrawal rights of the members of a building and loan association. "Such an interference with the right of contract," said the Court, "cannot be justified by saying that in the public interest the operations of building associations may be controlled and regulated, or that in the same interest their charters may be amended."

. . .

III.

In applying these principles to the present case, the first inquiry must be whether the state law has, in fact, operated as a substantial impairment of a contractual relationship.[16] The severity of the impairment measures the height of the hurdle the state legislation must clear. Minimal alteration of contractual obligations may end the inquiry at its first stage. Severe impairment, on the other hand, will push the inquiry to a careful examination of the nature and purpose of the state legislation.

The severity of an impairment of contractual obligations can be measured by the factors that reflect the high value the Framers placed on the protection of private contracts. Contracts enable individuals to order their personal and business affairs according to their particular needs and interests. Once arranged, those rights and obligations are binding under the law, and the parties are entitled to rely on them.

Here, the company's contracts of employment with its employees included as a fringe benefit or additional form of compensation, the pension plan. The

---

16. The novel construction of the Contract Clause expressed in the dissenting opinion is wholly contrary to the decisions of this Court. The narrow view that the Clause forbids only state laws that diminish the duties of a contractual obligor and not laws that increase them, a view arguably suggested by Satterlee v. Matthewson, 2 Pet. 380, has since been expressly repudiated.... Moreover, in any bilateral contract the diminution of duties on one side effectively increases the duties on the other.

The even narrower view that the Clause is limited in its application to state laws relieving debtors of obligations to their creditors is, as the dissent recognizes, ... completely at odds with this Court's decisions. See Dartmouth College v. Woodward, 4 Wheat. 518....

company's maximum obligation was to set aside each year an amount based on the plan's requirements for vesting. The plan satisfied the current federal income tax code and was subject to no other legislative requirements. And, of course, the company was free to amend or terminate the pension plan at any time. The company thus had no reason to anticipate that its employees' pension rights could become vested except in accordance with the terms of the plan. It relied heavily, and reasonably, on this legitimate contractual expectation in calculating its annual contributions to the pension fund.

The effect of Minnesota's Private Pension Benefits Protection Act on this contractual obligation was severe. The company was required in 1974 to have made its contributions throughout the pre–1974 life of its plan as if employees' pension rights had vested after 10 years, instead of vesting in accord with the terms of the plan. Thus a basic term of the pension contract—one on which the company had relied for 10 years—was substantially modified. The result was that although the company's past contributions were adequate when made, they were not adequate when computed under the 10–year statutory vesting requirement. The Act thus forced a current recalculation of the past 10 years' contributions based on the new, unanticipated 10–year vesting requirement.

Not only did the state law thus retroactively modify the compensation that the company had agreed to pay its employees from 1963 to 1974, but it did so by changing the company's obligations in an area where the element of reliance was vital—the funding of a pension plan. . . .

Moreover, the retroactive state-imposed vesting requirement was applied only to those employers who terminated their pension plans or who, like the company, closed their Minnesota offices. The company was thus forced to make all the retroactive changes in its contractual obligations at one time. . . .

Thus, the statute . . . nullifies express terms of the company's contractual obligations and imposes a completely unexpected liability in potentially disabling amounts [without] even any provision for gradual applicability or grace periods. . . . Yet there is no showing in the record . . . that this severe disruption of contractual expectations was necessary to meet an important general social problem. The presumption favoring "legislative judgment as to the necessity and reasonableness of a particular measure," . . . simply cannot stand in this case.

. . .

This Minnesota law simply does not possess the attributes of those state laws that in the past have survived challenge under the Contract Clause. . . . The law was not even purportedly enacted to deal with a broad, generalized economic or social problem. Cf. Home Building & Loan Assn. v. Blaisdell, 290 U.S., at 445. It did not operate in an area already subject to state regulation at the time the company's contractual obligations were originally undertaken, but invaded an area never before subject to regulation by the State. . . . It did not effect simply a temporary alteration of the contractual relationships of those within its coverage, but worked a severe, permanent, and immediate change in those relationships—irrevocably and retroactively. . . . And its narrow aim was levelled not at every Minnesota employer, not even at every Minnesota employer who left the State, . . . but only at those who had in the past been sufficiently enlightened as voluntarily to agree to establish pension plans for their employees.

"Not Blaisdell's case, but Worthen's (W.B. Worthen Co. v. Thomas, [292 U.S. 426])supplies the applicable rule" here. W.B. Worthen Co. v. Kavanaugh, 295 U.S. 56, 63. It is not necessary to hold that the Minnesota law impaired the obligation of the company's employment contracts "without moderation or reason or in a spirit of oppression." . . . But we do hold that if the Contract Clause means anything at all, it means that Minnesota could not constitutionally do what it tried to do to the company in this case.

The judgment of the District Court is reversed.

. . .

Mr. Justice Blackmun took no part in the consideration or decision of this case.

Mr. Justice Brennan, with whom Mr. Justice White and Mr. Justice Marshall join, dissenting.

. . .

Today's decision greatly expands the reach of the [Contract] Clause. The . . . Act . . . does not abrogate or dilute any obligation due a party to a private contract; rather, like all positive social legislation, the Act imposes new, additional obligations on a particular class of persons. In my view, any constitutional infirmity in the law must therefore derive, not from the Contract Clause, but from the Due Process Clause of the Fourteenth Amendment. I perceive nothing in the Act that works a denial of Due Process and therefore I dissent.

. . .

II.

The primary question in this case is whether the Contract Clause is violated by state legislation enacted to protect employees covered by a pension plan by requiring an employer to make outlays . . . to provide terminated employees with the equivalent of benefits reasonably to be expected under the plan. The Act does not relieve either the employer or his employees of any existing contract obligation. Rather, the Act simply creates an additional, supplemental duty of the employer, no different in kind from myriad duties created by a wide variety of legislative measures which defeat settled expectations but which have nonetheless been sustained by this Court. See, e.g., Usery v. Turner Elkhorn Mining Co., 428 U.S. 1 (1976); Hadacheck v. Sebastian, 239 U.S. 394 (1915). For this reason, the Minnesota Act . . . does not implicate the Contract Clause in any way. The basic fallacy of today's decision is its mistaken view that the Contract Clause protects all contract based expectations, including that of an employer that his obligations to his employees will not be legislatively enlarged beyond those explicitly provided in his pension plan.

. . .

C.

. . . [I]t is no more anomalous to give effect to the term "impairment" and deny a claimant protection under the Contract Clause when new duties are created than it is to give effect to the Clause's inapplicability to acts of the National Government and deny a Contract Clause remedy when an act of Congress denies a creditor the ability to enforce a contract right to payment. Both results are simply consequences of the fact that the Clause does not protect all contract based expectations.

More fundamentally, the Court's distortion of the meaning of the Contract Clause creates anomalies of its own and threatens to undermine the jurisprudence of property rights developed over the last 40 years. The Contract Clause, of course, is but one of several clauses in the Constitution that protect existing economic values from governmental interference. The Fifth Amendment's command that "private property [shall not] be taken for public use, without just compensation" is such a clause. A second is the Due Process Clause, which during the heyday of substantive due process, see Lochner v. New York, 198 U.S. 45 (1905), largely supplanted the Contract Clause in importance and operated as a potent limitation on Government's ability to interfere with economic expectations.... Decisions over the past 50 years have developed a coherent, unified interpretation of all the constitutional provisions that may protect economic expectations and these decisions have recognized a broad latitude in States to effect even severe interference with existing economic values when reasonably necessary to promote the general welfare. See Penn Central Transp. Co. v. New York City, 438 U.S. 104.... At the same time the prohibition of the Contract Clause, consistently with its wording and historic purposes, has been limited in application to state laws that diluted, with utter indifference to the legitimate interests of the beneficiary of a contract duty, the existing contract obligation....

Today's conversion of the Contract Clause ... must inevitably produce results difficult to square with any rational conception of a constitutional order. Under the Court's opinion, any law that may be characterized as "superimposing" new obligations on those provided for by contract is to be regarded as creating "sudden, substantial, and unanticipated burdens" and then to be subjected to the most exacting scrutiny. The validity of such a law will turn upon whether judges see it as a law that deals with a generalized social problem, whether it is temporary (as few will be) or permanent, whether it operates in an area previously subject to regulation, and, finally, whether its duties apply to a broad class of persons.... The necessary consequence of the extreme malleability of these rather vague criteria is to vest judges with broad subjective discretion to protect property interests that happen to appeal to them.

To permit this level of scrutiny of laws that interfere with contract based expectations is an anomaly. There is nothing sacrosanct about expectations rooted in contract that justify according them a constitutional immunity denied other property rights. Laws that interfere with settled expectations created by state property law (and which impose severe economic burdens) are uniformly held constitutional where reasonably related to the promotion of the general welfare. Hadacheck v. Sebastian, 239 U.S. 394 (1915), is illustrative. There a property owner had established on a particular parcel of land a perfectly lawful business of a brickyard, and, in reliance on the existing law, continued to operate that business for a number of years. However, a local ordinance was passed prohibiting the operation of brickyards in the particular locale and diminishing the value of the claimant's parcel and thus of his investment by nearly 90%. Notwithstanding the effect of the ordinance on the value of the investment, the ordinance was sustained against a taking claim. See also Miller v. Schoene, 276 U.S. 272 (1928) (statute required cutting down ornamental red cedar trees because they had cedar rust which would be harmful to apple trees in the vicinity).

There is no logical or rational basis for sustaining the duties created by the laws in *Miller* and *Hadacheck,* but invalidating the duty created by the Minnesota Act. Surely, the Act effects no greater interference with reasonable reliance interests than did these other laws. Moreover, the laws operate identically: they all create duties that burden one class of persons and benefit another. The only difference between the present case and *Hadacheck* or *Miller* is that here there was a prior contractual relationship between the members of the benefited and burdened classes. I simply cannot accept that this difference should possess constitutional significance. The only means of avoiding this anomaly is to construe the Contract Clause consistently with its terms and the original understanding and hold it is inapplicable to laws which create new duties.

. . .

ENERGY RESERVES GROUP, INC. v. KANSAS POWER & LIGHT CO., 459 U.S. 400 (1983). In 1975 Kansas Power & Light Co. (KPL) entered into two contracts with the predecessor-in-interest of Energy Reserves Group, Inc. (erg) to purchase natural gas from wells in Kansas. The initial price was $1.50 per thousand cubic feet (MCF) of gas but the contracts contained a government price escalation clause under which the price would rise to any price fixed by a governmental authority.

Congress passed the Natural Gas Policy Act of 1978. Section 102 of the Act fixed a gradually increasing price for newly discovered natural gas, which in December, 1978, was $2.078 per million British thermal units. Section 109 of the Act set a price for gas not otherwise covered at $1.63 per million Btus. The Act also regulated intrastate gas sales for the first time, fixing as a maximum price that under § 102 and permitting state regulation so long as prices fixed did not exceed the § 102 price. It was agreed that the gas contracts in dispute were intrastate and governed by this latter provision.

Kansas promptly passed a statute applicable to natural gas contracts entered before 1977 and controlling gas prices only until 1984. It specifically prohibited gas price contracts to operate so as to increase the prices of old intrastate gas beyond those set in § 109 of the federal act.

ERG took the position that under the contracts the price escalated to that of § 102 under the federal act and that the state could not change the contracts. KPL contended that the state act applied and the price should be that under § 109 of the federal act. ERG sued, but the Kansas courts held that the Kansas act applied and that the contract clause did not require otherwise. The Supreme Court, in an opinion written by Justice Blackmun, unanimously agreed with the Kansas courts.

A

"Although the language of the Contract Clause is facially absolute, its prohibition must be accommodated to the inherent police power of the State 'to safeguard the vital interests of its people.' Home Bldg. & Loan Ass'n v. Blaisdell, 290 U.S. 398, 434 (1934)....

. . .

"The threshold inquiry is 'whether the state law has, in fact, operated as a substantial impairment of a contractual relationship.' *Allied Structural Steel Co.,*.... See *United States Trust Co.,*..... The severity of the impairment is said to increase the level of scrutiny to which the legislation will be subjected. *Allied Structural Steel Co.,*..... Total destruction of contractual expectations is not necessary for a finding of substantial impairment. *United States Trust Co.,*.... On the other hand, state regulation that restricts a party to gains it reasonably expected from the contract does not necessarily constitute a substantial impairment. Id., at 31, citing El Paso v. Simmons, 379 U.S. 497, 515 (1965). In determining the extent of the impairment, we are to consider whether the industry the complaining party has entered has been regulated in the past. *Allied Structural Steel Co.,* ... citing Veix v. Sixth Ward Bldg. & Loan Ass'n, 310 U.S. 32, 38 (1940) ('When he purchased into an enterprise already regulated in the particular to which he now objects, he purchased subject to further legislation upon the same topic')....

"If the state regulation constitutes a substantial impairment, the State, in justification, must have a significant and legitimate public purpose behind the regulation, *United States Trust Co.,* ... such as the remedying of a broad and general social or economic problem. *Allied Structural Steel Co.,*.... Furthermore, since *Blaisdell,* the Court has indicated that the public purpose need not be addressed to an emergency or temporary situation. *United States Trust Co.,*.... One legitimate state interest is the elimination of unforeseen windfall profits. *United States Trust Co.,*.... The requirement of a legitimate public purpose guarantees that the State is exercising its police power, rather than providing a benefit to special interests.

"Once a legitimate public purpose has been identified, the next inquiry is whether the adjustment of 'the rights and responsibilities of contracting parties [is based] upon reasonable conditions and [is] of a character appropriate to the public purpose justifying [the legislation's] adoption.' *United States Trust Co.,*.... Unless the State itself is a contracting party,....[14] '[a]s is customary in reviewing economic and social regulation, ... courts properly defer to legislative judgment as to the necessity and reasonableness of a particular measure.' ...

B

"The threshold determination is whether the Kansas Act has impaired substantially ERG's contractual rights. Significant here is the fact that the parties are operating in a heavily regulated industry....

. . .

"Moreover, the contracts expressly recognize the existence of extensive regulation by providing that any contractual terms are subject to relevant present and future state and federal law. This latter provision could be interpreted to incorporate all future state price regulation, and thus dispose of the Contract Clause claim. Regardless of whether this interpretation is correct, the provision does suggest that ERG knew its contractual rights were subject to alteration by state price regulation. Price regulation existed and was foreseeable as the type of law that would alter contract obligations. Reading the Contract Clause as ERG does would mean that indefinite price escalator clauses could exempt ERG from any regulatory limitation of prices whatsoever. Such a result cannot be permitted. Hudson Water Co. v. McCarter, 209 U.S., at 357. In short, ERG's reasonable expectations have not been impaired by the Kansas Act. See El Paso v. Simmons, 379 U.S., at 515.

C

"To the extent, if any, the Kansas Act impairs ERG's contractual interests, the Kansas Act rests on, and is prompted by, significant and legitimate state interests....

"... There can be little doubt about the legitimate public purpose behind the Act.

---

14. See, generally, Note, A Process–Oriented Approach to the Contract Clause, 89 Yale L.J. 1623, 1647–1648 (1980) (distinguishing public from private contracts). In United States Trust Co., but not in Allied Structural Steel Co., the State was one of the contracting parties. When a State itself enters into a contract, it cannot simply walk away from its financial obligations. In almost every case, the Court has held a governmental unit to its contractual obligations when it enters financial or other markets. See United States Trust Co.,.... When the State is a party to the contract, "complete deference to a legislative assessment of reasonableness and necessity is not appropriate because the State's self-interest is at stake." United States Trust Co.,.... In the present case, of course, the stricter standard of United States Trust Co. does not apply because Kansas has not altered its own contractual obligations.

"Nor are the means chosen to implement these purposes deficient, particularly in light of the deference to which the Kansas Legislature's judgment is entitled.

"We thus resolve the constitutional issue against ERG."

. . .

"Justice Powell, with whom The Chief Justice and Justice Rehnquist join, concurring.

"I concur in the judgment and all of the Court's opinion except Part II–C. The Court concludes in Part II–B that there has been no substantial impairment of ERG's contractual rights. The closing sentence states that 'ERG's reasonable expectations have not been impaired by the Kansas Act.' This conclusion is dispositive, and it is unnecessary for the Court to address the question of whether, if there were an impairment of contractual rights, it would constitute a violation of the Contract Clause. See Allied Structural Steel Co. v. Spannaus, 438 U.S. 234, 245 (1978)."

EXXON CORP. v. EAGERTON, 462 U.S. 176 (1983). Alabama increased its severance tax on oil and gas and prohibited passing on the increase to purchasers. Some producers of oil and gas were parties to contracts made before the tax increase under which they were permitted to include in their price to customers any increase in severance taxes. The Court held unanimously that application of the pass-through prohibition to those contracts did not violate the contract clause. The Court said: "the prohibition applied to all oil and gas producers, regardless of whether they happened to be parties to sale contracts that contained a provision permitting them to pass tax increases through to their purchasers. The effect of the pass-through prohibition on existing contracts that did contain such a provision was incidental to its main effect of shielding consumers from the burden of the tax increase."[a]

C. THE JUST COMPENSATION CLAUSE OF THE FIFTH AMENDMENT—WHAT DOES IT ADD TO DUE PROCESS?

Introduction. The Fifth Amendment commands that "private property [not] be taken for public use, without just compensation." The primary focus of this section (subsections 1. and 2.) is not on the explicit exercise of the power of eminent domain, but on the frequently disputed issue of what kind of government regulation affecting the use of property constitutes a "taking" of it. Some attention is also given to the issues of what constitutes "property" protected by the amendment and, in subsection 3., what government's obligation is in the event of a taking.

A fourth issue, addressed here, arises because property may not be taken, even if compensation is offered, unless the taking is for a "public use." Missouri Pacific R. Co. v. Nebraska, 164 U.S. 403 (1896). Judicial scrutiny of

---

a. The contract clause is a restraint on state law only. Federal legislation impairing the obligation of contracts is subject to review under the due process clause of the Fifth Amendment, but, as the Court said in Pension Benefit Guaranty Corp. v. R.A. Gray & Co., 467 U.S. 717 (1984), the standard of review is "less searching." The Court said little more but emphasized that it had "never held ... that the principles embodied in the Fifth Amendment's Due Process Clause are coextensive with prohibitions existing against state impairments of pre-existing contracts." In National Railroad Passenger Corp. v. Atchison, Topeka and Santa Fe Railway Co., 470 U.S. 451 (1985), the Court did say that judicial scrutiny of federal legislation impairing a private contract should be "quite minimal" and added: "The party asserting a Fifth Amendment due process violation must overcome a presumption of constitutionality and 'establish that the legislature has acted in an arbitrary and irrational way.' "

the "public use" requirement has been quite limited, however. In Berman v. Parker, 348 U.S. 26 (1954), for example, the Court held that taking a private, decently maintained commercial property located in an otherwise blighted area for transfer to a private redevelopment agency to build private housing as part of an area redevelopment plan satisfied the public use requirement. The Court said: "The role of the judiciary in determining whether that power [of eminent domain] is being exercised for a public purpose is an extremely narrow one." That generous approach was followed in Hawaii Housing Authority v. Midkiff, 467 U.S. 229 (1984), which allowed eminent domain to be used to force the sale of fee simple title by Hawaiian land owners to their tenants. Hawaii's historically extraordinary concentration of private land ownership in a few hands had been found by the legislature to distort the residential ownership market, and reduction of the harms of oligopoly was a sufficient public purpose to justify the taking. Although the Court found the " 'public use' requirement ... coterminous with the scope of a sovereign's police powers," it reiterated nonetheless that there is "a role for courts to play in reviewing a legislature's judgment of what constitutes a public use," and stated that "where the exercise of the eminent domain power is rationally related to a conceivable public purpose, the Court has never held a compensated taking to be proscribed by the Public Use Clause."

In Brown v. Legal Foundation of Washington, 538 U.S. 216 (2003), the Court determined that paying for legal services for the needy using interest earned on pooled client funds that lawyers hold in trust accounts "unquestionably satisfied" the "public use" requirement:

"If the State had imposed a special tax, or perhaps a system of user fees, to generate the funds to finance the legal services supported by the Foundation, there would be no question as to the legitimacy of the use of the public's money. The fact that public funds might pay the legal fees of a lawyer representing a tenant in a dispute with a landlord who was compelled to contribute to the program would not undermine the public character of the 'use' of the funds. Provided that she receives just compensation for the taking of her property, a conscientious pacifist has no standing to object to the government's decision to use the property she formerly owned for the production of munitions. Even if there may be occasional misuses of IOLTA [Interest On Lawyer Trust Account] funds, the overall, dramatic success of these programs in serving the compelling interest in providing legal services to literally millions of needy Americans certainly qualifies the Foundation's distribution of these funds as a 'public use' within the meaning of the Fifth Amendment."

A footnote in Justice Scalia's dissenting opinion for four Justices objected to the Court having "announce[d] a new criterion for 'public use' ... [that] reduces the ... requirement to a negligible impediment indeed, since I am unaware of *any* use to which state taxes cannot constitutionally be devoted.... Taxes and user fees, since they are not 'takings,' see *United States v. Sperry Corp.*, 493 U.S. 52 (1989), are simply not subject to the 'public use' requirement, and so their constitutional legitimacy is entirely irrelevant to the existence *vel non* of a public use."

1.   RESTRICTIONS ON PROPERTY USE

Lucas v. South Carolina Coastal Council

505 U.S. 1003, 112 S.Ct. 2886, 120 L.Ed.2d 798 (1992).

Justice Scalia delivered the opinion of the Court.

In 1986, petitioner ... paid $975,000 for two residential lots on the Isle of Palms ... intend[ing] to build single-family homes. In 1988, however, the

South Carolina Legislature enacted the Beachfront Management Act ... (Act), which had the direct effect of barring petitioner from erecting any permanent habitable structures on his two parcels.... A state trial court found that this prohibition rendered Lucas's parcels "valueless." ... This case requires us to decide whether the Act's dramatic effect on the economic value of Lucas's lots accomplished a taking of private property under the Fifth and Fourteenth Amendments requiring the payment of "just compensation." ...

. . .

III

A

Prior to Justice Holmes' exposition in Pennsylvania Coal Co. v. Mahon, 260 U.S. 393 (1922), it was generally thought that the Takings Clause reached only a "direct appropriation" of property, ... or the functional equivalent of a "practical ouster of [the owner's] possession." ... Justice Holmes recognized in *Mahon,* however, that if the protection against physical appropriations of private property was to be meaningfully enforced, the government's power to redefine the range of interests included in the ownership of property was necessarily constrained by constitutional limits.... If, instead, the uses of private property were subject to unbridled, uncompensated qualification under the police power, "the natural tendency of human nature [would be] to extend the qualification more and more until at last private property disappear[ed]." ... These considerations gave birth in that case to the oft-cited maxim that, "while property may be regulated to a certain extent, if regulation goes too far it will be recognized as a taking." ...

... *Mahon* offered little insight into when, and under what circumstances, a given regulation would be seen as going "too far" for purposes of the Fifth Amendment. In 70–odd years of succeeding "regulatory takings" jurisprudence, we have generally eschewed any " 'set formula' " for determining how far is too far, preferring to "engag[e] in ... essentially ad hoc, factual inquiries," Penn Central Transportation Co. v. New York City, 438 U.S. 104, 124 (1978).... We have, however, described at least two discrete categories of regulatory action as compensable without case-specific inquiry into the public interest advanced in support of the restraint. The first encompasses regulations that compel the property owner to suffer a physical "invasion" of his property. In general (at least with regard to permanent invasions), no matter how minute the intrusion, and no matter how weighty the public purpose behind it, we have required compensation. For example, in Loretto v. Teleprompter Manhattan CATV Corp., 458 U.S. 419 (1982), we determined that New York's law requiring landlords to allow television cable companies to emplace cable facilities in their apartment buildings constituted a taking, ... even though the facilities occupied at most only 1 ½ cubic feet of the landlords' property.... See also United States v. Causby, 328 U.S. 256, 265, and n. 10 (1946) (physical invasions of airspace); cf. Kaiser Aetna v. United States, 444 U.S. 164 (1979) (imposition of navigational servitude upon private marina).

The second ... is where regulation denies all economically beneficial or productive use of land.... As we have said on numerous occasions, the Fifth Amendment is violated when land-use regulation "does not substantially advance legitimate state interests *or denies an owner economically viable use of his land.*" Agins . . .[7]

We have never set forth the justification for this rule. Perhaps . . ., as Justice Brennan suggested, . . . total deprivation of beneficial use is, from the landowner's point of view, the equivalent of a physical appropriation. . . . Surely, at least, in the extraordinary circumstance when *no* productive or economically beneficial use of land is permitted, it is less realistic to indulge our usual assumption that the legislature is simply "adjusting the benefits and burdens of economic life," Penn Central Transportation Co., . . . in a manner that secures an "average reciprocity of advantage" to everyone concerned. *Pennsylvania Coal Co. v. Mahon.* . . . And the *functional* basis for permitting the government, by regulation, to affect property values without compensation—that "Government hardly could go on if to some extent values incident to property could not be diminished without paying for every such change in the general law"—does not apply to the relatively rare situations where the government has deprived a landowner of all economically beneficial uses.

On the other side of the balance, affirmatively supporting a compensation requirement, is the fact that regulations that leave the owner of land without economically beneficial or productive options for its use—typically, as here, by requiring land to be left substantially in its natural state—carry with them a heightened risk that private property is being pressed into some form of public service under the guise of mitigating serious public harm. . . . The many statutes on the books, both state and federal, that provide for the use of eminent domain to impose servitudes on private scenic lands preventing developmental uses, or to acquire such lands altogether, suggest the practical equivalence in this setting of negative regulation and appropriation. . . .

We think, in short, that there are good reasons for our frequently expressed belief that when the owner of real property has been called upon to sacrifice all economically beneficial uses in the name of the common good, that is, to leave his property economically idle, he has suffered a taking.[8]

---

7. Regrettably, the rhetorical force of our "deprivation of all economically feasible use" rule is greater than its precision, since the rule does not make clear the "property interest" against which the loss of value is to be measured. When, for example, a regulation requires a developer to leave 90% of a rural tract in its natural state, it is unclear whether we would analyze the situation as one in which the owner has been deprived of all economically beneficial use of the burdened portion of the tract, or as one in which the owner has suffered a mere diminution in value of the tract as a whole. . . . Unsurprisingly, this uncertainty regarding the composition of the denominator in our "deprivation" fraction has produced inconsistent pronouncements by the Court. Compare Pennsylvania Coal Co. v. Mahon, 260 U.S. 393, 414 (1922) (law restricting subsurface extraction of coal held to effect a taking), with Keystone Bituminous Coal Assn. v. DeBenedictis, 480 U.S. 470, 497–502 (1987) (nearly identical law held not to effect a taking) . . . The answer to this difficult question may lie in how the owner's reasonable expectations have been shaped by the State's law of prop-

erty—i.e., whether and to what degree the State's law has accorded legal recognition and protection to the particular interest in land with respect to which the takings claimant alleges a diminution in (or elimination of) value. In any event, we avoid this difficulty in the present case, since the "interest in land" that Lucas has pleaded (a fee simple interest) is an estate with a rich tradition of protection at common law, and since the South Carolina Court of Common Pleas found that the Beachfront Management Act left each of Lucas's beachfront lots without economic value.

8. Justice Stevens criticizes the "deprivation of all economically beneficial use" rule as "wholly arbitrary," in that "[the] landowner whose property is diminished in value 95% recovers nothing," while the landowner who suffers a complete elimination of value "recovers the land's full value." This analysis errs in its assumption that the landowner whose deprivation is one step short of complete is not entitled to compensation. Such an owner might not be able to claim the benefit of our categorical formulation, but, as we have acknowledged time and again, "[t]he economic impact of the regulation on the

B

. . .

[M]any of our prior opinions have suggested that "harmful or noxious uses" of property may be proscribed by government regulation without the requirement of compensation.... "Harmful or noxious use" analysis was, [however], simply the progenitor of our more contemporary statements that "land-use regulation does not effect a taking if it 'substantially advance[s] legitimate state interests'...." *Nollan*....

The transition from our early focus on control of "noxious" uses to our contemporary understanding of the broad realm within which government may regulate without compensation was an easy one, since the distinction between "harm-preventing" and "benefit-conferring" regulation is often in the eye of the beholder. [F]or example, ... [o]ne could say that imposing a servitude on Lucas's land is necessary in order to prevent his use of it from "harming" South Carolina's ecological resources; or, instead, in order to achieve the "benefits" of an ecological preserve.... Whether Lucas's construction of single-family residences on his parcels should be described as bringing "harm" to South Carolina's adjacent ecological resources ... depends principally upon whether the describer believes that the State's use interest in nurturing those resources is so important that any competing adjacent use must yield.

... [N]oxious-use logic [thus] cannot serve as a touchstone to distinguish regulatory "takings"—which require compensation—from regulatory deprivations that do not require compensation. *A fortiori* the legislature's recitation of a noxious-use justification cannot be the basis for departing from our categorical rule that total regulatory takings must be compensated.... None of [our cases] that employed the logic of "harmful use" prevention to sustain a regulation involved an allegation that the regulation wholly eliminated the value of the claimant's land....

Where the State seeks to sustain regulation that deprives land of all economically beneficial use, we think it may resist compensation only if the logically antecedent inquiry into the nature of the owner's estate shows that the proscribed use interests were not part of his title to begin with. This accords, we think, with our "takings" jurisprudence, which has traditionally been guided by the understandings of our citizens regarding the content of, and the State's power over, the "bundle of rights" that they acquire when they obtain title to property. [T]he property owner necessarily expects the uses of his property to be restricted, from time to time, by various measures newly enacted by the State in legitimate exercise of its police powers; "[a]s long recognized, some values are enjoyed under an implied limitation and must yield to the police power." *Pennsylvania Coal Co. v. Mahon*.... And in the case of personal property, by reason of the State's traditionally high degree of control over commercial dealings, he ought to be aware of the possibility that new regulation might even render his property economically worthless.... In the case of land, however, ... the notion ... that title is somehow held subject to

claimant and ... the extent to which the regulation has interfered with distinct investment-backed expectations" are keenly relevant to takings analysis generally. Penn Central Transportation Co. v. New York City, 438 U.S. 104, 124 (1978). It is true that in at least some cases the landowner with 95% loss will get nothing, while the landowner with total loss will recover in full. But that occa-

sional result is no more strange than the gross disparity between the landowner whose premises are taken for a highway (who recovers in full) and the landowner whose property is reduced to 5% of its former value by the highway (who recovers nothing). Takings law is full of these "all-or-nothing" situations....

the "implied limitation" that the State may subsequently eliminate all economically valuable use is inconsistent with the historical compact recorded in the Takings Clause that has become part of our constitutional culture.

Where "permanent physical occupation" of land is concerned, we have refused to allow the government to decree it anew (without compensation), no matter how weighty the asserted "public interests" involved, *Loretto* ... — though we assuredly *would* permit the government to assert a permanent easement that was a pre-existing limitation upon the landowner's title. Compare Scranton v. Wheeler ... (1900) (interests of "riparian owner in the submerged lands ... bordering on a public navigable water" held subject to Government's navigational servitude), with *Kaiser Aetna v. United States* ... (imposition of navigational servitude on marina created and rendered navigable at private expense held to constitute a taking). We believe similar treatment must be accorded confiscatory regulations, i.e., regulations that prohibit all economically beneficial use of land: Any limitation so severe cannot be newly legislated or decreed (without compensation), but must inhere in the title itself, in the restrictions that background principles of the State's law of property and nuisance already place upon land ownership. A law or decree with such an effect must, in other words, do no more than duplicate the result that could have been achieved in the courts—by adjacent landowners (or other uniquely affected persons) under the State's law of private nuisance, or by the State under its complementary power to abate nuisances that affect the public generally, or otherwise.

On this analysis, the owner of a lake bed, for example, would not be entitled to compensation when he is denied the requisite permit to engage in a landfilling operation that would have the effect of flooding others' land. Nor the corporate owner of a nuclear generating plant, when it is directed to remove all improvements from its land upon discovery that the plant sits astride an earthquake fault. Such regulatory action may well have the effect of eliminating the land's only economically productive use, but it does not proscribe a productive use that was previously permissible under relevant property and nuisance principles. The use of these properties for what are now expressly prohibited purposes was always unlawful, and (subject to other constitutional limitations) it was open to the State at any point to make the implication of those background principles of nuisance and property law explicit.... When, however, a regulation that declares "off-limits" all economically productive or beneficial uses of land goes beyond what the relevant background principles would dictate, compensation must be paid to sustain it.

The "total taking" inquiry we require today will ordinarily entail (as the application of state nuisance law ordinarily entails) analysis of, among other things, the degree of harm to public lands and resources, or adjacent private property, posed by the claimant's proposed activities, ... the social value of the claimant's activities and their suitability to the locality in question, ... and the relative ease with which the alleged harm can be avoided through measures taken by the claimant and the government (or adjacent private landowners) alike.... The fact that a particular use has long been engaged in by similarly situated owners ordinarily imports a lack of any common-law prohibition (though changed circumstances or new knowledge may make what was previously permissible no longer so ...). So also does the fact that other landowners, similarly situated, are permitted to continue the use denied to the claimant.

It seems unlikely that common-law principles would have prevented the erection of any habitable or productive improvements on petitioner's land; they rarely support prohibition of the "essential use" of land.... The question, however, is one of state law to be dealt with on remand. We emphasize that to win its case South Carolina must do more than proffer the legislature's declaration that the uses Lucas desires are inconsistent with the public interest, or the conclusory assertion that they violate a common-law maxim. . . . Instead, as it would be required to do if it sought to restrain Lucas in a common-law action for public nuisance, South Carolina must identify background principles of nuisance and property law that prohibit the uses he now intends in the circumstances in which the property is presently found. Only on this showing can the State fairly claim that, in proscribing all such beneficial uses, the Beachfront Management Act is taking nothing.

. . .

Justice Kennedy, concurring in the judgment.

. . .

. . . I share the reservations of some of my colleagues about a finding that a beach front lot loses all value because of a development restriction. . . .

The finding of no value must be considered under the Takings Clause by reference to the owner's reasonable, investment-backed expectations. . . . Property is bought and sold, investments are made, subject to the State's power to regulate. Where a taking is alleged from regulations which deprive the property of all value, the test must be whether the deprivation is contrary to reasonable, investment-backed expectations.

There is an inherent tendency towards circularity in this synthesis, of course; for if the owner's reasonable expectations are shaped by what courts allow as a proper exercise of governmental authority, property tends to become what courts say it is. Some circularity must be tolerated in these matters, however. . . . The definition, moreover, is not circular in its entirety. The expectations protected by the Constitution are based on objective rules and customs that can be understood as reasonable by all parties involved.

[R]easonable expectations must be understood in light of the whole of our legal tradition. The common law of nuisance is too narrow a confine for the exercise of regulatory power in a complex and interdependent society. . . . The State should not be prevented from enacting new regulatory initiatives in response to changing conditions, and courts must consider all reasonable expectations whatever their source. The Takings Clause does not require a static body of state property law; it protects private expectations to ensure private investment. I agree with the Court that nuisance prevention accords with the most common expectations of property owners who face regulation, but I do not believe this can be the sole source of state authority to impose severe restrictions. Coastal property may present such unique concerns for a fragile land system that the State can go further in regulating its development and use than the common law of nuisance might otherwise permit.

The Supreme Court of South Carolina erred . . . by reciting the general purposes for which the state regulations were enacted without a determination that they were in accord with the owner's reasonable expectations and therefore sufficient to support a severe restriction on specific parcels of property. . . . The promotion of tourism, for instance, ought not to suffice to deprive specific property of all value without a corresponding duty to compensate. Furthermore, the means as well as the ends of regulation must accord with the owner's reasonable expectations. Here, the State did not act until after the property had been zoned for individual lot development and most other parcels had been improved, throwing the whole burden of the regulation on the remaining lots. . . .

. . .

Justice Blackmun, dissenting.

. . .

The South Carolina Supreme Court . . . decision rested on two premises that until today were unassailable—that the State has the power to prevent any use of property it finds to be harmful to its citizens, and that a state statute is entitled to a presumption of constitutionality.

. . .

Nothing in the record undermines the General Assembly's assessment that prohibitions on building in front of the setback line are necessary to protect people and property from storms, high tides, and beach erosion. Because that legislative determination cannot be disregarded in the absence of such evidence, . . . and because its determination of harm to life and property from building is sufficient to prohibit that use under this Court's cases, the South Carolina Supreme Court correctly found no taking.

. . .

. . . [C]laimants have the burden of showing a state law constitutes a taking. . . .

[T]he Court decides the State has the burden to convince the courts that its legislative judgments are correct. . . .

IV

The Court . . . create[s] a new scheme for regulations that eliminate all economic value[—]a categorical rule finding these regulations to be a taking unless the use they prohibit is a background common-law nuisance or property principle.

A

. . . If one fact about the Court's taking jurisprudence can be stated without contradiction, it is that "the particular circumstances of each case" determine whether a specific restriction will be rendered invalid by the government's failure to pay compensation. . . . When the government regulation prevents the owner from any economically valuable use of his property, the private interest is unquestionably substantial, but we have never before held that no public interest can outweigh it. . . .

This Court repeatedly has recognized the ability of government, in certain circumstances, to regulate property without compensation no matter how adverse the financial effect on the owner may be. . . .

. . .

The Court . . . claim[s] that [prior cases] never . . . upheld a regulation when the owner alleged the loss of all economic value. Even if th[at] factual premise were correct, its understanding of the Court's cases is distorted. In none . . . did the Court suggest that the right of a State to prohibit certain activities without paying compensation turned on the availability of some residual valuable use. Instead, the cases depended on whether the government interest was sufficient to prohibit the activity, given the significant private cost.

These cases rest on the principle that the State has full power to prohibit an owner's use of property if it is harmful to the public. . . .

B

. . .

. . . [T]he Court has relied in the past . . . on legislative judgments of what constitutes a harm.

. . .

. . . In determining what is a nuisance at common law, state courts make exactly the decision that the Court finds so troubling when made by the South Carolina General Assembly today: they determine whether the use is harmful. Common-law public and private nuisance law is simply a determination whether a particular use causes harm. . . . If judges in the 18th and 19th centuries can distinguish a harm from a benefit, why not judges in the 20th century, and if judges can, why not legislators? . . .

C

. . .

[H]istory [does not] indicate any common-law limit on the State's power to regulate harmful uses even to the point of destroying all economic value. Nothing in the discussions in Congress concerning the Taking Clause indicates that the Clause was limited by the common-law nuisance doctrine. . . .

In short, I find no clear and accepted "historical compact" or "understanding of our citizens" justifying the Court's new taking doctrine. . . . If the Court decided that the early common law provides the background principles for interpreting the Taking Clause, then regulation, as opposed to physical confiscation, would not be compensable. If the Court decided that the law of a later period provides the background principles, then regulation might be compensable, but the Court would have to confront the fact that legislatures regularly determined which uses were prohibited, independent of the common law, and independent of whether the uses were lawful when the owner purchased. What makes the Court's analysis unworkable is its attempt to package the law of two incompatible eras and peddle it as historical fact.

. . .

Justice Stevens, dissenting.

. . .

[T]he Court is doubly in error. The categorical rule the Court establishes is an unsound and unwise addition to the law and the Court's formulation of the exception to that rule is too rigid and too narrow.

The Categorical Rule

. . .

. . . We have frequently—and recently—held that, in some circumstances, a law that renders property valueless may nonetheless not constitute a taking. . . .

In addition to lacking support in past decisions, the Court's new rule is wholly arbitrary. A landowner whose property is diminished in value 95%

recovers nothing, while an owner whose property is diminished 100% recovers the land's full value. . . .

Moreover, because of the elastic nature of property rights, the Court's new rule will also prove unsound in practice. In response to the rule, courts may define "property" broadly and only rarely find regulations to effect total takings. . . .[3]

On the other hand, developers and investors may market specialized estates to take advantage of the Court's new rule. The smaller the estate, the more likely that a regulatory change will effect a total taking. Thus, an investor may, for example, purchase the right to build a multi-family home on a specific lot, with the result that a zoning regulation that allows only single-family homes would render the investor's property interest "valueless." In short, the categorical rule will likely have one of two effects: Either courts will alter the definition of the "denominator" in the takings "fraction," rendering the Court's categorical rule meaningless, or investors will manipulate the relevant property interests, giving the Court's rule sweeping effect. [N]either . . . is desirable or appropriate, and both are distortions of our takings jurisprudence.

Finally, the Court's justification for its new categorical rule is remarkably thin. . . . First, . . . that "total deprivation of feasible use is, from the landowner's point of view, the equivalent of a physical appropriation[,]" proves too much. From the "landowner's point of view," a regulation that diminishes a lot's value by 50% is as well "the equivalent" of the condemnation of half of the lot. Yet, it is well established that a 50% diminution in value does not by itself constitute a taking. See Euclid v. Ambler Realty Co., . . . (1926) (75% diminution in value). Thus, the landowner's perception of the regulation cannot justify the Court's new rule.

Second, . . . that because total takings are "relatively rare" [the Court's] new rule will not adversely affect the government's ability to "go on[,]" proves too little. . . . The Court's suggestion only begs the question of why regulations of *this* particular class should always be found to effect takings.

Finally, . . . the risks of . . . singling out [certain private property] do not justify a *per se* rule for total regulatory takings. There is no necessary correlation between "singling out" and total takings: a regulation may single out a property owner without depriving him of all of his property . . . ; and it may deprive him of all of his property without singling him out. . . . What matters . . . is not the degree of diminution of value, but rather the specificity of the expropriating act. . . .

In short, the Court's new rule is unsupported by prior decisions, arbitrary and unsound in practice, and theoretically unjustified. . . .

The Nuisance Exception

. . .

---

3. . . . [Even here] Lucas may put his land to "other uses"—fishing or camping, for example—or may sell his land to his neighbors as a buffer. In either event, his land is far from "valueless." This highlights a fundamental weakness in the Court's analysis: its failure to explain why only the impairment of "*economically* beneficial or productive use" of property is relevant in takings analysis. I should think that a regulation arbitrarily prohibiting an owner from continuing to use her property for bird-watching or sunbathing might constitute a taking under some circumstances; and, conversely, that such uses are of value to the owner. Yet the Court offers no basis for its assumption that the only uses of property cognizable under the Constitution are *developmental* uses.

The Court's holding today effectively freezes the State's common law, denying the legislature much of its traditional power to revise the law governing the rights and uses of property. . . .

. . . [That is] profoundly unwise. The human condition is one of constant learning and evolution—both moral and practical. Legislatures implement that new learning; in doing so they must often revise the definition of property and the rights of property owners. . . . New appreciation of the significance of endangered species, . . . the importance of wetlands, . . . and the vulnerability of coastal lands . . . shapes our evolving understandings of property rights.

. . . .

The Court's categorical approach rule will, I fear, greatly hamper the efforts of local officials and planners who must deal with increasingly complex problems in land-use and environmental regulation. . . . Viewed more broadly, the Court's new rule and exception conflict with the very character of our takings jurisprudence. We have frequently and consistently recognized that the definition of a taking cannot be reduced to a "set formula" and that determining whether a regulation is a taking is "essentially [an] ad hoc, factual inquir[y]." *Penn Central Transportation Co.* . . . This is unavoidable, for the determination whether a law effects a taking is ultimately a matter of "fairness and justice," . . . and "necessarily requires a weighing of private and public interests." . . . The rigid rules fixed by the Court today clash with this enterprise: "fairness and justice" are often disserved by categorical rules.

III

It is well established that a takings case "entails inquiry into [several factors:] the character of the governmental action, its economic impact, and its interference with reasonable investment-backed expectations." *PruneYard* . . . The Court's analysis today focuses on the last two of these three factors: the categorical rule addresses a regulation's "economic impact," while the nuisance exception recognizes that ownership brings with it only certain "expectations." Neglected by the Court today is the first, and in some ways, the most important factor in takings analysis: the character of the regulatory action.

The Just Compensation Clause "was designed to bar Government from forcing some people alone to bear public burdens which, in all fairness and justice, should be borne by the public as a whole." . . . We have, therefore, in our takings law frequently looked to the generality of a regulation of property.

. . . Perhaps the most familiar application of this principle of generality arises in zoning cases. A diminution in value caused by a zoning regulation is far less likely to constitute a taking if it is part of a general and comprehensive land-use plan, see *Euclid v. Amber Realty Co.,* . . . ; conversely, "spot zoning" is far more likely to constitute a taking, see *Penn Central.* . . .

The presumption that a permanent physical occupation, no matter how slight, effects a taking is wholly consistent with this principle. A physical taking entails a certain amount of "singling out." . . .

In analyzing takings claims, courts have long recognized the difference between a regulation that targets one or two parcels of land and a regulation that enforces a state-wide policy. . . .

In considering Lucas' claim, the generality of the Beachfront Management Act is significant. The Act does not target particular landowners, but rather regulates the use of the coastline of the entire State. . . . Moreover, the Act did not single out owners of undeveloped land. The Act also prohibited owners of developed land from rebuilding if their structures were destroyed.... In short, the South Carolina Act imposed substantial burdens on owners of developed and undeveloped land alike. This generality indicates that the Act is not an effort to expropriate owners of undeveloped land.

. . .

The impact of the ban on developmental uses must also be viewed in light of the purposes of the Act....

In view of all of these factors, even assuming that petitioner's property was rendered valueless, the risk inherent in investments of the sort made by petitioner, the generality of the Act, and the compelling purpose motivating the South Carolina Legislature persuade me that the Act did not effect a taking of petitioner's property.

Accordingly, I respectfully dissent.[a]

PALAZZOLO v. RHODE ISLAND, 533 U.S. 606 (2001). The owner of waterfront land contended that the application of state coastal wetland regulations to his property would constitute a taking. It was clear that he would *not* be allowed to develop the protected wetland portion of his property but he *would* be allowed to build a residence on the upland portion. In an opinion by Justice Kennedy, the Court first held that a takings claim is not automatically barred by the fact that the owner acquires the property after the restrictive regulation is enacted: "The Takings Clause ... in certain circumstances allows a landowner to assert that a particular exercise of the State's regulatory power is so unreasonable or onerous as to compel compensation" and that it "do[es] not become less so through passage of time or title." Because the upland portion of the property retained $200,000 in development value, however, the Court rejected Palazzolo's categorical *Lucas* claim for "fail[ure] to establish a deprivation of all economic value." The Court remanded for further consideration of whether there had been a taking under *Penn Central*'s multi-factored analysis.

TAHOE–SIERRA PRESERVATION COUNCIL, INC. v. TAHOE REGIONAL PLANNING AGENCY, 535 U.S. 302 (2002). Property owners surrounding Lake Tahoe brought a facial challenge claiming that two moratoria effectively prohibiting all development in the area for 32 months had "taken" their property. Pursuant to a congressionally-approved Compact between California and Nevada, the Tahoe Regional Planning Agency (TRPA) had imposed the moratoria while formulating a comprehensive regional land-use plan for environmentally sound growth.[b] The Court distinguished *Lucas* and held that the moratoria did not constitute "*per se* taking[s] of property." Justice Stevens wrote for the majority, saying in part:

"Petitioners ... contend that the mere enactment of a temporary regulation that, while in effect, denies a property owner all viable economic use of her property gives rise to an unqualified constitutional obligation to compensate her for the value of its use during that period.... Under their proposed rule, there is no need to evaluate[—as the regulatory takings approach of Penn Central Transportation Co. v. New York City, 438 U.S. 104 (1978), would

a. Justice Souter voted to dismiss the writ as improvidently granted; his separate statement is omitted.

b. Although the moratoria expired in mid–1984 when the anticipated plan was adopted, the development ban continued un-
til 1987 because California secured an injunction to stop the plan on the grounds that it was insufficiently stringent to protect the Tahoe Basin. The Court majority assumed that the 1984 injunction and the completely revised 1987 plan were not before them, however.

evaluate—]the landowners' investment-backed expectations, the actual impact of the regulation on any individual, the importance of the public interest served by the regulation, or the reasons for imposing the temporary restriction. . . .

". . . In our view the answer to the abstract question whether a temporary moratorium effects a taking is neither 'yes, always' nor 'no, never'; the answer depends upon the particular circumstances of the case[, which] are best analyzed within the *Penn Central* framework.

IV

". . . Our jurisprudence involving condemnations and physical takings . . . , for the most part, involves the straightforward application of *per se* rules. Our regulatory takings jurisprudence, in contrast, . . . is characterized by 'essentially ad hoc, factual inquiries,' . . . designed to allow 'careful examination and weighing of all the relevant circumstances.' . . .

". . .

"This longstanding distinction between acquisitions of property for public use, on the one hand, and regulations prohibiting private uses, on the other, makes it inappropriate to treat cases involving physical takings as controlling precedents for the evaluation of a claim that there has been a 'regulatory taking,' and vice versa. For the same reason that we do not ask whether a physical appropriation advances a substantial government interest or whether it deprives the owner of all economically valuable use, we do not apply our precedent from the physical takings context to regulatory takings claims. Land-use regulations are ubiquitous and most of them impact property values in some tangential way—often in completely unanticipated ways. Treating them all as *per se* takings would transform government regulation into a luxury few governments could afford. By contrast, physical appropriations are relatively rare, easily identified, and usually represent a greater affront to individual property rights. . . .

". . .

". . . *Penn Central* did . . . make it clear that even though multiple factors are relevant in the analysis of regulatory takings claims, in such cases we must focus on 'the parcel as a whole'. . . . This requirement that 'the aggregate must be viewed in its entirety' explains why, for example, a regulation that prohibited commercial transactions in eagle feathers, but did not bar other uses or impose any physical invasion or restraint upon them, was not a taking. Andrus v. Allard, 444 U.S. 51, 66 (1979). It also clarifies why restrictions on the use of only limited portions of the parcel, such as set-back ordinances, Gorieb v. Fox, 274 U.S. 603 (1927), or a requirement that coal pillars be left in place to prevent mine subsidence, *Keystone Bituminous Coal* . . . , were not considered regulatory takings. In each of these cases, we affirmed that 'where an owner possesses a full "bundle" of property rights, the destruction of one "strand" of the bundle is not a taking.' . . .

". . . [T]he separate remedial question of how compensation is measured once a regulatory taking is established . . . [was the issue] in *First English [Evangelical Lutheran Church v. County of Los Angeles*, 482 U.S. 304 (1987).] . . . *First English* . . . did not address . . . the quite different and logically prior question whether the temporary regulation at issue had in fact constituted a taking.

". . .

". . . *First English* . . . identified two reasons why a regulation temporarily denying an owner all use of her property might not constitute a taking. First,

... 'the county might avoid the conclusion that a compensable taking had occurred by establishing that the denial of all use was insulated as a part of the State's authority to enact safety regulations.' ... Second, we limited our holding 'to the facts presented' and recognized 'the quite different questions that would arise in the case of normal delays in obtaining building permits, changes in zoning ordinances, variances, and the like which [were] not before us.' ... Thus, our decision in *First English* surely did not approve, and implicitly rejected, the categorical submission that petitioners are now advocating.

"Similarly, our decision in *Lucas* is not dispositive of the question presented....

"...

"[O]ur holding that the permanent 'obliteration of the value' of a fee simple estate constitutes a categorical taking does not answer the question whether a regulation prohibiting any economic use of land for a 32–month period has the same legal effect. Petitioners seek to bring this case under the rule announced in *Lucas* by arguing that we can effectively sever a 32–month segment from the remainder of each landowner's fee simple estate, and then ask whether that segment has been taken in its entirety by the moratoria. Of course, defining the property interest taken in terms of the very regulation being challenged is circular. With property so divided, every delay would become a total ban; the moratorium and the normal permit process alike would constitute categorical takings. Petitioners' 'conceptual severance' argument is unavailing because it ignores *Penn Central's* admonition that in regulatory takings cases we must focus on 'the parcel as a whole.' ... We have consistently rejected such an approach to the 'denominator' question.... Thus, the District Court erred when it disaggregated petitioners' property into temporal segments corresponding to the regulations at issue and then analyzed whether petitioners were deprived of all economically viable use during each period.... The starting point for the court's analysis should have been to ask whether there was a total taking of the entire parcel; if not, then *Penn Central* was the proper framework.[26]

"An interest in real property is defined by the metes and bounds that describe its geographic dimensions and the term of years that describes the temporal aspect of the owner's interest. See *Restatement of Property* §§ 7–9 (1936). Both dimensions must be considered if the interest is to be viewed in its entirety. Hence, a permanent deprivation of the owner's use of the entire area is a taking of 'the parcel as a whole,' whereas a temporary restriction that merely causes a diminution in value is not. Logically, a fee simple estate cannot be rendered valueless by a temporary prohibition on economic use, because the property will recover value as soon as the prohibition is lifted....

"... [T]he categorical rule in *Lucas* was carved out for the 'extraordinary case' in which a regulation permanently deprives property of all value; the default rule remains that, in the regulatory taking context, we require a more fact specific inquiry...."

Justice Stevens then considered, nevertheless, whether a new *per se* rule should be established in one of three forms potentially applicable to this case. With respect to each,

---

26. The Chief Justice's dissent makes the same mistake by carving out a 6–year interest in the property, rather than considering the parcel as a whole, and treating the regulations covering that segment as analogous to a total taking under *Lucas*.

"the ultimate constitutional question is whether the concepts of 'fairness and justice' that underlie the Takings Clause will be better served by one of these categorical rules or by a *Penn Central* inquiry into all of the relevant circumstances in particular cases. From that perspective, the extreme categorical rule that any deprivation of all economic use, no matter how brief, constitutes a compensable taking surely cannot be sustained. Petitioners' broad submission would apply to numerous 'normal delays in obtaining building permits, changes in zoning ordinances, variances, and the like,' . . . as well as to orders temporarily prohibiting access to crime scenes, businesses that violate health codes, fire-damaged buildings, or other areas that we cannot now foresee. Such a rule would undoubtedly require changes in numerous practices that have long been considered permissible exercises of the police power. . . . A rule that required compensation for every delay in the use of property would render routine government processes prohibitively expensive or encourage hasty decisionmaking. Such an important change in the law should be the product of legislative rulemaking rather than adjudication.

"More importantly, . . . we are persuaded that the better approach to claims that a regulation has effected a temporary taking 'requires careful examination and weighing of all the relevant circumstances.' . . . In rejecting petitioners' *per se* rule, we do not hold that the temporary nature of a land-use restriction precludes finding that it effects a taking; we simply recognize that it should not be given exclusive significance one way or the other.

"A narrower rule that excluded the normal delays associated with processing permits, or that covered only delays of more than a year, would certainly have a less severe impact on prevailing practices, but it would still impose serious financial constraints on the planning process. Unlike the 'extraordinary circumstance' in which the government deprives a property owner of all economic use, *Lucas* . . ., moratoria like [those challenged here] are used widely among land-use planners to preserve the status quo while formulating a more permanent development strategy. In fact, the consensus in the planning community appears to be that moratoria, or 'interim development controls' as they are often called, are an essential tool of successful development. Yet even the weak version of petitioners' categorical rule would treat these interim measures as takings regardless of the good faith of the planners, the reasonable expectations of the landowners, or the actual impact of the moratorium on property values.[34]

"The interest in facilitating informed decisionmaking by regulatory agencies counsels against adopting a *per se* rule that would impose such severe costs on their deliberations. Otherwise, the financial constraints of compensating property owners during a moratorium may force officials to rush through the planning process or to abandon the practice altogether. To the extent that communities are forced to abandon using moratoria, landowners will have incentives to develop their property quickly before a comprehensive plan can be enacted, thereby fostering inefficient and ill-conceived growth. . . .

". . .

"Indeed, the interest in protecting the decisional process is even stronger when an agency is developing a regional plan than when it is considering a permit for a single parcel. In the proceedings involving the Lake Tahoe Basin,

---

34. The Chief Justice . . . suggest[s] that delays of six years or more should be treated as *per se* takings. However his dissent offers no explanation for why 6 years should be the cut-off point rather than 10 days, 10 months, or 10 years. . . .

for example, the moratoria enabled TRPA to obtain the benefit of comments and criticisms from interested parties, such as the petitioners, during its deliberations. Since a categorical rule tied to the length of deliberations would likely create added pressure on decisionmakers to reach a quick resolution of land-use questions, it would only serve to disadvantage those landowners and interest groups who are not as organized or familiar with the planning process. Moreover, with a temporary ban on development there is a lesser risk that individual landowners will be 'singled out' to bear a special burden that should be shared by the public as a whole.... At least with a moratorium there is a clear 'reciprocity of advantage,' ... because it protects the interests of all affected landowners against immediate construction that might be inconsistent with the provisions of the plan that is ultimately adopted.... In fact, there is reason to believe property values often will continue to increase despite a moratorium.... Such an increase makes sense in this context because property values throughout the Basin can be expected to reflect the added assurance that Lake Tahoe will remain in its pristine state....

"It may well be true that any moratorium that lasts for more than one year should be viewed with special skepticism. But given the fact that the District Court found that the 32 months required by TRPA to formulate the 1984 Regional Plan was not unreasonable, we could not possibly conclude that every delay of over one year is constitutionally unacceptable. Formulating a general rule of this kind is a suitable task for state legislatures.[37] In our view, the duration of the restriction is one of the important factors that a court must consider in the appraisal of a regulatory takings claim, but with respect to that factor as with respect to other factors, the 'temptation to adopt what amount to *per se* rules in either direction must be resisted.' *Palazzolo* ... (O'Connor, J., concurring).... We conclude, therefore, that the interest in 'fairness and justice' will be best served by relying on the familiar *Penn Central* approach when deciding cases like this, rather than by attempting to craft a new categorical rule."

Chief Justice Rehnquist, joined by Justices Scalia and Thomas, dissented "because the Takings Clause requires the government to pay compensation when it deprives owners of all economically viable use of their land, ... and because a ban on all development lasting almost six years does not resemble any traditional land-use planning device...." They considered TRPA responsible for the owners' "inability to use their land from 1981 through 1987" and rejected the Court's "distinction between 'temporary' and 'permanent' prohibitions...." Such a distinction, they said,

> "is tenuous. The 'temporary' prohibition in this case that the Court finds is not a taking lasted almost six years. The 'permanent' prohibition that the Court held to be a taking in *Lucas* lasted less than two years ... because the law, as it often does, changed.... Land-use regulations are not irrevocable. And the government can even abandon condemned land.... Under the Court's decision today, the takings question turns entirely on the initial label given a regulation.... There is every incentive for government to simply label any prohibition on development 'temporary,' or to fix a set number of years. As in this case, this initial designation does not preclude the government from repeatedly extending the 'temporary' prohibition into a long-term ban on all development. The Court now holds that such a designation by the government is conclusive even though in fact the

37.   Several States already have statutes authorizing interim zoning ordinances with   specific time limits....

moratorium greatly exceeds the time initially specified. Apparently, the Court would not view even a 10–year moratorium as a taking under *Lucas* because the moratorium is not 'permanent.'

"Our opinion in [*First English*] rejects any distinction between temporary and permanent takings when a landowner is deprived of all economically beneficial use of his land.... *First English* stated that 'temporary takings which, as here, deny a landowner all use of his property, are not different in kind from permanent takings, for which the Constitution clearly requires compensation.' ...

"More fundamentally, ... the justification for the *Lucas* rule ... is derived from the fact that a 'total deprivation of use is, from the landowner's point of view, the equivalent of a physical appropriation.' ... The regulation in *Lucas* was the 'practical equivalence' of a long-term physical appropriation, *i.e.,* a condemnation, so the Fifth Amendment required compensation. The 'practical equivalence,' from the landowner's point of view, of a 'temporary' ban on all economic use is a forced leasehold....

"... From petitioners' standpoint, what happened in this case is no different than if the government had taken a 6–year lease of their property....

"... [A] regulation denying all productive use of land does not implicate the traditional justification for differentiating between regulations and physical appropriations. In 'the extraordinary circumstance when *no* productive or economically beneficial use of land is permitted,' it is less likely that 'the legislature is simply "adjusting the benefits and burdens of economic life" in a manner that secures an "average reciprocity of advantage" to everyone concerned,' ... and more likely that the property 'is being pressed into some form of public service under the guise of mitigating serious public harm,' *Lucas*....

"The Court also reads *Lucas* as being fundamentally concerned with value, rather than with the denial of 'all economically beneficial or productive use of land,'.... But *Lucas* repeatedly discusses its holding as applying where '*no* productive or economically beneficial use of land is permitted.' ... Moreover, the Court's position that value is the *sine qua non* of the *Lucas* rule proves too much. Surely, the land at issue in *Lucas* retained some market value based on the contingency, which soon came to fruition, that the development ban would be amended.

"... Because the rationale for the *Lucas* rule applies just as strongly in this case, the 'temporary' denial of all viable use of land for six years is a taking.

"...

"When a regulation merely delays a final land use decision, we have recognized that there are other background principles of state property law that prevent the delay from being deemed a taking.... Thus, the short-term delays attendant to zoning and permit regimes are a longstanding feature of state property law and part of a landowner's reasonable investment-backed expectations....

"...

"But this case does not require us to decide as a categorical matter whether moratoria prohibiting all economic use are an implied limitation of state property law, because the duration of this 'moratorium' far exceeds that of ordinary moratoria ... [and] cannot be said to resemble any 'implied limitation' of state property law...."

Justice Thomas' separate dissent, joined by Justice Scalia, added this:

"I would hold that regulations prohibiting all productive uses of property are subject to *Lucas*' *per se* rule, regardless of whether the property so burdened retains theoretical useful life and value if, and when, the 'temporary' moratorium is lifted. To my mind, such potential future value bears on the amount of compensation due and has nothing to do with the question whether there was a taking in the first place...."

2. MANDATED ACCESS TO PROPERTY

A "taking" by regulation rather than by exercise of the power of eminent domain not only may occur when regulation excessively prohibits certain uses of property, but sometimes may occur when regulation requires that property be made physically available for public use. The Court readily acknowledges that regulation mandating access to private property affects a recognizable form of "property" interest.[1] Whether it amounts to a "taking" of the property interest, however, has been disputed in several cases.

1. A wide variety of other interests have been recognized as "property" within the meaning of the Just Compensation Clause. Interest earnings on a fund deposited in court for the benefit of creditors were held to be "incidents of ownership of the fund itself and ... property just as the fund itself is property" in Webb's Fabulous Pharmacies, Inc. v. Beckwith, 449 U.S. 155 (1980). The Court held that a state statute authorizing the court clerk to retain the fund's earnings for clerk services effected a taking of "private property": "A State, by *ipse dixit,* may not transform private property into public property without compensation, even for the limited duration of the deposit in court." This common law rule that "interest follows principal" was later followed by a 5–4 majority of the Court in the context of individually nominal interest amounts earned on client trust funds held by lawyers for short periods, which in normal practice could not earn interest under federal regulations but could do so pursuant to the Interest on Lawyers Trust Account (IOLTA) programs, used to fund nonprofit legal services organizations serving the poor. Phillips v. Washington Legal Foundation, 524 U.S. 156 (1998). The majority ruled that the interest remained the "property" of the clients, despite not having "economically realizable value to its owner," since "possession, control, and disposition are nonetheless valuable rights that inhere in the property." Justice Breyer's dissent urged that the interest was not the client's "property," because without the IOLTA program no interest could have been earned on these client funds and thus "the most that Texas law could have taken from the client is ... a right to prevent the principal from being put to productive use by others."

In Ruckelshaus v. Monsanto Co., 467 U.S. 986 (1984), the Court held that the Fifth Amendment safeguards against uncompensated federal takings "intangible property rights protected by state law"—in that case "health, safety, and environmental data cognizable as a trade-secret property right under Missouri law." And the right to pass on very small undivided interests in land to one's heirs was protected against complete abrogation without payment in Hodel v. Irving, 481 U.S. 704 (1987), even though Congress' ban was designed to consolidate inalienable Indian allotments for the future benefit of the tribe. Still, the Court did "reaffirm the continuing vitality of the long line of cases recognizing the States', and where appropriate, the United States', broad authority to adjust the rules governing the descent and devise of property without implicating the guarantees of the Just Compensation Clause."

Preseault v. Interstate Commerce Commission, 494 U.S. 1 (1990), raised the issue of the relationship between federal regulatory power and state property law in defining "property" subject to the guarantees of the Just Compensation Clause. Adjacent landowners claiming a reversionary interest in a railroad right-of-way challenged as a "taking" federal Trails Act amendments that authorized the ICC to preserve for possible future railroad use rights-of-way not currently in service and to allow interim use of the land as recreational trails. The Court found the challenge premature, holding that Congress had provided a Tucker Act remedy in the United States Claims Court for any takings claims arising from application of the amendments, a remedy the landowners had failed to pursue. In a concurring opinion, Justice O'Connor, joined by Justices Scalia and Kennedy, criticized the Court of Appeals for having concluded that "even if petitioners held the reversionary interest they claim, no taking occurred because 'no reversionary interest can or would vest' until the ICC determines that abandonment [not just discontinuance of the railroad right-of-way] is appropriate." Justice O'Connor said that "[t]his view conflates the scope of the ICC's

In PruneYard Shopping Center v. Robins, 447 U.S. 74 (1980), for example, the Court pursued "an inquiry into such factors as the character of the governmental action, its economic impact, and its interference with reasonable investment backed expectations," and concluded that an interpretation of the California Constitution's free speech provision requiring the owner of a multi-block shopping center open to the public to allow a group of students to set up a table in a corner of the central courtyard to solicit support for a petition did not constitute an unconstitutional taking. Conceding that "one of the essential sticks in the bundle of property rights is the right to exclude others," the Court declined to find the fact that the students "physically invaded" the property "determinative." It distinguished Kaiser Aetna v. United States, 444 U.S. 164 (1979), which found a taking where the Federal Government sought to compel free public use of an exclusive private marina (open only to fee-paying members) that had been developed at great cost, along with a complete marina community, by dredging a shallow private pond to connect it with navigable water. The primary distinction drawn was the greater extent of interference with the property owner's "reasonable investment backed expectations."

In a decision the dissent thought departed from the Court's usual analysis, however, a majority found a taking by a New York law designed to facilitate tenant access to cable TV, which required property owners to permit installation of cable facilities on their properties at a one-time payment of $1. Loretto v. Teleprompter Manhattan CATV Corp., 458 U.S. 419 (1982). Stating that its holding was "very narrow" and did not "question . . . a State's broad power to impose appropriate restrictions upon an owner's *use* of his property," the Court concluded "that a permanent physical occupation authorized by government is a taking without regard to the public interests that it may serve." The dissent criticized the "strained and untenable distinction between 'temporary physical invasions,' whose constitutionality concededly 'is subject to a balancing process,' and 'permanent physical occupations,' which are 'taking[s] without regard to other factors that a court might ordinarily examine.'"

What does the following case add?

Dolan v. City of Tigard

512 U.S. 374, 114 S.Ct. 2309, 129 L.Ed.2d 304 (1994).

Chief Justice Rehnquist delivered the opinion of the Court.

Petitioner challenges the decision of the Oregon Supreme Court which held that the city of Tigard could condition the approval of her building permit on the dedication of a portion of her property for flood control and traffic improvements. . . . We granted certiorari to resolve a question left open by our decision in Nollan v. California Coastal Comm'n, 483 U.S. 825 (1987), of what

power with the existence of a compensable taking and threatens to read the Just Compensation Clause out of the Constitution." She insisted that the "scope of the Commission's authority to regulate abandonments . . . is an issue quite distinct from whether the Commission's exercise of power over matters within its jurisdiction effected a taking of petitioners' property." In particular, "state law determines what property interest petitioners possess and . . . traditional [feder-al] takings doctrine will determine whether the Government must compensate petitioners for the burden imposed on any property interest they possess." Thus, "[t]he ICC may possess the power to postpone enjoyment of [state-created] reversionary interests, but the Fifth Amendment and well-established doctrine indicate that in certain circumstances the Government must compensate owners of those property interests when it exercises that power."

is the required degree of connection between the exactions imposed by the city and the projected impacts of the proposed development.

I

... [The City's] Community Development Code (CDC) ... requires property owners in the area zoned Central Business District to comply with a 15% open space and landscaping requirement [and also] requires that new development facilitate [the city's plan for a pedestrian/bicycle pathway intended to encourage alternatives to automobile transportation for short trips] by dedicating land ... where provided for in the ... plan.

The city['s] ... Master Drainage Plan ... noted that flooding occurred in several areas along Fanno Creek, including areas near petitioner's property[, and] established that the increase in impervious surfaces associated with continued urbanization would exacerbate these flooding problems. To combat these risks, the Drainage Plan suggested a series of improvements to the Fanno Creek Basin, including channel excavation in the area next to petitioner's property.... Other recommendations included ensuring that the floodplain remains free of structures and that it be preserved as greenways to minimize flood damage to structures....

Petitioner Florence Dolan owns a plumbing and electric supply store ... in the Central Business District ... [on a 1.67–acre lot, through and along part of which Fanno Creek flows.] The year-round flow of the creek renders the area within the creek's 100–year floodplain virtually unusable for commercial development. The city's comprehensive plan includes the Fanno Creek floodplain as part of the city's greenway system.

Petitioner applied to the city for a permit to ... nearly doubl[e] the size of the store to 17,600 square feet, ... pav[e] a 39–space parking lot[, and in a] second phase of the project, ... to build an additional structure ... for complementary businesses, and to provide more parking. The proposed expansion and intensified use are consistent with the city's zoning scheme in the Central Business District....

The City Planning Commission granted petitioner's permit application subject to conditions imposed by the city's CDC, [including requirements] that petitioner dedicate the portion of her property lying within the 100–year floodplain for improvement of a storm drainage system along Fanno Creek and that she dedicate an additional 15–foot strip of land adjacent to the floodplain as a pedestrian/bicycle pathway. The dedication required ... encompasses approximately 7,000 square feet, or roughly 10% of the property. In accordance with city practice, petitioner could rely on the dedicated property to meet the 15% open space and landscaping requirement mandated by the city's zoning scheme....

Petitioner requested variances from the CDC standards[,] ... argu[ing] that her proposed development would not conflict with the policies of the comprehensive plan.... The Commission denied the request.

The Commission made a series of findings concerning the relationship between the dedicated conditions and the projected impacts of petitioner's project. First, the Commission noted that "[i]t is reasonable to assume that customers and employees of the future uses of this site could utilize a pedestrian/bicycle pathway adjacent to this development for their transportation and recreational needs." ... The Commission noted that the site plan has provided for bicycle parking in a rack in front of the proposed building and "[i]t is reasonable to expect that some of the users of the bicycle parking provided for by the site plan will use the pathway adjacent to Fanno Creek if it is constructed." ... In addition, the Commission found that creation of a convenient, safe pedestrian/bicycle pathway system as an alternative means of transportation "could offset some of the traffic demand on [nearby] streets and lessen the increase in traffic congestion." ...

The Commission went on to note that the required floodplain dedication would be reasonably related to petitioner's request to intensify the use of the site given the increase in the impervious surface. The Commission stated that the "anticipated increased storm water flow from the subject property to an already strained creek and drainage basin can only add to the public need to manage the stream channel and floodplain for drainage purposes." ... Based on this anticipated increased storm water flow, the Commission concluded that "the requirement of dedication of the floodplain area on the site is related to the applicant's plan to intensify development on the site." ...

[Petitioner's administrative and state court appeals were unsuccessful.]

II

The Takings Clause of the Fifth Amendment [was] made applicable to the States through the Fourteenth Amendment, Chicago, B. & Q. R. Co. v. Chicago, 166 U. S. 226, 239 (1897)....[5] One of the principal purposes of the Takings Clause is "to bar Government from forcing some people alone to bear public burdens which, in all fairness and justice, should be borne by the public as a whole." Armstrong v. United States, 364 U.S. 40, 49 (1960). Without question, had the city simply required petitioner to dedicate a strip of land along Fanno Creek for public use, rather than conditioning the grant of her permit to redevelop her property on such a dedication, a taking would have occurred. Nollan, supra, at 831. Such public access would deprive petitioner of the right to exclude others, "one of the most essential sticks in the bundle of rights that are commonly characterized as property." Kaiser Aetna v. United States, 444 U.S. 164, 176 (1979).

On the other side of the ledger, the authority of state and local governments to engage in land use planning has been sustained against constitutional challenge as long ago as our decision in Euclid v. Ambler Realty Co., 272 U. S. 365 (1926).... A land use regulation does not effect a taking if it "substantially advance[s] legitimate state interests" and does not "den[y] an owner economically viable use of his land." Agins v. Tiburon, 447 U.S. 255, 260 (1980).

The sort of land use regulations discussed in the cases just cited, however, differ in two relevant particulars from the present case. First, they involved essentially legislative determinations classifying entire areas of the city, whereas here the city made an adjudicative decision to condition petitioner's application for a building permit on an individual parcel. Second, the conditions imposed were not simply a limitation on the use petitioner might make of her own parcel, but a requirement that she deed portions of the property to the city. In *Nollan*, supra, we held that governmental authority to exact such a condition was circumscribed by the Fifth and Fourteenth Amendments. Under the well-settled doctrine of "unconstitutional conditions," the government may

5. Justice Stevens' dissent suggests that this case is actually grounded in "substantive" due process, rather than in the view that the Takings Clause of the Fifth Amendment was made applicable to the States by the Fourteenth Amendment. But there is no doubt that later cases have held that the Fourteenth Amendment does make the Takings Clause of the Fifth Amendment applicable to the States, see Penn Central Transp. Co. v. New York City, 438 U.S. 104, 122 (1978); Nollan v. California Coastal Comm'n, 483 U.S. 825, 827 (1987)....

not require a person to give up a constitutional right—here the right to receive just compensation when property is taken for a public use—in exchange for a discretionary benefit conferred by the government where the property sought has little or no relationship to the benefit. See Perry v. Sindermann, 408 U.S. 593 (1972); Pickering v. Board of Ed. of Township High School Dist., 391 U.S. 563, 568 (1968).

Petitioner contends that the city has forced her to choose between the building permit and her right under the Fifth Amendment to just compensation for the public easements. Petitioner does not quarrel with the city's authority to exact some forms of dedication as a condition for the grant of a building permit, but challenges the showing made by the city to justify these exactions. She argues that the city has identified "no special benefits" conferred on her, and has not identified any "special quantifiable burdens" created by her new store that would justify the particular dedications required from her which are not required from the public at large.

III

[W]e must first determine whether the "essential nexus" exists between the "legitimate state interest" and the permit condition exacted by the city. Nollan, . . . If we find that a nexus exists, we must then decide the required degree of connection between the exactions and the projected impact of the proposed development. We were not required to reach this question in *Nollan*, because we concluded that the connection did not meet even the loosest standard. . . . Here, however, we must decide this question.

A

We addressed the essential nexus question in *Nollan*. The California Coastal Commission demanded a lateral public easement across the Nollan's beachfront lot in exchange for a permit to demolish an existing bungalow and replace it with a three-bedroom house. . . . The public easement was designed to connect two public beaches that were separated by the Nollan's property. The Coastal Commission had asserted that the public easement condition was imposed to promote the legitimate state interest of diminishing the "blockage of the view of the ocean" caused by construction of the larger house.

We agreed that the Coastal Commission's concern with protecting visual access to the ocean constituted a legitimate public interest. . . . We also agreed that the permit condition would have been constitutional "even if it consisted of the requirement that the Nollans provide a viewing spot on their property for passersby with whose sighting of the ocean their new house would inter-fere." . . . We resolved, however, that the Coastal Commission's regulatory authority was set completely adrift from its constitutional moorings when it claimed that a nexus existed between visual access to the ocean and a permit condition requiring lateral public access along the Nollan's beachfront lot. . . . How enhancing the public's ability to "traverse to and along the shorefront" served the same governmental purpose of "visual access to the ocean" from the roadway was beyond our ability to countenance. The absence of a nexus left the Coastal Commission in the position of simply trying to obtain an easement through gimmickry, which converted a valid regulation of land use into "an out-and-out plan of extortion." . . .

No such gimmicks are associated with the permit conditions imposed by the city in this case. Undoubtedly, the prevention of flooding along Fanno Creek and the reduction of traffic congestion in the Central Business District qualify as the type of legitimate public purposes we have upheld. . . . It seems equally obvious that a nexus exists between preventing flooding along Fanno Creek and limiting development within the creek's 100–year floodplain. Petitioner proposes to ... expand[] the impervious surface on the property and [thus] increas[e] the amount of stormwater run-off into Fanno Creek.

The same may be said for the city's attempt to reduce traffic congestion by providing for alternative means of transportation. In theory, a pedestrian/bicycle pathway provides a useful alternative means of transportation for workers and shoppers. . . .

B

The second part of our analysis requires us to determine whether the degree of the exactions demanded by the city's permit conditions bear the required relationship to the projected impact of petitioner's proposed development. Nollan, supra, at 834, quoting Penn Central, 438 U.S. 104, 127 (1978) ("[A] use restriction may constitute a taking if not reasonably necessary to the effectuation of a substantial government purpose"). Here the Oregon Supreme Court deferred to what it termed the "city's unchallenged factual findings" supporting the dedication conditions and found them to be reasonably related to the impact of the expansion of petitioner's business. . . .

. . . The city relies on the Commission's rather tentative findings that increased stormwater flow from petitioner's property "can only add to the public need to manage the [floodplain] for drainage purposes" to support its conclusion that the "requirement of dedication of the floodplain area on the site is related to the applicant's plan to intensify development on the site." . . .

The city made the following specific findings relevant to the pedestrian/bicycle pathway:

"In addition, the proposed expanded use of this site is anticipated to generate additional vehicular traffic thereby increasing congestion on nearby collector and arterial streets. Creation of a convenient, safe pedestrian/bicycle pathway system as an alternative means of transportation could offset some of the traffic demand on these nearby streets and lessen the increase in traffic congestion." . . .

The question for us is whether these findings are constitutionally sufficient to justify the conditions imposed by the city on petitioner's building permit. Since state courts have been dealing with this question a good deal longer than we have, we turn to representative decisions made by them.

In some States, very generalized statements as to the necessary connection between the required dedication and the proposed development seem to suffice. . . . We think this standard is too lax to adequately protect petitioner's right to just compensation if her property is taken for a public purpose.

Other state courts require a very exacting correspondence, described as the "specifi[c] and uniquely attributable" test. . . . Under this standard, if the local government cannot demonstrate that its exaction is directly proportional to the specifically created need, the exaction becomes "a veiled exercise of the power of eminent domain and a confiscation of private property behind the defense of police regulations." . . . We do not think the Federal Constitution requires such exacting scrutiny, given the nature of the interests involved.

A number of state courts have taken an intermediate position, requiring the municipality to show a "reasonable relationship" between the required dedication and the impact of the proposed development. . . .

. . .

We think the "reasonable relationship" test adopted by a majority of the state courts is closer to the federal constitutional norm than either of those previously discussed. But we do not adopt it as such, partly because the term "reasonable relationship" seems confusingly similar to the term "rational basis" which describes the minimal level of scrutiny under the Equal Protection Clause of the Fourteenth Amendment. We think a term such as "rough proportionality" best encapsulates what we hold to be the requirement of the Fifth Amendment. No precise mathematical calculation is required, but the city must make some sort of individualized determination that the required dedication is related both in nature and extent to the impact of the proposed development.[8]

. . . We turn now to analysis of whether the findings relied upon by the city here, first with respect to the floodplain easement, and second with respect to the pedestrian/bicycle path, satisfied these requirements.

. . . [K]eeping the floodplain open and free from development would likely confine the pressures on Fanno Creek created by petitioner's development. In fact, because petitioner's property lies within the Central Business District, the Community Development Code already required that petitioner leave 15% of it as open space and the undeveloped floodplain would have nearly satisfied that requirement. . . . But the city demanded more—it not only wanted petitioner not to build in the floodplain, but it also wanted petitioner's property along Fanno Creek for its Greenway system. The city has never said why a public greenway, as opposed to a private one, was required in the interest of flood control.

The difference to petitioner, of course, is the loss of her ability to exclude others. As we have noted, this right to exclude others is "one of the most essential sticks in the bundle of rights that are commonly characterized as property." Kaiser Aetna, 444 U.S., at 176. It is difficult to see why recreational visitors trampling along petitioner's floodplain easement are sufficiently related to the city's legitimate interest in reducing flooding problems along Fanno Creek, and the city has not attempted to make any individualized determination to support this part of its request.

The city contends that recreational easement along the Greenway is only ancillary to the city's chief purpose in controlling flood hazards. It further asserts that unlike the residential property at issue in *Nollan*, petitioner's property is commercial in character and therefore, her right to exclude others is compromised. . . . The city maintains that "[t]here is nothing to suggest that preventing [petitioner] from prohibiting [the easements] will unreasonably impair the value of [her] property as a [retail store]." PruneYard Shopping Center v. Robins, 447 U.S. 74, 83 (1980).

Admittedly, petitioner wants to build a bigger store to attract members of the public to her property. She also wants, however, to be able to control the time and manner in which they enter. The recreational easement on the Greenway is different in character from the exercise of state-protected rights of free expression and petition that we permitted in *PruneYard*. In *PruneYard*, we

---

8. Justice Stevens' dissent takes us to task for placing the burden on the city to justify the required dedication. He is correct in arguing that in evaluating most generally applicable zoning regulations, the burden properly rests on the party challenging the regulation to prove that it constitutes an arbitrary regulation of property rights. See, e.g., Euclid v. Ambler Realty Co., 272 U.S. 365 (1926). Here, by contrast, the city made an adjudicative decision to condition petitioner's application for a building permit on an individual parcel. In this situation, the burden properly rests on the city. See Nollan, 483 U.S., at 836. . . .

held that a major private shopping center that attracted more than 25,000 daily patrons had to provide access to persons exercising their state constitutional rights to distribute pamphlets and ask passersby to sign their petitions.... We based our decision, in part, on the fact that the shopping center "may restrict expressive activity by adopting time, place, and manner regulations that will minimize any interference with its commercial functions." ... By contrast, the city wants to impose a permanent recreational easement upon petitioner's property that borders Fanno Creek. Petitioner would lose all rights to regulate the time in which the public entered onto the Greenway, regardless of any interference it might pose with her retail store. Her right to exclude would not be regulated, it would be eviscerated.

If petitioner's proposed development had somehow encroached on existing greenway space in the city, it would have been reasonable to require petitioner to provide some alternative greenway space for the public either on her property or elsewhere. ... But that is not the case here. We conclude that the findings upon which the city relies do not show the required reasonable relationship between the floodplain easement and the petitioner's proposed new building.

With respect to the pedestrian/bicycle pathway, we have no doubt that the city was correct in finding that the larger retail sales facility proposed by petitioner will increase traffic on the streets of the Central Business District. The city estimates that the proposed development would generate roughly 435 additional trips per day. Dedications for streets, sidewalks, and other public ways are generally reasonable exactions to avoid excessive congestion from a proposed property use. But on the record before us, the city has not met its burden of demonstrating that the additional number of vehicle and bicycle trips generated by the petitioner's development reasonably relate to the city's requirement for a dedication of the pedestrian/bicycle pathway easement. The city simply found that the creation of the pathway "could offset some of the traffic demand ... and lessen the increase in traffic congestion."

... No precise mathematical calculation is required, but the city must make some effort to quantify its findings in support of the dedication for the pedestrian/bicycle pathway beyond the conclusory statement that it could offset some of the traffic demand generated.

. . .

The judgment ... is reversed, and the case is remanded for further proceedings consistent with this opinion.

Justice Stevens, with whom Justice Blackmun and Justice Ginsburg join, dissenting.

. . .

... The Court is correct ... that the city may not attach arbitrary conditions to a building permit or to a variance even when it can rightfully deny the application outright.... Yet the Court's description of the doctrinal underpinnings of its decision, the phrasing of its fledgling test of "rough proportionality," and the application of that test to this case run contrary to the traditional treatment of these cases and break considerable and unpropitious new ground.

I

... The state cases the Court consults ... either fail to support or decidedly undermine the Court's conclusions in key respects.

. . .

Not one of the state cases cited by the Court announces anything akin to a "rough proportionality" requirement....

In addition, the Court ignores the state courts' willingness to consider what the property owner gains from the exchange in question.... Dolan's acceptance of the permit, with its attached conditions, would provide her with benefits that may well go beyond any advantage she gets from expanding her business. As the United States pointed out at oral argument, the improvement that the city's drainage plan contemplates would widen the channel and reinforce the slopes to increase the carrying capacity during serious floods, "confer[ring] considerable benefits on the property owners immediately adjacent to the creek." ...

The state court decisions also are enlightening in the extent to which they required that the *entire parcel* be given controlling importance.... None ... identified the surrender of the fee owner's "power to exclude" as having any special significance. Instead, the courts uniformly examined the character of the entire economic transaction.

II

[O]ur own cases as well ... require the analysis to focus on the impact of the city's action on the entire parcel of private property.... Although limitation of the right to exclude others undoubtedly constitutes a significant infringement upon property ownership, Kaiser Aetna v. United States, 444 U.S. 164, 179–180 (1979), restrictions on that right do not alone constitute a taking, and do not do so in any event unless they "unreasonably impair the value or use" of the property. PruneYard Shopping Center v. Robins, 447 U.S. 74, 82–84 (1980).

The Court's narrow focus on one strand in the property owner's bundle of rights is particularly misguided in a case involving the development of commercial property.... The exactions associated with the development of a retail business are ... a species of business regulation that heretofore warranted a strong presumption of constitutional validity.

... The city of Tigard has demonstrated that its plan is rational and impartial and that the conditions at issue are "conducive to fulfillment of authorized planning objectives." Dolan, on the other hand, has offered no evidence that her burden of compliance has any impact at all on the value or profitability of her planned development. Following the teaching of the cases on which it purports to rely, the Court should not isolate the burden associated with the loss of the power to exclude from an evaluation of the benefit to be derived from the permit to enlarge the store and the parking lot.

... Under the Court's approach, a city must not only "quantify its findings," and make "individualized determination[s]" with respect to the nature and the extent of the relationship between the conditions and the impact, but also demonstrate "proportionality." The correct inquiry should instead concentrate on whether the required nexus is present and venture beyond considerations of a condition's nature or germaneness only if the developer establishes that a concededly germane condition is so grossly disproportionate to the proposed development's adverse effects that it manifests motives other than land use regulation on the part of the city....

III

Applying its new standard, the Court finds two defects in the city's case.... [B]oth ... are, at most, nothing more than harmless error.

... Given the commercial character of both the existing and the proposed use of the property as a retail store, it seems likely that potential customers "trampling along petitioner's floodplain," are more valuable than a useless parcel of vacant land. Moreover, the duty to pay taxes and the responsibility for potential tort liability may well make ownership of the fee interest in useless land a liability rather than an asset. . . .

The Court's rejection of the bike path condition amounts to nothing more than a play on words. Everyone agrees that the bike path "could" offset some of the increased traffic flow that the larger store will generate, but the findings do not unequivocally state that it *will* do so, or tell us just how many cyclists will replace motorists. Predictions on such matters are inherently nothing more than estimates. Certainly the assumption that there will be an offsetting benefit here is entirely reasonable and should suffice whether it amounts to 100 percent, 35 percent, or only 5 percent of the increase in automobile traffic that would otherwise occur. If the Court proposes to have the federal judiciary micromanage state decisions of this kind, it is indeed extending its welcome mat to a significant new class of litigants. . . . [P]roperty owners have surely found a new friend today.

IV

... Even more consequential than its incorrect disposition of this case ... is the Court's resurrection of a species of substantive due process analysis that it firmly rejected decades ago.

... The so-called "regulatory takings" doctrine ... has an obvious kinship with the line of substantive due process cases that *Lochner* exemplified. Besides having similar ancestry, both doctrines are potentially open-ended sources of judicial power to invalidate state economic regulations that Members of this Court view as unwise or unfair.

This case inaugurates an even more recent judicial innovation than the regulatory takings doctrine: the application of the "unconstitutional conditions" label to a mutually beneficial transaction between a property owner and a city. . . . Dolan has no right to be compensated for a taking unless the city acquires the property interests that she has refused to surrender. . . .

Even if Dolan should accept the city's conditions in exchange for the benefit that she seeks, it would not necessarily follow that she had been denied "just compensation" since it would be appropriate to consider the receipt of that benefit in any calculation of "just compensation." . . . Particularly in the absence of any evidence on the point, we should not presume that the discretionary benefit the city has offered is less valuable than the property interests that Dolan can retain or surrender at her option. But even if that discretionary benefit were so trifling that it could not be considered just compensation when it has "little or no relationship" to the property, the Court fails to explain why the same value would suffice when the required nexus is present. In this respect, the Court's reliance on the "unconstitutional conditions" doctrine is assuredly novel, and arguably incoherent. . . .

. . .

... If the government can demonstrate that the conditions it has imposed in a land-use permit are rational, impartial and conducive to fulfilling the aims of a valid land-use plan, a strong presumption of validity should attach to those conditions. The burden of demonstrating that those conditions have unreasonably impaired the economic value of the proposed improvement belongs squarely on the shoulders of the party challenging the state action's constitutionality....

I respectfully dissent.

Justice Souter, dissenting.

... *Nollan* declared the need for a nexus between the nature of an exaction of an interest in land (a beach easement) and the nature of governmental interests. The Court treats this case as raising a further question, not about the nature, but about the degree, of connection required between such an exaction and the adverse effects of development. The Court's opinion announces a test to address this question, but as I read the opinion, the Court does not apply that test to these facts, which do not raise the question the Court addresses.

First, as to the floodplain and Greenway, the Court acknowledges that an easement of this land for open space (and presumably including the five feet required for needed creek channel improvements) is reasonably related to flood control, but argues that the "permanent recreational easement" for the public on the Greenway is not so related. If that is so, it is not because of any lack of proportionality between permit condition and adverse effect, but because of a lack of any rational connection at all between exaction of a public recreational area and the governmental interest in providing for the effect of increased water runoff. That is merely an application of *Nollan*'s nexus analysis.... But ... the city of Tigard never sought to justify the public access portion of the dedication as related to flood control. It merely argued that whatever recreational uses were made of the bicycle path and the one foot edge on either side, were incidental to the permit condition requiring dedication of the 15–foot easement for an 8–foot-wide bicycle path and for flood control, including open space requirements and relocation of the bank of the river by some five feet. It seems to me such incidental recreational use can stand or fall with the bicycle path, which the city justified by reference to traffic congestion. As to the relationship the Court examines, between the recreational easement and a purpose never put forth as a justification by the city, the Court unsurprisingly finds a recreation area to be unrelated to flood control.

Second, as to the bicycle path, the Court ... only faults the city for saying that the bicycle path "could" rather than "would" offset the increased traffic from the store. That again ... is an application of *Nollan*, for the Court holds that the stated connection ("could offset") between traffic congestion and bicycle paths is too tenuous; only if the bicycle path "would" offset the increased traffic by some amount, could the bicycle path be said to be related to the city's legitimate interest in reducing traffic congestion.

I cannot agree that the application of *Nollan* is a sound one here, since it appears that the Court has placed the burden of producing evidence of relationship on the city, despite the usual rule in cases involving the police power that the government is presumed to have acted constitutionally.... Dolan has put forward no evidence that the burden of granting a dedication for the bicycle path is unrelated in kind to the anticipated increase in traffic congestion, nor, if there exists a requirement that the relationship be related in degree, has Dolan shown that the exaction fails any such test. The city, by contrast, calculated the increased traffic flow that would result from Dolan's proposed development to be 435 trips per day, and its Comprehensive Plan, applied here, relied on studies showing the link between alternative modes of transportation, including bicycle paths, and reduced street traffic congestion.... *Nollan*, therefore, is satisfied, and on that assumption the city's conditions should not be held to fail a further rough proportionality test or any other that might be devised to give meaning to the constitutional limits. . . .

. . .

CITY OF MONTEREY v. DEL MONTE DUNES, 526 U.S. 687 (1999). The city repeatedly denied permission to develop an ocean-front parcel, imposing increasingly restrictive conditions with each new application. The developer challenged the city's actions as a regulatory taking. Justice Kennedy's opinion, speaking for all nine Justices, contained the following passage:

"Although in a general sense concerns for proportionality animate the Takings Clause, . . . we have not extended the rough-proportionality test of *Dolan* beyond the special context of exactions—land-use decisions conditioning approval of development on the dedication of property to public use. . . . The rule applied in *Dolan* considers whether dedications demanded as conditions of development are proportional to the development's anticipated impacts. It was not designed to address, and is not readily applicable to, the much different questions arising where, as here, the landowner's challenge is based not on excessive exactions but on denial of development. We believe, accordingly, that the rough-proportionality test of *Dolan* is inapposite to a case such as this one."

YEE v. CITY OF ESCONDIDO, 503 U.S. 519 (1992). The Court rejected a claim by owners of a mobile home park that a local rent control ordinance, taken together with a state law significantly restricting the grounds for evicting current tenants from the park and for rejecting new tenants who purchase a mobile home in the park from a current tenant with an unexpired lease, effected a *per se* physical taking of their property. The park owners argued that the laws increased the saleable value of the tenants' mobile homes in the form of a transferable "right to occupy a pad at below-market rent indefinitely," and thus effectively transferred "from park owner to mobile home owner . . . A right of physical occupation of the park owner's land." the court concluded, however, that whatever the relevance of the owners' arguments to a *regulatory* taking claim based on use restrictions—a claim the Court decided was not properly before it—there had been no *physical* invasion of their property:

". . . The government effects a physical taking only where it *requires* the landowner to submit to the physical occupation of his land. . . .

". . . Petitioners voluntarily rented their land to mobile home owners. At least on the face of the regulatory scheme, neither the City nor the State compels petitioners, once they have rented their property to tenants, to continue doing so. . . . [The] tenants were invited by the petitioners, not forced upon them by the government. . . .

". . . A different case would be presented were the statute, on its face or as applied, to compel a landowner over objection to rent his property or to refrain in perpetuity from terminating a tenancy.

". . . When a landowner decides to rent his land to tenants, the government may place ceilings on the rents the landowner can charge . . . or require the landowner to accept tenants he does not like, . . . without automatically having to pay compensation. . . . Such forms of regulation are analyzed by engaging in the 'essentially ad hoc, factual inquiries' necessary to determine whether a regulatory taking has occurred."

3. REMEDIES FOR TAKINGS

FIRST ENGLISH EVANGELICAL LUTHERAN CHURCH OF GLENDALE v. COUNTY OF LOS ANGELES, 482 U.S. 304 (1987). Shortly after a flood destroyed the Church's creek-side buildings and campground, the County adopted an Interim Ordinance prohibiting replacement or construction of structures in a flood protection area encompassing the Church's property. The Church sued for damages for loss of all use, but the California courts held that even if all use had been denied, no damages could be recovered until the ordinance was finally declared unconstitutional, and then only for any period after that declaration for which the County continued to enforce it. The Supreme Court reversed in an opinion by Chief Justice Rehnquist that said in part:

" . . . The Court has recognized in more than one case that the government may elect to abandon its intrusion or discontinue regulations. . . . Similarly, a governmental body may acquiesce in a judicial declaration that one of its ordinances has effected an unconstitutional taking of property; the landowner has no right under the Just Compensation Clause to insist that a 'temporary' taking be deemed a permanent taking. But we have not resolved whether abandonment by the government requires payment of compensation for the period of time during which regulations deny a landowner all use of his land.

"In considering this question, we find substantial guidance in cases where the government has only temporarily exercised its right to use private property. . . .

"These cases reflect the fact that 'temporary' takings which, as here, deny a landowner all use of his property, are not different in kind from permanent takings, for which the Constitution clearly requires compensation. . . . In the present case the interim ordinance was adopted by the county of Los Angeles in January 1979, and became effective immediately. Appellant filed suit within a month after the effective date of the ordinance and yet when the Supreme Court of California denied a hearing in the case on October 17, 1985, the merits of appellant's claim had yet to be determined. The United States has been required to pay compensation for leasehold interests of shorter duration than this. The value of a leasehold interest in property for a period of years may be substantial, and the burden on the property owner in extinguishing such an interest for a period of years may be great indeed. . . . Where this burden results from governmental action that amounted to a taking, the Just Compensation Clause of the Fifth Amendment requires that the government pay the landowner for the value of the use of the land during this period. Cf. United States v. Causby, 328 U.S., at 261 ('It is the owner's loss, not the taker's gain, which is the measure of the value of the property taken'). Invalidation of the ordinance or its successor ordinance after this period of time, though converting the taking into a 'temporary' one, is not a sufficient remedy to meet the demands of the Just Compensation Clause.

" . . . Once a court determines that a taking has occurred, the government retains the whole range of options already available—amendment of the regulation, withdrawal of the invalidated regulation, or exercise of eminent domain. . . . We merely hold that where the government's activities have already worked a taking of all use of property, no subsequent action by the government can relieve it of the duty to provide compensation for the period during which the taking was effective.

" . . . We . . . do not deal with the quite different questions that would arise in the case of normal delays in obtaining building permits, changes in zoning ordinances, variances, and the like which are not before us. We realize that even our present holding will undoubtedly lessen to some extent the freedom and flexibility of land-use planners and governing bodies of municipal corporations when enacting land-use regulations. But such consequences necessarily flow from any decision upholding a claim of constitutional right; many of the provisions of the Constitution are designed to limit the flexibility and freedom of governmental authorities and the Just Compensation Clause of the Fifth Amendment is one of them. . . ."

Justice Stevens dissented. He noted that a taking by regulation leaves government with a choice of abandoning the regulation or compensating the property owner, and he suggested that "repeal will, in virtually all cases, mitigate the overall effect of the regulation so substantially that the slight diminution in value that the regulation caused while in effect cannot be classified as a taking of property." He conceded that in "some situations . . . even the temporary existence of a regulation has such severe consequences that invalidation or repeal will not mitigate the damage enough to remove the 'taking' label[,]" but he argued that "contrary to the Court's implications, the fact that a regulation would constitute a taking if allowed to remain in effect permanently is by no means dispositive of . . . whether the effect that the regulation has already had on the property is so severe that a taking occurred during the period before the regulation was invalidated."

Justice Stevens also noted the "possibility that land-use planning, like other forms of regulation, will deprive a citizen of the right to develop his property at the time and in the manner that will best serve his economic interests[,]" but said in part:

"... In my opinion, . . . it is the Due Process Clause rather than [the 'regulatory taking'] doctrine that protects the property owner from improperly motivated, unfairly conducted, or unnecessarily protracted governmental decision-making. Violation of the procedural safeguards mandated by the Due Process Clause will give rise to actions for damages under 42 U.S.C. § 1983, but I am not persuaded that delays in the development of property that are occasioned by fairly conducted administrative or judicial proceedings are compensable, except perhaps in the most unusual circumstances. On the contrary, I am convinced that the public interest in having important governmental decisions made in an orderly, fully informed way amply justifies the temporary burden on the citizen that is the inevitable by-product of democratic government."

JUST COMPENSATION

The problem of according the just compensation directed to be paid upon a taking for a public use presents great difficulties. The ground rules—that the owner's loss and not the taker's gain is the measure of compensation, United States v. Miller, 317 U.S. 369, 375 (1943); that where fair market value can be determined it is the normal measure of recovery, United States ex rel. T.V.A. v. Powelson, 319 U.S. 266, 275 (1943); and that fair market value is "what a willing buyer would pay in cash to a willing seller," *United States v. Miller,* supra—are suggestive of the varying considerations present in determining just compensation. Problems of peculiar value to the owner, of consequential damages, of enhanced value brought about by the project for which the land is condemned, of compensation for interests less than a fee, and myriads of others complicate the determination of what is just compensation. For a comprehensive study see 4 Nichols, *The Law of Eminent Domain* (rev. 4th ed. 1995).

One peculiar difficulty in determining the proper measure of just compensation arises when the measuring stick of the owner's loss, and the measuring stick of the fair market value of the property taken, arguably lead to different results. In Brown v. Legal Foundation of Washington, 538 U.S. 216 (2003), the Court addressed a just compensation claim directed at the uniform state practice that developed rapidly after 1980 (when Congress permitted federally insured banks to begin paying interest on certain checking accounts) of requiring lawyers to place in interest-bearing trust accounts client funds they are required to hold for short periods of time, and to transfer the interest the trust accounts earn to charitable entities providing legal services for the poor. In the aggregate the interest earned on IOLTA's (Interest on Lawyer Trust Accounts) exceeded $200 million nationwide in 2001, but for each individual client the cost of distributing the interest in most cases would exceed the interest earned on the client's funds. The Court previously had ruled that the interest on a client's funds are the "property" of the client, see Phillips v. Washington Legal Foundation, discussed supra at p. 568 n. 1, and this case involved whether the property had been "taken," and, if so, what compensation was due. The Court majority assumed the interest had been taken by the transfer, but it held that just compensation in this case was zero. Justice Stevens relied on the rule that "the 'just compensation' required by the Fifth Amendment is measured by the property owner's loss rather than the government's gain." He concluded that because, under the rules adopted by the Washington Supreme Court governing Washington's IOLTA program, client funds must be deposited "in non-IOLTA accounts whenever those funds could generate net earnings for the client[,]" the "owner's pecuniary loss ... is zero whenever the Washington law is obeyed...." Any "mistakes" in placing client funds in IOLTA accounts when they could have generated net income for the client would be "the consequence of the [lawyers'] incorrect private decisions rather than any state action" that "would provide ... support for a claim for compensation from the State...."

Justice Scalia, joined by Chief Justice Rehnquist and Justices Kennedy and Thomas, concluded, by contrast, that "petitioners are entitled to the fair market value of the interest generated by their funds held in interest on lawyers' trust accounts...." He relied on precedents articulating the just compensation requirement as "the amount of the market value of the property on the date it is appropriated" and emphasized that "*after* the interest has been generated in the pooled accounts ... it is at *that* point that just compensation for the taking must be assessed." (Emphasis in original). As for the transaction costs that would reduce the interest earned that could be returned to the client to zero or less, Justice Scalia found no precedent for the Court's "net value" approach instead of the actual interest earned, which was both what the client lost and the government gained: "[W]e have repeatedly held that just compensation is the 'market value" of the confiscated property, rather than the 'net loss' to the owner. 'Market value' is not reduced by what the owner would have lost in taxes or other exactions." In his view, the majority may have been resting "on the unfounded assumption that the State must return the interest directly to petitioners[, whereas t]he State could satisfy its obligation to pay just compensation by simply returning petitioners' money to the IOLTA account from which it was seized, leaving others to incur the accounting costs in the event petitioners seek to extract their interest from the account."

SECTION 2.   PROTECTION OF PERSONAL LIBERTIES

A.   INTRODUCTION

In Section 1 of this chapter we saw how the Court determined that the word "liberty" in the due process clause gave special protection to the liberty to contract so that restrictions on that liberty, especially as reflected in labor legislation, were invalid unless specially justified by the state.

The liberty of contract cases have long since been overruled. But more recently the Court has derived from the word liberty a special constitutional protection for privacy, personal autonomy, and some family relationships requiring special justification for state infringements on those interests. The process by which an interest is singled out by the Court for special constitutional protection is worthy of examination as a means of understanding how general constitutional phrases become limitations on the power of legislatures.

Some issues that relate to privacy are governed by special constitutional language. The fourth amendment (incorporated by the fourteenth amendment against the states) protects persons, places, and possessions against indiscriminate searches and seizures. The fifth amendment protects against self-incrimination. But no language in the Constitution talks about privacy, family life, or personal autonomy.

In reading these cases ask yourself whether the Court adduces a principled basis for singling out these particular interests from all the other aspects of liberty that similarly might be protected.

Try also to determine what is the scope of this special protection. What kinds of regulations can be brought within the privacy rubric so as to require special state justification?

For useful general discussion, see Dixon, *The "New" Substantive Due Process and the Democratic Ethic: A Prolegomenon,* 1976 B.Y.U.L.Rev. 43; Henkin, *Privacy and Autonomy,* 74 Colum.L.Rev. 1410 (1974).

Two early cases from the *Lochner* era are frequently cited in current opinions. In Meyer v. Nebraska, 262 U.S. 390 (1923), a parochial school language teacher had been convicted of violating a law prohibiting the teaching of any subject in a language other than English in the first eight grades of public and private schools. In reversing his conviction, the Court said that the liberty protected by due process "denotes not merely freedom from bodily restraint, but also the right of the individual to contract, to engage in any of the common occupations of life, to acquire useful knowledge, to marry, establish a home and bring up children, to worship God according to the dictates of his own conscience, and, generally, to enjoy those privileges long recognized at common law as essential to the orderly pursuit of happiness by free men." The right of Meyer to teach German and the right of parents to engage him were within that zone of constitutionally-protected liberty. The Court concluded that, because no justifications for the complete abolition of the right to teach foreign languages had been shown, "the statute as applied is arbitrary, and without reasonable relation to any end within the competency of the state."

In Pierce v. Society of Sisters, 268 U.S. 510 (1925), the Court upheld a trial court injunction against the enforcement of an Oregon statute requiring parents to send children between the ages of 8 and 16 to a public school. The suit was brought by a Catholic society operating a school and a private corporation operating a military academy. The Court noted that the effect of the act would be to force private schools out of business. It then said that under the doctrine of *Meyer* "we think it entirely plain that the [statute] unreasonably interferes with the liberty of parents and guardians to direct the upbringing and education of children under their control.... The fundamental theory of liberty upon which all governments in this Union repose excludes any general power of the state to standardize its children by forcing them to accept instruction from public teachers only. The child is not the mere creature of the state; those who nurture him and direct his destiny have the right, coupled with the high duty, to recognize and prepare him for additional obligations."

Another case prior to Griswold v. Connecticut that referred to special constitutional protection for interests relating to personal autonomy and family relationships was Skinner v. Oklahoma, 316 U.S. 535 (1942). The Court held invalid under equal protection a statute providing for compulsory sterilization of criminals convicted two or more times of crimes of moral turpitude. Since the statute made grand larceny a felony of moral turpitude, while embezzlement was not, it violated the equal protection clause. The Court, in an opinion by Justice Douglas, began its discussion of the equal protection issue by saying: "We are dealing here with legislation which involves one of the basic civil rights of man. Marriage and procreation are fundamental to the very existence and survival of the race. The power to sterilize, if exercised, may have subtle, far-reaching and devastating effects.... There is no redemption for the individual whom the law touches. Any experiment which the State conducts is to his irreparable injury. He is forever deprived of a basic liberty. We mention these matters not to reexamine the scope of the police power of the States. We advert to them merely in emphasis of our view that strict scrutiny of the classification which a State makes in a sterilization law is essential...."

Griswold v. Connecticut

381 U.S. 479, 85 S.Ct. 1678, 14 L.Ed.2d 510 (1965).

Mr. Justice Douglas delivered the opinion of the Court.

Appellant Griswold is Executive Director of the Planned Parenthood League of Connecticut. Appellant Buxton is a licensed physician and a professor at the Yale Medical School who served as Medical Director for the League at its Center in New Haven—a center open and operating from November 1 to November 10, 1961, when appellants were arrested.

They gave information, instruction, and medical advice to *married persons* as to the means of preventing conception. They examined the wife and prescribed the best contraceptive device or material for her use. Fees were usually charged, although some couples were serviced free.

The statutes whose constitutionality is involved in this appeal are §§ 53–32 and 54–196 of the General Statutes of Connecticut (1938). The former provides:

"Any person who uses any drug, medicinal article or instrument for the purpose of preventing conception shall be fined not less than fifty dollars or imprisoned not less than sixty days nor more than one year or be both fined and imprisoned."

Section 54–196 provides:

"Any person who assists, abets, counsels, causes, hires or commands another to commit any offense may be prosecuted and punished as if he were the principal offender."

The appellants were found guilty as accessories and fined $100 each, against the claim that the accessory statute as so applied violated the Fourteenth Amendment. The Appellate Division of the Circuit Court affirmed. The Court of Errors affirmed that judgment....

. . .

Coming to the merits, we are met with a wide range of questions that implicate the Due Process Clause of the Fourteenth Amendment. Overtones of some arguments suggest that Lochner v. State. of New York, 198 U.S. 45, should be our guide. But we decline that invitation as we did in West Coast Hotel Co. v. Parrish, 300 U.S. 379; Olsen v. State of Nebraska, 313 U.S. 236; Lincoln Federal Labor Union v. Northwestern Co., 335 U.S. 525; Williamson v. Lee Optical Co., 348 U.S. 483; Giboney v. Empire Storage Co., 336 U.S. 490. We do not sit as a super-legislature to determine the wisdom, need, and propriety of laws that touch economic problems, business affairs, or social conditions. This law, however, operates directly on an intimate relation of husband and wife and their physician's role in one aspect of that relation.

The association of people is not mentioned in the Constitution nor in the Bill of Rights. The right to educate a child in a school of the parents' choice— whether public or private or parochial—is also not mentioned. Nor is the right to study any particular subject or any foreign language. Yet the First Amendment has been construed to include certain of those rights.

By *Pierce v. Society of Sisters,* supra, the right to educate one's children as one chooses is made applicable to the States by the force of the First and Fourteenth Amendments. By *Meyer v. State of Nebraska,* supra, the same dignity is given the right to study the German language in a private school. In other words, the State may not, consistently with the spirit of the First Amendment, contract the spectrum of available knowledge. The right of freedom of speech and press includes not only the right to utter or to print, but the right to distribute, the right to receive, the right to read (Martin v. City of Struthers, 319 U.S. 141, 143) and freedom of inquiry, freedom of thought, and freedom to teach (see Wieman v. Updegraff, 344 U.S. 183, 195)—indeed the freedom of the entire university community. Sweezy v. State of New Hampshire, 354 U.S. 234, 249–250, 261–263; Barenblatt v. United States, 360 U.S. 109, 112; Baggett v. Bullitt, 377 U.S. 360, 369. Without those peripheral rights the specific rights would be less secure. And so we reaffirm the principle of the *Pierce* and the *Meyer* cases.

. . .

The foregoing cases suggest that specific guarantees in the Bill of Rights have penumbras, formed by emanations from those guarantees that help give them life and substance. See Poe v. Ullman, 367 U.S. 497, 516–522 (dissenting opinion). Various guarantees create zones of privacy. The right of association contained in the penumbra of the First Amendment is one, as we have seen. The Third Amendment in its prohibition against the quartering of soldiers "in any house" in time of peace without the consent of the owner is another facet of that privacy. The Fourth Amendment explicitly affirms the "right of the people to be secure in their persons, houses, papers, and effects, against unreasonable searches and seizures." The Fifth Amendment in its Self–Incrimination Clause enables the citizen to create a zone of privacy which government may not force him to surrender to his detriment. The Ninth Amendment provides: "The enumeration in the Constitution, of certain rights, shall not be construed to deny or disparage others retained by the people."

The Fourth and Fifth Amendments were described in Boyd v. United States, 116 U.S. 616, 630, as protection against all governmental invasions "of the sanctity of a man's home and the privacies of life." We recently referred in Mapp v. Ohio, 367 U.S. 643, 656, to the Fourth Amendment as creating a "right to privacy, no less important than any other right carefully and particularly reserved to the people." See Beaney, The Constitutional Right to Privacy, 1962 Sup.Ct.Rev. 212; Griswold, The Right to be Let Alone, 55 N.W.U.L.Rev. 216 (1960).

We have had many controversies over these penumbral rights of "privacy and repose." . . . These cases bear witness that the right of privacy which presses for recognition here is a legitimate one.

The present case, then, concerns a relationship lying within the zone of privacy created by several fundamental constitutional guarantees. And it concerns a law which, in forbidding the *use* of contraceptives rather than regulating their manufacture or sale, seeks to achieve its goals by means having a maximum destructive impact upon that relationship. Such a law cannot stand in light of the familiar principle, so often applied by this Court, that a "governmental purpose to control or prevent activities constitutionally subject to state regulation may not be achieved by means which sweep unnecessarily broadly and thereby invade the area of protected freedoms." NAACP v. Alabama, 377 U.S. 288, 307. Would we allow the police to search the sacred precincts of marital bedrooms for telltale signs of the use of contraceptives? The very idea is repulsive to the notions of privacy surrounding the marriage relationship.

We deal with a right of privacy older than the Bill of Rights—older than our political parties, older than our school system. Marriage is a coming together for better or for worse, hopefully enduring, and intimate to the degree of being sacred. It is an association that promotes a way of life, not causes; a harmony in living, not political faiths; a bilateral loyalty, not commercial or social projects. Yet it is an association for as noble a purpose as any involved in our prior decisions.

Reversed.

Reversed verdict of guilty

Mr. Justice Goldberg, whom The Chief Justice and Mr. Justice Brennan join, concurring.

I agree with the Court that Connecticut's birth control law unconstitutionally intrudes upon the right of marital privacy, and I join in its opinion and judgment. Although I have not accepted the view that " 'due process' as used in the Fourteenth Amendment includes all of the first eight Amendments," id., 367 U.S. at 516 (see my concurring opinion in Pointer v. Texas, 380 U.S. 400, 410, and the dissenting opinion of Mr. Justice Brennan in Cohen v. Hurley, 366 U.S. 117), I do agree that the concept of liberty protects those personal rights that are fundamental, and is not confined to the specific terms of the Bill of Rights. My conclusion that the concept of liberty is not so restricted and that it embraces the right of marital privacy though that right is not mentioned explicitly in the Constitution is supported both by numerous decisions of this Court, referred to in the Court's opinion, and by the language and history of the Ninth Amendment. In reaching the conclusion that the right of marital privacy is protected, as being within the protected penumbra of specific guarantees of the Bill of Rights, the Court refers to the Ninth Amendment. I add these words to emphasize the relevance of that Amendment to the Court's holding.

. . .

The Ninth Amendment reads, "The enumeration in the Constitution, of certain rights, shall not be construed to deny or disparage others retained by the people." . . .

While this Court has had little occasion to interpret the Ninth Amendment,[6] "[i]t cannot be presumed that any clause in the constitution is intended

6. This Amendment has been referred to as "The Forgotten Ninth Amendment," in a book with that title by Bennet B. Patterson (1955). Other commentary on the Ninth to be without effect." Marbury v. Madison, 1 Cranch 137, 174. In interpreting the Constitution, "real effect should be given to all the words it uses." Myers v. United States, 272 U.S. 52, 151. The Ninth Amendment to the Constitution may be regarded by some as a recent discovery but since 1791 it has been a basic part of the Constitution which we are sworn to uphold. To hold that a right so basic and fundamental and so deep-rooted in our society as the right of privacy in marriage may be infringed because that right is not guaranteed in so many words by the first eight amendments to the Constitution is to ignore the Ninth Amendment and to give it no effect whatsoever. Moreover, a judicial construction that this fundamental right is not protected by the Constitution because it is not mentioned in explicit terms by one of the first eight amendments or elsewhere in the Constitution would violate the Ninth Amendment, which specifically states that "[t]he enumeration in the Constitution, of certain rights shall not be *construed* to deny or disparage others retained by the people." (Emphasis added.)

. . .

The entire fabric of the Constitution and the purposes that clearly underlie its specific guarantees demonstrate that the rights to marital privacy and to marry and raise a family are of similar order and magnitude as the fundamental rights specifically protected.

Although the Constitution does not speak in so many words of the right of privacy in marriage, I cannot believe that it offers these fundamental rights no protection. The fact that no particular provision of the Constitution explicitly forbids the State from disrupting the traditional relation of the family—a relation as old and as fundamental as our entire civilization—surely does not show that the Government was meant to have the power to do so. Rather, as the Ninth Amendment expressly recognizes, there are fundamental personal rights such as this one, which are protected from abridgment by the Government though not specifically mentioned in the Constitution.

. . .

The logic of the dissents would sanction federal or state legislation that seems to me even more plainly unconstitutional than the statute before us. . . . [I]f upon a showing of a slender basis of rationality, a law outlawing voluntary birth control by married persons is valid, then, by the same reasoning, a law requiring compulsory birth control also would seem to be valid. In my view, however, both types of law would unjustifiably intrude upon rights of marital privacy which are constitutionally protected.

. . .

In sum, I believe that the right of privacy in the marital relation is fundamental and basic—a personal right "retained by the people" within the meaning of the Ninth Amendment. Connecticut cannot constitutionally abridge this fundamental right, which is protected by the Fourteenth Amendment from infringement by the States. I agree with the Court that petitioners' convictions must therefore be reversed.

Amendment includes Redlich, Are There "Certain Rights . . . Retained by the People"? 37 N.Y.U.L.Rev. 787 (1962), and Kelsey, The Ninth Amendment of the Federal Constitution, 11 Ind.L.J. 309 (1936). As far as I am aware, until today this Court has referred to the Ninth Amendment only in United Public Workers v. Mitchell, 330 U.S. 75, 94–95; Tennessee Electric Power Co. v. TVA, 306 U.S. 118, 143–144; and Ashwander v. TVA, 297 U.S. 288, 330–331. See also Calder v. Bull, 3 Dall. 386, 388; Loan Ass'n v. City of Topeka, 20 Wall. 655, 662–663. . . .

Mr. Justice Harlan, concurring in the judgment.

I fully agree with the judgment of reversal, but find myself unable to join the Court's opinion. The reason is that it seems to me to evince an approach to this case very much like that taken by my Brothers Black and Stewart in dissent, namely: the Due Process Clause of the Fourteenth Amendment does not touch this Connecticut statute unless the enactment is found to violate some right assured by the letter or penumbra of the Bill of Rights.

In other words, what I find implicit in the Court's opinion is that the "incorporation" doctrine may be used to *restrict* the reach of Fourteenth Amendment Due Process. For me this is just as unacceptable constitutional doctrine as is the use of the "incorporation" approach to *impose* upon the States all the requirements of the Bill of Rights as found in the provisions of the first eight amendments and in the decisions of this Court interpreting them. . . .

Mr. Justice White, concurring in the judgment.

In my view this Connecticut law as applied to married couples deprives them of "liberty" without due process of law, as that concept is used in the Fourteenth Amendment. I therefore concur in the judgment of the Court reversing these convictions under Connecticut's aiding and abetting statute.

. . .

Mr. Justice Black, with whom Mr. Justice Stewart joins, dissenting.

I agree with my Brother Stewart's dissenting opinion. And like him I do not to any extent whatever base my view that this Connecticut law is constitutional on a belief that the law is wise or that its policy is a good one. In order that there may be no room at all to doubt why I vote as I do, I feel constrained to add that the law is every bit as offensive to me as it is to my Brethren of the majority and my Brothers Harlan, White and Goldberg who, reciting reasons why it is offensive to them, hold it unconstitutional. There is no single one of the graphic and eloquent strictures and criticisms fired at the policy of this Connecticut law either by the Court's opinion or by those of my concurring Brethren to which I cannot subscribe—except their conclusion that the evil qualities they see in the law make it unconstitutional.

. . .

The Court talks about a constitutional "right of privacy" as though there is some constitutional provision or provisions forbidding any law ever to be passed which might abridge the "privacy" of individuals. But there is not. . . .

. . .

I realize that many good and able men have eloquently spoken and written, sometimes in rhapsodical strains, about the duty of this Court to keep the Constitution in tune with the times. The idea is that the Constitution must be changed from time to time and that this Court is charged with a duty to make those changes. For myself, I must with all deference reject that philosophy. The Constitution makers knew the need for change and provided for it. Amendments suggested by the people's elected representatives can be submitted to the people or their selected agents for ratification. That method of change was good for our Fathers, and being somewhat old-fashioned I must add it is good enough for me. And so, I cannot rely on the Due Process Clause or the Ninth Amendment or any mysterious and uncertain natural law concept as a reason for striking down this state law. The Due Process Clause with an "arbitrary and capricious" or "shocking to the conscience" formula was liberally used by this Court to strike down economic legislation in the early decades of this century, threatening, many people thought, the tranquility and stability of the nation. See, e.g., Lochner v. State. of New York, 198 U.S. 45. That formula, based on subjective considerations of "natural justice," is no less dangerous when used to enforce this Court's views about personal rights than those about economic rights. I had thought that we had laid that formula, as a means for striking down state legislation, to rest once and for all in cases like West Coast Hotel Co. v. Parrish, 300 U.S. 379; Olsen v. State of Nebraska ex rel. Western Reference & Bond Assn., 313 U.S. 236, and many other opinions. . . .

. . . The late Judge Learned Hand, after emphasizing his view that judges should not use the due process formula suggested in the concurring opinions today or any other formula like it to invalidate legislation offensive to their "personal preferences,"[22] made the statement, with which I fully agree, that:

> "For myself it would be most irksome to be ruled by a bevy of Platonic Guardians, even if I knew how to choose them, which I assuredly do not."

So far as I am concerned, Connecticut's law as applied here is not forbidden by any provision of the Federal Constitution as that Constitution was written, and I would therefore affirm.

Mr. Justice Stewart, whom Mr. Justice Black joins, dissenting.

Since 1879 Connecticut has had on its books a law which forbids the use of contraceptives by anyone. I think this is an uncommonly silly law. As a practical matter, the law is obviously unenforceable, except in the oblique context of the present case. As a philosophical matter, I believe the use of contraceptives in the relationship of marriage should be left to personal and private choice, based upon each individual's moral, ethical, and religious beliefs. As a matter of social policy, I think professional counsel about methods of birth control should be available to all, so that each individual's choice can be meaningfully made. But we are not asked in this case to say whether we think this law is unwise, or even asinine. We are asked to hold that it violates the United States Constitution. And that I cannot do.

. . .

What provisions of the Constitution, then, does make this state law invalid? The Court says it is the right of privacy "created by several fundamental constitutional guarantees." With all deference, I can find no such general right of privacy in the Bill of Rights, in any other part of the Constitution, or in any case ever before decided by this Court.[a]

. . .

PRIVACY AS AUTONOMY VERSUS PRIVACY AS FREEDOM FROM INTRUSION AND DISCLOSURE

In *Griswold* the Court appeared to use the term "privacy" in the sense of protecting private matters from disclosure. It emphasized intrusion into "the sacred precincts of marital bedrooms." But in Roe v. Wade, infra p. 621, the

---

22. Hand, The Bill of Rights (1958) 70. . . .

a. Helpful discussion of the Court's approach to the Griswold case may be found in: *Symposium on the Griswold Case and the Right of Privacy,* 64 Mich.L.Rev. 197 (1965); Beaney, *The Griswold Case and the Expand-* *ing Right to Privacy,* 1966 Wis.L.Rev. 979; Katin, *Griswold v. Connecticut: The Justices and Connecticut's "Uncommonly Silly Law,"* 42 Notre Dame L. 680 (1967); Franklin, *The Ninth Amendment as Civil Law Method and Its Implications for a Republican Form of Government,* 40 Tul.L.Rev. 487 (1966).

Court gave the term a broader meaning protecting personal autonomy. In fact, in Carey v. Population Services Int'l., 431 U.S. 678, 687 (1977), the Court said that later decisions had "put *Griswold* in proper perspective. *Griswold* may no longer be read as holding only that a State may not prohibit a married couple's use of contraceptives. Read in the light of its progeny, the teaching of *Griswold* is that the Constitution protects individual decisions in matters of childbearing from unjustified intrusion by the State."

Since *Griswold* the Court has decided very few claims that the state had unconstitutionally invaded privacy in the sense of requiring disclosure of personal matters. Whalen v. Roe, 429 U.S. 589 (1977), presented the question whether a state could record, in a centralized computer file, the names and addresses of all persons who had obtained, pursuant to a doctor's prescription, certain drugs for which there was both a lawful and an unlawful market. In response to an argument that the state requirement invaded a constitutionally protected zone of privacy, the Court noted: "The cases sometimes characterized as protecting 'privacy' have in fact involved at least two different kinds of interests. One is the individual interest in avoiding disclosure of personal matters, and another is the interest in independence in making certain kinds of important decisions." The Court upheld the statute on the ground that the state protections against public disclosure of the data were sufficient to avoid a serious threat to either interest. It concluded its opinion with the following paragraph:

> "A final word about issues we have not decided. We are not unaware of the threat to privacy implicit in the accumulation of vast amounts of personal information in computerized data banks or other massive government files. The collection of taxes, the distribution of welfare and social security benefits, the supervision of public health, the direction of our armed forces and the enforcement of the criminal laws, all require the orderly preservation of great quantities of information, much of which is personal in character and potentially embarrassing or harmful if disclosed. The right to collect and use such data for public purposes is typically accompanied by a concomitant statutory or regulatory duty to avoid unwarranted disclosures. Recognizing that in some circumstances that duty arguably has its roots in the Constitution, nevertheless New York's statutory scheme, and its implementing administrative procedures, evidence a proper concern with, and protection of, the individual's interest in privacy. We therefore need not, and do not, decide any question which might be presented by the unwarranted disclosure of accumulated private data—whether intentional or unintentional—or by a system that did not contain comparable security provisions. We simply hold that this record does not establish an invasion of any right or liberty protected by the Fourteenth Amendment."

B.   FAMILY AND MARITAL RELATIONSHIPS

Moore v. City of East Cleveland, Ohio
431 U.S. 494, 97 S.Ct. 1932, 52 L.Ed.2d 531 (1977).

Mr. Justice Powell announced the judgment of the Court, and delivered an opinion in which Mr. Justice Brennan, Mr. Justice Marshall, and Mr. Justice Blackmun joined.

East Cleveland's housing ordinance, like many throughout the country, limits occupancy of a dwelling unit to members of a single family. § 1351.02.

[handwritten margin note: limit occupancy of a dwelling to single family]

But the ordinance contains an unusual and complicated definitional section that recognizes as a "family" only a few categories of related individuals, § 1341.08.[2] Because her family, living together in her home, fits none of those categories, appellant stands convicted of a criminal offense. The question in this case is whether the ordinance violates the Due Process Clause of the Fourteenth Amendment.

strict def. of family

I.

Appellant, Mrs. Inez Moore, lives in her East Cleveland home together with her son, Dale Moore Sr., and her two grandsons, Dale, Jr., and John Moore, Jr. The two boys are first cousins rather than brothers; we are told that John came to live with his grandmother and with the elder and younger Dale Moores after his mother's death.

In early 1973, Mrs. Moore received a notice of violation from the city, stating that John was an "illegal occupant" and directing her to comply with the ordinance. When she failed to remove him from her home, the city filed a criminal charge. Mrs. Moore moved to dismiss, claiming that the ordinance was constitutionally invalid on its face. Her motion was overruled, and upon conviction she was sentenced to five days in jail and a $25 fine. The Ohio Court of Appeals affirmed after giving full consideration to her constitutional claims, and the Ohio Supreme Court denied review. . . .

II.

The city argues that our decision in Village of Belle Terre v. Boraas, 416 U.S. 1 (1974), requires us to sustain the ordinance attacked here. Belle Terre, like East Cleveland, imposed limits on the types of groups that could occupy a single dwelling unit. Applying the constitutional standard announced in this Court's leading land-use case, Euclid v. Ambler Realty Co., 272 U.S. 365 (1926), we sustained the Belle Terre ordinance on the ground that it bore a rational relationship to permissible state objectives.

But one overriding factor sets this case apart from *Belle Terre*. The ordinance there affected only *unrelated* individuals. It expressly allowed all who were related by "blood, adoption, or marriage" to live together, and in sustaining the ordinance we were careful to note that it promoted "family needs" and "family values." East Cleveland, in contrast, has chosen to regulate the

---

2. Section 1341.08 (1966) provides:

" 'Family' means a number of individuals related to the nominal head of the household or to the spouse of the nominal head of the household living as a single housekeeping unit in a single dwelling unit, but limited to the following:

"(a) Husband or wife of the nominal head of the household.

"(b) Unmarried children of the nominal head of the household or of the spouse of the nominal head of the household, provided, however, that such unmarried children have no children residing with them.

"(c) Father or mother of the nominal head of the household or of the spouse of the nominal head of the household.

"(d) Notwithstanding the provisions of subsection (b) hereof, a family may include not more than one dependent married or unmarried child of the nominal head of the household or of the spouse of the nominal head of the household and the spouse and dependent children of such dependent child. For the purpose of this subsection, a dependent person is one who has more than fifty percent of his total support furnished for him by the nominal head of the household and the spouse of the nominal head of the household.

"(e) A family may consist of one individual."

slices & divides into the family itself

occupancy of its housing by slicing deeply into the family itself. This is no mere incidental result of the ordinance. On its face it selects certain categories of relatives who may live together and declares that others may not. In particular, it makes a crime of a grandmother's choice to live with her grandson in circumstances like those presented here.

When a city undertakes such intrusive regulation of the family, neither *Belle Terre* nor *Euclid* governs; the usual judicial deference to the legislature is inappropriate. "This Court has long recognized that freedom of personal choice in matters of marriage and family life is one of the liberties protected by the Due Process Clause of the Fourteenth Amendment." ... A host of cases, tracing their lineage to Meyer v. Nebraska, 262 U.S. 390, 399–401 (1923), and Pierce v. Society of Sisters, 268 U.S. 510, 534–535 (1925), have consistently acknowledged a "private realm of family life which the state cannot enter." Prince v. Massachusetts, 321 U.S. 158, 166 (1944).... Of course, the family is not beyond regulation. See Prince v. Massachusetts. But when the government intrudes on choices concerning family living arrangements, this Court must examine carefully the importance of the governmental interests advanced and the extent to which they are served by the challenged regulation. See *Poe v. Ullman* (Harlan, J., dissenting).

purpose of legislation:

When thus examined, this ordinance cannot survive. The city seeks to justify it as a means of preventing overcrowding, minimizing traffic and parking congestion, and avoiding an undue financial burden on East Cleveland's school system. Although these are legitimate goals, the ordinance before us serves them marginally, at best. For example, the ordinance permits any family consisting only of husband, wife, and unmarried children to live together, even if the family contains a half-dozen licensed drivers, each with his or her own car. At the same time it forbids an adult brother and sister to share a household, even if both faithfully use public transportation. The ordinance would permit a grandmother to live with a single dependent son and children, even if his school-age children number a dozen, yet it forces Mrs. Moore to find another dwelling for her grandson John, simply because of the presence of his uncle and cousin in the same household. We need not labor the point. Section 1341.08 has but a tenuous relation to alleviation of the conditions mentioned by the city.

III.

The city would distinguish the cases based on *Meyer* and *Pierce.* It points out that none of them "gives grandmothers any fundamental rights with respect to grandsons," and suggests that any constitutional right to live together as a family extends only to the nuclear family—essentially a couple and its dependent children.

To be sure, these cases did not expressly consider the family relationship presented here. They were immediately concerned with freedom of choice with respect to childbearing, e.g., *LaFleur, Roe v. Wade, Griswold,* supra, or with the rights of parents to the custody and companionship of their own children, Stanley v. Illinois, supra, or with traditional parental authority in matters of child rearing and education. *Yoder, Ginsberg, Pierce, Meyer,* supra. But unless we close our eyes to the basic reasons why certain rights associated with the family have been accorded shelter under the Fourteenth Amendment's Due Process Clause, we cannot avoid applying the force and rationale of these precedents to the family choice involved in this case.

. . .

Substantive due process has at times been a treacherous field for this Court. There *are* risks when the judicial branch gives enhanced protection to certain substantive liberties without the guidance of the more specific provisions of the Bill of Rights. As the history of the *Lochner* era demonstrates, there is reason for concern lest the only limits to such judicial intervention become the predilections of those who happen at the time to be Members of this Court. That history counsels caution and restraint. But it does not counsel abandonment, nor does it require what the city urges here: cutting off any protection of family rights at the first convenient, if arbitrary boundary—the boundary of the nuclear family.

Appropriate limits on substantive due process come not from drawing arbitrary lines but rather from careful "respect for the teachings of history [and] solid recognition of the basic values that underlie our society." Griswold v. Connecticut, 381 U.S., at 501 (Harlan, J., concurring).... Our decisions establish that the Constitution protects the sanctity of the family precisely because the institution of the family is deeply rooted in this Nation's history and tradition. It is through the family that we inculcate and pass down many of our most cherished values, moral and cultural.

Ours is by no means a tradition limited to respect for the bonds uniting the members of the nuclear family. The tradition of uncles, aunts, cousins, and especially grandparents sharing a household along with parents and children has roots equally venerable and equally deserving of constitutional recognition. Over the years millions of our citizens have grown up in just such an environment, and most, surely, have profited from it. Even if conditions of modern society have brought about a decline in extended family households, they have not erased the accumulated wisdom of civilization, gained over the centuries and honored throughout our history, that supports a larger conception of the family. Out of choice, necessity, or a sense of family responsibility, it has been common for close relatives to draw together and participate in the duties and the satisfactions of a common home. Decisions concerning child rearing, which *Yoder, Meyer, Pierce* and other cases have recognized as entitled to constitutional protection, long have been shared with grandparents or other relatives who occupy the same household—indeed who may take on major responsibility for the rearing of the children. Especially in times of adversity, such as the death of a spouse or economic need, the broader family has tended to come together for mutual sustenance and to maintain or rebuild a secure home life. This is apparently what happened here.

Whether or not such a household is established because of personal tragedy, the choice of relatives in this degree of kinship to live together may not lightly be denied by the State. *Pierce* struck down an Oregon law requiring all children to attend the State's public schools, holding that the Constitution "excludes any general power of the State to standardize its children by forcing them to accept instruction from public teachers only." 268 U.S., at 535. By the same token the Constitution prevents East Cleveland from standardizing its children—and its adults—by forcing all to live in certain narrowly defined family patterns.

Reversed.

Mr. Justice Brennan, with whom Mr. Justice Marshall joins, concurring.

I join the plurality's opinion....

In today's America, the "nuclear family" is the pattern so often found in much of white suburbia. Sanden, Sociology: A Systematic Approach, p. 320

(1965). The Constitution cannot be interpreted, however, to tolerate the imposition by government upon the rest of us of white suburbia's preference in patterns of family living. The "extended family" that provided generations of early Americans with social services and economic and emotional support in times of hardship, and was the beachhead for successive waves of immigrants who populated our cities, remains not merely still a pervasive living pattern, but under the goad of brutal economic necessity, a prominent pattern— virtually a means of survival—for large numbers of the poor and deprived minorities of our society. For them compelled pooling of scant resources requires compelled sharing of a household.

The "extended" form is especially familiar among black families. . . .

I do not wish to be understood as implying that East Cleveland's enforcement of its ordinance is motivated by a racially discriminatory purpose: the record of this case would not support that implication. But the prominence of other than nuclear families among ethnic and racial minority groups, including our black citizens, surely demonstrates that the "extended family" pattern remains a vital tenet of our society. It suffices that in prohibiting this pattern of family living as a means of achieving its objectives, appellee city has chosen a device that deeply intrudes into family associational rights that historically have been central, and today remain central, to a large proportion of our population.

. . .

Mr. Justice Stevens, concurring in the judgment.

In my judgment the critical question presented by this case is whether East Cleveland's housing ordinance is a permissible restriction on appellant's right to use her own property as she sees fit.

. . .

Mr. Justice Stewart, with whom Mr. Justice Rehnquist joins, dissenting.

. . .

. . . The question presented, as I view it, is whether the decision in *Belle Terre* is controlling, or whether the Constitution compels a different result because East Cleveland's definition of "family" is more restrictive than that before us in the *Belle Terre* case.

. . . The *Belle Terre* decision disposes of the appellant's contentions to the extent they focus not on her blood relationships with her sons and grandsons but on more general notions about the "privacy of the home." Her suggestion that every person has a constitutional right permanently to share his residence with whomever he pleases, and that such choices are "beyond the province of legitimate governmental intrusion," amounts to the same argument that was made and found unpersuasive in *Belle Terre*.

To be sure, the ordinance involved in *Belle Terre* did not prevent blood relatives from occupying the same dwelling, and the Court's decision in that case does not, therefore, foreclose the appellant's arguments based specifically on the ties of kinship present in this case. Nonetheless, I would hold, for the reasons that follow, that the existence of those ties does not elevate either the appellant's claim of associational freedom or her claim of privacy to a level invoking constitutional protection.

. . .

The "association" in this case is not for any purpose relating to the promotion of speech, assembly, the press, or religion. And wherever the outer boundaries of constitutional protection of freedom of association may eventually turn out to be, they surely do not extend to those who assert no interest other than the gratification, convenience, and economy of sharing the same residence.

The appellant is considerably closer to the constitutional mark in asserting that the East Cleveland ordinance intrudes upon "the private realm of family life which the state cannot enter." . . .

Although the appellant's desire to share a single-dwelling unit also involves "private family life" in a sense, that desire can hardly be equated with any of the interests protected in [previous cases.] The ordinance . . . did not impede her choice to have or not to have children, and it did not dictate to her how her own children were to be nurtured and reared. The ordinance clearly does not prevent parents from living together or living with their unemancipated offspring.

. . .[7]

. . . When the Court has found that the Fourteenth Amendment placed a substantive limitation on a State's power to regulate, it has been in those rare cases in which the personal interests at issue have been deemed "implicit in the concept of ordered liberty." See Roe v. Wade, supra, at 152, quoting Palko v. Connecticut, 302 U.S. 319, 325. The interest that the appellant may have in permanently sharing a single kitchen and a suite of contiguous rooms with some of her relatives simply does not rise to that level. To equate this interest with the fundamental decisions to marry and to bear and raise children is to extend the limited substantive contours of the Due Process Clause beyond recognition.

The appellant also challenges the single-family occupancy ordinance on equal protection grounds. Her claim is that the city has drawn an arbitrary and irrational distinction between groups of people who may live together as a "family" and those who may not. . . .

Obviously, East Cleveland might have as easily and perhaps as effectively hit upon a different definition of "family." But a line could hardly be drawn that would not sooner or later become the target of a challenge like the appellant's. If "family" included all of the householder's grandchildren there would doubtless be the hard case of an orphaned niece or nephew. If, as the appellant suggests, a "family" must include all blood relatives, what of long-time friends? The point is that any definition would produce hardships in some cases without materially advancing the legislative purpose. . . .

. . .

Mr. Justice White, dissenting.

. . .

. . . Realizing that the present construction of the Due Process Clause represents a major judicial gloss on its terms, as well as on the anticipation of

---

7. The opinion of Mr. Justice Powell and Mr. Justice Brennan's concurring opinion both emphasize the traditional importance of the extended family in American life. But I fail to understand why it follows that the residents of East Cleveland are constitutionally prevented from following what Mr. Justice Brennan calls the "pattern" of "white suburbia," even though that choice may reflect "cultural myopia." In point of fact, East Cleveland is a predominantly Negro community, with a Negro City Manager and City Commission.

the Framers, and that much of the underpinning for the broad, substantive application of the Clause disappeared in the conflict between the executive and the judiciary in the 1930's and 1940's, the Court should be extremely reluctant to breathe still further substantive content into the Due Process Clause so as to strike down legislation adopted by a State or city to promote its welfare. Whenever the judiciary does so, it unavoidably pre-empts for itself another part of the governance of the country without express constitutional authority.

Accepting the cases as they are and the Due Process Clause as construed by them, however, I think it evident that the threshold question in any due process attack on legislation, whether the challenge is procedural or substantive, is whether there is a deprivation of life, liberty or property. . . .

It seems to me that Mr. Justice Douglas was closest to the mark in Poe v. Ullman, supra, at 517, when he said that the trouble with the holdings of the "old Court" was not in its definition of liberty but in its definition of the protections guaranteed to that liberty—"not in entertaining inquiries concerning the constitutionality of social legislation but in applying the standards that it did."

The term "liberty" is not, therefore, to be given a crabbed construction. I have no more difficulty than Mr. Justice Powell apparently does in concluding that petitioner in this case properly asserts a liberty interest within the meaning of the Due Process Clause. The question is not one of liberty, *vel non*. Rather, there being no procedural issue at stake, the issue is whether the precise interest involved—the interest in having more than one set of grandchildren live in her home—is entitled to such substantive protection under the Due Process Clause that this ordinance must be held invalid.

. . .

[T]he general principle [is] that "liberty may not be interfered with, under the guise of protecting the public interest, by legislative action which is arbitrary or without reasonable relation to some purpose within the competency of the state to effect." Meyer v. Nebraska, supra, at 399–400. This means-end test appears to require that any statute restrictive of liberty have an ascertainable purpose and represent a rational means to achieve that purpose, whatever the nature of the liberty interest involved. . . .

There are various "liberties," however, which require that infringing legislation be given closer judicial scrutiny, not only with respect to existence of a purpose and the means employed, but also with respect to the importance of the purpose itself relative to the invaded interest. Some interests would appear almost impregnable to invasion, such as the freedoms of speech, press, and religion, and the freedom from cruel and unusual punishments. Other interests, for example, the right of association, the right to vote, and various claims sometimes referred to under the general rubric of the right to privacy, also weigh very heavily against state claims of authority to regulate. It is this category of interests which, as I understand it, Mr. Justice Stewart refers to as "implicit in the concept of ordered liberty." Because he would confine the reach of substantive due process protection to interests such as these and because he would not classify in this category the asserted right to share a house with the relatives involved here, he rejects the due process claim.

Given his premise, he is surely correct. Under our cases, the Due Process Clause extends substantial protection to various phases of family life, but none requires that the claim made here be sustained. I cannot believe that the interest in residing with more than one set of grandchildren is one that calls for any kind of heightened protection under the Due Process Clause. . . .

Mr. Justice Powell would apparently construe the Due Process Clause to protect from all but quite important state regulatory interests any right or privilege that in his estimate is deeply rooted in the country's traditions. For me, this suggests a far too expansive charter for this Court and a far less meaningful and less confining guiding principle than Mr. Justice Stewart would use for serious substantive due process review. . . .

. . . Had it been our task to legislate, we might have approached the problem in a different manner than did the drafters of this ordinance; but I have no trouble in concluding that the normal goals of zoning regulation are present here and that the ordinance serves these goals by limiting, in identifiable circumstances, the number of people who can occupy a single household. The ordinance does not violate the Due Process Clause.

For very similar reasons, the equal protection claim must fail, since it is not to be judged by the strict scrutiny standard employed when a fundamental interest or suspect classification is involved. . . .

[A dissenting opinion by Chief Justice Burger is omitted.]ª

Zablocki v. Redhail

434 U.S. 374, 98 S.Ct. 673, 54 L.Ed.2d 618 (1978).

Mr. Justice Marshall delivered the opinion of the Court.

[A Wisconsin statute, §§ 245.10(1), (4), (5), required any "Wisconsin resident having minor issue not in his custody and which he is under an obligation to support by any court order or judgment" to obtain court permission to marry. The marriage applicant had to demonstrate compliance with the support obligation and that the children covered by the support order "are not then and are not likely thereafter to become public charges."

[handwritten margin note: contesting wisconsin statute]

In a paternity action, Redhail, an unmarried high school student, was ordered to pay $109 per month support until his child reached 18. From the date of the order in May 1972 until August 1974 he was unemployed, indigent, and consequently unable to make any support payments. His application for a marriage license the next month was denied for failure to obtain the requisite court order granting him permission to marry. It was stipulated that Redhail had not satisfied his support obligations (by December 1974, he was more than $3,700 in arrears), that his child had been a public charge since birth, and "that she would have been a public charge even if appellee had been current in his support payments."

Redhail brought a class action in federal district court, challenging the statute as violative of "equal protection and due process rights secured by the First, Fifth, Ninth, and Fourteenth Amendments." He alleged that he and the woman he wished to marry were expecting a child in March 1975 and wanted to be lawfully married before then. The district court held the statute invalid under the Equal Protection Clause, and the Supreme Court agreed.]

[handwritten margin note: violations of EP & due process]

II.

In evaluating §§ 245.10(1), (4), (5) under the Equal Protection Clause, "we must first determine what burden of justification the classification created thereby must meet, by looking to the nature of the classification and the

a. For a full discussion, see *Developments in the Law—The Constitution and the* *Family,* 93 Harv.L.Rev. 1156 (1980).

critical examination is the burden of justification that should be used

individual interests affected." . . . Since our past decisions make clear that the right to marry is of fundamental importance, and since the classification at issue here significantly interferes with the exercise of that right, we believe that "critical examination" of the state interests advanced in support of the classification is required. . . .

The leading decision of this Court on the right to marry is Loving v. Virginia, 388 U.S. 1 (1967). In that case, an interracial couple who had been convicted of violating Virginia's miscegenation laws challenged the statutory scheme on both equal protection and due process grounds. The Court's opinion could have rested solely on the ground that the statutes discriminated on the basis of race in violation of the Equal Protection Clause. But the Court went on to hold that the laws arbitrarily deprived the couple of a fundamental liberty protected by the Due Process Clause, the freedom to marry. The Court's language on the latter point bears repeating:

Loving v. virginia right to marry is a fundamental right

"The freedom to marry has long been recognized as one of the vital personal rights essential to the orderly pursuit of happiness by free men.

"Marriage is one of the 'basic civil rights of man,' fundamental to our very existence and survival." . . .

Although *Loving* arose in the context of racial discrimination, prior and subsequent decisions of this Court confirm that the right to marry is of fundamental importance for all individuals. . . .

More recent decisions have established that the right to marry is part of the fundamental "right of privacy" implicit in the Fourteenth Amendment's Due Process Clause. In Griswold v. Connecticut, 381 U.S. 479 (1965), the Court observed:

Griswold v. connecticut classifies is a right to privacy

"We deal with a right of privacy older than the Bill of Rights—older than our political parties, older than our school system. Marriage is a coming together for better or for worse, hopefully enduring, and intimate to the degree of being sacred. It is an association that promotes a way of life, not causes; a harmony in living, not political faiths; a bilateral loyalty, not commercial or social projects. Yet it is an association for as noble a purpose as any involved in our prior decisions."

. . .

Cases subsequent to *Griswold* and *Loving* have routinely categorized the decision to marry as among the personal decisions protected by the right of privacy. . . .

recognize abortion & procreation — must recognize marriage

It is not surprising that the decision to marry has been placed on the same level of importance as decisions relating to procreation, childbirth, child-rearing, and family relationships. As the facts of this case illustrate, it would make little sense to recognize a right of privacy with respect to other matters of family life and not with respect to the decision to enter the relationship that is the foundation of the family in our society. The woman whom appellee desired to marry had a fundamental right to seek an abortion of their expected child, see Roe v. Wade, supra, or to bring the child into life to suffer the myriad social, if not economic, disabilities that the status of illegitimacy brings. . . . Surely, a decision to marry and raise the child in a traditional family setting must receive equivalent protection. And, if appellee's right to procreate means anything at all, it must imply some right to enter the only relationship in which the State of Wisconsin allows sexual relations legally to take place.

By reaffirming the fundamental character of the right to marry, we do not mean to suggest that every state regulation which relates in any way to the incidents of or prerequisites for marriage must be subjected to rigorous scrutiny. To the contrary, reasonable regulations that do not significantly interfere with decisions to enter into the marital relationship may legitimately be imposed. See Califano v. Jobst, 434 U.S. 47 (1977). The statutory classification at issue here, however, clearly does interfere directly and substantially with the right to marry.

Under the challenged statute, no Wisconsin resident in the affected class may marry in Wisconsin or elsewhere without a court order, and marriages contracted in violation of the statute are both void and punishable as criminal offenses. Some of those in the affected class, like appellee, will never be able to obtain the necessary court order, because they either lack the financial means to meet their support obligations or cannot prove that their children will not become public charges. These persons are absolutely prevented from getting married. Many others, able in theory to satisfy the statute's requirements, will be sufficiently burdened by having to do so that they will in effect be coerced into foregoing their right to marry. And even those who can be persuaded to meet the statute's requirements suffer a serious intrusion into their freedom of choice in an area in which we have held such freedom to be fundamental.

III.

When a statutory classification significantly interferes with the exercise of a fundamental right, it cannot be upheld unless it is supported by sufficiently important state interests and is closely tailored to effectuate only those interests.... Appellant asserts that two interests are served by the challenged statute: the permission-to-marry proceeding furnishes an opportunity to counsel the applicant as to the necessity of fulfilling his prior support obligations; and the welfare of the out-of-custody children is protected. We may accept for present purposes that these are legitimate and substantial interests, but, since the means selected by the State for achieving these interests unnecessarily impinge on the right to marry, the statute cannot be sustained.

... The statute actually enacted ... does not expressly require or provide for any counselling whatsoever, nor for any automatic granting of permission to marry by the court, and thus it can hardly be justified as a means for ensuring counselling of the persons within its coverage. Even [if] counselling does take place ... this interest obviously cannot support the withholding of court permission to marry once counselling is completed.

With regard to safeguarding the welfare of the out-of-custody children, ... [at oral] argument, appellant's counsel suggested that ... the statute provides incentive for the applicant to make support payments to his children.... This "collection device" rationale cannot justify the statute's broad infringement on the right to marry.

First, with respect to individuals who are unable to meet the statutory requirements, the statute merely prevents the applicant from getting married, without delivering any money at all into the hands of the applicant's prior children. More importantly, regardless of the applicant's ability or willingness to meet the statutory requirements, the State already has numerous other means for exacting compliance with support obligations, means that are at least as effective as the instant statute's and yet do not impinge upon the right to marry. Under Wisconsin law, whether the children are from a prior marriage or were born out of wedlock, court-determined support obligations may be enforced directly via wage assignments, civil contempt proceedings, and criminal penalties. And, if the State believes that parents of children out of their custody should be responsible for ensuring that those children do not become public charges, this interest can be achieved by adjusting the criteria used for determining the amounts to be paid under their support orders.

There is also some suggestion that § 245.10 protects the ability of marriage applicants to meet support obligations to prior children by preventing the applicants from incurring new support obligations. But the challenged provisions of § 245.10 are grossly underinclusive with respect to this purpose, since they do not limit in any way new financial commitments by the applicant other than those arising out of the contemplated marriage. The statutory classification is substantially overinclusive as well: given the possibility that the new spouse will actually better the applicant's financial situation, by contributing income from a job or otherwise, the statute in many cases may prevent affected individuals from improving their ability to satisfy their prior support obligations. And, although it is true that the applicant will incur support obligations to any children born during the contemplated marriage, preventing the marriage may only result in the children being born out of wedlock, as in fact occurred in appellee's case. Since the support obligation is the same whether the child is born in or out of wedlock, the net result of preventing the marriage is simply more illegitimate children.

The statutory classification ... cannot be justified by the interests advanced in support of it. The judgment of the District Court is, accordingly, affirmed.

Mr. Chief Justice Burger, concurring.

I join Mr. Justice Marshall's opinion for the Court....

Mr. Justice Stewart, concurring in the judgment.

I cannot join the opinion of the Court. To hold, as the Court does, that the Wisconsin statute violates the Equal Protection Clause seems to me to misconceive the meaning of that constitutional guarantee. The Equal Protection Clause deals not with substantive rights or freedoms but with invidiously discriminatory classifications.... The paradigm of its violation is, of course, classification by race....

Like almost any law, the Wisconsin statute now before us affects some people and does not affect others. But to say that it thereby creates "classifications" in the equal protection sense strikes me as little short of fantasy. The problem in this case is not one of discriminatory classifications, but of unwarranted encroachment upon a constitutionally protected freedom. I think that the Wisconsin statute is unconstitutional because it exceeds the bounds of permissible state regulation of marriage, and invades the sphere of liberty protected by the Due Process Clause of the Fourteenth Amendment.

I.

I do not agree with the Court that there is a "right to marry" in the constitutional sense. That right, or more accurately, that privilege is under our federal system peculiarly one to be defined and limited by state law. Sosna v. Iowa, 419 U.S. 393, 404. A State may not only "significantly interfere with decisions to enter into the marriage relationship," but may in many circumstances absolutely prohibit it. Surely, for example, a State may legitimately say that no one can marry his or her sibling, that no one can marry who is not at least 14 years old, that no one can marry without first passing an examination for venereal disease, or that no one can marry who has a living husband or wife. But, just as surely, in regulating the intimate human relationship of marriage, there is a limit beyond which a State may not constitutionally go.

The Constitution does not specifically mention freedom to marry, but it is settled that the "liberty" protected by the Due Process Clause of the Fourteenth Amendment embraces more than those freedoms expressly enumerated in the Bill of Rights.... And the decisions of this Court have made clear that freedom of personal choice in matters of marriage and family life is one of the liberties so protected....

It is evident that the Wisconsin law now before us directly abridges that freedom. The question is whether the state interests that support the abridgment can overcome the substantive protections of the Constitution.

. . .

If Wisconsin had said that no one could marry who had not paid all of the fines assessed against him for traffic violations, I suppose the constitutional invalidity of the law would be apparent. For while the state interest would certainly be legitimate, that interest would be both disproportionate and unrelated to the restriction of liberty imposed by the State. But the invalidity of the law before us is hardly so clear, because its restriction of liberty seems largely to be imposed only on those who have abused the same liberty in the past.

. . .

On several occasions this Court has held that a person's inability to pay money demanded by the State does not justify the total deprivation of a constitutionally protected liberty....

The principle of those cases applies here as well. The Wisconsin law makes no allowance for the truly indigent....

As directed against either the indigent or the delinquent parent, the law is substantially more rational if viewed as a means of assuring the financial viability of future marriages. In this context, it reflects a plausible judgment that those who have not fulfilled their financial obligations and have not kept their children off the welfare rolls in the past are likely to encounter similar difficulties in the future. But the State's legitimate concern with the financial soundness of prospective marriages must stop short of telling people they may not marry because they are too poor or because they might persist in their financial irresponsibility. The invasion of constitutionally protected liberty and the chance of erroneous prediction are simply too great. A legislative judgment so alien to our traditions and so offensive to our shared notions of fairness offends the Due Process Clause of the Fourteenth Amendment.

II.

In an opinion of the Court half a century ago, Mr. Justice Holmes described an equal protection claim as "the usual last resort of constitutional arguments." Buck v. Bell, 274 U.S. 200, 208. Today equal protection doctrine has become the Court's chief instrument for invalidating state laws. Yet, in a case like this one, the doctrine is no more than substantive due process by another name.

Although the Court purports to examine the bases for legislative classifications and to compare the treatment of legislatively defined groups, it actually erects substantive limitations on what States may do. Thus, the effect of the Court's decision in this case is not to require Wisconsin to draw its legislative classifications with greater precision or to afford similar treatment to similarly situated persons. Rather, the message of the Court's opinion is that Wisconsin may not use its control over marriage to achieve the objectives of the state statute. Such restrictions on basic governmental power are at the heart of substantive due process.

The Court is understandably reluctant to rely on substantive due process. See Roe v. Wade, 410 U.S., at 167–168 (concurring opinion). But to embrace the essence of that doctrine under the guise of equal protection serves no purpose but obfuscation. . . .

To conceal this appropriate inquiry invites mechanical or thoughtless application of misfocused doctrine. To bring it into the open forces a healthy and responsible recognition of the nature and purpose of the extreme power we wield when, in invalidating a state law in the name of the Constitution, we invalidate *pro tanto* the process of representative democracy in one of the Sovereign States of the Union.

Mr. Justice Powell, concurring in the judgment.

I concur in the judgment of the Court . . . [but] write separately because the majority's rationale sweeps too broadly in an area which traditionally has been subject to pervasive state regulation. . . .

I.

. . .

. . . Thus, *Loving* involved a denial of a "fundamental freedom" on a wholly unsupportable basis—the use of classifications "directly subversive of the principle of equality at the heart of the Fourteenth Amendment. . . ." It does not speak to the level of judicial scrutiny of, or governmental justification for, "supportable" restrictions on the "fundamental freedom" of individuals to marry or divorce.

In my view, analysis must start from the recognition of domestic relations as "an area that has long been regarded as a virtually exclusive province of the States." Sosna v. Iowa, 419 U.S. 393, 404 (1975). The marriage relation traditionally has been subject to regulation, initially by the ecclesiastical authorities, and later by the secular state. . . . State regulation has included bans on incest, bigamy, and homosexuality, as well as various preconditions to marriage, such as blood tests. Likewise, a showing of fault on the part of one of the partners traditionally has been a prerequisite to the dissolution of an unsuccessful union. A "compelling state purpose" inquiry would cast doubt on the network of restrictions that the States have fashioned to govern marriage and divorce.

II.

State power over domestic relations is not without constitutional limits. The Due Process Clause requires a showing of justification "when the government intrudes on choices concerning family living arrangements" in a manner which is contrary to deeply rooted traditions. . . .

. . .

. . . I do not agree with the suggestion in the Court's opinion that a State may never condition the right to marry on satisfaction of existing support obligations simply because the State has alternative methods of compelling such payments. To the extent this restriction applies to persons who are able to make the required support payments but simply wish to shirk their moral and legal obligation, the Constitution interposes no bar to this additional collection mechanism. The vice inheres not in the collection concept, but in the failure to make provision for those without the means to comply with child-support obligations. . . .

. . .

The marriage applicant not only is required . . . to submit proof of compliance with his support obligation, but also to demonstrate—in some unspecified way—that his children "are not then and are not likely thereafter to become public charges." . . . Apparently, no other jurisdiction has embraced this approach as a method of reducing the number of children on public assistance. Because the State has not established a justification for this unprecedented foreclosure of marriage to many of its citizens solely because of their indigency, I concur in the judgment of the Court.

State can but hasn't shown enough justification

Mr. Justice Stevens, concurring in the judgment.

. . .

In sum, the public charge provision is either futile or perverse insofar as it applies to childless couples, couples who will have illegitimate children if they are forbidden to marry, couples whose economic status will be improved by marriage, and couples who are so poor that the marriage will have no impact on the welfare status of their children in any event. Even assuming that the right to marry may sometimes be denied on economic grounds, this clumsy and deliberate legislative discrimination between the rich and the poor is irrational in so many ways that it cannot withstand scrutiny under the Equal Protection Clause of the Fourteenth Amendment.

Mr. Justice Rehnquist, dissenting.

. . . I would view this legislative judgment in the light of the traditional presumption of validity. I think that under the Equal Protection Clause the statute need pass only the "rational basis test," Dandridge v. Williams, 397 U.S. 471, 485 (1970), and that under the Due Process Clause it need only be shown that it bears a rational relation to a constitutionally permissible objective. Williamson v. Lee Optical Co., 348 U.S. 483, 491 (1955); Ferguson v. Skrupa, 372 U.S. 726, 733 (1963) (Harlan, J., concurring). The statute so viewed is a permissible exercise of the State's power to regulate family life and to assure the support of minor children, despite its possible imprecision in the extreme cases envisioned in the concurring opinions.

Should use rational basis test

. . .

DOES EQUAL PROTECTION ANALYSIS ADD ANYTHING?

For examples of other cases where the Court has applied equal protection analysis to cases controlled by other constitutional provisions, see Carey v. Brown, 447 U.S. 455 (1980) (first amendment); Logan v. Zimmerman Brush Co., 455 U.S. 422 (1982) (procedural due process). In any of these cases, do the analysis and result differ if equal protection standards are disregarded and the case is determined under the applicable constitutional provisions? For an extended argument that they do not, see Westen, *The Empty Idea of Equality,* 95 Harv.L.Rev. 537 (1982). See also Cohen, *Is Equal Protection Like Oakland? Equality as a Surrogate for Other Rights,* 59 Tulane L.Rev. 884 (1985).

Michael H. v. Gerald D.

491 U.S. 110, 109 S.Ct. 2333, 105 L.Ed.2d 91 (1989).

Justice Scalia announced the judgment of the Court and delivered an opinion, in which The Chief Justice joins, and in all but note 6 of which Justice O'Connor and Justice Kennedy join.

Under California law, a child born to a married woman living with her husband is presumed to be a child of the marriage. Cal.Evid.Code Ann. § 621 *child born to married couple living together is presumed to be their child*

(West Supp.1989). The presumption of legitimacy may be rebutted only by the husband or wife, and then only in limited circumstances. Ibid. The instant appeal presents the claim that this presumption infringes upon the due process rights of a man who wishes to establish his paternity of a child born to the wife of another man, and the claim that it infringes upon the constitutional right of the child to maintain a relationship with her natural father.

infringes upon due process right of father; const. right of child

I

The facts of this case are, we must hope, extraordinary....

[In 1978, two years after Carole D. and Gerald D. married and began living in California, Carole began "an adulterous affair with her neighbor, Michael H." Three years later she gave birth to Victoria. Blood tests "showed a 98.07% probability that Michael was Victoria's father." Victoria always lived with Carole, but during her first three years they lived intermittently with Gerald in New York, with Michael in St. Thomas or Los Angeles, and with another man in California. Whenever they were with Michael, he "held Victoria out as his daughter."]

In November 1982, [when first] rebuffed in his attempts to visit Victoria, Michael filed a filiation action in California Superior Court to establish his paternity and right to visitation.... [Victoria's court-appointed attorney later] filed a cross-complaint asserting that if she had more than one psychological or de facto father, she was entitled to maintain her filial relationship, with all of the attendant rights, duties, and obligations, with both. In May 1983, Carole filed a motion for summary judgment.... In August, however, she returned to California, became involved once again with Michael, and instructed her attorneys to remove the summary judgment motion from the calendar.

... In April 1984, Carole and Michael signed a stipulation that Michael was Victoria's natural father. Carole left Michael the next month, however, and instructed her attorneys not to file the stipulation. In June 1984, Carole reconciled with Gerald and joined him in New York, where they now live with Victoria and two other children since born into the marriage.

In May 1984, Michael and Victoria ... sought visitation rights for Michael pendente lite.... [Based on a court-appointed psychologist's recommendation, the court] ordered ... limited visitation privileges pendente lite.

Denied because of statute presuming that Gerald is the father

presumption may be rebutted if..

On October 19, 1984, Gerald, who had intervened in the action, [successfully] moved for summary judgment on the ground that under Cal.Evid.Code § 621 there were no triable issues of fact as to Victoria's paternity. This law provides that "the issue of a wife cohabiting with her husband, who is not impotent or sterile, is conclusively presumed to be a child of the marriage." ... The presumption may be rebutted by blood tests, but only if a motion for such tests is made, within two years from the date of the child's birth, either by the husband or, if the natural father has filed an affidavit acknowledging paternity, by the wife....

On January 28, 1985, having found that affidavits submitted by Carole and Gerald sufficed to demonstrate that the two were cohabiting at conception and birth and that Gerald was neither sterile nor impotent, the Superior Court granted Gerald's motion for summary judgment, rejecting Michael's and Victoria's challenges to the constitutionality of § 621. The court also denied ... motions for continued visitation pending the appeal under Cal.Civ.Code § 4601, which provides that a court may, in its discretion, grant "reasonable visitation rights . . . to any . . . person having an interest in the welfare of the child." . . .

. . . [T]he California Court of Appeal affirmed the judgment . . . and upheld the constitutionality of the statute. . . . It interpreted that judgment, moreover, as having denied permanent visitation rights under § 4601. . . .

. . . [T]he California Supreme Court denied discretionary review. . . .

II

The California statute . . . is, in substance, more than a century old. . . . In 1980, the legislature . . . amended the statute to provide the husband an opportunity to introduce blood-test evidence in rebuttal of the presumption, . . . and in 1981 amended it to provide the mother such an opportunity. . . .

III

. . . [I]t is necessary to clarify what [Michael] sought and what he was denied. California law, like nature itself, makes no provision for dual fatherhood. Michael was seeking to be declared *the* father of Victoria. The immediate benefit he evidently sought to obtain from that status was visitation rights. See Cal.Civ.Code Ann. § 4601 (West 1983) (parent has statutory right to visitation "unless it is shown that such visitation would be detrimental to the best interests of the child"). But if Michael were successful in being declared the father, other rights would follow—most importantly, the right to be considered as the parent who should have custody, . . . a status which "embrace[s] the sum of parental rights with respect to the rearing of a child, including the child's care; the right to the child's services and earnings; the right to direct the child's activities; the right to make decisions regarding the control, education, and health of the child; and the right, as well as the duty, to prepare the child for additional obligations, which includes the teaching of moral standards, religious beliefs, and elements of good citizenship." 4 California Family Law § 60.02[1][b]. . . . All parental rights, including visitation, were automatically denied by denying Michael status as the father. While Cal.Civ.Code Ann. § 4601 places it within the discretionary power of a court to award visitation rights to a nonparent, the Superior Court here, affirmed by the Court of Appeal, held that California law denies visitation, against the wishes of the mother, to a putative father who has been prevented by § 621 from establishing his paternity.

Michael raises two related challenges to the constitutionality of § 621. First, he asserts that requirements of procedural due process prevent the State from terminating his liberty interest in his relationship with his child without affording him an opportunity to demonstrate his paternity in an evidentiary hearing. We believe this claim derives from a fundamental misconception of the nature of the California statute. While § 621 is phrased in terms of a presumption, that rule of evidence is the implementation of a substantive rule of law. California declares it to be, except in limited circumstances, *irrelevant* for paternity purposes whether a child conceived during and born into an existing marriage was begotten by someone other than the husband and had a prior relationship with him. As the Court of Appeal phrased it:

"The conclusive presumption is actually a substantive rule of law based upon a determination by the Legislature as a matter of overriding social policy, that given a certain relationship between the husband and wife, the husband is to be held responsible for the child, and that the integrity of the family unit should not be impugned." . . .

Of course the conclusive presumption not only expresses the State's substantive policy but also furthers it, excluding inquiries into the child's paternity that would be destructive of family integrity and privacy.

This Court has struck down as illegitimate certain "irrebuttable presumptions." See, e.g., Stanley v. Illinois, 405 U.S. 645 (1972); Vlandis v. Kline, 412 U.S. 441 (1973); Cleveland Board of Education v. LaFleur, 414 U.S. 632 (1974). Those holdings did not, however, rest upon *procedural* due process. A conclusive presumption does, of course, foreclose the person against whom it is invoked from demonstrating, in a particularized proceeding, that applying the presumption to him will in fact not further the lawful governmental policy the presumption is designed to effectuate. But the same can be said of any legal rule that establishes general classifications, whether framed in terms of a presumption or not. In this respect there is no difference between a rule which says that the marital husband shall be irrebuttably presumed to be the father, and a rule which says that the adulterous natural father shall not be recognized as the legal father. *Both* rules deny someone in Michael's situation a hearing on whether, in the particular circumstances of his case, California's policies would best be served by giving him parental rights. Thus ... our "irrebuttable presumption" cases must ultimately be analyzed as calling into question not the adequacy of procedures but ... the adequacy of the "fit" between the classification and the policy that the classification serves. See LaFleur, supra, at 652 (Powell, J., concurring in result); Vlandis, supra, at 456–459 (White, J., concurring), 466–469 (Rehnquist, J., dissenting); Weinberger v. Salfi, 422 U.S. 749 (1975). We therefore reject Michael's procedural due process challenge and proceed to his substantive claim.

Michael contends as a matter of substantive due process that because he has established a parental relationship with Victoria, protection of Gerald's and Carole's marital union is an insufficient state interest to support termination of that relationship. This argument is, of course, predicated on the assertion that Michael has a constitutionally protected liberty interest in his relationship with Victoria.

It is an established part of our constitutional jurisprudence that the term "liberty" in the Due Process Clause extends beyond freedom from physical restraint. See, e.g., Pierce v. Society of Sisters, 268 U.S. 510 (1925); Meyer v. Nebraska, 262 U.S. 390 (1923). Without that core textual meaning as a limitation, defining the scope of the Due Process Clause "has at times been a treacherous field for this Court," giving "reason for concern lest the only limits to ... judicial intervention become the predilections of those who happen at the time to be Members of this Court." Moore v. East Cleveland, 431 U.S. 494, 502 (1977)....

In an attempt to limit and guide interpretation of the Clause, we have insisted not merely that the interest denominated as a "liberty" be "fundamental" (a concept that, in isolation, is hard to objectify), but also that it be an interest traditionally protected by our society.[2] As we have put it, the Due Process Clause affords only those protections "so rooted in the traditions and conscience of our people as to be ranked as fundamental." Snyder v. Massachusetts, 291 U.S. 97, 105 (1934) (Cardozo, J.). Our cases reflect "continual insistence upon respect for the teachings of history [and] solid recognition of

---

2. We do not understand what Justice Brennan has in mind by an interest "that society traditionally has thought important ... without protecting it." The protection need not take the form of an explicit constitutional provision or statutory guarantee, but it must at least exclude (all that is necessary to decide the present case) a societal tradition of enacting laws *denying* the interest....

the basic values that underlie our society...." Griswold v. Connecticut, 381 U.S. 479, 501 (1965) (Harlan, J., concurring in judgment).

This insistence that the asserted liberty interest be rooted in history and tradition is evident, as elsewhere, in our cases according constitutional protection to certain parental rights. Michael reads the landmark case of Stanley v. Illinois, 405 U.S. 645 (1972), and the subsequent cases of Quilloin v. Walcott, 434 U.S. 246 (1978), Caban v. Mohammed, 441 U.S. 380 (1979) and Lehr v. Robertson, 463 U.S. 248 (1983), as establishing that a liberty interest is created by biological fatherhood plus an established parental relationship—factors that exist in the present case as well. We think that distorts the rationale of those cases. As we view them, they rest not upon such isolated factors but upon the historic respect—indeed, sanctity would not be too strong a term—traditionally accorded to the relationships that develop within the unitary family.... In *Stanley,* for example, we forbade the destruction of such a family when, upon the death of the mother, the state had sought to remove children from the custody of a father who had lived with and supported them and their mother for 18 years. As Justice Powell stated for the plurality in *Moore v. East Cleveland,* ...: "Our decisions establish that the Constitution protects the sanctity of the family precisely because the institution of the family is deeply rooted in this Nation's history and tradition."

Thus, the legal issue in the present case reduces to whether the relationship between persons in the situation of Michael and Victoria has been treated as a protected family unit under the historic practices of our society, or whether on any other basis it has been accorded special protection. We think it impossible to find that it has. In fact, quite to the contrary, our traditions have protected the marital family (Gerald, Carole, and the child they acknowledge to be theirs) against the sort of claim Michael asserts.

The presumption of legitimacy was a fundamental principle of the common law ... rebutt[able] only by proof that a husband was incapable of procreation or had had no access to his wife during the relevant period.... The primary policy rationale ... appears to have been an aversion to declaring children illegitimate, ... thereby depriving them of rights of inheritance and succession, 2 Kent's Commentaries 175 (1827), and likely making them wards of the state. A secondary policy concern was the interest in promoting the "peace and tranquillity of States and families," ... a goal that is obviously impaired by facilitating suits against husband and wife asserting that their children are illegitimate. Even though, as bastardy laws became less harsh, "[j]udges in both [England and the United States] gradually widened the acceptable range of evidence that could be offered by spouses, the law retained a strong bias against ruling the children of married women illegitimate." ...

We have found nothing in the older sources, nor in the older cases, addressing specifically the power of the natural father to assert parental rights over a child born into a woman's existing marriage with another man. Since it is Michael's burden to establish that such a power (at least where the natural father has established a relationship with the child) is so deeply embedded within our traditions as to be a fundamental right, the lack of evidence alone might defeat his case. But the evidence shows that even in modern times ... the ability of a person in Michael's position to claim paternity has not been generally acknowledged....

Moreover, even if it were clear that one in Michael's position generally possesses, and has generally always possessed, standing to challenge the marital child's legitimacy, that would still not establish Michael's case.... What he must establish ... is not that our society has traditionally allowed a natural father in his circumstances to establish paternity, but that it has traditionally accorded such a father parental rights, or at least has not traditionally denied them.... What counts is whether the States in fact award substantive parental rights to the natural father of a child conceived within and born into an extant marital union that wishes to embrace the child. We are not aware of a single case, old or new, that has done so. This is not the stuff of which fundamental rights qualifying as liberty interests are made.[6]

In Lehr v. Robertson, a case involving a natural father's attempt to block his child's adoption by the unwed mother's new husband, we observed that "[t]he significance of the biological connection is that it offers the natural father an opportunity that no other male possesses to develop a relationship with his offspring," ... and we assumed that the Constitution might require some protection of that opportunity.... Where, however, the child is born into an extant marital family, the natural father's unique opportunity conflicts with the similarly unique opportunity of the husband of the marriage; and it is not

---

6. Justice Brennan criticizes our methodology in using historical traditions specifically relating to the rights of an adulterous natural father, rather than inquiring more generally "whether parenthood is an interest that historically has received our attention and protection." There seems to us no basis for the contention that this methodology is "nove[l]." For example, in Bowers v. Hardwick, 478 U.S. 186 (1986), we noted that at the time the Fourteenth Amendment was ratified all but 5 of the 37 States had criminal sodomy laws, that all 50 of the States had such laws prior to 1961, and that 24 States and the District of Columbia continued to have them; and we concluded from that record, regarding that very specific aspect of sexual conduct, that "to claim that a right to engage in such conduct is 'deeply rooted in this Nation's history and tradition' or 'implicit in the concept of ordered liberty' is, at best, facetious." ... In Roe v. Wade, 410 U.S. 113 (1973), we spent about a fifth of our opinion negating the proposition that there was a longstanding tradition of laws proscribing abortion.... We do not understand why, having rejected our focus upon the societal tradition regarding the natural father's rights vis-a-vis a child whose mother is married to another man, Justice Brennan would choose to focus instead upon "parenthood." Why should the relevant category not be even more general—perhaps "family relationships"; or "personal relationships"; or even "emotional attachments in general"? Though the dissent has no basis for the level of generality it would select, we do: We refer to the most specific level at which a relevant tradition protecting, or denying protection to, the asserted right can be identified. If, for example, there were no societal tradition, either way, regarding the rights of the natural father of a child adulterously conceived, we would have to consult, and (if possible) reason from, the traditions regarding natural fathers in general. But there is such a more specific tradition, and it unqualifiedly denies

protection to such a parent. One would think that Justice Brennan would appreciate the value of consulting the most specific tradition available, since he acknowledges that "[e]ven if we can agree ... that 'family' and 'parenthood' are part of the good life, it is absurd to assume that we can agree on the content of those terms and destructive to pretend that we do." Because such general traditions provide such imprecise guidance, they permit judges to dictate rather than discern the society's views. The need, if arbitrary decision-making is to be avoided, to adopt the most specific tradition as the point of reference—or at least to announce, as Justice Brennan declines to do, some other criterion for selecting among the innumerable relevant traditions that could be consulted—is well enough exemplified by the fact that in the present case Justice Brennan's opinion and Justice O'Connor's opinion, which disapproves this footnote, *both* appeal to tradition, but on the basis of the tradition they select reach opposite results. Although assuredly having the virtue (if it be that) of leaving judges free to decide as they think best when the unanticipated occurs, a rule of law that binds neither by text nor by any particular, identifiable tradition, is no rule of law at all. Finally, we may note that this analysis is not inconsistent with the result in cases such as Griswold v. Connecticut, 381 U.S. 479 (1965), or Eisenstadt v. Baird, 405 U.S. 438 (1972). None of those cases acknowledged a longstanding and still extant societal tradition withholding the very right pronounced to be the subject of a liberty interest and then rejected it. Justice Brennan must do so here. In this case, the existence of such a tradition, continuing to the present day, refutes any possible contention that the alleged right is "so rooted in the traditions and conscience of our people as to be ranked as fundamental," Snyder v. Massachusetts, 291 U.S. 97, 105 (1934), or "implicit in the concept of ordered liberty," Palko v. Connecticut, 302 U.S. 319, 325 (1937).

[handwritten margin note:] Both "fathers" should have rights to establish relationships with the child

unconstitutional for the State to give categorical preference to the latter. In *Lehr* we quoted approvingly from Justice Stewart's dissent in Caban v. Mohammed, 441 U.S., at 397, to the effect that although "[i]n some circumstances the actual relationship between father and child may suffice to create in the unwed father parental interests comparable to those of the married father," "the absence of a legal tie with the mother may in such circumstances appropriately place a limit on whatever substantive constitutional claims might otherwise exist." ... In accord with our traditions, a limit is also imposed by the circumstance that the mother is, at the time of the child's conception and birth, married to and cohabitating with another man, both of whom wish to raise the child as the offspring of their union.[7] It is a question of legislative policy and not constitutional law whether California will allow the presumed parenthood of a couple desiring to retain a child conceived within and born into their marriage to be rebutted.

We do not accept Justice Brennan's criticism that this result "squashes" the liberty that consists of "the freedom not to conform." It seems to us that reflects the erroneous view that there is only one side to this controversy—that one disposition can expand a "liberty" of sorts without contracting an equivalent "liberty" on the other side. Such a happy choice is rarely available. Here, to *provide* protection to an adulterous natural father is to *deny* protection to a marital father, and vice versa. If Michael has a "freedom not to conform" (whatever that means), Gerald must equivalently have a "freedom to conform." One of them will pay a price for asserting that "freedom"—Michael by being unable to act as father of the child he has adulterously begotten, or Gerald by being unable to preserve the integrity of the traditional family unit he and Victoria have established. Our disposition does not choose between these two "freedoms," but leaves that to the people of California. Justice Brennan's approach chooses one of them as the constitutional imperative, on no apparent basis except that the unconventional is to be preferred.

IV

We have never had occasion to decide whether a child has a liberty interest, symmetrical with that of her parent, in maintaining her filial relationship. We need not do so here because, even assuming that such a right exists, Victoria's claim must fail. Victoria's due process challenge is, if anything, weaker than Michael's.... [S]he claims a due process right to maintain filial relationships with both Michael and Gerald. This assertion merits little discussion, for, whatever the merits of the guardian ad litem's belief that such an arrangement can be of great psychological benefit to a child, the claim that a State must recognize multiple fatherhood has no support in the history or traditions of this country. Moreover, even if [her claim is only that] she has a liberty interest in maintaining a filial relationship with her natural father, Michael, we find that, at best, her claim is the obverse of Michael's and fails for the same reasons.

. . .

The judgment of the California Court of Appeal is Affirmed.

Michael must give up rights [handwritten annotation]

---

7. Justice Brennan chides us for thus limiting our holding to situations in which ... the husband and wife wish to raise her child jointly.... We limit our pronouncement to the relevant facts of this case because it is at least possible that our traditions lead to a different conclusion with regard to adulter-ous fathering of a child whom the marital parents do not wish to raise as their own. It seems unfair for those who disagree with our holding to include among their criticisms that we have not extended the holding more broadly.

Justice O'Connor, with whom Justice Kennedy joins, concurring in part.

I concur in all but footnote 6 of Justice Scalia's opinion. This footnote sketches a mode of historical analysis to be used when identifying liberty interests protected by the Due Process Clause of the Fourteenth Amendment that may be somewhat inconsistent with our past decisions in this area. See Griswold v. Connecticut, 381 U.S. 479 (1965); Eisenstadt v. Baird, 405 U.S. 438 (1972). On occasion the Court has characterized relevant traditions protecting asserted rights at levels of generality that might not be "the most specific level" available. See Loving v. Virginia, 388 U.S. 1, 12 (1967); Turner v. Safley, 482 U.S. 78, 94 (1987).... I would not foreclose the unanticipated by the prior imposition of a single mode of historical analysis. Poe v. Ullman, 367 U.S. 497, 542, 544 (1961) (Harlan, J., dissenting).

Justice Stevens, concurring in the judgment.

As I understand this case, it raises two different questions about the validity of California's statutory scheme. First, is [§ 621] unconstitutional because it prevents Michael and Victoria from obtaining a judicial determination that he is her biological father—even if no legal rights would be affected by that determination? Second, does the California statute deny appellants a fair opportunity to prove that Victoria's best interests would be served by granting Michael visitation rights?

On the first issue I agree with Justice Scalia that the Federal Constitution imposes no obligation upon a State to "declare facts unless some legal consequence hinges upon the requested declaration." ...

On the second issue I do not agree with Justice Scalia's analysis. He seems to reject the possibility that a natural father might ever have a constitutionally protected interest in his relationship with a child whose mother was married to and cohabiting with another man at the time of the child's conception and birth. I think cases like Stanley v. Illinois, 405 U.S. 645 (1972) and Caban v. Mohammed, 441 U.S. 380 (1979), demonstrate that enduring "family" relationships may develop in unconventional settings. I therefore would not foreclose the possibility that a constitutionally protected relationship between a natural father and his child might exist in a case like this. Indeed, I am willing to assume for the purpose of deciding this case that Michael's relationship with Victoria is strong enough to give him a constitutional right to try to convince a trial judge that Victoria's best interest would be served by granting him visitation rights. I am satisfied, however, that the California statute, as applied in this case, gave him that opportunity.

Section 4601 ... plainly gave the trial judge the authority to grant Michael "reasonable visitation rights."

I recognize that my colleagues have interpreted § 621 as creating an absolute bar that would prevent a California trial judge from regarding the natural father as either a "parent" within the meaning of the first sentence of § 4601 or as "any other person" within the meaning of the second sentence. That is not only an unnatural reading of the statute's plain language, but it is also not consistent with the California courts' reading of the statute....

... [T]he trial judge ... considered the effect of § 4601 and expressly found "that, at the present time, it is not in the best interests of the child that the Plaintiff have visitation. The Court believes that the existence of two (2) 'fathers' as male authority figures will confuse the child and be counterproductive to her best interests." ...

[Margin note, handwritten:] Agrees except with deciding which liberties are protected by the constitution

. . . Because I am convinced that the trial judge had the authority under state law both to hear Michael's plea for visitation rights and to grant him such rights if Victoria's best interests so warranted, I am satisfied that the California statutory scheme is consistent with the Due Process Clause of the Fourteenth Amendment.

. . .

Justice Brennan, with whom Justice Marshall and Justice Blackmun join, dissenting.

In a case that has yielded so many opinions as has this one, it is fruitful to begin by emphasizing the common ground shared by a majority of this Court. Five Members of the Court refuse to foreclose "the possibility that a natural father might ever have a constitutionally protected interest in his relationship with a child whose mother was married to and cohabiting with another man at the time of the child's conception and birth." (Stevens, J., concurring in judgment). Five Justices agree that the flaw inhering in a conclusive presumption that terminates a constitutionally protected interest without any hearing whatsoever is a *procedural* one. See infra; (White, J., dissenting); (Stevens, J., concurring in judgment). Four Members of the Court agree that Michael H. has a liberty interest in his relationship with Victoria, see infra; (White, J., dissenting), and one assumes for purposes of this case that he does, (Stevens, J., concurring in judgment).

In contrast, only two Members of the Court fully endorse Justice Scalia's view of the proper method of analyzing questions arising under the Due Process Clause. See O'Connor, J., concurring in part. . . .

I

. . . [T]he plurality pretends that tradition places a discernible border around the Constitution. The pretense is seductive; it would be comforting to believe that a search for "tradition" involves nothing more idiosyncratic or complicated than poring through dusty volumes on American history. Yet, as Justice White observed in his dissent in Moore v. East Cleveland, 431 U.S. 494, 549 (1977): "What the deeply rooted traditions of the country are is arguable." Indeed, wherever I would begin to look for an interest "deeply rooted in the country's traditions," one thing is certain: I would not stop (as does the plurality) at Bracton, or Blackstone, or Kent, or even the American Law Reports in conducting my search. Because reasonable people can disagree about the content of particular traditions, and because they can disagree even about which traditions are relevant to the definition of "liberty," the plurality has not found the objective boundary that it seeks.

Even if we could agree, moreover, on the content and significance of particular traditions, we still would be forced to identify the point at which a tradition becomes firm enough to be relevant to our definition of liberty and the moment at which it becomes too obsolete to be relevant any longer. The plurality supplies no objective means by which we might make these determinations. Indeed, as soon as the plurality sees signs that the tradition upon which it bases its decision (the laws denying putative fathers like Michael standing to assert paternity) is crumbling, it shifts ground and says that the case has nothing to do with that tradition, after all. "What is at issue here," the plurality asserts after canvassing the law on paternity suits, "is not entitlement to a state pronouncement that Victoria was begotten by Michael." But that is precisely what is at issue here, and the plurality's last-minute denial of this fact dramatically illustrates the subjectivity of its own analysis.

It is ironic that an approach so utterly dependent on tradition is so indifferent to our precedents. Citing barely a handful of this Court's numerous decisions defining the scope of the liberty protected by the Due Process Clause to support its reliance on tradition, the plurality acts as though English legal treatises and the American Law Reports always have provided the sole source for our constitutional principles. They have not. Just as common-law notions no longer define the "property" that the Constitution protects, see Goldberg v. Kelly, 397 U.S. 254 (1970), neither do they circumscribe the "liberty" that it guarantees. On the contrary, " '[l]iberty' and 'property' are broad and majestic terms. They are among the '[g]reat [constitutional] concepts ... purposely left to gather meaning from experience.... [T]hey relate to the whole domain of social and economic fact, and the statesmen who founded this Nation knew too well that only a stagnant society remains unchanged.' " Board of Regents of State Colleges v. Roth, 408 U.S. 564, 571 (1972)....

It is not that tradition has been irrelevant to our prior decisions. Throughout our decisionmaking in this important area runs the theme that certain interests and practices—freedom from physical restraint, marriage, childbearing, childrearing, and others—form the core of our definition of "liberty." Our solicitude for these interests is partly the result of the fact that the Due Process Clause would seem an empty promise if it did not protect them, and partly the result of the historical and traditional importance of these interests in our society. In deciding cases arising under the Due Process Clause, therefore, we have considered whether the concrete limitation under consideration impermissibly impinges upon one of these more generalized interests.

Today's plurality, however, does not ask whether parenthood is an interest that historically has received our attention and protection; the answer to that question is too clear for dispute. Instead, the plurality asks whether the specific variety of parenthood under consideration—a natural father's relationship with a child whose mother is married to another man—has enjoyed such protection.

If we had looked to tradition with such specificity in past cases, many a decision would have reached a different result. Surely the use of contraceptives by unmarried couples, Eisenstadt v. Baird, 405 U.S. 438 (1972), or even by married couples, Griswold v. Connecticut, 381 U.S. 479 (1965); the freedom from corporal punishment in schools, Ingraham v. Wright, 430 U.S. 651 (1977); the freedom from an arbitrary transfer from a prison to a psychiatric institution, Vitek v. Jones, 445 U.S. 480 (1980); and even the right to raise one's natural but illegitimate children, Stanley v. Illinois, 405 U.S. 645 (1972), were not "interest[s] traditionally protected by our society," at the time of their consideration by this Court. If we had asked, therefore, in *Eisenstadt, Griswold, Ingraham, Vitek,* or *Stanley* itself whether the specific interest under consideration had been traditionally protected, the answer would have been a resounding "no." That we did not ask this question in those cases highlights the novelty of the interpretive method that the plurality opinion employs today.

. . .

... We are not an assimilative, homogeneous society, but a facilitative, pluralistic one, in which we must be willing to abide someone else's unfamiliar or even repellant practice because the same tolerant impulse protects our own idiosyncracies.... "[L]iberty" must include the freedom not to conform. The

[handwritten margin note: Does not ask if parenthood is a liberty but if that relationship is one protected in the past.]

plurality today squashes this freedom by requiring specific approval from history before protecting anything in the name of liberty.

. . .

II

. . . . /

. . . The better approach . . . is to ask whether the specific parent-child relationship under consideration is close enough to the interests that we already have protected to be deemed an aspect of "liberty" as well. [T]he question is not what "level of generality" should be used to describe the relationship between Michael and Victoria, but whether the relationship under consideration is sufficiently substantial to qualify as a liberty interest under our prior cases.

Proposed approach

. . . [Those] cases have produced a unifying theme: although an unwed father's biological link to his child does not, in and of itself, guarantee him a constitutional stake in his relationship with that child, such a link combined with a substantial parent-child relationship will do so. . . .

. . .

The plurality's . . . language suggests that if Carole or Gerald alone wished to raise Victoria, or if both were dead and the State wished to raise her, Michael and Victoria might be found to have a liberty interest in their relationship with each other. But that would be to say that whether Michael and Victoria have a liberty interest varies with the State's interest in recognizing that interest, for it is the State's interest in protecting the marital family—and not Michael and Victoria's interest in their relationship with each other—that varies with the status of Carole and Gerald's relationship. It is a bad day for due process when the State's interest in terminating a parent-child relationship is reason to conclude that that relationship is not part of the "liberty" protected by the Fourteenth Amendment.

. . .

. . . [Also, i]n announcing that what matters is not the father's ability to claim paternity, but his ability to obtain "substantive parental rights," the plurality turns procedural due process upside down. Michael's challenge in this Court does not depend on his ability ultimately to obtain visitation rights; it would be strange indeed if, before one could be granted a hearing, one were required to prove that one would prevail on the merits. The point of procedural due process is to give the litigant a fair chance at prevailing, not to ensure a particular substantive outcome. . . .

III

Because the plurality decides that Michael and Victoria have no liberty interest in their relationship with each other, it need consider neither the effect of § 621 on their relationship nor the State's interest in bringing about that effect. It is obvious, however, that the effect of § 621 is to terminate the relationship between Michael and Victoria before affording any hearing whatsoever on the issue whether Michael is Victoria's father. This refusal to hold a hearing is properly analyzed under our procedural due process cases, which instruct us to consider the State's interest in curtailing the procedures accompanying the termination of a constitutionally protected interest. California's interest, minute in comparison with a father's interest in his relationship with his child, cannot justify its refusal to hear Michael out on his claim that he is Victoria's father.

A

. . . What Michael wants is a chance to show that he is Victoria's father. By depriving him of this opportunity, California prevents Michael from taking advantage of the best-interest standard embodied in § 4601 of California's Civil Code, which directs that *parents* be given visitation rights unless "the visitation would be detrimental to the best interests of the child." . . .

As interpreted by the California courts, . . . § 621 . . . also deprives him of any chance of maintaining his relationship with the child he claims to be his own. When, as a result of § 621, a putative father may not establish his paternity, neither may he obtain discretionary visitation rights as a "nonparent" under § 4601. . . . Justice Stevens' assertion to the contrary is mere wishful thinking. . . .

. . .

Section 621 as construed by the California courts thus cuts off the relationship between Michael and Victoria—a liberty interest protected by the Due Process Clause—without affording the least bit of process. This case, in other words, involves a conclusive presumption that is used to terminate a constitutionally protected interest—the kind of rule that our preoccupation with procedural fairness has caused us to condemn. See, e.g., Vlandis v. Kline, 412 U.S. 441 (1973); Cleveland Board of Education v. LaFleur, 414 U.S. 632 (1974); Weinberger v. Salfi, 422 U.S. 749, 770–772 (1975).

Gerald D. and the plurality . . . protest [ ]that, instead of being a conclusive presumption, it is a "substantive rule of law." . . . It may be that all conclusive presumptions are, in a sense, substantive rules of law; but § 621 then belongs in that special category of substantive rules that presumes a fact relevant to a certain class of litigation, and it is that feature that renders § 621 suspect under our prior cases. To put the point differently, a conclusive presumption takes the form of "no X's are Y's," and is typically accompanied by a rule such as, ". . . and only Y's may obtain a driver's license." . . . Ignoring the fact that § 621 takes the form of "no X's are Y's," Gerald D. and the plurality fix upon the rule following § 621—only Y's may assert parental rights—and call § 621 a substantive rule of law. . . .

In a further effort to show that § 621 is not a conclusive presumption, Gerald D. claims—and the plurality agrees—that whether a man is the biological father of a child whose family situation places the putative father within § 621 is simply irrelevant to the State. This is, I surmise, an attempt to avoid the implications of our cases condemning the presumption of a fact that a State has made relevant or decisive to a particular decision. See, e.g., Bell v. Burson, 402 U.S. 535 (1971). Yet the claim that California does not care about factual paternity is patently false. California cares very much about factual paternity when the husband is impotent or sterile . . .; it cares very much about it when the wife and husband do not share the same home . . .; and it cares very much about it when the husband himself declares that he is not the father. . . . Indeed, under California law as currently structured, paternity is decisive in choosing the standard that will be used in granting or denying custody or visitation. The State, though selective in its concern for factual paternity, certainly is not *indifferent* to it.[9] More fundamentally, . . . [t]o say that

---

9. In this respect, the plurality is mistaken in suggesting that "there is no differ-   ence between a rule which says that the marital husband shall be irrebuttably pre-

California does not care about factual paternity in the limited circumstances of this case—where the husband is neither impotent nor sterile nor living apart from his wife—is simply another way of describing its conclusive presumption.

... [T]he plurality goes on to argue that a challenge to a conclusive presumption must rest on substantive rather than procedural due process. This is simply not so. In Weinberger v. Salfi, supra, the Court identified two lines of cases involving challenges to social-welfare legislation: those in which a legislative classification was challenged as arbitrary, and those in which a conclusive presumption was attacked. The Court fit the complaint in *Salfi* into the former category on the ground that the challenged law did not deprive anyone of a constitutionally protected interest.... Today's plurality, in contrast, classifies this case as one invoking substantive due process *before* it considers the nature of the interest at stake.... [The plurality fails] to recognize that the defect from which conclusive presumptions suffer is a *procedural* one: the State has declared a certain fact relevant, indeed controlling, yet has denied a particular class of litigants a hearing to establish that fact. This is precisely the kind of flaw that procedural due process is designed to correct.

B

. . .

[T]o say that the State must provide Michael with a hearing to prove his paternity is not to express any opinion of the ultimate state of affairs between Michael and Victoria and Carole and Gerald.... Michael first must convince a court that he is Victoria's father, and even if he is able to do this, he will be denied visitation rights if that would be in Victoria's best interests. See Cal.Civ.Code Ann. § 4601 (West Supp.1989). It is elementary that a determination that a State must afford procedures before it terminates a given right is not a prediction about the end result of those procedures.

. . .

Justice White, with whom Justice Brennan joins, dissenting.

California law, as the plurality describes it, tells us that, except in limited circumstances, California declares it to be *"irrelevant* for paternity purposes whether a child conceived during and born into a lawful marriage was begotten by someone other than the husband," (emphasis in original). This I do not accept, for the fact that Michael H. is the biological father of Victoria is to me highly relevant to whether he has rights, as a father or otherwise, with respect to the child. Because I believe that Michael H. has a liberty interest that cannot be denied without due process of the law, I must dissent.

I

Like Justices Brennan, Marshall, Blackmun and Stevens, I do not agree with the plurality opinion's conclusion that a natural father can never "have a constitutionally protected interest in his relationship with a child whose mother was married to and cohabiting with another man at the time of the child's conception and birth." (Stevens, J., concurring in judgment). ... The basic principle enunciated in the Court's unwed father cases is that an unwed father

sumed to be the father, and a rule which says that the adulterous natural father shall not be recognized as the legal father." In the latter case, the State has not made paternity the predominant concern in child-custody disputes and then told some putative fathers that they may not prove their paternity.

who has demonstrated a sufficient commitment to his paternity by way of personal, financial, or custodial responsibilities has a protected liberty interest in a relationship with his child.

We have not before faced the question of a biological father's relationship with his child when the child was born while the mother was married to another man. On several occasions however, we have considered whether a biological father has a constitutionally cognizable interest in an opportunity to establish paternity. Stanley v. Illinois, 405 U.S. 645 (1972), recognized the biological father's right to a legal relationship with his illegitimate child, holding that the Due Process Clause of the Fourteenth Amendment entitled the biological father to a hearing on his fitness before his illegitimate children could be removed from his custody....

Quilloin v. Walcott, 434 U.S. 246, 255 (1978), also expressly recognized due process rights in the biological father, even while holding that those rights were not impermissibly burdened by the State's application of a "best interests of the child" standard. Caban v. Mohammed, 441 U.S. 380 (1979), invalidated on equal protection grounds a statute under which a man's children could be adopted by their natural mother and her husband without the natural father's consent.

In Lehr v. Robertson, 463 U.S. 248, 261–262 (1983), ... the Court said clearly that fathers who have participated in raising their illegitimate children and have developed a relationship with them have constitutionally protected parental rights. Indeed, ... Lehr suggested that States must provide a biological father of an illegitimate child the means by which he may establish his paternity so that he may have the opportunity to develop a relationship with his child. The Court upheld a stepparent adoption over the natural father's objections, but acknowledged that "the existence or nonexistence of a substantial relationship between parent and child is a relevant criterion in evaluating both the rights of the parent and the best interests of the child." ... [H]owever, the father had never established a custodial, personal or financial relationship with his child....

In the case now before us, Michael H. is ... a father who has asserted his interests in raising and providing for his child since the very time of the child's birth.... Michael and Victoria lived together (albeit intermittently, given Carole's itinerant life style.) There is a personal and emotional relationship between Michael and Victoria, who grew up calling him "Daddy." Michael H. held Victoria out as his daughter and contributed to the child's financial support. The mother has never denied, and indeed has admitted that Michael H. is Victoria's father.... "When an unwed father demonstrates a full commitment to the responsibilities of parenthood by 'com[ing] forward to participate in the rearing of his child,' Caban, 441 U.S., at 392, his interest in personal contact with his child acquires substantial protection under the Due Process Clause." Lehr, supra, at 261. The facts in this case satisfy the Lehr criteria, which focused on the relationship between father and child, not on the relationship between father and mother. Under Lehr a "mere biological relationship" is not enough, but in light of Carole's vicissitudes, what more could Michael H. have done? It is clear enough that Michael H. ... has a liberty interest entitled to protection under the Due Process Clause of the Fourteenth Amendment.

II

California plainly denies Michael this protection.... California law not only deprives Michael H. of a legal parent-child relationship with his daughter

Victoria but even denies him the opportunity to introduce blood-test evidence to rebut the demonstrable fiction that Gerald is Victoria's father.[3] Unlike *Lehr*, Michael H. has not been denied notice. He has, most definitely, however, been denied any real opportunity to be heard. The grant of summary judgment against Michael H. was based on the conclusive presumption of Cal.Evid.Code Ann. § 621 (West Supp.1989), which denied him the opportunity to prove that he is Victoria's biological father. The Court gives its blessing to § 621 by relying on the State's asserted interests in the integrity of the family (defined as Carole and Gerald) and in protecting Victoria from the stigma of illegitimacy and by balancing away Michael's interest in establishing that he is the father of the child.

The interest in protecting a child from the social stigma of illegitimacy lacks any real connection to the facts of a case where a father is seeking to establish, rather than repudiate, paternity. The "stigma of illegitimacy" argument harks back to ancient common law when there were no blood tests to ascertain that the husband could not "by the laws of nature" be the child's father. Judicial process refused to declare that a child born in wedlock was illegitimate unless the proof was positive. The only such proof was physical absence or impotency.... [W]hatever stigma remains in today's society is far less compelling in the context of a child of a married mother, especially when there is a father asserting paternity and seeking a relationship with his child. It is hardly rare in this world of divorce and remarriage for a child to live with the "father" to whom her mother is married, and still have a relationship with her biological father.

The State's professed interest in the preservation of the existing marital unit is a more significant concern. To be sure, the intrusion of an outsider asserting that he is the father of a child whom the husband believes to be his own would be disruptive to say the least. On the facts of this case, however, Gerald was well aware of the liaison between Carole and Michael. The conclusive presumption of evidentiary rule § 621 virtually eliminates the putative father's chances of succeeding in his effort to establish paternity, but it by no means prevents him from asserting the claim. It may serve as a deterrent to such claims but does not eliminate the threat. Further, the argument that the conclusive presumption preserved the sanctity of the marital unit had more sway in a time when the husband was similarly prevented from challenging paternity.[4]

. . .

As the Court has said: "The significance of the biological connection is that it offers the natural father an opportunity that no other male possesses to develop a relationship with his offspring. If he grasps that opportunity and accepts some measure of responsibility for the child's future, he may enjoy the blessings of the parent-child relationship and make uniquely valuable contributions to the child's development." *Lehr*.... Michael H. eagerly grasped the opportunity to have a relationship with his daughter (he lived with her; he

3. While the ultimate resolution of Michael's case, were he permitted to introduce such evidence, might well be visitation rights or even custody of the child, it is important to keep in mind that the question at issue here is not whether he should be granted visitation or custody but simply whether he can take the first step in any such proceeding....

4. ... In 1980, the California Legislature amended § 621 of its Evidence Code in order to permit the husband an opportunity to overcome the presumption that he is the father of his wife's child if he raises the notice of motion for blood tests not later than two years from the birth of the child. (So much for the State's interest in protecting the child from the stigma of illegitimacy!)

declared her to be his child; he provided financial support for her) and still, with today's opinion, his opportunity has vanished. He has been rendered a stranger to his child.

. . .

TROXEL v. GRANVILLE, 530 U.S. 57 (2000). A Washington statute permitted "[a]ny person" to petition a superior court for visitation rights "at any time" and authorized the court to grant visitation whenever "visitation may serve the best interest of the child." the unwed father of two daughters separated from their mother in 1991, moved in with his parents, and regularly brought the girls for weekend visitation at their home until he committed suicide in 1993. After the girls' mother, Granville, informed the paternal grandparents, the Troxels, that she wanted to limit them to one short visit per month, they petitioned for two weekends of over-night visitation per month and two weeks each summer. Granville asked the court to order just one day of visitation per month with no overnight stay, but the Superior Court awarded the grandparents one weekend a month, one week in the summer and four hours on their birthdays, finding (on a subsequent remand) that the visitation order was in the best interest of the children. When the case reached the Washington Supreme Court, it held that the statute's text authorized the grandparents to seek visitation but, with four justices dissenting, that the statute was unconstitutional on its face for infringing the fundamental right of parents to rear their children, because it allowed visitation to non-parents without a finding that denying visitation would harm the child, and also because it allowed visitation in favor of any person at any time when a court found that to be in the best interest of the child.

With no majority opinion, the Supreme Court affirmed. Justice O'Connor's plurality opinion, joined by Chief Justice Rehnquist and Justices Ginsburg and Breyer, found that the "breathtakingly broad" nonparental visitation statute, "as applied in this case," violated the mother's fundamental "due process right to make decisions concerning the care, custody, and control of her daughters." The statute's failure to accord any deference to "a parent's decision that visitation would not be in the child's best interest" meant that, "in practical effect, in the State of Washington a court can disregard and overturn any decision by a fit custodial parent concerning visitation whenever a third party affected by the decision files a visitation petition, based solely on the judge's determination of the child's best interests." As applied in this case, the Superior Court not only "gave no special weight at all to Granville's determination of her daughters' best interests[,]" but "the judge placed on Granville, the fit custodial parent, the burden of disproving that visitation would be in the best interest of her daughters....":

> "The decisional framework employed by the Superior Court directly contravened the traditional presumption that a fit parent will act in the best interest of his or her child.... In that respect, the court's presumption failed to provide any protection for Granville's fundamental constitutional right to make decisions concerning the rearing of her own daughters.... [I]f a fit parent's decision of the kind at issue here becomes subject to judicial review, the court must accord at least some special weight to the parent's own determination."

After noting "that there is no allegation that Granville ever sought to cut off visitation entirely[,]" the plurality said in part:

> "... The [court's] slender findings, in combination with [its] announced presumption in favor of grandparent visitation and its failure to accord significant weight to Granville's already having offered meaningful

visitation to the Troxels, show that this case involves nothing more than a simple disagreement between the Washington Superior Court and Granville concerning her children's best interests.... [T]he Due Process Clause does not permit a State to infringe on the fundamental right of parents to make childrearing decisions simply because a state judge believes a 'better' decision could be made....

"Because we rest our decision on the sweeping breadth of § 26.10.160(3) and the application of that broad, unlimited power in this case, we do not consider the primary constitutional question passed on by the Washington Supreme Court—whether the Due Process Clause requires all nonparental visitation statutes to include a showing of harm or potential harm to the child as a condition precedent to granting visitation. We do not, and need not, define today the precise scope of the parental due process right in the visitation context. In this respect, we agree with Justice Kennedy that the constitutionality of any standard for awarding visitation turns on the specific manner in which that standard is applied and that the constitutional protections in this area are best 'elaborated with care.' Because much state-court adjudication in this context occurs on a case-by-case basis, we would be hesitant to hold that specific nonparental visitation statutes violate the Due Process Clause as a per se matter.*

"... Like the Washington Supreme Court, ... we are presented with an actual visitation order and the reasons why the Superior Court believed entry of the order was appropriate in this case. Faced with the Superior Court's application of § 26.10.160(3) to Granville and her family, the Washington Supreme Court chose ... to give the statute ... a literal and expansive interpretation ... that ... plainly encompassed the Superior Court's application of the statute.

"There is thus no reason to remand ... [T]he entry of the visitation order in this case violated the Constitution. We should say so now, without forcing the parties into additional litigation that would further burden Granville's parental right...."

Justice Souter concurred only in the judgment affirming the Washington Supreme Court's "facial invalidation of its own state statute" and declined to address issues of the statute's application. It sufficed that the Court's "repeatedly recognized right of upbringing would be a sham if it failed to encompass the right to be free of judicially compelled visitation by 'any party' at 'any time' a judge believed he 'could make a "better" decision' than the objecting parent had done." Hence, "there is no need to decide whether harm is required or to consider the precise scope of the parent's right or its necessary protections." Justice Thomas also concurred in the judgment. He left "for another day" whether "the original understanding of the Due Process Clause precludes judicial enforcement of unenumerated rights under that constitutional provision[,]" agreed "with the plurality that this Court's recognition of a fundamental right of parents to direct the upbringing of their children resolves this case[,]" and articulated that he "would apply strict scrutiny to infringements of fundamental rights."

souter concurs in judgment

There were three individual dissents. Justice Stevens, believing that the state appellate courts, who had not reviewed the trial court's application of the state statute, should do so before the Court addressed those questions, and also believing that the "State Supreme Court opinion ... significantly misstates the effect of the Federal Constitution upon any construction of that statute[,]"

3 dissents: Stevens

* All 50 States have statutes that provide for grandparent visitation in some form....

thought "the Court should identify and correct the two flaws in the reasoning of the state court's majority opinion, and remand for further review of the trial court's disposition of this specific case." First, he thought the facial challenge should fail because the statute had

"'a "plainly legitimate sweep," '. . . . Under the Washington statute, there are plainly any number of cases—indeed, one suspects, the most common to arise—in which the 'person' among 'any' seeking visitation is a once-custodial caregiver, an intimate relation, or even a genetic parent. Even the Court would seem to agree that in many circumstances, it would be constitutionally permissible for a court to award some visitation of a child to a parent or previous caregiver in cases of parental separation or divorce, cases of disputed custody, cases involving temporary foster care or guardianship, and so forth. . . . [T]he State Supreme Court majority incorrectly concluded that a statute authorizing 'any person' to file a petition seeking visitation privileges would invariably run afoul of the Fourteenth Amendment.

"[S]econd[,] the Washington Supreme Court's holding—that the Federal Constitution requires a showing of actual or potential 'harm' to the child before a court may order visitation continued over a parent's objections—finds no support in this Court's case law. . . . [W]e have never held that the parent's liberty interest in [the parent-child] relationship is so inflexible as to establish a rigid constitutional shield, protecting every arbitrary parental decision from any challenge absent a threshold finding of harm. . . .

". . .

"[W]e should recognize that there may be circumstances in which a child has a stronger interest at stake than mere protection from serious harm caused by the termination of visitation by a 'person' other than a parent. . . . Far from guaranteeing that parents' interests will be trammeled in the sweep of cases arising under the statute, the Washington law merely gives an individual—with whom a child may have an established relationship—the procedural right to ask the State to act as arbiter, through the entirely well-known best-interests standard, between the parent's protected interests and the child's. [T]he Due Process Clause of the Fourteenth Amendment leaves room for States to consider the impact on a child of possibly arbitrary parental decisions that neither serve nor are motivated by the best interests of the child."

Justice Scalia's dissent said:

Dissent: Scalia

"Only three holdings of this Court rest in whole or in part upon a substantive constitutional right of parents to direct the upbringing of their children—two of them from an era rich in substantive due process holdings that have since been repudiated. See Meyer v. Nebraska, 262 U.S. 390, 399, 401 (1923); Pierce v. Society of Sisters, 268 U.S. 510, 534–535 (1925); Wisconsin v. Yoder, 406 U.S. 205, 232–233 (1972). . . . While I would not now overrule those earlier cases (that has not been urged), neither would I extend the theory upon which they rested to this new context.

". . . If we embrace this unenumerated right, . . . we will be ushering in a new regime of judicially prescribed, and federally prescribed, family law. I have no reason to believe that federal judges will be better at this than state legislatures. . . ."

Kennedy Dissent

Finally, Justice Kennedy's dissent found the Washington Supreme Court's "sweeping ruling requiring the harm to the child standard" in error, and "so central" to its decision that he would have vacated and remanded on that "sole ground"—without addressing any application of the visitation statute or "whether, under the correct constitutional standards, the Washington statute can be invalidated on its face." His criticism of the ruling "that a parent has a constitutional right to prevent visitation in all cases not involving harm" included the following:

> "My principal concern is that the holding seems to proceed from the assumption that the parent or parents who resist visitation have always been the child's primary caregivers and that the third parties who seek visitation have no legitimate and established relationship with the child. . . .

> "Cases are sure to arise—perhaps a substantial number of cases—in which a third party, by acting in a caregiving role over a significant period of time, has developed a relationship with a child which is not necessarily subject to absolute parental veto. . . .

> ". . .

> "In light of the inconclusive historical record and case law, as well as the almost universal adoption of the best interests standard for visitation disputes, I would be hard pressed to conclude the right to be free of such review in all cases is itself ' "implicit in the concept of ordered liberty." ' . . . [I]t would be more appropriate to conclude that the constitutionality of the application of the best interests standard depends on more specific factors. In short, a fit parent's right vis-a-vis a complete stranger is one thing; her right vis-a-vis another parent or a de facto parent may be another. The protection the Constitution requires, then, must be elaborated with care, using the discipline and instruction of the case law system. . . ."

C. PERSONAL AUTONOMY

EISENSTADT v. BAIRD, 405 U.S. 438 (1972). In a prosecution of a defendant for giving a contraceptive to an unmarried person the Court had before it, among others, the question whether it was a denial of equal protection of the laws to permit the distribution of contraceptives to married persons but not to unmarried. One argument made to sustain the classification was that contraceptives were considered immoral. The counter argument was that under Griswold v. Connecticut it would be a denial of due process to prohibit the distribution of contraceptives. The Court said it did not need to decide the issue, but did make the following observation: "if the right of privacy means anything, it is the right of the *individual,* married or single, to be free from unwarranted governmental intrusion into matters so fundamentally affecting a person as the decision whether to bear or beget a child."

Roe v. Wade

410 U.S. 113, 93 S.Ct. 705, 35 L.Ed.2d 147 (1973).

Mr. Justice Blackmun delivered the opinion of the Court.

This Texas federal appeal and its Georgia companion, Doe v. Bolton, post, 410 U.S. 179, present constitutional challenges to state criminal abortion legislation. The Texas statutes under attack here are typical of those that have been in effect in many States for approximately a century. The Georgia statutes, in contrast, have a modern cast and are a legislative product that, to an extent at least, obviously reflects the influences of recent attitudinal change, of advancing medical knowledge and techniques, and of new thinking about an old issue.

We forthwith acknowledge our awareness of the sensitive and emotional nature of the abortion controversy, of the vigorous opposing views, even among physicians, and of the deep and seemingly absolute convictions that the subject inspires. One's philosophy, one's experiences, one's exposure to the raw edges of human existence, one's religious training, one's attitudes toward life and family and their values, and the moral standards one establishes and seeks to observe, are all likely to influence and to color one's thinking and conclusions about abortion.

In addition, population growth, pollution, poverty, and racial overtones tend to complicate and not to simplify the problem.

Our task, of course, is to resolve the issue by constitutional measurement free of emotion and of predilection. We seek earnestly to do this, and, because we do, we have inquired into, and in this opinion place some emphasis upon, medical and medical-legal history and what that history reveals about man's attitudes toward the abortive procedure over the centuries. We bear in mind, too, Mr. Justice Holmes' admonition in his now vindicated dissent in Lochner v. New York, 198 U.S. 45, 76 (1905):

> "It [the Constitution] is made for people of fundamentally differing views, and the accident of our finding certain opinions natural and familiar, or novel, and even shocking, ought not to conclude our judgment upon the question whether statutes embodying them conflict with the Constitution of the United States."

I.

Debating Texas statutes that make abortion illegal except to save mothers life

The Texas statutes that concern us here are Arts. 1191–1194 and 1196 of the State's Penal Code, Vernon's Ann.P.C. These make it a crime to "procure an abortion," as therein defined, or to attempt one, except with respect to "an abortion procured or attempted by medical advice for the purpose of saving the life of the mother." Similar statutes are in existence in a majority of the States.

. . .

V.

violation of personal liberty given by 14th amd. woman's right to choose to terminate pregnancy

The principal thrust of appellant's attack on the Texas statutes is that they improperly invade a right, said to be possessed by the pregnant woman, to choose to terminate her pregnancy. Appellant would discover this right in the concept of personal "liberty" embodied in the Fourteenth Amendment's Due Process Clause; or in personal, marital, familial, and sexual privacy said to be protected by the Bill of Rights or its penumbras, see Griswold v. Connecticut, 381 U.S. 479 (1965); Eisenstadt v. Baird, 405 U.S. 438 (1972); id., at 460 (White, J., concurring); or among those rights reserved to the people by the Ninth Amendment, Griswold v. Connecticut, 381 U.S., at 486 (Goldberg, J., concurring). Before addressing this claim, we feel it desirable briefly to survey, in several aspects, the history of abortion, for such insight as that history may afford us, and then to examine the state purposes and interests behind the criminal abortion laws.

. . .

[The Court's long historical discussion is omitted.]

VII.

Three reasons have been advanced to explain historically the enactment of criminal abortion laws in the 19th century and to justify their continued existence.

It has been argued occasionally that these laws were the product of a Victorian social concern to discourage illicit sexual conduct. Texas, however, does not advance this justification in the present case, and it appears that no court or commentator has taken the argument seriously. . . .

A second reason is concerned with abortion as a medical procedure. When most criminal abortion laws were first enacted, the procedure was a hazardous one for the woman. . . .

Modern medical techniques have altered this situation. Appellants and various *amici* refer to medical data indicating that abortion in early pregnancy, that is, prior to the end of first trimester, although not without its risk, is now relatively safe. Mortality rates for women undergoing early abortions, where the procedure is legal, appear to be as low as or lower than the rates for normal childbirth. Consequently, any interest of the State in protecting the woman from an inherently hazardous procedure, except when it would be equally dangerous for her to forgo it, has largely disappeared. Of course, important state interests in the area of health and medical standards do remain. The State has a legitimate interest in seeing to it that abortion, like any other medical procedure, is performed under circumstances that insure maximum safety for the patient. This interest obviously extends at least to the performing physician and his staff, to the facilities involved, to the availability of aftercare, and to adequate provision for any complication or emergency that might arise. The prevalence of high mortality rates at illegal "abortion mills" strengthens, rather than weakens, the State's interest in regulating the conditions under which abortions are performed. Moreover, the risk to the woman increases as her pregnancy continues. Thus the State retains a definite interest in protecting the woman's own health and safety when an abortion is proposed at a late stage of pregnancy.

The third reason is the State's interest—some phrase it in terms of duty—in protecting prenatal life. Some of the argument for this justification rests on the theory that a new human life is present from the moment of conception. The State's interest and general obligation to protect life then extends, it is argued, to prenatal life. Only when the life of the pregnant mother herself is at stake, balanced against the life she carries within her, should the interest of the embryo or fetus not prevail. Logically, of course, a legitimate state interest in this area need not stand or fall on acceptance of the belief that life begins at conception or at some other point prior to live birth. In assessing the State's interest, recognition may be given to the less rigid claim that as long as at least *potential* life is involved, the State may assert interests beyond the protection of the pregnant woman alone.

Parties challenging state abortion laws have sharply disputed in some courts the contention that a purpose of these laws, when enacted, was to protect prenatal life. Pointing to the absence of legislative history to support the contention, they claim that most state laws were designed solely to protect the woman. Because medical advances have lessened this concern, at least with respect to abortion in early pregnancy, they argue that with respect to such abortions the laws can no longer be justified by any state interest. There is some scholarly support for this view of original purpose. The few state courts called upon to interpret their laws in the late 19th and early 20th centuries did focus on the State's interest in protecting the woman's health rather than in preserving the embryo and fetus. Proponents of this view point out that in many States, including Texas, by statute or judicial interpretation, the pregnant woman herself could not be prosecuted for self-abortion or for cooperating in an abortion performed upon her by another. They claim that adoption of the "quickening" distinction through received common law and state statutes tacitly recognizes the greater health hazards inherent in late abortion and impliedly repudiates the theory that life begins at conception.

It is with these interests, and the weight to be attached to them, that this case is concerned.

VIII.

The Constitution does not explicitly mention any right of privacy. In a line of decisions, however, going back perhaps as far as Union Pacific R. Co. v. Botsford, 141 U.S. 250, 251 (1891), the Court has recognized that a right of personal privacy, or a guarantee of certain areas or zones of privacy, does exist under the Constitution. In varying contexts the Court or individual Justices have indeed found at least the roots of that right in the First Amendment, Stanley v. Georgia, 394 U.S. 557, 564 (1969); in the Fourth and Fifth Amendments, Terry v. Ohio, 392 U.S. 1, 8–9 (1968), Katz v. United States, 389 U.S. 347, 350 (1967); Boyd v. United States, 116 U.S. 616 (1886), see Olmstead v. United States, 277 U.S. 438, 478 (1928) (Brandeis, J., dissenting); in the penumbras of the Bill of Rights, Griswold v. Connecticut, 381 U.S. 479, 484–485 (1965); in the Ninth Amendment, id., at 486 (Goldberg, J., concurring); or in the concept of liberty guaranteed by the first section of the Fourteenth Amendment, see Meyer v. Nebraska, 262 U.S. 390, 399 (1923). These decisions make it clear that only personal rights that can be deemed "fundamental" or "implicit in the concept of ordered liberty," Palko v. Connecticut, 302 U.S. 319, 325 (1937), are included in this guarantee of personal privacy. They also make it clear that the right has some extension to activities relating to marriage, Loving v. Virginia, 388 U.S. 1, 12 (1967), procreation, Skinner v. Oklahoma, 316 U.S. 535 (1942), contraception, Eisenstadt v. Baird, 405 U.S. 438, 453–454 (1972); id., at 460, 463–465 (White, J., concurring), family relationships, Prince v. Massachusetts, 321 U.S. 158, 166 (1944), and child rearing and education, Pierce v. Society of Sisters, 268 U.S. 510, 535 (1925), Meyer v. Nebraska, supra.

This right of privacy, whether it be founded in the Fourteenth Amendment's concept of personal liberty and restrictions upon state action, as we feel it is, or, as the District Court determined, in the Ninth Amendment's reservation of rights to the people, is broad enough to encompass a woman's decision whether or not to terminate her pregnancy. The detriment that the State would impose upon the pregnant woman by denying this choice altogether is apparent. Specific and direct harm medically diagnosable even in early pregnancy may be involved. Maternity, or additional offspring, may force upon the woman a distressful life and future. Psychological harm may be imminent. Mental and physical health may be taxed by child care. There is also the distress, for all concerned, associated with the unwanted child, and there is the problem of bringing a child into a family already unable, psychologically and otherwise, to care for it. In other cases, as in this one, the additional difficulties and continuing stigma of unwed motherhood may be involved. All these are factors the woman and her responsible physician necessarily will consider in consultation.

On the basis of elements such as these, appellants and some *amici* argue that the woman's right is absolute and that she is entitled to terminate her pregnancy at whatever time, in whatever way, and for whatever reason she alone chooses. With this we do not agree. Appellants' arguments that Texas either has no valid interest at all in regulating the abortion decision, or no interest strong enough to support any limitation upon the woman's sole determination, is unpersuasive. The Court's decisions recognizing a right of privacy also acknowledge that some state regulation in areas protected by that right is appropriate. As noted above, a state may properly assert important interests in safeguarding health, in maintaining medical standards, and in protecting potential life. At some point in pregnancy, these respective interests become sufficiently compelling to sustain regulation of the factors that govern the abortion decision. The privacy right involved, therefore, cannot be said to be absolute. In fact, it is not clear to us that the claim asserted by some *amici* that one has an unlimited right to do with one's body as one pleases bears a close relationship to the right of privacy previously articulated in the Court's decisions. The Court has refused to recognize an unlimited right of this kind in the past. Jacobson v. Massachusetts, 197 U.S. 11 (1905) (vaccination); Buck v. Bell, 274 U.S. 200 (1927) (sterilization).

We therefore conclude that the right of personal privacy includes the abortion decision, but that this right is not unqualified and must be considered against important state interests in regulation.

We note that those federal and state courts that have recently considered abortion law challenges have reached the same conclusion. A majority, in addition to the District Court in the present case, have held state laws unconstitutional, at least in part, because of vagueness or because of over-breadth and abridgment of rights. . . .

Although the results are divided, most of these courts have agreed that the right of privacy, however based, is broad enough to cover the abortion decision; that the right, nonetheless, is not absolute and is subject to some limitations; and that at some point the state interests as to protection of health, medical standards, and prenatal life, become dominant. We agree with this approach.

Where certain "fundamental rights" are involved, the Court has held that regulation limiting these rights may be justified only by a "compelling state interest," Kramer v. Union Free School District, 395 U.S. 621, 627 (1969); Shapiro v. Thompson, 394 U.S. 618, 634 (1969); Sherbert v. Verner, 374 U.S. 398, 406 (1963), and that legislative enactments must be narrowly drawn to express only the legitimate state interests at stake. Griswold v. Connecticut, 381 U.S. 479, 485 (1965); Aptheker v. Secretary of State, 378 U.S. 500, 508 (1964); Cantwell v. Connecticut, 310 U.S. 296, 307–308 (1940); see Eisenstadt v. Baird, 405 U.S. 438, 460, 463–464 (1972) (White, J., concurring).

In the recent abortion cases . . . courts have recognized these principles. Those striking down state laws have generally scrutinized the State's interest in protecting health and potential life and have concluded that neither interest justified broad limitations on the reasons for which a physician and his pregnant patient might decide that she should have an abortion in the early stages of pregnancy. Courts sustaining state laws have held that the State's determinations to protect health or prenatal life are dominant and constitution-ally justifiable.

IX.

The District Court held that the appellee failed to meet his burden of demonstrating that the Texas statute's infringement upon Roe's rights was necessary to support a compelling state interest, and that, although the defendant presented "several compolling justifications for state presence in the area of abortions," the statutes outstripped these justifications and swept "far

[margin handwritten note:] Do not agree that woman can whenever & for whatever terminate

[margin handwritten note:] Right is not absolute, subject to limitation by state

beyond any areas of compelling state interest." 314 F.Supp., at 1222–1223. Appellant and appellee both contest that holding. Appellant ... claims an absolute right that bars any state imposition of criminal penalties in the area. Appellee argues that the State's determination to recognize and protect prenatal life from and after conception constitutes a compelling state interest. As noted above, we do not agree fully with either formulation.

A.   The appellee and certain *amici* argue that the fetus is a "person" within the language and meaning of the Fourteenth Amendment. In support of this they outline at length and in detail the well-known facts of fetal development. If this suggestion of personhood is established, the appellant's case, of course, collapses, for the fetus' right to life is then guaranteed specifically by the Amendment. The appellant conceded as much on reargument. On the other hand, the appellee conceded on reargument that no case could be cited that holds that a fetus is a person within the meaning of the Fourteenth Amendment.

The Constitution does not define "person" in so many words. Section 1 of the Fourteenth Amendment contains three references to "person." The first, in defining "citizens," speaks of "persons born or naturalized in the United States." The word also appears both in the Due Process Clause and in the Equal Protection Clause. "Person" is used in other places in the Constitution: in the listing of qualifications for representatives and senators, Art. I, § 2, cl. 2, and § 3, cl. 3; in the Apportionment Clause, Art. I, § 2, cl. 3; in the Migration and Importation provision, Art. I, § 9, cl. 1; in the Emolument Clause, Art. I, § 9, cl. 8; in the Electors provisions, Art. II, § 1, cl. 2, and the superseded cl. 3; in the provision outlining qualifications for the office of President, Art. II, § 1, cl. 5; in the Extradition provisions, Art. IV, § 2, cl. 2, and the superseded Fugitive Slave cl. 3; and in the Fifth, Twelfth, and Twenty-second Amendments as well as in §§ 2 and 3 of the Fourteenth Amendment. But in nearly all these instances, the use of the word is such that it has application only postnatally. None indicates, with any assurance, that it has any possible prenatal application.[54]

All this, together with our observation, supra, that throughout the major portion of the 19th century prevailing legal abortion practices were far freer than they are today, persuades us that the word "person," as used in the Fourteenth Amendment, does not include the unborn....

This conclusion, however, does not of itself fully answer the contentions raised by Texas, and we pass on to other considerations.

B.   The pregnant woman cannot be isolated in her privacy. She carries an embryo and, later, a fetus, if one accepts the medical definitions of the developing young in the human uterus. See Dorland's Illustrated Medical

54. When Texas urges that a fetus is entitled to Fourteenth Amendment protection as a person, it faces a dilemma. Neither in Texas nor in any other State are all abortions prohibited. Despite broad proscription, an exception always exists. The exception contained in Art. 1196, for an abortion procured or attempted by medical advice for the purpose of saving the life of the mother, is typical. But if the fetus is a person who is not to be deprived of life without due process of law, and if the mother's condition is the sole determinant, does not the Texas exception appear to be out of line with the Amendment's command?

There are other inconsistencies between Fourteenth Amendment status and the typical abortion statute. [I]n Texas the woman is not a principal or an accomplice with respect to an abortion upon her. If the fetus is a person, why is the woman not a principal or an accomplice? Further, the penalty for criminal abortion specified by Art. 1195 is significantly less than the maximum penalty for murder prescribed by Art. 1257 of the Texas Penal Code. If the fetus is a person, may the penalties be different?

Dictionary, 478–479, 547 (24th ed. 1965). The situation therefore is inherently different from marital intimacy, or bedroom possession of obscene material, or marriage, or procreation, or education, with which *Eisenstadt, Griswold, Stanley, Loving, Skinner, Pierce,* and *Meyer* were respectively concerned. As we have intimated above, it is reasonable and appropriate for a State to decide that at some point in time another interest, that of health of the mother or that of potential human life, becomes significantly involved. The woman's privacy is no longer sole and any right of privacy she possesses must be measured accordingly.

Texas urges that, apart from the Fourteenth Amendment, life begins at conception and is present throughout pregnancy, and that, therefore, the State has a compelling interest in protecting that life from and after conception. We need not resolve the difficult question of when life begins. When those trained in the respective disciplines of medicine, philosophy, and theology are unable to arrive at any consensus, the judiciary, at this point in the development of man's knowledge, is not in a position to speculate as to the answer.

It should be sufficient to note briefly the wide divergence of thinking on this most sensitive and difficult question. There has always been strong support for the view that life does not begin until live birth. This was the belief of the Stoics. It appears to be the predominant, though not the unanimous, attitude of the Jewish faith. It may be taken to represent also the position of a large segment of the Protestant community, insofar as that can be ascertained; organized groups that have taken a formal position on the abortion issue have generally regarded abortion as a matter for the conscience of the individual and her family. [T]he common law found greater significance in quickening. Physicians and their scientific colleagues have regarded that event with less interest and have tended to focus either upon conception or upon live birth or upon the interim point at which the fetus becomes "viable," that is, potentially able to live outside the mother's womb, albeit with artificial aid.[59] Viability is usually placed at about seven months (28 weeks) but may occur earlier, even at 24 weeks.[60] The Aristotelian theory of "mediate animation," that held sway throughout the Middle Ages and the Renaissance in Europe, continued to be official Roman Catholic dogma until the 19th century, despite opposition to this "ensoulment" theory from those in the Church who would recognize the existence of life from the moment of conception. The latter is now, of course, the official belief of the Catholic Church. As one of the briefs *amicus* discloses, this is a view strongly held by many non-Catholics as well, and by many physicians. Substantial problems for precise definition of this view are posed, however, by new embryological data that purport to indicate that conception is a "process" over time, rather than an event, and by new medical techniques such as menstrual extraction, the "morning-after" pill, implantation of embryos, artificial insemination, and even artificial wombs.

In areas other than criminal abortion the law has been reluctant to endorse any theory that life, as we recognize it, begins before live birth or to accord legal rights to the unborn except in narrowly defined situations and except when the rights are contingent upon live birth. For example, the traditional rule of tort law had denied recovery for prenatal injuries even though the child was born alive. That rule has been changed in almost every jurisdiction. In most States recovery is said to be permitted only if the fetus was

---

59. L. Hellman & J. Pritchard, Williams Obstetrics 493 (14th ed. 1971); Dorland's Illustrated Medical Dictionary 1689 (24th ed. 1965).

60. Hellman & Pritchard, supra, n. 59, at 493.

viable, or at least quick, when the injuries were sustained, though few courts have squarely so held. In a recent development, generally opposed by the commentators, some States permit the parents of a stillborn child to maintain an action for wrongful death because of prenatal injuries. Such an action, however, would appear to be one to vindicate the parents' interest and is thus consistent with the view that the fetus, at most, represents only the potentiality of life. Similarly, unborn children have been recognized as acquiring rights or interests by way of inheritance or other devolution of property, and have been represented by guardians *ad litem*. Perfection of the interests involved, again, has generally been contingent upon live birth. In short, the unborn have never been recognized in the law as persons in the whole sense.

X.

In view of all this, we do not agree that, by adopting one theory of life, Texas may override the rights of the pregnant woman that are at stake. We repeat, however, that the State does have an important and legitimate interest in preserving and protecting the health of the pregnant woman, whether she be a resident of the State or a non-resident who seeks medical consultation and treatment there, and that it has still *another* important and legitimate interest in protecting the potentiality of human life. These interests are separate and distinct. Each grows in substantiality as the woman approaches term and, at a point during pregnancy, each becomes "compelling."

With respect to the State's important and legitimate interest in the health of the mother, the "compelling" point, in the light of present medical knowledge, is at approximately the end of the first trimester. This is so because of the now established medical fact, referred to above ... that until the end of the first trimester mortality in abortion is less than mortality in normal childbirth. It follows that, from and after this point, a State may regulate the abortion procedure to the extent that the regulation reasonably relates to the preservation and protection of maternal health. Examples of permissible state regulation in this area are requirements as to the qualifications of the person who is to perform the abortion; as to the licensure of that person; as to the facility in which the procedure is to be performed, that is, whether it must be a hospital or may be a clinic or some other place of less-than-hospital status; as to the licensing of the facility; and the like.

This means, on the other hand, that, for the period of pregnancy prior to this "compelling" point, the attending physician, in consultation with his patient, is free to determine, without regulation by the State, that in his medical judgment the patient's pregnancy should be terminated. If that decision is reached, the judgment may be effectuated by an abortion free of interference by the State.

With respect to the State's important and legitimate interest in potential life, the "compelling" point is at viability. This is so because the fetus then presumably has the capability of meaningful life outside the mother's womb. State regulation protective of fetal life after viability thus has both logical and biological justifications. If the State is interested in protecting fetal life after viability, it may go so far as to proscribe abortion during that period except when it is necessary to preserve the life or health of the mother.

Measured against these standards, Art. 1196 of the Texas Penal Code, in restricting legal abortions to those "procured or attempted by medical advice for the purpose of saving the life of the mother," sweeps too broadly. The statute makes no distinction between abortions performed early in pregnancy and those performed later, and it limits to a single reason, "saving" the mother's life, the legal justification for the procedure. The statute, therefore, cannot survive the constitutional attack made upon it here.

statute doesn't survive

This conclusion makes it unnecessary for us to consider the additional challenge to the Texas statute asserted on grounds of vagueness. See United States v. Vuitch, 402 U.S. 62, 67–72 (1971).

XI.

To summarize and to repeat:

1. A state criminal abortion statute of the current Texas type, that excepts from criminality only a *life saving* procedure on behalf of the mother, without regard to pregnancy stage and without recognition of the other interests involved, is violative of the Due Process Clause of the Fourteenth Amendment.

(a) For the stage prior to approximately the end of the first trimester, the abortion decision and its effectuation must be left to the medical judgment of the pregnant woman's attending physician.

End of 1st tri - physician

(b) For the stage subsequent to approximately the end of the first trimester, the State, in promoting its interest in the health of the mother, may, if it chooses, regulate the abortion procedure in ways that are reasonably related to maternal health.

2nd tri - state may reg. procedures

(c) For the stage subsequent to viability the State, in promoting its interest in the potentiality of human life, may, if it chooses, regulate, and even proscribe, abortion except where it is necessary, in appropriate medical judgment, for the preservation of the life or health of the mother.

3rd - after viability state may reg or proscribe abortion when necessary

2. The State may define the term "physician," as it has been employed in the preceding numbered paragraphs of this Part XI of this opinion, to mean only a physician currently licensed by the State, and may proscribe any abortion by a person who is not a physician as so defined.

In Doe v. Bolton, 410 U.S. 179, procedural requirements contained in one of the modern abortion statutes are considered. That opinion and this one, of course, are to be read together.

This holding, we feel, is consistent with the relative weights of the respective interests involved, with the lessons and example of medical and legal history, with the lenity of the common law, and with the demands of the profound problems of the present day. The decision leaves the State free to place increasing restrictions on abortion as the period of pregnancy lengthens, so long as those restrictions are tailored to the recognized state interests. The decision vindicates the right of the physician to administer medical treatment according to his professional judgment up to the points where important state interests provide compelling justifications for intervention. Up to those points the abortion decision in all its aspects is inherently, and primarily, a medical decision, and basic responsibility for it must rest with the physician. If an individual practitioner abuses the privilege of exercising proper medical judgment, the usual remedies, judicial and intra-professional, are available.

. . .

Mr. Justice Stewart, concurring.

. . .

Mr. Justice Rehnquist, dissenting.

The Court's opinion brings to the decision of this troubling question both extensive historical fact and a wealth of legal scholarship. While its opinion thus commands my respect, I find myself nonetheless in fundamental disagreement with those parts of it which invalidate the Texas statute in question, and therefore dissent.

. . .

I have difficulty in concluding, as the Court does, that the right of "privacy" is involved in this case. Texas by the statute here challenged bars the performance of a medical abortion by a licensed physician on a plaintiff such as Roe. A transaction resulting in an operation such as this is not "private" in the ordinary usage of that word. Nor is the "privacy" which the Court finds here even a distant relative of the freedom from searches and seizures protected by the Fourth Amendment to the Constitution which the Court has referred to as embodying a right to privacy. Katz v. United States, 389 U.S. 347 (1967).

. . .

The Court eschews the history of the Fourteenth Amendment in its reliance on the "compelling state interest" test. See Weber v. Aetna Cas. & Sur. Co., 406 U.S. 164, 179 (1972) (dissenting opinion). But the Court adds a new wrinkle to this test by transposing it from the legal considerations associated with the Equal Protection Clause of the Fourteenth Amendment to this case arising under the Due Process Clause of the Fourteenth Amendment. Unless I misapprehend the consequences of this transplanting of the "compelling state interest test," the Court's opinion will accomplish the seemingly impossible feat of leaving this area of the law more confused than it found it.

While the Court's opinion quotes from the dissent of Mr. Justice Holmes in Lochner v. New York, 198 U.S. 45 (1905), the result it reaches is more closely attuned to the majority opinion of Mr. Justice Peckham in that case. As in *Lochner* and similar cases, applying substantive due process standards to economic and social welfare legislation, the adoption of the compelling state interest standard will inevitably require this Court to examine the legislative policies and pass on the wisdom of these policies in the very process of deciding whether a particular state interest put forward may or may not be "compelling." The decision here to break the term of pregnancy into three distinct terms and to outline the permissible restrictions the State may impose in each one, for example, partakes more of judicial legislation than it does of a determination of the intent of the drafters of the Fourteenth Amendment.

The fact that a majority of the States, reflecting after all the majority sentiment in those States, have had restrictions on abortions for at least a century is a strong indication, it seems to me, that the asserted right to an abortion is not "so rooted in the traditions and conscience of our people as to be ranked as fundamental," Snyder v. Massachusetts, 291 U.S. 97, 105 (1934). Even today, when society's views on abortion are changing, the very existence of the debate is evidence that the "right" to an abortion is not so universally accepted as the appellants would have us believe.[a]

a. For an early view criticizing the method by which the Court reached its result in the original abortion decisions, see Ely, *The Wages of Crying Wolf: A Comment on Roe v. Wade,* 82 Yale L.J. 920 (1973). For other useful commentary at the time see Epstein, *Substantive Due Process by Any Other Name: The Abortion Cases,* 1973 Sup.Ct.Rev. 159; Tribe, *Foreword: Toward a Model of Roles in the Due Process of Life and Law,* 87 Harv.L.Rev. 1 (1973).

[In the companion case of Doe v. Bolton, 410 U.S. 179 (1973), the Court held invalid a number of provisions of the Georgia statute regulating medical practice in abortion cases. The concurring and dissenting opinions which follow were addressed to both cases.]

Mr. Chief Justice Burger, concurring [in *Wade* and *Bolton*].

I agree that, under the Fourteenth Amendment to the Constitution, the abortion statutes of Georgia and Texas impermissibly limit the performance of abortions necessary to protect the health of pregnant women, using the term health in its broadest medical context. See United States v. Vuitch, 402 U.S. 62, 71–72 (1971). I am somewhat troubled that the Court has taken notice of various scientific and medical data in reaching its conclusion; however, I do not believe that the Court has exceeded the scope of judicial notice accepted in other contexts.

. . .

I do not read the Court's holding today as having the sweeping consequences attributed to it by the dissenting Justices; the dissenting views discount the reality that the vast majority of physicians observe the standards of their profession, and act only on the basis of carefully deliberated medical judgments relating to life and health. Plainly, the Court today rejects any claim that the Constitution requires abortion on demand.

Mr. Justice Douglas, concurring [in *Wade* and *Bolton*].

While I join the opinion of the Court, I add a few words.

The questions presented in the present cases go far beyond the issues of vagueness, which we considered in United States v. Vuitch, 402 U.S. 62. They involve the right of privacy, one aspect of which we considered in Griswold v. Connecticut, 381 U.S. 479, 484, when we held that various guarantees in the Bill of Rights create zones of privacy. . . .

The Ninth Amendment obviously does not create federally enforceable rights. It merely says, "The enumeration in the Constitution of certain rights, shall not be construed to deny or disparage others retained by the people." But a catalogue of these rights includes customary, traditional, and time-honored rights, amenities, privileges, and immunities that come within the sweep of "the Blessings of Liberty" mentioned in the preamble to the Constitution. Many of them in my view come within the meaning of the term "liberty" as used in the Fourteenth Amendment.

First is the autonomous control over the development and expression of one's intellect, interests, tastes, and personality.

These are rights protected by the First Amendment and in my view they are absolute, permitting of no exceptions. . . .

Second is freedom of choice in the basic decisions of one's life respecting marriage, divorce, procreation, contraception, and the education and upbringing of children.

These rights, unlike those protected by the First Amendment, are subject to some control by the police power. Thus the Fourth Amendment speaks only of "unreasonable searches and seizures" and of "probable cause." These rights are "fundamental" and we have held that in order to support legislative action the statute must be narrowly and precisely drawn and that a "compelling state interest" must be shown in support of the limitation. . . .

The liberty to marry a person of one's own choosing, Loving v. Virginia, 388 U.S. 1; the right of procreation, Skinner v. Oklahoma, 316 U.S. 535; the liberty to direct the education of one's children, Pierce v. Soc'y of Sisters, 268 U.S. 510, and the privacy of the marital relation, Griswold v. Connecticut, supra, are in this category. . . .

This right of privacy was called by Mr. Justice Brandeis the right "to be let alone." Olmstead v. United States, 277 U.S. 438, 478. That right includes the privilege of an individual to plan his own affairs, for, "outside areas of plainly harmful conduct, every American is left to shape his own life as he thinks best, do what he pleases, go where he pleases." Kent v. Dulles, 357 U.S. 116, 126.

Third is the freedom to care for one's health and person, freedom from bodily restraint or compulsion, freedom to walk, stroll, or loaf.

These rights, though fundamental, are likewise subject to regulation on a showing of "compelling state interest." . . .

The present statute has struck the balance between the woman and the State's interests wholly in favor of the latter. I am not prepared to hold that a State may equate, as Georgia has done, all phases of maturation preceding birth. . . .

In summary, the enactment is overbroad. It is not closely correlated to the aim of preserving pre-natal life. In fact, it permits its destruction in several cases, including pregnancies resulting from sex acts in which unmarried females are below the statutory age of consent. At the same time, however, the measure broadly proscribes aborting other pregnancies which may cause severe mental disorders. Additionally, the statute is overbroad because it equates the value of embryonic life immediately after conception with the worth of life immediately before birth. . . .

I also agree that the superstructure of medical supervision which Georgia has erected violates the patient's right of privacy inherent in her choice of her own physician.

Mr. Justice White, with whom Mr. Justice Rehnquist joins, dissenting [in *Wade* and *Bolton*]. . . .

With all due respect, I dissent. I find nothing in the language or history of the Constitution to support the Court's judgment. The Court simply fashions and announces a new constitutional right for pregnant mothers and, with scarcely any reason or authority for its action, invests that right with sufficient substance to override most existing state abortion statutes. The upshot is that the people and the legislatures of the 50 States are constitutionally disentitled to weigh the relative importance of the continued existence and development of the fetus on the one hand against a spectrum of possible impacts on the mother on the other hand. As an exercise of raw judicial power, the Court perhaps has authority to do what it does today; but in my view its judgment is an improvident and extravagant exercise of the power of judicial review which the Constitution extends to this Court.

The Court apparently values the convenience of the pregnant mother more than the continued existence and development of the life or potential life which she carries. Whether or not I might agree with that marshalling of values, I can in no event join the Court's judgment because I find no constitutional warrant for imposing such an order of priorities on the people and legislatures of the States. In a sensitive area such as this, involving as it does issues over which reasonable men may easily and heatedly differ, I cannot accept the Court's exercise of its clear power of choice by interposing a constitutional barrier to state efforts to protect human life and by investing mothers and doctors with the constitutionally protected right to exterminate it. This issue, for the most part, should be left with the people and to the political processes the people have devised to govern their affairs.

It is my view, therefore, that the Texas statute is not constitutionally infirm because it denies abortions to those who seek to serve only their convenience rather than to protect their life or health. . . .

Planned Parenthood of Southeastern Pennsylvania v. Casey

505 U.S. 833, 112 S.Ct. 2791, 120 L.Ed.2d 674 (1992).

Justice O'Connor, Justice Kennedy, and Justice Souter announced the judgment of the Court and delivered the opinion of the Court with respect to Parts I, II, III, V–A, V–C, and VI, an opinion with respect to Part V–E, in which Justice Stevens joins, and an opinion with respect to Parts IV, V–B, and V–D.

I

Liberty finds no refuge in a jurisprudence of doubt. Yet 19 years after our holding that the Constitution protects a woman's right to terminate her pregnancy in its early stages, Roe v. Wade, 410 U.S. 113 (1973), that definition of liberty is still questioned. [T]he United States, as it has done in five other cases in the last decade, again asks us to overrule *Roe*. . . .

[Five abortion clinics, and physicians providing abortion services, challenged each of] five provisions of the Pennsylvania Abortion Control Act [on its face]. . . . The Act requires that a woman seeking an abortion give her informed consent prior to the abortion procedure, and specifies that she be provided with certain information at least 24 hours before the abortion is performed. § 3205. For a minor to obtain an abortion, the Act requires the informed consent of one of her parents, but provides for a judicial bypass option if the minor does not wish to or cannot obtain a parent's consent. § 3206. [T]he Act requires that, unless certain exceptions apply, a married woman seeking an abortion must sign a statement indicating that she has notified her husband of her intended abortion. § 3209. The Act exempts compliance with these three requirements in the event of a "medical emergency," which is defined in § 3203 of the Act. . . . [It also] imposes certain reporting requirements on facilities that provide abortion services. . . .

. . . The District Court . . . held all [the provisions] unconstitutional. . . . The Court of Appeals . . . [upheld all but] the husband notification requirement. . . .

. . .

After considering the fundamental constitutional questions resolved by *Roe,* principles of institutional integrity, and the rule of *stare decisis*, we are led to conclude this: the essential holding of *Roe v. Wade* should be retained and once again reaffirmed.

. . . *Roe*'s essential holding, the holding we reaffirm, has three parts. First is a recognition of the right of the woman to choose to have an abortion before viability and to obtain it without undue interference from the State. Before viability, the State's interests are not strong enough to support a prohibition of abortion or the imposition of a substantial obstacle to the woman's effective right to elect the procedure. Second is a confirmation of the State's power to restrict abortions after fetal viability, if the law contains exceptions for pregnancies which endanger a woman's life or health. And third is the principle that the State has legitimate interests from the outset of the pregnancy in protecting the health of the woman and the life of the fetus that may become a child. These principles do not contradict one another; and we adhere to each.

II

. . .

Neither the Bill of Rights nor the specific practices of States at the time of the adoption of the Fourteenth Amendment marks the outer limits of the substantive sphere of liberty which the Fourteenth Amendment protects. See U.S. Const., Amend. 9. . . .

The inescapable fact is that adjudication of substantive due process claims may call upon the Court in interpreting the Constitution to exercise that same capacity which by tradition courts always have exercised: reasoned judgment. Its boundaries are not susceptible of expression as a simple rule. That does not mean we are free to invalidate state policy choices with which we disagree; yet neither does it permit us to shrink from the duties of our office. . . .

Men and women of good conscience can disagree, and we suppose some always shall disagree, about the profound moral and spiritual implications of terminating a pregnancy, even in its earliest stage. Some of us as individuals find abortion offensive to our most basic principles of morality, but that cannot control our decision. Our obligation is to define the liberty of all, not to mandate our own moral code. The underlying constitutional issue is whether the State can resolve these philosophic questions in such a definitive way that a woman lacks all choice in the matter, except perhaps in those rare circumstances in which the pregnancy is itself a danger to her own life or health, or is the result of rape or incest.

. . .

Our law affords constitutional protection to personal decisions relating to marriage, procreation, contraception, family relationships, child rearing, and education. . . . These matters, involving the most intimate and personal choices a person may make in a lifetime, choices central to personal dignity and autonomy, are central to the liberty protected by the Fourteenth Amendment. At the heart of liberty is the right to define one's own concept of existence, of meaning, of the universe, and of the mystery of human life. Beliefs about these matters could not define the attributes of personhood were they formed under compulsion of the State.

These considerations begin our analysis of the woman's interest in terminating her pregnancy but cannot end it, for this reason: though the abortion decision may originate within the zone of conscience and belief, it is more than a philosophic exercise. Abortion is a unique act. It is an act fraught with consequences for others: for the woman who must live with the implications of her decision; for the persons who perform and assist in the procedure; for the spouse, family, and society which must confront the knowledge that these procedures exist, procedures some deem nothing short of an act of violence against innocent human life; and, depending on one's beliefs, for the life or potential life that is aborted. Though abortion is conduct, it does not follow that the State is entitled to proscribe it in all instances. That is because the liberty of the woman is at stake in a sense unique to the human condition and so unique to the law. The mother who carries a child to full term is subject to anxieties, to physical constraints, to pain that only she must bear. That these sacrifices have from the beginning of the human race been endured by woman with a pride that ennobles her in the eyes of others and gives to the infant a bond of love cannot alone be grounds for the State to insist she make the sacrifice. Her suffering is too intimate and personal for the State to insist, without more, upon its own vision of the woman's role, however dominant that vision has been in the course of our history and our culture. The destiny of the woman must be shaped to a large extent on her own conception of her spiritual imperatives and her place in society.

[I]n some critical respects the abortion decision is of the same character as the decision to use contraception, to which *Griswold v. Connecticut, Eisenstadt v. Baird,* and *Carey v. Population Services International,* afford constitutional protection. We have no doubt as to the correctness of those decisions. They support the reasoning in *Roe* relating to the woman's liberty because they involve personal decisions concerning not only the meaning of procreation but also human responsibility and respect for it. . . .

. . .

While we appreciate the weight of the arguments made on behalf of the State . . ., arguments which in their ultimate formulation conclude that *Roe* should be overruled, the reservations any of us may have in reaffirming the central holding of *Roe* are outweighed by the explication of individual liberty we have given combined with the force of *stare decisis.* We turn now to that doctrine.

III

A

. . .

. . . [W]hen this Court reexamines a prior holding, its judgment is customarily informed by a series of prudential and pragmatic considerations designed to test the consistency of overruling a prior decision with the ideal of the rule of law, and to gauge the respective costs of reaffirming and overruling a prior case. . . .

. . .

1

Although *Roe* has engendered opposition, it has in no sense proven "unworkable," see Garcia v. San Antonio Metropolitan Transit Authority . . . (1985), representing as it does a simple limitation beyond which a state law is unenforceable. . . . [T]he required determinations fall within judicial competence.

2

. . .

. . . [F]or two decades of economic and social developments, people have organized intimate relationships and made choices that define their views of themselves and their places in society, in reliance on the availability of abortion in the event that contraception should fail. The ability of women to participate equally in the economic and social life of the Nation has been facilitated by their ability to control their reproductive lives. . . .

3

No evolution of legal principle has left *Roe*'s doctrinal footings weaker than they were in 1973. . . .

. . . *Roe* stands at an intersection of two lines of decisions. . . . [In the *Griswold* line,] *Roe* is clearly in no jeopardy, since subsequent constitutional developments have neither disturbed, nor do they threaten to diminish, the scope of recognized protection accorded to the liberty relating to intimate relationships, the family, and decisions about whether or not to beget or bear a child. . . .

[A]s a rule (whether or not mistaken) of personal autonomy and bodily integrity, with doctrinal affinity to cases recognizing limits on governmental power to mandate medical treatment or to bar its rejection . . ., our cases since *Roe* accord with *Roe*'s view that a State's interest in the protection of life falls short of justifying any plenary override of individual liberty claims. Cruzan v. Director, Missouri Dept. of Health . . . (1990); . . . .

Finally, [viewed] as *sui generis* . . . there clearly has been no erosion of its central determination. The original holding . . . was expressly affirmed by a majority of six in 1983, see Akron v. Akron Center for Reproductive Health, Inc., 462 U.S. 416 (1983)(*Akron I*), and by a majority of five in 1986, see Thornburgh v. American College of Obstetricians and Gynecologists, 476 U.S. 747 (1986). . . . More recently, in Webster v. Reproductive Health Services, 492 U.S. 490 (1989), although two of the present authors questioned the trimester framework in a way consistent with our judgment today, . . . a majority of the Court either decided to reaffirm or declined to address the constitutional validity of the central holding of *Roe*. . . .

. . . Even on the assumption that the central holding of *Roe* was in error, that error would go only to the strength of the state interest in fetal protection, not to the recognition afforded by the Constitution to the woman's liberty. . . .

The soundness of this prong of the *Roe* analysis is apparent from a consideration of the alternative. If indeed the woman's interest in deciding whether to bear and beget a child had not been recognized as in *Roe,* the State might as readily restrict a woman's right to choose to carry a pregnancy to term as to terminate it, to further asserted state interests in population control, or eugenics, for example. . . .

4

. . . [D]ivergences from the factual premises of 1973 have no bearing on the validity of *Roe*'s central holding, that viability marks the earliest point at which the State's interest in fetal life is constitutionally adequate to justify a legislative ban on nontherapeutic abortions. . . . Whenever it may occur, the attainment of viability may continue to serve as the critical fact. . . . [N]o change in *Roe*'s factual underpinning has left its central holding obsolete, and none supports an argument for overruling it.

5

. . . Within the bounds of normal *stare decisis* analysis, then, . . . the stronger argument is for affirming *Roe*'s central holding, with whatever degree of personal reluctance any of us may have, not for overruling it.

B

In a less significant case, *stare decisis* analysis could, and would, stop at the point we have reached. But the sustained and widespread debate *Roe* has provoked calls for some comparison between that case and others of comparable dimension.... Only two ... from the past century present themselves for examination, and in each instance the result reached by the Court accorded with the principles we apply today.

The first example is that line of cases identified with Lochner v. New York ... (1905).... West Coast Hotel Co. v. Parrish ... (1937), signalled the demise of *Lochner*.... In the meantime, the Depression had come and, with it, the lesson that seemed unmistakable to most people by 1937, that the interpretation of contractual freedom protected in *Adkins* rested on fundamentally false factual assumptions about the capacity of a relatively unregulated market to satisfy minimal levels of human welfare.... [T]he clear demonstration that the facts of economic life were different from those previously assumed warranted the repudiation of the old law.

The second comparison ... is with the cases employing the separate-but-equal rule.... They began with Plessy v. Ferguson ... (1896), ... [which] reject[ed] the argument that racial separation enforced by the legal machinery of American society treats the black race as inferior....

The Court in *Brown* ... observ[ed] that whatever may have been the understanding in *Plessy*'s time of the power of segregation to stigmatize those who were segregated with a "badge of inferiority," it was clear by 1954 that legally sanctioned segregation had just such an effect.... Society's understanding of the facts ... in 1954 was thus fundamentally different from the basis claimed for the decision in 1896. While we think *Plessy* was wrong the day it was decided, ... we must also recognize that the *Plessy* Court's explanation for its decision was so clearly at odds with the facts apparent to the Court in 1954 that the decision to reexamine *Plessy* was on this ground alone not only justified but required.

... In constitutional adjudication as elsewhere in life, changed circumstances may impose new obligations, and the thoughtful part of the Nation could accept each decision to overrule a prior case as a response to the Court's constitutional duty.

... Because neither the factual underpinnings of *Roe*'s central holding nor our understanding of it has changed (and because no other indication of weakened precedent has been shown) the Court could not pretend to be reexamining the prior law with any justification beyond a present doctrinal disposition to come out differently from the Court of 1973. To overrule prior law for no other reason than that would run counter to the view repeated in our cases, that a decision to overrule should rest on some special reason over and above the belief that a prior case was wrongly decided....

C

The examination of the conditions justifying the repudiation of *Adkins* by *West Coast Hotel* and *Plessy* by *Brown* is enough to suggest the terrible price that would have been paid if the Court had not overruled as it did. In the present case, however, ... the terrible price would be paid for overruling. [In addition,] overruling *Roe*'s central holding ... would seriously weaken the Court's capacity to exercise the judicial power and to function as the Supreme Court of a Nation dedicated to the rule of law....

... The Court's power lies ... in its legitimacy, a product of substance and perception....

... The Court must take care to speak and act in ways that allow people to accept its decisions on the terms the Court claims for them, as grounded truly in principle, not as compromises with social and political pressures having, as such, no bearing on the principled choices that the Court is obliged to make. . . .

The need for principled action to be perceived as such is implicated to some degree whenever this, or any other appellate court, overrules a prior case. . . .

. . . Where . . . the Court decides a case in such a way as to resolve the sort of intensely divisive controversy reflected in *Roe* and those rare, comparable cases, its decision has a dimension that the resolution of the normal case does not carry. It is the dimension present whenever the Court's interpretation of the Constitution calls the contending sides of a national controversy to end their national division by accepting a common mandate rooted in the Constitution.

The Court is not asked to do this very often, having thus addressed the Nation only twice in our lifetime, in the decisions of *Brown* and *Roe*. But when the Court does act in this way, its decision requires an equally rare precedential force to counter the inevitable efforts to overturn it. . . . [O]nly the most convincing justification . . . could suffice to demonstrate that a later decision overruling the first was anything but a surrender to political pressure, and an unjustified repudiation of the principle on which the Court staked its authority in the first instance. So to overrule under fire in the absence of the most compelling reason to reexamine a watershed decision would subvert the Court's legitimacy beyond any serious question. . . .

. . .

. . . A decision to overrule *Roe*'s essential holding under the existing circumstances would address error, if error there was, at the cost of both profound and unnecessary damage to the Court's legitimacy, and to the Nation's commitment to the rule of law. It is therefore imperative to adhere to the essence of *Roe*'s original decision, and we do so today.

IV

. . . [Although] much criticism has been directed at *Roe*['s line-drawing], a criticism that always inheres when the Court draws a specific rule from what in the Constitution is but a general standard[,] . . . [l]iberty must not be extinguished for want of a line that is clear. . . .

We conclude the line should be drawn at viability, so that before that time the woman has a right to choose to terminate her pregnancy. We adhere to this principle for two reasons. First, . . . *stare decisis* . . . .

[S]econd[,] the concept of viability . . . is the time at which there is a realistic possibility of maintaining and nourishing a life outside the womb, so that the independent existence of the second life can in reason and all fairness be the object of state protection that now overrides the rights of the woman. . . . The viability line also has, as a practical matter, an element of fairness. In some broad sense it might be said that a woman who fails to act before viability has consented to the State's intervention on behalf of the developing child.

The woman's right to terminate her pregnancy before viability is the most central principle of *Roe v. Wade*. It is a rule of law and a component of liberty we cannot renounce.

On the other side of the equation is the interest of the State in the protection of potential life. . . . The weight to be given this state interest, not the strength of the woman's interest, was the difficult question faced in *Roe*. We do not need to say whether each of us, . . . as an original matter, would have concluded, as the *Roe* Court did, that its weight is insufficient to justify a ban on abortions prior to viability even when it is subject to certain exceptions. The . . . immediate question is not the soundness of *Roe*'s resolution of the issue, but the precedential force that must be accorded to its holding. And we have concluded that the essential holding of *Roe* should be reaffirmed.

Yet it must be remembered that *Roe v. Wade* speaks with clarity in establishing not only the woman's liberty but also the State's "important and legitimate interest in potential life." . . . That portion of the decision in *Roe* has been given too little acknowledgement and implementation by the Court in its subsequent cases[, which] decided that any regulation touching upon the abortion decision must survive strict scrutiny, to be sustained only if drawn in narrow terms to further a compelling state interest. . . . Not all of the cases decided under that formulation can be reconciled with the holding in *Roe* itself that the State has legitimate interests in the health of the woman and in protecting the potential life within her. . . .

. . .

The trimester framework no doubt was erected to ensure that the woman's right to choose not become so subordinate to the State's interest in promoting fetal life that her choice exists in theory but not in fact. We do not agree, however, that the trimester approach is necessary to accomplish this objective. A framework of this rigidity was unnecessary and in its later interpretation sometimes contradicted the State's permissible exercise of its powers.

Though the woman has a right to choose to terminate or continue her pregnancy before viability, it does not at all follow that the State is prohibited from taking steps to ensure that this choice is thoughtful and informed. Even in the earliest stages of pregnancy, the State may enact rules and regulations designed to encourage her to know that there are philosophic and social arguments of great weight that can be brought to bear in favor of continuing the pregnancy to full term and that there are procedures and institutions to allow adoption of unwanted children as well as a certain degree of state assistance if the mother chooses to raise the child herself. . . .

We reject the trimester framework, which we do not consider to be part of the essential holding of *Roe*. . . . Measures aimed at ensuring that a woman's choice contemplates the consequences for the fetus do not necessarily interfere with the right recognized in *Roe*, although those measures have been found to be inconsistent with the rigid trimester framework announced in that case. . . . The trimester framework suffers from these basic flaws: in its formulation it misconceives the nature of the pregnant woman's interest; and in practice it undervalues the State's interest in potential life, as recognized in *Roe*.

. . .

. . . The fact that a law which serves a valid purpose, one not designed to strike at the right itself, has the incidental effect of making it more difficult or more expensive to procure an abortion cannot be enough to invalidate it. Only where state regulation imposes an undue burden on a woman's ability to make this decision does the power of the State reach into the heart of the liberty protected by the Due Process Clause. . . .

. . . [T]he Court's experience applying the trimester framework has led to the striking down of some abortion regulations which in no real sense deprived women of the ultimate decision. . . . [T]he other basic flaw in the trimester framework [is that] even in *Roe*'s terms, in practice it undervalues the State's interest in the potential life within the woman.

. . .

The very notion that the State has a substantial interest in potential life leads to the conclusion that not all regulations must be deemed unwarranted. Not all burdens on the right to decide whether to terminate a pregnancy will be undue. In our view, the undue burden standard is the appropriate means of reconciling the State's interest with the woman's constitutionally protected liberty.

. . .

A finding of an undue burden is a shorthand for the conclusion that a state regulation has the purpose or effect of placing a substantial obstacle in the path of a woman seeking an abortion of a nonviable fetus. A statute with this purpose is invalid because the means chosen by the State to further the interest in potential life must be calculated to inform the woman's free choice, not hinder it. And a statute which, while furthering the interest in potential life or some other valid state interest, has the effect of placing a substantial obstacle in the path of a woman's choice cannot be considered a permissible means of serving its legitimate ends.... [A]n undue burden is an unconstitutional burden.... [A] law designed to further the State's interest in fetal life which imposes an undue burden on the woman's decision before fetal viability [is un]constitutional....

Some guiding principles should emerge.... Regulations which do no more than create a structural mechanism by which the State, or the parent or guardian of a minor, may express profound respect for the life of the unborn are permitted, if they are not a substantial obstacle to the woman's exercise of the right to choose.... Unless it has that effect on her right of choice, a state measure designed to persuade her to choose childbirth over abortion will be upheld if reasonably related to that goal. Regulations designed to foster the health of a woman seeking an abortion are valid if they do not constitute an undue burden.

standard of review {

Even when jurists reason from shared premises, some disagreement is inevitable.... That is to be expected in the application of any legal standard which must accommodate life's complexity. We do not expect it to be otherwise with respect to the undue burden standard. We give this summary:

(a) To protect the central right recognized by *Roe v. Wade* while at the same time accommodating the State's profound interest in potential life, we will employ the undue burden analysis as explained in this opinion. An undue burden exists, and therefore a provision of law is invalid, if its purpose or effect is to place a substantial obstacle in the path of a woman seeking an abortion before the fetus attains viability.

(b) We reject the rigid trimester framework of *Roe v. Wade*. To promote the State's profound interest in potential life, throughout pregnancy the State may take measures to ensure that the woman's choice is informed, and measures designed to advance this interest will not be invalidated as long as their purpose is to persuade the woman to choose childbirth over abortion. These measures must not be an undue burden on the right.

(c) As with any medical procedure, the State may enact regulations to further the health or safety of a woman seeking an abortion. Unnecessary health regulations that have the purpose or effect of presenting a substantial obstacle to a woman seeking an abortion impose an undue burden on the right.

(d) Our adoption of the undue burden analysis does not disturb the central holding of *Roe v. Wade,* and we reaffirm that holding. Regardless of whether exceptions are made for particular circumstances, a State may not prohibit any woman from making the ultimate decision to terminate her pregnancy before viability.

(e) We also reaffirm *Roe*'s holding that "subsequent to viability, the State in promoting its interest in the potentiality of human life may, if it chooses, regulate, and even proscribe, abortion except where it is necessary, in appropriate medical judgment, for the preservation of the life or health of the mother." . . .

These principles control our assessment of the . . . challenged provisions.

V

. . .

A

Because it is central to the operation of various other requirements, we begin with the statute's definition of medical emergency. . . .

Petitioners argue that the definition is too narrow, contending that it forecloses the possibility of an immediate abortion despite some significant health risks. If . . . correct, we would be required to invalidate the restrictive operation of the provision, for the essential holding of *Roe* forbids a State from interfering with a woman's choice . . . if continuing her pregnancy would constitute a threat to her health. . . .

. . . While the definition could be interpreted in an unconstitutional manner, . . . [w]e . . . conclude that, as construed by the Court of Appeals, the medical emergency definition imposes no undue burden on a woman's abortion right.

B

We next consider the informed consent requirement. . . .

Our prior decisions establish that as with any medical procedure, the State may require a woman to give her written informed consent to an abortion. . . . In this respect, the statute is unexceptional. Petitioners challenge the statute's definition of informed consent because it includes the provision of specific information by the doctor and the mandatory 24–hour waiting period. The conclusions reached by a majority of the Justices in the separate opinions filed today and the undue burden standard adopted in this opinion require us to overrule in part some of the Court's past decisions. . . .

In *Akron I,* . . . we invalidated an ordinance which required that a woman seeking an abortion be provided by her physician with specific information "designed to influence the woman's informed choice between abortion or childbirth." . . .

To the extent *Akron I* and *Thornburgh* find a constitutional violation when the government requires, as it does here, the giving of truthful, nonmisleading information about the nature of the procedure, the attendant health risks and those of childbirth, and the "probable gestational age" of the fetus, those cases go too far, are inconsistent with *Roe*'s acknowledgment of an important interest in potential life, and are overruled. . . . [M]ost women considering an abortion would deem the impact on the fetus relevant, if not dispositive, to the decision. In attempting to ensure that a woman apprehend the full consequences of her decision, the State furthers the legitimate purpose of reducing the risk that a woman may elect an abortion, only to discover later, with devastating psychological consequences, that her decision was not fully informed. If the information the State requires to be made available to the woman is truthful and not misleading, the requirement may be permissible.

We also see no reason why the State may not require doctors to inform a woman seeking an abortion of the availability of materials relating to the consequences to the fetus, even when those consequences have no direct relation to her health.... We would think it constitutional for the State to require that in order for there to be informed consent to a kidney transplant operation the recipient must be supplied with information about risks to the donor as well as risks to himself or herself. A [similar] requirement ... was described in *Thornburgh* as "an outright attempt to wedge the Commonwealth's message discouraging abortion into the privacy of the informed-consent dialogue between the woman and her physician." ... We conclude, however, that informed choice need not be defined in such narrow terms that all considerations of the effect on the fetus are made irrelevant.... In short, requiring that the woman be informed of the availability of information relating to fetal development and the assistance available should she decide to carry the pregnancy to full term is a reasonable measure to insure an informed choice, one which might cause the woman to choose childbirth over abortion. This requirement cannot be considered a substantial obstacle to obtaining an abortion, and, it follows, there is no undue burden.

Our prior cases also suggest that the "straitjacket," *Thornburgh* ..., of particular information which must be given in each case interferes with a constitutional right of privacy between a pregnant woman and her physician. [T]he statute now before us does not require a physician to comply with the informed consent provisions "if he or she can demonstrate by a preponderance of the evidence, that he or she reasonably believed that furnishing the information would have resulted in a severely adverse effect on the physical or mental health of the patient." ... In this respect, the statute does not prevent the physician from exercising his or her medical judgment.

Whatever constitutional status the doctor-patient relation may have as a general matter, in the present context it is derivative of the woman's position.... Thus, a requirement that a doctor give a woman certain information as part of obtaining her consent to an abortion is, for constitutional purposes, no different from a requirement that a doctor give certain specific information about any medical procedure.

> *Informed consent is no diff from any other medical procedure.*

. . .

The Pennsylvania statute also requires us to reconsider the holding in *Akron I* that the State may not require that a physician, as opposed to a qualified assistant, provide information relevant to a woman's informed consent.... Since there is no evidence on this record that requiring a doctor to give the information as provided by the statute would amount in practical terms to a substantial obstacle to a woman seeking an abortion, we conclude that it is not an undue burden....

> *no undue burden*

Our analysis of Pennsylvania's 24–hour waiting period between the provision of the information deemed necessary to informed consent and the performance of an abortion under the undue burden standard requires us to reconsider the premise behind the decision in *Akron I* invalidating a parallel requirement. In *Akron I* we said: "Nor are we convinced that the State's legitimate concern that the woman's decision be informed is reasonably served by requiring a 24–hour delay as a matter of course." ... We consider that conclusion to be wrong. The idea that important decisions will be more informed and deliberate if they follow some period of reflection does not strike us as unreasonable, particularly where the statute directs that important information become part of the background of the decision. The statute, as construed by the Court of Appeals, permits avoidance of the waiting period in the event of a medical emergency and the record evidence shows that in the vast majority of cases, a 24–hour delay does not create any appreciable health risk. In theory, at least, the waiting period is a reasonable measure to implement the State's interest in protecting the life of the unborn, a measure that does not amount to an undue burden.

Whether the mandatory 24–hour waiting period is nonetheless invalid because in practice it is a substantial obstacle to a woman's choice to terminate her pregnancy is a closer question. The findings of fact by the District Court indicate that because of the distances many women must travel to reach an abortion provider, the practical effect will often be a delay of much more than a day because the waiting period requires that a woman seeking an abortion make at least two visits to the doctor. The District Court also found that in many instances this will increase the exposure of women seeking abortions to "the harassment and hostility of anti-abortion protestors demonstrating outside a clinic." . . . As a result, the District Court found that for those women who have the fewest financial resources, those who must travel long distances, and those who have difficulty explaining their whereabouts to husbands, employers, or others, the 24–hour waiting period will be "particularly burdensome." . . .

These findings are troubling in some respects, but they do not demonstrate that the waiting period constitutes an undue burden. We do not doubt that . . . the waiting period has the effect of "increasing the cost and risk of delay of abortions," . . . but the District Court did not conclude that the increased costs and potential delays amount to substantial obstacles. Rather, applying the trimester framework[, it] concluded that the waiting period does not further the state "interest in maternal health" and "infringes the physician's discretion to exercise sound medical judgment." . . . Yet, . . . under the undue burden standard a State is permitted to enact persuasive measures which favor childbirth over abortion, even if those measures do not further a health interest. . . .

We also disagree with the District Court's conclusion that the "particularly burdensome" effects of the waiting period on some women require its invalidation. A particular burden is not of necessity a substantial obstacle. Whether a burden falls on a particular group is a distinct inquiry from whether it is a substantial obstacle even as to the women in that group. And the District Court did not conclude that the waiting period is such an obstacle even for the women who are most burdened by it. Hence, on the record before us, and in the context of this facial challenge, we are not convinced that the 24–hour waiting period constitutes an undue burden.

We are left with the argument that the various aspects of the informed consent requirement are unconstitutional because they place barriers in the way of abortion on demand. Even the broadest reading of *Roe,* however, has not suggested that there is a constitutional right to abortion on demand. . . . Rather, the right protected by *Roe* is a right to decide to terminate a pregnancy free of undue interference by the State. Because the informed consent requirement facilitates the wise exercise of that right it cannot be classified as an interference with the right *Roe* protects. The informed consent requirement is not an undue burden on that right.

Next provision:

spousal consent

Lots of women subject to abuse

C

Section 3209 of Pennsylvania's abortion law provides, except in cases of medical emergency, that no physician shall perform an abortion on a married woman without receiving a signed statement from the woman that she has notified her spouse that she is about to undergo an abortion. The woman has the option of providing an alternative signed statement certifying that her husband is not the man who impregnated her; that her husband could not be located; that the pregnancy is the result of spousal sexual assault which she has reported; or that the woman believes that notifying her husband will cause him or someone else to inflict bodily injury upon her. A physician who performs an abortion on a married woman without receiving the appropriate signed statement will have his or her license revoked, and is liable to the husband for damages.

[The opinion here recounted at length the district court's findings with respect to the widespread incidence and dynamics of wife-battering, marital rape, and other coerced sexual activity, as well as studies of the frequency of psychological and physical abuse of women, including homicides, by their husbands or male partners.]

... In well-functioning marriages, spouses discuss important intimate decisions such as whether to bear a child. But there are millions of women in this country who are the victims of regular physical and psychological abuse at the hands of their husbands. Should these women become pregnant, they may have very good reasons for not wishing to inform their husbands of their decision to obtain an abortion. Many may have justifiable fears of physical abuse, but may be no less fearful of the consequences of reporting prior abuse to the Commonwealth of Pennsylvania. Many may have a reasonable fear that notifying their husbands will provoke further instances of child abuse; these women are not exempt from § 3209's notification requirement. Many may fear devastating forms of psychological abuse from their husbands, including verbal harassment, threats of future violence, the destruction of possessions, physical confinement to the home, the withdrawal of financial support, or the disclosure of the abortion to family and friends. These methods of psychological abuse may act as even more of a deterrent to notification than the possibility of physical violence, but women who are the victims of the abuse are not exempt from § 3209's notification requirement. And many women who are pregnant as a result of sexual assaults by their husbands will be unable to avail themselves of the exception for spousal sexual assault, § 3209(b)(3), because the exception requires that the woman have notified law enforcement authorities within 90 days of the assault, and her husband will be notified of her report once an investigation begins. § 3128(c). If anything in this field is certain, it is that victims of spousal sexual assault are extremely reluctant to report the abuse to the government; hence, a great many spousal rape victims will not be exempt from the notification requirement imposed by § 3209.

The spousal notification requirement is thus likely to prevent a significant number of women from obtaining an abortion. It does not merely make abortions a little more difficult or expensive to obtain; for many women, it will impose a substantial obstacle. We must not blind ourselves to the fact that the significant number of women who fear for their safety and the safety of their children are likely to be deterred from procuring an abortion as surely as if the Commonwealth had outlawed abortion in all cases.

... Respondents argue that ... the statute affects fewer than one percent of women seeking abortions [and thus] the statute cannot be invalid on its face.... We disagree....

... The proper focus of constitutional inquiry is the group for whom the law is a restriction, not the group for whom the law is irrelevant.

... [S]ection 3209's real target is narrower even than the class of women seeking abortions identified by the State: it is married women seeking abortions who do not wish to notify their husbands of their intentions and who do not qualify for one of the statutory exceptions to the notice requirement. The unfortunate yet persisting conditions we document above will mean that in a large fraction of the cases in which § 3209 is relevant, it will operate as a substantial obstacle to a woman's choice to undergo an abortion. It is an undue burden, and therefore invalid.

This conclusion is in no way inconsistent with our decisions upholding parental notification or consent requirements.... Those enactments, and our judgment that they are constitutional, are based on the quite reasonable assumption that minors will benefit from consultation with their parents and that children will often not realize that their parents have their best interests at heart. We cannot adopt a parallel assumption about adult women.

We recognize that a husband has a "deep and proper concern and interest ... in his wife's pregnancy and in the growth and development of the fetus she is carrying." ... If this case concerned a State's ability to require the mother to notify the father before taking some action with respect to a living child raised by both, therefore, it would be reasonable to conclude as a general matter that the father's interest in the welfare of the child and the mother's interest are equal.

Before birth, however, the issue takes on a very different cast. It is an inescapable biological fact that state regulation with respect to the child a woman is carrying will have a far greater impact on the mother's liberty than on the father's....

[N]ot so long ago ... a different understanding of the family and of the Constitution prevailed. In Bradwell v. Illinois, 16 Wall. 130 (1873), three Members of this Court reaffirmed the common-law principle that "a woman had no legal existence separate from her husband...." ... Only one generation has passed since this Court observed that "woman is still regarded as the center of home and family life," with attendant "special responsibilities" that precluded full and independent legal status under the Constitution ... These views, of course, are no longer consistent with our understanding of the family, the individual, or the Constitution.

... For the great many women who are victims of abuse inflicted by their husbands, or whose children are the victims of such abuse, a spousal notice requirement enables the husband to wield an effective veto over his wife's decision. Whether the prospect of notification itself deters such women from seeking abortions, or whether the husband, through physical force or psychological pressure or economic coercion, prevents his wife from obtaining an abortion until it is too late, the notice requirement will often be tantamount to the veto found unconstitutional in *Danforth*. The women most affected by this law—those who most reasonably fear the consequences of notifying their husbands that they are pregnant—are in the gravest danger.

The husband's interest in the life of the child his wife is carrying does not permit the State to empower him with this troubling degree of authority over his wife.... A State may not give to a man the kind of dominion over his wife that parents exercise over their children.

... Women do not lose their constitutionally protected liberty when they marry....

D

We next consider the parental consent provision. Except in a medical emergency, an unemancipated young woman under 18 may not obtain an abortion unless she and one of her parents (or guardian) provides consent.... If neither a parent nor a guardian provides consent, a court may authorize the performance of an abortion upon a determination that the young woman is mature and capable of giving informed consent and has in fact given her informed consent, or that an abortion would be in her best interests.

... Our cases establish, and we reaffirm today, that a State may require a minor seeking an abortion to obtain the consent of a parent or guardian, provided that there is an adequate judicial bypass procedure....

E

Under the recordkeeping and reporting requirements of the statute, every facility which performs abortions is required to file a report stating its name and address as well as the name and address of any related entity, such as a controlling or subsidiary organization. In the case of state-funded institutions, the information becomes public.

For each abortion performed, a report must be filed identifying: the physician (and the second physician where required); the facility; the referring physician or agency; the woman's age; the number of prior pregnancies and prior abortions she has had; gestational age; the type of abortion procedure; the date of the abortion; whether there were any pre-existing medical conditions which would complicate pregnancy; medical complications with the abortion; where applicable, the basis for the determination that the abortion was medically necessary; the weight of the aborted fetus; and whether the woman was married, and if so, whether notice was provided or the basis for the failure to give notice. Every abortion facility must also file quarterly reports showing the number of abortions performed broken down by trimester.... [T]he identity of each woman who has had an abortion remains confidential.

In *Danforth,* ... we held that recordkeeping and reporting provisions "that are reasonably directed to the preservation of maternal health and that properly respect a patient's confidentiality and privacy are permissible." [U]nder this standard, all the provisions at issue here except that relating to spousal notice are constitutional.... The collection of information with respect to actual patients is a vital element of medical research, and so it cannot be said that the requirements serve no purpose other than to make abortions more difficult. Nor do we find that the requirements impose a substantial obstacle to a woman's choice. At most they might increase the cost of some abortions by a slight amount. While at some point increased cost could become a substantial obstacle, there is no such showing on the record before us.

Subsection (12) ... requires the reporting of ... a married woman's "reason for failure to provide notice" to her husband.... Like the spousal notice requirement itself, this provision places an undue burden on a woman's choice, and must be invalidated for that reason.

VI

Our Constitution is a covenant running from the first generation of Americans to us and then to future generations.... We accept our responsibility not to retreat from interpreting the full meaning of the covenant in light of all our precedents. We invoke it once again to define the freedom guaranteed by the Constitution's own promise, the promise of liberty.

. . .

Justice Stevens, concurring in part and dissenting in part.

The portions of the Court's opinion that I have joined are more important than those with which I disagree. . . .

I

. . .

I . . . accept what is implicit in the Court's analysis, namely, a reaffirmation of *Roe*'s explanation of why the State's obligation to protect the life or health of the mother must take precedence over any duty to the unborn. The Court in *Roe* carefully considered, and rejected, the State's argument "that the fetus is a 'person' within the language and meaning of the Fourteenth Amendment." . . . Thus, as a matter of federal constitutional law, a developing organism that is not yet a "person" does not have what is sometimes described as a "right to life." This has been and, by the Court's holding today, remains a fundamental premise of our constitutional law governing reproductive autonomy.

II

. . . Contrary to . . . the joint opinion, it is not a "contradiction" to recognize that the State may have a legitimate interest in potential human life and, at the same time, to conclude that that interest does not justify the regulation of abortion before viability (although other interests, such as maternal health, may). [T]hat the State's interest is legitimate does not tell us when, if ever, that interest outweighs the pregnant woman's interest in personal liberty. . . .

. . .

Identifying the State's interests . . . makes clear that the interest in protecting potential life is not grounded in the Constitution. It is, instead, an indirect interest supported by both humanitarian and pragmatic concerns. Many of our citizens believe that any abortion reflects an unacceptable disrespect for potential human life and that the performance of more than a million abortions each year is intolerable; many find third-trimester abortions performed when the fetus is approaching personhood particularly offensive. The State has a legitimate interest in minimizing such offense. The State may also have a broader interest in expanding the population. . . .

In counterpoise is the woman's constitutional interest in liberty. One aspect of this liberty is a right to bodily integrity, a right to control one's person. . . . This right is neutral on the question of abortion: The Constitution would be equally offended by an absolute requirement that all women undergo abortions as by an absolute prohibition on abortions. . . .

The woman's constitutional liberty interest also involves her freedom to decide matters of the highest privacy and the most personal nature. . . . The authority to make such traumatic and yet empowering decisions is an element of basic human dignity. As the joint opinion so eloquently demonstrates, a woman's decision to terminate her pregnancy is nothing less than a matter of conscience.

Weighing the State's interest in potential life and the woman's liberty interest, I agree with the joint opinion that the State may " 'expres[s] a preference for normal childbirth,' " that the State may take steps to ensure that a woman's choice "is thoughtful and informed," and that "States are free to enact laws to provide a reasonable framework for a woman to make a decision that has such profound and lasting meaning." Serious questions arise, however, when a State attempts to "persuade the woman to choose childbirth over abortion." Decisional autonomy must limit the State's power to inject into a woman's most personal deliberations its own views of what is best. The State may promote its preferences by funding childbirth, by creating and maintaining alternatives to abortion, and by espousing the virtues of family; but it must respect the individual's freedom to make such judgments.

. . .

. . . [T]he Pennsylvania statute . . . require[s] a physician or counselor to provide the woman with a range of materials clearly designed to persuade her to choose not to undergo the abortion. While the State is free . . . to produce and disseminate such material, the State may not inject such information into the woman's deliberations just as she is weighing such an important choice.

. . . [By contrast, r]equir[ing] the physician to inform a woman of the nature and risks of the abortion procedure and the medical risks of carrying to term, are neutral requirements comparable to those imposed in other medical procedures. Those sections indicate no effort by the State to influence the woman's choice in any way. If anything, such requirements enhance, rather than skew, the woman's decisionmaking.

III

The 24–hour waiting period . . . raises even more serious concerns. . . .

. . . [T]here is no evidence that the mandated delay benefits women or that it is necessary to enable the physician to convey any relevant information to the patient. The mandatory delay thus appears to rest on outmoded and unacceptable assumptions about the decisionmaking capacity of women. While there are well-established and consistently maintained reasons for the State to view with skepticism the ability of minors to make decisions, . . . none of those reasons applies to an adult woman's decisionmaking ability. Just as we have left behind the belief that a woman must consult her husband before undertaking serious matters, so we must reject the notion that a woman is less capable of deciding matters of gravity. Cf. Reed v. Reed . . . (1971).

[T]he delay requirement may be premised on the belief that the decision to terminate a pregnancy is presumptively wrong. This premise is illegitimate. . . . States may not presume that a woman has failed to reflect adequately merely because her conclusion differs from the State's preference. . . .

Part of the constitutional liberty to choose is the equal dignity to which each of us is entitled. A woman who decides to terminate her pregnancy is entitled to the same respect as a woman who decides to carry the fetus to term. The mandatory waiting period denies women that equal respect.

IV

In my opinion, a correct application of the "undue burden" standard leads to the same conclusion. . . . A state-imposed burden on the exercise of a constitutional right is measured both by its effects and by its character: A burden may be "undue" either because the burden is too severe or because it lacks a legitimate, rational justification.

The 24–hour delay requirement fails both parts of this test. The findings of the District Court establish the severity of the burden.... [E]ven [when] the delay is not especially onerous, it is ... "undue" because there is no evidence [it] serves a useful and legitimate purpose. [T]here is no legitimate reason to require a woman who has agonized over her decision to leave the clinic or hospital and return again another day.... [A] rigid requirement that all patients wait 24 hours or (what is true in practice) much longer to evaluate the significance of information that is either common knowledge or irrelevant is an irrational and, therefore, "undue" burden.

The counseling provisions are similarly infirm.... [The mandated information must] be given to all women seeking abortions, including those for whom such information is clearly useless, such as those who are married, those who have undergone the procedure in the past and are fully aware of the options, and those who are fully convinced that abortion is their only reasonable option. Moreover, ... information [of probable gestational age] is of little decisional value in most cases, because 90% of all abortions are performed during the first trimester when fetal age has less relevance than when the fetus nears viability.... I conclude that the information requirements ... do not serve a useful purpose and thus constitute an unnecessary—and therefore undue—burden on the woman's constitutional liberty to decide to terminate her pregnancy.

Accordingly, while I disagree with Parts IV, V–B, and V–D of the joint opinion, I join the remainder of the Court's opinion.

Justice Blackmun, concurring in part, concurring in the judgment in part, and dissenting in part.

I join parts I, II, III, V–A, V–C, and VI of the joint opinion of Justices O'Connor, Kennedy, and Souter.

. . .

I

Make no mistake, the joint opinion of Justices O'Connor, Kennedy, and Souter is an act of personal courage and constitutional principle....

. . .

[W]hile ... the joint opinion errs in failing to invalidate the other regulations, I am pleased that [it] has not ruled out the possibility that these regulations may be shown to impose an unconstitutional burden. The joint opinion makes clear that its specific holdings are based on the insufficiency of the record before it....

II

. . .

... *Roe*'s requirement of strict scrutiny as implemented through a trimester framework should not be disturbed. No other approach has gained a majority, and no other is more protective of the woman's fundamental right. Lastly, no other approach properly accommodates the woman's constitutional right with the State's legitimate interests.

. . .

Application of the strict scrutiny standard results in the invalidation of all the challenged provisions. Indeed, as this Court has invalidated virtually identical provisions in prior cases, *stare decisis* requires that we again strike them down.

. . .

III

. . .

The Chief Justice's criticism of *Roe* follows from his stunted conception of individual liberty.... [He] construe[s] this Court's personal-liberty cases as establishing only a laundry list of particular rights, rather than a principled account of how these particular rights are grounded in a more general right of privacy. This constricted view is reinforced by The Chief Justice's exclusive reliance on tradition as a source of fundamental rights....

Even more shocking than The Chief Justice's cramped notion of individual liberty is his complete omission of any discussion of the effects that compelled childbirth and motherhood have on women's lives.... [His] view of the State's compelling interest in maternal health has less to do with health than it does with compelling women to be maternal.

. . .

IV

In one sense, the Court's approach is worlds apart from that of The Chief Justice and Justice Scalia. And yet ... the distance between the two approaches is ... but a single vote.

I am 83 years old. I cannot remain on this Court forever, and when I do step down, the confirmation process for my successor well may focus on the issue before us today. That, I regret, may be exactly where the choice between the two worlds will be made.

Chief Justice Rehnquist, with whom Justice White, Justice Scalia, and Justice Thomas join, concurring in the judgment in part and dissenting in part.

The joint opinion, following its newly-minted variation on *stare decisis*, retains the outer shell of *Roe v. Wade,* ... but beats a wholesale retreat from the substance of that case. We believe that *Roe* was wrongly decided, and that it can and should be overruled consistently with our traditional approach to *stare decisis* in constitutional cases. We would adopt the approach of the plurality in *Webster* ... and uphold the challenged provisions of the Pennsylvania statute in their entirety.

I

. . .

... Although they reject the trimester framework ..., Justices O'Connor, Kennedy, and Souter adopt a revised undue burden standard to analyze the challenged regulations. We conclude, however, that such an outcome is an unjustified constitutional compromise, one which [allows] the Court ... to closely scrutinize all types of abortion regulations despite the fact that it lacks the power to do so under the Constitution.

. . .

We have held that a liberty interest protected under the Due Process Clause of the Fourteenth Amendment will be deemed fundamental if it is "implicit in the concept of ordered liberty." Palko v. Connecticut ... (1937). Three years earlier, in Snyder v. Massachusetts ... (1934), we referred to a "principle of justice so rooted in the traditions and conscience of our people as to be ranked as fundamental." ... These expressions are admittedly not precise, but our decisions implementing this notion of "fundamental" rights do not afford any more elaborate basis on which to base such a classification.

In construing the phrase "liberty" incorporated in the Due Process Clause of the Fourteenth Amendment, we have recognized that its meaning extends beyond freedom from physical restraint.... But [our] opinions ... do not endorse any all-encompassing "right of privacy."

... Unlike marriage, procreation and contraception, abortion "involves the purposeful termination of potential life." Harris v. McRae ... (1980). The abortion decision must therefore "be recognized as *sui generis*, different in kind from the others that the Court has protected under the rubric of personal or family privacy and autonomy." ...

Nor do the historical traditions of the American people support the view that the right to terminate one's pregnancy is "fundamental." ... At the time of the adoption of the Fourteenth Amendment, statutory prohibitions or restrictions on abortion were commonplace; in 1868, at least 28 of the then 37 States and 8 Territories had statutes banning or limiting abortion.... By the turn of the century virtually every State had a law prohibiting or restricting abortion on its books. By the middle of the present century, a liberalization trend had set in. But 21 of the restrictive abortion laws in effect in 1868 were still in effect in 1973 when *Roe* was decided, and an overwhelming majority of the States prohibited abortion unless necessary to preserve the life or health of the mother.... On this record, it can scarcely be said that any deeply rooted tradition of relatively unrestricted abortion in our history supported the classification of the right to abortion as "fundamental" under the Due Process Clause of the Fourteenth Amendment.

. . .

II

The joint opinion['s] ... discussion of the principle of *stare decisis* appears to be almost entirely dicta, because [it] does not apply that principle in dealing with *Roe*. *Roe* decided that a woman had a fundamental right to an abortion. The joint opinion rejects that view. *Roe* decided that abortion regulations were to be subjected to "strict scrutiny" and could be justified only in the light of "compelling state interests." The joint opinion rejects that view.... *Roe* analyzed abortion regulation under a rigid trimester framework, a framework which has guided this Court's decisionmaking for 19 years. The joint opinion rejects that framework.

... Decisions following *Roe,* such as *Akron* ... (1983), and *Thornburgh* ... (1986), are frankly overruled in part under the "undue burden" standard expounded in the joint opinion.

In our view, authentic principles of *stare decisis* do not require that any portion of the reasoning in *Roe* be kept intact....

. . .

... [O]ne might inquire how the joint opinion can view the "central holding" of *Roe* as so deeply rooted in our constitutional culture, when it so casually uproots and disposes of that same decision's trimester framework. Furthermore, ... the same could have been said about this Court's erroneous decisions that the Constitution allowed "separate but equal" treatment of minorities, see Plessy v. Ferguson . . . (1896), or that "liberty" under the Due Process Clause protected "freedom of contract." . . . The "separate but equal" doctrine lasted 58 years after *Plessy,* and *Lochner*'s protection of contractual freedom lasted 32 years. However, the simple fact that a generation or more had grown used to these major decisions did not prevent the Court from correcting its errors in those cases, nor should it prevent us from correctly interpreting the Constitution here. . . .

Apparently realizing that conventional *stare decisis* principles do not support its position, the joint opinion advances a belief that retaining a portion of *Roe* is necessary to protect the "legitimacy" of this Court. . . .

[T]he joint opinion goes on to state that when the Court "resolve[s] the sort of intensely divisive controversy reflected in *Roe* and those rare, comparable cases," its decision is exempt from reconsideration under established principles of *stare decisis* in constitutional cases. . . .

[Distinguishing]   cases which are "intensely divisive" . . . from those that are not . . . is entirely subjective. . . .

. . . It [is] very odd indeed that the joint opinion chooses as benchmarks two cases in which the Court chose not to adhere to erroneous constitutional precedent, but instead enhanced its stature by acknowledging and correcting its error, apparently in violation of the joint opinion's "legitimacy" principle. See *West Coast Hotel Co. v. Parrish,* supra; *Brown v. Board of Education,* supra. . . . [Moreover,] . . . [p]ublic protests should not alter the normal application of *stare decisis*, lest perfectly lawful protest activity be penalized by the Court itself.

Taking the joint opinion on its own terms, we doubt that its distinction between *Roe,* on the one hand, and *Plessy* and *Lochner,* on the other, withstands analysis. The joint opinion acknowledges that the Court improved its stature by overruling *Plessy* in *Brown* on a deeply divisive issue. And our decision in *West Coast Hotel,* which overruled *Adkins v. Children's Hospital,* supra, and *Lochner,* was rendered at a time when Congress was considering President Franklin Roosevelt's proposal to "reorganize" this Court and enable him to name six additional Justices in the event that any member of the Court over the age of 70 did not elect to retire. It is difficult to imagine a situation in which the Court would face more intense opposition to a prior ruling than it did at that time, and, under the general principle proclaimed in the joint opinion, the Court seemingly should have responded to this opposition by stubbornly refusing to reexamine the *Lochner* rationale, lest it lose legitimacy by appearing to "overrule under fire."

. . . But the [joint] opinion contends that the Court was entitled to overrule *Plessy* and *Lochner* . . . only because both the Nation and the Court had learned new lessons in the interim. This is at best a feebly supported, *post hoc* rationalization for those decisions.

. . .

When the Court finally recognized its error in *West Coast Hotel,* it did not . . . state that *Lochner* had been based on an economic view that had fallen into disfavor. . . . [T]he theme of the opinion is that the Court had been mistaken as a matter of constitutional law when it embraced "freedom of contract" 32 years previously.

. . . [As for *Brown,*] adherence to *Roe* today under the guise of "legitimacy" would seem to resemble more closely adherence to *Plessy* on the same ground.

Fortunately, the Court did not choose that option in *Brown,* and instead frankly repudiated *Plessy....* [T]he same arguments made before the Court in *Brown* were made in *Plessy* as well. The Court in *Brown* simply recognized, as Justice Harlan had recognized beforehand, that the Fourteenth Amendment does not permit racial segregation. The rule of *Brown* is not tied to popular opinion about the evils of segregation; it is a judgment that the Equal Protection Clause does not permit racial segregation, no matter whether the public might come to believe that it is beneficial. On that ground it stands, and on that ground alone the Court was justified in properly concluding that the *Plessy* Court had erred.

[The] suggestion ... that the propriety of overruling a "divisive" decision depends in part on whether "most people" would now agree that it should be overruled ... is totally at war with the idea of "legitimacy" in whose name it is invoked.... The doctrine of *stare decisis* ... should be no more subject to the vagaries of public opinion than is the basic judicial task.

... [T]he joint opinion forgets that there are two sides to any controversy.... The decision in *Roe* has engendered large demonstrations, including repeated marches on this Court and on Congress, both in opposition to and in support of that opinion. A decision either way on *Roe* can therefore be perceived as favoring one group or the other. But this perceived dilemma arises only if one assumes, as the joint opinion does, that the Court should make its decisions with a view toward speculative public perceptions. If one assumes instead, as the Court surely did in both *Brown* and *West Coast Hotel,* that the Court's legitimacy is enhanced by faithful interpretation of the Constitution irrespective of public opposition, such self-engendered difficulties may be put to one side.

... The joint opinion's message to ... protesters appears to be that they must cease their activities in order to serve their cause, because their protests will only cement in place a decision which by normal standards of *stare decisis* should be reconsidered.... Strong and often misguided criticism of a decision should not render the decision immune from reconsideration, lest a fetish for legitimacy penalize freedom of expression.

... *Roe*['s "fundamental right"-"strict scrutiny"] standard ... at least had a recognized basis in constitutional law.... The same cannot be said for the "undue burden" standard, which is created largely out of whole cloth by the authors of the joint opinion. It is a standard which even today does not command the support of a majority of this Court. And it will not, we believe, result in the sort of "simple limitation," easily applied, which the joint opinion anticipates. In sum, it is a standard ... not built to last.

... [T]his standard is based even more on a judge's subjective determinations than was the trimester framework....

... [T]he undue burden standard presents nothing more workable than the trimester framework which it discards today. Under the guise of the Constitution, this Court will still impart its own preferences on the States in the form of a complex abortion code.

. . .

... A woman's interest in having an abortion is a form of liberty protected by the Due Process Clause, but States may regulate abortion procedures in ways rationally related to a legitimate state interest....

III

A

. . .

Section 3205(a)(1) requires a physician to disclose certain information about the abortion procedure and its risks and alternatives.... [T]his information "clearly is related to maternal health and to the State's legitimate purpose in requiring informed consent." *Akron*.... [Furthermore,] a State "may rationally decide that physicians are better qualified than counselors to impart this information and answer questions about the medical aspects of the available alternatives." ...

Section 3205(a)(2) compels the disclosure, by a physician or a counselor, of information concerning the availability of paternal child support and state-funded alternatives if the woman decides to proceed with her pregnancy.... [P]etitioners do not claim that the information required to be disclosed ... is in any way false or inaccurate.... We conclude that this required presentation of "balanced information" is rationally related to the State's legitimate interest in ensuring that the woman's consent is truly informed, ... and in addition furthers the State's interest in preserving unborn life. That the information might create some uncertainty and persuade some women to forgo abortions does not [mean] the Constitution forbids [providing it]. Indeed, it only demonstrates that this information might very well make a difference, and that it is therefore relevant to a woman's informed choice.... We acknowledge that in *Thornburgh* this Court struck down informed consent requirements similar to the ones at issue here.... In light of our rejection of *Roe*'s "fundamental right" approach to this subject, we do not regard *Thornburgh* as controlling.

For the same reason, we do not feel bound to follow this Court's previous holding that a State's 24–hour mandatory waiting period is unconstitutional. See *Akron* ... [Though] such a provision will result in delays for some women that might not otherwise exist, therefore placing a burden on their liberty[, it] in no way prohibits abortions, and the informed consent and waiting period requirements do not apply in the case of a medical emergency.... [I]n providing time for reflection and reconsideration, the waiting period helps ensure that a woman's decision to abort is a well-considered one, and reasonably furthers the State's legitimate interest in maternal health and in the unborn life of the fetus....

B

. . .

We think it beyond dispute that a State "has a strong and legitimate interest in the welfare of its young citizens, whose immaturity, inexperience, and lack of judgment may sometimes impair their ability to exercise their rights wisely." *Hodgson v. Minnesota* ... (opinion of Stevens, J.). A requirement of parental consent to abortion ... is reasonably designed to further this important and legitimate state interest....

C

... [I]t is not enough for petitioners to show that, in some "worst-case" circumstances, the [spousal] notice provision will operate as a grant of veto power to husbands.... Because they are making a facial challenge to the provision, they must "show that no set of circumstances exists under which the [provision] would be valid." ... This they have failed to do.

The ... spousal notification requirement rationally furthers ... legitimate state interests.... First, a husband's interests in procreation within marriage and in the potential life of his unborn child are certainly substantial ones.... The State itself has legitimate interests both in protecting these interests of the father and in protecting the potential life of the fetus, and the spousal notification requirement is reasonably related to advancing those state interests....

The State also has a legitimate interest in promoting "the integrity of the marital relationship." ... [T]he spousal notice requirement is a rational attempt by the State to improve truthful communication between spouses and encourage collaborative decision-making, and thereby fosters marital integrity....

D

... The District Court found that the[required] reports are kept completely confidential.... We ... conclude that the[] reporting requirements rationally further the State's legitimate interests in advancing the state of medical knowledge concerning maternal health and prenatal life, in gathering statistical information with respect to patients, and in ensuring compliance with other provisions of the Act.

... Petitioners ... contend ... that the forced public disclosure of the information given by facilities receiving public funds serves no legitimate state interest. We disagree.... As the Court of Appeals observed, "[w]hen a state provides money to a private commercial enterprise, there is a legitimate public interest in informing taxpayers who the funds are benefiting and what services the funds are supporting." ... These reporting requirements rationally further this legitimate state interest.

E

Finally, petitioners challenge the medical emergency exception provided for by the Act....

. . .

... [Under] the interpretation of the Court of Appeals in this case ... the provision ... should be upheld. When a woman is faced with any condition that poses a "significant threat to [her] life or health," she is exempted from the Act's consent and notice requirements and may proceed immediately with her abortion.

IV

[W]e would hold that each of the challenged provisions of the Pennsylvania statute is consistent with the Constitution. It bears emphasis that our conclusion in this regard does not carry with it any necessary approval of these regulations. Our task is, as always, to decide only whether the challenged provisions of a law comport with the United States Constitution. If, as we believe, these do, their wisdom as a matter of public policy is for the people of Pennsylvania to decide.

Justice Scalia, with whom The Chief Justice, Justice White, and Justice Thomas join, concurring in the judgment in part and dissenting in part.

... The States may, if they wish, permit abortion-on-demand, but the Constitution does not require them to do so. The permissibility of abortion, and the limitations upon it, are to be resolved like most important questions in our democracy: by citizens trying to persuade one another and then voting....

[T]he issue in this case [is] not whether the power of a woman to abort her unborn child is a "liberty" in the absolute sense; or even whether it is a liberty of great importance to many women. Of course it is both. The issue is whether it is a liberty protected by the Constitution of the United States. I am sure it is not. I reach that conclusion not because of anything so exalted as my views concerning the "concept of existence, of meaning, of the universe, and of the mystery of human life." Rather, I reach it ... because of two simple facts: (1) the Constitution says absolutely nothing about it, and (2) the longstanding traditions of American society have permitted it to be legally proscribed.[1] ...

. . .

... [A]pplying the rational basis test, I would uphold the Pennsylvania statute in its entirety. I must, however, respond to a few of the more outrageous arguments in today's opinion, which it is beyond human nature to leave unanswered....

. . .

... "[R]easoned judgment" does not begin by begging the question, as *Roe* and subsequent cases unquestionably did by assuming that what the State is protecting is the mere "potentiality of human life." ... The whole argument of abortion opponents is that what the Court calls the fetus and what others call the unborn child is a human life. Thus, whatever answer *Roe* came up with after conducting its "balancing" is bound to be wrong, unless it is correct that the human fetus is in some critical sense merely potentially human. There is of course no way to determine that as a legal matter; it is in fact a value judgment....

. . .

... [T]he best the Court can do to explain how it is that the word "liberty" must be thought to include the right to destroy human fetuses is to rattle off a collection of adjectives that simply decorate a value judgment and conceal a political choice.... But it is obvious to anyone applying "reasoned judgment" that the same adjectives can be applied to many forms of conduct that this Court ... has held are not entitled to constitutional protection—because, like abortion, they are forms of conduct that have long been criminalized in American society. Those adjectives might be applied, for example, to homosexual sodomy, polygamy, adult incest, and suicide, all of which are equally "intimate" and "deep[ly] personal" decisions involving "personal autonomy and bodily integrity," and all of which can constitutionally be proscribed

---

1. The Court's suggestion that adherence to tradition would require us to uphold laws against interracial marriage is entirely wrong. Any tradition in that case was contradicted by a text—an Equal Protection Clause that explicitly establishes racial equality as a constitutional value.... The enterprise launched in *Roe,* by contrast, sought to establish—in the teeth of a clear, contrary tradition—a value found nowhere in the constitutional text. There is, of course, no comparable tradition barring recognition of a "liberty interest" in carrying one's child to term free from state efforts to kill it. For that reason, it does not follow that the Constitution does not protect childbirth simply because it does not protect abortion. The Court's contention that the only way to protect childbirth is to protect abortion shows the utter bankruptcy of constitutional analysis deprived of tradition as a validating factor. It drives one to say that the only way to protect the right to eat is to acknowledge the constitutional right to starve oneself to death.

because it is our unquestionable constitutional tradition that they are proscribable. . . .

. . .

. . . The shortcomings of *Roe* did not include lack of clarity; Virtually all regulation of abortion before the third trimester was invalid. But . . . the joint opinion . . . calls upon federal district judges to apply an "undue burden" standard as doubtful in application as it is unprincipled in origin. . . .

. . .

The rootless nature of the "undue burden" standard . . . is . . . reflected in the fact that the joint opinion finds it necessary expressly to repudiate the more narrow formulations used in Justice O'Connor's earlier opinions. Those opinions stated that a statute imposes an "undue burden" if it imposes "absolute obstacles or severe limitations on the abortion decision," *Akron I*, . . . (O'Connor, J., dissenting). . . . Those strong adjectives are conspicuously missing from the joint opinion, whose authors have for some unexplained reason now determined that a burden is "undue" if it merely imposes a "substantial" obstacle to abortion decisions. Justice O'Connor has also abandoned (again without explanation) the view she expressed in . . . *Ashcroft* . . . (1983) (dissenting opinion), that a medical regulation which imposes an "undue burden" could nevertheless be upheld if it "reasonably relate[s] to the preservation and protection of maternal health," . . . . In today's version, even health measures will be upheld only "if they do not constitute an undue burden." Gone too is Justice O'Connor's statement that "the State possesses compelling interests in the protection of potential human life . . . throughout pregnancy," *Akron I* . . .; instead, the State's interest in unborn human life is stealthily downgraded to a merely "substantial" or "profound" interest. (That had to be done, of course, since designating the interest as "compelling" throughout pregnancy would have been, shall we say, a "substantial obstacle" to the joint opinion's determined effort to reaffirm what it views as the "central holding" of *Roe*.) . . . And "viability" is no longer the "arbitrary" dividing line previously decried by Justice O'Connor in *Akron I* . . .; the Court now announces that "the attainment of viability may continue to serve as the critical fact." It is difficult to maintain the illusion that we are interpreting a Constitution rather than inventing one, when we amend its provisions so breezily.

. . . [O]ne must turn to the 23 pages applying that standard to the present facts for further guidance. . . . [T]he joint opinion relies extensively on the factual findings of the District Court, and repeatedly qualifies its conclusions by noting that they are contingent upon the record. . . .

. . .

To the extent I can discern any meaningful content in the "undue burden" standard as applied in the joint opinion, . . . a State may not regulate abortion in such a way as to reduce significantly its incidence. . . . [D]espite flowery rhetoric about the State's "substantial" and "profound" interest in "potential human life," and criticism of *Roe* for undervaluing that interest, the joint opinion permits the State to pursue that interest only so long as it is not too successful. . . .

. . .

The Court's reliance upon *stare decisis* can best be described as contrived. . . . I confess never to have heard of this new, keep-what-you-want-and-throw-away-the-rest version. . . .

... [T]he arbitrary trimester framework, which the Court today discards, was quite as central to *Roe* as the arbitrary viability test, which the Court today retains....

. . .

The Court's description of the place of *Roe* in the social history of the United States is unrecognizable. Not only did *Roe* not ... resolve the deeply divisive issue of abortion; it did more than anything else to nourish it, by elevating it to the national level where it is infinitely more difficult to resolve. National politics were not plagued by abortion protests, national abortion lobbying, or abortion marches on Congress, before *Roe v. Wade* was decided. Profound disagreement existed ... but that disagreement was being worked out at the state level. As with many other issues, the division of sentiment within each State was not as closely balanced as it was among the population of the Nation as a whole, meaning not only that more people would be satisfied with the results of state-by-state resolution, but also that those results would be more stable. Pre–*Roe,* moreover, political compromise was possible.

Roe's mandate for abortion-on-demand destroyed the compromises of the past, rendered compromise impossible for the future, and required the entire issue to be resolved uniformly, at the national level. At the same time, *Roe* created a vast new class of abortion consumers and abortion proponents by eliminating the moral opprobrium that had attached to the act.... Many favor all of those developments, and it is not for me to say that they are wrong. But to portray *Roe* as the statesmanlike "settlement" of a divisive issue ... is nothing less than Orwellian. *Roe* fanned into life an issue that has inflamed our national politics in general, and has obscured with its smoke the selection of Justices to this Court in particular, ever since. And by keeping us in the abortion-umpiring business, it is the perpetuation of that disruption, rather than of any *pax Roeana,* that the Court's new majority decrees.

. . .

It is particularly difficult ... to sit still for the Court's lengthy lecture upon the virtues of "constancy," of "remain[ing] steadfast," of adhering to "principle." Among the five Justices who purportedly adhere to *Roe,* at most three agree upon the principle that constitutes adherence (the joint opinion's "undue burden" standard)—and that principle is inconsistent with *Roe*.... To make matters worse, two of the three, in order thus to remain steadfast, had to abandon previously stated positions....

I cannot agree with, indeed I am appalled by, the Court's suggestion that the decision whether to stand by an erroneous constitutional decision must be strongly influenced—against overruling, no less—by the substantial and continuing public opposition the decision has generated....

[T]he notion that we would decide a case differently from the way we otherwise would have in order to show that we can stand firm against public disapproval is frightening....

. . .

... I am as distressed as the Court is ... about the "political pressure" directed to the Court.... The Court would profit, I think, from giving less attention to the fact of this distressing phenomenon, and more attention to the cause of it ...: a new mode of constitutional adjudication that relies not upon text and traditional practice to determine the law, but upon what the Court calls "reasoned judgment," which turns out to be nothing but philosophical predilection and moral intuition. . . .

. . . If . . . the "liberties" protected by the Constitution are, as the Court says, undefined and unbounded, then the people should demonstrate, to protest that we do not implement their values instead of ours. Not only that, but confirmation hearings for new Justices should deteriorate into question-and-answer sessions in which Senators go through a list of their constituents' most favored and most disfavored alleged constitutional rights, and seek the nominee's commitment to support or oppose them. Value judgments, after all, should be voted on, not dictated; and if our Constitution has somehow accidently committed them to the Supreme Court, at least we can have a sort of plebiscite each time a new nominee to that body is put forward. Justice Blackmun not only regards this prospect with equanimity, he solicits it.

. . .

STENBERG v. CARHART, 530 U.S. 914 (2000). The Court chose "not [to] revisit [the] legal principles" of *Roe* and *Casey*, but to "apply them[,]" and held unconstitutional a Nebraska criminal statute banning "partial birth abortion . . ., unless . . . Necessary to save the life of the mother. . . ." The statute defined "partial birth abortion" as "an abortion procedure in which the person performing the abortion partially delivers vaginally a living unborn child before killing the unborn child and completing the delivery" and further defined the phrase "partially delivers vaginally a living unborn child before killing the unborn child" to mean "deliberately and intentionally delivering into the vagina a living unborn child, or a substantial portion thereof, for the purpose of performing a procedure that the person performing such procedure knows will kill the unborn child and does kill the unborn child."

[handwritten margin note: partial birth abortion definitions]

Justice Breyer's majority opinion observed that "[b]ecause Nebraska law seeks to ban one method of aborting a pregnancy, we must describe and then discuss several different abortion procedures." Indeed, the majority thought that "the outcome of this case depends" upon "technical distinctions among different abortion methods and related factual matters[.]" During the first trimester of pregnancy, when about 90% of all abortions are performed, the most common method is " 'vacuum aspiration,' which involves insertion of a vacuum tube . . . into the uterus to evacuate the contents." During the second trimester (12 to 24 weeks), when approximately 10% of abortions are performed, the most common procedure is "dilation and evacuation" (D & E), the varying forms of which all include dilating the cervix, removing some fetal tissue using nonvacuum instruments, and possibly dismembering the fetus or collapsing fetal parts "to facilitate evacuation from the uterus"—a dismemberment the Court said "typically occurs as the doctor pulls a portion of the fetus through the cervix into the birth canal." One variation, the "intact D & E" method, is "used after 16 weeks at the earliest, as . . . the fetal skull becomes too large to pass through the cervix"; it "involves removing the fetus from the uterus through the cervix 'intact,' *i.e.*, in one pass, rather than in several passes." Further, the "intact D & E proceeds in one of two ways. . . . If the fetus presents head first . . ., the doctor collapses the skull . . . and . . . then extracts the entire fetus through the cervix. If the fetus presents feet first (a breech presentation), the doctor pulls the fetal body through the cervix, collapses the skull, and extracts the fetus through the cervix. . . . The breech extraction version . . . is also known commonly as 'dilation and extraction,' or D & X." To reduce maternal health risks, "Dr. Carhart testified he attempts to use the intact D & E procedure during weeks 16 to 20. . . ." The majority also noted the District Court's conclusion "that 'the evidence is both clear and convincing that Carhart's D & X procedure is superior to, and safer than, the ... other abortion procedures used during the relevant gestational period in the 10 to 20 cases a year" he confronts.

The Court held the statute unconstitutional

"for at least two independent reasons. First, the law lacks any exception ' "for the preservation of the ... health of the mother.' " Casey, ... (joint opinion of O'Connor, Kennedy, and Souter, JJ.). Second, it "imposes an undue burden on a woman's ability" to choose a D & E abortion, thereby unduly burdening the right to choose abortion itself. . . .

A

"The Casey joint opinion reiterated what the Court held in Roe; that ' "subsequent to viability, the State in promoting its interest in the potentiality of human life may, if it chooses, regulate, and even proscribe, abortion *except where it is necessary, in appropriate medical judgment, for the preservation of the life or health of the mother.*' " ... (quoting Roe ...) (emphasis added).

". . . Since the law requires a health exception in order to validate even a postviability abortion regulation, it at a minimum requires the same in respect to previability regulation. . . .

"The quoted standard also depends on the state regulations 'promoting [the State's] interest in the potentiality of human life.' The Nebraska law, of course, does not directly further an interest 'in the potentiality of human life' by saving the fetus in question from destruction, as it regulates only a *method* of performing abortion. Nebraska describes its interests differently. It says the law ' "shows concern for the life of the unborn," "prevents cruelty to partially born children,' and 'preserves the integrity of the medical profession.' ... But we cannot see how the interest-related differences could make any difference to ... the application of the 'health' requirement.

". . .

". . . Our cases have repeatedly invalidated statutes that in the process of regulating the *methods* of abortion, imposed significant health risks. They make clear that a risk to a woman's health is the same whether it happens to arise from regulating a particular method of abortion, or from barring abortion entirely."

The Court rejected Nebraska's argument that no health exception was needed because its ban left safe alternatives and created no health risk to women. The Court believed "the findings and evidence support Dr. Carhart. The State fails to demonstrate that banning D & X without a health exception may not create significant health risks for women, because the record shows that significant medical authority supports the proposition that in some circumstances, D & X would be the safest procedure." Though "[b]y no means must a State grant physicians 'unfettered discretion' in their selection of abortion methods[,] ... where substantial medical authority supports the proposition that banning a particular abortion procedure could endanger women's health, Casey requires the statute to include a health exception when the procedure is ' "necessary, in appropriate medical judgment, for the preservation of the life or health of the mother.' "

With respect to the majority's alternative basis for finding the statute invalid, "Nebraska does not deny that the statute imposes an 'undue burden' [on a woman's right to terminate her pregnancy before viability] *if* it applies to the more commonly used D & E procedure as well as to D & X." In the Court's view, the statute's plain language, not reasonably subject to a narrowing interpretation, did not permit distinguishing "between D & E (where a foot or arm is drawn through the cervix) and D & X (where the body up to the head is drawn through the cervix)" and "[t]he dissents cannot explain how introduction of a substantial portion of a fetus into the vagina pursuant to D & X is a 'delivery,' while introduction pursuant to D & E is not.":

> "In sum, using this law some present prosecutors and future Attorneys General may choose to pursue physicians who use D & E procedures, the most commonly used method for performing previability second trimester abortions.... The result is an undue burden upon a woman's right to make an abortion decision."

A concurring opinion by Justice Stevens, joined by Justice Ginsburg, said in part:

> "... [D]uring the past 27 years, the central holding of Roe v. Wade, 410 U.S. 113 (1973), has been endorsed by all but 4 of the 17 Justices who have addressed the issue. That holding ... makes it impossible for me to understand how a State has any legitimate interest in requiring a doctor to follow any procedure other than the one that he or she reasonably believes will best protect the woman in her exercise of this constitutional liberty. But one need not even approach this view today to conclude that Nebraska's law must fall. For the notion that either of these two equally gruesome procedures performed at this late stage of gestation is more akin to infanticide than the other, or that the State furthers any legitimate interest by banning one but not the other, is simply irrational."

By contrast, Justice O'Connor's concurring opinion declared that "a ban on partial-birth abortion that only proscribed the D & X method of abortion and that included an exception to preserve the life and health of the mother would be constitutional in my view."

In her concurrence, Justice Ginsburg, joined by Justice Stevens, wrote that the statute "does not save any fetus from destruction" nor "seek to protect the lives or health of pregnant women[,]" and that, "as Justice Stevens points out, the most common method of performing previability second trimester abortions is no less distressing or susceptible to gruesome description." This led her to suggest that "the law prohibits the procedure because the State legislators seek to chip away at the private choice shielded by Roe v. Wade, even as modified by *Casey*" and in that way imposes an undue burden.

There were four dissents. Chief Justice Rehnquist continued to disagree with *Casey* and also joined the dissents of Justices Kennedy and Thomas, who "have correctly applied *Casey*'s principles." Justice Scalia wrote separately to urge that "*Casey* must be overruled[,]" saying in part that "those who believe that a 5–to–4 vote on a policy matter by unelected lawyers should not overcome the judgment of 30 state legislatures have a problem, not with the *application* of *Casey*, but with its *existence*." Justice Kennedy's lengthy dissent, joined by the Chief Justice, complained that Nebraska sought "only to ban the D & X" and that the Court gave too little recognition to *Casey*'s premise that "the States hav[e] an important constitutional role in defining their interests in the abortion debate." He wrote in part:

> "Nebraska was entitled to find the existence of a consequential moral difference between the procedures. We are referred to substantial medical authority that D & X perverts the natural birth process to a greater degree than D & E, commandeering the live birth process until the skull is pierced. American Medical Association (AMA) publications describe the D & X abortion method as 'ethically wrong.' ... D & X's stronger resem-

D&X is more like infanticide

what is the dissent's stand?

blance to infanticide means Nebraska could conclude the procedure presents a greater risk of disrespect for life and a consequent greater risk to the profession and society, which depend for their sustenance upon reciprocal recognition of dignity and respect. The Court is without authority to second-guess this conclusion.

"... [A]s an ethical and moral matter D & X is distinct from D & E and is a more serious concern for medical ethics and the morality of the larger society the medical profession must serve.... By its regulation, Nebraska instructs all participants in the abortion process, including the mother, of its moral judgment that all life, including the life of the unborn, is to be respected. The participants, Nebraska has determined, cannot be indifferent to the procedure used and must refrain from using the natural delivery process to kill the fetus. The differentiation between the procedures is itself a moral statement, serving to promote respect for human life...."

Justice Kennedy also thought the Court deferred too much to the physician's judgment about safety and that, under *Casey*, "Nebraska ... was entitled to conclude that its ban, while advancing important interests regarding the sanctity of life, deprived no woman of a safe abortion and therefore did not impose a substantial obstacle on the rights of any woman." He found "[s]ubstantial evidence support[ing] Nebraska's conclusion that its law denies no woman a safe abortion" and that at most "the D & X ... may present an unquantified lower risk of complication for a particular patient but that other proven safe procedures remain available even for this patient." Moreover, he thought it "important to recognize that the D & X is effective only when the fetus is close to viable or, in fact, viable; thus the State is regulating the process at the point where its interest in life is nearing its peak." State legislatures "have superior factfinding capabilities" over courts in "evaluat[ing] the relative worth of particular surgical procedures[,]" and, under *Casey*, "[r]ather than exalting the right of a physician to practice medicine with unfettered discretion, ... [t]he question ... is whether there was substantial and objective medical evidence to demonstrate the State had considerable support for its conclusion that the ban created a substantial risk to no woman's health." Moreover, Justice O'Connor's concurring "assurance is meaningless[,]" because a "ban which depends on the 'appropriate medical judgment' of Dr. Carhart is no ban at all"—"the vice of a health exception resting in the physician's discretion." Especially because a "commonsense understanding" of the statutory text "must be that the statute covers only the D & X" and concluding otherwise "ignore[s] the settled rule against deciding unnecessary constitutional questions[,]" the "immense constitutional holding" that "the statute requires a health exception which, for all practical purposes and certainly in the circumstances of this case, allows the physician to make the determination in his own professional judgment ... is unnecessary" as well as "incorrect."

Justice Thomas also dissented, joined by the Chief Justice and Justice Scalia. Apart from his view that the "standard set forth in the *Casey* joint opinion ... is ... as illegitimate as the standard it purported to replace[,]" he criticized the majority for "giv[ing] the lie to the promise of *Casey* that regulations that do no more than 'express profound respect for the life of the unborn are permitted, if they are not a substantial obstacle to the woman's exercise of the right to choose' whether or not to have an abortion." Justice Thomas argued at length—based on the statutory language, the common use of the term "partial birth abortion" to refer only to the D & X procedure, and what he perceived as the statute's susceptibility to any narrowing construction needed—"that the Nebraska statute does not prohibit the D & E procedure."

He readily concluded that the "States have a legitimate interest in banning" partial birth abortion, and he interpreted *"Roe* and *Casey"* to have "addressed only the situation in which a woman must obtain an abortion because of some threat to her health from continued pregnancy"—not "cases in which a physician considers one prohibited method of abortion to be preferable to permissible methods." According to Justice Thomas, "[t]oday's majority and Justice O'Connor twist *Roe* and *Casey* to apply to the situation in which a woman desires—for whatever reason—an abortion and wishes to obtain the abortion by some particular method." Furthermore, he complained,

> "... the majority expands the health exception rule articulated in *Casey* in one additional and equally pernicious way. Although *Roe* and *Casey* mandated a health exception for cases in which abortion is 'necessary' for a woman's health, the majority concludes that a procedure is 'necessary' if it has any comparative health benefits.... In effect, no regulation of abortion procedures is permitted because there will always be *some* support for a procedure and there will always be some doctors who conclude that the procedure is preferable.... This Court has now expressed its own conclusion that there is 'highly plausible' support for the view that partial birth abortion is safer, which, in the majority's view, means that the procedure is therefore 'necessary.' ... Therefore, Justice O'Connor's assurance that the constitutional failings of Nebraska's statute can be easily fixed is illusory. The majority's insistence on a health exception is a fig leaf barely covering its hostility to any abortion regulation by the States—a hostility that *Casey* purported to reject."

Finally, Justice Thomas argued that "prohibiting partial birth abortion without a health exception" did not pose "a substantial obstacle to obtaining an abortion"—the inquiry he thought *Casey* articulated. He wrote in part:

> "The *Casey* joint opinion makes clear that the Court should not strike down state regulations of abortion based on the fact that some women might face a marginally higher health risk from the regulation. In *Casey*, the Court upheld a 24–hour waiting period even though the Court credited evidence that for some women the delay would, in practice, be much longer than 24 hours, and even though it was undisputed that any delay in obtaining an abortion would impose additional health risks....

> "...

> "Like the *Casey* 24–hour waiting period, ... any increased health risk to women imposed by the partial birth abortion ban is minimal at most.... A select committee of ACOG 'could identify no circumstances under which this procedure ... would be the only option to save the life or preserve the health of the woman.' ... And, an ad hoc coalition of doctors, including former Surgeon General Koop, concluded that there are no medical conditions that require use of the partial birth abortion procedure to preserve the mother's health ...

> "In fact, there was evidence before the Nebraska Legislature that partial birth abortion *increases* health risks relative to other procedures....

> "...

> "... [E]ven if I were to assume credible evidence on both sides of the debate, that fact should resolve the undue-burden question in favor of allowing Nebraska to legislate. Where no one knows whether a regulation of abortion poses any burden at all, the burden surely does not amount to a

'substantial obstacle.' Under *Casey*, in such a case we should defer to the legislative judgment...."

Lawrence v. Texas

539 U.S. 558, 123 S.Ct. 2472, 156 L.Ed.2d 508 (2003).

Justice Kennedy delivered the opinion of the Court.

Liberty protects the person from unwarranted government intrusions into a dwelling or other private places. In our tradition the State is not omnipresent in the home. And there are other spheres of our lives and existence, outside the home, where the State should not be a dominant presence. Freedom extends beyond spatial bounds. Liberty presumes an autonomy of self that includes freedom of thought, belief, expression, and certain intimate conduct. The instant case involves liberty of the person both in its spatial and more transcendent dimensions.

I

The question before the Court is the validity of a Texas statute making it a crime for two persons of the same sex to engage in certain intimate sexual conduct.

In Houston, Texas, officers ... respon[ding] to a reported weapons disturbance ... entered an apartment where ... Lawrence ... resided [and] observed Lawrence and another man, Tyron Garner, engaging in a sexual act. The two petitioners were arrested ... and [later] convicted....

The complaints described their crime as "deviate sexual intercourse, namely anal sex, with a member of the same sex (man)." ... The applicable state law is Tex. Penal Code Ann. § 21.06(a) (2003). It provides: "A person commits an offense if he engages in deviate sexual intercourse with another individual of the same sex." The statute defines "[d]eviate sexual intercourse" as follows:

[handwritten margin note: Defined as deviate sexual intercourse]

"(A) any contact between any part of the genitals of one person and the mouth or anus of another person; or

"(B) the penetration of the genitals or the anus of another person with an object." § 21.01(1).

... The petitioners ... were each fined $200 and assessed court costs of $141.25....

The Court of Appeals for the Texas Fourteenth District ... en banc ..., in a divided opinion, ... affirmed the convictions[,] consider[ing] our decision in *Bowers v. Hardwick,* 478 U.S. 186 (1986), to be controlling on the federal due process aspect of the case....

. . .

II

We conclude the case should be resolved by determining whether the petitioners were free as adults to engage in the private conduct in the exercise of their liberty under the Due Process Clause of the Fourteenth Amendment to the Constitution. For this inquiry we deem it necessary to reconsider the Court's holding in *Bowers.*

. . .

The facts in *Bowers* had some similarities to the instant case.... One difference ... is that the Georgia statute prohibited the conduct whether or not the participants were of the same sex, while the Texas statute ... applies only to participants of the same sex.... [In *Bowers*, t]he Court, in an opinion by Justice White, sustained the Georgia law. Four Justices dissented....

The Court began its substantive discussion in *Bowers* as follows: "The issue presented is whether the Federal Constitution confers a fundamental right upon homosexuals to engage in sodomy and hence invalidates the laws of the many States that still make such conduct illegal and have done so for a very long time." That statement, we now conclude, discloses the Court's own failure to appreciate the extent of the liberty at stake. To say that the issue in *Bowers* was simply the right to engage in certain sexual conduct demeans the claim the individual put forward, just as it would demean a married couple were it to be said marriage is simply about the right to have sexual intercourse. The laws involved in *Bowers* and here are, to be sure, statutes that purport to do no more than prohibit a particular sexual act. Their penalties and purposes, though, have more far-reaching consequences, touching upon the most private human conduct, sexual behavior, and in the most private of places, the home. The statutes do seek to control a personal relationship that, whether or not entitled to formal recognition in the law, is within the liberty of persons to choose without being punished as criminals.

This, as a general rule, should counsel against attempts by the State, or a court, to define the meaning of the relationship or to set its boundaries absent injury to a person or abuse of an institution the law protects. It suffices for us to acknowledge that adults may choose to enter upon this relationship in the confines of their homes and their own private lives and still retain their dignity as free persons. When sexuality finds overt expression in intimate conduct with another person, the conduct can be but one element in a personal bond that is more enduring. The liberty protected by the Constitution allows homosexual persons the right to make this choice.

Having misapprehended the claim [as one of] a fundamental right to engage in consensual sodomy, the *Bowers* Court said: "Proscriptions against that conduct have ancient roots." ... In academic writings, and in many of the scholarly *amicus* briefs filed to assist the Court in this case, there are fundamental criticisms of the historical premises relied upon by the majority and concurring opinions in *Bowers*.... We need not enter this debate in the attempt to reach a definitive historical judgment, but the following considerations counsel against adopting the definitive conclusions upon which *Bowers* placed such reliance.

[T]here is no longstanding history in this country of laws directed at homosexual conduct as a distinct matter. Beginning in colonial times there were prohibitions of sodomy derived from the English criminal laws.... The English prohibition was understood to include relations between men and women as well as relations between men and men.... Nineteenth-century commentators similarly read American sodomy, buggery, and crime-against-nature statutes as criminalizing certain relations between men and women and between men and men.... The absence of legal prohibitions focusing on homosexual conduct may be explained in part by noting that according to some scholars the concept of the homosexual as a distinct category of person did not emerge until the late 19th century.... Thus early American sodomy laws were not directed at homosexuals as such but instead sought to prohibit nonprocreative sexual activity more generally. This does not suggest approval of homosexual conduct. It does tend to show that this particular form of conduct was not thought of as a separate category from like conduct between heterosexual persons.

Laws prohibiting sodomy do not seem to have been enforced against consenting adults acting in private.... Instead ..., 19th-century sodomy prosecutions typically involved relations between men and minor girls or minor boys, relations between adults involving force, relations between adults implicating disparity in status, or relations between men and animals.

... The longstanding criminal prohibition of homosexual sodomy upon which the *Bowers* decision placed such reliance is as consistent with a general condemnation of nonprocreative sex as it is with an established tradition of prosecuting acts because of their homosexual character.

... [F]ar from possessing "ancient roots," *Bowers....*, American laws targeting same-sex couples did not develop until the last third of the 20th century. The reported decisions concerning the prosecution of consensual, homosexual sodomy between adults for the years 1880–1995 are not always clear in the details, but a significant number involved conduct in a public place....

It was not until the 1970's that any State singled out same-sex relations for criminal prosecution, and only nine States have done so.... Post-*Bowers* even some of these States did not adhere to the policy of suppressing homosexual conduct. Over the course of the last decades, States with same-sex prohibitions have moved toward abolishing them....

In summary, the historical grounds relied upon in *Bowers* are more complex than the majority opinion and the concurring opinion by Chief Justice Burger indicate....

[O]f course, ... the Court in *Bowers* was making the broader point that for centuries there have been powerful voices to condemn homosexual conduct as immoral. The condemnation has been shaped by religious beliefs, conceptions of right and acceptable behavior, and respect for the traditional family. For many persons these are not trivial concerns but profound and deep convictions accepted as ethical and moral principles to which they aspire and which thus determine the course of their lives. These considerations do not answer the question before us, however. The issue is whether the majority may use the power of the State to enforce these views on the whole society through operation of the criminal law. "Our obligation is to define the liberty of all, not to mandate our own moral code." *Planned Parenthood of Southeastern Pa. v. Casey,* 505 U.S. 833, 850 (1992).

Chief Justice Burger joined the opinion for the Court in *Bowers* and further explained his views as follows: "Decisions of individuals relating to homosexual conduct have been subject to state intervention throughout the history of Western civilization. Condemnation of those practices is firmly rooted in Judeao–Christian moral and ethical standards." ... As with Justice White's assumptions about history, scholarship casts some doubt on the sweeping nature of the statement by Chief Justice Burger as it pertains to private homosexual conduct between consenting adults.... In all events we think that our laws and traditions in the past half century are of most relevance here. These references show an emerging awareness that liberty gives substantial protection to adult persons in deciding how to conduct their private lives in matters pertaining to sex. "[H]istory and tradition are the starting point but not in all cases the ending point of the substantive due process inquiry." *County of Sacramento v. Lewis,* 523 U.S. 833, 857 (1998) (Kennedy, J., concurring).

This emerging recognition should have been apparent when *Bowers* was decided. In 1955 the American Law Institute promulgated the Model Penal Code and made clear that it did not recommend or provide for "criminal penalties for consensual sexual relations conducted in private." ALI, Model Penal Code § 213.2, Comment 2, p. 372 (1980). It justified its decision on three grounds: (1) The prohibitions undermined respect for the law by penalizing conduct many people engaged in; (2) the statutes regulated private conduct not harmful to others; and (3) the laws were arbitrarily enforced and thus invited the danger of blackmail.... In 1961 Illinois changed its laws to conform to the Model Penal Code. Other States soon followed....

In *Bowers* the Court referred to the fact that before 1961 all 50 States had outlawed sodomy, and that at the time of the Court's decision 24 States and the District of Columbia had sodomy laws.... Justice Powell pointed out that these prohibitions often were being ignored, however. Georgia, for instance, had not sought to enforce its law for decades....

... A committee advising the British Parliament recommended in 1957 repeal of laws punishing homosexual conduct.... Parliament enacted the substance of those recommendations 10 years later....

Of even more importance, almost five years before *Bowers* was decided the European Court of Human Rights ... held that [Northern Ireland] laws proscribing [consensual homosexual] conduct were invalid under the European Convention on Human Rights. *Dudgeon v. United Kingdom*, 45 Eur. Ct. H. R. (1981).... Authoritative in all countries that are members of the Council of Europe (21 nations then, 45 nations now), the decision is at odds with the premise in *Bowers* that the claim put forward was insubstantial in our Western civilization.

In our own constitutional system the deficiencies in *Bowers* became even more apparent in the years following its announcement. The 25 States with laws prohibiting the relevant conduct referenced in the *Bowers* decision are reduced now to 13, of which 4 enforce their laws only against homosexual conduct. In those States where sodomy is still proscribed, whether for same-sex or heterosexual conduct, there is a pattern of nonenforcement with respect to consenting adults acting in private. The State of Texas admitted in 1994 that as of that date it had not prosecuted anyone under those circumstances....

Two principal cases decided after *Bowers* cast its holding into even more doubt. In *Planned Parenthood of Southeastern Pa. v. Casey,* 505 U.S. 833 (1992), the Court reaffirmed ... that our laws and tradition afford constitutional protection to personal decisions relating to marriage, procreation, contraception, family relationships, child rearing, and education.... [W]e stated as follows:

"These matters, involving the most intimate and personal choices a person may make in a lifetime, choices central to personal dignity and autonomy, are central to the liberty protected by the Fourteenth Amendment. At the heart of liberty is the right to define one's own concept of existence, of meaning, of the universe, and of the mystery of human life. Beliefs about these matters could not define the attributes of personhood were they formed under compulsion of the State."

Persons in a homosexual relationship may seek autonomy for these purposes, just as heterosexual persons do. The decision in *Bowers* would deny them this right.

[S]econd[, in] *Romer v. Evans,* 517 U.S. 620 (1996)[,] the Court struck down class-based legislation directed at homosexuals as a violation of the Equal

Protection Clause. *Romer* invalidated an amendment to Colorado's constitution which named as a solitary class persons who were homosexuals, lesbians, or bisexual either by "orientation, conduct, practices or relationships," . . ., and deprived them of protection under state antidiscrimination laws. We concluded that the provision was "born of animosity toward the class of persons affected" and further that it had no rational relation to a legitimate governmental purpose. . . .

[A]n alternative argument . . . contend[s] that *Romer* provides the basis for declaring the Texas statute invalid under the Equal Protection Clause. That is a tenable argument, but we conclude the instant case requires us to address whether *Bowers* itself has continuing validity. Were we to hold the statute invalid under the Equal Protection Clause some might question whether a prohibition would be valid if drawn differently, say, to prohibit the conduct both between same-sex and different-sex participants.

Equality of treatment and the due process right to demand respect for conduct protected by the substantive guarantee of liberty are linked in important respects, and a decision on the latter point advances both interests. If protected conduct is made criminal and the law which does so remains unexamined for its substantive validity, its stigma might remain even if it were not enforceable as drawn for equal protection reasons. When homosexual conduct is made criminal by the law of the State, that declaration in and of itself is an invitation to subject homosexual persons to discrimination both in the public and in the private spheres. The central holding of *Bowers* has been brought in question by this case, and it should be addressed. Its continuance as precedent demeans the lives of homosexual persons.

The stigma this criminal statute imposes, moreover, is not trivial. The offense, to be sure, is but a class C misdemeanor, a minor offense in the Texas legal system. Still, it remains a criminal offense with all that imports for the dignity of the persons charged[—a] record[, . . . possible] registration [as] sex offenders . . . [in] at least four States [and] the other collateral consequences always following a conviction, such as notations on job application forms. . . .

The foundations of *Bowers* have sustained serious erosion from our recent decisions in *Casey* and *Romer*. When our precedent has been thus weakened, criticism from other sources is of greater significance. In the United States criticism of *Bowers* has been substantial and continuing, disapproving of its reasoning in all respects, not just as to its historical assumptions. See, *e.g.,* C. Fried, Order and Law: Arguing the Reagan Revolution—A Firsthand Account 81B84 (1991); R. Posner, Sex and Reason 341B350 (1992). The courts of five different States have declined to follow it in interpreting provisions in their own state constitutions parallel to the Due Process Clause of the Fourteenth Amendment. . . .

To the extent *Bowers* relied on values we share with a wider civilization, it should be noted that the reasoning and holding in *Bowers* have been rejected elsewhere. The European Court of Human Rights has followed not *Bowers* but its own decision in *Dudgeon v. United Kingdom* . . . . Other nations, too, have taken action consistent with an affirmation of the protected right of homosexual adults to engage in intimate, consensual conduct. . . . The right the petitioners seek in this case has been accepted as an integral part of human freedom in many other countries. There has been no showing that in this country the governmental interest in circumscribing personal choice is somehow more legitimate or urgent.

The doctrine of *stare decisis* is essential to the respect accorded to the judgments of the Court and to the stability of the law. It is not, however, an inexorable command.... In *Casey* we noted that when a Court is asked to overrule a precedent recognizing a constitutional liberty interest, individual or societal reliance on the existence of that liberty cautions with particular strength against reversing course.... The holding in *Bowers*, however, has not induced detrimental reliance comparable to some instances where recognized individual rights are involved. Indeed, there has been no individual or societal reliance on *Bowers* of the sort that could counsel against overturning its holding once there are compelling reasons to do so. *Bowers* itself causes uncertainty, for the precedents before and after its issuance contradict its central holding.

The rationale of *Bowers* does not withstand careful analysis. In his dissenting opinion in *Bowers* Justice Stevens came to these conclusions:

"Our prior cases make two propositions abundantly clear. First, the fact that the governing majority in a State has traditionally viewed a particular practice as immoral is not a sufficient reason for upholding a law prohibiting the practice; neither history nor tradition could save a law prohibiting miscegenation from constitutional attack. Second, individual decisions by married persons, concerning the intimacies of their physical relationship, even when not intended to produce offspring, are a form of 'liberty' protected by the Due Process Clause of the Fourteenth Amendment. Moreover, this protection extends to intimate choices by unmarried as well as married persons." ...

Justice Stevens' analysis, in our view, should have been controlling in *Bowers* and should control here.

Bowers was not correct when it was decided, and it is not correct today. It ought not to remain binding precedent. *Bowers v. Hardwick* should be and now is overruled.

The present case does not involve minors. It does not involve persons who might be injured or coerced or who are situated in relationships where consent might not easily be refused. It does not involve public conduct or prostitution. It does not involve whether the government must give formal recognition to any relationship that homosexual persons seek to enter. The case does involve two adults who, with full and mutual consent from each other, engaged in sexual practices common to a homosexual lifestyle. The petitioners are entitled to respect for their private lives. The State cannot demean their existence or control their destiny by making their private sexual conduct a crime. Their right to liberty under the Due Process Clause gives them the full right to engage in their conduct without intervention of the government. "It is a promise of the Constitution that there is a realm of personal liberty which the government may not enter." *Casey*,.... The Texas statute furthers no legitimate state interest which can justify its intrusion into the personal and private life of the individual.

Had those who drew and ratified the Due Process Clauses of the Fifth Amendment or the Fourteenth Amendment known the components of liberty in its manifold possibilities, they might have been more specific. They did not presume to have this insight. They knew times can blind us to certain truths and later generations can see that laws once thought necessary and proper in fact serve only to oppress. As the Constitution endures, persons in every generation can invoke its principles in their own search for greater freedom.

[R]eversed ... and ... remanded for further proceedings not inconsistent with this opinion.

Justice O'Connor, concurring in the judgment.

... I joined *Bowers*, and do not join the Court in overruling it. Nevertheless, I agree ... that Texas' statute banning same-sex sodomy is unconstitutional ... base[d] on the Fourteenth Amendment's Equal Protection Clause.

. . .

[handwritten margin note: says it is an equal protection issue.]

... We have consistently held ... that some objectives, such as "a bare ... desire to harm a politically unpopular group," are not legitimate state interests.... When a law exhibits such a desire to harm a politically unpopular group, we have applied a more searching form of rational basis review to strike down such laws under the Equal Protection Clause.

We have been most likely to [do so] where, as here, the challenged legislation inhibits personal relationships. In *Department of Agriculture v. Moreno*, for example, we held that a law preventing those households containing an individual unrelated to any other member of the household from receiving food stamps violated equal protection because the purpose of the law was to " 'discriminate against hippies.' " ... The asserted governmental interest in preventing food stamp fraud was not deemed sufficient to satisfy rational basis review.... In *Eisenstadt v. Baird*, 405 U.S. 438, 447–455 (1972), we refused to sanction a law that discriminated between married and unmarried persons by prohibiting the distribution of contraceptives to single persons. Likewise, in *Cleburne v. Cleburne Living Center,* ... we held that it was irrational for a State to require a home for the mentally disabled to obtain a special use permit when other residences—like fraternity houses and apartment buildings—did not have to obtain such a permit. And in *Romer v. Evans,* we disallowed a state statute that "impos[ed] a broad and undifferentiated disability on a single named group"—specifically, homosexuals....

... Sodomy between opposite-sex partners ... is not a crime in Texas. That is, Texas treats the same conduct differently based solely on the participants. Those harmed by this law are people who have a same-sex sexual orientation and thus are more likely to engage in behavior prohibited by § 21.06.

The Texas statute makes homosexuals unequal in the eyes of the law by making particular conduct—and only that conduct—subject to criminal sanction....

... Texas' sodomy law brands all homosexuals as criminals, thereby making it more difficult for homosexuals to be treated in the same manner as everyone else....

Texas attempts to justify its law, and the effects of the law, by arguing that the statute satisfies rational basis review because it furthers the legitimate governmental interest of the promotion of morality. In *Bowers*, we held that a state law criminalizing sodomy as applied to homosexual couples did not violate substantive due process. We rejected the argument that no rational basis existed to justify the law, pointing to the government's interest in promoting morality.... The only question in front of the Court in *Bowers* was whether the substantive component of the Due Process Clause protected a right to engage in homosexual sodomy.... *Bowers* did not hold that moral disapproval of a group is a rational basis under the Equal Protection Clause to criminalize homosexual sodomy when heterosexual sodomy is not punished.

This case raises a different issue than *Bowers:* whether, under the Equal Protection Clause, moral disapproval is a legitimate state interest to justify by itself a statute that bans homosexual sodomy, but not heterosexual sodomy. It is not. Moral disapproval of this group, like a bare desire to harm the group, is an interest that is insufficient to satisfy rational basis review under the Equal

Protection Clause.... Indeed, we have never held that moral disapproval, without any other asserted state interest, is a sufficient rationale under the Equal Protection Clause to justify a law that discriminates among groups of persons.

Moral disapproval of a group cannot be a legitimate governmental interest under the Equal Protection Clause because legal classifications must not be "drawn for the purpose of disadvantaging the group burdened by the law." ... Texas' invocation of moral disapproval as a legitimate state interest proves nothing more than Texas' desire to criminalize homosexual sodomy. But the Equal Protection Clause prevents a State from creating "a classification of persons undertaken for its own sake." ... And because Texas so rarely enforces its sodomy law as applied to private, consensual acts, the law serves more as a statement of dislike and disapproval against homosexuals than as a tool to stop criminal behavior. The Texas sodomy law "raise[s] the inevitable inference that the disadvantage imposed is born of animosity toward the class of persons affected." ...

Texas argues, however, that the sodomy law does not discriminate against homosexual persons ...[—]only against homosexual conduct. [But] the conduct targeted by this law is conduct that is closely correlated with being homosexual. Under such circumstances, Texas' sodomy law is targeted at more than conduct. It is instead directed toward gay persons as a class.... When a State makes homosexual conduct criminal, and not "deviate sexual intercourse" committed by persons of different sexes, "that declaration in and of itself is an invitation to subject homosexual persons to discrimination both in the public and in the private spheres."

Indeed, Texas law confirms that the sodomy statute is directed toward homosexuals as a class. In Texas, calling a person a homosexual is slander *per se* because the word "homosexual" "impute[s] the commission of a crime." ... The State has admitted that because of the sodomy law, *being* homosexual carries the presumption of being a criminal. See *State v. Morales*, 826 S. W. 2d, at 202–203 ("[T]he statute brands lesbians and gay men as criminals and thereby legally sanctions discrimination against them in a variety of ways unrelated to the criminal law"). Texas' sodomy law therefore results in discrimination against homosexuals as a class in an array of areas outside the criminal law.... In *Romer v. Evans,* we refused to sanction a law that singled out homosexuals "for disfavored legal status." ... The same is true here. The Equal Protection Clause " 'neither knows nor tolerates classes among citizens.' " ... (quoting *Plessy v. Ferguson,* 163 U.S. 537, 559 (1896) (Harlan, J. dissenting)).

A State can of course assign certain consequences to a violation of its criminal law. But the State cannot single out one identifiable class of citizens for punishment that does not apply to everyone else, with moral disapproval as the only asserted state interest for the law....

Whether a sodomy law ... neutral both in effect and application, see *Yick Wo v. Hopkins,* 118 U.S. 356 (1886), would violate the substantive component of the Due Process Clause is an issue that need not be decided today. I am confident, however, that so long as the Equal Protection Clause requires a sodomy law to apply equally to the private consensual conduct of homosexuals and heterosexuals alike, such a law would not long stand in our democratic society....

That this law as applied to private, consensual conduct is unconstitutional under the Equal Protection Clause does not mean that other laws distinguishing between heterosexuals and homosexuals would similarly fail under rational basis review. Texas cannot assert any legitimate state interest here, such as national security or preserving the traditional institution of marriage. Unlike the moral disapproval of same-sex relations—the asserted state interest in this case—other reasons exist to promote the institution of marriage beyond mere moral disapproval of an excluded group.

. . .

Justice Scalia, with whom the Chief Justice and Justice Thomas join, dissenting.

. . .

. . . [N]owhere does the Court's opinion declare that homosexual sodomy is a "fundamental right" under the Due Process Clause; nor does it subject the Texas law to the standard of review that would be appropriate (strict scrutiny) if homosexual sodomy *were* a "fundamental right." Thus, while overruling the *outcome* of *Bowers*, the Court leaves strangely untouched its central legal conclusion: "[R]espondent would have us announce . . . a fundamental right to engage in homosexual sodomy. This we are quite unwilling to do." . . . Instead the Court simply describes petitioners' conduct as "an exercise of their liberty"—which it undoubtedly is—and proceeds to apply an unheard-of form of rational-basis review that will have far-reaching implications beyond this case. . . .

I

. . . [T]hree Members of today's majority[,] in *Planned Parenthood v. Casey* . . . when *stare decisis* meant preservation of judicially invented abortion rights, [found] the widespread criticism of *Roe* . . . strong reason to *reaffirm* it. . . .

Today, however, the widespread opposition to *Bowers*, a decision resolving an issue as "intensely divisive" as the issue in *Roe*, is offered as a reason in favor of *overruling* it. . . .

Today's approach to *stare decisis* invites us to overrule an erroneously decided precedent . . . *if:* (1) its foundations have been "eroded" by subsequent decisions; (2) it has been subject to "substantial and continuing" criticism.; and (3) it has not induced "individual or societal reliance" that counsels against overturning. The problem is that *Roe* itself—which today's majority surely has no disposition to overrule—satisfies these conditions to at least the same degree as *Bowers*.

(1) . . .

I do not quarrel with the Court's claim that *Romer v. Evans*, 517 U.S. 620 (1996), "eroded" the "foundations" of *Bowers'* rational-basis holding. See *Romer*, . . . (Scalia, J., dissenting). But *Roe* and *Casey* have been equally "eroded" by *Washington v. Glucksberg*, 521 U.S. 702, 721 (1997), which held that *only* fundamental rights which are " 'deeply rooted in this Nation's history and tradition' " qualify for anything other than rational basis scrutiny under the doctrine of "substantive due process." *Roe* and *Casey*, of course, subjected the restriction of abortion to heightened scrutiny without even attempting to establish that the freedom to abort *was* rooted in this Nation's tradition.

(2) *Bowers*, the Court says, has been subject to "substantial and continuing [criticism], disapproving of its reasoning in all respects, not just as to its historical assumptions." . . . Of course, *Roe* too (and by extension *Casey*) had been (and still is) subject to unrelenting criticism. . . .

(3) ... [T]he "societal reliance" on the principles confirmed in *Bowers* and discarded today has been overwhelming. Countless judicial decisions and legislative enactments have relied on the ancient proposition that a governing majority's belief that certain sexual behavior is "immoral and unacceptable" constitutes a rational basis for regulation.... State laws against bigamy, same-sex marriage, adult incest, prostitution, masturbation, adultery, fornication, bestiality, and obscenity are likewise sustainable only in light of *Bowers*' validation of laws based on moral choices. Every single one of these laws is called into question by today's decision; the Court makes no effort to cabin the scope of its decision to exclude them from its holding.... The impossibility of distinguishing homosexuality from other traditional "morals" offenses is precisely why *Bowers* rejected the rational-basis challenge....

What a massive disruption of the current social order, therefore, the overruling of *Bowers* entails. Not so the overruling of *Roe*, which would simply have restored the regime that existed for centuries before 1973, in which the permissibility of and restrictions upon abortion were determined legislatively State-by-State....

. . .

II

. . .

Texas Penal Code Ann. § 21.06(a) (2003) undoubtedly imposes constraints on liberty. So do laws prohibiting prostitution, recreational use of heroin, and, for that matter, working more than 60 hours per week in a bakery. But ... [t]he Fourteenth Amendment *expressly allows* States to deprive their citizens of "liberty," *so long as "due process of law" is provided* ....

Our opinions applying the doctrine known as "substantive due process" hold that the Due Process Clause prohibits States from infringing *fundamental* liberty interests, unless the infringement is narrowly tailored to serve a compelling state interest.... All other liberty interests may be abridged or abrogated pursuant to a validly enacted state law if that law is rationally related to a legitimate state interest.

Bowers held, first, that criminal prohibitions of homosexual sodomy are not subject to heightened scrutiny because they do not implicate a "fundamental right" under the Due Process Clause.... *Bowers* concluded that a right to engage in homosexual sodomy was not " 'deeply rooted in this Nation's history and tradition,' "....

The Court today does not overrule this holding. Not once does it describe homosexual sodomy as a "fundamental right" or a "fundamental liberty interest," nor does it subject the Texas statute to strict scrutiny. Instead, ... the Court concludes that the application of Texas's statute to petitioners' conduct fails the rational-basis test, and overrules *Bowers*' holding to the contrary....

III

. . .

... [T]he "definitive [historical] conclusion," ... on which *Bowers* relied [is] that our Nation has a longstanding history of laws prohibiting *sodomy in general*—regardless of whether it was performed by same-sex or opposite-sex couples:

"It is obvious to us that neither of these formulations would extend a fundamental right to homosexuals to engage in acts of consensual sodomy. Proscriptions against that conduct have ancient roots. *Sodomy* was a criminal offense at common law and was forbidden by the laws of the original 13 States when they ratified the Bill of Rights. In 1868, when the Fourteenth Amendment was ratified, all but 5 of the 37 States in the Union had *criminal sodomy laws*. In fact, until 1961, all 50 States outlawed *sodomy*, and today, 24 States and the District of Columbia continue to provide criminal penalties for *sodomy* performed in private and between consenting adults. Against this background, to claim that a right to engage in such conduct is 'deeply rooted in this Nation's history and tradition' or 'implicit in the concept of ordered liberty' is, at best, facetious." . . . (. . . emphasis added).

It is (as *Bowers* recognized) entirely irrelevant whether the laws in our long national tradition criminalizing homosexual sodomy were "directed at homosexual conduct as a distinct matter." . . . [T]he only relevant point is that [homosexual sodomy] *was* criminalized—which suffices to establish that homosexual sodomy is not a right "deeply rooted in our Nation's history and tradition." . . .

. . .

[T]he Court . . . says: "[O]ur laws and traditions in the past half century are of most relevance here [and] show *an emerging awareness* that liberty gives substantial protection to adult persons in deciding how to conduct their private lives *in matters pertaining to sex*." (emphasis added). Apart from the fact that such an "emerging awareness" does not establish a "fundamental right," the statement is factually false. States continue to prosecute all sorts of crimes by adults "in matters pertaining to sex": prostitution, adult incest, adultery, obscenity, and child pornography. Sodomy laws, too, have been enforced "in the past half century," in which there have been 134 reported cases involving prosecutions for consensual, adult, homosexual sodomy. . . . In relying . . . upon the American Law Institute's 1955 recommendation not to criminalize " 'consensual sexual relations conducted in private,' " the Court ignores the fact that this recommendation was "a point of resistance in most of the states that considered adopting the Model Penal Code." Gaylaw 159.

In any event, an "emerging awareness" is by definition not "deeply rooted in this Nation's history and tradition[s]," as we have said "fundamental right" status requires. Constitutional entitlements do not spring into existence because some States choose to lessen or eliminate criminal sanctions on certain behavior. Much less do they spring into existence, as the Court seems to believe, because *foreign nations* decriminalize conduct. . . .

IV

[T]he contention that there is no rational basis for the law here under attack . . . is so out of accord with our jurisprudence—indeed, with the jurisprudence of *any* society we know—that it requires little discussion.

The Texas statute undeniably seeks to further the belief of its citizens that certain forms of sexual behavior are "immoral and unacceptable," *Bowers* . . .—the same interest furthered by criminal laws against fornication, bigamy, adultery, adult incest, bestiality, and obscenity. . . . The Court . . . effectively decrees the end of all morals legislation. If, as the Court asserts, the promotion of majoritarian sexual morality is not even a *legitimate* state interest, none of the above-mentioned laws can survive rational-basis review.

V

Finally, I turn to petitioners' equal-protection challenge, which no Member of the Court save Justice O'Connor . . . embraces. . . .

. . .

Justice O'Connor simply decrees application of "a more searching form of rational basis review" to the Texas statute. The cases she cites do not recognize such a standard, and reach their conclusions only after finding, as required by conventional rational-basis analysis, that no conceivable legitimate state interest supports the classification at issue. . . . [She] must at least mean, however, that laws exhibiting " 'a . . . desire to harm a politically unpopular group' " are invalid *even though* there may be a conceivable rational basis to support them.

This reasoning leaves on pretty shaky grounds state laws limiting marriage to opposite-sex couples. Justice O'Connor seeks to preserve them by the conclusory statement that "preserving the traditional institution of marriage" is a legitimate state interest. But "preserving the traditional institution of marriage" is just a kinder way of describing the State's *moral disapproval* of same-sex couples. Texas's interest in § 21.06 could be recast in similarly euphemistic terms: "preserving the traditional sexual mores of our society." In the jurisprudence Justice O'Connor has seemingly created, judges can validate laws by characterizing them as "preserving the traditions of society" (good); or invalidate them by characterizing them as "expressing moral disapproval" (bad).

* * *

Today's opinion is the product of a Court, which is the product of a law-profession culture, that has largely signed on to the so-called homosexual agenda, by which I mean the agenda promoted by some homosexual activists directed at eliminating the moral opprobrium that has traditionally attached to homosexual conduct. . . .

. . . [T]he Court has taken sides in the culture war, departing from its role of assuring, as neutral observer, that the democratic rules of engagement are observed. . . . So imbued is the Court with the law profession's anti-anti-homosexual culture, that it is seemingly unaware that . . . in most States what the Court calls "discrimination" against those who engage in homosexual acts is perfectly legal; that proposals to ban such "discrimination" under Title VII have repeatedly been rejected by Congress, see Employment Non–Discrimination Act of 1994, S. 2238, 103d Cong., 2d Sess. (1994); Civil Rights Amendments, H. R. 5452, 94th Cong., 1st Sess. (1975); that in some cases such "discrimination" is *mandated* by federal statute, see 10 U.S.C. § 654(b)(1) (mandating discharge from the armed forces of any service member who engages in or intends to engage in homosexual acts); and that in some cases such "discrimination" is a constitutional right, see *Boy Scouts of America v. Dale*, 530 U.S. 640 (2000).

Let me be clear that I have nothing against homosexuals, or any other group, promoting their agenda through normal democratic means. . . . But persuading one's fellow citizens is one thing, and imposing one's views in absence of democratic majority will is something else. . . . What Texas has chosen to do is well within the range of traditional democratic action, and its hand should not be stayed through the invention of a brand-new "constitutional right" by a Court that is impatient of democratic change. . . .

One of the benefits of leaving regulation of this matter to the people rather than to the courts is that the people, unlike judges, need not carry things to their logical conclusion. The people may feel that their disapprobation of homosexual conduct is strong enough to disallow homosexual marriage, but not strong enough to criminalize private homosexual acts—and may legislate accordingly.... Today's opinion dismantles the structure of constitutional law that has permitted a distinction to be made between heterosexual and homosexual unions, insofar as formal recognition in marriage is concerned. If moral disapprobation of homosexual conduct is "no legitimate state interest" for purposes of proscribing that conduct; and if, ... "[w]hen sexuality finds overt expression in intimate conduct with another person, the conduct can be but one element in a personal bond that is more enduring"; what justification could there possibly be for denying the benefits of marriage to homosexual couples exercising "[t]he liberty protected by the Constitution"? ...

. . .

Justice Thomas, dissenting.

... I write separately to note that the law before the Court today "is ... uncommonly silly." *Griswold v. Connecticut*, 381 U.S. 479, 527 (1965) (Stewart, J., dissenting). If I were a member of the Texas Legislature, I would vote to repeal it. Punishing someone for expressing his sexual preference through noncommercial consensual conduct with another adult does not appear to be a worthy way to expend valuable law enforcement resources.

Notwithstanding this, ... just like Justice Stewart, I "can find [neither in the Bill of Rights nor any other part of the Constitution a] general right of privacy," ..., or as the Court terms it today, the "liberty of the person both in its spatial and more transcendent dimensions."

Washington v. Glucksberg

521 U.S. 702, 117 S.Ct. 2258, 138 L.Ed.2d 772 (1997).

Chief Justice Rehnquist delivered the opinion of the Court.

The question presented in this case is whether Washington's prohibition against "caus[ing]" or "aid[ing]" a suicide offends the Fourteenth Amendment to the United States Constitution. We hold that it does not.

... Washington law provides: "A person is guilty of promoting a suicide attempt when he knowingly causes or aids another person to attempt suicide." Wash. Rev. Code 9A.36.060(1) (1994).... At the same time, Washington's Natural Death Act, enacted in 1979, states that the "withholding or withdrawal of life-sustaining treatment" at a patient's direction "shall not, for any purpose, constitute a suicide." Wash. Rev. Code § 70.122.070(1)....

... [P]hysicians who practice in Washington[,] occasionally treat terminally ill, suffering patients, and declare that they would assist these patients in ending their lives if not for Washington's assisted-suicide ..., along with three gravely ill, pseudonymous plaintiffs who have since died and Compassion in Dying, a nonprofit organization that counsels people considering physician-assisted suicide, sued ... seeking a declaration that Wash Rev. Code 9A.36.060(1) (1994) is, on its face, unconstitutional....

The plaintiffs asserted "the existence of a liberty interest protected by the Fourteenth Amendment which extends to a personal choice by a mentally competent, terminally ill adult to commit physician-assisted suicide." ... Relying primarily on Planned Parenthood v. Casey, 505 U.S. 833 (1992), and Cruzan v. Director, Missouri Dept. of Health, 497 U.S. 261 (1990), the District

Court agreed ... and concluded that Washington's assisted-suicide ban is unconstitutional because it "places an undue burden on the exercise of [that] constitutionally protected liberty interest." ...

... The Ninth Circuit ... en banc ... affirmed ... [,] conclud[ing] that "the Constitution encompasses a due process liberty interest in controlling the time and manner of one's death—that there is, in short, a constitutionally-recognized 'right to die.'" ... After "[w]eighing and then balancing" this interest against Washington's various interests, the court held that the State's assisted-suicide ban was unconstitutional "as applied to terminally ill competent adults who wish to hasten their deaths with medication prescribed by their physicians."[6] We ... reverse.

I

We begin, as we do in all due-process cases, by examining our Nation's history, legal traditions, and practices. See, e.g., Casey, 505 U.S., at 849–850; Cruzan, 497 U.S., at 269–279; Moore v. East Cleveland, 431 U.S. 494, 503 (1977) (plurality opinion) (noting importance of "careful 'respect for the teachings of history'"). In almost every State—indeed, in almost every western democracy—it is a crime to assist a suicide....

More specifically, for over 700 years, the Anglo–American common-law tradition has punished or otherwise disapproved of both suicide and assisting suicide....

· · ·

... And the prohibitions against assisting suicide never contained exceptions for those who were near death....

... By the time the Fourteenth Amendment was ratified, it was a crime in most States to assist a suicide.... In this century, the Model Penal Code also prohibited "aiding" suicide, prompting many States to enact or revise their assisted-suicide bans. The Code's drafters observed that "the interests in the sanctity of life that are represented by the criminal homicide laws are threatened by one who expresses a willingness to participate in taking the life of another, even though the act may be accomplished with the consent, or at the request, of the suicide victim." American Law Institute, Model Penal Code § 210.5, Comment 5, p. 100 (Official Draft and Revised Comments 1980).

Though deeply rooted, the States' assisted-suicide bans have in recent years been reexamined and, generally, reaffirmed. Because of advances in medicine and technology, Americans today are increasingly likely to die in institutions, from chronic illnesses.... Public concern and democratic action are therefore sharply focused on how best to protect dignity and independence at the end of life, with the result that there have been many significant changes in state laws and in the attitudes these laws reflect. Many States, for example, now permit "living wills," surrogate health-care decisionmaking, and the withdrawal or refusal of life-sustaining medical treatment.... At the same time, however, voters and legislators continue for the most part to reaffirm their States' prohibitions on assisting suicide.

The Washington statute at issue in this case ... was enacted in 1975 as part of a revision of that State's criminal code. Four years later, Washington passed its Natural Death Act, which specifically stated that the "withholding or

---

6. It is ... the court's holding that Washington's physician-assisted suicide statute is unconstitutional as applied to the "class of terminally ill, mentally competent patients" that is before us today.

withdrawal of life-sustaining treatment . . . shall not, for any purpose, constitute a suicide" and that "[n]othing in this chapter shall be construed to condone, authorize, or approve mercy killing. . . ." . . . In 1991, Washington voters rejected a ballot initiative which, had it passed, would have permitted a form of physician-assisted suicide. Washington then added a provision to the Natural Death Act expressly excluding physician-assisted suicide. . . .

California voters rejected an assisted-suicide initiative similar to Washington's in 1993. On the other hand, in 1994, voters in Oregon enacted, also through ballot initiative, that State's "Death With Dignity Act," which legalized physician-assisted suicide for competent, terminally ill adults. Since the Oregon vote, many proposals to legalize assisted-suicide have been and continue to be introduced in the States' legislatures, but none has been enacted. And just last year, Iowa and Rhode Island joined the overwhelming majority of States explicitly prohibiting assisted suicide. . . . Also, on April 30, 1997, President Clinton signed the Federal Assisted Suicide Funding Restriction Act of 1997, which prohibits the use of federal funds in support of physician-assisted suicide. . . . [16]

Thus, the States are currently engaged in serious, thoughtful examinations of physician-assisted suicide and other similar issues. For example, New York State's Task Force on Life and the Law—an ongoing, blue-ribbon commission composed of doctors, ethicists, lawyers, religious leaders, and interested laymen—was convened in 1984 and commissioned with "a broad mandate to recommend public policy on issues raised by medical advances." . . . After studying physician-assisted suicide, however, the Task Force unanimously concluded that "[l]egalizing assisted suicide and euthanasia would pose profound risks to many individuals who are ill and vulnerable. . . . [T]he potential dangers of this dramatic change in public policy would outweigh any benefit that might be achieved." . . .

Attitudes toward suicide itself have changed since Bracton, but our laws have consistently condemned, and continue to prohibit, assisting suicide. Despite changes in medical technology and notwithstanding an increased emphasis on the importance of end-of-life decisionmaking, we have not retreated from this prohibition. Against this backdrop of history, tradition, and practice, we now turn to respondents' constitutional claim.

II

The Due Process Clause guarantees more than fair process, and the "liberty" it protects includes more than the absence of physical restraint. . . . The Clause also provides heightened protection against government interference with certain fundamental rights and liberty interests. . . . We have also assumed, and strongly suggested, that the Due Process Clause protects the traditional right to refuse unwanted lifesaving medical treatment. *Cruzan*, 497 U.S., at 278–279.

But we "ha[ve] always been reluctant to expand the concept of substantive due process because guideposts for responsible decisionmaking in this unchartered area are scarce and open-ended." . . . By extending constitutional protection to an asserted right or liberty interest, we, to a great extent, place the matter outside the arena of public debate and legislative action. We must therefore "exercise the utmost care whenever we are asked to break new ground in this field," . . . lest the liberty protected by the Due Process Clause

16. Other countries are embroiled in similar debates. . . .

be subtly transformed into the policy preferences of the members of this Court, *Moore*, 431 U.S., at 502 (plurality opinion).

Our established method of substantive-due-process analysis has two primary features: First, we have regularly observed that the Due Process Clause specially protects those fundamental rights and liberties which are, objectively, "deeply rooted in this Nation's history and tradition," id., at 503 (plurality opinion); Snyder v. Massachusetts, 291 U.S. 97, 105 (1934) ("so rooted in the traditions and conscience of our people as to be ranked as fundamental"), and "implicit in the concept of ordered liberty," such that "neither liberty nor justice would exist if they were sacrificed," Palko v. Connecticut, 302 U.S. 319, 325, 326 (1937). Second, we have required in substantive-due-process cases a "careful description" of the asserted fundamental liberty interest.... Our Nation's history, legal traditions, and practices thus provide the crucial "guideposts for responsible decisionmaking," that direct and restrain our exposition of the Due Process Clause....

Justice Souter, relying on Justice Harlan's dissenting opinion in *Poe v. Ullman*, would largely abandon this restrained methodology, and instead ask "whether [Washington's] statute sets up one of those 'arbitrary impositions' or 'purposeless restraints' at odds with the Due Process Clause of the Fourteenth Amendment" (quoting Poe, 367 U.S. 497, 543 (1961) (Harlan, J., dissenting)). In our view, however, the development of this Court's substantive-due-process jurisprudence ... has been a process whereby the outlines of the "liberty" specially protected by the Fourteenth Amendment—never fully clarified, to be sure, and perhaps not capable of being fully clarified—have at least been carefully refined by concrete examples involving fundamental rights found to be deeply rooted in our legal tradition. This approach tends to rein in the subjective elements that are necessarily present in due-process judicial review. In addition, by establishing a threshold requirement—that a challenged state action implicate a fundamental right—before requiring more than a reasonable relation to a legitimate state interest to justify the action, it avoids the need for complex balancing of competing interests in every case.

... [W]e have a tradition of carefully formulating the interest at stake in substantive-due-process cases. For example, although *Cruzan* is often described as a "right to die" case, ... we were, in fact, more precise: we assumed that the Constitution granted competent persons a "constitutionally protected right to refuse lifesaving hydration and nutrition." ... The Washington statute at issue in this case prohibits "aid[ing] another person to attempt suicide," ... and, thus, the question before us is whether the "liberty" specially protected by the Due Process Clause includes a right to commit suicide which itself includes a right to assistance in doing so.

... [A] consistent and almost universal tradition ... has long rejected the asserted right, and continues explicitly to reject it today, even for terminally ill, mentally competent adults. To hold for respondents, we would have to reverse centuries of legal doctrine and practice, and strike down the considered policy choice of almost every State....

Respondents contend, however, ... [p]ointing to *Casey* and *Cruzan*, ... that the "liberty" protected by the Due Process Clause includes "basic and intimate exercises of personal autonomy," ... [and] protects the "liberty of competent, terminally ill adults to make end-of-life decisions free of undue government interference." ... The question presented in this case, however, is whether the protections of the Due Process Clause include a right to commit suicide with another's assistance. With this "careful description" of respondents' claim in mind, we turn to *Casey* and *Cruzan*.

In *Cruzan*, we considered whether Nancy Beth Cruzan, who had been severely injured in an automobile accident and was in a persistive vegetative state, "ha[d] a right under the United States Constitution which would require the hospital to withdraw life-sustaining treatment" at her parents' request.... We began with the observation that "[a]t common law, even the touching of one person by another without consent and without legal justification was a battery." ... We then discussed the related rule that "informed consent is generally required for medical treatment." ... After reviewing a long line of relevant state cases, we concluded that "the common-law doctrine of informed consent is viewed as generally encompassing the right of a competent individual to refuse medical treatment." ... Next, we reviewed our own cases on the subject, and stated that "[t]he principle that a competent person has a constitutionally protected liberty interest in refusing unwanted medical treatment may be inferred from our prior decisions." ... Therefore, "for purposes of [that] case, we assume[d] that the United States Constitution would grant a competent person a constitutionally protected right to refuse lifesaving hydration and nutrition." ... We concluded that, notwithstanding this right, the Constitution permitted Missouri to require clear and convincing evidence of an incompetent patient's wishes concerning the withdrawal of life-sustaining treatment....

. . . .

The right assumed in *Cruzan* ... was not simply deduced from abstract concepts of personal autonomy. Given the common-law rule that forced medication was a battery, and the long legal tradition protecting the decision to refuse unwanted medical treatment, our assumption was entirely consistent with this Nation's history and constitutional traditions. The decision to commit suicide with the assistance of another may be just as personal and profound as the decision to refuse unwanted medical treatment, but it has never enjoyed similar legal protection. Indeed, the two acts are widely and reasonably regarded as quite distinct. See Vacco v. Quill, [521 U.S. 793 (1997)].[a] In *Cruzan* itself,

a. In *Quill*, decided with *Glucksberg*, the Court reversed a decision of the Second Circuit Court of Appeals holding that New York's prohibition on assisted suicide violated the Equal Protection Clause insofar as it prevented prescribing lethal medication for mentally competent, terminally ill patients, because New York law allowed such patients to refuse life-sustaining medical treatment, and the distinction was "not rationally related to any legitimate state interest." Chief Justice Rehnquist's majority opinion concluded that "the distinction between assisting suicide and withdrawing life-sustaining treatment, a distinction widely recognized and endorsed in the medical profession and in our legal traditions, is both important and logical; it is certainly rational." The Chief Justice continued:

"The distinction comports with fundamental legal principles of causation and intent. First, when a patient refuses life-sustaining medical treatment, he dies from an underlying fatal disease or pathology; but if a patient ingests lethal medication prescribed by a physician, he is killed by that medication....

"Furthermore, a physician who withdraws, or honors a patient's refusal to begin, life-sustaining medical treatment purposefully intends, or may so intend, only to respect his patient's wishes and 'to cease doing useless and futile or degrading things to the patient when [the patient] no longer stands to benefit from them.' ... The same is true when a doctor provides aggressive palliative care; in some cases, painkilling drugs may hasten a patient's death, but the physician's purpose and intent is, or may be, only to ease his patient's pain. A doctor who assists a suicide, however, 'must, necessarily and indubitably, intend primarily that the patient be made dead.' ... Similarly, a patient who commits suicide with a doctor's aid necessarily has the specific intent to end his or her own life, while a patient who refuses or discontinues treatment might not....

"The law has long used actors' intent or purpose to distinguish between two acts that may have the same result.... Put differently, the law distinguishes actions taken "because of" a given end from actions taken "in spite of" their unintended but foreseen consequences....

we recognized that most States outlawed assisted suicide—and even more do today—and we certainly gave no intimation that the right to refuse unwanted medical treatment could be somehow transmuted into a right to assistance in committing suicide. . . .

Respondents also rely on *Casey*. . . .

. . .

[They] emphasize the statement in *Casey* that:

"At the heart of liberty is the right to define one's own concept of existence, of meaning, of the universe, and of the mystery of human life. Beliefs about these matters could not define the attributes of personhood were they formed under compulsion of the State." . . .

By choosing this language, the Court's opinion in *Casey* described, in a general way and in light of our prior cases, those personal activities and decisions that this Court has identified as so deeply rooted in our history and traditions, or so fundamental to our concept of constitutionally ordered liberty, that they are protected by the Fourteenth Amendment. . . . That many of the rights and liberties protected by the Due Process Clause sound in personal autonomy does not warrant the sweeping conclusion that any and all important, intimate, and personal decisions are so protected, . . . and *Casey* did not suggest otherwise.

The history of the law's treatment of assisted suicide in this country has been and continues to be one of the rejection of nearly all efforts to permit it. That being the case, our decisions lead us to conclude that the asserted "right" to assistance in committing suicide is not a fundamental liberty interest protected by the Due Process Clause. The Constitution also requires, however, that Washington's assisted-suicide ban be rationally related to legitimate government interests. . . . This requirement is unquestionably met here. . . .

"... [M]any courts, including New York courts, have carefully distinguished refusing life-sustaining treatment from suicide. . . .

"Similarly, the overwhelming majority of state legislatures have drawn a clear line between assisting suicide and withdrawing or permitting the refusal of unwanted lifesaving medical treatment by prohibiting the former and permitting the latter. . . .

" . . .

"This Court has also recognized, at least implicitly, the distinction between letting a patient die and making that patient die. In [*Cruzan*], . . . our assumption of a right to refuse treatment was grounded not, as the Court of Appeals supposed, on the proposition that patients have a general and abstract 'right to hasten death,' but on well established, traditional rights to bodily integrity and freedom from unwanted touching. . . . *Cruzan* therefore provides no support for the notion that refusing life-sustaining medical treatment is 'nothing more nor less than suicide.'

"... Logic and contemporary practice support New York's judgment that the two acts are different, and New York may therefore, consistent with the Constitution, treat them differently. . . .

"New York's reasons for recognizing and acting on this distinction ... are discussed in greater detail in our opinion in *Glucksberg* [and] easily satisfy the constitutional requirement that a legislative classification bear a rational relation to some legitimate end."

Each of the concurring opinions in *Glucksberg* also applied to this case, except that Justice Souter here said this:

"Even though I do not conclude that assisted suicide is a fundamental right entitled to recognition at this time, I accord the claims raised by the patients and physicians in this case and Washington v. Glucksberg a high degree of importance, requiring a commensurate justification. . . . The reasons that lead me to conclude in *Glucksberg* that the prohibition on assisted suicide is not arbitrary under the due process standard also support the distinction between assistance to suicide, which is banned, and practices such as termination of artificial life support and death-hastening pain medication, which are permitted. I accordingly concur in the judgment of the Court."

First, Washington has an "unqualified interest in the preservation of human life." Cruzan, 497 U.S., at 282. The State's prohibition on assisted suicide, like all homicide laws, both reflects and advances its commitment to this interest....

... Washington ... insists that all persons' lives, from beginning to end, regardless of physical or mental condition, are under the full protection of the law.... As we have previously affirmed, the States "may properly decline to make judgments about the 'quality' of life that a particular individual may enjoy," Cruzan, 497 U.S., at 282. This remains true, as *Cruzan* makes clear, even for those who are near death.

Relatedly, all admit that suicide is a serious public-health problem, especially among persons in otherwise vulnerable groups....

Those who attempt suicide—terminally ill or not—often suffer from depression or other mental disorders.... Research indicates, however, that many people who request physician-assisted suicide withdraw that request if their depression and pain are treated. H. Hendin, Seduced by Death: Doctors, Patients and the Dutch Cure 24–25 (1997) (suicidal, terminally ill patients "usually respond well to treatment for depressive illness and pain medication and are then grateful to be alive"); New York Task Force 177–178. The New York Task Force, however, expressed its concern that, because depression is difficult to diagnose, physicians and medical professionals often fail to respond adequately to seriously ill patients' needs. Id., at 175. Thus, legal physician-assisted suicide could make it more difficult for the State to protect depressed or mentally ill persons, or those who are suffering from untreated pain, from suicidal impulses.

The State also has an interest in protecting the integrity and ethics of the medical profession.... [T]he American Medical Association, like many other medical and physicians' groups, has concluded that "[p]hysician-assisted suicide is fundamentally incompatible with the physician's role as healer." ... And physician-assisted suicide could, it is argued, undermine the trust that is essential to the doctor-patient relationship by blurring the time-honored line between healing and harming....

Next, the State has an interest in protecting vulnerable groups—including the poor, the elderly, and disabled persons—from abuse, neglect, and mistakes.... We have recognized ... the real risk of subtle coercion and undue influence in end-of-life situations. *Cruzan*, 497 U.S., at 281.... If physician-assisted suicide were permitted, many might resort to it to spare their families the substantial financial burden of end-of-life health-care costs.

The State's interest here goes beyond protecting the vulnerable from coercion; it extends to protecting disabled and terminally ill people from prejudice, negative and inaccurate stereotypes, and "societal indifference." ... The State's assisted-suicide ban reflects and reinforces its policy that the lives of terminally ill, disabled, and elderly people must be no less valued than the lives of the young and healthy, and that a seriously disabled person's suicidal impulses should be interpreted and treated the same way as anyone else's....

Finally, the State may fear that permitting assisted suicide will start it down the path to voluntary and perhaps even involuntary euthanasia.... [W]hat is couched as a limited right to "physician-assisted suicide" is likely, in effect, a much broader license, which could prove extremely difficult to police and contain. Washington's ban on assisting suicide prevents such erosion.

This concern is further supported by evidence about the practice of euthanasia in the Netherlands ... suggest[ing] that, despite the existence of various reporting procedures, euthanasia in the Netherlands has not been limited to competent, terminally ill adults who are enduring physical suffering, and that regulation of the practice may not have prevented abuses in cases involving vulnerable persons, including severely disabled neonates and elderly persons suffering from dementia. . . . Washington, like most other States, reasonably ensures against this risk by banning, rather than regulating, assisting suicide. . . .

We need not weigh exactingly the relative strengths of these various interests. They are unquestionably important and legitimate, and Washington's ban on assisted suicide is at least reasonably related to their promotion and protection. We therefore hold that Wash. Rev. Code § 9A.36.060(1) (1994) does not violate the Fourteenth Amendment, either on its face or "as applied to competent, terminally ill adults who wish to hasten their deaths by obtaining medication prescribed by their doctors." . . .[24]

* * *

Throughout the Nation, Americans are engaged in an earnest and profound debate about the morality, legality, and practicality of physician-assisted suicide. Our holding permits this debate to continue, as it should in a democratic society. . . .

Justice O'Connor, concurring.[*]

. . .

. . . I join the Court's opinions because I agree that there is no generalized right to "commit suicide." But respondents urge us to address the narrower question whether a mentally competent person who is experiencing great suffering has a constitutionally cognizable interest in controlling the circumstances of his or her imminent death. I see no need to reach that question in the context of the facial challenges to the New York and Washington laws at issue here. . . . The parties and *amici* agree that in these States a patient who is suffering from a terminal illness and who is experiencing great pain has no legal barriers to obtaining medication, from qualified physicians, to alleviate that suffering, even to the point of causing unconsciousness and hastening death. . . . In this light, even assuming that we would recognize such an interest, I agree that the State's interests in protecting those who are not truly competent or facing imminent death, or those whose decisions to hasten death would not truly be voluntary, are sufficiently weighty to justify a prohibition against physician-assisted suicide.

Every one of us at some point may be affected by our own or a family member's terminal illness. There is no reason to think the democratic process will not strike the proper balance between the interests of terminally ill, mentally competent individuals who would seek to end their suffering and the

---

24. . . . We emphasize that we today reject the Court of Appeals' specific holding that the statute is unconstitutional "as applied" to a particular class. See n. 6, supra. Justice Stevens agrees with this holding, but would not "foreclose the possibility that an individual plaintiff seeking to hasten her death, or a doctor whose assistance was sought, could prevail in a more particularized challenge." Our opinion does not absolutely foreclose such a claim. However, given our holding that the Due Process Clause of the Fourteenth Amendment does not provide heightened protection to the asserted liberty interest in ending one's life with a physician's assistance, such a claim would have to be quite different from the ones advanced . . . here.

* Justice Ginsburg concurs in the Court's judgments substantially for the reasons stated in this opinion. Justice Breyer joins this opinion except insofar as it joins the opinions of the Court.

State's interests in protecting those who might seek to end life mistakenly or under pressure. . . .

. . .

Justice Stevens, concurring in the judgments.

. . .

. . . The State has an interest in preserving and fostering the benefits that every human being may provide to the community. . . . The value to others of a person's life is far too precious to allow the individual to claim a constitutional entitlement to complete autonomy in making a decision to end that life. Thus, I fully agree with the Court that the "liberty" protected by the Due Process Clause does not include a categorical "right to commit suicide which itself includes a right to assistance in doing so."

But . . . a decision upholding a general statutory prohibition of assisted suicide does not mean that every possible application of the statute would be valid. . . .

II

. . . In most cases, the individual's constitutionally protected interest in his or her own physical autonomy, including the right to refuse unwanted medical treatment, will give way to the State's interest in preserving human life.

Cruzan, however, was not the normal case. . . . I insist that the source of Nancy Cruzan's right to refuse treatment was not just a common-law rule [but] an aspect of a far broader and more basic concept of freedom . . . older than the common law. This freedom embraces, not merely a person's right to refuse a particular kind of unwanted treatment, but also her interest in dignity, and in determining the character of the memories that will survive long after her death. . . .

. . .

. . . The now-deceased plaintiffs in this action may in fact have had a liberty interest even stronger than Nancy Cruzan's because, not only were they terminally ill, they were suffering constant and severe pain. Avoiding intolerable pain and the indignity of living one's final days incapacitated and in agony is certainly "[a]t the heart of [the] liberty . . . to define one's own concept of existence, of meaning, of the universe, and of the mystery of human life." Casey, 505 U.S., at 851.

. . . *Cruzan* [gave] recognition, not just to vague, unbridled notions of autonomy, but to the more specific interest in making decisions about how to confront an imminent death. . . . The liberty interest at stake in a case like this differs from, and is stronger than, both the common-law right to refuse medical treatment and the unbridled interest in deciding whether to live or die. It is an interest in deciding how, rather than whether, a critical threshold shall be crossed.

III

. . .

. . . Although as a general matter the State's interest in the contributions each person may make to society outweighs the person's interest in ending her life, this interest does not have the same force for a terminally ill patient faced not with the choice of whether to live, only of how to die. Allowing the individual, rather than the State, to make judgments " 'about the "quality" of life that a particular individual may enjoy,' " does not mean that the lives of terminally-ill, disabled people have less value than the lives of those who are healthy. Rather, it gives proper recognition to the individual's interest in choosing a final chapter that accords with her life story, rather than one that demeans her values and poisons memories of her. . . .

. . . I agree that the State has a compelling interest in preventing persons from committing suicide because of depression, or coercion by third parties. But the State's legitimate interest in preventing abuse does not apply to an individual who is not victimized by abuse, who is not suffering from depression, and who makes a rational and voluntary decision to seek assistance in dying. . . .

. . . [P]alliative care . . . cannot alleviate all pain and suffering. . . . An individual adequately informed of the care alternatives thus might make a rational choice for assisted suicide. For such an individual, the State's interest in preventing potential abuse and mistake is only minimally implicated.

The final major interest asserted by the State is its interest in preserving the traditional integrity of the medical profession. . . . But for some patients, it would be a physician's refusal to dispense medication to ease their suffering and make their death tolerable and dignified that would be inconsistent with the healing role. . . . Furthermore, because physicians are already involved in making decisions that hasten the death of terminally ill patients—through termination of life support, withholding of medical treatment, and terminal sedation—there is in fact significant tension between the traditional view of the physician's role and the actual practice in a growing number of cases.[12]

. . . Although, as the Court concludes today, the[] potential harms are sufficient to support the State's general public policy against assisted suicide, they will not always outweigh the individual liberty interest of a particular patient. . . . I do not . . . foreclose the possibility that an individual plaintiff seeking to hasten her death, or a doctor whose assistance was sought, could prevail in a more particularized challenge. . . .

IV

In New York, a doctor must respect a competent person's decision to refuse or to discontinue medical treatment even though death will thereby ensue, but the same doctor would be guilty of a felony if she provided her patient assistance in committing suicide. Today we hold that the Equal Protection Clause is not violated by the resulting disparate treatment of two classes of terminally ill people who may have the same interest in hastening death. I agree that the distinction between permitting death to ensue from an underlying fatal disease and causing it to occur by the administration of medication or other means provides a constitutionally sufficient basis for the State's classification. Unlike the Court, however, I am not persuaded that in all cases there will in fact be a significant difference between the intent of the physicians, the patients or the families in the two situations.

. . . The illusory character of any differences in intent or causation is confirmed by the fact that the American Medical Association unequivocally endorses the practice of terminal sedation—the administration of sufficient dosages of pain-killing medication to terminally ill patients to protect them from excruciating pain even when it is clear that the time of death will be

---

12. [T]here is evidence that a signifi- tice of hastening death in particular situa-
cant number of physicians support the prac- tions. . . .

advanced. The purpose of terminal sedation is to ease the suffering of the patient and comply with her wishes, and the actual cause of death is the administration of heavy doses of lethal sedatives. This same intent and causation may exist when a doctor complies with a patient's request for lethal medication to hasten her death.

. . . Our holding today in Vacco v. Quill that the Equal Protection Clause is not violated by New York's classification, just like our holding in Washington v. Glucksberg that the Washington statute is not invalid on its face, does not foreclose the possibility that some applications of the New York statute may impose an intolerable intrusion on the patient's freedom.

. . .

Justice Souter, concurring in the judgment.

. . . The question is whether the statute sets up one of those "arbitrary impositions" or "purposeless restraints" at odds with the Due Process Clause of the Fourteenth Amendment. Poe v. Ullman, 367 U.S. 497, 543 (1961) (Harlan, J., dissenting). . . .

. . .

III

. . .

This approach calls for a court to assess the relative "weights" or dignities of the contending interests, [a] judicial method . . . familiar to the common law. Common law method is subject, however, to two important constraints in the hands of a court engaged in substantive due process review. First, such a court is bound to confine the values that it recognizes to those truly deserving constitutional stature, either to those expressed in constitutional text, or those exemplified by "the traditions from which [the Nation] developed," or revealed by contrast with "the traditions from which it broke." . . .

[S]econd[,] . . . [i]t is no justification for judicial intervention merely to identify a reasonable resolution of contending values that differs from the terms of the legislation under review. It is only when the legislation's justifying principle, critically valued, is so far from being commensurate with the individual interest as to be arbitrarily or pointlessly applied that the statute must give way. . . .

The *Poe* dissent . . . reminds us that the process of substantive review by reasoned judgment . . . is one of close criticism going to the details of the opposing interests and to their relationships with the historically recognized principles that lend them weight or value.

. . . Exact analysis and characterization of any due process claim is critical to the method and to the result.

. . .

. . . [H]ere we are faced with an individual claim not to a right on the part of just anyone to help anyone else commit suicide under any circumstances, but to the right of a narrow class to help others also in a narrow class under a set of limited circumstances. And the claimants are met with the State's assertion, among others, that rights of such narrow scope cannot be recognized without jeopardy to individuals whom the State may concededly protect through its regulations.

IV

A

Respondents claim that a patient facing imminent death, who anticipates physical suffering and indignity, and is capable of responsible and voluntary choice, should have a right to a physician's assistance in providing counsel and drugs to be administered by the patient to end life promptly....

. . .

It is ... in the abortion cases that the most telling recognitions of the importance of bodily integrity and the concomitant tradition of medical assistance have occurred. In Roe v. Wade, ... we stressed the importance of the relationship between patient and physician....

The analogies between the abortion cases and this one are several. Even though the State has a legitimate interest in discouraging abortion, ... the Court recognized a woman's right to a physician's counsel and care. Like the decision to commit suicide, the decision to abort potential life can be made irresponsibly and under the influence of others, and yet the Court has held in the abortion cases that physicians are fit assistants. Without physician assistance in abortion, the woman's right would have too often amounted to nothing more than a right to self-mutilation, and without a physician to assist in the suicide of the dying, the patient's right will often be confined to crude methods of causing death, most shocking and painful to the decedent's survivors.

[F]inally,.... the good physician ... ministers to the patient. This idea of the physician as serving the whole person is a source of the high value traditionally placed on the medical relationship. Its value is surely as apparent here as in the abortion cases, for just as the decision about abortion is not directed to correcting some pathology, so the decision in which a dying patient seeks help is not so limited. The patients here sought not only an end to pain (which they might have had, although perhaps at the price of stupor) but an end to their short remaining lives with a dignity that they believed would be denied them by powerful pain medication, as well as by their consciousness of dependency and helplessness as they approached death. In that period when the end is imminent, they said, the decision to end life is closest to decisions that are generally accepted as proper instances of exercising autonomy over one's own body, instances recognized under the Constitution and the State's own law, instances in which the help of physicians is accepted as falling within the traditional norm.

. . .

In my judgment, the importance of the individual interest here, as within that class of "certain interests" demanding careful scrutiny of the State's contrary claim, see *Poe*, supra, at 543, cannot be gainsaid. Whether that interest might in some circumstances, or at some time, be seen as "fundamental" to the degree entitled to prevail is not, however, a conclusion that I need draw here, for I am satisfied that the State's interests described in the following section are sufficiently serious to defeat the present claim that its law is arbitrary or purposeless.

B

The State has put forward several interests to justify the Washington law as applied to physicians treating terminally ill patients, even those competent to make responsible choices: protecting life generally, ... discouraging suicide even if knowing and voluntary, . . . and protecting terminally ill patients from involuntary suicide and euthanasia, both voluntary and nonvoluntary. . . .

[T]he third is dispositive for me. That third justification is different from the first two, for it addresses specific features of respondents' claim, and it opposes that claim not with a moral judgment contrary to respondents', but with a recognized state interest in the protection of nonresponsible individuals and those who do not stand in relation either to death or to their physicians as do the patients whom respondents describe. . . . [M]istaken decisions may result from inadequate palliative care or a terminal prognosis that turns out to be error; coercion and abuse may stem from the large medical bills that family members cannot bear or unreimbursed hospitals decline to shoulder. Voluntary and involuntary euthanasia may result once doctors are authorized to prescribe lethal medication in the first instance, for they might find it pointless to distinguish between patients who administer their own fatal drugs and those who wish not to, and their compassion for those who suffer may obscure the distinction between those who ask for death and those who may be unable to request it. The argument is that a progression would occur, obscuring the line between the ill and the dying, and between the responsible and the unduly influenced, until ultimately doctors and perhaps others would abuse a limited freedom to aid suicides by yielding to the impulse to end another's suffering under conditions going beyond the narrow limits the respondents propose. The State thus argues, essentially, that respondents' claim is not as narrow as it sounds, simply because no recognition of the interest they assert could be limited to vindicating those interests and affecting no others. . . .

. . .

. . . Whether acting from compassion or under some other influence, a physician who would provide a drug for a patient to administer might well go the further step of administering the drug himself; so, the barrier between assisted suicide and euthanasia could become porous, and the line between voluntary and involuntary euthanasia as well. The case for the slippery slope is fairly made out here, not because recognizing one due process right would leave a court with no principled basis to avoid recognizing another, but because there is a plausible case that the right claimed would not be readily containable by reference to facts about the mind that are matters of difficult judgment, or by gatekeepers who are subject to temptation, noble or not.

Respondents propose . . . the answer of state regulation with teeth. . . .

But at least at this moment there are reasons for caution in predicting the effectiveness of the teeth proposed. Respondents' proposals . . . sound much like the guidelines now in place in the Netherlands, the only place where experience with physician-assisted suicide and euthanasia has yielded empirical evidence about how such regulations might affect actual practice. . . . Some commentators marshall evidence that the Dutch guidelines have in practice failed to protect patients from involuntary euthanasia and have been violated with impunity. . . . This evidence is contested. . . . The day may come when we can say with some assurance which side is right, but for now it is the substantiality of the factual disagreement, and the alternatives for resolving it, that matter. They are, for me, dispositive of the due process claim at this time.

. . .

Legislatures . . . have superior opportunities to obtain the facts necessary for a judgment about the present controversy. . . .

. . .

... The experimentation that should be out of the question in constitution-al adjudication displacing legislative judgments is entirely proper, as well as highly desirable, when the legislative power addresses an emerging issue like assisted suicide. The Court should accordingly stay its hand to allow reasonable legislative consideration. While I do not decide for all time that respondents' claim should not be recognized, I acknowledge the legislative institutional competence as the better one to deal with that claim at this time.

Justice Ginsburg, concurring in the judgments.

I concur in the Court's judgments in these cases substantially for the reasons stated by Justice O'Connor in her concurring opinion.

Justice Breyer, concurring in the judgments.

I believe that Justice O'Connor's views, which I share, have greater legal significance than the Court's opinion suggests. I join her separate opinion, except insofar as it joins the majority....

I agree with the Court in Vacco v. Quill that the articulated state interests justify the distinction drawn between physician assisted suicide and withdrawal of life-support. I also agree with the Court that the critical question in both of the cases before us is whether "the 'liberty' specially protected by the Due Process Clause includes a right" of the sort that the respondents assert.... I do not agree, however, with the Court's formulation of that claimed "liberty" interest. The Court describes it as a "right to commit suicide with another's assistance." But I would not reject the respondents' claim without considering a different formulation, for which our legal tradition may provide greater support. That formulation would use words roughly like a "right to die with dignity." But irrespective of the exact words used, at its core would lie personal control over the manner of death, professional medical assistance, and the avoidance of unnecessary and severe physical suffering—combined.

As Justice Souter points out, Justice Harlan's dissenting opinion in Poe v. Ullman, 367 U.S. 497 (1961), offers some support for such a claim....

... [R]espondents ... argue that one can find a "right to die with dignity" by examining the protection the law has provided for related, but not identical, interests relating to personal dignity, medical treatment, and freedom from state-inflicted pain....

I do not believe, however, that this Court need or now should decide whether or a not such a right is "fundamental." That is because, in my view, the avoidance of severe physical pain (connected with death) would have to comprise an essential part of any successful claim and because, as Justice O'Connor points out, the laws before us do not force a dying person to undergo that kind of pain. Rather, the laws of New York and of Washington do not prohibit doctors from providing patients with drugs sufficient to control pain despite the risk that those drugs themselves will kill.... And under these circumstances the laws of New York and Washington would overcome any remaining significant interests and would be justified, regardless.

. . .

Were the legal circumstances different—for example, were state law to prevent the provision of palliative care, including the administration of drugs as needed to avoid pain at the end of life—then the law's impact upon serious and otherwise unavoidable physical pain (accompanying death) would be more directly at issue. And as Justice O'Connor suggests, the Court might have to revisit its conclusions in those cases.

CHAPTER 10

THE EQUAL PROTECTION CLAUSE AND THE REVIEW OF THE REASONABLENESS OF LEGISLATION

SECTION 1 INTRODUCTION—THE SCOPE OF EQUAL PROTECTION

The fourteenth amendment provision that no state shall "deny to any person within its jurisdiction the equal protection of the laws," raises a host of difficult analytical problems. It can hardly be taken to be a guarantee that every law shall treat every person the same, for almost all legislation involves classifications placing special burdens on or granting special benefits to individuals or groups. But if laws may classify, what content can be given to a guarantee of "equal protection of the laws"?

THE ORIGINAL UNDERSTANDING

The Supreme Court originally took a narrow view of the scope of the equal protection clause. In the Slaughter–House Cases, 83 U.S. (16 Wall.) 36, 81 (1872), the Court said: "We doubt very much whether any action of a State not directed by way of discrimination against the negroes as a class, or on account of their race, will ever be held to come within the purview of this provision. It is so clearly a provision for that race and that emergency, that a strong case would be necessary for its application to any other." In Strauder v. West Virginia, 100 U.S. 303, 306, 307 (1880), which invalidated a statute limiting jury service to whites, the Court said: "[The fourteenth amendment] was designed to assure to the colored race the enjoyment of all the civil rights that under the law are enjoyed by white persons, and to give to that race the protection of the General Government, in that enjoyment, whenever it should be denied by the States." In referring to the equal protection clause the Court said: "What is this but declaring that the law in the States shall be the same for the black as for the white; that all persons whether colored or white, shall stand equal before the laws of the States and, in regard to the colored race, for whose protection the Amendment was primarily designed, that no discrimination shall be made against them by law because of their color."

However, the Court shortly expanded its view and brought the full range of legislative classification within the restrictions of the clause. In Barbier v. Connolly, 113 U.S. 27 (1884), the Court upheld a statute prohibiting the operation of laundries from 10 p.m. to 6 a.m., but assumed that the equal protection clause applied. The Court said that the equal protection clause guaranteed, inter alia, that "all persons should be equally entitled to pursue their happiness and acquire and enjoy property;" that "no impediment should be interposed to the pursuits of any one except as applied to the same pursuits by others under like circumstances;" and that "no greater burdens should be laid upon one than are laid upon others in the same calling or condition." The promise of *Barbier* that the equal protection clause would be applied to economic regulations was fulfilled in the following case.

GULF, COLORADO & SANTA FE RAILROAD CO. v. ELLIS, 165 U.S. 150 (1897). The Court invalidated a statute providing that successful plaintiffs in certain kinds of suits against railroad companies should receive in addition to costs reasonable attorney's fees "not to exceed $10." the following passages suggest its reasoning:

"... The act singles out a certain class of debtors and punishes them when for like delinquencies it punishes no others. They are not treated as other debtors, or equally with other debtors. They cannot appeal to the courts as other litigants under like conditions and with like protection. If litigation terminates adversely to them, they are mulcted in the attorney's fees of the successful plaintiff; if it terminates in their favor, they recover no attorney's fees. It is no sufficient answer to say that they are punished only when adjudged to be in the wrong. They do not enter the courts upon equal terms. They must pay attorney's fees if wrong; they do not recover any if right; while their adversaries recover if right and pay nothing if wrong. In the suits, therefore, to which they are parties they are discriminated against, and are not treated as others. They do not stand equal before the law. They do not receive its equal protection. All this is obvious from a mere inspection of the statute.

. . .

"While good faith and a knowledge of existing conditions on the part of a legislature is to be presumed, yet to carry that presumption to the extent of always holding that there must be some undisclosed and unknown reason for subjecting certain individuals or corporations to hostile and discriminating legislation is to make the protecting clauses of the Fourteenth Amendment a mere rope of sand, in no manner restraining state action.

. . .

"But it is said that it is not within the scope of the Fourteenth Amendment to withhold from States the power of classification, and that if the law deals alike with all of a certain class it is not obnoxious to the charge of a denial of equal protection. While, as a general proposition, this is undeniably true, ... yet it is equally true that such classification cannot be made arbitrarily. The State may not say that all white men shall be subjected to the payment of the attorney's fees of parties successfully suing them and all black men not. It may not say that all men beyond a certain age shall be alone thus subjected, or all men possessed of a certain wealth. These are distinctions which do not furnish any proper basis for the attempted classification. That must always rest upon some difference which bears a reasonable and just relation to the act in respect to which the classification is proposed, and can never be made arbitrarily and without any such basis."

. . .

THE DOCTRINE OF REASONABLE CLASSIFICATION

In *Ellis* the Court articulated a doctrine of reasonable classification. To be valid a classification must be reasonably related to the object of the legislation and cannot be arbitrary. But what determines whether a classification is reasonable?

To determine reasonableness of the law

↓

similarily situated be similarily treated

Look to purpose of the law

The following classic discussion of equal protection theory provides a framework of analysis. Tussman and tenBroek, *The Equal Protection of the Laws,* 37 Calif.L.Rev. 341 (1949):

"Here, then, is a paradox: The equal protection of the laws is a 'pledge of the protection of equal laws.' But laws may classify. And 'the very idea of classification is that of inequality.' In tackling this paradox the Court has neither abandoned the demand for equality nor denied the legislative right to classify. It has taken a middle course. It has resolved the contradictory demands of legislative specialization and constitutional generality by a doctrine of reasonable classification.

"The essence of that doctrine can be stated with deceptive simplicity. The Constitution does not require that things different in fact be treated in law as though they were the same. But it does require, in its concern for equality, that those who are similarly situated be similarly treated. The measure of the reasonableness of a classification is the degree of its success in treating similarly those similarly situated....

. . .

"... [W]here are we to look for the test of similarity of situation which determines the reasonableness of a classification? The inescapable answer is that we must look beyond the classification to the purpose of the law. A reasonable classification is one which includes all persons who are similarly situated with respect to the purpose of the law.

"The purpose of a law may be either the elimination of a public 'mischief' or the achievement of some positive public good. To simplify the discussion we shall refer to the purpose of a law in terms of the elimination of mischief, since the same argument holds in either case. We shall speak of the defining character or characteristics of the legislative classification as the trait. We can thus speak of the relation of the classification to the purpose of the law as the relation of the Trait to the Mischief.

. . .

"In other words, we are really dealing with the relation of two classes to each other. The first class consists of all individuals possessing the defining Trait; the second class consists of all individuals possessing, or rather, tainted by, the Mischief at which the law aims. The former is the legislative classification; the latter is the class of those similarly situated with respect to the purpose of the law. We shall refer to these two classes as T and M respectively.

"Now, since the reasonableness of any class T depends entirely upon its relation to a class M, it is obvious that it is impossible to pass judgment on the reasonableness of a classification without taking into consideration, or identifying, the purpose of the law....

"There are five possible relationships between the class defined by the Trait and the class defined by the Mischief. These relationships can be indicated by the following diagrams:

ex. T = japanese
M - spy for Japan

(1) : All *T*'s are *M*'s and all *M*'s are *T*'s

(2) : No *T*'s are *M*'s

(3) : All *T*'s are *M*'s but some *M*'s are not *T*'s

(4) : All *M*'s are *T*'s but some *T*'s are not *M*'s

(5) : Some *T*'s are *M*'s; some *T*'s are not *M*'s; and some *M*'s are not *T*'s

[handwritten margin note: T= possess the trait]

[handwritten margin note: M= tainted by the mischief at which the law aims]

One of these five relationships holds in fact in any case of legislative classification, and we will consider each from the point of view of its "reasonableness."

"The first two situations represent respectively the ideal limits of reasonableness and unreasonableness. . . .

[handwritten margin note: 1) reasonable 2) unreasonable 3) violation under-inclusive]

"Classification of the third type may be called 'under-inclusive.' All who are included in the class are tainted with the mischief, but there are others also tainted whom the classification does not include. Since the classification does not include all who are similarly situated with respect to the purpose of the law, there is a prima facie violation of the equal protection requirement of reasonable classification.

"But the Court has recognized the very real difficulties under which legislatures operate—difficulties arising out of both the nature of the legislative process and of the society which legislation attempts perennially to reshape—and it has refused to strike down indiscriminately all legislation embodying the classificatory inequality here under consideration.

"In justifying this refusal, the Court has defended under-inclusive classifications on such grounds as: the legislature may attack a general problem in a piecemeal fashion; 'some play must be allowed for the joints of the machine'; 'a statute aimed at what is deemed an evil, and hitting it presumably where experience shows it to be most felt, is not to be upset . . .'; 'the law does all that is needed when it does all that it can . . .'; and—perhaps with some impatience—the equal protection clause is not 'a pedagogic requirement of the impracticable.'

"These generalities, while expressive of judicial tolerance, are not, however, very helpful. They do not constitute a clear statement of the circumstances and conditions which justify such tolerance—which justify a departure from the strict requirements of the principle of equality. . . .

"The fourth type of classification imposes a burden upon a wider range of individuals than are included in the class of those tainted with the mischief at which the law aims. It can thus be called 'over-inclusive.' Herod, ordering the death of all male children born on a particular day because one of them would some day bring about his downfall, employed such a classification. It is exemplified by the quarantine and the dragnet. The wartime treatment of American citizens of Japanese ancestry is a striking recent instance of the imposition of burdens upon a large class of individuals because some of them were believed to be disloyal.

[handwritten margin note: 4) over-inclusive]

"The prima facie case against such departures from the ideal standards of reasonable classification is stronger than the case against under-inclusiveness. For in the latter case, all who are included in the class are at least tainted by the mischief at which the law aims; while over-inclusive classifications reach out to the innocent bystander, the hapless victim of circumstance or association."[a]

APPLICATION OF THE EQUAL PROTECTION LIMITATION TO THE FEDERAL GOVERNMENT THROUGH THE DUE PROCESS CLAUSE OF THE FIFTH AMENDMENT

Originally 5th has no equal protection clause like 14th

Originally the Supreme Court took the position that "[u]nlike the Fourteenth Amendment, the Fifth contains no equal protection clause and it provides no guaranty against discriminatory legislation by Congress." Detroit Bank v. United States, 317 U.S. 329, 337 (1943). At the same time the Court indicated that discriminatory legislation "may be so arbitrary and injurious in character as to violate the due process clause of the Fifth Amendment." Id. at 338.

However, in Bolling v. Sharpe, 347 U.S. 497, 499 (1954) (a companion case to Brown v. Board of Educ. of Topeka, 347 U.S. 483 (1954)) the Court, in invalidating racial segregation in the District of Columbia schools, said:

"Equal protection of the laws = 14th amd"

"The Fifth Amendment which is applicable in the District of Columbia does not contain an equal protection clause as does the Fourteenth Amendment which applies only to the states. But the concepts of equal protection and due process, both stemming from our American ideal of fairness, are not mutually exclusive. The 'equal protection of the laws' is a more explicit safeguard of prohibited unfairness than 'due process of law,' and, therefore, we do not imply that the two are always interchangeable phrases. But, as this Court has recognized, discrimination may be so unjustifiable as to be violative of due process."

By 1975 the Court went so far as to say, in invalidating a gender classification in the Social Security Act: "This Court's approach to Fifth Amendment equal protection claims has always been precisely the same as to equal protection claims under the Fourteenth Amendment." Weinberger v. Wiesenfeld, 420 U.S. 636, 639, n. 2 (1975). However, the next year the Court, in holding invalid a federal regulation barring resident aliens from employment in the federal competitive civil service, distinguished decisions holding similar state laws to be a violation of equal protection by saying: "The concept of equal justice under law is served by the Fifth Amendment's guarantee of due process, as well as by the Equal Protection Clause of the Fourteenth Amendment. Although both Amendments require the same type of analysis, ... the Court of Appeals correctly stated that the two protections are not always coextensive. Not only does the language of the two Amendments differ, but more importantly, there may be overriding national interests which justify selective federal legislation that would be unacceptable for an individual State." Hampton v. Mow Sun Wong, 426 U.S. 88, 100 (1976).

Vance v. Bradley

In Vance v. Bradley, 440 U.S. 93, 94 (1979), the Court said regarding a federal statute that the "issue presented is whether Congress violates the equal protection component of the Fifth Amendment's Due Process Clause." In a footnote to that statement the Court said: "Concern with assuring equal protection was part of the fabric of our Constitution even before the Fourteenth Amendment expressed it most directly in applying it to the States.... Accordingly, the Court has held that the Due Process Clause of the Fifth Amendment

a. Copyright (c), 1949, California Law Review, Inc. Reprinted by Permission.

Also see generally Note, *Developments in the Law—Equal Protection,* 82 Harv.L.Rev. 1065 (1969).

forbids the Federal Government from denying equal protection of the laws."
Yet more recently the Court asserted that benign "race-conscious classifications
adopted by Congress to address racial and ethnic discrimination are subject to a
different standard than such classifications prescribed by state and local
governments." Metro Broadcasting, Inc. v. Federal Communications Commission, 497 U.S. 547, 565 (1990). That portion of *Metro Broadcasting* was
specifically overruled in Adarand Constructors, Inc. v. Pena, 515 U.S. 200, 231–
32 (1995), however, where the Court declared "that the Constitution imposes
upon federal, state, and local government actors the same obligation to respect
the personal right to equal protection of the laws."[a]

THE STANDARD OF REVIEW

The Tussman and tenBroek excerpt does not address directly the question
of the standard of review to be applied in equal protection cases. How closely
must a classification be related to the purpose? How important must the
purpose be? Who has the burden of proof on the issue of reasonableness of the
classification?

In Lindsley v. Natural Carbonic Gas Co., 220 U.S. 61, 78 (1911), the Court
stated a standard which gave substantial deference to the legislative judgment
in making classifications:

> "The rules by which [the contention that a statutory classification
> violates the equal protection clause] must be tested, as is shown by
> repeated decisions of this court, are these: 1. The equal protection clause of
> the 14th Amendment does not take from the state the power to classify in
> the adoption of police laws, but admits of the exercise of a wide scope of
> discretion in that regard, and avoids what is done only when it is without
> any reasonable basis, and therefore is purely arbitrary. 2. A classification
> having some reasonable basis does not offend against that clause merely
> because it is not made with mathematical nicety, or because in practice it
> results in some inequality. 3. When the classification in such a law is called
> in question, if any state of facts reasonably can be conceived that would
> sustain it, the existence of that state of facts at the time the law was
> enacted must be assumed. 4. One who assails the classification in such a
> law must carry the burden of showing that it does not rest upon any
> reasonable basis, but is essentially arbitrary."

However, in the 1920s and early 1930s the Court invalidated a substantial
number of statutes under equal protection—particularly statutes discriminating against corporations and statutes making unusual tax classifications. In
many of these cases the Court, as in the due process cases of the period set out
in Chapter 9, supra, appeared to be placing the burden of justifying the
classifications on the state, without specifying how great that burden was. In
Quaker City Cab Co. v. Pennsylvania, 277 U.S. 389, 402 (1928), e.g., the Court
invalidated a law imposing a tax on corporations but not on individuals engaged
in the transportation business. The Court said: "The tax is imposed merely
because the owner is a corporation. The discrimination is not justified by any
difference in the source of the receipts or in the situation or character of the
property employed. It follows that the section fails to meet the requirement
that a classification to be consistent with the equal protection clause must be
based on a real and substantial difference having reasonable relation to the

---

a. See generally Karst, *The Fifth   55 N.C.L.Rev. 541 (1977).
Amendment's Guarantee of Equal Protection,*

subject of the legislation . . . In no view can [the classification] be held to have more than an arbitrary basis. . . ."

Two cases decided on the same day in 1936 further illustrate the failure of the Court to articulate a consistent standard of review in equal protection cases. In Borden's Farm Products Co. v. Ten Eyck, 297 U.S. 251, 263 (1936), the Court upheld a provision of the New York Milk Control Law that allowed milk dealers lacking a well-advertised trade name to sell to stores at one cent per quart lower than the price fixed for those who had one: "In the light of the facts found the legislature might reasonably have thought trade conditions existed justifying the fixing of a differential. Judicial inquiry does not concern itself with the accuracy of the legislative finding, but only with the question whether it so lacks any reasonable basis as to be arbitrary." In Mayflower Farms, Inc. v. Ten Eyck, 297 U.S. 266, 274 (1936), however, the Court invalidated another provision of the New York law which limited the one cent per quart differential to milk dealers who had been continuously in business since April 10, 1933, saying:

> "The challenged provision . . . is not a regulation of a business or activity in the interest of, or for the protection of, the public, but an attempt to give an economic advantage to those engaged in a given business at an arbitrary date as against all those who enter the industry after that date. The appellees do not intimate that the classification bears any relation to the public health or welfare generally; that the provision will discourage monopoly; or that it was aimed at any abuse, cognizable by law, in the milk business. In the absence of any such showing, we have no right to conjure up possible situations which might justify the discrimination. The classification is arbitrary and unreasonable and denies the appellant the equal protection of the law."

In 1937 the Court's approach to the application of equal protection changed as did its approach to the application of due process. With respect to ordinary social and economic legislation, the standard of review is low and the cases will be reviewed in Section 2. Higher standards of review are applied to cases in which the bases of classification—race, nationality, alienage, gender, legitimacy—are held to be "suspect" and to require special justification. These cases will be reviewed in Section 3. And finally in Section 4 we will examine cases in which the Court holds that legislative classifications which burden constitutionally protected interests are invalid if not closely related to important or substantial governmental interests.

As we pursue the three strands of equal protection through this chapter, it may be helpful to have a brief overview of the analytical differences among them. Consider the implications of the following three cases.

In the first, a statute excluding resident aliens from the receipt of welfare benefits was held invalid because "classifications based on alienage, like those based on nationality or race, are inherently suspect and subject to close judicial scrutiny." Graham v. Richardson, 403 U.S. 365, 372 (1971). In the second, a statute denying welfare assistance to residents who had not resided within the state for a year was held invalid because it served "to penalize the exercise" of the constitutionally protected "right" to travel and the state had not shown that the statutory scheme was "necessary to promote a *compelling* governmental interest." Shapiro v. Thompson, 394 U.S. 618, 634 (1969). In the third, a statute providing lower welfare payments for dependent children than for the aged was upheld because it did not use a suspect classification, burden a constitutionally protected interest, or fail the general test of rationality—there was some relationship between the classification and the state objective. Jefferson v. Hackney, 406 U.S. 535, 546, 549 (1972).

SECTION 2.   SOCIAL AND ECONOMIC REGULATORY LEGISLATION

Railway Express Agency v. New York

336 U.S. 106, 69 S.Ct. 463, 93 L.Ed. 533 (1949).

Mr. Justice Douglas delivered the opinion of the Court.

Section 124 of the Traffic Regulations of the City of New York promulgated by the Police Commissioner provides:

> "No person shall operate, or cause to be operated, in or upon any street an advertising vehicle; provided that nothing herein contained shall prevent the putting of business notices upon business delivery vehicles, so long as such vehicles are engaged in the usual business or regular work of the owner and not used merely or mainly for advertising."

Appellant is engaged in a nation-wide express business. It operates about 1,900 trucks in New York City and sells the space on the exterior sides of these trucks for advertising. That advertising is for the most part unconnected with its own business. It was convicted in the magistrates court and fined. The judgment of conviction was sustained in the Court of Special Sessions.... The Court of Appeals affirmed without opinion by a divided vote....

The Court of Special Sessions concluded that advertising on vehicles using the streets of New York City constitutes a distraction to vehicle drivers and to pedestrians alike and therefore affects the safety of the public in the use of the streets. We do not sit to weigh evidence on the due process issue in order to determine whether the regulation is sound or appropriate; nor is it our function to pass judgment on its wisdom. See Olsen v. State of Nebraska, 313 U.S. 236. We would be trespassing on one of the most intensely local and specialized of all municipal problems if we held that this regulation had no relation to the traffic problem of New York City. It is the judgment of the local authorities that it does have such a relation. And nothing has been advanced which shows that to be palpably false.

The question of equal protection of the laws is pressed more strenuously on us. It is pointed out that the regulation draws the line between advertisements of products sold by the owner of the truck and general advertisements. It is argued that unequal treatment on the basis of such a distinction is not justified by the aim and purpose of the regulation. It is said, for example, that one of appellant's trucks carrying the advertisement of a commercial house would not cause any greater distraction of pedestrians and vehicle drivers than if the commercial house carried the same advertisement on its own truck. Yet the regulation allows the latter to do what the former is forbidden from doing. It is therefore contended that the classification which the regulation makes has no relation to the traffic problem since a violation turns not on what kind of advertisements are carried on trucks but on whose trucks they are carried.

That, however, is a superficial way of analyzing the problem, even if we assume that it is premised on the correct construction of the regulation. The local authorities may well have concluded that those who advertised their own wares on their trucks do not present the same traffic problem in view of the nature or extent of the advertising which they use. It would take a degree of omniscience which we lack to say that such is not the case. If that judgment is correct, the advertising displays that are exempt have less incidence on traffic than those of appellants.

We cannot say that that judgment is not an allowable one. Yet if it is, the classification has relation to the purpose for which it is made and does not contain the kind of discrimination against which the Equal Protection Clause affords protection. It is by such practical considerations based on experience rather than by theoretical inconsistencies that the question of equal protection is to be answered. Patsone v. Commonwealth of Pennsylvania, 232 U.S. 138, 144.... And the fact that New York City sees fit to eliminate from traffic this kind of distraction but does not touch what may be even greater ones in a different category, such as the vivid displays on Times Square, is immaterial. It is no requirement of equal protection that all evils of the same genus be eradicated or none at all....

Affirmed.

Mr. Justice Rutledge acquiesces in the Court's opinion and judgment, dubitante on the question of equal protection of the laws.

Mr. Justice Jackson, concurring.

There are two clauses of the Fourteenth Amendment which this Court may invoke to invalidate ordinances by which municipal governments seek to solve their local problems. One says that no state shall "deprive any person of life, liberty, or property, without due process of law". The other declares that no state shall "deny to any person within its jurisdiction the equal protection of the laws."

My philosophy as to the relative readiness with which we should resort to these two clauses is almost diametrically opposed to the philosophy which prevails on this Court. While claims of denial of equal protection are frequently asserted, they are rarely sustained. But the Court frequently uses the due process clause to strike down measures taken by municipalities to deal with activities in their streets and public places which the local authorities consider to create hazards, annoyances or discomforts to their inhabitants....

The burden should rest heavily upon one who would persuade us to use the due process clause to strike down a substantive law or ordinance. Even its provident use against municipal regulations frequently disables all government—state, municipal and federal—from dealing with the conduct in question because the requirement of due process is also applicable to State and Federal Governments. Invalidation of a statute or an ordinance on due process grounds leaves ungoverned and ungovernable conduct which many people find objectionable.

Invocation of the equal protection clause, on the other hand, does not disable any governmental body from dealing with the subject at hand. It merely means that the prohibition or regulation must have a broader impact. I regard it as a salutary doctrine that cities, states and the Federal Government must exercise their powers so as not to discriminate between their inhabitants except upon some reasonable differentiation fairly related to the object of regulation. This equality is not merely abstract justice. The framers of the Constitution knew, and we should not forget today, that there is no more effective practical guaranty against arbitrary and unreasonable government than to require that the principles of law which officials would impose upon a minority must be imposed generally. Conversely, nothing opens the door to arbitrary action so effectively as to allow those officials to pick and choose only a few to whom they will apply legislation and thus to escape the political retribution that might be visited upon them if larger numbers were affected. Courts can take no better measure to assure that laws will be just than to require that laws be equal in operation. . . .

In this case, if the City of New York should assume that display of any advertising on vehicles tends and intends to distract the attention of persons using the highways and to increase the dangers of its traffic, I should think it fully within its constitutional powers to forbid it all. The same would be true if the City should undertake to eliminate or minimize the hazard by any generally applicable restraint, such as limiting the size, color, shape or perhaps to some extent the contents of vehicular advertising. Instead of such general regulation of advertising, however, the City seeks to reduce the hazard only by saying that while some may, others may not exhibit such appeals. The same display, for example, advertising cigarettes, which this appellant is forbidden to carry on its trucks, may be carried on the trucks of a cigarette dealer and might on the trucks of this appellant if it dealt in cigarettes. And almost an identical advertisement, certainly one of equal size, shape, color and appearance, may be carried by this appellant if it proclaims its own offer to transport cigarettes. But it may not be carried so long as the message is not its own but a cigarette dealer's offer to sell the same cigarettes.

. . .

The question in my mind comes to this. Where individuals contribute to an evil or danger in the same way and to the same degree, may those who do so for hire be prohibited, while those who do so for their own commercial ends but not for hire be allowed to continue? I think the answer has to be that the hireling may be put in a class by himself and may be dealt with differently than those who act on their own. But this is not merely because such a discrimination will enable the lawmaker to diminish the evil. That might be done by many classifications, which I should think wholly unsustainable. It is rather because there is a real difference between doing in self-interest and doing for hire, so that it is one thing to tolerate action from those who act on their own and it is another thing to permit the same action to be promoted for a price.

. . .

WILLIAMSON v. LEE OPTICAL OF OKLAHOMA, INC., 348 U.S. 483 (1955). The due process portions of this case are set out supra, p. 529. The Court disposed of an equal protection challenge to the portion of the law exempting sellers of ready-to-wear glasses from regulations imposed on opticians as follows:

statute upheld

"The problem of legislative classification is a perennial one, admitting of no doctrinaire definition. Evils in the same field may be of different dimensions and propositions, requiring different remedies. Or so the legislature may think. . . . Or the reform may take one step at a time, addressing itself to the phase of the problem which seems most acute to the legislative mind. . . . The legislature may select one phase of one field, and apply a remedy there, neglecting the others. . . . The prohibition of the Equal Protection Clause goes no further than the invidious discrimination. We cannot say that that point has been reached here. For all this record shows, the ready-to-wear branch of this business may not loom large in Oklahoma or may present problems of regulation distinct from the other branch."

SCOPE AND LEGITIMACY OF JUDICIAL REFIEW OF THE RATIONALITY OF LEGISLATION UNDER EQUAL PROTECTION

Constitutional law scholars are sharply divided on the question whether the courts should examine ordinary economic legislation under the equal protection clause to insure that such legislation is at least minimally related to some general good. Three general views are identifiable.

3 views to equal protection & assessing laws.

Some scholars assert the view that courts should examine both the means and the ends of legislation. They argue that courts cannot escape the burden of examining the outcomes of the legislative process to determine whether the regulations are reasonably related to legitimate public purposes. See, e.g. Tribe, *American Constitutional Law* 582–5, 1440, 1451 (2d ed. 1988); Tussman and tenBroek, *Equal Protection of the Laws,* 37 Calif.L.Rev. 341, 350 (1949). One such scholar, building on a Madisonian republican vision that legitimate policy must be formulated by representatives deliberating to further the public good rather than simply reflecting interest-group pressures, suggests that "[j]udicial scrutiny of the legislative process might take the form of a more serious inquiry into both process and outcome, designed to ensure that what emerges is genuinely public rather than a reflection of existing relations of private power." Sunstein, *Interest Groups in American Public Law,* 38 Stan.L.Rev. 29, 86 (1985).

Others assert that courts should not reexamine legislative choices as to the ends to be served by legislation but should engage in a real inquiry to determine whether the means selected have a real and substantial relation to the object sought to be attained. See, e.g., Gunther, *Forward: In Search of Evolving Doctrine on a Changing Court: A Model for a Newer Equal Protection,* 86 Harv.L.Rev. 1 (1972).

A third view is that the proper role of the courts is to police the structural and procedural limitations the Constitution imposes on the legislative process but not to scrutinize the outcomes for reasonableness. The proponents of this view state that, except for those constitutional provisions which place substantive limits on legislative outcomes by extending special protection to interests against the legislative process, the reach and limits of otherwise valid laws are assumed to be adequately explained by the conflicting forces within the legislative process which shaped them. See, e.g., Linde, *Due Process of Lawmaking,* 55 Neb.L.Rev. 197 (1975); Barrett, *The Rational Basis Standard for Equal Protection Review of Ordinary Legislative Classifications,* 68 Ky.L.Rev. 845 (1980).

To what extent are these views reflected in the following cases?

Federal Communications Commission v. Beach Communications, Inc.

508 U.S. 307, 113 S.Ct. 2096, 124 L.Ed.2d 211 (1993).

Justice Thomas delivered the opinion of the Court.

In providing for the regulation of cable television facilities, Congress has drawn a distinction between facilities that serve separately owned and managed buildings and those that serve one or more buildings under common ownership or management. Cable facilities in the latter category are exempt from regulation as long as they provide services without using public rights-of-way. The question ... is whether there is any conceivable rational basis justifying this distinction for purposes of the Due Process Clause of the Fifth Amendment.

I

The Cable Communications Policy Act of 1984 (Cable Act) ... provided for the franchising of cable systems by local governmental authorities.... Section 602(7) ... determines the reach of the franchise requirement by defining the operative term "cable system[]" [as] any facility designed to provide video programming to multiple subscribers through "closed transmission paths," but ... not ...

"a facility that serves only subscribers in 1 or more multiple unit dwellings under common ownership, control, or management, unless such facility or facilities us[e] any public right-of-way." § 602(7)(B)....

In part, this provision tracks a regulatory "private cable" exemption previously promulgated by the Federal Communications Commission (FCC or Commission) pursuant to pre-existing authority under the Communications Act....

[The] FCC ... clarif[ied] the agency's interpretation of the term "cable system" ... [i]n [a] proceeding [that] addressed the application of the exemption codified in § 602(7)(B) to satellite master antenna television (SMATV) facilities. Unlike a traditional cable television system, which delivers video programming to a large community of subscribers through coaxial cables laid under city streets or along utility lines, an SMATV system typically receives a signal from a satellite through a small satellite dish located on a rooftop and then retransmits the signal by wire to units within a building or complex of buildings.... The Commission ruled that an SMATV system that serves multiple buildings via a network of interconnected physical transmission lines is a cable system, unless it falls within the § 602(7)(B) exemption.... Consistent with the plain terms of the statutory exemption, the Commission concluded that such an SMATV system is subject to the franchise requirement if its transmission lines interconnect separately owned and managed buildings or if its lines use or cross any public right-of-way....

Respondents ...—SMATV operators that would be subject to franchising under the Cable Act as construed by the Commission—petitioned the Court of Appeals for review.... [A] majority ... found merit in the claim that § 602(7) violates the implied equal protection guarantee of the Due Process Clause.... [A]bsen[t] what it termed "the predominant rationale for local franchising" (use of public rights-of-way), the court saw no rational basis "[o]n the record," and was "unable to imagine" any conceivable basis, for distinguishing between those facilities exempted by the statute and those SMATV cable systems that link separately owned and managed buildings....

... We now reverse.

II

Whether embodied in the Fourteenth Amendment or inferred from the Fifth, equal protection is not a license for courts to judge the wisdom, fairness, or logic of legislative choices. In areas of social and economic policy, a statutory classification that neither proceeds along suspect lines nor infringes fundamental constitutional rights must be upheld against equal protection challenge if there is any reasonably conceivable state of facts that could provide a rational basis for the classification. See Sullivan v. Stroop, 496 U. S. 478, 485 (1990); Bowen v. Gilliard, 483 U. S. 587, 600–603 (1987); United States Railroad Retirement Bd. v. Fritz, 449 U. S. 166, 174–179 (1980); Dandridge v. Williams, 397 U. S. 471, 484–485 (1970). Where there are "plausible reasons" for Congress' action, "our inquiry is at an end." United States Railroad Retirement Bd. v. Fritz.... This standard of review is a paradigm of judicial restraint. "The Constitution presumes that, absent some reason to infer antipathy, even improvident decisions will eventually be rectified by the democratic process and that judicial intervention is generally unwarranted no matter how unwisely we may think a political branch has acted." Vance v. Bradley, 440 U. S. 93, 97 (1979) (footnote omitted).

On rational-basis review, a classification in a statute such as the Cable Act comes to us bearing a strong presumption of validity, see Lyng v. Automobile Workers, 485 U. S. 360, 370 (1988), and those attacking the rationality of the legislative classification have the burden "to negative every conceivable basis which might support it," Lehnhausen v. Lake Shore Auto Parts Co., 410 U. S. 356, 364 (1973).... Moreover, because we never require a legislature to articulate its reasons for enacting a statute, it is entirely irrelevant for constitutional purposes whether the conceived reason for the challenged distinction actually motivated the legislature. United States Railroad Retirement Bd. v. Fritz.... Thus, the absence of "legislative facts" explaining the distinction "[o]n the record," ... has no significance in rational-basis analysis.... [A] legislative choice is not subject to courtroom fact-finding and may be based on rational speculation unsupported by evidence or empirical data....

These restraints on judicial review have added force "where the legislature must necessarily engage in a process of line-drawing." ... Defining the class of persons subject to a regulatory requirement—much like classifying governmental beneficiaries—"inevitably requires that some persons who have an almost equally strong claim to favored treatment be placed on different sides of the line, and the fact [that] the line might have been drawn differently at some points is a matter for legislative, rather than judicial, consideration." ... The distinction ... here represents such a line: By excluding from the definition of "cable system" those facilities that serve commonly owned or managed buildings without using public rights-of-way, § 602(7)(B) delineates the bounds of the regulatory field. Such scope-of-coverage provisions are unavoidable components of most economic or social legislation. In establishing the franchise requirement, Congress had to draw the line somewhere [and] choose which facilities to franchise. This necessity renders the precise coordinates of the resulting legislative judgment virtually unreviewable, since the legislature must be allowed leeway to approach a perceived problem incrementally. See, e. g., Williamson v. Lee Optical of Okla., Inc., 348 U. S. 483 (1955)....

Applying these principles, we conclude that the common-ownership distinction is constitutional. There are at least two possible bases for the distinction; either one suffices. First, ... it is plausible that Congress ... adopted the FCC's earlier rationale[, under which] common ownership was thought to be indicative of those systems for which the costs of regulation would outweigh the benefits to consumers. Because the number of subscribers was a similar indicator, the Commission also exempted cable facilities that served fewer than 50 subscribers....

This regulatory-efficiency model ... provides a conceivable basis for the common-ownership exemption. A legislator might rationally assume that systems serving only commonly owned or managed buildings without crossing public rights-of-way would typically be limited in size or would share some other attribute affecting their impact on the welfare of cable viewers such that regulators could "safely ignor[e]" these systems.

Respondents argue that Congress did not intend common ownership to be a surrogate for small size, since Congress simultaneously rejected the FCC's 50–subscriber exemption by omitting it from the Cable Act.... Whether the posited reason . . . actually motivated Congress is "constitutionally irrelevant," . . . and, in any event, the FCC's explanation indicates that both common ownership and number of subscribers were considered indicia of "very small" cable systems. Respondents also contend that an SMATV operator could increase his subscription base and still qualify for the exemption simply by installing a separate satellite dish on each building served. . . . The additional cost of multiple dishes and associated transmission equipment, however, would impose an independent constraint on system size.

Furthermore, small size is only one plausible ownership-related factor contributing to consumer welfare. Subscriber influence is another. Where an SMATV system serves a complex of buildings under common ownership or management, individual subscribers could conceivably have greater bargaining power vis-a-vis the cable operator (even if the number of dwelling units were large), since all the subscribers could negotiate with one voice through the common owner or manager. Such an owner might have substantial leverage, because he could withhold permission to operate the SMATV system on his property. He would also have an incentive to guard the interests of his tenants. Thus, there could be less need to establish regulatory safeguards for subscribers in commonly owned complexes. Respondents acknowledge such possibilities, . . . and we certainly cannot say that these assumptions would be irrational.

There is a second conceivable basis for the statutory distinction. Suppose competing SMATV operators wish to sell video programming to subscribers in a group of contiguous buildings, such as a single city block, which can be interconnected by wire without crossing a public right-of-way. If all the buildings belong to one owner or are commonly managed, that owner or manager could freely negotiate a deal for all subscribers on a competitive basis. But if the buildings are separately owned and managed, the first SMATV operator who gains a foothold by signing a contract and installing a satellite dish and associated transmission equipment on one of the buildings would enjoy a powerful cost advantage in competing for the remaining subscribers: he could connect additional buildings for the cost of a few feet of cable, whereas any competitor would have to recover the cost of his own satellite headend facility. Thus, the first operator could charge rates well above his cost and still undercut the competition. This potential for effective monopoly power might theoretically justify regulating the latter class of SMATV systems and not the former.

III

. . . [T]here are plausible rationales unrelated to the use of public rights-of-way for regulating cable facilities serving separately owned and managed buildings. The assumptions underlying these rationales may be erroneous, but the very fact that they are "arguable" is sufficient, on rational-basis review, to "immuniz[e]" the congressional choice from constitutional challenge. Vance v. Bradley, 440 U. S., at 112.

The judgment of the Court of Appeals is reversed. . . .

Justice Stevens, concurring in the judgment.

. . .

. . . In my opinion the interest in the free use of one's own property provides adequate support for an exception from burdensome regulation and franchising requirements even when the property is occupied not only by family members and guests, but by lessees and co-owners as well, and even when the property complex encompasses multiple buildings.

The master antenna serving multiple units in an apartment building is less unsightly than a forest of individual antennas, each serving a separate apartment. It was surely sensible to allow owners to make use of such an improvement without incurring the costs of franchising and economic regulation....

That brings us to the "private cable" exemption.... A justification for [it] that rests on the presumption that an owner of property should be allowed to use an improvement on his own property as he sees fit unless there is a sufficient public interest in denying him that right simply does not apply [where] the improvement—here, the satellite antenna—is being used to distribute signals to subscribers on other people's property. In that situation, the property owner, or the SMATV operator, has reached out beyond the property line and is seeking to employ the satellite antenna in the broader market for television programming. While the crossing of that line need not trigger regulatory intervention, and the absence of such a crossing may not prevent such intervention, it certainly cannot be said that government is disabled, by the Constitution, from regulating in the case of the former and abstaining in the case of the latter....

Thus, while I am not fully persuaded that the "private cable" exemption is justified by the size of the market which it encompasses,[1] or by the Court's "monopoly" rationale,[2] ... it is reasonable to presume[3] that Congress was motivated by an interest in allowing property owners to exercise freedom in the use of their own property. Legislation so motivated surely does not violate the sovereign's duty to govern impartially. See Hampton v. Mow Sun Wong, 426 U. S. 88, 100 (1976)....

HELLER v. DOE, 509 U.S. 312 (1993). The Court rejected an equal protection challenge by adult mentally retarded people to Kentucky statutes (1) authorizing their involuntary civil commitment on a clear and convincing standard of proof, while requiring proof beyond a reasonable doubt for involuntary commitment of mentally ill persons, and (2) allowing close relatives and guardians of the mentally retarded, but not the mentally ill, to participate in commitment proceedings as parties entitled to present evidence and appeal. Confining itself to "rational-basis review" because that is how the case had been litigated, the Court, per Justice Kennedy, cited much of its discussion of that standard in *Beach Communications* and noted that in neither City of Cleburne v. Cleburne Living Center, infra, page 918, nor Schweiker v. Wilson, infra, page 710, "did we purport to apply a different standard of rational-basis review from that just described." although "even the standard of rationality ... must find some footing in the realities of the subject addressed by the legislation ... Kentucky has proffered more than adequate justifications for the differences in treatment between the mentally retarded and the mentally ill."

---

1. Approximately 25% of all multiple dwellings units are in complexes large enough to support an SMATV system.... Furthermore, whereas the FCC had, prior to [the Cable Act], exempted from regulation cable systems of less than 50 subscribers as well as those serving commonly owned multiple unit dwellings, Congress exempted only the latter when it passed the Cable Act, leaving out the exemption based on system size. Respondent thus makes a strong argument that Congress may have rejected the very rationale upon which the FCC, and the Court, rely.

2. ... [T]he Court's analysis overlooks the competitive presence of traditional cable as a potential constraint on an SMATV operator's capacity to extract monopoly rents from landlords.

3. The Court['s] ... formulation sweeps too broadly.... Judicial review under the "conceivable set of facts" test is tantamount to no review at all.... [W]hen the actual rationale for the legislative classification is unclear, we should inquire whether the classification is rationally related to "a legitimate purpose that we may reasonably presume to have motivated an impartial legislature." ...

The lower standard of proof for involuntary commitment of the mentally retarded "follows from the fact that mental retardation is easier to diagnose than is mental illness[,]" because it "tends to equalize the risks of an erroneous determination that the subject of a commitment proceeding has the condition in question." Moreover, there is a "reasonably conceivable state of facts ... from which Kentucky could conclude that the second prerequisite to commitment"—dangerousness to self or others—"is established more easily, as a general rule, in the case of the mentally retarded." That is so, because "retardation is a permanent, relatively stable condition," allowing reliance on the record of previous behavior, whereas "[m]anifestations of mental illness may be sudden, and past behavior may not be an adequate predictor of future actions" and prediction is "complicated as well by the difficulties inherent in diagnosis of mental illness." Finally, a "more far-reaching rationale justifying the different burdens of proof" is that the "prevailing methods of treatment for the mentally retarded, as a general rule, are much less invasive than are those given the mentally ill." Whereas the ill typically receive psychotropic drugs and psychiatric treatment involving "intrusive inquiries into the patient's innermost thoughts," the retarded more typically receive training for self-care and self-sufficiency. Although "the loss of liberty ... may be similar in many respects" for both groups, and "some persons committed for mental retardation are subjected to more intrusive treatments ..., it would have been plausible for the Kentucky legislature to believe that most mentally retarded individuals who are committed receive treatment which is different from, and less invasive than, that to which the mentally ill are subjected." The question being "at least debatable, ... rational-basis review permits a legislature to use just this sort of generalization." In sum, "[e]ach of these rationales, 'standing on its own, would suffice to establish a rational basis' " for the differential burden of proof.

As for the differential rights of close relatives and guardians to participate in the commitment proceeding, retardation "has its onset during a person's developmental period" and mental illness "may arise or manifest itself ... only after minority when the afflicted person's immediate family members have no knowledge of the medical condition and have long ceased to provide care and support." Moreover, adults diagnosed as mentally ill "may have a need for privacy that justifies ... confining a commitment proceeding to the smallest group compatible with due process." Hence, "Kentucky may have concluded that close relatives and guardians, both of whom likely have intimate knowledge of a mentally retarded person's abilities and experiences, have valuable insights which should be considered during the involuntary commitment process." By contrast, Kentucky also "may have concluded that participation as parties by relatives and guardians of the mentally ill would not in most cases have been of sufficient help to the trier of fact to justify the additional burden and complications of granting party status."

Justice Souter's dissent, joined in full by Justices Blackmun and Stevens, found both distinctions "not supported by any rational justification."[a] He, too, declined to address whether "heightened scrutiny" should apply, but only because it was unnecessary since the distinctions failed "rational-basis scrutiny, ... which we have previously applied to a classification on the basis of mental disability, see Cleburne v. Cleburne Living Center." He "would follow

a. Justice O'Connor also joined the dissent insofar as it found the differential standard of proof for commitment "irrational," but she agreed with the Court that "there are sufficiently plausible and legitimate reasons for the legislative determination" to differentiate regarding party status for close relatives and guardians.

Cleburne here" and thought the Court's opinion left *"Cleburne's* status … uncertain."[b]

With respect to the burden of proof differential, Justice Souter first argued that rationality is not satisfied "if burdens of proof rise simply with difficulties of proof," because "burdens of proof are assigned and risks of error are allocated not to reflect the mere difficulty of avoiding error, but the importance of avoiding it as judged after a thorough consideration of those respective interests of the parties that will be affected by the allocation"—in this case the State's "interests of protecting society from those posing dangers and protecting the ill or helpless individual from his own incapacities" and the individual's interests in "freedom from restraint and freedom from the stigma that restraint and its justifications impose on an institutionalized person." Justice Souter could find no "differences in the respective interests of the public and the subjects of the commitment proceedings" that provided a rational basis for differentiating between the ill and the retarded:

"… Both the ill and the retarded may be dangerous, each may require care, and the State's interest is seemingly of equal strength in each category of cases. No one has or would argue that the value of liberty varies somehow depending on whether one is alleged to be ill or retarded, and a mentally retarded person has as much to lose by civil commitment to an institution as a mentally ill counterpart … Even assuming, then, that the assertion of different degrees of difficulty of proof both of mental illness and mental retardation and of the dangerousness inherent in each condition is true (an assertion for which there is no support in the record), it lends not a shred of rational support to the decision to discriminate against the retarded in allocating the risk of erroneous curtailment of liberty."

He also disagreed with the Court that "it would have been plausible for the Kentucky legislature to believe that most mentally retarded individuals who are committed receive treatment which is … less invasive tha[n] that to which the mentally ill are subjected." Studies conducted nationally and in neighboring states indicated widespread use—and frequent abuse—of "mind-altering medication" and "intrusive psychiatric therapy" with respect to the mentally retarded as well as the mentally ill, and "[t]here being nothing in the record to suggest that Kentucky's institutions are free from these practices, and no reason whatever to assume so, there simply is no plausible basis for the Court's assumption that the institutional response to mental retardation is in the main less intrusive … than treatment of mental illness." Based on the "available literature … there are no apparent differences of therapeutic regimes that would plausibly explain less rigorous commitment standards for those alleged to be mentally retarded than for those alleged to be mentally ill."

As for the involvement of family members and guardians in the commitment proceeding, Justice Souter thought that although the differences cited by the Court "might justify a scheme in which immediate relatives and guardians were automatically called as witnesses in cases seeking institutionalization on the basis of mental retardation, they are completely unrelated to … permitting these immediate relatives and guardians to be involved 'as parties' so as to give them, among other things, the right to appeal as 'adverse' a decision not to institutionalize the individual…." Virtually all the State's involuntary com-

---

b. Justice Blackmun added a separate dissenting statement to express his "continuing adherence to the view that laws that discriminate against individuals with mental retardation," City of Cleburne v. Cleburne Living Center, Inc., 473 U.S. 432, 455 (1985) (opinion of Marshall, J., joined by Brennan and Blackmun, JJ.) … are subject to heightened review.

mitments of the retarded are promoted by relatives or guardians, and making them parties subjects "someone . . . alleged to be retarded" to "a second prosecutor." The import of this was clear to Justice Souter:

"The Court simply points to no characteristic of mental retardation that could rationally justify imposing this burden of a second prosecutor on those alleged to be mentally retarded where the State has decided not to impose it upon those alleged to be mentally ill. Even if we assumed a generally more regular connection between the relatives and guardians of those alleged to be retarded than those said to be mentally ill, it would not explain why the former should be subject to a second prosecutor when the latter are not.

"The same may be said about the Court's second suggested justification, that the mentally ill may have a need for privacy not shown by the retarded. Even assuming the ill need some additional privacy, and that participation of others in the commitment proceeding should therefore be limited 'to the smallest group compatible with due process,' why should the retarded be subject to a second prosecutor? The Court provides no answer.

"Without plausible justification, Kentucky is being allowed to draw a distinction that is difficult to see as resting on anything other than the stereotypical assumption that the retarded are 'perpetual children,' an assumption that has historically been taken to justify the disrespect and 'grotesque mistreatment' to which the retarded have been subjected. See Cleburne . . . (Stevens, J., concurring). . . ."

CENTRAL STATE UNIVERSITY v. AMERICAN ASSOCIATION OF UNIVERSITY PROFESSORS, 526 U.S. 124 (1999). An Ohio statute, designed to increase the time that public university professors spent teaching, mandated an instructional workload policy that would be exempt from collective bargaining. In a suit by the professors' collective bargaining agent, a majority of the Ohio Supreme Court held that the statute denied the professors equal protection of the laws, because no evidence in the record linked collective bargaining to a decline in teaching and the State had failed to demonstrate "any rational basis for singling out university faculty members as the only public employees . . . Precluded from bargaining over their workload." the Supreme Court summarily reversed per curiam, finding the mandate "an entirely rational step to accomplish" the statute's objective. The Court said:

". . . The legislature could quite reasonably have concluded that the policy animating the law would have been undercut and likely varied if it were subject to collective bargaining.

"The fact that the record before the Ohio courts did not show that collective bargaining in the past had lead to the decline in classroom time for faculty does not detract from the rationality of the legislative decision. . . . The legislature wanted a uniform workload policy to be in place by a certain date. It could properly conclude that collective bargaining about that policy in the future would interfere with the attainment of this end. Under our precedent, this is sufficient to sustain the exclusion of university professors from the otherwise general collective-bargaining scheme for public employees."

A concurring opinion by Justice Ginsburg, joined by Justice Breyer noted "that a summary disposition is not a fit occasion for elaborate discussion of our rational basis standard of review." A dissent by Justice Stevens that also objected to summary disposition said in part:

"The question . . . is whether there is a rational basis for discriminating against faculty members by depriving them of bargaining assistance that is available to all other public employees in the State of Ohio. Even the Court's speculation about the possible adverse consequences of collective bargaining about faculty workload does not explain why collective bargaining about the workloads of all other public employees might not give rise to the same adverse consequences arising from lack of state-wide uniformity. Indeed, I would suppose that the interest in protecting the academic freedom of university faculty members might provide a rational basis for giving them more bargaining assistance than other public employees. In any event, no one has explained why there is a rational basis for concluding that they should receive less."

ASCERTAINING LEGISLATIVE PURPOSE FOR RATIONAL BASIS REVIEW

The Court's consistent refusal to require that legislative bodies articulate the purpose of a statutory classification, or be held to an identifiable "actual" or even "reasonably presumable" purpose, in order to have the classification survive judicial review for reasonableness, has in some circumstances provoked vigorous methodological dissent. Two decisions rejecting attacks on distinctions in benefits legislation are noteworthy in this regard.

In United States Railroad Retirement Board v. Fritz, 449 U.S. 166 (1980), Congress discontinued dual railroad retirement and social security benefits for some but not all former rail employees, in part drawing a line on the basis of how recent rather than how long an employee's railroad service had been. Justice Rehnquist's majority opinion, applying the rational basis standard, stated that "the plain language of [the provision drawing the distinction] marks the beginning and end of our inquiry" into purpose. Nor was that purpose "achieved ... in a patently arbitrary or irrational way[,]" because "Congress could assume that those who had a current connection with the railroad industry when the Act was passed in 1974, or who returned to the industry before their retirement, were more likely than those who had left the industry prior to 1974, and who never returned, to be among the class of persons who pursue careers in the railroad industry, the class for whom the Railroad Retirement Act was designed." Having found "plausible reasons for Congress' action, our inquiry is at an end." Finally, the majority:

> "disagree[d] with the District Court's conclusion that Congress was unaware of what it accomplished or that it was misled by the groups that appeared before it. If this test were applied literally to every member of any legislature that ever voted on a law, there would be very few laws which would survive it. The language of the statute is clear, and we have historically assumed that Congress intended what it enacted."

In dissent, Justice Brennan, joined by Justice Marshall, objected to the majority's "tautological approach to statutory purpose[,]" arguing that "the 'plain language' of the statute can tell us only what the classification is; it can tell us nothing about the purpose of the classification, let alone the relationship between the classification and that purpose." He continued:

> "... It may always be said that Congress intended to do what it in fact did. If that were the extent of our analysis, we would find every statute, no matter how arbitrary or irrational, perfectly tailored to achieve its purpose. But equal protection scrutiny under the rational basis test requires the courts first to deduce the independent objectives of the statute, usually from statements of purpose and other evidence in the statute and legislative history, and second to analyze whether the challenged classification rationally furthers achievement of those objectives...."

Justice Brennan found in the legislative history "a 'principal purpose' ... explicitly stated by Congress ... to preserve the vested earned benefits of retirees who had already qualified for them." In his view, the classification, "which deprives some retirees of vested dual benefits that they had earned prior to 1974, directly conflicts with Congress' stated purpose" and, hence, is "not only rationally unrelated to the congressional purpose [but] inimical to it." In general, "[w]here Congress has expressly stated the purpose of a piece of legislation, but where the challenged classification is either irrelevant to or counter to that purpose, we must view any *post hoc* justifications proffered by Government attorneys with skepticism. A challenged classification may be sustained only if it is rationally related to achievement of an *actual* legitimate governmental purpose." Here, moreover, Congress had "asked railroad management and labor representatives to negotiate and submit a bill to restructure the Railroad Retirement system" and testimony "at congressional hearings perpetuated the inaccurate impression that all retirees with earned vested dual benefits under prior law would retain their benefits unchanged." While "a misstatement or several misstatements by witnesses before Congress would not ordinarily lead us to conclude that Congress misapprehended what it was doing ..., where complex legislation was drafted by outside parties and Congress relied on them to explain it, where the misstatements are frequent and unrebutted, and where no Member of Congress can be found to have stated the effect of the classification correctly, we are entitled to suspect that Congress may have been misled." Accordingly, "I do not think that this classification was rationally related to an *actual* governmental purpose."

Justice Stevens, concurring in the judgment, shared Justice Brennan's concern that "judicial review [not] constitute a mere tautological recognition of the fact that Congress did what it intended to do" and urged that "[w]hen Congress deprives a small class of persons of vested rights that are protected ... for others who are in a similar though not identical position, I believe the Constitution requires something more than merely a 'conceivable' or a 'plausible' explanation for the unequal treatment." But he did not

> "share Justice Brennan's conclusion that every statutory classification must further an objective that can be confidently identified as the 'actual purpose' of the legislature. Actual purpose is sometimes unknown. Moreover, undue emphasis on actual motivation may result in identically worded statutes being held valid in one State and invalid in a neighboring State. I therefore believe that we must discover a correlation between the classification and either the actual purpose of the statute or a legitimate purpose that we may reasonably presume to have motivated an impartial legislature. If the adverse impact on the disfavored class is an apparent aim of the legislature, its impartiality would be suspect. If, however, the adverse impact may reasonably be viewed as an acceptable cost of achieving a larger goal, an impartial lawmaker could rationally decide that that cost should be incurred."

Here, though "Congress originally intended to protect *all* vested benefits, ... it ultimately sacrificed some benefits in the interest of achieving other objectives"—ending dual benefits and "protecting the solvency of the entire railroad retirement program." As "any distinction ... within the class of vested beneficiaries would involve a difference of degree rather than a difference in entitlement[,]" Justice Stevens was "satisfied that a distinction based upon currency of railroad employment represents an impartial method of identifying that sort of difference."

The following year the Court divided 5–4 over an equal protection challenge by residents of mental institutions denied a small welfare allowance Congress had authorized for inmates of only those public institutions receiving Medicaid payments on their behalf. Schweiker v. Wilson, 450 U.S. 221 (1981). The majority concluded that adopting the Medicaid eligibility criterion "must be considered Congress' deliberate, considered choice" and reasoned that Congress "may rationally limit the grant to Medicaid recipients, for whose care the Federal Government already has assumed the major portion of the expense" and leave it to the States, who "Congress believed ... have a 'traditional' responsibility to care for those institutionalized in public mental institutions[,] to provide an equivalent."

Justice Powell's dissent, joined by Justices Brennan, Marshall, and Stevens, said in part:

"The deference to which legislative accommodation of conflicting interests is entitled rests in part upon the principle that the political process of our majoritarian democracy responds to the wishes of the people. Accordingly, an important touchstone for equal protection review of statutes is how readily a policy can be discerned which the legislature intended to serve.... [W]hether a statutory classification discriminates arbitrarily cannot be divorced from whether it was enacted to serve an identifiable purpose. When a legislative purpose can be suggested only by the ingenuity of a government lawyer litigating the constitutionality of a statute, a reviewing court may be presented not so much with a legislative policy choice as its absence.

"In my view, the Court should receive with some skepticism *post hoc* hypotheses about legislative purpose, unsupported by the legislative history.[6] When no indication of legislative purpose appears other than the current position of the Secretary, the Court should require that the classification bear a 'fair and substantial relation' to the asserted purpose. See F.S. Royster Guano Co. v. Virginia, 253 U.S. 412, 415 (1920). This marginally more demanding scrutiny indirectly would test the plausibility of the tendered purpose....

"I conclude that Congress had no rational reason for refusing to pay a comfort allowance to appellees, while paying it to numerous otherwise identically situated disabled indigents. This unexplained difference in treatment must have been a legislative oversight...."

[Margin note: In this case: must bear a fair & substantial relation to the asserted purpose]

MODERN RATIONAL BASIS REVIEW

Despite occasional dissenting expressions of discomfort with the "toothlessness" of rational basis review as applied in the realms of purely economic regulation and the provision of government benefits, the Court consistently has refused to invalidate any such measure, with one notable exception, for more than 50 years. In Morey v. Doud, 354 U.S. 457 (1957), the Court, with three dissenters, held that an Illinois statute imposing licensing and financial requirements on sellers and issuers of all money orders, except those of the "American Express Company[,]" violated equal protection. In reaching this conclusion, the Court took "all of these factors in conjunction—the remote

---

6. Some of our cases suggest that the actual purpose of a statute is irrelevant, Flemming v. Nestor, 363 U.S. 603, 612 (1960), and that the statute must be upheld "if any state of facts reasonably may be conceived to justify" its discrimination, McGowan v. Maryland, 366 U.S. 420, 426 (1961). Although these cases preserve an important caution, they do not describe the importance of actual legislative purpose in our analysis. We recognize that a legislative body rarely acts with a single mind and that compromises blur purpose.... Ascertainment of actual purpose to the extent feasible, however, remains an essential step in equal protection.

relationship of the statutory classification to the Act's purpose or to business characteristics, and the creation of a closed class by the singling out of the money orders of a named company, with accompanying economic advantages."

Nearly twenty years later in a brief per curiam opinion, however, the Court concluded without dissent that *Morey* "was a needlessly intrusive judicial infringement on the State's legislative powers" and "so far departs from proper equal protection analysis in cases of exclusively economic regulation that it should be, and is, overruled." New Orleans v. Dukes, 427 U.S. 297 (1976). *Dukes,* which the Court found "essentially indistinguishable" from *Morey,* upheld an ordinance that exempted from a general prohibition against the selling of foodstuffs from pushcarts in New Orleans' French Quarter "vendors who have continually operated the same business [there] for eight years prior to January 1, 1972." The Court concluded that "[t]he city's classification rationally furthers the purpose ... the city had identified as its objective ...[;] that is, as a means 'to preserve the appearance and custom valued by the Quarter's residents and attractive to tourists.' " As for the "grandfather provision," the Court decided that "the city could rationally choose initially to eliminate vendors of more recent vintage" and gave the following rationale: "The city could reasonably decide that newer businesses were less likely to have built up substantial reliance interests in continued operations ... and that the two vendors which qualified under the 'grandfather clause'—both of which had operated in the area for over 20 years ...—had themselves become part of the distinctive character and charm that distinguishes the Vieux Carre."

The Court, purporting to apply the rational basis standard, has invalidated a number of legislative classifications in the modern era, but none involved solely economic regulation or distribution of government benefits.[a] For example, the Court invoked rational basis review in striking down a gender distinction in Reed v. Reed, 404 U.S. 71 (1971), infra, page 754. Similarly, in City of Cleburne v. Cleburne Living Center, 473 U.S. 432 (1985), infra, page 918, despite Justice Marshall's dissenting criticism that it was engaging in " 'second order' rational basis review," the Court held that a city ordinance, as applied to deny a special use permit for the operation of a group home for the mentally retarded, failed rational basis scrutiny and revealed "an irrational prejudice" against that group. Of like import but without reference to *Cleburne,* the Court later invalidated an amendment to the Colorado Constitution precluding any level of state government from protecting the status of persons on the basis of their "homosexual, lesbian or bisexual orientation, conduct, practices or relationships," because "its sheer breadth is so discontinuous with the reasons offered for it that the amendment seems inexplicable by anything but animus toward the class that it affects; it lacks a rational relationship to legitimate state interests." Romer v. Evans, 517 U.S. 620, 632 (1996), infra page 926. Further examples include the Court's professed use of rational basis review

a. Addressing allegations that a municipality unconstitutionally demanded a 33-foot easement as a condition of connecting a particular owner's property to the municipal water supply when only a 15-foot easement was demanded from other similarly situated property owners, the Court held the complaint "sufficient to state a claim for relief under traditional equal protection analysis," even if "brought by a 'class of one,' where the plaintiff alleges that she has been intentionally treated differently from others similarly situated and that there is no rational basis for the difference in treatment." Village of Wil-

lowbrook v. Olech, 528 U.S. 562 (2000). The Court so ruled, "quite apart from the Village's subjective motivation," which the plaintiff claimed was "ill will resulting from the ... previous filing of an unrelated, successful lawsuit against the Village...." For Justice Breyer, concurring in the result, only that "added factor" of vindictiveness ameliorated the concern that the Court not interpret the Equal Protection Clause "in a way that would transform many ordinary violations of city or state law[, such as common instances of faulty zoning decisions,] into violations of the Constitution."

when invalidating legislative distinctions between newly-arrived and long-term state residents, as in Zobel v. Williams, 457 U.S. 55 (1982), infra, page 1024, and classifications disadvantaging nonresidents of a State, as in Metropolitan Life Insurance Co. v. Ward, 470 U.S. 869 (1985), infra, page 1047. In these and similar cases one might ask whether and in what ways the Court may be applying a different form of rational basis review than in the opinions presented in this section, and why the Court might invoke the rational basis standard but apply it differently rather than invoke a different standard.

SECTION 3.   SUSPECT CLASSIFICATIONS

Introduction. This section presents the cases where the classifying factor rather than the burden on a fundamental interest gives rise to a heightened standard of review. Subsection A deals with the most clearly suspect classifications—those disadvantaging racial minorities. Subsection B involves a special application of the racial classification doctrine to official racial segregation of schools and other public facilities. Subsection C addresses classifications dealing with gender, where the Court uses the classifying factor to justify a heightened standard of review but one not as rigorous as that applied to racial classifications.

The cases in Subsection D typically involve legislation lacking facially suspect classifications but having a differential impact on particular groups. The question addressed is whether "suspectness" turns on the "impact" of laws or the "intent" with which they are enacted.

Subsection E discusses the most controversial and divisive issue before the Court under the equal protection clause—the validity of the use of gender and racial classifications for the purpose of aiding women or minority groups.

Subsection F deals with classifications involving aliens, and Subsection G with other classifying factors that may trigger heightened scrutiny, such as illegitimacy, mental retardation, sexual orientation, age, and poverty.

A.   CLASSIFICATIONS DISADVANTAGING RACIAL MINORITIES

Loving v. Virginia

388 U.S. 1, 87 S.Ct. 1817, 18 L.Ed.2d 1010 (1967).

Mr. Chief Justice Warren delivered the opinion of the Court.

This case presents a constitutional question never addressed by this Court: whether a statutory scheme adopted by the State of Virginia to prevent marriages between persons solely on the basis of racial classifications violates the Equal Protection and Due Process Clauses of the Fourteenth Amendment. For reasons which seem to us to reflect the central meaning of those constitutional commands, we conclude that these statutes cannot stand consistently with the Fourteenth Amendment.

In June 1958, two residents of Virginia, Mildred Jeter, a Negro woman, and Richard Loving, a white man, were married in the District of Columbia pursuant to its laws. Shortly after their marriage, the Lovings returned to Virginia and established their marital abode in Caroline County. ... [A County] grand jury issued an indictment charging the Lovings with violating Virginia's ban on interracial marriages. On January 6, 1959, the Lovings

Ban on interracial marriage

pleaded guilty to the charge and were sentenced to one year in jail; however, the trial judge suspended the sentence for a period of 25 years on the condition that the Lovings leave the State and not return to Virginia together for 25 years, stating that:

> "Almighty God created the races white, black, yellow, malay, and red, and he placed them on separate continents. And but for the interference with his arrangement there would be no cause for such marriages. The fact that he separated the races shows that he did not intend for the races to mix."

After their convictions the Lovings took up residence in the District of Columbia. On November 6, 1963, they filed a motion in the state trial court to vacate the judgment and set aside the sentence on the ground that the statutes which they had violated were repugnant to the Fourteenth Amendment. The motion not having been decided by October 28, 1964, the Lovings instituted a class action in the United States District Court for the Eastern District of Virginia requesting that a three-judge court be convened to declare the Virginia antimiscegenation statutes unconstitutional and to enjoin state officials from enforcing their convictions. On January 22, 1965, the state trial judge denied the motion to vacate the sentences, and the Lovings perfected an appeal to the Supreme Court of Appeals of Virginia. On February 11, 1965, the three-judge District Court continued the case to allow the Lovings to present their constitutional claims to the highest state court.

The Supreme Court of Appeals upheld the constitutionality of the antimiscegenation statutes and, after modifying the sentence, affirmed the convictions. The Lovings appealed this decision, and we noted probable jurisdiction on December 12, 1966.

The two statutes under which appellants were convicted and sentenced are part of a comprehensive statutory scheme aimed at prohibiting and punishing interracial marriages. The Lovings were convicted of violating § 20–58 of the Virginia Code:

> "*Leaving State to Evade Law*. If any white person and colored person shall go out of this State, for the purpose of being married, and with the intention of returning, and be married out of it, and afterwards return to and reside in it, cohabiting as man and wife, they shall be punished as provided in § 20–59, and the marriage shall be governed by the same law as if it had been solemnized in this State. The fact of their cohabitation here as man and wife shall be evidence of their marriage."

Section 20–59, which defines the penalty for miscegenation, provides:

> "*Punishment for Marriage*. If any white person intermarry with a colored person, or any colored person intermarry with a white person, he shall be guilty of a felony and shall be punished by confinement in the penitentiary for not less than one nor more than five years."

Other central provisions in the Virginia statutory scheme are § 20–57, which automatically voids all marriages between "a white person and a colored person" without any judicial proceeding, and §§ 20–54 and 1–14 which, respectively, define "white persons" and "colored persons and Indians" for purposes of the statutory prohibitions. The Lovings have never disputed in the course of this litigation that Mrs. Loving is a "colored person" or that Mr. Loving is a "white person" within the meanings given those terms by the Virginia statutes.

Virginia is now one of 16 States which prohibit and punish marriages on the basis of racial classifications.[5] Penalties for miscegenation arose as an

---

5. ... Over the past 15 years, 14 States have repealed laws outlawing interracial marriage....

incident to slavery and have been common in Virginia since the colonial period. The present statutory scheme dates from the adoption of the Racial Integrity Act of 1924, passed during the period of extreme nativism which followed the end of the First World War. The central features of this Act, and current Virginia law, are the absolute prohibition of a "white person" marrying other than another "white person," a prohibition against issuing marriage licenses until the issuing official is satisfied that the applicants' statements as to their race are correct, certificates of "racial composition" to be kept by both local and state registrars, and the carrying forward of earlier prohibitions against racial intermarriage.

I.

In upholding the constitutionality of these provisions in the decision below, the Supreme Court of Appeals of Virginia referred to its 1955 decision in Naim v. Naim, 197 Va. 80, 87 S.E.2d 749, as stating the reasons supporting the validity of these laws. In *Naim,* the state court concluded that the State's legitimate purposes were "to preserve the racial integrity of its citizens," and to prevent "the corruption of blood," "a mongrel breed of citizens," and "the obliteration of racial pride," obviously an endorsement of the doctrine of White Supremacy.... The court also reasoned that marriage has traditionally been subject to state regulation without federal intervention, and, consequently, the regulation of marriage should be left to exclusive state control by the Tenth Amendment.

While the state court is no doubt correct in asserting that marriage is a social relation subject to the State's police power, ... the State does not contend ... that its powers to regulate marriage are unlimited notwithstanding the commands of the Fourteenth Amendment. Nor could it do so in light of Meyer v. State of Nebraska, 262 U.S. 390 (1923), and Skinner v. State of Oklahoma, 316 U.S. 535 (1942). Instead, the State argues that the meaning of the Equal Protection Clause, as illuminated by the statements of the Framers, is only that state penal laws containing an interracial element as part of the definition of the offense must apply equally to whites and Negroes in the sense that members of each race are punished to the same degree. Thus, the State contends that, because its miscegenation statutes punish equally both the white and the Negro participants in an interracial marriage, these statutes, despite their reliance on racial classifications, do not constitute an invidious discrimination based upon race. The second argument advanced by the State assumes the validity of its equal application theory. The argument is that, if the Equal Protection Clause does not outlaw miscegenation statutes because of their reliance on racial classifications, the question of constitutionality would thus become whether there was any rational basis for a State to treat interracial marriages differently from other marriages. On this question, the State argues, the scientific evidence is substantially in doubt and, consequently, this Court should defer to the wisdom of the state legislature in adopting its policy of discouraging interracial marriages.

Because we reject the notion that the mere "equal application" of a statute containing racial classifications is enough to remove the classifications from the Fourteenth Amendment's proscription of all invidious racial discriminations, we do not accept the State's contention that these statutes should be upheld if there is any possible basis for concluding that they serve a rational purpose. The mere fact of equal application does not mean that our analysis of this statute should follow the approach we have taken in cases involving no racial discrimination where the Equal Protection Clause has been arrayed against a statute discriminating between the kinds of advertising which may be displayed on trucks in New York City, Railway Express Agency, Inc. v. People of State of New York, 336 U.S. 106 (1949), or an exemption in Ohio's ad valorem tax for merchandise owned by a non-resident in a storage warehouse, Allied Stores of Ohio, Inc. v. Bowers, 358 U.S. 522 (1959). In these cases, involving distinctions not drawn according to race, the Court has merely asked whether there is any rational foundation for the discriminations, and has deferred to the wisdom of the state legislatures. In the case at bar, however, we deal with statutes containing racial classifications, and the fact of equal application does not immunize the statute from the very heavy burden of justification which the Fourteenth Amendment has traditionally required of state statutes drawn according to race.

Equal application doesnt bar from heavy justification

The State argues that statements in the Thirty-ninth Congress about the time of the passage of the Fourteenth Amendment indicate that the Framers did not intend the Amendment to make unconstitutional state miscegenation laws. Many of the statements alluded to by the State concern the debates over the Freedmen's Bureau Bill, which President Johnson vetoed, and the Civil Rights Act of 1866, enacted over his veto. While these statements have some relevance to the intention of Congress in submitting the Fourteenth Amendment, it must be understood that they pertained to the passage of specific statutes and not to the broader, organic purpose of a constitutional amendment. As for the various statements directly concerning the Fourteenth Amendment, we have said in connection with a related problem, that although these historical sources "cast some light" they are not sufficient to resolve the problem; "[a]t best, they are inconclusive. The most avid proponents of the post-War Amendments undoubtedly intended them to remove all legal distinctions among 'all persons born or naturalized in the United States.' Their opponents, just as certainly, were antagonistic to both the letter and the spirit of the Amendments and wished them to have the most limited effect." Brown et al. v. Board of Education of Topeka, et al., 347 U.S. 483 (1954). See also Strauder v. West Virginia, 100 U.S. 303, 310 (1880). We have rejected the proposition that the debates in the Thirty-ninth Congress or in the state legislatures which ratified the Fourteenth Amendment supported the theory advanced by the State, that the requirement of equal protection of the laws is satisfied by penal laws defining offenses based on racial classifications so long as white and Negro participants in the offense were similarly punished. McLaughlin et al. v. State of Florida, 379 U.S. 184 (1964).

The State finds support for its "equal application" theory in the decision of the Court in Pace v. Alabama, 106 U.S. 583 (1882). In that case, the Court upheld a conviction under an Alabama statute forbidding adultery or fornication between a white person and a Negro which imposed a greater penalty than that of a statute proscribing similar conduct by members of the same race. The Court reasoned that the statute could not be said to discriminate against Negroes because the punishment for each participant in the offense was the same. However, as recently as the 1964 Term, in rejecting the reasoning of that case, we stated "*Pace* represents a limited view of the Equal Protection Clause which has not withstood analysis in the subsequent decisions of this Court." *McLaughlin et al. v. Florida,* ... As we there demonstrated, the Equal Protection Clause requires the consideration of whether the classifications drawn by any statute constitute an arbitrary and invidious discrimination. The clear and central purpose of the Fourteenth Amendment was to eliminate all official state sources of invidious racial discrimination in the States. Slaughter–House Cases, 16 Wall. 36, 71 (1873); Strauder v. State of West Virginia, 100 U.S. 303, 307–308 (1880); Ex parte Virginia, 100 U.S. 339, 344–345 (1880); Shelley v. Kraemer, 334 U.S. 1 (1948); Burton v. Wilmington Parking Authority, 365 U.S. 715 (1961).

There can be no question but that Virginia's miscegenation statutes rest solely upon distinctions drawn according to race. The statutes proscribe generally accepted conduct if engaged in by members of different races. Over the years, this Court has consistently repudiated "[d]istinctions between citizens solely because of their ancestry" as being "odious to a free people whose institutions are founded upon the doctrine of equality." Hirabayashi v. United States, 320 U.S. 81, 100 (1943). At the very least, the Equal Protection Clause demands that racial classifications, especially suspect in criminal statutes, be subjected to the "most rigid scrutiny," Korematsu v. United States, 323 U.S. 214, 216 (1944), and, if they are ever to be upheld, they must be shown to be necessary to the accomplishment of some permissible state objective, independent of the racial discrimination which it was the object of the Fourteenth Amendment to eliminate. Indeed, two members of this Court have already stated that they "cannot conceive of a valid legislative purpose ... which makes the color of a person's skin the test of whether his conduct is a criminal offense." McLaughlin v. Florida, supra, 379 U.S. at 198 (Stewart, J., joined by Douglas, J., concurring).

[handwritten margin note: subject to rigid standards]

There is patently no legitimate overriding purpose independent of invidious racial discrimination which justifies this classification. The fact that Virginia only prohibits interracial marriages involving white persons demonstrates that the racial classifications must stand on their own justification, as measures designed to maintain White Supremacy.[11] We have consistently denied the constitutionality of measures which restrict the rights of citizens on account of race. There can be no doubt that restricting the freedom to marry solely because of racial classifications violates the central meaning of the Equal Protection Clause.

. . .

These convictions must be reversed. It is so ordered.

Mr. Justice Stewart, concurring.

I have previously expressed the belief that "it is simply not possible for a state law to be valid under our Constitution which makes the criminality of an act depend upon the race of the actor." McLaughlin v. State of Florida, 379 U.S. 184, 198 (concurring opinion). Because I adhere to that belief, I concur in the judgment of the Court.

Palmore v. Sidoti

466 U.S. 429, 104 S.Ct. 1879, 80 L.Ed.2d 421 (1984).

Chief Justice Burger delivered the opinion of the Court.

We granted certiorari to review a judgment of a state court divesting a natural mother of the custody of her infant child because of her remarriage to a person of a different race.

---

11. Appellants point out that the State's concern in these statutes, as expressed in the words of the 1924 Act's title, "An Act to Preserve Racial Integrity," extends only to the integrity of the white race. While Virginia prohibits whites from marrying any nonwhite (subject to the exception for the descendants of Pocahontas), Negroes, Orientals, and any other racial class may intermarry without statutory interference.

Appellants contend that this distinction renders Virginia's miscegenation statutes arbitrary and unreasonable even assuming the constitutional validity of an official purpose to preserve "racial integrity." We need not reach this contention because we find the racial classifications in these statutes repugnant to the Fourteenth Amendment, even assuming an even-handed state purpose to protect the "integrity" of all races.

I

When petitioner Linda Sidoti Palmore and respondent Anthony J. Sidoti, both Caucasians, were divorced in May 1980 in Florida, the mother was awarded custody of their three-year-old daughter.

In September 1981 the father sought custody of the child by filing a petition to modify the prior judgment because of changed conditions. The change was that the child's mother was then cohabiting with a Negro, Clarence Palmore, Jr., whom she married two months later. Additionally, the father made several allegations of instances in which the mother had not properly cared for the child.

After hearing testimony from both parties and considering a court counselor's investigative report, the court noted that the father had made allegations about the child's care, but the court made no findings with respect to these allegations. On the contrary, the court made a finding that "there is no issue as to either party's devotion to the child, adequacy of housing facilities, or respect[a]bility of the new spouse of either parent."

The court then addressed the recommendations of the court counselor, who had made an earlier report "in [another] case coming out of this circuit also involving the social consequences of an interracial marriage. Niles v. Niles, 299 So.2d 162." From this vague reference to that earlier case, the court turned to the present case and noted the counselor's recommendation for a change in custody because "[t]he wife [petitioner] has chosen for herself and for her child, a life-style unacceptable to her father *and to society*. . . . The child . . . is, or at school age will be, subject to environmental pressures not of choice."

The court then concluded that the best interests of the child would be served by awarding custody to the father. The court's rationale is contained in the following:

> "The father's evident resentment of the mother's choice of a black partner is not sufficient to wrest custody from the mother. It is of some significance, however, that the mother did see fit to bring a man into her home and carry on a sexual relationship with him without being married to him. Such action tended to place gratification of her own desires ahead of her concern for the child's future welfare. *This Court feels that despite the strides that have been made in bettering relations between the races in this country, it is inevitable that Melanie will, if allowed to remain in her present situation and attains school age and thus more vulnerable to peer pressures, suffer from the social stigmatization that is sure to come.*"

The Second District Court of Appeal affirmed without opinion, thus denying the Florida Supreme Court jurisdiction to review the case. . . . We . . . reverse.

II

The judgment of a state court determining or reviewing a child custody decision is not ordinarily a likely candidate for review by this Court. However, the court's opinion, after stating that the "father's evident resentment of the mother's choice of a black partner is not sufficient" to deprive her of custody, then turns to what it regarded as the damaging impact on the child from remaining in a racially-mixed household. This raises important federal concerns arising from the Constitution's commitment to eradicating discrimination based on race.

The Florida court did not focus directly on the parental qualifications of the natural mother or her present husband, or indeed on the father's qualifications to have custody of the child. The court found that "there is no issue as to either party's devotion to the child, adequacy of housing facilities, or respect[a]bility of the new spouse of either parent." This, taken with the absence of any negative finding as to the quality of the care provided by the mother, constitutes a rejection of any claim of petitioner's unfitness to continue the custody of her child.

The court correctly stated that the child's welfare was the controlling factor. But that court was entirely candid and made no effort to place its holding on any ground other than race. Taking the court's findings and rationale at face value, it is clear that the outcome would have been different had petitioner married a Caucasian male of similar respectability.

A core purpose of the Fourteenth Amendment was to do away with all governmentally-imposed discrimination based on race. See Strauder v. West Virginia, 100 U.S. 303, 307–308, 310 (1880). Classifying persons according to their race is more likely to reflect racial prejudice than legitimate public concerns; the race, not the person, dictates the category. See Personnel Administrator v. Feeney, 442 U.S. 256, 272 (1979). Such classifications are subject to the most exacting scrutiny; to pass constitutional muster, they must be justified by a compelling governmental interest and must be "necessary ... to the accomplishment" of its legitimate purpose, McLaughlin v. Florida, 379 U.S. 184, 196 (1964). See Loving v. Virginia, 388 U.S. 1, 11 (1967).

The State, of course, has a duty of the highest order to protect the interests of minor children, particularly those of tender years. In common with most states, Florida law mandates that custody determinations be made in the best interests of the children involved. Fla.Stat. § 61.13(2)(b)(1) (1983). The goal of granting custody based on the best interests of the child is indisputably a substantial governmental interest for purposes of the Equal Protection Clause.

It would ignore reality to suggest that racial and ethnic prejudices do not exist or that all manifestations of those prejudices have been eliminated. There is a risk that a child living with a step-parent of a different race may be subject to a variety of pressures and stresses not present if the child were living with parents of the same racial or ethnic origin.

The question, however, is whether the reality of private biases and the possible injury they might inflict are permissible considerations for removal of an infant child from the custody of its natural mother. We have little difficulty concluding that they are not. The Constitution cannot control such prejudices but neither can it tolerate them. Private biases may be outside the reach of the law, but the law cannot, directly or indirectly, give them effect. "Public officials sworn to uphold the Constitution may not avoid a constitutional duty by bowing to the hypothetical effects of private racial prejudice that they assume to be both widely and deeply held." Palmer v. Thompson, 403 U.S. 217, 260–261 (1971) (White, J., dissenting).

This is by no means the first time that acknowledged racial prejudice has been invoked to justify racial classifications. In Buchanan v. Warley, 245 U.S. 60 (1917), for example, this Court invalidated a Kentucky law forbidding Negroes from buying homes in white neighborhoods.

"It is urged that this proposed segregation will promote the public peace by preventing race conflicts. Desirable as this is, and important as is the preservation of the public peace, this aim cannot be accomplished by laws or ordinances which deny rights created or protected by the Federal Constitution.''

Whatever problems racially-mixed households may pose for children in 1984 can no more support a denial of constitutional rights than could the stresses that residential integration was thought to entail in 1917. The effects of racial prejudice, however real, cannot justify a racial classification removing an infant child from the custody of its natural mother found to be an appropriate person to have such custody.

uncanst.

The judgment of the District Court of Appeal is reversed.

It is so ordered.

THE JAPANESE CURFEW AND EVACUATION CASES

At the outset of World War II, some military authorities asserted that citizens as well as aliens of Japanese ancestry on the West Coast posed a security threat; that there was among them an actual or incipient fifth column. On February 19, 1942, President Roosevelt, acting as President and Commander-in-Chief, issued Executive Order No. 9066 authorizing such military commanders as he might designate to prescribe military areas from which any or all persons might be excluded as a security measure. Pursuant to this order he designated General DeWitt as Military Commander of the Western Defense Command. Acting under the Executive Order, the General, on March 2, 1942, established Military Area No. 1 which included the Pacific Coast states. Not willing to have these security measures entirely a matter of executive and military power, Congress, by the Act of March 21, 1942, made criminal the violation of enforcement orders issued under Executive Order 9066. Beginning on March 24, 1942, General DeWitt issued a series of orders applying to persons of Japanese ancestry residing in Military Area No. 1. One of these established a curfew for such persons between the hours of 8:00 p.m. and 6:00 a.m.; others were "exclusion orders" requiring persons of Japanese ancestry to remove from designated districts in the Military Area to "relocation centers" established further inland.

Established curfew for Japanese ? removed from designated districts

HIRABAYASHI v. UNITED STATES, 320 U.S. 81 (1943). Appellant, an American citizen of Japanese ancestry, was convicted in a federal district court of violating the curfew order and therefore the Act of March 21, 1942, by failing to remain in his residence between the hours of 8:00 p.m. and 6:00 a.m. the Court affirmed in an opinion by Chief Justice Stone, saying: "distinctions between citizens solely because of their ancestry are by their very nature odious to a free people whose institutions are founded upon the doctrine of equality." However, the Court held that while racial discriminations are in most cases irrelevant, there was an adequate showing in this case that persons of Japanese descent presented a special danger to the community in the context of the war with Japan and that it was not feasible to determine loyalty on an individual basis.

violated curfew but ct. held usually not ok, this time is because of danger due to war

KOREMATSU v. UNITED STATES, 323 U.S. 214 (1944). Petitioner, an American citizen of Japanese descent, was convicted in a federal district court for remaining in San Leandro, California, contrary to General Dewitt's Civilian Exclusion Order no. 34. No question was raised as to petitioner's loyalty to the United States. The Court upheld the conviction. It refused to rule on the validity of other orders which required the detention of excluded persons in relocation centers. Justice Black, speaking for the Court, said: "[a]ll legal restrictions which curtail the civil rights of a single racial group are immediate-

convicted for not relocating

Public neccessity justifies such restrictions

ly suspect. That is not to say that all such restrictions are unconstitutional. It is to say that courts must subject them to the most rigid scrutiny. Pressing public necessity may sometimes justify the existence of such restrictions; racial antagonism never can." He concluded his opinion by saying:

> "To cast this case into outlines of racial prejudice, without reference to the real military dangers which were presented, merely confuses the issue. Korematsu was not excluded from the Military Area because of hostility to him or his race. He *was* excluded because we are at war with the Japanese Empire, because the properly constituted military authorities feared an invasion of our West Coast and felt constrained to take proper security measures, because they decided that the military urgency of the situation demanded that all citizens of Japanese ancestry be segregated from the West Coast temporarily, and finally, because Congress, reposing its confidence in this time of war in our military leaders—as inevitably it must— determined they should have the power to do just this. There was evidence of disloyalty on the part of some, the military authorities considered that the need for action was great, and time was short. We cannot—by availing ourselves of the calm perspective of hindsight—now say that at that time these actions were unjustified."

Dissent: slippery slope

Justices Roberts, Murphy, and Jackson all dissented on the ground that the order constituted unjustified discrimination against loyal Japanese citizens on the basis of race. Justice Jackson noted the practical inability of the courts to interfere with military actions of this kind taken during times of war but said: "[O]nce a judicial opinion . . . rationalizes the Constitution to show that the Constitution sanctions such an order, the Court for all time has validated the principle of racial discrimination in criminal procedure and of transplanting American citizens. The principle then lies about like a loaded weapon ready for the hand of any authority that can bring forward a plausible claim of an urgent need."

EX PARTE MITSUYE ENDO, 323 U.S. 283 (1944). This case was decided the same day as *Korematsu* and involved a later phase of the Japanese relocation program, i.e., the continued detention of concededly loyal persons of Japanese ancestry in the relocation centers. This raised a question which had been expressly left open in *Korematsu*. Appellant, an American citizen of Japanese ancestry and unquestioned loyalty, was evacuated from Sacramento, California in 1942 and placed in an evacuation center, first in Modoc County, California, and then in Utah. In July, 1942, she filed a petition for writ of habeas corpus in the district court which denied it in July, 1943. An appeal was taken to the circuit court of appeals which certified certain questions to the Supreme Court. Justice Douglas, for the Court, said that whatever power the war relocation authority had to detain persons of Japanese ancestry initially, or to detain those whose loyalty was questioned, it had no authority to subject concededly loyal citizens to its "leave" procedure. The detainee seeking "indefinite leave" had to meet a number of conditions, including a showing that "public sentiment" at the detainee's "proposed destination" had been investigated and approved. The Court rested on the conclusion that the detention of a loyal citizen under these circumstances exceeded what was authorized by the Act of March 21, 1942, and the President's executive orders, but there were constitutional overtones in the opinion: ". . . We must assume that the Chief Executive and members of Congress, as well as the courts, are sensitive to and respectful of the liberties of the citizen. In interpreting a wartime measure we must assume that their purpose was to allow for the greatest possible accommodation between those liberties and the exigencies of war. . . . The purpose and objective of the act and of these orders are plain. Their single aim was the protection of the war effort against espionage and sabotage. It is in light of that one objective that the powers conferred by the orders must be construed.... A citizen who is concededly loyal presents no problem of espionage or sabotage.... When the power to detain is derived from the power to protect the war effort against espionage and sabotage, detention which has no relationship to that objective is unauthorized.... If we assume (as we do) that the original evacuation was justified, its lawful character was derived from the fact that it was an espionage and sabotage measure, not that there was community hostility to this group of American citizens. The evacuation program rested explicitly on the former ground not on the latter as the underlying legislation shows. The authority to detain a citizen or to grant him a conditional release as protection against espionage or sabotage is exhausted at least when his loyalty is conceded...."

The district court was reversed; Roberts and Murphy, JJ., concurred but stressed their view that the entire evacuation program was unconstitutional.[a]

WHAT GROUPS ARE SPECIALLY PROTECTED AGAINST DISCRIMINATION?

In the Slaughter–House Cases, 83 U.S. (16 Wall.) 36 (1872), set out supra, p. 474, the Court said: "We doubt very much whether any action of a State not directed by way of discrimination against the negroes as a class, or on account of their race, will ever be held to come within the purview of this provision. It is

a. The Japanese evacuation cases have been subject to great criticism: Girdner & Loftis, *The Great Betrayal* (1969); Rostow, *The Japanese–American Cases—A Disaster,* in *The Sovereign Prerogative* 193 (1962); Dembitz, *Racial Discrimination and the Military Judgment,* 45 Colum.L.Rev. 175 (1945).

Cf. Chief Justice Warren, *The Bill of Rights and the Military,* in *Great Rights* 89 (Cahn ed. 1963).

For a comprehensive study of Japanese–American evacuation, see tenBroek, Barnhart & Matson, *Prejudice, War and the Constitution* (1954).

The 1980's witnessed a legal reconsideration of this historical chapter. In 1980 Congress established a Commission on Wartime Relocation and Internment of Civilians to review the evacuation episode and recommend appropriate remedies. Its report, *Personal Justice Denied* (1982), concluded that military necessity did not justify exclusion and internment and that a grave injustice had occurred. Further research published in Irons, *Justice at War* (1983), an account of the original trials and how they were prosecuted and defended, revealed internal memoranda indicating that when the government presented its arguments in these cases it deliberately misled the Court about the military judgments that actually had been made. Using these sources, Fred Korematsu and Gordon Hirabayashi successfully challenged their original convictions. Korematsu's conviction was vacated in 1984 based on a correction of "errors of fact." Korematsu v.

United States, 584 F.Supp. 1406, 1420 (N.D.Cal.1984). Hirabayashi's convictions for violating the curfew and exclusion orders were later vacated "to make the judgments of the courts conform to the judgments of history." Hirabayashi v. United States, 828 F.2d 591, 593 (9th Cir.1987). The Court of Appeals concluded that the subsequent research "demonstrate[s] that there could have been no reasonable military assessment of an emergency at the time, that the orders were based upon racial stereotypes, and that the orders caused needless suffering and shame for thousands of American citizens." Congress subsequently enacted the Civil Liberties Act of 1988, 50 U.S.C.App. §§ 1989–1989d, which declared an official apology, urged the President to pardon those convicted who had refused to accept the discriminatory treatment, and appropriated funds for restitution of $20,000. to each individual of Japanese ancestry who, during the evacuation, relocation, and internment period, was a citizen or permanent resident alien, and was confined, held in custody, relocated, or otherwise deprived of liberty or property. An equal protection challenge to the Act by a citizen of German ancestry, interned with his father during the War after his father had received an individualized hearing, was rejected in Jacobs v. Barr, 959 F.2d 313 (D.C.Cir.1992), because "Congress's finding that Japanese Americans were the victims of prejudice, while German Americans were not" was "amply supported by historical evidence" and justified compensating "interns of Japanese but not German descent."

so clearly a provision for that race and that emergency, that a strong case would be necessary for its application to any other." A decade and a half later, however, the Court in Yick Wo v. Hopkins, 118 U.S. 356 (1886), invalidated a classification found to discriminate against aliens of Chinese ancestry, saying: "[The provisions of the fourteenth amendment] are universal in their application, to all persons within the territorial jurisdiction, without regard to any differences of race, or color, or of nationality." In Hernandez v. Texas, 347 U.S. 475 (1954) it was held a violation of the equal protection clause to subject a person of Mexican descent to trial before a jury from which persons of similar ancestry had been systematically excluded. In response to an argument by the state that the equal protection clause contemplated only two classes—white and Negro—the Court said:

> "Throughout our history differences in race and color have defined easily identifiable groups which have at times required the aid of the courts in securing equal treatment under the laws. But community prejudices are not static, and from time to time other differences from the community norm may define other groups which need the same protection. Whether such a group exists within a community is a question of fact. When the existence of a distinct class is demonstrated, and it is further shown that the laws, as written or as applied, single out that class for different treatment not based on some reasonable classification, the guarantees of the Constitution have been violated. The Fourteenth Amendment is not directed solely against discrimination due to a 'two-class theory'—that is, based upon differences between 'white' and Negro."

ASCERTAINING THE EXISTENCE OF A RACIAL CLASSIFICATION

When a statute on its face classifies by race, as in *Loving*, no problem arises. But under what circumstances may racial discrimination be found even though a statute on its face makes no racial classification? Two distinct situations are involved.

① First, a statute fair on its face may be administered in a way that results in racial discrimination. In Yick Wo v. Hopkins, supra, for example, the Court had before it an ordinance making it unlawful to operate a laundry in a wooden building without a permit from the board of supervisors. A laundryman of Chinese descent who had been denied a permit to operate his laundry in a wooden building showed that the board had denied permits to the 200 Chinese who had petitioned but granted them to 80 non-Chinese. In holding that this constituted a violation of equal protection the Court said: "Though the law itself be fair on its face, and impartial in appearance, yet, if it is applied and administered by public authority with an evil eye and an unequal hand, so as practically to make unjust and illegal discriminations between persons in similar circumstances, material to their rights, the denial of equal justice is still within the prohibition of the constitution."

② Second, the contention may be that a statute which does not on its face make a racial classification in fact was designed to discriminate against a racial group. At one extreme are cases where it is apparent from the face of the statute that an ostensibly nondiscriminatory classification in fact is based on race. See, e.g., Guinn v. United States, 238 U.S. 347 (1915). The Oklahoma Constitution was amended in 1910 to provide that no person shall be registered to vote unless able to read and write a section of that Constitution, but that no person who on Jan. 1, 1866, or any time prior thereto was entitled to vote under any form of government, and no lineal descendant of such person, shall be denied the right to vote because of inability to read and write a section of the Constitution. In holding the provision invalid as a forbidden racial discrimination in voting, the Court said that the discrimination appears from the mere statement of the text. "It is true it contains no express words of an exclusion from the standard which is established of any person on account of race, color, or previous condition of servitude, prohibited by the 15th Amendment, but the standard itself inherently brings that result into existence since it is based purely upon a period of time before the enactment of the 15th Amendment, and makes that period the controlling and dominant test of the right of suffrage." Similarly, saying in part that "[a]ncestry can be a proxy for race" and "[i]t is that proxy here[,]" a majority of the Court examined in context, and then invalidated as an impermissible racial discrimination, a voting qualification favoring the descendants of those who lived in Hawaii in 1778. Rice v. Cayetano, 528 U.S. 495 (2000), set forth infra at p. 1007.

At the other extreme are cases where a statute which does not make a racial classification is shown to have a disproportionate impact on a particular racial group. See, e.g., Jefferson v. Hackney, 406 U.S. 535 (1972), in which the Court upheld a state welfare statute which funded old age assistance at 100% of recognized need but aid to dependent children at 75% of such need. The Court held that a showing that 40% of the recipients of old age assistance were Negroes and Mexican–Americans while 87% of the recipients of aid to dependent children were from such groups was not sufficient to establish that the classification was based on race.

Because the problem of establishing the existence of the discrimination also arises in cases involving classifications based on gender, the cases dealing with proof of discriminatory purpose are postponed for consideration to page 800, infra.

B. RACIAL SEGREGATION IN SCHOOLS AND OTHER PUBLIC FACILITIES

Plessy v. Ferguson

163 U.S. 537, 16 S.Ct. 1138, 41 L.Ed. 256 (1896).

Mr. Justice Brown delivered the opinion of the court.

This case turns upon the constitutionality of an act of the general assembly of the state of Louisiana, passed in 1890, providing for separate railway carriages for the white and colored races. . . .

. . .

The petition for the writ of prohibition averred that petitioner was seven-eighths Caucasian and one-eighth African blood; that the mixture of colored blood was not discernible in him; and that he was entitled to every right, privilege, and immunity secured to citizens of the United States of the white race; and that, upon such theory, he took possession of a vacant seat in a coach where passengers of the white race were accommodated, and was ordered by the conductor to vacate said coach, and take a seat in another, assigned to persons of the colored race, and, having refused to comply with such demand, he was forcibly ejected, with the aid of a police officer, and imprisoned in the parish jail to answer a charge of having violated the above act.

The constitutionality of this act is attacked upon the ground that it conflicts ... with ... the fourteenth amendment....

. . .

The object of the amendment was undoubtedly to enforce the absolute equality of the two races before the law, but, in the nature of things, it could not have been intended to abolish distinctions based upon color, or to enforce social, as distinguished from political, equality, or a commingling of the two races upon terms unsatisfactory to either. Laws permitting, and even requiring, their separation, in places where they are liable to be brought into contact, do not necessarily imply the inferiority of either race to the other, and have been generally, if not universally, recognized as within the competency of the state legislatures in the exercise of their police power. The most common instance of this is connected with the establishment of separate schools for white and colored children, which have been held to be a valid exercise of the legislative power even by courts of states where the political rights of the colored race have been longest and most earnestly enforced.

. . .

Laws forbidding the intermarriage of the two races may be said in a technical sense to interfere with the freedom of contract, and yet have been universally recognized as within the police power of the state....

. . .

In this connection, it is also suggested by the learned counsel for the plaintiff in error that the same argument that will justify the state legislature in requiring railways to provide separate accommodations for the two races will also authorize them to require separate cars to be provided for people whose hair is of a certain color, or who are aliens, or who belong to certain nationalities, or to enact laws requiring colored people to walk upon one side of the street, and white people upon the other, or requiring white men's houses to be painted white, and colored men's black, or their vehicles or business signs to be of different colors, upon the theory that one side of the street is as good as the other, or that a house or vehicle of one color is as good as one of another color. The reply to all this is that every exercise of the police power must be reasonable, and extend only to such laws as are enacted in good faith for the promotion of the public good, and not for the annoyance or oppression of a particular class....

So far, then, as a conflict with the fourteenth amendment is concerned, the case reduces itself to the question whether the statute of Louisiana is a reasonable regulation, and with respect to this there must necessarily be a large discretion on the part of the legislature. In determining the question of reasonableness, it is at liberty to act with reference to the established usages, customs, and traditions of the people, and with a view to the promotion of their comfort, and the preservation of the public peace and good order. Gauged by this standard, we cannot say that a law which authorizes or even requires the separation of the two races in public conveyances is unreasonable, or more obnoxious to the fourteenth amendment than the acts of congress requiring separate schools for colored children in the District of Columbia, the constitutionality of which does not seem to have been questioned or the corresponding acts of state legislatures.

We consider the underlying fallacy of the plaintiff's argument to consist in the assumption that the enforced separation of the two races stamps the colored race with a badge of inferiority. If this be so, it is not by reason of anything found in the act, but solely because the colored race chooses to put that construction upon it. The argument necessarily assumes that if, as has been more than once the case, and is not unlikely to be so again, the colored race should become the dominant power in the state legislature, and should enact a law in precisely similar terms, it would thereby relegate the white race to an inferior position. We imagine that the white race, at least, would not acquiesce in this assumption. The argument also assumes that social prejudices may be overcome by legislation, and that equal rights cannot be secured to the negro except by an enforced commingling of the two races. We cannot accept this proposition. If the two races are to meet upon terms of social equality, it must be the result of natural affinities, a mutual appreciation of each other's merits, and a voluntary consent of individuals. . . . Legislation is powerless to eradicate racial instincts, or to abolish distinctions based upon physical differences, and the attempt to do so can only result in accentuating the difficulties of the present situation. If the civil and political rights of both races be equal, one cannot be inferior to the other civilly or politically. If one race be inferior to the other socially, the constitution of the United States cannot put them upon the same plane. . . .

legislation cannot fix social inequality

The judgment of the court below is therefore affirmed.

Mr. Justice Brewer did not hear the argument or participate in the decision of this case.

Mr. Justice Harlan dissenting. . . .

In respect of civil rights, common to all citizens, the constitution of the United States does not, I think, permit any public authority to know the race of those entitled to be protected in the enjoyment of such rights. Every true man has pride of race, and under appropriate circumstances, when the rights of others, his equals before the law, are not to be affected, it is his privilege to express such pride and to take such action based upon it as to him seems proper. But I deny that any legislative body or judicial tribunal may have regard to the race of citizens when the civil rights of those citizens are involved. Indeed, such legislation as that here in question is inconsistent not only with that equality of rights which pertains to citizenship, national and state, but with the personal liberty enjoyed by every one within the United States. . . .

cant refer to race when civil rights are involved

[The thirteenth, fourteenth, and fifteenth amendments] were welcomed by the friends of liberty throughout the world. They removed the race line from our governmental systems. . . .

It was said in argument that the statute of Louisiana does not discriminate against either race, but prescribes a rule applicable alike to white and colored citizens. But this argument does not meet the difficulty. Everyone knows that the statute in question had its origin in the purpose, not so much to exclude white persons from railroad cars occupied by blacks; as to exclude colored people from coaches occupied by or assigned to white persons. Railroad corporations of Louisiana did not make discrimination among whites in the matter of accommodation for travelers. The thing to accomplish was, under the guise of giving equal accommodation for whites and blacks, to compel the latter to keep to themselves while traveling in railroad passenger coaches. No one would be so wanting in candor as to assert the contrary. The fundamental objection, therefore, to the statute, is that it interferes with the personal freedom of citizens. . . . If a white man and a black man choose to occupy the same public conveyance on a public highway, it is their right to do so; and no government, proceeding alone on grounds of race, can prevent it without infringing the personal liberty of each. . . .

The white race deems itself to be the dominant race in this country. And so it is, in prestige, in achievements, in education, in wealth, and in power. So, I doubt not, it will continue to be for all time, if it remains true to its great heritage, and holds fast to the principles of constitutional liberty. But in view of the constitution, in the eye of the law, there is in this country no superior, dominant, ruling class of citizens. There is no caste here. Our constitution is color-blind, and neither knows nor tolerates classes among citizens. In respect of civil rights, all citizens are equal before the law. The humblest is the peer of the most powerful. The law regards man as man, and takes no account of his surroundings or of his color when his civil rights as guaranteed by the supreme law of the land are involved. It is therefore to be regretted that this high tribunal, the final expositor of the fundamental law of the land, has reached the conclusion that it is competent for a state to regulate the enjoyment by citizens of their civil rights solely upon the basis of race.

. . .

If evils will result from the commingling of the two races upon public highways established for the benefit of all, they will be infinitely less than those that will surely come from state legislation regulating the enjoyment of civil rights upon the basis of race. We boast of the freedom enjoyed by our people above all other peoples. But it is difficult to reconcile that boast with a state of the law which, practically, puts the brand of servitude and degradation upon a large class of our fellow citizens,—our equals before the law. The thin disguise of "equal" accommodations for passengers in railroad coaches will not mislead any one, nor atone for the wrong this day done. . . .

Brown v. Board of Education of Topeka

347 U.S. 483, 74 S.Ct. 686, 98 L.Ed. 873 (1954).

Mr. Chief Justice Warren delivered the opinion of the Court.

These cases come to us from the States of Kansas, South Carolina, Virginia, and Delaware. They are premised on different facts and different local conditions, but a common legal question justifies their consideration together in this consolidated opinion.

In each of the cases, minors of the Negro race, through their legal representatives, seek the aid of the courts in obtaining admission to the public schools of their community on a nonsegregated basis. In each instance, they have been denied admission to schools attended by white children under laws requiring or permitting segregation according to race. This segregation was alleged to deprive the plaintiffs of the equal protection of the laws under the Fourteenth Amendment. In each of the cases other than the Delaware case, a three-judge federal district court denied relief to the plaintiffs on the so-called "separate but equal" doctrine announced by this Court in Plessy v. Ferguson, 163 U.S. 537. Under that doctrine, equality of treatment is accorded when the races are provided substantially equal facilities, even though these facilities be separate. In the Delaware case, the Supreme Court of Delaware adhered to that doctrine, but ordered that the plaintiffs be admitted to the white schools because of their superiority to the Negro schools.

The plaintiffs contend that segregated public schools are not "equal" and cannot be made "equal," and that hence they are deprived of the equal protection of the laws. Because of the obvious importance of the question presented, the Court took jurisdiction. Argument was heard in the 1952 Term, and reargument was heard this Term on certain questions propounded by the Court.

Reargument was largely devoted to the circumstances surrounding the adoption of the Fourteenth Amendment in 1868. It covered exhaustively consideration of the Amendment in Congress, ratification by the states, then existing practices in racial segregation, and the views of proponents and opponents of the Amendment. This discussion and our own investigation convince us that, although these sources cast some light, it is not enough to resolve the problem with which we are faced. At best, they are inconclusive. The most avid proponents of the post-War Amendments undoubtedly intended them to remove all legal distinctions among "all persons born or naturalized in the United States." Their opponents, just as certainly were antagonistic to both the letter and the spirit of the Amendments and wished them to have the most limited effect. What others in Congress and the state legislatures had in mind cannot be determined with any degree of certainty.

An additional reason for the inconclusive nature of the Amendment's history, with respect to segregated schools, is the status of public education at that time. In the South, the movement toward free common schools, supported by general taxation, had not yet taken hold. Education of white children was largely in the hands of private groups. Education of Negroes was almost nonexistent, and practically all of the race were illiterate. In fact, any education of Negroes was forbidden by law in some states. Today, in contrast, many Negroes have achieved outstanding success in the arts and sciences as well as in the business and professional world. It is true that public school education at the time of the Amendment had advanced further in the North, but the effect of the Amendment on Northern States was generally ignored in the congressional debates. Even in the North, the conditions of public education did not approximate those existing today. The curriculum was usually rudimentary; ungraded schools were common in rural areas; the school term was but three months a year in many states; and compulsory school attendance was virtually unknown. As a consequence, it is not surprising that there should be so little in the history of the Fourteenth Amendment relating to its intended effect on public education.

little history after and concerning the schools.

In the first cases in this Court construing the Fourteenth Amendment, decided shortly after its adoption, the Court interpreted it as proscribing all state-imposed discriminations against the Negro race. The doctrine of "separate but equal" did not make its appearance in this Court until 1896 in the case of *Plessy v. Ferguson,* supra, involving not education but transportation. American courts have since labored with the doctrine for over half a century. In this Court, there have been six cases involving the "separate but equal" doctrine in the field of public education. In Cumming v. Board of Education of Richmond County, 175 U.S. 528, and Gong Lum v. Rice, 275 U.S. 78, the validity of the doctrine itself was not challenged. In more recent cases, all on the graduate school level, inequality was found in that specific benefits enjoyed by white students were denied to Negro students of the same educational qualifications. State of Missouri ex rel. Gaines v. Canada, 305 U.S. 337; Sipuel v. Board of Regents of University of Oklahoma, 332 U.S. 631; Sweatt v. Painter, 339 U.S. 629; McLaurin v. Oklahoma State Regents, 339 U.S. 637. In none of these cases was it necessary to reexamine the doctrine to grant relief to the Negro plaintiff. And in *Sweatt v. Painter,* supra, the Court expressly reserved decision on the question whether *Plessy v. Ferguson* should be held inapplicable to public education.

only cases precedent upheld notion of seperate but equal

Not look at separation itself but the effects of it.

In the instant cases, that question is directly presented. Here, unlike *Sweatt v. Painter,* there are findings below that the Negro and white schools involved have been equalized, or are being equalized, with respect to buildings, curricula, qualifications and salaries of teachers, and other "tangible" factors. Our decision, therefore, cannot turn on merely a comparison of these tangible factors in the Negro and white schools involved in each of the cases. We must look instead to the effect of segregation itself on public education.

In approaching this problem, we cannot turn the clock back to 1868 when the Amendment was adopted, or even to 1896 when *Plessy v. Ferguson* was written. We must consider public education in the light of its full development and its present place in American life throughout the Nation. Only in this way can it be determined if segregation in public schools deprives these plaintiffs of the equal protection of the laws.

Today, education is perhaps the most important function of state and local governments. Compulsory school attendance laws and the great expenditures for education both demonstrate our recognition of the importance of education to our democratic society. It is required in the performance of our most basic public responsibilities, even service in the armed forces. It is the very foundation of good citizenship. Today it is a principal instrument in awakening the child to cultural values, in preparing him for later professional training, and in helping him to adjust normally to his environment. In these days, it is doubtful that any child may reasonably be expected to succeed in life if he is denied the opportunity of an education. Such an opportunity, where the state has undertaken to provide it, is a right which must be made available to all on equal terms.

Deprives child of valuable education

We come then to the question presented: Does segregation of children in public schools solely on the basis of race, even though the physical facilities and other "tangible" factors may be equal, deprive the children of the minority group of equal educational opportunities? We believe that it does.

In *Sweatt v. Painter,* supra, in finding that a segregated law school for Negroes could not provide them equal educational opportunities, this Court relied in large part on "those qualities which are incapable of objective measurement but which make for greatness in a law school." In *McLaurin v. Oklahoma State Regents,* supra, the Court, in requiring that a Negro admitted to a white graduate school be treated like all other students, again resorted to intangible considerations: "... his ability to study, to engage in discussions and exchange views with other students, and, in general, to learn his profession." Such considerations apply with added force to children in grade and high schools. To separate them from others of similar age and qualifications solely because of their race generates a feeling of inferiority as to their status in the community that may affect their hearts and minds in a way unlikely ever to be undone. The effect of this separation on their educational opportunities was well stated by a finding in the Kansas case by a court which nevertheless felt compelled to rule against the Negro plaintiffs:

"Segregation of white and colored children in public schools has a detrimental effect upon the colored children. The impact is greater when it has the sanction of the law; for the policy of separating the races is usually interpreted as denoting the inferiority of the negro group. A sense of inferiority affects the motivation of a child to learn. Segregation with the sanction of law, therefore, has a tendency to [retard] the educational and mental development of negro children and to deprive them of some of the benefits they would receive in a racial[ly] integrated school system."

Whatever may have been the extent of psychological knowledge at the time of *Plessy v. Ferguson,* this finding is amply supported by modern authority.[11] Any language in *Plessy v. Ferguson* contrary to this finding is rejected.

We conclude that in the field of public education the doctrine of "separate but equal" has no place. Separate educational facilities are inherently unequal. Therefore, we hold that the plaintiffs and others similarly situated for whom the actions have been brought are, by reason of the segregation complained of, deprived of the equal protection of the laws guaranteed by the Fourteenth Amendment. This disposition makes unnecessary any discussion whether such segregation also violates the Due Process Clause of the Fourteenth Amendment.

In field of public education, seperate is not equal

Because these are class actions, because of the wide applicability of this decision, and because of the great variety of local conditions, the formulation of decrees in these cases presents problems of considerable complexity. On reargument, the consideration of appropriate relief was necessarily subordinated to the primary question—the constitutionality of segregation in public education. We have now announced that such segregation is a denial of the equal protection of the laws. In order that we may have the full assistance of the parties in formulating decrees, the cases will be restored to the docket, and the parties are requested to present further argument on Questions 4 and 5 previously propounded by the Court for the reargument this Term. The Attorney General of the United States is again invited to participate. The Attorneys General of the states requiring or permitting segregation in public education will also be permitted to appear as *amici curiae* upon request to do so by September 15, 1954, and submission of briefs by October 1, 1954.

It is so ordered.

Bolling v. Sharpe

347 U.S. 497, 74 S.Ct. 693, 98 L.Ed. 884 (1954).

Mr. Chief Justice Warren delivered the opinion of the Court.

This case challenges the validity of segregation in the public schools of the District of Columbia. The petitioners, minors of the Negro race, allege that such segregation deprives them of due process of law under the Fifth Amendment. They were refused admission to a public school attended by white children solely because of their race. They sought the aid of the District Court for the District of Columbia in obtaining admission. That court dismissed their complaint. The Court granted a writ of certiorari before judgment in the Court of Appeals because of the importance of the constitutional question presented. 344 U.S. 873.

We have this day held that the Equal Protection Clause of the Fourteenth Amendment prohibits the states from maintaining racially segregated public schools. The legal problem in the District of Columbia is somewhat different,

Have held that segregation is unconstitutional

---

11. K.B. Clark, Effect of Prejudice and Discrimination on Personality Development (Midcentury White House Conference on Children and Youth, 1950); Wittmer and Kotinsky, Personality in the Making (1952), c. VI; Deutscher and Chein, The Psychological Effects of Enforced Segregation: A Survey of Social Science Opinion, 26 J.Psychol. 259 (1948); Chein, What are the Psychological Effects of Segregation Under Conditions of Equal Facilities?, 3 Int.J.Opinion and Attitude Res. 229 (1949); Brameld, Educational Costs, in Discrimination and National Welfare (MacIver, ed., 1949), 44–48; Frazier, The Negro in the United States (1949), 674–681. And see generally Myrdal, An American Dilemma (1944).

This case involves 5th amendment

however. The Fifth Amendment, which is applicable in the District of Columbia, does not contain an equal protection clause as does the Fourteenth Amendment which applies only to the states. But the concepts of equal protection and due process, both stemming from our American ideal of fairness, are not mutually exclusive. The "equal protection of the laws" is a more explicit safeguard of prohibited unfairness than "due process of law," and, therefore, we do not imply that the two are always interchangeable phrases. But, as this Court has recognized, discrimination may be so unjustifiable as to be violative of due process.

Classifications based solely upon race must be scrutinized with particular care, since they are contrary to our traditions and hence constitutionally suspect. As long ago as 1896, this Court declared the principle "that the constitution of the United States, in its present form, forbids, so far as civil and political rights are concerned, discrimination by the general government, or by the states, against any citizen because of his race." And in Buchanan v. Warley, 245 U.S. 60, the Court held that a statute which limited the right of a property owner to convey his property to a person of another race was, as an unreasonable discrimination, a denial of due process of law.

Although the Court has not assumed to define "liberty" with any great precision, that term is not confined to mere freedom from bodily restraint. Liberty under law extends to the full range of conduct which the individual is free to pursue, and it cannot be restricted except for a proper governmental objective. Segregation in public education is not reasonably related to any proper governmental objective, and thus it imposes on Negro children of the District of Columbia a burden that constitutes an arbitrary deprivation of their liberty in violation of the Due Process Clause.

In view of our decision that the Constitution prohibits the states from maintaining racially segregated public schools, it would be unthinkable that the same Constitution would impose a lesser duty on the Federal Government. We hold that racial segregation in the public schools of the District of Columbia is a denial of the due process of law guaranteed by the Fifth Amendment to the Constitution.

For the reasons set out in *Brown v. Board of Education,* this case will be restored to the docket for reargument on Questions 4 and 5 previously propounded by the Court. 345 U.S. 972.

It is so ordered.

BROWN AND THE RELEVANCE OF SOCIAL SCIENCE AND HISTORICAL MATERIALS

The Court in *Brown* relied to some extent on studies by psychologists and social scientists to support the conclusion that placing Negro children in separate schools generates feelings of inferiority unlikely to be undone. The Court's reference to this data generated immediate controversy among lawyers as to its propriety and relevance. Compare Cahn, *Science or Common Sense? A Dangerous Myth, in 1954 Annual Survey of American Law: Jurisprudence,* 30 N.Y.U.L.Rev. 150 (1955) with Honnold, *Book Review,* 33 Ind.L.J. 612, 614 (1958). More recent and elaborate consideration will be found in two symposia: *The Courts, Social Science, and School Desegregation,* 39 Law & Contemp.Prob. (No. 1, Winter, 1975, and No. 2, Spring, 1975); *School Desegregation: Lessons of the First Twenty–Five Years,* 42 Law & Contemp.Prob. (Summer 1978 and Autumn 1978).

The Court in *Brown* also directed attention to the historical background of the fourteenth amendment. For a discussion of the historical record, see Bickel, *The Original Understanding and the Segregation Decisions,* 69 Harv.L.Rev. 1 (1955), *Selected Essays on Constitutional Law,* 1938–1962 (1963) 853.

For some of the voluminous literature which followed the desegregation cases and probed their implications, see Wechsler, *Toward Neutral Principles of Constitutional Law,* 73 Harv.L.Rev. 1 (1959); Black, *The Lawfulness of the Segregation Decisions,* 69 Yale L.J. 421 (1960); Pollak, *Racial Discrimination and Judicial Integrity,* 108 U.Pa.L.Rev. 1 (1959). These articles are reprinted in *Selected Essays on Constitutional Law,* 1938–1962 (1963) at 463, 844, and 819.

SEGREGATION IN PUBLIC FACILITIES OTHER THAN SCHOOLS

In *Brown* the Court emphasized the importance of education and gave reasons why segregation in schools was inherently unequal. When presented with the question whether the same reasoning would serve to invalidate segregation in other public facilities, the Court held such segregation invalid in a series of per curiam orders without explanatory opinions. In Mayor and City Council of Baltimore City v. Dawson, 350 U.S. 877 (1955), it summarily affirmed an order enjoining racial segregation in public beaches and bathhouses. In Holmes v. Atlanta, 350 U.S. 879 (1955) the Court summarily reversed a lower court order which appeared to permit the city to allocate a municipal golf course to different races on alternate days. In Gayle v. Browder, 352 U.S. 903 (1956) it summarily affirmed a judgment enjoining enforcement of racial segregation on city buses. Similar dispositions were made in cases involving other public facilities in New Orleans City Park Improvement Ass'n v. Detiege, 358 U.S. 54 (1958) (golf course and parks); State Athletic Comm'n v. Dorsey, 359 U.S. 533 (1959) (participation in athletic contests); Schiro v. Bynum, 375 U.S. 395 (1964) (municipal auditorium).

Eventually started applying it to everything [handwritten marginal note]

In Johnson v. Virginia, 373 U.S. 61 (1963), the Court wrote a brief per curiam opinion reversing a conviction of a defendant for sitting in a section of a segregated courtroom reserved for whites. The Court said, without further elaboration: "Such a conviction cannot stand for it is no longer open to question that a State may not constitutionally require segregation of public facilities."[7]

REMEDYING DE JURE SEGREGATION

As the Court's opinions in *Brown* and *Bolling* indicate, the "problems of considerable complexity" involved in the formulation of remedies to desegregate public schools that previously had operated under laws requiring or permitting racial segregation were postponed for separate consideration. A year later in Brown v. Board of Education, 349 U.S. 294 (1955) (*Brown II*), Chief Justice Warren authored another unanimous opinion, this time remanding the cases with these comments:

Brown II [handwritten marginal note]

"Full implementation ... may require solution of varied local school problems. School authorities have the primary responsibility for elucidating, assessing, and solving these problems; courts will have to consider whether the action of school authorities constitutes good faith implementation of the governing constitutional principles...."

---

7. For observations on the extent to which the Court uses per curiam decisions, see Brown, *Process of Law,* 72 Harv.L.Rev. 77 (1958).

"In fashioning and effectuating the decrees, the courts will be guided by equitable principles. Traditionally, equity has been characterized by a practical flexibility in shaping its remedies and by a facility for adjusting and reconciling public and private needs. These cases call for the exercise of these traditional attributes of equity power. At stake is the personal interest of the plaintiffs in admission to public schools as soon as practicable on a nondiscriminatory basis. To effectuate this interest may call for elimination of a variety of obstacles in making the transition to school systems operated in accordance with the constitutional principles set forth in our May 17, 1954, decision. Courts of equity may properly take into account the public interest in the elimination of such obstacles in a systematic and effective manner. But it should go without saying that the vitality of these constitutional principles cannot be allowed to yield simply because of disagreement with them.

"While giving weight to these public and private considerations, the courts will require that the defendants make a prompt and reasonable start toward full compliance with our May 17, 1954, ruling. Once such a start has been made, the courts may find that additional time is necessary to carry out the ruling in an effective manner. The burden rests upon the defendants to establish that such time is necessary in the public interest and is consistent with good faith compliance at the earliest practicable date. To that end, the courts may consider problems related to administration, arising from the physical condition of the school plant, the school transportation system, personnel, revision of school districts and attendance areas into compact units to achieve a system of determining admission to the public schools on a nonracial basis, and revision of local laws and regulations which may be necessary in solving the foregoing problems. They will also consider the adequacy of any plans the defendants may propose to meet these problems and to effectuate a transition to a racially nondiscriminatory school system. During this period of transition, the courts will retain jurisdiction of these cases.

"The . . . District Courts [shall] enter such orders and decrees consistent with this opinion as are necessary and proper to admit to public schools on a racially nondiscriminatory basis with all deliberate speed the parties to these cases. . . ."

During the half century following *Brown II*, in the face of substantial resistance, foot-dragging, and demographic and social change, the Court repeatedly confronted remedial questions involving how quickly desegregation must occur; what school authority responses were and were not adequate to satisfy the remedial obligation; the scope of judicial authority to formulate and enforce desegregation measures when those responses were deemed inadequate; and under what circumstances school authorities had satisfied their remedial obligations so that the district courts should no longer retain jurisdiction. Within the limited space available in a casebook, the events of this period cannot be described fully, but some of the central developments are key to understanding the meaning of *Brown* and the Court's ability to enforce it.[a]

Little change in the extent of racial segregation in Southern public schools occurred in the first decade following *Brown II*.[b] Some movement began with

a. For an excellent brief account of the first two decades, see Read, *Judicial Evolution of the Law of School Integration Since Brown v. Board of Education,* 39 Law & Contemp.Prob. 7 (No. 1, Winter, 1975).

b. For a comprehensive study that tracks changes in the extent of interracial contact during the half century following *Brown* in the context of the legal developments set forth in this set of notes, see Clotfelter, *After Brown: The Rise and Retreat of School Desegregation* (2004).

passage of The Civil Rights Act of 1964, which authorized the Attorney General of the United States to intervene in desegregation cases and prohibited racial discrimination by schools receiving federal funds. Still, progress was exceedingly slow, so that by 1968 the Court found constitutionally inadequate a common desegregation plan that allowed students freedom of choice in what school they attended but that in practical operation preserved a "dual system." **Green v. County School Board,** 391 U.S. 430 (1968).[c] *Green* established that although a freedom-of-choice program "could be a valid remedial measure in some circumstances"—if effective—"[t]he burden on a school board today is to come forward with a plan that promises realistically to work . . . *now* . . . until it is clear that state-imposed segregation has been completely removed." Three years later, acknowledging the struggle the lower federal courts had experienced implementing *Brown II* in the "hundreds of cases" from states having a long history of *de jure* racial segregation, the Court decided in the following case to "defin[e] in more precise terms . . . the scope of the duty of school authorities and district courts in implementing *Brown I* and the mandate to eliminate dual systems and establish unitary systems at once."

SWANN v. CHARLOTTE–MECKLENBURG BOARD OF EDUCATION, 402 U.S. 1 (1971). The Charlotte–Mecklenburg school system encompassed the city of Charlotte and surrounding Mecklenburg County, North Carolina—an area of 550 square miles. During the 1968–1969 school year the system served more than 84,000 pupils in 107 schools, about 71% of whom were white and 29% black. Of the 24,000 black students, 21,000 attended schools within the city of Charlotte, two-thirds of them in 21 schools "which were either totally Negro or more than 99% Negro." Pursuant to a federal district court order, the school board adopted a desegregation plan for elementary schools that included grouping two or three outlying schools with one black inner city school, transporting black students from grades one through four to the outlying white schools, and transporting white students from the fifth and sixth grades to the inner city black school. Chief Justice Burger's unanimous opinion contained the following excerpts, which addressed other aspects of the plan as well:

"The objective today remains to eliminate from the public schools all vestiges of state-imposed segregation. . . . That was the basis for the holding in *Green* that school authorities are 'clearly charged with the affirmative duty to take whatever steps might be necessary to convert to a unitary system in which racial discrimination would be eliminated root and branch'. . . .

"If school authorities fail in their affirmative obligations under these holdings, judicial authority may be invoked. Once a right and a violation have been shown, the scope of a district court's equitable powers to remedy past wrongs is broad, for breadth and flexibility are inherent in equitable remedies. . . .

"   . . .

"[J]udicial powers may be exercised only on the basis of a constitutional violation. Remedial judicial authority does not put judges automatically in the shoes of school authorities whose powers are plenary. Judicial authority enters only when local authority defaults.

"School authorities are traditionally charged with broad power to formulate and implement educational policy and might well conclude, for example,

c. For an insightful general discussion of desegregation "choice" plans, see Gewirtz, *Choice in the Transition: School Desegrega-* *tion and the Corrective Ideal*, 86 Colum. L. Rev. 728 (1986).

should
"redistribute"
schools

that in order to prepare students to live in a pluralistic society each school should have a prescribed ratio of Negro to white students reflecting the proportion for the district as a whole. To do this as an educational policy is within the broad discretionary powers of school authorities; absent a finding of a constitutional violation, however, that would not be within the authority of a federal court. As with any equity case, the nature of the violation determines the scope of the remedy. In default by the school authorities of their obligation to proffer acceptable remedies, a district court has broad power to fashion a remedy that will assure a unitary school system.

"...

"In *Green,* we pointed out that existing policy and practice with regard to faculty, staff, transportation, extracurricular activities, and facilities were among the most important indicia of a segregated system.... Independent of student assignment, where it is possible to identify a 'white school' or a 'Negro school' simply by reference to the racial composition of teachers and staff, the quality of school buildings and equipment, or the organization of sports activities, a *prima facie* case of violation of substantive constitutional rights under the Equal Protection Clause is shown.

"When a system has been dual in these respects, the first remedial responsibility of school authorities is to eliminate invidious racial distinctions. With respect to such matters as transportation, supporting personnel, and extracurricular activities, no more than this may be necessary. Similar corrective action must be taken with regard to the maintenance of buildings and the distribution of equipment. In these areas, normal administrative practice should produce schools of like quality, facilities, and staffs. Something more must be said, however, as to faculty assignment and new school construction.

"In the companion *Davis* case, the Mobile school board has argued that the Constitution requires that teachers be assigned on a 'color blind' basis. It also argues that the Constitution prohibits district courts from using their equity power to order assignment of teachers to achieve a particular degree of faculty desegregation. We reject that contention.

"...

"The construction of new schools and the closing of old ones is one of the most important functions of local school authorities and also one of the most complex. They must decide questions of location and capacity in light of population growth, finances, land values, site availability, through an almost endless list of factors to be considered. The result of this will be a decision which, when combined with one technique or another of student assignment, will determine the racial composition of the student body in each school in the system. Over the long run, the consequences of the choices will be far reaching. People gravitate toward school facilities, just as schools are located in response to the needs of people. The location of schools may thus influence the patterns of residential development of a metropolitan area and have important impact on composition of inner city neighborhoods.

"In the past, choices in this respect have been used as a potent weapon for creating or maintaining a state-segregated school system....

"In ascertaining the existence of legally imposed school segregation, the existence of a pattern of school construction and abandonment is thus a factor of great weight. In devising remedies where legally imposed segregation has been established, it is the responsibility of local authorities and district courts to see to it that future school construction and abandonment is not used and does not serve to perpetuate or re-establish the dual system. When necessary,

district courts should retain jurisdiction to assure that these responsibilities are carried out. . . .

V.

"The central issue . . . is . . . student assignment, and there are essentially four problem areas:

(1) to what extent racial balance or racial quotas may be used as an implement in a remedial order to correct a previously segregated system;

(2) whether every all-Negro and all-white school must be eliminated as an indispensable part of a remedial process of desegregation;

(3) what are the limits, if any, on the rearrangement of school districts and attendance zones, as a remedial measure; and

(4) what are the limits, if any, on the use of transportation facilities to correct state-enforced racial school segregation.

"(1) *Racial Balances or Racial Quotas.* . . .

[The Court reviewed the district court's direction "that efforts should be made to reach a 71–29 ratio in the various schools so that there will be no basis for contending that one school is racially different from the others . . ., that no school [should] be operated with an all-black or predominantly black student body, [and] that pupils of all grades [should] be assigned in such a way that as nearly as practicable the various schools at various grade levels have about the same proportion of black and white students." The opinion said in part:]

". . . If we were to read the holding of the District Court to require, as a matter of substantive constitutional right, any particular degree of racial balance or mixing, that approach would be disapproved and we would be obliged to reverse. The constitutional command to desegregate schools does not mean that every school in every community must always reflect the racial composition of the school system as a whole.

" . . .

"[However,] the use made of mathematical ratios was not more than a starting point in the process of shaping a remedy, rather than an inflexible requirement. . . . Awareness of the racial composition of the whole school system is likely to be a useful starting point in shaping a remedy to correct past constitutional violations. In sum, the very limited use made of mathematical ratios was within the equitable remedial discretion of the District Court.

"(2) *One–Race Schools.* [I]n metropolitan areas minority groups are often found concentrated in one part of the city. In some circumstances certain schools may remain all or largely of one race until new schools can be provided or neighborhood patterns change. Schools all or predominantly of one race in a district of mixed population will require close scrutiny to determine that school assignments are not part of state-enforced segregation.

"[T]he existence of some small number of one-race, or virtually one-race, schools within a district is not in and of itself the mark of a system which still practices segregation by law. The district judge or school authorities should make every effort to achieve the greatest possible degree of actual desegregation and will thus necessarily be concerned with the elimination of one-race schools. No *per se* rule can adequately embrace all the difficulties of reconciling the competing interests involved; but in a system with a history of segregation the need for remedial criteria of sufficient specificity to assure a school authority's compliance with its constitutional duty warrants a presumption against schools that are substantially disproportionate in their racial composition. Where the school authority's proposed plan for conversion from a dual to a unitary system contemplates the continued existence of some schools that are all or predominately of one race, they have the burden of showing that such school assignments are genuinely nondiscriminatory. The court should scrutinize such schools, and the burden upon the school authorities will be to satisfy the court that their racial composition is not the result of present or past discriminatory action on their part.

"An optional majority-to-minority transfer provision has long been recognized as a useful part of every desegregation plan. Provision for optional transfer of those in the majority racial group of a particular school to other schools where they will be in the minority is an indispensable remedy for those students willing to transfer to other schools in order to lessen the impact on them of the state-imposed stigma of segregation. In order to be effective, such a transfer arrangement must grant the transferring student free transportation and space must be made available in the school to which he desires to move.... The court orders in this and the companion *Davis* case now provide such an option.

"(3) *Remedial Altering of Attendance Zones.* The maps submitted in these cases graphically demonstrate that one of the principal tools employed by school planners and by courts to break up the dual school system has been a frank—and sometimes drastic—gerrymandering of school districts and attendance zones. An additional step was pairing, 'clustering,' or 'grouping' of schools with attendance assignments made deliberately to accomplish the transfer of Negro students out of formerly segregated Negro schools and transfer of white students to formerly all-Negro schools. More often than not, these zones are neither compact nor contiguous; indeed they may be on opposite ends of the city. As an interim corrective measure, this cannot be said to be beyond the broad remedial powers of a court.

"Absent a constitutional violation there would be no basis for judicially ordering assignment of students on a racial basis. All things being equal, with no history of discrimination, it might well be desirable to assign pupils to schools nearest their homes. But all things are not equal in a system that has been deliberately constructed and maintained to enforce racial segregation. The remedy for such segregation may be administratively awkward, inconvenient and even bizarre in some situations and may impose burdens on some; but all awkwardness and inconvenience cannot be avoided in the interim period when remedial adjustments are being made to eliminate the dual school systems.

". . .

"(4) *Transportation of Students.* ... No rigid guidelines as to student transportation can be given for application to the infinite variety of problems presented in thousands of situations. Bus transportation has been an integral part of the public education system for years.... Eighteen million of the nation's public school children, approximately 39%, were transported to their schools by bus in 1969–1970 in all parts of the country.

"The importance of bus transportation as a normal and accepted tool of educational policy is readily discernible in this and the companion case. The Charlotte school authorities did not purport to assign students on the basis of geographically drawn zones until 1965 and then they allowed almost unlimited transfer privileges. The District Court's conclusion that assignment of children to the school nearest their home serving their grade would not produce an effective dismantling of the dual system is supported by the record.

"Thus the remedial techniques used in the District Court's order were within the court's power to provide equitable relief; implementation of the decree is well within the capacity of the school authority.'

"The decree provided that the buses used to implement the plan would operate on direct routes. Students would be picked up at schools near their homes and transported to the schools they were to attend. The trips for elementary school pupils average about seven miles and the District Court found that they would take 'not over 35 minutes at the most.' This system compares favorably with the transportation plan previously operated in Charlotte under which each day 23,600 students on all grade levels were transported an average of 15 miles one way for an average trip requiring over an hour. In these circumstances, we find no basis for holding that the local school authorities may not be required to employ bus transportation as one tool of school desegregation. . . .

"An objection to transportation of students may have validity when the time or distance of travel is so great as to risk either the health of the children or significantly impinge on the educational process. . . . [T]he limits on time of travel will vary with many factors, but probably with none more than the age of the students. The reconciliation of competing values in a desegregation case is, of course, a difficult task with many sensitive facets but fundamentally no more so than remedial measures courts of equity have traditionally employed.

" . . .

"At some point . . . school authorities . . . should have achieved full compliance with this Court's decision in *Brown I*. The systems will then be 'unitary' in the sense required by . . . *Green* and *Alexander*.

"It does not follow that the communities served by such systems will remain demographically stable, for in a growing, mobile society, few will do so. Neither school authorities nor district courts are constitutionally required to make year-by-year adjustments of the racial composition of student bodies once the affirmative duty to desegregate has been accomplished and racial discrimination through official action is eliminated from the system. This does not mean that federal courts are without power to deal with future problems; but in the absence of a showing that either the school authorities or some other agency of the State has deliberately attempted to fix or alter demographic patterns to affect the racial composition of the schools, further intervention by a district court should not be necessary."

. . .[a]

---

a. In North Carolina State Bd. of Ed. v. Swann, 402 U.S. 43 (1971), the Court held unconstitutional a state statute providing that "No student shall be assigned or compelled to attend any school on account of race, creed, color or national origin, or for the purpose of creating a balance or ratio of race, religion or national origins." The Court said that the statute would obstruct the remedies utilized in the *Swann* case and added: "Just as the race of students must be considered in determining whether a constitutional violation has occurred, so also must race be considered in formulating a remedy. To forbid, at this stage, all assignments made on the basis of race would deprive school authorities of the one tool absolutely essential to fulfillment of their constitutional obligation to eliminate existing dual school systems." See also Davis v. Board of Sch. Comm'rs, 402 U.S. 33 (1971); McDaniel v. Barresi, 402 U.S. 39 (1971).

See generally Carter, *An Evaluation of Past and Current Legal Approaches to Vindication of the Fourteenth Amendment's Guarantee of Equal Educational Opportunity,* 1972 Wash.U.L.Q. 479; Karst, *Not One Law at Rome and Another at Athens: The Fourteenth Amendment in Nationwide Application,* 1972 Wash.U.L.Q. 383.

DE JURE SEGREGATION IN NORTHERN SCHOOLS AND THE APPLICATION OF DESEGREGATION REMEDIES NATIONWIDE

In the South schools had been desegregated by law. In the North the law did not require segregation, but some school districts had acted intentionally to separate students on racial grounds, and patterns of segregation were common in any event. In Keyes v. School District No. 1, Denver, Colo., 413 U.S. 189 (1973), the Court explored problems of northern desegregation for the first time. No legally based segregation had existed in Denver—in fact, the Colorado Constitution prohibited "any classification of pupils ... on account of race or color." Instead, the school board allegedly had taken certain actions intentionally for the purpose of creating or maintaining segregated schools in the district. Much of Justice Brennan's opinion for the Court addressed questions that arise when the plaintiff proves intentional acts of segregation in one part of a school district and seeks to use them as a basis for obtaining an order desegregating the schools in another part of the district. On this issue the Court held that "a finding of intentionally segregative school board actions in a meaningful portion of a school system, as in this case, creates a presumption that other segregated schooling within the system is not adventitious. It establishes, in other words, a prima facie case of unlawful segregative design on the part of school authorities, and shifts to those authorities the burden of proving that other segregated schools within the system are not also the results of intentionally segregative actions."

The opinion made the assumption (not challenged by the parties) that in a school district without a history of legally imposed segregation the initial burden of a plaintiff seeking a desegregation order is to establish (1) intentional acts by the school board designed to create or maintain racially segregated schools and (2) the existence of currently segregated schools resulting from those acts. The Court approved district court findings that the school board had engaged in deliberate racial segregation based on the construction of a new, relatively small elementary school in the middle of the black community, the gerrymandering of student attendance zones, the use of so-called "optional zones," and the excessive use of mobile classroom units. The Court also discussed how to establish the existence of segregated schools: "What is or is not a segregated school will necessarily depend on the facts of each particular case. In addition to the racial and ethnic composition of a school's student body, other factors such as the racial and ethnic composition of faculty and staff and the community and administration attitudes toward the school must be taken into consideration." In the context of Denver's "tri-ethnic" community—whose public schools were "66% Anglo, 14% Negro and 20% Hispano"—the Court concluded "that the District Court erred in separating Negroes and Hispanos for purposes of defining a 'segregated' school." Citing United States Commission on Civil Rights Reports on Hispano education in the Southwest, which concluded that Hispanos suffer from the same educational inequities as Negroes and American Indians, together with findings of shared economic and cultural deprivation and discrimination, the Court found "petitioners ... entitled to have schools with a combined predominance of Negroes and Hispanos included in the category of 'segregated' schools." As for defending against the prima facie case made once the plaintiff establishes intentional acts of segregation plus the existence of segregated schools, "if respondent School Board cannot disprove segregative intent, it can rebut the prima facie case only by showing that its past segregative acts did not create or contribute to the current segregated condition of the core city schools." The Court also said this:

"The respondent School Board invoked at trial its 'neighborhood school policy' as explaining racial and ethnic concentrations within the core city schools, arguing that since the core city area population had long been Negro and Hispano, the concentrations were necessarily the result of residential patterns and not of purposefully segregative policies. We have no occasion to consider in this case whether a 'neighborhood school policy' of itself will justify racial or ethnic concentrations in the absence of a finding that school authorities have committed acts constituting *de jure* segregation. It is enough that we hold that the mere assertion of such a policy is not dispositive where, as in this case, the school authorities have been found to have practiced *de jure* segregation in a meaningful portion of the school system by techniques that indicate that the 'neighborhood school' concept has not been maintained free of manipulation."[a]

Justice Powell, concurring in part and dissenting in part, disagreed with the Court's assumption that northern schools should be free of any obligation to desegregate in the absence of a showing of intentional segregative acts. He urged that "if our national concern is for those who attend [segregated] schools, rather than for perpetuating a legalism rooted in history rather than present reality, we must recognize that the evil of operating separate schools is no less in Denver than in Atlanta." He concluded on this point:

"... I would not ... perpetuate the *de jure de facto* distinction nor ... leave to petitioners the initial tortuous effort of identifying 'segregative acts' and deducing 'segregatory intent.' I would hold, quite simply, that where segregated public schools exist within a school district to a substantial degree, there is a prima facie case that the duly constituted public authorities ... are sufficiently responsible to impose ... a nationally applicable burden to demonstrate they nevertheless are operating a genuinely integrated school system."

Justice Powell then discussed the limits he would impose upon remedial orders by the courts, North or South. Brief excerpts from his long opinion follow:

"Where school authorities have defaulted in their duty to operate an integrated school system, district courts must insure that affirmative desegregative steps ensue. Many of these can be taken effectively without damaging state and parental interests in having children attend schools within a reasonable vicinity of home. Where desegregative steps are possible within the framework of a system of 'neighborhood education' school authorities must pursue them. . . .

". . . School boards would, of course, be free to develop and initiate further plans to promote school desegregation. In a pluralistic society such as ours, it is essential that no racial minority feel demeaned or discriminated against and that students of all races learn to play, work, and cooperate with one another in their common pursuits and endeavors. Nothing in this opinion is meant to discourage school boards from exceeding minimal constitutional standards in promoting the values of an integrated school experience.

"A *constitutional requirement* of extensive student transportation solely to achieve integration presents a vastly more complex problem. It promises on the one hand a greater degree of actual desegregation, while it infringes on what may fairly be regarded as other important community aspirations and personal rights. Such a requirement is further likely to divert attention and resources

a. Chief Justice Burger concurred in the result without opinion, and Justice White took no part in the decision.

from the foremost goal of any school system: the best quality education for all pupils. The Equal Protection Clause does indeed command that racial discrimination not be tolerated in the decisions of public school authorities. But it does not require that school authorities undertake widespread student transportation solely for the sake of maximizing integration.

". . . .

". . . The single most disruptive element in education today is the widespread use of compulsory transportation, especially at elementary grade levels. This has risked distracting and diverting attention from basic educational ends, dividing and embittering communities, and exacerbating rather than ameliorating inter-racial friction and misunderstanding. It is time to return to a more balanced evaluation of the recognized interests of our society in achieving desegregation with other educational and societal interests a community may legitimately assert. . . ."

Justice Douglas, concurring in the opinion of the Court, also agreed with Justice Powell that cases from the North and the South should be treated the same. Justice Rehnquist dissented.

The consequences of intentional actions that created virtually segregated school systems were examined again, this time involving two Ohio cities whose segregative acts had occurred before *Brown* was decided, in Columbus Bd. of Educ. v. Penick, 443 U.S. 449 (1979), and Dayton Bd. of Educ. v. Brinkman, 443 U.S. 526 (1979). The Court upheld the conclusion of the court of appeals that the cities since the *Brown* case had been under a duty to disestablish the dual system and had not done so. The five-Justice majority opinion included the following excerpt from the *Dayton* case:

"Petitioners next contend that, even if a dual system did exist a quarter of a century ago, the Court of Appeals erred in finding any widespread violations of constitutional duty since that time.

"Given intentionally segregated schools in 1954, however, the Court of Appeals was quite right in holding that the Board was thereafter under a continuing duty to eradicate the effects of that system and that the systemwide nature of the violation furnished prima facie proof that current segregation in the Dayton schools was caused at least in part by prior intentionally segregative official acts. Thus, judgment for the plaintiffs was authorized and required absent sufficient countervailing evidence by the defendant school officials. *Keyes* . . .; *Swann*. . . . At the time of trial, Dunbar High School and the three black elementary schools, or the schools that succeeded them, remained black schools; and most of the schools in Dayton were virtually one-race schools, as were 80% of the classrooms. 'Every school which was 90 percent or more black in 1951–52 *or* 1963–64 *or* 1971–72 and which is still in use today remains 90 percent or more black. Of the 25 white schools in 1972–73, *all* opened 90 percent or more white and, if open, were 90 percent or more white in 1971–72, 1963–64 and 1951–52.' 583 F.2d, at 254 (emphasis in original), . . . Against this background, the Court of Appeals held that '[t]he evidence of record demonstrates convincingly that defendants have failed to eliminate the continuing systemwide effects of their prior discrimination and have intentionally maintained a segregated school system down to the time the complaint was filed in the present case.' At the very least, defendants had failed to come forward with evidence to deny 'that the current racial composition of the school population reflects the systemwide impact' of the Board's prior discriminatory conduct.

"Part of the affirmative duty imposed by our cases . . . is the obligation not to take any action that would impede the process of disestablishing the dual system and its effects.... The Dayton Board, however, had engaged in many post-*Brown I* actions that had the effect of increasing or perpetuating segregation.... But the measure of the post-*Brown I* conduct of a school board under an unsatisfied duty to liquidate a dual system is the effectiveness, not the purpose, of the actions in decreasing or increasing the segregation caused by the dual system.... As was clearly established in *Keyes* and *Swann,* the Board had to do more than abandon its prior discriminatory purpose.... The Board has had an affirmative responsibility to see that pupil assignment policies and school construction and abandonment practices 'are not used and do not serve to perpetuate or re-establish the dual school system,' ... and the Board has a 'heavy burden' of showing that actions that increased or continued the effects of the dual system serve important and legitimate ends.''

MAY SCHOOL DESEGREGATION ORDERS EXTEND BEYOND SCHOOL DISTRICT LINES?

MILLIKEN v. BRADLEY, 418 U.S. 717 (1974). Litigation commenced in 1970 sought desegregation of the Detroit school district. At that time there were 86 school districts in the Detroit metropolitan area enrolling a million children, with about 275,000 in the Detroit district alone. The racial composition of the area school population was 81% white, 19% black. The racial composition of the Detroit district was 64% black and 34% white. Within the Detroit district most of the schools were either predominantly black or predominantly white. The trial judge found numerous actions by the Detroit School Board taken for the purpose of maintaining segregation of the schools within the district. He also found a number of actions by the State that contributed to the segregation, including a failure to provide funds for busing within Detroit while providing them in the suburbs. Eventually the judge found that it would not be possible to desegregate the schools by any remedy confined to Detroit alone, and that any remedy possible would simply create a system composed all of predominantly black schools and cause further movement of white pupils out of the public school system. The judge then determined that only an interdistrict remedy would solve the problem. Relying on the involvement of the State and requiring no showing of any segregative acts by the suburban school districts (and providing only minimal opportunity for those districts to appear and contest the ruling) the court ordered an interdistrict remedy. He designated 53 of the 85 suburban school districts plus Detroit as the "desegregation area" and appointed a panel to prepare a plan. The plan was to be based on 15 clusters containing part of the Detroit system and two or more suburban districts to "achieve the greatest degree of actual desegregation to the end that, upon implementation, no school, grade or classroom [would be] substantially disproportionate to the overall pupil racial composition." He also ordered the State to purchase or lease at least 295 buses to provide transportation under an interim plan. The Court of Appeals affirmed. It said that the harm to black pupils from being confined to predominantly black schools surrounded by white schools was the same whether within a single district or within a multi-district metropolitan area. It also said that the State's general responsibility for education and the acts of segregation it had committed justified the interdistrict order without showing violations by the suburban districts.

Supreme ct. reversed decision calling for an interdistrict remedy

The Supreme Court reversed. Chief Justice Burger, writing for the Court, noted that "the use of significant racial imbalance in schools within an autonomous school district as a signal which operates simply to shift the burden of proof, is a very different matter from equating racial imbalance with a constitutional violation calling for a remedy." As to the propriety of the interdistrict remedy, he said:

"Here the District Court's approach to what constituted 'actual desegregation' raises the fundamental question, not presented in *Swann,* as to the circumstances in which a federal court may order desegregation relief that embraces more than a single school district. The court's analytical starting point was its conclusion that school district lines are no more than arbitrary lines on a map 'drawn for political convenience.' Boundary lines may be bridged where there has been a constitutional violation calling for inter-district relief, but the notion that school district lines may be casually ignored or treated as a mere administrative convenience is contrary to the history of public education in our country. No single tradition in public education is more deeply rooted than local control over the operation of schools. . . .

". . . [T]he inter-district remedy approved by the two courts could disrupt and alter the structure of public education in Michigan. The metropolitan remedy would require, in effect, consolidation of 54 independent school districts historically administered as separate units into a vast new super school district. . . . Entirely apart from the logistical and other serious problems attending large-scale transportation of students, the consolidation would give rise to an array of other problems in financing and operating this new school system. Some of the more obvious questions would be: What would be the status and authority of the present popularly elected school boards? Would the children of Detroit be within the jurisdiction and operating control of a school board elected by the parents and residents of other districts? What board or boards would levy taxes for school operations in these 54 districts constituting the consolidated metropolitan area? What provisions could be made for assuring substantial equality in tax levies among the 54 districts, if this were deemed requisite? What provisions would be made for financing? Would the validity of long-term bonds be jeopardized unless approved by all of the component districts as well as the State? What body would determine that portion of the curricula now left to the discretion of local school boards? Who would establish attendance zones, purchase school equipment, locate and construct new schools, and indeed attend to all the myriad day-to-day decisions that are necessary to school operations affecting potentially more than three quarters of a million pupils? . . .

. . .

"Of course, no state law is above the Constitution. School district lines and the present laws with respect to local control, are not sacrosanct and if they conflict with the Fourteenth Amendment federal courts have a duty to prescribe appropriate remedies. See, e.g., Wright v. Council of City of Emporia, 407 U.S. 451; United States v. Scotland Neck Board of Education, 407 U.S. 484 (state or local officials prevented from carving out a new school district from an existing district that was in process of dismantling a dual school system); . . . But our prior holdings have been confined to violations and remedies within a single school district. We therefore turn to address, for the first time, the validity of a remedy mandating cross-district or inter-district consolidation to remedy a condition of segregation found to exist in only one district.

"The controlling principle consistently expounded in our holdings is that the scope of the remedy is determined by the nature and extent of the constitutional violation. *Swann.* . . . Before the boundaries of separate and autonomous school districts may be set aside by consolidating the separate units for remedial purposes or by imposing a cross-district remedy, it must first be shown that there has been a constitutional violation within one district that produces a significant segregative effect in another district. Specifically it must be shown that racially discriminatory acts of the state or local school districts, or of a single school district have been a substantial cause of inter-district segregation. Thus an inter-district remedy might be in order where the racially discriminatory acts of one or more school districts caused racial segregation in an adjacent district, or where district lines have been deliberately drawn on the basis of race. In such circumstances an inter-district remedy would be appropriate to eliminate the inter-district segregation directly caused by the constitutional violation. Conversely, without an inter-district violation and inter-district effect, there is no constitutional wrong calling for an inter-district remedy.

. . .

"In dissent Mr. Justice White and Mr. Justice Marshall undertake to demonstrate that agencies having statewide authority participated in maintaining the dual school system found to exist in Detroit. They are apparently of the view that once such participation is shown, the District Court should have a relatively free hand to reconstruct school districts outside of Detroit in fashioning relief. Our assumption, *arguendo* ... that state agencies did participate in the maintenance of the Detroit system, should make it clear that it is not on this point that we part company. The difference between us arises instead from established doctrine laid down by our cases. *Brown,* supra, *Green,* supra, *Swann,* supra, *Scotland Neck,* supra, and *Emporia,* supra, each addressed the issue of constitutional wrong in terms of an established geographic and administrative school system populated by both Negro and White children. In such a context, terms such as 'unitary' and 'dual' systems, and 'racially identifiable schools,' have meaning, and the necessary federal authority to remedy the constitutional wrong is firmly established. But the remedy is necessarily designed, as all remedies are, to restore the victims of discriminatory conduct to the position they would have occupied in the absence of such conduct. Disparate treatment of White and Negro students occurred within the Detroit school system, and not elsewhere, and on this record the remedy must be limited to that system. *Swann,* supra, at 16.

"The constitutional right of the Negro respondents residing in Detroit is to attend a unitary school system in that district.... The view of the dissenters, that the existence of a dual system *in Detroit* can be made the basis for a decree requiring cross-district transportation of pupils cannot be supported on the grounds that it represents merely the devising of a suitably flexible remedy for the violation of rights already established by our prior decisions. It can be supported only by drastic expansion of the constitutional right itself, an expansion without any support in either constitutional principle or precedent."

Justice Stewart concurred in the opinion of the Court and wrote a separate opinion which included in a footnote the observation that it is the "essential fact of a predominantly Negro school population in Detroit—caused by unknown and perhaps unknowable factors such as immigration, birth rates, economic changes, or cumulative acts of private racial fears—that accounts for the 'growing core of Negro schools,' a 'core' that had grown to include virtually the entire city." He then said that the courts have no authority to attempt to change this situation in the absence of proof that it was in any significant measure caused by governmental activity.

Justices White, Douglas, Brennan, and Marshall dissented. Justice White, writing for all the dissenters, thought the Court was, in the name of administrative convenience, permitting the state to insulate itself "from its duty to provide effective desegregation remedies by vesting sufficient power over its

[handwritten margin note:] Before you can impose a cross district remedy, you must show that a violation has been made

public schools in its local school districts." Justice Marshall, also writing for all the dissenters, observed:

"After 20 years of small, often difficult steps . . . , the Court today takes a giant step backwards. Notwithstanding a record showing widespread and pervasive racial segregation in the educational system provided by the State of Michigan for children in Detroit, this Court holds that the District Court was powerless to require the State to remedy its constitutional violation in any meaningful fashion. Ironically purporting to base its result on the principle that the scope of the remedy in a desegregation case should be determined by the nature and the extent of the constitutional violation, the Court's answer is to provide no remedy at all for the violation proved in this case, thereby guaranteeing that Negro children in Detroit will receive the same separate and inherently unequal education in the future as they have been unconstitutionally afforded in the past.

. . .

"Because of the already high and rapidly increasing percentage of Negro students in the Detroit system, as well as the prospect of white flight, a Detroit-only plan simply has no hope of achieving actual desegregation. Under such a plan white and Negro students will not go to school together. Instead, Negro children will continue to attend all-Negro schools. The very evil that *Brown I* was aimed at will not be cured, but will be perpetuated for the future. . . .

". . . Today's holding, I fear, is more a reflection of a perceived public mood that we have gone far enough in enforcing the Constitution's guarantee of equal justice than it is the product of neutral principles of law. . . ."[a]

MILLIKEN v. BRADLEY (MILLIKEN II), 433 U.S. 267 (1977). On remand, the district court included in its decree remedial or compensatory education programs, including in-service training for teachers and administrators, guidance and counseling programs, and revised testing procedures. The cost of these programs was to be borne equally by the Detroit Board of Education and the State of Michigan. That portion of the district court's order was affirmed by the Court of Appeals, and the State defendants appealed. They argued that, since the constitutional violation was unlawful segregation, under the principles of *Milliken I* the court's decree must be limited to redressing that violation by pupil assignments. The Supreme Court rejected that argument and affirmed. Chief Justice Burger said, for the Court:

"In a word, discriminatory student assignment policies can themselves manifest and breed other inequalities built into a dual system founded on racial discrimination. Federal courts need not, and cannot, close their eyes to inequalities, shown by the record, which flow from a longstanding segregated system."

MISSOURI v. JENKINS, 495 U.S. 33 (1990). After finding that the State of Missouri and the Kansas City, Missouri, School District (KCMSD) had operated a segregated school system within KCMSD, the district court ordered the implementation of a plan, largely offered by KCMSD, calling for a magnet school program costing over $200 million and capital improvements to the school system costing over $250 million. ("Magnet schools" are "public schools of voluntary enrollment designed to promote integration by drawing students

---

a. For a careful argument to the effect that the Court should extend federal remedies across school district boundaries so as to achieve maximum racial mixing in metropolitan areas, see Strickman, *School Desegregation at the Crossroads,* 70 Nw.U.L.Rev. 725 (1975). See also Sedler, *Metropolitan Desegregation in the Wake of Milliken—On Losing Big Battles and Winning Small Wars: The View Largely from Within,* 1975 Wash. U.L.Rev. 535.

away from their neighborhoods and private schools through distinctive curricula and high quality.") Various state law provisions effectively prevented KCMSD from raising taxes sufficient to finance the 25% portion of desegregation costs for which the district court held it liable. When KCMSD was unable to secure the funding from the voters, the city council or the state legislature, and the district court became convinced that KCMSD had exhausted its funding possibilities, the court itself ordered a significant increase in KCMSD property tax rates, notwithstanding the state law limitations. On the State's appeal, the Court of Appeals upheld the remedial orders and agreed, given the constitutional violations, that state law could not prevent KCMSD from raising funds sufficient to implement the desegregation remedy. The Court of Appeals concluded as a matter of "federal-state comity," however, that in the future the district court should not set the property tax rate itself but should authorize KCMSD to do so and should enjoin the operation of state laws hindering KCMSD from adequately funding the remedy.

The Supreme Court overturned the tax increase imposed directly by the district court but upheld the power of the district court to direct KCMSD to levy its own taxes and to enjoin state laws limiting or reducing such levies. Finding it "unnecessary to reach the difficult constitutional issues" of whether the tax increase the district court imposed directly violated Article III or the Tenth Amendment, the Court agreed "with the State that the tax increase contravened the principles of comity that must govern the exercise of the District Court's equitable discretion in this area." With respect to "financing desegregation," as with other aspects of solving desegregation problems, "local officials should at least have the opportunity to devise their own solutions." Justice White's majority opinion affirmed, however, that consistent with the Tenth Amendment and Article III the district courts possess equitable power to apportion desegregation costs between States and local school districts and to "set aside state laws preventing local governments from raising funds sufficient to satisfy their constitutional obligations [even though] those funds could also be obtained from the States." The Court concluded that "where (as here) it has been found that a particular remedy is required, the State cannot hinder the process by preventing a local government from implementing that remedy."

Justice Kennedy, joined by Chief Justice Rehnquist and Justices O'Connor and Scalia, concurred in the judgment, but strongly disagreed with the Court's approval of the "judicial taxation" in this case, arguing that "[a]ny purported distinction between direct imposition of a tax by the federal court and an order commanding the school district to impose the tax is but a formalism where the court's action is predicated on elimination of state law limitations on the school district's taxing authority." Under Article III "taxation is not a judicial function." The taxpayers were not parties and received no notice of taxation or opportunity to be heard, as judicial due process requires, and unlike taxation by a legislature "a district court order that overrides the citizens' state law protection against taxation without referendum approval can in no sense provide representational due process." Federal judges by design are "not representative or responsible to the people in a political sense" and "operation of tax systems . . . is not a function the judiciary as an institution is designed to exercise."

WHEN IS DESEGREGATION ACHIEVED AND JUDICIAL AUTHORITY AT AN END?

In Pasadena City Bd. of Educ. v. Spangler, 427 U.S. 424 (1976), the district court had entered a desegregation order requiring in part that by 1970 there

Pasadena
v. &
Spangler

should be no school in the district "with a majority of any minority students." The school board implemented the plan in 1970, fully carrying out its terms. Over the next several years as a result of demographic changes 5 out of 32 schools in the district came to have more than 50% black students. The school board returned to the district court and sought to have the decree modified to eliminate the requirement that there be no school with a majority of minority students. The district court refused and the court of appeals affirmed. The Supreme Court reversed. It noted that there was no contention that the post–1971 changes in the racial mix of the schools resulted from any segregative acts chargeable to the school district. Instead, the changes appeared to be the result of people moving into, out of, and around the district. It concluded:

"[T]he District Court approved a plan designed to obtain racial neutrality in the attendance of students at Pasadena's public schools. No one disputes that the initial implementation of this plan accomplished *that* objective. That being the case, the District Court was not entitled to require the School District to rearrange its attendance zones each year so as to ensure that the racial mix desired by the court was maintained in perpetuity. For having once implemented a racially neutral attendance pattern in order to remedy the perceived constitutional violations on the part of the defendants, the District Court had fully performed its function of providing the appropriate remedy for previous racially discriminatory attendance patterns."

Oklahoma v. Dowell

In Board of Education of Oklahoma City Public Schools v. Dowell, 498 U.S. 237 (1991), the district court in 1963 had found that over a long period Oklahoma City intentionally had segregated schools and housing, and based on subsequent findings of insufficient school board efforts to desegregate the city's schools, in 1972 had ordered the board to adopt a particular desegregation plan. In 1977 the district court granted the Board's "Motion to Close Case" based on a finding that the school system had operated the plan properly and had achieved unitary status. Although the 1977 order was not appealed, the black plaintiffs moved to reopen the case in 1985 following the Board's adoption of a neighborhood school Student Reassignment Plan (SRP) that reduced the length of bus rides of young black students but left half the 64 elementary schools in the district more than 90% black or 90% white. The district court concluded that the school district's unitary status had been maintained, that the SRP was not designed with discriminatory intent, and that the 1972 injunctive decree should be vacated. The Court of Appeals reversed, holding that by itself compliance with the injunction would not justify its dissolution.

The Supreme Court, Justice Souter not participating, unanimously agreed that the 1977 order terminating the case had not itself dissolved the desegregation decree, because there was ambiguity about whether "unitary" meant that all vestiges of past discrimination were completely remedied, or just that the school system currently was desegregated. The Court also unanimously agreed that the standard for whether dissolution of the decree is appropriate is whether "the purposes of the desegregation litigation [have] been fully achieved." The Court was divided, however, on what would satisfy that standard. Chief Justice Rehnquist's majority opinion held that "a finding by the District Court that the Oklahoma City School District was being operated in compliance with the commands of the Equal Protection Clause ... and that it was unlikely that the school board would return to its former ways" would meet the standard. The Court reversed the Court of Appeals, because "federal supervision of local school systems was intended as a temporary measure to remedy past discrimination" and desegregation decrees "are not intended to operate in perpetuity" or to condemn school districts that have complied in good faith for a reasonable period of time "to judicial tutelage for the indefinite future." The Court remanded, however, for the district court to "decide, in accordance with this opinion, whether the Board made a sufficient showing of constitutional compliance as of 1985, when the SRP was adopted, to allow the injunction to be dissolved." In particular, the district court "should address itself to whether the Board had complied in good faith with the desegregation decree since it was entered, and whether the vestiges of past discrimination had been eliminated to the extent practicable." Only after the district court decided whether the decree should be terminated should it then decide the challenge to the SRP, because if released from the desegregation plan the Board no longer would require court approval for such policy changes and a successful challenge to the SRP would require new proof that its adoption was an act of *de jure* segregation.

In dissent Justice Marshall, joined by Justices Blackmun and Stevens, would have affirmed the Court of Appeals' reinstatement of the decree based on the judgment that "feasible steps could be taken to avoid one-race schools" and that it was therefore "clear that the purposes of the decree have not yet been achieved." He stressed that "stigmatic injury" underlies the Court's insistence that all vestiges of *de jure* segregation be eliminated and that "[a]lthough the Court has never explicitly defined what constitutes a 'vestige' of state-enforced segregation, ... it extends to any condition that is likely to convey the message of inferiority implicit in a policy of segregation." In his view, "our school-desegregation jurisprudence establishes that the *effects* of past discrimination remain chargeable to the school district regardless of its lack of continued enforcement of segregation, and the remedial decree is required until those effects have been eliminated." The implication was this: "Against the background of former state-sponsorship of one-race schools, the persistence of racially identifiable schools perpetuates the message of racial inferiority associated with segregation. Therefore, such schools must be eliminated whenever feasible." Although "[r]etaining the decree does not require a return to active supervision" and "modification" might be "appropriate" to "improve its effectiveness and give the school district more flexibility in minimizing busing[,]" dissolving the decree would be inappropriate when the purposes of the decree had not fully been achieved.

A year later, in Freeman v. Pitts, 503 U.S. 467 (1992), the Court held that "a district court is permitted to withdraw judicial supervision with respect to discrete categories in which the school district has achieved compliance with a court-ordered desegregation plan" and "need not retain active control over every aspect of school administration until a school district has demonstrated unitary status in all facets of its system." Against a backdrop of decades of legally-mandated school segregation before *Brown v. Board of Education* and district court desegregation orders beginning in 1969, Georgia's DeKalb County School System ("DCSS") made efforts that the district court found to have "achieved maximum practical desegregation [of students] from 1969 to 1986." During that period, however, the black student population increased from 5.6% to 47%, the County experienced demographic shifts resulting in a high degree of residential segregation, and the schools, after first achieving a reasonable measure of racial balance, again became racially imbalanced. The district court "examined the interaction between DCSS policy and demographic shifts in DeKalb County" but found "no evidence that the school system's previous unconstitutional conduct may have contributed" to the pattern of residential segregation by race. Overall, the district court found DCSS "a unitary system with regard to student assignments, transportation, physical facilities, and extracurricular activities, and ruled that it would order no further relief in those areas." It also found, however, "that vestiges of the dual system remain

Freeman v. Pitts

in the areas of teacher and principal assignments, resource allocation, and quality of education" (assessed primarily on the basis of per pupil expenditures and teacher competence), and it ordered spending equalization and other remedial measures.

The Supreme Court held "that, in the course of supervising desegregation plans, federal courts have the authority to relinquish supervision and control of school districts in incremental stages, before full compliance has been achieved in every area of school operations." Justice Kennedy's majority opinion said in part: "Among the factors which must inform the sound discretion of the court in ordering partial withdrawal are the following: whether there has been full and satisfactory compliance with the decree in those aspects of the system where supervision is to be withdrawn; whether retention of judicial control is necessary or practicable to achieve compliance with the decree in other facets of the school system; and whether the school district has demonstrated . . . its good faith commitment to the whole of the court's decree and to those provisions of the law and the Constitution that were the predicate for judicial involvement in the first instance."

Regarding racial imbalance in student assignments, the Court emphasized that the "school district bears the burden of showing that any current imbalance is not traceable, in a proximate way, to the prior violation"; that "[a]s the *de jure* violation becomes more remote in time and these demographic changes intervene, it becomes less likely that a current racial imbalance in a school district is a vestige of the prior *de jure* system"; that "[t]he causal link between current conditions and the prior violation is even more attenuated if the school district has demonstrated its good faith"; and thus that given its findings "the District Court was correct to entertain the suggestion that DCSS had no duty to achieve systemwide racial balance in the student population." The Court noted that "a continuing violation in one area may need to be addressed by remedies in another" but found "no showing that racial balancing was an appropriate mechanism to cure other deficiencies in this case." The Court nonetheless remanded for specific findings that student reassignments would not be a feasible or practical way to solve the faculty assignment problem and that the school district had satisfied its "requirement [of] show[ing] its good faith commitment to the entirety of a desegregation plan so that parents, students and the public have assurance against further injuries or stigma[.]"

Finally, in Missouri v. Jenkins, 515 U.S. 70 (1995) (Jenkins III) (a subsequent stage of review of the district court plan the Court considered in Missouri v. Jenkins, supra p. 744), the Court, 5–4, found that the district court had exceeded its constitutional remedial authority by ordering the State (1) to fund salary increases for nearly all of KCMSD's instructional and noninstructional employees and (2) to continue to fund remedial quality education programs because student achievement levels remained "at or below national norms at many grade levels." The district court's "admittedly broad discretion" still had to be confined to eliminating "to the extent practicable the vestiges of prior de jure segregation within the KCMSD: a systemwide reduction in student achievement and the existence of 25 racially identifiable schools with a population of over 90% black students." Moreover, the district court's "end purpose" was to restore state and local control of a school system operating in compliance with the Constitution.

The district court had ordered salary increases and the quality education programs in order to improve the "desegregative attractiveness" of KCMSD as a means of remedying the vestiges of segregation, but Chief Justice Rehnquist noted that remedies designed to induce interdistrict transfer of nonminority students for redistribution within KCMSD exceeded the scope of the district court's broad remedial authority. The lower courts having found no interdistrict constitutional violations, no interdistrict relief was warranted under *Milliken I*, and the district court had "devised a remedy to accomplish indirectly what it admittedly lacks the remedial authority to mandate directly." De jure segregation had not "led to white flight from the KCMSD to suburban districts[,]" and "[a] district court seeking to remedy an intradistrict violation that has not 'directly caused' significant interdistrict effects ... exceeds its remedial authority if it orders a remedy with an interdistrict purpose." Because the district court's pursuit of "desegregative attractiveness" would justify remedial orders limitless in expenditure and duration, involve "many imponderables," and be "far removed from the task of eliminating the racial identifiability of the schools within the KCMSD," the Court concluded that the salary increase order "is simply too far removed from an acceptable implementation of a permissible means to remedy previous legally mandated segregation."

As for the State's challenge to "the requirement of indefinite funding of a quality education program until national norms are met," the Court noted that the district court's authority extended no further than to remedy to the extent practicable "the incremental effect that segregation has had on minority student achievement." Not just de jure segregation, but "external factors beyond the control of the KCMSD and the State affect minority student achievement," so the district court on remand "should sharply limit, if not dispense with, its reliance on" test scores. The Court's underlying concern was that "[i]nsistence upon academic goals unrelated to the effects of legal segregation unwarrantably postpones the day when the KCMSD will be able to operate on its own."

In one concurring opinion, Justice Thomas questioned whether continuing high black enrollments in KCMSD schools were vestiges of pre–1954 de jure segregation. He sharply criticized the district court's finding "that racial imbalances constituted an ongoing constitutional violation that continued to inflict harm on black students" as premised on "the idea that any school that is black is inferior, and that blacks cannot succeed without the benefit of the company of whites." He also urged that the equitable powers of the federal courts be more circumscribed by precise federalism and separation of powers restraints than they previously have been, and he argued that "absen[t] special circumstances, the remedy for de jure segregation ordinarily should not include educational programs for students who were not in school (or were even alive) during the period of segregation."

Justice Souter, joined by Justices Stevens, Ginsburg and Breyer, dissented. He contended that the salary orders were designed not only to draw students into the district's schools but to raise the level of student achievement in the KCMSD and thus that "to the extent that the District Court concludes on remand that its salary orders are justified by reference to the quality of education alone, nothing in the Court's opinion precludes those orders from remaining in effect." He also interpreted *Milliken I* not to preclude remedial orders whose purpose is to induce interdistrict student transfers as such, but only to prevent remedies that bind "the authorities of other governmental units that are free of violations and segregative effects." Because the "District Court's remedial measures go only to the operation and quality of schools within the KCMSD, and the burden of those measures accordingly falls only on the two proven constitutional wrongdoers in this case, the KCMSD and the State," in his view the district court had not exceeded its authority under *Milliken I.*

DISMANTLING DE JURE SEGREGATION OF STATE UNIVERSITIES

The extensive body of judicial opinions addressing state and local obligations to dismantle *de jure* segregation of public elementary and secondary schools has no counterpart when the issue is the nature and extent of the obligation to remedy de jure segregation of state institutions of higher education. The Court addressed that question in United States v. Fordice, 505 U.S. 717 (1992). Between 1848 and 1950, Mississippi created five state universities exclusively for whites and three exclusively for blacks. Despite Brown v. Board of Education, federal efforts begun in 1969, and 12 years of attempting to settle this action (filed in 1975), "[b]y the mid–1980's ... more than 99 percent of Mississippi's white students were enrolled" at the former group of campuses, whose student bodies "remained predominantly white, averaging between 80 and 91 percent white students[,]" and 71% of the State's black students attended the latter group, "where the racial composition ranged from 92 to 99 percent black." When the case finally went to trial, the state argued that it "had fulfilled its duty to disestablish its state-imposed segregative system by implementing and maintaining good-faith, nondiscriminatory race-neutral policies and practices in student admission, faculty hiring, and operations" and "that the mere continued existence of racially identifiable universities was not unlawful given the freedom of students to choose which institution to attend and the varying objectives and features of the State's universities." The district court "concluded that in the higher education context, 'the affirmative duty to desegregate does not contemplate either restricting choice or the achievement of any degree of racial balance.'" The Court of Appeals affirmed, but the Supreme Court reversed and remanded.

Writing for the Court, Justice White noted that all parties accepted Mississippi's constitutional duty to dismantle its formerly *de jure* dual system of higher education. He observed that prior decisions required the state to "eradicate[] policies and practices traceable to its prior *de jure* dual system that continue to foster segregation[.]" Although the Court agreed that universities differ from primary and secondary schools in student choice to seek higher education, no assignment to particular institutions, and the range of different educational missions served by different campuses, it did "not agree ... that the adoption and implementation of race-neutral policies alone suffice to demonstrate that the State has completely abandoned its prior dual system." It held that "[i]f policies traceable to the *de jure* system are still in force and have discriminatory effects, those policies too must be reformed to the extent practicable and consistent with sound educational practices."

Nor did the Court agree that Bazemore v. Friday, 478 U.S. 385 (1986), suggested otherwise:

"*Bazemore* raised the issue whether the financing and operational assistance provided by a state university's extension service to voluntary 4–H and Homemaker Clubs was inconsistent with the Equal Protection Clause because of the existence of numerous all-white and all-black clubs. Though prior to 1965 the clubs were supported on a segregated basis, the District Court had found that the policy of segregation had been completely abandoned and that no evidence existed of any lingering discrimination in either services or membership; any racial imbalance resulted from the wholly voluntary and unfettered choice of private individuals.... In this context, we held inapplicable the *Green* Court's judgment that a voluntary choice program was insufficient to dismantle a *de jure* dual system in public primary and secondary schools, but only after satisfying ourselves that the State had not fostered segregation by playing a part in the decision of which club an individual chose to join.

"*Bazemore* plainly does not excuse inquiry into whether Mississippi has left in place certain aspects of its prior dual system that perpetuate the racially segregated higher education system. If the State perpetuates policies and practices traceable to its prior system that continue to have segregative effects—whether by influencing student enrollment decisions or by fostering segregation in other facets of the university system—and such policies are without sound educational justification and can be practicably eliminated, the State has not satisfied its burden of proving that it has dismantled its prior system...."

Without "identify[ing] an exclusive list of unconstitutional remnants of Mississippi's prior *de jure* system[,]" the Court identified "four policies" that had to be justified or eliminated: "admission standards, program duplication, institutional mission assignments, and continued operation of all eight public universities." The requirement of higher standardized test scores for automatic admission to the historically white institutions, when proportionately more blacks than whites did not achieve those scores, was "not only traceable to the *de jure* system and ... originally adopted for a discriminatory purpose, but ... also ha[d] present discriminatory effects." So, too, "the differential admissions requirements between universities with dissimilar programmatic missions" was "inadequately justified" given that they "are remnants of the dual system with a continuing discriminatory effect, and the mission assignments 'to some degree follow the historical racial assignments.' " And the refusal to consider high school grades in determining automatic admission when "the disparity between black and white students' high school grade averages was much narrower than the gap between their average ACT scores" was not justified by a concern "with grade inflation and the lack of comparability in grading practices and course offerings among the State's diverse high schools ... because the ACT requirement was originally adopted for discriminatory purposes, the current requirement is traceable to that decision and seemingly continues to have segregative effects, and the State has so far failed to show that the 'ACT-only' admission standard is not susceptible to elimination without eroding sound educational policy."

Second, the "widespread duplication" of noncore programs at different campuses "was part and parcel of the prior dual system of higher education—the whole notion of 'separate but equal' required duplicative programs in two sets of schools—and ... the present unnecessary duplication is a continuation of that practice." The district "court's holding that petitioners could not establish the constitutional defect of unnecessary duplication ... improperly shifted the burden away from the State" and that "court failed to consider the combined effects of unnecessary program duplication with other policies, such as differential admissions standards, in evaluating whether the State had met its duty to dismantle its prior *de jure* segregated system."

Third, the "institutional mission designations adopted in 1981 ha[d] as their antecedents the policies enacted to perpetuate racial separation during the *de jure* segregated regime"—the historically white campuses being the best funded, with "the most advanced and specialized programs" and "the widest range of curricular functions." Given that background and the Court of Appeals' finding " 'that the mission designations had the effect of maintaining the more limited program scope at the historically black universities' " Justice White said:

"... We do not suggest that absent discriminatory purpose the assignment of different missions to various institutions in a State's higher education system would raise an equal protection issue where one or more of the institutions become or remain predominantly black or white. But here the issue is whether the State has sufficiently dismantled its prior dual system; and when combined with the differential admission practices and unnecessary program duplication, it is likely that the mission designations interfere with student choice and tend to perpetuate the segregated system. On remand, the court should inquire whether it would be practicable and consistent with sound educational practices to eliminate any such discriminatory effects of the State's present policy of mission assignments."

Finally, with respect to "continuing to ... operate all eight higher educational institutions[,]" although "certainly closure of one or more ... would decrease the discriminatory effects of the present system, ... based on the present record we are unable to say whether such action is constitutionally required":

"Elimination of program duplication and revision of admissions criteria may make institutional closure unnecessary. However, on remand this issue should be carefully explored by inquiring and determining whether retention of all eight institutions itself affects student choice and perpetuates the segregated higher education system, whether maintenance of each of the universities is educationally justifiable, and whether one or more of them can be practicably closed or merged with other existing institutions.

"... That an institution is predominantly white or black does not in itself make out a constitutional violation. But surely the State may not leave in place policies rooted in its prior officially-segregated system that serve to maintain the racial identifiability of its universities if those policies can practicably be eliminated without eroding sound educational policies."

At the end of his opinion, Justice White added this:

"If we understand private petitioners to press us to order the upgrading of [the three historically black institutions] solely so that they may be publicly financed, exclusively black enclaves by private choice, we reject that request. The State provides these facilities for all its citizens and it has not met its burden under *Brown* to take affirmative steps to dismantle its prior *de jure* system when it perpetuates a separate, but 'more equal' one. Whether such an increase in funding is necessary to achieve a full dismantlement under the standards we have outlined, however, is a different question, and one that must be addressed on remand."

Justice O'Connor, concurring, wrote in part:

"... [T]he circumstances in which a State may maintain a policy or practice traceable to *de jure* segregation that has segregative effects are narrow.... Where the State can accomplish legitimate educational objectives through less segregative means, the courts may infer lack of good faith.... [Also,] if the State shows that maintenance of certain remnants of its prior system is essential to accomplish its legitimate goals, then it still must prove that it has counteracted and minimized the segregative impact of such policies to the extent possible. Only by eliminating a remnant that unnecessarily continues to foster segregation or by negating insofar as possible its segregative impact can the State satisfy its constitutional obligation to dismantle the discriminatory system that should, by now, be only a distant memory."

In another concurring opinion, Justice Thomas wrote "separately to emphasize that ... because [the Court's standard] does not compel the elimination of all observed racial imbalance, it portends neither the destruction of historically black colleges nor the severing of those institutions from their distinctive histories and traditions." When a challenged policy "began during the prior *de jure* era, produces adverse impacts, and persists without sound educational justification ... we are justified in not requiring proof of a present specific intent to discriminate[,] ... both because the State has created the dispute through its own prior unlawful conduct, ... and because discriminatory intent does tend to persist through time." Yet "we do not foreclose the possibility that there exists 'sound educational justification' for maintaining historically black colleges *as such*." Rather,

"I think it undisputable that these institutions have succeeded in part because of their distinctive histories and traditions; for many, historically black colleges have become 'a symbol of the highest attainments of black culture.' ... Obviously, a State cannot maintain such traditions by closing particular institutions, historically white or historically black, to particular racial groups. Nonetheless, it hardly follows that a State cannot operate a diverse assortment of institutions—including historically black institutions—open to all on a race-neutral basis, but with established traditions and programs that might disproportionately appeal to one race or another. No one, I imagine, would argue that such institutional *diversity* is without 'sound educational justification,' or that it is even remotely akin to program *duplication*, which is designed to separate the races for the sake of separating the races ... Although I agree that a State is not constitutionally *required* to maintain its historically black institutions as such, I do not understand our opinion to hold that a State is *forbidden* from doing so. It would be ironic, to say the least, if the institutions that sustained blacks during segregation were themselves destroyed in an effort to combat its vestiges."

Justice Scalia concurred in the judgment in part, but dissented in part. In his view, only practices

"that limit access on discriminatory bases ... have the potential to generate the [stigmatic] harm *Brown I* condemned, and only they have the potential to deny students equal access to the best public education a State has to offer. Legacies of the dual system that permit (or even incidentally facilitate) free choice of racially identifiable schools—while still assuring each individual student the right to attend whatever school he wishes—do not have these consequences.

" . . .

"*Bazemore's* standard for dismantling a dual system ought to control here: discontinuation of discriminatory practices and adoption of a neutral admissions policy. [M]odern racial imbalance remains a 'vestige' of past segregative practices in Mississippi's universities, in that the previously mandated racial identification continues to affect where students choose to enroll—just as it surely affected which clubs students chose to join in *Bazemore*. ... Like the club attendance in *Bazemore* (and unlike the school attendance in *Green*), attending college is voluntary, not a legal obligation, and which institution particular students attend is determined by their own choice....

"It is my view that the requirement of compelled integration ... does not apply to higher education. Only one aspect of an historically segregated university system need be eliminated: discriminatory admissions standards...."

Justice Scalia, although agreeing that "the Constitution does not *require* equal funding" of HBI's and HWI's, also expressed concern that the Court's test might "*prohibit*[] it." He inferred that "the Court's test is designed to achieve . . . the elimination of predominantly black institutions" and objected in the following terms:

". . . There is nothing unconstitutional about a 'black' school in the sense, not of a school that blacks *must* attend and that whites *cannot*, but of a school that, as a consequence of private choice in residence or in school selection, contains, and has long contained, a large black majority. . . . In a perverse way, in fact, the insistence, whether explicit or implicit, that such institutions not be permitted to endure perpetuates the very stigma of black inferiority that *Brown I* sought to destroy. Not only Mississippi but Congress itself seems out of step with the drum that the Court beats today, judging by its passage of an Act entitled 'Strengthening Historically Black Colleges and Universities,' which authorizes the Education Department to provide money grants to historically black colleges. . . ."

C.   CLASSIFICATIONS BASED ON GENDER

Reed v. Reed

404 U.S. 71, 92 S.Ct. 251, 30 L.Ed.2d 225 (1971).

[Section 15–314C of the Idaho Code provided that in the choice of persons to administer an intestate estate "[o]f several persons claiming and equally entitled to administer, males must be preferred to females." Solely because of this statute an Idaho court appointed the father rather than the mother of a deceased child as administrator. The mother appealed the decision.]

Mr. Chief Justice Burger delivered the opinion of the Court.

. . .

Section 15–314 is restricted in its operation to those situations where competing applications for letters of administration have been filed by both male and female members of the same entitlement class established by § 15–312. In such situations, § 15–314 provides that different treatment be accorded to the applicants on the basis of their sex; it thus establishes a classification subject to scrutiny under the Equal Protection Clause.

In applying that clause, this Court has consistently recognized that the Fourteenth Amendment does not deny to States the power to treat different classes of persons in different ways. Barbier v. Connolly, 113 U.S. 27; Lindsley v. Natural Carbonic Gas Co., 220 U.S. 61 (1911); Railway Express Agency, Inc. v. New York, 336 U.S. 106 (1949); McDonald v. Board of Election Commissioners, 394 U.S. 802 (1969). The Equal Protection Clause of that Amendment does, however, deny to States the power to legislate that different treatment be accorded to persons placed by a statute into different classes on the basis of criteria wholly unrelated to the objective of that statute. A classification "must be reasonable, not arbitrary, and must rest upon some ground of difference having a fair and substantial relation to the object of the legislation, so that all persons similarly circumstanced shall be treated alike." Royster Guano Co. v. Virginia, 253 U.S. 412, 415 (1920). The question presented by this case, then, is whether a difference in the sex of competing applicants for letters of administration bears a rational relationship to a state objective that is sought to be advanced by the operation of §§ 15–312 and 15–314.

In upholding the latter section, the Idaho Supreme Court concluded that its objective was to eliminate one area of controversy when two or more persons, equally entitled under § 15–312, seek letters of administration and thereby present the probate court "with the issue of which one should be named." The court also concluded that where such persons are not of the same sex, the elimination of females from consideration "is neither an illogical nor arbitrary method devised by the legislature to resolve an issue that would otherwise require a hearing as to the relative merits ... of the two or more petitioning relatives...." ...

Clearly the objective of reducing the workload on probate courts by eliminating one class of contests is not without some legitimacy. The crucial question, however, is whether § 15–314 advances that objective in a manner consistent with the command of the Equal Protection Clause. We hold that it does not. To give a mandatory preference to members of either sex over members of the other, merely to accomplish the elimination of hearings on the merits, is to make the very kind of arbitrary legislative choice forbidden by the Equal Protection Clause of the Fourteenth Amendment; and whatever may be said as to the positive values of avoiding intrafamily controversy, the choice in this context may not lawfully be mandated solely on the basis of sex.

violation of EP.

. . .

The judgment of the Idaho Supreme Court is reversed and the case remanded for further proceedings not inconsistent with this opinion.

Frontiero v. Richardson

411 U.S. 677, 93 S.Ct. 1764, 36 L.Ed.2d 583 (1973).

Mr. Justice Brennan announced the judgment of the Court in an opinion in which Mr. Justice Douglas, Mr. Justice White, and Mr. Justice Marshall join.

The question before us concerns the right of a female member of the uniformed services to claim her spouse as a "dependent" for the purposes of obtaining increased quarters allowances and medical and dental benefits under 37 U.S.C. §§ 401, 403, and 10 U.S.C. §§ 1072, 1076, on an equal footing with male members. Under these statutes, a serviceman may claim his wife as a "dependent" without regard to whether she is in fact dependent upon him for any part of her support.... A servicewoman, on the other hand, may not claim her husband as a "dependent" under these programs unless he is in fact dependent upon her for over one-half of his support.... Thus, the question for decision is whether this difference in treatment constitutes an unconstitutional discrimination against servicewomen in violation of the Due Process Clause of the Fifth Amendment. A three-judge District Court for the Middle District of Alabama, one judge dissenting, rejected this contention ... We reverse.

Man can only be dependant if it can be proven so.

Hold as violation

I.

In an effort to attract career personnel through reenlistment, Congress established ... fringe benefits [for] members of the uniformed services on a competitive basis with business and industry. Thus, under 37 U.S.C. § 403, a member of the uniformed services with dependents is entitled to an increased "basic allowance for quarters" and, under 10 U.S.C. § 1076, a member's dependents are provided comprehensive medical and dental care.

Appellant Sharron Frontiero, a lieutenant in the United States Air Force, sought increased quarters allowances, and housing and medical benefits for her husband ... on the ground that he was her "dependent." Although such benefits would automatically have been granted with respect to the wife of a male member of the uniformed services, appellant's application was denied because she failed to demonstrate that her husband was dependent on her for more than one-half of his support. Appellants then commenced this suit, contending that, by making this distinction, the statutes unreasonably discriminate on the basis of sex in violation of the Due Process Clause of the Fifth Amendment. In essence, appellants asserted that the discriminatory impact of the statutes is two-fold: first, as a procedural matter, a female member is required to demonstrate her spouse's dependency, while no such burden is imposed upon male members; and second, as a substantive matter, a male member who does not provide more than one-half of his wife's support receives benefits, while a similarly situated female member is denied such benefits. . . .

Although the legislative history of these statutes sheds virtually no light on the purposes underlying the differential treatment accorded male and female members, a majority of the three-judge District Court surmised that Congress might reasonably have concluded that, since the husband in our society is generally the "breadwinner" in the family—and the wife typically the "dependent" partner—"it would be more economical to require married female members claiming husbands to prove actual dependency than to extend the presumption of dependency to such members." 341 F.Supp., at 207. Indeed, given the fact that approximately 99% of all members of the uniformed services are male, the District Court speculated that such differential treatment might conceivably lead to a "considerable saving of administrative expense and manpower." Ibid.

II.

At the outset, appellants contend that classifications based upon sex, like classifications based upon race, alienage, and national origin, are inherently suspect and must therefore be subjected to close judicial scrutiny. We agree and, indeed, find at least implicit support for such an approach in our unanimous decision only last Term in Reed v. Reed, 404 U.S. 71 (1971). . . .

There can be no doubt that our Nation has had a long and unfortunate history of sex discrimination. Traditionally, such discrimination was rationalized by an attitude of "romantic paternalism" which, in practical effect, put women not on a pedestal, but in a cage. Indeed, this paternalistic attitude became so firmly rooted in our national consciousness that, exactly 100 years ago, a distinguished member of this Court was able to proclaim:

"Man is, or should be, woman's protector and defender. The natural and proper timidity and delicacy which belongs to the female sex evidently unfits it for many of the occupations of civil life. The constitution of the family organization, which is founded in the divine ordinance, as well as in the nature of things, indicates the domestic sphere as that which properly belongs to the domain and functions of womanhood. The harmony, not to say identity, of interests and views which belong, or should belong, to the family institution is repugnant to the ideas of a woman adopting a distinct and independent career from that of her husband. . . .

". . . The paramount destiny and mission of women are to fulfil the noble and benign offices of wife and mother. This is the law of the Creator." Bradwell v. Illinois, 83 U.S. [16 Wall.] 130, 141 (1873) (Bradley, J., concurring).

As a result of notions such as these, our statute books gradually became laden with gross, stereotypical distinctions between the sexes and, indeed, throughout much of the 19th century the position of women in our society was, in many respects, comparable to that of blacks under the pre-Civil War slave codes. Neither slaves nor women could hold office, serve on juries, or bring suit in their own names, and married women traditionally were denied the legal capacity to hold or convey property or to serve as legal guardians of their own children. See generally, L. Kanowitz, Women and the Law: The Unfinished Revolution 5–6 (1969); G. Mydral, An American Dilemma 1073 (2d ed. 1962). And although blacks were guaranteed the right to vote in 1870, women were denied even that right—which is itself "preservative of other basic civil and political rights"—until adoption of the Nineteenth Amendment half a century later.

It is true, of course, that the position of women in America has improved markedly in recent decades. Nevertheless, it can hardly be doubted that, in part because of the high visibility of the sex characteristic, women still face pervasive, although at times more subtle, discrimination in our educational institutions, on the job market and, perhaps most conspicuously, in the political arena.[17] See generally, K. Amundsen, The Silenced Majority: Women and American Democracy (1971); The President's Task Force on Women's Rights and Responsibilities, A Matter of Simple Justice (1970).

Moreover, since sex, like race and national origin, is an immutable characteristic determined solely by the accident of birth, the imposition of special disabilities upon the members of a particular sex because of their sex would seem to violate "the basic concept of our system that legal burdens should bear some relationship to individual responsibility. . . ." Weber v. Aetna Casualty & Surety Co., 406 U.S. 164, 175 (1972). And what differentiates sex from such nonsuspect statuses as intelligence or physical disability, and aligns it with the recognized suspect criteria, is that the sex characteristic frequently bears no relation to ability to perform or contribute to society. As a result, statutory distinctions between the sexes often have the effect of invidiously relegating the entire class of females to inferior legal status without regard to the actual capabilities of its individual members.

We might also note that, over the past decade, Congress has itself manifested an increasing sensitivity to sex-based classifications. In Tit. VII of the Civil Rights Act of 1964, for example, Congress expressly declared that no employer, labor union, or other organization subject to the provisions of the Act shall discriminate against any individual on the basis of "race, color, religion, *sex,* or national origin." Similarly, the Equal Pay Act of 1963 provides that no employer covered by the Act "shall discriminate . . . between employees on the basis of sex." And § 1 of the Equal Rights Amendment, passed by Congress on March 22, 1972, and submitted to the legislatures of the States for ratification, declares that "[e]quality of rights under the law shall not be denied or abridged by the United States or by any State on account of sex." Thus, Congress has itself concluded that classifications based upon sex are inherently invidious, and this conclusion of a coequal branch of Government is not without significance to the question presently under consideration. . . .

With these considerations in mind, we can only conclude that classifications based upon sex, like classifications based upon race, alienage, or national origin, are inherently suspect, and must therefore be subjected to strict judicial

---

17. It is true, of course, that when viewed in the abstract, women do not constitute a small and powerless minority. Nevertheless, in part because of past discrimination, women are vastly underrepresented in this Nation's decisionmaking councils. There has never been a female President, nor a female member of this Court. Not a single woman presently sits in the United States Senate, and only 14 women hold seats in the House of Representatives. And, as appellants point out, this underrepresentation is present throughout all levels of our State and Federal Government.

scrutiny. Applying the analysis mandated by that stricter standard of review, it is clear that the statutory scheme now before us is constitutionally invalid.

III.

The sole basis of the classification established in the challenged statutes is the sex of the individuals involved....

Moreover, the Government concedes that the differential treatment accorded men and women under these statutes serves no purpose other than mere "administrative convenience." In essence, the Government maintains that, as an empirical matter, wives in our society frequently are dependent upon their husbands, while husbands rarely are dependent upon their wives. Thus, the Government argues that Congress might reasonably have concluded that it would be both cheaper and easier simply conclusively to presume that wives of male members are financially dependent upon their husbands, while burdening female members with the task of establishing dependency in fact.[22]

The Government offers no concrete evidence, however, tending to support its view that such differential treatment in fact saves the Government any money. In order to satisfy the demands of strict judicial scrutiny, the Government must demonstrate, for example, that it is actually cheaper to grant increased benefits with respect to *all* male members, than it is to determine which male members are in fact entitled to such benefits and to grant increased benefits only to those members whose wives actually meet the dependency requirement. Here, however, there is substantial evidence that, if put to the test, many of the wives of male members would fail to qualify for benefits. And in light of the fact that the dependency determination with respect to the husbands of female members is presently made solely on the basis of affidavits rather than through the more costly hearing process, the Government's explanation of the statutory scheme is, to say the least, questionable.

In any case, our prior decisions make clear that, although efficacious administration of governmental programs is not without some importance, "the Constitution recognizes higher values than speed and efficiency." Stanley v. Illinois, 405 U.S. 645, 656 (1972). And when we enter the realm of "strict judicial scrutiny," there can be no doubt that "administrative convenience" is not a shibboleth, the mere recitation of which dictates constitutionality. See Shapiro v. Thompson, 394 U.S. 618 (1969); Carrington v. Rash, 380 U.S. 89 (1965). On the contrary, any statutory scheme which draws a sharp line between the sexes, *solely* for the purpose of achieving administrative convenience, necessarily commands "dissimilar treatment for men and women who are ... similarly situated," and therefore involves the "very kind of arbitrary legislative choice forbidden by the [Constitution]...." Reed v. Reed.... We therefore conclude that, by according differential treatment to male and female members of the uniformed services for the sole purpose of achieving administrative convenience, the challenged statutes violate the Due Process Clause of the Fifth Amendment insofar as they require a female member to prove the dependency of her husband.

Reversed.

22. It should be noted that these statutes are not in any sense designed to rectify the effects of past discrimination against women.... On the contrary, these statutes seize upon a group—women—who have historically suffered discrimination in employment, and rely on the effects of this past discrimination as a justification for heaping on additional economic disadvantages....

Mr. Justice Stewart concurs in the judgment, agreeing that the statutes before us work an invidious discrimination in violation of the Constitution. Reed v. Reed, 404 U.S. 71.

Mr. Justice Rehnquist dissents for the reasons stated by Judge Rives in his opinion for the District Court, Frontiero v. Laird, 341 F.Supp. 201 (1972).

Mr. Justice Powell, with whom The Chief Justice and Mr. Justice Blackmun join, concurring in the judgment.

I agree that the challenged statutes constitute an unconstitutional discrimination against service women in violation of the Due Process Clause of the Fifth Amendment, but I cannot join the opinion of Mr. Justice Brennan, which would hold that all classifications based upon sex, "like classifications based upon race, alienage, and national origin," are "inherently suspect and must therefore be subjected to close judicial scrutiny." . . . It is unnecessary for the Court in this case to characterize sex as a suspect classification, with all of the far-reaching implications of such a holding. Reed v. Reed, 404 U.S. 71 (1971), which abundantly supports our decision today, did not add sex to the narrowly limited group of classifications which are inherently suspect. In my view, we can and should decide this case on the authority of *Reed* and reserve for the future any expansion of its rationale.

There is another, and I find compelling, reason for deferring a general categorizing of sex classifications as invoking the strictest test of judicial scrutiny. The Equal Rights Amendment, which if adopted will resolve the substance of this precise question, has been approved by the Congress and submitted for ratification by the States. If this Amendment is duly adopted, it will represent the will of the people accomplished in the manner prescribed by the Constitution. By acting prematurely and unnecessarily, as I view it, the Court has assumed a decisional responsibility at the very time when state legislatures, functioning within the traditional democratic process, are debating the proposed Amendment. It seems to me that this reaching out to preempt by judicial action a major political decision which is currently in process of resolution does not reflect appropriate respect for duly prescribed legislative processes.

There are times when this Court, under our system, cannot avoid a constitutional decision on issues which normally should be resolved by the elected representatives of the people. But democratic institutions are weakened, and confidence in the restraint of the Court is impaired, when we appear unnecessarily to decide sensitive issues of broad social and political importance at the very time they are under consideration within the prescribed constitutional processes.

Craig v. Boren

429 U.S. 190, 97 S.Ct. 451, 50 L.Ed.2d 397 (1976).

Mr. Justice Brennan delivered the opinion of the Court.

The interaction of two sections of an Oklahoma statute . . . prohibits the sale of "nonintoxicating" 3.2% beer to males under the age of 21 and to females under the age of 18. The question to be decided is whether such a gender-based differential constitutes a denial to males 18–20 years of age of the Equal Protection of the Laws in violation of the Fourteenth Amendment.

This action . . . by appellant Craig, a male then between 18 and 21 years of age, and by appellant Whitener, a licensed vendor of 3.2% beer . . . sought

Not
constitutional

declaratory and injunctive relief against enforcement of the gender-based differential on the ground that it constituted invidious discrimination against males 18–20 years of age. A three-judge court ... sustained [its] constitutionality and dismissed the action.... We reverse.

. . . .

II.

A.

... To withstand constitutional challenge, previous cases establish that classifications by gender must serve important governmental objectives and must be substantially related to achievement of those objectives. Thus, in *Reed,* the objectives of "reducing the workload on probate courts," ... and "avoiding intra-family controversy," ... were deemed of insufficient importance to sustain use of an overt gender criterion in the appointment of intestate administrators. Decisions following *Reed* similarly have rejected administrative ease and convenience as sufficiently important objectives to justify gender-based classifications. See, e.g., Stanley v. Illinois, 405 U.S. 645, 656 (1972); Frontiero v. Richardson, 411 U.S. 677, 690 (1973); cf. Schlesinger v. Ballard, 419 U.S. 498, 506–507 (1975). And only two Terms ago Stanton v. Stanton, 421 U.S. 7 (1975), expressly stating that *Reed v. Reed* was "controlling," id., at 13, held that *Reed* required invalidation of a Utah differential age-of-majority statute, notwithstanding the statute's coincidence with and furtherance of the State's purpose of fostering "old notions" of role-typing and preparing boys for their expected performance in the economic and political worlds. Id., at 14–15.[6]

past cases
have shot
down statutes
that
discriminate

Reed v. Reed has also provided the underpinning for decisions that have invalidated statutes employing gender as an inaccurate proxy for other, more germane bases of classification. Hence, "archaic and overbroad" generalizations, *Schlesinger v. Ballard,* ... concerning the financial position of servicewomen, *Frontiero v. Richardson,* ... and working women, Weinberger v. Wiesenfeld, 420 U.S. 636, 643 (1975), could not justify use of a gender line in determining eligibility for certain governmental entitlements. Similarly, increasingly outdated misconceptions concerning the role of females in the home rather than in the "marketplace and world of ideas" were rejected as loose-fitting characterizations incapable of supporting state statutory schemes that were premised upon their accuracy.... In light of the weak congruence between gender and the characteristic or trait that gender purported to represent, it was necessary that the legislatures choose either to realign their substantive laws in a gender-neutral fashion, or to adopt procedures for identifying those instances where the sex-centered generalization actually comported to fact. See, e.g., Stanley v. Illinois, ...; cf. Cleveland Board of Educ. v. LaFleur, 414 U.S. 632, 650 (1974).

Reed is
controlling
authority

In this case, too, "*Reed* we feel, is controlling ... ," *Stanton v. Stanton.*.... We turn then to the question whether, under *Reed,* the difference between males and females with respect to the purchase of 3.2% beer warrants the

---

6. Kahn v. Shevin, 416 U.S. 351 (1974) and Schlesinger v. Ballard, 419 U.S. 498 (1975), upholding the use of gender-based classifications, rested upon the Court's perception of the laudatory purposes of those laws as remedying disadvantageous conditions suffered by women in economic and military life. See 416 U.S., at 353–354; 419 U.S., at 508. Needless to say, in this case Oklahoma does not suggest that the age-sex differential was enacted to ensure the availability of 3.2% beer for women as compensation for previous deprivations.

differential in age drawn by the Oklahoma statute. We conclude that it does not.

. . .

C.

We accept for purposes of discussion the District Court's identification of the objective underlying §§ 241 and 245 as the enhancement of traffic safety.[7] Clearly, the protection of public health and safety represents an important function of state and local governments. However, appellees' statistics in our view cannot support the conclusion that the gender-based distinction closely serves to achieve that objective and therefore the distinction cannot under *Reed* withstand equal protection challenge.

The appellees introduced a variety of statistical surveys. First, an analysis of arrest statistics for 1973 demonstrated that 18–20–year–old male arrests for "driving under the influence" and "drunkenness" substantially exceeded female arrests for that same age period.[8] Similarly, youths aged 17–21 were found to be overrepresented among those killed or injured in traffic accidents, with males again numerically exceeding females in this regard.[9] Third, a random roadside survey in Oklahoma City revealed that young males were more inclined to drive and drink beer than were their female counterparts.[10] Fourth, Federal Bureau of Investigation nationwide statistics exhibited a notable increase in arrests for "driving under the influence."[11] Finally, statistical evidence gathered in other jurisdictions, particularly Minnesota and Michigan, was offered to corroborate Oklahoma's experience by indicating the pervasiveness of youthful participation in motor vehicle accidents following the imbibing of alcohol. Conceding that "the case is not free from doubt," . . . the District Court nonetheless concluded that this statistical showing substantiated "a rational basis for the legislative judgment underlying the challenged classification." . . .

Even were this statistical evidence accepted as accurate, it nevertheless offers only a weak answer to the equal protection question presented here. The most focused and relevant of the statistical surveys, arrests of 18–20–year–olds for alcohol-related driving offenses, exemplifies the ultimate unpersuasiveness of this evidentiary record. Viewed in terms of the correlation between sex and the actual activity that Oklahoma seeks to regulate—driving while under the

---

7. That this was the true purpose is not at all self-evident. The purpose is not apparent from the face of the statute and the Oklahoma Legislature does not preserve statutory history materials capable of clarifying the objectives served by its legislative enactments. . . . [We] leav[e] for another day consideration of whether the statement of the State's Assistant Attorney General should suffice to inform this Court of the legislature's objectives, or whether the Court must determine if the litigant simply is selecting a convenient, but false, *post-hoc* rationalization.

8. The disparities in 18–20–year–old male-female arrests were substantial for both categories of offenses: 427 versus 24 for driving under the influence of alcohol and 966 versus 102 for drunkenness. Even if we assume that a legislature may rely on such

arrest data in some situations, these figures do not offer support for a differential age line, for the disproportionate arrests of males persisted at older ages; indeed, in the case of arrests for drunkenness, the figures for all ages indicated "even more male involvement in such arrests at later ages." 399 F.Supp., at 1309. See also n. 14, infra.

9. This survey drew no correlation between the accident figures for any age group and levels of intoxication found in those killed or injured.

10. For an analysis of the results of this exhibit, see n. 16, infra.

11. The FBI made no attempt to relate these arrest figures either to beer drinking or to an 18–21 age differential, but rather found that male arrests for all ages exceeded 90% of the total.

influence of alcohol—the statistics broadly establish that .18% of females and 2% of males in that age group were arrested for that offense. While such a disparity is not trivial in a statistical sense, it hardly can form the basis for employment of a gender line as a classifying device. Certainly if maleness is to serve as a proxy for drinking and driving a correlation of 2% must be considered an unduly tenuous "fit." Indeed, prior cases have consistently rejected the use of sex as a decisionmaking factor even though the statutes in question certainly rested on far more predictive empirical relationships than this.[13]

Moreover, the statistics exhibit a variety of other shortcomings. . . . Setting aside the obvious methodological problems,[14] the surveys do not adequately justify the salient features of Oklahoma's gender-based traffic-safety law. None purports to measure the use and dangerousness of 3.2% beer as opposed to alcohol generally, a detail that is of particular importance since, in light of its low alcohol level, Oklahoma apparently considers the 3.2% beverage to be "non-intoxicating." 37 Okla.Stat. § 163.1 (1971); see State ex rel. Springer v. Bliss, 199 Okla. 198, 185 P.2d 220 (1947). Moreover, many of the studies, while graphically documenting the unfortunate increase in driving while under the influence of alcohol, make no effort to relate their findings to age-sex differentials as involved here. Indeed, the only survey that explicitly centered its attention upon young drivers and their use of beer—albeit apparently not of the diluted 3.2% variety—reached results that hardly can be viewed as impressive in justifying either a gender or age classification.[16]

[left margin handwritten note:] Didn't specifically consider 3.2% alcohol

13. For example, we can conjecture that in *Reed,* Idaho's apparent premise that women lacked experience in formal business matters (particularly compared to men) would have proved to be accurate in substantially more than 2% of all cases. And in both *Frontiero* and *Wiesenfeld,* we expressly found the government's empirical defense of mandatory dependency tests for men but not women to be unsatisfactory, even though we recognized that husbands still are far less likely to be dependent on their wives than vice versa. . . .

14. The very social stereotypes that find reflection in age differential laws, see Stanton v. Stanton, . . . are likely substantially to distort the accuracy of these comparative statistics. Hence "reckless" young men who drink and drive are transformed into arrest statistics, whereas their female counterparts are chivalrously escorted home. See, e.g., W. Reckless & B. Kay, The Female Offender 4, 7, 13, 16–17 (Report to Pres. Comm'n on Law Enforcement & Admin. of Justice, 1967). Moreover, the Oklahoma surveys, gathered under a regime where the age-differential law in question has been in effect, are lacking in controls necessary for appraisal of the actual effectiveness of the male 3.2% beer prohibition. In this regard, the disproportionately high arrest statistics for young males—and, indeed, the growing alcohol-related arrest figures for all ages and sexes—simply may be taken to document the relative futility of controlling driving behavior by the 3.2 beer statute and like legislation, although

we obviously have no means of estimating how many individuals, if any, actually were prevented from drinking by these laws.

16. The random roadside survey of drivers conducted in Oklahoma City during August of 1972 found that 78% of drivers under 20 were male. Turning to an evaluation of their drinking habits and factoring out nondrinkers, 84% of the males versus 77% of the females expressed a preference for beer. Further 16.5% of the men and 11.4% of the women had consumed some alcoholic beverage within two hours of the interview. Finally, a blood alcohol concentration greater than .1% was discovered in 14.6% of the males compared to 11.5% of the females. "The 1973 figures, although they contain some variations, reflect essentially the same pattern." 399 F.Supp., at 1309. Plainly these statistical disparities between the sexes are not substantial. Moreover, when the 18–20 age boundaries are lifted and all drivers analyzed, the 1972 roadside survey indicates that male drinking rose slightly whereas female exposure to alcohol remained relatively constant. Again, in 1973, the survey established that "compared to all drivers interviewed, . . . the under–20 age group generally showed a lower involvement with alcohol in terms of having drunk within the past two hours or having a significant BAC (blood alcohol content)." Id., at 1309. In sum, this survey provides little support for a gender line among teenagers and actually runs counter to the imposition of drinking restrictions based upon age.

There is no reason to belabor this line of analysis. It is unrealistic to expect either members of the judiciary or state officials to be well versed in the rigors of experimental or statistical technique. But this merely illustrates that proving broad sociological propositions by statistics is a dubious business, and one that inevitably is in tension with the normative philosophy that underlies the Equal Protection Clause. Suffice to say that the showing offered by the appellees does not satisfy us that sex represents a legitimate, accurate proxy for the regulation of drinking and driving. In fact, when it is further recognized that Oklahoma's statute prohibits only the selling of 3.2% beer to young males and not their drinking the beverage once acquired (even after purchase by their 18–20–year–old female companions), the relationship between gender and traffic safety becomes far too tenuous to satisfy *Reed's* requirement that the gender-based difference be substantially related to achievement of the statutory objective.

We hold, therefore, that under *Reed*, Oklahoma's 3.2% beer statute invidiously discriminates against males 18–20 years of age.

Discriminates

D.

Appellees argue, however, that §§ 241 and 245 enforce state policies concerning the sale and distribution of alcohol and by force of the Twenty-first Amendment should therefore be held to withstand the equal protection challenge. . . . The Twenty-first Amendment . . . primarily created an exception to the normal operation of the Commerce Clause. See, e.g., Hostetter v. Idlewild Bon Voyage Liquor Corp., 377 U.S. 324, 330 (1964); . . . .

Argue that they enforce state policies under 21st amd.

[Its] relevance . . . to other constitutional provisions becomes increasingly doubtful. . . .

[B]oth federal and state courts uniformly have declared the unconstitutionality of gender lines that restrain the activities of customers of state-regulated liquor establishments irrespective of the operation of the Twenty-first Amendment. . . . Even when state officials have posited sociological or empirical justifications for these gender-based differentiations, the courts have struck down discriminations aimed at an entire class under the guise of alcohol regulation. In fact, social science studies that have uncovered quantifiable differences in drinking tendencies dividing along both racial and ethnic lines strongly suggest the need for application of the Equal Protection Clause in preventing discriminatory treatment that almost certainly would be perceived as invidious.[22] In sum, the principles embodied in the Equal Protection Clause are not to be rendered inapplicable by statistically measured but loose-fitting generalities concerning the drinking tendencies of aggregate groups. We thus hold that the operation of the Twenty-first Amendment does not alter the application of equal protection standards that otherwise govern this case.

We conclude that the gender-based differential contained in 37 Okla.Stat. § 245 constitutes a denial of the Equal Protection of the Laws to males aged

22. Thus, if statistics were to govern the permissibility of state alcohol regulation without regard to the Equal Protection Clause as a limiting principle, it might follow that States could freely favor Jews and Italian Catholics at the expense of all other Americans, since available studies regularly demonstrate that the former two groups exhibit the lowest rates of problem drinking. . . .

In the past, . . . several States established criminal sanctions for the sale of alcohol to an Indian or "half or quarter breed Indian." . . . [S]tate alcohol beverage prohibitions also have been directed at other groups, notably German, Italian, and Catholic immigrants. . . . The repeal of most of these laws signals society's perception of the unfairness and questionable constitutionality of singling out groups to bear the brunt of alcohol regulation.

18–20[23] and reverse the judgment of the District Court.[24]

Mr. Justice Stewart, concurring.

. . .

Mr. Justice Blackmun, concurring.

I join the Court's opinion except Part II–D thereof. I agree, however, that the Twenty-first Amendment does not save the challenged Oklahoma statute.

Mr. Justice Powell, concurring.

I join the opinion of the Court [but] have reservations as to some of the discussion concerning the appropriate standard for equal protection analysis and the relevance of the statistical evidence. . . .

. . . I agree that Reed v. Reed, 404 U.S. 71 (1971), is the most relevant precedent. But I find it unnecessary . . . to read that decision as broadly as some of the Court's language may imply. *Reed* and subsequent cases involving gender-based classifications make clear that the Court subjects such classifications to a more critical examination than is normally applied when "fundamental" constitutional rights and "suspect classes" are not present.*

. . .

Mr. Justice Stevens, concurring.

There is only one Equal Protection Clause. It requires every State to govern impartially. It does not direct the courts to apply one standard of review in some cases and a different standard in other cases. Whatever criticism may be levelled at a judicial opinion implying that there are at least three such standards applies with the same force to a double standard.

I am inclined to believe that what has become known as the two-tiered analysis of equal protection claims does not describe a completely logical method of deciding cases, but rather is a method the Court has employed to explain decisions that actually apply a single standard in a reasonably consistent fashion. I also suspect that a careful explanation of the reasons motivating particular decisions may contribute more to an identification of that standard than an attempt to articulate it in all-encompassing terms. . . .

---

23. Insofar as Goesaert v. Cleary, 335 U.S. 464 (1948), may be inconsistent, that decision is disapproved. . . .

24. As noted in Stanton v. Stanton, . . . the Oklahoma Legislature is free to redefine any cutoff age for the purchase and sale of 3.2 beer that it may choose, provided that the redefinition operates in a gender-neutral fashion.

* As is evident from our opinions, the Court has had difficulty in agreeing upon a standard of equal protection analysis that can be applied consistently to the wide variety of legislative classifications. There are valid reasons for dissatisfaction with the "two-tier" approach that has been prominent in the Court's decisions in the past decade. Although viewed by many as a result-oriented substitute for more critical analysis, that approach—with its narrowly limited "upper-tier"—now has substantial precedential support. As has been true of *Reed* and its progeny, our decision today will be viewed by some as a "middle-tier" approach. While I would not endorse that characterization and would not welcome a further subdividing of equal protection analysis, candor compels the recognition that the relatively deferential "rational basis" standard of review normally applied takes on a sharper focus when we address a gender-based classification. So much is clear from our recent cases. For thoughtful discussions of equal protection analysis, see, e.g., Gunther, The Supreme Court, 1971 Term—Foreword: In Search of Evolving Doctrine on a Changing Court: A Model for Newer Equal Protection, 86 Harv.L.Rev. 1 (1972); Wilkinson, The Supreme Court, the Equal Protection Clause, and the Three Faces of Constitutional Equality, 61 Va.L.Rev. 945 (1975).

In this case, the classification is not as obnoxious as some the Court has condemned, nor as inoffensive as some the Court has accepted. It is objectionable because it is based on an accident of birth, because it is a mere remnant of the now almost universally rejected tradition of discriminating against males in this age bracket, and because, to the extent it reflects any physical difference between males and females, it is actually perverse. The question then is whether the traffic safety justification put forward by the State is sufficient to make an otherwise offensive classification acceptable.

The classification is not totally irrational. For the evidence does indicate that there are more males than females in this age bracket who drive and also more who drink. Nevertheless, . . . [i]t is difficult to believe that the statute was actually intended to cope with the problem of traffic safety, since it has only a minimal effect on access to a not-very-intoxicating beverage and does not prohibit its consumption. Moreover, the empirical data submitted by the State accentuates the unfairness of treating all 18–21–year–old males as inferior to their female counterparts. The legislation imposes a restraint on one hundred percent of the males in the class allegedly because about 2% of them have probably violated one or more laws relating to the consumption of alcoholic beverages. It is unlikely that this law will have a significant deterrent effect either on that 2% or on the law-abiding 98%. But even assuming some such slight benefit, it does not seem to me that an insult to all of the young men of the State can be justified by visiting the sins of the 2% on the 98%.

Mr. Chief Justice Burger, dissenting.

I am in general agreement with Mr. Justice Rehnquist's dissent. . . .

. . .

Though today's decision does not go so far as to make gender-based classifications "suspect," it makes gender a disfavored classification. Without an independent constitutional basis supporting the right asserted or disfavoring the classification adopted, I can justify no substantive constitutional protection other than the normal McGowan v. Maryland, 366 U.S., at 425–426, protection afforded by the Equal Protection Clause.

. . .

Mr. Justice Rehnquist, **dissenting.**

The Court's disposition of this case is objectionable on two grounds. First is its conclusion that *men* challenging a gender-based statute which treats them less favorably than women may invoke a more stringent standard of judicial review than pertains to most other types of classifications. Second is the Court's enunciation of this standard, without citation to any source, as being that "classifications by gender must serve *important* governmental objectives and must be *substantially* related to achievement of those objectives." (emphasis added). The only redeeming feature of the Court's opinion, to my mind, is that it apparently signals a retreat by those who joined the plurality opinion in Frontiero v. Richardson, 411 U.S. 677 (1973), from their view that sex is a "suspect" classification for purposes of equal protection analysis. I think the Oklahoma statute challenged here need pass only the "rational basis" equal protection analysis expounded in cases such as McGowan v. Maryland, 366 U.S. 420 (1961), and Williamson v. Lee Optical Co., 348 U.S. 483 (1955), and I believe that it is constitutional under that analysis.

. . .

CLASSIFICATIONS ADVANTAGING FEMALES

The Court in Craig v. Boren (in footnote 6) refers to cases such as Kahn v. Shevin, 416 U.S. 351 (1974), upholding classifications designed to remedy past discrimination against women. That case and others will be discussed in Subsection E, infra, dealing with "benign" discrimination in cases involving gender and in cases involving race.

WHAT CONSTITUTES DISCRIMINATION BASED ON GENDER?

In Geduldig v. Aiello, 417 U.S. 484 (1974) the Court rejected a challenge to the California disability insurance program which excluded from its coverage disabilities resulting from normal pregnancy. Justice Stewart, speaking for the Court, said, in part:

"The State has a legitimate interest in maintaining the self-supporting nature of its insurance program. Similarly, it has an interest in distributing the available resources in such a way as to keep benefit payments at an adequate level for disabilities that are covered, rather than to cover all disabilities inadequately. Finally, California has a legitimate concern in maintaining the contribution rate at a level that will not unduly burden participating employees, particularly low-income employees who may be most in need of the disability insurance.

"These policies provide an objective and wholly non-invidious basis for the State's decision not to create a more comprehensive insurance program than it has. There is no evidence in the record that the selection of the risks insured by the program worked to discriminate against any definable group or class in terms of the aggregate risk protection derived by that group or class from the program.[20] There is no risk from which men are protected and women are not. Likewise, there is no risk from which women are protected and men are not.[21]

"The appellee simply contends that, although she has received insurance protection equivalent to that provided all other participating employees, she has suffered discrimination because she encountered a risk that was outside the program's protection. For the reasons we have stated, we hold that this

---

20. The dissenting opinion to the contrary, this case is thus a far cry from cases like Reed v. Reed, 404 U.S. 71, and Frontiero v. Richardson, 411 U.S. 677, involving discrimination based upon gender as such. The California insurance program does not exclude anyone from benefit eligibility because of gender but merely removes one physical condition—pregnancy—from the list of compensable disabilities. While it is true that only women can become pregnant, it does not follow that every legislative classification concerning pregnancy is a sex-based classification like those considered in Reed, supra, and Frontiero, supra. Normal pregnancy is an objectively identifiable physical condition with unique characteristics. Absent a showing that distinctions involving pregnancy are mere pretexts designed to effect an invidious discrimination against the members of one sex or the other, lawmakers are constitutionally free to include or exclude pregnancy from the coverage of legislation such as this on any reasonable basis, just as with respect to any other physical condition.

The lack of identity between the excluded disability and gender as such under this insurance program becomes clear upon the most cursory analysis. The program divides potential recipients into two groups—pregnant women and nonpregnant persons. While the first group is exclusively female, the second includes members of both sexes. The fiscal and actuarial benefits of the program thus accrue to members of both sexes.

21. Indeed, the appellant submitted to the District Court data that indicated that both the annual claim rate and the annual claim cost are greater for women than for men. As the District Court acknowledged, "women contribute 28 per cent of the total disability insurance fund and receive back about 38 per cent of the fund in benefits." 359 F.Supp., at 800. Several *amici curiae* have represented to the Court that they have had a similar experience under private disability insurance programs.

contention is not a valid one under the Equal Protection Clause of the Fourteenth Amendment."

Justices Brennan, Douglas, and Marshall dissented on the ground that the *Reed* and *Frontiero* cases "mandate a stricter standard of scrutiny which the State's classification fails to satisfy."

In General Elec. Co. v. Gilbert, 429 U.S. 125 (1976), the Court held that a private company's disability plan which excluded disabilities arising from pregnancy did not violate Title VII of the Civil Rights Act of 1964, because, as in *Geduldig,* the classification did not involve discrimination based on sex. Justice Stevens disagreed, arguing in dissent that the classification was sex-based because "[t]he classification is between persons who face a risk of pregnancy and those who do not."

In Nashville Gas Co. v. Satty, 434 U.S. 136 (1977), the Court held that Title VII did not prohibit a private company policy providing sick leave pay for nonoccupational disabilities other than pregnancy, but did prohibit a policy that denied female employees returning to work after a pregnancy leave the accumulated seniority it granted others returning from sick leave. The Court said that the loss of seniority for pregnancy leaves differed from the failure to pay during the leave, because "petitioner has not merely refused to extend to women a benefit that men cannot and do not receive, but has imposed on women a substantial burden that men need not suffer." It also said that "[t]he distinction between burdens and benefits is more than one of semantics[,]" and that Title VII does not "permit an employer to burden female employees in such a way as to deprive them of employment opportunities because of their different roles."[a]

With these cases involving the question whether classifications based on pregnancy shall be treated as gender classifications for the purpose of determining the appropriate standard of review, compare Mathews v. Lucas, 427 U.S. 495 (1976). In that case the Social Security Act provided a presumption of dependency on a deceased father for all legitimate children and for some (but not all) illegitimate children. The Court said: "That the statutory classifications challenged here discriminate among illegitimate children does not mean, of course, that they are not also properly described as discriminating between legitimate and illegitimate children."

The cases addressing whether disparate treatment of pregnancy from other conditions constitutes gender discrimination also usefully may be compared with those where men and women receive disparate treatment based on accurate generalizations about the respective classes. In City of Los Angeles v. Manhart, 435 U.S. 702 (1978), the Court held that Title VII prohibited the Los Angeles Department of Water and Power from requiring its female employees to make larger contributions to its pension fund than its male employees, even though it assumed the truth of the generalization, based on mortality tables, that women as a class live longer than men and thus on average would receive pension benefits for a longer time. Justice Stevens wrote for the Court that the

---

a. In 1978 Congress amended Title VII of the Civil Rights Act of 1964 to provide: "The terms 'because of sex' or 'on the basis of sex' include, but are not limited to, because of or on the basis of pregnancy, childbirth, or related medical conditions; and women affected by pregnancy, childbirth, or related medical conditions shall be treated the same for all employment-related purposes, including receipt of benefits under fringe benefit programs, as other persons not so affected but similar in their ability or inability to work, ..." 42 U.S.C. § 2000e(k). The Court later applied this statute to hold invalid a health plan which gave lesser benefits for pregnancy-related conditions to spouses of male employees than it gave to female employees. Newport News Shipbuilding and Dry Dock Co. v. EEOC, 462 U.S. 669 (1983).

statute "precludes treatment of individuals as simply components of a racial, religious, sexual, or national class[,]" and that "[e]ven a true generalization about the class is an insufficient reason for disqualifying an individual to whom the generalization does not apply." Unlike the classification between "pregnant women and nonpregnant persons" at issue in *Gilbert* and *Geduldig,* "each of the two groups in this case is composed entirely and exclusively of members of the same sex." Consequently, "[o]n its face, this plan discriminates on the basis of sex whereas [those plans] discriminated on the basis of a special physical disability." This approach was followed in Arizona Governing Committee v. Norris, 463 U.S. 1073 (1983), which held that Arizona's pension plan providing for equal contributions from state employees of both sexes but lower pension benefits to female employees based on gender-based mortality tables violated the gender discrimination provisions of Title VII. The Court had "no hesitation in holding ... that the classification of employees on the basis of sex is no more permissible at the pay-out stage of a retirement plan than at the pay-in stage."

A separate problem arises when a statute that on its face does not make a gender classification is challenged on the ground that it has a disparate impact on one sex. See, e.g., Personnel Adm'r of Massachusetts v. Feeney, 442 U.S. 256 (1979), in which a law providing job preferences to veterans was challenged by a showing that 98% of veterans were male. *Feeney* will be considered along with similar cases involving race in Subsection D dealing with the requirement of showing a discriminatory purpose.

Michael M. v. Superior Court

450 U.S. 464, 101 S.Ct. 1200, 67 L.Ed.2d 437 (1981).

Justice Rehnquist announced the judgment of the Court and delivered an opinion in which The Chief Justice, Justice Stewart, and Justice Powell joined.

The question presented ... is whether California's "statutory rape" law, § 261.5 of the Cal. Penal Code Ann. ... violates the Equal Protection Clause of the Fourteenth Amendment. Section 261.5 defines unlawful sexual intercourse as "an act of sexual intercourse accomplished with a female not the wife of the perpetrator, where the female is under the age of 18 years." The statute thus makes men alone criminally liable for the act of sexual intercourse.

In July 1978, a complaint was filed ... alleging that petitioner, then a 17½–year–old male, had had unlawful sexual intercourse with a female under the age of 18, in violation of § 261.5.... Prior to trial, petitioner sought to set aside the information on both state and federal constitutional grounds, asserting that § 261.5 unlawfully discriminated on the basis of gender. The trial court and the California Court of Appeal denied petitioner's request for relief and petitioner sought review in the Supreme Court of California.

The Supreme Court held that "section 261.5 discriminates on the basis of sex because only females may be victims, and only males may violate the section." The court then subjected the classification to "strict scrutiny," stating that it must be justified by a compelling state interest. It found that the classification was "supported not by mere social convention but by the immutable physiological fact that it is the female exclusively who can become pregnant." Canvassing "the tragic human cost of illegitimate teenage pregnancies," including the large number of teenage abortions, the increased medical risk associated with teenage pregnancies, and the social consequences of teenage childbearing, the court concluded that the State has a compelling interest in

[handwritten margin notes:]

statutory rape law challenged because it makes men alone culpable

Supreme ct used strict scrutiny, saying it was justified only by compelling state interest

This ct. affirms

preventing such pregnancies. Because males alone can "physiologically cause the result which the law properly seeks to avoid," the court further held that the gender classification was readily justified as a means of identifying offender and victim. For the reasons stated below, we affirm the judgment....

... Unlike the California Supreme Court, we have not held that gender-based classifications are "inherently suspect" and thus we do not apply so-called "strict scrutiny" to those classifications.... Our cases have held, however, that the traditional minimum rationality test takes on a somewhat "sharper focus" when gender-based classifications are challenged. See Craig v. Boren, 429 U.S. 190, 210 n *(1976) (Powell, J., concurring). In Reed v. Reed, 404 U.S. 71 (1971), for example, the Court stated that a gender-based classification will be upheld if it bears a "fair and substantial relationship" to legitimate state ends, while in *Craig v. Boren,* ... the Court restated the test to require the classification to bear a "substantial relationship" to "important governmental objectives."

Underlying these decisions is the principle that a legislature may not "make overbroad generalizations based on sex which are entirely unrelated to any differences between men and women or which demean the ability or social status of the affected class." Parham v. Hughes, 441 U.S. 347, 354 (1979) (plurality opinion of Stewart, J.). But because the Equal Protection Clause does not "demand that a statute necessarily apply equally to all persons" or require " 'things which are different in fact ... to be treated in law as though they were the same,' " Rinaldi v. Yeager, 384 U.S. 305, 309 (1966), ... this Court has consistently upheld statutes where the gender classification is not invidious, but rather realistically reflects the fact that the sexes are not similarly situated in certain circumstances. Parham v. Hughes, supra; Califano v. Webster, 430 U.S. 313 (1977); Schlesinger v. Ballard, 419 U.S. 498 (1975); Kahn v. Shevin, 416 U.S. 351 (1974). As the Court has stated, a legislature may "provide for the special problems of women." Weinberger v. Wiesenfeld, 420 U.S. 636, 653 (1975).

... [T]hat the California Legislature criminalized the act of illicit sexual intercourse with a minor female is a sure indication of its intent or purpose to discourage that conduct. Precisely why the legislature desired that result is of course somewhat less clear. This Court has long recognized that "[i]nquiries into congressional motives or purposes are a hazardous matter," United States v. O'Brien, 391 U.S. 367, 383–384 (1968); Palmer v. Thompson, 403 U.S. 217, 224 (1971), and the search for the "actual" or "primary" purpose of a statute is likely to be elusive. Arlington Heights v. Metropolitan Housing Dev. Corp., 429 U.S. 252, 265 (1977).... Here, for example, the individual legislators may have voted for the statute for a variety of reasons. Some legislators may have been concerned about preventing teenage pregnancies, others about protecting young females from physical injury or from the loss of "chastity," and still others about promoting various religious and moral attitudes towards premarital sex.

The justification for the statute offered by the State, and accepted by the Supreme Court of California, is that the legislature sought to prevent illegitimate teenage pregnancies. That finding, of course, is entitled to great deference. Reitman v. Mulkey, 387 U.S. 369, 373–374 (1967). And although our cases establish that the State's asserted reason for the enactment of a statute may be rejected, if it "could not have been a goal of the legislation," *Weinberger v. Wiesenfeld,* ... this is not such a case.

We are satisfied not only that the prevention of illegitimate pregnancy is at least one of the "purposes" of the statute, but that the State has a strong interest in preventing such pregnancy. At the risk of stating the obvious, teenage pregnancies, which have increased dramatically over the last two decades, have significant social, medical and economic consequences for both the mother and her child, and the State. Of particular concern to the State is that approximately half of all teenage pregnancies end in abortion. And of those children who are born, their illegitimacy makes them likely candidates to become wards of the State.[6]

We need not be medical doctors to discern that young men and young women are not similarly situated with respect to the problems and the risks of sexual intercourse. Only women may become pregnant, and they suffer disproportionately the profound physical, emotional, and psychological consequences of sexual activity. The statute at issue here protects women from sexual intercourse at an age when those consequences are particularly severe.[7]

The question thus boils down to whether a State may attack the problem of sexual intercourse and teenage pregnancy directly by prohibiting a male from having sexual intercourse with a minor female. We hold that such a statute is sufficiently related to the State's objectives to pass constitutional muster.

Because virtually all of the significant harmful and inescapably identifiable consequences of teenage pregnancy fall on the young female, a legislature acts well within its authority when it elects to punish only the participant who, by nature, suffers few of the consequences of his conduct. It is hardly unreasonable for a legislature acting to protect minor females to exclude them from punishment. Moreover, the risk of pregnancy itself constitutes a substantial deterrence to young females. No similar natural sanctions deter males. A criminal sanction imposed solely on males thus serves to roughly "equalize" the deterrents on the sexes.

[margin handwriting: acting within its capacity when it tends to punish only the participant who suffers few]

We are unable to accept petitioner's contention that the statute is impermissibly underinclusive and must, in order to pass judicial scrutiny, be *broadened* so as to hold the female as criminally liable as the male. It is argued that this statute is not *necessary* to deter teenage pregnancy because a gender-neutral statute, where both male and female would be subject to prosecution, would serve that goal equally well. The relevant inquiry, however, is not whether the statute is drawn as precisely as it might have been, but whether

---

6. . . .

Subsequent to the decision below, the California Legislature considered and rejected proposals to render § 261.5 gender neutral, thereby ratifying the judgment of the California Supreme Court. That is enough to answer petitioner's contention that the statute was the "accidental byproduct of a traditional way of thinking about women." Califano v. Webster, 430 U.S. 313 (1977) (quoting Califano v. Goldfarb, 430 U.S. 199 (1977) (Stevens, J., concurring)). Certainly this decision of the California Legislature is as good a source as is this Court in deciding what is "current" and what is "outmoded" in the perception of women.

7. Although petitioner concedes that the State has a "compelling" interest in preventing teenage pregnancy, he contends that the "true" purpose of § 261.5 is to protect the virtue and chastity of young women. As such, the statute is unjustifiable because it rests on archaic stereotypes. . . . Even if the

preservation of female chastity were one of the motives of the statute, and even if that motive be impermissible, petitioner's argument must fail because "[i]t is a familiar practice of constitutional law that this court will not strike down an otherwise constitutional statute on the basis of an alleged illicit legislative motive." United States v. O'Brien, 391 U.S. 367, 383 (1968). In Orr v. Orr, 440 U.S. 268 (1979), for example, the Court rejected one asserted purpose as impermissible, but then considered other purposes to determine if they could justify the statute. Similarly, in Washington v. Davis, 426 U.S. 229, 243 (1976) the Court distinguished Palmer v. Thompson, 403 U.S. 217 (1971), on the grounds that the purposes of the ordinance there were not open to impeachment by evidence that the legislature was actually motivated by an impermissible purpose. See also Arlington Heights v. Metropolitan Housing Dev. Corp., 429 U.S. 252, 270, n. 21 (1977); Mobile v. Bolden, 446 U.S. 55, 91 (1980) (Stevens, J., concurring in judgment).

the line chosen by the California Legislature is within constitutional limitations....

In any event, we cannot say that a gender-neutral statute would be as
effective as the statute California has chosen to enact. The State persuasively
contends that a gender-neutral statute would frustrate its interest in effective
enforcement. Its view is that a female is surely less likely to report violations of
the statute if she herself would be subject to criminal prosecution. In an area
already fraught with prosecutorial difficulties, we decline to hold that the Equal
Protection Clause requires a legislature to enact a statute so broad that it may
well be incapable of enforcement.[10]

We similarly reject petitioner's argument that § 261.5 is impermissibly
overbroad because it makes unlawful sexual intercourse with prepubescent
females, who are, by definition, incapable of becoming pregnant. Quite apart
from the fact that the statute could well be justified on the grounds that very
young females are particularly susceptible to physical injury from sexual
intercourse, ... it is ludicrous to suggest that the Constitution requires the
California Legislature to limit the scope of its rape statute to older teenagers
and exclude young girls.

There remains only petitioner's contention that the statute is unconstitutional as it is applied to him because he, like Sharon, was under 18 at the time
of sexual intercourse. Petitioner argues that the statute is flawed because it
presumes that as between two persons under 18, the male is the culpable
aggressor. We find petitioner's contentions unpersuasive. Contrary to his
assertions, the statute does not rest on the assumption that males are generally
the aggressors. It is instead an attempt by a legislature to prevent illegitimate
teenage pregnancy by providing an additional deterrent for men. The age of the
man is irrelevant since young men are as capable as older men of inflicting the
harm sought to be prevented.

In upholding the California statute we also recognize that this is not a case
where a statute is being challenged on the grounds that it "invidiously
discriminates" against females. To the contrary, the statute places a burden on
males which is not shared by females. But we find nothing to suggest that men,
because of past discrimination or peculiar disadvantages, are in need of the
special solicitude of the courts. Nor is this a case where the gender classification is made "solely for ... administrative convenience," as in Frontiero v.
Richardson, 411 U.S. 677, 690 (1973) (emphasis omitted), or rests on "the
baggage of sexual stereotypes" as in Orr v. Orr, 440 U.S., at 283. As we have
held, the statute instead reasonably reflects the fact that the consequences of
sexual intercourse and pregnancy fall more heavily on the female than on the
male.

---

10. The question whether a statute is
substantially related to its asserted goals is at
best an opaque one. It can be plausibly argued that a gender-neutral statute would produce fewer prosecutions than the statute at
issue here. The dissent argues, on the other
hand, that "even assuming that a gender-
neutral statute would be more difficult to
enforce.... [c]ommon sense ... suggests
that a gender-neutral statutory rape law is
potentially a greater deterrent of sexual activity than a gender-based law, for the simple
reason that a gender-neutral law subjects
both men and women to criminal sanctions

and thus arguably has a deterrent effect on
twice as many potential violators."

Where such differing speculations as to
the effect of a statute are plausible, we think
it appropriate to defer to the decision of the
California Supreme Court, "armed as it was
with the knowledge of the facts and circumstances concerning the passage and potential
impact of [the statute], and familiar with the
milieu in which that provision would operate." Reitman v. Mulkey, 387 U.S. 369, 378–
379 (1967).

. . .

statute is upheld

Accordingly the judgment of the California Supreme Court is Affirmed.

Justice Stewart, concurring.

. . .

The Constitution is violated when government, state or federal, invidiously classifies similarly situated people on the basis of the immutable characteristics with which they were born. Thus, detrimental racial classifications by government always violate the Constitution, for the simple reason that, so far as the Constitution is concerned, people of different races are always similarly situated.... By contrast, while detrimental gender classifications by government often violate the Constitution, they do not always do so, for the reason that there are differences between males and females that the Constitution necessarily recognizes. In this case we deal with the most basic of these differences: females can become pregnant as the result of sexual intercourse; males cannot.

. . .

... Experienced observation confirms the common sense notion that adolescent males disregard the possibility of pregnancy far more than do adolescent females. And to the extent that § 261.5 may punish males for intercourse with prepubescent females, that punishment is justifiable because of the substantial physical risks for prepubescent females that are not shared by their male counterparts.

. . .

In short, the Equal Protection Clause does not mean that the physiological differences between men and women must be disregarded. While those differences must never be permitted to become a pretext for invidious discrimination, no such discrimination is presented by this case....

Justice Blackmun, concurring in the judgment.

It is gratifying that the plurality recognizes that "[a]t the risk of stating the obvious, teenage pregnancies ... have increased dramatically over the last two decades" and "have significant social, medical, and economic consequences for both the mother and her child, and the State." There have been times when I have wondered whether the Court was capable of this perception, particularly when it has struggled with the different but not unrelated problems that attend abortion issues. See, for example, ... today's opinion in *H.L. v. Matheson*....

Some might conclude that the two uses of the criminal sanction—here flatly to forbid intercourse in order to forestall teenage pregnancies, and in *Matheson* to prohibit a physician's abortion procedure except upon notice to the parents of the pregnant minor—are vastly different proscriptions. But the basic social and privacy problems are much the same. Both Utah's statute in *Matheson* and California's statute in this case are legislatively created tools intended to achieve similar ends and addressed to the same societal concerns: the control and direction of young people's sexual activities....

I, however, cannot vote to strike down the California statutory rape law, for I think it is a sufficiently reasoned and constitutional effort to control the problem at its inception.... I am persuaded that, although a minor has substantial privacy rights in intimate affairs connected with procreation, California's efforts to prevent teenage pregnancy are to be viewed differently from Utah's efforts to inhibit a woman from dealing with pregnancy once it has become an inevitability.

Craig v. Boren, 429 U.S. 190 (1976), was an opinion which, in large part, I joined. The plurality opinion in the present case points out the Court's respective phrasings of the applicable test in Reed v. Reed ... and in Craig v. Boren.... I vote to ... uphold the State's gender-based classification on that test and as exemplified by those two cases and by Schlesinger v. Ballard, 419 U.S. 498 (1975); Weinberger v. Wiesenfeld, 420 U.S. 636 (1975); and Kahn v. Shevin, 416 U.S. 351 (1974).

. . . .

Justice Brennan, with whom Justices White and Marshall join, dissenting.

I

It is disturbing to find the Court so splintered on a case that presents such a straightforward issue: whether the admittedly gender-based classification in Cal.Penal Code Ann. § 261.5 ... bears a sufficient relationship to the State's asserted goal of preventing teenage pregnancies to survive the "mid-level" constitutional scrutiny mandated by Craig v. Boren, 429 U.S. 190 (1976). Applying ... our precedents, ... the classification must be declared unconstitutional. I fear that the plurality and Justices Stewart and Blackmun reach the opposite result by placing too much emphasis on the desirability of achieving the State's asserted statutory goal—prevention of teenage pregnancy—and not enough emphasis on the fundamental question of whether the sex-based discrimination in the California statute is *substantially* related to the achievement of that goal.

[handwritten margin note: not enough emphasis if disc. is substantially related to achieve that goal.]

. . . .

... [E]ven assuming that prevention of teenage pregnancy is an important governmental objective and that it is in fact an objective of § 261.5, California still has the burden of proving that there are fewer teenage pregnancies under its gender-based statutory rape law than there would be if the law were gender neutral.... [It] must show that because its statutory rape law punishes only males, and not females, it more effectively deters minor females from having sexual intercourse.

. . . .

... [T]here are at least two serious flaws in the State's assertion that law enforcement problems created by a gender-neutral statutory rape law would make such a statute less effective than a gender-based statute in deterring sexual activity.

[handwritten margin note: Flaws in argument that gender neutral law will be less effective]

First, the experience of other jurisdictions, and California itself, belies the plurality's conclusion that a gender-neutral statutory rape law "may well be incapable of enforcement." ...

. . . .

[S]econd[,] ... even assuming that a gender-neutral statute would be more difficult to enforce, the State has still not shown that those enforcement problems would make such a statute less effective than a gender-based statute in deterring minor females from engaging in sexual intercourse. Common sense, however, suggests that a gender-neutral statutory rape law is potentially a *greater* deterrent of sexual activity than a gender-based law, for the simple reason that a gender-neutral law subjects both men and women to criminal sanctions and thus arguably has a deterrent effect on twice as many potential violators....

III

History shows different purpose

Until very recently, no California court or commentator had suggested that the purpose of California's statutory rape law was to protect young women from the risk of pregnancy. Indeed, the historical development of § 261.5 demonstrates that the law was initially enacted on the premise that young women, in contrast to young men, were to be deemed legally incapable of consenting to an act of sexual intercourse. Because their chastity was considered particularly precious, those young women were felt to be uniquely in need of the State's protection. In contrast, young men were assumed to be capable of making such decisions for themselves; the law therefore did not offer them any special protection.

It is perhaps because the gender classification in California's statutory rape law was initially designed to further these outmoded sexual stereotypes, rather than to reduce the incidence of teenage pregnancies, that the State has been unable to demonstrate a substantial relationship between the classification and its newly asserted goal.... But whatever the reason, the State has not shown that Cal.Penal Code § 261.5 is any more effective than a gender-neutral law would be in deterring minor females from engaging in sexual intercourse. It has therefore not met its burden of proving that the statutory classification is substantially related to the achievement of its asserted goal.

Has not met its burden of showing substantial relation

I would hold that § 261.5 violates the Equal Protection Clause....

Justice Stevens, dissenting.

Local custom and belief—rather than statutory laws of venerable but doubtful ancestry—will determine the volume of sexual activity among unmarried teenagers. The empirical evidence cited by the plurality demonstrates the futility of the notion that a statutory prohibition will significantly affect the volume of that activity or provide a meaningful solution to the problems created by it. Nevertheless, as a matter of constitutional power, unlike my Brother Brennan, I would have no doubt about the validity of a state law prohibiting all unmarried teenagers from engaging in sexual intercourse. The societal interests in reducing the incidence of venereal disease and teenage pregnancy are sufficient, in my judgment, to justify a prohibition of conduct that increases the risk of those harms.

My conclusion that a nondiscriminatory prohibition would be constitutional does not help me answer the question whether a prohibition applicable to only half of the joint participants in the risk-creating conduct is also valid. It cannot be true that the validity of a total ban is an adequate justification for a selective prohibition; otherwise, the constitutional objection to discriminatory rules would be meaningless. The question ... is whether the difference between males and females justifies this statutory discrimination based entirely on sex.

... I think the plurality is quite correct in making the assumption that the joint act that this law seeks to prohibit creates a greater risk of harm for the female than for the male....

. . .

Should prohibit her if she is the greater risk

[However,] that a female confronts a greater risk of harm than a male is a reason for applying the prohibition to her—not a reason for granting her a license to use her own judgment on whether or not to assume the risk....

. . .

Finally, even if ... there actually is some speculative basis for treating equally guilty males and females differently, ... any such speculative justification would be outweighed by the paramount interest in evenhanded enforcement of the law. A rule that authorizes punishment of only one of two equally guilty wrongdoers violates the essence of the constitutional requirement that the sovereign must govern impartially.

I respectfully dissent.

ROSTKER v. GOLDBERG, 453 U.S. 57 (1981). In 1980 President Carter recommended that Congress reactivate the draft registration process and provide for the registration of women as well as men. When Congress provided funds only for the registration of males, men subject to the draft sued as a class, claiming a violation of the Fifth Amendment's Due Process Clause. A District Court judgment in their favor was reversed by the Supreme Court. For the Court, Justice Rehnquist emphasized "[t]he customary deference accorded the judgments of congress ... When, as here, Congress specifically considered the question of the Act's constitutionality"; an even greater "healthy deference to legislative and executive judgments in the area of military affairs"; and a judicial "lack of competence" in this area that was "marked." Finding the District Court's "efforts to divorce registration from the military and national defense context, with all the deference called for in that context, singularly unpersuasive[,]" the Court nonetheless declined to adopt the Solicitor General's argument that it should apply the "rational relation" standard "and should not examine the Act under the heightened scrutiny with which we have approached gender-based discrimination, see Michael M. v. Superior Court of Sonoma County, 450 U.S. 464 (1981); Craig v. Boren, 429 U.S. 190; *reed v. Reed,* supra[,]" saying in part:

recommended draft of women (handwritten margin note)

"We do not think that the substantive guarantee of due process or certainty in the law will be advanced by any further 'refinement' in the applicable tests as suggested by the Government. Announced degrees of 'deference' to legislative judgments, just as levels of 'scrutiny' which this Court announces that it applies to particular classifications made by a legislative body, may all too readily become facile abstractions used to justify a result.... Simply labelling the legislative decision 'military' on the one hand or 'gender-based' on the other does not automatically guide a court to the correct constitutional result."

The majority found this case to be

"quite different from several of the gender-based discrimination cases we have considered in that ... Congress did not act 'unthinkingly' or 'reflexively and not for any considered reason.' the question of registering women for the draft not only received considerable national attention and was the subject of wide-ranging public debate, but also was extensively considered by Congress in hearings, floor debate, and in committee. ...

"The foregoing clearly establishes that the decision to exempt women from registration was not the 'accidental by-product of a traditional way of thinking about women.' Califano v. Webster, 430 U.S. 313, 320 (1977) (quoting Califano v. Goldfarb, 430 U.S. 199, 233 (1977) (Stevens, J., concurring)). In Michael M., 450 U.S., at 471, n. 6 (plurality), we rejected a similar argument because of action by the California Legislature considering and rejecting proposals to make a statute challenged on discrimination grounds gender-neutral. The cause for rejecting the argument is considerably stronger here. The issue was considered at great length, and Congress clearly expressed its purpose and intent. Contrast Califano v. Westcott, 443 U.S. 76, 87 (1979) ('the gender qualification ... escaped virtually unnoticed in the hearings and floor debates')."

After identifying the "purpose of registration [to be] to prepare for a draft *of combat troops*[,]" the Court noted that by statute or policy women "as a group ... are not eligible for combat" and that "Congress specifically recognized and endorsed the exclusion of women from combat in exempting women from registration." Accordingly, "[m]en and women, because of the combat restrictions on women, are simply not similarly situated for purposes of a draft or registration for a draft[,]" and "[t]he exemption of women from registration is not only sufficiently but also closely related to Congress' purpose in authorizing registration."

Finally, the Court thought the District Court had erred in "rel[ying] heavily on the President's decision to seek authority to register women and the testimony of members of the Executive Branch and the military in support of that decision[,]" including "testimony that in the event of a draft of 650,000 the military could absorb some 80,000 female inductees ... to fill noncombat positions, freeing men to go to the front." In doing so, "the District Court palpably exceeded its authority when it ignored Congress' considered response to this line of reasoning." First, "assuming that a small number of women could be drafted for noncombat roles, Congress simply did not consider it worth the added burdens of including women in draft and registration plans." Second, "Congress also concluded that whatever the need for women for noncombat roles during mobilization, ... it could be met by volunteers." And, "[m]ost significantly, Congress determined that staffing noncombat positions with women during a mobilization would be positively detrimental to the important goal of military flexibility." Rather than "undertaking an independent evaluation of this evidence," the District Court should have adopted "an appropriately deferential examination of *Congress'* evaluation of that evidence."

A dissent by Justice White, joined by Justice Brennan, "assume[d] what has not been challenged in this case—that excluding women from combat positions does not offend the constitution." But "[a]s I understand the record, ... the Government cannot rely on volunteers and must register and draft not only to fill combat positions and those noncombat positions that must be filled by combat-trained men, but also to secure the personnel needed for jobs that can be performed by persons ineligible for combat without diminishing military effectiveness." Justice White could "discern no adequate justification" for "discrimination between men and women" with respect to "the latter category of positions[.]"

In a separate dissent, also joined by Justice Brennan, Justice Marshall objected to the Court upholding a statute that "categorically excludes women from a fundamental civic obligation." He, too, emphasized that "this case does not involve a challenge to the statutes or policies that prohibit female members of the Armed Forces from serving in combat." His review of "the discussion and findings contained in the Senate Report" led him to conclude that at most the Report "demonstrates that drafting *very large numbers* of women would frustrate the achievement of a number of important [military] objectives[,] ... [b]ut ... do[es] not enable the Government to carry its burden of demonstrating that *completely* excluding women from the draft by excluding them from registration substantially furthers important governmental objectives."

MISSISSIPPI UNIVERSITY FOR WOMEN v. HOGAN, 458 U.S. 718 (1982). The Court held invalid a state statute that excluded males from enrolling in a state-supported professional nursing school. Justice O'Connor, writing for the Court, said that the "test for determining the validity of a gender-based classification is straightforward." without citing either *Michael M.* or *Rostker* she said: "Our decisions ... establish that the party seeking to uphold a statute that classifies individuals on the basis of their gender must carry the burden of showing an 'exceedingly persuasive justification' for the classification.... The burden is met only by showing at least that the classification serves 'important governmental objectives and that the discriminatory means employed' are 'substantially related to the achievement of those objectives.' " She also noted that the "policy of excluding males from admission to the school of nursing tends to perpetuate the stereotyped view of nursing as an exclusively women's job."

For a fuller treatment of this case, see infra p. 830. Compare with its formulation of the test for measuring the constitutionality of sex-based classifications the approach taken in each of the next two decisions.

J.E.B. v. ALABAMA EX REL. T. B., 511 U.S. 127 (1994). Beginning with Batson v. Kentucky, 476 U.S. 79 (1986), the Court had restricted the exercise of race-based peremptory challenges so that "whether the trial is criminal or civil, potential jurors, as well as litigants, have an equal protection right to jury selection procedures that are free from state-sponsored group stereotypes rooted in, and reflective of, historical prejudice." In this paternity and child support action, in which the State "used 9 of its 10 peremptory strikes to remove male jurors" (and "petitioner used all but one of his strikes to remove female jurors")—leaving the jury all-female due to a predominantly female pool—the Court extended *Batson* to "hold that gender, like race, is an unconstitutional proxy for juror competence and impartiality." It "reaffirm[ed]" that "[i]ntentional discrimination on the basis of gender by state actors violates the Equal Protection Clause, particularly where, as here, the discrimination serves to ratify and perpetuate invidious, archaic, and overbroad stereotypes about the relative abilities of men and women."

Justice Blackmun's majority opinion recounted the history of systematic discrimination against women serving on juries, from total exclusion well into the twentieth century to exemptions from mandatory jury service for women only, which the Court upheld as late as Hoyt v. Florida, 368 U.S. 57 (1961), on "the ground that women, unlike men, occupied a unique position 'as the center of home and family life.' " Then, noting the "heightened scrutiny afforded distinctions based on gender" that began in the 1970's, the Court rejected the argument that unlike racial discrimination, "gender discrimination in the selection of the petit jury should be permitted," because " 'gender discrimination in this country ... has never reached the level of discrimination' against African–Americans":

"While the prejudicial attitudes toward women in this country have not been identical to those held toward racial minorities, the similarities between the experiences of racial minorities and women, in some contexts, 'overpower those differences.' Note, Beyond Batson: Eliminating Gender–Based Peremptory Challenges, 105 Harv. L. Rev. 1920, 1921 (1992).... Certainly, with respect to jury service, African–Americans and women share a history of total exclusion, a history which came to an end for women many years after the embarrassing chapter in our history came to an end for African–Americans."

In any event, it sufficed "to acknowledge" the history of sex discrimination,

"a history which warrants the heightened scrutiny we afford all gender-based classifications today. Under our equal protection jurisprudence, gender-based classifications require 'an exceedingly persuasive justification' in order to survive constitutional scrutiny.... Thus, the only question is whether discrimination on the basis of gender in jury selection substantially furthers the State's legitimate interest in achieving a fair and impartial trial.[6] . . .

"Far from proffering an exceptionally persuasive justification for its gender-based peremptory challenges, respondent maintains that its decision to strike virtually all the males from the jury in this case 'may reasonably have been based upon the perception, supported by history, that men otherwise totally qualified to serve upon a jury might be more sympathetic and receptive to the arguments of a man alleged in a paternity action to be the father of an out-of-wedlock child, while women equally qualified to serve upon a jury might be more sympathetic and receptive to the arguments of the complaining witness who bore the child.' . . .

"We shall not accept as a defense to gender-based peremptory challenges 'the very stereotype the law condemns.' . . . Respondent offers virtually no support for the conclusion that gender alone is an accurate predictor of juror's attitudes; yet it urges this Court to condone the same stereotypes that justified the wholesale exclusion of women from juries and the ballot box.[11] Respondent seems to assume that gross generalizations that would be deemed impermissible if made on the basis of race are somehow permissible when made on the basis of gender.

"Discrimination in jury selection, whether based on race or on gender, causes harm to the litigants, the community, and the individual jurors who are wrongfully excluded from participation in the judicial process. The litigants are harmed by the risk that the prejudice which motivated the discriminatory selection of the jury will infect the entire proceedings. . . . The community is harmed by the State's participation in the perpetuation of invidious group stereotypes and the inevitable loss of confidence in our judicial system that state-sanctioned discrimination in the courtroom engenders.

"When state actors exercise peremptory challenges in reliance on gender stereotypes, they ratify and reinforce prejudicial views of the relative abilities of men and women. Because these stereotypes have wreaked injustice in so many other spheres of our country's public life, active discrimination by litigants on the basis of gender during jury selection 'invites cynicism respecting the jury's neutrality and its obligation to adhere to the law.' . . . The potential for cynicism is particularly acute in cases where gender-related issues are prominent, such as cases involving rape, sexual harassment, or paternity. . . .

"In recent cases we have emphasized that individual jurors themselves have a right to nondiscriminatory jury selection procedures. . . . Striking individual jurors on the assumption that they hold particular views simply because

6. Because we conclude that gender-based peremptory challenges are not substantially related to an important government objective, we once again need not decide whether classifications based on gender are inherently suspect. . . .

11. Even if a measure of truth can be found in some of the gender stereotypes used to justify gender-based peremptory challenges, that fact alone cannot support discrimination on the basis of gender in jury selection. We have made abundantly clear in past cases that gender classifications that rest on impermissible stereotypes violate the Equal Protection Clause, even when some statistical support can be conjured up for the generalization. . . . The generalization ad-

vanced by Alabama in support of its asserted right to discriminate on the basis of gender is, at the least, overbroad, and serves only to perpetuate the same "outmoded notions of the relative capabilities of men and women," Cleburne v. Cleburne Living Center, Inc., 473 U.S. 432, 441 (1985), that we have invalidated in other contexts. . . . The Equal Protection Clause, as interpreted by decisions of this Court, acknowledges that a shred of truth may be contained in some stereotypes, but requires that state actors look beyond the surface before making judgments about people that are likely to stigmatize as well as to perpetuate historical patterns of discrimination.

of their gender is 'practically a brand upon them, affixed by law, an assertion of their inferiority.' Strauder v. West Virginia, 100 U.S. 303, 308 (1880). It denigrates the dignity of the excluded juror, and, for a woman, reinvokes a history of exclusion from political participation.[14] The message it sends to all those in the courtroom, and all those who may later learn of the discriminatory act, is that certain individuals, for no reason other than gender, are presumed unqualified by state actors to decide important questions upon which reasonable persons could disagree."

Justice Blackmun observed that the Court's conclusion did "not imply the elimination of all peremptory challenges." Rather, "gender simply may not serve as a proxy for bias." In fact, "[p]arties may ... exercise their peremptory challenges to remove from the venire any group or class of individuals normally subject to 'rational basis' review." He also emphasized, in conclusion, the importance of equal opportunity in this context, because jury service constitutes direct "participation in our democratic processes[.]"

In a concurring opinion, Justice O'Connor urged that "today's holding should be limited to the government's use of gender-based peremptory strikes." It gave her "pause" that the decision would "increase the possibility that biased jurors will be allowed onto the jury, because sometimes a lawyer will be unable to provide an acceptable gender-neutral explanation even though the lawyer is in fact correct that the juror is unsympathetic." She elaborated:

"... We know that like race, gender matters. A plethora of studies make clear that in rape cases, for example, female jurors are somewhat more likely to vote to convict than male jurors.... Moreover, though there have been no similarly definitive studies regarding, for example, sexual harassment, child custody, or spousal or child abuse, one need not be a sexist to share the intuition that in certain cases a person's gender and resulting life experience will be relevant to his or her view of the case....

"Today's decision severely limits a litigant's ability to act on this intuition.... But to say that gender makes no difference as a matter of law is not to say that gender makes no difference as a matter of fact. I previously have said with regard to *Batson*: 'That the Court will not tolerate prosecutors' racially discriminatory use of the peremptory challenge, in effect, is a special rule of relevance, a statement about what this Nation stands for, rather than a statement of fact.' Brown v. North Carolina, 479 U.S. 940, 941–942 (1986) (O'Connor, J., concurring in denial of certiorari). Today's decision is a statement that, in an effort to eliminate the potential discriminatory use of the peremptory, ... gender is now governed by the special rule of relevance formerly reserved for race. Though we gain much from this statement, we cannot ignore what we lose. In extending *Batson* to gender we have added an additional burden to the state and federal trial process, taken a step closer to eliminating the peremptory challenge, and diminished the ability of litigants to act on sometimes accurate gender-based assumptions about juror attitudes."

These concerns led Justice O'Connor to the "position that the Equal Protection Clause does not limit the exercise of peremptory challenges by

---

14. The popular refrain is that all peremptory challenges are based on stereotypes of some kind, expressing various intuitive and frequently erroneous biases. But where peremptory challenges are made on the basis of group characteristics other than race or gender (like occupation, for example), they do not reinforce the same stereotypes about the group's competence or predispositions that have been used to prevent them from voting, participating on juries, pursuing their chosen professions, or otherwise contributing to civic life. See B. Babcock, A Place in the Palladium, Women's Rights and Jury Service, 61 U. Cinn. L. Rev. 1139, 1173 (1993).

private civil litigants and criminal defendants." She asked whether the Court later might preclude "the battered wife—on trial for wounding her abusive husband— ... from using her peremptory challenges to ensure that the jury of her peers contains as many women members as possible?" Her own reply was: "I assume we will, but I hope we will not."

Concurring in the judgment, Justice Kennedy said in part:

" ... For purposes of the Equal Protection Clause, an individual denied jury service because of a peremptory challenge exercised against her on account of her sex is no less injured than the individual denied jury service because of a law banning members of her sex from serving as jurors.... The injury is to personal dignity and to the individual's right to participate in the political process....

" ...

"[I]t is important to recognize that a juror sits not as a representative of a racial or sexual group but as an individual citizen. Nothing would be more pernicious to the jury system than for society to presume that persons of different backgrounds go to the jury room to voice prejudice.... The jury pool must be representative of the community, but that is a structural mechanism for preventing bias, not enfranchising it...."

Chief Justice Rehnquist dissented, finding "sufficient differences between race and gender discrimination such that the principle of *Batson* should not be extended to peremptory challenges to potential jurors based on sex." Those differences include a "less searching standard of review" for gender classifications; that, unlike women, "[r]acial groups comprise numerical minorities in our society"; that "racial equality has proved a more challenging goal to achieve on many fronts than gender equality"; and that "*Batson* is best understood as a recognition that race lies at the core of the commands of the Fourteenth Amendment." Accordingly, "[u]nder the Equal Protection Clause, these differences mean that the balance should tilt in favor of peremptory challenges when sex, not race, is the issue." The Chief Justice also made these observations:

" ... The two sexes differ, both biologically and, to a diminishing extent, in experience. It is not merely 'stereotyping' to say that these differences may produce a difference in outlook which is brought to the jury room. Accordingly, use of peremptory challenges on the basis of sex is generally not the sort of derogatory and invidious act which peremptory challenges directed at black jurors may be."

In a separate dissent, Justice Scalia, joined by the Chief Justice and Justice Thomas, argued that the Court's objection to "the use of sex as a proxy for particular views or sympathies ... seems to place the Court in opposition to its earlier Sixth Amendment 'fair cross-section' cases[.]" Furthermore, "if men and women jurors are (as the Court thinks) fungible, then the only arguable injury from the prosecutor's 'impermissible' use of male sex as the basis for his peremptories is injury to the stricken juror, not to the defendant." Justice Scalia also faulted the Court for "focusing unrealistically upon individual exercises of the peremptory challenge, and ignoring the totality of the practice." That all sides can exercise peremptories

"explains why peremptory challenges coexisted with the Equal Protection Clause for 120 years.... The situation would be different if both sides systematically struck individuals of one group, so that the strikes evinced group-based animus and served as a proxy for segregated venire lists.... The pattern here, however, displays not a systemic sex-based animus but

each side's desire to get a jury favorably disposed to its case. That is why the Court's characterization of respondent's argument as 'reminiscent of the arguments advanced to justify the total exclusion of women from juries,' is patently false. Women were categorically excluded from juries because of doubt that they were competent; women are stricken from juries by peremptory challenge because of doubt that they are well disposed to the striking party's case.... There is discrimination and dishonor in the former, and not in the latter...."

United States v. Virginia

518 U.S. 515, 116 S.Ct. 2264, 135 L.Ed.2d 735 (1996).

Justice Ginsburg delivered the opinion of the Court.

Virginia's public institutions of higher learning include an incomparable military college, Virginia Military Institute (VMI). The United States maintains that the Constitution's equal protection guarantee precludes Virginia from reserving exclusively to men the unique educational opportunities VMI affords. We agree.

cant prohibit~~ allow exclusive educational opp. to VMI

I

Founded in 1839, VMI is today the sole single-sex school among Virginia's 15 public institutions of higher learning. VMI's distinctive mission is to produce "citizen-soldiers," men prepared for leadership in civilian life and in military service. VMI pursues this mission through pervasive training of a kind not available anywhere else in Virginia[—] ... an "adversative method" [that] constantly endeavors to instill physical and mental discipline in its cadets and impart to them a strong moral code. ...

. . .

Neither the goal of producing citizen-soldiers nor VMI's implementing methodology is inherently unsuitable to women. And the school's impressive record in producing leaders has made admission desirable to some women. ...

II

. . .

VMI today enrolls about 1,300 men as cadets. ...

VMI['s] ... "... adversative, or doubting, model of education" ... features "[p]hysical rigor, mental stress, absolute equality of treatment, absence of privacy, minute regulation of behavior, and indoctrination in desirable values." ...

VMI cadets live in spartan barracks where surveillance is constant and privacy nonexistent; they wear uniforms, eat together in the mess hall, and regularly participate in drills. ... Entering students are incessantly exposed to the rat line, "an extreme form of the adversative model," comparable in intensity to Marine Corps boot camp. ...

. . .

[The United States, prompted by a female applicant's complaint, sued Virginia and VMI in 1990. The District Court ruled in favor of VMI but the Fourth Circuit reversed and remanded,] suggest[ing] these options for the State: Admit women to VMI; establish parallel institutions or programs; or

3 options

opened parallel school for women

abandon state support, leaving VMI free to pursue its policies as a private institution. . . .

. . . Virginia proposed a parallel program for women: Virginia Women's Institute for Leadership (VWIL). The 4–year, state-sponsored undergraduate program would be located at Mary Baldwin College, a private liberal arts school for women, and would be open, initially, to about 25 to 30 students. Although VWIL would share VMI's mission—to produce "citizen-soldiers"—the VWIL program would differ, as does Mary Baldwin College, from VMI in academic offerings, methods of education, and financial resources. . . .

. . .

[T]he District Court . . . decided the plan met the requirements of the Equal Protection Clause. . . .

A divided Court of Appeals affirmed. . . .

. . .

III

[T]his case present[s] two ultimate issues. First, does Virginia's exclusion of women from the educational opportunities provided by VMI—extraordinary opportunities for military training and civilian leadership development—deny to women "capable of all of the individual activities required of VMI cadets," . . . the equal protection of the laws guaranteed by the Fourteenth Amendment? Second, if VMI's "unique" situation . . . as Virginia's sole single-sex public institution of higher education . . . offends the Constitution's equal protection principle, what is the remedial requirement?

IV

We note, once again, the core instruction of this Court's pathmarking decisions in J.E.B. v. Alabama ex rel. T. B., . . . and *Mississippi Univ. for Women*, . . . : Parties who seek to defend gender-based government action must demonstrate an "exceedingly persuasive justification" for that action.

. . .

. . . Since *Reed*, the Court has repeatedly recognized that neither federal nor state government acts compatibly with the equal protection principle when a law or official policy denies to women, simply because they are women, full citizenship stature—equal opportunity to aspire, achieve, participate in and contribute to society based on their individual talents and capacities. . . .

. . . To summarize the Court's current directions for cases of official classification based on gender: Focusing on the differential treatment or denial of opportunity for which relief is sought, the reviewing court must determine whether the proffered justification is "exceedingly persuasive." The burden of justification is demanding and it rests entirely on the State. . . . The State must show "at least that the [challenged] classification serves 'important governmental objectives and that the discriminatory means employed' are 'substantially related to the achievement of those objectives.' " . . . The justification must be genuine, not hypothesized or invented *post hoc* in response to litigation. And it must not rely on overbroad generalizations about the different talents, capacities, or preferences of males and females. . . .

The heightened review standard our precedent establishes does not make sex a proscribed classification. . . . Physical differences between men and women . . . are enduring. . . .

"Inherent differences" between men and women ... remain cause for celebration, but not for denigration of the members of either sex or for artificial constraints on an individual's opportunity. Sex classifications may be used to compensate women "for particular economic disabilities [they have] suffered," ... to "promot[e] equal employment opportunity," ... to advance full development of the talent and capacities of our Nation's people. ... But such classifications may not be used, as they once were, ... to create or perpetuate the legal, social, and economic inferiority of women.

[W]e conclude that Virginia has shown no "exceedingly persuasive justification" for excluding all women from the citizen-soldier training afforded by VMI. ... Because the remedy proffered by Virginia—the Mary Baldwin VWIL program—does not cure the constitutional violation, i.e., it does not provide equal opportunity, we reverse. ...

V

... Virginia ... asserts two justifications in defense of VMI's exclusion of women. First, ... "single-sex education provides important educational benefits," ... and the option of single-sex education contributes to "diversity in educational approaches,". ... Second, ... "the unique VMI method of character development and leadership training," the school's adversative approach, would have to be modified were VMI to admit women. ...

A

Single-sex education affords pedagogical benefits to at least some students, ... and that reality is uncontested in this litigation. Similarly, it is not disputed that diversity among public educational institutions can serve the public good. But Virginia has not shown that VMI was established, or has been maintained, with a view to diversifying, by its categorical exclusion of women, educational opportunities within the State. In cases of this genre, our precedent instructs that "benign" justifications proffered in defense of categorical exclusions will not be accepted automatically; a tenable justification must describe actual state purposes, not rationalizations for actions in fact differently grounded. ...

. . .

Neither recent nor distant history bears out Virginia's alleged pursuit of diversity through single-sex educational options....

. . .

Virginia describes the current absence of public single-sex higher education for women as "an historical anomaly." ... But the historical record indicates action more deliberate than anomalous: First, protection of women against higher education; next, schools for women far from equal in resources and stature to schools for men; finally, conversion of the separate schools to coeducation....

Our 1982 decision in *Mississippi Univ. for Women* prompted VMI to reexamine its male-only admission policy.... A Mission Study Committee ... studied the problem from October 1983 until May 1986, and in that month counseled against "change of VMI status as a single-sex college." ... [W]e can hardly extract from that effort any state policy evenhandedly to advance diverse educational options. As the District Court observed, the Committee's analysis "primarily focuse[d] on anticipated difficulties in attracting females to VMI," and the report, overall, supplied "very little indication of how th[e] conclusion was reached."

In sum, we find no persuasive evidence in this record that VMI's male-only admission policy "is in furtherance of a state policy of 'diversity.'" ... A purpose genuinely to advance an array of educational options ... is not served by VMI's historic and constant plan—a plan to "affor[d] a unique educational benefit only to males." ... However "liberally" this plan serves the State's sons, it makes no provision whatever for her daughters. That is not equal protection.

B

[handwritten margin note: argue not possible to provide training unmodified to women]

Virginia next argues that VMI's adversative method of training provides educational benefits that cannot be made available, unmodified, to women. Alterations to accommodate women would necessarily be ... so "drastic," ... as to transform, indeed "destroy," VMI's program. ... Neither sex would be favored ...: Men would be deprived of the unique opportunity currently available to them; women would not gain that opportunity because their participation would "eliminat[e] the very aspects of [the] program that distinguish [VMI] ..." ...

The District Court forecast from expert witness testimony, and the Court of Appeals accepted, that coeducation would materially affect "at least these three aspects of VMI's program—physical training, the absence of privacy, and the adversative approach." ... And it is uncontested that women's admission would require accommodations, primarily in arranging housing assignments and physical training programs for female cadets. ... It is also undisputed, however, that "the VMI methodology could be used to educate women." ... The District Court even allowed that some women may prefer it to the methodology a women's college might pursue. ... ["S]ome women," the expert testimony established, "are capable of all of the individual activities required of VMI cadets," [and t]he parties ... agree that "some women can meet the physical standards [VMI] now impose[s] on men." ... In sum, as the Court of Appeals stated, "neither the goal of producing citizen soldiers," VMI's *raison d'etre*, "nor VMI's implementing methodology is inherently unsuitable to women." ...

... [T]he District Court made "findings" on "gender-based developmental differences[,]" [that] restate the opinions of Virginia's expert witnesses, opinions about typically male or typically female "tendencies." ... For example, "[m]ales tend to need an atmosphere of adversativeness," while "[f]emales tend to thrive in a cooperative atmosphere." ...

The United States does not challenge any expert witness estimation on average capacities or preferences of men and women. Instead, the United States emphasizes that ... we have cautioned reviewing courts to take a "hard look" at generalizations or "tendencies" of the kind pressed by Virginia, and relied upon by the District Court. ... State actors controlling gates to opportunity, we have instructed, may not exclude qualified individuals based on "fixed notions concerning the roles and abilities of males and females." ...

It may be assumed ... that most women would not choose VMI's adversative method. ... [H]owever, ... it is also probable that "many men would not want to be educated in such an environment." ... The issue, however, is not whether "women—or men—should be forced to attend VMI" [but] whether the State can constitutionally deny to women who have the will and capacity, the training and attendant opportunities that VMI uniquely affords. ...

The notion that admission of women would downgrade VMI's stature, destroy the adversative system and, with it, even the school, is a judgment hardly proved, a prediction hardly different from other "self-fulfilling prophec[ies]," ... once routinely used to deny rights or opportunities. When women first sought admission to the bar and access to legal education, concerns of the same order were expressed. ...

Medical faculties similarly resisted men and women as partners in the study of medicine. ...

Women's successful entry into the federal military academies, and their participation in the Nation's military forces, indicate that Virginia's fears for the future of VMI may not be solidly grounded. ... The State's justification for excluding all women from "citizen-soldier" training for which some are qualified, in any event, cannot rank as "exceedingly persuasive," as we have explained and applied that standard.

. . .

... Surely ... the State's great goal is not substantially advanced by women's categorical exclusion, in total disregard of their individual merit, from the State's premier "citizen-soldier" corps. Virginia, in sum, "has fallen far short of establishing the 'exceedingly persuasive justification,'" ... that must be the solid base for any gender-defined classification.

VI

In the second phase of the litigation, Virginia presented its remedial plan—maintain VMI as a male-only college and create VWIL as a separate program for women. The plan met District Court approval. The Fourth Circuit ... deferentially reviewed the State's proposal and decided that the two single-sex programs directly served Virginia's reasserted purposes: single-gender education, and "achieving the results of an adversative method in a military environment." ... [T]he Court of Appeals concluded that Virginia had arranged for men and women opportunities "sufficiently comparable" to survive equal protection evaluation....

Lower cts held that remedy was adequate

A

A remedial decree ... must closely fit the constitutional violation; it must be shaped to place persons unconstitutionally denied an opportunity or advantage in "the position they would have occupied in the absence of [discrimination]." See Milliken v. Bradley, 433 U.S. 267, 280 (1977). ... The constitutional violation in this case is the categorical exclusion of women from an extraordinary educational opportunity afforded men. A proper remedy for an unconstitutional exclusion, we have explained, aims to "eliminate [so far as possible] the discriminatory effects of the past" and to "bar like discrimination in the future." ...

remedy must fit violation

Virginia chose not to eliminate, but to leave untouched, VMI's exclusionary policy. For women only, however, Virginia proposed a separate program, different in kind from VMI and unequal in tangible and intangible facilities. ...

VWIL affords women no opportunity to experience the rigorous military training for which VMI is famed. ... Instead, the VWIL program "deemphasize[s]" military education, ... and uses a "cooperative method" of education "which reinforces self-esteem,". ...

VWIL students participate in ROTC and a "largely ceremonial" Virginia Corps of Cadets, ... but Virginia deliberately did not make VWIL a military institute. The VWIL House is not a military-style residence and VWIL students need not live together throughout the 4–year program, eat meals together, or wear uniforms during the school day. ... VWIL students thus do not experi-

Is not the same experience

ence the "barracks" life "crucial to the VMI experience," the spartan living arrangements designed to foster an "egalitarian ethic." ... Virginia deemed that core experience nonessential, indeed inappropriate, for training its female citizen-soldiers.

VWIL students ... [are k]ept away from the pressures, hazards, and psychological bonding characteristic of VMI's adversative training, [and thus] will not know the "feeling of tremendous accomplishment" commonly experienced by VMI's successful cadets. ...

Virginia maintains that these methodological differences are "justified pedagogically," based on "important differences between men and women in learning and developmental needs," "psychological and sociological differences" Virginia describes as "real" and "not stereotypes." ...

... [G]eneralizations about "the way women are," estimates of what is appropriate for *most women*, no longer justify denying opportunity to women whose talent and capacity place them outside the average description. Notably, Virginia never asserted that VMI's method of education suits *most men*. It is also revealing that Virginia accounted for its failure to make the VWIL experience "the entirely militaristic experience of VMI" on the ground that VWIL "is planned for women who do not necessarily expect to pursue military careers." ... By that reasoning, VMI's "entirely militaristic" program would be inappropriate for men in general or *as a group*, for "[o]nly about 15% of VMI cadets enter career military service." ...

cant stereotype women, some do fine under those circumstances

In contrast to the generalizations about women on which Virginia rests, we note again these dispositive realities: VMI's "implementing methodology" is not "inherently unsuitable to women," ...; "some women ... do well under [the] adversative model," ...; "some women, at least, would want to attend [VMI] if they had the opportunity," ...; "some women are capable of all of the individual activities required of VMI cadets," ... and "can meet the physical standards [VMI] now impose[s] on men,". ... It is on behalf of these women that the United States has instituted this suit, and it is for them that a remedy must be crafted,[19] a remedy that will end their exclusion from a state-supplied educational opportunity for which they are fit, a decree that will "bar like discrimination in the future." ...

B

In myriad respects other than military training, VWIL does not qualify as VMI's equal. VWIL's student body, faculty, course offerings, and facilities hardly match VMI's. Nor can the VWIL graduate anticipate the benefits associated with VMI's 157–year history, the school's prestige, and its influential alumni network.

... [T]he ... VWIL program [is] fairly appraised as a "pale shadow" of VMI in terms of the range of curricular choices and faculty stature, funding, prestige, alumni support and influence. ...

Virginia's VWIL solution is reminiscent of ... Sweatt v. Painter, 339 U.S. 629 (1950). Reluctant to admit African Americans to its flagship University of Texas Law School, the State set up a separate school for Herman Sweatt and other black law students. ...

---

19. Admitting women to VMI would undoubtedly require alterations necessary to afford members of each sex privacy from the other sex in living arrangements, and to adjust aspects of the physical training programs. ... Experience shows such adjustments are manageable. See U.S. Military Academy, ... Report of Admission of Women ... (1977–1980) (4–year longitudinal study of the admission of women to West Point). ...

... This Court contrasted resources at the new school with those at the school from which Sweatt had been excluded. ...

More important than the tangible features, the Court emphasized, are "those qualities which are incapable of objective measurement but which make for greatness" in a school, including "reputation of the faculty, experience of the administration, position and influence of the alumni, standing in the community, traditions and prestige." ... [T]he Court unanimously ruled that Texas had not shown "substantial equality in the [separate] educational opportunities" the State offered. ... In line with *Sweatt*, we rule here that Virginia has not shown substantial equality in the separate educational opportunities the State supports at VWIL and VMI.

C

. . .

The Fourth Circuit plainly erred in exposing Virginia's VWIL plan to a deferential analysis, for "all gender-based classifications today" warrant "heightened scrutiny." ... [T]he State has shown no "exceedingly persuasive justification" for withholding from women qualified for the experience premier training of the kind VMI affords.

. . .

Justice Thomas took no part in the consideration or decision of this case.

Chief Justice Rehnquist, concurring in the judgment.

. . .

I

Two decades ago in Craig v. Boren, 429 U.S. 190, 197 (1976), we announced that "[t]o withstand constitutional challenge, ... classifications by gender must serve important governmental objectives and must be substantially related to achievement of those objectives." We have adhered to that standard of scrutiny ever since. ... While the majority adheres to this test today, it also says that the State must demonstrate an " 'exceedingly persuasive justification' " to support a gender-based classification. It is unfortunate that the Court thereby introduces an element of uncertainty respecting the appropriate test.

While terms like "important governmental objective" and "substantially related" are hardly models of precision, they have more content and specificity than does the phrase "exceedingly persuasive justification." That phrase is best confined, as it was first used, as an observation on the difficulty of meeting the applicable test, not as a formulation of the test itself. ...

Our cases dealing with gender discrimination also require that the proffered purpose for the challenged law be the actual purpose. [O]n this ground ... the Court rejects the first of two justifications Virginia offers[—]the goal of diversity among its public educational institutions. While I ultimately agree that the State has not carried the day with this justification, I disagree with the Court's method of analyzing the issue.

. . .

... [Not until the 1982 *Mississippi University for Women* decision was] Virginia [placed] on notice that VMI's men-only admissions policy was open to serious question.

. . . .

... I agree with the Court that there is scant evidence in the record that [diversity in education with room for single-sex institutions] was the real reason that Virginia decided to maintain VMI as men only.* But, unlike the majority, I would consider only evidence that postdates ... *Hogan*, and would draw no negative inferences from the State's actions before that time. [A]fter *Hogan*, the State was entitled to reconsider its policy with respect to VMI, and to not have earlier justifications, or lack thereof, held against it.

Even if diversity in educational opportunity were the State's actual objective, the State's position would still be problematic[, because] ... the diversity benefited only one sex; there was single-sex public education available for men at VMI, but no corresponding single-sex public education available for women. . . .

I do not think, however, that the State's options were as limited as the majority may imply. . . . Had Virginia made a genuine effort to devote comparable public resources to a facility for women, and followed through on such a plan, it might well have avoided an equal protection violation. . . .

But ... neither the governing board of VMI nor the State took any action after 1982. If diversity in the form of single-sex, as well as coeducational, institutions of higher learning were to be available to Virginians, that diversity had to be available to women as well as to men.

The dissent criticizes me for "disregarding the four all-women's private colleges in Virginia (generously assisted by public funds)." The private women's colleges are treated by the State exactly as all other private schools are treated, which includes the provision of tuition-assistance grants to Virginia residents. Virginia gives no special support to the women's single-sex education. But obviously, the same is not true for men's education. Had the State provided the kind of support for the private women's schools that it provides for VMI, this may have been a very different case. For in so doing, the State would have demonstrated that its interest in providing a single-sex education for men, was to some measure matched by an interest in providing the same opportunity for women.

Virginia offers a second justification for the single-sex admissions policy: maintenance of the adversative method. I agree with the Court that this justification does not serve an important governmental objective. A State does not have substantial interest in the adversative methodology unless it is pedagogically beneficial[, and] ... there is no ... evidence in the record that an adversative method is pedagogically beneficial or is any more likely to produce character traits than other methodologies.

---

* The dissent equates our conclusion that VMI's "asserted interest in promoting diversity" is not " 'genuine,' " with a "charge" that the diversity rationale is "a pretext for discriminating against women." Of course, those are not the same thing. I do not read the Court as saying that the diversity rationale is a pretext for discrimination, and I would not endorse such a proposition. We may find that diversity was not the State's real reason without suggesting, or having to show, that the real reason was "antifeminism." Our cases simply require that the proffered purpose ... be the actual purpose, although not necessarily recorded. The dissent also says that the interest in diversity is so transparent that having to articulate it is "absurd on its face." Apparently, that rationale was not obvious to the Mission Study Committee which failed to list it among its reasons for maintaining VMI's all-men admission policy.

II

... [I]t is not the "exclusion of women" that violates the Equal Protection Clause, but the maintenance of an all-men school without providing any—much less a comparable—institution for women.

Accordingly, the remedy should not necessarily require either the admission of women to VMI, or the creation of a VMI clone for women. An adequate remedy ... might be a demonstration by Virginia that its interest in educating men in a single-sex environment is matched by its interest in educating women in a single-sex institution. ... It would ... suffic[e] if the two institutions offered the same quality of education and were of the same overall calibre.

If a state decides to create single-sex programs, [it] would, I expect, consider the public's interest and demand in designing curricula. And rightfully so. But the state should avoid assuming demand based on stereotypes; it must not assume *a priori*, without evidence, that there would be no interest in a women's school of civil engineering, or in a men's school of nursing.

In the end, ... VWIL ... fails as a remedy, because it is distinctly inferior to the existing men's institution and will continue to be for the foreseeable future. VWIL simply is not, in any sense, the institution that VMI is. In particular, VWIL is ... appended to a private college, not a self-standing institution; and VWIL is substantially underfunded as compared to VMI. I therefore ultimately agree with the Court that Virginia has not provided an adequate remedy.

Justice Scalia, dissenting.

Today the Court ... rejects ... the factual findings of two courts below, sweeps aside the precedents of this Court, and ignores the history of our people. As to facts: it explicitly rejects the finding that there exist "gender-based developmental differences" supporting Virginia's restriction of the "adversative" method to only a men's institution, and the finding that the all-male composition of ... VMI is essential to [its] character. As to precedent: it drastically revises our established standards for reviewing sex-based classifications. And as to history: it counts for nothing the long tradition ... of men's military colleges supported by both States and the Federal Government.

I

. . .

... [I]n my view the function of this Court is to preserve our society's values regarding (among other things) equal protection, not to revise them; to prevent backsliding from the degree of restriction the Constitution imposed upon democratic government, not to prescribe, on our own authority, progressively higher degrees. For that reason, it is my view that, whatever abstract tests we ... devise, they cannot supersede—and indeed ought to be crafted *so as to reflect*—those constant and unbroken national traditions that embody the people's understanding of ambiguous constitutional texts....

... [T]he tradition of having government-funded military schools for men is as well rooted in the traditions of this country as the tradition of sending only men into military combat. The people may decide to change the[m] through democratic processes; but the assertion that either tradition has been unconstitutional through the centuries is not law, but politics-smuggled-into-law.

And the same applies, more broadly, to single-sex education in general, which ... is threatened by today's decision with the cut-off of all state and federal support. ...

. . .

II

Only the amorphous "exceedingly persuasive justification" phrase, and not the standard elaboration of intermediate scrutiny, can be made to yield th[e] conclusion that VMI's single-sex composition is unconstitutional because there exist several women (or, one would have to conclude under the Court's reasoning, a single woman) willing and able to undertake VMI's program. Intermediate scrutiny has never required a least-restrictive-means analysis, but only a "substantial relation" between the classification and the state interests that it serves. ... There is simply no support in our cases for the notion that a sex-based classification is invalid unless it relates to characteristics that hold true in every instance.

[I]f the ... applicable standard of review for sex-based classifications were ... reconsider[ed], the stronger argument would be not for elevating the standard to strict scrutiny, but for reducing it to rational-basis review. The latter certainly has a firmer foundation in our past jurisprudence: Whereas no majority of the Court has ever applied strict scrutiny in a case involving sex-based classifications, we routinely applied rational-basis review until the 1970's. ... And of course normal, rational-basis review of sex-based classifications would be much more in accord with the genesis of heightened standards of judicial review, the famous footnote in United States v. Carolene Products Co., 304 U.S. 144 (1938). ... It is hard to consider women a "discrete and insular minorit[y]" unable to employ the "political processes ordinarily to be relied upon," when they constitute a majority of the electorate. And the suggestion that they are incapable of exerting that political power smacks of the same paternalism that the Court so roundly condemns. Moreover, a long list of legislation proves the proposition false. See, e.g., Equal Pay Act of 1963 ...; Title VII of the Civil Rights Act of 1964 ...; Title IX of the Education Amendments of 1972. ...; Women's Business Ownership Act of 1988. ...; Violence Against Women Act of 1994. ...

III

... [T]he question ... is whether the exclusion of women from VMI is "substantially related to an important governmental objective."

A

... Virginia has an important state interest in providing effective college education for its citizens. That single-sex instruction is an approach substantially related to that interest should be evident enough from the long and continuing history in this country of men's and women's colleges....

. . .

... [S]o too a State's decision to maintain within its system one school that provides the adversative method is "substantially related" to its goal of good education. Moreover, it was uncontested that "if the state were to establish a women's VMI-type [i.e., adversative] program, the program would attract an insufficient number of participants to make the program work," ...; and it was found by the District Court that if Virginia were to include women in VMI, the school "would eventually find it necessary to drop the adversative system altogether,". . . . Thus, Virginia's options were an adversative method that excludes women or no adversative method at all.

[S]ingle-sex education and a distinctive educational method "represent legitimate contributions to diversity in the Virginia higher education system." . . .

. . . Substantial evidence in the District Court [also] demonstrated that the Commonwealth has long proceeded on the principle that " '[h]igher education resources should be viewed as a whole—public and private' "—because such an approach enhances diversity and because " 'it is academic and economic waste to permit unwarranted duplication.' " . . . (quoting 1974 Report of the General Assembly Commission on Higher Education to the General Assembly of Virginia). It is thus significant that, whereas there are "four all-female private [colleges] in Virginia," there is only "one private all-male college," which "indicates that the private sector is providing for th[e] [former] form of education to a much greater extent that it provides for all-male education." . . . In these circumstances, Virginia's election to fund one public all-male institution and one on the adversative model—and to concentrate its resources in a single entity that serves both these interests in diversity—is substantially related to the State's important educational interests.

B

. . .

. . . [T]hat VMI would not have to change very much if it were to admit women . . . is irrelevant. . . .

But if . . . relevant, the Court would certainly be on the losing side[, given] . . . findings by two courts below, amply supported by the evidence, . . . that VMI would be fundamentally altered if it admitted women. . . .[5]

. . . Finally, the absence of a precise "all-women's analogue" to VMI is irrelevant. In Mississippi Univ. for Women v. Hogan, 458 U.S. 718 (1982), we attached no constitutional significance to the absence of an all-male nursing school. . . .

. . . VWIL [also] is, under our established test, irrelevant, so long as VMI's all-male character is "substantially related" to an important state goal. . . .

. . .

C

[T]he concurrence . . . finds VMI unconstitutional on a basis that is more moderate than the Court's but only at the expense of being even more implausible. . . . First, . . . it is absurd on its face even to *demand* "evidence" to prove that the Commonwealth's reason for maintaining a men's military academy is that a men's military academy provides a distinctive type of educational experience (i.e., fosters diversity). What other purpose *would* the Commonwealth have? . . .

Second, the . . . pedagogical benefits of VMI's adversative approach were not only proved, but were a given in this litigation. The reason the woman

---

5. The Court's do-it-yourself approach to factfinding . . . is exemplified by its invocation of the experience of the federal military academies to prove that not much change would occur. In fact, the District Court noted that "the West Point experience" supported the theory that a coeducational VMI would have to "adopt a [different] system," for West Point found it necessary upon becoming coeducational to "move away" from its adversative system. . . .

applicant who prompted this suit wanted to enter VMI was . . . [that s]he wanted the distinctive adversative education that VMI provided. . . .

[T]hird[, as for the view of the] concurrence . . . that after our decision in *Hogan* . . . the Commonwealth should have known that what this Court expected of it was . . . the creation of a state all-women's program[, a]ny lawyer who gave that advice . . . ought to have been either disbarred or committed. . . .

In any event, "diversity in the form of single-sex, as well as coeducational, institutions of higher learning," *is* "available to women as well as to men" in Virginia. The concurrence is able to assert the contrary only by disregarding the four all-women's private colleges in Virginia (generously assisted by public funds) and the Commonwealth's longstanding policy of coordinating public with private educational offerings. . . .

IV

. . .

Under the constitutional principles announced and applied today, single-sex public education is unconstitutional . . . [even though] the Court creates the illusion that government officials in some future case will have a clear shot at justifying some sort of single-sex public education. . . .

. . .

. . . [T]he Court indicates that if any program restricted to one sex is "uniqu[e]," it must be opened to members of the opposite sex "who have the will and capacity" to participate in it. [T]he single-sex program [in]capable of being characterized as "unique" is . . . nonexistent.

. . .

There are few extant single-sex public educational programs. The potential of today's decision for widespread disruption of existing institutions lies in its application to private single-sex education. . . .

. . .

NGUYEN v. IMMIGRATION AND NATURALIZATION SERVICE, 533 U.S. 53 (2001). Born in Vietnam in 1969 to an American citizen father and a Vietnamese citizen mother who never married each other, Nguyen came to the United States at age six, became a lawful permanent resident, and was raised in Texas by his father. At 22, he pleaded guilty to state child sexual assault charges and was sent to prison. During his confinement the INS successfully brought deportation proceedings against him as an alien convict, despite his father having obtained a DNA-based paternity declaration from a state court when Nguyen was 28. The Board of Immigration Appeals rejected his citizenship claim for noncompliance with 8 U.S.C. § 1409(a), which provides that a child born outside the United States to unmarried parents is not a citizen if his mother is an alien and his father is a citizen, unless

"(1) a blood relationship between the person and the father is established by clear and convincing evidence,

"(2) the father had the nationality of the United States at the time of the person's birth,

"(3) the father (unless deceased) has agreed in writing to provide financial support for the person until the person reaches the age of 18 years, and

"(4) while the person is under the age of 18 years—

"(A) the person is legitimated under the law of the person's residence or domicile,

"(B) the father acknowledges paternity of the person in writing under oath, or

"(C) the paternity of the person is established by adjudication of a competent court."

Although it was conceded that his father's paternity had not been established before he was 18, as § 1409(a)(4) required, Nguyen asserted that the requirement denied "the equal protection guarantee embedded in the Due Process Clause of the Fifth Amendment[,]" because children born abroad to an unwed alien father and citizen mother, notwithstanding § 1409(a), are automatically citizens at birth "if the mother had the nationality of the United States at the time of such person's birth, and if the mother had previously been physically present in the United States or one of its outlying possessions for a continuous period of one year...." § 1409(c). The Court of Appeals rejected the equal protection challenge, and the Supreme Court affirmed. Justice Kennedy's opinion for the Court said in part:

Automatically citizen if Born to citizen mother

"For a gender-based classification to withstand equal protection scrutiny, it must be established ' "at least that the [challenged] classification serves 'important governmental objectives and that the discriminatory means employed' are 'substantially related to the achievement of those objectives.' " ' United States v. Virginia.... § 1409 satisfies this standard. Given that determination, we need not decide whether some lesser degree of scrutiny pertains because the statute implicates Congress' immigration and naturalization power....

"[Two preliminary] observations concerning the operation of the provision are in order. First, a citizen mother expecting a child and living abroad has the right to re-enter the United States so the child can be born here and be a 14th Amendment citizen. From one perspective, then, the statute simply ensures equivalence between two expectant mothers who are citizens abroad if one chooses to reenter for the child's birth and the other chooses not to return, or does not have the means to do so.... [U]nlike the unmarried mother, the unmarried father as a general rule cannot control where the child will be born.

"Second, although § 1409(a)(4) requires certain conduct to occur before the child of a citizen father, born out of wedlock and abroad, reaches 18 years of age, it imposes no limitations on when an individual who qualifies under the statute can claim citizenship. The statutory treatment of citizenship is identical in this respect whether the citizen parent is the mother or the father. A person born to a citizen parent of either gender may assert citizenship, assuming compliance with statutory preconditions, regardless of his or her age. And while the conditions necessary for a citizen mother to transmit citizenship under § 1409(c) exist at birth, citizen fathers and/or their children have 18 years to satisfy the requirements of § 1409(a)(4)....

"... Congress' decision to impose requirements on unmarried fathers that differ from those on unmarried mothers is based on the significant difference between their respective relationships to the potential citizen at the time of birth. Specifically, the imposition of the requirement for a paternal relationship, but not a maternal one, is justified by two important governmental objectives....

"The first ... is the importance of assuring that a biological parent-child relationship exists. In the case of the mother, the relation is verifiable from the birth itself. The mother's status is documented in most instances by the birth certificate or hospital records and the witnesses who attest to her having given birth.

"In the case of the father, the uncontestable fact is that he need not be present at the birth. . . . If he is present, furthermore, that circumstance is not incontrovertible proof of fatherhood. Fathers and mothers are not similarly situated with regard to the proof of biological parenthood. The imposition of a different set of rules for making that legal determination with respect to fathers and mothers is neither surprising nor troublesome from a constitutional perspective. . . . Section 1409(a)(4)'s provision of three options for a father seeking to establish paternity—legitimation, paternity oath, and court order of paternity—is designed to ensure an acceptable documentation of paternity.

"Petitioners argue that the requirement of § 1409(a)(1), that a father provide clear and convincing evidence of parentage, is sufficient to achieve the end of establishing paternity, given the sophistication of modern DNA tests. . . . [T]he expense, reliability, and availability of such testing in various parts of the world may have been of particular concern to Congress. . . . The requirement of § 1409(a)(4) represents a reasonable conclusion by the legislature that the satisfaction of one of several alternatives will suffice to establish the blood link between father and child required as a predicate to the child's acquisition of citizenship. . . . Given the proof of motherhood that is inherent in birth itself, it is unremarkable that Congress did not require the same affirmative steps of mothers.

"Finally, to require Congress to speak without reference to the gender of the parent with regard to its objective of ensuring a blood tie between parent and child would be to insist on a hollow neutrality. . . . Congress could have required both mothers and fathers to prove parenthood within 30 days or, for that matter, 18 years, of the child's birth. . . . The differential treatment is inherent in a sensible statutory scheme, given the unique relationship of the mother to the event of birth.

"The second important governmental interest furthered in a substantial manner by § 1409(a)(4) is the determination to ensure that the child and the citizen parent have some demonstrated opportunity or potential to develop not just a relationship that is recognized, as a formal matter, by the law, but one that consists of the real, everyday ties that provide a connection between child and citizen parent and, in turn, the United States. . . . In the case of a citizen mother and a child born overseas, the opportunity for a meaningful relationship between citizen parent and child inheres in the very event of birth, an event so often critical to our constitutional and statutory understandings of citizenship. . . .

"The same opportunity does not result from the event of birth, as a matter of biological inevitability, in the case of the unwed father. [I]t is not always certain that a father will know that a child was conceived, nor is it always clear that even the mother will be sure of the father's identity. . . . One concern in this context has always been with young people, men for the most part, who are on duty with the Armed Forces in foreign countries. . . .

" . . .

" . . . [E]specially in light of the number of Americans who take short sojourns abroad, the prospect that a father might not even know of the conception is a realistic possibility. . . . Even if a father knows of the fact of conception, moreover, it does not follow that he will be present at the birth of the child. . . . Without an initial point of contact with the child by a father who knows the child is his own, there is no opportunity for father and child to begin a relationship. Section 1409 takes the unremarkable step of ensuring that such an opportunity, inherent in the event of birth as to the mother-child relationship, exists between father and child before citizenship is conferred upon the latter.

". . . [S]cientific proof of biological paternity does nothing, by itself, to ensure contact between father and child during the child's minority.

". . . It should be unobjectionable for Congress to require some evidence of a minimal opportunity for the development of a relationship with the child in terms the male can fulfill.

" . . .

". . . [T]he difference does not result from some stereotype, defined as a frame of mind resulting from irrational or uncritical analysis. There is nothing irrational or improper in the recognition that at the moment of birth—a critical event in the statutory scheme and in the whole tradition of citizenship law—the mother's knowledge of the child and the fact of parenthood have been established in a way not guaranteed in the case of the unwed father. This is not a stereotype. . . ."

With respect to the means inquiry, Justice Kennedy responded as follows to the argument "that, although a mother will know of her child's birth, 'knowledge that one is a parent, no matter how it is acquired, does not guarantee a relationship with one's child' " and thus to impose "the additional requirements of § 1409(a)(4) only on the children of citizen fathers must reflect a stereotype that women are more likely than men to actually establish a relationship with their children":

"This line of argument misconceives the nature of both the governmental interest at issue and the manner in which we examine statutes alleged to violate equal protection. As to the former, Congress would of course be entitled to advance the interest of ensuring an actual, meaningful relationship in every case before citizenship is conferred. Or Congress could excuse compliance with the formal requirements when an actual father-child relationship is proved. It did neither here, perhaps because of the subjectivity, intrusiveness, and difficulties of proof that might attend an inquiry into any particular bond or tie. Instead, Congress enacted an easily administered scheme to promote the different but still substantial interest of ensuring at least an opportunity for a parent-child relationship to develop. Petitioners' argument confuses the means and ends of the equal protection inquiry; § 1409(a)(4) should not be invalidated because Congress elected to advance an interest that is less demanding to satisfy than some other alternative.

"Even if one conceives of the interest Congress pursues as the establishment of a real, practical relationship of considerable substance between parent and child in every case, as opposed simply to ensuring the potential for the relationship to begin, . . . [i]t is almost axiomatic that a policy which seeks to foster the opportunity for meaningful parent-child bonds to develop has a close and substantial bearing on the governmental interest in the actual formation of that bond. None of our gender-based classification equal protection cases have required that the statute under consideration must be capable of achieving its ultimate objective in every instance.

"In this difficult context of conferring citizenship on vast numbers of persons, the means adopted by Congress are in substantial furtherance of important governmental objectives. The fit between the means and the important end is 'exceedingly persuasive.' . . ."

Justice Kennedy emphasized that "the obligation [§ 1409(a)(4)] imposes ... is minimal" and that an "individual who fails to comply with § 1409(a), but who has substantial ties to the United States, can seek citizenship in his or her own right, rather than via reliance on ties to a citizen parent." He noted that "[i]n light of our holding that there is no equal protection violation, ... we need not assess the implications of statements in our earlier cases regarding the wide deference afforded to Congress in the exercise of its immigration and naturalization power." He concluded his opinion this way:

"To fail to acknowledge even our most basic biological differences—such as the fact that a mother must be present at birth but the father need not be—risks making the guarantee of equal protection superficial, and so disserving it. Mechanistic classification of all our differences as stereotypes would operate to obscure those misconceptions and prejudices that are real. The distinction embodied in the statutory scheme here at issue is not marked by misconception and prejudice, nor does it show disrespect for either class. The difference between men and women in relation to the birth process is a real one, and the principle of equal protection does not forbid Congress to address the problem at hand in a manner specific to each gender."[a]

Justice O'Connor dissented, joined by Justices Souter, Ginsburg, and Breyer. They found no "exceedingly persuasive justification for the sex-based classification" and faulted the Court's analysis:

"[T]he majority hypothesizes about the interests served by the statute and fails adequately to inquire into [its] actual purposes .... The Court also does not always explain adequately the importance of the interests that it claims to be served by the provision. The majority also fails carefully to consider whether the sex-based classification is being used impermissibly 'as a "proxy for other, more germane bases of classification,"' Mississippi Univ. for Women, ... and instead casually dismisses the relevance of available sex-neutral alternatives. And ... the fit between the means and ends of § 1409(a)(4) is far too attenuated for the provision to survive heightened scrutiny. In all, the majority opinion represents far less than the rigorous application of heightened scrutiny that our precedents require."

In the dissenters' view, the majority failed both to "elaborate on the importance of th[e] interest [in assuring that a biological parent-child relationship exists], which presumably lies in preventing fraudulent conveyances of citizenship" and to "demonstrate that this is one of the actual purposes of § 1409(a)(4)." The "gravest defect in the Court's reliance on this interest, however, is the insufficiency of the fit between § 1409(a)(4)'s discriminatory means and the asserted end." Because § 1409(a)(1) requires that "a blood relationship between the person and the father [be] established by clear and convincing evidence[,]" and given the "virtual certainty of a biological link that modern DNA testing affords[,]" § 1409(a)(4) is not needed to further this interest. Nor does "§ 1409(a)(4)'s limitation of the time allowed for obtaining proof of paternity substantially further[] the assurance of a blood relationship[,]" for "[m]odern DNA testing ... essentially negates the evidentiary significance of the passage of time." In short, "[b]ecause § 1409(a)(4) adds little to the work that § 1409(a)(1) does on its own, it is difficult to say that § 1409(a)(4) 'substantially furthers' an important governmental interest."

Since "a mother will not always have formal legal documentation of birth because a birth certificate may not issue or may subsequently be lost [and c]onversely, a father's name may well appear on a birth certificate[,] ... the

---

a. Justice Scalia's concurring opinion, joined by Justice Thomas, is omitted.

majority has not shown that a mother's birth relation is uniquely verifiable by the INS, much less that any greater verifiability warrants a sex-based, rather than a sex-neutral, statute." Thus, requiring both mothers and fathers to prove parenthood would be a superior, sex-neutral alternative: "Far from being 'hollow,' the avoidance of gratuitous sex-based distinctions is the hallmark of equal protection." It did not matter that "it will likely be easier for mothers to satisfy a sex-neutral proof of parentage requirement" considering "that the differential impact of a facially neutral law does not trigger heightened scrutiny, see, e.g., Washington v. Davis, 426 U.S. 229 (1976), whereas we apply heightened scrutiny to laws that facially classify individuals on the basis of their sex."

The majority's focus on the second interest—" 'some demonstrated opportunity or potential to develop . . . real, everyday ties,'[—]appears to be the type of hypothesized rationale that is insufficient under heightened scrutiny." In any event, "it is questionable whether such an opportunity qualifies as an 'important' governmental interest apart from the existence of an actual relationship." Although "focusing on 'opportunity' rather than reality . . . presumably improves the chances of a sufficient means-end fit[,] in doing so, it dilutes significantly the weight of the interest." The dissent questioned "how . . . anyone profits from a 'demonstrated opportunity' for a relationship in the absence of the fruition of an actual tie. Children who have an 'opportunity' for such a tie with a parent . . . may never develop an actual relationship with that parent. . . . Likewise, where there is an actual relationship, it . . . does all the work in rendering appropriate a grant of citizenship, regardless of when and how the opportunity for that relationship arose." The dissent continued:

". . . Even if it is important 'to require that an opportunity for a parent-child relationship occur during the formative years of the child's minority,' it is difficult to see how the requirement that proof of such opportunity be obtained before the child turns 18 substantially furthers the asserted interest. As the facts of this case demonstrate, it is entirely possible that a father and child will have the opportunity to develop a relationship and in fact will develop a relationship without obtaining the proof of the opportunity during the child's minority. . . .

"Further underscoring the gap between the discriminatory means and the asserted end is the possibility that 'a child might obtain an adjudication of paternity "absent any affirmative act by the father, and perhaps even over his express objection."' [T]hat the means-end fit can break down so readily in theory, and not just in practice, is hardly characteristic of a 'substantial' means-end relationship.

"Moreover, available sex-neutral alternatives would at least replicate, and could easily exceed, whatever fit there is. . . . Congress could simply substitute for § 1409(a)(4) a requirement that the parent be present at birth or have knowledge of birth. . . . Congress could at least allow proof of such presence or knowledge to be one way of demonstrating an opportunity for a relationship. Under the present law, the statute on its face accords different treatment to a mother who is by nature present at birth and a father who is by choice present at birth even though those two individuals are similarly situated with respect to the 'opportunity' for a relationship. The mother can transmit her citizenship at birth, but the father cannot do so in the absence of at least one other affirmative act. The different statutory treatment is solely on account of the sex of the similarly situated individuals. This type of treatment is patently inconsistent with the promise of equal protection of the laws. See, e.g., *Reed* . . . .

"Indeed, the idea that a mother's presence at birth supplies adequate assurance of an opportunity to develop a relationship while a father's presence at birth does not would appear to rest only on an overbroad sex-based generalization. A mother may not have an opportunity for a relationship if the child is removed from his or her mother on account of alleged abuse or neglect, or if the child and mother are separated by tragedy, such as disaster or war, of the sort apparently present in this case. There is no reason, other than stereotype, to say that fathers who are present at birth lack an opportunity for a relationship on similar terms. The '[p]hysical differences between men and women,' *Virginia*, ... therefore do not justify § 1409(a)(4)'s discrimination."

"... Far from being a virtual axiom, the relationship between the intent to foster an opportunity and the fruition of the desired effect is merely a contingent proposition.

"The question that then remains is the sufficiency of the fit between § 1409(a)(4)'s discriminatory means and the goal of 'establish[ing] ... a real, practical relationship of considerable substance.' If Congress wishes to advance this end, it could easily do so by employing a sex-neutral classification that is a far 'more germane bas[i]s of classification' than sex, *Craig*.... For example, Congress could require some degree of regular contact between the child and the citizen parent over a period of time....

"... The Court admits that 'Congress could excuse compliance with the formal requirements when an actual father-child relationship is proved,' but speculates that Congress did not do so 'perhaps because of the subjectivity, intrusiveness, and difficulties of proof that might attend an inquiry into any particular bond or tie.' We have repeatedly rejected efforts to justify sex-based classifications on the ground of administrative convenience.... And to the extent Congress might seek simply to ensure an 'opportunity' for a relationship, little administrative inconvenience would seem to accompany a sex-neutral requirement of presence at birth, knowledge of birth, or contact between parent and child prior to a certain age.

"The claim that § 1409(a)(4) substantially relates to the achievement of the goal of a 'real, practical relationship' thus finds support not in biological differences but instead in a stereotype—i.e., 'the generalization that mothers are significantly more likely than fathers ... to develop caring relationships with their children.' ... Such a claim relies on 'the very stereotype the law condemns,' *J.E.B.* ..., 'lends credibility' to the generalization, *Mississippi Univ. for Women* ..., and helps to convert that 'assumption' into 'a self-fulfilling prophecy,' ibid. ... Indeed, contrary to this stereotype, [his father] has reared Nguyen, while Nguyen apparently has lacked a relationship with his mother.

"...

"In denying petitioner's claim that § 1409(a)(4) rests on stereotypes, the majority articulates a misshapen notion of 'stereotype' and its significance in our equal protection jurisprudence.... This Court has long recognized ... that an impermissible stereotype may enjoy empirical support and thus be in a sense 'rational.' ... Indeed, the stereotypes that underlie a sex-based classification 'may hold true for many, even most, individuals.' ... But in numerous cases where a measure of truth has inhered in the generalization, 'the Court has rejected official actions that classify unnecessarily and overbroadly by gender when more accurate and impartial functional lines can be drawn.' ...

"Nor do stereotypes consist only of those overbroad generalizations that ... 'show disrespect' for a class.... The hallmark of a stereotypical sex-based classification under this Court's precedents is not whether the classification is insulting, but whether it 'relie[s] upon the simplistic, outdated assumption that gender could be used as a "proxy for other, more germane bases of classification."' ...

"...

"... The history of sex discrimination in laws governing the transmission of citizenship and with respect to parental responsibilities for children born out of wedlock counsels at least some circumspection in discerning legislative purposes in this context....

"...

"Section 1409(a)(4) is ... paradigmatic of a historic regime that left women with responsibility, and freed men from responsibility, for nonmarital children.... The majority, however, rather than confronting the stereotypical notion that mothers must care for these children and fathers may ignore them, quietly condones the 'very stereotype the law condemns,' *J.E.B.* ..."[a]

WHO ARE DISCRIMINATED AGAINST—MALES OR FEMALES?

In *Frontiero v. Richardson,* supra, it was clear that the discrimination was against females. A serviceman who was married received increased quarters allowances and medical and dental benefits whether or not his wife was dependent on him while a married servicewoman received the benefits only if her husband was dependent on her.

But what of statutes like the one in Weinberger v. Wiesenfeld, 420 U.S. 636 (1975)? Social Security Act benefits of a deceased husband and father covered by the Act were payable both to the widow and the minor children in her care. Such benefits on the basis of the earnings of a deceased wife and mother covered by the Act however were paid only to the children and not to the father. Is this a discrimination against males because they receive no payments when the covered wife dies while the wife receives payments when the covered husband dies? Or is this a discrimination against women because women workers covered by the Act received less protection for their families than men workers? In *Wiesenfeld* the Court held that the discrimination was against women and held it unconstitutional.

The issue next arose in Califano v. Goldfarb, 430 U.S. 199 (1977). Under the Federal Old–Age, Survivors, and Disability Insurance Benefits program survivors benefits were paid to the widow of a deceased husband covered by the Act but were payable to a widower whose wife was covered only if he received one-half or more of his support from his deceased wife. The Court held the classification invalid—four Justices regarded it as discriminating against female workers and invalid, while Justice Stevens, concurring, regarded it as discriminating against male survivors but still invalid. The four dissenters analyzed the law as benefitting female survivors.

a. Regarding "the implications of statements in our earlier cases regarding the wide deference afforded to Congress in the exercise of its immigration and naturalization power," the dissent said in relevant part:

"The instant case is not about the admission of aliens but instead concerns the logically prior question whether an individual is a citizen in the first place. A predicate for application of the deference commanded by *Fiallo* is that the individuals concerned be aliens. But whether that predicate obtains is the very matter at issue in this case.... Because §§ 1401 and 1409 govern the conferral of citizenship at birth, and not the admission of aliens, the ordinary standards of equal protection review apply...."

In Wengler v. Druggists Mutual Insurance Co., 446 U.S. 142 (1980), the Court held that a Missouri workers' compensation law unconstitutionally discriminated "against both men and women." The law provided death benefits to widows of men who died in work-related accidents without requiring proof of dependency on the husband's earnings, but did not provide such benefits to a widower unless he demonstrated actual dependence on his wife's earnings or mental or physical incapacity to earn wages. Justice White's opinion for seven Justices reasoned that the law discriminated against working women by devaluing the importance of their efforts as family providers and also discriminated against surviving husbands by withholding benefits unless they proved incapacity or dependency. The discrimination was unjustified as a means of providing for needy spouses, the Court said, because "the discriminatory means employed—discrimination against women wage earners and surviving male spouses" failed to substantially serve that important governmental objective. The claim that administrative convenience justified using gender as a proxy for dependency also was rejected. The case was remanded to allow the Missouri Supreme Court to determine "whether the defect should be cured by extending the presumption of dependence to widowers or by eliminating it for widows." Justice Stevens again concurred, arguing that the law discriminated only against males, although unjustifiably so. Males were disadvantaged whether the focus was on the requirement that a surviving dependent male had to prove dependency when a woman did not, on the fact that nondependent women could receive benefits whereas nondependent men could not, or on the wife's lesser need for life insurance on her husband's life. Justice Rehnquist dissented.

EQUAL RIGHTS AMENDMENT PROPOSED

On March 22, 1972, Congress passed and submitted to the legislatures of the states for ratification an amendment to the Constitution reading as follows:

"Section 1. Equality of rights under the law shall not be denied or abridged by the United States or by any State on account of sex.

"Section 2. The Congress shall have the power to enforce, by appropriate legislation, the provisions of this article.

"Section 3. This amendment shall take effect two years after the date of ratification."

The statute proposing the amendment provided that the ratifications must occur within seven years. By 1978, 35 states (3 less than the required three-fourths) had ratified, but three of them had rescinded their previous ratification. Congress then passed a statute extending the time for ratification to June 30, 1982. The necessary number of states did not ratify by that deadline.

D.   THE REQUIREMENT OF A DISCRIMINATORY PURPOSE—THE RELEVANCE OF DISCRIMINATORY IMPACT

Washington v. Davis

426 U.S. 229, 96 S.Ct. 2040, 48 L.Ed.2d 597 (1976).

Mr. Justice White delivered the opinion of the Court.

This case involves the validity of a qualifying test administered to applicants for positions as police officers in the District of Columbia Metropolitan

Police Department. The test was sustained by the District Court but invalidated by the Court of Appeals. We ... reverse... .

I.

[Rejected applicants complained in the District Court] that the Department's recruiting procedures discriminated on the basis of race against black applicants by a series of practices including, but not limited to, a written personnel test which excluded a disproportionately high number of Negro applicants. These practices were asserted to violate respondents' rights "under the due process clause of the Fifth Amendment to the United States Constitution, under 42 U.S.C. § 1981 and under D.C.Code § 1–320." ... [On cross-motions for summary judgment, the] District Court granted petitioners' and denied respondents' motions....

According to the findings and conclusions of the District Court, to be accepted by the Department and to enter an intensive 17–week training program, the police recruit was required to satisfy certain physical and character standards, to be a high school graduate or its equivalent and to receive a grade of at least 40 on "Test 21," which is "an examination that is used generally throughout the federal service," which "was developed by the [United States] Civil Service Commission not the Police Department" and which was "designed to test verbal ability, vocabulary, reading and comprehension."

The validity of Test 21 was the sole issue before the court on the motions for summary judgment. The District Court noted that there was no claim of "an intentional discrimination or purposeful discriminatory actions" but only a claim that Test 21 bore no relationship to job performance and "has a highly discriminatory impact in screening out black candidates." Petitioners' evidence, the District Court said, warranted three conclusions: "(a) The number of black police officers, while substantial, is not proportionate to the population mix of the city. (b) A higher percentage of blacks fail the Test than whites. (c) The Test has not been validated to establish its reliability for measuring subsequent job performance." Ibid. This showing was deemed sufficient to shift the burden of proof to the defendants in the action, petitioners here; but the court nevertheless concluded that on the undisputed facts respondents were not entitled to relief. The District Court relied on several factors. Since August 1969, 44% of new police force recruits had been black; that figure also represented the proportion of blacks on the total force and was roughly equivalent to 20–29–year–old blacks in the 50–mile radius in which the recruiting efforts of the Police Department had been concentrated. It was undisputed that the Department had systematically and affirmatively sought to enroll black officers many of whom passed the test but failed to report for duty. The District Court rejected the assertion that Test 21 was culturally slanted to favor whites and was "satisfied that the undisputable facts prove the test to be reasonably and directly related to the requirements of the police recruit training program and that it is neither so designed nor operated to discriminate against otherwise qualified blacks." It was thus not necessary to show that Test 21 was not only a useful indicator of training school performance but had also been validated in terms of job performance—"the lack of job performance validation does not defeat the test, given its direct relationship to recruiting and the valid part it plays in this process." The District Court ultimately concluded that "the proof is wholly lacking that a police officer qualifies on the color of his skin rather than ability" and that the Department "should not be required on this showing to lower standards or to abandon efforts to achieve excellence."

Having lost on both constitutional and statutory issues in the District Court, respondents brought the case to the Court of Appeals claiming that their summary judgment motion, which rested on purely constitutional grounds, should have been granted. The tendered constitutional issue was whether the use of Test 21 invidiously discriminated against Negroes and hence denied them due process of law contrary to the commands of the Fifth Amendment. The Court of Appeals, addressing that issue, announced that it would be guided by Griggs v. Duke Power Co., 401 U.S. 424 (1971), a case involving the interpretation and application of Title VII of the Civil Rights Act of 1964, and held that the statutory standards elucidated in that case were to govern the due process question tendered in this one.... The court went on to declare that lack of discriminatory intent in designing and administering Test 21 was irrelevant; the critical fact was rather that a far greater proportion of blacks—four times as many—failed the test than did whites. This disproportionate impact, standing alone and without regard to whether it indicated a discriminatory purpose, was held sufficient to establish a constitutional violation, absent proof by petitioners that the test was an adequate measure of job performance in addition to being an indicator of probable success in the training program, a burden which the court ruled petitioners had failed to discharge.[a]

. . . .

II.

Because the Court of Appeals erroneously applied the legal standards applicable to Title VII cases in resolving the constitutional issue before it, we reverse its judgment in respondents' favor. Although the petition for certiorari did not present this ground for reversal, our Rule 40(1)(d)(2) provides that we "may notice a plain error not presented"; and this is an appropriate occasion to invoke the rule.

As the Court of Appeals understood Title VII, employees or applicants proceeding under it need not concern themselves with the employer's possibly discriminatory purpose but instead may focus solely on the racially differential impact of the challenged hiring or promotion practices. This is not the constitutional rule. We have never held that the constitutional standard for adjudicating claims of invidious racial discrimination is identical to the standards applicable under Title VII, and we decline to do so today.

The central purpose of the Equal Protection Clause of the Fourteenth Amendment is the prevention of official conduct discriminating on the basis of race. It is also true that the Due Process Clause of the Fifth Amendment contains an equal protection component prohibiting the United States from invidiously discriminating between individuals or groups. Bolling v. Sharpe, 347 U.S. 497 (1954). But our cases have not embraced the proposition that a law or

a. In Wards Cove Packing Co. v. Atonio, 490 U.S. 642 (1989), the Court interpreted *Griggs* narrowly by holding that once a plaintiff demonstrates that a particular employment practice caused an adverse disproportionate impact on nonwhites, the burden imposed on the employer is only a burden to "produce" a "legitimate business justification" for the practice, not a burden of "proof" of that or any higher level of justification. A plaintiff unable to persuade a trier of fact that a business necessity defense is illegitimate could only prevail by showing that the employer refused to adopt an equally effective alternate employment practice with less disparate impact. In the Civil Rights Act of 1991, P.L. 102–166, 105 Stat. 1071, Congress overrode *Wards Cove,* at least partially, by making the employer, not the challenger, carry the burden of "persuasion" in disparate impact cases that "the challenged practice is job related ... and consistent with business necessity." The Act also forbids using an employer's "demonstration that an employment practice is required by business necessity ... as a defense against a claim of intentional discrimination...."

other official act, without regard to whether it reflects a racially discriminatory purpose, is unconstitutional *solely* because it has a racially disproportionate impact.

Almost 100 years ago, Strauder v. West Virginia, 100 U.S. 303 (1879), established that the exclusion of Negroes from grand and petit juries in criminal proceedings violated the Equal Protection Clause, but the fact that a particular jury or a series of juries does not statistically reflect the racial composition of the community does not in itself make out an invidious discrimination forbidden by the Clause. "A purpose to discriminate must be present which may be proven by systematic exclusion of eligible jurymen of the prescribed race or by an unequal application of the law to such an extent as to show intentional discrimination." Akins v. Texas, 325 U.S. 398, 403–404 (1945). A defendant in a criminal case is entitled "to require that the State not deliberately and systematically deny to the members of his race the right to participate as jurors in the administration of justice." See also Carter v. Jury Commission, 396 U.S. 320, 335–337, 339 (1970); Cassell v. Texas, 339 U.S. 282, 287–290 (1950); Patton v. Mississippi, 332 U.S. 463, 468–469 (1947).

The rule is the same in other contexts. Wright v. Rockefeller, 376 U.S. 52 (1964), upheld a New York congressional apportionment statute against claims that district lines had been racially gerrymandered. The challenged districts were made up predominantly of whites or of minority races, and their boundaries were irregularly drawn. The challengers did not prevail because they failed to prove that the New York legislature "was either motivated by racial considerations or in fact drew the districts on racial lines"; the plaintiffs had not shown that the statute "was the product of a state contrivance to segregate on the basis of race or place of origin." ... The dissenters were in agreement that the issue was whether the "boundaries ... were purposefully drawn on racial lines." ...

The school desegregation cases have also adhered to the basic equal protection principle that the invidious quality of a law claimed to be racially discriminatory must ultimately be traced to a racially discriminatory purpose. That there are both predominantly black and predominantly white schools in a community is not alone violative of the Equal Protection Clause. The essential element of *de jure* segregation is "a current condition of segregation resulting from intentional state action ... the differentiating factor between *de jure* segregation and so-called *de facto* segregation ... is *purpose* or *intent* to segregate." Keyes v. School District No. 1, 413 U.S. 189, 205, 208 (1973). The Court has also recently rejected allegations of racial discrimination based solely on the statistically disproportionate racial impact of various provisions of the Social Security Act because "the acceptance of appellant's constitutional theory would render suspect each difference in treatment among the grant classes, however lacking the racial motivation and however rational the treatment might be." Jefferson v. Hackney, 406 U.S. 535, 548 (1972). And compare Hunter v. Erickson, 393 U.S. 385 (1969), with James v. Valtierra, 402 U.S. 137 (1971).

This is not to say that the necessary discriminatory racial purpose must be express or appear on the face of the statute, or that a law's disproportionate impact is irrelevant in cases involving Constitution-based claims of racial discrimination. A statute, otherwise neutral on its face, must not be applied so as invidiously to discriminate on the basis of race. Yick Wo v. Hopkins, 118 U.S. 356 (1886). It is also clear from the cases dealing with racial discrimination in the selection of juries that the systematic exclusion of Negroes is itself such an "unequal application of the law ... as to show intentional discrimination."

[handwritten margin note: purpose to discriminate must be present. solely impact is not enough]

[handwritten margin note: purpose doesnt have to be express or on its face]

Akins v. Texas, supra, at 404. Smith v. Texas, 311 U.S. 128 (1940); Pierre v. Louisiana, 306 U.S. 354 (1939); Neal v. Delaware, 103 U.S. 370 (1881). A prima facie case of discriminatory purpose may be proved as well by the absence of Negroes on a particular jury combined with the failure of the jury commissioners to be informed of eligible Negro jurors in a community, Hill v. Texas, 316 U.S. 400, 404 (1942), or with racially nonneutral selection procedures, Alexander v. Louisiana, 405 U.S. 625 (1972); Avery v. Georgia, 345 U.S. 559 (1953); Whitus v. Georgia, 385 U.S. 545 (1967). With a prima facie case made out, "the burden of proof shifts to the State to rebut the presumption of unconstitutional action by showing that permissible racially neutral selection criteria and procedures have produced the monochromatic result." Alexander, supra, at 632. See also Turner v. Fouche, 396 U.S. 346, 361 (1970); Eubanks v. Louisiana, 356 U.S. 584, 587 (1958).

Necessarily, an invidious discriminatory purpose may often be inferred from the totality of the relevant facts, including the fact, if it is true, that the law bears more heavily on one race than another. It is also not infrequently true that the discriminatory impact—in the jury cases for example, the total or seriously disproportionate exclusion of Negroes from jury venires—may for all practical purposes demonstrate unconstitutionality because in various circumstances the discrimination is very difficult to explain on nonracial grounds. Nevertheless, we have not held that a law, neutral on its face and serving ends otherwise within the power of government to pursue, is invalid under the Equal Protection Clause simply because it may affect a greater proportion of one race than of another. Disproportionate impact is not irrelevant, but it is not the sole touchstone of an invidious racial discrimination forbidden by the Constitution. Standing alone, it does not trigger the rule, McLaughlin v. Florida, 379 U.S. 184 (1964), that racial classifications are to be subjected to the strictest scrutiny and are justifiable only by the weightiest of considerations.

There are some indications to the contrary in our cases. In Palmer v. Thompson, 403 U.S. 217 (1971), the city of Jackson, Miss., following a court decree to this effect, desegregated all of its public facilities save five swimming pools which had been operated by the city and which, following the decree, were closed by ordinance pursuant to a determination by the city council that closure was necessary to preserve peace and order and that integrated pools could not be economically operated. Accepting the finding that the pools were closed to avoid violence and economic loss, this Court rejected the argument that the abandonment of this service was inconsistent with the outstanding desegregation decree and that the otherwise seemingly permissible ends served by the ordinance could be impeached by demonstrating that racially invidious motivations had prompted the city council's action. The holding was that the city was not overtly or covertly operating segregated pools and was extending identical treatment to both whites and Negroes. The opinion warned against grounding decision on legislative purpose or motivation, thereby lending support for the proposition that the operative effect of the law rather than its purpose is the paramount factor. But the holding of the case was that the legitimate purposes of the ordinance—to preserve peace and avoid deficits— were not open to impeachment by evidence that the councilmen were actually motivated by racial considerations. Whatever dicta the opinion may contain, the decision did not involve, much less invalidate, a statute or ordinance having neutral purposes but disproportionate racial consequences.

Wright v. Council of the City of Emporia, 407 U.S. 451 (1972), also indicates that in proper circumstances, the racial impact of a law, rather than its discriminatory purpose, is the critical factor. That case involved the division of a school district. The issue was whether the division was consistent with an outstanding order of a federal court to desegregate the dual school system found to have existed in the area. The constitutional predicate for the District Court's invalidation of the divided district was "the enforcement until 1969 of racial segregation in the public school system of which Emporia had always been a part." Id., at 459. There was thus no need to find "an independent constitutional violation." Ibid. Citing *Palmer v. Thompson,* we agreed with the District Court that the division of the district had the effect of interfering with the federal decree and should be set aside.

That neither *Palmer* nor *Wright* was understood to have changed the prevailing rule is apparent from *Keyes v. School District No. 1,* supra, where the principal issue in litigation was whether and to what extent there had been purposeful discrimination resulting in a partially or wholly segregated school system. Nor did other later cases, *Alexander v. Louisiana,* supra, and *Jefferson v. Hackney,* supra, indicate that either *Palmer* or *Wright* had worked a fundamental change in equal protection law.[11]

Both before and after *Palmer v. Thompson,* however, various Courts of Appeals have held in several contexts, including public employment, that the substantially disproportionate racial impact of a statute or official practice standing alone and without regard to discriminatory purpose, suffices to prove racial discrimination violating the Equal Protection Clause absent some justification going substantially beyond what would be necessary to validate most other legislative classifications. The cases impressively demonstrate that there is another side to the issue; but, with all due respect, to the extent that those cases rested on or expressed the view that proof of discriminatory racial purpose is unnecessary in making out an equal protection violation, we are in disagreement.

As an initial matter, we have difficulty understanding how a law establishing a racially neutral qualification for employment is nevertheless racially discriminatory and denies "any person equal protection of the laws" simply because a greater proportion of Negroes fail to qualify than members of other racial or ethnic groups. Had respondents, along with all others who had failed Test 21, whether white or black, brought an action claiming that the test denied each of them equal protection of the laws as compared with those who had passed with high enough scores to qualify them as police recruits, it is most unlikely that their challenge would have been sustained. Test 21, which is administered generally to prospective government employees, concededly seeks to ascertain whether those who take it have acquired a particular level of verbal skill; and it is untenable that the Constitution prevents the government from seeking modestly to upgrade the communicative abilities of its employees rather than to be satisfied with some lower level of competence, particularly where the job requires special ability to communicate orally and in writing. Respondents, as Negroes, could no more successfully claim that the test denied them equal protection than could white applicants who also failed. The conclusion would not be different in the face of proof that more Negroes than whites had been disqualified by Test 21. That other Negroes also failed to score well would, alone, not demonstrate that respondents individually were being denied

---

11. To the extent that *Palmer* suggests a generally applicable proposition that legislative purpose is irrelevant in constitutional adjudication, our prior cases—as indicated in the text—are to the contrary; and very shortly after *Palmer,* all Members of the Court majority in that case joined the Court's opinion in Lemon v. Kurtzman, 403 U.S. 602 (1971), which dealt with the issue of public financing for private schools and which announced, as the Court had several times before, that the validity of public aid to church-related schools includes close inquiry into the purpose of the challenged statute.

equal protection of the laws by the application of an otherwise valid qualifying test being administered to prospective police recruits.

Nor on the facts of the case before us would the disproportionate impact of Test 21 warrant the conclusion that it is a purposeful device to discriminate against Negroes and hence an infringement of the constitutional rights of respondents as well as other black applicants. As we have said, the test is neutral on its face and rationally may be said to serve a purpose the government is constitutionally empowered to pursue. Even agreeing with the District Court that the differential racial effect of Test 21 called for further inquiry, we think the District Court correctly held that the affirmative efforts of the Metropolitan Police Department to recruit black officers, the changing racial composition of the recruit classes and of the force in general, and the relationship of the test to the training program negated any inference that the Department discriminated on the basis of race or that "a police officer qualifies on the color of his skin rather than ability." 348 F.Supp., at 18.

Under Title VII, Congress provided that when hiring and promotion practices disqualifying substantially disproportionate numbers of blacks are challenged, discriminatory purpose need not be proved, and that it is an insufficient response to demonstrate some rational basis for the challenged practices. It is necessary, in addition, that they be "validated" in terms of job performance in any one of several ways, perhaps by ascertaining the minimum skill, ability or potential necessary for the position at issue and determining whether the qualifying tests are appropriate for the selection of qualified applicants for the job in question. However this process proceeds, it involves a more probing judicial review of, and less deference to, the seemingly reasonable acts of administrators and executives than is appropriate under the Constitution where special racial impact, without discriminatory purpose, is claimed. We are not disposed to adopt this more rigorous standard for the purposes of applying the Fifth and the Fourteenth Amendments in cases such as this.

A rule that a statute designed to serve neutral ends is nevertheless invalid, absent compelling justification, if in practice it benefits or burdens one race more than another would be far reaching and would raise serious questions about, and perhaps invalidate, a whole range of tax, welfare, public service, regulatory, and licensing statutes that may be more burdensome to the poor and to the average black than to the more affluent white.[14]

Given that rule, such consequences would perhaps be likely to follow. However, in our view, extension of the rule beyond those areas where it is already applicable by reason of statute, such as in the field of public employment, should await legislative prescription.

As we have indicated, it was error to direct summary judgment for respondents based on the Fifth Amendment.

III.

[The Court also rejected the statutory claims.]

---

14. Goodman, De Facto School Segregation: Constitutional and Empirical Analysis, 60 Cal.L.Rev. 275, 300 (1972), suggests that disproportionate impact analysis might invalidate "tests and qualifications for voting, draft deferment, public employment, jury service and other government-conferred benefits and opportunities ...; [s]ales taxes, bail schedules, utility rates, bridge tolls, license fees, and other state-imposed charges." It has also been argued that minimum wage and usury laws as well as professional licensing requirements would require major modifications in light of the unequal impact rule. Silverman, Equal Protection, Economic Legislation and Racial Discrimination, 25 Vand. L.Rev. 1183 (1972). See also Demsetz, Minorities in the Market Place, 43 N.C.L.Rev. 271.

... Based on the evidence before him, the District Judge concluded that Test 21 was directly related to the requirements of the police training program and that a positive relationship between the test and training course performance was sufficient to validate the former, wholly aside from its possible relationship to actual performance as a police officer. . . .

. . .

The judgment of the Court of Appeals accordingly is reversed.

So ordered.

Mr. Justice Stewart joins Parts I and II of the Court's opinion.

Mr. Justice Stevens, concurring.

While I agree with the Court's disposition of this case, I add these comments on the constitutional issue discussed in Part II. . . .

Frequently the most probative evidence of intent will be objective evidence of what actually happened rather than evidence describing the subjective state of mind of the actor. . . .

My point in making this observation is to suggest that the line between discriminatory purpose and discriminatory impact is not nearly as bright, and perhaps not quite as critical, as the reader of the Court's opinion might assume. I agree, of course, that a constitutional issue does not arise every time some disproportionate impact is shown. On the other hand, when the disproportion is as dramatic as in *Gomillion* or *Yick Wo*, it really does not matter whether the standard is phrased in terms of purpose or effect. Therefore, although I accept the statement of the general rule in the Court's opinion, I am not yet prepared to indicate how that standard should be applied in the many cases which have formulated the governing standard in different language.

Line between purpose & impact is vague

. . .

Mr. Justice Brennan, with whom Mr. Justice Marshall joins, dissenting. . . .

[This opinion addressed only the statutory issues explored in Part III of the Court's opinion.]

VILLAGE OF ARLINGTON HEIGHTS v. METROPOLITAN HOUSING DEVELOPMENT CORP., 429 U.S. 252 (1977). Metropolitan Housing submitted a request for the rezoning of a 15–acre parcel from single-family to multiple-family classification for the purpose of building apartments for low and moderate income families. The apartments were to be constructed under a federal program requiring an affirmative marketing plan to assure that the development would be racially integrated. Public hearings were held. Some persons objected to the introduction of low income racially integrated housing in the area. Many focused on the fact that the surrounding land had always been zoned for and occupied by single-family housing and neighboring citizens built or purchased their homes relying on the classification. They also noted that the city's consistent policy had been to zone for multiple-family housing only in areas that would serve as a buffer between single-family and commercial developments, whereas the parcel involved here did not adjoin any commercial district. The zoning request was denied and a suit was brought in the federal district court seeking declaratory and injunctive relief. The trial judge ruled for the city but the Court of Appeals reversed, finding that the "ultimate effect" of the denial was racially discriminatory. The Supreme Court reversed the Court of Appeals.

Denied zoning

Mr. Justice Powell, speaking for the Court, said, in part:

III.

"Our decision last Term in Washington v. Davis, 426 U.S. 229 (1976), made it clear that official action will not be held unconstitutional solely because it results in a racially disproportionate impact. . . .

"*Davis* does not require a plaintiff to prove that the challenged action rested solely on racially discriminatory purposes. Rarely can it be said that a legislature or administrative body operating under a broad mandate made a decision motivated solely by a single concern, or even that a particular purpose was the 'dominant' or 'primary' one. In fact, it is because legislators and administrators are properly concerned with balancing numerous competing considerations that courts refrain from reviewing the merits of their decisions, absent a showing of arbitrariness or irrationality. But racial discrimination is not just another competing consideration. When there is a proof that a discriminatory purpose has been a motivating factor in the decision, this judicial deference is no longer justified.[12]

"Determining whether invidious discriminatory purpose was a motivating factor demands a sensitive inquiry into such circumstantial and direct evidence of intent as may be available. The impact of the official action—whether it 'bears more heavily on one race than another,' Washington v. Davis, 426 U.S., at 242—may provide an important starting point. Sometimes a clear pattern, unexplainable on grounds other than race, emerges from the effect of the state action even when the governing legislation appears neutral on its face. Yick Wo v. Hopkins, 118 U.S. 356 (1886); Guinn v. United States, 238 U.S. 347 (1915); Lane v. Wilson, 307 U.S. 268 (1939); Gomillion v. Lightfoot, 364 U.S. 339 (1960). The evidentiary inquiry is then relatively easy.[13] But such cases are rare. Absent a pattern as stark as that in *Gomillion* or *Yick Wo,* impact alone is not determinative,[14] and the Court must look to other evidence.[15]

"The historical background of the decision is one evidentiary source, particularly if it reveals a series of official actions taken for invidious purposes. . . . The specific sequence of events leading up to the challenged decision also may shed some light on the decisionmaker's purposes. . . . For example, if the property involved here always had been zoned R–5 but suddenly was changed to R–3 when the town learned of MHDC's plans to erect integrated housing, we would have a far different case. Departures from the normal procedural sequence also might afford evidence that improper purposes are playing a role. Substantive departures too may be relevant, particularly if the

Factors {

---

12.   For a scholarly discussion of legislative motivation, see Brest, Palmer v. Thompson: An Approach to the Problem of Unconstitutional Legislative Motive, 1971 Sup.Ct. Rev. 95, 116–118.

13.   Several of our jury selection cases fall into this category. Because of the nature of the jury selection task, however, we have permitted a finding of constitutional violation even when the statistical pattern does not approach the extremes of *Yick Wo* or *Gomillion.* See, e.g., Turner v. Fouche, 396 U.S. 346, 359 (1970); Sims v. Georgia, 389 U.S. 404, 407 (1967).

14.   This is not to say that a consistent pattern of official racial discrimination is a necessary predicate to a violation of the equal protection clause. A single invidiously discriminatory governmental act—in the exercise of the zoning power as elsewhere—would not necessarily be immunized by the absence of such discrimination in the making of other comparable decisions. See City of Richmond v. United States, 422 U.S. 358, 378 (1975).

15.   In many instances, to recognize the limited probative value of disproportionate impact is merely to acknowledge the "heterogeneity" of the nation's population. Jefferson v. Hackney, 406 U.S. 535, 548 (1972); see also Washington v. Davis, 426 U.S., at 248.

factors usually considered important by the decisionmaker strongly favor a decision contrary to the one reached.

"The legislative or administrative history may be highly relevant, especially where there are contemporary statements by members of the decision-making body, minutes of its meetings, or reports. In some extraordinary instances the members might be called to the stand at trial to testify concerning the purpose of the official action, although even then such testimony frequently will be barred by privilege.... [18]

"The foregoing summary identifies, without purporting to be exhaustive, subjects of proper inquiry in determining whether racially discriminatory intent existed. With these in mind, we now address the case before us.

IV.

. . .

"We also have reviewed the evidence. The impact of the Village's decision does arguably bear more heavily on racial minorities. Minorities comprise 18% of the Chicago area population, and 40% of the income groups said to be eligible for Lincoln Green. But there is little about the sequence of events leading up to the decision that would spark suspicion. The area around the Victorian property has been zoned R–3 since 1959, the year when Arlington Heights first adopted a zoning map. Single-family homes surround the 80–acre site, and the Village is undeniably committed to single-family homes as its dominant residential land use. The rezoning request progressed according to the usual procedures. The Plan Commission even scheduled two additional hearings, at least in part to accommodate MHDC and permit it to supplement its presentation with answers to questions generated at the first hearing.

"The statements by the Plan Commission and Village Board members, as reflected in the official minutes, focused almost exclusively on the zoning aspects of the MHDC petition, and the zoning factors on which they relied are not novel criteria in the Village's rezoning decisions. There is no reason to doubt that there has been reliance by some neighboring property owners on the maintenance of single-family zoning in the vicinity. The Village originally adopted its buffer policy long before MHDC entered the picture and has applied the policy too consistently for us to infer discriminatory purpose from its application in this case. Finally, MHDC called one member of the Village Board to the stand at trial. Nothing in her testimony supports an inference of invidious purpose.

"In sum, the evidence does not warrant overturning the concurrent findings of both courts below. Respondents simply failed to carry their burden of proving that discriminatory purpose was a motivating factor in the Village's decision.[21] This conclusion ends the constitutional inquiry. The Court of Ap-

---

18. This Court has recognized, ever since *Fletcher v. Peck,* 6 Cranch 87, 130–131 (1810), that judicial inquiries into legislative or executive motivation represent a substantial intrusion into the workings of other branches of government. Placing a decision-maker on the stand is therefore "usually to be avoided." *Citizens to Preserve Overton Park v. Volpe,* 401 U.S. 402, 420 (1971). The problems involved have prompted a good deal of scholarly commentary. See *Tussman & TenBroek, The Equal Protection of the Laws,*

37 Calif.L.Rev. 341, 356–361 (1949); A. Bickel, The Least Dangerous Branch, 208–221 (1962); Ely, Legislative and Administrative Motivation in Constitutional Law, 79 Yale L.J. 1205 (1970); Brest supra, n. 8.

21. Proof that the decision by the Village was motivated in part by a racially discriminatory purpose would not necessarily have required invalidation of the challenged decision. Such proof would, however, have shifted to the Village the burden of establishing that the same decision would have resultpeals' further finding that the Village's decision carried a discriminatory 'ultimate effect' is without independent constitutional significance.''

Justices Marshall and Brennan concurred in Part III of the opinion set out above but indicated that in their view the case should be remanded to the court of appeals for it to reassess the evidence on discriminatory purpose. Justice White also dissented, calling for a remand to the court of appeals. Justice Stevens took no part in the decision.

PERSONNEL ADMINISTRATOR OF MASSACHUSETTS v. FEE-NEY, 442 U.S. 256 (1979). Massachusetts' veterans' preference for state civil service positions was challenged as unconstitutional gender discrimination. Under the law, all veterans had an ''absolute lifetime preference''; veterans with passing scores for classified civil service jobs were ranked above *all* other candidates. Since 98% of veterans were male, and the preference for veterans with passing scores was absolute, the impact of the law was, obviously, to disqualify female eligibles from consideration in much greater proportion than male eligibles. The Court rejected the argument that Massachusetts had discriminated against women in violation of the Equal Protection Clause. Justice Stewart's opinion for the Court said, in part:

''The cases of *Washington v. Davis,* and *Village of Arlington Heights v. Metropolitan Housing Development Corp.,* recognize that when a neutral law has a disparate impact upon a group that has historically been the victim of discrimination, an unconstitutional purpose may still be at work. But those cases signalled no departure from the settled rule that the Fourteenth Amendment guarantees equal laws, not equal results. . . .

''When a statute gender-neutral on its face is challenged on the ground that its effects upon women are disproportionately adverse, a two-fold inquiry is thus appropriate. The first question is whether the statutory classification is indeed neutral in the sense that it is not gender-based. If the classification itself, covert or overt, is not based upon gender, the second question is whether the adverse effect reflects invidious gender-based discrimination. . . . In this second inquiry, impact provides an 'important starting point,' but purposeful discrimination is 'the condition that offends the Constitution.' . . .

. . .

''The question whether ch. 31, § 23 establishes a classification that is overtly or covertly based upon gender must first be considered. The appellee has conceded that ch. 31, § 23 is neutral on its face. . . .

''. . . Apart from the fact that the definition of 'veterans' in the statute has always been neutral as to gender and that Massachusetts has consistently defined veteran status in a way that has been inclusive of women who have served in the military, this is not a law that can plausibly be explained only as a gender-based classification. Indeed, it is not a law that can rationally be explained on that ground. Veteran status is not uniquely male. Although few women benefit from the preference, the nonveteran class is not substantially all-female. To the contrary, significant numbers of nonveterans are men, and all nonveterans—male as well as female—are placed at a disadvantage. Too

ed even had the impermissible purpose not been considered. If this were established, the complaining party in a case of this kind no longer fairly could attribute the injury complained of to improper consideration of a discriminatory purpose. In such circum-

stances, there would be no justification for judicial interference with the challenged decision. But in this case respondents failed to make the required threshold showing. See Mt. Healthy City School Dist. Bd. of Education v. Doyle, 429 U.S. 274.

many men are affected to permit the inference that the statute is but a pretext for preferring men over women.

"Moreover, as the District Court implicitly found, the purposes of the statute provide the surest explanation for its impact. Just as there are cases in which impact alone can unmask an invidious classification, cf. *Yick Wo v. Hopkins,* there are others, in which—notwithstanding impact—the legitimate noninvidious purposes of a law cannot be missed. This is one. The distinction . . . is, as it seems to be, quite simply between veterans and nonveterans, not between men and women.

"The dispositive question, then, is whether the appellee has shown that a gender-based discriminatory purpose has, at least in some measure, shaped the Massachusetts veterans' preference legislation. . . .

"The contention that this veterans' preference is 'inherently non-neutral' or 'gender-based' presumes that the State, by favoring veterans, intentionally incorporated into its public employment policies the panoply of sex-based and assertedly discriminatory federal laws that have prevented all but a handful of women from becoming veterans. There are two serious difficulties with this argument. First, it is wholly at odds with the District Court's central finding that Massachusetts has not offered a preference to veterans for the purpose of discriminating against women. Second, it cannot be reconciled with the assumption made by both the appellee and the District Court that a more limited hiring preference for veterans could be sustained. Taken together, these difficulties are fatal.

. . .

"To be sure, this case is unusual in that it involves a law that by design is not neutral. The law overtly prefers veterans as such. As opposed to the written test at issue in *Davis,* it does not purport to define a job related characteristic. To the contrary, it confers upon a specifically described group—perceived to be particularly deserving—a competitive head start. But the District Court found, and the appellee has not disputed, that this legislative choice was legitimate. The basic distinction between veterans and nonveterans, having been found not gender-based, and the goals of the preference having been found worthy, Ch. 31 must be analyzed as is any other neutral law that casts a greater burden upon women as a group than upon men as a group. The enlistment policies of the armed services may well have discriminated on the basis of sex. See Frontiero v. Richardson, 411 U.S. 677; cf. Schlesinger v. Ballard, 419 U.S. 498. But the history of discrimination against women in the military is not on trial in this case.

"The appellee's ultimate argument rests upon the presumption, common to the criminal and civil law, that a person intends the natural and foreseeable consequences of his voluntary actions. . . .

". . . [I]t cannot seriously be argued that the legislature of Massachusetts could have been unaware that most veterans are men. It would thus be disingenuous to say that the adverse consequences of this legislation for women were unintended, in the sense that they were not volitional or in the sense that they were not foreseeable.

" 'Discriminatory purpose,' however, implies more than intent as volition or intent as awareness of consequences. . . . It implies that the decisionmaker, in this case a state legislature, selected or reaffirmed a particular course of action at least in part 'because of,' not merely 'in spite of,' its adverse effects upon an identifiable group. Yet nothing in the record demonstrates that this preference for veterans was originally devised or subsequently re-enacted

[handwritten margin note: excludes all non veterens men & women]

because it would accomplish the collateral goal of keeping women in a stereotypic and predefined place in the Massachusetts Civil Service.''

Justice Stevens' concurring opinion, joined by Justice White, said:

''While I concur in the Court's opinion, I confess that I am not at all sure that there is any difference between the two questions posed. . . . If a classification is not overtly based on gender, I am inclined to believe the question whether it is covertly gender-based is the same as the question whether its adverse effects reflect invidious gender-based discrimination. However the question is phrased, for me the answer is largely provided by the fact that the number of males disadvantaged by Massachusetts' Veterans Preference (1,867,-000) is sufficiently large—and sufficiently close to the number of disadvantaged females (2,954,000)—to refute the claim that the rule was intended to benefit males as a class over females as a class.''

Justice Marshall's dissent, joined by Justice Brennan, concluded that Massachusetts' veterans' preference system constituted ''intentional'' gender-based discrimination. The foreseeable impact of the law had such a disproportionate impact that the State should have the burden to establish that ''sex-based considerations played no part in the choice of the particular legislative scheme.''

''Clearly, that burden was not sustained here. The legislative history of the statute reflects the Commonwealth's patent appreciation of the impact the preference system would have on women, and an equally evident desire to mitigate that impact only with respect to certain traditionally female occupations. Until 1971, the statute and implementing civil service regulations exempted from operation of the preference any job requisitions 'especially calling for women.' . . . In practice, this exemption, coupled with the absolute preference for veterans, has created a gender-based civil service hierarchy, with women occupying low grade clerical and secretarial jobs and men holding more responsible and remunerative positions.

''Thus, for over 70 years, the Commonwealth has maintained, as an integral part of its veteran's preference system, an exemption relegating female civil service applicants to occupations traditionally filled by women. Such a statutory scheme both reflects and perpetuates precisely the kind of archaic assumptions about women's roles which we have previously held invalid. . . .''

COLUMBUS BOARD OF EDUCATION v. PENICK, 443 U.S. 449 (1979). The Court upheld a finding that schools were intentionally segregated based in large measure on a finding that the schools had been intentionally segregated in 1954 when *Brown* was decided and that they had failed in the intervening years to disestablish the dual system. It rejected an argument that the lower courts had not found an intention to discriminate, concluding that the District Court ''was amply cognizant of the controlling cases'' and ''recognized that under those cases disparate impact and foreseeable consequences, without more, do not establish a constitutional violation [but] are relevant evidence to prove the ultimate fact, forbidden purpose.'' The Court elaborated: ''adherence to a particular policy or practice, 'with full knowledge of the predictable effects of such adherence upon racial imbalance in a school system is one factor among many others which may be considered by a court in determining whether an inference of segregative intent should be drawn.' ''

CASTANEDA v. PARTIDA, 430 U.S. 482 (1977). Partida sued in a federal district court challenging his state court criminal conviction on the ground that the grand jury that indicted him resulted from a state grand jury selection process that discriminated against Mexican–Americans. The district judge found that Partida had made out a bare prima facie case of invidious discrimination based on a statistical showing that Mexican–Americans made up 79% of the county population in the 1970 census but over an overlapping 11 year period made up only 39% of those summoned to be grand jurors. However, he held that this was overcome by the State's showing that Mexican–Americans constituted the governing majority in the county, and dismissed the petition. The Court of Appeals reversed and the Supreme Court affirmed the court of appeals.

Justice Blackmun, speaking for the Court, reviewed the statistical evidence and concluded that Partida established a prima facie case of discrimination against Mexican–Americans. He then went on to hold that the state did not dispel the presumption of purposeful discrimination by its governing majority showing, saying:

"Because of the many facets of human motivation, it would be unwise to presume as a matter of law that human beings of one definable group will not discriminate against other members of their group . . . .[20]

"Furthermore, the relevance of a governing majority of elected officials to the grand jury selection process is questionable. The fact that certain elected officials are Mexican–American demonstrates nothing about the motivations and methods of the grand jury commissioners who select persons for grand jury lists. The only arguably relevant fact in this record on the issue is that three of the five jury commissioners in respondent's case were Mexican–American. Knowing only this, we would be forced to rely on the reasoning that we have rejected—that human beings would not discriminate against their own kind—in order to find that the presumption of purposeful discrimination was rebutted. Without the benefit of this simple behavioral presumption, discriminatory intent can be rebutted only with evidence in the record about the way in which the commissioners operated and their reasons for doing so. It was the State's burden to supply such evidence, once respondent established his prima facie case . . . .

"Finally, even if a 'governing majority' theory has general applicability in cases of this kind, the inadequacy of the record in this case does not permit such an approach. Among the evidentiary deficiencies are the lack of any indication of how long the Mexican–Americans have enjoyed 'governing majori- ty' status, the absence of information about the relative power inherent in the elective offices held by Mexican–Americans, and the uncertain relevance of the general political power to the specific issue in this case. Even for the most recent time period, when presumably the political power of Mexican–Americans was at its greatest, the discrepancy between the number of Mexican–Americans in the total population and the number on the grand jury lists was substantial. Thus, under the facts presented in this case, the 'governing majority' theory is not developed fully enough to satisfy the State's burden of rebuttal."

Justice Marshall concurred "to express [his] profound disagreement with the views expressed by Mr. Justice Powell in his dissent":

" . . . Justice Powell's assumptions about human nature, plausible as they may sound, fly in the face of a great deal of social science theory and research. Social scientists agree that members of minority groups frequently respond to discrimination and prejudice by attempting to disassociate themselves from the group, even to the point of adopting the majority's negative attitudes towards

---

20. This is not a case where a majority is practicing benevolent discrimination in fa- vor of a traditionally disfavored minority, al- though that situation illustrates that motiva- tions not immediately obvious might enter into discrimination against "one's own kind."

the minority. Such behavior occurs with particular frequency among members of minority groups who have achieved some measure of economic or political success and thereby have gained some acceptability among the dominant group.

"But even if my Brother Powell's behavioral assumptions were more valid, I still could not agree to making them the foundation for a constitutional ruling. It seems to me that especially in reviewing claims of intentional discrimination, this Court has a solemn responsibility to avoid basing its decisions on broad generalizations concerning minority groups. If history has taught us anything, it is the danger of relying on such stereotypes. The question for decision here is not how Mexican–Americans treat other Mexican–Americans, but how the particular grand jury commissioners in Hidalgo County acted. The only reliable way to answer that question ... is for the State to produce testimony concerning the manner in which the selection process operated...."

Justice Powell, joined by The Chief Justice and Justice Rehnquist, dissented. With respect to the governing majority issue, he said:

"In this case, the following critical facts are beyond dispute: the judge who appointed the jury commissioners and later presided over respondent's trial was Mexican–American; three of the five jury commissioners were Mexican–American; 10 of the 20 members of the grand jury array were Mexican–American; five of the 12 grand jurors who returned the indictment, including the foreman, were Mexican–American, and seven of the 12 petit jurors who returned the verdict of guilt were Mexican–American. In the year in which respondent was indicted, 52.5% of the persons on the grand jury list were Mexican–American. In addition, a majority of the elected officials in Hidalgo County were Mexican–American, as were a majority of the judges. That these positions of power and influence were so held is not surprising in a community where 80% of the population is Mexican–American. As was emphasized by District Judge Garza, the able Mexican–American jurist who presided over the habeas proceedings in the District Court, this case is unique. Every other jury discrimination case reaching this Court has involved a situation where the governing majority, and the resulting power over the jury selection process, was held by a white electorate and white officials.[6]

"The most significant fact in this case, all but ignored in the Court's opinion, is that a majority of the jury commissioners were Mexican–American. The jury commission is the body vested by Texas law with the authority to select grand jurors. Under the Texas selection system, as noted by the Court, the jury commission has the opportunity to identify in advance those potential jurors who have Spanish surnames. In these circumstances, where Mexican–Americans control both the selection of jurors and the political process, rational

---

6. I do not suggest, of course, that the mere fact that Mexican–Americans constitute a majority in Hidalgo County is dispositive. There are many communities in which, by virtue of historical or other reasons, a majority of the population may not be able at a particular time to control or significantly influence political decisions or the way the system operates. See *Turner v. Fouche,* supra. But no one can contend seriously that Hidalgo County is such a community. The classic situation in which a "minority group" may suffer discrimination in a community is where it is "relegated to ... a position of political powerlessness." San Antonio Independent School District v. Rodriguez, 411 U.S. 1, 28 (1973). Here the Mexican–Americans are not politically "powerless"; they are the majoritarian political element of the community, with demonstrated capability to elect and protect their own.

Nor do I suggest that persons in positions of power can never be shown to have discriminated against other members of the same ethnic or racial group. I would hold only that respondent's statistical evidence, without more, is insufficient to prove a claim of discrimination in this case.

inferences from the most basic facts in a democratic society render improbable respondent's claim of an intent to discriminate against him and other Mexican–Americans. As Judge Garza observed, 'If people in charge can choose whom they want, it is unlikely they will discriminate against themselves.' 384 F.Supp. 79, 90.

"That individuals are more likely to discriminate in favor of, than against, those who share their own identifiable attributes is the premise that underlies the cases recognizing that the criminal defendant has a personal right under the Fourteenth Amendment not to have members of his own class excluded from jury service. Discriminatory exclusion of members of the defendant's class has been viewed as unfairly excluding persons who may be inclined to favor the defendant. See Strauder v. West Virginia, 100 U.S., at 309. Were it not for the perceived likelihood that jurors will favor defendants of their own class, there would be no reason to suppose that a jury selection process that systematically excluded persons of a certain race would be the basis of any legitimate complaint by criminal defendants of that race. Only the individuals excluded from jury service would have a personal right to complain.

" . . . With all respect, I am compelled to say that the Court today has 'lightly' concluded that the grand jury commissioners of this county have disregarded not only their sworn duty but also their likely inclination to assure fairness to Mexican–Americans.[7]"

Chief Justice Burger, joined by Justice Powell and Justice Rehnquist, wrote a dissenting opinion challenging the adequacy of the statistical showing to make out a prima facie case of discrimination. Justice Stewart also dissented indicating that he was "in substantial agreement" with the other two dissenting opinions.

Rogers v. Lodge

458 U.S. 613, 102 S.Ct. 3272, 73 L.Ed.2d 1012 (1982).

Justice White delivered the opinion of the Court.

The issue in this case is whether the at-large system of elections in Burke County, Georgia violates the Fourteenth Amendment rights of Burke County's black citizens.

I

Burke County is a large, predominately rural county located in eastern Georgia[,] approximately two-thirds the size of the State of Rhode Island. According to the 1980 Census, Burke County had a total population of 19,349, of whom 10,385, or 53.6% were black. The average age of blacks living there is lower than the average age of whites and therefore whites constitute a slight majority of the voting age population. As of 1978, 6,373 persons were registered to vote in Burke County, of whom 38% were black.

---

7. I agree with Mr. Justice Marshall that stereotypes concerning identifiable classes in our society have no place in the decisions of this Court. For that reason, I consider it inappropriate to characterize the Mexican–American majority in Hidalgo County as a "minority group" and on that basis to suggest that these Mexican–Americans may have "adopt[ed] the majority's negative attitudes towards the minority." This type of speculation illustrates the lengths to which one must go to buttress a holding of purposeful discrimination that otherwise is based solely on a lack of proportional representation.

The Burke County Board of Commissioners governs the county. It was created in 1911 ... and consists of five members elected at large to concurrent four-year terms by all qualified voters in the county. The county has never been divided into districts, either for the purpose of imposing a residency requirement on candidates or for the purpose of requiring candidates to be elected by voters residing in a district. In order to be nominated or elected, a candidate must receive a majority of the votes cast in the primary or general election, and a runoff must be held if no candidate receives a majority in the first primary or general election.... Each candidate must run for a specific seat on the Board, ... and a voter may vote only once for any candidate. No Negro has ever been elected to the Burke County Board of Commissioners.

Eight black citizens of Burke County filed this [federal district court] suit in 1976 ... on behalf of all black citizens in Burke County. The complaint alleged that the County's system of at-large elections violates appellees' First, Thirteenth, Fourteenth and Fifteenth Amendment rights, as well as their rights under 42 U.S.C. §§ 1971, 1973, and 1983 by diluting the voting power of black citizens. Following a bench trial at which both sides introduced extensive evidence, the court issued an order on September 29, 1978 stating that appellees were entitled to prevail and ordering that Burke County be divided into five districts for purposes of electing County Commissioners. The court later issued detailed findings of fact and conclusions of law in which it stated that while the present method of electing County Commissioners was "racially neutral when adopted, [it] is being *maintained* for invidious purposes" in violation of appellees' Fourteenth and Fifteenth Amendment rights.

The Court of Appeals affirmed.... It stated that while the proceedings in the District Court took place prior to ... Mobile v. Bolden, 446 U.S. 55 (1980), the District Court correctly anticipated *Mobile* and required appellees to prove that the at-large voting system was maintained for a discriminatory purpose. The Court of Appeals also held that the District Court's findings not only were not clearly erroneous, but its conclusion that the at-large system was maintained for invidious purposes was "virtually mandated by the overwhelming proof." We ... affirm.

II

At-large voting schemes and multimember districts tend to minimize the voting strength of minority groups by permitting the political majority to elect *all* representatives of the district. A distinct minority, whether it be a racial, ethnic, economic, or political group, may be unable to elect any representatives in an at-large election, yet may be able to elect several representatives if the political unit is divided into single-member districts. The minority's voting power in a multimember district is particularly diluted when bloc voting occurs and ballots are cast along strict majority-minority lines. While multimember districts have been challenged for "their winner-take-all aspects, their tendency to submerge minorities and to overrepresent the winning party," Whitcomb v. Chavis, 403 U.S. 124, 158–159 (1971), this Court has repeatedly held that they are not unconstitutional *per se*. Mobile v. Bolden ...; White v. Regester, 412 U.S. 755, 765 (1973); Whitcomb v. Chavis, supra, 403 U.S. at 142. The Court has recognized, however, that multimember districts violate the Fourteenth Amendment if "conceived or operated as purposeful devices to further racial ... discrimination" by minimizing, cancelling out or diluting the voting strength of racial elements in the voting population. Whitcomb v. Chavis.... Cases charging that multimember districts unconstitutionally dilute the voting strength of racial minorities are thus subject to the standard of proof generally applicable to Equal Protection Clause cases. Washington v. Davis, 426 U.S. 229

(1976), and Village of Arlington Heights v. Metropolitan Housing Development Corp., 429 U.S. 252 (1977), made it clear that in order for the Equal Protection Clause to be violated, "the invidious quality of a law claimed to be racially discriminatory must ultimately be traced to a racially discriminatory purpose." ... Neither case involved voting dilution, but in both cases the Court observed that the requirement that racially discriminatory purpose or intent be proven applies to voting cases by relying upon, among others, Wright v. Rockefeller, 376 U.S. 52 (1964), a districting case, to illustrate that a showing of discriminatory intent has long been required in *all* types of equal protection cases charging racial discrimination....[5]

Arlington Heights and *Washington v. Davis* both rejected the notion that a law is invalid under the Equal Protection Clause simply because it may affect a greater proportion of one race than another.... However, both cases recognized that discriminatory intent need not be proven by direct evidence. "Necessarily, an invidious discriminatory purpose may often be inferred from the totality of the relevant facts, including the fact, if it is true, that the law bears more heavily on one race than another." Ibid. Thus determining the existence of a discriminatory purpose "demands a sensitive inquiry into such circumstantial and direct evidence of intent as may be available." *Arlington Heights,* supra, 429 U.S. at 266.

In *Mobile v. Bolden,* ... the Court was called upon to apply these principles to the at-large election system in Mobile, Alabama. Mobile is governed by three commissioners who exercise all legislative, executive, and administrative power in the municipality. Each candidate for the City Commission runs for one of three numbered posts in an at-large election and can only be elected by a majority vote. Plaintiffs brought a class action on behalf of all Negro citizens of Mobile alleging that the at-large scheme diluted their voting strength in violation of several statutory and constitutional provisions. The District Court concluded that the at-large system "violates the constitutional rights of the plaintiffs by improperly restricting their access to the political process," and ordered that the commission form of government be replaced by a mayor and a nine-member City Council elected from single-member districts. The Court of Appeals affirmed. This Court reversed.

Justice Stewart, writing for himself and three other Justices, noted that to prevail in their contention that the at-large voting system violates the Equal Protection Clause of the Fourteenth Amendment, plaintiffs had to prove the system was "conceived or operated as [a] purposeful devic[e] to further racial ... discrimination." ...[6]

5. Purposeful racial discrimination invokes the strictest scrutiny of adverse differential treatment. Absent such purpose, differential impact is subject only to the test of rationality. Washington v. Davis, supra, at 247–248.

6. With respect to the Fifteenth Amendment, the plurality held that the Amendment prohibits only direct, purposefully discriminatory interference with the freedom of Negroes to vote. "Having found that Negroes in Mobile 'register and vote without hindrance,' the District Court and Court of Appeals were in error in believing that the appellants invaded the protection of [the Fifteenth] Amendment in the present case."

Mobile v. Bolden, 446 U.S. 55, 65 (1980). Three Justices disagreed with the plurality's basis for putting aside the Fifteenth Amendment. Id., at 84, n. 3, (Stevens, J., concurring); Id., at 102 (White, J., dissenting); Id., at 125–135 (Marshall, J., dissenting). We express no view on the application of the Fifteenth Amendment to this case.

The plurality noted that plaintiffs' claim under § 2 of the Voting Rights Act, 79 Stat. 437, as amended, 42 U.S.C. § 1973, added nothing to their Fifteenth Amendment claim because the "legislative history of § 2 makes clear that it was intended to have an effect no different from that of the Fifteenth Amendment itself." Id., at 60–61.

The plurality went on to conclude that the District Court had failed to comply with this standard. The District Court had analyzed plaintiffs' claims in light of the standard ... set forth in Zimmer v. McKeithen, 485 F.2d 1297 (C.A.5 1973), aff'd on other grounds *sub nom.* East Carroll Parish School Bd. v. Marshall, 424 U.S. 636 (1976) *(per curiam). Zimmer* set out a list of factors[8] gleaned from *Whitcomb v. Chavis,* supra, and *White v. Regester,* supra, that a court should consider in assessing the constitutionality of at-large and multi-member district voting schemes. Under *Zimmer,* voting dilution is established "upon proof of the existence of an aggregate of these factors."

The plurality in *Mobile* was of the view that *Zimmer* was "decided upon the misunderstanding that it is not necessary to show a discriminatory purpose in order to prove a violation of the Equal Protection Clause—that proof of a discriminatory effect is sufficient." The plurality observed that while "the presence of the indicia relied on in *Zimmer* may afford some evidence of a discriminatory purpose," the mere existence of those criteria is not a substitute for a finding of discriminatory purpose. The District Court's standard in *Mobile* was likewise flawed....

Because the District Court in the present case employed the evidentiary factors outlined in *Zimmer,* it is urged that its judgment is infirm for the same reasons that led to the reversal in *Mobile.* We do not agree. First, and fundamentally, we are unconvinced that the District Court in this case applied the wrong legal standard. Not only was the District Court's decision rendered a considerable time after *Washington v. Davis* and *Arlington Heights,* but the trial judge also had the benefit of Nevett v. Sides, 571 F.2d 209 (C.A.5 1978), where the Court of Appeals for the Fifth Circuit assessed the impact of *Washington v. Davis* and *Arlington Heights* and held that "a showing of racially motivated discrimination is a necessary element in an equal protection voting dilution claim ..." The court stated that "[t]he ultimate issue in a case alleging unconstitutional dilution of the votes of a racial group is whether the districting plan under attack exists because it was intended to diminish or dilute the political efficacy of that group." Id., at 226. The Court of Appeals also explained that although the evidentiary factors outlined in *Zimmer* were important considerations in arriving at the ultimate conclusion of discriminatory intent, the plaintiff is not limited to those factors. "The task before the fact finder is to determine, under all the relevant facts, in whose favor the 'aggregate' of the evidence preponderates. This determination is peculiarly dependent upon the facts of each case."

The District Court referred to *Nevett v. Sides* and demonstrated its understanding of the controlling standard by observing that a determination of discriminatory intent is "a requisite to a finding of unconstitutional vote dilution" under the Fourteenth and Fifteenth Amendments. Furthermore, while recognizing that the evidentiary factors identified in *Zimmer* were to be considered, the District Court was aware that it was "not limited in its determination only to the *Zimmer* factors" but could consider other relevant factors as well. The District Court then proceeded to deal with what it considered to be the relevant proof and concluded that the at-large scheme of electing commissioners, "although racially neutral when adopted, is being

---

8. The primary factors listed in *Zimmer* include a lack of minority access to the candidate selection process, unresponsiveness of elected officials to minority interests, a tenuous state policy underlying the preference for multi-member or at-large districting, and the existence of past discrimination which pre-cludes effective participation in the elector process.... Factors which enhance the proof of voting dilution are the existence of large districts, anti-single shot voting provisions, and the absence of any provision for at-large candidates to run from geographic subdistricts....

maintained for invidious purposes." That system "while neutral in origin . . . has been subverted to invidious purposes." For the most part, the District Court dealt with the evidence in terms of the factors set out in *Zimmer* and its progeny, but as the Court of Appeals stated:

> "Judge Alaimo employed the constitutionally required standard . . . [and] did not treat the *Zimmer* criteria as absolute, but rather considered them only to the extent they were relevant to the question of discriminatory intent."

Although a tenable argument can be made to the contrary, we are not inclined to disagree with the Court of Appeals' conclusion that the District Court applied the proper legal standard.

III

A

We are also unconvinced that we should disturb the District Court's finding that the at-large system in Burke County was being maintained for the invidious purpose of diluting the voting strength of the black population. In *White v. Regester,* . . . we stated that we were not inclined to overturn the District Court's factual findings, "representing as they do a blend of history and an intensely local appraisal of the design and impact of the Bexar County multimember district in the light of past and present reality, political and otherwise." . . . We are of the view that the same clearly-erroneous standard applies to the trial court's finding in this case that the at-large system in Burke County is being maintained for discriminatory purposes, as well as to the court's subsidiary findings of fact. The Court of Appeals did not hold any of the District Court's findings of fact to be clearly erroneous, and this Court has frequently noted its reluctance to disturb findings of fact concurred in by two lower courts. . . . We agree with the Court of Appeals that on the record before us, none of the factual findings are clearly erroneous.

B

The District Court found that blacks have always made up a substantial majority of the population in Burke County, but that they are a distinct minority of the registered voters. There was also overwhelming evidence of bloc voting along racial lines. Hence, although there had been black candidates, no black had ever been elected to the Burke County commission. These facts bear heavily on the issue of purposeful discrimination. Voting along racial lines allows those elected to ignore black interests without fear of political consequences, and without bloc voting the minority candidates would not lose elections solely because of their race. Because it is sensible to expect that at least some blacks would have been elected in Burke County, the fact that none have ever been elected is important evidence of purposeful exclusion. See White v. Regester, supra, at 766.

Under our cases, however, such facts are insufficient in themselves to prove purposeful discrimination absent other evidence such as proof that blacks have less opportunity to participate in the political processes and to elect candidates of their choice. . . . Both the District Court and the Court of Appeals thought the supporting proof in this case was sufficient to support an inference of intentional discrimination. . . .

The District Court began by determining the impact of past discrimination on the ability of blacks to participate effectively in the political process. Past discrimination was found to contribute to low black voter registration because prior to the Voting Rights Act of 1965, blacks had been denied access to the political process by means such as literacy tests, poll taxes, and white primaries. The result was that "black suffrage in Burke County was virtually nonexistent." Black voter registration in Burke County has increased following the Voting Rights Act to the point that some 38 per cent of blacks eligible to vote are registered to do so. On that basis the District Court inferred that "past discrimination has had an adverse effect on black voter registration which lingers to this date." Past discrimination against blacks in education also had the same effect. Not only did Burke County schools discriminate against blacks as recently as 1969, but some schools still remain essentially segregated and blacks as a group have completed less formal education than whites.

The District Court found further evidence of exclusion from the political process. Past discrimination had prevented blacks from effectively participating in Democratic Party affairs and in primary elections. Until this law suit was filed, there had never been a black member of the County Executive Committee of the Democratic Party. There were also property ownership requirements that made it difficult for blacks to serve as chief registrar in the county. There had been discrimination in the selection of grand jurors, the hiring of county employees, and in the appointments to boards and committees which oversee the county government. The District Court thus concluded that historical discrimination had restricted the present opportunity of blacks effectively to participate in the political process. Evidence of historical discrimination is relevant to drawing an inference of purposeful discrimination, particularly in cases such as this one where the evidence shows that discriminatory practices were commonly utilized, that they were abandoned when enjoined by courts or made illegal by civil rights legislation, and that they were replaced by laws and practices which, though neutral on their face, serve to maintain the status quo.

Extensive evidence was cited by the District Court to support its finding that elected officials of Burke County have been unresponsive and insensitive to the needs of the black community, which increases the likelihood that the political process was not equally open to blacks. . . .

The District Court also considered the depressed socio-economic status of Burke County blacks. It found that proportionately more blacks than whites have incomes below the poverty level. . . .

Although finding that the state policy behind the at-large electoral system in Burke County was "neutral in origin," the District Court concluded that the policy "has been subverted to invidious purposes." As a practical matter, maintenance of the state statute providing for at-large elections in Burke County is determined by Burke County's state representatives, for the legislature defers to their wishes on matters of purely local application. The court found that Burke County's state representatives "have retained a system which has minimized the ability of Burke County Blacks to participate in the political system."

The trial court considered, in addition, several factors which this Court has indicated enhance the tendency of multimember districts to minimize the voting strength of racial minorities. See *Whitcomb v. Chavis,* . . . . It found that the sheer geographic size of the county . . . "has made it more difficult for Blacks to get to polling places or to campaign for office." The court concluded, as a matter of law, that the size of the county tends to impair the access of blacks to the political process. The majority vote requirement, Ga.Code § 34–1513 (1980), was found "to submerge the will of the minority" and thus "deny the minority's access to the system." The court also found the requirement that candidates run for specific seats, Ga.Code § 34–1015 (1980), enhances respondent's lack of access because it prevents a cohesive political group from concentrating on a single candidate. Because Burke County has no residency requirement, "[a]ll candidates could reside in Waynesboro, or in 'lily-white' neighborhoods. To that extent, the denial of access becomes enhanced."

None of the District Court's findings underlying its ultimate finding of intentional discrimination appears to us to be clearly erroneous; and as we have said, we decline to overturn the essential finding of the District Court, agreed to by the Court of Appeals, that the at-large system in Burke County has been maintained for the purpose of denying blacks equal access to the political processes in the county. As in *White v. Regester,* ... the District Court's findings were "sufficient to sustain [its] judgment ... and, on this record, we have no reason to disturb them."

IV

We also find no reason to overturn the relief ordered by the District Court. Neither the District Court nor the Court of Appeals discerned any special circumstances that would militate against utilizing single-member districts....

The judgment of the Court of Appeals is

Affirmed.

Justice Powell, with whom Justice Rehnquist joins, dissenting.

I

... In *Mobile* we reversed a finding of unconstitutional vote dilution because the lower courts had relied on factors insufficient as a matter of law to establish discriminatory intent. ... The District Court and Court of Appeals in this case based their findings of unconstitutional discrimination on the same factors held insufficient in *Mobile.* Yet the Court now finds their conclusion unexceptionable. The *Mobile* plurality also affirmed that the concept of "intent" was no mere fiction, and held that the District Court had erred in "its failure to identify the state officials whose intent it considered relevant." ... Although the courts below did not answer that question in this case, the Court today affirms their decision.

Whatever the wisdom of *Mobile,* the Court's opinion cannot be reconciled persuasively with that case. There are some variances in the largely sociological evidence presented in the two cases. But *Mobile* held that this *kind* of evidence was not enough. Such evidence, we found in *Mobile,* did not merely fall short, but "fell *far* short[,] of showing that [an at-large electoral scheme was] 'conceived or operated [as a] purposeful devic[e] to further racial ... discrimination.'" ... Because I believe that *Mobile* controls this case, I dissent.

II

The Court's decision today relies heavily on the capacity of the federal district courts—essentially free from any standards propounded by this Court—to determine whether at-large voting systems are "being maintained for the invidious purpose of diluting the voting strength of the black population." Federal courts thus are invited to engage in deeply subjective inquiries into the motivations of local officials in structuring local governments. Inquiries of this kind not only can be "unseemly," see Karst, The Costs of Motive–Centered Inquiry, 15 San Diego Law Rev. 1163, 1164 (1978); they intrude the federal courts—with only the vaguest constitutional direction—into an area of intensely local and political concern.

Emphasizing these considerations, Justice Stevens argues forcefully that the Court's focus of inquiry is seriously mistaken. I agree with much of what he says. As I do not share his views entirely, however, I write separately.

A

As I understand it, Justice Stevens' critique of the Court's approach rests on three principles with which I am in fundamental agreement.

First, it is appropriate to distinguish between "state action that inhibits an individual's right to vote and state action that affects the political strength of various groups." Mobile v. Bolden, 446 U.S. 55, 83 (Stevens, J., concurring). Under this distinction, this case is fundamentally different from cases involving direct barriers to voting. There is no claim here that blacks may not register freely and vote for whom they choose. This case also differs from one-man, one-vote cases, in which districting practices make a person's vote less weighty in some districts than in others.

Second, I agree with Justice Stevens that vote dilution cases of this kind are difficult if not impossible to distinguish—especially in their remedial aspect—from other actions to redress gerrymanders.

Finally, Justice Stevens clearly is correct in arguing that the standard used to identify unlawful racial discrimination in this area should be defined in terms that are judicially manageable and reviewable. In the absence of compelling reasons of both law and fact, the federal judiciary is unwarranted in undertaking to restructure state political systems. This is inherently a political area, where the identification of a seeming violation does not necessarily suggest an enforceable judicial remedy—or at least none short of a system of quotas or group representation. Any such system, of course, would be antithetical to the principles of our democracy.

B

Justice Stevens would accommodate these principles by holding that subjective intent is irrelevant to the establishment of a case of racial vote dilution under the Fourteenth Amendment. Despite sharing the concerns from which his position is developed, I would not accept this view. . . .

Nonetheless, I do agree with him that what he calls "objective" factors should be the focus of inquiry in vote-dilution cases. Unlike the considerations on which the lower courts relied in this case and in *Mobile,* the factors identified by Justice Stevens as "objective" in fact are direct, reliable, and unambiguous indices of discriminatory *intent.* If we held, as I think we should, that the district courts must place primary reliance on these factors to establish discriminatory intent, we would prevent federal court inquiries into the *subjective* thought processes of local officials—at least until enough objective evidence had been presented to warrant discovery into subjective motivations in this complex, politically charged area. By prescribing such a rule we would hold federal courts to a standard that was judicially manageable. And we would remain faithful to the central protective purpose of the Equal Protection Clause.

. . . I would hold that the factors cited by the Court of Appeals are too attenuated as a matter of law to support an inference of discriminatory intent [and] reverse its judgment on that basis.

Justice Stevens, dissenting.

. . .

[Justice Stevens' long and interesting opinion is omitted.]

NOTE

On June 29, the day before the opinion was announced in *Rogers,* Congress passed the following amended version of Section 2 of the Voting Rights Act of 1965:

"Sec. 2(a) No voting qualification or prerequisite to voting or standard, practice, or procedure shall be imposed or applied by any State or political subdivision in a manner which results in a denial or abridgement of the right of any citizen of the United States to vote on account of race or color, or in contravention of the guarantees set forth in section 4(f)(2), as provided in subsection (b).

"(b) A violation of subsection (a) is established if, based on the totality of circumstances, it is shown that the political processes leading to nomination or election in the State or political subdivision are not equally open to participation by members of a class of citizens protected by subsection (a) in that its members have less opportunity than other members of the electorate to participate in the political process and to elect representatives of their choice. The extent to which members of a protected class have been elected to office in the State or political subdivision is one circumstance which may be considered: Provided, That nothing in this section establishes a right to have members of a protected class elected in numbers equal to their proportion in the population."

The report of the Senate Committee on the Judiciary accompanying the bill made clear that it was intended to restore the legal standard governing voting discrimination cases before the Supreme Court's decision in City of Mobile, Ala. v. Bolden, 446 U.S. 55 (1980). The Court applied the 1982 amendments in Thornburg v. Gingles, 478 U.S. 30 (1986), to hold a legislative redistricting plan using multimember districts invalid. Deciding no constitutional issues, the Court concluded that the amendments eliminated any requirement of establishing that the contested electoral practice was adopted or maintained with the intent to discriminate against minority voters. The opinions in the case contain elaborate discussion of the problems involved in showing that multimember districts operate to prejudice the voting rights of minorities.

HUNTER v. UNDERWOOD, 471 U.S. 222 (1985). Section 182 of the Alabama Constitution, adopted at a convention in 1901, disenfranchised persons convicted of, among other offenses, "any crime ... Involving moral turpitude." Edwards, a black, and Underwood, a white, were blocked from the voter roles because they each had been convicted of presenting a worthless check. Their federal district court suit contended that § 182 had been intentionally adopted to disenfranchise blacks on account of their race. On this issue the district court treated Edwards as the representative of a class of black members and ruled for the defendants. The Court of Appeals reversed, holding that the evidence showed that § 182 had disenfranchised 10 times as many blacks as whites, and that it had been adopted for the purpose of preventing blacks from voting. The Supreme Court affirmed, all joining an opinion by Justice Rehnquist (Justice Powell not participating).

The Court said first that a neutral state law producing racially disproportionate effects will be invalidated only if it is shown that racially discriminatory intent or purpose was a substantial factor behind enacting the law.

"Proving the motivation behind official action is often a problematic undertaking. See Rogers v. Lodge, 458 U.S. 613 (1982). When we move from an examination of a board of county commissioners such as was involved in *Rogers* to a body the size of the Alabama Constitutional Convention of 1901, the difficulties in determining the actual motivations of the various legislators that produced a given decision increase." But no such difficulties were present here. Evidence from historians and from speeches at the Convention made it clear that zeal for white supremacy ran rampant at the convention. Indeed, the appellants did not seriously dispute that fact. What appellants did argue was that the real purpose behind § 182 was to disenfranchise both poor whites and blacks.

"Even were we to accept this explanation as correct, it hardly saves § 182 from invalidity. The explanation concedes both that discrimination against blacks, as well as against poor whites, was a motivating factor for the provision and that § 182 certainly would not have been adopted by the convention or ratified by the electorate in the absence of the racially discriminatory motivation.

"Citing Palmer v. Thompson, 403 U.S., at 224, and Michael M. v. Superior Court of Sonoma County, 450 U.S. 464, 472, n. 7 (1981) (plurality opinion), appellants make the further argument that the existence of a permissible motive for § 182, namely the disenfranchisement of poor whites, trumps any proof of a parallel impermissible motive. Whether or not intentional disenfranchisement of poor whites would qualify as a 'permissible motive' within the meaning of *Palmer* and *Michael M.*, it is clear that where both impermissible racial motivation and racially discriminatory impact are demonstrated, *Arlington Heights* and *Mt. Healthy* supply the proper analysis. Under the view that the Court of Appeals could properly take of the evidence, an additional purpose to discriminate against poor whites would not render nugatory the purpose to discriminate against all blacks, and it is beyond peradventure that the latter was a 'but-for' motivation for the enactment of § 182.

. . .

"At oral argument in this Court, the State suggested that, regardless of the original purpose of § 182, events occurring in the succeeding 80 years had legitimated the provision. . . . Without deciding whether § 182 would be valid if enacted today without any impermissible motivation, we simply observe that its original enactment was motivated by a desire to discriminate against blacks on account of race and the section continues to this day to have that effect. As such, it violates equal protection under *Arlington Heights*.

"Finally, appellants contend that the State is authorized by the Tenth Amendment and § 2 of the Fourteenth Amendment to deny the franchise to persons who commit misdemeanors involving moral turpitude. For the reasons we have stated, the enactment of § 182 violated the Fourteenth Amendment, and the Tenth Amendment cannot save legislation prohibited by the subsequently enacted Fourteenth Amendment. The single remaining question is whether § 182 is excepted from the operation of the Equal Protection Clause of § 1 of the Fourteenth Amendment by the 'other crime' provision of § 2 of that Amendment. Without again considering the implicit authorization of § 2 to deny the vote to citizens 'for participation in rebellion, or other crime,' see Richardson v. Ramirez, 418 U.S. 24 (1974), we are confident that § 2 was not designed to permit the purposeful racial discrimination attending the enactment and operation of § 182 which otherwise violates § 1 of the Fourteenth Amendment. Nothing in our opinion in *Richardson v. Ramirez* . . . suggests the contrary."

E. "Benign" Discrimination: Affirmative Action, Quotas, Preferences Based on Gender or Race

1. CLASSIFICATIONS ADVANTAGING FEMALES

Kahn v. Shevin

416 U.S. 351, 94 S.Ct. 1734, 40 L.Ed.2d 189 (1974).

Mr. Justice Douglas delivered the opinion of the Court.

Since at least 1885, Florida has provided for some form of property tax exemption for widows. The current law granting all widows an annual $500 exemption, Fla.Stat. § 196.191(7), F.S.A., has been essentially unchanged since 1941. Appellant Kahn is a widower who lives in Florida and applied for the exemption to the Dade County Tax Assessor's Office. It was denied because the statute offers no analogous benefit for widowers. Kahn then sought a declaratory judgment in the Circuit Court for Dade County, Florida, and that court held the statute violative of the Equal Protection Clause of the Fourteenth Amendment because the classification "widow" was based upon gender. The Florida Supreme Court reversed, finding the classification valid because it has a "fair and substantial relation to the object of the legislation," that object being the reduction of "the disparity between the economic capabilities of a man and a woman." Kahn appealed here.... We affirm.

There can be no dispute that the financial difficulties confronting the lone woman in Florida or in any other State exceed those facing the man. Whether from overt discrimination or from the socialization process of a male dominated culture, the job market is inhospitable to the woman seeking any but the lowest paid jobs. There are of course efforts underway to remedy this situation. On the federal level Title VII of the Civil Rights Act of 1964 prohibits covered employers and labor unions from discrimination on the basis of sex, 42 U.S.C. § 2000e-2(a), (b), (c), as does the Equal Pay Act of 1963, 29 U.S.C. § 206(d). But firmly entrenched practices are resistant to such pressures, and indeed, data compiled by the Women's Bureau of the United States Department of Labor shows that in 1972 women working full time had a median income which was only 57.9% of the male median—a figure actually six points lower than had been achieved in 1955. Other data points in the same direction. The disparity is likely to be exacerbated for the widow. While the widower can usually continue in the occupation which preceded his spouse's death in many cases the widow will find herself suddenly forced into a job market with which she is unfamiliar, and in which, because of her former economic dependency, she will have fewer skills to offer.

There can be no doubt therefore that Florida's differing treatment of widows and widowers "rest[s] upon some ground of difference having a fair and substantial relation to the object of the legislation." Reed v. Reed, 404 U.S. 71, 76....

This is not a case like Frontiero v. Richardson, 411 U.S. 677, where the Government denied its female employees both substantive and procedural benefits granted males "*solely* for administrative convenience." Id., at 690 (emphasis in original).[8] We deal here with a state tax law reasonably designed

---

8. And in *Frontiero* the plurality opinion also noted that the statutes there were "not in any sense designed to rectify the effects of past discrimination against women. On the contrary, these statutes seize upon a group—women—who have historically sufto further the state policy of cushioning the financial impact of spousal loss upon the sex for whom that loss imposes a disproportionately heavy burden. We have long held that "[w]here taxation is concerned and no specific federal right, apart from equal protection, is imperilled, the States have large leeway in making classifications and drawing lines which in their judgment produce reasonable systems of taxation." Lehnhausen v. Lake Shore Auto Parts Co., 410 U.S. 356, 359. A state tax law is not arbitrary although it "discriminate[s] in favor of a certain class ... if the discrimination is founded upon a reasonable distinction, or difference in state policy," not in conflict with the Federal Constitution. Allied Stores v. Bowers, 358 U.S. 522, 528. This principle has weathered nearly a century of Supreme Court adjudication, and it applies here as well. The statute before us is well within those limits.[10]

Affirmed.

Mr. Justice Brennan, with whom Mr. Justice Marshall joins, dissenting.

... In my view ... a legislative classification that distinguishes potential beneficiaries solely by reference to their gender-based status as widows or widowers, like classifications based upon race, alienage, and national origin, must be subjected to close judicial scrutiny, because it focuses upon generally immutable characteristics over which individuals have little or no control, and also because gender-based classifications too often have been inexcusably utilized to stereotype and stigmatize politically powerless segments of society. See Frontiero v. Richardson, 411 U.S. 677 (1973). The Court is not therefore free to sustain the statute on the ground that it rationally promotes legitimate governmental interests; rather, such suspect classifications can be sustained only when the State bears the burden of demonstrating that the challenged legislation serves overriding or compelling interests that cannot be achieved either by a more carefully tailored legislative classification or by the use of feasible less drastic means. While ... the statute serves a compelling governmental interest by "cushioning the financial impact of spousal loss upon the sex for whom that loss imposes a disproportionately heavy burden," I think [it] is invalid because the State's interest can be served equally well by a more narrowly drafted statute.

Gender-based classifications cannot be sustained merely because they promote legitimate governmental interests, such as efficacious administration of government. *Frontiero v. Richardson,* supra; Reed v. Reed, 404 U.S. 71 (1971).... On the contrary, any statutory scheme which draws a sharp line between the sexes, *solely* for the purpose of achieving administrative convenience, necessarily commands "dissimilar treatment for men and women who are ... similarly situated," and therefore involves the "very kind of arbitrary

---

fered discrimination in employment, and rely on the effects of this past discrimination as a justification for heaping on additional economic disadvantages." ... 411 U.S. 677, 689 n. 22....

   10. The dissents argue that the Florida Legislature could have drafted the statute differently, so that its purpose would have been accomplished more precisely. But the issue of course is not whether the statute could have been drafted more wisely, but whether the lines chosen by the Florida Legislature are within constitutional limitations. The dissent would use the Equal Protection Clause as a vehicle for reinstating notions of

substantive due process that have been repudiated....

   Gender has never been rejected as an impermissible classification in all instances. Congress has not so far drafted women into the Armed Services. 50 App.U.S.C. § 454. The famous Brandeis Brief in Muller v. Oregon, 208 U.S. 412, on which the court specifically relied, id., at 419–420, emphasized that the special physical organization of women has a bearing on the "conditions under which she should be permitted to toil." Id., at 420. These instances are pertinent to the problem in the tax field....

legislative choice forbidden by the [constitution]...." Reed v. Reed, 404 U.S., at 77, 76. "*Frontiero v. Richardson,*.... But Florida's justification of § 196.191(7) is not that it serves administrative convenience or helps to preserve the public fisc. Rather, the asserted justification is that § 196.191(7) is an affirmative step toward alleviating the effects of past economic discrimination against women."

I agree that, in providing special benefits for a needy segment of society long the victim of purposeful discrimination and neglect, the statute serves the compelling state interest of achieving equality for such groups. No one familiar with this country's history of pervasive sex discrimination against women can doubt the need for remedial measures to correct the resulting economic imbalances. Indeed, the extent of the economic disparity between men and women is dramatized by the data cited by the Court. By providing a property tax exemption for widows, § 196.01(7) assists in reducing that economic disparity for a class of women particularly disadvantaged by the legacy of economic discrimination. In that circumstance, the purpose and effect of the suspect classification is ameliorative; the statute neither stigmatizes nor denigrates widowers not also benefited by the legislation. Moreover, inclusion of needy widowers within the class of beneficiaries would not further the State's overriding interest in remedying the economic effects of past sex discrimination for needy victims of that discrimination. While doubtless some widowers are in financial need, no one suggests that such need results from sex discrimination as in the case of widows.

The statute nevertheless fails to satisfy the requirements of equal protection, since the State has not borne its burden of proving that its compelling interest could not be achieved by a more precisely tailored statute or by use of feasible less drastic means. Section 196.191(7) is plainly overinclusive, for the $500 property tax exemption may be obtained by a financially independent heiress as well as by an unemployed widow with dependent children. The State has offered nothing to explain why inclusion of widows of substantial economic means was necessary to advance the State's interest in ameliorating the effects of past economic discrimination against women.

Moreover, alternative means of classification, narrowing the class of widow beneficiaries, appear readily available. The exemption is granted only to widows who complete and file with the tax assessor a form application establishing their status as widows. By merely redrafting that form to exclude widows who earn annual incomes, or possess assets, in excess of specified amounts, the State could readily narrow the class of beneficiaries to those widows for whom the effects of past economic discrimination against women have been a practical reality.

Mr. Justice White, dissenting.

The Florida tax exemption at issue here is available to all widows but not to widowers. The presumption is that all widows are financially more needy and less trained or less ready for the job market than men. It may be that most widows have been occupied as housewife, mother and homemaker and are not immediately prepared for employment. But there are many rich widows who need no largess from the State; many others are highly trained and have held lucrative positions long before the death of their husbands. At the same time, there are many widowers who are needy and who are in more desperate financial straits and have less access to the job market than many widows. Yet none of them qualifies for the exemption.

I find the discrimination invidious and violative of the Equal Protection Clause. There is merit in giving poor widows a tax break, but gender-based classifications are suspect and require more justification than the State has offered.

I perceive no purpose served by the exemption other than to alleviate current economic necessity, but the State extends the exemption to widows who do not need the help and denies it to widowers who do. It may be administratively inconvenient to make individual determinations of entitlement and to extend the exemption to needy men as well as needy women, but administrative efficiency is not an adequate justification for discriminations based purely on sex. Frontiero v. Richardson, 411 U.S. 677 (1973); Reed v. Reed, 404 U.S. 71 (1971).

It may be suggested that the State is entitled to prefer widows over widowers because their assumed need is rooted in past and present economic discrimination against women. But this is not a credible explanation of Florida's tax exemption; for if the State's purpose was to compensate for past discrimination against females, surely it would not have limited the exemption to women who are widows. Moreover, even if past discrimination is considered to be the criterion for current tax exemption, the State nevertheless ignores all those widowers who have felt the effects of economic discrimination, whether as a member of a racial group or as one of the many who cannot escape the cycle of poverty. It seems to me that the State in this case is merely conferring an economic benefit in the form of a tax exemption and has not adequately explained why women should be treated differently than men.

I dissent.

CALIFANO v. WEBSTER, 430 U.S. 313 (1977). A complex formula for computing retirement benefits under social security permitted a female wage earner to exclude from the computation of her "average monthly wage" three more lower earning years than a similarly situated male wage earner could exclude. This resulted in a higher level of monthly old-age benefits for the retired female wage earner. In a Per Curiam opinion the Court held the classification valid, saying, in part:

"To withstand scrutiny under the equal protection component of the Fifth Amendment's Due Process Clause, 'classifications by gender must serve important governmental objectives and must be substantially related to achievement of those objectives.' Craig v. Boren, 429 U.S. 190, 197 (1976). Reduction of the disparity in economic condition between men and women caused by the long history of discrimination against women has been recognized as such an important governmental objective. Schlesinger v. Ballard, 419 U.S. 498 (1975); Kahn v. Shevin, 416 U.S. 351 (1974). But 'the mere recitation of a benign, compensatory purpose is not an automatic shield which protects against any inquiry into the actual purposes underlying a statutory scheme.' Weinberger v. Wiesenfeld, 420 U.S. 636, 648 (1975). Accordingly, we have rejected attempts to justify gender classifications as compensation for past discrimination against women when the classifications in fact penalized women wage earners, Califano v. Goldfarb, 430 U.S. 199, Weinberger v. Wiesenfeld, supra, at 645, or when the statutory structure and its legislative history revealed that the classification was not enacted as compensation for past discrimination. . . .

"The statutory scheme involved here is more analogous to those upheld in *Kahn* and *Ballard* than to those struck down in *Wiesenfeld* and *Goldfarb*. The more favorable treatment of the female wage earner enacted here was not a result of 'archaic and overbroad generalizations' about women, *Schlesinger v. Ballard* ... or of 'the role-typing society has long imposed' upon women, Stanton v. Stanton, 421 U.S. 7, 15 (1975), such as casual assumptions that women are 'the weaker sex' or are more likely to be child-rearers or dependents. Cf. Califano v. Goldfarb, supra; Weinberger v. Wiesenfeld, supra. Rather, 'the only discernible purpose of [§ 215's more favorable treatment is] the permissible one of redressing our society's longstanding disparate treatment of women.' Califano v. Goldfarb. . . .

"The challenged statute operated directly to compensate women for past economic discrimination. Retirement benefits under the Act are based on past earnings. But as we have recognized: 'Whether from overt discrimination or from the socialization process of a male-dominated culture, the job market is inhospitable to the woman seeking any but the lowest paid jobs.' Kahn v. Shevin, 416 U.S. at 353. . . . Thus, allowing women, who as such have been unfairly hindered from earning as much as men, to eliminate additional low-earning years from the calculation of their retirement benefits works directly to remedy some part of the effect of past discrimination. Cf. Schlesinger v. Ballard, supra, at 508.

"The legislative history of § 215(b)(3) also reveals that Congress directly addressed the justification for differing treatment of men and women in the former version of that section and purposely enacted the more favorable treatment for female wage earners to compensate for past employment discrimination against women. . . . "

Chief Justice Burger, joined by Justices Stewart, Blackmun, and Rehnquist concurred in the judgment.

ORR v. ORR, 440 U.S. 268 (1979). The Court held unconstitutional Alabama's statutory scheme imposing alimony obligations on husbands but not wives. It rejected the argument that the gender distinction was justified, because of the disparity between the economic condition of men and women, to provide support for needy wives of broken marriages. Justice Brennan's opinion for the Court said in part:

"Ordinarily, we would begin the analysis of the 'needy spouse' objective by considering whether sex is a sufficiently 'accurate proxy' for dependency to establish that the gender classification rests 'upon some ground of difference having a fair and substantial relation to the object of the legislation.' Similarly, we would initially approach the 'compensation' rationale by asking whether women had in fact been significantly discriminated against in the sphere to which the statute applied a sex-based classification, leaving the sexes '*not* similarly situated with respect to opportunities' in that sphere.[11]

"But in this case, even if sex were a reliable proxy for need, and even if the institution of marriage did discriminate against women, these factors still would 'not adequately justify the salient features of' Alabama's statutory scheme. Under the statute, individualized hearings at which the parties' relative financial circumstances are considered *already* occur. There is no reason, therefore, to use sex as a proxy for need. Needy males could be helped along with needy females with little if any additional burden on the State. In such circumstances, not even an administrative convenience rationale exists to justify operating by generalization or proxy. Similarly, since individualized hearings can determine which women were in fact discriminated against vis-a-vis their husbands, as well as which family units defied the stereotype and left the husband dependent on the wife, Alabama's alleged compensatory purpose may be effectuated without placing burdens solely on husbands. Progress toward fulfilling such a purpose would not be hampered, and it would cost the

---

11. We would also consider whether the purportedly compensatory "classifications in fact penalized women," and whether "the statutory structure and its legislative history revealed that the classification was not enacted as compensation for past discrimination."

State nothing more, if it were to treat men and women equally by making alimony burdens independent of sex. 'Thus, the gender-based distinction is gratuitous; without it the statutory scheme would only provide benefits to those men who are in fact similarly situated to the women the statute aids,' and the effort to help those women would not in any way be compromised.

"Moreover, use of a gender classification actually produces perverse results in this case. As compared to a gender-neutral law placing alimony obligations on the spouse able to pay, the present Alabama statutes give an advantage only to the financially secure wife whose husband is in need. Although such a wife might have to pay alimony under a gender-neutral statute, the present statutes exempt her from that obligation. Thus, '[t]he [wives] who benefit from the disparate treatment are those who were ... nondependent on their husbands.' They are precisely those who are not 'needy spouses' and who are 'least likely to have been victims of ... discrimination,' by the institution of marriage. A gender-based classification which, as compared to a gender-neutral one, generates additional benefits only for those it has no reason to prefer cannot survive equal protection scrutiny.

"Legislative classifications which distribute benefits and burdens on the basis of gender carry the inherent risk of reinforcing the stereotypes about the 'proper place' of women and their need for special protection. Thus, even statutes purportedly designed to compensate for and ameliorate the effects of past discrimination must be carefully tailored. Where, as here, the State's compensatory and ameliorative purposes are as well served by a gender-neutral classification as one that gender-classifies and therefore carries with it the baggage of sexual stereotypes, the State cannot be permitted to classify on the basis of sex. And this is doubly so where the choice made by the State appears to redound—if only indirectly—to the benefit of those without need for special solicitude.

"Having found Alabama's alimony statutes unconstitutional, we reverse the judgment below and remand the cause for further proceedings not inconsistent with this opinion. That disposition, of course, leaves the state courts free ... on remand to consider whether Mr. Orr's stipulated agreement to pay alimony, or other grounds of gender-neutral state law, bind him to continue his alimony payments."

Chief Justice Burger, Justice Powell, and Justice Rehnquist, dissenting on other issues, did not reach the equal protection question.

Mississippi University for Women v. Hogan

458 U.S. 718, 102 S.Ct. 3331, 73 L.Ed.2d 1090 (1982).

Justice O'Connor delivered the opinion of the Court.

This case presents the narrow issue of whether a state statute that excludes males from enrolling in a state-supported professional nursing school violates the Equal Protection Clause of the Fourteenth Amendment.

I

The facts are not in dispute. In 1884, the Mississippi legislature created the Mississippi Industrial Institute and College for the Education of White Girls of the State of Mississippi, now the oldest state-supported all-female college in the United States.... The school, known today as Mississippi University for Women (MUW), has from its inception limited its enrollment to women.

In 1971, MUW established a School of Nursing, initially offering a two-year associate degree. Three years later, the school instituted a four-year baccalaureate program in nursing and today also offers a graduate program. The School of Nursing has its own faculty and administrative officers and establishes its own criteria for admission.

Respondent, Joe Hogan, is a registered nurse but does not hold a baccalaureate degree in nursing. Since 1974, he has worked as a nursing supervisor in a medical center in Columbus, the city in which MUW is located. In 1979, Hogan applied for admission to the MUW School of Nursing's baccalaureate program. Although he was otherwise qualified, he was denied admission to the School of Nursing solely because of his sex. School officials informed him that he could audit the courses in which he was interested, but could not enroll for credit.

Hogan [sued in federal district], claiming the single-sex admissions policy of MUW's School of Nursing violated the Equal Protection Clause of the Fourteenth Amendment. . . .

[T]he District Court denied preliminary injunctive relief. . . .

The . . . Fifth Circuit reversed, holding that, because the admissions policy discriminates on the basis of gender, the District Court improperly used a "rational relationship" test to judge the constitutionality of the policy. . . .

We . . . affirm. . . .[7]

II

We begin our analysis aided by several firmly-established principles. Because the challenged policy expressly discriminates among applicants on the basis of gender, it is subject to scrutiny under the Equal Protection Clause of the Fourteenth Amendment. Reed v. Reed, 404 U.S. 71, 75 (1971). That this statute discriminates against males rather than against females does not exempt it from scrutiny or reduce the standard of review.[8] Caban v. Mohammed, 441 U.S. 380, 394 (1979); Orr v. Orr, 440 U.S. 268, 279 (1979). Our decisions also establish that the party seeking to uphold a statute that classifies individuals on the basis of their gender must carry the burden of showing an "exceedingly persuasive justification" for the classification. Kirchberg v. Feenstra, 450 U.S. 455, 461 (1981); Personnel Administrator of Massachusetts v. Feeney, 442 U.S. 256, 273 (1979). The burden is met only by showing at least that the classification serves "important governmental objectives and that the discriminatory means employed" are "substantially related to the achievement

7. Although some statements in the Court of Appeals' decision refer to all schools within MUW, . . . the factual underpinning of Hogan's claim for relief involved only his exclusion from the nursing program, and the Court of Appeals' holding applies only to Hogan's individual claim for relief. . . . Additionally, during oral argument, counsel verified that Hogan sought only admission to the School of Nursing. . . . [W]e decline to address . . . whether MUW's admissions policy, as applied to males seeking admission to schools other than the School of Nursing, violates the Fourteenth Amendment.

8. Without question, MUW's admissions policy worked to Hogan's disadvantage. Although Hogan could have attended classes and received credit in one of Mississippi's state-supported coeducational nursing programs, none of which was located in Columbus, he could attend only by driving a considerable distance from his home. A similarly situated female would not have been required to choose between foregoing credit and bearing that inconvenience. Moreover, since many students enrolled in the School of Nursing hold full-time jobs, Hogan's female colleagues had available an opportunity, not open to Hogan, to obtain credit for additional training. The policy of denying males the right to obtain credit toward a baccalaureate degree thus imposed upon Hogan "a burden he would not bear were he female." Orr v. Orr, 440 U.S. 268, 273 (1979).

of those objectives." Wengler v. Druggists Mutual Insurance Co., 446 U.S. 142, 150 (1980).

Although the test . . . is straightforward, it must be applied free of fixed notions concerning the roles and abilities of males and females. Care must be taken in ascertaining whether the statutory objective itself reflects archaic and stereotypic notions. Thus, if the statutory objective is to exclude or "protect" members of one gender because they are presumed to suffer from an inherent handicap or to be innately inferior, the objective itself is illegitimate. See Frontiero v. Richardson . . . (1973) (plurality opinion).

If the State's objective is legitimate and important, we next determine whether the requisite direct, substantial relationship between objective and means is present. The purpose of requiring that close relationship is to assure that the validity of a classification is determined through reasoned analysis rather than through the mechanical application of traditional, often inaccurate, assumptions about the proper roles of men and women. The need for the requirement is amply revealed by reference to the broad range of statutes already invalidated by this Court, statutes that relied upon the simplistic, outdated assumption that gender could be used as a "proxy for other, more germane bases of classification," Craig v. Boren, 429 U.S. 190, 198 (1976), to establish a link between objective and classification.

. . . .

III

A

The State's primary justification for maintaining the single-sex admissions policy of MUW's School of Nursing is that it compensates for discrimination against women and, therefore, constitutes educational affirmative action. As applied to the School of Nursing, we find the State's argument unpersuasive.

In limited circumstances, a gender-based classification favoring one sex can be justified if it intentionally and directly assists members of the sex that is disproportionately burdened. See Schlesinger v. Ballard, 419 U.S. 498 (1975). However, we consistently have emphasized that "the mere recitation of a benign, compensatory purpose is not an automatic shield which protects against any inquiry into the actual purposes underlying a statutory scheme." Weinberger v. Wiesenfeld, 420 U.S. 636, 648 (1975). The same searching analysis must be made, regardless of whether the State's objective is to eliminate family controversy, Reed v. Reed, supra, to achieve administrative efficiency, Frontiero v. Richardson, supra, or to balance the burdens borne by males and females.

It is readily apparent that a State can evoke a compensatory purpose to justify an otherwise discriminatory classification only if members of the gender benefited by the classification actually suffer a disadvantage related to the classification. We considered such a situation in Califano v. Webster, 430 U.S. 313 (1977), which involved a challenge to a statutory classification that allowed women to eliminate more low-earning years than men for purposes of computing Social Security retirement benefits. Although the effect of the classification was to allow women higher monthly benefits than were available to men with the same earning history, we upheld the statutory scheme, noting that it took into account that women "as such have been unfairly hindered from earning as much as men" and "work[ed] directly to remedy" the resulting economic disparity.

A similar pattern of discrimination against women influenced our decision in Schlesinger v. Ballard, 419 U.S. 498 (1975). There, we considered a federal statute that granted female Naval officers a 13–year tenure of commissioned service before mandatory discharge, but accorded male officers only a nine-year tenure. We recognized that, because women were barred from combat duty, they had had fewer opportunities for promotion than had their male counterparts. By allowing women an additional four years to reach a particular rank before subjecting them to mandatory discharge, the statute directly compensated for other statutory barriers to advancement.

In sharp contrast, Mississippi has made no showing that women lacked opportunities to obtain training in the field of nursing or to attain positions of leadership in that field when the MUW School of Nursing opened its door or that women currently are deprived of such opportunities. In fact, in 1970, the year before the School of Nursing's first class enrolled, women earned 94 percent of the nursing baccalaureate degrees conferred in Mississippi and 98.6 percent of the degrees earned nationwide. . . . As one would expect, the labor force reflects the same predominance of women in nursing. When MUW's School of Nursing began operation, nearly 98 percent of all employed registered nurses were female. . . .

Rather than compensate for discriminatory barriers faced by women, MUW's policy of excluding males from admission to the School of Nursing tends to perpetuate the stereotyped view of nursing as an exclusively women's job. By assuring that Mississippi allots more openings in its state-supported nursing schools to women than it does to men, MUW's admissions policy lends credibility to the old view that women, not men, should become nurses, and makes the assumption that nursing is a field for women a self-fulfilling prophecy. See Stanton v. Stanton, 421 U.S. 7 (1975). Thus, we conclude that, although the State recited a "benign, compensatory purpose," it failed to establish that the alleged objective is the actual purpose underlying the discriminatory classification.

The policy is invalid also because it fails the second part of the equal protection test, for the State has made no showing that the gender-based classification is substantially and directly related to its proposed compensatory objective. To the contrary, MUW's policy of permitting men to attend classes as auditors fatally undermines its claim that women, at least those in the School of Nursing, are adversely affected by the presence of men.

MUW permits men who audit to participate fully in classes. Additionally, both men and women take part in continuing education courses offered by the School of Nursing, in which regular nursing students also can enroll. The uncontroverted record reveals that admitting men to nursing classes does not affect teaching style, that the presence of men in the classroom would not affect the performance of the female nursing students, and that men in coeducational nursing schools do not dominate the classroom. In sum, the record . . . is flatly inconsistent with the claim that excluding men from the School of Nursing is necessary to reach any of MUW's educational goals.

Thus, considering both the asserted interest and the relationship between the interest and the methods used by the State, we conclude that the State has fallen far short of establishing the "exceedingly persuasive justification" needed to sustain the gender-based classification. Accordingly, we hold that MUW's policy denying males the right to enroll for credit in its School of Nursing violates the Equal Protection Clause of the Fourteenth Amendment.

. . .

Chief Justice Burger, dissenting.

I agree generally with Justice Powell's dissenting opinion. I write separately, however, to emphasize that the Court's holding today is limited to the context of a professional nursing school. Since the Court's opinion relies heavily on its finding that women have traditionally dominated the nursing profession, it suggests that a State might well be justified in maintaining, for example, the option of an all-women's business school or liberal arts program.

Justice Blackmun, dissenting.

. . .

I have come to suspect that it is easy to go too far with rigid rules in this area of claimed sex discrimination, and to lose—indeed destroy—values that mean much to some people by forbidding the State from offering them a choice while not depriving others of an alternate choice. . . .

. . .

I hope that we do not lose all values that some think are worthwhile (and are not based on differences of race or religion) and relegate ourselves to needless conformity. . . .

Justice Powell, with whom Justice Rehnquist joins, dissenting.

The Court's opinion bows deeply to conformity. Left without honor— indeed, held unconstitutional—is an element of diversity that has characterized much of American education and enriched much of American life. The Court in effect holds today that no State now may provide even a single institution of higher learning open only to women students. . . .

. . .

II

The issue in this case is whether a State transgresses the Constitution when—within the context of a public system that offers a diverse range of campuses, curricula, and educational alternatives—it seeks to accommodate the legitimate personal preferences of those desiring the advantages of an all-women's college. In my view, the Court errs seriously by assuming—without argument or discussion—that the equal protection standard generally applicable to sex discrimination is appropriate here. That standard was designed to free women from "archaic and overbroad generalizations. . . ." Schlesinger v. Ballard, 419 U.S. 498, 508 (1975). In no previous case have we applied it to invalidate state efforts to *expand* women's choices. Nor are there prior sex discrimination decisions by this Court in which a male plaintiff, as in this case, had the choice of an equal benefit. . . .

By applying heightened equal protection analysis to this case, the Court frustrates the liberating spirit of the Equal Protection Clause. It forbids the States from providing women with an opportunity to choose the type of university they prefer. And yet it is these women whom the Court regards as the *victims* of an illegal, stereotyped perception of the role of women in our society. The Court reasons this way in a case in which no woman has complained, and the only complainant is a man who advances no claims on behalf of anyone else. His claim, it should be recalled, is not that he is being denied a substantive educational opportunity, or even the right to attend an all-male or a coeducational college. It is *only* that the colleges open to him are located at inconvenient distances.

. . .

IV

A distinctive feature of America's tradition has been respect for diversity. This has been characteristic of the peoples from numerous lands who have built our country. It is the essence of our democratic system. At stake in this case as I see it is the preservation of a small aspect of this diversity. But that aspect is by no means insignificant, given our heritage of available choice between single-sex and coeducational institutions of higher learning. The Court answers that there is discrimination—not just that which may be tolerable, as for example between those candidates for admission able to contribute most to an educational institution and those able to contribute less—but discrimination of constitutional dimension. But, having found "discrimination," the Court finds it difficult to identify the victims. It hardly can claim that women are discriminated against. A constitutional case is held to exist solely because one man found it inconvenient to travel to any of the other institutions made available to him by the State of Mississippi. In essence he insists that he has a right to attend a college in his home community. This simply is not a sex discrimination case. The Equal Protection Clause was never intended to be applied to this kind of case.

JOHNSON v. TRANSPORTATION AGENCY, SANTA CLARA COUNTY, 480 U.S. 616 (1987). A white male passed over for promotion in favor of a female employee with lower test scores sued under Title VII of the 1964 Civil Rights Act. He raised no constitutional issues, and the court decided the case entirely under Title VII. After much discussion the Court held "that the agency appropriately took into account as one factor the sex of Diane Joyce in determining that she should be promoted to the road dispatcher position. The decision to do so was made pursuant to an affirmative action plan that represents a moderate, flexible, case-by-case approach to effecting a gradual improvement in the representation of minorities and women in the Agency's work force." Three justices dissented.

2. CLASSIFICATIONS ADVANTAGING RACIAL MINORITIES

RACE-CONSCIOUS AFFIRMATIVE ACTION, 1974–1989

During the last quarter of the 20th century the Court began to address the constitutionality of voluntary use of racial criteria for the avowed purpose of benefiting, rather than disadvantaging, racial minorities in the competition for valuable but finite opportunities such as public university admissions; government contracts, jobs and licenses; and voter representation. Earlier, in Swann v. Charlotte–Mecklenburg Board of Education, 402 U.S. 1 (1971), in the course of contrasting the legitimate scope of judicially-imposed race-conscious remedies for proven *de jure* school segregation with the broader scope of voluntary school board efforts, the Court had noted that "[s]chool authorities ... traditionally charged with broad power to formulate and implement educational policy ... might well conclude ... that in order to prepare students to live in a pluralistic society each school should have a prescribed ratio of Negro to white students reflecting the proportion for the district as a whole."

The first case that came to the Court squarely involving the constitutionality of a voluntary affirmative action program, however, was DeFunis v. Odegaard, 416 U.S. 312 (1974), but a majority of the Court dismissed as moot the action brought by a rejected white applicant to the University of Washington Law School, because by the time of the Court's opinion he was about to graduate by virtue of lower court proceedings.[a] Justice Douglas dissented, addressed the merits, and said in part that "a finding that the state school employed a racial classification in selecting its students subjects it to the strictest scrutiny under the Equal Protection Clause." What is "key," he argued, "is the consideration of each application *in a racially neutral way*." (Emphasis in original.) That meant first that because the Law School Admissions Test (LSAT) "reflects questions touching on cultural backgrounds, the Admissions Committee acted properly . . . in setting minority applications apart for separate processing . . . in order better to probe their capacities and potentials." That meant second, however, that the "reason for the separate treatment of minorities as a class is to make more certain that racial factors do not militate *against an applicant or on his behalf*" (emphasis in original) and, specifically, that "[w]hatever [DeFunis'] race, he had a constitutional right to have his application considered on its individual merits in a racially neutral manner." Justice Douglas was concerned that "[t]he reservation of a proportion of the law school class for members of selected minority groups is fraught with . . . dangers, for one must immediately determine which groups are to receive such favored treatment and which are to be excluded, the proportions of the class that are to be allocated to each, and even the criteria by which to determine whether an individual is a member of a favored group." He also objected that the "State . . . may not proceed by racial classification to force strict population equivalencies for every group in every occupation, overriding individual preferences"; that "a segregated admissions process creates suggestions of stigma and caste no less than a segregated classroom, and in the end it may produce that result despite its contrary intentions"; and that since "[a]ll races can compete fairly at all professional levels . . ., any state-sponsored preference to one race over another in that competition is . . . 'invidious' and violative of the Equal Protection Clause."

A majority of the Court addressed the constitutional merits of a voluntary race-conscious affirmative action program for the first time in Regents of the University of California v. Bakke, 438 U.S. 265 (1978), although the Court could not muster consensus on a majority opinion—a frequent occurrence in affirmative action cases. Without reaching the constitutional question, Justice Stevens, joined by Chief Justice Burger and Justices Stewart and Rehnquist, concluded that the special admissions program of the Medical School of the University of California at Davis—which reserved 16 out of 100 places in the first year class for applicants who were either Black, Chicano, Asian or American Indian and were selected by a separate special admissions committee—violated Title VI of the Civil Rights Act of 1964. Of the five Justices who relied on the Constitution, one (Justice Powell) applied the "most exacting scrutiny" to the racial classification and concluded that the Davis special admissions program denied Bakke his "individual" equal protection rights by making him ineligible for consideration for any of the 16 seats reserved for minority applicants. Five Justices thus agreed that the particular Davis program was unlawful. Justice Powell also concluded, however, that unlike the Davis set-aside program, "a properly devised admissions program involving the competitive consideration of race and ethnic origin" for all seats in the class could be used by an institution of higher education to assemble "a diverse student body"—a "goal that is of paramount importance in the fulfillment of its mission." The remaining four Justices (Brennan, White, Marshall, and Blackmun) concluded in a joint opinion that "a state government may adopt race-conscious programs if the purpose . . . is to remove the disparate racial impact its actions might otherwise have and if there is reason to believe that

---

a. The full report is set forth supra, p. 89.

the disparate impact is itself the product of past discrimination, whether its own or that of society at large"—and that there was "no question that Davis' program [was] valid under this test." The "articulated purpose of remedying the effects of past societal discrimination" was "sufficiently important to justify the use of race-conscious admissions programs where there is a substantial basis for concluding that minority underrepresentation is substantial and chronic, and that the handicap of past discrimination is impeding access of minorities to the medical school." And the "second prong of our test—whether the Davis program stigmatizes any discrete group or individual and whether race is reasonably used in light of the program's objectives—is clearly satisfied by the Davis program." The "use of racial preferences for remedial purposes does not inflict a pervasive injury upon individual whites in the sense that wherever they go or whatever they do there is a significant likelihood that they will be treated as second-class citizens because of their color.... Nor can the program reasonably be regarded as stigmatizing the program's beneficiaries or their race as inferior." (Justice Powell thought the "pliable notion of 'stigma' " was a standardless "subjective judgment," noting that "*[a]ll* state-imposed classifications that rearrange burdens and benefits on the basis of race are likely to be viewed with deep resentment by the individuals burdened" and thus "may outrage" them and "be perceived as invidious.") Taking Justice Powell's opinion together with their joint opinion, the four adherents to the joint opinion identified the constitutional common ground of a Court majority as having the following "central meaning": "Government may take race into account when it acts not to demean or insult any racial group but to remedy disadvantages cast on minorities by past racial prejudice, at least when appropriate findings have been made by judicial, legislative, or administrative bodies with competence to act in this area." (Many of the features of Justice Powell's influential opinion in *Bakke*, which have been widely employed since that decision in the formulation and administration of race-conscious affirmative action programs throughout higher education, are recounted in Grutter v. Bollinger, infra p. 876, and Gratz v. Bollinger, infra p. 898.)

In the 1980's voluntary affirmative action plans beyond the sphere of higher education were challenged. In Fullilove v. Klutznick, 448 U.S. 448 (1980), the Court, again with no majority opinion, upheld the "Minority Business Enterprise" (MBE) provision of the Public Works Employment Act of 1977, which appropriated federal funds for state and local public works projects. The MBE provision required the Secretary of Commerce, absent administrative waiver, to deny grant applications that did not include assurances that at least 10% of the grant amount would be expended for businesses owned 50% or more by minority group members, defined as "citizens of the United States who are Negroes, Spanish-speaking, Orientals, Indians, Eskimos and Aleuts." Administrative exceptions were available to eliminate MBE's that were not "bonafide" or that attempted price exploitation, or if grantees demonstrated that their best efforts had not and would not achieve the 10% target. Chief Justice Burger's opinion, joined by Justices White and Powell, invoked "appropriate deference to the Congress" but also "recognize[d] the need for careful judicial evaluation to assure that any congressional program that employs racial or ethnic criteria to accomplish the objective of remedying the present effects of past discrimination is narrowly tailored to the achievement of that goal." Applying the "most searching examination," however, he was satisfied that Congress' "comprehensive remedial power ... to enforce equal protection guarantees" supported the "clear objective" of ensuring that grantees "would not employ procurement practices that Congress had decided might result in perpetuation of the effects of prior discrimination which had impaired or

Fullilove v. Klutznick

foreclosed access by minority business to public contracting opportunities." He also was satisfied that this limited preference (affecting only 0.25% of annual construction work expenditures in the United States), and the flexibility provided by the waiver and exemption provisions, supported the conclusion that the MBE program was a constitutionally permissible means of achieving that objective. Hence, Congress had not violated "the equal protection component of the Due Process Clause of the Fifth Amendment." A concurring opinion by Justice Marshall, joined by Justices Brennan and Blackmun, reiterated their view in *Bakke* that the "proper inquiry is whether racial classifications designed to further remedial purposes serve important governmental objectives and are substantially related to achievement of those objectives"—a standard he found easily satisfied in this case. Justice Stewart, Justice Rehnquist, and Justice Stevens dissented, the latter urging that "[r]acial classifications are simply too pernicious to permit any but the most exact connection between justification and classification."

Wygant
v. Jackson

By contrast, the Court next invalidated a race-sensitive collective bargaining provision explicitly protecting recently hired minority school teachers from being laid off in the customary reverse order of seniority. Wygant v. Jackson Board of Education, 476 U.S. 267 (1986). The policy required that "at no time will there be a greater percentage of minority personnel laid off than the current percentage of minority personnel employed at the time of the layoff." Justice Powell's plurality opinion, joined by Chief Justice Burger and Justices Rehnquist and O'Connor, criticized the lower courts' holding "that the Board's interest in providing minority role models for its minority students, as an attempt to alleviate the effects of societal discrimination, was sufficiently important to justify the racial classification embodied in the layoff provision." Neither "societal discrimination alone," nor the role model theory used by the lower courts (which compared the percentage of minority teachers to the percentage of minority students), sufficed. Societal discrimination was "too amorphous"; remedial racial classifications had to be supported by "convincing evidence" of "prior discrimination by the governmental unit involved" and that was absent here. The role model rationale had "no logical stopping point" and did "not necessarily bear a relationship to the harm caused by prior discriminatory hiring practices," especially where there was "no apparent connection" between the percentage of minority students and the percentage of minority faculty. In any event, in a portion of his opinion that Justice O'Connor did not join, Justice Powell found the means chosen to serve these ends inadequately justified. With layoffs, the "burden to be borne by innocent individuals" is "too intrusive," for in contrast to hiring goals, which "impose a diffuse burden, often foreclosing only one of several opportunities, layoffs impose the entire burden of achieving racial equality on particular individuals, often resulting in serious disruption of their lives." Justice White concurred in the judgment, saying in part: "Whatever the legitimacy of hiring goals or quotas may be, the discharge of white teachers to make room for blacks, none of whom has been shown to be a victim of any racial discrimination, is quite a different matter. I cannot believe that in order to integrate a work force, it would be permissible to discharge whites and hire blacks until the latter comprise a suitable percentage of the work force." Justice Marshall, joined by Justices Brennan and Blackmun, dissented, "believ[ing] that a public employer, with the full agreement of its employees, should be permitted to preserve the benefits of a legitimate and constitutional affirmative-action hiring plan even while reducing its work force ...." Justice Stevens dissented separately, believing it "not necessary to find that the Board of Education has been guilty of racial discrimination in the past to support the conclusion that it has a legitimate interest in employing more black teachers in the future." Although the "Equal Protection Clause absolutely prohibits the use of race in many governmental contexts" (such as "who may serve on juries, who may use public services, who may marry, and who may be fit parents"), "race is not always irrelevant to sound governmental decisionmaking." For example, "in law enforcement, if an undercover agent is needed to infiltrate a group suspected of ongoing criminal behavior—and if the members of the group are all of the same race—it would seem perfectly rational to employ an agent of that race ...." Similarly, employing and retaining more minority teachers was "rational and unquestionably legitimate" to serve the "valid public purpose" of having "an integrated faculty ... able to provide benefits to the student body that could not be provided by an all white, or nearly all white, faculty."

City of Richmond v. J.A. Croson Company

488 U.S. 469, 109 S.Ct. 706, 102 L.Ed.2d 854 (1989).

Justice O'Connor announced the judgment of the Court and delivered the opinion of the Court with respect to Parts I, III–B, and IV, an opinion with respect to Part II, in which The Chief Justice and Justice White join, and an opinion with respect to Parts III–A and V, in which The Chief Justice, Justice White and Justice Kennedy join.

In this case, we confront once again the tension between the Fourteenth Amendment's guarantee of equal treatment to all citizens, and the use of race-based measures to ameliorate the effects of past discrimination on the opportunities enjoyed by members of minority groups in our society.... We ... consider the applicability of our decision in *Wygant* to a minority set-aside program adopted by the city of Richmond, Virginia.

I

On April 11, 1983, the Richmond City Council adopted the Minority Business Utilization Plan ... requir[ing] prime contractors to whom the city awarded construction contracts to subcontract at least 30% of the dollar amount of the contract to one or more Minority Business Enterprises (MBEs).... The 30% set-aside did not apply to city contracts awarded to minority-owned prime contractors....

The Plan defined an MBE as "[a] business at least fifty-one (51) percent of which is owned and controlled ... by minority group members." ... "Minority group members" were defined as "[c]itizens of the United States who are Blacks, Spanish-speaking, Orientals, Indians, Eskimos, or Aleuts." ... There was no geographic limit to the Plan; an otherwise qualified MBE from anywhere in the United States could avail itself of the 30% set-aside. The Plan declared that it was "remedial" in nature, and enacted "for the purpose of promoting wider participation by minority business enterprises in the construction of public projects." ... The Plan expired on June 30, 1988, and was in effect for approximately five years....

[The Plan authorized "waivers" on proof that the set-aside "cannot be achieved" and allowed] a bidder denied an award for failure to comply with the MBE requirements ... a general right of protest....

The Plan was adopted by the Richmond City Council after a public hearing....

There was no direct evidence of race discrimination on the part of the city in letting contracts or any evidence that the city's prime contractors had discriminated against minority-owned subcontractors....

[Croson, a plumbing and heating contractor, submitted the only bid on a city project to provide and install toilet fixtures at the city jail. Croson had concluded that an MBE would have to supply the fixtures to meet the 30% set-aside and had contacted 5 or 6 potential MBE suppliers, only one of which–on the day bids were due–expressed a desire to participate. At the bid opening the next day, that local MBE informed Croson's manager that "difficulty in obtaining credit approval had hindered his submission of a bid." Six days later, still having not received a bid, Croson asked for a waiver of the 30% set-aside, saying the interested MBE was "unqualified" and others contacted "had been unresponsive or unable to quote." The interested MBE later submitted a bid 7% over the market price and higher than the fixtures price Croson had included in its bid. The MBE also informed city procurement officials that it could supply the fixtures. T]he city denied Croson's waiver request, indicating that Croson had 10 days to submit an MBE Utilization Commitment Form, and warned that failure to do so could result in its bid being considered unresponsive.

. . . Croson [sued in federal district court], arguing that the Richmond ordinance was unconstitutional on its face and as applied in this case.

The District Court upheld the Plan in all respects. . . . [A] divided panel of the Fourth Circuit Court of Appeals affirmed. . . . Relying on the great deference which this Court accorded Congress' findings of past discrimination in *Fullilove,* the panel majority indicated its view that the same standard should be applied to the Richmond City Council . . .

. . . We granted [review], vacated the opinion of the Court of Appeals, and remanded the case for further consideration in light of our intervening decision in Wygant v. Jackson Board of Education, 476 U.S. 267 (1986).

On remand, a divided . . . Court of Appeals struck down the Richmond set-aside program as violating both prongs of strict scrutiny under the Equal Protection Clause of the Fourteenth Amendment. . . .

. . .

. . . [W]e now affirm the judgment.

II

The parties and their supporting *amici* fight an initial battle over the scope of the city's power to adopt legislation designed to address the effects of past discrimination. Relying on our decision in *Wygant,* appellee argues that the city must limit any race-based remedial efforts to eradicating the effects of its own prior discrimination . . . Appellant argues that . . . *Fullilove* is controlling, [so] that . . . Richmond enjoys sweeping legislative power to define and attack the effects of prior discrimination in its local construction industry. We find that neither of these two rather stark alternatives can withstand analysis.

. . .

Appellant and its supporting *amici* rely heavily on *Fullilove* for the proposition that a city council, like Congress, need not make specific findings of discrimination to engage in race-conscious relief. Thus, appellant argues "[i]t would be a perversion of federalism to hold that the federal government has a compelling interest in remedying the effects of racial discrimination in its own public works program, but a city government does not." . . .

What appellant ignores is that Congress, unlike any State or political subdivision, has a specific constitutional mandate to enforce the dictates of the Fourteenth Amendment. The power to "enforce" may at times also include the power to define situations which *Congress* determines threaten principles of equality and to adopt prophylactic rules to deal with those situations. See Katzenbach v. Morgan, . . . ("Correctly viewed, section 5 is a positive grant of legislative power authorizing Congress to exercise its discretion in determining whether and what legislation is needed to secure the guarantees of the Fourteenth Amendment"). See also South Carolina v. Katzenbach, 383 U.S. 301, 326 (1966) (similar interpretation of congressional power under section 2 of the Fifteenth Amendment). The Civil War Amendments themselves worked a dramatic change in the balance between congressional and state power over matters of race. Speaking of the Thirteenth and Fourteenth Amendments in Ex parte Virginia, 100 U.S. 339, 345 (1880), the Court stated: "They were intended to be, what they really are, limitations of the powers of the States and enlargements of the power of Congress."

That Congress may identify and redress the effects of society-wide discrimination does not mean that, *a fortiori*, the States and their political subdivisions are free to decide that such remedies are appropriate. Section 1 of the Fourteenth Amendment is an explicit *constraint* on state power, and the States must undertake any remedial efforts in accordance with that provision. To hold otherwise would be to cede control over the content of the Equal Protection Clause to the 50 state legislatures and their myriad political subdivisions. The mere recitation of a benign or compensatory purpose for the use of a racial classification would essentially entitle the States to exercise the full power of Congress under section 5 of the Fourteenth Amendment and insulate any racial classification from judicial scrutiny under section 1. We believe that such a result would be contrary to the intentions of the Framers of the Fourteenth Amendment, who desired to place clear limits on the States' use of race as a criterion for legislative action. . . .

. . .

It would seem equally clear, however, that a state or local subdivision (if delegated the authority from the State) has the authority to eradicate the effects of private discrimination within its own legislative jurisdiction. This authority must, of course, be exercised within the constraints of section 1 of the Fourteenth Amendment. Our decision in *Wygant* is not to the contrary. *Wygant* addressed the constitutionality of the use of racial quotas by local school authorities pursuant to an agreement reached with the local teachers' union. It was in the context of addressing the school board's power to adopt a race-based layoff program affecting its own work force that the *Wygant* plurality indicated that the Equal Protection Clause required "some showing of prior discrimination by the governmental unit involved." . . . As a matter of state law, the city of Richmond has legislative authority over its procurement policies, and can use its spending powers to remedy private discrimination, if it identifies the discrimination with the particularity required by the Fourteenth Amendment. . . .

Thus, if the city could show that it had essentially become a "passive participant" in a system of racial exclusion practiced by elements of the local construction industry, we think it clear that the city could take affirmative steps to dismantle such a system. It is beyond dispute that any public entity, state or federal, has a compelling interest in assuring that public dollars, drawn from the tax contributions of all citizens, do not serve to finance the evil of private prejudice. . . .

III

A

The Equal Protection Clause of the Fourteenth Amendment provides that "[N]o State shall ... deny to *any person* within its jurisdiction the equal protection of the laws" (emphasis added). As this Court has noted in the past, the "rights created by the first section of the Fourteenth Amendment are, by its terms, guaranteed to the individual. The rights established are personal rights." Shelley v. Kraemer, 334 U.S. 1, 22 (1948). The Richmond Plan denies certain citizens the opportunity to compete for a fixed percentage of public contracts based solely upon their race. To whatever racial group these citizens belong, their "personal rights" to be treated with equal dignity and respect are implicated by a rigid rule erecting race as the sole criterion in an aspect of public decisionmaking.

Absent searching judicial inquiry into the justification for such race-based measures, there is simply no way of determining what classifications are "benign" or "remedial" and what classifications are in fact motivated by illegitimate notions of racial inferiority or simple racial politics. Indeed, the purpose of strict scrutiny is to "smoke out" illegitimate uses of race by assuring that the legislative body is pursuing a goal important enough to warrant use of a highly suspect tool. The test also ensures that the means chosen "fit" this compelling goal so closely that there is little or no possibility that the motive for the classification was illegitimate racial prejudice or stereotype.

Classifications based on race carry a danger of stigmatic harm. Unless they are strictly reserved for remedial settings, they may in fact promote notions of racial inferiority and lead to a politics of racial hostility. See University of California Regents v. Bakke, 438 U.S., at 298 (opinion of Powell, J.) ("[P]referential programs may only reinforce common stereotypes holding that certain groups are unable to achieve success without special protection based on a factor having no relation to individual worth"). We thus reaffirm the view expressed by the plurality in *Wygant* that the standard of review under the Equal Protection Clause is not dependent on the race of those burdened or benefited by a particular classification....

· · ·

Even were we to accept a reading of the guarantee of equal protection under which the level of scrutiny varies according to the ability of different groups to defend their interests in the representative process, heightened scrutiny would still be appropriate in the circumstances of this case. One of the central arguments for applying a less exacting standard to "benign" racial classifications is that such measures essentially involve a choice made by dominant racial groups to disadvantage themselves. If one aspect of the judiciary's role under the Equal Protection Clause is to protect "discrete and insular minorities" from majoritarian prejudice or indifference, see United States v. Carolene Products Co., 304 U.S. 144, 153 n. 4 (1938), some maintain that these concerns are not implicated when the "white majority" places burdens upon itself. See J. Ely, Democracy and Distrust 170 (1980).

In this case, blacks comprise approximately 50% of the population of the city of Richmond. Five of the nine seats on the City Council are held by blacks. The concern that a political majority will more easily act to the disadvantage of a minority based on unwarranted assumptions or incomplete facts would seem to militate for, not against, the application of heightened judicial scrutiny in this case. See Ely, The Constitutionality of Reverse Racial Discrimination, 41 U.Chi.L.Rev. 723, 739, n. 58 (1974) ("Of course it works both ways: a law that favors Blacks over Whites would be suspect if it were enacted by a predominantly Black legislature'').

. . .

Justice Powell's opinion [in *Bakke*] . . . indicated that for the governmental interest in remedying past discrimination to be triggered "judicial, legislative, or administrative findings of constitutional or statutory violations" must be made. . . . Only then does the Government have a compelling interest in favoring one race over another.

In *Wygant*, . . . four Members of the Court applied heightened scrutiny to a race-based system of employee layoffs. Justice Powell, writing for the plurality, again drew the distinction between "societal discrimination" which is an inadequate basis for race-conscious classifications, and the type of identified discrimination that can support and define the scope of race-based relief. . . .

The role model theory . . . failed for two reasons. First, the statistical disparity between students and teachers had no probative value in demonstrating the kind of prior discrimination in hiring or promotion that would justify race-based relief. . . . Second, because the role model theory had no relation to some basis for believing a constitutional or statutory violation had occurred, it could be used to "justify" race-based decisionmaking essentially limitless in scope and duration. . . .

III

B

We think it clear that the factual predicate offered in support of the Richmond Plan suffers from the same two defects identified as fatal in *Wygant*. The District Court found the city council's "findings sufficient to ensure that, in adopting the Plan, it was remedying the present effects of past discrimination in the *construction industry*." . . . (emphasis added). Like the "role model" theory employed in *Wygant*, a generalized assertion that there has been past discrimination in an entire industry provides no guidance for a legislative body to determine the precise scope of the injury it seeks to remedy. It "has no logical stopping point." *Wygant*, ... Relief for such an ill-defined wrong could extend until the percentage of public contracts awarded to MBEs in Richmond mirrored the percentage of minorities in the population as a whole.

Appellant argues that it is attempting to remedy various forms of past discrimination that are alleged to be responsible for the small number of minority businesses in the local contracting industry. Among these the city cites the exclusion of blacks from skilled construction trade unions and training programs. This past discrimination has prevented them "from following the traditional path from laborer to entrepreneur." The city also lists a host of nonracial factors which would seem to face a member of any racial group attempting to establish a new business enterprise, such as deficiencies in working capital, inability to meet bonding requirements, unfamiliarity with bidding procedures, and disability caused by an inadequate track record.

While there is no doubt that the sorry history of both private and public discrimination in this country has contributed to a lack of opportunities for black entrepreneurs, this observation, standing alone, cannot justify a rigid racial quota in the awarding of public contracts in Richmond, Virginia. Like the claim that discrimination in primary and secondary schooling justifies a rigid racial preference in medical school admissions, an amorphous claim that there has been past discrimination in a particular industry cannot justify the use of an unyielding racial quota.

It is sheer speculation how many minority firms there would be in Richmond absent past societal discrimination, just as it was sheer speculation how many minority medical students would have been admitted to the medical school at Davis absent past discrimination in educational opportunities. Defining these sorts of injuries as "identified discrimination" would give local governments license to create a patchwork of racial preferences based on statistical generalizations about any particular field of endeavor.

These defects are readily apparent in this case. The 30% quota cannot in any realistic sense be tied to any injury suffered by anyone. The District Court relied upon five predicate "facts" in reaching its conclusion that there was an adequate basis for the 30% quota: (1) the ordinance declares itself to be remedial; (2) several proponents of the measure stated their views that there had been past discrimination in the construction industry; (3) minority businesses received .67% of prime contracts from the city while minorities constituted 50% of the city's population; (4) there were very few minority contractors in local and state contractors' associations; and (5) in 1977, Congress made a determination that the effects of past discrimination had stifled minority participation in the construction industry nationally.

None of these "findings," singly or together, provide the city of Richmond with a "strong basis in evidence for its conclusion that remedial action was necessary." *Wygant*, ... There is nothing approaching a prima facie case of a constitutional or statutory violation by *anyone* in the Richmond construction industry. . . .

The District Court accorded great weight to the fact that the city council designated the Plan as "remedial." But the mere recitation of a "benign" or legitimate purpose for a racial classification, is entitled to little or no weight. . . . Racial classifications are suspect, and that means that simple legislative assurances of good intention cannot suffice.

The District Court also relied on the highly conclusionary statement of a proponent of the Plan that there was racial discrimination in the construction industry "in this area, and the State, and around the nation." It also noted that the city manager had related his view that racial discrimination still plagued the construction industry in his home city of Pittsburg. These statements are of little probative value in establishing identified discrimination in the Richmond construction industry. The factfinding process of legislative bodies is generally entitled to a presumption of regularity and deferential review by the judiciary. See Williamson v. Lee Optical of Oklahoma, Inc., 348 U.S. 483, 488–489 (1955). But when a legislative body chooses to employ a suspect classification, it cannot rest upon a generalized assertion as to the classification's relevance to its goals. . . . A governmental actor cannot render race a legitimate proxy for a particular condition merely by declaring that the condition exists. . . . The history of racial classifications in this country suggests that blind judicial deference to legislative or executive pronouncements of necessity has no place in equal protection analysis. See Korematsu v. United States, 323 U.S. 214, 235–240 (1944) (Murphy, J., dissenting).

Reliance on the disparity between the number of prime contracts awarded to minority firms and the minority population of the city of Richmond is similarly misplaced. . . .

In the employment context, we have recognized that for certain entry level positions or positions requiring minimal training, statistical comparisons of the racial composition of an employer's workforce to the racial composition of the relevant population may be probative of a pattern of discrimination. . . . But where special qualifications are necessary, the relevant statistical pool for purposes of demonstrating discriminatory exclusion must be the number of minorities qualified to undertake the particular task....

In this case, the city does not even know how many MBEs in the relevant market are qualified to undertake prime or subcontracting work in public construction projects.... Nor does the city know what percentage of total city construction dollars minority firms now receive as subcontractors on prime contracts let by the city.

To a large extent, the set-aside of subcontracting dollars seems to rest on the unsupported assumption that white prime contractors simply will not hire minority firms.... Indeed, there is evidence in this record that overall minority participation in city contracts in Richmond is seven to eight percent, and that minority contractor participation in Community Block Development Grant *construction* projects is 17% to 22%. Without any information on minority participation in subcontracting, it is quite simply impossible to evaluate overall minority representation in the city's construction expenditures.

The city and the District Court also relied on evidence that MBE membership in local contractors' associations was extremely low. Again, standing alone this evidence is not probative of any discrimination in the local construction industry. There are numerous explanations for this dearth of minority participation, including past societal discrimination in education and economic opportunities as well as both black and white career and entrepreneurial choices. Blacks may be disproportionately attracted to industries other than construction.... The mere fact that black membership in these trade organizations is low, standing alone, cannot establish a prima facie case of discrimination....

For low minority membership in these associations to be relevant, the city would have to link it to the number of local MBEs eligible for membership. If the statistical disparity between eligible MBEs and MBE membership were great enough, an inference of discriminatory exclusion could arise. In such a case, the city would have a compelling interest in preventing its tax dollars from assisting these organizations in maintaining a racially segregated construction market....

Finally, the city and the District Court relied on Congress' finding in connection with the set-aside approved in *Fullilove* that there had been nationwide discrimination in the construction industry. The probative value of these findings for demonstrating the existence of discrimination in Richmond is extremely limited. By its inclusion of a waiver procedure in the national program addressed in *Fullilove,* Congress explicitly recognized that the scope of the problem would vary from market area to market area....

Moreover, as noted above, Congress was exercising its powers under section 5 of the Fourteenth Amendment in making a finding that past discrimination would cause federal funds to be distributed in a manner which reinforced prior patterns of discrimination. While the States and their subdivisions may take remedial action when they possess evidence that their own spending practices are exacerbating a pattern of prior discrimination, they must identify that discrimination, public or private, with some specificity before they may use race-conscious relief. Congress has made national findings that there has been societal discrimination in a host of fields. If all a state or local government need do is find a congressional report on the subject to enact a set-aside program, the constraints of the Equal Protection Clause will, in effect, have been rendered a nullity. See Days 480–481 ("[I]t is essential that state and local agencies also establish the presence of discrimination in their own bailiwicks, based either upon their own fact-finding processes or upon determinations made by other competent institutions").

. . .

In sum, none of the evidence presented by the city points to any identified discrimination in the Richmond construction industry. We, therefore, hold that the city has failed to demonstrate a compelling interest in apportioning public contracting opportunities on the basis of race. To accept Richmond's claim that past societal discrimination alone can serve as the basis for rigid racial preferences would be to open the door to competing claims for "remedial relief" for every disadvantaged group. The dream of a Nation of equal citizens in a society where race is irrelevant to personal opportunity and achievement would be lost in a mosaic of shifting preferences based on inherently unmeasurable claims of past wrongs. . . . We think such a result would be contrary to both the letter and spirit of a constitutional provision whose central command is equality.

The foregoing analysis applies only to the inclusion of blacks within the Richmond set-aside program. There is *absolutely no evidence* of past discrimination against Spanish-speaking, Oriental, Indian, Eskimo, or Aleut persons in any aspect of the Richmond construction industry. The District Court took judicial notice of the fact that the vast majority of "minority" persons in Richmond were black. It may well be that Richmond has never had an Aleut or Eskimo citizen. The random inclusion of racial groups that, as a practical matter, may never have suffered from discrimination in the construction industry in Richmond, suggests that perhaps the city's purpose was not in fact to remedy past discrimination.

If a 30% set-aside was "narrowly tailored" to compensate black contractors for past discrimination, one may legitimately ask why they are forced to share this "remedial relief" with an Aleut citizen who moves to Richmond tomorrow? The gross overinclusiveness of Richmond's racial preference strongly impugns the city's claim of remedial motivation. . . . [S]ee . . . Days 482 ("Such programs leave one with the sense that the racial and ethnic groups favored by the set-aside were added without attention to whether their inclusion was justified by evidence of past discrimination").

IV

[I]t is almost impossible to assess whether the Richmond Plan is narrowly tailored to remedy prior discrimination since it is not linked to identified discrimination in any way. We limit ourselves to two observations in this regard.

First, there does not appear to have been any consideration of the use of race-neutral means to increase minority business participation in city contracting. . . . Many of the barriers to minority participation in the construction industry relied upon by the city to justify a racial classification appear to be race neutral. If MBEs disproportionately lack capital or cannot meet bonding requirements, a race-neutral program of city financing for small firms would, a fortiori, lead to greater minority participation. The principal opinion in *Fullilove* found that Congress had carefully examined and rejected race-neutral alternatives before enacting the MBE set-aside. . . .

Second, the 30% quota cannot be said to be narrowly tailored to any goal, except perhaps outright racial balancing. It rests upon the "completely unrealistic" assumption that minorities will choose a particular trade in lockstep proportion to their representation in the local population. . . .

Since the city must already consider bids and waivers on a case-by-case basis, it is difficult to see the need for a rigid numerical quota. As noted above, the congressional scheme upheld in *Fullilove* allowed for a waiver of the set-aside provision where an MBE's higher price was not attributable to the effects of past discrimination. Based upon proper findings, such programs are less problematic from an equal protection standpoint because they treat all candidates individually, rather than making the color of an applicant's skin the sole relevant consideration. Unlike the program upheld in *Fullilove*, the Richmond Plan's waiver system focuses solely on the availability of MBEs; there is no inquiry into whether or not the particular MBE seeking a racial preference has suffered from the effects of past discrimination by the city or prime contractors.

Given the existence of an individualized procedure, the city's only interest in maintaining a quota system rather than investigating the need for remedial action in particular cases would seem to be simple administrative convenience. But the interest in avoiding the bureaucratic effort necessary to tailor remedial relief to those who truly have suffered the effects of prior discrimination cannot justify a rigid line drawn on the basis of a suspect classification.... Under Richmond's scheme, a successful black, Hispanic, or Oriental entrepreneur from anywhere in the country enjoys an absolute preference over other citizens based solely on their race. We think it obvious that such a program is not narrowly tailored to remedy the effects of prior discrimination.

V

Nothing we say today precludes a state or local entity from taking action to rectify the effects of identified discrimination within its jurisdiction. If the City of Richmond had evidence before it that nonminority contractors were systematically excluding minority businesses from subcontracting opportunities it could take action to end the discriminatory exclusion. Where there is a significant statistical disparity between the number of qualified minority contractors willing and able to perform a particular service and the number of such contractors actually engaged by the locality or the locality's prime contractors, an inference of discriminatory exclusion could arise.... Under such circumstances, the city could act to dismantle the closed business system by taking appropriate measures against those who discriminate on the basis of race or other illegitimate criteria.... In the extreme case, some form of narrowly tailored racial preference might be necessary to break down patterns of deliberate exclusion.

Nor is local government powerless to deal with individual instances of racially motivated refusals to employ minority contractors. Where such discrimination occurs, a city would be justified in penalizing the discriminator and providing appropriate relief to the victim of such discrimination.... Moreover, evidence of a pattern of individual discriminatory acts can, if supported by appropriate statistical proof, lend support to a local government's determination that broader remedial relief is justified....

Even in the absence of evidence of discrimination, the city has at its disposal a whole array of race-neutral devices to increase the accessibility of city contracting opportunities to small entrepreneurs of all races.... The city may also act to prohibit discrimination in the provision of credit or bonding by local suppliers and banks....

In the case at hand, the city has not ascertained how many minority enterprises are present in the local construction market nor the level of their participation in city construction projects. The city points to no evidence that qualified minority contractors have been passed over for city contracts or subcontracts, either as a group or in any individual case....

Proper findings in this regard are necessary to define both the scope of the injury and the extent of the remedy necessary to cure its effects. Such findings also serve to assure all citizens that the deviation from the norm of equal treatment of all racial and ethnic groups is a temporary matter, a measure taken in the service of the goal of equality itself. Absent such findings, there is a danger that a racial classification is merely the product of unthinking stereotypes or a form of racial politics.... Because the city of Richmond has failed to identify the need for remedial action in the awarding of its public construction contracts, its treatment of its citizens on a racial basis violates the dictates of the Equal Protection Clause....

Affirmed.

Justice Stevens, concurring in part and concurring in the judgment.

... I ... do not agree with the premise that seems to underlie today's decision, as well as the decision in Wygant v. Jackson Board of Education, 476 U.S. 267 (1986), that a governmental decision that rests on a racial classification is never permissible except as a remedy for a past wrong. I do, however, agree with the Court's explanation of why the Richmond ordinance cannot be justified as a remedy for past discrimination, and therefore join Parts I, III–B, and IV of its opinion. I write separately to emphasize three aspects of the case that are of special importance to me.

First, the city makes no claim that the public interest in the efficient performance of its construction contracts will be served by granting a preference to minority-business enterprises. This case is therefore completely unlike *Wygant,* in which I thought it quite obvious that the School Board had reasonably concluded that an integrated faculty could provide educational benefits to the entire student body that could not be provided by an all-white, or nearly all-white faculty....

Second, this litigation involves an attempt by a legislative body, rather than a court, to fashion a remedy for a past wrong.... It is the judicial system, rather than the legislative process, that is best equipped to identify past wrongdoers and to fashion remedies that will create the conditions that presumably would have existed had no wrong been committed....

Third, instead of engaging in a debate over the proper standard of review to apply in affirmative-action litigation, I believe it is more constructive to try to identify the characteristics of the advantaged and disadvantaged classes that may justify their disparate treatment.... In this case that approach convinces me that, instead of carefully identifying the characteristics of the two classes of contractors that are respectively favored and disfavored by its ordinance, the Richmond City Council has merely engaged in the type of stereotypical analysis that is a hallmark of violations of the Equal Protection Clause. Whether we look at the class of persons benefited by the ordinance or at the disadvantaged class, the same conclusion emerges.

The justification for the ordinance is the fact that in the past white contractors—and presumably other white citizens in Richmond—have discriminated against black contractors. The class of persons benefited by the ordinance is not, however, limited to victims of such discrimination—it encompasses persons who have never been in business in Richmond as well as minority contractors who may have been guilty of discriminating against members of other minority groups. Indeed, for all the record shows, all of the minority-business enterprises that have benefited from the ordinance may be firms that have prospered not-withstanding the discriminatory conduct that may have harmed other minority firms years ago. Ironically, minority firms that have survived in the competitive struggle, rather than those that have perished, are most likely to benefit from an ordinance of this kind. . . .

There is a special irony in the stereotypical thinking that prompts legislation of this kind. Although it stigmatizes the disadvantaged class with the unproven charge of past racial discrimination, it actually imposes a greater stigma on its supposed beneficiaries. . . .

Justice Kennedy, concurring in part and concurring in the judgment.

I join all but Part II of Justice O'Connor's opinion. . . .

Part II examines our caselaw upholding Congressional power to grant preferences based on overt and explicit classification by race. See Fullilove v. Klutznick, 448 U.S. 448 (1980). With the acknowledgment that the summary in Part II is both precise and fair, I must decline to join it. The process by which a law that is an equal protection violation when enacted by a State becomes transformed to an equal protection guarantee when enacted by Congress poses a difficult proposition for me; but as it is not before us, any reconsideration of that issue must await some further case. For purposes of the ordinance challenged here, it suffices to say that the State has the power to eradicate racial discrimination and its effects in both the public and private sectors, and the absolute duty to do so where those wrongs were caused intentionally by the State itself. The Fourteenth Amendment ought not to be interpreted to reduce a State's authority in this regard, unless, of course, there is a conflict with federal law or a state remedy is itself a violation of equal protection. The latter is the case presented here.

The moral imperative of racial neutrality is the driving force of the Equal Protection Clause. Justice Scalia's opinion underscores that proposition, quite properly in my view. . . . His opinion would make it crystal clear to the political branches, at least those of the States, that legislation must be based on criteria other than race.

Nevertheless, given that a rule of automatic invalidity for racial preferences in almost every case would be a significant break with our precedents that require a case-by-case test, I am not convinced we need adopt it at this point. On the assumption that it will vindicate the principle of race neutrality found in the Equal Protection Clause, I accept the less absolute rule contained in Justice O'Connor's opinion, a rule based on the proposition that any racial preference must face the most rigorous scrutiny by the courts. My reasons for doing so are as follows. First, I am confident that, in application, the strict scrutiny standard will operate in a manner generally consistent with the imperative of race neutrality, because it forbids the use even of narrowly drawn racial classifications except as a last resort. Second, the rule against race-conscious remedies is already less than an absolute one, for that relief may be the only adequate remedy after a judicial determination that a State or its instrumentality has violated the Equal Protection Clause. I note, in this connection, that evidence which would support a judicial finding of intentional discrimination may suffice also to justify remedial legislative action, for it diminishes the constitutional responsibilities of the political branches to say they must wait to act until ordered to do so by a court. Third, the strict scrutiny rule is consistent with our precedents, as Justice O'Connor's opinion demonstrates.

The ordinance before us falls far short of the standard we adopt. The nature and scope of the injury that existed; its historical or antecedent causes; the extent to which the City contributed to it, either by intentional acts or by passive complicity in acts of discrimination by the private sector; the necessity for the response adopted, its duration in relation to the wrong, and the precision with which it otherwise bore on whatever injury in fact was addressed, were all matters unmeasured, unexplored, unexplained by the City Council. We are left with an ordinance and a legislative record open to the fair charge that it is not a remedy but is itself a preference which will cause the same corrosive animosities that the Constitution forbids in the whole sphere of government and that our national policy condemns in the rest of society as well. This ordinance is invalid under the Fourteenth Amendment.

Justice Scalia, concurring in the judgment.

I agree with much of the Court's opinion, and, in particular, with its conclusion that strict scrutiny must be applied to all governmental classification by race, whether or not its asserted purpose is "remedial" or "benign." I do not agree, however, with the Court's dicta suggesting that, despite the Fourteenth Amendment, state and local governments may in some circumstances discriminate on the basis of race in order (in a broad sense) "to ameliorate the effects of past discrimination." The benign purpose of compensating for social disadvantages, whether they have been acquired by reason of prior discrimination or otherwise, can no more be pursued by the illegitimate means of racial discrimination than can other assertedly benign purposes we have repeatedly rejected.... The difficulty of overcoming the effects of past discrimination is as nothing compared with the difficulty of eradicating from our society the source of those effects, which is the tendency—fatal to a nation such as ours—to classify and judge men and women on the basis of their country of origin or the color of their skin. A solution to the first problem that aggravates the second is no solution at all....

We have in some contexts approved the use of racial classifications by the Federal Government to remedy the effects of past discrimination. I do not believe that we must or should extend those holdings to the States.... [W]ithout revisiting what we held in *Fullilove* (or trying to derive a rationale from the three separate opinions supporting the judgment, none of which commanded more than three votes ...), I do not believe our decision in that case controls the one before us here.

A sound distinction between federal and state (or local) action based on race rests not only upon the substance of the Civil War Amendments, but upon social reality and governmental theory.... What the record shows ... is that racial discrimination against any group finds a more ready expression at the state and local than at the federal level. To the children of the Founding Fathers, this should come as no surprise. An acute awareness of the heightened danger of oppression from political factions in small, rather than large, political units dates to the very beginning of our national history....

... Richmond [enacted] a set-aside clearly and directly beneficial to the dominant political group, which happens also to be the dominant racial group. The same thing has no doubt happened before in other cities (though the racial basis of the preference has rarely been made textually explicit)—and blacks have often been on the receiving end of the injustice. Where injustice is the game, however, turn-about is not fair play.

In my view there is only one circumstance in which the States may act *by race* to "undo the effects of past discrimination": where that is necessary to eliminate their own maintenance of a system of unlawful racial classification.

If, for example, a state agency has a discriminatory pay scale compensating black employees in all positions at 20% less than their nonblack counterparts, it may assuredly promulgate an order raising the salaries of "all black employees" by 20%.... This distinction explains our school desegregation cases, in which we have made plain that States and localities sometimes have an obligation to adopt race-conscious remedies. While there is no doubt that those cases have taken into account the continuing "effects" of previously mandated racial school assignment, we have held those effects to justify a race-conscious remedy only because we have concluded, in that context, that they perpetuate a "dual school system." ...

. . .

I agree with the Court's dictum that a fundamental distinction must be drawn between the effects of "societal" discrimination and the effects of "identified" discrimination, and that the situation would be different if Richmond's plan were "tailored" to identify those particular bidders who "suffered from the effects of past discrimination by the city or prime contractors." In my view, however, the reason that would make a difference is not, as the Court states, that it would justify race-conscious action—but rather that it would enable race-neutral remediation. Nothing prevents Richmond from according a contracting preference to identified victims of discrimination. While most of the beneficiaries might be black, neither the beneficiaries nor those disadvantaged by the preference would be identified *on the basis of their race*. In other words, far from justifying racial classification, identification of actual victims of discrimination makes it less supportable than ever, because more obviously unneeded.

. . .

It is plainly true that in our society blacks have suffered discrimination immeasurably greater than any directed at other racial groups. But those who believe that racial preferences can help to "even the score" display, and reinforce, a manner of thinking by race that was the source of the injustice and that will, if it endures within our society, be the source of more injustice still. The relevant proposition is not that it was blacks, or Jews, or Irish who were discriminated against, but that it was individual men and women, "created equal," who were discriminated against. And the relevant resolve is that that should never happen again. Racial preferences appear to "even the score" (in some small degree) only if one embraces the proposition that our society is appropriately viewed as divided into races, making it right that an injustice rendered in the past to a black man should be compensated for by discriminating against a white. Nothing is worth that embrace. Since blacks have been disproportionately disadvantaged by racial discrimination, any race-neutral remedial program aimed at the disadvantaged *as such* will have a disproportionately beneficial impact on blacks. Only such a program, and not one that operates on the basis of race, is in accord with the letter and the spirit of our Constitution.

. . .

Justice Marshall, with whom Justice Brennan and Justice Blackmun join, dissenting.

It is a welcome symbol of racial progress when the former capital of the Confederacy acts forthrightly to confront the effects of racial discrimination in its midst. In my view, nothing in the Constitution can be construed to prevent Richmond, Virginia, from allocating a portion of its contracting dollars for businesses owned or controlled by members of minority groups. Indeed, Richmond's set-aside program is indistinguishable in all meaningful respects from—and in fact was patterned upon—the federal set-aside plan which this Court upheld in Fullilove v. Klutznick, 448 U.S. 448 (1980).

. . .

. . . [T]oday's decision marks a deliberate and giant step backward in this Court's affirmative action jurisprudence. . . . The majority's unnecessary pronouncements will inevitably discourage or prevent governmental entities, particularly States and localities, from acting to rectify the scourge of past discrimination. . . .

I

As an initial matter, the majority takes an exceedingly myopic view of the factual predicate on which the Richmond City Council relied when it passed the Minority Business Utilization Plan. . . . It is only against th[e] backdrop of documented national discrimination . . . that the local evidence adduced by Richmond can be properly understood. The majority's refusal to recognize that Richmond has proven itself no exception to the dismaying pattern of national exclusion which Congress so painstakingly identified infects its entire analysis of this case.

Six years before Richmond acted, Congress passed, and the President signed, the Public Works Employment Act of 1977 . . .

Th[is] congressional program upheld in *Fullilove* [in 1980] was based upon an array of congressional and agency studies which documented the powerful influence of racially exclusionary practices in the business world. [Justice Marshall here quoted from a 1975 and a 1977 report by the House Committee on Small Business.]

Thus, as of 1977, there was "abundant evidence" in the public domain "that minority businesses ha[d] been denied effective participation in public contracting opportunities by procurement practices that perpetuated the effects of prior discrimination." *Fullilove,* . . . . Significantly, this evidence demonstrated that discrimination had prevented existing or nascent minority-owned businesses from obtaining not only federal contracting assignments, but state and local ones as well. See *Fullilove,* supra, at 478.

The members of the Richmond City Council were well aware of these exhaustive congressional findings, a point the majority, tellingly, elides. . . .

. . .

. . . So long as one views Richmond's local evidence of discrimination against the backdrop of systematic nationwide racial discrimination which Congress had so painstakingly identified in this very industry, this case is readily resolved.

II

. . . My view has long been that race-conscious classifications designed to further remedial goals "must serve important governmental objectives and must be substantially related to achievement of those objectives" in order to withstand constitutional scrutiny. . . . Analyzed in terms of this two-prong standard, Richmond's set-aside, like the federal program on which it was modeled, is "plainly constitutional." . . .

A

1

... Richmond has two powerful interests in setting aside a portion of public contracting funds for minority-owned enterprises. The first is the city's interest in eradicating the effects of past racial discrimination. It is far too late in the day to doubt that remedying such discrimination is a compelling, let alone an important, interest....

Richmond['s] second compelling interest ... is ... preventing the city's own spending decisions from reinforcing and perpetuating the exclusionary effects of past discrimination....

. . .

... When government channels all its contracting funds to a white-dominated community of established contractors whose racial homogeneity is the product of private discrimination, it does more than place its imprimatur on the practices which forged and which continue to define that community. It also provides a measurable boost to those economic entities that have thrived within it, while denying important economic benefits to those entities which, but for prior discrimination, might well be better qualified to receive valuable government contracts. In my view, the interest in ensuring that the government does not reflect and reinforce prior private discrimination in dispensing public contracts is every bit as strong as the interest in eliminating private discrimination—an interest which this Court has repeatedly deemed compelling....

2

The remaining question with respect to the "governmental interest" prong of equal protection analysis is whether Richmond has proffered satisfactory proof of past racial discrimination to support its twin interests in remediation and in governmental nonperpetuation....

. . .

The varied body of evidence on which Richmond relied provides a "strong," "firm," and "unquestionably legitimate" basis upon which the City Council could determine that the effects of past racial discrimination warranted a remedial and prophylactic governmental response. As I have noted, Richmond acted against a backdrop of congressional and Executive Branch studies which demonstrated with such force the nationwide pervasiveness of prior discrimination that Congress presumed that " 'present economic inequities' " in construction contracting resulted from " 'past discriminatory systems.' " The city's local evidence confirmed that Richmond's construction industry did not deviate from this pernicious national pattern. The fact that just .67% of public construction expenditures over the previous five years had gone to minority-owned prime contractors, despite the city's racially mixed population, strongly suggests that construction contracting in the area was rife with "present economic inequities." To the extent this enormous disparity did not itself demonstrate that discrimination had occurred, the descriptive testimony of Richmond's elected and appointed leaders drew the necessary link between the pitifully small presence of minorities in construction contracting and past exclusionary practices. That *no one* who testified challenged this depiction of widespread racial discrimination in area construction contracting lent significant weight to these accounts. The fact that area trade associations had virtually no minority members dramatized the extent of present inequities and suggested the lasting power of past discriminatory systems. In sum, to suggest that the facts on which Richmond has relied do not provide a sound basis for its finding of past racial discrimination simply blinks credibility.

. . .

. . . [W]here the issue is not present discrimination but rather whether *past* discrimination has resulted in the *continuing exclusion* of minorities from an historically tight-knit industry, a contrast between population and work force is entirely appropriate to help gauge the degree of the exclusion. . . . This contrast is especially illuminating in cases like this, where a main avenue of introduction into the work force—here, membership in the trade associations whose members presumably train apprentices and help them procure subcontracting assignments—is itself grossly dominated by nonminorities. The majority's assertion that the city "does not even know how many MBE's in the relevant market are qualified," is thus entirely beside the point. If Richmond indeed has a monochromatic contracting community . . . this most likely reflects the lingering power of past exclusionary practices. Certainly this is the explanation Congress has found persuasive at the national level. See *Fullilove,* . . . . The city's requirement that prime public contractors set aside 30% of their subcontracting assignments for minority-owned enterprises, subject to the ordinance's provision for waivers where minority-owned enterprises are unavailable or unwilling to participate, is designed precisely to ease minority contractors into the industry.

. . .

Had the majority paused for a moment on the facts of the Richmond experience, it would have discovered that the city's leadership is deeply familiar with what racial discrimination is. The members of the Richmond City Council have spent long years witnessing multifarious acts of discrimination, including, but not limited to, the deliberate diminution of black residents' voting rights, resistance to school desegregation, and publicly sanctioned housing discrimination. Numerous decisions of federal courts chronicle this disgraceful recent history. . . .

. . .

When the legislatures and leaders of cities with histories of pervasive discrimination testify that past discrimination has infected one of their industries, armchair cynicism like that exercised by the majority has no place. . . .

Finally, I vehemently disagree with the majority's dismissal of the congressional and Executive Branch findings noted in *Fullilove* as having "extremely limited" probative value in this case. The majority concedes that Congress established nothing less than a "presumption" that minority contracting firms have been disadvantaged by prior discrimination. The majority, inexplicably, would forbid Richmond to "share" in this information, and permit only Congress to take note of these ample findings. In thus requiring that Richmond's local evidence be severed from the context in which it was prepared, the majority would require cities seeking to eradicate the effects of past discrimination within their borders to reinvent the evidentiary wheel and engage in unnecessarily duplicative, costly, and time-consuming factfinding.

No principle of federalism or of federal power, however, forbids a state or local government from drawing upon a nationally relevant historical record prepared by the Federal Government. . . .

B

In my judgment, Richmond's set-aside plan also comports with the second prong of the equal protection inquiry, for it is substantially related to the interests it seeks to serve in remedying past discrimination and in ensuring that municipal contract procurement does not perpetuate that discrimination. The most striking aspect of the city's ordinance is the similarity it bears to the "appropriately limited" federal set-aside provision upheld in *Fullilove*.... Like the federal provision, Richmond's is limited to five years in duration, ibid., and was not renewed when it came up for reconsideration in 1988. Like the federal provision, Richmond's contains a waiver provision freeing from its subcontracting requirements those nonminority firms that demonstrate that they cannot comply with its provisions.... Like the federal provision, Richmond's has a minimal impact on innocent third parties. While the measure affects 30% of public contracting dollars, that translates to only 3% of overall Richmond area contracting....

Finally, like the federal provision, Richmond's does not interfere with any vested right of a contractor to a particular contract; instead it operates entirely prospectively. Ibid. Richmond's initiative affects only future economic arrangements and imposes only a diffuse burden on nonminority competitors—here, businesses owned or controlled by nonminorities which seek subcontracting work on public construction projects. The plurality in *Wygant* emphasized the importance of this not disrupting the settled and legitimate expectations of innocent parties....

... The majority takes issue ... with two aspects of Richmond's tailoring: the city's refusal to explore the use of race-neutral measures to increase minority business participation in contracting, and the selection of a 30% set-aside figure. The majority's first criticism is flawed in two respects. First, the majority overlooks the fact that since 1975, Richmond has barred both discrimination by the city in awarding public contracts and discrimination by public contractors[, but] this ban has not succeeded in redressing the impact of past discrimination or in preventing city contract procurement from reinforcing racial homogeneity. Second, ... race-neutral measures ..., while theoretically appealing, have been discredited by Congress as ineffectual in eradicating the effects of past discrimination in this very industry....

As for Richmond's 30% target, the majority ... ignores two important facts. First, the set-aside measure affects only 3% of overall city contracting; thus, any imprecision in tailoring has far less impact than the majority suggests. But more important, the majority ignores the fact that Richmond's 30% figure was patterned directly on the *Fullilove* precedent. Congress' 10% figure fell "roughly halfway between the present percentage of minority contractors and the percentage of minority group members in the Nation." *Fullilove*, ... (Powell, J., concurring). The Richmond City Council's 30% figure similarly falls roughly halfway between the present percentage of Richmond-based minority contractors (almost zero) and the percentage of minorities in Richmond (50%). In faulting Richmond for not presenting a different explanation for its choice of a set-aside figure, the majority honors *Fullilove* only in the breach.

III

I would ordinarily end my analysis at this point and conclude that Richmond's ordinance satisfies both the governmental interest and substantial relationship prongs of our Equal Protection Clause analysis. However, ... the majority has gone beyond the facts of this case to announce a set of principles which unnecessarily restrict the power of governmental entities to take race-conscious measures to redress the effects of prior discrimination.

A

Today, for the first time, a majority of this Court has adopted strict scrutiny as its standard of Equal Protection Clause review of race-conscious remedial measures. This is an unwelcome development. A profound difference separates governmental actions that themselves are racist, and governmental actions that seek to remedy the effects of prior racism or to prevent neutral governmental activity from perpetuating the effects of such racism . . .

Racial classifications "drawn on the presumption that one race is inferior to another or because they put the weight of government behind racial hatred and separatism" warrant the strictest judicial scrutiny because of the very irrelevance of these rationales. . . . By contrast, racial classifications drawn for the purpose of remedying the effects of discrimination that itself was race-based have a highly pertinent basis: the tragic and indelible fact that discrimination against blacks and other racial minorities in this Nation has pervaded our Nation's history and continues to scar our society. . . .

> . . .

B

I am also troubled by the majority's assertion that, even if it did not believe generally in strict scrutiny of race-based remedial measures, "the circumstances of this case" require this Court to look upon the Richmond City Council's measure with the strictest scrutiny. The sole such circumstance which the majority cites, however, is the fact that blacks in Richmond are a "dominant racial grou[p]" in the city. . . .

While . . . the numerical and political supremacy of a given racial group is a factor bearing upon the level of scrutiny to be applied, this Court has never held that numerical inferiority, standing alone, makes a racial group "suspect" and thus entitled to strict scrutiny review. Rather, we have identified other "traditional indicia of suspectness": whether a group has been "saddled with such disabilities, or subjected to such a history of purposeful unequal treatment, or relegated to such a position of political powerlessness as to command extraordinary protection from the majoritarian political process." San Antonio Independent School District v. Rodriguez, 411 U.S. 1, 28 (1973).

It cannot seriously be suggested that nonminorities in Richmond have any "history of purposeful unequal treatment." Ibid. Nor is there any indication that they have any of the disabilities that have characteristically afflicted those groups this Court has deemed suspect. Indeed, the numerical and political dominance of nonminorities within the State of Virginia and the Nation as a whole provide an enormous political check against the "simple racial politics" at the municipal level which the majority fears. If the majority really believes that groups like Richmond's nonminorities, which comprise approximately half the population but which are outnumbered even marginally in political fora, are deserving of suspect class status for these reasons alone, this Court's decisions denying suspect status to women, . . . and to persons with below-average incomes, . . . stand on extremely shaky ground. . . .

> . . .

. . . The majority's view that remedial measures undertaken by municipalities with black leadership must face a stiffer test of Equal Protection Clause scrutiny than remedial measures undertaken by municipalities with white leadership implies a lack of political maturity on the part of this Nation's elected minority officials that is totally unwarranted. Such insulting judgments have no place in constitutional jurisprudence.

C

. . .

Nothing in the Constitution or in the prior decisions of this Court supports limiting state authority to confront the effects of past discrimination to those situations in which a prima facie case of a constitutional or statutory violation can be made out. . . .

. . .

To the degree that this parsimonious standard is grounded on a view that either section 1 or section 5 of the Fourteenth Amendment substantially disempowered States and localities from remedying past racial discrimination, the majority is seriously mistaken. . . . Certainly *Fullilove* did not view section 5 either as limiting the traditionally broad police powers of the States to fight discrimination, or as mandating a zero-sum game in which state power wanes as federal power waxes. On the contrary, the *Fullilove* plurality invoked section 5 only because it provided specific and certain authorization for the Federal Government's attempt to impose a race-conscious condition on the dispensation of federal funds by state and local grantees. . . .

. . .

. . . To interpret any aspect of these Amendments as proscribing state remedial responses . . . turns the Amendments on their heads. . . .

. . . [18]

Adarand Constructors, Inc. v. Pena

515 U.S. 200, 115 S.Ct. 2097, 132 L.Ed.2d 158 (1995).

Justice O'Connor announced the judgment of the Court and delivered an opinion with respect to Parts I, II, III–A, III–B, III–D, and IV, which is for the Court except insofar as it might be inconsistent with the views expressed in Justice Scalia's concurrence, and an opinion with respect to Part III–C in which Justice Kennedy joins.

Petitioner Adarand Constructors, Inc., claims that the Federal Government's practice of giving general contractors on government projects a financial incentive to hire subcontractors controlled by "socially and economically disadvantaged individuals," and in particular, the Government's use of race-based presumptions in identifying such individuals, violates the equal protection component of the Fifth Amendment's Due Process Clause. The Court of Appeals rejected Adarand's claim. We conclude, however, that courts should analyze cases of this kind under a different standard of review than the one the Court of Appeals applied. We therefore vacate the Court of Appeals' judgment and remand the case for further proceedings.

---

18. A separate dissenting opinion by   is omitted.
Justice Blackmun, joined by Justice Brennan,

I

[In 1989 an agency of the United States Department of Transportation (DOT) awarded the prime contract for a highway construction project in Colorado to Mountain Gravel & Construction Company. Mountain Gravel subcontracted the guardrail portion of the contract to Gonzales Construction Company rather than to Adarand, the low bidder, because the prime contract authorized additional compensation for hiring subcontractors certified as small businesses controlled by "socially and economically disadvantaged individuals."] Federal law requires [such] a subcontracting clause ... in most federal agency contracts, and it also requires the clause to state that "[t]he contractor shall presume that socially and economically disadvantaged individuals include Black Americans, Hispanic Americans, Native Americans, Asian Pacific Americans, and other minorities, or any other individual found to be disadvantaged by the [Small Business] Administration [SBA] pursuant to section 8(a) of the Small Business Act." 15 U.S.C. §§ 637(d)(2), (3). Adarand claims that the presumption set forth in that statute discriminates on the basis of race in violation of the Federal Government's Fifth Amendment obligation not to deny anyone equal protection of the laws.

These fairly straightforward facts implicate a complex scheme of federal statutes and regulations. The Small Business Act ... defines "socially disadvantaged individuals" as "those who have been subjected to racial or ethnic prejudice or cultural bias because of their identity as a member of a group without regard to their individual qualities," § 8(a)(5), ... and it defines "economically disadvantaged individuals" as "those socially disadvantaged individuals whose ability to compete in the free enterprise system has been impaired due to diminished capital and credit opportunities as compared to others in the same business area who are not socially disadvantaged." § 8(a)(6)(A)....

    . . .

[Two SBA programs were relevant. The "8(a) program" confers numerous benefits, including automatic eligibility for the challenged subcontractor compensation provisions, on small businesses 51% owned by individuals who qualify as "socially and economically disadvantaged." The SBA presumes that Black, Hispanic, Asian Pacific, Subcontinent Asian, and Native Americans, as well as "members of other groups designated from time to time by SBA," are "socially disadvantaged," but it allows any other individual to prove social disadvantage. Every 8(a) participant must also prove "economic disadvantage." The "8(d) subcontracting program" is limited to eligibility for such subcontracting provisions, and it operates like the 8(a) program, except that the Court felt "some uncertainty ... whether participation in the 8(d) subcontracting program requires an individualized showing of economic disadvantage." For particular participants in both the 8(a) and 8(d) programs, third parties can rebut the presumptions of economic or social disadvantage.

Funds for the highway project were appropriated in the Surface Transportation and Uniform Relocation Assistance Act of 1987 (STURAA), which required no less than 10% of those funds to be spent with certified disadvantaged small businesses. STURAA incorporated the Small Business Act's definitions, including the race-based presumptions, and required the Transportation Secretary to set minimum criteria for State governments to use in certifying eligible businesses. The Secretary's regulations required certifying authorities to use rebuttable race-based presumptions of both social and economic disadvantage. The record did not reveal whether Gonzales had been certified under these regulations or under either the SBA's 8(a) or 8(d) program.]

Adarand [sued] various federal officials ..., claiming that the race-based presumptions involved in the use of subcontracting compensation clauses violate Adarand's right to equal protection. The District Court granted the Government's motion for summary judgment.... The ... Tenth Circuit affirmed.... It understood our decision in Fullilove v. Klutznick, 448 U.S. 448 (1980), to have adopted "a lenient standard, resembling intermediate scrutiny, in assessing" the constitutionality of federal race-based action.... Applying that "lenient standard," as further developed in Metro Broadcasting, Inc. v. FCC, 497 U.S. 547 (1990), the Court of Appeals upheld the use of subcontractor compensation clauses....

. . .

III

The Government urges that "[t]he Subcontracting Compensation Clause program is ... a program based on disadvantage, not on race," and thus that it is subject only to "the most relaxed judicial scrutiny." ... To the extent that the statutes and regulations involved in this case are race neutral, we agree. The Government concedes, however, that "the race-based rebuttable presumption used in some certification determinations under the Subcontracting Compensation Clause" is subject to some heightened level of scrutiny....

Adarand's claim arises under the Fifth Amendment [Due Process Clause.] Although this Court has always understood that Clause to provide some measure of protection against arbitrary treatment by the Federal Government, it is not as explicit a guarantee of equal treatment as the Fourteenth Amendment [Equal Protection Clause].... Our cases have accorded varying degrees of significance to the difference in the language of those two Clauses....

A

Through the 1940s, this Court had routinely taken the view in non-race-related cases that, "[u]nlike the Fourteenth Amendment, the Fifth contains no equal protection clause and it provides no guaranty against discriminatory legislation by Congress." Detroit Bank v. United States, 317 U.S. 329, 337 (1943).... When the Court first faced a Fifth Amendment equal protection challenge to a federal racial classification, it adopted a similar approach, with most unfortunate results. In Hirabayashi v. United States, 320 U.S. 81 (1943), the Court considered a curfew applicable only to persons of Japanese ancestry. The Court observed—correctly—that "[d]istinctions between citizens solely because of their ancestry are by their very nature odious to a free people whose institutions are founded upon the doctrine of equality," and that "racial discriminations are in most circumstances irrelevant and therefore prohibited." ... But it also cited *Detroit Bank* for the proposition that the Fifth Amendment "restrains only such discriminatory legislation by Congress as amounts to a denial of due process," ... and upheld the curfew....

... Korematsu v. United States, 323 U.S. 214 (1944), ... did not address the view ... that the Federal Government's obligation to provide equal protection differs significantly from that of the States. Instead, it began by noting that "all legal restrictions which curtail the civil rights of a single racial group are immediately suspect ... [and] courts must subject them to the most rigid scrutiny." ... That promising dictum might be read to undermine the view that the Federal Government is under a lesser obligation to avoid injurious racial classifications than are the States.... But ... the Court ... inexplicably relied on "the principles we announced in the *Hirabayashi* case" ... to conclude that, although "exclusion from the area in which one's home is located is a far greater deprivation than constant confinement to the home from 8 p. m. to 6 a. m.," . . . the racially discriminatory order was nonetheless within the Federal Government's power.

In Bolling v. Sharpe, 347 U.S. 497 (1954), the Court for the first time explicitly questioned the existence of any difference between the obligations of the Federal Government and the States to avoid racial classifications. . . .

Bolling's facts concerned school desegregation, but its reasoning was not so limited. . . .

Later cases in contexts other than school desegregation did not distinguish between the duties of the States and the Federal Government to avoid racial classifications. . . .

. . . Thus, in 1975, the Court stated explicitly that "[t]his Court's approach to Fifth Amendment equal protection claims has always been precisely the same as to equal protection claims under the Fourteenth Amendment." Weinberger v. Wiesenfeld, 420 U.S. 636, 638, n. 2 (1975). . . . We do not understand a few contrary suggestions appearing in cases in which we found special deference to the political branches of the Federal Government to be appropriate, e. g., Hampton v. Mow Sun Wong . . . (1976) (federal power over immigration), to detract from this general rule.

B

Most of the cases discussed above involved classifications burdening groups that have suffered discrimination in our society. In 1978, the Court confronted the question whether race-based governmental action designed to benefit such groups should also be subject to "the most rigid scrutiny." Regents of Univ. of California v. Bakke . . . did not produce an opinion for the Court. . . .

Two years after *Bakke*, the Court faced another challenge to remedial race-based action, this time involving action undertaken by the Federal Government. In Fullilove v. Klutznick, 448 U.S. 448 (1980), the Court upheld Congress' inclusion of a 10% set-aside for minority-owned businesses in the Public Works Employment Act of 1977. As in *Bakke*, there was no opinion for the Court. Chief Justice Burger, in an opinion joined by Justices White and Powell, observed that "[a]ny preference based on racial or ethnic criteria must necessarily receive a most searching examination to make sure that it does not conflict with constitutional guarantees." . . . That opinion, however, "d[id] not adopt, either expressly or implicitly, the formulas of analysis articulated in such cases as [*Bakke*]." . . . It employed instead a two-part test which asked, first, "whether the objectives of th[e] legislation are within the power of Congress," and second, "whether the limited use of racial and ethnic criteria, in the context presented, is a constitutionally permissible means for achieving the congressional objectives." . . . It then upheld the program under that test, adding at the end of the opinion that the program also "would survive judicial review under either 'test' articulated in the several *Bakke* opinions." . . . Justice Powell wrote separately to express his view that the plurality opinion had essentially applied "strict scrutiny" as described in his *Bakke* opinion—i. e., it had determined that the set-aside was "a necessary means of advancing a compelling governmental interest"—and had done so correctly. . . . Justice Stewart (joined by then-Justice Rehnquist) dissented, arguing that the Constitution required the Federal Government to meet the same strict standard as the States when enacting racial classifications, . . . and that the program before the Court failed that standard. Justice Stevens also dissented, arguing that "[r]acial classifications are simply too pernicious to permit any but the most exact connection between justification and classification," . . . and that the program before the Court could not be characterized "as a 'narrowly tailored' remedial measure." ... Justice Marshall (joined by Justices Brennan and Blackmun) concurred in the judgment, reiterating the view of four Justices in *Bakke* that any race-based governmental action designed to "remed[y] the present effects of past racial discrimination" should be upheld if it was "substantially related" to the achievement of an "important governmental objective"—i. e., such action should be subjected only to what we now call "intermediate scrutiny." ...

In Wygant v. Jackson Board of Ed., 476 U.S. 267 (1986), the Court considered ... whether a school board could adopt race-based preferences in determining which teachers to lay off. . . .

The Court's failure to produce a majority opinion in *Bakke*, *Fullilove*, and *Wygant* left unresolved the proper analysis for remedial race-based governmental action. . . .

The Court resolved the issue, at least in part, in 1989. Richmond v. J.A. Croson Co., 488 U.S. 469 (1989), concerned a city's determination that 30% of its contracting work should go to minority-owned businesses. A majority of the Court in *Croson* held that "the standard of review under the Equal Protection Clause is not dependent on the race of those burdened or benefited by a particular classification," and that the single standard of review for racial classifications should be "strict scrutiny." ...

With *Croson*, the Court finally agreed that the Fourteenth Amendment requires strict scrutiny of all race-based action by state and local governments. But *Croson* of course had no occasion to declare what standard of review the Fifth Amendment requires for such action taken by the Federal Government. *Croson* observed simply that the Court's "treatment of an exercise of congressional power in *Fullilove* cannot be dispositive here," because *Croson*'s facts did not implicate Congress' broad power under § 5 of the Fourteenth Amendment. . . .

Despite lingering uncertainty in the details, however, the Court's cases through *Croson* had established three general propositions with respect to governmental racial classifications. First, skepticism: " '[a]ny preference based on racial or ethnic criteria must necessarily receive a most searching examination,' " ... Second, consistency: "the standard of review under the Equal Protection Clause is not dependent on the race of those burdened or benefited by a particular classification," Croson ..., i. e., all racial classifications reviewable under the Equal Protection Clause must be strictly scrutinized. And third, congruence: "[e]qual protection analysis in the Fifth Amendment area is the same as that under the Fourteenth Amendment,". . . . Taken together, these three propositions lead to the conclusion that any person, of whatever race, has the right to demand that any governmental actor subject to the Constitution justify any racial classification subjecting that person to unequal treatment under the strictest judicial scrutiny. . . .

A year later, however, the Court took a surprising turn. Metro Broadcasting, Inc. v. FCC, 497 U.S. 547 (1990), involved a Fifth Amendment challenge to two race-based policies of the Federal Communications Commission. In *Metro Broadcasting*, the Court repudiated the long-held notion that "it would be unthinkable that the same Constitution would impose a lesser duty on the Federal Government" than it does on a State to afford equal protection of the laws ... by holding that "benign" federal racial classifications need only satisfy intermediate scrutiny, even though *Croson* had recently concluded that such classifications enacted by a State must satisfy strict scrutiny. "[B]enign" federal racial classifications, the Court said, "—even if those measures are not 'remedial' in the sense of being designed to compensate victims of past governmental or societal discrimination—are constitutionally permissible to the extent that they serve important governmental objectives within the power of Congress and are substantially related to achievement of those objectives." . . . The Court did not explain how to tell whether a racial classification should be deemed "benign," other than to express "confiden[ce] that an 'examination of the legislative scheme and its history' will separate benign measures from other types of racial classifications." . . .

Applying this test, the Court first noted that the FCC policies at issue did not serve as a remedy for past discrimination. . . . Proceeding on the assumption that the policies were nonetheless "benign," it concluded that they served the "important governmental objective" of "enhancing broadcast diversity," . . . and that they were "substantially related" to that objective. . . . It therefore upheld the policies.

By adopting intermediate scrutiny as the standard of review for congressionally mandated "benign" racial classifications, *Metro Broadcasting* departed from prior cases in two significant respects. First, it turned its back on *Croson*'s explanation of why strict scrutiny of all governmental racial classifications is essential:

> "Absent searching judicial inquiry into the justification for such race-based measures, there is simply no way of determining what classifications are 'benign' or 'remedial' and what classifications are in fact motivated by illegitimate notions of racial inferiority or simple racial politics. Indeed, the purpose of strict scrutiny is to 'smoke out' illegitimate uses of race by assuring that the legislative body is pursuing a goal important enough to warrant use of a highly suspect tool. The test also ensures that the means chosen 'fit' this compelling goal so closely that there is little or no possibility that the motive for the classification was illegitimate racial prejudice or stereotype." . . . We adhere to that view today, despite the surface appeal of holding "benign" racial classifications to a lower standard, because "it may not always be clear that a so-called preference is in fact benign," *Bakke* . . . (opinion of Powell, J.). . . .

Second, *Metro Broadcasting* squarely rejected one of the three propositions established by the Court's earlier equal protection cases, namely, congruence between the standards applicable to federal and state racial classifications, and in so doing also undermined the other two—skepticism of all racial classifications, and consistency of treatment irrespective of the race of the burdened or benefited group. . . . Under *Metro Broadcasting*, certain racial classifications ("benign" ones enacted by the Federal Government) should be treated less skeptically than others; and the race of the benefited group is critical to the determination of which standard of review to apply. *Metro Broadcasting* was thus a significant departure from much of what had come before it.

The three propositions undermined by *Metro Broadcasting* all derive from the basic principle that the Fifth and Fourteenth Amendments to the Constitution protect persons, not groups. It follows . . . that all governmental action based on race . . . should be subjected to detailed judicial inquiry to ensure that the personal right to equal protection of the laws has not been infringed. . . . Accordingly, we hold today that all racial classifications, imposed by whatever federal, state, or local governmental actor, must be analyzed by a reviewing court under strict scrutiny. In other words, such classifications are constitutional only if they are narrowly tailored measures that further compelling governmental interests. To the extent that *Metro Broadcasting* is inconsistent with that holding, it is overruled.

In dissent, Justice Stevens['s] . . . criticisms reflect a serious misunderstanding of our opinion.

. . . What he fails to recognize is that strict scrutiny does take "relevant differences" into account—indeed, that is its fundamental purpose. The point of carefully examining the interest asserted by the government in support of a racial classification, and the evidence offered to show that the classification is needed, is precisely to distinguish legitimate from illegitimate uses of race in governmental decisionmaking. And Justice Stevens concedes that "some cases may be difficult to classify"; all the more reason, in our view, to examine all racial classifications carefully. Strict scrutiny does not "trea[t] dissimilar race-based decisions as though they were equally objectionable"; to the contrary, it evaluates carefully all governmental race-based decisions in order to decide which are constitutionally objectionable and which are not. By requiring strict scrutiny of racial classifications, we require courts to make sure that a governmental classification based on race . . . is legitimate, before permitting unequal treatment based on race to proceed.

Justice Stevens chides us for our "supposed inability to differentiate between 'invidious' and 'benign' discrimination," because it is in his view sufficient that "people understand the difference between good intentions and bad." But . . . the point of strict scrutiny is to "differentiate between" permissible and impermissible governmental use of race. And Justice Stevens himself has already explained in his dissent in *Fullilove* why "good intentions" alone are not enough . . .: "[E]ven though it is not the actual predicate for this legislation, a statute of this kind inevitably is perceived by many as resting on an assumption that those who are granted this special preference are less qualified in some respect that is identified purely by their race. Because that perception—especially when fostered by the Congress of the United States—can only exacerbate rather than reduce racial prejudice, it will delay the time when race will become a truly irrelevant, or at least insignificant, factor . . .; see also id., at 537 ('Racial classifications are simply too pernicious to permit any but the most exact connection between justification and classification' "); Croson, supra, at 516–517 (Stevens, J., concurring in part and concurring in judgment) ("Although [the legislation at issue] stigmatizes the disadvantaged class with the unproven charge of past racial discrimination, it actually imposes a greater stigma on its supposed beneficiaries"). . . . These passages make a persuasive case for requiring strict scrutiny of congressional racial classifications.

Perhaps it is not the standard of strict scrutiny itself, but our use of the concepts of "consistency" and "congruence" in conjunction with it, that leads Justice Stevens to dissent. According to Justice Stevens, our view of consistency "equate[s] remedial preferences with invidious discrimination," and ignores the difference between "an engine of oppression" and an effort "to foster equality in society," or, more colorfully, "between a 'No Trespassing' sign and a welcome mat." It does nothing of the kind. The principle of consistency simply means that whenever the government treats any person unequally because of his or her race, that person has suffered an injury that falls squarely within the language and spirit of the Constitution's guarantee of equal protection. It says nothing about the ultimate validity of any particular law; that determination is the job of the court applying strict scrutiny. The principle of consistency explains the circumstances in which the injury requiring strict scrutiny occurs. The application of strict scrutiny, in turn, determines whether a compelling governmental interest justifies the infliction of that injury.

Consistency does recognize that any individual suffers an injury when he or she is disadvantaged by the government because of his or her race, whatever that race may be. This Court clearly stated that principle in *Croson*.... Justice Stevens does not explain how his views square with *Croson*, or with the long line of cases understanding equal protection as a personal right.

Justice Stevens also claims that we have ignored any difference between federal and state legislatures. But requiring that Congress, like the States, enact racial classifications only when doing so is necessary to further a "compelling interest" does not contravene any principle of appropriate respect for a co-equal Branch of the Government. [T]rue[,] various Members of this Court have taken different views of the authority § 5 of the Fourteenth Amendment confers upon Congress to deal with the problem of racial discrimination, and the extent to which courts should defer to Congress' exercise of that authority.... We need not, and do not, address these differences today. For now, it is enough to observe that Justice Stevens' suggestion that any Member of this Court has repudiated in this case his or her previously expressed views on the subject is incorrect.

C

. . .

It is worth pointing out the difference between the applications of *stare decisis* in this case and in Planned Parenthood of Southeastern Pa. v. Casey, 505 U.S. 833 (1992). *Casey* explained how considerations of *stare decisis* inform the decision whether to overrule a long-established precedent that has become integrated into the fabric of the law. Overruling precedent of that kind naturally may have consequences for "the ideal of the rule of law".... In addition, such precedent is likely to have engendered substantial reliance, as was true in *Casey* itself.... But ... we do not face a precedent of that kind, because *Metro Broadcasting* itself departed from our prior cases—and did so quite recently. By refusing to follow *Metro Broadcasting*, then, we do not depart from the fabric of the law; we restore it. [A]lso[,] reliance on a case that has recently departed from precedent is likely to be minimal, particularly where, as here, the rule ... in that case is unlikely to affect primary conduct in any event....

... [W]e think that well-settled legal principles pointed toward a conclusion different from that reached in *Metro Broadcasting*, and we therefore disagree with Justice Stevens that "the law at the time of that decision was entirely open to the result the Court reached." ... There is nothing new about the notion that Congress, like the States, may treat people differently because of their race only for compelling reasons.

"The real problem ... is whether a principle shall prevail over its later misapplications." ... *Metro Broadcasting*'s untenable distinction between state and federal racial classifications lacks support in our precedent, and undermines the fundamental principle of equal protection as a personal right. In this case, as between that principle and "its later misapplications," the principle must prevail.

D

Our action today makes explicit what Justice Powell thought implicit in the *Fullilove* lead opinion: federal racial classifications, like those of a State, must serve a compelling governmental interest, and must be narrowly tailored to further that interest.... [I]t follows that to the extent (if any) that *Fullilove* held federal racial classifications to be subject to a less rigorous standard, it is no longer controlling. But we need not decide today whether the program upheld in *Fullilove* would survive strict scrutiny as our more recent cases have defined it.

Some have questioned the importance of debating the proper standard of review of race-based legislation.... But we agree with Justice Stevens that, "[b]ecause racial characteristics so seldom provide a relevant basis for disparate treatment, and because classifications based on race are potentially so harmful to the entire body politic, it is especially important that the reasons for any such classification be clearly identified and unquestionably legitimate," and that "[r]acial classifications are simply too pernicious to permit any but the most exact connection between justification and classification." *Fullilove* ... (dissenting opinion).... We think that requiring strict scrutiny is the best way to ensure that courts will consistently give racial classifications that kind of detailed examination, both as to ends and as to means. *Korematsu* demonstrates vividly that even "the most rigid scrutiny" can sometimes fail to detect an illegitimate racial classification.... Any retreat from the most searching judicial inquiry can only increase the risk of another such error occurring in the future.

Finally, we wish to dispel the notion that strict scrutiny is "strict in theory, but fatal in fact." ... The unhappy persistence of both the practice and the lingering effects of racial discrimination against minority groups in this country is an unfortunate reality, and government is not disqualified from acting in response to it. As recently as 1987, for example, every Justice of this Court agreed that the Alabama Department of Public Safety's "pervasive, systematic, and obstinate discriminatory conduct" justified a narrowly tailored race-based remedy. See United States v. Paradise, 480 U. S., at 167 (plurality opinion of Brennan, J.); id., at 190 (Stevens, J., concurring in judgment); id., at 196 (O'Connor, J., dissenting). When race-based action is necessary to further a compelling interest, such action is within constitutional constraints if it satisfies the "narrow tailoring" test this Court has set out in previous cases.

IV

Because our decision today alters the playing field in some important respects, we think it best to remand ... for further consideration in light of the principles we have announced. The Court of Appeals, following *Metro Broadcasting* and *Fullilove*, analyzed the case in terms of intermediate scrutiny. It ... did not decide ... whether the interests served by the use of subcontractor compensation clauses are properly described as "compelling." It also did not address the question of narrow tailoring in terms of our strict scrutiny cases, by asking, for example, whether there was "any consideration of the use of race-neutral means to increase minority business participation" in government contracting, *Croson* ..., or whether the program was appropriately limited such that it "will not last longer than the discriminatory effects it is designed to eliminate," *Fullilove* ... (Powell, J., concurring).

Moreover, unresolved questions remain concerning the details of the complex regulatory regimes implicated by the use of subcontractor compensation clauses. For example, the SBA's 8(a) program requires an individualized inquiry into the economic disadvantage of every participant, ... whereas the DOT's regulations implementing STURAA § 106(c) do not.... And the regulations seem unclear as to whether 8(d) subcontractors must make individualized showings, or instead whether the race-based presumption applies both to social and economic disadvantage.... We also note an apparent discrepancy between the definitions of which socially disadvantaged individuals qualify as economically disadvantaged for the 8(a) and 8(d) programs; the former requires a showing that such individuals' ability to compete has been impaired "as compared to others in the same or similar line of business who are not socially disadvantaged," ... while the latter requires that showing only "as compared to others in the same or similar line of business," .... The question whether any of the ways in which the Government uses subcontractor compensation clauses can survive strict scrutiny, and any relevance distinctions such as these may have to that question, should be addressed in the first instance by the lower courts.

. . .

Justice Scalia, concurring in part and concurring in the judgment.

I join the opinion of the Court, except Part III–C, and except insofar as it may be inconsistent with the following: In my view, government can never have a "compelling interest" in discriminating on the basis of race in order to "make up" for past racial discrimination in the opposite direction.... Individuals who have been wronged by unlawful racial discrimination should be made whole; but under our Constitution there can be no such thing as either a creditor or a debtor race. That concept is alien to the Constitution's focus upon the individual ... and its rejection of dispositions based on race, see Amdt. 15, § 1 (prohibiting abridgment of the right to vote "on account of race") or based on blood, see Art. III, § 3 ("[N]o Attainder of Treason shall work Corruption of Blood"); Art. I, § 9 ("No Title of Nobility shall be granted by the United States"). To pursue the concept of racial entitlement—even for the most admirable and benign of purposes—is to reinforce and preserve for future mischief the way of thinking that produced race slavery, race privilege and race hatred. In the eyes of government, we are just one race here. It is American.

It is unlikely, if not impossible, that the challenged program would survive under this understanding of strict scrutiny, but I am content to leave that to be decided on remand.

Justice Thomas, concurring in part and concurring in the judgment.

I agree with the majority's conclusion that strict scrutiny applies to all government classifications based on race. I write separately, however, to express my disagreement with the premise underlying Justice Stevens' and Justice Ginsburg's dissents: that there is a racial paternalism exception to the principle of equal protection. I believe that there is a "moral [and] constitutional equivalence" (Stevens, J., dissenting) between laws designed to subjugate a race and those that distribute benefits on the basis of race in order to foster some current notion of equality. Government cannot make us equal; it can only recognize, respect, and protect us as equal before the law.

That these programs may have been motivated, in part, by good intentions cannot provide refuge from the principle that under our Constitution, the government may not make distinctions on the basis of race. As far as the Constitution is concerned, it is irrelevant whether a government's racial classifications are drawn by those who wish to oppress a race or by those who have a sincere desire to help those thought to be disadvantaged. There can be no doubt that the paternalism that appears to lie at the heart of this program is at war with the principle of inherent equality that underlies and infuses our Constitution....

These programs ... also undermine the moral basis of the equal protection principle. Purchased at the price of immeasurable human suffering, the equal protection principle reflects our Nation's understanding that such classifications ultimately have a destructive impact on the individual and our society....

[T]here can be no doubt that racial paternalism and its unintended consequences can be as poisonous and pernicious as any other form of discrimination. So-called "benign" discrimination teaches many that because of chronic
and apparently immutable handicaps, minorities cannot compete with them
without their patronizing indulgence. Inevitably, such programs engender
attitudes of superiority or, alternatively, provoke resentment among those who
believe that they have been wronged by the government's use of race. These
programs stamp minorities with a badge of inferiority and may cause them to
develop dependencies or to adopt an attitude that they are "entitled" to
preferences....

In my mind, government-sponsored racial discrimination based on benign
prejudice is just as noxious as discrimination inspired by malicious prejudice. In
each instance, it is racial discrimination, plain and simple.

Justice Stevens, with whom Justice Ginsburg joins, dissenting.

. . .

II

The Court's concept of "consistency" assumes that there is no significant
difference between a decision by the majority to impose a special burden on the
members of a minority race and a decision by the majority to provide a benefit
to certain members of that minority notwithstanding its incidental burden on
some members of the majority. [T]hat assumption is untenable. There is no
moral or constitutional equivalence between a policy that is designed to
perpetuate a caste system and one that seeks to eradicate racial subordination.
Invidious discrimination is an engine of oppression, subjugating a disfavored
group to enhance or maintain the power of the majority. Remedial race-based
preferences reflect the opposite impulse: a desire to foster equality in society.
No sensible conception of the Government's constitutional obligation to "govern impartially" . . . should ignore this distinction.[1]

. . .

The consistency that the Court espouses would disregard the difference
between a "No Trespassing" sign and a welcome mat. It would treat a
Dixiecrat Senator's decision to vote against Thurgood Marshall's confirmation
in order to keep African Americans off the Supreme Court as on a par with
President Johnson's evaluation of his nominee's race as a positive factor. It
would equate a law that made black citizens ineligible for military service with
a program aimed at recruiting black soldiers. An attempt by the majority to
exclude members of a minority race from a regulated market is fundamentally
different from a subsidy that enables a relatively small group of newcomers to
enter that market....

The Court's explanation for treating dissimilar race-based decisions as
though they were equally objectionable is a supposed inability to differentiate
between "invidious" and "benign" discrimination. But the term "affirmative
action" is common and well understood. Its presence in everyday parlance
shows that people understand the difference between good intentions and
bad....

1. ... The Court suggests today that
"strict scrutiny" means something different—something less strict—when applied to
benign racial classifications. Although I agree
that benign programs deserve different treatment than invidious programs, there is a
danger that the fatal language of "strict scrutiny" will skew the analysis and place well-
crafted benign programs at unnecessary risk.

Indeed, our jurisprudence has made the standard to be applied in cases of invidious discrimination turn on whether the discrimination is "intentional," or whether, by contrast, it merely has a discriminatory "effect." Washington v. Davis, 426 U.S. 229 (1976). Surely this distinction is at least as subtle, and at least as difficult to apply . . . as the usually obvious distinction between a measure intended to benefit members of a particular minority race and a measure intended to burden a minority race. A state actor inclined to subvert the Constitution might easily hide bad intentions in the guise of unintended "effects"; but I should think it far more difficult to enact a law intending to preserve the majority's hegemony while casting it plausibly in the guise of affirmative action for minorities.

. . . [A] single standard that purports to equate remedial preferences with invidious discrimination cannot be defended in the name of "equal protection."

Moreover, the Court['s] new "consistency" approach to race-based classifications is difficult to square with its insistence upon rigidly separate categories for discrimination against different classes of individuals. For example, as the law currently stands, the Court will apply "intermediate scrutiny" to cases of invidious gender discrimination and "strict scrutiny" to cases of invidious race discrimination, while applying the same standard for benign classifications as for invidious ones. If this remains the law, then today's lecture about "consistency" will produce the anomalous result that the Government can more easily enact affirmative-action programs to remedy discrimination against women than it can enact affirmative-action programs to remedy discrimination against African Americans—even though the primary purpose of the Equal Protection Clause was to end discrimination against the former slaves. . . . When a court becomes preoccupied with abstract standards, it risks sacrificing common sense at the altar of formal consistency.

As a matter of constitutional and democratic principle, a decision by representatives of the majority to discriminate against the members of a minority race is fundamentally different from those same representatives' decision to impose incidental costs on the majority of their constituents in order to provide a benefit to a disadvantaged minority.[5] Indeed, . . . the former is virtually always repugnant to the principles of a free and democratic society, whereas the latter is, in some circumstances, entirely consistent with the ideal of equality. . . .

5. . . . Justice Thomas argues that the most significant cost associated with an affirmative-action program is its adverse stigmatic effect on its intended beneficiaries. Although I agree that this cost may be more significant than many people realize, . . . I do not think it applies to the facts of this case. First, . . . [n]o beneficiaries of the specific program . . . have challenged its constitutionality—perhaps because they do not find the preferences stigmatizing, or perhaps because their ability to opt out of the program provides them all the relief they would need. Second, . . . Justice Thomas' extreme proposition—that there is a moral and constitutional equivalence between an attempt to subjugate and an attempt to redress the effects of a caste system—[is not] at all persuasive. It is one thing to question the wisdom of affirmative-action programs. . . . It is another thing altogether to equate the many well-

meaning and intelligent lawmakers and their constituents—whether members of majority or minority races—who have supported affirmative action over the years, to segregationists and bigots. Finally, although Justice Thomas is more concerned about the potential effects of these programs than the intent of those who enacted them . . . , I am not persuaded that the psychological damage brought on by affirmative action is as severe as that engendered by racial subordination. That, in any event, is a judgment the political branches can be trusted to make. In enacting affirmative action programs, a legislature intends to remove obstacles that have unfairly placed individuals of equal qualifications at a competitive disadvantage. . . . I do not believe such action, whether wise or unwise, deserves such an invidious label as "racial paternalism." . . .

III

The Court's concept of "congruence" assumes ... no significant difference between a decision by the Congress ... to adopt an affirmative-action program and such a decision by a State or a municipality. [T]hat assumption ... ignores important practical and legal differences between federal and state or local decisionmakers.

These differences have been identified repeatedly and consistently both in opinions of the Court and in separate opinions authored by members of today's majority. Thus, in Metro Broadcasting, Inc. v. FCC, 497 U.S. 547 (1990), ... we identified the special "institutional competence" of our National Legislature.... We recalled the several opinions in *Fullilove* that admonished this Court to "approach our task with appropriate deference to the Congress, a co-equal branch charged by the Constitution with the power to 'provide for the ... general Welfare of the United States' and 'to enforce, by appropriate legislation,' the equal protection guarantees of the Fourteenth Amendment. ...'" ...

... In his separate opinion in Richmond v. J.A. Croson Co., 488 U.S. 469, 520–524 (1989), Justice Scalia discussed the basis for this distinction....

In her plurality opinion in *Croson*, Justice O'Connor also emphasized the importance of this distinction when she responded to the City's argument that *Fullilove* was controlling. She wrote: "What appellant ignores is that Congress, unlike any State or political subdivision, has a specific constitutional mandate to enforce the dictates of the Fourteenth Amendment. The power to 'enforce' may at times also include the power to define situations which Congress determines threaten principles of equality and to adopt prophylactic rules to deal with those situations. The Civil War Amendments themselves worked a dramatic change in the balance between congressional and state power over matters of race." ...

An additional reason for giving greater deference to the National Legislature than to a local law-making body is that federal affirmative-action programs represent the will of our entire Nation's elected representatives, whereas a state or local program may have an impact on nonresident entities who played no part in the decision to enact it. Thus, in the state or local context, individuals who were unable to vote for the local representatives who enacted a race-conscious program may nonetheless feel the effects of that program. This difference recalls the goals of the Commerce Clause, U.S. Const., Art. I, § 8, cl. 3, which permits Congress to legislate on certain matters of national importance while denying power to the States in this area for fear of undue impact upon out-of-state residents....

Ironically, after all of the time, effort, and paper this Court has expended in differentiating between federal and state affirmative action, the majority today virtually ignores the issue.... Such silence, however, cannot erase the difference between Congress' institutional competence and constitutional authority to overcome historic racial subjugation and the States' lesser power to do so.

. . . .

... In the programs challenged in this case, Congress has acted both with respect to private individuals and, as in *Fullilove*, with respect to the States themselves.[9] When Congress does this, it draws its power directly from § 5 of

---

9. The funding for the preferences challenged in this case comes from ... STURAA ..., in which Congress has granted funds to the States in exchange for a commitment to the Fourteenth Amendment.... The Fourteenth Amendment directly empowers Congress at the same time it expressly limits the States.[11] This is no accident. It represents our Nation's consensus, achieved after hard experience throughout our sorry history of race relations, that the Federal Government must be the primary defender of racial minorities against the States, some of which may be inclined to oppress such minorities. A rule of "congruence" that ignores a purposeful "incongruity" so fundamental to our system of government is unacceptable.

. . .

IV

The Court's concept of *stare decisis* treats some of the language we have used in explaining our decisions as though it were more important than our actual holdings....

This is the third time in the Court's entire history that it has considered the constitutionality of a federal affirmative-action program. On each of the two prior occasions, the first in 1980, Fullilove v. Klutznick, 448 U.S. 448, and the second in 1990, Metro Broadcasting, Inc. v. FCC, 497 U.S. 547, the Court upheld the program....

In the Court's view, our decision in *Metro Broadcasting* was inconsistent with the rule announced in Richmond v. J.A. Croson Co., 488 U.S. 469 (1989). But two decisive distinctions separate those two cases. First, *Metro Broadcasting* involved a federal program, whereas *Croson* involved a city ordinance. *Metro Broadcasting* thus drew primary support from *Fullilove*, which predated *Croson* and which *Croson* distinguished on the grounds of the federal-state dichotomy that the majority today discredits. Although members of today's majority trumpeted the importance of that distinction in *Croson*, they now reject it in the name of "congruence." It is therefore quite wrong for the Court to suggest today that overruling *Metro Broadcasting* merely restores the *status quo ante*, for the law at the time of that decision was entirely open to the result the Court reached. *Today's* decision is an unjustified departure from settled law.

foster subcontracting by disadvantaged business enterprises, or "DBE's." STURAA is also the source of funding for DBE preferences in federal highway contracting. Approximately 98% of STURAA's funding is allocated to the States.... Moreover, under STURAA States are empowered to certify businesses as "disadvantaged" for purposes of receiving subcontracting preferences in both state and federal contracts.... In this case, Adarand has sued only the federal officials responsible for implementing federal highway contracting policy; it has not directly challenged DBE preferences granted in state contracts funded by STURAA. It is not entirely clear, then, whether the majority's "congruence" rationale would apply to federally regulated state contracts, which may conceivably be within the majority's view of Congress' § 5 authority even if the federal contracts are not. See Metro Broadcasting, 497 U. S., at 603–604 (O'Connor, J., dissenting). As I read the majority's opinion, however, it draws no distinctions between direct federal preferences and federal preferences achieved through subsidies to States. The extent to which STURAA intertwines elements of direct federal regulations with elements of federal conditions on grants to the States would make such a distinction difficult to sustain.

11. We have read § 5 as a positive grant of authority to Congress, not just to punish violations, but also to define and expand the scope of the Equal Protection Clause. Katzenbach v. Morgan, 384 U.S. 641 (1966). In *Katzenbach*, this meant that Congress under § 5 could require the States to allow non-English-speaking citizens to vote, even if denying such citizens a vote would not have been an independent violation of § 1.... Congress, then, can expand the coverage of § 1 by exercising its power under § 5 when it acts to foster equality. Congress has done just that here; it has decided that granting certain preferences to minorities best serves the goals of equal protection.

Second, *Metro Broadcasting*'s holding rested on more than its application of "intermediate scrutiny." . . . What truly distinguishes *Metro Broadcasting* from our other affirmative-action precedents is the distinctive goal of the federal program in that case. Instead of merely seeking to remedy past discrimination, the FCC program was intended to achieve future benefits in the form of broadcast diversity. . . .

[P]rior to *Metro Broadcasting*, the interest in diversity had been mentioned in a few opinions, but it is perfectly clear that the Court had not yet decided whether that interest had sufficient magnitude to justify a racial classification. *Metro Broadcasting*, of course, answered that question in the affirmative. The majority today overrules *Metro Broadcasting* only insofar as it is "inconsistent with [the] holding" that strict scrutiny applies to "benign" racial classifications promulgated by the Federal Government. The proposition that fostering diversity may provide a sufficient interest to justify such a program is *not* inconsistent with the Court's holding today—indeed, the question is not remotely presented in this case—and I do not take the Court's opinion to diminish that aspect of our decision in *Metro Broadcasting*.

The Court's suggestion that it may be necessary in the future to overrule *Fullilove* in order to restore the fabric of the law is even more disingenuous than its treatment of *Metro Broadcasting*. For the Court endorses the "strict scrutiny" standard that Justice Powell applied in *Bakke* and acknowledges that he applied that standard in *Fullilove* as well. Moreover, Chief Justice Burger also expressly concluded that the program we considered in *Fullilove* was valid under any of the tests articulated in *Bakke*, which of course included Justice Powell's. . . . The Court thus adopts a standard applied in *Fullilove* at the same time it questions that case's continued vitality and accuses it of departing from prior law. . . . As was true of *Metro Broadcasting*, the Court in *Fullilove* decided an important, novel, and difficult question. Providing a different answer to a similar question today cannot fairly be characterized as merely "restoring" previously settled law.

V

The Court's holding in *Fullilove* surely governs the result in this case. The Public Works Employment Act of 1977 (1977 Act) . . . is different in several critical respects from the portions of the Small Business Act (SBA) . . . and STURAA . . . challenged in this case. Each of those differences makes the current program . . . significantly less objectionable than the 1977 categorical grant of $400 million in exchange for a 10% set-aside in public contracts to "a class of investors defined solely by racial characteristics." *Fullilove*, 448 U. S., at 532 (Stevens, J., dissenting). In no meaningful respect is the current scheme more objectionable than the 1977 Act. Thus, if the 1977 Act was constitutional, then so must be the SBA and STURAA. Indeed, even if my dissenting views in *Fullilove* had prevailed, this program would be valid.

Unlike the 1977 Act, the present statutory scheme does not make race the sole criterion of eligibility for participation in the program. Race does give rise to a rebuttable presumption of social disadvantage which, at least under STURAA, gives rise to a second rebuttable presumption of economic disadvantage. . . . But a small business may qualify as a DBE, by showing that it is both socially and economically disadvantaged, even if it receives neither of these presumptions. . . . Thus, the current preference is more inclusive than the 1977 Act because it does not make race a necessary qualification.

More importantly, race is not a sufficient qualification. Whereas a millionaire with a long history of financial successes . . . would have qualified for a preference under the 1977 Act merely because he was an Asian American or an African American, ... neither the SBA nor STURAA creates any such anomaly. The DBE program excludes members of minority races who are not, in fact, socially or economically disadvantaged. . . . The presumption of social disadvantage reflects the unfortunate fact that irrational racial prejudice—along with its lingering effects—still survives. The presumption of economic disadvantage embodies a recognition that success in the private sector of the economy is often attributable, in part, to social skills and relationships. Unlike the 1977 set-asides, the current preference is designed to overcome the social and economic disadvantages that are often associated with racial characteristics. If, in a particular case, these disadvantages are not present, the presumptions can be rebutted. . . . The program is thus designed to allow race to play a part in the decisional process only when there is a meaningful basis for assuming its relevance.

[I]t is particularly significant that the current program targets the negotiation of subcontracts between private firms. The 1977 Act applied entirely to the award of public contracts, an area of the economy in which social relationships should be irrelevant and in which proper supervision of government contracting officers should preclude any discrimination against particular bidders on account of their race. [Here], the program seeks to overcome barriers of prejudice between private parties—specifically, between general contractors and subcontractors. The SBA and STURAA embody Congress' recognition that such barriers may actually handicap minority firms seeking business as subcontractors from established leaders in the industry that have a history of doing business with their golfing partners. Indeed, minority subcontractors may face more obstacles than direct, intentional racial prejudice: they may face particular barriers simply because they are more likely to be new in the business and less likely to know others in the business. Given such difficulties, Congress could reasonably find that a minority subcontractor is less likely to receive favors from the entrenched businesspersons who award subcontracts only to people with whom—or with whose friends—they have an existing relationship. This program, then, if in part a remedy for past discrimination, is most importantly a forward-looking response to practical problems faced by minority subcontractors.

The current program contains another forward-looking component that the 1977 set-asides did not share. Section 8(a) of the SBA provides for periodic review of the status of DBE's, ... and DBE status can be challenged by a competitor at any time under any of the routes to certification. . . . Such review prevents ineligible firms from taking part in the program solely because of their minority ownership, even when those firms were once disadvantaged but have since become successful. The emphasis on review also indicates the Administration's anticipation that after their presumed disadvantages have been overcome, firms will "graduate" into a status in which they will be able to compete for business, including prime contracts, on an equal basis. . . . As with other phases of the statutory policy of encouraging the formation and growth of small business enterprises, this program is intended to facilitate entry and increase competition in the free market.

Significantly, the current program, unlike the 1977 set-aside, does not establish any requirement—numerical or otherwise—that a general contractor must hire DBE subcontractors. The program we upheld in *Fullilove* required that 10% of the federal grant for every federally funded project be expended on minority business enterprises. In contrast, the current program contains no quota. Although it provides monetary incentives to general contractors to hire DBE subcontractors, it does not require them to hire DBE's, and they do not lose their contracts if they fail to do so. The importance of this incentive to general contractors (who always seek to offer the lowest bid) should not be underestimated; but the preference here is far less rigid, and thus more narrowly tailored, than the 1977 Act. Cf. *Bakke*, 438 U. S., at 319–320 (opinion of Powell, J.) (distinguishing between numerical set-asides and consideration of race as a factor).

Finally, the record shows a dramatic contrast between the sparse deliberations that preceded the 1977 Act ... and the extensive hearings conducted in several Congresses before the current program was developed.... If the 1977 program of race-based set-asides satisfied the strict scrutiny dictated by Justice Powell's vision of the Constitution—a vision the Court expressly endorses today—it must follow as night follows the day that the Court of Appeals' judgment upholding this more carefully crafted program should be affirmed.

. . .

Justice Souter, with whom Justice Ginsburg and Justice Breyer join, dissenting.

. . .

... The statutory scheme must be treated as constitutional if Fullilove v. Klutznick, 448 U.S. 448 (1980), is applied, and petitioners did not identify any of the factual premises on which *Fullilove* rested as having disappeared since that case was decided.

. . .

In these circumstances, I agree with Justice Stevens's conclusion that stare decisis compels the application of *Fullilove*.... *Fullilove* ... produced a result on shared grounds that petitioner does not attack: that discrimination in the construction industry had been subject to government acquiescence, with effects that remain and that may be addressed by some preferential treatment falling within the congressional power under § 5 of the Fourteenth Amendment.[11] ... [T]he statutes in question here (which are substantially better tailored to the harm being remedied than the statute endorsed in *Fullilove*....) pass muster under Fifth Amendment due process and Fourteenth Amendment equal protection.

The Court ... does not reach the application of *Fullilove* ..., and on remand ... the Government and petitioner [must] address anew the facts upon which statutes like these must be judged on the Government's remedial theory of justification: facts about the current effects of past discrimination, the necessity for a preferential remedy, and the suitability of this particular preferential scheme.... [I]t seems fair to ask whether the statutes will meet a different fate from what *Fullilove* would have decreed. The answer is, quite probably not, though of course there will be some interpretive forks in the road before the significance of strict scrutiny for congressional remedial statutes becomes entirely clear.

... Indeed, the Court's very recognition today that strict scrutiny can be compatible with the survival of a classification so reviewed demonstrates that

11. If the statutes are within the § 5 power, they are just as enforceable when the national government makes a construction contract directly as when it funnels construction money through the states. In any event, as Justice Stevens has noted, it is not clear whether the current challenge implicates only Fifth Amendment due process or Fourteenth Amendment equal protection as well.

our concepts of equal protection enjoy a greater elasticity than the standard categories might suggest. . . .

In assessing the degree to which today's holding portends a departure from past practice, it is also worth noting that nothing in today's opinion implies any view of Congress's § 5 power and the deference due its exercise that differs from the views expressed by the *Fullilove* plurality. . . . Thus, today's decision should leave § 5 exactly where it is as the source of an interest of the national government sufficiently important to satisfy the corresponding requirement of the strict scrutiny test.

Finally, . . . I do not understand that today's decision will necessarily have any effect on the . . . long accepted . . . view that constitutional authority to remedy past discrimination is not limited to the power to forbid its continuation, but extends to eliminating those effects that would otherwise persist and skew the operation of public systems even in the absence of current intent to practice any discrimination. . . . This is so whether the remedial authority is exercised by a court, . . . the Congress, . . . or some other legislature. . . . Indeed, a majority of the Court today reiterates that there are circumstances in which Government may, consistently with the Constitution, adopt programs aimed at remedying the effects of past invidious discrimination. . . .

When the extirpation of lingering discriminatory effects is thought to require a catch-up mechanism, like the racially preferential inducement under the statutes considered here, the result may be that some members of the historically favored race are hurt by that remedial mechanism, however innocent they may be of any personal responsibility for any discriminatory conduct. When this price is considered reasonable, it is in part because it is a price to be paid only temporarily; if the justification for the preference is eliminating the effects of a past practice, the assumption is that the effects will themselves recede into the past, becoming attenuated and finally disappearing. . . .

Surely the transition from the *Fullilove* plurality view (in which Justice Powell joined) to today's strict scrutiny (which will presumably be applied as Justice Powell employed it) does not signal a change in the standard by which the burden of a remedial racial preference is to be judged as reasonable or not at any given time. If in the District Court Adarand had chosen to press a challenge to the reasonableness of the burden of these statutes, more than a decade after *Fullilove* had examined such a burden, I doubt that the claim would have fared any differently from the way it will now be treated on remand from this Court.

Justice Ginsburg, with whom Justice Breyer joins, dissenting.

For the reasons stated by Justice Souter, and in view of the attention the political branches are currently giving the matter of affirmative action, I see no compelling cause for the intervention the Court has made in this case. I further agree with Justice Stevens that . . . large deference is owed by the Judiciary to "Congress' institutional competence and constitutional authority to overcome historic racial subjugation." I write separately to underscore . . . the considerable field of agreement . . . revealed in opinions that together speak for a majority of the Court.

I

. . .

The divisions in this difficult case should not obscure the Court's recognition of the persistence of racial inequality and a majority's acknowledgement of Congress' authority to act affirmatively, not only to end discrimination, but also to counteract discrimination's lingering effects.... Those effects, reflective of a system of racial caste only recently ended, are evident in our workplaces, markets, and neighborhoods....

Given this history and its practical consequences, Congress surely can conclude that a carefully designed affirmative action program may help to realize, finally, the "equal protection of the laws" the Fourteenth Amendment has promised since 1868.

II

The lead opinion uses one term, "strict scrutiny," to describe the standard of judicial review for all governmental classifications by race. But that opinion's elaboration strongly suggests that the strict standard announced is indeed "fatal" for classifications burdening groups that have suffered discrimination in our society. That seems to me, and, I believe, to the Court, the enduring lesson one should draw from Korematsu v. United States, 323 U.S. 214 (1944).... A *Korematsu*-type classification, as I read the opinions in this case, will never again survive scrutiny....

For a classification made to hasten the day when "we are just one race," (Scalia, J., concurring in part and concurring in judgment), however, the lead opinion has dispelled the notion that "strict scrutiny" is " 'fatal in fact.' " ... Properly, a majority of the Court calls for review that is searching, in order to ferret out classifications in reality malign, but masquerading as benign. The Court's once lax review of sex-based classifications demonstrates the need for such suspicion. See, e.g., Hoyt v. Florida, 368 U.S. 57, 60 (1961) (upholding women's "privilege" of automatic exemption from jury service)....

Close review also is in order for this further reason.... [S]ome members of the historically favored race can be hurt by catch-up mechanisms designed to cope with the lingering effects of entrenched racial subjugation. Court review can ensure that preferences are not so large as to trammel unduly upon the opportunities of others or interfere too harshly with legitimate expectations of persons in once-preferred groups....

* * *

While I would not disturb the programs challenged in this case, and would leave their improvement to the political branches, I see today's decision as one that allows our precedent to evolve, still to be informed by and responsive to changing conditions.

Miller v. Johnson

515 U.S. 900, 115 S.Ct. 2475, 132 L.Ed.2d 762 (1995).

[The report in this case appears infra at p. 960.]

RACIAL GERRYMANDERING AND THE VOTING RIGHTS ACT

[This Note appears infra at p. 972.]

HUNT v. CROMARTIE, 526 U.S. 541 (1999). The report in this case appears, infra, at p. 978.

EASLEY v. CROMARTIE, 532 U.S. 234 (2001). The report in this case appears, infra, at p. 979.

RICE v. CAYETANO, 528 U.S. 495 (2000). The report in this case appears, infra, at p. 1007.

Grutter v. Bollinger

539 U.S. 306, 123 S.Ct. 2325, 156 L.Ed.2d 304 (2003).

Justice O'Connor delivered the opinion of the Court.

This case requires us to decide whether the use of race as a factor in student admissions by the University of Michigan Law School ... is unlawful.

I

A

The Law School['s admissions policy seeks an academically capable, diverse student body through efforts that sought to] compl[y] with this Court's most recent ruling on the use of race in university admissions. See *Regents of Univ. of Cal. v. Bakke,* 438 U.S. 265 (1978)....

The hallmark of that policy is its focus on academic ability coupled with a flexible assessment of applicants' talents, experiences, and potential "to contribute to the learning of those around them." ... The policy requires admissions officials to evaluate each applicant based on all the information available in the file, including a personal statement, letters of recommendation, and an essay describing the ways in which the applicant will contribute to the life and diversity of the Law School.... In reviewing an applicant's file, admissions officials must consider the applicant's undergraduate grade point average (GPA) and Law School Admissions Test (LSAT) score because they are important (if imperfect) predictors of academic success in law school.... The policy stresses that "no applicant should be admitted unless we expect that applicant to do well enough to graduate with no serious academic problems." ...

The policy makes clear, however, that even the highest possible score does not guarantee admission.... Nor does a low score automatically disqualify an applicant.... Rather, the policy requires admissions officials to look beyond grades and test scores to other criteria that are important to the Law School's educational objectives.... So-called " 'soft' variables" such as "the enthusiasm of recommenders, the quality of the undergraduate institution, the quality of the applicant's essay, and the areas and difficulty of undergraduate course selection" are all brought to bear in assessing an "applicant's likely contributions to the intellectual and social life of the institution." ...

The policy aspires to "achieve that diversity which has the potential to enrich everyone's education and thus make a law school class stronger than the sum of its parts." ... The policy does not restrict the types of diversity contributions eligible for "substantial weight" in the admissions process, but instead recognizes "many possible bases for diversity admissions." ... The policy does, however, reaffirm the Law School's longstanding commitment to "one particular type of diversity," that is, "racial and ethnic diversity with special reference to the inclusion of students from groups which have been historically discriminated against, like African–Americans, Hispanics and Native Americans, who without this commitment might not be represented in our student body in meaningful numbers." ... By enrolling a " 'critical mass' of [underrepresented] minority students," the Law School seeks to "ensur[e] their ability to make unique contributions to the character of the Law School." ...

. . .

B

Petitioner Barbara Grutter is a white Michigan resident who applied to the Law School in 1996 with a 3.8 grade point average and 161 LSAT score. The Law School [eventually] rejected her application [and she sued,] ... alleg[ing] that respondents discriminated against her on the basis of race in violation of the Fourteenth Amendment; Title VI of the Civil Rights Act of 1964, ... 42 U.S.C. § 2000d; and ... 42 U.S.C. § 1981.

Petitioner further alleged that her application was rejected because the Law School uses race as a "predominant" factor, giving applicants who belong to certain minority groups "a significantly greater chance of admission than students with similar credentials from disfavored racial groups." ...

. . .

... The District Court ... conduct[ed] a bench trial on the extent to which race was a factor in the Law School's admissions decisions, and whether the Law School's consideration of race in admissions decisions constituted a race-based double standard.

... [The] Director of Admissions ... testified that he did not direct his staff to admit a particular percentage or number of minority students, but rather to consider an applicant's race along with all other factors.... [He] testified that at the height of the admissions season, he would frequently consult the so-called "daily reports" that kept track of the racial and ethnic composition of the class (along with other information such as residency status and gender) ... to ensure that a critical mass of underrepresented minority students would be reached so as to realize the educational benefits of a diverse student body.... [He] stressed, however, that he did not seek to admit any particular number or percentage of underrepresented minority students....

[A successor] Director of Admissions ... testified that " 'critical mass' " means " 'meaningful numbers' " or " 'meaningful representation,' " which she understood to mean a number that encourages underrepresented minority students to participate in the classroom and not feel isolated.... [She] stated there is no number, percentage, or range of numbers or percentages that constitute critical mass [and] that she must consider the race of applicants because a critical mass of underrepresented minority students could not be enrolled if admissions decisions were based primarily on undergraduate GPAs and LSAT scores....

The ... Dean of the Law School ... indicated that critical mass means numbers such that underrepresented minority students do not feel isolated or like spokespersons for their race.... In some cases, [he testified,] an applicant's race may play no role, while in others it may be a " 'determinative' " factor....

. . .

In an attempt to quantify the extent to which the Law School actually considers race in making admissions decisions, the parties introduced voluminous evidence at trial. [P]etitioner's expert ... generated and analyzed "admissions grids" for ... 1995–2000 ... show[ing] the number of applicants and the number of admittees for all combinations of GPAs and LSAT scores.... He concluded that membership in certain minority groups " 'is an extremely strong factor in the decision for acceptance,' " and that applicants from these minority groups " 'are given an extremely large allowance for admission' " as compared to applicants who are members of nonfavored groups.... [He] conceded, however, that race is not the predominant factor in the Law School's admissions calculus. . . .

[T]he Law School's expert . . . focused on the predicted effect of eliminating race as a factor in the Law School's admission process [and concluded that] a race-blind admissions system would have a " 'very dramatic,' " negative effect on underrepresented minority admissions. . . . He testified that in 2000, 35 percent of underrepresented minority applicants were admitted [and] predicted that if race were not considered, only 10 percent of those applicants would have been admitted. . . . Under this scenario, underrepresented minority students would have comprised 4 percent of the entering class in 2000 instead of the actual figure of 14.5 percent. . . .

In the end, the District Court concluded that the Law School's use of race as a factor in admissions decisions was unlawful. . . .

Sitting en banc, the Court of Appeals reversed[, four judges dissenting.] . . .

. . .

We granted certiorari . . . to resolve the disagreement among the Courts of Appeals on a question of national importance: Whether diversity is a compelling interest that can justify the narrowly tailored use of race in selecting applicants for admission to public universities. . . .

II

A

We last addressed the use of race in public higher education over 25 years ago. In the landmark *Bakke* case, we reviewed a racial set-aside program that reserved 16 out of 100 seats in a medical school class for members of certain minority groups. 438 U.S. 265 (1978). . . . The only holding for the Court in *Bakke* was that a "State has a substantial interest that legitimately may be served by a properly devised admissions program involving the competitive consideration of race and ethnic origin." . . . Thus, we reversed that part of the lower court's judgment that enjoined the university "from any consideration of the race of any applicant." . . .

Since this Court's splintered decision in *Bakke*, Justice Powell's opinion announcing the judgment of the Court has served as the touchstone for constitutional analysis of race-conscious admissions policies. Public and private universities across the Nation have modeled their own admissions programs on Justice Powell's views on permissible race-conscious policies. . . . We therefore discuss Justice Powell's opinion in some detail.

. . . In Justice Powell's view, when governmental decisions "touch upon an individual's race or ethnic background, he is entitled to a judicial determination that the burden he is asked to bear on that basis is precisely tailored to serve a compelling governmental interest." . . . Under this exacting standard, only one of the interests asserted by the university survived Justice Powell's scrutiny.

First, Justice Powell rejected an interest in " 'reducing the historic deficit of traditionally disfavored minorities in medical schools and in the medical profession' " as an unlawful interest in racial balancing. . . . Second, Justice Powell rejected an interest in remedying societal discrimination because such measures would risk placing unnecessary burdens on innocent third parties "who bear no responsibility for whatever harm the beneficiaries of the special admissions program are thought to have suffered." . . . Third, Justice Powell rejected an interest in "increasing the number of physicians who will practice in communities currently underserved," concluding that even if such an interest could be compelling in some circumstances the program under review was not "geared to promote that goal." ...

Justice Powell approved the university's use of race to further only one interest: "the attainment of a diverse student body." ... With the important proviso that "constitutional limitations protecting individual rights may not be disregarded," Justice Powell grounded his analysis in the academic freedom that "long has been viewed as a special concern of the First Amendment." ... Justice Powell emphasized that nothing less than the " 'nation's future depends upon leaders trained through wide exposure' to the ideas and mores of students as diverse as this Nation of many peoples." ... In seeking the "right to select those students who will contribute the most to the 'robust exchange of ideas,' " a university seeks "to achieve a goal that is of paramount importance in the fulfillment of its mission." ... Both "tradition and experience lend support to the view that the contribution of diversity is substantial." ...

Justice Powell was, however, careful to emphasize that in his view race "is only one element in a range of factors a university properly may consider in attaining the goal of a heterogeneous student body." ... For Justice Powell, "[i]t is not an interest in simple ethnic diversity, in which a specified percentage of the student body is in effect guaranteed to be members of selected ethnic groups," that can justify the use of race.... Rather, "[t]he diversity that furthers a compelling state interest encompasses a far broader array of qualifications and characteristics of which racial or ethnic origin is but a single though important element." ...

. . .

... [F]or the reasons set out below, today we endorse Justice Powell's view that student body diversity is a compelling state interest that can justify the use of race in university admissions.

B

... Because the Fourteenth Amendment "protect[s] *persons, not groups*," all "governmental action based on race—a *group* classification long recognized as in most circumstances irrelevant and therefore prohibited—should be subjected to detailed judicial inquiry to ensure that the *personal* right to equal protection of the laws has not been infringed." *Adarand Constructors, Inc. v. Peã,* 515 U.S. 200, 227 (1995) (emphasis in original ...). ...

We have held that all racial classifications imposed by government "must be analyzed by a reviewing court under strict scrutiny." ... This means that such classifications are constitutional only if they are narrowly tailored to further compelling governmental interests. "Absent searching judicial inquiry into the justification for such race-based measures," we have no way to determine what "classifications are 'benign' or 'remedial' and what classifications are in fact motivated by illegitimate notions of racial inferiority or simple racial politics." *Richmond v. J. A. Croson Co.,* 488 U.S. 469, 493 (1989) (plurality opinion). We apply strict scrutiny to all racial classifications to " 'smoke out' illegitimate uses of race by assuring that [government] is pursuing a goal important enough to warrant use of a highly suspect tool." ...

Strict scrutiny is not "strict in theory, but fatal in fact." *Adarand* ... Although all governmental uses of race are subject to strict scrutiny, not all are invalidated by it. ... When race-based action is necessary to further a compelling governmental interest, such action does not violate the constitutional guarantee of equal protection so long as the narrow-tailoring requirement is also satisfied.

Context matters when reviewing race-based governmental action under the Equal Protection Clause.... Not every decision influenced by race is equally objectionable and strict scrutiny is designed to provide a framework for carefully examining the importance and the sincerity of the reasons advanced by the governmental decisionmaker for the use of race in that particular context.

III

A

With these principles in mind, we turn to the question whether the Law School's use of race is justified by a compelling state interest. [R]espondents assert only one justification for their use of race in the admissions process: obtaining "the educational benefits that flow from a diverse student body." ... In other words, the Law School asks us to recognize, in the context of higher education, a compelling state interest in student body diversity.

... [S]ome language in [our affirmative-action cases decided since *Bakke*] might be read to suggest that remedying past discrimination is the only permissible justification for race-based governmental action.... But we have never held that .... Today, we hold that the Law School has a compelling interest in attaining a diverse student body.

The Law School's educational judgment that such diversity is essential to its educational mission is one to which we defer. The Law School's assessment that diversity will, in fact, yield educational benefits is substantiated by respondents and their *amici*. Our scrutiny of the interest asserted by the Law School is no less strict for taking into account complex educational judgments in an area that lies primarily within the expertise of the university. Our holding today is in keeping with our tradition of giving a degree of deference to a university's academic decisions, within constitutionally prescribed limits....

We have long recognized that, given the important purpose of public education and the expansive freedoms of speech and thought associated with the university environment, universities occupy a special niche in our constitutional tradition.... In announcing the principle of student body diversity as a compelling state interest, Justice Powell invoked our cases recognizing a constitutional dimension, grounded in the First Amendment, of educational autonomy: "The freedom of a university to make its own judgments as to education includes the selection of its student body." *Bakke* .... From this premise, Justice Powell reasoned that by claiming "the right to select those students who will contribute the most to the 'robust exchange of ideas,' a university 'seek[s] to achieve a goal that is of paramount importance in the fulfillment of its mission.' ... Our conclusion that the Law School has a compelling interest in a diverse student body is informed by our view that attaining a diverse student body is at the heart of the Law School's proper institutional mission, and that 'good faith' on the part of a university is 'presumed' absent 'a showing to the contrary.' " ...

As part of its goal of "assembling a class that is both exceptionally academically qualified and broadly diverse," the Law School seeks to "enroll a 'critical mass' of minority students." ... The Law School's interest is not simply "to assure within its student body some specified percentage of a particular group merely because of its race or ethnic origin." *Bakke*, ... (opinion of Powell, J.). That would amount to outright racial balancing, which is patently unconstitutional.... Rather, the Law School's concept of critical mass is defined by reference to the educational benefits that diversity is designed to produce.

These benefits are substantial. As the District Court emphasized, the Law School's admissions policy promotes "cross-racial understanding," helps to break down racial stereotypes, and "enables [students] to better understand persons of different races." ... These benefits are "important and laudable," because "classroom discussion is livelier, more spirited, and simply more enlightening and interesting" when the students have "the greatest possible variety of backgrounds." ...

The Law School's claim of a compelling interest is further bolstered by its *amici*, who point to the educational benefits that flow from student body diversity. In addition to the expert studies and reports entered into evidence at trial, numerous studies show that student body diversity promotes learning outcomes, and "better prepares students for an increasingly diverse workforce and society, and better prepares them as professionals." Brief for American Educational Research Association et al. as *Amici Curiae* 3; see, *e.g.*, W. Bowen & D. Bok, The Shape of the River (1998); Diversity Challenged: Evidence on the Impact of Affirmative Action (G. Orfield & M. Kurlaender eds. 2001); Compelling Interest: Examining the Evidence on Racial Dynamics in Colleges and Universities (M. Chang, D. Witt, J. Jones, & K. Hakuta eds. 2003).

These benefits are not theoretical but real, as major American businesses have made clear that the skills needed in today's increasingly global marketplace can only be developed through exposure to widely diverse people, cultures, ideas, and viewpoints. Brief for 3M et al. as *Amici Curiae* 5; Brief for General Motors Corp. as *Amicus Curiae* 3–4. What is more, high-ranking retired officers and civilian leaders of the United States military assert that, "[b]ased on [their] decades of experience," a "highly qualified, racially diverse officer corps ... is essential to the military's ability to fulfill its principle mission to provide national security." Brief for Julius W. Becton, Jr. et al. as *Amici Curiae* 27. The primary sources for the Nation's officer corps are the service academies and the Reserve Officers Training Corps (ROTC), the latter comprising students already admitted to participating colleges and universities.... At present, "the military cannot achieve an officer corps that is *both* highly qualified *and* racially diverse unless the service academies and the ROTC used limited race-conscious recruiting and admissions policies." *Ibid.* (emphasis in original). To fulfill its mission, the military "must be selective in admissions for training and education for the officer corps, *and* it must train and educate a highly qualified, racially diverse officer corps in a racially diverse setting." ... (emphasis in original). We agree that "[i]t requires only a small step from this analysis to conclude that our country's other most selective institutions must remain both diverse and selective." *Ibid.*

We have repeatedly acknowledged the overriding importance of preparing students for work and citizenship, describing education as pivotal to "sustaining our political and cultural heritage" with a fundamental role in maintaining the fabric of society. *Plyler v. Doe*, 457 U.S. 202, 221 (1982). This Court has long recognized that "education ... is the very foundation of good citizenship." *Brown v. Board of Education*, 347 U.S. 483, 493 (1954). For this reason, the diffusion of knowledge and opportunity through public institutions of higher education must be accessible to all individuals regardless of race or ethnicity. The United States, as *amicus curiae*, affirms that "[e]nsuring that public institutions are open and available to all segments of American society, including people of all races and ethnicities, represents a paramount government objective." ... And, "[n]owhere is the importance of such openness more acute than in the context of higher education." ... Effective participation by members of all racial and ethnic groups in the civic life of our Nation is essential if the dream of one Nation, indivisible, is to be realized.

Moreover, universities, and in particular, law schools, represent the training ground for a large number of our Nation's leaders.... Individuals with law degrees occupy roughly half the state governorships, more than half the seats in the United States Senate, and more than a third of the seats in the United States House of Representatives.... The pattern is even more striking when it comes to highly selective law schools. A handful of these schools accounts for 25 of the 100 United States Senators, 74 United States Courts of Appeals judges, and nearly 200 of the more than 600 United States District Court judges ....

In order to cultivate a set of leaders with legitimacy in the eyes of the citizenry, it is necessary that the path to leadership be visibly open to talented and qualified individuals of every race and ethnicity. All members of our heterogeneous society must have confidence in the openness and integrity of the educational institutions that provide this training. [L]aw schools "cannot be effective in isolation from the individuals and institutions with which the law interacts." See *Sweatt v. Painter*.... Access to legal education (and thus the legal profession) must be inclusive of talented and qualified individuals of every race and ethnicity, so that all members of our heterogeneous society may participate in the educational institutions that provide the training and education necessary to succeed in America.

The Law School does not premise its need for critical mass on "any belief that minority students always (or even consistently) express some characteristic minority viewpoint on any issue." ... To the contrary, diminishing the force of such stereotypes is both a crucial part of the Law School's mission, and one that it cannot accomplish with only token numbers of minority students. Just as growing up in a particular region or having particular professional experiences is likely to affect an individual's views, so too is one's own, unique experience of being a racial minority in a society, like our own, in which race unfortunately still matters. The Law School has determined, based on its experience and expertise, that a "critical mass" of underrepresented minorities is necessary to further its compelling interest in securing the educational benefits of a diverse student body.

B

Even in the limited circumstance when drawing racial distinctions is permissible to further a compelling state interest, government is still "constrained in how it may pursue that end: [T]he means chosen to accomplish the [government's] asserted purpose must be specifically and narrowly framed to accomplish that purpose." *Shaw v. Hunt,* 517 U.S. 899, 908 (1996).... The purpose of the narrow tailoring requirement is to ensure that "the means chosen 'fit' ... th[e] compelling goal so closely that there is little or no possibility that the motive for the classification was illegitimate racial prejudice or stereotype." *Richmond v. J. A. Croson Co.,* 488 U.S., at 493 (plurality opinion).

Since *Bakke,* we have had no occasion to define the contours of the narrow-tailoring inquiry with respect to race-conscious university admissions programs. That inquiry must be calibrated to fit the distinct issues raised by the use of race to achieve student body diversity in public higher education. Contrary to Justice Kennedy's assertions, we do not "abandon[] strict scrutiny." Rather, ... we adhere to *Adarand*'s teaching that the very purpose of strict scrutiny is to take such "relevant differences into account." ...

To be narrowly tailored, a race-conscious admissions program cannot use a quota system—it cannot "insulat[e] each category of applicants with certain desired qualifications from competition with all other applicants." *Bakke,* ...

(opinion of Powell, J.). Instead, a university may consider race or ethnicity only as a " 'plus' in a particular applicant's file," without "insulat[ing] the individual from comparison with all other candidates for the available seats." . . . In other words, an admissions program must be "flexible enough to consider all pertinent elements of diversity in light of the particular qualifications of each applicant, and to place them on the same footing for consideration, although not necessarily according them the same weight." . . .

We find that the Law School's admissions program bears the hallmarks of a narrowly tailored plan. As Justice Powell made clear in *Bakke*, truly individualized consideration demands that race be used in a flexible, nonmechanical way. It follows from this mandate that universities cannot establish quotas for members of certain racial groups or put members of those groups on separate admissions tracks. . . . Nor can universities insulate applicants who belong to certain racial or ethnic groups from the competition for admission. . . . Universities can, however, consider race or ethnicity more flexibly as a "plus" factor in the context of individualized consideration of each and every applicant. . . .

We are satisfied that the Law School's admissions program, like the Harvard plan described by Justice Powell, does not operate as a quota. Properly understood, a "quota" is a program in which a certain fixed number or proportion of opportunities are "reserved exclusively for certain minority groups." . . . Quotas " 'impose a fixed number or percentage which must be attained, or which cannot be exceeded,' " . . . and "insulate the individual from comparison with all other candidates for the available seats." . . . In contrast, "a permissible goal . . . require[s] only a good-faith effort . . . to come within a range demarcated by the goal itself," . . . and permits consideration of race as a "plus" factor in any given case while still ensuring that each candidate "compete[s] with all other qualified applicants," . . . .

. . .

The Law School's goal of attaining a critical mass of underrepresented minority students does not transform its program into a quota. As the Harvard plan described by Justice Powell recognized, there is of course "some relationship between numbers and achieving the benefits to be derived from a diverse student body, and between numbers and providing a reasonable environment for those students admitted." . . . "[S]ome attention to numbers," without more, does not transform a flexible admissions system into a rigid quota. . . . Nor, as Justice Kennedy posits, does the Law School's consultation of the "daily reports,' "which keep track of the racial and ethnic composition of the class (as well as of residency and gender), "suggest [] there was no further attempt at individual review save for race itself" during the final stages of the admissions process. To the contrary, the Law School's admissions officers testified without contradiction that they never gave race any more or less weight based on the information contained in these reports. . . . Moreover, as Justice Kennedy concedes, between 1993 and 2000, the number of African–American, Latino, and Native–American students in each class at the Law School varied from 13.5 to 20.1 percent, a range inconsistent with a quota.

The Chief Justice believes that the Law School's policy conceals an attempt to achieve racial balancing, and cites admissions data to contend that the Law School discriminates among different groups within the critical mass. But, as the Chief Justice concedes, the number of underrepresented minority students who ultimately enroll in the Law School differs substantially from their representation in the applicant pool and varies considerably for each group from year to year. . . .

That a race-conscious admissions program does not operate as a quota does not, by itself, satisfy the requirement of individualized consideration. When using race as a "plus" factor in university admissions, a university's admissions program must remain flexible enough to ensure that each applicant is evaluated as an individual and not in a way that makes an applicant's race or ethnicity the defining feature of his or her application. The importance of this individualized consideration in the context of a race-conscious admissions program is paramount. . . .

Here, the Law School engages in a highly individualized, holistic review of each applicant's file, giving serious consideration to all the ways an applicant might contribute to a diverse educational environment. The Law School affords this individualized consideration to applicants of all races. There is no policy, either *de jure* or *de facto*, of automatic acceptance or rejection based on any single "soft" variable. Unlike the program at issue in *Gratz v. Bollinger*, [539 U.S. 244 (2003),] the Law School awards no mechanical, predetermined diversity "bonuses" based on race or ethnicity. See [*Gratz*] (distinguishing a race-conscious admissions program that automatically awards 20 points based on race from the Harvard plan, which considered race but "did not contemplate that any single characteristic automatically ensured a specific and identifiable contribution to a university's diversity"). Like the Harvard plan, the Law School's admissions policy "is flexible enough to consider all pertinent elements of diversity in light of the particular qualifications of each applicant, and to place them on the same footing for consideration, although not necessarily according them the same weight." . . .

We also find that, like the Harvard plan Justice Powell referenced in *Bakke*, the Law School's race-conscious admissions program adequately ensures that all factors that may contribute to student body diversity are meaningfully considered alongside race in admissions decisions. With respect to the use of race itself, all underrepresented minority students admitted by the Law School have been deemed qualified. By virtue of our Nation's struggle with racial inequality, such students are both likely to have experiences of particular importance to the Law School's mission, and less likely to be admitted in meaningful numbers on criteria that ignore those experiences. . . .

The Law School does not, however, limit in any way the broad range of qualities and experiences that may be considered valuable contributions to student body diversity. . . .

What is more, the Law School actually gives substantial weight to diversity factors besides race. The Law School frequently accepts nonminority applicants with grades and test scores lower than underrepresented minority applicants (and other nonminority applicants) who are rejected. . . . This shows that the Law School seriously weighs many other diversity factors besides race that can make a real and dispositive difference for nonminority applicants as well. By this flexible approach, the Law School sufficiently takes into account, in practice as well as in theory, a wide variety of characteristics besides race and ethnicity that contribute to a diverse student body. . . .

Petitioner and the United States argue that the Law School's plan is not narrowly tailored because race-neutral means exist to obtain the educational benefits of student body diversity that the Law School seeks. We disagree. Narrow tailoring does not require exhaustion of every conceivable race-neutral alternative. Nor does it require a university to choose between maintaining a reputation for excellence or fulfilling a commitment to provide educational opportunities to members of all racial groups. . . . Narrow tailoring does, however, require serious, good faith consideration of workable race-neutral alternatives that will achieve the diversity the university seeks. . . .

We agree with the Court of Appeals that the Law School sufficiently considered workable race-neutral alternatives. The District Court took the Law School to task for failing to consider race-neutral alternatives such as "using a lottery system" or "decreasing the emphasis for all applicants on undergraduate GPA and LSAT scores." . . . But these alternatives would require a dramatic sacrifice of diversity, the academic quality of all admitted students, or both.

The Law School's current admissions program considers race as one factor among many, in an effort to assemble a student body that is diverse in ways broader than race. Because a lottery would make that kind of nuanced judgment impossible, it would effectively sacrifice all other educational values, not to mention every other kind of diversity. So too with the suggestion that the Law School simply lower admissions standards for all students, a drastic remedy that would require the Law School to become a much different institution and sacrifice a vital component of its educational mission. The United States advocates "percentage plans," recently adopted by public undergraduate institutions in Texas, Florida, and California to guarantee admission to all students above a certain class-rank threshold in every high school in the State. . . . The United States does not, however, explain how such plans could work for graduate and professional schools. Moreover, even assuming such plans are race-neutral, they may preclude the university from conducting the individualized assessments necessary to assemble a student body that is not just racially diverse, but diverse along all the qualities valued by the university. We are satisfied that the Law School adequately considered race-neutral alternatives currently capable of producing a critical mass without forcing the Law School to abandon the academic selectivity that is the cornerstone of its educational mission.

We acknowledge that "there are serious problems of justice connected with the idea of preference itself" *Bakke,* . . . (opinion of Powell, J.). Narrow tailoring, therefore, requires that a race-conscious admissions program not unduly harm members of any racial group. . . .

We are satisfied that the Law School's admissions program does not. Because the Law School considers "all pertinent elements of diversity," it can (and does) select nonminority applicants who have greater potential to enhance student body diversity over underrepresented minority applicants. . . . As Justice Powell recognized in *Bakke,* so long as a race-conscious admissions program uses race as a "plus" factor in the context of individualized consideration, a rejected applicant

"will not have been foreclosed from all consideration for that seat simply because he was not the right color or had the wrong surname. . . . His qualifications would have been weighed fairly and competitively, and he would have no basis to complain of unequal treatment under the Fourteenth Amendment." . . .

We agree that, in the context of its individualized inquiry into the possible diversity contributions of all applicants, the Law School's race-conscious admissions program does not unduly harm nonminority applicants.

We are mindful, however, that "[a] core purpose of the Fourteenth Amendment was to do away with all governmentally imposed discrimination based on race." *Palmore v. Sidoti,* 466 U.S. 429, 432 (1984). Accordingly, race-conscious admissions policies must be limited in time. This requirement reflects that racial classifications, however compelling their goals, are potentially so danger-ous that they may be employed no more broadly than the interest demands. Enshrining a permanent justification for racial preferences would offend this fundamental equal protection principle. We see no reason to exempt race-conscious admissions programs from the requirement that all governmental use of race must have a logical end point. The Law School, too, concedes that all "race-conscious programs must have reasonable durational limits."....

In the context of higher education, the durational requirement can be met by sunset provisions in race-conscious admissions policies and periodic reviews to determine whether racial preferences are still necessary to achieve student body diversity. Universities in California, Florida, and Washington State, where racial preferences in admissions are prohibited by state law, are currently engaged in experimenting with a wide variety of alternative approaches. Uni-versities in other States can and should draw on the most promising aspects of these race-neutral alternatives as they develop. . . .

The requirement that all race-conscious admissions programs have a termination point "assure[s] all citizens that the deviation from the norm of equal treatment of all racial and ethnic groups is a temporary matter, a measure taken in the service of the goal of equality itself." *Richmond v. J. A. Croson Co.,* . . . .

We take the Law School at its word that it would "like nothing better than to find a race-neutral admissions formula" and will terminate its race-conscious admissions program as soon as practicable.... It has been 25 years since Justice Powell first approved the use of race to further an interest in student body diversity in the context of public higher education. Since that time, the number of minority applicants with high grades and test scores has indeed increased.... We expect that 25 years from now, the use of racial preferences will no longer be necessary to further the interest approved today.

IV

In summary, the Equal Protection Clause does not prohibit the Law School's narrowly tailored use of race in admissions decisions to further a compelling interest in obtaining the educational benefits that flow from a diverse student body. Consequently, petitioner's statutory claims based on Title VI and 42 U.S.C. § 1981 also fail. See *Bakke, supra,* at 287 (opinion of Powell, J.) ("Title VI . . . proscribe[s] only those racial classifications that would violate the Equal Protection Clause or the Fifth Amendment"); *General Building Contractors Assn., Inc. v. Pennsylvania,* 458 U.S. 375, 389–391 (1982) (the prohibition against discrimination in § 1981 is co-extensive with the Equal Protection Clause). The judgment of the Court of Appeals for the Sixth Circuit, accordingly, is affirmed.

. . .

Justice Ginsburg, with whom Justice Breyer joins, concurring.

. . .

The Court . . . observes that "[i]t has been 25 years since Justice Powell [in *Regents of Univ. of Cal. v. Bakke,* 438 U.S. 265 (1978)] first approved the use of race to further an interest in student body diversity in the context of public higher education." For at least part of that time, however, the law could not fairly be described as "settled," and in some regions of the Nation, overtly race-conscious admissions policies have been proscribed.... Moreover, it was only 25 years before *Bakke* that this Court declared public school segregation unconstitutional, a declaration that, after prolonged resistance, yielded an end to a law-enforced racial caste system, itself the legacy of centuries of slavery. . . .

It is well documented that conscious and unconscious race bias, even rank discrimination based on race, remain alive in our land, impeding realization of our highest values and ideals. . . . As to public education, data for the years 2000–2001 show that 71.6% of African–American children and 76.3% of Hispanic children attended a school in which minorities made up a majority of the student body. . . . And schools in predominantly minority communities lag far behind others measured by the educational resources available to them. . . .

However strong the public's desire for improved education systems may be, . . . it remains the current reality that many minority students encounter markedly inadequate and unequal educational opportunities. Despite these inequalities, some minority students are able to meet the high threshold requirements set for admission to the country's finest undergraduate and graduate educational institutions. As lower school education in minority communities improves, an increase in the number of such students may be anticipated. From today's vantage point, one may hope, but not firmly forecast, that over the next generation's span, progress toward nondiscrimination and genuinely equal opportunity will make it safe to sunset affirmative action.

Chief Justice Rehnquist, with whom Justice Scalia, Justice Kennedy, and Justice Thomas join, dissenting.

. . . I do not believe . . . that the University of Michigan Law School's . . . means are narrowly tailored to the interest it asserts. The Law School claims it must take the steps it does to achieve a " 'critical mass' " of underrepresented minority students. . . . But its actual program bears no relation to this asserted goal. Stripped of its "critical mass" veil, the Law School's program is revealed as a naked effort to achieve racial balancing.

. . . Our cases establish that . . . respondents must demonstrate that their methods of using race " 'fit' " a compelling state interest "with greater precision than any alternative means." . . .

Before the Court's decision today, we consistently applied the same strict scrutiny analysis regardless of the government's purported reason for using race and regardless of the setting in which race was being used. . . . Indeed, even in the specific context of higher education, we emphasized that "constitutional limitations protecting individual rights may not be disregarded." *Bakke*, ...

Although the Court recites the language of our strict scrutiny analysis, its application of that review is unprecedented in its deference.

.   .   .

In practice, the Law School's program bears little or no relation to its asserted goal of achieving "critical mass." Respondents explain that the Law School seeks to accumulate a "critical mass" of *each* underrepresented minority group. . . . But the record demonstrates that the Law School's admissions practices with respect to these groups differ dramatically and cannot be defended under any consistent use of the term "critical mass."

From 1995 through 2000, the Law School admitted between 1,130 and 1,310 students. Of those, between 13 and 19 were Native American, between 91 and 108 were African–Americans, and between 47 and 56 were Hispanic. If the Law School is admitting between 91 and 108 African–Americans in order to achieve "critical mass," thereby preventing African–American students from feeling "isolated or like spokespersons for their race," one would think that a number of the same order of magnitude would be necessary to accomplish the same purpose for Hispanics and Native Americans. Similarly, even if all of the Native American applicants admitted in a given year matriculate, which the record demonstrates is not at all the case, how can this possibly constitute a "critical mass" of Native Americans in a class of over 350 students? In order for this pattern of admission to be consistent with the Law School's explanation of "critical mass," one would have to believe that the objectives of "critical mass" offered by respondents are achieved with only half the number of Hispanics and one-sixth the number of Native Americans as compared to African–Americans. But respondents offer no race-specific reasons for such disparities. Instead, they simply emphasize the importance of achieving "critical mass," without any explanation of why that concept is applied differently among the three underrepresented minority groups.

These different numbers, moreover, come only as a result of substantially different treatment among the three underrepresented minority groups, as is apparent in an example offered by the Law School and highlighted by the Court: The school asserts that it "frequently accepts nonminority applicants with grades and test scores lower than underrepresented minority applicants (and other nonminority applicants) who are rejected." . . . Specifically, the Law School states that "[s]ixty-nine minority applicants were rejected between 1995 and 2000 with at least a 3.5 [Grade Point Average (GPA)] and a [score of] 159 or higher on the [Law School Admissions Test (LSAT)]" while a number of Caucasian and Asian–American applicants with similar or lower scores were admitted. . . .

Review of the record reveals only 67 such individuals. Of these 67 individuals, *56* were Hispanic, while only 6 were African–American, and only 5 were Native American. This discrepancy reflects a consistent practice. For example, in 2000, 12 Hispanics who scored between a 159–160 on the LSAT and earned a GPA of 3.00 or higher applied for admission and only 2 were admitted. . . . Meanwhile, 12 African–Americans in the same range of qualifications applied for admission and all 12 were admitted. . . . Likewise, that same year, 16 Hispanics who scored between a 151–153 on the LSAT and earned a 3.00 or higher applied for admission and only 1 of those applicants was admitted. . . . Twenty-three similarly qualified African–Americans applied for admission and 14 were admitted. . . .

These statistics have a significant bearing on petitioner's case. Respondents have *never* offered any race-specific arguments explaining why significantly more individuals from one underrepresented minority group are needed in order to achieve "critical mass" or further student body diversity. They certainly have not explained why Hispanics, who they have said are among "the groups most isolated by racial barriers in our country," should have their admission capped out in this manner. . . . [T]he Law School's disparate admissions practices with respect to these minority groups demonstrate that its alleged goal of "critical mass" is simply a sham. . . . Surely strict scrutiny cannot permit these sort of disparities without at least some explanation.

Only when the "critical mass" label is discarded does a likely explanation for these numbers emerge. . . .

[T]he correlation between the percentage of the Law School's pool of applicants who are members of the three minority groups and the percentage of the admitted applicants who are members of these same groups is far too precise to be dismissed as merely the result of the school paying "some attention to [the] numbers." . . . [F]rom 1995 through 2000 the percentage of admitted applicants who were members of these minority groups closely tracked the percentage of individuals in the school's applicant pool who were from the same groups.

. . .

For example, in 1995, when 9.7% of the applicant pool was African–American, 9.4% of the admitted class was African–American. By 2000, only 7.5% of the applicant pool was African–American, and 7.3% of the admitted class was African–American. This correlation is striking. Respondents themselves emphasize that the number of underrepresented minority students admitted to the Law School would be significantly smaller if the race of each applicant were not considered. . . . But, as the examples above illustrate, the measure of the decrease would differ dramatically among the groups. The tight correlation between the percentage of applicants and admittees of a given race, therefore, must result from careful race based planning by the Law School. It suggests a formula for admission based on the aspirational assumption that all applicants are equally qualified academically, and therefore that the proportion of each group admitted should be the same as the proportion of that group in the applicant pool. . . .

Not only do respondents fail to explain this phenomenon, they attempt to obscure it. . . . ("The Law School's minority enrollment percentages . . . diverged from the percentages in the applicant pool by as much as 17.7% from 1995–2000"). But the divergence between the percentages of underrepresented minorities in the applicant pool and in the *enrolled* classes is not the only relevant comparison. In fact, it may not be the most relevant comparison. The Law School cannot precisely control which of its admitted applicants decide to attend the university. But it can and, as the numbers demonstrate, clearly does employ racial preferences in extending offers of admission. Indeed, the ostensibly flexible nature of the Law School's admissions program that the Court finds appealing appears to be, in practice, a carefully managed program designed to ensure proportionate representation of applicants from selected minority groups.

I do not believe that the Constitution gives the Law School such free rein in the use of race. The Law School has offered no explanation for its actual admissions practices and, unexplained, we are bound to conclude that the Law School has managed its admissions program, not to achieve a "critical mass," but to extend offers of admission to members of selected minority groups in proportion to their statistical representation in the applicant pool. But this is precisely the type of racial balancing that the Court itself calls "patently unconstitutional."

Finally, I believe that the Law School's program fails strict scrutiny because it is devoid of any reasonably precise time limit on the Law School's use of race in admissions. . . .

The Court suggests a possible 25–year limitation on the Law School's current program. Respondents, on the other hand, remain more ambiguous, explaining that "the Law School of course recognizes that race-conscious programs must have reasonable durational limits, and the Sixth Circuit properly found such a limit in the Law School's resolve to cease considering race when genuine race-neutral alternatives become available." . . . These discussions of a time limit are the vaguest of assurances. In truth, they permit the Law School's use of racial preferences on a seemingly permanent basis. Thus, an important component of strict scrutiny—that a program be limited in time—is casually subverted.

The Court, in an unprecedented display of deference under our strict scrutiny analysis, upholds the Law School's program despite its obvious flaws. We have said that when it comes to the use of race, the connection between the ends and the means used to attain them must be precise. But here the flaw is deeper than that; it is not merely a question of "fit" between ends and means. Here the means actually used are forbidden by the Equal Protection Clause of the Constitution.

Justice Kennedy, dissenting.

The separate opinion by Justice Powell in *Regents of Univ. of Cal. v. Bakke* is based on the principle that a university admissions program may take account of race as one, nonpredominant factor in a system designed to consider each applicant as an individual, provided the program can meet the test of strict scrutiny by the judiciary. ... This is a unitary formulation. If strict scrutiny is abandoned or manipulated to distort its real and accepted meaning, the Court lacks authority to approve the use of race even in this modest, limited way. The opinion by Justice Powell, in my view, states the correct rule for resolving this case. The Court, however, does not apply strict scrutiny. By trying to say otherwise, it undermines both the test and its own controlling precedents.

Justice Powell's approval of the use of race in university admissions reflected a tradition, grounded in the First Amendment, of acknowledging a university's conception of its educational mission.... Our precedents provide a basis for the Court's acceptance of a university's considered judgment that racial diversity among students can further its educational task, when supported by empirical evidence....

... [B]ut deference is not to be given with respect to the methods by which it is pursued....

. . .

About 80 to 85 percent of the places in the entering class are given to applicants in the upper range of Law School Admissions Test scores and grades[, who] likely will be admitted without consideration of race or ethnicity. With respect to the remaining 15 to 20 percent of the seats, race is likely outcome determinative for many members of minority groups. That is where the competition becomes tight and where any given applicant's chance of admission is far smaller if he or she lacks minority status. At this point the numerical concept of critical mass has the real potential to compromise individual review.

The Law School has not demonstrated how individual consideration is, or can be, preserved at this stage of the application process given the instruction to attain what it calls critical mass. In fact the evidence shows otherwise. There was little deviation among admitted minority students during the years from 1995 to 1998. The percentage of enrolled minorities fluctuated only by 0.3%, from 13.5% to 13.8%. The number of minority students to whom offers were extended varied by just a slightly greater magnitude of 2.2%, from the high of 15.6% in 1995 to the low of 13.4% in 1998.

The District Court relied on this uncontested fact to draw an inference that the Law School's pursuit of critical mass mutated into the equivalent of a quota.... Admittedly, there were greater fluctuations among enrolled minorities in the preceding years, 1987–1994, by as much as 5 or 6%. The percentage of minority offers, however, at no point fell below 12%, historically defined by the Law School as the bottom of its critical mass range. The greater variance during the earlier years, in any event, does not dispel suspicion that the school engaged in racial balancing. The data would be consistent with an inference that the Law School modified its target only twice, in 1991 (from 13% to 19%), and then again in 1995 (back from 20% to 13%). The intervening year, 1993, when the percentage dropped to 14.5%, could be an aberration, caused by the school's miscalculation as to how many applicants with offers would accept or by its redefinition, made in April 1992, of which minority groups were entitled to race-based preference. . . .

The narrow fluctuation band raises an inference that the Law School subverted individual determination, and strict scrutiny requires the Law School to overcome the inference. . . .

. . . At the very least, the constancy of admitted minority students and the close correlation between the racial breakdown of admitted minorities and the composition of the applicant pool . . . require the Law School either to produce a convincing explanation or to show it has taken adequate steps to ensure individual assessment. The Law School does neither.

The obvious tension between the pursuit of critical mass and the require-ment of individual review increased by the end of the admissions season. Most of the decisions where race may decide the outcome are made during this period. . . .

The consultation of daily reports during the last stages in the admissions process suggests there was no further attempt at individual review save for race itself. The admissions officers could use the reports to recalibrate the plus factor given to race depending on how close they were to achieving the Law School's goal of critical mass. The bonus factor of race would then become divorced from individual review; it would be premised instead on the numerical objective set by the Law School.

The Law School made no effort to guard against this danger. It provided no guidelines to its admissions personnel on how to reconcile individual assess-ment with the directive to admit a critical mass of minority students. . . .

To be constitutional, a university's compelling interest in a diverse student body must be achieved by a system where individual assessment is safeguarded through the entire process. . . .

. . . By deferring to the law schools' choice of minority admissions pro-grams, the courts will lose the talents and resources of the faculties and administrators in devising new and fairer ways to ensure individual consider-ation. Constant and rigorous judicial review forces the law school faculties to undertake their responsibilities as state employees in this most sensitive of areas with utmost fidelity to the mandate of the Constitution. . . . Prospective students, the courts, and the public can demand that the State and its law schools prove their process is fair and constitutional in every phase of imple-mentation.

. . . Deference is antithetical to strict scrutiny, not consistent with it.

. . .

If universities are given the latitude to administer programs that are tantamount to quotas, they will have few incentives to make the existing minority admissions schemes transparent and protective of individual review. The unhappy consequence will be to perpetuate the hostilities that proper consideration of race is designed to avoid. . . .

It is regrettable the Court's important holding allowing racial minorities to have their special circumstances considered in order to improve their educational opportunities is accompanied by a suspension of the strict scrutiny which was the predicate of allowing race to be considered in the first place.... [T]hough I reiterate my approval of giving appropriate consideration to race in this one context, I must dissent in the present case.

Justice Scalia, with whom Justice Thomas joins, concurring in part and dissenting in part.

I join the opinion of the Chief Justice. As he demonstrates, the University of Michigan Law School's mystical "critical mass" justification for its discrimination by race challenges even the most gullible mind. The admissions statistics show it to be a sham to cover a scheme of racially proportionate admissions.

I also join Parts I through VII of Justice Thomas's opinion. I find particularly unanswerable his central point: that the allegedly "compelling state interest" at issue here is not the incremental "educational benefit" that emanates from the fabled "critical mass" of minority students, but rather Michigan's interest in maintaining a "prestige" law school whose normal admissions standards disproportionately exclude blacks and other minorities. If that is a compelling state interest, everything is.

. . .

Unlike a clear constitutional holding that racial preferences in state educational institutions are impermissible, or even a clear anticonstitutional holding that racial preferences in state educational institutions are OK, today's *Grutter-Gratz* split double header seems perversely designed to prolong the controversy and the litigation. Some future lawsuits will presumably focus on whether the discriminatory scheme in question contains enough evaluation of the applicant "as an individual" and sufficiently avoids "separate admissions tracks" to fall under *Grutter* rather than *Gratz*. Some will focus on whether a university has gone beyond the bounds of a " 'good faith effort' " and has so zealously pursued its "critical mass" as to make it an unconstitutional *de facto* quota system, rather than merely " 'a permissible goal.' " ... Other lawsuits may focus on whether, in the particular setting at issue, any educational benefits flow from racial diversity.... Still other suits may challenge the bona fides of the institution's expressed commitment to the educational benefits of diversity that immunize the discriminatory scheme in *Grutter*.... And still other suits may claim that the institution's racial preferences have gone below or above the mystical *Grutter*-approved "critical mass." Finally, litigation can be expected on behalf of minority groups intentionally short changed in the institution's composition of its generic minority "critical mass." I do not look forward to any of these cases. The Constitution proscribes government discrimination on the basis of race, and state-provided education is no exception.

Justice Thomas, with whom Justice Scalia joins as to Parts I–VII, concurring in part and dissenting in part.

... I believe blacks can achieve in every avenue of American life without the meddling of university administrators....

... The Law School, of its own choosing, and for its own purposes, maintains an exclusionary admissions system that it knows produces racially disproportionate results. Racial discrimination is not a permissible solution to the self-inflicted wounds of this elitist admissions policy.

. . .

I

The majority agrees that the Law School's racial discrimination should be subjected to strict scrutiny. . . .

. . . A majority of the Court has validated only two circumstances where "pressing public necessity" or a "compelling state interest" can possibly justify racial discrimination by state actors. First, the lesson of *Korematsu* is that national security constitutes a "pressing public necessity," though the government's use of race to advance that objective must be narrowly tailored. Second, the Court has recognized as a compelling state interest a government's effort to remedy past discrimination for which it is responsible. *Richmond v. J. A. Croson Co.,* 488 U.S. 469, 504 (1989).

. . .

. . . In *Palmore v. Sidoti,* 466 U.S. 429 (1984), the Court held that even the best interests of a child did not constitute a compelling state interest that would allow a state court to award custody to the father because the mother was in a mixed-race marriage. . . .

. . .

Where the Court has accepted only national security, and rejected even the best interests of a child, as a justification for racial discrimination, I conclude that only those measures the State must take to provide a bulwark against anarchy, or to prevent violence, will constitute a "pressing public necessity." . . .

. . .

II

. . .

. . . It is the *educational benefits* that are the end, or allegedly compelling state interest, not "diversity."

. . . [T]he Law School seeks to improve marginally the education it offers without sacrificing too much of its exclusivity and elite status.[4]

. . .

III

. . .

Under the proper standard, there is no pressing public necessity in maintaining a public law school at all and, it follows, certainly not an elite law school. Likewise, marginal improvements in legal education do not qualify as a compelling state interest.

. . .

4. The Law School believes both that the educational benefits of a racially engineered student body are large and that adjusting its overall admissions standards to achieve the same racial mix would require it to sacrifice its elite status. If the Law School is correct that the educational benefits of "diversity" are so great, then achieving them by altering admissions standards should not compromise its elite status. The Law School's reluctance to do this suggests that the educational benefits it alleges are not significant or do not exist at all.

... [E]ven assuming that a State may, under appropriate circumstances, demonstrate a cognizable interest in having an elite law school, Michigan has failed to do so here.

. . .

... The only interests that can satisfy the Equal Protection Clause's demands are those found within a State's jurisdiction.

The only cognizable state interests vindicated by operating a public law school are, therefore, the education of that State's citizens and the training of that State's lawyers. . . .

The Law School today, however, does precious little training of those attorneys who will serve the citizens of Michigan. In 2002, graduates of the University of Michigan Law School made up less than 6% of applicants to the Michigan bar. . . .

In sum, the Law School trains few Michigan residents and overwhelmingly serves students, who, as lawyers, leave the State of Michigan. By contrast, Michigan's other public law school, Wayne State University Law School, sends 88% of its graduates on to serve the people of Michigan. . . . It does not take a social scientist to conclude that it is precisely the Law School's status as an elite institution that causes it to be a way-station for the rest of the country's lawyers, rather than a training ground for those who will remain in Michigan. The Law School's decision to be an elite institution does little to advance the welfare of the people of Michigan or any cognizable interest of the State of Michigan.

[Also,] that few States choose to maintain elite law schools raises a strong inference that there is nothing compelling about elite status. . . .

. . .

IV

The interest in remaining elite and exclusive that the majority thinks so obviously critical requires the use of admissions "standards" that, in turn, create the Law School's "need" to discriminate on the basis of race. . . .

With the adoption of different admissions methods, such as accepting all students who meet minimum qualifications, see Brief for United States as *Amicus Curiae* 13–14, the Law School could achieve its vision of the racially aesthetic student body without the use of racial discrimination. . . . [O]ther top law schools have [done so].

. . .

The Court's deference ... will ... have serious collateral consequences. The Court relies heavily on social science evidence to justify its deference. . . . The Court never acknowledges, however, the growing evidence that racial (and other sorts) of heterogeneity actually impairs learning among black students. See, *e.g.,* Flowers & Pascarella, Cognitive Effects of College Racial Composition on African American Students After 3 Years of College, 40 J. of College Student Development 669, 674 (1999) (concluding that black students experience superior cognitive development at Historically Black Colleges (HBCs) and that, even among blacks, "a substantial diversity moderates the cognitive effects of attending an HBC"); Allen, The Color of Success: African–American College Student Outcomes at Predominantly White and Historically Black Public Colleges and Universities, 62 Harv. Educ. Rev. 26, 35 (1992) (finding that black students attending HBCs report higher academic achievement than those attending predominantly white colleges).

. . .

The majority grants deference to the Law School's "assessment that diversity will, in fact, yield educational benefits." It follows, therefore, that an HBC's assessment that racial homogeneity will yield educational benefits would similarly be given deference. An HBC's rejection of white applicants in order to maintain racial homogeneity seems permissible, therefore, under the majority's view of the Equal Protection Clause. . . .

Moreover one would think, in light of the Court's decision in *United States v. Virginia,* 518 U.S. 515 (1996), that before being given license to use racial discrimination, the Law School would be required to radically reshape its admissions process, even to the point of sacrificing some elements of its character. In *Virginia,* a majority of the Court, without a word about academic freedom, accepted the all-male Virginia Military Institute's (VMI) representation that some changes in its "adversative" method of education would be required with the admission of women, . . . but did not defer to VMI's judgment that these changes would be too great. Instead, the Court concluded that they were "manageable." . . . That case involved sex discrimination, which is subjected to intermediate, not strict, scrutiny. . . . So in *Virginia,* where the standard of review dictated that greater flexibility be granted to VMI's educational policies than the Law School deserves here, this Court gave no deference. Apparently where the status quo being defended is that of the elite establishment—here the Law School—rather than a less fashionable Southern military institution, the Court will defer without serious inquiry and without regard to the applicable legal standard.

. . .

Virginia is also notable for the fact that the Court relied on the "experience" of formerly single-sex institutions, such as the service academies, to conclude that admission of women to VMI would be "manageable." . . . Today, however, the majority ignores the "experience" of those institutions that have been forced to abandon explicit racial discrimination in admissions.

The sky has not fallen at Boalt Hall at the University of California, Berkeley, for example. Prior to Proposition 209's adoption of Cal. Const., Art. 1, § 31(a), which bars the State from "grant[ing] preferential treatment . . . on the basis of race . . . in the operation of . . . public education," Boalt Hall enrolled 20 blacks and 28 Hispanics in its first-year class for 1996. In 2002, without deploying express racial discrimination in admissions, Boalt's entering class enrolled 14 blacks and 36 Hispanics. . . . Total underrepresented minority student enrollment at Boalt Hall now exceeds 1996 levels. Apparently [Michigan] Law School cannot be counted on to be as resourceful. The Court is willfully blind to the very real experience in California and elsewhere, which raises the inference that institutions with "reputation[s] for excellence" rivaling the Law School's have satisfied their sense of mission without resorting to prohibited racial discrimination.

V

. . .

[T]here is nothing ancient, honorable, or constitutionally protected about "selective" admissions . . .

... Since its inception, selective admissions has been the vehicle for racial, ethnic, and religious tinkering and experimentation by university administrators.... Columbia, Harvard, and others infamously determined that they had "too many" Jews, just as today the Law School argues it would have "too many" whites if it could not discriminate in its admissions process. ...

Columbia employed intelligence tests precisely because Jewish applicants, who were predominantly immigrants, scored worse on such tests.... In other words, the tests were adopted with full knowledge of their disparate impact. Cf. *DeFunis v. Odegaard*, 416 U.S. 312, 335 (1974) *(per curiam)* (Douglas, J., dissenting).

Similarly no modern law school can claim ignorance of the poor performance of blacks, relatively speaking, on the Law School Admissions Test (LSAT). Nevertheless, law schools continue to use the test and then attempt to "correct" for black underperformance by using racial discrimination in admissions so as to obtain their aesthetic student body. The Law School's continued adherence to measures it knows produce racially skewed results is not entitled to deference by this Court....

Having decided to use the LSAT, the Law School must accept the constitutional burdens that come with this decision. The Law School may freely continue to employ the LSAT and other allegedly merit-based standards in whatever fashion it likes. What the Equal Protection Clause forbids, but the Court today allows, is the use of these standards hand-in-hand with racial discrimination....

. . .

VI

... I believe what lies beneath the Court's decision today are the benighted notions that one can tell when racial discrimination benefits (rather than hurts) minority groups, ... and that racial discrimination is necessary to remedy general societal ills. [T]he majority still cannot commit to the principle that racial classifications are *per se* harmful and that almost no amount of benefit in the eye of the beholder can justify such classifications.

Putting aside what I take to be the Court's implicit rejection of *Adarand*'s holding that beneficial and burdensome racial classifications are equally invalid, I must contest the notion that the Law School's discrimination benefits those admitted as a result of it.... [N]owhere in any of the filings in this Court is any evidence that the purported "beneficiaries" of this racial discrimination prove themselves by performing at (or even near) the same level as those students who receive no preferences. Cf. Thernstrom & Thernstrom, Reflections on the Shape of the River, 46 UCLA L. Rev. 1583, 1605–1608 (1999) (discussing the failure of defenders of racial discrimination in admissions to consider the fact that its "beneficiaries" are underperforming in the classroom).

The silence in this case is deafening to those of us who view higher education's purpose as imparting knowledge and skills to students, rather than a communal, rubber-stamp, credentialing process. The Law School is not looking for those students who, despite a lower LSAT score or undergraduate grade point average, will succeed in the study of law. The Law School seeks only a facade—it is sufficient that the class looks right, even if it does not perform right.

. . .

Beyond the harm the Law School's racial discrimination visits upon its test subjects, no social science has disproved the notion that this discrimination "engender[s] attitudes of superiority or, alternatively, provoke[s] resentment among those who believe that they have been wronged by the government's use of race." *Adarand*, ... (Thomas, J., concurring in part and concurring in judgment). "These programs stamp minorities with a badge of inferiority and may cause them to develop dependencies or to adopt an attitude that they are 'entitled' to preferences." ...

... The majority of blacks are admitted to the Law School because of discrimination, and because of this policy all are tarred as undeserving. This problem of stigma does not depend on determinacy as to whether those stigmatized are actually the "beneficiaries" of racial discrimination. When blacks take positions in the highest places of government, industry, or academia, it is an open question today whether their skin color played a part in their advancement. The question itself is the stigma—because either racial discrimination did play a role, in which case the person may be deemed "otherwise unqualified," or it did not, in which case asking the question itself unfairly marks those blacks who would succeed without discrimination. Is this what the Court means by "visibly open"?

. . .

VII

As the foregoing makes clear, I believe the Court's opinion to be, in most respects, erroneous. I do, however, find two points on which I agree.

A

First, I note that the issue of unconstitutional racial discrimination among the groups the Law School prefers is not presented in this case, because petitioner has never argued that the Law School engages in such a practice, and the Law School maintains that it does not.... I join the Court's opinion insofar as it confirms that this type of racial discrimination remains unlawful.... [T]he Law School may not discriminate in admissions between similarly situated blacks and Hispanics, or between whites and Asians. This is so because preferring black to Hispanic applicants, for instance, does nothing to further the interest recognized by the majority today. Indeed, the majority describes such racial balancing as "patently unconstitutional." Like the Court, I express no opinion as to whether the Law School's current admissions program runs afoul of this prohibition.

B

... While I agree that in 25 years the practices of the Law School will be illegal, they are, for the reasons I have given, illegal now....

. . .

I ... understand the imposition of a 25–year time limit only as a holding that the deference the Court pays to the Law School's educational judgments and refusal to change its admissions policies will itself expire.... The Court defines this time limit in terms of narrow tailoring, but I believe this arises from its refusal to define rigorously the broad state interest vindicated today. ... With these observations, I join the last sentence of Part III of the opinion of the Court.

. . .

GRATZ v. BOLLINGER, 539 U.S. 244 (2003). In this companion case to *Grutter*, two white residents of Michigan who had been denied admission to the University of Michigan's undergraduate College of Literature, Science, and the Arts (LSA) brought a class action challenging the University's use of race in its admissions system. That system considered a number of factors in making admissions decisions, including high school grades, standardized test scores, high school quality, curriculum strength, geography, alumni relationships, leadership, and race. It employed a selection index that assigned points for the various factors considered; provided that 100 points would virtually assure admission; and assigned 20 points for being an underrepresented minority applicant. It was "undisputed that the University admits 'virtually every qualified ... applicant' from" the groups the University considered to be "underrepresented minorities," namely, "African–Americans, Hispanics, and Native Americans." Chief Justice Rehnquist, speaking for a Court majority that included the four dissenters in *Grutter* plus Justice O'Connor, concluded "that because the University's use of race in its current freshman admissions policy is not narrowly tailored to achieve [its] asserted compelling interest in diversity, the admissions policy violates the Equal Protection Clause of the Fourteenth Amendment" as well as "Title VI and 42 U.S.C. § 1981." Responding to the argument "that 'diversity as a basis for employing racial preferences is simply too open-ended, ill-defined, and indefinite to constitute a compelling interest capable of supporting narrowly-tailored means[,]' " the Chief Justice wrote that "for the reasons set forth today in *Grutter v. Bollinger,* the Court has rejected these arguments ...." But, applying strict scrutiny, the majority found "that the University's policy, which automatically distributes 20 points, or one-fifth of the points needed to guarantee admission, to every single 'underrepresented minority' applicant solely because of race, is not narrowly tailored to achieve the interest in educational diversity that respondents claim justifies their program." The opinion said in pertinent part:

"Justice Powell's opinion in *Bakke* emphasized the importance of considering each particular applicant as an individual, assessing all of the qualities that individual possesses, and in turn, evaluating that individual's ability to contribute to the unique setting of higher education. The admissions program Justice Powell described, however, did not contemplate that any single characteristic automatically ensured a specific and identifiable contribution to a university's diversity. ... Instead, under the approach Justice Powell described, each characteristic of a particular applicant was to be considered in assessing the applicant's entire application.

"The current LSA policy does not provide such individualized consideration.... The only consideration that accompanies [its] distribution of points is a factual review of an application to determine whether an individual is a member of one of these minority groups. Moreover, unlike Justice Powell's example, where the race of a 'particular black applicant' could be considered without being decisive, ... the LSA's automatic distribution of 20 points has the effect of making 'the factor of race ... decisive' for virtually every minimally qualified underrepresented minority applicant...."

The "fact that the LSA has created the possibility of an applicant's file being flagged for individualized consideration ... only emphasizes the flaws of the University's system as a whole when compared to that described by Justice Powell[,]" because "automatically awarding 20 points" virtually guaranteed that "every qualified underrepresented minority applicant [was] admitted" without needing to resort to individualized review (which was available "only ... *after* admissions counselors automatically distribute the University's version of a 'plus' ''), and individualized consideration was "the exception and not the rule" in any event. Finally, that the volume of undergraduate applications might make it impractical "to use the admissions system ... upheld by the Court today in *Grutter*" did not matter, because "the fact that the implementation of a program capable of providing individualized consideration might present administrative challenges does not render constitutional an otherwise problematic system."

Justice O'Connor wrote a separate concurring opinion, which Justice Breyer joined except insofar as it joined the Court's opinion, contrasting the law school admissions process upheld in *Grutter* with the undergraduate policy invalidated in *Gratz*:

> "... The law school considers the various diversity qualifications of each applicant, including race, on a case-by-case basis.... By contrast, [the College] relies on the selection index to assign *every* underrepresented minority applicant the same, *automatic* 20–point bonus without consideration of the particular background, experiences, or qualities of each individual applicant. And this mechanized selection index score, by and large, automatically determines the admissions decision for each applicant. The selection index thus precludes admissions counselors from conducting the type of individualized consideration the Court's opinion in *Grutter* ... requires: consideration of each applicant's individualized qualifications, including the contribution each individual's race or ethnic identity will make to the diversity of the student body, taking into account diversity within and among all racial and ethnic groups...."

Justice Thomas also wrote a separate concurrence, saying that he "join[ed] the Court's opinion because ... it correctly applies our precedents, including today's decision in *Grutter v. Bollinger*[, though he] would hold that a State's use of racial discrimination in higher education admissions is categorically prohibited by the Equal Protection Clause." He noted that the "admissions policy that the Court today invalidates does not suffer from the additional constitutional defect of allowing racial 'discriminat[ion] among [the] groups' included within its definition of underrepresented minorities, ... because it awards all underrepresented minorities the same racial preference." But "[u]nder today's decisions," it did fail to "allow for consideration of ... nonracial distinctions among applicants on both sides of the single permitted racial classification."

Justice Breyer concurred in the judgment, agreeing with Justice O'Connor except for joining the Court's opinion, and with part of Justice Ginsburg's dissenting opinion. He specifically "agree[d] with Justice Ginsburg that ... government decisionmakers may properly distinguish between policies of inclusion and exclusion, for the former are more likely to prove consistent with the basic constitutional obligation that the law respect each individual equally ...."

Justice Souter dissented, joined on the merits by Justice Ginsburg.[a] He found "the freshman admissions system here ... closer to what *Grutter* approves than to [the quota system] *Bakke* condemns," because it "lets all applicants compete for all places and values an applicant's offering for any place not only on grounds of race, but on ... all of the characteristics that the college thinks relevant to student diversity ..." He noted that "[n]onminority students may receive 20 points for athletic ability, socioeconomic disadvantage,

---

a. Justice Souter also joined a separate dissenting opinion by Justice Stevens, who urged dismissal for lack of jurisdiction and did not reach the merits.

attendance at a socioeconomically disadvantaged or predominantly minority high school, or at the Provost's discretion; they may also receive 10 points for being residents of Michigan, 6 for residence in an underrepresented Michigan county, 5 for leadership and service, and so on.'' He continued:

"The very nature of a college's permissible practice of awarding value to racial diversity means that race must be considered in a way that increases some applicants' chances for admission. Since college admission is not left entirely to inarticulate intuition, it is hard to see what is inappropriate in assigning some stated value to a relevant characteristic, whether it be reasoning ability, writing style, running speed, or minority race. Justice Powell's plus factors necessarily are assigned some values. The college simply does by a numbered scale what the law school accomplishes in its 'holistic review,' *Grutter* ...; the distinction does not imply that applicants to the undergraduate college are denied individualized consideration or a fair chance to compete on the basis of all the various merits their applications may disclose.

"Nor is it possible to say that the 20 points convert race into a decisive factor comparable to reserving minority places as in Bakke .... The present record obviously shows that nonminority applicants may achieve higher selection point totals than minority applicants owing to characteristics other than race, and the fact that the university admits 'virtually every qualified under-represented minority applicant,' ... may reflect nothing more than the likelihood that very few qualified minority applicants apply, ... as well as the possibility that self-selection results in a strong minority applicant pool. It suffices ... that there are no *Bakke*-like set-asides and that consideration of an applicant's whole spectrum of ability is no more ruled out by giving 20 points for race than by giving the same points for athletic ability or socioeconomic disadvantage.

. . .

"... Drawing on admissions systems used at public universities in California, Florida, and Texas, the United States contends that Michigan could get student diversity in satisfaction of its compelling interest by guaranteeing admission to a fixed percentage of the top students from each high school in Michigan....

"While there is nothing unconstitutional about such a practice, ...[4] [t]he 'percentage plans' are just as race conscious as the point scheme (and fairly so), but they get their racially diverse results without saying directly what they are doing or why they are doing it. In contrast, Michigan states its purpose directly .... Equal protection cannot become an exercise in which the winners are the ones who hide the ball.''

Another dissent, by Justice Ginsburg, joined by Justice Souter, first asserted that "government decisionmakers may properly distinguish between policies of exclusion and inclusion"; that "[a]ctions designed to burden groups long denied full citizenship stature are not sensibly ranked with measures taken to hasten the day when entrenched discrimination and its after effects have been extirpated"; and that "[c]ontemporary human rights documents draw just this line; they distinguish between policies of oppression and measures designed to accelerate *de facto* equality. See ... the United Nations-initiated Conventions on the Elimination of All Forms of Racial Discrimination and on the Elimina-

---

4. Of course it might be pointless in the State of Michigan, where minorities are a much smaller fraction of the population than in California, Florida, or Texas....

tion of All Forms of Discrimination against Women. . . ." (Justice Breyer joined this portion of the opinion.) Justice Ginsburg then argued as follows:

". . . Every applicant admitted under the current plan, petitioners do not here dispute, is qualified to attend the College. . . . The racial and ethnic groups to which the College accords special consideration . . . historically have been relegated to inferior status by law and social practice; their members continue to experience class-based discrimination to this day. . . . There is no suggestion that the College adopted its current policy in order to limit or decrease enrollment by any particular racial or ethnic group, and no seats are reserved on the basis of race. . . . Nor has there been any demonstration that the College's program unduly constricts admissions opportunities for students who do not receive special consideration based on race. . . .[10]

". . . [C]olleges and universities will seek to maintain their minority enrollment—and the networks and opportunities thereby opened to minority graduates—whether or not they can do so in full candor through adoption of affirmative action plans of the kind here at issue. Without recourse to such plans, [they] may resort to camouflage . . . . If honesty is the best policy, surely Michigan's accurately described, fully disclosed College affirmative action program is preferable to achieving similar numbers through winks, nods, and disguises."[a]

F. CLASSIFICATIONS DISADVANTAGING ALIENS

Graham v. Richardson

403 U.S. 365, 91 S.Ct. 1848, 29 L.Ed.2d 534 (1971).

Mr. Justice Blackmun delivered the opinion of the Court.

These are welfare cases. They provide yet another aspect of the widening litigation in this area. The issue here is whether the Equal Protection Clause of the Fourteenth Amendment prevents a State from conditioning welfare benefits either (a) upon the beneficiary's possession of United States citizenship, or

10. The United States points to the "percentage plans" used in California, Florida, and Texas as one example of a "race-neutral alternativ[e]" that would permit the College to enroll meaningful numbers of minority students. . . . Calling such 10 or 20% plans "race-neutral" seems to me disingenuous, for they "unquestionably were adopted with the specific purpose of increasing representation of African–Americans and Hispanics in the public higher education system." . . . Percentage plans depend for their effectiveness on continued racial segregation at the secondary school level: They can ensure significant minority enrollment in universities only if the majority-minority high school population is large enough to guarantee that, in many schools, most of the students in the top 10 or 20% are minorities. Moreover, because such plans link college admission to a single criterion—high school class rank—they create perverse incentives. They encourage parents to keep their children in low-per-

forming segregated schools, and discourage students from taking challenging classes that might lower their grade point averages. . . . And even if percentage plans could boost the sheer numbers of minority enrollees at the undergraduate level, they do not touch enrollment in graduate and professional schools.

a. Chief Justice Rehnquist's majority opinion found Justice Ginsburg's "observations" in this paragraph "remarkable for two reasons. First, they suggest that universities—to whose academic judgment we are told in *Grutter v. Bollinger* we should defer—will pursue their affirmative-action programs whether or not they violate the United States Constitution. Second, they recommend that these violations should be dealt with, not by requiring the universities to obey the Constitution, but by changing the Constitution so that it conforms to the conduct of the universities."

(b) if the beneficiary is an alien, upon his having resided in this country for a specified number of years. . . .

I.

. . .

[Aliens denied welfare benefits challenged an Arizona law that provided welfare to citizens but not to aliens unless they had resided in the United States for 15 years and a Pennsylvania law that excluded aliens from certain state funded welfare benefits. In each case a three-judge district court ruled that the statute violated equal protection.]

II.

The appellants argue initially that the States, consistent with the Equal Protection Clause, may favor United States citizens over aliens in the distribution of welfare benefits. It is said that this distinction involves no "invidious discrimination" . . . for the State is not discriminating with respect to race or nationality.

The Fourteenth Amendment provides, "[N]or shall any State deprive any person of life, liberty, or property, without due process of law; nor deny to any person within its jurisdiction the equal protection of the laws." It has long been settled, and it is not disputed here, that the term "person" in this context encompasses lawfully admitted resident aliens as well as citizens of the United States and entitles both citizens and aliens to the equal protection of the laws of the State in which they reside. Yick Wo v. Hopkins, 118 U.S. 356, 369 (1886); Truax v. Raich, 239 U.S. 33, 39 (1915); Takahashi v. Fish & Game Commission, 334 U.S., at 420. Nor is it disputed that the Arizona and Pennsylvania statutes in question create two classes of needy persons, indistinguishable except with respect to whether they are or are not citizens of this country. Otherwise qualified United States citizens living in Arizona are entitled to federally funded categorical assistance benefits without regard to length of national residency, but aliens must have lived in this country for 15 years in order to qualify for aid. United States citizens living in Pennsylvania, unable to meet the requirements for federally funded benefits, may be eligible for state supported general assistance, but resident aliens as a class are precluded from that assistance.

Under traditional equal protection principles, a State retains broad discretion to classify as long as its classification has a reasonable basis. . . . This is so in "the area of economics and social welfare." Dandridge v. Williams, 397 U.S. 471, 485 (1970). But the Court's decisions have established that classifications based on alienage, like those based on nationality or race, are inherently suspect and subject to close judicial scrutiny. Aliens as a class are a prime example of a "discrete and insular" minority (see United States v. Carolene Products Co., 304 U.S. 144, 152–153 n. 4 (1938)) for whom such heightened judicial solicitude is appropriate. Accordingly, it was said in Takahashi, 334 U.S., at 420, that ". . . the power of a state to apply its laws exclusively to its alien inhabitants as a class is confined within narrow limits."

Arizona and Pennsylvania seek to justify their restrictions on the eligibility of aliens for public assistance solely on the basis of a State's "special public interest" in favoring its own citizens over aliens in the distribution of limited resources such as welfare benefits. . . .

. . . [W]e conclude that a State's desire to preserve limited welfare benefits for its own citizens is inadequate to justify Pennsylvania's making noncitizens ineligible for public assistance, and Arizona's restricting benefits to citizens and longtime resident aliens....

. . .

We agree with the three-judge court in the Pennsylvania case that the "justification of limiting expenses is particularly inappropriate and unreasonable when the discriminated class consists of aliens...." There can be no "special public interest" in tax revenues to which aliens have contributed on an equal basis with the residents of the State.

Accordingly, we hold that a state statute that denies welfare benefits to resident aliens and one that denies them to aliens who have not resided in the United States for a specified number of years violates the Equal Protection Clause.

III.

An additional reason why the state statutes at issue in these cases do not withstand constitutional scrutiny emerges from the area of federal-state relations. The National Government has "broad constitutional powers in determining what aliens shall be admitted to the United States, the period they may remain, regulation of their conduct before naturalization, and the terms and conditions of their naturalization." Takahashi v. Fish & Game Commission, 334 U.S., at 419; Hines v. Davidowitz, 312 U.S. 52, 66 (1941); see also Chinese Exclusion Case, 130 U.S. 581 (1889); United States ex rel. Turner v. Williams, 194 U.S. 279 (1904); Fong Yue Ting v. United States, 149 U.S. 698 (1893); Harisiades v. Shaughnessy, 342 U.S. 580 (1952). Pursuant to that power, Congress has provided, as part of a comprehensive plan for the regulation of immigration and naturalization, that "[A]liens who are paupers, professional beggars, or vagrants" or aliens who "are likely at any time to become public charges" shall be excluded from admission into the United States, 8 U.S.C. §§ 1182(a)(8) and 1182(a)(15), and that any alien lawfully admitted shall be deported who "has within five years after entry become a public charge from causes not affirmatively shown to have arisen after entry...." 8 U.S.C. § 1251(a)(8). Admission of aliens likely to become public charges may be conditioned upon the posting of a bond or cash deposit. 8 U.S.C. § 1138. But Congress has not seen fit to impose any burden or restriction on aliens who become indigent after their entry into the United States. Rather, it has broadly declared that "All persons within the jurisdiction of the United States shall have the same right in every State and Territory ... to the full and equal benefit of all laws and proceedings for the security of persons and property as is enjoyed by white citizens...." 42 U.S.C. § 1981. The protection of this statute has been held to extend to aliens as well as to citizens. Takahashi.... Moreover, this Court has made it clear that, whatever may be the scope of the constitutional right of interstate travel, aliens lawfully within this country have a right to enter and abide in any State in the Union "on an equality of legal privileges with all citizens under nondiscriminatory laws." Takahashi....

State laws that restrict the eligibility of aliens for welfare benefits merely because of their alienage conflict with these overriding national policies in an area constitutionally entrusted to the Federal Government.... State alien residency requirements, that either deny welfare benefits to noncitizens or condition them on longtime residency, equate with the assertion of a right, inconsistent with federal policy, to deny entrance and abode. Since such laws encroach upon exclusive federal power, they are constitutionally impermissible.

. . .

The judgments appealed from are affirmed.

It is so ordered.

Mr. Justice Harlan joins in Parts III and IV of the Court's opinion, and in the judgment of the Court.

Bernal v. Fainter

467 U.S. 216, 104 S.Ct. 2312, 81 L.Ed.2d 175 (1984).

Justice Marshall delivered the opinion of the Court.

The question ... is whether a statute of the State of Texas violates the Equal Protection Clause of the Fourteenth Amendment ... by denying aliens the opportunity to become notaries public. The Court of Appeals for the Fifth Circuit held that the statute does not offend the Equal Protection Clause. We ... reverse.

I

Petitioner, a native of Mexico, is a resident alien who has lived in the United States since 1961. He works as a paralegal for Texas Rural Legal Aid, Inc., helping migrant farm workers on employment and civil rights matters. In order to administer oaths to these workers and to notarize their statements for use in civil litigation, petitioner applied in 1978 to become a notary public. Under Texas law, notaries public authenticate written instruments, administer oaths, and take out-of-court depositions. The Texas Secretary of State denied petitioner's application because he failed to satisfy the statutory requirement that a notary public be a citizen of the United States. Tex.Civ.Stat.Ann., Art. 5949(2).... After an unsuccessful administrative appeal, petitioner brought suit in the federal district court, claiming that the citizenship requirement mandated by Article 5942(2) violated the federal Constitution.

The District Court ruled in favor of petitioner.... A divided panel of the Court of Appeals for the Fifth Circuit reversed, concluding that the proper standard for review was the rational relationship test and that Article 5949(2) satisfied that test because it "bears a rational relationship to the state's interest in the proper and orderly handling of a countless variety of legal documents of importance to the state." Vargas v. Strake, 710 F.2d 190, 195 (C.A.5 1983).

II

As a general matter, a State law that discriminates on the basis of alienage can be sustained only if it can withstand strict judicial scrutiny. In order to withstand strict scrutiny, the law must advance a compelling State interest by the least restrictive means available. Applying this principle, we have invalidated an array of State statutes that denied aliens the right to pursue various occupations. In Sugarman v. Dougall, 413 U.S. 634 (1973), we struck down a State statute barring aliens from employment in permanent positions in the competitive class of the State civil service. In In re Griffiths, 413 U.S. 717 (1973), we nullified a State law excluding aliens from eligibility for membership in the State bar. And in Examining Board v. Flores de Otero, 426 U.S. 572 (1976), we voided a State law that excluded aliens from the practice of civil engineering.

We have, however, developed a narrow exception to the rule that discrimination based on alienage triggers strict scrutiny. This exception has been labelled the "political function" exception and applies to laws that exclude aliens from positions intimately related to the process of democratic self-government. The contours of the "political function" exception are outlined by our prior decisions. In Foley v. Connelie, 435 U.S. 291 (1978), we held that a State may require police to be citizens because, in performing a fundamental obligation of government, police "are clothed with authority to exercise an almost infinite variety of discretionary powers" often involving the most sensitive areas of daily life. In Ambach v. Norwick, 441 U.S. 68 (1979), we held that a State may bar aliens who have not declared their intent to become citizens from teaching in the public schools because teachers, like police, possess a high degree of responsibility and discretion in the fulfillment of a basic governmental obligation. They have direct, day-to-day contact with students, exercise unsupervised discretion over them, act as role models and influence their students about the government and the political process. Finally, in Cabell v. Chavez–Salido, 454 U.S. 432 (1982), we held that a State may bar aliens from positions as probation officers because they, like police and teachers, routinely exercise discretionary power, involving a basic governmental function, that places them in a position of direct authority over other individuals.

The rationale behind the political function exception is that within broad boundaries a State may establish its own form of government and limit the right to govern to those who are full-fledged members of the political community. Some public positions are so closely bound up with the formulation and implementation of self-government that the State is permitted to exclude from those positions persons outside the political community, hence persons who have not become part of the process of democratic self-determination.

> "The exclusion of aliens from basic governmental processes is not a deficiency in the democratic system but a necessary consequence of the community's process of political self-definition. Self-government, whether direct or through representatives, begins by defining the scope of the community of the governed and thus of the governors as well: Aliens are by definition those outside of this community."

We have therefore lowered our standard of review when evaluating the validity of exclusions that entrust only to citizens important elective and nonelective positions whose operations "go to the heart of representative government." Sugarman v. Dougall, supra, 413 U.S., at 647. "While not retreating from the position that restrictions on lawfully resident aliens that primarily affect economic interests are subject to heightened judicial scrutiny . . . we have concluded that strict scrutiny is out of place when the restriction primarily serves a political function. . . ." Cabell v. Chavez–Salido, supra, 454 U.S., at 439.

To determine whether a restriction based on alienage fits within the narrow political function exception, we devised in *Cabell* a two-part test.

> "First, the specificity of the classification will be examined: a classification that is substantially overinclusive or underinclusive tends to undercut the governmental claim that the classification serves legitimate political ends. . . . Second, even if the classification is sufficiently tailored, it may be applied in the particular case only to 'persons holding state elective or important nonelective executive, legislative, and judicial positions,' those officers who 'participate directly in the formulation, execution, or review of

[handwritten margin note: 2 part test]

broad public policy' and hence 'perform functions that go right to the heart of representative government.' "[7]

III

We now turn to Article 5949(2) to determine whether it satisfies the *Cabell* test. The statute provides that "[t]o be eligible for appointment as a Notary Public, a person shall be a resident citizen of the United States and of this state...." Unlike the statute invalidated in *Sugarman,* Article 5949(2) does not indiscriminately sweep within its ambit a wide range of offices and occupations but specifies only one particular post with respect to which the State asserts a right to exclude aliens. Clearly, then, the statute is not overinclusive; it applies narrowly to only one category of persons: those wishing to obtain appointments as notaries. Less clear is whether Article 5942(2) is fatally underinclusive. Texas does not require court reporters to be United States citizens even though they perform some of the same services as notaries. Nor does Texas require that its Secretary of State be a citizen, even though he holds the highest appointive position in the State and performs many important functions, including supervision of the licensing of all notaries public. We need not decide this issue, however, because of our decision with respect to the second prong of the *Cabell* test.

In support of the proposition that notaries public fall within that category of officials who perform functions that "go to the heart of representative government," the State emphasizes that notaries are designated as public officers by the Texas Constitution. Texas maintains that this designation indicates that the State views notaries as important officials occupying posts central to the State's definition of itself as a political community. This Court, however, has never deemed the *source* of a position—whether it derives from a State's statute or its Constitution—as the dispositive factor in determining whether a State may entrust the position only to citizens. Rather, this Court has always looked to the actual *function* of the position as the dispositive factor. The focus of our inquiry has been whether a position was such that the officeholder would necessarily exercise broad discretionary power over the formulation or execution of public policies importantly affecting the citizen population—power of the sort that a self-governing community could properly entrust only to full-fledged members of that community. As the Court noted in *Cabell,* in determining whether the function of a particular position brings the position within the narrow ambit of the exception, "the Court will look to the importance of the function as a factor giving substance to the concept of democratic self-government."

The State maintains that even if the actual function of a post is the touchstone of a proper analysis, Texas notaries public should still be classified among those positions from which aliens can properly be excluded because the duties of Texas notaries entail the performance of functions sufficiently consequential to be deemed "political." ...

We recognize the critical need for a notary's duties to be carried out correctly and with integrity. But a notary's duties, important as they are, hardly implicate responsibilities that go to the heart of representative government. Rather, these duties are essentially clerical and ministerial. In contrast

---

7. We emphasize, as we have in the past, that the political-function exception must be narrowly construed; otherwise the exception will swallow the rule and depreciate the significance that should attach to the designation of a group as a "discrete and insular" minority for whom heightened judicial solicitude is appropriate. See Nyquist v. Mauclet, 432 U.S. 1, 11 (1977).

to state troopers, *Foley v. Connelie,* notaries do not routinely exercise the State's monopoly of legitimate coercive force. Nor do notaries routinely exercise the wide discretion typically enjoyed by public school teachers when they present materials that educate youth respecting the information and values necessary for the maintenance of a democratic political system. See Ambach v. Norwick, 441 U.S., at 77. To be sure, considerable damage could result from the negligent or dishonest performance of a notary's duties. But the same could be said for the duties performed by cashiers, building inspectors, the janitors who clean up the offices of public officials, and numerous other categories of personnel upon whom we depend for careful, honest service. What distinguishes such personnel from those to which the political function exception is properly applied is that the latter are either invested with policy-making responsibility or broad discretion in the execution of public policy that requires the routine exercise of authority over individuals. Neither of these characteristics pertain to the functions performed by Texas notaries.

The inappropriateness of applying the political function exception to Texas notaries is further underlined by our decision in *In re Griffiths* ... in which we subjected to strict scrutiny a Connecticut statute that prohibited non-citizens from becoming members of the State bar. Along with the usual powers and privileges accorded to members of the bar, Connecticut gave to members of its bar additional authority that encompasses the very duties performed by Texas notaries—authority to "sign writs and subpoenas, take recognizances, administer oaths and take depositions and acknowledgement of deeds." In striking down Connecticut's citizenship requirement, we concluded that "[i]t in no way denigrates a lawyer's high responsibility to observe that [these duties] hardly involve matters of state policy or acts of such unique responsibility as to entrust them only to citizens." If it is improper to apply the political function exception to a citizenship requirement governing eligibility for membership in a State bar, it would be anomalous to apply the exception to the citizenship requirement that governs eligibility to become a Texas notary. We conclude, then, that the "political function" exception is inapplicable to Article 5949(2) and that the statute is therefore subject to strict judicial scrutiny.

IV

To satisfy strict scrutiny, the State must show that Article 5949(2) furthers a compelling State interest by the least restrictive means practically available. Respondent maintains that Article 5949(2) serves its "legitimate concern that notaries be reasonably familiar with state law and institutions" and "that notaries may be called upon years later to testify to acts they have performed." However both of these asserted justifications utterly fail to meet the stringent requirements of strict scrutiny. There is nothing in the record that indicates that resident aliens, as a class, are so incapable of familiarizing themselves with Texas law as to justify the State's absolute and class-wide exclusion. The possibility that some resident aliens are unsuitable for the position cannot justify a wholesale ban against all resident aliens. Furthermore, if the State's concern with ensuring a notary's familiarity with state law were truly "compelling," one would expect the State to give some sort of test actually measuring a person's familiarity with the law. The State, however, administers no such test. To become a notary public in Texas, one is merely required to fill out an application that lists one's name and address and that answers four questions pertaining to one's age, citizenship, residency and criminal record—nothing that reflects the State's asserted interest in insuring that notaries are familiar with Texas law. Similarly inadequate is the State's purported interest in insuring the later availability of notaries' testimony. This justification fails because the State fails to advance a factual showing that the unavailability of notaries' testimony presents a real, as opposed to a merely speculative, problem to the State. Without a factual underpinning, the State's asserted interest lacks the weight we have required of interests properly denominated as compelling.

V

We conclude that Article 5949(2) violates the Fourteenth Amendment.... Accordingly the judgment . . . is reversed, and the case is remanded for further proceedings consistent with this opinion.

Justice Rehnquist, dissenting.

I dissent for the reasons stated in my dissenting opinion in Sugarman v. Dougall, 413 U.S. 634, 649 (1973).

Mathews v. Diaz

426 U.S. 67, 96 S.Ct. 1883, 48 L.Ed.2d 478 (1976).

Mr. Justice Stevens delivered the opinion of the Court.

The question presented by the Secretary's appeal is whether Congress may condition an alien's eligibility for participation in a federal medical insurance program on continuous residence in the United States for a five-year period and admission for permanent residence. The District Court held that the first condition was unconstitutional and that it could not be severed from the second. Since we conclude that both conditions are constitutional, we reverse.

Each of the appellees is a resident alien who was lawfully admitted to the United States less than five years ago. Appellees Diaz and Clara are Cuban refugees who remain in this country at the discretion of the Attorney General; appellee Espinosa has been admitted for permanent residence. All three are over 65 years old and have been denied enrollment in the Medicare Part B supplemental medical insurance program established by . . . the Social Security Act.... They brought this action to challenge the statutory basis for that denial. Specifically, they attack 42 U.S.C. § 1395o(2), which grants eligibility to resident citizens who are 65 or older but denies eligibility to such aliens unless they have been admitted for permanent residence and also have resided in the United States for at least five years....

. . .

II.

There are literally millions of aliens within the jurisdiction of the United States. The Fifth Amendment, as well as the Fourteenth Amendment, protects every one of these persons from deprivation of life, liberty or property without due process of law. Wong Yang Sung v. McGrath, 339 U.S. 33, 48–51; Wong Wing v. United States, 163 U.S. 228, 238; see Russian Volunteer Fleet v. United States, 282 U.S. 481, 489. Even one whose presence in this country is unlawful, involuntary, or transitory, is entitled to that constitutional protection. *Wong Yang Sung,* supra; *Wong Wing,* supra.

The fact that all persons, aliens and citizens alike, are protected by the Due Process Clause does not lead to the further conclusion that all aliens are entitled to enjoy all the advantages of citizenship or, indeed, to the conclusion that all aliens must be placed in a single homogenous legal classification. For a host of constitutional and statutory provisions rest on the premise that a legitimate distinction between citizens and aliens may justify attributes and benefits for one class not accorded to the other;[12] and the class of aliens is itself a heterogenous multitude of persons with a wide-ranging variety of ties to this country.

In the exercise of its broad power over naturalization and immigration, Congress regularly makes rules that would be unacceptable if applied to citizens. The exclusion of aliens and the reservation of the power to deport have no permissible counterpart in the Federal Government's power to regulate the conduct of its own citizenry. The fact that an act of Congress treats aliens differently from citizens does not in itself imply that such disparate treatment is "invidious."

In particular, the fact that Congress has provided some welfare benefits for citizens does not require it to provide like benefits for *all aliens*. Neither the overnight visitor, the unfriendly agent of a hostile foreign power, the resident diplomat, nor the illegal entrant, can advance even a colorable constitutional claim to a share in the bounty that a conscientious sovereign makes available to its own citizens and *some* of its guests. The decision to share that bounty with our guests may take into account the character of the relationship between the alien and this country: Congress may decide that as the alien's tie grows stronger, so does the strength of his claim to an equal share of that munificence.

The real question presented by this case is not whether discrimination between citizens and aliens is permissible; rather, it is whether the statutory discrimination *within* the class of aliens—allowing benefits to some aliens but not to others—is permissible. We turn to that question.

III.

For reasons long recognized as valid, the responsibility for regulating the relationship between the United States and our alien visitors has been committed to the political branches of the Federal Government. Since decisions in these matters may implicate our relations with foreign powers, and since a wide variety of classifications must be defined in the light of changing political and economic circumstances, such decisions are frequently of a character more appropriate to either the legislature or the executive than to the judiciary. This very case illustrates the need for flexibility in policy choices rather than the rigidity often characteristic of constitutional adjudication. Appellees Diaz and Clara are but two of over 440,000 Cuban refugees who arrived in the United States between 1961 and 1972. And the Cuban parolees are but one of several categories of aliens who have been admitted in order to make a humane response to a natural catastrophe or an international political situation. Any rule of constitutional law that would inhibit the flexibility of the political branches of government to respond to changing world conditions should be adopted only with the greatest caution. The reasons that preclude judicial review of political questions also dictate a narrow standard of review of decisions made by the Congress or the President in the area of immigration and naturalization.

---

12. The Constitution protects the privileges and immunities only of citizens, Amend. XIV, § 1; see Art. IV, § 2, cl. 1, and the right to vote only of citizens. Amends. XV, XIX, XXIV, XXVI. It requires that Representatives have been citizens for seven years, Art. I, § 2, cl. 2, and Senators citizens for nine, Art. I, § 3, cl. 3, and that the President be a "natural born Citizen." Art. II, § 1, cl. 5.

A multitude of federal statutes distinguish between citizens and aliens. The whole of Title 8 of the United States Code, regulating aliens and nationality, is founded on the legitimacy of distinguishing citizens and aliens. A variety of other federal statutes provide for disparate treatment of aliens and citizens. . . .

Since it is obvious that Congress has no constitutional duty to provide *all aliens* with the welfare benefits provided to citizens, the party challenging the constitutionality of the particular line Congress has drawn has the burden of advancing principled reasoning that will at once invalidate that line and yet tolerate a different line separating some aliens from others. In this case the appellees have challenged two requirements, first that the alien be admitted as a permanent resident, and second that his residence be of a duration of at least five years. But if these requirements were eliminated, surely Congress would at least require that the alien's entry be lawful; even then, unless mere transients are to be held constitutionally entitled to benefits, *some* durational requirement would certainly be appropriate. In short, it is unquestionably reasonable for Congress to make an alien's eligibility depend on both the character and the duration of his residence. Since neither requirement is wholly irrational, this case essentially involves nothing more than a claim that it would have been more reasonable for Congress to select somewhat different requirements of the same kind.

We may assume that the five-year line drawn by Congress is longer than necessary to protect the fiscal integrity of the program. We may also assume that unnecessary hardship is incurred by persons just short of qualifying. But it remains true that some line is essential, that any line must produce some harsh and apparently arbitrary consequences, and, of greatest importance, that those who qualify under the test Congress has chosen may reasonably be presumed to have a greater affinity to the United States than those who do not. In short, citizens and those who are most like citizens qualify. Those who are less like citizens do not.

The task of classifying persons for medical benefits, like the task of drawing lines for federal tax purposes, inevitably requires that some persons who have an almost equally strong claim to favored treatment be placed on different sides of the line; the differences between the eligible and the ineligible are differences in degree rather than differences in the character of their respective claims. When this kind of policy choice must be made, we are especially reluctant to question the exercise of congressional judgment. In this case, since appellees have not identified a principled basis for prescribing a different standard than the one selected by Congress, they have, in effect, merely invited us to substitute our judgment for that of Congress in deciding which aliens shall be eligible to participate in the supplementary insurance program on the same conditions as citizens. We decline the invitation.

IV.

The cases on which appellees rely are consistent with our conclusion that this statutory classification does not deprive them of liberty or property without due process of law.

Graham v. Richardson, 403 U.S. 365, provides the strongest support for appellees' position. That case holds that state statutes that deny welfare benefits to resident aliens, or to aliens not meeting a requirement of durational residence within the United States, violate the Equal Protection Clause of the Fourteenth Amendment and encroach upon the exclusive federal power over the entrance and residence of aliens. Of course, the latter ground of decision actually supports our holding today that it is the business of the political branches of the Federal Government, rather than that of either the States or the federal judiciary, to regulate the conditions of entry and residence of aliens. The equal protection analysis also involves significantly different considerations because it concerns the relationship between aliens and the States rather than between aliens and the Federal Government.

Insofar as state welfare policy is concerned, there is little, if any, basis for treating persons who are citizens of another State differently from persons who are citizens of another country. Both groups are noncitizens as far as the State's interests in administering its welfare programs are concerned. Thus, a division by a State of the category of persons who are not citizens of that State into subcategories of United States citizens and aliens has no apparent justification, whereas, a comparable classification by the Federal Government is a routine and normally legitimate part of its business. Furthermore, whereas the Constitution inhibits every State's power to restrict travel across its own borders, Congress is explicitly empowered to exercise that type of control over travel across the borders of the United States.

We hold that § 1395o(2)(B) has not deprived appellees of liberty or property without due process of law.

The judgment of the District Court is reversed.

NGUYEN v. IMMIGRATION AND NATURALIZATION SERVICE, 533 U.S. 53 (2001). The report in this case appears, supra at p. 792.

G. WHAT OTHER CLASSIFICATIONS WILL PROVOKE HEIGHTENED SCRUTINY?

1. CLASSIFICATIONS DISADVANTAGING NON–MARITAL CHILDREN

THE STANDARD OF REVIEW FOR LEGITIMACY CLASSIFICATIONS

In Levy v. Louisiana, 391 U.S. 68 (1968), the Court held invalid a state statute permitting legitimate but not illegitimate children to sue for wrongful death of their mother. The Court indicated that the classification did not meet the lowest standard of review. "Legitimacy or illegitimacy of birth has no relation to the nature of the wrong allegedly inflicted on the mother." In Labine v. Vincent, 401 U.S. 532 (1971), the Court upheld a statute under which illegitimate children acknowledged but not legitimated by the father could not take by intestate succession from the father. The next year, in Weber v. Aetna Cas. and Sur. Co., 406 U.S. 164 (1972), the Court held invalid a statute that did not permit dependent, unacknowledged children of a father to recover workers' compensation benefits for death of the father, saying that the classification "is justified by no legitimate state interest, compelling or otherwise." In the next three cases to come before it the Court invalidated legitimacy classifications: Gomez v. Perez, 409 U.S. 535 (1973) (father obligated to support legitimate but not illegitimate children); New Jersey Welfare Rights Organization v. Cahill, 411 U.S. 619 (1973) (state welfare statute); Jimenez v. Weinberger, 417 U.S. 628 (1974) (federal classification that did not permit some illegitimate children to obtain benefits under parent's disability insurance).

In Mathews v. Lucas, 427 U.S. 495 (1976), the Court upheld a provision of the Social Security Act that gave a survivor's benefit to a minor dependent child of a deceased parent, but extended a presumption of dependency to all children except certain classes of illegitimate children. Justice Blackmun, speaking for the Court, said that the trial judge was wrong in treating the classification as suspect requiring strict scrutiny:

"It is true, of course, that the legal status of illegitimacy, however defined, is like race or national origin, a characteristic determined by causes not within the control of the illegitimate individual, and it bears no relation to the individual's ability to participate in and contribute to society. The Court recognized in *Weber* that visiting condemnation upon the child in order to express society's disapproval of the parents' liaisons

> 'is illogical and unjust. Moreover, imposing disabilities on the illegitimate child is contrary to the basic concept of our system that legal burdens should bear some relationship to individual responsibility or wrongdoing. Obviously, no child is responsible for his birth and penalizing the illegitimate child is an ineffectual—as well as an unjust—way of deterring the parent.' . . .

"But where the law is arbitrary in such a way, we have had no difficulty in finding the discrimination impermissible on less demanding standards than those advocated here. New Jersey Welfare Rights Organization v. Cahill, 411 U.S. 619 (1973); Richardson v. Davis, 409 U.S. 1069 (1972); Richardson v. Griffin, 409 U.S. 1069 (1972); *Weber,* supra; Levy v. Louisiana, 391 U.S. 68 (1968). And such irrationality in some classifications does not in itself demonstrate that other, possibly rational, distinctions made in part on the basis of legitimacy are inherently untenable. Moreover, while the law has long placed the illegitimate child in an inferior position relative to the legitimate in certain circumstances, particularly in regard to obligations of support or other aspects of family law, see generally, e.g., H. Krause, *Illegitimacy: Law and Social Policy* 21–42 (1971); Gray & Rudovsky, *The Court Acknowledges the Illegitimate: Levy v. Louisiana and Glona v. American Guarantee & Liability Insurance Co.,* 118 U.Pa.L.Rev. 1, 19–38 (1969), perhaps in part because the roots of the discrimination rest in the conduct of the parents rather than the child, and perhaps in part because illegitimacy does not carry an obvious badge, as race or sex do, this discrimination against illegitimates has never approached the severity or pervasiveness of the historic legal and political discrimination against women and Negroes. See Frontiero v. Richardson, 411 U.S. 677, 684–686 (1973) (plurality opinion).

"We therefore adhere to our earlier view, see Labine v. Vincent, 401 U.S. 532 (1971), that the Act's discrimination between individuals on the basis of their legitimacy does not 'command extraordinary protection from the majoritarian political process,' San Antonio Independent School District v. Rodriguez, 411 U.S. 1, 28 (1973), which our most exacting scrutiny would entail."

Later in the opinion he referred to the showing necessary to demonstrate that the relationship between the statutory classifications and the likelihood of dependency was not sufficiently material: "[T]he scrutiny by which their showing is to be judged is not a toothless one" but "the burden remains upon the appellees to demonstrate the insubstantiality of that relation."

LALLI v. LALLI, 439 U.S. 259 (1978). In order to inherit from their fathers by intestate succession, New York law requires illegitimate children to secure a judicial paternity order during the father's lifetime. The New York courts rejected an equal protection claim by a man who had not obtained such an order, but who tried to submit evidence in support of his petition to share in his putative father's estate that included a notarized document from the decedent consenting to his marriage and referring to him as "my son," and several affidavits by persons who stated that his putative father had acknowledged him openly and often as his child. The Supreme Court affirmed 5–4, but with no majority opinion.

Justice Powell's plurality opinion, joined by Chief Justice Burger and Justice Stewart, distinguished this case from Trimble v. Gordon, 430 U.S. 762 (1977), where the Court held that an Illinois statute denied equal protection because it was "not substantially related to permissible state interests." The Illinois law "provid[ed] that a child born out of wedlock could inherit from his intestate father only if the father had 'acknowledged' the child and the child had been legitimated by the intermarriage of the parents." The father in *Trimble* "had neither acknowledged [the daughter] nor married her mother" but he had "been found to be her father in a judicial decree ordering him to contribute to her support." The statute bore " 'only the most attenuated relationship to the asserted goal' " of encouraging "legitimate family relationships." Moreover, although "the often difficult problem of proving the paternity of illegitimate children and the related danger of spurious claims against intestate estates 'might justify a more demanding standard for illegitimate children claiming under their fathers' estates than that required either for illegitimate children claiming under their mothers' estates or for legitimate children generally[,]' [t]he Illinois statute ... was constitutionally flawed, because, by insisting upon not only an acknowledgment by the father, but also the marriage of the parents, it excluded 'at least some significant categories of illegitimate children of intestate men [whose] inheritance rights can be recognized without jeopardizing the orderly settlement of estates or the dependability of titles of property passing under intestacy laws.' " The Court in *Trimble* thus "concluded that the Equal Protection Clause required that a statute placing exceptional burdens on illegitimate children in the furtherance of proper State objectives must be more 'carefully tuned to alternative considerations,' than was true of the broad disqualification in the Illinois law."

By contrast, under the New York statute "the marital status of the parents is irrelevant" and the State did not seek to defend it as a means of encouraging legitimate family relationships. Rather, the "primary state goal ... is to provide for the just and orderly disposition of property at death[,]" where "the States have an interest of considerable magnitude" and where practical problems of estate administration "counsel against treating illegitimate children identically to all other heirs of an intestate father": "Even where an individual claiming to be the illegitimate child of a deceased man makes himself known, the difficulties facing an estate are likely to persist. Because of the particular problems of proof, spurious claims may be difficult to expose." Accordingly, New York's "interests" in protecting " 'innocent adults and those rightfully interested in their estates from fraudulent claims of heirship and harassing litigation instituted by those seeking to establish themselves as illegitimate heirs' ... are substantial." Finally, "the means adopted by New York" were found to be "substantially related to the important state interests the statute is intended to promote":

"The administration of an estate will be facilitated, and the possibility of delay and uncertainty minimized, where the entitlement of an illegitimate child to notice and participation is a matter of judicial record before the administration commences. Fraudulent assertions of paternity will be much less likely to succeed, or even to arise, where the proof is put before a court of law at a time when the putative father is available to respond, rather than first brought to light when the distribution of the assets of an estate is in the offing.

"Appellant contends that § 4–1.2, like the statute at issue in *Trimble,* excludes 'significant categories of illegitimate children' who could be allowed to inherit 'without jeopardizing the orderly settlement' of their intestate fathers' estates. He urges that 'known' illegitimate children who, despite the absence of an order of filiation obtained during their fathers' lifetimes, can present convincing proof of paternity ... cannot rationally be denied inheritance as they pose none of the risks § 4–1.2 was intended to minimize.

"We do not question that there will be some illegitimate children who would be able to establish their relationship to their deceased fathers without serious disruption of the administration of estates and that, as applied to such individuals, § 4–1.2 appears to operate unfairly. But few statutory classifications are entirely free from the criticism that they sometimes produce inequitable results. Our inquiry under the Equal Protection Clause does not focus on the abstract 'fairness' of a state law, but on whether the statute's relation to the state interests it is intended to promote is so tenuous that it lacks the rationality contemplated by the Fourteenth Amendment."

Justice Rehnquist concurred in the judgment for the reasons stated in his dissent in *Trimble.* Justice Blackmun also concurred in the judgment, because although he found the plurality's attempt to distinguish it "unconvincing," he "would overrule *Trimble.*" Justice Brennan dissented, joined by Justices White, Marshall, and Stevens. They understood *Trimble* as having "declar[ed] that the state interest in the accurate and efficient determination of paternity can be adequately served by requiring the illegitimate child to offer into evidence a 'formal acknowledgment of paternity.'" Because the "New York statute ... like the Illinois statute in *Trimble,* excludes 'forms of proof which do not compromise the State['s] interests[,] it discriminates against illegitimates through means not substantially related to the legitimate interests that the statute purports to promote....'"

CLARK v. JETER, 486 U.S. 456 (1988). Pennsylvania law required an illegitimate child to prove paternity before seeking support from his or her father. Although legitimate children could seek parental support at any time, illegitimate children were required to bring suits to establish paternity within six years of birth. The Court unanimously held that this six year limitation denied illegitimate children the equal protection of the laws.[a] Justice O'Connor's opinion said that "intermediate scrutiny ... generally has been applied to discriminatory classifications based on sex or illegitimacy" and that "[t]o withstand intermediate scrutiny, a statutory classification must be substantially related to an important governmental objective." Relying on Mills v. Habluetzel, 456 U.S. 91 (1982), and Pickett v. Brown, 462 U.S. 1 (1983), which respectively invalidated a one-year and a two-year statute of limitations for such suits, the Court concluded that "[e]ven six years does not necessarily provide a reasonable opportunity to assert a claim on behalf of an illegitimate child" but indicated that even if six years might be reasonable that period was "not substantially related to Pennsylvania's interest in avoiding the litigation of stale or fraudulent claims." In concluding that the statute "does not withstand heightened scrutiny," the Court noted that Pennsylvania places no limits on when paternity issues may be litigated in other kinds of cases, that the new law extended the period to 18 years, and that increasingly sophisticated scientific technology had become available.

a. While the paternity suit was pending in this case, Pennsylvania amended its law to conform to federal legislation requiring all states participating in the federal child support program to have procedures to establish the paternity of any child under 18. The Court declined to address a federal preemption claim, however, because it had not been adequately raised in the state courts, which applied the six–year statute of limitations to this case.

PARENTAL RIGHTS OF FATHERS OF ILLEGITIMATE CHILDREN

It is a common statutory pattern for the father of an illegitimate child to be given fewer parental rights than the child's mother, or than the father of a child born in wedlock or legitimated. That statutory pattern has raised substantive due process questions concerning state regulation of the relationship between parent and child, as well as questions of procedural due process and equal protection.

In Stanley v. Illinois, 405 U.S. 645 (1972), the unmarried parents of three children lived together for 18 years before the mother's death. Illinois law provided that illegitimate children become wards of the State upon the mother's death. The Court held that denying Stanley a hearing on his fitness as a parent denied him procedural due process and equal protection. As to the equal protection claim, "all Illinois parents are constitutionally entitled to a hearing on their fitness before their children are removed from their custody"; hence the distinction between unmarried fathers on the one hand, and unmarried mothers, married parents and divorced parents on the other, was contrary to the equal protection clause.

In Quilloin v. Walcott, 434 U.S. 246 (1978), the natural father had neither lived with the child's mother, nor had custody of the child. The child's mother consented to the child's adoption by her husband. State courts dismissed the father's objection to the adoption under a law requiring only the mother's consent for adoption of an illegitimate child. The Court's conclusion that the father had not been denied substantive due process was limited to the facts of the case—the father had not sought custody of the child, and the adoption recognized "a family unit already in existence." The Court also rejected an equal protection challenge based on the argument that a married father who was separated or divorced would have been permitted to veto the adoption. An argument that an unmarried father should, as matter of equal protection, be given the same rights as an unmarried mother, was not considered because it had not been properly presented.

That argument, however, proved crucial in Caban v. Mohammed, 441 U.S. 380 (1979). The father had lived with the children as their father in their early years. At the time of the petition for adoption by the children's mother and her husband, the father and mother were engaged in a legal battle for the children's custody. The Court held that New York's law, which permitted an unwed mother to block her child's adoption but gave no similar right to the father, was an unconstitutional distinction on the basis of gender. Although Justice Powell's opinion for the Court rejected the argument that the gender distinction could be justified by the difference in maternal and paternal roles, it conceded that the distinction could be applied constitutionally in cases of adoption at birth or in cases where the father had not participated in the rearing of the child. Chief Justice Burger, and Justices Stewart, Rehnquist and Stevens dissented.

On the same day the *Caban* case was decided, Justice Powell concurred with the dissenters in that case to sustain a distinction between unwed mothers and fathers. Parham v. Hughes, 441 U.S. 347 (1979), involved a Georgia law permitting the mother of an illegitimate child to sue for the wrongful death of a child, while denying that right to the child's father. The four *Caban* dissenters, in an opinion by Justice Stewart, argued that the gender based distinction was not invidious—the father's right to sue was not denied solely because of his male sex, but because he had taken no steps to legitimate the child. Justice Powell concurred in the result on the narrower ground that the gender-based distinction was justified by problems of proving paternity after an illegitimate child's death. Justice White's dissent, joined by Justices Brennan, Marshall and Blackmun, argued that Georgia's interest in rejecting spurious claims could not justify categorically eliminating all claims of fathers of illegitimate children "on the basis of sex."

The Court returned to the problem in Lehr v. Robertson, 463 U.S. 248 (1983). Lehr, an unmarried father, had lived with the mother before the child was born, visited the mother and child in the hospital, but thereafter had little contact, neither providing support nor offering to marry the mother. The mother married another man eight months after the child's birth and when the child was two years old the mother and her husband sought to adopt the child. Without notice to Lehr, the court granted the adoption after it had become aware that Lehr had filed a paternity and visitation proceeding in another county. Lehr sued to set aside the adoption proceeding as violating the due process and equal protection clauses. The New York courts denied his claim and the Supreme Court affirmed.

Justice Stevens, writing for the majority, noted that New York maintains a "putative father registry" in which a person claiming to be the father may enter his name and have the right to receive notice of any proceeding to adopt the child. The law also provides notice to men who have been adjudicated to be fathers, who have been identified as fathers on the child's birth certificate, who live openly with the child and the child's mother and hold themselves out as fathers, who have been identified as father by the mother in a sworn written statement, and who were married to the child's mother before the child was six months old. This law, the Court said, adequately protected the opportunity of the putative father to establish a relationship with the illegitimate child. Lehr had not complied with that statute and had not established any relationship with the child. Under these circumstances it was not a denial of due process to enter the order of adoption without notice to Lehr, even though the judge in the adoption proceeding had knowledge of the paternity petition filed by Lehr. "Since the New York statutes adequately protected appellant's inchoate interest in establishing a relationship with ... [the child], we find no merit in the claim that his constitutional rights were offended because the family court strictly complied with the notice provisions of the statute."

The Court also held that there was no denial of equal protection. It said that the parents here were in a different position than those in *Caban v. Mohammed*. Lehr never established any custodial, personal, or financial relations with the child. "If one parent has an established custodial relationship with the child and the other parent has either abandoned or never established a relationship, the Equal Protection Clause does not prevent a state from according the two parents different legal rights."

Justices White, Marshall and Blackmun dissented, arguing that it was a denial of due process to deny notice and an opportunity to be heard in an adoption proceeding to a putative father when the state has actual notice of his existence, whereabouts, and interest in the child.

In Michael H. v. Gerald D., 491 U.S. 110 (1989), the Court was confronted with a variety of constitutional challenges to a California law establishing a conclusive presumption, as against all but husband and wife, that a child born to a married woman cohabiting with her husband is a child of the marriage. The California courts had applied the presumption to bar a claim of paternity and visitation rights by Michael, a man who wished to offer blood tests showing to a 98% probability that he is the biological father of Victoria, whose mother was married to and cohabiting with her husband at Victoria's conception and

1981 birth, but who had then had an affair with, and later intermittently lived with, Michael. The child had always lived with her mother, which meant sometimes with Michael and sometimes (and eventually) with Gerald, the husband. The Court addressed Michael's procedural and substantive due process claims to a relationship with Victoria and Victoria's due process and equal protection claims to a relationship with her natural father.

Justice Scalia, joined by the Chief Justice and Justices O'Connor and Kennedy, rejected Michael's procedural due process claims on the view that conclusive presumption problems raise issues of substantive, not procedural, due process. After extended discussion, they concluded that Michael lacked "a constitutionally protected liberty interest in his relationship with Victoria[,]" at least in circumstances where "the husband and wife wish to raise her child jointly." As to Victoria, the plurality concluded that she had no "due process right to maintain a filial relationship with both Michael and Gerald[,]" because "the claim that a State must recognize multiple fatherhood has no support in the traditions or history of this country." Her claim of "a liberty interest in maintaining a filial relationship with her natural father" failed "for the same reasons" as Michael's claim. The plurality also rejected her claim that allowing the presumption of her legitimacy to be rebutted by her mother and presumed father, but not by her, violated equal protection. Victoria was treated as legitimate, not illegitimate, by California law and thus "the ordinary 'rational relationship' standard" applied. Preventing "the child—or, more accurately, ... a court-appointed guardian ad litem—" from rebutting the presumption of legitimacy rationally served the legitimate end of protecting the integrity of the marital union; it differed rationally from allowing husband or wife to contest the child's legitimacy, because in such cases "the stability of the marriage has already been shaken."

Justice Stevens concurred in the judgment. He "would not foreclose the possibility that a constitutionally protected relationship between a natural father and his child might exist in a case like this[,]" but concluded, based on his reading of California law and the determination of the California courts in this case, that "Michael was given a fair opportunity to show that he is Victoria's natural father, that he had developed a relationship with her, and that her interests would be served by granting him visitation rights." He found "nothing fundamentally unfair about the exercise of a judge's discretion that, in the end, allows the mother to decide whether her child's best interest would be served by allowing the natural father visitation privileges."

Justice Brennan's dissent, joined by Justices Marshall and Blackmun, dismissed Justice Stevens' reading of California law as "wishful thinking." Disagreeing sharply with the plurality's interpretive sources and method, he concluded that "unwed fathers have a constitutionally protected interest in their relationships with their children"; that the case was "properly analyzed under our procedural due process cases[,]" because the statute's "effect ... is to terminate the relationship ... before affording any hearing whatsoever on the issue whether Michael is Victoria's father"; and that California's interest in preserving family privacy could not justify terminating the parent-child relationship without a hearing.

In a separate dissent, Justice White, joined by Justice Brennan, concluded that the "basic principle enumerated in the Court's unwed father cases is that an unwed father who has demonstrated a sufficient commitment to his paternity by way of personal, financial, or custodial responsibilities has a protected liberty interest in a relationship with his child." Michael had done all he could to establish his relationship with Victoria, and he was denied procedural due process, because "he is foreclosed from establishing his paternity and is ultimately precluded, by the State, from developing a relationship with his child" without ever being allowed to present the blood test evidence of his paternity.

For the full report of this case, see supra, p. 603.

2. CLASSIFICATIONS DISADVANTAGING THE RETARDED, HOMOSEXUALS, THE ELDERLY, THE POOR, ETC.

City of Cleburne v. Cleburne Living Center

473 U.S. 432, 105 S.Ct. 3249, 87 L.Ed.2d 313 (1985).

Justice White delivered the opinion of the Court.

A Texas city denied a special use permit for the operation of a group home for the mentally retarded, acting pursuant to a municipal zoning ordinance requiring permits for such homes. The Court of Appeals for the Fifth Circuit held that mental retardation is a "quasi-suspect" classification and that the ordinance violated the Equal Protection Clause because it did not substantially further an important governmental purpose. We hold that a lesser standard of scrutiny is appropriate, but conclude that under that standard the ordinance is invalid as applied in this case.

I

... [The] anticipated [group] home would house 13 retarded men and women ... under the constant supervision of CLC staff members....

... [A] special use permit, renewable annually, was required for the construction of "[h]ospitals for the insane or feeble-minded, or alcoholic [sic] or drug addicts, or penal or correctional institutions." The city had determined that the proposed group home should be classified as a "hospital for the feeble-minded." After holding a public hearing on CLC's application, the city council voted three to one to deny a special use permit.

CLC [sued] ... alleging, *inter alia*, that the zoning ordinance was invalid on its face and as applied because it discriminated against the mentally retarded.... The [district] court deemed the ordinance, as written and applied, to be rationally related to the City's legitimate interests in "the legal responsibility of CLC and its residents, ... the safety and fears of residents in the adjoining neighborhood," and the number of people to be housed....

The ... Fifth Circuit reversed, ... [applying] intermediate-level scrutiny.... [It] held that the ordinance was invalid on its face because it did not substantially further any important governmental interests [and] that the ordinance was also invalid as applied....

II

. . . .

We have declined ... to extend heightened review to differential treatment based on age:

"While the treatment of the aged in this Nation has not been wholly free of discrimination, such persons, unlike, say, those who have been discriminated against on the basis of race or national origin, have not experienced a 'history of purposeful unequal treatment' or been subjected to unique disabilities on the basis of stereotyped characteristics not truly indicative of their abilities." Massachusetts Board of Retirement v. Murgia, 427 U.S. 307, 313 (1976).[a]

The lesson of *Murgia* is that where individuals in the group affected by a law have distinguishing characteristics relevant to interests the state has the authority to implement, the courts have been very reluctant, as they should be in our federal system and with our respect for the separation of powers, to closely scrutinize legislative choices as to whether, how and to what extent those interests should be pursued. In such cases, the Equal Protection Clause requires only a rational means to serve a legitimate end.

III

[W]e conclude for several reasons that the Court of Appeals erred in holding mental retardation a quasi-suspect classification calling for a more exacting standard of judicial review than is normally accorded economic and social legislation. First, ... th[e] mentally retarded have a reduced ability to cope with and function in the everyday world.... They are thus different, immutably so, in relevant respects, and the states' interest in dealing with and providing for them is plainly a legitimate one.[10] How this large and diversified group is to be treated under the law is a difficult and often a technical matter, very much a task for legislators guided by qualified professionals and not by the perhaps ill-informed opinions of the judiciary. Heightened scrutiny inevitably involves substantive judgments about legislative decisions, and we doubt that

a. *Murgia* applied a rational basis standard and upheld a Massachusetts compulsory retirement law for state police officers who attained age fifty, rejecting the challenge of an officer who had passed an annual physical examination administered four months before he was retired involuntarily. The Court concluded that the objective of assuring physical fitness was rationally furthered by a maximum age limitation and that it was not necessary for the state to use individualized testing after age 50 even if that might determine fitness more precisely. The state did not have to choose the "best means" to accomplish its purpose, only a rational one.

The Court similarly has upheld a mandatory retirement age of 60 for Foreign Service officers, Vance v. Bradley, 440 U.S. 93 (1979), and a provision of the Missouri Constitution requiring nearly all state judges to retire at age 70. Gregory v. Ashcroft, 111 S.Ct. 2395 (1991). In *Gregory* the Court rejected arguments "that the mandatory retirement provision makes two irrational distinctions: between judges who have reached age 70 and younger judges, and between judges 70 and over and other state employees of the same age who are not subject to mandatory retirement." The age distinction was rationally related to Missouri's "legitimate, indeed compelling, interest in maintaining a judiciary fully capable of performing the demanding tasks that judges must perform." The alternatives of voluntary retirement, impeachment, and retention elections rationally could be perceived as inadequate checks on judges

whose performance has declined with advancing age. That judges serve longer terms, often run unopposed, and are less scrutinized by the public rationally explained "the distinction between judges and other state employees, in whom a deterioration in performance is more readily discernible and who are more easily removed." Although it is "probably not true that most" judges "suffer significant deterioration in performance at age 70" and "may not be true at all[,]" the "people of Missouri rationally could conclude that the threat of deterioration at age 70 is sufficiently great, and the alternatives for removal sufficiently inadequate, that they will require all judges to step aside at age 70."

10. As Dean Ely has observed:

"Surely one has to feel sorry for a person disabled by something he or she can't do anything about, but I'm not aware of any reason to suppose that elected officials are unusually unlikely to share that feeling. Moreover, classifications based on physical disability and intelligence are typically accepted as legitimate, even by judges and commentators who assert that immutability is relevant. The explanation, when one is given, is that *those* characteristics (unlike the one the commentator is trying to render suspect) are often relevant to legitimate purposes. At that point there's not much left of the immutability theory, is there?" J. Ely, Democracy and Distrust 150 (1980) (footnote omitted). See also id., at 154–155.

the predicate for such judicial oversight is present where the classification deals with mental retardation.

Second, . . . lawmakers have been addressing their difficulties in a manner that belies a continuing antipathy or prejudice and a corresponding need for more intrusive oversight by the judiciary. Thus, the federal government has not only outlawed discrimination against the mentally retarded in federally funded programs, see § 504 of the Rehabilitation Act of 1973, 29 U.S.C. § 794, but it has also provided the retarded with the right to receive "appropriate treatment, services, and habilitation" in a setting that is "least restrictive of [their] personal liberty." Developmental Disabilities Assistance and Bill of Rights Act, 42 U.S.C. §§ 6010(1), (2). In addition, the government has conditioned federal education funds on a State's assurance that retarded children will enjoy an education that, "to the maximum extent appropriate," is integrated with that of non-mentally retarded children. Education of the Handicapped Act, 20 U.S.C. § 1412(5)(B). The government has also facilitated the hiring of the mentally retarded into the federal civil service by exempting them from the requirement of competitive examination. . . . Texas has similarly enacted legislation that acknowledges the special status of the mentally retarded by conferring certain rights upon them, such as "the right to live in the least restrictive setting appropriate to [their] individual needs and abilities," including "the right to live . . . in a group home." Mentally Retarded Persons Act of 1977. . . .

. . . That a civilized and decent society expects and approves such legislation indicates that governmental consideration of those differences in the vast majority of situations is not only legitimate but desirable. It may be, as CLC contends, that legislation designed to benefit, rather than disadvantage, the retarded would generally withstand examination under a test of heightened scrutiny. The relevant inquiry, however, is whether heightened scrutiny is constitutionally mandated in the first instance. [M]erely requiring the legislature to justify its efforts in these terms may lead it to refrain from acting at all. Much recent legislation intended to benefit the retarded also assumes the need for measures that might be perceived to disadvantage them. The Education of the Handicapped Act, for example, requires an "appropriate" education, not one that is equal in all respects to the education of non-retarded children; clearly, admission to a class that exceeded the abilities of a retarded child would not be appropriate. Similarly, the Developmental Disabilities Assistance Act and the Texas act give the retarded the right to live only in the "least restrictive setting" appropriate to their abilities, implicitly assuming the need for at least some restrictions that would not be imposed on others. Especially given the wide variation in the abilities and needs of the retarded themselves, governmental bodies must have a certain amount of flexibility and freedom from judicial oversight in shaping and limiting their remedial efforts.

Third, the legislative response . . . negates any claim that the mentally retarded are politically powerless in the sense that they have no ability to attract the attention of the lawmakers. . . .

Fourth, if the large and amorphous class of the mentally retarded were deemed quasi-suspect . . ., it would be difficult to find a principled way to distinguish a variety of other groups who have perhaps immutable disabilities setting them off from others, who cannot themselves mandate the desired legislative responses, and who can claim some degree of prejudice from at least part of the public at large. One need mention . . . only the aging, the disabled, the mentally ill, and the infirm. We are reluctant to set out on that course. . . .

. . . Because mental retardation is a characteristic that the government may legitimately take into account in a wide range of decisions, and because both state and federal governments have recently committed themselves to assisting the retarded, we will not presume that any given legislative action, even one that disadvantages retarded individuals, is rooted in considerations that the Constitution will not tolerate.

Our refusal to recognize the retarded as a quasi-suspect class does not leave them entirely unprotected from invidious discrimination[;] legislation that distinguishes between the mentally retarded and others must be rationally related to a legitimate governmental purpose. . . .

IV

. . . We inquire first whether requiring a special use permit . . . in the circumstances here deprives respondents of the equal protection of the laws. If it does, there will be no occasion to decide whether the special use permit provision is facially invalid where the mentally retarded are involved. . . . This is the preferred course of adjudication since it enables courts to avoid making unnecessarily broad constitutional judgments. . . .

. . . The City does not require a special use permit in an R–3 zone for apartment houses, multiple dwellings, boarding and lodging houses, fraternity or sorority houses, dormitories, apartment hotels, hospitals, sanitariums, nursing homes for convalescents or the aged (other than for the insane or feeble-minded or alcoholics or drug addicts), private clubs or fraternal orders, and other specified uses. . . . May the city require the permit for this facility when other care and multiple dwelling facilities are freely permitted?

. . . Because in our view the record does not reveal any rational basis for believing that the . . . home would pose any special threat to the city's legitimate interests, we affirm the judgment below insofar as it holds the ordinance invalid as applied. . . .

The District Court found that the City Council's insistence on the permit rested on several factors. First, the Council was concerned with the negative attitude of the majority of property owners located within 200 feet of the Featherston facility, as well as with the fears of elderly residents of the neighborhood. But mere negative attitudes, or fear, unsubstantiated by factors which are properly cognizable in a zoning proceeding, are not permissible bases for treating a home for the mentally retarded differently from apartment houses, multiple dwellings, and the like. . . . [T]he City may not . . . defer[] to the wishes or objections of some fraction of the body politic. "Private biases may be outside the reach of the law, but the law cannot, directly or indirectly, give them effect." Palmore v. Sidoti, 466 U.S. 429, 433 (1984).

Second, the Council had two objections to the location of the facility. [It] was across the street from a junior high school, and [the Council] feared that the students might harass the occupants. . . . But the school itself is attended by about 30 mentally retarded students, and denying a permit based on such vague, undifferentiated fears is again permitting some portion of the community to validate what would otherwise be an equal protection violation. The other objection to the home's location was that it was located on "a five hundred year flood plain." This concern . . ., however, can hardly be based on a distinction between the Featherston home and, for example, nursing homes, homes for convalescents or the aged, or sanitariums or hospitals. . . . The same may be said of another concern of the Council—doubts about the legal responsibility for actions which the mentally retarded might take. If there is no concern about legal responsibility with respect to other uses . . . such as boarding and fraternity houses, it is difficult to believe that . . . mildly or moderately mentally retarded individuals . . . would present any different or special hazard.

Fourth, . . . [given that] there would be no restrictions on the number of people who could occupy this home as a boarding house, nursing home, family dwelling, fraternity house, or dormitory[,] . . . this record does not clarify how . . . the characteristics of the intended occupants . . . rationally justify denying [them] what would be permitted to groups occupying the same site for different purposes. Th[ey] are the type of individuals who, with supporting staff, satisfy federal and state standards for group housing in the community; and there is no dispute that the home would meet the federal square-footage-per-resident requirement for facilities of this type. . . . In the words of the Court of Appeals, "The City never justifies its apparent view that other people can live under such 'crowded' conditions when mentally retarded persons cannot."

In the courts below the city also urged that the ordinance is aimed at avoiding concentration of population and at lessening congestion of the streets. These concerns obviously fail to explain why apartment houses, fraternity and sorority houses, hospitals and the like, may freely locate in the area without a permit. So, too, the expressed worry about fire hazards, the serenity of the neighborhood, and the avoidance of danger to other residents fail rationally to justify singling out [this] home . . . for the special use permit. . . .

The short of it is that requiring the permit in this case appears to us to rest on an irrational prejudice against the mentally retarded. . . .

The judgment . . . is affirmed insofar as it invalidates the zoning ordinance as applied to the . . . home [and] is otherwise vacated.

It is so ordered.

Justice Stevens, with whom The Chief Justice joins, concurring.

. . . [O]ur cases reflect a continuum of judgmental responses to differing classifications . . . ranging from "strict scrutiny" at one extreme to "rational basis" at the other. I have never been persuaded that these so called "standards" adequately explain the decisional process. Cases involving classifications based on alienage, illegal residency, illegitimacy, gender, age, or—as in this case—mental retardation, do not fit well into sharply defined classifications.

. . .

Every law that places the mentally retarded in a special class is not presumptively irrational. The differences between mentally retarded persons and those with greater mental capacity are obviously relevant to certain legislative decisions. An impartial lawmaker—indeed, even a member of a class of persons defined as mentally retarded—could rationally vote in favor of a law providing funds for special education and special treatment for the mentally retarded. A mentally retarded person could also recognize that he is a member of a class that might need special supervision in some situations, both to protect himself and to protect others. Restrictions on his right to drive cars or to operate hazardous equipment might well seem rational even though they deprived him of employment opportunities and the kind of freedom of travel enjoyed by other citizens. . . .

Even so, the Court of Appeals correctly observed that through ignorance and prejudice the mentally retarded "have been subjected to a history of unfair and often grotesque mistreatment." . . . The record convinces me that this permit was required because of the irrational fears of neighboring property owners, rather than for the protection of the mentally retarded persons who would reside in respondent's home.

. . . In this Court, the city has argued that the discrimination was really motivated by a desire to protect the mentally retarded from the hazards presented by the neighborhood. Zoning ordinances are not usually justified on any such basis, and in this case, for the reasons explained by the Court, I find that justification wholly unconvincing. I cannot believe that a rational member of this disadvantaged class could ever approve of the discriminatory application of the city's ordinance in this case.

Accordingly, I join the opinion of the Court.

Justice Marshall, with whom Justice Brennan and Justice Blackmun join, concurring in the judgment in part and dissenting in part.

. . .

I cannot agree ... with the way in which the Court reaches its result or with the narrow, as-applied remedy it provides.... The Court ... disclaims that anything special, in the form of heightened scrutiny, is taking place. Yet Cleburne's ordinance surely would be valid under the traditional rational basis test applicable to economic and commercial regulation. In my view, it is important to articulate, as the Court does not, the facts and principles that justify subjecting this zoning ordinance to the searching review—the heightened scrutiny—that actually leads to its invalidation. Moreover, in invalidating Cleburne's exclusion of the "feebleminded" only as applied ..., rather than on its face, the Court radically departs from our equal protection precedents....

I

. . .

I share the Court's criticisms of the overly broad lines that Cleburne's zoning ordinance has drawn. But if the ordinance is to be invalidated for its imprecise classifications, it must be pursuant to more powerful scrutiny than the minimal rational-basis test used to review classifications affecting only economic and commercial matters. The same imprecision in a similar ordinance that required opticians but not optometrists to be licensed to practice, see *Williamson v. Lee Optical Co.,* supra, or that excluded new but not old businesses from parts of a community, see *New Orleans v. Dukes,* supra, would hardly be fatal to the statutory scheme.

The refusal to acknowledge that something more than minimum rationality review is at work here is ... unfortunate in at least two respects. [It] creates precedent ... to subject economic and commercial classifications to similar and searching "ordinary" rational basis review—a small and regrettable step back toward the days of Lochner v. New York, 198 U.S.45 (1905). Moreover, by failing to articulate the factors that justify today's "second order" rational basis review, the Court provides no principled foundation for determining when more searching inquiry is to be invoked....

II

I have long believed the level of scrutiny employed in an equal protection case should vary with "the constitutional and societal importance of the interest adversely affected and the recognized invidiousness of the basis upon which the particular classification is drawn." San Antonio Independent School District v. Rodriguez, 411 U.S. 1, 99 (1973) (Marshall, J., dissenting).... When a zoning ordinance works to exclude the retarded from all residential districts in a community, these two considerations require that the ordinance be convincingly justified as substantially furthering legitimate and important purposes....

First, the interest of the retarded in establishing group homes is substantial. The right to "establish a home" has long been cherished as one of the fundamental liberties embraced by the Due Process Clause. See Meyer v. Nebraska, 262 U.S. 390, 399 (1923). For retarded adults, this right means living together in group homes, for as deinstitutionalization has progressed, group homes have become the primary means by which retarded adults can enter life in the community. . . .

Second, the mentally retarded have been subject to a "lengthy and tragic history," University of California Regents v. Bakke, 438 U.S. 265, 303 (1978) (opinion of Powell, J.), of segregation and discrimination that can only be called grotesque. During much of the nineteenth century, mental retardation was viewed as neither curable nor dangerous and the retarded were largely left to their own devices. By the latter part of the century and during the first decades of the new one, however, social views of the retarded underwent a radical transformation. Fueled by the rising tide of Social Darwinism, the "science" of eugenics, and the extreme xenophobia of those years, leading medical authorities and others began to portray the "feeble minded" as a "menace to society and civilization . . . responsible in a large degree for many, if not all, of our social problems." A regime of state-mandated segregation and degradation soon emerged that in its virulence and bigotry rivaled, and indeed paralleled, the worst excesses of Jim Crow. Massive custodial institutions were built to warehouse the retarded for life; the aim was to halt reproduction of the retarded and "nearly extinguish their race." Retarded children were categorically excluded from public schools, based on the false stereotype that all were ineducable and on the purported need to protect nonretarded children from them. State laws deemed the retarded "unfit for citizenship."

Segregation was accompanied by eugenic marriage and sterilization laws that extinguished for the retarded one of the "basic civil rights of man"—the right to marry and procreate. Skinner v. Oklahoma, 316 U.S. 535, 541 (1942). Marriages of the retarded were made, and in some states continue to be, not only voidable but also often a criminal offense. The purpose of such limitations, which frequently applied only to women of child bearing age, was unabashedly eugenic: to prevent the retarded from propagating. To assure this end, 29 states enacted compulsory eugenic sterilization laws between 1907 and 1931. J. Landman, Human Sterilization 302–303 (1932). See Buck v. Bell, 274 U.S. 200, 207 (1927) (Holmes, J.); cf. Plessy v. Ferguson, 163 U.S. 537 (1896); Bradwell v. Illinois, 16 Wall. 130, 141 (1873) (Bradley, J., concurring in judgment).

Prejudice, once let loose, is not easily cabined. . . . As of 1979, most states still categorically disqualified "idiots" from voting, without regard to individual capacity and with discretion to exclude left in the hands of low-level election officials. Not until Congress enacted the Education of the Handicapped Act . . . were "the door[s] of public education" opened wide to handicapped children. Hendrick Hudson District Board of Education v. Rowley, 458 U.S. 176, 192 (1982). But most important, lengthy and continuing isolation of the retarded has perpetuated the ignorance, irrational fears, and stereotyping that long have plagued them.

In light of the importance of the interest at stake and the history of discrimination the retarded have suffered, the Equal Protection Clause requires us to do more than review the distinctions drawn by Cleburne's zoning ordinance as if they appeared in a taxing statute or in economic or commercial legislation.[17] The searching scrutiny I would give to restrictions on the ability

---

17. This history of discrimination may well be directly relevant to the issue before the Court. . . . [Its] genealogy strongly suggests that Cleburne's current exclusion of the of the retarded to establish community group homes leads me to conclude that Cleburne's vague generalizations for classifying the "feeble minded" with drug addicts, alcoholics, and the insane, and excluding them where the elderly, the ill, the boarder, and the transient are allowed, are not substantial or important enough to overcome the suspicion that the ordinance rests on impermissible assumptions or outmoded and perhaps invidious stereotypes....

III

. . .

The Court downplays the lengthy "history of purposeful unequal treatment" of the retarded, ... by pointing to recent legislative action that is said to "beli[e] a continuing antipathy or prejudice." ...

... Shifting cultural, political, and social patterns at times come to make past practices appear inconsistent with fundamental principles upon which American society rests, an inconsistency legally cognizable under the Equal Protection Clause. It is natural that evolving standards of equality come to be embodied in legislation. When that occurs, courts should look to the fact of such change as a source of guidance on evolving principles of equality....

. . .

[L]egislative change ... certainly does not eviscerate the underlying constitutional principle. The Court, for example, has never suggested that race-based classifications became any less suspect once extensive legislation had been enacted on the subject. See Palmore v. Sidoti, 466 U.S. 429 (1984).

For the retarded, just as for Negroes and women, much has changed in recent years, but much remains the same; out-dated statutes are still on the books, and irrational fears or ignorance, traceable to the prolonged social and cultural isolation of the retarded, continue to stymie recognition of the dignity and individuality of retarded people. Heightened judicial scrutiny of action appearing to impose unnecessary barriers to the retarded is required in light of increasing recognition that such barriers are inconsistent with evolving principles of equality embedded in the Fourteenth Amendment.

. . .

IV

In light of the scrutiny that should be applied here, Cleburne's ordinance sweeps too broadly to dispel the suspicion that it rests on a bare desire to treat the retarded as outsiders, pariahs who do not belong in the community.... [H]owever, the Court invalidates it merely as applied.... I must dissent from the novel proposition that "the preferred course of adjudication" is to leave standing a legislative act resting on "irrational prejudice" thereby forcing individuals in the group discriminated against to continue to run the act's gauntlet.

. . .

"feeble minded" was written in the darkest days of segregation and stigmatization of the retarded and simply carried over to the current ordinance. Recently we held that extant laws originally motivated by a discriminatory purpose continue to violate the Equal Protection Clause, even if they would be permissible were they reenacted without a discriminatory motive. See Hunter v. Underwood, 471 U.S. 222, 233 (1985). But in any event, the roots of a law that by its terms excludes from a community the "feeble minded" are clear....

Invalidating on its face the ordinance's special treatment of the "feeble-minded", in contrast, would place the responsibility for tailoring and updating Cleburne's unconstitutional ordinance where it belongs: with the legislative arm of the City of Cleburne.... [It] might separate group homes (presently treated nowhere in the ordinance) from hospitals, and it might define a narrow sub-class of the retarded for whom even group homes could legitimately be excluded. Special treatment of the retarded might be ended altogether. But whatever the contours such an ordinance might take, the city should not be allowed to keep its ordinance on the books intact and thereby shift to the courts the responsibility to confront the complex empirical and policy questions involved in updating statutes affecting the mentally retarded. A legislative solution would yield standards and provide the sort of certainty to retarded applicants and administrative officials that case-by-case judicial rulings cannot provide. Retarded applicants should not have to continue to attempt to surmount Cleburne's vastly overbroad ordinance.

. . .

HELLER v. DOE, 509 U.S. 312 (1993). The report in this case appears *supra* at p. 704.

Romer v. Evans

517 U.S. 620, 116 S.Ct. 1620, 134 L.Ed.2d 855 (1996).

Justice Kennedy delivered the opinion of the Court.

One century ago, the first Justice Harlan admonished this Court that the Constitution "neither knows nor tolerates classes among citizens." Plessy v. Ferguson, 163 U.S. 537, 559 (1896) (dissenting opinion). Unheeded then, those words now are understood to state a commitment to the law's neutrality where the rights of persons are at stake. The Equal Protection Clause enforces this principle and today requires us to hold invalid a provision of Colorado's Constitution.

I

[A]n amendment to the Constitution of ... Colorado, adopted in a 1992 statewide referendum ... as "Amendment 2," ... [stemmed] in large part from ordinances that had been passed in various Colorado municipalities[,] bann[ing] discrimination in many transactions and activities, including housing, employment, education, public accommodations, and health and welfare services.... What gave rise to the statewide controversy was the protection ... afforded to persons discriminated against by reason of their sexual orientation....

Yet Amendment 2, in explicit terms, does more than repeal or rescind these provisions. It prohibits all legislative, executive or judicial action at any level of state or local government designed to protect the named class, a class we shall refer to as homosexual persons or gays and lesbians. The amendment reads:

"No Protected Status Based on Homosexual, Lesbian, or Bisexual Orientation. Neither the State of Colorado, through any of its branches or departments, nor any of its agencies, political subdivisions, municipalities or school districts, shall enact, adopt or enforce any statute, regulation, ordinance or policy whereby homosexual, lesbian or bisexual orientation, conduct, practices or relationships shall constitute or otherwise be the basis of or entitle any person or class of persons to have or claim any minority status, quota preferences, protected status or claim of discrimination. This Section of the Constitution shall be in all respects self-executing." ...

Soon after Amendment 2 was adopted, this litigation to declare its invalidity and enjoin its enforcement was commenced in [state court by] homosexual persons, some of them government employees[, and by] governmental entities which had acted earlier to protect homosexuals from discrimination but would be prevented by Amendment 2 from continuing to do so.....

The trial court granted a preliminary injunction.... [On appeal, s]ustaining the interim injunction and remanding the case for further proceedings, the State Supreme Court held that Amendment 2 was subject to strict scrutiny under the Fourteenth Amendment because it infringed the fundamental right of gays and lesbians to participate in the political process.... To reach this conclusion, the state court relied on our voting rights cases, e.g., Reynolds v. Sims, 377 U.S. 533 (1964); Carrington v. Rash, 380 U.S. 89 (1965); Harper v. Virginia Bd. of Elections, 383 U.S. 663 (1966); Williams v. Rhodes, 393 U.S. 23 (1968), and on our precedents involving discriminatory restructuring of governmental decisionmaking, see, e.g., Hunter v. Erickson, 393 U.S. 385 (1969); Reitman v. Mulkey, 387 U.S. 369 (1967); Washington v. Seattle School Dist. No. 1, 458 U.S. 457 (1982); Gordon v. Lance, 403 U.S. 1 (1971). On remand, the State advanced various arguments in an effort to show that Amendment 2 was narrowly tailored to serve compelling interests, but the trial court found none sufficient. It enjoined enforcement of Amendment 2, and the Supreme Court of Colorado ... affirmed.... We ... affirm ..., but on a rationale different from that adopted by the State Supreme Court.

II

The State's principal argument in defense of Amendment 2 is that it puts gays and lesbians in the same position as all other persons. So, the State says, the measure does no more than deny homosexuals special rights. This reading of the amendment's language is implausible. We rely ... upon the authoritative construction of Colorado's Supreme Court[, which] ... found it invalid even on a modest reading of its implications....

"The immediate objective of Amendment 2 is, at a minimum, to repeal existing statutes, regulations, ordinances, and policies of state and local entities that barred discrimination based on sexual orientation....

"The 'ultimate effect' of Amendment 2 is to prohibit any governmental entity from adopting similar, or more protective statutes, regulations, ordinances, or policies in the future unless the state constitution is first amended to permit such measures." ...

Sweeping and comprehensive is the change in legal status effected by this law.... Homosexuals, by state decree, are put in a solitary class with respect to transactions and relations in both the private and governmental spheres. The amendment withdraws from homosexuals, but no others, specific legal protection from the injuries caused by discrimination, and it forbids reinstatement of these laws and policies.

The change that Amendment 2 works in the legal status of gays and lesbians in the private sphere is far-reaching, both on its own terms and when considered in light of the structure and operation of modern anti-discrimination laws.... [M]ost States have chosen to counter discrimination by enacting detailed statutory schemes....

Colorado's state and municipal laws typify this emerging tradition of statutory protection.... The laws first enumerate the persons or entities subject to a duty not to discriminate.... The Boulder ordinance, for example, has a comprehensive definition of entities deemed places of "public accommodation." ... The Denver ordinance is of similar breadth, applying, for example, to hotels, restaurants, hospitals, dental clinics, theaters, banks, common carriers, travel and insurance agencies, and "shops and stores dealing with goods or services of any kind,"....

These statutes and ordinances also depart from the common law by enumerating the groups or persons within their ambit of protection.... Colorado's state and local governments have not limited anti-discrimination laws to groups that have so far been given the protection of heightened equal protection scrutiny under our cases.... Rather, they set forth an extensive catalogue of traits which cannot be the basis for discrimination, including age, military status, marital status, pregnancy, parenthood, custody of a minor child, political affiliation, physical or mental disability of an individual or of his or her associates—and, in recent times, sexual orientation....

Amendment 2 bars homosexuals from securing protection against the injuries that these public-accommodations laws address ... [and] nullifies specific legal protections for this targeted class in all transactions in housing, sale of real estate, insurance, health and welfare services, private education, and employment....

Not confined to the private sphere, Amendment 2 also operates to repeal and forbid all laws or policies providing specific protection for gays or lesbians from discrimination by every level of Colorado government. The State Supreme Court cited two examples[—]... Colorado Executive Order D0035 (1990), which forbids employment discrimination against " 'all state employees, classified and exempt' on the basis of sexual orientation[,]" [and] "various provisions prohibiting discrimination based on sexual orientation at state colleges." ... The repeal of these measures and the prohibition against their future reenactment demonstrates that Amendment 2 has the same force and effect in Colorado's governmental sector as it does elsewhere and that it applies to policies as well as ordinary legislation.

Amendment 2's reach may not be limited to specific laws passed for the benefit of gays and lesbians. It is a fair, if not necessary, inference from the broad language of the amendment that it deprives gays and lesbians even of the protection of general laws and policies that prohibit arbitrary discrimination in governmental and private settings.... At some point in the systematic administration of these laws, an official must determine whether homosexuality is an arbitrary and thus forbidden basis for decision. Yet a decision to that effect would itself amount to a policy prohibiting discrimination on the basis of homosexuality, and so would appear to be no more valid under Amendment 2 than the specific prohibitions against discrimination the state court held invalid.

If this consequence follows from Amendment 2, as its broad language suggests, it would compound the constitutional difficulties the law creates. The state court did not decide whether the amendment has this effect, however, and neither need we. In the course of rejecting the argument that Amendment 2 is intended to conserve resources to fight discrimination against suspect classes, the Colorado Supreme Court made the limited observation that the amendment is not intended to affect many anti-discrimination laws protecting non-suspect classes.... In our view that does not resolve the issue. In any event, even if, as we doubt, homosexuals could find some safe harbor in laws of general application, we cannot accept the view that Amendment 2's prohibition on specific legal protections does no more than deprive homosexuals of special rights. To the contrary, the amendment imposes a special disability upon those persons alone. Homosexuals are forbidden the safeguards that others enjoy or may seek without constraint. They can obtain specific protection against discrimination only by enlisting the citizenry of Colorado to amend the state constitution or perhaps, on the State's view, by trying to pass helpful laws of general applicability. This is so no matter how local or discrete the harm, no matter how public and widespread the injury. We find nothing special in the protections Amendment 2 withholds. These are protections taken for granted by most people either because they already have them or do not need them; these are protections against exclusion from an almost limitless number of transactions and endeavors that constitute ordinary civic life in a free society.

III

The Fourteenth Amendment's promise that no person shall be denied the equal protection of the laws must co-exist with the practical necessity that most legislation classifies for one purpose or another, with resulting disadvantage to various groups or persons.... We have attempted to reconcile the principle with the reality by stating that, if a law neither burdens a fundamental right nor targets a suspect class, we will uphold the legislative classification so long as it bears a rational relation to some legitimate end. See, e.g., Heller v. Doe, 509 U.S. 312, 319–320 (1993).

Amendment 2 fails, indeed defies, even this conventional inquiry. First, the amendment has the peculiar property of imposing a broad and undifferentiated disability on a single named group, an exceptional and, as we shall explain, invalid form of legislation. Second, its sheer breadth is so discontinuous with the reasons offered for it that the amendment seems inexplicable by anything but animus toward the class that it affects; it lacks a rational relationship to legitimate state interests.

Taking the first point, even in the ordinary equal protection case calling for the most deferential of standards, we insist on knowing the relation between the classification adopted and the object to be attained. The search for the link between classification and objective gives substance to the Equal Protection Clause; it provides guidance and discipline for the legislature, which is entitled to know what sorts of laws it can pass; and it marks the limits of our own authority. In the ordinary case, a law will be sustained if it can be said to advance a legitimate government interest, even if the law seems unwise or works to the disadvantage of a particular group, or if the rationale for it seems tenuous. See New Orleans v. Dukes, 427 U.S. 297 (1976) ...; Williamson v. Lee Optical of Okla., Inc., 348 U.S. 483 (1955) ...; Railway Express Agency, Inc. v. New York, 336 U.S. 106 (1949).... The laws challenged in the cases just cited were narrow enough in scope and grounded in a sufficient factual context for us to ascertain that there existed some relation between the classification and the purpose it served. By requiring that the classification bear a rational relationship to an independent and legitimate legislative end, we ensure that classifications are not drawn for the purpose of disadvantaging the group burdened by the law....

Amendment 2 confounds this normal process of judicial review. It is at once too narrow and too broad. It identifies persons by a single trait and then denies them protection across the board. The resulting disqualification of a class of persons from the right to seek specific protection from the law is unprecedented in our jurisprudence....

It is not within our constitutional tradition to enact laws of this sort. Central both to the idea of the rule of law and to our own Constitution's guarantee of equal protection is the principle that government and each of its parts remain open on impartial terms to all who seek its assistance.... Respect for this principle explains why laws singling out a certain class of citizens for disfavored legal status or general hardships are rare. A law declaring that in general it shall be more difficult for one group of citizens than for all others to seek aid from the government is itself a denial of equal protection of the laws in the most literal sense....

Davis v. Beason, 133 U.S. 333 (1890), not cited by the parties but relied upon by the dissent, is not evidence that Amendment 2 is within our constitutional tradition, and any reliance upon it as authority for sustaining the amendment is misplaced. In *Davis*, the Court approved an Idaho territorial statute denying Mormons, polygamists, and advocates of polygamy the right to vote and to hold office because, as the Court construed the statute, it "simply excludes from the privilege of voting, or of holding any office of honor, trust or profit, those who have been convicted of certain offences, and those who advocate a practical resistance to the laws of the Territory and justify and approve the commission of crimes forbidden by it." ... To the extent *Davis* held that persons advocating a certain practice may be denied the right to vote, it is no longer good law. Brandenburg v. Ohio, 395 U.S. 444 (1969) (per curiam). To the extent it held that the groups designated in the statute may be deprived of the right to vote because of their status, its ruling could not stand without surviving strict scrutiny, a most doubtful outcome.... To the extent *Davis* held that a convicted felon may be denied the right to vote, its holding is not implicated by our decision and is unexceptionable. See Richardson v. Ramirez, 418 U.S. 24 (1974).

A second and related point is that laws of the kind now before us raise the inevitable inference that the disadvantage imposed is born of animosity toward the class of persons affected. "[I]f the constitutional conception of 'equal protection of the laws' means anything, it must at the very least mean that a bare ... desire to harm a politically unpopular group cannot constitute a legitimate governmental interest." Department of Agriculture v. Moreno, 413 U.S. 528, 534 (1973). Even laws enacted for broad and ambitious purposes often can be explained by reference to legitimate public policies which justify the incidental disadvantages they impose on certain persons. Amendment 2, however, in making a general announcement that gays and lesbians shall not have any particular protections from the law, inflicts on them immediate, continuing, and real injuries that outrun and belie any legitimate justifications that may be claimed for it. We conclude that, in addition to the far-reaching deficiencies of Amendment 2 that we have noted, the principles it offends, in another sense, are conventional and venerable; a law must bear a rational relationship to a legitimate governmental purpose, ... and Amendment 2 does not.

The primary rationale the State offers for Amendment 2 is respect for other citizens' freedom of association, and in particular the liberties of landlords or employers who have personal or religious objections to homosexuality. Colorado also cites its interest in conserving resources to fight discrimination against other groups. The breadth of the Amendment is so far removed from these particular justifications that we find it impossible to credit them. We cannot say that Amendment 2 is directed to any identifiable legitimate purpose or discrete objective. It is a status-based enactment divorced from any factual context from which we could discern a relationship to legitimate state interests; it is a classification of persons undertaken for its own sake, something the Equal Protection Clause does not permit....

We must conclude that Amendment 2 classifies homosexuals not to further a proper legislative end but to make them unequal to everyone else. This Colorado cannot do. A State cannot so deem a class of persons a stranger to its laws. Amendment 2 violates the Equal Protection Clause, and the judgment of the Supreme Court of Colorado is affirmed.

. . .

Justice Scalia, with whom The Chief Justice and Justice Thomas join, dissenting.

The Court has mistaken a Kulturkampf for a fit of spite. The constitutional amendment before us here is not the manifestation of a " 'bare . . . desire to harm' " homosexuals, but is rather a modest attempt by seemingly tolerant Coloradans to preserve traditional sexual mores against the efforts of a politically powerful minority to revise those mores through use of the laws. That objective, and the means chosen to achieve it, are not only unimpeachable under any constitutional doctrine hitherto pronounced . . .; they have been specifically approved by the Congress of the United States and by this Court.

In holding that homosexuality cannot be singled out for disfavorable treatment, the Court contradicts a decision, unchallenged here, pronounced only 10 years ago, see Bowers v. Hardwick, 478 U.S. 186 (1986), and places the prestige of this institution behind the proposition that opposition to homosexuality is as reprehensible as racial or religious bias. Whether it is or not is precisely the cultural debate that gave rise to the Colorado constitutional amendment (and to the preferential laws against which the amendment was directed). Since the Constitution of the United States says nothing about this subject, it is left to be resolved by normal democratic means, including the democratic adoption of provisions in state constitutions. This Court has no business imposing upon all Americans the resolution favored by the elite class from which the Members of this institution are selected, pronouncing that "animosity" toward homosexuality is evil. I vigorously dissent.

I

. . .

. . . The clear import of the Colorado court's [decision] is that "general laws and policies that prohibit arbitrary discrimination" would continue to prohibit discrimination on the basis of homosexual conduct as well. . . . The amendment prohibits *special treatment* of homosexuals, and nothing more. It would not affect, for example, a requirement of state law that pensions be paid to all retiring state employees with a certain length of service; homosexual employees, as well as others, would be entitled to that benefit. But it would prevent the State or any municipality from making death-benefit payments to the "life partner" of a homosexual when it does not make such payments to the long-time roommate of a nonhomosexual employee. Or again, it does not affect the requirement of the State's general insurance laws that customers be afforded coverage without discrimination unrelated to anticipated risk. Thus, homosexuals could not be denied coverage, or charged a greater premium, with respect to auto collision insurance; but neither the State nor any municipality could require that distinctive health insurance risks associated with homosexuality (if there are any) be ignored.

[T]he Court's opinion ultimately does not dispute all this, but assumes it to be true. The only denial of equal treatment it contends homosexuals have suffered is this: They may not obtain *preferential treatment* without amending the state constitution. That is to say, the principle underlying the Court's opinion is that one who is accorded equal treatment under the laws, but cannot as readily as others obtain *preferential treatment* under the laws, has been denied equal protection of the laws. If merely stating this alleged "equal protection" violation does not suffice to refute it, our constitutional jurisprudence has achieved terminal silliness.

The central thesis of the Court's reasoning is that any group is denied equal protection when, to obtain advantage (or, presumably, to avoid disadvantage), it must have recourse to a more general and hence more difficult level of political decisionmaking than others. The world has never heard of such a principle.... And it seems to me most unlikely that any multilevel democracy can function under such a principle. For whenever a disadvantage is imposed, or conferral of a benefit is prohibited, at one of the higher levels of democratic decisionmaking (i.e., by the state legislature rather than local government, or by the people at large in the state constitution rather than the legislature), the affected group has (under this theory) been denied equal protection. [C]onsider a state law prohibiting the award of municipal contracts to relatives of mayors or city councilmen. Once ... passed, ... relatives must, in order to get the benefit of city contracts, persuade the state legislature—unlike all other citizens, who need only persuade the municipality. It is ridiculous to consider this a denial of equal protection....

The Court might reply that the example I have given is *not* a denial of equal protection only because the same "rational basis" (avoidance of corruption) which renders constitutional the *substantive discrimination* against relatives (i.e., the fact that they alone cannot obtain city contracts) also automatically suffices to sustain what might be called the *electoral-procedural discrimination* against them (i.e., the fact that they must go to the state level to get this changed). This is of course a perfectly reasonable response, and would explain why "electoral-procedural discrimination" has not hitherto been heard of: a law that is valid in its substance is automatically valid in its level of enactment. But the Court cannot afford to make this argument, for as I shall discuss next, there is no doubt of a rational basis for the substance of the prohibition at issue here. The Court's entire novel theory rests upon the proposition that there is something *special*—something that cannot be justified by normal "rational basis" analysis—in making a disadvantaged group (or a nonpreferred group) resort to a higher decisionmaking level. That proposition finds no support in law or logic.

II

I turn next to whether there was a legitimate rational basis for the substance of the constitutional amendment—for the prohibition of special protection for homosexuals.[18] It is unsurprising that the Court avoids discussion of this question, since the answer is so obviously yes. The case most relevant to the issue before us today is not even mentioned in the Court's opinion: In Bowers v. Hardwick, 478 U.S. 186 (1986), we held that the Constitution does not prohibit what virtually all States had done from the founding of the Republic until very recent years—making homosexual conduct a crime.... If it is constitutionally permissible for a State to make homosexual conduct criminal, surely it is constitutionally permissible for a State to enact

---

18. The Court evidently agrees that "rational basis" ... is the governing standard. The trial court rejected respondents' argument that homosexuals constitute a "suspect" or "quasi-suspect" class, and respondents elected not to appeal that ruling to the Supreme Court of Colorado.... And the Court implicitly rejects the Supreme Court of Colorado's holding ... that Amendment 2 infringes upon a "fundamental right" of "independently identifiable class[es]" to "participate equally in the political process."

other laws merely *disfavoring* homosexual conduct.... And *a fortiori* it is constitutionally permissible for a State to adopt a provision *not even* disfavoring homosexual conduct, but merely prohibiting all levels of state government from bestowing *special protections* upon homosexual conduct. Respondents ... counter *Bowers* with the argument that a greater-includes-the-lesser rationale cannot justify Amendment 2's application to individuals who do not engage in homosexual acts, but are merely of homosexual "orientation." ...

But assuming that, in Amendment 2, a person of homosexual "orientation" is someone who does not engage in homosexual conduct but merely has a tendency or desire to do so, *Bowers* still suffices to establish a rational basis for the provision. If it is rational to criminalize the conduct, surely it is rational to deny special favor and protection to those with a self-avowed tendency or desire to engage in the conduct. Indeed, where criminal sanctions are not involved, homosexual "orientation" is an acceptable stand-in for homosexual conduct.... Just as a policy barring the hiring of methadone users as transit employees does not violate equal protection simply because some methadone users pose no threat to passenger safety, see New York City Transit Authority v. Beazer, 440 U.S. 568 (1979), ... Amendment 2 is not constitutionally invalid simply because it could have been drawn more precisely so as to withdraw special antidiscrimination protections only from those of homosexual "orientation" who actually engage in homosexual conduct....

Moreover, even if the provision regarding homosexual "orientation" *were* invalid, respondents' challenge to Amendment 2—which is a facial challenge— must fail.... It would not be enough ... that Amendment 2 is unconstitutional as applied to those of homosexual "orientation"; since, under *Bowers*, Amendment 2 is unquestionably constitutional as applied to those who engage in homosexual conduct, the facial challenge cannot succeed....

III

... What [Colorado] has done is not only unprohibited, but eminently reasonable, with close, congressionally approved precedent in earlier constitutional practice.

First, ... I had thought that one could consider certain conduct reprehensible—murder, for example, or polygamy, or cruelty to animals—and could exhibit even "animus" toward such conduct. Surely that is the only sort of "animus" at issue here: moral disapproval of homosexual conduct, the same sort of moral disapproval that produced the centuries-old criminal laws that we held constitutional in *Bowers*. The Colorado amendment does not, to speak entirely precisely, prohibit giving favored status to people who are *homosexuals*; they can be favored for many reasons—for example, because they are senior citizens or members of racial minorities. But it prohibits giving them favored status *because of their homosexual conduct*—that is, it prohibits favored status *for homosexuality*.

But ... the degree of hostility reflected by Amendment 2 is the smallest conceivable. The Court's portrayal of Coloradans as a society fallen victim to pointless, hate-filled "gay-bashing" is so false as to be comical. Colorado not only is one of the 25 States that have repealed their antisodomy laws, but was among the first to do so.... But the society that eliminates criminal punishment for homosexual acts does not necessarily abandon the view that homosexuality is morally wrong and socially harmful; often, abolition simply reflects the view that enforcement of such criminal laws involves unseemly intrusion into the intimate lives of citizens....

... The problem ... for those who wish to retain social disapprobation of homosexuality ... is that, because those who engage in homosexual conduct tend to reside in disproportionate numbers in certain communities, ... have high disposable income, ... and of course care about homosexual-rights issues much more ardently than the public at large, they possess political power much greater than their numbers, both locally and statewide. Quite understandably, they devote this political power to achieving not merely a grudging social toleration, but full social acceptance, of homosexuality....

By the time Coloradans were asked to vote on Amendment 2, ... Aspen, Boulder, and Denver ... had enacted ordinances that listed "sexual orientation" as an impermissible ground for discrimination, equating the moral disapproval of homosexual conduct with racial and religious bigotry.... The ... Governor ... had signed an executive order pronouncing that "in the State of Colorado we recognize the diversity in our pluralistic society and strive to bring an end to discrimination in any form," and directing state agency-heads to "ensure non-discrimination" in hiring and promotion based on, among other things, "sexual orientation." ... I do not mean to be critical of these legislative successes; homosexuals are as entitled to use the legal system for reinforcement of their moral sentiments as are the rest of society. But they are subject to being countered by lawful, democratic countermeasures as well.

... Amendment 2 ... sought to counter both the geographic concentration and the disproportionate political power of homosexuals by (1) resolving the controversy at the statewide level, and (2) making the election a single-issue contest for both sides.... The Court today asserts that this most democratic of procedures ... *must* be unconstitutional, because it has never happened before.... [T]his is proved false every time a state law prohibiting or disfavoring certain conduct is passed, because such a law prevents the adversely affected group—whether drug addicts, or smokers, or gun owners, or motorcyclists—from changing the policy thus established in "each of [the] parts" of the State....

But ... a much closer analogy ... involves precisely the effort by the majority of citizens to preserve its view of sexual morality statewide, against the efforts of a geographically concentrated and politically powerful minority to undermine it. The constitutions of ... Arizona, Idaho, New Mexico, Oklahoma, and Utah *to this day* contain provisions stating that polygamy is "forever prohibited." ... Polygamists, and those who have a polygamous "orientation," have been "singled out" by these provisions for much more severe treatment than merely denial of favored status; and that treatment can only be changed by achieving amendment of the state constitutions. The Court's disposition today suggests that these provisions are unconstitutional, and that polygamy must be permitted in these States on a state-legislated, or perhaps even local-option, basis—unless, of course, polygamists for some reason have fewer constitutional rights than homosexuals.

... Congress ... *required* the inclusion of ... antipolygamy provisions in the constitutions ... as a condition of their admission to statehood.... Thus, this "singling out" of the sexual practices of a single group for statewide, democratic vote ... has not only happened, but has received the explicit approval of ... Congress.

I cannot say that this Court has explicitly approved any of these state constitutional provisions; but it has approved a territorial statutory provision that went even further, depriving polygamists of the ability even to achieve a constitutional amendment, by depriving them of the power to vote. In Davis v. Beason, 133 U.S. 333 (1890), Justice Field wrote for a unanimous Court[,] ...

reject[ing] the argument that "such discrimination is a denial of the equal protection of the laws." ...[3]

This Court cited *Beason* with approval as recently as 1993, in an opinion authored by the same Justice who writes for the Court today. That opinion said: "[A]dverse impact will not always lead to a finding of impermissible targeting. For example, a social harm may have been a legitimate concern of government for reasons quite apart from discrimination.... See, e.g., ... Davis v. Beason, 133 U.S. 333 (1890)." Church of Lukumi Babalu Aye, Inc. v. Hialeah, 508 U.S. 520, 535 (1993). It remains to be explained how § 501 of the Idaho Revised Statutes was not an "impermissible targeting" of polygamists, but (the much more mild) Amendment 2 is an "impermissible targeting" of homosexuals. Has the Court concluded that the perceived social harm of polygamy is a "legitimate concern of government," and the perceived social harm of homosexuality is not?

. . .

Lawrence v. Texas

539 U.S. 558, 123 S.Ct. 2472, 156 L.Ed.2d 508 (2003).

[The report in this case appears supra at p. 664.]

WEALTH CLASSIFICATIONS

Legislative classifications disadvantaging the poor most frequently take the form of financial charges applied to the indigent as well as the relatively more affluent, or withholding of welfare or other assistance from some indigents but not others. As a result, the issues normally involve disproportionate impact on the poor rather than explicit disadvantaging of them. Implicitly, these issues may involve whether equal protection not only requires treating similarly situated people similarly, but differently situated people differently, and whether the Constitution imposes affirmative obligations to assist the poor. The due process and equal protection dimensions of issues of poverty and the provision of government benefits and services are more fully discussed infra in section 4. D. (p. 1055).

The Court generally states, however, that wealth classifications are not suspect. In Harper v. Virginia State Board of Elections, 383 U.S. 663 (1966) (set out fully infra p. 998), the Court did hold it a denial of equal protection to condition the right to vote in state elections on payment of a poll tax. Justice Douglas' opinion for the Court said: "Lines drawn on the basis of wealth or property, like those of race ..., are traditionally disfavored." But subsequently, in other contexts, the Court has not followed this approach. In Ortwein v. Schwab, 410 U.S. 656 (1973), for example, the Court upheld a $25 state

---

3. ... The Court ... claim[s] that "[t]o the extent [*Beason*]held that the groups designated in the statute may be deprived of the right to vote because of their status, its ruling could not stand without surviving strict scrutiny, a most doubtful outcome." But if that is so, it is only because we have declared the right to vote to be a "fundamental political right," see, e.g., Dunn v. Blumstein, 405 U.S. 330, 336 (1972), deprivation of which triggers strict scrutiny. Amendment 2, of course, does not deny the fundamental right to vote, and the Court rejects the Colorado court's view that there exists a fundamental right to participate in the political process. Strict scrutiny is thus not in play here. Finally, the Court's suggestion that § 501 of the Revised Statutes of Idaho, and Amendment 2, deny rights on account of "status" (rather than conduct) opens up a broader debate involving the significance of *Bowers* to this case, a debate which the Court is otherwise unwilling to join.

appellate court filing fee as applied to an indigent challenging a welfare agency determination. The Court said: "No suspect classification, such as race, nationality, or alienage, is present.... The applicable standard is that of rational justification." Similarly, in Harris v. McRae, 448 U.S. 297 (1980) (set out fully infra p. 1065), the Court rejected an equal protection challenge to a federal statute prohibiting the expenditure of federal funds for abortions, despite conceding that the principal impact "falls on the indigent." The Court said that "that fact does not itself render the funding restriction constitutionally invalid, for this Court has held repeatedly that poverty, standing alone, is not a suspect classification. See, e.g., James v. Valtierra, 402 U.S. 137." Most recently, in Kadrmas v. Dickinson Public Schools, 487 U.S. 450 (1988), the Court rejected an indigent's equal protection challenge to a fee for bus service from a student's home to school. The Court declined "to apply a form of strict or 'heightened' scrutiny" and said: "We have previously rejected the suggestion that statutes having different effects on the wealthy and the poor should on that account alone be subjected to strict equal protection scrutiny. See, e.g., Harris v. McRae ...; Ortwein v. Schwab...."

SECTION 4. PROTECTION OF PERSONAL LIBERTIES

A. EQUAL PROTECTION AND RIGHTS SECURED BY OTHER CONSTITUTIONAL PROVISIONS

Zablocki v. Redhail

434 U.S. 374, 98 S.Ct. 673, 54 L.Ed.2d 618 (1978).

[The report in this case appears supra at p. 597.]

DOES EQUAL PROTECTION ANALYSIS ADD ANYTHING?

[This note appears supra at p. 603.]

B. VOTING AND ELECTIONS

1. INTRODUCTION

THE CONSTITUTION AND THE FRANCHISE

(1) **The Constitution of 1789.** As originally adopted the Constitution left it to the States to determine who should have the right to vote in national as well as state elections. Art. II, § 1 provided for the selection of the President by electors appointed in each state "in such Manner as the Legislature thereof may direct"—a provision that has remained unchanged. Art. 1, § 2, cl. 1 provided that the persons voting for members of the House of Representatives "shall have the Qualifications requisite for Electors of the most numerous Branch of the State Legislature." Art. 1, § 3, cl. 1 provided that the members of the Senate should be chosen by the legislature of each State. It was not until the adoption of the seventeenth amendment in 1913 that it was provided that members of the Senate should be elected "by the people" of the respective States. That amendment also provided that the persons voting for members of the Senate "shall have the qualifications requisite for electors of the most numerous branch of the State legislatures." Art. I, § 4, cl. 1 provided that the "Times, Places and Manner of holding Elections for Senators and Representatives shall be prescribed in each State by the Legislature thereof; but the Congress may at any time by Law make or alter such Regulations, except as to the Places of choosing Senators."

(2) The Civil War Amendments. Before the Civil War all but six States discriminated against Negroes in establishing qualifications to vote. Stephanson, *Race Distinctions in American Law* 285 (1910). The fourteenth amendment did not directly forbid discrimination in voting. Section 2 of the amendment did provide for a reduction in representation in the House of Representatives in proportion to the number of "male inhabitants" who were not permitted to vote. However, the fifteenth amendment was soon adopted providing that the "right of citizens of the United States to vote shall not be denied or abridged by the United States or by any State on account of race, color, or previous condition of servitude." (For a modern interpretation of the Fifteenth Amendment, see the report of Rice v. Cayetano, 528 U.S. 495 (2000), infra at p. 1007.)

(3) The Nineteenth, Twenty–Fourth, and Twenty–Sixth Amendments. The Civil War amendments did not extend the franchise to all. Women were, of course, citizens but citizenship did not carry the right to vote. Minor v. Happersett, 88 U.S. (21 Wall.) 162 (1875). Only after a long campaign for women's suffrage was the Nineteenth Amendment ratified in 1920 providing that the right of citizens to vote "shall not be denied or abridged by the United States or by any State on account of sex." In 1964 the Twenty–Fourth Amendment was adopted providing that the right of any citizen to vote for the President, Vice–President, or members of Congress "shall not be denied or abridged by the United States or any State by reason of failure to pay any poll tax or other tax." Finally the Twenty–Sixth Amendment was adopted in 1971 providing that the right of any citizen eighteen years or older to vote "shall not be denied or abridged by the United States or by any State on account of age."

THE EQUAL PROTECTION CLAUSE AS THE SOURCE OF A RIGHT TO VOTE AND RUN FOR ELECTIVE OFFICE

In reading the cases in this section two general questions should be considered: (1) Does the court use the general language of the equal protection clause to establish a substantive right to vote and participate in elections that goes beyond the specific constitutional provisions summarized above? (2) Is there special constitutional justification for the Court to go beyond the express language of the Constitution to guarantee the broadest access to the political processes? Cf. Ely, *Democracy and Distrust* 117 (1980): "[u]nblocking stoppages in the democratic process is what judicial review ought preeminently to be about, and denial of the vote seems the quintessential stoppage."

The cases will be discussed in two groups: (1) Those relating to legislative districting; and (2) those relating to qualifications of voters.

2.   LEGISLATIVE DISTRICTING

Reynolds v. Sims

377 U.S. 533, 84 S.Ct. 1362, 12 L.Ed.2d 506 (1964).

Mr. Chief Justice Warren delivered the opinion of the Court.

Involved in these cases are an appeal and two cross-appeals from a decision of the Federal District Court ... holding invalid, under the Equal Protection Clause of the Federal Constitution, the existing and two legislatively proposed plans for the apportionment of seats in the two houses of the Alabama

Legislature, and ordering into effect a temporary reapportionment plan comprised of parts of the proposed but judicially disapproved measures.

. . .

[Under the existing plan, in the Senate one county of 15,417 population had a Senate seat and another county of over 600,000 people also had only a single seat. In the House one county with a population of 13,462 had two seats while another of 314,301 had only three seats. The two proposed plans reduced these disparities somewhat but still had a House in which the population for a seat in one district was 5 times that of another district and a Senate still in the neighborhood of 59 to 1.]

Undeniably the Constitution of the United States protects the right of all qualified citizens to vote, in state as well as in federal elections. A consistent line of decisions by this Court in cases involving attempts to deny or restrict the right of suffrage has made this indelibly clear. It has been repeatedly recognized that all qualified voters have a constitutionally protected right to vote, Ex parte Yarbrough, 110 U.S. 651, and to have their votes counted, United States v. Mosley, 238 U.S. 383. In *Mosley* the Court stated that it is "as equally unquestionable that the right to have one's vote counted is as open to protection . . . as the right to put a ballot in a box." . . . The right to vote can neither be denied outright, . . . nor can it be destroyed by alteration of ballots, see United States v. Classic, 313 U.S. 299, 315, nor diluted by ballot-box stuffing. . . . As the Court stated in *Classic,* "Obviously included within the right to choose, secured by the Constitution, is the right of qualified voters within a state to cast their ballots and have them counted. . . ." . . . Racially based gerrymandering, Gomillion v. Lightfoot, 364 U.S. 339, and the conducting of white primaries, Nixon v. Herndon, 273 U.S. 536, Nixon v. Condon, 286 U.S. 73, Smith v. Allwright, 321 U.S. 649, Terry v. Adams, 345 U.S. 461, both of which result in denying to some citizens their right to vote, have been held to be constitutionally impermissible. And history has seen a continuing expansion of the scope of the right of suffrage in this country. The right to vote freely for the candidate of one's choice is of the essence of a democratic society, and any restrictions on that right strike at the heart of representative government. And the right of suffrage can be denied by a debasement or dilution of the weight of a citizen's vote just as effectively as by wholly prohibiting the free exercise of the franchise.

. . .

In Gray v. Sanders, 372 U.S. 368, we held that the Georgia county unit system, applicable in statewide primary elections, was unconstitutional since it resulted in a dilution of the weight of the votes of certain Georgia voters merely because of where they resided. . . .

In Wesberry v. Sanders, 376 U.S. 1, decided earlier this Term, we held that attacks on the constitutionality of congressional districting plans enacted by state legislatures do not present nonjusticiable questions and should not be dismissed generally for "want of equity." We determined that the constitutional test for the validity of congressional districting schemes was one of substantial equality of population among the various districts established by a state legislature for the election of members of the Federal House of Representatives.

. . .

Gray and *Wesberry* are of course not dispositive of or directly controlling on our decision in these cases involving state legislative apportionment controversies. Admittedly, those decisions, in which we held that, in statewide and in congressional elections, one person's vote must be counted equally with those of all other voters in a State, were based on different constitutional considerations and were addressed to rather distinct problems. But neither are they wholly inapposite. *Gray,* though not determinative here since involving the weighting of votes in statewide elections, established the basic principle of equality among voters within a State, and held that voters cannot be classified, constitutionally, on the basis of where they live, at least with respect to voting in statewide elections. And our decision in *Wesberry* was of course grounded on that language of the Constitution which prescribes that members of the Federal House of Representatives are to be chosen "by the People," while attacks on state legislative apportionment schemes, such as that involved in the instant cases, are principally based on the Equal Protection Clause of the Fourteenth Amendment. Nevertheless, *Wesberry* clearly established that the fundamental principle of representative government in this country is one of equal representation for equal numbers of people, without regard to race, sex, economic status, or place of residence within a State. Our problem, then, is to ascertain, in the instant cases, whether there are any constitutionally cognizable principles which would justify departures from the basic standard of equality among voters in the apportionment of seats in state legislatures.

III.

A predominant consideration in determining whether a State's legislative apportionment scheme constitutes an invidious discrimination violative of rights asserted under the Equal Protection Clause is that the rights allegedly impaired are individual and personal in nature....

Legislators represent people, not trees or acres. Legislators are elected by voters, not farms or cities or economic interests. As long as ours is a representative form of government, and our legislatures are those instruments of government elected directly by and directly representative of the people, the right to elect legislators in a free and unimpaired fashion is a bedrock of our political system. It could hardly be gainsaid that a constitutional claim had been asserted by an allegation that certain otherwise qualified voters had been entirely prohibited from voting for members of their state legislature. And, if a State should provide that the votes of citizens in one part of the State should be given two times, or five times, or 10 times the weight of votes of citizens in another part of the State, it could hardly be contended that the right to vote of those residing in the disfavored areas had not been effectively diluted. It would appear extraordinary to suggest that a state could be constitutionally permitted to enact a law providing that certain of the state's voters could vote two, five, or 10 times for their legislative representatives, while voters living elsewhere could vote only once. And it is inconceivable that a state law to the effect that, in counting votes for legislators, the votes of citizens in one part of the State would be multiplied by two, five, or 10, while the votes of persons in another area would be counted only at face value, could be constitutionally sustainable. Of course, the effect of state legislative districting schemes which give the same number of representatives to unequal numbers of constituents is identical. Overweighting and overvaluation of the votes of those living here has the certain effect of dilution and undervaluation of the votes of those living there. The resulting discrimination against those individual voters living in disfavored areas is easily demonstrable mathematically. Their right to vote is simply not the same right to vote as that of those living in a favored part of the State. Two, five, or 10 of them must vote before the effect of their voting is equivalent to that of their favored neighbor. Weighting the votes of citizens differently, by any method or means, merely because of where they happen to reside, hardly seems justifiable....

... Since the achieving of fair and effective representation for all citizens is concededly the basic aim of legislative apportionment, we conclude that the Equal Protection Clause guarantees the opportunity for equal participation by all voters in the election of state legislators. Diluting the weight of votes because of place of residence impairs basic constitutional rights under the Fourteenth Amendment just as much as invidious discriminations based upon factors such as race, Brown v. Board of Education, 347 U.S. 483, or economic status, Griffin v. People of State of Illinois, 351 U.S. 12.... Our constitutional system amply provides for the protection of minorities by means other than giving them majority control of state legislatures. And the democratic ideals of equality and majority rule, which have served this Nation so well in the past, are hardly of any less significance for the present and the future.

We are told that the matter of apportioning representation in a state legislature is a complex and many-faceted one. We are advised that States can rationally consider factors other than population in apportioning legislative representation. We are admonished not to restrict the power of the States to impose differing views as to political philosophy on their citizens. We are cautioned about the dangers of entering into political thickets and mathematical quagmires. Our answer is this: a denial of constitutionally protected rights demands judicial protection; our oath and our office require no less of us.

... Population is, of necessity, the starting point for consideration and the controlling criterion for judgment in legislative apportionment controversies. A citizen, a qualified voter, is no more nor no less so because he lives in the city or on the farm. This is the clear and strong command of our Constitution's Equal Protection Clause. This is an essential part of the concept of a government of laws and not men. This is at the heart of Lincoln's vision of "government of the people, by the people, [and] for the people." The Equal Protection Clause demands no less than substantially equal state legislative representation for all citizens, of all places as well as of all races.

IV.

We hold that, as a basic constitutional standard, the Equal Protection Clause requires that the seats in both houses of a bicameral state legislature must be apportioned on a population basis. Simply stated, an individual's right to vote for state legislators is unconstitutionally impaired when its weight is in a substantial fashion diluted when compared with votes of citizens living in other parts of the State. Since, under neither the existing apportionment provisions nor under either of the proposed plans was either of the houses of the Alabama Legislature apportioned on a population basis, the District Court correctly held that all three of these schemes were constitutionally invalid.

V.

. . .

The system of representation in the two Houses of the Federal Congress is one ingrained in our Constitution, as part of the law of the land. It is one conceived out of compromise and concession indispensable to the establishment of our federal republic. Arising from unique historical circumstances, it is based on the consideration that in establishing our type of federalism a group of formerly independent States bound themselves together under one national government....

Political subdivisions of States—counties, cities, or whatever—never were and never have been considered as sovereign entities. Rather, they have been traditionally regarded as subordinate governmental instrumentalities created by the State to assist in the carrying out of state governmental functions.... The relationship of the States to the Federal Government could hardly be less analogous.

. . .

Since we find the so-called federal analogy inapposite to a consideration of the constitutional validity of state legislative apportionment schemes, we necessarily hold that the Equal Protection Clause requires both houses of a state legislature to be apportioned on a population basis....

VI.

By holding that as a federal constitutional requisite both houses of a state legislature must be apportioned on a population basis, we mean that the Equal Protection Clause requires that a State make an honest and good faith effort to construct districts, in both houses of its legislature, as nearly of equal population as is practicable. We realize that it is a practical impossibility to arrange legislative districts so that each one has an identical number of residents, or citizens, or voters. Mathematical exactness or precision is hardly a workable constitutional requirement....

. . .

A State may legitimately desire to maintain the integrity of various political subdivisions, insofar as possible, and provide for compact districts of contiguous territory in designing a legislative apportionment scheme. Valid considerations may underlie such aims. Indiscriminate districting, without any regard for political subdivision or natural or historical boundary lines, may be little more than an open invitation to partisan gerrymandering. Single-member districts may be the rule in one State, while another State might desire to achieve some flexibility by creating multimember or floterial districts. Whatever the means of accomplishment, the overriding objective must be substantial equality of population among the various districts, so that the vote of any citizen is approximately equal in weight to that of any other citizen in the State....

But neither history alone, nor economic or other sorts of group interests, are permissible factors in attempting to justify disparities from population-based representation. Citizens, not history or economic interests, cast votes. Considerations of area alone provide an insufficient justification for deviations from the equal-population principle. Again, people, not land or trees or pastures, vote. Modern developments and improvements in transportation and communications make rather hollow, in the mid–1960's, most claims that deviations from population-based representation can validly be based solely on geographical considerations. Arguments for allowing such deviations in order to insure effective representation for sparsely settled areas and to prevent legislative districts from becoming so large that the availability of access of citizens to their representatives is impaired are today, for the most part, unconvincing.

A consideration that appears to be of more substance in justifying some deviations from population-based representation in state legislatures is that of insuring some voice to political subdivisions, as political subdivisions. Several factors make more than insubstantial claims that a State can rationally consider according political subdivisions some independent representation in at least one body of the state legislature, as long as the basic standard of equality of population among districts is maintained. . . .

VIII.

That the Equal Protection Clause requires that both houses of a state legislature be apportioned on a population basis does not mean that States cannot adopt some reasonable plan for periodic revision of their apportionment schemes. Decennial reapportionment appears to be a rational approach to readjustment of legislative representation in order to take into account population shifts and growth. . . . In substance, we do not regard the Equal Protection Clause as requiring daily, monthly, annual or biennial reapportionment, so long as a State has a reasonably conceived plan for periodic readjustment of legislative representation. . . .

. . .

Affirmed and remanded.

[Justices Clark and Stewart concurred. Justice Harlan filed a lengthy dissenting opinion.]

REYNOLDS AND THE FIRST ROUND OF REAPPORTIONMENT

(1) Along with *Reynolds* the Court decided cases involving five other States. One is worth special note. In Colorado the voters in 1962 had defeated a proposed constitutional amendment providing for apportionment of both houses of the legislature on a population basis and adopted another amendment providing for a lower house based on population and an upper house based on a combination of population and other factors. In Lucas v. Forty–Fourth General Assembly of Colorado, 377 U.S. 713 (1964), the Court held this plan invalid despite the fact that it had been adopted by a majority of the voters, saying: "An individual's constitutionally protected right to cast an equally weighted vote cannot be denied even by a vote of a majority of the State's electorate, if the apportionment scheme adopted by the voters fails to measure up to the requirements of the Equal Protection Clause."

(2) *Reynolds* touched off a nation-wide effort to reapportion legislatures in accordance with its standards based on the 1960 census. In many States the political processes were incapable of achieving such a result and the federal courts found themselves faced with the duty of prescribing apportionment plans. Judicial doctrine developed rapidly towards the point that only mathematically equal districts would be approved—one-person, one-vote became a constitutional standard—and various state limitations on the construction of legislative districts were invalidated as interfering with mathematical equality. Little or no attention was paid in the cases to the realities of political representation. Legislators discovered that with the aid of computers mathematically equal districts could be created in ways which would favor incumbents or give undue representation in the legislatures to particular parties or interest groups. For an elaborate and useful discussion of the background of *Reynolds* and its companion cases and of the litigation up to 1968, see Dixon, *Democratic Representation: Reapportionment in Law and Politics* (1968). The literature on reapportionment during this period was enormous. Aside from innumerable articles, there were, in addition to Dixon's, the following significant books:

Baker, *The Reapportionment Revolution* (1966); Cortner, *The Apportionment Cases* (1970); Lee, *One Man, One Vote: WMCA and the Struggle for Equal Representation* (1967); McKay, *The Law and Politics of Equal Representation*

(1965); McKay, *Reapportionment Reappraisal: A Report on the One Man, One Vote Principle in Practice* (1968); Polsby (Ed.), *Reapportionment in the 1970s* (1971).

(3) The Court decided several more cases based on the reapportionments of the 1960s. Since they are referred to in the more recent cases set out below, no attempt will be made here to cite or discuss them.

THE 1970 CENSUS AND THE SECOND ROUND OF REAPPORTIONMENT

The 1970 census set off a second round of reapportionment struggles in the legislatures and in the courts. The legislatures faced the problem on the assumption that the Supreme Court would hold them very close to the goal of mathematical equality and would not inquire too deeply into the political and other consequences of apportionments meeting the numerical standard. A mathematical standard could be easily quantified and measured. To determine whether a particular apportionment scheme produced a fair representation of the various political groups or served to dilute the political power of particular minority groups was much more difficult.

The Supreme Court, perhaps influenced by the spate of literature and the presence of more sophisticated advocates, surprised many by shifting away from its almost exclusive reliance on equal numbers as the constitutional test when the 1970 cases began to come to it.

MAHAN v. HOWELL, 410 U.S. 315 (1973). A Virginia statute apportioned the House of Delegates so that the maximum percentage variation from the ideal was 16.4%—one district being 6.8% under the ideal and another 9.6% over. The minimum population percentage necessary to elect a majority of the House was 49.29%. The districts followed political jurisdictional lines of the counties and cities, except for Fairfax County, which was divided into two five-member districts. In a suit challenging this plan the district court held it violated constitutional standards and ordered into effect its own plan, which reduced the maximum percentage variation to 10% but extended districts across subdivision lines in 12 instances. The Supreme Court reversed and reinstated the statutory plan. Justice Rehnquist, for the Court, said that the strict standards applicable to congressional districting did not apply to state legislatures and stated the standard of review to be applied as follows:

"We are not prepared to say that the decision of the people of Virginia to grant the General Assembly the power to enact local legislation dealing with the political subdivisions is irrational. And if that be so, the decision of the General Assembly to provide representation to subdivisions *qua* subdivisions in order to implement that constitutional power is likewise valid when measured against the Equal Protection Clause of the Fourteenth Amendment. The inquiry then becomes whether it can reasonably be said that the state policy urged by Virginia to justify the divergences in the legislative reapportionment plan of the House is indeed furthered by the plan adopted by the legislature, and whether if so justified the divergences are also within tolerable limits. For a State's policy urged in justification of disparity in district population, however rational, cannot constitutionally be permitted to emasculate the goal of substantial equality."

He applied this standard as follows:

"We hold that the legislature's plan for apportionment of the House of Delegates may reasonably be said to advance the rational state policy of respecting the boundaries of political subdivisions. The remaining inquiry is whether the population disparities among the districts which have resulted from the pursuit of this plan exceed constitutional limits. We conclude that they do not.

. . . .

"Neither courts nor legislatures are furnished any specialized calipers which enable them to extract from the general language of the Equal Protection Clause of the Fourteenth Amendment the mathematical formula which establishes what range of percentage deviations are permissible, and what are not. The 16–odd percent maximum deviation which the District Court found to exist in the legislative plan for the reapportionment of the House is substantially less than the percentage deviations which have been found invalid in the previous decisions of this Court. While this percentage may well approach tolerable limits, we do not believe it exceeds them. Virginia has not sacrificed substantial equality to justifiable deviations."

Justices Brennan, Douglas, and Marshall, dissenting, stated their view of the constitutional standards to be applied:

"The holdings of our prior decisions can be restated in two unequivocal propositions. First the paramount goal of reapportionment must be the drawing of district lines so as to achieve precise equality in the population of each district. . . . The Constitution does not permit a State to relegate considerations of equality to secondary status and reserve as the primary goal of apportionment the service of some other state interest.

"Second, it is open to the State, in the event that it should fail to achieve the goal of population equality, to attempt to justify its failure by demonstrating that precise equality could not be achieved without jeopardizing some critical governmental interest. The Equal Protection Clause does not exalt the principle of equal representation to the point of nullifying every competing interest of the State. But we have held firmly to the view that variations in weight accorded each vote can be approved only where the State meets its burden of presenting cogent reasons in explanation of the variations, and even then only where the variations are small."

GAFFNEY v. CUMMINGS, 412 U.S. 735 (1973). Pursuant to the Connecticut Constitution, after the state legislature, and then an eight-member bipartisan commission, could not agree on a reapportionment plan following the 1970 census, a three-member Apportionment Board, consisting of one judge chosen by the Democratic Speaker of the House of Representatives, another judge chosen by the Republican Minority Leader of the House, and a third judge chosen by the other two, filed a reapportionment plan in 1971, with one member dissenting. The plan was soon challenged in federal court as a denial of equal protection because (1) the numerical deviations from population equality (a maximum deviation of 1.81% between the largest and smallest senatorial districts and of 7.83% between the largest and smallest House districts) were too great, and (2) the Board deliberately followed "a policy of 'political fairness,' which aimed at a rough scheme of proportional representation of the two major political parties" by using "the party voting results in the preceding three statewide elections" to create "a proportionate number of Republican and Democratic legislative seats." The Supreme Court rejected both claims.

Justice White's majority opinion said that prior cases had established "that the larger variations from substantial equality are too great to be justified by any state interest so far suggested[,]" although "as *Mahan v. Howell* demonstrates, population deviations among districts may be sufficiently large to require justification but nonetheless be justifiable and legally sustainable." It was, however, "now time to recognize that minor deviations from mathematical equality among state legislative districts are insufficient to make out a prima facie case of invidious discrimination under the Fourteenth Amendment so as to require justification by the State." Because "the basic statistical materials which legislatures and courts usually have to work with are the results of the United States census taken at 10–year intervals" and "they are inherently less than absolutely accurate[,]" "it makes little sense to conclude from relatively minor 'census population' variations among legislative districts that any person's vote is being substantially diluted." Constant changes in district populations and the fact that " 'census persons' are not voters" also argued against exact insistence on census population equality. The opinion went further:

"More fundamentally, *Reynolds* recognized that 'the achieving of fair and effective representation for all citizens is ... the basic aim of legislative apportionment', and it was for that reason that the decision insisted on substantial equality of populations among districts.

"... Fair and effective representation may be destroyed by gross population variations among districts, but it is apparent that such representation does not depend solely on mathematical equality among district populations. There are other relevant factors to be taken into account and other important interests that States may legitimately be mindful of.... An unrealistic overemphasis on raw population figures, a mere nose count in the districts, may submerge these other considerations and itself furnish a ready tool for ignoring factors that in day-to-day operation are important to an acceptable representation and apportionment arrangement.

"Nor is the goal of fair and effective representation furthered by making the standards of reapportionment so difficult to satisfy that the reapportionment task is recurringly removed from legislative hands and performed by federal courts who themselves must make the political decisions necessary to formulate a plan or accept those made by reapportionment plaintiffs, who may have wholly different goals than those embodied in the official plan...."

The majority also rejected the claim "that even if acceptable population-wise, the Apportionment Board's plan was invidiously discriminatory because a 'political fairness principle' was followed in making up the districts":

"... The very essence of districting is to produce a different—a more 'politically fair'—result than would be reached with elections at large, in which the winning party would take 100% of the legislative seats. Politics and political considerations are inseparable from districting and apportionment.... The reality is that districting inevitably has and is intended to have substantial political consequences.

"It may be suggested that those who redistrict and reapportion should work with census, not political, data and achieve population equality without regard for political impact. But this politically mindless approach may produce, whether intended or not, the most grossly gerrymandered results; and, in any event, it is most unlikely that the political impact of such a plan would remain undiscovered by the time it was proposed or adopted, in which event the results would be both known and, if not changed, intended.

"... [M]ultimember districts may be vulnerable, if racial or political groups have been fenced out of the political process and their voting strength invidiously minimized. See White v. Regester, 412 U.S. 755; *Whitcomb v. Chavis,* supra.... Beyond this, we have not ventured far or attempted the impossible task of extirpating politics from what are the essentially political processes of the sovereign States. Even more plainly, judicial interest should be at its lowest ebb when a State purports fairly to allocate political power to the parties in accordance with their voting strength and, within quite tolerable limits, succeeds in doing so. . . ."

[Justices Brennan, Douglas and Marshall dissented.]

Karcher v. Daggett

462 U.S. 725, 103 S.Ct. 2653, 77 L.Ed.2d 133 (1983).

Justice Brennan delivered the opinion of the Court.

The question presented . . . is whether an apportionment plan for congressional districts satisfies Art. I, § 2 without need for further justification if the population of the largest district is less than one percent greater than the population of the smallest district. A three-judge District Court declared New Jersey's 1982 reapportionment plan unconstitutional on the authority of Kirkpatrick v. Preisler, 394 U.S. 526 (1969), and White v. Weiser, 412 U.S. 783 (1973), because the population deviations among districts, although small, were not the result of a good-faith effort to achieve population equality. We affirm.

I

[The New Jersey Legislature adopted] the Feldman Plan contain[ing] 14 districts, with an average population per district (as determined by the 1980 census) of 526,059. . . . On the average, each district differed from the "ideal" figure by 0.1384%, or about 726 people. The largest . . . had a population of 527,472, and the smallest . . . a population of 523,798. The difference . . . was 3,674 people, or 0.6984% of the average district. The populations of the other districts also varied. . . .

The Legislature had before it other plans with appreciably smaller population deviations between the largest and smallest districts. . . . [One] had a maximum population difference of 2,375, or 0.4514% of the average figure.

Almost immediately after the Feldman Plan became law, a group of individuals with varying interests, including all incumbent Republican members of Congress from New Jersey, sought a declaration that the apportionment plan violated Article I, § 2 of the Constitution and an injunction against proceeding with the primary election for United States Representatives under the plan. . . .

. . . .

II

Article I, § 2, establishes a "high standard of justice and common sense" for the apportionment of congressional districts: "equal representation for equal numbers of people." Wesberry v. Sanders, 376 U.S. 1, 18 (1964). Precise mathematical equality, however, may be impossible to achieve in an imperfect world; therefore the "equal representation" standard is enforced only to the extent of requiring that districts be apportioned to achieve population equality "as nearly as is practicable." . . .

Thus two basic questions shape litigation over population deviations in state legislation apportioning congressional districts. First, the court must consider whether the population differences among districts could have been reduced or eliminated altogether by a good-faith effort to draw districts of equal population. Parties challenging apportionment legislation must bear the burden of proof on this issue, and if they fail to show that the differences could have been avoided the apportionment scheme must be upheld. If, however, the plaintiffs can establish that the population differences were not the result of a good-faith effort to achieve equality, the State must bear the burden of proving that each significant variance between districts was necessary to achieve some legitimate goal. *Kirkpatrick*....

III

Appellants' principal argument ... contend[s] that the Feldman Plan should be regarded *per se* as the product of a good-faith effort to achieve population equality because the maximum population deviation among districts is smaller than the predictable undercount in available census data.

A

Kirkpatrick squarely rejected a nearly identical argument. "The whole thrust of the 'as nearly as practicable' approach is inconsistent with adoption of fixed numerical standards which excuse population variances without regard to the circumstances of each particular case." ...; see *White v. Weiser*.... Adopting any standard other than population equality, using the best census data available, ... would subtly erode the Constitution's ideal of equal representation. If state legislators knew that a certain *de minimis* level of population differences were acceptable, they would doubtless strive to achieve that level rather than equality.... Furthermore, choosing a different standard would import a high degree of arbitrariness into the process of reviewing apportionment plans.... In this case, appellants argue that a maximum deviation of approximately 0.7% should be considered *de minimis*. If we accept that argument, how are we to regard deviations of 0.8%, 0.95%, 1%, or 1.1%?

Any standard, including absolute equality, involves a certain artificiality. As appellants point out, even the census data are not perfect, and the well-known restlessness of the American people means that population counts for particular localities are outdated long before they are completed. Yet problems with the data at hand apply equally to any population-based standard we could choose. As between two standards—equality or something-less-than equality—only the former reflects the aspirations of Art. 1, § 2.

To accept the legitimacy of unjustified, though small population deviations in this case would mean to reject the basic premise of *Kirkpatrick* and *Wesberry*. We decline ... to go that far. The unusual rigor of their standard has been noted several times. Because of that rigor, we have required that absolute population equality be the paramount objective of apportionment only in the case of congressional districts, for which the command of Art. I, § 2, as regards the National Legislature outweighs the local interests that a State may deem relevant in apportioning districts for representatives to state and local legislatures, but we have not questioned the population equality standard for congressional districts.... The principle of population equality for congressional districts has not proved unjust or socially or economically harmful in experience.... If anything, this standard should cause less difficulty now for state legislatures than it did when we adopted it in *Wesberry*. The rapid advances in computer technology and education during the last two decades make it relatively simple to draw contiguous districts of equal population and at the same time to further whatever secondary goals the State has.... We thus reaffirm that there are no *de minimis* population variations, which could practicably be avoided, but which nonetheless meet the standard of Art. I, § 2 without justification.[6]

. . .

B

The sole difference between appellants' theory and the argument we rejected in *Kirkpatrick* is that appellants have proposed a *de minimis* line that gives the illusion of rationality and predictability: the "inevitable statistical imprecision of the census." . . .

. . .

The census may systematically undercount population, and the rate of undercounting may vary from place to place. Those facts, however, do not render meaningless the differences in population between congressional districts, as determined by uncorrected census counts. To the contrary, the census data provide the only reliable—albeit less than perfect—indication of the districts' "real" relative population levels. . . . Furthermore, because the census count represents the "best population data available," . . . it is the only basis for good-faith attempts to achieve population equality. Attempts to explain population deviations on the basis of flaws in census data must be supported with a precision not achieved here. . . .

C

Given that the census-based population deviations in the Feldman Plan reflect real differences among the districts, it is clear that they could have been avoided or significantly reduced with a good-faith effort to achieve population equality. For that reason alone, it would be inappropriate to accept the Feldman Plan as "functionally equivalent" to a plan with districts of equal population.

. . .

IV

. . . [A]ppellees' success in proving that the Feldman Plan was not the product of a good-faith effort to achieve population equality means only that the burden shifted to the State to prove that the population deviations in its plan were necessary to achieve some legitimate state objective. *White v. Weiser* demonstrates that we are willing to defer to state legislative policies, so long as they are consistent with constitutional norms, even if they require small differences in the population of congressional districts. . . . Any number of consistently applied legislative policies might justify some variance, including,

---

6. Justice White objects that "the rule of absolute equality is perfectly compatible with 'gerrymandering' of the worst sort," Wells v. Rockefeller, 394 U.S. 542, 551 (1969) (Harlan, J., dissenting). That may certainly be true to some extent: beyond requiring States to justify population deviations with explicit, precise reasons, which might be expected to have some inhibitory effect, *Kirkpatrick* does little to prevent what is known as gerrymandering. . . . *Kirkpatrick*'s object, achieving population equality, is far less ambitious than what would be required to address gerrymandering on a constitutional level.

In any event, the additional claim that *Kirkpatrick* actually promotes gerrymandering (as opposed to merely failing to stop it) is completely empty. A federal principle of population equality does not prevent any State from taking steps to inhibit gerrymandering, so long as a good-faith effort is made to achieve population equality as well. See, e.g., Colo. Const. art. V, § 47 (guidelines as to compactness, contiguity, boundaries of political subdivisions, and communities of interest); Mass. Const. art. CI, § 1 (boundaries); N.Y.Elec.Law § 4–100(b) (McKinney 1978) (compactness and boundaries).

. . .

for instance, making districts compact, respecting municipal boundaries, preserving the cores of prior districts, and avoiding contests between incumbent Representatives. As long as the criteria are nondiscriminatory, . . . these are all legitimate objectives that on a proper showing could justify minor population deviations. . . . The State must, however, show with some specificity that a particular objective required the specific deviations in its plan, rather than simply relying on general assertions. The showing required to justify population deviations is flexible, depending on the size of the deviations, the importance of the State's interests, the consistency with which the plan as a whole reflects those interests, and the availability of alternatives that might substantially vindicate those interests yet approximate population equality more closely. By necessity, whether deviations are justified requires case-by-case attention to these factors.

. . .

The District Court properly found that appellants did not justify the population deviations in this case.

V

The District Court properly applied the two-part test of *Kirkpatrick v. Preisler*. . . . It correctly held that the population deviations in the plan were not functionally equal as a matter of law, and it found that the plan was not a good-faith effort to achieve population equality using the best available census data. It also correctly rejected appellants' attempt to justify the population deviations as not supported by the evidence. [Its] judgment . . . is affirmed.

Justice Stevens, concurring.

As an alternative ground for affirmance, the appellees contended at oral argument that the bizarre configuration of New Jersey's congressional districts is sufficient to demonstrate that the plan was not adopted in "good faith." This argument, as I understand it, is a claim that the district boundaries are unconstitutional because they are the product of political gerrymandering. Since my vote is decisive in this case, it seems appropriate to explain how this argument influences my analysis of the question that divides the Court. As I have previously pointed out, political gerrymandering is one species of "vote dilution" that is proscribed by the Equal Protection Clause. . . .

I

. . . It can be demonstrated . . . that the holding in *Wesberry*, as well as our holding today, has firmer roots in the Constitution than those provided by Article I, § 2.

. . .

The Equal Protection Clause requires every State to govern impartially. [R]ules governing its election machinery or defining electoral boundaries . . . must serve the interests of the entire community. See Reynolds v. Sims. . . . If they serve no purpose other than to favor one segment—whether racial, ethnic, religious, economic, or political—that may occupy a position of strength at a particular point in time, or to disadvantage a politically weak segment of the community, they violate the constitutional guarantee of equal protection.

. . . [P]rotection against vote dilution cannot be confined to racial groups. As long as [the Equal Protection Clause] proscribes gerrymandering against such groups, its proscription must provide comparable protection for other cognizable groups of voters as well. . . .

II

Like Justice White, I am convinced that judicial preoccupation with the goal of perfect population equality is an inadequate method of judging the constitutionality of an apportionment plan. I would not hold that an obvious gerrymander is wholly immune from attack simply because it comes closer to perfect population equality than every competing plan. On the other hand, I do not find any virtue in the proposal to relax the standard set forth in *Wesberry* and subsequent cases, and to ignore population disparities after some arbitrarily defined threshold has been crossed. . . .

. . .

III

In this case it is not necessary to go beyond the reasoning in the Court's opinions in Wesberry v. Sanders, 376 U.S. 1 (1964), Kirkpatrick v. Preisler, 394 U.S. 526 (1969), and White v. Weiser, 412 U.S. 783 (1973), to reach the correct result. . . . [T]he plan's shortcomings regarding shape and compactness, subdivision boundaries, and neutral decisionmaking . . . strengthen my conclusion that [it] violates the Equal Protection Clause.

A glance at the map shows district configurations well deserving the kind of descriptive adjectives—"uncouth" and "bizarre"—that have traditionally been used to describe acknowledged gerrymanders. . . . [W]hile disregarding geographical compactness, the redistricting scheme wantonly disregards county boundaries. . . .

Such a map prompts an inquiry into the process that led to its adoption. . . . [T]he record indicates that [it] was far from neutral. It was designed to increase the number of Democrats, and to decrease the number of Republicans, that New Jersey's voters would send to Congress in future years. . . .

Because I have not made a comparative study of other districting plans, and because the State has not had the opportunity to offer justifications specifically directed toward the additional concerns I have discussed, I cannot conclude with absolute certainty that the New Jersey plan was an unconstitutional partisan gerrymander. But I am in full agreement with the Court's holding that, because the plan embodies deviations from population equality that have not been justified by any neutral state objective, it cannot stand. . . .

Justice White, with whom The Chief Justice, Justice Powell, and Justice Rehnquist join, dissenting.

. . .

I respectfully dissent from the Court's unreasonable insistence on an unattainable perfection in the equalizing of congressional districts. The Court's decision today is not compelled by Kirkpatrick v. Preisler, 394 U.S. 526 (1969), and White v. Weiser, 412 U.S. 783 (1973), and if the Court is convinced that our cases demand the result reached today, the time has arrived to reconsider these precedents. . . .

I

"The achieving of fair and effective representation for all citizens is concededly the basic aim of legislative apportionment." Reynolds v. Sims, 377 U.S. 533, 566 (1964). One must suspend credulity to believe that the Court's draconian response to a trifling 0.6984% maximum deviation promotes "fair and effective representation" for the people of New Jersey. The requirement that "as nearly as is practicable one man's vote in a congressional election is to be worth as much as another's," Wesberry v. Sanders, 376 U.S. 1, 7–8 (1964), must be understood in light of the malapportionment in the states at the time *Wesberry* was decided. The plaintiffs in *Wesberry* were voters in a congressional district (pop. 823,680) encompassing Atlanta that was three times larger than Georgia's smallest district (272,154) and more than double the size of an average district. Because the state had not reapportioned for 30 years, the Atlanta District possessing one-fifth of Georgia's population had only one-tenth of the Congressmen. Georgia was not atypical; congressional districts throughout the country had not been redrawn for decades and deviations of over 50% were the rule. These substantial differences in district size diminished, in a real sense, the representativeness of congressional elections. The Court's invalidation of these profoundly unequal districts should not be read as a demand for precise mathematical equality between the districts. Indeed, the Court sensibly observed that "it may not be possible [for the states] to draw Congressional districts with mathematical precision." . . .

. . .

. . . I fear that the Court's [ruling] invites further litigation of virtually every congressional redistricting plan in the nation. At least twelve states which have completed redistricting on the basis of the 1980 census have adopted plans with a higher deviation than that presented here, and four others have deviations quite similar to New Jersey's. [U]nder the Court's rationale, even Rhode Island's plan—whose two districts have a deviation of 0.02% or about 95 people—would be subject to constitutional attack.

In all such cases, state legislatures will be hard pressed to justify their preference for the selected plan. . . . When the state fails to sustain its burden, the result will generally be that a court must select an alternative plan. . . .

The only way a legislature or bipartisan commission can hope to avoid litigation will be to dismiss all other legitimate concerns and opt automatically for the districting plan with the smallest deviation. Yet no one can seriously contend that such an inflexible insistence upon mathematical exactness will serve to promote "fair and effective representation." The more likely result of today's extension of *Kirkpatrick* is to move closer to fulfilling Justice Fortas' prophecy that "a legislature might have to ignore the boundaries of common sense, running the congressional district line down the middle of the corridor of an apartment house or even dividing the residents of a single-family house between two districts." 394 U.S., at 538. Such sterile and mechanistic application only brings the principle of "one man, one vote" into disrepute.

II

. . . [T]he Court offers no positive virtues that will follow from its decision. . . .

Instead the Court is purely defensive. . . .

. . .

Yet today the Court—with no mention of the contrary holdings in *Kirkpatrick*—opines: "Any number of consistently applied legislative policies might justify some variance, including for instance, making districts compact, respecting municipal boundaries, preserving the cores of prior districts, and avoiding contests between incumbent Representatives." I, of course, welcome the Court's overruling of these ill-considered holdings of *Kirkpatrick*. There should be no question but that state legislatures may account for political and geographic boundaries in order to preserve traditional subdivisions and achieve compact and contiguous districts. Justice Stevens recognizes that courts should "give greater weight to the importance of the State's interests and the consistency with which those interests are served than to the size of the deviations." Thus, a majority of the Court appears ready to apply this new standard "with a strong measure of deference to the legitimate concerns of the State." Post, (Powell, J., dissenting).

In order that legislatures have room to accommodate these legitimate noncensus factors, a range of *de minimis* population deviation, like that permitted in the legislative reapportionment cases, is required. The Court's insistence that every deviation, no matter how small, be justified with specificity discourages legislatures from considering these "legitimate" factors in making their plans, lest the justification be found wanting, the plan invalidated, and a judicially drawn substitute put in its place. Moreover, the requirement of precise mathematical equality continues to invite those who would bury their political opposition to employ equipopulous gerrymanders. A *de minimis* range would not preclude such gerrymanders but would at least force the political cartographer to justify his work on its own terms.

III

Our cases dealing with state legislative apportionment have taken a more sensible approach. We have recognized that certain small deviations do not, in themselves, ordinarily constitute a *prima facie* constitutional violation. Gaffney v. Cummings, 412 U.S. 735 (1973); White v. Regester, 412 U.S. 755 (1973). Moreover, we have upheld plans with reasonable variances that were necessary to account for political subdivisions, Mahan v. Howell, 410 U.S. 315 (1973), to preserve the voting strength of minority groups, and to insure political fairness, *Gaffney v. Cummings,* supra....

Bringing together our legislative and congressional cases does not imply overlooking relevant differences between the two. States normally draw a larger number of legislative districts, which accordingly require a greater margin to account for geographical and political boundaries. "[C]ongressional districts are not so intertwined and freighted with strictly local interests as are state legislative districts." *White v. Weiser....* Furthermore, because Congressional districts are generally much larger than State Legislative districts, each percentage point of variation represents a commensurately greater number of people. But these are differences of degree. They suggest that the level at which courts should entertain challenges to districting plans, absent unusual circumstances, should be lower in the congressional cases, but not altogether nonexistent. Although I am not wedded to a precise figure, in light of the current range of population deviations, a 5% cutoff appears reasonable. I would not entertain judicial challenges, absent extraordinary circumstances, where the maximum deviation is less than 5%. Somewhat greater deviations, if rationally related to an important state interest, may also be permissible. Certainly, the maintaining of compact, contiguous districts, the respecting of political subdivisions, and efforts to assure political fairness, e.g., *Gaffney v. Cummings,* ... constitute such interests.

I would not hold up New Jersey's plan as a model reflection of such interests. Nevertheless, the deviation involved here is *de minimis,* and, regardless of what other infirmities the plan may have, constitutional or otherwise, there is no violation of Art. I, § 2—the sole issue before us. It would, of course, be a different matter if appellees could demonstrate that New Jersey's plan invidiously discriminated against a racial or political group....

. . . .

Justice Powell, dissenting.

I join Justice White's excellent dissenting opinion, and reaffirm my previously expressed doubt that "the Constitution—a vital and living charter after nearly two centuries because of the wise flexibility of its key provisions—could be read to require a rule of mathematical exactitude in legislative reapportionment." ... I write separately to express some additional thoughts on gerrymandering and its relation to apportionment factors that presumably were not thought relevant under Kirkpatrick v. Preisler, 394 U.S. 526 (1969).

. . .

I ... am prepared to entertain constitutional challenges to partisan gerrymandering that reaches the level of discrimination described by Justice Stevens.

. . .

... Because this precise issue was not addressed by the District Court, however, it need not be reached here. . . .

BROWN v. THOMSON, 462 U.S. 835 (1983). The Wyoming Constitution provides that its House of Representatives shall be apportioned according to population, except that each county shall have at least one representative. In 1981 the apportionment statute provided a representative for Niobrara County even though its population was 60% below the mean. Overall the plan provided a maximum deviation of 89% and an average deviation of 16%. The statute also provided that if the allocation of a seat to Niobrara County was held invalid its population should be added to another county and the number of seats in the House reduced from 64 to 63. In a suit brought to challenge this scheme the court upheld the statute as applied to Niobrara County. Justice Powell's majority opinion said that only its receiving a seat was challenged and hence it was not necessary to consider whether adherence to county boundaries justified the population deviations that exist throughout Wyoming districts. Looking only at the marginal effects of the grant to the one county, the court found that "this case presents an unusually strong example of an apportionment plan the population variations of which are entirely the result of the consistent and nondiscriminatory application of a legitimate state policy." The Court found that Wyoming's interest in maintaining county representation in the legislature was not outweighed by the marginal impact giving a seat to Niobrara County had on representation in the entire House.

Justice O'Connor, joined by Justice Stevens, both of whom had voted with the majority in *Karcher v. Daggett,* added a statement noting that the Court was deciding only the additional deviation caused by the allocation of a seat to Niobrara County and saying: "I have the gravest doubts that a statewide legislative plan with an 85% maximum deviation would survive constitutional scrutiny despite the presence of the State's strong interest in preserving county boundaries. I join the Court's opinion on the understanding that nothing in it suggests that this Court would uphold such a scheme."

[Justices Brennan, White, Marshall, and Blackmun dissented.]

REYNOLDS AND LOCAL GOVERNMENTAL UNITS

In Hadley v. Junior College Dist., 397 U.S. 50 (1970), eight school districts had combined to form a junior college district governed by six trustees. The governing statute provided that if no school district had more than 33 ⅓% of the population all trustees were elected at large; if a district had between 33 ⅓%

and 50% of the population it would elect two trustees with the rest elected at large from the remaining districts; if a district had between 50% and 66 ⅔% it would elect three trustees; and if over 66 ⅔% it would elect four. In a suit by residents of a school district having 60% of the population but permitted to elect only 50% of the trustees, the Court held this scheme invalid. Justice Black, for the majority, said, in part: "[In Avery v. Midland County, 390 U.S. 474 (1968), we held that] a qualified voter in a local election also has a constitutional right to have his vote counted with substantially the same weight as that of any other voter in a case where the elected officials exercised 'general governmental powers over the entire geographic area served by the body.'

"... Appellants argue that since the trustees can levy and collect taxes, issue bonds with certain restrictions, hire and fire teachers, make contracts, collect fees, supervise and discipline students, pass on petitions to annex school districts, acquire property by condemnation, and in general manage the operations of the junior college, their powers are equivalent, for apportionment purposes, to those exercised by the county commissioners in *Avery*. We feel that these powers, while not fully as broad as those of the Midland County Commissioners,[6] certainly show that the trustees perform important governmental functions within the districts, and we think these powers are general enough and have sufficient impact throughout the district ... that the principle ... applied in *Avery* should also be applied here....

    . . .

"When a court is asked to decide whether a State is required by the Constitution to give each qualified voter the same power in an election open to all, there is no discernible, valid reason why constitutional distinctions should be drawn on the basis of the purpose of the election. If one person's vote is given less weight through unequal apportionment, his right to equal voting participation is impaired just as much when he votes for a school board member as when he votes for a state legislator....

"It has also been urged that we distinguish for apportionment purposes between elections for 'legislative' officials and those for 'administrative' officers. Such a suggestion would leave courts with an equally unmanageable principle since governmental activities 'cannot easily be classified in the neat categories favored by civics texts', *Avery*, ... and it must also be rejected. We therefore hold today that as a general rule, whenever a state or local government decides to select persons by popular election to perform governmental functions, the Equal Protection Clause of the Fourteenth Amendment requires that each qualified voter must be given an equal opportunity to participate in that election, and when members of an elected body are chosen from separate districts, each district must be established on a basis that will insure, as far as is practicable, that equal numbers of voters can vote for proportionally equal numbers of officials. It is of course possible that there might be some case in which a State elects certain functionaries whose duties are so far removed from normal governmental activities and so disproportionately affect different groups that a popular election in compliance with *Reynolds*, ... might not be required, but certainly we see nothing in the present case that indicates that

---

6. The Midland County Commissioners established and maintained the county jail, appointed numerous county officials, made contracts, built roads and bridges, administered the county welfare system, performed duties in connection with elections, set the county tax rate, issued bonds, adopted the county budget, built and ran hospitals, airports, and libraries, fixed school district boundaries, established a housing authority, and determined the election districts for county commissioners. *Avery*, supra, at 476–477.

the activities of these trustees fit in that category. Education has traditionally been a vital governmental function, and these trustees, whose election the State has opened to all qualified voters, are governmental officials in every relevant sense of that term. . . .

". . . [T]he Act necessarily results in a systematic discrimination against voters in the more populous school districts[,] . . . because whenever a large district's percentage of the total enumeration falls within a certain percentage range it is always allocated the number of trustees corresponding to the bottom of that range. . . . Such built-in discrimination against voters in large districts cannot be sustained as a sufficient compliance with the constitutional mandate that each person's vote count as much as another's, as far as practicable. . . .

"In holding that the guarantee of equal voting strength for each voter applies in all elections of governmental officials, we do not feel that the States will be inhibited in finding ways to insure that legitimate political goals of representation are achieved. We have previously upheld against constitutional challenge an election scheme that required that candidates be residents of certain districts that did not contain equal numbers of people. Dusch v. Davis, 387 U.S. 112 (1967). Since all the officials in that case were elected at large, the right of each voter was given equal treatment.[a] We have also held that where a State chooses to select members of an official body by appointment rather than election, and that choice does not itself offend the Constitution, the fact that each official does not 'represent' the same number of people does not deny those people equal protection of the laws. Sailors v. Board of Education, 387 U.S. 105 (1967); cf. Fortson v. Morris, 385 U.S. 231 (1966).[b] And a State may, in certain cases, limit the right to vote to a particular group or class of people. As we said before, '[v]iable local governments may need many innovations, numerous combinations of old and new devices, great flexibility in municipal arrangements to meet changing urban conditions. We see nothing in the Constitution to prevent experimentation.' Sailors. . . . But once a State has decided to use the process of popular election and 'once the class of voters is chosen and their qualifications specified, we see no constitutional way by which equality of voting power may be evaded.' Gray v. Sanders, 372 U.S. 368, 381 (1963)."

In Lockport v. Citizens for Community Action, 430 U.S. 259 (1977), a New York law provided that a new county charter would go into effect only if approved in a referendum election by separate majorities of the voters who live in the cities within the county, and of those who live outside the cities. The

---

a. See also Dallas County, Ala. v. Reese, 421 U.S. 477 (1975), in which the Court upheld a requirement that county commissioners be elected by countywide balloting but with a requirement that a member be elected from each of four districts having substantial population disparities. The Court said such a scheme could be overturned only on a showing that it "in fact operates impermissibly to dilute the voting strength of an identifiable element of the voting population."

b. In Fortson the Court upheld a provision of the Constitution of Georgia that when no candidate for the office of Governor receives a majority of votes cast in the general election the Governor shall be elected by a majority of the members of the Georgia General Assembly from the two persons having

the highest number of votes. The Court said: "There is no provision of the United States Constitution or any of its amendments which either expressly or impliedly dictates the method a State must use to select its Governor. A method which would be valid if initially employed is equally valid when employed as an alternative."

The Court relied on Fortson in Rodriguez v. Popular Democratic Party, 457 U.S. 1 (1982), sustaining a Puerto Rico statute permitting the political party of an incumbent legislator to appoint an interim replacement when the legislator vacates the position. The Court rejected an argument that the Constitution requires election of state legislators. The Constitution confers no "right to vote, per se," but a right to participate on an equal basis when elections are held.

Court held that this arrangement did not violate the equal protection clause in a case where there were many more voters in the cities than in the county outside the cities and where the charter was rejected, despite a majority of all the voters in the entire county having voted in favor, because of its failure to secure a majority of the noncity voters. The Court noted that the interests of the city and the noncity voters were likely to be quite different with respect to the adoption of a new county charter, and concluded:

"The provisions of New York law here in question no more than recognize the realities of these substantially differing electoral interests. Granting to these provisions the presumption of constitutionality to which every duly enacted state and federal law is entitled, we are unable to conclude that they violate the Equal Protection Clause of the Fourteenth Amendment."

In Salyer Land Co. v. Tulare Lake Basin Water Storage Dist., 410 U.S. 719 (1973), the defendant water storage district was organized under a California law providing for elections for directors in which only the holders of title to land in the district were entitled to vote and in which each such voter was entitled to cast one vote for each $100 value of land and improvements in the district. 77 persons resided within the district. 189 persons owned land in amounts up to 80 acres each. Four large operators owned 85% of the land, with one corporation owning enough to give it a majority of the board of directors. A landowner, a lessee, and a resident of the district asserted that the restriction of voting to landowners and the weighting of votes according to valuation of land owned were unconstitutional. The trial court ruled for the defendant and the Supreme Court affirmed.

Justice Rehnquist, for the Court, distinguished earlier cases invalidating restricting voting to landowners on the ground that those cases involved residents of local government units exercising general governmental power, whereas the district here "by reason of its special limited purpose and of the disproportionate effect of its activities on landowners as a group" is an exception to the rule of *Reynolds* and *Hadley*.

"The appellee district in this case ... has relatively limited authority. [T]he reason for its existence, is to provide for the acquisition, storage, and distribution of water for farming in the Tulare Lake Basin. It provides no other general public services such as schools, housing, transportation, utilities, roads or anything else of the type ordinarily financed by a municipal body. There are no towns, shops, hospitals or other facilities designed to improve the quality of life within the district boundaries and it does not have a fire department, police, buses, or trains.

"Not only does the district not exercise what might be thought of as 'normal governmental' authority, but its actions disproportionately affect land-owners. All of the costs of district projects are assessed against land by assessors in proportion to the benefits received. Likewise, charges for services rendered are collectible from persons receiving their benefit in proportion to the services. When such persons are delinquent in payment, just as in the case of delinquency in payments of assessments, such charges become a lien on the land. Calif. Water Code §§ 47183, 46280. In short, there is no way that the economic burdens of district operations can fall on residents *qua* residents, and the operations of the districts primarily affect the land within their boundaries.

"Under these circumstances it is quite understandable that the statutory framework for election of directors of the appellee focuses on the land benefit-ed, rather than on people as such."

As to the argument that weighting the vote according to assessed valuation denied equal protection, he noted that the benefits and burdens to each landowner in the district are in proportion to the assessed value of the land. Thus, in a recent district project a small landowner with one vote was assessed $46 as his share of the cost while the large corporate farm with 37,825 votes was assessed $817,685 as its share. "We cannot say that the California legislative decision to permit voting in the same proportion is not rationally based."

Justices Douglas, Brennan and Marshall dissented.

In Ball v. James, 451 U.S. 355 (1981), the Court applied *Salyer Land* to uphold the system under which the Salt River Project Agricultural Improvement and Power District in Arizona elects its directors, with voting limited to landowners and voting power apportioned according to the amount of land the voter owns. The Salt River District encompasses almost half the population of Arizona, including large parts of Phoenix and other cities. While all of its water is allocated according to land ownership, 25% goes for urban uses. The District generates and sells electric power, with 98% of its revenues coming from such sales. Despite these facts demonstrating that the District plays a major role in the lives of most Arizonans, Justice Stewart, writing for the majority, said:

> "[T]he District simply does not exercise the sort of governmental powers that invoke the strict demands of *Reynolds*. The District cannot impose ad valorem property taxes or sales taxes. It cannot enact any laws governing the conduct of citizens, nor does it administer such normal functions of government as the maintenance of streets, the operations of schools, or sanitation, health, or welfare services."

He concluded that limiting the vote to landowners and making the weight of their vote dependent on the number of acres owned was valid because it bears "a reasonable relationship to its statutory objectives."

Justice Powell concurred in the Court's opinion and added that in this case the public was adequately protected by the fact that the Arizona legislature could control the electoral composition of the District. Justices White, Brennan, Marshall, and Blackmun dissented.

Salyer Land and *Ball v. James* were distinguished in Quinn v. Millsap, 491 U.S. 95 (1989), which held unanimously that a property ownership requirement, for membership on a "board of freeholders" responsible for proposing to the voters a plan of reorganization of the governments of the City of St. Louis and St. Louis County, violated equal protection. The Court first rejected the Missouri Supreme Court's interpretation of *Salyer* and *Ball* as having held that the equal protection clause is completely inapplicable to government units lacking general governmental powers: "On the contrary, the Court expressly applied equal protection analysis and concluded that the voting qualifications at issue passed constitutional scrutiny." Nor did the fact that the board only "recommend[ed] a plan of reorganization to the voters ... immunize [it] from equal protection scrutiny[,]" for "the Equal Protection Clause protects the 'right to be considered for public service without the burden of invidiously discriminatory disqualifications.'" Finding it unnecessary to apply any more than "rationality review[,]" the Court concluded that neither an understanding of community issues nor a stake in the community's future depended on property ownership. Finally, "the mere fact that the board of freeholders considers land-use issues cannot suffice to sustain a land-ownership requirement in this case." Unlike the water district cases, the "purpose of the board ... is not so directly linked with land ownership." Its "mandate is far more encompassing: it has the power to draft and submit a plan to reorganize the entire governmental structure of St. Louis city and county." Its "work ... thus affects all citizens of the city and county, regardless of land ownership."[a]

In Board of Estimate v. Morris, 489 U.S. 688 (1989), the Court held that New York City's electoral scheme for the Board of Estimate violated the "one person, one vote" apportionment requirements of equal protection. The Board of Estimate is composed of eight elected officials who automatically become members of the Board upon election to their respective primary positions. Three officials—the Mayor, the comptroller, and the president of the City Council—are elected in city-wide elections and cast two votes each on matters before the Board (except that the Mayor has no vote on the acceptance or modification of his budget proposal). The remaining five—the presidents of each of the City's 5 boroughs—are elected by the voters in their respective boroughs and cast one vote each. Voters from Brooklyn, the most populous borough, challenged the method of constituting the Board, citing the substantial disparity in population among the various boroughs, which include the Bronx, Brooklyn, Manhattan, Queens, and Richmond (Staten Island).

The Court first found that the range of the Board's fiscal responsibilities and land use, franchise, and contracting powers over the City's seven million inhabitants, together with the legislative functions it shares with the City Council in approving or modifying the Mayor's proposed budget, "situate the Board comfortably within the category of governmental bodies whose 'powers are general enough and have sufficient impact throughout the district' to require that elections to the body comply with Equal Protection strictures. See *Hadley v. Junior College Dist.*" The Court then rejected the city's claim that "the Board's composition survives constitutional challenge because the city-wide members cast a 6–5 majority of board votes and hence are in a position to control the outcome of board actions." The votes of the borough presidents are sometimes determinative, and thus voters in some boroughs retain more power than voters in other boroughs, because the at-large Board members "often do not vote together" and, given that "the Mayor has no vote on budget issues, the citywide members alone cannot control budgetary decisions."

Excepting Justices Brennan and Stevens, who concurred separately on this point, the Court did fault the Court of Appeals for failing to factor the presence of at-large members on the board into the calculation of the deviation between the more and less populous boroughs, because "the voters in each borough vote for the at-large members as well as their borough president, and they are also represented by those members." The correct method of calculation only reduced the maximum percentage deviation from 132% to 78%, however, and the Court could find no justification for "such a substantial departure from the one-person, one-vote ideal."

THE EQUAL PROTECTION CLAUSE AND THE REQUIREMENT OF SUPER–MAJORITIES

In Gordon v. Lance, 403 U.S. 1 (1971), the Court upheld a state constitutional provision requiring the approval of 60% of the voters in a referendum election before political subdivisions could incur bonded indebtedness or in-

---

a. In Rice v. Cayetano, 528 U.S. 495 1044 (2000), infra at p. 1007, the Court also distinguished *Salyer Land* and *Ball v. James* in the context of upholding a Fifteenth Amendment challenge to a voting qualification favoring the descendants of those who lived in Hawaii in 1778: "Our special purpose district cases have not suggested that compliance with the one-person, one-vote rule of the Fourteenth Amendment somehow excuses compliance with the Fifteenth Amendment ... [, which] has independent meaning and force."

crease tax rates. The case resulted from a school election in which a bond issue and a tax increase received 51.5% of the vote but were declared defeated. The Court said, in part:

"Although West Virginia has not denied any group access to the ballot, it has indeed made it more difficult for some kinds of governmental actions to be taken. Certainly any departure from strict majority rule gives disproportionate power to the minority. But there is nothing in the language of the Constitution, our history or our cases that requires that a majority always prevail on every issue.

. . .

"The Federal Constitution itself provides that a simple majority vote is insufficient on some issues; the provisions on impeachment and ratification of treaties are but two examples. Moreover, the Bill of Rights removes entire areas of legislation from the concept of majoritarian supremacy. . . ."

CONGRESSIONAL APPORTIONMENT OF REPRESENTATIVES AMONG THE SEVERAL STATES

In contrast to the usual suit challenging a state's scheme of intrastate apportionment of congressional or state legislative districts, U.S. Department of Commerce v. Montana, 503 U.S. 442 (1992), concerned Montana's challenge to a 1941 Act of Congress directing the use of a particular method for apportioning among the 50 States, after each decennial census, the 435 seats in the House of Representatives. Application of that method following the 1990 census reduced Montana's congressional delegation from two representatives to one. A lower federal court "decided that the principle of equal representation for equal numbers of people that was applied to intrastate districting in Wesberry v. Sanders, 376 U.S. 1 (1964), should also be applied to the apportionment of seats among the States" and invalidated the Act for producing a "variance between the population of Montana's single district and the ideal district" that "could not be justified[.]"

A unanimous Supreme Court reversed. Justice Stevens' opinion first set forth these basic constitutional parameters:

"The general admonition in Article I, § 2, that Representatives shall be apportioned among the several States 'according to their respective numbers' is constrained by three requirements. The number of representatives shall not exceed one for every 30,000 persons; each State shall have at least one Representative; and district boundaries may not cross state lines. . . ."

The opinion examined the nature and effects of the various apportionment methods Congress had used before 1941 and the expert studies and reports upon which Congress relied in adopting the current method. It then rejected the suggestion that Congress' choice of apportionment method is a judicially unreviewable political question. On the merits, the Court noted that, unlike reducing population variances among districts within a State, reducing absolute population differences among districts located in different States increases relative differences from the nationwide average and worsens another State's deviation from the ideal size district at the same time that it lessens the deviation of a complaining State. The Court found no "substantive principle of commanding constitutional significance" in the various "alternative measures of inequality" from among which Congress chose its preferred method of apportionment. It noted that "[t]he constitutional guarantee of one Representative for each State inexorably compels a significant departure from the ideal" and that "the need to allocate a fixed number of indivisible Representatives among 50 States of varying populations makes it virtually impossible to have the same size district in any pair of States, let alone in all 50." Invoking the "spirit of compromise that provided two Senators for every State and Representatives of the People 'according to their respective Numbers' in the House[,]" Justice Stevens explained that "some compromise between the interests of larger and smaller States must be made to achieve a fair apportionment for the entire country." Given these premises:

> "The constitutional framework that generated the need for compromise in the apportionment process must also delegate to Congress a measure of discretion that is broader than that accorded the States in the much easier task of determining district sizes within State borders.... Its apparently good-faith choice of a method of apportionment ... commands far more deference than a state districting decision that is capable of being reviewed under a relatively rigid mathematical standard."

A footnote at this point in the Court's opinion noted that "Montana does not contend that the [Act's chosen] method systematically favors a particular party, nor that its retention over a 50–year period reflects efforts to maintain partisan political advantage." The Court concluded that "Congress had ample power to enact the statutory procedure in 1941 and to apply the method ... after the 1990 census."[a]

Miller v. Johnson

515 U.S. 900, 115 S.Ct. 2475, 132 L.Ed.2d 762 (1995).

Justice Kennedy delivered the opinion of the Court.

The constitutionality of Georgia's congressional redistricting plan is at issue here. In Shaw v. Reno, 509 U.S. 630 (1993), we held that a plaintiff states a claim under the Equal Protection Clause by alleging that a state redistricting plan, on its face, has no rational explanation save as an effort to separate voters on the basis of race. The question we now decide is whether Georgia's new Eleventh District gives rise to a valid equal protection claim under the principles announced in *Shaw*, and, if so, whether it can be sustained nonetheless as narrowly tailored to serve a compelling governmental interest.

I

A

The Equal Protection Clause['s] ... central mandate is racial neutrality in governmental decisionmaking. See, e.g., Loving v. Virginia, 388 U.S. 1, 11

a. The Court subsequently held that even more deference was due decisions concerning "the Federal Government's conduct of the census—a context even further removed from intrastate districting than is congressional apportionment." Wisconsin v. City of New York, 517 U.S. 1, 18 (1996). The Court unanimously rejected a claim that the Secretary of Commerce acted unconstitutionally when he decided not to use a particular statistical adjustment designed to correct an undercount (and the accompanying differential undercount of racial minorities) in the initial 1990 census enumeration. The Secretary had concluded that since the primary purpose of the census was to apportion political representation among the States, it was more important to achieve "distributive accuracy"—having the proportions of people in different areas most accurate—than to achieve the best "numerical accuracy." The Court found "no constitutional basis ... for preferring numerical accuracy to distributive accuracy, or for preferring gross accuracy to some particular measure of accuracy." Given "the Constitution's broad grant of authority to Congress, the Secretary's decision not to adjust need bear only a reasonable relationship to the accomplishment of an actual enumeration of the population, keeping in mind the constitutional purpose of the census"—a standard the Secretary had met by his focus on distributive accuracy.

(1967); McLaughlin v. Florida, 379 U.S. 184, 191–192 (1964); see also Brown v. Board of Education, 347 U.S. 483 (1954).... Laws classifying citizens on the basis of race cannot be upheld unless they are narrowly tailored to achieving a compelling state interest. See, e.g., Adarand....

In *Shaw v. Reno* ... we recognized that these equal protection principles govern a State's drawing of congressional districts, though, as our cautious approach there discloses, application of these principles to electoral districting is a most delicate task.... [W]e held that "redistricting legislation that is so bizarre on its face that it is 'unexplainable on grounds other than race,' ... demands the same close scrutiny that we give other state laws that classify citizens by race." ...

. . .

B

In 1965, the Attorney General designated Georgia a covered jurisdiction under § 4(b) of the Voting Rights Act.... In consequence, § 5 of the Act requires Georgia to obtain either administrative preclearance by the Attorney General or approval by the United States District Court for the District of Columbia of any change in a "standard, practice, or procedure with respect to voting" made after November 1, 1964.... The preclearance mechanism applies to congressional redistricting plans, see, e.g., Beer v. United States, 425 U.S. 130, 133 (1976), and requires that the proposed change "not have the purpose and will not have the effect of denying or abridging the right to vote on account of race or color." ... "[T]he purpose of § 5 has always been to insure that no voting-procedure changes would be made that would lead to a retrogression in the position of racial minorities with respect to their effective exercise of the electoral franchise." ...

Between 1980 and 1990, one of Georgia's 10 congressional districts was a majority-black district, that is, a majority of the district's voters were black. The 1990 Decennial Census indicated that Georgia's population of 6,478,216 persons, 27% of whom are black, entitled it to an additional eleventh congressional seat, ... prompting Georgia's General Assembly to redraw the State's congressional districts. Both the House and the Senate adopted redistricting guidelines which, among other things, required single-member districts of equal population, contiguous geography, nondilution of minority voting strength, fidelity to precinct lines where possible, and compliance with §§ 2 and 5 of the Act.... Only after these requirements were met did the guidelines permit drafters to consider other ends, such as maintaining the integrity of political subdivisions, preserving the core of existing districts, and avoiding contests between incumbents....

[Two successive redistricting plans submitted to the Attorney General for preclearance, each containing two majority-minority districts, were rejected because the Justice Department, "relying on alternative plans proposing three majority-minority districts"—one alternative being "the so-called 'max-black' plan ... drafted by the American Civil Liberties Union (ACLU) for the General Assembly's black caucus"—"concluded that Georgia had 'failed to explain adequately' its failure to create a third majority-minority district."] The State did not seek a declaratory judgment from the District Court for the District of Columbia....

Twice spurned, the General Assembly set out to create three majority-minority districts to gain preclearance.... Using the ACLU's "max-black" plan as its benchmark, ... the General Assembly enacted a plan that "bore all the signs of [the Justice Department's] involvement...." The Eleventh District lost the black population of Macon, but picked up Savannah, thereby connecting the black neighborhoods of metropolitan Atlanta and the poor black populace of coastal Chatham County, though 260 miles apart in distance and worlds apart in culture. In short, the social, political and economic makeup of the Eleventh District tells a tale of disparity, not community.... As the attached appendices attest,

> "[t]he populations of the Eleventh are centered around four discrete, widely spaced urban centers that have absolutely nothing to do with each other, and stretch the district hundreds of miles across rural counties and narrow swamp corridors." ...

> "The dense population centers ... were all majority-black, all at the periphery of the district, and in the case of Atlanta, Augusta and Savannah, all tied to a sparsely populated rural core by even less populated land bridges. Extending from Atlanta to the Atlantic, the Eleventh covered 6,748.2 square miles, splitting eight counties and five municipalities along the way." ...

Georgia's plan included three majority-black districts, though, and received Justice Department preclearance....

Elections were held under the new congressional redistricting plan on November 4, 1992, and black candidates were elected to Congress from all three majority-black districts.... [F]ive white voters from the Eleventh District [sued,] ... alleg[ing] that Georgia's Eleventh District was a racial gerrymander and so a violation of the Equal Protection Clause as interpreted in *Shaw v. Reno*.... A majority of the [three-judge] District Court [held] the Eleventh District ... invalid under *Shaw*, with one judge dissenting....

II

A

Finding that the "evidence of the General Assembly's intent to racially gerrymander the Eleventh District is overwhelming, and practically stipulated by the parties involved," the District Court held that race was the predominant, overriding factor in drawing the Eleventh District.... Appellants do not take issue with the court's factual finding of this racial motivation. Rather, they contend that evidence of a legislature's deliberate classification of voters on the basis of race cannot alone suffice to state a claim under *Shaw*. They argue that, regardless of the legislature's purposes, a plaintiff must demonstrate that a district's shape is so bizarre that it is unexplainable other than on the basis of race, and that appellees failed to make that showing here. Appellants' conception of the constitutional violation misapprehends our holding in *Shaw* and the Equal Protection precedent upon which *Shaw* relied.

Shaw recognized a claim "analytically distinct" from a vote dilution claim.... Whereas a vote dilution claim alleges that the State has enacted a particular voting scheme as a purposeful device "to minimize or cancel out the voting potential of racial or ethnic minorities," Mobile v. Bolden, 446 U.S. 55, 66 (1980) ..., an action disadvantaging voters of a particular race, the essence of the equal protection claim recognized in *Shaw* is that the State has used race as a basis for separating voters into districts. Just as the State may not, absent extraordinary justification, segregate citizens on the basis of race in its public parks, ... buses, ... golf courses, ... beaches, ... and schools, ... it may not separate its citizens into different voting districts on the basis of race. The idea is a simple one: "At the heart of the Constitution's guarantee of equal protection lies the simple command that the Government must treat citizens 'as individuals', not 'as simply components of a racial, religious, sexual or national class.' " ... When the State assigns voters on the basis of race, it engages in the offensive and demeaning assumption that voters of a particular race, because of their race, "think alike, share the same political interests, and will prefer the same candidates at the polls." *Shaw*.... Race-based assignments ... also cause society serious harm. As we concluded in *Shaw*: "Racial classifications with respect to voting carry particular dangers. Racial gerrymandering, even for remedial purposes, may balkanize us into competing racial factions; it threatens to carry us further from the goal of a political system in which race no longer matters—a goal that the Fourteenth and Fifteenth Amendments embody, and to which the Nation continues to aspire. It is for these reasons that race-based districting by our state legislatures demands close judicial scrutiny." ...

Our observation in *Shaw* of the consequences of racial stereotyping was not meant to suggest that a district must be bizarre on its face before there is a constitutional violation.... Shape is relevant not because bizarreness is a necessary element of the constitutional wrong or a threshold requirement of proof, but because it may be persuasive circumstantial evidence that race for its own sake, and not other districting principles, was the legislature's dominant and controlling rationale in drawing its district lines. The logical implication ... is that parties may rely on evidence other than bizarreness to establish race-based districting....

... We recognized in *Shaw* that, outside the districting context, statutes are subject to strict scrutiny under the Equal Protection Clause ... when, though race neutral on their face, they are motivated by a racial purpose or object.... [In prior cases,] the presumed racial purpose of state action, not its stark manifestation, [was] the constitutional violation....

Shaw applied these same principles to redistricting....

Appellants and some of their amici argue that the Equal Protection Clause's general proscription on race-based decisionmaking does not obtain in the districting context because redistricting by definition involves racial considerations. Underlying their argument are the very stereotypical assumptions the Equal Protection Clause forbids. It is true that redistricting in most cases will implicate a political calculus in which various interests compete for recognition, but it does not follow from this that individuals of the same race share a single political interest. The view that they do is "based on the demeaning notion that members of the defined racial groups ascribe to certain 'minority views' that must be different from those of other citizens," ... the precise use of race as a proxy the Constitution prohibits....

In sum, ... parties alleging that a State has assigned voters on the basis of race are neither confined in their proof to evidence regarding the district's geometry and makeup nor required to make a threshold showing of bizarreness. Today's case requires us further to consider the requirements of the proof necessary to sustain this equal protection challenge.

B

... Redistricting legislatures will ... almost always be aware of racial demographics; but it does not follow that race predominates in the redistricting process.... The distinction between being aware of racial considerations and being motivated by them may be difficult to make. This evidentiary difficulty, together with the sensitive nature of redistricting and the presumption of good faith that must be accorded legislative enactments, requires courts to exercise extraordinary caution in adjudicating claims that a state has drawn district lines on the basis of race. The plaintiff's burden is to show, either through circumstantial evidence of a district's shape and demographics or more direct evidence going to legislative purpose, that race was the predominant factor motivating the legislature's decision to place a significant number of voters within or without a particular district. To make this showing, a plaintiff must prove that the legislature subordinated traditional race-neutral districting principles, including but not limited to compactness, contiguity, respect for political subdivisions or communities defined by actual shared interests, to racial considerations. . . .

In our view, the District Court applied the correct analysis, and its finding that race was the predominant factor motivating the drawing of the Eleventh District was not clearly erroneous. The court found it was "exceedingly obvious" from the shape of the Eleventh District, together with the relevant racial demographics, that the drawing of narrow land bridges to incorporate within the District outlying appendages containing nearly 80% of the district's total black population was a deliberate attempt to bring black populations into the district. . . . Although by comparison with other districts the geometric shape of the Eleventh District may not seem bizarre on its face, when its shape is considered in conjunction with its racial and population densities, the story of racial gerrymandering seen by the District Court becomes much clearer. . . . Although this evidence is quite compelling, we need not determine whether it was, standing alone, sufficient to establish a *Shaw* claim. . . . The District Court had before it considerable additional evidence showing that the General Assembly was motivated by a predominant, overriding desire to assign black populations to the Eleventh District. . . .

The court found that "it became obvious," both from the Justice Department's objection letters and the three preclearance rounds in general, "that [the Justice Department] would accept nothing less than abject surrender to its maximization agenda." . . . It further found that the General Assembly acquiesced and as a consequence was driven by its overriding desire to comply with the Department's maximization demands. The court supported its conclusion . . . with the State's own concessions. . . . [I]n its brief to this Court, the State concedes that "[i]t is undisputed that Georgia's eleventh is the product of a desire by the General Assembly to create a majority black district." . . . On this record, we fail to see how the District Court could have reached any conclusion other than that race was the predominant factor in drawing Georgia's Eleventh District; and in any event we conclude the court's finding is not clearly erroneous. . . .

In light of its well-supported finding, the District Court was justified in rejecting the various alternative explanations offered for the District. Although a legislature's compliance with "traditional districting principles such as compactness, contiguity, and respect for political subdivisions" may well suffice to refute a claim of racial gerrymandering, *Shaw* . . ., appellants cannot make such a refutation where, as here, those factors were subordinated to racial objectives. . . .

Nor can the State's districting legislation be rescued by mere recitation of purported communities of interest. The evidence was compelling "that there are no tangible 'communities of interest' spanning the hundreds of miles of the Eleventh District." . . . [N]ot alleged shared interests but rather the object of maximizing the District's black population and obtaining Justice Department approval . . . explained the General Assembly's actions. . . . A State is free to recognize communities that have a particular racial makeup, provided its action is directed toward some common thread of relevant interests. "[W]hen members of a racial group live together in one community, a reapportionment plan that concentrates members of the group in one district and excludes them from others may reflect wholly legitimate purposes." *Shaw*.... But where the State assumes from a group of voters' race that they "think alike, share the same political interests, and will prefer the same candidates at the polls," it engages in racial stereotyping at odds with equal protection mandates....

. . .

III

To satisfy strict scrutiny, the State must demonstrate that its districting legislation is narrowly tailored to achieve a compelling interest.... There is a "significant state interest in eradicating the effects of past racial discrimination." *Shaw*.... The State does not argue, however, that it created the Eleventh District to remedy past discrimination, and with good reason: there is little doubt that the State's true interest in designing the Eleventh District was creating a third majority-black district to satisfy the Justice Department's preclearance demands.... Whether or not in some cases compliance with the Voting Rights Act, standing alone, can provide a compelling interest independent of any interest in remedying past discrimination, it cannot do so here. As we suggested in *Shaw*, compliance with federal antidiscrimination laws cannot justify race-based districting where the challenged district was not reasonably necessary under a constitutional reading and application of those laws.... The congressional plan challenged here was not required by the Voting Rights Act under a correct reading of the statute.

. . .

We do not accept the contention that the State has a compelling interest in complying with whatever preclearance mandates the Justice Department issues.... Where a State relies on the Department's determination that race-based districting is necessary to comply with the Voting Rights Act, the judiciary retains an independent obligation in adjudicating consequent equal protection challenges to ensure that the State's actions are narrowly tailored to achieve a compelling interest....

... [W]e have rejected agency interpretations to which we would otherwise defer where they raise serious constitutional questions.... When the Justice Department's interpretation of the Act compels race-based districting, it by definition raises a serious constitutional question, ... and should not receive deference.

Georgia's drawing of the Eleventh District was not required under the Act because there was no reasonable basis to believe that Georgia's earlier enacted plans violated § 5. Wherever a plan is "ameliorative," a term we have used to describe plans increasing the number of majority-minority districts, it "cannot violate § 5 unless the new apportionment itself so discriminates on the basis of race or color as to violate the Constitution." *Beer*.... Georgia's first and second proposed plans increased the number of majority-black districts from 1 out of 10 (10%) to 2 out of 11 (18.18%). These plans were "ameliorative" and could not have violated § 5's non-retrogression principle.... Acknowledging as much, ... the United States [objects] that Georgia failed to proffer a nondiscriminatory purpose for its refusal in the first two submissions to take the steps necessary to create a third majority-minority district.

The Government's position is insupportable.... Although ... the State has the burden to prove a nondiscriminatory purpose under § 5, ... Georgia's Attorney General provided a detailed explanation for the State's initial decision not to enact the max-black plan.... The District Court accepted this explanation ... and found an absence of any discriminatory intent.... The State's policy of adhering to other districting principles instead of creating as many majority-minority districts as possible does not support an inference that the plan "so discriminates on the basis of race or color as to violate the Constitution," *Beer* ..., and thus cannot provide any basis under § 5 for the Justice Department's objection.

Instead of grounding its objections on evidence of a discriminatory purpose, it would appear the Government was driven by its policy of maximizing majority-black districts.... In utilizing § 5 to require States to create majority-minority districts wherever possible, the Department of Justice expanded its authority under the statute beyond what Congress intended and we have upheld.

. . .

[W]e recognized in *Beer* that "the purpose of § 5 has always been to insure that no voting-procedure changes would be made that would lead to a retrogression in the position of racial minorities with respect to their effective exercise of the electoral franchise." ... The Justice Department's maximization policy seems quite far removed from this purpose. We are especially reluctant to conclude that § 5 justifies that policy given the serious constitutional concerns it raises. In South Carolina v. Katzenbach, 383 U.S. 301 (1966), we upheld § 5 as a necessary and constitutional response to some states' "extraordinary stratagem[s] of contriving new rules of various kinds for the sole purpose of perpetuating voting discrimination in the face of adverse federal court decrees." ... But our belief in *Katzenbach* that the federalism costs exacted by § 5 preclearance could be justified by those extraordinary circumstances does not mean they can be justified in the circumstances of this case. And the Justice Department's implicit command that States engage in presumptively unconstitutional race-based districting brings the Voting Rights Act, once upheld as a proper exercise of Congress' authority under § 2 of the Fifteenth Amendment, *Katzenbach* ..., into tension with the Fourteenth Amendment.... We need not, however, resolve these troubling and difficult constitutional questions today. There is no indication Congress intended such a far-reaching application of § 5, so we reject the Justice Department's interpretation of the statute and avoid the constitutional problems that interpretation raises....

IV

The Voting Rights Act, and its grant of authority to the federal courts to uncover official efforts to abridge minorities' right to vote, has been of vital importance in eradicating invidious discrimination from the electoral process and enhancing the legitimacy of our political institutions. Only if our political system and our society cleanse themselves of that discrimination will all members of the polity share an equal opportunity to gain public office regardless of race. As a Nation we share both the obligation and the aspiration of working toward this end. The end is neither assured nor well served, however, by carving electorates into racial blocs.... It takes a shortsighted and unauthorized view of the Voting Rights Act to invoke that statute, which has played a decisive role in redressing some of our worst forms of discrimination, to demand the very racial stereotyping the Fourteenth Amendment forbids.

* * *

The judgment of the District Court is affirmed, and the case is remanded for further proceedings consistent with this decision.

It is so ordered.

Justice O'Connor, concurring.

I understand the threshold standard the Court adopts—"that the legislature subordinated traditional race-neutral districting principles ... to racial considerations"—to be a demanding one. To invoke strict scrutiny, a plaintiff must show that the State has relied on race in substantial disregard of customary and traditional districting practices. Those practices provide a crucial frame of reference and therefore constitute a significant governing principle in cases of this kind. The standard would be no different if a legislature had drawn the boundaries to favor some other ethnic group; certainly the standard does not treat efforts to create majority-minority districts less favorably than similar efforts on behalf of other groups. Indeed, the driving force behind the adoption of the Fourteenth Amendment was the desire to end legal discrimination against blacks.

Application of the Court's standard does not throw into doubt the vast majority of the Nation's 435 congressional districts, where presumably the States have drawn the boundaries in accordance with their customary districting principles. That is so even though race may well have been considered in the redistricting process. See Shaw v. Reno.... But application of the Court's standard helps achieve *Shaw*'s basic objective of making extreme instances of gerrymandering subject to meaningful judicial review. I therefore join the Court's opinion.

Justice Stevens, dissenting.

... I believe the respondents ... have not suffered any legally cognizable injury.

In [*Shaw*] the Court crafted a new cause of action with two novel, troubling features. First, the Court misapplied the term "gerrymander," previously used to describe grotesque line-drawing by a dominant group to maintain or enhance its political power at a minority's expense, to condemn the efforts of a majority (whites) to share its power with a minority (African Americans). Second, the Court dispensed with its previous insistence in vote dilution cases on a showing of injury to an identifiable group of voters, but it failed to explain adequately what showing a plaintiff must make to establish standing to litigate the newly minted *Shaw* claim. Neither in *Shaw* itself nor in the cases decided today has the Court coherently articulated what injury this cause of action is designed to redress....

Even assuming the validity of *Shaw*, I cannot see how respondents ... could assert the injury the Court attributes to them.... The Court's conclusion [regarding] standing ... appears to rest on a theory that their placement in the Eleventh District caused them " 'representational harms.' " ... *Shaw* ... explained the concept of "representational harms" as follows: "When a district obviously is created solely to effectuate the perceived common interests of one racial group, elected officials are more likely to believe that their primary obligation is to represent only the members of that group, rather than their constituency as a whole." ... [R]epresentational harms ... can only come about ... if all or most black voters support the same candidate, and ... if the successful candidate ignores the interests of her white constituents. Respondents' standing, in other words, ultimately depends on the very premise the Court purports to abhor: that voters of a particular race " 'think alike, share the same political interests, and will prefer the same candidates at the polls.' " ... This generalization, as the Court recognizes, is "offensive and demeaning."

[A] vote dilution claim ... allows voters to allege that gerrymandered district lines have impaired their ability to elect a candidate of their own race. The Court emphasizes, however, that a so-called *Shaw* claim is " 'analytically distinct' from a vote dilution claim." [But] the Court [has not] answered the question its analytic distinction raises: If the *Shaw* injury does not flow from an increased probability that white candidates will lose, then how can the increased probability that black candidates will win cause white voters, such as respondents, cognizable harm?

The Court attempts an explanation ... by equating the injury it imagines respondents have suffered with the injuries African Americans suffered under segregation.... [But o]ur desegregation cases redressed the *exclusion* of black citizens from public facilities reserved for whites. In this case, in contrast, any voter, black or white, may live in the Eleventh District. What respondents contest is the *inclusion* of too many black voters in the District as drawn. [I]f respondents allege no vote dilution, that inclusion can cause them no conceivable injury.[a]

[Also,] legal segregation frustrated the public interest in diversity and tolerance by barring African Americans from joining whites in the activities at issue. The districting plan here, in contrast, serves the interest in diversity and tolerance by increasing the likelihood that a meaningful number of black representatives will add their voices to legislative debates....

... I do not see how a districting plan that favors a politically weak group can violate equal protection....

The Court's refusal to distinguish an enactment that helps a minority group from enactments that cause it harm is especially unfortunate at the intersection of race and voting, given that African Americans and other

---

a. In the companion case of United States v. Hays, 515 U.S. 737 (1995), the Court declined to rule on the merits of a "racial gerrymander" challenge to a Louisiana congressional districting plan, because the challengers lacked standing to raise it: they did not live in the majority-minority district that was the "primary focus of their racial gerrymandering claim, and they have not otherwise demonstrated that they, personally, have been subjected to a racial classification." Justice O'Connor's opinion for the Court, rejecting the claim that "anybody in the State has a claim," observed in part:

"We discussed the harms caused by racial classifications in *Shaw*. We noted that, in general, '[t]hey threaten to stigmatize individuals by reason of their membership in a racial group and to incite racial hostility.' ... We also noted 'representational harms'.... Any citizen able to demonstrate that he or she, personally, has been injured by that kind of racial classification has standing to challenge the classification in federal court.

"Demonstrating the individualized harm our standing doctrine requires may not be easy in the racial gerrymandering context.... Where a plaintiff resides in a racially gerrymandered district, however, the plaintiff has been denied equal treatment because of the legislature's reliance on racial criteria, and therefore has standing to challenge the legislature's action.... Voters in such districts may suffer the special representational harms racial classifications can cause in the voting context. On the other hand, where a plaintiff does not live in such a district, he or she does not suffer those special harms, and any inference that the plaintiff has personally been subjected to a racial classification would not be justified absent specific evidence tending to support that inference...."

Justice Breyer, joined by Justice Souter "join[ed] the Court's opinion to the extent that it discusses voters ... who do not reside within the district that they challenge." Justice Ginsburg concurred in the judgment without comment, and Justice Stevens did so in an opinion objecting to the Court's willingness to recognize that residents of racially gerrymandered districts may suffer individualized harms:

"... What I do not understand is the majority's view that these racially diverse respondents should fare better if they resided in black-majority districts instead of white-majority districts...."

disadvantaged groups have struggled so long and so hard for inclusion in that most central exercise of our democracy.... [T]reating racial groups differently from other identifiable groups of voters, as the Court does today, is itself an invidious racial classification. Racial minorities should receive neither more nor less protection than other groups against gerrymanders. *A fortiori*, racial minorities should not be less eligible than other groups to benefit from districting plans the majority designs to aid them.

I respectfully dissent.

Justice Ginsburg, with whom Justices Stevens and Breyer join, and with whom Justice Souter joins except as to Part III–B, dissenting.

. . .

... Because I do not endorse the Court's new standard and would not upset Georgia's plan, I dissent.

I

. . .

... [T]hat the Georgia General Assembly took account of race in drawing district lines—a fact not in dispute—does not render the State's plan invalid. To offend the Equal Protection Clause, all agree, the legislature had to do more than consider race. How much more, is the issue that divides the Court today.

. . .

II

A

. . .

In *Shaw*, the Court ... wrote cautiously, emphasizing that judicial intervention is exceptional.... The problem in *Shaw* was ..., in the Court's estimation, ... race alone steering placement of district lines.

B

The record before us does not show that race similarly overwhelmed traditional districting practices in Georgia....

In contrast to the snake-like North Carolina district inspected in *Shaw*, Georgia's Eleventh District is hardly "bizarre," "extremely irregular," or "irrational on its face." ... Instead, [its] design reflects significant consideration of "traditional districting factors (such as keeping political subdivisions intact) and the usual political process of compromise and trades for a variety of nonracial reasons." ... (S.D.Ga.1994) (Edmondson, J., dissenting).... The District covers a core area in central and eastern Georgia, and its total land area of 6,780 square miles is about average for the State....

Nor does [it] disrespect the boundaries of political subdivisions. Of the 22 counties in the District, 14 are intact and 8 are divided[—]about the state average in divided counties.... Seventy-one percent of [its] boundaries track the borders of political subdivisions.... Of the State's 11 districts, 5 score worse than the Eleventh District on this criterion, and 5 score better.... Eighty-three percent of [its] geographic area is composed of intact counties, above average for the State's congressional districts.... And notably, the Eleventh District's boundaries largely follow precinct lines.

Evidence at trial similarly shows that considerations other than race went into determining the Eleventh District's boundaries. For a "political reason" ... the DeKalb County portion of the Eleventh District was drawn to include a particular (largely white) precinct.... The corridor through Effingham County was substantially narrowed at the request of a (white) State Representative.... In Chatham County, the District was trimmed to exclude a heavily black community in Garden City because a State Representative wanted to keep the city intact inside the neighboring First District.... The Savannah extension was configured by "the narrowest means possible" to avoid splitting the city of Port Wentworth....

Georgia's Eleventh District, in sum, is not an outlier district shaped without reference to familiar districting techniques. Tellingly, the District that the Court's decision today unsettles is not among those on a statistically calculated list of the 28 most bizarre districts in the United States, a study prepared in the wake of our decision in *Shaw*....

C

The Court suggests that ... the U.S. Department of Justice ... effectively drew the lines ... with nothing but race in mind. Yet the "Max–Black" plan advanced by the Attorney General was not the plan passed by the Georgia General Assembly....

And ... Georgia could have demanded relief from the Department's objections by instituting a civil action in the United States District Court for the District of Columbia, with ultimate review in this Court. Instead ... the State chose to adopt the plan [it] forcefully defends before us....

D

[T]he Court recognizes as an appropriate districting principle, "respect for ... communities defined by actual shared interests." ...

But ethnicity itself can tie people together, as volumes of social science literature have documented—even people with divergent economic interests. For this reason, ethnicity is a significant force in political life....

[L]egislatures have long drawn voting districts along ethnic lines. Our Nation's cities are full of districts identified by their ethnic character—Chinese, Irish, Italian, Jewish, Polish, Russian, for example.... The creation of ethnic districts reflecting felt identity is not ordinarily viewed as offensive or demeaning to those included in the delineation.

III

... [T]he Court orders strict scrutiny for districting plans "predominantly motivated" by race. No longer can a State avoid judicial oversight by giving ... genuine and measurable consideration to traditional districting practices.... This invitation to litigate against the State seems to me neither necessary nor proper.

A

The Court derives its test from diverse opinions on the relevance of race in contexts distinctly unlike apportionment....

In adopting districting plans, however, States do not treat people as individuals. Apportionment schemes, by their very nature, assemble people in groups. States do not assign voters to districts based on merit or achievement, standards States might use in hiring employees or engaging contractors....

That ethnicity defines some of these groups is a political reality.... Until now, no constitutional infirmity has been seen in districting Irish or Italian voters together, for example, so long as the delineation does not abandon familiar apportionment practices.... If Chinese–Americans and Russian–Americans may seek and secure group recognition in the delineation of voting districts, then African–Americans should not be dissimilarly treated. Otherwise, in the name of equal protection, we would shut out "the very minority group whose history in the United States gave birth to the Equal Protection Clause." See *Shaw* ... (Stevens, J., dissenting).[12]

B

Under the Court's approach, judicial review of the same intensity, *i.e.*, strict scrutiny, is in order once it is determined that an apportionment is predominantly motivated by race. It matters not at all ... whether the apportionment dilutes or enhances minority voting strength. [H]owever, "[t]here is no moral or constitutional equivalence between a policy that is designed to perpetuate a caste system and one that seeks to eradicate racial subordination." ...

Special circumstances justify vigilant judicial inspection to protect minority voters—circumstances that do not apply to majority voters. A history of exclusion from state politics left racial minorities without clout to extract provisions for fair representation in the lawmaking forum.... The equal protection rights of minority voters thus could have remained unrealized absent the Judiciary's close surveillance.... The majority, by definition, encounters no such blockage. White voters in Georgia do not lack means to exert strong pressure on their state legislators. The force of their numbers is itself a powerful determiner of what the legislature will do that does not coincide with perceived majority interests.

State legislatures ... today operate under federal constraints imposed by the Voting Rights Act—constraints justified by history and designed by Congress to make once-subordinated people free and equal citizens. But these federal constraints do not leave majority voters in need of extraordinary judicial solicitude. The Attorney General ... is herself a political actor. She ... is no doubt aware of the political cost of venturing too far to the detriment of majority voters. Majority voters, furthermore, can press the State to seek judicial review if the Attorney General refuses to preclear a plan that the voters favor. Finally, the Act is itself a political measure, subject to modification in the political process.

C

The Court's disposition renders redistricting perilous work for state legislatures. Statutory mandates and political realities may require States to consider race when drawing district lines.... But today's decision is a counterforce; it opens the way for federal litigation if "traditional ... districting principles" arguably were accorded less weight than race.... Genuine attention to traditional districting practices and avoidance of bizarre configurations seemed, under *Shaw*, to provide a safe harbor.... In view of today's decision, that is no longer the case.

12. Race-conscious practices a State may elect to pursue, of course, are not as limited as those it may be required to pursue. See Voinovich v. Quilter, 507 U.S. 146, 156 (1993) ("[F]ederal courts may not order the creation of majority-minority districts unless necessary to remedy a violation of federal law. But that does not mean that the State's powers are similarly limited. Quite the opposite is true....").

Only after litigation—under either the Voting Rights Act, the Court's new *Miller* standard, or both—will States now be assured that plans conscious of race are safe. Federal judges in large numbers may be drawn into the fray. This enlargement of the judicial role is unwarranted. The reapportionment plan that resulted from Georgia's political process merited this Court's approbation, not its condemnation. Accordingly, I dissent.

RACIAL GERRYMANDERING AND THE VOTING RIGHTS ACT

A year after Miller v. Johnson, the Court, by the same 5–4 alignment, invalidated four more majority-minority districts—one from North Carolina and three from Texas—constructed after the 1990 census with attention to the perceived requirements of the Voting Rights Act ("VRA") and the Justice Department's ("DOJ") enforcement of it. The new companion cases again addressed the nature of the cause of action first recognized in Shaw v. Reno, 509 U.S. 630 (1993) (*Shaw I*); the threshold showing required to trigger strict scrutiny of congressional districts configured in race-conscious fashion; compliance with the Voting Rights Act as a compelling state interest; and the elements of narrow tailoring necessary to satisfy strict scrutiny.

The North Carolina case, Shaw v. Hunt, 517 U.S. 899 (1996) (*Shaw II*), reversed a decision of the District Court, on remand of *Shaw I*, that the State's two majority-minority districts, though deliberately drawn to produce a certain racial composition, were "constitutional, nonetheless, because ... narrowly tailored to further the State's compelling interests in complying with §§ 2 and 5 of the Voting Rights Act...." Refusing to address the challenge to one of the majority-minority districts, because no plaintiffs resided within it nor "provided specific evidence that they personally were assigned to their voting districts on the basis of race[,]" the Court held the other district unconstitutional as "not narrowly tailored to serve a compelling state interest."

The State's initial districting plan had included only one majority-minority district, but when DOJ refused preclearance under VRA § 5 for failure "to give effect to black and Native American voting strength" in a *southern* part of the State for reasons DOJ considered "pretextual," the State submitted, and received preclearance for, a revised plan with a second majority-black district (District 12) in a *northern* part of the State. Applying *Miller*, Chief Justice Rehnquist's majority opinion first found race to be the "predominant factor in drawing" District 12, requiring strict scrutiny to be satisfied. The State could not rely on a compelling interest in remedying past or present racial discrimination, because the District Court had found that such an interest "did not actually precipitate the use of race in the redistricting plan." As for the claim "that the race-based redistricting was constitutionally justified by the State's duty to comply with the Voting Rights Act[,]" the Court "once again" did "not reach" the "question whether under the proper circumstances compliance with the Voting Rights Act, on its own, could be a compelling interest[,] ... because we find that creating an additional majority-black district was not required under a correct reading of § 5 and that District 12, as drawn, is not a remedy narrowly tailored to the State's professed interest in avoiding § 2 liability." Since the State's "first plan ... was ameliorative, having created the first majority-black district in recent history[,]" *Miller* made clear that the plan would not violate § 5 and its "nonretrogression" standard absent independently unconstitutional racial discrimination.

The argument in favor of District 12 based on avoiding § 2 liability elicited this response:

"... Our precedent establishes that a plaintiff may allege a § 2 violation in a single-member district if the manipulation of districting lines fragments politically cohesive minority voters among several districts or packs them into one district or a small number of districts, and thereby dilutes the voting strength of members of the minority population.... To prevail on such a claim, a plaintiff must prove that the minority group 'is sufficiently large and geographically compact to constitute a majority in a single-member district'; that the minority group 'is politically cohesive'; and that 'the white majority votes sufficiently as a bloc to enable it ... usually to defeat the minority's preferred candidate.' Thornburg v. Gingles, 478 U.S. 30, 50–51 (1986).... A court must also consider all other relevant circumstances and must ultimately find based on the totality of those circumstances that members of a protected class 'have less opportunity than other members of the electorate to participate in the political process and to elect representatives of their choice.' [§ 2(b)]....

"We assume, *arguendo*, ... that compliance with § 2 could be a compelling interest, and we likewise assume, *arguendo*, that the General Assembly believed a second majority-minority district was needed in order not to violate § 2, and that the legislature at the time it acted had a strong basis in evidence to support that conclusion. [Still,] the North Carolina plan does not survive strict scrutiny because the remedy—the creation of District 12—is not narrowly tailored to the asserted end."

The reason was that the legislature "must, at a minimum, remedy the anticipated [§ 2] violation or achieve compliance to be narrowly tailored." Here, however, District 12 did not "contain[] a 'geographically compact' population of any race" and the "vote dilution injuries suffered by [people in one area of the State] are not remedied by creating a safe majority-black district somewhere else in the State." It was "a misconception of the vote-dilution claim" to believe that it "belongs to the minority as a group and not to its individual members."

The companion Texas case, Bush v. Vera, 517 U.S. 952 (1996), affirmed invalidation of three districts under *Shaw I* and *Miller* but revealed important disagreements among the five majority Justices regarding (1) the level of race-consciousness in districting that will provoke strict scrutiny and (2) their willingness to announce that compliance with the results test of § 2 is a compelling state interest. A plurality opinion by Justice O'Connor, joined by Chief Justice Rehnquist and Justice Kennedy, expressly noted that "[s]trict scrutiny does not apply merely because redistricting is performed with consciousness of race ... [nor] to all cases of intentional creation of majority-minority districts[, but only where] ... legitimate districting principles were 'subordinated' to race." They "differ[ed] from Justice Thomas, who would apparently hold that it suffices that racial considerations be *a* motivation for the drawing of a majority-minority district." They thought further inquiry necessary for "mixed motive case[s]" like this one, involving "other goals, particularly incumbency protection...." Nonetheless, the combination of the District Court's "findings—that the State substantially neglected traditional districting criteria such as compactness, that it was committed from the outset to creating majority-minority districts, and that it manipulated district lines to exploit unprecedentedly detailed racial data—together weigh in favor of the application of strict scrutiny[, although w]e do not hold that any one of these factors is independently sufficient to require strict scrutiny."

Justice Thomas, joined by Justice Scalia, concurred only in the judgment to disagree "with Justice O'Connor's assertion that strict scrutiny is not invoked by the intentional creation of majority-minority districts":

"... [T]he intentional creation of a majority-minority district certainly means more than mere awareness that application of traditional, race-neutral districting principles will result in the creation of a district in which a majority of the district's residents are members of a particular minority group. See Personnel Administrator of Mass. v. Feeney, 442 U.S. 256, 279 (1979) (distinguishing discriminatory intent from 'intent as volition' or 'intent as awareness of consequences'). In my view, it means that the legislature affirmatively undertakes to create a majority-minority district that would not have existed but for the express use of racial classifications—in other words, that a majority-minority district is created 'because of,' and not merely 'in spite of,' racial demographics. See ibid. When that occurs, traditional race-neutral districting principles are necessarily subordinated (and race necessarily predominates), and the legislature has classified persons on the basis of race. The resulting redistricting must be viewed as a racial gerrymander."

Because "Texas readily admits that it intentionally created majority-minority districts and that those districts would not have existed but for its affirmative use of racial demographics ... strict scrutiny" was appropriate.

The plurality, by contrast, undertook individualized examination of each district and ultimately concluded that race predominated in the drawing of the "bizarre shapes" of all three. With respect to the majority-black District 30 in Dallas County, the plurality acknowledged that "[i]n some circumstances, incumbency protection might explain as well as, or better than, race a State's decision to depart from other traditional districting principles, such as compactness, in the drawing of bizarre district lines[,]" but it emphasized that "to the extent that race is used as a proxy for political characteristics [i.e., assuming that to include blacks is to include Democrats], a racial stereotype requiring strict scrutiny is in operation." With respect to the interlocking majority-black and majority-Hispanic districts in the Houston area—"two of the three least regular districts in the country"—the influence of incumbency protection was "overwhelmed ... by the State's efforts to maximize racial divisions"—especially given "the intricacy of the lines drawn, separating Hispanic voters from African–American voters on a block-by-block basis, betray[ing] the critical impact of the block-by-block racial data available on the [computer software] program."

As in *Shaw II*, each of the districts was "not narrowly tailored" to a compelling state interest. The plurality again assumed without deciding that compliance with the results test of § 2 "can be a compelling state interest[,]" though Justice O'Connor went further and separately concurred in her own plurality opinion to join the dissenters in affirming for a different Court majority that "the States have a compelling interest in complying with the results test as this Court has interpreted it." The plurality "also reaffirm[ed] that the 'narrow tailoring' requirement of strict scrutiny allows the States a limited degree of leeway" and leaves the States "flexibility that federal courts enforcing § 2 lack, ... insofar as deference is due to their reasonable fears of, and to their reasonable efforts to avoid, § 2 liability." But "§ 2 does not require a State to create, on predominantly racial lines, a district that is not 'reasonably compact.' ... If, because of the dispersion of the minority population, a reasonably compact majority-minority district cannot be created, § 2 does not require a majority-minority district; if a reasonably compact district can be created, nothing in § 2 requires the race-based creation of a district that is far from compact." The plurality continued:

"... Significant deviations from traditional districting principles, such as the bizarre shape and noncompactness demonstrated by the districts here, cause constitutional harm insofar as they convey the message that political identity is, or should be, predominantly racial. [B]izarre shaping ... is part of the constitutional problem insofar as it disrupts nonracial bases of political identity and thus intensifies the emphasis on race.

" ... The districts before us exhibit a level of racial manipulation that exceeds what § 2 could justify."

The plurality concluded by rejecting the dissenters' calls for reconsidering the *Shaw I* cause of action, stating in part:

"Legislators and district courts nationwide have modified their practices— or, rather, reembraced the traditional districting practices that were almost universally followed before the 1990 census—in response to *Shaw I*. Those practices and our precedents, which acknowledge voters as more than mere racial statistics, play an important role in defining the political identity of the American voter. Our Fourteenth Amendment jurisprudence evinces a commitment to eliminate unnecessary and excessive governmental use and reinforcement of racial stereotypes.... We decline to retreat from that commitment today."

Justice O'Connor's separate opinion also addressed the dissenters:

"Although I agree with the dissenters about § 2's role as part of our national commitment to racial equality, I differ from them in my belief that that commitment can and must be reconciled with the complementary commitment of our Fourteenth Amendment jurisprudence to eliminate the unjustified use of racial stereotypes....

" ... The Voting Rights Act requires the States and the courts to take action to remedy the reality of racial inequality in our political system, sometimes necessitating race-based action, while the Fourteenth Amendment requires us to look with suspicion on the excessive use of racial considerations by the government. But I believe that the States, playing a primary role, and the courts, in their secondary role, are capable of distinguishing the appropriate and reasonably necessary uses of race from its unjustified and excessive uses."

Justice Stevens, joined by Justices Ginsburg and Breyer, filed separate, extended dissents in *Shaw II* and *Vera*.[c] Justice Souter's lengthy dissent, filed in *Vera* but applicable to both cases, was also joined by Justices Ginsburg and Breyer. It called on the Court "to admit *Shaw*'s failure" and abandon the *Shaw* cause of action altogether.

Justice Stevens contended in *Shaw II* that "the record reveals that two race-neutral, traditional districting criteria determined District 12's shape: the interest in ensuring that incumbents would remain residents of the districts they have previously represented; and the interest in placing predominantly rural voters in one district and predominantly urban voters in another." In any event, insofar as the majority assumed that the State had drawn District 12 to avoid § 2 liability, "it cannot be correct to say that a racially discriminatory purpose controlled its line-drawing. A more accurate conclusion would be that

c. Justices Ginsburg and Breyer did not join that portion of Justice Stevens' dissent in *Shaw II* elaborating his criticism in *Miller* and *Hays* that the Court's conception of "standing" and "injury" in its "emerging and misguided race-based districting jurisprudence" was fundamentally flawed. Justice Stevens urged in part that "the constitutional claim ... ultimately depends for its success on little more than speculative judicial suppositions about the societal message that is to be gleaned from race-based districting. I know of no workable constitutional principle, however, that can discern whether the message conveyed is a distressing endorsement of racial separatism, or an inspiring call to integrate the political process."

the State took race into account only to the extent necessary to meet the requirements of a carefully thought out federal statute.... The majority's implicit equation of the intentional consideration of race in order to comply with the Voting Rights Act with intentional racial discrimination reveals the inadequacy of the framework it adopts for considering the constitutionality of race-based districting."

In *Vera*, he argued that "the fair implications of the District Court's findings" were "that Texas' entire map is a political, not a racial gerrymander"—even though it was "clear that race also played a role...." He noted and reinforced the Court's endorsement of the view that a State constitutionally may consider race in the deliberate creation of majority-minority districts, reasoning that "when the state action (i) has neither the intent nor effect of harming any particular group, (ii) is not designed to give effect to irrational prejudices held by its citizens but to break them down, and (iii) uses race as a classification because race is 'relevant' to the benign goal of the classification, ... we need not view the action with the typically fatal skepticism that we have used to strike down the most pernicious forms of state behavior." He found "overwhelming evidence that incumbency protection was the critical motivating factor in the creation of the bizarre Texas districts," and thought it "neither irrational, nor invidious ... to assume that a black resident of a particular community is a Democrat if reliable statistical evidence discloses that 97% of the blacks in that community vote in Democratic primary elections."

Even assuming the applicability of strict scrutiny, Justice Stevens thought the challenged districts were narrowly tailored to the compelling interest of compliance with the VRA. In *Shaw II*, he thought it irrelevant that District 12 "did not 'remedy' any potential violation of § 2" in southern North Carolina, because a second majority-minority district anywhere in the State would have precluded § 2 liability. As for the Texas districts in *Vera*, Justice Stevens objected to the Court's "insist[ence] that the lack of compactness in the districts prevent them from being 'narrowly tailored'[,]" because "if there is no independent constitutional duty to create compact districts in the first place, and the Court suggests none, there is no reason why noncompact districts should not be a permissible method of avoiding violations of law. The fact that they might be unacceptable judicial remedies does not speak to the question whether they may be acceptable when adopted by a state legislature...."

He concluded with these statements:

"... Perhaps minority candidates, forced to run in majority-white districts, will be able to overcome the long history of stereotyping and discrimination that has heretofore led the vast majority of majority-white districts to reject minority candidacies. Perhaps not. I am certain only that bodies of elected federal and state officials are in a far better position than anyone on this Court to assess whether the Nation's long history of discrimination has been overcome, and that nothing in the Constitution requires this unnecessary intrusion into the ability of States to negotiate solutions to political differences while providing long-excluded groups the opportunity to participate effectively in the democratic process...."

Justice Souter's dissent urged the Court "to recognize that *Shaw*'s problems result from a basic misconception about the relation between race and districting principles ... that no amount of case-by-case tinkering can eliminate." The idea "that racial groups, like all other groups, play a real and legitimate role in political decisionmaking ... involves nothing more than an acknowledgement of the reality that our concepts of common interest, geography, and personal allegiances are in many places simply too bound up with race to deny some room for a theory of representative democracy allowing for the consideration of racially conceived interests." This "use of race ... conveys no message about the inferiority or outsider status of members of the white majority excluded from a district ... [and] implies nothing about the capacity or value of the minority to which it gives the chance of electoral success." Moreover, *Shaw* has the "further conceptual inadequacy [that w]hereas it defines injury as the reinforcement of the notion that members of a racial group will prefer the same candidates at the polls, the immediate object of the constitutional prohibition against the intentional dilution of minority voting strength is to protect the right of minority voters to make just such a preference effective."

Justice Souter raised special objection to the unmanageability of *Miller*'s "predominant motive" standard, "not merely" because "the very nature of districting decisions makes it difficult to identify whether any particular consideration, racial or otherwise," predominated, but "more fundamental[ly,]" because "in the political environment in which race can affect election results, many of these traditional districting principles cannot be applied without taking race into account and are thus, as a practical matter, inseparable from the supposedly illegitimate racial considerations":

"If ... a legislature may draw district lines to preserve the integrity of a given community, ... this objective is inseparable from preserving the community's racial identity when the community is characterized, or even self-defined, by the race of the majority of those who live there...

"Or take the traditional principle of providing protection for incumbents.... [I]f the incumbent has drawn support largely for racial reasons [or] was elected in a majority-minority district created to remedy vote dilution that resulted from racial bloc voting[, i]t would be sheer fantasy to assume that consideration of race in these circumstances is somehow separable from application of the traditional principle of incumbency protection, and sheer incoherence to think that the consideration of race that is constitutionally required to remedy Fourteenth and Fifteenth Amendment vote dilution somehow becomes unconstitutional when aimed at protecting the incumbent the next time the census requires redistricting."

In Abrams v. Johnson, 521 U.S. 74 (1997), the district court, on remand from Miller v. Johnson, supra, adopted a new congressional reapportionment plan providing for one majority-minority district after the Georgia legislature deadlocked, with the House having provided for two and the Senate just one. This time black voters, joined by the United States, challenged the court's remedial plan for "making more changes than necessary to cure constitutional defects in the previous plan [and for] violating §§ 2 and 5 of the Voting Rights Act of 1965...." By the same 5–4 vote as in *Miller*, the Supreme Court rejected this attack.

Justice Kennedy's majority opinion emphasized, among other things, that "[i]nterference by the Justice Department, leading the state legislature to act based on an overriding concern with race," rendered deference to post–1990 census state redistricting plans inappropriate. He concluded that "the trial court acted well within its discretion in deciding it could not draw two majority-black districts without itself engaging in racial gerrymandering." Because "the District Court found, without clear error, that the black population was not sufficiently compact for a second majority-black district" and that there was "insufficient racial polarization in voting to meet the *Gingles* requirements"—a conclusion supported by the fact that "[a]ll three black incumbents won elections under the court plan, two in majority-white districts running against white candidates"—there was no § 2 violation. As for § 5, there was no showing "that black voters in any particular district suffered a retrogression in their voting strength under the court plan . . . ."

Justice Breyer's dissent argued that the Georgia legislature had expressed a preference for at least two majority-black districts and that, because a "two-district plan is not unconstitutional[,]" the majority was wrong not to follow that preference. He thought the district court and the majority improperly had discounted Georgia's plans as tainted by Justice Department interference, whereas the Department's pressure on the Georgia legislature was no more objectionable than other "political pressures" routinely applied in the redistricting process. Moreover, he disagreed with what he understood to be the majority's view "that a two-district plan . . . would violate the Constitution as interpreted in *Miller*." He contended that a second compact majority-black district could have been created; noted that the district court had conceded "some degree of vote polarization"; and suggested that the district court had "asked the wrong question":

"... The question is not about whether the evidence proves § 2 *in fact requires* two majority-minority districts. The question is whether the evidence is strong enough to justify a legislature's reasonable belief that that was so. The record rather clearly demonstrates a 'strong basis in the evidence' for *believing* that § 2 or § 5 required two majority-minority districts. . . .

"This legal distinction—between whether a plan really violates § 2 or might well violate § 2—may seem technical. But it is not. A legal rule that permits legislatures to take account of race only when § 2 *really* requires them to do so is a rule that shifts the power to redistrict from legislatures to federal courts (for only the latter can say what § 2 *really* requires). A rule that rests upon a reasonable view of the evidence (i.e., that permits the legislature to use race if it has a *'strong basis' for believing* it necessary to do so) is a rule that leaves at least a modicum of discretionary (race-related) redistricting authority in the hands of legislators. . . ."

HUNT v. CROMARTIE, 526 U.S. 541 (1999). After the Supreme Court ruled in *Shaw II* that North Carolina's Twelfth Congressional District constituted an unconstitutional racial gerrymander, the State redrew District 12 in 1997, reducing its black population below a majority, splitting fewer counties, and making it smaller. In a new suit challenging the redrawn district on the same ground, the district court granted the challengers' summary judgment motion, finding as "uncontroverted material facts" that "District 12 was drawn to collect precincts with high racial identification rather than political identification," that "more heavily Democratic precincts . . . were bypassed in the drawing of District 12 and included in the surrounding congressional districts," and that "[t]he legislature disregarded traditional districting criteria."

The Supreme Court reversed in an opinion by Justice Thomas. Although the circumstantial "evidence tends to support an inference that the State drew its district lines with an impermissible racial motive[,] . . . [t]he District Court nevertheless was only partially correct in stating that the material facts before it were uncontroverted." The "legislature's motivation is itself a factual question[,]" and data analysis had been submitted supporting "an inference that the General Assembly did no more than create a district of strong partisan Democrats." On motion for summary judgment the District Court was required to accept the "political motivation explanation as true," meaning that "appellees were not entitled to judgment as a matter of law." Specifically, "[e]vidence that blacks constitute even a supermajority in one congressional district while amounting to less than a plurality in a neighboring district will not, by itself, suffice to prove that a jurisdiction was motivated by race in drawing its district lines when the evidence also shows a high correlation between race and party preference." The "evidence might allow the District Court to find that the State acted with an impermissible racial motivation, despite the State's explanation ..., [but] it does not require that the court do so. All that can be said on the record before us is that motivation was in dispute...." After trial, the evidence might "support a finding that race was the State's predominant motive," but the case "was not suited for summary disposition."

In an opinion concurring in the judgment, Justice Stevens, joined by Justices Souter, Ginsburg and Breyer, wrote in part:

"[A]ppellees' evidence may include nothing more than (i) a bizarre shape, which is equally consistent with either political or racial motivation, (ii) registration data, which are virtually irrelevant when actual voting results were available and which point in a different direction, and (iii) knowledge of the racial composition of the district. Because we do not have before us the question whether the District Court erred in denying the State's motion for summary judgment, I need not decide whether that circumstantial evidence even raises an inference of improper motive."

In a responsive footnote to Justice Stevens, Justice Thomas stated:

"... We do not necessarily quarrel with the proposition that a district's unusual shape can give rise to an inference of political motivation. But we doubt that a bizarre shape equally supports a political inference and a racial one...."

EASLEY v. CROMARTIE, 532 U.S. 234 (2001). On remand from the reversal of summary judgment in Hunt v. Cromartie, the three-judge District Court held a 3–day trial and again concluded, over one dissent, that the North Carolina legislature unconstitutionally had used race as the "predominant factor" in drawing the 1997 boundaries of its 12th Congressional District. On direct appeal, the Supreme Court again reversed, this time finding the District Court's findings "clearly erroneous." Calling the issue "evidentiary," and engaging in "extensive review," Justice Breyer's majority opinion "concede[d that] the record contains a modicum of evidence offering support for the District Court's conclusion[,]" but concluded that the "evidence, taken together, ... does not show that racial considerations predominated in the drawing of District 12's boundaries ... because race in this case correlates closely with political behavior." He continued:

"The basic question is whether the legislature drew District 12's boundaries because of race *rather than* because of political behavior (coupled with traditional, nonracial districting considerations). It is not, as the dissent contends, whether a legislature may defend its districting decisions based on a 'stereotype' about African–American voting behavior. And given the fact that the party attacking the legislature's decision bears the burden of proving that racial considerations are 'dominant and controlling,' *Miller* ..., given the 'demanding' nature of that burden of proof, id. ... (O'Connor, J., concurring), and given the sensitivity, the 'extraordinary caution,' that district courts must show to avoid treading upon legislative prerogatives, id. ... (majority opinion), the attacking party has not successfully shown that race, rather than politics, predominantly accounts for the result. The record leaves us with the 'definite and firm conviction,' ... that the District Court erred in finding to the contrary....

"... [M]ore generally ...: In a case such as this one where majority-minority districts (or the approximate equivalent) are at issue and where racial identification correlates highly with political affiliation, the party attacking the legislatively drawn boundaries must show at the least that the legislature could have achieved its legitimate political objectives in alternative ways that are comparably consistent with traditional districting principles. That party must also show that those districting alternatives would have brought about significantly greater racial balance. Appellees failed to make any such showing here...."

Justice Thomas, joined by Chief Justice Rehnquist and Justices Scalia and Kennedy, dissented. Objecting that "the Court ignores its role as a reviewing court and engages in its own factfinding enterprise[,]" he concluded that "[i]f I were the District Court, I might have reached the same conclusion that the Court does[,]" but that "[i]n light of the direct evidence of racial motive and the inferences that may be drawn from the circumstantial evidence, I am satisfied that the District Court's finding was permissible, even if not compelled by the record." In the course of his opinion, he expressed the view that it was "[un]necessary to impose a new burden on appellees to show districting alternatives would have brought about 'significantly greater racial balance.'" He also said that

> "the District Court was assigned the task of determining *whether*, not *why*, race predominated. As I see it, this inquiry is sufficient to answer the constitutional question because racial gerrymandering offends the Constitution whether the motivation is malicious or benign. It is not a defense that the legislature merely may have drawn the district based on the stereotype that blacks are reliable Democratic voters."

Vieth v. Jubelirer

541 U.S. 267, 124 S.Ct. 1769, 158 L.Ed.2d 546 (2004).

Justice Scalia announced the judgment of the Court and delivered an opinion, in which The Chief Justice, Justice O'Connor, and Justice Thomas join.

Plaintiffs-appellants ... challenge a map drawn by the Pennsylvania General Assembly establishing districts for the election of congressional Representatives, on the ground that the districting constitutes an unconstitutional political gerrymander. In *Davis v. Bandemer,* 478 U.S. 109 (1986), this Court held that political gerrymandering claims are justiciable, but could not agree upon a standard to adjudicate them. The present appeal ... questions whether ... *Bandemer* was in error, and, if not, what the standard should be.

I

[Following the 2000 census, Pennsylvania's delegation in Congress decreased from 21 to 19 Representatives. Democratic voters challenged the subsequent redistricting plan, alleging that—under pressure from prominent national figures in the Republican Party to adopt a partisan redistricting plan as a punitive measure against Democrats for having enacted pro-Democrat redistricting plans elsewhere—the Republican controlling majorities in both houses of Pennsylvania's legislature, together with the Republican Governor, had adopted a politically gerrymandered plan in violation of Article I and the Equal Protection Clause of the Fourteenth Amendment. The new congressional districts were said to be "meandering and irregular," and to "ignor[e] all traditional redistricting criteria, including the preservation of local government boundaries, solely for the sake of partisan advantage." A three-judge District

Court dismissed the political gerrymandering claim, and the Supreme Court noted probable jurisdiction.]

II

Political gerrymanders are not new to the American scene. One scholar traces them back to the Colony of Pennsylvania at the beginning of the 18th century.... [A]t the time of the framing [t]here were allegations that Patrick Henry attempted (unsuccessfully) to gerrymander James Madison out of the First Congress.... And in 1812 ... there occurred the notoriously outrageous political districting in Massachusetts that gave the gerrymander its name—an amalgam of the names of Massachusetts Governor Elbridge Gerry and the creature ("salamander") which the outline of an election district he was credited with forming was thought to resemble. ... "By 1840 the gerrymander was a recognized force in party politics and was generally attempted in all legislation enacted for the formation of election districts. It was generally conceded that each party would attempt to gain power which was not proportionate to its numerical strength." ...

It is significant that the Framers provided a remedy for such practices in the Constitution. Article 1, § 4, while leaving in state legislatures the initial power to draw districts for federal elections, permitted Congress to "make or alter" those districts if it wished....

The power bestowed on Congress ... to restrain the practice of political gerrymandering ... has not lain dormant. In the Apportionment Act of 1842, Congress provided that Representatives must be elected from single-member districts "composed of contiguous territory." ... (... "an attempt to forbid the practice of the gerrymander"). Congress again imposed these requirements in the Apportionment Act of 1862, ... and in 1872 further required that districts "contai[n] as nearly as practicable an equal number of inhabitants,".... In the Apportionment Act of 1901, Congress imposed a compactness requirement.... The requirements of contiguity, compactness, and equality of population were repeated in the 1911 apportionment legislation, but were not thereafter continued. Today, only the single-member-district-requirement remains.... Recent history, however, attests to Congress's awareness of the sort of districting practices appellants protest, and of its power under Article I, § 4 to control them. Since 1980, no fewer than five bills have been introduced to regulate gerrymandering in congressional districting....

Eighteen years ago, we held that the Equal Protection Clause grants judges the power—and duty—to control political gerrymandering, see *Davis v. Bandemer*.... It is to consideration of this precedent that we now turn.

III

... Sometimes ... the judicial department has no business entertaining [a] claim of unlawfulness—because the question is entrusted to one of the political branches or involves no judicially enforceable rights. See, *e.g., Nixon v. United States,* 506 U.S. 224 (1993) (challenge to procedures used in Senate impeachment proceedings); *Pacific States Telephone & Telegraph Co. v. Oregon,* 223 U.S. 118 (1912) (claims arising under the Guaranty Clause of Article IV, § 4). Such questions are said to be "nonjusticiable," or "political questions."

... "The judicial Power" created by Article III, § 1 ... is the power to act in the manner traditional for English and American courts. One of the most obvious limitations imposed by that requirement is that judicial action must be governed by *standard,* by *rule.* Laws promulgated by the Legislative Branch can be inconsistent, illogical, and ad hoc; law pronounced by the courts must be principled, rational, and based upon reasoned distinctions.

Over the dissent of three Justices, the Court held in *Davis v. Bandemer* that, since it was "not persuaded that there are no judicially discernible and manageable standards by which political gerrymander cases are to be decided," . . . such cases *were* justiciable. The clumsy shifting of the burden of proof for the premise (the Court was "not persuaded" that standards do not exist, rather than "persuaded" that they do) was necessitated by the uncomfortable fact that the six-Justice majority could not discern what the judicially discernable standards might be. There was no majority on that point. Four of the Justices finding justiciability believed that the standard was one thing . . . (plurality opinion of White, J., joined by Brennan, Marshall, and Blackmun, JJ.); two believed it was something else . . . (Powell, J., joined by Stevens, J., concurring in part and dissenting in part). The lower courts have lived with that assurance of a standard (or more precisely, lack of assurance that there is no standard), coupled with that inability to specify a standard, for the past 18 years. In that time, they have considered numerous political gerrymandering claims; this Court has never revisited the unanswered question of what standard governs.

Nor can it be said that the lower courts have, over 18 years, succeeded in shaping the standard that this Court was initially unable to enunciate. They have simply applied the standard set forth in *Bandemer's* four-Justice plurality opinion. This might be thought to prove that the four-Justice plurality standard has met the test of time—but for the fact that its application has almost invariably produced the same result . . . as would have obtained if the question were nonjusticiable: judicial intervention has been refused. . . . The one case in which relief was provided . . . did *not* involve the drawing of district lines; in *all* of the cases we are aware of involving that most common form of political gerrymandering, relief was denied. . . . To think that this lower-court jurisprudence has brought forth "judicially discernible and manageable standards" would be fantasy.

Eighteen years of judicial effort with virtually nothing to show for it justify us in revisiting the question whether the standard promised by *Bandemer* exists. As the following discussion reveals, no judicially discernible and manageable standards for adjudicating political gerrymandering claims have emerged. Lacking them, we must conclude that political gerrymandering claims are nonjusticiable and that *Bandemer* was wrongly decided.

A

We begin our review of possible standards with that proposed by Justice White's plurality opinion in *Bandemer* because, as the narrowest ground for our decision in that case, it has been the standard employed by the lower courts. The plurality concluded that a political gerrymandering claim could succeed only where plaintiffs showed "both intentional discrimination against an identifiable political group and an actual discriminatory effect on that group." . . . As to the intent element, the plurality acknowledged that "[a]s long as redistricting is done by a legislature, it should not be very difficult to prove that the likely political consequences of the reapportionment were intended." . . . However, the effects prong was significantly harder to satisfy. Relief could not be based merely upon the fact that a group of persons banded together for political purposes had failed to achieve representation commensurate with its numbers, or that the apportionment scheme made its winning of elections more difficult. . . . Rather, it would have to be shown that, taking into account a variety of historic factors and projected election results, the group had been "denied its chance to effectively influence the political process" as a whole, which could be achieved even without electing a candidate. . . . [I]n a challenge to an individual district the inquiry would focus "on the opportunity of members of the group to participate in party deliberations in the slating and nomination of candidates, their opportunity to register and vote, and hence their chance to directly influence the election returns and to secure the attention of the winning candidate." . . . A statewide challenge, by contrast, would involve an analysis of "the voters' direct *or indirect* influence on the elections of the state legislature as a whole." . . . With what has proved to be a gross understatement, the plurality acknowledged this was "of necessity a difficult inquiry." . . .

In her *Bandemer* concurrence, Justice O'Connor predicted that the plurality's standard "will over time either prove unmanageable and arbitrary or else evolve towards some loose form of proportionality." . . . A similar prediction of unmanageability was expressed in Justice Powell's opinion, making it the prognostication of a majority of the Court. . . . That prognostication has been amply fulfilled.

In the lower courts, the legacy of the plurality's test is one long record of puzzlement and consternation. . . . The test has been criticized for its indeterminacy by a host of academic commentators. See, *e.g.,* L. Tribe, American Constitutional Law § 13–9, p. 1083 (2d ed. 1988) ("Neither Justice White's nor Justice Powell's approach to the question of partisan apportionment gives any real guidance to lower courts forced to adjudicate this issue . . ."); . . . Because this standard was misguided when proposed, has not been improved in subsequent application, and is not even defended before us today by the appellants, we decline to affirm it as a constitutional requirement.

B

Appellants . . . propose[to] retain[] the two-pronged framework of the *Bandemer* plurality—intent plus effect—but modif[y] the type of showing sufficient to satisfy each.

To satisfy appellants' intent standard, a plaintiff must "show that the mapmakers acted with a *predominant intent* to achieve partisan advantage," which can be shown "by direct evidence or by circumstantial evidence that other neutral and legitimate redistricting criteria were subordinated to the goal of achieving partisan advantage." . . . As compared with the *Bandemer* plurality's test of mere intent to disadvantage the plaintiff's group, this proposal seemingly makes the standard more difficult to meet—but only at the expense of making the standard more indeterminate.

"Predominant intent" to disadvantage the plaintiff political group refers to the relative importance of that goal as compared with all the other goals that the map seeks to pursue—contiguity of districts, compactness of districts, observance of the lines of political subdivision, protection of incumbents of all parties, cohesion of natural racial and ethnic neighborhoods, compliance with requirements of the Voting Rights Act of 1965 regarding racial distribution, etc. Appellants contend that their intent test *must* be discernible and manageable because it has been borrowed from our racial gerrymandering cases. See *Miller v. Johnson,* 515 U.S. 900 (1995); *Shaw v. Reno,* 509 U.S. 630 (1993). To begin with, in a very important respect that is not so. In the racial gerrymandering context, the predominant intent test has been applied to the challenged district in which the plaintiffs voted. . . . Here, however, appellants do not assert that an apportionment fails their intent test if any single district does so. Since "it would be quixotic to attempt to bar state legislatures from considering politics as they redraw district lines," Brief for Appellants 3, appellants propose a test that is satisfied only when "partisan advantage was the predominant motivation *behind the entire statewide plan*," . . . (emphasis added). Vague as the "predominant motivation" test might be when used to evaluate single districts, it all but evaporates when applied statewide. Does it mean, for instance, that partisan intent must outweigh all other goals—contiguity, compactness, preservation of neighborhoods, etc.—*statewide?* And how is the statewide "outweighing" to be determined? If three-fifths of the map's districts forgo the pursuit of partisan ends in favor of strictly observing political-subdivision lines, and only two-fifths ignore those lines to disadvantage the plaintiffs, is the observance of political subdivisions the "predominant" goal between those two? We are sure appellants do not think so.

Even within the narrower compass of challenges to a single district, applying a "predominant intent" test to *racial* gerrymandering is easier and less disruptive. The Constitution clearly contemplates districting by political entities, see Article I, § 4, and unsurprisingly that turns out to be root-and-branch a matter of politics. . . . By contrast, the purpose of segregating voters on the basis of race is not a lawful one, and is much more rarely encountered. Determining whether the shape of a particular district is so substantially affected by the presence of a rare and constitutionally suspect motive as to invalidate it is quite different from determining whether it is so substantially affected by the excess of an ordinary and lawful motive as to invalidate it. Moreover, the fact that partisan districting is a lawful and common practice means that there is almost *always* room for an election-impeding lawsuit contending that partisan advantage was the predominant motivation; not so for claims of racial gerrymandering. Finally, courts might be justified in accepting a modest degree of unmanageability to enforce a constitutional command which (like the Fourteenth Amendment obligation to refrain from racial discrimination) is clear; whereas they are not justified in inferring a judicially enforceable constitutional obligation (the obligation not to apply *too much* partisanship in districting) which is both dubious and severely unmanageable. For these reasons, to the extent that our racial gerrymandering cases represent a model of discernible and manageable standards, they provide no comfort here.

The effects prong of appellants' proposal replaces the *Bandemer* plurality's vague test of "denied its chance to effectively influence the political process," . . . with criteria that are seemingly more specific. The requisite effect is established when "(1) the plaintiffs show that the districts systematically 'pack' and 'crack' the rival party's voters,[7] *and* (2) the court's examination of the 'totality of circumstances' confirms that the map can thwart the plaintiffs' ability to translate a majority of votes into a majority of seats." . . . This test is loosely based on our cases applying § 2 of the Voting Rights Act . . . to discrimination by race. . . . But a person's politics is rarely as readily discernible—and *never* as permanently discernible—as a person's race. Political affiliation is not an immutable characteristic, but may shift from one election to the next; and even within a given election, not all voters follow the party line. We dare say (and hope) that the political party which puts forward an utterly incompetent candidate will lose even in its registration stronghold. These facts make it impossible to assess the effects of partisan gerrymandering, to fashion a standard for evaluating a violation, and finally to craft a remedy. . . .

---

7. "Packing" refers to the practice of filling a district with a supermajority of a given group or party. "Cracking" involves the splitting of a group or party among several districts to deny that group or party a majority in any of those districts.

Assuming, however, that the effects of partisan gerrymandering can be determined, appellants' test would invalidate the districting only when it prevents a majority of the electorate from electing a majority of representatives. Before considering whether this particular standard is judicially manageable we question whether it is judicially discernible in the sense of being relevant to some constitutional violation. Deny it as appellants may (and do), this standard rests upon the principle that groups (or at least political-action groups) have a right to proportional representation. But the Constitution contains no such principle. It guarantees equal protection of the law to persons, not equal representation in government to equivalently sized groups. It nowhere says that farmers or urban dwellers, Christian fundamentalists or Jews, Republicans or Democrats, must be accorded political strength proportionate to their numbers.

Even if the standard were relevant, however, it is not judicially manageable. To begin with, how is a party's majority status to be established? Appellants propose using the results of statewide races as the benchmark of party support. But as their own complaint describes, in the 2000 Pennsylvania statewide elections some Republicans won and some Democrats won.... Moreover, to think that majority status in statewide races establishes majority status for district contests, one would have to believe that the only factor determining voting behavior at all levels is political affiliation. That is assuredly not true....

But if we could identify a majority party, we would find it impossible to assure that that party wins a majority of seats—unless we radically revise the States' traditional structure for elections. In any winner-take-all district system, there can be no guarantee, no matter how the district lines are drawn, that a majority of party votes statewide will produce a majority of seats for that party.... Whether by reason of partisan districting or not, party constituents may always wind up "packed" in some districts and "cracked" throughout others.... [P]olitical groups that tend to cluster (as is the case with Democratic voters in cities) would be systematically affected by what might be called a "natural" packing effect....

Our one-person, one-vote cases ... have no bearing upon this question, neither in principle nor in practicality. Not in principle, because to say that each individual must have an equal say in the selection of representatives, and hence that a majority of individuals must have a majority say, is not at all to say that each discernable group, whether farmers or urban dwellers or political parties, must have representation equivalent to its numbers. And not in practicality, because the easily administrable standard of population equality adopted by *Wesberry* and *Reynolds* enables judges to decide whether a violation has occurred (and to remedy it) essentially on the basis of three readily determined factors—where the plaintiff lives, how many voters are in his district, and how many voters are in other districts; whereas requiring judges to decide whether a districting system will produce a statewide majority for a majority party casts them forth upon a sea of imponderables, and asks them to make determinations that not even election experts can agree upon.

For these reasons, we find appellants' proposed standards neither discernible nor manageable.

C

For many of the same reasons, we also reject the standard suggested by Justice Powell in *Bandemer*. He agreed with the plurality that a plaintiff should show intent and effect, but believed that the ultimate inquiry ought to focus on whether district boundaries had been drawn solely for partisan ends to the exclusion of "all other neutral factors relevant to the fairness of redistricting." . . .

. . . [His] is essentially a totality-of-the-circumstances analysis, where all conceivable factors, none of which is dispositive, are weighed with an eye to ascertaining whether the particular gerrymander has gone too far—or, in Justice Powell's terminology, whether it is not "fair." "Fairness" does not seem to us a judicially manageable standard. Fairness is compatible with noncontiguous districts, it is compatible with districts that straddle political subdivisions, and it is compatible with a party's not winning the number of seats that mirrors the proportion of its vote. Some criterion more solid and more demonstrably met than that seems to us necessary to enable the state legislatures to discern the limits of their districting discretion, to meaningfully constrain the discretion of the courts, and to win public acceptance for the courts' intrusion into a process that is the very foundation of democratic decisionmaking.

IV

We turn next to consideration of the standards proposed by today's dissenters. We preface it with the observation that the mere fact that these four dissenters come up with three different standards—all of them different from the two proposed in *Bandemer* and the one proposed here by appellants—goes a long way to establishing that there is no constitutionally discernible standard.

A

Justice Stevens concurs in the judgment that we should not address plaintiffs' statewide political gerrymandering challenges. Though he reaches that result via standing analysis, while we reach it through political-question analysis, our conclusions are the same: these statewide claims are nonjusticiable.

Justice Stevens would, however, require courts to consider political gerrymandering challenges at the individual-district level. Much of his dissent is addressed to the incompatibility of severe partisan gerrymanders with democratic principles. We do not disagree with that judgment. . . . The issue . . . is not whether severe partisan gerrymanders violate the Constitution, but whether it is for the courts to say when a violation has occurred, and to design a remedy. On that point, Justice Stevens's dissent is less helpful, saying, essentially, that if we can do it in the racial gerrymandering context we can do it here.

We have examined the many reasons why that is not so. . . .

Justice Stevens's confidence that what courts have done with racial gerrymandering can be done with political gerrymandering rests in part upon his belief that "the same standards should apply." But in fact the standards are quite different. A purpose to discriminate on the basis of race receives the strictest scrutiny under the Equal Protection Clause, while a similar purpose to discriminate on the basis of politics does not. . . .

Justice Stevens relies on *First Amendment cases* to suggest that politically discriminatory gerrymanders are subject to strict scrutiny under the *Equal Protection Clause*. It is elementary that scrutiny levels are claim specific. An action that triggers a heightened level of scrutiny for one claim may receive a very different level of scrutiny for a different claim because the underlying rights, and consequently constitutional harms, are not comparable. To say that suppression of political speech (a claimed First Amendment violation) triggers strict scrutiny is not to say that failure to give political groups equal representation (a claimed equal protection violation) triggers strict scrutiny. Only an equal protection claim is before us in the present case—perhaps for the very good reason that a First Amendment claim, if it were sustained, would render unlawful *all* consideration of political affiliation in districting, just as it renders unlawful *all* consideration of political affiliation in hiring for non-policy-level government jobs....

Having failed to make the case for strict scrutiny of political gerrymandering, Justice Stevens falls back on the argument that scrutiny levels simply do not matter for purposes of justiciability. He asserts that a standard imposing a strong presumption of invalidity (strict scrutiny) is no more discernible and manageable than a standard requiring an evenhanded balancing of all considerations with no thumb on the scales (ordinary scrutiny). To state this is to refute it. As is well known, strict scrutiny readily, and almost always, results in invalidation. Moreover, the mere fact that there exist standards which this Court could apply—the proposition which much of Justice Stevens's opinion is devoted to establishing—does not mean that those standards are discernible in the Constitution. This Court may not willy-nilly apply standards—even manageable standards—having no relation to constitutional harms....

B

Justice Souter, like Justice Stevens, would restrict these plaintiffs, on the allegations before us, to district-specific political gerrymandering claims. Unlike Justice Stevens, however, Justice Souter recognizes that there is no existing workable standard for adjudicating such claims. He proposes a "fresh start": a newly constructed standard loosely based in form on our Title VII cases, ... and complete with a five-step prima facie test sewn together from parts of, among other things, our Voting Rights Act jurisprudence, law review articles, and apportionment cases. Even if these self-styled "clues" to unconstitutionality could be manageably applied, which we doubt, there is no reason to think they would detect the constitutional crime which Justice Souter is investigating—an "extremity of unfairness" in partisan competition.

Under Justice Souter's proposed standard, in order to challenge a particular district, a plaintiff must show (1) that he is a member of a "cohesive political group"; (2) "that the district of his residence ... paid little or no heed" to traditional districting principles; (3) that there were "specific correlations between the district's deviations from traditional districting principles and the distribution of the population of his group"; (4) that a hypothetical district exists which includes the plaintiff's residence, remedies the packing or cracking of the plaintiff's group, and deviates less from traditional districting principles; and (5) that "the defendants acted intentionally to manipulate the shape of the district in order to pack or crack his group." When those showings have been made, the burden would shift to the defendants to justify the district "by reference to objectives other than naked partisan advantage."

While this five-part test seems eminently scientific, upon analysis one finds that each of the last four steps requires a quantifying judgment that is unguided and ill suited to the development of judicial standards: *How much* disregard of traditional districting principles? *How many* correlations between deviations and distribution? *How much* remedying of packing or cracking by the hypothetical district? *How many legislators* must have had the intent to pack and crack—and *how efficacious* must that intent have been (must it have been, for example, a *sine qua non* cause of the districting, or a *predominant* cause)? At step two, for example, Justice Souter would require lower courts to assess whether mapmakers paid "little or no heed to . . . traditional districting principles." What is a lower court to do when, as will often be the case, the district adheres to some traditional criteria but not others? Justice Souter's only response to this question is to evade it: "It is not necessary now to say exactly how a district court would balance a good showing on one of these indices against a poor showing on another, for that sort of detail is best worked out case by case." But the devil lurks precisely in such detail. The central problem is determining when political gerrymandering has gone too far. It does not solve that problem to break down the original unanswerable question (How much political motivation and effect is too much?) into four more discrete but equally unanswerable questions.

Justice Souter's proposal is doomed to failure for a more basic reason: No test . . . can possibly be successful unless one knows what he is testing *for*. In the present context, the test ought to identify deprivation of that minimal degree of representation or influence to which a political group is constitutionally entitled. As we have seen, the *Bandemer* test sought . . . to specify what that minimal degree was: "[a] chance to effectively influence the political process." . . . So did the appellants' proposed test: "[the] ability to translate a majority of votes into a majority of seats." . . . Justice Souter avoids the difficulties of those formulations by never telling us what his test is looking for, other than the utterly unhelpful "extremity of unfairness." He vaguely describes the harm he is concerned with as vote dilution, a term which usually implies some actual effect on the weight of a vote. But no element of his test looks to the effect of the gerrymander on the electoral success, the electoral opportunity, or even the political influence, of the plaintiff group. We do not know the precise constitutional deprivation his test is designed to identify and prevent.

. . .

Like us, Justice Souter acknowledges and accepts that "some intent to gain political advantage is inescapable whenever political bodies devise a district plan, and some effect results from the intent." Thus, again like us, he recognizes that "the issue is one of how much is too much." And once those premises are conceded, the only line that can be drawn must be based, as Justice Souter again candidly admits, upon a substantive "notio[n] of fairness." This is the same flabby goal that deprived Justice Powell's test of all determinacy. To be sure, Justice Souter frames it somewhat differently: courts must intervene, he says, when "partisan competition has reached an *extremity* of unfairness." We do not think the problem is solved by adding the modifier.

C

We agree with much of Justice Breyer's dissenting opinion, which convincingly demonstrates that "political considerations will likely play an important, and proper, role in the drawing of district boundaries." This places Justice Breyer, like the other dissenters, in the difficult position of drawing the line between good politics and bad politics. Unlike them, he would tackle this problem at the statewide level.

The criterion Justice Breyer proposes is nothing more precise than "the *unjustified* use of political factors to entrench a minority in power." While he invokes in passing the Equal Protection Clause, it should be clear to any reader that what constitutes *unjustified* entrenchment depends on his own theory of "effective government." While one must agree with Justice Breyer's incredibly abstract starting point that our Constitution sought to create a "basically democratic" form of government, that is a long and impassable distance away from the conclusion that the judiciary may assess whether a group (somehow defined) has achieved a level of political power (somehow defined) commensurate with that to which they would be entitled absent *unjustified* political machinations (whatever that means).

Justice Breyer provides no real guidance for the journey. [H]e never tells us what he is testing for, beyond the unhelpful *"unjustified* entrenchment." . . .

But perhaps the most surprising omission from Justice Breyer's dissent . . . is the absence of any cost-benefit analysis. . . . He gives no instance (and we know none) of permanent frustration of majority will. . . . Is the regular insertion of the judiciary into districting, with the delay and uncertainty that brings to the political process and the partisan . . . enmity it brings upon the courts, worth the benefit to be achieved—an accelerated (by some unknown degree) effectuation of the majority will? We think not.

V

Justice Kennedy recognizes that we have "demonstrat[ed] the shortcomings of the other standards that have been considered to date." He acknowledges, moreover, that we "lack . . . comprehensive and neutral principles for drawing electoral boundaries"; and that there is an "absence of rules to limit and confine judicial intervention." From these premises, one might think that Justice Kennedy would reach the conclusion that political gerrymandering claims are nonjusticiable. Instead, however, he concludes that courts should continue to adjudicate such claims because a standard *may* one day be discovered.

. . . Justice Kennedy's disposition is . . . not legally available. . . .

. . .

. . . [T]he lower court has held the claim *justiciable* but unsupported by the facts. We must either enunciate the standard that causes us to agree or disagree with that merits judgment, or else affirm that the claim is beyond our competence to adjudicate.

. . .

. . . We can affirm because political districting presents a nonjusticiable question; or we can affirm because we believe the correct standard which identifies unconstitutional political districting has not been met; we cannot affirm because we do not know what the correct standard is. Reduced to its essence, Justice Kennedy's opinion boils down to this: "As presently advised, I know of no discernible and manageable standard that can render this claim justiciable. I am unhappy about that, and hope that I will be able to change my opinion in the future." What are the lower courts to make of this pronouncement? We suggest that they must treat it as a reluctant fifth vote against justiciability at district and statewide levels—a vote that may change in some future case but that holds, for the time being, that this matter is nonjusticiable.

VI

We conclude that neither Article I, § 2, nor the Equal Protection Clause, nor . . . Article I, § 4, provides a judicially enforceable limit on the political considerations that the States and Congress may take into account when districting.

Considerations of *stare decisis* do not compel us to allow *Bandemer* to stand.... [I]n *Bandemer* ... the majority's inability to enunciate the judicially discernible and manageable standard that it thought existed (or did not think did not exist) presaged the need for reconsideration in light of subsequent experience. [I]t is hard to imagine how any action taken in reliance upon *Bandemer* could conceivably be frustrated—except the bringing of lawsuits, which is not the sort of primary conduct that is relevant.

While we do not lightly overturn one of our own holdings, "when governing decisions are unworkable or are badly reasoned, 'this Court has never felt constrained to follow precedent.' " ... Eighteen years of essentially pointless litigation have persuaded us that *Bandemer* is incapable of principled application. We would therefore overrule that case, and decline to adjudicate these political gerrymandering claims.

... [A]ffirmed.

Justice Kennedy, concurring in the judgment.

... I would not foreclose all possibility of judicial relief if some limited and precise rationale were found to correct an established violation of the Constitution in some redistricting cases.

When presented with a claim of injury from partisan gerrymandering, courts confront two obstacles. First is the lack of comprehensive and neutral principles for drawing electoral boundaries.... Second is the absence of rules to limit and confine judicial intervention. With uncertain limits, intervening courts ... would risk assuming political, not legal, responsibility for a process that often produces ill will and distrust.

That courts can grant relief in districting cases where race is involved does not answer our need for fairness principles here. Those controversies ... involve sorting permissible classifications in the redistricting context from impermissible ones. Race is an impermissible classification.... Politics is quite a different matter....

A determination that a gerrymander violates the law must rest on something more than the conclusion that political classifications were applied. It must rest instead on a conclusion that the classifications, though generally permissible, were applied in an invidious manner or in a way unrelated to any legitimate legislative objective.

. . .

... Because there are yet no agreed upon substantive principles of fairness in districting, we have no basis on which to define clear, manageable, and politically neutral standards for measuring the particular burden a given partisan classification imposes on representational rights....

... The fairness principle appellants propose is that a majority of voters in the Commonwealth should be able to elect a majority of the Commonwealth's congressional delegation. There is no authority for this precept.... The plurality demonstrates the shortcomings of the other standards that have been considered to date.... Our attention has not been drawn to statements of principled, well-accepted rules of fairness that should govern districting, or to helpful formulations of the legislator's duty in drawing district lines.

. . .

There are, then, weighty arguments for holding cases like these to be nonjusticiable; and those arguments may prevail in the long run. In my view, however, the arguments are not so compelling that they require us now to bar all future claims of injury from a partisan gerrymander. It is not in our tradition to foreclose the judicial process from the attempt to define standards and remedies where it is alleged that a constitutional right is burdened or denied. Nor is it alien to the Judiciary to draw or approve election district lines. Courts, after all, already do so in many instances. A determination by the Court to deny all hopes of intervention could erode confidence in the courts as much as would a premature decision to intervene.

Our willingness to enter the political thicket of the apportionment process with respect to one-person, one-vote claims makes it particularly difficult to justify a categorical refusal to entertain claims against this other type of gerrymandering. The plurality's conclusion that absent an "easily administrable standard" the appellants' claim must be nonjusticiable contrasts starkly with the more patient approach of *Baker v. Carr,* 369 U.S. 186 (1962), not to mention the controlling precedent on the question of justiciability of *Davis v. Bandemer, supra,* the case the plurality would overrule.

... Whether a manageable standard made the right at issue in *Baker* enforceable was as much a necessary inquiry there as it is here.....

Even putting *Baker* to the side—and so assuming that the existence of a workable standard for measuring a gerrymander's burden on representational rights distinguishes one-person, one-vote claims from partisan gerrymandering claims for justiciability purposes—I would still reject the plurality's conclusions as to nonjusticiability. Relying on the distinction between a claim having or not having a workable standard of that sort involves a difficult proof ... that no standard could exist[—]a difficult proposition to establish, for proving a negative is a challenge in any context.

That no such standard has emerged in this case should not be taken to prove that none will emerge in the future. Where important rights are involved, the impossibility of full analytical satisfaction is reason to err on the side of caution.... If a State passed an enactment that declared "All future apportionment shall be drawn so as most to burden Party X's rights to fair and effective representation, though still in accord with one-person, one-vote principles," we would surely conclude the Constitution had been violated. If that is so, we should admit the possibility remains that a legislature might attempt to reach the same result without that express directive. This possibility suggests that in another case a standard might emerge that suitably demonstrates how an apportionment's *de facto* incorporation of partisan classifications burdens rights of fair and effective representation (and so establishes the classification is unrelated to the aims of apportionment and thus is used in an impermissible fashion).

The plurality says that 18 years, in effect, prove the negative. As Justice Souter is correct to point out, however, during these past 18 years the lower courts could do no more than follow *Davis v. Bandemer,* which formulated a single, apparently insuperable standard. Moreover, by the timeline of the law 18 years is rather a short period. In addition, the rapid evolution of technologies in the apportionment field suggests yet unexplored possibilities. Computer assisted districting has become so routine and sophisticated that legislatures, experts, and courts can use databases to map electoral districts in a matter of hours, not months.... Technology is both a threat and a promise. On the one hand, if courts refuse to entertain any claims of partisan gerrymandering, the temptation to use partisan favoritism in districting in an unconstitutional manner will grow. On the other hand, these new technologies may produce new methods of analysis that make more evident the precise nature of the burdens gerrymanders impose on the representational rights of voters and parties. That would facilitate court efforts to identify and remedy the burdens, with judicial intervention limited by the derived standards.

. . .

. . . [A]ppellants' complaint alleges no impermissible use of political classifications and so states no valid claim on which relief may be granted. . . .

The plurality thinks I resolve this case with reference to no standard, but that is wrong. The Fourteenth Amendment standard governs; and there is no doubt of that. My analysis only notes that if a subsidiary standard could show how an otherwise permissible classification, as applied, burdens representational rights, we could conclude that appellants' evidence states a provable claim under the Fourteenth Amendment standard.

. . . The First Amendment may be the more relevant constitutional provision in future cases that allege unconstitutional partisan gerrymandering. After all, these allegations involve the First Amendment interest of not burdening or penalizing citizens because of their participation in the electoral process, their voting history, their association with a political party, or their expression of political views. . . . First Amendment concerns arise where a State enacts a law that has the purpose and effect of subjecting a group of voters or their party to disfavored treatment by reason of their views. . . .

. . . If a court were to find that a State did impose burdens and restrictions on groups or persons by reason of their views, there would likely be a First Amendment violation, unless the State shows some compelling interest. . . .

. . . [T]he First Amendment may offer a sounder and more prudential basis for intervention than does the Equal Protection Clause. The equal protection analysis puts its emphasis on the permissibility of an enactment's classifications. This works where race is involved since classifying by race is almost never permissible. It presents a more complicated question when the inquiry is whether a generally permissible classification has been used for an impermissible purpose. That question can only be answered in the affirmative by the subsidiary showing that the classification as applied imposes unlawful burdens. The First Amendment analysis concentrates on whether the legislation burdens the representational rights of the complaining party's voters for reasons of ideology, beliefs, or political association. The analysis allows a pragmatic or functional assessment that accords some latitude to the States. . . .

. . .

Justice Stevens, dissenting.

The central question . . . is whether political gerrymandering claims are justiciable. Although our reasons . . . differ, five Members of the Court are convinced that the plurality's answer to that question is erroneous. Moreover, . . . we share the view that, even if these appellants are not entitled to prevail, it would be contrary to precedent and profoundly unwise to foreclose all judicial review of similar claims that might be advanced in the future. . . .

The concept of equal justice under law requires the State to govern impartially. . . . In my view, when partisanship is the legislature's sole motivation—when any pretense of neutrality is forsaken unabashedly and all traditional districting criteria are subverted for partisan advantage—the governing body cannot be said to have acted impartially.

. . . I would decide this case on a narrow ground. Plaintiff-appellants urge us to craft new rules that in effect would authorize judicial review of statewide election results to protect the democratic process from a transient majority's abuse of its power to define voting districts. I agree with the Court's refusal to undertake that ambitious project. I am persuaded, however, that [the resident voter's district-specific challenge alleging that the new districting plan was created "solely" to effectuate the interests of Republicans, and that the General Assembly relied "exclusively" on a principle of "maximum partisan advantage" when drawing the plan,] establish[ed] . . . that she has stated a claim that, at least with respect to District 6, Pennsylvania's redistricting plan violates the equal protection principles enunciated in our voting rights cases both before and after *Bandemer*. . . .

I

. . .

. . . [T]he plurality does not argue that the judicially manageable standards that have been used to adjudicate racial gerrymandering claims would not be equally manageable in political gerrymandering cases. Instead, its distinction of those cases rests on its view that race as a districting criterion is "much more rarely encountered" than partisanship, and that determining whether race—"a rare and constitutionally suspect motive"—dominated a districting decision "is quite different from determining whether [such a decision] is so substantially affected by the excess of an ordinary and lawful motive as to [be] invali[d]." But those considerations are wholly irrelevant to the issue of justiciability.

To begin with, the plurality errs in assuming that politics is "an ordinary and lawful motive." . . . [P]olitical affiliation is not an appropriate standard for excluding voters from a congressional district.

. . . [P]artisanship is not always as benign a consideration as the plurality appears to assume. . . .

State action that discriminates against a political minority for the sole and unadorned purpose of maximizing the power of the majority plainly violates the decisionmaker's duty to remain impartial. . . . Thus, the critical issue in both racial and political gerrymandering cases is the same: whether a single non-neutral criterion controlled the districting process to such an extent that the Constitution was offended. . . .

II

. . .

The risk of representational harms identified in the *Shaw* cases is equally great, if not greater, in the context of partisan gerrymanders. *Shaw I* was borne of the concern that an official elected from a racially gerrymandered district will feel beholden only to a portion of her constituents, and that those constituents will be defined by race. . . . The parallel danger of a partisan gerrymander is that the representative will perceive that the people who put her in power are those who drew the map rather than those who cast ballots, and she will feel beholden not to a subset of her constituency, but to no part of her constituency at all. The . . . will of the cartographers rather than the will of the people will govern. . . .

III

. . .

In sum, in evaluating a challenge to a specific district, I would . . . ask whether the legislature allowed partisan considerations to dominate and control the lines drawn, forsaking all neutral principles. [I]f no neutral criterion can be identified to justify the lines drawn, and if the only possible explanation for a district's bizarre shape is a naked desire to increase partisan strength, then no rational basis exists to save the district from an equal protection challenge. Such a narrow test would cover only a few meritorious claims, but it would preclude extreme abuses, . . . and it would perhaps shorten the time period in which the pernicious effects of such a gerrymander are felt. This test would mitigate the current trend under which partisan considerations are becoming the be-all and end-all in apportioning representatives.

IV

. . .

Quite obviously, . . . several standards for identifying impermissible partisan influence are available to judges who have the will to enforce them. We could hold that every district boundary must have a neutral justification; we could apply Justice Powell's three-factor approach in *Bandemer;* we could apply the predominant motivation standard fashioned by the Court in its racial gerrymandering cases; or we could endorse either of the approaches advocated today by Justice Souter and Justice Breyer. What is clear is that it is not the unavailability of judicially manageable standards that drives today's decision. It is, instead, a failure of judicial will to condemn even the most blatant violations of a state legislature's fundamental duty to govern impartially.

. . .

Justice Souter, with whom Justice Ginsburg joins, dissenting.

. . .

I

. . . [T]he issue is . . . how much is too much, and we can be no more exact in stating a verbal test for too much partisanship than we can be in defining too much race consciousness when some is inevitable and legitimate. . . . Instead of coming up with a verbal formula for too much, . . . the Court's job must be to identify clues, as objective as we can make them, indicating that partisan competition has reached an extremity of unfairness.

. . .

II

[I]t is up to us to make a fresh start. [I]n the years since *Davis,* the increasing efficiency of partisan redistricting has damaged the democratic process to a degree that our predecessors only began to imagine. . . .

I would therefore preserve *Davis's* holding that political gerrymandering is a justiciable issue, but otherwise start anew. I would adopt a political gerrymandering test analogous to the summary judgment standard crafted in *McDonnell Douglas Corp. v. Green,* 411 U.S. 792 (1973), calling for a plaintiff to satisfy elements of a prima facie cause of action, at which point the State would have the opportunity not only to rebut the evidence supporting the plaintiff's case, but to offer an affirmative justification for the districting choices, even assuming the proof of the plaintiff's allegations. . . . [I]n the . . . interest of threshold simplicity, I would stick to problems of single-member districts; if we could not devise a workable scheme for dealing with claims about these, we would have to forget the complications posed by multimember districts.

III

A

For a claim based on a specific single-member district, I would require the plaintiff to make out a *prima facie* case with five elements. First, the resident plaintiff would identify a cohesive political group to which he belonged, which would normally be a major party. . . .

Second, a plaintiff would need to show that the district of his residence . . . paid little or no heed to those traditional districting principles whose disregard can be shown straightforwardly: contiguity, compactness, respect for political subdivisions, and conformity with geographic features like rivers and mountains. . . .

. . .

Third, the plaintiff would need to establish specific correlations between the district's deviations from traditional districting principles and the distribution of the population of his group. . . .

Fourth, a plaintiff would need to present the court with a hypothetical district including his residence, one in which the proportion of the plaintiff's group was lower (in a packing claim) or higher (in a cracking one) and which at the same time deviated less from traditional districting principles than the actual district. . . .

Fifth, and finally, the plaintiff would have to show that the defendants acted intentionally to manipulate the shape of the district in order to pack or crack his group. . . .

. . .

B

A plaintiff who got this far would have shown that his State intentionally acted to dilute his vote, having ignored reasonable alternatives consistent with traditional districting principles. I would then shift the burden to the defendants to justify their decision by reference to objectives other than naked partisan advantage. . . .

. . .[7]

This is not . . . the time or place for a comprehensive list of legitimate objectives a State might present. The . . . Constitution should not petrify traditional districting objectives as exclusive, and it is enough to say that the State would be required to explain itself, to demonstrate that whatever reasons it gave were more than a mere pretext for an old-fashioned gerrymander.

C

. . . [F]or now I would limit consideration of a statewide claim to one built upon a number of district-specific ones. . . .

---

7. . . . I agree with this Court's earlier statements that the Constitution guarantees no right to proportional representation. . . . It does not follow that the Constitution permits every state action intended to achieve any extreme form of disproportionate representation.

D

... The enquiries I am proposing are not ... as hard-edged as I wish they could be, but neither do they have a degree of subjectivity inconsistent with the judicial function.

... The harm from partisan gerrymandering is ... a species of vote dilution.... To devise a judicial remedy for that harm, ... it is not necessary to adopt a full-blown theory of fairness.... It is sufficient ... to agree that gerrymandering is ... unfair, as the plurality does not dispute; to observe the traditional methods of the gerrymanderer, which the plurality summarizes; and to adopt a test aimed at detecting and preventing the use of those methods, which, I think, mine is.... My test would no doubt leave substantial room for a party in power to seek advantage through its control of the districting process; the only way to prevent all opportunism would be to remove districting wholly from legislative control, which I am not prepared to say the Constitution requires. But that does not make it impossible for courts to identify at least the worst cases of gerrymandering, and to provide a remedy. The most the plurality can show is that my approach would not catch them all....

IV

... I would ... vacate ... and remand for further proceedings....

Justice Breyer, dissenting.

... Sometimes purely political "gerrymandering" will fail to advance any plausible democratic objective while simultaneously threatening serious democratic harm. And sometimes when that is so, courts can identify an equal protection violation and provide a remedy. Because the plaintiffs could claim (but have not yet proved) that such circumstances exist here, I would reverse the District Court's dismissal of their complaint.

. . .

... [T]he legislature's use of political boundary drawing considerations ordinarily does *not* violate the Constitution's Equal Protection Clause. The reason lies not simply in the difficulty of identifying abuse or finding an appropriate judicial remedy. The reason is more fundamental: Ordinarily, there simply is no abuse. The use of purely political boundary-drawing factors, even where harmful to the members of one party, will often nonetheless find justification in other desirable democratic ends, such as maintaining relatively stable legislatures in which a minority party retains significant representation.

. . .

At the same time, [there is] at least one circumstance where use of purely political boundary-drawing factors can amount to a serious, and remediable, abuse, namely the *unjustified* use of political factors to entrench a minority in power. By entrenchment I mean a situation in which a party that enjoys only minority support among the populace has nonetheless contrived to take, and hold, legislative power. By *unjustified* entrenchment I mean that the minority's hold on power is purely the result of partisan manipulation and not other factors. These "other" factors that could lead to "justified" (albeit temporary) minority entrenchment include sheer happenstance, the existence of more than two major parties, the unique constitutional requirements of certain representational bodies such as the Senate, or reliance on traditional (geographic, communities of interest, etc.) districting criteria.

... Where unjustified entrenchment takes place, voters find it far more difficult to remove those responsible for a government they do not want; ... democratic values are dishonored.

... [W]hether political gerrymandering does, or does not, violate the Constitution in other instances, gerrymandering that leads to entrenchment amounts to an abuse that violates the Constitution's Equal Protection Clause.

. . .

Courts need not intervene often to prevent the kind of abuse I have described, because those harmed constitute a political majority, and a majority normally can work its political will.... And where a State has improperly gerrymandered congressional districts, Congress retains the power to revise the State's districting determinations. See U.S. Const., Art. I, § 4....

Moreover, voters in some States ... have found a procedural solution, confiding the task to a commission that is limited in the extent to which it may base districts on partisan concerns. According to the National Conference of State Legislatures, 12 States currently give "first and final authority for [state] legislative redistricting to a group other than the legislature." ...

But ... the political advantages of a gerrymander may become ever greater in the future.... The combination of increasingly precise map-drawing technology and increasingly frequent map drawing means that a party may be able to bring about a gerrymander that is not only precise, but virtually impossible to dislodge. Thus, court action may prove necessary.

. . .

[C]ourts should be able to identify the presence of one important gerrymandering evil, the unjustified entrenching in power of a political party that the voters have rejected. They should be able to separate the unjustified abuse of partisan boundary-drawing considerations to achieve that end from their more ordinary and justified use. And they should be able to design a remedy for extreme cases.

. . .

I do not claim that the problem of identification and separation is easily solved, even in extreme instances. But courts can identify a number of strong indicia of abuse. The presence of actual entrenchment, while not always unjustified ... is such a sign, particularly when accompanied by the use of partisan boundary drawing criteria in the way that Justice Stevens describes, *i.e.*, a use that both departs from traditional criteria and cannot be explained other than by efforts to achieve partisan advantage. [Abusive] scenarios fall along a continuum: The more permanently entrenched the minority's hold on power becomes, the less evidence courts will need that the minority engaged in gerrymandering to achieve the desired result.

. . .

The presence of ... circumstances ... where the risk of entrenchment is demonstrated, where partisan considerations render the traditional district-drawing compromises irrelevant, where no justification other than party advantage can be found ... seem to me extreme enough to set off a constitutional alarm. The risk of harm to basic democratic principle is serious; identification is possible; and remedies can be found.

. . .

3. QUALIFICATIONS OF VOTERS

Harper v. Virginia State Board of Elections

383 U.S. 663, 86 S.Ct. 1079, 16 L.Ed.2d 169 (1966).

Mr. Justice Douglas delivered the opinion of the Court.[a]

These are suits by Virginia residents to have declared unconstitutional Virginia's poll tax. The three-judge District Court, feeling bound by our decision in Breedlove v. Suttles, 302 U.S. 277, dismissed the complaint....

While the right to vote in federal elections is conferred by Art. I, § 2, of the Constitution ... the right to vote in state elections is nowhere expressly mentioned. It is argued that the right to vote in state elections is implicit, particularly by reason of the First Amendment and that it may not constitutionally be conditioned upon the payment of a tax or fee.... We do not stop to canvass the relation between voting and political expression. For it is enough to say that once the franchise is granted to the electorate, lines may not be drawn which are inconsistent with the Equal Protection Clause of the Fourteenth Amendment. That is to say, the right of suffrage "is subject to the imposition of state standards which are not discriminatory and which do not contravene any restriction that Congress, acting pursuant to its constitutional powers, has imposed." Lassiter v. Northampton County Board of Elections, 360 U.S. 45, 51. We were speaking there of a state literacy test which we sustained, warning that the result would be different if a literacy test, fair on its face, were used to discriminate against a class.... But the *Lassiter* case does not govern the result here, because, unlike a poll tax, the "ability to read and write ... has some relation to standards designed to promote intelligent use of the ballot." ...

We conclude that a State violates the Equal Protection Clause of the Fourteenth Amendment whenever it makes the affluence of the voter or payment of any fee an electoral standard. Voter qualifications have no relation to wealth nor to paying or not paying this or any other tax. Our cases demonstrate that the Equal Protection Clause of the Fourteenth Amendment restrains the States from fixing voter qualifications which invidiously discriminate. Thus without questioning the power of a State to impose reasonable residence restrictions on the availability of the ballot ..., we held in Carrington v. Rash, 380 U.S. 89, that a State may not deny the opportunity to vote to a bona fide resident merely because he is a member of the armed services. "By forbidding a soldier ever to controvert the presumption of non-residence, the Texas Constitution imposes an invidious discrimination in violation of the Fourteenth Amendment." ... Previously we had said that neither homesite nor occupation "affords a permissible basis for distinguishing between qualified voters within the State." ... We think the same must be true of requirements of wealth or affluence or payment of a fee.

Long ago in Yick Wo v. Hopkins, 118 U.S. 356, 370, the Court referred to "the political franchise of voting" as a "fundamental political right, because

---

a. In the two decades 1934–1954, five states abolished the poll tax: Louisiana, Florida, Georgia, South Carolina and Tennessee. This voluntary action then stopped—probably because of feelings stirred by the 1954 *Brown* decision. As of 1963, payment of a poll tax was a prerequisite to voting in five states: Alabama, Arkansas, Mississippi, Texas and Virginia. Burke Marshall reported: "By now the tax is a negligible, bi-racial deterrent to voting." 27 Law & Contemp.Pr. 455, 464 (1962). In 1962 Congress proposed, and by 1964 the requisite number of States had ratified, the Twenty-fourth Amendment outlawing the "poll tax or other tax" as a condition for voting in federal elections.

preservative of all rights." Recently in Reynolds v. Sims, 377 U.S. 533, 561–562, we said: "Undoubtedly, the right of suffrage is a fundamental matter in a free and democratic society. Especially since the right to exercise the franchise in a free and unimpaired manner is preservative of other basic civil and political rights, any alleged infringement of the right of citizens to vote must be carefully and meticulously scrutinized." ...

It is argued that a State may exact fees from citizens for many different kinds of licenses; that if it can demand from all an equal fee for a driver's license, it can demand from all an equal poll tax for voting. But we must remember that the interest of the State, when it comes to voting, is limited to the power to fix qualifications. Wealth, like race, creed, or color, is not germane to one's ability to participate intelligently in the electoral process. Lines drawn on the basis of wealth or property, like those of race ..., are traditionally disfavored.... To introduce wealth or payment of a fee as a measure of a voter's qualifications is to introduce a capricious or irrelevant factor. The degree of the discrimination is irrelevant. In this context—that is, as a condition of obtaining a ballot—the requirement of fee paying causes an "invidious" discrimination ... that runs afoul of the Equal Protection Clause. Levy "by the poll," as stated in Breedlove v. Suttles, ... is an old familiar form of taxation; and we say nothing to impair its validity so long as it is not made a condition to the exercise of the franchise. *Breedlove v. Suttles* sanctioned its use as "a prerequisite of voting." ... To that extent the *Breedlove* case is over-ruled.

We agree, of course, with Mr. Justice Holmes that the Due Process Clause of the Fourteenth Amendment "does not enact Mr. Herbert Spencer's Social Statics".... Likewise, the Equal Protection Clause is not shackled to the political theory of a particular era. In determining what lines are unconstitutionally discriminatory, we have never been confined to historic notions of equality, any more than we have restricted due process to a fixed catalogue of what was at a given time deemed to be the limits of fundamental rights.... Notions of what constitutes equal treatment for purposes of the Equal Protection Clause *do* change. This Court in 1896 held that laws providing for separate public facilities for white and Negro citizens did not deprive the latter of the equal protection and treatment that the Fourteenth Amendment commands.... Seven of the eight Justices then sitting subscribed to the Court's opinion, thus joining in expressions of what constituted unequal and discriminatory treatment that sound strange to a contemporary ear. When, in 1954—more than a half-century later—we repudiated the "separate-but-equal" doctrine of *Plessy* as respects public education we stated: "In approaching this problem, we cannot turn the clock back to 1868 when the Amendment was adopted, or even to 1896 when Plessy v. Ferguson was written." Brown v. Board of Education....

In a recent searching re-examination of the Equal Protection Clause, we held ... that "the opportunity for equal participation by all voters in the election of state legislators" is required. Reynolds v. Sims.... We decline to qualify that principle by sustaining this poll tax. Our conclusion, like that in *Reynolds v. Sims,* is founded not on what we think governmental policy should be, but on what the Equal Protection Clause requires.

We have long been mindful that where fundamental rights and liberties are asserted under the Equal Protection Clause, classifications which might invade or restrain them must be closely scrutinized and carefully confined....

Those principles apply here. For to repeat, wealth or fee paying has, in our view, no relation to voting qualifications; the right to vote is too precious, too fundamental to be so burdened or conditioned.

Reversed.

Mr. Justice Black, dissenting.

... The Court ... overrules *Breedlove* in part, but its opinion reveals that it does so not by using its limited power to interpret the original meaning of the Equal Protection Clause, but by giving that clause a new meaning which it believes represents a better governmental policy. From this action I dissent.

. . .

The Court's justification for consulting its own notions rather than following the original meaning of the Constitution, as I would, apparently is based on the belief of the majority of the Court that for this Court to be bound by the original meaning of the Constitution is an intolerable and debilitating evil; that our Constitution should not be "shackled to the political theory of a particular era," and that to save the country from the original Constitution the Court must have constant power to renew it and keep it abreast with this Court's more enlightening theories of what is best for our society. It seems to me that this is not only an attack on the great value of our Constitution itself but also on the concept of a written constitution which is to survive through the years as originally written unless changed through the amendment process which the Framers wisely provided. Moreover, when a "political theory" embodied in our Constitution becomes outdated, it seems to me that a majority of the nine members of this Court are not only without constitutional power but are far less qualified to choose a new constitutional political theory than the people of this country proceeding in the manner provided by Article V.

The people have not found it impossible to amend their Constitution to meet new conditions. The Equal Protection Clause itself is the product of the peoples' desire to use their constitutional power to amend the Constitution to meet new problems....

Mr. Justice Harlan, whom Mr. Justice Stewart joins, dissenting.

The final demise of state poll taxes, already totally proscribed by the Twenty–Fourth Amendment with respect to federal elections and abolished by the States themselves in all but four States with respect to state elections, is perhaps in itself not of great moment. But the fact that the *coup de grace* has been administered by this Court instead of being left to the affected States or to the federal political process should be a matter of continuing concern to all interested in maintaining the proper role of this tribunal under our scheme of government.

. . .

DUNN v. BLUMSTEIN, 405 U.S. 330 (1972). In holding invalid a statute imposing as a condition of voting residence in the state for one year and the county for three months before the election, the Court said:

A.

"Durational residence requirements completely bar from voting all residents not meeting the fixed durational standards. By denying some citizens the right to vote, such laws deprive them of 'a fundamental political right, ... preservative of all rights.' Reynolds v. Sims, 377 U.S. 533, 562 (1964). There is no need to repeat now the labors undertaken in earlier cases to analyze this right to vote and to explain in detail the judicial role in reviewing state statutes which selectively distribute the franchise. In decision after decision, this Court has made clear that a citizen has a constitutionally protected right to participate in elections on an equal basis with other citizens in the jurisdiction. See, e.g., Evans v. Cornman, 398 U.S. 419, 421–422 (1970);[a] Kramer v. Union Free School District No. 15, 395 U.S. 621, 626–628 (1969);[b] Cipriano v. City of Houma, 395 U.S. 701, 706 (1969);[c] Harper v. Virginia State Board of Elections, 383 U.S. 663, 667 (1966); Carrington v. Rash, 380 U.S. 89, 93–94 (1965);[d] Reynolds v. Sims, supra. This 'equal right to vote,' *Evans v. Cornman, . . .* is not absolute; the States have the power to impose voter qualifications, and to regulate access to the franchise in other ways. . . . But, as a general matter, 'before that right [to vote] can be restricted, the purpose of the restriction and the assertedly overriding interests served by it must meet close constitutional scrutiny.' *Evans v. Cornman* . . .; see Bullock v. Carter, 405 U.S. 134 (1972).[e]

"Tennessee urges that this case is controlled by Drueding v. Devlin, 380 U.S. 125 (1965). *Drueding* was a decision upholding Maryland's durational residence requirements. The District Court tested those requirements by the equal protection standard applied to ordinary state regulations: whether the exclusions are reasonably related to a permissible state interest. . . . We summarily affirmed *per curiam* without the benefit of argument. But if it was not clear then, it is certainly clear now that a more exacting test is required for any statute which 'place[s] a condition on the exercise of the right to vote.' Bullock v. Carter. . . . This development in the law culminated in Kramer v. Union Free School District No. 15, supra, 395 U.S. 621 (1969). There we canvassed in detail the reasons for strict review of statutes distributing the franchise, . . . noting *inter alia* that such statutes 'constitute the foundation of our representative society.' We concluded that if a challenged statute grants the right to vote to some citizens and denies the franchise to others, 'the Court must determine whether the exclusions are *necessary* to promote a *compelling* state interest.'

a. Persons living on the grounds of the National Institutes of Health, a federal reservation or enclave located within the boundaries of Maryland, were denied the right to vote in Maryland elections on the ground that they were not residents of Maryland. The Court held the denial unconstitutional: "In nearly every election, federal, state, and local, for offices from the Presidency to the school board, and on the entire variety of ballot propositions, appellees have a stake equal to that of other Maryland residents. As the District Court concluded, they are entitled under the Fourteenth Amendment to protect that stake by exercising the equal right to vote."

b. A New York law provided that residents of school districts could vote in school district elections only if they (1) own or lease taxable real property in the district, or (2) are parents or have custody of children enrolled in the local public schools. The Court noted that the statute was to be given "a close and exacting examination" because "statutes distributing the franchise constitute the foundation of our representative society." The Court then held the statute unconstitutional because the state had not demonstrated a "compelling state interest" justifying the limitation on the franchise.

c. A state provision giving only "property taxpayers" the right to vote in elections called to approve the issuance of revenue bonds by a municipal utility was held unconstitutional. The Court found no basis for the limitation since "the benefits and burdens of the bond issue fall indiscriminately on the property owner and nonproperty owner alike."

d. The Court held invalid a Texas constitutional provision prohibiting a member of the armed forces who moves his home to Texas from voting in any election so long as he is a member of the armed forces.

e. A Texas law requiring candidates to pay large filing fees in order to have their names placed on the ballot in primary elections was held invalid. The Court said:

"Because the Texas filing fee scheme has a real and appreciable impact on the exercise of the franchise, and because this impact is related to the resources of the voters supporting a particular candidate, we conclude, as in *Harper,* that the laws must be 'closely scrutinized' and found reasonably necessary to the accomplishment of legitimate state objectives in order to pass constitutional muster."

Id., at 627 (emphasis added); Cipriano v. City of Houma, 395 U.S. 701, 704 (1969); City of Phoenix v. Kolodziejski, 399 U.S. 204, 205, 209 (1970).[f] Cf. Harper v. Virginia State Board of Elections, supra, 383 U.S., at 670. This is the test we apply here."

MARSTON v. LEWIS, 410 U.S. 679 (1973). Arizona required a voter to have resided in the State for 50 days before an election and also to register at least 50 days prior. The Court held this requirement valid in light of a state showing that it would be difficult to do the necessary paper work in any shorter period before the election, stating: "In the present case, we are confronted with a recent and amply justifiable legislative judgment that 50 days rather than 30 is necessary to promote the State's important interest in accurate voter lists. The Constitution is not so rigid that that determination and others like it may not stand." A dissent argued that the Court had fixed in *Dunn* the line of 30 days as that beyond which reliance on administrative convenience is extremely questionable and "we can avoid an unprincipled numbers game only if we insist that any deviations from the line we have drawn, after mature consideration, be justified by far more substantial evidence than that produced" in this case.

HILL v. STONE, 421 U.S. 289 (1975). Issuance of bonds to finance construction of a city library was defeated in a Fort Worth election. Residents brought this federal court action challenging the provision of Texas law limiting the right to vote in city bond issue elections to persons who have "rendered" or listed real, mixed, or personal property for taxation in the election district. Under the law mere listing of the property—not the payment of any tax—was the prerequisite to voting. The Court, by a vote of five to three, held the statute invalid under the Equal Protection Clause, stating, in part:

"The basic principle . . . is that as long as the election in question is not one of special interest, any classification restricting the franchise on grounds other than residence, age, and citizenship cannot stand unless the district or State can demonstrate that the classification serves a compelling state interest. See *Kramer* . . .; *Cipriano* . . . .

"The appellant's claim that the Ft. Worth election was one of special interest and thus outside the principles of the *Kramer* case runs afoul of our decision in *City of Phoenix v. Kolodziejski,* supra. In the *Phoenix* case, we expressly stated that a general obligation bond issue—even where the debt service will be paid entirely out of property taxes as in Ft. Worth—is a matter of general interest, and that the principles of *Kramer* apply to classifications limiting eligibility among registered voters.

"In making the alternative contentions that the 'rendering requirement' creates no real 'classification,' or that the classification created should be upheld as being reasonable, the appellant misconceives the rationale of *Kramer* and its successors. Appellant argues that since all property is required to be rendered for taxation, and since anyone can vote in a bond election if he renders any property, no matter how little, the Texas scheme does not discriminate on the basis of wealth or property. Our cases, however, have not held or intimated that only property-based classifications are suspect; in an election of general interest, restrictions on the franchise of any character must meet a stringent test of justification. The Texas scheme creates a classification based on rendering, and it in effect disfranchises those who have not rendered their property for taxation in the year of the bond election. Mere reasonableness will therefore not suffice to sustain the classification created in this case.

f. The Court held that a State could not restrict to real property taxpayers the vote in elections to approve the issuance of general obligation bonds.

B.

"The appellant has sought to justify the State's rendering requirement solely on the ground that it extends some protection to property owners, who will bear the direct burden of retiring the city's bonded indebtedness. The *Phoenix* case, however, rejected this analysis of the 'direct' imposition of costs on property owners. Even under a system in which the responsibility of retiring the bonded indebtedness falls directly on property taxpayers, all members of the community share in the cost in various ways. Moreover, the construction of a library is not likely to be of special interest to a particular, well-defined portion of the electorate. . . .

"The appellee city officials argue that the rendering qualifications furthers another state interest: it encourages prospective voters to render their property and thereby helps enforce the State's tax laws. This argument is difficult to credit. The use of the franchise to compel compliance with other, independent state objectives is questionable in any context. . . .

"In sum, the Texas rendering requirement erects a classification that impermissibly disenfranchises persons otherwise qualified to vote, solely because they have not rendered some property for taxation. The *Phoenix* case establishes that Ft. Worth's election was not a 'special interest' election, and the state interests proffered by appellant and the city officials fall far short of meeting the 'compelling state interest' test consistently applied in *Kramer, Cipriano,* and *Phoenix.*"

NOTE

In Richardson v. Ramirez, 418 U.S. 24 (1974), the Court held valid California constitutional provisions and implementing statutes disenfranchising persons convicted of an "infamous crime." The Court said, in part:

"As we have seen, however, the exclusion of felons from the vote has an affirmative sanction in § 2 of the Fourteenth Amendment, a sanction which was not present in the case of the other restrictions on the franchise which were invalidated in the cases on which respondents rely. We hold that the understanding of those who adopted the Fourteenth Amendment, as reflected in the express language of § 2 and in the historical and judicial interpretation of the Amendment's applicability to state laws disenfranchising felons, is of controlling significance in distinguishing such laws from those other state limitations on the franchise which have been held invalid under the Equal Protection Clause by this Court."

EQUAL PROTECTION AND BALLOT EVALUATION

The Court has interpreted the Equal Protection Clause to restrict not only the setting of qualifications for eligibility to vote, but, at least in some circumstances, the standards and processes employed for determining which among disputed ballots in contested elections shall be counted, and how. It did so in the immediate, politically charged aftermath of the extremely close 2000 Presidential election, which hinged on Florida's 25 electoral votes. Just several hundred of nearly 6 million Florida votes cast separated Governor George W. Bush—the winner of the initial machine count and the state-mandated machine recount—and Vice President Albert Gore, Jr., who, among other legal actions, sued and eventually secured from the Florida Supreme Court on December 8 a judgment mandating, *inter alia*, an immediate statewide manual recounting of ballots on which vote tabulation machines had failed to detect a vote for

President ("undervotes"). A bare majority of the Court stayed that judgment on December 9 and, in Bush v. Gore, 531 U.S. 98 (2000), reversed it on December 12, holding that the judgment contemplated "standardless manual recounts" in "violation of the Equal Protection Clause." Moreover, because the Court majority understood the Florida Supreme Court to have said that the Florida legislature intended to have Florida's electors selected by December 12 in accordance with the "safe harbor provision" of the federal Electoral Count Act of 1887, 3 U.S.C. § 5–which requires any controversy or contest designed to lead to a conclusive selection of electors to be completed by that date–the Court concluded that it was too late to devise a constitutionally proper hand count.

The per curiam majority of five Justices said in part:

"The individual citizen has no federal constitutional right to vote for electors for the President of the United States unless and until the state legislature chooses a statewide election as the means to implement its power to appoint members of the Electoral College. U.S. Const., Art. II, § 1.... [I]t may ... select the electors itself, which ... State legislatures in several States [did] for many years after the Framing of our Constitution.... [N]ow ... in each of the several States the citizens themselves vote for Presidential electors. When the state legislature vests the right to vote for President in its people, the right to vote as the legislature has prescribed is fundamental; and one source of its fundamental nature lies in the equal weight accorded to each vote and the equal dignity owed to each voter....

"The right to vote is protected in more than the initial allocation of the franchise. Equal protection applies as well to the manner of its exercise. Having once granted the right to vote on equal terms, the State may not, by later arbitrary and disparate treatment, value one person's vote over that of another. See, e.g., Harper v. Virginia Bd. of Elections, 383 U.S. 663, 665 (1966).... It must be remembered that 'the right of suffrage can be denied by a debasement or dilution of the weight of a citizen's vote just as effectively as by wholly prohibiting the free exercise of the franchise.' Reynolds v. Sims, 377 U.S. 533, 555 (1964)."

Finding "[m]uch of the controversy" focused on incompletely punched ballot cards with the "chads" hanging or just indented and hence unreadable by machine, the majority found the Florida Supreme Court's direction

"that the intent of the voter be discerned from such ballots ... unobjectionable as an abstract proposition and a starting principle. The problem inheres in the absence of specific standards to ensure its equal application. The formulation of uniform rules to determine intent based on these recurring circumstances is practicable and, we conclude, necessary.

"... The search for intent can be confined by specific rules designed to ensure uniform treatment.

"The want of those rules here has led to unequal evaluation of ballots in various respects.... [T]he standards for accepting or rejecting contested ballots might vary not only from county to county but indeed within a single county from one recount team to another.

"The record provides some examples. A monitor ... observed that three members of [a] county canvassing board applied different standards in defining a legal vote.... [A]t least one county changed its evaluative standards during the counting process.... This is not a process with sufficient guarantees of equal treatment.

"... [I]n the context of the Presidential selection process in Moore v. Ogilvie, 394 U.S. 814 (1969), ... we invalidated a county-based procedure that diluted the influence of citizens in larger counties in the nominating process[,] observing that '[t]he idea that one group can be granted greater voting strength than another is hostile to the one man, one vote basis of our representative government.'

"The State Supreme Court ratified this uneven treatment.... [E]ach of the counties used varying standards to determine what was a legal vote. Broward County used a more forgiving standard than Palm Beach County, and uncovered almost three times as many new votes, a result markedly disproportionate to the difference in population between the counties."

The Court also objected to the Florida Supreme Court's failure to require the hand count to assess overvotes (ballots containing more than one fully punched chad) as well as undervotes; its willingness "to include whatever partial counts are done by the time of final certification"; and its failure to "specify who would recount the ballots"—forcing "county canvassing boards ... to pull together ad hoc teams comprised of judges from various Circuits who had no previous training in handling and interpreting ballots." The Court then said:

"The recount process, in its features here described, is inconsistent with the minimum procedures necessary to protect the fundamental right of each voter in the special instance of a statewide recount under the authority of a single state judicial officer. Our consideration is limited to the present circumstances, for the problem of equal protection in election processes generally presents many complexities.

"The question ... is not whether local entities, in the exercise of their expertise, may develop different systems for implementing elections. Instead, ... a state court with the power to assure uniformity has ordered a statewide recount with minimal procedural safeguards. When a court orders a statewide remedy, there must be at least some assurance that the rudimentary requirements of equal treatment and fundamental fairness are satisfied."[a]

There were four separate dissents. Justice Stevens, joined by Justices Ginsburg and Breyer, concluded that "the failure of the Florida Supreme Court to specify in detail the precise manner in which the 'intent of the voter,' ... is to be determined" did not "rise[] to the level of a constitutional violation." The Court had "never before called into question the substantive standard by which a State determines that a vote has been legally cast" and there was "no reason to think that the guidance provided to the factfinders, specifically the various canvassing boards, by the 'intent of the voter' standard" was insufficient. Although "[a]dmittedly, the use of differing substandards for determining voter intent in different counties employing similar voting systems may raise serious concerns[, t]hose concerns are alleviated—if not eliminated—by the fact that a single impartial magistrate will ultimately adjudicate all objections arising from the recount process." In any event, under the majority's "own reasoning, the appropriate course of action would be to remand to allow more specific procedures for implementing the legislature's uniform general standard to be established" rather than to "disenfranchise[] ... an unknown number of voters whose [uncounted] ballots reveal their intent[.]" December 12 was not a

---

a. A concurring opinion by Chief Justice Rehnquist, joined by Justices Scalia and Thomas, found "additional grounds to reverse the Florida Supreme Court's decision"—namely, that its post-election decisions interpreting Florida's election statutes had so departed from the Florida legislature's scheme for appointing presidential electors, including the "legislative desire to attain the 'safe harbor' provided by § 5[,]" as to violate Art. II, § 1, cl.2. The four dissenters strongly disagreed, finding the Article II challenge to the Florida Supreme Court's statutory interpretations "not substantial."

fixed deadline, because the "safe harbor provisions" only "provide rules of decision for Congress to follow when selecting among conflicting slates of electors" and "do not prohibit a State from counting what the majority concedes to be legal votes until a bona fide winner is determined."

Justice Souter's dissent was joined by Justices Breyer, Stevens and Ginsburg, insofar as it criticized the Court's intervention at all rather than "allow[ing] the State to follow the course indicated by the opinions of its own Supreme Court" (which might have obviated any need for Supreme Court review), and insofar as it rejected any claimed violations of The Electoral Count Act or Article II. Only Justice Breyer joined that portion of his dissent that said in part:

"... It is true that the Equal Protection Clause does not forbid the use of a variety of voting mechanisms within a jurisdiction, even though different mechanisms will have different levels of effectiveness in recording voters' intentions; local variety can be justified by concerns about cost, the potential value of innovation, and so on. But evidence in the record here suggests that a different order of disparity obtains under rules for determining a voter's intent that have been applied (and could continue to be applied) to identical types of ballots used in identical brands of machines and exhibiting identical physical characteristics (such as 'hanging' or 'dimpled' chads).... I can conceive of no legitimate state interest served by these differing treatments of the expressions of voters' fundamental rights. The differences appear wholly arbitrary."

He would have "remand[ed] the case ... with instructions to establish uniform standards for evaluating the several types of ballots that have prompted differing treatments, to be applied within and among counties when passing on such identical ballots in any further recounting[,]" however, and he found "no justification for denying the State the opportunity to try to count all disputed ballots now."

Justice Ginsburg's dissent, in the portion addressing equal protection that was joined only by Justice Stevens, could not "agree that the recount adopted by the Florida court, flawed as it may be, would yield a result any less fair or precise than the certification that preceded that recount." She felt that "the Court's conclusion that a constitutionally adequate recount is impractical is a prophecy the Court's own judgment will not allow to be tested" and that "[s]uch an untested prophecy should not decide the Presidency of the United States."

Finally, Justice Breyer's dissent argued primarily—joined by Justices Stevens, Souter and Ginsburg—that the "Court was wrong to take this case[,] wrong to grant a stay [and] should now vacate that stay and permit the Florida Supreme Court to decide whether the recount should resume." With respect to the equal protection issues, joined only by Justice Souter, he rejected the complaints of failure to include overvotes and of recounts of all ballots, not just undervotes, in some but not all counties, because petitioner Bush had "presented no evidence ... that a manual recount of overvotes would identify additional legal votes." However, the "absence of a uniform, specific standard to guide the recounts" did "implicate principles of fundamental fairness" and "in these very special circumstances, ... may well have counseled the adoption of a uniform standard to address the problem." Given "the majority's disposition," he declined to "decide whether, or the extent to which, as a remedial matter, the Constitution would place limits upon the content of the uniform standard[,]" but he found "no justification for the majority's remedy" of "halt[ing] the recount entirely" rather than remanding to permit a recount "in accordance with a single-uniform substandard."[a]

THE FIFTEENTH AMENDMENT AS A LIMITATION ON STATE (AND FEDERAL) POWER TO FIX QUALIFICATIONS FOR VOTERS

By its terms, the fifteenth amendment prohibits the United States or any State from denying or abridging the right of United States citizens to vote "on account of race, color, or previous condition of servitude." In Guinn v. United States, 238 U.S. 347 (1915), the Court found impermissible racial discrimination in a 1910 amendment to the Oklahoma Constitution that imposed a literacy requirement for voting but exempted all who were entitled to vote on or before January 1, 1866, and their lineal descendants. The Court also addressed the fifteenth amendment in the following modern case.

RICE v. CAYETANO, 528 U.S. 495 (2000). In 1978 Hawaii amended its Constitution to create a state agency, the Office of Hawaiian Affairs (OHA), to administer programs benefiting two groups: (1) "native Hawaiians" (defined by statute "as descendants of not less than one-half part of the races inhabiting the Hawaiian islands prior to 1778"—the date when England's Captain Cook first landed in Hawaii), and (2) "Hawaiians" (defined more broadly as those descended from "the aboriginal peoples" inhabiting Hawaii in 1778). OHA is governed by nine trustees who "shall be Hawaiians" and who shall be "elected by qualified voters who are Hawaiians" in a statewide election. In a suit by a Hawaiian citizen lacking the ancestry required to vote in the trustee election, the Court found "a clear violation of the Fifteenth Amendment." Justice Kennedy's opinion for the majority first rejected the argument that the voting classification was not based on race but on whether one had an ancestor in Hawaii at a particular time, thus excluding fully Polynesian Hawaiians with no ancestors who lived there in 1778 and including those who could trace as little as 1/64th of their ancestry to a Hawaiian inhabitant from 1778. He wrote in part:

> "Ancestry can be a proxy for race. It is that proxy here. Even if the residents of Hawaii in 1778 had been of more diverse ethnic backgrounds and cultures, it is far from clear that a voting test favoring their descendants would not be a race-based qualification. But that is not this case. For centuries Hawaii was isolated from migration.... The inhabitants shared common physical characteristics, and by 1778 they had a common culture.... The provisions before us reflect the State's effort to preserve that commonality of people to the present day.... The very object of the statutory definition in question and of its earlier congressional counterpart in the Hawaiian Homes Commission Act is to treat the early Hawaiians as a distinct people, commanding their own recognition and respect. The State, in enacting the legislation before us, has used ancestry as a racial definition and for a racial purpose."

a. The Court's decision in Bush v. Gore called forth a torrent of commentary addressing the nature and propriety of the Court's intervention. For one sample of a wide range of views on many of the facets of the decision, including its equal protection analysis, see the various contributions to Symposium, *The Law of Presidential Elections: Issues in the Wake of Florida 2000*, 29 Florida State University Law Review 325–1029 (2001). For a general treatment of election disputes using the 2000 election in general, and Bush v. Gore in particular, as the organizing theme, see Issacharoff, Karlan & Pildes, *When Elections Go Bad: The Law of Democracy and the Presidential Election of 2000* (2001).

Justice Kennedy found confirmation of this conclusion in the "history of the State's definition" and he went on to say:

"... Simply because a class defined by ancestry does not include all members of the race does not suffice to make the classification race neutral. Here, the State's argument is undermined by its express racial purpose and by its actual effects.

"The ancestral inquiry mandated by the State implicates the same grave concerns as a classification specifying a particular race by name. One of the principal reasons race is treated as a forbidden classification is that it demeans the dignity and worth of a person to be judged by ancestry instead of by his or her own merit and essential qualities. An inquiry into ancestral lines is not consistent with respect based on the unique personality each of us possesses, a respect the Constitution itself secures in its concern for persons and citizens.

"The ancestral inquiry mandated by the State is forbidden by the Fifteenth Amendment for the further reason that the use of racial classifications is corruptive of the whole legal order democratic elections seek to preserve. The law itself may not become the instrument for generating the prejudice and hostility all too often directed against persons whose particular ancestry is disclosed by their ethnic characteristics and cultural traditions...."

Justice Kennedy then rejected Hawaii's "three principal defenses of its voting law." First, based on the special mission of the OHA trustees to protect the interests of native Hawaiians and afford them a measure of self-governance, Hawaii invoked Morton v. Mancari, 417 U.S. 535 (1974), which upheld employment preferences at the federal Bureau of Indian Affairs for individuals who were "one-fourth or more degree Indian blood and ... member[s] of a Federally-recognized tribe." The BIA preference could be "tied rationally to the fulfillment of Congress' unique obligation toward the Indians," and was "reasonably and rationally designed to further Indian self-government." Without addressing "whether Congress may treat the native Hawaiians as it does the Indian tribes[,]" however, Justice Kennedy said that *Mancari*, which treated the BIA preference as "political rather than racial in nature," did not permit Congress to "authorize a State to establish a voting scheme that limits the electorate for its public officials to a class of tribal Indians, to the exclusion of all non-Indian citizens."

"... If a non-Indian lacks a right to vote in tribal elections, it is for the reason that such elections are the internal affair of a quasi-sovereign. The OHA elections, by contrast, are the affair of the State of Hawaii. OHA is a state agency, established by the State Constitution, responsible for the administration of state laws and obligations....

" ...

"The validity of the voting restriction is the only question before us. [W]e assume the validity of the underlying administrative structure and trusts, without intimating any opinion on that point. Nonetheless, the elections for OHA trustee are elections of the State, not of a separate quasi-sovereign, and they are elections to which the Fifteenth Amendment applies...."

Second, the majority rejected Hawaii's defense based on "cases holding that the rule of one person, one vote does not pertain to certain special purpose districts such as water or irrigation districts. See Ball v. James, 451 U.S. 355 (1981); Salyer Land Co. v. Tulare Lake Basin Water Storage Dist., 410 U.S. 719 (1973)." Finding it "far from clear that the *Salyer* line of cases would be at all applicable to statewide elections for an agency with the powers and responsibilities of OHA[,]" the Court "would not find those cases dispositive in any event[,]" because "compliance with the one-person, one-vote rule of the Four-teenth Amendment" would not "excuse[] compliance with the Fifteenth Amendment[,]" which "has independent meaning and force." Nor, third, did Hawaii's argument that the "restriction is based on beneficiary status rather than race" succeed. Not only was there a mismatch between the bulk of the funds being earmarked to benefit "native Hawaiians" and the eligible voting group extending to the broader group of "Hawaiians," but "more essential[ly, t]he State's position rests . . . on the demeaning premise that citizens of a particular race are somehow more qualified than others to vote on certain matters."

Concurring in the result, Justice Breyer, joined by Justice Souter, saw "no need . . . to decide this case on the basis of so vague a concept as 'quasi-sovereign,' " and he would "not subscribe to the Court's consequently sweeping prohibition." Instead, he thought the Court "should reject Hawaii's effort to justify its rules through analogy to a trust for an Indian tribe because the record makes clear that (1) there is no 'trust' for native Hawaiians here, and (2) OHA's electorate, as defined in the statute, does not sufficiently resemble an Indian tribe." As to (1), OHA administers revenues from public lands granted by the United States at statehood for the benefit of all the people of Hawaii, receives funding by ordinary legislation, and does not spend all its money to benefit native Hawaiians, so that "OHA is simply a special purpose department of Hawaii's state government." As to (2), the State, not a tribe or its equivalent, defined the electorate to include, not just native Hawaiians (who might be "analogous to tribes of other Native Americans"), but "Hawaiians" who might be "less than one five-hundredth original Hawaiian (assuming nine generations between 1778 and the present)"—a definition "well beyond any reasonable limit." Although these factors "destroy[ed] the analogy on which Hawaii's justification must depend[, t]his is not to say that Hawaii's definitions themselves independently violated the Constitution . . .; it is only to say that the analogies they here offer are too distant to save a race-based voting definition that in their absence would clearly violate the Fifteenth Amendment."

Justice Stevens dissented, emphasizing the Federal Government's "wide latitude in carrying out its obligations arising from the special relationship it has with the aboriginal peoples, a category that includes the native Hawaiians, . . . the State's own fiduciary responsibility—arising from its establishment of a public trust—for administering assets granted it by the Federal Government in part for the benefit of native Hawaiians[,]" and the absence of "invidious discrimination present in this effort to see that indigenous peoples are compensated for past wrongs, and to preserve a distinct and vibrant culture. . . ." The "well-established federal trust relationship with the native Hawaiians" made *Mancari* relevant and allowed "special benefits designed to restore a measure of native self-governance. . . ." With respect to the majority's concern "that we are confronted here with a state constitution and legislative enactment—passed by a majority of the entire population of Hawaii—rather than a law passed by Congress or a tribe itself[,] . . . OHA and its trustee elections can hardly be characterized simply as an 'affair of the State' alone; they are the instruments for implementing the Federal Government's trust relationship with a once sovereign indigenous people. This Court has held more than once that the federal power to pass laws fulfilling its trust relationship with the Indians may be delegated to the States." From that perspective, "as with the BIA preferences in *Mancari*, the OHA voting requirement is certainly reasonably designed to promote 'self-government' by the descendants of the indigenous Hawaiians, and to make OHA 'more responsive to the needs of its constituent groups.' "

These reasons were "more than sufficient to justify the OHA trust system and trustee election provision under the Fourteenth Amendment."

As for the Fifteenth Amendment, Justice Stevens noted that it does not prohibit the use of ancestry per se, and he argued that in this case ancestry was not "a proxy for race, or a pretext for invidious racial discrimination." *Guinn* and like cases involved voting systems "designed to exclude one racial class (at least) from voting" and "have no application to a system designed to empower politically the remaining members of a class of once sovereign, indigenous people." That all of the eligible voters "are beneficiaries of the public trust created by the State and administered by OHA, and ... have at least one ancestor who was a resident of Hawaii in 1778" established an acceptable trust scheme "whose terms provide that the trustees shall be elected by a class including beneficiaries"—a "classification th[at] exists wholly apart from race." Justice Stevens also said:

"... [T]here is surely nothing racially invidious about a decision to enlarge the class of eligible voters to include 'any descendant' of a 1778 resident of the Islands. The broader category of eligible voters serves quite practically to ensure that, regardless how 'dilute' the race of native Hawaiians becomes[,] ... there will remain a voting interest whose ancestors were a part of a political, cultural community, and who have inherited through participation and memory the set of traditions the trust seeks to protect. The putative mismatch only underscores the reality that it cannot be purely a racial interest that either the trust or the election provision seeks to secure; the political and cultural interests served are—unlike racial survival—shared by both native Hawaiians and Hawaiians.[14]

"... The OHA voting qualification—part of a statutory scheme put in place by democratic vote of a multiracial majority of all state citizens, including those non-'Hawaiians' who are not entitled to vote in OHA trustee elections—appropriately includes every resident of Hawaii having at least one ancestor who lived in the Islands in 1778.... Unlike a class including only full-blooded Polynesians—as one would imagine were the class strictly defined in terms of race—the OHA election provision excludes all full-blooded Polynesians currently residing in Hawaii who are not descended from a 1778 resident of Hawaii. Conversely, unlike many of the old southern voting schemes in which any potential voter with a 'taint' of non-Hawaiian blood would be excluded, the OHA scheme excludes no descendant of a 1778 resident because he or she is also part European, Asian, or African as a matter of race. The classification here is thus both too inclusive and not inclusive enough to fall strictly along racial lines.

"...

"... [T]he classification here is not 'demeaning' at all.... It is based on the permissible assumption in this context that families with 'any' ancestor who lived in Hawaii in 1778, and whose ancestors thereafter continued to live in Hawaii, have a claim to compensation and self-determination that others do not. For the multiracial majority of the citizens of the State of Hawaii to recognize that deep reality is not to demean their own interests but to honor those of others.

"... Our traditional understanding of democracy and voting preferences makes it difficult to conceive that the majority of the State's voting population

---

14. ...

... It is ... culture, rather than the Polynesian race, that is uniquely Hawaiian and in need of protection.

would have enacted a measure that discriminates against, or in any way represents prejudice and hostility toward, that self-same majority. . . . "

Justice Ginsburg dissented separately "for the reasons stated by Justice Stevens in [that part] of his dissenting opinion . . . relying on established federal authority over Native Americans. . . . "

THE FIRST AMENDMENT AS A LIMITATION ON STATE POWER TO FIX QUALIFICATIONS FOR VOTERS

The first amendment may also be a restriction on state power to set voter qualifications. In Kusper v. Pontikes, 414 U.S. 51 (1973), the Court held invalid a provision of the Illinois Election Code prohibiting a person from voting in the primary election of a political party if that person has voted in another party's primary within the preceding 23 months. The Court said: "There can no longer be any doubt that freedom to associate with others for the common advancement of political beliefs and ideas is a form of 'orderly group activity' protected by the First and Fourteenth Amendments. . . . The right to associate with the political party of one's choice is an integral part of this basic constitutional freedom. . . . To be sure, administration of the electoral process is a matter that the Constitution largely entrusts to the States. But, in exercising their powers of supervision over elections and in setting qualifications for voters, the States may not infringe upon basic constitutional protections." The Court went on to hold that the state had not shown that the restriction on voting in primary elections was closely related to a compelling state interest and hence it was invalid.

ACCESS TO THE BALLOT AND OTHER ELECTION LAWS

In addition to determining voter qualifications, states have extensively regulated the electoral process. Regulations relating to the following major areas exist: (1) Access of political parties and independent candidates to the ballot. (2) Political party nominating procedures. (3) Eligibility requirements for candidates. (4) Campaign regulations. See *Developments in the Law— Elections*, 88 Harv.L.Rev. 1111 (1975).

These laws have been attacked both as violations of equal protection and of the first amendment. For a discussion of the first amendment problems, see p. 1606 infra.

The following cases are among those relying principally on the equal protection clause.

BULLOCK v. CARTER, 405 U.S. 134 (1972). Texas imposed very high filing fees as a condition of becoming a candidate in a primary election. They were challenged by prospective candidates who asserted they were financially unable to pay the fees. The Court held the statute unconstitutional. In determining the standard of review to be applied, the Court said:

"The initial and direct impact of filing fees is felt by aspirants for office, rather than voters, and the Court has not heretofore attached such fundamental status to candidacy as to invoke a rigorous standard of review. However, the rights of voters and the rights of candidates do not lend themselves to neat separation; laws that affect candidates always have at least some theoretical, correlative effect on voters. Of course, not every limitation or incidental burden on the exercise of voting rights is subject to a stringent standard of review."

The Court then went on to note that the statute would exclude candidates without personal wealth or affluent backers. Not only would this limit the voters in their choice of candidates but also it would likely fall more heavily on the less affluent segments of society. Hence, because the scheme has a significant impact on the exercise of the franchise and because the impact is related to the resources of the voters, the Court concluded "that the laws must be 'closely scrutinized' and found reasonably necessary to the accomplishment of legitimate state objectives...." The Court went on to hold that the state interests, including that of regulating the number of candidates on the ballot, did not justify the regulation.

LUBIN v. PANISH, 415 U.S. 709 (1974). California imposed modest filing fees for primary elections fixed at one to two percent of the annual salary for the office. The Court upheld a challenge by a candidate who alleged that he could not afford to pay any filing fee, concluding:

"The absence of any alternative means of gaining access to the ballot inevitably renders the California system exclusionary as to some aspirants.... [T]he payment of a fee is an absolute, not an alternative, condition, and failure to meet it is a disqualification from running for office. Thus, California has chosen to achieve the important and legitimate interest of maintaining the integrity of elections by means which can operate to exclude some potentially serious candidates from the ballot without providing them with any alternative means of coming before the voters. Selection of candidates solely on the basis of ability to pay a fixed fee without providing any alternative means is not reasonably necessary to the accomplishment of the State's legitimate election interests. Accordingly, we hold that in the absence of reasonable alternative means of ballot access, a State may not ... require from an indigent candidate filing fees he cannot pay."

CLEMENTS v. FASHING, 457 U.S. 957 (1982). A Texas statute provided that judges and other office holders could not cut short their existing terms of office in order to serve in the Texas legislature. A Justice of the Peace claimed that this statute violated equal protection. The Court rejected the claim 5 to 4 but without a majority opinion. The plurality opinion by Justice Rehnquist said that the statute "need only rest on a rational predicate in order to survive challenge under the Equal Protection Clause" and that it met this challenge. Justice Stevens, concurring, objected to the plurality's discussion of levels of scrutiny. The Court also upheld the statute against a claim based on the first amendment.

C.   TRAVEL AND INTERSTATE MIGRATION, LENGTH OF STATE RESIDENCE, AND DISADVANTAGING NONRESIDENTS

Introduction. Section A. addressed whether equal protection analysis is sometimes used to decide cases involving rights secured by other constitutional provisions. This section addresses a set of cases, all analyzed in the equal protection framework, that involve constitutional claims of freedom to seek opportunity through interstate movement, migration, or trade, without being disadvantaged relative to those who already live where the opportunity is sought. Moreover, these cases not only implicate constitutional values of federalism in interstate relationships, but they combine, as do many other equal protection cases, concern about highly valued personal liberty with concern about the nature of the disadvantaging classification. Thus they may usefully be compared with cases like Harper v. Virginia State Board of Elections, supra p. 998, which focused on both voting as a specially protected interest and wealth as a classification; the cases in Section D. infra on poverty and welfare; and many others.

Although the cases do not divide neatly into those emphasizing the liberty of interstate opportunity and those emphasizing distinctions based on the fact or length of residency, they are divided here into three subsections. The first addresses interstate travel and migration, the second distinctions among state residents based on their length of residence, and the third distinctions between residents and nonresidents.

1. TRAVEL AND INTERSTATE MIGRATION

Shapiro v. Thompson

394 U.S. 618, 89 S.Ct. 1322, 22 L.Ed.2d 600 (1969).

Mr. Justice Brennan delivered the opinion of the Court.

These three appeals were restored to the calendar for reargument.... Each is an appeal from a decision of a three-judge District Court holding unconstitutional a State or District of Columbia statutory provision which denies welfare assistance to residents of the State or District who have not resided within their jurisdictions for at least one year immediately preceding their applications for such assistance. We affirm....

II.

There is no dispute that the effect of the waiting-period requirement in each case is to create two classes of needy resident families indistinguishable from each other except that one is composed of residents who have resided a year or more, and the second of residents who have resided less than a year, in the jurisdiction. On the basis of this sole difference the first class is granted and the second class is denied welfare aid upon which may depend the ability of the families to obtain the very means to subsist—food, shelter, and other necessities of life. In each case, the District Court found that appellees met the test for residence in their jurisdictions, as well as all other eligibility requirements except the requirement of residence for a full year prior to their applications. On reargument, appellees' central contention is that the statutory prohibition of benefits to residents of less than a year creates a classification which constitutes an invidious discrimination denying them equal protection of the laws. We agree. The interests which appellants assert are promoted by the classification either may not constitutionally be promoted by government or are not compelling governmental interests.

III.

Primarily, appellants justify the waiting-period requirement as a protective device to preserve the fiscal integrity of state public assistance programs. It is asserted that people who require welfare assistance during their first year of residence in a State are likely to become continuing burdens on state welfare programs. Therefore, the argument runs, if such people can be deterred from entering the jurisdiction by denying them welfare benefits during the first year, state programs to assist long-time residents will not be impaired by a substantial influx of indigent newcomers.

There is weighty evidence that exclusion from the jurisdiction of the poor who need or may need relief was the specific objective of these provisions....

We do not doubt that the one-year waiting period device is well suited to discourage the influx of poor families in need of assistance. An indigent who desires to migrate, resettle, find a new job, start a new life will doubtless hesitate if he knows that he must risk making the move without the possibility of falling back on state welfare assistance during his first year of residence, when his need may be most acute. But the purpose of inhibiting migration by needy persons into the State is constitutionally impermissible.

This Court long ago recognized that the nature of our Federal Union and our constitutional concepts of personal liberty unite to require that all citizens be free to travel throughout the length and breadth of our land uninhibited by statutes, rules or regulations which unreasonably burden or restrict this movement....

We have no occasion to ascribe the source of this right to travel interstate to a particular constitutional provision. It suffices that, as Mr. Justice Stewart said for the Court in United States v. Guest, 383 U.S. 745, 757–758 (1966):

"The constitutional right to travel from one State to another ... occupies a position fundamental to the concept of our Federal Union. It is a right that has been firmly established and repeatedly recognized.

"[The] right finds no explicit mention in the Constitution. The reason, it has been suggested, is that a right so elementary was conceived from the beginning to be a necessary concomitant of the stronger Union the Constitution created. In any event, freedom to travel throughout the United States has long been recognized as a basic right under the Constitution."

Thus, the purpose of deterring the in-migration of indigents cannot serve as justification for the classification created by the one-year waiting period, since that purpose is constitutionally impermissible....

Alternatively, appellants argue that even if it is impermissible for a State to attempt to deter the entry of all indigents, the challenged classification may be justified as a permissible state attempt to discourage those indigents who would enter the State solely to obtain larger benefits. We observe first that none of the statutes before us is tailored to serve that objective....

More fundamentally, a State may no more try to fence out those indigents who seek higher welfare benefits than it may try to fence out indigents generally. Implicit in any such distinction is the notion that indigents who enter a State with the hope of securing higher welfare benefits are somehow less deserving than indigents who do not take this consideration into account. But we do not perceive why a mother who is seeking to make a new life for herself and her children should be regarded as less deserving because she considers, among other factors, the level of a State's public assistance. Surely such a mother is no less deserving than a mother who moves into a particular State in order to take advantage of its better educational facilities.

Appellants argue further that the challenged classification may be sustained as an attempt to distinguish between new and old residents on the basis of the contribution they have made to the community through the payment of taxes. We have difficulty seeing how long-term residents who qualify for welfare are making a greater present contribution to the State in taxes than indigent residents who have recently arrived. If the argument is based on contributions made in the past by the long-term residents, there is some question, as a factual matter, whether this argument is applicable in Pennsylvania where the record suggests that some 40% of those denied public assistance because of the waiting period had lengthy prior residence in the State. But we need not rest on the particular facts of these cases. Appellants' reasoning would logically permit the State to bar new residents from schools, parks, and libraries or deprive them of police and fire protection. Indeed it would permit the State to apportion all benefits and services according to the past tax contributions of its citizens. The Equal Protection Clause prohibits such an apportionment of state services.[10]

We recognize that a State has a valid interest in preserving the fiscal integrity of its programs. It may legitimately attempt to limit its expenditures, whether for public assistance, public education, or any other program. But a State may not accomplish such a purpose by invidious distinctions between classes of its citizens. It could not, for example, reduce expenditures for education by barring indigent children from its schools. Similarly, in the cases before us, appellants must do more than show that denying welfare benefits to new residents saves money. The saving of welfare costs cannot be an independent ground for an invidious classification.

In sum, neither deterrence of indigents from migrating to the State nor limitation of welfare benefits to those regarded as contributing to the State is a constitutionally permissible state objective.

IV.

Appellants next advance as justification certain administrative and related governmental objectives allegedly served by the waiting-period requirement. They argue that the requirement (1) facilitates the planning of the welfare budget; (2) provides an objective test of residency; (3) minimizes the opportunity for recipients fraudulently to receive payments from more than one jurisdiction; and (4) encourages early entry of new residents into the labor force.

At the outset, we reject appellants' argument that a mere showing of a rational relationship between the waiting period and these four admittedly permissible state objectives will suffice to justify the classification.... The waiting-period provision denies welfare benefits to otherwise eligible applicants solely because they have recently moved into the jurisdiction. But in moving from State to State or to the District of Columbia appellees were exercising a constitutional right, and any classification which serves to penalize the exercise of that right, unless shown to be necessary to promote a *compelling* governmental interest, is unconstitutional....

The argument that the waiting-period requirement facilitates budget predictability is wholly unfounded. The records in all three cases are utterly devoid of evidence that either State or the District of Columbia in fact uses the one-year requirement as a means to predict the number of people who will require assistance in the budget year....

The argument that the waiting period serves as an administratively efficient rule of thumb for determining residency similarly will not withstand scrutiny. The residence requirement and the one-year waiting-period requirement are distinct and independent prerequisites for assistance under these three statutes, and the facts relevant to the determination of each are directly examined by the welfare authorities. Before granting an application, the welfare authorities investigate the applicant's employment, housing, and family situation and in the course of the inquiry necessarily learn the facts upon which to determine whether the applicant is a resident.

Similarly, there is no need for a State to use the one-year waiting period as a safeguard against fraudulent receipt of benefits; for less drastic means are available, and are employed, to minimize that hazard. Of course, a State has a valid interest in preventing fraud by any applicant, whether a newcomer or a long-time resident. It is not denied however that the investigations now

---

10. We are not dealing here with state insurance programs which may legitimately tie the amount of benefits to the individual's contributions.

conducted entail inquiries into facts relevant to that subject. In addition, cooperation among state welfare departments is common. The District of Columbia, for example, provides interim assistance to its former residents who have moved to a State which has a waiting period. As a matter of course, District officials send a letter to the welfare authorities in the recipient's new community "to request the information needed to continue assistance." A like procedure would be an effective safeguard against the hazard of double payments. Since double payments can be prevented by a letter or a telephone call, it is unreasonable to accomplish this objective by the blunderbuss method of denying assistance to all indigent newcomers for an entire year.

Pennsylvania suggests that the one-year waiting period is justified as a means of encouraging new residents to join the labor force promptly. But this logic would also require a similar waiting period for long-term residents of the State. A state purpose to encourage employment provides no rational basis for imposing a one-year waiting-period restriction on new residents only.

We conclude therefore that appellants in these cases do not use and have no need to use the one-year requirement for the governmental purposes suggested. Thus, even under traditional equal protection tests a classification of welfare applicants according to whether they have lived in the State for one year would seem irrational and unconstitutional. But, of course, the traditional criteria do not apply in these cases. Since the classification here touches on the fundamental right of interstate movement, its constitutionality must be judged by the stricter standard of whether it promotes a *compelling* state interest. Under this standard, the waiting period requirement clearly violates the Equal Protection Clause.

V.

Connecticut and Pennsylvania argue, however, that the constitutional challenge to the waiting period requirements must fail because Congress expressly approved the imposition of the requirement by the States as part of the jointly funded AFDC program. . . .

But even if we were to assume, *arguendo,* that Congress did approve the imposition of a one-year waiting period, it is the responsive *state* legislation which infringes constitutional rights. By itself § 402(b) has absolutely no restrictive effect. It is therefore not that statute but only the state requirements which pose the constitutional question.

Finally, even if it could be argued that the constitutionality of § 402(b) is somehow at issue here, it follows from what we have said that the provision, insofar as it permits the one-year waiting-period requirement, would be unconstitutional. Congress may not authorize the States to violate the Equal Protection Clause. Perhaps Congress could induce wider state participation in school construction if it authorized the use of joint funds for the building of segregated schools. But could it seriously be contended that Congress would be constitutionally justified in such authorization by the need to secure state cooperation? Congress is without power to enlist state cooperation in a joint federal-state program by legislation which authorizes the States to violate the Equal Protection Clause. Katzenbach v. Morgan, 384 U.S. 641, 651 (1966).

VI.

The waiting-period requirement in the District of Columbia Code . . . is also unconstitutional even though it was adopted by Congress as an exercise of federal power. In terms of federal power, the discrimination created by the one-year requirement violates the Due Process Clause of the Fifth Amendment.

"[W]hile the Fifth Amendment contains no equal protection clause, it does forbid discrimination that is 'so unjustifiable as to be violative of due process.' " Schneider v. Rusk, 377 U.S. 163, 168 (1964); Bolling v. Sharpe, 347 U.S. 497 (1954). For the reasons we have stated in invalidating the Pennsylvania and Connecticut provisions, the District of Columbia provision is also invalid—the Due Process Clause of the Fifth Amendment forbids Congress from denying public assistance to poor persons otherwise eligible solely on the ground that they have not been residents of the District of Columbia for one year at the time their applications are filed.

. . .

Affirmed.

Mr. Justice Stewart, concurring.

In joining the opinion of the Court, I add a word in response to the dissent of my Brother Harlan, who, I think, has quite misapprehended what the Court's opinion says.

The Court today does *not* "pick out particular human activities, characterize them as 'fundamental,' and give them added protection. . . ." To the contrary, the Court simply recognizes, as it must, an established constitutional right, and gives to that right no less protection than the Constitution itself demands. . . .

Mr. Chief Justice Warren, with whom Mr. Justice Black joins, dissenting.

In my opinion the issue before us can be simply stated: may Congress, acting under one of its enumerated powers, impose minimal nationwide residence requirements or authorize the States to do so? Since I believe that Congress does have this power and has constitutionally exercised it in these cases, I must dissent. . . .

Mr. Justice Harlan, dissenting. . . .

In upholding the equal protection argument, the Court has applied an equal protection doctrine of relatively recent vintage: the rule that statutory classifications which either are based upon certain "suspect" criteria or affect "fundamental rights" will be held to deny equal protection unless justified by a "compelling" governmental interest. . . .

The "compelling interest" doctrine, which today is articulated more explicitly than ever before, constitutes an increasingly significant exception to the long-established rule that a statute does not deny equal protection if it is rationally related to a legitimate governmental objective. The "compelling interest" doctrine has two branches. The branch which requires that classifications based upon "suspect" criteria be supported by a compelling interest apparently had its genesis in cases involving racial classifications, which have at least since Korematsu v. United States, 323 U.S. 214, 216 (1944), been regarded as inherently "suspect." The criterion of "wealth" apparently was added to the list of "suspects" as an alternative justification for the rationale in Harper v. Virginia Bd. of Elections, 383 U.S. 663, 668 (1966), in which Virginia's poll tax was struck down. The criterion of political allegiance may have been added in Williams v. Rhodes, 393 U.S. 23 (1968). Today the list apparently has been further enlarged to include classifications based upon recent interstate movement, and perhaps those based upon the exercise of *any* constitutional right, . . .

I think that this branch of the "compelling interest" doctrine is sound when applied to racial classifications, for historically the Equal Protection Clause was largely a product of the desire to eradicate legal distinctions founded upon race. However, I believe that the more recent extensions have been unwise....

The second branch of the "compelling interest" principle is even more troublesome. For it has been held that a statutory classification is subject to the "compelling interest" test if the result of the classification may be to affect a "fundamental right," regardless of the basis of the classification....

I think this branch of the "compelling interest" doctrine particularly unfortunate and unnecessary. It is unfortunate because it creates an exception which threatens to swallow the standard equal protection rule. Virtually every state statute affects important rights. This Court has repeatedly held, for example, that the traditional equal protection standard is applicable to statutory classifications affecting such fundamental matters as the right to pursue a particular occupation, the right to receive greater or smaller wages or to work more or less hours, and the right to inherit property. Rights such as these are in principle indistinguishable from those involved here, and to extend the "compelling interest" rule to all cases in which such rights are affected would go far toward making this Court a "super-legislature." This branch of the doctrine is also unnecessary. When the right affected is one assured by the federal Constitution, any infringement can be dealt with under the Due Process Clause. But when a statute affects only matters not mentioned in the federal Constitution and is not arbitrary or irrational, I must reiterate that I know of nothing which entitles this Court to pick out particular human activities, characterize them as "fundamental," and give them added protection under an unusually stringent equal protection test. ...

DUNN v. BLUMSTEIN, 405 U.S. 330 (1972). In this case the Court upheld a challenge to a Tennessee law providing that in order to vote one must be a resident of the state for one year and of the county for three months before the election. The Court, in an opinion by Justice Marshall, held that the residence requirement had to meet the *Shapiro* compelling state interest test because (1) it burdened the right to vote, and (2) it burdened the right to travel. The aspects of the case dealing with voting were considered *supra*, p. 1000. The Court responded to the state's argument that durational residence requirements do not abridge the right to travel because they neither seek to deter travel nor actually do deter travel as follows:

"This view represents a fundamental misunderstanding of the law. It is irrelevant whether disenfranchisement or denial of welfare is the more potent deterrent to travel. *Shapiro* did not rest upon a finding that denial of welfare actually deterred travel. Nor have other 'right to travel' cases in this Court always relied on the presence of actual deterrence. In *Shapiro* we explicitly stated that the compelling state interest test would be triggered by 'any classification which serves to *penalize* the exercise of that right [to travel]....'

"Of course it is true that the two individual interests affected by Tennessee's durational residence requirements are affected in different ways. Travel is permitted, but only at a price; voting is prohibited. The right to travel is merely penalized, while the right to vote is absolutely denied. But these differences are irrelevant for present purposes....

"The right to travel is 'an *unconditional* personal right,' a right whose exercise may not be conditioned.... Durational residence laws impermissibly condition and penalize the right to travel by imposing their prohibitions on only those persons who have recently exercised that right. In the present case, such laws force a person who wishes to travel and change residences to choose between travel and the basic right to vote.... Absent a compelling state interest, a State may not burden the right to travel in this way."

The Court also restated what the State must show to justify a statute burdening the right to travel or the right to vote:

"It is not sufficient for the State to show that durational residence requirements further a very substantial state interest. In pursuing that important interest, the State cannot choose means which unnecessarily burden or restrict constitutionally protected activity. Statutes affecting constitutional rights must be drawn with 'precision,' ... and must be 'tailored' to serve their legitimate objectives. *Shapiro v. Thompson*.... And if there are other, reasonable ways to achieve those goals with a lesser burden on constitutionally protected activity, a State may not choose the way of greater interference. If it acts at all, it must choose 'less drastic means.' "

It then went on to hold that while the State had identified important and presumably "compelling" state interests—prevention of fraudulent voting and assuring knowledgeable voters—the durational residence requirement was not closely enough related to either of those interests.

Chief Justice Burger dissented. Justice Blackmun concurred in the result. Justices Powell and Rehnquist took no part in the decision.

MEMORIAL HOSPITAL v. MARICOPA COUNTY, 415 U.S. 250 (1974). Applying *Shapiro* and *Dunn,* the Court held invalid an Arizona statute requiring a year's residence in a county as a condition to receiving nonemergency hospitalization or medical care at the county's expense. The challenge was brought by an indigent suffering from a chronic asthmatic and bronchial illness who suffered a severe respiratory attack within a month after he moved from New Mexico to Phoenix, Arizona. Justice Marshall's majority opinion said in part:

"The right of interstate travel has repeatedly been recognized as a basic constitutional freedom. Whatever its ultimate scope, however, the right to travel was involved in only a limited sense in *Shapiro.* The Court was there concerned only with the right to '[migrate], with intent to settle and abide' or, as the Court put it, 'to migrate, resettle, find a new job and start a new life.' Even a bona fide residence requirement would burden the right to travel, if travel meant merely movement. But, in *Shapiro,* the Court explained that '[t]he residence requirement and the one-year waiting-period requirement are distinct and independent prerequisites' for assistance and only the latter was held to be unconstitutional.... Later, in invalidating a durational residency requirement for voter registration on the basis of *Shapiro,* we cautioned that our decision was not intended to 'cast doubt on the validity of appropriately defined and uniformly applied bona fide residence requirements.' Dunn v. Blumstein....

The opinion later said:

"Although any durational residence requirement impinges to some extent on the right to travel, the Court in *Shapiro* did not declare such requirements to be *per se* unconstitutional....

" . . .

"Thus, *Shapiro* and *Dunn* stand for the proposition that a classification which 'operates to *penalize* those persons ... who have exercised their constitutional right of interstate migration,' must be justified by a compelling state interest.... Although any durational residency requirement imposes a potential cost on migration, the Court, in *Shapiro,* cautioned that some 'waiting-periods . . . may not be penalties.' . . . In *Dunn v. Blumstein,* supra, the Court found that the denial of the franchise, 'a fundamental political right,' . . . was a penalty requiring application of the compelling state interest test. In *Shapiro,* the Court found denial of the basic 'necessities of life' to be a penalty. Nonetheless, the Court has declined to strike down state statutes requiring one year of residence as a condition to lower tuition at state institutions of higher education. [Citing Vlandis v. Kline, 412 U.S. 441, 452–453 n. 9 (1973).]

"Whatever the ultimate parameters of the *Shapiro* penalty analysis, it is at least clear that medical care is as much 'a basic necessity of life' to an indigent as welfare assistance. And, governmental privileges or benefits necessary to basic sustenance have often been viewed as being of greater constitutional significance than less essential forms of governmental entitlements. See, e.g., *Shapiro,* supra; Goldberg v. Kelly, 397 U.S. 254, 264 (1970). . . . It would be odd, indeed, to find that the State of Arizona was required to afford Evaro welfare assistance to keep him from discomfort of inadequate housing or the pangs of hunger but could deny him the medical care necessary to relieve him from the wheezing and gasping for breath that attend his illness.

"   . . .

"Not unlike the admonition of the Bible that, 'Ye shall have one manner of law, as well for the stranger as for one of your country.' Leviticus, 24:22, the right of interstate travel must be seen as insuring new residents the same right to vital government benefits and privileges in the States to which they migrate as are enjoyed by other residents. The State of Arizona's durational residency requirement for free medical care penalizes indigents for exercising their right to migrate to and settle in that State. Accordingly, the classification created by the residency requirement, 'unless shown to be necessary to promote a *compelling* [state] interest, is unconstitutional.' *Shapiro,* . . . (Emphasis original.)"

Using an analysis like that in *Shapiro,* Justice Marshall concluded that "[a]ppellees have not met their heavy burden of justification, nor demonstrated that the State, in pursuing legitimate objectives, has chosen means which do not unnecessarily impinge on constitutionally protected interests." Chief Justice Burger and Justice Blackmun concurred in the result.

Justice Douglas wrote separately to say that "[s]o far as interstate travel *per se* is considered, I share the doubts of my Brother Rehnquist" but that "in the setting of this case the invidious discrimination against the poor, Harper v. Virginia Board of Elections, 383 U.S. 663 (1966), not the right to travel interstate is . . . the critical issue."

Justice Rehnquist dissented, saying in part:

"The legal question in this case is simply whether the State of Arizona has acted arbitrarily in determining that access to local hospital facilities for nonemergency medical care should be denied to persons until they have established residency for one year. The impediment which this quite rational determination has placed on petitioner Evaro's 'right to travel' is so remote as to be negligible: so far as the record indicates Evaro moved from New Mexico to Arizona three years ago and has remained ever since. The eligibility requirement has not the slightest resemblance to the actual barriers to the right of free ingress and egress protected by the Constitution, and struck down in cases such as *Crandall* and *Edwards.* And unlike *Shapiro* it does not involve an urgent need for the necessities of life or a benefit funded from current revenues to which the claimant may well have contributed. It is a substantial broadening of, and departure from, all of these holdings, all the more remarkable for the lack of explanation which accompanies the result."

Sosna v. Iowa

419 U.S. 393, 95 S.Ct. 553, 42 L.Ed.2d 532 (1975).

Mr. Justice Rehnquist delivered the opinion of the Court.

Appellant Carol Sosna married Michael Sosna on September 5, 1964, in Michigan. They lived together in New York between October 1967 and August 1971, after which date they separated but continued to live in New York. In August 1972, appellant moved to Iowa with her three children, and the following month she petitioned the District Court of Jackson County, Iowa, for a dissolution of her marriage.... The Iowa court dismissed the petition for lack of jurisdiction, finding that Michael Sosna was not a resident of Iowa and appellant had not been a resident of the State of Iowa for one year preceding the filing of her petition. In so doing the Iowa court applied the provisions of Iowa Code § 598.6 requiring that the petitioner in such an action be "for the last year a resident of the state."

Instead of appealing this ruling to the Iowa appellate courts, appellant filed a complaint in [federal court] asserting that Iowa's durational residency requirement for invoking its divorce jurisdiction violated the ... Constitution....

A three-judge court ... held that the Iowa durational residency requirement was constitutional.... We ... decide that this case is not moot, and [up]hold the Iowa durational residency requirement for divorce....

The durational residency requirement ... is a part of Iowa's comprehensive statutory regulation of domestic relations, an area that has long been regarded as a virtually exclusive province of the States....

The imposition of a durational residency requirement for divorce is scarcely unique to Iowa, since 48 States impose such a requirement as a condition for maintaining an action for divorce. As might be expected, the periods vary among the States and range from six weeks to two years. The one-year period selected by Iowa is the most common length of time prescribed.

Appellant contends that the Iowa requirement of one year's residence is unconstitutional ... because it establishes two classes of persons and discriminates against those who have recently exercised their right to travel to Iowa, thereby contravening the Court's holdings in Shapiro v. Thompson, 394 U.S. 618 (1969); Dunn v. Blumstein, 405 U.S. 330 (1972), and Memorial Hospital v. Maricopa County, 415 U.S. 250 (1974); ...

State statutes imposing durational residency requirements were of course invalidated when imposed by States as a qualification for welfare payments, *Shapiro,* supra, for voting, *Dunn,* supra, and for medical care, *Maricopa County,* supra. But none of those cases intimated that the States might never impose durational residency requirements, and such a proposition was in fact expressly disclaimed. What those cases had in common was that the durational residency requirements they struck down were justified on the basis of budgetary or record-keeping considerations which were held insufficient to outweigh the constitutional claims of the individuals. But Iowa's divorce residency requirement is of a different stripe. Appellant was not irretrievably foreclosed from obtaining some part of what she sought, as was the case with the welfare recipients in *Shapiro,* the voters in *Dunn,* or the indigent patient in *Maricopa County.* She would eventually qualify for the same sort of adjudication which she demanded virtually upon her arrival in the State. Iowa's requirement delayed her access to the courts, but, by fulfilling it, a plaintiff could ultimately obtain the same opportunity for adjudication which she asserts ought to be hers at an earlier point in time.

Iowa's residency requirement may reasonably be justified on grounds other than purely budgetary considerations or administrative convenience.... A decree of divorce is not a matter in which the only interested parties are the State as a sort of "grantor," and a plaintiff such as appellant in the role of "grantee." Both spouses are obviously interested in the proceedings, since it will affect their marital status and very likely their property rights. Where a married couple has minor children, a decree of divorce would usually include provisions for their custody and support. With consequences of such moment riding on a divorce decree issued by its courts, Iowa may insist that one seeking to initiate such a proceeding have the modicum of attachment to the State required here.

Such a requirement additionally furthers the State's parallel interests in both avoiding officious intermeddling in matters in which another State has a paramount interest, and in minimizing the susceptibility of its own divorce decrees to collateral attack. A State such as Iowa may quite reasonably decide that it does not wish to become a divorce mill for unhappy spouses who have lived there as short a time as appellant had when she commenced her action in the state court after having long resided elsewhere. Until such time as Iowa is convinced that appellant intends to remain in the State, it lacks the "nexus between person and place of such permanence as to control the creation of legal relations and responsibilities of the utmost significance." Williams v. North Carolina, 325 U.S. 226, 229 (1945). Perhaps even more importantly, Iowa's interests extend beyond its borders and include the recognition of its divorce decrees by other States under the Full Faith and Credit Clause of the Constitution, Art. IV, § 1. For that purpose, this Court has often stated that "judicial power to grant a divorce—jurisdiction, strictly speaking—is founded on domicil." *Williams,*.... Where a divorce decree is entered after a finding of domicile in *ex parte* proceedings, this Court has held that the finding of domicile is not binding upon another State and may be disregarded in the face of "cogent evidence" to the contrary.... For that reason, the State asked to enter such a decree is entitled to insist that the putative divorce plaintiff satisfy something more than the bare minimum of constitutional requirements before a divorce may be granted. The State's decision to exact a one-year residency requirement as a matter of policy is therefore buttressed by a quite permissible inference that this requirement not only effectuates state substantive policy but likewise provides a greater safeguard against successful collateral attack than would a requirement of bona fide residence alone. This is precisely the sort of determination that a State in the exercise of its domestic relations jurisdiction is entitled to make.

We therefore hold that the state interest in requiring that those who seek a divorce from its courts be genuinely attached to the State, as well as a desire to insulate divorce decrees from the likelihood of collateral attack, requires a different resolution of the constitutional issue presented than was the case in *Shapiro,* supra, *Dunn,* supra, and *Maricopa County,* supra.

.   .   .

[The Court also held that the statute did not violate due process by invoking a permanent and irrebuttable presumption of non-residence.]

Affirmed.

Mr. Justice White, dissenting.

. . .

Because I find that the case before the Court has become moot, I must respectfully dissent.

Mr. Justice Marshall, with whom Mr. Justice Brennan joins, dissenting.

The Court today departs sharply from the course we have followed in analyzing durational residency requirements since Shapiro v. Thompson, 394 U.S. 618 (1969). Because I think the principles set out in that case and its progeny compel reversal here, I respectfully dissent.

As we have made clear in *Shapiro* and subsequent cases, any classification that penalizes exercise of the constitutional right to travel is invalid unless it is justified by a compelling governmental interest. . . .

The Court's failure to address the instant case in these terms suggests a new distaste for the mode of analysis we have applied to this corner of equal protection law. In its stead, the Court has employed what appears to be an *ad hoc* balancing test, under which the State's putative interest in ensuring that its divorce plaintiffs establish some roots in Iowa is said to justify the one-year residency requirement. I am concerned not only about the disposition of this case, but also about the implications of the majority's analysis for other divorce statutes and for durational residency requirement cases in general.

JONES v. HELMS, 452 U.S. 412 (1981). A Georgia statute provided that parental abandonment of a child is a misdemeanor, but is a felony if the parent thereafter leaves the State. The lower federal court held the statute invalid because it infringed upon the right to travel, and the State's interests could be protected by less drastic means. On appeal, the Supreme Court unanimously reversed. Justice Stevens' opinion for the Court concluded that defendant's criminal conduct "necessarily qualified his right" to travel interstate. He noted, moreover, that this case did not involve, as did earlier "right to travel" cases, disparate treatment of residents and non-residents, or old and new residents. The question was the narrower one whether a State could enhance criminal punishment if the offender left the State after committing the crime. "Thus, although a simple penalty for leaving a State is plainly impermissible, if departure aggravates the consequences of conduct that is otherwise punishable, the State may treat the entire sequence of events, from the initial offense to departure from the State, as more serious than its separate components."

BONA FIDE RESIDENCE REQUIREMENTS

In McCarthy v. Philadelphia Civil Service Commission, 424 U.S. 645 (1976), the Court summarily rejected a city fire department employee's challenge to a requirement that city employees be residents of the city. The per curiam opinion distinguished *Shapiro, Dunn,* and *Memorial Hospital:*

". . . Neither in those cases, nor in any others, have we questioned the validity of a condition placed upon municipal employment that a person be a resident *at the time* of his application. In this case appellant claims a constitutional right to be employed by the city of Philadelphia *while* he is living elsewhere. There is no support in our cases for such a claim.

"We have previously differentiated between a requirement of continuing residency and a requirement of prior residency of a given duration. Thus in *Shapiro,* . . . we stated '[t]he residence requirement and the one-year waiting-period requirement are distinct and independent prerequisites'. And in *Memorial Hospital,* ... quoting *Dunn,* ... the Court explained that *Shapiro* and *Dunn* did not question 'the validity of appropriately defined and uniformly applied bona fide residence requirements.'

"This case involves that kind of bona fide continuing residence requirement. The judgment of the Commonwealth Court of Pennsylvania is therefore affirmed."

In Martinez v. Bynum, 461 U.S. 321 (1983), the Supreme Court upheld on its face a Texas law that permits a school district to deny tuition-free admission to a minor who lives apart from a parent or guardian, if the minor's presence in the school district is for the primary purpose of attending public schools. The durational residence cases permit "bona fide residence requirements." In Vlandis v. Kline, 412 U.S. 441, 453–454 (1973), the Court had stated that a state's interest in preserving the right of residents to attend state universities on a preferential tuition basis permits a state to "establish such reasonable criteria for in-state status as to make virtually certain that students who are not, in fact, bona fide residents of the State, but who have come there solely for educational purposes, cannot take advantage of the in-state rates." A school district would thus be justified in denying admission to all minor children whose parents did not satisfy traditional criteria of residency. The Texas statute was not invalid because it went further and allowed enrollment by children whose parents were present in the district, without intent to remain indefinitely, or children who were present in the district for some purpose other than attending school. Justice Marshall dissented. (A fuller report in this case appears infra, p. 1121.)

Saenz v. Roe

526 U.S. 489, 119 S.Ct. 1518, 143 L.Ed.2d 689 (1999).

[The report in this case appears, infra p. 1035]

2.   LENGTH OF STATE RESIDENCE DISTINCTIONS

Zobel v. Williams

457 U.S. 55, 102 S.Ct. 2309, 72 L.Ed.2d 672 (1982).

Chief Justice Burger, delivered the opinion of the Court.

The question ... is whether a statutory scheme by which a State distributes income derived from its natural resources to the adult citizens of the State in varying amounts, based on the length of each citizen's residence, violates the equal protection rights of newer state citizens. The Alaska Supreme Court sustained the constitutionality of the statute....

We reverse.

I

The 1967 discovery of large oil reserves on state-owned land in the Prudhoe Bay area of Alaska resulted in a windfall to the State. The State, which had a total budget of $124 million in 1969, before the oil revenues began to flow into the state coffers, received $3.7 billion in petroleum revenues during the 1981 fiscal year. This income will continue, and most likely grow for some years in the future. Recognizing that its mineral reserves, although large, are finite and that the resulting income will not continue in perpetuity, the State took steps to assure that its current good fortune will bring long range benefits. To accomplish this Alaska in 1976 adopted a constitutional amendment establishing the Permanent Fund into which the State must deposit at least 25% of its mineral income each year. Alaska Const., Art. IX, § 15. The amendment prohibits the legislature from appropriating any of the principal of the fund but permits use of the fund's earnings for general governmental purposes.

In 1980, the legislature enacted a dividend program to distribute annually a portion of the Fund's earnings directly to the State's adult residents. Under the plan, each citizen 18 years of age or older receives one dividend unit for each year of residency subsequent to 1959, the first year of statehood. The statute fixed the value of each dividend unit at $50 for the 1979 fiscal year; a one-year resident thus would receive one unit, or $50, while a resident of Alaska since it became a State in 1959 would receive 21 units, or $1,050. The value of a dividend unit will vary each year depending on the income of the Permanent Fund and the amount of that income the State allocates for other purposes. The State now estimates that the 1985 fiscal year dividend will be nearly four times as large as that for 1979.

Appellants, residents of Alaska since 1978, brought this suit in 1980 challenging the dividend distribution plan as violative of their right to equal protection guarantees and their constitutional right to migrate to Alaska, to establish residency there and thereafter to enjoy the full rights of Alaska citizenship on the same terms as all other citizens of the State....

II

The Alaska dividend distribution law is quite unlike the durational residency requirements we examined in Sosna v. Iowa, 419 U.S. 393 (1975); Memorial Hospital v. Maricopa County, 415 U.S. 250 (1974); Dunn v. Blumstein, 405 U.S. 330 (1972); and Shapiro v. Thompson, 394 U.S. 618 (1969). Those cases involved laws which required new residents to reside in the State a fixed minimum period to be eligible for certain benefits available on an equal basis to all other residents. The asserted purpose of the durational residency requirements was to assure that only persons who had established *bona fide* residence received rights and benefits provided for residents.

The Alaska statute does not impose any threshold waiting period on those seeking dividend benefits; persons with less than a full year of residency are entitled to share in the distribution. Alaska Stat. § 43.23.010. Nor does the statute purport to establish a test of the *bona fides* of state residence. Instead, the dividend statute creates fixed, permanent distinctions between an ever increasing number of perpetual classes of concededly *bona fide* residents, based on how long they have been in the State.

Appellants established residence in Alaska two years before the dividend law was passed. The distinction they complain of is not one which the State makes between those who arrived in Alaska after the enactment of the dividend distribution law and those who were residents prior to its enactment. Appellants instead challenge the distinctions made within the class of persons who were residents when the dividend scheme was enacted in 1980. The distinctions appellants attack include the preference given to persons who were residents when Alaska became a State in 1959 over all those who have arrived since then, as well as the distinctions made between all *bona fide* residents who settled in Alaska at different times during the 1959 to 1980 period.[5]

---

5. . . .

The statute does not involve the kind of discrimination which the Privileges and Im-

munities Clause of Art. IV was designed to prevent. That Clause "was designed to insure

... Appellants claim that the distinctions made by the Alaska law should be subjected to the higher level of scrutiny applied to the durational residency requirements in Shapiro v. Thompson, supra and Memorial Hospital v. Maricopa County, supra. The State, on the other hand, asserts that the law need only meet the minimum rationality test. In any event, if the statutory scheme cannot pass even the minimal test proposed by the State, we need not decide whether any enhanced scrutiny is called for.

A

The State advanced and the Alaska Supreme Court accepted three purposes justifying the distinctions made by the dividend program: (a) creation of a financial incentive for individuals to establish and maintain residence in Alaska; (b) encouragement of prudent management of the Permanent Fund; and (c) apportionment of benefits in recognition of undefined "contributions of various kinds, both tangible and intangible, which residents have made during their years of residency."

As the Alaska Supreme Court apparently realized, the first two state objectives—creating a financial incentive for individuals to establish and maintain Alaska residence, and assuring prudent management of the Permanent Fund and the State's natural and mineral resources—are not rationally related to the distinctions Alaska seeks to make between newer residents and those who have been in the State since 1959. Assuming *arguendo* that granting increased dividend benefits for each year of continued Alaska residence might give some residents an incentive to stay in the state in order to reap increased dividend benefits in the future, the State's interest is not in any way served by granting greater dividends to persons for their residency during the 21 years prior to the enactment.

Nor does the State's purpose of furthering the prudent management of the Permanent Fund and the state's resources support retrospective application of its plan to the date of statehood. On this score the state's contention is straightforward:

"... If residents believed that twenty years from now they would be required to share permanent fund income on a per capita basis with the large population that Alaska will no doubt have by then, the temptation would be great to urge the legislature to provide immediately for the highest possible return on the investments of the permanent fund principal, which would require investments in riskier ventures."

The State similarly argues that equal per capita distribution would encourage rapacious development of natural resources. Even if we assume that the state interest is served by increasing the dividend for each year of residency beginning with the date of enactment, is it rationally served by granting greater dividends in varying amounts to those who resided in Alaska during the 21 years prior to enactment? We think not.

The last of the State's objectives—to reward citizens for past contributions—alone was relied upon by the Alaska Supreme Court to support the retrospective application of the law to 1959. However, that objective is not a legitimate state purpose. A similar "past contributions" argument was made and rejected in *Shapiro v. Thompson* ...: ... Similarly, in Vlandis v. Kline, 412

to a citizen of State A who ventures into State B the same privileges which the citizens of State B enjoy." Toomer v. Witsell, 334 U.S. 385, 395 (1948). The Clause is thus not applicable to this case.

U.S. 441 (1973), we noted that "apportion[ment] of tuition rates on the basis of old and new residency ... would give rise to grave problems under the Equal Protection Clause of the Fourteenth Amendment."

If the States can make the amount of a cash dividend depend on length of residence, what would preclude varying university tuition on a sliding scale based on years of residence—or even limiting access to finite public facilities, eligibility for student loans, for civil service jobs, or for government contracts by length of domicile? Could States impose different taxes based on length of residence? Alaska's reasoning could open the door to state apportionment of other rights, benefits and services according to length of residency. It would permit the states to divide citizens into expanding numbers of permanent classes. Such a result would be clearly impermissible.

B

We need not consider whether the State could enact the dividend program prospectively only....

III

.   .   .

We hold that the Alaska dividend distribution plan violates the ... Equal Protection Clause.... [T]he judgment ... is reversed and the case is remanded for further proceedings not inconsistent with this opinion.

Justice Brennan, with whom Justice Marshall, Justice Blackmun, and Justice Powell join, concurring.

I join the opinion of the Court, and agree with its conclusion that the retrospective aspects of Alaska's dividend-distribution law are not rationally related to a legitimate state purpose. I write separately only to emphasize that the pervasive discrimination embodied in the Alaska distribution scheme gives rise to constitutional concerns of somewhat larger proportions than may be evident on a cursory reading of the Court's opinion. In my view, these concerns might well preclude even the prospective operation of Alaska's scheme.

.   .   .

... In my view, it is difficult to escape from the recognition that underlying any scheme of classification on the basis of duration of residence, we shall almost invariably find the unstated premise that "some citizens are more equal than others." We rejected that premise and, I believe, implicitly rejected most forms of discrimination based upon length of residence, when we adopted the Equal Protection Clause.

Justice O'Connor, concurring in the judgment.

The Court strikes Alaska's distribution scheme, purporting to rely solely upon the Equal Protection Clause of the Fourteenth Amendment. The phrase "right to travel" appears only fleetingly in the Court's analysis, dismissed with an observation that "right to travel analysis refers to little more than a particular application of equal protection analysis." The Court's reluctance to rely explicitly on a right to travel is odd, because its holding depends on the assumption that Alaska's desire "to reward citizens for past contributions ... is not a legitimate state purpose." Nothing in the Equal Protection Clause itself, however, declares this objective illegitimate. Instead, as a full reading of Shapiro v. Thompson, 394 U.S. 618 (1969) and Vlandis v. Kline, 412 U.S. 441 (1973), reveals, the Court has rejected this objective only when its implementation would abridge an interest in interstate travel or migration.

I respectfully suggest, therefore, that the Court misdirects its criticism when it labels Alaska's objective illegitimate. A desire to compensate citizens for their prior contributions is neither inherently invidious nor irrational. Under some circumstances, the objective may be wholly reasonable....

Alaska's distribution plan distinguishes between long-term residents and recent arrivals. Stripped to its essentials, the plan denies non-Alaskans settling in the State the same privileges afforded longer-term residents. The Privileges and Immunities Clause of Article IV, which guarantees "[t]he Citizens of each State ... all Privileges and Immunities of Citizens in the several States," addresses just this type of discrimination. Accordingly, I would measure Alaska's scheme against the principles implementing the Privileges and Immunities Clause. In addition to resolving the particular problems raised by Alaska's scheme, this analysis supplies a needed foundation for many of the "right to travel" claims discussed in the Court's prior opinions.

I

. . .

... Surely this scheme imposes one of the "disabilities of alienage" prohibited by Article IV's Privileges and Immunities Clause. See Paul v. Virginia, 8 Wall. 168, 180 (1869).

It could be argued that Alaska's scheme does not trigger the Privileges and Immunities Clause because it discriminates among classes of residents, rather than between residents and nonresidents. This argument, however, misinterprets the force of Alaska's distribution system.... Each group of citizens who migrated to Alaska in the past, or chooses to move there in the future, lives in the State on less favorable terms than those who arrived earlier. The circumstance that some of the disfavored citizens already live in Alaska does not negate the fact that "the citizen of State A who ventures into [Alaska]" to establish a home labors under a continuous disability.

If the Privileges and Immunities Clause applies to Alaska's distribution system, then our prior opinions describe the proper standard of review....

Once the Court ascertains that discrimination burdens an "essential activity," it will test the constitutionality of the discrimination under a two-part test. First, there must be "something to indicate that noncitizens constitute a peculiar source of the evil at which the statute is aimed." Hicklin v. Orbeck, 437 U.S. 518, 525–526 (1978) (quoting Toomer v. Witsell, 334 U.S. 385, 398 (1948)). Second, the Court must find a "substantial relationship" between the evil and the discrimination practiced against the noncitizens.

Certainly the right infringed in this case is "fundamental." Alaska's statute burdens those nonresidents who choose to settle in the State. It is difficult to imagine a right more essential to the Nation as a whole than the right to establish residence in a new State....

Alaska has not shown that its new residents are the "peculiar source" of any evil addressed by its disbursement scheme....

Even if new residents were the peculiar source of these evils, Alaska has not chosen a cure that bears a "substantial relationship" to the malady....

For these reasons, I conclude that Alaska's disbursement scheme violates Article IV's Privileges and Immunities Clause. I thus reach the same destination as the Court, but along a course that more precisely identifies the evils of the challenged statute.

. . .

Justice Rehnquist, dissenting.

Alaska's dividend distribution scheme represents one State's effort to apportion unique economic benefits among its citizens. Although the wealth received from the oil deposits of Prudhoe Bay may be quite unlike the economic resources enjoyed by most States, Alaska's distribution of that wealth is in substance no different from any other State's allocation of economic benefits. The distribution scheme being in the nature of economic regulation, I am at a loss to see the rationality behind the Court's invalidation of it as a denial of equal protection. This Court has long held that state economic regulations are presumptively valid, and violate the Fourteenth Amendment only in the rarest of circumstances: . . .

. . . [T]he illegitimacy of a State's recognizing the past contributions of its citizens has been established by the Court only in certain cases considering an infringement of the right to travel, and the majority itself rightly declines to apply the strict scrutiny analysis of those right-to-travel cases. The distribution scheme at issue in this case impedes no person's right to travel to and settle in Alaska; if anything, the prospect of receiving annual cash dividends would encourage immigration to Alaska. The State's third justification cannot, therefore, be dismissed simply by quoting language about its legitimacy from right-to-travel cases which have no relevance to the question before us.

. . . .

Attorney General of New York v. Soto–Lopez

476 U.S. 898, 106 S.Ct. 2317, 90 L.Ed.2d 899 (1986).

Justice Brennan announced the judgment of the Court and delivered an opinion in which Justice Marshall, Justice Blackmun, and Justice Powell joined.

The question . . . is whether a preference in civil service employment opportunities offered by the State of New York solely to resident veterans who lived in the State at the time they entered military service violates the constitutional rights of resident veterans who lived outside the State when they entered military service.

I

The State of New York, through its Constitution, N.Y. Const., Art. V, § 6, and its Civil Service Law, N.Y.Civ.Serv.Law § 85 . . . grants a civil service employment preference, in the form of points added to examination scores, to New York residents who are honorably-discharged veterans of the United States armed forces, who served during time of war, and who were residents of New York when they entered military service. This preference may be exercised only once, either for original hiring or for one promotion. . . .

Appellees . . . are veterans of the United States Army and long-time residents of New York. Both men claim to have met all the eligibility criteria for the New York State civil service preference except New York residence when they entered the Army. Both . . . passed New York City civil service examinations, but were denied the veterans' preference by the New York City Civil Service Commission because they were residents of Puerto Rico at the time they joined the military. Appellees sued the City in Federal District Court, alleging that the requirement of residence when they joined the military violated the Equal Protection Clause of the Fourteenth Amendment and the constitutionally protected right to travel. . . .

The District Court dismissed appellees' complaint.... The Court of Appeals for the Second Circuit reversed.... It ... held that the prior residence requirement of the New York civil service preference offends both the Equal Protection Clause and the right to travel.... We affirm.

"[F]reedom to travel throughout the United States has long been recognized as a basic right under the Constitution." *Dunn v. Blumstein*.... And, it is clear that the freedom to travel includes the "freedom to enter and abide in any State in the Union." *Dunn* ...

The textual source of the constitutional right to travel, or, more precisely, the right of free interstate migration, though, has proven elusive. It has been variously assigned to the Privileges and Immunities Clause of Art. IV, ... to the Commerce Clause, ... and to the Privileges and Immunities Clause of the Fourteenth Amendment,.... The right has also been inferred from the federal structure of government adopted by our Constitution.... However, in light of the unquestioned historic acceptance of the principle of free interstate migration, and of the important role that principle has played in transforming many States into a single Nation, we have not felt impelled to locate this right definitively in any particular constitutional provision.... Whatever its origin, the right to migrate is firmly established and has been repeatedly recognized by our cases. See, e.g., Hooper v. Bernalillo County Assessor, 472 U.S. 612, 618, n. 6 (1985); *Zobel,* ...

A state law implicates the right to travel when it actually deters such travel, ... when impeding travel is its primary objective, ..., or when it uses " 'any classification which serves to penalize the exercise of that right.' " ... Our right to migrate cases have principally involved the latter, indirect manner of burdening the right. More particularly, our recent cases have dealt with state laws that, by classifying residents according to the time they established residence, resulted in the unequal distribution of rights and benefits among otherwise qualified bona fide residents.[3]

Because the creation of different classes of residents raises equal protection concerns, we have also relied upon the Equal Protection Clause in these cases. Whenever a state law infringes a constitutionally protected right, we undertake intensified equal protection scrutiny of that law.... Thus, in several cases, we asked expressly whether the distinction drawn by the State between older and newer residents burdens the right to migrate. Where we found such a burden, we required the State to come forward with a compelling justification.... In other cases, where we concluded that the contested classifications did not survive even rational basis scrutiny, we had no occasion to inquire whether enhanced scrutiny was appropriate. *Hooper,* supra; *Zobel,* supra. The analysis in all of these cases, however, is informed by the same guiding principle—the right to migrate protects residents of a State from being disadvantaged, or from being treated differently, simply because of the timing of their migration, from other similarly situated residents.[4] ...

---

3. We have always carefully distinguished between bona fide residence requirements, which seek to differentiate between residents and nonresidents, and residence requirements, such as durational, fixed date, and fixed point residence requirements, which treat established residents differently based on the time they migrated into the State....

4. Of course, regardless of the label we place on our analysis—right to migrate or equal protection—once we find a burden on the right to migrate the standard of review is the same. Laws which burden that right must be necessary to further a compelling state interest. See, e.g., *Memorial Hospital,* supra; *Dunn,* supra; *Shapiro,* supra.

New York's eligibility requirements for its civil service preference conditions a benefit on New York residence at a particular past time in an individual's life. It favors those veterans who were New York residents at a past fixed point over those who were not New York residents at the same point in their lives. Our cases have established that similar methods of favoring "prior" residents over "newer" ones, such as limiting a benefit to those who resided in the State by a fixed past date, *Hooper,* supra; granting incrementally greater benefits for each year of residence, *Zobel,* supra; and conditioning eligibility for certain benefits on completion of a fixed period of residence, see, e.g., *Memorial Hospital,* supra; Dunn v. Blumstein, 405 U.S. 330 (1972); *Shapiro,* supra, warrant careful judicial review.[5] But, our cases have also established that only where a State's law "operates to penalize those persons . . . who have exercised their constitutional right of interstate migration" is heightened scrutiny triggered. *Memorial Hospital. . . .*

Our task in this case, then, is first to determine whether New York's restriction of its civil service preference to veterans who entered the armed forces while residing in New York operates to penalize those persons who have exercised their right to migrate. If we find that it does, appellees must prevail unless New York can demonstrate that its classification is necessary to accomplish a compelling state interest.[6] . . .

III

A

In previous cases, we have held that even temporary deprivations of very important benefits and rights can operate to penalize migration. For example, in *Shapiro,* supra, and in *Memorial Hospital,* supra, we found that recently arrived indigent residents were deprived of life's necessities by durational residence requirements for welfare assistance and for free, nonemergency medical care, respectively, which were available to other poor residents. In *Dunn,* supra, we held that new residents were denied a basic right by a durational residence requirement for establishing eligibility to vote. The fact that these deprivations were temporary did not offset the Court's conclusions that they were so severe and worked such serious inequities among otherwise

---

5. We have cautioned, however, that not all waiting periods are impermissible. See, e.g., *Memorial Hospital,* supra, at 258–259; *Shapiro,* supra, at 638, n. 21. Indeed, in Sosna v. Iowa, 419 U.S. 393 (1975), we upheld a 1–year residency condition for maintaining an action for divorce. We noted the State's strong, traditional interest in setting the terms of and procedures for marriage and divorce. Weighing the fact that appellant's access to the desired state procedure was only temporarily delayed, against the State's important interest, we concluded that her right to migrate was not violated.

We have also sustained domicile requirements, which incorporated 1–year waiting periods, for resident tuition at state universities. Starns v. Malkerson, 401 U.S. 985 (1971), summarily aff'g 326 F.Supp. 234 (Minn.1970) (three-judge court); Sturgis v. Washington, 414 U.S. 1057 (1973), summarily aff'g 368 F.Supp. 38 W.D. (Wash.) (three-judge court). See also Vlandis v. Kline, 412 U.S. 441, 452–454 (1973).

6. In his concurrence, The Chief Justice takes the Court to task for asking in the first instance what is the appropriate standard of review to employ in evaluating New York's laws. The Chief Justice argues that we should initially run the laws through a rational basis analysis and then, if they survive that level of scrutiny, ask whether a higher level is appropriate.

We disagree. The logical first question to ask when presented with an equal protection claim, and the one we usually ask first, is what level of review is appropriate. . . .

It is true, as The Chief Justice suggests, that in *Hooper,* supra, and *Zobel,* supra, the Court did not follow this same logical sequence of analysis. We think that the better approach is that which the Court has employed in other equal protection cases—to inquire first as to the proper level of scrutiny and then to apply it.

qualified residents that they effectively penalized new residents for the exercise of their rights to migrate.

More recently, in Hooper v. Bernalillo, 472 U.S. 612 (1985), and *Zobel v. Williams,* supra, we struck down state laws that created permanent distinctions among residents based on the length or timing of their residence in the State. At issue in *Hooper* was a New Mexico statute that granted a tax exemption to Vietnam veterans who resided in the State before May 8, 1976. *Zobel* concerned an Alaska statute granting residents one state mineral income dividend unit for each year of residence subsequent to 1959. Because we employed rational basis equal protection analysis in those cases, we did not face directly the question whether the contested laws operated to penalize interstate migration. Nonetheless, the conclusion that they did penalize migration may be inferred from our determination that "the Constitution will not tolerate a state benefit program that 'creates fixed, permanent distinctions . . . between . . . classes of concededly bona fide residents, based on how long they have been in the State.' " *Hooper* . . . (quoting *Zobel* . . .).

[Appellees] have been denied a significant benefit that is granted to all veterans similarly situated except for state of residence at the time of their entry into the military. While the benefit sought here may not rise to the same level of importance as the necessities of life and the right to vote, it is unquestionably substantial. The award of bonus points can mean the difference between winning or losing civil service employment, with its attendant job security, decent pay, and good benefits. . . . Furthermore, appellees have been permanently deprived of the veterans' credits that they seek. As the Court of Appeals observed, "[t]he veteran's ability to satisfy the New York residence requirement is . . . fixed. He either was a New York resident at the time of his initial induction or he was not; he cannot earn a change in status." 755 F.2d, at 275. Such a permanent deprivation of a significant benefit, based only on the fact of nonresidence at a past point in time, clearly operates to penalize appellees for exercising their rights to migrate.

B

New York offers four interests in justification of its fixed point residence requirement: (1) the encouragement of New York residents to join the armed services; (2) the compensation of residents for service in time of war by helping these veterans reestablish themselves upon coming home; (3) the inducement of veterans to return to New York after wartime service; and (4) the employment of a "uniquely valuable class of public servants" who possess useful experience acquired through their military service. All four justifications fail to withstand heightened scrutiny on a common ground—each of the State's asserted interests could be promoted fully by granting bonus points to *all* otherwise qualified veterans. New York residents would still be encouraged to join the services. Veterans who served in time of war would be compensated. And, both former New Yorkers and prior residents of other States would be drawn to New York after serving the Nation, thus providing the State with an even larger pool of potentially valuable public servants.

. . .

IV

. . . The State has not met its heavy burden of proving that it has selected a means of pursuing a compelling state interest which does not impinge unnecessarily on constitutionally protected interests. Consequently, we conclude that New York's veterans' preference violates appellees' constitutionally protected rights to migrate and to equal protection of the law.

. . .

Affirmed.

Chief Justice Burger, concurring in the judgment.

. . . Both *Zobel* and *Hooper* held that the classifications used by the States to award preferences to certain citizens failed to pass a rational basis test *under the Equal Protection Clause.* As a result, we had no occasion to reach the issues whether the classifications would survive heightened scrutiny or whether the right to travel was violated. . . .

The Court's opinion, however, instead *begins* the analysis by addressing the "right to migrate." Moreover, heightened scrutiny is employed without first determining whether the challenged New York classification would survive even rational basis analysis. . . .

. . .

I would affirm the judgment of the Court of Appeals based on our reasoning and holdings in *Hooper* and *Zobel,* rather than adding dicta concerning the right to travel.

Justice White, concurring in the judgment.

I agree with Justice O'Connor that the right to travel is not sufficiently implicated in this case to require heightened scrutiny. Hence, I differ with Justice Brennan in this respect. But I agree with The Chief Justice that the New York statute at issue denies equal protection of the laws because the classification it employs is irrational. I therefore concur in the judgment.

Justice Stevens, dissenting.

. . .

Justice O'Connor, with whom Justice Rehnquist and Justice Stevens join, dissenting.

. . . Because I believe that New York's veterans' preference scheme is not constitutionally offensive under the Equal Protection Clause, does not penalize some free-floating "right to migrate," and does not violate the Privileges and Immunities Clause of Art. IV, § 2, of the Constitution, I dissent.

I

The Court's constitutional analysis runs generally as follows: because the classification imposed by New York's limited, one-time veterans' civil service preference "penalizes" appellees' constitutional "right to migrate," the preference program must be subjected to heightened scrutiny, which it does not survive because it is insufficiently narrowly tailored to serve its asserted purposes. On the strength of this reasoning, the Court concludes that the preference program violates both appellees' constitutional "right to migrate" and their right to equal protection of the law, although it does not make clear how much of its analysis is necessary or sufficient to find a violation of the "right to migrate" independently of an Equal Protection Clause violation.

In pursuing this new dual analysis, the Court simply rejects the equal protection approach the Court has previously employed in similar cases, see, e.g., Hooper v. Bernalillo County Assessor, 472 U.S. 612 (1985), without bothering to explain why its novel use of both "right to migrate" analysis and strict equal protection scrutiny is more appropriate, necessary or doctrinally coherent.... Indeed, the Court does not even feel "impelled to locate ['the right to migrate'] definitively in any particular constitutional provision," despite the fact that its ruling rests in major part on its determination that the preference scheme penalizes that right....

. . .

It is unfortunate that the Court has once again failed to articulate and justify by reference to textual sources a single constitutional principle or analysis upon which it can rely in deciding cases such as this. I adhere to my belief that the Privileges and Immunities Clause of Art. IV, § 2, of the Constitution supplies the relevant basis for analysis in evaluating claims like appellees', where the principal allegation is that the state scheme impermissibly distinguishes between state residents, allegedly imposing a relative burden on those who have more recently exercised their right to establish residence in the State. See Zobel v. Williams ... (O'Connor, J., concurring in judgment). I also continue to believe that a State's desire to compensate its citizens for their prior contributions is "neither inherently invidious nor irrational," either under the Court's "right to migrate" or under some undefined, substantive component of the Equal Protection Clause.... This case presents one of those instances in which the recognition of state citizens' past sacrifices constitutes a valid state interest that does not infringe any constitutionally protected interest, including the fundamental right to settle in another State which is protected by the Privileges and Immunities Clause of Art. IV, § 2....

II

. . .

The New York law certainly does not directly restrict or burden appellees' freedom to move to New York and to establish residence there by imposing discriminatory fees, taxes, or other direct restraints....

Finally, the New York scheme does not effectively penalize those who exercise their fundamental right to settle in the State of their choice by requiring newcomers to accept a status inferior to that of all oldtime residents of New York upon their arrival. Cf. Zobel v. Williams, 457 U.S., at 74 (O'Connor, J., concurring in judgment). Those veterans who were not New York residents when they joined the United States Armed Forces, who subsequently move to New York, and who endeavor to secure civil service employment are treated exactly the same as the vast majority of New York citizens; they are in no sense regarded as "second-class citizens" when compared with the vast majority of New Yorkers or even the majority of the candidates against whom they must compete in obtaining civil employment. Cf. Hicklin v. Orbeck, 437 U.S. 518 (1978). To the extent that persons such as appellees labor under any practical disability, it is a disability that they share in equal measure with countless other New York residents, including New York residents who joined the Armed Forces from New York but are ineligible for the veterans' preference for other reasons.

... New York's veterans' preference scheme requires that veterans satisfy a number of preconditions, of which prior residency is only one, before they qualify for the preference. Moreover, the preference only increases the possibility of securing a civil service appointment; it does not guarantee it. Those newly arrived veterans who achieve a sufficiently high score on the exam may not be disadvantaged at all by the preference program; conversely, the chances of those who receive a very low score may not be affected by the fact that their competitors received bonus points. Finally, the bonus program is a one-time benefit. Veterans who join the service in New York, who satisfy the other statutory requirements, and who achieve a sufficiently high score on the exam to bring them within range of securing employment may only use the bonus points on one examination for appointment and in one job for promotion. Thus, persons such as appellees are not forced to labor under a "continuous disability" by comparison even to this discrete group of New York citizens. Zobel v. Williams, supra, at 75 (O'Connor, J., concurring in judgment).

. . .

In sum, finding that this scheme in theory or practical effect constitutes a "penalty" on appellees' fundamental right to settle in New York or on their "right to migrate" seems to me ephemeral, and completely unnecessary to safeguard the constitutional purpose of "maintaining a Union rather than a mere 'league of States.'" Zobel v. Williams, supra, at 73 (O'Connor, J., concurring in judgment).... Thus, heightened scrutiny, either under the "right to migrate" or the Equal Protection Clause is inappropriate.

Under rational basis review, New York's program plainly passes constitutional muster....

. . .

Whether this issue is tested under the "right to migrate," the Equal Protection Clause, or the Privileges and Immunities Clause of Art. IV, § 2, something more than the minimal effect on the right to travel or migrate that exists in this case must be required to trigger heightened scrutiny or the Court's right to travel analysis will swallow all the traditional deference shown to state economic and social regulation. The modest scheme at issue here does not penalize in a constitutional sense veterans who joined the Armed Forces in other States for choosing to eventually settle in New York, and does not deny them equal protection....[a]

Saenz v. Roe

526 U.S. 489, 119 S.Ct. 1518, 143 L.Ed.2d 689 (1999).

Justice Stevens delivered the opinion of the Court.

In 1992, California enacted a statute limiting the maximum welfare benefits available to newly arrived residents. The scheme limits the amount payable to a family that has resided in the State for less than 12 months to the amount payable by the State of the family's prior residence. The questions presented by this case are whether the 1992 statute was constitutional when it was enacted and, if not, whether an amendment to the Social Security Act enacted by Congress in 1996 affects that determination.

I

. . .

... In 1992, in order to make a relatively modest reduction in its vast welfare budget, the California Legislature enacted § 11450.03 of the state Welfare and Institutions Code ... to change the California AFDC program by limiting new residents, for the first year they live in California, to the benefits

---

a. See generally Cohen, *Equal Treatment for Newcomers: The Core Meaning of*   *National and State Citizenship,* 1 Const.Commentary 9 (1984).

they would have received in the State of their prior residence. Because in 1992 a state program either had to conform to federal specifications or receive a waiver from the Secretary of Health and Human Services in order to qualify for federal reimbursement, § 11450.03 required approval by the Secretary to take effect. In October 1992, the Secretary issued a waiver purporting to grant such approval.

... [T]hree California residents who were eligible for AFDC benefits challeng[ed] the constitutionality of the durational residency requirement[, each] alleg[ing] that she had recently moved to California to live with relatives in order to escape abusive family circumstances [and] that her monthly AFDC grant for the ensuing 12 months would be substantially lower under § 11450.03 than if the statute were not in effect....

The District Court ... preliminarily enjoined implementation of the statute. The Court of Appeals summarily affirmed....

We granted the State's petition for certiorari [but] were ... unable to reach the merits because the Secretary's approval of § 11450.03 had been invalidated in a separate proceeding, and the State had acknowledged that the Act would not be implemented without further action by the Secretary. We vacated the judgment and directed that the case be dismissed. Anderson v. Green, 513 U.S. 557 (1995) (per curiam). Accordingly, § 11450.03 remained inoperative until after Congress enacted the Personal Responsibility and Work Opportunity Reconciliation Act of 1996 PRWORA, 110 Stat. 2105.

PRWORA replaced the AFDC program with TANF [Temporary Assistance to Needy Families]. The new statute expressly authorizes any State that receives a block grant under TANF to "apply to a family the rules (including benefit amounts) of the [TANF] program ... of another State if the family has moved to the State from the other State and has resided in the State for less than 12 months." 42 U.S.C. § 604(c) (1994 ed., Supp. II). With this federal statutory provision in effect, California no longer needed specific approval from the Secretary to implement § 11450.03....

... [Under the California rules,] the lower level of benefits applies regardless of whether the family was on welfare in the State of prior residence and regardless of the family's motive for moving to California. The instructions also explain that the residency requirement is inapplicable to families that recently arrived from another country.

II

[T]his action ... [presents] essentially the same claims asserted by the plaintiffs in *Anderson v. Green*, but also challeng[es] the constitutionality of PRWORA's approval of the durational residency requirement....

. . .

... [The District Court] again enjoined the implementation of the statute. [T]he Court of Appeals affirmed.... We now affirm.

III

The word "travel" is not found in the text of the Constitution. Yet the "constitutional right to travel from one State to another" is firmly embedded in our jurisprudence. United States v. Guest, 383 U.S. 745, 757 (1966). Indeed, as Justice Stewart reminded us in Shapiro v. Thompson, 394 U.S. 618 (1969), the right is so important that it is "assertable against private interference as well as governmental action . . . a virtually unconditional personal right, guaranteed by the Constitution to us all." Id., at 643 (concurring opinion).

. . .

In this case California argues that § 11450.03 was not enacted for the impermissible purpose of inhibiting migration by needy persons and that, unlike the legislation reviewed in *Shapiro*, it does not penalize the right to travel because new arrivals are not ineligible for benefits during their first year of residence. California submits that, instead of being subjected to the strictest scrutiny, the statute should be upheld if it is supported by a rational basis and that the State's legitimate interest in saving over $10 million a year satisfies that test. [T]he United States . . . has advanced the novel argument that the enactment of PRWORA allows the States to adopt a "specialized choice-of-law-type provision" that "should be subject to an intermediate level of constitutional review," merely requiring that durational residency requirements be "substantially related to an important governmental objective." The debate about the appropriate standard of review, together with the potential relevance of the federal statute, persuades us that it will be useful to focus on the source of the constitutional right on which respondents rely.

IV

The "right to travel" discussed in our cases embraces at least three different components. It protects the right of a citizen of one State to enter and to leave another State, the right to be treated as a welcome visitor rather than an unfriendly alien when temporarily present in the second State, and, for those travelers who elect to become permanent residents, the right to be treated like other citizens of that State.

. . . Given that § 11450.03 imposed no obstacle to respondents' entry into California, we think the State is correct when it argues that the statute does not directly impair the exercise of the right to free interstate movement. For the purposes of this case, therefore, we need not identify the source of that particular right in the text of the Constitution. The right of "free ingress and regress to and from" neighboring States, which was expressly mentioned in the text of the Articles of Confederation, may simply have been "conceived from the beginning to be a necessary concomitant of the stronger Union the Constitution created." Id., at 758.

The second component of the right to travel is, however, expressly protected by the text of the Constitution. The first sentence of Article IV, § 2, provides:

"The Citizens of each State shall be entitled to all Privileges and Immunities of Citizens in the several States."

Thus, by virtue of a person's state citizenship, a citizen of one State who travels in other States, intending to return home at the end of his journey, is entitled to enjoy the "Privileges and Immunities of Citizens in the several States" that he visits. This provision . . . provides important protections for nonresidents who enter a State whether to obtain employment, Hicklin v. Orbeck, 437 U.S. 518 (1978), to procure medical services, Doe v. Bolton, 410 U.S. 179, 200 (1973), or even to engage in commercial shrimp fishing, Toomer v. Witsell, 334 U.S. 385 (1948). Those protections are not "absolute," but the Clause "does bar discrimination against citizens of other States where there is no substantial reason for the discrimination beyond the mere fact that they are citizens of other States." Id., at 396. There may be a substantial reason for requiring the nonresident to pay more than the resident for a hunting license, see Baldwin v.

Fish and Game Comm'n of Mont., 436 U.S. 371, 390–391 (1978), or to enroll in the state university, see Vlandis v. Kline, 412 U.S. 441, 445 (1973), but our cases have not identified any acceptable reason for qualifying the protection afforded by the Clause for "the 'citizen of State A who ventures into State B' to settle there and establish a home." *Zobel*, 457 U.S., at 74 (O'Connor, J., concurring in judgment). Permissible justifications for discrimination between residents and nonresidents are simply inapplicable to a nonresident's exercise of the right to move into another State and become a resident of that State.

What is at issue in this case, then, is this third aspect of the right to travel—the right of the newly arrived citizen to the same privileges and immunities enjoyed by other citizens of the same State. That right is protected not only by the new arrival's status as a state citizen, but also by her status as a citizen of the United States. That additional source of protection is plainly identified in the opening words of the Fourteenth Amendment:

> "All persons born or naturalized in the United States, and subject to the jurisdiction thereof, are citizens of the United States and of the State wherein they reside. No State shall make or enforce any law which shall abridge the privileges or immunities of citizens of the United States; . . . ."

Despite fundamentally differing views concerning the coverage of the Privileges or Immunities Clause of the Fourteenth Amendment, most notably expressed in the majority and dissenting opinions in the Slaughter–House Cases, 16 Wall. 36 (1872), it has always been common ground that this Clause protects the third component of the right to travel. Writing for the majority in the *Slaughter-House Cases*, Justice Miller explained that one of the privileges conferred by this Clause "is that a citizen of the United States can, of his own volition, become a citizen of any State of the Union by a *bona fide* residence therein, with the same rights as other citizens of that State." Id., at 80. Justice Bradley, in dissent, used even stronger language to make the same point:

> "The states have not now, if they ever had, any power to restrict their citizenship to any classes or persons. A citizen of the United States has a perfect constitutional right to go to and reside in any State he chooses, and to claim citizenship therein, and an equality of rights with every other citizen; and the whole power of the nation is pledged to sustain him in that right. He is not bound to cringe to any superior, or to pray for any act of grace, as a means of enjoying all the rights and privileges enjoyed by other citizens." Id., at 112–113.

That newly arrived citizens "have two political capacities, one state and one federal," adds special force to their claim that they have the same rights as others who share their citizenship. Neither mere rationality nor some intermediate standard of review should be used to judge the constitutionality of a state rule that discriminates against some of its citizens because they have been domiciled in the State for less than a year. The appropriate standard may be more categorical than that articulated in *Shapiro*, see supra, at 1524–1525, but it is surely no less strict.

V

Because this case involves discrimination against citizens who have completed their interstate travel, the State's argument that its welfare scheme affects the right to travel only "incidentally" is beside the point. Were we concerned solely with actual deterrence to migration, we might be persuaded that a partial withholding of benefits constitutes a lesser incursion on the right to travel than an outright denial of all benefits. See Dunn v. Blumstein, 405 U.S. 330, 339 (1972). But since the right to travel embraces the citizen's right to be treated equally in her new State of residence, the discriminatory classification is itself a penalty.

It is undisputed that respondents and the members of the class that they represent are citizens of California and that their need for welfare benefits is unrelated to the length of time that they have resided in California. We thus have no occasion to consider what weight might be given to a citizen's length of residence if the bona fides of her claim to state citizenship were questioned. Moreover, because whatever benefits they receive will be consumed while they remain in California, there is no danger that recognition of their claim will encourage citizens of other States to establish residency for just long enough to acquire some readily portable benefit, such as a divorce or a college education, that will be enjoyed after they return to their original domicile. See, e.g., Sosna v. Iowa, 419 U.S. 393 (1975); Vlandis v. Kline, 412 U.S. 441 (1973).

The classifications challenged in this case—and there are many—are defined entirely by (a) the period of residency in California and (b) the location of the prior residences of the disfavored class members. The favored class of beneficiaries includes all eligible California citizens who have resided there for at least one year, plus those new arrivals who last resided in another country or in a State that provides benefits at least as generous as California's. Thus, within the broad category of citizens who resided in California for less than a year, there are many who are treated like lifetime residents. And within the broad sub-category of new arrivals who are treated less favorably, there are many smaller classes whose benefit levels are determined by the law of the States from whence they came. To justify § 11450.03, California must therefore explain not only why it is sound fiscal policy to discriminate against those who have been citizens for less than a year, but also why it is permissible to apply such a variety of rules within that class.

These classifications may not be justified by a purpose to deter welfare applicants from migrating to California for three reasons. First, although it is reasonable to assume that some persons may be motivated to move for the purpose of obtaining higher benefits, the empirical evidence reviewed by the District Judge, which takes into account the high cost of living in California, indicates that the number of such persons is quite small—surely not large enough to justify a burden on those who had no such motive. Second, California has represented to the Court that the legislation was not enacted for any such reason.[19] Third, even if it were, as we squarely held in Shapiro v. Thompson, 394 U.S. 618 (1969), such a purpose would be unequivocally impermissible.

[Handwritten margin note: Reasons why not justified in detering applicants]

Disavowing any desire to fence out the indigent, California has instead advanced an entirely fiscal justification for its multitiered scheme. The enforcement of § 11450.03 will save the State approximately $10.9 million a year. The question is not whether such saving is a legitimate purpose but whether the State may accomplish that end by the discriminatory means it has chosen. An evenhanded, across-the-board reduction of about 72 cents per month for every beneficiary would produce the same result. But our negative answer to the question does not rest on the weakness of the State's purported fiscal justification. It rests on the fact that the Citizenship Clause of the Fourteenth Amendment expressly equates citizenship with residence: "That Clause does not provide for, and does not allow for, degrees of citizenship based on length of residence." *Zobel*, 457 U.S., at 69. It is equally clear that the Clause does not tolerate a hierarchy of 45 subclasses of similarly situated citizens based on the

---

19. The District Court and the Court of Appeals concluded, however, that the "apparent purpose of § 11450.03 was to deter migration of poor people to California." Roe v. Anderson, 134 F.3d 1400, 1404 (C.A.9 1998).

reason does not save money does not justify discrimination

location of their prior residence.[20] Thus § 11450.03 is doubly vulnerable: Neither the duration of respondents' California residence, nor the identity of their prior States of residence, has any relevance to their need for benefits. Nor do those factors bear any relationship to the State's interest in making an equitable allocation of the funds to be distributed among its needy citizens.... In short, the State's legitimate interest in saving money provides no justification for its decision to discriminate among equally eligible citizens.

VI

The question that remains is whether congressional approval of durational residency requirements in the 1996 amendment to the Social Security Act somehow resuscitates the constitutionality of § 11450.03. That question is readily answered, for we have consistently held that Congress may not authorize the States to violate the Fourteenth Amendment. Moreover, the protection afforded to the citizen by the Citizenship Clause of that Amendment is a limitation on the powers of the National Government as well as the States.

... Congress has no affirmative power to authorize the States to violate the Fourteenth Amendment and is implicitly prohibited from passing legislation that purports to validate any such violation....

The Solicitor General does not unequivocally defend the constitutionality of § 11450.03. But he has argued that two features of PRWORA may provide a sufficient justification for state durational requirements to warrant further inquiry before finally passing on the section's validity, or perhaps that it is only invalid insofar as it applies to new arrivals who were not on welfare before they arrived in California.

He first points out that because the TANF program gives the States broader discretion than did AFDC, there will be significant differences among the States which may provide new incentives for welfare recipients to change their residences. He does not, however, persuade us that the disparities under the new program will necessarily be any greater than the differences under AFDC.... Moreover, we are not convinced that a policy of eliminating incentives to move to California provides a more permissible justification for classifying California citizens than a policy of imposing special burdens on new arrivals to deter them from moving into the State. Nor is the discriminatory impact of § 11450.03 abated by repeatedly characterizing it as "a sort of specialized choice-of-law rule." California law alone discriminates among its own citizens on the basis of their prior residence.

The Solicitor General also suggests that we should recognize the congressional concern addressed in the legislative history of PRWORA that the "States might engage in a 'race to the bottom' in setting the benefit levels in their TANF programs." Again, it is difficult to see why that concern should be any greater under TANF than under AFDC. The evidence reviewed by the District Court indicates that the savings resulting from the discriminatory policy, if spread equitably throughout the entire program, would have only a miniscule impact on benefit levels. Indeed, as one of the legislators apparently interpreted this concern, it would logically prompt the States to reduce benefit levels sufficiently "to encourage emigration of benefit recipients." But speculation about such an unlikely eventuality provides no basis for upholding § 11450.03.

---

20. See Cohen, Discrimination Against New State Citizens: An Update, 11 Const. Comm. 73, 79 (1994) ("[J]ust as it would violate the Constitution to deny these new arrivals state citizenship, it would violate the Constitution to concede their citizenship in name only while treating them as if they were still citizens of other states").

Finally, the Solicitor General suggests that the State's discrimination might be acceptable if California had limited the disfavored subcategories of new citizens to those who had received aid in their prior State of residence at any time within the year before their arrival in California. The suggestion is ironic for at least three reasons: It would impose the most severe burdens on the neediest members of the disfavored classes; it would significantly reduce the savings that the State would obtain, thus making the State's claimed justification even less tenable; and, it would confine the effect of the statute to what the Solicitor General correctly characterizes as "the invidious purpose of discouraging poor people generally from settling in the State."

* * *

Citizens of the United States, whether rich or poor, have the right to choose to be citizens "of the State wherein they reside." U.S. Const., Amdt. 14, § 1. The States, however, do not have any right to select their citizens. The Fourteenth Amendment, like the Constitution itself, was, as Justice Cardozo put it, "framed upon the theory that the peoples of the several states must sink or swim together, and that in the long run prosperity and salvation are in union and not division." Baldwin v. G.A.F. Seelig, Inc., 294 U.S. 511, 523 (1935).

. . .

Chief Justice Rehnquist, with whom Justice Thomas joins, dissenting.

The Court today breathes new life into the previously dormant Privileges or Immunities Clause of the Fourteenth Amendment . . . to strike down what I believe is a reasonable measure falling under the head of a "good-faith residency requirement." Because I do not think any provision of the Constitution—and surely not a provision relied upon for only the second time since its enactment 130 years ago—requires this result, I dissent.

I

Much of the Court's opinion is unremarkable and sound. The right to travel clearly embraces the right to go from one place to another, and prohibits States from impeding the free interstate passage of citizens.... The Court wisely holds that because Cal. Welf. & Inst.Code Ann. § 11450.03 (West Supp.1999) imposes no obstacle to respondents' entry into California, the statute does not infringe upon the right to travel. Thus, the traditional conception of the right to travel is simply not an issue in this case.

I also have no difficulty with aligning the right to travel with the protections afforded by the Privileges and Immunities Clause of Article IV, § 2, to nonresidents who enter other States "intending to return home at the end of [their] journey." . . . Like the traditional right-to-travel guarantees discussed above, however, this Clause has no application here, because respondents expressed a desire to stay in California and become citizens of that State. Respondents therefore plainly fall outside the protections of Article IV, § 2.

Finally, I agree with the proposition that a "citizen of the United States can, of his own volition, become a citizen of any State of the Union by a *bona fide* residence therein, with the same rights as other citizens of that State." Slaughter–House Cases, 16 Wall. 36, 80 (1872).

But I cannot see how the right to become a citizen of another State is a necessary "component" of the right to travel, or why the Court tries to marry these separate and distinct rights. A person is no longer "traveling" in any sense of the word when he finishes his journey to a State which he plans to make his home. Indeed, under the Court's logic, the protections of the Privileges or Immunities Clause recognized in this case come into play only when an individual stops traveling with the intent to remain and become a citizen of a new State. The right to travel and the right to become a citizen are distinct, their relationship is not reciprocal, and one is not a "component" of the other. Indeed, the same dicta from the *Slaughter-House Cases* quoted by the Court actually treats the right to become a citizen and the right to travel as separate and distinct rights under the Privileges or Immunities Clause of the Fourteenth Amendment. See id., at 79–80. At most, restrictions on an individual's right to become a citizen indirectly affect his calculus in deciding whether to exercise his right to travel in the first place, but such an attenuated and uncertain relationship is no ground for folding one right into the other.

No doubt the Court has, in the past 30 years, essentially conflated the right to travel with the right to equal state citizenship in striking down durational residence requirements similar to the one challenged here. . . .

[T]he Court in these cases held that restricting the provision of welfare benefits, votes, or certain medical benefits to new citizens for a limited time impermissibly "penalized" them under the Equal Protection Clause of the Fourteenth Amendment for having exercised their right to travel. . . . In other cases, the Court recognized that laws dividing new and old residents had little to do with the right to travel and merely triggered an inquiry into whether the resulting classification rationally furthered a legitimate government purpose. See Zobel v. Williams, 457 U.S. 55, 60, n. 6 (1982); Hooper v. Bernalillo County Assessor, 472 U.S. 612, 618 (1985).[2] While *Zobel* and *Hooper* reached the wrong result in my view, they at least put the Court on the proper track in identifying exactly what interests it was protecting; namely, the right of individuals not to be subject to unjustifiable classifications as opposed to infringements on the right to travel.

The Court today tries to clear much of the underbrush created by these prior right-to-travel cases, abandoning its effort to define what residence requirements deprive individuals of "important rights and benefits" or "penalize" the right to travel. Under its new analytical framework, a State, outside certain ill-defined circumstances, cannot classify its citizens by the length of their residence in the State without offending the Privileges or Immunities Clause of the Fourteenth Amendment. The Court thus departs from *Shapiro* and its progeny, and, while paying lipservice to the right to travel, the Court does little to explain how the right to travel is involved at all. Instead, as the Court's analysis clearly demonstrates, this case is only about respondents' right to immediately enjoy all the privileges of being a California citizen in relation to that State's ability to test the good-faith assertion of this right. The Court has thus come full circle by effectively disavowing the analysis of *Shapiro*, segregating the right to travel and the rights secured by Article IV from the right to become a citizen under the Privileges or Immunities Clause, and then testing the residence requirement here against this latter right. For all its misplaced efforts to fold the right to become a citizen into the right to travel, the Court has essentially returned to its original understanding of the right to travel.

2. As Chief Justice Burger aptly stated in *Zobel*: "In reality, right to travel analysis refers to little more than a particular application of equal protection analysis. Right to travel cases have examined, in equal protection terms, state distinctions between newcomers and longer term residents." 457 U.S., at 60, n. 6.

II

In unearthing from its tomb the right to become a state citizen and to be treated equally in the new State of residence, however, the Court ignores a State's need to assure that only persons who establish a bona fide residence receive the benefits provided to current residents of the State.

. . .

While the physical presence element of a bona fide residence is easy to police, the subjective intent element is not. It is simply unworkable and futile to require States to inquire into each new resident's subjective intent to remain. Hence, States employ objective criteria such as durational residence requirements to test a new resident's resolve to remain before these new citizens can enjoy certain in-state benefits. Recognizing the practical appeal of such criteria, this Court has repeatedly sanctioned the State's use of durational residence requirements before new residents receive in-state tuition rates at state universities. Starns v. Malkerson, 401 U.S. 985 (1971), summarily aff'g 326 F.Supp. 234 (D.Minn.1970) (upholding 1–year residence requirement for in-state tuition)... The Court has declared: "The State can establish such reasonable criteria for in-state status as to make virtually certain that students who are not, in fact, *bona fide* residents of the State, but have come there solely for educational purposes, cannot take advantage of the in-state rates." See Vlandis v. Kline, 412 U.S. 441, 453–454 (1973). The Court has done the same in upholding a 1–year residence requirement for eligibility to obtain a divorce in state courts, see Sosna v. Iowa, 419 U.S. 393, 406–409 (1975), and in upholding political party registration restrictions that amounted to a durational residency requirement for voting in primary elections, see Rosario v. Rockefeller, 410 U.S. 752, 760–762 (1973).

If States can require individuals to reside in-state for a year before exercising the right to educational benefits, the right to terminate a marriage, or the right to vote in primary elections that all other state citizens enjoy, then States may surely do the same for welfare benefits. Indeed, there is no material difference between a 1–year residence requirement applied to the level of welfare benefits given out by a State, and the same requirement applied to the level of tuition subsidies at a state university. The welfare payment here and in-state tuition rates are cash subsidies provided to a limited class of people, and California's standard of living and higher education system make both subsidies quite attractive. Durational residence requirements were upheld when used to regulate the provision of higher education subsidies, and the same deference should be given in the case of welfare payments....

The Court today recognizes that States retain the ability to determine the bona fides of an individual's claim to residence, but then tries to avoid the issue.... I do not understand how the absence of a link between need and length of residency bears on the State's ability to objectively test respondents' resolve to stay in California. There is no link between the need for an education or for a divorce and the length of residence, and yet States may use length of residence as an objective yardstick to channel their benefits to those whose intent to stay is legitimate.

In one respect, the State has a greater need to require a durational residence for welfare benefits than for college eligibility. The impact of a large number of new residents who immediately seek welfare payments will have a far greater impact on a State's operating budget than the impact of new residents seeking to attend a state university. In the case of the welfare recipients, a modest durational residence requirement to allow for the completion of an annual legislative budget cycle gives the State time to decide how to finance the increased obligations.

The Court tries to distinguish education and divorce benefits by contending that the welfare payment here will be consumed in California, while a college education or a divorce produces benefits that are "portable" and can be enjoyed after individuals return to their original domicile. But this "you can't take it with you" distinction is more apparent than real, and offers little guidance to lower courts who must apply this rationale in the future. Welfare payments are a form of insurance, giving impoverished individuals and their families the means to meet the demands of daily life while they receive the necessary training, education, and time to look for a job. The cash itself will no doubt be spent in California, but the benefits from receiving this income and having the opportunity to become employed or employable will stick with the welfare recipient if they stay in California or go back to their true domicile. Similarly, tuition subsidies are "consumed" in-state but the recipient takes the benefits of a college education with him wherever he goes. A welfare subsidy is thus as much an investment in human capital as is a tuition subsidy, and their attendant benefits are just as "portable." More importantly, this foray into social economics demonstrates that the line drawn by the Court borders on the metaphysical, and requires lower courts to plumb the policies animating certain benefits like welfare to define their "essence" and hence their "portability." . . .

. . .

Finally, Congress' express approval in 42 U.S.C. § 604(c) of durational residence requirements for welfare recipients like the one established by California only goes to show the reasonableness of a law like § 11450.03. The National Legislature, where people from Mississippi as well as California are represented, has recognized the need to protect state resources in a time of experimentation and welfare reform. As States like California revamp their total welfare packages, . . . they should have the authority and flexibility to ensure that their new programs are not exploited. Congress has decided that it makes good welfare policy to give the States this power. California has reasonably exercised it through an objective, narrowly tailored residence requirement. I see nothing in the Constitution that should prevent the enforcement of that requirement.

Justice Thomas, with whom The Chief Justice joins, dissenting.

. . . In my view, the majority attributes a meaning to the Privileges or Immunities Clause that likely was unintended when the Fourteenth Amendment was enacted and ratified.

. . .

The [American] colonists' repeated assertions that they maintained the rights, privileges and immunities of persons "born within the realm of England" and "natural born" persons suggests that, at the time of the founding, the terms "privileges" and "immunities" (and their counterparts) were understood to refer to those fundamental rights and liberties specifically enjoyed by English citizens, and more broadly, by all persons. Presumably members of the Second Continental Congress so understood these terms when they employed them in the Articles of Confederation. . . . The Constitution . . . similarly guarantees that "[t]he Citizens of each State shall be entitled to all Privileges and Immunities of Citizens in the several States." Art. IV, § 2, cl. 1.

Justice Bushrod Washington's landmark opinion in Corfield v. Coryell, 6 Fed. Cas. 546 (No. 3, 230) (CCED Pa. 1825), reflects this historical understanding. . . .

Washington rejected the proposition that the Privileges and Immunities Clause guaranteed equal access to all public benefits (such as the right to harvest oysters in public waters) that a State chooses to make available. Instead, he endorsed the colonial-era conception of the terms "privileges" and "immunities," concluding that Article IV encompassed only fundamental rights that belong to all citizens of the United States. . . .

Justice Washington's opinion in *Corfield* indisputably influenced the Members of Congress who enacted the Fourteenth Amendment. . . .

. . . [R]epeated references to the *Corfield* decision [by Members of the 39th Congress], combined with what appears to be the historical understanding of the Clause's operative terms, supports the inference that, at the time the Fourteenth Amendment was adopted, people understood that "privileges or immunities of citizens" were fundamental rights, rather than every public benefit established by positive law. Accordingly, the majority's conclusion—that a State violates the Privileges or Immunities Clause when it "discriminates" against citizens who have been domiciled in the State for less than a year in the distribution of welfare benefits—appears contrary to the original understanding and is dubious at best.

. . . Because I believe that the demise of the Privileges or Immunities Clause has contributed in no small part to the current disarray of our Fourteenth Amendment jurisprudence, I would be open to reevaluating its meaning in an appropriate case. Before invoking the Clause, however, we should endeavor to understand what the framers of the Fourteenth Amendment thought that it meant. We should also consider whether the Clause should displace, rather than augment, portions of our equal protection and substantive due process jurisprudence. The majority's failure to consider these important questions raises the specter that the Privileges or Immunities Clause will become yet another convenient tool for inventing new rights, limited solely by the "predilections of those who happen at the time to be Members of this Court." Moore v. East Cleveland, 431 U.S. 494, 502 (1977).

I respectfully dissent.

WILLIAMS v. VERMONT, 472 U.S. 14 (1985). A majority of the Court understood state law to exempt from the motor vehicle use tax imposed when cars are registered in Vermont, not only those who had already paid sales tax on cars purchased in Vermont, but those who were Vermont residents when they purchased and first registered a car in another, reciprocating State to the extent they had paid a sales or use tax there. The Court upheld an equal protection claim by new residents of Vermont denied the exemption because they had bought and registered a car in such a State before moving to Vermont. Justice White's majority opinion noted that it was still "unnecessary to reach" a question the Court previously had "expressly reserved"—"whether a State must credit a sales tax paid to another State against its own use tax"—because "[w]hatever the general rule may be, to provide a credit only to those who were residents at the time they paid the sales tax is an arbitrary distinction that violates the Equal Protection Clause." After noting that normally this kind of tax exemption "will be sustained if the legislature could reasonably have concluded that the challenged classification would promote a legitimate state purpose[,]" the opinion continued:

"We perceive no legitimate purpose, however, that is furthered by this discriminatory exemption. As we said in holding that the use tax base cannot be broader than the sales tax base, 'equal treatment for in-state and out-of-state taxpayers similarly situated is the condition precedent for a valid use tax on goods imported from out-of-state.' Halliburton Oil Well Co. v. Reily, 373 U.S. 64, 70 (1963).[7] A State may not treat those within its borders unequally solely on the basis of their different residences or States of incorporation.... In the present case, residence at the time of purchase is a wholly arbitrary basis on which to distinguish among present Vermont registrants—at least among those who used their cars elsewhere before coming to Vermont.[8] Having registered a car in Vermont they are similarly situated for all relevant purposes. Each is a Vermont resident, using a car in Vermont, with an equal obligation to pay for the maintenance and improvement of Vermont's roads. The purposes of the statute would be identically served, and with an identical burden, by taxing each. The distinction between them bears no relation to the statutory purpose. See Zobel v. Williams, 457 U.S. 55, 61 (1982)....

"In sum, we can see no relevant difference between motor vehicle registrants who purchased their cars out-of-state while they were Vermont residents and those who only came to Vermont after buying a car elsewhere. To free one group and not the other from the otherwise applicable tax burden violates the Equal Protection Clause."

Justice Powell took no part in the decision of the case. Justice Brennan concurred, stating:

"I join the Court's opinion for the reasons stated therein and in my concurring opinion in Zobel v. Williams, 457 U.S. 55, 65 (1982). General application of distinctions of the kind made by the Vermont statute would clearly, though indirectly, threaten the 'federal interest in free interstate migration.' Id., at 66. In addition, the statute makes distinctions among residents that are not 'supported by a valid state interest independent of the discrimination itself.' Id., at 70."

Justice Blackmun, joined by Justices Rehnquist and O'Connor, dissented. He first accused the majority of "imagin[ing] a fanciful, hypothetical discrimination" in favor of a "phantom beneficiary"—the "Vermont resident who leaves the State to purchase an automobile, pays the sales tax and registers the car in the foreign State of purchase, lives there for a while, and then returns to Vermont and registers the car there." Assuming the Court correctly had identified a real issue, however, Justice Blackmun continued:

"The reason nonresidents who purchase cars out-of-state are taxed if they subsequently relocate in Vermont, while resident out-of-state purchasers are not, is that it was presumed that people will use their cars primarily in the States in which they reside. Most people who do not reside in Vermont and do not purchase their cars in that State, will not use their cars primarily in

---

7. *Halliburton* was decided under the Commerce Clause and is not dispositive. We do not consider in what way, if any, the failure to give appellants a credit might burden interstate commerce. The critical point is the Court's emphasis on the need for equal treatment of taxpayers who can be distinguished only on the basis of residence. See also Henneford v. Silas Mason Co., 300 U.S. 577, 583–584 (1937).

8. The dissent does not disagree that such people are similarly situated, nor does it

identify any justification for preferential treatment of the resident. It merely argues that the inequity is the acceptable result of the imprecision of a generally rational classification. Under rational-basis scrutiny, legislative classifications are of course allowed some play in the joints. But the choice of a proxy criterion—here, residence for State of use—cannot be so casual as this, particularly when a more precise and direct classification is easily drawn.

Vermont. If at some time in the future they move to Vermont and register their automobiles there, the assumption is that they will have used their cars in two different States. On the other hand, most people who reside in Vermont and purchase their cars out-of-state will return to Vermont immediately with their cars. Thus, the out-of-state purchaser is taxed, while the Vermont purchaser is exempted to the extent that he already has paid a sales tax. This distinction is hardly irrational, and the fact that there may be a Vermont resident who both purchases and uses his car out-of-state ... surely does not render the scheme irrational. A tax classification does not violate the demands of equal protection simply because it may not perfectly identify the class of people it wishes to single out....

"... The Court ... ignores the purpose of the tax and of the classification. Vermont does not wish to 'distinguish among present Vermont registrants,' but to distinguish those who will likely use Vermont's roads immediately after they have purchased cars out-of-state from those who will not. Residency is not an irrational way to enact such a classification ..."

3.   CLASSIFICATIONS DISADVANTAGING NONRESIDENTS

Metropolitan Life Insurance Co. v. Ward

470 U.S. 869, 105 S.Ct. 1676, 84 L.Ed.2d 751 (1985).

Justice Powell delivered the opinion of the Court.

This case presents the question whether Alabama's domestic preference tax statute, Ala.Code §§ 27–4–4 and 27–4–5 (1975), that taxes out-of-state insurance companies at a higher rate than domestic insurance companies, violates the Equal Protection Clause.

I

... [F]oreign life insurance companies pay a tax on their gross premiums received from business conducted in Alabama at a rate of 3 percent, and foreign companies selling other types of insurance pay at a rate of 4 percent. Ala.Code § 27–4–4(a) (1975). All domestic insurance companies, in contrast, pay at a rate of only 1 percent on all types of insurance premiums. § 27–4–5(a)....

. . . .

II

Appellants, a group of insurance companies incorporated outside of the State of Alabama, filed claims with the Alabama Department of Insurance in 1981, contending that the domestic preference tax statute, as applied to them, violated the Equal Protection Clause....

... Relying on this Court's opinion in Western & Southern Life Ins. Co. v. State Board of Equalization of California, 451 U.S. 648 (1981), the [trial] court ruled that the Alabama statute did not violate the Equal Protection Clause because it served "at least two purposes, in addition to raising revenue: (1) encouraging the formation of new insurance companies in Alabama, and (2) encouraging capital investment by foreign insurance companies in the Alabama assets and governmental securities set forth in the statute." The court also found that the distinction the statute created between foreign and domestic companies was rationally related to those two purposes and that the Alabama Legislature reasonably could have believed that the classification would have promoted those purposes.

... [T]he Court of Civil Appeals ... affirmed ... as to the existence of the two legitimate state purposes, but remanded for an evidentiary hearing on the issue of rational relationship, concluding that summary judgment was inappropriate on that question because the evidence was in conflict.... Appellants petitioned the Supreme Court of Alabama ... on ... the legitimate state purpose issue, and the State and the intervenors petitioned for review of the remand order.... The Supreme Court denied certiorari on all claims. [Because appellants] waived their rights to an evidentiary hearing on the rational relationship issue ..., judgment was entered for the State and the intervenors....

III

Prior to our decision in Western & Southern Life Ins. Co. v. State Board of Equalization of California, supra, the jurisprudence of the applicability of the Equal Protection Clause to discriminatory tax statutes had a somewhat checkered history. Lincoln National Life Ins. Co. v. Read, 325 U.S. 673 (1945), held that so-called "privilege" taxes, required to be paid by a foreign corporation before it would be permitted to do business within a State, were immune from equal protection challenge. That case stood in stark contrast, however, to the Court's prior decisions ..., as well as to later decisions, in which the Court had recognized that the Equal Protection Clause placed limits on other forms of discriminatory taxation imposed on out-of-state corporations solely because of their residence....

In *Western & Southern,* ... we reviewed all of these cases for the purpose of deciding whether to permit an equal protection challenge to a California statute imposing a retaliatory tax on foreign insurance companies doing business within the State, when the home States of those companies imposed a similar tax on California insurers entering their borders. We concluded that *Lincoln* was no more than "a surprising throwback" to the days before enactment of the Fourteenth Amendment and in which incorporation of a domestic corporation or entry of a foreign one had been granted only as a matter of privilege by the State in its unfettered discretion.... We therefore rejected the longstanding but "anachronis[tic]" rule of *Lincoln* and explicitly held that the Equal Protection Clause imposes limits upon a State's power to condition the right of a foreign corporation to do business within its borders.... We held that "[w]e consider it now established that, whatever the extent of a State's authority to exclude foreign corporations from doing business within its boundaries, that authority does not justify imposition of more onerous taxes or other burdens on foreign corporations than those imposed on domestic corporations, unless the discrimination between foreign and domestic corporations bears a rational relation to a legitimate state purpose." ...

Because appellants waived their right to an evidentiary hearing on the issue whether the classification in the Alabama domestic preference tax statute bears a rational relation to the two purposes upheld by the Circuit Court, the only question before us is whether those purposes are legitimate.[5]

A

(1)

The first of the purposes found by the trial court to be a legitimate reason for the statute's classification between foreign and domestic corporations is

---

5. The State and the intervenors advanced some 15 additional purposes in support of the Alabama statute. As neither the Circuit Court nor the Court of Civil Appeals ruled on the legitimacy of those purposes, that question is not before us, and we express no view as to it. On remand, the State will be free to advance again its arguments relating to the legitimacy of those purposes.

. . .

that it encourages the formation of new domestic insurance companies in Alabama....

... In *Western & Southern,* ... we did not hold as a general rule that promotion of domestic industry is a legitimate state purpose under equal protection analysis.[6] Rather, we held that California's purpose in enacting the retaliatory tax—to promote the *interstate* business of domestic insurers by deterring *other States* from enacting discriminatory or excessive taxes—was a legitimate one.... In contrast, Alabama asks us to approve its purpose of promoting the business of its domestic insurers *in Alabama* by penalizing foreign insurers who also want to do business in the State. Alabama has made no attempt, as California did, to influence the policies of other States in order to enhance its domestic companies' ability to operate interstate; rather, it has erected barriers to foreign companies who wish to do interstate business in order to improve its domestic insurers' ability to compete at home.

The crucial distinction between the two cases lies in the fact that Alabama's aim to promote domestic industry is purely and completely discriminatory, designed only to favor domestic industry within the State, no matter what the cost to foreign corporations also seeking to do business there. Alabama's purpose, contrary to California's, constitutes the very sort of parochial discrimination that the Equal Protection Clause was intended to prevent.... Unlike the retaliatory tax involved in *Western & Southern,* which only burdens residents of a State that imposes its own discriminatory tax on outsiders, the domestic preference tax gives the "home team" an advantage by burdening *all* foreign corporations seeking to do business within the State, no matter what they or their States do.

The validity of the view that a State may not constitutionally favor its own residents by taxing foreign corporations at a higher rate solely because of their residence is confirmed by a long line of this Court's cases so holding.... As the Court stated ... with respect to general tax burdens on business, "the foreign corporation stands equal, and is to be classified with domestic corporations of the same kind." ... In all of these cases, the discriminatory tax was imposed by the State on foreign corporations doing business within the State solely because of their residence, presumably to promote domestic industry within the State. In relying on these cases and rejecting *Lincoln* in *Western & Southern,* we reaffirmed the continuing viability of the Equal Protection Clause as a means of challenging a statute that seeks to benefit domestic industry within the State only by grossly discriminating against foreign competitors.

. . .

(2)

The State argues nonetheless that it is impermissible to view a discriminatory tax such as the one at issue here as violative of the Equal Protection Clause. This approach, it contends, amounts to no more than "Commerce Clause rhetoric in equal protection clothing." The State maintains that because

---

6. We find the other cases on which the State relies also to be inapposite to this inquiry. *Bacchus Imports, Pike,* and *Parker* discussed whether promotion of local industry is a valid state purpose under the Commerce Clause. The Commerce Clause, unlike the Equal Protection Clause, is integrally concerned with whether a state purpose implicates local or national interests. The Equal Protection Clause, in contrast, is concerned with whether a state purpose is impermissibly discriminatory; whether the discrimination involves local or other interests is not central to the inquiry to be made. Thus, the fact that promotion of local industry is a legitimate state interest in the Commerce Clause context says nothing about its validity under equal protection analysis....

. . .

Congress, in enacting the McCarran–Ferguson Act, 15 U.S.C. §§ 1011–1015, intended to authorize States to impose taxes that burden interstate commerce in the insurance field, the tax at issue here must stand. Our concerns are much more fundamental.... Although the McCarran–Ferguson Act exempts the insurance industry from Commerce Clause restrictions, it does not purport to limit in any way the applicability of the Equal Protection Clause. As noted above, our opinion in *Western & Southern* expressly reaffirmed the viability of equal protection restraints on discriminatory taxes in the insurance context.

Moreover, the State's view ignores the differences between Commerce Clause and equal protection analysis and the consequent different purposes those two constitutional provisions serve. Under Commerce Clause analysis, the State's interest, if legitimate, is weighed against the burden the state law would impose on interstate commerce. In the equal protection context, however, if the State's purpose is found to be legitimate, the state law stands as long as the burden it imposes is found to be rationally related to that purpose, a relationship that is not difficult to establish....

The two constitutional provisions perform different functions in the analysis of the permissible scope of a State's power—one protects interstate commerce, and the other protects persons from unconstitutional discrimination by the States.... The effect of the statute at issue here is to place a discriminatory tax burden on foreign insurers who desire to do business within the State, thereby also incidentally placing a burden on interstate commerce. Equal protection restraints are applicable even though the effect of the discrimination in this case is similar to the type of burden with which the Commerce Clause also would be concerned. We reaffirmed the importance of the Equal Protection Clause in the insurance context in *Western & Southern* and see no reason now for reassessing that view.

In whatever light the State's position is cast, acceptance of its contention that promotion of domestic industry is always a legitimate state purpose under equal protection analysis would eviscerate the Equal Protection Clause in this context. A State's natural inclination frequently would be to prefer domestic business over foreign. If we accept the State's view here, then any discriminatory tax would be valid if the State could show it reasonably was intended to benefit domestic business.[10] A discriminatory tax would stand or fall depending primarily on how a State framed its purpose—as benefiting one group or as harming another. This is a distinction without a difference, and one that we rejected last term in an analogous context arising under the Commerce Clause. Bacchus Imports, Ltd. v. Dias, 468 U.S., at 273. We hold that under the circumstances of this case, promotion of domestic business by discriminating against nonresident competitors is not a legitimate state purpose.

B

The second purpose found by the courts below to be legitimate was the encouragement of capital investment in the Alabama assets and governmental securities specified in the statute. We do not agree that this is a legitimate state purpose when furthered by discrimination. Domestic insurers remain entitled to the more favorable rate of tax regardless of whether they invest in Alabama

---

10. Indeed, under the State's analysis, *any* discrimination subject to the rational relation level of scrutiny could be justified simply on the ground that it favored one group at the expense of another. This case does not involve or question, as the dissent suggests, the broad authority of a State to promote and regulate its own economy. We hold only that such regulation may not be accomplished by imposing discriminatorily higher taxes on nonresident corporations solely because they are nonresidents.

assets. Moreover, the investment incentive provision of the Alabama statute does not enable foreign insurance companies to eliminate the discriminatory effect of the statute. No matter how much of their assets they invest in Alabama, foreign insurance companies are still required to pay a higher gross premiums tax than domestic companies. The State's investment incentive provision therefore does not cure, but reaffirms, the statute's impermissible classification based solely on residence. We hold that encouraging investment in Alabama assets and securities in this plainly discriminatory manner serves no legitimate state purpose.

IV

We conclude that neither of the two purposes furthered by the Alabama domestic preference tax statute and addressed by the Circuit Court for Montgomery County ... is legitimate under the Equal Protection Clause to justify the imposition of the discriminatory tax at issue here. The judgment of the Alabama Supreme Court accordingly is reversed, and the case is remanded for further proceedings not inconsistent with this opinion.

It is so ordered.

Justice O'Connor, with whom Justice Brennan, Justice Marshall and Justice Rehnquist join, dissenting.

This case presents a simple question: Is it legitimate for a state to use its taxing power to promote a domestic insurance industry and to encourage capital investment within its borders? In a holding that can only be characterized as astonishing, the Court determines that these purposes are illegitimate. This holding is unsupported by precedent and subtly distorts the constitutional balance, threatening the freedom of both state and federal legislative bodies to fashion appropriate classifications in economic legislation. Because I disagree with both the Court's method of analysis and its conclusion, I respectfully dissent.

I

... Appellants rely on the Equal Protection Clause because, as corporations, they are not "citizens" protected by the privileges and immunities clauses of the Constitution.... Similarly, they cannot claim Commerce Clause protection because Congress in the McCarran–Ferguson ... explicitly suspended Commerce Clause restraints on state taxation of insurance and placed insurance regulation firmly within the purview of the several States....

... [T]he Court ... meld[s] the proper two-step inquiry regarding the State's purpose and the classification's relationship to that purpose into a single unarticulated judgment. This tactic enables the Court to characterize State goals that have been legitimated by Congress itself as improper solely because it disagrees with the concededly rational means of differential taxation selected by the legislature. This unorthodox approach leads to further error. The Court gives only the most cursory attention to the factual and legal bases supporting the State's purposes and ignores both precedent and significant evidence in the record establishing their legitimacy. Most troubling, the Court discovers in the Equal Protection Clause an implied prohibition against classifications whose purpose is to give the "home team" an advantage over interstate competitors even where Congress has authorized such advantages.

... Judicial deference is strongest where a tax classification is alleged to infringe the right to equal protection.... As the Court emphatically noted in *Allied Stores of Ohio, Inc. v. Bowers:*

"[I]t has repeatedly been held and appears to be entirely settled that a statute which encourages the location within the State of needed and useful industries by exempting them, though not also others, from its taxes is not arbitrary and does not violate the Equal Protection Clause of the Fourteenth Amendment. Similarly, it has long been settled that a classification, though discriminatory, is not arbitrary or violative of the Equal Protection Clause of the Fourteenth Amendment if any state of facts reasonably can be conceived that would sustain it." . . .

. . .

III

. . .

. . . Alabama does *not* tax at a higher rate solely on the basis of residence; it taxes insurers, domestic as well as foreign, who do not maintain a principal place of business or substantial assets in Alabama, based on conceded distinctions in the contributions of these insurers *as a class* to the State's insurance objectives. The majority obscures the issue by observing that a given "foreign insurance company doing the same type and volume of business in Alabama as a domestic company" will pay a higher tax. . . . Rational basis scrutiny does not require that the classification be mathematically precise or that *every* foreign insurer or *every* domestic company fit to perfection the general profile on which the classification is based. . . .

IV

. . . The Court[,] by a remarkable evasive tactic[,] simply declares that the ends of promoting a domestic insurance industry and attracting investments to the State *when accomplished through the means of discriminatory taxation* are not legitimate state purposes. . . . By collapsing the two prongs of the rational basis test into one, the Court arrives at the ultimate issue—whether the *means* are constitutional—without ever engaging in the deferential inquiry we have adopted as a brake on judicial impeachment of legislative policy choices. In addition to unleashing an undisciplined form of Equal Protection Clause scrutiny, the Court's approach today has serious implications for the authority of Congress under the Commerce Clause. . . .

. . .

. . . Favoring local business as an end in itself might be "rational" but would be antithetical to federalism. Accepting arguendo this interpretation, we have shown that the measure at issue here does not benefit local business as an end in itself but serves important ulterior goals. Moreover, any federalism component of equal protection is fully vindicated where Congress has explicitly validated a parochial focus. Surely the Equal Protection Clause was not intended to supplant the Commerce Clause, foiling Congress' decision under its commerce powers to "affirmatively permit [some measure of] parochial favoritism" when necessary to a healthy federation. White v. Massachusetts Council of Construction Employers, 460 U.S. 204, 212 (1983). Such a view of the Equal Protection Clause cannot be reconciled with the McCarran–Ferguson Act and our decisions in *Western & Southern* and *Benjamin*.

Western & Southern established that a state may validly tax out-of-state corporations at a higher rate if its goal is to promote the ability of its domestic businesses to compete in *interstate* markets. Nevertheless, the Court today concludes that the converse policy is forbidden, striking down legislation whose purpose is to encourage the *intrastate* activities of local business concerns by permitting them to compete effectively on their home turf. In essence, the Court declares "We will excuse an unequal burden on foreign insurers if the State's purpose is to foster its domestic insurer's activities in *other* States, but the same unequal burden will be unconstitutional when employed to further a policy that places a higher social value on the domestic insurer's *homestate* than interstate activities." This conclusion is not drawn from the Commerce Clause, the textual source of constitutional restrictions on State interference with interstate competition. Reliance on the Commerce Clause would, of course, be unavailing here in view of the McCarran–Ferguson Act. Instead the Court engrafts its own economic values on the Equal Protection Clause. Beyond guarding against arbitrary or irrational discrimination, as interpreted by the Court today this Clause now prohibits the effectuation of economic policies, even where sanctioned by Congress, that elevate local concerns over interstate competition. . . .

. . . This newly unveiled power of the Equal Protection Clause would come as a surprise to the Congress that passed the McCarran–Ferguson Act and the Court that sustained the Act against constitutional attack. In the McCarran–Ferguson Act, Congress expressly sanctioned such economic parochialism in the context of state regulation and taxation of insurance.

The doctrine adopted by the majority threatens the freedom not only of the States but also of the Federal Government to formulate economic policy. The dangers in discerning in the Equal Protection Clause a prohibition against barriers to interstate business irrespective of the Commerce Clause should be self-evident. The Commerce Clause is a flexible tool of economic policy that Congress may use as it sees fit, letting it lie dormant or invoking it to limit as well as promote the free flow of commerce. Doctrines of equal protection are constitutional limits that constrain the acts of federal and state legislatures alike. See, e.g., Califano v. Webster, 430 U.S. 313 (1977); Cohen, Congressional Power to Validate Unconstitutional State Laws: A Forgotten Solution to an Old Enigma, 35 Stan.L.Rev. 387, 400–413 (1983). The Court's analysis casts a shadow over numerous congressional enactments that adopted as federal policy "the type of parochial favoritism" the Court today finds unconstitutional. White v. Massachusetts Council of Construction Employers, 460 U.S., at 213. Contrary to the reasoning in *Benjamin,* the Court today indicates the Equal Protection Clause stands as an independent barrier if courts should determine that either Congress or a State has ventured the "wrong" direction down what has become, by judicial fiat, the one-way street of the Commerce Clause. Nothing in the Constitution or our past decisions supports forcing such an economic straight-jacket on the federal system.

V

Today's opinion charts an ominous course. I can only hope this unfortunate adventure . . . will be an isolated episode. . . .[a]

NORTHEAST BANCORP, INC. v. BOARD OF GOVERNORS OF THE FEDERAL RESERVE SYSTEM, 472 U.S. 159 (1985). The Bank Holding Company Act, enacted by Congress in 1965, prohibits approval of an application of a bank holding company or a bank located in one state to acquire a bank or a bank holding company located in another State unless the acquisition "is specifically authorized by the statute laws of the State in which such bank is located by language to that effect and not merely by implication." In 1982 Massachusetts enacted a statute permitting an out-of-state bank

---

a. See generally, Cohen, *Federalism in Equality Clothing: A Comment on Metropoli-* *tan Life Insurance Company v. Ward,* 38 Stan.L.Rev. 1 (1985).

holding company with its principal place of business in one of the other New England states to establish or acquire a Massachusetts based bank or bank holding company, provided that the other New England state accords equivalent reciprocal privileges to Massachusetts banking organizations. Connecticut enacted a similar statute in 1983. A Connecticut bank holding company sought permission from the Federal Reserve Board to purchase a bank holding company in Massachusetts and a Massachusetts bank holding company sought permission to acquire a Connecticut bank holding company. The board approved the acquisitions and the Court of Appeals affirmed.

Justice Rehnquist, writing for the Court, said first that there was no commerce clause objection because Congress had specifically consented to the kind of state regulations involved here. He also addressed as follows the contention that under *Metropolitan Life Insurance Co. v. Ward* to permit the States to favor banks from the New England region as opposed to those outside of that region denied equal protection:

"In *Metropolitan Life* we held that encouraging the formation of new domestic insurance companies within a State and encouraging capital investment in the State's assets and governmental securities were not, standing alone, legitimate state purposes which could permissibly be furthered by discriminating against out-of-state corporations in favor of local corporations. There we said:

'This case does not involve or question, as the dissent suggests, the broad authority of a State, to promote and regulate its own economy. We hold only that such regulation may not be accomplished by imposing discriminatorily higher taxes on nonresident corporations solely because they are nonresidents.'

"Here the States in question—Massachusetts and Connecticut—are not favoring local corporations at the expense of out-of-state corporations. They are favoring out-of-state corporations domiciled within the New England region over out-of-state corporations from other parts of the country, and to this extent their laws may be said to 'discriminate' against the latter. But with respect to the business of banking, we do not write on a clean slate; recently . . . we said that 'banking and related financial activities are of profound local concern.' This statement is a recognition of the historical fact that our country traditionally has favored widely dispersed control of banking. While many other western nations are dominated by a handful of centralized banks, we have some 15,000 commercial banks attached to a greater or lesser degree to the communities in which they are located. The Connecticut legislative Commission that recommended adoption of the Connecticut statute in question considered interstate banking on a regional basis to combine the beneficial effect of increasing the number of banking competitors with the need to preserve a close relationship between those in the community who need credit and those who provide credit. The debates in the Connecticut Legislature preceding the enactment of the Connecticut law evince concern that immediate acquisition of Connecticut banks by holding companies headquartered outside the New England region would threaten the independence of local banking institutions. No doubt similar concerns motivated the Massachusetts Legislature.

"We think that the concerns which spurred Massachusetts and Connecticut to enact the statutes here challenged, different as they are from those which motivated the enactment of the Alabama statute in *Metropolitan,* meet the traditional rational basis for judging equal protection claims under the Fourteenth Amendment. . . ."

Justice O'Connor, concurring, said:

"I agree that the state banking statutes at issue here do not violate the Commerce Clause, the Compact Clause, or the Equal Protection Clause. I write separately to note that I see no meaningful distinction for Equal Protection Clause purposes between the Massachusetts and Connecticut statutes we uphold today and the Alabama statute at issue in Metropolitan Life Insurance Co. v. Ward, 470 U.S. 869 (1985).

"The Court distinguishes this case from *Metropolitan Life* on the ground that Massachusetts and Connecticut favor neighboring out-of-state banks over all other out-of-state banks. It is not clear to me why completely barring the banks of 44 States from doing business is less discriminatory than Alabama's scheme of taxing the insurance companies from 49 States at a slightly higher rate. Nor is it clear why the Equal Protection Clause should tolerate a regional 'home team' when it condemns a state 'home team.'

"The Court emphasizes that here we do not write on a clean slate as the business of banking is 'of profound local concern.' The business of insurance is also of uniquely local concern.... Both industries historically have been regulated by the States in recognition of the critical part they play in securing the financial well-being of local citizens and businesses.... States have regulated insurance since 1851. Like the local nature of banking, the local nature of insurance is firmly ensconced in federal law....

. . . .

"Especially where Congress has sanctioned the barriers to commerce that fostering of local industries might engender, this Court has no authority under the Equal Protection Clause to invalidate classifications designed to encourage local businesses because of their special contributions. Today's opinion is consistent with the longstanding doctrine that the Equal Protection Clause permits economic regulation that distinguishes between groups that *are* legitimately different—as local institutions so often are—in ways relevant to the proper goals of the State."

Justice Powell took no part in deciding the case.

D.   COURT ACCESS, WELFARE, AND THE POOR

Introduction. The Court has addressed arguments for heightened scrutiny based on both the nature of the liberty interest affected and the nature of the disadvantaged class in a number of contexts. Here the emphasis is on two sets of claims: that fees for representation in, and resolution of, legal disputes unconstitutionally have deprived the poor of access to appropriate judicial services; and that the poor unconstitutionally have been denied welfare benefits. As suggested in the Note on Wealth Classifications, supra p. 935, the issues generally arise in the context of differential impact on the poor, rather than in the context of explicit disadvantaging of them for being poor as such. Another common thread linking these two groups of cases is that the basis of the claims may be due process, equal protection, or both. The court access and welfare cases are presented together to allow for consideration of these complexities and connections.

THE RIGHTS OF THE POOR DEFENDANT IN THE CRIMINAL JUSTICE SYSTEM

During the past 40 years the Court has had before it a number of cases involving the criminal appellate process. It invalidated a series of state statutes that by requiring filing fees and transcripts barred access to appeal by a defendant who was indigent. See, e.g., Griffin v. Illinois, 351 U.S. 12 (1956); Draper v. Washington, 372 U.S. 487 (1963). In Douglas v. California, 372 U.S. 353 (1963), the Court also held that a state had a duty to furnish counsel to an indigent taking his first appeal as of right. In Ross v. Moffitt, 417 U.S. 600 (1974), however, the Court held that an indigent defendant was not entitled to have counsel provided in taking a discretionary appeal to the highest state court or in petitioning for certiorari in the United States Supreme Court.

The Court said:

"The precise rationale for the *Griffin* and *Douglas* line of cases has never been explicitly stated, some support being derived from the Equal Protection Clause of the Fourteenth Amendment, and some from the Due Process Clause of that Amendment. Neither clause by itself provides an entirely satisfactory basis for the result reached, each depending on a different inquiry which emphasizes different factors. 'Due process' emphasizes fairness between the State and the individual dealing with the State, regardless of how other individuals in the same situation may be treated. 'Equal protection,' on the other hand, emphasizes disparity in treatment by a State between classes of individuals whose situations are arguably indistinguishable."

The Court went on to hold that the denial of counsel in this case was constitutional under either clause. The Court concluded:

"[T]he fact that a particular service might be of benefit to an indigent defendant does not mean that the service is constitutionally required. The duty of the State under our cases is not to duplicate the legal arsenal that may be privately retained by a criminal defendant in a continuing effort to reverse his conviction, but only to assure the indigent defendant an adequate opportunity to present his claims fairly in the context of the State's appellate process."

Justices Douglas, Brennan, and Marshall dissented.

In Pennsylvania v. Finley, 481 U.S. 551 (1987) the Court reaffirmed *Ross v. Moffitt,* holding that the state has no constitutional duty under either the due process or equal protection clauses to provide counsel to a defendant in postconviction proceedings.

In Murray v. Giarratano, 492 U.S. 1 (1989), indigent prisoners sentenced to death argued that due process and the Eighth Amendment ban on cruel and unusual punishment required the state to provide them with counsel in postconviction proceedings. Four Justices (Rehnquist, White, O'Connor, and Scalia) rejected these claims outright, finding no greater obligation to provide counsel on collateral review in capital cases than in any others. Justice Kennedy concurred in the judgment, concluding that the due process require-ment of "meaningful access" to court recognized in Bounds v. Smith, 430 U.S. 817 (1977), was satisfied in this case. He rejected a categorical requirement of appointed counsel in every case, because the meaningful court access obligation "can be satisfied in various ways[.]" He also asserted that "collateral relief proceedings are a central part of the review process for prisoners sentenced to death" and that the "complexity of our jurisprudence in this area ... makes it unlikely that capital defendants will be able to file successful petitions for collateral relief without the assistance of persons learned in the law." In this case, however, he was not prepared to find a violation of the meaningful court access right, because "no prisoner on death row in Virginia has been unable to obtain counsel to represent him in postconviction proceedings, and Virginia's prison system is staffed with institutional lawyers to assist in preparing petitions for postconviction relief."

In dissent, Justice Stevens, joined by Justices Brennan, Marshall and Blackmun, would have required the "appointment of counsel for indigent death row inmates who wish to pursue state postconviction relief."

ACCESS OF THE POOR TO THE COURTS IN CIVIL CASES

BODDIE v. CONNECTICUT, 401 U.S. 371 (1971). A welfare recipient challenged the state procedures under which a plaintiff in a divorce action was required to pay fees of about $60 in order to file the action. The Court discussed the case as one involving procedural due process, concluding "that the State's refusal to admit these appellants to its courts, the sole means in Connecticut for obtaining a divorce, must be regarded as the equivalent of denying them an opportunity to be heard upon their claimed right to a dissolution of their marriages, and, in the absence of a sufficient countervailing justification for the state's action, a denial of due process." Justices Douglas and Brennan in concurring opinions argued that the decision should have been rested on the equal protection clause because of discrimination against the poor. Justice Black dissented. For a discussion which preceded *Boddie,* see Goodpaster, *The Integration of Equal Protection, Due Process Standards, and the Indigent's Right of Free Access to the Courts,* 56 Iowa L.Rev. 223 (1970).

UNITED STATES v. KRAS, 409 U.S. 434 (1973). An indigent petitioner seeking voluntary bankruptcy sought to proceed without paying the fees (not more than $50 in this case) that were a condition of discharge. The district court found for the petitioner, relying on *Boddie.* The Supreme Court reversed. Justice Blackmun, speaking for the Court, said, in part:

"We agree with the Government that our decision in *Boddie* does not control the disposition of this case and that the District Court's reliance upon *Boddie* is misplaced.

"A. *Boddie* was based on the notion that a State cannot deny access, simply because of one's poverty, to a 'judicial proceeding [that is] the only effective means of resolving the dispute at hand.' 401 U.S., at 376. Throughout the opinion there is constant and recurring reference to Connecticut's exclusive control over the establishment, enforcement, and dissolution of the marital relationship. The Court emphasized that 'marriage involves interests of basic importance in our society' ibid., and spoke of 'state monopolization of the means for legally dissolving this relationship.' '[R]esort to the state courts [was] the only avenue to dissolution of ... marriages,' which was 'not only the paramount dispute-settlement technique, but, in fact the only available one.' ... In the light of all this, we concluded that resort to the judicial process was 'no more voluntary in a realistic sense than that of the defendant called upon to defend his interests in court' and we resolved the case 'in light of the principles enunciated in our due process decisions that delimit rights of defendants compelled to litigate their differences in the judicial forum.'

"B. The appellants in *Boddie,* on the one hand, and Robert Kras, on the other stand in materially different postures. The denial of access to the judicial forum in *Boddie* touched directly, as has been noted, on the marital relationship and on the associational interests that surround the establishment and dissolution of that relationship. On many occasions we have recognized the fundamental importance of these interests under our Constitution. See, for example, Loving v. Virginia, 388 U.S. 1 (1967).... The *Boddie* appellants' inability to dissolve their marriages seriously impaired their freedom to pursue other protected associational activities. Kras' alleged interest in the elimination of his debt burden, and in obtaining his desired new start in life, although important and so recognized by the enactment of the Bankruptcy Act, does not rise to the same constitutional level. See Dandridge v. Williams, 397 U.S. 471 (1970); Richardson v. Belcher, 404 U.S. 78 (1971). If Kras is not discharged in bankruptcy, his position will not be materially altered in any constitutional sense. Gaining or not gaining a discharge will effect no change with respect to basic necessities. We see no fundamental interest that is gained or lost depending on the availability of a discharge in bankruptcy.

"C. Nor is the government's control over the establishment, enforcement, or dissolution of debts nearly so exclusive as Connecticut's control over the marriage relationship in *Boddie*. In contrast with divorce, bankruptcy is not the only method available to a debtor for the adjustment of his legal relationship with his creditors. The utter exclusiveness of court access and court remedy, as has been noted, was a potent factor in *Boddie*. But '[w]ithout a prior judicial imprimatur, individuals may freely enter into and rescind commercial contracts....' 401 U.S., at 376.

"However unrealistic the remedy may be in a particular situation, a debtor, in theory, and often in actuality, may adjust his debts by negotiated agreement with his creditors. At times the happy passage of the applicable limitation period, or other acceptable creditor arrangement, will provide the answer. Government's role with respect to the private commercial relationship is qualitatively and quantitatively different than its role in the establishment, enforcement, and dissolution of marriage.

"Resort to the Court, therefore, is not Kras' sole path to relief. *Boddie's* emphasis on exclusivity finds no counterpart in the bankrupt's situation....

"D. We are also of the opinion that the filing fee requirement does not deny Kras the equal protection of the laws. Bankruptcy is hardly akin to free speech or marriage or to those other rights, so many of which are imbedded in the First Amendment, that the Court has come to regard as fundamental and that demand the lofty requirement of a compelling governmental interest before they may be significantly regulated. See Shapiro v. Thompson, 394 U.S. 618, 638 (1969). Neither does it touch upon what has been said to be the suspect criteria of race, nationality or alienage. Graham v. Richardson, 403 U.S. 365, 375 (1971). Instead, bankruptcy legislation is in the area of economics and social welfare. See Dandridge v. Williams, 397 U.S., at 484–485; Richardson v. Belcher, 404 U.S., at 81; Lindsey v. Normet, 405 U.S. 56, 74 (1972); Jefferson v. Hackney, 406 U.S. 535, 546 (1972). This being so, the applicable standard, in measuring the propriety of Congress' classification, is that of rational justification."

Justices Stewart, Douglas, and Marshall, dissented.

ORTWEIN v. SCHWAB, 410 U.S. 656 (1973). Ortwein, a recipient of old-age assistance, had his award reduced by the county welfare agency. As provided by state law he appealed to the state public welfare agency, which held a hearing and upheld the county agency's decision. Judicial review of the state agency decision was provided by law in the state appellate court. Ortwein sought to appeal without paying the $25 filing fee required in all civil cases filed in that court, alleging that he was indigent and unable to pay the fee. The state court denied this contention and refused to hear the appeal without the fee. The Supreme Court, in a *per curiam* opinion, affirmed, indicating that *Kras* rather than *Boddie* was the controlling precedent. The Court gave three principal reasons for its decision:

(1) The interest in increased welfare benefits "has far less constitutional significance" than the inability to dissolve one's marriage except through the courts.

(2) Ortwein did receive a pre-termination evidentiary hearing (the required due process minimum) not conditioned on the payment of a fee. "This Court has long recognized that, even in criminal cases, due process does not require a State to provide an appellate system."

(3) The filing fee does not violate the Equal Protection Clause by discriminating against the poor. The litigation, which deals with welfare payments, is in the area of economics and social welfare. "No suspect classification, such as race, nationality, or alienage, is present.... The applicable standard is that of rational justification." The filing fee makes a contribution toward the cost of operating the court system, hence the "requirement of rationality is met."

Justices Stewart, Douglas, Brennan and Marshall dissented.

LITTLE v. STREATER, 452 U.S. 1 (1981). A unanimous Court concluded that refusal to furnish blood grouping tests to an indigent defendant in a civil paternity case denied that defendant "a meaningful opportunity to be heard" within the rationale of *Boddie v. Connecticut*. The Court relied on these factors: this action was not simply a civil proceeding between private parties since the child's mother was compelled to bring the action by state welfare officials and the State Attorney General was a party to the action; under State Law, the defendant's testimony in a paternity action, standing alone, was insufficient to overcome the mother's testimony.

LASSITER v. DEPARTMENT OF SOCIAL SERVICES, 452 U.S. 18 (1981). A majority of the Court concluded that due process required the appointment of counsel, for an indigent parent in a proceeding brought by the state to terminate parental status, only in appropriate circumstances. The majority held that in this case, those special factors requiring the appointment of counsel were not present in that: no allegations of neglect or abuse had been made; no expert witness testified; and the presence of counsel could not have made a determinative difference in the result. The four dissenting Justices (Blackmun, Brennan, Marshall and Stevens) argued that due process should require the appointment of counsel for indigents in all proceedings brought by the state to terminate parental rights.

M.L.B. v. S.L.J., 519 U.S. 102 (1996). The Court held that Mississippi could not deny an indigent mother the right to appeal the sufficiency of the evidence supporting a trial court's decision terminating all her parental rights based on her inability to pay substantial costs for preparing the trial record necessary to enable effective appellate review. The majority observed "that the Court's decisions concerning access to judicial processes ... Reflect both equal protection and due process concerns[,]" but that most had relied on equal protection, "as M.L.B.'s plea heavily does, for ... Due process does not independently require that the state provide a right to appeal." Though not controlled by precedent because this was a *civil* case involving indigency related to *appellate* review rather than any court access at all, the majority emphasized that a State must have strong justification when a matter of family association so fundamental as that of mother and child is at stake in a way as irrevocable as complete termination of any parental right. It also stressed the "considerable" risk of error evidenced by the frequency of appellate reversal of Mississippi trial court determinations to terminate parental rights, and the relative insignificance of the State's countervailing financial interest "in the tightly circumscribed category of parental status termination cases [where] appeals are few, and not likely to impose an undue burden on the State."

Unlike precedents holding that the Constitution does not mandate affirmative subsidies to exercise fundamental rights, such as freedom to speak or to choose an abortion procedure, which involved requests for "state aid to subsidize their privately initiated action or to alleviate the consequences of differences in economic circumstances that existed apart from state action[,]" here the objective was "to defend against the State's destruction of ... family bonds, and to resist the brand associated with a parental unfitness adjudication." Unlike cases holding that otherwise neutral laws do not presumptively violate equal protection simply because of disproportionate adverse effects on a racial minority, much less on the poor, here the rules were "wholly contingent on one's ability to pay, and thus 'visit different consequences on two categories of persons,' ...; they apply to all indigents and do not reach anyone outside that class." As for concern that the Court's ruling inevitably would implicate greater financial obligations on the State to pay for transcripts in aid of appellate review in other important civil cases, the Court emphasized that the unique deprivation associated with terminating parental status set this case apart "even from other domestic relations matters such as divorce, paternity, and child custody."

Justice Kennedy concurred in the judgment, asserting that "due process is quite a sufficient basis for our holding." Justice Thomas dissented, joined in full by Justice Scalia and in part by Chief Justice Rehnquist (except for the portion of the opinion declaring Justice Thomas' "inclin[ation] to vote to overrule *Griffin* and its progeny").

PROVISION OF ESSENTIAL GOVERNMENTAL BENEFITS AND SERVICES TO THE POOR

The general question raised here is whether the Constitution provides a basis for a higher level of judicial scrutiny of legislation that relates to the provision by government to the poor of basic human necessities—food, medical care, education, housing—than it does to economic regulations. Three separate constitutional arguments may be made to support an affirmative answer to that question.

(1) Does the constitution (through the due process clause or otherwise) guarantee some minimum entitlement by the poor to the basic necessities of life? Is the due process clause not only a shield against governmental deprivations of liberty and property but also a sword which imposes affirmative obligations on government? Professor Michelman, *On Protecting the Poor Through the Fourteenth Amendment*, 83 Harv.L.Rev. 7, 9 (1969), argues that the purposes of the Supreme Court decisions dealing with equal protection and wealth classifications "could be more soundly and satisfyingly understood as vindication of a state's duty to protect against certain hazards which are endemic in an unequal society, rather than vindication of a duty to avoid complicity in unequal treatment." He goes on to elaborate the proposition that the Court should be talking of "minimum protection against economic hazard" rather than "equal protection." Professor Tribe refers to "[e]merging notions that government has an affirmative obligation somehow to provide at least a minimally decent subsistence with respect to the most basic human needs, subject to all of the familiar difficulties with judicial enforcement of affirmative duties." *American Constitutional Law*, 1336 (2d ed. 1988). Professor Michelman restated his thesis in *Welfare Rights in a Constitutional Democracy*, 1979 Wash.U.L.Q. 659. In commentary on that restatement Professor Bork asserted "that the argument for welfare rights is unconnected with either the Constitution or its history" and therefore "offers inadequate guidelines and so requires

political decision making by the judiciary." *The Impossibility of Finding Welfare Rights in the Constitution,* 1979 Wash.U.L.Q. 695. See also Appleton, *Professor Michelman's Quest for a Constitutional Welfare Right,* 1979 Wash. U.L.Q. 715.

(2) Should classifications in statutes providing governmental services to the poor be subject to a heightened standard of review under the equal protection clause because they involve the basic economic needs of impoverished human beings?

(3) Should classifications based on wealth be held to be constitutionally "suspect" and hence to require special justification in order to be valid? This argument was discussed supra p. 935.

WELFARE AS A FUNDAMENTAL RIGHT CALLING FOR STRICT SCRUTINY

A conscious attempt was made by lawyers involved in legal services programs to deal with what they regarded as inadequate welfare grants by persuading the Court to read a "right to life" into the equal protection clause that would guarantee an adequate minimum payment for every needy individual in society. The story of this attempt is told in Krislov, *The OEO Lawyers Fail to Constitutionalize a Right to Welfare: A Study in the Uses and Limits of the Judicial Process,* 58 Minn.L.Rev. 211 (1973); Sparer, *The Right to Welfare* in *The Rights of Americans* 65 (N. Dorsen, ed. 1971).

Dandridge v. Williams

397 U.S. 471, 90 S.Ct. 1153, 25 L.Ed.2d 491 (1970).

[Maryland participated in the federal Aid to Families with Dependent Children program (AFDC), providing grants of a certain amount for each child but imposing an upper limit of $250 per month that any family could receive. Recipients with large families that received less aid per child than smaller families not affected by the maximum challenged the regulation in federal district court. They contended that the state limit contravened the federal statute and discriminated against them merely because of the size of their families in violation of the equal protection clause. The Court upheld the state limit, rejecting both the statutory and the constitutional claims. Portions of the opinions relating to the constitutional issues are printed below.]

Mr. Justice Stewart delivered the opinion of the Court.

. . . .

II.

Although a State may adopt a maximum grant system in allocating its funds available for AFDC payments without violating the Act, it may not, of course, impose a regime of invidious discrimination in violation of the Equal Protection Clause of the Fourteenth Amendment. Maryland says that its maximum grant regulation is wholly free of any invidiously discriminatory purpose or effect, and that the regulation is rationally supportable on at least four entirely valid grounds. The regulation can be clearly justified, Maryland argues, in terms of legitimate state interests in encouraging gainful employment, in maintaining an equitable balance in economic status as between welfare families and those supported by a wage-earner, in providing incentives for family planning, and in allocating available public funds in such a way as fully to meet the needs of the largest possible number of families. The District Court, while apparently recognizing the validity of at least some of these state concerns, nonetheless held that the regulation "is invalid on its face for overreaching,"—that it violates the Equal Protection Clause "[b]ecause it cuts too broad a swath on an indiscriminate basis as applied to the entire group of AFDC eligibles to which it purports to apply,...."

If this were a case involving government action claimed to violate the First Amendment guarantee of free speech, a finding of "overreaching" would be significant and might be crucial. For when otherwise valid governmental regulation sweeps so broadly as to impinge upon activity protected by the First Amendment, its very overbreadth may make it unconstitutional.... But the concept of "overreaching" has no place in this case. For here we deal with state regulation in the social and economic field, not affecting freedoms guaranteed by the Bill of Rights, and claimed to violate the Fourteenth Amendment only because the regulation results in some disparity in grants of welfare payments to the largest AFDC families.[16] For this Court to approve the invalidation of state economic or social regulation as "overreaching" would be far too reminiscent of an era when the Court thought the Fourteenth Amendment gave it power to strike down state laws "because they may be unwise, improvident, or out of harmony with a particular school of thought." Williamson v. Lee Optical of Oklahoma, Inc., 348 U.S. 483, 488. That era long ago passed into history. Ferguson v. Skrupa, 372 U.S. 726.

In the area of economics and social welfare, a State does not violate the Equal Protection Clause merely because the classifications made by its laws are imperfect. If the classification has some "reasonable basis," it does not offend the Constitution simply because the classification "is not made with mathematical nicety or because in practice it results in some inequality." Lindsley v. Natural Carbonic Gas Co., 220 U.S. 61, 78.... "A statutory discrimination will not be set aside if any state of facts reasonably may be conceived to justify it." McGowan v. Maryland, 366 U.S. 420, 426.

To be sure, the cases cited, and many others enunciating this fundamental standard under the Equal Protection Clause, have in the main involved state regulation of business or industry. The administration of public welfare assistance, by contrast, involves the most basic economic needs of impoverished human beings. We recognize the dramatically real factual difference between the cited cases and this one, but we can find no basis for applying a different constitutional standard.[17] ... It is a standard that has consistently been applied to state legislation restricting the availability of employment opportunities. Goesaert v. Cleary, 335 U.S. 464; Kotch v. Board of River Port Pilot Comm'rs, 330 U.S. 552.... And it is a standard that is true to the principle that the Fourteenth Amendment gives the federal courts no power to impose upon the States their views of what constitutes wise economic or social policy.

Under this long-established meaning of the Equal Protection Clause, it is clear that the Maryland maximum grant regulation is constitutionally valid. We need not explore all the reasons that the State advances in justification of the regulation. It is enough that a solid foundation for the regulation can be found in the State's legitimate interest in encouraging employment and in avoiding

16. Cf. Shapiro v. Thompson, 394 U.S. 618, where by contrast, the Court found state interference with the constitutionally protected freedom of interstate travel.

17. It is important to note that there is no contention that the Maryland regulation is infected with a racially discriminatory purpose or effect such as to make it inherently suspect. Cf. McLaughlin v. Florida, 379 U.S. 184.

discrimination between welfare families and the families of the working poor. By combining a limit on the recipient's grant with permission to retain money earned, without reduction in the amount of the grant, Maryland provides an incentive to seek gainful employment. And by keying the maximum family AFDC grants to the minimum wage a steadily employed head of a household receives, the State maintains some semblance of an equitable balance between families on welfare and those supported by an employed breadwinner.

It is true that in some AFDC families there may be no person who is employable. It is also true that with respect to AFDC families whose determined standard of need is below the regulatory maximum, and who therefore receive grants equal to the determined standard, the employment incentive is absent. But the Equal Protection Clause does not require that a State must choose between attacking every aspect of a problem or not attacking the problem at all.... It is enough that the State's action be rationally based and free from invidious discrimination. The regulation before us meets that test.

We do not decide today that the Maryland regulation is wise, that it best fulfills the relevant social and economic objectives that Maryland might ideally espouse, or that a more just and humane system could not be devised. Conflicting claims of morality and intelligence are raised by opponents and proponents of almost every measure, certainly including the one before us. But the intractable economic, social, and even philosophical problems presented by public welfare assistance programs are not the business of this Court. The Constitution may impose certain procedural safeguards upon systems of welfare administration, Goldberg v. Kelly, 397 U.S. 254. But the Constitution does not empower this Court to second-guess state officials charged with the difficult responsibility of allocating limited public welfare funds among the myriad of potential recipients.

The judgment is reversed.

[Justice Black, joined by Chief Justice Burger, and Justice Harlan filed concurring opinions. Justice Douglas dissented on the statutory issue.]

Mr. Justice Marshall, whom Mr. Justice Brennan joins, dissenting.

. . .

This classification process effected by the maximum grant regulation produces a basic denial of equal treatment. Persons who are concededly similarly situated (dependent children and their families), are not afforded equal, or even approximately equal, treatment under the maximum grant regulation. Subsistence benefits are paid with respect to some needy dependent children; nothing is paid with respect to others. Some needy families receive full subsistence assistance as calculated by the State; the assistance paid to other families is grossly below their similarly calculated needs.

Yet, as a general principle, individuals should not be afforded different treatment by the State unless there is a relevant distinction between them and "a statutory discrimination must be based on differences that are reasonably related to the purposes of the Act in which it is found." Morey v. Doud, 354 U.S. 457, 465 (1957).... Consequently, the State may not, in the provision of important services or the distribution of governmental payments, supply benefits to some individuals while denying them to others who are similarly situated....

In the instant case, the only distinction between those children with respect to whom assistance is granted and those children who are denied such assistance is the size of the family into which the child permits himself to be born. The class of individuals with respect to whom payments are actually made (the first four or five eligible dependent children in a family), is grossly underinclusive in terms of the class that the AFDC program was designed to assist, namely, *all* needy dependent children. Such underinclusiveness manifests "a prima facie violation of the equal protection requirement of reasonable classification," compelling the State to come forward with a persuasive justification for the classification.

The Court never undertakes to inquire for such a justification; rather it avoids the task by focusing upon the abstract dichotomy between two different approaches to equal protection problems that have been utilized by this Court.

Under the so-called "traditional test," a classification is said to be permissible under the Equal Protection Clause unless it is "without any reasonable basis." Lindsley v. Natural Carbonic Gas Co., 220 U.S. 61, 78 (1911). On the other hand, if the classification affects a "fundamental right," then the state interest in perpetuating the classification must be "compelling" in order to be sustained. See, e.g., *Shapiro v. Thompson*, supra; . . . .

This case simply defies easy characterization in terms of one or the other of these "tests." The cases relied on by the Court, in which a "mere rationality" test was actually used, e.g., Williamson v. Lee Optical of Oklahoma, Inc., 348 U.S. 483 (1955), are most accurately described as involving the application of equal protection reasoning to the regulation of business interests. The extremes to which the Court has gone in dreaming up rational bases for state regulation in that area may in many instances be ascribed to a healthy revulsion from the Court's earlier excesses in using the Constitution to protect interests that have more than enough power to protect themselves in the legislative halls. This case, involving the literally vital interests of a powerless minority—poor families without breadwinners—is far removed from the area of business regulation, as the Court concedes. Why then is the standard used in those cases imposed here? We are told no more than that this case falls in "the area of economics and social welfare," with the implication that from there the answer is obvious.

In my view, equal protection analysis of this case is not appreciably advanced by the *a priori* definition of a "right," fundamental or otherwise. Rather, concentration must be placed upon the character of the classification in question, the relative importance to individuals in the class discriminated against of the governmental benefits that they do not receive, and the asserted state interests in support of the classification. . . .

It is the individual interests here at stake that, as the Court concedes, most clearly distinguish this case from the "business regulation" equal protection cases. AFDC support to needy dependent children provides the stuff that sustains those children's lives: food, clothing, shelter. And this Court has already recognized several times that when a benefit, even a "gratuitous" benefit, is necessary to sustain life, stricter constitutional standards, both procedural and substantive, are applied to the deprivation of that benefit.

. . .

In any event, it cannot suffice merely to invoke the spectre of the past and to recite from *Lindsley v. Natural Carbonic Gas Co.* and *Williamson v. Lee Optical of Oklahoma, Inc.* to decide the case. Appellees are not a gas company or an optical dispenser; they are needy dependent children and families who are discriminated against by the State. The basis of that discrimination—the classification of individuals into large and small families—is too arbitrary and too unconnected to the asserted rationale, the impact on those discriminated against—the denial of even a subsistence existence—too great, and the supposed interests served too contrived and attenuated to meet the requirements of the Constitution. . . .

I would affirm the judgment of the District Court.

Harris v. McRae

448 U.S. 297, 100 S.Ct. 2671, 65 L.Ed.2d 784 (1980).

Mr. Justice Stewart delivered the opinion of the Court.

This case presents statutory and constitutional questions concerning the public funding of abortions under Title XIX of the Social Security Act, commonly known as the "Medicaid" Act, and recent annual appropriations acts containing the so-called "Hyde Amendment." The statutory question is whether Title XIX requires a State that participates in the Medicaid program to fund the cost of medically necessary abortions for which federal reimbursement is unavailable under the Hyde Amendment. The constitutional question, which arises only if Title XIX imposes no such requirement, is whether the Hyde Amendment, by denying public funding for certain medically necessary abortions, contravenes the liberty or equal protection guarantees of the Due Process Clause of the Fifth Amendment, or either of the Religion Clauses of the First Amendment.

I.

. . .

Since September 1976, Congress has prohibited . . . the use of any federal funds to reimburse the cost of abortions under the Medicaid program except under certain specified circumstances. This funding restriction is commonly known as the "Hyde Amendment," after its original congressional sponsor, Representative Hyde. The current version of the Hyde Amendment, applicable for fiscal year 1980, provides:

> "[N]one of the funds provided by this joint resolution shall be used to perform abortions except where the life of the mother would be endangered if the fetus were carried to term; or except for such medical procedures necessary for the victims of rape or incest when such rape or incest has been reported promptly to a law enforcement agency or public health service." Pub.L. No. 96–123, § 109, 93 Stat. 926. See also Pub.L. No. 96–86, § 118, 93 Stat. 662.

. . .

[T]he District Court . . . invalidat[ed] all versions of the Hyde Amendment on constitutional grounds. . . .

. . .

II.

. . .

. . . [W]e conclude that Title XIX does not require a participating State to pay for those medically necessary abortions for which federal reimbursement is unavailable under the Hyde Amendment.[16]

---

16. A participating State is free, if it so chooses, to include in its Medicaid plan those medically necessary abortions for which federal reimbursement is unavailable. . . . We hold only that a State *need* not include such abortions in its Medicaid plan.

III.

[Hence,] we must consider the constitutional validity of the Hyde Amendment. The appellees assert that the funding restrictions of the Hyde Amendment violate several rights secured by the Constitution—(1) the right of a woman, implicit in the Due Process Clause of the Fifth Amendment, to decide whether to terminate a pregnancy, (2) the prohibition under the Establishment Clause of the First Amendment against any "law respecting an establishment of religion," and (3) the right to freedom of religion protected by the Free Exercise Clause of the First Amendment. The appellees also contend that, quite apart from substantive constitutional rights, the Hyde Amendment violates the equal protection component of the Fifth Amendment.

. . .

A.

We address first the appellees' argument that the Hyde Amendment, by restricting the availability of certain medically necessary abortions under Medicaid, impinges on the "liberty" protected by the Due Process Clause as recognized in Roe v. Wade, 410 U.S. 113, and its progeny.

In the *Wade* case, this Court held ... that the "liberty" protected by the Due Process Clause of the Fourteenth Amendment ... includes the freedom of a woman to decide whether to terminate a pregnancy.

But the Court ... also recognized that a State has legitimate interests during a pregnancy in both ensuring the health of the mother and protecting potential human life. These state interests, which were found to be "separate and distinct" and to "grow[ ]in substantiality as the woman approaches term," pose a conflict with a woman's untrammeled freedom of choice....

In Maher v. Roe, 432 U.S. 464, the Court was presented with the question whether the scope of personal constitutional freedom recognized in *Roe v. Wade* included an entitlement to Medicaid payments for abortions that are not medically necessary. At issue in *Maher* was a Connecticut welfare regulation under which Medicaid recipients received payments for medical services incident to childbirth, but not for medical services incident to nontherapeutic abortions. The District Court held that the regulation violated the Equal Protection Clause of the Fourteenth Amendment because the unequal subsidization of childbirth and abortion impinged on the "fundamental right to abortion" recognized in *Wade* and its progeny.

It was the view of this Court that "the District Court misconceived the nature and scope of the fundamental right recognized in *Roe*." 432 U.S., at 471. The doctrine of *Roe v. Wade,* the Court held in *Maher,* "protects the woman from unduly burdensome interference with her freedom to decide whether to terminate her pregnancy," such as the severe criminal sanctions at issue in *Roe v. Wade,* supra, or the absolute requirement of spousal consent for an abortion challenged in Planned Parenthood of Central Missouri v. Danforth, 428 U.S. 52.

But the constitutional freedom recognized in *Wade* and its progeny, the *Maher* Court explained, did not prevent Connecticut from making "a value judgment favoring childbirth over abortion, and ... implement[ing] that judgment by the allocation of public funds." As the Court elaborated:

"The Connecticut regulation before us is different in kind from the laws invalidated in our previous abortion decisions. The Connecticut regulation places no obstacles—absolute or otherwise—in the pregnant woman's path to an abortion. An indigent woman who desires an abortion suffers no disadvantage as a consequence of Connecticut's decision to fund childbirth; she continues as before to be dependent on private sources for the service she desires. The State may have made childbirth a more attractive alternative, thereby influencing the woman's decision, but it has imposed no restriction on access to abortions that was not already there. The indigency that may make it difficult—and in some cases, perhaps, impossible—for some women to have abortions is neither created nor in any way affected by the Connecticut regulation."

... In explaining why the constitutional principle recognized in *Wade* and later cases ... did not translate into a constitutional obligation of Connecticut to subsidize abortions, the Court cited the "basic difference between direct state interference with a protected activity and state encouragement of an alternative activity consonant with legislative policy. Constitutional concerns are greatest when the State attempts to impose its will by force of law; the State's power to encourage actions deemed to be in the public interest is necessarily far broader." Thus, even though the Connecticut regulation favored childbirth over abortion by means of subsidization of one and not the other, the Court in *Maher* concluded that the regulation did not impinge on the constitutional freedom recognized in *Wade* because it imposed no governmental restriction on access to abortions.

The Hyde Amendment, like the Connecticut welfare regulation at issue in *Maher,* places no governmental obstacle in the path of a woman who chooses to terminate her pregnancy, but rather, by means of unequal subsidization of abortion and other medical services, encourages alternative activity deemed in the public interest. The present case does differ factually from *Maher* insofar as that case involved a failure to fund nontherapeutic abortions, whereas the Hyde Amendment withholds funding of certain medically necessary abortions. Accordingly, the appellees argue that because the Hyde Amendment affects a significant interest not present or asserted in *Maher*—the interest of a woman in protecting her health during pregnancy—and because that interest lies at the core of the personal constitutional freedom recognized in *Wade;* the present case is constitutionally different from *Maher.* ...

... [True,] *Wade* emphasized ... that the woman's decision carries with it significant personal health implications—both physical and psychological. In fact, ... the Court held that even after fetal viability a State may not prohibit abortions "necessary to preserve the life or health of the mother." Because even the compelling interest of the State in protecting potential life after fetal viability was held to be insufficient to outweigh a woman's decision to protect her life or health, it could be argued that the freedom of a woman to decide whether to terminate her pregnancy for health reasons does in fact lie at the core of the constitutional liberty identified in *Wade.*

But, ... it simply does not follow that a woman's freedom of choice carries with it a constitutional entitlement to the financial resources to avail herself of the full range of protected choices. The reason why was explained in *Maher:* although government may not place obstacles in the path of a woman's exercise of her freedom of choice, it need not remove those not of its own creation. Indigency falls in the latter category. The financial constraints that restrict an indigent woman's ability to enjoy the full range of constitutionally protected freedom of choice are the product not of governmental restrictions on access to abortions, but rather of her indigency. Although Congress has opted to subsidize medically necessary services generally, but not certain medically necessary abortions, the fact remains that the Hyde Amendment leaves an indigent woman with at least the same range of choice in deciding whether to obtain a medically necessary abortion as she would have had if Congress had chosen to subsidize no health care costs at all. We are thus not persuaded that the Hyde Amendment impinges on the constitutionally protected freedom of choice recognized in *Wade*.[19]

Although the liberty protected by the Due Process Clause affords protection against unwarranted government interference with freedom of choice in the context of certain personal decisions, it does not confer an entitlement to such funds as may be necessary to realize all the advantages of that freedom. To hold otherwise would mark a drastic change in our understanding of the Constitution. It cannot be that because government may not prohibit the use of contraceptives, Griswold v. Connecticut, 381 U.S. 479, or prevent parents from sending their child to a private school, Pierce v. Society of Sisters, 268 U.S. 510, government, therefore, has an affirmative constitutional obligation to ensure that all persons have the financial resources to obtain contraceptives or send their children to private schools. To translate the limitation on governmental power implicit in the Due Process Clause into an affirmative funding obligation would require Congress to subsidize the medically necessary abortion of an indigent woman even if Congress had not enacted a Medicaid program to subsidize other medically necessary services. Nothing in the Due Process Clause supports such an extraordinary result. Whether freedom of choice that is constitutionally protected warrants federal subsidization is a question for Congress to answer, not a matter of constitutional entitlement. Accordingly, we conclude that the Hyde Amendment does not impinge on the due process liberty recognized in *Wade*.

B.

The appellees also argue that the Hyde Amendment contravenes rights secured by the Religion Clauses of the First Amendment. . . .

. . .

[The Court held that the Hyde Amendment did not contravene the establishment clause of the first amendment and that the parties lacked standing to raise a challenge under the free exercise clause.]

---

19. The appellees argue that the Hyde Amendment is unconstitutional because it "penalizes" the exercise of a woman's choice to terminate a pregnancy by abortion. See Memorial Hospital v. Maricopa County, 415 U.S. 250; Shapiro v. Thompson, 394 U.S. 618. This argument falls short of the mark. In *Maher*, the Court found only a "semantic difference" between the argument that Connecticut's refusal to subsidize nontherapeutic abortions "unduly interfere[d]" with the exercise of the constitutional liberty recognized in *Wade* and the argument that it "penalized" the exercise of that liberty. And, regardless of how the claim was characterized, the *Maher* Court rejected the argument that Connecticut's refusal to subsidize protected conduct, without more, impinged on the constitutional freedom of choice. This reasoning is equally applicable in the present case. A substantial constitutional question would arise if Congress had attempted to withhold all Medicaid benefits from an otherwise eligible candidate simply because that candidate had exercised her constitutionally protected freedom to terminate her pregnancy by abortion. This would be analogous to Sherbert v. Verner, 374 U.S. 398, where this Court held that a State may not, consistent with the First and Fourteenth Amendments, withhold *all* unemployment compensation benefits from a claimant who would otherwise be eligible for such benefits but for the fact that she is unwilling to work one day per week on her Sabbath. But the Hyde Amendment, unlike the statute at issue in *Sherbert*, does not provide for such a broad disqualification from receipt of public benefits. Rather, the Hyde Amendment, like the Connecticut welfare provision at issue in *Maher*, represents simply a refusal to subsidize certain protected conduct. A refusal to fund protected activity, without more, cannot be equated with the imposition of a "penalty" on that activity.

C.

It remains to be determined whether the Hyde Amendment violates the equal protection component of the Fifth Amendment. This challenge is premised on the fact that, although federal reimbursement is available under Medicaid for medically necessary services generally, the Hyde Amendment does not permit federal reimbursement of all medically necessary abortions. The District Court held, and the appellees argue here, that this selective subsidization violates the constitutional guarantee of equal protection.

The guarantee of equal protection under the Fifth Amendment is not a source of substantive rights or liberties,[25] but rather a right to be free from invidious discrimination in statutory classifications and other governmental activity. It is well-settled that where a statutory classification does not itself impinge on a right or liberty protected by the Constitution, the validity of classification must be sustained unless "the classification rests on grounds wholly irrelevant to the achievement of [any legitimate governmental] objective." McGowan v. Maryland, supra, 366 U.S., at 425. This presumption of constitutional validity, however, disappears if a statutory classification is predicated on criteria that are, in a constitutional sense, "suspect," the principal example of which is a classification based on race, e.g., Brown v. Board of Education, 347 U.S. 483.

1.

For the reasons stated above, we have already concluded that the Hyde Amendment violates no constitutionally protected substantive rights. We now conclude as well that it is not predicated on a constitutionally suspect classification. In reaching this conclusion, we again draw guidance from the Court's decision in *Maher v. Roe.* As to whether the Connecticut welfare regulation providing funds for childbirth but not for nontherapeutic abortions discriminated against a suspect class, the Court in *Maher* observed:

> "An indigent woman desiring an abortion does not come within the limited category of disadvantaged classes so recognized by our cases. Nor does the fact that the impact of the regulation falls upon those who cannot pay lead to a different conclusion. In a sense, every denial of welfare to an indigent creates a wealth classification as compared to nonindigents who are able to pay for the desired goods or services. But this Court has never held that financial need alone identifies a suspect class for purposes of equal protection analysis." . . .

Thus, the Court in *Maher* found no basis for concluding that the Connecticut regulation was predicated on a suspect classification.

[T]he present case is indistinguishable from *Maher* in this respect. Here, as in *Maher,* the principal impact of the Hyde Amendment falls on the indigent. But that fact does not itself render the funding restriction constitutionally invalid, for this Court has held repeatedly that poverty, standing alone, is not a suspect classification. See, e.g., James v. Valtierra, 402 U.S. 137. That *Maher* involved the refusal to fund nontherapeutic abortions, whereas the present case involves the refusal to fund medically necessary abortions, has no bearing on

---

25. An exception to this statement is to be found in Reynolds v. Sims, 377 U.S. 533, and its progeny. Although the Constitution of the United States does not confer the right to vote in state elections, see Minor v. Happersett, 21 Wall. 162, 178, *Reynolds* held that if a State adopts an electoral system, the Equal Protection Clause of the Fourteenth Amendment confers upon a qualified voter a substantive right to participate in the electoral process equally with other qualified voters. See, e.g., Dunn v. Blumstein, 405 U.S. 330, 336.

the factors that render a classification "suspect" within the meaning of the constitutional guarantee of equal protection.

2.

The remaining question then is whether the Hyde Amendment is rationally related to a legitimate governmental objective. It is the Government's position that the Hyde Amendment bears a rational relationship to its legitimate interest in protecting the potential life of the fetus. We agree.

. . .

. . . By subsidizing the medical expenses of indigent women who carry their pregnancies to term while not subsidizing the comparable expenses of women who undergo abortions (except those whose lives are threatened), Congress has established incentives that make childbirth a more attractive alternative than abortion for persons eligible for Medicaid. These incentives bear a direct relationship to the legitimate congressional interest in protecting potential life. Nor is it irrational that Congress has authorized federal reimbursement for medically necessary services generally, but not for certain medically necessary abortions. Abortion is inherently different from other medical procedures, because no other procedure involves the purposeful termination of a potential life.

. . .

. . . It is not the mission of this Court or any other to decide whether the balance of competing interests reflected in the Hyde Amendment is wise social policy. If that were our mission, not every Justice who has subscribed to the judgment of the Court today could have done so. But we cannot, in the name of the Constitution, overturn duly enacted statutes simply "because they may be unwise, improvident, or out of harmony with a particular school of thought." . . . Rather, "when an issue involves policy choices as sensitive as those implicated [here] . . . , the appropriate forum for their resolution in a democracy is the legislature." Maher v. Roe. . . .

. . .

. . . [T]he judgment . . . is reversed, and the case is remanded . . . for further proceedings consistent with this opinion.

It is so ordered.

Mr. Justice White, concurring.

. . .

Mr. Justice Brennan, with whom Mr. Justice Marshall and Mr. Justice Blackmun join, dissenting.

I agree entirely with my Brother Stevens that the State's interest in protecting the potential life of the fetus cannot justify the exclusion of financially and medically needy women from the benefits to which they would otherwise be entitled solely because the treatment that a doctor has concluded is medically necessary involves an abortion. I write separately to express my continuing disagreement with the Court's mischaracterization of the nature of the fundamental right recognized in Roe v. Wade, 410 U.S. 113 (1973), and its misconception of the manner in which that right is infringed by federal and state legislation withdrawing all funding for medically necessary abortions.

. . . *Roe* and its progeny established that the pregnant woman has a right to be free from state interference with her choice to have an abortion . . . The proposition for which these cases stand thus is not that the State is under an affirmative obligation to ensure access to abortions for all who may desire them; it is that the State must refrain from wielding its enormous power and influence in a manner that might burden the pregnant woman's freedom to choose whether to have an abortion. The Hyde Amendment's denial of public funds for medically necessary abortions plainly intrudes upon this constitutionally protected decision, for both by design and in effect it serves to coerce indigent pregnant women to bear children that they would otherwise elect not to have.[4]

. . . [T]he Hyde Amendment is nothing less than an attempt by Congress to . . . achieve indirectly what *Roe v. Wade* said it could not do directly. Under Title XIX of the Social Security Act, the Federal Government reimburses participating States for virtually all medically necessary services it provides to the categorically needy. The sole limitation of any significance is the Hyde Amendment's prohibition against the use of any federal funds to pay for the costs of abortions (except where the life of the mother would be endangered if the fetus were carried to term). As my Brother Stevens persuasively demonstrates, exclusion of medically necessary abortions from Medicaid coverage cannot be justified as a cost-saving device. Rather, the Hyde Amendment is a transparent attempt by the Legislative Branch to impose the political majority's judgment of the morally acceptable and socially desirable preference on a sensitive and intimate decision that the Constitution entrusts to the individual. Worse yet, the Hyde Amendment does not foist that majoritarian viewpoint with equal measure upon everyone in our Nation, rich and poor alike; rather, it imposes that viewpoint only upon that segment of our society which, because of its position of political powerlessness, is least able to defend its privacy rights from the encroachments of state-mandated morality. The instant legislation thus calls for more exacting judicial review than in most other cases. . . .

Moreover, it is clear that the Hyde Amendment not only was designed to inhibit, but does in fact inhibit the woman's freedom to choose abortion over childbirth. . . . [U]nder the Hyde Amendment, the Government will fund only those procedures incidental to childbirth. By thus injecting coercive financial incentives favoring childbirth into a decision that is constitutionally guaranteed to be free from governmental intrusion, the Hyde Amendment deprives the indigent woman of her freedom to choose abortion over maternity, thereby impinging on the due process liberty right recognized in *Roe v. Wade*.

. . . [T]he Court fails to appreciate . . . that it is not simply the woman's indigency that interferes with her freedom of choice, but the combination of her own poverty and the government's unequal subsidization of abortion and childbirth.

. . . By funding all of the expenses associated with childbirth and none of the expenses incurred in terminating pregnancy, the government literally makes an offer that the indigent woman cannot afford to refuse. It matters not that in this instance the government has used the carrot rather than the stick. What is critical is the realization that as a practical matter, many poverty-stricken women will choose to carry their pregnancy to term simply because the government provides funds for the associated medical services, even though

---

4. My focus throughout this opinion is upon the coercive impact of the congressional decision to fund one outcome of pregnancy—childbirth—while not funding the other—abortion. Because I believe this alone renders the Hyde Amendment unconstitutional, I do not dwell upon the other disparities that the Amendment produces in the treatment of rich and poor, pregnant and nonpregnant. I concur completely, however, in my Brother Stevens' discussion of those disparities. . . .

these same women would have chosen to have an abortion if the government had also paid for that option, or indeed if the government had stayed out of the picture altogether and had defrayed the costs of neither procedure.

The fundamental flaw in the Court's due process analysis, then, is its failure to acknowledge that the discriminatory distribution of the benefits of governmental largesse can discourage the exercise of fundamental liberties just as effectively as can an outright denial of those rights through criminal and regulatory sanctions. . . .

. . .

The Medicaid program cannot be distinguished from . . . other statutory schemes that unconstitutionally burdened fundamental rights.[6] . . .

I respectfully dissent.

Mr. Justice Marshall, dissenting.

. . .

. . . The Court's decision today marks a retreat from *Roe v. Wade* and represents a cruel blow to the most powerless members of our society. I dissent.

. . .

I.

The record developed below reveals that the standards set forth in the Hyde Amendment exclude the majority of cases in which the medical profession would recommend abortion as medically necessary. Indeed, in States that have adopted a standard more restrictive than the "medically necessary" test of the Medicaid Act, the number of funded abortions has decreased by over 98%.

. . .

An optimistic estimate indicates that as many as 100 excess deaths may occur each year as a result of the Hyde Amendment. The record contains no estimate of the health damage that may occur to poor women, but it shows that it will be considerable.

II.

. . .

A.

This case is perhaps the most dramatic illustration to date of the deficiencies in the Court's obsolete "two-tiered" approach to the Equal Protection Clause. . . . With all deference, I am unable to understand how the Court can afford the same level of scrutiny to the legislation involved here—whose cruel impact falls exclusively on indigent pregnant women—that it has given to

---

6. . . . [I]t is no answer to assert that no "penalty" is being imposed because the State is only refusing to pay for the specific costs of the protected activity rather than withholding other Medicaid benefits to which the recipient would be entitled or taking some other action more readily characterized as "punitive." Surely the government could not provide free transportation to the polling booths only for those citizens who vote for Democratic candidates, even though the fail- ure to provide the same benefit to Republicans "represents simply a refusal to subsidize certain protected conduct," ibid., and does not involve the denial of any other governmental benefits. Whether the State withholds only the special costs of a disfavored option or penalizes the individual more broadly for the manner in which she exercises her choice, it cannot interfere with a constitutionally protected decision through the coercive use of governmental largesse.

legislation distinguishing opticians from ophthalmologists, or to other legislation that makes distinctions between economic interests more than able to protect themselves in the political process.... Heightened scrutiny of legislative classifications has always been designed to protect groups "saddled with such disabilities or subjected to such a history of purposeful unequal treatment, or relegated to such a position of political powerlessness as to command extraordinary protection from the majoritarian political process." San Antonio School District v. Rodriguez, supra, at 28 (1973).[4] And while it is now clear that traditional "strict scrutiny" is unavailable to protect the poor against classifications that disfavor them, Dandridge v. Williams, 397 U.S. 471 (1970), I do not believe that legislation that imposes a crushing burden on indigent women can be treated with the same deference given to legislation distinguishing among business interests.

B.

. . .

The class burdened by the Hyde Amendment consists of indigent women, a substantial proportion of whom are members of minority races. As I observed in *Maher,* nonwhite women obtain abortions at nearly double the rate of whites.... In my view, the fact that the burden of the Hyde Amendment falls exclusively on financially destitute women suggests "a special condition, which tends seriously to curtail the operation of those political processes ordinarily to be relied upon to protect minorities, and which may call for a correspondingly more searching judicial inquiry." United States v. Carolene Products, 304 U.S. 144, 152–153, n. 4 (1938). For this reason, I continue to believe that "a showing that state action has a devastating impact on the lives of minority racial groups must be relevant" for purposes of equal protection analysis. Jefferson v. Hackney, 406 U.S. 535, 575–576 (1972) (Marshall, J., dissenting).

As I explained in *Maher,* the asserted state interest in protecting potential life is insufficient to "outweigh the deprivation or serious discouragement of a vital constitutional right of especial importance to poor and minority women."
. . .

C.

Although I would abandon the strict-scrutiny-rational-basis dichotomy in equal protection analysis, it is by no means necessary to [do so] to conclude ... that the Hyde Amendment is a denial of equal protection. My Brother Brennan has demonstrated that the Amendment is unconstitutional because it impermissibly infringes upon the individual's constitutional right to decide whether to terminate a pregnancy. And as my Brother Stevens demonstrates the Government's interest in protecting fetal life is not a legitimate one when it is in conflict with "the preservation of the life or health of the mother," *Roe v. Wade,* ... and when the Government's effort to make serious health damage to the mother "a more attractive alternative than abortion" does not rationally promote the governmental interest in encouraging normal childbirth.

... *Maher* turned on the fact that the legislation there under consideration discouraged only nontherapeutic, or medically unnecessary, abortions. In the Court's view, denial of Medicaid funding for nontherapeutic abortions was not a

---

4. For this reason the Court has on occasion suggested that classifications discriminating against the poor are subject to special scrutiny under the Fifth and Four-teenth Amendments. See McDonald v. Board of Election, 394 U.S. 802, 807 (1969); Harper v. Virginia Bd. of Elections, 383 U.S. 663, 668 (1966).

denial of equal protection because Medicaid funds were available only for medically necessary procedures. Thus the plaintiffs were seeking benefits which were not available to others similarly situated. I continue to believe that *Maher* was wrongly decided. But it is apparent that while the plaintiffs in *Maher* were seeking a benefit not available to others similarly situated, respondents are protesting their exclusion from a benefit that is available to all others similarly situated[—]a crucial difference for equal protection purposes.

. . .

III.

. . .

Ultimately, the result reached today may be traced to the Court's unwillingness to apply the constraints of the Constitution to decisions involving the expenditure of governmental funds....

. . .

In this case, the Federal Government has taken upon itself the burden of financing practically all medically necessary expenditures. One category of medically necessary expenditure has been singled out for exclusion, and the sole basis for the exclusion is a premise repudiated for purposes of constitutional law in *Roe v. Wade*. The consequence is a devastating impact on the lives and health of poor women. I do not believe that a Constitution committed to the equal protection of the laws can tolerate this result. I dissent.

Mr. Justice Blackmun, dissenting.

. . . [W]hat I said in dissent in Beal v. Doe, 432 U.S. 438, 442 (1977), and its two companion cases, Maher v. Roe, 432 U.S. 464 (1977), and Poelker v. Doe, 432 U.S. 519 (1977), continues for me to be equally pertinent and equally applicable in these Hyde Amendment cases. There is "condescension" in the Court's holding "that she may go elsewhere for her abortion"; this is "disingenuous and alarming"; the Government "punitively impresses upon a needy minority its own concepts of the socially desirable, the publicly acceptable, and the morally sound"; the "financial argument, of course, is specious"; there truly is "another world 'out there,' the existence of which the Court, I suspect, either chooses to ignore or fears to recognize"; the "cancer of poverty will continue to grow"; and "the lot of the poorest among us," once again, and still, is not to be bettered.

Mr. Justice Stevens, dissenting.

. . .

This case involves a special exclusion of women who, by definition, are confronted with a choice between two serious harms: serious health damage to themselves on the one hand and abortion on the other. The competing interests are the interest in maternal health and the interest in protecting potential human life. It is now part of our law that the pregnant woman's decision as to which of these conflicting interests shall prevail is entitled to constitutional protection.

. . .

. . . The Hyde Amendments not only exclude financially and medically needy persons from the pool of benefits for a constitutionally insufficient reason; they also require the expenditure of millions and millions of dollars in order to thwart the exercise of a constitutional right, thereby effectively inflicting serious and long lasting harm on impoverished women who want and need abortions for valid medical reasons. In my judgment, these amendments constitute an unjustifiable, and indeed blatant, violation of the sovereign's duty to govern impartially.

I respectfully dissent.

LYNG v. CASTILLO, 477 U.S. 635 (1986). In two steps Congress amended the Federal Food Stamp Program, which determines eligibility and benefit levels on a "household" rather than an individual basis, to treat as a single household parents and children (1981), or siblings (1982), who live together, whether or not they usually eat together. Families fitting these profiles, except that they generally bought their food and prepared their meals as separate economic units, sued in federal district court to prevent the consequent loss or reduction of food stamps and to be treated as separate households, contending that "the statutory distinction between parents, children, and siblings, and all other groups of individuals violates the guarantee of equal treatment in the Due Process Clause of the Fifth Amendment." The district court, "persuaded that the statutory definition had a rational basis[,]" nonetheless applied "a stricter standard of review" based "primarily on United States Department of Agriculture v. Moreno, 413 U.S. 528, 534 (1973), ... Which it construed as holding that a 'Congressional desire to harm a politically unpopular group' could not justify the exclusion of household groups which contained unrelated persons," and from which it "reasoned that 'if the Supreme Court is willing to protect unpopular political groups it should even be more willing to protect the traditional family value of living together.' " The Supreme Court reversed. For the court, Justice Stevens said in part:

"The District Court erred in [using] 'heightened scrutiny.' The disadvantaged class [of] parents, children, and siblings [is] not a 'suspect' or 'quasi-suspect' class. As a historical matter, they have not been subjected to discrimination; they do not exhibit obvious, immutable, or distinguishing characteristics that define them as a discrete group; and they are not a minority or politically powerless. See, e.g., Massachusetts Board of Retirement v. Murgia, 427 U.S. 307, 313–314 (1976) (per curiam). In fact, quite the contrary is true.

"Nor does the statutory classification 'directly and substantially' interfere with family living arrangements and thereby burden a fundamental right. Zablocki v. Redhail, 434 U.S. 374, 386–387, and n. 12 (1978).... The 'household' definition does not order or prevent any group of persons from dining together. Indeed, in the overwhelming majority of cases it probably has no effect at all. It is exceedingly unlikely that close relatives would choose to live apart simply to increase their allotment of food stamps, for the cost of separate housing would almost certainly exceed the incremental value of the additional stamps.... Thus, just as in *United States Department of Agriculture v. Moreno*—the decision which the District Court read to require 'heightened scrutiny'—the 'legislative classification must be sustained if the classification itself is rationally related to a legitimate governmental interest.' ...[3]

---

3. In United States Department of Agriculture v. Moreno, 413 U.S. 528 (1973), we held that the definition of the term "household" in the Food Stamp Act as amended in 1971, 84 Stat. 2048, was unconstitutional. That definition drew a distinction between households composed entirely of persons who are related to one another and households containing one or more members who are unrelated to the rest. Unlike the present statute, the 1971 definition completely disqualified all households in the latter category. Not only were all groups of unrelated persons ineligible for benefits, but even groups of related persons would lose their benefits if they admitted one nonrelative to their household. We concluded that this definition did not further the interest in preventing fraud, or any other legitimate purpose of the Food Stamp Program....

For several reasons the Court was "persuaded that Congress could rationally conclude that the two categories merited differential treatment":

". . . Congress could reasonably determine that close relatives sharing a home—almost by definition—tend to purchase and prepare meals together while distant relatives and unrelated individuals might not be so inclined. In that event, even though close relatives are undoubtedly as honest as other food stamp recipients, the potential for mistaken or misstated claims of separate dining would be greater in the case of close relatives than would be true for those with weaker communal ties, simply because a greater percentage of the former category in fact prepare meals jointly than the comparable percentage in the latter category. The additional fact that close relatives represent by far the largest proportion of food stamp recipients, might well have convinced Congress that limited funds would not permit the accommodation given distant relatives and unrelated persons to be stretched to embrace close relatives as well. Finally, Congress might have reasoned that it would be somewhat easier for close relatives—again, almost by definition—to accommodate their living habits to a federal policy favoring common meal preparation than it would be for more distant relatives or unrelated persons to do so. . . ."

Three Justices each dissented, finding the classification "irrational." One, Justice Marshall, first complained that "the Court's rigid, bipolar approach, which purports to apply rational basis scrutiny unless a suspect classification is involved or the exercise of a fundamental right is impeded puts legislative classifications impinging upon sensitive issues of family structure and survival on the same plane as a refusal to let a merchant hawk his wares on a particular street corner." Since "food stamp benefits . . . are necessary for the affected families' very survival, and the Federal Government denies that benefit to families who do not, by preparing their meals together, structure themselves in a manner that the Government believes will minimize unnecessary expenditures[,] . . . the Government is . . . directly and substantially influencing the living arrangements of families whose resources are so low that they must rely on their relatives for shelter. The Government has thus chosen to intrude into the family dining room . . . where . . . the right to privacy exists in its strongest form." As the "challenged classifications amount to a conclusive presumption that related families living under the same roof do all of their cooking together[,] the regulation [also] affect[s] the even more vital interest in survival[,]" because "some separate families liv[ing] in the same house . . . cannot prepare meals together because of different work schedules or lack of cooking or eating utensils."

In a later portion of his opinion, with which Justice White agreed, Justice Marshall also found "Congress' undeniably legitimate desire to prevent fraud and waste in the food stamp program . . . related at best tenuously to the achievement of those goals." He had

"some doubt that the classification used here could pass even a rational-basis test. In United States Dept. of Agriculture v. Moreno, 413 U.S. 528 (1973), we held that a definition of 'household' that excluded any living group containing an individual unrelated to any other member of the group did not rationally further the Government's interest in preventing fraud in the food stamp program. Despite the Court's attempts to distinguish this case from *Moreno*, the critical fact in both cases is that the statute drew a distinction that bears no necessary relation to the prevention of fraud. . . . In the present case, the Government has provided no justification for the conclusion that related

The 1971 definition was, therefore, "wholly without any rational basis" and "in-   valid under the Due Process Clause of the Fifth Amendment." 413 U.S., at 538.

individuals living together are more likely to lie about their living arrangements than are unrelated individuals. Nor has it demonstrated that fraudulent conduct by related households is more difficult to detect than similar abuses by unrelated households.

"Congress . . . cite[d] no hard evidence that related persons living together were in fact significant sources of fraud. . . .

". . . Congress . . . recogniz[ed] that distinct families living together often are genuinely separate households, and that the food stamp program should permit separate families that are not related to live together but maintain separate households. . . . Congress nevertheless assumed that related families are less likely to be genuinely separate households than are unrelated families, and failed even to provide related families a chance to rebut the legislative presumption."

E. EDUCATION

San Antonio Independent School Dist. v. Rodriguez

411 U.S. 1, 93 S.Ct. 1278, 36 L.Ed.2d 16 (1973).

Mr. Justice Powell delivered the opinion of the Court.

This suit attacking the Texas system of financing public education was initiated by Mexican–American parents whose children attend the elementary and secondary schools in the Edgewood Independent School District, an urban school district in San Antonio, Texas. They brought a class action on behalf of school children throughout the State who are members of minority groups or who are poor and reside in school districts having a low property tax base [against] the State Board of Education, the Commissioner of Education, the State Attorney General, and the Bexar County (San Antonio) Board of Trustees. . . . [The three-judge district court held] the Texas school finance system unconstitutional under the Equal Protection Clause of the Fourteenth Amendment. . . . [W]e reverse. . . .

[handwritten: alleging that the Texas school finances system is violating EP]

I.

. . .

[The Court described at length the Texas system of school financing. For present purposes it is enough to note that half of the total educational expenditures in Texas came from the Texas Minimum Foundation School Program. State revenues financed 80% of the Program, with the remaining 20% (known as the Local Fund Assignment) coming from the local districts under a formula designed to reflect each district's relative taxpaying ability. Each school district imposed a property tax to raise funds to satisfy its Local Fund Assignment and to provide the revenues needed above those received under the Foundation Program.]

The school district in which appellees reside, the Edgewood Independent School District, has been compared throughout this litigation with the Alamo Heights Independent School District. This comparison between the least and most affluent districts in the San Antonio area serves to illustrate the manner in which the dual system of finance operates and to indicate the extent to which substantial disparities exist despite the State's impressive progress in recent years. Edgewood is one of seven public school districts in the metropolitan area. Approximately 22,000 students are enrolled in its 25 elementary and

[handwritten: Edgewood is compared to Alamo throughout case]

secondary schools. The district is situated in the core-city sector of San Antonio in a residential neighborhood that has little commercial or industrial property. The residents are predominantly of Mexican–American descent: approximately 90% of the student population is Mexican–American and over 6% is Negro. The average assessed property value per pupil is $5,960—the lowest in the metropolitan area—and the median family income ($4,686) is also the lowest. At an equalized tax rate of $1.05 per $100 of assessed property—the highest in the metropolitan area—the district contributed $26 to the education of each child for the 1967–1968 school year above its Local Fund Assignment for the Minimum Foundation Program. The Foundation Program contributed $222 per pupil for a state-local total of $248. Federal funds added another $108 for a total of $356 per pupil.

Alamo Heights is the most affluent school district in San Antonio. Its six schools, housing approximately 5,000 students, are situated in a residential community quite unlike the Edgewood District. The school population is predominantly Anglo, having only 18% Mexican–Americans and less than 1% Negroes. The assessed property value per pupil exceeds $49,000 and the median family income is $8,001. In 1967–1968 the local tax rate of $.85 per $100 of valuation yielded $333 per pupil over and above its contribution to the Foundation Program. Coupled with the $225 provided from that Program, the district was able to supply $558 per student. Supplemented by a $36 per pupil grant from federal sources, Alamo Heights spent $594 per pupil.

. . . [1970–1971] figures also reveal the extent to which these two districts' allotments were funded from their own required contributions to the Local Fund Assignment. Alamo Heights, because of its relative wealth, was required to contribute out of its local property tax collections approximately $100 per pupil, or about 20% of its Foundation grant. Edgewood, on the other hand, paid only $8.46 per pupil, which is about 2.4% of its grant. It does appear then that, at least as to these two districts, the Local Fund Assignment does reflect a rough approximation of the relative taxpaying potential of each.

Despite . . . recent increases, substantial interdistrict disparities in school expenditures found by the District Court to prevail in San Antonio and in varying degrees throughout the State still exist. And it was these disparities, largely attributable to differences in the amounts of money collected through local property taxation, that led the District Court to conclude that Texas' dual system of public school finance violated the Equal Protection Clause. . . .

Texas virtually concedes that its historically rooted dual system of financing education could not withstand the strict judicial scrutiny that this Court has found appropriate in reviewing legislative judgments that interfere with fundamental constitutional rights or that involve suspect classifications. If, as previous decisions have indicated, strict scrutiny means that the State's system is not entitled to the usual presumption of validity, that the State rather than the complainants must carry a "heavy burden of justification," that the State must demonstrate that its educational system has been structured with "precision" and is "tailored" narrowly to serve legitimate objectives and that it has selected the "least drastic means" for effectuating its objectives, the Texas financing system and its counterpart in virtually every other State will not pass muster. The State candidly admits that "[n]o one familiar with the Texas system would contend that it has yet achieved perfection." Apart from its concession that educational finance in Texas has "defects" and "imperfections," the State defends the system's rationality with vigor and disputes the District Court's finding that it lacks a "reasonable basis."

This, then, establishes the framework for our analysis. We must decide, first, whether the Texas system of financing public education operates to the disadvantage of some suspect class or impinges upon a fundamental right explicitly or implicitly protected by the Constitution, thereby requiring strict judicial scrutiny. If so, the judgment of the District Court should be affirmed. If not, the Texas scheme must still be examined to determine whether it rationally furthers some legitimate, articulated state purpose and therefore does not constitute an invidious discrimination in violation of the Equal Protection Clause of the Fourteenth Amendment.

Decide if suspect then use strict standard, otherwise use rational basis

II.

. . .

A.

The wealth discrimination discovered by the District Court in this case, and by several other courts that have recently struck down school financing laws in other States,[48] is quite unlike any of the forms of wealth discrimination heretofore reviewed by this Court. Rather than focusing on the unique features of the alleged discrimination, the courts in these cases have virtually assumed their findings of a suspect classification through a simplistic process of analysis: since, under the traditional systems of financing public schools, some poorer people receive less expensive educations than other more affluent people, these systems discriminate on the basis of wealth. This approach largely ignores the hard threshold questions, including whether it makes a difference for purposes of consideration under the Constitution that the class of disadvantaged "poor" cannot be identified or defined in customary equal protection terms, and whether the relative—rather than absolute—nature of the asserted deprivation is of significant consequence. Before a State's laws and the justifications for the classifications they create are subjected to strict judicial scrutiny, we think these threshold considerations must be analyzed more closely than they were in the court below.

Threshold questions before subjected to strict scrutiny

. . .

However described, it is clear that appellees' suit asks this Court to extend its most exacting scrutiny to review a system that allegedly discriminates against a large, diverse, and amorphous class, unified only by the common factor of residence in districts that happen to have less taxable wealth than other districts. The system of alleged discrimination and the class it defines have none of the traditional indicia of suspectness: the class is not saddled with such disabilities, or subjected to such a history of purposeful unequal treatment, or relegated to such a position of political powerlessness as to command extraordinary protection from the majoritarian political process.

class doesn't have usual indicia of suspect

We thus conclude that the Texas system does not operate to the peculiar disadvantage of any suspect class. But in recognition of the fact that this Court has never heretofore held that wealth discrimination alone provides an adequate basis for invoking strict scrutiny, appellees have not relied solely on this contention. They also assert that the State's system impermissibly interferes with the exercise of a "fundamental" right and that accordingly the prior decisions of this Court require the application of the strict standard of judicial review. . . . It is this question—whether education is a fundamental right, in

48.   Serrano v. Priest, 96 Cal.Rptr. 601, 487 P.2d 1241, 5 Cal.3d 584 (1971); Van Dusartz v. Hatfield, 334 F.Supp. 870 (D.Minn.1971); Robinson v. Cahill, 118 N.J.Super. 223, 287 A.2d 187 (1972); Milliken v. Green, No. 53, 809 (Mich. 1973).

[handwritten margin note: wealth dist. has not given strict scrutiny but fundamental right of education has.]

the sense that it is among the rights and liberties protected by the Constitution—which has so consumed the attention of courts and commentators in recent years.

B.

In Brown v. Board of Education, 347 U.S. 483 (1954), a unanimous Court recognized that "education is perhaps the most important function of state and local governments." . . .

Nothing this Court holds today in any way detracts from our historic dedication to public education. We are in complete agreement with the conclusion of the three-judge panel below that "the grave significance of education both to the individual and to our society" cannot be doubted. But the importance of a service performed by the State does not determine whether it must be regarded as fundamental for purposes of examination under the Equal Protection Clause. Mr. Justice Harlan, dissenting from the Court's application of strict scrutiny to a law impinging upon the right of interstate travel, admonished that "[v]irtually every state statute affects important rights." Shapiro v. Thompson, 394 U.S. 618, 655, 661 (1969). In his view, if the degree of judicial scrutiny of state legislation fluctuated depending on a majority's view of the importance of the interest affected, we would have gone "far toward making this Court a 'super-legislature.' " We would indeed then be assuming a legislative role and one for which the Court lacks both authority and competence. But Mr. Justice Stewart's response in *Shapiro* to Mr. Justice Harlan's concern correctly articulates the limits of the fundamental rights rationale employed in the Court's equal protection decisions:

[handwritten margin note: criticizing saying they can pick any right & make it an imp. right]

"The Court today does *not* 'pick out particular human activities, characterize them as' fundamental, 'and give them added protection. . . .' To the contrary, the Court simply recognizes, as it must, an established constitutional right, and gives to that right no less protection than the Constitution itself demands." 394 U.S., at 642. (Emphasis from original.)

. . .

. . . The right to interstate travel had long been recognized as a right of constitutional significance, and the Court's decision therefore did not require an *ad hoc* determination as to the social or economic importance of that right.

. . .

[handwritten margin note: cant create substantive const. rights by looking at precedent cases & comparing. Must do it by assessing wether it is a explicit or implicit right gauranteed by the constitution]

The lesson of these cases . . . is plain. It is not the province of this Court to create substantive constitutional rights in the name of guaranteeing equal protection of the laws. Thus the key to discovering whether education is "fundamental" is not to be found in comparisons of the relative societal significance of education as opposed to subsistence or housing. Nor is it to be found by weighing whether education is as important as the right to travel. Rather, the answer lies in assessing whether there is a right to education explicitly or implicitly guaranteed by the Constitution. Eisenstadt v. Baird, 405 U.S. 438 (1972);[73] Dunn v. Blumstein, 405 U.S. 330 (1972);[74] Police Department

73. In *Eisenstadt*, the Court struck down a Massachusetts statute that prohibited the distribution of contraceptive devices, finding that the law failed "to satisfy even the more lenient equal protection standard." . . . Nevertheless, in *dictum*, the Court recited the correct form of equal protection analysis: "if we were to conclude that the Massachusetts statute impinges upon fundamental

freedoms under Griswold [v. Connecticut, 381 U.S. 479 (1965)], the statutory classification would have to be not merely *rationally related* to a valid public purpose but *necessary* to the achievement of a *compelling* state interest." . . . (emphasis from original).

74. *Dunn* fully canvasses this Court's voting rights cases and explains that "this of the City of Chicago v. Mosley, 408 U.S. 92 (1972);[75] Skinner v. Oklahoma, 316 U.S. 535 (1942).[76]

Education, of course, is not among the rights afforded explicit protection under our Federal Constitution. Nor do we find any basis for saying it is implicitly so protected....

We have carefully considered each of the arguments supportive of the District Court's finding that education is a fundamental right or liberty and have found those arguments unpersuasive. In one further respect we find this a particularly inappropriate case in which to subject state action to strict judicial scrutiny.... Each of our prior cases involved legislation which "deprived," "infringed," or "interfered" with the free exercise of some such fundamental personal right or liberty. See Skinner v. Oklahoma ...; Shapiro v. Thompson ...; Dunn v. Blumstein.... A critical distinction between those cases and the one now before us lies in what Texas is endeavoring to do with respect to education.... The Texas system of school finance ... was implemented in an effort to *extend* public education and to improve its quality. Of course, every reform that benefits some more than others may be criticized for what it fails to accomplish. But we think it plain that, in substance, the thrust of the Texas system is affirmative and reformatory and, therefore, should be scrutinized under judicial principles sensitive to the nature of the State's efforts and to the rights reserved to the States under the Constitution.

C.

. . .

We need not rest our decision, however, solely on the inappropriateness of the strict scrutiny test. A century of Supreme Court adjudication under the Equal Protection Clause affirmatively supports the application of the traditional standard of review, which requires only that the State's system be shown to bear some rational relationship to legitimate state purposes. This case represents far more than a challenge to the manner in which Texas provides for the education of its children. We have here nothing less than a direct attack on the way in which Texas has chosen to raise and disburse state and local tax revenues. We are asked to condemn the State's judgment in conferring on political subdivisions the power to tax local property to supply revenues for local interests. In so doing, appellees would have the Court intrude in an area in which it has traditionally deferred to state legislatures. This Court has often

Court has made clear that a citizen has a *constitutionally protected right* to participate in elections on an equal basis with other citizens in the jurisdiction." ... (emphasis supplied). The constitutional underpinnings of the right to equal treatment in the voting process can no longer be doubted even though, as the Court noted in Harper v. Virginia Bd. of Elections, 383 U.S. 663, 665 (1966), "the right to vote in state elections is nowhere expressly mentioned." ...

75. In *Mosley,* the Court struck down a Chicago antipicketing ordinance that exempted labor picketing from its prohibitions. The ordinance was held invalid under the Equal Protection Clause after subjecting it to careful scrutiny and finding that the ordinance was not narrowly drawn. The stricter standard of review was appropriately applied since the ordinance was one "affecting First Amendment interests." ...

76. *Skinner* applied the standard of close scrutiny to a state law permitting forced sterilization of "habitual criminals." Implicit in the Court's opinion is the recognition that the right of procreation is among the rights of personal privacy protected under the Constitution. See Roe v. Wade, 410 U.S. 113 (1973).

admonished against such interferences with the State's fiscal policies under the Equal Protection Clause. . . .

Thus we stand on familiar ground when we continue to acknowledge that the Justices of this Court lack both the expertise and the familiarity with local problems so necessary to the making of wise decisions with respect to the raising and disposition of public revenues. . . .

In addition to matters of fiscal policy, this case also involves the most persistent and difficult questions of educational policy, another area in which this Court's lack of specialized knowledge and experience counsels against premature interference with the informed judgments made at the state and local levels. . . .

. . .

The foregoing considerations buttress our conclusion that Texas' system of public school finance is an inappropriate candidate for strict judicial scrutiny. These same considerations are relevant to the determination whether that system, with its conceded imperfections, nevertheless bears some rational relationship to a legitimate state purpose. It is to this question that we next turn our attention.

III.

. . .

In sum, to the extent that the Texas system of school finance results in unequal expenditures between children who happen to reside in different districts, we cannot say that such disparities are the product of a system that is so irrational as to be invidiously discriminatory. Texas has acknowledged its shortcomings and has persistently endeavored—not without some success—to ameliorate the differences in levels of expenditures without sacrificing the benefits of local participation. The Texas plan is not the result of hurried, ill-conceived legislation. It certainly is not the product of purposeful discrimination against any group or class. On the contrary, it is rooted in decades of experience in Texas and elsewhere, and in major part is the product of responsible studies by qualified people. In giving substance to the presumption of validity to which the Texas system is entitled, . . . it is important to remember that at every stage of its development it has constituted a "rough accommodation" of interests in an effort to arrive at practical and workable solutions. . . . One also must remember that the system here challenged is not peculiar to Texas or to any other State. In its essential characteristics the Texas plan for financing public education reflects what many educators for a half century have thought was an enlightened approach to a problem for which there is no perfect solution. We are unwilling to assume for ourselves a level of wisdom superior to that of legislators, scholars, and educational authorities in 49 States, especially where the alternatives proposed are only recently conceived and nowhere yet tested. . . .

upheld financial system

. . .

Reversed.

Mr. Justice Stewart, concurring.

. . .

Unlike other provisions of the Constitution, the Equal Protection Clause confers no substantive rights and creates no substantive liberties.[2] The function

2. There is one notable exception to the above statement: It has been established in recent years that the Equal Protection Clause confers the substantive right to participate on an equal basis with other qualified voters whenever the State has adopted an electoral

of the Equal Protection Clause, rather, is simply to measure the validity of *classifications* created by state laws.

There is hardly a law on the books that does not affect some people differently from others. But the basic concern of the Equal Protection Clause is with state legislation whose purpose or effect is to create discrete and objectively identifiable classes. And with respect to such legislation, it has long been settled that the Equal Protection Clause is offended only by laws that are invidiously discriminatory—only by classifications that are wholly arbitrary or capricious....

. . .

Mr. Justice Brennan, dissenting.

Although I agree with my Brother White that the Texas statutory scheme is devoid of any rational basis, and for that reason is violative of the Equal Protection Clause, I also record my disagreement with the Court's rather distressing assertion that a right may be deemed "fundamental" for the purposes of equal protection analysis only if it is "explicitly or implicitly guaranteed by the Constitution." ... As my Brother Marshall convincingly demonstrates, our prior cases stand for the proposition that "fundamentality" is, in large measure, a function of the right's importance in terms of the effectuation of those rights which are in fact constitutionally guaranteed. Thus, "[a]s the nexus between the specific constitutional guarantee and the nonconstitutional interest draws closer, the nonconstitutional interest becomes more fundamental and the degree of judicial scrutiny applied when the interest is infringed on a discriminatory basis must be adjusted accordingly." ...

Here, there can be no doubt that education is inextricably linked to the right to participate in the electoral process and to the rights of free speech and association guaranteed by the First Amendment.... This being so, any classification affecting education must be subjected to strict judicial scrutiny, and since even the State concedes that the statutory scheme now before us cannot pass constitutional muster under this stricter standard of review, I can only conclude that the Texas school financing scheme is constitutionally invalid.

Mr. Justice White, with whom Mr. Justice Douglas and Mr. Justice Brennan join, dissenting.

. . .

The Equal Protection Clause permits discriminations between classes but requires that the classification bear some rational relationship to a permissible object sought to be attained by the statute. It is not enough that the Texas system before us seeks to achieve the valid, rational purpose of maximizing local initiative; the means chosen by the State must also be rationally related to the end sought to be achieved....

Neither Texas nor the majority heeds this rule. If the State aims at maximizing local initiative and local choice, by permitting school districts to resort to the real property tax if they choose to do so, it utterly fails in achieving its purpose in districts with property tax bases so low that there is

process for determining who will represent any segment of the State's population. See, e.g., Reynolds v. Sims, 377 U.S. 533; Kramer v. Union School District, 395 U.S. 621; Dunn v. Blumstein, 405 U.S. 330, 336. But there is no constitutional right to vote, as such. Minor v. Happersett, 88 U.S. 162. If there were such a right, both the Fifteenth Amendment and the Nineteenth Amendment would have been wholly unnecessary.

little if any opportunity for interested parents, rich or poor, to augment school district revenues. Requiring the State to establish only that unequal treatment is in furtherance of a permissible goal, without also requiring the State to show that the means chosen to effectuate that goal are rationally related to its achievement, makes equal protection analysis no more than an empty gesture. In my view, the parents and children in Edgewood, and in like districts, suffer from an invidious discrimination violative of the Equal Protection Clause.

. . . .

Mr. Justice Marshall, with whom Mr. Justice Douglas concurs, dissenting.

. . .

. . . I must once more voice my disagreement with the Court's rigidified approach to equal protection analysis. See Dandridge v. Williams, 397 U.S. 471, 519–521 (1970) (dissenting opinion). . . . The Court apparently seeks to establish today that equal protection cases fall into one of two neat categories which dictate the appropriate standard of review—strict scrutiny or mere rationality. But this Court's decisions in the field of equal protection defy such easy categorization. A principled reading of what this Court has done reveals that it has applied a spectrum of standards in reviewing discrimination allegedly violative of the Equal Protection Clause. This spectrum clearly comprehends variations in the degree of care with which the Court will scrutinize particular classifications, depending, I believe, on the constitutional and societal importance of the interest adversely affected and the recognized invidiousness of the basis upon which the particular classification is drawn. I find in fact that many of the Court's recent decisions embody the very sort of reasoned approach to equal protection analysis for which I previously argued—that is, an approach in which "concentration [is] placed upon the character of the classification in question, the relative importance to the individuals in the class discriminated against of the governmental benefits they do not receive, and the asserted state interests in support of the classification." Dandridge v. Williams. . . .

I therefore cannot accept the majority's labored efforts to demonstrate that fundamental interests, which call for strict scrutiny of the challenged classification, encompass only established rights which we are somehow bound to recognize from the text of the Constitution itself. To be sure, some interests which the Court has deemed to be fundamental for purposes of equal protection analysis are themselves constitutionally protected rights. . . . But it will not do to suggest that the "answer" to whether an interest is fundamental for purposes of equal protection analysis is *always* determined by whether that interest "is a right . . . explicitly or implicitly guaranteed by the Constitution." . . .

. . . .

The majority is, of course, correct when it suggests that the process of determining which interests are fundamental is a difficult one. But I do not think the problem is insurmountable. And I certainly do not accept the view that the process need necessarily degenerate into an unprincipled, subjective "picking-and-choosing" between various interests or that it must involve this Court in creating "substantive constitutional rights in the name of guaranteeing equal protection of the laws." . . . Although not all fundamental interests are constitutionally guaranteed, the determination of which interests are fundamental should be firmly rooted in the text of the Constitution. The task in every case should be to determine the extent to which constitutionally guaranteed rights are dependent on interests not mentioned in the Constitution. As the nexus between the specific constitutional guarantee and the nonconstitutional interest draws closer, the nonconstitutional interest becomes more fundamental and the degree of judicial scrutiny applied when the interest is infringed on a discriminatory basis must be adjusted accordingly. Thus, it cannot be denied that interests such as procreation, the exercise of the state franchise, and access to criminal appellate processes are not fully guaranteed to the citizen by our Constitution. But these interests have nonetheless been afforded special judicial consideration in the face of discrimination because they are, to some extent, interrelated with constitutional guarantees. Procreation is now understood to be important because of its interaction with the established constitutional right of privacy. The exercise of the state franchise is closely tied to basic civil and political rights inherent in the First Amendment. And access to criminal appellate processes enhances the integrity of the range of rights implicit in the Fourteenth Amendment guarantee of due process of law. Only if we closely protect the related interests from state discrimination do we ultimately ensure the integrity of the constitutional guarantee itself. This is the real lesson that must be taken from our previous decisions involving interests deemed to be fundamental.

. . .

. . . The majority suggests . . . that a variable standard of review would give this Court the appearance of a "super-legislature." . . . I cannot agree. Such an approach seems to me a part of the guarantees of our Constitution and of the historic experiences with oppression of and discrimination against discrete, powerless minorities which underlie that document. In truth, the Court itself will be open to the criticism raised by the majority so long as it continues on its present course of effectively selecting in private which cases will be afforded special consideration without acknowledging the true basis of its action.[67] . . .

. . .

As the Court points out, . . . no previous decision has deemed the presence of just a wealth classification to be sufficient basis to call forth "rigorous judicial scrutiny" of allegedly discriminatory state action. Compare, e.g., *Harper v. Virginia Board of Elections,* supra, with e.g., James v. Valtierra, 402 U.S. 137 (1971). That wealth classifications alone have not necessarily been considered to bear the same high degree of suspectness as have classifications based on, for instance, race or alienage may be explainable on a number of grounds. The "poor" may not be seen as politically powerless as certain discrete and insular minority groups. Personal poverty may entail much the same social stigma as historically attached to certain racial or ethnic groups. But personal poverty is not a permanent disability; its shackles may be escaped. Perhaps, most importantly, though, personal wealth may not necessarily share the general irrelevance as basis for legislative action that race or nationality is recognized to have. While the "poor" have frequently been a legally disadvantaged group, it cannot be ignored that social legislation must frequently take cognizance of the economic status of our citizens. Thus, we have generally gauged the invidiousness of wealth classifications with an awareness of the importance of the interests being affected and the relevance of personal wealth to those interests. See *Harper v. Virginia Board of Elections,* supra.

---

67. See generally Gunther, The Supreme Court, 1971 Term: Foreword, In Search of Evolving Doctrine on a Changing Court: A Model for a Newer Equal Protection, 86 Harv.L.Rev. 1 (1972).

When evaluated with these considerations in mind, it seems to me that discrimination on the basis of group wealth in this case likewise calls for careful judicial scrutiny. . . .

. . .

Plyler v. Doe

457 U.S. 202, 102 S.Ct. 2382, 72 L.Ed.2d 786 (1982).

Justice Brennan delivered the opinion of the Court.

The question presented by these cases is whether, consistent with the Equal Protection Clause of the Fourteenth Amendment, Texas may deny to undocumented school-age children the free public education that it provides to children who are citizens of the United States or legally admitted aliens.

I

Since the late nineteenth century, the United States has restricted immigration into this country. Unsanctioned entry into the United States is a crime, 8 U.S.C. § 1325, and those who have entered unlawfully are subject to deportation, 8 U.S.C. §§ 1251–1252. But despite the existence of these legal restrictions, a substantial number of persons have succeeded in unlawfully entering the United States. . . .

In May 1975, the Texas legislature revised its education laws to withhold from local school districts any state funds for the education of children who were not "legally admitted" into the United States. The 1975 revision also authorized local school districts to deny enrollment in their public schools to children not "legally admitted" to the country. . . . These cases involve constitutional challenges to those provisions.

. . .

II

The Fourteenth Amendment provides that "No State shall . . . deprive any person of life, liberty, or property, without due process of law; nor deny to *any person within its jurisdiction* the equal protection of the laws." Appellants argue at the outset that undocumented aliens, because of their immigration status, are not "persons within the jurisdiction" of the State of Texas, and that they therefore have no right to the equal protection of Texas law. We reject this argument. Whatever his status under the immigration laws, an alien is surely a "person" in any ordinary sense of that term. Aliens, even aliens whose presence in this country is unlawful, have long been recognized as "persons" guaranteed due process of law by the Fifth and Fourteenth Amendments. Shaughnessy v. Mezei, 345 U.S. 206, 212 (1953); Wong Wing v. United States, 163 U.S. 228, 238 (1896); Yick Wo v. Hopkins, 118 U.S. 356, 369 (1886). Indeed, we have clearly held that the Fifth Amendment protects aliens whose presence in this country is unlawful from invidious discrimination by the Federal Government. Mathews v. Diaz, 426 U.S. 67, 77 (1976).

. . .

III

. . .

. . . [W]e have treated as presumptively invidious those classifications that disadvantage a "suspect class,"[14] or that impinge upon the exercise of a "fundamental right."[15] With respect to such classifications, [we] requir[e] the State to demonstrate that its classification has been precisely tailored to serve a compelling governmental interest. In addition, we have recognized that certain forms of legislative classification, while not facially invidious, nonetheless give rise to recurring constitutional difficulties; in these limited circumstances we have sought the assurance that the classification reflects a reasoned judgment consistent with the ideal of equal protection by inquiring whether it may fairly be viewed as furthering a substantial interest of the State.[16] We turn to a consideration of the standard appropriate for the evaluation of § 21.031.

A

Sheer incapability or lax enforcement of the laws barring entry into this country, coupled with the failure to establish an effective bar to the employment of undocumented aliens, has resulted in the creation of a substantial "shadow population" of illegal migrants—numbering in the millions—within our borders. This situation raises the specter of a permanent caste of undocumented resident aliens, encouraged by some to remain here as a source of cheap labor, but nevertheless denied the benefits that our society makes available to citizens and lawful residents. The existence of such an underclass presents most difficult problems for a Nation that prides itself on adherence to principles of equality under law.[19]

14. Several formulations might explain our treatment of certain classifications as "suspect." Some classifications are more likely than others to reflect deep-seated prejudice rather than legislative rationality in pursuit of some legitimate objective. Legislation predicated on such prejudice is easily recognized as incompatible with the constitutional understanding that each person is to be judged individually and is entitled to equal justice under the law. Classifications treated as suspect tend to be irrelevant to any proper legislative goal. See McLaughlin v. Florida, 379 U.S. 184, 192 (1964); Hirabayashi v. United States, 320 U.S. 81, 100 (1943). Finally, certain groups, indeed largely the same groups, have historically been "relegated to such a position of political powerlessness as to command extraordinary protection from the majoritarian political process." San Antonio School District v. Rodriguez, 411 U.S. 1, 28 (1973); Graham v. Richardson, 403 U.S. 365, 372 (1971); see United States v. Carolene Products Co., 304 U.S. 144, 152–153, n. 4 (1938). The experience of our Nation has shown that prejudice may manifest itself in the treatment of some groups. Our response to that experience is reflected in the Equal Protection Clause of the Fourteenth Amendment. Legislation imposing special disabilities upon groups disfavored by virtue of circumstances beyond their control suggests the kind of "class or caste" treatment that the Fourteenth Amendment was designed to abolish.

15. In determining whether a class-based denial of a particular right is deserving of strict scrutiny under the Equal Protection Clause, we look to the Constitution to see if the right infringed has its source, explicitly or implicitly, therein. But we have also recognized the fundamentality of participation in state "elections on an equal basis with other citizens in the jurisdiction," Dunn v. Blumstein ... , even though "the right to both, *per se,* is not a constitutionally protected right." San Antonio School District, 411 U.S., at 35, n. 78. With respect to suffrage, we have explained the need for strict scrutiny as arising from the significance of the franchise as the guardian of all other rights. See Harper v. Virginia Bd. of Elections, 383 U.S. 663, 667 (1966); Reynolds v. Sims, 377 U.S. 533, 562 (1964). . . .

16. See Craig v. Boren, 429 U.S. 190 (1976); Lalli v. Lalli, 439 U.S. 259 (1978). This technique of "intermediate" scrutiny permits us to evaluate the rationality of the legislative judgment with reference to well-settled constitutional principles. . . . Only when concerns sufficiently absolute and enduring can be clearly ascertained from the Constitution and our cases do we employ this standard to aid us in determining the rationality of the legislative choice.

19. We reject the claim that "illegal aliens" are a "suspect class." No case in which we have attempted to define a suspect class, see e.g., n. 14 supra, has addressed the status of persons unlawfully in our country. Unlike most of the classifications that we have recognized as suspect, entry into this class, by virtue of entry into this country, is *cant punish kids for the actions of their parents*

The children who are plaintiffs in these cases are special members of this underclass. Persuasive arguments support the view that a State may withhold its beneficence from those whose very presence within the United States is the product of their own unlawful conduct. These arguments do not apply with the same force to classifications imposing disabilities on the minor *children* of such illegal entrants. At the least, those who elect to enter our territory by stealth and in violation of our law should be prepared to bear the consequences, including, but not limited to, deportation. But the children of those illegal entrants are not comparably situated. Their "parents have the ability to conform their conduct to societal norms," and presumably the ability to remove themselves from the State's jurisdiction; but the children who are plaintiffs in these cases "can affect neither their parents' conduct nor their own status." Trimble v. Gordon, 430 U.S. 762, 770 (1977). Even if the State found it expedient to control the conduct of adults by acting against their children, legislation directing the onus of a parent's misconduct against his children does not comport with fundamental conceptions of justice....

Is not immutable, but is for the children

Of course, undocumented status is not irrelevant to any proper legislative goal. Nor is undocumented status an absolutely immutable characteristic since it is the product of conscious, indeed unlawful, action. But § 21.031 is directed against children, and imposes its discriminatory burden on the basis of a legal characteristic over which children can have little control. It is thus difficult to conceive of a rational justification for penalizing these children for their presence within the United States. Yet that appears to be precisely the effect of § 21.031.

Public education is not a "right" granted to individuals by the Constitution. San Antonio School District.... But neither is it merely some governmental "benefit" indistinguishable from other forms of social welfare legislation. Both the importance of education in maintaining our basic institutions, and the lasting impact of its deprivation on the life of the child, mark the distinction. The "American people have always regarded education and the acquisition of knowledge as matters of supreme importance." Meyer v. Nebraska, 262 U.S. 390, 400 (1923). We have recognized "the public school as a most vital civic institution for the preservation of a democratic system of government," Abington School District v. Schempp, 374 U.S. 203, 230 (1963) (Brennan, J., concurring), and as the primary vehicle for transmitting "the values on which our society rests." Ambach v. Norwick, 441 U.S. 68, 76 (1979).... In addition, education provides the basic tools by which individuals might lead economically productive lives to the benefit of us all. In sum, education has a fundamental role in maintaining the fabric of our society. We cannot ignore the significant social costs borne by our Nation when select groups are denied the means to absorb the values and skills upon which our social order rests.

In addition to the pivotal role of education in sustaining our political and cultural heritage, denial of education to some isolated group of children poses an affront to one of the goals of the Equal Protection Clause: the abolition of

the product of voluntary action. Indeed, entry into the class is itself a crime. In addition, it could hardly be suggested that undocumented status is a "constitutional irrelevancy." With respect to the actions of the federal government, alienage classifications may be intimately related to the conduct of foreign policy, to the federal prerogative to control access to the United States, and to the plenary federal power to determine who has suffi-

ciently manifested his allegiance to become a citizen of the Nation. No State may independently exercise a like power. But if the Federal Government has by uniform rule prescribed what it believes to be appropriate standards for the treatment of an alien subclass, the States may, of course, follow federal direction. See De Canas v. Bica, 424 U.S. 351 (1976).

governmental barriers presenting unreasonable obstacles to advancement on the basis of individual merit. Paradoxically, by depriving the children of any disfavored group of an education, we foreclose the means by which that group might raise the level of esteem in which it is held by the majority. But more directly, "education prepares individuals to be self-reliant and self-sufficient participants in society." Wisconsin v. Yoder.... Illiteracy is an enduring disability. The inability to read and write will handicap the individual deprived of a basic education each and every day of his life. The inestimable toll of that deprivation on the social, economic, intellectual and psychological well-being of the individual, and the obstacle it poses to individual achievement, makes it most difficult to reconcile the cost or the principle of a status-based denial of basic education with the framework of equality embodied in the Equal Protection Clause. What we said 28 years ago in Brown v. Board of Education, 347 U.S. 483 (1954), still holds true:

> "... In these days, it is doubtful that any child may reasonably be expected to succeed in life if he is denied the opportunity of an education. Such an opportunity, where the state has undertaken to provide it, is a right which must be made available to all on equal terms."

B

These well-settled principles allow us to determine the proper level of deference to be afforded § 21.031. Undocumented aliens cannot be treated as a suspect class because their presence in this country in violation of federal law is not a "constitutional irrelevancy." Nor is education a fundamental right; a State need not justify by compelling necessity every variation in the manner in which education is provided to its population. See San Antonio School Dist. v. Rodriguez, 411 U.S. 1, 28–39 (1973). But more is involved in this case than the abstract question whether § 21.031 discriminates against a suspect class, or whether education is a fundamental right. Section 21.031 imposes a lifetime hardship on a discrete class of children not accountable for their disabling status. The stigma of illiteracy will mark them for the rest of their lives. By denying these children a basic education, we deny them the ability to live within the structure of our civic institutions, and foreclose any realistic possibility that they will contribute in even the smallest way to the progress of our Nation. In determining the rationality of § 21.031, we may appropriately take into account its costs to the Nation and to the innocent children who are its victims. In light of these countervailing costs, the discrimination contained in § 21.031 can hardly be considered rational unless it furthers some substantial goal of the State.

IV

It is the State's principal argument, and apparently the view of the dissenting Justices, that the undocumented status of these children *vel non* establishes a sufficient rational basis for denying them benefits that a State might choose to afford other residents. The State notes that while other aliens are admitted "on an equality of legal privileges with all citizens under non-discriminatory laws," Takahashi v. Fish & Game Comm'n, 334 U.S. 410, 420 (1948), the asserted right of these children to an education can claim no implicit congressional imprimatur. Indeed, on the State's view, Congress' apparent disapproval of the presence of these children within the United States, and the evasion of the federal regulatory program that is the mark of undocumented status, provides authority for its decision to impose upon them special disabilities. Faced with an equal protection challenge respecting the treatment of aliens, we agree that the courts must be attentive to congressional policy; the exercise of congressional power might well affect the State's preroga-tives to afford differential treatment to a particular class of aliens. But we are unable to find in the congressional immigration scheme any statement of policy that might weigh significantly in arriving at an equal protection balance concerning the State's authority to deprive these children of an education.

. . .

To be sure, like all persons who have entered the United States unlawfully, these children are subject to deportation. 8 U.S.C. §§ 1251–1252. But there is no assurance that a child subject to deportation will ever be deported. An illegal entrant might be granted federal permission to continue to reside in this country, or even to become a citizen. See, e.g., 8 U.S.C. §§ 1252, 1253(h), 1254. In light of the discretionary federal power to grant relief from deportation, a State cannot realistically determine that any particular undocumented child will in fact be deported until after deportation proceedings have been complet-ed. It would of course be most difficult for the State to justify a denial of education to a child enjoying an inchoate federal permission to remain.

We are reluctant to impute to Congress the intention to withhold from these children, for so long as they are present in this country through no fault of their own, access to a basic education. In other contexts, undocumented status, coupled with some articulable federal policy, might enhance State authority with respect to the treatment of undocumented aliens. But in the area of special constitutional sensitivity presented by this case, and in the absence of any contrary indication fairly discernible in the present legislative record, we perceive no national policy that supports the State in denying these children an elementary education. The State may borrow the federal classifica-tion. But to justify its use as a criterion for its own discriminatory policy, the State must demonstrate that the classification is reasonably adapted to *"the purposes for which the state desires to use it."* Oyama v. California, 332 U.S. 633, 664–665 (1948) (Murphy, J., concurring) (emphasis added). We therefore turn to the state objectives that are said to support § 21.031.

V

Appellants argue that the classification at issue furthers an interest in the "preservation of the state's limited resources for the education of its lawful residents." Of course, a concern for the preservation of resources standing alone can hardly justify the classification used in allocating those resources. . . . The State must do more than justify its classification with a concise expression of an intention to discriminate. . . . Apart from the asserted state prerogative to act against undocumented children solely on the basis of their undocumented status—an asserted prerogative that carries only minimal force in the circum-stances of this case—we discern three colorable state interests that might support § 21.031.

First, appellants appear to suggest that the State may seek to protect the State from an influx of illegal immigrants. While a State might have an interest in mitigating the potentially harsh economic effects of sudden shifts in popula-tion, § 21.031 hardly offers an effective method of dealing with an urgent demographic or economic problem. There is no evidence in the record suggest-ing that illegal entrants impose any significant burden on the State's economy. To the contrary, the available evidence suggests that illegal aliens underutilize public services, while contributing their labor to the local economy and tax money to the State fisc. . . .

Second, ... appellants suggest that undocumented children are appropriately singled out for exclusion because of the special burdens they impose on the State's ability to provide high quality public education. But the record in no way supports the claim that exclusion of undocumented children is likely to improve the overall quality of education in the State....

Finally, appellants suggest that undocumented children are appropriately singled out because their unlawful presence within the United States renders them less likely than other children to remain within the boundaries of the State, and to put their education to productive social or political use within the State. Even assuming that such an interest is legitimate, it is an interest that is most difficult to quantify. The State has no assurance that any child, citizen or not, will employ the education provided by the State within the confines of the State's borders. In any event, the record is clear that many of the undocumented children disabled by this classification will remain in this country indefinitely, and that some will become lawful residents or citizens of the United States. It is difficult to understand precisely what the State hopes to achieve by promoting the creation and perpetuation of a subclass of illiterates within our boundaries, surely adding to the problems and costs of unemployment, welfare, and crime. It is thus clear that whatever savings might be achieved by denying these children an education, they are wholly insubstantial in light of the costs involved to these children, the State, and the Nation.

VI

If the State is to deny a discrete group of innocent children the free public education that it offers to other children residing within its borders, that denial must be justified by a showing that it furthers some substantial state interest. No such showing was made here. Accordingly, the judgment of the Court of Appeals in each of these cases is

Affirmed.

Justice Marshall, concurring.

While I join the Court opinion, ... I continue to believe that an individual's interest in education is fundamental.... Furthermore, I believe that the facts of these cases demonstrate the wisdom of rejecting a rigidified approach to equal protection analysis, and of employing an approach that allows for varying levels of scrutiny depending upon "the constitutional and societal importance of the interest adversely affected and the recognized invidiousness of the basis upon which the particular classification is drawn." ...

Justice Blackmun, concurring.

I join the opinion and judgment of the Court.

Like Justice Powell, I believe that the children involved in this litigation "should not be left on the streets uneducated." I write separately, however, because in my view the nature of the interest at stake is crucial to the proper resolution of this case.

The "fundamental rights" aspect of the Court's equal protection analysis—the now-familiar concept that governmental classifications bearing on certain interests must be closely scrutinized—has been the subject of some controversy....

. . .

I joined Justice Powell's opinion for the Court in *Rodriguez,* and I continue to believe that it provides the appropriate model for resolving most equal protection disputes. Classifications infringing substantive constitutional rights necessarily will be invalid, if not by force of the Equal Protection Clause, then through operation of other provisions of the Constitution. Conversely, classifications bearing on nonconstitutional interests—even those involving "the most basic economic needs of impoverished human beings," Dandridge v. Williams, 397 U.S. 471, 485 (1970)—generally are not subject to special treatment under the Equal Protection Clause, because they are not distinguishable in any relevant way from other regulations in "the area of economics and social welfare." Ibid.

With all this said, however, I believe the Court's experience has demonstrated that the *Rodriguez* formulation does not settle every issue of "fundamental rights" arising under the Equal Protection Clause. Only a pedant would insist that there are *no* meaningful distinctions among the multitude of social and political interests regulated by the States, and *Rodriguez* does not stand for quite so absolute a proposition. . . .

. . .

In my view, when the State provides an education to some and denies it to others, it immediately and inevitably creates class distinctions of a type fundamentally inconsistent with . . . the Equal Protection Clause. Children denied an education are placed at a permanent and insurmountable competitive disadvantage, for an uneducated child is denied even the opportunity to achieve. And when those children are members of an identifiable group, that group—through the State's action—will have been converted into a discrete underclass. Other benefits provided by the State, such as housing and public assistance, are of course important; to an individual in immediate need, they may be more desirable than the right to be educated. But classifications involving the complete denial of education are in a sense unique, for they strike at the heart of equal protection values by involving the State in the creation of permanent class distinctions. . . . In a sense, then, denial of an education is the analogue of denial of the right to vote: the former relegates the individual to second-class social status; the latter places him at a permanent political disadvantage.

This conclusion is fully consistent with *Rodriguez*[, which] reserved judgment on the constitutionality of a state system that "occasioned an absolute denial of educational opportunities to any of its children," noting that "no charge fairly could be made that the system [at issue in *Rodriguez*]fails to provide each child with an opportunity to acquire . . . basic minimal skills." . . .

. . . Whatever the State's power to classify deportable aliens, . . . and whatever the Federal Government's ability to draw more precise and more acceptable alienage classifications, the statute at issue here sweeps within it a substantial number of children who will in fact, and who may well be entitled to, remain in the United States. Given the extraordinary nature of the interest involved, this makes the classification here fatally imprecise. And, as the Court demonstrates, the Texas legislation is not otherwise supported by any substantial interests.

. . .

Justice Powell, concurring.

I join the opinion of the Court, and write separately to emphasize the unique character of the case before us.

. . .

Although the analogy is not perfect, our holding today does find support in decisions of this Court with respect to the status of illegitimates. In Weber v. Aetna Casualty & Surety Co., 406 U.S. 164, 175 (1972) we said: "visiting . . . condemnation on the head of an infant" for the misdeeds of the parents is illogical, unjust, and "contrary to the basic concept of our system that legal burdens should bear some relationship to individual responsibility or wrongdoing."

. . .

In my view, the State's denial of education to these children bears no substantial relation to any substantial state interest. Both of the district courts found that an uncertain but significant percentage of illegal alien children will remain in Texas as residents and many eventually will become citizens. . . .

. . . [I]t hardly can be argued rationally that anyone benefits from the creation within our borders of a subclass of illiterate persons many of whom will remain in the State, adding to the problems and costs of both State and National Governments attendant upon unemployment, welfare and crime.

Chief Justice Burger, with whom Justice White, Justice Rehnquist, and Justice O'Connor join, dissenting.

Were it our business to set the Nation's social policy, I would agree without hesitation that it is senseless for an enlightened society to deprive any children—including illegal aliens—of an elementary education. I fully agree that it would be folly—and wrong—to tolerate creation of a segment of society made up of illiterate persons, many having a limited or no command of our language. However, the Constitution does not constitute us as "Platonic Guardians" nor does it vest in this Court the authority to strike down laws because they do not meet our standards of desirable social policy, "wisdom," or "common sense." . . . We trespass on the assigned function of the political branches under our structure of limited and separated powers when we assume a policy making role as the court does today.

The Court makes no attempt to disguise that it is acting to make up for Congress' lack of "effective leadership" in dealing with the serious national problems caused by the influx of uncountable millions of illegal aliens across our borders. . . . However, it is not the function of the judiciary to provide "effective leadership" simply because the political branches of government fail to do so.

. . .

Once it is conceded—as the Court does—that illegal aliens are not a suspect class, and that education is not a fundamental right, our inquiry should focus on and be limited to whether the legislative classification at issue bears a rational relationship to a legitimate state purpose. . . .

. . .

. . . [T]hat there are sound *policy* arguments against the Texas legislature's choice does not render that choice an unconstitutional one.

. . .

Congress, "vested by the Constitution with the responsibility of protecting our borders and legislating with respect to aliens," bears primary responsibility for addressing the problems occasioned by the millions of illegal aliens flooding across our southern border. . . . While the "specter of a permanent caste" of illegal Mexican residents of the United States is indeed a disturbing one, it is but one segment of a larger problem, which is for the political branches to solve. I find it difficult to believe that Congress would long tolerate such a self-destructive result—that it would fail to deport these illegal alien families or to provide for the education of their children. Yet instead of allowing the political processes to run their course—albeit with some delay—the Court seeks to do Congress' job for it, compensating for congressional inaction. It is not unreasonable to think that this encourages the political branches to pass their problems to the judiciary.

The solution to this seemingly intractable problem is to defer to the political processes, unpalatable as that may be to some.

MARTINEZ v. BYNUM, 461 U.S. 321 (1983). A child born in Texas (and thus a United States citizen) lived with his parents in Mexico, where they were citizens, until he returned to Texas at age 8 to live with his sister in order to attend public school there. He challenged the constitutionality on its face of a Texas law denying tuition-free admission to local public schools to minors who live apart from their parents or guardians, if the minor's presence in the school district is "for the primary purpose of attending the public free schools." The Court rejected the facial attack. Justice Powell's majority opinion said that a "bona fide residence requirement, appropriately defined and uniformly applied, furthers the substantial state interest in assuring that services provided for its residents are enjoyed only by residents." As discussed in the report of this case supra p. 1024, the Court concluded that the law "does not burden or penalize the constitutional right of interstate travel[.]" By granting "the benefits of residency to everyone who satisfies the traditional residence definition [of physical presence and an intention to remain indefinitely] and to some who legitimately could be classified as nonresidents"—those who do not intend to remain indefinitely in the district but currently reside there other than for the sole purpose of attending school—the State adopted a legitimate bona fide residence requirement. Justice Powell also found an "independent justification for local residence requirements in the public-school context" in the maintenance of school quality: "Absent residence requirements, . . . The proper planning and operation of the schools would suffer significantly."

Justice Brennan concurred separately "to stress that this case involves only a facial challenge." Justice Marshall dissented, concluding that "the statutory classification, which deprives some children of an education because of their motive for residing in Texas, is not adequately justified by the asserted state interests."

FINANCIAL INEQUALITY BETWEEN AND WITHIN SCHOOL DISTRICTS

In two decisions that distinguished *Rodriguez* and *Plyler,* respectively, the Court addressed further claims of impermissible state favoritism of some local school districts over others or of impermissible distinctions among students within school districts. Papasan v. Allain, 478 U.S. 265 (1986), involved a challenge to Mississippi's unequal distribution between the State's northern and southern counties of money derived from different assets the Federal Government had conveyed for the use of the State's schools. In the course of remanding the case to the lower courts to consider whether federal requirements or variations in local management responsibilities concerning the federal assets might provide a rational basis for the funding disparities, the Court noted that *Rodriguez* and *Plyler* had "not yet definitively settled . . . whether a minimally adequate education is a fundamental right and whether a statute alleged to discriminatorily infringe that right should be accorded heightened equal protection review." Those issues still did not have to be resolved, however, because the complaint did not allege facts supporting an assertion that the students had been denied a minimally adequate education. Nor, unlike *Rodriguez,* was "the overall organization of the Mississippi public school financing program" challenged. Instead, Justice White's majority opinion indicated that because Mississippi decided "to divide state resources unequally among school districts[,]" whereas the unequal financing in *Rodriguez* was "traceable to school district funds available from local real estate taxation," the "rationality of the disparity in *Rodriguez,*" which was based on "allowing meaningful local control over school funding, [did] not settle the constitutionality of disparities alleged in this case." A dissent by Justice Powell, joined by Chief Justice Burger and Justice Rehnquist, objected to the Court's remand. He emphasized that the federally derived funds "account for only 1 ½% of overall funds provided for schools" and argued that "[t]he Equal Protection Clause, at least in the context of state funding of schools, is concerned with *substance,* not with the *de minimis* variations of funding among the districts."

Kadrmas v. Dickinson Public Schools, 487 U.S. 450 (1988), involved a North Dakota law authorizing "nonreorganized" school districts to charge a fee for transporting students to school. A student who was refused bus service when her parents did not pay fees imposed by such a district challenged both the statute's authorization to charge a fee and its distinction between reorganized and nonreorganized districts. The Court, 5–4, rejected both challenges.

With respect to charging for bus service per se, Justice O'Connor's majority opinion declined to apply any form of " 'heightened' scrutiny[,]" whether the argument was "that the busing fee unconstitutionally places a greater obstacle to education in the path of the poor than it does in the path of wealthier families[,]" or "that the Equal Protection Clause affirmatively requires government to provide free transportation to school, at least for some class of students that would include Sarita Kadrmas." The Court declined to "extend" *Plyler* and did not find it controlling, as Kadrmas "has not been penalized by the government for illegal conduct by her parents" and the user fee did not threaten to create or perpetuate a sub-class of illiterates. Precedents holding "that government may not withhold certain especially important services from those . . . unable to pay for them" were also inapposite, because unlike those cases "the Kadrmas family could and did find a private alternative to the public school bus service for which Dickinson charged a fee." Because the "Constitution does not require that such service be provided at all," it sufficed that allowing "local school boards the option of charging patrons a user fee" rationally encouraged them "to provide school bus service."

The Court also upheld the rationality of the distinction between reorganized and nonreorganized school districts. Much of North Dakota being thinly populated, reorganized districts are those consolidated into larger districts and that thus entail larger distances from home to school. Under state law, reorganization plans must contain transportation provisions that only voter approval subsequently can change. The Court thought state law might allow a reorganized district to charge a transportation fee as well, so that the only "definitely established difference between reorganized and nonreorganized districts is this: in the latter, local school boards may impose a bus service user fee on their own authority, while the direct approval of the voters would be required in reorganized districts." Because "[t]hat difference . . . simply reflects voluntary agreements made during the history of North Dakota's reorganization process, . . . it could scarcely be thought to make the State's laws arbitrary or irrational." Even assuming reorganized districts were forbidden to charge for bus service, the Court thought it "evident that the legislature could conceivably have believed that such a policy would serve the legitimate purpose of fulfilling the reasonable expectations of those residing in districts with free busing arrangements imposed by reorganization plans"—a purpose having "no application to nonreorganized districts."

A dissent by Justice Marshall, joined by Justice Brennan, asserted that, for poor children, "imposing a fee for transportation is no different in practical effect from imposing a fee directly for education" and thus the case presented "the question whether a State may discriminate against the poor in providing access to education." In prior cases he discerned "a deep distrust of policies that specially burden the access of disadvantaged persons to the governmental institutions and processes that offer members of our society an opportunity to improve their status and better their lives." Citing *Plyler,* he noted the "intent of the Fourteenth Amendment ... to abolish caste legislation" and urged that "exacting scrutiny" be applied. He found *Plyler*'s "reasoning ... fully applicable[,]" because the State had "acted to burden the educational opportunities of a disadvantaged group of children, who need an education to become full participants in society." The State's fiscal interest in failing to exempt "indigent families from the busing fee" was "insubstantial" and could not justify the challenged discrimination.

In a separate dissent, Justice Stevens, joined by Justice Blackmun, argued that the distinction between reorganized and nonreorganized districts was irrational. Looking only to the "actual purpose of the geographic discrimination" identified by the North Dakota Supreme Court—to encourage reorganization "by alleviating parental concerns regarding the cost of student transportation in the reorganized district"—he thought it plain that "free bus transportation is an important component of public education in a sparsely populated State" and that "after the voters in a school district have had a fair opportunity to decide whether or not to reorganize, there is no longer any justification at all for allowing the nonreorganized districts to place an obstacle in the path of poor children seeking an education in some parts of the State that has been removed in other parts...."

CHAPTER 11

DEFINING THE SCOPE OF "LIBERTY" AND "PROPERTY" PROTECTED BY THE DUE PROCESS CLAUSE—THE PROCEDURAL DUE PROCESS CASES

Introduction. In Chapter 8 we examined whether the due process clause was intended to provide more than a requirement of fair procedure. In Chapter 9 we examined at length the substantive interests that are protected under the due process clause. The purpose of this chapter is to return to the issue of procedure in order to pursue the general question whether the interests protected by a requirement of fair procedure are the same as those protected by commands of fairness in substance. No attempt is made in this chapter to present a complete picture of the constitutional requirements of fair procedure in criminal, civil, and administrative proceedings. Those requirements are discussed at length in separate courses.

Section 1 deals with whether there is, or ought to be, a difference in the interests protected by "substantive" and "procedural" due process. The question arises in two contexts. First, is every interest that is given substantive protection also accorded procedural protection? Does a determination that a particular interest is "liberty" or "property" that is substantively protected (in the sense that the state must establish some reason for imposing a burden on it) carry with it a correlative right to some kind of a hearing in which it can be determined whether the particular burden is justified? Second, does the requirement of fair procedure extend beyond those interests given substantive protection by the Constitution? When government extends protection to an interest it is not constitutionally required to recognize, is there a constitutionally imposed right to a hearing in which it can be determined that the particular burden on the interest is justified? For example, if a state provides for the payment of welfare to persons meeting certain criteria, may it also provide for the removal of individual recipients from the welfare rolls without some form of a hearing in which it can be determined whether the recipients meet the statutory criteria?

A second problem is what constitutes "deprivation" of a protectible liberty or property interest, and a third relates to the nature and timing of the hearing required. To some degree decisions determining whether a hearing is required have been influenced by the timing and formality of the hearing contemplated. No attempt is made here to pursue this issue systematically, though a summary discussion is presented at the end of the cases in Section 1.

Section 2 presents the "irrebuttable presumption" cases that deal with the analytically separate question of the extent to which the due process clause limits the legislative power to classify by imposing a requirement of individualized hearings.

SECTION 1.   WHEN DOES DUE PROCESS MANDATE CONSTITUTIONAL PROCEDURES?

A.   WHAT "PROPERTY" AND "LIBERTY" IS PROTECTED?

Board of Regents of State Colleges v. Roth

408 U.S. 564, 92 S.Ct. 2701, 33 L.Ed.2d 548 (1972).

Mr. Justice Stewart delivered the opinion of the Court.

In 1968 the respondent, David Roth, was hired for his first teaching job as assistant professor of political science at Wisconsin State University–Oshkosh. He was hired for a fixed term of one academic year. The notice of his faculty appointment specified that his employment would begin on September 1, 1968, and would end on June 30, 1969. The respondent completed that term. But he was informed that he would not be rehired for the next academic year.

The respondent had no tenure rights to continued employment. Under Wisconsin statutory law a state university teacher can acquire tenure as a "permanent" employee only after four years of year-to-year employment. Having acquired tenure, a teacher is entitled to continued employment "during efficiency and good behavior." A relatively new teacher without tenure, however, is under Wisconsin law entitled to nothing beyond his one-year appointment. There are no statutory or administrative standards defining eligibility for re-employment. State law thus clearly leaves the decision whether to rehire a nontenured teacher for another year to the unfettered discretion of University officials.

The procedural protection afforded a Wisconsin State University teacher before he is separated from the University corresponds to his job security. As a matter of statutory law, a tenured teacher cannot be "discharged except for cause upon written charges" and pursuant to certain procedures. A nontenured teacher, similarly, is protected to some extent *during* his one-year term. Rules promulgated by the Board of Regents provide that a nontenured teacher "dismissed" before the end of the year may have some opportunity for review of the "dismissal." But the Rules provide no real protection for a nontenured teacher who simply is not re-employed for the next year. He must be informed by February first "concerning retention or non-retention for the ensuing year." But "no reason for non-retention need be given. No review or appeal is provided in such case."

In conformance with these Rules, the President of Wisconsin State University–Oshkosh informed the respondent before February 1, 1969, that he would not be rehired for the 1969–1970 academic year. He gave the respondent no reason for the decision and no opportunity to challenge it at any sort of hearing.

The respondent then brought this action in a federal district court alleging that the decision not to rehire him for the next year infringed his Fourteenth Amendment rights. He attacked the decision both in substance and procedure. First, he alleged that the true reason for the decision was to punish him for certain statements critical of the University administration, and that it therefore violated his right to freedom of speech. Second, he alleged that the failure of University officials to give him notice of any reason for nonretention and an opportunity for a hearing violated his right to procedural due process of law.

The District Court granted summary judgment for the respondent on the procedural issue, ordering the University officials to provide him with reasons and a hearing. The Court of Appeals, with one judge dissenting, affirmed this partial summary judgment. We granted certiorari. The only question presented to us at this stage in the case is whether the respondent had a constitutional right to a statement of reasons and a hearing on the University's decision not to rehire him for another year. We hold that he did not.

I.

The requirements of procedural due process apply only to the deprivation of interests encompassed within the Fourteenth Amendment's protection of liberty and property. When protected interests are implicated the right to some kind of prior hearing is paramount. But the range of interests protected by procedural due process is not infinite.

. . .

"Liberty" and "property" are broad and majestic terms. They are among the "[g]reat [constitutional] concepts . . . purposely left to gather meaning from experience. . . . [T]hey relate to the whole domain of social and economic fact, and the statesmen who founded this Nation knew too well that only a stagnant society remains unchanged." National Ins. Co. v. Tidewater Co., 337 U.S. 582, 646 (Frankfurter, J., dissenting). For that reason the Court has fully and finally rejected the wooden distinction between "rights" and "privileges" that once seemed to govern the applicability of procedural due process rights. The Court has also made clear that the property interests protected by procedural due process extend well beyond actual ownership of real estate, chattels, or money. By the same token, the Court has required due process protection for deprivations of liberty beyond the sort of formal constraints imposed by the criminal process.

. . .

Yet, while the Court has eschewed rigid or formalistic limitations on the protection of procedural due process, it has at the same time observed certain boundaries. For the words "liberty" and "property" in the Due Process Clause of the Fourteenth Amendment must be given some meaning.

II.

. . .

There might be cases in which a State refused to re-employ a person under such circumstances that interests in liberty would be implicated. But this is not such a case.

The State, in declining to rehire the respondent, did not make any charge against him that might seriously damage his standing and associations in his community. It did not base the nonrenewal of his contract on a charge, for example, that he had been guilty of dishonesty, or immorality. Had it done so, this would be a different case. . . . In such a case, due process would accord an opportunity to refute the charge before University officials.[12] In the present

---

12. The purpose of such notice and hearing is to provide the person an opportunity to clear his name. Once a person has cleared his name at a hearing, his employer, of course, may remain free to deny him future employment for other reasons.

case, however, there is no suggestion whatever that the respondent's interest in his "good name, reputation, honor or integrity" is at stake.

Similarly, there is no suggestion that the State, in declining to reemploy the respondent, imposed on him a stigma or other disability that foreclosed his freedom to take advantage of other employment opportunities. The State, for example, did not invoke any regulations to bar the respondent from all other public employment in State universities. Had it done so, this, again, would be a different case....

To be sure, the respondent has alleged that the non-renewal of his contract was based on his exercise of his right to freedom of speech. But this allegation is not now before us. The District Court stayed proceedings on this issue, and the respondent has yet to prove that the decision not to rehire him was, in fact, based on his free speech activities.[14]

Hence, on the record before us, all that clearly appears is that the respondent was not rehired for one year at one University. It stretches the concept too far to suggest that a person is deprived of "liberty" when he simply is not rehired in one job but remains as free as before to seek another....

III.

The Fourteenth Amendment's procedural protection of property is a safeguard of the security of interests that a person has already acquired in specific benefits. These interests—property interests—may take many forms.

. . .

Certain attributes of "property" interests protected by procedural due process emerge from these decisions. To have a property interest in a benefit, a person clearly must have more than an abstract need or desire for it. He must have more than a unilateral expectation of it. He must, instead, have a legitimate claim of entitlement to it. It is a purpose of the ancient institution of property to protect those claims upon which people rely in their daily lives, reliance that must not be arbitrarily undermined. It is a purpose of the constitutional right to a hearing to provide an opportunity for a person to vindicate those claims.

Property interests, of course, are not created by the Constitution. Rather, they are created and their dimensions are defined by existing rules or understandings that stem from an independent source such as state law—rules or understandings that secure certain benefits and that support claims of entitle-

---

14. ...

When a State would directly impinge upon interests in free speech or free press, this Court has on occasion held that opportunity for a fair adversary hearing must precede the action, whether or not the speech or press interest is clearly protected under substantive First Amendment standards. Thus we have required fair notice and opportunity for an adversary hearing before an injunction is issued against the holding of rallies and public meetings. Carroll v. Princess Anne, 393 U.S. 175. Similarly, we have indicated the necessity of procedural safeguards before a State makes a large-scale seizure of a per-

son's allegedly obscene books, magazines and so forth. A Quantity of Books v. Kansas, 378 U.S. 205; Marcus v. Search Warrant, 367 U.S. 717. See Freedman v. Maryland, 380 U.S. 51; Bantam Books v. Sullivan, 372 U.S. 58. See generally Monaghan, First Amendment "Due Process," 83 Harv.L.Rev. 518.

In the respondent's case, however, the State has not directly impinged upon interests in free speech or free press in any way comparable to a seizure of books or an injunction against meetings. Whatever may be a teacher's rights of free speech, the interest in holding a teaching job at a state university, *simpliciter*, is not itself a free speech interest.

ment to those benefits. Thus the welfare recipients in *Goldberg v. Kelly,* supra, had a claim of entitlement to welfare payments that was grounded in the statute defining eligibility for them. The recipients had not yet shown that they were, in fact, within the statutory terms of eligibility. But we held that they had a right to a hearing at which they might attempt to do so.

Just as the welfare recipients' "property" interest in welfare payments was created and defined by statutory terms, so the respondent's "property" interest in employment at the Wisconsin State University–Oshkosh was created and defined by the terms of his appointment. Those terms secured his interest in employment up to June 30, 1969. But the important fact in this case is that they specifically provided that the respondent's employment was to terminate on June 30. They did not provide for contract renewal absent "sufficient cause." Indeed, they made no provision for renewal whatsoever.

Thus the terms of the respondent's appointment secured absolutely no interest in re-employment for the next year. They supported absolutely no possible claim of entitlement to re-employment. Nor, significantly, was there any state statute or University rule or policy that secured his interest in re-employment or that created any legitimate claim to it.[16] In these circumstances, the respondent surely had an abstract concern in being rehired, but he did not have a *property* interest sufficient to require the University authorities to give him a hearing when they declined to renew his contract of employment.

IV.

. . .

... [T]he respondent has not shown that he was deprived of liberty or property protected by the Fourteenth Amendment. The judgment of the Court of Appeals, accordingly, is reversed and the case is remanded for further proceedings consistent with this opinion.

It is so ordered.

Mr. Justice Marshall, dissenting.

. . .

In my view, every citizen who applies for a government job is entitled to it unless the government can establish some reason for denying the employment. This is the "property" right that I believe is protected by the Fourteenth Amendment and that cannot be denied "without due process of law." And it is also liberty—liberty to work—which is the "very essence of the personal freedom and opportunity" secured by the Fourteenth Amendment.

. . .

It may be argued that to provide procedural due process to all public employees or prospective employees would place an intolerable burden on the machinery of government. Cf. Goldberg v. Kelly, supra. The short answer to that argument is that it is not burdensome to give reasons when reasons exist. Whenever an application for employment is denied, an employee is discharged, or a decision not to rehire an employee is made, there should be some reason

---

16. To be sure, the respondent does suggest that most teachers hired on a year-to-year basis by the Wisconsin State University–Oshkosh are, in fact, rehired. But the District Court has not found that there is anything approaching a "common law" of re-employment, see Perry v. Sindermann, post, at 602, so strong as to require University officials to give the respondent a statement of reasons and a hearing on their decision not to rehire him.

for the decision. It can scarcely be argued that government would be crippled by a requirement that the reason be communicated to the person most directly affected by the government's action.

Where there are numerous applicants for jobs, it is likely that few will choose to demand reasons for not being hired. But, if the demand for reasons is exceptionally great, summary procedures can be devised that would provide fair and adequate information to all persons. As long as the government has a good reason for its actions it need not fear disclosure. It is only where the government acts improperly that procedural due process is truly burdensome. And that is precisely when it is most necessary....[a]

AMERICAN MANUFACTURERS MUTUAL INSURANCE CO. v. SULLIVAN, 526 U.S. 40 (1999). Amendments to Pennsylvania's Workers' Compensation scheme created a "utilization review" procedure that allows insurers to request review of the "reasonableness and necessity" of medical treatment for injured employees before having to pay their medical bills. Rejecting a claim "that medical benefits are a state-created entitlement, and thus an insurer cannot withhold payment of medical benefits without affording an injured worker due process[,]" the Court reasoned as follows:

"... Under Pennsylvania law, an employee is not entitled to payment for *all* medical treatment once the employer's initial liability is established, as respondents' argument assumes. Instead, the law expressly limits an employee's entitlement to 'reasonable' and 'necessary' medical treatment, and requires that disputes over the reasonableness and necessity of particular treatment must be resolved *before* an employer's obligation to pay—and an employee's entitlement to benefits—arise.... Thus, for an employee's property interest in the payment of medical benefits to attach under state law, the employee must clear two hurdles: First, he must prove that an employer is liable for a work-related injury, and second, he must establish that the particular medical treatment at issue is reasonable and necessary. Only then does the employee's interest parallel that of the beneficiary of welfare assistance in *Goldberg [v. Kelly*, 397 U.S. 254 (1970),] and the recipient of disability benefits in *Mathews [v. Eldridge*, 424 U.S. 319 (1976)].

"... While [respondents] indeed have established their initial *eligibility* for medical treatment, they have yet to make good on their claim that the particular medical treatment they received was reasonable and necessary. Consequently, they do not have a property interest—under the logic of their

---

a. Dissenting opinions by Justice Douglas and Brennan are omitted. Justice Powell took no part in the decision.

In Perry v. Sindermann, 408 U.S. 593 (1972) a teacher's employment was terminated without notice of reasons or hearing after being employed by the college for four successive years under a series of one-year contracts. In his suit he alleged that the decision not to rehire him was based on his public criticism of policies of the college administration and thus infringed his right to free speech and that the failure to give him notice and hearing violated procedural due process. The trial court granted summary judgment for the defendant college on the basis of affidavits denying that plaintiff's criticism was involved and asserting no need to provide a hearing. The Court held that this decision was in error for two reasons: (1)

Plaintiff was entitled to a full hearing on his free speech claim because "a teacher's public criticism of his superiors on matters of public concern may be constitutionally protected and may, therefore, be an impermissible basis for termination of his employment." (2) Plaintiff was also entitled to a hearing on his allegation that he had in fact some form of tenure under the practices of the college. There "may be an unwritten 'common law' in a particular university that certain employees shall have the equivalent of tenure." Plaintiff was entitled to show whether that existed in this case and, if it did, he would be entitled to an order obligating college officials to give him a hearing.

See Simon, *Liberty and Property in the Supreme Court: A Defense of Roth and Perry*, 71 Calif.L.Rev. 146 (1983).

own argument—in having their providers paid for treatment that has yet to be found reasonable and necessary. . . .

"Having concluded that respondents' due process claim falters for lack of a property interest in the payment of benefits, we need go no further. . . . [13]"

Justice Ginsburg "join[ed] Part III of the Court's opinion on the understanding that the Court rejects specifically, and only, respondents' demands for constant payment of each medical bill, within 30 days of receipt, pending determination of the necessity or reasonableness of the medical treatment. See *ante*, n. 13. I do not doubt, however, that due process requires fair procedures for the adjudication of respondents' claims for workers' compensation benefits, including medical care."

Justice Breyer, joined by Justice Souter, also "agree[d] with Part III insofar as it rejects respondents' facial attack on the statute and also points out that respondents 'do not contend that they have a property interest in their claims for payment, as distinct from the payments themselves.' *Ante*, n. 13. I would add, however, that there may be individual circumstances in which the receipt of earlier payments leads an injured person reasonably to expect their continuation, in which case that person may well possess a constitutionally protected 'property' interest. See, e.g., Board of Regents of State Colleges v. Roth, 408 U.S. 564, 577 (1972). . . ."

Justice Stevens, concurring in part and dissenting in part, remarked:

"Because the individual respondents suffered work-related injuries, they are entitled to have their employers, or the employers' insurers, pay for whatever 'reasonable' and 'necessary' treatment they may need. . . . That right—whether described as a 'claim' for payment or a 'cause of action'—is unquestionably a species of property protected by the Due Process Clause of the Fourteenth Amendment. . . . Because the resolution of . . . disputes [over the reasonableness or necessity of particular treatments] determines the scope of the claimants' property interests, the Constitution requires that the procedure be fair. . . . It is equally clear that the State's duty to establish and administer a fair procedure for resolving the dispute obtains whether the dispute is initiated by the filing of a claim or by an insurer's decision to withhold payment until the reasonableness issue is resolved."

LAW THAT DEFINES SUBSTANTIVE ENTITLEMENTS TOGETHER WITH PROCEDURAL QUALIFICATIONS

Not long after *Roth* and *Sindermann*, the Court divided over the proper treatment of statutes that simultaneously appeared to create legitimate expectations of continued employment absent some kind of cause for dismissal and limited procedures for determining the existence of such cause. Should the entitlement provisions be thought to stand alone as creating a "property" interest whose deprivation required procedural protections mandated by the Due Process clauses? Or should the procedural qualification provisions be understood to define a more circumscribed "property" interest whose deprivation only required compliance with the requirements of the entitlement granting law?

13. Respondents do not contend that they have a property interest in their claims for payment, as distinct from the payments themselves, such that the State, the argument goes, could not finally reject their claims without affording them appropriate procedural protections.

In Arnett v. Kennedy, 416 U.S. 134 (1974), six Justices writing in separate concurring and dissenting opinions, seemed to take the former approach. In Bishop v. Wood, 426 U.S. 341 (1976), four of those dissented from a majority's decision that a discharged policeman was not deprived "of a property interest protected by the Fourteenth Amendment." Justice Stevens' majority opinion concluded that a "tenable" interpretation of state law by the lower federal courts was that the local ordinance, which provided that a permanent employee could be discharged for failing to perform work up to the standard of his classification, or for negligence, inefficiency or unfitness, might "be construed as granting no right to continued employment but merely conditioning an employee's removal on compliance with certain specified procedures" and thus "that petitioner 'held his position at the will and pleasure of the city.'" On that construction *Arnett* was irrelevant, the Court said, for there "the Court concluded that because the employee could only be discharged for cause, he had a property interest . . . entitled to constitutional protection."

Justice White's dissent, joined by Justices Brennan, Marshall and Blackmun, thought *Arnett* indistinguishable, for he understood the ordinance to contain "unequivocal language . . . that [petitioner] may be dismissed only for certain kinds of cause[,]" so that the majority's holding "rests . . . on the fact that state law provides no *procedures* for assuring that the City Manager dismiss him only for cause. The right to his job apparently given by the first two sentences of the ordinance is thus redefined, according to the majority, by the procedures provided for in the third sentence and as redefined is infringed only if the procedures are not followed." In a footnote, Justice White said that he did "not disagree with the majority or the courts below on the meaning of the state law"—that "as a matter of state law petitioner has no remedy no matter how arbitrarily or erroneously the City Manager has acted." Rather, "I differ . . . only with respect to the constitutional significance of an unambiguous state law. A majority of the Justices in Arnett v. Kennedy . . . stood on the proposition that the Constitution required procedures *not* required by state law when the state conditions dismissal on 'cause.'"

Nearly a decade later, the Court addressed this problem more definitively in the following case.

CLEVELAND BOARD OF EDUCATION v. LOUDERMILL, 470 U.S. 532 (1985). An Ohio statute provided that classified civil service employees were entitled to retain their positions "during good behavior and efficient service" and could not be dismissed except for "misfeasance, malfeasance, or nonfeasance in office." It also required that an employee dismissed for cause be provided with an order of removal giving the reasons therefor and allowed an appeal to a state administrative board whose judgment could be reviewed in the state trial court.

A state security guard stated on his job application that he had never been convicted of a felony. Several months after he was hired the Board of Education discovered that he had been convicted of grand larceny, discharged him, and gave him a letter stating this reason. He appealed to the Civil Service Commission, which upheld his dismissal. He then filed this case in the federal district court, arguing that the state statute was unconstitutional on its face because it did not give him a chance to respond to charges before dismissal. A bus mechanic fired by the Parma Board of Education after failing an eye examination filed a similar suit after the Civil Service Commission ordered his reinstatement but without back pay. The district court rejected both claims, but the court of appeals reversed and the Supreme Court affirmed.

Justice White's opinion for the Court said:

"... The statute plainly supports the conclusion, reached by both lower courts, that respondents possessed property rights in continued employment....

"The Parma Board argues, however, that the property right is defined by, and conditioned on, the legislature's choice of procedures for its deprivation.... The procedures were adhered to in these cases. According to petitioner, '[t]o require additional procedures would in effect expand the scope of the property interest itself'....

"This argument ... has its genesis in the plurality opinion in *Arnett v. Kennedy*.... *Arnett* involved a challenge by a former federal employee to the procedures by which he was dismissed. The plurality reasoned that where the legislation conferring the substantive right also sets out the procedural mechanism for enforcing that right, the two cannot be separated:

'The employee's statutorily defined right is not a guarantee against removal without cause in the abstract, but such a guarantee as enforced by the procedures which Congress has designated for the determination of cause.

  . . .

'... [W]here the grant of a substantive right is inextricably intertwined with the limitations on the procedures which are to be employed in determining that right, a litigant in the position of appellee must take the bitter with the sweet.' ...

After pointing out that six Justices in *Arnett* had specifically rejected this view and discussing subsequent cases, Justice White wrote:

"In light of these holdings, it is settled that the 'bitter with the sweet' approach misconceives the constitutional guarantee. If a clearer holding is needed, we provide it today. The point is straightforward: the Due Process Clause provides that certain substantive rights—life, liberty, and property—cannot be deprived except pursuant to constitutionally adequate procedures. The categories of substance and procedure are distinct. Were the rule otherwise, the Clause would be reduced to a mere tautology. 'Property' cannot be defined by the procedures provided for its deprivation any more than can life or liberty. The right to due process 'is conferred, not be legislative grace, but by constitutional guarantee. While the legislature may elect not to confer a property interest in [public] employment, it may not constitutionally authorize the deprivation of such an interest, once conferred, without appropriate procedural safeguards.' Arnett v. Kennedy, supra, 416 U.S., at 167 (Powell, J., concurring in part and concurring in result in part); see id., at 185 (White, J., concurring in part and dissenting in part).

"In short, once it is determined that the Due Process Clause applies, 'the question remains what process is due.' Morrissey v. Brewer, 408 U.S. 471, 481 (1972). The answer to that question is not to be found in the Ohio statute."

The Court then held that an employee must have some kind of hearing before discharge when he has a constitutionally protected property interest in his employment. But when a full administrative hearing and judicial review is available after termination, the employee does not have a right to a full adversarial evidentiary hearing before discharge. "The tenured public employee is entitled to oral or written notice of the charges against him, an explanation of the employer's evidence, and an opportunity to present his side of the story.... To require more than this prior to termination would intrude to an unwarranted extent on the government's interest in quickly removing an unsatisfactory employee."

Justice Marshall argued that the employee should receive a full adversarial evidentiary pre-termination hearing.

Justice Rehnquist dissented alone on the issue raised in *Arnett:*

"We ought to recognize the totality of the State's definition of the property right in question, and not merely seize upon one of several paragraphs in a unitary statute to proclaim that in that paragraph the State has inexorably conferred upon a civil service employee something which it is powerless under the United States Constitution to qualify in the next paragraph of the statute. This practice ignores our duty under *Roth* to rely on state law as the source of property interests for purposes of applying the Due Process Clause of the Fourteenth Amendment. While it does not impose a federal definition of property, the Court departs from the full breadth of the holding in *Roth* by its selective choice from among the sentences the Ohio legislature chooses to use in establishing and qualifying a right."

THE INTERRELATIONSHIPS OF SUBSTANTIVE AND PROCEDURAL DUE PROCESS

What is the relationship between the constitutional requirements of "fair substance" and "fair procedure"? In theory, the procedural requirement is conceptually distinct from any constitutional limit on the substance of government policy.

Hearings reinforce the rule of law by insuring official regularity and minimizing the scope for arbitrary decision-making. The procedural requirement may also serve, however, as a means for forcing the state to take more seriously than it might otherwise the substantive issues at stake. In Fuentes v. Shevin, 407 U.S. 67 (1972), the Court held invalid a state law which permitted summary seizure of property under a writ of replevin without prior notice or hearing to the possessor of the property. As part of its justification for requiring a prior hearing the Court said:

"The constitutional right to be heard is a basic aspect of the duty of government to follow a fair process of decisionmaking when it acts to deprive a person of his possessions. The purpose of this requirement is not only to ensure abstract fair play to the individual. Its purpose, more particularly, is to protect his use and possession of property from arbitrary encroachment—to minimize substantively unfair or mistaken deprivations of property, a danger that is especially great when the State seizes goods simply upon the application of and for the benefit of a private party. So viewed, the prohibition against the deprivation of property without due process of law reflects the high value, embedded in our constitutional and political history, that we place on a person's right to enjoy what is his, free of governmental interference. See Lynch v. Household Finance Corp., 405 U.S. 538.

"The requirement of notice and an opportunity to be heard raises no impenetrable barrier to the taking of a person's possessions. But the fair process of decisionmaking that it guarantees works, by itself, to protect against arbitrary deprivation of property. For when a person has an opportunity to speak up in his own defense, and when the State must listen to what he has to say, substantively unfair and simply mistaken deprivations of property interests can be prevented."

The problem of distinguishing substance and procedure is most complex where the state provides benefits it is not constitutionally compelled to provide. What are the procedural requirements, if any, when the state discharges an employee or terminates welfare benefits? Three situations must be distinguished:

(1) The state in creating the benefit also creates standards to govern its termination. For example, a state provides that certain government employees can be discharged only for "good cause". Even though the government is not obligated to provide the job, is it required by procedural due process to provide a fair hearing in applying its own standards to take a job away?

(2) The state in creating the benefit provides that it may be taken away at will. For example, a state provides that particular government employees may be fired in their superiors' discretion. The question now is whether the state may terminate a job in the unconstrained discretion of an administrative official. Is that question one of substantive due process? Or of procedural due process? If it is decided that the state can use standardless discretion to terminate the benefit, can there be any requirement of fair procedure? Or is the necessity for a hearing obviated in these situations because, as Justice Stevens observed in Codd v. Velger, 429 U.S. 624 (1977), "a hearing would [be] pointless because nothing plaintiff [can] prove [will] entitle him to keep his job"?

(3) The state creates the benefit, establishes standards to govern its termination, and provides the procedures to be used in determining whether the standards for termination have been met. If those procedures do not meet the minimum standards of fairness required by due process, will they be held invalid? *Loudermill* says yes. Can that be reconciled with the view that the state may avoid any hearing requirement when it authorizes standardless discretion for termination of employment?

Michael H. v. Gerald D.

491 U.S. 110, 109 S.Ct. 2333, 105 L.Ed.2d 91 (1989).

[The report in this case appears, supra at p. 603.]

Sandin v. Conner

515 U.S. 472, 115 S.Ct. 2293, 132 L.Ed.2d 418 (1995).

Chief Justice Rehnquist delivered the opinion of the Court.

We granted certiorari to reexamine the circumstances under which state prison regulations afford inmates a liberty interest protected by the Due Process Clause.

I

[While serving an indeterminate sentence of 30 years to life in a Hawaii prison, Conner reacted angrily to a strip-search and was charged with "high misconduct" for physical interference with a correctional function and "low moderate misconduct" for using abusive or obscene language and for harassing employees. An adjustment committee held a hearing at which Conner appeared but was not allowed to present witnesses. The committee found him guilty and sentenced him, inter alia, to 30 days disciplinary segregation for the physical obstruction charge. On appeal, months after serving this punishment, the deputy administrator found unsupported, and so expunged, the high misconduct charge. In the interim, Conner had sued in federal court, claiming that the refusal to allow him to present witnesses deprived him of procedural due process.] The District Court granted summary judgment in favor of the prison officials.

The Court of Appeals ... reversed.... It concluded that Conner had a liberty interest in remaining free from disciplinary segregation ... based ... on a prison regulation that instructs the committee to find guilt when a charge of misconduct is supported by substantial evidence.... [It] reasoned from Kentucky Department of Corrections v. Thompson, 490 U.S. 454 (1989), that the committee's duty to find guilt was nondiscretionary. From the language of the regulation, it drew a negative inference that the committee may not impose segregation if it does not find substantial evidence of misconduct.... It viewed this as a state-created liberty interest.... We ... reverse.

II

Our due process analysis begins with Wolff [v. McDonnell, 418 U.S. 539 (1974), where] Nebraska inmates challenged the decision of prison officials to revoke good time credits without adequate procedures.... Inmates earned good time credits under a state statute that bestowed mandatory sentence reductions for good behavior, ... revocable only for "flagrant or serious misconduct[.]" ... We held that the Due Process Clause itself does not create a liberty interest in credit for good behavior, but that the statutory provision created a liberty interest in a "shortened prison sentence" which resulted from good time credits, credits which were revocable only if the prisoner was guilty of serious misconduct.... The Court characterized this liberty interest as one of "real substance".…

Inmates in Meachum [v. Fano, 427 U.S. 215 (1976), challenged] transfers from a Massachusetts medium security prison to a maximum security facility with substantially less favorable conditions.... The Court began with the proposition that the Due Process Clause does not protect every change in the conditions of confinement having a substantial adverse impact on the prisoner. It then held that the Due Process Clause did not itself create a liberty interest in prisoners to be free from intrastate prison transfers.... It reasoned that transfer to a maximum security facility, albeit one with more burdensome conditions, was "within the normal limits or range of custody which the conviction has authorized the State to impose." ... The Court distinguished *Wolff* by noting that there the protected liberty interest in good time credit had been created by state law; here no comparable Massachusetts law stripped officials of the discretion to transfer prisoners to alternate facilities "for whatever reason or for no reason at all." ...

Shortly after *Meachum*, the Court embarked on a different approach to defining state-created liberty interests. Because dictum in *Meachum* distinguished *Wolff* by focusing on whether state action was mandatory or discretionary, the Court in later cases laid ever greater emphasis on this somewhat mechanical dichotomy....

[In Hewitt v. Helms, 459 U.S. 460 (1983), the Court] evaluat[ed] the claims of inmates who had been confined to administrative segregation[. I]t first rejected the inmates' claim of a right to remain in the general population.... The Due Process Clause standing alone confers no liberty interest in freedom from state action taken " 'within the sentence imposed[.]' " It then concluded that the transfer to less amenable quarters for nonpunitive reasons was "ordinarily contemplated by a prison sentence." ... Examination of the possibility that the State had created a liberty interest by virtue of its prison regulations followed. Instead of looking to whether the State created an interest of "real substance" comparable to the good time credit scheme of *Wolff*, the Court asked whether the State had gone beyond issuing mere procedural guidelines and had used "language of an unmistakably mandatory character" such that the incursion on liberty would not occur "absent specified substantive predicates." ... Finding such mandatory directives in the regulations before it, the Court decided that the State had created a protected liberty interest....

As this methodology took hold, no longer did inmates need to rely on a showing that they had suffered a " 'grievous loss' " of liberty retained even after sentenced to terms of imprisonment. Morrissey v. Brewer, 408 U.S. 471, 481 (1972).... For the Court had ceased to examine the "nature" of the interest with respect to interests allegedly created by the State.... In a series of cases since *Hewitt*, the Court has wrestled with the language of intricate, often rather routine prison guidelines to determine whether mandatory language and substantive predicates created an enforceable expectation that the state would produce a particular outcome with respect to the prisoner's conditions of confinement.

. . .

By shifting the focus of the liberty interest inquiry to one based on the language of a particular regulation, and not the nature of the deprivation, the Court encouraged prisoners to comb regulations in search of mandatory language on which to base entitlements to various state-conferred privileges. Courts have, in response, and not altogether illogically, drawn negative inferences from mandatory language in the text of prison regulations. The Court of Appeals' approach in this case is typical: it inferred from the mandatory directive that a finding of guilt "shall" be imposed under certain conditions the conclusion that the absence of such conditions prevents a finding of guilt.

Such a conclusion may be entirely sensible in the ordinary task of construing a statute defining rights and remedies available to the general public. It is a good deal less sensible in the case of a prison regulation primarily designed to guide correctional officials in the administration of a prison....

Hewitt has produced at least two undesirable effects. First, it creates disincentives for States to codify prison management procedures in the interest of uniform treatment.... States may avoid creation of "liberty" interests by having scarcely any regulations, or by conferring standardless discretion on correctional personnel.

Second, the *Hewitt* approach has led to the involvement of federal courts in the day-to-day management of prisons, often squandering judicial resources with little offsetting benefit to anyone....

[W]e believe that the search for a negative implication from mandatory language in prisoner regulations has strayed from the real concerns undergirding the liberty protected by the Due Process Clause. The time has come to return to the due process principles ... in *Wolff* and *Meachum*. Following *Wolff*, we recognize that States may under certain circumstances create liberty interests which are protected by the Due Process Clause. ... But these interests will be generally limited to freedom from restraint which, while not exceeding the sentence in such an unexpected manner as to give rise to protection by the Due Process Clause of its own force, see, e.g., Vitek, 445 U. S., at 493 (transfer to mental hospital), and Washington, 494 U. S., at 221–222 (involuntary administration of psychotropic drugs), nonetheless imposes atypical and significant hardship on the inmate in relation to the ordinary incidents of prison life.

Conner asserts, incorrectly, that any state action taken for a punitive reason encroaches upon a liberty interest under the Due Process Clause even in the absence of any state regulation. Neither Bell v. Wolfish, 441 U.S. 520 (1979), nor Ingraham v. Wright, 430 U.S. 651 (1977), requires such a rule. *Bell* dealt with the interests of pretrial detainees and not convicted prisoners....

... *Ingraham* ... addressed the rights of schoolchildren to remain free from arbitrary corporal punishment. The Court noted that the Due Process Clause historically encompassed the notion that the state could not "physically punish an individual except in accordance with due process of law" and so found schoolchildren sheltered....

The punishment of incarcerated prisoners, on the other hand, serves different aims than those found invalid in *Bell* and *Ingraham*. The process does not impose retribution in lieu of a valid conviction, nor does it maintain physical control over free citizens forced by law to subject themselves to state control over the educational mission. It effectuates prison management and prisoner rehabilitative goals.... Admittedly, prisoners do not shed all constitutional rights at the prison gate, ... but " '[l]awful incarceration brings about the necessary withdrawal or limitation of many privileges and rights, a retraction justified by the considerations underlying our penal system.' " ... Discipline by prison officials in response to a wide range of misconduct falls within the expected parameters of the sentence imposed by a court of law.

This case, though concededly punitive, does not present a dramatic departure from the basic conditions of Conner's indeterminate sentence. Although Conner points to dicta in cases implying that solitary confinement automatically triggers due process protection, ... this Court has not had the opportunity to address in an argued case the question whether disciplinary confinement of inmates itself implicates constitutional liberty interests. We hold that Conner's discipline in segregated confinement did not present the type of atypical, significant deprivation in which a state might conceivably create a liberty interest. The record shows that ... disciplinary segregation ... mirrored those conditions imposed upon inmates in administrative segregation and protective custody. We note also that the State expunged Conner's disciplinary record with respect to the "high misconduct" charge 9 months after Conner served time in segregation. Thus, Conner's confinement did not exceed similar, but totally discretionary confinement in either duration or degree of restriction.... Based on a comparison between inmates inside and outside disciplinary segregation, the State's actions in placing him there for 30 days did not work a major disruption in his environment.

Nor does Conner's situation present a case where the State's action will inevitably affect the duration of his sentence....

We hold, therefore, that neither the Hawaii prison regulation in question, nor the Due Process Clause itself, afforded Conner a protected liberty interest that would entitle him to the procedural protections set forth in *Wolff*. The regime to which he was subjected as a result of the misconduct hearing was within the range of confinement to be normally expected for one serving an indeterminate term of 30 years to life.

The judgment of the Court of Appeals is accordingly

Reversed.

Justice Ginsburg, with whom Justice Stevens joins, dissenting.

. . .

Unlike the Court, I conclude that Conner had a liberty interest, protected by the Fourteenth Amendment's Due Process Clause, in avoiding the disciplinary confinement he endured. As Justice Breyer details, Conner's prison punishment effected a severe alteration in the conditions of his incarceration. Disciplinary confinement as punishment for "high misconduct" not only deprives prisoners of privileges for protracted periods; unlike administrative segregation and protective custody, disciplinary confinement also stigmatizes them and diminishes parole prospects. Those immediate and lingering consequences should suffice to qualify such confinement as liberty-depriving for purposes of Due Process Clause protection....[1]

I see the Due Process Clause itself, not Hawaii's prison code, as the wellspring of the protection due Conner. Deriving protected liberty interests from mandatory language in local prison codes would make of the fundamental right something more in certain States, something less in others....[2]

Deriving the prisoner's due process right from the code for his prison, moreover, yields this practical anomaly: a State that scarcely attempts to control the behavior of its prison guards may, for that very laxity, escape constitutional accountability; a State that tightly cabins the discretion of its prison workers may, for that attentiveness, become vulnerable to constitutional claims. An incentive for ruleless prison management disserves the State's penological goals and jeopardizes the welfare of prisoners.

. . .

Justice Breyer, with whom Justice Souter joins, dissenting.

. . .

II

... In determining whether state officials have deprived an inmate ... of a procedurally protected "liberty," this Court traditionally has looked either (1) to the nature of the deprivation (how severe, in degree or kind) or (2) to the State's rules governing the imposition of that deprivation (whether they, in effect, give the inmate a "right" to avoid it). See, e.g., Kentucky Department of Corrections v. Thompson, 490 U.S. 454, 460–461, 464–465 (1989). Thus, this Court has said that certain changes in conditions may be so severe or so different from ordinary conditions of confinement that, whether or not state law gives state authorities broad discretionary power to impose them, the state authorities may not do so "without complying with minimum requirements of due process." Vitek v. Jones, 445 U.S. 480, 491–494 (1980) ("involuntary commitment to a mental hospital"); Washington v. Harper, 494 U.S. 210, 221–222 (1990) ("unwanted administration of antipsychotic drugs"). The Court has also said that deprivations that are less severe or more closely related to the original terms of confinement nonetheless will amount to deprivations of

---

1. ... The Court notes ... that the State eventually expunged Conner's disciplinary record as a result of his successful administrative appeal. But hindsight cannot tell us whether a liberty interest existed at the outset. One must ... know at the start the character of the interest at stake in order to determine then what process, if any, is constitutionally due....

2. The Court describes a category of liberty interest that is something less than the one the Due Process Clause itself shields, something more than anything a prison code provides. The State may create a liberty interest, the Court tells us, when "atypical and significant hardship [would be borne by] the inmate in relation to the ordinary incidents of prison life." What design lies beneath these key words? The Court ventures no examples, leaving consumers of the Court's work at sea, unable to fathom what would constitute an "atypical, significant deprivation" and yet not trigger protection under the Due Process Clause directly.

procedurally protected liberty, provided that state law (including prison regulations) narrowly cabins the legal power of authorities to impose the deprivation (thereby giving the inmate a kind of right to avoid it). See Hewitt v. Helms. . . .

If we apply these general pre-existing principles to the relevant facts before us, it seems fairly clear . . . that the prison punishment . . . deprived Conner of constitutionally protected "liberty." For one thing, the punishment worked a fairly major change in Conner's conditions. . . .

Moreover, irrespective of whether this punishment amounts to a deprivation of liberty independent of state law, here the prison's own disciplinary rules severely cabin the authority of prison officials to impose this kind of punishment. They . . . (1) impose a punishment that is substantial, (2) restrict its imposition as a punishment to instances in which an inmate has committed a defined offense, and (3) prescribe nondiscretionary standards for determining whether or not an inmate committed that offense.

Accordingly, under this Court's liberty-defining standards, imposing the punishment would "deprive" Conner of "liberty" within the meaning of the Due Process Clause. . . .

III

The majority . . . seeks to change, or to clarify, [those] "liberty" defining standards in one important respect[: by] . . . impos[ing] a minimum standard, namely that a deprivation falls within the Fourteenth Amendment's definition of "liberty" only if it "imposes atypical and significant hardship on the inmate in relation to the ordinary incidents of prison life."

I am not certain whether or not the Court means this standard to change prior law radically. . . . There is no need, however, for . . . significant change . . . to read the Constitution's Due Process Clause to protect inmates against deprivations of freedom that are important, not comparatively insignificant. Rather, . . . this concern simply requires elaborating, and explaining, the Court's present standards (without radical revision) [so as] not [to] create procedurally protected "liberty" interests where only minor matters are at stake.

Three sets of considerations, taken together, support my conclusion. . . . First, . . . it is not easy to specify just when, or how much of, a loss triggers . . . protection. There is a broad middle category of imposed restraints or deprivations that, considered by themselves, are neither obviously so serious as to fall within, nor obviously so insignificant as to fall without, the Clause's protection.

Second, the difficult line-drawing task that this middle category implies helps to explain why this Court developed its additional liberty-defining standard, which looks to local law (examining whether that local law creates a "liberty" by significantly limiting the discretion of local authorities to impose a restraint). . . . Despite its similarity to the way in which the Court determines the existence, or nonexistence, of "property" for Due Process Clause purposes, the justification for looking at local law is not the same in the prisoner liberty context. In protecting property, the Due Process Clause often aims to protect reliance, say, reliance upon an "entitlement" that local (i.e., nonconstitutional) law itself has created or helped to define. . . . In protecting liberty, however, the Due Process Clause protects . . . an absence of government restraint, the very absence of restraint that we call freedom. . . .

Nevertheless, there are several other important reasons, in the prison context, to consider the provisions of state law. The fact that a further deprivation of an inmate's freedom takes place under local rules that cabin the authorities' discretionary power to impose the restraint suggests, other things being equal, that the matter is more likely to have played an important role in the life of the inmate.... It suggests, other things being equal, that the matter is more likely of a kind to which procedural protections historically have applied, and where they normally prove useful, for such rules often single out an inmate and condition a deprivation upon the existence, or nonexistence, of particular facts.... It suggests, other things being equal, that the matter will not involve highly judgmental administrative matters that call for the wise exercise of discretion—matters where courts reasonably should hesitate to second-guess prison administrators.... It suggests, other things being equal, that the inmate will have thought that he himself, through control of his own behavior, could have avoided the deprivation, and thereby have believed that (in the absence of his misbehavior) the restraint fell outside the "sentence imposed" upon him.... Finally, courts can identify the presence or absence of cabined discretion fairly easily and objectively, at least much of the time.... These characteristics of "cabined discretion" mean that courts can use it as a kind of touchstone that can help them, when they consider the broad middle category of prisoner restraints, to separate those kinds of restraints that, in general, are more likely to call for constitutionally guaranteed procedural protection, from those that more likely do not.... I believe courts will continue to find this touchstone helpful as they seek to apply the majority's middle category standard.

Third, there is, therefore, no need to apply the "discretion-cabining" approach ... where a deprivation is unimportant enough (or so similar in nature to ordinary imprisonment) that it rather clearly falls outside that middle category.... [T]his Court has never held that comparatively unimportant prisoner "deprivations" fall within the scope of the Due Process Clause even if local law limits the authority of prison administrators to impose such minor deprivations.... And ... it should now simply specify that they do not.

I recognize that, as a consequence, courts must separate the unimportant from the potentially significant, without the help of the more objective "discretion-cabining" test. Yet, making that judicial judgment seems no more difficult than many other judicial tasks.... It seems to me possible to separate less significant matters such as television privileges ... from more significant matters, such as the solitary confinement at issue here. Indeed, prison regulations themselves may help in this respect, such as the regulations here which separate (from more serious matters) "low moderate" and "minor" misconduct....

[T]he problems that the majority identifies suggest ... mak[ing] explicit the lower definitional limit, in the prison context, of "liberty" under the Due Process Clause—a limit ... already implicit in this Court's precedent.... Th[ey] do not require abandoning that precedent....

IV

The Court today reaffirms that the "liberty" protected by the Fourteenth Amendment includes interests that state law may create. It excludes relatively minor matters from that protection.... And, it does not question the vast body of case law ... recognizing that segregation can deprive an inmate of constitutionally-protected "liberty." ... That being so, it is difficult to see why the Court reverses, rather than affirms, the Court of Appeals in this case.

. . .

I agree [that the] conditions in administrative and disciplinary segregation are relatively similar in Hawaii [and that] the rules governing administrative segregation do, indeed, provide prison officials with broad leeway. But, I disagree with the majority's assertion about the relevance of the expungement. How can a later decision of prison authorities transform Conner's segregation for a violation of a specific disciplinary rule into a term of segregation under the administrative rules? How can a later expungement restore to Conner the liberty that, in fact, he had already lost? . . .

In sum, expungement or no, Conner suffered a deprivation that was significant, not insignificant. And, that deprivation took place under disciplinary rules that . . . do cabin official discretion sufficiently. I would therefore hold that Conner was deprived of "liberty" within the meaning of the Due Process Clause.

. . .

WASHINGTON v. HARPER, 494 U.S. 210 (1990). A mentally ill but not incompetent prisoner challenged, *inter alia,* the state's failure to provide him with a judicial hearing before administering antipsychotic medication against his will. The Washington Supreme Court held that due process required this and other procedural safeguards. It also held that the substance of the state's policy violated due process, because it allowed forced medication of any inmate found to be mentally ill and "gravely disabled" or dangerous to himself, others or their property, without also requiring proof that the state has a compelling interest in administering the medication and that the administration of the drugs is necessary and effective to further that interest. The Supreme Court overturned both holdings. Justice Kennedy's majority opinion said, in part:

"The Washington Supreme Court's decision . . . has both substantive and procedural aspects. It is axiomatic that procedural protections must be examined in terms of the substantive rights at stake. But identifying the contours of the substantive right remains a task distinct from deciding what procedural protections are necessary to protect that right. '[T]he substantive issue involves a definition of th[e] protected constitutional interest, as well as identification of the conditions under which competing state interests might outweigh it. The procedural issue concerns the minimum procedures required by the Constitution for determining that the individual's liberty interest actually is outweighed in a particular instance.' . . .

"Restated in the terms of this case, the substantive issue is what factual circumstances must exist before the State may administer antipsychotic drugs to the prisoner against his will; the procedural issue is whether the State's nonjudicial mechanisms used to determine the facts in a particular case are sufficient. . . .

"As a matter of state law, the Policy itself undoubtedly confers . . . a right to be free from the arbitrary administration of antipsychotic drugs. . . . By permitting a psychiatrist to treat an inmate with antipsychotic drugs against his wishes only if he is found to be (1) mentally ill and (2) gravely disabled or dangerous, the Policy creates a justifiable expectation on the part of the inmate that the drugs will not be administered unless those conditions exist. . . .

"We have no doubt that, in addition to the liberty interest created by the State's Policy, respondent possesses a significant liberty interest in avoiding the unwanted administration of antipsychotic drugs under the Due Process Clause of the Fourteenth Amendment. . . . Upon full consideration of the administrative scheme, however, we find that the Due Process Clause confers upon respondent no greater right than that recognized under state law.

"Respondent contends that the State, under the mandate of the Due Process Clause, may not override his choice to refuse antipsychotic drugs unless he has been found to be incompetent, and then only if the factfinder makes a substituted judgment that he, if competent, would consent to drug treatment. We disagree. The extent of a prisoner's right ... must be defined in the context of the inmate's confinement. The Policy ... requires the State to establish, by a medical finding, that a mental disorder exists which is likely to cause harm if not treated. Moreover, the fact that the medication must first be prescribed by a psychiatrist, and then approved by a reviewing psychiatrist, ensures that the treatment in question will be ordered only if it is in the prisoner's medical interests, given the legitimate needs of his institutional confinement. These standards, which recognize both the prisoner's medical interests and the State's interests, meet the demands of the Due Process Clause.

"... [T]he proper standard for determining the validity of a prison regulation claimed to infringe on an inmate's constitutional rights is to ask whether the regulation is 'reasonably related to legitimate penological interests.' ... This is true even when the constitutional right claimed to have been infringed is fundamental, and the State under other circumstances would have been required to satisfy a more rigorous standard of review.... The [Washington Supreme Court] erred in refusing to apply the standard of reasonableness."

Applying the reasonableness standard, the Court held "that, given the requirements of the prison environment, the Due Process Clause permits the State to treat a prison inmate who has a serious mental illness with antipsychotic drugs against his will, if the inmate is dangerous to himself or others and the treatment is in the inmate's medical interest." Then, "[h]aving determined that state law recognizes a liberty interest, also protected by the Due Process Clause, which permits refusal of antipsychotic drugs unless certain preconditions are met," the Court addressed "what procedural protections are necessary to ensure the decision to medicate ... is neither arbitrary nor erroneous under the standards we have discussed above." Despite concluding that "[t]he forcible injection of medication into a nonconsenting person's body represents a substantial interference with that person's liberty" and that "[w]hile the therapeutic benefits of antipsychotic drugs are well documented, it is also true that the drugs can have serious, even fatal, side effects[,]" the Court held that a judicial hearing was unnecessary and that the particular administrative hearing procedures provided by the State satisfied procedural due process.

Justice Stevens dissented in an opinion joined by Justices Brennan and Marshall. He thought the majority had undervalued the liberty interest it had acknowledged:

"[T]he several dimensions of the liberty ... are both physical and intellectual. Every violation of a person's bodily integrity is an invasion of his or her liberty. The invasion is particularly intrusive if it creates a substantial risk of permanent injury and premature death. Moreover, any such action is degrading if it overrides a competent person's choice to reject a specific form of medical treatment. And when the purpose or effect of forced drugging is to alter the will and the mind of the subject, it constitutes a deprivation of liberty in the most literal and fundamental sense."

Justice Stevens had "no doubt ... that a competent individual's right to refuse such medication is a fundamental liberty interest deserving the highest order of protection." He found the state's policy invalid, because it "sweepingly sacrifices the inmate's substantive liberty interest to refuse psychotropic drugs, regardless of his medical interests, to institutional and administrative concerns." He also criticized the Court's opinion for failing to separate sufficiently the state's interest in institutional convenience from its interest in helping the inmate's medical condition. Finally, in view of the strength of the liberty interest implicated, he found the state's procedures constitutionally deficient for failing "to have the treatment decision made or reviewed by an impartial person or tribunal."

B.   WHAT CONSTITUTES A DEPRIVATION?

Daniels v. Williams

474 U.S. 327, 106 S.Ct. 662, 88 L.Ed.2d 662 (1986).

Justice Rehnquist delivered the opinion of the Court.

In Parratt v. Taylor, 451 U.S. 527 (1981), a state prisoner sued under 42 U.S.C. § 1983, claiming that prison officials had negligently deprived him of his property without due process of law. After deciding that § 1983 contains no independent state-of-mind requirement, we concluded that although petitioner had been "deprived" of property within the meaning of the Due Process Clause of the Fourteenth Amendment, the State's postdeprivation tort remedy provided the process that was due. Petitioner's claim in this case, which also rests on an alleged Fourteenth Amendment "deprivation" caused by the negligent conduct of a prison official, leads us to reconsider our statement in Parratt that "the alleged loss, even though negligently caused, amounted to a deprivation." . . . We conclude that the Due Process Clause is simply not implicated by a *negligent* act of an official causing unintended loss of or injury to life, liberty or property.

In this § 1983 action, petitioner seeks to recover damages for back and ankle injuries allegedly sustained when he fell on a prison stairway. He claims that, while an inmate at the city jail in Richmond, Virginia, he slipped on a pillow negligently left on the stairs by respondent, a correctional deputy stationed at the jail. Respondent's negligence, the argument runs, "deprived" petitioner of his "liberty" interest in freedom from bodily injury . . .; because respondent maintains that he is entitled to the defense of sovereign immunity in a state tort suit, petitioner is without an "adequate" state remedy. . . . Accordingly, the deprivation of liberty was without "due process of law."

. . .

In *Parratt,* before concluding that Nebraska's tort remedy provided all the process that was due, we said that the loss of the prisoner's hobby kit, "even though negligently caused, amounted to a deprivation [under the Due Process Clause]." . . . Justice Powell, concurring in the result, criticized the majority for "pass[ing] over" this important question of the state of mind required to constitute a "deprivation" of property. . . . He argued that negligent acts by state officials, though causing loss of property, are not actionable under the Due Process Clause. To Justice Powell, mere negligence could not "wor[k] a deprivation in the *constitutional sense.*" . . . Not only does the word "deprive" in the Due Process Clause connote more than a negligent act, but we should not "open the federal courts to lawsuits where there has been no affirmative abuse of power." . . . Upon reflection, we agree and overrule *Parratt* to the extent that it states that mere lack of due care by a state official may "deprive" an individual of life, liberty or property under the Fourteenth Amendment.

The Due Process Clause of the Fourteenth Amendment provides: "[N]or shall any State deprive any person of life, liberty, or property, without due process of law." Historically, this guarantee of due process has been applied to *deliberate* decisions of government officials to deprive a person of life, liberty or property.... No decision of this Court before *Parratt* supported the view that negligent conduct by a state official, even though causing injury, constitutes a deprivation under the Due Process Clause. This history reflects the traditional and common-sense notion that the Due Process Clause, like its forebear in the Magna Carta, ... was " 'intended to secure the individual from the arbitrary exercise of the powers of government,' " Hurtado v. California, 110 U.S. 516, 527 (1884). By requiring the government to follow appropriate procedures when its agents decide to "deprive any person of life, liberty, or property," the Due Process Clause promotes fairness in such decisions. And by barring certain government actions regardless of the fairness of the procedures used to implement them, ... it serves to prevent governmental power from being "used for purposes of oppression," Murray's Lessee v. Hoboken Land & Improvement Co., 59 U.S. (18 How.) 272, 277 (1856) (discussing Due Process Clause of Fifth Amendment).

We think that the actions of prison custodians in leaving a pillow on the prison stairs, or mislaying an inmate's property, are quite remote from the concerns just discussed. Far from an abuse of power, lack of due care suggests no more than a failure to measure up to the conduct of a reasonable person. To hold that injury caused by such conduct is a deprivation within the meaning of the Fourteenth Amendment would trivialize the centuries-old principle of due process of law.

... Our Constitution deals with the large concerns of the governors and the governed, but it does not purport to supplant traditional tort law in laying down rules of conduct to regulate liability for injuries that attend living together in society. We have previously rejected reasoning that "would make of the Fourteenth Amendment a font of tort law to be superimposed upon whatever systems may already be administered by the States," Paul v. Davis, 424 U.S. 693, 701 (1976), quoted in Parratt v. Taylor, 451 U.S., at 544.

The only tie between the facts of this case and anything governmental in nature is the fact that respondent was a sheriff's deputy at the Richmond city jail and petitioner was an inmate confined in that jail. But while the Due Process Clause of the Fourteenth Amendment obviously speaks to some facets of this relationship, see e.g., Wolff v. McDonnell, 418 U.S. 539 (1974), we do not believe its protections are triggered by lack of due care by prison officials. "Medical malpractice does not become a constitutional violation merely because the victim is a prisoner," Estelle v. Gamble, 429 U.S. 97, 106 (1976), and "false imprisonment does not become a violation of the Fourteenth Amendment merely because the defendant is a state official." Baker v. McCollan, 443 U.S. 137, 146 (1979). Where a government official's act causing injury to life, liberty or property is merely negligent, "no procedure for compensation is *constitutionally* required." *Parratt,* 451 U.S., at 548 (Powell, J., concurring in result) (emphasis added.)[1]

That injuries inflicted by governmental negligence are not addressed by the United States Constitution is not to say that they may not raise significant legal concerns and lead to the creation of protectible legal interests. The enactment of tort claim statutes, for example, reflects the view that injuries caused by such negligence should generally be redressed. It is no reflection on

---

1. Accordingly, we need not decide whether, as petitioner contends, the possibility of a sovereign immunity defense in a Virginia tort suit would render that remedy "inadequate" under *Parratt* and Hudson v. Palmer, 468 U.S. 517 (1984).

either the breadth of the United States Constitution or the importance of traditional tort law to say that they do not address the same concerns.

In support of his claim that negligent conduct can give rise to a due process "deprivation," petitioner makes several arguments, none of which we find persuasive . . . .[3]

. . .

Affirmed.

Justice Marshall concurs in the result.

Justice Blackmun, concurring in the judgment.

I concur in the result . . . .[a]

DAVIDSON v. CANNON, 474 U.S. 344 (1986), was a companion case to Daniels v. Williams. A prisoner sent a note to prison authorities reporting a threat from another prisoner. The note was put aside and forgotten, and the prisoner was assaulted. Justice Rehnquist's opinion for the Court treated the prisoner's § 1983 suit as involving simple negligence by prison officials, which, under *Daniels,* did not implicate due process concerns. "respondents' lack of due care in this case led to serious injury, but that lack of care simply does not approach the sort of abusive government conduct that the Due Process Clause was designed to prevent."

Justice Brennan dissented. He took the view "that official conduct which causes personal injury due to recklessness or deliberate indifference, does deprive the victim of liberty within the meaning of the Fourteenth Amendment[,]" and he urged a remand for review of "the District Court's holding that respondents' conduct was not reckless."

Justice Blackmun also dissented, joined by Justice Marshall. In addition to agreeing with Justice Brennan's position, he argued that "[i]n some cases . . . governmental negligence is an abuse of power." In particular, "when a State assumes sole responsibility for one's physical security and then ignores his call for help," due process is implicated. "In the context of prisons, this means that once the State has taken away an inmate's means of protecting himself from attack by other inmates, a prison official's negligence in providing protection can amount to a deprivation of the inmate's liberty, at least absent extenuating circumstances."

Justice Stevens concurred in the judgments in both *Daniels* and *Davidson* on the ground that in each case the state had provided adequate procedures for the vindication of the plaintiff's claims. But he rejected the conclusion that due process was not required for official negligence. He wrote:

"... 'Deprivation,' ... identifies, not the actor's state of mind, but the victim's infringement or loss. The harm to a prisoner is the same whether a pillow is left negligently, recklessly, or intentionally; so too, the harm resulting to a prisoner from an attack is the same whether his request for protection is ignored negligently, recklessly, or deliberately. In each instance, the prisoner is losing—being 'deprived' of—an aspect of liberty as the result, in part, of a form of state action."

3. [P]etitioner concedes that respondent was at most negligent. Accordingly, this case affords us no occasion to consider whether something less than intentional conduct, such as recklessness or "gross negligence," is enough to trigger the protections of the Due Process Clause.

a. An opinion by Justice Stevens concurring in the judgment in this case and in *Davidson v. Cannon* is omitted here but described below.

C.   WHAT PROCESS IS DUE AND WHEN?

The determination that due process requires compliance with procedural safeguards before government deprives a person of a protected interest triggers a further inquiry into what the timing and nature of the constitutionally required procedures must be. Those often complex questions cannot be explored in depth here, but some flavor of the kinds of considerations that are implicated may be gathered from a brief discussion.

As the Court indicated in Parratt v. Taylor, 451 U.S. 527 (1981), "[t]he fundamental requirement of due process is the opportunity to be heard and it is an 'opportunity which must be granted at a meaningful time and in a meaningful manner.'" As to timing, this normally but not always means that the opportunity must be made available before the deprivation occurs. *Parratt* reaffirmed that due process necessitates "some kind of hearing ... at some time before a State finally deprives a person of his property interests," but it held that "either the necessity of quick action by the State or the impracticability of providing any meaningful predeprivation process can, when coupled with the availability of some meaningful means by which to assess the propriety of the State's action at some time after the initial taking, satisfy the requirements of procedural due process." As applied in *Parratt,* the impracticality of requiring a predeprivation hearing before prison officials negligently lost an inmate's property in an unauthorized random act, together with the availability of a state postdeprivation tort remedy for damages, satisfied the demands of due process. (As Daniels v. Williams, supra p. 1116, indicates, *Parratt* had assumed that negligent loss of a prisoner's hobby kit amounted to a "deprivation.")

Parratt's willingness to accept a subsequent judicial tort remedy in place of a predeprivation hearing was extended in Hudson v. Palmer, 468 U.S. 517 (1984), to random and unauthorized, but intentional, deprivations of property—in that case the intentional destruction by prison officials of a prisoner's property during a search. The Court said that the underlying rationale was the same for both negligent and intentional acts: "[W]hen deprivations of property are effected through random and unauthorized conduct of a state employee, predeprivation procedures are simply 'impracticable' since the state cannot know when such deprivations will occur." Accordingly, a subsequent intentional tort remedy against the employee satisfied due process. The Court also held, however, that the ability to obtain relief in a subsequent independent tort action does not justify omitting a predeprivation hearing when deprivation of a protected interest results from some established state procedure rather than from a state employee's random and unauthorized act. Logan v. Zimmerman Brush Co., 455 U.S. 422 (1982). See generally, Smolla, *The Displacement of Federal Due Process Claims by State Tort Remedies: Parratt v. Taylor and Logan v. Zimmerman Brush Company,* 1982 U.Ill.L.Rev. 831.

A postdeprivation damages remedy also was held insufficient to satisfy due process in Zinermon v. Burch, 494 U.S. 113 (1990), a suit by a person who, after having been found disoriented and hurt, was admitted to a mental health care facility and detained for five months, pursuant to state procedures for consenting, "voluntary" treatment of the mentally ill. He claimed that the hospital staff knew or should have known that he was incapable of voluntary, understanding informed consent and that they wilfully and recklessly deprived him of his liberty without due process by not following the state's more elaborate procedures for "involuntary" admission and treatment. The Court rejected the categorical contention that deprivations of liberty always require a predeprivation hearing, observing that "the reasoning of *Parratt* and *Hudson* emphasizes the State's inability to provide predeprivation process because of the random and unpredictable nature of the deprivation, not the fact that only property losses were at stake." But the Court also held those cases distinguishable for three reasons. First, the liberty deprivation was predictable, because "[i]t is hardly unforeseeable that a person requesting treatment for mental illness might be incapable of informed consent, and that state officials with the power to admit patients might take their apparent willingness to be admitted at face value and not initiate involuntary placement procedures." Second, predeprivation process was possible by having the State limit and guide the power to admit patients so that the established procedures for involuntary admission are afforded not only to "those who are unwilling" but also "those who are unable to give consent." Third, the staff's conduct was not "unauthorized" in the same sense as in *Parratt* and *Hudson,* because "[t]he State delegated to them the power and authority to effect the very deprivation complained of here . . . and also delegated to them the concomitant duty to initiate the procedural safeguards set up by state law to guard against unlawful confinement." Four Justices dissented, taking the view that since Burch had not attacked the state's commitment procedures, but only the staff's reckless and wanton failure to employ them, the allegations amounted to the same kind of unpredictable, wrongful departure from established state policy for which a postdeprivation tort action satisfied due process under *Parratt* and *Hudson.*

The procedural demands of due process not only raise issues of timing, but also of the nature of the hearing that must be provided in different contexts, ranging from what kind of notice is needed, to whether counsel and a judicial or less formal decisionmaker are required, to whether informal process on written submissions or more formal proceedings involving the availability of oral and evidentiary presentation and rights of confrontation and cross-examination is the minimum process due. The Court's classic general formulation of what is required in particular contexts is found in Mathews v. Eldridge, 424 U.S. 319 (1976), which said "that identification of the specific dictates of due process generally requires consideration of three distinct factors: First, the private interest that will be affected by the official action; second, the risk of an erroneous deprivation of such interest through the procedures used, and the probable value, if any, of additional or substitute procedural safeguards; and finally, the Government's interest, including the function involved and the fiscal and administrative burdens that the additional or substitute procedural requirement would entail." For a general critique, see Mashaw, *Due Process in the Administrative State* (1985). For a sharply contested application of the *Mathews* approach in the context of the process that must be made available to citizens seeking to challenge their indefinite detention pursuant to Presidential designation as "enemy combatants," see Hamdi v. Rumsfeld, supra p. 404.

SECTION 2.   PROCEDURAL DUE PROCESS AND IRREBUTTABLE PRESUMPTIONS

Introduction. In Vance v. Bradley, 440 U.S. 93 (1979), the Court had before it a challenge under the equal protection clause to a statute requiring all foreign service officers to retire at age 60. In upholding the age classification the Court found it rational because Congress could reasonably believe that *many* employees at age 60 would be unfit to perform some of the tasks required of foreign service officers.

The cases in this section raise a potentially separate constitutional challenge to a classification such as that in *Bradley*. Congress could not reasonably believe that *all* employees were unfit at age 60. Can the due process clause then be read to require an individual hearing for each foreign service employee on the question of that employee's fitness? Or does the resolution of the equal protection issue limit the hearing right to the issue whether the employee has attained age 60?

Would the question be different if the statute read that all foreign service officers shall be subject to compulsory retirement when they become unfit to perform the relevant tasks and that it shall be conclusively presumed that any officer 60 years of age or older is unfit? Does casting the statute in that form give each employee who is retired at age 60 a due process right to a hearing on the issue of fitness?

Vlandis v. Kline

412 U.S. 441, 93 S.Ct. 2230, 37 L.Ed.2d 63 (1973).

[Connecticut required non-residents who enrolled in the state university system to pay tuition and other fees at higher rates than residents. It defined an unmarried student as a non-resident if his or her legal address for any part of the one-year period before to applying for admission was outside of Connecticut. It defined a married student as a non-resident if his or her legal address at the time of application for admission was outside of Connecticut. It then provided that a student's residency status at the time of admission should continue for the student's entire period of attendance.

Two students, one married and one unmarried, were classified as non-residents at the time of application to the state university, but later became residents. They brought suit in the federal district court challenging the conclusive presumption of nonresidence as applied to force them to pay higher fees than other residents of the state. The district court ruled in their favor. The state appealed.]

Mr. Justice Stewart delivered the opinion of the Court.

. . .

Statutes creating permanent irrebuttable presumptions have long been disfavored under the Due Process Clause of the Fifth and Fourteenth Amendments. . . .

The . . . case of Bell v. Burson, 402 U.S. 535 (1971), involved a Georgia statute which provided that if an uninsured motorist was involved in an accident and could not post security for the amount of damages claimed, his driver's license must be suspended without any hearing on the question of fault or responsibility. The Court held that since the State purported to be concerned with fault in suspending a driver's license, it could not, consistent with procedural due process, conclusively presume fault from the fact that the uninsured motorist was involved in an accident, and could not, therefore, suspend his driver's license without a hearing on that crucial factor.

Likewise, in Stanley v. Illinois, 405 U.S. 645 (1972), the Court struck down, as violative of the Due Process Clause, Illinois' irrebuttable statutory presumption that all unmarried fathers are unqualified to raise their children. . . .

The same considerations obtain here. It may be that most applicants to Connecticut's university system who apply from outside the State or within a year of living out of State have no real intention of becoming Connecticut residents and will never do so. But it is clear that not all of the applicants from out of State inevitably fall in this category. Indeed, in the present case, both appellees possess many of the indicia of Connecticut residency, such as year-round Connecticut homes, Connecticut driver's licenses, car registrations, voter registrations, etc.; and both were found by the District Court to have become bona fide residents of Connecticut before the 1972 Spring semester. Yet, under the State's statutory scheme, neither was permitted any opportunity to demonstrate the bona fides of her Connecticut residency for tuition purposes, and neither will ever have such an opportunity in the future so long as she remains a student. . . .

In sum, since Connecticut purports to be concerned with residency in allocating the rates for tuition and fees at its university system, it is forbidden by the Due Process Clause to deny an individual the resident rates on the basis of a permanent and irrebuttable presumption of nonresidence, when that presumption is not necessarily or universally true in fact, and when the State has reasonable alternative means of making the crucial determination. Rather, standards of due process require that the State allow such an individual the opportunity to present evidence showing that he is a bona fide resident entitled to the in-state rates. Since § 126 precluded the appellees from ever rebutting the presumption that they were nonresidents of Connecticut, that statute operated to deprive them of a significant amount of their money without due process of law.

We are aware, of course, of the special problems involved in determining the bona fide residence of college students who come from out of State to attend that State's public university. Our holding today should in no wise be taken to mean that Connecticut must classify the students in its university system as residents, for purposes of tuition and fees, just because they go to school there. Nor should our decision be construed to deny a State the right to impose on a student, as one element in demonstrating bona fide residence, a reasonable durational residency requirement, which can be met while in student status. We fully recognize that a State has a legitimate interest in protecting and preserving the quality of its colleges and universities and the right of its own bona fide residents to attend such institutions on a preferential tuition basis.

We hold only that a permanent irrebuttable presumption of nonresidence— the means adopted by Connecticut to preserve that legitimate interest—is violative of the Due Process Clause, because it provides no opportunity for students who applied from out of State to demonstrate that they have become bona fide Connecticut residents. The State can establish such reasonable criteria for in-state status as to make virtually certain that students who are not, in fact, bona fide residents of the State, but who have come there solely for educational purposes, cannot take advantage of the in-state rates. . . .

Judgment affirmed.

Mr. Justice Marshall, with whom Mr. Justice Brennan joins, concurring.

I join the opinion of the Court except insofar as it suggests that a State may impose a one-year residency requirement as a prerequisite to qualifying for in-state tuition benefits. . . . That question is not presented by this case since here we deal with a permanent, irrebuttable presumption of nonresidency based on the fact that a student was a nonresident at the time he applied for admission to the state university system. . . .

Mr. Justice White, concurring in the judgment. . . .

Mr. Chief Justice Burger, with whom Mr. Justice Rehnquist joins, dissenting.

. . .

Mr. Justice Rehnquist, with whom The Chief Justice and Mr. Justice Douglas join, dissenting.

The Court's opinion relegates to the limbo of unconstitutionality a Connecticut law that requires higher tuition from those who come from out of State to attend its state universities than from those who come from within the State. The opinion accomplishes this result by a highly theoretical analysis that relies heavily on notions of substantive due process that have been authoritatively repudiated by subsequent decisions of the Court. Believing as I do that the Connecticut statutory scheme is a constitutionally permissible means of dealing with an increasingly acute problem facing state systems of higher education, I dissent. . . .

Cleveland Board of Education v. LaFleur

414 U.S. 632, 94 S.Ct. 791, 39 L.Ed.2d 52 (1974).

Mr. Justice Stewart delivered the opinion of the Court.

[LaFleur and Nelson brought suit challenging a school board rule requiring every pregnant teacher to take maternity leave without pay at least five months before the expected birth of her child, with application filed two weeks prior to date of departure. Despite their wish to finish the school year they were forced to take leave in March. Their babies were born in late July and August. Cohen challenged the rule in another district requiring leave without pay four months before the expected birth with written notice six months before the date of expected birth. She was required to leave her job in December, and her baby was born in May. The Court found the regulations unconstitutional.]

. . .

II.

This Court has long recognized that freedom of personal choice in matters of marriage and family life is one of the liberties protected by the Due Process Clause of the Fourteenth Amendment. Roe v. Wade, 410 U.S. 113 (1973); Loving v. Virginia, 388 U.S. 1, 12 (1967); Griswold v. Connecticut, 381 U.S. 479 (1965); Pierce v. Society of Sisters, 268 U.S. 510 (1925); Meyer v. Nebraska, 262 U.S. 390 (1923). . . . As we noted in Eisenstadt v. Baird, 405 U.S. 438, 453 (1972), there is a right "to be free from unwarranted governmental intrusion into matters so fundamentally affecting a person as the decision whether to bear or beget a child."

By acting to penalize the pregnant teacher for deciding to bear a child, overly restrictive maternity leave regulations can constitute a heavy burden on the exercise of these protected freedoms. Because public school maternity leave rules directly affect "one of the basic civil rights of man," Skinner v. Oklahoma . . ., the Due Process Clause of the Fourteenth Amendment requires that such rules must not needlessly, arbitrarily, or capriciously impinge upon this vital area of a teacher's constitutional liberty. The question before us in these cases is whether the interests advanced in support of the rules of the Cleveland and Chesterfield County School Boards can justify the particular procedures they have adopted.

The school boards in these cases have offered two essentially overlapping explanations for their mandatory maternity leave rules. First, they contend that the firm cut-off dates are necessary to maintain continuity of classroom instruction, since advance knowledge of when a pregnant teacher must leave facilitates the finding and hiring of a qualified substitute. Secondly, the school boards seek to justify their maternity rules by arguing that at least some teachers become physically incapable of adequately performing certain of their duties during the latter part of pregnancy. By keeping the pregnant teacher out of the classroom during these final months, the maternity leave rules are said to protect the health of the teacher and her unborn child, while at the same time assuring that students have a physically capable instructor in the classroom at all times.

It cannot be denied that continuity of instruction is a significant and legitimate educational goal. Regulations requiring pregnant teachers to provide early notice of their condition to school authorities undoubtedly facilitate administrative planning toward the important objective of continuity. . . .

Thus, while the advance notice provisions in the Cleveland and Chesterfield County rules are wholly rational and may well be necessary to serve the objective of continuity of instruction, the absolute requirements of termination at the end of the fourth or fifth month of pregnancy are not. Were continuity the only goal, cut-off dates much later during pregnancy would serve as well or better than the challenged rules, providing that ample advance notice requirements were retained. Indeed, continuity would seem just as well attained if the teacher herself were allowed to choose the date upon which to commence her leave, at least so long as the decision were required to be made and notice given of it well in advance of the date selected.

. . .

We thus conclude that the arbitrary cut-off dates embodied in the mandatory leave rules before us have no rational relationship to the valid state interest of preserving continuity of instruction. As long as the teacher is required to give substantial advance notice of her condition, the choice of firm dates later in pregnancy would serve the boards' objectives just as well, while imposing a far lesser burden on the women's exercise of constitutionally protected freedom.

The question remains as to whether the fifth and sixth month cut-off dates can be justified on the other ground advanced by the school boards—the necessity of keeping physically unfit teachers out of the classroom. There can be no doubt that such an objective is perfectly legitimate, both on educational and safety grounds. And, despite the plethora of conflicting medical testimony in these cases, we can assume *arguendo* that at least some teachers become physically disabled from effectively performing their duties during the latter stages of pregnancy.

The mandatory termination provisions of the Cleveland and Chesterfield County rules surely operate to insulate the classroom from the presence of potentially incapacitated pregnant teachers. But . . . the rules sweep too broadly . . ., for the provisions amount to a conclusive presumption that every pregnant teacher who reaches the fifth or sixth month of pregnancy is physically incapable of continuing. There is no individualized determination by the teacher's doctor—or the school board's—as to any particular teacher's ability to continue at her job. The rules contain an irrebuttable presumption of physical incompetency, and that presumption applies even when the medical evidence as to an individual woman's physical status might be wholly to the contrary.

As the Court noted last Term in Vlandis v. Kline, 412 U.S. 441, 446 (1973), "permanent irrebuttable presumptions have long been disfavored under the Due Process Clause of the Fifth and Fourteenth Amendments." . . .

. . .

. . . [T]he medical experts in these cases differed on many points, [but] they unanimously agreed on one—the ability of any particular pregnant woman to continue at work past any fixed time in her pregnancy is very much an individual matter. Even assuming *arguendo* that there are some women who would be physically unable to work past the particular cut-off dates embodied in the challenged rules, it is evident that there are large numbers of teachers who are fully capable of continuing work for longer than the Cleveland and Chesterfield County regulations will allow. Thus, the conclusive presumption embodied in these rules, like that in *Vlandis,* is neither "necessarily nor universally true," and is violative of the Due Process Clause.

The school boards have argued that the mandatory termination dates serve the interest of administrative convenience, since there are many instances of teacher pregnancy, and the rules obviate the necessity for case-by-case determinations. Certainly, the boards have an interest in devising prompt and efficient procedures to achieve their legitimate objectives in this area. . . .

While it might be easier for the school boards to conclusively presume that all pregnant women are unfit to teach past the fourth or fifth month or even the first month, of pregnancy, administrative convenience alone is insufficient to make valid what otherwise is a violation of due process of law.[13] The Fourteenth Amendment requires the school boards to employ alternative administrative means, which do not so broadly infringe upon basic constitutional liberty, in support of their legitimate goals.

We conclude, therefore, that neither the necessity for continuity of instruction nor the state interest in keeping physically unfit teachers out of the classroom can justify the sweeping mandatory leave regulations that the Cleveland and Chesterfield County School Boards have adopted. While the regulations no doubt represent a good-faith attempt to achieve a laudable goal, they cannot pass muster under the Due Process Clause of the Fourteenth Amendment, because they employ irrebuttable presumptions that unduly penalize a female teacher for deciding to bear a child.

. . .

Mr. Justice Douglas concurs in the result.

Mr. Justice Powell (concurring in the result).

I concur in the Court's result, but I am unable to join its opinion. In my view these cases should not be decided on the ground that the mandatory maternity leave regulations impair any right to bear children or create an

---

13. This is not to say that the only means for providing appropriate protection for the rights of pregnant teachers is an individualized determination in each case and in every circumstance. We are not dealing in these cases with maternity leave regulations requiring a termination of employment at some firm date during the last few weeks of pregnancy. We therefore have no occasion to decide whether such regulations might be justified by considerations not presented in these records—for example, widespread medical consensus about the "disabling" effect of pregnancy on a teacher's job performance during these latter days, or evidence showing that such firm cutoffs were the only reasonable method of avoiding the possibility of labor beginning while some teacher was in the classroom, or proof that adequate substitutes could not be procured without at least some minimal lead time and certainty as to the dates upon which their employment was to begin.

"irrebuttable presumption." It seems to me that equal protection analysis is the appropriate frame of reference....

. . .

Mr. Justice Rehnquist, with whom The Chief Justice joins (dissenting).

The Court rests its invalidation of the school regulations involved in these cases on the Due Process Clause of the Fourteenth Amendment, rather than on any claim of sexual discrimination under the Equal Protection Clause of that Amendment. My Brother Stewart thereby enlists the Court in another quixotic engagement in his apparently unending war on irrebuttable presumptions. In this case we are told that although a regulation "requiring a termination of employment at some firm date during the last few weeks of pregnancy" (n. 13, opinion of the Court), might pass muster, the regulations here challenged requiring termination at the end of the fourth or fifth month of pregnancy violate due process of law....

The lines drawn by the school boards ... in these cases require pregnant teachers to take forced leave at a stage of their pregnancy when medical evidence seems to suggest that a majority of them might well be able to continue teaching without any significant possibility of physical impairment. But ... the medical evidence also suggests that in some cases there may be physical impairment at the stage of pregnancy fastened on by the regulations in question, and that the probability of physical impairment increases as the pregnancy advances. If legislative bodies are to be permitted to draw a general line anywhere short of the delivery room, I can find no judicial standard of measurement which says the ones drawn here were invalid. I therefore dissent.[a]

Weinberger v. Salfi

422 U.S. 749, 95 S.Ct. 2457, 45 L.Ed.2d 522 (1975).

Mr. Justice Rehnquist delivered the opinion of the Court.

Appellants, the Department of Health, Education, and Welfare, its Secretary, the Social Security Administration and various of its officials, appeal from a [district court] decision ... invalidating duration-of-relationship Social Security eligibility requirements for surviving wives and stepchildren of deceased wage earners....

I.

Appellee Salfi married the deceased wage earner, Londo L. Salfi, on May 27, 1972. Despite his alleged apparent good health at the time of the marriage, he suffered a heart attack less than a month later, and died on November 21, 1972, less than six months after the marriage. Appellee filed applications for mother's insurance benefits for herself and child's insurance benefits for her daughter by a previous marriage.... These applications were denied by the Social Security Administration, both initially and on reconsideration at the regional level, solely on the basis of the duration-of-relationship requirements

---

a. In Turner v. Department of Employment, 423 U.S. 44 (1975), the Court invalidated a Utah law making pregnant women ineligible for unemployment benefits for a period extending from 12 weeks before the expected date of childbirth until a date six weeks after childbirth. The Court relied on the conclusive presumption analysis in the *Cleveland Board* case.

of §§ 416(c)(5) and (e)(2), which define "widow" and "child." The definitions exclude surviving wives and stepchildren who had their respective relationships to a deceased wage earner for less than nine months prior to his death.

The named appellees then filed this action. . . .

A three-judge District Court . . . on cross-motions for summary judgment . . . granted substantially all of the relief prayed for by appellees. . . .

III.

The District Court relied on congressional history for the proposition that the duration-of-relationship requirement was intended to prevent the use of sham marriages to secure Social Security payments. As such, . . . "the requirement constitutes a presumption that marriages like Mrs. Salfi's, which did not precede the wage earner's death by at least nine months, were entered into for the purpose of securing Social Security benefits." The presumption was moreover, conclusive, because applicants were not afforded an opportunity to disprove the presence of the illicit purpose. The court held that under our decisions in Cleveland Board of Education v. LaFleur, 414 U.S. 632 (1974), Vlandis v. Kline, 412 U.S. 441 (1973), and Stanley v. Illinois, 405 U.S. 645 (1972), the requirement was unconstitutional, because it presumed a fact which was not necessarily or universally true.

. . .

We hold that these cases are not controlling on the issue before us now. Unlike the claims involved in *Stanley* and *LaFleur,* a noncontractual claim to receive funds from the public treasury enjoys no constitutionally protected status, *Dandridge v. Williams,* supra, though of course Congress may not invidiously discriminate among such claimants on the basis of a "bare congressional desire to harm a politically unpopular group," U.S. Dept. of Agriculture v. Moreno, 413 U.S. 528, 534 (1973), or on the basis of criteria which bear no rational relation to a legitimate legislative goal. Jimenez v. Weinberger, 417 U.S. 628, 636 (1974); U.S. Dept. of Agriculture v. Murry, 413 U.S. 508, 513–514 (1973). Unlike the statutory scheme in *Vlandis* . . . the Social Security Act does not purport to speak in terms of the bona fides of the parties to a marriage, but then make plainly relevant evidence of such bona fides inadmissible. . . .

We think that the District Court's extension of the holdings of *Stanley, Vlandis* and *LaFleur* to the eligibility requirement in issue here would turn the doctrine of those cases into a virtual engine of destruction of countless legislative judgments which have heretofore been thought wholly consistent with the Fifth and Fourteenth Amendments to the Constitution. . . .

. . .

More recently, in Mourning v. Family Publications Service, Inc., 411 U.S. 356 (1973), the Court sustained the constitutionality of a regulation promulgated under the Truth in Lending Act which made the Act's disclosure provisions applicable whenever credit is offered to a consumer "for which either a finance charge is or may be imposed or which pursuant to an agreement, is or may be payable in more than four installments." Id., at 362. The regulation was challenged because it was said to conclusively presume that payments made under an agreement providing for more than four installments necessarily included a finance charge, when in fact that might not be the case. The Court rejected the constitutional challenge in this language:

> "The rule was intended as a prophylactic measure; it does not presume that all creditors who are within its ambit assess finance charges, but

rather, imposes a disclosure requirement on all members of a defined class in order to discourage evasion by a substantial portion of that class."

If the Fifth and Fourteenth Amendments permit this latitude to legislative decisions regulating the private sector of the economy, they surely allow no less latitude in prescribing the conditions upon which funds shall be dispensed from the public treasury. Dandridge v. Williams, supra. With these principles in mind, we turn to consider the statutory provisions which the District Court held invalid.

. . .

Under those standards, the question raised is not whether a statutory provision precisely filters out those, and only those, who are in the factual position which generated the congressional concern reflected in the statute. Such a rule would ban all prophylactic provisions, and would be directly contrary to our holding in *Mourning,* supra. Nor is the question whether the provision filters out a substantial part of the class which caused congressional concern, or whether it filters out more members of the class than nonmembers. The question is whether Congress, its concern having been reasonably aroused by the possibility of an abuse which it legitimately desired to avoid, could rationally have concluded both that a particular limitation or qualification would protect against its occurrence, and that the expense and other difficulties of individual determinations justified the inherent imprecision of a prophylactic rule. We conclude that the duration-of-relationship test meets this constitutional standard.

The danger of persons entering a marriage relationship not to enjoy its traditional benefits, but instead to enable one spouse to claim benefits upon the anticipated early death of the wage earner, has been recognized from the very beginning of the Social Security program. . . .

Undoubtedly the concerns reflected in this congressional material are legitimate, involving as they do the integrity of both the Social Security Trust Fund and the marriage relationship. It is also undoubtedly true that the duration-of-relationship requirement operates to lessen the likelihood of abuse through sham relationships entered in contemplation of imminent death. We also think that Congress could rationally have concluded that any imprecision from which it might suffer was justified by its ease and certainty of operation.

. . .

The administrative difficulties of individual eligibility determinations are without doubt matters which Congress may consider when determining whether to rely on rules which sweep more broadly than the evils with which they seek to deal. In this sense, the duration-of-relationship requirement represents not merely a substantive policy determination that benefits should be awarded only on the basis of genuine marital relationships, but also a substantive policy determination that limited resources would not be well spent in making individual determinations. It is an expression of Congress' policy choice that the Social Security system, and its millions of beneficiaries, would be best served by a prophylactic rule which bars claims arising from the bulk of sham marriages which are actually entered, which discourages such marriages from ever taking place, and which is also objective and easily administered.

The Constitution does not preclude such policy choices as a price for conducting programs for the distribution of social insurance benefits. Cf. Geduldig v. Aiello, supra, at 496. Unlike criminal prosecutions, or the custody proceedings at issue in *Stanley v. Illinois,* such programs do not involve affirmative government action which seriously curtails important liberties cognizable under the Constitution. There is thus no basis for our requiring individualized determinations when Congress can rationally conclude not only that generalized rules are appropriate to its purposes and concerns, but also that the difficulties of individual determinations outweigh the marginal increments in the precise effectuation of congressional concern which they might be expected to produce.

The judgment of the District Court is

Reversed.

Mr. Justice Douglas, dissenting.

. . .

On the merits, I believe that the main problem with these legislatively created presumptions is that they frequently invade the right to a jury trial. See Tot v. United States, 319 U.S. 463, 473 (1943) (concurring opinion). The present law was designed to bar payment of certain Social Security benefits when the purpose of the marriage was to obtain such benefits. Whether this was the aim of a particular marriage is a question of fact, to be decided by the jury in an appropriate case. I therefore would vacate and remand the case to give Mrs. Salfi the right to show that her marriage did not offend the statutory scheme, that it was not a sham.

Mr. Justice Brennan, with whom Mr. Justice Marshall joins, dissenting.

. . .

The merits of this case can be dealt with very briefly. For it is, I believe, apparent on the face of the Court's opinion that today's holding is flatly contrary to several recent decisions, specifically Vlandis v. Kline, 412 U.S. 441 (1973); U.S. Dept. of Agriculture v. Murry, 413 U.S. 508 (1973), and Jimenez v. Weinberger, 417 U.S. 628 (1974).

. . .

USERY v. TURNER ELKHORN MINING CO., 428 U.S. 1 (1976). Section 411(c)(3) of the Federal Coal Mine Health and Safety Act provides that a miner shown by x-ray or other clinical evidence to be afflicted with complicated pneumoconiosis is "irrebuttably presumed" to be totally disabled due to pneumoconiosis; if he has died, it is irrebuttably presumed that he was totally disabled by pneumoconiosis at the time of his death, and that his death was due to pneumoconiosis. In rejecting a challenge by coal mine operators to this provision the Court said:

". . . We think the District Court erred in equating this case with those in the mold of *Stanley* and *Vlandis*.

"As an operational matter, the effect of § 411(c)(3)'s 'irrebuttable presumption' of total disability is simply to establish entitlement in the case of a miner who is clinically diagnosable as extremely ill with pneumoconiosis arising out of coal mine employment. Indeed, the legislative history discloses that it was precisely this advanced and progressive stage of the disease that Congress sought most certainly to compensate. Were the Act phrased simply and directly to provide that operators were bound to provide benefits for all miners clinically demonstrating their affliction with complicated pneumoconiosis arising out of employment in the mines, we think it clear that there could be no due process objection to it. For, as we have already observed, destruction of earning capacity is not the sole legitimate basis for compulsory compensation of employees by their employers. New York Central R.R. Co. v. Bianc, 250 U.S. 596 (1919). We cannot say that it would be irrational for Congress to conclude that impairment of health alone warrants compensation. Since Congress can clearly draft a statute to accomplish precisely what it has accomplished through § 411(c)(3)'s presumption of disability, the argument is essentially that Congress has accomplished its result in an impermissible manner—by defining eligibility in terms of 'total disability' and erecting an 'irrebuttable presumption' of total disability upon a factual showing that does not necessarily satisfy the statutory definition of total disability. But in a statute such as this, regulating purely economic matters, we do not think that Congress' choice of statutory language can invalidate the enactment when its operation and effect are clearly permissible. Cf. Weinberger v. Salfi, 422 U.S. 749, 767–785 (1975); McDonald v. Board of Election, 394 U.S. 802, 809 (1969); United States v. Carolene Products Co., 304 U.S. 144, 154 (1938)."

Michael H. v. Gerald D.

491 U.S. 110, 109 S.Ct. 2333, 105 L.Ed.2d 91 (1989).

[The report in this case appears, supra at p. 603]

CHAPTER 12

APPLICATION OF THE POST CIVIL WAR AMENDMENTS TO PRIVATE CONDUCT: CONGRESSIONAL POWER TO ENFORCE THE AMENDMENTS

Introduction This chapter presents a mixture of issues that can best be described as those involved in the Civil Rights Cases with which this chapter begins. That 1883 decision took a narrow view of the reach of section 1 of the thirteenth amendment and section 1 of the fourteenth amendment in their application to private racial discrimination. The decision also adopted a correspondingly narrow view of Congressional power to enforce the amendments. After setting out the decision in the Civil Rights Cases in section 1, the remainder of this chapter explores the question whether its basic conceptions are still valid. Section 2, dealing with the "state action" concept, includes those cases concerning the application of constitutional limits of governmental action to private conduct. The subject of the rest of the chapter is Congressional power to enforce the Civil War Amendments, focusing particularly on the extent of the power to prohibit both private and state action that would be lawful in the absence of federal legislation. Section 3 presents a brief review of the surviving fragments of Reconstruction era legislation, and contemporary federal legislation protecting civil rights. Section 4 addresses the issue of Congressional power to prohibit private racial discrimination in enforcing the thirteenth amendment's prohibition of slavery and involuntary servitude. Section 5 focuses on Congressional power under the fourteenth amendment to prohibit private racial, and non-racial, discrimination. Section 6 broadens the focus beyond issues of private discrimination, examining the extent of Congressional power to prohibit state laws and practices that violate neither section 1 of the fourteenth amendment nor section 1 of the fifteenth amendment. This last section considers both the scope of Congressional power to provide broad remedies for conceded constitutional violations and, most controversial, to modify the substantive content of constitutional rights.

SECTION 1. EARLY INTERPRETATION

Civil Rights Cases

109 U.S. 3, 3 S.Ct. 18, 27 L.Ed. 835 (1883).

Bradley, J. These cases are all founded on the first and second sections of the act of congress known as the "Civil Rights Act," passed March 1, 1875, entitled "An act to protect all citizens in their civil and legal rights." 18 Stat.

335. Two of the cases, those against Stanley and Nichols, are indictments for denying to persons of color the accommodations and privileges of an inn or hotel; two of them, those against Ryan and Singleton, are, one an information, the other an indictment, for denying to individuals the privileges and accommodations of a theater, the information against Ryan being for refusing a colored person a seat in the dress circle of Maguire's theater in San Francisco; and the indictment against Singleton being for denying to another person, whose color is not stated, the full enjoyment of the accommodations of the theater known as the Grand Opera House in New York, "said denial not being made for any reasons by law applicable to citizens of every race and color, and regardless of any previous condition of servitude." The case of Robinson and wife against the Memphis & Charleston Railroad Company was an action brought in the circuit court of the United States for the western district of Tennessee, to recover the penalty of $500 given by the second section of the act; and the *gravamen* was the refusal by the conductor of the railroad company to allow the wife to ride in the ladies' car, for the reason, as stated in one of the counts, that she was a person of African descent. The jury rendered a verdict for the defendants in this case upon the merits under a charge of the court, to which a bill of exceptions was taken by the plaintiffs....

It is obvious that the primary and important question in all the cases is the constitutionality of the law; for if the law is unconstitutional none of the prosecutions can stand.

The sections of the law referred to provide as follows:

"Section 1. That all persons within the jurisdiction of the United States shall be entitled to the full and equal enjoyment of the accommodations, advantages, facilities, and privileges of inns, public conveyances on land or water, theaters, and other places of public amusement; subject only to the conditions and limitations established by law, and applicable alike to citizens of every race and color, regardless of any previous condition of servitude.

"Section 2. That any person who shall violate the foregoing section by denying to any citizen, except for reasons by law applicable to citizens of every race and color, and regardless of any previous condition of servitude, the full enjoyment of any of the accommodations, advantages, facilities, or privileges in said section enumerated, or by aiding or inciting such denial, shall, for every such offense, forfeit and pay the sum of $500 to the person aggrieved thereby, to be recovered in an action of debt, with full costs; and shall, also, for every such offense, be deemed guilty of a misdemeanor, and upon conviction thereof shall be fined not less than $500 nor more than $1,000, or shall be imprisoned not less than 30 days nor more than one year...."

Has congress constitutional power to make such a law? Of course, no one will contend that the power to pass it was contained in the constitution before the adoption of the last three amendments. The power is sought, first, in the fourteenth amendment, and the views and arguments of distinguished senators, advanced while the law was under consideration, claiming authority to pass it by virtue of that amendment, are the principal arguments adduced in favor of the power....

The first section of the fourteenth amendment,—which is the one relied on,—after declaring who shall be citizens of the United States, and of the several states, is prohibitory in its character, and prohibitory upon the states. It declares that "no state shall make or enforce any law which shall abridge the privileges or immunities of citizens of the United States; nor shall any state deprive any person of life, liberty, or property without due process of law; nor deny to any person within its jurisdiction the equal protection of the laws." It is state action of a particular character that is prohibited. Individual invasion of individual rights is not the subject-matter of the amendment. It has a deeper and broader scope. It nullifies and makes void all state legislation, and state action of every kind, which impairs the privileges and immunities of citizens of the United States, or which injures them in life, liberty, or property without due process of law, or which denies to any of them the equal protection of the laws. It not only does this, but, in order that the national will, thus declared, may not be a mere *brutum fulmen,* the last section of the amendment invests congress with power to enforce it by appropriate legislation. To enforce what? To enforce the prohibition. To adopt appropriate legislation for correcting the effects of such prohibited state laws and state acts, and thus to render them effectually null, void, and innocuous. This is the legislative power conferred upon congress, and this is the whole of it. It does not invest congress with power to legislate upon subjects which are within the domain of state legislation; but to provide modes of relief against state legislation, or state action, of the kind referred to. It does not authorize congress to create a code of municipal law for the regulation of private rights; but to provide modes of redress against the operation of state laws, and the action of state officers, executive or judicial, when these are subversive of the fundamental rights specified in the amendment....

In this connection it is proper to state that civil rights, such as are guaranteed by the constitution against state aggression, cannot be impaired by the wrongful acts of individuals, unsupported by state authority in the shape of laws, customs, or judicial or executive proceedings. The wrongful act of an individual, unsupported by any such authority, is simply a private wrong, or a crime of that individual; an invasion of the rights of the injured party, it is true, whether they affect his person, his property, or his reputation; but if not sanctioned in some way by the state, or not done under state authority, his rights remain in full force, and may presumably be vindicated by resort to the laws of the state for redress. An individual cannot deprive a man of his right to vote, to hold property, to buy and to sell, to sue in the courts, or to be a witness or a juror; he may, by force or fraud, interfere with the enjoyment of the right in a particular case; he may commit an assault against the person, or commit murder, or use ruffian violence at the polls, or slander the good name of a fellow-citizen; but unless protected in these wrongful acts by some shield of state law or state authority, he cannot destroy or injure the right; he will only render himself amenable to satisfaction or punishment; and amenable therefor to the laws of the state where the wrongful acts are committed....

Of course, these remarks do not apply to those cases in which congress is clothed with direct and plenary powers of legislation over the whole subject, accompanied with an express or implied denial of such power to the states, as in the regulation of commerce with foreign nations, among the several states, and with the Indian tribes, the coining of money, the establishment of post-offices and post-roads, the declaring of war, etc. In these cases congress has power to pass laws for regulating the subjects specified, in every detail and the conduct and transactions of individuals in respect thereof.

. . .

... [T]he power of congress to adopt direct and primary, as distinguished from corrective, legislation on the subject in hand, is sought, in the second place, from the thirteenth amendment, which abolishes slavery. This amendment declares "that neither slavery, nor involuntary servitude, except as a punishment for crime, whereof the party shall have been duly convicted, shall exist within the United States, or any place subject to their jurisdiction;" and it gives congress power to enforce the amendment by appropriate legislation. . . .

It is true that slavery cannot exist without law any more than property in lands and goods can exist without law, and therefore the thirteenth amendment may be regarded as nullifying all state laws which establish or uphold slavery. But it has a reflex character also, establishing and decreeing universal civil and political freedom throughout the United States; and it is assumed that the power vested in congress to enforce the article by appropriate legislation, clothes congress with power to pass all laws necessary and proper for abolishing all badges and incidents of slavery in the United States; and upon this assumption it is claimed that this is sufficient authority for declaring by law that all persons shall have equal accommodations and privileges in all inns, public conveyances, and places of public amusement; the argument being that the denial of such equal accommodations and privileges is in itself a subjection to a species of servitude within the meaning of the amendment. . . .

It may be that by the black code, (as it was called), in the times when slavery prevailed, the proprietors of inns and public conveyances were forbidden to receive persons of the African race, because it might assist slaves to escape from the control of their masters. This was merely a means of preventing such escapes, and was no part of the servitude itself. A law of that kind could not have any such object now, however justly it might be deemed an invasion of the party's legal right as a citizen, and amenable to the prohibitions of the fourteenth amendment.

The long existence of African slavery in this country gave us very distinct notions of what it was, and what were its necessary incidents. Compulsory service of the slave for the benefit of the master, restraint of his movements except by the master's will, disability to hold property, to make contracts, to have a standing in court, to be a witness against a white person, and such like burdens and incapacities were the inseparable incidents of the institution. Severer punishments for crimes were imposed on the slave than on free persons guilty of the same offenses. Congress, as we have seen, by the civil rights bill of 1866, passed in view of the thirteenth amendment, before the fourteenth was adopted, undertook to wipe out these burdens and disabilities, the necessary incidents of slavery, constituting its substance and visible form; and to secure to all citizens of every race and color, and without regard to previous servitude, those fundamental rights which are the essence of civil freedom, namely, the same right to make and enforce contracts, to sue, be parties, give evidence, and to inherit, purchase, lease, sell, and convey property, as is enjoyed by white citizens. Whether this legislation was fully authorized by the thirteenth amendment alone, without the support which it afterwards received from the fourteenth amendment, after the adoption of which it was re-enacted with some additions, it is not necessary to inquire. It is referred to for the purpose of showing that at that time (in 1866) congress did not assume, under the authority given by the thirteenth amendment, to adjust what may be called the social rights of men and races in the community; but only to declare and vindicate those fundamental rights which appertain to the essence of citizenship, and the enjoyment or deprivation of which constitutes the essential distinction between freedom and slavery. . . .

The only question under the present head, therefore, is, whether the refusal to any persons of the accommodations of an inn, or a public conveyance, or a place of public amusement, by an individual, and without any sanction or support from any state law or regulation, does inflict upon such persons any manner of servitude, or form of slavery, as those terms are understood in this country? . . .

Now, conceding, for the sake of the argument, that the admission to an inn, a public conveyance, or a place of public amusement, on equal terms with all other citizens, is the right of every man and all classes of men, is it any more than one of those rights which the states by the Fourteenth Amendment are forbidden to deny to any person? And is the Constitution violated until the denial of the right has some State sanction or authority? Can the act of a mere individual, the owner of the inn, the public conveyance, or place of amusement, refusing the accommodation, be justly regarded as imposing any badge of slavery or servitude upon the applicant, or only as inflicting an ordinary civil injury, properly cognizable by the laws of the state, and presumably subject to redress by those laws until the contrary appears?

After giving to these questions all the consideration which their importance demands, we are forced to the conclusion that such an act of refusal has nothing to do with slavery or involuntary servitude, and that if it is violative of any right of the party, his redress is to be sought under the laws of the state; or, if those laws are adverse to his rights and do not protect him, his remedy will be found in the corrective legislation which congress has adopted, or may adopt, for counteracting the effect of state laws, or state action, prohibited by the fourteenth amendment. It would be running the slavery argument into the ground to make it apply to every act of discrimination which a person may see fit to make as to the guests he will entertain, or as to the people he will take into his coach or cab or car, or admit to his concert or theater, or deal with in other matters of intercourse or business. Innkeepers and public carriers, by the laws of all the states, so far as we are aware, are bound, to the extent of their facilities, to furnish proper accommodation to all unobjectionable persons who in good faith apply for them. If the laws themselves make any unjust discrimination, amenable to the prohibitions of the fourteenth amendment, congress has full power to afford a remedy under that amendment and in accordance with it.

When a man has emerged from slavery, and by the aid of beneficent legislation has shaken off the inseparable concomitants of that state, there must be some stage in the progress of his elevation when he takes the rank of a mere citizen, and ceases to be the special favorite of the laws, and when his rights as a citizen, or a man, are to be protected in the ordinary modes by which other men's rights are protected. There were thousands of free colored people in this country before the abolition of slavery, enjoying all the essential rights of life, liberty, and property the same as white citizens; yet no one, at that time, thought that it was any invasion of their personal *status* as freemen because they were not admitted to all the privileges enjoyed by white citizens, or because they were subjected to discriminations in the enjoyment of accommodations in inns, public conveyances, and places of amusement. Mere discriminations on account of race or color were not regarded as badges of slavery. If, since that time, the enjoyment of equal rights in all these respects has become established by constitutional enactment, it is not by force of the thirteenth amendment, (which merely abolishes slavery,) but by force of the fourteenth and fifteenth amendments.

On the whole, we are of opinion that no countenance of authority for the passage of the law in question can be found in either the thirteenth or fourteenth amendment of the constitution; and no other ground of authority for its passage being suggested, it must necessarily be declared void, at least so far as its operation in the several states is concerned. . . .

Mr. Justice Harlan dissenting:

The opinion in these cases proceeds, it seems to me, upon grounds entirely too narrow and artificial. I cannot resist the conclusion that the substance and spirit of the recent Amendments of the Constitution have been sacrificed by a subtle and ingenious verbal criticism. "It is not the words of the law but the internal sense of it that makes the law; the letter of the law is the body; the sense and reason of the law is the soul." Constitutional provisions, adopted in the interest of liberty, and for the purpose of securing, through national legislation, if need be, rights inhering in a state of freedom, and belonging to American citizenship, have been so construed as to defeat the ends the people desired to accomplish, which they attempted to accomplish, and which they supposed they had accomplished by changes in their fundamental law....

[In a long opinion Justice Harlan argued that both the 13th and 14th Amendments gave Congress power to legislate directly with reference to private individuals engaged in such quasi-public businesses as those involved in this case.]

My brethren say, that when a man has emerged from slavery, and by the aid of beneficient legislation has shaken off the inseparable concomitants of that state, there must be some stage in the progress of his elevation when he takes the rank of a mere citizen, and ceases to be the special favorite of the laws, and when his rights as a citizen, or a man, are to be protected in the ordinary modes by which other men's rights are protected. It is, I submit, scarcely just to say that the colored race has been the special favorite of the laws. The Statute of 1875, now adjudged to be unconstitutional, is for the benefit of citizens of every race and color. What the Nation, through Congress, has sought to accomplish in reference to that race, is—what had already been done in every State of the Union for the white race—to secure and protect rights belonging to them as freemen and citizens; nothing more. It was not deemed enough "to help the feeble up, but to support him after." The one underlying purpose of congressional legislation has been to enable the black race to take the rank of mere citizens. The difficulty has been to compel a recognition of the legal right of the black race to take the rank of citizens, and to secure the enjoyment of privileges belonging, under the law, to them as a component part of the people for whose welfare and happiness government is ordained. At every step, in this direction, the Nation has been confronted with class tyranny, which a contemporary English historian says is, of tyrannies, the most intolerable, "For it is ubiquitous in its operation, and weighs, perhaps, most heavily on those whose obscurity or distance would withdraw them from the notice of a single despot." Today, it is the colored race which is denied, by corporations and individuals wielding public authority, rights fundamental in their freedom and citizenship. At some future time, it may be that some other race will fall under the ban of race discrimination. If the constitutional Amendments be enforced, according to the intent with which, as I conceive, they were adopted, there cannot be in this Republic, any class of human beings in practical subjection to another class, with power in the latter to dole out to the former just such privileges as they may choose to grant. The supreme law of the land has decreed that no authority shall be exercised in this country upon the basis of discrimination, in respect of civil rights, against freemen and citizens because of their race, color or previous condition of servitude. To that decree—for the due enforcement of which, by appropriate legislation, Congress has been invested with express power—every one must bow, whatever may have been, or whatever now are, his individual views as to the wisdom or policy, either of the recent changes in the fundamental law, or of the legislation which has been enacted to give them effect.

For the reasons stated I feel constrained to withhold my assent to the opinion of the court.

THE RELATIONSHIP BETWEEN CONGRESSIONAL POWER TO ENFORCE THE CONSTITUTION AND SELF–ENFORCING PROVISIONS OF THE CONSTITUTION

While the ultimate issue in the Civil Rights Cases concerned the constitutional validity of a federal statute prohibiting private discrimination, the bulk of the opinion discusses the question whether private racial discrimination would violate the Constitution had there been no federal legislation. The case was a major decision concerning the application of the Constitution to private conduct only because the Court's rationale was that Congressional power to enforce the thirteenth and fourteenth amendments necessarily tracked the self-executing provisions of those amendments. The next section of this chapter will explore the extent to which the fourteenth amendment applies of its own force to private conduct. Sections 4 through 6 will return to the issue of Congressional power. It is appropriate at this point to entertain a preliminary inquiry whether the interpretations of section one of the thirteenth amendment and section one of the fourteenth amendment should mark the outer limits of Congress' power to "enforce" those amendments.

Consider the facts of one of the cases grouped for decision in the Civil Rights Cases—the owner of a private theater enforcing a racially discriminatory policy in the selection of patrons. What are the consequences of a judicial decision that section one of the fourteenth amendment requires preferring the rights of the excluded patrons to those of the owner? What are the consequences of a judicial decision that Congress has the power under section five of the fourteenth amendment to require the theater owner to desist from racial discrimination in choice of patrons? Do those different consequences suggest that there should be differences in the reach of the self-enforcing provisions of section one and Congressional power under section five? Can major differences in the reach of section one and Congressional power under section five be recognized without giving Congress limitless power no longer tied to any limitation that it be directed to "enforcing" the fourteenth amendment?

SECTION 2.   APPLICATION OF THE CONSTITUTION TO PRIVATE CONDUCT

Introduction to the State Action Concept. With the exception of the thirteenth amendment the Constitution is a restraint on governmental action and does not provide one private citizen with rights against another. The Bill of Rights restrains the action of the federal government. The fourteenth amendment provides that "no state shall" deprive any person of due process or equal protection. The fifteenth amendment prohibits denial of voting rights "by the United States or by any State...." The same verbal formula appears in the voting right protections of the nineteenth, twenty-fourth and twenty-sixth amendments.

A basic conception of the opinion in the Civil Rights Cases was that "civil rights, such as are guaranteed by the Constitution against state aggression, cannot be impaired by the wrongful acts of individuals, unsupported by state authority in the shape of laws, customs, or judicial or executive proceedings." In a general sense, however, all private action is "supported by state authority" if the state has not chosen to make that private action illegal. It has proved to be extremely difficult to determine when state involvement with private action, beyond mere failure to prohibit it, brings into play the constitutional limitations on governmental action.

It has also proved to be difficult to organize the cases that involve the problem. Subsection A deals with the argument that constitutional limits apply because a private party is performing a function normally performed by government. Subsection B collects the cases where it is claimed that government has enforced the racially discriminatory decisions of private parties. Subsection C includes, quite simply, the rest of the cases where the argument has been made that government has "supported" the conduct of private parties by approving it, regulating it, or providing financial support to it.

From the end of World War II through 1968, all Supreme Court decisions that reached the question whether unconstitutional state action was present decided that it was. Since 1970, most Supreme Court decisions considering the same issue have not found unconstitutional state action. Part of the explanation may be found in significant changes in the Court's membership. (Compare Evans v. Newton, 382 U.S. 296(1966), infra p. 1124, with Evans v. Abney, 396 U.S. 435 (1970); infra p. 1138, Amalgamated Food Employees Union Local 590 v. Logan Valley Plaza, Inc., 391 U.S. 308 (1968), with Lloyd Corp., Ltd. v. Tanner, 407 U.S. 551 (1972), both discussed infra p. 1124.) Other explanations may stem from the fact that nearly all of the cases prior to 1968 dealt with racial discrimination. Since 1970, issues such as first amendment rights of access to private property and due process rights of fair procedure have been prominent. Is the extent of governmental action required to invoke constitutional protection less where racial discrimination is claimed than when other forms of discrimination, or other constitutional rights, are involved?

A related question concerns the impact of the growing body of federal legislation prohibiting private racial discrimination. (See sections 3, 4, 5 and 6 of this chapter.) The Civil Rights Act of 1964 prohibits private racial discrimination in places of public accommodation, employment, and activities—including private education—receiving Federal financial assistance. The 1968 Civil Rights Act prohibits racial discrimination in the private housing market, and provides criminal penalties for many forms of private racial violence. And, in 1968, the Court discovered that remaining fragments of the Civil Rights Act of 1866 reached broad areas of private racial discrimination. (See section 4 of this chapter.) There are few cases now where the issue whether federal law prohibits private racial discrimination will turn on whether sufficient indicia of state action are present to invoke the provisions of the fourteenth amendment. Does this suggest legitimate reasons for limiting state action doctrines, even as applied to racial discrimination?

A.   PRIVATE PERFORMANCE OF "GOVERNMENT" FUNCTIONS

THE WHITE PRIMARY CASES

Despite the clear terms of the fifteenth amendment, for three-quarters of a century an effective means to block voting by Blacks was their exclusion from the Democratic Party in Southern States. Initially, it was argued that primary voting was beyond constitutional protection, even if state law mandated exclusion of Black voters from participation in the Democratic primaries. In Nixon v. Herndon, 273 U.S. 536 (1927), however, a Texas statute excluding Blacks from Democratic primaries was held to be unconstitutional as racial discrimination by the state. Texas' response was to repeal the offending statute, and to provide that a party's executive committee had the power to determine the party's membership. Exclusion of Blacks from the Democratic primary was again held unconstitutional on the ground that the new Texas statute had made the committee an agent of the state. Nixon v. Condon, 286 U.S. 73 (1932). When the Texas Democratic Party once again excluded Blacks from party membership, however, the exclusion survived constitutional attack on the ground that it was not state action, but the action of a private group. Grovey v. Townsend, 295 U.S. 45 (1935). Grovey v. Townsend was overruled in Smith v. Allwright, 321 U.S. 649 (1944), because "the place of the primary in the electoral scheme makes clear that state delegation to a party of the power to fix the qualifications of primary elections is delegation of a state function that may make the party's action the action of the state." That the Constitution prohibited exclusion of Blacks from participating in elections, whatever form the election took, was dramatized in Terry v. Adams, 345 U.S. 461 (1953), where Blacks were excluded from voting in a pre-primary straw vote of a Texas county political organization called the Jaybird Democratic Organization. Because winners in the Jaybird primary ran unopposed in the formal Democratic primaries, the Court decided that exclusion of Blacks from the Jaybird primary was a violation of the fifteenth amendment, despite the absence of formal state involvement in their exclusion.

STEELE v. LOUISVILLE AND NASHVILLE RAILROAD CO., 323 U.S. 192 (1944). The Brotherhood of Locomotive Firemen and Enginemen, under the terms of the Railway Labor Act, was exclusive bargaining representative for the railway firemen. Blacks who constituted a substantial minority of the labor force, were excluded from membership in the brotherhood. As a result of negotiations an agreement was made in 1941 between the railroad and the brotherhood providing for restrictions on the hiring and promotion of blacks with the ultimate aim of their exclusion from work as firemen. Steele, a black fireman, brought suit against the railroad and the brotherhood based on the foregoing facts. The Supreme Court of Alabama affirmed the dismissal of the complaint. the United States Supreme Court, speaking through Chief Justice Stone, said:

"If, as the state court has held, the Act confers this power on the bargaining representative of a craft or class of employees without any commensurate statutory duty toward its members, constitutional questions arise. For the representative is clothed with power not unlike that of a legislature which is subject to constitutional limitations on its power to deny, restrict, destroy or discriminate against the rights of those for whom it legislates and which is also under an affirmative constitutional duty equally to protect those rights....

"We think that the Railway Labor Act imposes upon the statutory representatives of a craft at least as exacting a duty to protect equally the interests of the members of the craft as the Constitution imposes upon a legislature to give equal protection to the interests of those for whom it legislates. Congress has seen fit to clothe the bargaining representative with powers comparable to those possessed by a legislative body both to create and restrict the rights of those whom it represents, ... but it has also imposed on the representative a corresponding duty....

"Reversed."

Justice Murphy, concurring, stated that the case presented "a grave constitutional issue that should be squarely faced." The Railway Labor Act must be construed to bar this discrimination: "Otherwise the Act would bear the stigma of unconstitutionality under the Fifth Amendment in this respect."

[handwritten margin note: Holding]

[handwritten margin note: must bar Act's discrimination]

ACCESS TO COMPANY TOWNS AND SHOPPING CENTERS

marsh v. Alabama [handwritten margin note]

Marsh v. Alabama, 326 U.S. 501 (1946), was one of two pre–1970 Supreme Court decisions, that presented the state action issue in some context other than racial discrimination. A member of Jehovah's Witnesses was prosecuted for trespass when she distributed religious literature on the streets of a company-owned town and refused to leave when ordered to do so. The town involved was described by the Court as being accessible to and freely used by the public in general with nothing to distinguish it from any other town except the fact that the title to the property belonged to a private corporation. In reversing the conviction the Court talked primarily about first amendment issues. It stated that had the corporation owned the segment of the state highway that paralleled the business street of the company town and operated that segment it would "have been the performance of a public function." The opinion then continued:

> "We do not think it makes any significant constitutional difference as to the relationship between the rights of the owner and those of the public that here the State, instead of permitting the corporation to operate a highway, permitted it to use its property as a town, operate a 'business block' in the town and a street and sidewalk on that business block.... Whether a corporation or a municipality owns or possesses the town the public in either case has an identical interest in the functioning of the community in such manner that the channels of communication remain free."

The other pre–1970 case not involving racial discrimination was Amalgamated Food Employees Union Local 590 v. Logan Valley Plaza, Inc., 391 U.S. 308 (1968), which extended *Marsh* to require that picketers be given access to a large privately-owned shopping center. Justice Marshall's opinion for the majority concluded that there was no reason to draw a distinction between a privately owned business district surrounded by residential property under the same ownership, and one surrounded by property under other ownership. Justice Black, the author of the *Marsh* opinion but one of three dissenters in *Logan Valley,* argued that the company town in *Marsh* had all the attributes of a conventional municipality, but that the shopping center had only one— ownership of the business block. *Logan Valley* was criticized, but distinguished, in Lloyd Corp., Ltd. v. Tanner, 407 U.S. 551 (1972), where anti-war leafletters were held not to have a constitutional right of access to a large privately-owned shopping center. The four Justices in the *Logan Valley* majority who were still on the Court dissented in *Lloyd.* In Hudgens v. NLRB, 424 U.S. 507 (1976), the Court concluded that *Lloyd* had overruled *Logan Valley* and that speakers had no constitutional right of access to large privately-owned shopping centers.

EVANS v. NEWTON, 382 U.S. 296 (1966). In 1911, Senator Augustus O. Bacon executed a will devising land to the city of Macon, Georgia, for a park for whites only. The city kept the park segregated for decades, but in some years prior to this suit permitted blacks to use it on the ground that the city could not constitutionally maintain a segregated park. (See Pennsylvania v. Board of City Trusts, infra, p. 1136) This suit sought to remove the city as trustee. Black citizens of Macon intervened, asking the state court to refuse to appoint new private trustees. State courts accepted the resignation of the city as trustee and appointed private trustees. . The united states supreme court reversed, holding that the park could not be maintained on a segregated basis, despite the city's resignation as trustee. Justice Douglas' opinion for the court gave two reasons. First, his opinion read the record below as showing that the city remained "entwined in the management or control of the park." Second, the opinion stated:

> "This conclusion [that the substitution of trustees did not transfer the park to the 'private sector'] is buttressed by the nature of the service rendered the community by a park. The service rendered even by a private park of this character is municipal in nature. It is open to every white person, there being no selective element other than race. Golf clubs, social centers, luncheon clubs, schools such as Tuskegee was at least in origin, and other like organizations in the private sector are often racially orient- ed. A park, on the other hand, is more like a fire department or police department that traditionally serves the community. Mass recreation through the use of parks is plainly in the public domain, Watson v. Memphis, 373 U.S. 526; and state courts that aid private parties to perform that public function on a segregated basis implicate the State in conduct proscribed by the Fourteenth Amendment. Like the streets of the company town in Marsh v. Alabama, supra, the elective process of Terry v. Adams, supra, and the transit system of Public Util. Comm'n v. Pollak, supra, the predominant character and purpose of this park are municipal."

Justice White concurred in the result. Justices Black, Harlan and Stewart dissented.

Flagg Brothers, Inc. v. Brooks

436 U.S. 149, 98 S.Ct. 1729, 56 L.Ed.2d 185 (1978).

Mr. Justice Rehnquist delivered the opinion of the Court.

The question presented by this litigation is whether a warehouseman's proposed sale of goods entrusted to him for storage, as permitted by New York Uniform Commercial Code § 7–210, is an action properly attributable to the State of New York. . . .

I.

According to her complaint, the allegations of which we must accept as true, respondent Shirley Brooks and her family were evicted from their apart- ment in Mount Vernon, N.Y., on June 13, 1973. The City Marshal arranged for Brooks' possessions to be stored by petitioner Flagg Brothers, Inc., in its warehouse. Respondent was informed of the cost of moving and storage, and she instructed the workmen to proceed, although she found the price too high. On August 25, 1973, after a series of disputes over the validity of the charges being claimed by petitioner, Flagg Brothers, Brooks received a letter demanding that her account be brought up to date within 10 days "or your furniture will be sold." . . . A series of subsequent letters from respondent and her attorneys produced no satisfaction.

Brooks thereupon initiated this class action in the District Court under 42 U.S.C. § 1983, seeking damages, an injunction against the threatened sale of her belongings, and the declaration that such a sale pursuant to § 7–210 would violate the Due Process and Equal Protection Clauses of the Fourteenth Amendment. . . . [T]he District Court, dismissed the complaint for failure to state a claim for relief under § 1983.

A divided panel of the Court of Appeals reversed.

. . .

II.

A claim upon which relief may be granted to respondents against Flagg Brothers under § 1983 must embody at least two elements. Respondents are first bound to show that they have been deprived of a right "secured by the Constitution and the laws" of the United States. They must secondly show that Flagg Brothers deprived them of this right acting "under color of any statute" of the State of New York. It is clear that these two elements denote two separate areas of inquiry. . . .

It must be noted that respondents have named no public officials as defendants in this action. The city marshal, who supervised their evictions, was dismissed from the case by the consent of all the parties. This total absence of overt official involvement plainly distinguishes this case from earlier decisions imposing procedural restrictions on creditors' remedies. . . . While as a factual matter any person with sufficient physical power may deprive a person of his property, only a State or a private person whose action "may fairly be treated as that of the State itself," . . . may deprive him of "an interest encompassed within the Fourteenth Amendment's protection," . . . Thus, the only issue presented by this case is whether Flagg Brothers' action may fairly be attributed to the State of New York. We conclude that it may not.

III.

Respondents' primary contention is that New York has delegated to Flagg Brothers a power "traditionally exclusively reserved to the State." . . . They argue that the resolution of private disputes is a traditional function of civil government, and that the State in § 7–210 has delegated this function to Flagg Brothers. Respondents, however, have read too much into the language of our previous cases. While many functions have been traditionally performed by governments, very few have been "exclusively reserved to the State."

One such area has been elections. While the Constitution protects private rights of association and advocacy with regard to the election of public officials, our cases make it clear that the conduct of the elections themselves is an exclusively public function. . . .

A second line of cases under the public function doctrine originated with Marsh v. Alabama . . . Just as the Texas Democratic Party in *Smith* and the Jaybird Democratic Association in *Terry* effectively performed the entire public function of selecting public officials, so too the Gulf Shipbuilding Corp. performed all the necessary municipal functions in the town of Chickasaw, Ala., which it owned. . . .

These two branches of the public function doctrine have in common the feature of exclusivity.[8] Although the elections held by the Democratic Party and its affiliates were the only meaningful elections in Texas, and the streets owned by the Gulf Shipbuilding Corp. were the only streets in Chickasaw, the

---

8. Respondents also contend that Evans v. Newton, 382 U.S. 296 (1966), establishes that the operation of a park for recreational purposes is an exclusively public function. We doubt that *Newton* intended to establish any such broad doctrine in the teeth of the experience of several American entrepreneurs who amassed great fortunes by operating parks for recreational purposes. We think *Newton* rests on a finding of ordinary state action under extraordinary circumstances. The Court's opinion emphasizes that the record showed "no change in the municipal maintenance and concern over this facility," id., at 301, after the transfer of title to private trustees. That transfer had not been shown to have eliminated the actual involvement of the city in the daily maintenance and care of the park.

proposed sale by Flagg Brothers under § 7–210 is not the only means of resolving this purely private dispute. . . .

Whatever the particular remedies available under New York law, we do not consider a . . . detailed description of them necessary to our conclusion that the settlement of disputes between debtors and creditors is not traditionally an exclusive public function. . . .

Modern Rule

Thus, even if we were inclined to extend the sovereign function doctrine outside of its present carefully confined bounds, the field of private commercial transactions would be a particularly inappropriate area into which to expand it. We conclude that our sovereign function cases do not support a finding of state action here.

. . . [T]here are a number of state and municipal functions not covered by our election cases nor governed by the reasoning of *Marsh* which have been administered with a greater degree of exclusivity by States and municipalities than has the function of so-called "dispute resolution." Among these are such functions as education, fire and police protection, and tax collection. We express no view as to the extent, if any, to which a city or State might be free to delegate to private parties the performance of such functions and thereby avoid the strictures of the Fourteenth Amendment. The mere recitation of these possible permutations and combinations of factual situations suffices to caution us that their resolution should abide the necessity of deciding them.

IV.

Respondents further urge that Flagg Brothers' proposed action is properly attributable to the State because the State has authorized and encouraged it in enacting § 7–210. Our cases state "that a State is responsible for the . . . act of a private party when the State, by its law, has compelled the act." . . . This Court, however, has never held that a State's mere acquiescence in a private action converts that action into that of the State. . . .

. . .

Here, the State of New York has not compelled the sale of a bailor's goods, but has merely announced the circumstances under which its courts will not interfere with a private sale. Indeed, the crux of respondents' complaint is not that the State *has* acted, but that it has *refused* to act. This statutory refusal to act is no different in principle from an ordinary statute of limitations whereby the State declines to provide a remedy for private deprivations of property after the passage of a given period of time.

. . .

Reversed.

Mr. Justice Brennan took no part in the consideration or decision of this case.

Mr. Justice Stevens, with whom Mr. Justice White and Mr. Justice Marshall join, dissenting.

. . . In my judgment the Court's holding is fundamentally inconsistent with, if not foreclosed by, our prior decisions which have imposed procedural restrictions on the State's authorization of certain creditors' remedies. . . .

There is no question in this case but that respondents have a property interest in the possessions that the warehouseman proposes to sell. It is also clear that, whatever power of sale the warehouseman has, it does not derive from the consent of the respondents. The claimed power derives solely from the

State, and specifically from § 7–210 of the New York Uniform Commercial Code. The question is whether a state statute which authorizes a private party to deprive a person of his property without his consent must meet the requirements of the Due Process Clause of the Fourteenth Amendment. This question must be answered in the affirmative unless the State has virtually unlimited power to transfer interests in private property without any procedural protections.

In determining that New York's statute cannot be scrutinized under the Due Process Clause, the Court reasons that the warehouseman's proposed sale is solely private action because the state statute *"permits* but does not compel" the sale, . . . (emphasis added), and because the warehouseman has not been delegated a power *"exclusively* reserved to the State," . . . (emphasis added). Under this approach a State could enact laws authorizing private citizens to use self-help in countless situations without any possibility of federal challenge. . . . [T]he distinctions between "permission" and "compulsion" on the one hand, and "exclusive" and "non-exclusive," on the other, cannot be determinative factors in state-action, analysis. . . . In this case, the State of New York, by enacting § 7–210 of the Uniform Commercial Code, has acted in the most effective and unambiguous way a State can act. This section specifically authorizes petitioner to sell respondents' possessions; it details the procedures that petitioner must follow; and it grants petitioner the power to convey good title to goods that are now owned by respondents to a third party.

While Members of this Court have suggested that statutory authorization alone may be sufficient to establish state action, it is not necessary to rely on those suggestions in this case because New York has authorized the warehouseman to perform what is clearly a state function. The test of what is a state function for purposes of the Due Process Clause has been variously phrased. Most frequently the issue is presented in terms of whether the State has delegated a function traditionally and historically associated with sovereignty. . . . In this Court, petitioners have attempted to argue that the nonconsensual transfer of property rights is not a traditional function of the sovereign. The overwhelming historical evidence is to the contrary, however, and the Court wisely does not adopt this position. Instead, the Court reasons that state action cannot be found because the State has not delegated to the warehouseman an *exclusive* sovereign function. This distinction, however, is not consistent with our prior decisions on state action[9]. . . .

. . .

Whether termed "traditional," "exclusive," or "significant," the state power to order binding, nonconsensual resolution of a conflict between debtor and creditor is exactly the sort of power with which the Due Process Clause is concerned. And the State's delegation of that power to a private party is, accordingly, subject to due process scrutiny. . . .

It is important to emphasize that, contrary to the Court's apparent fears, this conclusion does not even remotely suggest that "all private deprivations of property [will] be converted into public acts whenever the State, for whatever reason, denies relief sought by the putative property owner." . . . The focus is not on the private deprivation but on the state authorization. "[W]hat is always

---

9. The Court, for instance, attempts to distinguish Evans v. Newton, . . . *Newton* concededly involved a function which is not exclusively sovereign—the operation of a park, but the Court claims that *Newton* actually rested on a determination that the City was still involved in the "daily maintenance and care of the park." This stark attempt to rewrite the rationale of the *Newton* opinion is fully answered by Mr. Justice White's opinion in that case. . . .

vital to remember is that it is the *state's* conduct, whether action or inaction, not the *private* conduct, that gives rise to constitutional attack." H. Friendly, The Dartmouth College Case and The Public–Private Penumbra, p. 17 (emphasis in original). The State's conduct in this case takes the concrete form of a statutory enactment, and it is that statute that may be challenged.

My analysis in this case thus assumes that petitioner's proposed sale will conform to the procedure specified by the state legislature and that respondents' challenge therefore will be to the constitutionality of that process. It is only what the State itself has enacted that they may ask the federal court to review in a § 1983 case. If there should be a deviation from the state statute— such as a failure to give the notice required by the state law—the defect could be remedied by a state court and there would be no occasion for § 1983 relief. . . .

On the other hand, if there is compliance with the New York statute, the state legislative action which enabled the deprivation to take place must be subject to constitutional challenge in a federal court. Under this approach, the federal courts do not have jurisdiction to review every foreclosure proceeding in which the debtor claims that there has been a procedural defect constituting a denial of due process of law. Rather, the Federal District Court's jurisdiction under § 1983 is limited to challenges to the constitutionality of the state procedure itself. . . .

Finally, it is obviously true that the overwhelming majority of disputes in our society are resolved in the private sphere. But it is no longer possible, if it ever was, to believe that a sharp line can be drawn between private and public actions. The Court today holds that our examination of state delegations of power should be limited to those rare instances where the State has ceded one of its "exclusive" powers. As indicated, I believe that this limitation is neither logical nor practical. More troubling, this description of what is state action does not even attempt to reflect the concerns of the Due Process Clause, for the state action doctrine is, after all, merely one aspect of this broad constitutional protection.

In the broadest sense, we expect government "to provide a reasonable and fair framework of rules which facilitate commercial transactions. . . ." Mitchell v. W.T. Grant, . . . 416 U.S., at 624 (Powell, J., concurring). This "framework of rules" is premised on the assumption that the State will control nonconsensual deprivations of property and that the State's control will, in turn, be subject to the restrictions of the Due Process Clause. The power to order legally binding surrenders of property and the constitutional restrictions on that power are necessary correlatives in our system. In effect, today's decision allows the State to divorce these two elements by the simple expedient of transferring the implementation of its policy to private parties. Because the Fourteenth Amendment does not countenance such a division of power and responsibility, I respectfully dissent.[a]

SAN FRANCISCO ARTS & ATHLETICS, INC. v. UNITED STATES OLYMPIC COMMITTEE, 483 U.S. 522 (1987). Section 110 of the Amateur Sports Act of 1978 grants the committee the right to prohibit commercial and promotional uses of the word "olympic." The court rejected an argument that the committee violated the equal protection component of the Fifth Amendment by discriminatory enforcement of its exclusive right. The committee was

---

a. See Brest, *State Action and Liberal Theory: A Casenote on* Flagg Brothers v. Brooks, 130 U.Pa.L.Rev. 96 (1982).

not a governmental actor and did not perform functions that have been traditionally the exclusive prerogative of the federal government. There was no evidence of governmental involvement in the committee's choice of how it enforced its right. Four dissenters argued that the committee was a governmental actor because there was a "symbiotic relationship" between the committee and the federal government in coordinating amateur athletics in international competition. Two of the four dissenters argued, in addition, that the committee performed a public function in governing international amateur athletics.

B.   GOVERNMENTAL ENFORCEMENT OF "PRIVATE" DECISIONS

Shelley v. Kraemer

334 U.S. 1, 68 S.Ct. 836, 92 L.Ed. 1161 (1948).

Mr. Chief Justice Vinson delivered the opinion of the Court.

These cases present for our consideration questions relating to the validity of court enforcement of private agreements, generally described as restrictive covenants, which have as their purpose the exclusion of persons of designated race or color from the ownership or occupancy of real property. Basic constitutional issues of obvious importance have been raised.

The first of these cases comes to this Court on certiorari to the Supreme Court of Missouri. On February 16, 1911, thirty out of a total of thirty-nine owners of property fronting both sides of Labadie Avenue between Taylor Avenue and Cora Avenue in the city of St. Louis, signed an agreement, which was subsequently recorded providing in part:

"... the said property is hereby restricted to the use and occupancy for the term of Fifty (50) years from this date, so that it shall be a condition all the time and whether recited and referred to as [sic] not in subsequent conveyances and shall attach to the land, as a condition precedent to the sale of the same, that hereafter no part of said property or any portion thereof shall be, for said term of Fifty-years, occupied by any person not of the Caucasian race, it being intended hereby to restrict the use of said property for said period of time against the occupancy as owners or tenants of any portion of said property for resident or other purpose by people of the Negro or Mongolian Race."

The entire district described in the agreement included fifty-seven parcels of land. The thirty owners who signed the agreement held title to forty-seven parcels, including the particular parcel involved in this case. ...

On August 11, 1945, pursuant to a contract of sale, petitioners Shelley, who are Negroes, for valuable consideration received from one Fitzgerald a warranty deed to the parcel in question. The trial court found that petitioners had no actual knowledge of the restrictive agreement at the time of the purchase.

On October 9, 1945, respondents, as owners of other property subject to the terms of the restrictive covenant, brought suit in the Circuit Court of the city of St. Louis praying that petitioners Shelley be restrained from taking possession of the property and that judgment be entered divesting title out of petitioners Shelley and revesting title in the immediate grantor or in such other person as the court should direct. The trial court denied the requested relief on the ground that the restrictive agreement, upon which respondents based their action, had never become final and complete. ...

The Supreme Court of Missouri sitting *en banc* reversed and directed the trial court to grant the relief for which respondents had prayed. That court held the agreement effective and concluded that enforcement of its provisions violated no rights guaranteed to petitioners by the Federal Constitution. At the time the court rendered its decision, petitioners were occupying the property in question.

The second of the cases under consideration comes to this Court from the Supreme Court of Michigan. The circumstances presented do not differ materially from the Missouri case. . . .

Petitioners have placed primary reliance on their contentions, first raised in the state courts, that judicial enforcement of the restrictive agreements in these cases has violated rights guaranteed to petitioners by the Fourteenth Amendment of the Federal Constitution and Acts of Congress passed pursuant to that Amendment. Specifically, petitioners urge that they have been denied the equal protection of the laws, deprived of property without due process of law, and have been denied privileges and immunities of citizens of the United States. We pass to a consideration of those issues.

I.

Whether the equal protection clause of the Fourteenth Amendment inhibits judicial enforcement by state courts of restrictive covenants based on race or color is a question which this Court has not heretofore been called upon to consider. . . .

. . .

It should be observed that these covenants do not seek to proscribe any particular use of the affected properties. Use of the properties for residential occupancy, as such, is not forbidden. The restrictions of these agreements, rather are directed toward a designated class of persons and seek to determine who may and who may not own or make use of the properties for residential purposes. The excluded class is defined wholly in terms of race or color; "simply that and nothing more."

It cannot be doubted that among the civil rights intended to be protected from discriminatory state action by the Fourteenth Amendment are the rights to acquire, enjoy, own and dispose of property. . . .

It is likewise clear that restrictions on the right of occupancy of the sort sought to be created by the private agreements in these cases could not be squared with the requirements of the Fourteenth Amendment if imposed by state statute or local ordinance. We do not understand respondents to urge the contrary. In the case of Buchanan v. Warley [245 U.S. 60] a unanimous Court declared unconstitutional the provisions of a city ordinance which denied to colored persons the right to occupy houses in blocks in which the greater number of houses were occupied by white persons, and imposed similar restrictions on white persons with respect to blocks in which the greater number of houses were occupied by colored persons. During the course of the opinion in that case, this Court stated: "The Fourteenth Amendment and these statutes enacted in furtherance of its purpose operate to qualify and entitle a colored man to acquire property without state legislation discriminating against him solely because of color."

In Harmon v. Tyler, 273 U.S. 668 (1927), a unanimous court, on the authority of *Buchanan v. Warley,* supra, declared invalid an ordinance which forbade any Negro to establish a home on any property in a white community or any white person to establish a home in a Negro community, "except on the written consent of a majority of the persons of the opposite race inhabiting such community or portion of the City to be affected.''

But the present cases, unlike those just discussed, do not involve action by state legislatures or city councils. Here the particular patterns of discrimination and the areas in which the restrictions are to operate, are determined, in the first instance, by the terms of agreements among private individuals. Participation of the State consists in the enforcement of the restrictions so defined. The crucial issue with which we are here confronted is whether this distinction removes these cases from the operation of the prohibitory provisions of the Fourteenth Amendment.

Since the decision of this Court in the Civil Rights Cases, 109 U.S. 3 (1883), the principle has become firmly embedded in our constitutional law that the action inhibited by the first section of the Fourteenth Amendment is only such action as may fairly be said to be that of the States. That Amendment erects no shield against merely private conduct, however discriminatory or wrongful.

We conclude, therefore, that the restrictive agreements standing alone cannot be regarded as a violation of any rights guaranteed to petitioners by the Fourteenth Amendment. So long as the purposes of those agreements are effectuated by voluntary adherence to their terms, it would appear clear that there has been no action by the State and the provisions of the Amendment have not been violated. . . .

But here there was more. These are cases in which the purposes of the agreements were secured only by judicial enforcement by state courts of the restrictive terms of the agreements. The respondents urge that judicial enforcement of private agreements does not amount to state action; or, in any event, the participation of the State is so attenuated in character as not to amount to state action within the meaning of the Fourteenth Amendment. Finally, it is suggested, even if the States in these cases may be deemed to have acted in the constitutional sense, their action did not deprive petitioners of rights guaranteed by the Fourteenth Amendment. We move to a consideration of these matters.

II.

That the action of state courts and of judicial officers in their official capacities is to be regarded as action of the State within the meaning of the Fourteenth Amendment, is a proposition which has long been established by decisions of this Court. That principle was given expression in the earliest cases involving the construction of the terms of the Fourteenth Amendment. . . .

One of the earliest applications of the prohibitions contained in the Fourteenth Amendment to action of state judicial officials occurred in cases in which Negroes had been excluded from jury service in criminal prosecutions by reason of their race or color. These cases demonstrate, also, the early recognition by this Court that state action in violation of the Amendment's provisions is equally repugnant to the constitutional commands whether directed by state statute or taken by a judicial official in the absence of statute. . . .

The action of state courts in imposing penalties or depriving parties of other substantive rights without providing adequate notice and opportunity to defend, has, of course, long been regarded as a denial of the due process of law guaranteed by the Fourteenth Amendment. . . .

In numerous cases, this Court has reversed criminal convictions in state courts for failure of those courts to provide the essential ingredients of a fair hearing. . . .

But the examples of state judicial action which have been held by this Court to violate the Amendment's commands are not restricted to situations in which the judicial proceedings were found in some manner to be procedurally unfair. It has been recognized that the action of state courts in enforcing a substantive common-law rule formulated by those courts, may result in the denial of rights guaranteed by the Fourteenth Amendment, even though the judicial proceedings in such cases may have been in complete accord with the most rigorous conceptions of procedural due process. Thus in American Federation of Labor v. Swing, 1941, 312 U.S. 321, enforcement by state courts of the common-law policy of the State, which resulted in the restraining of peaceful picketing, was held to be state action of the sort prohibited by the Amendment's guaranties of freedom of discussion. . . .

The short of the matter is that from the time of the adoption of the Fourteenth Amendment until the present, it has been the consistent ruling of this Court that the action of the States to which the Amendment has reference, includes action of state courts and state judicial officials. Although, in construing the terms of the Fourteenth Amendment, differences have from time to time been expressed as to whether particular types of state action may be said to offend the Amendment's prohibitory provisions, it has never been suggested that state court action is immunized from the operation of those provisions simply because the act is that of the judicial branch of the state government.

III.

Against this background of judicial construction, extending over a period of some three-quarters of a century, we are called upon to consider whether enforcement by state courts of the restrictive agreements in these cases may be deemed to be the acts of those States; and, if so, whether that action has denied these petitioners the equal protection of the laws which the Amendment was intended to insure.

We have no doubt that there has been state action in these cases in the full and complete sense of the phrase. The undisputed facts disclose that petitioners were willing purchasers of properties upon which they desired to establish homes. The owners of the properties were willing sellers; and contracts of sale were accordingly consummated. It is clear that but for the active intervention of the state courts, supported by the full panoply of state power, petitioners would have been free to occupy the properties in question without restraint.

These are not cases, as has been suggested, in which the States have merely abstained from action, leaving private individuals free to impose such discriminations as they see fit. Rather, these are cases in which the States have made available to such individuals the full coercive power of government to deny to petitioners, on the grounds of race or color, the enjoyment of property rights in premises which petitioners are willing and financially able to acquire and which the grantors are willing to sell. The difference between judicial enforcement and nonenforcement of the restrictive covenants is the difference to petitioners between being denied rights of property available to other members of the community and being accorded full enjoyment of those rights on an equal footing.

The enforcement of the restrictive agreements by the state courts in these cases was directed pursuant to the common-law policy of the States as formulated by those courts in earlier decisions. In the Missouri case, enforcement of the covenant was directed in the first instance by the highest court of the State after the trial court had determined the agreement to be invalid for want of the requisite number of signatures. In the Michigan case, the order of enforcement by the trial court was affirmed by the highest state court. The judicial action in each case bears the clear and unmistakable imprimatur of the State. We have noted that previous decisions of this Court have established the proposition that judicial action is not immunized from the operation of the Fourteenth Amendment simply because it is taken pursuant to the state's common-law policy. Nor is the Amendment ineffective simply because the particular pattern of discrimination, which the State has enforced, was defined initially by the terms of a private agreement. State action, as that phrase is understood for the purposes of the Fourteenth Amendment, refers to exertions of state power in all forms. And when the effect of that action is to deny rights subject to the protection of the Fourteenth Amendment, it is the obligation of this Court to enforce the constitutional commands.

We hold that in granting judicial enforcement of the restrictive agreements in these cases, the States have denied petitioners the equal protection of the laws and that, therefore, the action of the state courts cannot stand. We have noted that freedom from discrimination by the States in the enjoyment of property rights was among the basic objectives sought to be effectuated by the framers of the Fourteenth Amendment. That such discrimination has occurred in these cases is clear. Because of the race or color of these petitioners they have been denied rights of ownership or occupancy enjoyed as a matter of course by other citizens of different race or color. . . .

Respondents urge, however, that since the state courts stand ready to enforce restrictive covenants excluding white persons from the ownership or occupancy of property covered by such agreements, enforcement of covenants excluding colored persons may not be deemed a denial of equal protection of the laws to the colored persons who are thereby affected. This contention does not bear scrutiny. The parties have directed our attention to no case in which a court, state or federal, has been called upon to enforce a covenant excluding members of the white majority from ownership or occupancy of real property on grounds of race or color. But there are more fundamental considerations. The rights created by the first section of the Fourteenth Amendment are, by its terms, guaranteed to the individual. The rights established are personal rights. It is, therefore, no answer to these petitioners to say that the courts may also be induced to deny white persons rights of ownership and occupancy on grounds of race or color. Equal protection of the laws is not achieved through indiscriminate imposition of inequalities. . . .

. . .

For the reasons stated, the judgment of the Supreme Court of Missouri and the judgment of the Supreme Court of Michigan must be reversed.

Reversed.

Mr. Justice Reed, Mr. Justice Jackson, and Mr. Justice Rutledge took no part in the consideration or decision of these cases.

RESTRICTIVE COVENANTS

Restrictive covenants directed against minorities were used widely prior to the *Shelley* case, particularly in large cities in the North and West. These covenants were not only against Blacks but also Armenians, Jews, Mexicans, Syrians, Japanese, Chinese and American Indians. It has been estimated that

80% of the land in Chicago was restricted. *To Secure These Rights—The Report of the President's Committee on Civil Rights* 67–70 (1947).

The use of these covenants prior to *Shelley* contributed to the isolation of Blacks in congested and substandard housing. Partly as a result of limitations of Blacks' access to housing, they often were forced to pay higher rentals than Whites. Helfield & Groner, *Race Discrimination in Housing,* 57 Yale L.J. 426, 426–33 (1948). Would such evidence have been relevant to the *Shelley* decision? See Martin, *Segregation of Residences of Negroes,* 32 Mich.L.Rev. 721 (1934).[1]

BARROWS v. JACKSON, 346 U.S. 249 (1953). Plaintiff's predecessor and defendant, owners of real estate in the same neighborhood, entered into an agreement, recorded on the deeds and running against subsequent takers, that their property would be occupied only by caucasians. Plaintiff sued defendant for damages alleging that, in violation of their agreement, defendant had sold his property without including the agreed restriction in the deed, and had permitted non–caucasians to move in and occupy the premises. The California courts sustained a demurrer to the complaint on the authority of *Shelley.*

The United States Supreme Court affirmed California's denial of relief. Justice Minton, for the Court, wrote: "This Court will not permit or require California to coerce respondent to respond in damages for failure to observe a restrictive covenant that this Court would deny California the right to enforce in equity. . . ."

PROSECUTION OF "SIT–IN" DEMONSTRATORS IN THE 1960S

A significant phase of the civil rights struggle was the use of "sit-in" demonstrations at Southern restaurants or lunch counters where Blacks were segregated or refused service. Typically, Blacks would sit at a table or counter, be asked to leave, and be arrested and convicted of trespass when they refused. The Supreme Court reviewed the constitutionality of the convictions of literally hundreds of sit-in demonstrators in the early sixties. While the convictions were reversed, a majority of the Court never faced squarely the question whether enforcement of a private property owner's discrimination was unconstitutional state action under Shelley v. Kraemer. In some cases, convictions were reversed on the ground that the state trespass statute gave inadequate warning as to whether it prohibited remaining on private property after being asked to leave as well as unauthorized "entry." Bouie v. City of Columbia, 378 U.S. 347 (1964). Where convictions were reversed because of unconstitutional state action, the grounds were narrow. E.g., Robinson v. Florida, 378 U.S. 153 (1964) (city ordinance required segregation although restaurant manager stated that Blacks were excluded for business reasons); Griffin v. Maryland, 378 U.S. 130 (1964) (amusement park employee who asked Blacks to leave and arrested them was also deputized as a sheriff).

The *Griffin* case is particularly interesting. The state argued that the constitutional issues in the case were indistinguishable from those where the trespass arrest had been made by a police officer not employed by the park. The Court did not resolve the state's broad contention that no constitutional violation followed from a police arrest and state conviction for trespass of a person refusing to leave private property. The Court noted that Collins, the

---

1. See also: Karst & Van Alstyne, *State Action,* 14 Stan.L.Rev. 3 (1961); Henkin, *Shelley v. Kraemer: Notes for a Revised Opinion,* 110 U.Pa.L.Rev. 473 (1962); *Effect of State Court Interpretation of a Contract,* 55 Mich.L.Rev. 871 (1957); *Police Enforcement* *of Private Discrimination,* 52 N.W.U.L.Rev. 774 (1958); *Criminal Penalties to Enforce Private Discrimination,* 57 Mich.L.Rev. 122 (1958); *Impact of Shelley v. Kraemer on the State Action Concept,* 44 Cal.L.Rev. 718 (1956).

park employee who asked the defendants to leave, wore a sheriff's badge and "consistently identified himself as a deputy sheriff" when asking defendants to leave and placing them under arrest. Collins had a contractual obligation to enforce the park's policy. The case thus fell within the rule that a state (Collins) could not undertake an obligation to enforce a private policy of racial discrimination. The three dissenters conceded that Collins was exercising state authority, but argued that "the involvement of the State is no different from what it would have been had the arrests been made by a regular policeman dispatched from police headquarters." Suppose Collins had not worn his badge nor identified himself as a sheriff when he asked defendants to leave the amusement park. When they refused, he called a regular policeman who arrived and made the arrest. Can you think of a tenable theory that supports a conclusion that there was unconstitutional state action on the facts in *Griffin,* but that there would not be on the supposed facts?

The sit-in cases came to an end with the enactment of Title II of the Civil Rights Act of 1964 which prohibited discrimination in places of public accommodation. (The Court held that the statute abated sit-in prosecutions that had occurred prior to its enactment. Hamm v. City of Rock Hill, 379 U.S. 306 [1964].) In one of the last of the sit-in cases, five Justices did reach the broader issue of the application of Shelley v. Kraemer to the sit-in situation. Bell v. Maryland, 378 U.S. 226 (1964). Justice Douglas, joined by Justice Goldberg, argued that *Shelley* should govern when trespass convictions were used to enforce private discrimination that represented business preferences rather than personal prejudices. (Justice Goldberg, joined by Chief Justice Warren and Justice Douglas, also argued that access to public accommodations was a privilege of national citizenship). Justice Black's dissent, joined by Justices Harlan and White, argued that *Shelley* was inapplicable. A citizen who sought the law's protection of his property rights was not cast outside the law's protection because he called on law officers to enforce those rights. Shelley v. Kraemer was a case, according to Justice Black, where enforcement of a restrictive covenant operated to prohibit a willing seller from conveying to a Black purchaser and its principle did not apply to cases where the property owner was unwilling to permit occupation of his property by Blacks.

Pennsylvania v. Board of City Trusts

353 U.S. 230, 77 S.Ct. 806, 1 L.Ed.2d 792 (1957).

Per Curiam.

The motion to dismiss the appeal for want of jurisdiction is granted, 28 U.S.C. § 1257(2). Treating the papers whereon the appeal was taken as a petition for writ of certiorari, 28 U.S.C. § 2103, the petition is granted. 28 U.S.C. § 1257(3).

Stephen Girard, by a will probated in 1831, left a fund in trust for the erection, maintenance, and operation of a "college." The will provided that the college was to admit "as many poor white male orphans, between the ages of six and ten years, as the said income shall be adequate to maintain." The will named as trustee the City of Philadelphia. The provisions of the will were carried out by the State and City and the college was opened in 1848. Since 1869, by virtue of an act of the Pennsylvania Legislature, the trust has been administered and the college operated by the "Board of Directors of City Trusts of the City of Philadelphia." . . . [a]

a. The Board is composed of 15 persons, including the mayor, the president of the City Council and twelve other citizens appointed by the judges of the Court of Com-

In February 1954, the petitioners Foust and Felder applied for admission to the college. They met all qualifications except that they were Negroes. For this reason the Board refused to admit them. They petitioned the Orphans' Court of Philadelphia County for an order directing the Board to admit them, alleging that their exclusion because of race violated the Fourteenth Amendment to the Constitution. The State of Pennsylvania and the City of Philadelphia joined in the suit also contending the Board's action violated the Fourteenth Amendment. The Orphans' Court rejected the constitutional contention and refused to order the applicants' admission. . . . This was affirmed by the Pennsylvania Supreme Court. . . .

The Board which operates Girard College is an agency of the State of Pennsylvania. Therefore, even though the Board was acting as a trustee, its refusal to admit Foust and Felder to the college because they were Negroes was discrimination by the State. Such discrimination is forbidden by the Fourteenth Amendment. . . . Accordingly, the judgment of the Supreme Court of Pennsylvania is reversed and the cause is remanded for further proceedings not inconsistent with this opinion.

It is so ordered.

STATE ENFORCEMENT OF CHARITABLE TRUSTS

After the decision in Pennsylvania v. Board of City Trusts, Pennsylvania courts substituted private trustees to effectuate Stephen Girard's "dominant purpose" to limit the College to White orphans. In re Girard College Trusteeship, 391 Pa. 434, 138 A.2d 844 (1958). The Supreme Court never reached the merits of the questions whether Girard College could be administered by private trustees and continue to exclude Blacks or whether the state court's substitution of trustees to permit continued exclusion of Blacks was itself unconstitutional state action. (The appeal was dismissed for lack of jurisdiction and certiorari was denied. 357 U.S. 570 (1958).) The grounds of decision in Evans v. Newton, supra p. 1124, made it unnecessary to decide whether state enforcement of discriminatory testamentary trusts was in all cases unconstitutional state action.

Charitable trusts do not have identifiable beneficiaries and are enforced, at least nominally, by state officials. States will not enforce such trusts unless they serve worthy purposes. Finally, charitable trusts are exempt from taxation, and are free from otherwise applicable restrictions on indefinite accumulation of trust property. (The Girard trust grew from 2 to 98 million dollars.) Do these elements of state contact impose a constitutional obligation on all private trusts to avoid racial discrimination? See Clark, *Charitable Trusts, the Fourteenth Amendment and the Will of Stephen Girard,* 66 Yale L.J. 979 (1957). An additional issue presented in both the Girard trust litigation and Evans v. Newton was whether, under the doctrine of Shelley v. Kraemer, the action of a state court in replacing a government trustee with a private trustee, for the purpose of effectuating a testator's desire to discriminate, was in itself unconstitutional state action.

mon Pleas of the County of Philadelphia. The treasurer of the city serves as treasurer of the board. Pursuant to the terms of the will the funds of the trust were held and invested by the city treasurer and an annual accounting made to the legislature. The expenses of operating the school were defrayed wholly from the trust fund. It appears that the Board of City Trusts took an active role in directing the administration of the School. See In re Girard's Estate, 386 Pa. 548, 127 A.2d 287 (1956), certiorari granted, judgment reversed 353 U.S. 230 (1957).

Lower federal courts have dealt with some of these issues in the context of educational testamentary trusts. The Court of Appeals for the Third Circuit held the state courts' substitution of private trustees in the *Girard College* case was unconstitutional state action. Commonwealth of Pennsylvania v. Brown, 392 F.2d 120 (3d Cir.1968), cert. denied 391 U.S. 921 (1968). Earlier, a United States District Court decided that the terms of an 1833 bequest limiting Tulane University to the education of Whites were no longer binding. Guillory v. Administrators of Tulane University of La., 212 F.Supp. 674 (E.D.La.1962). Does the Supreme Court's decision in Evans v. Abney, which follows, cast doubt on the soundness of those lower court decisions?

EVANS v. ABNEY, 396 U.S. 435 (1970). After the decision in Evans v. Newton, the Supreme Court of Georgia ruled that Senator Bacon's intention to provide a park for Whites only had become impossible to fulfill and that accordingly the trust had failed and the parkland and other trust property had reverted by operation of Georgia law to the heirs of the senator. The Supreme Court upheld this action. Justice Black, writing for the Court, said, in part:

"When a city park is destroyed because the Constitution required it to be integrated, there is reason for everyone to be disheartened. We agree with petitioners that in such a case it is not enough to find that the state court's result was reached through the application of established principles of state law.... Here, however, the action of the Georgia Supreme Court declaring the Baconsfield trust terminated presents no violation of constitutionally protected rights, and any harshness that may have resulted from the State court's decision can be attributed solely to its intention to effectuate as nearly as possible the explicit terms of Senator Bacon's will.

"Petitioners first argue that the action of the Georgia court violates the United States Constitution in that it imposes a drastic 'penalty,' the 'forfeiture' of the park, merely because of the city's compliance with the constitutional mandate expressed by this Court in Evans v. Newton. Of course, Evans v. Newton did not speak to the problem of whether Baconsfield should or could continue to operate as a park; it held only that its continued operation as a park had to be without racial discrimination. But petitioners now want to extend that holding to forbid the Georgia courts from closing Baconsfield on the ground that such a closing would penalize the city and its citizens for complying with the Constitution. We think, however, that the will of Senator Bacon and Georgia law provide all the justification necessary for imposing such a 'penalty.' The construction of wills is essentially a state-law question ... and in this case the Georgia Supreme Court, as we read its opinion, interpreted Senator Bacon's will as embodying a preference for termination of the park rather than its integration. Given this, the Georgia court had no alternative under its relevant trust laws, which are long standing and neutral with regard to race, but to end the Baconsfield trust and return the property to the Senator's heirs."

PEREMPTORY CHALLENGES TO EXCLUDE JURORS ON ACCOUNT OF RACE

In Powers v. Ohio, 499 U.S. 400 (1991), the Court held that a prosecutor's exclusion of petit jurors through race-based peremptory challenges denied the excluded jurors equal protection, and that the criminal defendant had third-party standing to raise that issue. In two subsequent cases, the principal issue was whether there was state action in juror challenges by a private litigant and a criminal defendant.

Edmonson v. Leesville Concrete Co., Inc., 500 U.S. 614 (1991), held that the Constitution prohibited juror challenges by a private litigant. The Court applied a two part test to determine the state action question. First, did a private party's exercise of a right or privilege have its "source in state authority"? Peremptory challenges are permitted only when government allows them through statute or decisional law. Second, can the private party charged with constitutional violation "be described in all fairness as a state actor"? Private parties could not exercise juror challenges "absent the overt, significant assistance of the court," and juror challenges involved the performance of a traditional public function—selecting an entity (the jury) that is a "quintessential governmental body." The Court distinguished Polk County v. Dodson, 454 U.S. 312 (1981), which had held that a public defender, although employed by government, was not a state actor in a case claiming constitutionally inadequate representation. A defense lawyer in a criminal case is ethically committed to be an adversary to the government, while there is no adversarial relationship between the private litigant and government in the jury selection process.

Dodson was harder to distinguish in Georgia v. McCollum, 505 U.S. 42 (1992), where the Court held that it is unconstitutional for a criminal defense lawyer to use race-based peremptory challenges. Whether a public defender is a state actor "depends on the nature and context of the function he is performing." The public defender's function in exercising a peremptory challenge is different from other actions taken in the accused's defense, because it involves "the power to choose a quintessential governmental body."

Brentwood Academy v. Tennessee Secondary School Athletic Association

531 U.S. 288, 121 S.Ct. 924, 148 L.Ed.2d 807 (2001).

Justice Souter delivered the opinion of the Court.

The issue is whether a statewide association incorporated to regulate interscholastic athletic competition among public and private secondary schools may be regarded as engaging in state action when it enforces a rule against a member school. ... We hold that the association's regulatory activity may and should be treated as state action owing to the pervasive entwinement of state school officials in the structure of the association, there being no offsetting reason to see the association's acts in any other way.

I

Respondent Tennessee Secondary School Athletic Association (Association) is a not-for-profit membership corporation organized to regulate interscholastic sport among the public and private high schools in Tennessee that belong to it. No school is forced to join, but without any other authority actually regulating interscholastic athletics, it enjoys the memberships of almost all the State's public high schools (some 290 of them or 84% of the Association's voting membership), far outnumbering the 55 private schools that belong. A member school's team may play or scrimmage only against the team of another member, absent a dispensation.

The Association's rulemaking arm is its legislative council, while its board of control tends to administration. The voting membership of each of these nine-person committees is limited under the Association's bylaws to high school principals, assistant principals, and superintendents elected by the member schools, and the public school administrators who so serve typically attend meetings during regular school hours. Although the Association's staff members are not paid by the State, they are eligible to join the State's public retirement system for its employees. Member schools pay dues to the Association, though the bulk of its revenue is gate receipts at member teams' football and basketball tournaments, many of them held in public arenas rented by the Association.

The constitution, bylaws, and rules of the Association set standards of school membership and the eligibility of students to play in interscholastic games. . . .

Ever since the Association was incorporated in 1925, Tennessee's State Board of Education (State Board) has (to use its own words) acknowledged the corporation's functions "in providing standards, rules and regulations for interscholastic competition in the public schools of Tennessee," . . . More recently, . . . in 1972, it went so far as to adopt a rule expressly "designat[ing]" the Association as "the organization to supervise and regulate the athletic activities in which the public junior and senior high schools in Tennessee participate on an interscholastic basis." . . . In 1996, however, the State Board dropped the original Rule . . . expressly designating the Association as regulator; it substituted a statement "recogniz[ing] the value of participation in interscholastic athletics and the role of [the Association] in coordinating interscholastic athletic competition," while "authoriz[ing] the public schools of the state to voluntarily maintain membership in [the Association]." . . .

The action before us responds to a 1997 regulatory enforcement proceeding brought against petitioner, Brentwood Academy, a private parochial high school member of the Association. The Association's board of control found that Brentwood violated a rule prohibiting "undue influence" in recruiting athletes, when it wrote to incoming students and their parents about spring football practice. The Association accordingly placed Brentwood's athletic program on probation for four years, declared its football and boys' basketball teams ineligible to compete in playoffs for two years, and imposed a $3,000 fine. When these penalties were imposed, all the voting members of the board of control and legislative council were public school administrators.

Brentwood sued the Association and its executive director in federal court under . . . 42 U.S.C. § 1983, claiming that enforcement of the Rule was state action and a violation of the First and Fourteenth Amendments. The District Court entered summary judgment for Brentwood. . . .

The United States Court of Appeals for the Sixth Circuit reversed. . . . Rehearing en banc was later denied over the dissent of two judges. . . .

We granted certiorari, . . . and now reverse.

Our cases try to plot a line between state action subject to Fourteenth Amendment scrutiny and private conduct (however exceptionable) that is not. . . . If the Fourteenth Amendment is not to be displaced . . . its ambit cannot be a simple line between States and people operating outside formally governmental organizations, and the deed of an ostensibly private organization or individual is to be treated sometimes as if a State had caused it to be performed. . . .

What is fairly attributable is a matter of normative judgment, and the criteria lack rigid simplicity. From the range of circumstances that could point toward the State behind an individual face, no one fact can function as a necessary condition across the board for finding state action; nor is any set of circumstances absolutely sufficient, for there may be some countervailing reason against attributing activity to the government. . . .

Our cases have identified a host of facts that can bear on the fairness of such an attribution. . . .

Amidst such variety, examples may be the best teachers, and examples from our cases are unequivocal in showing that the character of a legal entity is determined neither by its expressly private characterization in statutory law, nor by the failure of the law to acknowledge the entity's inseparability from recognized government officials or agencies. . . . Pennsylvania v. Board of Directors of City Trusts of Philadelphia . . . held the privately endowed Gerard College to be a state actor and enforcement of its private founder's limitation of admission to whites attributable to the State, because, consistent with the terms of the settlor's gift, the college's board of directors was a state agency established by state law. Ostensibly the converse situation occurred in Evans v. Newton, . . . which held that private trustees to whom a city had transferred a park were nonetheless state actors barred from enforcing racial segregation, since the park served the public purpose of providing community recreation, and "the municipality remain[ed] entwined in [its] management [and] control,"
. . .

These examples of public entwinement in the management and control of ostensibly separate trusts or corporations foreshadow this case, as this Court itself anticipated in [National Collegiate Athletic Assn. v. Tarkanian, 488 U.S. 179 (1988)]. *Tarkanian* arose when an undoubtedly state actor, the University of Nevada, suspended its basketball coach, Tarkanian, in order to comply with rules and recommendations of the National Collegiate Athletic Association (NCAA). The coach charged the NCAA with state action, arguing that the state university had delegated its own functions to the NCAA, clothing the latter with authority to make and apply the university's rules, the result being joint action making the NCAA a state actor.

. . .

B

. . . The nominally private character of the Association is overborne by the pervasive entwinement of public institutions and public officials in its composition and workings, and there is no substantial reason to claim unfairness in applying constitutional standards to it.

The Association is not an organization of natural persons acting on their own, but of schools, and of public schools to the extent of 84% of the total. . . .

. . . Interscholastic athletics obviously play an integral part in the public education of Tennessee. . . . Since a pickup system of interscholastic games would not do, these public teams need some mechanism to produce rules and regulate competition. The mechanism is an organization overwhelmingly composed of public school officials who select representatives (all of them public officials at the time in question here), who in turn adopt and enforce the rules that make the system work. Thus, by giving these jobs to the Association, the 290 public schools of Tennessee belonging to it can sensibly be seen as exercising their own authority to meet their own responsibilities. Unsurprisingly, then, the record indicates that half the council or board meetings documented here were held during official school hours, and that public schools have largely provided for the Association's financial support. A small portion of the Association's revenue comes from membership dues paid by the schools, and the principal part from gate receipts at tournaments among the member schools. Unlike mere public buyers of contract services, whose payments for services rendered do not convert the service providers into public actors, . . . the schools here obtain membership in the service organization and give up sources of their own income to their collective association. The Association thus exercises the authority of the predominantly public schools to charge for admission to their games; the Association does not receive this money from the schools, but enjoys the schools' moneymaking capacity as its own.

In sum, to the extent of 84% of its membership, the Association is an organization of public schools represented by their officials acting in their official capacity to provide an integral element of secondary public schooling. There would be no recognizable Association, legal or tangible, without the public school officials, who do not merely control but overwhelmingly perform all but the purely ministerial acts by which the Association exists and functions in practical terms. Only the 16% minority of private school memberships prevents this entwinement of the Association and the public school system from being total and their identities totally indistinguishable.

To complement the entwinement of public school officials with the Association from the bottom up, the State of Tennessee has provided for entwinement from top down. State Board members are assigned ex officio to serve as members of the board of control and legislative council, and the Association's ministerial employees are treated as state employees to the extent of being eligible for membership in the state retirement system.

. . .

C

Entwinement is also the answer to the Association's several arguments offered to persuade us that the facts would not support a finding of state action under various criteria applied in other cases. These arguments are beside the point, simply because the facts justify a conclusion of state action under the criterion of entwinement, a conclusion in no sense unsettled merely because other criteria of state action may not be satisfied by the same facts.

The Association places great stress, for example, on the application of a public function test, as exemplified in Rendell–Baker v. Kohn, 457 U.S. 830 (1982). There, an apparently private school provided education for students whose special needs made it difficult for them to finish high school. ... [W]e held that the performance of such a public function did not permit a finding of state action on the part of the school unless the function performed was exclusively and traditionally public, as it was not in that case. The Association argues that application of the public function criterion would produce the same result here, and we will assume, arguendo, that it would. But this case does not turn on a public function test, any more than Rendell–Baker had anything to do with entwinement of public officials in the special school.

For the same reason, it avails the Association nothing to stress that the State neither coerced nor encouraged the actions complained of. "Coercion" and "encouragement" are like "entwinement" in referring to kinds of facts that can justify characterizing an ostensibly private action as public instead. Facts that address any of these criteria are significant, but no one criterion must necessarily be applied. When, therefore, the relevant facts show pervasive entwinement to the point of largely overlapping identity, the implication of state action is not affected by pointing out that the facts might not loom large under a different test.

D

This is not to say that all of the Association's arguments are rendered beside the point by the public officials' involvement in the Association, for after application of the entwinement criterion, or any other, there is a further potential issue.... Even facts that suffice to show public action (or, standing alone, would require such a finding) may be outweighed in the name of some value at odds with finding public accountability in the circumstances. ...

. . .

The judgment of the Court of Appeals for the Sixth Circuit is reversed, and the case is remanded for further proceedings consistent with this opinion.

It is so ordered.

Justice Thomas, with whom the Chief Justice, Justice Scalia, and Justice Kennedy join, dissenting.

We have never found state action based upon mere "entwinement." Until today, we have found a private organization's acts to constitute state action only when the organization performed a public function; was created, coerced, or encouraged by the government; or acted in a symbiotic relationship with the government. ... I respectfully dissent.

... Although we have used many different tests to identify state action, they all have a common purpose. Our goal in every case is to determine whether an action "can fairly be attributed to the State." ...

A

Regardless of these various tests for state action, common sense dictates that the TSSAA's actions cannot fairly be attributed to the State, and thus cannot constitute state action.... The TSSAA's rules are enforced not by a state agency but by its own board of control, which comprises high school principals, assistant principals, and superintendents, none of whom must work at a public school. Of course, at the time the recruiting rule was enforced in this case, all of the board members happened to be public school officials. However, each board member acts in a representative capacity on behalf of all the private and public schools in his region of Tennessee, and not simply his individual school.

The State of Tennessee did not create the TSSAA. The State does not fund the TSSAA and does not pay its employees. ... The only state pronouncement acknowledging the TSSAA's existence is a rule providing that the State Board of Education permits public schools to maintain membership in the TSSAA if they so choose.

Moreover, the State of Tennessee has never had any involvement in the particular action taken by the TSSAA in this case: the enforcement of the TSSAA's recruiting rule prohibiting members from using "undue influence" on students or their parents or guardians "to secure or to retain a student for athletic purposes." There is no indication that the State has ever had any interest in how schools choose to regulate recruiting. ...

B

. . .

The TSSAA has not performed a function that has been "traditionally exclusively reserved to the State." ... The TSSAA no doubt serves the public, particularly the public schools, but the mere provision of a service to the public does not render such provision a traditional and exclusive public function. ...

... It is also obvious that the TSSAA is not an entity created and controlled by the government for the purpose of fulfilling a government objective.... Indeed, no one claims that the State of Tennessee played any role in the creation of the TSSAA as a private corporation in 1925. ...

In addition, the State of Tennessee has not "exercised coercive power or ... provided such significant encouragement [to the TSSAA], either overt or covert," ... To be sure, public schools do provide a small portion of the TSSAA's funding through their membership dues, but no one argues that these dues are somehow conditioned on the TSSAA's enactment and enforcement of recruiting rules. Likewise, even if the TSSAA were dependent on state funding to the extent of 90%, as was the case in Blum, instead of less than 4%, mere financial dependence on the State does not convert the TSSAA's actions into acts of the State.... Furthermore, there is no evidence of "joint participation," ... between the State and the TSSAA in the TSSAA's enforcement of its recruiting rule. The TSSAA's board of control enforces its recruiting rule solely in accordance with the authority granted to it under the contract that each member signs.

. . .

Because I do not believe that the TSSAA's action of enforcing its recruiting rule is fairly attributable to the State of Tennessee, I would affirm.

II

Although the TSSAA's enforcement activities cannot be considered state action as a matter of common sense or under any of this Court's existing theories of state action, the majority presents a new theory. Under this theory, the majority holds that the combination of factors it identifies evidences "entwinement" of the State with the TSSAA, and that such entwinement converts private action into state action. ...

. . .

* * *

Because the majority never defines "entwinement," the scope of its holding is unclear. If we are fortunate, the majority's fact-specific analysis will have little bearing beyond this case. But if the majority's new entwinement test develops in future years, it could affect many organizations that foster activities, enforce rules, and sponsor extracurricular competition among high schools—not just in athletics, but in such diverse areas as agriculture, mathematics, music, marching bands, forensics, and cheerleading. Indeed, this entwinement test may extend to other organizations that are composed of, or controlled by, public officials or public entities, such as firefighters, policemen, teachers, cities, or counties. I am not prepared to say that any private organization that permits public entities and public officials to participate acts as the State in anything or everything it does, and our state-action jurisprudence has never reached that far. The state-action doctrine was developed to reach only those actions that are truly attributable to the State, not to subject private citizens to the control of federal courts hearing § 1983 actions.

I respectfully dissent.

C.   GOVERNMENT FINANCING, REGULATION AND AUTHORIZATION OF PRIVATE CONDUCT

1.   PRIVATE ACTIVITY ON GOVERNMENT PROPERTY

Burton v. Wilmington Parking Authority

365 U.S. 715, 81 S.Ct. 856, 6 L.Ed.2d 45 (1961).

[The Eagle Coffee Shoppe is a restaurant located within an offstreet automobile parking building in Wilmington, Delaware. The parking building is owned and operated by the Wilmington Parking Authority, an agency of the State of Delaware, and the restaurant is the Authority's lessee. Before it began actual construction of the facility, the Authority was advised by its retained experts that the anticipated revenue from the parking of cars and proceeds from sale of its bonds would not be sufficient to finance the construction costs of the facility. Moreover, the bonds were not expected to be marketable if payable solely out of parking revenues. To secure additional capital needed for its "debt-service" requirements, and thereby to make bond financing practicable, the Authority decided it was necessary to enter long-term leases with responsible tenants for commercial use of some of the space available in the projected "garage building." The public was invited to bid for these leases.

[In April 1957 such a private lease, for 20 years and renewable for another 10 years, was made with Eagle Coffee Shoppe, Inc., for use as a "restaurant, dining room, banquet hall, cocktail lounge and bar and for no other use and purpose." Other portions of the structure were leased to other tenants, including a bookstore, a retail jeweler, and a food store. Upon completion of the building, the Authority located at appropriate places thereon official signs indicating the public character of the building, and flew from mastheads on the roof both the state and national flags.

[In August 1958 Burton parked his car in the building and walked around to enter the restaurant by its front door on Ninth Street. He was refused service. He then filed this action seeking a declaratory judgment, alleging that he was refused service solely because he was a Negro. On motions for summary judgment the trial court ruled for Burton. The Delaware Supreme Court reversed on the ground that Eagle Coffee Shoppe was under no duty to serve because of a state statute providing: "No keeper of an inn, tavern, hotel, or restaurant, or other place of public entertainment or refreshment of travelers, guests, or customers shall be obliged, by law, to furnish entertainment or refreshment to persons whose reception or entertainment by him would be offensive to the major part of his customers and would injure his business. . . ."]

Mr. Justice Clark delivered the opinion of the Court.

. . .

It is clear, as it always has been since the Civil Rights Cases . . . that "Individual invasion of individual rights is not the subject-matter of the amendment," and that private conduct abridging individual rights does no violence to the Equal Protection Clause unless to some significant extent the State in any of its manifestations has been found to have become involved in it. Because the virtue of the right to equal protection of the laws could lie only in the breadth of its application, its constitutional assurance was reserved in terms whose imprecision was necessary if the right were to be enjoyed in the variety of individual-state relationships which the Amendment was designed to embrace. For the same reason, to fashion and apply a precise formula for recognition of state responsibility under the Equal Protection Clause is an "impossible task" . . . Only by sifting facts and weighing circumstances can the nonobvious involvement of the State in private conduct be attributed its true significance. . . .

Addition of all these activities, obligations and responsibilities of the Authority, the benefits mutually conferred, together with the obvious fact that the restaurant is operated as an integral part of a public building devoted to a public parking service, indicates that degree of state participation and involvement in discriminatory action which it was the design of the Fourteenth

Amendment to condemn. It is irony amounting to grave injustice that in one part of a single building, erected and maintained with public funds by an agency of the State to serve a public purpose, all persons have equal rights, while in another portion, also serving the public, a Negro is a second-class citizen, offensive because of his race, without rights and unentitled to service, but at the same time fully enjoys equal access to nearby restaurants in wholly privately owned buildings. As the Chancellor pointed out, in its lease with Eagle the Authority could have affirmatively required Eagle to discharge the responsibilities under the Fourteenth Amendment imposed upon the private enterprise as a consequence of state participation. But no State may effectively abdicate its responsibilities by either ignoring them or by merely failing to discharge them whatever the motive may be. It is of no consolation to an individual denied the equal protection of the laws that it was done in good faith. Certainly the conclusions drawn in similar cases by the various Courts of Appeals do not depend upon such a distinction. By its inaction, the Authority, and through it the State, has not only made itself a party to the refusal of service, but has elected to place its power, property and prestige behind the admitted discrimination. The State has so far insinuated itself into a position of interdependence with Eagle that it must be recognized as a joint participant in the challenged activity, which, on that account, cannot be considered to have been so "purely private" as to fall without the scope of the Fourteenth Amendment.

Because readily applicable formulae may not be fashioned, the conclusions drawn from the facts and circumstances of this record are by no means declared as universal truths on the basis of which every state leasing agreement is to be tested.... Specifically defining the limits of our inquiry, what we hold today is that when a State leases public property in the manner and for the purpose shown to have been the case here, the proscriptions of the Fourteenth Amendment must be complied with by the lessee as certainly as though they were binding covenants written into the agreement itself.

The judgment of the Supreme Court of Delaware is reversed and the cause remanded for further proceedings consistent with this opinion.

[Justice Stewart concurred. Justices Frankfurter, Harlan, and Whittaker, dissented.]

REALITY v. APPEARANCE OF STATE ACTION

Consider the following hypothesis. In cases concerning racial discrimination, an important factor of decision is whether all of the circumstances create a public perception that the state approves the private discriminatory decision. Are appearances of state approval more important than an inquiry whether, appearances aside, racial discrimination can be traced to governmental decisions? The suggested hypothesis would support the results in the preceding cases of Pennsylvania v. Board of Trusts and Burton v. Wilmington Parking Authority. So long as the city ran the school, it appeared that the city and not the testator was making the choice to engage in a policy of racial discrimination. So long as the city operated the parking garage, it would appear that it approved racial discrimination by tenants in the parking structure. It can also be argued that the hypothesis explains the disparate results in the two cases concerning Senator Bacon's will—Evans v. Newton, supra p. 1124, and Evans v. Abney, supra p. 1138. The city had operated the park for so long as a segregated park that merely turning it over to a private trustee for continued segregated operation would not remove the appearance of a segregated city park. On the other hand, terminating the operation of the park because the city could no longer follow Senator Bacon's wish that it be segregated did not give the appearance that the city approved the testator's choice. (Consider the case of a private university refusing to accept a bequest because it *disapproves* conditions attached to it.)

Are you persuaded that *Abney* and *Newton* are both appropriately decided under the hypothesis suggested here? Do you think that the hypothesis is useful in marking the limits of state action doctrine? Is the hypothesis useful in explaining the disparate state-action and no-state-action conclusions in the cases that follow?

GILMORE v. MONTGOMERY, ALA., 417 U.S. 556 (1974). The case involved actions by a city in permitting the use of public park recreational facilities by private segregated school groups and any other non–school groups that allegedly discriminate in their membership on the basis of race. The Court held it invalid for the city to allocate use of park facilities to private segregated school groups where that action facilitated the avoidance of an outstanding school desegregation order. With respect to the use by other segregated groups the Court found the facts insufficiently developed to permit a ruling and sent the case back to the district court. In concluding its opinion the Court said:

"We close with this word of caution. It should be obvious that the exclusion of any person or group—all-Negro, all-oriental, or all-white—from public facilities infringes upon the freedom of the individual to associate as he chooses. Mr. Justice Douglas emphasized this in his dissent, joined by Mr. Justice Marshall, in *Moose Lodge*. He observed, 'The associational rights which our system honors permit all white, all black, all brown and all yellow clubs to be formed. They also permit all Catholic, all Jewish, or all agnostic clubs to be established. Government may not tell a man or woman who his or her associates must be. The individual can be as selective as he desires.' ... The freedom to associate applies to the beliefs we share, and to those we consider reprehensible. It tends to produce the diversity of opinion that oils the machine of democratic government and insures peaceful, orderly change. Because its exercise is largely dependent on the right to own or use property, ... any denial of access to public facilities must withstand close scrutiny and be carefully circumscribed. Certainly, a person's mere membership in an organization which possesses a discriminatory admissions policy would not alone be ground for his exclusion from public facilities. Having said this, however, we must also be aware that the very exercise of the freedom to associate by some may serve to infringe that freedom for others. Invidious discrimination takes its own toll on the freedom to associate, and it is not subject to affirmative constitutional protection when it involves state action. Norwood v. Harrison, 413 U.S., at 470.'"

2. GOVERNMENT FINANCIAL ASSISTANCE TO PRIVATE ACTIVITIES

NORWOOD v. HARRISON, 413 U.S. 455 (1973). Mississippi had a statutory program under which textbooks were purchased by the state and lent to students in both public and private schools. A suit was brought challenging the application of this statute in lending textbooks to students attending schools with racially discriminatory admission policies. The Court held the statute invalid as applied to such schools. The Court said:

court held statute invalid

"This Court has consistently affirmed decisions enjoining state tuition grants to students attending racially discriminatory private schools. A textbook lending program is not legally distinguishable from the forms of state assistance foreclosed by the prior cases. Free textbooks, like tuition grants directed to private school students, are a form of financial assistance inuring to the benefit of the private schools themselves. An inescapable educational cost for students in both public and private schools is the expense of providing all necessary learning materials. When, as here, that necessary expense is borne by the State, the economic consequence is to give aid to the enterprise; if the school engages in discriminatory practices the State by tangible aid in the form of textbooks thereby gives support to such discrimination. Racial discrimination in state-operated schools is barred by the Constitution and '[i]t is also axiomatic that a state may not induce, encourage or promote private persons to accomplish what it is constitutionally forbidden to accomplish.' . . .

"We do not suggest that a State violates its constitutional duty merely because it has provided *any* form of state service that benefits private schools said to be racially discriminatory. Textbooks are a basic educational tool and, like tuition grants, they are provided only in connection with schools; they are to be distinguished from generalized services government might provide to schools in common with others. Moreover, the textbooks provided to private school students by the State in this case are a form of assistance readily available from sources entirely independent of the State—unlike, for example, 'such necessities of life as electricity, water, and police and fire protection.' Moose Lodge No. 107 v. Irvis, 407 U.S. 163, 173 (1972). The State has neither an absolute nor operating monopoly on the procurement of school textbooks; anyone can purchase them on the open market.

"The District Court laid great stress on the absence of showing by appellants that 'any child enrolled in private school, if deprived of free textbooks, would withdraw from private school and subsequently enroll in the public schools.' We can accept this factual assertion; we cannot and do not know, on this record at least, whether state textbook assistance is the determinative factor in the enrollment of any students in any of the private schools in Mississippi. We do not agree with the District Court in its analysis of the legal consequences of this uncertainty, for the Constitution does not permit the State to aid discrimination even when there is no precise causal relationship between state financial aid to a private school and the continued well-being of that school. A State may not grant the type of tangible financial aid here involved if that aid has a significant tendency to facilitate, reinforce, and support private discrimination."

BLUM v. YARETSKY, 457 U.S. 991 (1982). A class of medicaid patients brought suit claiming that private nursing homes violated their rights to procedural due process in transferring them to lower levels of care, or discharging them. The nursing homes receive reimbursement from the state for their services in caring for medicaid patients. Decisions by the nursing home result in lower medicaid benefits. The Court held that there was no state action that would trigger the fourteenth amendment's requirement of procedural due process. Justice Rehnquist's opinion for the court said, in part:

"Respondents . . . argue that the State 'affirmatively commands' the summary discharge or transfer of Medicaid patients who are thought to be inappropriately placed in their nursing facilities. Were this characterization accurate, we would have a different question before us. However, our review of the statutes and regulations identified by respondents does not support respondents' characterization of them.

. . .

". . . [R]espondents' complaint is about nursing home decisions to discharge or transfer, not to admit, Medicaid patients. But we are not satisfied that the State is responsible for those decisions.... The regulations cited by respondents require [nursing homes] 'to make all efforts possible to transfer patients to the appropriate level of care or home as indicated by the patient's medical condition or needs' ... The nursing homes are required to complete patient care assessment forms designed by the State and 'provide the receiving facility or provider with a current copy of same at the time of discharge to an alternate level of care facility or home.' ...

"These regulations do not require the nursing homes to rely on the forms in making discharge or transfer decisions, nor do they demonstrate that the State is responsible for the decision to discharge or transfer particular patients. Those decisions ultimately turn on medical judgments made by private parties according to professional standards that are not established by the State. This case, therefore, is not unlike Polk County v. Dodson, 454 U.S. 312 (1981), in which the question was whether a public defender acts 'under color of' state law within the meaning of 42 U.S.C. § 1983 when representing an indigent defendant in a state criminal proceeding. Although the public defender was employed by the State and appointed by the State to represent the respondent, we concluded that '[t]his assignment entailed functions and obligations in no way dependent on state authority.' ... The decisions made by the public defender in the course of representing his client were framed in accordance with professional canons of ethics, rather than dictated by any rule of conduct imposed by the State. The same is true of nursing home decisions to discharge or transfer particular patients because the care they are receiving is medically inappropriate."

Justices Brennan and Marshall dissented.

RENDELL–BAKER v. KOHN, 457 U.S. 830 (1982). Plaintiffs were discharged teachers, previously employed by a private school for maladjusted high school students. Most of the school's students had been referred to it by city and state agencies. Public funds account for 90 to 99% of the school's operating budget. Plaintiffs brought suit under 42 u.s.c. § 1983, claiming that their discharges were for constitutionally protected speech, in violation of the First Amendment, and that they had been denied procedural due process. The Court held that the private school did not act under color of state law in dismissing the plaintiffs. Chief Justice Burger's opinion said, in part:

"The school ... is not fundamentally different from many private corporations whose business depends primarily on contracts to build roads, bridges, dams, ships, or submarines for the government. Acts of such private contractors do not become acts of the government by reason of their significant or even total engagement in performing public contracts."

Justices Marshall and Brennan dissented.

3.   GOVERNMENT REGULATION OF PRIVATE ACTIVITY

Moose Lodge No. 107 v. Irvis

407 U.S. 163, 92 S.Ct. 1965, 32 L.Ed.2d 627 (1972).

Mr. Justice Rehnquist delivered the opinion of the Court.

Appellee Irvis, a Negro ... , was refused service by appellant Moose Lodge, a local branch of the national fraternal organization located in Harrisburg, Pennsylvania. Appellee then brought this action under 42 U.S.C. § 1983 for injunctive relief in the United States District Court for the Middle District of

State action because the state had sold him a liquor license

Pennsylvania. He claimed that because the Pennsylvania liquor board had issued appellant Moose Lodge a private club license that authorized the sale of alcoholic beverages on its premises, the refusal of service to him was "state action" for the purposes of the Equal Protection Clause of the Fourteenth Amendment. He named both Moose Lodge and the Pennsylvania Liquor Authority as defendants, seeking injunctive relief that would have required the defendant liquor board to revoke Moose Lodge's license so long as it continued its discriminatory practices. Appellee sought no damages.

Revoked lic. for disc. practice. Moose lodge appealed

A three-judge district court, convened at appellee's request, upheld his contention on the merits, and entered a decree declaring invalid the liquor license issued to Moose Lodge "as long as it follows a policy of racial discrimination in its membership or operating policies or practices." Moose Lodge alone appealed from the decree ...

I.

The District Court in its opinion found that "a Caucasian member in good standing brought plaintiff, a Negro, to the Lodge's dining room and bar as his guest and requested service of food and beverages. The Lodge through its employees refused service to plaintiff solely because he is a Negro." It is undisputed that each local Moose Lodge is bound by the constitution and general by-laws of the Supreme Lodge, the latter of which contains a provision limiting membership in the lodges to white male Caucasians. The District Court in this connection found that "[t]he lodges accordingly maintain a policy and practice of restricting membership to the Caucasian race and permitting members to bring only Caucasian guests on lodge premises, particularly to the dining room and bar."

. . .

He did not seek to be a member so he doesn't have standing. But their guest services did.

Any injury to appellee from the conduct of Moose Lodge stemmed not from the lodge's membership requirements, but from its policies with respect to the serving of guests of members. Appellee has standing to seek redress for injuries done to him, but may not seek redress for injuries done to others. ... [A]ppellee was not injured by Moose Lodge's membership policy since he never sought to become a member....

Because appellee had no standing to litigate a constitutional claim arising out of Moose Lodge's membership practices, the District Court erred in reaching that issue on the merits. But it did not err in reaching the constitutional claim of appellee that Moose Lodge's guest service practices under these circumstances violated the Fourteenth Amendment....

II.

Moose Lodge is a private club in the ordinary meaning of that term. It is a local chapter of a national fraternal organization having well defined requirements for membership. It conducts all of its activities in a building that is owned by it. It is not publicly funded. Only members and guests are permitted in any lodge of the order; one may become a guest only by invitation of a member or upon invitation of the house committee.

Appellee, while conceding the right of private clubs to choose members upon a discriminatory basis, asserts that the licensing of Moose Lodge to serve liquor by the Pennsylvania Liquor Control Board amounts to such State involvement with the club's activities as to make its discriminatory practices forbidden by the Equal Protection Clause of the Fourteenth Amendment. The relief sought and obtained by appellee in the District Court was an injunction forbidding the licensing by the liquor authority of Moose Lodge until it ceased its discriminatory practices. We conclude that Moose Lodge's refusal to serve food and beverages to a guest by reason of the fact that he was a Negro does not, under the circumstances here presented, violate the Fourteenth Amendment.

Holding: No violation

. . .

While the principle is easily stated, the question of whether particular discriminatory conduct is private, on the one hand, or amounts to "state action," on the other hand, frequently admits of no easy answer. . . .

Our cases make clear that the impetus for the forbidden discrimination need not originate with the State if it is state action that enforces privately originated discrimination. Shelley v. Kraemer, supra. . . .

The Court has never held, of course, that discrimination by an otherwise private entity would be violative of the Equal Protection Clause if the private entity receives any sort of benefit or service at all from the State, or if it is subject to state regulation in any degree whatever. Since state-furnished services include such necessities of life as electricity, water, and police and fire protection, such a holding would utterly emasculate the distinction between private as distinguished from state conduct set forth in The Civil Rights Cases, supra, and adhered to in subsequent decisions. Our holdings indicate that where the impetus for the discrimination is private, the State must have "significantly involved itself with invidious discriminations," Reitman v. Mulkey, 387 U.S. 369, 380 (1967), in order for the discriminatory action to fall within the ambit of the constitutional prohibition.

State provides lots to private entities

. . .

Here there is nothing approaching the symbiotic relationship between lessor and lessee that was present in *Burton,* where the private lessee obtained the benefit of locating in a building owned by the state created parking authority, and the parking authority was enabled to carry out its primary public purpose of furnishing parking space by advantageously leasing portions of the building constructed for that purpose to commercial lessees such as the owner of the Eagle Restaurant. Unlike *Burton,* the Moose Lodge building is located on land owned by it, not by any public authority. Far from apparently holding itself out as a place of public accommodation, Moose Lodge quite ostentatiously proclaims the fact that it is not open to the public at large. Nor is it located and operated in such surroundings that although private in name, it discharges a function or performs a service that would otherwise in all likelihood be performed by the State. In short, while Eagle was a public restaurant in a public building, Moose Lodge is a private social club in a private building.

With the exception hereafter noted, the Pennsylvania Liquor Control Board plays absolutely no part in establishing or enforcing the membership or guest policies of the club that it licenses to serve liquor. There is no suggestion in this record that the Pennsylvania law, either as written or as applied, discriminates against minority groups either in their right to apply for club licenses themselves or in their right to purchase and be served liquor in places of public accommodation. The only effect that the state licensing of Moose Lodge to serve liquor can be said to have on the right of any other Pennsylvanian to buy or be served liquor on premises other than those of Moose Lodge is that for some purposes club licenses are counted in the maximum number of licenses which may be issued in a given municipality. Basically each municipality has a quota of one retail license for each 1,500 inhabitants. Licenses issued to hotels, municipal golf courses and airport restaurants are not counted in this quota, nor are club licenses until the maximum number of retail licenses is reached. Beyond that point, neither additional retail licenses nor additional club licenses may be issued so long as the number of issued and outstanding retail licenses remains at or above the statutory maximum.

The District Court was at pains to point out in its opinion what it considered to be the "pervasive" nature of the regulation of private clubs by the Pennsylvania Liquor Control Board. . . .

However detailed this type of regulation may be in some particulars, it cannot be said to in any way foster or encourage racial discrimination. Nor can it be said to make the State in any realistic sense a partner or even a joint venturer in the club's enterprise. The limited effect of the prohibition against obtaining additional club licenses when the maximum number of retail licenses allotted to a municipality has been issued, when considered together with the availability of liquor from hotel, restaurant, and retail licensees falls far short of conferring upon club licensees a monopoly in the dispensing of liquor in any given municipality or in the State as a whole. We therefore hold that, with the exception hereafter noted, the operation of the regulatory scheme enforced by the Pennsylvania Liquor Control Board does not sufficiently implicate the State in the discriminatory guest policies of Moose Lodge so as to make the latter "state action" within the ambit of the Equal Protection Clause of the Fourteenth Amendment.

The District Court found that the regulations of the Liquor Control Board adopted pursuant to statute affirmatively require that "every club licensee shall adhere to all the provisions of its Constitution and By-Laws." Appellant argues that the purpose of this provision "is purely and simply and plainly the prevention of subterfuge," pointing out that the *bona fides* of a private club, as opposed to a place of public accommodation masquerading as a private club, is a matter with which the State Liquor Control Board may legitimately concern itself. Appellee concedes this to be the case, and expresses disagreement with the District Court on this point. There can be no doubt that the label "private club" can and has been used to evade both regulations of state and local liquor authorities, and statutes requiring places of public accommodation to serve all persons without regard to race, color, religion, or national origin. This Court in Daniel v. Paul, 395 U.S. 298 (1969), had occasion to address this issue in connection with the application of Title II of the Civil Rights Act of 1964, 78 Stat. 243, 42 U.S.C. § 2000a et seq.

. . .

Even though the Liquor Control Board regulation in question is neutral in its terms, the result of its application in a case where the constitution and by-laws of a club required racial discrimination would be to invoke the sanctions of the State to enforce a concededly discriminatory private rule. State action, for purposes of the Equal Protection Clause, may emanate from rulings of administrative and regulatory agencies as well as from legislative or judicial action. . . . Shelley v. Kraemer . . . makes it clear that the application of state sanctions to enforce such a rule would violate the Fourteenth Amendment. Although the record before us is not as clear as one would like, appellant has not persuaded us that the District Court should have denied any and all relief.

Appellee was entitled to a decree enjoining the enforcement of § 113.09 of the regulations promulgated by the Pennsylvania Liquor Control Board insofar as that regulation requires compliance by Moose Lodge with provisions of its constitution and by-laws containing racially discriminatory provisions. He was entitled to no more. The judgment of the District Court is reversed, and the cause remanded with instructions to enter a decree in conformity with this opinion.

Mr. Justice Douglas, with whom Mr. Justice Marshall joins, dissenting.

. . .

Were this regulation [enforcing the discriminatory membership clause] the only infirmity in Pennsylvania's licensing scheme, I would perhaps agree with the majority that the appropriate relief would be a decree enjoining its enforcement. But there is another flaw in the scheme not so easily cured. Liquor licenses in Pennsylvania, unlike driver's licenses, or marriage licenses, are not freely available to those who meet racially neutral qualifications. There is a complex quota system, which the majority accurately describes. What the majority neglects to say is that the Harrisburg quota, where Moose Lodge No. 107 is located, has been full for many years. No more club licenses may be issued in that city.

This state-enforced scarcity of licenses restricts the ability of blacks to obtain liquor, for liquor is commercially available *only* at private clubs for a significant portion of each week. Access by blacks to places that serve liquor is further limited by the fact that the state quota is filled. A group desiring to form a nondiscriminatory club which would serve blacks must purchase a license held by an existing club, which can exact a monopoly price for the transfer. The availability of such a license is speculative at best, however, for, as Moose Lodge itself concedes, without a liquor license a fraternal organization would be hard-pressed to survive.

Thus, the State of Pennsylvania is putting the weight of its liquor license, concededly a valued and important adjunct to a private club, behind racial discrimination. . . .

I would affirm the judgment below.

Mr. Justice Brennan, with whom Mr. Justice Marshall joins, dissenting.

When Moose Lodge obtained its liquor license, the State of Pennsylvania became an active participant in the operation of the Lodge bar. Liquor licensing laws are only incidentally revenue measures; they are primarily pervasive regulatory schemes under which the State dictates and continually supervises virtually every detail of the operation of the licensee's business. Very few, if any, other licensed businesses experience such complete state involvement. Yet the Court holds that that involvement does not constitute "state action" making the Lodge's refusal to serve a guest liquor solely because of his race a violation of the Fourteenth Amendment. The vital flaw in the Court's reasoning is its complete disregard of the fundamental value underlying the "state action" concept. . . .

Plainly, the State of Pennsylvania's liquor regulations intertwine the State with the operation of the Lodge bar in a "significant way [and] lend [the State's] authority to the sordid business of racial discrimination." . . .

This is thus a case requiring application of the principle that until today has governed our determinations of the existence of "state action": "Our prior decisions leave no doubt that the mere existence of efforts by the State, through legislation or otherwise, to authorize, encourage, or otherwise support racial discrimination in a particular facet of life constitutes illegal state involvement in those pertinent private acts of discrimination that subsequently occur." . . .

I therefore dissent and would affirm the final decree entered by the District Court.

Jackson v. Metropolitan Edison Co.

419 U.S. 345, 95 S.Ct. 449, 42 L.Ed.2d 477 (1974).

[Plaintiff brought suit against defendant, a privately owned and operated utility corporation which holds a certificate of public convenience issued by the Pennsylvania Utilities Commission, seeking damages and injunctive relief under 42 U.S.C. § 1983 for termination of her electric service allegedly before she had been afforded notice, a hearing, and an opportunity to pay any amounts due. Plaintiff claimed that under state law she was entitled to reasonably continuous electric service and that respondent's termination for alleged nonpayment, permitted by a provision of its general tariff filed with the Commission, was state action depriving her of her property without due process of law. The Court of Appeals affirmed the District Court's dismissal of her complaint. The Supreme Court affirmed.]

Mr. Justice Rehnquist delivered the opinion of the Court.

. . .

Here the action complained of was taken by a utility company which is privately owned and operated, but which in many particulars of its business is subject to extensive state regulation. The mere fact that a business is subject to state regulation does not by itself convert its action into that of the State for purposes of the Fourteenth Amendment. Moose Lodge No. 107 v. Irvis, supra, 407 U.S. at 176–177. Nor does the fact that the regulation is extensive and detailed, as in the case of most public utilities, do so. Public Utilities Comm'n v. Pollak, 343 U.S. 451, 462 (1952). It may well be that acts of a heavily regulated utility with at least something of a governmentally protected monopoly will more readily be found to be "state" acts than will the acts of an entity lacking these characteristics. But the inquiry must be whether there is a sufficiently close nexus between the State and the challenged action of the regulated entity so that the action of the latter may be fairly treated as that of the State itself. . . . The true nature of the State's involvement may not be immediately obvious, and detailed inquiry may be required in order to determine whether the test is met. . . .

Petitioner advances a series of contentions which, in her view, lead to the conclusion that this case should fall on the *Burton* side of the line drawn in the *Civil Rights Cases,* supra, rather than on the *Moose Lodge* side of that line. We find none of them persuasive.

Petitioner first argues that "state action" is present because of the monopoly status allegedly conferred upon Metropolitan by the State of Pennsylvania. As a factual matter, it may well be doubted that the State ever granted or guaranteed Metropolitan a monopoly. But assuming that it had, this fact is not determinative in considering whether Metropolitan's termination of service to petitioner was "state action" for purposes of the Fourteenth Amendment. In *Pollak,* supra, where the Court dealt with the activities of the District of Columbia Transit Company, a congressionally established monopoly, we expressly disclaimed reliance on the monopoly status of the transit authority. Id., . . . Similarly, although certain monopoly aspects were presented in *Moose Lodge No. 107,* supra, we found that the Lodge's action was not subject to the provisions of the Fourteenth Amendment. In each of those cases, there was insufficient relationship between the challenged actions of the entities involved and their monopoly status. There is no indication of any greater connection here.

Petitioner next urges that state action is present because respondent provides an essential public service required to be supplied on a reasonably continuous basis by 66 Pa.Stat. § 1171, and hence performs a "public function." We have of course found state action present in the exercise by a private entity of powers traditionally exclusively reserved to the State. See, e.g., Nixon v. Condon, 286 U.S. 73 (1931) (election); Terry v. Adams, 345 U.S. 461 (1953) (election); Marsh v. Alabama, 326 U.S. 501 (1946) (company town); Evans v. Newton, 382 U.S. 296 (1966) (municipal park). If we were dealing with the exercise by Metropolitan of some power delegated to it by the State which is traditionally associated with sovereignty, such as eminent domain, our case would be quite a different one. But while the Pennsylvania statute imposes an obligation to furnish service on regulated utilities, it imposes no such obligation on the State. The Pennsylvania courts have rejected the contention that the furnishing of utility services is either a state function or a municipal duty. . . .

[margin note: P's 2nd arg.]

Perhaps in recognition of the fact that the supplying of utility service is not traditionally the exclusive prerogative of the State, petitioner invites the expansion of the doctrine of this limited line of cases into a broad principle that all businesses "affected with the public interest" are state actors in all their actions.

We decline the invitation for reasons stated long ago in Nebbia v. New York, 291 U.S. 502 (1934), in the course of rejecting a substantive due process attack on state legislation: . . .

Doctors, optometrists, lawyers, Metropolitan, and Nebbia's upstate New York grocery selling a quart of milk are all in regulated businesses, providing arguably essential goods and services, "affected with a public interest." We do not believe that such a status converts their every action, absent more, into that of the State.

We also reject the notion that Metropolitan's termination is state action because the State "has specifically authorized and approved" the termination practice. In the instant case, Metropolitan filed with the Public Utilities Commission a general tariff—a provision of which states Metropolitan's right to terminate service for nonpayment. This provision has appeared in Metropolitan's previously filed tariffs for many years and has never been the subject of a hearing or other scrutiny by the Commission. . . .

[margin note: P's 3rd arg.]

. . . [T]he sole connection of the Commission with this regulation was Metropolitan's simple notice filing with the Commission and the lack of any Commission action to prohibit it.

The case most heavily relied on by petitioner is Public Utilities Comm'n v. Pollak, supra. There the Court dealt with the contention that Capital Transit's installation of a piped music system on its buses violated the First Amendment rights of the bus riders. It is not entirely clear whether the Court alternatively held that Capital Transit's action was action of the "State" for First Amendment purposes, or whether it merely assumed *arguendo* that it was and went on to resolve the First Amendment question adversely to the bus riders. In either event, the nature of the state involvement there was quite different than it is here. The District of Columbia Public Utilities Commission, on its own motion, commenced an investigation of the effects of the piped music, and after a full hearing concluded not only that Capital Transit's practices were "not inconsistent with public convenience, comfort, and safety," . . . but also that the practice "in fact through the creation of better will among passengers, . . .

tends to improve the conditions under which the public rides." ... Here, on the other hand, there was no such imprimatur placed on the practice of Metropolitan about which petitioner complains. The nature of governmental regulation of private utilities is such that a utility may frequently be required by the state regulatory scheme to obtain approval for practices a business regulated in less detail would be free to institute without any approval from a regulatory body. Approval by a state utility commission of such a request from a regulated utility, where the commission has not put its own weight on the side of the proposed practice by ordering it, does not transmute a practice initiated by the utility and approved by the commission into "state action." At most, the Commission's failure to overturn this practice amounted to no more than a determination that a Pennsylvania utility was authorized to employ such a practice if it so desired. Respondent's exercise of the choice allowed by state law where the initiative comes from it and not from the State, does not make its action in doing so "state action" for purposes of the Fourteenth Amendment.

We also find absent in the instant case the symbiotic relationship presented in Burton v. Wilmington Parking Authority, 365 U.S. 715 (1961). ...

Metropolitan is a privately owned corporation, and it does not lease its facilities from the State of Pennsylvania. It alone is responsible for the provision of power to its customers. In common with all corporations of the State it pays taxes to the State, and it is subject to a form of extensive regulation by the State in a way that most other business enterprises are not. But this was likewise true of the appellant club in Moose Lodge No. 107 v. Irvis, ...

All of petitioner's arguments taken together show no more than that Metropolitan was a heavily regulated private utility, enjoying at least a partial monopoly in the providing of electrical service within its territory, and that it elected to terminate service to petitioner in a manner which the Pennsylvania Public Utilities Commission found permissible under state law. Under our decision this is not sufficient to connect the State of Pennsylvania with respondent's action so as to make the latter's conduct attributable to the State for purposes of the Fourteenth Amendment.

We conclude that the State of Pennsylvania is not sufficiently connected with respondent's action in terminating petitioner's service so as to make respondent's conduct in so doing attributable to the State for purposes of the Fourteenth Amendment. We therefore have no occasion to decide whether petitioner's claim to continued service was "property" for purposes of that Amendment, or whether "due process of law" would require a State taking similar action to accord petitioner the procedural rights for which she contends. The judgment of the Court of Appeals for the Third Circuit is therefore

Affirmed.

Mr. Justice Douglas, dissenting.

I reach the opposite conclusion from that reached by the majority on the state action issue. ...

Mr. Justice Brennan, dissenting.

I do not think that a controversy existed between petitioner and respondent entitling petitioner to be heard in this action. ...

Mr. Justice Marshall, dissenting.

I agree with my Brother Brennan that this case is a very poor vehicle for resolving the difficult and important questions presented today. ... Since the

[handwritten margin note: not a sufficient condition to state]

Court has disposed of the case by finding no state action, however, I think it appropriate to register my dissent on that point....

. . .

The fact that the Metropolitan Edison Company supplies an essential public service that is in many communities supplied by the government weighs more heavily for me than for the majority....

Private parties performing functions affecting the public interest can often make a persuasive claim to be free of the constitutional requirements applicable to governmental institutions because of the value of preserving a private sector in which the opportunity for individual choice is maximized.... Maintaining the private status of parochial schools, cited by the majority, advances just this value.... But it is hard to imagine any such interests that are furthered by protecting public utility companies from meeting the constitutional standards that would apply if the companies were state-owned. The values of pluralism and diversity are simply not relevant when the private company is the only electric company in town.

. . .

What is perhaps most troubling about the Court's opinion is that it would appear to apply to a broad range of claimed constitutional violations by the company. The Court has not adopted the notion, accepted elsewhere, that different standards should apply to state action analysis when different constitutional claims are presented. ... Thus, the majority's analysis would seemingly apply as well to a company that refused to extend service to Negroes, welfare recipients, or any other group that the company preferred, for its own reasons, not to serve. I cannot believe that this Court would hold that the State's involvement with the utility company was not sufficient to impose upon the company an obligation to meet the constitutional mandate of nondiscrimination. Yet nothing in the analysis of the majority opinion suggests otherwise.

I dissent.

4.   GOVERNMENT APPROVAL OF PRIVATE ACTIVITY

Reitman v. Mulkey

387 U.S. 369, 87 S.Ct. 1627, 18 L.Ed.2d 830 (1967).

Mr. Justice White delivered the opinion of the Court.

The question here is whether Art. I, § 26 of the California Constitution denies "to any person ... the equal protection of the laws" within the meaning of the Fourteenth Amendment of the Constitution of the United States. Section 26 of Art. I, an initiated measure submitted to the people as Proposition 14 in a statewide ballot in 1964, provides in part as follows:

> "Neither the State nor any subdivision or agency thereof shall deny, limit or abridge, directly or indirectly, the right of any person, who is willing or desires to sell, lease or rent any part or all of his real property, to decline to sell, lease or rent such property to such person or persons as he, in his absolute discretion, chooses."

The real property covered by § 26 is limited to residential property and contains an exception for state-owned real estate.

... [T]he Mulkeys who are husband and wife and respondents here, sued under § 51 and § 52 of the California Civil Code alleging that petitioners had refused to rent them an apartment solely on account of their race. An injunction and damages were demanded. Petitioners moved for summary judgment on the ground that §§ 51 and 52, insofar as they were the basis for the Mulkeys' action, had been rendered null and void by the adoption of Proposition 14 after the filing of the complaint. The trial court granted the motion and respondents took the case to the California Supreme Court.

... [That court reversed, holding] that Art. I, § 26, was invalid as denying the equal protection of the laws guaranteed by the Fourteenth Amendment. ...

We affirm the judgment of the California Supreme Court. We first turn to the opinion of that court ... , which quite properly undertook to examine the constitutionality of § 26 in terms of its "immediate objective," its "ultimate effect" and its "historical context and the conditions existing prior to its enactment." Judgments such as these we have frequently undertaken ourselves.... But here the California Supreme Court has addressed itself to these matters and we should give careful consideration to its views because they concern the purpose, scope, and operative effect of a provision of the California Constitution.

First, the court considered whether § 26 was concerned at all with private discriminations in residential housing. This involved a review of past efforts by the California Legislature to regulate such discriminations. The Unruh Act ... on which respondents based their cases, was passed in 1959. The Hawkins Act ... followed and prohibited discriminations in publicly assisted housing. In 1961, the legislature enacted proscriptions against restrictive covenants. Finally, in 1963, came the Rumford Fair Housing Act, ... superseding the Hawkins Act and prohibiting racial discriminations in the sale or rental of any private dwelling containing more than four units. That act was enforceable by the State Fair Employment Practice Commission.

It was against this background that Proposition 14 was enacted. Its immediate design and intent, the California court said, was "to overturn state laws that bore on the right of private sellers and lessors to discriminate," the Unruh and Rumford Acts, and "to forestall future state action that might circumscribe this right." This aim was successfully achieved: the adoption of Proposition 14 "generally nullifies both the Rumford and Unruh Acts as they apply to the housing market," and establishes "a purported constitutional right to *privately* discriminate on grounds which admittedly would be unavailable under the Fourteenth Amendment *should state action* be involved."

Second, the court conceded that the State was permitted a neutral position with respect to private racial discriminations and that the State was not bound by the Federal Constitution to forbid them. But, because a significant state involvement in private discriminations could amount to unconstitutional state action, Burton v. Wilmington Parking Authority, 365 U.S. 715, the court deemed it necessary to determine whether Proposition 14 invalidly involved the State in racial discriminations in the housing market. Its conclusion was that it did.

To reach this result, the state court examined certain prior decisions in this Court in which discriminatory state action was identified. Based on these cases, ... it concluded that a prohibited state involvement could be found "even where the state can be charged with only encouraging," rather than commanding discrimination.... To the California court "[t]he instant case presents an undeniably analogous situation" wherein the State had taken affirmative action designed to make private discriminations legally possible.

Section 26 was said to have changed the situation from one in which discriminatory practices were restricted "to one wherein it is encouraged, within the meaning of the cited decisions"; § 26 was legislative action "which authorized private discrimination" and made the State "at least a partner in the instant act of discrimination. . . ." The court could "conceive of no other purpose for an application of section 26 aside from authorizing the perpetration of a purported private discrimination. . . ." The judgment of the California court was that § 26 unconstitutionally involves the State in racial discriminations and is therefore invalid under the Fourteenth Amendment.

There is no sound reason for rejecting this judgment. Petitioners contend that the California court has misconstrued the Fourteenth Amendment since the repeal of any statute prohibiting racial discrimination, which is constitutionally permissible, may be said to "authorize" and "encourage" discrimination because it makes legally permissible that which was formerly proscribed. But as we understand the California court, it did not posit a constitutional violation on the mere repeal of the Unruh and Rumford Acts. It did not read either our cases or the Fourteenth Amendment as establishing an automatic constitutional barrier to the repeal of an existing law prohibiting racial discriminations in housing; nor did the court rule that a State may never put in statutory form an existing policy of neutrality with respect to private discriminations. What the court below did was first to reject the notion that the State was required to have a statute prohibiting racial discriminations in housing. Second, it held the purpose and intent of § 26 was to authorize private racial discriminations in the housing market, to repeal the Unruh and Rumford Acts and to create a constitutional right to discriminate on racial grounds in the sale and leasing of real property. Hence, the court dealt with § 26 as though it expressly authorized and constitutionalized the private right to discriminate. Third, the court assessed the ultimate impact of § 26 in the California environment and concluded that the section would encourage and significantly involve the State in private racial discrimination contrary to the Fourteenth Amendment.

The California court could very reasonably conclude that § 26 would and did have wider impact than a mere repeal of existing statutes. Section 26 mentioned neither the Unruh nor Rumford Acts in so many words. Instead, it announced the constitutional right of any person to decline to sell or lease his real property to anyone to whom he did not desire to sell or lease. Unruh and Rumford were thereby *pro tanto* repealed. But the section struck more deeply and more widely. Private discriminations in housing were now not only free from Rumford and Unruh but they also enjoyed a far different status than was true before the passage of those statutes. The right to discriminate, including the right to discriminate on racial grounds, was now embodied in the State's basic charter, immune from legislative, executive, or judicial regulation at any level of the state government. Those practicing racial discriminations need no longer rely solely on their personal choice. They could now invoke express constitutional authority, free from censure or interference of any kind from official sources. All individuals, partnerships, corporations and other legal entities, as well as their agents and representatives, could now discriminate with respect to their residential real property, which is defined as any interest in real property of any kind or quality, "irrespective of how obtained or financed," and seemingly irrespective of the relationship of the State to such interests in real property. Only the State is excluded with respect to property owned by it.

. . . Here the California court, armed as it was with the knowledge of the facts and circumstances concerning the passage and potential impact of § 26, and familiar with the milieu in which that provision would operate, has determined that the provision would involve the State in private racial discriminations to an unconstitutional degree. We accept this holding of the California court.

The assessment of § 26 by the California court is similar to what this Court has done in appraising state statutes or other official actions in other contexts....

None of these cases squarely controls the case we now have before us. But they do illustrate the range of situations in which discriminatory state action has been identified. They do exemplify the necessity for a court to assess the potential impact of official action in determining whether the State has significantly involved itself with invidious discriminations. Here we are dealing with a provision which does not just repeal an existing law forbidding private racial discriminations. Section 26 was intended to authorize, and does authorize, racial discrimination in the housing market. The right to discriminate is now one of the basic policies of the State. The California Supreme Court believes that the section will significantly encourage and involve the State in private discriminations. We have been presented with no persuasive considerations indicating that this judgment should be overturned.

Affirmed.

Mr. Justice Douglas, concurring.

While I join the opinion of the Court, I add a word to indicate the dimensions of our problem.

.   .   .

Since the real estate brokerage business is one that can be and is state regulated and since it is state licensed, it must be dedicated, like the telephone companies and the carriers and the hotels and motels to the requirements of service to all without discrimination—a standard that in its modern setting is conditioned by the demands of the Equal Protection Clause of the Fourteenth Amendment.

Mr. Justice Harlan, whom Mr. Justice Black, Mr. Justice Clark, and Mr. Justice Stewart join, dissenting.

I consider that this decision, which cuts deeply into state political processes, is supported neither by anything "found" by the Supreme Court of California nor by any of our past cases decided under the Fourteenth Amendment. In my view today's holding, salutary as its result may appear at first blush, may in the long run actually serve to handicap progress in the extremely difficult field of racial concerns. I must respectfully dissent....

.   .   .

In the case at hand California, acting through the initiative and referendum, has decided to remain "neutral" in the realm of private discrimination affecting the sale or rental of private residential property; in such transactions private owners are now free to act in a discriminatory manner previously forbidden to them. In short, all that has happened is that California has effected a *pro tanto* repeal of its prior statutes forbidding private discrimination. This runs no more afoul of the Fourteenth Amendment than would have California's failure to pass any such antidiscrimination statutes in the first instance. The fact that such repeal was also accompanied by a constitutional prohibition against future enactment of such laws by the California Legislature cannot well be thought to affect, from a federal constitutional standpoint, the validity of what California has done. The Fourteenth Amendment does not reach such state constitutional action any more than it does a simple legislative repeal of legislation forbidding private discrimination.

I.

The Court attempts to fit § 26 within the coverage of the Equal Protection Clause by characterizing it as in effect an affirmative call to residents of California to discriminate. The main difficulty with this viewpoint is that it depends upon a characterization of § 26 that cannot fairly be made. The provision is neutral on its face, and it is only by in effect asserting that this requirement of passive official neutrality is camouflage that the Court is able to reach its conclusion. In depicting the provision as tantamount to active state encouragement of discrimination the Court essentially relies on the fact that the California Supreme Court so concluded. It is said that the findings of the highest court of California as to the meaning and impact of the enactment are entitled to great weight. I agree, of course, that *findings of fact* by a state court should be given great weight, but this familiar proposition hardly aids the Court's holding in this case. . . .

. . . Put in another way, I cannot transform the California court's conclusion of law into a finding of fact that the State through the adoption of § 26 is actively promoting racial discrimination. It seems to me manifest that the state court decision rested entirely on what that court conceived to be the compulsion of the Fourteenth Amendment, not on any fact-finding by the state courts.

II.

There is no question that the adoption of § 26, repealing the former state antidiscrimination laws and prohibiting the enactment of such state laws in the future, constituted "state action" within the meaning of the Fourteenth Amendment. The only issue is whether this provision impermissibly deprives any person of equal protection of the laws . . . .

A moment of thought will reveal the far-reaching possibilities of the Court's new doctrine, which I am sure the Court does not intend. Every act of private discrimination is either forbidden by state law or permitted by it. There can be little doubt that such permissiveness—whether by express constitutional or statutory provision, or implicit in the common law—to some extent "encourages" those who wish to discriminate to do so. Under this theory "state action" in the form of laws that do nothing more than passively permit private discrimination could be said to tinge *all* private discrimination with the taint of unconstitutional state encouragement.

. . . I believe the state action required to bring the Fourteenth Amendment into operation must be affirmative and purposeful, actively fostering discrimination. Only in such a case is ostensibly "private" action more properly labeled "official." I do not believe that the mere enactment of § 26, on the showing made here, falls within this class of cases.

III.

I think that this decision is not only constitutionally unsound, but in its practical potentialities short-sighted. Opponents of state antidiscrimination statutes are now in a position to argue that such legislation should be defeated because, if enacted, it may be unrepealable. More fundamentally, the doctrine underlying this decision may hamper, if not preclude, attempts to deal with the delicate and troublesome problems of race relations through the legislative process. . . .[a]

PRECURSORS AND SUCCESSORS TO REITMAN v. MULKEY

The theory of Reitman v. Mulkey had been anticipated in two individual concurring opinions in significant state action cases. In Burton v. Wilmington Parking Auth., infra p. 1160, Justice Stewart concurred because the Delaware Supreme Court had relied on a statute which authorized restaurant proprietors to refuse to serve persons whose presence would be offensive to a majority of customers. Justice Harlan's dissent in the same case conceded that if the Delaware court had construed the statute to authorize discriminatory classification based exclusively on race, he would "certainly agree" that the statute violated the Fourteenth Amendment. In Evans v. Newton, supra p. 1140, Justice White's concurrence was premised on a Georgia statute which had been enacted in 1905, six years before Senator Bacon's will was executed. That statute explicitly authorized charitable trusts for public parks for the use of one race. While the statute did not compel trust settlors to discriminate, "if the validity of the racial condition in Senator Bacon's trust would have been in doubt but for the 1904 statute and if the statute removed such doubt only for racial restrictions, leaving the validity of nonracial restrictions still in question. . . . such a statute would depart from a policy of strict neutrality in matters of private discrimination. . . ."

Is the disagreement between the majority and dissenting opinions in Reitman v. Mulkey applicable to those cases where a statute validating private conduct uses an express racial classification? In Hunter v. Erickson, 393 U.S. 385 (1969), the Court held invalid a city charter provision which prevented the city council from implementing any ordinance dealing with racial, religious, or ancestral discrimination in housing without the approval of the majority of the city voters. Justices Harlan and Stewart concurred, noting that since the challenged provision was discriminatory on its face, it bore a far heavier burden of justification than was required in *Reitman*. Justice Black was the sole dissenter.

Justice Black, however, wrote the Court's opinion in James v. Valtierra, 402 U.S. 137 (1971), which upheld a provision of the California constitution requiring a referendum for publicly supported low-rent housing projects, because "California's entire history demonstrates the repeated use of referendums to give citizens a voice on questions of public policy." Three Justices dissented, arguing that the challenged provision rested on the explicit suspect classification of poverty. Without challenging the dissent's argument that explicit de jure classifications based on wealth were suspect, the Court concluded that the challenged provision could be invalidated only by extending the rationale of *Hunter* beyond cases where racial classifications were used, "and this we decline to do."[1]

---

a. For discussion of the issues in Reitman v. Mulkey, see Black, *"State Action," Equal Protection, and California's Proposition 14,* 81 Harv.L.Rev. 69 (1967); Note, *The Unconstitutionality of Proposition 14,* 19 Stan.L.Rev. 232 (1966); Comments, 14 U.C.L.A.L.Rev. 1 (1966).

1. In Romer v. Evans, 517 U.S. 620, 116 S.Ct. 1620 (1996), the Court dealt with an amendment to the Colorado Constitution that precluded any level of state government from protecting the status of persons based on their "homosexual, lesbian or bisexual orientation, conduct, practices or relationships." The Colorado Supreme Court held the measure unconstitutional, relying in part on Hunter v. Erickson. The Supreme Court affirmed, but did not rely upon or cite *Hunter*, nor did the Court advert to the issue of state action. The full report of this case appears infra, p. 926. For discussion of the *Hunter* line of cases see Vikram D. Amar and

The Court relied on Hunter v. Erickson in Washington v. Seattle Sch. Dist. No. 1, 458 U.S. 457 (1982). A voter initiative of the State of Washington was passed shortly after Seattle adopted a mandatory busing program to achieve desegregation. The initiative's terms prohibited local school boards from requiring students to attend schools other than those nearest the students' homes. The provision also barred seven methods of "indirect student assignment" by school boards, including the redefinition of attendance zones, pairing of schools, and the use of feeder schools. The initiative permitted assignment of pupils to distant schools for purposes of special education, because of health or safety hazards, or physical barriers or obstacles between residence and school, or if the nearest school was overcrowded or lacked physical facilities. Finally, the initiative expressly permitted busing for racial balance if ordered by a court of competent jurisdiction "adjudicating constitutional issues." Holding the initiative unconstitutional, Justice Blackmun's opinion for the Court summarized the principle of Hunter v. Erickson as follows:

> . . . "As Justice Harlan noted while concurring in the Court's opinion in *Hunter,* laws structuring political institutions or allocating political power according to 'neutral principles'—such as the executive veto, or the typically burdensome requirements for amending state constitutions—are not subject to equal protection attack, though they may 'make it more difficult for minorities to achieve favorable legislation.' . . . Because such laws make it more difficult for *every* group in the community to enact comparable laws, they 'provid[e] a just framework within which the diverse political groups in our society may fairly compete.' . . . Thus, the political majority may generally restructure the political process to place obstacles in the path of everyone seeking to secure the benefits of governmental action. But a different analysis is required when the State allocates governmental power non-neutrally, by explicitly using the *racial* nature of a decision to determine the decisionmaking process. State action of this kind, the Court said, 'places *special* burdens on racial minorities within the governmental process,' . . . thereby 'making it *more* difficult for certain racial and religious minorities [than for other members of the community] to achieve legislation that is in their interest.' . . . Such a structuring of the political process, the Court said, was 'no more permissible than [is] denying [members of a racial minority] the vote, on an equal basis with others.' . . . "

In this case, the initiative dealt only with desegregation of public schools, which "at bottom inures primarily to the benefit of the minority." And, by placing the power over desegregation at the state level, the initiative restructured the State's political process on the basis of a classification that differentiated between "racial matters and . . . other problems in the same area." Finally, the Court held that no inquiry was required into the question whether there was an "intent" to discriminate, under the doctrine of Washington v. Davis, 426 U.S. 229 (1976). When "racially conscious" political decisionmaking "is singled out for peculiar and disadvantageous treatment, the government action plainly rests on distinctions based on race." Justice Powell, joined by Chief Justice Burger, Justice Rehnquist, and Justice O'Connor, dissented. Justice Powell argued that "racial minorities are not uniquely or comparatively burdened by the State's adoption of a policy that would be lawful if adopted by any School District in the State. . . . The Constitution does not dictate to the

Evan H. Caminker; "Equal Protection, Unequal Political Burdens and the CCRI," 23 Hastings Const. L.Q. 1019 (1996).

States at what level of government decisions affecting the public schools must be taken."

Compare the decision in Crawford v. Los Angeles Board of Education, 458 U.S. 527 (1982). California courts had required mandatory busing in the Los Angeles school district, interpreting the California Constitution to require alleviation of de facto, as well as de jure, school segregation. An initiative amended the California Constitution to forbid California courts to order busing unless required by the United States Constitution. The Court held that the initiative was constitutional. Justice Powell's opinion for the Court explained that the initiative employed no racial classification, and no discriminatory purpose had been shown. "[T]he simple repeal or modification of desegregation or anti-discrimination laws, without more, never has been viewed as embodying a presumptively invalid racial classification." Justice Blackmun, concurring, argued that Washington v. Seattle Sch. Dist. No. 1 differed from *Crawford* because "the people of California—the same entity that put in place the State Constitution, and created the enforceable obligation to desegregate—have made the desegregation obligation judicially unenforceable." Justice Marshall dissented, stating: "I fail to see how a fundamental redefinition of the governmental decisionmaking structure with respect to the same racial issue can be unconstitutional when the State seeks to remove the authority from local school boards, yet constitutional when the State attempts to achieve the same result by limiting the power of its courts."

SECTION 3.   Federal Civil Rights Legislation

A.   The Reconstruction Legacy

From 1866 to 1875 Congressional leaders attached great importance to national legislation in aid of civil rights. State action which violated the new constitutional rights of freedmen could be resisted in court; but this means of vindicating constitutional guaranties depended on successful litigation by ex-slaves, and carried no sanction to deter unconstitutional action in those cases where private litigation could not succeed. Hence Congress added the possibility of federal criminal prosecution, directed not only against state officials but also against private individuals who interfered with the liberty of the new freedmen.

Only the following fragments remain.

REMAINING RECONSTRUCTION ERA—FEDERAL CIVIL RIGHTS STATUTES

1.   Criminal Provisions:

18 U.S.C. § 241.[1] "*Conspiracy Against Rights of Citizens.* If two or more persons conspire to injure, oppress, threaten, or intimidate any citizen in the free exercise or enjoyment of any right or privilege secured to him by the Constitution or laws of the United States, or because of his having so exercised the same; or

"If two or more persons go in disguise on the highway, or on the premises of another, with intent to prevent or hinder his free exercise or enjoyment of any right or privilege so secured—

---

1.   From § 6 of the 1870 Act.

[handwritten margin note: possibility to prosecute state? private ind. who interfered with freedmen -]

"They shall be fined not more than $10,000 or imprisoned not more than ten years, or both; and if death results, they shall be subject to imprisonment for any term of years or for life."

18 U.S.C. § 242.[2] *"Deprivation of Rights under Color of Law.* Whoever, under color of any law, statute, ordinance, regulation, or custom, willfully subjects any inhabitant of any State, Territory, or District to the deprivation of any rights, privileges, or immunities secured or protected by the Constitution or laws of the United States, or to different punishments, pains, or penalties, on account of such inhabitant being an alien, or by reason of his color, or race, than are prescribed for the punishment of citizens, shall be fined not more than $1,000 or imprisoned not more than one year, or both; and if bodily injury results shall be fined under this title and imprisoned not more than ten years, or both; and if death results shall be subject to imprisonment for any term of years or for life."

2. Civil Provisions:

42 U.S.C. § 1981.[3] *"Equal Rights under the Law."*

"(a) All persons within the jurisdiction of the United States shall have the same right in every State and Territory to make and enforce contracts, to sue, be parties, give evidence, and to the full and equal benefit of all laws and proceedings for the security of persons and property as is enjoyed by white citizens, and shall be subject to like punishment, pains, penalties, taxes, licenses, and exactions of every kind, and to no other."

"(b) For purposes of this section, the term 'make and enforce contracts' includes the making, performance, modification, and termination of contracts, and the enjoyment of all benefits, privileges, terms, and conditions of the contractual relationship."

"(c) The rights protected by this section are protected against impairment by nongovernmental discrimination and impairment under color of State law."

42 U.S.C. § 1982.[4] *"Property Rights of Citizens.* All citizens of the United States shall have the same right, in every State and Territory, as is enjoyed by white citizens thereof to inherit, purchase, lease, sell, hold, and convey real and personal property."

42 U.S.C. § 1983.[5] *"Civil Action for Deprivation of Rights.* Every person who, under color of any statute, ordinance, regulation, custom, or usage, of any State or Territory or the District of Columbia, subjects, or causes to be subjected, any citizen of the United States or other persons within the jurisdiction thereof to the deprivation of any rights, privileges or immunities secured by the Constitution and laws, shall be liable to the person injured in an action of law, suit in equity, or other proper proceedings for redress...."

42 U.S.C. § 1985.[6] *"Conspiracy to Interfere with Civil Rights.* (1) [conspiracies to prevent federal officers from performing duties].... (2) [obstructing justice].... (3) If two or more persons in any State or Territory conspire or go in disguise on the highway or on the premises of another, for the purpose of depriving ... any person or class of persons of the equal protection of the laws, or of equal privileges and immunities under the laws; or for the purpose of preventing or hindering the constituted authorities of any State or Territory

---

2. From § 2 of the 1866 Act, as amended by § 17 of the 1870 Act.

3. From the 1866 and 1870 Acts.

4. From the 1866 Act.

5. From § 1 of the 1871 Act.

6. From the 1871 Act.

from giving or securing to all persons within such State or Territory the equal protection of the laws ... the party so injured or deprived may have an action for the recovery of damages, occasioned by such injury or deprivation, against any one or more of the conspirators."

ENFORCING AND INTERPRETING THE CIVIL RIGHTS STATUTES

Sections 4 and 5 of this chapter will focus on issues of interpretation of these Reconstruction statutes that are relevant to issues of the scope of Congressional power to protect civil rights against the conduct of private individuals. These represent, however, only a fraction of the issues surrounding contemporary application of these statutes.

The civil rights acts were enforced vigorously during Reconstruction. In the peak year of 1873 there were 1271 prosecutions under their criminal provisions in Southern federal courts. Even before the decision in the Civil Rights Cases, the end of Reconstruction and the withdrawal of federal troops marked a significant change in enforcement. In 1878, there were 25 criminal cases. The change in national mood was reflected both in Congress and the Supreme Court. The last of the federal civil rights laws was enacted in 1875, and Congress retired from the scene for more than three quarters of a century. One year later the Court decided in United States v. Cruikshank, 92 U.S. (2 Otto) 542 (1876), that an indictment against members of a lynch mob accused of killing two Blacks failed to state an offense under the 1870 Act. Other provisions of the civil rights acts were invalidated prior to the decision in the Civil Rights Cases. United States v. Reese, 92 U.S. (2 Otto) 214 (1876), held provisions of the 1870 Act dealing with voting rights invalid because they were not limited to interference with voting on account of race, color or previous condition of servitude. United States v. Harris, 106 U.S. (16 Otto) 629 (1883), invalidated the antilynching provisions of the 1871 Act, holding that Congress lacked power to punish private persons who removed Black prisoners from state custody and abused or killed them.

The decision in the Civil Rights Cases was followed by later decisions curtailing the power of the federal government to protect Blacks from private violence. For example, Hodges v. United States, 203 U.S. 1 (1906), held that Congress lacked power to protect Blacks from private violence that interfered with their employment. From 1909 to 1939, the criminal provisions of the federal civil rights acts lay dormant until Attorney General Frank Murphy established a Civil Rights Section in the Department of Justice.

One target of prosecution was unlawful violence against prisoners and arrestees. In those prosecutions under the predecessor of 18 U.S.C. § 242, two problems arose. First, it was contended that the lawless and unauthorized conduct of the police was not "under color of ... law"; second, it was claimed that the uncertain contours of constitutional rights rendered the criminal punishment of state officials for violating those rights unconstitutionally vague. Screws v. United States, 325 U.S. 91 (1945), held that state officials who wielded state power acted under color of law whether or not their conduct was illegal under state law. The problem of vagueness was addressed by requiring that the federal constitutional rights denied by the defendant be specifically defined by prior law or court decisions, and that the defendant be proved to have acted "wilfully" with specific intent to deprive the victim of those rights.

Vigorous enforcement of the criminal provisions of the remaining fragments of Reconstruction civil rights acts also led to rediscovery of their civil provisions. 42 U.S.C. § 1983 has become the primary vehicle for litigation requiring state officials to obey the commands of federal constitutional or statutory law. (See Chapter 3, page 1151.) Problems of interpretation have been numerous, particularly where the complaint under § 1983 seeks the award of damages. In Monroe v. Pape, 365 U.S. 167 (1961), the Court held that damages were available under § 1983 against police officers who engaged in an unlawful search and seizure. The Court adopted the definition of "color of law" from Screws v. United States, supra, but held the requirement of that case, that the defendant act "wilfully," inapplicable since § 1983 provided a civil remedy and was not a criminal statute. Thus, damages could be awarded although the constitutional right denied was not specifically defined and the defendant did not act with specific intent to deny that right.

The potential for damage awards against legislators who enacted laws later determined to be unconstitutional, judges who applied those laws, and state prosecutors who enforced them, has led to an elaborate body of judicially developed immunities from liability for damages under § 1983. An example of a controversial decision concerning the scope of the immunity from damage awards is Stump v. Sparkman, 435 U.S. 349 (1978), where a divided Court held that a judge was not liable for ordering the involuntary sterilization of a minor despite the "clear absence of all jurisdiction." In addition, individual defendants not entitled to absolute immunity have been allowed the defense that their action was taken in "good faith." In Wood v. Strickland, 420 U.S. 308 (1975), the Court divided 5–4 on the definition of good faith in a suit against school officials who expelled students without an adequate hearing. The potential for damage liability may also have resulted, in some cases, in a narrow definition of constitutional rights.

Section 1983 provides no basis for an action against state governments as such. Quern v. Jordan, 440 U.S. 332, 341 (1979). *Monroe v. Pape,* supra, had also held that local governments were not subject to suit under § 1983. That aspect of *Monroe* was overruled in Monell v. New York City Dept. of Social Services, 436 U.S. 658 (1978). Municipalities are not liable under *Monell,* however, on a respondeat superior theory for acts of their employees. Municipal liability for damages is limited to the denial of federal rights by "official policy." On the other hand, municipalities are not entitled to defend a § 1983 action based on the good faith of their officials. Owen v. City of Independence, Mo., 445 U.S. 622 (1980).

B.   CONTEMPORARY FEDERAL CIVIL RIGHTS LEGISLATION

The Civil Rights Act of 1964. The most comprehensive of contemporary federal civil rights laws is the Civil Rights Act of 1964 (78 Stat. 241). Title II on Discrimination in Places of Public Accommodation (42 U.S.C. § 2000a) sets forth elaborate provisions for injunctive relief against racial discrimination by hotels, restaurants, theaters and similar establishments. The scope and constitutional support for these provisions have already been examined in Chapter 4. Katzenbach v. McClung, 379 U.S. 294 (1964), page 174, supra. Title III authorizes civil actions by the Attorney General against discrimination in public facilities; Title IV (*inter alia*) authorizes similar remedial action by the Attorney General against continued discrimination in public education (42 U.S.C. §§ 2000b–2000c). Title VI prohibits "discrimination under any program or activity receiving Federal financial assistance" (42 U.S.C. § 2000d)—a provision of sweeping potential in view of the widespread dependence on federal spending.[7] Title VII on Equal Employment Opportunity broadly prohibits discrimination in employment. (42 U.S.C. § 2000e).

---

7. In Grove City College v. Bell, 465 U.S. 555 (1984), the Court held that Title VI applied only to programs receiving Federal assistance. 1987 legislation, passed over President Reagan's veto, extends coverage to substantially all activities of an institution receiving Federal assistance.

The Voting Rights Act of 1965. The confrontation at the bridge in Selma, Alabama crystallized support that led to the Voting Rights Act of 1965 (79 Stat. 437, 42 U.S.C. § 1973). The central theory of the Act was to move beyond the case-by-case litigation strategy of prior legislation, which had accomplished little in enforcing the command of the Fifteenth Amendment. The Act made special provision for "covered jurisdictions"—states or political subdivisions that on November 1, 1964, had used literacy tests as a qualification for voting, and where less than half of the voting-age residents voted in the 1964 presidential election. Literacy tests were suspended in covered jurisdictions and the Attorney General could appoint federal voting registrars. Any electoral changes in covered jurisdictions were made inoperative, unless precleared by the Attorney General, on a finding that the changes would not perpetuate voting discrimination. The preclearance procedures were extended by the 1970, 1975, and 1982 Acts, the 1982 Act extending them for an additional 25 years. The 1982 Act also provided for judicial challenges to existing voting legislation and voting laws of non-covered jurisdictions, that had the effect of denying voting rights to racial minorities. (As to the last-mentioned provision, see p. 808, supra.)

The only provision of the 1965 Act dealing with literacy tests beyond those in covered jurisdictions was § 4(e)—not part of the original bill, but introduced from the floor. New York excused from its literacy test for voting persons who had completed six grades of schooling in the English language. The effect of § 4(e) was to require New York to exempt also those who had successfully completed six grades in a school in Puerto Rico, even though the language of instruction was Spanish.

The 1965 provisions suspending literacy tests in covered jurisdictions, and § 4(e), were made obsolete in the 1970 Act. Congress suspended literacy tests for voting nationwide for a period of five years. The suspension was made permanent in the 1975 Act. The 1970 Act also contained a significant provision going beyond racial discrimination in voting, lowering the minimum age for voters in state and federal elections to 18. That provision was superseded by the twenty-sixth amendment in 1971.

The Civil Rights Act of 1968. The assassination of Dr. Martin Luther King on April 4, 1968, released emotions and pressures that speeded the enactment on April 11, 1968, of a further Civil Rights Act (P.L. 90–284; 90th Cong., H.R. 2516). The most controversial subject reached by the 1968 Act was racial discrimination in housing. But this is only one part (Title VIII) of a complex piece of legislation embracing ten Titles.

Title I establishes heavy criminal penalties for the use of force or threats to interfere with "federally protected activities" (18 U.S.C. § 245)—generally those activities that have been blocked or deterred by racial discrimination.

Title VIII (Secs. 801–819) prohibits discrimination "because of race, color, religion or national origin" in sales or rentals of housing. 1988 amendments provide for enhanced enforcement, as well as adding to the categories of prohibited discrimination.

SECTION 4. FEDERAL POWER TO REGULATE PRIVATE CONDUCT UNDER THE THIRTEENTH AMENDMENT

Introduction. It will be recalled that the decision in the Civil Rights Cases conceded that Congressional power to enforce the thirteenth amendment extended to private racial discrimination that could be described as a badge of slavery. Its narrow construction of that concept, however, led to a narrow definition of Congressional power under the thirteenth amendment to regulate private racial discrimination. The cases discussed in this section, all decided since 1968, raise two questions. First, under the modern decisions, are there any forms of private racial discrimination that are *not* within Congressional power to prohibit? Second, to the extent that the thirteenth amendment empowers Congress to prohibit private *racial* discrimination, would the thirteenth amendment power sustain prohibition of similar *non-racial* discrimination, such as discrimination based on national origin, religion, gender, age or physical handicap?

Jones v. Alfred H. Mayer Co.

392 U.S. 409, 88 S.Ct. 2186, 20 L.Ed.2d 1189 (1968).

Mr. Justice Stewart delivered the opinion of the Court.

In this case we are called upon to determine the scope and the constitutionality of an Act of Congress, 42 U.S.C. § 1982, which provides that:

> "All citizens of the United States shall have the same right, in every State and Territory, as is enjoyed by white citizens thereof to inherit, purchase, lease, sell, hold, and convey real and personal property."

On September 2, 1965, the petitioners filed a complaint in the District Court for the Eastern District of Missouri, alleging that the respondents had refused to sell them a home in the Paddock Woods community of St. Louis County for the sole reason that petitioner Joseph Lee Jones is a Negro. Relying in part upon § 1982, the petitioners sought injunctive and other relief. The District Court sustained the respondents' motion to dismiss the complaint, and the Court of Appeals for the Eighth Circuit affirmed, concluding that § 1982 applies only to state action and does not reach private refusals to sell. We granted certiorari to consider the questions thus presented. For the reasons that follow, we reverse the judgment of the Court of Appeals. We hold that § 1982 bars *all* racial discrimination, private as well as public, in the sale or rental of property, and that the statute, thus construed, is a valid exercise of the power of Congress to enforce the Thirteenth Amendment.

I.

At the outset, it is important to make clear precisely what this case does *not* involve. Whatever else it may be, 42 U.S.C. § 1982 is not a comprehensive open housing law. In sharp contrast to the Fair Housing Title (Title VIII) of the Civil Rights Act of 1968 ... the statute in this case deals only with racial discrimination and does not address itself to discrimination on grounds of religion or national origin. It does not deal specifically with discrimination in the provision of services or facilities in connection with the sale or rental of a dwelling. It does not prohibit advertising or other representations that indicate discriminatory preferences. It does not refer explicitly to discrimination in financing arrangements or in the provision of brokerage services. It does not empower a federal administrative agency to assist aggrieved parties. It makes no provision for intervention by the Attorney General. And, although it can be enforced by injunction, it contains no provision expressly authorizing a federal court to order the payment of damages.

Thus, although § 1982 contains none of the exemptions that Congress included in the Civil Rights Act of 1968, it would be a serious mistake to suppose that § 1982 in any way diminishes the significance of the law recently enacted by Congress. . . .

. . .

III.

Look at lang. to see if it prohibits disc. by state & public, or just state . . . .

We begin with the language of the statute itself. In plain and unambiguous terms, § 1982 grants to all citizens, without regard to race or color, "the same right" to purchase and lease property "as is enjoyed by white citizens." As the Court of Appeals in this case evidently recognized, that right can be impaired as effectively by "those who place property on the market" as by the State itself. For, even if the State and its agents lend no support to those who wish to exclude persons from their communities on racial grounds, the fact remains that, whenever property "is placed on the market for whites only, whites have a right denied to Negroes." So long as a Negro citizen who wants to buy or rent a home can be turned away simply because he is not white, he cannot be said to enjoy "the *same* right . . . as is enjoyed by white citizens . . . to . . . purchase [and] lease . . . real and personal property." 42 U.S.C. § 1982. (Emphasis added.)

On its face, therefore, § 1982 appears to prohibit *all* discrimination against Negroes in the sale or rental of property—discrimination by private owners as well as discrimination by public authorities. Indeed, even the respondents seem to concede that, if § 1982 "means what it says"—to use the words of the respondents' brief—then it must encompass every racially motivated refusal to sell or rent and cannot be confined to officially sanctioned segregation in housing. Stressing what they consider to be the revolutionary implications of so literal a reading of § 1982, the respondents argue that Congress cannot possibly have intended any such result. Our examination of the relevant history, however, persuades us that Congress meant exactly what it said.

. . .

V.

The remaining question is whether Congress has power under the Constitution to do what § 1982 purports to do: to prohibit all racial discrimination, private and public, in the sale and rental of property. Our starting point is the Thirteenth Amendment, for it was pursuant to that constitutional provision that Congress originally enacted what is now § 1982. . . .

As its text reveals, the Thirteenth Amendment "is not a mere prohibition of State laws establishing or upholding slavery, but an absolute declaration that slavery or involuntary servitude shall not exist in any part of the United States." Civil Rights Cases, 109 U.S. 3, 20. It has never been doubted, therefore, "that the power vested in Congress to enforce the article by appropriate legislation," ibid., includes the power to enact laws "direct and primary, operating upon the acts of individuals, whether sanctioned by State legislation or not." Id., at 23.

Thus, the fact that § 1982 operates upon the unofficial acts of private individuals, whether or not sanctioned by state law, presents no constitutional problem. If Congress has power under the Thirteenth Amendment to eradicate conditions that prevent Negroes from buying and renting property because of their race or color, then no federal statute calculated to achieve that objective can be thought to exceed the constitutional power of Congress simply because it reaches beyond state action to regulate the conduct of private individuals. The constitutional question in this case, therefore, comes to this: Does the authority of Congress to enforce the Thirteenth Amendment "by appropriate legislation" include the power to eliminate all racial barriers to the acquisition of real and personal property? We think the answer to that question is plainly yes.

"By its own unaided force and effect," the Thirteenth Amendment "abolished slavery, and established universal freedom." Civil Rights Cases, 109 U.S. 3, 20. Whether or not the Amendment *itself* did any more than that—a question not involved in this case—it is at least clear that the Enabling Clause of that Amendment empowered Congress to do much more. For that clause clothed "Congress with power to pass *all laws necessary and proper for abolishing all badges and incidents of slavery in the United States.*" Ibid. (Emphasis added.)

. . . .

. . . Surely Congress has the power under the Thirteenth Amendment rationally to determine what are the badges and the incidents of slavery, and the authority to translate that determination into effective legislation. Nor can we say that the determination Congress has made is an irrational one. For this Court recognized long ago that, whatever else they may have encompassed, the badges and incidents of slavery—its "burdens and disabilities"—included restraints upon "those fundamental rights which are the essence of civil freedom, namely, the same right . . . to inherit, purchase, lease, sell and convey property, as is enjoyed by white citizens." Civil Rights Cases, 109 U.S. 3, 22. Just as the Black Codes, enacted after the Civil War to restrict the free exercise of those rights, were substitutes for the slave system, so the exclusion of Negroes from white communities became a substitute for the Black Codes. And when racial discrimination herds men into ghettos and makes their ability to buy property turn on the color of their skin, then it too is a relic of slavery.

Negro citizens North and South, who saw in the Thirteenth Amendment a promise of freedom—freedom to "go and come at pleasure" and to "buy and sell when they please"—would be left with "a mere paper guarantee" if Congress were powerless to assure that a dollar in the hands of a Negro will purchase the same thing as a dollar in the hands of a white man. At the very least, the freedom that Congress is empowered to secure under the Thirteenth Amendment includes the freedom to buy whatever a white man can buy, the right to live wherever a white man can live. If Congress cannot say that being a free man means at least this much, then the Thirteenth Amendment made a promise the Nation cannot keep.

Representative Wilson of Iowa was the floor manager in the House for the Civil Rights Act of 1866. In urging that Congress had ample authority to pass the pending bill, he recalled the celebrated words of Chief Justice Marshall in McCulloch v. Maryland, 4 Wheat. 316, 421:

"Let the end be legitimate, let it be within the scope of the constitution, and all means which are appropriate, which are plainly adapted to that end, which are not prohibited, but consist with the letter and spirit of the constitution, are constitutional."

"The end is legitimate," the Congressman said, "because it is defined by the Constitution itself. The end is the maintenance of freedom. . . . A man who enjoys the civil rights mentioned in this bill cannot be reduced to slavery. . . . This settles the appropriateness of this measure, and that settles its constitutionality."

We agree. The judgment is reversed.[a]

a. A concurring opinion by Justice Douglas is omitted.

Mr. Justice Harlan, whom Mr. Justice White joins, dissenting.

The decision in this case appears to me to be most ill-considered and ill-advised.

. . .

For reasons which follow, I believe that the Court's construction of § 1982 as applying to purely private action is almost surely wrong, and at the least is open to serious doubt. The issue of the constitutionality of § 1982, as construed by the Court, and of liability under the Fourteenth Amendment alone, also present formidable difficulties. Moreover, the political processes of our own era have, since the date of oral argument in this case, given birth to a civil rights statute embodying "fair housing" provisions which would at the end of this year make available to others, though apparently not to the petitioners themselves, the type of relief which the petitioners now seek. It seems to me that this latter factor so diminishes the public importance of this case that by far the wisest course would be for this Court to refrain from decision and to dismiss the writ as improvidently granted.

. . .

Statute only refers to state

Like the Court, I began analysis of § 1982 by examining its language. . . . The Court finds it "plain and unambiguous" that this language forbids purely private as well as state-authorized discrimination. With all respect, I do not find it so. For me, there is an inherent ambiguity in the term "right," as used in § 1982. The "right" referred to may either be a right to equal status under the law, in which case the statute operates only against state-sanctioned discrimination, or it may be an "absolute" right enforceable against private individuals. To me, the words of the statute, taken alone, suggest the former interpretation, not the latter.[9]

. . .

In sum, the most which can be said with assurance about the intended impact of the 1866 Civil Rights Act upon purely private discrimination is that the Act probably was envisioned by most members of Congress as prohibiting official, community-sanctioned discrimination in the South, engaged in pursuant to local "customs" which in the recent time of slavery probably were embodied in laws or regulations. Acts done under the color of such "customs" were, of course, said by the Court in the Civil Rights Cases . . . to constitute "state action" prohibited by the Fourteenth Amendment. . . . Adoption of a "state action" construction of the Civil Rights Act would therefore have the additional merit of bringing its interpretation into line with that of the Fourteenth Amendment, which this Court has consistently held to reach only "state action." This seems especially desirable in light of the wide agreement that a major purpose of the Fourteenth Amendment, at least in the minds of its

---

9. . . . In the Civil Rights Cases, 109 U.S. 3, the Court said of identical language in the predecessor statute to § 1982:

"[C]ivil rights, such as are guaranteed by the constitution against state aggression, cannot be impaired by the wrongful acts of individuals, unsupported by state authority. . . . The wrongful act of an individual, unsupported by any such authority, is simply a private wrong, or a crime of that individual; an invasion of the rights of the injured party, it is true . . . ; but if not sanctioned in some

way by the state, or not done under State authority, his rights remain in full force, and may presumably be vindicated by resort to the laws of the State for redress. An individual cannot deprive a man of his right . . . to hold property, to buy and sell . . . ; he may, by force or fraud, interfere with the enjoyment of the right in a particular case; . . . but, unless protected in these wrongful acts by some shield of state law or state authority, he cannot destroy or injure the right. . . ." 109 U.S., at 17.

congressional proponents, was to assure that the rights conferred by the then recently enacted Civil Rights Act could not be taken away by a subsequent Congress.

.   .   .

OTHER INTERPRETATIONS OF RECONSTRUCTION ERA— CIVIL RIGHTS LEGISLATION PREMISED ON THE THIRTEENTH AMENDMENT

Since the decision in Jones v. Alfred H. Mayer Co., the Court has interpreted or re-interpreted a number of Reconstruction-era federal civil rights laws. Consider the implications of these decisions on the issue of the scope of Congressional enforcement power under § 2 of the thirteenth amendment.

(1) Application of 42 U.S.C. §§ 1981 and 1982 to conduct of private parties. In addition to § 1982, involved in Jones v. Alfred H. Mayer Co., another fragment of § 1 of the Civil Rights Act of 1866 is § 1981, providing that "all persons within the jurisdiction of the United States" have the same right "as is enjoyed by white citizens," to "make and enforce contracts." The Court has reaffirmed that the right to purchase property under § 1982 is a prohibition of private discrimination, and has extended that rationale to the right to make and enforce contracts under § 1981. Runyon v. McCrary, 427 U.S. 160 (1976).

(2) Application of § 1982 to "property." In Sullivan v. Little Hunting Park, Inc., 396 U.S. 229 (1969), the Court held that § 1982 applied to refusal by a residents' association, running a community swimming pool, to approve assignment of a membership share from a white owner to a black tenant. Since the tenant paid part of his monthly rental for assignment of the membership share, refusal to approve the membership transfer was an interference with his right to "lease" the house. In City of Memphis v. Greene, 451 U.S. 100 (1981), however, the Court concluded that closing a street through a white residential community did not give rise to a cause of action, under § 1982, for black residents of a nearby predominantly black neighborhood. Plaintiffs' injury was not an impairment of their "property interests."

(3) Application of § 1981 to discrimination in private employment and admission to private schools. McDonald v. Santa Fe Trail Transportation Co., 427 U.S. 273 (1976), confirmed earlier decisions that the equal right to "make and enforce contracts" affords a remedy against discrimination in private employment on the basis of race. Runyon v. McCrary, supra, held that § 1981 reaches a private schools' racial discrimination in admission.

(4) Redress of private racial violence under 42 U.S.C. § 1985(3). This statute provides an action for damages for private conspiracies "for the purpose of depriving . . . any person or class of persons of the equal protection of the laws, or of equal privileges and immunities under the laws." Collins v. Hardyman, 341 U.S. 651 (1951), had held that this provision was applicable only to conspiracies under color of state law. Griffin v. Breckenridge, 403 U.S. 88 (1971), overruled Collins v. Hardyman on this point, holding that § 1985(3) applied to conspiratorial private violence based on "racial, or perhaps otherwise class-based, invidious discriminatory animus." The *Collins* decision had reasoned that narrow construction of the statute was necessary to avoid constitutional problems. As applied to private racial violence, the perceived constitutional problems "simply do not exist" because "Congress was wholly within its powers under § 2 of the Thirteenth Amendment in creating a statutory cause of action for Negro citizens who have been the victims of conspiratorial, racially discriminatory private action aimed at depriving them of the basic rights that the law secures to all free men.''

In Bray v. Alexandria Women's Health Clinic, 506 U.S. 263 (1993), the Court held that § 1985(3) did not provide a federal cause of action against defendants who obstructed access to abortion clinics. Defendants' opposition to abortion was not ''class-based invidiously discriminatory animus'' because it did not focus on women ''by reason of their sex.'' (The Court did not decide the question left open in *Griffin*—whether § 1985(3) was limited to cases involving racial animus.)

(5) Application of §§ 1981 and 1982 to situations exempted from modern federal civil rights statutes. The Court's expansive interpretation of §§ 1981 and 1982 has extended these fragments of the Civil Rights Act of 1866 to areas of private racial discrimination that are the subject of modern federal civil rights acts, such as housing, employment, and public accommodations. As the Court notes in its opinion in Jones v. Alfred H. Mayer Co., for example, the prohibition of housing discrimination in § 1982 ''contains none of the exemptions that Congress included in the Civil Rights Act of 1968.'' Consider, particularly, the exemption for the ''private club or other [private] establishment'' in the public accommodation provisions of the Civil Rights Act of 1964. If an institution that meets the definition of a ''private club'' excludes racial minorities from its dining facilities, its conduct is not prohibited by the 1964 Act. Is that conduct also beyond the reach of § 1981? The Court has not yet squarely faced the question of how far exemptions in modern civil rights statutes should be read as an ''implied repeal'' of the unqualified provisions of §§ 1981 and 1982. In Sullivan v. Little Hunting Park, supra, the Court concluded that the defendant residents' association was not a ''private club,'' since its membership was open to all residents of the geographic area without exclusiveness other than race. And, in Runyon v. McCrary, supra, the private club exemption of the 1964 Act, applicable only to discrimination in public accommodations, was irrelevant to discrimination in admission to a private school.

(6) Application of § 1981 to ''private'' associational or contractual relationships. The broad definition of the right to be free from discrimination in making ''contracts'' has raised the concern that § 1981 will be applied to a variety of ''private associational relationships'' where persons are excluded on the ground of race. In Runyon v. McCrary, supra, the argument was made that § 1981, as applied to a private school's admissions policy, would violate ''constitutionally protected rights of free association and privacy, or a parent's right to direct the education of his children.'' The Court did not resolve the question whether § 1981 should be interpreted as inapplicable to certain ''private'' relationships. It rejected the argument on the ground that the rights of parents to send children to private schools, and the rights of parents and schools to determine the content of instruction, did not confer a right on private schools to operate ''unfettered by reasonable government regulations''. (The Court's opinion stated that the case did not present the question of the right of a private social organization to limit its membership on racial grounds.)

Justices White and Rehnquist, dissenting, suggested that future cases would involve the issue of private associational rights.

''Imaginative judicial construction of the word 'contract' is foreseeable; Thirteenth Amendment limitations on Congress' power to ban 'badges and incidents of slavery' may be discovered; the doctrine of the right to association may be bent to cover a specific situation. In any event, courts will be called upon to balance sensitive policy considerations against each other—which considerations have never been addressed by any Congress—all under the guise of 'construing' a statute. This is a task appropriate for the Legislature, not for the Judiciary."

Concurring, Justice Powell saw fewer difficulties in identifying contracts beyond the reach of § 1981 because they were "so personal as to have a discernible rule of exclusivity which is inoffensive to § 1981."

"§ 1981, as interpreted by our prior decisions, does reach certain acts that are 'private' in the sense that they involve no *state* action. But choices, including those involved in entering into a contract, that are 'private' in the sense that they are not part of a commercial relationship offered generally or widely, and that reflect the selectivity exercised by an individual entering into a personal relationship, certainly were not intended to be restricted by the 19th Century Civil Rights Acts."

For a discussion of the range of possible constitutional issues that might arise in the application of §§ 1981 and 1982 to "private" associations, see the majority and concurring opinions in Roberts v. United States Jaycees, infra page 1584.

(7) Application of § 1981 to discrimination against white persons. In McDonald v. Santa Fe Trail Transportation Co., supra, the Court rejected an argument that § 1981 was inapplicable to private racial discrimination against white persons. The Court conceded that the rejected argument was supported by a "mechanical reading" of the language granting all persons the same rights "as is enjoyed by white citizens." The legislative history of the 1866 Act, however, showed that it was not intended solely for the protection of nonwhites.

The Court also relied on the legislative history of the 1866 Act in Shaare Tefila Congregation v. Cobb, 481 U.S. 615 (1987) and Saint Francis College v. Al–Khazraji, 481 U.S. 604 (1987). Sections 1981 and 1982 are limited to "racial" discrimination, and do not reach discrimination on the basis of national origin or religion. The concept of "race" used by Congress in 1866, however, was not based on the modern scientific understanding of the term. Thus, the Court held that actions by an Arab under § 1981 and by Jews under § 1982 stated claims for "racial" discrimination. "Congress intended to protect from discrimination identifiable classes of persons who are subjected to intentional discrimination solely because of their ancestry or ethnic characteristics."

SECTION 5.   FEDERAL POWER TO REGULATE PRIVATE CONDUCT UNDER THE FOURTEENTH AMENDMENT

CIVIL RIGHTS LEGISLATION AND THE COMMERCE AND SPENDING POWERS

Whatever the scope of Congressional power under the thirteenth amendment to prohibit private racial discrimination, current decisions have not addressed the question of the reach of that power to other forms of discrimination. While the equal protection component of the fourteenth amendment has been extended beyond issues of racial discrimination, there are still unanswered questions about the reach of the fourteenth amendment enforcement power as applied to private conduct. It may be asked, however, whether it will ever be necessary to resolve those questions to sustain Congressional legislation prohibiting private discrimination. Modern civil rights laws have often been based upon Congress' power to regulate the economy and to control the conduct of federal grantees, and not upon the enforcement powers under the Reconstruction Amendments. The public accommodation provisions of the 1964 Civil Rights Act were based squarely upon the commerce power, for example, and were sustained by the Court in Heart of Atlanta Motel v. United States, supra p. 172, and Katzenbach v. McClung, supra p. 174, on that basis. In United Brotherhood of Carpenters v. Scott, 463 U.S. 825 (1983), the Court held that a private conspiracy to infringe first amendment rights, not motivated by racial bias, was not a violation of 42 U.S.C. § 1985(3). The four dissenters (Justice Blackmun, joined by Justices Brennan, Marshall and O'Connor) interpreted § 1985(3) to provide a cause of action for private conspiracies to interfere with first amendment rights. Both the majority and the dissent stated that if § 1985(3) were interpreted to reach private interference with first amendment rights, Congress would have power to ban such conspiracies under the commerce clause. Under those decisions, can you think of any case where it would be necessary to determine the reach of Congress' power under section 5 of the fourteenth amendment in order to define Congress' power to regulate private conduct? Consider, particularly, those cases in Section 2 of this Chapter that have found insufficient state action to subject private conduct to the provisions of section one of the fourteenth amendment. Would any of those situations be beyond Congressional regulatory power under the commerce clause?

PRIVILEGES OF NATIONAL CITIZENSHIP

Curiously, one long established source of federal power to control private conduct stems from the concept of privileges of national citizenship recognized by the Slaughter–House Cases, supra p. 460. The curiosity is that the only express constitutional recognition of privileges of national citizenship is contained in section one of the fourteenth amendment. Nevertheless, the rationale of the Civil Rights Cases—that since section one of the fourteenth amendment prohibited only state action the enforcement power under section five did not extend to private conduct—was never held applicable to Congressional legislation that protected privileges of national citizenship from private interference. That is because the Slaughter–House Cases defined privileges of national citizenship as those "which owe their existence to the Federal government, its National character, its Constitution, or its laws." Under that definition, privileges of national citizenship did not "owe their existence" to their inclusion in the fourteenth amendment, and Congressional power to protect them stemmed from implied federal power that was not limited to the enforcement power under the fourteenth amendment.

The decision in the Slaughter–House Cases doomed much of the Reconstruction legislation by its narrow interpretation of the privileges and immunities clause. But, within that narrow interpretation, portions of those laws that were directed at purely private conduct were upheld as applied, and those provisions have survived. In this connection, the provisions of 18 U.S.C. § 241, penalizing private conspiracies to injure "any citizen in the free exercise or enjoyment of any right or privilege secured to him by the Constitution or laws of the United States," and of 42 U.S.C. § 1985(3), providing a civil action for private conspiracies to deny any person "equal privileges or immunities under the law," continue to be relevant.

A list of the privileges of national citizenship is contained in Justice Moody's opinion in Twining v. New Jersey, 211 U.S. 78, 97 (1908). Dicta or holdings in prosecutions under § 241 have identified these privileges of national citizenship, with concomitant federal power to protect them from private conduct. In United States v. Cruikshank, 92 U.S. 542 (1876), the Court held that the general rights of speech and assembly were not within the privileges of national citizenship, but announced in dicta that there was a federal right to assemble to petition Congress for a redress of grievances. Ex parte Yarbrough (Ku Klux Cases), 110 U.S. 651 (1884), added the right to vote in federal elections. (A more modern case, United States v. Classic, 313 U.S. 299 [1941], extended the right to primary elections for federal officers.) Logan v. United States, 144 U.S. 263 (1892), sustained prosecution of members of a lynch mob conspiring to injure a prisoner in custody of a United States Marshal. (Compare the decision nine years earlier, United States v. Harris, 106 U.S. 629 [1883], which declared unconstitutional a provision of the 1875 Act as applied to a lynch mob killing a state prisoner.) In re Quarles, 158 U.S. 532 (1895) decided that one right of federal citizenship was the right to inform federal officials of a violation of federal law.

In more recent cases, the "right to pass freely from State to State," which appeared first in Justice Moody's list of national privileges in *Twining*, has been prominent. One aspect of the decision in United States v. Guest, 383 U.S. 745 (1966), sustained an indictment under § 241 that alleged that defendants conspired to intimidate "Negro citizens of the United States" in their right to "travel freely to and from the State of Georgia." (That case grew out of the murder of Lemuel Penn, a nationally prominent incident involving Southern violence by Whites against Blacks, in 1964. Other aspects of the *Guest* decision will be discussed in the two notes that follow this one.) The Court concluded that not only did Congress have power under the commerce clause to protect free interstate travel, but that the right was one of those privileges protected by § 241. The *Guest* holding was reaffirmed in Griffin v. Breckenridge, 403 U.S. 88 (1971), which held that a private conspiracy to prevent persons from traveling interstate was actionable under § 1985(3).

Whether § 241 is applicable to other yet undefined privileges beyond those discussed in the preceding paragraphs is doubtful. The Court's opinion in *Guest* noted that criminal prosecution under § 241 was permissible for a conspiracy to interfere with interstate travel only because the right had been specifically defined in previous cases, and a specific intent by defendants to interfere with that right must be proved. (See Screws v. United States, discussed supra, p. 1161) Justice Brennan, in his separate opinion, noted that § 241 was not "model legislation," and that relying on courts to "determine on a case-by-case basis whether the right purportedly threatened is a federal right ... brings § 241 close to the danger line of being void for vagueness." 18 U.S.C. § 245, enacted two years later as part of the 1968 Civil Rights Act, is more specific. Among the private violence and intimidation made criminal by that statute are intended interferences with participation in programs, facilities or activities provided or administered by the United States, with federal employment, with service as a federal juror, and with participation in programs receiving federal financial assistance. Section 245 also punishes private interference with voting or campaigning in *any* election. The concept of privileges of national citizenship would sustain that statute as applied to federal elections. What theory sustains its application to elections for state and local offices? (See the note on *Private Interference With Fourteenth Amendment Rights* below, p. 1173.)

DENIAL OF FOURTEENTH AMENDMENT RIGHTS UNDER COLOR OF LAW OR CUSTOM

Even under the narrowest interpretation of the Civil Rights Cases, federal legislation can reach private conduct interfering with fourteenth amendment rights when that conduct contains sufficient indicia of state action to be prohibited by section one of the fourteenth amendment. Two important fragments of Reconstruction legislation explicitly reach denial of constitutional rights under color of law or "custom." Criminal penalties are provided by 18 U.S.C. § 242, and a civil action by 42 U.S.C. § 1983.

The two leading cases construing these statutes both involved allegations of unlawful police conduct. In Screws v. United States, 325 U.S. 91 (1945), the indictment under § 242 alleged that Screws, who held a grudge against his Black victim and had threatened to "get" him, had beaten him to death after arresting him and bringing him to the courthouse square where the jail was located. Monroe v. Pape, 365 U.S. 167 (1961), was a civil action under § 1983, alleging that the defendant police illegally invaded the plaintiff's home and searched it. In both cases, the Court rejected arguments that the police did not act "under color of law" if their conduct violated state law.

United States v. Price, 383 U.S. 787 (1966), for example, grew out of the widely publicized murder of three civil rights workers, Chaney, Goodman and Schwerner, outside Philadelphia, Mississippi in 1964. The indictment alleged a conspiracy between three law enforcement officials and fifteen private individuals to deprive the victims of their fourteenth amendment rights not to be "punished" without due process of law. The lower court had dismissed the indictments against the private defendants on the ground that they had not acted under color of law. The Court reversed and reinstated the indictments, holding that private parties jointly engaged with state officials in prohibited action are acting under color of law within the meaning of § 242. More recently, in Lugar v. Edmondson Oil Co., Inc., 457 U.S. 922 (1982), the same rationale was applied to a creditor using unconstitutional judicial procedures to collect a private debt, because he "acted in joint participation with state officials in seizure of the disputed property."

In United States v. Guest, supra, the indictment charged that defendants conspired to deprive Blacks of fourteenth amendment rights by, among other things, causing their arrest by false reports that they had committed criminal acts. The indictment was held to be a sufficient allegation of state involvement which could be proved by showing active connivance of state agents in making of the false reports "or other conduct amounting to official discrimination." (The opinion, although ambiguous, can be read to conclude by implication that there would be no state action if the proof merely showed that private individuals had made the false reports, without any involvement by public officials, and public officials had acted on those reports in good faith. The Court did state, however, that the case did not require, in order to sustain the indictment, any "determination of the threshold level that state action must attain in order to create rights under the Equal Protection Clause.")

Adickes v. Kress & Co., 398 U.S. 144 (1970), was a civil action under 42 U.S.C. § 1983 by a white woman who had been refused service in a lunch counter that she entered in the company of Blacks. Plaintiff claimed that the defendant had refused her service pursuant to a "custom of the community to segregate the races in public eating places." The majority of the Court interpreted the statute as requiring a showing of "state involvement" and "not simply a practice that reflects longstanding social habits, generally observed by the people in a locality." Hence, the plaintiff was required to show that custom "have the force of law by virtue of persistent practices of state officials." Justice Douglas, dissenting, asserted that it should be sufficient for plaintiff to show a custom in the sense of "the unwritten commitment, stronger than ordinances, statutes and regulations, by which men live and arrange their lives." Justice Brennan's dissent said it "means custom of the people of a State, not custom of state officials."

PRIVATE INTERFERENCE WITH FOURTEENTH AMENDMENT RIGHTS

It is time to return, once more, to a basic conception of the Civil Rights Cases. It will be recalled that the Court reasoned that, because section one of the fourteenth amendment prohibited only discrimination by the state, Congress lacked power under section five to prohibit private discrimination in public accommodations. Would that still be true? Could Congress have passed Title II of the 1964 Act (public accommodations), Title VII of the 1964 Act (employment), and Title VIII of the 1968 Act (housing), under its power to enforce the fourteenth amendment's guarantee of equal protection of the laws? (Note that all three statutes reach beyond racial discrimination, unlike the public accommodations law invalidated in the Civil Rights Cases.) While six Justices in *United States v. Guest,* supra, agreed to an important dictum that section five of the fourteenth amendment empowers Congress to enact laws punishing private interference with fourteenth amendment rights, the answers to the questions posed are still not clear.

To understand the ambiguity, it is necessary to analyze the *Guest* decision in some detail. The indictment alleged that the defendants, all private individuals, had conspired to deny Blacks the right to "equal utilization, without discrimination upon the basis of race" of state owned facilities. The district court had dismissed the indictment on the ground that the criminal provisions of § 241, which contain no requirement that defendants act under color of law, were limited to privileges of national citizenship and did not reach fourteenth amendment rights. In the *Price* case, supra, decided the same day, the Court had held that conspiracies under color of law to deprive victims of fourteenth amendment rights were punishable under § 241. In *Guest,* a majority of the Court concluded that a conspiracy to deny victims' fourteenth amendment rights could not be prosecuted under § 241 in the absence of proof of state action. (As indicated in the previous note, dismissal of the indictment was reversed on the ground that the indictment could be read to allege state action.)

Justice Brennan, Chief Justice Warren and Justice Douglas dissented from the Court's conclusion that all conspiracies to deprive persons of fourteenth amendment rights were beyond the reach of § 241 unless state involvement in the conspiracy was proved. Justice Brennan concluded that Congress had the power to enact § 241, if it were construed to reach private conspiracies to deny fourteenth amendment rights, and criticized the Court's opinion as casting doubt on that Congressional power. That, in turn, led three members of the majority (Justices Clark, Black and Fortas) to write separately, stressing that the majority had merely construed the statute, and had decided no questions concerning the scope of Congress' power to "punish private conspiracies that interfere with fourteenth amendment rights, such as the right to utilize public facilities." They concluded summarily that there was "no doubt" that Congress had that power. Justice Brennan then responded that a majority of the Court had expressed the view that Congress could control private conduct interfering with the exercise of fourteenth amendment rights.

It should be emphasized that the portion of the indictment at issue in *Guest* alleged that the private defendants had conspired to deny their victims equal access to state facilities. The focus of the constitutional discussion in Justice Brennan's dissent and Justice Clark's separate opinion was the power to reach that conduct. Justice Brennan's rationale was that, in order to protect the constitutional right to equal utilization of state facilities, it was appropriate for Congress to punish private individuals who made it impossible for their victims to exercise those rights. (Contrast that with the position of the Civil Rights Cases that individuals who made it impossible for others to exercise their rights had not deprived them of those rights, and that Congress could not reach that individual conduct.) Would the theory also authorize Congress to control private conduct unrelated to any relationship between the victim and the state?

UNITED STATES v. MORRISON, 529 U.S. 598 (2000). The Court held that 42 U.S.C. § 13981, which provided a federal civil remedy for victims of gender–motivated violence, could not be sustained under § 5 of the fourteenth amendment. (That portion of the opinion concluding that the statute could not be sustained under the commerce clause appears supra, page 177.) Plaintiff argued that, because of pervasive bias against victims of gender–motivated violence, state justice systems failed to protect those victims. Chief Justice Rehnquist's opinion, joined by Justices O'Connor, Scalia, Kennedy and Thomas, rejected the argument that Congress acted appropriately under § 5 of the Fourteenth Amendment to remedy state bias and deter discrimination in state courts.

"[T]he language and purpose of the Fourteenth Amendment place certain limitations on the manner in which Congress may attack discriminatory conduct. These limitations are necessary to prevent the Fourteenth Amendment from obliterating the Framers' carefully crafted balance of power between the States and the National Government.... Foremost among these limitations is the time-honored principle that the Fourteenth Amendment, by its very terms, prohibits only state action....

. . .

"[I]n the Civil Rights Cases ... , we held that the public accommodation provisions of the Civil Rights Act of 1875, which applied to purely private conduct, were beyond the scope of the § 5 enforcement power....

"Petitioners ... rely on United States v. Guest ... for the proposition that the rule laid down in the Civil Rights Cases is no longer good law. In *Guest*, the Court reversed the construction of an indictment under 18 U.S.C. § 241, saying in the course of its opinion that 'we deal here with issues of statutory construction, not with issues of constitutional power.' ... Three Members of the Court, in a separate opinion by Justice Brennan, expressed the view that the Civil Rights Cases were wrongly decided, and that Congress could under § 5 prohibit actions by private individuals.... Three other Members of the Court, who joined the opinion of the Court, joined a separate opinion by Justice Clark which in two or three sentences stated the conclusion that Congress could 'punis[h] all conspiracies—with or without state action—that interfere with Fourteenth Amendment rights.'
. . .

"Though these three Justices saw fit to opine on matters not before the Court in *Guest*, the Court had no occasion to revisit the Civil Rights Cases ... , having determined 'the indictment [charging private individuals with conspiring to deprive blacks of equal access to state facilities] in fact contain[ed] an express allegation of state involvement.' ...

"To accept petitioners' argument, moreover, one must add to the three Justices joining Justice Brennan's reasoned explanation for his belief that the Civil Rights Cases were wrongly decided, the three Justices joining Justice Clark's opinion who gave no explanation whatever for their similar view. This is simply not the way that reasoned constitutional adjudication proceeds. We accordingly have no hesitation in saying that it would take more than the naked dicta contained in Justice Clark's opinion, when added to Justice Brennan's opinion, to cast any doubt upon the enduring vitality of the Civil Rights Cases ...

. . .

"Petitioners alternatively argue that, unlike the situation in the Civil Rights Cases, here there has been gender-based disparate treatment by state authorities, whereas in those cases there was no indication of such state action. There is abundant evidence, however, to show that the Congresses that enacted the Civil Rights Acts of 1871 and 1875 had a purpose similar to that of Congress in enacting § 13981 ...

"But even if that distinction were valid, we do not believe it would save § 13981's civil remedy. For the remedy is simply not 'corrective in its character, adapted to counteract and redress the operation of such prohibited [s]tate laws or proceedings of [s]tate officers.' Civil Rights Cases, 109 U.S., at 18.... Section 13981 is not aimed at proscribing discrimination by officials which the Fourteenth Amendment might not itself proscribe; it is directed not at any State or state actor, but at individuals who have committed criminal acts motivated by gender bias.

"In the present cases, for example, § 13981 visits no consequence whatever on any Virginia public official ... "

Justice Breyer's dissent was joined by Justice Stevens:

"Given my conclusion on the Commerce Clause question, I need not consider Congress' authority under § 5 of the Fourteenth Amendment. Nonetheless, I doubt the Court's reasoning rejecting that source of authority....

. . .

"[W]hy can Congress not provide a remedy against private actors? Those private actors, of course, did not themselves violate the Constitution. But this Court has held that Congress at least sometimes can enact remedial '[l]egislation ... [that] prohibits conduct which is not itself unconstitutional.' ... The statutory remedy ... intrudes little upon either States or private parties. It may lead state actors to improve their own remedial systems, primarily through example. It restricts private actors only by imposing liability for private conduct that is, in the main, already forbidden by state law. Why is the remedy 'disproportionate'? And given the relation between remedy and violation—the creation of a federal remedy to substitute for constitutionally inadequate state remedies—where is the lack of 'congruence'?"

. . .

"Despite my doubts about the majority's § 5 reasoning, I need not, and do not, answer the § 5 question, which I would leave for more thorough analysis if necessary on another occasion. Rather, in my view, the Commerce Clause provides an adequate basis for the statute before us...."

SECTION 6.   THE SCOPE OF CONGRESSIONAL POWER TO REDEFINE THE AMENDMENTS

A.   "REMEDIAL" POWER

City of Rome v. United States

446 U.S. 156, 100 S.Ct. 1548, 64 L.Ed.2d 119 (1980).

Mr. Justice Marshall delivered the opinion of the Court.

At issue in this case is the constitutionality of the Voting Rights Act of 1965 and its applicability to electoral changes and annexations made by the city of Rome, Ga.

I.

This is a declaratory judgment action brought by appellant city of Rome, a municipality in northwestern Georgia, under the Voting Rights Act of 1965, 42 U.S.C. § 1971 et seq. (1976). In 1970 the city had a population of 30,759, the racial composition of which was 76.6% white and 23.4% Negro. The voting-age population in 1970 was 79.4% white and 20.6% Negro.

The governmental structure of the city is established by a charter enacted in 1918 by the General Assembly of Georgia. Before the amendments at issue in this case, Rome's city charter provided for a nine-member city commission and a five-member board of education to be elected concurrently on an at-large basis by a plurality of the vote. The city was divided into nine wards, with one city commissioner from each ward to be chosen in the citywide election. There was no residency requirement for board of education candidates.

In 1966, the General Assembly of Georgia passed several laws of local application that extensively amended the electoral provisions of the city's charter. These enactments altered the Rome electoral scheme in the following ways:

(1) the number of wards was reduced from nine to three;

(2) each of the nine commissioners would henceforth be elected at-large to one of three numbered posts established within each ward;

(3) each commissioner would be elected by majority rather than plurality vote, and if no candidate for a particular position received a majority, a run-off election would be held between the two candidates who had received the largest number of votes;

(4) the terms of the three commissioners from each ward would be staggered;

(5) the board of education was expanded from five to six members;

(6) each board member would be elected at-large, by majority vote, for one of two numbered posts created in each of the three wards, with runoff procedures identical to those applicable to city commission elections;

(7) board members would be required to reside in the wards from which they were elected;

(8) the terms of the two members from each ward would be staggered.

Section 5 of the Voting Rights Act of 1965 requires preclearance by the Attorney General or the United States District Court for the District of Columbia of any change in a "standard, practice, or procedure with respect to voting," ... made after November 1, 1964, by jurisdictions that fall within the coverage formula set forth in § 4(b) of the Act ... In 1965, the Attorney General designated Georgia a covered jurisdiction under the Act ... and the municipalities of that State must therefore comply with the preclearance procedure ...

. . . .

... The Attorney General declined to preclear the provisions for majority vote, numbered posts, and staggered terms for city commission and board of education elections, as well as the residency requirement for board elections.

He concluded that in a city such as Rome, in which the population is predominately white and racial bloc voting has been common, these electoral changes would deprive Negro voters of the opportunity to elect a candidate of their choice....

. . .

The city and two of its officials then filed this action, seeking relief from the Act based on a variety of claims. A three-judge court ... rejected the city's arguments and granted summary judgment for the defendants. We ... affirm.

A.

The appellants contend that the city may exempt itself from the coverage of the Act. To evaluate this argument, we must examine the provisions of the Act in some detail.

... As we have noted, the city of Rome comes within the preclearance requirement because it is a political unit in a covered jurisdiction, the State of Georgia. ...

Section 4(a) also provides, however, a procedure for exemption from the Act. This so-called "bail out" provision allows a covered jurisdiction to escape the preclearance requirement of § 5 by bringing a declaratory judgment action before a three-judge panel of the United States District Court for the District of Columbia and proving that no "test or device" has been used in the jurisdiction "during the seventeen years preceding the filing of the action for the purpose or with the effect of denying or abridging the right to vote on account of race or color." The District Court refused to allow the city to "bail out" of the Act's coverage, holding that the political units of a covered jurisdiction cannot independently bring a § 4(a) bailout action. We agree.

... Under the plain language of the statute, it appears that any bailout action to exempt the city must be filed by, and seek to exempt all of, the State of Georgia.

III.

The appellants raise five issues of law in support of their contention that the Act may not properly be applied to the electoral changes and annexations disapproved by the Attorney General.

A.

The District Court found that the disapproved electoral changes and annexations had not been made for any discriminatory purpose, but did have a discriminatory effect. The appellants argue that § 5 of the Act may not be read as prohibiting voting practices that have only a discriminatory effect. The appellants do not dispute that the plain language of § 5 commands that the Attorney General may clear a practice only if it "does not have the purpose *and* will not have the effect of denying or abridging the right to vote on account of race or color." ... By describing the elements of discriminatory purpose and effect in the conjunctive, Congress plainly intended that a voting practice not be precleared unless *both* discriminatory purpose and effect are absent....

The appellants urge that we abandon this settled interpretation because in their view § 5, to the extent that it prohibits voting changes that have only a discriminatory effect, is unconstitutional. Because the statutory meaning and congressional intent are plain, however, we are required to reject the appellants' suggestion that we engage in a saving construction and avoid the constitutional issues they raise.... Instead we now turn to their constitutional contentions.

B.

Congress passed the Act under the authority accorded it by the Fifteenth Amendment. The appellants contend that the Act is unconstitutional because it exceeds Congress' power to enforce that Amendment. They claim that § 1 of the Amendment prohibits only purposeful racial discrimination in voting, and that in enforcing that provision pursuant to § 2, Congress may not prohibit voting practices lacking discriminatory intent even if they are discriminatory in effect. We hold that, even if § 1 of the Amendment prohibits only purposeful discrimination, the prior decisions of this Court foreclose any argument that Congress may not, pursuant to § 2, outlaw voting practices that are discriminatory in effect.

The appellants are asking us to do nothing less than overrule our decision in South Carolina v. Katzenbach, 383 U.S. 301 (1966), in which we upheld the constitutionality of the Act. The Court in that case observed that, after making an extensive investigation, Congress had determined that its earlier attempts to remedy the "insidious and pervasive evil" of racial discrimination in voting had failed because of "unremitting and ingenious defiance of the Constitution" in some parts of this country. ... Case-by-case adjudication had proved too ponderous a method to remedy voting discrimination, and, when it had produced favorable results, affected jurisdictions often "merely switched to discriminatory devices not covered by the federal decrees." ... In response to its determination that "sterner and more elaborate measures" were necessary, ... Congress adopted the Act, a "complex scheme of stringent remedies aimed at areas where voting discrimination has been most flagrant," ...

The Court then turned to the question whether the Fifteenth Amendment empowered Congress to impose the rigors of the Act upon the covered jurisdictions. The Court examined the interplay between the judicial remedy created by § 1 of the Amendment and the legislative authority conferred by § 2:

> "By adding this authorization [in § 2], the Framers indicated that Congress was to be chiefly responsible for implementing the rights created by § 1. 'It is the power of Congress which has been enlarged. Congress is authorized to *enforce* the prohibitions by appropriate legislation. Some legislation is contemplated to make the [civil war] amendments fully effective.' Ex parte Virginia, 100 U.S. 339, 345. Accordingly, in addition to the courts, Congress has full remedial powers to effectuate the constitutional prohibition against racial discrimination in voting." ...

Congress' authority under § 2 of the Fifteenth Amendment, we held, was no less broad than its authority under the Necessary and Proper Clause, see McCulloch v. Maryland,.... This authority, as applied by longstanding precedent to congressional enforcement of the Civil War Amendments, is defined in these terms:

> " 'Whatever legislation is appropriate, that is, adapted to carry out the objects the [civil war] amendments have in view, whatever tends to enforce submission to the prohibitions they contain, and to secure to all persons the enjoyment of perfect equality of civil rights and the equal protection of the laws against State denial or invasion, if not prohibited, is brought within the domain of congressional power.' Ex parte Virginia, 100 U.S. [339,] 345–346." South Carolina v. Katzenbach, supra, at 327.

Applying this standard, the Court held that the coverage formula of § 4(b), the ban on the use of literacy tests and related devices, the requirement that new voting rules must be precleared and must lack both discriminatory purpose and effect, and the use of federal examiners were all appropriate methods for Congress to use to enforce the Fifteenth Amendment. . . .

The Court's treatment in South Carolina v. Katzenbach of the Act's ban on literacy tests demonstrates that, under the Fifteenth Amendment, Congress may prohibit voting practices that have only a discriminatory effect. The Court had earlier held in Lassiter v. Northampton County Board of Elections, 360 U.S. 45 (1959), that the use of a literacy test that was fair on its face and was not employed in a discriminatory fashion did not violate § 1 of the Fifteenth Amendment. In upholding the Act's *per se* ban on such tests in *South Carolina v. Katzenbach,* the Court found no reason to overrule *Lassiter.* Instead, the Court recognized that the prohibition was an appropriate method of enforcing the Fifteenth Amendment because for many years most of the covered jurisdictions had imposed such tests to effect voting discrimination and the continued use of even nondiscriminatory, fairly administered literacy tests would "freeze the effect" of past discrimination by allowing white illiterates to remain on the voting rolls while excluding illiterate Negroes. South Carolina v. Katzenbach, supra, 383 U.S., at 334. This holding makes clear that Congress may, under the authority of § 2 of the Fifteenth Amendment, prohibit state action that, though in itself not violative of § 1, perpetuates the effects of past discrimination.

Other decisions of this Court also recognize Congress' broad power to enforce the Civil War Amendments. In Katzenbach v. Morgan, 384 U.S. 641 (1966), the Court held that legislation enacted under authority of § 5 of the Fourteenth Amendment would be upheld so long as the Court could find that the enactment " 'is plainly adapted to [the] end' " of enforcing the Equal Protection Clause and "is not prohibited by but is consistent with 'the letter and spirit of the constitution,' " regardless of whether the practices outlawed by Congress in themselves violated the Equal Protection Clause. . . . The Court stated that, "[c]orrectly viewed, § 5 is a positive grant of legislative power authorizing Congress to exercise its discretion in determining whether and what legislation is needed to secure the guarantees of the Fourteenth Amendment." . . . Four years later, in Oregon v. Mitchell, 400 U.S. 112 (1970), the Court unanimously upheld a provision of the Voting Rights Act Amendments of 1970 . . . imposing a five-year nationwide ban on literacy tests and similar requirements for registering to vote in state and federal elections. The Court concluded that Congress could rationally have determined that these provisions were appropriate methods of attacking the perpetuation of earlier, purposeful racial discrimination, regardless of whether the practices they prohibited were discriminatory only in effect. . . .

It is clear, then, that under § 2 of the Fifteenth Amendment Congress may prohibit practices that in and of themselves do not violate § 1 of the Amendment, so long as the prohibitions attacking racial discrimination in voting are "appropriate," as that term is defined in McCulloch v. Maryland and Ex parte Virginia. In the present case, we hold that the Act's ban on electoral changes that are discriminatory in effect is an appropriate method of promoting the purposes of the Fifteenth Amendment, even if it is assumed that § 1 of the Amendment prohibits only intentional discrimination in voting. Congress could rationally have concluded that, because electoral changes by jurisdictions with a demonstrable history of intentional racial discrimination in voting create the risk of purposeful discrimination, it was proper to prohibit changes that have a discriminatory impact. . . . We find no reason, then, to disturb Congress' considered judgment that banning electoral changes that have a discriminatory impact is an effective method of preventing States from " 'undo[ing] or defeat[ing] the rights recently won' by Negroes." . . . .

C.

The appellants next assert that, even if the Fifteenth Amendment authorized Congress to enact the Voting Rights Act, that legislation violates principles of federalism articulated in National League of Cities v. Usery, 426 U.S. 833 (1976). . . .

. . .

We agree with the court below that [Fitzpatrick v. Bitzer, 427 U.S. 445 (1976)] stands for the proposition that principles of federalism that might otherwise be an obstacle to congressional authority are necessarily overridden by the power to enforce the Civil War Amendments "by appropriate legislation." Those Amendments were specifically designed as an expansion of federal power and an intrusion on state sovereignty. . . .

. . .

Mr. Justice Stevens, concurring.

Although I join the Court's opinion, the dissenting opinions prompt me to emphasize two points . . . (1) whether, as a statutory matter, Congress has prescribed a statewide remedy that denies local political units within a covered State the right to "bail out" separately; and (2) if so, whether, as a constitutional matter, such statewide relief exceeds the enforcement powers of Congress. If, as I believe, Congress could properly impose a statewide remedy and in fact did so in the Voting Rights Act, then the fact that the city of Rome has been innocent of any wrongdoing for the last 17 years is irrelevant; indeed, we may assume that there has never been any racial discrimination practiced in the city of Rome. If racially discriminatory voting practices elsewhere in the State of Georgia were sufficiently pervasive to justify the statewide remedy Congress prescribed, that remedy may be applied to each and every political unit within the State, including the city of Rome.

. . .

. . . [R]emedies for discriminatory practices that were widespread within a State may be applied to every governmental unit within the State even though some of those local units may have never engaged in purposeful discrimination themselves. In short, Congress has the constitutional power to regulate voting practices in Rome, so long as it has the power to regulate such practices in the entire State of Georgia. Since there is no claim that the entire State is entitled to relief from the federal restrictions, Rome's separate claim must fail.

I therefore join the Court's opinion.

Mr. Justice Powell dissenting.

Two years ago this Court held that the term "State" in § 4(a) of the Voting Rights Act includes all political subdivisions that control election processes, and that those subdivisions are subject to the requirement in § 5 of the Act that federal authorities preclear changes in voting procedures. United States v. Board of Commissioners of Sheffield, Alabama, 435 U.S. 110 (1978) (*Sheffield*). Today the Court concludes that those subdivisions are within the term "State" when it comes to an action to "bail out" from the preclearance requirement. Because this decision not only conflicts with *Sheffield* but also raises grave questions as to the constitutionality of the Act, I dissent.

. . .

III.

There is . . . more involved here than incorrect construction of the statute. The Court's interpretation of § 4(a) renders the Voting Rights Act unconstitutional as applied to the city of Rome. The preclearance requirement both intrudes on the prerogatives of state and local governments and abridges the voting rights of all citizens in States covered under the Act. Under § 2 of the Fifteenth Amendment, Congress may impose such constitutional deprivations only if it is acting to remedy violations of voting rights. . . . In view of the District Court finding that Rome has not denied or abridged the voting rights of blacks, the Fifteenth Amendment provides no authority for continuing those deprivations until the entire State of Georgia satisfies the bailout standards of § 4(a).

When this Court first sustained the Voting Rights Act of 1965, it conceded that the legislation was "an uncommon exercise of congressional power." South Carolina v. Katzenbach, supra, 383 U.S., at 334. The Court recognized that preclearance under the Act implicates serious federalism concerns. . . . As Mr. Justice Stevens noted in *Sheffield,* the statute's "encroachment on state sovereignty is significant and undeniable." . . . (dissenting opinion). That encroachment is especially troubling because it destroys local control of the means of self-government, one of the central values of our policy. Unless the federal structure provides some protection for a community's ordering of its own democratic procedures, the right of each community to determine its own course within the boundaries marked by the Constitution is at risk. Preclearance also operates at an individual level to diminish the voting rights of residents of covered areas. Federal review of local voting practices reduces the influence that citizens have over policies directly affecting them, and strips locally elected officials of their autonomy to chart policy.

The Court in South Carolina v. Katzenbach . . . upheld the imposition of preclearance as a prophylactic measure based on the remedial power of Congress to enforce the Fifteenth Amendment. . . .

The Court in South Carolina v. Katzenbach emphasized, however, that a government subjected to preclearance could be relieved of federal oversight if voting discrimination in fact did not continue or materialize during the prescribed period. . . . As long as the bailout option is available, there is less cause for concern that the Voting Rights Act may overreach congressional powers by imposing preclearance on a nondiscriminating government. Without bailout, the problem of constitutional authority for preclearance becomes acute.

IV.

If there were reason to believe that today's decision would protect the voting rights of minorities in any way, perhaps this case could be viewed as one where the Court's ends justify dubious analytical means. But the District Court found, and no one denies, that for at least 17 years there has been no voting discrimination by the city of Rome. Despite this record, the Court today continues federal rule over the most local decisions made by this small city in Georgia. Such an outcome must vitiate the incentive for any local government in a State covered by the Act to meet diligently the Act's requirements. Neither the Framers of the Fifteenth Amendment nor the Congress that enacted the Voting Rights Act could have intended that result.

Mr. Justice Rehnquist, with whom Mr. Justice Stewart joins, dissenting.

We have only today held that the city of Mobile does not violate the Constitution by maintaining an at-large system of electing city officials unless voters can prove that system is a product of purposeful discrimination. City of Mobile v. Bolden, 446 U.S. 55 (1980). This result is reached even though the black residents of Mobile have demonstrated that racial "bloc" voting has prevented them from electing a black representative to the city government. The Court correctly concluded that a city has no obligation under the Constitution to structure its representative system in a manner that maximizes the black community's ability to elect a black representative. Yet in the instant case, the city of Rome is prevented from instituting precisely the type of structural changes which the Court says Mobile may maintain consistently with the Civil War Amendments, so long as their purpose be legitimate, because Congress has prohibited these changes under the Voting Rights Act as an exercise of its "enforcement" power conferred by those Amendments.

It is not necessary to hold that Congress is limited to merely providing a forum in which aggrieved plaintiffs may assert rights under the Civil War Amendments in order to disagree with the Court's decision permitting Congress to strait-jacket the city of Rome in this manner. Under § 5 of the Fourteenth Amendment and § 2 of the Fifteenth Amendment, Congress is granted only the power to "enforce" by "appropriate" legislation the limitations on state action embodied in those Amendments. While the presumption of constitutionality is due to any act of a coordinate branch of the Federal Government or of one of the States, it is this Court which is ultimately responsible for deciding challenges to the exercise of power by those entities. Marbury v. Madison ... Today's decision is nothing less than a total abdication of that authority, rather than an exercise of the deference due to a coordinate branch of the government.

. . .

II.

... While I agree with Mr. Justice Powell's conclusion that requiring localities to *submit* to preclearance is a significant intrusion on local autonomy, it is an even greater intrusion on that autonomy to *deny* preclearance sought.

... There are three theories of congressional enforcement power relevant to this case. First, it is clear that if the proposed changes would violate the Constitution, Congress could certainly prohibit their implementation. It has never been seriously maintained, however, that Congress can do no more than the judiciary to enforce the Amendments' commands. Thus, if the electoral changes in issue do not violate the Constitution, as judicially interpreted, it must be determined whether Congress could nevertheless appropriately prohibit these changes under the other two theories of congressional power. Under the second theory, Congress can act remedially to enforce the judicially established substantive prohibitions of the Amendments. If not properly remedial, the exercise of this power could be sustained only if this Court accepts the premise of the third theory that Congress has the authority under its enforcement powers to determine, without more, that electoral changes with a disparate impact on race violate the Constitution, in which case Congress by a legislative Act could effectively amend the Constitution.

I think it is apparent that neither of the first two theories for sustaining the exercise of congressional power support this application of the Voting Rights Act. After our decision in *City of Mobile* there is little doubt that Rome has not engaged in *constitutionally* prohibited conduct. I also do not believe that prohibition of these changes can genuinely be characterized as a remedial exercise of congressional enforcement powers. Thus, the result of the Court's holding is that Congress effectively has the power to determine for itself that this conduct violates the Constitution. This result violates previously well-established distinctions between the Judicial Branch and the Legislative or Executive Branches of the Federal Government. See ... Marbury v. Madison ...

A.

If the enforcement power is construed as a "remedial" grant of authority, it is this Court's duty to ensure that a challenged congressional act does no more than "enforce" the limitations on state power established in the Fourteenth and Fifteenth Amendments. Marbury v. Madison. The Court has not resolved the question of whether it is an appropriate exercise of remedial power for Congress to prohibit local governments from instituting structural changes in their government, which although not racially motivated, will have the effect of decreasing the ability of a black voting bloc to elect a black candidate.

. . .

The precedent on which the Court relies simply does not support its remedial characterization. Neither Oregon v. Mitchell, 400 U.S. 112 (1970), nor South Carolina v. Katzenbach, supra, legitimize the use of an irrebuttable presumption that "vote diluting" changes are motivated by a discriminatory animus. The principal electoral practice in issue in those cases was the use of literacy tests. . . .

The presumption that the literacy tests were either being used to purposefully discriminate, or that the disparate effects of those tests were attributable to discrimination in state-administered education was not very wide of the mark. . . .

The nationwide ban was also found necessary to effectively remedy past constitutional violations. . . .

Presumptive prohibition of vote diluting procedures is not similarly an "appropriate" means of exacting state compliance with the Civil War Amendments. First, these prohibitions are quite unlike the literacy ban, where the disparate effects were traceable to the discrimination of governmental bodies in education even if their present desire to use the tests was legitimate. Any disparate impact associated with the nondiscriminatory electoral changes in issue here results from bloc voting—private rather than governmental discrimination. . . .

It is also clear that while most States still utilizing literacy tests may have been doing so to discriminate, a similar generalization could not be made about all government structures which have some disparate impact on black voting strength. . . .

Nor does the prohibition of all practices with a disparate impact enhance congressional prevention of purposeful discrimination. The changes in issues are not, like literacy tests, though fair on their face, subject to discriminatory application by local authorities. See Yick Wo v. Hopkins, 118 U.S. 356 (1886). They are either discriminatory from the outset or not.

Finally, the advantages supporting the imposition of a nationwide ban are simply not implicated in this case. No added administrative burdens are in issue since Congress has provided the mechanism for preclearance suits in any event, and the burden of proof for this issue is on the locality. And it is certain that the only constitutional wrong implicated—purposeful dilution—can be effectively remedied by prohibiting it where it occurs. For all these reasons, I do not think that the present case is controlled by the result in *Oregon*. By prohibiting all electoral changes with a disparate impact, Congress has attempted to prevent disparate impacts—not purposeful discrimination.

Congress unquestionably has the power to prohibit and remedy state action which intentionally deprives citizens of Fourteenth and Fifteenth Amendment rights. But unless these powers are to be wholly uncanalized, it cannot be appropriate remedial legislation for Congress to prohibit Rome from structuring its government in the manner as its population sees fit absent a finding or unrebutted presumption that Rome has been, or is, intentionally discriminating against its black citizens. Rome has simply committed no constitutional violations, as this Court has defined them.

B.   "INTERPRETIVE" POWER

Through 2004, the Court decided a number of important cases addressing what role, if any, Congress has in interpreting and defining the specific content of constitutional provisions. Many of them construed Congress' power under Section 5 of the Fourteenth Amendment. In reading them, consider how much of the Court's reasoning is grounded in separation of powers concerns, and how much is grounded in federalism considerations.

City of Boerne v. Flores

521 U.S. 507, 117 S.Ct. 2157, 138 L.Ed.2d 624 (1997).

Justice Kennedy delivered the opinion of the Court.*

A decision by local zoning authorities to deny a church a building permit was challenged under the Religious Freedom Restoration Act of 1993 (RFRA) ... The case calls into question the authority of Congress to enact RFRA. We conclude the statute exceeds Congress' power.

I

[A church in Texas was denied permission to alter and enlarge its building to accommodate more worshippers under a Boerne City Council ordinance designed to protect historic landmarks or buildings in a historic district. The church's Archbishop sued in federal court, invoking its rights under the RFRA. The district court found that RFRA was unconstitutional because Congress lacked power under Section 5 of the Fourteenth Amendment to enact it. The Fifth Circuit reversed, and the Supreme Court reversed the Court of Appeals.]

II

Congress enacted RFRA in direct response to the Court's decision in Employment Div., Dept. of Human Resources of Ore. v. Smith, 494 U.S. 872 (1990). There we considered a Free Exercise Clause claim brought by members of the Native American Church who were denied unemployment benefits when they lost their jobs because they had used peyote. Their practice was to ingest peyote for sacramental purposes, and they challenged an Oregon statute of general applicability which made use of the drug criminal. In evaluating the claim, we declined to apply the balancing test set forth in Sherbert v. Verner,

* Justice Scalia joins all but Part III–A–1 of this opinion.

374 U.S. 398 (1963), under which we would have asked whether Oregon's prohibition substantially burdened a religious practice and, if it did, whether the burden was justified by a compelling government interest. We stated: "[G]overnment's ability to enforce generally applicable prohibitions of socially harmful conduct . . . cannot depend on measuring the effects of a governmental action on a religious objector's spiritual development. . . ." . . .

. . .

. . . *Smith* held that neutral, generally applicable laws may be applied to religious practices even when not supported by a compelling governmental interest.

Four Members of the Court disagreed. They argued the law placed a substantial burden on the Native American Church members so that it could be upheld only if the law served a compelling state interest and was narrowly tailored to achieve that end. . . .

These points of constitutional interpretation were debated by Members of Congress in hearings and floor debates. Many criticized the Court's reasoning, and this disagreement resulted in the passage of RFRA. Congress announced:

"(1) [T]he framers of the Constitution, recognizing free exercise of religion as an unalienable right, secured its protection in the First Amendment to the Constitution;

"(2) laws 'neutral' toward religion may burden religious exercise as surely as laws intended to interfere with religious exercise;

"(3) governments should not substantially burden religious exercise without compelling justification;

"(4) in Employment Division v. Smith, 494 U.S. 872 (1990), the Supreme Court virtually eliminated the requirement that the government justify burdens on religious exercise imposed by laws neutral toward religion; and

"(5) the compelling interest test as set forth in prior Federal court rulings is a workable test for striking sensible balances between religious liberty and competing prior governmental interests." 42 U.S.C. § 2000bb(a).

The Act's stated purposes are:

"(1) to restore the compelling interest test as set forth in Sherbert v. Verner, 374 U.S. 398 (1963) and Wisconsin v. Yoder, 406 U.S. 205 (1972) and to guarantee its application in all cases where free exercise of religion is substantially burdened; and

"(2) to provide a claim or defense to persons whose religious exercise is substantially burdened by government." § 2000bb(b).

RFRA prohibits "[g]overnment" from "substantially burden[ing]" a person's exercise of religion even if the burden results from a rule of general applicability unless the government can demonstrate the burden "(1) is in furtherance of a compelling governmental interest; and (2) is the least restrictive means of furthering that compelling governmental interest." . . . The Act's mandate applies to any "branch, department, agency, instrumentality, and official (or other person acting under color of law) of the United States," as well as to any "State, or . . . subdivision of a State." . . . The Act's universal coverage is confirmed in § 2000bb–3(a), under which RFRA "applies to all Federal and State law, and the implementation of that law, whether statutory or otherwise, and whether adopted before or after [RFRA's enactment]." In accordance with RFRA's usage of the term, we shall use "state law" to include local and municipal ordinances.

III

A

Under our Constitution, the Federal Government is one of enumerated powers. McCulloch v. Maryland ... The judicial authority to determine the constitutionality of laws, in cases and controversies, is based on the premise that the "powers of the legislature are defined and limited; and that those limits may not be mistaken, or forgotten, the constitution is written." Marbury v. Madison ...

Congress relied on its Fourteenth Amendment enforcement power in enacting the most far reaching and substantial of RFRA's provisions, those which impose its requirements on the States....

In defense of the Act respondent contends, with support from the United States as *amicus*, that RFRA is permissible enforcement legislation. Congress, it is said, is only protecting by legislation one of the liberties guaranteed by the Fourteenth Amendment's Due Process Clause, the free exercise of religion, beyond what is necessary under *Smith*. It is said the congressional decision to dispense with proof of deliberate or overt discrimination and instead concentrate on a law's effects accords with the settled understanding that § 5 includes the power to enact legislation designed to prevent as well as remedy constitutional violations. It is further contended that Congress' § 5 power is not limited to remedial or preventive legislation.

... Legislation which deters or remedies constitutional violations can fall within the sweep of Congress' enforcement power even if in the process it prohibits conduct which is not itself unconstitutional and intrudes into "legislative spheres of autonomy previously reserved to the States." ... For example, the Court upheld a suspension of literacy tests and similar voting requirements under Congress' parallel power to enforce the provisions of the Fifteenth Amendment ... as a measure to combat racial discrimination in voting, South Carolina v. Katzenbach, 383 U.S. 301, 308 (1966), despite the facial constitutionality of the tests under Lassiter v. Northampton County Bd. of Elections, 360 U.S. 45 (1959). We have also concluded that other measures protecting voting rights are within Congress' power to enforce the Fourteenth and Fifteenth Amendments, despite the burdens those measures placed on the States. ...

It is also true, however, that "[a]s broad as the congressional enforcement power is, it is not unlimited." ... In assessing the breadth of § 5's enforcement power, we begin with its text. Congress has been given the power "to enforce" the "provisions of this article." We agree with respondent, of course, that Congress can enact legislation under § 5 enforcing the constitutional right to the free exercise of religion. ...

Congress' power under § 5, however, extends only to "enforc[ing]" the provisions of the Fourteenth Amendment. The Court has described this power as "remedial," ... The design of the Amendment and the text of § 5 are inconsistent with the suggestion that Congress has the power to decree the substance of the Fourteenth Amendment's restrictions on the States. Legislation which alters the meaning of the Free Exercise Clause cannot be said to be enforcing the Clause. Congress does not enforce a constitutional right by changing what the right is. It has been given the power "to enforce," not the power to determine what constitutes a constitutional violation. Were it not so, what Congress would be enforcing would no longer be, in any meaningful sense, the "provisions of [the Fourteenth Amendment]."

While the line between measures that remedy or prevent unconstitutional actions and measures that make a substantive change in the governing law is not easy to discern, and Congress must have wide latitude in determining where it lies, the distinction exists and must be observed. There must be a congruence and proportionality between the injury to be prevented or remedied and the means adopted to that end. Lacking such a connection, legislation may become substantive in operation and effect. History and our case law support drawing the distinction, one apparent from the text of the Amendment.

1

. . .

The design of the Fourteenth Amendment has proved significant . . . in maintaining the traditional separation of powers between Congress and the Judiciary. . . . As enacted, the Fourteenth Amendment confers substantive rights against the States which, like the provisions of the Bill of Rights, are self-executing. . . . The power to interpret the Constitution in a case or controversy remains in the Judiciary.

2

The remedial and preventive nature of Congress' enforcement power, and the limitation inherent in the power, were confirmed in our earliest cases on the Fourteenth Amendment. In the Civil Rights Cases, 109 U.S. 3 (1883), the Court invalidated sections of the Civil Rights Act of 1875 which prescribed criminal penalties for denying to any person "the full enjoyment of" public accommodations and conveyances, on the grounds that it exceeded Congress' power by seeking to regulate private conduct. The Enforcement Clause, the Court said, did not authorize Congress to pass "general legislation upon the rights of the citizen, but corrective legislation; that is, such as may be necessary and proper for counteracting such laws as the States may adopt or enforce, and which, by the amendment, they are prohibited from making or enforcing. . . ." . . . Although the specific holdings of these early cases might have been superseded or modified, see, e.g., Heart of Atlanta Motel, Inc. v. United States, 379 U.S. 241 (1964); United States v. Guest, 383 U.S. 745 (1966), their treatment of Congress' § 5 power as corrective or preventive, not definitional, has not been questioned.

Recent cases have continued to revolve around the question of whether § 5 legislation can be considered remedial. In South Carolina v. Katzenbach . . . we upheld various provisions of the Voting Rights Act of 1965, finding them to be "remedies aimed at areas where voting discrimination has been most flagrant," . . . and necessary to "banish the blight of racial discrimination in voting, which has infected the electoral process in parts of our country for nearly a century," . . . . We noted evidence in the record reflecting the subsisting and pervasive discriminatory—and therefore unconstitutional—use of literacy tests. . . . The Act's new remedies, which used the administrative resources of the Federal Government, included the suspension of both literacy tests and, pending federal review, all new voting regulations in covered jurisdictions, as well as the assignment of federal examiners to list qualified applicants enabling those listed to vote. The new, unprecedented remedies were deemed necessary given the ineffectiveness of the existing voting rights laws, . . . and the slow costly character of case-by-case litigation. . . .

After South Carolina v. Katzenbach, the Court continued to acknowledge the necessity of using strong remedial and preventive measures to respond to the widespread and persisting deprivation of constitutional rights resulting from this country's history of racial discrimination....

3

Any suggestion that Congress has a substantive, non-remedial power under the Fourteenth Amendment is not supported by our case law. In Oregon v. Mitchell, ... a majority of the Court concluded Congress had exceeded its enforcement powers by enacting legislation lowering the minimum age of voters from 21 to 18 in state and local elections. The five Members of the Court who reached this conclusion explained that the legislation intruded into an area reserved by the Constitution to the States....

There is language in our opinion in Katzenbach v. Morgan, 384 U.S. 641 (1966), which could be interpreted as acknowledging a power in Congress to enact legislation that expands the rights contained in § 1 of the Fourteenth Amendment. This is not a necessary interpretation, however, or even the best one. In *Morgan*, the Court considered the constitutionality of § 4(e) of the Voting Rights Act of 1965, which provided that no person who had successfully completed the sixth primary grade in a public school in, or a private school accredited by, the Commonwealth of Puerto Rico in which the language of instruction was other than English could be denied the right to vote because of an inability to read or write English. New York's Constitution, on the other hand, required voters to be able to read and write English. The Court provided two related rationales for its conclusion that § 4(e) could "be viewed as a measure to secure for the Puerto Rican community residing in New York nondiscriminatory treatment by government." ... Under the first rationale, Congress could prohibit New York from denying the right to vote to large segments of its Puerto Rican community, in order to give Puerto Ricans "enhanced political power" that would be "helpful in gaining nondiscriminatory treatment in public services for the entire Puerto Rican community." ... Section 4(e) thus could be justified as a remedial measure to deal with "discrimination in governmental services." ... The second rationale, an alternative holding, did not address discrimination in the provision of public services but "discrimination in establishing voter qualifications." ... The Court perceived a factual basis on which Congress could have concluded that New York's literacy requirement "constituted an invidious discrimination in violation of the Equal Protection Clause." ... Both rationales for upholding § 4(e) rested on unconstitutional discrimination by New York and Congress' reasonable attempt to combat it. As Justice Stewart explained in Oregon v. Mitchell, ... interpreting *Morgan* to give Congress the power to interpret the Constitution "would require an enormous extension of that decision's rationale."

If Congress could define its own powers by altering the Fourteenth Amendment's meaning, no longer would the Constitution be "superior paramount law, unchangeable by ordinary means." It would be "on a level with ordinary legislative acts, and, like other acts, ... alterable when the legislature shall please to alter it." Marbury v. Madison ... Under this approach, it is difficult to conceive of a principle that would limit congressional power.... Shifting legislative majorities could change the Constitution and effectively circumvent the difficult and detailed amendment process contained in Article V.

We now turn to consider whether RFRA can be considered enforcement legislation under § 5 of the Fourteenth Amendment.

B

Respondent contends that RFRA is a proper exercise of Congress' remedial or preventive power. The Act, it is said, is a reasonable means of protecting the free exercise of religion as defined by *Smith*. It prevents and remedies laws which are enacted with the unconstitutional object of targeting religious beliefs and practices.... If Congress can prohibit laws with discriminatory effects in order to prevent racial discrimination in violation of the Equal Protection Clause, ... then it can do the same, respondent argues, to promote religious liberty.

While preventive rules are sometimes appropriate remedial measures, there must be a congruence between the means used and the ends to be achieved. The appropriateness of remedial measures must be considered in light of the evil presented.... Strong measures appropriate to address one harm may be an unwarranted response to another, lesser one....

A comparison between RFRA and the Voting Rights Act is instructive. In contrast to the record which confronted Congress and the judiciary in the voting rights cases, RFRA's legislative record lacks examples of modern instances of generally applicable laws passed because of religious bigotry. The history of persecution in this country detailed in the hearings mentions no episodes occurring in the past 40 years. ... Rather, the emphasis of the hearings was on laws of general applicability which place incidental burdens on religion.... It is difficult to maintain that they are examples of legislation enacted or enforced due to animus or hostility to the burdened religious practices or that they indicate some widespread pattern of religious discrimination in this country. Congress' concern was with the incidental burdens imposed, not the object or purpose of the legislation.... This lack of support in the legislative record, however, is not RFRA's most serious shortcoming. Judicial deference, in most cases, is based not on the state of the legislative record Congress compiles but "on due regard for the decision of the body constitutionally appointed to decide." ... As a general matter, it is for Congress to determine the method by which it will reach a decision.

Regardless of the state of the legislative record, RFRA cannot be considered remedial, preventive legislation, if those terms are to have any meaning. RFRA is so out of proportion to a supposed remedial or preventive object that it cannot be understood as responsive to, or designed to prevent, unconstitutional behavior. It appears, instead, to attempt a substantive change in constitutional protections. Preventive measures prohibiting certain types of laws may be appropriate when there is reason to believe that many of the laws affected by the congressional enactment have a significant likelihood of being unconstitutional. ...

RFRA is not so confined. Sweeping coverage ensures its intrusion at every level of government, displacing laws and prohibiting official actions of almost every description and regardless of subject matter. RFRA's restrictions apply to every agency and official of the Federal, State, and local Governments.... RFRA applies to all federal and state law, statutory or otherwise, whether adopted before or after its enactment ... RFRA has no termination date or termination mechanism. Any law is subject to challenge at any time by any individual who alleges a substantial burden on his or her free exercise of religion.

The reach and scope of RFRA distinguish it from other measures passed under Congress' enforcement power, even in the area of voting rights. In South Carolina v. Katzenbach, the challenged provisions were confined to those regions of the country where voting discrimination had been most flagrant, ...

and affected a discrete class of state laws, i.e., state voting laws. Furthermore, to ensure that the reach of the Voting Rights Act was limited to those cases in which constitutional violations were most likely (in order to reduce the possibility of overbreadth), the coverage under the Act would terminate "at the behest of States and political subdivisions in which the danger of substantial voting discrimination has not materialized during the preceding five years." ... The provisions restricting and banning literacy tests, upheld in Katzenbach v. Morgan, ... and Oregon v. Mitchell, ... attacked a particular type of voting qualification, one with a long history as a "notorious means to deny and abridge voting rights on racial grounds." ... In *City of Rome*, ... the Court rejected a challenge to the constitutionality of a Voting Rights Act provision which required certain jurisdictions to submit changes in electoral practices to the Department of Justice for preimplementation review. The requirement was placed only on jurisdictions with a history of intentional racial discrimination in voting.... Like the provisions at issue in South Carolina v. Katzenbach, this provision permitted a covered jurisdiction to avoid preclearance requirements under certain conditions and, moreover, lapsed in seven years. This is not to say, of course, that § 5 legislation requires termination dates, geographic restrictions or egregious predicates. Where, however, a congressional enactment pervasively prohibits constitutional state action in an effort to remedy or to prevent unconstitutional state action, limitations of this kind tend to ensure Congress' means are proportionate to ends legitimate under § 5.

The stringent test RFRA demands of state laws reflects a lack of proportionality or congruence between the means adopted and the legitimate end to be achieved. If an objector can show a substantial burden on his free exercise, the State must demonstrate a compelling governmental interest and show that the law is the least restrictive means of furthering its interest. Claims that a law substantially burdens someone's exercise of religion will often be difficult to contest.... Requiring a State to demonstrate a compelling interest and show that it has adopted the least restrictive means of achieving that interest is the most demanding test known to constitutional law.... Laws valid under *Smith* would fall under RFRA without regard to whether they had the object of stifling or punishing free exercise. We make these observations not to reargue the position of the majority in *Smith* but to illustrate the substantive alteration of its holding attempted by RFRA. Even assuming RFRA would be interpreted in effect to mandate some lesser test, say one equivalent to intermediate scrutiny, the statute nevertheless would require searching judicial scrutiny of state law with the attendant likelihood of invalidation. This is a considerable congressional intrusion into the States' traditional prerogatives and general authority to regulate for the health and welfare of their citizens.

The substantial costs RFRA exacts, both in practical terms of imposing a heavy litigation burden on the States and in terms of curtailing their traditional general regulatory power, far exceed any pattern or practice of unconstitutional conduct under the Free Exercise Clause as interpreted in *Smith*. Simply put, RFRA is not designed to identify and counteract state laws likely to be unconstitutional because of their treatment of religion. In most cases, the state laws to which RFRA applies are not ones which will have been motivated by religious bigotry. If a state law disproportionately burdened a particular class of religious observers, this circumstance might be evidence of an impermissible legislative motive.... RFRA's substantial burden test, however, is not even a discriminatory effects or disparate impact test. It is a reality of the modern regulatory state that numerous state laws, such as the zoning regulations at issue here, impose a substantial burden on a large class of individuals. When the exercise of religion has been burdened in an incidental way by a law of general application, it does not follow that the persons affected have been burdened any more than other citizens, let alone burdened because of their religious beliefs. In addition, the Act imposes in every case a least restrictive means requirement—a requirement that was not used in the pre-*Smith* jurisprudence RFRA purported to codify—which also indicates that the legislation is broader than is appropriate if the goal is to prevent and remedy constitutional violations.

When Congress acts within its sphere of power and responsibilities, it has not just the right but the duty to make its own informed judgment on the meaning and force of the Constitution. This has been clear from the early days of the Republic. In 1789, when a Member of the House of Representatives objected to a debate on the constitutionality of legislation based on the theory that "it would be officious" to consider the constitutionality of a measure that did not affect the House, James Madison explained that "it is incontrovertibly of as much importance to this branch of the Government as to any other, that the constitution should be preserved entire. It is our duty." Were it otherwise, we would not afford Congress the presumption of validity its enactments now enjoy.

Our national experience teaches that the Constitution is preserved best when each part of the government respects both the Constitution and the proper actions and determinations of the other branches. When the Court has interpreted the Constitution, it has acted within the province of the Judicial Branch, which embraces the duty to say what the law is. Marbury v. Madison. When the political branches of the Government act against the background of a judicial interpretation of the Constitution already issued, it must be understood that in later cases and controversies the Court will treat its precedents with the respect due them under settled principles, including stare decisis, and contrary expectations must be disappointed. RFRA was designed to control cases and controversies, such as the one before us; but as the provisions of the federal statute here invoked are beyond congressional authority, it is this Court's precedent, not RFRA, which must control.

It is for Congress in the first instance to "determin[e] whether and what legislation is needed to secure the guarantees of the Fourteenth Amendment," and its conclusions are entitled to much deference. Katzenbach v. Morgan, 384 U.S., at 651. Congress' discretion is not unlimited, however, and the courts retain the power, as they have since Marbury v. Madison, to determine if Congress has exceeded its authority under the Constitution. Broad as the power of Congress is under the Enforcement Clause of the Fourteenth Amendment, RFRA contradicts vital principles necessary to maintain separation of powers and the federal balance. The judgment of the Court of Appeals sustaining the Act's constitutionality is reversed.

It is so ordered.

Justice Stevens, concurring.

In my opinion, the Religious Freedom Restoration Act of 1993 (RFRA) is a "law respecting an establishment of religion" that violates the First Amendment to the Constitution.

If the historic landmark on the hill in Boerne happened to be a museum or an art gallery owned by an atheist, it would not be eligible for an exemption from the city ordinances that forbid an enlargement of the structure. Because the landmark is owned by the Catholic Church, it is claimed that RFRA gives its owner a federal statutory entitlement to an exemption from a generally applicable, neutral civil law. Whether the Church would actually prevail under the statute or not, the statute has provided the Church with a legal weapon that no atheist or agnostic can obtain. This governmental preference for religion, as opposed to irreligion, is forbidden by the First Amendment. . . .

Justice Scalia, with whom Justice Stevens joins, concurring in part.

I write to respond briefly to the claim of Justice O'Connor's dissent . . . that historical materials support a result contrary to the one reached in Employment Div., Dept. of Human Resources of Ore. v. Smith, 494 U.S. 872 (1990). . . .

Justice O'Connor, with whom Justice Breyer joins except as to a portion of Part I, dissenting.

I dissent from the Court's disposition of this case. I agree with the Court that the issue before us is whether the Religious Freedom Restoration Act (RFRA) is a proper exercise of Congress' power to enforce § 5 of the Fourteenth Amendment. But as a yardstick for measuring the constitutionality of RFRA, the Court uses its holding in Employment Div., Dept. of Human Resources of Ore. v. Smith, 494 U.S. 872 (1990), the decision that prompted Congress to enact RFRA as a means of more rigorously enforcing the Free Exercise Clause. I remain of the view that *Smith* was wrongly decided, and I would use this case to reexamine the Court's holding there. . . .

I

I agree with much of the reasoning set forth in Part III–A of the Court's opinion. Indeed, if I agreed with the Court's standard in *Smith*, I would join the opinion. . . .

The Court's analysis of whether RFRA is a constitutional exercise of Congress' § 5 power, set forth in Part III–B of its opinion, is premised on the assumption that *Smith* correctly interprets the Free Exercise Clause. This is an assumption that I do not accept. I continue to believe that *Smith* adopted an improper standard for deciding free exercise claims. . . .

. . .

Justice Souter, dissenting.

To decide whether the Fourteenth Amendment gives Congress sufficient power to enact the Religious Freedom Restoration Act, the Court measures the legislation against the free-exercise standard of Employment Div., Dept. of Human Resources of Ore. v. Smith, 494 U.S. 872 (1990). For the reasons stated in my opinion in Church of Lukumi Babalu Aye, Inc. v. Hialeah, 508 U.S. 520, 564–577 (1993) . . . I have serious doubts about the precedential value of the *Smith* rule and its entitlement to adherence. . . . [W]ithout briefing and argument on the merits of that rule . . . , I am not now prepared to join Justice O'Connor in rejecting it or the majority in assuming it to be correct. In order to provide full adversarial consideration, this case should be set down for reargument permitting plenary reexamination of the issue. . . .

Justice Breyer, dissenting.

I agree with Justice O'Connor that the Court should direct the parties to brief the question whether Employment Div., Dept. of Human Resources of Ore. v. Smith, 494 U.S. 872 (1990) was correctly decided, and set this case for reargument. I do not, however, find it necessary to consider the question whether, assuming *Smith* is correct, § 5 of the Fourteenth Amendment would authorize Congress to enact the legislation before us. . . . I therefore join Justice O'Connor's dissent, with the exception of the first paragraph of Part I.

KIMEL v. FLORIDA BOARD OF REGENTS, 528 U.S. 62 (2000). The Age Discrimination in Employment Act (ADEA) prohibits employment discrimination because of age. The Court held that ADEA was not authorized by § 5 of the Fourteenth Amendment. Justice O'Connor wrote the opinion for the Court.

"Applying the ... 'congruence and proportionality' test ... , we conclude that the ADEA is not 'appropriate legislation' under § 5 of the Fourteenth Amendment....

"States may discriminate on the basis of age without offending the Fourteenth Amendment if the age classification in question is rationally related to a legitimate state interest. The rationality commanded by the Equal Protection Clause does not require States to match age distinctions and the legitimate interests they serve with razorlike precision....

. . .

"Judged against the backdrop of our equal protection jurisprudence, it is clear that the ADEA is 'so out of proportion to a supposed remedial or preventive object that it cannot be understood as responsive to, or designed to prevent, unconstitutional behavior.' City of Boerne, 521 U.S., at 532. The Act, through its broad restriction on the use of age as a discriminating factor, prohibits substantially more state employment decisions and practices than would likely be held unconstitutional under the applicable equal protection, rational basis standard. ... "

Board of Trustees of the University of Alabama v. Garrett

531 U.S. 356, 121 S.Ct. 955, 148 L.Ed.2d 866 (2001).

Chief Justice Rehnquist delivered the opinion of the Court.

We decide here whether employees of the State of Alabama may recover money damages by reason of the State's failure to comply with the provisions of Title I of the Americans with Disabilities Act of 1990 (ADA or Act)....[1] We hold that such suits are barred by the Eleventh Amendment.

The ADA prohibits certain employers, including the States, from "discriminat[ing] against a qualified individual with a disability because of the disability of such individual in regard to job application procedures, the hiring, advancement, or discharge of employees, employee compensation, job training, and other terms, conditions, and privileges of employment." ... To this end, the Act requires employers to "mak[e] reasonable accommodations to the known physical or mental limitations of an otherwise qualified individual with a disability who is an applicant or employee, unless [the employer] can demonstrate that the accommodation would impose an undue hardship on the operation of the [employer's] business." ...

Respondent Patricia Garrett, a registered nurse, was employed as the Director of Nursing, OB/Gyn/Neonatal Services, for the University of Alabama in Birmingham Hospital. In 1994, Garrett was diagnosed with breast cancer and subsequently underwent a lumpectomy, radiation treatment, and chemotherapy. Garrett's treatments required her to take substantial leave from work.

---

1. ... Title II of the ADA, [deals with the "services, programs, or activities of a public entity," ... We are not disposed to decide the constitutional issue whether Title II, which has somewhat different remedial provisions from Title I, is appropriate legislation under § 5 of the Fourteenth Amendment....

Upon returning to work in July 1995, Garrett's supervisor informed Garrett that she would have to give up her Director position. Garrett then applied for and received a transfer to another, lower paying position as a nurse manager.

Respondent Milton Ash worked as a security officer for the Alabama Department of Youth Services (Department). Upon commencing this employment, Ash informed the Department that he suffered from chronic asthma and that his doctor recommended he avoid carbon monoxide and cigarette smoke, and Ash requested that the Department modify his duties to minimize his exposure to these substances. Ash was later diagnosed with sleep apnea and requested, again pursuant to his doctor's recommendation, that he be reassigned to daytime shifts to accommodate his condition. Ultimately, the Department granted none of the requested relief. Shortly after Ash filed a discrimination claim with the Equal Employment Opportunity Commission, he noticed that his performance evaluations were lower than those he had received on previous occasions.

Garrett and Ash filed separate lawsuits in the District Court, both seeking money damages under the ADA. Petitioners moved for summary judgment, claiming that the ADA exceeds Congress' authority to abrogate the State's Eleventh Amendment immunity. ... [T]he District Court agreed with petitioners' position and granted their motions for summary judgment.... The Court of Appeals reversed....

. . .

I

. . .

We have recognized ... that Congress may abrogate the States' Eleventh Amendment immunity when it both unequivocally intends to do so and "act[s] pursuant to a valid grant of constitutional authority." ...

Congress may not ... base its abrogation of the States' Eleventh Amendment immunity upon the powers enumerated in Article I. ... Congress may subject nonconsenting States to suit in federal court when it does so pursuant to a valid exercise of its [Fourteenth Amendment] § 5 power. ... Accordingly, the ADA can apply to the States only to the extent that the statute is appropriate § 5 legislation.[3]

. . .

City of Boerne ... confirmed ... the long-settled principle that it is the responsibility of this Court, not Congress, to define the substance of constitutional guarantees. ... Accordingly, § 5 legislation reaching beyond the scope of § 1's actual guarantees must exhibit "congruence and proportionality between the injury to be prevented or remedied and the means adopted to that end." ...

II

The first step in applying these now familiar principles is to identify with some precision the scope of the constitutional right at issue. Here, that inquiry requires us to examine the limitations § 1 of the Fourteenth Amendment places upon States' treatment of the disabled. As we did last Term in *Kimel*,

---

3. It is clear that Congress intended to invoke § 5 as one of its bases for enacting the ADA....

... we look to our prior decisions under the Equal Protection Clause dealing with this issue.

In Cleburne v. Cleburne Living Center, Inc., 473 U.S. 432 (1985), we considered an equal protection challenge to a city ordinance requiring a special use permit for the operation of a group home for the mentally retarded. The specific question before us was whether ... mental retardation qualified as a "quasi-suspect" classification under our equal protection jurisprudence.... We ... [concluded] instead that such legislation incurs only the minimum "rational-basis" review applicable to general social and economic legislation.[4] ... In a statement that today seems quite prescient, we explained that

> "if the large and amorphous class of the mentally retarded were deemed quasi-suspect for the reasons given by the Court of Appeals, it would be difficult to find a principled way to distinguish a variety of other groups who have perhaps immutable disabilities setting them off from others, who cannot themselves mandate the desired legislative responses, and who can claim some degree of prejudice from at least part of the public at large. One need mention in this respect only the aging, the disabled, the mentally ill, and the infirm. We are reluctant to set out on that course, and we decline to do so." ...

Under rational-basis review, where a group possesses "distinguishing characteristics relevant to interests the State has the authority to implement," a State's decision to act on the basis of those differences does not give rise to a constitutional violation. ...

Justice Breyer suggests that *Cleburne* stands for the broad proposition that state decisionmaking reflecting "negative attitudes" or "fear" necessarily runs afoul of the Fourteenth Amendment. Although such biases may often accompany irrational (and therefore unconstitutional) discrimination, their presence alone does not a constitutional violation make. As we noted in *Cleburne*: "[M]ere negative attitudes, or fear, unsubstantiated by factors which are properly cognizable in a zoning proceeding, are not permissible bases for treating a home for the mentally retarded differently...." ... This language, read in context, simply states the unremarkable and widely acknowledged tenet of this Court's equal protection jurisprudence that state action subject to rational-basis scrutiny does not violate the Fourteenth Amendment when it "rationally furthers the purpose identified by the State." Massachusetts Bd. of Retirement v. Murgia, 427 U.S. 307 (1976) (per curiam).

Thus, the result of *Cleburne* is that States are not required by the Fourteenth Amendment to make special accommodations for the disabled, so long as their actions towards such individuals are rational. They could quite hard headedly—and perhaps hardheartedly—hold to job-qualification requirements which do not make allowance for the disabled. If special accommodations for the disabled are to be required, they have to come from positive law and not through the Equal Protection Clause.[5]

---

4. Applying the basic principles of rationality review, *Cleburne* struck down the city ordinance in question. ... The Court's reasoning was that the city's purported justifications for the ordinance made no sense in light of how the city treated other groups similarly situated ...

5. It is worth noting that by the time that Congress enacted the ADA in 1990, every State in the Union had enacted such measures. At least one Member of Congress remarked that "this is probably one of the few times where the States are so far out in front of the Federal Government, it's not funny." ... A number of these provisions, however, did not go as far as the ADA did in requiring accommodation.

III

Once we have determined the metes and bounds of the constitutional right in question, we examine whether Congress identified a history and pattern of unconstitutional employment discrimination by the States against the disabled. Just as § 1 of the Fourteenth Amendment applies only to actions committed "under color of state law," Congress' § 5 authority is appropriately exercised only in response to state transgressions. ... The legislative record of the ADA, however, simply fails to show that Congress did in fact identify a pattern of irrational state discrimination in employment against the disabled.

Respondents contend that the inquiry as to unconstitutional discrimination should extend not only to States themselves, but to units of local governments, such as cities and counties. All of these, they say, are "state actors" for purposes of the Fourteenth Amendment. This is quite true, but the Eleventh Amendment does not extend its immunity to units of local government. ... These entities are subject to private claims for damages under the ADA without Congress' ever having to rely on § 5 of the Fourteenth Amendment to render them so. It would make no sense to consider constitutional violations on their part, as well as by the States themselves, when only the States are the beneficiaries of the Eleventh Amendment.

Congress made a general finding in the ADA that "historically, society has tended to isolate and segregate individuals with disabilities, and, despite some improvements, such forms of discrimination against individuals with disabilities continue to be a serious and pervasive social problem." ... The record assembled by Congress includes many instances to support such a finding. But the great majority of these incidents do not deal with the activities of States.

Respondents in their brief cite half a dozen examples from the record that did involve States. A department head at the University of North Carolina refused to hire an applicant for the position of health administrator because he was blind; similarly, a student at a state university in South Dakota was denied an opportunity to practice teach because the dean at that time was convinced that blind people could not teach in public schools. A microfilmer at the Kansas Department of Transportation was fired because he had epilepsy; deaf workers at the University of Oklahoma were paid a lower salary than those who could hear. The Indiana State Personnel Office informed a woman with a concealed disability that she should not disclose it if she wished to obtain employment.

Several of these incidents undoubtedly evidence an unwillingness on the part of state officials to make the sort of accommodations for the disabled required by the ADA. Whether they were irrational under our decision in *Cleburne* is more debatable, particularly when the incident is described out of context. But even if it were to be determined that each incident upon fuller examination showed unconstitutional action on the part of the State, these incidents taken together fall far short of even suggesting the pattern of unconstitutional discrimination on which § 5 legislation must be based. ... In 1990, the States alone employed more than 4.5 million people. ... It is telling, we think, that given these large numbers, Congress assembled only such minimal evidence of unconstitutional state discrimination in employment against the disabled.

Justice Breyer maintains that Congress applied Title I of the ADA to the States in response to a host of incidents representing unconstitutional state discrimination in employment against persons with disabilities. A close review of the relevant materials, however, undercuts that conclusion. Justice Breyer's Appendix C consists not of legislative findings, but of unexamined, anecdotal accounts of "adverse, disparate treatment by state officials." Of course, as we have already explained, "adverse, disparate treatment" often does not amount to a constitutional violation where rational-basis scrutiny applies. These accounts, moreover, were submitted not directly to Congress but to the Task Force on the Rights and Empowerment of Americans with Disabilities, which made no findings on the subject of state discrimination in employment. . . . And, had Congress truly understood this information as reflecting a pattern of unconstitutional behavior by the States, one would expect some mention of that conclusion in the Act's legislative findings. There is none. . . .

Even were it possible to squeeze out of these examples a pattern of unconstitutional discrimination by the States, the rights and remedies created by the ADA against the States would raise the same sort of concerns as to congruence and proportionality as were found in *City of Boerne*, supra. For example, whereas it would be entirely rational (and therefore constitutional) for a state employer to conserve scarce financial resources by hiring employees who are able to use existing facilities, the ADA requires employers to "mak[e] existing facilities used by employees readily accessible to and usable by individuals with disabilities." . . . The ADA does except employers from the "reasonable accommodatio[n]" requirement where the employer "can demonstrate that the accommodation would impose an undue hardship on the operation of the business of such covered entity." . . . However, even with this exception, the accommodation duty far exceeds what is constitutionally required in that it makes unlawful a range of alternate responses that would be reasonable but would fall short of imposing an "undue burden" upon the employer. . . .

The ADA also forbids "utilizing standards, criteria, or methods of administration" that disparately impact the disabled, without regard to whether such conduct has a rational basis. . . . Although disparate impact may be relevant evidence of racial discrimination, . . . such evidence alone is insufficient even where the Fourteenth Amendment subjects state action to strict scrutiny. . . .

The ADA's constitutional shortcomings are apparent when the Act is compared to Congress' efforts in the Voting Rights Act of 1965 to respond to a serious pattern of constitutional violations. In South Carolina v. Katzenbach, 383 U.S. 301 (1966), . . . we noted that "[b]efore enacting the measure, Congress explored with great care the problem of racial discrimination in voting." . . .

In that Act, Congress documented a marked pattern of unconstitutional action by the States. State officials, Congress found, routinely applied voting tests in order to exclude African–American citizens from registering to vote. . . . Congress also determined that litigation had proved ineffective and that there persisted an otherwise inexplicable 50–percentage-point gap in the registration of white and African–American voters in some States. . . . Congress' response was to promulgate in the Voting Rights Act a detailed but limited remedial scheme designed to guarantee meaningful enforcement of the Fifteenth Amendment in those areas of the Nation where abundant evidence of States' systematic denial of those rights was identified.

. . . The contrast between this kind of evidence, and the evidence that Congress considered in the present case, is stark. Congressional enactment of the ADA represents its judgment that there should be a "comprehensive national mandate for the elimination of discrimination against individuals with disabilities." . . . Congress is the final authority as to desirable public policy, but in order to authorize private individuals to recover money damages against the States, there must be a pattern of discrimination by the States which violates the Fourteenth Amendment, and the remedy imposed by Congress must be congruent and proportional to the targeted violation. Those requirements are not met here, and to uphold the Act's application to the States would allow Congress to rewrite the Fourteenth Amendment law laid down by this Court in Cleburne. Section 5 does not so broadly enlarge congressional authority. The judgment of the Court of Appeals is therefore Reversed.

Justice Kennedy, with whom Justice O'Connor joins, concurring.

Prejudice, we are beginning to understand, rises not from malice or hostile animus alone. ... There can be little doubt ... that persons with mental or physical impairments are confronted with prejudice which can stem from indifference or insecurity as well as from malicious ill will.

... I do not doubt that the Americans with Disabilities Act of 1990 will be a milestone on the path to a more decent, tolerant, progressive society.

It is a question of quite a different order, however, to say that the States in their official capacities, the States as governmental entities, must be held in violation of the Constitution on the assumption that they embody the misconceived or malicious perceptions of some of their citizens. ... The failure of a State to revise policies now seen as incorrect under a new understanding of proper policy does not always constitute the purposeful and intentional action required to make out a violation of the Equal Protection Clause. ...

. . .

It must be noted, moreover, that what is in question is not whether the Congress, acting pursuant to a power granted to it by the Constitution, can compel the States to act. What is involved is only the question whether the States can be subjected to liability in suits brought not by the Federal Government (to which the States have consented, ... but by private persons seeking to collect moneys from the state treasury without the consent of the State). The predicate for money damages against an unconsenting State in suits brought by private persons must be a federal statute enacted upon the documentation of patterns of constitutional violations committed by the State in its official capacity. That predicate ... has not been established. With these observations, I join the Court's opinion.

Justice Breyer, with whom Justice Stevens, Justice Souter and Justice Ginsberg join, dissenting.

. . .

... In my view, Congress reasonably could have concluded that the remedy before us constitutes an "appropriate" way to enforce this basic equal protection requirement. And that is all the Constitution requires.

I

The Court says that its primary problem with this statutory provision is one of legislative evidence. It says that "Congress assembled only ... minimal evidence of unconstitutional state discrimination in employment." In fact, Congress compiled a vast legislative record documenting " 'massive, society-wide discrimination' " against persons with disabilities....

The powerful evidence of discriminatory treatment throughout society in general, including discrimination by private persons and local governments, implicates state governments as well, for state agencies form part of that same larger society. There is no particular reason to believe that they are immune from the "stereotypic assumptions" and pattern of "purposeful unequal treatment" that Congress found prevalent. The Court claims that it "make[s] no sense" to take into consideration constitutional violations committed by local governments. But the substantive obligation that the Equal Protection Clause creates applies to state and local governmental entities alike. . . . Local governments often work closely with, and under the supervision of, state officials, and in general, state and local government employers are similarly situated. . . .

. . .

The congressionally appointed task force collected numerous specific examples, provided by persons with disabilities themselves, of adverse, disparate treatment by state officials. They reveal, not what the Court describes as "half a dozen" instances of discrimination, but hundreds of instances of adverse treatment at the hands of state officials—instances in which a person with a disability found it impossible to obtain a state job, to retain state employment, to use the public transportation that was readily available to others in order to get to work, or to obtain a public education, which is often a prerequisite to obtaining employment. . . .

As the Court notes, those who presented instances of discrimination rarely provided additional, independent evidence sufficient to prove in court that, in each instance, the discrimination they suffered lacked justification from a judicial standpoint. Perhaps this explains the Court's view that there is "minimal evidence of unconstitutional state discrimination." But a legislature is not a court of law. And Congress, unlike courts, must, and does, routinely draw general conclusions . . .

Regardless, Congress expressly found substantial unjustified discrimination against persons with disabilities. . . . In making these findings, Congress followed our decision in *Cleburne*, which established that not only discrimination against persons with disabilities that rests upon "a bare . . . desire to harm a politically unpopular group," . . . violates the Fourteenth Amendment, but also discrimination that rests solely upon "negative attitude [s]," "fea[r]," . . . or "irrational prejudice,". . . .

The evidence in the legislative record bears out Congress' finding that the adverse treatment of persons with disabilities was often arbitrary or invidious in this sense, and thus unjustified. . . .

II

The Court's failure to find sufficient evidentiary support may well rest upon its decision to hold Congress to a strict, judicially created evidentiary standard, particularly in respect to lack of justification. . . .

The problem with the Court's approach is that neither the "burden of proof" that favors States nor any other rule of restraint applicable to judges applies to Congress when it exercises its § 5 power. "Limitations stemming from the nature of the judicial process . . . have no application to Congress." . . . Rational-basis review—with its presumptions favoring constitutionality—is "a paradigm of judicial restraint." . . . And the Congress of the United States is not a lower court.

Indeed, the Court in *Cleburne* drew this very institutional distinction. We emphasized that "courts have been very reluctant, as they should be in our federal system and with our respect for the separation of powers, to closely scrutinize legislative choices." . . .

There is simply no reason to require Congress, seeking to determine facts relevant to the exercise of its § 5 authority, to adopt rules or presumptions that reflect a court's institutional limitations. Unlike courts, Congress can readily gather facts from across the Nation, assess the magnitude of a problem, and more easily find an appropriate remedy.... Unlike courts, Congress directly reflects public attitudes and beliefs, enabling Congress better to understand where, and to what extent, refusals to accommodate a disability amount to behavior that is callous or unreasonable to the point of lacking constitutional justification. Unlike judges, Members of Congress can directly obtain information from constituents who have first-hand experience with discrimination and related issues.

Moreover, unlike judges, Members of Congress are elected. ... To apply a rule designed to restrict courts as if it restricted Congress' legislative power is to stand the underlying principle—a principle of judicial restraint—on its head. But without the use of this burden of proof rule or some other unusually stringent standard of review, it is difficult to see how the Court can find the legislative record here inadequate. Read with a reasonably favorable eye, the record indicates that state governments subjected those with disabilities to seriously adverse, disparate treatment. And Congress could have found, in a significant number of instances, that this treatment violated the substantive principles of justification—shorn of their judicial-restraint-related presumptions—that this Court recognized in *Cleburne*.

III

The Court argues in the alternative that the statute's damage remedy is not "congruent" with and "proportional" to the equal protection problem that Congress found. ...

[W]hat is wrong with a remedy that, in response to unreasonable employer behavior, requires an employer to make accommodations that are reasonable? Of course, what is "reasonable" in the statutory sense and what is "unreasonable" in the constitutional sense might differ. In other words, the requirement may exceed what is necessary to avoid a constitutional violation. But it is just that power—the power to require more than the minimum that § 5 grants to Congress, as this Court has repeatedly confirmed. ...

. . .

... [E]ven today, the Court purports to apply, not to depart from, these standards. But the Court's analysis and ultimate conclusion deprive its declarations of practical significance. The Court "sounds the word of promise to the ear but breaks it to the hope."

IV

The Court's harsh review of Congress' use of its § 5 power is reminiscent of the similar (now-discredited) limitation that it once imposed upon Congress' Commerce Clause power. Compare Carter v. Carter Coal Co., 298 U.S. 238 (1936), with United States v. Darby, 312 U.S. 100 (1941) (rejecting *Carter Coal's* rationale). I could understand the legal basis for such review were we judging a statute that discriminated against those of a particular race or gender ... , or a statute that threatened a basic constitutionally protected liberty such as free speech, ... The legislation before us, however, does not discriminate against anyone, nor does it pose any threat to basic liberty. And it is difficult to understand why the Court, which applies "minimum 'rational-basis' review" to statutes that burden persons with disabilities, subjects to far stricter scrutiny a statute that seeks to help those same individuals.

... Rules for interpreting § 5 that would provide States with special protection ... run counter to the very object of the Fourteenth Amendment.

... I doubt that today's decision serves any constitutionally based federalism interest.

The Court, through its evidentiary demands, its non-deferential review, and its failure to distinguish between judicial and legislative constitutional competencies, improperly invades a power that the Constitution assigns to Congress. ... Whether the Commerce Clause does or does not enable Congress to enact this provision, ... in my view, § 5 gives Congress the necessary authority.

For the reasons stated, I respectfully dissent.

Nevada Department of Human Resources v. Hibbs

538 U.S. 721, 123 S.Ct. 1972, 155 L.Ed.2d 953 (2003).

Chief Justice Rehnquist delivered the opinion of the Court.

The Family and Medical Leave Act of 1993 (FMLA or Act) entitles eligible employees to take up to 12 work weeks of unpaid leave annually for any of several reasons, including the onset of a "serious health condition" in an employee's spouse, child, or parent. ... The Act creates a private right of action to seek both equitable relief and money damages "against any employer (including a public agency) in any Federal or State court of competent jurisdiction," ... should that employer "interfere with, restrain, or deny the exercise of" FMLA rights ... We hold that employees of the State of Nevada may recover money damages in the event of the State's failure to comply with the family-care provision of the Act.

... Respondent ... worked for the Department's Welfare Division. In April and May 1997, he sought leave under the FMLA to care for his ailing wife, who was recovering from a car accident and neck surgery. The Department granted his request for the full 12 weeks of FMLA leave.... In October 1997, the Department informed respondent that he had exhausted his FMLA leave, that no further leave would be granted, and that he must report to work by November 12, 1997. Respondent failed to do so and was terminated.

Respondent sued petitioners in the United States District Court seeking damages and injunctive and declaratory relief for ... violations of [FMLA]. The District Court awarded petitioners summary judgment on the grounds that the FMLA claim was barred by the Eleventh Amendment and that respondent's Fourteenth Amendment rights had not been violated. ... The Ninth Circuit reversed.

. . .

Congress may ... abrogate ... immunity in federal court if it makes its intention to abrogate unmistakably clear in the language of the statute and acts pursuant to a valid exercise of its power under § 5 of the Fourteenth Amendment. ... This case turns, then, on whether Congress acted within its constitutional authority when it sought to abrogate the States' immunity for purposes of the FMLA's family-leave provision.

In enacting the FMLA, Congress relied on two of the powers vested in it by the Constitution: its Article I commerce power and its power under § 5 of the Fourteenth Amendment to enforce that Amendment's guarantees. Congress may not abrogate the States' sovereign immunity pursuant to its Article I power over commerce. ... Congress may, however, abrogate States' sovereign immunity through a valid exercise of its § 5 power ...

Two provisions of the Fourteenth Amendment are relevant here: Section 5 grants Congress the power "to enforce" the substantive guarantees of § 1— among them, equal protection of the laws—by enacting "appropriate legislation." Congress may, in the exercise of its § 5 power, do more than simply proscribe conduct that we have held unconstitutional. "Congress' power 'to enforce' the Amendment includes the authority both to remedy and to deter violation of rights guaranteed thereunder by prohibiting a somewhat broader swath of conduct, including that which is not itself forbidden by the Amendment's text." . . . In other words, Congress may enact so-called prophylactic legislation that proscribes facially constitutional conduct, in order to prevent and deter unconstitutional conduct.

City of Boerne also confirmed, however, that it falls to this Court, not Congress, to define the substance of constitutional guarantees. . . . We distinguish appropriate prophylactic legislation from "substantive redefinition of the Fourteenth Amendment right at issue," . . . by applying the test set forth in *City of Boerne:* Valid § 5 legislation must exhibit "congruence and proportionality between the injury to be prevented or remedied and the means adopted to that end." . . .

The FMLA aims to protect the right to be free from gender-based discrimination in the workplace. We have held that statutory classifications that distinguish between males and females are subject to heightened scrutiny. . . . For a gender-based classification to withstand such scrutiny, it must "serv[e] important governmental objectives," and "the discriminatory means employed [must be] substantially related to the achievement of those objectives." . . . The State's justification for such a classification "must not rely on overbroad generalizations about the different talents, capacities, or preferences of males and females." . . . We now inquire whether Congress had evidence of a pattern of constitutional violations on the part of the States in this area.

The history of the many state laws limiting women's employment opportunities is chronicled in—and, until relatively recently, was sanctioned by—this Court's own opinions.

. . .

Congress responded to this history of discrimination by abrogating States' sovereign immunity in Title VII of the Civil Rights Act of 1964 . . . But state gender discrimination did not cease. . . . According to evidence that was before Congress when it enacted the FMLA, States continue to rely on invalid gender stereotypes in the employment context, specifically in the administration of leave benefits. Reliance on such stereotypes cannot justify the States' gender discrimination in this area. . . . The long and extensive history of sex discrimination prompted us to hold that measures that differentiate on the basis of gender warrant heightened scrutiny; here . . . the persistence of such unconstitutional discrimination by the States justifies Congress' passage of prophylactic § 5 legislation.

As the FMLA's legislative record reflects, a 1990 Bureau of Labor Statistics (BLS) survey stated that 37 percent of surveyed private-sector employees were covered by maternity leave policies, while only 18 percent were covered by paternity leave policies. . . .

Congress also heard testimony that "[p]arental leave for fathers . . . is rare. Even . . . [w]here child-care leave policies do exist, men, *both in the public and private sectors*, receive notoriously discriminatory treatment in their requests for such leave." . . .

Finally, Congress had evidence that, even where state laws and policies were not facially discriminatory, they were applied in discriminatory ways. . . .

In spite of all of the above evidence, Justice Kennedy argues in dissent that Congress' passage of the FMLA was unnecessary because "the States appear to have been ahead of Congress in providing gender-neutral family leave benefits," and points to Nevada's leave policies in particular. However, it was only "[s]ince Federal family leave legislation was first introduced" that the States had even "begun to consider similar family leave initiatives." . . .

Furthermore, the dissent's statement that some States "had adopted some form of family-care leave" before the FMLA's enactment glosses over important shortcomings of some state policies. First, seven States had childcare leave provisions that applied to women only. . . . These laws reinforced the very stereotypes that Congress sought to remedy through the FMLA. Second, 12 States provided their employees no family leave, beyond an initial childbirth or adoption, to care for a seriously ill child or family member. Third, many States provided no statutorily guaranteed right to family leave, offering instead only voluntary or discretionary leave programs. Three States left the amount of leave time primarily in employers' hands. Congress could reasonably conclude that such discretionary family-leave programs would do little to combat the stereotypes about the roles of male and female employees that Congress sought to eliminate. Finally, four States provided leave only through administrative regulations or personnel policies, which Congress could reasonably conclude offered significantly less firm protection than a federal law. Against the above backdrop of limited state leave policies, no matter how generous petitioner's own may have been, Congress was justified in enacting the FMLA as remedial legislation.

In sum, the States' record of unconstitutional participation in, and fostering of, gender-based discrimination in the administration of leave benefits is weighty enough to justify the enactment of prophylactic § 5 legislation.

We reached the opposite conclusion in *Garrett* and *Kimel*. In those cases, the § 5 legislation under review responded to a purported tendency of state officials to make age-or disability-based distinctions. Under our equal protection case law, discrimination on the basis of such characteristics is not judged under a heightened review standard . . .

Here, however, Congress directed its attention to state gender discrimination, which triggers a heightened level of scrutiny. . . . Because the standard for demonstrating the constitutionality of a gender-based classification is more difficult to meet than our rational-basis test . . . it was easier for Congress to show a pattern of state constitutional violations. Congress was similarly successful in South Carolina v. Katzenbach, 383 U.S. 301, 308–313 (1966), where we upheld the Voting Rights Act of 1965: Because racial classifications are presumptively invalid, most of the States' acts of race discrimination violated the Fourteenth Amendment.

. . .

Stereotypes about women's domestic roles are reinforced by parallel stereotypes presuming a lack of domestic responsibilities for men. Because employers continued to regard the family as the woman's domain, they often denied men similar accommodations or discouraged them from taking leave. These mutually reinforcing stereotypes created a self-fulfilling cycle of discrimination that forced women to continue to assume the role of primary family caregiver, and fostered employers' stereotypical views about women's commitment to work and their value as employees. Those perceptions, in turn, Congress reasoned, lead to subtle discrimination that may be difficult to detect on a case-by-case basis.

. . .

By creating an across-the-board, routine employment benefit for all eligible employees, Congress sought to ensure that family-care leave would no longer be stigmatized as an inordinate drain on the workplace caused by female employees, and that employers could not evade leave obligations simply by hiring men. By setting a minimum standard of family leave for *all* eligible employees, irrespective of gender, the FMLA attacks the formerly state-sanctioned stereotype that only women are responsible for family caregiving, thereby reducing employers' incentives to engage in discrimination by basing hiring and promotion decisions on stereotypes.

The dissent characterizes the FMLA as a "substantive entitlement program" rather than a remedial statute because it establishes a floor of 12 weeks' leave. In the dissent's view, in the face of evidence of gender-based discrimination by the States in the provision of leave benefits, Congress could do no more in exercising its § 5 power than simply proscribe such discrimination. But this position cannot be squared with our recognition that Congress "is not confined to the enactment of legislation that merely parrots the precise wording of the Fourteenth Amendment," but may prohibit "a somewhat broader swath of conduct, including that which is not itself forbidden by the Amendment's text." . . . For example, this Court has upheld certain prophylactic provisions of the Voting Rights Act as valid exercises of Congress' § 5 power, including the literacy test ban and preclearance requirements for changes in States' voting procedures. . . .

Indeed, in light of the evidence before Congress, a statute mirroring Title VII, that simply mandated gender equality in the administration of leave benefits, would not have achieved Congress' remedial object. Such a law would allow States to provide for no family leave at all. Where "[t]wo-thirds of the nonprofessional caregivers for older, chronically ill, or disabled persons are working women," . . . and state practices continue to reinforce the stereotype of women as caregivers, such a policy would exclude far more women than men from the workplace.

Unlike the statutes at issue in *City of Boerne*, *Kimel*, and *Garrett*, which applied broadly to every aspect of state employers' operations, the FMLA is narrowly targeted at the fault line between work and family—precisely where sex-based overgeneralization has been and remains strongest—and affects only one aspect of the employment relationship. . . .

. . .

For the above reasons, we conclude that [FMLA] is congruent and proportional to its remedial object, and can "be understood as responsive to, or designed to prevent, unconstitutional behavior." . . .

The judgment of the Court of Appeals is therefore

Affirmed.

Justice Souter, with whom Justice Ginsburg and Justice Breyer join, concurring.

. . . I join the Court's opinion here without conceding the dissenting . . . views expressed in Seminole Tribe of Fla. v. Florida . . .

Justice Stevens, concurring in the judgment.

Because I have never been convinced that an Act of Congress can amend the Constitution and because I am uncertain whether the congressional enactment before us was truly " 'needed to secure the guarantees of the Fourteenth Amendment,' " I write separately to explain why I join the Court's judgment. . . .

. . . As long as it clearly expresses its intent, Congress may abrogate that common-law defense pursuant to its power to regulate commerce "among the several States." . . . The family-care provision of the Family and Medical Leave Act of 1993 is unquestionably a valid exercise of a power that is "broad enough to support federal legislation regulating the terms and conditions of state employment." . . .

Justice Scalia, dissenting.

I join Justice Kennedy's dissent, and add one further observation: The constitutional violation that is a prerequisite to "prophylactic" congressional action to "enforce" the Fourteenth Amendment is a violation *by the State against which the enforcement action is taken.* There is no guilt by association, enabling the sovereignty of one State to be abridged under § 5 of the Fourteenth Amendment because of violations by another State, or by most other States, or even by 49 other States. Congress has sometimes displayed awareness of this self-evident limitation. That is presumably why the most sweeping provisions of the Voting Rights Act of 1965—which we upheld in *City of Rome v. United States,* 446 U.S. 156 (1980), as a valid exercise of congressional power under § 2 of the Fifteenth Amendment—were restricted to States "with a demonstrable history of intentional racial discrimination in voting," . . .

Today's opinion for the Court does not even attempt to demonstrate that each one of the 50 States . . . was in violation of the Fourteenth Amendment. It treats "the States" as some sort of collective entity which is guilty or innocent as a body. . . .

. . . [T]he court may, if asked, proceed to analyze whether the statute . . . can be validly applied to the litigant. In the context of § 5 prophylactic legislation applied against a State, this would entail examining whether the State has itself engaged in discrimination sufficient to support the exercise of Congress's prophylactic power.

. . . I think Nevada will be entitled to assert that the mere facts that (1) it is a State, and (2) some States are bad actors, is not enough; it can demand that *it* be shown to have been acting in violation of the Fourteenth Amendment.

Justice Kennedy, with whom Justice Scalia and Justice Thomas join, dissenting.

. . . [T]he family leave provision of the Act . . . is invalid to the extent it allows for private suits against the unconsenting States.

Congress does not have authority to define the substantive content of the Equal Protection Clause; it may only shape the remedies warranted by the violations of that guarantee. *City of Boerne, supra* . . . This requirement has special force in the context of the Eleventh Amendment, which protects a State's fiscal integrity from federal intrusion by vesting the States with immunity from private actions for damages pursuant to federal laws. The Commerce Clause likely would permit the National Government to enact an entitlement program such as this one; but when Congress couples the entitlement with the authorization to sue the States for monetary damages, it blurs the line of accountability the State has to its own citizens. . . .

The Court is unable to show that States have engaged in a pattern of unlawful conduct which warrants the remedy of opening state treasuries to private suits. The inability to adduce evidence of alleged discrimination, coupled with the inescapable fact that the federal scheme is not a remedy but a benefit program, demonstrate the lack of the requisite link between any problem Congress has identified and the program it mandated.

... All would agree that women historically have been subjected to conditions in which their employment opportunities are more limited than those available to men. As the Court acknowledges, however, Congress responded to this problem by abrogating States' sovereign immunity in Title VII of the Civil Rights Act of 1964 ... The provision now before us ... has a different aim than Title VII. It seeks to ensure that eligible employees, irrespective of gender, can take a minimum amount of leave time to care for an ill relative.

The relevant question, as the Court seems to acknowledge, is whether, notwithstanding the passage of Title VII and similar state legislation, the States continued to engage in widespread discrimination on the basis of gender in the provision of family leave benefits. ... The evidence to substantiate this charge must be far more specific, however, than a simple recitation of a general history of employment discrimination against women. ...

Respondents fail to make the requisite showing. ...

As the Court seems to recognize, the evidence considered by Congress concerned discriminatory practices of the private sector, not those of state employers. ...

. . .

The Court's reliance on evidence suggesting States provided men and women with the parenting leave of different length ... concerns the Act's grant of parenting leave, ... and is too attenuated to justify the family leave provision. The Court of Appeals' conclusion to the contrary was based on an assertion that "if states discriminate along gender lines regarding the one kind of leave, then they are likely to do so regarding the other." The charge that a State has engaged in a pattern of unconstitutional discrimination against its citizens is a most serious one. It must be supported by more than conjecture.

The Court maintains the evidence pertaining to the parenting leave is relevant because both parenting and family leave provisions respond to "the same gender stereotype: that women's family duties trump those of the workplace." This sets the contours of the inquiry at too high a level of abstraction. The question is not whether the family leave provision is a congruent and proportional response to general gender-based stereotypes in employment ... ; the question is whether it is a proper remedy to an alleged pattern of unconstitutional discrimination by States in the grant of family leave. The evidence of gender-based stereotypes is too remote to support the required showing.

The Court next argues that "even where state laws and policies were not facially discriminatory, they were applied in discriminatory ways."

Even if there were evidence that individual state employers, in the absence of clear statutory guidelines, discriminated in the administration of leave benefits, this circumstance alone would not support a finding of a state-sponsored pattern of discrimination. The evidence could perhaps support the charge of disparate impact, but not a charge that States have engaged in a pattern of intentional discrimination prohibited by the Fourteenth Amendment. ...

The federal-state equivalence upon which the Court places such emphasis is a deficient rationale at an even more fundamental level, however; for the States appear to have been ahead of Congress in providing gender-neutral family leave benefits. Thirty States, the District of Columbia, and Puerto Rico had adopted some form of family-care leave in the years preceding the Act's adoption. ... At the very least, the history of the Act suggests States were in the process of solving any existing gender-based discrimination in the provision of family leave.

The Court acknowledges that States have adopted family leave programs prior to federal intervention, but argues these policies suffered from serious imperfections. Even if correct, this observation proves, at most, that programs more generous and more effective than those operated by the States were feasible. That the States did not devise the optimal programs is not, however, evidence that the States were perpetuating unconstitutional discrimination. Given that the States assumed a pioneering role in the creation of family leave schemes, it is not surprising these early efforts may have been imperfect. This is altogether different, however, from purposeful discrimination.

. . .

Our concern with gender discrimination, which is subjected to heightened scrutiny, as opposed to age-or disability-based distinctions, which are reviewed under rational standard, ... does not alter this conclusion. The application of heightened scrutiny is designed to ensure gender-based classifications are not based on the entrenched and pervasive stereotypes which inhibit women's progress in the workplace.... Given the insufficiency of the evidence that States discriminated in the provision of family leave, the unfortunate fact that stereotypes about women continue to be a serious and pervasive social problem would not alone support the charge that a State has engaged in a practice designed to deny its citizens the equal protection of the laws.

The paucity of evidence to support the case the Court tries to make demonstrates that Congress was not responding with a congruent and proportional remedy to a perceived course of unconstitutional conduct. Instead, it enacted a substantive entitlement program of its own. If Congress had been concerned about different treatment of men and women with respect to family leave, a congruent remedy would have sought to ensure the benefits of any leave program enacted by a State are available to men and women on an equal basis. Instead, the Act imposes, across the board, a requirement that States grant a minimum of 12 weeks of leave per year. ...

. . .

To be sure, the Nevada scheme did not track that devised by the Act in all respects. The provision of unpaid leave was discretionary and subject to a possible reporting requirement. ... A congruent remedy to any discriminatory exercise of discretion, however, is the requirement that the grant of leave be administered on a gender-equal basis, not the displacement of the State's scheme by a federal one. The scheme enacted by the Act does not respect the States' autonomous power to design their own social benefits regime.

Were more proof needed to show that this is an entitlement program, not a remedial statute, it should suffice to note that the Act does not even purport to bar discrimination in some leave programs the States do enact and administer. Under the Act, a State is allowed to provide women with, say, 24 weeks of family leave per year but provide only 12 weeks of leave to men. As the counsel for the United States conceded during the argument, a law of this kind might run afoul of the Equal Protection Clause or Title VII, but it would not constitute a violation of the Act. The Act on its face is not drawn as a remedy to gender-based discrimination in family leave.

. . . The dual requirement that Congress identify a pervasive pattern of unconstitutional state conduct and that its remedy be proportional and congruent to the violation is designed to separate permissible exercises of congressional power from instances where Congress seeks to enact a substantive entitlement under the guise of its § 5 authority.

The Court's precedents upholding the Voting Rights Act of 1965 as a proper exercise of Congress' remedial power are instructive. In South Carolina *v. Katzenbach*, 383 U.S. 301 (1966), the Court concluded that the Voting Rights Act's prohibition on state literacy tests was an appropriate method of enforcing the constitutional protection against racial discrimination in voting. This measure was justified because "Congress documented a marked pattern of unconstitutional action by the States." This scheme was both congruent, because it "aimed at areas where voting discrimination has been most flagrant," . . . and proportional, because it was necessary to "banish the blight of racial discrimination in voting, which has infected the electoral process in parts of our country for nearly a century," . . .

. . .

. . . The family leave benefit conferred by the Act is, by contrast, a substantive benefit Congress chose to confer upon state employees. . . .

. . .

Tennessee v. Lane

541 U.S. 509, 124 S.Ct. 1978, 158 L.Ed.2d 820 (2004).

Justice Stevens delivered the opinion of the Court.

Disability Act

Title II of the Americans with Disabilities Act of 1990 (ADA or Act) . . . provides that "no qualified individual with a disability shall, by reason of such disability, be excluded from participation in or be denied the benefits of the services, programs or activities of a public entity, or be subjected to discrimination by any such entity." . . . The question presented in this case is whether Title II exceeds Congress' power under § 5 of the Fourteenth Amendment.

I

In August 1998, respondents George Lane and Beverly Jones filed this action against the State of Tennessee and a number of Tennessee counties, alleging past and ongoing violations of Title II. Respondents, both of whom are paraplegics who use wheelchairs for mobility, claimed that they were denied access to, and the services of, the state court system by reason of their disabilities. Lane alleged that he was compelled to appear to answer a set of criminal charges on the second floor of a county courthouse that had no elevator. At his first appearance, Lane crawled up two flights of stairs to get to the courtroom. When Lane returned to the courthouse for a hearing, he refused to crawl again or to be carried by officers to the courtroom; he consequently was arrested and jailed for failure to appear. Jones, a certified court reporter, alleged that she has not been able to gain access to a number of county courthouses, and, as a result, has lost both work and an opportunity to participate in the judicial process. Respondents sought damages and equitable relief.

The State moved to dismiss the suit on the ground that it was barred by the Eleventh Amendment. The District Court denied the motion without opinion . . . [and] the Court of Appeals for the Sixth Circuit entered an order holding the case in abeyance pending our decision in Board of Trustees of Ala. v. Garrett, 531 U.S. 356 (2001).

In *Garrett*, we concluded that the Eleventh Amendment bars private suits seeking money damages for state violations of Title I of the ADA. We left open, however, the question whether the Eleventh Amendment permits suits for money damages under Title II. . . . Following the *Garrett* decision, the Court of Appeals [in another case] . . . interpreted *Garrett* to bar private ADA suits against States based on equal protection principles, but not those that rely on due process principles. . . .

. . . [T]he Court of Appeals [then] entered an order affirming the District Court's denial of the State's motion to dismiss in this case. . . . The order explained that respondents' claims were not barred because they were based on due process principles. . . . We granted certiorari . . . and now affirm.

II

The ADA was passed by large majorities in both Houses of Congress after decades of deliberation and investigation into the need for comprehensive legislation to address discrimination against persons with disabilities. In the years immediately preceding the ADA's enactment, Congress held 13 hearings and created a special task force that gathered evidence from every State in the Union. . . . Central among the[] conclusions was Congress' finding that

> "individuals with disabilities are a discrete and insular minority who have been faced with restrictions and limitations, subjected to a history of purposeful unequal treatment, and relegated to a position of political powerlessness in our society, based on characteristics that are beyond the control of such individuals and resulting from stereotypic assumptions not truly indicative of the individual ability of such individuals to participate in, and contribute to, society." 42 U.S.C. § 12101(a)(7).

. . . [The Act] forbids discrimination against persons with disabilities in three major areas of public life: employment, which is covered by Title I of the statute; public services, programs, and activities, which are the subject of Title II; and public accommodations, which are covered by Title III.

Title II, § § 12131–12134, prohibits any public entity from discriminating against "qualified" persons with disabilities in the provision or operation of public services, programs, or activities. The Act defines the term "public entity" to include state and local governments, as well as their agencies and instrumentalities. § 12131(1). Persons with disabilities are "qualified" if they, "with or without reasonable modifications to rules, policies, or practices, the removal of architectural, communication, or transportation barriers, or the provision of auxiliary aids and services, mee[t] the essential eligibility requirements for the receipt of services or the participation in programs or activities provided by a public entity." . . .

III

. . . Our cases have . . . held that Congress may abrogate the State's Eleventh Amendment immunity. To determine whether it has done so in any given case, we "must resolve two predicate questions: first, whether Congress unequivocally expressed its intent to abrogate that immunity; and second, if it did, whether Congress acted pursuant to a valid grant of constitutional authority." ...

The first question is easily answered in this case. The Act specifically provides: "A State shall not be immune under the eleventh amendment to the Constitution of the United States from an action in Federal or State court of competent jurisdiction for a violation of this chapter." ... The question, then, is whether Congress had the power to give effect to its intent.

In Fitzpatrick v. Bitzer, 427 U.S. 445 (1976), we held that Congress can abrogate a State's sovereign immunity when it does so pursuant to a valid exercise of its power under § 5 of the Fourteenth Amendment to enforce the substantive guarantees of that Amendment.... This enforcement power, as we have often acknowledged, is a "broad power indeed." ... It includes "the authority both to remedy and to deter violation of rights guaranteed [[by the Fourteenth Amendment]] by prohibiting a somewhat broader swath of conduct, including that which is not itself forbidden by the Amendment's text." ... We have thus repeatedly affirmed that "Congress may enact so-called prophylactic legislation that proscribes facially constitutional conduct, in order to prevent and deter unconstitutional conduct." Nevada Dept. of Human Resources v. Hibbs, 538 U.S. 721, 727–728, (2003).... The most recent affirmation of the breadth of Congress' § 5 power came in *Hibbs*, in which we considered whether a male state employee could recover money damages against the State for its failure to comply with the family-care leave provision of the Family and Medical Leave Act of 1993 (FMLA).... We upheld the FMLA as a valid exercise of Congress' § 5 power to combat unconstitutional sex discrimination, even though there was no suggestion that the State's leave policy was adopted or applied with a discriminatory purpose that would render it unconstitutional under the rule of Personnel Administrator of Mass. v. Feeney, 442 U.S. 256 (1979)....

Congress' § 5 power is not, however, unlimited. While Congress must have a wide berth in devising appropriate remedial and preventative measures for unconstitutional actions, those measures may not work a "substantive change in the governing law." [City of Boerne v. Flores, 521 U.S. 507, 519 (1997)]. In *Boerne*, we recognized that the line between remedial legislation and substantive redefinition is "not easy to discern," and that "Congress must have wide latitude in determining where it lies." ... But we also confirmed that "the distinction exists and must be observed," and set forth a test for so observing it: Section 5 legislation is valid if it exhibits "a congruence and proportionality between the injury to be prevented or remedied and the means adopted to that end." ...

. . .

Applying the *Boerne* test in *Garrett*, we concluded that Title I of the ADA was not a valid exercise of Congress' § 5 power to enforce the Fourteenth Amendment's prohibition on unconstitutional disability discrimination in public employment.... [W]e concluded Congress' exercise of its prophylactic § 5 power was unsupported by a relevant history and pattern of constitutional violations.... Although the dissent pointed out that Congress had before it a great deal of evidence of discrimination by the States against persons with disabilities, ... the Court's opinion noted that the "overwhelming majority" of that evidence related to "the provision of public services and public accommodations, which areas are addressed in Titles II and III," rather than Title I.... We [also] emphasized that the House and Senate Committee Reports on the ADA focused on " 'discrimination [in] ... employment in the private sector,' " and made no mention of discrimination in public employment. ... Finally, we concluded that Title I's broad remedial scheme was insufficiently targeted to remedy or prevent unconstitutional discrimination in public employment....

In view of the significant differences between Titles I and II, however, *Garrett* left open the question whether Title II is a valid exercise of Congress' § 5 enforcement power. It is to that question that we now turn.

IV

The first step of the *Boerne* inquiry requires us to identify the constitutional right or rights that Congress sought to enforce when it enacted Title II.... In *Garrett* we identified Title I's purpose as enforcement of the Fourteenth Amendment's command that "all persons similarly situated should be treated alike." ... As we observed, classifications based on disability violate that constitutional command if they lack a rational relationship to a legitimate governmental purpose....

Title II, like Title I, seeks to enforce this prohibition on irrational disability discrimination. But it also seeks to enforce a variety of other basic constitutional guarantees, infringements of which are subject to more searching judicial review.... These rights include some, like the right of access to the courts at issue in this case, that are protected by the Due Process Clause of the Fourteenth Amendment. The Due Process Clause and the Confrontation Clause of the Sixth Amendment, as applied to the States via the Fourteenth Amendment, both guarantee to a criminal defendant such as respondent Lane the "right to be present at all stages of the trial where his absence might frustrate the fairness of the proceedings." Faretta v. California, 422 U.S. 806, 819, n.15 (1975). The Due Process Clause also requires the States to afford certain civil litigants a "meaningful opportunity to be heard" by removing obstacles to their full participation in judicial proceedings. Boddie v. Connecticut, 401 U.S. 371, 379 (1971); M.L.B. v. S. L. J., 519 U.S. 102 (1996). We have held that the Sixth Amendment guarantees to criminal defendants the right to trial by a jury composed of a fair cross section of the community, noting that the exclusion of "identifiable segments playing major roles in the community cannot be squared with the constitutional concept of jury trial." Taylor v. Louisiana, 419 U.S. 522, 530 (1975). And, finally, we have recognized that members of the public have a right of access to criminal proceedings secured by the First Amendment. Press–Enterprise Co. v. Superior Court of Cal., County of Riverside, 478 U.S. 1, 8–15 (1986).

... While § 5 authorizes Congress to enact reasonably prophylactic remedial legislation, the appropriateness of the remedy depends on the gravity of the harm it seeks to prevent. "Difficult and intractable problems often require powerful remedies," *Kimel*, 528 U.S. at 88, but it is also true that "[s]trong measures appropriate to address one harm may be an unwarranted response to another, lesser one[]"....

It is not difficult to perceive the harm that Title II is designed to address. Congress enacted Title II against a backdrop of pervasive unequal treatment in the administration of state services and programs, including systematic deprivations of fundamental rights. For example, "[a]s of 1979, most States ... categorically disqualified 'idiots' from voting, without regard to individual capacity." The majority of these laws remain on the books, and have been the subject of legal challenge as recently as 2001. Similarly, a number of States have prohibited and continue to prohibit persons with disabilities from engaging in activities such as marrying and serving as jurors. The historical experience that Title II reflects is also documented in this Court's cases, which have identified unconstitutional treatment of disabled persons by state agencies in a

[margin note: rational basis review for disabilities]

variety of settings, including unjustified commitment, . . . the abuse and neglect of persons committed to state mental health hospitals, . . . and irrational discrimination in zoning decisions. . . . The decisions of other courts, too, document a pattern of unequal treatment in the administration of a wide range of public services, programs, and activities, including the penal system, public education, and voting. Notably, these decisions also demonstrate a pattern of unconstitutional treatment in the administration of justice.

This pattern of disability discrimination persisted despite several federal and state legislative efforts to address it. In the deliberations that led up to the enactment of the ADA, Congress identified important shortcomings in existing laws that rendered them "inadequate to address the pervasive problems of discrimination that people with disabilities are facing." . . .

With respect to the particular services at issue in this case, Congress learned that many individuals, in many States across the country, were being excluded from courthouses and court proceedings by reason of their disabilities. A report before Congress showed that some 76% of public services and programs housed in state-owned buildings were inaccessible to and unusable by persons with disabilities, even taking into account the possibility that the services and programs might be restructured or relocated to other parts of the buildings. U.S. Civil Rights Commission, Accommodating the Spectrum of Individual Abilities 39 (1983). Congress itself heard testimony from persons with disabilities who described the physical inaccessibility of local courthouses. Oversight Hearing on H.R. 4468 before the House Subcommittee on Select Education of the Committee on Education and Labor, 100th Cong., 2d Sess., 40–41, 48 (1988). And its appointed task force heard numerous examples of the exclusion of persons with disabilities from state judicial services and programs, including exclusion of persons with visual impairments and hearing impairments from jury service, failure of state and local governments to provide interpretive services for the hearing impaired, failure to permit the testimony of adults with developmental disabilities in abuse cases, and failure to make courtrooms accessible to witnesses with physical disabilities. . . .[16]

. . . Just last Term in *Hibbs*, we approved the family-care leave provision of the FMLA as valid § 5 legislation based primarily on evidence of disparate provision of parenting leave, little of which concerned unconstitutional state conduct. . . . We explained that because the FMLA was targeted at sex-based classifications, which are subject to a heightened standard of judicial scrutiny, "it was easier for Congress to show a pattern of state constitutional violations" than in *Garrett* or *Kimel*, both of which concerned legislation that targeted classifications subject to rational-basis review. . . . Title II is aimed at the enforcement of a variety of basic rights, including the right of access to the courts at issue in this case, that call for a standard of judicial review at least as searching, and in some cases more searching, than the standard that applies to

---

16. The Chief Justice dismisses as "irrelevant" the portions of this evidence that concern the conduct of nonstate governments. . . . This argument rests on the mistaken' premise that a valid exercise of Congress' § 5 power must always be predicated solely on evidence of constitutional violations by the States themselves. To operate on that premise in this case would be particularly inappropriate because this case concerns the provision of judicial services, an area in which local governments are typically treated as "arm [s] of the State" for Eleventh

Amendment purposes . . . and thus enjoy precisely the same immunity from unconsented suit as the States. . . .

In any event, our cases have recognized that evidence of constitutional violations on the part of nonstate governmental actors is relevant to the § 5 inquiry. . . . Moreover, . . . [in *Hibbs*] the evidence before the Congress that enacted the FMLA related primarily to the practices of private-sector employers and the Federal Government. . . .

sex-based classifications. And in any event, the record of constitutional violations in this case—including judicial findings of unconstitutional state action, and statistical, legislative, and anecdotal evidence of the widespread exclusion of persons with disabilities from the enjoyment of public services—far exceeds the record in *Hibbs*.

. . .

V

The only question that remains is whether Title II is an appropriate response to this history and pattern of unequal treatment. At the outset, we must determine the scope of that inquiry. Title II . . . reaches a wide array of official conduct in an effort to enforce an equally wide array of constitutional guarantees. Petitioner urges us both to examine the broad range of Title II's applications all at once, and to treat that breadth as a mark of the law's invalidity. According to petitioner, the fact that Title II applies not only to public education and voting-booth access but also to seating at state-owned hockey rinks indicates that Title II is not appropriately tailored to serve its objectives. But nothing in our case law requires us to consider Title II, with its wide variety of applications, as an undifferentiated whole. Whatever might be said about Title II's other applications, the question presented in this case is not whether Congress can validly subject the States to private suits for money damages for failing to provide reasonable access to hockey rinks, or even to voting booths, but whether Congress had the power under § 5 to enforce the constitutional right of access to the courts. Because we find that Title II unquestionably is valid § 5 legislation as it applies to the class of cases implicating the accessibility of judicial services, we need go no further. . . .

Congress' chosen remedy for the pattern of exclusion and discrimination described above, Title II's requirement of program accessibility, is congruent and proportional to its object of enforcing the right of access to the courts. The unequal treatment of disabled persons in the administration of judicial services has a long history, and has persisted despite several legislative efforts to remedy the problem of disability discrimination. . . .

The remedy Congress chose is nevertheless a limited one. Recognizing that failure to accommodate persons with disabilities will often have the same practical effect as outright exclusion, Congress required the States to take reasonable measures to remove architectural and other barriers to accessibility. . . . But Title II does not require States to employ any and all means to make judicial services accessible to persons with disabilities, and it does not require States to compromise their essential eligibility criteria for public programs. It requires only "reasonable modifications" that would not fundamentally alter the nature of the service provided, and only when the individual seeking modification is otherwise eligible for the service. . . .

. . .

For these reasons, we conclude that Title II, as it applies to the class of cases implicating the fundamental right of access to the courts, constitutes a valid exercise of Congress' § 5 authority to enforce the guarantees of the Fourteenth Amendment. The judgment of the Court of Appeals is therefore affirmed.

It is so ordered.

Justice Souter, with whom Justice Ginsburg joins, concurring.

I join the Court's opinion subject to the same caveats about the Court's recent cases on the Eleventh Amendment and § 5 of the Fourteenth that I noted in *Hibbs*, 538 U.S. at 740 (Souter, J. concurring).

Although I concur in the Court's approach applying the congruence-and-proportionality criteria to Title II of the Americans with Disabilities Act of 1990 as a guarantee of access to courts and related rights, I note that if the Court engaged in a more expansive enquiry as the Chief Justice suggests, ... the evidence to be considered would underscore the appropriateness of action under § 5 to address the situation of disabled individuals before the courts, for that evidence would show that the judiciary itself has endorsed the basis for some of the very discrimination subject to congressional remedy under § 5. Buck v. Bell, 274 U.S. 200 (1927), was not grudging in sustaining the constitutionality of the once-pervasive practice of involuntarily sterilizing those with mental disabilities. See id. at 207 ("It is better for all the world, if instead of waiting to execute degenerate offspring for crime, or to let them starve for their imbecility, society can prevent those who are manifestly unfit from continuing their kind.... Three generations of imbeciles are enough"). Laws compelling sterilization were often accompanied by others indiscriminately requiring institutionalization, and prohibiting certain individuals with disabilities from marrying, from voting, from attending public schools, and even from appearing in public. One administrative action along these lines was judicially sustained in part as a justified precaution against the very sight of a child with cerebral palsy, lest he "produc[e] a depressing and nauseating effect" upon others....

... In sustaining the application of Title II today, the Court takes a welcome step away from the judiciary's prior endorsement of blunt instruments imposing legal handicaps.

Justice Ginsburg, with whom Justice Souter and Justice Breyer join, concurring.

For the reasons stated by the Court, and mindful of Congress' objective in enacting the Americans with Disabilities Act—the elimination or reduction of physical and social structures that impede people with some present, past, or perceived impairments from contributing, according to their talents, to our Nation's social, economic, and civic life—I join the Court's opinion.

The ... ADA ... is a measure expected to advance equal-citizenship stature for persons with disabilities....

. . .

Legislation calling upon all government actors to respect the dignity of individuals with disabilities is entirely compatible with our Constitution's commitment to federalism, properly conceived. It seems to me not conducive to a harmonious federal system to require Congress, before it exercises authority under § 5 of the Fourteenth Amendment, essentially to indict each State for disregarding the equal-citizenship stature of persons with disabilities.... Members of Congress are understandably reluctant to condemn their own States as constitutional violators, complicit in maintaining the isolated and unequal status of persons with disabilities. I would not disarm a National Legislature for resisting an adversarial approach to lawmaking better suited to the courtroom.

Chief Justice Rehnquist, with whom Justice Kennedy and Justice Thomas join, dissenting.

... Because today's decision is irreconcilable with *Garrett* and the well-established principles it embodies, I dissent.

. . .

In *Garrett*, we conducted the three-step inquiry first enunciated in *City of Boerne* to determine whether Title I of the ADA satisfied the congruence-and-proportionality test. A faithful application of that test to Title II reveals that it too " 'substantively redefine[s],' " rather than permissibly enforces, the rights protected by the Fourteenth Amendment....

The first step is to "identify with some precision the scope of the constitutional right at issue." ...

... In this case, the task of identifying the scope of the relevant constitutional protection is ... difficult because Title II purports to enforce a panoply of constitutional rights of disabled persons: not only the equal protection right against irrational discrimination, but also certain rights protected by the Due Process Clause.... However, because the Court ultimately upholds Title II "as it applies to the class of cases implicating the fundamental right of access to the courts," ... the proper inquiry focuses on the scope of those due process rights. The Court cites four access-to-the-courts rights that Title II purportedly enforces: (1) the right of the criminal defendant to be present at all critical stages of the trial, ... ; (2) the right of litigants to have a "meaningful opportunity to be heard" in judicial proceedings, ... ; (3) the right of the criminal defendant to trial by a jury composed of a fair cross section of the community, ... ; and (4) the public right of access to criminal proceedings....

Having traced the "metes and bounds" of the constitutional rights at issue, the next step in the congruence-and-proportionality inquiry requires us to examine whether Congress "identified a history and pattern" of violations of these constitutional rights by the States with respect to the disabled.... This step is crucial to determining whether Title II is a legitimate attempt to remedy or prevent actual constitutional violations by the States or an illegitimate attempt to rewrite the constitutional provisions it purports to enforce.... But the majority identifies nothing in the legislative record that shows Congress was responding to widespread violations of the due process rights of disabled persons.

Rather than limiting its discussion of constitutional violations to the due process rights on which it ultimately relies, the majority sets out on a wide-ranging account of societal discrimination against the disabled.... This digression recounts historical discrimination against the disabled through institutionalization laws, restrictions on marriage, voting, and public education, conditions in mental hospitals, and various other forms of unequal treatment in the administration of public programs and services. Some of this evidence would be relevant if the Court were considering the constitutionality of the statute as a whole; but the Court rejects that approach in favor of a narrower "as-applied" inquiry. We discounted much the same type of outdated, generalized evidence in *Garrett* as unsupportive of Title I's ban on employment discrimination....

Even if it were proper to consider this broader category of evidence, much of it does not concern unconstitutional action by the States. The bulk of the Court's evidence concerns discrimination by nonstate governments, rather than the States themselves.... Therefore, even outside the "access to the courts" context, the Court identifies few, if any, constitutional violations perpetrated by the States against disabled persons.

With respect to the due process "access to the courts" rights on which the Court ultimately relies, Congress' failure to identify a pattern of actual constitutional violations by the States is even more striking. Indeed, there is nothing in the legislative record or statutory findings to indicate that disabled persons were systematically denied the right to be present at criminal trials, denied the meaningful opportunity to be heard in civil cases, unconstitutionally excluded from jury service, or denied the right to attend criminal trials.

. . .

The near-total lack of actual constitutional violations in the congressional record is reminiscent of *Garrett*, wherein we found that the same type of minimal anecdotal evidence "f[e]ll far short of even suggesting the pattern of unconstitutional [state action] on which § 5 legislation must be based." . . .

. . .

The third step of our congruence-and-proportionality inquiry removes any doubt as to whether Title II is valid § 5 legislation. At this stage, we ask whether the rights and remedies created by Title II are congruent and proportional to the constitutional rights it purports to enforce and the record of constitutional violations adduced by Congress. . . .

. . .

. . . By requiring special accommodation and the elimination of programs that have a disparate impact on the disabled, Title II prohibits far more state conduct than does the equal protection ban on irrational discrimination. We invalidated Title I's similar requirements in *Garrett*, observing that "[i]f special accommodations for the disabled are to be required, they have to come from positive law and not through the Equal Protection Clause." . . .

The majority, however, claims that Title II also vindicates fundamental rights protected by the Due Process Clause—in addition to access to the courts—that are subject to heightened Fourteenth Amendment scrutiny [such as voting, the right to move to a new jurisdiction, and the right to marriage and procreation.]. . . . But Title II is not tailored to provide prophylactic protection of these rights; instead, it applies to any service, program, or activity provided by any entity. Its provisions affect transportation, health, education, and recreation programs, among many others, all of which are accorded only rational-basis scrutiny under the Equal Protection Clause. A requirement of accommodation for the disabled at a state-owned amusement park or sports stadium, for example, bears no permissible prophylactic relationship to enabling disabled persons to exercise their fundamental constitutional rights. . . . Viewed as a whole, then, there is little doubt that Title II of the ADA does not validly abrogate state sovereign immunity.

The majority concludes that Title II's massive overbreadth can be cured by considering the statute only "as it applies to the class of cases implicating the accessibility of judicial services." . . . I have grave doubts about importing an "as applied" approach into the § 5 context. While the majority is of course correct that this Court normally only considers the application of a statute to a particular case, the proper inquiry under *City of Boerne* and its progeny is somewhat different. In applying the congruence-and-proportionality test, we ask whether Congress has attempted to statutorily redefine the constitutional rights protected by the Fourteenth Amendment. This question can only be answered by measuring the breadth of a statute's coverage against the scope of the constitutional rights it purports to enforce and the record of violations it purports to remedy.

In conducting its as-applied analysis, however, the majority posits a hypothetical statute, never enacted by Congress, that applies only to courthouses. The effect is to rig the congruence-and-proportionality test by artificially constricting the scope of the statute to closely mirror a recognized constitutional right. But Title II is not susceptible of being carved up in this manner; it applies indiscriminately to all "services," "programs," or "activities" of any "public entity." . . .

Our § 5 precedents do not support this as-applied approach. In each case, we measured the full breadth of the statute or relevant provision that Congress enacted against the scope of the constitutional right it purported to enforce. If we had arbitrarily constricted the scope of the statutes to match the scope of a core constitutional right, those cases might have come out differently. In *Garrett*, for example, Title I might have been upheld "as applied" to irrational employment discrimination. . . .

. . .

For the foregoing reasons, I respectfully dissent.

Justice Scalia, dissenting.

. . .

I joined the Court's opinion in *Boerne* with some misgiving. I have generally rejected tests based on such malleable standards as "proportionality," because they have a way of turning into vehicles for the implementation of individual judges' policy preferences. . . . Even so, I signed on to the "congruence and proportionality" test in *Boerne*, and adhered to it in later cases. . . .

But these cases were soon followed by [*Hibbs*], in which the Court held that the Family and Medical Leave Act of 1993 . . . , which required States to provide their employees up to 12 work weeks of unpaid leave (for various purposes) annually, was "congruent and proportional to its remedial object [of preventing sex discrimination], and can be understood as responsive to, or designed to prevent, unconstitutional behavior." . . . And now we have today's decision, holding that Title II of the ADA is congruent and proportional to the remediation of constitutional violations, in the face of what seems to me a compelling demonstration of the opposite by the Chief Justice's dissent.

I yield to the lessons of experience. The "congruence and proportionality" standard, like all such flabby tests, is a standing invitation to judicial arbitrariness and policy-driven decisionmaking. Worse still, it casts this Court in the role of Congress's taskmaster. Under it, the courts (and ultimately this Court) must regularly check Congress's homework to make sure that it has identified sufficient constitutional violations to make its remedy congruent and proportional. As a general matter, we are ill advised to adopt or adhere to constitutional rules that bring us into constant conflict with a coequal branch of Government. And when conflict is unavoidable, we should not come to do battle with the United States Congress armed only with a test ("congruence and proportionality") that has no demonstrable basis in the text of the Constitution and cannot objectively be shown to have been met or failed. . . .

I would replace "congruence and proportionality" with another test—one that provides a clear, enforceable limitation supported by the text of § 5. Section 5 grants Congress the power "*to enforce*, by appropriate legislation," the other provisions of the Fourteenth Amendment. U.S. Const., Amdt. 14 (emphasis added). . . . [O]ne does not, within any normal meaning of the term, "enforce" a prohibition by issuing a still broader prohibition directed to the same end. One does not, for example, "enforce" a 55–mile-per-hour speed limit by imposing a 45–mile-per-hour speed limit—even though that is indeed directed to the same end of automotive safety and will undoubtedly result in many fewer violations of the 55–mile-per-hour limit. And one does not "enforce" the right of access to the courts at issue in this case ... by requiring that disabled persons be provided access to all of the "services, programs, or activities" furnished or conducted by the State.... That is simply not what the power to enforce means—or ever meant. The 1860 edition of Noah Webster's American Dictionary of the English Language, current when the Fourteenth Amendment was adopted, defined "enforce" as: "To put in execution; to cause to take effect; as, to enforce the laws." Id., at 396. See also J. Worcester, Dictionary of the English Language 484 (1860) ("To put in force; to cause to be applied or executed; as, 'To enforce a law' "). Nothing in § 5 allows Congress to go beyond the provisions of the Fourteenth Amendment to proscribe, prevent, or "remedy" conduct that does not itself violate any provision of the Fourteenth Amendment. So-called "prophylactic legislation" is reinforcement rather than enforcement.

. . .

The major impediment to the approach I have suggested is stare decisis. A lot of water has gone under the bridge since *Morgan*, and many important and well-accepted measures, such as the Voting Rights Act, assume the validity of *Morgan* and *South Carolina*....

However, *South Carolina* and *Morgan*, all of our later cases except *Hibbs* that give an expansive meaning to "enforce" in § 5 of the Fourteenth Amendment, and all of our earlier cases that even suggest such an expansive meaning in dicta, involved congressional measures that were directed exclusively against, or were used in the particular case to remedy, racial discrimination....

Giving § 5 more expansive scope with regard to measures directed against racial discrimination by the States accords to practices that are distinctively violative of the principal purpose of the Fourteenth Amendment a priority of attention that this Court envisioned from the beginning, and that has repeatedly been reflected in our opinions. In the Slaughter–House Cases, 16 Wall. 36 (1873), the Court's first confrontation with the Fourteenth Amendment, we said the following with respect to the Equal Protection Clause:

> "We doubt very much whether any action of a State not directed by way of discrimination against the negroes as a class, or on account of their race, will ever be held to come within the purview of this provision. It is so clearly a provision for that race and that emergency, that a strong case would be necessary for its application to any other." ...

. . .

Thus, principally for reasons of stare decisis, I shall henceforth apply the permissive *McCulloch* standard to congressional measures designed to remedy racial discrimination by the States. I would not, however, abandon the requirement that Congress may impose prophylactic § 5 legislation only upon those particular States in which there has been an identified history of relevant constitutional violations.... I would also adhere to the requirement that the prophylactic remedy predicated upon such state violations must be directed against the States or state actors rather than the public at large.... When those requirements have been met, however, I shall leave it to Congress, under constraints no tighter than those of the Necessary and Proper Clause, to decide what measures are appropriate under § 5 to prevent or remedy racial discrimination by the States.

I shall also not subject to "congruence and proportionality" analysis congressional action under § 5 that is not directed to racial discrimination. Rather, I shall give full effect to that action when it consists of "enforcement" of the provisions of the Fourteenth Amendment, within the broad but not unlimited meaning of that term I have described above. When it goes beyond enforcement to prophylaxis, however, I shall consider it ultra vires. The present legislation is plainly of the latter sort.

Requiring access for disabled persons to all public buildings cannot remotely be considered a means of "enforcing" the Fourteenth Amendment.... For these reasons, I respectfully dissent from the judgment of the Court.

Justice Thomas, dissenting.

I join the Chief Justice's dissent.... Because I joined the dissent in [*Hibbs*], and continue to believe that *Hibbs* was wrongly decided, I write separately only to disavow any reliance on *Hibbs* in reaching this conclusion.

Dickerson v. United States

530 U.S. 428, 120 S.Ct. 2326, 147 L.Ed.2d 405 (2000).

Chief Justice Rehnquist delivered the opinion of the Court.

In Miranda v. Arizona, 384 U.S. 436 (1966), we held that certain warnings must be given before a suspect's statement made during custodial interrogation could be admitted in evidence. In the wake of that decision, Congress enacted 18 U.S.C. § 3501, which in essence laid down a rule that the admissibility of such statements should turn only on whether or not they were voluntarily made. We hold that *Miranda*, being a constitutional decision of this Court, may not be in effect overruled by an Act of Congress, and we decline to overrule *Miranda* ourselves. We therefore hold that *Miranda* and its progeny in this Court govern the admissibility of statements made during custodial interrogation in both state and federal courts.

Petitioner Dickerson was indicted for bank robbery, conspiracy to commit bank robbery, and using a firearm in the course of committing a crime of violence, all in violation of the applicable provisions of Title 18 of the United States Code. Before trial, Dickerson moved to suppress a statement he had made at a Federal Bureau of Investigation field office, on the grounds that he had not received "Miranda warnings" before being interrogated. The District Court granted his motion ... [T]he United States Court of Appeals for the Fourth Circuit ... reversed ... It [held] that § 3501 ... was satisfied in this case. It then concluded that our decision in *Miranda* was not a constitutional holding, and that therefore Congress could by statute have the final say on the question of admissibility.

... [W]e ... reverse.

. . .

In *Miranda*, we ... concluded that the coercion inherent in custodial interrogation blurs the line between voluntary and involuntary statements, and thus heightens the risk that an individual will not be "accorded his privilege under the Fifth Amendment ... not to be compelled to incriminate himself.".... Accordingly, we laid down "concrete constitutional guidelines for law enforcement agencies and courts to follow." ... Those guidelines established that the admissibility in evidence of any statement given during custodial interrogation of a suspect would depend on whether the police provided the suspect with four warnings. . . .

Two years after *Miranda* was decided, Congress enacted § 3501. That section provides, in relevant part:

"(a) In any criminal prosecution brought by the United States or by the District of Columbia, a confession . . . shall be admissible in evidence if it is voluntarily given. Before such confession is received in evidence, the trial judge shall, out of the presence of the jury, determine any issue as to voluntariness. If the trial judge determines that the confession was voluntarily made it shall be admitted in evidence and the trial judge shall permit the jury to hear relevant evidence on the issue of voluntariness and shall instruct the jury to give such weight to the confession as the jury feels it deserves under all the circumstances.

"(b) The trial judge in determining the issue of voluntariness shall take into consideration all the circumstances surrounding the giving of the confession, including (1) the time elapsing between arrest and arraignment of the defendant making the confession, if it was made after arrest and before arraignment, (2) whether such defendant knew the nature of the offense with which he was charged or of which he was suspected at the time of making the confession, (3) whether or not such defendant was advised or knew that he was not required to make any statement and that any such statement could be used against him, (4) whether or not such defendant had been advised prior to questioning of his right to the assistance of counsel; and (5) whether or not such defendant was without the assistance of counsel when questioned and when giving such confession.

"The presence or absence of any of the above-mentioned factors to be taken into consideration by the judge need not be conclusive on the issue of voluntariness of the confession."

. . . Congress intended by its enactment to overrule *Miranda*. . . . [W]e must address whether Congress has constitutional authority to thus supersede *Miranda*. If Congress has such authority, § 3501's totality-of-the-circumstances approach must prevail over *Miranda*'s requirement of warnings; if not, that section must yield to *Miranda*'s more specific requirements.

. . . This Court has supervisory authority over the federal courts, and we may use that authority to prescribe rules of evidence and procedure that are binding in those tribunals. . . . Congress retains the ultimate authority to modify or set aside any judicially created rules of evidence and procedure that are not required by the Constitution.

But Congress may not legislatively supersede our decisions interpreting and applying the Constitution. See, e.g., City of Boerne v. Flores . . . This case therefore turns on whether the *Miranda* Court announced a constitutional rule or merely exercised its supervisory authority to regulate evidence in the absence of congressional direction. . . .

. . . [F]irst and foremost of the factors . . . [supporting the conclusion] that *Miranda* is a constitutional decision—is that both *Miranda* and two of its companion cases applied the rule to proceedings in state courts . . . [W]e do not hold a supervisory power over the courts of the several States. . . . With respect to proceedings in state courts, our "authority is limited to enforcing the commands of the United States Constitution." . . .

The *Miranda* opinion itself begins by stating that the Court granted certiorari "to explore some facets of the problems . . . of applying the privilege against self-incrimination to in-custody interrogation, and to give concrete constitutional guidelines for law enforcement agencies and courts to follow.''.... In fact, the majority opinion is replete with statements indicating that the majority thought it was announcing a constitutional rule. Indeed, the Court's ultimate conclusion was that the unwarned confessions obtained in the four cases before the Court in *Miranda* "were obtained from the defendant under circumstances that did not meet constitutional standards for protection of the privilege." ...

Additional support for our conclusion that *Miranda* is constitutionally based is found in the *Miranda* Court's invitation for legislative action to protect the constitutional right against coerced self-incrimination. ... [T]he *Miranda* Court concluded that, "[i]n order to combat these pressures and to permit a full opportunity to exercise the privilege against self-incrimination, the accused must be adequately and effectively appraised of his rights and the exercise of those rights must be fully honored." ... However, the Court ... opined that the Constitution would not preclude legislative solutions that differed from the prescribed *Miranda* warnings but which were "at least as effective in apprising accused persons of their right of silence and in assuring a continuous opportunity to exercise it."....

. . .

... [T]he court-invited amicus curiae contends that the section complies with the requirement that a legislative alternative to *Miranda* be equally as effective in preventing coerced confessions. See Brief for Paul G. Cassell as Amicus Curiae. We agree with the amicus' contention that there are more remedies available for abusive police conduct than there were at the time *Miranda* was decided.... But we do not agree that these additional measures supplement § 3501's protections sufficiently to meet the constitutional minimum. *Miranda* requires procedures that will warn a suspect in custody of his right to remain silent and which will assure the suspect that the exercise of that right will be honored. ... As discussed above, § 3501 explicitly eschews a requirement of pre-interrogation warnings in favor of an approach that looks to the administration of such warnings as only one factor in determining the voluntariness of a suspect's confession. The additional remedies cited by amicus do not, in our view, render them, together with § 3501 an adequate substitute for the warnings required by *Miranda*.

The dissent argues that it is judicial overreaching for this Court to hold § 3501 unconstitutional unless we hold that the *Miranda* warnings are required by the Constitution, in the sense that nothing else will suffice to satisfy constitutional requirements. But we need not go farther than *Miranda* to decide this case. In *Miranda*, the Court noted that reliance on the traditional totality-of-the-circumstances test raised a risk of overlooking an involuntary custodial confession, ... , a risk that the Court found unacceptably great when the confession is offered in the case in chief to prove guilt. The Court therefore concluded that something more than the totality test was necessary. ...

Whether or not we would agree with *Miranda*'s reasoning and its resulting rule, were we addressing the issue in the first instance, the principles of *stare decisis* weigh heavily against overruling it now. ...

We do not think there is such justification for overruling *Miranda*. *Miranda* has become embedded in routine police practice to the point where the warnings have become part of our national culture. ... [O]ur subsequent cases have reduced the impact of the *Miranda* rule on legitimate law enforcement while reaffirming the decision's core ruling that unwarned statements may not be used as evidence in the prosecution's case in chief.

The disadvantage of the *Miranda* rule is that statements which may be by no means involuntary, made by a defendant who is aware of his "rights," may nonetheless be excluded and a guilty defendant go free as a result. But experience suggests that the totality-of-the-circumstances test which § 3501 seeks to revive is more difficult than *Miranda* for law enforcement officers to conform to, and for courts to apply in a consistent manner. . . .

In sum, we conclude that *Miranda* announced a constitutional rule that Congress may not supersede legislatively. . . . [W]e decline to overrule *Miranda* ourselves. The judgment of the Court of Appeals is therefore

Reversed.

Justice Scalia, with whom Justice Thomas joins, dissenting.

. . . [T]oday's decision is not a reaffirmation of *Miranda*, but a radical revision of the most significant element of *Miranda* (as of all cases): the rationale that gives it a permanent place in our jurisprudence.

Marbury v. Madison, 1 Cranch 137 (1803), held that an Act of Congress will not be enforced by the courts if what it prescribes violates the Constitution of the United States. . . . One will search today's opinion in vain, however, for a statement . . . that what 18 U.S.C. § 3501 prescribes . . . violates the Constitution. The reason the statement does not appear is . . . that Justices whose votes are needed to compose today's majority are on record as believing that a violation of Miranda is not a violation of the Constitution. . . . And so, to justify today's agreed-upon result, the Court must adopt a significant new, if not entirely comprehensible, principle of constitutional law. As the Court chooses to describe that principle, statutes of Congress can be disregarded, not only when what they prescribe violates the Constitution, but when what they prescribe contradicts a decision of this Court that "announced a constitutional rule." . . . [T]he only thing that can possibly mean in the context of this case is that this Court has the power, not merely to apply the Constitution but to expand it, imposing what it regards as useful "prophylactic" restrictions upon Congress and the States. That is an immense and frightening antidemocratic power, and it does not exist.

. . . [The Court cannot say that] custodial interrogation that is not preceded by *Miranda* warnings or their equivalent violates the Constitution of the United States . . . because a majority of the Court does not believe it. The Court therefore acts in plain violation of the Constitution when it denies effect to this Act of Congress.

I

. . .

It was once possible to characterize the so-called *Miranda* rule as resting (however implausibly) upon the proposition that what the statute here before us permits—the admission at trial of un-Mirandized confessions—violates the Constitution. That is the fairest reading of the *Miranda* case itself. . . .

. . .

. . . [T]he decision in *Miranda*, if read as an explication of what the Constitution requires, is preposterous. There is, for example, simply no basis in reason for concluding that a response to the very first question asked, by a suspect who already knows all of the rights described in the *Miranda* warning,

is anything other than a volitional act. . . . And even if one assumes that the elimination of compulsion absolutely requires informing even the most knowledgeable suspect of his right to remain silent, it cannot conceivably require the right to have counsel present. . . .

. . .

II

[S]ince *Miranda* we have explicitly, and repeatedly, interpreted that decision as having announced, not the circumstances in which custodial interrogation runs afoul of the Fifth or Fourteenth Amendment, but rather only "prophylactic" rules that go beyond the right against compelled self-incrimination. . . . The Court has squarely concluded that it is possible—indeed not uncommon—for the police to violate *Miranda* without also violating the Constitution.

. . .

. . . In light of these cases, . . . it is simply no longer possible for the Court to conclude . . . that a violation of *Miranda*'s rules is a violation of the Constitution. . . . [T]hat is what is required before the Court may disregard a law of Congress governing the admissibility of evidence in federal court. . . .

. . .

Finally, the Court asserts that *Miranda* must be a "constitutional decision" announcing a "constitutional rule," and thus immune to congressional modification, because we have since its inception applied it to the States. . . . If . . . the argument is meant as an appeal to logic rather than stare decisis, it is a classic example of begging the question . . .

III

There was available to the Court a means of reconciling the established proposition that a violation of *Miranda* does not itself offend the Fifth Amendment with the Court's assertion of a right to ignore the present statute. . . .

Petitioner and the United States contend that there is nothing at all exceptional, much less unconstitutional, about the Court's adopting prophylactic rules to buttress constitutional rights, and enforcing them against Congress and the States. . . .

. . .

. . . [W]hat the Court did in *Miranda* . . . is in fact extraordinary. That the Court has, on rare and recent occasion, repeated the mistake does not transform error into truth . . . The power with which the Court would endow itself under a "prophylactic" justification for *Miranda* goes far beyond what it has permitted Congress to do under authority of that text. Whereas we have insisted that congressional action under § 5 of the Fourteenth Amendment must be "congruent" with, and "proportional" to, a constitutional violation, see City of Boerne v. Flores, . . . the *Miranda* nontextual power to embellish confers authority to prescribe preventive measures against not only constitutionally prohibited compelled confessions, but also . . . foolhardy ones.

I applaud, therefore, the refusal of the Justices in the majority to enunciate this boundless doctrine of judicial empowerment . . . Since there is in fact no other principle that can reconcile today's judgment with the post-*Miranda* cases that the Court refuses to abandon, what today's decision will stand for

... is the power of the Supreme Court to write a prophylactic, extraconstitutional Constitution, binding on Congress and the States.

IV

Thus, while I agree with the Court that § 3501 cannot be upheld without also concluding that *Miranda* represents an illegitimate exercise of our authority to review state-court judgments, I do not share the Court's hesitation in reaching that conclusion. ...

. . .

FEDERALISM AND CONGRESSIONAL APPROVAL OF "UNCONSTITUTIONAL" STATE LAWS

A number of constitutional limitations—the contract clause of Article I, Section 10, and the privileges and immunities clause of Article IV, Section 2, for example—apply only as limitations on the states. Other constitutional limitations that restrict both the national government and the states do so in different ways. Despite the "incorporation" of equal protection standards into the fifth amendment, Congress can adopt policies for the treatment of aliens that would be unconstitutional if contained in state legislation.[1] Limits on state territorial jurisdiction, such as the rules under the due process clause of the fourteenth amendment concerning the scope of in personam jurisdiction of state courts,[2] will not apply to a national government with nationwide territorial jurisdiction.

In one context, it is clear beyond dispute that Congress can "consent" to state laws that would otherwise violate a constitutional limit applicable to the states, but inapplicable to the national government. By ordinary legislation, Congress can validate state laws that would be unconstitutional unreasonable burdens on interstate commerce.[3] The traditional explanation for the power to consent has been two-fold: the limitation on state power is not express, but an implication from Congressional power to regulate interstate commerce; the limitation stems from an assumption that, if Congress is silent, it is presumed that Congress desired an unburdened interstate market.[4] Notice that those explanations are inapplicable to other constitutional limitations on state power that are express, and not merely implied from the existence of federal power. Justice Rutledge's opinion for the Court in Prudential Ins. Co. v. Benjamin, 328 U.S. 408 (1946) stated, however, that the conventional explanations "did not go to the heart of the matter," and do not explain the power of Congress to consent to state laws unreasonably burdening commerce.

1. See Mathews v. Diaz, 426 U.S. 67 (1976), supra p. 908; Hampton v. Mow Sun Wong, 426 U.S. 88 (1976); Plyler v. Doe, 457 U.S. 202 (1982), supra p. 1086.

2. The Court described the inability of a state court to bind an absent defendant as stemming from the due process clause of the fourteenth amendment in Pennoyer v. Neff, 95 U.S. (5 Otto) 714, 733–734 (1878). Even before the adoption of the fourteenth amendment, however, the Court enforced limitations on state judicial jurisdiction without tying them to any particular clause of the constitution. See page 473, supra. Commerce clause limitations on state power have sometimes been concerned with the extraterritorial impact of state laws. See Baldwin v. G.A.F. Seelig, Inc., 294 U.S. 511 (1935). Most recent cases limiting state power to tax interstate business have relied more on limits of territorial power imposed by the due process clause of the fourteenth amendment than on the limitations imposed by the commerce clause.

3. These cases are discussed at pages 161–162, supra.

4. See Dowling, *Interstate Commerce and State Power—Revised Version,* 47 Colum.L.Rev. 547 (1947).

Benjamin involved the McCarran–Ferguson Act of 1945, which provided that "silence on the part of the Congress shall not be construed to impose any barrier" to state regulation or taxation of insurance.[5] The Court held that the Act validated discriminatory state taxes on out-of-state insurance companies that would otherwise violate the commerce clause. Justice Rutledge's opinion explained that:

> "The power of Congress over commerce exercised without reference to coordinated action of the states is not restricted ... by any limitation which forbids it to discriminate against interstate commerce and in favor of local trade.... This broad authority Congress may exercise alone [subject to constitutional limits on Congress' power], or in conjunction with coordinated action by the states, in which case limitations imposed for the preservation of their powers become inoperative and only those designed to forbid action altogether by any power or combination of powers in our governmental system remain effective.... Clear and gross must be the evil which would nullify such an exertion, one which could arise only by exceeding ... limitation[s] imposed by a constitutional provision or provisions designed and intended to outlaw the action entirely from our constitutional framework."

Does this mean that Congress can validate any state law, so long as Congress would have had the power to enact an identical or analogous law? For an argument along those lines, see W. Cohen, *Congressional Power to Validate Unconstitutional State Laws: A Forgotten Solution to an Old Enigma,* 35 Stan.L.Rev. 387 (1983).

In Metropolitan Life Insurance Co. v. Ward, 470 U.S. 869 (1985), supra page 1047, the Court held that a discriminatory tax identical to that in *Benjamin,* was unconstitutional as a violation of the equal protection clause. The Court concluded that Congress had not intended to validate laws that violated the due process or equal protection clause. If Congress had specifically provided that discriminatory taxes on out-of-state insurance companies were valid as against an equal protection challenge, would this have changed the outcome in *Ward*? For an argument that it would, see W. Cohen, *Federalism in Equality Clothing: A Comment on* Metropolitan Life Insurance Company v. Ward, 38 Stan.L.Rev. 1 (1985). Compare Northeast Bancorp, Inc. v. Board of Governors of the Federal Reserve System, 472 U.S. 159 (1985), supra page 1037 (state legislation excluding out-of-state banks, with Congressional permission, does not violate the equal protection clause).

Saenz v. Roe

526 U.S. 489, 119 S.Ct. 1518, 143 L.Ed.2d 689 (1999).

[The report in this case appears, supra page 1035.]

---

5. The Act was a response to the decision in United States v. South–Eastern Underwriters Ass'n, 322 U.S. 533 (1944).

*

PART IV

Constitutional Protection of Expression and Conscience

The first four chapters in this part provide a detailed look at issues of freedom of expression. Chapter 13 examines the definition of constitutionally protected speech, and focuses on doctrine dealing with prohibition of expression because of its content. Chapter 14 deals with government restriction that purports to control the time, place, or manner of speaking rather than the content of expression. Chapter 15 concerns indirect government restrictions on expression and the definition of peripheral first amendment rights. (Specific topics include the control of communicative conduct, compelled affirmation and disclosure, denial of government employment because of an employee's speech or association, denial of other government benefits, and freedom of political association.) Chapter 16 pulls together cases concerning the printed and electronic media. That chapter examines whether the guarantee of freedom of the press imposes restrictions on government independent of, and in addition to, those imposed by the guarantee of freedom of speech. The protection of religious conscience and conduct is reserved for Chapter 17.

CHAPTER 13

GOVERNMENTAL CONTROL OF THE CONTENT OF EXPRESSION

Introduction. This chapter focuses on the core problem in defining the contours of freedom of expression—the extent to which speech can be punished by government because of its content. Section 1 deals at length with speech advocating the violent overthrow of government. Section 2 is a deliberate digression, examining judicial techniques for avoiding decision whether speech can be controlled because of its content. This section examines the doctrine of prior restraint, and the doctrines of vagueness and overbreadth. Section 3 returns to the problem of content control, examining the Court's efforts to draw the distinction between protected and unprotected speech in four different contexts—defamation and privacy, obscenity, fighting words and offensive speech, and commercial speech.

SECTION 1. AN INTRODUCTION TO PROBLEMS OF CONTENT CONTROL OF SPEECH

A. HISTORICAL INTRODUCTION—THE STATUS OF FREE SPEECH UP TO THE 1920's

1. THE ENGLISH BACKGROUND

Freedom of thought and expression is taken so much as a matter of course in most western societies today that we are apt to forget how recently it has come to be accepted. As the distinguished English historian, J.B. Bury, emphasized in *A History of Freedom of Thought* (1913), "human societies (there are some brilliant exceptions) have been generally opposed to freedom of thought" and "it has taken centuries to persuade the most enlightened peoples that liberty to publish one's opinions and to discuss all questions is a good and not a bad thing" (Home University Library Ed., 1952, p. 2). This is due in part to the persistent inclination of people to cling to familiar and accepted opinion, and to dislike what is new, but other reasons are not difficult to discover.

Both the society and outlook of the Middle Ages were authoritarian; truth was divinely revealed and error was sin. Consequently to extirpate erroneous views was not only permissible but a high moral obligation and the unifying structure of the medieval Church provided the central authority for determining what was true and what was false. Thus the churchmen who in 1633 condemned Galileo to live the rest of his life in seclusion because he insisted that the earth was not the stationary center of the universe were only performing their duty as determined by the standards under which they had lived.[1]

---

1. This incident is told in detail in De Santillana, *The Crime of Galileo* (1955).

Even after the impact of the Renaissance and Reformation, the rebirth of learning, and the development of nation-states, the modern concept of freedom of thought was slow to develop. Diversity replaced the unity of the Middle Ages and the invention of the printing press brought a new and previously unequaled medium of communication. But on the whole, the dissenters and reformers sought only to establish a new brand of truth (their own) and did not recognize the value of general freedom of thought and speech as the means of arriving at truth.

The three centuries that elapsed between the appearance of the first book printed in England, by Caxton in 1476, and the Declaration of Independence in 1776 provide the immediate background of the American constitutional system, and the struggles of this period are particularly relevant in the area of freedom of thought and expression. They concerned two issues above all others, the separation of the English Church from that of Rome and the limitation of the prerogative of the Crown. Neither of these developments assured the freedom of the individual, but supplanted one religious establishment with another and made parliament supreme in areas that theretofore had been the province of the King. Dispute and domestic turmoil fomented discussion, as they always do, but the very limited freedom permitted to thought and speech is shown by the position of the press.

The invention of printing was almost as frightening to the mind of the fifteenth century as has been the discovery of atomic fission to the mind of the twentieth. The printing press, unless rigidly controlled, gave to dissident groups a powerful medium for "dangerous doctrine." No friend of the established order could view this situation with complacency at a time when religious truth, then an all-consuming subject, was deemed a matter of prior revelation and when political controversy was entering the crisis of the life-and-death struggle between King and Parliament. Three instruments for the legal control of discussion were used: (1) the concept of constructive treason; (2) the doctrine of seditious libel; and (3) the domination of the press through state monopoly and licensing.

The law of treason was based on the Statute 25 Edward III (1351), which defined the crime to include (1) compassing or imagining the King's death, (2) levying war against the King, or (3) adhering to his enemies. These three clauses, strictly construed, did not offer complete protection for the security of the monarch and of the state, or so it was believed. Hence there arose in the seventeenth century that judicial extension of the statute known as constructive treason. Compassing or imagining the King's death, like intending to wage war against him, being a mental state, could be proved only by overt acts. During the latter part of the seventeenth century the judges ruled that printed and sometimes spoken words could constitute overt acts. Thus John Twyn was convicted of treason and hanged, drawn, and quartered in 1664 for printing a book asserting that the King was accountable to the people who were entitled to revolt and take the government into their own hands.[2]

However, prosecutions for constructive treason were rare, only two printers being executed for the crime during the seventeenth century and one during the eighteenth.[3] A more effective method of suppression was available, the law of seditious libel, under which convictions ran into the hundreds. Conviction for this crime did not bring death but the penalties were often severe, including indefinite imprisonment and heavy fines. The law of seditious

2. This and similar cases are recounted in Siebert, *Freedom of the Press in England, 1476–1776* (1952), p. 267.

3. Siebert, op. cit., p. 365.

libel was developed in prosecutions before the Court of Star Chamber in the late sixteenth century, and when that body was abolished in 1641, the rules were taken over by the common law courts. The original theory of the offense was that the King was the fountainhead of justice and law whose acts were beyond popular criticism and that consequently it was wrong to censure him openly.[4] This doctrine was carried to such lengths that any reflection on the government in written or printed form might be held seditious libel. In 1704 Chief Justice Holt declared: "If people should not be called to account for possessing the people with an ill opinion of the government, no government can subsist. For it is very necessary for all governments that the people should have a good opinion of it. And nothing can be worse to any government than to endeavour to procure animosities as to the management of it; this has always been looked upon as a crime, and no government can be safe without it."[5]

As the eighteenth century progressed juries became less inclined to bring in verdicts of guilty in seditious libel cases. The judges then took the position that truth was no defense and that the only issue to be submitted to the jury was whether or not the defendant had published the allegedly seditious statements. Whether or not the statements constituted a libel was a matter of law to be determined by the judge. This trend was strenuously opposed by the distinguished English barrister Thomas Erskine, among others, who contended that the jury should be asked to bring in a general verdict of guilty or not guilty and to determine the defendant's criminal intent as in other criminal cases. The final result of this struggle was the passage in 1792 of Fox's Libel Act which established Erskine's views and gave the jury the power to render a general verdict on the whole issue in a libel case rather than merely on the issue of publication.

The French revolution brought a flurry of seditious libel cases, including the prosecution of Thomas Paine in 1792 for the publication of his "Rights of Man", but these prosecutions and the enactment of Fox's Libel Act marked the end of seditious libel as an instrument for the suppression of free speech in England.[6]

The third method of controlling expression of opinion, and on the whole the most effective one, was the elaborate system of printing monopolies and licensing. The authority to regulate the printing press in England was claimed by the Crown as one of its prerogative rights until the supremacy of Parliament was established by the revolution of 1688. Beginning with Henry VIII (1509–1547) the press was held in check through royal proclamations, licenses, patents of monopoly, orders in Council, and Star Chamber decrees. The first English index of prohibited "heretical and blasphemous" books was created by royal proclamation in 1529 and a licensing system for all books was established in 1538 by a proclamation designed to stamp out "seditious opinions" as well as heretical views. Licensors were appointed and no book could lawfully be printed and distributed without their prior approval. The system was modified and extended by the charter granted the Stationers Company in 1557. Members of the Company were given extensive control over the press by the provision of the Charter prohibiting all printing within the realm except by members of the Company or by those having special license from the Crown. The Company enforced both its own licensing ordinances and those issued by the Crown; all

---

4. Stephen, *History of Criminal Law in England* (1883) Vol. II, p. 299.

5. Rex v. Tutchin, 14 *State Trials*, p. 1095, quoted in Siebert, op. cit., p. 271.

6. The efforts of Thomas Erskine on behalf of liberalism in eighteenth century England, including his defense of Thomas Paine, are told in Lloyd Paul Stryker's biography of Erskine, *For the Defense* (1947).

member printers were required to obtain a license from the officers of the Company before printing any works and all presses were required to be registered with the Company.

The seventeenth century brought great changes to England in the form of the Puritan Revolution, the Commonwealth, and the triumph of Parliament through the revolution of 1688, but it did not bring freedom of the press, although eloquent voices, such as John Milton's,[7] were raised in its behalf. The licensing and other controls became less effective during this century, but the principal change was the shift in power from the Crown to Parliament. The objection of the Puritans to the control of the press was not so much to the control as to the fact that it was exercised by the King. With the fall of Charles I (1649) power passed to Parliament, and after the struggles of the Commonwealth (1649–1653), the Protectorate (1653–1659), and the Stuart restoration (1660–1689), the supremacy of Parliament was confirmed by the Revolution of 1688 and the Bill of Rights of 1689. However, that great document of English constitutional development did not contain any statement espousing general freedom of speech or the press. Its only provision on the subject merely stated: "That the freedom of speech and debates or proceedings in parliament ought not to be impeached or questioned in any court or place out of parliament". It was freedom of speech *in* Parliament, *not outside,* that was recognized.

The control of the press exercised by Parliament gradually relaxed during the century following the Bill of Rights. At the end of the seventeenth century the power of the Stationers Company was broken by the refusal of Parliament to continue its monopolies and special privileges. The methods of control then shifted from licensing to subsidization and taxation. The government resorted to subsidization in order to promote the opinion it desired; such literary figures as Defoe, Swift, Addison, Steele, and Fielding all engaged in political pamphleteering or journalism for which they were compensated in one form or another by the government or political leaders. In 1712, newspapers, pamphlets, advertisements, and paper were subjected to taxes which had the effect of suppressing many of the smaller ephemeral publications then sniping at the policies of the government. That this was the purpose of the taxes is suggested by the fact that books were exempted. These taxes were continued with varying degrees of effectiveness until the first half of the nineteenth century.

It was in the light of this background that Blackstone discussed freedom of thought and expression in his Commentaries, first published in 1765. It is important to note that he wrote at a time when licensing had been abandoned but the law of seditious libel was still in full vigor. His comments are as follows:

"The liberty of the press is indeed essential to the nature of a free state; but this consists in laying no *previous* restraints upon publications, and not

---

7. Milton had difficulties with the Stationers Company and the authorities over the publication of his pamphlets on divorce. He made his reply in Areopagitica (1644) which was a plea for the abolition of the licensing system. See Siebert, op. cit., p. 195. Milton's argument for freedom of the press cannot be given here, but the following sentences deserve quotation: "Where there is much desire to learn, there is of necessity will be much arguing, much writing, many opinions; for opinion in good men is but knowledge in the making.... And though all the winds of doctrine were let loose to play upon the earth, so Truth be in the field we do injuriously, by licensing and prohibiting, to misdoubt her strength. Let her and Falsehood grapple; whoever knew Truth put to the worse, in a free and open encounter? Her confuting is the best and surest suppressing...." However, apparently Milton had reservations about complete freedom of expression, for he also said he would not tolerate "popery and open superstition."? Furthermore that "which is impious or evil absolutely either against faith or manners no law can possibly permit, that intends not to unlaw itself...." *The Tradition of Freedom* (Mayer ed. 1957) pp. 26, 28, 29.

in freedom from censure for criminal matter when published. Every freeman has an undoubted right to lay what sentiments he pleases before the public: to forbid this, is to destroy the freedom of the press; but if he publishes what is improper, mischievous, or illegal, he must take the consequence of his own temerity. To subject the press to the restrictive power of a licenser, as was formerly done, both before and since the revolution, is to subject all freedom of sentiment to the prejudices of one man, and make him the arbitrary and infallible judge of all controverted points in learning, religion, and government. But to punish (as the law does at present) any dangerous or offensive writings, which, when published, shall on a fair and impartial trial be adjudged of a pernicious tendency, is necessary for the preservation of peace and good order, of government and religion, the only solid foundations of civil liberty. Thus the will of individuals is still left free; the abuse only of that free will is the object of legal punishment. Neither is any restraint hereby laid upon freedom of thought or inquiry: liberty of private sentiment is still left; the disseminating, or making public, of bad sentiments, destructive of the ends of society, is the crime which society corrects." (*Commentaries*, Book IV, pp. 151–152.)[8]

2. THE ADOPTION OF THE FIRST AMENDMENT AND THE CONTROVERSY OVER THE ALIEN AND SEDITION LAWS

(1) **The Original Intent.** Scholars have not been able to agree as to the purpose intended to be served by the first amendment. The basic question is whether it was intended as a charter of freedom or as no more than a determination that regulation of speech and press according to common law principles should be reserved to the states. The most recent scholarship supports the latter position. Leonard Levy concludes, for example, that the amendment was intended only as a restraint on Congress and not on the courts in enforcing the common law crime of seditious libel and "that the prohibition on Congress was motivated far less by a desire to give immunity to political expression than by a solicitude for states' rights and the federal principle. The primary purpose of the first amendment was to reserve to the states an exclusive authority, as far as legislation was concerned, in the field of speech and press." *Freedom of Press from Zenger v. Jefferson* lix (1966).[1] For a different view, see Brant, *The Bill of Rights* 223–236 (1965).

(2) **The Sedition Act.** The Sedition Act (part of a package known as the Alien and Sedition Laws), passed in 1798, made it a crime carrying imprisonment up to two years to write, utter, or publish "any false, scandalous and malicious writing ... against the government of the United States, or either house of the congress ... or the President ... with intent to defame [them] ... or to bring them ... into contempt or disrepute; or to excite against them ... the hatred of the good people of the United States, or to stir up sedition within the United States, or to excite any unlawful combinations therein, for opposing or resisting any law of the United States, or any act of the President of the

8. For a general review of the English background of our Bill of Rights, see Brant, *The Bill of Rights,* 3–219 (1965). See also Chafee, *How Human Rights Got into the Constitution* (1952) and *Three Human Rights in the Constitution of 1787* (1956). For a convenient collection of the documentary sources, see Perry and Cooper, *Sources of our Liberties* (1959).

1. Professor Levy in *Legacy of Suppression* (1960) reviews freedom of expression in early American history and concludes that in colonial America the people did not understand that freedom of thought means equal freedom for the other fellow, especially the one with hated ideas.

United States, done in pursuance of any such law, or of the powers vested in him by the constitution of the United States, or to resist, oppose, or defeat any such law or act...." The Act also provided that truth could be offered in defense and that the jury "shall have a right to determine the law and the fact, under the direction of the court, as in other cases." 1 Stat. 596 (1798).

The Sedition Act became the center of an enormous political controversy. Much attention was paid to the question whether it violated the first amendment. Levy contends that in this controversy there was a sudden breakthrough in libertarian thought with the Jeffersonian Republicans abandoning common law notions, arguing that free government required freedom of discussion, and asserting that only injurious conduct as manifested by deeds rather than words should be subjected to criminal punishment. *Freedom of the Press from Zenger to Jefferson* lxx–lxxix (1966).[2]

The Sedition Act by its own terms was to be in force only until March 3, 1801. One of Jefferson's first acts as President was to pardon all persons convicted under the act. Jefferson's own view of the first amendment, however, seemed to be one of federalism rather than freedom—at least in his role as President subject to scurrilous attacks in opposition newspapers. In 1803 he wrote a letter to Governor McKean of Pennsylvania referring to the licentiousness and lying of the press and then asserting: "This is a dangerous state of things, and the press ought to be restored to its credibility if possible. The restraints provided by the laws of the states are sufficient for this if applied. And I have therefore long thought that a few prosecutions of the most prominent offenders would have a wholesome effect in restoring the integrity of the presses. Not a general prosecution, for that would look like persecution: but a selected one. The paper I now inclose appears to me to offer as good an instance in every respect to make an example of, as can be selected."[3]

In 1806 a common law prosecution of Connecticut editors for libel of President Jefferson and the Congress was brought in the federal courts. That avenue for controlling the press was eliminated by the Supreme Court on appeal from the conviction in that case—not because the prosecution violated the first amendment, but rather on the general proposition that federal courts had no common law criminal jurisdiction. *United States v. Hudson* and *Goodwin*, 11 U.S. (7 Cranch) 32 (1812).[4]

3.   FREEDOM OF SPEECH AND PRESS IN THE NINETEENTH CENTURY

(1) **Introduction.** The Supreme Court did not begin to elaborate the protection accorded by the first amendment until the time of World War I. One should not draw from that fact the conclusion that there were no intrusions on freedom of speech and the press during this period of time. Developments in the states were unaffected by the first amendment. It was not until 1925 that the Court indicated that the fourteenth amendment had made the first applica-

---

2. More recently another author contends that the opposition to the Sedition Act was founded primarily on notions of states' rights rather than civil liberties with a primary motivation being the preservation of slavery. Berns, *Freedom of the Press and the Alien and Sedition Laws: A Reappraisal,* 1970 Sup.Ct.Rev. 109.

3. The letter is set out in Levy, *Freedom of the Press from Zenger to Jefferson* 364

(1966). In a letter to Abigail Adams in 1804 he also said: "While we deny that Congress have a right to control the freedom of the press, we have ever asserted the right of the States, and their exclusive right, to do so." Id. at 366, 367.

4. For the story of the case and Jefferson's somewhat belated disapproval of the prosecution, see Levy, *Jefferson and Civil Liberties—The Darker Side* 61 (1963).

ble to the states. But there were episodes involving federal control, particularly of the press, that were not subjected to testing by the Supreme Court.[1]

(2) **Punishment for Contempt of Court.** Under the Judiciary Act of 1789 which authorized federal courts to punish "all contempts of authority in any cause or hearing" before them, federal courts early asserted the authority to punish newspapers and others who criticized court decisions. In one early case a federal district judge, James H. Peck, had one Lawless imprisoned and disbarred for publishing a criticism of a decision by Peck which was on appeal. Lawless had powerful political friends and as a result impeachment proceedings were brought against Judge Peck. Peck was acquitted but immediately thereafter Congress amended the statute to limit the contempt power to "misbehaviour of any person or persons in the presence of the said courts, or so near thereto as to obstruct the administration of justice." The story of this episode is told in Nye v. United States, 313 U.S. 33, 45 (1941). As a result of the change in the statute the federal courts for a long time did not assert the power to punish critics. (State courts, however, began increasingly to use contempt to punish comments outside the court on the ground that they tended to interfere with the administration of justice.) In 1918 in Toledo Newspaper Co. v. United States, 247 U.S. 402 (1918), the Supreme Court interpreted the federal statute as not applying a geographical limitation on the contempt power of the federal courts and said that the test under the statute was "the character of the act done and its direct tendency to prevent and obstruct the discharge of judicial duty." The Court also rejected the claim that freedom of the press was violated when contempt was used to punish under this test. To state that proposition was to answer it, the Court said, "since it involves in its very statement the contention that the freedom of the press is the freedom to do wrong with impunity, and implies the right to frustrate and defeat the discharge of those governmental duties upon the performance of which the freedom of all, including that of the press, depends." By 1928 the judicial use of the contempt power to punish the press was widespread with most of the cases involving comments impugning the fairness, independence, or integrity of the judge.[2]

(3) **Control of Public Discussion of the Slavery Question.** Antislavery speech was regarded in the South as presenting a very real danger to the institution of slavery. While local dissenters were easily dealt with, the South also sought to exclude from the South any antislavery publications. In 1835 President Jackson asked Congress to enact a law prohibiting the circulation in the South through the mails "of incendiary publications intended to instigate the slaves to insurrection." Calhoun opposed this as a violation of freedom of the press, as being similar to the Sedition Act, but then he proposed a statute making it unlawful for a postmaster to receive and put into the mail any paper "touching the subject of slavery" and addressed to any person in a state which forbade by law the circulation of such materials. Neither of these bills passed but in practice postmasters in the South responded to local pressures and refused to deliver antislavery materials. By 1863 the Postmaster General was asserting the power—which was not challenged for a long time—to remove from the mails or prevent delivery of anti-Union writings or material considered to be obscene. This restraint on discussion of slavery carried over into Congress in which the House by a series of gag rules refused from 1836 to 1845 to entertain or to discuss any petition relating to slavery.[3]

---

1. For an excellent brief general account of this period see Nelson, *Freedom of the Press from Hamilton to the Warren Court* xix-xxxvii (1967).

2. For an account of the times, see Nelles & King, *Contempt by Publication in the United States,* 28 Colum.L.Rev. 401, 524 (1928).

3. For a fuller treatment of these epi-

(4) **The Civil War.** During the war there existed both a substantial amount of freedom by the press and a substantial amount of suppression by the military and the President. In one case President Lincoln went so far as to suppress newspapers and order trials of the publishers before military tribunals. For the documents in that case see Nelson, supra note 1, at 232–247. For a fuller account of the relationships between Lincoln and the press, see Randall, *Constitutional Problems Under Lincoln* 477–510 (1951).

(5) **Obscenity, and Control of the Mails.** In 1873 Congress passed the "Comstock law" providing for punishment of those who used the mails to transport obscene materials. State and federal prosecutions for obscenity reached new highs after the turn of the century.[4]

(6) **Civil and Criminal Libel under State Law.** Even if the Sedition Act controversy were viewed as excluding federal libel laws, states remained free of federal constitutional restraint. As late as 1922, the Supreme Court maintained that "neither the Fourteenth Amendment nor any other provision of the Constitution of the United States imposes upon the States any restrictions about 'freedom of speech'...." Prudential Ins. Co. v. Cheek, 259 U.S. 530, 543 (1922). While decisional law established truth as a complete defense in civil libel cases, the press was subject to practically strict liability for statements that were innocently false. Criminal libel laws often provided only a qualified defense of truth. Prosecutions for criminal libel in the state courts increased sharply in the later 1800's and stayed high through World War I. In 1918, a law review author could still assert:

"There is no such thing as an unlimited right to print whatever one may choose to print, regardless of its character and effect. Without law there can be no liberty, and freedom of the press does not mean irresponsibility for what is printed. All right-thinking men will join with Alexander Hamilton in his reprobation of 'the pestilential doctrine of an unchecked press,' and agree with him that ill-fated would be our country were this doctrine to prevail.

"It is for the state to say what publications are harmful, what use of the press is permissible. It would be an act of tyranny under normal conditions to deprive a citizen of the right to own a gun, but it is essential to public safety to prevent him from using it to the injury of others. So it is with the printing press, an instrument not less dangerous than a shot gun. It is not tyrannous nor inconsistent with the freedom of the press that its owner should be held accountable for any improper use he may make of it."[5]

B. WORLD WAR I AND THE POST-WAR YEARS: PENALIZING THE ADVOCACY OF THE OVERTHROW OF GOVERNMENT BY FORCE OR VIOLENCE

THE CONCERN FOR RADICAL SPEECH IN THE FIRST QUARTER OF THE TWENTIETH CENTURY

In the early years, principal free speech and press disputes had involved the role of newspapers and periodicals—typically those of a different political

sodes, see Berns, *Freedom of the Press and the Alien and Sedition Laws: A Reappraisal,* 1970, Sup.Ct.Rev. 109, 142, 150; Nelson, *Freedom of the Press from Hamilton to the Warren Court* xxii-xxvi (1967); Miller, *Arguing About Slavery: The Great Battle in the United States Congress* (1995).

4. See generally on this period, Nelson, *Freedom of the Press from Hamilton to the Warren Court* xxviii-xxxii (1967). For an account of postal censorship see Deutsch, *The Freedom of the Press and of the Mails,* 36 Mich.L.Rev. 703 (1938).

5. Long, *The Freedom of the Press,* 5 Va.L.Rev. 225, 228, 229 (1918).

persuasion than the party in power—in acting as critics of government. A rising concern with radicals began to surface at the turn of the century. Following President McKinley's assassination, the New York Criminal Anarchy law, which became a model for later state and federal legislation, made it a crime to belong to an organization that taught the doctrine that government should be overthrown by force of violence. The Immigration Act of 1903 provided that persons who believed in or advocated the overthrow of government by force and violence should be barred from entering the country, or deported if already here.

The fear of radicals was brought to a head, and fused with concern over enemy sympathizers, by the country's entry into the First World War.

In 1917 Congress passed the Espionage Act. This act made it a crime when the country was at war to "willfully make or convey false reports or false statements with intent to interfere" with the prosecution of the war or to promote the success of enemies, or willfully to "cause or attempt to cause" insubordination, disloyalty, mutiny, or refusal of duty, in the military or naval forces of the United States, or willfully to "obstruct the recruiting or enlistment service of the United States." Another provision of the act forbade the mailing of any material in violation of the provisions of the act or "advocating or urging treason, insurrection, or forcible resistance to any law of the United States...." In 1918 the statute was amended to make criminal the utterance of language "intended to bring the form of government of the United States into contempt, scorn, contumely, or disrepute." This 1918 version of the Sedition Act was repealed in 1921. There were nearly 2,000 prosecutions under the 1917 and 1918 Acts, many publications were excluded from the mails, and a series of challenges under the first amendment came quickly to the Supreme Court.[1]

The antiradical sentiment of the war years became more intense after the war ended. The country was plagued by rumors of radical takeover of government. There was labor unrest, and the news featured incidents of riots and bombings. Radical leaders were prosecuted under state laws modeled after the 1902 New York Criminal Anarchy Law. Some of these cases, too, reached the Supreme Court and renewed the judicial debate concerning the meaning of free speech in the context of attempts to punish the advocates of radical doctrines.[2]

MASSES PUBLISHING CO. v. PATTEN, 244 Fed. 535 (S.D.N.Y.1917). The publisher of a revolutionary journal called "The Masses" brought suit to enjoin the postmaster of New York from refusing to accept the magazine in the mails. The postmaster argued that the magazine was nonmailable under the provision of the espionage act making nonmailable any publication that violated the other provisions of the act. Part of the focus here was on the provisions of the act penalizing the willful causing of disaffection in the military services and the willful obstruction of recruitment. On these points judge learned hand construed the statute[3] as follows:

"The next phrase relied upon is that which forbids any one from willfully causing insubordination, disloyalty, mutiny, or refusal of duty in the military or naval forces of the United States. The defendant's position is that to arouse discontent and disaffection among the people with the prosecution of the war and with the draft tends to promote a mutinous and insubordinate temper

---

1. See generally Chafee, *Freedom of Speech* (1920) for an account of the period.

2. For a review of the cases from *Schenck* to *Whitney,* see Cover, *The Left, The Right and the First Amendment,* 40 Md. L.Rev. 349 (1981).

3. Hand's grant of an injunction, based on that construction, was reversed by the Court of Appeals. 246 Fed. 24 (2d Cir.1917).

among the troops. This, too, is true; men who become satisfied that they are engaged in an enterprise dictated by the unconscionable selfishness of the rich, and effectuated by a tyrannous disregard for the will of those who must suffer and die, will be more prone to insubordination than those who have faith in the cause and acquiesce in the means. Yet to interpret the word 'cause' so broadly would, as before, involve necessarily as a consequence the suppression of all hostile criticism, and of all opinion except what encouraged and supported the existing policies, or which fell within the range of temperate argument. It would contradict the normal assumption of democratic government that the suppression of hostile criticism does not turn upon the justice of its substance or the decency and propriety of its temper. Assuming that the power to repress such opinion may rest in Congress in the throes of a struggle for the very existence of the state, its exercise is so contrary to the use and wont of our people that only the clearest expression of such a power justifies the conclusion that it was intended.

"The defendant's position, therefore, in so far as it involves the suppression of the free utterance of abuse and criticism of the existing law, or of the policies of the war, is not, in my judgment, supported by the language of the statute. Yet there has always been a recognized limit to such expressions, incident indeed to the existence of any compulsive power of the state itself. One may not counsel or advise others to violate the law as it stands. Words are not only the keys of persuasion, but the triggers of action, and those which have no purport but to counsel the violation of law cannot by any latitude of interpretation be a part of that public opinion which is the final source of government in a democratic state. The defendant asserts not only that the magazine indirectly through its propaganda leads to a disintegration of loyalty and a disobedience of law, but that in addition it counsels and advises resistance to existing law, especially to the draft. The consideration of this aspect of the case more properly arises under the third phrase of section 3, which forbids any willful obstruction of the recruiting or enlistment service of the United States, but, as the defendant urges that the magazine falls within each phrase, it is as well to take it up now. To counsel or advise a man to an act is to urge upon him either that it is his interest or his duty to do it. While, of course, this may be accomplished as well by indirection as expressly, since words carry the meaning that they impart, the definition is exhaustive, I think, and I shall use it. Political agitation, by the passions it arouses or the convictions it engenders, may in fact stimulate men to the violation of law. Detestation of existing policies is easily transformed into forcible resistance of the authority which puts them in execution, and it would be folly to disregard the causal relation between the two. Yet to assimilate agitation, legitimate as such, with direct incitement to violent resistance, is to disregard the tolerance of all methods of political agitation which in normal times is a safeguard of free government. The distinction is not a scholastic subterfuge, but a hard-bought acquisition in the fight for freedom, and the purpose to disregard it must be evident when the power exists. If one stops short of urging upon others that it is their duty or their interest to resist the law, it seems to me one should not be held to have attempted to cause its violation. If that be not the test, I can see no escape from the conclusion that under this section every political agitation which can be shown to be apt to create a seditious temper is illegal. I am confident that by such language Congress had no such revolutionary purpose in view.

"It seems to me, however, quite plain that none of the language and none of the cartoons in this paper can be thought directly to counsel or advise insubordination or mutiny, without a violation of their meaning quite beyond any tolerable understanding. I come, therefore, to the third phrase of the section, which forbids any one from willfully obstructing the recruiting or enlistment service of the United States. I am not prepared to assent to the plaintiff's position that this only refers to acts other than words, nor that the act thus defined must be shown to have been successful. One may obstruct without preventing, and the mere obstruction is an injury to the service; for it throws impediments in its way. Here again, however, since the question is of the expression of opinion, I construe the sentence, so far as it restrains public utterance, as I have construed the other two, and as therefore limited to the direct advocacy of resistance to the recruiting and enlistment service. If so, the inquiry is narrowed to the question whether any of the challenged matter may be said to advocate resistance to the draft, taking the meaning of the words with the utmost latitude which they can bear."

SCHENCK v. UNITED STATES, 249 U.S. 47 (1919). Section 3 of title I of the Espionage Act of 1917 established three offenses: "[1] whoever, when the United States is at war, shall willfully make or convey false reports or false statements with intent to interfere with the operation or success of the military or naval forces of the United States or to promote the success of its enemies and [2] whoever, when the United States is at war, shall willfully cause or attempt to cause insubordination, disloyalty, mutiny, or refusal of duty, in the military or naval forces of the United States, or [3] shall willfully obstruct the recruiting or enlistment service of the United States, to the injury of the service or of the United States, shall be punished by a fine of not more than $10,000 or imprisonment for not more than twenty years, or both."[a] section 4 of the same title punished persons conspiring to violate section 3, if any one of them did any act to effect the object of the conspiracy. Schenck and the other defendants were indicted and convicted of a conspiracy to violate section 3, by sending to drafted men, circulars calculated to cause insubordination in the armed services and to obstruct the recruiting and enlistment service of the United States. The circulars asserted that conscription violated the idea of the thirteenth amendment and was despotism in the interest of Wall Street's chosen few. Although the message "in form at least confined itself to peaceful measures," it urged the conscript not to "submit to intimidation" and denied the power of the government to send citizens abroad to shoot persons of other lands. Defendant did not deny that the tendency of the circulars was to influence persons to obstruct the draft, but contended that any such tendency was protected by the first amendment.

Justice Holmes' unanimous opinion for the Supreme Court contains the following statement:

"We admit that in many places and in ordinary times the defendants in saying all that was said in the circular would have been within their constitutional rights. But the character of every act depends upon the circumstances in which it is done. . . . The most stringent protection of free speech would not protect a man in falsely shouting fire in a theatre and causing a panic. It does not even protect a man from an injunction against uttering words that may have all the effect of force. . . . The question in every case is whether the words used are used in such circumstances and are of such a nature as to create a clear and present danger that they will bring about the substantive evils that Congress has a right to prevent. It is a question of proximity and degree. When a nation is at war many things that might be said in time of peace are such a hindrance to its effort that their utterance will not be endured so long as men fight and that no Court could regard them as protected by any constitutional right. It seems to be

a. 40 Stat. 219, which became 50 U.S.C. § 33, repealed June 25, 1948 when the present United States Code was enacted. The numbers have been inserted to indicate the different clauses of the provision.

admitted that if an actual obstruction of the recruiting service were proved, liability for words that produced that effect might be enforced. The statute of 1917 in § 4 punishes conspiracies to obstruct as well as actual obstruction. If the act, (speaking, or circulating a paper,) its tendency and the intent with which it is done are the same, we perceive no ground for saying that success alone warrants making the act a crime."

The convictions were affirmed.[b]

ABRAMS v. UNITED STATES, 250 U.S. 616 (1919), involved the 1918 amendment to the Espionage Act. Offenses under the act included uttering, printing, writing, or publishing any disloyal, profane, scurrilous or abusive language or language intended to cause contempt, scorn, contumely or disrepute as regards the form of government of the United States; any language intended to incite resistance to the United States or promote the cause of its enemies; or any language urging curtailment of production of any things necessary to the prosecution of war with intent to hinder such prosecution. Abrams and his fellow defendants were indicted and convicted of conspiring to violate these provisions of the 1918 amendment, in that they printed and distributed some 5000 circulars in New York City on about August 22, 1918, which circulars were intended to bring the form of government of the United States into contempt; to encourage resistance to the United States in World War I; and to incite curtailment of war production. In the circulars, President Wilson was denounced as a hypocrite and a coward for sending troops into Russia to support the anti–Bolshevik forces; the workers of the world were urged to awake and put down the common enemy—capitalism; the general strike was advocated as the necessary reply to the "barbaric intervention" in Russia; and the toilers of America were to pledge themselves "to create so great a disturbance that the autocrats of America shall be compelled to keep their armies at home, and not be able to spare any for Russia."

The majority concluded that any question regarding the constitutionality of the Espionage Act as a whole had been disposed of by *Schenck* and related cases, leaving, as the major issue, the sufficiency of the evidence to sustain the guilty verdict. They held that it had been proved that the defendants published their circulars with intent to encourage resistance to the war with Germany and to incite curtailment of war production.[a]

Justice Holmes, joined by Justice Brandeis, wrote a dissenting opinion in which he concluded that the circulars did not show the requisite intent to provoke resistance to the war with Germany or to curtail production in order to cripple the war effort. The opinion concludes with the following paragraphs.

"In this case sentences of twenty years imprisonment have been imposed for the publishing of two leaflets that I believe the defendants had as much right to publish as the Government has to publish the Constitution of the United States now vainly invoked by them. Even if I am technically wrong and

---

b. One week later, on the authority of the *Schenck* decision, the Court sustained the conviction of a prominent socialist, *Eugene V. Debs,* under the same statute. In the course of a general address on socialism and opposition to the war, Debs praised draft resisters and stated: "You need to know that you are fit for something better than slavery and cannon fodder." Debs' 10 year sentence was affirmed because the jury could find that his remarks had a tendency to obstruct recruiting, and Debs had that intent. Justice Holmes stated that, even if the tendency of the speech and Debs' intent were incidental to Debs' main point in his speech—opposition to the war—his speech was not "protected by reason of its being part of a general program and expressions of a general and conscientious belief." Debs v. United States, 249 U.S. 211, 215 (1919).

a. The majority found it unnecessary to review defendants' conviction on the count charging that the circulars were intended to bring the form of government of the United States into contempt.

enough can be squeezed from these poor and puny anonymities to turn the color of legal litmus paper; I will add, even if what I think the necessary intent were shown; the most nominal punishment seems to me all that possibly could be inflicted, unless the defendants are to be made to suffer not for what the indictment alleges but for the creed that they avow—a creed that I believe to be the creed of ignorance and immaturity when honestly held, as I see no reason to doubt that it was held here, but which, although made the subject of examination at the trial, no one has a right even to consider in dealing with the charges before the Court.

"Persecution for the expression of opinions seems to me perfectly logical. If you have no doubt of your premises or your power and want a certain result with all your heart you naturally express your wishes in law and sweep away all opposition. To allow opposition by speech seems to indicate that you think the speech impotent, as when a man says that he has squared the circle, or that you do not care whole-heartedly for the result, or that you doubt either your power or your premises. But when men have realized that time has upset many fighting faiths, they may come to believe even more than they believe the very foundations of their own conduct that the ultimate good desired is better reached by free trade in ideas—that the best test of truth is the power of the thought to get itself accepted in the competition of the market, and that truth is the only ground upon which their wishes safely can be carried out. That at any rate is the theory of our Constitution. It is an experiment, as all life is an experiment. Every year if not every day we have to wager our salvation upon some prophecy based upon imperfect knowledge. While that experiment is part of our system I think that we should be eternally vigilant against attempts to check the expression of opinions that we loathe and believe to be fraught with death, unless they so imminently threaten immediate interference with the lawful and pressing purposes of the law that an immediate check is required to save the country. I wholly disagree with the argument of the Government that the First Amendment left the common law as to seditious libel in force. History seems to me against the notion. I had conceived that the United States through many years had shown its repentance for the Sedition Act of 1798, by repaying fines that it imposed. Only the emergency that makes it immediately dangerous to leave the correction of evil counsels to time warrants making any exception to the sweeping command, 'Congress shall make no law ... abridging the freedom of speech.' Of course I am speaking only of expressions of opinion and exhortations, which were all that were uttered here, but I regret that I cannot put into more impressive words my belief that in their conviction upon this indictment the defendants were deprived of their rights under the Constitution of the United States."[b]

HAND'S "ADVOCACY" TEST VS. HOLMES' "CLEAR AND PRESENT" TEST

Professor Corwin summarized the holdings of the *Schenck* and *Abrams* cases as follows:

b. The Abrams case was the only one under the 1918 Act to reach the Supreme Court. That Act was repealed in 1921 (41 Stat. 1359), leaving the original 1917 Act to become what is now 18 U.S.C. § 2388. There have been intermittent prosecutions under the legislation. See Hartzel v. United States, 322 U.S. 680 (1944); United States v. Powell, 156 F.Supp. 526 (N.D.Cal.1957). The 1917 Act (by its original terms and as carried into 18 U.S.C. § 2388) applies only "when the United States is at war."

Related to the above legislation is a provision of the Universal Military Training and Service Act of 1948 which provides that one "who knowingly counsels, aids, or abets another to refuse or evade registration or service in the armed forces or any of the requirements of this title" is guilty of a crime. 50 U.S.C.App. § 462(a). Under this section, a dean of a college was convicted for telling a

"To sum up, the following propositions seem to be established with respect to constitutional freedom of speech and press: first, Congress is not limited to forbidding words which are of a nature 'to create a clear and present danger' to national interest, but it may forbid words which are intended to endanger those interests if in the exercise of a fair legislative discretion it finds it 'necessary and proper' to do so; second, the intent of the accused in uttering the alleged forbidden words may be presumed from the reasonable consequences of such words, though the presumption is a rebuttable one; third, the court will not scrutinize on appeal the findings of juries in this class of cases more strictly than in other penal cases. In short, the cause of freedom of speech and press is largely in the custody of legislative majorities and of juries, which, so far as there is evidence to show, is just where the framers of the Constitution intended it to be." Corwin, *Freedom of Speech and Press Under the First Amendment: A Resume,* 30 Yale L.J. 48, 55 (1920), reprinted in 2 Selected Essays on Constitutional Law 1060, 1067 (1938).

Gunther, *Learned Hand and the Origins of Modern First Amendment Doctrine: Some Fragments of History,* 27 Stan.L.Rev. 719 (1975), sets forth contemporary correspondence between Judge Hand and Justice Holmes, making it clear that they had quite different points of view as to the appropriate limits on the punishment of radical speech. Holmes, in fact, started with the observation that "free speech stands no differently than freedom from vaccination." In a letter to Professor Chafee in 1921 Hand summarized his objections to the Holmes approach as set forth in *Schenck* and *Abrams:*

"I am not wholly in love with Holmesy's test and the reason is this. Once you admit that the matter is one of degree, while you may put it where it genuinely belongs, you so obviously make it a matter of administration, i.e. you give to Tomdickandharry, D.J., so much latitude that the jig is at once up. Besides their ineffabilities, the Nine Elder Statesmen, have not shown themselves wholly immune from the 'herd instinct' and what seems 'immediate and direct' today may seem very remote next year even though the circumstances surrounding the utterance be unchanged. I own I should prefer a qualitative formula, hard, conventional, difficult to evade." Id. at 770.

The *Abrams* case suggested a somewhat different problem than *Schenck.* In *Schenck,* the statutory language prohibited conduct. *Abrams* involved a statute making criminal "language intended to incite resistance to the United States" and "language urging curtailment of production of any things necessary to the prosecution of war with intent to hinder such prosecution." In Gitlow v. New York, which is set out below, New York's statute penalized the advocacy of the "duty, necessity, or propriety" of overturning the government by force or violence.

Gitlow v. New York

268 U.S. 652, 45 S.Ct. 625, 69 L.Ed. 1138 (1925).

Mr. Justice Sanford delivered the opinion of the Court.

Benjamin Gitlow was indicted in the Supreme Court of New York, with three others, for the statutory crime of criminal anarchy. New York Penal Law

student who was refusing to register, "Do not let them coerce you into registering." Gara v. United States, 178 F.2d 38 (6th Cir.1949), affirmed by an equally divided vote, 340 U.S. 857 (1950).

§§ 160, 161. He was separately tried, convicted, and sentenced to imprisonment. The judgment was affirmed by the Appellate Division and by the Court of Appeals. . . .

The contention here is that the statute, by its terms and as applied in this case, is repugnant to the due process clause of the Fourteenth Amendment. Its material provisions are:

"§ 160. *Criminal anarchy defined.* Criminal anarchy is the doctrine that organized government should be overthrown by force or violence, or by assassination of the executive head or of any of the executive officials of government, or by any unlawful means. The advocacy of such doctrine either by word of mouth or writing is a felony.

"§ 161. *Advocacy of criminal anarchy.* Any person who:

"1. By word of mouth or writing advocates, advises or teaches the duty, necessity or propriety of overthrowing or overturning organized government by force or violence, or by assassination of the executive head or of any of the executive officials of government, or by any unlawful means; or,

"2. Prints, publishes, edits, issues or knowingly circulates, sells, distributes or publicly displays any book, paper, document, or written or printed matter in any form, containing or advocating, advising or teaching the doctrine that organized government should be overthrown by force, violence or any unlawful means, . . .

"Is guilty of a felony and punishable" by imprisonment or fine, or both.

The indictment was in two counts. The first charged that the defendant had advocated, advised and taught the duty, necessity and propriety of overthrowing and overturning organized government by force, violence and unlawful means, by certain writings therein set forth entitled "The Left Wing Manifesto"; the second that he had printed, published and knowingly circulated and distributed a certain paper called "The Revolutionary Age," containing the writings set forth in the first count advocating, advising and teaching the doctrine that organized government should be overthrown by force, violence and unlawful means.

The following facts were established on the trial by undisputed evidence and admissions: . . . It was admitted that the defendant signed a card subscribing to the Manifesto and Program of the Left Wing, which all applicants were required to sign before being admitted to membership; that he went to different parts of the State to speak to branches of the Socialist Party about the principles of the Left Wing and advocated their adoption; and that he was responsible for the Manifesto as it appeared, that "he knew of the publication, in a general way and he knew of its publication afterwards, and is responsible for its circulation."

There was no evidence of any effect resulting from the publication and circulation of the Manifesto.

No witnesses were offered in behalf of the defendant.

. . .

The court, among other things, charged the jury, in substance, that they must determine what was the intent, purpose and fair meaning of the Manifesto; that its words must be taken in their ordinary meaning, as they would be understood by people whom it might reach; that a mere statement or analysis of social and economic facts and historical incidents, in the nature of an essay, accompanied by prophecy as to the future course of events, but with no teaching, advice or advocacy of action, would not constitute the advocacy, advice or teaching of a doctrine for the overthrow of government within the meaning of the statute; that a mere statement that unlawful acts might accomplish such a purpose would be insufficient, unless there was a teaching, advising and advocacy of employing such unlawful acts for the purpose of overthrowing government; and that if the jury had a reasonable doubt that the Manifesto did teach, advocate or advise the duty, necessity or propriety of using unlawful means for the overthrowing of organized government, the defendant was entitled to an acquittal.

The defendant's counsel submitted two requests to charge which embodied in substance the statement that to constitute criminal anarchy within the meaning of the statute it was necessary that the language used or published should advocate, teach or advise the duty, necessity or propriety of doing "some definite or immediate act or acts" of force, violence or unlawfulness directed toward the overthrowing of organized government. These were denied further than had been charged. Two other requests to charge embodied in substance the statement that to constitute guilt the language used or published must be "reasonably and ordinarily calculated to incite certain persons" to acts of force, violence or unlawfulness, with the object of overthrowing organized government. These were also denied.

. . .

. . . The sole contention here is, essentially, that as there was no evidence of any concrete result flowing from the publication of the Manifesto or of circumstances showing the likelihood of such result, the statute as construed and applied by the trial court penalizes the mere utterance, as such, of "doctrine" having no quality of incitement, without regard either to the circumstances of its utterance or to the likelihood of unlawful sequences; and that, as the exercise of the right of free expression with relation to government is only punishable "in circumstances involving likelihood of substantive evil," the statute contravenes the due process clause of the Fourteenth Amendment. . . .

. . .

The statute does not penalize the utterance or publication of abstract "doctrine" or academic discussion having no quality of incitement to any concrete action. It is not aimed against mere historical or philosophical essays. It does not restrain the advocacy of changes in the form of government by constitutional and lawful means. What it prohibits is language advocating, advising or teaching the overthrow of organized government by unlawful means. These words imply urging to action. . . .

The Manifesto, plainly, is neither the statement of abstract doctrine nor, as suggested by counsel, mere prediction that industrial disturbances and revolutionary mass strikes will result spontaneously in an inevitable process of evolution in the economic system. It advocates and urges in fervent language mass action which shall progressively foment industrial disturbances and through political mass strikes and revolutionary mass action overthrow and destroy organized parliamentary government. It concludes with a call to action in these words:

"The proletariat revolution and the Communist reconstruction of society—*the struggle for these*—is now indispensable.... The Communist International calls the proletariat of the world to the final struggle!"

This is not the expression of philosophical abstraction, the mere prediction of future events; it is the language of direct incitement.

The means advocated for bringing about the destruction of organized parliamentary government, namely, mass industrial revolts usurping the functions of municipal government, political mass strikes directed against the parliamentary state, and revolutionary mass action for its final destruction, necessarily imply the use of force and violence, and in their essential nature are inherently unlawful in a constitutional government of law and order. That the jury were warranted in finding that the Manifesto advocated not merely the abstract doctrine of overthrowing organized government by force, violence and unlawful means, but action to that end, is clear.

For present purposes we may and do assume that freedom of speech and of the press—which are protected by the First Amendment from abridgment by Congress—are among the fundamental personal rights and "liberties" protected by the due process clause of the Fourteenth Amendment from impairment by the States....

. . .

By enacting the present statute the State has determined, through its legislative body, that utterances advocating the overthrow of organized government by force, violence and unlawful means, are so inimical to the general welfare and involve such danger of substantive evil that they may be penalized in the exercise of its police power. That determination must be given great weight.... That utterances inciting to the overthrow of organized government by unlawful means, present a sufficient danger of substantive evil to bring their punishment within the range of legislative discretion, is clear. Such utterances, by their very nature, involve danger to the public peace and to the security of the State. They threaten breaches of the peace and ultimate revolution. And the immediate danger is none the less real and substantial, because the effect of a given utterance cannot be accurately foreseen. The State cannot reasonably be required to measure the danger from every such utterance in the nice balance of a jeweler's scale. A single revolutionary spark may kindle a fire that, smouldering for a time, may burst into a sweeping and destructive conflagration. It cannot be said that the State is acting arbitrarily or unreasonably when in the exercise of its judgment as to the measures necessary to protect the public peace and safety, it seeks to extinguish the spark without waiting until it has enkindled the flame or blazed into the conflagration. It cannot reasonably be required to defer the adoption of measures for its own peace and safety until the revolutionary utterances lead to actual disturbances of the public peace or imminent and immediate danger of its own destruction; but it may, in the exercise of its judgment, suppress the threatened danger in its incipiency....

We cannot hold that the present statute is an arbitrary or unreasonable exercise of the police power of the State unwarrantably infringing the freedom of speech or press; and we must and do sustain its constitutionality.

This being so it may be applied to every utterance—not too trivial to be beneath the notice of the law—which is of such a character and used with such intent and purpose as to bring it within the prohibition of the statute.... In other words, when the legislative body has determined generally, in the constitutional exercise of its discretion, that utterances of a certain kind involve such danger of substantive evil that they may be punished, the question whether any specific utterance coming within the prohibited class is likely, in and of itself, to bring about the substantive evil, is not open to consideration. It is sufficient that the statute itself be constitutional and that the use of the language comes within its prohibition.

It is clear that the question in such cases is entirely different from that involved in those cases where the statute merely prohibits certain acts involving the danger of substantive evil, without any reference to language itself, and it is sought to apply its provisions to language used by the defendant for the purpose of bringing about the prohibited results. There, if it be contended that the statute cannot be applied to the language used by the defendant because of its protection by the freedom of speech or press, it must necessarily be found, as an original question, without any previous determination by the legislative body, whether the specific language used involved such likelihood of bringing about the substantive evil as to deprive it of the constitutional protection. In such cases it has been held that the general provisions of the statute may be constitutionally applied to the specific utterance of the defendant if its natural tendency and probable effect was to bring about the substantive evil which the legislative body might prevent. Schenck v. United States ...; Debs v. United States ... And the general statement in the *Schenck Case,* ... that the "question in every case is whether the words used are used in such circumstances and are of such a nature as to create a clear and present danger that they will bring about the substantive evils,"—upon which great reliance is placed in the defendant's argument—was manifestly intended, as shown by the context, to apply only in cases of this class, and has no application to those like the present, where the legislative body itself has previously determined the danger of substantive evil arising from utterances of a specified character....

And finding, for the reasons stated, that the statute is not in itself unconstitutional, and that it has not been applied in the present case in derogation of any constitutional right, the judgment of the Court of Appeals is

Affirmed.

Mr. Justice Holmes, dissenting. Mr. Justice Brandeis and I are of opinion that this judgment should be reversed. The general principle of free speech, it seems to me, must be taken to be included in the Fourteenth Amendment, in view of the scope that has been given to the word "liberty" as there used, although perhaps it may be accepted with a somewhat larger latitude of interpretation than is allowed to Congress by the sweeping language that governs or ought to govern the laws of the United States. If I am right then I think that the criterion sanctioned by the full Court in Schenck v. United States ... applies.... It is true that in my opinion this criterion was departed from in Abrams v. United States, 250 U.S. 616, but the convictions that I expressed in that case are too deep for it to be possible for me as yet to believe that it ... settled the law. If what I think the correct test is applied, it is manifest that there was no present danger of an attempt to overthrow the government by force on the part of the admittedly small minority who shared the defendant's views. It is said that this manifesto was more than a theory, that it was an incitement. Every idea is an incitement. It offers itself for belief and if believed it is acted on unless some other belief outweighs it or some failure of energy stifles the movement at its birth. The only difference between the expression of an opinion and an incitement in the narrower sense is the speaker's enthusiasm for the result. Eloquence may set fire to reason. But whatever may be thought of the redundant discourse before us it had no chance of starting a present conflagration. If in the long run the beliefs expressed in proletarian dictatorship are destined to be accepted by the dominant forces of the community, the only meaning of free speech is that they should be given their chance and have their way.

If the publication of this document had been laid as an attempt to induce an uprising against government at once and not at some indefinite time in the future it would have presented a different question. The object would have been one with which the law might deal, subject to the doubt whether there was any danger that the publication could produce any result, or in other words whether it was not futile and too remote from possible consequences. But the indictment alleges the publication and nothing more.

WHITNEY v. CALIFORNIA, 274 U.S. 357 (1927), arose under the California criminal syndicalism act that defined "criminal syndicalism" as any doctrine advocating, teaching or abetting sabotage or other unlawful acts of violence as a means of accomplishing industrial or political change. It was a crime for any person to organize, assist in organizing, or knowingly become a member of any organization or group of persons associated to advocate, teach or abet criminal syndicalism.

Ms. Whitney was a socialist who in 1919 became a temporary member of the new Communist Labor Party and went as a delegate to a convention for organizing a California branch. There she supported a resolution which would have committed the organization to the use of peaceful and lawful methods of change, but this resolution lost and the convention adopted a program resembling Gitlow's Left Wing Manifesto. Whitney was found guilty under the act in that she assisted in organizing and knowingly became a member of a group formed to advocate criminal syndicalism.

The United States Supreme Court sustained the conviction. The majority opinion made two principal points: (a) Whether or not Miss Whitney helped organize and became a member of the Communist Labor Party with knowledge of its program of criminal syndicalism was a question of fact upon which the verdict of the jury was conclusive. (b) The California act "may not be declared unconstitutional unless it is an arbitrary or unreasonable attempt to exercise the authority vested in the state in the public interest." Because of the danger to the public peace and security from an organization advocating violent and unlawful methods of change, the act could not be regarded as an unreasonable exercise of the police power, unwarrantably infringing any right of free speech and assembly.

Justice Brandeis, although concurring in affirmance for procedural reasons, wrote a major opinion, joined by Justice Holmes, disagreeing with the Court's analysis. He said in part:

"Those who won our independence believed that the final end of the State was to make men free to develop their faculties, and that in its government the deliberative forces should prevail over the arbitrary. They valued liberty both as an end and as a means. They believed liberty to be the secret of happiness and courage to be the secret of liberty. They believed that freedom to think as you will and to speak as you think are means indispensable to the discovery and spread of political truth; that without free speech and assembly discussion would be futile; that with them, discussion affords ordinarily adequate protection against the dissemination of noxious doctrine; that the greatest menace to freedom is an inert people; that public discussion is a political duty; and that this should be a fundamental principle of the American government. They recognized the risks to which all human institutions are subject. But they knew that order cannot be secured merely through fear of punishment for its infraction; that it is hazardous to discourage thought, hope and imagination; that fear breeds repression; that repression breeds hate; that hate menaces stable government; that the path of safety lies in the opportunity to discuss freely supposed grievances and proposed remedies; and that the fitting remedy for evil counsels is good ones. Believing in the power of reason as applied through public discussion, they eschewed silence coerced by law—the argument of force in its worst form. Recognizing the occasional tyrannies of governing majorities, they amended the Constitution so that free speech and assembly should be guaranteed.

"Fear of serious injury cannot alone justify suppression of free speech and assembly. Men feared witches and burnt women. It is the function of speech to free men from the bondage of irrational fears. To justify suppression of free speech there must be reasonable ground to fear that serious evil will result if free speech is practiced. There must be reasonable ground to believe that the danger apprehended is imminent. There must be reasonable ground to believe that the evil to be prevented is a serious one. Every denunciation of existing law tends in some measure to increase the probability that there will be a violation of it. Condonation of a breach enhances the probability. Expressions of approval add to the probability. Propagation of the criminal state of mind by teaching syndicalism increases it. Advocacy of law-breaking heightens it still further. But even advocacy of violation, however reprehensible morally, is not a justification for denying free speech where the advocacy falls short of incitement and there is nothing to indicate that the advocacy would be immediately acted on. The wide difference between advocacy and incitement, between preparation and attempt, between assembling and conspiracy, must be borne in mind. In order to support a finding of clear and present danger it must be shown either that immediate serious violence was to be expected or was advocated, or that the past conduct furnished reason to believe that such advocacy was then contemplated."

"Those who won our independence by revolution were not cowards. They did not fear political change. They did not exalt order at the cost of liberty. To courageous, self-reliant men, with confidence in the power of free and fearless reasoning applied through the processes of popular government, no danger flowing from speech can be deemed clear and present, unless the incidence of the evil apprehended is so imminent that it may befall before there is opportunity for full discussion. If there be time to expose through discussion the falsehood and fallacies, to avert the evil by the processes of education, the remedy to be applied is more speech, not enforced silence. Only an emergency can justify repression. Such must be the rule if authority is to be reconciled with freedom. Such, in my opinion, is the command of the Constitution. It is therefore always open to Americans to challenge a law abridging free speech and assembly by showing that there was no emergency justifying it.

"Moreover, even imminent danger cannot justify resort to prohibition of these functions essential to effective democracy, unless the evil apprehended is relatively serious. Prohibition of free speech and assembly is a measure so stringent that it would be inappropriate as the means for averting a relatively trivial harm to society. A police measure may be unconstitutional merely because the remedy, although effective as means of protection, is unduly harsh or oppressive. Thus, a State might, in the exercise of its police power, make any trespass upon the land of another a crime, regardless of the results or of the intent or purpose of the trespasser. It might, also, punish an attempt, a conspiracy, or an incitement to commit the trespass. But it is hardly conceivable that this Court would hold constitutional a statute which punished as a felony the mere voluntary assembly with a society formed to teach that pedestrians had the moral right to cross unenclosed, unposted, waste lands and to advocate their doing so, even if there was imminent danger that advocacy would lead to a trespass. The fact that speech is likely to result in some violence or in destruction of property is not enough to justify its suppression. There must be the probability of serious injury to the State. Among free men, the deterrents ordinarily to be applied to prevent crime are education and punishment for violations of the law, not abridgement of the rights of free speech and assembly. . . ."[a]

THE BASIS OF THE BRANDEIS CONCURRENCE IN THE WHITNEY CASE

Because Justice Brandeis' opinion in *Whitney* is both the most articulate and passionate defense of the clear and present danger test, it is often forgotten that he and Justice Holmes voted to affirm Anita Whitney's conviction. The reason for concurrence was explained as follows:

"Whether in 1919, when Miss Whitney did the things complained of, there was in California such clear and present danger of serious evil, might have been made the important issue in the case. She might have required that the issue be determined either by the court or the jury. She claimed below that the statute as applied to her violated the Federal Constitution; but she did not claim that it was void because there was no clear and present danger of serious evil, nor did she request that the existence of these conditions of a valid measure thus restricting the rights of free speech and assembly be passed upon by the court or a jury. On the other hand, there was evidence on which the court or jury might have found that such danger existed. I am unable to assent to the suggestion in the opinion of the Court that assembling with a political party, formed to advocate the desirability of a proletarian revolution by mass action at some date necessarily far in the future, is not a right within the protection of the Fourteenth Amendment. In the present case, however, there was other testimony which tended to establish the existence of a conspiracy, on the part of members of the International Workers of the World, to commit present serious crimes; and likewise to show that such a conspiracy would be furthered by the activity of the society of which Miss Whitney was a member. Under these circumstances the judgment of the state court cannot be disturbed."

Note that the defendant was not charged with illegal advocacy, but was convicted for organizing and being a member of a group engaged in unlawful advocacy. Moreover, there was no evidence that she engaged personally in the unlawful advocacy. To the contrary, she had sponsored a competing resolution at the group's organizing meeting calling for peaceful and lawful change. Suppose the clear and present danger defense had been raised at the criminal trial, but it had been found, on sufficient evidence, that the party advocated present serious crimes, and that there was a clear and present danger that those crimes would be committed. Under the position of Justices Brandeis and Holmes, would the fact that defendant disagreed with the advocacy of criminal conduct and did not personally participate in that advocacy be the basis of a viable first amendment defense? Would it be sufficient for conviction that she remained as an active party member, knowing of its illegal advocacy?

DE JONGE v. OREGON, 299 U.S. 353 (1937). De Jonge was convicted on an indictment charging violation of the Oregon criminal syndicalism law that defined "criminal syndicalism" as "the doctrine which advocates crime, physi-

---

a. The Whitney case and its background are discussed in Chafee, *Free Speech in the United States* (1941), pp. 343–354. Shortly after the Supreme Court's decision, she was pardoned by Governor Young of California, who in giving reasons for his action made reference to the opinion of Justice Brandeis.

cal violence, sabotage or any unlawful acts or methods as a means of accomplishing or effecting industrial or political change or revolution." Among the offenses created were the teaching of criminal syndicalism, the printing or distribution of material advocating the doctrine, the organization of a society or group which advocates it, and presiding at or assisting in conducting a meeting of such an organization, society or group.

The indictment charged that the defendant had unlawfully presided at, and assisted in conducting "an assemblage of persons", to wit, the Communist Party, "which said assemblage of persons" did then and there unlawfully teach and advocate the doctrine of criminal syndicalism.

The evidence showed that De Jonge was a member of the Communist Party; that he presided over and otherwise participated in the public meeting held in Portland, Oregon, under the auspices of the Communist Party; that the meeting was held to protest against illegal raids on workers' halls and homes, and against the shooting of striking longshoremen by the Portland police; and at the meeting there were no unlawful acts done, nor any advocacy of criminal syndicalism. The Supreme Court of Oregon affirmed the conviction on the ground that in addition to the above evidence, there was evidence to show, as the indictment had charged, that the Communist Party at other times and places in Oregon, had taught and advocated criminal syndicalism.

Chief Justice Hughes, speaking for a unanimous Court, delivered an opinion containing the following paragraphs:

"Conviction upon a charge not made would be sheer denial of due process. It thus appears that, while defendant was a member of the Communist Party, he was not indicted for participating in its organization, or for joining it, or for soliciting members or for distributing its literature. He was not charged with teaching or advocating criminal syndicalism or sabotage or any unlawful acts, either at the meeting or elsewhere. He was accordingly deprived of the benefit of evidence as to the orderly and lawful conduct of the meeting and that it was not called or used for the advocacy of criminal syndicalism or sabotage or any unlawful action. His sole offense as charged, and for which he was convicted and sentenced to imprisonment for seven years, was that he had assisted in the conduct of a public meeting, albeit otherwise lawful, which was held under the auspices of the Communist Party.

". . .

"Freedom of speech and of the press are fundamental rights which are safeguarded by the due process clause of the Fourteenth Amendment of the Federal Constitution. . . . The right of peaceable assembly is a right cognate to those of free speech and free press and is equally fundamental. As this Court said in United States v. Cruikshank, 92 U.S. 542, 552: 'The very idea of a government, republican in form, implies a right on the part of its citizens to meet peaceably for consultation in respect to public affairs and to petition for a redress of grievances.' The First Amendment of the Federal Constitution expressly guarantees that right against abridgment by Congress. But explicit mention there does not argue exclusion elsewhere. For the right is one that cannot be denied without violating those fundamental principles of liberty and justice which lie at the base of all civil and political institutions—principles which the Fourteenth Amendment embodies in the general terms of its due process clause. . . .

". . .

"It follows from these considerations that, consistently with the Federal Constitution, peaceable assembly for lawful discussion cannot be made a crime.

The holding of meetings for peaceable political action cannot be proscribed. Those who assist in the conduct of such meetings cannot be branded as criminals on that score. The question, if the rights of free speech and peaceable assembly are to be preserved, is not as to the auspices under which the meeting is held but as to its purpose; not as to the relations of the speakers, but whether their utterances transcend the bounds of the freedom of speech which the Constitution protects. If the persons assembling have committed crimes elsewhere, if they have formed or are engaged in a conspiracy against the public peace and order, they may be prosecuted for their conspiracy or other violation of valid laws. But it is a different matter when the State, instead of prosecuting them for such offenses, seizes upon mere participation in a peaceable assembly and a lawful public discussion as the basis for a criminal charge.

"We are not called upon to review the findings of the state court as to the objectives of the Communist Party. Notwithstanding those objectives, the defendant still enjoyed his personal right of free speech and to take part in a peaceable assembly having a lawful purpose, although called by that Party. The defendant was none the less entitled to discuss the public issues of the day and thus in a lawful manner, without incitement to violence or crime, to seek redress of alleged grievances. That was of the essence of his guaranteed personal liberty."

C.   THE POST WORLD WAR II COLD WAR ERA: PROSECUTION OF COMMUNISTS UNDER THE SMITH ACT

THE SMITH ACT

During the years that followed the Second World War, anti-radical hysteria surpassed that of the Great Red Scare of the 1920's. The focus this time was the Russian threat, and the specific concern was espionage and subversion by the Communist Party of the United States. The output of both the national and state legislatures, passing laws dealing with loyalty and security, was enormous during this period. So too, were the number of cases, many decided by the United States Supreme Court. The cases that follow are only a small part of the story of the Supreme Court's treatment of anti-Communist legislation during the years of the cold war and after. They are, however, an important part since they continue the debate begun in *Schenck, Abrams, Gitlow* and *Whitney*.

The *Dennis* case, which follows, resulted from federal prosecution of the Communist Party's top national leaders. The *Yates* and *Scales* cases involved prosecutions of lower level Communist Party officials, that followed in the wake of the Court's affirmance of the convictions in *Dennis*. Ironically, the legislation under which the prosecutions were initiated had been enacted prior to the war. The Smith Act was passed in 1940 as a rider to other legislation and received little attention in or out of Congress until it was employed, after the war, as the vehicle for prosecution of Communist Party officials. The Smith Act was patterned on the New York Criminal Anarchy Act which had been sustained in Gitlow v. New York.

DENNIS v. UNITED STATES, 341 U.S. 494 (1951). Petitioners, leaders of the Communist Party, were prosecuted and convicted in a federal district court in New York of violating the Smith Act. The Act provided:

"Sec. 2(a). It shall be unlawful for any person?

"(1) to knowingly or willfully advocate, abet, advise, or teach the duty, necessity, desirability, or propriety of overthrowing or destroying any government in the United States by force or violence, or by the assassination of any officer of any such government;

". . .

"(3) to organize or help to organize any society, group, or assembly of persons who teach, advocate, or encourage the overthrow or destruction of any government in the United States by force or violence; or to be or become a member of, or affiliate with, any such society, group, or assembly of persons, knowing the purposes thereof. . . .

"Sec. 3. It shall be unlawful for any person to attempt to commit, or to conspire to commit, any of the acts prohibited by the provisions of this title."

The indictment charged petitioners with conspiring (1) to organize as the Communist Party of the United States a group of persons who teach and advocate the overthrow of the Government of the United States by force and violence, and (2) to advocate and teach the duty and necessity of overthrowing the government of the United States by force and violence. After a protracted trial, the judge gave the jury instructions which included the following:

"In further construction and interpretation of the statute I charge you that it is not the abstract doctrine of overthrowing or destroying organized government by unlawful means which is denounced by this law, but the teaching and advocacy of action for the accomplishment of that purpose, by language reasonably and ordinarily calculated to incite persons to such action. Accordingly, you cannot find the defendants or any of them guilty of the crime charged unless you are satisfied beyond a reasonable doubt that they conspired to organize a society, group and assembly of persons who teach and advocate the overthrow or destruction of the Government of the United States by force and violence and to advocate and teach the duty and necessity of overthrowing or destroying the Government of the United States by force and violence, with the intent that such teaching and advocacy be of a rule or principle of action and by language reasonably and ordinarily calculated to incite persons to such action, all with the intent to cause the overthrow or destruction of the Government of the United States by force and violence as speedily as circumstances would permit.

". . .

"If you are satisfied that the evidence establishes beyond a reasonable doubt that the defendants, or any of them, are guilty of a violation of the statute, as I have interpreted it to you, I find as matter of law that there is sufficient danger of a substantive evil that the Congress has a right to prevent to justify the application of the statute under the First Amendment of the Constitution.

"This is [a] matter of law about which you have no concern. It is a finding on a matter of law which I deem essential to support my ruling that the case should be submitted to you to pass upon the guilt or innocence of the defendants."

The convictions were affirmed by the Court of Appeals and the Supreme Court granted certiorari limited to the question of the constitutionality of the Smith Act as construed and applied. Several opinions were written, none of which obtained the approval of sufficient Justices to make it the opinion of the Court.

The opinion receiving the greatest assent was by Chief Justice Vinson, joined by Justices Reed, Burton and Minton. "The obvious purpose of the statute," said the Chief Justice, "is to protect existing Government, not from change by peaceable, lawful and constitutional means, but from change by violence, revolution and terrorism." Although the statute was inapplicable to "peaceful studies and discussions or teaching and advocacy in the realm of ideas," it did limit speech. Therefore, the case "squarely presented" the Court with the application of the "clear and present danger" test and required a decision as to "what that phrase imports."[a]

"Obviously, the words cannot mean that before the Government may act, it must wait until the *putsch* is about to be executed, the plans have been laid and the signal is awaited. If Government is aware that a group aiming at its overthrow is attempting to indoctrinate its members and to commit them to a course whereby they will strike when the leaders feel the circumstances permit, action by the Government is required. The argument that there is no need for Government to concern itself, for Government is strong, it possesses ample powers to put down a rebellion, it may defeat the revolution with ease needs no answer. For that is not the question. Certainly an attempt to overthrow the Government by force, even though doomed from the outset because of inadequate numbers or power of the revolutionists, is a sufficient evil for Congress to prevent. . . .

"The situation with which Justices Holmes and Brandeis were concerned in *Gitlow* was a comparatively isolated event, bearing little relation in their minds to any substantial threat to the safety of the community. . . . They were not confronted with any situation comparable to the instant one—the development of an apparatus designed and dedicated to the overthrow of the Government, in the context of world crisis after crisis.

"Chief Judge Learned Hand, writing for the majority below, interpreted the phrase as follows: 'In each case [courts] must ask whether the gravity of the "evil," discounted by its improbability, justifies such invasion of free speech as is necessary to avoid the danger.' 183 F.2d at 212. We adopt this statement of the rule. As articulated by Chief Judge Hand, it is as succinct and inclusive as any other we might devise at this time. It takes into consideration those factors which we deem relevant, and relates their significances. More we cannot expect from words.

"Likewise, we are in accord with the court below, which affirmed the trial court's finding that the requisite danger existed. The mere fact that from the period 1945 to 1948 petitioners' activities did not result in an attempt to overthrow the Government by force and violence is of course no answer to the fact that there was a group that was ready to make the attempt. The formation by petitioners of such a highly organized conspiracy, with rigidly disciplined members subject to call when the leaders, these petitioners, felt that the time had come for action, coupled with the inflammable nature of world conditions, similar uprisings in other countries, and the touch-and-go nature of our relations with countries with whom petitioners were in the very least ideologically attuned, convince us that their convictions were justified on this score. And this analysis disposes of the contention that a conspiracy to advocate, as distinguished from the advocacy itself, cannot be constitutionally restrained,

---

a. The Chief Justice made it clear that he regarded the views of Holmes and Brandeis as having won the acceptance of the Court. "Although no case subsequent to *Whitney* and *Gitlow* has expressly overruled the majority opinions in those cases, there is little doubt that subsequent opinions have inclined toward the Holmes–Brandeis rationale."

because it comprises only the preparation. It is the existence of the conspiracy which creates the danger. . . . If the ingredients of the reaction are present, we cannot bind the Government to wait until the catalyst is added."

The Chief Justice also approved of the ruling below that withheld the issue of clear and present danger from the jury. "Bearing, as it does, the marks of a 'question of law,' the issue is properly one for the judge to decide."

He concluded that the convictions should be affirmed.

Justice Frankfurter wrote an extensive concurring opinion in which he emphasized the importance of a careful examination of the conflicting interests of national security and free speech which the Court was required to assess in order to arrive at its decision. He believed that the prior decisions resolving conflicts between speech and competing interests, when viewed as a whole, expressed an attitude toward the judicial function and a standard of values which were decisive of the case. "Free-speech cases are not an exception to the principle that we are not legislators, that direct policy-making is not our province. How best to reconcile competing interests is the business of legislatures, and the balance they strike is a judgment not to be displaced by ours, but to be respected unless outside the pale of fair judgment."

Justice Jackson's concurring opinion contended that the clear and present danger test was inapplicable since the prosecution was for conspiracy and under circumstances greatly different from those in *Gitlow, Whitney,* and earlier cases. "I would save it, unmodified, for application as a 'rule of reason' in the kind of case for which it was devised. When the issue is criminality of a hot-headed speech on a street corner, or circulation of a few incendiary pamphlets, or parading by some zealots behind a red flag, or refusal of a handful of school children to salute our flag, it is not beyond the capacity of the judicial process to gather, comprehend, and weigh the necessary materials for decision whether it is a clear and present danger of substantive evil or a harmless letting off of steam."

Justice Black's dissenting opinion emphasized that petitioners were not charged with an attempt to overthrow the Government, or with overt acts designed to overthrow the Government, or even with saying anything or writing anything designed to overthrow the Government. He argued that section 3 of the Smith Act was unconstitutional as a "virulent form of prior censorship of speech and press" in violation of the First Amendment. Justice Douglas also dissented, warning against the dangers of basing a prosecution for seditious conspiracy on speech alone. To make the criminality of the teaching of doctrine turn solely on the intent with which it is taught, made the offense similar to the old English crime of constructive treason. As to the clear and present danger rule, he observed:

"There comes a time when even speech loses its constitutional immunity. Speech innocuous one year may at another time fan such destructive flames that it must be halted in the interests of the safety of the Republic. That is the meaning of the clear and present danger test. When conditions are so critical that there will be no time to avoid the evil that the speech threatens, it is time to call a halt. Otherwise, free speech which is the strength of the Nation will be the cause of its destruction.

"Yet free speech is the rule, not the exception. The restraint to be constitutional must be based on more than fear, on more than passionate opposition against the speech, on more than a revolted dislike for its contents. There must be some immediate injury to society that is likely if speech is allowed."

Justice Clark did not participate in the disposition of the case. The convictions were affirmed by a vote of six to two.

CLEAR AND PRESENT DANGER AS A TEST FOR THE VALIDITY OF LEGISLATION

It will be recalled that the Court in Gitlow v. New York rejected the clear and present danger test, noting that it had been used in Schenck v. United States only for the purpose of deciding when a defendant's speech violated a law that punished conduct. The *Gitlow* majority held that clear and present danger was an irrelevant concept when a law criminally punished certain categories of speech. Chief Justice Vinson's plurality opinion in Dennis v. United States conceded that the *Gitlow* rationale would make the clear and present danger test inapplicable to the Smith Act convictions reviewed by the Court, but he concluded that intervening Court opinions "have inclined toward the Holmes–Brandeis rationale." Accordingly, he interpreted that rationale as requiring an inquiry as to whether a clear and present danger justified application of the Smith Act to the particular facts. (The Court did not, however, review the sufficiency of the evidence to sustain the convictions, since that question had been removed from the case by the Court's limited grant of certiorari.)

Hans Linde argues that, although the decision was wrong in its result, the *Gitlow* Court was right in rejecting clear and present danger as a test for determining the validity of laws that punish speech. Linde, *"Clear and Present Danger" Reexamined: Dissonance in the Brandenburg Concerto*, 22 Stan.L.Rev. 1163 (1970). He summarizes his position as follows: "The objective conditions under which the particular expression occurs . . .—whether stated as 'clear and present danger' or some other formula—can be a factor at the time when suppression of that particular occurrence is before a court. It cannot easily be an element in the constitutionality of the decision to make a law proscribing a kind of speech or publication for the future." (Linde would reserve the clear and present danger test for cases, like *Schenck,* where the statute punished conduct and the defendant's speech was claimed to be a violation. He would invalidate the Smith Act under his standard for reviewing legislation directed against the communicative content of speech or press, arguing that the first amendment invalidates a law punishing speech if the proscribed content falls *under any circumstances* within the protection of the first amendment.)

Yates v. United States

354 U.S. 298, 77 S.Ct. 1064, 1 L.Ed.2d 1356 (1957).

Mr. Justice Harlan delivered the opinion of the Court.

We brought these cases here to consider certain questions arising under the Smith Act . . . and otherwise to review the convictions of these petitioners for conspiracy to violate that Act. Among other things, the convictions are claimed to rest upon an application of the Smith Act which is hostile to the principles upon which its constitutionality was upheld in Dennis v. United States, 341 U.S. 494.

These 14 petitioners stand convicted, after a jury trial in the United States District Court for the Southern District of California, upon a single count indictment charging them with conspiring (1) to advocate and teach the duty and necessity of overthrowing the Government of the United States by force and violence, and (2) to organize, as the Communist Party of the United States, a society of persons who so advocate and teach, all with the intent of causing the overthrow of the Government by force and violence as speedily as circumstances would permit. . . .

. . .

Petitioners contend that the instructions to the jury were fatally defective in that the trial court refused to charge that, in order to convict, the jury must find that the advocacy which the defendants conspired to promote was of a kind calculated to "incite" persons to action for the forcible overthrow of the Government. It is argued that advocacy of forcible overthrow as mere *abstract doctrine* is within the free speech protection of the First Amendment; that the Smith Act, consistently with that constitutional provision, must be taken as proscribing only the sort of advocacy which incites to illegal *action;* and that the trial court's charge, by permitting conviction for mere advocacy, unrelated to its tendency to produce forcible action, resulted in an unconstitutional application of the Smith Act. The Government, which at the trial also requested the court to charge in terms of "incitement," now takes the position, however, that the true constitutional dividing line is not between inciting and abstract advocacy of forcible overthrow, but rather between advocacy as such, irrespective of its inciting qualities, and the mere discussion or exposition of violent overthrow as an abstract theory. . . .

There can be no doubt from the record that in so instructing the jury the court regarded as immaterial, and intended to withdraw from the jury's consideration, any issue as to the character of the advocacy in terms of its capacity to stir listeners to forcible action. . . .

We are thus faced with the question whether the Smith Act prohibits advocacy and teaching of forcible overthrow as an abstract principle, divorced from any effort to instigate action to that end, so long as such advocacy or teaching is engaged in with evil intent. We hold that it does not.

The distinction between advocacy of abstract doctrine and advocacy directed at promoting unlawful action is one that has been consistently recognized in the opinions of this Court, beginning with Fox v. Washington, 236 U.S. 273; and Schenck v. United States, 249 U.S. 47. This distinction was heavily underscored in Gitlow v. New York, 268 U.S. 652. . . .

We need not, however, decide the issue before us in terms of constitutional compulsion, for our first duty is to construe this statute. In doing so we should not assume that Congress chose to disregard a constitutional danger zone so clearly marked, or that it used the words "advocate" and "teach" in their ordinary dictionary meanings when they had already been construed as terms of art carrying a special and limited connotation. . . .

. . .

In failing to distinguish between advocacy of forcible overthrow as an abstract doctrine and advocacy of action to that end, the District Court appears to have been led astray by the holding in *Dennis* that advocacy of violent action to be taken at some future time was enough. It seems to have considered that, since "inciting" speech is usually thought of as something calculated to induce immediate action, and since *Dennis* held advocacy of action for future overthrow sufficient, this meant that advocacy, irrespective of its tendency to generate action, is punishable, provided only that it is uttered with a specific intent to accomplish overthrow. In other words, the District Court apparently thought that *Dennis* obliterated the traditional dividing line between advocacy of abstract doctrine and advocacy of action.

This misconceives the situation confronting the Court in *Dennis* and what was held there. Although the jury's verdict, interpreted in light of the trial court's instructions, did not justify the conclusion that the defendants' advocacy was directed at, or created any danger of, immediate overthrow, it did establish that the advocacy was aimed at building up a seditious group and maintaining it in readiness for action at a propitious time.... The essence of the *Dennis* holding was that indoctrination of a group in preparation for future violent action, as well as exhortation to immediate action, by advocacy found to be directed to "action for the accomplishment" of forcible overthrow, to violence as "a rule or principle of action," and employing "language of incitement," ... is not constitutionally protected when the group is of sufficient size and cohesiveness, is sufficiently oriented towards action, and other circumstances are such as reasonably to justify apprehension that action will occur. This is quite a different thing from the view of the District Court here that mere doctrinal justification of forcible overthrow, if engaged in with the intent to accomplish overthrow, is punishable *per se* under the Smith Act. That sort of advocacy, even though uttered with the hope that it may ultimately lead to violent revolution, is too remote from concrete action to be regarded as the kind of indoctrination preparatory to action which was condemned in *Dennis*. As one of the concurring opinions in *Dennis* put it: "Throughout our decisions there has recurred a distinction between the statement of an idea which may prompt its hearers to take unlawful action, and advocacy that such action be taken." ... There is nothing in *Dennis* which makes that historic distinction obsolete.

. . .

In light of the foregoing we are unable to regard the District Court's charge upon this aspect of the case as adequate. The jury was never told that the Smith Act does not denounce advocacy in the sense of preaching abstractly the forcible overthrow of the Government. We think that the trial court's statement that the proscribed advocacy must include the "urging," "necessity," and "duty" of forcible overthrow, and not merely its "desirability" and "propriety," may not be regarded as a sufficient substitute for charging that the Smith Act reaches only advocacy of action for the overthrow of government by force and violence. The essential distinction is that those to whom the advocacy is addressed must be urged to *do* something, now or in the future, rather than merely to *believe* in something....

. . .

[The Court ordered an acquittal of five of the 14 petitioners,[a] finding "no adequate evidence in the record" to sustain their convictions on retrial.][b]

Mr. Justice Brennan and Mr. Justice Whittaker took no part in the consideration or decision of this case.

Mr. Justice Black, with whom Mr. Justice Douglas joins, concurring in part and dissenting in part.

[a] Upon remand of the *Yates* case, the lower court dismissed the indictments against the remaining defendants who had not been acquitted by the Supreme Court. This action was "reluctantly" requested by the Government because it could not "satisfy the evidentiary requirements laid down by the Supreme Court in its opinion reversing the conviction in this matter." New York Times, Dec. 3, 1957, p. 71.

[b] The types of evidence that led the Court to order the five acquitted, and not the remaining nine, are summarized in *Scales v. United States,* infra.

I would reverse every one of these convictions and direct that all the defendants be acquitted. In my judgment the statutory provisions on which these prosecutions are based abridge freedom of speech, press and assembly in violation of the First Amendment to the United States Constitution. See my dissent and that of Mr. Justice Douglas in Dennis v. United States, 341 U.S. 494, 579, 581. . . .

. . .

Mr. Justice Clark, dissenting.

The petitioners, principal organizers and leaders of the Communist Party in California, have been convicted for a conspiracy covering the period 1940 to 1951. They were engaged in this conspiracy with the defendants in Dennis v. United States, 341 U.S. 494 (1951). . . .

. . .

The conspiracy includes the same group of defendants as in the *Dennis* case though petitioners here occupied a lower echelon in the party hierarchy. . . . The convictions here were based upon evidence closely paralleling that adduced in *Dennis* . . .

I would affirm the convictions. . . .

. . .

Scales v. United States

367 U.S. 203, 81 S.Ct. 1469, 6 L.Ed.2d 782 (1961).

[Petitioner, Chairman of the North and South Carolina Districts of the Communist Party, was convicted of violating the membership clause of the Smith Act (18 U.S.C. § 2385), which made it a crime to become a member of an organization advocating the overthrow of the government by force or violence, knowing the purposes of such organization.[1] The trial court had instructed the jury that in order to convict it must find that (1) the Communist Party advocated the violent overthrow of the government, in the sense of present "advocacy of action" to accomplish that end as soon as circumstances were propitious; and (2) petitioner was an "active" member of the Party, and not merely "a nominal, passive, inactive, or purely technical" member with knowledge of the Party's illegal advocacy and a specific intent to bring about overthrow "as speedily as circumstances would permit." The Supreme Court affirmed the conviction.]

Mr. Justice Harlan delivered the opinion of the Court.

. . .

1. Section 2385 (whose membership clause we place in italics) reads: . . .

"Whoever organizes or helps or attempts to organize any society, group, or assembly of persons who teach, advocate, or encourage the overthrow or destruction of any such government by force or violence; *or becomes or is a member of,* or affiliates with, *any such society, group, or assembly of persons, knowing the purposes thereof?*

"Shall be fined not more than $20,000 or imprisoned not more than twenty years, or both, and shall be ineligible for employment by the United States or any department or agency thereof, for the five years next following his conviction." . . .

[Court's footnote.]

1. Constitutional Challenge to the Membership Clause on Its Face. ...

Any thought that due process puts beyond the reach of the criminal law all individual associational relationships, unless accompanied by the commission of specific acts of criminality, is dispelled by familiar concepts of the law of conspiracy and complicity.... In this instance it is an organization which engages in criminal activity, and we can perceive no reason why one who actively and knowingly works in the ranks of that organization, intending to contribute to the success of those specifically illegal activities, should be any more immune from prosecution than he to whom the organization has assigned the task of carrying out the substantive criminal act ...

... It must indeed be recognized that a person who merely becomes a member of an illegal organization, by that "act" alone need be doing nothing more than signifying his assent to its purposes and activities on one hand, and providing, on the other, only the sort of moral encouragement which comes from the knowledge that others believe in what the organization is doing....

... [T]hese factors have weight and must be found to be overborne in a total constitutional assessment of the statute. We think, however, they are duly met when the statute is found to reach only "active" members having also a guilty knowledge and intent, and which therefore prevents a conviction on what otherwise might be regarded as merely an expression of sympathy with the alleged criminal enterprise, unaccompanied by any significant action in its support or any commitment to undertake such action.

. . .

... It was settled in *Dennis* that the advocacy with which we are here concerned is not constitutionally protected speech, and it was further established that a combination to promote such advocacy, albeit under the aegis of what purports to be a political party, is not such association as is protected by the First Amendment. We can discern no reason why membership, when it constitutes a purposeful form of complicity in a group engaging in this same forbidden advocacy, should receive any greater degree of protection from the guarantees of that Amendment....

2. Evidentiary Challenge

. . .

On this phase of the case petitioner's principal contention is that the evidence was insufficient to establish that the Communist Party was engaged in present advocacy of violent overthrow of the Government in the sense required by the Smith Act, that is, in "advocacy of action" for the accomplishment of such overthrow either immediately or as soon as circumstances proved propitious, and uttered in terms reasonably calculated to "incite" to such action.... This contention rests largely on the proposition that the evidence on this aspect of the case does not differ materially from that which the Court in *Yates* stated was inadequate to establish that sort of Party advocacy there.

. . .

We agree with petitioner that the evidentiary question here is controlled in large part by *Yates*. The decision in *Yates* rested on the view (not articulated in the opinion, though perhaps it should have been) that the Smith Act offenses, involving as they do subtler elements than are present in most other crimes, call for strict standards in assessing the adequacy of the proof needed to make out a case of illegal advocacy. This premise is as applicable to prosecutions under the membership clause of the Smith Act as it is to conspiracy prosecutions under that statute as we had in *Yates.*

The impact of *Yates* with respect to this petitioner's evidentiary challenge is not limited, however, to that decision's requirement of strict standards of proof. *Yates* also articulates general criteria for the evaluation of evidence in determining whether this requirement is met. The *Yates* opinion, through its characterizations of large portions of the evidence which were either described in detail or referred to by reference to the record, indicates what type of evidence is needed to permit a jury to find that (a) there was "advocacy of action" and (b) the Party was responsible for such advocacy.

First, *Yates* makes clear what type of evidence is not *in itself* sufficient to show illegal advocacy. This category includes evidence of the following: the teaching of Marxism–Leninism and the connected use of Marxist "classics" as textbooks; the official general resolutions and pronouncements of the Party at past conventions; dissemination of the Party's general literature, including the standard outlines on Marxism; the Party's history and organizational structure; the secrecy of meetings and the clandestine nature of the Party generally; statements by officials evidencing sympathy for and alliance with the U.S.S.R. It was the predominance of evidence of this type which led the Court to order the acquittal of several *Yates* defendants, with the comment that they had not themselves "made a single remark or been present when someone else made a remark which would tend to prove the charges against them." However, this kind of evidence, while insufficient in itself to sustain a conviction, is not irrelevant. Such evidence in the context of other evidence, may be of value in showing illegal advocacy.

Second, the *Yates* opinion also indicates what kind of evidence is sufficient. There the Court pointed to two series of events which justified the denial of directed acquittals as to nine of the *Yates* defendants. The Court noted that with respect to seven of the defendants, meetings in San Francisco ... might be considered to be "the systematic teaching and advocacy of illegal action which is condemned by the statute." ... In those meetings, a small group of members were not only taught that violent revolution was inevitable, but they were also taught techniques for achieving that end. For example, the *Yates* record reveals that members were directed to be prepared to convert a general strike into a revolution and to deal with Negroes so as to prepare them specifically for revolution. In addition to the San Francisco meetings, the Court referred to certain activities in the Los Angeles area "which might be considered to amount to 'advocacy of action'" and with which two *Yates* defendants were linked. ... Thus, one member was "surreptitiously indoctrinated in methods ... of moving 'masses of people in time of crisis'"; others were told to adopt such Russian prerevolutionary techniques as the development of a special communication system through a newspaper similar to Pravda.... Viewed together, these events described in *Yates* indicate at least two patterns of evidence sufficient to show illegal advocacy: (a) the teaching of forceful overthrow, accompanied by directions as to the type of illegal action which must be taken when the time for the revolution is reached; and (b) the teaching of forceful overthrow, accompanied by a contemporary, though legal, course of conduct clearly undertaken for the specific purpose of rendering effective the later illegal activity which is advocated....

Finally, *Yates* is also relevant here in indicating, at least by implication, the type and quantum of evidence necessary to attach liability for illegal advocacy to the Party. In discussing the Government's "conspiratorial-nexus theory" the Court found that the evidence there was insufficient because the incidents of illegal advocacy were infrequent, sporadic, and not fairly related to the period covered by the indictment. In addition, the Court indicated that the illegal advocacy was not sufficiently tied to officials who spoke for the Party as such.

Thus, in short, *Yates* imposes a strict standard of proof, and indicates the kind of evidence that is insufficient to show illegal advocacy under that standard, the kind of evidence that is sufficient, and what pattern of evidence is necessary to hold the Party responsible for such advocacy. With these criteria in mind, we now proceed to an examination of the evidence in this case.

[The Court's summary of the evidence is omitted.]

We conclude that this evidence sufficed to make a case for the jury on the issue of illegal Party advocacy. *Dennis* and *Yates* have definitely laid at rest any doubt that present advocacy of *future* action for violent overthrow satisfies statutory and constitutional requirements equally with advocacy of *immediate* action to that end.... Hence this record cannot be considered deficient because it contains no evidence of advocacy for immediate overthrow.

Since the evidence amply showed that Party leaders were continuously preaching during the indictment period the inevitability of eventual forcible overthrow, the first and basic question is a narrow one: whether the jury could permissibly infer that such preaching, in whole or in part, "was aimed at building up a seditious group and maintaining it in readiness for action at a propitious time ... the kind of indoctrination preparatory to action which was condemned in *Dennis.*" ... On this score, we think that the jury, under instructions which fully satisfied the requirements of *Yates,* was entitled to infer from this systematic preaching ... that "advocacy of action" was engaged in.

. . .

Affirmed.

Mr. Justice Black, dissenting.

. . .

... I think it is important to point out the manner in which this case re-emphasizes the freedom-destroying nature of the "balancing test" presently in use by the Court to justify its refusal to apply specific constitutional protections of the Bill of Rights. ... Petitioner is being sent to jail for the express reason that he has associated with people who have entertained unlawful ideas and said unlawful things, and that of course is a *direct* abridgment of his freedoms of speech and assembly—under any definition that has ever been used for that term. ...

. . .

Mr. Justice Douglas, dissenting.

. . .

The case is not saved by showing that petitioner was an active member. None of the activity constitutes a crime....

Not one single illegal act is charged to petitioner. That is why the essence of the crime covered by the indictment is merely belief—belief in the proletarian revolution, belief in Communist creed.

. . .

Mr. Justice Brennan, with whom The Chief Justice and Mr. Justice Douglas join, dissenting.

[These justices argued that in § 4(f) of the Internal Security Act Congress legislated immunity from prosecution under the membership clause of the Smith Act.][a]

AFTERMATH OF THE YATES, SCALES AND NOTO CASES

Of 141 people indicted under the Smith Act, 29 served prison terms. These included the 11 defendants in *Dennis,* 17 defendants in two cases prior to *Yates* that the Court declined to review, and the single defendant in *Scales.* Emerson, *The System of Freedom of Expression* 124 (1970). The government had turned to membership clause prosecutions after *Yates,* because it concluded that it would be unable to satisfy the Court's requirement that each defendant be proved to have personally advocated specific illegal acts or have participated in such advocacy by others. While the Court sustained the constitutionality of the membership clause in *Scales,* and also sustained the conviction, the *Scales* case marked the end of Smith Act prosecutions. Under the *Scales* and *Noto* cases, was the government required, in a membership clause case, to satisfy the same proof requirements imposed by *Yates?*

Consider, also, whether proof meeting the criteria imposed by the *Yates, Scales* and *Noto* cases would also sustain conviction under two older statutes contained in the federal criminal code, United States Code, Title 18:

§ 2383.   Rebellion or Insurrection

Whoever incites, sets on foot, assists, or engages in any rebellion or insurrection against the authority of the United States or the laws thereof, or gives aid or comfort thereto, shall be fined not more than $10,000 or imprisoned not more than ten years, or both; and shall be incapable of holding any office under the United States.

§ 2384.   Seditious Conspiracy

If two or more persons in any State or Territory, or in any place subject to the jurisdiction of the United States, conspire to overthrow, put down, or to destroy by force the Government of the United States, or to levy war against them, or to oppose by force the authority thereof, or by force to prevent, hinder, or delay the execution of any law of the United States, or by force to seize, take, or possess any property of the United States contrary to the authority thereof, they shall each be fined not more than $20,000 or imprisoned not more than twenty years, or both.

a. Decided the same day as *Scales,* Noto v. United States, 367 U.S. 290 (1961), involved another prosecution under the membership clause of the Smith Act. The conviction was reversed because there was insufficient evidence of illegal Communist Party advocacy. Dicta stated that there must also be proof of the defendant's personal criminal purpose. "This element of the membership crime, like its others, must be judged *strictissimi juris,* for otherwise there is a danger that one in sympathy with the legitimate aims of such an organization, but not specifically intending to accomplish them by resort to violence, might be punished for his adherence to lawful and constitutionally protected purposes, because of other and unprotected purposes which he does not necessarily share." See United States v. Spock, 416 F.2d 165 (1st Cir.1969), reversing the conviction of Dr. Spock and others for conspiracy to counsel, aid, and abet registrants to resist the draft.

D.   THE CURRENT STATUS OF THE CLEAR AND PRESENT DANGER TEST—THE "BRANDENBURG CONCERTO"[1]

Brandenburg v. Ohio

395 U.S. 444, 89 S.Ct. 1827, 23 L.Ed.2d 430 (1969).

Per Curiam.

The appellant, a leader of a Ku Klux Klan group, was convicted under the Ohio Criminal Syndicalism statute for "advocat[ing] ... the duty, necessity, or propriety of crime, sabotage, violence, or unlawful methods of terrorism as a means of accomplishing industrial or political reform" and for "voluntarily assembl[ing] with any society, group, or assemblage of persons formed to teach or advocate the doctrines of criminal syndicalism." Ohio Rev. Code Ann. § 2923.13. He was fined $1,000 and sentenced to one to 10 years' imprisonment. The appellant challenged the constitutionality of the criminal syndicalism statute under the First and Fourteenth Amendments to the United States Constitution, but the intermediate appellate court of Ohio affirmed his conviction without opinion. The Supreme Court of Ohio dismissed his appeal, *sua sponte,* "for the reason that no substantial constitutional question exists herein." ... Appeal was taken to this Court, ... We reverse.

The record shows that a man, identified at trial as the appellant, telephoned an announcer-reporter on the staff of a Cincinnati television station and invited him to come to a Ku Klux Klan "rally" to be held at a farm in Hamilton County. With the cooperation of the organizers, the reporter and a cameraman attended the meeting and filmed the events. Portions of the films were later broadcast on the local station and on a national network.

The prosecution's case rested on the films and on testimony identifying the appellant as the person who communicated with the reporter and who spoke at the rally. The State also introduced into evidence several articles appearing in the film, including a pistol, a rifle, a shotgun, ammunition, a Bible, and a red hood worn by the speaker in the films.

One film showed 12 hooded figures, some of whom carried firearms. They were gathered around a large wooden cross, which they burned. No one was present other than the participants and the newsmen who made the film. Most of the words uttered during the scene were incomprehensible when the film was projected, but scattered phrases could be understood that were derogatory of Negroes and, in one instance, of Jews.[1] Another scene on the same film showed the appellant, in Klan regalia, making a speech. The speech, in full, was as follows:

1. Linde, supra, p. 1276.

1. The significant portions that could be understood were:

"How far is the nigger going to—yeah."

"This is what we are going to do to the niggers."

"A dirty nigger."

"Send the Jews back to Israel."

"Let's give them back to the dark garden."

"Save America."

"Let's go back to constitutional betterment."

"Bury the niggers."

"We intend to do our part."

"Give us our state rights."

"Freedom for the whites."

"Nigger will have to fight for every inch he gets from now on."

"This is an organizers' meeting. We have had quite a few members here today which are—we have hundreds, hundreds of members throughout the State of Ohio. I can quote from a newspaper clipping from the Columbus, Ohio Dispatch, five weeks ago Sunday morning. The Klan has more members in the State of Ohio than does any other organization. We're not a revengent organization, but if our President, our Congress, our Supreme court, continues to suppress the white, Caucasian race, it's possible that there might have to be some revengeance taken.

"We are marching on Congress July the Fourth, four hundred thousand strong. From there we are dividing into two groups, one group to march on St. Augustine, Florida, the other group to march into Mississippi. Thank you."

The second film showed six hooded figures one of whom, later identified as the appellant, repeated a speech very similar to that recorded on the first film. The reference to the possibility of "revengeance" was omitted, and one sentence was added: "Personally, I believe the nigger should be returned to Africa, the Jew returned to Israel." Though some of the figures in the films carried weapons, the speaker did not.

The Ohio Criminal Syndicalism Statute was enacted in 1919. From 1917 to 1920, identical or quite similar laws were adopted by 20 States and two territories. E. Dowell, A History of Criminal Syndicalism Legislation in the United States 21 (1939). In 1927, this Court sustained the constitutionality of California's Criminal Syndicalism Act, . . . the text of which is quite similar to that of the laws of Ohio. Whitney v. California, 274 U.S. 357 (1927). The Court upheld the statute on the ground that, without more, "advocating" violent means to effect political and economic change involves such danger to the security of the State that the State may outlaw it. Cf. Fiske v. Kansas, 274 U.S. 380 (1927). But *Whitney* has been thoroughly discredited by later decisions. See Dennis v. United States, 341 U.S. 494, at 507 (1951). These later decisions have fashioned the principle that the constitutional guarantees of free speech and free press do not permit a State to forbid or proscribe advocacy of the use of force or of law violation except where such advocacy is directed to inciting or producing imminent lawless action and is likely to incite or produce such action.[2] As we said in Noto v. United States, 367 U.S. 290, 297–298 (1961), "the mere abstract teaching . . . of the moral propriety or even moral necessity for a resort to force and violence, is not the same as preparing a group for violent action and steeling it to such action." See also Herndon v. Lowry, 301 U.S. 242, 259–261 (1937); Bond v. Floyd, 385 U.S. 116, 134 (1966). A statute which fails to draw this distinction impermissibly intrudes upon the freedoms guaranteed by the First and Fourteenth Amendments. It sweeps within its condemnation speech which our Constitution has immunized from governmental control. Cf. Yates v. United States, 354 U.S. 298 (1957); De Jonge v. Oregon, 299 U.S. 353 (1937); Stromberg v. California, 283 U.S. 359 (1931). . . .

Measured by this test, Ohio's Criminal Syndicalism Act cannot be sustained. The Act punishes persons who "advocate or teach the duty necessity, or propriety" of violence "as a means of accomplishing industrial or political

[handwritten margin note: Principle used to uphold statute]

---

2. It was on the theory that the Smith Act, 54 Stat. 670, 18 U.S.C. § 2385, embodied such a principle and that it had been applied only in conformity with it that this Court sustained the Act's constitutionality. Dennis v. United States, 341 U.S. 494 (1951). That this was the basis for *Dennis* was emphasized in Yates v. United States, 354 U.S. 298, 320– 324 (1957), in which the Court overturned convictions for advocacy of the forcible overthrow of the Government under the Smith Act, because the trial judge's instructions had allowed conviction for mere advocacy, unrelated to its tendency to produce forcible action.

reform"; or who publish or circulate or display any book or paper containing such advocacy; or who "justify" the commission of violent acts "with intent to exemplify, spread or advocate the propriety of the doctrines of criminal syndicalism"; or who "voluntarily assemble" with a group formed "to teach or advocate the doctrines of criminal syndicalism." Neither the indictment nor the trial judge's instructions to the jury in any way refined the statute's bald definition of the crime in terms of mere advocacy not distinguished from incitement to imminent lawless action.[3]

Accordingly, we are here confronted with a statute which, by its own words and as applied, purports to punish mere advocacy and to forbid, on pain of criminal punishment, assembly with others merely to advocate the described type of action.[4] Such a statute falls within the condemnation of the First and Fourteenth Amendments. The contrary teaching of Whitney v. California, supra, cannot be supported, and that decision is therefore overruled.

Reversed.

Mr. Justice Black, concurring.

I agree with the views expressed by Mr. Justice Douglas in his concurring opinion in this case that the "clear and present danger" doctrine should have no place in the interpretation of the First Amendment. I join the Court's opinion, which, as I understand it, simply cites Dennis v. United States, 341 U.S. 494 (1951), but does not indicate any agreement on the Court's part with the "clear and present danger" doctrine on which *Dennis* purported to rely.

Mr. Justice Douglas, concurring.

While I join the opinion of the Court, I desire to enter a *caveat*.

. . .

. . . I see no place in the regime of the First Amendment for any "clear and present danger" test, whether strict and tight as some would make it, or freewheeling as the Court in *Dennis* rephrased it.

When one reads the opinions closely and sees when and how the "clear and present danger" test has been applied, great misgivings are aroused. First, the threats were often loud but always puny and made serious only by judges so wedded to the *status quo* that critical analysis made them nervous. Second, the test was so twisted and perverted in *Dennis* as to make the trial of those teachers of Marxism an all-out political trial which was part and parcel of the cold war that has eroded substantial parts of the First Amendment.

. . .

3. The first count of the indictment charged that appellant "did unlawfully by word of mouth advocate the necessity, or propriety of crime, violence, or unlawful methods of terrorism as a means of accomplishing political reform...." The second count charged that appellant "did unlawfully voluntarily assemble with a group or assemblage of persons formed to advocate the doctrines of criminal syndicalism...." The trial judge's charge merely followed the language of the indictment. No construction of the statute by the Ohio courts has brought it within constitutionally permissible limits. The Ohio Supreme Court has considered the statute in only one previous case, State v. Kassay, 126 Ohio St. 177, 184 N.E. 521 (1932), where the constitutionality of the statute was sustained.

4. Statutes affecting the right of assembly, like those touching on freedom of speech, must observe the established distinctions between mere advocacy and incitement to imminent lawless action, for as Chief Justice Hughes wrote in De Jonge v. Oregon, supra, at 364: "The right of peaceable assembly is a right cognate to those of free speech and free press and is equally fundamental." ...

The line between what is permissible and not subject to control and what may be made impermissible and subject to regulation is the line between ideas and overt acts.

The example usually given by those who would punish speech is the case of one who falsely shouts fire in a crowded theatre.

This is, however, a classic case where speech is brigaded with action. They are indeed inseparable and a prosecution can be launched for the overt acts actually caused. Apart from rare instances of that kind, speech is, I think, immune from prosecution. Certainly there is no constitutional line between advocacy of abstract ideas as in *Yates* and advocacy of political action as in *Scales*. The quality of advocacy turns on the depth of the conviction; and government has no power to invade that sanctuary of belief and conscience.[a]

THE CONSTITUTIONAL LAW IMPLICATIONS OF THE COURT'S SMITH ACT INTERPRETATION

Despite the fact that it is a *per curiam* decision[1] and despite possible arguments that much of the discussion of clear and present danger is dicta, *Brandenburg* has been read as an authoritative statement of the Court's position on the minimum protection afforded speech.[2] Subsequent cases have converted other aspects of the Court's construction of the Smith Act in the *Yates* and *Scales* cases into constitutional doctrine.

Even under the position taken by Justices Brandeis and Holmes, people could be punished for knowing membership in an organization advocating the commission of serious crimes, if there was a clear and present danger that those crimes would be committed. Justice Brandeis' *Whitney* concurrence did not require proof that the defendant participated in the advocacy or shared the organization's illegal purposes. Dicta in the *Scales* and *Noto* cases, however, required that there be proof, beyond defendant's knowledge of illegal advocacy by the organization, of the defendant's "active membership" and specific intent to accomplish the organization's illegal aims. Application of those requirements would have required the acquittal of the defendant in the *Whitney* case, even upon proof that her organization advocated specific criminal conduct and that there was a clear and present danger. Those requirements have, however, been converted from interpretations of the Smith Act to first amendment doctrine. The development occurred in a series of cases dealing with government requests for information, qualification for government employment and loyalty oaths; none of the cases involved criminal punishment.[3]

a. For a review of the development of clear and present danger doctrine from prior to World War I through *Brandenburg,* see Rabban, *The Emergence of Modern First Amendment Doctrine,* 50 U.Chi.L.Rev. 1205 (1983).

1. It is unusual that the Court's major expression of contemporary first amendment doctrine is contained in an unsigned opinion. The editors have been informed by a reliable source that the opinion had been written by Justice Fortas, who resigned prior to the Court's announcement of the decision. The same source states that the case was regarded as easy in its result, and very little attention was paid to what the opinion said.

2. E.g., a state conviction for disorderly conduct based on an intemperate speech at a campus anti-war demonstration was reversed, on the authority of *Brandenburg,* in Hess v. Indiana, 414 U.S. 105 (1973). Specifically, the Court held that the *Brandenburg* criteria had not been met both because the defendant's speech did not advocate specific unlawful action, and there was insufficient evidence that his words were likely to produce imminent disorder.

3. Elfbrandt v. Russell, 384 U.S. 11, 15–16 (1966); Keyishian v. Board of Regents, 385 U.S. 589, 606 (1967); Law Students Civil Rights Research Council, Inc. v. Wadmond, 401 U.S. 154, 165 (1971).

DEFERENCE TO LEGISLATIVE JUDGMENT CONCERNING THE PRESENCE AND EXTENT OF DANGER

A major issue in the clear and present danger debate is whether courts should defer to legislative judgments concerning the danger posed by classes of speech or the defendant's speech. It will be recalled that, in *Gitlow,* the Court noted the New York legislature's implicit determination that *all* revolutionary speech was dangerous, and concluded "it must be given great weight." Justice Frankfurter's concurring opinion in *Dennis* argued that the case presented a clash of interests "[i]t is not for us to decide" since Congress had decided that the danger created by Communist Party speech justified its restriction. 341 U.S. at 550. Chief Justice Vinson's plurality opinion accepted clear and present danger as the appropriate standard, with the obligation of courts to examine whether there is a clear and present danger to justify application of the statute to the specific situation, and thus did not articulately refer to sustaining of legislative judgments. (The rejection of any requirement of imminence allowed the plurality to discover the requisite danger. The Court had, moreover, not granted certiorari to consider the sufficiency of the evidence, so the Court was not required to determine whether any particular Communist Party speech created danger.) Chief Justice Vinson's opinion can be read as implicitly deferring to contemporary legislative and executive judgments concerning the danger to internal security presented by the Communist Party.

The Court discussed the issue of deference to legislative judgment in Landmark Communications, Inc. v. Virginia, 435 U.S. 829 (1978). Chief Justice Burger's opinion for the Court said, in part:

". . . Properly applied, the test requires a court to make its own inquiry into the imminence and magnitude of the danger said to flow from the particular utterance and then to balance the character of the evil, as well as its likelihood, against the need for free and unfettered expression. The possibility that other measures will serve the State's interests should also be weighed.

. . .

"A legislature appropriately inquires into and may declare the reasons impelling legislative action but the judicial function commands analysis of whether the specific conduct charged falls within the reach of the statute and if so whether the legislation is consonant with the Constitution. Were it otherwise, the scope of freedom of speech and of the press would be subject to legislative definition and the function of the First Amendment as a check on legislative power would be nullified."

THE CLEAR AND PRESENT DANGER DEBATE—SOME GENERAL CONSIDERATIONS

The earlier debate, in an extensive literature, argued whether a tightly-drawn clear and present danger test was a *necessary* condition for protection of freedom of speech.[1] The Court's current adherence to it has muted that debate, and brought to the fore the question whether any version of the clear and present danger test is a *sufficient* condition for protection of freedom of speech.[2]

---

1. The most articulate defense of the clear and present danger test is contained in Chafee, *Free Speech in the United States* (1941). For a contemporary defense, see Redish, *Advocacy of Unlawful Conduct and The* *First Amendment: In Defense of Clear and Present Danger,* 70 Calif.L.Rev. 1159 (1982).

2. The earliest critical scholarly attack on the test as insufficiently protective of speech is Meiklejohn, *Free Speech and Its Relation to Self–Government* (1948).

Before turning to some of the arguments made in the debate, however, it is important to note that clear and present danger is not a doctrine for all first amendment seasons. In its focus on the danger of illegal conduct, at most its literal application is limited to those cases where the only societal interest asserted for restricting speech is that danger. As will be seen in Section 3 of this chapter, and in the following two chapters, whether or not clear and present danger is the appropriate test for speech urging violation of the law, it is not helpful in other problem areas.[3] Some general themes in the debate are, however, of broader application. Some of those themes are singled out for brief mention, below.

(1) Political Speech Contrasted with Other Forms of Speech. While the clear and present danger test is by its terms directed at any speech advocating the commission of a crime, all of the Supreme Court's cases have, in fact, involved some form of political speech—whether the general platform of a radical organization or a hot-tempered street-corner protest speech. A major criticism of the clear and present danger approach is that it permits stifling of radical political speech based on problematic assessments of public danger, while it over-protects dangerous speech in a non-political context.

The application of first amendment principles to criminal defendants who incite or solicit others, or agree among themselves to commit specific, serious crimes in a non-political context has not been much explored.[4] Professor Chafee, the most ardent defender of Holmes' clear and present danger approach, argued that its source could be found in the general criminal law of attempt, which required that the defendant had made "dangerous progress toward the consummation" of the crime.[5] It will be recalled, however, that Holmes' opinions in *Schenck* and *Abrams* focused at least as much on the speakers' "intent" as on their "dangerous progress." The requirement of progress toward consummation of the criminal conduct urged by speech seems not to be clearly reflected in criminal law doctrines of solicitation and conspiracy, which also focus primarily on issues of proof of the defendant's intent. The Model Penal Code, § 5.02, provides that a person is guilty of solicitation to commit a crime "if with the purpose of facilitating its commission he commands, encourages or requests another person to engage in specific conduct which would constitute such crime." No requirement that the person solicited is likely to commit the crime has been imposed. The crime of conspiracy,

---

3. Prior to the *Dennis* case, the Court had employed the clear and present danger test in the context of a state contempt of court conviction of a newspaper and a labor leader for allegedly prejudicial statements concerning pending cases. Justice Black's opinion for the Court in Bridges v. California, 314 U.S. 252 (1941), held that these publications could not constitutionally constitute contempt in the absence of a clear and present danger to the administration of justice. Later cases involving contempt prosecutions for media criticism of judicial decisions have continued to reverse the convictions using the idiom of clear and present danger. Pennekamp v. Florida, 328 U.S. 331 (1946); Craig v. Harney, 331 U.S. 367 (1947); Wood v. Georgia, 370 U.S. 375 (1962). Those cases, however, can be read as imposing an absolute ban on contempt prosecution for media statements concerning pending cases, or criticism of judicial action. See Baltimore Radio Show,

Inc. v. State, 193 Md. 300, 67 A.2d 497 (1949), cert. denied 338 U.S. 912 (1950).

Bridges, Pennekamp and *Craig* were prominent among the cases cited by Chief Justice Vinson in his opinion in the *Dennis* case for the proposition that the Court had "inclined toward the Holmes–Brandeis rationale." 341 U.S. at 507.

4. Compare, however, State v. Robertson, 293 Or. 402, 649 P.2d 569 (1982). The Oregon Supreme Court, in an opinion by Justice Linde, invalidated a statute making "criminal coercion" a crime. The challenged statute concerned compelling or inducing a person to do something he has a legal right not to do by making a threat to inflict specific harms, including exposing a secret. For extended comment on the decision, see Greenawalt, *Criminal Coercion and Freedom of Speech,* 78 Northwestern L.Rev. 1081 (1983).

5. Chafee, supra note 1, at 47.

whether or not it requires the commission of an overt act as well as the agreement, has similarly not required a showing that the ultimate object of the conspiracy would occur.

The argument that clear and present danger affords too little protection in the arena of political speech was first put forward by Alexander Meiklejohn.[6] He argued that the principle of freedom of speech was rooted in principles of self-government, and that there should be absolute protection for the discussion of public issues, but considerably less protection for speech that did not discuss issues of public interest.[7] Critics of the Meiklejohn approach have questioned the ability to draw the distinction between political and other forms of speech, and have objected to the low level of protection afforded non-political speech under his theory.[8] Advocates of a political speech principle have disagreed with Meiklejohn's assessment of the level of protection to be afforded political speech[9] or with his conclusion that the first amendment was inapplicable to non-political speech.[10] It is, however, a useful inquiry to consider whether the pattern of the Court's decisions reflects a distinction between speech discussing public affairs and other kinds of communication.

(2) Absolutes and Balances. Justice Black was a consistent opponent of balancing competing interests as a technique of judicial adjudication. While his early opinions spoke of clear and present danger, he indicated in his *Dennis* dissent that he believed clear and present danger did not mark the outer boundaries of protected expression. For him, clear and present danger had become simply another technique for balancing competing interests. (Justice Frankfurter's *Dennis* concurrence, by contrast, criticized clear and present danger as too wooden a standard to permit the sensitive balancing of competing interests.) The position adopted by Justices Black and Douglas was that the first amendment forbids any government restriction on "speech" but permits the government to regulate "conduct." In their opinions in a number of cases, Justices Black and Harlan debated the question whether freedom of speech was absolutely protected[11] with Justice Black consistently maintaining that "the men who drafted our Bill of Rights did all the 'balancing' that was to be done in this field."[12]

Criticisms of both the balancers and the absolutists should be obvious. Given the intractable problem of assigning values to competing interests, it is claimed that balancing is not a process but simply a convenient method of rationalizing subjective conclusions. Moreover, it often has been employed with excessive deference to the interests that justify suppression of speech. Absolute protection, it is argued, over-protects intolerable speech, or requires sophistry in drawing speech-conduct distinctions, or both.[13] The clash of contentions

---

6. Meiklejohn, supra note 2.

7. Specifically, Meiklejohn argued that "freedom of speech" protected by the first amendment was non-abridgable, but that "liberty of speech" was protected only by the concept of due process and could be regulated for sufficient reasons. Id. at 37–39.

8. E.g., Emerson, *The System of Freedom of Expression* 541 (1970); Chafee, *Book Review of Meiklejohn's Free Speech and its Relation to Self–Government,* 62 Harv.L.Rev. 891 (1949).

9. Bork, *Neutral Principles and Some First Amendment Problems,* 47 Ind.L.J. 1 (1971).

10. Be Vier, *The First Amendment and Political Speech: An Inquiry into the Substance and Limits of Principle,* 30 Stan.L.Rev. 299 (1978).

11. E.g., Barenblatt v. United States, 360 U.S. 109 (1959); Konigsberg v. State Bar, 366 U.S. 36 (1961); cf. Cohen v. California, 403 U.S. 15 (1971).

12. 366 U.S. at 61.

13. A sampling of the law review discussion includes Griswold, *Absolute is in the Dark—A Discussion of the Approach of the Supreme Court to Constitutional Questions,* 8 Utah L.Rev. 167 (1963); Frantz, *The First Amendment in the Balance,* 71 Yale L.J. 1424

about absolutism and balancing has abated in contemporary free speech cases, but some of the competing arguments may have re-appeared in a new form.

(3) Ad Hoc and Definitional Balancing. A major dispute in the debate surrounding clear and present danger was whether it was appropriate to focus on the danger of all revolutionary speech, or the danger of the defendant's particular speech in its context.[14] An analogous argument concerns the method for reconciling free speech values with competing governmental interests. Ad hoc balancing requires weighing the value of particular speech against the strength of competing interests in the particular case. Definitional balancing suggests that the competing interests should result not in ad hoc decisions but the framing of rules of general application.[15] For a "definitional balancer," the proper rule in a particular context may be one of absolute protection for speech, which may trigger at least part of the controversy between absolutism and balancing. Moreover, the distinction between ad hoc and definitional balancing is itself slippery, since it turns on the level of generality at which a balance is struck or whether there is predictable content in a rule. The student should be alert, in the materials that follow, to the question whether particular free speech issues have been resolved by ad hoc or definitional balancing. A final question is whether the results reached, or the reasons given, represent a single, coherent theory of freedom of expression.

SECTION 2.   INTERMEZZO: AN INTRODUCTION TO THE CONCEPTS OF VAGUENESS, OVERBREADTH AND PRIOR RESTRAINT

Introduction. Section 3 of this chapter will continue the inquiry begun in Section 1—exploring the societal interests that justify government control of the content of expression. This section involves judicial techniques that permit

---

(1962); Mendelson, *On the Meaning of the First Amendment: Absolutes in the Balance,* 50 Calif.L.Rev. 821 (1962); Frantz, *Is the First Amendment Law—A Reply to Professor Mendelson,* 51 Calif.L.Rev. 729 (1963); Kalven, *Upon Re-reading Mr. Justice Black on the First Amendment,* 14 U.C.L.A.L.Rev. 428 (1967); Gunther, *In Search of Judicial Quality on a Changing Court: The Case of Justice Powell,* 24 Stanf.L.Rev. 1001 (1972); Powe, *Evolution to Absolutism: Justice Douglas and the First Amendment,* 74 Colum.L.Rev. 371 (1974).

It can be argued that Justice Black was forced to manipulate the boundaries separating expression and action. In Giboney v. Empire Storage and Ice Co., 336 U.S. 490 (1949), he wrote the opinion for a unanimous court sustaining a restraint of trade conviction of union picketers whose placards urged an ice distributor to stop selling ice to nonunion peddlers. His opinion stated that the placards were to effectuate an unlawful purpose, and the defendants had engaged in illegal conduct "carried out by means of language." In Cohen v. California, 403 U.S. 15 (1971), infra, p. 1311, the Court overturned a breach of the peace conviction of a person who wore a

jacket in a courthouse bearing the words "Fuck the Draft." Justice Black joined Justice Blackmun's dissent, which stated that the defendant's "antic ... was mainly conduct and little speech."

14.   See Linde, supra page 1276.

15.   The term "definitional balancing" first appears in Nimmer, *The Right to Speak from Times to Time: First Amendment Theory Applied to Libel and Misapplied to Privacy,* 56 Cal.L.Rev. 935 (1968), which still contains the most lucid description of the distinction between definitional and ad hoc balancing. Id. at 939–948. The most comprehensive treatment of freedom of expression issues which rejects both absolutism and ad hoc balancing is contained in Emerson, supra note 8. Another attempt to construct a general structure avoiding ad hoc balancing is contained in a series of articles by Professor C. Edwin Baker. They are cited in Shiffrin, *The First Amendment and Economic Regulation: Away from a General Theory of the First Amendment,* 78 Northwestern L.Rev. 1212, 1224 n. 83 (1983), and Baker's approach is both explained and criticized, id. at 1239–1251.

courts to reverse a defendant's conviction, or invalidate a statute, without deciding whether or not the content of expression or publication is constitutionally protected. The question to be asked is whether these techniques, as they are employed, respond to legitimate constitutional concerns or whether they are devices to avoid or postpone harder decisions concerning the limits of constitutionally protected speech. This section will not exhaust the study of vagueness, overbreadth and prior restraint. Decisions included in the remainder of this chapter, and the succeeding three chapters, are often based on these concepts.

A.   VAGUENESS AND OVERBREADTH

HERNDON v. LOWRY, 301 U.S. 242 (1937). Herndon, an African American, had gone to Alabama as a paid organizer for the Communist Party during the depression years of the 1930's. He enrolled at least five members and held some meetings. When he was arrested he had in his possession Communist literature, including a pamphlet urging self determination for blacks and advocating strikes, boycotts and a revolutionary struggle for power. It did not appear that he had distributed the literature found in his possession nor that he had advocated anything other than relief for the needy. Herndon received a heavy sentence under a Georgia statute that had been aimed at slave insurrections in its earlier form, before the civil war. (The statute would have permitted imposition of the death penalty in Herndon's case.) The statute defined "attempt to incite insurrection" as "any attempt, by persuasion or otherwise, to induce others to join in any combined resistance to the lawful authority of the state." Herndon appealed his conviction to the Georgia Supreme Court, arguing that the evidence was insufficient to sustain his conviction, because there was no proof that immediate serious violence was expected or advocated. The Georgia Supreme Court affirmed the conviction, ruling that such proof was unnecessary. A defendant did not have to intend that an insurrection should follow "instantly or at any given time, but it would be sufficient that he intended it to happen at any time, as a result of his influence, by those whom he sought to incite."

Herndon's major argument in the Supreme Court was that the insurrection statute as construed was unconstitutional, since no clear and present danger was required for conviction. The Court, however, reversed the conviction without overruling the holding of Gitlow v. New York, 268 U.S. 652 (1925), that a legislature could make revolutionary speech a crime without requiring proof of clear and present danger. The Court first analyzed the evidence, and concluded that Herndon had been convicted for merely talking about unemployment relief, since there was no proof he had distributed the single copies of the more inflammatory literature in his possession. Relying in part on De Jonge v. Oregon, 299 U.S. 353 (1937) (Section 1, supra), the Court held on these facts that Herndon's conviction was an "unwarranted invasion of the right of freedom of speech." The Court's second ground of decision was that the insurrection statute was unconstitutional. Portions of Justice Roberts' discussion of that ground follow:

"The statute, as construed and applied in the appellant's trial, does not furnish a sufficiently ascertainable standard of guilt. . . .

" . . . To be guilty under the law, as construed, a defendant need not advocate resort to force. He need not teach any particular doctrine to come within its purview. Indeed, he need not be active in the formation of a combination or group if he agitate for a change in the frame of government, however peaceful his own intent. If, by the exercise of prophesy, he can forecast

that, as a result of a chain of causation, following his proposed action a group may arise at some future date which will resort to force, he is bound to make the prophesy and abstain, under pain of punishment, possibly of execution. Every person who attacks existing conditions, who agitates for a change in the form of government, must take the risk that if a jury should be of opinion he ought to have foreseen that his utterances might contribute in any measure to some future forcible resistance to the existing government he may be convicted of the offense of inciting insurrection. Proof that the accused in fact believed that his effort would cause a violent assault upon the state would not be necessary to conviction. It would be sufficient if the jury thought he reasonably might foretell that those he persuaded to join the party might, at some time in the indefinite future, resort to forcible resistance of government. The question thus proposed to a jury involves pure speculation as to future trends of thought and action. Within what time might one reasonably expect that an attempted organization of the Communist Party in the United States would result in violent action by that party? If a jury returned a special verdict saying twenty years or even fifty years the verdict could not be shown to be wrong. The law, as thus construed, licenses the jury to create its own standard in each case....

"...

"The statute as construed and applied, amounts merely to a dragnet which may enmesh any one who agitates for a change of government if a jury can be persuaded that he ought to have foreseen his words would have some effect in the future conduct of others. No reasonably ascertainable standard of guilt is prescribed. So vague and indeterminate are the boundaries thus set to the freedom of speech and assembly that the law necessarily violates the guarantees of liberty embodied in the Fourteenth Amendment."[a]

Coates v. Cincinnati

402 U.S. 611, 91 S.Ct. 1686, 29 L.Ed.2d 214 (1971).

Mr. Justice Stewart delivered the opinion of the Court.

A Cincinnati, Ohio, ordinance makes it a criminal offense for "three or more persons to assemble ... on any of the sidewalks ... and there conduct themselves in a manner annoying to persons passing by...." The issue before us is whether this ordinance is unconstitutional on its face.

The appellants were convicted of violating the ordinance, and the convictions were ultimately affirmed by a closely divided vote in the Supreme Court of Ohio, upholding the constitutional validity of the ordinance. An appeal from that judgment was brought here.... The record brought before the reviewing courts tells us no more than that the appellant Coates was a student involved in a demonstration and the other appellants were pickets involved in a labor dispute. For throughout this litigation it has been the appellants' position that the ordinance on its face violates the First and Fourteenth Amendments of the Constitution. ...

In rejecting this claim and affirming the convictions the Ohio Supreme Court did not give the ordinance any construction at variance with the apparent plain import of its language....

. . .

a. For an interesting discussion of *Herndon v. Lowry*, see Chafee, *Free Speech in the United States* 388–398 (1941).

statute is vague

We are thus relegated, at best, to the words of the ordinance itself. If three or more people meet together on a sidewalk or street corner, they must conduct themselves so as not to annoy any police officer or other person who should happen to pass by. In our opinion this ordinance is unconstitutionally vague because it subjects the exercise of the right of assembly to an unascertainable standard, and unconstitutionally broad because it authorizes the punishment of constitutionally protected conduct.

no standard of conduct is specified at all

Conduct that annoys some people does not annoy others. Thus, the ordinance is vague not in the sense that it requires a person to conform his conduct to an imprecise but comprehensible normative standard, but rather in the sense that no standard of conduct is specified at all. As a result, "men of common intelligence must necessarily guess at its meaning." . . .

It is said that the ordinance is broad enough to encompass many types of conduct clearly within the city's constitutional power to prohibit. And so, indeed, it is. The city is free to prevent people from blocking sidewalks, obstructing traffic, littering streets, committing assaults, or engaging in countless other forms of anti-social conduct. It can do so through the enactment and enforcement of ordinances directed with reasonable specificity toward the conduct to be prohibited. . . . It cannot constitutionally do so through the enactment and enforcement of an ordinance whose violation may entirely depend upon whether or not a policeman is annoyed.

But the vice of the ordinance lies not alone in its violation of the due process standard of vagueness. The ordinance also violates the constitutional right of free assembly and association. Our decisions establish that mere public intolerance or animosity cannot be the basis for abridgment of these constitutional freedoms. . . . The First and Fourteenth Amendments do not permit a State to make criminal the exercise of the right of assembly simply because its exercise may be "annoying" to some people. If this were not the rule, the right of the people to gather in public places for social or political purposes would be continually subject to summary suspension through the good-faith enforcement of a prohibition against annoying conduct. And such a prohibition, in addition, contains an obvious invitation to discriminatory enforcement against those whose association together is "annoying" because their ideas, their lifestyle or their physical appearance is resented by the majority of their fellow citizens.

statute held invalid

The ordinance before us makes a crime out of what under the Constitution cannot be a crime. It is aimed directly at activity protected by the Constitution. We need not lament that we do not have before us the details of the conduct found to be annoying. It is the ordinance on its face that sets the standard of conduct and warns against transgression. The details of the offense could no more serve to validate this ordinance than could the details of an offense charged under an ordinance suspending unconditionally the right of assembly and free speech.

The judgment is reversed.

Mr. Justice White, with whom The Chief Justice and Mr. Justice Blackmun join, dissenting.

The claim in this case, in part, is that the Cincinnati ordinance is so vague that it may not constitutionally be applied to any conduct. But the ordinance prohibits persons from assembling with others and "conduct[ing] themselves in a manner annoying to persons passing by. . . ." . . . Any man of average comprehension should know that some kinds of conduct, such as assault or blocking passage on the street, will annoy others and are clearly covered by the "annoying conduct" standard of the ordinance. It would be frivolous to say that

these and many other kinds of conduct are not within the foreseeable reach of the law.

It is possible that a whole range of other acts, defined with unconstitutional imprecision, is forbidden by the ordinance. But as a general rule, when a criminal charge is based on conduct constitutionally subject to proscription and clearly forbidden by a statute, it is no defense that the law would be unconstitutionally vague if applied to other behavior. Such a statute is not vague on its face. It may be vague as applied in some circumstances, but ruling on such a challenge obviously requires knowledge of the conduct with which a defendant is charged.

. . .

So . . . in United States v. National Dairy Corp., 372 U.S. 29 (1963), where we considered a statute forbidding sales of goods at "unreasonably" low prices to injure or eliminate a competitor, 15 U.S.C. § 13a, we thought the statute gave a seller adequate notice that sales below costs were illegal. The statute was therefore not facially vague, although it might be difficult to tell whether certain other kinds of conduct fell within this language. . . . This approach is consistent with the host of cases holding that "one to whom application of a statute is constitutional will not be heard to attack the statute on the ground that impliedly it might also be taken as applying to other persons or other situations in which its application might be unconstitutional." United States v. Raines, 362 U.S. 17, 21 (1960), and cases there cited.

Our cases, however, including *National Dairy,* recognize a different approach where the statute at issue purports to regulate or proscribe rights of speech or press protected by the First Amendment. . . . Although a statute may be neither vague, overbroad, nor otherwise invalid as applied to the conduct charged against a particular defendant, he is permitted to raise its vagueness or unconstitutional overbreadth as applied to others. And if the law is found deficient in one of these respects, it may not be applied to him either, until and unless a satisfactory limiting construction is placed on the statute. . . . The statute, in effect, is stricken down on its face. This result is deemed justified since the otherwise continued existence of the statute in unnarrowed form would tend to suppress constitutionally protected rights. . . .

Even accepting the overbreadth doctrine with respect to statutes clearly reaching speech, the Cincinnati ordinance does not purport to bar or regulate speech as such. It prohibits persons from assembling and "conduct[ing]" themselves in a manner annoying to other persons. Even if the assembled defendants in this case were demonstrating and picketing, we have long recognized that picketing is not solely a communicative endeavor and has aspects which the State is entitled to regulate even though there is incidental impact on speech. In Cox v. Louisiana, 379 U.S. 559 (1965), the Court held valid on its face a statute forbidding picketing and parading near a courthouse. This was deemed a valid regulation of conduct rather than pure speech. . . .

In the case before us, I would deal with the Cincinnati ordinance as we would with the ordinary criminal statute. The ordinance clearly reaches certain conduct but may be illegally vague with respect to other conduct. The statute is not infirm on its face and since we have no information from this record as to what conduct was charged against these defendants, we are in no position to judge the statute as applied. That the ordinance may confer wide discretion in a wide range of circumstances is irrelevant when we may be dealing with conduct at its core.

I would therefore affirm the judgment of the Ohio Supreme Court.

Mr. Justice Black.

. . .

. . . [T]he First Amendment which forbids the State to abridge freedom of speech, would invalidate this city ordinance if it were used to punish the making of a political speech, even if that speech were to annoy other persons. In contrast, however, the ordinance could properly be applied to prohibit the gathering of persons in the mouths of alleys to annoy passersby by throwing rocks or by some other conduct not at all connected with speech. It is a matter of no little difficulty to determine when a law can be held void on its face and when such summary action is inappropriate. This difficulty has been aggravated in this case, because the record fails to show in what conduct these defendants had engaged to annoy other people. In my view, a record showing the facts surrounding the conviction is essential to adjudicate the important constitutional issues in this case. I would therefore, vacate the judgment and remand the case to the court below to give both parties an opportunity to supplement the record so that we may determine whether the conduct actually punished is the kind of conduct which it is within the power of the State to punish.

BROADRICK v. OKLAHOMA, 413 U.S. 601 (1973). An Oklahoma statute proscribed partisan political activity by state civil servants. Plaintiffs, who had engaged in partisan political activities (including solicitation of money) among their co–workers, brought suit to enjoin enforcement of the statute. They conceded that the statute validly could prohibit the conduct they had engaged in but sought to have it declared unconstitutional because it forbade the wearing of political buttons and displaying bumper stickers—activity they had not engaged in. They argued that the statute was overbroad because buttons and stickers were protected expression.

Justice White, writing for the Court rejected this contention:

"[T]he Court has altered its traditional rules of standing to permit—in the First Amendment area—'attacks on overly broad statutes with no requirement that the person making the attack demonstrate that his own conduct could not be regulated by a statute drawn with the requisite specificity.' Dombrowski v. Pfister, 380 U.S. 479, 486 (1965). Litigants, therefore, are permitted to challenge a statute not because their own rights of free expression are violated, but because of a judicial prediction or assumption that the statute's very existence may cause others not before the court to refrain from constitutionally protected speech or expression.

"Such claims of facial overbreadth have been entertained in cases involving statutes which, by their terms, seek to regulate 'only spoken words.' Gooding v. Wilson, 405 U.S. 518, 520 (1972). . . . In such cases, it has been the judgment of this Court that the possible harm to society in permitting some unprotected speech to go unpunished is outweighed by the possibility that protected speech of others may be muted and perceived grievances left to fester because of the possible inhibitory effects of overly broad statutes. Overbreadth attacks have also been allowed where the Court thought rights of association were ensnared in statutes which, by their broad sweep, might result in burdening innocent associations. . . . Facial overbreadth claims have also been entertained where statutes, by their terms, purport to regulate the time, place and manner of expressive or communicative conduct, . . . and where such conduct has required official approval under laws that delegated standardless discretionary power to local functionaries, resulting in virtually unreviewable prior restraints on First Amendment rights. . . .

"The consequence of our departure from traditional rules of standing in the First Amendment area is that any enforcement of a statute thus placed at issue is totally forbidden until and unless a limiting construction or partial invalidation so narrows it as to remove the seeming threat or deterrence to constitutionally protected expression. Application of the overbreadth doctrine in this manner is, manifestly, strong medicine. It has been employed by the Court sparingly and only as a last resort. . . .

"It remains a 'matter of no little difficulty' to determine when a law may properly be held void on its face and when 'such summary action' is inappropriate. . . . But the plain import of our cases is, at the very least, that facial overbreadth adjudication is an exception to our traditional rules of practice and that its function, a limited one at the outset, attenuates as the otherwise unprotected behavior that it forbids the State to sanction moves from 'pure speech' towards conduct and that conduct—even if expressive—falls within the scope of otherwise valid criminal laws that reflect legitimate state interests in maintaining comprehensive controls over harmful, constitutionally unprotected conduct. Although such laws, if too broadly worded, may deter protected speech to some unknown extent, there comes a point where that effect—at best a prediction—cannot, with confidence, justify invalidating a statute on its face and so prohibiting a State from enforcing the statute against conduct that is admittedly within its power to proscribe. . . . To put the matter another way, particularly where conduct and not merely speech is involved, we believe that the overbreadth of a statute must not only be real, but substantial as well, judged in relation to the statute's plainly legitimate sweep. It is our view that § 818 is not substantially overbroad and that whatever overbreadth may exist should be cured through case-by-case analysis of the fact situations to which its sanctions, assertedly, may not be applied.[14]"

Justice Douglas dissented on the ground that the whole statute violated the first amendment. Justice Brennan concluded a dissenting opinion joined by Justices Stewart and Marshall as follows:

"At this stage, it is obviously difficult to estimate the probable impact of today's decision. If the requirement of 'substantial' overbreadth is construed to mean only that facial review is inappropriate where the likelihood of an impermissible application of the statute is too small to generate a 'chilling effect' on protected speech or conduct, then the impact is likely to be small. On the other hand, if today's decision necessitates the drawing of artificial distinctions between protected speech and protected conduct, and if the 'chill' on protected conduct is rarely, if ever, found sufficient to require the facial invalidation of an overbroad statute, then the effect could be very grave indeed. In my view, the principles set forth in Coates v. City of Cincinnati, are essential to the preservation and enforcement of the First Amendment guarantees. Since no subsequent development has persuaded me that the principles are ill-founded or that *Coates* was incorrectly decided, I would reverse the judgment of the District Court on the strength of that decision and hold . . . the Oklahoma Merit Act unconstitutional on its face."

BROCKETT v. SPOKANE ARCADES, INC., 472 U.S. 491 (1985). The court concluded that a state obscenity statute was overbroad because it used

[handwritten margin note: claimed statute was overbroad]

---

14. . . . The dissent . . . insists that Coates v. City of Cincinnati, 402 U.S. 611 (1971), must be taken as overruled. But we are unpersuaded that *Coates* stands as a barrier to a rule that would invalidate statutes for overbreadth only when the flaw is a sub-stantial concern in the context of the statute as a whole. Our judgment is that the Oklahoma statute, when authoritative administrative constructions are accepted, is not invalid under such a rule.

vagueness of term "lust"

the term "lust" in defining obscene matter. (The definition included materials that appealed to "only normal sexual appetites," and were thus constitutionally protected.) The court decided, however, that the lower federal court had erred in declaring the statute invalid as a whole. On this issue, the court's opinion said:

"For its holding that in First Amendment cases an overbroad statute must be stricken down on its face, the Court of Appeals relied on that line of cases exemplified by Thornhill v. Alabama, 310 U.S. 88 (1940), and more recently by Village of Schaumburg v. Citizens for a Better Environment, 444 U.S. 620 (1980). In those cases, an individual whose own speech or expressive conduct may validly be prohibited or sanctioned is permitted to challenge a statute on its face because it also threatens others not before the court—those who desire to engage in legally protected expression but who may refrain from doing so rather than risk prosecution or undertake to have the law declared partially invalid. If the overbreadth is 'substantial,'[12] the law may not be enforced against anyone, including the party before the court, until it is narrowed to reach only unprotected activity, whether by legislative action or by judicial construction or partial invalidation. Broadrick v. Oklahoma, 413 U.S. 601 (1973).

"It is otherwise where the parties challenging the statute are those who desire to engage in protected speech that the overbroad statute purports to punish, or who seek to publish both protected and unprotected material. There is then no want of a proper party to challenge the statute, no concern that an attack on the statute will be unduly delayed or protected speech discouraged. The statute may forthwith be declared invalid to the extent that it reaches too far, but otherwise left intact.

"The cases before us are ones governed by the normal rule that partial, rather than facial, invalidation is the required course. The Washington statute was faulted by the Court of Appeals only because it reached material that incited normal as well as unhealthy interest in sex, and appellees, or some of them, desiring to publish this sort of material, claimed that they faced punishment if they did so. Unless there are countervailing considerations, the Washington law should have been invalidated only insofar as the word 'lust' is to be understood as reaching protected materials.

. . .

"Partial invalidation would be improper if it were contrary to legislative intent in the sense that the legislature had passed an inseverable Act or would not have passed it had it known the challenged provision was invalid. . . . It would be frivolous to suggest, and no one does, that the Washington Legislature, if it could not proscribe materials that appealed to normal as well as abnormal sexual appetites, would have refrained from passing the moral nuisance statute. And it is quite evident that the remainder of the statute retains its effectiveness as a regulation of obscenity. In these circumstances, the issue of severability is no obstacle to partial invalidation, which is the course the Court of Appeals should have pursued."

FEDERAL COURT INJUNCTIONS AGAINST VAGUE AND OVERBROAD STATUTES

It is accurate to say that laws are judged for vagueness and overbreadth on their "face" only in the sense, as Justice Stewart points out in *Coates,* that it is

---

12. The Court of Appeals erred in holding that the substantial overbreadth requirement is inapplicable where pure speech rather than conduct is at issue. . . .

unnecessary to know the details of the defendant's conduct, or to determine whether it was constitutionally protected. It is a mistake to conclude that statutes are judged for vagueness and overbreadth only with reference to their literal statutory language. A statute may appear to be vague and overbroad, but those problems may disappear if judicial construction clarifies its prohibitions and limits its potentially overbroad applications. A good example is the Smith Act, considered at length in Section 1 of this chapter. Were it not for the limiting constructions given the statute in the *Yates, Scales* and *Noto* cases, its literal application would require a conclusion that it is overbroad. State courts, too, can remove potential issues of vagueness and overbreadth by a limiting construction of the statute involved. Thus, in reviewing a case that originated in a state court, the issue before the Supreme Court is whether the statute, as construed by the state courts, is vague or overbroad. (Notice that in *Herndon* the vagueness problem stemmed, in part, from the state court's construction and, in *Coates,* the state court had not construed the statute beyond its plain language.)

In any case in which issues of first amendment vagueness and overbreadth are raised there are difficult questions of degree—determining the degree of vagueness or overbreadth that will be fatal and deciding whether a party can raise the challenge that the statute is vague or overbroad as to other persons. Those problems are, however, further complicated when the challenges are raised in a federal court suit to enjoin enforcement of the law as opposed to Supreme Court review of a state criminal conviction. The first problem for the federal court is that it can only guess whether state courts would give an apparently vague or overbroad law a narrowing construction that would obviate the problem. That can be particularly troublesome when the law sought to be enjoined is newly enacted and has never been construed in the state courts. The second problem is to define standing to raise the challenges—obviously less of a problem where a defendant seeking Supreme Court review is attempting to overturn the very statutory provision under which he was convicted. Allowing a defendant in a state criminal action to enjoin a pending prosecution can create inordinate delay in the state criminal process or create a mechanism by which state court decisions on federal issues are reviewed and "reversed" by lower federal courts and not by the Supreme Court. On the other hand, permitting suit by any person who alleges a future intent to engage in behavior arguably within the statutory prohibition practically allows anyone to mount a vagueness or overbreadth challenge to a state law. Allowing anyone alleging a subjective "chill" to ask a federal court to strike down a state law on the basis that there are some hypothetical uncertainties or applications to protected speech produces litigation with many of the undesirable features of advisory opinions. The complex federal jurisdiction rules addressed to these problems were explored, in general terms, earlier in Chapter 3. They will be examined here with reference to their impact on litigation of vagueness and overbreadth challenges.

(1) Postponing Decision. A technique for addressing the possibility that state courts might narrow the statute's apparent vagueness or overbreadth is for the federal court to stay the action before it, allowing the parties to obtain an "authoritative" state court construction of the law. In Baggett v. Bullitt, 377 U.S. 360 (1964), the Court invalidated, as impermissibly vague, a Washington loyalty oath for teachers requiring affirmation that the teacher was not a "subversive person." In Dombrowski v. Pfister, 380 U.S. 479 (1965), a Louisiana law requiring registration of "subversive organizations" was invalidated for vagueness and overbreadth. In both cases, the Court refused to postpone exercise of jurisdiction to allow state court interpretation. Portions of Justice

Brennan's opinion in *Dombrowski* can be read as suggesting that abstention to clarify state law is never appropriate when the law is challenged on vagueness and overbreadth grounds. He emphasized that a major premise of vagueness and overbreadth doctrine was that such laws operated to chill constitutionally protected speech by those not "hardy enough to risk criminal prosecution." He further pointed out that the abstention process was time consuming and, in the intervening time, those affected remained subject to the statute's "chilling effect." Both opinions, however, also emphasized that the challenged laws presented a multitude of issues of interpretation that were not likely to be resolved in any single proceeding. Babbitt v. United Farm Workers Nat'l Union, 442 U.S. 289 (1979) held that abstention to allow state court interpretation is required where the uncertainty of a challenged statute concerns a single issue that can be resolved by state courts in a single proceeding.

(2) **Dismissal.** Justice Brennan's discussion in *Dombrowski* of the "chilling effect" of vague and overbroad statutes upon parties not before the court led lower federal courts to permit a proliferation of vagueness and overbreadth challenges to state criminal statutes. Younger v. Harris, 401 U.S. 37 (1971), substantially curbed that litigation. At issue in the case was the constitutional validity of the California criminal syndicalism law which had been upheld in Whitney v. California, 274 U.S. 357 (1927) (supra Section 1). Harris had been indicted under the act, and sued to enjoin his state prosecution. Other parties plaintiff were allowed to intervene—Progressive Labor Party members who alleged that Harris' prosecution inhibited them from advocacy of Party programs, and a college instructor who claimed he was uncertain whether he could teach about Marxism. The lower federal courts enjoined Harris' prosecution, holding the law unconstitutional. The Supreme Court reversed, concluding that the federal injunction suit should have been dismissed. The intervenors had not alleged a credible threat they would be prosecuted, and as to them there was no "live controversy." Allowing Harris to sue presented the opposite problem— undue interference with a pending state criminal proceeding. Harris could raise his constitutional defense in the pending prosecution. More broadly, Justice Black's opinion for the Court stated: "Procedures for testing the constitutionality of a statute 'on its face' in the manner apparently contemplated by *Dombrowski,* and for then enjoining all action to enforce the statute until the State can obtain court approval for a modified version, are fundamentally at odds with the function of . . . federal courts in our constitutional plan." Among the difficulties, he listed the "speculative and amorphous nature of the required line-by-line analysis of detailed statutes [which] ordinarily results in a kind of case that is wholly unsatisfactory for deciding constitutional questions."

The seed of *Younger v. Harris* has grown into a luxuriant forest of rules. Barring suit by persons actually prosecuted and those not threatened with prosecution has left a narrow corridor for bringing federal court actions to determine the constitutionality of state criminal laws. Suit for declaratory judgment of unconstitutionality (as opposed to an injunction) is permitted where the plaintiff shows a credible threat of prosecution, but has not been prosecuted. Steffel v. Thompson, 415 U.S. 452 (1974). Further, a temporary injunction against prosecution *pendente lite* may be issued on a sufficient showing of irreparable harm and likely success on the merits. Doran v. Salem Inn, Inc., 422 U.S. 922 (1975). If a temporary injunction is not entered, and state prosecution is begun before "proceedings of substance on the merits" have occurred in the federal declaratory judgment action, the federal action must be dismissed. Hicks v. Miranda, 422 U.S. 332 (1975). If a federal declaratory judgment of unconstitutionality is issued, it is an open question whether subsequent state prosecutions can then be enjoined by the federal court. (Justices White and Rehnquist expressed polar positions on that issue in concurring opinions in Hicks v. Miranda.) The question may be particularly perplexing if the statute is declared unconstitutional for vagueness and overbreadth, but there is a possibility that state court construction of the statute in the subsequent state prosecution might narrow the statute's interpretation. Shapiro, *State Courts and Federal Declaratory Judgments,* 74 N.W.U.L.Rev. 759 (1979).

An interesting situation occurs when the defendant has been prosecuted in a state court, and the conviction has become final. The defendant wishes to continue the conduct that resulted in conviction, and, without seeking to set aside the past conviction, asks a federal court to bar future prosecution. In that situation, a federal court may enjoin future state criminal prosecutions. Since the federal plaintiff is willing to let the past criminal conviction stand, there is no interference with state criminal actions and, in form, the federal trial court is not exercising quasi-appellate review of a state court decision. Wooley v. Maynard, 430 U.S. 705 (1977), infra, p. 1450; Carey v. Brown, 447 U.S. 455 (1980). Neither *Wooley* nor *Carey* was decided on vagueness or overbreadth grounds. The implications of those cases, however, for vagueness and overbreadth challenges should be noted. The past state conviction gives some concreteness to the federal litigation. It is known what the defendant has done and intends to do in the future. The particular features of the statute at issue are defined by the previous conviction. And, most significant, a state court has had a prior opportunity to construe the statute and narrow its interpretation.

Virginia v. Hicks

539 U.S. 113, 123 S.Ct. 2191, 156 L.Ed.2d 148 (2003).

Justice Scalia delivered the opinion of the Court.

The issue presented in this case is whether the Richmond Redevelopment and Housing Authority's trespass policy is facially invalid under the First Amendment's overbreadth doctrine.

I

A

The Richmond Redevelopment and Housing Authority (RRHA) owns and operates a housing development for low-income residents called Whitcomb Court. Until June 23, 1997, the city of Richmond owned the streets within Whitcomb Court. The city council decided, however, to "privatize" these streets in an effort to combat rampant crime and drug dealing in Whitcomb Court— much of it committed and conducted by nonresidents. ... The city then conveyed these streets by a recorded deed to the RRHA (which is a political subdivision of the Commonwealth of Virginia). ... [T]he RRHA posted red-and-white signs on each apartment building—and every 100 feet along the streets— of Whitcomb Court, which state: "NO TRESPASSING[.] PRIVATE PROPER-TY[.] ..." The RRHA also enacted a policy authorizing the Richmond police

> "to serve notice, either orally or in writing, to any person who is found on Richmond Redevelopment and Housing Authority property when such person is not a resident, employee, or such person cannot demonstrate *a legitimate business or social purpose* for being on the premises. Such notice shall forbid the person from returning to the property. Finally, Richmond Redevelopment and Housing Authority authorizes Richmond Police Department officers to arrest any person for trespassing after such person,

having been duly notified, either stays upon or returns to Richmond Redevelopment and Housing Authority property."

Persons who trespass after being notified not to return are subject to prosecution under Va. Code Ann. § 18.2B119 (1996):

"If any person without authority of law goes upon or remains upon the lands, buildings or premises of another, or any portion or area thereof, after having been forbidden to do so, either orally or in writing, by the owner, lessee, custodian or other person lawfully in charge thereof ... he shall be guilty of a Class 1 misdemeanor."

B

Respondent Kevin Hicks, a nonresident of Whitcomb Court, has been convicted on two prior occasions of trespassing there and once of damaging property there. Those convictions are not at issue in this case. While the property-damage charge was pending, the RRHA gave Hicks written notice barring him from Whitcomb Court, and Hicks signed this notice in the presence of a police officer. Twice after receiving this notice Hicks asked for permission to return; twice the Whitcomb Court housing manager said "no." That did not stop Hicks; in January 1999 he again trespassed at Whitcomb Court and was arrested and convicted under § 18.2B119.

At trial, Hicks maintained that the RRHA's policy limiting access to Whitcomb Court was both unconstitutionally overbroad and void for vagueness. On appeal of his conviction, ... the Virginia Supreme Court ... found the policy defective because it vested too much discretion in Whitcomb Court's manager to determine whether an individual's presence at Whitcomb Court is "authorized," allowing her to "prohibit speech that she finds personally distasteful or offensive even though such speech may be protected by the First Amendment." ...

II

A

Hicks does not contend that he was engaged in constitutionally protected conduct when arrested; nor does he challenge the validity of the trespass *statute* under which he was convicted. Instead he claims that the RRHA *policy* barring him from Whitcomb Court is overbroad under the First Amendment, and cannot be applied to him—or anyone else. The First Amendment doctrine of overbreadth is an exception to our normal rule regarding the standards for facial challenges. ...

. . .

B

Petitioner asks this Court to impose restrictions on "the use of overbreadth standing," limiting the availability of facial overbreadth challenges to those whose *own conduct* involved some sort of expressive activity. The United States as *amicus curiae* makes the same proposal, and urges that Hicks' facial challenge to the RRHA trespass policy "should not have been entertained." The problem with these proposals is that we are reviewing here the decision of a *State* Supreme Court; our standing rules limit only the *federal* courts' jurisdiction over certain claims. "[S]tate courts are not bound by the limitations of a case or controversy or other federal rules of justiciability even when they address issues of federal law." ... Whether Virginia's courts should have *entertained* this overbreadth challenge is entirely a matter of state law.

This Court may, however, review the Virginia Supreme Court's holding that the RRHA policy violates the First Amendment. We may examine, in particular, whether the claimed overbreadth in the RRHA policy is sufficiently "substantial" to produce facial invalidity. These questions involve not standing, but "the determination of [a] First Amendment challenge on the merits." ... Because it is the Commonwealth of Virginia, not Hicks, that has invoked the authority of the federal courts by petitioning for a writ of certiorari, our jurisdiction to review the First Amendment merits question is clear ... The Commonwealth has suffered, as a consequence of the Virginia Supreme Court's "final judgment altering tangible legal rights," an actual injury in fact—inability to prosecute Hicks for trespass—that is sufficiently "distinct and palpable" to confer standing under Article III ... We accordingly proceed to that merits inquiry, leaving for another day the question whether our ordinary rule that a litigant may not rest a claim to relief on the legal rights or interests of third parties ... would exclude a case such as this from initiation in federal court.

C

The Virginia Supreme Court found that the RRHA policy allowed Gloria S. Rogers, the manager of Whitcomb Court, to exercise "unfettered discretion" in determining who may use the RRHA's property. ... Specifically, the court faulted an "unwritten" rule that persons wishing to hand out flyers on the sidewalks of Whitcomb Court need to obtain Rogers' permission. This unwritten portion of the RRHA policy, the court concluded, unconstitutionally allows Rogers to "prohibit speech that she finds personally distasteful or offensive."

... The Virginia Supreme Court, based on its objection to the "unwritten" requirement that demonstrators and leafleters obtain advance permission, declared the *entire* RRHA trespass policy overbroad and void—including the written rule that those who return after receiving a barment notice are subject to arrest. Whether these provisions are severable is of course a matter of state law, ... and the Virginia Supreme Court has implicitly decided that they are not—that all components of the RRHA trespass policy must stand or fall together. It could not properly decree that they fall by reason of the overbreadth doctrine, however, unless the trespass policy, *taken as a whole*, is substantially overbroad judged in relation to its plainly legitimate sweep. ...

Hicks has not made such a showing with regard to the RRHA policy taken as a whole ... Consider the "no-return" notice served on nonresidents who have no "legitimate business or social purpose" in Whitcomb Court: Hicks has failed to demonstrate that this notice would even be given to anyone engaged in constitutionally protected speech. ... Hicks has failed to demonstrate that *any* First Amendment activity falls outside the "legitimate business or social purpose[s]" that permit entry. As far as appears, until one receives a barment notice, entering for a First Amendment purpose is not a trespass.

As for the written provision authorizing the police to arrest those who return to Whitcomb Court after receiving a barment notice: That certainly does not violate the First Amendment as applied to persons whose postnotice entry is not for the purpose of engaging in constitutionally protected speech. And Hicks has not even established that it would violate the First Amendment as applied to persons whose postnotice entry *is* for that purpose. ... [T]he notice-barment rule subjects to arrest those who reenter after trespassing and after being warned not to return—*regardless* of whether, upon their return, they seek to engage in speech. Neither the basis for the barment sanction (the prior trespass) nor its purpose (preventing future trespasses) has anything to do with the First Amendment. Punishing its violation by a person who wishes to engage in free speech no more implicates the First Amendment than would the punishment of a person who has (pursuant to lawful regulation) been banned from a public park after vandalizing it, and who ignores the ban in order to take part in a political demonstration. Here, as there, it is Hicks' nonexpressive *conduct*—his entry in violation of the notice-barment rule—not his speech, for which he is punished as a trespasser.

Most importantly, both the notice-barment rule and the 'legitimate business or social purpose' rule apply to *all* persons who enter the streets of Whitcomb Court, not just to those who seek to engage in expression. . . . Applications of the RRHA policy that violate the First Amendment can still be remedied through as-applied litigation, but the Virginia Supreme Court should not have used the "strong medicine" of overbreadth to invalidate the entire RRHA trespass policy. Whether respondent may challenge his conviction on other grounds—and whether those claims have been properly preserved—are issues we leave open on remand.

. . .

Justice Souter, with whom Justice Breyer joins, concurring.

I join the Court's opinion and add this afterword to flag an issue of no consequence here, but one on which a future case might turn. In comparing invalid applications against valid ones for purposes of the First Amendment overbreadth doctrine, the Supreme Court of Virginia apparently assumed that the appropriate focus of the analysis was the "unwritten" element of the housing authority's trespass policy, that is, the requirement that nonresidents distributing literature or demonstrating on the property obtain prior authorization. . . . We, on the other hand, take a broader view of the relevant law, by looking to the potential applications of the entire trespass policy, written and unwritten. It does not matter here, however, which position one takes on the appropriate "law" whose overbreadth is to be assessed, for there is no substantial overbreadth either way. . . . But in other circumstances, the scope of the law chosen for comparison with invalid applications might decide the case. It might be dispositive whether, say, a city's speech ordinance for a public park is analyzed alone or as one element of the combined policies governing expression in public schoolyards, municipal cemeteries, and the city council chamber. Suffice it to say that today's decision does not address how to go about identifying the scope of the relevant law for purposes of overbreadth analysis.

B.   PRIOR RESTRAINT

Introduction. The historical introduction to this chapter referred to the English history of licensed presses and Blackstone's conclusion in 1765 that liberty of the press consisted in an absence of prior restraints upon publication, but imposed no limit on punishing the publisher after publication. (Section 1, Subsection A, 1.) As late as 1907, Justice Holmes, on first encountering the problem, repeated the Blackstone proposition that the Constitution forbade "all such *previous restraints* upon publication, as had been practiced by other governments" but not "the subsequent punishment of such as may be deemed contrary to the public welfare."[1] It is now obvious that the Constitution does impose serious limits on the punishment of speech and publications. The prior

---

1.   Patterson v. Colorado, 205 U.S. 454, 462 (1907). It was not until 1919 that Holmes announced: "I wholly disagree with the argument . . . that the First Amendment left the common law as to seditious libel in force." Abrams v. United States, 250 U.S. 616, 630 (1919) (dissenting opinion).

restraint concept is not obsolete, however. A person, whose publication or speech is not constitutionally protected from punishment, under a properly drawn criminal statute, can still complain if it is inhibited by an unconstitutional prior restraint.

The traditional system of prior restraint was an administrative licensing mechanism, with the publisher forbidden to publish without prior approval of an executive official. The Court has upheld administrative licensing systems, where official permission in advance has been required for expressive activities conducted on public property. (The problems posed by requirements for parade permits are discussed below, beginning at page 1309.) The Court has sustained an administrative licensing system in only one context not involving use of public property. In Times Film Corp. v. City of Chicago, 365 U.S. 43 (1961), the Court concluded that a motion picture licensing ordinance was not invalid "on its face." The nation's existing motion picture licensing systems, however, did not survive the decision four years later in Freedman v. Maryland, 380 U.S. 51 (1965). The Court concluded that the motion picture licensing system under review was invalid because: (1) it did not require the administrative censor to seek judicial review if a permit was refused; (2) if the exhibitor sought judicial review, exhibition of the film was not permitted pending review; (3) there was no assurance of prompt judicial determination. The Court explained that there were important differences between judicial and administrative proceedings. "Unlike a prosecution for obscenity, a censorship proceeding puts the initial burden on the exhibitor or distributor. Because the censor's business is to censor, there inheres the danger that he may well be less responsive than a court—part of an independent branch of government—to the constitutionally protected interests in free expression."

The next case does not involve administrative censorship but a court injunction. *Near v. Minnesota,* the Court's seminal decision on prior restraint, equated injunctions with administrative censorship. Is an injunction any more "prior" than a criminal statute forbidding the same conduct?

Near v. Minnesota

283 U.S. 697, 51 S.Ct. 625, 75 L.Ed. 1357 (1931).

Mr. Chief Justice Hughes delivered the opinion of the Court.

Chapter 285 of the Session Laws of Minnesota for the year 1925 provides for the abatement, as a public nuisance, of a "malicious, scandalous and defamatory newspaper, magazine or other periodical." ...

. . .

Under this statute ... the county attorney of Hennepin county brought this action to enjoin the publication of what was described as a "malicious, scandalous and defamatory newspaper, magazine or other periodical," known as The Saturday Press, published by the defendants in the city of Minneapolis. . . .

... [T]he articles charged, in substance, that a Jewish gangster was in control of gambling, bootlegging, and racketeering in Minneapolis, and that law enforcing officers and agencies were not energetically performing their duties.... There is no question but that the articles made serious accusations against the public officers named and others in connection with the prevalence of crimes and the failure to expose and punish them....

... The court ... found that the defendants through these publications "did engage in the business of regularly and customarily producing, publishing and circulating a malicious, scandalous and defamatory newspaper," and that "the said publication under said name of The Saturday Press, or any other name, constitutes a public nuisance under the laws of the State." Judgment was thereupon entered adjudging that "the newspaper, magazine and periodical known as The Saturday Press," as a public nuisance, "be and is hereby abated." The judgment perpetually enjoined the defendants "from producing, editing, publishing, circulating, having in their possession, selling or giving away any publication whatsoever which is a malicious, scandalous or defamatory newspaper, as defined by law," and also "from further conducting said nuisance under the name and title of said The Saturday Press or any other name or title."

[The judgment was affirmed by the State Supreme Court.]

This statute, for the suppression as a public nuisance of a newspaper or periodical, is unusual, if not unique, and raises questions of grave importance transcending the local interests involved in the particular action. It is no longer open to doubt that the liberty of the press, and of speech, is within the liberty safeguarded by the due process clause of the Fourteenth Amendment from invasion by state action....

First. The statute is not aimed at the redress of individual or private wrongs. Remedies for libel remain available and unaffected. The statute, said the state court, "is not directed at threatened libel but at an existing business which, generally speaking, involves more than libel." It is aimed at the distribution of scandalous matter as "detrimental to public morals and to the general welfare," tending "to disturb the peace of the community" and "to provoke assaults and the commission of crime." ...

Second. The statute is directed not simply at the circulation of scandalous and defamatory statements with regard to private citizens, but at the continued publication by newspapers and periodicals of charges against public officers of corruption, malfeasance in office, or serious neglect of duty. Such charges by their very nature create a public scandal. They are scandalous and defamatory within the meaning of the statute, which has its normal operation in relation to publications dealing prominently and chiefly with the alleged derelictions of public officers.

Third. The object of the statute is not punishment, in the ordinary sense, but suppression of the offending newspaper or periodical. The reason for the enactment, as the state court has said, is that prosecutions to enforce penal statutes for libel do not result in "efficient repression or suppression of the evils of scandal." ...

This suppression is accomplished by enjoining publication and that restraint is the object and effect of the statute.

Fourth. The statute not only operates to suppress the offending newspaper or periodical, but to put the publisher under an effective censorship. When a newspaper or periodical is found to be "malicious, scandalous and defamatory," and is suppressed as such, resumption of publication is punishable as a contempt of court by fine or imprisonment. Thus where a newspaper or periodical has been suppressed because of the circulation of charges against public officers of official misconduct, it would seem to be clear that the renewal of the publication of such charges would constitute a contempt, and that the judgment would lay a permanent restraint upon the publisher, to escape which he must satisfy the court as to the character of a new publication. Whether he would be permitted again to publish matter deemed to be derogatory to the same or other public officers would depend upon the court's ruling....

If we cut through mere details of procedure, the operation and effect of the statute in substance is that public authorities may bring the owner or publisher of a newspaper or periodical before a judge upon a charge of conducting a business of publishing scandalous and defamatory matter—in particular that the matter consists of charges against public officers of official dereliction—and unless the owner or publisher is able and disposed to bring competent evidence to satisfy the judge that the charges are true and are published with good motives and for justifiable ends, his newspaper or periodical is suppressed and further publication is made punishable as a contempt. This is of the essence of censorship.

The question is whether a statute authorizing such proceedings in restraint of publication is consistent with the conception of the liberty of the press as historically conceived and guaranteed. In determining the extent of the constitutional protection, it has been generally, if not universally, considered that it is the chief purpose of the guaranty to prevent previous restraints upon publication....

. . .

The objection has ... been made that the principle as to immunity from previous restraint is stated too broadly, if every such restraint is deemed to be prohibited. That is undoubtedly true; the protection even as to previous restraint is not absolutely unlimited. But the limitation has been recognized only in exceptional cases: "When a nation is at war many things that might be said in time of peace are such a hindrance to its effort that their utterance will not be endured so long as men fight and that no Court could regard them as protected by any constitutional right." Schenck v. United States, 249 U.S. 47, 52. No one would question but that a government might prevent actual obstruction to its recruiting service or the publication of the sailing dates of transports or the number and location of troops. On similar grounds, the primary requirements of decency may be enforced against obscene publications. The security of the community life may be protected against incitements to acts of violence and the overthrow by force of orderly government.... These limitations are not applicable here. Nor are we now concerned with questions as to the extent of authority to prevent publications in order to protect private rights according to the principles governing the exercise of the jurisdiction of courts of equity.

The exceptional nature of its limitations places in a strong light the general conception that liberty of the press, historically considered and taken up by the Federal Constitution, has meant, principally although not exclusively, immunity from previous restraints or censorship....

. . .

The statute in question cannot be justified by reason of the fact that the publisher is permitted to show, before injunction issues, that the matter published is true and is published with good motives and for justifiable ends....

. . .

For these reasons we hold the statute, so far as it authorized the proceedings in this action under clause (b) of section one, to be an infringement of the liberty of the press guaranteed by the Fourteenth Amendment. We should add that this decision rests upon the operation and effect of the statute, without regard to the question of the truth of the charges contained in the particular periodical. The fact that the public officers named in this case, and those associated with the charges of official dereliction, may be deemed to be impeccable, cannot affect the conclusion that the statute imposes an unconstitutional restraint upon publication.

Judgement reversed.

Mr. Justice Butler, dissenting.

. . .

The Court quotes Blackstone in support of its condemnation of the statute as imposing a previous restraint upon publication. But the *previous restraints* referred to by him subjected the press to the arbitrary will of an administrative officer. . . .

. . .

The Minnesota statute does not operate as a *previous* restraint on publication within the proper meaning of that phrase. It does not authorize administrative control in advance such as was formerly exercised by the licensers and censors but prescribes a remedy to be enforced by a suit in equity. In this case there was previous publication made in the course of the business of regularly producing malicious, scandalous and defamatory periodicals. The business and publications unquestionably constitute an abuse of the right of free press. The statute denounces the things done as a nuisance on the ground, as stated by the state supreme court, that they threaten morals, peace, and good order. There is no question of the power of the state to denounce such transgressions. The restraint authorized is only in respect of continuing to do what has been duly adjudged to constitute a nuisance. . . . It is fanciful to suggest similarity between the granting or enforcement of the decree authorized by this statute to prevent *further* publication of malicious, scandalous, and defamatory articles and the *previous restraint* upon the press by licensers as referred to by Blackstone and described in the history of the times to which he alludes.

. . .

The judgment should be affirmed.

Mr. Justice Van Devanter, Mr. Justice McReynolds, and Mr. Justice Sutherland concur in this opinion.

INJUNCTIONS AND PRIOR RESTRAINT

In Pittsburgh Press Co. v. Pittsburgh Commission on Human Relations, 413 U.S. 376, 389–390 (1973), the Court noted that not all injunctions against future publications were invalid prior restraints. "The special vice of a prior restraint is that communication will be suppressed, either directly or by inducing excessive caution in the speaker, before an adequate determination that it is protected by the First Amendment." The Court indicated that the challenged order—which required the newspaper to desist from segregating "help wanted" advertisements by gender—was not a prior restraint for two reasons: there was a continuing course of past conduct identical to that enjoined, making it unnecessary "to speculate as to the effect of publication"; the publication enjoined was clearly defined and not constitutionally protected.

A restraining order issued *ex parte,* prohibiting speech without notice or hearing, obviously can create substantial constitutional questions. E.g., Carroll

v. President and Commissioners of Princess Anne, 393 U.S. 175 (1968) (*ex parte* order forbidding rally is unconstitutional where no showing that it was impossible to notify opposing parties and provide hearing); Fort Wayne Books, Inc. v. Indiana, 489 U.S. 46 (1989) (pre-trial seizure of adult bookstore under state racketeering law is unconstitutional prior restraint). If the injunction in *Near* had forbidden the defendants to publish any newspaper, the overbroad remedy might violate the first amendment.

In *Near,* does the constitutionality of the challenged injunction procedures depend on the question whether a contempt action for violation of the injunction would permit a defense that the alleged contempt was a constitutionally protected publication or exhibition? In Near v. Minnesota, Justice Butler's dissent made the point that in a contempt action the newspaper publisher would have available all defenses available in a criminal libel action. 283 U.S. at 730. Chief Justice Hughes' opinion did not challenge that assertion. If one assumes that a criminal libel law is constitutional, and that only publications that constituted criminal libel could be punished as contempt, should an injunction against future libelous publications still be characterized as a prior restraint?

See Blasi, *Toward a Theory of Prior Restraint: The Central Linkage,* 66 Minn.L.Rev. 11 (1981); Mayton, *Toward a Theory of First Amendment Process: Injunctions of Speech, Subsequent Punishment and the Costs of Prior Restraint Doctrine,* 67 Corn.L.Q. 245 (1982); Jeffries, *Rethinking Prior Restraint,* 92 Yale L.J. 409 (1983).

PARADE AND DEMONSTRATION PERMIT SYSTEMS

Despite traditional prior restraint law, systems requiring official permission in advance for parades and demonstrations have been upheld. In Cox v. New Hampshire, 312 U.S. 569 (1941), the Court sustained a licensing system for parades on public streets, designed to prevent traffic congestion and overlapping parades at the same time and place, and to give authorities notice in advance to afford opportunity for proper policing. A parade or demonstration permit ordinance is unconstitutional, however, if it allows the administrative official standardless discretion to deny permission, or if it authorizes denial on the basis of impermissible standards.[1] In Shuttlesworth v. Birmingham, 394 U.S. 147 (1969), for example, a parade ordinance was unconstitutional because it authorized denial of a permit if "the public welfare, peace, safety, health, decency, good order, morals, or convenience require that it be refused." A number of complex issues have arisen, however, with reference to the appropriate procedures for testing the constitutional validity of parade and demonstration permit ordinances and of individual decisions denying permits.

It is clear that if the ordinance is unconstitutional because it provides inadequate standards for granting or denial of permits, the defense is available in a prosecution for parading or demonstrating without a permit. The defendant need not have sought a permit, nor, if a permit were sought, have taken steps to review the official decision denying permission. The issue of the

---

1. In Forsyth County v. Nationalist Movement, 505 U.S. 123 (1992), the Court did not resolve the question whether the first amendment limits the amount of any fee for a parade permit to a "nominal sum." The Court held invalid an ordinance that allowed the administrator to "adjust the amount to be paid [up to a maximum of $1,000 per day] in order to meet the expense incident to the administration of the ordinance and to the maintenance of public order in the matter licensed." The court concluded that the ordinance gave the administrator unbridled discretion to set fees, and that assessing the fee with reference to security costs would increase permit fees based on content, because the fee would include the projected cost of controlling hostile crowds.

validity of the ordinance is open, too, whether or not permission could have been denied under a properly drafted provision.[2] The rationale has been that the unconstitutional ordinance is "void" and therefore it is appropriate to contest its validity without first seeking a permit under it. Lovell v. Griffin, Ga., 303 U.S. 444 (1938).

Suppose, however, that the ordinance is valid but the licensing official denies permission for unconstitutional reasons. Poulos v. New Hampshire, 345 U.S. 395 (1953), establishes that a state can require that the applicant seek review of the invalid denial of the permit under a valid ordinance. *Poulos* reasoned that the rationale for requiring permission in advance for a parade or demonstration allowed the state to insist that the disappointed applicant not ignore the official denial of permission, and to require challenge through appropriate procedures before the parade or demonstration is held. *Poulos* presents a real dilemma to the applicant unconstitutionally denied permission.[3] The ordinance in *Poulos* required the applicant to seek judicial review of the denial and precluded him from holding his planned meeting pending those judicial proceedings. Justice Reed's opinion in that case rejected the argument that judicial review would be so time-consuming as to make it impossible to hold the planned meeting, stating that while delay was "unfortunate," it was "a price citizens must pay for life in an orderly society." In Freedman v. Maryland, 380 U.S. 51 (1965), however, a motion picture censorship ordinance was held unconstitutional because it did not require the licensing official to go to court after denying a license, and did not provide for prompt judicial review. Southeastern Promotions v. Conrad, 420 U.S. 546 (1975), required the directors of a municipal auditorium to follow the *Freedman* procedures upon denial of permission to use the auditorium. Thomas v. Chicago Park District, 534 U.S. 316 (2002), held that *Freedman*'s requirement that licensing officials seek prompt judicial review was not applicable to content-neutral denial of parade and demonstration permits. ("Such a traditional exercise of authority does not raise the censorship concerns that prompted us to impose the extraordinary procedural safeguards on the film licensing process in *Freedman*.") On the other hand, in City of Littleton v. Z.J. Gifts, 541 U.S. 774 (2004), the Court concluded that an "adult business" licensing ordinance would need to provide assurance of prompt judicial review if the denial of the license was content-based. *Freedman*'s judicial review safeguard was meant to prevent "undue delay," and requires prompt judicial decision.

In Walker v. Birmingham, 388 U.S. 307 (1967), the Court reviewed the criminal contempt conviction of Black ministers who had been enjoined by a state court from holding a Good Friday march to protest racial discrimination.

---

2. In Kunz v. New York, 340 U.S. 290 (1951), for example, defendant's license application was denied because he had in the past ridiculed and denounced the religious beliefs of others, and there had been disorder. His conviction for holding a public worship meeting on the streets without a permit was reversed because the ordinance lacked standards for permit denials.

3. The dilemma is exacerbated if there is uncertainty concerning the constitutional validity of the underlying ordinance. In Cox v. New Hampshire, 312 U.S. 569 (1941), the parade permit ordinance under which the defendants were convicted was silent about the standards for granting or denying permits. The convictions were affirmed, however, because the New Hampshire Supreme Court interpreted the ordinance, on the defendants' appeal, to allow denial only upon considerations such as traffic congestion, overlapping parades, and risks of disorder. In Shuttlesworth v. Birmingham, Ala., 394 U.S. 147 (1969), the Court reversed a conviction for parading without a license despite a similar limiting construction of the ordinance under which the defendants were convicted. Given the language of the ordinance, and past administrative practice, it "would have taken extraordinary clairvoyance" for defendants to have foreseen, when they held their parade, the "remarkable job of plastic surgery" by the state court four years later.

The Court's decision in Shuttlesworth v. Birmingham, note 3 supra, two years later made clear that the parade permit ordinance on which the injunction was based was unconstitutional, and that the clearly stated position of police commissioner Eugene "Bull" Conner, that no permit would be issued, rested on unconstitutional considerations. Moreover, the grant of an *ex parte* injunction, without notice or opportunity to participate in the proceedings, probably also violated the first amendment.[4] Alabama, however, was among the states following the rule that an injunction must be obeyed, even if erroneous, until it is set aside on appellate review.[5] Accordingly, the Alabama Supreme Court refused to consider constitutional attacks on the injunction or the underlying parade ordinance. The Supreme Court affirmed, by a vote of five to four. Justice Stewart's opinion for the Court said that the "case would arise in quite a different constitutional posture if the petitioners, before disobeying the injunction, had challenged it in the Alabama courts, and had been met with delay or frustration of their constitutional claims." In United States v. Ryan, 402 U.S. 530, 532 n. 4 (1971), the Court said: "Our holding [in Walker v. Birmingham] that the claims there sought to be asserted were not open on review of petitioners' contempt convictions was based [upon] the availability of review of those claims at an earlier stage."

Watchtower Bible and Tract Society of New York v. Village of Stratton

536 U.S. 150, 122 S.Ct. 2080, 153 L.Ed.2d 205 (2002).

Justice Stevens delivered the opinion of the Court.

Petitioners contend that a village ordinance making it a misdemeanor to engage in door-to-door advocacy without first registering with the mayor and receiving a permit violates the First Amendment. Through this facial challenge, we consider the door-to-door canvassing regulation not only as it applies to religious proselytizing, but also to anonymous political speech and the distribution of handbills.

I

Petitioner Watchtower Bible and Tract Society of New York, Inc., coordinates the preaching activities of Jehovah's Witnesses throughout the United States and publishes Bibles and religious periodicals that are widely distributed. Petitioner Wellsville, Ohio, Congregation of Jehovah's Witnesses, Inc., supervises the activities of approximately 59 members in a part of Ohio that includes the Village of Stratton (Village). Petitioners offer religious literature without cost to anyone interested in reading it. They allege that they do not solicit contributions or orders for the sale of merchandise or services, but they do accept donations.

Petitioners brought this action against the Village and its mayor in the United States District Court for the Southern District of Ohio, seeking an injunction against the enforcement of several sections of Ordinance No. 1998–5 regulating uninvited peddling and solicitation on private property in the Village. Petitioners' complaint alleged that the ordinance violated several constitutional rights, including the free exercise of religion, free speech, and the freedom of the press. The District Court conducted a bench trial at which

---

4. Carroll v. President and Comm'rs of Princess Anne, 393 U.S. 175 (1968).

5. The rule is the same in the federal courts. United States v. United Mine Workers of America, 330 U.S. 258 (1947).

evidence of the administration of the ordinance and its effect on petitioners was introduced.

Section 116.01 prohibits "canvassers" and others from "going in and upon" private residential property for the purpose of promoting any "cause" without first having obtained a permit pursuant to § 116.03. That section provides that any canvasser who intends to go on private property to promote a cause, must obtain a "Solicitation Permit" from the office of the mayor; there is no charge for the permit, and apparently one is issued routinely after an applicant fills out a fairly detailed "Solicitor's Registration Form." The canvasser is then authorized to go upon premises that he listed on the registration form, but he must carry the permit upon his person and exhibit it whenever requested to do so by a police officer or by a resident. The ordinance sets forth grounds for the denial or revocation of a permit, but the record before us does not show that any application has been denied or that any permit has been revoked. Petitioners did not apply for a permit.

A section of the ordinance that petitioners do not challenge establishes a procedure by which a resident may prohibit solicitation even by holders of permits. If the resident files a "No Solicitation Registration Form" with the mayor, and also posts a "No Solicitation" sign on his property, no uninvited canvassers may enter his property, unless they are specifically authorized to do so in the "No Solicitation Registration Form" itself. Only 32 of the Village's 278 residents filed such forms. Each of the forms in the record contains a list of 19 suggested exceptions; on one form, a resident checked 17 exceptions, thereby excluding only "Jehovah's Witnesses" and "Political Candidates" from the list of invited canvassers. Although Jehovah's Witnesses do not consider themselves to be "solicitors" because they make no charge for their literature or their teaching, leaders of the church testified at trial that they would honor "no solicitation" signs in the Village. They also explained at trial that they did not apply for a permit because they derive their authority to preach from Scripture. "For us to seek a permit from a municipality to preach we feel would almost be an insult to God."

Petitioners introduced some evidence that the ordinance was the product of the mayor's hostility to their ministry, but the District Court credited the mayor's testimony that it had been designed to protect the privacy rights of the Village residents, specifically to protect them "from 'flim flam' con artists who prey on small town populations." Nevertheless, the court concluded that the terms of the ordinance applied to the activities of petitioners as well as to "business or political canvassers."

The District Court ... held the ordinance constitutionally valid as applied to petitioners and dismissed the case.

The Court of Appeals for the Sixth Circuit affirmed. ...

. . .

We granted certiorari to decide the following question: "Does a municipal ordinance that requires one to obtain a permit prior to engaging in the door-to-door advocacy of a political cause and to display upon demand the permit, which contains one's name, violate the First Amendment protection accorded to anonymous pamphleteering or discourse?"

II

For over 50 years, the Court has invalidated restrictions on door-to-door canvassing and pamphleteering. It is more than historical accident that most of these cases involved First Amendment challenges brought by Jehovah's Witnesses, because door-to-door canvassing is mandated by their religion. As we noted in *Murdock v. Pennsylvania*, 319 U.S. 105, 108 (1943), the Jehovah's Witnesses "claim to follow the example of Paul, teaching 'publicly, and from house to house.' . . . In doing so they believe that they are obeying a commandment of God." . . .

Although our past cases involving Jehovah's Witnesses, most of which were decided shortly before and during World War II, do not directly control the question we confront today, they provide both a historical and analytical backdrop for consideration of petitioners' First Amendment claim that the breadth of the Village's ordinance offends the First Amendment. Those cases involved petty offenses that raised constitutional questions of the most serious magnitude—questions that implicated the free exercise of religion, the freedom of speech, and the freedom of the press. From these decisions, several themes emerge that guide our consideration of the ordinance at issue here.

First, the cases emphasize the value of the speech involved. For example, in *Murdock v. Pennsylvania*, the Court noted that "hand distribution of religious tracts is an age-old form of missionary evangelism—as old as the history of printing presses. . . . It has the same claim to protection as the more orthodox and conventional exercises of religion. It also has the same claim as the others to the guarantees of freedom of speech and freedom of the press." . . .

In addition, the cases discuss extensively the historical importance of door-to-door canvassing and pamphleteering as vehicles for the dissemination of ideas. In *Schneider v. State (Town of Irvington)*, 308 U.S. 147 (1939), the petitioner was a Jehovah's Witness who had been convicted of canvassing without a permit based on evidence that she had gone from house to house offering to leave books or booklets. Writing for the Court, Justice Roberts stated that "pamphlets have proved most effective instruments in the dissemination of opinion. . . . To require a censorship through license which makes impossible the *free and unhampered* distribution of pamphlets strikes at the very heart of the constitutional guarantees." . . .

Despite the emphasis on the important role that door-to-door canvassing and pamphleteering has played in our constitutional tradition of free and open discussion, these early cases also recognized the interests a town may have in some form of regulation, particularly when the solicitation of money is involved. In *Cantwell v. Connecticut*, 310 U.S. 296 (1940), the Court held that an ordinance requiring Jehovah's Witnesses to obtain a license before soliciting door to door was invalid because the issuance of the license depended on the exercise of discretion by a city official. Our opinion recognized that "a State may protect its citizens from fraudulent solicitation by requiring a stranger in the community, before permitting him publicly to solicit funds for any purpose, to establish his identity and his authority to act for the cause which he purports to represent." *Id.*, at 306. Similarly, in Martin v. City of Struthers, the Court recognized crime prevention as a legitimate interest served by these ordinances and noted that "burglars frequently pose as canvassers, either in order that they may have a pretense to discover whether a house is empty and hence ripe for burglary, or for the purpose of spying out the premises in order that they may return later." 319 U.S., at 144. Despite recognition of these interests as legitimate, our precedent is clear that there must be a balance between these interests and the effect of the regulations on First Amendment rights. . . .

Finally, the cases demonstrate that efforts of the Jehovah's Witnesses to resist speech regulation have not been a struggle for their rights alone. In *Martin*, after cataloging the many groups that rely extensively upon this method of communication, the Court summarized that "[d]oor to door distribution of circulars is essential to the poorly financed causes of little people." 319 U.S., at 144–146.

That the Jehovah's Witnesses are not the only "little people" who face the risk of silencing by regulations like the Village's is exemplified by our cases involving nonreligious speech. . . . In *Thomas* [v. Collins, 323 U. S. 516 (1945)], the issue was whether a labor leader could be required to obtain a permit before delivering a speech to prospective union members. After reviewing the Jehovah's Witnesses cases discussed above, the Court observed:

> "As a matter of principle a requirement of registration in order to make a public speech would seem generally incompatible with an exercise of the rights of free speech and free assembly. . . .
>
> . . .
>
> "If the exercise of the rights of free speech and free assembly cannot be made a crime, we do not think this can be accomplished by the device of requiring previous registration as a condition for exercising them and making such a condition the foundation for restraining in advance their exercise and for imposing a penalty for violating such a restraining order. So long as no more is involved than exercise of the rights of free speech and free assembly, it is immune to such a restriction. If one who solicits support for the cause of labor may be required to register as a condition to the exercise of his right to make a public speech, so may he who seeks to rally support for any social, business, religious or political cause. We think a requirement that one must register before he undertakes to make a public speech to enlist support for a lawful movement is quite incompatible with the requirements of the First Amendment." *Id.*, at 539–540.

Although these World War II-era cases provide guidance for our consideration of the question presented, they do not answer one preliminary issue that the parties adamantly dispute. That is, what standard of review ought we use in assessing the constitutionality of this ordinance. We find it unnecessary, however, to resolve that dispute because the breadth of speech affected by the ordinance and the nature of the regulation make it clear that the Court of Appeals erred in upholding it.

III

The Village argues that three interests are served by its ordinance: the prevention of fraud, the prevention of crime, and the protection of residents' privacy. We have no difficulty concluding, in light of our precedent, that these are important interests that the Village may seek to safeguard through some form of regulation of solicitation activity. We must also look, however, to the amount of speech covered by the ordinance and whether there is an appropriate balance between the affected speech and the governmental interests that the ordinance purports to serve.

The text of the Village's ordinance prohibits "canvassers" from going on private property for the purpose of explaining or promoting any "cause," unless they receive a permit and the residents visited have not opted for a "no solicitation" sign. Had this provision been construed to apply only to commercial activities and the solicitation of funds, arguably the ordinance would have been tailored to the Village's interest in protecting the privacy of its residents and preventing fraud. Yet, even though the Village has explained that the ordinance was adopted to serve those interests, it has never contended that it should be so narrowly interpreted. To the contrary, the Village's administration of its ordinance unquestionably demonstrates that the provisions apply to a significant number of noncommercial "canvassers" promoting a wide variety of "causes." Indeed, on the "No Solicitation Forms" provided to the residents, the canvassers include "Camp Fire Girls," "Jehovah's Witnesses," "Political Candidates," "Trick or Treaters during Halloween Season," and "Persons Affiliated with Stratton Church." The ordinance unquestionably applies, not only to religious causes, but to political activity as well. It would seem to extend to "residents casually soliciting the votes of neighbors," or ringing doorbells to enlist support for employing a more efficient garbage collector.

The mere fact that the ordinance covers so much speech raises constitutional concerns. It is offensive—not only to the values protected by the First Amendment, but to the very notion of a free society—that in the context of everyday public discourse a citizen must first inform the government of her desire to speak to her neighbors and then obtain a permit to do so. Even if the issuance of permits by the mayor's office is a ministerial task that is performed promptly and at no cost to the applicant, a law requiring a permit to engage in such speech constitutes a dramatic departure from our national heritage and constitutional tradition. Three obvious examples illustrate the pernicious effect of such a permit requirement.

First, as our cases involving distribution of unsigned handbills demonstrate, there are a significant number of persons who support causes anonymously. ..., the Court of Appeals erred in concluding that the ordinance does not implicate anonymity interests. ... The badge requirement that we invalidated in *Buckley* [v. American Constitutional Law Foundation, Inc., 525 U.S. 182 (1999)] applied to petition circulators seeking signatures in face-to-face interactions. ... In the Village, strangers to the resident certainly maintain their anonymity, and the ordinance may preclude such persons from canvassing for unpopular causes. Such preclusion may well be justified in some situations—for example, by the special state interest in protecting the integrity of a ballot-initiative process, see *ibid.*, or by the interest in preventing fraudulent commercial transactions. The Village ordinance, however, sweeps more broadly, covering unpopular causes unrelated to commercial transactions or to any special interest in protecting the electoral process.

Second, requiring a permit as a prior condition on the exercise of the right to speak imposes an objective burden on some speech of citizens holding religious or patriotic views. As our World War II-era cases dramatically demonstrate, there are a significant number of persons whose religious scruples will prevent them from applying for such a license. There are no doubt other patriotic citizens, who have such firm convictions about their constitutional right to engage in uninhibited debate in the context of door-to-door advocacy, that they would prefer silence to speech licensed by a petty official.

Third, there is a significant amount of spontaneous speech that is effectively banned by the ordinance. A person who made a decision on a holiday or a weekend to take an active part in a political campaign could not begin to pass out handbills until after he or she obtained the required permit. Even a spontaneous decision to go across the street and urge a neighbor to vote against the mayor could not lawfully be implemented without first obtaining the mayor's permission. ...

The breadth and unprecedented nature of this regulation does not alone render the ordinance invalid. ... [I]t is not tailored to the Village's stated interests. Even if the interest in preventing fraud could adequately support the ordinance insofar as it applies to commercial transactions and the solicitation of funds, that interest provides no support for its application to petitioners, to political campaigns, or to enlisting support for unpopular causes. The Village, however, argues that the ordinance is nonetheless valid because it serves the two additional interests of protecting the privacy of the resident and the prevention of crime.

With respect to the former, it seems clear that § 107 of the ordinance, which provides for the posting of "No Solicitation" signs and which is not challenged in this case, coupled with the resident's unquestioned right to refuse to engage in conversation with unwelcome visitors, provides ample protection for the unwilling listener. *Schaumburg*, 444 U.S., at 639 ("[T]he provision permitting homeowners to bar solicitors from their property by posting [no solicitation] signs ... suggest[s] the availability of less intrusive and more effective measures to protect privacy"). The annoyance caused by an uninvited knock on the front door is the same whether or not the visitor is armed with a permit.

With respect to the latter, it seems unlikely that the absence of a permit would preclude criminals from knocking on doors and engaging in conversations not covered by the ordinance. They might, for example, ask for directions or permission to use the telephone, or pose as surveyers or census takers. Or they might register under a false name with impunity because the ordinance contains no provision for verifying an applicant's identity or organizational credentials. Moreover, the Village did not assert an interest in crime prevention below, and there is an absence of any evidence of a special crime problem related to door-to-door solicitation in the record before us.

The rhetoric used in the World War II-era opinions that repeatedly saved petitioners' co-religionists from petty prosecutions reflected the Court's evaluation of the First Amendment freedoms that are implicated in this case. The value judgment that then motivated a united democratic people fighting to defend those very freedoms from totalitarian attack is unchanged. It motivates our decision today.

The judgment of the Court of Appeals is reversed, and the case is remanded for further proceedings consistent with this opinion.

It is so ordered.

Justice Breyer, with whom Justice Souter and Justice Ginsburg join, concurring.

While joining the Court's opinion, I write separately to note that the dissent's "crime prevention" justification for this ordinance is not a strong one. For one thing, there is no indication that the legislative body that passed the ordinance considered this justification. ...

... I can only conclude that if the village of Stratton thought preventing burglaries and violent crimes was an important justification for this ordinance, it would have said so.

. . .

Justice Scalia, with whom Justice Thomas joins, concurring in the judgment.

I concur in the judgment, for many but not all of the reasons set forth in the opinion for the Court. I do not agree, for example, that one of the causes of the invalidity of Stratton's ordinance is that some people have a religious objection to applying for a permit ...

. . .

As for the Court's fairy-tale category of "patriotic citizens," who would rather be silenced than licensed in a manner that the Constitution (but for their "patriotic" objection) would permit: If our free-speech jurisprudence is to be determined by the predicted behavior of such crackpots, we are in a sorry state indeed.

Chief Justice Rehnquist, dissenting.

Stratton is a village of 278 people located along the Ohio River where the borders of Ohio, West Virginia, and Pennsylvania converge. It is strung out along a multilane highway connecting it with the cities of East Liverpool to the north and Steubenville and Weirton, West Virginia, to the south. One may doubt how much legal help a village of this size has available in drafting an ordinance such as the present one, but even if it had availed itself of a battery of constitutional lawyers, they would have been of little use in the town's effort. For the Court today ignores the cases on which those lawyers would have relied, and comes up with newly fashioned doctrine. . . .

More than half a century ago we recognized that canvassers, "whether selling pots or distributing leaflets, may lessen the peaceful enjoyment of a home," and that "burglars frequently pose as canvassers, either in order that they may have a pretense to discover whether a house is empty and hence ripe for burglary, or for the purpose of spying out the premises in order that they may return later." *Martin v. City of Struthers,* 319 U.S. 141, 144 (1943). These problems continue to be associated with door-to-door canvassing, as are even graver ones.

. . .

The town had little reason to suspect that the negligible burden of having to obtain a permit runs afoul of the First Amendment. For over 60 years, we have categorically stated that a permit requirement for door-to-door canvassers, which gives no discretion to the issuing authority, is constitutional. The District Court and Court of Appeals, relying on our cases, upheld the ordinance. The Court today, however, abruptly changes course and invalidates the ordinance.

. . . Our early decisions in this area expressly sanction a law that merely requires a canvasser to register. In *Cantwell v. Connecticut,* 310 U.S. 296, 306 (1940), we stated that "[w]ithout doubt a State may protect its citizens from fraudulent solicitation by requiring a stranger in the community, before permitting him publicly to solicit funds for any purpose, to establish his identity and his authority to act for the cause which he purports to represent." In *Murdock v. Pennsylvania,* 319 U.S. 105, 116 (1943), we contrasted the license tax struck down in that case with "merely a registration ordinance calling for an identification of the solicitors so as to give the authorities some basis for investigating strangers coming into the community." And *Martin, supra,* at 148, states that a "city can punish those who call at a home in defiance of the previously expressed will of the occupant and, in addition, can by identification devices control the abuse of the privilege by criminals posing as canvassers."

It is telling that Justices Douglas and Black, perhaps the two Justices in this Court's history most identified with an expansive view of the First Amendment, authored, respectively, *Murdock* and *Martin.* Their belief in the constitutionality of the permit requirement that the Court strikes down today demonstrates just how far the Court's present jurisprudence has strayed from the core concerns of the First Amendment.

. . .

The Stratton ordinance suffers from none of the defects deemed fatal in these earlier decisions. The ordinance does not prohibit door-to-door canvassing; it merely requires that canvassers fill out a form and receive a permit. Cf. *Martin, supra*. The mayor does not exercise any discretion in deciding who receives a permit; approval of the permit is automatic upon proper completion of the form. Cf. *Cantwell, supra*. And petitioners do not contend in this Court that the ordinance is vague. . . .

Just as troubling . . . is the difficulty of discerning from the Court's opinion what exactly it is about the Stratton ordinance that renders it unconstitutional. It is not clear what test the Court is applying, or under which part of that indeterminate test the ordinance fails. . . . Under a straightforward application of the applicable First Amendment framework, however, the ordinance easily passes muster.

There is no support in our case law for applying anything more stringent than intermediate scrutiny to the ordinance. The ordinance is content neutral and does not bar anyone from going door-to-door in Stratton. It merely regulates the manner in which one must canvass: A canvasser must first obtain a permit. . . . Earlier this Term, the Court reaffirmed that this test applies to content-neutral time, place, or manner restrictions on speech in public forums. See Thomas v. Chicago Park Dist., 534 U.S. 316 (2002).

. . . [I]t would be puzzling if regulations of speech taking place on *another citizen's* private property warranted greater scrutiny than regulations of speech taking place in public forums. Common sense and our precedent say just the opposite. . . .

. . .

The next question is whether the ordinance serves the important interests of protecting privacy and preventing fraud and crime. With respect to the interest in protecting privacy, the Court concludes that "[t]he annoyance caused by an uninvited knock on the front door is the same whether or not the visitor is armed with a permit." True, but that misses the key point: the permit requirement results in fewer uninvited knocks. Those who have complied with the permit requirement are less likely to visit residences with no trespassing signs, as it is much easier for the authorities to track them down.

The Court also fails to grasp how the permit requirement serves Stratton's interest in preventing crime. We have approved of permit requirements for those engaging in protected First Amendment activity because of a common-sense recognition that their existence both deters and helps detect wrongdoing. . . .

The ordinance prevents and detects serious crime by making it a crime not to register. . . .

Of course, the Stratton ordinance does not guarantee that no canvasser will ever commit a burglary or violent crime. . . . In order to survive intermediate scrutiny, however, a law need not solve the crime problem, it need only further the interest in preventing crime. Some deterrence of serious criminal activity is more than enough to survive intermediate scrutiny.

. . .

. . . A discretionless permit requirement for canvassers does not violate the First Amendment. Today, the Court elevates its concern with what is, at most, a negligible burden on door-to-door communication above this established proposition. Ironically, however, today's decision may result in less of the door-to-door communication that the Court extols. As the Court recognizes, any homeowner may place a "No Solicitation" sign on his or her property, and it is a crime to violate that sign. In light of today's decision depriving Stratton residents of the degree of accountability and safety that the permit requirement provides, more and more residents may decide to place these signs in their yards and cut off door-to-door communication altogether.

SECTION 3.   SPEECH CONFLICTING WITH OTHER COMMUNITY VALUES: GOVERNMENT CONTROL OF THE CONTENT OF SPEECH

Introduction. Section 1 of this chapter examined the lengthy controversy concerning speech that advocates the commission of a crime, and speech advocating the violent overthrow of existing government. This section returns to the inquiry whether there are legitimate government interests that will justify punishing the speaker because of speech content. The four areas examined here—defamation and privacy, obscenity, fighting words and offensive speech, and commercial speech—have one thing in common. In the early 1940's, the Court stated categorically that they were outside the area of constitutional protection normally afforded by the first amendment. In Chaplinsky v. New Hampshire, 315 U.S. 568, 571–572 (1942), Justice Murphy's opinion for a unanimous court said:

> "There are certain well-defined and narrowly limited classes of speech, the prevention and punishment of which has never been thought to raise any Constitutional problem. These include the lewd and obscene, the profane, the libelous, and the insulting or 'fighting' words—those which by their very utterance inflict injury or tend to incite an immediate breach of the peace. It has been well observed that such utterances are no essential part of any exposition of ideas, and are of such slight social value as a step to truth that any benefit that may be derived from them is clearly outweighed by the social interest in order and morality."

Barely more than a month later, in Valentine v. Chrestensen, 316 U.S. 52 (1942), the Court added "purely commercial advertising" to the list of subjects outside the realm of first amendment protection.

Definitional problems to one side (and definitional problems have been particularly serious in the obscenity field), the approach of *Chaplinsky* and *Valentine* has not proved enduring. Within these areas of expression, the Court has imposed significant first amendment barriers to government control of the content of expression. At the same time, the Court has recognized legitimate governmental interests in these cases that permit some control of content. The most important question to be asked is whether the Court has drawn the lines that define constitutionally protected speech content in the right places. A second question is whether the first amendment law that has crystallized in each of these four categories is consistent with that in the other three.

A.   PROTECTION OF INDIVIDUAL REPUTATION AND PRIVACY

BEAUHARNAIS v. ILLINOIS, 343 U.S. 250 (1952). An Illinois statute made criminal any publication which "portrays depravity, criminality, unchastity, or lack of virtue of a class of citizens, of any race, color, creed or religion which said publication ... exposes the citizens of any race, color, creed or religion to contempt, derision, or obloquy or which is productive of breach of the peace or riots." Beauharnais was convicted under this statute for passing out leaflets in the form of a petition to the mayor and city council of Chicago "to halt the further encroachment, harassment and invasion of white people, their property, neighborhoods and persons, by the Negro." It also included a statement: "if persuasion and the need to prevent the white race from becoming mongrelized by the negro will not unite us, then the aggressions . . . rapes, robberies, knives, guns and marijuana of the negro, surely will." The Supreme Court upheld his conviction with four Justices dissenting. Justice Frankfurter, speaking for the court, examined in detail the status of libel laws in the states and referred to earlier statements to the effect that punishment for libel presents no constitutional problem. He then said: "[i]f an utterance directed at an individual may be the object of criminal sanctions, we cannot deny to a state power to punish the same utterance directed at a defined group, unless we can say this is a wilful and purposeless restriction unrelated to the peace and well-being of the state." After discussing problems in the cities he concluded that "we would deny experience to say that the Illinois legislature was without reason" in enacting the law.

At the end of his opinion he included the following paragraph: "Libelous utterances not being within the area of constitutionally protected speech, it is unnecessary, either for us or for the State courts, to consider the issues behind the phrase 'clear and present danger.' Certainly no one would contend that obscene speech, for example, may be punished only upon a showing of such circumstances. Libel, as we have seen, is in the same class."

Justice Black, in dissent, complained that the Court was degrading first amendment freedoms to the "rational basis" level. He concluded as follows: "To say that a legislative body can, with this Court's approval, make it a crime to petition for and publicly discuss proposed legislation seems as far-fetched to me as it would be to say that a valid law could be enacted to punish a candidate for President for telling the people his views. I think the First Amendment, with the Fourteenth, 'absolutely' forbids such laws without any 'ifs' or 'buts' or 'whereases.' Whatever the danger, if any, in such public discussions, it is a danger the Founders deemed outweighed by the danger incident to the stifling of thought and speech. The Court does not act on this view of the Founders. It calculates what it deems to be the danger of public discussion, holds the scales are tipped on the side of state suppression, and upholds state censorship. . . . If there be minority groups who hail this holding as their victory, they might consider the possible relevancy of this ancient remark: 'Another such victory and I am undone.' "

New York Times Co. v. Sullivan

376 U.S. 254, 84 S.Ct. 710, 11 L.Ed.2d 686 (1964).

Mr. Justice Brennan delivered the opinion of the Court.

We are required in this case to determine for the first time the extent to which the constitutional protections for speech and press limit a State's power to award damages in a libel action brought by a public official against critics of his official conduct.

Respondent L.B. Sullivan is one of the three elected Commissioners of the City of Montgomery, Alabama. He testified that he was "Commissioner of Public Affairs and the duties are supervision of the Police Department, Fire Department, Department of Cemetery and Department of Scales." He brought this civil libel action against the four individual petitioners, who are Negroes and Alabama clergymen, and against petitioner the New York Times Company, a New York corporation which publishes the New York Times, a daily newspaper. A jury in the Circuit Court of Montgomery County awarded him damages of $500,000, the full amount claimed, against all the petitioners, and the Supreme Court of Alabama affirmed....

Respondent's complaint alleged that he had been libeled by statements in a full-page advertisement that was carried in the New York Times on March 29, 1960. Entitled "Heed Their Rising Voices," the advertisement [charged that peaceful demonstrations of Southern Negro students in behalf of their rights guaranteed by the Constitution] "... are being met by an unprecedented wave of terror by those who would deny and negate that document which the whole world looks upon as setting the pattern for modern freedom...." Succeeding paragraphs purported to illustrate the "wave of terror" by describing certain alleged events. The text concluded with an appeal for funds for three purposes: support of the student movement, "the struggle for the right-to-vote," and the legal defense of Dr. Martin Luther King, Jr., leader of the movement, against a perjury indictment then pending in Montgomery....

Of the 10 paragraphs of text in the advertisement, the third and a portion of the sixth were the basis of respondent's claim of libel. They read as follows:

> Third paragraph:
>
> "In Montgomery, Alabama, after students sang 'My Country, 'Tis of Thee' on the State Capitol steps, their leaders were expelled from school, and truckloads of police armed with shotguns and tear-gas ringed the Alabama State College Campus. When the entire student body protested to state authorities by refusing to re-register, their dining hall was padlocked in an attempt to starve them into submission."
>
> Sixth paragraph:
>
> "Again and again the Southern violators have answered Dr. King's peaceful protests with intimidation and violence. They have bombed his home almost killing his wife and child. They have assaulted his person. They have arrested him seven times—for 'speeding,' 'loitering' and similar 'offenses.' And now they have charged him with 'perjury'—a *felony* under which they could imprison him for *ten years*...."

[margin note: Basis for suit of libel]

Although neither of these statements mentions respondent by name, he contended that the word "police" in the third paragraph referred to him as the Montgomery Commissioner who supervised the Police Department, so that he was being accused of "ringing" the campus with police. He further claimed that the paragraph would be read as imputing to the police, and hence to him, the padlocking of the dining hall in order to starve the students into submission. As to the sixth paragraph, he contended that since arrests are ordinarily made by the police, the statement "They have arrested [Dr. King] seven times" would be read as referring to him; he further contended that the "They" who did the arresting would be equated with the "They" who committed the other described acts and with the "Southern violators." ...

It is uncontroverted that some of the statements contained in the two paragraphs were not accurate descriptions of events which occurred in Montgomery. Although Negro students staged a demonstration on the State Capitol steps, they sang the National Anthem and not "My Country, 'Tis of Thee." Although nine students were expelled by the State Board of Education, this was not for leading the demonstration at the Capitol, but for demanding service at a lunch counter in the Montgomery County Courthouse on another day. Not the entire student body, but most of it, had protested the expulsion, not by refusing *contradictions*

to register, but by boycotting classes on a single day; virtually all the students did register for the ensuing semester. The campus dining hall was not padlocked on any occasion, and the only students who may have been barred from eating there were the few who had neither signed a preregistration application nor requested temporary meal tickets. Although the police were deployed near the campus in large numbers on three occasions, they did not at any time "ring" the campus, and they were not called to the campus in connection with the demonstration on the State Capitol steps, as the third paragraph implied. Dr. King had not been arrested seven times, but only four; and although he claimed to have been assaulted some years earlier in connection with his arrest for loitering outside a courtroom, one of the officers who made the arrest denied that there was such an assault.

On the premise that the charges in the sixth paragraph could be read as referring to him, respondent was allowed to prove that he had not participated in the events described. Although Dr. King's home had in fact been bombed twice when his wife and child were there, both of these occasions antedated respondent's tenure as Commissioner, and the police were not only not implicated in the bombings, but had made every effort to apprehend those who were. Three of Dr. King's four arrests took place before respondent became Commissioner. Although Dr. King had in fact been indicted (he was subsequently acquitted) on two counts of perjury, each of which carried a possible five-year sentence, respondent had nothing to do with procuring the indictment.

Respondent made no effort to prove that he suffered actual pecuniary loss as a result of the alleged libel. One of his witnesses, a former employer, testified that if he had believed the statements, he doubted whether he "would want to be associated with anybody who would be a party to such things that are stated in that ad," and that he would not re-employ respondent if he believed "that he allowed the Police Department to do the things that the paper say he did." But neither this witness nor any of the others testified that he had actually believed the statements in their supposed reference to respondent. . . .

The trial judge submitted the case to the jury under instructions that the statements in the advertisement were "libelous per se" and were not privileged, so that petitioners might be held liable if the jury found that they had published the advertisement and that the statements were made "of and concerning" respondent. . . .

. . .

We reverse the judgment. We hold that the rule of law applied by the Alabama courts is constitutionally deficient for failure to provide the safeguards for freedom of speech and of the press that are required by the First and Fourteenth Amendments in a libel action brought by a public official against critics of his official conduct. We further hold that under the proper safeguards the evidence presented in this case is constitutionally insufficient to support the judgment for respondent. . . .

Under Alabama law as applied in this case, a publication is "libelous per se" if the words "tend to injure a person . . . in his reputation" or to "bring [him] into public contempt"; the trial court stated that the standard was met if the words are such as to "injure him in his public office, or impute misconduct to him in his office, or want of official integrity, or want of fidelity to a public trust. . . ." The jury must find that the words were published "of and concerning" the plaintiff, but where the plaintiff is a public official his place in the governmental hierarchy is sufficient evidence to support a finding that his reputation has been affected by statements that reflect upon the agency of which he is in charge. Once "libel per se" has been established, the defendant has no defense as to stated facts unless he can persuade the jury that they were true in all their particulars.... Unless he can discharge the burden of proving truth, general damages are presumed, and may be awarded without proof of pecuniary injury....

The question before us is whether this rule of liability, as applied to an action brought by a public official against critics of his official conduct, abridges the freedom of speech and of the press that is guaranteed by the First and Fourteenth Amendments.

Respondent relies heavily, as did the Alabama courts, on statements of this Court to the effect that the Constitution does not protect libelous publications. Those statements do not foreclose our inquiry here. None of the cases sustained the use of libel laws to impose sanctions upon expression critical of the official conduct of public officials.... Like insurrection, contempt, advocacy of unlawful acts, breach of the peace, obscenity, solicitation of legal business, and the various other formulae for the repression of expression that have been challenged in this Court, libel can claim no talismanic immunity from constitutional limitations. It must be measured by standards that satisfy the First Amendment.

The general proposition that freedom of expression upon public questions is secured by the First Amendment has long been settled by our decisions. The constitutional safeguard, we have said, "was fashioned to assure unfettered interchange of ideas for the bringing about of political and social changes desired by the people." Roth v. United States, 354 U.S. 476, 484....

Thus we consider this case against the background of a profound national commitment to the principle that debate on public issues should be uninhibited, robust, and wide-open, and that it may well include vehement, caustic, and sometimes unpleasantly sharp attacks on government and public officials. See Terminiello v. Chicago, 337 U.S. 1, 4; De Jonge v. Oregon, 299 U.S. 353, 365. The present advertisement, as an expression of grievance and protest on one of the major public issues of our time, would seem clearly to qualify for the constitutional protection. The question is whether it forfeits that protection by the falsity of some of its factual statements and by its alleged defamation of respondent.

Authoritative interpretations of the First Amendment guarantees have consistently refused to recognize an exception for any test of truth—whether administered by judges, juries, or administrative officials—and especially not one that puts the burden of proving truth on the speaker. ...

Injury to official reputation affords no more warrant for repressing speech that would otherwise be free than does factual error. Where judicial officers are involved, this Court has held that concern for the dignity and reputation of the courts does not justify the punishment as criminal contempt of criticism of the judge or his decision. Bridges v. California, 314 U.S. 252....

If neither factual error nor defamatory content suffices to remove the constitutional shield from criticism of official conduct, the combination of the two elements is no less inadequate. This is the lesson to be drawn from the great controversy over the Sedition Act of 1798 ...

Although the Sedition Act was never tested in this Court, the attack upon its validity has carried the day in the court of history.... These views reflect a broad consensus that the Act, because of the restraint it imposed upon criticism of government and public officials, was inconsistent with the First Amendment.

. . .

What a State may not constitutionally bring about by means of a criminal statute is likewise beyond the reach of its civil law of libel. The fear of damage awards under a rule such as that invoked by the Alabama courts here may be markedly more inhibiting than the fear of prosecution under a criminal statute.... The judgment awarded in this case—without the need for any proof of actual pecuniary loss—was one thousand times greater than the maximum fine provided by the Alabama criminal statute, and one hundred times greater than that provided by the Sedition Act. And since there is no double-jeopardy limitation applicable to civil lawsuits, this is not the only judgment that may be awarded against petitioners for the same publication. Whether or not a newspaper can survive a succession of such judgments, the pall of fear and timidity imposed upon those who would give voice to public criticism is an atmosphere in which the First Amendment freedoms cannot survive. Plainly the Alabama law of civil libel is "a form of regulation that creates hazards to protected freedoms markedly greater than those that attend reliance upon the criminal law." Bantam Books, Inc. v. Sullivan, 372 U.S. 58, 70.

The state rule of law is not saved by its allowance of the defense of truth.... Allowance of the defense of truth, with the burden of proving it on the defendant, does not mean that only false speech will be deterred.... Under such a rule, would-be critics of official conduct may be deterred from voicing their criticism, even though it is believed to be true and even though it is in fact true, because of doubt whether it can be proved in court or fear of the expense of having to do so. They tend to make only statements which "steer far wider of the unlawful zone." ... The rule thus dampens the vigor and limits the variety of public debate. It is inconsistent with the First and Fourteenth Amendments.

The constitutional guarantees require, we think, a federal rule that prohibits a public official from recovering damages for a defamatory falsehood relating to his official conduct unless he proves that the statement was made with "actual malice"—that is, with knowledge that it was false or with reckless disregard of whether it was false or not....

. . .

... We think the evidence against the Times supports at most a finding of negligence in failing to discover the misstatements, and is constitutionally insufficient to show the recklessness that is required for a finding of actual malice....

We also think the evidence was constitutionally defective in another respect: it was incapable of supporting the jury's finding that the allegedly libelous statements were made "of and concerning" respondent. Respondent relies on the words of the advertisement and the testimony of six witnesses to establish a connection between it and himself....

Reversed and remanded.

Mr. Justice Black, with whom Mr. Justice Douglas joins, concurring.

... "Malice," even as defined by the Court, is an elusive, abstract concept, hard to prove and hard to disprove. The requirement that malice be proved provides at best an evanescent protection for the right critically to discuss public affairs and certainly does not measure up to the sturdy safeguard embodied in the First Amendment. Unlike the Court, therefore, I vote to reverse exclusively on the ground that the Times and the individual defendants had an absolute, unconditional constitutional right to publish in the Times advertisement their criticisms of the Montgomery agencies and officials. . . .

. . .

Mr. Justice Goldberg, with whom Mr. Justice Douglas joins (concurring in the result).

. . .

In my view, the First and Fourteenth Amendments to the Constitution afford to the citizen and to the press an absolute, unconditional privilege to criticize official conduct despite the harm which may flow from excesses and abuses. . . .

NEW YORK TIMES AND "THE CENTRAL MEANING OF THE FIRST AMENDMENT"

The relationship of *New York Times* to the old law of seditious libel and its potential importance for the future is explored in Kalven, *The New York Times Case: A note on "the Central Meaning of the First Amendment,"* 1964 Sup.Ct. Rev. 191, 209. Professor Kalven contended that freedom from prosecutions for seditious libel—freedom to criticize government—is essential to the existence of a free society. After careful examination he concluded that a major purpose of the opinion was to make it clear that the "central meaning" of the first amendment was that seditious libel cannot be sanctioned: "Although the total structure of the opinion is not without its difficulties, it seems to me to convey, however imperfectly, the following crucial syllogism: The central meaning of the Amendment is that seditious libel cannot be made the subject of government sanction. The Alabama rule on fair comment is closely akin to making seditious libel an offense. The Alabama rule therefore violated the central meaning of the Amendment."

Gertz v. Robert Welch, Inc.

418 U.S. 323, 94 S.Ct. 2997, 41 L.Ed.2d 789 (1974).

Mr. Justice Powell delivered the opinion of the Court.

This Court has struggled for nearly a decade to define the proper accommodation between the law of defamation and the freedoms of speech and press protected by the First Amendment. With this decision we return to that effort. We granted certiorari to reconsider the extent of a publisher's constitutional privilege against liability for defamation of a private citizen. 410 U.S. 925 (1973).

I.

In 1968 a Chicago policeman named Nuccio shot and killed a youth named Nelson. The state authorities prosecuted Nuccio for the homicide and ultimately obtained a conviction for murder in the second degree. The Nelson family retained petitioner Elmer Gertz, a reputable attorney, to represent them in civil litigation against Nuccio.

Respondent publishes American Opinion, a monthly outlet for the views of the John Birch Society. Early in the 1960's the magazine began to warn of a nationwide conspiracy to discredit local law enforcement agencies and create in their stead a national police force capable of supporting a Communist dictatorship. As part of the continuing effort to alert the public to this assumed danger, the managing editor of American Opinion commissioned an article on the murder trial of Officer Nuccio. For this purpose he engaged a regular contributor to the magazine. In March of 1969 respondent published the resulting article under the title "FRAME–UP: Richard Nuccio And The War On Police." The article purports to demonstrate that the testimony against Nuccio at his criminal trial was false and that his prosecution was part of the Communist campaign against the police.

In his capacity as counsel for the Nelson family in the civil litigation, petitioner attended the coroner's inquest into the boy's death and initiated actions for damages, but he neither discussed Officer Nuccio with the press nor played any part in the criminal proceeding. Notwithstanding petitioner's remote connection with the prosecution of Nuccio, respondent's magazine portrayed him as an architect of the "frame-up." According to the article, the police file on petitioner took "a big, Irish cop to lift." The article stated that petitioner had been an official of the "Marxist League for Industrial Democracy, originally known as the Intercollegiate Socialist Society, which has advocated the violent seizure of our government." It labelled Gertz a "Leninist" and a "Communist-fronter." It also stated that Gertz had been an officer of the National Lawyers Guild, described as a Communist organization that "probably did more than any other outfit to plan the Communist attack on the Chicago police during the 1968 Democratic convention."

These statements contained serious inaccuracies. The implication that petitioner had a criminal record was false. Petitioner had been a member and officer of the National Lawyers Guild some 15 years earlier, but there was no evidence that he or that organization had taken any part in planning the 1968 demonstrations in Chicago. There was also no basis for the charge that petitioner was a "Leninist" or a "Communist-fronter." And he had never been a member of the "Marxist League for Industrial Democracy" or the "Intercollegiate Socialist Society."

The managing editor of American Opinion made no effort to verify or substantiate the charges against petitioner. Instead, he appended an editorial introduction stating that the author had "conducted extensive research into the Richard Nuccio case." And he included in the article a photograph of petitioner and wrote the caption that appeared under it: "Elmer Gertz of Red Guild harasses Nuccio." Respondent placed the issue of American Opinion containing the article on sale at newsstands throughout the country and distributed reprints of the article on the streets of Chicago.

Petitioner filed a diversity action for libel in the United States District Court for the Northern District of Illinois. ...

. . .

... [T]he District Court concluded that the *New York Times* standard should govern this case even though petitioner was not a public official or public figure. ...

Petitioner appealed to contest the applicability of the *New York Times* standard to this case. ... The Court of Appeals ... affirmed. ... [W]e reverse.

II.

. . .

Three years after *New York Times,* a majority of the Court agreed to extend the constitutional privilege to defamatory criticism of "public figures." This extension was announced in Curtis Publishing Co. v. Butts and its companion Associated Press v. Walker, 388 U.S. 130, 162 (1967). The first case involved the Saturday Evening Post's charge that Coach Wally Butts of the University of Georgia had conspired with Coach Bear Bryant of the University of Alabama to fix a football game between their respective schools. *Walker* involved an erroneous Associated Press account of former Major General Edwin Walker's participation in a University of Mississippi campus riot. Because Butts was paid by a private alumni association and Walker had resigned from the Army, neither could be classified as a "public official" under *New York Times*. Although Mr. Justice Harlan announced the result in both cases, a majority of the Court agreed with Mr. Chief Justice Warren's conclusion that the *New York Times* test should apply to criticism of "public figures" as well as "public officials." The Court extended the constitutional privilege announced in that case to protect defamatory criticism of nonpublic persons who "are nevertheless intimately involved in the resolution of important public questions or, by reason of their fame, shape events in areas of concern to society at large." ...

. . .

III.

We begin with the common ground. Under the First Amendment there is no such thing as a false idea. However pernicious an opinion may seem, we depend for its correction not on the conscience of judges and juries but on the competition of other ideas. But there is no constitutional value in false statements of fact. Neither the intentional lie nor the careless error materially advances society's interest in "uninhibited, robust, and wide-open" debate on public issues. ...

Although the erroneous statement of fact is not worthy of constitutional protection, it is nevertheless inevitable in free debate.... And punishment of error runs the risk of inducing a cautious and restrictive exercise of the constitutionally guaranteed freedoms of speech and press. Our decisions recognize that a rule of strict liability that compels a publisher or broadcaster to guarantee the accuracy of his factual assertions may lead to intolerable self-censorship. Allowing the media to avoid liability only by proving the truth of all injurious statements does not accord adequate protection to First Amendment liberties....

The need to avoid self-censorship by the news media is, however, not the only societal value at issue. If it were, this Court would have embraced long ago the view that publishers and broadcasters enjoy an unconditional and indefeasible immunity from liability for defamation.... Such a rule would indeed obviate the fear that the prospect of civil liability for injurious falsehood might dissuade a timorous press from the effective exercise of First Amendment freedoms. Yet absolute protection for the communications media requires a total sacrifice of the competing value served by the law of defamation.

The legitimate state interest underlying the law of libel is the compensation of individuals for the harm inflicted on them by defamatory falsehood. We would not lightly require the State to abandon this purpose....

. . .

The *New York Times* standard defines the level of constitutional protection appropriate to the context of defamation of a public person. Those who, by reason of the notoriety of their achievements or the vigor and success with which they seek the public's attention, are properly classed as public figures and those who hold governmental office may recover for injury to reputation only on clear and convincing proof that the defamatory falsehood was made with knowledge of its falsity or with reckless disregard for the truth. This standard administers an extremely powerful antidote to the inducement to media self-censorship of the common law rule of strict liability for libel and slander. And it exacts a correspondingly high price from the victims of defamatory falsehood.... For the reasons stated below, we conclude that the state interest in compensating injury to the reputation of private individuals requires that a different rule should obtain with respect to them.

. . .

... [W]e have no difficulty in distinguishing among defamation plaintiffs. The first remedy of any victim of defamation is self-help—using available opportunities to contradict the lie or correct the error and thereby to minimize its adverse impact on reputation. Public officials and public figures usually enjoy significantly greater access to the channels of effective communication and hence have a more realistic opportunity to counteract false statements than private individuals normally enjoy. Private individuals are therefore more vulnerable to injury, and the state interest in protecting them is correspondingly greater.

More important than the likelihood that private individuals will lack effective opportunities for rebuttal, there is a compelling normative consideration underlying the distinction between public and private defamation plaintiffs. An individual who decides to seek governmental office must accept certain necessary consequences of that involvement in public affairs. He runs the risk of closer public scrutiny than might otherwise be the case. And society's interest in the officers of government is not strictly limited to the formal discharge of official duties....

Those classed as public figures stand in a similar position. Hypothetically, it may be possible for someone to become a public figure through no purposeful action of his own, but the instances of truly involuntary public figures must be exceedingly rare. For the most part those who attain this status have assumed roles of especial prominence in the affairs of society. Some occupy positions of such persuasive power and influence that they are deemed public figures for all purposes. More commonly, those classed as public figures have thrust themselves to the forefront of particular public controversies in order to influence the resolution of the issues involved. In either event, they invite attention and comment.

Even if the foregoing generalities do not obtain in every instance, the communications media are entitled to act on the assumption that public officials and public figures have voluntarily exposed themselves to increased risk of injury from defamatory falsehood concerning them. No such assumption is justified with respect to a private individual. He has not accepted public office nor assumed an "influential role in ordering society." Curtis Publishing Co. v. Butts, 388 U.S., at 164 (Warren, C.J., concurring in result). He has relinquished no part of his interest in the protection of his own good name, and consequently he has a more compelling call on the courts for redress of injury inflicted by defamatory falsehood. Thus, private individuals are not only more vulnerable to injury than public officials and public figures; they are also more deserving of recovery.

For these reasons we conclude that the States should retain substantial latitude in their efforts to enforce a legal remedy for defamatory falsehood injurious to the reputation of a private individual. The extension of the *New York Times* test proposed by the *Rosenbloom* plurality would abridge this legitimate state interest to a degree that we find unacceptable....

We hold that, so long as they do not impose liability without fault, the States may define for themselves the appropriate standard of liability for a publisher or broadcaster of defamatory falsehood injurious to a private individual. This approach provides a more equitable boundary between the competing concerns involved here. It recognizes the strength of the legitimate state interest in compensating private individuals for wrongful injury to reputation, yet shields the press and broadcast media from the rigors of strict liability for defamation. At least this conclusion obtains where, as here, the substance of the defamatory statement "makes substantial danger to reputation apparent." This phrase places in perspective the conclusion we announce today. Our inquiry would involve considerations somewhat different from those discussed above if a State purported to condition civil liability on a factual misstatement whose content did not warn a reasonably prudent editor or broadcaster of its defamatory potential. Cf. Time, Inc. v. Hill, 385 U.S. 374 (1967). Such a case is not now before us, and we intimate no view as to its proper resolution.

IV.

. . . For the reasons stated below, we hold that the States may not permit recovery of presumed or punitive damages, at least when liability is not based on a showing of knowledge of falsity or reckless disregard for the truth.

The common law of defamation is an oddity of tort law, for it allows recovery of purportedly compensatory damages without evidence of actual loss. Under the traditional rules pertaining to actions for libel, the existence of injury is presumed from the fact of publication. Juries may award substantial sums as compensation for supposed damage to reputation without any proof that such harm actually occurred. The largely uncontrolled discretion of juries to award damages where there is no loss unnecessarily compounds the potential of any system of liability for defamatory falsehood to inhibit the vigorous exercise of First Amendment freedoms. Additionally, the doctrine of presumed damages invites juries to punish unpopular opinion rather than to compensate individuals for injury sustained by the publication of a false fact. More to the point, the States have no substantial interest in securing for plaintiffs such as this petitioner gratuitous awards of money damages far in excess of any actual injury.

. . . It is necessary to restrict defamation plaintiffs who do not prove knowledge of falsity or reckless disregard for the truth to compensation for actual injury. We need not define "actual injury," as trial courts have wide experience in framing appropriate jury instructions in tort actions. Suffice it to say that actual injury is not limited to out-of-pocket loss. Indeed, the more customary types of actual harm inflicted by defamatory falsehood include impairment of reputation and standing in the community, personal humiliation, and mental anguish and suffering. Of course, juries must be limited by appropriate instructions, and all awards must be supported by competent evidence concerning the injury, although there need be no evidence which assigns an actual dollar value to the injury.

We also find no justification for allowing awards of punitive damages against publishers and broadcasters held liable under state-defined standards of liability for defamation. In most jurisdictions jury discretion over the amounts awarded is limited only by the gentle rule that they not be excessive. Consequently, juries assess punitive damages in wholly unpredictable amounts bearing no necessary relation to the actual harm caused. And they remain free to use their discretion selectively to punish expressions of unpopular views. Like the doctrine of presumed damages, jury discretion to award punitive damages unnecessarily exacerbates the danger of media self-censorship, but, unlike the former rule, punitive damages are wholly irrelevant to the state interest that justifies a negligence standard for private defamation actions. They are not compensation for injury. Instead, they are private fines levied by civil juries to punish reprehensible conduct and to deter its future occurrence. In short, the private defamation plaintiff who establishes liability under a less demanding standard than that stated by *New York Times* may recover only such damages as are sufficient to compensate him for actual injury.

V.

Notwithstanding our refusal to extend the *New York Times* privilege to defamation of private individuals, respondent contends that we should affirm the judgment below on the ground that petitioner is either a public official or a public figure. There is little basis for the former assertion. Several years prior to the present incident, petitioner had served briefly on housing committees appointed by the mayor of Chicago, but at the time of publication he had never held any remunerative governmental position. Respondent admits this but argues that petitioner's appearance at the coroner's inquest rendered him a "de facto public official." Our cases recognize no such concept. Respondent's suggestion would sweep all lawyers under the *New York Times* rule as officers of the court and distort the plain meaning of the "public official" category beyond all recognition. We decline to follow it.

Respondent's characterization of petitioner as a public figure raises a different question. That designation may rest on either of two alternative bases. In some instances an individual may achieve such pervasive fame or notoriety that he becomes a public figure for all purposes and in all contexts. More commonly, an individual voluntarily injects himself or is drawn into a particular public controversy and thereby becomes a public figure for a limited range of issues. In either case such persons assume special prominence in the resolution of public questions.

Petitioner has long been active in community and professional affairs. He has served as an officer of local civic groups and of various professional organizations, and he has published several books and articles on legal subjects. Although petitioner was consequently well-known in some circles, he had achieved no general fame or notoriety in the community. None of the prospective jurors called at the trial had ever heard of petitioner prior to this litigation, and respondent offered no proof that this response was atypical of the local population. We would not lightly assume that a citizen's participation in community and professional affairs rendered him a public figure for all purposes. Absent clear evidence of general fame or notoriety in the community, and pervasive involvement in the affairs of society, an individual should not be deemed a public personality for all aspects of his life. It is preferable to reduce the public figure question to a more meaningful context by looking to the nature and extent of an individual's participation in the particular controversy giving rise to the defamation.

In this context it is plain that petitioner was not a public figure. He played a minimal role at the coroner's inquest, and his participation related solely to his representation of a private client. He took no part in the criminal prosecution of Officer Nuccio. Moreover, he never discussed either the criminal or civil litigation with the press and was never quoted as having done so. He plainly did not thrust himself into the vortex of this public issue, nor did he engage the public's attention in an attempt to influence its outcome. We are persuaded that the trial court did not err in refusing to characterize petitioner as a public figure for the purpose of this litigation.

We therefore conclude that the *New York Times* standard is inapplicable to this case and that the trial court erred in entering judgment for respondent. Because the jury was allowed to impose liability without fault and was permitted to presume damages without proof of injury, a new trial is necessary. We reverse and remand for further proceedings in accord with this opinion.

It is so ordered.[a]

Mr. Justice Douglas, dissenting.

The Court describes this case as a return to the struggle of "defin[ing] the proper accommodation between the law of defamation and the freedoms of speech and press protected by the First Amendment." It is indeed a struggle, once described by Mr. Justice Black as "the same quagmire" in which the Court "is now helplessly struggling in the field of obscenity." Curtis Publishing Co. v. Butts, 388 U.S. 130, 171 (concurring opinion). I would suggest that the struggle is a quite hopeless one, for, in light of the command of the First Amendment, no "accommodation" of its freedoms can be "proper" except those made by the Framers themselves.

. . .

Mr. Justice Brennan, dissenting.

. . . [W]e strike the proper accommodation between avoidance of media self-censorship and protection of individual reputations only when we require States to apply the . . . knowing-or-reckless-falsity standard in civil libel actions concerning media reports of the involvement of private individuals in events of public or general interest.

. . .

Mr. Justice White, dissenting.

. . .

. . . As I see it, there are wholly insufficient grounds for scuttling the libel laws of the States in such wholesale fashion, to say nothing of deprecating the reputation interest of ordinary citizens and rendering them powerless to protect themselves. I do not suggest that the decision is illegitimate or beyond the bounds of judicial review, but it is an ill-considered exercise of the power entrusted to this Court, particularly when the Court has not had the benefit of briefs and argument addressed to most of the major issues which the Court now decides. I respectfully dissent.

. . .

Dun & Bradstreet, Inc. v. Greenmoss Builders, Inc.

472 U.S. 749, 105 S.Ct. 2939, 86 L.Ed.2d 593 (1985).

Justice Powell announced the judgment of the Court and delivered an opinion, in which Justice Rehnquist and Justice O'Connor joined.

a. A concurrence by Justice Blackmun and a dissent by Chief Justice Burger are omitted.

... The question presented in this case is whether [the] rule of *Gertz* applies when the false and defamatory statements do not involve matters of public concern.

I

Petitioner Dun & Bradstreet, a credit reporting agency, provides subscribers with financial and related information about businesses. All the information is confidential; under the terms of the subscription agreement the subscribers may not reveal it to anyone else. On July 26, 1976, petitioner sent a report to five subscribers indicating that respondent, a construction contractor, had filed a voluntary petition for bankruptcy. This report was false and grossly misrepresented respondent's assets and liabilities....

. . .

Respondent then brought this defamation action in Vermont state court. It alleged that the false report had injured its reputation and sought both compensatory and punitive damages....

After trial, the jury returned a verdict in favor of respondent and awarded $50,000 in compensatory or presumed damages and $300,000 in punitive damages. Petitioner moved for a new trial.... The trial court indicated some doubt as to whether *Gertz* applied to "nonmedia cases," but granted a new trial "[b]ecause of ... dissatisfaction with its charge and ... conviction that the interests of justice require[d]" it.

The Vermont Supreme Court reversed.... [T]he court held "that as a matter of federal constitutional law, the media protections outlined in *Gertz* are inapplicable to nonmedia defamation actions."

. . .

IV

We have never considered whether the *Gertz* balance obtains when the defamatory statements involve no issue of public concern. To make this determination, we must employ the approach approved in *Gertz* and balance the State's interest in compensating private individuals for injury to their reputation against the First Amendment interest in protecting this type of expression. This state interest is identical to the one weighed in *Gertz*....

The First Amendment interest, on the other hand, is less important than the one weighed in *Gertz*. We have long recognized that not all speech is of equal First Amendment importance. It is speech on " 'matters of public concern' " that is "at the heart of the First Amendment's protection." ... In contrast, speech on matters of purely private concern is of less First Amendment concern. ... As a number of state courts, including the court below, have recognized, the role of the Constitution in regulating state libel law is far more limited when the concerns that activated *New York Times* and *Gertz* are absent....

... [C]ourts for centuries have allowed juries to presume that some damage occurred from many defamatory utterances and publications.... This rule furthers the state interest in providing remedies for defamation by ensuring that those remedies are effective. In light of the reduced constitutional value of speech involving no matters of public concern, we hold that the state interest adequately supports awards of presumed and punitive damages—even absent a showing of "actual malice."

V

The only remaining issue is whether petitioner's credit report involved a matter of public concern. In a related context, we have held that "[w]hether ... speech addresses a matter of public concern must be determined by [the expression's] content, form, and context ... as revealed by the whole record." ... These factors indicate that petitioner's credit report concerns no public issue. It was speech solely in the individual interest of the speaker and its specific business audience. ... This particular interest warrants no special protection when—as in this case—the speech is wholly false and clearly damaging to the victim's business reputation. ... Moreover, since the credit report was made available to only five subscribers, who, under the terms of the subscription agreement, could not disseminate it further, it cannot be said that the report involves any "strong interest in the free flow of commercial information." ... There is simply no credible argument that this type of credit reporting requires special protection to ensure that "debate on public issues [will] be uninhibited, robust, and wide-open." ...

In addition, the speech here, like advertising, is hardy and unlikely to be deterred by incidental state regulation. ... It is solely motivated by the desire for profit, which, we have noted, is a force less likely to be deterred than others. Ibid. Arguably, the reporting here was also more objectively verifiable than speech deserving of greater protection. See ibid. In any case, the market provides a powerful incentive to a credit reporting agency to be accurate, since false credit reporting is of no use to creditors. Thus, any incremental "chilling" effect of libel suits would be of decreased significance.

VI

We conclude that permitting recovery of presumed and punitive damages in defamation cases absent a showing of "actual malice" does not violate the First Amendment when the defamatory statements do not involve matters of public concern. Accordingly, we affirm the judgment of the Vermont Supreme Court.

It is so ordered.

Chief Justice Burger, concurring in the judgment.

. . .

I continue to believe ... that *Gertz* was ill-conceived, and therefore agree with Justice White that *Gertz* should be overruled....

Justice White, concurring in the judgment.

. . .

... I remain convinced that *Gertz* was erroneously decided. I have also become convinced that the Court struck an improvident balance in the *New York Times* case between the public's interest in being fully informed about public officials and public affairs and the competing interest of those who have been defamed in vindicating their reputation.

. . .

The *New York Times* rule ... countenances two evils: first, the stream of information about public officials and public affairs is polluted and often remains polluted by false information; and second, the reputation and professional life of the defeated plaintiff may be destroyed by falsehoods that might have been avoided with a reasonable effort to investigate the facts. In terms of the First Amendment and reputational interests at stake, these seem grossly perverse results.

. . .

I still believe the common-law rules should have been retained where plaintiff is not a public official or public figure. . . .

It is interesting that Justice Powell declines to follow the *Gertz* approach in this case. I had thought that the decision in *Gertz* was intended to reach cases that involve any false statements of fact injurious to reputation, whether the statement is made privately or publicly and whether or not it implicates a matter of public importance. Justice Powell, however, distinguishes *Gertz* as a case that involved a matter of public concern, an element absent here. Wisely, in my view, Justice Powell does not rest his application of a different rule here on a distinction drawn between media and nonmedia defendants. On that issue, I agree with Justice Brennan that the First Amendment gives no more protection to the press in defamation suits than it does to others exercising their freedom of speech. None of our cases affords such a distinction; to the contrary, the Court has rejected it at every turn. It should be rejected again, particularly in this context, since it makes no sense to give the most protection to those publishers who reach the most readers and therefore pollute the channels of communication with the most misinformation and do the most damage to private reputation. If *Gertz* is to be distinguished from this case, on the ground that it applies only where the allegedly false publication deals with a matter of general or public importance, then where the false publication does not deal with such a matter, the common-law rules would apply whether the defendant is a member of the media or other public disseminator or a nonmedia individual publishing privately. Although Justice Powell speaks only of the inapplicability of the *Gertz* rule with respect to presumed and punitive damages, it must be that the *Gertz* requirement of some kind of fault on the part of the defendant is also inapplicable in cases such as this.

. . .

Justice Brennan, with whom Justice Marshall, Justice Blackmun and Justice Stevens join, dissenting.

. . .

II

The question presented here is narrow. Neither the parties nor the courts below have suggested that Respondent Greenmoss Builders should be required to show actual malice to obtain a judgment and actual compensatory damages. Nor do the parties question the requirement of *Gertz* that respondent must show fault to obtain a judgment and actual damages. The only question presented is whether a jury award of presumed and punitive damages based on less than a showing of actual malice is constitutionally permissible. *Gertz* provides a forthright negative answer. To preserve the jury verdict in this case, therefore, the opinions of Justice Powell and Justice White have cut away the protective mantle of *Gertz*.

A

Relying on the analysis of the Vermont Supreme Court, Respondent urged that this pruning be accomplished by restricting the applicability of *Gertz* to cases in which the defendant is a "media" entity. . . . First Amendment difficulties lurk in the definitional questions such an approach would generate.... Perhaps most importantly, the argument that *Gertz* should be limited to the media misapprehends our cases. We protect the press to ensure the vitality of First Amendment guarantees. This solicitude implies no endorsement of the principle that speakers other than the press deserve lesser First Amendment protection....

... [A]t least six Members of this Court (the four who join this opinion and Justice White and The Chief Justice) agree today that, in the context of defamation law, the rights of the institutional media are no greater and no less than those enjoyed by other individuals or organizations engaged in the same activities.[10]

B

. . .

... The credit reporting at issue here surely involves a subject matter of sufficient public concern to require the comprehensive protections of *Gertz*. Were this speech appropriately characterized as a matter of only private concern, moreover, the elimination of the *Gertz* restrictions on presumed and punitive damages would still violate basic First Amendment requirements.

The credit reports of Dun & Bradstreet bear few of the earmarks of commercial speech that might be entitled to somewhat less rigorous protection. In *every* case in which we have permitted more extensive state regulation on the basis of a commercial speech rationale the speech being regulated was pure advertising—an offer to buy or sell goods and services or encouraging such buying and selling. Credit reports are not commercial advertisements for a good or service or a proposal to buy or sell such a product. . . .

Of course, the commercial context of Dun & Bradstreet's reports is relevant to the constitutional analysis.... The special harms caused by inaccurate credit reports, the lack of public sophistication about or access to such reports, and the fact that such reports by and large contain statements that are fairly readily susceptible of verification, all may justify appropriate regulation designed to prevent the social losses caused by false credit reports. And in the libel context, the States' regulatory interest in protecting reputation is served by rules permitting recovery for actual compensatory damages upon a showing of fault. Any further interest in deterring potential defamation through case-by-case judicial imposition of presumed and punitive damage awards on less than a showing of actual malice simply exacts too high a toll on First Amendment values. Accordingly, Greenmoss Builders should be permitted to recover for any actual damage it can show resulted from Dun & Bradstreet's negligently false credit report, but should be required to show actual malice to receive presumed or punitive damages. Because the jury was not instructed in accordance with these principles, we would reverse and remand for further proceedings not inconsistent with this opinion.

The Florida Star v. B.J.F.

491 U.S. 524, 109 S.Ct. 2603, 105 L.Ed.2d 443 (1989).

Justice Marshall delivered the opinion of the Court.

Florida Stat. section 794.03 (1987) makes it unlawful to "print, publish, or broadcast ... in any instrument of mass communication" the name of the

---

10. Justice Powell's opinion does not expressly reject the media-nonmedia distinc- tion, but does expressly decline to apply that distinction to resolve this case.

victim of a sexual offense. Pursuant to this statute, appellant The Florida Star was found civilly liable for publishing the name of a rape victim which it had obtained from a publicly released police report. The issue presented here is whether this result comports with the First Amendment. We hold that it does not.

I

The Florida Star is a weekly newspaper which serves the community of Jacksonville, Florida, and which has an average circulation of approximately 18,000 copies. A regular feature of the newspaper is its "Police Reports" section. That section, typically two to three pages in length, contains brief articles describing local criminal incidents under police investigation.

On October 20, 1983, appellee B.J.F. reported to the Duval County, Florida, Sheriff's Department (the Department) that she had been robbed and sexually assaulted by an unknown assailant. The Department prepared a report on the incident which identified B.J.F., by her full name. The Department then placed the report in its press room. The Department does not restrict access either to the press room or to the reports made available therein.

A Florida Star reporter-trainee sent to the press room copied the police report verbatim, including B.J.F.'s full name, on a blank duplicate of the Department's forms. A Florida Star reporter then prepared a one-paragraph article about the crime, derived entirely from the trainee's copy of the police report. The article included B.J.F.'s full name. It appeared in the "Robberies" subsection of the "Police Reports" section on October 29, 1983, one of fifty-four police blotter stories in that day's edition. The article read:

"[B.J.F.] reported on Thursday, October 20, she was crossing Brentwood Park, which is in the 500 block of Golfair Boulevard, enroute to her bus stop, when an unknown black man ran up behind the lady and placed a knife to her neck and told her not to yell. The suspect then undressed the lady and had sexual intercourse with her before fleeing the scene with her 60 cents, Timex watch and gold necklace. Patrol efforts have been suspended concerning this incident because of a lack of evidence."

In printing B.J.F.'s full name, The Florida Star violated its internal policy of not publishing the names of sexual offense victims.

On September 26, 1984, B.J.F. filed suit in the Circuit Court of Duval County against the Department and The Florida Star, alleging that these parties negligently violated section 794.03. . . .

. . .

. . . The jury awarded B.J.F. $75,000 in compensatory damages and $25,000 in punitive damages. . . .

The First District Court of Appeal affirmed in a three-paragraph per curiam opinion. . . . The Supreme Court of Florida denied discretionary review.

. . . We . . . reverse.

II

The tension between the right which the First Amendment accords to a free press, on the one hand, and the protections which various statutes and common-law doctrines accord to personal privacy against the publication of truthful information, on the other, is a subject we have addressed several times in recent years. Our decisions in cases involving government attempts to sanction the accurate dissemination of information as invasive of privacy, have not, however, exhaustively considered this conflict. On the contrary, although our decisions have without exception upheld the press' right to publish, we have emphasized each time that we were resolving this conflict only as it arose in a discrete factual context.

The parties to this case frame their contentions in light of a trilogy of cases which have presented, in different contexts, the conflict between truthful reporting and state-protected privacy interests. In Cox Broadcasting Corp. v. Cohn, 420 U.S. 469 (1975), we found unconstitutional a civil damages award entered against a television station for broadcasting the name of a rape-murder victim which the station had obtained from courthouse records. In Oklahoma Publishing Co. v. District Court, 430 U.S. 308 (1977), we found unconstitutional a state court's pretrial order enjoining the media from publishing the name or photograph of an 11–year–old boy in connection with a juvenile proceeding involving that child which reporters had attended. Finally, in Smith v. Daily Mail Publishing Co., 443 U.S. 97 (1979), we found unconstitutional the indictment of two newspapers for violating a state statute forbidding newspapers to publish, without written approval of the juvenile court, the name of any youth charged as a juvenile offender. The papers had learned about a shooting by monitoring a police band radio frequency, and had obtained the name of the alleged juvenile assailant from witnesses, the police, and a local prosecutor.

. . .

We conclude that imposing damages on appellant for publishing B.J.F.'s name violates the First Amendment . . . Despite the strong resemblance this case bears to *Cox Broadcasting,* that case cannot fairly be read as controlling here. The name of the rape victim in that case was obtained from courthouse records that were open to public inspection, a fact which Justice White's opinion for the Court repeatedly noted. . . . Significantly, one of the reasons we gave in *Cox Broadcasting* for invalidating the challenged damages award was the important role the press plays in subjecting trials to public scrutiny and thereby helping guarantee their fairness. . . . That role is not directly compromised where, as here, the information in question comes from a police report prepared and disseminated at a time at which not only had no adversarial criminal proceedings begun, but no suspect had been identified.

Nor need we accept appellant's invitation to hold broadly that truthful publication may never be punished consistent with the First Amendment. Our cases have carefully eschewed reaching this ultimate question, mindful that the future may bring scenarios which prudence counsels our not resolving anticipatorily. . . . Indeed, in *Cox Broadcasting,* we pointedly refused to answer even the less sweeping question "whether truthful publications may ever be subjected to civil or criminal liability" for invading "an area of privacy" defined by the State. . . . Respecting the fact that press freedom and privacy rights are both "plainly rooted in the traditions and significant concerns of our society," we instead focused on the less sweeping issue of "whether the State may impose sanctions on the accurate publication of the name of a rape victim obtained from public records—more specifically, from judicial records which are maintained in connection with a public prosecution and which themselves are open to public inspection." . . . We continue to believe that the sensitivity and significance of the interests presented in clashes between First Amendment and privacy rights counsel relying on limited principles that sweep no more broadly than the appropriate context of the instant case.

In our view, this case is appropriately analyzed with reference to such a limited First Amendment principle. It is the one, in fact, which we articulated in *Daily Mail* in our synthesis of prior cases involving attempts to punish truthful publication:

> "[I]f a newspaper lawfully obtains truthful information about a matter of public significance then state officials may not constitutionally punish publication of the information, absent a need to further a state interest of the highest order." 443 U.S., at 103.

According the press the ample protection provided by that principle is supported by at least three separate considerations....

First, because the *Daily Mail* formulation only protects the publication of information which a newspaper has "lawfully obtain[ed]," ... the government retains ample means of safeguarding significant interests upon which publication may impinge, including protecting a rape victim's anonymity. To the extent sensitive information rests in private hands, the government may under some circumstances forbid its nonconsensual acquisition, thereby bringing outside of the *Daily Mail* principle the publication of any information so acquired. To the extent sensitive information is in the government's custody, it has even greater power to forestall or mitigate the injury caused by its release. The government may classify certain information, establish and enforce procedures ensuring its redacted release, and extend a damages remedy against the government or its officials where the government's mishandling of sensitive information leads to its dissemination. Where information is entrusted to the government, a less drastic means than punishing truthful publication almost always exists for guarding against the dissemination of private facts....[8]

A second consideration undergirding the *Daily Mail* principle is the fact that punishing the press for its dissemination of information which is already publicly available is relatively unlikely to advance the interests in the service of which the State seeks to act. It is not, of course, always the case that information lawfully acquired by the press is known, or accessible, to others. But where the government has made certain information publicly available, it is highly anomalous to sanction persons other than the source of its release.... The *Daily Mail* formulation reflects the fact that it is a limited set of cases indeed where, despite the accessibility of the public to certain information, a meaningful public interest is served by restricting its further release by other entities, like the press....

A third and final consideration is the "timidity and self-censorship" which may result from allowing the media to be punished for publishing certain truthful information.... *Cox Broadcasting* noted this concern with overdeterrence in the context of information made public through official court records, but the fear of excessive media self-suppression is applicable as well to other information released, without qualification, by the government. A contrary rule, depriving protection to those who rely on the government's implied representations of the lawfulness of dissemination, would force upon the media the onerous obligation of sifting through government press releases, reports, and pronouncements to prune out material arguably unlawful for publication. This situation could inhere even where the newspaper's sole object was to reproduce, with no substantial change, the government's rendition of the event in question.

---

8. The *Daily Mail* principle does not settle the issue of whether, in cases where information has been acquired *unlawfully* by a newspaper or by a source, government may ever punish not only the unlawful acquisition, but the ensuing publication as well. ... We have no occasion to address it here.

Applied to the instant case, the *Daily Mail* principle clearly commands reversal. The first inquiry is whether the newspaper "lawfully obtain[ed] truthful information about a matter of public significance." . . . It is undisputed that the news article describing the assault on B.J.F. was accurate. In addition, appellant lawfully obtained B.J.F.'s name. Appellee's argument to the contrary is based on the fact that under Florida law, police reports which reveal the identity of the victim of a sexual offense are not among the matters of "public record" which the public, by law, is entitled to inspect. But the fact that state officials are not required to disclose such reports does not make it unlawful for a newspaper to receive them when furnished by the government. Nor does the fact that the Department apparently failed to fulfill its obligation under section 794.03 not to "cause or allow to be . . . published" the name of a sexual offense victim make the newspaper's ensuing receipt of this information unlawful. Even assuming the Constitution permitted a State to proscribe *receipt* of information, Florida has not taken this step. It is, clear, furthermore, that the news article concerned "a matter of public significance," . . . in the sense in which the *Daily Mail* synthesis of prior cases used that term. That is, the article generally, as opposed to the specific identity contained within it, involved a matter of paramount public import: the commission, and investigation, of a violent crime which had been reported to authorities. . . .

The second inquiry is whether imposing liability on appellant pursuant to section 794.03 serves "a need to further a state interest of the highest order." . . . Appellee argues that a rule punishing publication furthers three closely related interests: the privacy of victims of sexual offenses; the physical safety of such victims, who may be targeted for retaliation if their names become known to their assailants; and the goal of encouraging victims of such crimes to report these offenses without fear of exposure.

At a time in which we are daily reminded of the tragic reality of rape, it is undeniable that these are highly significant interests, a fact underscored by the Florida Legislature's explicit attempt to protect these interests by enacting a criminal statute prohibiting much dissemination of victim identities. We accordingly do not rule out the possibility that, in a proper case, imposing civil sanctions for publication of the name of a rape victim might be so overwhelmingly necessary to advance these interests as to satisfy the Daily Mail standard. For three independent reasons, however, imposing liability for publication under the circumstances of this case is too precipitous a means of advancing these interests to convince us that there is a "need" within the meaning of the *Daily Mail* formulation for Florida to take this extreme step.

First is the manner in which appellant obtained the identifying information in question. As we have noted, where the government itself provides information to the media, it is most appropriate to assume that the government had, but failed to utilize, far more limited means of guarding against dissemination than the extreme step of punishing truthful speech. That assumption is richly borne out in this case. B.J.F.'s identity would never have come to light were it not for the erroneous, if inadvertent, inclusion by the Department of her full name in an incident report made available in a press room open to the public. Florida's policy against disclosure of rape victims' identities, reflected in section 794.03, was undercut by the Department's failure to abide by this policy. Where, as here, the government has failed to police itself in disseminating information, it is clear under *Cox Broadcasting, Oklahoma Publishing,* and *Landmark Communications* that the imposition of damages against the press for its subsequent publication can hardly be said to be a narrowly tailored means of safeguarding anonymity. Once the government has placed such information in the public domain, . . . hopes for restitution must rest upon the willingness of the government to compensate victims for their loss of privacy, and to protect them from the other consequences of its mishandling of the information which these victims provided in confidence.

That appellant gained access to the information in question through a government news release makes it especially likely that, if liability were to be imposed, self-censorship would result. Reliance on a news release is a paradigmatically "routine newspaper reporting techniqu[e]." ... The government's issuance of such a release, without qualification, can only convey to recipients that the government considered dissemination lawful, and indeed expected the recipients to disseminate the information further. Had appellant merely reproduced the news release prepared and released by the Department, imposing civil damages would surely violate the First Amendment. The fact that appellant converted the police report into a news story by adding the linguistic connecting tissue necessary to transform the report's facts into full sentences cannot change this result.

A second problem with Florida's imposition of liability for publication is the broad sweep of the negligence per se standard applied under the civil cause of action implied from section 794.03. Unlike claims based on the common law tort of invasion of privacy, ... civil actions based on section 794.03 require no case-by-case findings that the disclosure of a fact about a person's private life was one that a reasonable person would find highly offensive. On the contrary, under the per se theory of negligence adopted by the courts below, liability follows automatically from publication. This is so regardless of whether the identity of the victim is already known throughout the community; whether the victim has voluntarily called public attention to the offense; or whether the identity of the victim has otherwise become a reasonable subject of public concern—because, perhaps, questions have arisen whether the victim fabricated an assault by a particular person. Nor is there a scienter requirement of any kind under section 794.03, engendering the perverse result that truthful publications challenged pursuant to this cause of action are less protected by the First Amendment than even the least protected defamatory falsehoods: those involving purely private figures, where liability is evaluated under a standard, usually applied by a jury, of ordinary negligence. See Gertz v. Robert Welch, Inc., 418 U.S. 323 (1974)....

Third, and finally, the facial underinclusiveness of section 794.03 raises serious doubts about whether Florida is, in fact, serving, with this statute, the significant interests which appellee invokes ... Section 794.03 prohibits the publication of identifying information only if this information appears in an "instrument of mass communication," a term the statute does not define. Section 794.03 does not prohibit the spread by other means of the identities of victims of sexual offenses. An individual who maliciously spreads word of the identity of a rape victim is thus not covered, despite the fact that the communication of such information to persons who live near, or work with, the victim may have consequences equally devastating as the exposure of her name to large numbers of strangers....

When a State attempts the extraordinary measure of punishing truthful publication in the name of privacy, it must demonstrate its commitment to advancing this interest by applying its prohibition evenhandedly, to the small-time disseminator as well as the media giant. Where important First Amendment interests are at stake, the mass scope of disclosure is not an acceptable surrogate for injury. A ban on disclosures effected by "instrument[s] of mass communication" simply cannot be defended on the ground that partial prohibitions may effect partial relief.... Without more careful and inclusive precau-

tions against alternative forms of dissemination, we cannot conclude that Florida's selective ban on publication by the mass media satisfactorily accomplishes its stated purpose.

III

Our holding today is limited. We do not hold that truthful publication is automatically constitutionally protected, or that there is no zone of personal privacy within which the State may protect the individual from intrusion by the press, or even that a State may never punish publication of the name of a victim of a sexual offense. We hold only that where a newspaper publishes truthful information which it has lawfully obtained, punishment may lawfully be imposed, if at all, only when narrowly tailored to a state interest of the highest order, and that no such interest is satisfactorily served by imposing liability under section 794.03 to appellant under the facts of this case. The decision below is therefore

Reversed.

Justice Scalia concurring in part and concurring in the judgment.

I think it sufficient to decide this case to rely upon the third ground set forth in the Court's opinion: that a law cannot [justify] ... a restriction upon truthful speech, when it leaves appreciable damage to that supposedly vital interest unprohibited. In the present case, I would anticipate that the rape victim's discomfort at the dissemination of news of her misfortune among friends and acquaintances would be at least as great as her discomfort at its publication by the media to people to whom she is only a name. Yet the law in question does not prohibit the former in either oral or written form. Nor is it at all clear, as I think it must be to validate this statute, that Florida's general privacy law would prohibit such gossip....

This law has every appearance of a prohibition that society is prepared to impose upon the press but not upon itself....

Justice White, with whom the Chief Justice and Justice O'Connor join, dissenting.

. . .

I

The Court finds its result compelled, or at least supported in varying degrees, by three of our prior cases ... None of these cases requires the harsh outcome reached today.

. . .

These facts—that the disclosure came in judicial proceedings, which were open to the public—were critical to our analysis in *Cox Broadcasting*....

Cox Broadcasting stands for the proposition that the State cannot make the press its first line of defense in withholding private information from the public—it cannot ask the press to secrete private facts that the State makes no effort to safeguard in the first place....

Finding *Cox Broadcasting* inadequate to support its result, the Court relies on Smith v. Daily Mail Publishing Co. as its principal authority. But the flat rule from *Daily Mail* on which the Court places so much reliance ... was introduced in *Daily Mail* with the cautious qualifier that such a rule was "suggest[ed]" by our prior cases, "[n]one of [which] ... directly control[led]" . . .

More importantly, at issue in *Daily Mail* was the disclosure of the name of the perpetrator of an infamous murder of a 15–year–old student.... Surely the rights of those accused of crimes and those who are their victims must differ with respect to privacy concerns....

Consequently, I cannot agree that *Cox Broadcasting,* or *Oklahoma Publishing,* or *Daily Mail* require—or even substantially support—the result reached by the Court today.

II

We are left, then, to wonder whether the three "independent reasons" the Court cites for reversing the judgment for B.J.F. support its result.

The first of these reasons relied on by the Court is the fact "appellant gained access to [B.J.F.'s name] through a government news release." ... Here, the "release" of information provided by the government was not, as the Court says, "without qualification." As the Star's own reporter conceded at trial, the crime incident report that inadvertently included B.J.F.'s name was posted in a room that contained signs making it clear that the names of rape victims were not matters of public record, and were not to be published....

. . . .

Second, the Court complains that appellant was judged here under too strict a liability standard....

... Permitting liability under a negligence per se theory does not mean that defendants will be held liable without a showing of negligence, but rather, that the standard of care has been set by the legislature, instead of the courts.... [T]he legislature—reflecting popular sentiment—has determined that disclosure of the fact that a person was raped is categorically a revelation that reasonable people find offensive. And as for the Court's suggestion that the Florida courts' theory permits liability without regard for whether the victim's identity is already known, or whether she herself has made it known—these are facts that would surely enter into the calculation of damages in such a case....

Third, the Court faults the Florida criminal statute for being underinclusive ... But our cases which have struck down laws that limit or burden the press due to their underinclusiveness have involved situations where a legislature has singled out one segment of the news media or press for adverse treatment, ... or singled out the press for adverse treatment when compared to other similarly situated enterprises.... Here, the Florida law evenhandedly covers all "instrument[s] of mass communication" no matter their form, media, content, nature or purpose.... Florida wanted to prevent the widespread distribution of rape victim's names, and therefore enacted a statute tailored almost as precisely as possible to achieving that end.

. . .

Consequently, neither the State's "dissemination" of B.J.F.'s name, nor the standard of liability imposed here, nor the underinclusiveness of Florida tort law require setting aside the verdict for B.J.F.... I turn, therefore, to the more general principles at issue here to see if they recommend the Court's result.

III

At issue in this case is whether there is any information about people, which—though true—may not be published in the press. By holding that only "a state interest of the highest order" permits the State to penalize the

publication of truthful information, and by holding that protecting a rape victim's right to privacy is not among those state interests of the highest order, the Court accepts appellant's invitation to obliterate one of the most noteworthy legal inventions of the 20th–Century: the tort of the publication of private facts.... If the First Amendment prohibits wholly private persons (such as B.J.F.) from recovering for the publication of the fact that she was raped, I doubt that there remain any "private facts" which persons may assume will not be published in the newspapers, or broadcast on television.

Of course, the right to privacy is not absolute. Even the Article widely relied upon in cases vindicating privacy rights, Warren & Brandeis, The Right to Privacy, 4 Harv.L.Rev., at 193, recognized that this right inevitably conflicts with the public's right to know about matters of general concern—and that sometimes, the latter must trump the former. Id., at 214–215. Resolving this conflict is a difficult matter, and I do not fault the Court for attempting to strike an appropriate balance between the two, but rather, for according too little weight to B.J.F.'s side of equation, and too much on the other.

. . .

Bartnicki v. Vopper

532 U.S. 514, 121 S.Ct. 1753, 149 L.Ed.2d 787 (2001).

Justice Stevens delivered the opinion of the Court.

These cases raise an important question concerning what degree of protection, if any, the First Amendment provides to speech that discloses the contents of an illegally intercepted communication. . . .

The suit at hand involves the repeated intentional disclosure of an illegally intercepted cellular telephone conversation about a public issue. The persons who made the disclosures did not participate in the interception, but they did know—or at least had reason to know—that the interception was unlawful. Accordingly, these cases present a conflict between interests of the highest order—on the one hand, the interest in the full and free dissemination of information concerning public issues, and, on the other hand, the interest in individual privacy and, more specifically, in fostering private speech. . . . [W]e are firmly convinced that the disclosures made by respondents in this suit are protected by the First Amendment.

I

During 1992 and most of 1993, the Pennsylvania State Education Association, a union representing the teachers at the Wyoming Valley West High School, engaged in collective-bargaining negotiations with the school board. Petitioner Kane, then the president of the local union, testified that the negotiations were " 'contentious' and received 'a lot of media attention.' " In May 1993, petitioner Bartnicki, who was acting as the union's "chief negotiator," used the cellular phone in her car to call Kane and engage in a lengthy conversation about the status of the negotiations. An unidentified person intercepted and recorded that call.

. . . At one point, Kane said: "If they're not gonna move for three percent, we're gonna have to go to their, their homes.... To blow off their front porches, we'll have to do some work on some of those guys. (PAUSES). Really, uh, really and truthfully because this is, you know, this is bad news. (UNDECIPHERABLE)."

In the early fall of 1993, the parties accepted a non-binding arbitration proposal that was generally favorable to the teachers. In connection with news reports about the settlement, respondent Vopper, a radio commentator who had been critical of the union in the past, played a tape of the intercepted conversation on his public affairs talk show. Another station also broadcast the tape, and local newspapers published its contents. After filing suit against Vopper and other representatives of the media, Bartnicki and Kane (hereinafter petitioners) learned through discovery that Vopper had obtained the tape from Jack Yocum, the head of a local taxpayers' organization that had opposed the union's demands throughout the negotiations. Yocum, who was added as a defendant, testified that he had found the tape in his mailbox shortly after the interception and recognized the voices of Bartnicki and Kane. Yocum played the tape for some members of the school board, and later delivered the tape itself to Vopper.

II

In their amended complaint, petitioners alleged that their telephone conversation had been surreptitiously intercepted by an unknown person using an electronic device, that Yocum had obtained a tape of that conversation, and that he intentionally disclosed it to Vopper, as well as other individuals and media representatives. Thereafter, Vopper and other members of the media repeatedly published the contents of that conversation. The amended complaint alleged that each of the defendants "knew or had reason to know" that the recording of the private telephone conversation had been obtained by means of an illegal interception. Relying on both federal and Pennsylvania statutory provisions, petitioners sought actual damages, statutory damages, punitive damages, and attorney's fees and costs.

... [T]he District Court rejected respondents' First Amendment defense ...

Thereafter, the District Court granted a motion for an interlocutory appeal, [certifying] as controlling questions of law: "(1) whether the imposition of liability on the media Defendants under the [wiretapping statutes] solely for broadcasting the newsworthy tape on the Defendant [Vopper's] radio/public affairs program, when the tape was illegally intercepted and recorded by unknown persons who were not agents of [the] Defendants, violates the First Amendment; and (2) whether imposition of liability under the aforesaid [wiretapping] statutes on Defendant Jack Yocum solely for providing the anonymously intercepted and recorded tape to the media Defendants violates the First Amendment." ...

... [T]he majority [of the Court of Appeals] concluded that the statutes were invalid because they deterred significantly more speech than necessary to protect the privacy interests at stake. The court remanded the case with instructions to enter summary judgment for respondents. ...

III

... One of the stated purposes of [Title III of the Omnibus Crime Control and Safe Streets Act of 1968, entitled Wiretapping and Electronic Surveillance] was "to protect effectively the privacy of wire and oral communications." ... In addition to authorizing and regulating electronic surveillance for law enforcement purposes, Title III also regulated private conduct. ... Subsection (c), the original version of the provision most directly at issue in this case, applied to any person who "willfully discloses, or endeavors to disclose, to any other person the contents of any wire or oral communication, knowing or having reason to know that the information was obtained through the interception of a wire or oral communication in violation of this subsection." The oral communications protected by the Act were only those "uttered by a person exhibiting an expectation that such communication is not subject to interception under circumstances justifying such expectation." . . .

. . . As enacted in 1968, Title III did not apply to the monitoring of radio transmissions. In the Electronic Communications Privacy Act of 1986, . . . however, Congress enlarged the coverage of Title III to prohibit the interception of "electronic" as well as oral and wire communications. By reason of that amendment, as well as a 1994 amendment which applied to cordless telephone communications, . . . Title III now applies to the interception of conversations over both cellular and cordless phones. . . .

IV

The constitutional question before us concerns the validity of the statutes as applied to the specific facts of this case. Because of the procedural posture of the case, it is appropriate to make certain important assumptions about those facts. We accept petitioners' submission that the interception was intentional, and therefore unlawful, and that, at a minimum, respondents "had reason to know" that it was unlawful. Accordingly, the disclosure of the contents of the intercepted conversation by Yocum to school board members and to representatives of the media, as well as the subsequent disclosures by the media defendants to the public, violated the federal and state statutes. Under the provisions of the federal statute, as well as its Pennsylvania analog, petitioners are thus entitled to recover damages from each of the respondents. The only question is whether the application of these statutes in such circumstances violates the First Amendment.[8]

In answering that question, we accept respondents' submission on three factual matters that serve to distinguish most of the cases that have arisen under § 2511. First, respondents played no part in the illegal interception. Rather, they found out about the interception only after it occurred, and in fact never learned the identity of the person or persons who made the interception. Second, their access to the information on the tapes was obtained lawfully, even though the information itself was intercepted unlawfully by someone else. . . . Third, the subject matter of the conversation was a matter of public concern. If the statements about the labor negotiations had been made in a public arena—during a bargaining session, for example—they would have been newsworthy. This would also be true if a third party had inadvertently overheard Bartnicki making the same statements to Kane when the two thought they were alone.

V

We agree with petitioners that § 2511(1)(c), as well as its Pennsylvania analog, is in fact a content-neutral law of general applicability. . . . In determining whether a regulation is content based or content neutral, we look to the purpose behind the regulation . . . In this case, the basic purpose of the statute at issue is to "protec[t] the privacy of wire[, electronic,] and oral communications." . . . The statute does not distinguish based on the content of the intercepted conversations, nor is it justified by reference to the content of those conversations. Rather, the communications at issue are singled out by virtue of

---

8. In answering this question, we draw no distinction between the media respondents and Yocum. See, e.g., New York Times Co. v. Sullivan, 376 U.S. 254 (1964); First Nat. Bank of Boston v. Bellotti, 435 U.S. 765, 777 (1978).

the fact that they were illegally intercepted—by virtue of the source, rather than the subject matter.

On the other hand, the naked prohibition against disclosures is fairly characterized as a regulation of pure speech. Unlike the prohibition against the "use" of the contents of an illegal interception in § 2511(1)(d), subsection (c) is not a regulation of conduct. It is true that the delivery of a tape recording might be regarded as conduct, but given that the purpose of such a delivery is to provide the recipient with the text of recorded statements, it is like the delivery of a handbill or a pamphlet, and as such, it is the kind of "speech" that the First Amendment protects. . . . As a general matter, "state action to punish the publication of truthful information seldom can satisfy constitutional standards." Smith v. Daily Mail Publishing Co., 443 U.S. 97, 102 (1979). . . .

. . .

. . . New York Times Co. v. United States, 403 U.S. 713 (1971) . . . raised, but did not resolve the question "whether, in cases where information has been acquired unlawfully by a newspaper or by a source, government may ever punish not only the unlawful acquisition, but the ensuing publication as well." . . . The question here, however, is a narrower version of that still-open question. Simply put, the issue here is this: "Where the punished publisher of information has obtained the information in question in a manner lawful in itself but from a source who has obtained it unlawfully, may the government punish the ensuing publication of that information based on the defect in a chain?" . . .

. . .

The Government identifies two interests served by the statute—first, the interest in removing an incentive for parties to intercept private conversations, and second, the interest in minimizing the harm to persons whose conversations have been illegally intercepted. We assume that those interests adequately justify the prohibition in § 2511(1)(d) against the interceptor's own use of information that he or she acquired by violating § 2511(1)(a), but it by no means follows that punishing disclosures of lawfully obtained information of public interest by one not involved in the initial illegality is an acceptable means of serving those ends.

The normal method of deterring unlawful conduct is to impose an appropriate punishment on the person who engages in it. If the sanctions that presently attach to a violation of § 2511(1)(a) do not provide sufficient deterrence, perhaps those sanctions should be made more severe. But it would be quite remarkable to hold that speech by a law-abiding possessor of information can be suppressed in order to deter conduct by a non-law-abiding third party. . . . With only a handful of exceptions, the violations of § 2511(1)(a) that have been described in litigated cases have been motivated by either financial gain or domestic disputes. In virtually all of those cases, the identity of the person or persons intercepting the communication has been known. Moreover, petitioners cite no evidence that Congress viewed the prohibition against disclosures as a response to the difficulty of identifying persons making improper use of scanners and other surveillance devices and accordingly of deterring such conduct, and there is no empirical evidence to support the assumption that the prohibition against disclosures reduces the number of illegal interceptions.

Although this case demonstrates that there may be an occasional situation in which an anonymous scanner will risk criminal prosecution by passing on information without any expectation of financial reward or public praise, surely this is the exceptional case. Moreover, there is no basis for assuming that imposing sanctions upon respondents will deter the unidentified scanner from continuing to engage in surreptitious interceptions. Unusual cases fall far short of a showing that there is a "need of the highest order" for a rule supplementing the traditional means of deterring antisocial conduct.

The Government's second argument, however, is considerably stronger. Privacy of communication is an important interest, . . . and Title III's restrictions are intended to protect that interest, thereby "encouraging the uninhibited exchange of ideas and information among private parties. . . ." Moreover, the fear of public disclosure of private conversations might well have a chilling effect on private speech.

. . . [T]here are important interests to be considered on both sides of the constitutional calculus. In considering that balance, we acknowledge that some intrusions on privacy are more offensive than others, and that the disclosure of the contents of a private conversation can be an even greater intrusion on privacy than the interception itself. As a result, there is a valid independent justification for prohibiting such disclosures by persons who lawfully obtained access to the contents of an illegally intercepted message, even if that prohibition does not play a significant role in preventing such interceptions from occurring in the first place.

We need not decide whether that interest is strong enough to justify the application of § 2511(c) to disclosures of trade secrets or domestic gossip or other information of purely private concern. . . . In other words, the outcome of the case does not turn on whether § 2511(1)(c) may be enforced with respect to most violations of the statute without offending the First Amendment. The enforcement of that provision in this case, however, implicates the core purposes of the First Amendment because it imposes sanctions on the publication of truthful information of public concern.

. . . In this case, privacy concerns give way when balanced against the interest in publishing matters of public importance. As Warren and Brandeis stated in their classic law review article: "The right of privacy does not prohibit any publication of matter which is of public or general interest." The Right to Privacy, 4 Harv. L.Rev. 193, 214 (1890). One of the costs associated with participation in public affairs is an attendant loss of privacy. . . .

. . .

We think it clear that parallel reasoning requires the conclusion that a stranger's illegal conduct does not suffice to remove the First Amendment shield from speech about a matter of public concern. The months of negotiations over the proper level of compensation for teachers at the Wyoming Valley West High School were unquestionably a matter of public concern, and respondents were clearly engaged in debate about that concern. That debate may be more mundane than the Communist rhetoric that inspired Justice Brandeis' classic opinion in Whitney v. California, 274 U.S., at 372, but it is no less worthy of constitutional protection.

The judgment is affirmed.

It is so ordered.

Justice Breyer, with whom Justice O'Connor joins, concurring.

I join the Court's opinion because I agree with its "narrow" holding, limited to the special circumstances present here: (1) the radio broadcasters acted lawfully (up to the time of final public disclosure); and (2) the information publicized involved a matter of unusual public concern, namely a threat of potential physical harm to others. I write separately to explain why, in my view, the Court's holding does not imply a significantly broader constitutional immunity for the media.

. . .

I would ask whether the statutes strike a reasonable balance between their speech-restricting and speech-enhancing consequences. Or do they instead impose restrictions on speech that are disproportionate when measured against their corresponding privacy and speech-related benefits, taking into account the kind, the importance, and the extent of these benefits, as well as the need for the restrictions in order to secure those benefits? What this Court has called "strict scrutiny"—with its strong presumption against constitutionality—is normally out of place where, as here, important competing constitutional interests are implicated. . . .

The statutory restrictions before us directly enhance private speech. . . . The statutes ensure the privacy of telephone conversations much as a trespass statute ensures privacy within the home. That assurance of privacy helps to overcome our natural reluctance to discuss private matters when we fear that our private conversations may become public. And the statutory restrictions consequently encourage conversations that otherwise might not take place.

. . . At the same time, these statutes restrict public speech directly, deliberately, and of necessity. They include media publication within their scope not simply as a means, say, to deter interception, but also as an end. Media dissemination of an intimate conversation to an entire community will often cause the speakers serious harm over and above the harm caused by an initial disclosure to the person who intercepted the phone call. . . . And the threat of that widespread dissemination can create a far more powerful disincentive to speak privately than the comparatively minor threat of disclosure to an interceptor and perhaps to a handful of others. Insofar as these statutes protect private communications against that widespread dissemination, they resemble laws that would award damages caused through publication of information obtained by theft from a private bedroom. See generally Warren & Brandeis, The Right to Privacy, 4 Harv. L.Rev. 193 (1890) . . . See also Restatement (Second) of Torts § 652D (1977).

As a general matter, despite the statutes' direct restrictions on speech, the Federal Constitution must tolerate laws of this kind because of the importance of these privacy and speech-related objectives. . . . Rather than broadly forbid this kind of legislative enactment, the Constitution demands legislative efforts to tailor the laws in order reasonably to reconcile media freedom with personal, speech-related privacy.

Nonetheless, looked at more specifically, the statutes, as applied in these circumstances, do not reasonably reconcile the competing constitutional objectives. Rather, they disproportionately interfere with media freedom. For one thing, the broadcasters here engaged in no unlawful activity other than the ultimate publication of the information another had previously obtained. . . .

For another thing, the speakers had little or no legitimate interest in maintaining the privacy of the particular conversation. That conversation involved a suggestion about "blow[ing] off . . . front porches" and "do[ing] some work on some of these guys," thereby raising a significant concern for the safety of others. . . . Even where the danger may have passed by the time of publication, that fact cannot legitimize the speaker's earlier privacy expectation. Nor should editors, who must make a publication decision quickly, have to determine present or continued danger before publishing this kind of threat.

Further, the speakers themselves, the president of a teacher's union and the union's chief negotiator, were "limited public figures," for they voluntarily engaged in a public controversy. They thereby subjected themselves to somewhat greater public scrutiny and had a lesser interest in privacy than an individual engaged in purely private affairs. . . .

This is not to say that the Constitution requires anyone, including public figures, to give up entirely the right to private communication, i.e., communication free from telephone taps or interceptions. But the subject matter of the conversation at issue here is far removed from that in situations where the media publicizes truly private matters. . . .

Thus, in finding a constitutional privilege to publish unlawfully intercepted conversations of the kind here at issue, the Court does not create a "public interest" exception that swallows up the statutes' privacy-protecting general rule. Rather, it finds constitutional protection for publication of intercepted information of a special kind. Here, the speakers' legitimate privacy expectations are unusually low, and the public interest in defeating those expectations is unusually high. Given these circumstances, along with the lawful nature of respondents' behavior, the statutes' enforcement would disproportionately harm media freedom.

I emphasize the particular circumstances before us because, in my view, the Constitution permits legislatures to respond flexibly to the challenges future technology may pose to the individual's interest in basic personal privacy. Clandestine and pervasive invasions of privacy, unlike the simple theft of documents from a bedroom, are genuine possibilities as a result of continuously advancing technologies. Eavesdropping on ordinary cellular phone conversations in the street (which many callers seem to tolerate) is a very different matter from eavesdropping on encrypted cellular phone conversations or those carried on in the bedroom. But the technologies that allow the former may come to permit the latter. And statutes that may seem less important in the former context may turn out to have greater importance in the latter. Legislatures also may decide to revisit statutes such as those before us, creating better tailored provisions designed to encourage, for example, more effective privacy-protecting technologies.

For these reasons, we should avoid adopting overly broad or rigid constitutional rules, which would unnecessarily restrict legislative flexibility. I consequently agree with the Court's holding that the statutes as applied here violate the Constitution, but I would not extend that holding beyond these present circumstances.

Chief Justice Rehnquist, with whom Justice Scalia and Justice Thomas join, dissenting.

. . . In an attempt to prevent some of the most egregious violations of privacy, the United States, the District of Columbia, and 40 States have enacted laws prohibiting the intentional interception and knowing disclosure of electronic communications. The Court holds that all of these statutes violate the First Amendment insofar as the illegally intercepted conversation touches upon a matter of "public concern," an amorphous concept that the Court does not even attempt to define. But the Court's decision diminishes, rather than enhances, the purposes of the First Amendment: chilling the speech of the millions of Americans who rely upon electronic technology to communicate each day.

. . .

... [T]he *Daily Mail* cases upon which the Court relies do not address the question presented here. Our decisions themselves made this clear: "The *Daily Mail* principle does not settle the issue whether, in cases where information has been acquired unlawfully by a newspaper or by a source, the government may ever punish not only the unlawful acquisition, but the ensuing publication as well." ... The transmission of the intercepted communication from the eavesdropper to the third party is itself illegal; and where, as here, the third party then knowingly discloses that communication, another illegal act has been committed. The third party in this situation cannot be likened to the reporters in the *Daily Mail* cases, who lawfully obtained their information through consensual interviews or public documents.

. . .

Congress and the overwhelming majority of States reasonably have concluded that sanctioning the knowing disclosure of illegally intercepted communications will deter the initial interception itself, a crime which is extremely difficult to detect. ...

. . .

... Were there no prohibition on disclosure, an unlawful eavesdropper who wanted to disclose the conversation could anonymously launder the interception through a third party and thereby avoid detection. Indeed, demand for illegally obtained private information would only increase if it could be disclosed without repercussion. The law against interceptions, which the Court agrees is valid, would be utterly ineffectual without these antidisclosure provisions.

At base, the Court's decision to hold these statutes unconstitutional rests upon nothing more than the bald substitution of its own prognostications in place of the reasoned judgment of 41 legislative bodies and the United States Congress. ...

. . .

... The Constitution should not protect the involuntary broadcast of personal conversations. Even where the communications involve public figures or concern public matters, the conversations are nonetheless private and worthy of protection. Although public persons may have forgone the right to live their lives screened from public scrutiny in some areas, it does not and should not follow that they also have abandoned their right to have a private conversation without fear of it being intentionally intercepted and knowingly disclosed.

ZACCHINI v. SCRIPPS–HOWARD BROADCASTING CO., 433 U.S. 562 (1977). Hugo Zacchini was an entertainer, whose 15 second act consisted of being shot from a cannon into a net 200 feet away. A reporter for a local television station, attending the county fair where Zacchini was performing, was asked by Zacchini not to film his act. The reporter, however, returned the next day and videotaped the entire act. The tape, which ran 15 seconds, was shown on the 11:00 o'clock news that night. In the state trial court, Zacchini was awarded summary judgment in an action for appropriation of his "professional property." The Ohio Supreme Court reversed, relying on Time, Inc. v. Hill, 385 U.S. 374 (1967), for the proposition that the television station had a privilege to report the act as a newsworthy event. The Supreme Court reversed. the court's opinion, by Justice White, concluded that the *Hill* case was inapposite:

"Time, Inc. v. Hill, which was hotly contested and decided by a divided Court, involved an entirely different tort from the 'right of publicity' recognized by the Ohio Supreme Court. As the opinion reveals in Time, Inc. v. Hill, the Court was steeped in the literature of privacy law and was aware of the developing distinctions and nuances in this branch of the law. . . . The Court was aware that it was adjudicating a 'false light' privacy case involving a matter of public interest, not a case involving 'intrusion,' . . . 'appropriation' of a name or likeness for the purposes of trade, . . . or 'private details' about a non-newsworthy person or event. . . . It is also abundantly clear that Time, Inc. v. Hill did not involve a performer, a person with a name having commercial value, or any claim to a 'right of publicity.' This discrete kind of 'appropriation' case was plainly identified in the literature cited by the Court and had been adjudicated in the reported cases.

"'. . .

"'. . . Wherever the line in particular situations is to be drawn between media reports that are protected and those that are not, we are quite sure that the First and Fourteenth Amendments do not immunize the media when they broadcast a performer's entire act without his consent. The Constitution no more prevents a State from requiring respondent to compensate petitioner for broadcasting his act on television than it would privilege respondent to film and broadcast a copyrighted dramatic work without liability to the copyright owner. . . .'"

Justice Powell's dissent, joined by Justices Brennan and Marshall, emphasized that the case involved a 15 second clip that was part of a routine daily news program.

"In my view the First Amendment commands a different analytical starting point from the one selected by the Court. Rather than begin with a quantitative analysis of the performer's behavior—is this or is this not his entire act—we should direct initial attention to the actions of the news media: what use did the station make of the film footage? When a film is used, as here, for a routine portion of a regular news program, I would hold that the First Amendment protects the station from a 'right of publicity' or 'appropriation' suit, absent a strong showing by the plaintiff that the news broadcast was a subterfuge or cover for private or commercial exploitation."

Justice Stevens, dissenting, would have remanded the case to the Ohio Supreme Court for clarification as to whether its decision denying liability rested on the constitutional ground.

B.   CONTROL OF OBSCENITY AND PORNOGRAPHY

Paris Adult Theatre I v. Slaton

413 U.S. 49, 93 S.Ct. 2628, 37 L.Ed.2d 446 (1973).

Mr. Chief Justice Burger delivered the opinion of the Court.

Petitioners are two Atlanta, Georgia, movie theaters and their owners and managers, operating in the style of "adult" theaters. . . . [R]espondents, the local state district attorney and the solicitor for the local state trial court, filed civil complaints in that court alleging that petitioners were exhibiting to the public for paid admission two allegedly obscene films . . .

Respondents' complaints, made on behalf of the State of Georgia, demanded that the two films be declared obscene and that petitioners be enjoined from exhibiting the films. . . .

... Certain photographs, ... produced at trial, were stipulated to portray the single entrance to both Paris Adult Theatre I and Paris Adult Theatre II as it appeared at the time of the complaints. These photographs show a conventional, inoffensive theater entrance, without any pictures, but with signs indicating that the theaters exhibit "Atlanta's Finest Mature Feature Films." On the door itself is a sign saying: "Adult Theatre—You must be 21 and able to prove it. If viewing the nude body offends you, Please Do Not Enter."

... [T]he trial judge dismissed respondents' complaints.... On appeal, the Georgia Supreme Court unanimously reversed....

. . .

II

We categorically disapprove the theory, apparently adopted by the trial judge, that obscene, pornographic films acquire constitutional immunity from state regulation simply because they are exhibited for consenting adults only. This holding was properly rejected by the Georgia Supreme Court. Although we have often pointedly recognized the high importance of the state interest in regulating the exposure of obscene materials to juveniles and unconsenting adults, ... this Court has never declared these to be the only legitimate state interests permitting regulation of obscene material....

In particular, we hold that there are legitimate state interests at stake in stemming the tide of commercialized obscenity, even assuming it is feasible to enforce effective safeguards against exposure to juveniles and to passersby.... These include the interest of the public in the quality of life and the total community environment, the tone of commerce in the great city centers, and, possibly, the public safety itself.... [T]here is at least an arguable correlation between obscene material and crime. Quite apart from sex crimes, however, there remains one problem of large proportions aptly described by Professor Bickel:

"It concerns the tone of the society, the mode, or to use terms that have perhaps greater currency, the style and quality of life, now and in the future. A man may be entitled to read an obscene book in his room, or expose himself indecently there.... We should protect his privacy. But if he demands a right to obtain the books and pictures he wants in the market, and to foregather in public places—discreet, if you will, but accessible to all—with others who share his tastes, *then to grant him his right is to affect the world about the rest of us, and to impinge on other privacies.* Even supposing that each of us can, if he wishes, effectively avert the eye and stop the ear (which, in truth, we cannot), what is commonly read and seen and heard and done intrudes upon us all, want it or not." 22 The Public Interest 25–26 (Winter 1971). (Emphasis added.) ...

But, it is argued, there are no scientific data which conclusively demonstrate that exposure to obscene material adversely affects men and women or their society.... It is not for us to resolve empirical uncertainties underlying state legislation, save in the exceptional case where that legislation plainly impinges upon rights protected by the Constitution itself.... Although there is no conclusive proof of a connection between antisocial behavior and obscene material, the legislature of Georgia could quite reasonably determine that such a connection does or might exist....

. . .

If we accept the unprovable assumption that a complete education requires the reading of certain books, ... and the well nigh universal belief that good books, plays, and art lift the spirit, improve the mind, enrich the human personality, and develop character, can we then say that a state legislature may not act on the corollary assumption that commerce in obscene books, or public exhibitions focused on obscene conduct, have a tendency to exert a corrupting and debasing impact leading to antisocial behavior? . . . The sum of experience, including that of the past two decades, affords an ample basis for legislatures to conclude that a sensitive, key relationship of human existence, central to family life, community welfare, and the development of human personality, can be debased and distorted by crass commercial exploitation of sex. Nothing in the Constitution prohibits a State from reaching such a conclusion and acting on it legislatively simply because there is no conclusive evidence or empirical data.

It is argued that individual "free will" must govern, even in activities beyond the protection of the First Amendment and other constitutional guarantees of privacy, and that government cannot legitimately impede an individual's desire to see or acquire obscene plays, movies, and books. We do indeed base our society on certain assumptions that people have the capacity for free choice. Most exercises of individual free choice—those in politics, religion, and expression of ideas—are explicitly protected by the Constitution. Totally unlimited play for free will, however, is not allowed in our or any other society. . . .

. . .

It is asserted, however, that standards for evaluating state commercial regulations are inapposite in the present context, as state regulation of access by consenting adults to obscene material violates the constitutionally protected right to privacy enjoyed by petitioners' customers. . . . [I]t is unavailing to compare a theater, open to the public for a fee, with the private home of *Stanley v. Georgia,* [394 U.S.,] at 568, and the marital bedroom of *Griswold v. Connecticut, supra,* [381 U.S.,] at 485–486. . . .

. . .

. . . Where communication of ideas, protected by the First Amendment, is not involved, or the particular privacy of the home protected by *Stanley,* or any of the other "areas or zones" of constitutionally protected privacy, the mere fact that, as a consequence, some human "utterances" or "thoughts" may be incidentally affected does not bar the State from acting to protect legitimate state interests. . . .

Finally, petitioners argue that conduct which directly involves "consenting adults" only has, for that sole reason, a special claim to constitutional protection. Our Constitution establishes a broad range of conditions on the exercise of power by the States, but for us to say that our Constitution incorporates the proposition that conduct involving consenting adults only is always beyond state regulation, is a step we are unable to take. . . .

. . .

Mr. Justice Brennan, with whom Mr. Justice Stewart and Mr. Justice Marshall join, dissenting.

. . . I am convinced that the approach initiated 16 years ago in Roth v. United States, 354 U.S. 476 (1957), and culminating in the Court's decision today, cannot bring stability to this area of the law without jeopardizing fundamental First Amendment values, and I have concluded that the time has come to make a significant departure from that approach.

. . .

Our experience with the *Roth* approach has certainly taught us that the outright suppression of obscenity cannot be reconciled with the fundamental principles of the First and Fourteenth Amendments.... [W]e have failed to formulate a standard that sharply distinguishes protected from unprotected speech ...

... [A]fter 16 years of experimentation and debate I am reluctantly forced to the conclusion that none of the available formulas, including the one announced today, can reduce the vagueness to a tolerable level while at the same time striking an acceptable balance between the protections of the First and Fourteenth Amendments, on the one hand, and on the other the asserted state interest in regulating the dissemination of certain sexually oriented materials.... Although we have assumed that obscenity does exist and that we "know it when [we] see it," Jacobellis v. Ohio, [378 U.S.] at 197 (Stewart, J., concurring), we are manifestly unable to describe it in advance except by reference to concepts so elusive that they fail to distinguish clearly between protected and unprotected speech.

. . .

The problems of fair notice and chilling protected speech are very grave standing alone. But it does not detract from their importance to recognize that a vague statute in this area creates a third, although admittedly more subtle, set of problems. These problems concern the institutional stress that inevitably results where the line separating protected from unprotected speech is excessively vague....

... [A]lmost every case is "marginal." And since the "margin" marks the point of separation between protected and unprotected speech, we are left with a system in which almost every obscenity case presents a constitutional question of exceptional difficulty....

. . .

The Court evidently recognizes that difficulties with the *Roth* approach necessitate a significant change of direction. But the Court does not describe its understanding of those difficulties, nor does it indicate how the restatement of the *Memoirs* test is in any way responsive to the problems that have arisen. In my view, the restatement leaves unresolved the very difficulties that compel our rejection of the underlying *Roth* approach, while at the same time contributing substantial difficulties of its own. The modification of the *Memoirs* test may prove sufficient to jeopardize the analytic underpinnings of the entire scheme. And today's restatement will likely have the effect, whether or not intended, of permitting far more sweeping suppression of sexually oriented expression, including expression that would almost surely be held protected under our current formulation.

. . .

In any case, even if the Court's approach left undamaged the conceptual framework of *Roth,* and even if it clearly barred the suppression of works with at least some social value, I would nevertheless be compelled to reject it....

. . .

Ultimately, the reformulation must fail because it still leaves in this Court the responsibility of determining in each case whether the materials are protected by the First Amendment....

. . .

... I have considered the view, urged so forcefully since 1957 by our Brothers Black and Douglas, that the First Amendment bars the suppression of any sexually oriented expression. That position would effect a sharp reduction, although perhaps not a total elimination, of the uncertainty that surrounds our current approach. Nevertheless, I am convinced that it would achieve that desirable goal only by stripping the States of power to an extent that cannot be justified by the commands of the Constitution, at least so long as there is available an alternative approach that strikes a better balance between the guarantee of free expression and the States' legitimate interests.

. . .

In short, while I cannot say that the interests of the State—apart from the question of juveniles and unconsenting adults—are trivial or nonexistent, I am compelled to conclude that these interests cannot justify the substantial damage to constitutional rights and to this Nation's judicial machinery that inevitably results from state efforts to bar the distribution even of unprotected material to consenting adults.... I would hold, therefore, that at least in the absence of distribution to juveniles or obtrusive exposure to unconsenting adults, the First and Fourteenth Amendments prohibit the State and Federal Governments from attempting wholly to suppress sexually oriented materials on the basis of their allegedly "obscene" contents. Nothing in this approach precludes those governments from taking action to serve what may be strong and legitimate interests through regulation of the manner of distribution of sexually oriented material.

... Difficult questions must still be faced, notably in the areas of distribution to juveniles and offensive exposure to unconsenting adults. Whatever the extent of state power to regulate in those areas, it should be clear that the view I espouse today would introduce a large measure of clarity to this troubled area, would reduce the institutional pressure on this Court and the rest of the State and Federal Judiciary, and would guarantee fuller freedom of expression while leaving room for the protection of legitimate governmental interests....

Mr. Justice Douglas, dissenting.

My Brother Brennan is to be commended for seeking a new path through the thicket which the Court entered when it undertook to sustain the constitutionality of obscenity laws and to place limits on their application. I have expressed on numerous occasions my disagreement with the basic decision that held that "obscenity" was not protected by the First Amendment....

. . .

I applaud the effort of my Brother Brennan to forsake the low road which the Court has followed in this field. The new regime he would inaugurate is much closer than the old to the policy of abstention which the First Amendment proclaims. ... I see no constitutional basis for fashioning a rule that makes a publisher, producer, bookseller, librarian, or movie house operator criminally responsible, when he fails to take affirmative steps to protect the consumer against literature, books, or movies offensive to those who temporarily occupy the seats of the mighty.

. . .

Miller v. California

413 U.S. 15, 93 S.Ct. 2607, 37 L.Ed.2d 419 (1973).

Mr. Chief Justice Burger delivered the opinion of the Court.

This is one of a group of "obscenity-pornography" cases being reviewed by the Court in a re-examination of standards enunciated in earlier cases....

Appellant conducted a mass mailing campaign to advertise the sale of illustrated books, euphemistically called "adult" material. After a jury trial, he was convicted of violating California Penal Code § 311.2(a), a misdemeanor, by knowingly distributing obscene matter,[1] and the Appellate Department, Superior Court of California, County of Orange, summarily affirmed the judgment without opinion. Appellant's conviction was specifically based on his conduct in causing five unsolicited advertising brochures to be sent through the mail in an envelope addressed to a restaurant in Newport Beach, California. The envelope was opened by the manager of the restaurant and his mother. They had not requested the brochures; they complained to the police.

The brochures advertise four books entitled "Intercourse," "Man–Woman," "Sex Orgies Illustrated," and "An Illustrated History of Pornography," and a film entitled "Marital Intercourse." While the brochures contain some descriptive printed material, primarily they consist of pictures and drawings very explicitly depicting men and women in groups of two or more engaging in a variety of sexual activities, with genitals often prominently displayed.

I

. . . This Court has recognized that the States have a legitimate interest in prohibiting dissemination or exhibition of obscene material when the mode of dissemination carries with it a significant danger of offending the sensibilities of unwilling recipients or of exposure to juveniles. . . . It is in this context that we are called on to define the standards which must be used to identify obscene material that a State may regulate without infringing on the First Amendment as applicable to the States through the Fourteenth Amendment.

. . . In Roth v. United States, 354 U.S. 476 (1957), the Court sustained a conviction under a federal statute punishing the mailing of "obscene, lewd, lascivious or filthy . . ." materials. The key to that holding was the Court's rejection of the claim that obscene materials were protected by the First Amendment. . . .

Nine years later, in Memoirs v. Massachusetts, 383 U.S. 413 (1966), the Court . . . articulated a new test of obscenity. The plurality held that under the *Roth* definition

> "as elaborated in subsequent cases, three elements must coalesce: it must be established that (a) the dominant theme of the material taken as a whole appeals to a prurient interest in sex; (b) the material is patently offensive because it affronts contemporary community standards relating to the description or representation of sexual matters; and (c) the material is utterly without redeeming social value." . . .

While *Roth* presumed "obscenity" to be "utterly without redeeming social importance," *Memoirs* required that to prove obscenity it must be affirmatively established that the material is "utterly without redeeming social value." Thus,

---

1. At the time of the commission of the alleged offense, . . . § 311 of the California Penal Code read in relevant part:

. . .

"As used in this chapter:

"(a) 'Obscene' means that to the average person, applying contemporary standards, the predominant appeal of the matter, taken as a whole, is to prurient interest, i.e., a shameful or morbid interest in nudity, sex, or excretion, which goes substantially beyond customary limits of candor in description or representation of such matters and is matter which is utterly without redeeming social importance." . . .

... the *Memoirs* plurality [required] the prosecution to prove a negative, i.e., that the material was "utterly without redeeming social value"—a burden virtually impossible to discharge under our criminal standards of proof....

Apart from the initial formulation in the *Roth* case, no majority of the Court has at any given time been able to agree on a standard to determine what constitutes obscene, pornographic material subject to regulation under the States' police power....[3] ...

The case we now review was tried on the theory that the California Penal Code § 311 approximately incorporates the three-stage *Memoirs* test, supra. But now the *Memoirs* test has been abandoned as unworkable by its author, and no Member of the Court today supports the *Memoirs* formulation.

II

... [W]e now confine the permissible scope of [obscenity] regulation to works which depict or describe sexual conduct. That conduct must be specifically defined by the applicable state law, as written or authoritatively construed. A state offense must also be limited to works which, taken as a whole, appeal to the prurient interest in sex, which portray sexual conduct in a patently offensive way, and which, taken as a whole, do not have serious literary, artistic, political, or scientific value.

The basic guidelines for the trier of fact must be: (a) whether "the average person, applying contemporary community standards" would find that the work, taken as a whole, appeals to the prurient interest; (b) whether the work depicts or describes, in a patently offensive way, sexual conduct specifically defined by the applicable state law; and (c) whether the work, taken as a whole, lacks serious literary, artistic, political, or scientific value. We do not adopt as a constitutional standard the "utterly without redeeming social value" test of *Memoirs v. Massachusetts;* that concept has never commanded the adherence of more than three Justices at one time. If a state law that regulates obscene material is thus limited, as written or construed, the First Amendment values applicable to the States through the Fourteenth Amendment are adequately protected by the ultimate power of appellate courts to conduct an independent review of constitutional claims when necessary....

... [A] few plain examples of what a state statute could define for regulation under part (b) of the standard announced in this opinion [are]:

(a) Patently offensive representations or descriptions of ultimate sexual acts, normal or perverted, actual or simulated.

(b) Patently offensive representations or descriptions of masturbation, excretory functions, and lewd exhibition of the genitals.

... At a minimum, prurient, patently offensive depiction or description of sexual conduct must have serious literary, artistic, political, or scientific value to merit First Amendment protection.... For example, medical books ... necessarily use graphic illustrations and descriptions of human anatomy. In

---

3. In the absence of a majority view, this Court was compelled to embark on the practice of summarily reversing convictions for the dissemination of materials that at least five members of the Court, applying their separate tests, found to be protected by the First Amendment. Redrup v. New York, 386 U.S. 767 (1967). Thirty-one cases have been decided in this manner.... The *Redrup* procedure has cast us in the role of an unreviewable board of censorship for the 50 States, subjectively judging each piece of material brought before us.

resolving the inevitably sensitive questions of fact and law, we must continue to rely on the jury system ...

. . .

Under the holdings announced today, no one will be subject to prosecution for the sale or exposure of obscene materials unless these materials depict or describe patently offensive "hard core" sexual conduct specifically defined by the regulating state law, as written or construed. We are satisfied that these specific prerequisites will provide fair notice ...

III

Under a National Constitution, fundamental First Amendment limitations on the powers of the States do not vary from community to community, but this does not mean that there are, or should or can be, fixed, uniform national standards of precisely what appeals to the "prurient interest" or is "patently offensive." These are essentially questions of fact ... When triers of fact are asked to decide whether "the average person, applying contemporary community standards" would consider certain materials "prurient," it would be unrealistic to require that the answer be based on some abstract formulation.... To require a State to structure obscenity proceedings around evidence of a national "community standard" would be an exercise in futility.

We conclude that neither the State's alleged failure to offer evidence of "national standards," nor the trial court's charge that the jury consider state community standards, were constitutional errors....

... [T]he primary concern with requiring a jury to apply the standard of "the average person, applying contemporary community standards" is to be certain that, so far as material is not aimed at a deviant group, it will be judged by its impact on an average person, rather than a particularly susceptible or sensitive person—or indeed a totally insensitive one.... [T]he requirement that the jury evaluate the materials with reference to "contemporary standards of the State of California" serves this protective purpose and is constitutionally adequate.

. . .

Mr. Justice Douglas, dissenting.

. . .

My contention is that until a civil proceeding has placed a tract beyond the pale, no criminal prosecution should be sustained....

. . .

If a specific book, play, paper, or motion picture has in a civil proceeding been condemned as obscene and review of that finding has been completed, and thereafter a person publishes, shows, or displays that particular book or film, then a vague law has been made specific. There would remain the underlying question whether the First Amendment allows an implied exception in the case of obscenity. I do not think it does ... But at least a criminal prosecution brought at that juncture would not violate the time-honored void-for-vagueness test.

. . .

Mr. Justice Brennan, with whom Mr. Justice Stewart and Mr. Justice Marshall join, dissenting.

... [I]t is clear that under my dissent in *Paris Adult Theatre I,* the statute under which the prosecution was brought is unconstitutionally overbroad, and therefore invalid on its face....

Jenkins v. Georgia

418 U.S. 153, 94 S.Ct. 2750, 41 L.Ed.2d 642 (1974).

Mr. Justice Rehnquist delivered the opinion of the Court.

Appellant was convicted in Georgia of the crime of distributing obscene material. His conviction, in March 1972, was for showing the film "Carnal Knowledge" in a movie theater in Albany, Georgia....

... We conclude here that the film "Carnal Knowledge" is not obscene under the constitutional standards announced in Miller v. California, 413 U.S. 15 (1973), and that the First and Fourteenth Amendments therefore require that the judgment of the Supreme Court of Georgia affirming appellant's conviction be reversed.

. . .

Miller states that the questions of what appeals to the "prurient interest" and what is "patently offensive" under the obscenity test which it formulates are "essentially questions of fact." ...

But all of this does not lead us to agree with the Supreme Court of Georgia's apparent conclusion that the jury's verdict against appellant virtually precluded all further appellate review of appellant's assertion that his exhibition of the film was protected by the First and Fourteenth Amendments. Even though questions of appeal to the "prurient interest" or of patent offensiveness are "essentially questions of fact," it would be a serious misreading of *Miller* to conclude that juries have unbridled discretion in determining what is "patently offensive." ... [W]e made it plain that under that holding "no one will be subject to prosecution for the sale or exposure of obscene materials unless these materials depict or describe patently offensive 'hard core' sexual conduct...."

. . .

We also took pains in *Miller* to "give a few plain examples of what a state statute could define for regulation under part (b) of the standard announced," that is, the requirement of patent offensiveness. ... These examples include "representations or descriptions of ultimate sexual acts, normal or perverted, actual or simulated," and "representations or descriptions of masturbation, excretory functions, and lewd exhibition of the genitals." Ibid. While this did not purport to be an exhaustive catalog of what juries might find patently offensive, it was certainly intended to fix substantive constitutional limitations, deriving from the First Amendment, on the type of material subject to such a determination. It would be wholly at odds with this aspect of *Miller* to uphold an obscenity conviction based upon a defendant's depiction of a woman with a bare midriff, even though a properly charged jury unanimously agreed on a verdict of guilty.

Our own viewing of the film satisfies us that "Carnal Knowledge" could not be found under the *Miller* standards to depict sexual conduct in a patently offensive way. Nothing in the movie falls within either of the two examples given in *Miller* of material which may constitutionally be found to meet the "patently offensive" element of those standards, nor is there anything sufficiently similar to such material to justify similar treatment. While the subject matter of the picture is, in a broader sense, sex, and there are scenes in which sexual conduct including "ultimate sexual acts" is to be understood to be taking place, the camera does not focus on the bodies of the actors at such times. There is no exhibition whatever of the actors' genitals, lewd or otherwise, during these scenes. There are occasional scenes of nudity, but nudity alone is not enough to make material legally obscene under the *Miller* standards.

Appellant's showing of the film "Carnal Knowledge" is simply not the "public portrayal of hard core sexual conduct for its own sake, and for the ensuing commercial gain" which we said was punishable in *Miller* . . . We hold that the film could not, as a matter of constitutional law, be found to depict sexual conduct in a patently offensive way, and that it is therefore not outside the protection of the First and Fourteenth Amendments because it is obscene. . . .

Mr. Justice Brennan, with whom Mr. Justice Stewart and Mr. Justice Marshall join, concurring in the result.

. . . Today's decision confirms my observation in Paris Adult Theatre I v. Slaton . . . that the Court's new formulation does not extricate us from the mire of case-by-case determinations of obscenity. . . .

After the Court's decision today, there can be no doubt that *Miller* requires appellate courts—including this Court—to review independently the constitutional fact of obscenity. . . .

In order to make the review mandated by *Miller,* the Court was required to screen the film "Carnal Knowledge" and make an independent determination of obscenity *vel non* . . . .

. . .

Mr. Justice Douglas, being of the view that any ban on obscenity is prohibited by the First Amendment, . . . concurs in the reversal of this conviction. . . .

Ashcroft v. The Free Speech Coalition

535 U.S. 234, 122 S.Ct. 1389, 152 L.Ed.2d 403 (2002).

Justice Kennedy delivered the opinion of the Court.

We consider in this case whether the Child Pornography Prevention Act of 1996 (CPPA), 18 U.S.C. § 2251 et seq., abridges the freedom of speech. The CPPA extends the federal prohibition against child pornography to sexually explicit images that appear to depict minors but were produced without using any real children. The statute prohibits, in specific circumstances, possessing or distributing these images, which may be created by using adults who look like minors or by using computer imaging. The new technology, according to Congress, makes it possible to create realistic images of children who do not exist. . . .

By prohibiting child pornography that does not depict an actual child, the statute goes beyond New York v. Ferber, 458 U.S. 747 (1982), which distinguished child pornography from other sexually explicit speech because of the State's interest in protecting the children exploited by the production process. . . . As a general rule, pornography can be banned only if obscene, but under *Ferber*, pornography showing minors can be proscribed whether or not the images are obscene under the definition set forth in Miller v. California. . . .

While we have not had occasion to consider the question, we may assume that the apparent age of persons engaged in sexual conduct is relevant to whether a depiction offends community standards. Pictures of young children engaged in certain acts might be obscene where similar depictions of adults, or perhaps even older adolescents, would not. The CPPA, however, is not directed at speech that is obscene . . . Like the law in *Ferber*, the CPPA seeks to reach beyond obscenity, and it makes no attempt to conform to the *Miller* standard. For instance, the statute would reach visual depictions, such as movies, even if they have redeeming social value.

The principal question to be resolved, then, is whether the CPPA is constitutional where it proscribes a significant universe of speech that is neither obscene under *Miller* nor child pornography under *Ferber*.

I

Before 1996, Congress defined child pornography as the type of depictions at issue in *Ferber*, images made using actual minors. . . . The CPPA retains that prohibition at 18 U.S.C. § 2256(8)(A) and adds three other prohibited categories of speech, of which the first, § 2256(8)(B), and the third, § 2256(8)(D), are at issue in this case. Section 2256(8)(B) prohibits "any visual depiction, including any photograph, film, video, picture, or computer or computer-generated image or picture" that "is, or appears to be, of a minor engaging in sexually explicit conduct." The prohibition on "any visual depiction" does not depend at all on how the image is produced. The section captures a range of depictions, sometimes called "virtual child pornography," which include computer-generated images, as well as images produced by more traditional means. For instance, the literal terms of the statute embrace a Renaissance painting depicting a scene from classical mythology, a "picture" that "appears to be, of a minor engaging in sexually explicit conduct." The statute also prohibits Hollywood movies, filmed without any child actors, if a jury believes an actor "appears to be" a minor engaging in "actual or simulated . . . sexual intercourse." § 2256(2).

These images do not involve, let alone harm, any children in the production process; but Congress decided the materials threaten children in other, less direct, ways. Pedophiles might use the materials to encourage children to participate in sexual activity. . . . Furthermore, pedophiles might "whet their own sexual appetites" with the pornographic images, "thereby increasing the creation and distribution of child pornography and the sexual abuse and exploitation of actual children." . . . Under these rationales, harm flows from the content of the images, not from the means of their production. In addition, Congress identified another problem created by computer-generated images: Their existence can make it harder to prosecute pornographers who do use real minors. . . . As imaging technology improves, Congress found, it becomes more difficult to prove that a particular picture was produced using actual children. . . .

Section 2256(8)(C) prohibits a more common and lower tech means of creating virtual images, known as computer morphing. Rather than creating original images, pornographers can alter innocent pictures of real children so that the children appear to be engaged in sexual activity. Although morphed images may fall within the definition of virtual child pornography, they implicate the interests of real children and are in that sense closer to the images in *Ferber*. Respondents do not challenge this provision, and we do not consider it.

Respondents do challenge § 2256(8)(D). Like the text of the "appears to be" provision, the sweep of this provision is quite broad. Section 2256(8)(D) defines child pornography to include any sexually explicit image that was "advertised, promoted, presented, described, or distributed in such a manner that conveys the impression" it depicts "a minor engaging in sexually explicit conduct." One Committee Report identified the provision as directed at sexually explicit images pandered as child pornography. . . . The statute is not so limited in its reach, however, as it punishes even those possessors who took no part in pandering. Once a work has been described as child pornography, the taint remains on the speech in the hands of subsequent possessors, making possession unlawful even though the content otherwise would not be objectionable.

Fearing that the CPPA threatened the activities of its members, respondent Free Speech Coalition and others challenged the statute in the United States District Court for the Northern District of California. The Coalition, a California trade association for the adult-entertainment industry, alleged that its members did not use minors in their sexually explicit works, but they believed some of these materials might fall within the CPPA's expanded definition of child pornography. The other respondents are Bold Type, Inc., the publisher of a book advocating the nudist lifestyle; Jim Gingerich, a painter of nudes; and Ron Raffaelli, a photographer specializing in erotic images. Respondents alleged that the "appears to be" and "conveys the impression" provisions are overbroad and vague, chilling them from producing works protected by the First Amendment. The District Court disagreed and granted summary judgment to the Government. . . .

The Court of Appeals for the Ninth Circuit reversed. . . .

. . .

II

. . . [A] law imposing criminal penalties on protected speech is a stark example of speech suppression. The CPPA's penalties are indeed severe. A first offender may be imprisoned for 15 years. . . . A repeat offender faces a prison sentence of not less than 5 years and not more than 30 years in prison. . . . While even minor punishments can chill protected speech, . . . this case provides a textbook example of why we permit facial challenges to statutes that burden expression. With these severe penalties in force, few legitimate movie producers or book publishers, or few other speakers in any capacity, would risk distributing images in or near the uncertain reach of this law. The Constitution gives significant protection from overbroad laws that chill speech within the First Amendment's vast and privileged sphere. Under this principle, the CPPA is unconstitutional on its face if it prohibits a substantial amount of protected expression. . . .

. . .

. . . [S]peech may not be prohibited because it concerns subjects offending our sensibilities. . . .

As a general principle, the First Amendment bars the government from dictating what we see or read or speak or hear. The freedom of speech has its limits; it does not embrace certain categories of speech, including defamation, incitement, obscenity, and pornography produced with real children. . . . While these categories may be prohibited without violating the First Amendment, none of them includes the speech prohibited by the CPPA. . . .

As we have noted, the CPPA is much more than a supplement to the existing federal prohibition on obscenity. ... The CPPA ..., extends to images that appear to depict a minor engaging in sexually explicit activity without regard to the *Miller* requirements. ... Any depiction of sexually explicit activity, no matter how it is presented, is proscribed. The CPPA applies to a picture in a psychology manual, as well as a movie depicting the horrors of sexual abuse....

... The statute proscribes the visual depiction of an idea—that of teenagers engaging in sexual activity—that is a fact of modern society and has been a theme in art and literature throughout the ages. Under the CPPA, images are prohibited so long as the persons appear to be under 18 years of age. This is higher than the legal age for marriage in many States, as well as the age at which persons may consent to sexual relations. ...

... Both themes—teenage sexual activity and the sexual abuse of children—have inspired countless literary works. William Shakespeare created the most famous pair of teenage lovers, one of whom is just 13 years of age. ... The work has inspired no less than 40 motion pictures, some of which suggest that the teenagers consummated their relationship. ...

Contemporary movies pursue similar themes. Last year's Academy Awards featured the movie, *Traffic*, which was nominated for Best Picture. ... The film portrays a teenager, identified as a 16–year-old, who becomes addicted to drugs. The viewer sees the degradation of her addiction, which in the end leads her to a filthy room to trade sex for drugs. The year before, *American Beauty* won the Academy Award for Best Picture. ... In the course of the movie, a teenage girl engages in sexual relations with her teenage boyfriend, and another yields herself to the gratification of a middle-aged man. ...

... Whether or not the films we mention violate the CPPA, they explore themes within the wide sweep of the statute's prohibitions. If these films, or hundreds of others of lesser note that explore those subjects, contain a single graphic depiction of sexual activity within the statutory definition, the possessor of the film would be subject to severe punishment without inquiry into the work's redeeming value. This is inconsistent with an essential First Amendment rule: The artistic merit of a work does not depend on the presence of a single explicit scene. ...

The Government seeks to address this deficiency by arguing that speech prohibited by the CPPA is virtually indistinguishable from child pornography, which may be banned without regard to whether it depicts works of value. ... *Ferber* recognized that the State had an interest in stamping it out without regard to any judgment about its content. ... The production of the work, not its content, was the target of the statute. The fact that a work contained serious literary, artistic, or other value did not excuse the harm it caused to its child participants. ...

... First, as a permanent record of a child's abuse, the continued circulation itself would harm the child who had participated. Like a defamatory statement, each new publication of the speech would cause new injury to the child's reputation and emotional well-being. ... Second, because the traffic in child pornography was an economic motive for its production, the State had an interest in closing the distribution network.... Under either rationale, the speech had what the Court in effect held was a proximate link to the crime from which it came.

Later, in Osborne v. Ohio, 495 U.S. 103 (1990), the Court ruled that these same interests justified a ban on the possession of pornography produced by using children. . . . It did not suggest that, absent this concern, other governmental interests would suffice.

. . . [T]he CPPA prohibits speech that records no crime and creates no victims by its production. Virtual child pornography is not "intrinsically related" to the sexual abuse of children, as were the materials in *Ferber*. . . . While the Government asserts that the images can lead to actual instances of child abuse, . . . the causal link is contingent and indirect. The harm does not necessarily follow from the speech, but depends upon some unquantified potential for subsequent criminal acts.

The Government says these indirect harms are sufficient because, as *Ferber* acknowledged, child pornography rarely can be valuable speech. . . . This argument, however, suffers from two flaws. First, *Ferber*'s judgment about child pornography was based upon how it was made, not on what it communicated. . . .

The second flaw in the Government's position is that *Ferber* did not hold that child pornography is by definition without value. On the contrary, the Court recognized some works in this category might have significant value, . . . but relied on virtual images—the very images prohibited by the CPPA—as an alternative and permissible means of expression . . . *Ferber*, then, not only referred to the distinction between actual and virtual child pornography, it relied on it as a reason supporting its holding. *Ferber* provides no support for a statute that eliminates the distinction and makes the alternative mode criminal as well.

III

. . . The Government . . . argues that the CPPA is necessary because pedophiles may use virtual child pornography to seduce children. . . . The Government, of course, may punish adults who provide unsuitable materials to children, see Ginsberg v. New York, 390 U.S. 629 (1968), and it may enforce criminal penalties for unlawful solicitation. The precedents establish, however, that speech within the rights of adults to hear may not be silenced completely in an attempt to shield children from it. . . .

Here, the Government wants to keep speech from children not to protect them from its content but to protect them from those who would commit other crimes. The principle, however, remains the same: The Government cannot ban speech fit for adults simply because it may fall into the hands of children. The evil in question depends upon the actor's unlawful conduct, conduct defined as criminal quite apart from any link to the speech in question. This establishes that the speech ban is not narrowly drawn. The objective is to prohibit illegal conduct, but this restriction goes well beyond that interest by restricting the speech available to law-abiding adults.

The Government submits further that virtual child pornography whets the appetites of pedophiles and encourages them to engage in illegal conduct. This rationale cannot sustain the provision in question. The mere tendency of speech to encourage unlawful acts is not a sufficient reason for banning it. . . . First Amendment freedoms are most in danger when the government seeks to control thought or to justify its laws for that impermissible end. The right to think is the beginning of freedom, and speech must be protected from the government because speech is the beginning of thought.

. . . There is here no attempt, incitement, solicitation, or conspiracy. The Government has shown no more than a remote connection between speech that might encourage thoughts or impulses and any resulting child abuse. Without a significantly stronger, more direct connection, the Government may not prohibit speech on the ground that it may encourage pedophiles to engage in illegal conduct.

The Government next argues that its objective of eliminating the market for pornography produced using real children necessitates a prohibition on virtual images as well. Virtual images, the Government contends, are indistinguishable from real ones; they are part of the same market and are often exchanged. In this way, it is said, virtual images promote the trafficking in works produced through the exploitation of real children. The hypothesis is somewhat implausible. If virtual images were identical to illegal child pornography, the illegal images would be driven from the market by the indistinguishable substitutes. Few pornographers would risk prosecution by abusing real children if fictional, computerized images would suffice.

In the case of the material covered by *Ferber*, the creation of the speech is itself the crime of child abuse; the prohibition deters the crime by removing the profit motive. ... [H]ere, there is no underlying crime at all. Even if the Government's market deterrence theory were persuasive in some contexts, it would not justify this statute.

Finally, the Government says that the possibility of producing images by using computer imaging makes it very difficult for it to prosecute those who produce pornography by using real children. Experts, we are told, may have difficulty in saying whether the pictures were made by using real children or by using computer imaging. The necessary solution, the argument runs, is to prohibit both kinds of images. The argument, in essence, is that protected speech may be banned as a means to ban unprotected speech. This analysis turns the First Amendment upside down.

The Government may not suppress lawful speech as the means to suppress unlawful speech. Protected speech does not become unprotected merely because it resembles the latter. The Constitution requires the reverse.... The overbreadth doctrine prohibits the Government from banning unprotected speech if a substantial amount of protected speech is prohibited or chilled in the process.

To avoid the force of this objection, the Government would have us read the CPPA not as a measure suppressing speech but as a law shifting the burden to the accused to prove the speech is lawful. In this connection, the Government relies on an affirmative defense under the statute, which allows a defendant to avoid conviction for nonpossession offenses by showing that the materials were produced using only adults and were not otherwise distributed in a manner conveying the impression that they depicted real children. ...

The Government raises serious constitutional difficulties by seeking to impose on the defendant the burden of proving his speech is not unlawful.... If the evidentiary issue is a serious problem for the Government, as it asserts, it will be at least as difficult for the innocent possessor....

We need not decide, however, whether the Government could impose this burden on a speaker. Even if an affirmative defense can save a statute from First Amendment challenge, here the defense is incomplete and insufficient, even on its own terms.... A defendant charged with possessing, as opposed to distributing, proscribed works may not defend on the ground that the film depicts only adult actors. ... So while the affirmative defense may protect a movie producer from prosecution for the act of distribution, that same producer, and all other persons in the subsequent distribution chain, could be liable for possessing the prohibited work. Furthermore, the affirmative defense provides no protection to persons who produce speech by using computer imaging, or through other means that do not involve the use of adult actors who appear to be minors. ... In these cases, the defendant can demonstrate no children were harmed in producing the images, yet the affirmative defense would not bar the prosecution. For this reason, the affirmative defense cannot save the statute, for it leaves unprotected a substantial amount of speech not tied to the Government's interest in distinguishing images produced using real children from virtual ones.

. . .

IV

Respondents challenge § 2256(8)(D) as well. This provision bans depictions of sexually explicit conduct that are "advertised, promoted, presented, described, or distributed in such a manner that conveys the impression that the material is or contains a visual depiction of a minor engaging in sexually explicit conduct."....

... The CPPA prohibits sexually explicit materials that "conve[y] the impression" they depict minors. While that phrase may sound like the "appears to be" prohibition in § 2256(8)(B), it requires little judgment about the content of the image. Under § 2256(8)(D), the work must be sexually explicit, but otherwise the content is irrelevant. Even if a film contains no sexually explicit scenes involving minors, it could be treated as child pornography if the title and trailers convey the impression that the scenes would be found in the movie. The determination turns on how the speech is presented, not on what is depicted. ...

The Government does not offer a serious defense of this provision ... The materials, for instance, are not likely to be confused for child pornography in a criminal trial. The Court has recognized that pandering may be relevant, as an evidentiary matter, to the question whether particular materials are obscene. See Ginzburg v. United States, 383 U.S. 463, 474 (1966) ...

... Section 2256(8)(D), however, prohibits a substantial amount of speech that falls outside Ginzburg's rationale. Materials falling within the proscription are tainted and unlawful in the hands of all who receive it, though they bear no responsibility for how it was marketed, sold, or described. The statute, furthermore, does not require that the context be part of an effort at "commercial exploitation." ... § 2256(8)(D) is substantially overbroad ...

V

... [T]he prohibitions of §§ 2256(8)(B) and 2256(8)(D) are overbroad and unconstitutional. ...

The judgment of the Court of Appeals is affirmed.

. . .

Justice Thomas, concurring in the judgment.

In my view, the Government's most persuasive asserted interest in support of the [CCPA] is the prosecution rationale—that persons who possess and disseminate pornographic images of real children may escape conviction by claiming that the images are computer-generated, thereby raising a reasonable doubt as to their guilt. At this time, however, the Government asserts only that defendants raise such defenses, not that they have done so successfully. In fact, the Government points to no case in which a defendant has been acquitted based on a "computer-generated images" defense. While this speculative interest cannot support the broad reach of the CPPA, technology may evolve to the point where it becomes impossible to enforce actual child pornography laws because the Government cannot prove that certain pornographic images are of real children. In the event this occurs, the Government should not be foreclosed from enacting a regulation of virtual child pornography that contains an appropriate affirmative defense or some other narrowly drawn restriction.

... [I]f technological advances thwart prosecution of "unlawful speech," the Government may well have a compelling interest in barring or otherwise regulating some narrow category of "lawful speech" in order to enforce effectively laws against pornography made through the abuse of real children. ...

Justice O'Connor, with whom The Chief Justice and Justice Scalia join as to Part II, concurring in the judgment in part and dissenting in part.

. . .

This litigation involves a facial challenge to the CPPA's prohibitions of pornographic images that "appea[r] to be ... of a minor" and of material that "conveys the impression" that it contains pornographic images of minors. While I agree with the Court's judgment that the First Amendment requires that the latter prohibition be struck down, I disagree with its decision to strike down the former prohibition in its entirety. ... I would strike down the prohibition of pornography that "appears to be" of minors only insofar as it is applied to the class of youthful-adult pornography.

I

... The Government ... requests that the Court exclude youthful-adult and virtual-child pornography from the protection of the First Amendment.

I agree with the Court's decision not to grant this request. ... [W]hat the Government asks this Court to rule is that it may ... prohibit youthful-adult and virtual-adult pornography that is merely indecent.... Although such pornography looks like the material at issue in New York v. Ferber, ... no children are harmed in the process of creating such pornography. ... Therefore, *Ferber* does not support the Government's ban on youthful-adult and virtual-child pornography. ... The Court correctly concludes that the causal connection between pornographic images that "appear" to include minors and actual child abuse is not strong enough to justify withdrawing First Amendment protection for such speech.

I also agree with the Court's decision to strike down the CPPA's ban on material presented in a manner that "conveys the impression" that it contains pornographic depictions of actual children ("actual-child pornography"). ... The Court concludes that § 2256(8)(D) is overbroad, but its reasoning also persuades me that the provision is not narrowly tailored. The provision therefore fails strict scrutiny. ...

Finally, I agree with Court that that the CPPA's ban on youthful-adult pornography is overbroad. The Court provides several examples of movies that, although possessing serious literary, artistic or political value and employing only adult actors to perform simulated sexual conduct, fall under the CPPA's proscription ...

II

I disagree with the Court, however, that the CPPA's prohibition of virtual-child pornography is overbroad. Before I reach that issue, there are two preliminary questions: whether the ban on virtual-child pornography fails strict scrutiny and whether that ban is unconstitutionally vague. I would answer both in the negative.

... [G]iven the rapid pace of advances in computer-graphics technology, the Government's concern is reasonable....

Respondents argue that, even if the Government has a compelling interest to justify banning virtual-child pornography, the "appears to be ... of a minor" language is not narrowly tailored to serve that interest.... They assert that the CPPA would capture even cartoon-sketches or statues of children that were sexually suggestive. Such images surely could not be used, for instance, to seduce children. I agree. A better interpretation of "appears to be ... of" is "virtually indistinguishable from"—an interpretation that would not cover the examples respondents provide. ...

Reading the statute only to bar images that are virtually indistinguishable from actual children would not only assure that the ban on virtual-child pornography is narrowly tailored, but would also assuage any fears that the "appears to be ... of a minor" language is vague....

The Court concludes that the CPPA's ban on virtual-child pornography is overbroad. ... Respondents provide no examples of films or other materials that are wholly computer-generated and contain images that "appea[r] to be ... of minors" engaging in indecent conduct, but that have serious value or do not facilitate child abuse. Their overbreadth challenge therefore fails.

III

Although in my view the CPPA's ban on youthful-adult pornography appears to violate the First Amendment, the ban on virtual-child pornography does not. It is true that both bans are authorized by the same text.... Invalidating a statute due to overbreadth, however, is an extreme remedy, one that should be employed "sparingly and only as a last resort." ...

Heeding this caution, I would strike the "appears to be" provision only insofar as it is applied to the subset of cases involving youthful-adult pornography. ...

... Drawing a line around, and striking just, the CPPA's ban on youthful-child pornography ... preserves the CPPA's prohibition of the material that Congress found most dangerous to children.

. . .

Chief Justice Rehnquist, with whom Justice Scalia joins in part, dissenting.

I agree with Part II of Justice O'Connor's opinion ... Congress has a compelling interest in ensuring the ability to enforce prohibitions of actual child pornography, and we should defer to its findings that rapidly advancing technology soon will make it all but impossible to do so. ...

I also agree with Justice O'Connor that serious First Amendment concerns would arise were the Government ever to prosecute someone for simple distribution or possession of a film with literary or artistic value, such as "Traffic" or "American Beauty." I write separately, however, because the ... (CPPA) ... need not be construed to reach such materials.

We normally do not strike down a statute on First Amendment grounds "when a limiting instruction has been or could be placed on the challenged statute." ...

Other than computer generated images that are virtually indistinguishable from real children engaged in sexually explicitly conduct, the CPPA can be limited so as not to reach any material that was not already unprotected before the CPPA ...

Indeed, we should be loath to construe a statute as banning film portrayals of Shakespearian tragedies, without some indication—from text or legislative history—that such a result was intended. ...

. . .

United States v. Playboy Entertainment Group, Inc.

529 U.S. 803, 120 S.Ct. 1878, 146 L.Ed.2d 865 (2000).

Justice Kennedy delivered the opinion of the Court.

This case presents a challenge to § 505 of the Telecommunications Act of 1996 ... Section 505 requires cable television operators who provide channels "primarily dedicated to sexually-oriented programming" either to "fully scramble or otherwise fully block" those channels or to limit their transmission to hours when children are unlikely to be viewing, set by administrative regulation as the time between 10 p.m. and 6 a.m.... Even before enactment of the statute, signal scrambling was already in use. Cable operators used scrambling in the regular course of business, so that only paying customers had access to certain programs. Scrambling could be imprecise, however; and either or both audio and visual portions of the scrambled programs might be heard or seen, a phenomenon known as "signal bleed." The purpose of § 505 is to shield children from hearing or seeing images resulting from signal bleed.

To comply with the statute, the majority of cable operators adopted the second, or "time channeling," approach. The effect of the widespread adoption of time channeling was to eliminate altogether the transmission of the targeted programming outside the safe harbor period in affected cable service areas. In other words, for two thirds of the day no household in those service areas could receive the programming, whether or not the household or the viewer wanted to do so.

Appellee Playboy Entertainment Group, Inc., challenged the statute as unnecessarily restrictive content-based legislation violative of the First Amendment. After a trial, a three-judge District Court concluded that a regime in which viewers could order signal blocking on a household-by-household basis presented an effective, less restrictive alternative to § 505. Finding no error in this conclusion, we affirm.

I

. . .

The statute was enacted because not all scrambling technology is perfect. Analog cable television systems may use either "RF" or "baseband" scrambling systems, which may not prevent signal bleed, so discernible pictures may appear from time to time on the scrambled screen. Furthermore, the listener might hear the audio portion of the program.

... The problem is that at present it appears not to be economical to convert simpler RF or baseband scrambling systems to alternative scrambling technologies on a systemwide scale. Digital technology may one day provide another solution, as it presents no bleed problem at all. Indeed, digital systems are projected to become the technology of choice, which would eliminate the

signal bleed problem. Digital technology is not yet in widespread use, however.
. . .

. . . Section 505 was added by floor amendment, without significant debate, to the Telecommunications Act of 1996 (Act), a major legislative effort designed "to reduce regulation and encourage the rapid deployment of new telecommunications technologies." . . . Section 505 is found in Title V of the Act, which is itself known as the Communications Decency Act of 1996 (CDA). . . .

. . .

When the statute became operative, most cable operators had "no practical choice but to curtail [the targeted] programming during the [regulated] sixteen hours. . . . [T]he result was a significant restriction of communication, with a corresponding reduction in Playboy's revenues.

. . . [T]he District Court . . . concluded that § 505 violates the First Amendment. . . . One plausible, less restrictive alternative could be found in another section of the Act: § 504, which requires a cable operator, "[u]pon request by a cable service subscriber . . . without charge, [to] fully scramble or otherwise fully block" any channel the subscriber does not wish to receive. . . .

. . .

The United States filed a direct appeal in this Court . . . We . . . affirm.

II

Two essential points should be understood concerning the speech at issue here. First, we shall assume that many adults themselves would find the material highly offensive; and when we consider the further circumstance that the material comes unwanted into homes where children might see or hear it against parental wishes or consent, there are legitimate reasons for regulating it. Second, all parties bring the case to us on the premise that Playboy's programming has First Amendment protection. As this case has been litigated, it is not alleged to be obscene; adults have a constitutional right to view it; the Government disclaims any interest in preventing children from seeing or hearing it with the consent of their parents; and Playboy has concomitant rights under the First Amendment to transmit it. These points are undisputed.

The speech in question is defined by its content; and the statute which seeks to restrict it is content based. Section 505 applies only to channels primarily dedicated to "sexually explicit adult programming or other programming that is indecent." . . .

Not only does § 505 single out particular programming content for regulation, it also singles out particular programmers. The speech in question was not thought by Congress to be so harmful that all channels were subject to restriction. Instead, the statutory disability applies only to channels "primarily dedicated to sexually-oriented programming." . . . One sponsor of the measure even identified appellee by name. . . . Laws designed or intended to suppress or restrict the expression of specific speakers contradict basic First Amendment principles. . . .

. . . [T]he only reasonable way for a substantial number of cable operators to comply with the letter of § 505 is to time channel, which silences the protected speech for two-thirds of the day in every home in a cable service area . . . It is of no moment that the statute does not impose a complete prohibition. The distinction between laws burdening and laws banning speech is but a matter of degree. The Government's content-based burdens must satisfy the same rigorous scrutiny as its content-based bans.

... If a statute regulates speech based on its content, it must be narrowly tailored to promote a compelling Government interest. ... If a less restrictive alternative would serve the Government's purpose, the legislature must use that alternative. ...

Where the designed benefit of a content-based speech restriction is to shield the sensibilities of listeners, the general rule is that the right of expression prevails, even where no less restrictive alternative exists. ... Cohen v. California ...: The standard is strict scrutiny. This case involves speech alone; and even where speech is indecent and enters the home, the objective of shielding children does not suffice to support a blanket ban if the protection can be accomplished by a less restrictive alternative.

In [Sable Communications of Cal., Inc. v. FCC, 492 U.S. 115], for instance, the feasibility of a technological approach to controlling minors' access to "dial-a-porn" messages required invalidation of a complete statutory ban on the medium.... And, while mentioned only in passing [in Reno v. American Civil Liberties Union, 521 U.S. 844 (1997)], the mere possibility that user-based Internet screening software would "soon be widely available" was relevant to our rejection of an overbroad restriction of indecent cyberspeech. ...

. . .

There is, moreover, a key difference between cable television and the broadcasting media, which is the point on which this case turns: Cable systems have the capacity to block unwanted channels on a household-by-household basis. ... This is not to say that the absence of an effective blocking mechanism will in all cases suffice to support a law restricting the speech in question; but if a less restrictive means is available for the Government to achieve its goals, the Government must use it.

III

... No one disputes that § 504, which requires cable operators to block undesired channels at individual households upon request, is narrowly tailored to the Government's goal of supporting parents who want those channels blocked. The question is whether § 504 can be effective.

When a plausible, less restrictive alternative is offered to a content-based speech restriction, it is the Government's obligation to prove that the alternative will be ineffective to achieve its goals. The Government has not met that burden here. In support of its position, the Government cites empirical evidence showing that § 504, as promulgated and implemented before trial, generated few requests for household-by-household blocking. ... The uncomfortable fact is that § 504 was the sole blocking regulation in effect for over a year; and the public greeted it with a collective yawn.

. . .

... [T]he District Court explored three explanations for the lack of individual blocking requests. First, individual blocking might not be an effective alternative, due to technological or other limitations. Second, although an adequately advertised blocking provision might have been effective, § 504 as written did not require sufficient notice to make it so. Third, the actual signal bleed problem might be far less of a concern than the Government at first had supposed.

To sustain its statute, the Government was required to show that the first was the right answer. According to the District Court, however, the first and third possibilities were "equally consistent" with the record before it. As for the second, the record was "not clear" as to whether enough notice had been issued to give § 504 a fighting chance. The case, then, was at best a draw. Unless the District Court's findings are clearly erroneous, the tie goes to free expression.

. . . There is little hard evidence of how widespread or how serious the problem of signal bleed is. Indeed, there is no proof as to how likely any child is to view a discernible explicit image, and no proof of the duration of the bleed or the quality of the pictures or sound. . . . Under § 505, sanctionable signal bleed can include instances as fleeting as an image appearing on a screen for just a few seconds. . . .

. . .

. . . A rational cable operator, faced with the possibility of sanctions for intermittent bleeding, could well choose to time channel even if the bleeding is too momentary to pose any concern to most households. . . .

. . . [M]arket-based solutions such as programmable televisions, VCR's, and mapping systems (which display a blue screen when tuned to a scrambled signal) may eliminate signal bleed at the consumer end of the cable. . . .

No support for the restriction can be found in the near barren legislative record relevant to this provision. Section 505 was added to the Act by floor amendment, accompanied by only brief statements, and without committee hearing or debate. . . . One of the measure's sponsors did indicate she considered time channeling to be superior to voluntary blocking, which "put[s] the burden of action on the subscriber, not the cable company." . . . (statement of Sen. Feinstein). This sole conclusory statement, however, tells little about the relative efficacy of voluntary blocking versus time channeling, other than offering the unhelpful, self-evident generality that voluntary measures require voluntary action. . . .

. . . The Government also failed to prove § 504 with adequate notice would be an ineffective alternative to § 505. . . . There is no evidence that a well-promoted voluntary blocking provision would not be capable at least of informing parents about signal bleed (if they are not yet aware of it) and about their rights to have the bleed blocked (if they consider it a problem and have not yet controlled it themselves).

. . . [T]o the extent the District Court erred, it was only in attempting to implement the less restrictive alternative through judicial decree by requiring Playboy to provide for expanded notice in its cable service contracts. The appropriate remedy was not to repair the statute, it was to enjoin the speech restriction. Given the existence of a less restrictive means, if the Legislature wished to improve its statute, perhaps in the process giving careful consideration to other alternatives, it then could do so.

. . .

It is no response that voluntary blocking requires a consumer to take action, or may be inconvenient, or may not go perfectly every time. A court should not assume a plausible, less restrictive alternative would be ineffective; and a court should not presume parents, given full information, will fail to act. If unresponsive operators are a concern, moreover, a notice statute could give cable operators ample incentive, through fines or other penalties for noncompliance, to respond to blocking requests in prompt and efficient fashion.

. . .

There can be little doubt, of course, that under a voluntary blocking regime, even with adequate notice, some children will be exposed to signal bleed; and we need not discount the possibility that a graphic image could have a negative impact on a young child. It must be remembered, however, that children will be exposed to signal bleed under time channeling as well. Time channeling, unlike blocking, does not eliminate signal bleed around the clock. Just as adolescents may be unsupervised outside of their own households, it is hardly unknown for them to be unsupervised in front of the television set after 10 p.m. The record is silent as to the comparative effectiveness of the two alternatives.

* * *

... The history of the law of free expression is one of vindication in cases involving speech that many citizens may find shabby, offensive, or even ugly. It follows that all content-based restrictions on speech must give us more than a moment's pause. ...

The Government has failed to show that § 505 is the least restrictive means for addressing a real problem; and the District Court did not err in holding the statute violative of the First Amendment. ...

Justice Stevens, concurring.

Because Justice Scalia has advanced an argument that the parties have not addressed, a brief response is in order. Relying on Ginzburg v. United States, 383 U.S. 463 (1966), Justice Scalia would treat programs whose content is, he assumes, protected by the First Amendment as though they were obscene because of the way they are advertised. ...

... The very fact that the programs marketed by Playboy are offensive to many viewers provides a justification for protecting, not penalizing, truthful statements about their content.

Justice Thomas, concurring.

It would seem to me that, with respect to at least some of the cable programming affected by § 505 ..., the Government has ample constitutional and statutory authority to prohibit its broadcast entirely. ... Though perhaps not all of the programming at issue in the case is obscene ..., one could fairly conclude that, under the standards applicable in many communities, some of the programming meets the *Miller* test. ...

However, ... I am unwilling, in the absence of factual findings or advocacy of the position, to rely on the view that some of the relevant programming is obscene.

. . .

Justice Scalia, dissenting.

I agree with the principal dissent in this case.... I write separately to express my view that § 505 can be upheld in simpler fashion: by finding that it regulates the business of obscenity.

... I will assume for purposes of this discussion (though it is a highly fanciful assumption) that none of the transmissions at issue independently crosses the boundary we have established for obscenity, ... so that the individual programs themselves would enjoy First Amendment protection. In my view, however, that assumption does not put an end to the inquiry.

We have recognized that commercial entities which engage in "the sordid business of pandering" by "deliberately emphasiz[ing] the sexually provocative aspects of [their nonobscene products], in order to catch the salaciously disposed," engage in constitutionally unprotected behavior. Ginzburg v. United States, 383 U.S. 463, 467, 472 (1966) . . . This is so whether or not the products in which the business traffics independently meet the high hurdle we have established for delineating the obscene . . .

. . .

Thus, while I agree with Justice Breyer's child-protection analysis, it leaves me with the same feeling of true-but-inadequate as the conclusion that Al Capone did not accurately report his income. It is not only children who can be protected from occasional uninvited exposure to what appellee calls "adult-oriented programming"; we can all be. . . . In most contexts, contemporary American society has chosen to permit such commercial exploitation. That may be a wise democratic choice, if only because of the difficulty in many contexts (though not this one) of identifying the panderer to sex. It is, however, not a course compelled by the Constitution. Since the Government is entirely free to block these transmissions, it may certainly take the less drastic step of dictating how, and during what times, they may occur.

Justice Breyer, with whom the Chief Justice, Justice O'Connor and Justice Scalia join, dissenting.

. . .

II

The majority first concludes that the Government failed to prove the seriousness of the problem—receipt of adult channels by children whose parents did not request their broadcast. This claim is flat-out wrong. . . .

I would add to this empirical evidence the majority's own statement that "most cable operators had 'no practical choice but to curtail'" adult programming by switching to nighttime only transmission of adult channels. . . . I do not think it realistic to imagine that signal bleed occurs just enough to make cable operators skittish, without also significantly exposing children to these images.

If, as the majority suggests, the signal bleed problem is not significant, then there is also no significant burden on speech created by § 505. The majority cannot have this evidence both ways. . . .

III

The majority's second claim—that the Government failed to demonstrate the absence of a "less restrictive alternative"—presents a closer question. . . .

The words . . . "similarly and effective," are critical. . . .

These words imply a degree of leeway, however small, for the legislature when it chooses among possible alternatives in light of predicted comparative effects. Without some such empirical leeway, the undoubted ability of lawyers and judges to imagine some kind of slightly less drastic or restrictive an approach would make it impossible to write laws that deal with the harm that called the statute into being. . . .

. . .

. . . Unlike the majority, I believe the record makes clear that § 504's opt-out is not a similarly effective alternative. . . .

... Government has a compelling interest in helping parents by preventing minors from accessing sexually explicit materials in the absence of parental supervision....

By definition, § 504 does nothing at all to further the compelling interest. ... How then is it a similarly effective § 505 alternative?

The record, moreover, sets forth empirical evidence showing that the two laws are not equivalent with respect to the Government's objectives. ... I doubt that the public, though it may well consider the viewing habits of adults a matter of personal choice, would "yawn" when the exposure in question concerns young children, the absence of parental consent, and the sexually explicit material here at issue.

Neither is the record neutral in respect to the curative power of better notice. ... Better notice of § 504 rights does little to help parents discover their children's viewing habits ... And it does nothing at all in respect to steps three through five. Yet the record contains considerable evidence that those problems matter....

. . .

Of course, it is logically possible that "better notice" will bring about near perfect parental knowledge (of what children watch and § 504 opt-out rights), that cable operators will respond rapidly to blocking requests, and that still 94% of all informed parents will decided not to have adult channels blocked for free. But the probability that this remote possibility will occur is neither a "draw" nor a "tie." ...

. . .

IV

Section 505 raises the cost of adult channel broadcasting. In doing so, it restricts, but does not ban adult speech. ... The record shows no similarly effective, less restrictive alternative. Consequently § 505's restriction, viewed in light of the proposed alternative, is proportionate to need. That is to say, it restricts speech no more than necessary to further that compelling need. Taken together, these considerations lead to the conclusion that § 505 is lawful.

. . .

Ashcroft v. ACLU

535 U.S. 564, 122 S.Ct. 1700, 152 L.Ed.2d 771 (2002).

Justice Thomas announced the judgment of the Court and delivered the opinion of the Court with respect to Parts I, II, and IV, an opinion with respect to Parts III–A, III–C, and III–D, in which THE Chief Justice and Justice Scalia join, and an opinion with respect to Part III–B, in which THE Chief Justice, Justice O'Connor, and Justice Scalia join.

This case presents the narrow question whether the Child Online Protection Act's (COPA or Act) use of "community standards" to identify "material that is harmful to minors" violates the First Amendment. We hold that this aspect of COPA does not render the statute facially unconstitutional.

I

... While "surfing" the World Wide Web, ... individuals can access material about topics ranging from aardvarks to Zoroastrianism. One can use the Web to read thousands of newspapers published around the globe, purchase tickets for a matinee at the neighborhood movie theater, or follow the progress of any Major League Baseball team on a pitch-by-pitch basis.

The Web also contains a wide array of sexually explicit material, including hardcore pornography. ... In 1998, for instance, there were approximately 28,000 adult sites promoting pornography on the Web. ... [C]hildren may discover this pornographic material either by deliberately accessing pornographic Web sites or by stumbling upon them. ...

Congress first attempted to protect children from exposure to pornographic material on the Internet by enacting the Communications Decency Act of 1996 (CDA) ... The CDA prohibited the knowing transmission over the Internet of obscene or indecent messages to any recipient under 18 years of age. ... It also forbade any individual from knowingly sending over or displaying on the Internet certain "patently offensive" material in a manner available to persons under 18 years of age. ... The prohibition specifically extended to "any comment, request, suggestion, proposal, image, or other communication that, in context, depict [ed] or describ[ed], in terms patently offensive as measured by contemporary community standards, sexual or excretory activities or organs." ...

The CDA provided two affirmative defenses to those prosecuted under the statute. The first protected individuals who took "good faith, reasonable, effective, and appropriate actions" to restrict minors from accessing obscene, indecent, and patently offensive material over the Internet. ... The second shielded those who restricted minors from accessing such material "by requiring use of a verified credit card, debit account, adult access code, or adult personal identification number." ...

Notwithstanding these affirmative defenses, in Reno v. American Civil Liberties Union, [521 U.S. 844 (1997),] we held that the CDA's regulation of indecent transmissions, ... and the display of patently offensive material, ... ran afoul of the First Amendment. We concluded that "the CDA lack[ed] the precision that the First Amendment requires when a statute regulates the content of speech" because, "[i]n order to deny minors access to potentially harmful speech, the CDA effectively suppress[ed] a large amount of speech that adults ha[d] a constitutional right to receive and to address to one another." ...

Our holding was based on three crucial considerations. First, "existing technology did not include any effective method for a sender to prevent minors from obtaining access to its communications on the Internet without also denying access to adults." ... Second, "[t]he breadth of the CDA's coverage [was] wholly unprecedented." ... "Its open-ended prohibitions embrace[d]," not only commercial speech or commercial entities, but also "all nonprofit entities and individuals posting indecent messages or displaying them on their own computers in the presence of minors." *Ibid.* In addition, because the CDA did not define the terms "indecent" and "patently offensive," the statute "cover[ed] large amounts of nonpornographic material with serious educational or other value." ... As a result, regulated subject matter under the CDA extended to "discussions about prison rape or safe sexual practices, artistic images that include nude subjects, and arguably the card catalog of the Carnegie Library." ... Third, we found that neither affirmative defense set forth in the CDA "constitute[d] the sort of 'narrow tailoring' that [would] save an otherwise patently invalid unconstitutional provision." ... Consequently, only the CDA's ban on the knowing transmission of obscene messages survived scrutiny because obscene speech enjoys no First Amendment protection. ...

After our decision in Reno v. American Civil Liberties Union, Congress explored other avenues for restricting minors' access to pornographic material on the Internet. In particular, Congress passed and the President signed into law the Child Online Protection Act, 112 Stat. 2681–736 (codified in 47 U.S.C. § 231 (1994 ed., Supp. V)). COPA prohibits any person from "knowingly and with knowledge of the character of the material, in interstate or foreign commerce by means of the World Wide Web, mak[ing] any communication for commercial purposes that is available to any minor and that includes any material that is harmful to minors." 47 U.S.C. § 231(a)(1).

Apparently responding to our objections to the breadth of the CDA's coverage, Congress limited the scope of COPA's coverage in at least three ways. First, while the CDA applied to communications over the Internet as a whole, including, for example, e-mail messages, COPA applies only to material displayed on the World Wide Web. Second, unlike the CDA, COPA covers only communications made "for commercial purposes." ... And third, while the CDA prohibited "indecent" and "patently offensive" communications, COPA restricts only the narrower category of "material that is harmful to minors."
...

Drawing on the three-part test for obscenity set forth in *Miller v. California*, 413 U.S. 15, 93 S.Ct. 2607, 37 L.Ed.2d 419 (1973), COPA defines "material that is harmful to minors" as

"any communication, picture, image, graphic image file, article, recording, writing, or other matter of any kind that is obscene or that?

"(A) the average person, applying contemporary community standards, would find, taking the material as a whole and with respect to minors, is designed to appeal to, or is designed to pander to, the prurient interest;

"(B) depicts, describes, or represents, in a manner patently offensive with respect to minors, an actual or simulated sexual act or sexual contact, an actual or simulated normal or perverted sexual act, or a lewd exhibition of the genitals or post-pubescent female breast; and

"(C) taken as a whole, lacks serious literary, artistic, political, or scientific value for minors." 47 U.S.C. § 231(e)(6).

Like the CDA, COPA also provides affirmative defenses to those subject to prosecution under the statute. An individual may qualify for a defense if he, "in good faith, has restricted access by minors to material that is harmful to minors—(A) by requiring the use of a credit card, debit account, adult access code, or adult personal identification number; (B) by accepting a digital certificate that verifies age; or (C) by any other reasonable measures that are feasible under available technology." § 231(c)(1). Persons violating COPA are subject to both civil and criminal sanctions. A civil penalty of up to $50,000 may be imposed for each violation of the statute. Criminal penalties consist of up to six months in prison and/or a maximum fine of $50,000. An additional fine of $50,000 may be imposed for any intentional violation of the statute. § 231(a).

One month before COPA was scheduled to go into effect, respondents filed a lawsuit challenging the constitutionality of the statute in the United States District Court for the Eastern District of Pennsylvania. Respondents are a diverse group of organizations, most of which maintain their own Web sites. While the vast majority of content on their Web sites is available for free, respondents all derive income from their sites. Some, for example, sell advertising that is displayed on their Web sites, while others either sell goods directly over their sites or charge artists for the privilege of posting material. All respondents either post or have members that post sexually oriented material on the Web. Respondents' Web sites contain "resources on obstetrics, gynecology, and sexual health; visual art and poetry; resources designed for gays and lesbians; information about books and stock photographic images offered for sale; and online magazines."

In their complaint, respondents alleged that, although they believed that the material on their Web sites was valuable for adults, they feared that they would be prosecuted under COPA because some of that material "could be construed as 'harmful to minors' in some communities." ...

The District Court granted respondents' motion for a preliminary injunction, barring the Government from enforcing the Act until the merits of respondents' claims could be adjudicated. ...

... The United States Court of Appeals for the Third Circuit affirmed. ...

We ... now vacate the Court of Appeals' judgment.

II

. . .

Ending over a decade of turmoil, this Court in *Miller* set forth the governing three-part test for assessing whether material is obscene and thus unprotected by the First Amendment ...

... The Court preserved the use of community standards in formulating the *Miller* test, explaining that they furnish a valuable First Amendment safeguard: "[T]he primary concern ... is to be certain that ... [material] will be judged by its impact on an average person, rather than a particularly susceptible or sensitive person—or indeed a totally insensitive one." ...

III

The Court of Appeals, however, concluded that this Court's prior community standards jurisprudence "has no applicability to the Internet and the Web" because "Web publishers are currently without the ability to control the geographic scope of the recipients of their communications." We therefore must decide whether this technological limitation renders COPA's reliance on community standards constitutionally infirm.

A

In addressing this question, the parties first dispute the nature of the community standards that jurors will be instructed to apply when assessing, in prosecutions under COPA, whether works appeal to the prurient interest of minors and are patently offensive with respect to minors. Respondents contend that jurors will evaluate material using "local community standards," while petitioner maintains that jurors will not consider the community standards of any particular geographic area, but rather will be "instructed to consider the standards of the adult community as a whole, without geographic specification."

In the context of this case, which involves a facial challenge to a statute that has never been enforced, we do not think it prudent to engage in speculation as to whether certain hypothetical jury instructions would or would not be consistent with COPA, and deciding this case does not require us to do so. It is sufficient to note that community standards need not be defined by reference to a precise geographic area. . . .

B

Because juries would apply different standards across the country, and Web publishers currently lack the ability to limit access to their sites on a geographic basis, the Court of Appeals feared that COPA's "community standards" component would effectively force all speakers on the Web to abide by the "most puritan" community's standards.

In evaluating the constitutionality of the CDA, this Court expressed a similar concern over that statute's use of community standards to identify patently offensive material on the Internet. We noted that "the 'community standards' criterion as applied to the Internet means that any communication available to a nationwide audience will be judged by the standards of the community most likely to be offended by the message." *Reno,* . . .

The CDA's use of community standards to identify patently offensive material, however, was particularly problematic in light of that statute's unprecedented breadth and vagueness. The statute covered communications depicting or describing "sexual or excretory activities or organs" that were "patently offensive as measured by contemporary community standards"—a standard somewhat similar to the second prong of *Miller*'s three-prong test. But the CDA did not include any limiting terms resembling *Miller*'s additional two prongs. . . . It neither contained any requirement that restricted material appeal to the prurient interest nor excluded from the scope of its coverage works with serious literary, artistic, political, or scientific value. . . . The tremendous breadth of the CDA magnified the impact caused by differences in community standards across the country, restricting Web publishers from openly displaying a significant amount of material that would have constituted protected speech in some communities across the country but run afoul of community standards in others.

COPA, by contrast, does not appear to suffer from the same flaw because it applies to significantly less material than did the CDA and defines the harmful-to-minors material restricted by the statute in a manner parallel to the *Miller* definition of obscenity. To fall within the scope of COPA, works must not only "depic[t], describ[e], or rcprcscn[t], in a mannor patently offensive with respect to minors," particular sexual acts or parts of the anatomy, they must also be designed to appeal to the prurient interest of minors and "taken as a whole, lac[k] serious literary, artistic, political, or scientific value for minors." . . .

These additional two restrictions substantially limit the amount of material covered by the statute. Material appeals to the prurient interest, for instance, only if it is in some sense erotic. . . . Of even more significance, however, is COPA's exclusion of material with serious value for minors. . . . In *Reno,* we emphasized that the serious value "requirement is particularly important because, unlike the 'patently offensive' and 'prurient interest' criteria, it is not judged by contemporary community standards." . . .

C

When the scope of an obscenity statute's coverage is sufficiently narrowed by a "serious value" prong and a "prurient interest" prong, we have held that requiring a speaker disseminating material to a national audience to observe varying community standards does not violate the First Amendment. . . . Hamling v. United States, 418 U.S. 87 (1974). . . .

Like respondents here, the dissenting opinion in *Hamling* argued that it was unconstitutional for a federal statute to rely on community standards to regulate speech. . . .

This Court, however, rejected Justice Brennan's argument that the federal mail statute unconstitutionally compelled speakers choosing to distribute materials on a national basis to tailor their messages to the least tolerant community. . . .

Fifteen years later, *Hamling*'s holding was reaffirmed in Sable Communications of Cal., Inc. v. FCC, 492 U.S. 115 (1989). *Sable* addressed the constitutionality of . . . a statutory provision prohibiting the use of telephones to make obscene or indecent communications for commercial purposes. The petitioner in that case, a "dial-a-porn" operator, challenged, in part, that portion of the statute banning obscene phone messages. Like respondents here, the "dial-a-porn" operator argued that reliance on community standards to identify obscene material impermissibly compelled "message senders . . . to tailor all their messages to the least tolerant community." . . . Relying on *Hamling,* however, this Court once again rebuffed this attack on the use of community standards in a federal statute of national scope: "There is no constitutional barrier under *Miller* to prohibiting communications that are obscene in some communities under local standards even though they are not obscene in others. *If Sable's audience is comprised of different communities with different local standards, Sable ultimately bears the burden of complying with the prohibition on obscene messages."* . . . (emphasis added).

The Court of Appeals below concluded that *Hamling* and *Sable* "are easily distinguished from the present case" because in both of those cases "the defendants had the ability to control the distribution of controversial material with respect to the geographic communities into which they released it" whereas "Web publishers have no such comparable control." In neither *Hamling* nor *Sable,* however, was the speaker's ability to target the release of material into particular geographic areas integral to the legal analysis. In *Hamling,* the ability to limit the distribution of material to targeted communities was not mentioned, let alone relied upon, and in *Sable,* a dial-a-porn operator's ability to screen incoming calls from particular areas was referenced only as a supplemental point . . . In the latter case, this Court made no effort to evaluate how burdensome it would have been for dial-a-porn operators to tailor their messages to callers from thousands of different communities across the Nation, instead concluding that the burden of complying with the statute rested with those companies. . . .

While Justice Kennedy and Justice Stevens question the applicability of this Court's community standards jurisprudence to the Internet, we do not believe that the medium's "unique characteristics" justify adopting a different approach than that set forth in *Hamling* and *Sable.* If a publisher chooses to send its material into a particular community, this Court's jurisprudence teaches that it is the publisher's responsibility to abide by that community's standards. The publisher's burden does not change simply because it decides to distribute its material to every community in the Nation. . . . If a publisher wishes for its material to be judged only by the standards of particular communities, then it need only take the simple step of utilizing a medium that enables it to target the release of its material into those communities.

Respondents offer no other grounds upon which to distinguish this case from *Hamling* and *Sable.* While those cases involved obscenity rather than material that is harmful to minors, we have no reason to believe that the practical effect of varying community standards under COPA, given the statute's definition of "material that is harmful to minors," is significantly greater than the practical effect of varying community standards under federal obscenity statutes. ... [I]f we were to hold COPA unconstitutional *because of* its use of community standards, federal obscenity statutes would likely also be unconstitutional as applied to the Web. ...

D

... Because Congress has narrowed the range of content restricted by COPA in a manner analogous to *Miller*'s definition of obscenity, we conclude, consistent with our holdings in *Hamling* and *Sable,* that any variance caused by the statute's reliance on community standards is not substantial enough to violate the First Amendment.

IV

The scope of our decision today is quite limited. We hold only that COPA's reliance on community standards to identify "material that is harmful to minors" does not *by itself* render the statute substantially overbroad for purposes of the First Amendment. We do not express any view as to whether COPA suffers from substantial overbreadth for other reasons, whether the statute is unconstitutionally vague, or whether the District Court correctly concluded that the statute likely will not survive strict scrutiny analysis once adjudication of the case is completed below. While respondents urge us to resolve these questions at this time, prudence dictates allowing the Court of Appeals to first examine these difficult issues.

Petitioner does not ask us to vacate the preliminary injunction entered by the District Court, and in any event, we could not do so without addressing matters yet to be considered by the Court of Appeals. As a result, the Government remains enjoined from enforcing COPA absent further action by the Court of Appeals or the District Court.

. . .

Justice O'Connor, concurring in part and concurring in the judgment.

I agree with the plurality that even if obscenity on the Internet is defined in terms of local community standards, respondents have not shown that the Child Online Protection Act (COPA) is overbroad solely on the basis of the variation in the standards of different communities. Like Justice Breyer, however, I write separately to express my views on the constitutionality and desirability of adopting a national standard for obscenity for regulation of the Internet.

The plurality's opinion argues that, even under local community standards, the variation between the most and least restrictive communities is not so great with respect to the narrow category of speech covered by COPA as to, alone, render the statute substantially overbroad. I agree, given respondents' failure to provide examples of materials that lack literary, artistic, political, and scientific value for minors, which would nonetheless result in variation among communities judging the other elements of the test. ...

But respondents' failure to prove substantial overbreadth on a facial challenge in this case still leaves open the possibility that the use of local community standards will cause problems for regulation of obscenity on the Internet, for adults as well as children, in future cases. In an as-applied challenge, for instance, individual litigants may still dispute that the standards of a community more restrictive than theirs should apply to them. And in future facial challenges to regulation of obscenity on the Internet, litigants may make a more convincing case for substantial overbreadth. Where adult speech is concerned, for instance, there may in fact be a greater degree of disagreement about what is patently offensive or appeals to the prurient interest.

Nor do I think such future cases can be resolved by application of the approach we took in *Hamling* . . . and *Sable* . . . I agree with Justice Kennedy that, given Internet speakers' inability to control the geographic location of their audience, expecting them to bear the burden of controlling the recipients of their speech, as we did in *Hamling* and *Sable,* may be entirely too much to ask, and would potentially suppress an inordinate amount of expression. For these reasons, adoption of a national standard is necessary in my view for any reasonable regulation of Internet obscenity.

. . .

While I would prefer that the Court resolve the issue before it by explicitly adopting a national standard for defining obscenity on the Internet, given respondents' failure to demonstrate substantial overbreadth due solely to the variation between local communities, I join Parts I, II, III–B, and IV of Justice Thomas' opinion and the judgment.

Justice Breyer, concurring in part and concurring in the judgment.

I write separately because I believe that Congress intended the statutory word "community" to refer to the Nation's adult community taken as a whole, not to geographically separate local areas. The statutory language does not explicitly describe the specific "community" to which it refers. It says only that the "average person, applying contemporary community standards" must find that the "material as a whole and with respect to minors, is designed to appeal to, or is designed to pander to, the prurient interest. . . ." . . .

. . .

. . . [T]his view of the statute avoids the need to examine the serious First Amendment problem that would otherwise exist. . . . To read the statute as adopting the community standards of every locality in the United States would provide the most puritan of communities with a heckler's Internet veto affecting the rest of the Nation. The technical difficulties associated with efforts to confine Internet material to particular geographic areas make the problem particularly serious. . . .

. . . I do not join Part III of Justice Thomas' opinion, although I agree with much of the reasoning set forth in Parts III–B and III–D, insofar as it explains . . . that variation reflecting application of the same national standard by different local juries does not violate the First Amendment.

Justice Kennedy, with whom Justice Souter and Justice Ginsburg join, concurring in the judgment.

I

. . . COPA is a major federal statute, enacted in the wake of our previous determination that its predecessor violated the First Amendment. . . . Congress and the President were aware of our decision, and we should assume that in seeking to comply with it they have given careful consideration to the constitutionality of the new enactment. For these reasons, even if this facial challenge appears to have considerable merit, the Judiciary must proceed with caution and identify overbreadth with care before invalidating the Act.

. . .

... To observe only that community standards vary across the country is to ignore the antecedent question: community standards as to what? Whether the national variation in community standards produces overbreadth requiring invalidation of COPA, ... depends on the breadth of COPA's coverage and on what community standards are being invoked. Only by identifying the universe of speech burdened by COPA is it possible to discern whether national variation in community standards renders the speech restriction overbroad. ...

... Some examination of the group of covered speakers and the categories of covered speech is necessary in order to comprehend the extent of the alleged overbreadth.

... I join the judgment of the Court vacating the opinion of the Court of Appeals and remanding for consideration of the statute as a whole. Unlike Justice Thomas, however, I would not assume that the Act is narrow enough to render the national variation in community standards unproblematic. Indeed, if the District Court correctly construed the statute across its other dimensions, then the variation in community standards might well justify enjoining enforcement of the Act. I would leave that question to the Court of Appeals in the first instance.

II

... The nub of the problem is, as the Court has said, that "the 'community standards' criterion as applied to the Internet means that any communication available to a nationwide audience will be judged by the standards of the community most likely to be offended by the message." ... This observation was the linchpin of the Court of Appeals' analysis, and we must now consider whether it alone suffices to support the holding below.

The quoted sentence from *Reno* was not casual dicta; rather, it was one rationale for the holding of the case. ...Variation in community standards rendered the statute broader than the scope of the Government's own expressed compelling interest.

It is true, as Justice Thomas points out, that requiring a speaker addressing a national audience to meet varying community standards does not always violate the First Amendment. See *Hamling* ... ; *Sable* ... These cases, however, are of limited utility in analyzing the one before us, because each mode of expression has its own unique characteristics ... Indeed, when Congress purports to abridge the freedom of a new medium, we must be particularly attentive to its distinct attributes ... The economics and the technology of each medium affect both the burden of a speech restriction and the Government's interest in maintaining it.

... [I]n upholding a ban on obscene phone messages, we emphasized that the speaker could "hire operators to determine the source of the calls or engag[e] with the telephone company to arrange for the screening and blocking of out-of-area calls or fin[d] another means for providing messages compatible with community standards." ... And if we did not make the same point in *Hamling,* that is likely because it is so obvious that mailing lends itself to geographic restriction. ...

The economics and technology of Internet communication differ in important ways from those of telephones and mail. Paradoxically, as the District Court found, it is easy and cheap to reach a worldwide audience on the Internet, but expensive if not impossible to reach a geographic subset. A Web publisher in a community where avant garde culture is the norm may have no desire to reach a national market; he may wish only to speak to his neighbors;

nevertheless, if an eavesdropper in a more traditional, rural community chooses to listen in, there is nothing the publisher can do. As a practical matter, COPA makes the eavesdropper the arbiter of propriety on the Web. And it is no answer to say that the speaker should "take the simple step of utilizing a [different] medium." . . .

. . .

. . . [W]e need not decide whether the statute invokes local or national community standards to conclude that vacatur and remand are in order. If the statute does incorporate some concept of national community standards, the actual standard applied is bound to vary by community nevertheless, as the Attorney General concedes.

For this reason the Court of Appeals was correct to focus on COPA's incorporation of varying community standards; and it may have been correct as well to conclude that in practical effect COPA imposes the most puritanical community standard on the entire country. . . . In striking down COPA's predecessor, the *Reno* Court identified this precise problem, and if the *Hamling* and *Sable* Courts did not find the problem fatal, that is because those cases involved quite different media. The national variation in community standards constitutes a particular burden on Internet speech.

III

The question that remains is whether this observation *"by itself"* suffices to enjoin the Act. I agree with the Court that it does not. We cannot know whether variation in community standards renders the Act substantially overbroad without first assessing the extent of the speech covered and the variations in community standards with respect to that speech.

. . . As this case comes to us, once it is accepted that we cannot strike down the Act based merely on the phrase "contemporary community standards," we should go no further than to vacate and remand for a more comprehensive analysis of the Act.

. . .

Justice Stevens, dissenting.

Appeals to prurient interests are commonplace on the Internet, as in older media. Many of those appeals lack serious value for minors as well as adults. Some are offensive to certain viewers but welcomed by others. For decades, our cases have recognized that the standards for judging their acceptability vary from viewer to viewer and from community to community. Those cases developed the requirement that communications should be protected if they do not violate contemporary community standards. In its original form, the community standard provided a shield for communications that are offensive only to the least tolerant members of society. . . . In the context of the Internet, however, community standards become a sword, rather than a shield. If a prurient appeal is offensive in a puritan village, it may be a crime to post it on the World Wide Web.

. . .

We have . . . repeatedly rejected the position that the free speech rights of adults can be limited to what is acceptable for children. See . . . *Butler v. Michigan,* 352 U.S. 380, 383 (1957).

. . . Like the . . . ban against selling adult books found impermissible in *Butler,* COPA seeks to limit protected speech that is not targeted at children, simply because it can be obtained by them while surfing the Web. In evaluating the overbreadth of such a statute, we should be mindful of Justice Frankfurter's admonition not to "burn the house to roast the pig," *Butler,* 352 U.S., at 383.

COPA not only restricts speech that is made available to the general public, it also covers a medium in which speech cannot be segregated to avoid communities where it is likely to be considered harmful to minors. ...

If the material were forwarded through the mails, as in *Hamling,* or over the telephone, as in *Sable,* the sender could avoid destinations with the most restrictive standards. ... In light of this fundamental difference in technologies, the rules applicable to the mass mailing of an obscene montage or to obscene dial-a-porn should not be used to judge the legality of messages on the World Wide Web.

.   .   .

Justice Thomas points to several other provisions in COPA to argue that any overbreadth will be rendered insubstantial by the rest of the statute. These provisions afford little reassurance, however, as they only marginally limit the sweep of the statute. ...

.   .   .

Justice Kennedy makes a similar misstep when he ties the overbreadth inquiry to questions about the scope of the other provisions of the statute. ... These other provisions may reduce the absolute number of Web pages covered by the statute, but even the narrowest version of the statute abridges a substantial amount of protected speech that many communities would not find harmful to minors. Because Web speakers cannot limit access to those specific communities, the statute is substantially overbroad regardless of how its other provisions are construed.

Justice Thomas acknowledges, and petitioner concedes, that juries across the country will apply different standards and reach different conclusions about whether particular works are harmful to minors. ...

... Because communities differ widely in their attitudes toward sex, particularly when minors are concerned, the Court of Appeals was correct to conclude that, regardless of how COPA's other provisions are construed, applying community standards to the Internet will restrict a substantial amount of protected speech that would not be considered harmful to minors in many communities.

Whether that consequence is appropriate depends, of course, on the content of the message. The kind of hard-core pornography involved in *Hamling,* which I assume would be obscene under any community's standard, does not belong on the Internet. Perhaps "teasers" that serve no function except to invite viewers to examine hardcore materials, or the hidden terms written into a Web site's "metatags" in order to dupe unwitting Web surfers into visiting pornographic sites, deserve the same fate. But COPA extends to a wide range of prurient appeals in advertisements, online magazines, Web-based bulletin boards and chat rooms, stock photo galleries, Web diaries, and a variety of illustrations encompassing a vast number of messages that are unobjectionable in most of the country and yet provide no "serious value" for minors. It is quite wrong to allow the standards of a minority consisting of the least tolerant communities to regulate access to relatively harmless messages in this burgeoning market.

... I would affirm the judgment of the Court of Appeals ...

Ashcroft v. American Civil Liberties Union

__ U.S. __, 124 S.Ct. 2783, 159 L.Ed.2d 690 (2004).

Justice Kennedy delivered the opinion of the Court.

This case presents a challenge to a statute enacted by Congress to protect minors from exposure to sexually explicit materials on the Internet, the Child Online Protection Act (COPA). 112 Stat. 2681–736, codified at 47 U.S.C. § 231. We must decide whether the Court of Appeals was correct to affirm a ruling by the District Court that enforcement of COPA should be enjoined because the statute likely violates the First Amendment.

In enacting COPA, Congress gave consideration to our earlier decisions on this subject, in particular the decision in *Reno v. American Civil Liberties Union,* 521 U.S. 844, 117 S.Ct. 2329, 138 L.Ed.2d 874 (1997). ... The imperative of according respect to the Congress, however, does not permit us to depart from well-established First Amendment principles. Instead, we must hold the Government to its constitutional burden of proof.

Content-based prohibitions, enforced by severe criminal penalties, have the constant potential to be a repressive force in the lives and thoughts of a free people. To guard against that threat the Constitution demands that content-based restrictions on speech be presumed invalid ... and that the Government bear the burden of showing their constitutionality ... This is true even when Congress twice has attempted to find a constitutional means to restrict, and punish, the speech in question.

This case comes to the Court on certiorari review of an appeal from the decision of the District Court granting a preliminary injunction. ... The Government has failed, at this point, to rebut the plaintiffs' contention that there are plausible less restrictive alternatives to the statute. Substantial practical considerations, furthermore, argue in favor of upholding the injunction and allowing the case to proceed to trial. For those reasons, we affirm the decision of the Court of Appeals upholding the preliminary injunction, and we remand the case so that it may be returned to the District Court for trial on the issues presented.

I

A

COPA is the second attempt by Congress to make the Internet safe for minors by criminalizing certain Internet speech. ...

In response to the Court's decision in *Reno,* Congress passed COPA. COPA imposes criminal penalties of a $50,000 fine and six months in prison for the knowing posting, for "commercial purposes," of World Wide Web content that is "harmful to minors." § 231(a)(1). Material that is "harmful to minors" is defined as:

"any communication, picture, image, graphic image file, article, recording, writing, or other matter of any kind that is obscene or that?

"(A) the average person, applying contemporary community standards, would find, taking the material as a whole and with respect to minors, is designed to appeal to, or is designed to pander to, the prurient interest;

"(B) depicts, describes, or represents, in a manner patently offensive with respect to minors, an actual or simulated sexual act or sexual contact, an actual or simulated normal or perverted sexual act, or a lewd exhibition of the genitals or post-pubescent female breast; and

"(C) taken as a whole, lacks serious literary, artistic, political, or scientific value for minors." § 231(e)(6).

"Minors" are defined as "any person under 17 years of age." § 231(e)(7). A person acts for "commercial purposes only if such person is engaged in the business of making such communications." . . .

While the statute labels all speech that falls within these definitions as criminal speech, it also provides an affirmative defense to those who employ specified means to prevent minors from gaining access to the prohibited materials on their Web site. A person may escape conviction under the statute by demonstrating that he

"has restricted access by minors to material that is harmful to minors?

"(A) by requiring use of a credit card, debit account, adult access code, or adult personal identification number;

"(B) by accepting a digital certificate that verifies age, or

"(C) by any other reasonable measures that are feasible under available technology." § 231(c)(1).

Since the passage of COPA, Congress has enacted additional laws regulating the Internet in an attempt to protect minors. For example, it has enacted a prohibition on misleading Internet domain names . . . in order to prevent Web site owners from disguising pornographic Web sites in a way likely to cause uninterested persons to visit them. See Brief for Petitioner 7 (giving, as an example, the Web site "whitehouse.com"). It has also passed a statute creating a "Dot Kids" second-level Internet domain, the content of which is restricted to that which is fit for minors under the age of 13. . . .

. . .

II

A

This Court, like other appellate courts, has always applied the abuse of discretion standard on the review of a preliminary injunction. . . . If the underlying constitutional question is close, therefore, we should uphold the injunction and remand for trial on the merits. Applying this mode of inquiry, we agree with the Court of Appeals that the District Court did not abuse its discretion in entering the preliminary injunction. . . .

. . . When plaintiffs challenge a content-based speech restriction, the burden is on the Government to prove that the proposed alternatives will not be as effective as the challenged statute. . . .

The purpose of the test is to ensure that speech is restricted no further than necessary to achieve the goal, for it is important to assure that legitimate speech is not chilled or punished. For that reason, the test does not begin with the status quo of existing regulations, then ask whether the challenged restriction has some additional ability to achieve Congress' legitimate interest. Any restriction on speech could be justified under that analysis. Instead, the court should ask whether the challenged regulation is the least restrictive means among available, effective alternatives.

In deciding whether to grant a preliminary injunction stage, a district court must consider whether the plaintiffs have demonstrated that they are likely to prevail on the merits. . . . As the Government bears the burden of proof on the ultimate question of COPA's constitutionality, respondents must be deemed likely to prevail unless the Government has shown that respondents' proposed less restrictive alternatives are less effective than COPA. Applying that analysis, the District Court concluded that respondents were likely to prevail. That conclusion was not an abuse of discretion, because on this record there are a number of plausible, less restrictive alternatives to the statute.

The primary alternative considered by the District Court was blocking and filtering software. Blocking and filtering software is an alternative that is less restrictive than COPA, and, in addition, likely more effective as a means of restricting children's access to materials harmful to them. The District Court, in granting the preliminary injunction, did so primarily because the plaintiffs had proposed that filters are a less restrictive alternative to COPA and the Government had not shown it would be likely to disprove the plaintiffs' contention at trial.

Filters are less restrictive than COPA. They impose selective restrictions on speech at the receiving end, not universal restrictions at the source. Under a filtering regime, adults without children may gain access to speech they have a right to see without having to identify themselves or provide their credit card information. Even adults with children may obtain access to the same speech on the same terms simply by turning off the filter on their home computers. Above all, promoting the use of filters does not condemn as criminal any category of speech, and so the potential chilling effect is eliminated, or at least much diminished. All of these things are true, moreover, regardless of how broadly or narrowly the definitions in COPA are construed.

Filters also may well be more effective than COPA. First, a filter can prevent minors from seeing all pornography, not just pornography posted to the Web from America. ... COPA does not prevent minors from having access to those foreign harmful materials. That alone makes it possible that filtering software might be more effective in serving Congress' goals. Effectiveness is likely to diminish even further if COPA is upheld, because the providers of the materials that would be covered by the statute simply can move their operations overseas. It is not an answer to say that COPA reaches some amount of materials that are harmful to minors; the question is whether it would reach more of them than less restrictive alternatives. In addition, the District Court found that verification systems may be subject to evasion and circumvention, for example by minors who have their own credit cards. Finally, filters also may be more effective because they can be applied to all forms of Internet communication, including e-mail, not just communications available via the World Wide Web.

. . .

One argument to the contrary is worth mentioning—the argument that filtering software is not an available alternative because Congress may not require it to be used. That argument carries little weight, because Congress undoubtedly may act to encourage the use of filters. We have held that Congress can give strong incentives to schools and libraries to use them. It could also take steps to promote their development by industry, and their use by parents. It is incorrect, for that reason, to say that filters are part of the current regulatory status quo. The need for parental cooperation does not automatically disqualify a proposed less restrictive alternative. In enacting COPA, Congress said its goal was to prevent the "widespread availability of the Internet" from providing "opportunities for minors to access materials through the World Wide Web in a manner that can frustrate parental supervision or control." ... COPA presumes that parents lack the ability, not the will, to monitor what their children see. By enacting programs to promote use of filtering software, Congress could give parents that ability without subjecting protected speech to severe penalties.

The closest precedent on the general point is our decision in *Playboy Entertainment Group. Playboy Entertainment Group,* like this case, involved a content-based restriction designed to protect minors from viewing harmful materials. The choice was between a blanket speech restriction and a more specific technological solution that was available to parents who chose to implement it. ... Absent a showing that the proposed less restrictive alternative would not be as effective, we concluded, the more restrictive option preferred by Congress could not survive strict scrutiny ... In the instant case, too, the Government has failed to show, at this point, that the proposed less restrictive alternative will be less effective. ...

B

There are also important practical reasons to let the injunction stand pending a full trial on the merits. First, the potential harms from reversing the injunction outweigh those of leaving it in place by mistake ...

Second, there are substantial factual disputes remaining in the case. As mentioned above, there is a serious gap in the evidence as to the effectiveness of filtering software. ... By allowing the preliminary injunction to stand and remanding for trial, we require the Government to shoulder its full constitutional burden of proof respecting the less restrictive alternative argument, rather than excuse it from doing so.

Third, and on a related point, the factual record does not reflect current technological reality—a serious flaw in any case involving the Internet. The technology of the Internet evolves at a rapid pace. Yet the factfindings of the District Court were entered in February 1999, over five years ago. Since then, certain facts about the Internet are known to have changed. ... It is reasonable to assume that other technological developments important to the First Amendment analysis have also occurred during that time. More and better filtering alternatives may exist than when the District Court entered its findings. Indeed, we know that after the District Court entered its factfindings, a congressionally appointed commission issued a report that found that filters are more effective than verification screens.

. . .

Remand will also permit the District Court to take account of a changed legal landscape. Since the District Court made its factfindings, Congress has passed at least two further statutes that might qualify as less restrictive alternatives to COPA—a prohibition on misleading domain names, and a statute creating a minors-safe "Dot Kids" domain. Remanding for trial will allow the District Court to take into account those additional potential alternatives.

Justice Stevens, with whom Justice Ginsburg joins, concurring.

When it first reviewed the constitutionality of the Child Online Protection Act (COPA), the Court of Appeals held that the statute's use of "contemporary community standards" to identify materials that are "harmful to minors" was a serious, and likely fatal, defect. ... I continue to believe that the Government may not penalize speakers for making available to the general World Wide Web audience that which the least tolerant communities in America deem unfit for their children's consumption.

But COPA's use of community standards is not the statute's only constitutional defect. Today's decision points to another: that, as far as the record reveals, encouraging deployment of user-based controls, such as filtering software, would serve Congress' interest in protecting minors from sexually explicit Internet materials as well or better than attempting to regulate the vast content of the World Wide Web at its source, and at a far less significant cost to First Amendment values.

... [B]ecause implementation of the various adult-verification mechanisms described in the statute provides only an affirmative defense, ... even full compliance with COPA cannot guarantee freedom from prosecution. Speakers who dutifully place their content behind age screens may nevertheless find themselves in court, forced to prove the lawfulness of their speech on pain of criminal conviction....

Criminal prosecutions are, in my view, an inappropriate means to regulate the universe of materials classified as "obscene," ... [E]ven With Justice Breyer's guidance, I find it impossible to identify just how far past the already ill-defined territory of "obscenity" he thinks the statute extends. Attaching criminal sanctions to a mistaken judgment about the contours of the novel and nebulous category of "harmful to minors" speech clearly imposes a heavy burden....

. . .

Justice Scalia, dissenting.

I agree with Justice Breyer's conclusion that the Child Online Protection Act (COPA), 47 U.S.C. § 231, is constitutional. Both the Court and Justice Breyer err, however, in subjecting COPA to strict scrutiny. Nothing in the First Amendment entitles the type of material covered by COPA to that exacting standard of review. ...

There is no doubt that the commercial pornography covered by COPA fits this description. The statute applies only to a person who, "as a regular course of such person's trade or business, with the objective of earning a profit," ... and "with knowledge of the character of the material," § 231(a)(1), communicates material that depicts certain specified sexual acts and that "is designed to appeal to, or is designed to pander to, the prurient interest," ... Since this business could, consistent with the First Amendment, be banned entirely, COPA's lesser restrictions raise no constitutional concern.

Justice Breyer, with whom the Chief Justice and Justice O'Connor join, dissenting.

. . .

... [T]he Court is wrong. I cannot accept its conclusion that Congress could have accomplished its statutory objective—protecting children from commercial pornography on the Internet—in other, less restrictive ways.

I

... [T]he Act, properly interpreted, imposes a burden on protected speech that is no more than modest.

A

The Act's definitions limit the material it regulates to material that does not enjoy First Amendment protection, namely legally obscene material, and very little more. A comparison of this Court's definition of unprotected, "legally obscene," material with the Act's definitions makes this clear. . . .

. . .

B

The Act does not censor the material it covers. Rather, it requires providers of the "harmful to minors" material to restrict minors' access to it by verifying age. They can do so by inserting screens that verify age using a credit card, adult personal identification number, or other similar technology. See § 231(c)(1). In this way, the Act requires creation of an internet screen that minors, but not adults, will find difficult to bypass.

. . .

In addition to the monetary cost, and despite strict requirements that identifying information be kept confidential, . . . the identification requirements inherent in age-screening may lead some users to fear embarrassment. Both monetary costs and potential embarrassment can deter potential viewers and, in that sense, the statute's requirements may restrict access to a site. But this Court has held that in the context of congressional efforts to protect children, restrictions of this kind do not automatically violate the Constitution. And the Court has approved their use. . . .

In sum, the Act at most imposes a modest additional burden on adult access to legally obscene material, perhaps imposing a similar burden on access to some protected borderline obscene material as well.

II

I turn next to the question of "compelling interest," that of protecting minors from exposure to commercial pornography. No one denies that such an interest is "compelling." . . . Rather, the question here is whether the Act, given its restrictions on adult access, significantly advances that interest. In other words, is the game worth the candle?

The majority argues that it is not, because of the existence of "blocking and filtering software." The majority refers to the presence of that software as a "less restrictive alternative." But that is a misnomer—a misnomer that may lead the reader to believe that all we need do is look to see if the blocking and filtering software is less restrictive; and to believe that, because in one sense it is (one can turn off the software), that is the end of the constitutional matter.

But such reasoning has no place here. Conceptually speaking, the presence of filtering software is not an *alternative* legislative approach to the problem of protecting children from exposure to commercial pornography. Rather, it is part of the status quo, *i.e.,* the backdrop against which Congress enacted the present statute. It is always true, by definition, that the status quo is less restrictive than a new regulatory law. It is always less restrictive to do *nothing* than to do *something*. But "doing nothing" does not address the problem Congress sought to address—namely that, despite the availability of filtering software, children were still being exposed to harmful material on the Internet.

Thus, the relevant constitutional question is not the question the Court asks: Would it be less restrictive to do nothing? Of course it would be. Rather, the relevant question posits a comparison of (a) a status quo that includes filtering software with (b) a change in that status quo that adds to it an age-verification screen requirement. Given the existence of filtering software, does the problem Congress identified remain significant? Does the Act help to address it? These are questions about the relation of the Act to the compelling interest. Does the Act, compared to the status quo, significantly advance the ball? . . .

The answers to these intermediate questions are clear: Filtering software, as presently available, does not solve the "child protection" problem. It suffers from four serious inadequacies that prompted Congress to pass legislation instead of relying on its voluntary use. First, its filtering is faulty, allowing some pornographic material to pass through without hindrance. . . . [I]n the absence of words, the software alone cannot distinguish between the most obscene pictorial image and the Venus de Milo. . . .

Second, filtering software costs money. Not every family has the $40 or so necessary to install it.

. . .

Third, filtering software depends upon parents willing to decide where their children will surf the Web and able to enforce that decision. As to millions of American families, that is not a reasonable possibility. More than 28 million school age children have both parents or their sole parent in the work force, at least 5 million children are left alone at home without supervision each week, and many of those children will spend afternoons and evenings with friends who may well have access to computers and more lenient parents. . . .

. . .

American Booksellers Association, Inc. v. Hudnut

771 F.2d 323 (7th Cir.1985).

Before Cudahy and Easterbrook, Circuit Judges, and Swygert, Senior Circuit Judge.

Easterbrook, Circuit Judge.

Indianapolis enacted an ordinance defining "pornography" as a practice that discriminates against women. "Pornography" is to be redressed through the administrative and judicial methods used for other discrimination. The City's definition of "pornography" is considerably different from "obscenity," which the Supreme Court has held is not protected by the First Amendment.

To be "obscene" under Miller v. California, 413 U.S. 15 (1973), "a publication must, taken as a whole, appeal to the prurient interest, must contain patently offensive depictions or descriptions of specified sexual conduct, and on the whole have no serious literary, artistic, political, or scientific value." . . . Both offensiveness and an appeal to something other than "normal, healthy sexual desires" . . . are essential elements of "obscenity."

"Pornography" under the ordinance is "the graphic sexually explicit subordination of women, whether in pictures or in words, that also includes one or more of the following:

(1) Women are presented as sexual objects who enjoy pain or humiliation; or

(2) Women are presented as sexual objects who experience sexual pleasure in being raped; or

(3) Women are presented as sexual objects tied up or cut up or mutilated or bruised or physically hurt, or as dismembered or truncated or fragmented or severed into body parts; or

(4) Women are presented as being penetrated by objects or animals; or

(5) Women are presented in scenarios of degradation, injury, abasement, torture, shown as filthy or inferior, bleeding, bruised, or hurt in a context that makes these conditions sexual; or

(6) Women are presented as sexual objects for domination, conquest, violation, exploitation, possession, or use, or through postures or positions of servility or submission or display." . . .

The statute provides that the "use of men, children, or transsexuals in the place of women in paragraphs (1) through (6) above shall also constitute pornography under this section." The ordinance as passed in April 1984 defined "sexually explicit" to mean actual or simulated intercourse or the uncovered exhibition of the genitals, buttocks or anus. An amendment in June 1984 deleted this provision, leaving the term undefined.

The Indianapolis ordinance does not refer to the prurient interest, to offensiveness, or to the standards of the community. It demands attention to particular depictions, not to the work judged as a whole. It is irrelevant under the ordinance whether the work has literary, artistic, political, or scientific value. The City and many amici point to these omissions as virtues. They maintain that pornography influences attitudes, and the statute is a way to alter the socialization of men and women rather than to vindicate community standards of offensiveness. And as one of the principal drafters of the ordinance has asserted, "if a woman is subjected, why should it matter that the work has other value?" Catharine A. MacKinnon, Pornography, Civil Rights, and Speech, 20 Harv.Civ.Rts.—Civ.Lib.L.Rev. 1, 21 (1985).

Civil rights groups and feminists have entered this case as amici on both sides. Those supporting the ordinance say that it will play an important role in reducing the tendency of men to view women as sexual objects, a tendency that leads to both unacceptable attitudes and discrimination in the workplace and violence away from it. Those opposing the ordinance point out that much radical feminist literature is explicit and depicts women in ways forbidden by the ordinance and that the ordinance would reopen old battles. It is unclear how Indianapolis would treat works from James Joyce's *Ulysses* to Homer's *Iliad;* both depict women as submissive objects for conquest and domination.

We do not try to balance the arguments for and against an ordinance such as this. The ordinance discriminates on the ground of the content of the speech. Speech treating women in the approved way—in sexual encounters "premised on equality" (MacKinnon, supra, at 22)—is lawful no matter how sexually explicit. Speech treating women in the disapproved way—as submissive in matters sexual or as enjoying humiliation—is unlawful no matter how significant the literary, artistic, or political qualities of the work taken as a whole. The state may not ordain preferred viewpoints in this way. The Constitution forbids the state to declare one perspective right and silence opponents.

I

The ordinance contains four prohibitions. People may not "traffic" in pornography, "coerce" others into performing in pornographic works, or "force" pornography on anyone. Anyone injured by someone who has seen or read pornography has a right of action against the maker or seller.

Trafficking is defined in § 16–3(g)(4) as the "production, sale, exhibition, or distribution of pornography." The offense excludes exhibition in a public or educational library, but a "special display" in a library may be sex discrimination. Section 16–3(g)(4)(C) provides that the trafficking paragraph "shall not be construed to make isolated passages or isolated parts actionable."

"Coercion into pornographic performance" is defined in § 16–3(g)(5) as "[c]oercing, intimidating or fraudulently inducing any person . . . into performing for pornography. . . ." The ordinance specifies that proof of any of the following "shall not constitute a defense: I. That the person is a woman; . . . VI. That the person has previously posed for sexually explicit pictures . . . with anyone . . . ; . . . VIII. That the person actually consented to a use of the performance that is changed into pornography; . . . IX. That the person knew that the purpose of the acts or events in question was to make pornography; . . . XI. That the person signed a contract, or made statements affirming a willingness to cooperate in the production of pornography; XII. That no physical force, threats, or weapons were used in the making of the pornography; or XIII. That the person was paid or otherwise compensated."

"Forcing pornography on a person," according to § 16–3(g)(5), is the "forcing of pornography on any woman, man, child, or transsexual in any place of employment, in education, in a home, or in any public place." The statute does not define forcing, but one of its authors states that the definition reaches pornography shown to medical students as part of their education or given to language students for translation. MacKinnon, supra, at 40–41.

Section 16–3(g)(7) defines as a prohibited practice the "assault, physical attack, or injury of any woman, man, child, or transsexual in a way that is directly caused by specific pornography."

For purposes of all four offenses, it is generally "not . . . a defense that the respondent did not know or intend that the materials were pornography. . . ." Section 16–3(g)(8). But the ordinance provides that damages are unavailable in trafficking cases unless the complainant proves "that the respondent knew or had reason to know that the materials were pornography." It is a complete defense to a trafficking case that all of the materials in question were pornography only by virtue of category (6) of the definition of pornography. In cases of assault caused by pornography, those who seek damages from "a seller, exhibitor or distributor" must show that the defendant knew or had reason to know of the material's status as pornography. By implication, those who seek damages from an author need not show this.

A woman aggrieved by trafficking in pornography may file a complaint "as a woman acting against the subordination of women" with the office of equal opportunity. Section 16–17(b). A man, child, or transsexual also may protest trafficking "but must prove injury in the same way that a woman is injured. . . ." Ibid. Subsection (a) also provides, however, that "any person claiming to be aggrieved" by trafficking, coercion, forcing, or assault may complain against the "perpetrators." We need not decide whether § 16–17(b) qualifies the right of action in § 16–17(a).

. . .

The district court held the ordinance unconstitutional. . . .

II

The plaintiffs are a congeries of distributors and readers of books, magazines, and films. The American Booksellers Association comprises about 5,200 bookstores and chains. The Association for American Publishers includes most of the country's publishers. Video Shack, Inc., sells and rents video cassettes in Indianapolis. Kelly Bentley, a resident of Indianapolis, reads books and watches films. There are many more plaintiffs. Collectively the plaintiffs (or their members, whose interest they represent) make, sell, or read just about every kind of material that could be affected by the ordinance, from hard-core films to W.B. Yeats's poem "Leda and the Swan" (from the myth of Zeus in the form of a swan impregnating an apparently subordinate Leda), to the collected works of James Joyce, D.H. Lawrence, and John Cleland.

. . .

III

"If there is any fixed star in our constitutional constellation, it is that no official, high or petty, can prescribe what shall be orthodox in politics, nationalism, religion, or other matters of opinion or force citizens to confess by word or act their faith therein." West Virginia State Board of Education v. Barnette, 319 U.S. 624, 642 (1943). Under the First Amendment the government must leave to the people the evaluation of ideas. Bald or subtle, an idea is as powerful as the audience allows it to be. A belief may be pernicious—the beliefs of Nazis led to the death of millions, those of the Klan to the repression of millions. A pernicious belief may prevail. Totalitarian governments today rule much of the planet, practicing suppression of billions and spreading dogma that may enslave others. One of the things that separates our society from theirs is our absolute right to propagate opinions that the government finds wrong or even hateful.

. . .

Under the ordinance graphic sexually explicit speech is "pornography" or not depending on the perspective the author adopts. Speech that "subordinates" women and also, for example, presents women as enjoying pain, humiliation, or rape, or even simply presents women in "positions of servility or submission or display" is forbidden, no matter how great the literary or political value of the work taken as a whole. Speech that portrays women in positions of equality is lawful, no matter how graphic the sexual content. This is thought control. It establishes an "approved" view of women, of how they may react to sexual encounters, of how the sexes may relate to each other. Those who espouse the approved view may use sexual images; those who do not, may not.

Indianapolis justifies the ordinance on the ground that pornography affects thoughts. Men who see women depicted as subordinate are more likely to treat them so. Pornography is an aspect of dominance. It does not persuade people so much as change them. It works by socializing, by establishing the expected and the permissible. In this view pornography is not an idea; pornography is the injury. There is much to this perspective. Beliefs are also facts. People often act in accordance with the images and patterns they find around them. People raised in a religion tend to accept the tenets of that religion, often without independent examination. People taught from birth that black people are fit only for slavery rarely rebelled against that creed; beliefs coupled with the self-interest of the masters established a social structure that inflicted great harm while enduring for centuries. Words and images act at the level of the subconscious before they persuade at the level of the conscious. Even the truth has little chance unless a statement fits within the framework of beliefs that may never have been subjected to rational study.

Therefore we accept the premises of this legislation. Depictions of subordination tend to perpetuate subordination. The subordinate status of women in turn leads to affront and lower pay at work, insult and injury at home, battery and rape on the streets. In the language of the legislature, "[p]ornography is central in creating and maintaining sex as a basis of discrimination. Pornography is a systematic practice of exploitation and subordination based on sex which differentially harms women. The bigotry and contempt it produces, with the acts of aggression it fosters, harm women's opportunities for equality and rights [of all kinds]." Indianapolis Code § 16–1(a)(2).

Yet this simply demonstrates the power of pornography as speech. All of these unhappy effects depend on mental intermediation. Pornography affects how people see the world, their fellows, and social relations. If pornography is what pornography does, so is other speech. . . . The Alien and Sedition Acts passed during the administration of John Adams rested on a sincerely held belief that disrespect for the government leads to social collapse and revolution—a belief with support in the history of many nations. Most governments of the world act on this empirical regularity, suppressing critical speech. In the United States, however, the strength of the support for this belief is irrelevant. . . .

Racial bigotry, anti-semitism, violence on television, reporters' biases—these and many more influence the culture and shape our socialization. None is directly answerable by more speech, unless that speech too finds its place in the popular culture. Yet all is protected as speech, however insidious. Any other answer leaves the government in control of all of the institutions of culture, the great censor and director of which thoughts are good for us.

Sexual responses often are unthinking responses, and the association of sexual arousal with the subordination of women therefore may have a substantial effect. But almost all cultural stimuli provoke unconscious responses. Religious ceremonies condition their participants. Teachers convey messages by selecting what not to cover; the implicit message about what is off limits or unthinkable may be more powerful than the messages for which they present rational argument. Television scripts contain unarticulated assumptions. People may be conditioned in subtle ways. If the fact that speech plays a role in a process of conditioning were enough to permit governmental regulation, that would be the end of freedom of speech.

It is possible to interpret the claim that the pornography is the harm in a different way. Indianapolis emphasizes the injury that models in pornographic films and pictures may suffer. The record contains materials depicting sexual torture, penetration of women by red-hot irons and the like. These concerns have nothing to do with written materials subject to the statute, and physical injury can occur with or without the "subordination" of women. As we discuss in Part IV, a state may make injury in the course of producing a film unlawful independent of the viewpoint expressed in the film.

The more immediate point, however, is that the image of pain is not necessarily pain. In *Body Double,* a suspense film directed by Brian DePalma, a woman who has disrobed and presented a sexually explicit display is murdered by an intruder with a drill. The drill runs through the woman's body. The film is sexually explicit and a murder occurs—yet no one believes that the actress suffered pain or died. In *Barbarella* a character played by Jane Fonda is at times displayed in sexually explicit ways and at times shown "bleeding, bruised, [and] hurt in a context that makes these conditions sexual"—and again no one believes that Fonda was actually tortured to make the film. In *Carnal Knowledge* a woman grovels to please the sexual whims of a character played by Jack Nicholson; no one believes that there was a real sexual submission, and the Supreme Court held the film protected by the First Amendment. Jenkins v. Georgia, 418 U.S. 153 (1974). And this works both ways. The description of women's sexual domination of men in *Lysistrata* was not real dominance.

Depictions may affect slavery, war, or sexual roles, but a book about slavery is not itself slavery, or a book about death by poison a murder.

Much of Indianapolis's argument rests on the belief that when speech is "unanswerable," and the metaphor that there is a "marketplace of ideas" does not apply, the First Amendment does not apply either. The metaphor is honored; Milton's *Aeropagitica* and John Stewart Mill's *On Liberty* defend freedom of speech on the ground that the truth will prevail, and many of the most important cases under the First Amendment recite this position. The Framers undoubtedly believed it. As a general matter it is true. But the Constitution does not make the dominance of truth a necessary condition of freedom of speech. To say that it does would be to confuse an outcome of free speech with a necessary condition for the application of the amendment.

A power to limit speech on the ground that truth has not yet prevailed and is not likely to prevail implies the power to declare truth. . . . If the government may declare the truth, why wait for the failure of speech? Under the First Amendment, however, . . . the government may not restrict speech on the ground that in a free exchange truth is not yet dominant.

. . .

We come, finally, to the argument that pornography is "low value" speech, that it is enough like obscenity that Indianapolis may prohibit it. Some cases hold that speech far removed from politics and other subjects at the core of the Framers' concerns may be subjected to special regulation. E.g., FCC v. Pacifica Foundation, 438 U.S. 726 (1978); Young v. American Mini Theatres, Inc., 427 U.S. 50, 67–70 (1976) (plurality opinion); Chaplinsky v. New Hampshire, 315 U.S. 568, 571–72 (1942). These cases do not sustain statutes that select among viewpoints, however. In *Pacifica* the FCC sought to keep vile language off the air during certain times. The Court held that it may; but the Court would not have sustained a regulation prohibiting scatological descriptions of Republicans but not scatological descriptions of Democrats, or any other form of selection among viewpoints. . . .

At all events, "pornography" is not low value speech within the meaning of these cases. Indianapolis seeks to prohibit certain speech because it believes this speech influences social relations and politics on a grand scale, that it controls attitudes at home and in the legislature. This precludes a characterization of the speech as low value. True, pornography and obscenity have sex in common. But Indianapolis left out of its definition any reference to literary, artistic, political, or scientific value. The ordinance applies to graphic sexually explicit subordination in works great and small.[3] The Court sometimes balances the value of speech against the costs of its restriction, but it does this by category of speech and not by the content of particular works. . . . Indianapolis has created an approved point of view and so loses the support of these cases.

---

3. Indianapolis briefly argues that Beauharnais v. Illinois, 343 U.S. 250 (1952), which allowed a state to penalize "group libel," supports the ordinance. In Collin v. Smith, 578 F.2d at 1205, we concluded that cases such as *New York Times v. Sullivan* had so washed away the foundations of *Beauharnais* that it could not be considered authoritative. If we are wrong in this, however, the case still does not support the ordinance. It is not clear that depicting women as subordinate in sexually explicit ways, even combined with a depiction of pleasure in rape, would fit within the definition of a group libel. The well received film Swept Away used explicit sex, plus taking pleasure in rape, to make a political statement, not to defame. Work must be an insult or slur for its own sake to come within the ambit of *Beauharnais,* and a work need not be scurrilous at all to be "pornography" under the ordinance.

Any rationale we could imagine in support of this ordinance could not be limited to sex discrimination. Free speech has been on balance an ally of those seeking change. Governments that want stasis start by restricting speech. Culture is a powerful force of continuity; Indianapolis paints pornography as part of the culture of power. Change in any complex system ultimately depends on the ability of outsiders to challenge accepted views and the reigning institutions. Without a strong guarantee of freedom of speech, there is no effective right to challenge what is.

IV

The definition of "pornography" is unconstitutional. No construction or excision of particular terms could save it. The offense of trafficking in pornography necessarily falls with the definition....

... The district court came to the same conclusion. Its judgment is therefore

Affirmed.[a]

C. CONTROL OF "FIGHTING WORDS" AND OFFENSIVE SPEECH

CANTWELL v. CONNECTICUT, 310 U.S. 296 (1940). Cantwell, a member of the Jehovah's Witnesses, was engaged in proselytizing in the streets of New Haven. He was convicted of a common law breach of the peace based on a showing that he stopped two men in the street, asked, and received, permission to play an anti–Catholic phonograph record. Both listeners were incensed by the contents of the record and were tempted to strike Cantwell unless he went away. On being told to be on his way he left their presence. The court reversed his conviction. Justice Roberts, speaking for the court, said, in part:

"The offense known as breach of the peace embraces a great variety of conduct destroying or menacing public order and tranquility. It includes not only violent acts but acts and words likely to produce violence in others. No one would have the hardihood to suggest that the principle of freedom of speech sanctions incitement to riot or that religious liberty connotes the privilege to exhort others to physical attack upon those belonging to another sect. When clear and present danger of riot, disorder, interference with traffic upon the public streets, or other immediate threat to public safety, peace, or order, appears, the power of the state to prevent or punish is obvious. Equally obvious is it that a state may not unduly suppress free communication of views, religious or other, under the guise of conserving desirable conditions. Here we have a situation analogous to a conviction under a statute sweeping in a great variety of conduct under a general and indefinite characterization, and leaving to the executive and judicial branches too wide a discretion in its application.

". . .

"We find in the instant case no assault or threatening of bodily harm, no truculent bearing, no intentional discourtesy, no personal abuse. On the contrary, we find only an effort to persuade a willing listener to buy a book or to contribute money in the interest of what Cantwell, however misguided others may think him, conceived to be true religion.

". . .

a. A concurrence by Judge Swygert is omitted. The decision was summarily affirmed by the Supreme Court without argument or opinion. (Chief Justice Burger, and Justices Rehnquist and O'Connor dissented, stating that the case should be set for argument.) 475 U.S. 1001 (1986).

"Although the contents of the record not unnaturally aroused animosity, we think that, in the absence of a statute narrowly drawn to define and punish specific conduct as constituting a clear and present danger to a substantial interest of the State, the petitioner's communication, considered in the light of the constitutional guarantees, raised no such clear and present menace to public peace and order as to render him liable to conviction of the common law offense in question."

CHAPLINSKY v. NEW HAMPSHIRE, 315 U.S. 568 (1942). Defendant, a Jehovah's Witness, got into an altercation on a public sidewalk with the city marshal of Rochester, New Hampshire, and allegedly told the officer: "you are a God damned racketeer" and a "damned fascist." Defendant was convicted under a statute forbidding a person to address "any offensive, derisive or annoying word to any other person who is lawfully in any street or other public place." The statute was construed by the state court to ban only "such words, as ordinary men know, are likely to cause a fight," thus to prohibit "the face–to–face words plainly likely to cause a breach of the peace by the addressee." Justice Murphy's opinion for the Court stated that fighting words—"those which by their very utterance inflict injury or tend to incite an immediate breach of the peace"—were not protected by the Constitution. A unanimous Court sustained the conviction.

Cohen v. California

403 U.S. 15, 91 S.Ct. 1780, 29 L.Ed.2d 284 (1971).

[Defendant was convicted of violating a California statute that prohibited "maliciously and willfully disturb[ing] the peace or quiet of any neighborhood or person" by "offensive conduct." In a Los Angeles courthouse corridor he had worn a jacket bearing the plainly visible words "Fuck the Draft." Women and children were present in the corridor. He testified that he wore the jacket as a means of informing the public of the depth of his feelings against the Vietnam war and the draft. In affirming, the California Court of Appeals held that "offensive conduct" means "behavior which has a tendency to provoke *others* to acts of violence or to in turn disturb the peace"; it was "certainly reasonably foreseeable" that defendant's conduct might cause others to commit an act of violence against defendant or attempt to forcibly remove his jacket.]

Mr. Justice Harlan delivered the opinion of the Court.

. . .

... [A]s it comes to us, this case cannot be said to fall within those relatively few categories of instances where prior decisions have established the power of government to deal more comprehensively with certain forms of individual expression simply upon a showing that such a form was employed. This is not, for example, an obscenity case. Whatever else may be necessary to give rise to the States' broader power to prohibit obscene expression, such expression must be, in some significant way, erotic. ... It cannot plausibly be maintained that this vulgar allusion to the Selective Service System would conjure up such psychic stimulation in anyone likely to be confronted with Cohen's crudely defaced jacket.

This Court has also held that the States are free to ban the simple use, without a demonstration of additional justifying circumstances, of so-called "fighting words," those personally abusive epithets which, when addressed to the ordinary citizen, are, as a matter of common knowledge, inherently likely to provoke violent reaction. Chaplinsky v. New Hampshire.... While the four-letter word displayed by Cohen in relation to the draft is not uncommonly employed in a personally provocative fashion, in this instance it was clearly not "directed to the person of the hearer." Cantwell v. Connecticut ... No individual actually or likely to be present could reasonably have regarded the words on appellant's jacket as a direct personal insult. Nor do we have here an instance of the exercise of the State's police power to prevent a speaker from intentionally provoking a given group to hostile reaction. Cf. Feiner v. New York, 340 U.S. 315 (1951); Terminiello v. Chicago, 337 U.S. 1 (1949). There is ... no showing that anyone who saw Cohen was in fact violently aroused or that appellant intended such a result.

[handwritten margin note: no showing that jacket actually incited violence]

Finally, in arguments before this Court much has been made of the claim that Cohen's distasteful mode of expression was thrust upon unwilling or unsuspecting viewers, and that the State might therefore legitimately act as it did in order to protect the sensitive from otherwise unavoidable exposure to appellant's crude form of protest. Of course, the mere presumed presence of unwitting listeners or viewers does not serve automatically to justify curtailing all speech capable of giving offense. ... While this Court has recognized that government may properly act in many situations to prohibit intrusion into the privacy of the home of unwelcome views and ideas which cannot be totally banned from the public dialogue, e.g., Rowan v. Post Office Dept., 397 U.S. 728 (1970), we have at the same time consistently stressed that "we are often 'captives' outside the sanctuary of the home and subject to objectionable speech." Id., at 738. The ability of government, consonant with the Constitution, to shut off discourse solely to protect others from hearing it is, in other words, dependent upon a showing that substantial privacy interests are being invaded in an essentially intolerable manner. Any broader view of this authority would effectively empower a majority to silence dissidents simply as a matter of personal predilections.

[handwritten margin note: not enough~]

In this regard, persons confronted with Cohen's jacket were in a quite different posture than, say, those subjected to the raucous emissions of sound trucks blaring outside their residences. Those in the Los Angeles courthouse could effectively avoid further bombardment of their sensibilities simply by averting their eyes. And while it may be that one has a more substantial claim to a recognizable privacy interest when walking through a courthouse corridor than, for example, strolling through Central Park, surely it is nothing like the interest in being free from unwanted expression in the confines of one's own home.... Given the subtlety and complexity of the factors involved, if Cohen's "speech" was otherwise entitled to constitutional protection, we do not think the fact that some unwilling "listeners" in a public building may have been briefly exposed to it can serve to justify this breach of the peace conviction where, as here, there was no evidence that persons powerless to avoid appellant's conduct did in fact object to it, and where that portion of the statute upon which Cohen's conviction rests evinces no concern, either on its face or as construed by the California courts, with the special plight of the captive auditor, but, instead, indiscriminately sweeps within its prohibitions all "offensive conduct" that disturbs "any neighborhood or person."

Against this background, the issue flushed by this case stands out in bold relief. It is whether California can excise, as "offensive conduct," one particular scurrilous epithet from the public discourse, either upon the theory of the court below that its use is inherently likely to cause violent reaction or upon a more general assertion that the States, acting as guardians of public morality, may properly remove this offensive word from the public vocabulary.

The rationale of the California court is plainly untenable.... We have been shown no evidence that substantial numbers of citizens are standing ready to strike out physically at whoever may assault their sensibilities with execrations like that uttered by Cohen....

Admittedly, it is not so obvious that the First and Fourteenth Amendments must be taken to disable the States from punishing public utterance of this unseemly expletive in order to maintain what they regard as a suitable level of discourse within the body politic. We think, however, that examination and reflection will reveal the shortcomings of a contrary viewpoint.

. . .

Against this perception of the constitutional policies involved, we discern certain more particularized considerations that peculiarly call for reversal of this conviction. First, the principle contended for by the State seems inherently boundless. How is one to distinguish this from any other offensive word? ... For, while the particular four-letter word being litigated here is perhaps more distasteful than most others of its genre, it is nevertheless often true that one man's vulgarity is another's lyric. Indeed, we think it is largely because governmental officials cannot make principled distinctions in this area that the Constitution leaves matters of taste and style so largely to the individual.

Additionally, we cannot overlook the fact, because it is well illustrated by the episode involved here, that much linguistic expression serves a dual communicative function: it conveys not only ideas capable of relatively precise, detached explication, but otherwise inexpressible emotions as well. In fact, words are often chosen as much for their emotive as their cognitive force....

Finally, and in the same vein, we cannot indulge the facile assumption that one can forbid particular words without also running a substantial risk of suppressing ideas in the process. Indeed, governments might soon seize upon the censorship of particular words as a convenient guise for banning the expression of unpopular views....

It is, in sum, our judgment that, absent a more particularized and compelling reason for its actions, the State may not, consistently with the First and Fourteenth Amendments, make the simple public display here involved of this single four-letter expletive a criminal offense....

Reversed.[a]

Mr. Justice Blackmun, with whom The Chief Justice and Mr. Justice Black join.

I dissent....

Cohen's absurd and immature antic, in my view, was mainly conduct and little speech....

City of Houston, Texas v. Hill

482 U.S. 451, 107 S.Ct. 2502, 96 L.Ed.2d 398 (1987).

Justice Brennan delivered the opinion of the Court.

This case presents the question whether a municipal ordinance that makes it unlawful to interrupt a police officer in the performance of his or her duties is unconstitutionally overbroad under the First Amendment.

---

a. See Cohen, *A Look Back at* Cohen v. California, 34 U.C.L.A.L.Rev. 1595 (1987).

I

Appellee Raymond Wayne Hill is a lifelong resident of Houston, Texas. At the time this lawsuit began, he worked as a paralegal and as executive director of the Houston Human Rights League. A member of the board of the Gay Political Caucus, which he helped found in 1975, Hill was also affiliated with a Houston radio station, and had carried city and county press passes since 1975. He lived in Montrose, a "diverse and eclectic neighborhood" that is the center of gay political and social life in Houston.

The incident that sparked this lawsuit occurred in the Montrose area ... Hill observed a friend, Charles Hill, intentionally stopping traffic on a busy street, evidently to enable a vehicle to enter traffic. Two Houston police officers, one of whom was named Kelley, approached Charles and began speaking with him.... Hill began shouting at the officers "in an admitted attempt to divert Kelley's attention from Charles Hill." Hill first shouted: "Why don't you pick on somebody your own size?" After Officer Kelley responded: "Are you interrupting me in my official capacity as a Houston police officer?" Hill then shouted: "Yes, why don't you pick on somebody my size?" Hill was arrested under Houston Code of Ordinances section 34–11(a) for "wilfully or intentionally interrupting a city policeman ... by verbal challenge during an investigation." Charles Hill was not arrested. Hill was then acquitted after a nonjury trial in Municipal Court.

Code of Ordinances, City of Houston, Texas, § 34–11(a) (1984) reads:

"Sec. 34–11. Assaulting or interfering with policemen.

"(a) It shall be unlawful for any person to assault, strike or in any manner oppose, molest, abuse or interrupt any policeman in the execution of his duty, or any person summoned to aid in making an arrest."

Following his acquittal in the Charles Hill incident, Hill brought the suit in the Federal District Court for the Southern District of Texas seeking (1) a declaratory judgment that § 34–11(a) was unconstitutional both on its face and as it had been applied to him ...

At trial, Hill introduced records provided by the City regarding both the frequency with which arrests had been made for violation of the ordinance and the type of conduct with which those arrested had been charged. He also introduced evidence and testimony concerning the arrests of several reporters under the ordinance. Finally, Hill introduced evidence regarding his own experience with the ordinance, under which he has been arrested four times since 1975, but never convicted.

The District Court held that Hill's evidence did not demonstrate that the ordinance had been unconstitutionally applied....

... [T]he Court of Appeals, by a vote of 8–7, [reversed]....

. . .

... We ... affirm.

II

. . .

The City's principal argument is that the ordinance does not inhibit the exposition of ideas, and that it bans "core criminal conduct" not protected by the First Amendment. In its view, the application of the ordinance to Hill illustrates that the police employ it only to prohibit such conduct, and not "as a subterfuge to control or dissuade free expression." Since the ordinance is "content-neutral," and since there is no evidence that the City has applied the ordinance to chill particular speakers or ideas, the City concludes that the ordinance is not substantially overbroad.

We disagree with the city's characterization for several reasons. First, the enforceable portion of the ordinance deals not with core criminal conduct, but with speech. As the city has conceded, the language in the ordinance making it unlawful for any person to "assault" or "strike" a police officer is preempted by the Texas Penal Code.... Accordingly, the enforceable portion of the ordinance makes it "unlawful for any person to ... in any manner oppose, molest, abuse or interrupt any policeman in the execution of his duty," and thereby prohibits verbal interruptions of police officers.

Second, contrary to the city's contention, the First Amendment protects a significant amount of verbal criticism and challenge directed at police officers. "Speech is often provocative and challenging.... [But it] is nevertheless protected against censorship or punishment, unless shown likely to produce a clear and present danger of a serious substantive evil that rises far above public inconvenience, annoyance, or unrest." Terminiello v. Chicago, 337 U.S. 1, 4 (1949). In *Lewis v. City of New Orleans,* ... a municipal ordinance ... made it a crime " 'for any person wantonly to curse or revile or to use obscene or opprobrious language toward or with reference to any member of the city police while in the actual performance of his duty.' " ... We ... invalidated the ordinance as facially overbroad.... Moreover, in a concurring opinion in *Lewis,* Justice Powell suggested that even the "fighting words" exception recognized in Chaplinsky v. New Hampshire ... might require a narrower application in cases involving words addressed to a police officer, because "a properly trained officer may reasonably be expected to 'exercise a higher degree of restraint' than the average citizen, and thus be less likely to respond belligerently to 'fighting words.' " ...

The Houston ordinance is much more sweeping than the municipal ordinance struck down in *Lewis.* It is not limited to fighting words nor even to obscene or opprobrious language, but prohibits speech that "in any manner ... interrupt[s]" an officer. The Constitution does not allow such speech to be made a crime. The freedom of individuals verbally to oppose or challenge police action without thereby risking arrest is one of the principal characteristics by which we distinguish a free nation from a police state.

The city argues, however, that even if the ordinance encompasses some protected speech, its sweeping nature is both inevitable and essential to maintain public order. The City recalls this Court's observation in Smith v. Goguen, 415 U.S. 566, 581 (1974):

> "There are areas of human conduct where, by the nature of the problems presented, legislatures simply cannot establish standards with great precision. Control of the broad range of disorderly conduct that may inhibit a policeman in the performance of his official duties may be one such area requiring as it does an on-the-spot assessment of the need to keep order."

The city further suggests that its ordinance is comparable to the disorderly conduct statute upheld against a facial challenge in Colten v. Kentucky, 407 U.S. 104 (1972).

This Houston ordinance, however, is not narrowly tailored to prohibit only disorderly conduct or fighting words, and in no way resembles the law upheld in *Colten.* Although we appreciate the difficulties of drafting precise laws, we have repeatedly invalidated laws that provide the police with unfettered discretion to arrest individuals for words or conduct that annoy or offend them.... In *Lewis*, Justice Powell elaborated the basis for our concern with such sweeping, dragnet laws:

"This ordinance, as construed by the Louisiana Supreme Court, confers on police a virtually unrestrained power to arrest and charge persons with a violation.... The present type of ordinance tends to be invoked only where there is no other valid basis for arresting an objectionable or suspicious person. The opportunity for abuse, especially where a statute has received a virtually open-ended interpretation, is self-evident."

. . .

Houston's ordinance criminalizes a substantial amount of constitutionally protected speech, and accords the police unconstitutional discretion in enforcement. The ordinance's plain language is admittedly violated scores of times daily, yet only some individuals—those chosen by the police in their unguided discretion—are arrested.... We conclude that the ordinance is substantially overbroad, and that the Court of Appeals did not err in holding it facially invalid.

. . .

IV

Today's decision reflects the constitutional requirement that, in the face of verbal challenges to police action, officers and municipalities must respond with restraint. We are mindful that the preservation of liberty depends in part upon the maintenance of social order.... But the First Amendment recognizes, wisely we think, that a certain amount of expressive disorder not only is inevitable in a society committed to individual freedom, but must itself be protected if that freedom would survive. We therefore affirm the judgment of the Court of Appeals.

It is so ordered.[a]

Justice Blackmun, concurring.

I join the Court's opinion and its judgment except that I do not agree with any implication—if one exists—that Gooding v. Wilson, 405 U.S. 518 (1972), and Lewis v. City of New Orleans, 415 U.S. 130 (1974), are good law in the context of their facts, or that they lend any real support to the judgment under review in this case....

Justice Powell, with whom Justice O'Connor joins, and with whom The Chief Justice joins as to Parts I and II, and Justice Scalia joins as to Parts II and III, concurring in the judgment in part and dissenting in part.

... In my view, the Court should not have reached the merits of the constitutional claims, but instead should have certified a question to the Texas Court of Criminal Appeals.... Finally, although I agree that the ordinance as interpreted by the Court violates the Fourteenth Amendment, I write separately because I cannot join the Court's reasoning.

. . .

III

I agree with the Court's conclusion that the ordinance violates the Fourteenth Amendment, but do not join the Court's reasoning.

---

a. A concurring statement by Justice Scalia is omitted.

A

... Lewis v. City of New Orleans, 415 U.S. 130 (1974), is clearly distinguishable.... On its face, the New Orleans ordinance criminalizes only the use of language.... By contrast, the ordinance presented in this case could be applied to activity that involves no element of speech or communication. For example, the ordinance evidently would punish individuals who—without saying a single word—obstructed an officer's access to the scene of an ongoing public disturbance, or indeed the scene of a crime. Accordingly, I cannot agree with the Court that this ordinance punishes only speech.

... I have no doubt that a municipality constitutionally may punish an individual who chooses to stand near a police officer and persistently attempt to engage the officer in conversation while the officer is directing traffic at a busy intersection. Similarly, an individual, by contentious and abusive speech, could interrupt an officer's investigation of possible criminal conduct. A person observing an officer pursuing a person suspected of a felony could run beside him in a public street shouting at the officer. Similar tactics could interrupt a policeman lawfully attempting to interrogate persons believed to be witnesses to a crime.

. . .

B

Despite the concerns expressed above, I nevertheless agree that the ambiguous terms of this ordinance "confe[r] on police a virtually unrestrained power to arrest and charge persons with a violation.... The record contains a sampling of complaints filed under the ordinance in 1981 and 1982. People have been charged with such crimes as "Failure to remain silent and stationary," "Remaining," "Refusing to remain silent," and "Talking." ... Although some of these incidents may have involved unprotected conduct, the vagueness of these charges suggests that, with respect to this ordinance, Houston officials have not been acting with proper sensitivity to the constitutional rights of their citizens. ... Accordingly, I agree with the Court that the Houston ordinance is unconstitutional.

... In view of the difficulty of drafting precise language that never restrains speech and yet serves the public interest, the attempts of States and municipalities to draft laws of this type should be accorded some leeway. ... [I]t should be possible for the present ordinance to be reframed in a way that would limit the present broad discretion of officers and at the same time protect substantially the city's legitimate interests. For example, the ordinance could make clear that it applies to speech only if the purpose of the speech were to interfere with the performance by a police officer of his lawful duties. ...

. . .

Chief Justice Rehnquist, dissenting.

I join Parts I and II of Justice Powell's opinion concurring in the judgment in part and dissenting in part. I do not agree, however, that the Houston ordinance, in the absence of an authoritative construction by the Texas courts, is unconstitutional....

Virginia v. Black

538 U.S. 343, 123 S.Ct. 1536, 155 L.Ed.2d 535 (2003).

Justice O'Connor announced the judgment of the Court and delivered the opinion of the Court with respect to Parts I, II, and III, and

an opinion with respect to Parts IV and V, in which the Chief Justice, Justice Stevens, and Justice Breyer join.

In this case we consider whether the Commonwealth of Virginia's statute banning cross burning with "an intent to intimidate a person or group of persons" violates the First Amendment. Va.Code Ann. § 18.2–423 (1996). We conclude that while a State, consistent with the First Amendment, may ban cross burning carried out with the intent to intimidate, the provision in the Virginia statute treating any cross burning as prima facie evidence of intent to intimidate renders the statute unconstitutional in its current form.

I

Respondents Barry Black, Richard Elliott, and Jonathan O'Mara were convicted separately of violating Virginia's cross-burning statute, § 18.2–423. That statute provides:

> "It shall be unlawful for any person or persons, with the intent of intimidating any person or group of persons, to burn, or cause to be burned, a cross on the property of another, a highway or other public place. Any person who shall violate any provision of this section shall be guilty of a Class 6 felony.

> "Any such burning of a cross shall be prima facie evidence of an intent to intimidate a person or group of persons."

On August 22, 1998, Barry Black led a Ku Klux Klan rally in Carroll County, Virginia. Twenty-five to thirty people attended this gathering, which occurred on private property with the permission of the owner, who was in attendance. The property was located on an open field just off Brushy Fork Road (State Highway 690) in Cana, Virginia.

When the sheriff of Carroll County learned that a Klan rally was occurring in his county, he went to observe it from the side of the road. During the approximately one hour that the sheriff was present, about 40 to 50 cars passed the site, a "few" of which stopped to ask the sheriff what was happening on the property. Eight to ten houses were located in the vicinity of the rally. Rebecca Sechrist ... "sat and watched to see wha[t][was] going on" from the lawn of her in-laws' house. She looked on as the Klan prepared for the gathering and subsequently conducted the rally itself. During the rally, Sechrist heard Klan members speak about "what they were" and "what they believed in." The speakers "talked real bad about the blacks and the Mexicans." One speaker told the assembled gathering that "he would love to take a .30/.30 and just random[ly] shoot the blacks." The speakers also talked about "President Clinton and Hillary Clinton," and about how their tax money "goes to ... the black people." Sechrist testified that this language made her "very ... scared."

At the conclusion of the rally, the crowd circled around a 25–to 30–foot cross. The cross was between 300 and 350 yards away from the road. According to the sheriff, the cross "then all of a sudden ... went up in a flame." As the cross burned, the Klan played Amazing Grace over the loudspeakers. Sechrist stated that the cross burning made her feel "awful" and "terrible."

... The sheriff ... entered the rally, and asked "who was responsible for burning the cross." ... Black responded, "I guess I am because I'm the head of the rally." ...

Black was charged with burning a cross with the intent of intimidating a person or group of persons, in violation of § 18.2–423. At his trial, the jury was instructed that "intent to intimidate means the motivation to intentionally put a person or a group of persons in fear of bodily harm. Such fear must arise from the willful conduct of the accused rather than from some mere temperamental timidity of the victim." The trial court also instructed the jury that "the burning of a cross by itself is sufficient evidence from which you may infer the required intent." . . . The Court of Appeals of Virginia affirmed Black's conviction.

On May 2, 1998, respondents Richard Elliott and Jonathan O'Mara, as well as a third individual, attempted to burn a cross on the yard of James Jubilee. Jubilee, an African–American, was Elliott's next-door neighbor in Virginia Beach, Virginia. Four months prior to the incident, Jubilee and his family had moved from California to Virginia Beach. Before the cross burning, Jubilee spoke to Elliott's mother to inquire about shots being fired from behind the Elliott home. Elliott's mother explained to Jubilee that her son shot firearms as a hobby, and that he used the backyard as a firing range.

On the night of May 2, respondents drove a truck onto Jubilee's property, planted a cross, and set it on fire. Their apparent motive was to "get back" at Jubilee for complaining about the shooting in the backyard. Respondents were not affiliated with the Klan. The next morning, as Jubilee was pulling his car out of the driveway, he noticed the partially burned cross approximately 20 feet from his house. After seeing the cross, Jubilee was "very nervous" because he "didn't know what would be the next phase," and because "a cross burned in your yard . . . tells you that it's just the first round."

Elliott and O'Mara were charged with attempted cross burning and conspiracy to commit cross burning. O'Mara pleaded guilty to both counts, reserving the right to challenge the constitutionality of the cross-burning statute. The judge sentenced O'Mara to 90 days in jail and fined him $2,500. The judge also suspended 45 days of the sentence and $1,000 of the fine.

At Elliott's trial, the judge originally ruled that the jury would be instructed "that the burning of a cross by itself is sufficient evidence from which you may infer the required intent." At trial, however, the court instructed the jury that the Commonwealth must prove that "the defendant intended to commit cross burning," that "the defendant did a direct act toward the commission of the cross burning," and that "the defendant had the intent of intimidating any person or group of persons." . . . The jury found Elliott guilty of attempted cross burning and acquitted him of conspiracy to commit cross burning. It sentenced Elliott to 90 days in jail and a $2,500 fine. The Court of Appeals of Virginia affirmed the convictions of both Elliott and O'Mara.

Each respondent appealed to the Supreme Court of Virginia, arguing that § 18.2–423 is facially unconstitutional. The Supreme Court of Virginia consolidated all three cases, and held that the statute is unconstitutional on its face. It held that the Virginia cross-burning statute "is analytically indistinguishable from the ordinance found unconstitutional in *R.A.V.* [*v. St. Paul*, 505 U.S. 377 (1992)]." . . .

. . . .

II

. . .

Often, the Klan used cross burnings as a tool of intimidation and a threat of impending violence. . . .

. . .

Throughout the history of the Klan, cross burnings have also remained potent symbols of shared group identity and ideology. . . .

At Klan gatherings across the country, cross burning became the climax of the rally or the initiation. . . .

. . . In short, a burning cross has remained a symbol of Klan ideology and of Klan unity.

. . . [W]hile cross burning sometimes carries no intimidating message, at other times the intimidating message is the *only* message conveyed. For example, when a cross burning is directed at a particular person not affiliated with the Klan, the burning cross often serves as a message of intimidation, designed to inspire in the victim a fear of bodily harm. Moreover, the history of violence associated with the Klan shows that the possibility of injury or death is not just hypothetical. The person who burns a cross directed at a particular person often is making a serious threat, meant to coerce the victim to comply with the Klan's wishes unless the victim is willing to risk the wrath of the Klan. Indeed, as the cases of respondents Elliott and O'Mara indicate, individuals without Klan affiliation who wish to threaten or menace another person sometimes use cross burning because of this association between a burning cross and violence.

In sum, while a burning cross does not inevitably convey a message of intimidation, often the cross burner intends that the recipients of the message fear for their lives. And when a cross burning is used to intimidate, few if any messages are more powerful.

III

A

. . .

. . . The First Amendment permits "restrictions upon the content of speech in a few limited areas, which are 'of such slight social value as a step to truth that any benefit that may be derived from them is clearly outweighed by the social interest in order and morality.' " R.A.V. v. City of St. Paul, *supra,* at 382–383, (quoting Chaplinsky v. New Hampshire, [313 U.S. 568] at 572).

. . . [T]he First Amendment . . . permits a State to ban a "true threat." . . . ("[T]hreats of violence are outside the First Amendment"); Madsen v. Women's Health Center, Inc., 512 U.S. 753 (1994); Schenck v. Pro–Choice Network of Western N. Y., 519 U.S. 357, 373 (1997).

"True threats" encompass those statements where the speaker means to communicate a serious expression of an intent to commit an act of unlawful violence to a particular individual or group of individuals. . . . The speaker need not actually intend to carry out the threat. Rather, a prohibition on true threats "protect[s] individuals from the fear of violence" and "from the disruption that fear engenders," in addition to protecting people "from the possibility that the threatened violence will occur." . . . Intimidation in the constitutionally proscribable sense of the word is a type of true threat, where a speaker directs a threat to a person or group of persons with the intent of placing the victim in fear of bodily harm or death. Respondents do not contest that some cross burnings fit within this meaning of intimidating speech, and rightly so. As noted in Part II, *supra,* the history of cross burning in this country shows that cross burning is often intimidating, intended to create a pervasive fear in victims that they are a target of violence.

B

. . . It is true, as the Supreme Court of Virginia held, that the burning of a cross is symbolic expression. The reason why the Klan burns a cross at its rallies, or individuals place a burning cross on someone else's lawn, is that the burning cross represents the message that the speaker wishes to communicate. Individuals burn crosses as opposed to other means of communication because cross burning carries a message in an effective and dramatic manner.

The fact that cross burning is symbolic expression, however, does not resolve the constitutional question. The Supreme Court of Virginia relied upon R.A.V. v. City of St. Paul, *supra*, to conclude that once a statute discriminates on the basis of this type of content, the law is unconstitutional. We disagree.

In *R.A.V.*, we held that a local ordinance that banned certain symbolic conduct, including cross burning, when done with the knowledge that such conduct would " 'arouse anger, alarm or resentment in others on the basis of race, color, creed, religion or gender' " was unconstitutional ... We held that the ordinance did not pass constitutional muster because it discriminated on the basis of content by targeting only those individuals who "provoke violence" on a basis specified in the law. ... The ordinance did not cover "[t]hose who wish to use 'fighting words' in connection with other ideas—to express hostility, for example, on the basis of political affiliation, union membership, or homosexuality." ... This content-based discrimination was unconstitutional because it allowed the city "to impose special prohibitions on those speakers who express views on disfavored subjects." ...

We did not hold in *R.A.V.* that the First Amendment prohibits *all* forms of content-based discrimination within a proscribable area of speech. Rather, we specifically stated that some types of content discrimination did not violate the First Amendment:

"When the basis for the content discrimination consists entirely of the very reason the entire class of speech at issue is proscribable, no significant danger of idea or viewpoint discrimination exists. Such a reason, having been adjudged neutral enough to support exclusion of the entire class of speech from First Amendment protection, is also neutral enough to form the basis of distinction within the class." ...

Indeed, we noted that it would be constitutional to ban only a particular type of threat: "[T]he Federal Government can criminalize only those threats of violence that are directed against the President ... since the reasons why threats of violence are outside the First Amendment ... have special force when applied to the person of the President." ... And a State may "choose to prohibit only that obscenity which is the most patently offensive *in its prurience—i.e.,* that which involves the most lascivious displays of sexual activity." ... Consequently, while the holding of *R.A.V.* does not permit a State to ban only obscenity based on "offensive *political* messages," or "only those threats against the President that mention his policy on aid to inner cities," the First Amendment permits content discrimination "based on the very reasons why the particular class of speech at issue ... is proscribable," ...

Similarly, Virginia's statute does not run afoul of the First Amendment insofar as it bans cross burning with intent to intimidate. Unlike the statute at issue in *R.A.V.*, the Virginia statute does not single out for opprobrium only that speech directed toward "one of the specified disfavored topics." ... It does not matter whether an individual burns a cross with intent to intimidate because of the victim's race, gender, or religion, or because of the victim's "political affiliation, union membership, or homosexuality." Moreover, as a factual matter it is not true that cross burners direct their intimidating conduct solely to racial or religious minorities.... Indeed, in the case of Elliott and O'Mara, it is at least unclear whether the respondents burned a cross due to racial animus. ...

The First Amendment permits Virginia to outlaw cross burnings done with the intent to intimidate because burning a cross is a particularly virulent form of intimidation. Instead of prohibiting all intimidating messages, Virginia may choose to regulate this subset of intimidating messages in light of cross burning's long and pernicious history as a signal of impending violence. Thus, just as a State may regulate only that obscenity which is the most obscene due to its prurient content, so too may a State choose to prohibit only those forms of intimidation that are most likely to inspire fear of bodily harm. A ban on cross burning carried out with the intent to intimidate is fully consistent with our holding in *R.A.V.* and is proscribable under the First Amendment.

IV

The Supreme Court of Virginia ruled in the alternative that Virginia's cross-burning statute was unconstitutionally overbroad due to its provision stating that "[a]ny such burning of a cross shall be prima facie evidence of an intent to intimidate a person or group of persons." . . . In this Court, as in the Supreme Court of Virginia, respondents do not argue that the prima facie evidence provision is unconstitutional as applied to any one of them. Rather, they contend that the provision is unconstitutional on its face.

The Supreme Court of Virginia has not ruled on the meaning of the prima facie evidence provision. It has, however, stated that "the act of burning a cross alone, with no evidence of intent to intimidate, will nonetheless suffice for arrest and prosecution and will insulate the Commonwealth from a motion to strike the evidence at the end of its case-in-chief." The jury in the case of Richard Elliott did not receive any instruction on the prima facie evidence provision, and the provision was not an issue in the case of Jonathan O'Mara because he pleaded guilty. The court in Barry Black's case, however, instructed the jury that the provision means: "The burning of a cross, by itself, is sufficient evidence from which you may infer the required intent." . . .

The prima facie evidence provision, as interpreted by the jury instruction, renders the statute unconstitutional. Because this jury instruction is the Model Jury Instruction, and because the Supreme Court of Virginia had the opportunity to expressly disavow the jury instruction, the jury instruction's construction of the prima facie provision "is a ruling on a question of state law that is as binding on us as though the precise words had been written into" the statute. . . . As construed by the jury instruction, the prima facie provision strips away the very reason why a State may ban cross burning with the intent to intimidate. The prima facie evidence provision permits a jury to convict in every cross-burning case in which defendants exercise their constitutional right not to put on a defense. And even where a defendant like Black presents a defense, the prima facie evidence provision makes it more likely that the jury will find an intent to intimidate regardless of the particular facts of the case. The provision permits the Commonwealth to arrest, prosecute, and convict a person based solely on the fact of cross burning itself.

It is apparent that the provision as so interpreted " 'would create an unacceptable risk of the suppression of ideas.' " . . . The act of burning a cross may mean that a person is engaging in constitutionally proscribable intimidation. But that same act may mean only that the person is engaged in core political speech. The prima facie evidence provision in this statute blurs the line between these two meanings of a burning cross. As interpreted by the jury instruction, the provision chills constitutionally protected political speech because of the possibility that a State will prosecute—and potentially convict—

somebody engaging only in lawful political speech at the core of what the First Amendment is designed to protect.

As the history of cross burning indicates, a burning cross is not always intended to intimidate. Rather, sometimes the cross burning is a statement of ideology, a symbol of group solidarity. It is a ritual used at Klan gatherings, and it is used to represent the Klan itself. ... Indeed, occasionally a person who burns a cross does not intend to express either a statement of ideology or intimidation. Cross burnings have appeared in movies such as Mississippi Burning, and in plays such as the stage adaptation of Sir Walter Scott's The Lady of the Lake.

The prima facie provision makes no effort to distinguish among these different types of cross burnings. It does not distinguish between a cross burning done with the purpose of creating anger or resentment and a cross burning done with the purpose of threatening or intimidating a victim. It does not distinguish between a cross burning at a public rally or a cross burning on a neighbor's lawn. It does not treat the cross burning directed at an individual differently from the cross burning directed at a group of like-minded believers. ... I agree with Justice Souter that the prima facie evidence provision can "skew jury deliberations toward conviction in cases where the evidence of intent to intimidate is relatively weak and arguably consistent with a solely ideological reason for burning."

It may be true that a cross burning, even at a political rally, arouses a sense of anger or hatred among the vast majority of citizens who see a burning cross. But this sense of anger or hatred is not sufficient to ban all cross burnings. As Gerald Gunther has stated, "The lesson I have drawn from my childhood in Nazi Germany and my happier adult life in this country is the need to walk the sometimes difficult path of denouncing the bigot's hateful ideas with all my power, yet at the same time challenging any community's attempt to suppress hateful ideas by force of law." Casper, Gerry, 55 Stan. L.Rev. 647, 649 (2002) (internal quotation marks omitted). The prima facie evidence provision in this case ignores all of the contextual factors that are necessary to decide whether a particular cross burning is intended to intimidate. The First Amendment does not permit such a shortcut.

For these reasons, the prima facie evidence provision, as interpreted through the jury instruction and as applied in Barry Black's case, is unconstitutional on its face. ... Unlike Justice Scalia, we refuse to speculate on whether *any* interpretation of the prima facie evidence provision would satisfy the First Amendment. Rather, all we hold is that because of the interpretation of the prima facie evidence provision given by the jury instruction, the provision makes the statute facially invalid at this point. We also recognize the theoretical possibility that the court, on remand, could interpret the provision in a manner different from that so far set forth in order to avoid the constitutional objections we have described. We leave open that possibility. We also leave open the possibility that the provision is severable, and if so, whether Elliott and O'Mara could be retried under § 18.2–423.

V

With respect to Barry Black, we agree with the Supreme Court of Virginia that his conviction cannot stand, and we affirm the judgment of the Supreme Court of Virginia. With respect to Elliott and O'Mara, we vacate the judgment of the Supreme Court of Virginia, and remand the case for further proceedings.*

. . .

Justice Scalia, with whom Justice Thomas joins as to Parts I and II, concurring in part, concurring in the judgment in part, and dissenting in part.

I agree with the Court that, under our decision in *R.A.V. v. St. Paul,* 505 U.S. 377 (1992), a State may, without infringing the First Amendment, prohibit cross burning carried out with the intent to intimidate. Accordingly, I join Parts I–III of the Court's opinion. I also agree that we should vacate and remand the judgment of the Virginia Supreme Court so that that Court can have an opportunity authoritatively to construe the prima-facie-evidence provision . . . I write separately, however, to describe what I believe to be the correct interpretation of § 18.2–423, and to explain why I believe there is no justification for the plurality's apparent decision to invalidate that provision on its face.

I

Section 18.2–423 provides that the burning of a cross in public view "shall be prima facie evidence of an intent to intimidate." In order to determine whether this component of the statute violates the Constitution, it is necessary, first, to establish precisely what the presentation of prima facie evidence accomplishes.

The established meaning in Virginia, then, of the term "prima facie evidence" appears to be perfectly orthodox: It is evidence that suffices, on its own, to establish a particular fact. But . . . this is true only to the extent that the evidence goes unrebutted. . . .

. . .

It is important to note that the Virginia Supreme Court did not suggest (as did the trial court's jury instructions in respondent Black's case) that a jury may, in light of the prima-facie-evidence provision, ignore any rebuttal evidence that has been presented and, solely on the basis of a showing that the defendant burned a cross, find that he intended to intimidate. Nor, crucially, did that court say that the presentation of prima facie evidence is always sufficient to get a case to a jury . . . That is, presentation of evidence that a defendant burned a cross in public view is automatically sufficient, on its own, to support an inference that the defendant intended to intimidate *only until* the defendant comes forward with some evidence in rebuttal.

II

The question presented, then, is whether, given this understanding of the term "prima facie evidence," the cross-burning statute is constitutional. . . .

. . . We have never held that the mere threat that individuals who engage in protected conduct will be subject to arrest and prosecution suffices to render a statute overbroad. Rather, our overbreadth jurisprudence has consistently focused on whether *the prohibitory terms* of a particular statute extend to protected conduct; that is, we have inquired whether individuals who engage in

---

* A concurring opinion by Justice Stevens is omitted.

protected conduct can be *convicted* under a statute, not whether they might be subject to arrest and prosecution. . . .

. . .

. . . [T]he plurality cannot claim that improper convictions will result from the operation of the prima-facie-evidence provision *alone*. As the plurality concedes, the only persons who might impermissibly be convicted by reason of that provision are those who adopt a particular trial strategy, to wit, abstaining from the presentation of a defense.

. . .

Conceding (quite generously, in my view) that this class of persons exists, it cannot possibly give rise to a viable facial challenge, not even with the aid of our First Amendment overbreadth doctrine. For this Court has emphasized repeatedly that "where a statute regulates expressive conduct, the scope of the statute does not render it unconstitutional unless its overbreadth is not only real, but *substantial* as well, judged in relation to the statute's plainly legitimate sweep." Osborne v. Ohio, 495 U.S. 103, 112 (1990). . . .

. . .

. . . [T]he plurality holds out the possibility that the Virginia Supreme Court will offer some saving construction of the statute. It should go without saying that if a saving construction of § 18.2–423 is possible, then facial invalidation is inappropriate. . . . So, what appears to have happened is that the plurality has facially invalidated not § 18.2–423, but its own hypothetical interpretation of § 18.2–423, and has then remanded to the Virginia Supreme Court to learn the *actual* interpretation of § 18.2–423. Words cannot express my wonderment at this virtuoso performance.

III

. . . I believe the prima-facie-evidence provision in Virginia's cross-burning statute is constitutionally unproblematic. Nevertheless, because the Virginia Supreme Court has not yet offered an authoritative construction of § 18.2–423, I concur in the Court's decision to vacate and remand the judgment with respect to respondents Elliott and O'Mara. I also agree that respondent Black's conviction cannot stand. . . . Because I believe the constitutional defect in Black's conviction is rooted in a jury instruction and not in the statute itself, I would not dismiss the indictment and would permit the Commonwealth to retry Black if it wishes to do so. . . .

Justice Souter, with whom Justice Kennedy and Justice Ginsburg join, concurring in the judgment in part and dissenting in part.

I agree with the majority that the Virginia statute makes a content-based distinction within the category of punishable intimidating or threatening expression, the very type of distinction we considered in R.A.V. v. St. Paul, 505 U.S. 377 (1992). I disagree that any exception should save Virginia's law from unconstitutionality under the holding in *R.A.V.* or any acceptable variation of it.

I

The ordinance struck down in *R.A.V.,* as it had been construed by the State's highest court, prohibited the use of symbols (including but not limited to a burning cross) as the equivalent of generally proscribable fighting words, but the ordinance applied only when the symbol was provocative " 'on the basis of race, color, creed, religion or gender.' " Although the Virginia statute in issue here contains no such express "basis of" limitation on prohibited subject matter, the specific prohibition of cross burning with intent to intimidate selects a symbol with particular content from the field of all proscribable expression meant to intimidate. . . .

. . . [T]he *R.A.V.* . . . opinion [identified] an exception for content discrimination on a basis that "consists entirely of the very reason the entire class of speech at issue is proscribable." *R.A.V., supra,* at 388, 112 S.Ct. 2538. This is the exception the majority speaks of here as covering statutes prohibiting "particularly virulent" proscribable expression.

I do not think that the Virginia statute qualifies for this virulence exception as *R.A.V.* explained it. The statute fits poorly with the illustrative examples given in *R.A.V.,* none of which involves communication generally associated with a particular message. . . .

II

. . . I thus read *R.A.V.* . . . as covering prohibitions that are not clearly associated with a particular viewpoint, and that are consequently different from the Virginia statute. On that understanding of things, I necessarily read the majority opinion as treating *R.A.V.*'s virulence exception in a more flexible, pragmatic manner. . . .

III

My concern here, in any event, is not with the merit of a pragmatic doctrinal move. For whether or not the Court should conceive of exceptions to *R.A.V.*'s general rule in a more practical way, no content-based statute should survive even under a pragmatic recasting of *R.A.V.* without a high probability that no "official suppression of ideas is afoot," *R.A.V., supra,* at 390. I believe the prima facie evidence provision stands in the way of any finding of such a high probability here.

. . .

As I see the likely significance of the evidence provision, its primary effect is to skew jury deliberations toward conviction in cases where the evidence of intent to intimidate is relatively weak and arguably consistent with a solely ideological reason for burning. an initiation ceremony or political rally visible to the public. In such a case, if the factfinder is aware of the prima facie evidence provision, as the jury was in respondent Black's case, the provision will have the practical effect of tilting the jury's thinking in favor of the prosecution. What is significant is not that the provision permits a factfinder's conclusion that the defendant acted with proscribable and punishable intent without any further indication, because some such indication will almost always be presented. What is significant is that the provision will encourage a factfinder to err on the side of a finding of intent to intimidate when the evidence of circumstances fails to point with any clarity either to the criminal intent or to the permissible one. . . .

To the extent the prima facie evidence provision skews prosecutions, then, it skews the statute toward suppressing ideas. . . .

. . .

Justice Thomas, dissenting.

In every culture, certain things acquire meaning well beyond what outsiders can comprehend. That goes for both the sacred, see Texas v. Johnson, 491

U.S. 397, 422–429 (1989) (Rehnquist, C. J., dissenting) (describing the unique position of the American flag in our Nation's 200 years of history), and the profane. I believe that cross burning is the paradigmatic example of the latter.

I

... I believe that the majority errs in imputing an expressive component to the activity in question. In my view, whatever expressive value cross burning has, the legislature simply wrote it out by banning only intimidating conduct undertaken by a particular means. A conclusion that the statute prohibiting cross burning with intent to intimidate sweeps beyond a prohibition on certain conduct into the zone of expression overlooks not only the words of the statute but also reality.

A

... To me, the majority's brief history of the Ku Klux Klan only reinforces this common understanding of the Klan as a terrorist organization, which, in its endeavor to intimidate, or even eliminate those its dislikes, uses the most brutal of methods.

Such methods typically include cross burning—"a tool for the intimidation and harassment of racial minorities, Catholics, Jews, Communists, and any other groups hated by the Klan." ... For those not easily frightened, cross burning has been followed by more extreme measures, such as beatings and murder. ... As the Solicitor General points out, the association between acts of intimidating cross burning and violence is well documented in recent American history. ...

But the perception that a burning cross is a threat and a precursor of worse things to come is not limited to blacks. Because the modern Klan expanded the list of its enemies beyond blacks and "radical[s]," to include Catholics, Jews, most immigrants, and labor unions, a burning cross is now widely viewed as a signal of impending terror and lawlessness. ...

In our culture, cross burning has almost invariably meant lawlessness and understandably instills in its victims well-grounded fear of physical violence.

B

. . .

It strains credulity to suggest that a state legislature that adopted a litany of segregationist laws self-contradictorily intended to squelch the segregationist message. Even for segregationists, violent and terroristic conduct, the Siamese twin of cross burning, was intolerable. The ban on cross burning with intent to intimidate demonstrates that even segregationists understood the difference between intimidating and terroristic conduct and racist expression. It is simply beyond belief that, in passing the statute now under review, the Virginia legislature was concerned with anything but penalizing conduct it must have viewed as particularly vicious.

Accordingly, this statute prohibits only conduct, not expression. And, just as one cannot burn down someone's house to make a political point and then seek refuge in the First Amendment, those who hate cannot terrorize and intimidate to make their point. In light of my conclusion that the statute here addresses only conduct, there is no need to analyze it under any of our First Amendment tests.

II

Even assuming that the statute implicates the First Amendment, in my view, the fact that the statute permits a jury to draw an inference of intent to intimidate from the cross burning itself presents no constitutional problems. Therein lies my primary disagreement with the plurality.

. . .

B

... The plurality fears the chill on expression because, according to the plurality, the inference permits "the Commonwealth to arrest, prosecute and convict a person based solely on the fact of cross burning itself." First, it is, at the very least, unclear that the inference comes into play during arrest and initiation of a prosecution, that is, prior to the instructions stage of an actual trial. Second, ... the inference is rebuttable and, as the jury instructions given in this case demonstrate, Virginia law still requires the jury to find the existence of each element, including intent to intimidate, beyond a reasonable doubt.

Moreover, even in the First Amendment context, the Court has upheld such regulations where conduct that initially appears culpable, ultimately results in dismissed charges. A regulation of pornography is one such example. ... [P]ornographers trafficking in images of adults who look like minors, may be not only deterred but also arrested and prosecuted for possessing what a jury might find to be legal materials. This "chilling" effect has not, however, been a cause for grave concern with respect to overbreadth of such statutes among the members of this Court.

That the First Amendment gives way to other interests is not a remarkable proposition. What is remarkable is that, under the plurality's analysis, the determination of whether an interest is sufficiently compelling depends not on the harm a regulation in question seeks to prevent, but on the area of society at which it aims. For instance, in Hill v. Colorado, 530 U.S. 703 (2000), the Court upheld a restriction on protests near abortion clinics, explaining that the State had a legitimate interest, which was sufficiently narrowly tailored, in protecting those seeking services of such establishments "from unwanted advice" and "unwanted communication" ... In so concluding, the Court placed heavy reliance on the "vulnerable physical and emotional conditions" of patients. ... Thus, when it came to the rights of those seeking abortions, the Court deemed restrictions on "unwanted advice," which, notably, can be given only from a distance of at least 8 feet from a prospective patient, justified by the countervailing interest in obtaining abortion. Yet, here, the plurality strikes down the statute because one day an individual might wish to burn a cross, but might do so without an intent to intimidate anyone. That cross burning subjects its targets, and, sometimes, an unintended audience, ... to extreme emotional distress, and is virtually never viewed merely as "unwanted communication," but rather, as a physical threat, is of no concern to the plurality. Henceforth, under the plurality's view, physical safety will be valued less than the right to be free from unwanted communications.

III

Because I would uphold the validity of this statute, I respectfully dissent.

D.   REGULATION OF COMMERCIAL SPEECH

Virginia State Board of Pharmacy v. Virginia Citizens Consumer Council, Inc.

425 U.S. 748, 96 S.Ct. 1817, 48 L.Ed.2d 346 (1976).

Mr. Justice Blackmun delivered the opinion of the Court.

The plaintiff-appellees in this case attack, as violative of the First and Fourteenth Amendments, that portion of § 54–524.35 of Va.Code Ann. (1974), which provides that a pharmacist licensed in Virginia is guilty of unprofessional conduct if he "(3) publishes, advertises or promotes, directly or indirectly, in any manner whatsoever, any amount, price, fee, premium, discount, rebate or credit terms . . . for any drugs which may be dispensed only by prescription." The three-judge District Court declared the quoted portion of the statute "void and of no effect," . . .

I.

. . .

Inasmuch as only a licensed pharmacist may dispense prescription drugs in Virginia, . . . advertising or other affirmative dissemination of prescription drug price information is effectively forbidden in the State. . . . The prohibition does not extend to nonprescription drugs, but neither is it confined to prescriptions that the pharmacist compounds himself. Indeed, about 95% of all prescriptions now are filled with dosage forms prepared by the pharmaceutical manufacturer.

II.

. . .

The present . . . attack on the statute is one made not by one directly subject to its prohibition, that is, a pharmacist, but by prescription drug consumers who claim that they would greatly benefit if the prohibition were lifted and advertising freely allowed. The plaintiffs are an individual Virginia resident who suffers from diseases that require her to take prescription drugs on a daily basis, and two nonprofit organizations. Their claim is that the First Amendment entitles the user of prescription drugs to receive information that pharmacists wish to communicate to them through advertising and other promotional means, concerning the prices of such drugs.

Certainly that information may be of value. Drug prices in Virginia, for both prescription and nonprescription items, strikingly vary from outlet to outlet even within the same locality. . . .

III.

The question first arises whether, even assuming that First Amendment protection attaches to the flow of drug price information, it is a protection enjoyed by the appellees as recipients of the information, and not solely, if at all, by the advertisers themselves who seek to disseminate that information.

Freedom of speech presupposes a willing speaker. But where a speaker exists, as is the case here, the protection afforded is to the communication, to its source and to its recipients both. This is clear from the decided cases. In Lamont v. Postmaster General, 381 U.S. 301 (1965), the Court upheld the First Amendment rights of citizens to receive political publications sent from abroad. More recently, in Kleindienst v. Mandel, 408 U.S. 753, 762–763 (1972), we acknowledged that this Court has referred to a First Amendment right to "receive information and ideas," and that freedom of speech "necessarily protects the right to receive." And in Procunier v. Martinez, 416 U.S. 396, 408–409 (1974), where censorship of prison inmates' mail was under examination, we thought it unnecessary to assess the First Amendment rights of the inmates themselves, for it was reasoned that such censorship equally infringed the rights of nominates to whom the correspondence was addressed. . . . If there is a right to advertise, there is a reciprocal right to receive the advertising, and it may be asserted by these appellees.

IV.

The appellants contend that the advertisement of prescription drug prices is outside the protection of the First Amendment because it is "commercial speech." There can be no question that in past decisions the Court has given some indication that commercial speech is unprotected. In Valentine v. Chrestensen, [316 U.S. 52 (1942)], the Court upheld a New York statute that prohibited the distribution of any "handbill, circular . . . or other advertising matter whatsoever in or upon any street." The Court concluded that, although the First Amendment would forbid the banning of all communication by handbill in the public thoroughfares, it imposed "no such restraint on government as respects purely commercial advertising." . . . Further support for a "commercial speech" exception to the First Amendment may perhaps be found in Breard v. Alexandria, 341 U.S. 622 (1951), where the Court upheld a conviction for violation of an ordinance prohibiting door-to-door solicitation of magazine subscriptions. The Court reasoned: "The selling . . . brings into the transaction a commercial feature," and it distinguished *Martin v. Struthers*, . . . where it had reversed a conviction for door-to-door distribution of leaflets publicizing a religious meeting, as a case involving "no element of the commercial." . . .

. . .

Last Term, in Bigelow v. Virginia, 421 U.S. 809 (1975), the notion of unprotected "commercial speech" all but passed from the scene. . . .

Some fragment of hope for the continuing validity of a "commercial speech" exception arguably might have persisted because of the subject matter of the advertisement in *Bigelow*. We noted that in announcing the availability of legal abortions in New York, the advertisement "did more than simply propose a commercial transaction. It contained factual material of clear 'public interest.'" . . .

Here, in contrast, the question whether there is a First Amendment exception for "commercial speech" is squarely before us. Our pharmacist does not wish to editorialize on any subject, cultural, philosophical, or political. He does not wish to report any particularly newsworthy fact, or to make generalized observations even about commercial matters. The "idea" he wishes to communicate is simply this: "I will sell you the X prescription drug at the Y price." Our question, then, is whether this communication is wholly outside the protection of the First Amendment.

V.

. . .

If there is a kind of commercial speech that lacks all First Amendment protection . . . it must be distinguished by its content. Yet the speech whose content deprives it of protection cannot simply be speech on a commercial subject. No one would contend that our pharmacist may be prevented from being heard on the subject of whether, in general, pharmaceutical prices should be regulated, or their advertisement forbidden. Nor can it be dispositive that a commercial advertisement is noneditorial, and merely reports a fact. Purely factual matter of public interest may claim protection. . . .

Our question is whether speech which does "no more than propose a commercial transaction," ... is so removed from any "exposition of ideas," Chaplinsky v. New Hampshire ... that it lacks all protection. Our answer is that it is not.

Focusing first on the individual parties to the transaction that is proposed in the commercial advertisement, we may assume that the advertiser's interest is a purely economic one. That hardly disqualifies him for protection under the First Amendment. . . .

As to the particular consumer's interest in the free flow of commercial information, that interest may be as keen, if not keener by far, than his interest in the day's most urgent political debate. Appellees' case in this respect is a convincing one. Those whom the suppression of prescription drug price information hits the hardest are the poor, the sick, and particularly the aged. A disproportionate amount of their income tends to be spent on prescription drugs; yet they are the least able to learn, by shopping from pharmacist to pharmacist, where their scarce dollars are best spent. When drug prices vary as strikingly as they do, information as to who is charging what becomes more than a convenience. It could mean the alleviation of physical pain or the enjoyment of basic necessities.

Generalizing, society also may have a strong interest in the free flow of commercial information. Even an individual advertisement, though entirely "commercial," may be of general public interest. . . . Obviously, not all commercial messages contain the same or even a very great public interest element. There are few to which such an element, however, could not be added. Our pharmacist, for example, could cast himself as a commentator on store-to-store disparities in drug prices, giving his own and those of a competitor as proof. We see little point in requiring him to do so, and little difference if he does not.

. . . So long as we preserve a predominantly free enterprise economy, the allocation of our resources in large measure will be made through numerous private economic decisions. It is a matter of public interest that those decisions, in the aggregate, be intelligent and well informed. To this end, the free flow of commercial information is indispensable. . . . And if it is indispensable to the proper allocation of resources in a free enterprise system, it is also indispensable to the formation of intelligent opinions as to how that system ought to be regulated or altered. Therefore, even if the First Amendment were thought to be primarily an instrument to enlighten public decisionmaking in a democracy, we could not say that the free flow of information does not serve that goal.

Arrayed against these substantial individual and societal interests are a number of justifications for the advertising ban. These have to do principally with maintaining a high degree of professionalism on the part of licensed pharmacists. . . .

Price advertising, it is argued, will place in jeopardy the pharmacist's expertise and, with it, the customer's health. It is claimed that the aggressive price competition that will result from unlimited advertising will make it impossible for the pharmacist to supply professional services in the compounding, handling, and dispensing of prescription drugs. . . . Price advertising, it is said, will reduce the pharmacist's status to that of a mere retailer.

The strength of these proffered justifications is greatly undermined by the fact that high professional standards, to a substantial extent, are guaranteed by the close regulation to which pharmacists in Virginia are subject. And this case concerns the retail sale by the pharmacist more than it does his professional standards. Surely, any pharmacist guilty of professional dereliction that actually endangers his customer will promptly lose his license. At the same time, we cannot discount the Board's justifications entirely. The Court regarded justifications of this type sufficient to sustain the advertising bans challenged on due process and equal protection grounds in Head v. New Mexico Board, supra; Williamson v. Lee Optical Co., supra; and Semler v. Dental Examiners, supra.

The challenge now made, however, is based on the First Amendment. This casts the Board's justifications in a different light....

. . .

There is, of course, an alternative to this highly paternalistic approach. That alternative is to assume that this information is not in itself harmful, that people will perceive their own best interests if only they are well enough informed, and that the best means to that end is to open the channels of communication rather than to close them. If they are truly open, nothing prevents the "professional" pharmacist from marketing his own assertedly superior product, and contrasting it with that of the low-cost, high-volume prescription drug retailer. But the choice among these alternative approaches is not ours to make or the Virginia General Assembly's. It is precisely this kind of choice, between the dangers of suppressing information, and the dangers of its misuse if it is freely available, that the First Amendment makes for us. Virginia is free to require whatever professional standards it wishes of its pharmacists; it may subsidize them or protect them from competition in other ways. . . . But it may not do so by keeping the public in ignorance of the entirely lawful terms that competing pharmacists are offering. In this sense, the justifications Virginia has offered for suppressing the flow of prescription drug price information, far from persuading us that the flow is not protected by the First Amendment, have reinforced our view that it is. We so hold.

VI.

In concluding that commercial speech, like other varieties, is protected, we of course do not hold that it can never be regulated in any way. Some forms of commercial speech regulation are surely permissible. We mention a few only to make clear that they are not before us and therefore are not foreclosed by this case.

There is no claim, for example, that the prohibition on prescription drug price advertising is a mere time, place, and manner restriction. We have often approved restrictions of that kind provided that they are justified without reference to the content of the regulated speech, that they serve a significant governmental interest, and that in so doing they leave open ample alternative channels for communication of the information.... Whatever may be the proper bounds of time, place, and manner restrictions on commercial speech, they are plainly exceeded by this Virginia statute, which singles out speech of a particular content and seeks to prevent its dissemination completely.

Nor is there any claim that prescription drug price advertisements are forbidden because they are false or misleading in any way. Untruthful speech, commercial or otherwise, has never been protected for its own sake. ... Obviously, much commercial speech is not provably false, or even wholly false, but only deceptive or misleading. We foresee no obstacle to a State's dealing effectively with this problem.[24] The First Amendment, as we construe it today,

24. In concluding that commercial speech enjoys First Amendment protection, we have not held that it is wholly undifferen- tiable from other forms. There are common- sense differences between speech that does "no more than propose a commercial transacdoes not prohibit the State from insuring that the stream of commercial information flows cleanly as well as freely. . . .

Also, there is no claim that the transactions proposed in the forbidden advertisements are themselves illegal in any way. . . .

What is at issue is whether a State may completely suppress the dissemination of concededly truthful information about entirely lawful activity, fearful of that information's effect upon its disseminators and its recipients. Reserving other questions, we conclude that the answer to this one is in the negative.

The judgment of the District Court is affirmed.

It is so ordered.

Mr. Justice Stevens took no part in the consideration or decision of this case.

Mr. Chief Justice Burger, concurring.

. . . Our decision today . . . deals largely with the State's power to prohibit pharmacists from advertising the retail price of *prepackaged* drugs. . . . [Q]uite different factors would govern were we faced with a law regulating or even prohibiting advertising by the traditional learned professions of medicine or law. . . .

. . .

Mr. Justice Stewart, concurring.

. . .

. . . [T]he Court's decision calls into immediate question the constitutional legitimacy of every state and federal law regulating false or deceptive advertising. I write separately to explain why I think today's decision does not preclude such governmental regulation. . . .

. . .

Mr. Justice Rehnquist, dissenting.

The logical consequences of the Court's decision in this case, a decision which elevates commercial intercourse between a seller hawking his wares and a buyer seeking to strike a bargain to the same plane as has been previously reserved for the free marketplace of ideas, are far reaching indeed. Under the Court's opinion the way will be open not only for dissemination of price information but for active promotion of prescription drugs, liquor, cigarettes and other products the use of which it has previously been thought desirable to

---

tion" . . . and other varieties. Even if the differences do not justify the conclusion that commercial speech is valueless, and thus subject to complete suppression by the State, they nonetheless suggest that a different degree of protection is necessary to insure that the flow of truthful and legitimate commercial information is unimpaired. The truth of commercial speech, for example, may be more easily verifiable by its disseminator than, let us say, news reporting or political commentary, in that ordinarily the advertiser seeks to disseminate information about a specific product or service that he himself provides and presumably knows more about than anyone else. Also, commercial speech may be more durable than other kinds. Since adver-

tising is the sine qua non of commercial profits, there is little likelihood of its being chilled by proper regulation and foregone entirely.

Attributes such as these, the greater objectivity and hardiness of commercial speech, may make it less necessary to tolerate inaccurate statements for fear of silencing the speaker. . . . They may also make it appropriate to require that a commercial message appear in such a form, or include such additional information, warnings and disclaimers, as are necessary to prevent its being deceptive. . . . They may also make inapplicable the prohibition against prior restraints. . . .

discourage. Now, however, such promotion is protected by the First Amendment so long as it is not misleading or does not promote an illegal product or enterprise. In coming to this conclusion, the Court has overruled a legislative determination that such advertising should not be allowed and has done so on behalf of a consumer group which is not directly disadvantaged by the statute in question. This effort to reach a result which the Court obviously considers desirable is a troublesome one, for two reasons. It extends standing to raise First Amendment claims beyond the previous decisions of this Court. It also extends the protection of that Amendment to purely commercial endeavors which its most vigorous champions on this Court had thought to be beyond its pale.

. . .

ATTORNEY ADVERTISING

Chief Justice Burger's attempt, in his concurrence, to distinguish prohibitions on professional advertising, proved to be unavailing. In Bates v. State Bar of Arizona, 433 U.S. 350 (1977), the Court held 5–4 that lawyers could not be prohibited from advertising the price of "routine legal services." In subsequent cases, a number of other lines have been drawn. The Court has distinguished between commercial solicitation and solicitation of legal employment by advocacy organizations. Ohralik v. Ohio State Bar Ass'n, 436 U.S. 447 (1978), sustained discipline of an attorney for personal solicitation of contingent fee employment, while In re Primus, 436 U.S. 412 (1978), reversed discipline of an ACLU lawyer. The Court noted that Primus' letter (offering legal assistance to a woman who had been sterilized as a condition of receiving welfare) came within the "generous zone of First Amendment protection reserved for associational freedom." The Court has also distinguished between in-person solicitation, involved in the *Ohralik* decision, and solicitation by advertisement and letter. In Zauderer v. Office of Disciplinary Counsel, 471 U.S. 626 (1985), the Court struck down a categorical prohibition of attorney advertising containing information or advice about legal problems. In *Shapero v. Kentucky Bar Ass'n*, 486 U.S. 466 (1988), the Court held that a state rule, prohibiting attorney mailings of advertisements "precipitated by a specific event . . . involving or relating to the addressee," was invalid. Both newspaper and direct mail advertising posed less risk of "overreaching or undue influence" than in-person solicitation.

The Court distinguished *Shapero* in Florida Bar v. Went For It, Inc., 515 U.S. 618 (1995). *Shapero* had dealt with a rule imposing a ban on direct mail solicitation "whatever the time frame and whoever the recipient." Justice O'Connor's opinion for the Court concluded that a rule forbidding solicitation of accident victims during a 30–day period after the accident was constitutional. "The Bar has substantial interest both in protecting injured Floridians from invasive conduct by lawyers and in preventing the erosion of confidence in the profession that such repeated invasions have engendered. . . . The palliative devised by the Bar to address these harms is narrow both in scope and in duration." Justice Kennedy's dissent, joined by Justices Stevens, Souter and Ginsburg, argued that the rule prejudiced accident victims "to vindicate the State's purported desire for more dignity in the legal profession."

The Court has been divided on the question whether the contents of particular lawyer-advertisements were misleading. In *Zauderer,* a majority concluded that advertising a contingent fee was misleading because there was no disclosure that clients could be liable for significant litigation costs. In *Shapero,* a plurality concluded that a letter sent to persons against whom foreclosure suits had been filed could not be prohibited merely because it liberally used underscored, uppercase letters (e.g., "Call *NOW,* don't wait.... Remember it is *FREE* and there is *NO* charge for calling.") or contained subjective predictions of customer satisfaction (e.g., "It may surprise you what I may be able to do for you.") In Ibanez v. Florida Department of Business and Professional Regulation, Board of Accountancy, 512 U.S. 136 (1994), a lawyer was also a state-licensed Certified Public Accountant and was authorized to use the designation "Certified Financial Planner" by the Certified Financial Planner Board of Standards, a private organization. The Court held that she could not be disciplined for referring to those two credentials in her yellow pages listing, on her business cards, and on her law offices stationery, because neither was false or misleading.

The Court distinguished CPAs from attorneys in Edenfield v. Fane, 507 U.S. 761 (1993). As noted, the Court had held in *Ohralik* that in-person solicitation by attorneys could be prohibited. In *Edenfield*, the Court concluded that a ban on in-person solicitation by accountants violated the First Amendment. While lawyers are trained in the art of persuasion, accountants are trained to emphasize independence and objectivity. Moreover, an accountant's typical potential client is an experienced business executive. Therefore, CPA solicitation is not "inherently conducive to overreaching."

OVERBREADTH AND COMMERCIAL SPEECH

Justice Blackmun, for the Court, in Bates v. State Bar, 433 U.S. 350, 379–381 (1977):

"In the usual case involving a restraint on speech, a showing that the challenged rule served unconstitutionally to suppress speech would end our analysis. In the First Amendment context, the Court has permitted attacks on overly broad statutes without requiring that the person making the attack demonstrate that in fact his specific conduct was protected.... Having shown that the disciplinary rule interferes with protected speech, appellants ordinarily could expect to benefit regardless of the nature of their acts.

"The First Amendment overbreadth doctrine, however, represents a departure from the traditional rule that a person may not challenge a statute on the ground that it might be applied unconstitutionally in circumstances other than those before the court.... The reason for the special rule in First Amendment cases is apparent: an overbroad statute might serve to chill protected speech. First Amendment interests are fragile interests, and a person who contemplates protected activity might be discouraged by the *in terrorem* effect of the statute.... Indeed, such a person might choose not to speak because of uncertainty whether his claim of privilege would prevail if challenged. The use of overbreadth analysis reflects the conclusion that the possible harm to society from allowing unprotected speech to go unpunished is outweighed by the possibility that protected speech will be muted.

"But the justification for the application of overbreadth analysis applies weakly, if at all, in the ordinary commercial context. ... Since advertising is linked to commercial well-being, it seems unlikely that such speech is particularly susceptible to being crushed by overbroad regulation.... Moreover, concerns for uncertainty in determining the scope of protection are reduced; the advertiser seeks to disseminate information about a product or service that he provides, and presumably he can determine more readily than others whether his speech is truthful and protected. Ibid. Since overbreadth has been described by this Court as 'strong medicine,' which 'has been employed ... sparingly and only as a last resort,' Broadrick v. Oklahoma, ... we decline to apply it to professional advertising, a context where it is not necessary to further its intended objective."

Central Hudson Gas & Electric Corp. v. Public Service Commission

447 U.S. 557, 100 S.Ct. 2343, 65 L.Ed.2d 341 (1980).

Mr. Justice Powell delivered the opinion of the Court.

This case presents the question whether a regulation of the Public Service Commission of the State of New York violates the First and Fourteenth Amendments because it completely bans promotional advertising by an electrical utility.

I.

In December 1973, the Commission, appellee here, ordered electric utilities in New York State to cease all advertising that "promot[es] the use of electricity." The order was based on the Commission's finding that "the interconnected utility system in New York State does not have sufficient fuel stocks or sources of supply to continue furnishing all customer demands for the 1973–1974 winter."

Three years later, when the fuel shortage had eased, the Commission requested comments from the public on its proposal to continue the ban on promotional advertising. Central Hudson Gas & Electric Corp., the appellant in this case, opposed the ban on First Amendment grounds. After reviewing the public comments, the Commission extended the prohibition . . .

The Policy Statement divided advertising expenses "into two broad categories: promotional—advertising intended to stimulate the purchase of utility services—and institutional and informational, a broad category inclusive of all advertising not clearly intended to promote sales." The Commission declared all promotional advertising contrary to the national policy of conserving energy. It acknowledged that the ban is not a perfect vehicle for conserving energy. For example, the Commission's order prohibits promotional advertising to develop consumption during periods when demand for electricity is low. By limiting growth in "off-peak" consumption, the ban limits the "beneficial side effects" of such growth in terms of more efficient use of existing powerplants. And since oil dealers are not under the Commission's jurisdiction and thus remain free to advertise, it was recognized that the ban can achieve only "piecemeal conservationism." Still, the Commission adopted the restriction because it was deemed likely to "result in some dampening of unnecessary growth" in energy consumption.

The Commission's order explicitly permitted "informational" advertising designed to encourage "*shifts* of consumption" from peak demand times to periods of low electricity demand. Informational advertising would not seek to increase aggregate consumption, but would invite a leveling of demand throughout any given 24–hour period. The agency offered to review "specific proposals by the companies for specifically described [advertising] programs that meet these criteria."

. . .

Appellant challenged the order in state court, arguing that the Commission had restrained commercial speech in violation of the First and Fourteenth Amendments. The Commission's order was upheld by the trial court and at the intermediate appellate level. The New York Court of Appeals affirmed.... We ... reverse.

II.

The Commission's order restricts only commercial speech, that is, expression related solely to the economic interests of the speaker and its audience.... In applying the First Amendment to this area, we have rejected the "highly paternalistic" view that government has complete power to suppress or regulate commercial speech....

Nevertheless, our decisions have recognized "the 'commonsense' distinction between speech proposing a commercial transaction, which occurs in an area traditionally subject to government regulation and other varieties of speech." ...[5] The Constitution therefore accords a lesser protection to commercial speech than to other constitutionally guaranteed expression.... The protection available for particular commercial expression turns on the nature both of the expression and of the governmental interests served by its regulation.

. . .

If the communication is neither misleading nor related to unlawful activity, the government's power is more circumscribed. The State must assert a substantial interest to be achieved by restrictions on commercial speech. Moreover, the regulatory technique must be in proportion to that interest. The limitation on expression must be designed carefully to achieve the State's goal. Compliance with this requirement may be measured by two criteria. First, the restriction must directly advance the state interest involved; the regulation may not be sustained if it provides only ineffective or remote support for the government's purpose. Second, if the governmental interest could be served as well by a more limited restriction on commercial speech, the excessive restrictions cannot survive....[8]

. . .

In commercial speech cases, then, a four-part analysis has developed. At the outset, we must determine whether the expression is protected by the First Amendment. For commercial speech to come within that provision, it at least must concern lawful activity and not be misleading. Next, we ask whether the asserted governmental interest is substantial. If both inquiries yield positive answers, we must determine whether the regulation directly advances the governmental interest asserted, and whether it is not more extensive than is necessary to serve that interest.

---

5. ... [T]he concurring opinion of Mr. Justice Stevens views the Commission's order as suppressing more than commercial speech because it would outlaw, for example, advertising that promoted electricity consumption by touting the environmental benefits of such uses. Apparently the concurring opinion would accord full First Amendment protection to all promotional advertising that includes claims "relating to ... questions frequently discussed and debated by our political leaders."

Although this approach responds to the serious issues surrounding our national energy policy as raised in this case, we think it would blur further the line the Court has sought to draw in commercial speech cases. It would grant broad constitutional protection to any advertising that links a product to a current public debate. But many, if not most, products may be tied to public concerns with the environment, energy, economic policy, or individual health and safety. ...

8. This analysis is not an application of the "overbreadth" doctrine....

In this case, the Commission's prohibition acts directly against the promotional activities of Central Hudson, and to the extent the limitations are unnecessary to serve the State's interest, they are invalid.

III.

We now apply this four-step analysis for commercial speech to the Commission's arguments in support of its ban on promotional advertising.

A.

The Commission does not claim that the expression at issue either is inaccurate or relates to unlawful activity. Yet the New York Court of Appeals questioned whether Central Hudson's advertising is protected commercial speech. Because appellant holds a monopoly over the sale of electricity in its service area, the state court suggested that the Commission's order restricts no commercial speech of any worth. The court stated that advertising in a "noncompetitive market" could not improve the decisionmaking of consumers. The court saw no constitutional problem with barring commercial speech that it viewed as conveying little useful information.

This reasoning falls short of establishing that appellant's advertising is not commercial speech protected by the First Amendment. Monopoly over the supply of a product provides no protection from competition with substitutes for that product. Electric utilities compete with suppliers of fuel oil and natural gas in several markets, such as those for home heating and industrial power. . . .

. . .

B.

. . . The Commission argues, and the New York court agreed, that the State's interest in conserving energy is sufficient to support suppression of advertising designed to increase consumption of electricity. In view of our country's dependence on energy resources beyond our control, no one can doubt the importance of energy conservation. Plainly, therefore, the state interest asserted is substantial.

. . .

C.

Next, we focus on the relationship between the State's interests and the advertising ban. . . .

. . .

There is an immediate connection between advertising and demand for electricity. Central Hudson would not contest the advertising ban unless it believed that promotion would increase its sales. Thus, we find a direct link between the state interest in conservation and the Commission's order.

D.

We come finally to the critical inquiry in this case: whether the Commission's complete suppression of speech ordinarily protected by the First Amendment is no more extensive than necessary to further the State's interest in energy conservation. The Commission's order reaches all promotional advertising, regardless of the impact of the touted service on overall energy use. But the energy conservation rationale, as important as it is, cannot justify suppressing information about electric devices or services that would cause no net increase in total energy use. In addition, no showing has been made that a more limited restriction on the content of promotional advertising would not serve adequately the State's interests.

Appellant insists that but for the ban, it would advertise products and services that use energy efficiently. These include the "heat pump," which both parties acknowledge to be a major improvement in electric heating, and the use of electric heat as a "back-up" to solar and other heat sources. Although the Commission has questioned the efficiency of electric heating before this Court, neither the Commission's Policy Statement nor its order denying rehearing made findings on this issue. In the absence of authoritative findings to the contrary, we must credit as within the realm of possibility the claim that electric heat can be an efficient alternative in some circumstances.

The Commission's order prevents appellant from promoting electric services that would reduce energy use by diverting demand from less efficient sources, or that would consume roughly the same amount of energy as do alternative sources. In neither situation would the utility's advertising endanger conservation or mislead the public. To the extent that the Commission's order suppresses speech that in no way impairs the State's interest in energy conservation, the Commission's order violates the First and Fourteenth Amendments and must be invalidated. . . .

The Commission also has not demonstrated that its interest in conservation cannot be protected adequately by more limited regulation of appellant's commercial expression. To further its policy of conservation, the Commission could attempt to restrict the format and content of Central Hudson's advertising. It might, for example, require that the advertisements include information about the relative efficiency and expense of the offered service, both under current conditions and for the foreseeable future.... In the absence of a showing that more limited speech regulation would be ineffective, we cannot approve the complete suppression of Central Hudson's advertising.

IV.

Our decision today in no way disparages the national interest in energy conservation. We accept without reservation the argument that conservation, as well as the development of alternative energy sources, is an imperative national goal. Administrative bodies empowered to regulate electric utilities have the authority—and indeed the duty—to take appropriate action to further this goal. When, however, such action involves the suppression of speech, the First and Fourteenth Amendments require that the restriction be no more extensive than is necessary to serve the state interest. In this case, the record before us fails to show that the total ban on promotional advertising meets this requirement.

Accordingly, the judgment of the New York Court of Appeals is reversed.

. . .

Mr. Justice Blackmun with whom Mr. Justice Brennan joins, concurring in the judgment.

I agree with the Court that the Public Service Commission's ban on promotional advertising of electricity by public utilities is inconsistent with the First and Fourteenth Amendments. I concur only in the Court's judgment, however, because I believe the test now evolved and applied by the Court is not consistent with our prior cases and does not provide adequate protection for truthful, nonmisleading, noncoercive commercial speech.

. . .

I seriously doubt whether suppression of information concerning the availability and price of a legally offered product is ever a permissible way for the

State to "dampen" demand for or use of the product. Even though "commercial" speech is involved, such a regulatory measure strikes at the heart of the First Amendment. This is because it is a covert attempt by the State to manipulate the choices of its citizens, not by persuasion or direct regulation, but by depriving the public of the information needed to make a free choice....

. . .

It appears that the Court would permit the State to ban all direct advertising of air conditioning, assuming that a more limited restriction on such advertising would not effectively deter the public from cooling its homes. In my view, our cases do not support this type of suppression. If a governmental unit believes that use or overuse of air conditioning is a serious problem, it must attack that problem directly, by prohibiting air conditioning or regulating thermostat levels. . . .

Mr. Justice Stevens, with whom Mr. Justice Brennan joins, concurring in the judgment.

Because "commercial speech" is afforded less constitutional protection than other forms of speech, it is important that the commercial speech concept not be defined too broadly lest speech deserving of greater constitutional protection be inadvertently suppressed. The issue in this case is whether New York's prohibition on the promotion of the use of electricity through advertising is a ban on nothing but commercial speech.

In my judgment one of the two definitions the Court uses in addressing that issue is too broad and the other may be somewhat too narrow. The Court first describes commercial speech as "expression related solely to the economic interests of the speaker and its audience." Although it is not entirely clear whether this definition uses the subject matter of the speech or the motivation of the speaker as the limiting factor, it seems clear to me that it encompasses speech that is entitled to the maximum protection afforded by the First Amendment. Neither a labor leader's exhortation to strike, nor an economist's dissertation on the money supply, should receive any lesser protection because the subject matter concerns only the economic interests of the audience. Nor should the economic motivation of a speaker qualify his constitutional protection; even Shakespeare may have been motivated by the prospect of pecuniary reward. Thus, the Court's first definition of commercial speech is unquestionably too broad.

The Court's second definition refers to " 'speech proposing a commercial transaction.' " A salesman's solicitation, a broker's offer, and a manufacturer's publication of a price list or the terms of his standard warranty would unquestionably fit within this concept. Presumably, the definition is intended to encompass advertising that advises possible buyers of the availability of specific products at specific prices and describes the advantages of purchasing such items. Perhaps it also extends to other communications that do little more than make the name of a product or a service more familiar to the general public. Whatever the precise contours of the concept, and perhaps it is too early to enunciate an exact formulation, I am persuaded that it should not include the entire range of communication that is embraced within the term "promotional advertising."

This case involves a governmental regulation that completely bans promotional advertising by an electric utility. This ban encompasses a great deal more than mere proposals to engage in certain kinds of commercial transactions. It prohibits all advocacy of the immediate or future use of electricity. It curtails expression by an informed and interested group of persons of their point of view on questions relating to the production and consumption of electrical energy—questions frequently discussed and debated by our political leaders. For example, an electric company's advocacy of the use of electric heat for environmental reasons, as opposed to wood-burning stoves, would seem to fall squarely within New York's promotional advertising ban and also within the bounds of maximum First Amendment protection. The breadth of the ban thus exceeds the boundaries of the commercial speech concept, however that concept may be defined.

The justification for the regulation is nothing more than the expressed fear that the audience may find the utility's message persuasive. Without the aid of any coercion, deception, or misinformation, truthful communication may persuade some citizens to consume more electricity than they otherwise would. I assume that such a consequence would be undesirable and that government may therefore prohibit and punish the unnecessary or excessive use of electricity than they otherwise would. I assume that such a consequence would be undesirable and that government may therefore prohibit and punish the unnecessary or excessive use of electricity. But if the perceived harm associated with greater electrical usage is not sufficiently serious to justify direct regulation, surely it does not constitute the kind of clear and present danger that can justify the suppression of speech.

In sum I concur in the result because I do not consider this to be a "commercial speech" case. Accordingly, I see no need to decide whether the Court's four-part analysis, adequately protects commercial speech—as properly defined—in the face of a blanket ban of the sort involved in this case.

Mr. Justice Rehnquist, dissenting.

. . .

The Court's decision today fails to give due deference to [the] subordinate position of commercial speech. The Court in so doing returns to the bygone era of Lochner v. New York, 198 U.S. 45 (1905), in which it was common practice for this Court to strike down economic regulations adopted by a State based on the Court's own notions of the most appropriate means for the State to implement its considered policies.

. . . New York's order here is in my view more akin to an economic regulation to which virtually complete deference should be accorded by this Court.

I doubt there would be any question as to the constitutionality of New York's conservation effort if the Public Service Commission had chosen to raise the price of electricity, . . . to condition its sale on specified terms, . . . or to restrict its production, ... In terms of constitutional values, I think that such controls are virtually indistinguishable from the State's ban on promotional advertising.

. . .

THE DEFINITION OF COMMERCIAL SPEECH

The conventional definition of commercial speech is that it is speech "proposing a commercial transaction." Justice Powell's *Central Hudson* opinion also defines commercial speech as that "related solely to the economic interests of the speaker and its audience." Are there differences between those two definitions? In Bolger v. Youngs Drug Products Corp., 463 U.S. 60 (1983), the Court determined that "informational pamphlets" discussing the desirability of prophylactics in general and the manufacturer's products in particular were commercial speech even though they were linked to a public debate. On the other hand, the Court stated in Board of Trustees of the State University of New York v. Fox, 492 U.S. 469 (1989), that giving legal advice or medical consultation for a fee was not commercial speech—speech for a profit was not necessarily speech that proposes a commercial transaction.

Consider whether the speech involved in the following cases falls within the parameters of commercial speech doctrine. Dun & Bradstreet, Inc. v. Greenmoss Builders, Inc., 472 U.S. 749 (1985), page 1275, supra (commercial credit report); Lowe v. Securities and Exchange Commission, 472 U.S. 181 (1985) (newsletters containing investment advice and commentary); San Francisco Arts & Athletics, Inc. v. United States Olympic Committee, 483 U.S. 522 (1987) (federal statute granting Committee power to prohibit commercial and promotional uses of the word "Olympic"); City of Cincinnati v. Discovery Network, Inc., 507 U.S. 410 (1993) (free magazine, consisting primarily of promotional material relating to publisher's adult education program, also included information about current events of general interest; free magazine, consisting primarily of advertisements of real estate for sale, also included information about interest rates, market trends, and other real estate matters).

CHARITABLE SOLICITATION

Constitutionally protected commercial speech is not limited to advertising. In Schaumburg v. Citizens for a Better Environment, 444 U.S. 620 (1980), the Court invalidated an ordinance that prohibited solicitation for charities that received less than 75 percent of the receipts. Riley v. National Federation of Blind of N.C., Inc., 487 U.S. 781 (1988), held that it was unconstitutional to require solicitors to disclose the percentage of funds raised that would go to charities before asking for money. (The Court concluded that there were "less burdensome" alternatives available, such as state publication of financial disclosure forms that professional fundraisers were required to file. See also Secretary of State of Maryland v. Joseph H. Munson Co., 467 U.S. 947 (1984).) Illinois v. Telemarketing Associates, Inc., 538 U.S. 600 (2003), involved a state court action for fraud that the state attorney general filed against a corporation which retained more than 85 percent of the gross receipts from its solicitation of contributions to a charity. In permitting the action to proceed, the Court emphasized that the defendant was charged with making affirmatively false or misleading representations that were not protected by the First Amendment. The Court's earlier cases would be relevant if the complaint merely had alleged that the defendant's fundraising campaign was fraudulent only because so little money went to the charity. In this case, however, the complaint alleged that the defendant's telemarketers made affirmatively false statements to potential donors, leading them to believe that a substantial portion of their contributions would reach the charity.

44 Liquormart, Inc. v. Rhode Island

517 U.S. 484, 116 S.Ct. 1495, 134 L.Ed.2d 711 (1996).

Justice Stevens announced the judgment of the Court and delivered the opinion of the Court with respect to Parts I, II, VII, and VIII, an opinion with respect to Parts III and V, in which Justice Kennedy, Justice Souter, and Justice Ginsburg join, an opinion with respect to Part VI, in which Justice Kennedy, Justice Thomas, and Justice Ginsburg join, and an opinion with respect to Part IV, in which Justice Kennedy and Justice Ginsburg join.

Last Term we held that a federal law abridging a brewer's right to provide the public with accurate information about the alcoholic content of malt beverages is unconstitutional. Rubin v. Coors Brewing Co., 514 U.S. 476, 491 (1995). We now hold that Rhode Island's statutory prohibition against advertisements that provide the public with accurate information about retail prices of alcoholic beverages is also invalid. Our holding rests on the conclusion that such an advertising ban is an abridgment of speech protected by the First Amendment and that it is not shielded from constitutional scrutiny by the Twenty-first Amendment.

I

In 1956, the Rhode Island Legislature enacted two separate prohibitions against advertising the retail price of alcoholic beverages. The first applies to vendors licensed in Rhode Island as well as to out-of-state manufacturers, wholesalers, and shippers. It prohibits them from "advertising in any manner whatsoever" the price of any alcoholic beverage offered for sale in the State; the only exception is for price tags or signs displayed with the merchandise within licensed premises and not visible from the street. The second statute applies to the Rhode Island news media. It contains a categorical prohibition against the publication or broadcast of any advertisements—even those referring to sales in other States—that "make reference to the price of any alcoholic beverages."

. . .

II

Petitioners 44 Liquormart, Inc. (44 Liquormart), and Peoples Super Liquor Stores, Inc. (Peoples), are licensed retailers of alcoholic beverages. Petitioner 44 Liquormart operates a store in Rhode Island and petitioner Peoples operates several stores in Massachusetts that are patronized by Rhode Island residents. Peoples uses alcohol price advertising extensively in Massachusetts, where such advertising is permitted, but Rhode Island newspapers and other media outlets have refused to accept such ads.

Complaints from competitors about an advertisement placed by 44 Liquormart in a Rhode Island newspaper in 1991 generated enforcement proceedings that in turn led to the initiation of this litigation. The advertisement did not state the price of any alcoholic beverages. Indeed, it noted that "State law prohibits advertising liquor prices." The ad did, however, state the low prices at which peanuts, potato chips, and Schweppes mixers were being offered, identify various brands of packaged liquor, and include the word "WOW" in large letters next to pictures of vodka and rum bottles. Based on the conclusion that the implied reference to bargain prices for liquor violated the statutory ban on price advertising, the Rhode Island Liquor Control Administrator assessed a $400 fine.

After paying the fine, 44 Liquormart, joined by Peoples, filed this action . . . in the Federal District Court seeking a declaratory judgment that the two statutes and the administrator's implementing regulations violate the First Amendment. . . .

. . .

. . . [The District Court] concluded that the price advertising ban was unconstitutional. . . .

The Court of Appeals reversed. . . .

. . . .

III

. . .

In Central Hudson Gas & Elec. Corp. v. Public Serv. Comm'n of N. Y., 447 U.S. 557 (1980), we took stock of our developing commercial speech jurisprudence. . . .

. . .

. . . [T]he majority explained that although the special nature of commercial speech may require less than strict review of its regulation, special concerns arise from "regulations that entirely suppress commercial speech in order to pursue a nonspeech-related policy." . . . In those circumstances, "a ban on speech could screen from public view the underlying governmental policy." . . . As a result, the Court concluded that "special care" should attend the review of such blanket bans, and it pointedly remarked that "in recent years this Court has not approved a blanket ban on commercial speech unless the speech itself was flawed in some way, either because it was deceptive or related to unlawful activity." . . .

IV

. . . Rhode Island errs in concluding that all commercial speech regulations are subject to a similar form of constitutional review simply because they target a similar category of expression. The mere fact that messages propose commercial transactions does not in and of itself dictate the constitutional analysis that should apply to decisions to suppress them. . . .

When a State regulates commercial messages to protect consumers from misleading, deceptive, or aggressive sales practices, or requires the disclosure of beneficial consumer information, the purpose of its regulation is consistent with the reasons for according constitutional protection to commercial speech and therefore justifies less than strict review. However, when a State entirely prohibits the dissemination of truthful, nonmisleading commercial messages for reasons unrelated to the preservation of a fair bargaining process, there is far less reason to depart from the rigorous review that the First Amendment generally demands.

. . .

The special dangers that attend complete bans on truthful, nonmisleading commercial speech cannot be explained away by appeals to the "commonsense distinctions" that exist between commercial and noncommercial speech. . . . Regulations that suppress the truth are no less troubling because they target objectively verifiable information, nor are they less effective because they aim at durable messages. As a result, neither the "greater objectivity" nor the "greater hardiness" of truthful, nonmisleading commercial speech justifies reviewing its complete suppression with added deference. . . .

It is the State's interest in protecting consumers from "commercial harms" that provides "the typical reason why commercial speech can be subject to greater governmental regulation than noncommercial speech." . . . Yet bans that target truthful, nonmisleading commercial messages rarely protect consumers from such harms. Instead, such bans often serve only to obscure an "underlying governmental policy" that could be implemented without regulating speech. . . . In this way, these commercial speech bans not only hinder consumer choice, but also impede debate over central issues of public policy. . . .

Precisely because bans against truthful, nonmisleading commercial speech rarely seek to protect consumers from either deception or overreaching, they usually rest solely on the offensive assumption that the public will respond "irrationally" to the truth. . . . The First Amendment directs us to be especially skeptical of regulations that seek to keep people in the dark for what the government perceives to be their own good. That teaching applies equally to state attempts to deprive consumers of accurate information about their chosen products. . . .

V

In this case, there is no question that Rhode Island's price advertising ban constitutes a blanket prohibition against truthful, nonmisleading speech about a lawful product. There is also no question that the ban serves an end unrelated to consumer protection. Accordingly, we must review the price advertising ban with "special care," *Central Hudson* . . . mindful that speech prohibitions of this type rarely survive constitutional review. . . .

The State argues that the price advertising prohibition should nevertheless be upheld because it directly advances the State's substantial interest in promoting temperance, and because it is no more extensive than necessary. . . .

In evaluating the ban's effectiveness in advancing the State's interest, we note that a commercial speech regulation "may not be sustained if it provides only ineffective or remote support for the government's purpose." *Central Hudson* . . . For that reason, the State bears the burden of showing not merely that its regulation will advance its interest, but also that it will do so "to a material degree." . . . The need for the State to make such a showing is particularly great given the drastic nature of its chosen means—the wholesale suppression of truthful, nonmisleading information. Accordingly, we must determine whether the State has shown that the price advertising ban will significantly reduce alcohol consumption.

We can agree that common sense supports the conclusion that a prohibition against price advertising, like a collusive agreement among competitors to refrain from such advertising, will tend to mitigate competition and maintain prices at a higher level than would prevail in a completely free market. Despite the absence of proof on the point, we can even agree with the State's contention that it is reasonable to assume that demand, and hence consumption throughout the market, is somewhat lower whenever a higher, noncompetitive price level prevails. However, without any findings of fact, or indeed any evidentiary support whatsoever, we cannot agree with the assertion that the price advertising ban will significantly advance the State's interest in promoting temperance.

Although the record suggests that the price advertising ban may have some impact on the purchasing patterns of temperate drinkers of modest means, the State has presented no evidence to suggest that its speech prohibition will significantly reduce market-wide consumption. Indeed, the District Court's considered and uncontradicted finding on this point is directly to the contrary. Moreover, the evidence suggests that the abusive drinker will probably not be deterred by a marginal price increase, and that the true alcoholic may simply reduce his purchases of other necessities.

In addition, as the District Court noted, the State has not identified what price level would lead to a significant reduction in alcohol consumption, nor has it identified the amount that it believes prices would decrease without the ban. Thus, the State's own showing reveals that any connection between the ban and a significant change in alcohol consumption would be purely fortuitous.

As is evident, any conclusion that elimination of the ban would significantly increase alcohol consumption would require us to engage in the sort of "speculation or conjecture" that is an unacceptable means of demonstrating that a restriction on commercial speech directly advances the State's asserted interest. ... Such speculation certainly does not suffice when the State takes aim at accurate commercial information for paternalistic ends.

The State also cannot satisfy the requirement that its restriction on speech be no more extensive than necessary. It is perfectly obvious that alternative forms of regulation that would not involve any restriction on speech would be more likely to achieve the State's goal of promoting temperance. As the State's own expert conceded, higher prices can be maintained either by direct regulation or by increased taxation. Per capita purchases could be limited as is the case with prescription drugs. Even educational campaigns focused on the problems of excessive, or even moderate, drinking might prove to be more effective.

As a result, even under the less than strict standard that generally applies in commercial speech cases, the State has failed to establish a "reasonable fit" between its abridgment of speech and its temperance goal. ... It necessarily follows that the price advertising ban cannot survive the more stringent constitutional review that *Central Hudson* itself concluded was appropriate for the complete suppression of truthful, nonmisleading commercial speech. ...

VI

The State responds by arguing that it merely exercised appropriate "legislative judgment" in determining that a price advertising ban would best promote temperance. Relying on the *Central Hudson* analysis set forth in Posadas de Puerto Rico Associates v. Tourism Co. of P. R., 478 U.S. 328 (1986), and United States v. Edge Broadcasting Co., 509 U.S. 418 (1993), Rhode Island first argues that, because expert opinions as to the effectiveness of the price advertising ban "go both ways," the Court of Appeals correctly concluded that the ban constituted a "reasonable choice" by the legislature. The State next contends that precedent requires us to give particular deference to that legislative choice because the State could, if it chose, ban the sale of alcoholic beverages outright. ... Finally, the State argues that deference is appropriate because alcoholic beverages are so-called "vice" products. ... We consider each of these contentions in turn.

The State's first argument fails to justify the speech prohibition at issue. Our commercial speech cases recognize some room for the exercise of legislative judgment. ... However, Rhode Island errs in concluding that *Edge* and *Posadas* establish the degree of deference that its decision to impose a price advertising ban warrants.

In *Edge*, we upheld a federal statute that permitted only those broadcasters located in States that had legalized lotteries to air lottery advertising. The statute was designed to regulate advertising about an activity that had been deemed illegal in the jurisdiction in which the broadcaster was located.... Here, by contrast, the commercial speech ban targets information about entirely lawful behavior.

Posadas is more directly relevant. There, a five-Member majority held that, under the *Central Hudson* test, it was "up to the legislature" to choose to reduce gambling by suppressing in-state casino advertising rather than engaging in educational speech. ... Rhode Island argues that this logic demonstrates the constitutionality of its own decision to ban price advertising in lieu of raising taxes or employing some other less speech-restrictive means of promoting temperance.

The reasoning in *Posadas* does support the State's argument, but, on reflection, we are now persuaded that *Posadas* erroneously performed the First Amendment analysis. The casino advertising ban was designed to keep truthful, nonmisleading speech from members of the public for fear that they would be more likely to gamble if they received it. As a result, the advertising ban served to shield the State's antigambling policy from the public scrutiny that more direct, nonspeech regulation would draw. ...

Given our longstanding hostility to commercial speech regulation of this type, *Posadas* clearly erred in concluding that it was "up to the legislature" to choose suppression over a less speech-restrictive policy. The *Posadas* majority's conclusion on that point cannot be reconciled with the unbroken line of prior cases striking down similarly broad regulations on truthful, nonmisleading advertising when non-speech-related alternatives were available. ...

Because the 5-to-4 decision in Posadas marked such a sharp break from our prior precedent, and because it concerned a constitutional question about which this Court is the final arbiter, we decline to give force to its highly deferential approach. Instead, in keeping with our prior holdings, we conclude that a state legislature does not have the broad discretion to suppress truthful, nonmisleading information for paternalistic purposes that the *Posadas* majority was willing to tolerate. ...

We also cannot accept the State's second contention, which is premised entirely on the "greater-includes-the-lesser" reasoning endorsed toward the end of the majority's opinion in *Posadas*. There, the majority stated that "the greater power to completely ban casino gambling necessarily includes the lesser power to ban advertising of casino gambling." ... It went on to state that "because the government could have enacted a wholesale prohibition of [casino gambling] it is permissible for the government to take the less intrusive step of allowing the conduct, but reducing the demand through restrictions on advertising." ... The majority concluded that it would "surely be a strange constitutional doctrine which would concede to the legislature the authority to totally ban a product or activity, but deny to the legislature the authority to forbid the stimulation of demand for the product or activity through advertising on behalf of those who would profit from such increased demand." ... On the basis of these statements, the State reasons that its undisputed authority to ban alcoholic beverages must include the power to restrict advertisements offering them for sale.

In Rubin v. Coors Brewing Co., 514 U.S. 476 (1995), the United States advanced a similar argument as a basis for supporting a statutory prohibition against revealing the alcoholic content of malt beverages on product labels. We rejected the argument, noting that the statement in the *Posadas* opinion was made only after the majority had concluded that the Puerto Rican regulation "survived the *Central Hudson* test." ... Further consideration persuades us that the "greater-includes-the-lesser" argument should be rejected for the additional and more important reason that it is inconsistent with both logic and well-settled doctrine.

Although we do not dispute the proposition that greater powers include lesser ones, we fail to see how that syllogism requires the conclusion that the State's power to regulate commercial activity is "greater" than its power to ban truthful, nonmisleading commercial speech. Contrary to the assumption made in *Posadas*, we think it quite clear that banning speech may sometimes prove far more intrusive than banning conduct. . . . [W]e reject the assumption that words are necessarily less vital to freedom than actions, or that logic somehow proves that the power to prohibit an activity is necessarily "greater" than the power to suppress speech about it.

As a matter of First Amendment doctrine, the *Posadas* syllogism is even less defensible. The text of the First Amendment makes clear that the Constitution presumes that attempts to regulate speech are more dangerous than attempts to regulate conduct. That presumption accords with the essential role that the free flow of information plays in a democratic society. As a result, the First Amendment directs that government may not suppress speech as easily as it may suppress conduct, and that speech restrictions cannot be treated as simply another means that the government may use to achieve its ends.

These basic First Amendment principles clearly apply to commercial speech; indeed, the *Posadas* majority impliedly conceded as much by applying the *Central Hudson* test. Thus, it is no answer that commercial speech concerns products and services that the government may freely regulate. . . .

. . .

Thus, just as it is perfectly clear that Rhode Island could not ban all obscene liquor ads except those that advocated temperance, we think it equally clear that its power to ban the sale of liquor entirely does not include a power to censor all advertisements that contain accurate and nonmisleading information about the price of the product. As the entire Court apparently now agrees, the statements in the *Posadas* opinion on which Rhode Island relies are no longer persuasive.

Finally, we find unpersuasive the State's contention that, under *Posadas* and *Edge*, the price advertising ban should be upheld because it targets commercial speech that pertains to a "vice" activity. The appellees premise their request for a so-called "vice" exception to our commercial speech doctrine on language in *Edge* which characterized gambling as a "vice". . . . The respondents misread our precedent. Our decision last Term striking down an alcohol-related advertising restriction effectively rejected the very contention respondents now make. . . .

Moreover, the scope of any "vice" exception to the protection afforded by the First Amendment would be difficult, if not impossible, to define. Almost any product that poses some threat to public health or public morals might reasonably be characterized by a state legislature as relating to "vice activity". Such characterization, however, is anomalous when applied to products such as alcoholic beverages, lottery tickets, or playing cards, that may be lawfully purchased on the open market. The recognition of such an exception would also have the unfortunate consequence of either allowing state legislatures to justify censorship by the simple expedient of placing the "vice" label on selected lawful activities, or requiring the federal courts to establish a federal common law of vice. . . . For these reasons, a "vice" label that is unaccompanied by a corresponding prohibition against the commercial behavior at issue fails to provide a principled justification for the regulation of commercial speech about that activity.

VII

. . .

. . . [T]he text of the Twenty-first Amendment supports the view that, while it grants the States authority over commerce that might otherwise be reserved to the Federal Government, it places no limit whatsoever on other constitutional provisions. Nevertheless, Rhode Island argues ... that in this case the Twenty-first Amendment tilts the First Amendment analysis in the State's favor.

In reaching its conclusion, the Court of Appeals relied on our decision in California v. LaRue, 409 U.S. 109 (1972). In *LaRue*, five Members of the Court relied on the Twenty-first Amendment to buttress the conclusion that the First Amendment did not invalidate California's prohibition of certain grossly sexual exhibitions in premises licensed to serve alcoholic beverages. Specifically, the opinion stated that the Twenty-first Amendment required that the prohibition be given an added presumption in favor of its validity. ... We are now persuaded that the Court's analysis in *LaRue* would have led to precisely the same result if it had placed no reliance on the Twenty-first Amendment.

Entirely apart from the Twenty-first Amendment, the State has ample power to prohibit the sale of alcoholic beverages in inappropriate locations. Moreover, in subsequent cases the Court has recognized that the States' inherent police powers provide ample authority to restrict the kind of "bacchanalian revelries" described in the *LaRue* opinion regardless of whether alcoholic beverages are involved. ... As we recently noted: "*LaRue* did not involve commercial speech about alcohol, but instead concerned the regulation of nude dancing in places where alcohol was served." ...

Without questioning the holding in *LaRue*, we now disavow its reasoning insofar as it relied on the Twenty-first Amendment....

VIII

Because Rhode Island has failed to carry its heavy burden of justifying its complete ban on price advertising, we conclude that R.I. Gen. Laws §§ 3–8–7 and 3–8–8.1, as well as Regulation 32 of the Rhode Island Liquor Control Administration, abridge speech in violation of the First Amendment as made applicable to the States by the Due Process Clause of the Fourteenth Amendment. The judgment of the Court of Appeals is therefore reversed.

It is so ordered.

Justice Scalia, concurring in part and concurring in the judgment.

I share Justice Thomas's discomfort with the *Central Hudson* test, which seems to me to have nothing more than policy intuition to support it. I also share Justice Stevens' aversion towards paternalistic governmental policies that prevent men and women from hearing facts that might not be good for them. On the other hand, it would also be paternalism for us to prevent the people of the States from enacting laws that we consider paternalistic, unless we have good reason to believe that the Constitution itself forbids them. I will take my guidance as to what the Constitution forbids, with regard to a text as indeterminate as the First Amendment's preservation of "the freedom of speech," and where the core offense of suppressing particular political ideas is not at issue, from the long accepted practices of the American people. ...

The briefs and arguments of the parties in the present case provide no illumination on that point; understandably so, since both sides accepted *Central Hudson*. ... I consider ... relevant the state legislative practices prevalent at the time the First Amendment was adopted, since almost all of the States had free-speech constitutional guarantees of their own, whose meaning was not likely to have been different from the federal constitutional provision derived from them. Perhaps more relevant still are the state legislative practices at the time the Fourteenth Amendment was adopted, since it is most improbable that that adoption was meant to overturn any existing national consensus regarding free speech. . . . The parties and their amici provide no evidence on these points.

Since I do not believe we have before us the wherewithal to declare *Central Hudson* wrong—or at least the wherewithal to say what ought to replace it—I must resolve this case in accord with our existing jurisprudence, which all except Justice Thomas agree would prohibit the challenged regulation. I am not disposed to develop new law, or reinforce old, on this issue, and accordingly I merely concur in the judgment of the Court. . . .

Justice Thomas, concurring in Parts I, II, VI, and VII, and concurring in the judgment.

In cases such as this, in which the government's asserted interest is to keep legal users of a product or service ignorant in order to manipulate their choices in the marketplace, the balancing test adopted in Central Hudson . . . should not be applied, in my view. Rather, such an "interest" is per se illegitimate and can no more justify regulation of "commercial" speech than it can justify regulation of "noncommercial" speech.

. . .

II

I do not join the principal opinion's application of the *Central Hudson* balancing test because I do not believe that such a test should be applied to a restriction of "commercial" speech, at least when, as here, the asserted interest is one that is to be achieved through keeping would-be recipients of the speech in the dark. . . . Faulting the State for failing to show that its price advertising ban decreases alcohol consumption "significantly," as Justice Stevens does, seems to imply that if the State had been more successful at keeping consumers ignorant and thereby decreasing their consumption, then the restriction might have been upheld. This contradicts *Virginia Pharmacy Bd.*'s rationale for protecting "commercial" speech in the first instance.

. . . [T]he Court's holding will in fact be quite sweeping if applied consistently in future cases. The opinions would appear to commit the courts to striking down restrictions on speech whenever a direct regulation (i.e., a regulation involving no restriction on speech regarding lawful activity at all) would be an equally effective method of dampening demand by legal users. But it would seem that directly banning a product (or rationing it, taxing it, controlling its price, or otherwise restricting its sale in specific ways) would virtually always be at least as effective in discouraging consumption as merely restricting advertising regarding the product would be, and thus virtually all restrictions with such a purpose would fail the fourth prong of the *Central Hudson* test. . . .

The upshot of the application of the fourth prong in the opinions of Justice Stevens and of Justice O'Connor seems to be that the government may not, for the purpose of keeping would-be consumers ignorant and thus decreasing demand, restrict advertising regarding commercial transactions-or at least that it may not restrict advertising regarding commercial transactions except to the extent that it outlaws or otherwise directly restricts the same transactions within its own borders. I welcome this outcome; but, rather than "applying" the fourth prong of *Central Hudson* to reach the inevitable result that all or most such advertising restrictions must be struck down, I would [hold] that all attempts to dissuade legal choices by citizens by keeping them ignorant are impermissible.

. . .

Justice O'Connor, with whom the Chief Justice, Justice Souter, and Justice Breyer join, concurring in the judgment.

. . . I agree with the Court that Rhode Island's price-advertising ban is invalid. I would resolve this case more narrowly, however, by applying our established *Central Hudson* test to determine whether this commercial-speech regulation survives First Amendment scrutiny.

. . .

Both parties agree that the first two prongs of the *Central Hudson* test are met. Even if we assume arguendo that Rhode Island's regulation also satisfies the requirement that it directly advance the governmental interest, Rhode Island's regulation fails the final prong; that is, its ban is more extensive than necessary to serve the State's interest.

. . .

. . . Rhode Island says that the ban is intended to keep alcohol prices high as a way to keep consumption low. . . .

The fit between Rhode Island's method and this particular goal is not reasonable. If the target is simply higher prices generally to discourage consumption, the regulation imposes too great, and unnecessary, a prohibition on speech in order to achieve it. The State has other methods at its disposal-methods that would more directly accomplish this stated goal without intruding on sellers' ability to provide truthful, nonmisleading information to customers. Indeed, Rhode Island's own expert conceded that "the objective of lowering consumption of alcohol by banning price advertising could be accomplished by establishing minimum prices and/or by increasing sales taxes on alcoholic beverages." . . . The ready availability of such alternatives—at least some of which would far more effectively achieve Rhode Island's only professed goal, at comparatively small additional administrative cost—demonstrates that the fit between ends and means is not narrowly tailored. . . .

Respondents point for support to Posadas de Puerto Rico Associates v. Tourism Co. of P. R.,

. . .

It is true that *Posadas* accepted as reasonable, without further inquiry, Puerto Rico's assertions that the regulations furthered the government's interest and were no more extensive than necessary to serve that interest. Since *Posadas*, however, this Court has examined more searchingly the State's professed goal, and the speech restriction put into place to further it, before accepting a State's claim that the speech restriction satisfies First Amendment scrutiny. . . . The closer look that we have required since *Posadas* comports better with the purpose of the analysis set out in *Central Hudson*, by requiring the State to show that the speech restriction directly advances its interest and is narrowly tailored. Under such a closer look, Rhode Island's price-advertising ban clearly fails to pass muster.

Because Rhode Island's regulation fails even the less stringent standard set out in *Central Hudson*, nothing here requires adoption of a new analysis for the evaluation of commercial speech regulation. . . . I would not here undertake the question whether the test we have employed since *Central Hudson* should be displaced.

. . .

... While I agree with the Court's finding that the regulation is invalid, I would decide that issue on narrower grounds. I therefore concur in the judgment.

Greater New Orleans Broadcasting Association, Inc. v. United States

527 U.S. 173, 119 S.Ct. 1923, 144 L.Ed.2d 161 (1999).

Justice Stevens delivered the opinion of the Court.

Federal law prohibits some, but by no means all, broadcast advertising of lotteries and casino gambling. In United States v. Edge Broadcasting Co., 509 U.S. 418 (1993), we upheld the constitutionality of 18 U.S.C. § 1304 as applied to broadcast advertising of Virginia's lottery by a radio station located in North Carolina, where no such lottery was authorized. Today we hold that § 1304 may not be applied to advertisements of private casino gambling that are broadcast by radio or television stations located in Louisiana, where such gambling is legal.

I

Through most of the 19th and the first half of the 20th centuries, Congress adhered to a policy that not only discouraged the operation of lotteries and similar schemes, but forbade the dissemination of information concerning such enterprises by use of the mails, even when the lottery in question was chartered by a state legislature. ... [W]e found that the notion that "lotteries ... are supposed to have a demoralizing influence upon the people" provided sufficient justification for excluding circulars concerning such enterprises from the federal postal system. Ex parte Jackson, 96 U.S. 727, 736–737 (1878). We likewise deferred to congressional judgment in upholding the similar exclusion for newspapers that contained either lottery advertisements or prize lists. In re Rapier, 143 U.S. 110, 134–135 (1892) ... The current versions of these early antilottery statutes are now codified at 18 U.S.C. §§ 1301–1303.

Congress extended its restrictions on lottery-related information to broadcasting as communications technology made that practice both possible and profitable. It enacted the statute at issue in this case as § 316 of the Communications Act of 1934, 48 Stat. 1088. Now codified at 18 U.S.C. § 1304 ("Broadcasting lottery information"), the statute prohibits radio and television broadcasting, by any station for which a license is required, of

"any advertisement of or information concerning any lottery, gift enterprise, or similar scheme, offering prizes dependent in whole or in part upon lot or chance, or any list of the prizes drawn or awarded by means of any such lottery, gift enterprise, or scheme, whether said list contains any part or all of such prizes."

... Although § 1304 is a criminal statute, ... in practice, the provision traditionally has been enforced by the Federal Communications Commission (FCC), which imposes administrative sanctions on radio and television licensees for violations of the agency's implementing regulation. ...Petitioners now concede that the broadcast ban in § 1304 and the FCC's regulation encompasses advertising for privately owned casinos ...

During the second half of this century, Congress dramatically narrowed the scope of the broadcast prohibition in § 1304. The first inroad was minor: In 1950, certain not-for-profit fishing contests were exempted as "innocent pastimes ... far removed from the reprehensible type of gambling activity which it was paramount in the congressional mind to forbid." ...

Subsequent exemptions were more substantial. Responding to the growing popularity of State-run lotteries, in 1975 Congress enacted the provision that gave rise to our decision in *Edge.* ... With subsequent modifications, that amendment now exempts advertisements of State-conducted lotteries from the nationwide postal restrictions in §§ 1301 and 1302, and from the broadcast restriction in § 1304, when "broadcast by a radio or television station licensed to a location in ... a State which conducts such a lottery." ... The § 1304 broadcast restriction remained in place, however, for stations licensed in States that do not conduct lotteries. In *Edge,* we held that this remaining restriction on broadcasts from nonlottery States, such as North Carolina, supported the "laws against gambling" in those jurisdictions and properly advanced the "congressional policy of balancing the interests of lottery and nonlottery States."

In 1988, Congress enacted two additional statutes that significantly curtailed the coverage of § 1304. First, the Indian Gaming Regulatory Act (IGRA) ... exempted "any gaming conducted by an Indian tribe pursuant to" the Act from both the postal and transportation restrictions in 18 U.S.C. §§ 1301–1302, and the broadcast restriction in § 1304. ... Second, the Charity Games Advertising Clarification Act of 1988 ... extended the exemption from §§ 1301–1304 for state-run lotteries to include any other lottery, gift enterprise, or similar scheme—not prohibited by the law of the State in which it operates—when conducted by: (i) any governmental organization; (ii) any not-for-profit organization; or (iii) a commercial organization as a promotional activity "clearly occasional and ancillary to the primary business of that organization." [U]nlike the 1975 broadcast exemption for advertisements of and information concerning State-conducted lotteries, the exemptions in both of these 1988 statutes are not geographically limited; they shield messages from § 1304's reach in States that do not authorize such gambling as well as those that do.

A separate statute, the 1992 Professional and Amateur Sports Protection Act, ... proscribes most sports betting and advertising thereof. ... However, the Act also includes a variety of exemptions, some with obscured congressional purposes: (i) gambling schemes conducted by States or other governmental entities at any time between January 1, 1976, and August 31, 1990; (ii) gambling schemes authorized by statutes in effect on October 2, 1991; (iii) gambling "conducted exclusively in casinos" located in certain municipalities if the schemes were authorized within one year of the effective date of the Act and, for "commercial casino gaming scheme[s]," that had been in operation for the preceding ten years pursuant to a State constitutional provision and comprehensive State regulation applicable to that municipality; and (iv) gambling on parimutuel animal racing or jai-alai games. ... These exemptions make the scope of § 3702's advertising prohibition somewhat unclear, but the prohibition is not limited to broadcast media and does not depend on the location of a broadcast station or other disseminator of promotional materials.

Thus, unlike the uniform federal antigambling policy that prevailed in 1934 when 18 U.S.C. § 1304 was enacted, federal statutes now accommodate both pro-gambling and antigambling segments of the national polity.

II

Petitioners are an association of Louisiana broadcasters and its members who operate FCC-licensed radio and television stations in the New Orleans metropolitan area. But for the threat of sanctions . . . , petitioners would broadcast promotional advertisements for gaming available at private, for-profit casinos that are lawful and regulated in both Louisiana and neighboring Mississippi. According to an FCC official, however, "[u]nder appropriate conditions, some broadcast signals from Louisiana broadcasting stations may be heard in neighboring states including Texas and Arkansas," where private casino gambling is unlawful.

Petitioners brought this action against the United States and the FCC in the District Court for the Eastern District of Louisiana, praying for a declaration that § 1304 and the FCC's regulation violate the First Amendment as applied to them, and for an injunction preventing enforcement of the statute and the rule against them. [T]he District Court ruled in favor of the Government. . . .

A divided panel of the Court of Appeals for the Fifth Circuit . . . affirmed the grant of summary judgment to the Government. . . .

. . .

While the broadcasters' petition for certiorari was pending in this Court, we decided 44 Liquormart, Inc. v. Rhode Island, . . . [W]e . . . remanded the case for further consideration. . . .

On remand, the Fifth Circuit majority adhered to its prior conclusion. . . . We now reverse.

III

In a number of cases involving restrictions on speech that is "commercial" in nature, we have employed *Central Hudson's* four-part test to resolve First Amendment challenges . . .

. . . [P]etitioners as well as certain judges, scholars, and amici curiae have advocated repudiation of the *Central Hudson* standard and implementation of a more straightforward and stringent test for assessing the validity of governmental restrictions on commercial speech. As the opinions in *44 Liquormart* demonstrate, reasonable judges may disagree about the merits of such proposals. It is, however, an established part of our constitutional jurisprudence that we do not ordinarily reach out to make novel or unnecessarily broad pronouncements on constitutional issues when a case can be fully resolved on a narrower ground. . . . In this case, there is no need to break new ground. *Central Hudson*, as applied in our more recent commercial speech cases, provides an adequate basis for decision.

IV

All parties to this case agree that the messages petitioners wish to broadcast constitute commercial speech, and that these broadcasts would satisfy the first part of the *Central Hudson* test: Their content is not misleading and concerns lawful activities. . . .

The second part of the *Central Hudson* test asks whether the asserted governmental interest served by the speech restriction is substantial. The Solicitor General identifies two such interests: (1) reducing the social costs associated with "gambling" or " 'casino gambling,' " and (2) assisting States that "restrict gambling" or "prohibit casino gambling" within their own borders. . . .

We can accept the characterization of these two interests as "substantial," but that conclusion is by no means self-evident. . . . That Congress has generally exempted state-run lotteries and casinos from federal gambling legislation reflects a decision to defer to, and even promote, differing gambling policies in different States. . . . Whatever its character in 1934 when § 1304 was adopted, the federal policy of discouraging gambling in general, and casino gambling in particular, is now decidedly equivocal.

. . . Even though the Government has identified substantial interests, when we consider both their quality and the information sought to be suppressed, the crosscurrents in the scope and application of § 1304 become more difficult for the Government to defend.

V

The third part of the *Central Hudson* test asks whether the speech restriction directly and materially advances the asserted governmental interest. . . .

The fourth part of the test complements the direct-advancement inquiry of the third, asking whether the speech restriction is not more extensive than necessary to serve the interests that support it. . . .

. . . § 1304 cannot satisfy these standards. With regard to the first asserted interest—alleviating the social costs of casino gambling by limiting demand—the Government contends that its broadcasting restrictions directly advance that interest because "promotional" broadcast advertising concerning casino gambling increases demand for such gambling, which in turn increases the amount of casino gambling that produces those social costs. . . . [I]t does not necessarily follow that the Government's speech ban has directly and materially furthered the asserted interest. . . . [A]ny measure of the effectiveness of the Government's attempt to minimize the social costs of gambling cannot ignore Congress' simultaneous encouragement of tribal casino gambling, which may well be growing at a rate exceeding any increase in gambling or compulsive gambling that private casino advertising could produce. And, . . . the Government fails to "connect casino gambling and compulsive gambling with broadcast advertising for casino"—let alone broadcast advertising for non-Indian commercial casinos. . . .

We need not resolve the question whether any lack of evidence in the record fails to satisfy the standard of proof under *Central Hudson*, however, because the flaw in the Government's case is more fundamental: The operation of § 1304 and its attendant regulatory regime is so pierced by exemptions and inconsistencies that the Government cannot hope to exonerate it. . . . Under current law, a broadcaster may not carry advertising about privately operated commercial casino gambling, regardless of the location of the station or the casino. . . . On the other hand, advertisements for tribal casino gambling authorized by state compacts—whether operated by the tribe or by a private party pursuant to a management contract—are subject to no such broadcast ban, even if the broadcaster is located in or broadcasts to a jurisdiction with the strictest of antigambling policies. . . . Government-operated, nonprofit, and "occasional and ancillary" commercial casinos are likewise exempt. . . .

The FCC's interpretation and application of §§ 1304 and 1307 underscore the statute's infirmity. Attempting to enforce the underlying purposes and policy of the statute, the FCC has permitted broadcasters to tempt viewers with claims of "Vegas-style excitement" at a commercial "casino" if "casino" is part of the establishment's proper name and the advertisement can be taken to refer to the casino's amenities, rather than directly promote its gaming aspects. While we can hardly fault the FCC in view of the statute's focus on the suppression of certain types of information, the agency's practice is squarely at odds with the governmental interests asserted in this case.

From what we can gather, the Government is committed to prohibiting accurate product information, not commercial enticements of all kinds, and then only when conveyed over certain forms of media and for certain types of gambling—indeed, for only certain brands of casino gambling—and despite the fact that messages about the availability of such gambling are being conveyed over the airwaves by other speakers.

Even putting aside the broadcast exemptions for arguably distinguishable sorts of gambling that might also give rise to social costs about which the Federal Government is concerned—such as state lotteries and parimutuel betting on horse and dog races, . . .—the Government presents no convincing reason for pegging its speech ban to the identity of the owners or operators of the advertised casinos. The Government cites revenue needs of States and tribes that conduct casino gambling, and notes that net revenues generated by the tribal casinos are dedicated to the welfare of the tribes and their members. . . . Yet the Government admits that tribal casinos offer precisely the same types of gambling as private casinos. . . . The Government's suggestion that Indian casinos are too isolated to warrant attention is belied by a quick review of tribal geography and the Government's own evidence regarding the financial success of tribal gaming. If distance were determinative, Las Vegas might have remained a relatively small community, or simply disappeared like a desert mirage.

Ironically, the most significant difference identified by the Government between tribal and other classes of casino gambling is that the former are "heavily regulated." . . . If such direct regulation provides a basis for believing that the social costs of gambling in tribal casinos are sufficiently mitigated to make their advertising tolerable, one would have thought that Congress might have at least experimented with comparable regulation before abridging the speech rights of federally unregulated casinos. . . . There surely are practical and nonspeech-related forms of regulation—including a prohibition or supervision of gambling on credit; limitations on the use of cash machines on casino premises; controls on admissions; pot or betting limits; location restrictions; and licensing requirements—that could more directly and effectively alleviate some of the social costs of casino gambling.

. . .

Given the special federal interest in protecting the welfare of Native Americans, . . . we recognize that there may be valid reasons for imposing commercial regulations on non-Indian businesses that differ from those imposed on tribal enterprises. It does not follow, however, that those differences also justify abridging non-Indians' freedom of speech more severely than the freedom of their tribal competitors. For the power to prohibit or to regulate particular conduct does not necessarily include the power to prohibit or regulate speech about that conduct. . . . And to the extent that the purpose and operation of federal law distinguishes among information about tribal, governmental, and private casinos based on the identity of their owners or operators, the Government presents no sound reason why such lines bear any meaningful relationship to the particular interest asserted: minimizing casino gambling and its social costs by way of a (partial) broadcast ban. . . .

The second interest asserted by the Government—the derivative goal of "assisting" States with policies that disfavor private casinos—adds little to its case. We cannot see how this broadcast restraint, ambivalent as it is, might directly and adequately further any state interest in dampening consumer demand for casino gambling if it cannot achieve the same goal with respect to the similar federal interest.

Furthermore, even assuming that the state policies on which the Federal Government seeks to embellish are more coherent and pressing than their federal counterpart, § 1304 sacrifices an intolerable amount of truthful speech about lawful conduct. . . .

VI

. . . Had the Federal Government adopted a more coherent policy, or accommodated the rights of speakers in States that have legalized the underlying conduct, . . . this might be a different case. But under current federal law, as applied to petitioners and the messages that they wish to convey, the broadcast prohibition in 18 U.S.C. § 1304 . . . (1998) violates the First Amendment. The judgment of the Court of Appeals is therefore

Reversed.

Chief Justice Rehnquist, concurring.

. . .

Were Congress to undertake substantive regulation of the gambling industry, rather than simply the manner in which it may broadcast advertisements, "exemptions and inconsistencies'" such as those in § 1304 might well prove constitutionally tolerable. . . . Williamson v. Lee Optical. . . .

But when Congress regulates commercial speech, the *Central Hudson* test imposes a more demanding standard of review. I agree with the Court that that standard has not been met here and I join its opinion.

Justice Thomas, concurring in the judgment.

I continue to adhere to my view that . . . the *Central Hudson* test should not be applied because [it] can no more justify regulation of "commercial speech" than it can justify regulation of "noncommercial speech."

Lorillard Tobacco Co. v. Reilly

533 U.S. 525, 121 S.Ct. 2404, 150 L.Ed.2d 532 (2001).

Justice O'Connor delivered the opinion of the Court.

In January 1999, the Attorney General of Massachusetts promulgated comprehensive regulations governing the advertising and sale of cigarettes, smokeless tobacco, and cigars. . . . Petitioners, a group of cigarette, smokeless tobacco, and cigar manufacturers and retailers, filed suit in Federal District Court claiming that the regulations violate federal law and the United States Constitution. In large measure, the District Court determined that the regulations are valid and enforceable. The United States Court of Appeals for the First Circuit affirmed in part and reversed in part, concluding that the regulations are not pre empted by federal law and do not violate the First Amendment. The first question presented for our review is whether certain cigarette advertising regulations are pre-empted by the Federal Cigarette Labeling and Advertising Act (FCLAA), . . . 15 U.S.C. § 1331 et seq. The second question presented is whether certain regulations governing the advertising and sale of tobacco products violate the First Amendment.

I

In November 1998, Massachusetts, along with over 40 other States, reached a landmark agreement with major manufacturers in the cigarette industry. The signatory States settled their claims against these companies in exchange for monetary payments and permanent injunctive relief. ... At the press conference covering Massachusetts' decision to sign the agreement, then-Attorney General Scott Harshbarger announced that as one of his last acts in office, he would create consumer protection regulations to restrict advertising and sales practices for tobacco products. He explained that the regulations were necessary in order to "close holes" in the settlement agreement and "to stop Big Tobacco from recruiting new customers among the children of Massachusetts."

In January 1999, pursuant to his authority to prevent unfair or deceptive practices in trade, ... the Massachusetts Attorney General (Attorney General) promulgated regulations governing the sale and advertisement of cigarettes, smokeless tobacco, and cigars. ... The regulations have a broader scope than the master settlement agreement, reaching advertising, sales practices, and members of the tobacco industry not covered by the agreement. The regulations place a variety of restrictions on outdoor advertising, point-of-sale advertising, retail sales transactions, transactions by mail, promotions, sampling of products, and labels for cigars.

. . .

II

[The Court held that the State's outdoor and point-of-sale advertising regulations for cigarettes were pre-empted.]

III

By its terms, the FCLAA's pre-emption provision only applies to cigarettes. Accordingly, we must evaluate the smokeless tobacco and cigar petitioners' First Amendment challenges to the State's outdoor and point-of-sale advertising regulations. The cigarette petitioners did not raise a pre-emption challenge to the sales practices regulations. Thus, we must analyze the cigarette as well as the smokeless tobacco and cigar petitioners' claim that certain sales practices regulations for tobacco products violate the First Amendment.

A

. . .

Petitioners urge us to reject the *Central Hudson* analysis and apply strict scrutiny. ... But here, as in Greater New Orleans [Broadcasting Assn., Inc. v. United States], 527 U.S. 173, 184 (1999), we see "no need to break new ground. *Central Hudson*, as applied in our more recent commercial speech cases, provides an adequate basis for decision." ...

Only the last two steps of *Central Hudson*'s four-part analysis are at issue here. The Attorney General has assumed for purposes of summary judgment that petitioners' speech is entitled to First Amendment protection. With respect to the second step, none of the petitioners contests the importance of the State's interest in preventing the use of tobacco products by minors.

The third step of *Central Hudson* concerns the relationship between the harm that underlies the State's interest and the means identified by the State to advance that interest. ...

The last step of the *Central Hudson* analysis ... requires a reasonable " 'fit between the legislature's ends and the means chosen to accomplish those ends, ... a means narrowly tailored to achieve the desired objective.' " ... Focusing on the third and fourth steps of the *Central Hudson* analysis, we first address the outdoor advertising and point-of-sale advertising regulations for smokeless tobacco and cigars. We then address the sales practices regulations for all tobacco products.

B

The outdoor advertising regulations prohibit smokeless tobacco or cigar advertising within a 1,000–foot radius of a school or playground. ...

1

The smokeless tobacco and cigar petitioners contend that the Attorney General's regulations do not satisfy *Central Hudson*'s third step. They maintain that although the Attorney General may have identified a problem with underage cigarette smoking, he has not identified an equally severe problem with respect to underage use of smokeless tobacco or cigars. ... The cigar petitioners catalogue a list of differences between cigars and other tobacco products, including the characteristics of the products and marketing strategies. The petitioners finally contend that the Attorney General cannot prove that advertising has a causal link to tobacco use such that limiting advertising will materially alleviate any problem of underage use of their products.

In previous cases, we have acknowledged the theory that product advertising stimulates demand for products, while suppressed advertising may have the opposite effect. ... The Attorney General cites numerous studies to support this theory in the case of tobacco products.

. . .

Our review of the record reveals that the Attorney General has provided ample documentation of the problem with underage use of smokeless tobacco and cigars. In addition, we disagree with petitioners' claim that there is no evidence that preventing targeted campaigns and limiting youth exposure to advertising will decrease underage use of smokeless tobacco and cigars. On this record and in the posture of summary judgment, we are unable to conclude that the Attorney General's decision to regulate advertising of smokeless tobacco and cigars in an effort to combat the use of tobacco products by minors was based on mere "speculation [and] conjecture." ...

2

Whatever the strength of the Attorney General's evidence to justify the outdoor advertising regulations, however, we conclude that the regulations do not satisfy the fourth step of the *Central Hudson* analysis. The final step of the *Central Hudson* analysis, the "critical inquiry in this case," requires a reasonable fit between the means and ends of the regulatory scheme. ... The Attorney General's regulations do not meet this standard. The broad sweep of the regulations indicates that the Attorney General did not "carefully calculat[e] the costs and benefits associated with the burden on speech imposed" by the regulations. ...

The outdoor advertising regulations prohibit any smokeless tobacco or cigar advertising within 1,000 feet of schools or playgrounds. . . . [T]he Court of Appeals concluded that the regulations prohibit advertising in a substantial portion of the major metropolitan areas of Massachusetts. . . .

The substantial geographical reach of the Attorney General's outdoor advertising regulations is compounded by other factors. "Outdoor" advertising includes not only advertising located outside an establishment, but also advertising inside a store if that advertising is visible from outside the store. The regulations restrict advertisements of any size and the term advertisement also includes oral statements. . . .

In some geographical areas, these regulations would constitute nearly a complete ban on the communication of truthful information about smokeless tobacco and cigars to adult consumers. The breadth and scope of the regulations, and the process by which the Attorney General adopted the regulations, do not demonstrate a careful calculation of the speech interests involved.

First, the Attorney General did not seem to consider the impact of the 1,000-foot restriction on commercial speech in major metropolitan areas. . . . The uniformly broad sweep of the geographical limitation demonstrates a lack of tailoring.

In addition, the range of communications restricted seems unduly broad. For instance, it is not clear from the regulatory scheme why a ban on oral communications is necessary to further the State's interest. Apparently that restriction means that a retailer is unable to answer inquiries about its tobacco products if that communication occurs outdoors. Similarly, a ban on all signs of any size seems ill suited to target the problem of highly visible billboards, as opposed to smaller signs. To the extent that studies have identified particular advertising and promotion practices that appeal to youth, tailoring would involve targeting those practices while permitting others. As crafted, the regulations make no distinction among practices on this basis.

. . .

The State's interest in preventing underage tobacco use is substantial, and even compelling, but it is no less true that the sale and use of tobacco products by adults is a legal activity. We must consider that tobacco retailers and manufacturers have an interest in conveying truthful information about their products to adults, and adults have a corresponding interest in receiving truthful information about tobacco products. . . . As the State protects children from tobacco advertisements, tobacco manufacturers and retailers and their adult consumers still have a protected interest in communication. . . .

. . .

. . . [A] retailer in Massachusetts may have no means of communicating to passersby on the street that it sells tobacco products because alternative forms of advertisement, like newspapers, do not allow that retailer to propose an instant transaction in the way that onsite advertising does. The ban on any indoor advertising that is visible from the outside also presents problems in establishments like convenience stores, which have unique security concerns that counsel in favor of full visibility of the store from the outside. It is these sorts of considerations that the Attorney General failed to incorporate into the regulatory scheme.

We conclude that the Attorney General has failed to show that the outdoor advertising regulations for smokeless tobacco and cigars are not more extensive than necessary to advance the State's substantial interest in preventing underage tobacco use. Justice Stevens urges that the Court remand the case for further development of the factual record. We believe that a remand is inappropriate in this case because the State had ample opportunity to develop a record with respect to tailoring (as it had to justify its decision to regulate advertising), and additional evidence would not alter the nature of the scheme before the Court.

A careful calculation of the costs of a speech regulation does not mean that a State must demonstrate that there is no incursion on legitimate speech interests, but a speech regulation cannot unduly impinge on the speaker's ability to propose a commercial transaction and the adult listener's opportunity to obtain information about products. After reviewing the outdoor advertising regulations, we find the calculation in this case insufficient for purposes of the First Amendment.

C

Massachusetts has also restricted indoor, point-of-sale advertising for smokeless tobacco and cigars. Advertising cannot be "placed lower than five feet from the floor of any retail establishment which is located within a one thousand foot radius of" any school or playground. . . .

We conclude that the point-of-sale advertising regulations fail both the third and fourth steps of the *Central Hudson* analysis. . . . [T]he State's goal is to prevent minors from using tobacco products and to curb demand for that activity by limiting youth exposure to advertising. The 5 foot rule does not seem to advance that goal. Not all children are less than 5 feet tall, and those who are certainly have the ability to look up and take in their surroundings.

By contrast to Justice Stevens, we do not believe this regulation can be construed as a mere regulation of conduct under United States v. O'Brien, 391 U.S. 367 (1968). To qualify as a regulation of communicative action governed by the scrutiny outlined in *O'Brien*, the State's regulation must be unrelated to expression. . . . Here, Massachusetts' height restriction is an attempt to regulate directly the communicative impact of indoor advertising.

Massachusetts may wish to target tobacco advertisements and displays that entice children, much like floor-level candy displays in a convenience store, but the blanket height restriction does not constitute a reasonable fit with that goal. . . . There is no de minimis exception for a speech restriction that lacks sufficient tailoring or justification. We conclude that the restriction on the height of indoor advertising is invalid under *Central Hudson*'s third and fourth prongs.

D

The Attorney General also promulgated a number of regulations that restrict sales practices by cigarette, smokeless tobacco, and cigar manufacturers and retailers. Among other restrictions, the regulations bar the use of self-service displays and require that tobacco products be placed out of the reach of all consumers in a location accessible only to salespersons. Two of the cigarette petitioners . . . , petitioner U.S. Smokeless Tobacco Company, and the cigar petitioners challenge the sales practices regulations on First Amendment grounds. The cigar petitioners additionally challenge a provision that prohibits sampling or promotional giveaways of cigars or little cigars. . . .

. . . .

. . . As we read the regulations, they basically require tobacco retailers to place tobacco products behind counters and require customers to have contact with a salesperson before they are able to handle a tobacco product.

The cigarette and smokeless tobacco petitioners contend that "the same First Amendment principles that require invalidation of the outdoor and indoor advertising restrictions require invalidation of the display regulations at issue in this case." The cigar petitioners contend that self-service displays for cigars cannot be prohibited because each brand of cigar is unique and customers traditionally have sought to handle and compare cigars at the time of purchase.

We reject these contentions. Assuming that petitioners have a cognizable speech interest in a particular means of displaying their products, . . . these regulations withstand First Amendment scrutiny.

Massachusetts' sales practices provisions regulate conduct that may have a communicative component, but Massachusetts seeks to regulate the placement of tobacco products for reasons unrelated to the communication of ideas. . . . We conclude that the State has demonstrated a substantial interest in preventing access to tobacco products by minors and has adopted an appropriately narrow means of advancing that interest. . . .

. . . Unattended displays of tobacco products present an opportunity for access without the proper age verification required by law. Thus, the State prohibits self-service and other displays that would allow an individual to obtain tobacco products without direct contact with a salesperson. It is clear that the regulations leave open ample channels of communication. The regulations do not significantly impede adult access to tobacco products. Moreover, retailers have other means of exercising any cognizable speech interest in the presentation of their products. We presume that vendors may place empty tobacco packaging on open display, and display actual tobacco products so long as that display is only accessible to sales personnel. As for cigars, there is no indication in the regulations that a customer is unable to examine a cigar prior to purchase, so long as that examination takes place through a salesperson.

. . .

We conclude that the sales practices regulations withstand First Amendment scrutiny. The means chosen by the State are narrowly tailored to prevent access to tobacco products by minors, are unrelated to expression, and leave open alternative avenues for vendors to convey information about products and for would-be customers to inspect products before purchase.

IV

. . .

To the extent that federal law and the First Amendment do not prohibit state action, States and localities remain free to combat the problem of underage tobacco use by appropriate means. . . .

Justice Kennedy, with whom Justice Scalia joins, concurring in part and concurring in the judgment.

The obvious overbreadth of the outdoor advertising restrictions suffices to invalidate them under the fourth part of the test in *Central Hudson* . . . As a result, in my view, there is no need to consider whether the restrictions satisfy the third part of the test, a proposition about which there is considerable doubt. Neither are we required to consider whether Central Hudson should be retained in the face of the substantial objections that can be made to it. My continuing concerns that the test gives insufficient protection to truthful, nonmisleading commercial speech require me to refrain from expressing agreement with the Court's application of the third part of *Central Hudson*. . . . With the exception of Part III–B–1, then, I join the opinion of the Court.

Justice Thomas, concurring in part and concurring in the judgment.

I join the opinion of the Court (with the exception of Part III–B–1) because . . . I would subject all of the advertising restrictions to strict scrutiny and would hold that they violate the First Amendment.

I

. . .

. . . In my view, an asserted government interest in keeping people ignorant by suppressing expression "is per se illegitimate and can no more justify regulation of 'commercial' speech than it can justify regulation of 'noncommercial' speech." . . . That is essentially the interest asserted here, and, adhering to the views I expressed in *44 Liquormart*, I would subject the Massachusetts regulations to strict scrutiny.

B

Even if one accepts the premise that commercial speech generally is entitled to a lower level of constitutional protection than are other forms of speech, it does not follow that the regulations here deserve anything less than strict scrutiny. . . . Even when speech falls into a category of reduced constitutional protection, the government may not engage in content discrimination for reasons unrelated to those characteristics of the speech that place it within the category. . . .

. . .

C

. . .

Viewed as an effort to proscribe solicitation to unlawful conduct, these regulations clearly fail the *Brandenburg* test. A State may not "forbid or proscribe advocacy of the use of force or of law violation except where such advocacy is directed to inciting or producing imminent lawless action and is likely to incite or produce such action." . . . Even if Massachusetts could prohibit advertisements reading, "Hey kids, buy cigarettes here," these regulations sweep much more broadly than that. They cover "any . . . statement or representation . . . the purpose or effect of which is to promote the use or sale" of tobacco products, whether or not the statement is directly or indirectly addressed to minors. . . . On respondents' theory, all tobacco advertising may be limited because some of its viewers may not legally act on it.

. . .

At bottom, respondents' theory rests on the premise that an indirect solicitation is enough to empower the State to regulate speech, and that, as petitioners put it, even an advertisement directed at adults "will give any children who may happen to see it the wrong idea and therefore must be suppressed from public view." . . .

. . . Even if Massachusetts has a valid interest in regulating speech directed at children—who, it argues, may be more easily misled, and to whom the sale of tobacco products is unlawful—it may not pursue that interest at the expense of the free speech rights of adults.

. . .

We have held consistently that speech "cannot be suppressed solely to protect the young from ideas or images that a legislative body thinks unsuitable for them." . . . To be sure, in FCC v. Pacifica Foundation, 438 U.S. 726 (1978), we upheld the Federal Communications Commission's power to regulate indecent but nonobscene radio broadcasts. But *Pacifica* relied heavily on what it considered to be the "special justifications for regulation of the broadcast media that are not applicable to other speakers." Outside of the broadcasting context, we have adhered to the view that "the governmental interest in protecting children from harmful materials" does not "justify an unnecessarily broad suppression of speech addressed to adults." . . .

II

Under strict scrutiny, the advertising ban may be saved only if it is narrowly tailored to promote a compelling government interest. . . . If that interest could be served by an alternative that is less restrictive of speech, then the State must use that alternative instead. . . . Applying this standard, the regulations here must fail.

A

Massachusetts asserts a compelling interest in reducing tobacco use among minors. Applied to adults, an interest in manipulating market choices by keeping people ignorant would not be legitimate, let alone compelling. But assuming that there is a compelling interest in reducing underage smoking, and that the ban on outdoor advertising promotes this interest, I doubt that the same is true of the ban on point-of-sale advertising below five feet. . . . Far from serving a compelling interest, the ban on displays below five feet seems to lack even a minimally rational relationship to any conceivable interest.

There is also considerable reason to doubt that the restrictions on cigar and smokeless tobacco outdoor advertising promote any state interest. Outdoor advertising for cigars, after all, is virtually nonexistent. Cigar makers use no billboards in Massachusetts, and in fact their nationwide outdoor advertising budget is only about $50,000 per year. To the extent outdoor advertising exists, there is no evidence that it is targeted at youth or has a significant effect on youth. . . .

Much the same is true of smokeless tobacco. Here respondents place primary reliance on evidence that, in the late 1960's, the U.S. Smokeless Tobacco Company increased its sales through advertising targeted at young males. But this does nothing to show that advertising affecting minors is a problem today. . . .

B

In any case, even assuming that the regulations advance a compelling state interest, they must be struck down because they are not narrowly tailored. The Court is correct, that the arbitrary 1,000–foot radius demonstrates a lack of narrow tailoring, but the problem goes deeper than that. A prohibited zone defined solely by circles drawn around schools and playgrounds is necessarily overinclusive, regardless of the radii of the circles. Consider, for example, a billboard located within 1,000 feet of a school but visible only from an elevated freeway that runs nearby. Such a billboard would not threaten any of the interests respondents assert, but it would be banned anyway, because the regulations take no account of whether the advertisement could even be seen by children. The prohibited zone is even more suspect where, as here, it includes all but 10 percent of the area in the three largest cities in the State.

The loose tailoring of the advertising ban is displayed not only in its geographic scope but also in the nature of the advertisements it affects. The regulations define "advertisement" very broadly; the term includes any "written . . . statement or representation, made by" a person who sells tobacco products, "the purpose or effect of which is to promote the use or sale of the product." . . . Almost everything a business does has the purpose of promoting the sale of its products, so this definition would cover anything a tobacco retailer might say. Some of the prohibited speech would not even be commercial. If a store displayed a sign promoting a candidate for Attorney General who had promised to repeal the tobacco regulations if elected, it probably would be doing so with the long-term purpose of promoting sales, and the display of such a sign would be illegal.

Even if the definition of "advertisement" were read more narrowly so as to require a specific reference to tobacco products, it still would have Draconian effects. It would, for example, prohibit a tobacconist from displaying a sign reading "Joe's Cigar Shop." . . . Respondents assert no interest in cigar retailer anonymity, and it is difficult to conceive of any other interest to which this rule could be said to be narrowly tailored.

The regulations fail the narrow tailoring inquiry for another, more fundamental reason. In addition to examining a narrower advertising ban, the State should have examined ways of advancing its interest that do not require limiting speech at all. Here, respondents had several alternatives. Most obviously, they could have directly regulated the conduct with which they were concerned. . . . Massachusetts already prohibits the sale of tobacco to minors, but it could take steps to enforce that prohibition more vigorously. It also could enact laws prohibiting the purchase, possession, or use of tobacco by minors. And, if its concern is that tobacco advertising communicates a message with which it disagrees, it could seek to counteract that message with "more speech, not enforced silence," Whitney v. California, 274 U.S. 357, 377 (1927) (Brandeis, J., concurring).

III

Underlying many of the arguments of respondents and their amici is the idea that tobacco is in some sense sui generis—that it is so special, so unlike any other object of regulation, that application of normal First Amendment principles should be suspended. . . . [T]o uphold the Massachusetts tobacco regulations would be to accept a line of reasoning that would permit restrictions on advertising for a host of other products.

. . .

Respondents have identified no principle of law or logic that would preclude the imposition of restrictions on fast food and alcohol advertising similar to those they seek to impose on tobacco advertising. In effect, they seek a "vice" exception to the First Amendment. No such exception exists. . . . If it did, it would have almost no limit. . . .

No legislature has ever sought to restrict speech about an activity it regarded as harmless and inoffensive. . . . It is therefore no answer for the State to say that the makers of cigarettes are doing harm: perhaps they are. But in that respect they are no different from the purveyors of other harmful products, or the advocates of harmful ideas. When the State seeks to silence them, they are all entitled to the protection of the First Amendment.

Justice Stevens, with whom Justice Ginsburg and Justice Breyer join, and with whom Justice Souter joins as to Part I, concurring in part, concurring in the judgment in part, and dissenting in part.

Because I strongly disagree with the Court's conclusion that the Federal Cigarette Labeling and Advertising Act of 1965 (FCLAA or Act) ... precludes States and localities from regulating the location of cigarette advertising, I dissent from Parts II–A and II–B of the Court's opinion. On the First Amendment questions, I agree with the Court both that the outdoor advertising restrictions imposed by Massachusetts serve legitimate and important state interests and that the record does not indicate that the measures were properly tailored to serve those interests. Because the present record does not enable us to adjudicate the merits of those claims on summary judgment, I would vacate the decision upholding those restrictions and remand for trial on the constitutionality of the outdoor advertising regulations. Finally, because I do not believe that either the point-of-sale advertising restrictions or the sales practice restrictions implicate significant First Amendment concerns, I would uphold them in their entirety.

. . .

II

On the First Amendment issues raised by petitioners, my disagreements with the majority are less significant. I would, however, reach different dispositions as to the 1,000–foot rule and the height restrictions for indoor advertising, and my evaluation of the sales practice restrictions differs from the Court's.

The 1,000–Foot Rule

... [N]oble ends do not save a speech-restricting statute whose means are poorly tailored.

. . .

... I share the majority's concern as to whether the 1,000–foot rule unduly restricts the ability of cigarette manufacturers to convey lawful information to adult consumers. This, of course, is a question of line-drawing. ...

... Finding the appropriate balance is no easy matter. Though many factors plausibly enter the equation when calculating whether a child-directed location restriction goes too far in regulating adult speech, one crucial question is whether the regulatory scheme leaves available sufficient "alternative avenues of communication." ... Because I do not think the record contains sufficient information to enable us to answer that question, I would vacate the award of summary judgment upholding the 1,000–foot rule and remand for trial on that issue. ...

... The dearth of reliable statistical information as to the scope of the ban is problematic.

... More importantly, the Court lacks sufficient qualitative information as to the areas where cigarette advertising is prohibited and those where it is permitted....

Finally, the Court lacks information as to other avenues of communication available to cigarette manufacturers and retailers. ...

... While the ultimate question before us is one of law, the answer to that question turns on complicated factual questions relating to the practical effects of the regulations. As the record does not reveal the answer to these disputed questions of fact, the court should have denied summary judgment to both parties and allowed the parties to present further evidence.

. . .

The Sales Practice and Indoor Advertising Restrictions

... I ... write separately on this issue to make two brief points.

First, ... the sales practice restrictions are best analyzed as regulating conduct, not speech. See 218 F. 3d, at 53. While the decision how to display one's products no doubt serves a marginal communicative function, the same can be said of virtually any human activity performed with the hope or intention of evoking the interest of others. This Court has long recognized the need to differentiate between legislation that targets expression and legislation that targets conduct for legitimate non-speech-related reasons but imposes an incidental burden on expression. See, e.g., United States v. O'Brien, 391 U.S. 367 (1968). However difficult that line may be to draw, it seems clear to me that laws requiring that stores maintain items behind counters and prohibiting self-service displays fall squarely on the conduct side of the line. Restrictions as to the accessibility of dangerous or legally-restricted products are a common feature of the regulatory regime governing American retail stores. I see nothing the least bit constitutionally problematic in requiring individuals to ask for the assistance of a salesclerk in order to examine or purchase a handgun, a bottle of penicillin, or a package of cigarettes.

Second, though I admit the question is closer, I would, for similar reasons, uphold the regulation limiting tobacco advertising in certain retail establishments to the space five feet or more above the floor. When viewed in isolation, this provision appears to target speech. ... Nonetheless, I am ultimately persuaded that the provision is unobjectionable because it is little more than an adjunct to the other sales practice restrictions. As the Commonwealth of Massachusetts can properly legislate the placement of products and the nature of displays in its convenience stores, I would not draw a distinction between such restrictions and height restrictions on related product advertising. I would accord the Commonwealth some latitude in imposing restrictions that can have only the slightest impact on the ability of adults to purchase a poisonous product and may save some children from taking the first step on the road to addiction.

Thompson v. Western States Medical Center

535 U.S. 357, 122 S.Ct. 1497, 152 L.Ed.2d 563 (2002).

Justice O'Connor delivered the opinion of the Court.

Section 503A of the Food and Drug Administration Modernization Act of 1997 (FDAMA or Act), 111 Stat. 2328, 21 U.S.C. § 353a, exempts "compounded drugs" from the Food and Drug Administration's standard drug approval requirements as long as the providers of those drugs abide by several restrictions, including that they refrain from advertising or promoting particular compounded drugs. Respondents, a group of licensed pharmacies that specialize in compounding drugs, sought to enjoin enforcement of the subsections of the Act dealing with advertising and solicitation, arguing that those provisions violate the First Amendment's free speech guarantee. The District Court agreed with respondents and granted their motion for summary judgment. . . .

The Court of Appeals for the Ninth Circuit affirmed . . . We conclude, as did the courts below, that § 503A's provisions regarding advertisement and promotion amount to unconstitutional restrictions on commercial speech, and we therefore affirm.

I

Drug compounding is a process by which a pharmacist or doctor combines, mixes, or alters ingredients to create a medication tailored to the needs of an individual patient. Compounding is typically used to prepare medications that are not commercially available, such as medication for a patient who is allergic to an ingredient in a mass-produced product. It is a traditional component of the practice of pharmacy . . . Pharmacists may provide compounded drugs to patients only upon receipt of a valid prescription from a doctor or other medical practitioner licensed to prescribe medication. . . .

. . .

For approximately the first 50 years . . . the FDA generally left regulation of compounding to the States. . . . The FDA eventually became concerned, however, that some pharmacists were manufacturing and selling drugs under the guise of compounding, thereby avoiding the FDCA's new drug requirements. In 1992, in response to this concern, the FDA issued a Compliance Policy Guide. . . . It stated that the "FDA believes that an increasing number of establishments with retail pharmacy licenses are engaged in manufacturing, distributing, and promoting unapproved new drugs for human use in a manner that is clearly outside the bounds of traditional pharmacy practice and that constitute violations of the [FDCA]." . . .

. . . [T]he Guide announced that it was FDA policy to permit pharmacists to compound drugs after receipt of a valid prescription for an individual patient or to compound drugs in "very limited quantities" before receipt of a valid prescription if they could document a history of receiving valid prescriptions "generated solely within an established professional practitioner-patient-pharmacy relationship" . . .

Congress turned portions of this policy into law when it enacted the FDAMA in 1997. The FDAMA . . . exempts compounded drugs from the FDCA's "new drug" requirements and other requirements provided the drugs satisfy a number of restrictions. . . . [M]ost relevant for this litigation, the prescription must be "unsolicited," § 353a(a), and the pharmacy, licensed pharmacist, or licensed physician compounding the drug may "not advertise or promote the compounding of any particular drug, class of drug, or type of drug." § 353a(c). The pharmacy, licensed pharmacist, or licensed physician may, however, "advertise and promote the compounding service." *Ibid.*

Respondents are a group of licensed pharmacies that specialize in drug compounding. They have prepared promotional materials that they distribute by mail and at medical conferences to inform patients and physicians of the use and effectiveness of specific compounded drugs. . . .

. . .

II

The parties agree that the advertising and soliciting prohibited by the FDAMA constitute commercial speech. . . .

. . .

Neither party has challenged the appropriateness of applying the *Central Hudson* framework to the speech-related provisions at issue here. . . .

III

The Government does not attempt to defend the FDAMA's speech-related provisions under the first prong of the *Central Hudson* test; *i.e.,* it does not argue that the prohibited advertisements would be about unlawful activity or would be misleading. Instead, the Government argues that the FDAMA satisfies the remaining three prongs of the *Central Hudson* test.

The Government asserts that three substantial interests underlie the FDAMA. The first is an interest in "preserv[ing] the effectiveness and integrity of the FDCA's new drug approval process and the protection of the public health that it provides." The second is an interest in "preserv[ing] the availability of compounded drugs for those individual patients who, for particularized medical reasons, cannot use commercially available products that have been approved by the FDA." Finally, the Government argues that "[a]chieving the proper balance between those two independently compelling but competing interests is itself a substantial governmental interest."

Explaining these interests, the Government argues that the FDCA's new drug approval requirements are critical to the public health and safety. ...

... [T]he Government also acknowledges that "because obtaining FDA approval for a new drug is a costly process, requiring FDA approval of all drug products compounded by pharmacies for the particular needs of an individual patient would, as a practical matter, eliminate the practice of compounding, and [that this] would be undesirable because compounding is sometimes critical to the care of patients with drug allergies, patients who cannot tolerate particular drug delivery systems, and patients requiring special drug dosages."

... [T]he Government needs to be able to draw a line between small-scale compounding and large-scale drug manufacturing. That line must distinguish compounded drugs produced on such a small scale that they could not undergo safety and efficacy testing from drugs produced and sold on a large enough scale that they could undergo such testing and therefore must do so.

The Government argues that the FDAMA's speech-related provisions provide just such a line, *i.e.,* that, in the terms of *Central Hudson,* they "directly advanc[e] the governmental interest[s] asserted." ... The Government argues that advertising ... is "a fair proxy for actual or intended large-scale manufacturing," ...

... [T]he Government has failed to demonstrate that the speech restrictions are "not more extensive than is necessary to serve [those] interest[s]." ...

Several non-speech-related means of drawing a line between compounding and large-scale manufacturing might be possible here. First, it seems that the Government could use the very factors the FDA relied on to distinguish compounding from manufacturing in its 1992 Compliance Policy Guide. For example, the Government could ban the use of "commercial scale manufacturing or testing equipment for compounding drug products." It could prohibit pharmacists from compounding more drugs in anticipation of receiving prescriptions than in response to prescriptions already received. It could prohibit pharmacists from "[o]ffering compounded drugs at wholesale to other state licensed persons or commercial entities for resale." Alternately, it could limit the amount of compounded drugs, either by volume or by numbers of prescriptions, that a given pharmacist or pharmacy sells out of State. Another possibility not suggested by the Compliance Policy Guide would be capping the amount of any particular compounded drug, either by drug volume, number of prescriptions, gross revenue, or profit that a pharmacist or pharmacy may make or sell in a given period of time. It might even be sufficient to rely solely on the non-speech-related provisions of the FDAMA, such as the requirement that compounding only be conducted in response to a prescription or a history of receiving a prescription, . . . and the limitation on the percentage of a pharmacy's total sales that out-of-state sales of compounded drugs may represent . . .

. . . Nowhere in the legislative history of the FDAMA or petitioners' briefs is there any explanation of why the Government believed forbidding advertising was a necessary as opposed to merely convenient means of achieving its interests. . . . If the First Amendment means anything, it means that regulating speech must be a last—not first—resort. Yet here it seems to have been the first strategy the Government thought to try.

. . . The dissent describes another governmental interest—an interest in prohibiting the sale of compounded drugs to "patients who may not clearly need them," . . . Nowhere in its briefs, however, does the Government argue that this interest motivated the advertising ban. Although, for the reasons given by the dissent, Congress conceivably could have enacted the advertising ban to advance this interest, we have generally only sustained statutes on the basis of hypothesized justifications when reviewing statutes merely to determine whether they are rational. . . . The *Central Hudson* test is significantly stricter than the rational basis test, however, requiring the Government not only to identify specifically "a substantial interest to be achieved by [the] restrictio[n] on commercial speech," . . . but also to prove that the regulation "directly advances" that interest and is "not more extensive than is necessary to serve that interest," . . .

Even if the Government had argued that the FDAMA's speech-related restrictions were motivated by a fear that advertising compounded drugs would put people who do not need such drugs at risk by causing them to convince their doctors to prescribe the drugs anyway, that fear would fail to justify the restrictions. Aside from the fact that this concern rests on the questionable assumption that doctors would prescribe unnecessary medications (an assumption the dissent is willing to make based on one magazine article and one survey, neither of which was relied upon by the Government), this concern amounts to a fear that people would make bad decisions if given truthful information about compounded drugs. We have previously rejected the notion that the Government has an interest in preventing the dissemination of truthful commercial information in order to prevent members of the public from making bad decisions with the information. . . .

Even if the Government had asserted an interest in preventing people who do not need compounded drugs from obtaining those drugs, the statute does not directly advance that interest. . . . Although the advertising ban may reduce the demand for compounded drugs from those who do not need the drugs, it does nothing to prevent such individuals from obtaining compounded drugs other than requiring prescriptions. But if it is appropriate for the statute to rely on doctors to refrain from prescribing compounded drugs to patients who do not need them, it is not clear why it would not also be appropriate to rely on doctors to refrain from prescribing compounded drugs to patients who do not need them in a world where advertising was permitted.

. . . .

If the Government's failure to justify its decision to regulate speech were not enough to convince us that the FDAMA's advertising provisions were unconstitutional, the amount of beneficial speech prohibited by the FDAMA would be. . . . It would prevent pharmacists with no interest in mass-producing medications, but who serve clienteles with special medical needs, from telling the doctors treating those clients about the alternative drugs available through compounding. For example, a pharmacist serving a children's hospital where many patients are unable to swallow pills would be prevented from telling the children's doctors about a new development in compounding that allowed a drug that was previously available only in pill form to be administered another way. . . . The fact that the FDAMA would prohibit such seemingly useful speech even though doing so does not appear to directly further any asserted governmental objective confirms our belief that the prohibition is unconstitutional.

. . .

Justice Thomas, concurring.

I concur because I agree with the Court's application of the test set forth in *Central Hudson* . . . I continue, however, to adhere to my view that cases such as this should not be analyzed under the *Central Hudson* test. . . .

Justice Breyer, with whom The Chief Justice, Justice Stevens, and Justice Ginsburg join, dissenting.

. . .

. . . I believe that the Court seriously undervalues the importance of the Government's interest in protecting the health and safety of the American public.

I

In my view, the advertising restriction "directly advances" the statute's important safety objective . . . to confine the sale of untested, compounded, drugs to where they are medically needed. But to do so the statute must exclude from the area of permitted drug sales *both* (1) those drugs that traditional drug manufacturers might supply after testing—typically drugs capable of being produced in large amounts, *and* (2) those compounded drugs sought by patients who may not clearly need them—including compounded drugs produced in small amounts.

The . . . statute, in seeking to confine distribution of untested tailored drugs, must look both at the amount supplied (to help decide whether ordinary manufacturers might provide a tested alternative) and at the nature of demand (to help separate genuine need from simple convenience). . . .

This second intermediate objective is logically related to Congress' primary end—the minimizing of safety risks. The statute's basic exemption from testing requirements inherently creates risks simply by placing untested drugs in the hands of the consumer. Where an individual has a specific medical need for a specially tailored drug those risks are likely offset. But where an untested drug is a convenience, not a necessity, that offset is unlikely to be present.

That presumably is why neither the Food and Drug Administration (FDA) nor Congress anywhere suggests that all that matters is the total *amount* of a particular drug's sales. . . . That is why the statute itself, as well as the FDA policy that the statute reflects, lists several distinguishing factors, of which advertising is one. . . .

. . .

And that, in part, is why federal and state authorities have long permitted pharmacists to advertise the fact that they compound drugs, while forbidding the advertisement of individual compounds. . . .

These policies and statutory provisions reflect the view that individualized consideration is more likely present, and convenience alone is more likely absent, when demand for a compounding prescription originates with a doctor, not an advertisement. The restrictions try to assure that demand is generated doctor-to-patient-to-pharmacist, not pharmacist-to-advertisement-to-patient-to-doctor. And they do so in order to diminish the likelihood that those who do not genuinely need untested compounded drugs will not receive them.

There is considerable evidence that the relevant means—the advertising restrictions—directly advance this statutory objective. . . .

. . . [C]ompounded drugs carry with them special risks. After all, compounding is not necessarily a matter of changing a drug's flavor, but rather it is a matter of combining different ingredients in new, untested ways, say, adding a pain medication to an antihistamine to counteract allergies or increasing the ratio of approved ingredients in a salve to help the body absorb it at a faster rate. And the risks associated with the untested combination of ingredients or the quicker absorption rate or the working conditions necessary to change an old drug into its new form can, for some patients, mean infection, serious side effects, or even death. . . .

There is considerable evidence that consumer oriented advertising will create strong consumer-driven demand for a particular drug. . . .

And there is strong evidence that doctors will often respond affirmatively to a patient's request for a specific drug that the patient has seen advertised. . . .

In these circumstances, Congress could reasonably conclude that doctors will respond affirmatively to a patient's request for a compounded drug even if the doctor would not normally prescribe it. When a parent learns that a child's pill can be administered in liquid form, when a patient learns that a compounded skin cream has an enhanced penetration rate, or when an allergy sufferer learns that a compounded anti-inflammatory allergy medication can alleviate a sinus headache without the sedative effects of antihistamines, that parent or patient may well ask for the desired prescription. And the doctor may well write the prescription even in the absence of special need—at least if any risk likely to arise from lack of testing is so small that only *scientific testing*, not anecdote or experience, would reveal it. . . .

Of course, the added risks in any such individual case may be small. But those individual risks added together can significantly affect the public health. At least, the FDA and Congress could reasonably reach that conclusion. And that fact, along with the absence of any significant evidence that the advertising restrictions have prevented doctors from learning about, or obtaining, compounded drugs, means that the FDA and Congress could also conclude that the advertising restrictions "directly advance" the statute's safety goal. . . . There is no reason for this Court, as a matter of constitutional law, to reach a different conclusion.

II

I do not believe that Congress could have achieved its safety objectives in significantly less restrictive ways. Consider the several alternatives the Court suggests. . . .

. . .

The Court adds that "[t]he Government has not offered any reason why these possibilities, alone or in combination, would be insufficient." The Government's failure to do so may reflect the fact that only the Court, not any of the respondents, has here suggested that these "alternatives," alone or in combination, would prove sufficient. In fact, the FDA's Compliance Policy Guide, from which the Court draws its first four alternatives, specifically warned that these alternatives alone were insufficient to successfully distinguish traditional compounding from unacceptable manufacturing. . . .

III

The Court responds to the claim that advertising compounded drugs causes people to obtain drugs that do not promote their health, by finding it implausible given the need for a prescription and by suggesting that it is not relevant. The First Amendment, it says, does not permit the Government to control the content of advertising, where doing so flows from "fear" that "people would make bad decisions if given truthful information about compounded drugs." This response . . . fails to take account of considerations that make the claim more than plausible (if properly stated); and it is inconsistent with this Court's interpretation of the Constitution.

It is an oversimplification to say that the Government "fear[s]" that doctors or patients "would make bad decisions if given truthful information." Rather, the Government fears the safety consequences of multiple compound-drug prescription decisions initiated not by doctors but by pharmacist-to-patient advertising. Those consequences flow from the adverse cumulative effects of multiple individual decisions each of which may seem perfectly reasonable considered on its own. The Government fears that, taken together, these apparently rational individual decisions will undermine the safety testing system, thereby producing overall a net balance of harm . . . Consequently, the Government leaves pharmacists free to explain through advertisements what compounding is, to advertise that they engage in compounding, and to advise patients to discuss the matter with their physicians. And it forbids advertising the specific drug in question, not because it fears the "information" the advertisement provides, but because it fears the systematic effect . . . of advertisements that will not fully explain the complicated risks at issue. And this latter fear is more than plausible.

I do not deny that the statute restricts the circulation of some truthful information. . . . Nonetheless, this Court has not previously held that commercial advertising restrictions automatically violate the First Amendment. Rather, the Court has applied a more flexible test. It has examined the restriction's proportionality, the relation between restriction and objective, the fit between ends and means. . . . It has done so because it has concluded that, from a constitutional perspective, commercial speech does not warrant application of the Court's strictest speech-protective tests. And it has reached this conclusion in part because restrictions on commercial speech do not often repress individual self-expression; they rarely interfere with the functioning of democratic political processes; and they often reflect a democratically determined governmental decision to regulate a commercial venture in order to protect, for example, the consumer, the public health, individual safety, or the environment. . . .

. . . The Court, in my view, gives insufficient weight to the Government's regulatory rationale, and too readily assumes the existence of practical alternatives. It thereby applies the commercial speech doctrine too strictly. . . .

. . . [A]n overly rigid "commercial speech" doctrine will transform what ought to be a legislative or regulatory decision about the best way to protect the health and safety of the American public into a constitutional decision prohibiting the legislature from enacting necessary protections. As history in respect to the Due Process Clause shows, any such transformation would involve a tragic constitutional misunderstanding. . . .

. . .

CHAPTER 14

RESTRICTIONS ON TIME, PLACE, OR MANNER OF EXPRESSION

Introduction. The title of this chapter signals a shift in emphasis from controlling expression because of its content to restricting the time, place, or manner of expression. It is, however, a shift rather than a break in the analysis of freedom of speech. Time, place, or manner issues were prominent in some of the cases in the preceding chapter. Issues of speech content are often central to time, place, or manner restrictions. A repetitive question is whether any consistent principle can be formulated where government restrictions of expression blend considerations of time, place, or manner with considerations of content.

SECTION 1. THE TRADITIONAL PUBLIC FORUM: SPEECH ACTIVITIES IN STREETS AND PARKS

SCHNEIDER v. NEW JERSEY, TOWN OF IRVINGTON, 308 U.S. 147 (1939). The court had before it three cases involving city ordinances forbidding the distribution of handbills in the streets (and in one case in any public place). The cases involved convictions of persons distributing handbills giving notice of meetings on public issues in two cases and as an incident to labor picketing in the third. As to the question whether cities could forbid all distribution of handbills on public streets, the court held they could not. The court reversed the convictions in these three cases. Justice roberts, speaking for the court, said, in part:

"Municipal authorities, as trustees for the public, have the duty to keep their communities' streets open and available for movement of people and property, the primary purpose to which the streets are dedicated. So long as legislation to this end does not abridge the constitutional liberty of one rightfully upon the street to impart information through speech or the distribution of literature, it may lawfully regulate the conduct of those using the streets. For example, a person could not exercise this liberty by taking his stand in the middle of a crowded street, contrary to traffic regulations, and maintain his position to the stoppage of all traffic; a group of distributors could not insist upon a constitutional right to form a cordon across the street and to allow no pedestrian to pass who did not accept a tendered leaflet; nor does the guarantee of freedom of speech or of the press deprive a municipality of power to enact regulations against throwing literature broadcast in the streets. Prohibition of such conduct would not abridge the constitutional liberty since such activity bears no necessary relationship to the freedom to speak, write, print or distribute information or opinion.

. . .

"The motive of the legislation under attack in Numbers 13, 18 and 29 is held by the courts below to be the prevention of littering of the streets and, although the alleged offenders were not charged with themselves scattering paper in the streets, their convictions were sustained upon the theory that distribution by them encouraged or resulted in such littering. We are of opinion that the purpose to keep the streets clean and of good appearance is insufficient to justify an ordinance which prohibits a person rightfully on a public street from handing literature to one willing to receive it. Any burden imposed upon the city authorities in cleaning and caring for the streets as an indirect consequence of such distribution results from the constitutional protection of the freedom of speech and press. This constitutional protection does not deprive a city of all power to prevent street littering. There are obvious methods of preventing littering. Amongst these is the punishment of those who actually throw papers on the streets."

MINIMUM ACCESS v. EQUAL ACCESS TO THE PUBLIC FORUM

There are two famous quotations expressing polar positions. While sitting on the Massachusetts Supreme Judicial Court, Justice Holmes observed: "For the Legislature absolutely or conditionally to forbid public speaking in a highway or public park is no more an infringement of the rights of a member of the public than for the owner of a private house to forbid it in his house." Commonwealth v. Davis, 162 Mass. 510, 511, 39 N.E. 113 (1895), affirmed 167 U.S. 43, 47–48 (1897). Justice Roberts' plurality opinion in Hague v. C.I.O., 307 U.S. 496, 515–516 (1939) contains this often quoted dictum: "Wherever the title of streets and parks may rest, they have immemorially been held in trust for the use of public and, time out of mind, have been used for purposes of assembly, communicating thoughts between citizens, and discussing public questions. Such use of the streets and public places has, from ancient times, been a part of the privileges, immunities, rights, and liberties of citizens."

No Supreme Court decision has confronted the constitutionality of a municipality's decision to reserve its streets entirely for traffic and its parks as facilities for quiet rest and relaxation. In that context, the issue may be more theoretical than real. The cases before the Court have either involved time, place, or manner restrictions that did not totally preclude use of parks and streets for expression, or restrictions that denied equal access to the public facilities involved. Does resolution of the debate whether all parks and streets could be closed to expression affect the results in those cases? Does Justice Roberts' opinion in *Schneider* implicitly rest on accepting his dictum in *Hague*?

For discussion of these issues see Kalven, *The Concept of the Public Forum: Cox v. Louisiana*, 1965 Sup.Ct.Rev. 1.

Frisby v. Schultz

487 U.S. 474, 108 S.Ct. 2495, 101 L.Ed.2d 420 (1988).

Justice O'Connor delivered the opinion of the Court.

Brookfield, Wisconsin, has adopted an ordinance that completely bans picketing "before or about" any residence. This case presents a facial First Amendment challenge to that ordinance.

I

Brookfield, Wisconsin, is a residential suburb of Milwaukee with a population of approximately 4,300. The appellees, Sandra C. Schultz and Robert C.

Braun, are individuals strongly opposed to abortion and wish to express their views on the subject by picketing on a public street outside the Brookfield residence of a doctor who apparently performs abortions at two clinics in neighboring towns. Appellees and others engaged in precisely that activity, assembling outside the doctor's home on at least six occasions between April 20, 1985, and May 20, 1985, for periods ranging from one to one and a half hours. The size of the group varied from 11 to more than 40. The picketing was generally orderly and peaceful; the town never had occasion to invoke any of its various ordinances prohibiting obstruction of the streets, loud and unnecessary noises, or disorderly conduct. Nonetheless, the picketing generated substantial controversy and numerous complaints.

... On May 7, 1985, the town passed an ordinance that prohibited all picketing in residential neighborhoods except for labor picketing. But after reviewing this Court's decision in Carey v. Brown, 447 U.S. 455 (1980), which invalidated a similar ordinance as a violation of the Equal Protection Clause, the town attorney instructed the police not to enforce the new ordinance and advised the Town Board that the ordinance's labor picketing exception likely rendered it unconstitutional. This ordinance was repealed on May 15, 1985, and replaced with the following flat ban on all residential picketing:

> "It is unlawful for any person to engage in picketing before or about the residence or dwelling of any individual in the Town of Brookfield."

. . .

... [A]ppellees ceased picketing in Brookfield and filed this lawsuit in United States District Court for the Eastern District of Wisconsin [seeking] ... declaratory as well as preliminary and permanent injunctive relief on the grounds that the ordinance violated the First Amendment....

The District Court granted appellees' motion for a preliminary injunction....

A divided panel of the United States Court of Appeals for the Seventh Circuit affirmed....

. . .

II

The antipicketing ordinance operates at the core of the First Amendment by prohibiting appellees from engaging in picketing on an issue of public concern. ... [W]e have traditionally subjected restrictions on public issue picketing to careful scrutiny. ...

To ascertain what limits, if any, may be placed on protected speech, we have often focused on the "place" of that speech, considering the nature of the forum the speaker seeks to employ. Our cases have recognized that the standards by which limitations on speech must be evaluated "differ depending on the character of the property at issue." Perry Education Assn. v. Perry Local Educators' Assn., 460 U.S. 37, 44 (1983). Specifically, we have identified three types of fora: "the traditional public forum, the public forum created by government designation, and the nonpublic forum." ...

... [W]e have repeatedly referred to public streets as the archetype of a traditional public forum.... "[T]ime out of mind" public streets and sidewalks have been used for public assembly and debate, the hallmarks of a traditional public forum.... Hague v. CIO, 307 U.S. 496, 515 (1939) (Roberts, J.). Appellants, however, urge us to disregard these "clichés." They argue that the streets of Brookfield should be considered a nonpublic forum. Pointing to the physical narrowness of Brookfield's streets as well as to their residential character, appellants contend that such streets have not by tradition or designation been held open for public communication.

We reject this suggestion. Our prior holdings make clear that a public street does not lose its status as a traditional public forum simply because it runs through a residential neighborhood. . . .

In short, our decisions identifying public streets and sidewalks as traditional public fora are not accidental invocations of a "cliché," but recognition that "[w]herever the title of streets and parks may rest, they have immemorially been held in trust for the use of the public." Hague v. CIO, supra, at 515 (Roberts, J.). . . . The residential character of those streets may well inform the application of the relevant test, but it does not lead to a different test; the antipicketing ordinance must be judged against the stringent standards we have established for restrictions on speech in traditional public fora:

> "In these quintessential public for[a], the government may not prohibit all communicative activity. For the State to enforce a content-based exclusion it must show that its regulation is necessary to serve a compelling state interest and that it is narrowly drawn to achieve that end. . . . The State may also enforce regulations of the time, place, and manner of expression which are content-neutral, are narrowly tailored to serve a significant government interest, and leave open ample alternative channels of communication." *Perry*, [460 U.S.] at 45 (citations omitted).

As *Perry* makes clear, the appropriate level of scrutiny is initially tied to whether the statute distinguishes between prohibited and permitted speech on the basis of content. . . . [W]e accept the lower courts' conclusion that the Brookfield ordinance is content neutral. Accordingly, we turn to consider whether the ordinance is "narrowly tailored to serve a significant government interest" and whether it "leave[s] open ample alternative channels of communication." . . .

Because the last question is so easily answered, we address it first. . . . To the extent they endorsed a broad reading of the ordinance, the lower courts ran afoul of the well-established principle that statutes will be interpreted to avoid constitutional difficulties. . . . We instead construe the ordinance more narrowly. This narrow reading is supported by the representations of counsel for the town at oral argument, which indicate that the town takes, and will enforce, a limited view of the "picketing" proscribed by the ordinance. Thus, . . . "picketing would be having the picket proceed on a definite course or route in front of a home." The picket need not be carrying a sign, but in order to fall within the scope of the ordinance the picketing must be directed at a single residence. General marching through residential neighborhoods, or even walking a route in front of an entire block of houses, is not prohibited by this ordinance. Accordingly, we construe the ban to be a limited one; only focused picketing taking place solely in front of a particular residence is prohibited.

So narrowed, the ordinance permits the more general dissemination of a message. . . .

We readily agree that the ordinance preserves ample alternative channels of communication and thus move on to inquire whether the ordinance serves a significant government interest. We find that such an interest is identified within the text of the ordinance itself: the protection of residential privacy.

. . .

One important aspect of residential privacy is protection of the unwilling listener. Although in many locations, we expect individuals simply to avoid speech they do not want to hear, ... the home is different. ... [W]e have repeatedly held that individuals are not required to welcome unwanted speech into their own homes and that the government may protect this freedom. See, e.g., FCC v. Pacifica Foundation, 438 U.S. 726, 748–749 (1978) (offensive radio broadcasts); ... Kovacs v. Cooper, 336 U.S. 77, 86–87 (1949) (sound trucks).

. . .

It remains to be considered, however, whether the Brookfield ordinance is narrowly tailored to protect only unwilling recipients of the communications. A statute is narrowly tailored if it targets and eliminates no more than the exact source of the "evil" it seeks to remedy....

... The type of focused picketing prohibited by the Brookfield ordinance is fundamentally different from more generally directed means of communication that may not be completely banned in residential areas. ... In such cases "the flow of information [is not] into ... household[s], but to the public." Organization for a Better Austin v. Keefe, 402 U.S. 415, 420 (1971). Here, in contrast, the picketing is narrowly directed at the household, not the public. The type of picketers banned by the Brookfield ordinance generally do not seek to disseminate a message to the general public, but to intrude upon the targeted resident, and to do so in an especially offensive way. Moreover, even if some such picketers have a broader communicative purpose, their activity nonetheless inherently and offensively intrudes on residential privacy. The devastating effect of targeted picketing on the quiet enjoyment of the home is beyond doubt . . .

. . .

The First Amendment permits the government to prohibit offensive speech as intrusive when the "captive" audience cannot avoid the objectionable speech. ... The target of the focused picketing banned by the Brookfield ordinance is just such a "captive." The resident is figuratively, and perhaps literally, trapped within the home, and because of the unique and subtle impact of such picketing is left with no ready means of avoiding the unwanted speech. ... Accordingly, the Brookfield ordinance's complete ban of that particular medium of expression is narrowly tailored.

Of course, this case presents only a facial challenge to the ordinance. Particular hypothetical applications of the ordinance—to, for example, a particular resident's use of his or her home as a place of business or public meeting, or to picketers present at a particular home by invitation of the resident—may present somewhat different questions. ...

Because the picketing prohibited by the Brookfield ordinance is speech directed primarily at those who are presumptively unwilling to receive it, the State has a substantial and justifiable interest in banning it. The nature and scope of this interest make the ban narrowly tailored. The ordinance also leaves open ample alternative channels of communication and is content neutral. Thus, largely because of its narrow scope, the facial challenge to the ordinance must fail. The contrary judgment of the Court of Appeals is

Reversed.

Justice White, concurring in the judgment.

I agree with the Court that an ordinance which only forbade picketing before a single residence would not be unconstitutional on its face....

. . .

Justice Brennan, with whom Justice Marshall joins, dissenting.

The Court today sets out the appropriate legal tests and standards governing the question presented, and proceeds to apply most of them correctly. Regrettably, though, the Court errs in the final step of its analysis, and approves an ordinance banning significantly more speech than is necessary to achieve the government's substantial and legitimate goal. Accordingly, I must dissent.

. . .

... [S]ubstantial regulation is permitted to neutralize the intrusive or unduly coercive aspects of picketing around the home. But to say that picketing may be substantially regulated is not to say that it may be prohibited in its entirety. Once size, time, volume, and the like have been controlled to ensure that the picket is no longer intrusive or coercive, only the speech itself remains, conveyed perhaps by a lone, silent individual, walking back and forth with a sign.... Such speech, which no longer implicates the heightened governmental interest in residential privacy, is nevertheless banned by the Brookfield law. Therefore, the ordinance is not narrowly tailored.

. . .

Justice Stevens, dissenting.

. . .

I do not believe we advance the inquiry by rejecting ... the "... argument that residential streets are something less than public fora." ... The streets in a residential neighborhood that has no sidewalks are quite obviously a different type of forum than a stadium or a public park. Attaching the label "public forum" to the area in front of a single family dwelling does not help us decide whether the town's interest in the safe and efficient flow of traffic or its interest in protecting the privacy of its citizens justifies denying picketers the right to march up and down the streets at will.

. . .

... The scope of the ordinance gives the town officials far too much discretion in making enforcement decisions; while we sit by and await further developments, potential picketers must act at their peril. ... [I]t is a simple matter for the town to amend its ordinance and to limit the ban to conduct that unreasonably interferes with the privacy of the home and does not serve a reasonable communicative purpose. Accordingly, I respectfully dissent.

Capitol Square Review and Advisory Board v. Pinette
515 U.S. 753, 115 S.Ct. 2440, 132 L.Ed.2d 650 (1995).

[The report in this case appears infra, page 1760.]

Madsen v. Women's Health Center, Inc.
512 U.S. 753, 114 S.Ct. 2516, 129 L.Ed.2d 593 (1994).

Chief Justice Rehnquist delivered the opinion of the Court.

Petitioners challenge the constitutionality of an injunction entered by a Florida state court which prohibits antiabortion protestors from demonstrating in certain places and in various ways outside of a health clinic that performs abortions. We hold that the establishment of a 36–foot buffer zone on a public street from which demonstrators are excluded passes muster under the First Amendment, but that several other provisions of the injunction do not.

I

Respondents operate abortion clinics throughout central Florida. Petitioners and other groups and individuals are engaged in activities near the site of one such clinic in Melbourne, Florida. They picketed and demonstrated where the public street gives access to the clinic. ... [A] Florida state court permanently enjoined petitioners from blocking or interfering with public access to the clinic, and from physically abusing persons entering or leaving the clinic. Six months later, respondents sought to broaden the injunction, complaining that access to the clinic was still impeded by petitioners' activities and that such activities had also discouraged some potential patients from entering the clinic, and had deleterious physical effects on others. The trial court thereupon issued a broader injunction, which is challenged here.

The court found that, despite the initial injunction, protesters continued to impede access to the clinic by congregating on the paved portion of the street—Dixie Way—leading up to the clinic, and by marching in front of the clinic's driveways. It found that as vehicles heading toward the clinic slowed to allow the protesters to move out of the way, "sidewalk counselors" would approach and attempt to give the vehicle's occupants antiabortion literature. The number of people congregating varied from a handful to 400, and the noise varied from singing and chanting to the use of loudspeakers and bullhorns.

.   .   .

Doctors and clinic workers, in turn, were not immune even in their homes. Petitioners picketed in front of clinic employees' residences; shouted at passersby; rang the doorbells of neighbors and provided literature identifying the particular clinic employee as a "baby killer." Occasionally, the protestors would confront minor children of clinic employees who were home alone. This and similar testimony led the state court to conclude that its original injunction had proved insufficient.... The amended injunction prohibits petitioners from engaging in the following acts:

"(1) At all times on all days, from entering the premises and property of the Aware Woman Center for Choice [the Melbourne clinic]....

"(2) At all times on all days, from blocking, impeding, inhibiting, or in any other manner obstructing or interfering with access to, ingress into and egress from any building or parking lot of the Clinic.

"(3) At all times on all days, from congregating, picketing, patrolling, demonstrating or entering that portion of public right-of-way or private property within [36] feet of the property line of the Clinic.... An exception to the 36 foot buffer zone is the area immediately adjacent to the Clinic on the east.... The [petitioners] ... must remain at least [5] feet from the Clinic's east line. Another exception to the 36 foot buffer zone relates to the record title owners of the property to the north and west of the Clinic. The prohibition against entry into the 36 foot buffer zones does not apply to such persons and their invitees. The other prohibitions contained herein do apply, if such owners and their invitees are acting in concert with the [petitioners]....

"(4) During the hours of 7:30 a.m. through noon, on Mondays through Saturdays, during surgical procedures and recovery periods, from singing, chanting, whistling, shouting, yelling, use of bullhorns, auto horns, sound amplification equipment or other sounds or images observable to or within earshot of the patients inside the Clinic.

"(5) At all times on all days, in an area within [300] feet of the Clinic, from physically approaching any person seeking the services of the Clinic unless such person indicates a desire to communicate by approaching or by inquiring of the [petitioners]....

"(6) At all times on all days, from approaching, congregating, picketing, patrolling, demonstrating or using bullhorns or other sound amplification equipment within [300] feet of the residence of any of the [respondents'] employees, staff, owners or agents, or blocking or attempting to block, barricade, or in any other manner, temporarily or otherwise, obstruct the entrances, exits or driveways of the residences of any of the [respondents'] employees, staff, owners or agents. The [petitioners] and those acting in concert with them are prohibited from inhibiting or impeding or attempting to impede, temporarily or otherwise, the free ingress or egress of persons to any street that provides the sole access to the street on which those residences are located.

"(7) At all times on all days, from physically abusing, grabbing, intimidating, harassing, touching, pushing, shoving, crowding or assaulting persons entering or leaving, working at or using services at the [respondents'] Clinic or trying to gain access to, or leave, any of the homes of owners, staff or patients of the Clinic.

"(8) At all times on all days, from harassing, intimidating or physically abusing, assaulting or threatening any present or former doctor, health care professional, or other staff member, employee or volunteer who assists in providing services at the [respondents'] Clinic.

"(9) At all times on all days, from encouraging, inciting, or securing other persons to commit any of the prohibited acts listed herein."

The Florida Supreme Court upheld the constitutionality of the trial court's amended injunction. . . .

. . .

II

We begin by addressing petitioners' contention that the state court's order, because it is an injunction that restricts only the speech of antiabortion protesters, is necessarily content or viewpoint based. Accordingly, they argue, we should examine the entire injunction under the strictest standard of scrutiny. ... We disagree. To accept petitioners' claim would be to classify virtually every injunction as content or viewpoint based. An injunction, by its very nature, applies only to a particular group (or individuals) and regulates the activities, and perhaps the speech, of that group. It does so, however, because of the group's past actions in the context of a specific dispute between real parties. The parties seeking the injunction assert a violation of their rights; the court hearing the action is charged with fashioning a remedy for a specific deprivation, not with the drafting of a statute addressed to the general public.

The fact that the injunction in the present case did not prohibit activities of those demonstrating in favor of abortion is justly attributable to the lack of any similar demonstrations by those in favor of abortion, and of any consequent request that their demonstrations be regulated by injunction. There is no suggestion in this record that Florida law would not equally restrain similar conduct directed at a target having nothing to do with abortion; none of the restrictions imposed by the court were directed at the contents of petitioner's message.

Our principal inquiry in determining content neutrality is whether the government has adopted a regulation of speech "without reference to the content of the regulated speech." . . . We thus look to the government's purpose as the threshold consideration. Here, the state court imposed restrictions on petitioners incidental to their antiabortion message because they repeatedly violated the court's original order. That petitioners all share the same viewpoint regarding abortion does not in itself demonstrate that some invidious content or viewpoint-based purpose motivated the issuance of the order. It suggests only that those in the group whose conduct violated the court's order happen to share the same opinion regarding abortions being performed at the clinic. In short, the fact that the injunction covered people with a particular viewpoint does not itself render the injunction content or viewpoint based. . . .[2] Accordingly, the injunction issued in this case does not demand the level of heightened scrutiny set forth in Perry Education Assn., 460 U. S., at 45. And we proceed to discuss the standard which does govern.

III

If this were a content-neutral, generally applicable statute, instead of an injunctive order, its constitutionality would be assessed under the standard set forth in Ward v. Rock Against Racism, [491 U.S.] at 791, and similar cases. Given that the forum around the clinic is a traditional public forum . . . we would determine whether the time, place, and manner regulations were "narrowly tailored to serve a significant governmental interest." . . .

There are obvious differences, however, between an injunction and a generally applicable ordinance. Ordinances represent a legislative choice regarding the promotion of particular societal interests. Injunctions, by contrast, are remedies imposed for violations (or threatened violations) of a legislative or judicial decree. . . . Injunctions also carry greater risks of censorship and discriminatory application than do general ordinances. Injunctions, of course, have some advantages over generally applicable statutes in that they can be tailored by a trial judge to afford more precise relief than a statute where a violation of the law has already occurred. . . .

We believe that these differences require a somewhat more stringent application of general First Amendment principles in this context. . . . Accordingly, when evaluating a content-neutral injunction, we think that our standard time, place, and manner analysis is not sufficiently rigorous. We must ask

2. We also decline to adopt the prior restraint analysis urged by petitioners. Prior restraints do often take the form of injunctions. See, e.g., New York Times Co. v. United States, 403 U. S. 713 (1971) (refusing to enjoin publications of the "Pentagon Papers"); Vance v. Universal Amusement Co., 445 U. S. 308 (1980) (per curiam) (holding that Texas public nuisance statute which authorized state judges, on the basis of a showing that a theater had exhibited obscene films in the past, to enjoin its future exhibition of films not yet found to be obscene was unconstitutional as authorizing an invalid prior restraint.) Not all injunctions which may incidentally affect expression, however, are "prior restraints" in the sense that that term was used in New York Times Co., supra, or Vance, supra. Here petitioners are not prevented from expressing their message in any one of several different ways; they are simply prohibited from expressing it within the 36–foot buffer zone. Moreover, the injunction was issued not because of the content of petitioners' expression, as was the case in New York Times Co. and Vance, but because of their prior unlawful conduct.

instead whether the challenged provisions of the injunction burden no more speech than necessary to serve a significant government interest. . . .

Both Justice Stevens and Justice Scalia disagree with the standard we announce, for policy reasons. Justice Stevens believes that "injunctive relief should be judged by a more lenient standard than legislation," because injunctions are imposed on individuals or groups who have engaged in illegal activity. "Justice Scalia, by contrast, believes that content-neutral injunctions are 'at least as deserving of strict scrutiny as a statutory, content-based restriction.'" Justice Scalia bases his belief on the danger that injunctions, even though they might not "attack content as content," may be used to suppress particular ideas; that individual judges should not be trusted to impose injunctions in this context; and that an injunction is procedurally more difficult to challenge than a statute. We believe that consideration of all of the differences and similarities between statutes and injunctions supports, as a matter of policy, the standard we apply here.

Justice Scalia . . . cites a number of cases in which we have struck down, with little or no elaboration, prior restraints on free expression. As we have explained, however, we do not believe that this injunction constitutes a prior restraint, and we therefore believe that the "heavy presumption" against its constitutionality does not obtain here. See n. 2, supra.

. . .

. . . [T]he State has a strong interest in protecting a woman's freedom to seek lawful medical or counseling services in connection with her pregnancy. The State also has a strong interest in ensuring the public safety and order, in promoting the free flow of traffic on public streets and sidewalks, and in protecting the property rights of all its citizens. In addition, the [State has a] strong interest in residential privacy . . . applied by analogy to medical privacy. . . . We agree with the Supreme Court of Florida that the combination of these governmental interests is quite sufficient to justify an appropriately tailored injunction to protect them. We now examine each contested provision of the injunction to see if it burdens more speech than necessary to accomplish its goal.

A

1

We begin with the 36–foot buffer zone. . . . This speech-free buffer zone requires that petitioners move to the other side of Dixie Way and away from the driveway of the clinic, where the state court found that they repeatedly had interfered with the free access of patients and staff. . . .

. . .

The need for a complete buffer zone near the clinic entrances and driveway may be debatable, but some deference must be given to the state court's familiarity with the facts and the background of the dispute between the parties even under our heightened review. . . . On balance, we hold that the 36–foot buffer zone around the clinic entrances and driveway burdens no more speech than necessary to accomplish the governmental interest at stake.

. . .

2

The inclusion of private property on the back and side of the clinic in the 36–foot buffer zone raises different concerns. The accepted purpose of the buffer zone is to protect access to the clinic and to facilitate the orderly flow of traffic on Dixie Way. Patients and staff wishing to reach the clinic do not have to cross the private property abutting the clinic property on the north and west, and nothing in the record indicates that petitioners' activities on the private property have obstructed access to the clinic. . . . We hold that on the record before us the 36–foot buffer zone as applied to the private property to the north and west of the clinic burdens more speech than necessary to protect access to the clinic.

B

In response to high noise levels outside the clinic, the state court restrained the petitioners from "singing, chanting, whistling, shouting, yelling, use of bullhorns, auto horns, sound amplification equipment or other sounds or images observable to or within earshot of the patients inside the [c]linic" during the hours of 7:30 a.m. through noon on Mondays through Saturdays. . . . Noise control is particularly important around hospitals and medical facilities during surgery and recovery periods. . . .

We hold that the limited noise restrictions imposed by the state court order burden no more speech than necessary to ensure the health and well-being of the patients at the clinic. The First Amendment does not demand that patients at a medical facility undertake Herculean efforts to escape the cacophony of political protests. . . .

C

The same, however, cannot be said for the "images observable" provision of the state court's order. Clearly, threats to patients or their families, however communicated, are proscribable under the First Amendment. But rather than prohibiting the display of signs that could be interpreted as threats or veiled threats, the state court issued a blanket ban on all "images observable." This broad prohibition on all "images observable" burdens more speech than necessary to achieve the purpose of limiting threats to clinic patients or their families. Similarly, if the blanket ban on "images observable" was intended to reduce the level of anxiety and hypertension suffered by the patients inside the clinic, it would still fail. The only plausible reason a patient would be bothered by "images observable" inside the clinic would be if the patient found the expression contained in such images disagreeable. But it is much easier for the clinic to pull its curtains than for a patient to stop up her ears, and no more is required to avoid seeing placards through the windows of the clinic. This provision of the injunction violates the First Amendment.

D

The state court ordered that petitioners refrain from physically approaching any person seeking services of the clinic "unless such person indicates a desire to communicate" in an area within 300 feet of the clinic. The state court was attempting to prevent clinic patients and staff from being "stalked" or "shadowed" by the petitioners as they approached the clinic. . . .

But it is difficult, indeed, to justify a prohibition on all uninvited approaches of persons seeking the services of the clinic, regardless of how peaceful the contact may be, without burdening more speech than necessary to prevent intimidation and to ensure access to the clinic. . . .

E

The final substantive regulation challenged by petitioners relates to a prohibition against picketing, demonstrating, or using sound amplification equipment within 300 feet of the residences of clinic staff. [With reference to] the use of sound amplification equipment ... the government may simply demand that petitioners turn down the volume if the protests overwhelm the neighborhood. ...

. . .

... [T]he 300–foot zone around the residences in this case is much larger than the zone provided for in the ordinance which we approved in *Frisby*. ... The record before us does not contain sufficient justification for this broad a ban on picketing; it appears that a limitation on the time, duration of picketing, and number of pickets outside a smaller zone could have accomplished the desired result.

. . .

V

In sum, we uphold the noise restrictions and the 36–foot buffer zone around the clinic entrances and driveway because they burden no more speech than necessary to eliminate the unlawful conduct targeted by the state court's injunction. We strike down as unconstitutional the 36–foot buffer zone as applied to the private property to the north and west of the clinic, the "images observable" provision, the 300–foot no-approach zone around the clinic, and the 300–foot buffer zone around the residences, because these provisions sweep more broadly than necessary to accomplish the permissible goals of the injunction. Accordingly, the judgment of the Florida Supreme Court is

Affirmed in part, and reversed in part.[a]

Justice Stevens, concurring in part and dissenting in part.

... I ... join Parts II and IV of the Court's opinion ... I part company with the Court, however, on its ... enunciation of the applicable standard of review.

I

I agree with the Court that a different standard governs First Amendment challenges to generally applicable legislation than the standard that measures such challenges to judicial remedies for proven wrongdoing ..... Unlike the Court, however, I believe that injunctive relief should be judged by a more lenient standard than legislation. As the Court notes, legislation is imposed on an entire community, regardless of individual culpability. By contrast, injunctions apply solely to an individual or a limited group of individuals who, by engaging in illegal conduct, have been judicially deprived of some liberty-the normal consequence of illegal activity. Given this distinction, a statute prohibiting demonstrations within 36 feet of an abortion clinic would probably violate the First Amendment, but an injunction directed at a limited group of persons who have engaged in unlawful conduct in a similar zone might well be constitutional.

a. A brief concurring opinion by Justice Souter, who also joined the Court's opinion, is omitted.

The standard governing injunctions has two obvious dimensions. On the one hand, the injunction should be no more burdensome than necessary to provide complete relief, ... In a First Amendment context, as in any other, the propriety of the remedy depends almost entirely on the character of the violation and the likelihood of its recurrence. For this reason, standards fashioned to determine the constitutionality of statutes should not be used to evaluate injunctions.

. . .

II

. . .

Petitioners' "counseling" of the clinic's patients is a form of expression analogous to labor picketing. It is a mixture of conduct and communication. ... Just as it protects picketing, the First Amendment protects the speaker's right to offer "sidewalk counseling" to all passersby. That protection, however, does not encompass attempts to abuse an unreceptive or captive audience, at least under the circumstances of this case. ...

. . .

... I thus conclude that, under the circumstances of this case, the prohibition against "physically approaching" in the 300–foot zone around the clinic withstands petitioners' First Amendment challenge. I therefore dissent from Part III–D.

. . .

For the reasons stated, I concur in Parts I, II, III–E, and IV of the Court's opinion, and respectfully dissent from the remaining portions.

Justice Scalia, with whom Justice Kennedy and Justice Thomas join, concurring in the judgment in part and dissenting in part.

... The entire injunction in this case departs so far from the established course of our jurisprudence that in any other context it would have been regarded as a candidate for summary reversal.

But the context here is abortion. ... Today's decision ... makes it painfully clear that no legal rule or doctrine is safe from ad hoc nullification by this Court when an occasion for its application arises in a case involving state regulation of abortion. ...

. . .

II

A

. . .

... [A] restriction upon speech imposed by injunction (whether nominally content based or nominally content neutral) is at least as deserving of strict scrutiny as a statutory, content-based restriction.

That is so for several reasons: The danger of content-based statutory restrictions upon speech is that they may be designed and used precisely to suppress the ideas in question rather than to achieve any other proper governmental aim. But that same danger exists with injunctions. Although a speech-restricting injunction may not attack content as content ..., it lends itself just as readily to the targeted suppression of particular ideas. ... The proceedings before us here illustrate well enough what I mean. The injunction was sought against a single-issue advocacy group by persons and organizations with a business or social interest in suppressing that group's point of view.

The second reason speech-restricting injunctions are at least as deserving of strict scrutiny is obvious enough: they are the product of individual judges rather than of legislatures-and often of judges who have been chagrined by prior disobedience of their orders. . . . [P]ersons subject to a speech-restricting injunction who have not the money or not the time to lodge an immediate appeal face a Hobson's choice: they must remain silent, since if they speak their First Amendment rights are no defense in subsequent contempt proceedings. This is good reason to require the strictest standard for issuance of such orders.

. . .

III

. . .

B

I turn now to the Court's performance in the present case. I am content to evaluate it under the lax (intermediate-intermediate scrutiny) standard that the Court has adopted, because even by that distorted light it is inadequate.

. . .

. . . The interests assertedly protected by the supplementary injunction did not include any interest whose impairment was a violation of Florida law or of a Florida-court injunction. . . . [T]hat means that the interests cannot possibly qualify as "significant interests" under the Court's new standard.

C

Finally, I turn to the Court's application of the second part of its test: whether the provisions of the injunction "burden no more speech than necessary" to serve the significant interest protected.

. . . With regard to the 36–foot speech-free zone, . . . the test which the Court sets for itself has not been met.

Assuming a "significant state interest" . . . in both (1) keeping pedestrians off the paved portion of Dixie Way, and (2) enabling cars to cross the public sidewalk at the clinic's driveways without having to slow down or come to even a "momentary" stop, there are surely a number of ways to protect those interests short of banishing the entire protest demonstration from the 36–foot zone. . . .

. . .

For these reasons, I dissent from that portion of the judgment upholding parts of the injunction.

Hill v. Colorado

530 U.S. 703, 120 S.Ct. 2480, 147 L.Ed.2d 597 (2000).

Justice Stevens delivered the opinion of the Court.

At issue is the constitutionality of a 1993 Colorado statute that regulates speech-related conduct within 100 feet of the entrance to any health care facility. The specific section of the statute that is challenged, Colo. Rev. Stat.

§ 18–9–122(3) (1999), makes it unlawful within the regulated areas for any person to "knowingly approach" within eight feet of another person, without that person's consent, "for the purpose of passing a leaflet or handbill to, displaying a sign to, or engaging in oral protest, education, or counseling with such other person. . . ." Although the statute prohibits speakers from approaching unwilling listeners, it does not require a standing speaker to move away from anyone passing by. Nor does it place any restriction on the content of any message that anyone may wish to communicate to anyone else, either inside or outside the regulated areas. It does, however, make it more difficult to give unwanted advice, particularly in the form of a handbill or leaflet, to persons entering or leaving medical facilities.

The question is whether the First Amendment rights of the speaker are abridged by the protection the statute provides for the unwilling listener.

I

. . . [P]etitioners filed a complaint . . . praying for a declaration that § 18–9–122(3) was facially invalid and seeking an injunction against its enforcement. They stated that prior to the enactment of the statute, they had engaged in "sidewalk counseling" on the public ways and sidewalks within 100 feet of the entrances to facilities where human abortion is practiced or where medical personnel refer women to other facilities for abortions. . . .

. . .

The District Judge granted respondents' motion [for summary judgment] and dismissed the complaint. . . .

The Colorado Court of Appeals affirmed . . .

In 1996, the Supreme Court of Colorado denied review, and petitioners sought a writ of certiorari from our Court. While their petition was pending, we decided Schenck v. Pro–Choice Network of Western N.Y., 519 U.S. 357 (1997). Because we held in that case that an injunctive provision creating a speech-free "floating buffer zone" with a 15–foot radius violates the First Amendment, we . . . remanded the case . . . for further consideration in light of Schenck.

On remand the Court of Appeals reinstated its judgment upholding the statute.

The Colorado Supreme Court affirmed. . . .

. . . We now affirm.

II

. . . A brief review of both sides of the dispute reveals that each has legitimate and important concerns.

The First Amendment interests of petitioners are clear and undisputed. As a preface to their legal challenge, petitioners emphasize three propositions. First, . . . the areas protected by the statute encompass all the public ways within 100 feet of every entrance to every health care facility everywhere in the State of Colorado . . . even though the legislative history makes it clear that its enactment was primarily motivated by activities in the vicinity of abortion clinics. Second, . . . their leafleting, sign displays, and oral communications are protected by the First Amendment. . . . Third, the public sidewalks, streets, and ways affected by the statute are "quintessential" public forums for free speech. . . .

On the other hand, petitioners do not challenge the legitimacy of the state interests that the statute is intended to serve. It is a traditional exercise of the States' "police powers to protect the health and safety of their citizens." . . . That interest may justify a special focus on unimpeded access to health care facilities and the avoidance of potential trauma to patients associated with confrontational protests. . . .

It is also important when conducting this interest analysis to recognize the significant difference between state restrictions on a speaker's right to address a willing audience and those that protect listeners from unwanted communication. This statute deals only with the latter.

The right to free speech, of course, includes the right to attempt to persuade others to change their views, and may not be curtailed simply because the speaker's message may be offensive to his audience. But the protection afforded to offensive messages does not always embrace offensive speech that is so intrusive that the unwilling audience cannot avoid it. . . .

. . . None of our decisions has minimized the enduring importance of "the right to be free" from persistent "importunity, following and dogging" after an offer to communicate has been declined. . . . It is that right, as well as the right of "passage without obstruction," that the Colorado statute legitimately seeks to protect. The restrictions imposed by the Colorado statute only apply to communications that interfere with these rights rather than those that involve willing listeners.

The dissenters argue that we depart from precedent by recognizing a "right to avoid unpopular speech in a public forum." . . . The dissenters . . . consider recognizing any of the interests of unwilling listeners—let alone balancing those interests against the rights of speakers—to be unconstitutional. Our cases do not support this view.

III

. . . It is . . . appropriate to comment on the "content neutrality" of the statute. As we explained in Ward [v. Rock Against Racism, 491 U.S. 781 (1989)]:

> "The principal inquiry in determining content neutrality, in speech cases generally and in time, place, or manner cases in particular, is whether the government has adopted a regulation of speech because of disagreement with the message it conveys." . . .

The Colorado statute passes that test for three independent reasons. First, it is not a "regulation of speech." Rather, it is a regulation of the places where some speech may occur. Second, it was not adopted "because of disagreement with the message it conveys." . . . [T]he statute's "restrictions apply equally to all demonstrators, regardless of viewpoint, and the statutory language makes no reference to the content of the speech." Third, the State's interests in protecting access and privacy, and providing the police with clear guidelines, are unrelated to the content of the demonstrators' speech. . . .

Petitioners nevertheless argue that the statute is not content neutral insofar as it applies to some oral communication. The statute applies to all persons who "knowingly approach" within eight feet of another for the purpose of leafleting or displaying signs; for such persons, the content of their oral statements is irrelevant. With respect to persons who are neither leafletters nor sign carriers, however, the statute does not apply unless their approach is "for the purpose of . . . engaging in oral protest, education, or counseling." Petitioners contend that an individual near a health care facility who knowingly approaches a pedestrian to say "good morning" or to randomly recite lines from a novel would not be subject to the statute's restrictions. Because the content of the oral statements made by an approaching speaker must sometimes be examined to determine whether the knowing approach is covered by the statute, petitioners argue that the law is "content-based" . . .

. . .

. . . We have never held, or suggested, that it is improper to look at the content of an oral or written statement in order to determine whether a rule of law applies to a course of conduct. With respect to the conduct that is the focus of the Colorado statute, it is unlikely that there would often be any need to know exactly what words were spoken in order to determine whether "sidewalk counselors" are engaging in "oral protest, education, or counseling" rather than pure social or random conversation.

Theoretically, of course, cases may arise in which it is necessary to review the content of the statements made by a person approaching within eight feet of an unwilling listener to determine whether the approach is covered by the statute. But that review need be no more extensive than a determination of whether a general prohibition of "picketing" or "demonstrating" applies to innocuous speech.... [W]e have never suggested that the kind of cursory examination that might be required to exclude casual conversation from the coverage of a regulation of picketing would be problematic.

. . .

The Colorado statute's regulation of the location of protests, education, and counseling ... places no restrictions on—and clearly does not prohibit—either a particular viewpoint or any subject matter that may be discussed by a speaker. Rather, it simply establishes a minor place restriction on an extremely broad category of communications with unwilling listeners. Instead of drawing distinctions based on the subject that the approaching speaker may wish to address, the statute applies equally to used car salesmen, animal rights activists, fundraisers, environmentalists, and missionaries. Each can attempt to educate unwilling listeners on any subject, but without consent may not approach within eight feet to do so.

The dissenters, nonetheless, contend that the statute is not "content neutral" [because] "it lends itself" to being "used for invidious thought-control purposes." But a statute that restricts certain categories of speech only lends itself to invidious use if there is a significant number of communications, raising the same problem that the statute was enacted to solve, that fall outside the statute's scope, while others fall inside. ... The statute does not distinguish among speech instances that are similarly likely to raise the legitimate concerns to which it responds. Hence, the statute cannot be struck down for failure to maintain "content neutrality," or for "underbreadth."

Also flawed is Justice Kennedy's theory that a statute restricting speech becomes unconstitutionally content based because of its application "to the specific locations where that discourse occurs." A statute prohibiting solicitation in airports that was motivated by the aggressive approaches of Hari-Krishnas does not become content based solely because its application is confined to airports....

Similarly, the contention that a statute is "viewpoint based" simply because its enactment was motivated by the conduct of the partisans on one side of a debate is without support. The antipicketing ordinance upheld in Frisby v. Schultz, 487 U.S. 474 (1988), a decision in which both of today's dissenters joined, was obviously enacted in response to the activities of antiabortion protesters who wanted to protest at the home of a particular doctor to persuade him and others that they viewed his practice of performing abortions to be murder. We nonetheless summarily concluded that the statute was content neutral....

Justice Kennedy further suggests that a speaker who approaches a patient and "chants in praise of the Supreme Court and its abortion decisions, or hands out a simple leaflet saying, 'We are for abortion rights,'" would not be subject to the statute. But what reason is there to believe the statute would not apply to that individual? ...

... § 18–9–122(3) is content neutral.

IV

... § 18–9–122(3) is a valid time, place, and manner regulation under the test applied in *Ward* because it is "narrowly tailored." ... [W]hen a content-neutral regulation does not entirely foreclose any means of communication, it may satisfy the tailoring requirement even though it is not the least restrictive or least intrusive means of serving the statutory goal.

The three types of communication regulated ... are the display of signs, leafletting, and oral speech. The 8–foot separation between the speaker and the audience should not have any adverse impact on the readers' ability to read signs displayed by demonstrators....

With respect to oral statements, the distance certainly can make it more difficult for a speaker to be heard ... [T]his statute does not suffer from the failings that compelled us to reject the "floating buffer zone" in *Schenck* ... Unlike the 15–foot zone in *Schenck*, this 8–foot zone allows the speaker to communicate at a "normal conversational distance." ... Additionally, the statute allows the speaker to remain in one place, and other individuals can pass within eight feet of the protester without causing the protester to violate the statute. Finally, here there is a "knowing" requirement that protects speakers "who thought they were keeping pace with the targeted individual" at the proscribed distance from inadvertently violating the statute....

... [W]hether or not the 8–foot interval is the best possible accommodation of the competing interests at stake, we must accord a measure of deference to the judgment of the Colorado Legislature....

The burden on the ability to distribute handbills is more serious because it seems possible that an 8–foot interval could hinder the ability of a leafletter to deliver handbills to some unwilling recipients. The statute does not, however, prevent a leafletter from simply standing near the path of oncoming pedestrians and proffering his or her material, which the pedestrians can easily accept. ... In Heffron v. International Soc. for Krishna Consciousness, Inc., 452 U.S. 640 (1981), we upheld a state fair regulation that required a religious organization desiring to distribute literature to conduct that activity only at an assigned location—in that case booths. As in this case, the regulation primarily burdened the distributors' ability to communicate with unwilling readers. We concluded our opinion by emphasizing that the First Amendment protects the right of every citizen to "reach the minds of willing listeners and to do so there must be opportunity to win their attention." ... The Colorado statute adequately protects those rights.

Finally, in determining whether a statute is narrowly tailored, we ... "determin[e] whether these restrictions burden more speech than necessary."....

Persons who are attempting to enter health care facilities—for any purpose—are often in particularly vulnerable physical and emotional conditions. The State of Colorado has responded to its substantial and legitimate interest in protecting these persons from unwanted encounters, confrontations, and even assaults by enacting an exceedingly modest restriction on the speakers' ability to approach.

Justice Kennedy, however, argues that the statute leaves petitioners without adequate means of communication. . . . [T]he statute takes a prophylactic approach; it forbids all unwelcome demonstrators to come closer than eight feet. We recognize that by doing so, it will sometimes inhibit a demonstrator whose approach in fact would have proved harmless. But the statute's prophylactic aspect is justified by the great difficulty of protecting, say, a pregnant woman from physical harassment with legal rules that focus exclusively on the individual impact of each instance of behavior, demanding in each case an accurate characterization (as harassing or not harassing) of each individual movement within the 8–foot boundary. Such individualized characterization of each individual movement is often difficult to make accurately. A bright-line prophylactic rule may be the best way to provide protection, and, at the same time, by offering clear guidance and avoiding subjectivity, to protect speech itself.

. . . .

Finally, the 8–foot restriction occurs only within 100 feet of a health care facility—the place where the restriction is most needed. . . .

This restriction is thus reasonable and narrowly tailored.

V

. . . There are two parts to petitioners' "overbreadth" argument. On the one hand, they argue that the statute is too broad because it protects too many people in too many places, rather than just the patients at the facilities where confrontational speech had occurred. Similarly, it burdens all speakers, rather than just persons with a history of bad conduct. On the other hand, petitioners also contend that the statute is overbroad because it "bans virtually the universe of protected expression, including displays of signs, distribution of literature, and mere verbal statements"

The first part of the argument does not identify a constitutional defect. The fact that the coverage of a statute is broader than the specific concern that led to its enactment is of no constitutional significance. . . . Here, the comprehensiveness of the statute is a virtue, not a vice, because it is evidence against there being a discriminatory governmental motive. . . .

The second part of the argument is based on a misreading of the statute and an incorrect understanding of the overbreadth doctrine. . . . Petitioners have not persuaded us that the impact of the statute on the conduct of other speakers will differ from its impact on their own sidewalk counseling. . . . Like petitioners' own activities, the conduct of other protesters and counselors at all health care facilities are encompassed within the statute's "legitimate sweep." Therefore, the statute is not overly broad.

VI

Petitioners also claim that § 18–9–122(3) is unconstitutionally vague. They find a lack of clarity in three parts of the section: the meaning of "protest, education, or counseling"; the "consent" requirement; and the determination of whether one is "approaching" within eight feet of another.

A statute can be impermissibly vague for either of two independent reasons. First, if it fails to provide people of ordinary intelligence a reasonable opportunity to understand what conduct it prohibits. Second, if it authorizes or even encourages arbitrary and discriminatory enforcement. . . .

. . . In this case, the first concern is ameliorated by the fact that § 18–9–122(3) contains a scienter requirement.

Petitioners proffer hypertechnical theories as to what the statute covers, such as whether an outstretched arm constitutes "approaching." . . . [S]peculation about possible vagueness in hypothetical situations not before the Court will not support a facial attack on a statute when it is surely valid "in the vast majority of its intended applications," . . .

. . .

VII

. . .

The judgment of the Colorado Supreme Court is affirmed.

It is so ordered.

Justice Souter, with whom Justice O'Connor, Justice Ginsburg, and Justice Breyer join, concurring.

I join the opinion of the Court and add this further word. . . .

. . . There is always a correlation with subject and viewpoint when the law regulates conduct that has become the signature of one side of a controversy. But that does not mean that every regulation of such distinctive behavior is content based as First Amendment doctrine employs that term. The correct rule, rather, is captured in the formulation that a restriction is content based only if it is imposed because of the content of the speech, . . . and not because of offensive behavior identified with its delivery.

. . .

. . . The question is simply whether the ostensible reason for regulating the circumstances is really something about the ideas. Here, the evidence indicates that the ostensible reason is the true reason. . . . What is prohibited is a close encounter when the person addressed does not want to get close. . . . Hence the implausibility of any claim that an anti-abortion message, not the behavior of protesters, is what is being singled out.

. . .

. . . I would note the contrast between the operation of subsection (3) and that of the comparable portion of the injunction struck down in *Schenck* . . ., where . . . the floating bubble was larger (15 feet) and was associated with near-absolute prohibitions on speech. . . . Whether floating bubble zones are so inherently difficult to administer that only fixed, no-speech zones (or prohibitions on ambulatory counseling within a fixed zone) should pass muster is an issue neither before us nor well suited to consideration on a facial challenge . . .

Justice Scalia, with whom Justice Thomas joins, dissenting.

. . .

. . . Having deprived abortion opponents of the political right to persuade the electorate that abortion should be restricted by law, the Court today continues and expands its assault upon their individual right to persuade women contemplating abortion that what they are doing is wrong. . . .

I

... Whether a speaker must obtain permission before approaching within eight feet—and whether he will be sent to prison for failing to do so—depends entirely on what he intends to say when he gets there. I have no doubt that this regulation would be deemed content-based in an instant if the case before us involved antiwar protesters, or union members seeking to "educate" the public about the reasons for their strike. ... But the jurisprudence of this Court has a way of changing when abortion is involved.

. . .

... This Colorado law is no more targeted at used car salesmen, animal rights activists, fund raisers, environmentalists, and missionaries than French vagrancy law was targeted at the rich. ...

. . .

In sum, it blinks reality to regard this statute, in its application to oral communications, as anything other than a content-based restriction upon speech in the public forum. ...

II

... [E]ven a content-neutral, time, place, and manner restriction must be narrowly tailored to advance a significant state interest, and must leave open ample alternative means of communication. ...

This requires us to determine, first, what is the significant interest the State seeks to advance? ... Colorado has identified in the text of the statute itself the interest it sought to advance: to ensure that the State's citizens may "obtain medical counseling and treatment in an unobstructed manner" by "preventing the willful obstruction of a person's access to medical counseling and treatment at a health care facility." ... The Court nevertheless concludes that the Colorado provision is narrowly tailored to serve the State's interest in protecting its citizens' rights to be let alone from unwanted speech.

. . .

I shall discuss below the obvious invalidity of this statute assuming, first (in Part A), the fictitious state interest that the Court has invented, and then (in Part B), the interest actually recited in the statute and asserted by counsel for Colorado.

A

. . .

... [T]he "right to be let alone" ... is not an interest that may be legitimately weighed against the speakers' First Amendment rights ... We have consistently held that "the Constitution does not permit the government to decide which types of otherwise protected speech are sufficiently offensive to require protection for the unwilling listener or viewer." ...

... We have upheld limitations on a speaker's exercise of his right to speak on the public streets when that speech intrudes into the privacy of the home. ... The Court today elevates the abortion clinic to the status of the home.

. . .

B

I turn now to the real state interest at issue here?the one set forth in the statute and asserted in Colorado's brief: the preservation of unimpeded access to health care facilities. . . . In subsection (3), however, the State of Colorado has prohibited a vast amount of speech that cannot possibly be thought to correspond to that evil.

. . .

Justice Kennedy, dissenting.

. . .

I

. . .

A

. . . The law imposes content-based restrictions on speech by reason of the terms it uses, the categories it employs, and the conditions for its enforcement. It is content based, too, by its predictable and intended operation. Whether particular messages violate the statute is determined by their substance. The law is a prime example of a statute inviting screening and censoring of individual speech; and it is serious error to hold otherwise.

. . .

. . . The purpose and design of the statute—as everyone ought to know and as its own defenders urge in attempted justification—are to restrict speakers on one side of the debate: those who protest abortions. The statute applies only to medical facilities, a convenient yet obvious mask for the legislature's true purpose and for the prohibition's true effect. One need read no further than the statute's preamble to remove any doubt about the question. . . .

. . .

B

In a further glaring departure from precedent we learn today that citizens have a right to avoid unpopular speech in a public forum. . . .

. . .

III

Even aside from the erroneous, most disturbing assumptions that the statute is content neutral, viewpoint neutral, and neither vague nor overbroad, the Court falls into further serious error when it turns to the time, place, and manner rules set forth in *Ward*.

. . .

. . . Both the State and the Court attempt to sidestep the enactment's obvious content-based restriction by praising the statute's breadth, by telling us all topics of conversation, not just discourse on abortion, are banned within the statutory proscription. . . . Our precedents do not permit content censoring to be cured by taking even more protected speech within a statute's reach. . . .

. . .

Assuming Colorado enacted the statute to respond to incidents of disorder-ly and unlawful conduct near abortion clinics, there were alternatives to restricting speech. It is beyond dispute that pinching or shoving or hitting is a battery actionable under the criminal law and punishable as a crime. State courts have also found an actionable tort when there is a touching, done in an offensive manner, of an object closely identified with the body, even if it is not clothing or the body itself. . . .

The majority insists the statute aims to protect distraught women who are embarrassed, vexed, or harassed as they attempt to enter abortion clinics. If these are punishable acts, they should be prohibited in those terms. . . .

. . . The prophylactic theory seems to be based on a supposition that most citizens approaching a health care facility are unwilling to listen to a fellow citizen's message and that face-to-face communications will lead to lawless behavior within the power of the State to punish. These premises have no support in law or in fact. . . .

．　．　．

IV

．　．　．

The Court now strikes at the heart of the reasoned, careful balance I had believed was the basis for the joint opinion in *Casey*. The vital principle of the opinion was that in defined instances the woman's decision whether to abort her child was in its essence a moral one, a choice the State could not dictate. Foreclosed from using the machinery of government to ban abortions in early term, those who oppose it are remitted to debate the issue in its moral dimensions. In a cruel way, the Court today turns its back on that balance. It in effect tells us the moral debate is not so important after all and can be conducted just as well through a bullhorn from an 8–foot distance as it can through a peaceful, face-to-face exchange of a leaflet. The lack of care with which the Court sustains the Colorado statute reflects a most troubling abdication of our responsibility to enforce the First Amendment.

．　．　．

SECTION 2.   THE NON-TRADITIONAL FORUM—SPEECH ACTIVITIES IN PUBLIC PROPERTY OTHER THAN PARKS AND STREETS

Adderley v. Florida

385 U.S. 39, 87 S.Ct. 242, 17 L.Ed.2d 149 (1966).

Mr. Justice Black delivered the opinion of the Court.

Petitioners . . . were convicted on a charge of "trespass with a malicious and mischievous intent" upon the premises of the county jail . . . Petitioners, apparently all students of the Florida A. & M. University in Tallahassee, had gone from the school to the jail about a mile away, along with many other students, to "demonstrate" at the jail their protests of arrests of other protesting students the day before, and perhaps to protest more generally against state and local policies and practices of racial segregation, including segregation of the jail. The county sheriff . . . tried to persuade the students to leave the jail grounds. When this did not work, he notified them that they must leave, that if they did not leave he would arrest them for trespassing, and that if they resisted he would charge them with that as well. Some of the students left but others, including petitioners, remained and they were arrested. On appeal the convictions were affirmed....

Petitioners have insisted from the beginning of this case that it is controlled by and must be reversed because of our prior cases of Edwards v. South Carolina, 372 U.S. 229 ... We cannot agree.

... In *Edwards,* the demonstrators went to the South Carolina State Capitol grounds to protest. In this case they went to the jail. Traditionally, state capitol grounds are open to the public. Jails, built for security purposes, are not.... More importantly, South Carolina sought to prosecute its State Capitol demonstrators by charging them with the common-law crime of breach of the peace. The South Carolina breach-of-the-peace statute was ... struck down as being so broad and all-embracing as to jeopardize speech, press, assembly and petition,....

The Florida trespass statute under which these petitioners were charged cannot be challenged on this ground. It is aimed at conduct of one limited kind, that is, for one person or persons to trespass upon the property of another with a malicious and mischievous intent. There is no lack of notice in this law, nothing to entrap or fool the unwary.

. . .

... [T]he jury was authorized to find that the State had proven every essential element of the crime.... That [leaves] only the question of whether conviction ... unconstitutionally deprives petitioners of their rights to freedom of speech, press, assembly or petition. We hold it does not. The sheriff, as jail custodian, had power, as the state courts have here held, to direct that this large crowd of people get off the grounds. There is not a shred of evidence in this record that this power was exercised, or that its exercise was sanctioned by the lower courts, because the sheriff objected to what was being sung or said by the demonstrators or because he disagreed with the objectives of their protest. The record reveals that he objected only to their presence on that part of the jail grounds reserved for jail uses. There is no evidence at all that on any other occasion had similarly large groups of the public been permitted to gather on this portion of the jail grounds for any purpose. Nothing in the Constitution of the United States prevents Florida from even-handed enforcement of its general trespass statute against those refusing to obey the sheriff's order to remove themselves from what amounted to the curtilage of the jailhouse. The State, no less than a private owner of property, has power to preserve the property under its control for the use to which it is lawfully dedicated. For this reason there is no merit to the petitioners' argument that they had a constitutional right to stay on the property, over the jail custodian's objections, because this "area chosen for the peaceful civil rights demonstration was not only 'reasonable' but also particularly appropriate...." Such an argument has as its major unarticulated premise the assumption that people who want to propagandize protests or views have a constitutional right to do so whenever and however and wherever they please. ... The United States Constitution does not forbid a State to control the use of its own property for its own lawful nondiscriminatory purpose.

These judgments are affirmed.

Mr. Justice Douglas, with whom The Chief Justice, Mr. Justice Brennan, and Mr. Justice Fortas concur, dissenting.

. . .

The jailhouse, like an executive mansion, a legislative chamber, a courthouse, or the statehouse itself ... is one of the seats of government whether it be the Tower of London, the Bastille, or a small county jail. And when it houses political prisoners or those who many think are unjustly held, it is an obvious center for protest....

. . .

We do violence to the First Amendment when we permit this "petition for redress of grievances" to be turned into a trespass action....

. . .

There may be some public places which are so clearly committed to other purposes that their use for the airing of grievances is anomalous. There may be some instances in which assemblies and petitions for redress of grievances are not consistent with other necessary purposes of public property. A noisy meeting may be out of keeping with the serenity of the statehouse or the quiet of the courthouse.... But this is quite different from saying that all public places are off limits to people with grievances.... And it is farther yet from saying that the "custodian" of the public property in his discretion can decide when public places shall be used for the communication of ideas, especially the constitutional right to assemble and petition for redress of grievances....

VIEWPOINT—NEUTRAL RULES DENYING ACCESS TO NON-TRADITIONAL PUBLIC FORA

From the 1966 decision in *Adderley* until 1992 the Court consistently refused to classify any public property other than the parks and streets as a traditional public forum. Moreover, viewpoint-neutral rules restricting access to non-traditional public fora were nearly-consistently upheld under an approach that sustained those rules if reasonably consistent with the government's interest in preserving the property for non-speech uses. (The one extreme exception was Board of Airport Commrs. of Los Angeles v. Jews for Jesus, Inc., 482 U.S. 569 (1987), which struck down an airport rule forbidding "all First Amendment activities" in the terminal. The rule literally prohibited talking and reading.)

The cases include: Greer v. Spock, 424 U.S. 828 (1976) (regulation forbidding demonstrations and political speeches on military base); Heffron v. International Society for Krishna Consciousness, 452 U.S. 640 (1981) (state fair rule limiting sale or distribution of written materials to fixed locations); Perry Education Association v. Perry Local Educators' Association, 460 U.S. 37 (1983) (teachers' organization other than elected bargaining representative forbidden to use school mailboxes to communicate with teachers); Los Angeles v. Taxpayers for Vincent, 466 U.S. 789 (1984) (municipal ordinance forbids placing signs on public property); Cornelius v. NAACP Legal Defense and Educational Fund, 473 U.S. 788 (1985) (legal defense and advocacy organizations excluded from participating in federal employees' charity drive); Ward v. Rock Against Racism, 491 U.S. 781 (1989) (regulation of music volume at public amphitheater); United States v. Kokinda, 497 U.S. 720 (1990) (postal regulation forbids soliciting charitable contributions on postal premises).

International Society for Krishna Consciousness, Inc. v. Lee

505 U.S. 672, 112 S.Ct. 2701, 120 L.Ed.2d 541 (1992).

Chief Justice Rehnquist delivered the opinion of the Court.

In this case we consider whether an airport terminal operated by a public authority is a public forum and whether a regulation prohibiting solicitation in the interior of an airport terminal violates the First Amendment.

The relevant facts in this case are not in dispute. Petitioner International Society for Krishna Consciousness, Inc. (ISKCON) is a not-for-profit religious corporation whose members perform a ritual known as sankirtan. The ritual consists of " 'going into public places, disseminating religious literature and soliciting funds to support the religion.' " The primary purpose of this ritual is raising funds for the movement.

Respondent Walter Lee ... was the police superintendent of the Port Authority of New York and New Jersey and was charged with enforcing the regulation at issue. The Port Authority owns and operates three major airports in the greater New York City area. . . .

. . .

The Port Authority has adopted a regulation forbidding within the terminals the repetitive solicitation of money or distribution of literature. The regulation states:

"1. The following conduct is prohibited within the interior areas of buildings or structures at an air terminal if conducted by a person to or with passers-by in a continuous or repetitive manner:

"(a) The sale or distribution of any merchandise, including but not limited to jewelry, food stuffs, candles, flowers, badges and clothing.

"(b) The sale or distribution of flyers, brochures, pamphlets, books or any other printed or written material.

"(c) Solicitation and receipt of funds."

The regulation governs only the terminals; the Port Authority permits solicitation and distribution on the sidewalks outside the terminal buildings. The regulation effectively prohibits petitioner from performing sankirtan in the terminals. As a result, petitioner brought suit seeking declaratory and injunctive relief ... [T]he District Court granted petitioner summary judgment.

The Court of Appeals affirmed in part and reversed in part .. Relying on our recent decision in United States v. Kokinda, 497 U.S. 720 (1990), a divided panel concluded that the terminals are not public fora. ... The Court of Appeals then concluded that, presented with the issue, this Court would find that the ban on solicitation was reasonable, but the ban on distribution was not. Petitioner sought certiorari respecting the Court of Appeals' decision that the terminals are not public fora and upholding the solicitation ban. Respondent cross-petitioned respecting the court's holding striking down the distribution ban. . . .[3]

... Where the government is acting as a proprietor, managing its internal operations, rather than acting as lawmaker with the power to regulate or license, its action will not be subjected to the heightened review to which its actions as a lawmaker may be subject.... Thus, we have upheld a ban on political advertisements in city-operated transit vehicles, Lehman v. City of Shaker Heights, 418 U.S. 298 (1974), even though the city permitted other types of advertising on those vehicles. Similarly, we have permitted a school district to limit access to an internal mail system used to communicate with

3. We deal here only with ISKCON's petition raising the permissibility of solicitation. Respondent's cross-petition concerning the leafletting ban is disposed of in the companion case, *Lee v. International Society for Krishna Consciousness, Inc.*

teachers employed by the district. Perry Education Assn. v. Perry Local Educators' Ass'n, 460 U.S. 37 (1983).

These cases reflect, either implicitly or explicitly, a "forum-based" approach for assessing restrictions that the government seeks to place on the use of its property. . . . Under this approach, regulation of speech on government property that has traditionally been available for public expression is subject to the highest scrutiny. Such regulations survive only if they are narrowly drawn to achieve a compelling state interest. . . . The second category of public property is the designated public forum, whether of a limited or unlimited character—property that the state has opened for expressive activity by part or all of the public. . . . Regulation of such property is subject to the same limitations as that governing a traditional public forum. . . . Finally, there is all remaining public property. Limitations on expressive activity conducted on this last category of property must survive only a much more limited review. The challenged regulation need only be reasonable, as long as the regulation is not an effort to suppress the speaker's activity due to disagreement with the speaker's view. . . .

The parties do not disagree that this is the proper framework. Rather, they disagree whether the airport terminals are public fora or nonpublic fora. They also disagree whether the regulation survives the "reasonableness" review governing nonpublic fora, should that prove the appropriate category. Like the Court of Appeals, we conclude that the terminals are nonpublic fora and that the regulation reasonably limits solicitation.

. . .

. . . [A] traditional public forum is property that has as "a principal purpose . . . the free exchange of ideas." . . . Moreover, consistent with the notion that the government—like other property owners—"has power to preserve the property under its control for the use to which it is lawfully dedicated," . . . the government does not create a public forum by inaction. Nor is a public forum created "whenever members of the public are permitted freely to visit a place owned or operated by the Government." . . . The decision to create a public forum must instead be made "by intentionally opening a nontraditional forum for public discourse." . . . Finally, we have recognized that the location of property also has bearing because separation from acknowledged public areas may serve to indicate that the separated property is a special enclave, subject to greater restriction. . . .

. . . [T]he tradition of airport activity does not demonstrate that airports have historically been made available for speech activity. Nor can we say that these particular terminals, or airport terminals generally, have been intentionally opened by their operators to such activity; the frequent and continuing litigation evidencing the operators' objections belies any such claim. In short, there can be no argument that society's time-tested judgment, expressed through acquiescence in a continuing practice, has resolved the issue in petitioner's favor.

Petitioner attempts to circumvent the history and practice governing airport activity by pointing our attention to the variety of speech activity that it claims historically occurred at various "transportation nodes" such as rail stations, bus stations, wharves, and Ellis Island. Even if we were inclined to accept petitioner's historical account describing speech activity at these locations, an account respondent contests, we think that such evidence is of little import for two reasons. First, much of the evidence is irrelevant to public fora analysis, because sites such as bus and rail terminals traditionally have had private ownership. . . . The development of privately owned parks that ban speech activity would not change the public fora status of publicly held parks. But the reverse is also true. The practices of privately held transportation centers do not bear on the government's regulatory authority over a publicly owned airport.

Second, the relevant unit for our inquiry is an airport, not "transportation nodes" generally. . . . To make a category of "transportation nodes" . . . would unjustifiably elide what may prove to be critical differences of which we should rightfully take account. The "security magnet," for example, is an airport commonplace that lacks a counterpart in bus terminals and train stations. And public access to air terminals is also not infrequently restricted—just last year the Federal Aviation Administration required airports for a 4–month period to limit access to areas normally publicly accessible. . . . To blithely equate airports with other transportation centers, therefore, would be a mistake.

The differences among such facilities are unsurprising since . . . airports are commercial establishments funded by users fees and designed to make a regulated profit, and where nearly all who visit do so for some travel related purpose. As commercial enterprises, airports must provide services attractive to the marketplace. In light of this, it cannot fairly be said that an airport terminal has as a principal purpose "promoting the free exchange of ideas." . . . To the contrary, . . . Port Authority management considers the purpose of the terminals to be the facilitation of passenger air travel, not the promotion of expression. . . . Even if we look beyond the intent of the Port Authority to the manner in which the terminals have been operated, the terminals have never been dedicated (except under the threat of court order) to expression in the form sought to be exercised here: i.e., the solicitation of contributions and the distribution of literature.

The terminals here are far from atypical. Airport builders and managers focus their efforts on providing terminals that will contribute to efficient air travel. . . . Thus, we think that neither by tradition nor purpose can the terminals be described as satisfying the standards we have previously set out for identifying a public forum.

The restrictions here challenged, therefore, need only satisfy a requirement of reasonableness. . . . We have no doubt that under this standard the prohibition on solicitation passes muster.

We have on many prior occasions noted the disruptive effect that solicitation may have on business. . . . Passengers who wish to avoid the solicitor may have to alter their path, slowing both themselves and those around them. The result is that the normal flow of traffic is impeded. . . . This is especially so in an airport. . . .

In addition, face-to-face solicitation presents risks of duress that are an appropriate target of regulation. The skillful, and unprincipled, solicitor can target the most vulnerable, including those accompanying children or those suffering physical impairment and who cannot easily avoid the solicitation. . . . The unsavory solicitor can also commit fraud through concealment of his affiliation or through deliberate efforts to shortchange those who agree to purchase. . . . Compounding this problem is the fact that, in an airport, the targets of such activity frequently are on tight schedules. This in turn makes such visitors unlikely to stop and formally complain to airport authorities. As a result, the airport faces considerable difficulty in achieving its legitimate interest in monitoring solicitation activity to assure that travelers are not interfered with unduly.

The Port Authority has concluded that its interest in monitoring the activities can best be accomplished by limiting solicitation and distribution to the sidewalk areas outside the terminals. This sidewalk area is frequented by an overwhelming percentage of airport users. Thus the resulting access of those who would solicit the general public is quite complete. In turn we think it would be odd to conclude that the Port Authority's terminal regulation is unreasonable despite the Port Authority having otherwise assured access to an area universally traveled.

. . .

For the foregoing reasons, the judgment of the Court of Appeals sustaining the ban on solicitation in Port Authority terminals is

Affirmed.

Justice O'Connor, concurring. . .

In the decision below, the Court of Appeals upheld a ban on solicitation of funds within the airport terminals operated by the Port Authority of New York and New Jersey, but struck down a ban on the repetitive distribution of printed or written material within the terminals. I would affirm both parts of that judgment.

I . . . agree that publicly owned airports are not public fora. . . . I also agree with the Court that the Port Authority has not expressly opened its airports to the types of expression at issue here and therefore has not created a "limited" or "designated" public forum relevant to this case.

. . . That airports are not public fora, however, does not mean that the government can restrict speech in whatever way it likes. . . . For example, in Board of Airport Commrs. of Los Angeles v. Jews for Jesus, Inc., 482 U.S. 569 (1987), we unanimously struck down a regulation that prohibited "all First Amendment activities" in the Los Angeles International Airport (LAX) without even reaching the question whether airports were public fora. . . .

. . .

. . . In my view, the Port Authority is operating a shopping mall as well as an airport. The reasonableness inquiry, therefore, is not whether the restrictions on speech are "consistent with . . . preserving the property" for air travel, . . . but whether they are reasonably related to maintaining the multipurpose environment that the Port Authority has deliberately created.

Applying that standard, I agree with the Court . . . that the ban on solicitation is reasonable. . . .

In my view, however, the regulation banning leafletting . . . cannot be upheld as reasonable on this record. I therefore concur in the judgment . . . striking down that prohibition. . . . [I]t is difficult to point to any problems intrinsic to the act of leafletting that would make it naturally incompatible with a large, multipurpose forum such as those at issue here.

. . .

Moreover, the Port Authority has not offered any justifications or record evidence to support its ban on the distribution of pamphlets alone. Its argument is focused instead on the problems created when literature is distributed in conjunction with a solicitation plea . . . . . Because I cannot see how peaceful pamphleteering is incompatible with the multipurpose environment of the Port Authority airports, I cannot accept that a total ban on that activity is reasonable without an explanation as to why such a restriction "preserv[es] the property" for the several uses to which it has been put. . . .

. . .

Justice Kennedy, with whom Justice Blackmun, Justice Stevens, and Justice Souter join as to Part I, concurring in the judgment.

While I concur in the judgment affirming in this case, my analysis differs in substantial respects from that of the Court. In my view the airport corridors and shopping areas outside of the passenger security zones, areas operated by the Port Authority, are public forums. . . . The Port Authority's blanket prohibition on the distribution or sale of literature . . . is invalid under the First and Fourteenth Amendments. The Port Authority's rule disallowing in-person solicitation of money for immediate payment, however, is in my view a narrow and valid regulation of the time, place, and manner of protected speech in this forum, or else is a valid regulation of the nonspeech element of expressive conduct. I would sustain the Port Authority's ban on solicitation and receipt of funds.

I

. . .

. . . The Court today holds that traditional public forums are limited to public property which have as " 'a principal purpose . . . the free exchange of ideas' "; and that this purpose must be evidenced by a long-standing historical practice of permitting speech. The Court also holds that designated forums consist of property which the government intends to open for public discourse. All other types of property are, in the Court's view, nonpublic forums. . . .

This analysis is flawed at its very beginning. It leaves the government with almost unlimited authority to restrict speech on its property by doing nothing more than articulating a non-speech-related purpose for the area, and it leaves almost no scope for the development of new public forums absent the rare approval of the government. . . .

. . .

The Court's approach is contrary to the underlying purposes of the public forum doctrine. . . . Public places are of necessity the locus for discussion of public issues, as well as protest against arbitrary government action. . . .

. . .

The effect of the Court's narrow view of the first category of public forums is compounded by its description of the second purported category, the so-called "designated" forum. The requirements for such a designation are so stringent that I cannot be certain whether the category has any content left at all. . . .

The Court's answer to these objections appears to be a recourse to history as justifying its recognition of streets, parks, and sidewalks, but apparently no other types of government property, as traditional public forums. The Court ignores the fact that the purpose of the public forum doctrine is to give effect to the broad command of the First Amendment to protect speech from governmental interference. The jurisprudence is rooted in historic practice, but it is not tied to a narrow textual command limiting the recognition of new forums. In my view the policies underlying the doctrine cannot be given effect unless we recognize that open, public spaces and thoroughfares which are suitable for discourse may be public forums, whatever their historical pedigree and without concern for a precise classification of the property. . . . In a country where most citizens travel by automobile, and parks all too often become locales for crime rather than social intercourse, our failure to recognize the possibility that new types of government property may be appropriate forums for speech will lead to a serious curtailment of our expressive activity.

One of the places left in our mobile society that is suitable for discourse is a metropolitan airport. It is of particular importance to recognize that such spaces are public forums because in these days an airport is one of the few government-owned spaces where many persons have extensive contact with other members of the public. Given that private spaces of similar character are not subject to the dictates of the First Amendment, . . . it is critical that we preserve these areas for protected speech. In my view, our public forum doctrine must recognize this reality, and allow the creation of public forums which do not fit within the narrow tradition of streets, sidewalks, and parks. . . .

I agree with the Court that government property of a type which by history and tradition has been available for speech activity must continue to be recognized as a public forum. In my view, however, constitutional protection is not confined to these properties alone. Under the proper circumstances I would accord public forum status to other forms of property, regardless of its ancient or contemporary origins and whether or not it fits within a narrow historic tradition. . . .

The second category of the Court's jurisprudence, the so-called designated forum, provides little, if any, additional protection for speech. Where government property does not satisfy the criteria of a public forum, the government retains the power to dedicate the property for speech, whether for all expressive activity or for limited purposes only. . . . [W]hen property has been designated for a particular expressive use, the government may choose to eliminate that designation. But this increases the need to protect speech in other places, where discourse may occur free of such restrictions. . . .

Under this analysis, it is evident that the public spaces of the Port Authority's airports are public forums. First, . . . the public spaces in the airports are broad, public thoroughfares full of people and lined with stores and other commercial activities. An airport corridor is of course not a street, but that is not the proper inquiry. The question is one of physical similarities, sufficient to suggest that the airport corridor should be a public forum for the same reasons that streets and sidewalks have been treated as public forums by the people who use them.

Second, the airport areas involved here are open to the public without restriction. . . . It is the very breadth and extent of the public's use of airports that makes it imperative to protect speech rights there. [I]f the Port Authority allows the uses and open access to airports that is shown on this record, it cannot argue that some vestigial power to change its practices bars the conclusion that its airports are public forums, any more than the power to bulldoze a park bars a finding that a public forum exists so long as the open use does.

Third, and perhaps most important, it is apparent from the record, and from the recent history of airports, that when adequate time, place, and manner regulations are in place, expressive activity is quite compatible with the uses of major airports. . . .

The danger of allowing the government to suppress speech is shown in the case now before us. A grant of plenary power allows the government to tilt the dialogue heard by the public, to exclude many, more marginal voices. The first challenged Port Authority regulation establishes a flat prohibition on "[t]he sale or distribution of flyers, brochures, pamphlets, books or any other printed or written material," if conducted within the airport terminal, "in a continuous or repetitive manner." ... Justice O'Connor finds it void even under the standards applicable to government regulations in nonpublic forums. ...

II

It is my view, however, that the Port Authority's ban on the "solicitation and receipt of funds" within its airport terminals should be upheld under the standards applicable to speech regulations in public forums. The regulation may be upheld as either a reasonable time, place, and manner restriction, or as a regulation directed at the nonspeech element of expressive conduct. The two standards have considerable overlap in a case like this one.

... The confluence of the two tests is well demonstrated by a case like this, where the government regulation at issue can be described with equal accuracy as a regulation of the manner of expression, or as a regulation of conduct with an expressive component.

I am in full agreement with the statement of the Court that solicitation is a form of protected speech. ... If the Port Authority's solicitation regulation prohibited all speech which requested the contribution of funds, I would conclude that it was a direct, content-based restriction of speech in clear violation of the First Amendment. The Authority's regulation does not prohibit all solicitation, however; it prohibits the "solicitation and receipt of funds." I do not understand this regulation to prohibit all speech that solicits funds. It reaches only personal solicitations for immediate payment of money. ... In other words, the regulation permits expression that solicits funds, but limits the manner of that expression to forms other than the immediate receipt of money.

So viewed, I believe the Port Authority's rule survives our test for speech restrictions in the public forum. In-person solicitation of funds, when combined with immediate receipt of that money, creates a risk of fraud and duress which is well recognized, and which is different in kind from other forms of expression or conduct. Travelers who are unfamiliar with the airport, perhaps even unfamiliar with this country, its customs and its language, are an easy prey for the money solicitor. ... As the Court recounts, questionable practices associated with solicitation can include the targeting of vulnerable and easily coerced persons, misrepresentation of the solicitor's cause, and outright theft....

. . .

Much of what I have said about the solicitation of funds may seem to apply to the sale of literature, but the differences between the two activities are of sufficient significance to require they be distinguished for constitutional purposes. ... For one, the government interest in regulating the sales of literature is not as powerful as in the case of solicitation. ... And perhaps most important, the flat ban on sales of literature leaves open fewer alternative channels of communication than the Port Authority's more limited prohibition on the solicitation and receipt of funds. ... [T]he Port Authority's regulation allows no practical means for advocates and organizations to sell literature within the public forums which are its airports.

. . .

For these reasons I agree that the Court of Appeals should be affirmed in full in finding the Port Authority's ban on the distribution or sale of literature unconstitutional, but upholding the prohibition on solicitation and immediate receipt of funds.

Justice Souter, with whom Justice Blackmun and Justice Stevens join, concurring ... and dissenting....

I

I join in Part I of Justice Kennedy's opinion. ...

. . .

I also agree with Justice Kennedy's statement of the public forum principle: we should classify as a public forum any piece of public property that is "suitable for discourse" in its physical character, where expressive activity is "compatible" with the use to which it has actually been put....

II

From the Court's conclusion ... sustaining the total ban on solicitation of money for immediate payment, I respectfully dissent....

Even if I assume arguendo that the ban on the petitioners' activity at issue here is both content neutral and merely a restriction on the manner of communication, the regulation must be struck down for its failure to satisfy the requirements of narrow tailoring to further a significant state interest....

... Since there is here no evidence of any type of coercive conduct, over and above the merely importunate character of the open and public solicitation, that might justify a ban, ... the regulation cannot be sustained to avoid coercion.

As for fraud, our cases do not provide government with plenary authority to ban solicitation just because it could be fraudulent. ... The evidence of fraudulent conduct here is virtually nonexistent....

Even assuming a governmental interest adequate to justify some regulation, the present ban would fall when subjected to the requirement of narrow tailoring....

Finally, I do not think the Port Authority's solicitation ban leaves open the "ample" channels of communication required of a valid content-neutral time, place and manner restriction. A distribution of preaddressed envelopes is unlikely to be much of an alternative. The practical reality of the regulation, which this Court can never ignore, is that it shuts off a uniquely powerful avenue of communication for organizations like the International Society for Krishna Consciousness, and may, in effect, completely prohibit unpopular and poorly funded groups from receiving funds in response to protected solicitation....

. . .

LEE v. INTERNATIONAL SOCIETY FOR KRISHNA CONSCIOUS-NESS, INC., 505 U.S. 830 (1992). In the companion case to International Society for Krishna Consciousness, Inc. v. Lee, the court affirmed the judgment of the court of appeals that the ban on distribution of literature is invalid under the First Amendment. The Court's per curiam opinion stated that affirmance was "[f]or the reasons expressed in the opinions of Justice O'Connor, Justice Kennedy, and Justice Souter in *International Society for Kirshna Conscious-*

ness." Justice Rehnquist's dissent, joined by Justices White, Scalia and Thomas, also relied on his opinion in that case. He said, in addition:

"The risks and burdens posed by leafletting are quite similar to those posed by solicitation. The weary, harried, or hurried traveler may have no less desire and need to avoid the delays generated by having literature foisted upon him than he does to avoid delays from a financial solicitation. And while a busy passenger perhaps may succeed in fending off a leafletter with minimal disruption to himself by agreeing simply to take the proffered material, this does not completely ameliorate the dangers of congestion flowing from such leafletting. Others may choose not simply to accept the material but also to stop and engage the leafletter in debate, obstructing those who follow. Moreover, those who accept material may often simply drop it on the floor once out of the leafletter's range, creating an eyesore, a safety hazard, and additional clean-up work for airport staff."

Arkansas Educational Television Commission v. Forbes

523 U.S. 666, 118 S.Ct. 1633, 140 L.Ed.2d 875 (1998).

Justice Kennedy delivered the opinion of the Court.

A state-owned public television broadcaster sponsored a candidate debate from which it excluded an independent candidate with little popular support. The issue before us is whether, by reason of its state ownership, the station had a constitutional obligation to allow every candidate access to the debate. We conclude that, unlike most other public television programs, the candidate debate was subject to constitutional constraints applicable to nonpublic fora under our forum precedents. Even so, the broadcaster's decision to exclude the candidate was a reasonable, viewpoint-neutral exercise of journalistic discretion.

I

Petitioner, the Arkansas Educational Television Commission (AETC), is an Arkansas state agency owning and operating a network of five noncommercial television stations. . . .

In the spring of 1992, AETC staff began planning a series of debates between candidates for federal office in the November 1992 elections. AETC decided to televise a total of five debates, scheduling one for the Senate election and one for each of the four congressional elections in Arkansas. . . . AETC staff developed a debate format allowing about 53 minutes during each 1–hour debate for questions to and answers by the candidates. Given the time constraint, [AETC] "decided to limit participation in the debates to the major party candidates or any other candidate who had strong popular support."

On June 17, 1992, AETC invited the Republican and Democratic candidates for Arkansas' Third Congressional District to participate in the AETC debate for that seat. Two months later, after obtaining the 2,000 signatures required by Arkansas law, . . . respondent Ralph Forbes was certified as an independent candidate qualified to appear on the ballot for the seat. Forbes was a perennial candidate who had sought, without success, a number of elected offices in Arkansas. On August 24, 1992, he wrote to AETC requesting permission to participate in the debate for his district, scheduled for October 22, 1992. On September 4, AETC . . . denied Forbes' request, explaining that AETC had "made a bona fide journalistic judgement that our viewers would be best served by limiting the debate" to the candidates already invited.

On October 19, 1992, Forbes filed suit against AETC, ... claiming that he was entitled to participate in the debate under ... the First Amendment ... The District Court ... dismissed Forbes' action for failure to state a claim.

Sitting en banc, the Court of Appeals ... reversed ...

On remand, the District Court found as a matter of law that the debate was a nonpublic forum, and the issue became whether Forbes' views were the reason for his exclusion. At trial, ... [t]he jury made express findings that AETC's decision to exclude Forbes had not been influenced by political pressure or disagreement with his views. The District Court entered judgment for AETC.

The Court of Appeals again reversed. ...

... We now reverse.

II

... At the outset ... it is instructive to ask whether public forum principles apply to the case at all.

Having first arisen in the context of streets and parks, the public forum doctrine should not be extended in a mechanical way to the very different context of public television broadcasting. ... [B]road rights of access for outside speakers would be antithetical, as a general rule, to the discretion that stations and their editorial staff must exercise to fulfill their journalistic purpose and statutory obligations.

Congress has rejected the argument that "broadcast facilities should be open on a nonselective basis to all persons wishing to talk about public issues." Columbia Broadcasting System, Inc. v. Democratic National Committee, 412 U.S. 94, 105 (1973). Instead, television broadcasters enjoy the "widest journalistic freedom" consistent with their public responsibilities. ... Among the broadcaster's responsibilities is the duty to schedule programming that serves the "public interest, convenience, and necessity." 47 U.S.C. § 309(a). Public and private broadcasters alike are not only permitted, but indeed required, to exercise substantial editorial discretion in the selection and presentation of their programming.

As a general rule, the nature of editorial discretion counsels against subjecting broadcasters to claims of viewpoint discrimination. Programming decisions would be particularly vulnerable to claims of this type because even principled exclusions rooted in sound journalistic judgment can often be characterized as viewpoint-based. To comply with their obligation to air programming that serves the public interest, broadcasters must often choose among speakers expressing different viewpoints. ... Much like a university selecting a commencement speaker, a public institution selecting speakers for a lecture series, or a public school prescribing its curriculum, a broadcaster by its nature will facilitate the expression of some viewpoints instead of others. Were the judiciary to require, and so to define and approve, pre-established criteria for access, it would risk implicating the courts in judgments that should be left to the exercise of journalistic discretion.

When a public broadcaster exercises editorial discretion in the selection and presentation of its programming, it engages in speech activity.... Although programming decisions often involve the compilation of the speech of third parties, the decisions nonetheless constitute communicative acts. ...

Claims of access under our public forum precedents could obstruct the legitimate purposes of television broadcasters....

In the absence of any congressional command to "[r]egimen[t] broadcasters" in this manner, ... we are disinclined to do so through doctrines of our own design. This is not to say the First Amendment would bar the legislative imposition of neutral rules for access to public broadcasting. Instead, we say that, in most cases, the First Amendment of its own force does not compel public broadcasters to allow third parties access to their programming.

Although public broadcasting as a general matter does not lend itself to scrutiny under the forum doctrine, candidate debates present the narrow exception to the rule. For two reasons, a candidate debate like the one at issue here is different from other programming. First, unlike AETC's other broadcasts, the debate was by design a forum ... to allow the candidates to express their views with minimal intrusion by the broadcaster. In this respect the debate differed even from a political talk show, whose host can express partisan views and then limit the discussion to those ideas.

Second, in our tradition, candidate debates are of exceptional significance in the electoral process. ... Deliberation on the positions and qualifications of candidates is integral to our system of government, and electoral speech may have its most profound and widespread impact when it is disseminated through televised debates. ...

As we later discuss, in many cases it is not feasible for the broadcaster to allow unlimited access to a candidate debate. Yet the requirement of neutrality remains; a broadcaster cannot grant or deny access to a candidate debate on the basis of whether it agrees with a candidate's views. ...

The special characteristics of candidate debates support the conclusion that the AETC debate was a forum of some type. The question of what type must be answered by reference to our public forum precedents, to which we now turn.

III

Forbes argues, and the Court of Appeals held, that the debate was a public forum to which he had a First Amendment right of access. Under our precedents, however, the debate was a nonpublic forum, from which AETC could exclude Forbes in the reasonable, viewpoint-neutral exercise of its journalistic discretion.

A

For our purposes, it will suffice to employ the categories of speech fora already established and discussed in our cases....

. . .

In summary, traditional public fora are open for expressive activity regardless of the government's intent. The objective characteristics of these properties require the government to accommodate private speakers. The government is free to open additional properties for expressive use by the general public or by a particular class of speakers, thereby creating designated public fora. Where the property is not a traditional public forum and the government has not chosen to create a designated public forum, the property is either a nonpublic forum or not a forum at all.

B

The parties agree the AETC debate was not a traditional public forum. The Court has rejected the view that traditional public forum status extends beyond its historic confines ... and even had a more expansive conception of traditional public fora been adopted, ..., the almost unfettered access of a traditional public forum would be incompatible with the programming dictates a television broadcaster must follow. The issue, then, is whether the debate was a designated public forum or a nonpublic forum.

Under our precedents, the AETC debate was not a designated public forum. To create a forum of this type, the government must intend to make the property "generally available," Widmar v. Vincent, 454 U.S. 263, 264 (1981), to a class of speakers. In *Widmar*, for example, a state university created a public forum for registered student groups by implementing a policy that expressly made its meeting facilities "generally open" to such groups. ...

A designated public forum is not created when the government allows selective access for individual speakers rather than general access for a class of speakers. ...

... On one hand, the government creates a designated public forum when it makes its property generally available to a certain class of speakers ... On the other hand, the government does not create a designated public forum when it does no more than reserve eligibility for access to the forum to a particular class of speakers, whose members must then, as individuals, "obtain permission," ... to use it. ...

The ... distinction between general and selective access furthers First Amendment interests. By recognizing the distinction, we encourage the government to open its property to some expressive activity in cases where, if faced with an all-or-nothing choice, it might not open the property at all. That this distinction turns on governmental intent does not render it unprotective of speech. Rather, it reflects the reality that, with the exception of traditional public fora, the government retains the choice of whether to designate its property as a forum for specified classes of speakers.

Here, the debate did not have an open-microphone format. Contrary to the assertion of the Court of Appeals, AETC did not make its debate generally available to candidates for Arkansas' Third Congressional District seat. Instead, ... AETC reserved eligibility for participation in the debate to candidates for the Third Congressional District seat (as opposed to some other seat). At that point, ... AETC made candidate-by-candidate determinations as to which of the eligible candidates would participate in the debate.... Thus the debate was a nonpublic forum.

... [T]he Court of Appeals' holding would result in less speech, not more. In ruling that the debate was a public forum open to all ballot-qualified candidates, the Court of Appeals would place a severe burden upon public broadcasters who air candidates' views. In each of the 1988, 1992, and 1996 Presidential elections, for example, no fewer than 22 candidates appeared on the ballot in at least one State.... In the 1996 congressional elections, it was common for 6 to 11 candidates to qualify for the ballot for a particular seat.... In the 1993 New Jersey gubernatorial election, to illustrate further, sample ballot mailings included the written statements of 19 candidates. ... On logistical grounds alone, a public television editor might, with reason, decide that the inclusion of all ballot-qualified candidates would "actually undermine the educational value and quality of debates."

. . .

C

The debate's status as a nonpublic forum, however, did not give AETC unfettered power to exclude any candidate it wished. ... To be consistent with the First Amendment, the exclusion of a speaker from a nonpublic forum must not be based on the speaker's viewpoint and must otherwise be reasonable in light of the purpose of the property. . . .

In this case, the jury found Forbes' exclusion was not based on "objections or opposition to his views." . . .

. . . AETC excluded Forbes because the voters lacked interest in his candidacy, not because AETC itself did.

The broadcaster's decision to exclude Forbes was a reasonable, viewpoint-neutral exercise of journalistic discretion consistent with the First Amendment. The judgment of the Court of Appeals is

Reversed.

Justice Stevens, with whom Justice Souter and Justice Ginsburg join, dissenting.

The Court has decided that a state-owned television network has no "constitutional obligation to allow every candidate access to" political debates that it sponsors. I do not challenge that decision. The judgment of the Court of Appeals should nevertheless be affirmed. . . . The ad hoc decision of the staff of the Arkansas Educational Television Commission (AETC) raises precisely the concerns . . . "that a law subjecting the exercise of First Amendment freedoms to the prior restraint of a license, without narrow, objective, and definite standards to guide the licensing authority, is unconstitutional."

In its discussion of the facts, the Court barely mentions the standardless character of the decision to exclude Forbes from the debate. In its discussion of the law, the Court understates the constitutional importance of the distinction between state ownership and private. . . .

I

. . .

Given the fact that the Republican winner in the Third Congressional District race in 1992 received only 50.22% of the vote and the Democrat received 47.20%, it would have been necessary for Forbes, who had made a strong showing in recent Republican primaries, to divert only a handful of votes from the Republican candidate to cause his defeat. Thus, even though the AETC staff may have correctly concluded that Forbes was "not a serious candidate," their decision to exclude him from the debate may have determined the outcome of the election in the Third District.

. . .

The apparent flexibility of AETC's purported standard suggests the extent to which the staff had nearly limitless discretion to exclude Forbes from the debate based on ad hoc justifications. . . .

II

. . . [T]he Court seriously underestimates the importance of the difference between private and public ownership of broadcast facilities. . . .

. . .

. . . Because AETC is owned by the State, deference to its interest in making ad hoc decisions about the political content of its programs necessarily increases the risk of government censorship and propaganda in a way that protection of privately owned broadcasters does not.

III

The ... First Amendment will not tolerate a state agency's arbitrary exclusion from a debate forum based, for example, on an expectation that the speaker might be critical of the Governor, or might hold unpopular views about abortion or the death penalty. Indeed, the Court so holds today.

It seems equally clear, however, that the First Amendment will not tolerate arbitrary definitions of the scope of the forum. ...

... [A] State's failure to set any meaningful boundaries at all cannot insulate the State's action from First Amendment challenge. The dispositive issue in this case, then, is not whether AETC created a designated public forum or a nonpublic forum, ... but whether AETC defined the contours of the debate forum with sufficient specificity to justify the exclusion of a ballot-qualified candidate.

AETC asks that we reject Forbes' constitutional claim on the basis of entirely subjective, ad hoc judgments about the dimensions of its forum. The First Amendment demands more ...

. . . .

... The importance of avoiding arbitrary or viewpoint-based exclusions from political debates militates strongly in favor of requiring the controlling state agency to use (and adhere to) pre-established, objective criteria to determine who among qualified candidates may participate. ...

Like the Court, I do not endorse the view of the Court of Appeals that all candidates who qualify for a position on the ballot are necessarily entitled to access to any state-sponsored debate. ... Requiring government employees to set out objective criteria by which they choose which candidates will benefit from the significant media exposure that results from state-sponsored political debates would alleviate some of the risk inherent in allowing government agencies—rather than private entities—to stage candidate debates.

Accordingly, I would affirm the judgment of the Court of Appeals.

SECTION 3.   SPEECH ON PRIVATE PREMISES

City of Ladue v. Gilleo

512 U.S. 43, 114 S.Ct. 2038, 129 L.Ed.2d 36 (1994).

Justice Stevens delivered the opinion of the Court.

An ordinance of the City of Ladue prohibits homeowners from displaying any signs on their property except "residence identification" signs, "for sale" signs, and signs warning of safety hazards. The ordinance permits commercial establishments, churches, and nonprofit organizations to erect certain signs that are not allowed at residences. The question presented is whether the ordinance violates a Ladue resident's right to free speech.

I

Respondent Margaret P. Gilleo owns one of the 57 single-family homes in the Willow Hill subdivision of Ladue. On December 8, 1990, she placed on her front lawn a 24 by 36 inch sign printed with the words "Say No to War in the Persian Gulf, Call Congress Now." After that sign disappeared, Gilleo put up another but it was knocked to the ground. When Gilleo reported these incidents to the police, they advised her that such signs were prohibited in Ladue. The City Council denied her petition for a variance. Gilleo then filed this action under 42 U. S. C. § 1983 against the City, the Mayor, and members of the City Council, alleging that Ladue's sign ordinance violated her First Amendment right of free speech.

The District Court issued a preliminary injunction against enforcement of the ordinance. Gilleo then placed an 8.5 by 11 inch sign in the second story window of her home stating, "For Peace in the Gulf." The Ladue City Council responded to the injunction by repealing its ordinance and enacting a replacement. Like its predecessor, the new ordinance contains a general prohibition of "signs" and defines that term broadly. The ordinance prohibits all signs except those that fall within one of ten exemptions. Thus, "residential identification signs" no larger than one square foot are allowed, as are signs advertising "that the property is for sale, lease or exchange" and identifying the owner or agent. Also exempted are signs "for churches, religious institutions, and schools," "[c]ommercial signs in commercially or industrial zoned districts," and on-site signs advertising "gasoline filling stations." Unlike its predecessor, the new ordinance contains a lengthy "Declaration of Findings, Policies, Interests, and Purposes," part of which recites that the "proliferation of an unlimited number of signs in private, residential, commercial, industrial, and public areas of the City of Ladue would create ugliness, visual blight and clutter, tarnish the natural beauty of the landscape as well as the residential and commercial architecture, impair property values, substantially impinge upon the privacy and special ambience of the community, and may cause safety and traffic hazards to motorists, pedestrians, and children[.]"

Gilleo amended her complaint to challenge the new ordinance, which explicitly prohibits window signs like hers. The District Court held the ordinance unconstitutional, and the Court of Appeals affirmed. . . .

We . . . affirm.

II

While signs are a form of expression protected by the Free Speech Clause, they pose distinctive problems that are subject to municipalities' police powers. Unlike oral speech, signs take up space and may obstruct views, distract motorists, displace alternative uses for land, and pose other problems that legitimately call for regulation. It is common ground that governments may regulate the physical characteristics of signs—just as they can, within reasonable bounds and absent censorial purpose, regulate audible expression in its capacity as noise. . . .

In Linmark Associates, Inc. v. Willingboro, 431 U. S. 85 (1977), we addressed an ordinance that sought to maintain stable, integrated neighborhoods by prohibiting homeowners from placing "For Sale" or "Sold" signs on their property. . . . [W]e held that the First Amendment prevented the township from "achieving its goal by restricting the free flow of truthful information." . . . In some respects Linmark is the mirror image of this case. For instead of prohibiting "For Sale" signs without banning any other signs, Ladue has exempted such signs from an otherwise virtually complete ban. Moreover, whereas in Linmark we noted that the ordinance was not concerned with the promotion of aesthetic values unrelated to the content of the prohibited speech, id., . . . here Ladue relies squarely on that content-neutral justification for its ordinance.

. . .

[There are] two analytically distinct grounds for challenging the constitutionality of a municipal ordinance regulating the display of signs. One is that the measure in effect restricts too little speech because its exemptions discriminate on the basis of the signs' messages. ... Alternatively, such provisions are subject to attack on the ground that they simply prohibit too much protected speech. ... The City of Ladue contends, first, that the Court of Appeals' reliance on the former rationale was misplaced because the City's regulatory purposes are content-neutral, and, second, that those purposes justify the comprehensiveness of the sign prohibition. A comment on the former contention will help explain why we ultimately base our decision on a rejection of the latter.

III

While surprising at first glance, the notion that a regulation of speech may be impermissibly underinclusive is firmly grounded in basic First Amendment principles. Thus, an exemption from an otherwise permissible regulation of speech may represent a governmental "attempt to give one side of a debatable public question an advantage in expressing its views to the people." ...

The City argues that [the] mix of prohibitions and exemptions in the ordinance ... reflects legitimate differences among the side effects of various kinds of signs. These differences are only adventitiously connected with content, and supply a sufficient justification, unrelated to the City's approval or disapproval of specific messages, for carving out the specified categories from the general ban ..... Because only a few residents will need to display "for sale" or "for rent" signs at any given time, permitting one such sign per marketed house does not threaten visual clutter. Because the City has only a few businesses, churches, and schools, the same rationale explains the exemption for on-site commercial and organizational signs. Moreover, some of the exempted categories (e.g., danger signs) respond to unique public needs to permit certain kinds of speech. Even if we assume the validity of these arguments, the exemptions in Ladue's ordinance nevertheless shed light on the separate question of whether the ordinance prohibits too much speech.

Exemptions from an otherwise legitimate regulation of a medium of speech may be noteworthy for a reason quite apart from the risks of viewpoint and content discrimination: they may diminish the credibility of the government's rationale for restricting speech in the first place. In this case, at the very least, the exemptions from Ladue's ordinance demonstrate that Ladue has concluded that the interest in allowing certain messages to be conveyed by means of residential signs outweighs the City's aesthetic interest in eliminating outdoor signs. Ladue has not imposed a flat ban on signs because it has determined that at least some of them are too vital to be banned.

Under the Court of Appeals' content discrimination rationale, the City might theoretically remove the defects in its ordinance by simply repealing all of the exemptions. If, however, the ordinance is also vulnerable because it prohibits too much speech, that solution would not save it. ... Therefore, we first ask whether Ladue may properly prohibit Gilleo from displaying her sign, and then, only if necessary, consider the separate question whether it was improper for the City simultaneously to permit certain other signs. In examining the propriety of Ladue's near-total prohibition of residential signs, we will assume, arguendo, the validity of the City's submission that the various exemptions are free of impermissible content or viewpoint discrimination.

IV

. . .

. . . Ladue has almost completely foreclosed a venerable means of communication that is both unique and important. It has totally foreclosed that medium to political, religious, or personal messages. . . . They may not afford the same opportunities for conveying complex ideas as do other media, but residential signs have long been an important and distinct medium of expression.

Our prior decisions have voiced particular concern with laws that foreclose an entire medium of expression. Thus, we have held invalid ordinances that completely banned the distribution of pamphlets within the municipality, Lovell v. Griffin, 303 U. S. 444, 451–452 (1938); handbills on the public streets, Jamison v. Texas, 318 U. S. 413, 416 (1943); the door-to-door distribution of literature, Martin v. Struthers, 319 U. S. 141, 145–149 (1943); Schneider v. State, 308 U. S. 147, 164–165 (1939), and live entertainment, Schad v. Mount Ephraim, 452 U. S. 61, 75–76 (1981). . . . Although prohibitions foreclosing entire media may be completely free of content or viewpoint discrimination, the danger they pose to the freedom of speech is readily apparent—by eliminating a common means of speaking, such measures can suppress too much speech.

Ladue contends, however, that its ordinance is a mere regulation of the "time, place, or manner" of speech because residents remain free to convey their desired messages by other means, such as hand-held signs, "letters, handbills, flyers, telephone calls, newspaper advertisements, bumper stickers, speeches, and neighborhood or community meetings." . However, even regulations that do not foreclose an entire medium of expression, but merely shift the time, place, or manner of its use, must "leave open ample alternative channels for communication." . . . In this case, we are not persuaded that adequate substitutes exist for the important medium of speech that Ladue has closed off.

Displaying a sign from one's own residence often carries a message quite distinct from placing the same sign someplace else, or conveying the same text or picture by other means. Precisely because of their location, such signs provide information about the identity of the "speaker." As an early and eminent student of rhetoric observed, the identity of the speaker is an important component of many attempts to persuade. A sign advocating "Peace in the Gulf" in the front lawn of a retired general or decorated war veteran may provoke a different reaction than the same sign in a 10–year-old child's bedroom window or the same message on a bumper sticker of a passing automobile. An espousal of socialism may carry different implications when displayed on the grounds of a stately mansion than when pasted on a factory wall or an ambulatory sandwich board.

Residential signs are an unusually cheap and convenient form of communication. Especially for persons of modest means or limited mobility, a yard or window sign may have no practical substitute. Even for the affluent, the added costs in money or time of taking out a newspaper advertisement, handing out leaflets on the street, or standing in front of one's house with a hand-held sign may make the difference between participating and not participating in some public debate. Furthermore, a person who puts up a sign at her residence often intends to reach neighbors, an audience that could not be reached nearly as well by other means.

A special respect for individual liberty in the home has long been part of our culture and our law . . .; that principle has special resonance when the government seeks to constrain a person's ability to speak there. . . . Most Americans would be understandably dismayed, given that tradition, to learn that it was illegal to display from their window an 8 by 11 inch sign expressing their political views. . . .

Our decision that Ladue's ban on almost all residential signs violates the First Amendment by no means leaves the City powerless to address the ills that may be associated with residential signs. It bears mentioning that individual residents themselves have strong incentives to keep their own property values up and to prevent "visual clutter" in their own yards and neighborhoods—incentives markedly different from those of persons who erect signs on others' land, in others' neighborhoods, or on public property. Residents' self-interest diminishes the danger of the "unlimited" proliferation of residential signs that concerns the City of Ladue. We are confident that more temperate measures could in large part satisfy Ladue's stated regulatory needs without harm to the First Amendment rights of its citizens. As currently framed, however, the ordinance abridges those rights.

Accordingly, the judgment of the Court of Appeals is Affirmed.

Justice O'Connor, concurring.

It is unusual for us, when faced with a regulation that on its face draws content distinctions, to "assume, arguendo, the validity of the City's submission that the various exemptions are free of impermissible content or viewpoint discrimination." With rare exceptions, content discrimination in regulations of the speech of private citizens on private property or in a traditional public forum is presumptively impermissible, and this presumption is a very strong one. . . . The normal inquiry that our doctrine dictates is, first, to determine whether a regulation is content-based or content-neutral, and then, based on the answer to that question, to apply the proper level of scrutiny. . . .

Over the years, some cogent criticisms have been leveled at our approach. See, e.g., . . . Farber, Content Regulation and the First Amendment: A Revisionist View, 68 Geo. L. J. 727 (1980); Stephan, The First Amendment and Content Discrimination, 68 Va. L. Rev. 203 (1982). And it is quite true that regulations are occasionally struck down because of their content-based nature, even though common sense may suggest that they are entirely reasonable. The content distinctions present in this ordinance may, to some, be a good example of this.

But though our rule has flaws, it has substantial merit as well. It is a rule, in an area where fairly precise rules are better than more discretionary and more subjective balancing tests. . . .

I would have preferred to apply our normal analytical structure in this case, which may well have required us to examine this law with the scrutiny appropriate to content-based regulations. Perhaps this would have forced us to confront some of the difficulties with the existing doctrine; perhaps it would have shown weaknesses in the rule, and led us to modify it to take into account the special factors this case presents. . . .

Nonetheless, I join the Court's opinion, because I agree with its conclusion in Part IV that even if the restriction were content-neutral, it would still be invalid, and because I do not think Part III casts any doubt on the propriety of our normal content discrimination inquiry.

City of Los Angeles v. Alameda Books, Inc.

535 U.S. 425, 122 S.Ct. 1728, 152 L.Ed.2d 670 (2002).

Justice O'Connor announced the judgment of the Court and delivered an opinion, in which The Chief Justice, Justice Scalia, and Justice Thomas join.

Los Angeles Municipal Code § 12.70(C) (1983), as amended, prohibits "the establishment or maintenance of more than one adult entertainment business in the same building, structure or portion thereof." Respondents, two adult establishments that each operated an adult bookstore and an adult video arcade in the same building, filed a suit ... alleging that § 12.70(C) violates the First Amendment and seeking declaratory and injunctive relief. The District Court granted summary judgment to respondents ... The Court of Appeals for the Ninth Circuit affirmed ... We reverse and remand. ...

I

In 1977, the city of Los Angeles conducted a comprehensive study of adult establishments and concluded that concentrations of adult businesses are associated with higher rates of prostitution, robbery, assaults, and thefts in surrounding communities. Accordingly, the city enacted an ordinance prohibiting the establishment, substantial enlargement, or transfer of ownership of an adult arcade, bookstore, cabaret, motel, theater, or massage parlor or a place for sexual encounters within 1,000 feet of another such enterprise or within 500 feet of any religious institution, school, or public park. See Los Angeles Municipal Code § 12.70(C) (1978).

There is evidence that the intent of the city council when enacting this prohibition was not only to disperse distinct adult establishments housed in separate buildings, but also to disperse distinct adult businesses operated under common ownership and housed in a single structure. The ordinance the city enacted, however, directed that "[t]he distance between any two adult entertainment businesses shall be measured in a straight line ... from the closest exterior structural wall of each business." ... Subsequent to enactment, the city realized that this method of calculating distances created a loophole permitting the concentration of multiple adult enterprises in a single structure.

Concerned that allowing an adult-oriented department store to replace a strip of adult establishments could defeat the goal of the original ordinance, the city council amended § 12.70(C) by adding a prohibition on "the establishment or maintenance of more than one adult entertainment business in the same building, structure or portion thereof." Los Angeles Municipal Code § 12.70(C) (1983). The amended ordinance defines an "Adult Entertainment Business" as an adult arcade, bookstore, cabaret, motel, theater, or massage parlor or a place for sexual encounters, and notes that each of these enterprises "shall constitute a separate adult entertainment business even if operated in conjunction with another adult entertainment business at the same establishment." ...

... Although respondents are located in different buildings, each operates its retail sales and rental operations in the same commercial space in which its video booths are located. There are no physical distinctions between the different operations within each establishment and each establishment has only one entrance. ...

. . .

II

In Renton v. Playtime Theatres, Inc., [475 U.S. 41 (1986)], this Court considered the validity of a municipal ordinance that prohibited any adult movie theater from locating within 1,000 feet of any residential zone, family dwelling, church, park, or school. Our analysis of the ordinance proceeded in three steps. First, we found that the ordinance did not ban adult theaters altogether, but merely required that they be distanced from certain sensitive locations. The ordinance was properly analyzed, therefore, as a time, place, and manner regulation. . . . We next considered whether the ordinance was content neutral or content based. If the regulation were content based, it would be considered presumptively invalid and subject to strict scrutiny. . . . We held, however, that the Renton ordinance was aimed not at the content of the films shown at adult theaters, but rather at the secondary effects of such theaters on the surrounding community, namely at crime rates, property values, and the quality of the city's neighborhoods. Therefore, the ordinance was deemed content neutral. . . . Finally, given this finding, we stated that the ordinance would be upheld so long as the city of Renton showed that its ordinance was designed to serve a substantial government interest and that reasonable alternative avenues of communication remained available. . . . We concluded that Renton had met this burden, and we upheld its ordinance. . . .

The Court of Appeals applied the same analysis to evaluate the Los Angeles ordinance challenged in this case. . . . It explained that, even if the Los Angeles ordinance were content neutral, the city had failed to demonstrate, as required by the third step of the *Renton* analysis, that its prohibition on multiple-use adult establishments was designed to serve its substantial interest in reducing crime. The Court of Appeals noted that the primary evidence relied upon by Los Angeles to demonstrate a link between combination adult businesses and harmful secondary effects was the 1977 study conducted by the city's planning department. The Court of Appeals found, however, that the city could not rely on that study because it did not "suppor[t] a reasonable belief that [the] combination [of] businesses . . . produced harmful secondary effects of the type asserted." . . .

. . .

The Court of Appeals found that the 1977 study did not reasonably support the inference that a concentration of adult operations within a single adult establishment produced greater levels of criminal activity because the study focused on the effect that a concentration of establishments—not a concentration of operations within a single establishment—had on crime rates. The Court of Appeals pointed out that the study treated combination adult bookstore/arcades as single establishments and did not study the effect of any separate-standing adult bookstore or arcade.

The Court of Appeals misunderstood the implications of the 1977 study. While the study reveals that areas with high concentrations of adult establishments are associated with high crime rates, areas with high concentrations of adult establishments are also areas with high concentrations of adult operations, albeit each in separate establishments. It . . . is rational for the city to infer that reducing the concentration of adult operations in a neighborhood, whether within separate establishments or in one large establishment, will reduce crime rates.

. . .

The error that the Court of Appeals made is that it required the city to prove that its theory about a concentration of adult operations attracting crowds of customers, much like a minimall or department store does, is a necessary consequence of the 1977 study. . . . The Court of Appeals simply replaced the city's theory—that having many different operations in close proximity attracts crowds—with its own—that the size of an operation attracts crowds. . . . The Court of Appeals' analysis . . . implicitly requires the city to prove that its theory is the only one that can plausibly explain the data because only in this manner can the city refute the Court of Appeals' logic.

. . .

In *Renton,* we specifically refused to set such a high bar for municipalities that want to address merely the secondary effects of protected speech. We held that a municipality may rely on any evidence that is "reasonably believed to be relevant" for demonstrating a connection between speech and a substantial, independent government interest. . . . This is not to say that a municipality can get away with shoddy data or reasoning. The municipality's evidence must fairly support the municipality's rationale for its ordinance. If plaintiffs fail to cast direct doubt on this rationale, either by demonstrating that the municipality's evidence does not support its rationale or by furnishing evidence that disputes the municipality's factual findings, the municipality meets the standard set forth in *Renton.* If plaintiffs succeed in casting doubt on a municipality's rationale in either manner, the burden shifts back to the municipality to supplement the record with evidence renewing support for a theory that justifies its ordinance. . . . This case is at a very early stage in this process. It arrives on a summary judgment motion by respondents defended only by complaints that the 1977 study fails to prove that the city's justification for its ordinance is necessarily correct. Therefore, we conclude that the city, at this stage of the litigation, has complied with the evidentiary requirement in *Renton.*

Justice Souter faults the city for relying on the 1977 study not because the study fails to support the city's theory that adult department stores, like adult minimalls, attract customers and thus crime, but because the city does not demonstrate that free-standing single-use adult establishments reduce crime. In effect, Justice Souter asks the city to demonstrate, not merely by appeal to common sense, but also with empirical data, that its ordinance will successfully lower crime. Our cases have never required that municipalities make such a showing, certainly not without actual and convincing evidence from plaintiffs to the contrary. . . . A municipality considering an innovative solution may not have data that could demonstrate the efficacy of its proposal because the solution would, by definition, not have been implemented previously. The city's ordinance banning multiple-use adult establishments is such a solution. Respondents contend that there are no adult video arcades in Los Angeles County that operate independently of adult bookstores. But without such arcades, the city does not have a treatment group to compare with the control group of multiple-use adult establishments. . . .

Our deference to the evidence presented by the city of Los Angeles is the product of a careful balance between competing interests. . . . We are also guided by the fact that *Renton* requires that municipal ordinances receive only intermediate scrutiny if they are content neutral. . . . There is less reason to be concerned that municipalities will use these ordinances to discriminate against unpopular speech. . . .

Justice Souter would have us rethink this balance, and indeed the entire *Renton* framework. In *Renton,* the Court distinguished the inquiry into whether a municipal ordinance is content neutral from the inquiry into whether it is "designed to serve a substantial government interest and do not unreasonably limit alternative avenues of communication." . . . The former requires courts to verify that the "predominate concerns" motivating the ordinance "were with the secondary effects of adult [speech], and not with the content of adult [speech]." . . . The latter inquiry goes one step further and asks whether the municipality can demonstrate a connection between the speech regulated by the ordinance and the secondary effects that motivated the adoption of the ordinance. Only at this stage did *Renton* contemplate that courts would examine evidence concerning regulated speech and secondary effects. . . . Justice Souter would either merge these two inquiries or move the evidentiary analysis into the inquiry on content neutrality, and raise the evidentiary bar that a municipality must pass. . . .

. . . Justice Souter does not clarify the sort of evidence upon which municipalities may rely to meet the evidentiary burden he would require. It is easy to say that courts must demand evidence when "common experiences" or "common assumptions" are incorrect, but it is difficult for courts to know ahead of time whether that condition is met. Municipalities will, in general, have greater experience with and understanding of the secondary effects that follow certain protected speech than will the courts. . . . For this reason our cases require only that municipalities rely upon evidence that is "reasonably believed to be relevant" to the secondary effects that they seek to address.

III

. . .

. . . [R]espondents argue, as an alternative basis to sustain the Court of Appeals' judgment, that the Los Angeles ordinance is not a typical zoning regulation. Rather, respondents explain, the prohibition on multiuse adult establishments is effectively a ban on adult video arcades because no such business exists independently of an adult bookstore. Respondents request that the Court hold that the Los Angeles ordinance is not a time, place, and manner regulation, and that the Court subject the ordinance to strict scrutiny. This also appears to be the theme of Justice Kennedy's concurrence. . . . We consider that . . . as simply a reformulation of the requirement that an ordinance warrants intermediate scrutiny only if it is a time, place, and manner regulation and not a ban. The Court of Appeals held, however, that the city's prohibition on the combination of adult bookstores and arcades is not a ban and respondents did not petition for review of that determination.

. . .

Justice Scalia, concurring.

I join the plurality opinion because I think it represents a correct application of our jurisprudence concerning regulation of the "secondary effects" of pornographic speech. As I have said elsewhere, however, in a case such as this our First Amendment traditions make "secondary effects" analysis quite unnecessary. The Constitution does not prevent those communities that wish to do so from regulating, or indeed entirely suppressing, the business of pandering sex. . . .

Justice Kennedy, concurring in the judgment.

Speech can produce tangible consequences. It can change minds. It can prompt actions. These primary effects signify the power and the necessity of free speech. Speech can also cause secondary effects, however, unrelated to the impact of the speech on its audience. A newspaper factory may cause pollution, and a billboard may obstruct a view. These secondary consequences are not always immune from regulation by zoning laws even though they are produced by speech.

Municipal governments know that high concentrations of adult businesses can damage the value and the integrity of a neighborhood. The damage is measurable; it is all too real. The law does not require a city to ignore these consequences if it uses its zoning power in a reasonable way to ameliorate them without suppressing speech. . . .

. . . In my view our precedents may allow the city to impose its regulation in the exercise of the zoning authority. The city is not, at least, to be foreclosed by summary judgment, so I concur in the judgment.

This separate statement seems to me necessary, however, for two reasons. First, *Renton* . . . described a similar ordinance as "content neutral," and I agree with the dissent that the designation is imprecise. Second, in my view, the plurality's application of *Renton* might constitute a subtle expansion, with which I do not concur.

I

In *Renton*, the Court determined that while the material inside adult bookstores and movie theaters is speech, the consequent sordidness outside is not. The challenge is to correct the latter while leaving the former, as far as possible, untouched. If a city can decrease the crime and blight associated with certain speech by the traditional exercise of its zoning power, and at the same time leave the quantity and accessibility of the speech substantially undiminished, there is no First Amendment objection. This is so even if the measure identifies the problem outside by reference to the speech inside—that is, even if the measure is in that sense content based.

On the other hand, a city may not regulate the secondary effects of speech by suppressing the speech itself. . . . Though the inference may be inexorable that a city could reduce secondary effects by reducing speech, this is not a permissible strategy. The purpose and effect of a zoning ordinance must be to reduce secondary effects and not to reduce speech.

A zoning measure can be consistent with the First Amendment if it is likely to cause a significant decrease in secondary effects and a trivial decrease in the quantity of speech. It is well documented that multiple adult businesses in close proximity may change the character of a neighborhood for the worse. Those same businesses spread across the city may not have the same deleterious effects. At least in theory, a dispersal ordinance causes these businesses to separate rather than to close, so negative externalities are diminished but speech is not.

The calculus is a familiar one to city planners, for many enterprises other than adult businesses also cause undesirable externalities. . . .

. . . If the validity of the legislative classification for zoning purposes be fairly debatable, the legislative judgment must be allowed to control.

True, the First Amendment protects speech and not slaughterhouses. But in both contexts, the inference of impermissible discrimination is not strong. An equally strong inference is that the ordinance is targeted not at the activity, but at its side effects. If a zoning ordinance is directed to the secondary effects of adult speech, the ordinance does not necessarily constitute impermissible content discrimination. A zoning law need not be blind to the secondary effects of adult speech, so long as the purpose of the law is not to suppress it.

The ordinance at issue in this case is not limited to expressive activities. It also extends, for example, to massage parlors, which the city has found to cause similar secondary effects. . . . This ordinance, moreover, is just one part of an elaborate web of land-use regulations in Los Angeles, all of which are intended to promote the social value of the land as a whole without suppressing some activities or favoring others. . . . All this further suggests that the ordinance is more in the nature of a typical land-use restriction and less in the nature of a law suppressing speech.

For these reasons, the ordinance is not so suspect that we must employ the usual rigorous analysis that content-based laws demand in other instances. The ordinance may be a covert attack on speech, but we should not presume it to be so. In the language of our First Amendment doctrine it calls for intermediate and not strict scrutiny, as we held in *Renton*.

II

In *Renton*, the Court began by noting that a zoning ordinance is a time, place, or manner restriction. The Court then proceeded to consider the question whether the ordinance was "content based." The ordinance "by its terms [was] designed to prevent crime, protect the city's retail trade, maintain property values, and generally protec[t] and preserv[e] the quality of [the city's] neighborhoods, commercial districts, and the quality of urban life, not to suppress the expression of unpopular views." On this premise, the Court designated the restriction "content neutral." . . .

The Court appeared to recognize, however, that the designation was something of a fiction, which, perhaps, is why it kept the phrase in quotes. After all, whether a statute is content neutral or content based is something that can be determined on the face of it; if the statute describes speech by content then it is content based. And the ordinance in *Renton* "treat[ed] theaters that specialize in adult films differently from other kinds of theaters." . . . The fiction that this sort of ordinance is content neutral—or "content neutral"—is perhaps more confusing than helpful . . . These ordinances are content based and we should call them so.

Nevertheless, for the reasons discussed above, the central holding of *Renton* is sound: A zoning restriction that is designed to decrease secondary effects and not speech should be subject to intermediate rather than strict scrutiny. . . . As a matter of common experience, these sorts of ordinances are more like a zoning restriction on slaughterhouses and less like a tax on unpopular newspapers. The zoning context provides a built-in legitimate rationale, which rebuts the usual presumption that content-based restrictions are unconstitutional. For this reason, we apply intermediate rather than strict scrutiny.

III

The narrow question presented in this case is whether the ordinance at issue is invalid "because the city did not study the negative effects of such combinations of adult businesses, but rather relied on judicially approved statutory precedent from other jurisdictions." This question is actually two questions. First, what proposition does a city need to advance in order to sustain a secondary-effects ordinance? Second, how much evidence is required to support the proposition? The plurality skips to the second question and gives the correct answer; but in my view more attention must be given to the first.

. . . [A] city must advance some basis to show that its regulation has the purpose and effect of suppressing secondary effects, while leaving the quantity and accessibility of speech substantially intact. . . . A city may not assert that it will reduce secondary effects by reducing speech in the same proportion. On this point, I agree with Justice Souter. The rationale of the ordinance must be that it will suppress secondary effects—and not by suppressing speech.

. . .

. . . [I]t does not suffice to say that inconvenience will reduce demand and fewer patrons will lead to fewer secondary effects. . . . It is no trick to reduce secondary effects by reducing speech or its audience; but a city may not attack secondary effects indirectly by attacking speech.

The analysis requires a few more steps. If two adult businesses are under the same roof, an ordinance requiring them to separate will have one of two results: One business will either move elsewhere or close. The city's premise cannot be the latter. . . .

. . . The claim, therefore, must be that this ordinance will cause two businesses to split rather than one to close, that the quantity of speech will be substantially undiminished, and that total secondary effects will be significantly reduced. This must be the rationale of a dispersal statute.

Only after identifying the proposition to be proved can we ask the second part of the question presented: is there sufficient evidence to support the proposition? As to this, we have consistently held that a city must have latitude to experiment, at least at the outset, and that very little evidence is required. . . . As a general matter, courts should not be in the business of second-guessing fact-bound empirical assessments of city planners. . . . The Los Angeles City Council knows the streets of Los Angeles better than we do. . . . It is entitled to rely on that knowledge; and if its inferences appear reasonable, we should not say there is no basis for its conclusion.

In this case the proposition to be shown is supported by a single study and common experience. The city's study shows a correlation between the concentration of adult establishments and crime. . . . This original ordinance is not challenged here, and we may assume that it is constitutional.

If we assume that the study supports the original ordinance, then most of the necessary analysis follows. We may posit that two adult stores next door to each other attract 100 patrons per day. The two businesses split apart might attract 49 patrons each. (Two patrons, perhaps, will be discouraged by the inconvenience of the separation—a relatively small cost to speech.) On the other hand, the reduction in secondary effects might be dramatic, because secondary effects may require a critical mass. Depending on the economics of vice, 100 potential customers/victims might attract a coterie of thieves, prostitutes, and other ne'er-do-wells; yet 49 might attract none at all. If so, a dispersal ordinance would cause a great reduction in secondary effects at very small cost to speech. Indeed, the very absence of secondary effects might increase the audience for the speech; perhaps for every two people who are discouraged by the inconvenience of two-stop shopping, another two are encouraged by hospitable surroundings. In that case, secondary effects might be eliminated at no cost to speech whatsoever, and both the city and the speaker will have their interests well served.

Only one small step remains to justify the ordinance at issue in this case. The city may next infer—from its study and from its own experience—that two adult businesses under the same roof are no better than two next door. The city could reach the reasonable conclusion that knocking down the wall between two adult businesses does not ameliorate any undesirable secondary effects of their proximity to one another. If the city's first ordinance was justified, therefore, then the second is too. Dispersing two adult businesses under one roof is reasonably likely to cause a substantial reduction in secondary effects while reducing speech very little.

IV

. . . [T]his ordinance . . . might not withstand intermediate scrutiny. The ordinance does, however, survive the summary judgment motion that the Court of Appeals ordered granted in this case.

Justice Souter, with whom Justice Stevens and Justice Ginsburg join, and with whom Justice Breyer joins as to Part II, dissenting.

. . . I assume that the ordinance was constitutional when adopted, . . . and assume for purposes of this case that the original ordinance remains valid today.

. . .

From a policy of dispersing adult establishments, the city has thus moved to a policy of dividing them in two. The justification claimed for this application of the new policy remains, however, the 1977 survey, . . . and the 1977 survey provides no support for the breakup policy. Its evidentiary insufficiency bears emphasis and is the principal reason that I respectfully dissent from the Court's judgment today.

I

This ordinance stands or falls on the results of what our cases speak of as intermediate scrutiny, generally contrasted with the demanding standard applied under the First Amendment to a content-based regulation of expression. . . .

. . . [S]trict scrutiny leaves few survivors.

The comparatively softer intermediate scrutiny is reserved for regulations justified by something other than content of the message, such as a straightforward restriction going only to the time, place, or manner of speech or other expression. . . .

Although this type of land-use restriction has even been called a variety of time, place, or manner regulation, . . . equating a secondary-effects zoning regulation with a mere regulation of time, place, or manner jumps over an important difference between them. A restriction on loudspeakers has no obvious relationship to the substance of what is broadcast, while a zoning regulation of businesses in adult expression just as obviously does. And while it may be true that an adult business is burdened only because of its secondary effects, it is clearly burdened only if its expressive products have adult content. Thus, the Court has recognized that this kind of regulation, though called content neutral, occupies a kind of limbo between full-blown, content-based restrictions and regulations that apply without any reference to the substance of what is said. . . .

It would in fact make sense to give this kind of zoning regulation a First Amendment label of its own, and if we called it content correlated, we would not only describe it for what it is, but keep alert to a risk of content-based regulation that it poses. The risk lies in the fact that when a law applies selectively only to speech of particular content, the more precisely the content is identified, the greater is the opportunity for government censorship. Adult speech refers not merely to sexually explicit content, but to speech reflecting a favorable view of being explicit about sex and a favorable view of the practices it depicts; a restriction on adult content is thus also a restriction turning on a particular viewpoint, of which the government may disapprove.

This risk of viewpoint discrimination is subject to a relatively simple safeguard, however. If combating secondary effects of property devaluation and crime is truly the reason for the regulation, it is possible to show by empirical evidence that the effects exist, that they are caused by the expressive activity subject to the zoning, and that the zoning can be expected either to ameliorate them or to enhance the capacity of the government to combat them (say, by concentrating them in one area), without suppressing the expressive activity itself. This capacity of zoning regulation to address the practical problems without eliminating the speech is, after all, the only possible excuse for speaking of secondary-effects zoning as akin to time, place, or manner regulations.

In examining claims that there are causal relationships between adult businesses and an increase in secondary effects (distinct from disagreement), and between zoning and the mitigation of the effects, stress needs to be placed on the empirical character of the demonstration available. . . . The weaker the demonstration of facts distinct from disapproval of the "adult" viewpoint, the greater the likelihood that nothing more than condemnation of the viewpoint drives the regulation.

Equal stress should be placed on the point that requiring empirical justification of claims about property value or crime is not demanding anything Herculean. Increased crime, like prostitution and muggings, and declining property values in areas surrounding adult businesses, are all readily observable, often to the untrained eye and certainly to the police officer and urban planner. These harms can be shown by police reports, crime statistics, and studies of market value, all of which are within a municipality's capacity or available from the distilled experiences of comparable communities. . . .

And precisely because this sort of evidence is readily available, reviewing courts need to be wary when the government appeals, not to evidence, but to an uncritical common sense in an effort to justify such a zoning restriction. It is not that common sense is always illegitimate in First Amendment demonstration. The need for independent proof varies with the point that has to be established, and zoning can be supported by common experience when there is no reason to question it. . . . It has become a commonplace, based on our own cases, that concentrating adult establishments drives down the value of neighboring property used for other purposes. . . . In fact, however, the city found that general assumption unjustified by its 1977 study.

. . . In this case, however, the government has not shown that bookstores containing viewing booths, isolated from other adult establishments, increase crime or produce other negative secondary effects in surrounding neighborhoods, and we are thus left without substantial justification for viewing the city's First Amendment restriction as content correlated but not simply content based. By the same token, the city has failed to show any causal relationship between the breakup policy and elimination or regulation of secondary effects.

II

. . .

. . . My concern is not with the assumption behind the [1983] amendment itself, that a conglomeration of adult businesses under one roof, as in a minimall or adult department store, will produce undesirable secondary effects comparable to what a cluster of separate adult establishments brings about. That may or may not be so. The assumption that is clearly unsupported, however, goes to the city's supposed interest in applying the amendment to the book and video stores in question, and in applying it to break them up. The city, of course, claims no interest in the proliferation of adult establishments, the ostensible consequence of splitting the sales and viewing activities so as to produce two stores where once there was one. Nor does the city assert any interest in limiting the sale of adult expressive material as such, or reducing the number of adult video booths in the city, for that would be clear content-based regulation, and the city was careful in its 1977 report to disclaim any such intent.

Rather, the city apparently assumes that a bookstore selling videos and providing viewing booths produces secondary effects of crime, and more crime than would result from having a single store without booths in one part of town and a video arcade in another. But the city neither says this in so many words nor proffers any evidence to support even the simple proposition that an otherwise lawfully located adult bookstore combined with video booths will produce any criminal effects. The Los Angeles study treats such combined stores as one, and draws no general conclusion that individual stores spread apart from other adult establishments (as under the basic Los Angeles ordinance) are associated with any degree of criminal activity above the general norm; nor has the city called the Court's attention to any other empirical study, or even anecdotal police evidence, that supports the city's assumption. In fact, if the Los Angeles study sheds any light whatever on the city's position, it is the light of skepticism, for we may fairly suspect that the study said nothing about the secondary effects of freestanding stores because no effects were observed. The reasonable supposition, then, is that splitting some of them up will have no consequence for secondary effects whatever.

. . . The bookstores involved here are not concentrations of traditionally separate adult businesses that have been studied and shown to have an association with secondary effects, and they exemplify no new form of concentration like a mall under one roof. They are combinations of selling and viewing activities that have commonly been combined, and . . . no study conducted by the city has reported that this type of traditional business, any more than any other adult business, has a correlation with secondary effects in the absence of concentration with other adult establishments in the neighborhood. . . .

. . . [In *Renton,* the] limitations on location required no further support than the factual basis tying location to secondary effects; the zoning approved . . . had no effect on the way the owners of the stores carried on their adult businesses beyond controlling location, and no heavier burden than the location limit was approved by this Court.

The Los Angeles ordinance, however, does impose a heavier burden, and one lacking any demonstrable connection to the interest in crime control. . . . [T]he government's freedom of experimentation cannot displace its burden under the intermediate scrutiny standard to show that the restriction on speech is no greater than essential to realizing an important objective, in this case policing crime. Since we cannot make even a best guess that the city's breakup policy will have any effect on crime or law enforcement, we are a very far cry from any assurance against covert content-based regulation.

And concern with content-based regulation targeting a viewpoint is right to the point here, as witness a fact that involves no guesswork. . . . [T]wo establishments in place of one will entail two business overheads in place of one: two monthly rents, two electricity bills, two payrolls. Every month business will be more expensive than it used to be, perhaps even twice as much. That sounds like a good strategy for driving out expressive adult businesses. It sounds, in other words, like a policy of content-based regulation.

I respectfully dissent.

Consolidated Edison Co. of New York v. Public Service Commission

447 U.S. 530, 100 S.Ct. 2326, 65 L.Ed.2d 319 (1980).

Mr. Justice Powell delivered the opinion of the Court.

The question in this case is whether the First Amendment, as incorporated by the Fourteenth Amendment, is violated by an order of the Public Service

Commission of the State of New York that prohibits the inclusion in monthly electric bills of inserts discussing controversial issues of public policy.

I

The Consolidated Edison Company of New York, appellant in this case, placed written material entitled "Independence Is Still a Goal, and Nuclear Power Is Needed To Win the Battle" in its January 1976 billing envelope. . . .

In March 1976, the Natural Resources Defense Council, Inc. (NRDC) requested Consolidated Edison to enclose a rebuttal prepared by NRDC in its next billing envelope. When Consolidated Edison refused, NRDC asked the Public Service Commission of the State of New York to open Consolidated Edison's billing envelopes to contrasting views on controversial issues of public importance.

On February 17, 1977, the Commission, appellee here, denied NRDC's request, but prohibited "utilities from using bill inserts to discuss political matters, including the desirability of future development of nuclear power." . . . Accordingly, the Commission barred utility companies from including bill inserts that express "their opinions or viewpoints on controversial issues of public policy." The Commission did not, however, bar utilities from sending bill inserts discussing topics that are not "controversial issues of public policy." . . .

Consolidated Edison sought review of the Commission's order in the New York state courts. . . . The Court of Appeals held that the order did not violate the Constitution because it was a valid time, place and manner regulation designed to protect the privacy of Consolidated Edison's customers. . . . We reverse.

II

. . .

. . . [T]he Commission's prohibition of discussion of controversial issues strikes at the heart of the freedom to speak.

III

. . . The Commission's arguments require us to consider three theories that might justify the state action. We must determine whether the prohibition is (i) a reasonable time, place, or manner restriction, (ii) a permissible subject-matter regulation, or (iii) a narrowly tailored means of serving a compelling state interest.

A

. . .

The Commission does not pretend that its action is unrelated to the content or subject matter of bill inserts. Indeed, it has undertaken to suppress certain bill inserts precisely because they address controversial issues of public policy. . . .

B

The Commission next argues that its order is acceptable because it applies to all discussion of nuclear power, whether pro or con, in bill inserts. The prohibition, the Commission contends, is related to subject matter rather than to the views of a particular speaker. Because the regulation does not favor either side of a political controversy, the Commission asserts that it does not unconstitutionally suppress freedom of speech.

The First Amendment's hostility to content-based regulation extends not only to restrictions on particular viewpoints, but also to prohibition of public discussion of an entire topic. . . .

. . .

C

. . . The Commission argues finally that its prohibition is necessary (i) to avoid forcing Consolidated Edison's views on a captive audience, (ii) to allocate limited resources in the public interest, and (iii) to ensure that ratepayers do not subsidize the cost of the bill inserts.

The State Court of Appeals largely based its approval of the prohibition upon its conclusion that the bill inserts intruded upon individual privacy. . . . But the Court of Appeals erred in its assessment of the seriousness of the intrusion.

Even if a short exposure to Consolidated Edison's views may offend the sensibilities of some consumers, the ability of government "to shut off discourse solely to protect others from hearing it [is] dependent upon a showing that substantial privacy interests are being invaded in an essentially intolerable manner." Cohen v. California, 403 U.S., at 21. . . . Where a single speaker communicates to many listeners, the First Amendment does not permit the government to prohibit speech as intrusive unless the "captive" audience cannot avoid objectionable speech.

. . .

The Commission contends that because a billing envelope can accommodate only a limited amount of information, political messages should not be allowed to take the place of inserts that promote energy conservation or safety, or that remind consumers of their legal rights. The Commission relies upon Red Lion Broadcasting Co. v. F.C.C., [395 U.S. 367 (1969)], in which the Court held that the regulation of radio and television broadcast frequencies permit the Federal Government to exercise unusual authority over speech. But billing envelopes differ from broadcast frequencies in two ways. First, a broadcaster communicates through use of a scarce, publicly owned resource. No person can broadcast without a license, whereas all persons are free to send correspondence to private homes through the mails. Thus, it cannot be said that billing envelopes are a limited resource comparable to the broadcast spectrum. Second, the Commission has not shown on the record before us that the presence of the bill inserts at issue would preclude the inclusion of other inserts that Consolidated Edison might be ordered lawfully to include in the billing envelope. . . .

Finally, the Commission urges that its prohibition would prevent ratepayers from subsidizing the costs of policy-oriented bill inserts. But the Commission did not base its order on an inability to allocate costs between the shareholders of Consolidated Edison and the ratepayers. . . . Accordingly, there is no basis on this record to assume that the Commission could not exclude the cost of these bill inserts from the utility's rate base. . . .

IV

The Commission's suppression of bill inserts that discuss controversial issues of public policy directly infringes the freedom of speech protected by the

First and Fourteenth Amendments. The state action is neither a valid time, place, or manner restriction, nor a permissible subject-matter regulation, nor a narrowly drawn prohibition justified by a compelling state interest. Accordingly, the regulation is invalid....

. . .

Mr. Justice Stevens, concurring in the judgment.

. . .

There are ... many situations in which the subject matter, or, indeed, even the point of view of the speaker, may provide a justification for a time, place and manner regulation. Perhaps the most obvious example is the regulation of oral argument in this Court; the appellant's lawyer precedes his adversary solely because he seeks reversal of a judgment. As is true of many other aspects of liberty, some forms of orderly regulation actually promote freedom more than would a state of total anarchy.

Instead of trying to justify our conclusion by reasoning from honey-combed premises, I prefer to identify the basis of decision in more simple terms. ... A regulation of speech that is motivated by nothing more than a desire to curtail expression of a particular point of view on controversial issues of general interest is the purest example of a "law ... abridging the freedom of speech, or of the press." A regulation that denies one group of persons the right to address a selected audience on "controversial issues of public policy" is plainly such a regulation.

The only justification for the regulation relied on by the New York Court of Appeals is that the utilities' bill inserts may be "offensive" to some of their customers. ... Since the Public Service Commission has candidly put forward this impermissible justification for its censorial regulation, it plainly violates the First Amendment.

Accordingly, I concur in the judgment of the Court.

Mr. Justice Blackmun, with whom Mr. Justice Rehnquist as to Parts I and II joins, dissenting.

. . .

... I cannot agree with the Court that the New York Public Service Commission's ban on the utility bill insert somehow deprives the utility of its First and Fourteenth Amendment rights. Because of Consolidated Edison's monopoly status and its rate structure, the use of the insert amounts to an exaction from the utility's customers by way of forced aid for the utility's speech. And, contrary to the Court's suggestion, an allocation of the insert's cost between the utility's shareholders and the ratepayers would not eliminate this coerced subsidy.

I

A public utility is a state-created monopoly.... Under the laws of New York and other States, ... a public utility cannot include in the rate base the costs of political advertising and lobbying.... These costs cannot be passed on to consumers because ratepayers derive no service-related benefits from political advertisements. The purpose of such advertising and lobbying is to benefit the utility's shareholders, and its cost must be deducted from profits otherwise available for the shareholders....

II

The Commission concluded, properly in my view, that use of the billing envelope to distribute management's pamphlets amounts to a forced subsidy of the utility's speech by the ratepayers. Consolidated Edison would counter this argument by pointing out that it is willing to allocate to shareholders the *additional* costs attributable to the inserts. . . .

. . .

. . . The Commission's ban on bill inserts does not restrict the utility from using the shareholders' resources to finance communication of its viewpoints on any topic. Consolidated Edison is completely free to use the mails and any other medium of communication on the same basis as any other speaker. . . .

. . .

SECTION 4. SPEECH IN THE PUBLIC SCHOOLS

THE GOVERNMENT AS SPEAKER

(1) The Role of Government Speech in Public Debate. No Supreme Court decision has interpreted the first amendment to require that government communications be neutral or present all sides of debate on controversial public issues, other than issues of religious doctrine. The Court's most relevant discussion was in Buckley v. Valeo, 424 U.S. 1, 92–93 (1976), where the Court rejected a first amendment challenge to provisions of the Federal Election Campaign Act of 1971 for public financing of presidential election campaigns. The Court's opinion stated:

> "Appellants next argue that 'by analogy' to the Religion Clauses of the First Amendment public financing of election campaigns, however meritorious, violates the First Amendment. We have of course held that the Religion Clauses—'Congress shall make no law respecting an establishment of religion, or prohibiting the free exercise thereof'—require Congress, and the States through the Fourteenth Amendment, to remain neutral in matters of religion. . . . The Government may not aid one religion to the detriment of others or impose a burden on one religion that is not imposed on others, and may not even aid all religions. . . . But the analogy is patently inapplicable to our issue here. Although 'Congress shall make no law . . . abridging the freedom of speech, or of the press,' Subtitle H is a congressional effort, not to abridge, restrict, or censor speech, but rather to use public money to facilitate and enlarge public discussion and participation in the electoral process, goals vital to a self-governing people. Thus, Subtitle H furthers, not abridges, pertinent First Amendment values.[127]"

127. The historical bases of the Religion and Speech Clauses are markedly different. Intolerable persecutions throughout history led to the Framers' firm determination that religious worship—both in method and belief—must be strictly protected from government intervention. . . . But the central purpose of the Speech and Press Clauses was to assure a society in which "uninhibited, robust, and wide-open" public debate concerning matters of public interest would thrive, for only in such a society can a healthy representative democracy flourish. . . . Legislation to enhance these First Amendment values is the rule, not the exception. Our statute books are replete with laws providing financial assistance to the exercise of free speech, such as aid to public broadcasting and other forms of educational media . . . and preferential postal rates and antitrust exemptions for newspapers. . . .

(2) The Issue of Neutrality in Connection with the Government Forum. In the traditional public forum cases, involving communication in parks and streets, the constitutional requirement of government content neutrality was established in a context where government was playing no part in communication. Where the government operates a forum whose primary purpose is communication, government may play a variety of communicative roles—ranging from choosing the communication and communicators allowed to use the forum, to editor, to active speaker. Is it possible to reconcile a constitutional requirement of government content neutrality in the public forum with a conception of government as a partisan communicator? Consider Columbia Broadcasting System, Inc. v. Democratic National Committee, 412 U.S. 94 (1973), infra, p. 1567. The Court rejected statutory and constitutional claims that radio and television stations could not refuse to sell editorial advertising time. Justice Brennan's dissent, joined by Justice Marshall, concluded that the scheme of federal regulation of the electronic media constituted sufficient governmental action to require application of the first amendment to decisions made by owners of radio and television stations. He argued that the fact that the broadcast forum was designed specifically for communication made arguments for applying constitutional requirements of equal access to that forum even stronger than in the case of parks and streets, since a requirement of access "would in no sense divert that spectrum from its intended use." He conceded that broadcasters have a first amendment interest in exercising "journalistic supervision," which would operate in "normal programming time," but concluded that the right of broadcasters to speak was less central to decisions that deal "only with the allocation of advertising time." Contrast Justice Douglas' assertion in his opinion concurring in the result in Lehman v. City of Shaker Heights, 418 U.S. 298, 306 (1974), that "[t]he First Amendment . . . draws no distinction between press privately owned, and press owned otherwise." (In the *C.B.S.* case, in polar contradiction to Justice Brennan, Justice Douglas argued that existing federal statutory requirements of broadcast impartiality and public access were unconstitutional.) Is it possible to reconcile an interpretation of the first amendment that overturns government requirements of neutrality for a privately owned communicative forum with another first amendment interpretation that imposes a constitutional requirement of neutrality for a similar governmentally owned forum?

Tinker v. Des Moines Independent Community School District

393 U.S. 503, 89 S.Ct. 733, 21 L.Ed.2d 731 (1969).

[In December, 1965, petitioners, Des Moines high school and junior high students, wore black armbands to school to publicize their objections to United States operations in Vietnam. Anticipating such action, the school authorities had adopted a policy that any student wearing an armband to school would be suspended until he or she returned without the armband. Petitioners refused to remove their armbands and were suspended. They sought a federal injunction restraining the school officials from disciplining them. The lower federal courts upheld the action of the school authorities.]

Mr. Justice Fortas delivered the opinion of the Court.

. . .

. . . [T]he wearing of armbands in the circumstances of this case was entirely divorced from actually or potentially disruptive conduct by those participating in it. It was closely akin to "pure speech" which, we have repeatedly held, is entitled to comprehensive protection under the First Amendment....

First Amendment rights, applied in light of the special characteristics of the school environment, are available to teachers and students. It can hardly be argued that either students or teachers shed their constitutional rights to freedom of speech or expression at the schoolhouse gate. This has been the unmistakable holding of this Court for almost 50 years. In Meyer v. Nebraska, 262 U.S. 390 (1923), and Bartels v. Iowa, 262 U.S. 404 (1923), this Court, in opinions by Mr. Justice McReynolds, held that the Due Process Clause of the Fourteenth Amendment prevents States from forbidding the teaching of a foreign language to young students. Statutes to this effect, the Court held, unconstitutionally interfere with the liberty of teacher, student, and parent.[2]

. . .

... On the other hand, the Court has repeatedly emphasized the need for affirming the comprehensive authority of the States and of school officials, consistent with fundamental constitutional safeguards, to prescribe and control conduct in the schools. ... Our problem lies in the area where students in the exercise of First Amendment rights collide with the rules of the school authorities.

The problem posed by the present case does not relate to regulation of the length of skirts or the type of clothing, to hair style or deportment.... It does not concern aggressive, disruptive action or even group demonstrations. Our problem involves direct, primary First Amendment rights akin to "pure speech."

The school officials banned and sought to punish petitioners for a silent, passive, expression of opinion, unaccompanied by any disorder or disturbance on the part of petitioners. There is here no evidence whatever of petitioners' interference, actual or nascent, with the school's work or of collision with the rights of other students to be secure and to be let alone....

. . .

In order for the State in the person of school officials to justify prohibition of a particular expression of opinion, it must be able to show that its action was caused by something more than a mere desire to avoid the discomfort and unpleasantness that always accompany an unpopular viewpoint....

... [O]ur independent examination of the record fails to yield evidence that the school authorities had reason to anticipate that the wearing of the armbands would substantially interfere with the work of the school or impinge upon the rights of other students....

On the contrary, the action of the school authorities appears to have been based upon an urgent wish to avoid the controversy which might result from

---

2. Hamilton v. Regents of Univ. of Cal., 293 U.S. 245 (1934) is sometimes cited for the broad proposition that the State may attach conditions to attendance at a state university that require individuals to violate their religious convictions. The case involved dismissal of members of a religious denomination from a land grant college for refusal to participate in military training. Narrowly viewed, the case turns upon the Court's con- clusion that merely requiring a student to participate in school training in military "sci- ence" could not conflict with his constitution- ally protected freedom of conscience. The de- cision cannot be taken as establishing that the State may impose and enforce any condi- tions that it chooses upon attendance at pub- lic institutions of learning ... See, e.g., West Virginia v. Barnette, 319 U.S. 624 (1943)....

the expression, even by the silent symbol of armbands, of opposition to this Nation's part in the conflagration of Vietnam. . . .

It is also relevant that the school authorities did not purport to prohibit the wearing of all symbols of political or controversial significance. The record shows that students in some of the schools wore buttons relating to national political campaigns, and some even wore the Iron Cross, traditionally a symbol of Nazism. The order prohibiting the wearing of armbands did not extend to these. . . .

. . .

The principal use to which the schools are dedicated is to accommodate students during prescribed hours for the purpose of certain types of activities. Among those activities is personal intercommunication among the students. This is not only an inevitable part of the process of attending school; it is also an important part of the educational process. A student's rights therefore, do not embrace merely the classroom hours. When he is in the cafeteria, or on the playing field, or on the campus during the authorized hours, he may express his opinions, even on controversial subjects like the conflict in Vietnam, if he does so without "materially and substantially interfer[ing] with . . . appropriate discipline in the operation of the school" and without colliding with the rights of others. . . . But conduct by the student, in class or out of it, which for any reason—whether it stems from time, place, or type of behavior—materially disrupts classwork or involves substantial disorder or invasion of the rights of others is, of course, not immunized by the constitutional guarantee of freedom of speech. . . .

. . .

Reversed and remanded.[a]

Mr. Justice Stewart, concurring.

Although I agree with much of what is said in the Court's opinion, and with its judgment in this case, I cannot share the Court's uncritical assumption that, school discipline aside, the First Amendment rights of children are co-extensive with those of adults. . . .

Mr. Justice Black, dissenting.

. . . I think the record overwhelmingly shows that the armbands did exactly what the elected school officials and principals foresaw they would, that is, took the students' minds off their classwork and diverted them to thoughts about the highly emotional subject of the Vietnam war. . . .

. . . [A] teacher of kindergarten, grammar school, or high school pupils no more carries into a school with him a complete right to freedom of speech and expression than an anti-Catholic or anti-Semite carries with him a complete freedom of speech and religion into a Catholic church or Jewish synagogue. Nor does a person carry with him into the United States Senate or House, or into the Supreme Court, or any other court, a complete constitutional right to go into those places contrary to their rules and speak his mind on any subject he pleases. It is a myth to say that any person has a constitutional right to say what he pleases, where he pleases, and when he pleases. . . .

. . .

a. A concurrence by Justice White and a dissent by Justice Harlan have been omitted.

Bethel School District No. 403 v. Fraser

478 U.S. 675, 106 S.Ct. 3159, 92 L.Ed.2d 549 (1986).

Chief Justice Burger delivered the opinion of the Court.

We granted certiorari to decide whether the First Amendment prevents a school district from disciplining a high school student for giving a lewd speech at a school assembly.

I

A

... [R]espondent Matthew N. Fraser, a student at Bethel High School in Pierce County, Washington, delivered a speech nominating a fellow student for student elective office. Approximately 600 high school students, many of whom were 14–year–olds, attended the assembly. Students were required to attend the assembly or to report to the study hall. ... During the entire speech, Fraser referred to his candidate in terms of an elaborate, graphic, and explicit sexual metaphor.

Two of Fraser's teachers, with whom he discussed the contents of his speech in advance, informed him that the speech was "inappropriate and that he probably should not deliver it," and that his delivery of the speech might have "severe consequences."

During Fraser's delivery of the speech, a school counselor observed the reaction of students to the speech. Some students hooted and yelled; some by gestures graphically simulated the sexual activities pointedly alluded to in respondent's speech. ...

A Bethel High School disciplinary rule prohibiting the use of obscene language in the school provides:

> "Conduct which materially and substantially interferes with the educational process is prohibited, including the use of obscene, profane language or gestures."

The morning after the assembly, the Assistant Principal called Fraser into her office and notified him that the school considered his speech to have been a violation of this rule. ... Fraser was then informed that he would be suspended for three days, and that his name would be removed from the list of candidates for graduation speaker at the school's commencement exercises.

. . .

B

Respondent, by his father as guardian ad litem, then brought this action in the United States District Court for the Western District of Washington. ... The District Court held that the school's sanctions violated respondent's right to freedom of speech under the First Amendment....

The Court of Appeals for the Ninth Circuit affirmed....

... We reverse.

II

. . .

The marked distinction between the political "message" of the armbands in *Tinker* and the sexual content of respondent's speech in this case seems to have been given little weight by the Court of Appeals. In upholding the students' right to engage in a nondisruptive, passive expression of a political viewpoint in *Tinker,* this Court was careful to note that the case did "not concern speech or action that intrudes upon the work of the schools or the rights of other students." ...

. . .

III

. . .

... [F]undamental values of "habits and manners of civility" essential to a democratic society must, of course, include tolerance of divergent political and religious views, even when the views expressed may be unpopular. But these "fundamental values" must also take into account consideration of the sensibilities of others, and, in the case of a school, the sensibilities of fellow students. The undoubted freedom to advocate unpopular and controversial views in schools and classrooms must be balanced against the society's countervailing interest in teaching students the boundaries of socially appropriate behavior. ...

In our Nation's legislative halls, where some of the most vigorous political debates in our society are carried on, there are rules prohibiting the use of expressions offensive to other participants in the debate. ... Can it be that what is proscribed in the halls of Congress is beyond the reach of school officials to regulate?

... It does not follow ... that simply because the use of an offensive form of expression may not be prohibited to adults making what the speaker considers a political point, that the same latitude must be permitted to children in a public school. ...

Surely it is a highly appropriate function of public school education to prohibit the use of vulgar and offensive terms in public discourse. ... The determination of what manner of speech in the classroom or in school assembly is inappropriate properly rests with the school board.

... The schools, as instruments of the state, may determine that the essential lessons of civil, mature conduct cannot be conveyed in a school that tolerates lewd, indecent, or offensive speech and conduct such as that indulged in by this confused boy.

. . .

We hold that petitioner School District acted entirely within its permissible authority in imposing sanctions upon Fraser in response to his offensively lewd and indecent speech. Unlike the sanctions imposed on the students wearing armbands in *Tinker,* the penalties imposed in this case were unrelated to any political viewpoint. ...

. . .

The judgment of the Court of Appeals for the Ninth Circuit is reversed.

Justice Blackmun concurs in the result.

Justice Brennan, concurring in the judgment.

Respondent gave the following speech at a high school assembly in support of a candidate for student government office:

"I know a man who is firm—he's firm in his pants, he's firm in his shirt, his character is firm—but most . . . of all, his belief in you, the students of Bethel, is firm.

"Jeff Kuhlman is a man who takes his point and pounds it in. If necessary, he'll take an issue and nail it to the wall. He doesn't attack things in spurts—he drives hard, pushing and pushing until finally—he succeeds.

"Jeff is a man who will go to the very end—even the climax, for each and every one of you.

"So vote for Jeff for A.S.B. vice-president—he'll never come between you and the best our high school can be."

The Court, referring to these remarks as "obscene," "vulgar," "lewd," and "offensively lewd," concludes that school officials properly punished respondent for uttering the speech. Having read the full text of respondent's remarks, I find it difficult to believe that it is the same speech the Court describes. . . .

. . . Respondent's speech may well have been protected had he given it in school but under different circumstances, where the school's legitimate interests in teaching and maintaining civil public discourse were less weighty.

. . .

Justice Marshall, dissenting.

I dissent from the Court's decision, however, because in my view the School District failed to demonstrate that respondent's remarks were indeed disruptive. . . .

Justice Stevens, dissenting.

. . .

It seems fairly obvious that respondent's speech would be inappropriate in certain classroom and formal social settings. On the other hand, in a locker room or perhaps in a school corridor the metaphor in the speech might be regarded as rather routine comment. If this be true, and if respondent's audience consisted almost entirely of young people with whom he conversed on a daily basis, can we—at this distance—confidently assert that he must have known that the school administration would punish him for delivering it?

. . .

Board of Education v. Pico

457 U.S. 853, 102 S.Ct. 2799, 73 L.Ed.2d 435 (1982).

Justice Brennan announced the judgment of the Court and delivered an opinion in which Justice Marshall and Justice Stevens joined, and in which Justice Blackmun joined except for Part II–A–(1).

The principal question presented is whether the First Amendment imposes limitations upon the exercise by a local school board of its discretion to remove library books from high school and junior high school libraries.

I

Petitioners are the Board of Education of the Island Trees Union Free School District No. 26, in New York, and [officers and members of the Board]. . . . Respondents . . . were students at the High School, and . . . a student at the Junior High School.

In September 1975 [3 officers and members of the board] attended a conference sponsored by Parents of New York United (PONYU), a politically conservative organization of parents concerned about education legislation in the State of New York. At the conference these petitioners obtained lists of books described ... as "objectionable," and ... as "improper fare for school students." It was later determined that the High School library contained nine of the listed books, and that another listed book was in the Junior High School library.[2] In February 1976, ... the Board gave an "unofficial direction" that the listed books be ... delivered to the Board's offices, so that Board members could read them. ... [T]he Board ... characterized the removed books as "anti-American, anti-Christian, anti-Semitic, and just plain filthy," and concluded that "[i]t is our duty, our moral obligation, to protect the children in our schools from this moral danger as surely as from physical and medical dangers."

A short time later, the Board appointed a "Book Review Committee," consisting of four Island Trees parents and four members of the Island Trees schools staff, to read the listed books and to recommend to the Board whether the books should be retained ... [T]he Committee ..., recommend[ed] that five of the listed books be retained and that two others be removed from the school libraries. As for the remaining four books, the Committee could not agree on two, took no position on one, and recommended that the last book be made available to students only with parental approval. The Board substantially rejected the Committee's report ..., deciding that only one book should be returned to the High School library without restriction, that another should be made available subject to parental approval, but that the remaining nine books should "be removed from elementary and secondary libraries and [from] use in the curriculum." The Board gave no reasons for rejecting the recommendations of the Committee that it had appointed.

Respondents reacted to the Board's decision by bringing the present action under 42 U.S.C. § 1983 in the United States District Court for the Eastern District of New York. ... They asked the court for a declaration that the Board's actions were unconstitutional, and for preliminary and permanent injunctive relief ordering the Board to return the nine books to the school libraries and to refrain from interfering with the use of those books in the schools' curricula.

. . .

II

We emphasize at the outset the limited nature of the substantive question presented by the case before us. Our precedents have long recognized certain constitutional limits upon the power of the State to control even the curriculum and classroom. For example, Meyer v. Nebraska, 262 U.S. 390 (1923), struck down a state law that forbade the teaching of modern foreign languages in public and private schools, and Epperson v. Arkansas, 393 U.S. 97 (1968), declared unconstitutional a state law that prohibited the teaching of the Darwinian theory of evolution in any state-supported school. But the current

2. The nine books in the High School library were: Slaughter House Five, by Kurt Vonnegut, Jr.; The Naked Ape, by Desmond Morris; Down These Mean Streets, by Piri Thomas; Best Short Stories of Negro Writers, edited by Langston Hughes; Go Ask Alice, of anonymous authorship; Laughing Boy, by Oliver LaFarge; Black Boy, by Richard Wright; A Hero Ain't Nothin' But A Sandwich, by Alice Childress; and Soul On Ice, by Eldridge Cleaver. The book in the Junior High School library was A Reader for Writers, edited by Jerome Archer. Still another listed book, The Fixer, by Bernard Malamud, was found to be included in the curriculum of a 12th–grade literature course.

action does not require us to re-enter this difficult terrain, which *Meyer* and *Epperson* traversed without apparent misgiving. For as this case is presented to us, it does not involve textbooks, or indeed any books that Island Trees students would be required to read. Respondents do not seek in this Court to impose limitations upon their school board's discretion to prescribe the curricula of the Island Trees schools. On the contrary, the only books at issue in this case are *library* books, books that by their nature are optional rather than required reading. Our adjudication of the present case thus does not intrude into the classroom, or into the compulsory courses taught there. Furthermore, even as to library books, the action before us does not involve the *acquisition* of books. ... Rather, the only action challenged in this case is the *removal* from school libraries of books originally placed there by the school authorities, or without objection from them.

The substantive question before us is still further constrained by the procedural posture of this case. Petitioners were granted summary judgment by the District Court. The Court of Appeals reversed that judgment, and remanded the action for a trial on the merits of respondents' claims. We can reverse the judgment of the Court of Appeals, and grant petitioners' request for reinstatement of the summary judgment in their favor, only if we determine that "there is no genuine issue as to any material fact," and that petitioners are "entitled to a judgment as a matter of law." Fed.Rule Civ.Proc. 56(c). In making our determination, any doubt as to the existence of a genuine issue of material fact must be resolved against petitioners as the moving party....

In sum, the issue before us in this case is a narrow one, both substantively and procedurally. It may best be restated as two distinct questions. First, Does the First Amendment impose *any* limitations upon the discretion of petitioners to remove library books from the Island Trees High School and Junior High School? Second, If so, do the affidavits and other evidentiary materials before the District Court, construed most favorably to respondents, raise a genuine issue of fact whether petitioners might have exceeded those limitations? If we answer either of these questions in the negative, then we must reverse the judgment of the Court of Appeals and reinstate the District Court's summary judgment for petitioners. If we answer both questions in the affirmative, then we must affirm the judgment below. We examine these questions in turn.

A

(1)

The Court has long recognized that local school boards have broad discretion in the management of school affairs. ... We are therefore in full agreement with petitioners that local school boards must be permitted "to establish and apply their curriculum in such a way as to transmit community values," and that "there is a legitimate and substantial community interest in promoting respect for authority and traditional values be they social, moral, or political."

At the same time, however, we have necessarily recognized that the discretion of the States and local school boards in matters of education must be exercised in a manner that comports with the transcendent imperatives of the First Amendment. ...

. . .

... [W]e think that the First Amendment rights of students may be directly and sharply implicated by the removal of books from the shelves of a school library. ... [W]e have held that in a variety of contexts "the Constitution protects the right to receive information and ideas." Stanley v. Georgia, 394 U.S. 557, 564 (1969) . . . This right is an inherent corollary of the rights of free speech and press. . . .

. . .

. . . Of course all First Amendment rights accorded to students must be construed "in light of the special characteristics of the school environment." . . . But the special characteristics of the school *library* make that environment especially appropriate for the recognition of the First Amendment rights of students.

. . . Petitioners emphasize the inculcative function of secondary education, and argue that they must be allowed *unfettered* discretion to "transmit community values" through the Island Trees schools. But that sweeping claim overlooks the unique role of the school library. . . . [T]he libraries afford [students] an opportunity at self-education and individual enrichment that is wholly optional. Petitioners might well defend their claim of absolute discretion in matters of *curriculum* by reliance upon their duty to inculcate community values. But we think that petitioners' reliance upon that duty is misplaced where, as here, they attempt to extend their claim of absolute discretion beyond the compulsory environment of the classroom, into the school library and the regime of voluntary inquiry that there holds sway.

(2)

In rejecting petitioners' claim of absolute discretion to remove books from their school libraries, we do not deny that local school boards have a substantial legitimate role to play in the determination of school library content. We thus must turn to the question of the extent to which the First Amendment places limitations upon the discretion of petitioners to remove books from their libraries. . . .

. . . Petitioners rightly possess significant discretion to determine the content of their school libraries. But that discretion may not be exercised in a narrowly partisan or political manner. If a Democratic school board, motivated by party affiliation, ordered the removal of all books written by or in favor of Republicans, few would doubt that the order violated the constitutional rights of the students denied access to those books. The same conclusion would surely apply if an all-white school board, motivated by racial animus, decided to remove all books authored by blacks or advocating racial equality and integration. Our Constitution does not permit the official suppression of *ideas*. Thus whether petitioners' removal of books from their school libraries denied respondents their First Amendment rights depends upon the motivation behind petitioners' action. If petitioners *intended* by their removal decision to deny respondents access to ideas with which petitioners disagreed, and if this intent was the decisive factor in petitioners' decision, then petitioners have exercised their discretion in violation of the Constitution. . . . On the other hand, respondents implicitly concede that an unconstitutional motivation would *not* be demonstrated if it were shown that petitioners had decided to remove the books at issue because those books were pervasively vulgar. And again, respondents concede that if it were demonstrated that the removal decision was based solely upon the "educational suitability" of the books in question, then their removal would be "perfectly permissible." In other words, in respondents' view such motivations, if decisive of petitioners' actions, would not carry the danger of an official suppression of ideas, and thus would not violate respondents' First Amendment rights.

As noted earlier, nothing in our decision today affects in any way the discretion of a local school board to choose books to *add* to the libraries of their schools. Because we are concerned in this case with the suppression of ideas, our holding today affects only the discretion to *remove* books. In brief, we hold that local school boards may not remove books from school library shelves simply because they dislike the ideas contained in those books. . . .

B

We now turn to the remaining question presented by this case: Do the evidentiary materials that were before the District Court, when construed most favorably to respondents, raise a genuine issue of material fact whether petitioners exceeded constitutional limitations in exercising their discretion to remove the books from the school libraries? We conclude that the materials do raise such a question, which forecloses summary judgment in favor of petitioners.

. . .

. . . The evidence plainly does not foreclose the possibility that petitioners' decision to remove the books rested decisively upon disagreement with constitutionally protected ideas in those books, or upon a desire on petitioners' part to impose upon the students of the Island Trees High School and Junior High School a political orthodoxy to which petitioners and their constituents adhered. Of course, some of the evidence before the District Court might lead a finder of fact to accept petitioners' claim that their removal decision was based upon constitutionally valid concerns. But that evidence at most creates a genuine issue of material fact on the critical question of the credibility of petitioners' justifications for their decision. . . .

The mandate shall issue forthwith.

Affirmed.

Justice Blackmun, concurring in part and concurring in the judgment.

While I agree with much in today's plurality opinion, and while I accept the standard laid down by the plurality to guide proceedings on remand, I write separately because I have a somewhat different perspective on the nature of the First Amendment right involved.

I

. . .

In my view, . . . the principle involved here is both narrower and more basic than the "right to receive information" identified by the plurality. I do not suggest that the State has any affirmative obligation to provide students with information or ideas, something that may well be associated with a "right to receive." And I do not believe, as the plurality suggests, that the right at issue here is somehow associated with the peculiar nature of the school library; if schools may be used to inculcate ideas, surely libraries may play a role in that process. Instead, I suggest that certain forms of state discrimination between ideas are improper. In particular, our precedents command the conclusion that the State may not act to deny access to an idea simply because state officials disapprove of that idea for partisan or political reasons.

. . .

II

. . .

Because I believe that the plurality has derived a standard similar to the one compelled by my analysis, I join all but Part II–A(1) of the plurality opinion.

Justice White, concurring in the judgment.

. . . The unresolved factual issue, as I understand it, is the reason or reasons underlying the school board's removal of the books. I am not inclined to disagree with the Court of Appeals on such a fact-bound issue and hence concur in the judgment of affirmance. Presumably this will result in a trial and the making of a full record and findings on the critical issues.

The plurality seems compelled to go further and issue a dissertation on the extent to which the First Amendment limits the discretion of the school board to remove books from the school library. I see no necessity for doing so at this point. When findings of fact and conclusions of law are made by the District Court, that may end the case. If, for example, the District Court concludes after a trial that the books were removed for their vulgarity, there may be no appeal. In any event, if there is an appeal, if there is dissatisfaction with the subsequent Court of Appeals' judgment, and if certiorari is sought and granted, there will be time enough to address the First Amendment issues that may then be presented.

. . . [a]

Chief Justice Burger, with whom Justice Powell, Justice Rehnquist, and Justice O'Connor join, dissenting.

. . .

Whatever role the government might play as a conduit of information, schools in particular ought not be made a slavish courier of the material of third parties. . . . [Since] schools may legitimately be used as vehicles for "inculcating fundamental values necessary to the maintenance of a democratic political system," . . . school authorities must have broad discretion to fulfill that obligation. Presumably all activity within a primary or secondary school involves the conveyance of information and at least an implied approval of the worth of that information. How are "fundamental values" to be inculcated except by having school boards make content-based decisions about the appropriateness of retaining materials in the school library and curriculum? . . .

. . .

Justice Rehnquist, with whom The Chief Justice and Justice Powell join, dissenting.

. . .

I

A

. . .

. . . Petitioners did not, for the reasons stated hereafter, run afoul of the First and Fourteenth Amendments by removing these particular books from the library in the manner in which they did. I would save for another day—

a. Dissenting opinions by Justices Powell and O'Connor are omitted.

feeling quite confident that that day will not arrive—the extreme examples posed in Justice Brennan's opinion.

B

Considerable light is shed on the correct resolution of the constitutional question in this case by examining the role played by petitioners. Had petitioners been the members of a town council, I suppose all would agree that, absent a good deal more than is present in this record, they could not have prohibited the sale of these books by private booksellers within the municipality. But we have also recognized that the government may act in other capacities than as sovereign, and when it does the First Amendment may speak with a different voice. . . .

. . . When it acts as an educator, at least at the elementary and secondary school level, the government is engaged in inculcating social values and knowledge in relatively impressionable young people. Obviously there are innumerable decisions to be made as to what courses should be taught, what books should be purchased, or what teachers should be employed. In every one of these areas the members of a school board will act on the basis of their own personal or moral values, will attempt to mirror those of the community, or will abdicate the making of such decisions to so-called "experts." . . . In the very course of administering the many-faceted operations of a school district, the mere decision to purchase some books will necessarily preclude the possibility of purchasing others. The decision to teach a particular subject may preclude the possibility of teaching another subject. A decision to replace a teacher because of ineffectiveness may by implication be seen as a disparagement of the subject matter taught. In each of these instances, however, the book or the exposure to the subject matter may be acquired elsewhere. The managers of the school district are not proscribing it as to the citizenry in general, but are simply determining that it will not be included in the curriculum or school library. In short, actions by the government as educator do not raise the same First Amendment concerns as actions by the government as sovereign.

II

. . .

A

Despite Justice Brennan's suggestion to the contrary, this Court has never held that the First Amendment grants junior high school and high school students a right of access to certain information in school. . . .

. . .

. . . Our past decisions are . . . unlike this case where the removed books are readily available to students and non students alike at the corner bookstore or the public library.

B

There are even greater reasons for rejecting Justice Brennan's analysis, however, than the significant fact that we have never adopted it in the past. . . . The idea that such students have a right of access, *in the school,* to information other than that thought by their educators to be necessary is contrary to the very nature of an inculcative education.

. . .

... Unlike university or public libraries, elementary and secondary school libraries are not designed for free-wheeling inquiry; they are tailored, as the public school curriculum is tailored, to the teaching of basic skills and ideas. Thus, Justice Brennan cannot rely upon the nature of school libraries to escape the fact that the First Amendment right to receive information simply has no application to the one public institution which, by its very nature, is a place for the selective conveyance of ideas.

After all else is said, however, the most obvious reason that petitioners' removal of the books did not violate respondents' right to receive information is the ready availability of the books elsewhere. . . .

C

Justice Brennan's own discomfort with the idea that students have a right to receive information from their elementary or secondary schools is demonstrated by the artificial limitations which he places upon the right. . . . The attempt to confine the right to the library is one such limitation, the fallacies of which have already been demonstrated.

As a second limitation, Justice Brennan distinguishes the act of removing a previously acquired book from the act of refusing to acquire the book in the first place: . . . The failure of a library to acquire a book denies access to its contents just as effectively as does the removal of the book from the library's shelf. As a result of either action the book cannot be found in the "principal locus" of freedom discovered by Justice Brennan.

. . .

The final limitation placed by Justice Brennan upon his newly discovered right is a motive requirement . . . But bad motives and good motives alike deny access to the books removed. If Justice Brennan truly recognizes a constitutional right to receive information, it is difficult to see why the reason for the denial makes any difference. Of course Justice Brennan's view is that intent matters because the First Amendment does not tolerate an officially prescribed orthodoxy. But this reasoning mixes First Amendment apples and oranges. The right to receive information differs from the right to be free from an officially prescribed orthodoxy. Not every educational denial of access to information casts a pall of orthodoxy over the classroom.

. . .

Hazelwood School District v. Kuhlmeier

484 U.S. 260, 108 S.Ct. 562, 98 L.Ed.2d 592 (1988).

Justice White delivered the opinion of the Court.

This case concerns the extent to which educators may exercise editorial control over the contents of a high school newspaper produced as part of the school's journalism curriculum.

I

. . . Respondents [three former Hazelwood East High School students who were staff members of Spectrum, the school newspaper] . . . contend that school officials violated their First Amendment rights by deleting two pages of articles from the May 13, 1983, issue of Spectrum.

Spectrum was written and edited by the Journalism II class at Hazelwood East. The newspaper was published every three weeks or so during the 1982–1983 school year. More than 4,500 copies of the newspaper were distributed during that year to students, school personnel, and members of the community.

The Board of Education allocated funds from its annual budget for the printing of Spectrum. These funds were supplemented by proceeds from sales of the newspaper. . . . The other costs associated with the newspaper—such as supplies, textbooks, and a portion of the journalism teacher's salary—were borne entirely by the Board.

. . .

The practice at Hazelwood East during the spring 1983 semester was for the journalism teacher to submit page proofs of each Spectrum issue to Principal Reynolds for his review prior to publication. On May 10, Emerson [the faculty newspaper adviser] delivered the proofs of the May 13 edition to Reynolds, who objected to two of the articles scheduled to appear in that edition. One of the stories described three Hazelwood East students' experiences with pregnancy; the other discussed the impact of divorce on students at the school.

Reynolds was concerned that, although the pregnancy story used false names "to keep the identity of these girls a secret," the pregnant students still might be identifiable from the text. He also believed that the article's references to sexual activity and birth control were inappropriate for some of the younger students at the school. In addition, Reynolds was concerned [with] a student identified by name in the divorce story. . . .

Reynolds believed that there was no time to make the necessary changes in the stories before the scheduled press run and that the newspaper would not appear before the end of the school year if printing were delayed to any significant extent. He concluded that his only options under the circumstances were to publish a four-page newspaper instead of the planned six-page newspaper, eliminating the two pages on which the offending stories appeared, or to publish no newspaper at all. . . .

Respondents subsequently commenced this action in the United States District Court for the Eastern District of Missouri seeking a declaration that their First Amendment rights had been violated, injunctive relief, and monetary damages. After a bench trial, the District Court denied an injunction, holding that no First Amendment violation had occurred.

. . .

The Court of Appeals for the Eighth Circuit reversed. . . .

. . .

We . . . reverse.

II

. . .

A

We deal first with the question whether Spectrum may appropriately be characterized as a forum for public expression. The public schools do not possess all of the attributes of streets, parks, and other traditional public forums. . . . Hence, school facilities may be deemed to be public forums only if school authorities have "by policy or by practice" opened those facilities "for indiscriminate use by the general public," . . . or by some segment of the public, such as student organizations. . . . If the facilities have instead been reserved for other intended purposes, "communicative or otherwise," then no public forum has been created . . .

The policy of school officials toward *Spectrum* was reflected in Hazelwood School Board Policy . . . that "[s]chool sponsored publications are developed within the adopted curriculum and its educational implications in regular classroom activities." The Hazelwood East Curriculum Guide described the Journalism II course as a "laboratory situation in which the students publish the school newspaper applying skills they have learned in Journalism I." . . . Students received grades and academic credit for their performance in the course.

. . .

. . . Accordingly, school officials were entitled to regulate the contents of *Spectrum* in any reasonable manner. . . . It is this standard, rather than our decision in *Tinker,* that governs this case.

B

The question whether the First Amendment requires a school to tolerate particular student speech—the question that we addressed in *Tinker*—is different from the question whether the First Amendment requires a school affirmatively to promote particular student speech. The former question addresses educators' ability to silence a student's personal expression that happens to occur on the school premises. The latter question concerns educators' authority over school-sponsored publications, theatrical productions, and other expressive activities that students, parents, and members of the public might reasonably perceive to bear the imprimatur of the school. These activities may fairly be characterized as part of the school curriculum, whether or not they occur in a traditional classroom setting, so long as they are supervised by faculty members and designed to impart particular knowledge or skills to student participants and audiences.[3]

Educators are entitled to exercise greater control over this second form of student expression to assure that participants learn whatever lessons the activity is designed to teach, that readers or listeners are not exposed to material that may be inappropriate for their level of maturity, and that the views of the individual speaker are not erroneously attributed to the school. . . .

Accordingly, we conclude that the standard articulated in *Tinker* for determining when a school may punish student expression need not also be the standard for determining when a school may refuse to lend its name and resources to the dissemination of student expression. Instead, we hold that educators do not offend the First Amendment by exercising editorial control over the style and content of student speech in school-sponsored expressive activities so long as their actions are reasonably related to legitimate pedagogical concerns.

. . . It is only when the decision to censor a school-sponsored publication, theatrical production, or other vehicle of student expression has no valid

---

3. The distinction that we draw between speech that is sponsored by the school and speech that is not is fully consistent with Papish v. Board of Curators of University of Missouri, 410 U.S. 667 (1973) (per curiam), which involved an off-campus "underground" newspaper that school officials merely had allowed to be sold on a state university campus.

educational purpose that the First Amendment ... require[s] judicial intervention to protect students' constitutional rights.

III

We also conclude that Principal Reynolds acted reasonably in requiring the deletion from the May 13 issue of Spectrum of the pregnancy article, the divorce article, and the remaining articles that were to appear on the same pages of the newspaper.

. . .

In sum, we cannot reject as unreasonable Principal Reynolds' conclusion that neither the pregnancy article nor the divorce article was suitable for publication in Spectrum. ... Finally, we conclude that the principal's decision to delete two pages of Spectrum, rather than to delete only the offending articles or to require that they be modified, was reasonable under the circumstances as he understood them. Accordingly, no violation of First Amendment rights occurred.

. . .

Justice Brennan, with whom Justice Marshall and Justice Blackmun join, dissenting.

. . .

I

. . .

[The Court has never] intimated a distinction between personal and school-sponsored speech in any other context. ...

II

Even if we were writing on a clean slate, I would reject the Court's rationale for abandoning *Tinker* in this case....

. . .

The mere fact of school sponsorship does not, as the Court suggests, license ... thought control in the high school, whether through school suppression of disfavored viewpoints or through official assessment of topic sensitivity. The former would constitute unabashed and unconstitutional viewpoint discrimination.... [S]chool officials may not, out of like motivation, discriminatorily excise objectionable ideas from a student publication. The State's prerogative to dissolve the student newspaper entirely (or to limit its subject matter) no more entitles it to dictate which viewpoints students may express on its pages, than the State's prerogative to close down the schoolhouse entitles it to prohibit the nondisruptive expression of antiwar sentiment within its gates.

. . .

SECTION 5. GOVERNMENT SUBSIDIES TO SPEECH

Rust v. Sullivan

500 U.S. 173, 111 S.Ct. 1759, 114 L.Ed.2d 233 (1991).

Chief Justice Rehnquist delivered the opinion of the Court.

These cases concern a facial challenge to Department of Health and Human Services (HHS) regulations which limit the ability of Title X fund recipients to engage in abortion-related activities....

I

A

In 1970, Congress enacted Title X of the Public Health Service Act (Act), ... which provides federal funding for family-planning services. The Act authorizes the Secretary to "make grants to and enter into contracts with public or nonprofit private entities to assist in the establishment and operation of voluntary family planning projects which shall offer a broad range of acceptable and effective family planning methods and services." ... Section 1008 of the Act ... provides that "[n]one of the funds appropriated under this subchapter shall be used in programs where abortion is a method of family planning." ... That restriction was intended to ensure that Title X funds would "be used only to support preventive family planning services, population research, infertility services, and other related medical, informational, and educational activities." ...

In 1988, the Secretary promulgated new regulations designed to provide " 'clear and operational guidance' to grantees about how to preserve the distinction between Title X programs and abortion as a method of family planning." ... The regulations clarify, through the definition of the term "family planning," that Congress intended Title X funds "to be used only to support preventive family planning services." ...

The regulations attach three principal conditions on the grant of federal funds for Title X projects. First, the regulations specify that a "Title X project may not provide counseling concerning the use of abortion as a method of family planning or provide referral for abortion as a method of family planning." ... Because Title X is limited to preconceptional services, the program does not furnish services related to childbirth. Only in the context of a referral out of the Title X program is a pregnant woman given transitional information ... Title X projects must refer every pregnant client "for appropriate prenatal and/or social services by furnishing a list of available providers that promote the welfare of the mother and the unborn child.". . . . The list may not be used indirectly to encourage or promote abortion, "such as by weighing the list of referrals in favor of health care providers which perform abortions, by including on the list of referral providers health care providers whose principal business is the provision of abortions, by excluding available providers who do not provide abortions, or by 'steering' clients to providers who offer abortion as a method of family planning." ... The Title X project is expressly prohibited from referring a pregnant woman to an abortion provider, even upon specific request. One permissible response to such an inquiry is that "the project does not consider abortion an appropriate method of family planning and therefore does not counsel or refer for abortion." ...

Second, the regulations broadly prohibit a Title X project from engaging in activities that "encourage, promote or advocate abortion as a method of family planning." ... Forbidden activities include lobbying for legislation that would increase the availability of abortion as a method of family planning, developing or disseminating materials advocating abortion as a method of family planning, providing speakers to promote abortion as a method of family planning, using legal action to make abortion available in any way as a method of family planning, and paying dues to any group that advocates abortion as a method of family planning as a substantial part of its activities. . . .

Third, the regulations require that Title X projects be organized so that they are "physically and financially separate" from prohibited abortion activities. . . .

B

Petitioners are Title X grantees and doctors who supervise Title X funds suing on behalf of themselves and their patients. Respondent is the Secretary of the Department of Health and Human Services. . . . [P]etitioners . . . [sought] declaratory and injunctive relief to prevent implementation of the regulations. . . . [T]he District Court . . . granted summary judgment in favor of the Secretary.

A panel of the Court of Appeals for the Second Circuit affirmed. . . .

. . .

II

We begin by pointing out the posture of the cases before us. Petitioners are challenging the facial validity of the regulations. Thus, we are concerned only with the question whether, on their face, the regulations are both authorized by the Act, and can be construed in such a manner that they can be applied to a set of individuals without infringing upon constitutionally protected rights. Petitioners face a heavy burden in seeking to have the regulations invalidated as facially unconstitutional. . . .

. . .

III

Petitioners contend that the regulations violate the First Amendment by impermissibly discriminating based on viewpoint because they prohibit "all discussion about abortion as a lawful option—including counseling, referral, and the provision of neutral and accurate information about ending a pregnancy—while compelling the clinic or counselor to provide information that promotes continuing a pregnancy to term." They assert that the regulations violate the "free speech rights of private health care organizations that receive Title X funds, of their staff, and of their patients" by impermissibly imposing "viewpoint-discriminatory conditions on government subsidies" and thus "penaliz[e] speech funded with non-Title X monies." . . . Relying on Regan v. Taxation With Representation of Wash., and Arkansas Writers Project, Inc. v. Ragland, 481 U.S. 221, 234 (1987), petitioners also assert that while the Government may place certain conditions on the receipt of federal subsidies, it may not "discriminate invidiously in its subsidies in such a way as to 'ai[m] at the suppression of dangerous ideas.' " . . .

There is no question but that the statutory prohibition contained in § 1008 is constitutional. . . . The Government can, without violating the Constitution, selectively fund a program to encourage certain activities it believes to be in the public interest, without at the same time funding an alternate program which seeks to deal with the problem in another way. In so doing, the Government has not discriminated on the basis of viewpoint; it has merely chosen to fund one activity to the exclusion of the other. . . .

The challenged regulations implement the statutory prohibition by prohibiting counseling, referral, and the provision of information regarding abortion as a method of family planning. They are designed to ensure that the limits of the federal program are observed. The Title X program is designed not for prenatal care, but to encourage family planning. A doctor who wished to offer prenatal care to a project patient who became pregnant could properly be prohibited from doing so because such service is outside the scope of the federally funded program. The regulations prohibiting abortion counseling and referral are of the same ilk; "no funds appropriated for the project may be used in programs where abortion is a method of family planning," and a doctor employed by the project may be prohibited in the course of his project duties from counseling abortion or referring for abortion. This is not a case of the Government "suppressing a dangerous idea," but of a prohibition on a project grantee or its employees from engaging in activities outside of its scope.

To hold that the Government unconstitutionally discriminates on the basis of viewpoint when it chooses to fund a program dedicated to advance certain permissible goals, because the program in advancing those goals necessarily discourages alternate goals, would render numerous government programs constitutionally suspect. When Congress established a National Endowment for Democracy to encourage other countries to adopt democratic principles, . . . it was not constitutionally required to fund a program to encourage competing lines of political philosophy such as Communism and Fascism. . . .

We believe that petitioners' reliance upon our decision in *Arkansas Writers' Project,* supra, is misplaced. That case involved a state sales tax which discriminated between magazines on the basis of their content. Relying on this fact, and on the fact that the tax "targets a small group within the press," contrary to our decision in Minneapolis Star & Tribune Co. v. Minnesota Comm'r of Revenue, 460 U.S. 575 (1983), the Court held the tax invalid. But we have here not the case of a general law singling out a disfavored group on the basis of speech content, but a case of the Government refusing to fund activities, including speech, which are specifically excluded from the scope of the project funded.

    . . .

Petitioners also contend that the restrictions on the subsidization of abortion-related speech contained in the regulations are impermissible because they condition the receipt of a benefit, in this case Title X funding, on the relinquishment of a constitutional right, the right to engage in abortion advocacy and counseling. Relying on Perry v. Sindermann, 408 U.S. 593, 597 (1972), and FCC v. League of Women Voters of Cal., 468 U.S. 364 (1984), petitioners argue that "even though the government may deny [a] . . . benefit for any number of reasons, there are some reasons upon which the government may not rely. It may not deny a benefit to a person on a basis that infringes his constitutionally protected interests—especially his interest in freedom of speech." . . .

Petitioners' reliance on these cases is unavailing, however, because here the government is not denying a benefit to anyone, but is instead simply insisting that public funds be spent for the purposes for which they were authorized. . . . The regulations govern the scope of the Title X project's activities, and leave the grantee unfettered in its other activities. The Title X grantee can continue to perform abortions, provide abortion-related services, and engage in abortion advocacy; it simply is required to conduct those activities through programs that are separate and independent from the project that receives Title X funds. . . .

In contrast, our "unconstitutional conditions" cases involve situations in which the government has placed a condition on the recipient of the subsidy rather than on a particular program or service, thus effectively prohibiting the recipient from engaging in the protected conduct outside the scope of the federally funded program. In FCC v. League of Women Voters of Cal., we invalidated a federal law providing that noncommercial television and radio stations that receive federal grants may not "engage in editorializing." Under that law, a recipient of federal funds was "barred absolutely from all editorializing" because it "is not able to segregate its activities according to the source of its funding" and thus "has no way of limiting the use of its federal funds to all noneditorializing activities." The effect of the law was that "a noncommercial educational station that receives only 1% of its overall income from [federal] grants is barred absolutely from all editorializing" and "barred from using even wholly private funds to finance its editorial activity." ... We expressly recognized, however, that were Congress to permit the recipient stations to "establish 'affiliate' organizations which could then use the station's facilities to editorialize with nonfederal funds, such a statutory mechanism would plainly be valid." ... Such a scheme would permit the station "to make known its views on matters of public importance through its nonfederally funded, editorializing affiliate without losing federal grants for its noneditorializing broadcast activities." ...

Similarly, in *Regan* we held that Congress could, in the exercise of its spending power, reasonably refuse to subsidize the lobbying activities of tax-exempt charitable organizations by prohibiting such organizations from using tax-deductible contributions to support their lobbying efforts. In so holding, we explained that such organizations remained free "to receive deductible contributions to support ... nonlobbying activit[ies]." ...

By requiring that the Title X grantee engage in abortion-related activity separately from activity receiving federal funding, Congress has, consistent with our teachings in *League of Women Voters* and *Regan,* not denied it the right to engage in abortion-related activities. Congress has merely refused to fund such activities out of the public fisc, and the Secretary has simply required a certain degree of separation from the Title X project in order to ensure the integrity of the federally funded program.

The same principles apply to petitioners' claim that the regulations abridge the free speech rights of the grantee's staff. ... The employees' freedom of expression is limited during the time that they actually work for the project; but this limitation is a consequence of their decision to accept employment in a project, the scope of which is permissibly restricted by the funding authority.

This is not to suggest that funding by the Government, even when coupled with the freedom of the fund recipients to speak outside the scope of the Government-funded project, is invariably sufficient to justify government control over the content of expression. For example, this Court has recognized that the existence of a Government "subsidy," in the form of Government-owned property, does not justify the restriction of speech in areas that have "been traditionally open to the public for expressive activity," ... Similarly, we have recognized that the university is a traditional sphere of free expression so fundamental to the functioning of our society that the Government's ability to control speech within that sphere by means of conditions attached to the expenditure of Government funds is restricted by the vagueness and overbreadth doctrines of the First Amendment, Keyishian v. Board of Regents, 385 U.S. 589, 603, 605–606 (1967). It could be argued by analogy that traditional relationships such as that between doctor and patient should enjoy protection under the First Amendment from government regulation, even when subsidized by the Government. We need not resolve that question here, however, because the Title X program regulations do not significantly impinge upon the doctor-patient relationship. Nothing in them requires a doctor to represent as his own any opinion that he does not in fact hold. Nor is the doctor-patient relationship established by the Title X program sufficiently all-encompassing so as to justify an expectation on the part of the patient of comprehensive medical advice. The program does not provide post-conception medical care, and therefore a doctor's silence with regard to abortion cannot reasonably be thought to mislead a client into thinking that the doctor does not consider abortion an appropriate option for her. The doctor is always free to make clear that advice regarding abortion is simply beyond the scope of the program. In these circumstances, the general rule that the Government may choose not to subsidize speech applies with full force.

. . .

Affirmed.

Justice Blackmun, with whom Justice Marshall joins, with whom Justice Stevens joins as to Parts II and III, and with whom Justice O'Connor joins as to Part I, dissenting.

. . . [T]he Court, for the first time, upholds viewpoint-based suppression of speech solely because it is imposed on those dependent upon the Government for economic support. . . . I dissent. . . .

. . .

II

. . .

A

Until today, the Court never has upheld viewpoint-based suppression of speech simply because that suppression was a condition upon the acceptance of public funds. . . .

. . . In *Regan,* the Court upheld a content-neutral provision of the Internal Revenue Code. . . . [T]he Court explained: "The case would be different if Congress were to discriminate invidiously in its subsidies in such a way as to 'ai[m]' at the suppression of dangerous ideas.' . . ." . . .

It cannot seriously be disputed that the counseling and referral provisions at issue in the present cases constitute content-based regulation of speech. Title X grantees may provide counseling and referral regarding any of a wide range of family planning and other topics, save abortion. . . .

The Regulations are also clearly viewpoint-based. While suppressing speech favorable to abortion with one hand, the Secretary compels anti-abortion speech with the other. . . .

. . .

B

The Court concludes that the challenged Regulations do not violate the First Amendment rights of Title X staff members because any limitation of the employees' freedom of expression is simply a consequence of their decision to accept employment at a federally funded project. But it has never been sufficient to justify an otherwise unconstitutional condition upon public employment that the employee may escape the condition by relinquishing his or her job. . . .

. . . Under the majority's reasoning, the First Amendment could be read to tolerate any governmental restriction upon an employee's speech so long as that restriction is limited to the funded workplace. This is a dangerous proposition, and one the Court has rightly rejected in the past.

. . .

The Government's articulated interest in distorting the doctor-patient dialogue—ensuring that federal funds are not spent for a purpose outside the scope of the program—falls far short of that necessary to justify the suppression of truthful information and professional medical opinion regarding constitutionally protected conduct. . . . By failing to balance or even to consider the free speech interests claimed by Title X physicians against the Government's asserted interest in suppressing the speech, the Court falters in its duty to implement the protection that the First Amendment clearly provides for this important message.

C

Finally, it is of no small significance that the speech the Secretary would suppress is truthful information regarding constitutionally protected conduct of vital importance to the listener. One can imagine no legitimate governmental interest that might be served by suppressing such information[a]. . . .

. . .

Rosenberger v. Rector and Visitors of the University of Virginia

515 U.S. 819, 115 S.Ct. 2510, 132 L.Ed.2d 700 (1995).

[The report in this case appears infra, page 1811.]

National Endowment for the Arts v. Finley

524 U.S. 569, 118 S.Ct. 2168, 141 L.Ed.2d 500 (1998).

Justice O'Connor delivered the opinion of the Court.

The National Foundation on the Arts and Humanities Act, as amended in 1990, requires the Chairperson of the National Endowment for the Arts (NEA) to ensure that "artistic excellence and artistic merit are the criteria by which [grant] applications are judged, taking into consideration general standards of decency and respect for the diverse beliefs and values of the American public." . . . In this case, we review the Court of Appeals' determination that § 954(d)(1), on its face, impermissibly discriminates on the basis of viewpoint and is void for vagueness under the First and Fifth Amendments. We conclude that § 954(d)(1) is facially valid, as it neither inherently interferes with First Amendment rights nor violates constitutional vagueness principles.

I

A

. . . The enabling statute vests the NEA with substantial discretion to award grants; it identifies only the broadest funding priorities, including "artistic and cultural significance, giving emphasis to American creativity and cultural diversity," "professional excellence," and the encouragement of "public knowledge, education, understanding, and appreciation of the arts." . . . .

a. Dissenting opinions by Justices Stevens and O'Connor are omitted.

Applications for NEA funding are initially reviewed by advisory panels composed of experts in the relevant field of the arts. ... The panels report to the 26–member National Council on the Arts (Council), which, in turn, advises the NEA Chairperson. The Chairperson has the ultimate authority to award grants but may not approve an application as to which the Council has made a negative recommendation. ...

Since 1965, the NEA has distributed over three billion dollars in grants to individuals and organizations, funding that has served as a catalyst for increased state, corporate, and foundation support for the arts. Congress has recently restricted the availability of federal funding for individual artists, confining grants primarily to qualifying organizations and state arts agencies, and constraining sub-granting. ...

Throughout the NEA's history, only a handful of the agency's roughly 100,000 awards have generated formal complaints about misapplied funds or abuse of the public's trust. Two provocative works, however, prompted public controversy in 1989 and led to congressional revaluation of the NEA's funding priorities and efforts to increase oversight of its grant-making procedures. The Institute of Contemporary Art at the University of Pennsylvania had used $30,000 of a visual arts grant it received from the NEA to fund a 1989 retrospective of photographer Robert Mapplethorpe's work. The exhibit, entitled The Perfect Moment, included homoerotic photographs that several Members of Congress condemned as pornographic. ... Members also denounced artist Andres Serrano's work Piss Christ, a photograph of a crucifix immersed in urine. ... Serrano had been awarded a $15,000 grant from the Southeast Center for Contemporary Art, an organization that received NEA support.

. . .

In the 1990 appropriations bill, Congress [created] an Independent Commission of constitutional law scholars to review the NEA's grant-making procedures and assess the possibility of more focused standards for public arts funding. The Commission ... concluded that there is no constitutional obligation to provide arts funding, but also ... cautioned against legislation setting forth any content restrictions. ...

... The House rejected the Crane Amendment, which would have virtually eliminated the NEA, ... and the Rohrabacher Amendment, which would have introduced a prohibition on awarding any grants that could be used to "promote, distribute, disseminate, or produce matter that has the purpose or effect of denigrating the beliefs, tenets, or objects of a particular religion" or "of denigrating an individual, or group of individuals, on the basis of race, sex, handicap, or national origin," .... Ultimately, Congress adopted the Williams/Coleman Amendment ... which directs the Chairperson, in establishing procedures to judge the artistic merit of grant applications, to "tak[e] into consideration general standards of decency and respect for the diverse beliefs and values of the American public."

The NEA has not promulgated any official interpretation of the provision ... John Frohnmayer, then Chairperson of the NEA, ... declared that he would "count on [the] procedures" ensuring diverse membership on the peer review panels to fulfill Congress' mandate.

B

The four individual respondents in this case ... are performance artists who applied for NEA grants before § 954(d)(1) was enacted. An advisory panel recommended approval of respondents' projects, ... A majority of the Council subsequently recommended disapproval, and in June 1990, the NEA informed respondents that they had been denied funding. Respondents filed suit, alleging that the NEA had violated their First Amendment rights by rejecting the applications on political grounds,.... When Congress enacted § 954(d)(1), respondents, now joined by the National Association of Artists' Organizations (NAAO), amended their complaint to challenge the provision as void for vagueness and impermissibly viewpoint based.

. . .

The District Court ... granted summary judgment in favor of respondents . . .

A divided panel of the Court of Appeals affirmed the District Court's ruling. ...

. . .

We ... reverse the judgment of the Court of Appeals.

II

A

Respondents raise a facial constitutional challenge to § 954(d)(1), and consequently they confront "a heavy burden" in advancing their claim. ...

Respondents argue that the provision is a paradigmatic example of viewpoint discrimination because it rejects any artistic speech that either fails to respect mainstream values or offends standards of decency. The premise of respondents' claim is that § 954(d)(1) constrains the agency's ability to fund certain categories of artistic expression. The NEA, however, reads the provision as merely hortatory, and contends that it stops well short of an absolute restriction. ... Indeed, the agency asserts that it has adequately implemented § 954(d)(1) merely by ensuring the representation of various backgrounds and points of view on the advisory panels that analyze grant applications. ... We do not decide whether the NEA's view—that the formulation of diverse advisory panels is sufficient to comply with Congress' command—is in fact a reasonable reading of the statute. It is clear, however, that the text of § 954(d)(1) imposes no categorical requirement. The advisory language stands in sharp contrast to congressional efforts to prohibit the funding of certain classes of speech. When Congress has in fact intended to affirmatively constrain the NEA's grant-making authority, it has done so in no uncertain terms. ...

. . .

That § 954(d)(1) admonishes the NEA merely to take "decency and respect" into consideration ... [undercuts] respondents' argument that the provision inevitably will be utilized as a tool for invidious viewpoint discrimination. ...

Respondents' claim that the provision is facially unconstitutional may be reduced to the argument that the criteria in § 954(d)(1) are sufficiently subjective that the agency could utilize them to engage in viewpoint discrimination. Given the varied interpretations of the criteria and the vague exhortation to "take them into consideration," it seems unlikely that this provision will introduce any greater element of selectivity than the determination of "artistic excellence" itself. And we are reluctant, in any event, to invalidate legislation

"on the basis of its hypothetical application to situations not before the Court."
. . .

. . .

. . . Any content-based considerations that may be taken into account in the grant-making process are a consequence of the nature of arts funding. The NEA has limited resources and it must deny the majority of the grant applications that it receives, including many that propose "artistically excellent" projects. The agency may decide to fund particular projects for a wide variety of reasons, "such as the technical proficiency of the artist, the creativity of the work, the anticipated public interest in or appreciation of the work, the work's contemporary relevance, its educational value, its suitability for or appeal to special audiences (such as children or the disabled), its service to a rural or isolated community, or even simply that the work could increase public knowledge of an art form.". . . .

Respondent's reliance on our decision in Rosenberger v. Rector and Visitors of Univ. of Va., 515 U.S. 819 (1995), is therefore misplaced. In *Rosenberger*, a public university declined to authorize disbursements from its Student Activities Fund to finance the printing of a Christian student newspaper. We held that by subsidizing the Student Activities Fund, the University had created a limited public forum, from which it impermissibly excluded all publications with religious editorial viewpoints . . . . . Although the scarcity of NEA funding does not distinguish this case from *Rosenberger*, . . . the competitive process according to which the grants are allocated does. . . . The NEA's mandate is to make aesthetic judgments, and the inherently content-based "excellence" threshold for NEA support sets it apart from the subsidy at issue in *Rosenberger*—which was available to all student organizations that were " 'related to the educational purpose of the University,' " . . . —and from comparably objective decisions on allocating public benefits, such as access to a school auditorium or a municipal theater, see Lamb's Chapel v. Center Moriches Union Free School Dist., 508 U.S. 384, 386 (1993); Southeastern Promotions, Ltd. v. Conrad, 420 U.S. 546, 555 (1975), or the second class mailing privileges available to " 'all newspapers and other periodical publications,' " see Hannegan v. Esquire, Inc., 327 U.S. 146, 148, n. 1 (1946).

Respondents do not allege discrimination in any particular funding decision. . . . Thus, we have no occasion here to address an as-applied challenge in a situation where the denial of a grant may be shown to be the product of invidious viewpoint discrimination. If the NEA were to leverage its power to award subsidies on the basis of subjective criteria into a penalty on disfavored viewpoints, then we would confront a different case. . . . Unless and until § 954(d)(1) is applied in a manner that raises concern about the suppression of disfavored viewpoints, however, we uphold the constitutionality of the provision. . . .

. . .

III

The lower courts also erred in invalidating § 954(d)(1) as unconstitutionally vague. . . . The terms of the provision are undeniably opaque, and if they appeared in a criminal statute or regulatory scheme, they could raise substantial vagueness concerns. . . .

In the context of selective subsidies, it is not always feasible for Congress to legislate with clarity. Indeed, if this statute is unconstitutionally vague, then so too are all government programs awarding scholarships and grants on the basis of subjective criteria such as "excellence." ... To accept respondents' vagueness argument would be to call into question the constitutionality of these valuable government programs and countless others like them.

Section 954(d)(1) merely adds some imprecise considerations to an already subjective selection process. ...

. . .

Justice Scalia with whom Justice Thomas joins, concurring in the judgment.

... I think that § 954(d)(1) must be evaluated as written ... By its terms, it establishes content-and-viewpoint-based criteria upon which grant applications are to be evaluated. And that is perfectly constitutional.

I

THE STATUTE MEANS WHAT IT SAYS

. . .

... [T]he presence of the "tak[e] into consideration" clause "cannot be regarded as mere surplusage; it means something," ... And the "something" is that the decisionmaker, all else being equal, will favor applications that display decency and respect, and disfavor applications that do not.

This unquestionably constitutes viewpoint discrimination. ... If viewpoint discrimination in this context is unconstitutional ..., the law is invalid....

. . .

II

WHAT THE STATUTE SAYS IS CONSTITUTIONAL

... With the enactment of § 954(d)(1), Congress did not abridge the speech of those who disdain the beliefs and values of the American public, nor did it abridge indecent speech. Those who wish to create indecent and disrespectful art are as unconstrained now as they were before the enactment of this statute. Avant-garde artistes such as respondents remain entirely free to epater les bourgeois; they are merely deprived of the additional satisfaction of having the bourgeoisie taxed to pay for it. ...

. . .

The nub of the difference between me and the Court is that I regard the distinction between "abridging" speech and funding it as a fundamental divide, on this side of which the First Amendment is inapplicable. The Court, by contrast, seems to believe that the First Amendment, despite its words, has some ineffable effect upon funding, imposing constraints of an indeterminate nature which it announces (without troubling to enunciate any particular test) are not violated by the statute here—or, more accurately, are not violated by the quite different, emasculated statute that it imagines. ...

. . .

Justice Souter, dissenting.

. . .

The decency and respect proviso mandates viewpoint-based decisions in the disbursement of government subsidies, and the Government has wholly failed to explain why the statute should be afforded an exemption from the fundamental rule of the First Amendment that viewpoint discrimination in the exercise of public authority over expressive activity is unconstitutional. ...

I

. . .

... [W]e characteristically begin by asking "whether the government has adopted a regulation of speech because of disagreement with the message it conveys. ..." ... The answer in this case is damning. One need do nothing more than read the text of the statute to conclude that Congress's purpose in imposing the decency and respect criteria was to prevent the funding of art that conveys an offensive message; the decency and respect provision on its face is quintessentially viewpoint based, and quotations from the Congressional Record merely confirm the obvious legislative purpose. ...

II

In the face of such clear legislative purpose, so plainly expressed, the Court has its work cut out for it in seeking a constitutional reading of the statute. ...

. . .

... Just as the statute cannot be read as anything but viewpoint based, or as requiring nothing more than diverse review panels, it cannot be read as tolerating awards to spread indecency or disrespect, so long as the review panel, the National Counsel on the Arts, and the Chairperson have given some thought to the offending qualities and decided to underwrite them anyway. That, after all, is presumably just what prompted the congressional outrage in the first place. . . .

But even if I found the Court's view of "consideration" plausible, that would make no difference at all on the question of constitutionality. ... [T]he First Amendment bars the government from considering viewpoint when it decides whether to subsidize private speech, and a statute that mandates the consideration of viewpoint is quite obviously unconstitutional. ...

III

A second basic strand in the Court's treatment of today's question, and the heart of Justice Scalia's, in effect assumes that whether or not the statute mandates viewpoint discrimination, there is no constitutional issue here because government art subsidies fall within a zone of activity free from First Amendment restraints. The Government calls attention to the roles of government-as-speaker and government-as-buyer, in which the government is of course entitled to engage in viewpoint discrimination: if the Food and Drug Administration launches an advertising campaign on the subject of smoking, it may condemn the habit without also having to show a cowboy taking a puff on the opposite page; and if the Secretary of Defense wishes to buy a portrait to decorate the Pentagon, he is free to prefer George Washington over George the Third.

The Government freely admits, however, that it neither speaks through the expression subsidized by the NEA, nor buys anything for itself with its NEA grants. On the contrary, ... the Government acts as a patron, financially underwriting the production of art by private artists and impresarios for independent consumption. Accordingly, the Government would have us liberate government-as-patron from First Amendment strictures not by placing it squarely within the categories of government-as-buyer or government-as-speaker, but by recognizing a new category by analogy to those accepted ones. The analogy is, however, a very poor fit, and this patronage falls embarrassingly on the wrong side of the line between government-as-buyer or-speaker and government-as-regulator-of-private-speech.

. . .

. . . I would not hesitate to reject the Government's plea to recognize a new, categorical patronage exemption from the requirement of viewpoint neutrality. . . .

. . .

IV

Although I, like the Court, recognize that "facial challenges to legislation are generally disfavored," . . . the proviso is the type of statute that most obviously lends itself to such an attack. The NEA does not offer a list of reasons when it denies a grant application, and an artist or exhibitor whose subject raises a hint of controversy can never know for sure whether the decency and respect criteria played a part in any decision by the NEA to deny funding. . . .

. . .

Legal Services Corporation v. Velazquez

531 U.S. 533, 121 S.Ct. 1043, 149 L.Ed.2d 63 (2001).

Justice Kennedy delivered the opinion of the Court.

In 1974, Congress enacted the Legal Services Corporation Act, . . . establish[ing] the Legal Services Corporation (LSC) as a District of Columbia nonprofit corporation. LSC's mission is to distribute funds appropriated by Congress to eligible local grantee organizations "for the purpose of providing financial support for legal assistance in noncriminal proceedings or matters to persons financially unable to afford legal assistance." . . .

. . . In many instances the grantees are funded by a combination of LSC funds and other public or private sources. The grantee organizations hire and supervise lawyers to provide free legal assistance to indigent clients. . . .

This suit requires us to decide whether one of the conditions imposed by Congress on the use of LSC funds violates the First Amendment rights of LSC grantees and their clients. . . . [T]he restriction . . . prohibits legal representation funded by recipients of LSC moneys if the representation involves an effort to amend or otherwise challenge existing welfare law. As interpreted by the LSC and by the Government, the restriction prevents an attorney from arguing to a court that a state statute conflicts with a federal statute or that either a state or federal statute by its terms or in its application is violative of the United States Constitution.

Lawyers employed by New York City LSC grantees, together with private LSC contributors, LSC indigent clients, and various state and local public officials whose governments contribute to LSC grantees, brought suit in the United States District Court for the Southern District of New York to declare the restriction . . . invalid. The United States Court of Appeals for the Second Circuit approved an injunction against enforcement of the provision as an impermissible viewpoint-based discrimination in violation of the First Amendment. . . . We agree that the restriction violates the First Amendment, and we affirm the judgment of the Court of Appeals.

I

From the inception of the LSC, Congress has placed restrictions on its use of funds. For instance, the LSC Act prohibits recipients from making available LSC funds, program personnel, or equipment to any political party, to any political campaign, or for use in "advocating or opposing any ballot measures." ... The Act further proscribes use of funds in most criminal proceedings and in litigation involving nontherapeutic abortions, secondary school desegregation, military desertion, or violations of the Selective Service statute. ... Fund recipients are barred from bringing class-action suits unless express approval is obtained from LSC. ...

The restrictions at issue were part of a compromise set of restrictions enacted in the Omnibus Consolidated Rescissions and Appropriations Act of 1996 ... The relevant portion of '504(a)(16) prohibits funding of any organization

> "that initiates legal representation or participates in any other way, in litigation, lobbying, or rulemaking, involving an effort to reform a Federal or State welfare system, except that this paragraph shall not be construed to preclude a recipient from representing an individual eligible client who is seeking specific relief from a welfare agency if such relief does not involve an effort to amend or otherwise challenge existing law in effect on the date of the initiation of the representation."

The prohibitions apply to all of the activities of an LSC grantee, including those paid for by non-LSC funds. ... We are concerned with the statutory provision which excludes LSC representation in cases which "involve an effort to amend or otherwise challenge existing law in effect on the date of the initiation of the representation."

In 1997, LSC adopted final regulations clarifying § 504(a)(16). ... LSC interpreted the statutory provision to allow indigent clients to challenge welfare agency determinations of benefit ineligibility under interpretations of existing law. For example, an LSC grantee could represent a welfare claimant who argued that an agency made an erroneous factual determination or that an agency misread or misapplied a term contained in an existing welfare statute. According to LSC, a grantee in that position could argue as well that an agency policy violated existing law. ... Under LSC's interpretation, however, grantees could not accept representations designed to change welfare laws, much less argue against the constitutionality or statutory validity of those laws. Even in cases where constitutional or statutory challenges became apparent after representation was well under way, LSC advised that its attorneys must withdraw. ...

. . .

II

The United States and LSC rely on Rust v. Sullivan, 500 U.S. 173 (1991), as support for the LSC program restrictions. In *Rust*, Congress established program clinics to provide subsidies for doctors to advise patients on a variety of family planning topics. Congress did not consider abortion to be within its family planning objectives, however, and it forbade doctors employed by the program from discussing abortion with their patients. ...

We upheld the law, reasoning that Congress had not discriminated against viewpoints on abortion, but had "merely chosen to fund one activity to the exclusion of the other." ... The restrictions were considered necessary "to ensure that the limits of the federal program [were] observed." ... Title X did not single out a particular idea for suppression because it was dangerous or disfavored; rather, Congress prohibited Title X doctors from counseling that was outside the scope of the project. . . .

The Court in *Rust* did not place explicit reliance on the rationale that the counseling activities of the doctors under Title X amounted to governmental speech; when interpreting the holding in later cases, however, we have explained *Rust* on this understanding. We have said that viewpoint-based funding decisions can be sustained in instances in which the government is itself the speaker, . . . or instances, like *Rust*, in which the government "used private speakers to transmit information pertaining to its own program." . . . As we said in Rosenberger [v. Rector & Visitors of Univ. of Va., 515 U.S. 819 (1995)], "[w]hen the government disburses public funds to private entities to convey a governmental message, it may take legitimate and appropriate steps to ensure that its message is neither garbled nor distorted by the grantee." . . . The latitude which may exist for restrictions on speech where the government's own message is being delivered flows in part from our observation that, "[w]hen the government speaks, for instance to promote its own policies or to advance a particular idea, it is, in the end, accountable to the electorate and the political process for its advocacy. If the citizenry objects, newly elected officials later could espouse some different or contrary position." Board of Regents of Univ. of Wis. System v. Southworth, [529 U.S. 217 (2000)].

Neither the latitude for government speech nor its rationale applies to subsidies for private speech in every instance, however. As we have pointed out, "[i]t does not follow . . . that viewpoint-based restrictions are proper when the [government] does not itself speak or subsidize transmittal of a message it favors but instead expends funds to encourage a diversity of views from private speakers." *Rosenberger* . . .

Although the LSC program differs from the program at issue in *Rosenberger* in that its purpose is not to "encourage a diversity of views," the salient point is that, like the program in *Rosenberger*, the LSC program was designed to facilitate private speech, not to promote a governmental message. . . . In . . . suits for benefits, an LSC-funded attorney speaks on the behalf of the client in a claim against the government for welfare benefits. The lawyer is not the government's speaker. The attorney defending the decision to deny benefits will deliver the government's message in the litigation. The LSC lawyer, however, speaks on the behalf of his or her private, indigent client. . . .

. . . The advice from the attorney to the client and the advocacy by the attorney to the courts cannot be classified as governmental speech even under a generous understanding of the concept. In this vital respect this suit is distinguishable from *Rust*.

The private nature of the speech involved here, and the extent of LSC's regulation of private expression, are indicated further by the circumstance that the Government seeks to use an existing medium of expression and to control it, in a class of cases, in ways which distort its usual functioning. Where the government uses or attempts to regulate a particular medium, we have been informed by its accepted usage in determining whether a particular restriction on speech is necessary for the program's purposes and limitations. In FCC v. League of Women Voters of Cal., 468 U.S. 364 (1984), the Court was instructed by its understanding of the dynamics of the broadcast industry in holding that prohibitions against editorializing by public radio networks were an impermissible restriction, even though the Government enacted the restriction to control the use of public funds. The First Amendment forbade the Government from using the forum in an unconventional way to suppress speech inherent in the nature of the medium. . . . In Arkansas Ed. Television Comm'n v. Forbes, 523 U.S. 666 (1998), the dynamics of the broadcasting system gave station programmers the right to use editorial judgment to exclude certain speech so that the broadcast message could be more effective. And in *Rosenberger*, the fact that student newspapers expressed many different points of view was an important foundation for the Court's decision to invalidate viewpoint-based restrictions. . . .

When the government creates a limited forum for speech, certain restrictions may be necessary to define the limits and purposes of the program. . . . The same is true when the government establishes a subsidy for specified ends. . . . As this suit involves a subsidy, limited forum cases . . . may not be controlling in a strict sense, yet they do provide some instruction. Here the program presumes that private, nongovernmental speech is necessary, and a substantial restriction is placed upon that speech. . . . [L]awyers funded in the Government program may not undertake representation in suits for benefits if they must advise clients respecting the questionable validity of a statute which defines benefit eligibility and the payment structure. The limitation forecloses advice or legal assistance to question the validity of statutes under the Constitution of the United States. It extends further, it must be noted, so that state statutes inconsistent with federal law under the Supremacy Clause may be neither challenged nor questioned.

. . . Restricting LSC attorneys in advising their clients and in presenting arguments and analyses to the courts distorts the legal system by altering the traditional role of the attorneys . . . Just as government . . . could not elect to use a broadcasting network or a college publication structure in a regime which prohibits speech necessary to the proper functioning of those systems, . . . it may not design a subsidy to effect this serious and fundamental restriction on advocacy of attorneys and the functioning of the judiciary.

. . .

Interpretation of the law and the Constitution is the primary mission of the judiciary when it acts within the sphere of its authority to resolve a case or controversy. Marbury v. Madison, 1 Cranch 137 (1803) ("It is emphatically the province and the duty of the judicial department to say what the law is"). An informed, independent judiciary presumes an informed, independent bar. Under § 504(a)(16), however, cases would be presented by LSC attorneys who could not advise the courts of serious questions of statutory validity. The disability is inconsistent with the proposition that attorneys should present all the reasonable and well-grounded arguments necessary for proper resolution of the case. By seeking to prohibit the analysis of certain legal issues and to truncate presentation to the courts, the enactment under review prohibits speech and expression upon which courts must depend for the proper exercise of the judicial power. . . .

The restriction imposed by the statute here threatens severe impairment of the judicial function. Section 504(a)(16) sifts out cases presenting constitutional challenges in order to insulate the Government's laws from judicial inquiry. If the restriction on speech and legal advice were to stand, the result would be two tiers of cases. In cases where LSC counsel were attorneys of record, there would be lingering doubt whether the truncated representation had resulted in complete analysis of the case, full advice to the client, and proper presentation to the court. The courts and the public would come to question the adequacy and fairness of professional representations when the attorney, either consciously to comply with this statute or unconsciously to continue the representation despite the statute, avoided all reference to questions of statutory validity and constitutional authority. A scheme so inconsistent with accepted separation-of-powers principles is an insufficient basis to sustain or uphold the restriction on speech.

It is no answer to say the restriction on speech is harmless because, under LSC's interpretation of the Act, its attorneys can withdraw. This misses the point. The statute is an attempt to draw lines around the LSC program to exclude from litigation those arguments and theories Congress finds unacceptable but which by their nature are within the province of the courts to consider.

The restriction on speech is even more problematic because in cases where the attorney withdraws from a representation, the client is unlikely to find other counsel. ... Thus, with respect to the litigation services Congress has funded, there is no alternative channel for expression of the advocacy Congress seeks to restrict. This is in stark contrast to *Rust*. There, a patient could receive the approved Title X family planning counseling funded by the Government and later could consult an affiliate or independent organization to receive abortion counseling. Unlike indigent clients who seek LSC representation, the patient in *Rust* was not required to forfeit the Government-funded advice when she also received abortion counseling through alternative channels. Because LSC attorneys must withdraw whenever a question of a welfare statute's validity arises, an individual could not obtain joint representation so that the constitutional challenge would be presented by a non-LSC attorney, and other, permitted, arguments advanced by LSC counsel.

Finally, LSC and the Government maintain that '504(a)(16) is necessary to define the scope and contours of the federal program, a condition that ensures funds can be spent for those cases most immediate to congressional concern. In support of this contention, they suggest the challenged limitation takes into account the nature of the grantees' activities and provides limited congressional funds for the provision of simple suits for benefits. In petitioners' view, the restriction operates neither to maintain the current welfare system nor insulate it from attack; rather, it helps the current welfare system function in a more efficient and fair manner by removing from the program complex challenges to existing welfare laws.

The effect of the restriction, however, is to prohibit advice or argumentation that existing welfare laws are unconstitutional or unlawful. Congress cannot recast a condition on funding as a mere definition of its program in every case, lest the First Amendment be reduced to a simple semantic exercise. Here, notwithstanding Congress' purpose to confine and limit its program, the restriction operates to insulate current welfare laws from constitutional scrutiny and certain other legal challenges, a condition implicating central First Amendment concerns. In no lawsuit funded by the Government can the LSC attorney, speaking on behalf of a private client, challenge existing welfare laws. As a result, arguments by indigent clients that a welfare statute is unlawful or unconstitutional cannot be expressed in this Government-funded program for petitioning the courts, even though the program was created for litigation involving welfare benefits, and even though the ordinary course of litigation involves the expression of theories and postulates on both, or multiple, sides of an issue.

... There can be little doubt that the LSC Act funds constitutionally protected expression; and in the context of this statute there is no programmatic message of the kind recognized in *Rust* and which sufficed there to allow the Government to specify the advice deemed necessary for its legitimate objectives. This serves to distinguish '504(a)(16) from any of the Title X program restrictions upheld in *Rust*, and to place it beyond any congressional funding condition approved in the past by this Court.

Congress was not required to fund an LSC attorney to represent indigent clients; and when it did so, it was not required to fund the whole range of legal representations or relationships. The LSC and the United States, however, in effect ask us to permit Congress to define the scope of the litigation it funds to exclude certain vital theories and ideas. The attempted restriction is designed to insulate the Government's interpretation of the Constitution from judicial challenge. The Constitution does not permit the Government to confine litigants and their attorneys in this manner. We must be vigilant when Congress imposes rules and conditions which in effect insulate its own laws from legitimate judicial challenge. Where private speech is involved, even Congress' antecedent funding decision cannot be aimed at the suppression of ideas thought inimical to the Government's own interest. . . .

For the reasons we have set forth, the funding condition is invalid. . . .

The judgment of the Court of Appeals is

Affirmed.

Justice Scalia, with whom the Chief Justice, Justice O'Connor, and Justice Thomas join, dissenting.

Section 504(a)(16) . . . defines the scope of a federal spending program. It does not directly regulate speech, and it neither establishes a public forum nor discriminates on the basis of viewpoint. The Court agrees with all this, yet applies a novel and unsupportable interpretation of our public-forum precedents to declare '504(a)(16) facially unconstitutional. This holding not only has no foundation in our jurisprudence; it is flatly contradicted by a recent decision that is on all fours with the present case. . . .

I

. . .

. . . Section 504(a)(16) . . . withholds LSC funds from every entity that "participates in any . . . way . . . in litigation, lobbying, or rulemaking . . . involving an effort to reform a Federal or State welfare system." It thus bans LSC-funded entities from participating on either side of litigation involving such statutes, from participating in rulemaking relating to the implementation of such legislation, and from lobbying Congress itself regarding any proposed changes to such legislation. . . .

The restrictions relating to rulemaking and lobbying . . . duplicate general prohibitions on the use of LSC funds for those activities found elsewhere in the Appropriations Act. . . . The restriction on litigation, however, is unique, and it contains a proviso specifying what the restriction does not cover. Funding recipients may "represen[t] an individual eligible client who is seeking specific relief from a welfare agency if such relief does not involve an effort to amend or otherwise challenge existing law in effect on the date of the initiation of the representation." The . . . LSC can sponsor neither challenges to nor defenses of existing welfare reform law. The litigation ban is symmetrical: Litigants challenging the covered statutes or regulations do not receive LSC funding, and neither do litigants defending those laws against challenge.

If a suit for benefits raises a claim outside the scope of the LSC program, the LSC-funded lawyer may not participate in the suit. . . .

II

The LSC Act is a federal subsidy program, not a federal regulatory program. . . . Regulations directly restrict speech; subsidies do not. Subsidies, it is true, may indirectly abridge speech, but only if the funding scheme is " 'manipulated' to have a 'coercive effect' " on those who do not hold the subsidized position. . . . Proving unconstitutional coercion is difficult enough when the spending program has universal coverage and excludes only certain speech—such as a tax exemption scheme excluding lobbying expenses. The Court has found such programs unconstitutional only when the exclusion was "aimed at the suppression of dangerous ideas." . . . The Court has found such selective spending unconstitutionally coercive only once, when the government created a public forum with the spending program but then discriminated in distributing funding within the forum on the basis of viewpoint. See Rosenberger v. Rector and Visitors of Univ. of Va. . . . When the limited spending program does not create a public forum, proving coercion is virtually impossible, because simply denying a subsidy "does not 'coerce' belief," . . .

In Rust v. Sullivan, . . . the Court applied these principles to a statutory scheme that is in all relevant respects indistinguishable from '504(a)(16). . . . We rejected a First Amendment free-speech challenge to the funding scheme, explaining that "[t]he Government can, without violating the Constitution, selectively fund a program to encourage certain activities it believes to be in the public interest, without at the same time funding an alternative program which seeks to deal with the problem another way." . . . This was not, we said, the type of "discriminat[ion] on the basis of viewpoint" that triggers strict scrutiny, . . . because the " 'decision not to subsidize the exercise of a fundamental right does not infringe the right,' " . . .

The same is true here. The LSC Act, like the scheme in *Rust*, . . . does not create a public forum. Far from encouraging a diversity of views, it has always, as the Court accurately states, "placed restrictions on its use of funds," . . . Nor does § 504(a)(16) discriminate on the basis of viewpoint, since it funds neither challenges to nor defenses of existing welfare law. The provision simply declines to subsidize a certain class of litigation, and under *Rust* that decision "does not infringe the right" to bring such litigation. . . . No litigant who, in the absence of LSC funding, would bring a suit challenging existing welfare law is deterred from doing so by '504(a)(16). *Rust* thus controls these cases and compels the conclusion that '504(a)(16) is constitutional.

The Court contends that *Rust* is different because the program at issue subsidized government speech, while the LSC funds private speech. . . . If the private doctors' confidential advice to their patients at issue in *Rust* constituted "government speech," it is hard to imagine what subsidized speech would not be government speech. Moreover, the majority's contention that the subsidized speech in these cases is not government speech because the lawyers have a professional obligation to represent the interests of their clients founders on the reality that the doctors in *Rust* had a professional obligation to serve the interests of their patients. . . .

The Court further asserts that these cases are different from *Rust* because the welfare funding restriction "seeks to use an existing medium of expression and to control it . . . in ways which distort its usual functioning." This is wrong on both the facts and the law. It is wrong on the law because there is utterly no precedent for the novel and facially implausible proposition that the First Amendment has anything to do with government funding that—though it does not actually abridge anyone's speech—"distorts an existing medium of expression." . . .

The Court's "nondistortion" principle is also wrong on the facts, since there is no basis for believing that § 504(a)(16), ... will distort the operation of the courts. It may well be that the bar of § 504(a)(16) will cause LSC-funded attorneys to decline or to withdraw from cases that involve statutory validity. But that means at most that fewer statutory challenges to welfare laws will be presented to the courts because of the unavailability of free legal services for that purpose. So what? The same result would ensue from excluding LSC-funded lawyers from welfare litigation entirely. It is not the mandated, nondistortable function of the courts to inquire into all "serious questions of statutory validity" in all cases. Courts must consider only those questions of statutory validity that are presented by litigants, and if the Government chooses not to subsidize the presentation of some such questions, that in no way "distorts" the courts' role. ...

Nor will the judicial opinions produced by LSC cases systematically distort the interpretation of welfare laws. Judicial decisions do not stand as binding "precedent" for points that were not raised, not argued, and hence not analyzed. ... The statutory validity that courts assume in LSC cases will remain open for full determination in later cases.

Finally, the Court is troubled "because in cases where the attorney withdraws from a representation, the client is unlikely to find other counsel." That is surely irrelevant, since it leaves the welfare recipient in no worse condition than he would have been in had the LSC program never been enacted. Respondents properly concede that even if welfare claimants cannot obtain a lawyer anywhere else, the Government is not required to provide one. ...

The only conceivable argument that can be made for distinguishing *Rust* is that there even patients who wished to receive abortion counseling could receive the nonabortion services that the Government-funded clinic offered, whereas here some potential LSC clients who wish to receive representation on a benefits claim that does not challenge the statutes will be unable to do so because their cases raise a reform claim that an LSC lawyer may not present. This difference, of course, is required by the same ethical canons that the Court elsewhere does not wish to distort. Rather than sponsor "truncated representation," Congress chose to subsidize only those cases in which the attorneys it subsidized could work freely. ... And it is impossible to see how this difference from *Rust* has any bearing upon the First Amendment question, which ... is whether the funding scheme is " 'manipulated' to have a 'coercive effect' " ... It could be claimed to have such an effect if the client in a case ineligible for LSC representation could eliminate the ineligibility by waiving the claim that the statute is invalid; but he cannot. No conceivable coercive effect exists.

This has been a very long discussion to make a point that is embarrassingly simple: The LSC subsidy neither prevents anyone from speaking nor coerces anyone to change speech, and is indistinguishable in all relevant respects from the subsidy upheld in Rust v. Sullivan....

. . .

... The Court's decision displays not only an improper special solicitude for our own profession; it also displays, I think, the very fondness for "reform through the courts"—the making of innumerable social judgments through judge-pronounced constitutional imperatives—that prompted Congress to restrict publicly funded litigation of this sort. ... I respectfully dissent.

United States v. American Library Association, Inc.

539 U.S. 194, 123 S.Ct. 2297, 156 L.Ed.2d 221 (2003).

Chief Justice Rehnquist announced the judgment of the Court and delivered an opinion, in which Justice O'Connor, Justice Scalia, and Justice Thomas joined.

... Under [the Children's Internet Protection Act (CIPA)], a public library may not receive federal assistance to provide Internet access unless it installs software to block images that constitute obscenity or child pornography, and to prevent minors from obtaining access to material that is harmful to them. The District Court held these provisions facially invalid on the ground that they induce public libraries to violate patrons' First Amendment rights. We now reverse.

To help public libraries provide their patrons with Internet access, Congress offers two forms of federal assistance. First, the E-rate program established by the Telecommunications Act of 1996 entitles qualifying libraries to buy Internet access at a discount.... In the year ending June 30, 2002, libraries received $58.5 million in such discounts.... Second, pursuant to the Library Services and Technology Act (LSTA), ... the Institute of Museum and Library Services makes grants to state library administrative agencies to "electronically lin[k] libraries with educational, social, or information services," "assis[t] libraries in accessing information through electronic networks," and "pa[y] costs for libraries to acquire or share computer systems and telecommunications technologies.".... In fiscal year 2002, Congress appropriated more than $149 million in LSTA grants. These programs have succeeded greatly in bringing Internet access to public libraries: By 2000, 95% of the Nation's libraries provided public Internet access. ...

By connecting to the Internet, public libraries provide patrons with a vast amount of valuable information. But there is also an enormous amount of pornography on the Internet, much of which is easily obtained. The accessibility of this material has created serious problems for libraries, which have found that patrons of all ages, including minors, regularly search for online pornography. Some patrons also expose others to pornographic images by leaving them displayed on Internet terminals or printed at library printers.

Upon discovering these problems, Congress became concerned that the E-rate and LSTA programs were facilitating access to illegal and harmful pornography. ... Congress learned that adults "us[e] library computers to access pornography that is then exposed to staff, passersby, and children," and that "minors acces[s] child and adult pornography in libraries."

But Congress also learned that filtering software that blocks access to pornographic Web sites could provide a reasonably effective way to prevent such uses of library resources. ... By 2000, before Congress enacted CIPA, almost 17% of public libraries used such software on at least some of their Internet terminals, and 7% had filters on all of them. ... A library can set such software to block categories of material, such as "Pornography" or "Violence." When a patron tries to view a site that falls within such a category, a screen appears indicating that the site is blocked. ... But a filter set to block pornography may sometimes block other sites that present neither obscene nor pornographic material, but that nevertheless trigger the filter. To minimize this problem, a library can set its software to prevent the blocking of material that falls into categories like "Education," "History," and "Medical." ... A library may also add or delete specific sites from a blocking category and anyone can ask companies that furnish filtering software to unblock particular sites....

... CIPA ... provides that a library may not receive E-rate or LSTA assistance unless it has "a policy of Internet safety for minors that includes the operation of a technology protection measure ... that protects against access" by all persons to "visual depictions" that constitute "obscen[ity]" or "child pornography," and that protects against access by minors to "visual depictions" that are "harmful to minors." ... The statute defines a "[t]echnology protection measure" as "a specific technology that blocks or filters Internet access to material covered by" CIPA. ... CIPA also permits the library to "disable" the filter "to enable access for bona fide research or other lawful purposes." ... Under the E-rate program, disabling is permitted "during use by an adult." ... Under the LSTA program, disabling is permitted during use by any person.

Appellees are a group of libraries, library associations, library patrons, and Web site publishers, including the American Library Association (ALA) and the Multnomah County Public Library in Portland, Oregon....

Congress has wide latitude to attach conditions to the receipt of federal assistance in order to further its policy objectives. South Dakota v. Dole, 483 U.S. 203, 206 (1987). But Congress may not "induce" the recipient "to engage in activities that would themselves be unconstitutional." ... To determine whether libraries would violate the First Amendment by employing the filtering software that CIPA requires, we must first examine the role of libraries in our society.

... To fulfill their traditional missions, public libraries must have broad discretion to decide what material to provide to their patrons. Although they seek to provide a wide array of information, their goal has never been to provide "universal coverage." ... Instead, public libraries seek to provide materials "that would be of the greatest direct benefit or interest to the community." ... To this end, libraries collect only those materials deemed to have "requisite and appropriate quality."

We have held in two analogous contexts that the government has broad discretion to make content-based judgments in deciding what private speech to make available to the public. In Arkansas Ed. Television Comm'n v. Forbes, 523 U.S. 666, 672B673 (1998), we held that public forum principles do not generally apply to a public television station's editorial judgments regarding the private speech it presents to its viewers. "[B]road rights of access for outside speakers would be antithetical, as a general rule, to the discretion that stations and their editorial staff must exercise to fulfill their journalistic purpose and statutory obligations." ...

Similarly, in National Endowment for Arts v. Finley, 524 U.S. 569 (1998), we upheld an art funding program that required the National Endowment for the Arts (NEA) to use content-based criteria in making funding decisions. We explained that "[a]ny content-based considerations that may be taken into account in the grant-making process are a consequence of the nature of arts funding." *Id.,* at 585. In particular, "[t]he very assumption of the NEA is that grants will be awarded according to the 'artistic worth of competing applicants,' and absolute neutrality is simply inconceivable." ...

The principles underlying *Forbes* and *Finley* also apply to a public library's exercise of judgment in selecting the material it provides to its patrons. Just as forum analysis and heightened judicial scrutiny are incompatible with the role of public television stations and the role of the NEA, they are also incompatible with the discretion that public libraries must have to fulfill their traditional missions. Public library staffs necessarily consider content in making collection decisions and enjoy broad discretion in making them.

... [P]ublic forum principles ... are out of place in the context of this case. Internet access in public libraries is neither a "traditional" nor a "designated" public forum. ... First, this resource—which did not exist until quite recently—has not "immemorially been held in trust for the use of the public and, time out of mind, ... been used for purposes of assembly, communication of thoughts between citizens, and discussing public questions." ... We have "rejected the view that traditional public forum status extends beyond its historic confines." ... The doctrines surrounding traditional public forums may not be extended to situations where such history is lacking.

Nor does Internet access in a public library satisfy our definition of a "designated public forum." To create such a forum, the government must make an affirmative choice to open up its property for use as a public forum. The government does not create a public forum by inaction or by permitting limited discourse, but only by intentionally opening a non-traditional forum for public discourse. ...

... A public library does not acquire Internet terminals in order to create a public forum for Web publishers to express themselves, any more than it collects books in order to provide a public forum for the authors of books to speak. It provides Internet access ... for the same reasons it offers other library resources: to facilitate research, learning, and recreational pursuits by furnishing materials of requisite and appropriate quality. ...

... A library's failure to make quality-based judgments about all the material it furnishes from the Web does not somehow taint the judgments it does make. ... Most libraries already exclude pornography from their print collections because they deem it inappropriate for inclusion. We do not subject these decisions to heightened scrutiny; it would make little sense to treat libraries' judgments to block online pornography any differently, when these judgments are made for just the same reason.

Moreover, because of the vast quantity of material on the Internet and the rapid pace at which it changes, libraries cannot possibly segregate, item by item, all the Internet material that is appropriate for inclusion from all that is not. While a library could limit its Internet collection to just those sites it found worthwhile, it could do so only at the cost of excluding an enormous amount of valuable information that it lacks the capacity to review. ...

... [T]he dissents fault the tendency of filtering software to "overblock"— that is, to erroneously block access to constitutionally protected speech that falls outside the categories that software users intend to block. Due to the software's limitations, "[m]any erroneously blocked [Web] pages contain content that is completely innocuous for both adults and minors, and that no rational person could conclude matches the filtering companies' category definitions, such as 'pornography' or 'sex.'" Assuming that such erroneous blocking presents constitutional difficulties, any such concerns are dispelled by the ease with which patrons may have the filtering software disabled. When a patron encounters a blocked site, he need only ask a librarian to unblock it or (at least in the case of adults) disable the filter. As the District Court found, libraries have the capacity to permanently unblock any erroneously blocked site, and the Solicitor General stated at oral argument that a "library may ... eliminate the filtering with respect to specific sites ... at the request of a patron." ... The Solicitor General confirmed that a "librarian can, in response to a request from a patron, unblock the filtering mechanism altogether," and further explained that a patron would not "have to explain ... why he was asking a site to be unblocked or the filtering to be disabled." ... [S]ome patrons may be too embarrassed to request them. But the Constitution does not guarantee the right to acquire information at a public library without any risk of embarrassment.

Appellees urge us to affirm the District Court's judgment on the alternative ground that CIPA imposes an unconstitutional condition on the receipt of federal assistance. Under this doctrine, "the government may not deny a benefit to a person on a basis that infringes his constitutionally protected ... freedom of speech" even if he has no entitlement to that benefit. ... Appellees argue that CIPA imposes an unconstitutional condition on libraries ... by requiring them, as a condition on their receipt of federal funds, to surrender their First Amendment right to provide the public with access to constitutionally protected speech.

We need not decide this question because, even assuming that appellees may assert an "unconstitutional conditions" claim, this claim would fail on the merits. Within broad limits, "when the Government appropriates public funds to establish a program it is entitled to define the limits of that program." ... In *Rust* [v. Sullivan, 500 U.S. 173 (1991)], Congress had appropriated federal funding for family planning services and forbidden the use of such funds in programs that provided abortion counseling. ... Recipients of these funds challenged this restriction, arguing that it impermissibly conditioned the receipt of a benefit on the relinquishment of their constitutional right to engage in abortion counseling. ... We rejected that claim, recognizing that "the Government [was] not denying a benefit to anyone, but [was] instead simply insisting that public funds be spent for the purposes for which they were authorized." ...

The same is true here. The E-rate and LSTA programs were intended to help public libraries fulfill their traditional role of obtaining material of requisite and appropriate quality for educational and informational purposes.... Especially because public libraries have traditionally excluded pornographic material from their other collections, Congress could reasonably impose a parallel limitation on its Internet assistance programs. ...

Justice Stevens asserts the premise that "[a] federal statute penalizing a library for failing to install filtering software on every one of its Internet-accessible computers would unquestionably violate [the First] Amendment." ... But—assuming again that public libraries have First Amendment rights— CIPA does not "penalize" libraries that choose not to install such software, or deny them the right to provide their patrons with unfiltered Internet access. Rather, CIPA simply reflects Congress' decision not to subsidize their doing so. ...

Appellees mistakenly contend, in reliance on Legal Services Corporation v. Velazquez, 531 U.S. 533 (2001), that CIPA's filtering conditions "[d]istor[t] the [u]sual [f]unctioning of [p]ublic [l]ibraries." In *Velazquez*, the Court concluded that a Government program of furnishing legal aid to the indigent differed from the program in *Rust* "[i]n th[e] vital respect" that the role of lawyers who represent clients in welfare disputes is to advocate *against* the Government, and there was thus an assumption that counsel would be free of state control. ... The Court concluded that the restriction on advocacy in such welfare disputes would distort the usual functioning of the legal profession and the federal and state courts before which the lawyers appeared. Public libraries, by contrast, have no comparable role that pits them against the Government, and there is no comparable assumption that they must be free of any conditions that their benefactors might attach to the use of donated funds or other assistance.

Because public libraries' use of Internet filtering software does not violate their patrons' First Amendment rights, CIPA does not induce libraries to violate the Constitution, and is a valid exercise of Congress' spending power. Nor does CIPA impose an unconstitutional condition on public libraries. Therefore, the judgment of the District Court for the Eastern District of Pennsylvania is

Reversed.

Justice Kennedy, concurring in the judgment.

If, on the request of an adult user, a librarian will unblock filtered material or disable the Internet software filter without significant delay, there is little to this case. The Government represents this is indeed the fact.

. . .

If some libraries do not have the capacity to unblock specific Web sites or to disable the filter or if it is shown that an adult user's election to view constitutionally protected Internet material is burdened in some other substantial way, that would be the subject for an as-applied challenge, not the facial challenge made in this case.

The interest in protecting young library users from material inappropriate for minors is legitimate, and even compelling, as all Members of the Court appear to agree. Given this interest, and the failure to show that the ability of adult library users to have access to the material is burdened in any significant degree, the statute is not unconstitutional on its face. For these reasons, I concur in the judgment of the Court.

Justice Breyer, concurring in the judgment.

. . . I reach the plurality's ultimate conclusion in a different way.

In ascertaining whether the statutory provisions are constitutional, I would apply a form of heightened scrutiny, examining the statutory requirements in question with special care. The Act directly restricts the public's receipt of information. . . . And it does so through limitations imposed by outside bodies (here Congress) upon two critically important sources of information—the Internet as accessed via public libraries. . . . [W]e should not examine the statute's constitutionality as if it raised no special First Amendment concern— as if, like tax or economic regulation, the First Amendment demanded only a "rational basis" for imposing a restriction. Nor should we accept the Government's suggestion that a presumption in favor of the statute's constitutionality applies.

At the same time, in my view, the First Amendment does not here demand application of the most limiting constitutional approach—that of "strict scrutiny." The statutory restriction in question is, in essence, a kind of "selection" restriction (a kind of editing). It affects the kinds and amount of materials that the library can present to its patrons. And libraries often properly engage in the selection of materials, either as a matter of necessity (*i.e.,* due to the scarcity of resources) or by design (*i.e.,* in accordance with collection development policies). . . . "[S]trict scrutiny" implies too limiting and rigid a test for me to believe that the First Amendment requires it in this context.

Instead, I would examine the constitutionality of the Act's restrictions here as the Court has examined speech-related restrictions in other contexts where circumstances call for heightened, but not "strict," scrutiny—where, for example, complex, competing constitutional interests are potentially at issue or speech-related harm is potentially justified by unusually strong governmental interests. Typically the key question in such instances is one of proper fit. . . .

In such cases the Court has asked whether the harm to speech-related interests is disproportionate in light of both the justifications and the potential alternatives. It has considered the legitimacy of the statute's objective, the extent to which the statute will tend to achieve that objective, whether there are other, less restrictive ways of achieving that objective, and ultimately whether the statute works speech-related harm that, in relation to that objective, is out of proportion. . . . This approach does not substitute a form of "balancing" for less flexible, though more speech-protective, forms of "strict scrutiny." Rather, it *supplements* the latter with an approach that is more flexible but nonetheless provides the legislature with less than ordinary leeway in light of the fact that constitutionally protected expression is at issue. . . .

The Act's restrictions satisfy these constitutional demands. . . . [T]he software filters both "overblock," screening out some perfectly legitimate material, and "underblock," allowing some obscene material to escape detection by the filter. But no one has presented any clearly superior or better fitting alternatives.

At the same time, the Act contains an important exception that limits the speech-related harm that "overblocking" might cause . . . [allowing] libraries to permit any adult patron access to an "overblocked" Web site; the adult patron need only ask a librarian to unblock the specific Web site or, alternatively, ask the librarian, "Please disable the entire filter."

. . .

Given the comparatively small burden that the Act imposes upon the library patron seeking legitimate Internet materials, I cannot say that any speech-related harm that the Act may cause is disproportionate when considered in relation to the Act's legitimate objectives. I therefore agree with the plurality that the statute does not violate the First Amendment, and I concur in the judgment.

Justice Stevens, dissenting.

. . . I agree with the plurality that it is neither inappropriate nor unconstitutional for a local library to experiment with filtering software as a means of curtailing children's access to Internet Web sites displaying sexually explicit images. I also agree with the plurality that the 7% of public libraries that decided to use such software on *all* of their Internet terminals in 2000 did not act unlawfully. Whether it is constitutional for the Congress of the United States to impose that requirement on the other 93%, however, raises a vastly different question. Rather than allowing local decisionmakers to tailor their responses to local problems, the Children's Internet Protection Act (CIPA) operates as a blunt nationwide restraint on adult access to "an enormous amount of" . . . constitutionally protected speech. In my view, this restraint is unconstitutional.

I

The unchallenged findings of fact made by the District Court reveal fundamental defects in the filtering software that is now available or that will be available in the foreseeable future. Because the software relies on key words or phrases to block undesirable sites, it does not have the capacity to exclude a precisely defined category of images. . . .

The effect of the overblocking is the functional equivalent of a host of individual decisions excluding hundreds of thousands of individual constitutionally protected messages from Internet terminals located in public libraries throughout the Nation. . . .

. . .

. . . The plurality . . . relies on the Solicitor General's assurance that the statute permits individual librarians to disable filtering mechanisms whenever a patron so requests. In my judgment, that assurance does not cure the constitutional infirmity in the statute.

Until a blocked site or group of sites is unblocked, a patron is unlikely to know what is being hidden and therefore whether there is any point in asking for the filter to be removed. It is as though the statute required a significant part of every library's reading materials to be kept in unmarked, locked rooms or cabinets, which could be opened only in response to specific requests. Some curious readers would in time obtain access to the hidden materials, but many would not. Inevitably, the interest of the authors of those works in reaching the widest possible audience would be abridged.

II

The plurality incorrectly argues that the statute does not impose "an unconstitutional condition on public libraries." On the contrary, it impermissibly conditions the receipt of Government funding on the restriction of significant First Amendment rights.

. . .

. . . [W]e have always assumed that libraries have discretion when making decisions regarding what to include in, and exclude from, their collections. . . . Given our Nation's deep commitment "to safeguarding academic freedom" and to the "robust exchange of ideas," . . . a library's exercise of judgment with respect to its collection is entitled to First Amendment protection.

A federal statute penalizing a library for failing to install filtering software on every one of its Internet-accessible computers would unquestionably violate that Amendment. . . . I think it equally clear that the First Amendment protects libraries from being denied funds for refusing to comply with an identical rule. An abridgment of speech by means of a threatened denial of benefits can be just as pernicious as an abridgment by means of a threatened penalty.

Our cases holding that government employment may not be conditioned on the surrender of rights protected by the First Amendment illustrate the point. . . .

The issue in this case does not involve governmental attempts to control the speech or views of its employees. It involves the use of its treasury to impose controls on an important medium of expression. In an analogous situation, we specifically held that when "the Government seeks to use an existing medium of expression and to control it, in a class of cases, in ways which distort its usual functioning," the distorting restriction must be struck down under the First Amendment. . . .

The plurality argues that the controversial decision in Rust v. Sullivan . . . requires rejection of appellees' unconstitutional conditions claim. But, as subsequent cases have explained, *Rust* only involved and only applies to instances of governmental speech—that is, situations in which the government seeks to communicate a specific message. . . . These programs thus are designed to provide access, particularly for individuals in low-income communities, ... to a vast amount and wide variety of private speech. They are not designed to foster or transmit any particular governmental message.

. . .

The plurality's reliance on National Endowment for Arts v. Finley ... is also misplaced. That case involved a challenge to a statute setting forth the criteria used by a federal panel of experts administering a federal grant program. Unlike this case, the Federal Government was not seeking to impose restrictions on the administration of a nonfederal program. ... *Rust* would appear to permit restrictions on a federal program such as the NEA arts grant program at issue in *Finley*.

Further, like a library, the NEA experts in *Finley* had a great deal of discretion to make judgments as to what projects to fund. But unlike this case, *Finley* did not involve a challenge by the NEA to a governmental restriction on its ability to award grants. Instead, the respondents were performance artists who had applied for NEA grants but were denied funding. ... If this were a case in which library patrons had challenged a library's decision to install and use filtering software, it would be in the same posture as *Finley*. Because it is not, *Finley* does not control this case.

Also unlike *Finley*, the Government does not merely seek to control a library's discretion with respect to computers purchased with Government funds or those computers with Government-discounted Internet access. ... [I]f a library attempts to provide Internet service for even *one* computer through an E-rate discount, that library must put filtering software on *all* of its computers with Internet access, not just the one computer with E-rate discount.

This Court should not permit federal funds to be used to enforce this kind of broad restriction of First Amendment rights, particularly when such a restriction is unnecessary to accomplish Congress' stated goal. ... The abridgment of speech is equally obnoxious whether a rule like this one is enforced by a threat of penalties or by a threat to withhold a benefit.

. . .

Justice Souter, with whom Justice Ginsburg joins, dissenting.

I agree in the main with Justice Stevens that the blocking requirements of the Children's Internet Protection Act ... impose an unconstitutional condition on the Government's subsidies to local libraries for providing access to the Internet. I also agree with the library appellees on a further reason to hold the blocking rule invalid in the exercise of the spending power under Article I, § 8: the rule mandates action by recipient libraries that would violate the First Amendment's guarantee of free speech if the libraries took that action entirely on their own. I respectfully dissent on this further ground.

I

Like the other Members of the Court, I have no doubt about the legitimacy of governmental efforts to put a barrier between child patrons of public libraries and the raw offerings on the Internet otherwise available to them there, and if the only First Amendment interests raised here were those of children, I would uphold application of the Act. ...

Nor would I dissent if I agreed with the majority of my colleagues, that an adult library patron could, consistently with the Act, obtain an unblocked terminal simply for the asking. I realize the Solicitor General represented this to be the Government's policy, and if that policy were communicated to every affected library as unequivocally as it was stated to us at argument, local librarians might be able to indulge the unblocking requests of adult patrons to the point of taking the curse off the statute for all practical purposes. But the Federal Communications Commission, in its order implementing the Act, pointedly declined to set a federal policy on when unblocking by local libraries would be appropriate under the statute. . . .

In any event, we are here to review a statute, and the unblocking provisions simply cannot be construed, even for constitutional avoidance purposes, to say that a library must unblock upon adult request, no conditions imposed and no questions asked. . . .

We therefore have to take the statute on the understanding that adults will be denied access to a substantial amount of nonobscene material harmful to children but lawful for adult examination, and a substantial quantity of text and pictures harmful to no one. . . .

We likewise have to examine the statute on the understanding that the restrictions on adult Internet access have no justification in the object of protecting children. Children could be restricted to blocked terminals, leaving other unblocked terminals in areas restricted to adults and screened from casual glances. And of course the statute could simply have provided for unblocking at adult request, with no questions asked. . . .

The question for me, then, is whether a local library could itself constitutionally impose these restrictions on the content otherwise available to an adult patron through an Internet connection, at a library terminal provided for public use. The answer is no. A library that chose to block an adult's Internet access to material harmful to children (and whatever else the undiscriminating filter might interrupt) would be imposing a content-based restriction on communication of material in the library's control that an adult could otherwise lawfully see. This would simply be censorship. . . .

II

The Court's plurality does not treat blocking affecting adults as censorship, but chooses to describe a library's act in filtering content as simply an instance of the kind of selection from available material that every library . . . must perform. . . . But this position does not hold up.

A

Public libraries are indeed selective in what they acquire to place in their stacks, as they must be. There is only so much money and so much shelf space . . . Selectivity is thus necessary and complex, and these two characteristics explain why review of a library's selection decisions must be limited. . . .

At every significant point, however, the Internet blocking here defies comparison to the process of acquisition. Whereas traditional scarcity of money and space require a library to make choices about what to acquire, and the choice to be made is whether or not to spend the money to acquire something, blocking is the subject of a choice made after the money for Internet access has been spent or committed. Since it makes no difference to the cost of Internet access whether an adult calls up material harmful for children or the Articles of Confederation, blocking (on facts like these) is not necessitated by scarcity of either money or space. In the instance of the Internet, what the library acquires is electronic access, and the choice to block is a choice to limit access that has already been acquired. Thus, deciding against buying a book means there is no book (unless a loan can be obtained), but blocking the Internet is merely blocking access purchased in its entirety and subject to unblocking if the librarian agrees. The proper analogy therefore is not to passing up a book that might have been bought; it is either to buying a book and then keeping it from adults lacking an acceptable "purpose," or to buying an encyclopedia and then cutting out pages with anything thought to be unsuitable for all adults.

B

... The plurality ... argues ... that the traditional responsibility of public libraries has called for denying adult access to certain books, or bowdlerizing the content of what the libraries let adults see. But, in fact, the plurality's conception of a public library's mission has been rejected by the libraries themselves. And no library that chose to block adult access in the way mandated by the Act could claim that the history of public library practice in this country furnished an implicit gloss on First Amendment standards, allowing for blocking out anything unsuitable for adults.

Institutional history of public libraries in America discloses an evolution toward a general rule, now firmly rooted, that any adult entitled to use the library has access to any of its holdings. To be sure, this freedom of choice was apparently not within the inspiration for the mid–19th century development of public libraries ... [There] was a growing understanding that a librarian's job was to guarantee that "all people had access to all ideas," ...

By the time McCarthyism began its assaults, appellee American Library Association had developed a Library Bill of Rights against censorship ... and an Intellectual Freedom Committee to maintain the position that beyond enforcing existing laws against obscenity, "there is no place in our society for extra-legal efforts to coerce the taste of others, to confine adults to the reading matter deemed suitable for adolescents, or to inhibit the efforts of writers to achieve artistic expression." ... So far as I have been able to tell, this statement expressed the prevailing ideal in public library administration after World War II, and it seems fair to say as a general rule that libraries by then had ceased to deny requesting adults access to any materials in their collections. ...

   . . .

... [I]n 1973, the ALA adopted a policy opposing the practice ... of keeping certain books off the open shelves, available only on specific request. ... The statement conceded that "closed shelf," "locked case," "adults only," or "restricted shelf" collections were "common to many libraries in the United States." ... The ALA nonetheless came out against it, in these terms: "While the limitation differs from direct censorship activities, such as removal of library materials or refusal to purchase certain publications, it nonetheless constitutes censorship, albeit a subtle form." ...

Amidst these and other ALA statements from the latter half of the 20th century, however, one subject is missing. There is not a word about barring requesting adults from any materials in a library's collection ... The silence bespeaks an American public library that gives any adult patron any material at hand, and a history without support for the plurality's reading of the First Amendment as tolerating a public library's censorship of its collection against adult enquiry.

C

... Quite simply, we can smell a rat when a library blocks material already in its control, just as we do when a library removes books from its shelves for reasons having nothing to do with wear and tear, obsolescence, or lack of demand. Content-based blocking and removal tell us something that mere absence from the shelves does not.

.   .   .

After a library has acquired material . . ., the variety of possible reasons that might legitimately support an initial rejection are no longer in play. Removal of books or selective blocking by controversial subject matter is not a function of limited resources and less likely than a selection decision to reflect an assessment of esthetic or scholarly merit. Removal (and blocking) decisions being so often obviously correlated with content, they tend to show up for just what they are, and because such decisions tend to be few, courts can examine them without facing a deluge. The difference between choices to keep out and choices to throw out is thus enormous, a perception that underlay the good sense of the plurality's conclusion in Board of Ed., Island Trees Union Free School Dist. No. 26 v. Pico, 457 U.S. 853 (1982), that removing classics from a school library in response to pressure from parents and school board members violates the Speech Clause.

.   .   .

CHAPTER 15

PROTECTION OF PENUMBRAL FIRST AMENDMENT RIGHTS

Introduction. The constitutional protection of expression, belief and association extends to "peripheral" areas beyond individual freedom to utter or print. It should be emphasized that the term "peripheral" does not suggest lesser importance. The terms "penumbras" and "peripheral rights" first appeared in Griswold v. Connecticut, 381 U.S. 479 (1965). In demonstrating that the protection of the first amendment was not confined to the right to utter or print, Justice Douglas explained that "[w]ithout those peripheral rights the specific rights would be less secure."

SECTION 1. SYMBOLIC SPEECH

United States v. O'Brien

391 U.S. 367, 88 S.Ct. 1673, 20 L.Ed.2d 672 (1968).

Mr. Chief Justice Warren delivered the opinion of the Court.

[O'Brien burned his selective service registration certificate on the steps of the South Boston Courthouse in the presence of a sizable crowd. He was convicted for violation of a federal statute that made it a crime to knowingly destroy or mutilate the certificate.]

. . .

II.

O'Brien first argues that the [statute] is unconstitutional as applied to him because his act of burning his registration certificate was protected "symbolic speech" . . .

We cannot accept the view that an apparently limitless variety of conduct can be labelled "speech" whenever the person engaging in the conduct intends thereby to express an idea. However, even on the assumption that the alleged communicative element in O'Brien's conduct is sufficient to bring into play the First Amendment, it does not necessarily follow that the destruction of a registration certificate is constitutionally protected activity. This Court has held that when "speech" and "nonspeech" elements are combined in the same course of conduct, a sufficiently important governmental interest in regulating the nonspeech element can justify incidental limitations on First Amendment freedoms. To characterize the quality of the governmental interest which must appear, the Court has employed a variety of descriptive terms: compelling; substantial; subordinating; paramount; cogent; strong. Whatever imprecision inheres in these terms, we think it clear that a government regulation is sufficiently justified if it is within the constitutional power of the Government;

if it furthers an important or substantial governmental interest; if the governmental interest is unrelated to the suppression of free expression; and if the incidental restriction on alleged First Amendment freedom is no greater than is essential to the furtherance of that interest. We find that the [statute] meets all of these requirements, and consequently that O'Brien can be constitutionally convicted for violating it.

. . .

The many functions performed by Selective Service certificates establish beyond doubt that Congress has a legitimate and substantial interest in preventing their wanton and unrestrained destruction and assuring their continuing availability by punishing people who knowingly and wilfully destroy or mutilate them. . . .

. . .

. . . The governmental interest and the scope of the [statute] are limited to preventing a harm to the smooth and efficient functioning of the Selective Service System. When O'Brien deliberately rendered unavailable his registration certificate, he wilfully frustrated this governmental interest. For this noncommunicative impact of his conduct, and for nothing else, he was convicted.

The case at bar is therefore unlike one where the alleged governmental interest in regulating conduct arises in some measure because the communication allegedly integral to the conduct is itself thought to be harmful. In Stromberg v. California, 283 U.S. 359 (1931), for example, this Court struck down a statutory phrase which punished people who expressed their "opposition to organized government" by displaying "any flag, badge, banner, or device." Since the statute there was aimed at suppressing communication it could not be sustained as a regulation of noncommunicative conduct. . . .

In conclusion, we find that because of the Government's substantial interest in assuring the continuing availability of issued Selective Service certificates, because [the statute] is an appropriately narrow means of protecting this interest and condemns only the independent noncommunicative impact of conduct within its reach, and because the noncommunicative impact of O'Brien's act of burning his registration certificate frustrated the Government's interest, a sufficient governmental interest has been shown to justify O'Brien's conviction.

III.

O'Brien finally argues that the 1965 Amendment is unconstitutional as enacted because what he calls the "purpose" of Congress was "to suppress freedom of speech." We reject this argument because under settled principles the purpose of Congress, as O'Brien uses that term, is not a basis for declaring this legislation unconstitutional.

It is a familiar principle of constitutional law that this Court will not strike down an otherwise constitutional statute on the basis of an alleged illicit legislative motive. . . .

Inquiries into congressional motives or purposes are a hazardous matter. When the issue is simply the interpretation of legislation, the Court will look to statements by legislators for guidance as to the purpose of the legislature, because the benefit to sound decision-making in this circumstance is thought sufficient to risk the possibility of misreading Congress' purpose. It is entirely a different matter when we are asked to void a statute that is, under well-settled criteria, constitutional on its face, on the basis of what fewer than a handful of Congressmen said about it. What motivates one legislator to make a speech about a statute is not necessarily what motivates scores of others to enact it, and the stakes are sufficiently high for us to eschew guesswork. We decline to void essentially on the ground that it is unwise legislation which Congress had the undoubted power to enact and which could be reenacted in its exact form if the same or another legislator made a "wiser" speech about it.

. . .

We think it not amiss, in passing, to comment upon O'Brien's legislative-purpose argument. There was little floor debate on this legislation in either House. Only Senator Thurmond commented on its substantive features in the Senate. . . . In the House debate only two Congressmen addressed themselves to the Amendment—Congressmen Rivers and Bray. . . . It is principally on the basis of the statements by these three Congressmen that O'Brien makes his congressional-"purpose" argument. We note that if we were to examine legislative purpose in the instant case, we would be obliged to consider not only these statements but also the more authoritative reports of the Senate and House Armed Services Committees. The portions of those reports explaining the purpose of the Amendment are reproduced in the Appendix in their entirety. While both reports make clear a concern with the "defiant" destruction of so-called "draft cards" and with "open" encouragement to others to destroy their cards, both reports also indicate that this concern stemmed from an apprehension that unrestrained destruction of cards would disrupt the smooth functioning of the Selective Service System.

IV.

. . . [T]he Court of Appeals should have affirmed the judgment of conviction entered by the District Court. . . . [a]

Mr. Justice Marshall took no part in the consideration or decision of these cases.

Mr. Justice Douglas, dissenting.

Justice Douglas' dissent was limited to the point that the case should be reargued to consider the issue of the validity of peacetime conscription. Later, however, in his concurring opinion in Brandenburg v. Ohio, 395 U.S. 444, 455 (1969), he said: "O'Brien was not prosecuted for not having his draft card available when asked for by a federal agent. He was indicted, tried, and convicted for burning the card. And this Court's affirmance of that conviction was not, with all respect, consistent with the First Amendment."]

Texas v. Johnson

491 U.S. 397, 109 S.Ct. 2533, 105 L.Ed.2d 342 (1989).

Justice Brennan delivered the opinion of the Court.

After publicly burning an American flag as a means of political protest, Gregory Lee Johnson was convicted of desecrating a flag in violation of Texas

---

a. A concurring opinion by Justice Harlan is omitted. On the issue of legislative motivation in O'Brien, see Ely, *Legislative and Administrative Motivation in Constitu-* *tional Law,* 79 Yale L.J. 1205 (1970), and Brest, *Palmer v. Thompson: An Approach to the Problem of Unconstitutional Legislative Motive,* 1971 Sup.Ct.Rev. 95.

law. This case presents the question whether his conviction is consistent with the First Amendment. We hold that it is not.

I

While the Republican National Convention was taking place in Dallas in 1984, respondent Johnson participated in a political demonstration dubbed the "Republican War Chest Tour." . . .

The demonstration ended in front of Dallas City Hall, where Johnson unfurled the American flag, doused it with kerosene, and set it on fire. While the flag burned, the protestors chanted, "America, the red, white, and blue, we spit on you." . . .

Of the approximately 100 demonstrators, Johnson alone was charged with . . . the desecration of a venerated object. . . .[1] After a trial, he was convicted, sentenced to one year in prison, and fined $2,000. The . . . Texas Court of Criminal Appeals reversed . . .

. . .

. . . We . . . affirm.

II

Johnson was convicted of flag desecration for burning the flag rather than for uttering insulting words. . . . We must first determine whether Johnson's burning of the flag constituted expressive conduct, permitting him to invoke the First Amendment in challenging his conviction. See, e.g., Spence v. Washington, 418 U.S. 405, 409–411 (1974). If his conduct was expressive, we next decide whether the State's regulation is related to the suppression of free expression. . . . If the State's regulation is not related to expression, then the less stringent standard we announced in United States v. O'Brien for regulations of noncommunicative conduct controls. . . . If it is, then we are outside of *O'Brien*'s test, and we must ask whether this interest justifies Johnson's conviction under a more demanding standard.[2] . . . A third possibility is that the State's asserted interest is simply not implicated on these facts, and in that event the interest drops out of the picture. . . .

. . .

---

1. Tex.Penal Code Ann. section 42.09 (1989) provides . . . :

"Section 42.09. Desecration of Venerated Object

"(a) A person commits an offense if he intentionally or knowingly desecrates:

(1) a public monument;

(2) a place of worship or burial; or

(3) a state or national flag.

"(b) For purposes of this section, 'desecrate' means deface, damage, or otherwise physically mistreat in a way that the actor knows will seriously offend one or more persons likely to observe or discover his action. . . ."

2. Although Johnson has raised a facial challenge to Texas' flag-desecration statute, we choose to resolve this case on the basis of his claim that the statute as applied to him violates the First Amendment. Section 42.09 regulates only physical conduct with respect to the flag, not the written or spoken word. . . . Because the prosecution of a person who had not engaged in expressive conduct would pose a different case, and because we are capable of disposing of this case on narrower grounds, we address only Johnson's claim that section 42.09 as applied to political expression like his violates the First Amendment.

In deciding whether particular conduct possesses sufficient communicative elements to bring the First Amendment into play, we have asked whether "[a]n intent to convey a particularized message was present, and [whether] the likelihood was great that the message would be understood by those who viewed it." 418 U.S., at 410–411. Hence, we have recognized the expressive nature of students' wearing of black armbands to protest American military involvement in Vietnam, Tinker v. Des Moines Independent Community School Dist., 393 U.S. 503, 505 (1969); of a sit-in by blacks in a "whites only" area to protest segregation, Brown v. Louisiana, 383 U.S. 131, 141–142 (1966); of the wearing of American military uniforms in a dramatic presentation criticizing American involvement in Vietnam, Schacht v. United States, 398 U.S. 58 (1970); and of picketing about a wide variety of causes. . . .

Especially pertinent to this case are our decisions recognizing the communicative nature of conduct relating to flags. Attaching a peace sign to the flag, *Spence,* . . . ; saluting the flag, *Barnette,* . . . ; and displaying a red flag, *Stromberg v. California,* . . . we have held, all may find shelter under the First Amendment. . . . That we have had little difficulty identifying an expressive element in conduct relating to flags should not be surprising. The very purpose of a national flag is to serve as a symbol of our country . . .

. . .

. . .

The State of Texas conceded for purposes of its oral argument in this case that Johnson's conduct was expressive conduct, and this concession seems to us . . . prudent . . . Johnson's burning of the flag was conduct "sufficiently imbued with elements of communication," . . . to implicate the First Amendment.

III

The Government generally has a freer hand in restricting expressive conduct than it has in restricting the written or spoken word. . . . It may not, however, proscribe particular conduct *because* it has expressive elements. . . . It is . . . not simply the verbal or nonverbal nature of the expression, but the governmental interest at stake, that helps to determine whether a restriction on that expression is valid.

. . . [W]e have limited the applicability of *O'Brien's* relatively lenient standard to those cases in which "the governmental interest is unrelated to the suppression of free expression." . . .

In order to decide whether *O'Brien's* test applies here, therefore, we must decide whether Texas has asserted an interest in support of Johnson's conviction that is unrelated to the suppression of expression. . . . The State offers two separate interests to justify this conviction: preventing breaches of the peace, and preserving the flag as a symbol of nationhood and national unity. We hold that the first interest is not implicated on this record and that the second is related to the suppression of expression.

A

Texas claims that its interest in preventing breaches of the peace justifies Johnson's conviction for flag desecration. . . . The only evidence offered by the State at trial to show the reaction to Johnson's actions was the testimony of several persons who had been seriously offended by the flag-burning.

The State's position, therefore, amounts to a claim that an audience that takes serious offense at particular expression is necessarily likely to disturb the peace and that the expression may be prohibited on this basis....

[W]e have not permitted the Government to assume that every expression of a provocative idea will incite a riot, but have instead required careful consideration of the actual circumstances surrounding such expression.... To accept Texas' arguments that it need only demonstrate "the potential for a breach of the peace," and that every flag-burning necessarily possesses that potential, would be to eviscerate our holding in *Brandenburg*. This we decline to do.

Nor does Johnson's expressive conduct fall within that small class of "fighting words" that are "likely to provoke the average person to retaliation, and thereby cause a breach of the peace." Chaplinsky v. New Hampshire, 315 U.S. 568, 574 (1942). No reasonable onlooker would have regarded Johnson's generalized expression of dissatisfaction with the policies of the Federal Government as a direct personal insult or an invitation to exchange fisticuffs....

. . .

B

The State also asserts an interest in preserving the flag as a symbol of nationhood and national unity. ... [T]his interest is related to expression ... The State, apparently, is concerned that such conduct will lead people to believe either that the flag does not stand for nationhood and national unity, but instead reflects other, less positive concepts, or that the concepts reflected in the flag do not in fact exist, that is, we do not enjoy unity as a Nation. These concerns blossom only when a person's treatment of the flag communicates some message, and thus are related "to the suppression of free expression" within the meaning of *O'Brien*. We are thus outside of *O'Brien*'s test altogether.

IV

It remains to consider whether the State's interest in preserving the flag as a symbol of nationhood and national unity justifies Johnson's conviction.

. . .

... Johnson was prosecuted because he knew that his politically charged expression would cause "serious offense." If he had burned the flag as a means of disposing of it because it was dirty or torn, he would not have been convicted of flag desecration under this Texas law ... The Texas law is thus not aimed at protecting the physical integrity of the flag in all circumstances, but is designed instead to protect it only against impairments that would cause serious offense to others....

Whether Johnson's treatment of the flag violated Texas law thus depended on the likely communicative impact of his expressive conduct....

... Johnson's political expression was restricted because of the content of the message he conveyed. We must therefore subject the State's asserted interest in preserving the special symbolic character of the flag to "the most exacting scrutiny." ...

Texas argues that its interest in preserving the flag as a symbol of nationhood and national unity survives this close analysis.... [T]he State's claim is that ... the message conveyed ... is a harmful one and therefore may be prohibited.

If there is a bedrock principle underlying the First Amendment, it is that the Government may not prohibit the expression of an idea simply because society finds the idea itself offensive or disagreeable. . . .

We have not recognized an exception to this principle even where our flag has been involved. In Street v. New York, 394 U.S. 576 (1969), we held that a State may not criminally punish a person for uttering words critical of the flag. . . .

. . . In *Spence,* we held that the same interest asserted by Texas here was insufficient to support a criminal conviction under a flag-misuse statute for the taping of a peace sign to an American flag. . . .

In short, nothing in our precedents suggests that a State may foster its own view of the flag by prohibiting expressive conduct relating to it. . . . The State's argument cannot depend here on the distinction between written or spoken words and nonverbal conduct. That distinction, we have shown, is of no moment where the nonverbal conduct is expressive, as it is here, and where the regulation of that conduct is related to expression, as it is here. . . .

. . . If we were to hold that a State may forbid flag-burning wherever it is likely to endanger the flag's symbolic role, but allow it wherever burning a flag promotes that role . . . we would be saying that when it comes to impairing the flag's physical integrity, the flag itself may be used as a symbol . . . only in one direction.

. . .

There is, moreover, no indication—either in the text of the Constitution or in our cases interpreting it—that a separate juridical category exists for the American flag alone. . . . We decline, therefore, to create for the flag an exception to the joust of principles protected by the First Amendment.

. . .

V

. . . The judgment of the Texas Court of Criminal Appeals is therefore

Affirmed.[a]

Chief Justice Rehnquist, with whom Justice White and Justice O'Connor join, dissenting.

In holding this Texas statute unconstitutional, the Court ignores Justice Holmes' familiar aphorism that "a page of history is worth a volume of logic." New York Trust Co. v. Eisner, 256 U.S. 345, 349 (1921). For more than 200 years, the American flag has occupied a unique position as the symbol of our Nation, a uniqueness that justifies a governmental prohibition against flag burning in the way respondent Johnson did here.

. . .

. . . [T]he public burning of the American flag by Johnson was no essential part of any exposition of ideas, and at the same time it had a tendency to incite a breach of the peace. Johnson was free to make any verbal denunciation of the flag that he wished; indeed, he was free to burn the flag in private. . . .

. . .

a.   A concurring opinion by Justice Ken-   Court, is omitted.
nedy, who also joined the opinion of the

... The Texas statute deprived Johnson of only one rather inarticulate symbolic form of protest—a form of protest that was profoundly offensive to many—and left him with a full panoply of other symbols and every conceivable form of verbal expression to express his deep disapproval of national policy. Thus, in no way can it be said that Texas is punishing him because his hearers—or any other group of people—were profoundly opposed to the message that he sought to convey. Such opposition is no proper basis for restricting speech or expression under the First Amendment. It was Johnson's use of this particular symbol, and not the idea that he sought to convey by it or by his many other expressions, for which he was punished.

. . .

... The Court decides that the American flag is just another symbol, about which not only must opinions pro and con be tolerated, but for which the most minimal public respect may not be enjoined. The government may conscript men into the Armed Forces where they must fight and perhaps die for the flag, but the government may not prohibit the public burning of the banner under which they fight. I would uphold the Texas statute as applied in this case.

Justice Stevens, dissenting.

... In my judgment rules that apply to a host of other symbols, such as state flags, armbands, or various privately promoted emblems of political or commercial identity, are not necessarily controlling. Even if flag burning could be considered just another species of symbolic speech under the logical application of the rules that the Court has developed in its interpretation of the First Amendment in other contexts, this case has an intangible dimension that makes those rules inapplicable.

. . .

UNITED STATES v. EICHMAN, 496 U.S. 310 (1990). After the decision in Texas v. Johnson, congress passed the Flag Protection Act of 1989, which provided criminal penalties for a person who "knowingly mutilates, defaces, physically defiles, burns, maintains on the floor or ground, or tramples upon any flag of the United States." Prosecuted for burning flags, defendants moved to dismiss the charges on the ground that the Act violated the First Amendment. Two United States District Courts held the Act unconstitutional. The Supreme Court affirmed.

The Court held that the case was governed by *Johnson,* rejecting an argument that *Johnson* should be reassessed in light of Congress' recognition of a national consensus favoring a prohibition on flag-burning.

"[A]ny suggestion that the Government's interest in suppressing speech becomes more weighty as popular opposition to that speech grows is foreign to the First Amendment."

Justice Stevens, joined by Chief Justice Rehnquist, Justice White and Justice O'Connor, dissented. Justice Stevens elaborated the argument in his *Johnson* dissent that Congress had a legitimate interest in preserving the symbolic value of the flag.

City of Erie v. Pap's A.M.

529 U.S. 277, 120 S.Ct. 1382, 146 L.Ed.2d 265 (2000).

Justice O'Connor announced the judgment of the Court and delivered the opinion of the Court with respect to Parts I and II, and an

opinion with respect to Parts III and IV, in which The Chief Justice, Justice Kennedy, and Justice Breyer join.

The city of Erie, Pennsylvania, enacted an ordinance banning public nudity. Respondent Pap's A.M. (hereinafter Pap's), which operated a nude dancing establishment in Erie, challenged the constitutionality of the ordinance and sought a permanent injunction against its enforcement. The Pennsylvania Supreme Court, although noting that this Court in Barnes v. Glen Theatre, Inc., 501 U.S. 560, (1991), had upheld an Indiana ordinance that was "strikingly similar" to Erie's, found that the public nudity sections of the ordinance violated respondent's right to freedom of expression under the United States Constitution. ... We hold that Erie's ordinance is a content-neutral regulation that satisfies the four-part test of United States v. O'Brien, ... Accordingly, we reverse the decision of the Pennsylvania Supreme Court....

I

On September 28, 1994, the city council for the city of Erie, Pennsylvania, enacted Ordinance 75–1994, a public indecency ordinance that makes it a summary offense to knowingly or intentionally appear in public in a "state of nudity." Respondent Pap's, a Pennsylvania corporation, operated an establishment in Erie known as "Kandyland" that featured totally nude erotic dancing performed by women. To comply with the ordinance, these dancers must wear, at a minimum, "pasties" and a "G-string." On October 14, 1994, two days after the ordinance went into effect, Pap's filed a complaint ... seeking declaratory relief and a permanent injunction against the enforcement of the ordinance.

    . . .

III

Being "in a state of nudity" is not an inherently expressive condition. As we explained in *Barnes*, however, nude dancing of the type at issue here is expressive conduct, although we think that it falls only within the outer ambit of the First Amendment's protection. ...

    . . .

In *Barnes*, we analyzed an almost identical statute, holding that Indiana's public nudity ban did not violate the First Amendment, although no five Members of the Court agreed on a single rationale for that conclusion. We now clarify that government restrictions on public nudity such as the ordinance at issue here should be evaluated under the framework set forth in *O'Brien* for content-neutral restrictions on symbolic speech.

    . . .

The ordinance here, like the statute in *Barnes*, is on its face a general prohibition on public nudity. By its terms, the ordinance regulates conduct alone. It does not target nudity that contains an erotic message; rather, it bans all public nudity, regardless of whether that nudity is accompanied by expressive activity. ...

    . . .

As Justice Souter noted in *Barnes*, "on its face, the governmental interest in combating prostitution and other criminal activity is not at all inherently related to expression." ... In that sense, this case is similar to *O'Brien*. ... [T]he Government regulation prohibiting the destruction of draft cards was aimed at maintaining the integrity of the Selective Service System and not at suppressing the message of draft resistance ... So too here, the ordinance prohibiting public nudity is aimed at combating crime and other negative secondary effects caused by the presence of adult entertainment establishments like Kandyland and not at suppressing the erotic message conveyed by this type of nude dancing. Put another way, the ordinance does not attempt to regulate the primary effects of the expression, i.e., the effect on the audience of watching nude erotic dancing, but rather the secondary effects, such as the impacts on public health, safety, and welfare, which we have previously recognized are "caused by the presence of even one such" establishment. ...

Although the Pennsylvania Supreme Court acknowledged that one goal of the ordinance was to combat the negative secondary effects associated with nude dancing establishments, the court concluded that the ordinance was nevertheless content based, relying on Justice White's position in dissent in *Barnes* for the proposition that a ban of this type necessarily has the purpose of suppressing the erotic message of the dance. ... A majority of the Court rejected that view in *Barnes*, and we do so again here.

... In light of the Pennsylvania court's determination that one purpose of the ordinance is to combat harmful secondary effects, the ban on public nudity here is no different from the ban on burning draft registration cards in *O'Brien*, ...

Justice Stevens argues that the ordinance enacts a complete ban on expression. We ... disagree ... The public nudity ban certainly has the effect of limiting one particular means of expressing the kind of erotic message being disseminated at Kandyland. But simply to define what is being banned as the "message" is to assume the conclusion. We did not analyze the regulation in *O'Brien* as having enacted a total ban on expression. ... Although there may be cases in which banning the means of expression so interferes with the message that it essentially bans the message, that is not the case here.

Even if we had not already rejected the view that a ban on public nudity is necessarily related to the suppression of the erotic message of nude dancing, we would do so now because the premise of such a view is flawed. The State's interest in preventing harmful secondary effects is not related to the suppression of expression. In trying to control the secondary effects of nude dancing, the ordinance seeks to deter crime and the other deleterious effects caused by the presence of such an establishment in the neighborhood. ...

... [E]ven if Erie's public nudity ban has some minimal effect on the erotic message by muting that portion of the expression that occurs when the last stitch is dropped, the dancers at Kandyland and other such establishments are free to perform wearing pasties and G-strings. Any effect on the overall expression is de minimis....

. . .

In [City of Renton v. Playtime Theatres, Inc., 475 U.S. 41 (1986)], the regulation explicitly treated "adult" movie theaters differently from other theaters, and defined "adult" theaters solely by reference to the content of their movies. ... We nonetheless treated the zoning regulation as content neutral because the ordinance was aimed at the secondary effects of adult theaters, a justification unrelated to the content of the adult movies themselves. ... Here, Erie's ordinance is on its face a content-neutral restriction on conduct. ...

... The ordinance prohibiting public nudity is therefore valid if it satisfies the four-factor test from *O'Brien* for evaluating restrictions on symbolic speech.

IV

Applying that standard here, we conclude that Erie's ordinance is justified under *O'Brien*. ... Because the nude dancing at Kandyland is of the same character as the adult entertainment at issue in *Renton*, ... it was reasonable for Erie to conclude that such nude dancing was likely to produce the same secondary effects. ... Regardless of whether Justice Souter now wishes to disavow his opinion in *Barnes* on this point, the evidentiary standard described in *Renton* controls here, and Erie meets that standard.

In any event, Erie also relied on its own findings. The preamble to the ordinance states that "the Council of the City of Erie has, at various times over more than a century, expressed its findings that certain lewd, immoral activities carried on in public places for profit are highly detrimental to the public health, safety and welfare, and lead to the debasement of both women and men, promote violence, public intoxication, prostitution and other serious criminal activity." ...

. . .

Justice Souter, however, would require Erie to develop a specific evidentiary record supporting its ordinance. ...

But whether the harm is evident to our "intuition," is not the proper inquiry. If it were, we would simply say there is no doubt that a regulation prohibiting public nudity would alleviate the harmful secondary effects associated with nude dancing. ...

As to the second point—whether the regulation furthers the government interest—it is evident that ... a ban on such nude dancing would further Erie's interest in preventing such secondary effects. To be sure, requiring dancers to wear pasties and G-strings may not greatly reduce these secondary effects, but *O'Brien* requires only that the regulation further the interest in combating such effects. ... It also may be true that a pasties and G-string requirement would not be as effective as, for example, a requirement that the dancers be fully clothed, but the city must balance its efforts to address the problem with the requirement that the restriction be no greater than necessary to further the city's interest.

... Justice Souter points out that zoning is an alternative means of addressing this problem. It is far from clear, however, that zoning imposes less of a burden on expression than the minimal requirement implemented here. In any event, since this is a content-neutral restriction, least restrictive means analysis is not required. ...

. . .

Justice Scalia, with whom Justice Thomas joins, concurring in the judgment.

. . .

II

... I agree that the decision of the Pennsylvania Supreme Court must be reversed, but disagree with the mode of analysis the Court has applied.

... In *Barnes*, I voted to uphold the challenged Indiana statute "not because it survives some lower level of First Amendment scrutiny, but because, as a general law regulating conduct and not specifically directed at expression, it is not subject to First Amendment scrutiny at all." ... Erie's ordinance, too, by its terms prohibits not merely nude dancing, but the act—irrespective of whether it is engaged in for expressive purposes—of going nude in public. ...

... When conduct other than speech itself is regulated, it is my view that the First Amendment is violated only "[w]here the government prohibits conduct precisely because of its communicative attributes." ... Here, even if one hypothesizes that the city's object was to suppress only nude dancing, that would not establish an intent to suppress what (if anything) nude dancing communicates. I do not feel the need, as the Court does, to identify some "secondary effects" associated with nude dancing that the city could properly seek to eliminate. (I am highly skeptical, to tell the truth, that the addition of pasties and g-strings will at all reduce the tendency of establishments such as Kandyland to attract crime and prostitution, and hence to foster sexually transmitted disease.) The traditional power of government to foster good morals (bonos mores), and the acceptability of the traditional judgment (if Erie wishes to endorse it) that nude public dancing itself is immoral, have not been repealed by the First Amendment.

Justice Souter, concurring in part and dissenting in part.

I ... agree with the analytical approach that the plurality employs in deciding this case. ... I do not believe, however, that the current record allows us to say that the city has made a sufficient evidentiary showing to sustain its regulation, and I would therefore vacate the decision of the Pennsylvania Supreme Court and remand the case for further proceedings.

I

. . .

... [T]he record before us today is deficient in its failure to reveal any evidence on which Erie may have relied, either for the seriousness of the threatened harm or for the efficacy of its chosen remedy. ... The plurality opinion in *Barnes* made no mention of evidentiary showings at all, and though my separate opinion did make a pass at the issue, I did not demand reliance on germane evidentiary demonstrations, whether specific to the statute in question or developed elsewhere. ...

... The final *O'Brien* requirement is that the incidental speech restriction be shown to be no greater than essential to achieve the government's legitimate purpose.... To deal with this issue, we have to ask what basis there is to think that the city would be unsuccessful in countering any secondary effects by the significantly lesser restriction of zoning to control the location of nude dancing, thus allowing for efficient law enforcement, restricting effects on property values, and limiting exposure of the public. The record shows that for 23 years there has been a zoning ordinance on the books to regulate the location of establishments like Kandyland, but the city has not enforced it....

. . .

Careful readers, and not just those on the Erie City Council, will of course realize that my partial dissent rests on a demand for an evidentiary basis that I failed to make when I concurred in *Barnes*, supra. I should have demanded the evidence then, too, and my mistake calls to mind Justice Jackson's foolproof explanation of a lapse of his own, when he quoted Samuel Johnson, " 'Ignorance, sir, ignorance.' " McGrath v. Kristensen, 340 U.S. 162, 178 (1950) (concurring opinion). I may not be less ignorant of nude dancing than I was nine years ago, but after many subsequent occasions to think further about the needs of the First Amendment, I have come to believe that a government must toe the mark more carefully than I first insisted. I hope it is enlightenment on my part, and acceptable even if a little late. . . .

. . .

Justice Stevens, with whom Justice Ginsburg joins, dissenting.

Far more important than the question whether nude dancing is entitled to the protection of the First Amendment are the dramatic changes in legal doctrine that the Court endorses today. Until now, the "secondary effects" of commercial enterprises featuring indecent entertainment have justified only the regulation of their location. For the first time, the Court has now held that such effects may justify the total suppression of protected speech. Indeed, the plurality opinion concludes that admittedly trivial advancements of a State's interests may provide the basis for censorship. The Court's commendable attempt to replace the fractured decision in Barnes v. Glen Theatre, Inc., . . . with a single coherent rationale is strikingly unsuccessful . . .

I

. . . Prior to the enactment of the ordinance, the dancers at Kandyland performed in the nude. . . . [A]fter its enactment they can perform precisely the same dances if they wear "pasties and G-strings." . . .

. . . If one assumes that the same erotic message is conveyed by nude dancers as by those wearing miniscule costumes, one means of expressing that message is banned; if one assumes that the messages are different, one of those messages is banned. In either event, the ordinance is a total ban.

The Court relies on the so-called "secondary effects" test to defend the ordinance. . . . Never before have we approved the use of that doctrine to justify a total ban on protected First Amendment expression. . . .

. . .

II

The Court's mishandling of our secondary effects cases is not limited to its approval of a total ban. It compounds that error by dramatically reducing the degree to which the State's interest must be furthered by the restriction imposed on speech . . .

In what can most delicately be characterized as an enormous understatement, the plurality concedes that "requiring dancers to wear pasties and G-strings may not greatly reduce these secondary effects." To believe that the mandatory addition of pasties and a G-string will have any kind of noticeable impact on secondary effects requires nothing short of a titanic surrender to the implausible. . . . It is one thing to say, however, that O'Brien is more lenient than the "more demanding standard" . . . It is quite another to say that the test can be satisfied by nothing more than the mere possibility of de minimis effects on the neighborhood.

. . .

SECTION 2.   COMPELLED AFFIRMATION OF BELIEF

WEST VIRGINIA STATE BOARD OF EDUCATION v. BARNETTE, 319 U.S. 624 (1943). A resolution of the Board of Education required all teachers and pupils to participate in the flag salute.

Justice Jackson's opinion for the Court concluded that the compulsory salute violated the First Amendment. Minersville School District v. Gobitis, 310 U.S. 586 (1940), which had sustained the validity of an identical requirement, was overruled. Justice Jackson noted that saluting the flag required "affirmation of a belief and an attitude of mind." His opinion included the following observations:

"It is now a commonplace that censorship or suppression of expression of opinion is tolerated by our Constitution only when the expression presents a clear and present danger of action of a kind the State is empowered to prevent and punish. It would seem that involuntary affirmation could be commanded only on even more immediate and urgent grounds than silence. But here the power of compulsion is invoked without any allegation that remaining passive during a flag salute ritual creates a clear and present danger that would justify an effort even to muffle expression. To sustain the compulsory flag salute we are required to say that a Bill of Rights which guards the individual's right to speak his own mind, left it open to public authorities to compel him to utter what is not in his mind.

. . .

"Nor does the issue as we see it turn on one's possession of particular religious views or the sincerity with which they are held. While religion supplies appellees' motive for enduring the discomforts of making the issue in this case, many citizens who do not share these religious views hold such a compulsory rite to infringe constitutional liberty of the individual. It is not necessary to inquire whether nonconformist beliefs will exempt from the duty to salute unless we first find power to make the salute a legal duty.

. . .

"If there is any fixed star in our constitutional constellation, it is that no official, high or petty, can prescribe what shall be orthodox in politics, nationalism, religion, or other matters of opinion or force citizens to confess by word or act their faith therein. If there are any circumstances which permit an exception, they do not now occur to us."

WOOLEY v. MAYNARD, 430 U.S. 705 (1977). George and Maxine Maynard were Jehovah's Witnesses, who had moral, religious and political objections to New Hampshire's license plate motto—"live free or die," which they covered up. Mr. Maynard was arrested and convicted under a law making it a misdemeanor to obscure the figures or letters on license plates. The United States Supreme Court affirmed a decision of a lower federal court enjoining enforcement of the ordinance against the Maynards.

Chief Justice Burger,'s opinion for the Court concluded that the case was controlled by *Barnette*.

"New Hampshire's statute in effect requires that appellees use their private property as a 'mobile billboard' for the State's ideological message—or suffer a penalty, as Maynard already has. As a condition to driving an automobile—a virtual necessity for most Americans—the Maynards must display 'Live Free or Die' to hundreds of people each day. The fact that most individuals agree with the thrust of New Hampshire's motto is not the test; most Americans also find the flag salute acceptable. The First Amendment protects the right of individuals to hold a point of view different from the majority and to refuse to foster, in the way New Hampshire commands, an idea they find morally objectionable.''

Justice Rehnquist, joined by Justice Blackmun, in dissent, argued that the Maynards had not been forced to advocate any point of view.

''The logic of the Court's opinion leads to startling, and I believe totally unacceptable, results. For example, the mottoes 'In God We Trust' and 'E Pluribus Unum' appear on the coin and currency of the United States. I cannot imagine that the statutes . . . proscribing defacement of U.S. currency impinge upon the First Amendment rights of an atheist. The fact that an atheist carries and uses United States currency does not, in any meaningful sense, convey any affirmation of belief on his part in the motto 'In God We Trust.' ''

SECTION 3.   FREEDOM OF ASSOCIATION

A.   INTRODUCTION

NAACP v. Alabama

357 U.S. 449, 78 S.Ct. 1163, 2 L.Ed.2d 1488 (1958).

[In 1956 the State Attorney General brought suit in a state court to enjoin the NAACP from conducting further activities within the State. It was alleged, among other things, that the Association had recruited members, solicited contributions and opened a regional office in the State; also it had assisted Negro students seeking admission to the State University and had supported the Negro boycott of the bus lines in Montgomery to compel the seating of passengers without regard to race. The State's pre-trial motion for the production of a large number of the Association's records, including the names and addresses of all of its Alabama "members" and "agents," was granted. The Association produced a large portion of the records, but refused to supply the membership lists, and was fined for contempt.]

Mr. Justice Harlan, delivered the opinion of the Court.

. . .

We think that the production order . . . must be regarded as entailing the likelihood of a substantial restraint upon the exercise by petitioner's members of their right to freedom of association. Petitioner has made an uncontroverted showing that on past occasions revelation of the identity of its rank-and-file members has exposed these members to economic reprisal, loss of employment, threat of physical coercion, and other manifestations of public hostility. Under these circumstances, we think it apparent that compelled disclosure of petitioner's Alabama membership is likely to affect adversely the ability of petitioner and its members to pursue their collective effort to foster beliefs which they admittedly have the right to advocate, in that it may induce members to withdraw from the Association and dissuade others from joining it because of fear of exposure of their beliefs shown through their associations and of the consequences of this exposure.

. . .

We turn to the final question whether Alabama has demonstrated an interest in obtaining the disclosures it seeks from petitioner which is sufficient to justify the deterrent effect which we have concluded these disclosures may well have on the free exercise by petitioner's members of their constitutionally protected right of association. . . .

. . .

Whether there was "justification" in this instance turns solely on the substantiality of Alabama's interest in obtaining the membership lists. . . . Without intimating the slightest view upon the merits of these issues, we are unable to perceive that the disclosure of the names of petitioner's rank-and-file members has a substantial bearing on either of them. . . .

. . .

We hold that the immunity from state scrutiny of membership lists which the Association claims on behalf of its members is here so related to the right of the members to pursue their lawful private interest privately and to associate freely with others in so doing as to come within the protection of the Fourteenth Amendment. And we conclude that Alabama has fallen short of showing a controlling justification for the deterrent effect on the free enjoyment of the right to associate which disclosure of membership lists is likely to have. Accordingly, the judgment of civil contempt and the $100,000 fine which resulted from petitioner's refusal to comply with the production order in this respect must fall. . . .

. . .

SPEECH AND NON–SPEECH ASSOCIATION

NAACP v. Button, 371 U.S. 415 (1963), concerned application of Virginia statutes, forbidding solicitation of legal business, to the NAACP's activities in litigating public school desegregation cases. The Court concluded that NAACP litigation was expression. It was "not a technique of resolving private differences" but a "means of achieving the lawful objectives of equality of treatment by all government." It was thus "a form of political expression." The Court held that restrictions imposed on the NAACP's litigation activities violated the first amendment.

Button emphasized that the first amendment rights involved stemmed from "[r]esort to the courts to seek vindication of constitutional rights" rather than "avaricious use of the legal process for purely private gain." In Brotherhood of R.R. Trainmen v. Virginia, 377 U.S. 1 (1964), however, the Court considered application of the Virginia prohibition of solicitation of legal business to the group legal services plan of a labor union. The plan channeled workers' personal injury suits to a group of lawyers. The Court concluded that the union's activities fell "just as clearly within the protection of the First Amendment" as those involved in *Button,* and application of the statute violated the first amendment.

NAACP v. Alabama had spoken of "association for the advancement of beliefs and ideas." NAACP v. Button stressed group activity seeking "through lawful means to achieve political ends." The *R.R. Trainmen* case, however, more broadly extended first amendment association rights to group activities "for the lawful purpose of helping and advising one another in asserting . . . rights." Does the first amendment's protection of freedom of association extend to all group activities of groups with political objectives? Does it extend to association for any purpose?

B.   LIMITS ON ASSOCIATION ACTIVITIES

NAACP v. Claiborne Hardware Co.

458 U.S. 886, 102 S.Ct. 3409, 73 L.Ed.2d 1215 (1982).

Justice Stevens delivered the opinion of the Court.

The term "concerted action" encompasses unlawful conspiracies and constitutionally protected assemblies. The "looseness and pliability" of legal doctrine applicable to concerted action led Justice Jackson to note that certain joint activities have a "chameleon-like" character. The boycott of white merchants in Claiborne County, Miss., that gave rise to this litigation had such a character; it included elements of criminality and elements of majesty. Evidence that fear of reprisals caused some black citizens to withhold their patronage from respondents' businesses convinced the Supreme Court of Mississippi that the entire boycott was unlawful and that each of the 92 petitioners was liable for all of its economic consequences. Evidence that persuasive rhetoric, determination to remedy past injustices, and a host of voluntary decisions by free citizens were the critical factors in the boycott's success presents us with the question whether the state court's judgment is consistent with the Constitution of the United States.

I

[The boycott, begun in 1966, led to this state court action, filed in 1969 by several merchants, for damages and injunctive relief. Defendants included the NAACP, Aaron Henry (President of the Mississippi NAACP), Charles Evers (Field Secretary for the Mississippi NAACP), and 144 individuals participating in the boycott. After a lengthy trial that concluded in 1976, the trial court found the defendants liable. A broad permanent injunction was entered, and damages in excess of one and one quarter million dollars were awarded. The Mississippi Supreme Court upheld the imposition of liability against most defendants on the common law tort theory of malicious interference with plaintiffs' business.]

II

... We consider first whether petitioners' activities are protected in any respect by the Federal Constitution and, if they are, what effect such protection has on a lawsuit of this nature.

A

The boycott of white merchants at issue in this case took many forms. The boycott was launched at a meeting of a local branch of the NAACP attended by several hundred persons. Its acknowledged purpose was to secure compliance by both civic and business leaders with a lengthy list of demands for equality and racial justice. The boycott was supported by speeches and nonviolent picketing. Participants repeatedly encouraged others to join in its cause.

Each of these elements of the boycott is a form of speech or conduct that is ordinarily entitled to protection under the First and Fourteenth Amendments. The black citizens named as defendants in this action banded together and collectively expressed their dissatisfaction with a social structure that had denied them rights to equal treatment and respect....

. . . .

Speech itself also was used to further the aims of the boycott. Nonpartici-
pants repeatedly were urged to join the common cause, both through public
address and through personal solicitation. These elements of the boycott
involve speech in its most direct form. In addition, names of boycott violators
were read aloud at meetings at the First Baptist Church and published in a
local black newspaper. Petitioners admittedly sought to persuade others to join
the boycott through social pressure and the "threat" of social ostracism. Speech
does not lose its protected character, however, simply because it may embarrass
others or coerce them into action....

. . .

In sum, the boycott clearly involved constitutionally protected activity....
Through exercise of these First Amendment rights, petitioners sought to bring
about political, social, and economic change. Through speech, assembly, and
petition—rather than through riot or revolution—petitioners sought to change
a social order that had consistently treated them as second-class citizens.

The presence of protected activity, however, does not end the relevant
constitutional inquiry. Governmental regulation that has an incidental effect on
First Amendment freedoms may be justified in certain narrowly defined instances. ... A nonviolent and totally voluntary boycott may have a disruptive
effect on local economic conditions. This Court has recognized the strong
governmental interest in certain forms of economic regulation, even though
such regulation may have an incidental effect on rights of speech and association. ... The right of business entities to "associate" to suppress competition
may be curtailed. ... Unfair trade practices may be restricted. Secondary
boycotts and picketing by labor unions may be prohibited, as part of "Congress'
striking of the delicate balance between union freedom of expression and the
ability of neutral employers, employees, and consumers to remain free from
coerced participation in industrial strife." ... See International Longshoremen's Assoc. v. Allied International, Inc., 456 U.S. 212 ...[a]

While States have broad power to regulate economic activity, we do not
find a comparable right to prohibit peaceful political activity such as that found
in the boycott in this case....

. . .

It is not disputed that a major purpose of the boycott in this case was to
influence governmental action.... Petitioners sought to vindicate rights of
equality and of freedom that lie at the heart of the Fourteenth Amendment
itself. The right of the States to regulate economic activity could not justify a
complete prohibition against a nonviolent, politically motivated boycott designed to force governmental and economic change and to effectuate rights
guaranteed by the Constitution itself.

... We hold that the nonviolent elements of petitioners' activities are
entitled to the protection of the First Amendment.

---

a. The cited case was decided two and
one-half months before *Claiborne Hardware*.
A unanimous Court held that a politically
motivated refusal by a longshoremen's union
to unload cargo from the Soviet Union was a
secondary boycott prohibited by the National
Labor Relations Act. A first amendment argument by the union was rejected summarily.
Secondary labor picketing was not protected
by the first amendment. "It would seem even
clearer that conduct designed not to communicate but to coerce merits still less consideration."

B

... [W]e consider here the effect of our holding that much of petitioners' conduct was constitutionally protected on the ability of the State to impose liability for elements of the boycott that were not so protected.

... [T]he presence of activity protected by the First Amendment imposes restraints on the grounds that may give rise to damage liability and on the persons who may be held accountable for those damages.

. . .

... Civil liability may not be imposed merely because an individual belonged to a group, some members of which committed acts of violence. For liability to be imposed by reason of association alone, it is necessary to establish that the group itself possessed unlawful goals and that the individual held a specific intent to further those illegal aims....

III

The chancellor awarded respondents damages for all business losses that were sustained during a 7 year period beginning in 1966 and ending December 31, 1972. With the exception of Aaron Henry, all defendants were held jointly and severally liable for these losses. The chancellor's findings were consistent with his view that voluntary participation in the boycott was a sufficient basis on which to impose liability. ... In light of the principles set forth above, it is evident that such a damage award may not be sustained in this case.

. . .

IV

. . .

... The use of speeches, marches, and threats of social ostracism cannot provide the basis for a damages award. But violent conduct is beyond the pale of constitutional protection.

The taint of violence colored the conduct of some of the petitioners. They, of course, may be held liable for the consequences of their violent deeds. The burden of demonstrating that it colored the entire collective effort, however, is not satisfied by evidence that violence occurred or even that violence contributed to the success of the boycott. ... The burden of demonstrating that fear rather than protected conduct was the dominant force in the movement is heavy. ... The findings of the chancellor ... are constitutionally insufficient to support the judgment that all petitioners are liable for all losses resulting from the boycott.

The judgment is reversed. The case is remanded for further proceedings not inconsistent with this opinion.

It is so ordered.

Justice Rehnquist concurs in the result.

Justice Marshall took no part in the consideration or decision of this case.

C.   LIMITS ON ASSOCIATION MEMBERSHIP POLICIES

ROBERTS v. UNITED STATES JAYCEES, 468 U.S. 609 (1984). After the Minneapolis and St. Paul chapters of the Jaycees began to admit women as regular members, the national organization advised the chapters that their charters would be revoked. The chapters filed charges of discrimination with the Minnesota Department of Human Rights, alleging that exclusion of women by the national organization violated the Minnesota Human Rights Act, which prohibits discrimination on the basis of gender by a business offering goods or services to the public. The national organization brought suit to enjoin enforcement of the Act against it. The court held that applying the Minnesota Statute to the Jaycees did not violate the Constitution. Justice Brennan's opinion described the two different freedoms of association:

> "Our decisions have referred to constitutionally protected 'freedom of association' in two distinct senses. In one line of decisions, the Court has concluded that choices to enter into and maintain certain intimate human relationships must be secured against undue intrusion by the State because of the role of such relationships in safeguarding the individual freedom that is central to our constitutional scheme. In this respect, freedom of association receives protection as a fundamental element of personal liberty. In another set of decisions, the Court has recognized a right to associate for the purpose of engaging in those activities protected by the First Amendment—speech, assembly, petition for the redress of grievances, and the exercise of religion. The Constitution guarantees freedom of association of this kind as an indispensable means of preserving other individual liberties."

There had been no violation of the freedom of intimate association:

> "[T]he local chapters of the Jaycees are neither small nor selective. Moreover, much of the activity central to the formation and maintenance of the association involves the participation of strangers to that relationship. Accordingly, we conclude that the Jaycees chapters lack the distinctive characteristics that might afford constitutional protection to the decision of its members to exclude women."

Nor had there been violation of the freedom of expressive association. The Jaycees did not demonstrate that there had been:

> "any serious burdens on the male members' freedom of expressive association.... To be sure, ... a 'not insubstantial part' of the Jaycees' activities constitutes protected expression on political, economic, cultural, and social affairs. ... There is, however, no basis in the record for concluding that admission of women as full voting members will impede the organization's ability to engage in these protected activities or to disseminate its preferred views"

BOARD OF DIRECTORS OF ROTARY INTERNATIONAL v. ROTARY CLUB OF DUARTE, 481 U.S. 537 (1987). The Court held that application of a State antidiscrimination law to require admission of women to membership in local rotary clubs did not deny freedom of intimate association or freedom of expressive association. As to freedom of intimate association, the critical factors were the organization's "size, purpose, selectivity, and whether others are excluded from critical aspects of the relationship." As to freedom of expressive association, rotary clubs do not take positions on "public questions" as a matter of policy. Even if the State antidiscrimination act "does work some slight infringement" on expressive association, it was justified by the "compelling interest in eliminating discrimination against women." In a footnote, the court said that it had not decided the extent of First Amendment protection of associational rights "in the many clubs and other entities with selective membership." Each case would require "a careful inquiry into the objective characteristics of the particular relationship at issue."

Boy Scouts of America v. Dale

530 U.S. 640, 120 S.Ct. 2446, 147 L.Ed.2d 554 (2000).

Chief Justice Rehnquist delivered the opinion of the Court.

Petitioners are the Boy Scouts of America and the Monmouth Council, a division of the Boy Scouts of America (collectively, Boy Scouts). . . . The Boy Scouts asserts that homosexual conduct is inconsistent with the values it seeks to instill. Respondent is James Dale, a former Eagle Scout whose adult membership in the Boy Scouts was revoked when the Boy Scouts learned that he is an avowed homosexual and gay rights activist. The New Jersey Supreme Court held that New Jersey's public accommodations law requires that the Boy Scouts admit Dale. This case presents the question whether applying New Jersey's public accommodations law in this way violates the Boy Scouts' First Amendment right of expressive association. We hold that it does.

I

. . .

II

In Roberts v. United States Jaycees . . . we observed that "implicit in the right to engage in activities protected by the First Amendment" is "a corresponding right to associate with others in pursuit of a wide variety of political, social, economic, educational, religious, and cultural ends." . . . . Forcing a group to accept certain members may impair the ability of the group to express those views, and only those views, that it intends to express. . . .

The forced inclusion of an unwanted person in a group infringes the group's freedom of expressive association if the presence of that person affects in a significant way the group's ability to advocate public or private viewpoints. New York State Club Assn., Inc. v. City of New York, 487 U.S. 1, 13 (1988). But the freedom of expressive association, like many freedoms, is not absolute. We have held that the freedom could be overridden "by regulations adopted to serve compelling state interests, unrelated to the suppression of ideas, that cannot be achieved through means significantly less restrictive of associational freedoms." . . .

To determine whether a group is protected by the First Amendment's expressive associational right, we must determine whether the group engages in "expressive association." The First Amendment's protection of expressive association is not reserved for advocacy groups. But to come within its ambit, a group must engage in some form of expression, whether it be public or private.

Because this is a First Amendment case where the ultimate conclusions of law are virtually inseparable from findings of fact, we are obligated to independently review the factual record to ensure that the state court's judgment does not unlawfully intrude on free expression. . . . The record reveals the following. The Boy Scouts is a private, nonprofit organization. According to its mission statement:

"It is the mission of the Boy Scouts of America to serve others by helping to instill values in young people and, in other ways, to prepare them to make ethical choices over their lifetime in achieving their full potential.

"The values we strive to instill are based on those found in the Scout Oath and Law:

"On my honor I will do my best to do my duty to God and my country and to obey the Scout Law; to help other people at all times; to keep myself physically strong, mentally awake, and morally straight.

"Scout Law

"A Scout is:

"Trustworthy Obedient Loyal Cheerful Helpful Thrifty Friendly Brave Courteous Clean Kind Reverent."

Thus, the general mission of the Boy Scouts is clear: "[T]o instill values in young people." The Boy Scouts seeks to instill these values by having its adult leaders spend time with the youth members, instructing and engaging them in activities like camping, archery, and fishing. During the time spent with the youth members, the scoutmasters and assistant scoutmasters inculcate them with the Boy Scouts' values—both expressly and by example. It seems indisputable that an association that seeks to transmit such a system of values engages in expressive activity. . . .

Given that the Boy Scouts engages in expressive activity, we must determine whether the forced inclusion of Dale as an assistant scoutmaster would significantly affect the Boy Scouts' ability to advocate public or private viewpoints. This inquiry necessarily requires us first to explore, to a limited extent, the nature of the Boy Scouts' view of homosexuality.

. . . The Boy Scouts asserts that homosexual conduct is inconsistent with the values embodied in the Scout Oath and Law, particularly with the values represented by the terms "morally straight" and "clean."

Obviously, the Scout Oath and Law do not expressly mention sexuality or sexual orientation. And the terms "morally straight" and "clean" are by no means self-defining. Different people would attribute to those terms very different meanings. . . .

The New Jersey Supreme Court analyzed the Boy Scouts' beliefs and found that the "exclusion of members solely on the basis of their sexual orientation is inconsistent with Boy Scouts' commitment to a diverse and 'representative' membership . . ." The court concluded that the exclusion of members like Dale "appears antithetical to the organization's goals and philosophy." But our cases reject this sort of inquiry; it is not the role of the courts to reject a group's expressed values because they disagree with those values or find them internally inconsistent. . . .

The Boy Scouts asserts that it "teach[es] that homosexual conduct is not morally straight," and that it does "not want to promote homosexual conduct as a legitimate form of behavior." We accept the Boy Scouts' assertion. We need not inquire further to determine the nature of the Boy Scouts' expression with respect to homosexuality. But because the record before us contains written evidence of the Boy Scouts' viewpoint, we look to it as instructive, if only on the question of the sincerity of the professed beliefs.

. . .

. . . at least as of 1978—the year James Dale entered Scouting—the official position of the Boy Scouts was that avowed homosexuals were not to be Scout leaders.

A position statement promulgated by the Boy Scouts in 1991 (after Dale's membership was revoked but before this litigation was filed) also supports its current view . . .

. . .

We must then determine whether Dale's presence as an assistant scoutmaster would significantly burden the Boy Scouts' desire to not "promote homosexual conduct as a legitimate form of behavior." As we give deference to an association's assertions regarding the nature of its expression, we must also give deference to an association's view of what would impair its expression. . . . Dale's presence in the Boy Scouts would, at the very least, force the organization to send a message, both to the youth members and the world, that the Boy Scouts accepts homosexual conduct as a legitimate form of behavior.

Hurley [v. Irish–American Gay, Lesbian and Bisexual Group of Boston, Inc., 515 U.S. 557 (1995)] is illustrative on this point. There we considered whether the application of Massachusetts' public accommodations law to require the organizers of a private St. Patrick's Day parade to include among the marchers an Irish–American gay, lesbian, and bisexual group, GLIB, violated the parade organizers' First Amendment rights. We noted that the parade organizers did not wish to exclude the GLIB members because of their sexual orientations, but because they wanted to march behind a GLIB banner. . . .

Here, we have found that the Boy Scouts believes that homosexual conduct is inconsistent with the values it seeks to instill in its youth members; it will not "promote homosexual conduct as a legitimate form of behavior." As the presence of GLIB in Boston's St. Patrick's Day parade would have interfered with the parade organizers' choice not to propound a particular point of view, the presence of Dale as an assistant scoutmaster would just as surely interfere with the Boy Scout's choice not to propound a point of view contrary to its beliefs.

The New Jersey Supreme Court determined that the Boy Scouts' ability to disseminate its message was not significantly affected by the forced inclusion of Dale as an assistant scoutmaster . . . We disagree . . .

First, associations do not have to associate for the "purpose" of disseminating a certain message in order to be entitled to the protections of the First Amendment. An association must merely engage in expressive activity that could be impaired in order to be entitled to protection. For example, the purpose of the St. Patrick's Day parade in *Hurley* was not to espouse any views about sexual orientation, but we held that the parade organizers had a right to exclude certain participants nonetheless.

Second, even if the Boy Scouts discourages Scout leaders from disseminating views on sexual issues—a fact that the Boy Scouts disputes . . .—the First Amendment protects the Boy Scouts' method of expression. If the Boy Scouts wishes Scout leaders to avoid questions of sexuality and teach only by example, this fact does not negate the sincerity of its belief discussed above.

Third, the First Amendment simply does not require that every member of a group agree on every issue in order for the group's policy to be "expressive association." The Boy Scouts takes an official position with respect to homosexual conduct, and that is sufficient for First Amendment purposes. In this same vein, Dale makes much of the claim that the Boy Scouts does not revoke the membership of heterosexual Scout leaders that openly disagree with the Boy Scouts' policy on sexual orientation. But if this is true, it is irrelevant. . . . The Boy Scouts has a First Amendment right to choose to send one message but not the other. . . .

Having determined that the Boy Scouts is an expressive association and that the forced inclusion of Dale would significantly affect its expression, we inquire whether the application of New Jersey's public accommodations law to require that the Boy Scouts accept Dale as an assistant scoutmaster runs afoul of the Scouts' freedom of expressive association. We conclude that it does.

State public accommodations laws were originally enacted to prevent discrimination in traditional places of public accommodation—like inns and trains.... Over time, the public accommodations laws have expanded to cover more places. ... As the definition of "public accommodation" has expanded from clearly commercial entities, such as restaurants, bars, and hotels, to membership organizations such as the Boy Scouts, the potential for conflict between state public accommodations laws and the First Amendment rights of organizations has increased.

. . .

Dale contends that we should apply the intermediate standard of review enunciated in United States v. O'Brien ... to evaluate the competing interests. There the Court enunciated a four-part test for review of a governmental regulation that has only an incidental effect on protected speech ... But New Jersey's public accommodations law directly and immediately affects associational rights, in this case associational rights that enjoy First Amendment protection. Thus, *O'Brien* is inapplicable.

In *Hurley*, we applied traditional First Amendment analysis to hold that the application of the Massachusetts public accommodations law to a parade violated the First Amendment rights of the parade organizers. ... [T]he analysis we applied there is similar to the analysis we apply here. ... The state interests embodied in New Jersey's public accommodations law do not justify such a severe intrusion on the Boy Scouts' rights to freedom of expressive association. That being the case, we hold that the First Amendment prohibits the State from imposing such a requirement through the application of its public accommodations law.

. . .

The judgment of the New Jersey Supreme Court is reversed, and the cause remanded for further proceedings not inconsistent with this opinion.

It is so ordered.

Justice Stevens, with whom Justice Souter, Justice Ginsburg and Justice Breyer join, dissenting.

... The New Jersey Supreme Court's construction of the statutory definition of a "place of public accommodation" has given its statute a more expansive coverage than most similar state statutes. ... The question in this case is whether that expansive construction trenches on the federal constitutional rights of the Boy Scouts of America (BSA).

. . .

... New Jersey's law ... does not "impos[e] any serious burdens" on BSA's "collective effort on behalf of [its] shared goals," ... nor does it force BSA to communicate any message that it does not wish to endorse. New Jersey's law, therefore, abridges no constitutional right of the Boy Scouts.

I

. . .

In this case, Boy Scouts of America contends that it teaches the young boys who are Scouts that homosexuality is immoral. ... This contention, quite plainly, requires us to look at what, exactly, are the values that BSA actually teaches.

. . .

It is plain as the light of day that neither one of these principles—"morally straight" and "clean"—says the slightest thing about homosexuality. Indeed, neither term in the Boy Scouts' Law and Oath expresses any position whatsoever on sexual matters.

. . .

II

. . .

... BSA's policy statements fail to establish any clear, consistent, and unequivocal position on homosexuality. Nor did BSA have any reason to think Dale's sexual conduct, as opposed to his orientation, was contrary to the group's values.

. . .

III

... [W]e have routinely and easily rejected assertions of this right by expressive organizations with discriminatory membership policies, such as private schools, law firms, and labor organizations. In fact, until today, we have never once found a claimed right to associate in the selection of members to prevail in the face of a State's antidiscrimination law. To the contrary, we have squarely held that a State's antidiscrimination law does not violate a group's right to associate simply because the law conflicts with that group's exclusionary membership policy.

. . .

... BSA has, at most, simply adopted an exclusionary membership policy and has no shared goal of disapproving of homosexuality. ... In short, Boy Scouts of America is simply silent on homosexuality. There is no shared goal or collective effort to foster a belief about homosexuality at all—let alone one that is significantly burdened by admitting homosexuals.

. . .

IV

... [T]he majority insists that we must "give deference to an association's assertions regarding the nature of its expression" and "we must also give deference to an association's view of what would impair its expression.". . . .

. . .

... An organization can adopt the message of its choice, and it is not this Court's place to disagree with it. But we must inquire whether the group is, in fact, expressing a message (whatever it may be) and whether that message (if one is expressed) is significantly affected by a State's antidiscrimination law.
. . .

Surely there are instances in which an organization that truly aims to foster a belief at odds with the purposes of a State's antidiscrimination laws will have a First Amendment right to association that precludes forced compliance with those laws. But that right is not a freedom to discriminate at will, nor is it a right to maintain an exclusionary membership policy simply out of fear of what the public reaction would be if the group's membership were opened up. . . .

. . .

V

. . .

Dale's inclusion in the Boy Scouts is nothing like the case in *Hurley*. His participation sends no cognizable message to the Scouts or to the world. Unlike GLIB, Dale did not carry a banner or a sign; he did not distribute any fact sheet; and he expressed no intent to send any message. If there is any kind of message being sent, then, it is by the mere act of joining the Boy Scouts. Such an act does not constitute an instance of symbolic speech under the First Amendment.

. . . [I]f merely joining a group did constitute symbolic speech . . . , then the right of free speech effectively becomes a limitless right to exclude for every organization, whether or not it engages in any expressive activities. . . .

The only apparent explanation for the majority's holding, then, is that homosexuals are simply so different from the rest of society that their presence alone—unlike any other individual's—should be singled out for special First Amendment treatment. . . .

. . .

VI

Unfavorable opinions about homosexuals "have ancient roots." . . .

. . . [S]uch prejudices are still prevalent and . . . have caused serious and tangible harm to countless members of the class New Jersey seeks to protect . . . That harm can only be aggravated by the creation of a constitutional shield for a policy that is itself the product of a habitual way of thinking about strangers. . . .

. . . I respectfully dissent.

Justice Souter, with whom Justice Ginsburg and Justice Breyer join, dissenting.

I join Justice Stevens' dissent but add this further word . . .

. . .

. . . I conclude that BSA has not made out an expressive association claim, . . . because of its failure to make sexual orientation the subject of any unequivocal advocacy, . . .

If, on the other hand, an expressive association claim has met the conditions Justice Stevens describes as necessary, there may well be circumstances in which the antidiscrimination law must yield, as he says. It is certainly possible for an individual to become so identified with a position as to epitomize it publicly. When that position is at odds with a group's advocated position, applying an antidiscrimination statute to require the group's acceptance of the individual in a position of group leadership could so modify or muddle or frustrate the group's advocacy as to violate the expressive associational right. While it is not our business here to rule on any such hypothetical, it is at least clear that our estimate of the progressive character of the group's position will be irrelevant to the First Amendment analysis if such a case comes to us for decision.

D.   COMPULSORY ASSOCIATION MEMBERSHIP

Keller v. State Bar of California

496 U.S. 1, 110 S.Ct. 2228, 110 L.Ed.2d 1 (1990).

Chief Justice Rehnquist delivered the opinion of the Court.

Petitioners, members of the State Bar of California, sued that body claiming its use of their membership dues to finance certain ideological or political activities to which they were opposed violated their rights under the First Amendment of the United States Constitution. The Supreme Court of California rejected this challenge on the grounds that respondent State Bar is a state agency, and as such may use the dues for any purpose within its broad statutory authority. We agree that lawyers admitted to practice in the State may be required to join and pay dues to the State Bar, but disagree as to the scope of permissible dues-financed activities in which respondent may engage.

Respondent State Bar is an organization created under California law to regulate the State's legal profession. It is an entity commonly referred to as an "integrated bar"—an association of attorneys in which membership and dues are required as a condition of practicing law in a State.... The association performs a variety of functions ... "[T]he State Bar for many years has lobbied the Legislature and other governmental agencies, filed amicus curiae briefs in pending cases, held an annual conference of delegates at which issues of current interest are debated and resolutions approved, and engaged in a variety of education programs." These activities are financed principally through the use of membership dues.

Petitioners, 21 members of the State Bar, sued in state court claiming that through these activities respondent expends mandatory dues payments to advance political and ideological causes to which they do not subscribe....

. . .

In Lathrop v. Donohue, 367 U.S. 820 (1961), a Wisconsin lawyer claimed that he could not constitutionally be compelled to join and financially support a state bar association which expressed opinions on, and attempted to influence, legislation. Six Members of this Court, relying on Railway Employees v. Hanson, 351 U.S. 225 (1956), rejected this claim. ...

. . .

The *Lathrop* plurality ... expressly reserved judgment on Lathrop's additional claim that his free speech rights were violated by the Wisconsin Bar's use of his mandatory dues to support objectionable political activities.... Petitioners here present this very claim for decision, contending that the use of their compulsory dues to finance political and ideological activities of the State Bar with which they disagree violates their rights of free speech guaranteed by the First Amendment.

In Abood v. Detroit Board of Education, 431 U.S. 209 (1977), the Court confronted the issue of whether, consistent with the First Amendment, agency-shop dues of nonunion public employees could be used to support political and ideological causes of the union which were unrelated to collective-bargaining activities. We held that while the Constitution did not prohibit a union from spending "funds for the expression of political views ... or toward the advancement of other ideological causes not germane to its duties as collective-bargaining representative," the Constitution did require that such expenditures be "financed from charges, dues, or assessments paid by employees who [did] not object to advancing those ideas and who [were] not coerced into doing so against their will by the threat of loss of governmental employment." ... [I]n the later case of Ellis v. Railway Clerks, 466 U.S. 435 (1984), the Court made it clear that the principles of *Abood* apply equally to employees in the private sector....

... [T]he California Supreme Court in this case held that respondent's status as a regulated state agency exempted it from any constitutional constraints on the use of its dues.... Respondent also urges this position, invoking the so-called "government speech" doctrine [arguing that] "[t]he government must take substantive positions and decide disputed issues to govern.... So long as it bases its actions on legitimate goals, government may speak despite citizen disagreement with its message, for government is not required to be content-neutral." ...

... The State Bar of California is a good deal different from most other entities that would be regarded in common parlance as "governmental agencies." Its principal funding comes not from appropriations made to it by the legislature, but from dues levied on its members by the Board of Governors. ...

There is, by contrast, a substantial analogy between the relationship of the State Bar and its members, on the one hand, and the relation of the employee unions and their members, on the other. The reason behind the legislative enactment of "agency shop" laws is to prevent "free riders" ... from avoiding their fair share of the cost of a process from which they benefit. The members of the State Bar concededly do not benefit as directly ..., but the position of the organized bars has generally been that they prefer a large measure of self-regulation to regulation conducted by a government body which has little or no connection with the profession. ... It is entirely appropriate that all of the lawyers who derive benefit from the unique status of being among those admitted to practice before the courts should be called upon to pay a fair share of the cost of the professional involvement in this effort.

But the very specialized characteristics of the State Bar of California discussed above served to distinguish it from the role of the typical government official or agency. Government officials are expected as a part of the democratic process to represent and to espouse the views of a majority of their constituents. ... If every citizen were to have a right to insist that no one paid by public funds express a view with which he disagreed, debate over issues of great concern to the public would be limited to those in the private sector, and the process of government as we know it radically transformed....

The State Bar of California was created, not to participate in the general government of the State, but to provide specialized professional advice to those with the ultimate responsibility of governing the legal profession. Its members and officers are such not because they are citizens or voters, but because they are lawyers. We think that these differences between the State Bar, on the one hand, and traditional government agencies and officials, on the other hand, render unavailing respondent's argument that it is not subject to the same constitutional rule with respect to the use of compulsory dues as are labor unions representing public and private employees.

. . .

Abood held that a union could not expend a dissenting individual's dues for ideological activities not "germane" to the purpose for which compelled association was justified: collective bargaining. Here the compelled association and integrated bar is justified by the State's interest in regulating the legal profession and improving the quality of legal services. The State Bar may therefore constitutionally fund activities germane to those goals out of the mandatory dues of all members. It may not, however, in such manner fund activities of an ideological nature which fall outside of those areas of activity. The difficult question, of course, is to define the latter class of activities.

. . .

. . . [T]he guiding standard must be whether the challenged expenditures are necessarily or reasonably incurred for the purpose of regulating the legal profession or "improving the quality of the legal service available to the people of the State." . . .

. . .

Precisely where the line falls between those State Bar activities in which the officials and members of the Bar are acting essentially as professional advisors to those ultimately charged with the regulation of the legal profession, on the one hand, and those activities having political or ideological coloration which are not reasonably related to the advancement of such goals, on the other, will not always be easy to discern. But the extreme ends of the spectrum are clear: Compulsory dues may not be expended to endorse or advance a gun control or nuclear weapons freeze initiative; at the other end of the spectrum petitioners have no valid constitutional objection to their compulsory dues being spent for activities connected with disciplining members of the bar or proposing ethical codes for the profession.

. . .

In addition to their claim for relief based on respondent's use of their mandatory dues, petitioners' complaint also requested an injunction prohibiting the State Bar from using its name to advance political and ideological causes or beliefs. This request for relief appears to implicate a much broader freedom of association claim than was at issue in *Lathrop*. Petitioners challenge not only their "compelled financial support of group activities," but urge that they cannot be compelled to associate with an organization that engages in political or ideological activities beyond those for which mandatory financial support is justified under the principles of *Lathrop* and *Abood*. The California courts did not address this claim, and we decline to do so in the first instance. The state courts remain free, of course, to consider this issue on remand.

The judgment of the Supreme Court of California is reversed, and the case is remanded for further proceedings not inconsistent with this opinion.

Reversed.

United States v. United Foods, Inc.

533 U.S. 405, 121 S.Ct. 2334, 150 L.Ed.2d 438 (2001).

Justice Kennedy delivered the opinion of the Court.

Four Terms ago, in Glickman v. Wileman Brothers & Elliott, Inc., 521 U. S. 457 (1997), the Court rejected a First Amendment challenge to the constitutionality of a series of agricultural marketing orders that, as part of a larger regulatory marketing scheme, required producers of certain California tree fruit to pay assessments for product advertising. In this case a federal statute mandates assessments on handlers of fresh mushrooms to fund advertising for the product. . . .

The statute in question, enacted by Congress in 1990, is the Mushroom Promotion, Research, and Consumer Information Act ... The Act authorizes the Secretary of Agriculture to establish a Mushroom Council to pursue the statute's goals. Mushroom producers and importers, as defined by the statute, submit nominations from among their group to the Secretary, who then designates the Council membership. ... To fund its programs, the Act allows the Council to impose mandatory assessments upon handlers of fresh mushrooms in an amount not to exceed one cent per pound of mushrooms produced or imported. ... The assessments can be used for "projects of mushroom promotion, research, consumer information, and industry information." ... It is undisputed, though, that most monies raised by the assessments are spent for generic advertising to promote mushroom sales.

Respondent United Foods, Inc., is a large agricultural enterprise based in Tennessee. It grows and distributes many crops and products, including fresh mushrooms. In 1996 respondent refused to pay its mandatory assessments under the Act. The forced subsidy for generic advertising, it contended, is a violation of the First Amendment. ... The United States filed an action in the United States District Court, ... seeking an order compelling respondent to pay....

After *Glickman* was decided,.... [t]he District Court, holding *Glickman* dispositive of the First Amendment challenge, granted the Government's motion for summary judgment. The Court of Appeals ... reversed ... We agree with the Court of Appeals and now affirm.

. . .

We have used standards for determining the validity of speech regulations which accord less protection to commercial speech than to other expression. ... That approach, in turn, has been subject to some criticism. ... We need not enter into the controversy, for even viewing commercial speech as entitled to lesser protection, we find no basis under either *Glickman* or our other precedents to sustain the compelled assessments sought in this case. It should be noted, moreover, that the Government itself does not rely upon *Central Hudson* to challenge the Court of Appeals decision, and we therefore do not consider whether the Governments interest could be considered substantial for purposes of the *Central Hudson* test. The question is whether the government may underwrite and sponsor speech with a certain viewpoint using special subsidies exacted from a designated class of persons, some of whom object to the idea being advanced.

... Our precedents concerning compelled contributions to speech provide the beginning point for our analysis. The fact that the speech is in aid of a commercial purpose does not deprive respondent of all First Amendment protection ... The subject matter of the speech may be of interest to but a small segment of the population; yet those whose business and livelihood depend in some way upon the product involved no doubt deem First Amendment protection to be just as important for them as it is for other discrete, little noticed groups in a society which values the freedom resulting from speech in all its diverse parts. First Amendment concerns apply here because of the requirement that producers subsidize speech with which they disagree.

... Here the disagreement could be seen as minor: Respondent wants to convey the message that its brand of mushrooms is superior to those grown by other producers. It objects to being charged for a message which seems to be favored by a majority of producers. The message is that mushrooms are worth consuming whether or not they are branded. First Amendment values are at serious risk if the government can compel a particular citizen, or a discrete group of citizens, to pay special subsidies for speech on the side that it favors; and there is no apparent principle which distinguishes out of hand minor debates about whether a branded mushroom is better than just any mushroom. As a consequence, the compelled funding for the advertising must pass First Amendment scrutiny.

In the Governments view the assessment in this case is permitted by *Glickman* because it is similar in important respects. It imposes no restraint on the freedom of an objecting party to communicate its own message; the program does not compel an objecting party (here a corporate entity) itself to express views it disfavors; and the mandated scheme does not compel the expression of political or ideological views. . . . The program sustained in *Glickman* differs from the one under review in a most fundamental respect. In *Glickman* the mandated assessments for speech were ancillary to a more comprehensive program restricting marketing autonomy. Here, for all practical purposes, the advertising itself, far from being ancillary, is the principal object of the regulatory scheme.

. . . In deciding [*Glickman*] we emphasized "the importance of the statutory context in which it arises." . . . The California tree fruits were marketed "pursuant to detailed marketing orders that ha[d] displaced many aspects of independent business activity." . . . The producers of tree fruit who were compelled to contribute funds for use in cooperative advertising "d[id] so as a part of a broader collective enterprise in which their freedom to act independently [wa]s already constrained by the regulatory scheme." . . . [T]heir mandated participation in an advertising program with a particular message was the logical concomitant of a valid scheme of economic regulation.

The features of the marketing scheme found important in *Glickman* are not present in the case now before us. . . . [A]lmost all of the funds collected under the mandatory assessments are for one purpose: generic advertising. Beyond the collection and disbursement of advertising funds, there are no marketing orders that regulate how mushrooms may be produced and sold, no exemption from the antitrust laws, and nothing preventing individual producers from making their own marketing decisions. . . .

It is true that the party who protests the assessment here is required simply to support speech by others, not to utter the speech itself. We conclude, however, that the mandated support is contrary to the First Amendment principles set forth in cases involving expression by groups which include persons who object to the speech, but who, nevertheless, must remain members of the group by law or necessity. . . .

. . . .

. . . [I]n *Glickman* . . ., the market for tree fruit was cooperative. . . . Though four Justices who join this opinion disagreed, the majority of the Court in *Glickman* found the compelled contributions were nothing more than additional economic regulation, which did not raise First Amendment concerns. . . .

The statutory mechanism as it relates to handlers of mushrooms is concededly different from the scheme in *Glickman*; here the statute does not require group action, save to generate the very speech to which some handlers object . . . . . We have not upheld compelled subsidies for speech in the context of a program where the principal object is speech itself. . . . [T]the expression respondent is required to support is not germane to a purpose related to an association independent from the speech itself ... [T]he assessments are not permitted under the First Amendment.

. . .

The Government argues the advertising here is government speech, and so immune from the scrutiny we would otherwise apply. . . .

The Governments failure to raise its argument in the Court of Appeals deprived respondent of the ability to address significant matters that might have been difficult points for the Government. For example, although the Government asserts that advertising is subject to approval by the Secretary of Agriculture, respondent claims the approval is pro forma. . . .

... Although in some instances we have allowed a respondent to defend a judgment on grounds other than those pressed or passed upon below, ... it is quite a different matter to allow a petitioner to assert new substantive arguments attacking, rather than defending, the judgment when those arguments were not pressed in the court whose opinion we are reviewing, or at least passed upon by it.

... [T]he judgment of the Court of Appeals is

Affirmed.

Justice Stevens, concurring.

Justice Breyer has correctly noted that the program at issue in this case, like that in Glickman ... "does not compel speech itself; it compels the payment of money." ... It does not follow, however, that the First Amendment is not implicated when a person is forced to subsidize speech to which he objects. ... The incremental impact on the liberty of a person who has already surrendered far greater liberty to the collective entity (either voluntarily or as a result of permissible compulsion) does not, in my judgment, raise a significant constitutional issue if it is ancillary to the main purpose of the collective program.

> This case, however, raises the open question whether such compulsion is constitutional when nothing more than commercial advertising is at stake. The naked imposition of such compulsion, like a naked restraint on speech itself, seems quite different to me. We need not decide whether other interests ... might justify a compelled subsidy like this, but surely the interest in making one entrepreneur finance advertising for the benefit of his competitors, including some who are not required to contribute, is insufficient.

Justice Thomas, concurring.

... I write separately ... to reiterate my views that ... [a]ny regulation that compels the funding of advertising must be subjected to the most stringent First Amendment scrutiny.

Justice Breyer, with whom Justice Ginsburg joins, and with whom Justice O'Connor joins as to Parts I and III, dissenting.

The Court, in my view, ... introduces into First Amendment law an unreasoned legal principle that may well pose an obstacle to the development of beneficial forms of economic regulation. I consequently dissent.

I

... [In *Glickman* we] ... gave the following reasons in support of our conclusion:

"First, the marketing orders impose no restraint on the freedom of any producer to communicate any message to any audience. Second, they do not compel any person to engage in any actual or symbolic speech. Third, they do not compel the producers to endorse or to finance any political or ideological views." . . .

This case, although it involves mushrooms rather than fruit, is identical in each of these three critical respects. . . .

The Court sees an important difference in what it says is the fact that Wilemans fruit producers were subject to regulation. . . .

. . . The Court in *Wileman* did not refer to the presence of price or output regulations. . . .

. . . [I]t is difficult to understand why the presence or absence of price and output regulations could make a critical First Amendment difference. The Court says that collective fruit advertising (unlike mushroom advertising) was the "logical concomitant" of the more comprehensive "economic" regulatory "scheme." . . . . But it does not explain how that could be so. . . .

. . . [T]he advertising here relates directly, not in an incidental or subsidiary manner, to the regulatory programs underlying goal of "maintain [ing] and expand[ing] existing markets and uses for mushrooms." . . . As the Mushroom Acts economic goals indicate, collective promotion and research is a perfectly traditional form of government intervention in the marketplace. And compelled payment may be needed to produce those benefits where, otherwise, some producers would take a free ride on the expenditures of others. . . .

Compared with traditional "command and control," price, or output regulation, this kind of regulation—which relies upon self-regulation through industry trade associations and upon the dissemination of information—is more consistent, not less consistent, with producer choice. It is difficult to see why a Constitution that seeks to protect individual freedom would consider the absence of "heavy regulation," to amount to a special, determinative reason for refusing to permit this less intrusive program. If the Court classifies the former, more comprehensive regulatory scheme as "economic regulation" for First Amendment purposes, it should similarly classify the latter, which does not differ significantly but for the comparatively greater degree of freedom that it allows.

. . .

II

. . . Nearly every human action that the law affects, and virtually all governmental activity, involves speech. . . .

That, I believe, is why it is important to understand that the regulatory program before us is a "species of economic regulation," . . . which does not "warrant special First Amendment scrutiny," . . . I would so characterize the program for three reasons.

First, the program does not significantly interfere with protected speech interests. It does not compel speech itself; it compels the payment of money. Money and speech are not identical. . . . Indeed, the contested requirement— that individual producers make a payment to help achieve a governmental objective—resembles a targeted tax. . . .

Second, this program furthers, rather than hinders, the basic First Amendment "commercial speech" objective. The speech at issue amounts to ordinary product promotion within the commercial marketplace—an arena typically characterized both by the need for a degree of public supervision and the absence of a special democratic need to protect the channels of public debate, i.e., the communicative process itself. ... No one here claims that the mushroom producers are restrained from contributing to a public debate, moving public opinion, writing literature, creating art, invoking the processes of democratic self-government, or doing anything else more central to the First Amendments concern with democratic self-government.

... Unlike many of the commercial speech restrictions this Court has previously addressed, the program before us promotes the dissemination of truthful information to consumers. And to sustain the objecting producers constitutional claim will likely make less information, not more information, available. Perhaps that is why this Court has not previously applied "compelled speech" doctrine to strike down laws requiring provision of additional commercial speech.

Third, there is no special risk of other forms of speech-related harm. ...[T]here is no risk of significant harm to an individuals conscience. The program does not censor producer views unrelated to its basic regulatory justification. And there is little risk of harming any "discrete, little noticed grou[p]." ...

Taken together, these circumstances lead me to classify this common example of government intervention in the marketplace as involving a form of economic regulation, not "commercial speech," for purposes of applying First Amendment presumptions. ...

The Courts decision converts "a question of economic policy for Congress and the Executive" into a "First Amendment issue," contrary to *Wileman*. For these reasons, I dissent.

BOARD OF REGENTS OF UNIVERSITY OF WISCONSIN SYSTEM v. SOUTHWORTH, 529 U.S. 217 (2000). The University of Wisconsin requires students to pay an activity fee, part of which is disbursed to registered student organizations. Students who objected to paying the fee on First Amendment grounds argued that they should be given the choice not to fund student groups that engage in ideological expression offensive to their personal beliefs. Justice Kennedy wrote the opinion of the Court, holding that the mandatory fee did not violate the First Amendment.

"The University may determine that its mission is well served if students have the means to engage in dynamic discussions of philosophical, religious, scientific, social, and political subjects in their extracurricular campus life outside the lecture hall. If the University reaches this conclusion, it is entitled to impose a mandatory fee to sustain an open dialogue to these ends.

"The University must provide some protection to its students' First Amendment interests, however. The proper measure, and the principal standard of protection for objecting students, we conclude, is the requirement of viewpoint neutrality in the allocation of funding support. Viewpoint neutrality was the obligation to which we gave substance in Rosenberger v. Rector and Visitors of Univ. of Va., 515 U.S. 819 (1995). There the University of Virginia feared that any association with a student newspaper advancing religious viewpoints would violate the Establishment Clause. We rejected the argument, holding that the school's adherence to a rule of viewpoint neutrality in administering its student fee program would prevent 'any mistaken impression that the student newspapers speak for the University.' ... When a university requires its students to pay fees to support the extracurricular speech of other students, all in the interest of open discussion, it may not prefer some viewpoints to others. There is symmetry then in our holding here and in *Rosenberger*. Viewpoint neutrality is the justification for requiring the student to pay the fee in the first instance and for ensuring the integrity of the program's operation once the funds have been collected. We conclude that the University of Wisconsin may sustain the extracurricular dimensions of its programs by using mandatory student fees with viewpoint neutrality as the operational principle."

E.   COMPULSORY SPEECH ACCESS FOR THIRD PARTIES

PRUNEYARD SHOPPING CENTER v. ROBINS, 447 U.S. 74 (1980). A group of high school students sought to solicit support for petitions opposing a United Nations resolution against "Zionism" at a large privately–owned shopping center. They were ordered by the owner of to leave the premises, and brought suit to enjoin the owner from denying them access. The California Supreme Court interpreted the California Constitution to require the owner to allow use of its shopping center for speech and petitioning. The United States Supreme Court rejected an argument that private property owners were being required to participate in disseminating ideological messages they might oppose. It was unlikely that the owner would be identified with the messages of others, and any false identification could be easily disavowed. Concurring in the result, Justices Powell and White argued that there would be serious First Amendment issues if speakers using the owner's premises expressed views strongly opposed by the owner.

Pacific Gas and Electric Company v. Public Utilities Commission of California

475 U.S. 1, 106 S.Ct. 903, 89 L.Ed.2d 1 (1986).

Justice Powell announced the judgment of the Court and delivered an opinion in which the Chief Justice, Justice Brennan, and Justice O'Connor join.

The question in this case is whether the California Public Utilities Commission may require a privately owned utility company to include in its billing envelopes speech of a third party with which the utility disagrees.

I

For the past 62 years, appellant Pacific Gas and Electric Company has distributed a newsletter in its monthly billing envelope. Appellant's newsletter, called *Progress*, reaches over three million customers. It has included political editorials, feature stories on matters of public interest, tips on energy conservation, and straightforward information about utility services and bills.

In 1980, appellee Toward Utility Rate Normalization (TURN), an intervenor in a ratemaking proceeding before California's Public Utilities Commission ... urged the Commission to forbid appellant to use the billing envelopes to distribute political editorials, on the ground that the appellant's customers should not bear the expense of appellant's own political speech. The Commission decided that the envelope space that appellant had used to disseminate *Progress* is the property of the ratepayers. This "extra space" was defined as "the space remaining in the billing envelope, after inclusion of the monthly bill and any required legal notices, for inclusion of other materials up to such total envelope weight as would not result in any additional postage cost."

In an effort to apportion this "extra space" between appellant and its customers, the Commission permitted TURN to use the "extra space" four times a year for the next two years. . . .

Appellant appealed the Commission's order to the California Supreme Court, arguing that it has a First Amendment right not to help spread a message with which it disagrees . . . The California Supreme Court denied discretionary review. We . . . reverse.

II

. . . [I]n Consolidated Edison Co. v. Public Service Comm'n of N.Y., 447 U.S. 530, 544 (1980), we invalidated a state order prohibiting a privately owned utility company from discussing controversial political issues in its billing envelopes. . . . [T]he critical considerations were that the State sought to abridge speech that the First Amendment is designed to protect, and that such prohibitions limited the range of information and ideas to which the public is exposed. . . .

There is no doubt that . . . appellant's newsletter *Progress* receives the full protection of the First Amendment. . . . In appearance no different from a small newspaper, *Progress'* contents range from energy-saving tips to stories about wildlife conservation, and from billing information to recipes. *Progress* thus extends well beyond speech that proposes a business transaction, . . . and includes the kind of discussion of "matters of public concern" that the First Amendment both fully protects and implicitly encourages. . . .

The Commission recognized as much, but concluded that requiring appellant to disseminate TURN's views did not infringe upon First Amendment rights. It reasoned that appellant remains free to mail its own newsletter except for the four months in which TURN is given access. The Commission's conclusion necessarily rests on one of two premises: (i) compelling appellant to grant TURN access to a hitherto private forum does not infringe appellant's right to speak; or (ii) appellant has no property interest in the relevant forum and therefore has no constitutionally protected right in restricting access to it. We now examine those propositions.

III

Compelled access like that ordered in this case both penalizes the expression of particular points of view and forces speakers to alter their speech to conform with an agenda they do not set. These impermissible effects are not remedied by the Commission's definition of the relevant property rights.

A

This Court has previously considered the question whether compelling a private corporation to provide a forum for views other than its own may infringe the corporation's freedom of speech. Miami Herald Publishing Co. v. Tornillo, 418 U.S. 241 (1974) . . . involved a challenge to Florida's right-of-reply statute. The Florida law provided that, if a newspaper assailed a candidate's character or record, the candidate could demand that the newspaper print a reply of equal prominence and space. . . .

We found that the right-of-reply statute directly interfered with the newspaper's right to speak in two ways. . . . First, the newspaper's expression of a particular viewpoint triggered an obligation to permit other speakers, with whom the newspaper disagreed, to use the newspaper's facilities to spread their own message. ... [B]y forcing the newspaper to disseminate opponents' views, the statute penalized the newspaper's own expression....[6]

Second, ... Florida's statute interfered with ... "editorial control and judgment" by forcing the newspaper to tailor its speech to an opponent's agenda, and to respond to candidates' arguments where the newspaper might prefer to be silent....

The concerns that caused us to invalidate the compelled access rule in *Tornillo* apply to appellant as well as to the institutional press....

The Court's decision in PruneYard Shopping Center v. Robins ... is not to the contrary.... Notably absent from *PruneYard* was any concern that access to this area might affect the shopping center owner's exercise of his own right to speak: the owner did not even allege that he objected to the content of the pamphlets; nor was the access right content based. *PruneYard* thus does not undercut the proposition that forced associations that burden protected speech are impermissible.[8]

B

The Commission's order ... does not simply award access to the public at large; rather, it discriminates on the basis of the viewpoints of the selected speakers. ... Access is limited to persons or groups—such as TURN—who disagree with appellant's views as expressed in *Progress* and who oppose appellant in Commission proceedings.

Such one-sidedness impermissibly burdens appellant's own expression. ...because access is awarded only to those who disagree with appellant's views and who are hostile to appellant's interests, appellant must contend with the fact that whenever it speaks out on a given issue, it may be forced—at TURN's discretion—to help disseminate hostile views....

Appellant does not, of course, have the right to be free from vigorous debate. But it *does* have the right to be free from government restrictions that abridge its own rights in order to "enhance the relative voice" of its opponents.... The Commission's order requires *appellant* to assist in disseminating *TURN*'s views; it does not equally constrain both sides of the debate about utility regulation. ...

The Commission's access order also impermissibly requires appellant to associate with speech with which appellant may disagree. The order on its face leaves TURN free to use the billing envelopes to discuss any issues it chooses. Should TURN choose, for example, to urge appellant's customers to vote for a particular slate of legislative candidates, or to argue in favor of legislation that could seriously affect the utility business, appellant may be forced either to appear to agree with TURN's views or to respond....

. . .

6. This Court has sustained a limited government-enforced right of access to broadcast media. Red Lion Broadcasting Co. v. FCC, 395 U.S. 367 (1969). ... Appellant's billing envelopes do not, however, present the same constraints that justify the result in *Red Lion:* "[A] broadcaster communicates through use of a scarce, publicly owned resource. No person can broadcast without a license, whereas all persons are free to send correspondence to private homes through the mails." ...

8. In addition, the relevant forum in *PruneYard* was the open area of the shopping center into which the general public was invited. This area was, almost by definition, peculiarly public in nature.... There is no correspondingly public aspect to appellant's billing envelopes.

C

The Commission has emphasized that appellant's customers own the "extra space" in the billing envelopes. According to appellees, it follows that appellant cannot have a constitutionally protected interest in restricting access to the envelopes. This argument misperceives both the relevant property rights and the nature of the State's First Amendment violation.

The Commission expressly declined to hold that under California law appellant's customers own the entire billing envelopes and everything contained therein. It decided only that the ratepayers own the "extra space" in the envelope, defined as that space left over after including the bill and required notices, up to a weight of one ounce. The envelopes themselves, the bills, and *Progress* all remain appellant's property. The Commission's access order thus clearly requires appellant to use its property as a vehicle for spreading a message with which it disagrees. In Wooley v. Maynard, . . . [t]he "private property" that was used to spread the unwelcome message was the automobile, not the license plates. Similarly, the Commission's order requires appellant to use its property—the billing envelopes—to distribute the message of another. This is so whoever is deemed to own the "extra space."

A different conclusion would necessarily imply that our decision in *Tornillo* rested on the Miami Herald's ownership of the space that would have been used to print candidate replies. . . . The constitutional difficulty with the right-of-reply statute was that it required the newspaper to disseminate a message with which the newspaper disagreed. This difficulty did not depend on whether the particular paper on which the replies were printed belonged to the newspaper or to the candidate.

. . . [F]orced association with potentially hostile views burdens the expression of views different from TURN's and risks forcing appellant to speak where it would prefer to remain silent. Those effects do not depend on who "owns" the "extra space."

IV

Notwithstanding that it burdens protected speech, the Commission's order could be valid if it were a narrowly tailored means of serving a compelling state interest. . . .

A

Appellees identify two assertedly compelling state interests that the access order is said to advance. First, appellees argue that the order furthers the State's interest in effective ratemaking proceedings. TURN has been a regular participant in those proceedings, and the Commission found that TURN has aided the Commission in performing its regulatory task. . . .

The State's interest in fair and effective utility regulation may be compelling. The difficulty with appellees' argument is that the State can serve that interest through means that would not violate appellant's First Amendment rights, such as awarding costs and fees. . . .

Second, appellees argue that the order furthers the State's interest in promoting speech by making a variety of views available to appellant's customers. . . . We have noted above that this interest is not furthered by an order that is not content neutral. Moreover, the means chosen to advance variety tend to inhibit expression of appellant's views in order to promote TURN's. . . .

It follows that the Commission's order is not a narrowly tailored means of furthering this interest.

. . .

V

We conclude that the Commission's order impermissibly burdens appellant's First Amendment rights because it forces appellant to associate with the views of other speakers, and because it selects the other speakers on the basis of their viewpoints. . . .

. . .

Justice Blackmun took no part in the consideration or decision of this case.

Chief Justice Burger, concurring.

I join Justice Powell's opinion, but think we need not go beyond the authority of Wooley v. Maynard . . . to decide this case. . . .

Justice Marshall, concurring in the judgment.

. . . Two significant differences between the State's grant of access in this case and the grant of access in *PruneYard* lead me to find a constitutional barrier here that I did not find in the earlier case.

The first difference is the degree of intrusiveness of the permitted access. . . .

In the present case . . . appellant has never opened up its billing envelope to the use of the public. . . . Were appellant to use its billing envelope as a sort of community billboard, regularly carrying the messages of third parties, its desire to exclude a particular speaker would be deserving of lesser solicitude . . .

The second difference between this case and *PruneYard* is that the State has chosen to give TURN a right to speak at the expense of appellant's ability to use the property in question as a forum for the exercise of its own First Amendment rights. While the shopping center owner in *PruneYard* wished to be free of unwanted expression, he nowhere alleged that his own expression was hindered in the slightest. In contrast, the present case involves a forum of inherently limited scope. . . .

. . .

Justice Rehnquist, with whom Justice White and Justice Stevens join as to Part I, dissenting.

. . . I believe that the right of access here is constitutionally indistinguishable from the right of access approved in PruneYard Shopping Center v. Robins, . . . and therefore I dissent.

I

. . .

. . . [T]he plurality stretches *Tornillo* to stand for the general proposition that the First Amendment prohibits any regulation that deters a corporation from engaging in some expressive behavior. But the deterrent effect of any statute is an empirical question of degree. When the potential deterrent effect of a particular state law is remote and speculative, the law simply is not subject to heightened First Amendment scrutiny. . . .

... The order does not prevent PG & E from using the billing envelopes in the future to distribute inserts whenever it wishes. ... The most that can be said about the connection between the inserts and the order is that the existence of the inserts quite probably brought to TURN's attention the possibility of requesting access.

Nor does the access order create any cognizable risk of deterring PG & E from expressing its views in the most candid fashion. Unlike the reply statute in *Tornillo,* which conditioned access upon discrete instances of certain expression, the right of access here bears no relationship to PG & E's future conduct. PG & E cannot prevent the access by remaining silent or avoiding discussion of controversial subjects....

II

The plurality argues, however, that the right of access also implicates PG & E's right not to speak or to associate with the speech of others, thereby triggering heightened scrutiny....

There is, however, a ... fundamental flaw in the plurality's analysis. This Court has recognized that natural persons enjoy negative free speech rights because of their interest in self-expression; an individual's right not to speak or to associate with the speech of others is a component of the broader constitutional interest of natural persons in freedom of conscience....

. . .

Extension of the individual freedom of conscience decisions to business corporations strains the rationale of those cases beyond the breaking point. To ascribe to such artificial entities an "intellect" or "mind" for freedom of conscience purposes is to confuse metaphor with reality. Corporations generally have not played the historic role of newspapers as conveyers of individual ideas and opinion....

. . .

III

... Because I think this case is governed by *PruneYard,* and not by *Tornillo,* or *Wooley,* I would affirm the judgment of the Supreme Court of California.

Justice Stevens, dissenting.

. . .

Given that the Commission can require the utility to make certain statements and to carry the Commission's own messages to its customers, it seems but a small step to acknowledge that the Commission can also require the utility to act as the conduit for a public interest group's message that bears a close relationship to the purpose of the billing envelope. An analog to this requirement appears in securities law: the Securities and Exchange Commission requires the incumbent board of directors to transmit proposals of dissident shareholders which it opposes. ... [A]lthough the analogy is far from perfect—it performs the same function as the Commission's rule by making accessible the relevant audience, whether it be shareholders investing in the corporation or consumers served by the utility, to individuals or groups with demonstrable interests in reaching that audience for certain limited and approved purposes.

If the California Public Utilities Commission had taken over company buildings and vehicles for propaganda purposes, or even engaged in viewpoint discrimination among speakers desirous of sending messages via the billing envelope, I would be concerned. But nothing in this case presents problems even remotely resembling or portending the ones just mentioned. . . .

SECTION 4.   APPLICATION OF THE FIRST AMENDMENT TO GOVERNMENT REGULATION OF ELECTIONS

A.   CHOOSING AND ELECTING CANDIDATES FOR PUBLIC OFFICE

POLITICAL ASSOCIATION AND SELECTION OF DELEGATES TO MAJOR NATIONAL PARTY CONVENTIONS

At one extreme, the activities of major political parties in candidate selection may be so influential in the election process that the activity will not be viewed as "private" political association at all. As the White Primary Cases demonstrate, a formally private political group that uniformly dictates the choice of the winning candidate performs a public function, and its freedom to bar participation in its election processes is limited by the fourteenth and fifteenth amendments. Even where political parties' candidate selection processes are not themselves "state action" for constitutional purposes, it is clear that a wide variety of state regulation of parties' delegate and candidate selection processes is justified as an indispensable part of regulation of elections.

Two cases raise the question whether there is a point where state legislation controlling the organization, delegate selection processes, and candidate selection processes, of political parties violates the rights of the party and its members to free political association. Both cases involved rules of the Democratic National Party concerning delegate selection for the Party's national convention. The Party's newly enacted rules, in both cases, conflicted with state law.

In Cousins v. Wigoda, 419 U.S. 477 (1975) the Court reviewed the decision of a state court that Illinois law governed seating of a state delegation at the 1972 Democratic National Convention. Illinois law was in conflict with party rules regarding, inter alia, inclusion of minorities, women, and young people, in the delegation. The Court decided that the Illinois law was unconstitutional. The Party's associational rights included the right to identify the people who comprised the Party and, subsidiary to that, the right to determine seating at the Convention. Illinois' interest in controlling electoral processes did not justify its insistence that the Convention seat the delegation chosen according to state law.

Primary elections, however, play an increasing role in the delegate selection process for major national party conventions. Democratic Party of United States v. Wisconsin ex rel. LaFollette, 450 U.S. 107 (1981), demonstrates that it is not easy to distinguish state interests in regulating primary elections and party interests in controlling delegate selection. Wisconsin's "open primary" law, enacted in 1903 and first applied to presidential primaries in 1906, allows voters to participate in any party's primary without regard to party affiliation and without public declaration of party preference. Delegates to party conventions are not chosen by the primary vote, but are bound to vote at national conventions in accord with the election results. In an action that was aimed at minimizing the cross-over voting in Wisconsin primaries, the National Democratic Party enacted a rule that participation in the delegate selection process for the 1980 Convention would be restricted to voters "who publicly declare their party preference." The Court held, 6–3, that Wisconsin could not compel the National Party to seat a delegation bound, under state law, to vote for candidates according to the results of the open primary.

Justice Stewart's opinion for the Court ... said:

> "The State has a substantial interest in the manner in which its elections are conducted, and the National Party has a substantial interest in the manner in which the delegates to its National Convention are selected. But these interests are not incompatible, and to the limited extent they clash in this case, both interests can be preserved. The National Party rules do not forbid Wisconsin to conduct an open primary. But if Wisconsin does open its primary, it cannot require that Wisconsin delegates to the National Party Convention vote there in accordance with the primary results, if to do so would violate Party rules."

Justice Powell's dissent (joined by Justices Blackmun and Rehnquist) characterized Wisconsin's law as directed to the conduct of the presidential preference primary, and only "indirectly" to the selection of delegates. Wisconsin's interest in open participation in primary elections, compared to the Party's minimal interest in requiring voters to formally identify with the Party before voting, justified that "indirect" infringement in requiring delegates to vote according to the primary results.

Tashjian v. Republican Party of Connecticut

479 U.S. 208, 107 S.Ct. 544, 93 L.Ed.2d 514 (1986).

Justice Marshall delivered the opinion of the Court.

Appellee Republican Party of the State of Connecticut (the Party) in 1984 adopted a Party rule which permits independent voters—registered voters not affiliated with any political party—to vote in Republican primaries for federal and statewide offices.... [T]he State's election statutes ... [require] voters in any party primary to be registered members of that party. ... Appellees ... challenged this eligibility provision on the ground that it deprives the Party of its First Amendment right to enter into political association with individuals of its own choosing. The District Court granted summary judgment in favor of appellees. The Court of Appeals affirmed. We ... affirm.

. . .

II

. . .

The Party here contends that § 9–431 impermissibly burdens the right of its members to determine for themselves with whom they will associate, and whose support they will seek, in their quest for political success. The Party's attempt to broaden the base of public participation in and support for its activities is conduct undeniably central to the exercise of the right of association. ...

. . .

Were the State to restrict by statute financial support of the Party's candidates to Party members, or to provide that only Party members might be selected as the Party's chosen nominees for public office, such a prohibition of potential association with nonmembers would clearly infringe upon the rights of the Party's members under the First Amendment to organize with like-minded citizens in support of common political goals.... The statute here places limits upon the group of registered voters whom the Party may invite to participate in the "basic function" of selecting the Party's candidates.... The State thus limits the Party's associational opportunities at the crucial juncture at which the appeal to common principles may be translated into concerted action, and hence to political power in the community.

It is, of course, fundamental to appellant's defense of the State's statute that this impingement upon the associational rights of the Party and its members occurs at the ballot box, for the Constitution grants to the States a broad power to prescribe the "Times, Places and Manner of holding Elections for Senators and Representatives," Art. I, § 4, cl. 1, which power is matched by state control over the election process for state offices. But this authority does not extinguish the State's responsibility to observe the limits established by the First Amendment rights of the State's citizens. ...

III

Appellant contends that § 9–431 is a narrowly tailored regulation which advances the State's compelling interests by ensuring the administrability of the primary system, preventing raiding, avoiding voter confusion, and protecting the responsibility of party government.

A

... [A]ppellant argues here that the administrative burden imposed by the Party rule is a sufficient ground on which to uphold the constitutionality of § 9–431. Appellant contends that the Party's rule would require the purchase of additional voting machines, the training of additional poll workers, and potentially the printing of additional ballot materials specifically intended for independents voting in the Republican primary....

... [T]he possibility of future increases in the cost of administering the election system is not a sufficient basis here for infringing appellees' First Amendment rights....

B

Appellant argues that § 9–431 is justified as a measure to prevent raiding, a practice "whereby voters in sympathy with one party designate themselves as voters of another party so as to influence or determine the results of the other party's primary." ... [T]hat interest is not implicated here.... [A] raid on the Republican Party primary by independent voters ... is not impeded by § 9–431.... Indeed, under Conn.Gen.Stat. § 9–56 (1985), which permits an independent to affiliate with the Party as late as noon on the business day preceding the primary, the State's election statutes actually *assist* a "raid" by independents, which could be organized and implemented at the 11th hour....

C

Appellant's next argument in support of § 9–431 is that the closed primary system avoids voter confusion. ...

... [A]ppellant's concern that candidates selected under the Party rule will be the nominees of an "amorphous" group using the Party's name is inconsistent with the facts. The Party is not proposing that independents be allowed to choose the Party's nominee without Party participation; on the contrary, to be listed on the Party's primary ballot continues to require, under a statute not challenged here, that the primary candidate have obtained at least 20% of the vote at a Party convention, which only Party members may attend. . . .

. . .

D

Finally, appellant contends that § 9–431 furthers the State's compelling interest in protecting the integrity of the two-party system and the responsibility of party government. . . .

The relative merits of closed and open primaries have been the subject of substantial debate since the beginning of this century, and no consensus has as yet emerged. . . . But our role is not to decide whether the state legislature was acting wisely in enacting the closed primary system in 1955, or whether the Republican Party makes a mistake in seeking to depart from the practice of the past 30 years.

We have previously recognized the danger that "splintered parties and unrestrained factionalism may do significant damage to the fabric of government." Storer v. Brown, 415 U.S., at 736. We upheld a California statute which denied access to the ballot to any independent candidate who had voted in a party primary or been registered as a member of a political party within one year prior to the immediately preceding primary election. . . .

The statute in *Storer* was designed to protect the parties and the party system against the disorganizing effect of independent candidacies launched by unsuccessful putative party nominees. . . . In the present case, the state statute is defended on the ground that it protects the integrity of the Party against the Party itself.

Under these circumstances, the views of the State, which to some extent represent the views of the one political party transiently enjoying majority power, as to the optimum methods for preserving party integrity lose much of their force. . . .

. . .

V

We conclude that § 9–431 impermissibly burdens the rights of the Party and its members protected by the First and Fourteenth Amendments. The interests asserted by appellant in defense of the statute are insubstantial. The judgment of the Court of Appeals is

Affirmed.

Justice Stevens, with whom Justice Scalia joins, dissenting.

The threshold issue presented by this case is whether, consistently with the Constitution, a State may permit a voter to participate in elections to the Congress while preventing that same person from voting for candidates to the most numerous branch of the state legislature. If we respect the plain language of Article I, § 2, cl. 1 of the Constitution and the Seventeenth Amendment, [and] the intent of the Framers, . . . we must answer that question in the negative.

. . .

Justice Scalia, with whom The Chief Justice and Justice O'Connor join, dissenting.

. . .

In my view, the Court's opinion exaggerates the importance of the associational interest at issue, if indeed it does not see one where none exists. . . . The

Connecticut voter who, while steadfastly refusing to register as a Republican, casts a vote in the Republican primary, forms no more meaningful an "association" with the Party than does the independent or the registered Democrat who responds to questions by a Republican Party pollster. If the concept of freedom of association is extended to such casual contacts, it ceases to be of any analytic use. . . .

. . . The Party is entirely free to put forward, if it wishes, that candidate who has the highest degree of support among Party members and independents combined. The State is under no obligation, however, to let its party primary be used, instead of a party-funded opinion poll, as the means by which the party identifies the relative popularity of its potential candidates among independents. Nor is there any reason apparent to me why the State cannot insist that this decision to support what might be called the independents' choice be taken *by the party membership in a democratic fashion,* rather than through a process that permits the members' votes to be diluted—and perhaps even absolutely outnumbered—by the votes of outsiders.

. . .

California Democratic Party v. Jones

530 U.S. 567, 120 S.Ct. 2402, 147 L.Ed.2d 502 (2000).

Justice Scalia delivered the opinion of the Court.

This case presents the question whether the State of California may, consistent with the First Amendment to the United States Constitution, use a so-called "blanket" primary to determine a political party's nominee for the general election.

I

Under California law, a candidate for public office has two routes to gain access to the general ballot for most state and federal elective offices. He may receive the nomination of a qualified political party by winning its primary, . . . or he may file as an independent by obtaining (for a statewide race) the signatures of one percent of the State's electorate or (for other races) the signatures of three percent of the voting population of the area represented by the office in contest . . .

Until 1996, to determine the nominees of qualified parties California held what is known as a "closed" partisan primary, in which only persons who are members of the political party—i.e., who have declared affiliation with that party when they register to vote . . .—can vote on its nominee . . . In 1996 the citizens of California adopted by initiative Proposition 198. Promoted largely as a measure that would "weaken party hard-liners" and ease the way for "moderate problem-solvers," Proposition 198 changed California's partisan primary from a closed primary to a blanket primary. Under the new system, "[a]ll persons entitled to vote, including those not affiliated with any political party, shall have the right to vote . . . for any candidate regardless of the candidate's political affiliation." . . . Whereas under the closed primary each voter received a ballot limited to candidates of his own party, as a result of Proposition 198 each voter's primary ballot now lists every candidate regardless of party affiliation and allows the voter to choose freely among them. It remains the case, however, that the candidate of each party who wins the greatest number of votes "is the nominee of that party at the ensuing general election." . . . [2]

Petitioners in this case are four political parties—the California Democratic Party, the California Republican Party, the Libertarian Party of California, and the Peace and Freedom Party—each of which has a rule prohibiting persons not members of the party from voting in the party's primary. Petitioners brought suit . . ., alleging, inter alia, that California's blanket primary violated their First Amendment rights of association . . . The District Court . . . held that the burden on petitioners' rights of association was not a severe one, and was justified by state interests. . . . The Ninth Circuit . . . affirmed. . . .

II

Respondents [contend that] primaries are public rather than private proceedings, and the States may and must play a role in ensuring that they serve the public interest. Proposition 198, respondents conclude, is simply a rather pedestrian example of a State's regulating its system of elections.

We have recognized, of course, that States have a major role to play in structuring and monitoring the election process, including primaries. . . .

What we have not held, however, is that the processes by which political parties select their nominees are, as respondents would have it, wholly public affairs that States may regulate freely. To the contrary, we have continually stressed that when States regulate parties' internal processes they must act within limits imposed by the Constitution. . . . In this regard, respondents' reliance on Smith v. Allwright, 321 U.S. 649 (1944), and Terry v. Adams, 345 U.S. 461 (1953), is misplaced. In *Allwright*, we invalidated the Texas Democratic Party's rule limiting participation in its primary to whites; in *Terry*, we invalidated the same rule promulgated by the Jaybird Democratic Association, a "self-governing voluntary club," . . . These cases held only that, when a State prescribes an election process that gives a special role to political parties, . . . the parties' discriminatory action becomes state action under the Fifteenth Amendment. . . . They do not stand for the proposition that party affairs are public affairs, free of First Amendment protections . . .

. . .

In no area is the political association's right to exclude more important than in the process of selecting its nominee. That process often determines the party's positions on the most significant public policy issues of the day, and even when those positions are predetermined it is the nominee who becomes the party's ambassador to the general electorate in winning it over to the party's views. . . .

Unsurprisingly, our cases vigorously affirm the special place the First Amendment reserves for, and the special protection it accords, the process by which a political party "select[s] a standard bearer who best represents the party's ideologies and preferences." . . .

. . .

2. California's new blanket primary system does not apply directly to the apportionment of presidential delegates. . . . Instead, the State tabulates the presidential primary in two ways: according to the number of votes each candidate received from the entire voter pool and according to the amount each received from members of his own party. The national parties may then use the latter figure to apportion delegates. Nor does it apply to the election of political party central or district committee members; only party members may vote in these elections. . . .

In [Democratic Party of United States v. Wisconsin ex rel. La Follette, . . . [w]e held that, whatever the strength of the state interests supporting the open primary itself, they could not justify this "substantial intrusion into the associational freedom of members of the National Party."[7] . . .

California's blanket primary violates the principles set forth in these cases. Proposition 198 forces political parties to associate with—to have their nominees, and hence their positions, determined by—those who, at best, have refused to affiliate with the party, and, at worst, have expressly affiliated with a rival. In this respect, it is qualitatively different from a closed primary. Under that system, even when it is made quite easy for a voter to change his party affiliation the day of the primary, and thus, in some sense, to "cross over," at least he must formally become a member of the party; and once he does so, he is limited to voting for candidates of that party.[8]

The evidence in this case demonstrates that under California's blanket primary system, the prospect of having a party's nominee determined by adherents of an opposing party is far from remote—indeed, it is a clear and present danger. . . .

The record also supports the obvious proposition that these substantial numbers of voters who help select the nominees of parties they have chosen not to join often have policy views that diverge from those of the party faithful. . . .

. . .

In any event, the deleterious effects of Proposition 198 are not limited to altering the identity of the nominee. Even when the person favored by a majority of the party members prevails, he will have prevailed by taking somewhat different positions—and, should he be elected, will continue to take somewhat different positions in order to be renominated. . . . [T]he whole purpose of Proposition 198 was to favor nominees with "moderate" positions. . . .

. . .

In sum, Proposition 198 forces petitioners to adulterate their candidate-selection process—the "basic function of a political party," . . .—by opening it up to persons wholly unaffiliated with the party. Such forced association has the likely outcome—indeed, in this case the intended outcome—of changing the parties' message. We can think of no heavier burden on a political party's associational freedom. Proposition 198 is therefore unconstitutional unless it is narrowly tailored to serve a compelling state interest. . . . It is to that question which we now turn.

III

Respondents proffer seven state interests they claim are compelling. Two of them—producing elected officials who better represent the electorate and expanding candidate debate beyond the scope of partisan concerns—are simply circumlocution for producing nominees and nominee positions other than those the parties would choose if left to their own devices. . . . Both of these supposed

---

7. . . . Of course La Follette involved the burden a state regulation imposed on a national party, but that factor affected only the weight of the State's interest, and had no bearing upon the existence vel non of a party's First Amendment right to exclude. . . .

8. In this sense, the blanket primary also may be constitutionally distinct from the open primary, see n. 6, supra, in which the voter is limited to one party's ballot. . . . This case does not require us to determine the constitutionality of open primaries.

interests, therefore, reduce to nothing more than a stark repudiation of freedom of political association ...

. . .

Respondents' third asserted compelling interest is that the blanket primary is the only way to ensure that disenfranchised persons enjoy the right to an effective vote. By "disenfranchised," respondents do not mean those who cannot vote; they mean simply independents and members of the minority party in "safe" districts. ... [E]ven if it were accurate to describe the plight of the non-party-member in a safe district as "disenfranchisement," Proposition 198 is not needed to solve the problem. The voter who feels himself disenfranchised should simply join the party. That may put him to a hard choice, but it is not a state-imposed restriction upon his freedom of association, whereas compelling party members to accept his selection of their nominee is a state-imposed restriction upon theirs.

Respondents' remaining four asserted state interests—promoting fairness, affording voters greater choice, increasing voter participation, and protecting privacy—are not, like the others, automatically out of the running; but neither are they, in the circumstances of this case, compelling. ...

The aspect of fairness addressed by Proposition 198 is presumably the supposed inequity of not permitting nonparty members in "safe" districts to determine the party nominee. If that is unfair at all (rather than merely a consequence of ... majority [rule]), it seems to us less unfair than permitting nonparty members to hijack the party. As for affording voters greater choice, it is obvious that the net effect of this scheme—indeed, its avowed purpose—is to reduce the scope of choice, by assuring a range of candidates who are all more "centrist." ... The interest in increasing voter participation is just a variation on the same theme (more choices favored by the majority will produce more voters).... As for the protection of privacy: the specific privacy interest at issue is ... confidentiality of one's party affiliation. ... [W]e do not think that the State's interest in assuring the privacy of this piece of information in all cases can conceivably be considered a "compelling" one. ...

Finally, we may observe that even if all these state interests were compelling ones, Proposition 198 is not a narrowly tailored means of furthering them. Respondents could protect them all by resorting to a nonpartisan blanket primary. Generally speaking, under such a system, the State determines what qualifications it requires for a candidate to have a place on the primary ballot— which may include nomination by established parties and voter-petition requirements for independent candidates. Each voter, regardless of party affiliation, may then vote for any candidate, and the top two vote getters (or however many the State prescribes) then move on to the general election. This system has all the characteristics of the partisan blanket primary, save the constitutionally crucial one: Primary voters are not choosing a party's nominee. Under a nonpartisan blanket primary, a State may ensure more choice, greater participation, increased "privacy," and a sense of "fairness"—all without severely burdening a political party's First Amendment right of association.

* * *

Respondents' legitimate state interests and petitioners' First Amendment rights are not inherently incompatible. To the extent they are in this case, the State of California has made them so by forcing political parties to associate with those who do not share their beliefs. And it has done this at the "crucial juncture" at which party members traditionally find their collective voice and select their spokesman. ... The burden Proposition 198 places on petitioners' rights of political association is both severe and unnecessary. The judgment for the Court of Appeals for the Ninth Circuit is reversed.

It is so ordered.

Justice Kennedy, concurring.

. . .

. . . [T]here is much to be said in favor of California's law; and I might find this to be a close case if it were simply a way to make elections more fair and open or addressed matters purely of party structure.

The true purpose of this law, however, is to force a political party to accept a candidate it may not want and, by so doing, to change the party's doctrinal position on major issues. . . . I agree with the Court's opinion.

I add this separate concurrence to say that Proposition 198 is doubtful for a further reason. In justification of its statute California tells us a political party has the means at hand to protect its associational freedoms. The party, California contends, can simply use its funds and resources to support the candidate of its choice . . . [B]y reason of the Court's denial of First Amendment protections to a political party's spending of its own funds and resources in cooperation with its preferred candidate, see Colorado Republican Federal Campaign Comm. v. Federal Election Comm'n, 518 U.S. 604 (1996), the Federal Government or the State has the power to prevent the party from using the very remedy California now offers up to defend its law.

. . .

Were the views of those who would uphold both California's blanket primary system and limitations on coordinated party expenditures to become prevailing law, the State could control political parties at two vital points in the election process. First, it could mandate a blanket primary to weaken the party's ability to defend and maintain its doctrinal positions by allowing nonparty members to vote in the primary. Second, it could impose severe restrictions on the amount of funds and resources the party could spend in efforts to counteract the State's doctrinal intervention. . . .

. . . With these observations, I join the opinion of the Court.

Justice Stevens, with whom Justice Ginsburg joins as to Part I, dissenting.

. . . I am convinced that California's adoption of a blanket primary pursuant to Proposition 198 does not violate the First Amendment, and that its use in primary elections for state offices is therefore valid. . . .

I

A State's power to determine how its officials are to be elected is a quintessential attribute of sovereignty. This case is about the State of California's power to decide who may vote in an election conducted, and paid for, by the State. The United States Constitution imposes constraints on the States' power to limit access to the polls, but we have never before held or suggested that it imposes any constraints on States' power to authorize additional citizens to participate in any state election for a state office. In my view, principles of federalism require us to respect the policy choice made by the State's voters in approving Proposition 198.

. . .

When a political party defines the organization and composition of its governing units, when it decides what candidates to endorse, and when it decides whether and how to communicate those endorsements to the public, it is engaged in the kind of private expressive associational activity that the First Amendment protects. . . .

. . . I think it clear—though the point has never been decided by this Court—"that a State may require parties to use the primary format for selecting their nominees." The reason a State may impose this significant restriction on a party's associational freedoms is that both the general election and the primary are quintessential forms of state action. It is because the primary is state action that an organization—whether it calls itself a political party or just a "Jaybird" association—may not deny non-Caucasians the right to participate in the selection of its nominees . . . . . The protections that the First Amendment affords to the "internal processes" of a political party, do not encompass a right to exclude nonmembers from voting in a state-required, state-financed primary election.

The so-called "right not to associate" that the Court relies upon, then, is simply inapplicable to participation in a state election. A political party, like any other association, may refuse to allow non-members to participate in the party's decisions when it is conducting its own affairs; California's blanket primary system does not infringe this principle. But an election, unlike a convention or caucus, is a public affair. . . . In my view, while state rules abridging participation in its elections should be closely scrutinized, the First Amendment does not inhibit the State from acting to broaden voter access to state-run, state-financed elections. . . .

. . .

The Court's reliance on a political party's "right not to associate" as a basis for limiting a State's power to conduct primary elections will inevitably require it either to draw unprincipled distinctions among various primary configurations or to alter voting practices throughout the Nation in fundamental ways. Assuming that a registered Democrat or independent who wants to vote in the Republican gubernatorial primary can do so merely by asking for a Republican ballot, the Republican Party's constitutional right "not to associate" is pretty feeble if the only cost it imposes on that Democrat or independent is a loss of his right to vote for non-Republican candidates for other offices. . . .

. . . Given that open primaries are supported by essentially the same state interests that the Court disparages today and are not as "narrow" as nonpartisan primaries, there is surely a danger that open primaries will fare no better against a First Amendment challenge than blanket primaries have.

. . . 3 States presently have blanket primaries, while an additional 21 States have open primaries and 8 States have semi-closed primaries in which independents may participate. This Court's willingness to invalidate the primary schemes of 3 States and cast serious constitutional doubt on the schemes of 29 others at the parties' behest is, as the District Court rightly observed, "an extraordinary intrusion into the complex and changing election laws of the States [that] . . . remove[s] from the American political system a method for candidate selection that many States consider beneficial and which in the uncertain future could take on new appeal and importance."

. . .

Even if the "right not to associate" did authorize the Court to review the State's policy choice, its evaluation of the competing interests at stake is seriously flawed. For example, the Court's conclusion that a blanket primary severely burdens the parties' associational interests in selecting their standard bearers does not appear to be borne out by experience with blanket primaries in Alaska and Washington....

. . .

B. POLITICAL FUNDRAISING AND EXPENDITURES

Buckley v. Valeo

424 U.S. 1, 96 S.Ct. 612, 46 L.Ed.2d 659 (1976).

Per Curiam.

These appeals present constitutional challenges to the key provisions of the Federal Election Campaign Act of 1971, ... as amended in 1974.

. . .

I. Contribution and Expenditure Limitations

The intricate statutory scheme adopted by Congress to regulate federal election campaigns includes restrictions on political contributions and expenditures that apply broadly to all phases of and all participants in the election process. The major contribution and expenditure limitations in the Act prohibit individuals from contributing more than $25,000 in a single year or more than $1,000 to any single candidate for an election campaign and from spending more than $1,000 a year "relative to a clearly identified candidate." Other provisions restrict a candidate's use of personal and family resources in his campaign and limit the overall amount that can be spent by a candidate in campaigning for federal office.

. . .

A. General Principles

The Act's contribution and expenditure limitations operate in an area of the most fundamental First Amendment activities. ...

. . .

We cannot share the view that the present Act's contribution and expenditure limitations are comparable to the restrictions on conduct upheld in *O'Brien.* The expenditure of money simply cannot be equated with such conduct as destruction of a draft card. Some forms of communication made possible by the giving and spending of money involve speech alone, some involve conduct primarily, and some involve a combination of the two. Yet this Court has never suggested that the dependence of a communication on the expenditure of money operates itself to introduce a nonspeech element or to reduce the exacting scrutiny required by the First Amendment....

Nor can the Act's contribution and expenditure limitations be sustained, as some of the parties suggest, by reference to the constitutional principles reflected in such decisions as Cox v. Louisiana, supra, Adderley v. Florida, 385 U.S. 39 (1966), and Kovacs v. Cooper, 336 U.S. 77 (1949). ... The critical difference between this case and those time, place and manner cases is that the present Act's contribution and expenditure limitations impose direct quantity restrictions on political communication and association by persons, groups, candidates and political parties in addition to any reasonable time, place, and manner regulations otherwise imposed.

A restriction on the amount of money a person or group can spend on political communication during a campaign necessarily reduces the quantity of expression by restricting the number of issues discussed, the depth of their exploration, and the size of the audience reached. This is because virtually every means of communicating ideas in today's mass society requires the expenditure of money. . . .

The expenditure limitations contained in the Act represent substantial rather than merely theoretical restraints on the quantity and diversity of political speech. The $1,000 ceiling on spending "relative to a clearly identified candidate," . . . would appear to exclude all citizens and groups except candidates, political parties and the institutional press from any significant use of the most effective modes of communication. Although the Act's limitations on expenditures by campaign organizations and political parties provide substantially greater room for discussion and debate, they would have required restrictions in the scope of a number of past congressional and Presidential campaigns and would operate to constrain campaigning by candidates who raise sums in excess of the spending ceiling.

By contrast with a limitation upon expenditures for political expression, a limitation upon the amount that any one person or group may contribute to a candidate or political committee entails only a marginal restriction upon the contributor's ability to engage in free communication. A contribution serves as a general expression of support for the candidate and his views, but does not communicate the underlying basis for the support. . . . While contributions may result in political expression if spent by a candidate or an association to present views to the voters, the transformation of contributions into political debate involves speech by someone other than the contributor.

Given the important role of contributions in financing political campaigns, contribution restrictions could have a severe impact on political dialogue if the limitations prevented candidates and political committees from amassing the resources necessary for effective advocacy. There is no indication, however, that the contribution limitations imposed by the Act would have any dramatic adverse effect on the funding of campaigns and political associations. The overall effect of the Act's contribution ceilings is merely to require candidates and political committees to raise funds from a greater number of persons and to compel people who would otherwise contribute amounts greater than the statutory limits to expend such funds on direct political expression, rather than to reduce the total amount of money potentially available to promote political expression.

The Act's contribution and expenditure limitations also impinge on protected associational freedoms. Making a contribution, like joining a political party, serves to affiliate a person with a candidate. In addition, it enables like-minded persons to pool their resources in furtherance of common political goals. The Act's contribution ceilings thus limit one important means of associating with a candidate or committee, but leave the contributor free to become a member of any political association and to assist personally in the association's efforts on behalf of candidates. And the Act's contribution limitations permit associations and candidates to aggregate large sums of money to promote effective advocacy. By contrast, the Act's $1,000 limitation on independent expenditures "relative to a clearly identified candidate" precludes most associations from effectively amplifying the voice of their adherents, the original basis for the recognition of First Amendment protection of the freedom of association. . . .

In sum, although the Act's contribution and expenditure limitations both implicate fundamental First Amendment interests, its expenditure ceilings impose significantly more severe restrictions on protected freedoms of political expression and association than do its limitations on financial contributions.

B.   Contribution Limitations

1.   The $1,000 Limitation on Contributions by Individuals and Groups to Candidates and Authorized Campaign Committees . . .

(A)

As the general discussion in Part I–A, supra, indicated, the primary First Amendment problem raised by the Act's contribution limitations is their restriction of one aspect of the contributor's freedom of political association. . . .

. . .

The Act's $1,000 contribution limitation focuses precisely on the problem of large campaign contributions—the narrow aspect of political association where the actuality and potential for corruption have been identified—while leaving persons free to engage in independent political expression, to associate actively through volunteering their services, and to assist to a limited but nonetheless substantial extent in supporting candidates and committees with financial resources. Significantly, the Act's contribution limitations in themselves do not undermine to any material degree the potential for robust and effective discussion of candidates and campaign issues by individual citizens, associations, the institutional press, candidates, and political parties.

We find that, under the rigorous standard of review established by our prior decisions, the weighty interests served by restricting the size of financial contributions to political candidates are sufficient to justify the limited effect upon First Amendment freedoms caused by the $1,000 contribution ceiling.

. . .

(C)

Apart from these First Amendment concerns, appellants argue that the contribution limitations work such an invidious discrimination between incumbents and challengers that the statutory provisions must be declared unconstitutional on their face. In considering this contention, it is important at the outset to note that the Act applies the same limitations on contributions to all candidates regardless of their present occupations, ideological views, or party affiliations. Absent record evidence of invidious discrimination against challengers as a class, a court should generally be hesitant to invalidate legislation which on its face imposes evenhanded restrictions. . . .

. . .

The charge of discrimination against minor-party and independent candidates is more troubling, but the record provides no basis for concluding that the Act invidiously disadvantages such candidates. As noted above, the Act on its face treats all candidates equally with regard to contribution limitations. And the restriction would appear to benefit minor-party and independent candidates relative to their major-party opponents because major-party candidates receive far more money in large contributions. Although there is some force to appellants' response that minor-party candidates are primarily concerned with their ability to amass the resources necessary to reach the electorate rather than with their funding position relative to their major-party opponents, the record is virtually devoid of support for the claim that the $1,000 contribution limitation will have a serious effect on the initiation and scope of minor-party and independent candidacies. Moreover, any attempt to exclude minor parties and independents en masse from the Act's contribution limitations overlooks the fact that minor-party candidates may win elective office or have a substantial impact on the outcome of an election.

In view of these considerations, we conclude that the impact of the Act's $1,000 contribution limitation on major-party challengers and on minor-party candidates does not render the provision unconstitutional on its face.

[The Court also upheld the $5,000 limit on contributions by political committees, limitations on volunteers' incidental expenses, and the $25,000 limitation on total contributions during any calendar year.]

C. Expenditure Limitations

The Act's expenditure ceilings impose direct and substantial restraints on the quantity of political speech.... It is clear that a primary effect of these expenditure limitations is to restrict the quantity of campaign speech by individuals, groups, and candidates. The restrictions, while neutral as to the ideas expressed, limit political expression "at the core of our electoral process and of the First Amendment freedoms." ...

1. The $1,000 Limitation on Expenditures "Relative to a Clearly Identified Candidate"

   . . .

   ... [T]he constitutionality of § 608(e)(1) turns on whether the governmental interests advanced in its support satisfy the exacting scrutiny applicable to limitations on core First Amendment rights of political expression.

We find that the governmental interest in preventing corruption and the appearance of corruption is inadequate to justify § 608(e)(1)'s ceiling on independent expenditures....

   . . .

It is argued, however, that the ancillary governmental interest in equalizing the relative ability of individuals and groups to influence the outcome of elections serves to justify the limitation on express advocacy of the election or defeat of candidates ... But the concept that government may restrict the speech of some elements of our society in order to enhance the relative voice of others is wholly foreign to the First Amendment ... The First Amendment's protection against governmental abridgment of free expression cannot properly be made to depend on a person's financial ability to engage in public discussion....

   . . .

2. Limitation on Expenditures by Candidates from Personal or Family Resources

   . . .

The ceiling on personal expenditures by candidates on their own behalf, like the limitations on independent expenditures contained in § 608(e)(1), imposes a substantial restraint on the ability of persons to engage in protected First Amendment expression....

. . .

The ancillary interest in equalizing the relative financial resources of candidates competing for elective office, therefore, provides the sole relevant rationale for § 608(a)'s expenditure ceiling. That interest is clearly not sufficient to justify the provision's infringement of fundamental First Amendment rights....

3. Limitations on Campaign Expenditures

Section 608(c) places limitations on overall campaign expenditures by candidates seeking nomination for election and election to federal office....

No governmental interest that has been suggested is sufficient to justify the restriction on the quantity of political expression imposed by § 608(c)'s campaign expenditure limitations. The major evil associated with rapidly increasing campaign expenditures is the danger of candidate dependence on large contributions. The interest in alleviating the corrupting influence of large contributions is served by the Act's contribution limitations and disclosure provisions rather than by § 608(c)'s campaign expenditure ceilings....

. . .

The campaign expenditure ceilings appear to be designed primarily to serve the governmental interests in reducing the allegedly skyrocketing costs of political campaigns.... The First Amendment denies government the power to determine that spending to promote one's political views is wasteful, excessive, or unwise. In the free society ordained by our Constitution it is not the government but the people—individually as citizens and candidates and collectively as associations and political committees—who must retain control over the quantity and range of debate on public issues in a political campaign.

For these reasons we hold that § 608(c) is constitutionally invalid.

In sum, the provisions of the Act that impose a $1,000 limitation on contributions to a single candidate, ... a $5,000 limitation on contributions by a political committee to a single candidate, ... and a $25,000 limitation on total contributions by an individual during any calendar year, ... are constitutionally valid. These limitations along with the disclosure provisions, constitute the Act's primary weapons against the reality or appearance of improper influence stemming from the dependence of candidates on large campaign contributions. ... By contrast, the First Amendment requires the invalidation of the Act's independent expenditure ceiling, ... its limitation on a candidate's expenditures from his own personal funds, ... and its ceilings on overall campaign expenditures ...

[Chief Justice Burger and Justice Blackmun dissented from the ruling upholding the contribution limitations. Justice Marshall dissented from the ruling that it was unconstitutional to limit expenditures from the candidate's personal or family funds. Justice White dissented from the ruling that the expenditure limitations were invalid.]

POLITICAL ACTION COMMITTEES

In California Medical Association v. Federal Election Commission, 453 U.S. 182 (1981), the Court upheld the $5000 political contribution limitation, as applied to a contribution by the association to its multi-candidate political action committee. The Court rejected the argument that, as applied, the restriction operated as a limit on expenditures rather than contributions. Only five Justices spoke to the merits, four dissenting on jurisdictional grounds. Four of the Justices reaching the merits stated that speech by proxy through an association's contributions to its political action committee was not "entitled to full First Amendment protection." The fifth Justice argued that the limitation should be tested by a "rigorous standard of review" but concluded that it was constitutional under that standard.

Federal Election Commission v. National Conservative Political Action Committee, 470 U.S. 480 (1985) held that section 9012(f) of the Presidential Election Campaign Fund Act was invalid. That section prohibited independent political committees from expending more than $1,000 to further the election of a presidential candidate who had opted to receive public financing. The Court rejected the argument that PAC spending presented a greater potential for corruption because the breadth of PAC organizations permitted expenditures larger than individual expenditures.

Austin v. Michigan Chamber of Commerce

494 U.S. 652, 110 S.Ct. 1391, 108 L.Ed.2d 652 (1990).

Justice Marshall delivered the opinion of the Court.

In this appeal, we must determine whether § 54(1) of the Michigan Campaign Finance Act violates either the First or the Fourteenth Amendment to the Constitution. Section 54(1) prohibits corporations from using corporate treasury funds for independent expenditures in support of or in opposition to any candidate in elections for state office.... Corporations are allowed, however, to make such expenditures from segregated funds used solely for political purposes.... In response to a challenge brought by the Michigan State Chamber of Commerce, the Sixth Circuit held that § 54(1) could not be applied to the Chamber, a Michigan nonprofit corporation, without violating the First Amendment. Although we agree that expressive rights are implicated in this case, we hold that application of § 54(1) to the Chamber is constitutional because the provision is narrowly tailored to serve a compelling state interest. Accordingly, we reverse the judgment of the Court of Appeals.

I

Section 54(1) of the Michigan Campaign Finance Act prohibits corporations from making contributions and independent expenditures in connection with state candidate elections.[1] The issue before us is only the constitutionality of the State's ban on independent expenditures. ... The Act exempts from this general prohibition against corporate political spending any expenditure made from a segregated fund.... A corporation may solicit contributions to its political fund only from an enumerated list of persons associated with the corporation....

The Michigan State Chamber of Commerce, a nonprofit Michigan corporation, challenges the constitutionality of this statutory scheme. The Chamber comprises more than 8,000 members, three-quarters of whom are for-profit corporations. The Chamber's general treasury is funded through annual dues required of all members....

---

1. Section 54(1) is modeled on a provision of the Federal Election Campaign Act of 1971 ... that requires corporations and labor unions to use segregated funds to finance independent expenditures made in federal elections....

In June 1985 Michigan scheduled a special election to fill a vacancy in the Michigan House of Representatives. Although the Chamber had established and funded a separate political fund, it sought to use its general treasury funds to place in a local newspaper an advertisement supporting a specific candidate. As the Act made such an expenditure punishable as a felony, ... the Chamber brought suit in District Court for injunctive relief against enforcement of the Act, arguing that the restriction on expenditures is unconstitutional under both the First and the Fourteenth Amendments.

. . .

II

To determine whether Michigan's restrictions on corporate political expenditures may constitutionally be applied to the Chamber, we must ascertain whether they burden the exercise of political speech and, if they do, whether they are narrowly tailored to serve a compelling state interest.... Certainly, the use of funds to support a political candidate is "speech" ... The mere fact that the Chamber is a corporation does not remove its speech from the ambit of the First Amendment. ...

A

This Court concluded in FEC v. Massachusetts Citizens for Life, Inc., 479 U.S. 238 (1986) *(MCFL),* that a federal statute requiring corporations to make independent political expenditures only through special segregated funds ... burdens corporate freedom of expression.... The Court reasoned that the small nonprofit corporation in that case would face certain organizational and financial hurdles in establishing and administering a segregated political fund. ... These hurdles "impose[d] administrative costs that many small entities [might] be unable to bear" and "create[d] a disincentive for such organizations to engage in political speech." ...

Despite the Chamber's success in administering its separate political fund, Michigan's segregated fund requirement still burdens the Chamber's exercise of expression because "the corporation is not free to use its general funds for campaign advocacy purposes." ... The Act imposes requirements similar to those in the federal statute involved in *MCFL:* a segregated fund must have a treasurer, ... and its administrators must keep detailed accounts of contributions, ... and file with state officials a statement of organization.... In addition, a nonprofit corporation like the Chamber may solicit contributions to its political fund only from members, stockholders of members, officers or directors of members, and the spouses of any of these persons.... Although these requirements do not stifle corporate speech entirely, they do burden expressive activity.... Thus, they must be justified by a compelling state interest.

B

The State contends that the unique legal and economic characteristics of corporations necessitate some regulation of their political expenditures to avoid corruption or the appearance of corruption. ... State law grants corporations special advantages—such as limited liability, perpetual life, and favorable treatment of the accumulation and distribution of assets—that enhance their ability to attract capital and to deploy their resources in ways that maximize the return on their shareholders' investments. These state-created advantages not only allow corporations to play a dominant role in the nation's economy, but also permit them to use "resources amassed in the economic marketplace" to obtain "an unfair advantage in the political marketplace." *MCFL* ...

We therefore have recognized that "the compelling governmental interest in preventing corruption support[s] the restriction of the influence of political war chests funneled through the corporate form." ...

... Although this Court has distinguished these expenditures from direct contributions in the context of federal laws regulating individual donors, *Buckley,* ... it has also recognized that a legislature might demonstrate a danger of real or apparent corruption posed by such expenditures when made by corporations to influence candidate elections ... Regardless of whether this danger of "financial quid pro quo" corruption ... may be sufficient to justify a restriction on independent expenditures, Michigan's regulation aims at a different type of corruption in the political arena: the corrosive and distorting effects of immense aggregations of wealth that are accumulated with the help of the corporate form and that have little or no correlation to the public's support for the corporation's political ideas. The Act ... ensures that expenditures reflect actual public support for the political ideas espoused by corporations. We emphasize that the mere fact that corporations may accumulate large amounts of wealth is not the justification for § 54; rather, the unique state-conferred corporate structure that facilitates the amassing of large treasuries warrants the limit on independent expenditures. Corporate wealth can unfairly influence elections when it is deployed in the form of independent expenditures, just as it can when it assumes the guise of political contributions. We therefore hold that the State has articulated a sufficiently compelling rationale to support its restriction on independent expenditures by corporations.

C

We next turn to the question whether the Act is sufficiently narrowly tailored to achieve its goal. We find that the Act is precisely targeted to eliminate the distortion caused by corporate spending while also allowing corporations to express their political views.... [T]he Act does not impose an *absolute* ban on all forms of corporate political spending but permits corporations to make independent political expenditures through separate segregated funds. Because persons contributing to such funds understand that their money will be used solely for political purposes, the speech generated accurately reflects contributors' support for the corporation's political views....

. . .

III

The Chamber contends that even if the Campaign Finance Act is constitutional with respect to for-profit corporations, it nonetheless cannot be applied to a nonprofit ideological corporation like a chamber of commerce. In *MCFL,* we held that the nonprofit organization there had "features more akin to voluntary political associations than business firms, and therefore should not have to bear burdens on independent spending solely because of [its] incorporated status." ... In reaching that conclusion, we enumerated three characteristics of the corporation that were "essential" to our holding. ... Because the Chamber does not share these crucial features, the Constitution does not require that it be exempted from the generally applicable provisions of § 54(1).

The first characteristic of Massachusetts Citizens for Life, Inc., that distinguished it from ordinary business corporations was that the organization "was formed for the express purpose of promoting political ideas, and cannot engage in business activities." ...

In contrast, the Chamber's bylaws set forth more varied purposes, several of which are not inherently political. . . . The Chamber's nonpolitical activities .. suffice to distinguish it from *MCFL* . . .

We described the second feature of MCFL as the absence of "shareholders or other persons affiliated so as to have a claim on its assets or earnings. This ensures that persons connected with the organization will have no economic disincentive for disassociating with it if they disagree with its political activity." . . . Although the Chamber also lacks shareholders, many of its members may be similarly reluctant to withdraw as members even if they disagree with the Chamber's political expression, because they wish to benefit from the Chamber's nonpolitical programs and to establish contacts with other members of the business community. . . .

The final characteristic upon which we relied in *MCFL* was the organization's independence from the influence of business corporations. . . . In striking contrast, more than three-quarters of the Chamber's members are business corporations. . . . Business corporations . . . could circumvent the Act's restrictions by funneling money through the Chamber's general treasury. Because the Chamber accepts money from for-profit corporations, it could, absent application of § 54(1), serve as a conduit for corporate political spending. . . .

IV

The Chamber also attacks § 54(1) as underinclusive because it does not regulate the independent expenditures of unincorporated labor unions.[4] Whereas unincorporated unions, and indeed individuals, may be able to amass large treasuries, they do so without the significant state-conferred advantages of the corporate structure. . . .

Moreover, labor unions differ from corporations in that union members who disagree with a union's political activities need not give up full membership in the organization to avoid supporting its political activities. . . . An employee who objects to a union's political activities . . . can decline to contribute to those activities, while continuing to enjoy the benefits derived from the union's performance of its duties as the exclusive representative of the bargaining unit on labor-management issues. As a result, the funds available for a union's political activities more accurately reflect members' support for the organization's political views than does a corporation's general treasury. . . .

V

Because we hold that § 54(1) does not violate the First Amendment, we must address the Chamber's contention that the provision infringes its rights under the Fourteenth Amendment. The Chamber argues that the statute treats similarly situated entities unequally. Specifically, it contends that the State should also restrict the independent expenditures of unincorporated associations with the ability to accumulate large treasuries and of corporations engaged in the media business.

. . . [T]he State's decision to regulate only corporations is precisely tailored to serve the compelling state interest of eliminating from the political process the corrosive effect of political "war chests" amassed with the aid of the legal advantages given to corporations.

---

4. The Federal Election Campaign Act restricts the independent expenditures of la- bor organizations as well as those of corporations. 2 U.S.C. § 441b(a).

Similarly, we find that the Act's exemption of media corporations from the expenditure restrictions does not render the statute unconstitutional....[5] ... [T]he exception will undoubtedly result in the imposition of fewer restrictions on the expression of corporations that are in the media business. Thus, it cannot be regarded as neutral, and the distinction must be justified by a compelling state purpose.

... Although the press' unique societal role may not entitle the press to greater protection under the Constitution, ... it does provide a compelling reason for the State to exempt media corporations from the scope of political expenditure limitations. We therefore hold that the Act does not violate the Equal Protection Clause.

. . .

Justice Stevens, concurring.

In my opinion the distinction between individual expenditures and individual contributions that the Court identified in Buckley v. Valeo ... should have little, if any, weight in reviewing corporate participation in candidate elections. In that context, I believe the danger of either the fact, or the appearance, of quid pro quo relationships provides an adequate justification for state regulation of both expenditures and contributions. ...

Justice Brennan, concurring.

I join the Court's opinion....

. . .

The PAC requirement may be unconstitutional as applied to some corporations because they do not present the dangers at which expenditure limitations are aimed. Indeed, we determined that Massachusetts Citizens for Life—the antiabortion advocacy organization at issue in *MCFL*—fell into this category....

The majority today persuasively demonstrates that the situation in this case is markedly different from that in *MCFL*....

. . .

Justice Scalia, dissenting.

... [T]he Court today endorses the principle that too much speech is an evil that the democratic majority can proscribe.... [T]hat principle is ... incompatible with the absolutely central truth of the First Amendment: that government cannot be trusted to assure, through censorship, the "fairness" of political debate.

I

A

. . .

... We held in Buckley v. Valeo ... that independent expenditures to express the political views of individuals and associations do not raise a sufficient threat of corruption to justify prohibition.... Neither the Court's

5. The Federal Election Campaign Act contains a similar exemption that excludes from the definition of expenditure "any news story, commentary, or editorial distributed through the facilities of any broadcasting station, newspaper, magazine, or other periodical publication, unless such facilities are owned or controlled by any political party, political committee, or candidate."....

opinion nor either of the concurrences makes any effort to distinguish that case ... The plaintiffs in the case included corporations....

Buckley v. Valeo should not be overruled, because it is entirely correct....

. . .

II

. . .

Perhaps the Michigan law before us here has an unqualifiedly noble objective—to "equalize" the political debate by preventing disproportionate expression of corporations' points of view.... The premise of our Bill of Rights, however, is that there are some things—even some seemingly *desirable* things—that government cannot be trusted to do. The very first of these is establishing the restrictions upon speech that will assure "fair" political debate.... Perhaps the Michigan legislature was genuinely trying to assure a "balanced" presentation of political views; on the other hand, perhaps it was trying to give unincorporated unions (a not insubstantial force in Michigan) political advantage over major employers. Or perhaps it was trying to assure a "balanced" presentation because it knows that with evenly balanced speech incumbent officeholders generally win. The fundamental approach of the First Amendment, I had always thought, was to assume the worst, and to rule the regulation of political speech "for fairness sake" simply out of bounds.

. . .

... [T]he object of the law we have approved today is not to prevent wrongdoing but to prevent speech. Since those private associations known as corporations have so much money, they will speak so much more, and their views will be given inordinate prominence in election campaigns. This is not an argument that our democratic traditions allow—neither with respect to individuals associated in corporations nor with respect to other categories of individuals whose speech may be "unduly" extensive (because they are rich) or "unduly" persuasive (because they are movie stars) or "unduly" respected (because they are clergymen). The premise of our system is that there is no such thing as too much speech—that the people are not foolish but intelligent, and will separate the wheat from the chaff....

. . .

Justice Kennedy, with whom Justice O'Connor and Justice Scalia join, dissenting.

The majority opinion validates not one censorship of speech but two. One is Michigan's content-based law which decrees it a crime for a nonprofit corporate speaker to endorse or oppose candidates for Michigan public office. . . .

The other censorship scheme, I most regret to say, is of our own creation. It is value-laden, content-based speech suppression that permits some nonprofit corporate groups but not others to engage in political speech. . . .

I

. . .

A

The State has conceded that among those communications prohibited by its statute are the publication by a nonprofit corporation of its own assessment of a candidate's voting record. With the imprimatur of this Court, it is now a felony in Michigan for the Sierra Club, or the American Civil Liberties Union, or the Michigan State Chamber of Commerce, to advise the public how a candidate voted on issues of urgent concern to their members. In both practice and theory, the prohibition aims at the heart of political debate.

. . .

B

The second censorship scheme validated by today's holding is the one imposed by the Court. In . . . *MCFL*, a First Amendment right to use corporate treasury funds was recognized for the nonprofit corporation then before us. . . .[S]mall, single issue nonprofit corporations . . . pass the Court's own vague test for determining who are the favored participants in the electoral process. There can be no doubt that if a State were to enact a statute empowering an administrative board to determine which corporations could place candidate advertisements in newspapers and which could not, with authority to enforce the guidelines the Court adopts today . . ., the statute would be held unconstitutional. The First Amendment does not permit courts to exercise speech suppression authority denied to legislatures.

. . .

II

The Act does not meet our standards for laws that burden fundamental rights. The State cannot demonstrate that a compelling interest supports its speech restriction, nor can it show that its law is narrowly tailored to the purported statutory end. . . .

A

. . .

The Court purports to distinguish *MCFL* on the ground that the nonprofit corporation permitted to speak in that case received no funds from profit-making corporations. . . . But this distinction rests on the fallacy that the source of the speaker's funds is somehow relevant to the speaker's right of expression or society's interest in hearing what the speaker has to say. . . . The principled approach is to acknowledge that where political speech is concerned, freedom to speak extends to all nonprofit corporations, not the special favorites of a majority of this Court.

B

. . .

That the censorship applies to the nonprofit corporate speaker itself and not to a PAC that it has organized, far from being a saving feature of the regulation, further condemns it. . . . The record in this case tended to show that between 25 and 50 percent of a PAC's funds are required to establish and administer the PAC. While the corporation can direct the PAC to make expenditures on behalf of candidates, the PAC can be funded only by contributions from shareholders, directors, officers, and managerial employees, and cannot receive corporate treasury funds. . . .

. . .

The majority relies on the state interest in protecting members from the use of nonprofit corporate funds to support candidates whom they may oppose. We should reject this interest as insufficient to save the Act here, just as we rejected the argument in *Bellotti*. . . .

. . . *Abood* does not apply here, as the disincentives to dissociate are not comparable. . . . One need not become a member of the Michigan Chamber of Commerce or the Sierra Club in order to earn a living. To the extent that members disagree with a nonprofit corporation's policies, they can seek change from within, withhold financial support, cease to associate with the group, or form a rival group of their own. . . .

To create second-class speakers that can be stifled on the subject of candidate qualifications is to silence some of the most significant participants in the American public dialogue, as evidenced by the amici briefs filed on behalf of the Chamber of Commerce by the American Civil Liberties Union, the Center for Public Interest Law, the American Medical Association, the National Association of Realtors, the American Insurance Association, the National Organization for Women, Greenpeace Action, the National Abortion Rights Action League, the National Right to Work Committee, the Planned Parenthood Federation of America, the Fund for the Feminist Majority, the Washington Legal Foundation, and the Allied Educational Foundation. . . .

. . .

III

An independent ground for invalidating this statute is the blanket exemption for media corporations. . . .

The web of corporate ownership that links media and nonmedia corporations is difficult to untangle for the purpose of any meaningful distinction. Newspapers, television networks, and other media may be owned by parent corporations with multiple business interests. . . . I can find no permissible basis under the First Amendment for the States to make this unsupported distinction among corporate speakers.

. . .

McConnell v. Federal Election Commission

540 U.S. 93, 124 S.Ct. 619, 157 L.Ed.2d 491 (2003).

Justice Stevens and Justice O'Connor delivered the opinion of the Court with respect to BCRA Titles I and II.[*]

The Bipartisan Campaign Reform Act of 2002 (BCRA) . . . contains a series of amendments to the Federal Election Campaign Act of 1971 (FECA) . . . and other portions of the United States Code . . . that are challenged in these cases. In this opinion we discuss Titles I and II of BCRA. The opinion of the Court delivered by the Chief Justice discusses Titles III and IV, and the opinion of the Court delivered by Justice Breyer discusses Title V.

I

More than a century ago the "sober-minded Elihu Root" advocated legislation that would prohibit political contributions by corporations in order to

---

[*] Justice Souter, Justice Ginsburg, and Justice Breyer join this opinion in its entirety.

prevent "the great aggregations of wealth, from using their corporate funds, directly or indirectly," to elect legislators who would "vote for their protection and the advancement of their interests as against those of the public." ... In Root's opinion, such legislation would "strik[e] at a constantly growing evil which has done more to shake the confidence of the plain people of small means of this country in our political institutions than any other practice which has ever obtained since the foundation of our Government" ... The Congress of the United States has repeatedly enacted legislation endorsing Root's judgment.

... [T]he first such enactment responded to President Theodore Roosevelt's call for legislation forbidding all contributions by corporations "to any political committee or for any political purpose." ... The resulting 1907 statute completely banned corporate contributions of "money ... in connection with" any federal election. ...

In 1925 Congress extended the prohibition of "contributions" to include "anything of value," and "made acceptance of a corporate contribution as well as the giving of such a contribution a crime." ... We upheld the amended statute against a constitutional challenge, observing that "[t]he power of Congress to protect the election of President and Vice President from corruption being clear, the choice of means to that end presents a question primarily addressed to the judgment of Congress." Burroughs v. United States, 290 U.S. 534, 547 (1934).

Congress' historical concern with the "political potentialities of wealth" and their "untoward consequences for the democratic process," ... has long reached beyond corporate money. During and shortly after World War II, Congress reacted to the "enormous financial outlays" made by some unions in connection with national elections. ... Congress first restricted union contributions in the Hatch Act ... and it later prohibited "union contributions in connection with federal elections ... altogether." ... Congress subsequently extended that prohibition to cover unions' election-related expenditures as well as contributions, and it broadened the coverage of federal campaigns to include both primary and general elections. ...

In early 1972 Congress continued its steady improvement of the national election laws by enacting FECA ... As first enacted, that statute required disclosure of all contributions exceeding $100 and of expenditures by candidates and political committees that spent more than $1,000 per year. ...

As the 1972 presidential elections made clear, however, FECA's passage did not deter unseemly fundraising and campaign practices. Evidence of those practices persuaded Congress to enact the Federal Election Campaign Act Amendments of 1974. ...

The 1974 amendments closed the loophole that had allowed candidates to use an unlimited number of political committees for fundraising purposes and thereby to circumvent the limits on individual committees' receipts and disbursements. They also limited individual political contributions to any single candidate to $1,000 per election, with an overall annual limitation of $25,000 by any contributor; imposed ceilings on spending by candidates and political parties for national conventions; required reporting and public disclosure of contributions and expenditures exceeding certain limits; and established the Federal Election Commission (FEC) to administer and enforce the legislation. ...

. . .

... This Court ... concluded that each set of limitations raised serious— though different—concerns under the First Amendment. Buckley v. Valeo, 424

U.S. 1, 14–23 (1976) *(per curiam)*. We treated the limitations on candidate and individual expenditures as direct restraints on speech, but we observed that the contribution limitations, in contrast, imposed only "a marginal restriction upon the contributor's ability to engage in free communication." . . . Considering the "deeply disturbing examples" of corruption related to candidate contributions discussed in the Court of Appeals' opinion, we determined that limiting contributions served an interest in protecting "the integrity of our system of representative democracy." . . . [T]he Act's primary purpose—"to limit the actuality and appearance of corruption resulting from large individual financial contributions"—provided "a constitutionally sufficient justification for the $1,000 contribution limitation." . . .

We prefaced our analysis of the $1,000 limitation on expenditures by observing that it broadly encompassed every expenditure " 'relative to a clearly identified candidate.' " . . . To avoid vagueness concerns we construed that phrase to apply only to "communications that in express terms advocate the election or defeat of a clearly identified candidate for federal office." . . . We concluded, however, that as so narrowed, the provision would not provide effective protection against the dangers of *quid pro quo* arrangements, because persons and groups could eschew expenditures that expressly advocated the election or defeat of a clearly identified candidate while remaining "free to spend as much as they want to promote the candidate and his views." . . . We also rejected the argument that the expenditure limits were necessary to prevent attempts to circumvent the Act's contribution limits, because FECA already treated expenditures controlled by or coordinated with the candidate as contributions, and we were not persuaded that independent expenditures posed the same risk of real or apparent corruption as coordinated expenditures. . . . We therefore held that Congress' interest in preventing real or apparent corruption was inadequate to justify the heavy burdens on the freedoms of expression and association that the expenditure limits imposed.

. . .

Three important developments in the years after our decision in *Buckley* persuaded Congress that further legislation was necessary to regulate the role that corporations, unions, and wealthy contributors play in the electoral process. As a preface to our discussion of the specific provisions of BCRA, we comment briefly on the increased importance of "soft money," the proliferation of "issue ads," and the disturbing findings of a Senate investigation into campaign practices related to the 1996 federal elections.

Soft Money

Under FECA, "contributions" must be made with funds that are subject to the Act's disclosure requirements and source and amount limitations. Such funds are known as "federal" or "hard" money. FECA defines the term "contribution," however, to include only the gift or advance of anything of value "made by any person for the purpose of influencing any election for *Federal* office." . . . Donations made solely for the purpose of influencing state or local elections are therefore unaffected by FECA's requirements and prohibitions. As a result, prior to the enactment of BCRA, federal law permitted corporations and unions, as well as individuals who had already made the maximum permissible contributions to federal candidates, to contribute "nonfederal money"—also known as "soft money"—to political parties for activities intended to influence state or local elections.

Shortly after *Buckley* was decided, questions arose concerning the treatment of contributions intended to influence both federal and state elections.

Although a literal reading of FECA's definition of "contribution" would have required such activities to be funded with hard money, the FEC ruled that political parties could fund mixed-purpose activities—including get-out-the-vote drives and generic party advertising—in part with soft money. In 1995 the FEC concluded that the parties could also use soft money to defray the costs of "legislative advocacy media advertisements," even if the ads mentioned the name of a federal candidate, so long as they did not expressly advocate the candidate's election or defeat. . . .

As the permissible uses of soft money expanded, the amount of soft money raised and spent by the national political parties increased exponentially. . . .

Many contributions of soft money were dramatically larger than the contributions of hard money permitted by FECA. For example, in 1996 the top five corporate soft-money donors gave, in total, more than $9 million in nonfederal funds to the two national party committees. In the most recent election cycle the political parties raised almost $300 million—60% of their total soft-money fundraising—from just 800 donors, each of which contributed a minimum of $120,000. Moreover, the largest corporate donors often made substantial contributions to both parties. Such practices corroborate evidence indicating that many corporate contributions were motivated by a desire for access to candidates and a fear of being placed at a disadvantage in the legislative process relative to other contributors, rather than by ideological support for the candidates and parties.

. . .

The solicitation, transfer, and use of soft money thus enabled parties and candidates to circumvent FECA's limitations on the source and amount of contributions in connection with federal elections.

Issue Advertising

In *Buckley* we construed FECA's disclosure and reporting requirements, as well as its expenditure limitations, "to reach only funds used for communications that expressly advocate the election or defeat of a clearly identified candidate." . . . As a result of that strict reading of the statute, the use or omission of "magic words" such as "Elect John Smith" or "Vote Against Jane Doe" marked a bright statutory line separating "express advocacy" from "issue advocacy." . . . So-called issue ads . . . not only could be financed with soft money, but could be aired without disclosing the identity of, or any other information about, their sponsors.

While the distinction between "issue" and express advocacy seemed neat in theory, the two categories of advertisements proved functionally identical in important respects. . . . Little difference existed, for example, between an ad that urged viewers to "vote against Jane Doe" and one that condemned Jane Doe's record on a particular issue before exhorting viewers to "call Jane Doe and tell her what you think." . . . [T]he conclusion that such ads were specifically intended to affect election results was confirmed by the fact that almost all of them aired in the 60 days immediately preceding a federal election. . . . Indeed, the ads were attractive to organizations and candidates precisely because they were beyond FECA's reach, enabling candidates and their parties to work closely with friendly interest groups to sponsor so-called issue ads when the candidates themselves were running out of money.

. . .

. . . As with soft-money contributions, political parties and candidates used the availability of so-called issue ads to circumvent FECA's limitations, asking donors who contributed their permitted quota of hard money to give money to nonprofit corporations to spend on "issue" advocacy.

Senate Committee Investigation

In 1998 the Senate Committee on Governmental Affairs issued a six-volume report summarizing the results of an extensive investigation into the campaign practices in the 1996 federal elections. The report gave particular attention to the effect of soft money on the American political system, including elected officials' practice of granting special access in return for political contributions.

The committee's principal findings relating to Democratic Party fundraising were set forth in the majority's report, while the minority report primarily described Republican practices. The two reports reached consensus, however, on certain central propositions. They agreed that the "soft money loophole" had led to a "meltdown" of the campaign finance system that had been intended "to keep corporate, union and large individual contributions from influencing the electoral process." One Senator stated that "the hearings provided overwhelming evidence that the twin loopholes of soft money and bogus issue advertising have virtually destroyed our campaign finance laws, leaving us with little more than a pile of legal rubble."

. . .

The report discussed potential reforms, including a ban on soft money at the national and state party levels and restrictions on sham issue advocacy by nonparty groups. The majority expressed the view that a ban on the raising of soft money by national party committees would effectively address the use of union and corporate general treasury funds in the federal political process only if it required that candidate-specific ads be funded with hard money. The minority similarly recommended the elimination of soft-money contributions to political parties from individuals, corporations, and unions, as well as "reforms addressing candidate advertisements masquerading as issue ads."

II

In BCRA, Congress enacted many of the committee's proposed reforms. BCRA's central provisions are designed to address Congress' concerns about the increasing use of soft money and issue advertising to influence federal elections. Title I regulates the use of soft money by political parties, officeholders, and candidates. Title II primarily prohibits corporations and labor unions from using general treasury funds for communications that are intended to, or have the effect of, influencing the outcome of federal elections.

Section 403 of BCRA provides special rules for actions challenging the constitutionality of any of the Act's provisions. . . . Eleven such actions were filed promptly after the statute went into effect in March 2002. As required by § 403, those actions were filed in the District Court for the District of Columbia and heard by a three-judge court. . . . The court . . . ultimately delivered a decision embodied in a two-judge *per curiam* opinion and three separate, lengthy opinions, . . . [holding] some parts of BCRA unconstitutional and [holding other parts constitutional]. . . .

. . .

III

Title I is Congress' effort to plug the soft-money loophole. The cornerstone of Title I is new FECA § 323(a), which prohibits national party committees and their agents from soliciting, receiving, directing, or spending any soft money. ... In short, § 323(a) takes national parties out of the soft-money business.

The remaining provisions of new FECA § 323 largely reinforce the restrictions in § 323(a). ...

Plaintiffs mount a facial First Amendment challenge to new FECA § 323, as well as challenges based on the Elections Clause, U.S. Const., Art. I, § 4, principles of federalism, and the equal protection component of the Due Process Clause. We address these challenges in turn.

A

In *Buckley* and subsequent cases, we have subjected restrictions on campaign expenditures to closer scrutiny than limits on campaign contributions. In these cases we have recognized that contribution limits, unlike limits on expenditures, "entai[l] only a marginal restriction upon the contributor's ability to engage in free communication." ...

Because the communicative value of large contributions inheres mainly in their ability to facilitate the speech of their recipients, we have said that contribution limits impose serious burdens on free speech only if they are so low as to "preven[t] candidates and political committees from amassing the resources necessary for effective advocacy." *Ibid.*

... The "overall effect" of dollar limits on contributions is "merely to require candidates and political committees to raise funds from a greater number of persons." ...

Our treatment of contribution restrictions ... also reflects the importance of the interests that underlie contribution limits—interests in preventing "both the actual corruption threatened by large financial contributions and the eroding of public confidence in the electoral process through the appearance of corruption." ... The less rigorous standard of review we have applied to contribution limits ... shows proper deference to Congress' ability to weigh competing constitutional interests in an area in which it enjoys particular expertise. It also provides Congress with sufficient room to anticipate and respond to concerns about circumvention of regulations designed to protect the integrity of the political process.

Our application of this less rigorous degree of scrutiny has given rise to significant criticism in the past from our dissenting colleagues. [citing dissenting opinions of Justices Kennedy and Thomas] ... [I]n its lengthy deliberations leading to the enactment of BCRA, Congress properly relied on the recognition of its authority contained in *Buckley* and its progeny. Considerations of *stare decisis,* buttressed by the respect that the Legislative and Judicial Branches owe to one another, provide additional powerful reasons for adhering to the analysis of contribution limits that the Court has consistently followed since *Buckley* ...

Like the contribution limits we upheld in *Buckley,* § 323's restrictions have only a marginal impact on the ability of contributors, candidates, officeholders, and parties to engage in effective political speech. ...

Plaintiffs contend that we must apply strict scrutiny to § 323 because many of its provisions restrict not only contributions but also the spending and solicitation of funds raised outside of FECA's contribution limits. But for purposes of determining the level of scrutiny, it is irrelevant that Congress chose in § 323 to regulate contributions on the demand rather than the supply side. . . . The relevant inquiry is whether the mechanism adopted to implement the contribution limit, or to prevent circumvention of that limit, burdens speech in a way that a direct restriction on the contribution itself would not. That is not the case here.

For example, while § 323(a) prohibits national parties from receiving or spending nonfederal money, and § 323(b) prohibits state party committees from spending nonfederal money on federal election activities, neither provision in any way limits the total amount of money parties can spend. . . . Rather, they simply limit the source and individual amount of donations. That they do so by prohibiting the spending of soft money does not render them expenditure limitations.

Similarly, the solicitation provisions of § 323(a) and § 323(e), which restrict the ability of national party committees, federal candidates, and federal officeholders to solicit nonfederal funds, leave open ample opportunities for soliciting federal funds on behalf of entities subject to FECA's source and amount restrictions. . . .

Section 323 thus shows "due regard for the reality that solicitation is characteristically intertwined with informative and perhaps persuasive speech seeking support for particular causes or for particular views." . . . The fact that party committees and federal candidates and officeholders must now ask only for limited dollar amounts or request that a corporation or union contribute money through its PAC in no way alters or impairs the political message "intertwined" with the solicitation. . . . And rather than chill such solicitations, . . . the restriction here tends to increase the dissemination of information by forcing parties, candidates, and officeholders to solicit from a wider array of potential donors. As with direct limits on contributions, therefore, § 323's spending and solicitation restrictions have only a marginal impact on political speech. . . .

Finally, plaintiffs contend that the type of associational burdens that § 323 imposes are fundamentally different from the burdens that accompanied *Buckley*'s contribution limits, and merit the type of strict scrutiny we have applied to attempts to regulate the internal processes of political parties. . . . In making this argument, plaintiffs greatly exaggerate the effect of § 323, contending that it precludes *any* collaboration among national, state, and local committees of the same party in fundraising and electioneering activities. We do not read the provisions in that way. Section 323 merely subjects a greater percentage of contributions to parties and candidates to FECA's source and amount limitations. . . . The modest impact that § 323 has on the ability of committees within a party to associate with each other does not independently occasion strict scrutiny. None of this is to suggest that the alleged associational burdens imposed on parties by § 323 have no place in the First Amendment analysis; it is only that we account for them in the application, rather than the choice, of the appropriate level of scrutiny.

With these principles in mind, we apply the less rigorous scrutiny applicable to contribution limits to evaluate the constitutionality of new FECA § 323. . . .

New FECA § 323(a)'s Restrictions on National Party Committees

The core of Title I is new FECA § 323(a), which provides that "national committee[s] of a political party . . . may not solicit, receive, or direct to another person a contribution, donation, or transfer of funds or any other thing of value, or spend any funds, that are not subject to the limitations, prohibitions, and reporting requirements of this Act." . . .

The main goal of § 323(a) is modest. In large part, it simply effects a return to the scheme that was approved in *Buckley* and that was subverted by the creation of the FEC's allocation regime, which permitted the political parties to fund federal electioneering efforts with a combination of hard and soft money. . . .

1.   *Governmental Interests Underlying New FECA § 323(a)*

The Government defends § 323(a)'s ban on national parties' involvement with soft money as necessary to prevent the actual and apparent corruption of federal candidates and officeholders. . . . We have not limited that interest to the elimination of cash-for-votes exchanges. . . .

Of "almost equal" importance has been the Government's interest in combating the appearance or perception of corruption engendered by large campaign contributions. . . . And because the First Amendment does not require Congress to ignore the fact that "candidates, donors, and parties test the limits of the current law," . . . these interests have been sufficient to justify not only contribution limits themselves, but laws preventing the circumvention of such limits, . . .

. . . The idea that large contributions to a national party can corrupt or, at the very least, create the appearance of corruption of federal candidates and officeholders is neither novel nor implausible. . . . [C]ontributions to a federal candidate's party in aid of that candidate's campaign threaten to create—no less than would a direct contribution to the candidate—a sense of obligation. . . . This is particularly true of contributions to national parties, with which federal candidates and officeholders enjoy a special relationship and unity of interest. . . .

The question for present purposes is whether large *soft-money* contributions to national party committees have a corrupting influence or give rise to the appearance of corruption. Both common sense and the ample record in these cases confirm Congress' belief that they do. . . . [C]orporate, union, and wealthy individual donors have been free to contribute substantial sums of soft money to the national parties, which the parties can spend for the specific purpose of influencing a particular candidate's federal election. It is not only plausible, but likely, that candidates would feel grateful for such donations and that donors would seek to exploit that gratitude.

. . . Thus, despite FECA's hard-money limits on direct contributions to candidates, federal officeholders have commonly asked donors to make soft-money donations . . .

          . . . .

Plaintiffs argue that without concrete evidence of an instance in which a federal officeholder has actually switched a vote (or, presumably, evidence of a specific instance where the public believes a vote was switched), Congress has not shown that there exists real or apparent corruption. But the record is to the contrary. The evidence connects soft money to manipulations of the legislative calendar, leading to Congress' failure to enact, among other things, generic drug legislation, tort reform, and tobacco legislation. . . . To claim that such actions do not change legislative outcomes surely misunderstands the legislative process.

More importantly, plaintiffs conceive of corruption too narrowly. Our cases have firmly established that Congress' legitimate interest extends beyond preventing simple cash-for-votes corruption to curbing "undue influence on an officeholder's judgment, and the appearance of such influence." ...

The record in the present case is replete with ... examples of national party committees peddling access to federal candidates and officeholders in exchange for large soft-money donations. ...

Despite this evidence ..., Justice Kennedy would limit Congress' regulatory interest *only* to the prevention of the actual or apparent *quid pro quo* corruption "inherent in" contributions made directly to, contributions made at the express behest of, and expenditures made in coordination with, a federal officeholder or candidate. Regulation of any other donation or expenditure—regardless of its size, the recipient's relationship to the candidate or officeholder, its potential impact on a candidate's election, its value to the candidate, or its unabashed and explicit intent to purchase influence—would, according to Justice Kennedy, simply be out of bounds. This crabbed view of corruption, and particularly of the appearance of corruption, ignores precedent, common sense, and the realities of political fundraising exposed by the record in this litigation.

Justice Kennedy's interpretation of the First Amendment would render Congress powerless to address more subtle but equally dispiriting forms of corruption. Just as troubling to a functioning democracy as classic *quid pro quo* corruption is the danger that officeholders will decide issues not on the merits or the desires of their constituencies, but according to the wishes of those who have made large financial contributions valued by the officeholder. ...

Justice Kennedy likewise takes too narrow a view of the appearance of corruption. ... In our view, however, Congress is not required to ignore historical evidence regarding a particular practice or to view conduct in isolation from its context. To be sure, mere political favoritism or opportunity for influence alone is insufficient to justify regulation. As the record demonstrates, it is the manner in which parties have *sold* access to federal candidates and officeholders that has given rise to the appearance of undue influence. Implicit (and, as the record shows, sometimes explicit) in the sale of access is the suggestion that money buys influence. It is no surprise then that purchasers of such access unabashedly admit that they are seeking to purchase just such influence. It was not unwarranted for Congress to conclude that the selling of access gives rise to the appearance of corruption.

. . .

2. *New FECA § 323(a)'s Restriction on Spending and Receiving Soft Money*

Plaintiffs and the Chief Justice contend that § 323(a) is impermissibly overbroad because it subjects *all* funds raised and spent by national parties to FECA's hard-money source and amount limits, including, for example, funds spent on purely state and local elections in which no federal office is at stake. ... As the record demonstrates, it is the close relationship between federal officeholders and the national parties, as well as the means by which parties have traded on that relationship, that have made all large soft-money contributions to national parties suspect.

. . .

... [N]ational parties [are] in a position to sell access to federal officeholders in exchange for soft-money contributions that the party can then use for its own purposes. Access to federal officeholders is the most valuable favor the national party committees are able to give in exchange for large donations. ...

[L]arge soft-money donations to national party committees are likely to buy donors preferential access to federal officeholders no matter the ends to which their contributions are eventually put. . . .

3. *New FECA § 323(a)'s Restriction on Soliciting or Directing Soft Money*

Plaintiffs also contend that § 323(a)'s prohibition on national parties' soliciting or directing soft-money contributions is substantially overbroad. The reach of the solicitation prohibition, however, is limited. It bars only solicitations of soft money by national party committees and by party officers in their official capacities. The committees remain free to solicit hard money on their own behalf, as well as to solicit hard money on behalf of state committees and state and local candidates. . . .

This limited restriction on solicitation follows sensibly from the prohibition on national committees' receiving soft money. . . .

4. *New FECA § 323(a)'s Application to Minor Parties*

The McConnell and political party plaintiffs contend that § 323(a) is substantially overbroad and must be stricken on its face because it impermissibly infringes the speech and associational rights of minor parties . . . which, owing to their slim prospects for electoral success and the fact that they receive few large soft-money contributions from corporate sources, pose no threat of corruption comparable to that posed by the RNC and DNC. In *Buckley,* we rejected a similar argument . . . [T]he relevance of the interest in avoiding actual or apparent corruption is not a function of the number of legislators a given party manages to elect. It applies as much to a minor party that manages to elect only one of its members to federal office as it does to a major party whose members make up a majority of Congress. It is therefore reasonable to require that all parties and all candidates follow the same set of rules designed to protect the integrity of the electoral process.

We add that . . . [o]nly when an organization has gained official status, which carries with it significant benefits for its members, will the proscriptions of § 323(a) apply. Even then, a nascent or struggling minor party can bring an as-applied challenge if § 323(a) prevents it from "amassing the resources necessary for effective advocacy."

. . .

New FECA § 323(b)'s Restrictions on State and Local Party Committees

In constructing a coherent scheme of campaign finance regulation, Congress recognized that, given the close ties between federal candidates and state party committees, BCRA's restrictions on national committee activity would rapidly become ineffective if state and local committees remained available as a conduit for soft-money donations. Section 323(b) . . . prevents donors from contributing nonfederal funds to state and local party committees to help finance "Federal election activity." . . . The term "Federal election activity" encompasses four distinct categories of electioneering: (1) voter registration activity during the 120 days preceding a regularly scheduled federal election; (2) voter identification, get-out-the-vote (GOTV), and generic campaign activity that is "conducted in connection with an election in which a candidate for Federal office appears on the ballot"; (3) any "public communication" that "refers to a clearly identified candidate for Federal office" and "promotes," "supports," "attacks," or "opposes" a candidate for that office; and (4) the services provided by a state committee employee who dedicates more than 25% of his or her time to "activities in connection with a Federal election." . . . All activities that fall within the statutory definition must be funded with hard money. . . .

Section 323(b)(2), the so-called Levin Amendment, carves out an exception to this general rule . . . [that] allows state and local party committees to pay for certain types of federal election activity with an allocated ratio of hard money and "Levin funds"—that is, funds raised within an annual limit of $10,000 per person. . . .

The scope of the Levin Amendment is limited in two ways. First, state and local parties can use Levin money to fund only activities that fall within categories (1) and (2) of the statute's definition of federal election activity— namely, voter registration activity, voter identification drives, GOTV drives, and generic campaign activities. . . . And not all of these activities qualify: Levin funds cannot be used to pay for any activities that refer to "a clearly identified candidate for Federal office"; they likewise cannot be used to fund broadcast communications unless they refer "solely to a clearly identified candidate for State or local office." . . .

Second, both the Levin funds and the allocated portion of hard money used to pay for such activities must be raised entirely by the state or local committee that spends them. § 441i(b)(2)(B)(iv). This means that a state party committee cannot use Levin funds transferred from other party committees to cover the Levin funds portion of a Levin Amendment expenditure. It also means that a state party committee cannot use hard money transferred from other party committees to cover the hard-money portion of a Levin Amendment expenditure. Furthermore, national committees, federal candidates, and federal office-holders generally may not solicit Levin funds on behalf of state committees, and state committees may not team up to raise Levin funds. . . . They can, however, jointly raise the hard money used to make Levin expenditures.

1. *Governmental Interests Underlying New FECA § 323(b)*

. . .

. . . Having been taught the hard lesson of circumvention by the entire history of campaign finance regulation, Congress knew that soft-money donors would react to § 323(a) by scrambling to find another way to purchase influence. . . .

2. *New FECA § 323(b)'s Tailoring*

Plaintiffs argue that even if some legitimate interest might be served by § 323(b), the . . . provision is substantially overbroad because it federalizes activities that pose no conceivable risk of corrupting or appearing to corrupt federal officeholders. Second, they argue that the Levin Amendment imposes an unconstitutional burden on the associational rights of political parties. Finally, they argue that the provision prevents them from amassing the resources they need to engage in effective advocacy. We address these points in turn.

a. *§ 323(b)'s Application to Federal Election Activity*

Plaintiffs assert that § 323(b) . . . goes well beyond Congress' concerns about the corruption of the federal electoral process. We disagree.

It is true that § 323(b) captures some activities that affect state campaigns for nonfederal offices. But these are the same sorts of activities that already were covered by the FEC's pre-BCRA allocation rules, and thus had to be funded in part by hard money, because they affect federal as well as state elections. . . .

Like the rest of Title I, § 323(b) is premised on Congress' judgment that if a large donation is capable of putting a federal candidate in the debt of the contributor, it poses a threat of corruption or the appearance of corruption. . . . § 323(b) is narrowly focused on regulating . . . contributions to state and local parties that can be used to benefit federal candidates directly. Further, these regulations all are reasonably tailored, with various temporal and substantive limitations designed to focus the regulations on the important anticorruption interests to be served. We conclude that § 323(b) is a closely-drawn means of countering both corruption and the appearance of corruption.

The first two categories of "Federal election activity," voter registration efforts . . . and generic campaign activities conducted in connection with a federal election, . . . clearly capture activity that benefits federal candidates. Common sense dictates . . . that a party's efforts to register voters sympathetic to that party directly assist the party's candidates for federal office. . . . It is equally clear that federal candidates reap substantial rewards from any efforts that increase the number of like-minded registered voters who actually go to the polls. . . .

. . .

Because voter registration, voter identification, GOTV, and generic campaign activity all confer substantial benefits on federal candidates, the funding of such activities creates a significant risk of actual and apparent corruption. . . . The prohibition on the use of soft money in connection with these activities is therefore closely drawn to meet the sufficiently important governmental interests of avoiding corruption and its appearance.

. . .

IV

. . .

BCRA § 201's Definition of "Electioneering Communication"

. . . § 201, comprehensively amends FECA § 304, which requires political committees to file detailed periodic financial reports with the FEC. The amendment coins a new term, "electioneering communication," to replace the narrowing construction . . . in *Buckley,* . . . [which] limited the coverage of FECA's disclosure requirement to communications expressly advocating the election or defeat of particular candidates. By contrast, the term "electioneering communication" is not so limited, but is defined to encompass any "broadcast, cable, or satellite communication" that

"(I) refers to a clearly identified candidate for Federal office;

"(II) is made within?

"(aa) 60 days before a general, special, or runoff election for the office sought by the candidate; or

"(bb) 30 days before a primary or preference election, or a convention or caucus of a political party that has authority to nominate a candidate, for the office sought by the candidate; and

"(III) in the case of a communication which refers to a candidate other than President or Vice President, is targeted to the relevant electorate."

. . .

New FECA § 304(f)(3)(C) further provides that a communication is "targeted to the relevant electorate" if it "can be received by 50,000 or more persons" in the district or State the candidate seeks to represent. . . .

. . . BCRA's use of this new term is not limited to the disclosure context. A later section . . . restricts corporations' and labor unions' funding of electioneering communications. Plaintiffs challenge the constitutionality of the new term as it applies in both the disclosure and the expenditure contexts.

The major premise of plaintiffs' challenge to BCRA's use of the term "electioneering communication" is that *Buckley* drew a constitutionally mandated line between express advocacy and so-called issue advocacy, and that speakers possess an inviolable First Amendment right to engage in the latter category of speech. Thus, plaintiffs maintain, Congress cannot constitutionally require disclosure of, or regulate expenditures for, "electioneering communications" without making an exception for those "communications" that do not meet *Buckley*'s definition of express advocacy.

. . . [T]he express advocacy restriction was an endpoint of statutory interpretation, not a first principle of constitutional law. . . .

. . .

. . . In narrowly reading the FECA provisions in *Buckley* to avoid problems of vagueness and overbreadth, we nowhere suggested that a statute that was neither vague nor overbroad would be required to toe the same express advocacy line. . . .

. . . *Buckley* . . . in no way drew a constitutional boundary that forever fixed the permissible scope of provisions regulating campaign-related speech.

Nor are we persuaded, independent of our precedents, that the First Amendment erects a rigid barrier between express advocacy and so-called issue advocacy. That notion cannot be squared with our longstanding recognition that the presence or absence of magic words cannot meaningfully distinguish electioneering speech from a true issue ad. . . . *Buckley*'s express advocacy line, in short, has not aided the legislative effort to combat real or apparent corruption, and Congress enacted BCRA to correct the flaws it found in the existing system.

Finally we observe that new FECA § 304(f)(3)'s definition of "electioneering communication" raises none of the vagueness concerns that drove our analysis in *Buckley*. . . .

BCRA § 201's Disclosure Requirements

. . . [W]henever any person makes disbursements totaling more than $10,000 during any calendar year for the direct costs of producing and airing electioneering communications, he must file a statement with the FEC identifying the pertinent elections and all persons sharing the costs of the disbursements. . . . If the disbursements are made from a corporation's or labor union's segregated account, or by a single individual who has collected contributions from others, the statement must identify all persons who contributed $1,000 or more to the account or the individual during the calendar year. . . . The statement must be filed within 24 hours of each "disclosure date"—a term defined to include the first date and all subsequent dates on which a person's aggregate undisclosed expenses for electioneering communications exceed $10,000 for that calendar year. . . .

... [P]laintiffs challenge [these] disclosure requirements as unnecessarily ... requiring disclosure of the names of persons who contributed $1,000 or more to the individual or group that paid for a communication ...

... [T]he important state interests that prompted the *Buckley* Court to uphold FECA's disclosure requirements—providing the electorate with information, deterring actual corruption and avoiding any appearance thereof, and gathering the data necessary to enforce more substantive electioneering restrictions—apply in full ...

... *Buckley* forecloses a facial attack on the new provision in § 304 that requires disclosure of the names of persons contributing $1,000 or more to segregated funds or individuals that spend more than $10,000 in a calendar year on electioneering communications. ... *Buckley* rejected the contention that FECA's disclosure requirements could not constitutionally be applied to minor parties and independent candidates because the Government's interest in obtaining information from such parties was minimal and the danger of infringing their rights substantial. In *Buckley*, ... we found no evidence that any party had been exposed to economic reprisals or physical threats as a result of the compelled disclosures. ... We acknowledged that such a case might arise in the future, however, and addressed the standard of proof that would then apply ...

A few years later we used that standard to resolve a minor party's challenge to the constitutionality of the State of Ohio's disclosure requirements. We held that the First Amendment prohibits States from compelling disclosures that would subject identified persons to "threats, harassment, and reprisals," and that the District Court's findings had established a "reasonable probability" of such a result. Brown v. Socialist Workers '74 Campaign Comm. (Ohio), 459 U.S. 87, 100 (1982).

. . .

BCRA § 202's Treatment of "Coordinated Communications" as Contributions

Section 202 of BCRA ... provide[s] that disbursements for "electioneering communication[s]" that are coordinated with a candidate or party will be treated as contributions to, and expenditures by, that candidate or party. ...The amendment clarifies the scope of the preceding subsection, ... which states more generally that "expenditures made by any person in cooperation, consultation, or concert, with, or at the request or suggestion of" a candidate or party will constitute contributions. ... In *Buckley* we construed the statutory term "expenditure" to reach only spending for express advocacy. ... BCRA § 202 pre-empts a possible claim that ... coordinated expenditures for communications that avoid express advocacy cannot be counted as contributions. As we explained above, *Buckley*'s narrow interpretation of the term "expenditure" was not a constitutional limitation on Congress' power to regulate federal elections. Accordingly, there is no reason why Congress may not treat coordinated disbursements for electioneering communications in the same way it treats all other coordinated expenditures. ...

BCRA § 203's Prohibition of Corporate and Labor Disbursements for Electioneering Communications

Since our decision in *Buckley,* Congress' power to prohibit corporations and unions from using funds in their treasuries to finance advertisements expressly advocating the election or defeat of candidates in federal elections has been firmly embedded in our law. The ability to form and administer separate segregated funds authorized by FECA § 316 ... has provided corporations and unions with a constitutionally sufficient opportunity to engage in express advocacy. That has been this Court's unanimous view, and it is not challenged in this litigation.

Section 203 of BCRA ... extend[s] this rule, which previously applied only to express advocacy, to all "electioneering communications" ... Because corporations can still fund electioneering communications with PAC money, it is "simply wrong" to view the provision as a "complete ban" on expression rather than a regulation. ...

. . .

In light of our precedents, plaintiffs do not contest that the Government has a compelling interest in regulating advertisements that expressly advocate the election or defeat of a candidate for federal office. Nor do they contend that the speech involved in so-called issue advocacy is any more core political speech than are words of express advocacy. ... Rather, plaintiffs argue that the justifications that adequately support the regulation of express advocacy do not apply to significant quantities of speech encompassed by the definition of electioneering communications.

... The precise percentage of issue ads that clearly identified a candidate and were aired during those relatively brief preelection time spans but had no electioneering purpose is a matter of dispute between the parties ... Nevertheless, the vast majority of ads clearly had such a purpose. ... Moreover, whatever the precise percentage may have been in the past, in the future corporations and unions may finance genuine issue ads during those time frames by simply avoiding any specific reference to federal candidates, or in doubtful cases by paying for the ad from a segregated fund.

... Even if we assumed that BCRA will inhibit some constitutionally protected corporate and union speech, that assumption would not "justify prohibiting all enforcement" of the law unless its application to protected speech is substantial, "not only in an absolute sense, but also relative to the scope of the law's plainly legitimate applications." ...

Plaintiffs also argue that FECA § 316(b)(2)'s segregated-fund requirement for electioneering communications is underinclusive because it does not apply to advertising in the print media or on the Internet. ... As we held in *Buckley,* "reform may take one step at a time, addressing itself to the phase of the problem which seems most acute to the legislative mind." ... One might just as well argue that the electioneering communication definition is underinclusive because it leaves advertising 61 days in advance of an election entirely unregulated. The record amply justifies Congress' line drawing.

In addition to arguing that § 316(b)(2)'s segregated-fund requirement is underinclusive, some plaintiffs contend that it unconstitutionally discriminates in favor of media companies [by excluding] from the definition of electioneering communications any "communication appearing in a news story, commentary, or editorial distributed through the facilities of any broadcasting station, unless such facilities are owned or controlled by any political party, political committee, or candidate." ... Plaintiffs argue this provision gives free rein to media companies to engage in speech without resort to PAC money. [The] effect, however, is much narrower than plaintiffs suggest. The provision excepts news items and commentary only; it does not afford *carte blanche* to media companies generally to ignore FECA's provisions. The statute's narrow exception is wholly consistent with First Amendment principles. "A valid distinction ... exists between corporations that are part of the media industry and other corporations that are not involved in the regular business of imparting news to the public." . . .

. . .

V

Many years ago we observed that "[t]o say that Congress is without power to pass appropriate legislation to safeguard . . . an election from the improper use of money to influence the result is to deny to the nation in a vital particular the power of self protection." . . . We abide by that conviction in considering Congress' most recent effort to confine the ill effects of aggregated wealth on our political system. We are under no illusion that BCRA will be the last congressional statement on the matter. Money, like water, will always find an outlet. What problems will arise, and how Congress will respond, are concerns for another day. In the main we uphold BCRA's two principal, complementary features: the control of soft money and the regulation of electioneering communications. . . .

Chief Justice Rehnquist delivered the opinion of the Court with respect to BCRA Titles III and IV*.

This opinion addresses issues involving miscellaneous Title III and IV provisions . . .

BCRA § 305

BCRA § 305 amends the federal Communications Act of 1934, . . . which requires that, 45 days before a primary or 60 days before a general election, broadcast stations must sell a qualified candidate the "lowest unit charge of the station for the same class and amount of time for the same period," . . . Section 305's amendment, in turn, denies a candidate the benefit of that lowest unit charge unless the candidate "provides written certification to the broadcast station that the candidate (and any authorized committee of the candidate) shall not make any direct reference to another candidate for the same office," or the candidate, in the manner prescribed in BCRA § 305(a)(3), clearly identifies herself at the end of the broadcast and states that she approves of the broadcast. . . .

The McConnell plaintiffs challenge § 305. They argue that Senator McConnell's testimony that he plans to run advertisements critical of his opponents in the future and that he had run them in the past is sufficient to establish standing. We think not.

. . .

. . . § 305 amended the Communication Act's requirements with respect to the lowest unit charge for broadcasting time. But this price is not available to qualified candidates until 45 days before a primary election or 60 days before a general election. Because Senator McConnell's current term does not expire until 2009, the earliest day he could be affected by § 305 is 45 days before the Republican primary election in 2008. This alleged injury in fact is too remote temporally to satisfy Article III standing. . . .

[The opinion concluded that plaintiffs similarly lacked standing to challenge a number of provisions in Titles III and IV.]

---

* Justice O'Connor, Justice Scalia, Justice Kennedy, and Justice Souter join this opinion in its entirety. Justice Stevens, Justice Ginsburg, and Justice Breyer join this opinion, except with respect to BCRA § 305. Justice Thomas joins this opinion with respect to BCRA §§ 304, 305, 307, 316, 319, and 403(b).

BCRA § 318

BCRA § 318 ... prohibits individuals "17 years old or younger" from making contributions to candidates and contributions or donations to political parties. ... The McConnell and Echols plaintiffs ... argue that § 318 violates the First Amendment rights of minors. We agree.

Minors enjoy the protection of the First Amendment. ... Limitations on the amount that an individual may contribute to a candidate or political committee impinge on the protected freedoms of expression and association. ... The Government asserts that the provision protects against corruption by conduit; that is, donations by parents through their minor children to circumvent contribution limits applicable to the parents. But the Government offers scant evidence of this form of evasion. ... Absent a more convincing case of the claimed evil, this interest is simply too attenuated for § 318 to withstand heightened scrutiny. ...

Even assuming, *arguendo,* the Government advances an important interest, the provision is overinclusive. The States have adopted a variety of more tailored approaches—*e.g.,* counting contributions by minors against the total permitted for a parent or family unit, imposing a lower cap on contributions by minors, and prohibiting contributions by very young children. Without deciding whether any of these alternatives is sufficiently tailored, we hold that the provision here sweeps too broadly. ...

. . .

Justice Breyer delivered the opinion of the Court with respect to BCRA Title V.*

We consider here the constitutionality of § 504 of [BICRA, which] requires broadcasters to keep publicly available records of politically related broadcasting requests. ... The McConnell plaintiffs, who include the National Association of Broadcasters, argue that § 504 imposes onerous administrative burdens, lacks any offsetting justification, and consequently violates the First Amendment. ... We disagree ...

I

BCRA § 504's key requirements are the following:

(1) A "candidate request" requirement calls for broadcasters to keep records of broadcast requests "made by or on behalf of" any "legally qualified candidate for public office." ...

(2) An "election message request" requirement calls for broadcasters to keep records of requests (made by anyone) to broadcast "message[s]" that refer either to a "legally qualified candidate" or to "any election to Federal office." ...

(3) An "issue request" requirement calls for broadcasters to keep records of requests (made by anyone) to broadcast "message[s]" related to a "national legislative issue of public importance," ... or otherwise relating to a "political matter of national importance," ...

* Justice Stevens, Justice O'Connor, Justice Souter, and Justice Ginsburg join this   opinion in its entirety.

II

BCRA § 504's "candidate request" requirements are virtually identical to those contained in a regulation that the Federal Communications Commission (FCC) promulgated as early as 1938 . . .

. . .

. . . Because we cannot, on the present record, find the longstanding FCC regulation unconstitutional, we likewise cannot strike down the "candidate request" provision in BCRA § 504; for the latter simply embodies the regulation in a statute, thereby blocking any agency attempt to repeal it.

III

BCRA § 504's "election message request" requirements call for broadcasters to keep records of requests (made by any member of the public) to broadcast a "message" about "a legally qualified candidate" or "any election to Federal office." . . .

Given the nature of many of the messages, recordkeeping can help both the regulatory agencies and the public evaluate broadcasting fairness, and determine the amount of money that individuals or groups, supporters or opponents, intend to spend to help elect a particular candidate. . . .

. . .

. . . If, as we have held, the "candidate request" requirements are constitutional, the "election message" requirements, which serve similar governmental interests and impose only a small incremental burden, must be constitutional as well.

IV

The "issue request" requirements call for broadcasters to keep records of requests (made by any member of the public) to broadcast "message[s]" about "a national legislative issue of public importance" or "any political matter of national importance." . . . These recordkeeping requirements seem likely to help the FCC determine whether broadcasters are carrying out their "obligations to afford reasonable opportunity for the discussion of conflicting views on issues of public importance," . . . and whether broadcasters are too heavily favoring entertainment, and discriminating against broadcasts devoted to public affairs . . .

. . .

The regulatory burden, in practice, will depend on how the FCC interprets and applies this provision. The FCC has adequate legal authority to write regulations that may limit, and make more specific, the provision's potential linguistic reach. . . . The parties remain free to challenge the provisions, as interpreted by the FCC in regulations, or as otherwise applied. Any such challenge will likely provide greater information about the provisions' justifications and administrative burdens. Without that additional information, we cannot now say that the burdens are so great, or the justifications so minimal, as to warrant finding the provisions unconstitutional on their face.

The McConnell plaintiffs and the Chief Justice make one final claim. They say that the "issue request" requirement will force them to disclose information that will reveal their political strategies to opponents, perhaps prior to a broadcast. We are willing to assume that the Constitution includes some form of protection against premature disclosure of campaign strategy—though, given the First Amendment interest in free and open discussion of campaign issues, we make this assumption purely for argument's sake. Nonetheless, even on that assumption we do not see how BCRA § 504 can be unconstitutional on its face.

. . .

Justice Kennedy, concurring in the judgment in part and dissenting in part with respect to BCRA Titles I and II.*

The First Amendment guarantees our citizens the right to judge for themselves the most effective means for the expression of political views and to decide for themselves which entities to trust as reliable speakers. Significant portions of Titles I and II . . . constrain that freedom. . . .

Today's decision upholding these laws purports simply to follow Buckley v. Valeo, . . . but the majority, to make its decision work, must abridge free speech where *Buckley* did not. . . . In so doing, it replaces discrete and respected First Amendment principles with new, amorphous, and unsound rules, rules which dismantle basic protections for speech.

. . . BCRA would have imposed felony punishment on Ross Perot's 1996 efforts to build the Reform Party. . . . BCRA makes it a felony for an environmental group to broadcast an ad, within 60 days of an election, exhorting the public to protest a Congressman's impending vote to permit logging in national forests. . . .

To the majority, all this is . . . part of Congress' "steady improvement of the national election laws." We should make no mistake. . . . It is an effort by Congress to ensure that civic discourse takes place only through the modes of its choosing. And BCRA is only the beginning . . .

. . . Government cannot be trusted to moderate its own rules for suppression of speech. The dangers posed by speech regulations have led the Court to insist upon principled constitutional lines and a rigorous standard of review. The majority now abandons these distinctions and limitations.

With respect, I dissent from the majority opinion upholding BCRA Titles I and II. . . .

I.   TITLE I AND COORDINATION PROVISIONS

. . . Even a cursory review of the speech and association burdens these laws create makes their First Amendment infirmities obvious: Title I bars individuals with shared beliefs from pooling their money above limits set by Congress to form a new third party . . . Title I bars national party officials from soliciting or directing soft money to state parties for use on a state ballot initiative. . . . Title I compels speech. Party officials who want to engage in activity such as fundraising must now speak magic words to ensure the solicitation cannot be interpreted as anything other than a solicitation for hard, not soft, money. . . . Title I prohibits the national parties from giving any sort of funds to nonprofit entities, even federally regulated hard money . . . By express terms, Title I imposes multiple different forms of spending caps on parties, candidates, and their agents. . . .

Until today . . . the Court has accepted but two principles to use in determining the validity of campaign finance restrictions. First is the anticor-

---

* The Chief Justice joins this opinion in its entirety. Justice Scalia joins this opinion except to the extent it upholds new FECA § 323(e) and BCRA § 202. Justice Thomas joins this opinion with respect to BCRA § 213.

ruption rationale. . . . Second, the Court . . . has said that the willing adoption of the entity form by corporations and unions justifies regulating them differently. . . .

. . . Most of the regulations at issue, notably all of the Title I soft money bans and the Title II coordination provisions, do not draw distinctions based on corporate or union status. . . . [T]he focus must be on *Buckley*'s anticorruption rationale and the First Amendment rights of individual citizens.

A. Constitutionally Sufficient Interest

In *Buckley,* the Court held that one, and only one, interest justified the significant burden on the right of association involved there: eliminating, or preventing, actual corruption or the appearance of corruption stemming from contributions to candidates. . . .

. . .

Thus, though *Buckley* subjected expenditure limits to strict scrutiny and contribution limits to less exacting review, it held neither could withstand constitutional challenge unless it was shown to advance the anticorruption interest. . . . If the interest is not advanced, the regulations cannot comport with the Constitution, quite apart from the standard of review.

Buckley made clear, by its express language and its context, that the corruption interest only justifies regulating candidates' and officeholders' receipt of what we can call the *"quids"* in the *quid pro quo* formulation. . . .

. . .

[T]he perception of corruption that the majority now asserts is somehow different from the *quid pro quo* potential . . . created by . . . contributions directly to a candidate.

. . .

The Court . . . interprets the anticorruption rationale to allow regulation not just of "actual or apparent *quid pro quo* arrangements," but of any conduct that wins goodwill from or influences a Member of Congress. . . .

. . .

Access in itself, however, shows only that in a general sense an officeholder favors someone or that someone has influence on the officeholder. . . .

The generic favoritism or influence theory articulated by the Court is at odds with standard First Amendment analyses because it is unbounded and susceptible to no limiting principle. Any given action might be favored by any given person, so by the Court's reasoning political loyalty of the purest sort can be prohibited. There is no remaining principled method for inquiring whether a campaign finance regulation does in fact regulate corruption in a serious and meaningful way. We are left to defer to a congressional conclusion that certain conduct creates favoritism or influence.

. . .

The majority attempts to mask its extension of *Buckley* under claims that BCRA prevents the appearance of corruption, even if it does not prevent actual corruption . . . [T]he inquiry does not turn on whether some persons assert that an appearance of corruption exists. . . . Instead, the Court asked whether the Government had proved that the regulated conduct, the expenditures, posed inherent *quid pro quo* corruption potential. . . .

. . .

1. New FECA §§ 323(a), (b), (d), and (f)

Sections 323(a), (b), (d), and (f) . . . cannot stand because they do not add regulation to conduct that poses a demonstrable *quid pro quo* danger. They do not further *Buckley*'s corruption interest.

. . .

On its face § 323(a) does not regulate federal candidates' or officeholders' receipt of *quids* because it does not regulate contributions to, or conduct by, candidates or officeholders. . . .

. . .

. . . The record confirms that soft money party contributions, without more, do not create *quid pro quo* corruption potential. As a conceptual matter, generic party contributions may engender good will from a candidate or officeholder . . . Still, no Member of Congress testified this favoritism changed voting behavior.

. . .

None of [the] other sections has an independent justifying interest. Section 323(b), for example, adds regulation only to activity undertaken by a state party. In the District Court two of the three judges found as fact that particular state and local parties exist primarily to participate in state and local elections, that they spend the majority of their resources on those elections, and that their voter registration and Get Out The Vote (GOTV) activities, in particular, are directed primarily at state and local elections. . . .

. . .

When one recognizes that §§ 323(a), (b), (d), and (f) do not serve the interest the anticorruption rationale contemplates, Title I's entirety begins to look very much like an incumbency protection plan. . . . That impression is worsened by the fact that Congress exempted its officeholders from the more stringent prohibitions imposed on party officials. Compare new FECA § 323(a) with new FECA § 323(e). Section 323(a) raises an inflexible bar against soft money solicitation, in any way, by parties or party officials. Section 323(e), in contrast, enacts exceptions to the rule for federal officeholders (the very centerpiece of possible corruption), and allows them to solicit soft money for various uses and organizations.

. . .

2. New FECA § 323(e)

Ultimately, only one of the challenged Title I provisions satisfies *Buckley*'s anticorruption rationale and the First Amendment's guarantee. It is § 323(e). This provision is the sole aspect of Title I that is a direct and necessary regulation of federal candidates' and officeholders' receipt of *quids*. Section 323(e) . . . and the regulations that follow, limit candidates' and their agents' solicitation of soft money. The regulation of a candidate's receipt of funds furthers a constitutionally sufficient interest. More difficult, however, is the question whether regulation of a candidate's solicitation of funds also furthers this interest if the funds are given to another.

I agree with the Court that the broader solicitation regulation does further a sufficient interest. The making of a solicited gift is a *quid* both to the recipient of the money and to the one who solicits the payment (by granting his request). Rules governing candidates' or officeholders' solicitation of contributions are, therefore, regulations governing their receipt of *quids*. This regulation fits under *Buckley*'s anticorruption rationale.

. . .

B.   Standard of Review

. . . In *Buckley,* we applied "closely drawn" scrutiny to contribution limitations and strict scrutiny to expenditure limitations. . . . [T]he majority assumes that because *Buckley* applied the rationale in the context of contribution and expenditure limits, its application gives Congress and the Court the capacity to classify any challenged campaign finance regulation as either a contribution or an expenditure limit. . . .

Title I's provisions prohibit the receipt of funds; and in most instances, but not all, this can be defined as a contribution limit. . . . They prohibit the giving of funds to nonprofit groups; and this falls within neither definition as we have ever defined it. Finally, they prohibit fundraising activity; and the parties dispute the classification of this regulation (the challengers say it is core political association, while the Government says it ultimately results only in a limit on contribution receipts).

. . .

Even if the laws could be classified in broad terms as only contribution limits, . . . that still leaves the question what "contribution limits" can include if they are to be upheld under *Buckley*. *Buckley*'s application of a less exacting review to contribution limits must be confined to the narrow category of money gifts that are directed, in some manner, to a candidate or officeholder. Any broader definition of the category contradicts *Buckley*'s *quid pro quo* rationale . . .

The Court, it must be acknowledged, both in *Buckley* and on other occasions, has described contribution limits due some more deferential review in less than precise terms. At times it implied that donations to political parties would also qualify as contributions whose limitation too would be subject to less exacting review. . . .

Buckley's underlying rationale is this: Less exacting review applies to Government regulations that "significantly interfere" with First Amendment rights of association. But any regulation of speech or associational rights creating "markedly greater interference" than such significant interference receives strict scrutiny. Unworkable and ill advised though it may be, *Buckley* unavoidably sets forth this test: Even a 'significant interference' with protected rights of political association" may be sustained if the State demonstrates [1] a sufficiently important interest and [2] employs means closely drawn to avoid unnecessary abridgment of associational freedoms. . . .

. . .

The majority makes *Buckley*'s already awkward and imprecise test all but meaningless in its application. . . .

. . .

Congress has undertaken this comprehensive reordering of association and speech rights in the name of enforcing contribution limitations. Here, however, as in *Buckley,* "[t]he markedly greater burden on basic freedoms caused by [BCRA's pervasive regulation] cannot be sustained simply by invoking the interest in maximizing the effectiveness of the less intrusive contribution limitations." ... BCRA fundamentally alters, and thereby burdens, protected speech and association throughout our society. Strict scrutiny ought apply to review of its constitutionality. Under strict scrutiny, the congressional scheme, for the most part, cannot survive....

. . .

Compared to the narrowly tailored effort of § 323(e), which addresses in direct and specific terms federal candidates' and officeholders' quest for dollars, these sections cast a wide net not confined to the critical categories of federal candidate or officeholder involvement. They are not narrowly tailored; they are not closely drawn; they flatly violate the First Amendment; and even if they do encompass some speech that poses a regulable *quid pro quo* danger, that little assurance does not justify or permit a regime which silences so many legitimate voices in this protected sphere.

. . .

The final aspect of BCRA that implicates *Buckley*'s anticorruption rationale is § 213, the forced choice provision. The majority concludes § 213 violates the Constitution. I agree and write on this aspect of the case to point out that the section's unlawfulness flows ... from its raw suppression of constitutionally protected speech.

Section 213 unconstitutionally forces the parties to surrender one of two First Amendment rights. I continue to believe ... that even under *Buckley* a political party has a protected right to make coordinated expenditures with its candidates.... Our well-established constitutional tradition respects the role parties play in the electoral process and in stabilizing our representative democracy. ... Section 213's command that the parties abandon one First Amendment right or the other offends the Constitution.

II. TITLE II PROVISIONS

A. Disclosure Provisions

... I agree with the Court's judgment upholding the disclosure provisions contained in § 201 of Title II, with one exception.

Section 201's advance disclosure requirement—the aspect of the provision requiring those who have contracted to speak to disclose their speech in advance—is, in my view, unconstitutional. Advance disclosure imposes real burdens on political speech that *post hoc* disclosure does not. It forces disclosure of political strategy by revealing where ads are to be run and what their content is likely to be (based on who is running the ad). It also provides an opportunity for the ad buyer's opponents to dissuade broadcasters from running ads. ... Against those tangible additional burdens, the Government identifies no additional interest uniquely served by advance disclosure. If Congress intended to ensure that advertisers could not flout these disclosure laws by running an ad before the election, but paying for it afterwards, then Congress should simply have required the disclosure upon the running of the ad. Burdening the First Amendment further by requiring advance disclosure is not a constitutionally acceptable alternative. To the extent § 201 requires advance disclosure, it finds no justification in its subordinating interests and imposes greater burdens than the First Amendment permits.

. . .

B. BCRA § 203

The majority permits a new and serious intrusion on speech when it upholds § 203, the key provision in Title II that prohibits corporations and labor unions from using money from their general treasury to fund electioneering communications. The majority compounds the error made in *Austin v. Michigan Chamber of Commerce,* 494 U.S. 652 (1990) . . . Instead of extending *Austin* to suppress new and vibrant voices, I would overrule it and return our campaign finance jurisprudence to principles consistent with the First Amendment.

1.

The Government and the majority are right about one thing: The express-advocacy requirement, with its list of magic words, is easy to circumvent. . . . What the Court and the Government call sham, however, are the ads speakers find most effective. Unlike express ads that leave nothing to the imagination, the record shows that issues ads are preferred by almost all candidates, even though politicians, unlike corporations, can lawfully broadcast express ads if they so choose. It is a measure of the Government's disdain for protected speech that it would label as a sham the mode of communication sophisticated speakers choose because it is the most powerful.

The Government's use of the pejorative label should not obscure § 203's practical effect: It prohibits a mass communication technique favored in the modern political process for the very reason that it is the most potent. That the Government would regulate it for this reason goes only to prove the illegitimacy of the Government's purpose. . . . The problem is that the majority uses *Austin,* a decision itself unfaithful to our First Amendment precedents, to justify banning a far greater range of speech. This has it all backwards. If protected speech is being suppressed, that must be the end of the inquiry.

. . .

Austin was the first and, until now, the only time our Court had allowed the Government to exercise the power to censor political speech based on the speaker's corporate identity. The majority's contrary contention is simply incorrect. . . . The distinction . . . between independent expenditures for commenting on issues, on the one hand, and supporting or opposing a candidate, on the other, has no First Amendment significance apart from *Austin*'s arbitrary line.

Austin was based on a faulty assumption. . . . [T]here is a general recognition now that discussions of candidates and issues are quite often intertwined in practical terms. . . . Just as arguments about immense aggregations of corporate wealth and concerns about protecting shareholders and union members do not justify a ban on issue ads, they cannot sustain a ban on independent expenditures for express ads. . . .

. . .

I surmise that even the majority . . . appreciates these problems with *Austin*. That is why it invents a new justification. We are now told that "the government also has a compelling interest in insulating federal elections from the type of corruption arising from the real or apparent creation of political debts." . . .

This rationale has no limiting principle. Were we to accept it, Congress would have the authority to outlaw even pure issue ads, because they, too, could endear their sponsors to candidates who adopt the favored positions.

Taken to its logical conclusion, the alleged Government interest "in insulating federal elections from ... the real or apparent creation of political debts" also conflicts with *Buckley*. ... The Government's position would eviscerate the line between expenditures and contributions and subject both to the same "complaisant review under the First Amendment." ...

    . . .

5.

Title II's vagueness and overbreadth demonstrate Congress' fundamental misunderstanding of the First Amendment. The Court, it must be said, succumbs to the same mistake. The majority begins with a denunciation of direct campaign contributions by corporations and unions. It then uses this rhetorical momentum as its leverage to uphold the Act. The problem, however, is that Title II's ban on electioneering communications covers general commentaries on political issues and is far removed from laws prohibiting direct contributions from corporate and union treasuries. The severe First Amendment burden of this ban on independent expenditures requires much stronger justifications than the majority offers. ...

The hostility toward corporations and unions that infuses the majority opinion is inconsistent with the viewpoint neutrality the First Amendment demands of all Government actors, including the members of this Court. Corporations, after all, are the engines of our modern economy. They facilitate complex operations on which the Nation's prosperity depends. ... Unions are also an established part of the national economic system. They, too, have their own unique insights to contribute to the political debate, but the law's impact on them is just as severe. The costs of the majority's misplaced concerns about the "corrosive and distorting effects of immense aggregations of wealth," ... moreover, will weigh most heavily on budget-strapped nonprofit entities upon which many of our citizens rely for political commentary and advocacy. These groups must now choose between staying on the sidelines in the next election or establishing a PAC against their institutional identities. PACs are a legal construct sanctioned by Congress. They are not necessarily the means of communication chosen and preferred by the citizenry.

    . . .

CONCLUSION

    . . .

The First Amendment ... cannot be read to allow Congress to provide for the imprisonment of those who attempt to establish new political parties and alter the civic discourse. Our pluralistic society is filled with voices expressing new and different viewpoints, speaking through modes and mechanisms that must be allowed to change in response to the demands of an interested public. ... The Court, upholding multiple laws that suppress both spontaneous and concerted speech, leaves us less free than before. Today's decision breaks faith with our tradition of robust and unfettered debate.

For the foregoing reasons, with respect, I dissent from the Court's decision upholding the main features of Titles I and II.

Justice Scalia, concurring with respect to BCRA Titles III and IV, dissenting with respect to BCRA Titles I and V, and concurring in the judgment in part and dissenting in part with respect to BCRA Title II.

... I cannot avoid adding to the many writings a few words of my own.

This is a sad day for the freedom of speech. Who could have imagined that the same Court which, within the past four years, has sternly disapproved of restrictions upon such inconsequential forms of expression as virtual child pornography, . . . tobacco advertising, . . . dissemination of illegally intercepted communications, . . . and sexually explicit cable programming, . . . would smile with favor upon a law that cuts to the heart of what the First Amendment is meant to protect: the right to criticize the government. For that is what the most offensive provisions of this legislation are all about. . . .

. . .

I wish to address three fallacious propositions that might be thought to justify some or all of the provisions of this legislation—only the last of which is explicitly embraced by the principal opinion for the Court, but all of which underlie, I think, its approach to these cases.

(a) Money is Not Speech

It was said by congressional proponents of this legislation, . . . that since this legislation regulates nothing but the expenditure of money for speech, as opposed to speech itself, the burden it imposes is not subject to full First Amendment scrutiny . . . Until today, however, that view has been categorically rejected by our jurisprudence. . . .

. . . [T]oday's cavalier attitude toward regulating the financing of speech (the "exacting scrutiny" test of *Buckley* is not uttered in any majority opinion, and is not observed in the ones from which I dissent) frustrates the fundamental purpose of the First Amendment. . . .

. . .

. . . [A] law limiting the amount a person can spend to broadcast his political views is a direct restriction on speech. That is no different from a law limiting the amount a newspaper can pay its editorial staff or the amount a charity can pay its leafletters. It is equally clear that a limit on the amount a candidate can *raise* from any one individual for the purpose of speaking is also a direct limitation on speech. . . .

(b) Pooling Money is Not Speech

Another proposition which could explain at least some of the results of today's opinion is that the First Amendment right to spend money for speech does not include the right to combine with others in spending money for speech. . . .

We have said that "implicit in the right to engage in activities protected by the First Amendment" is "a corresponding right to associate with others in pursuit of a wide variety of political, social, economic, educational, religious, and cultural ends." . . . That "right to associate . . . in pursuit" includes the right to pool financial resources.

. . .

(c) Speech by Corporations Can Be Abridged

. . .

. . . The First Amendment does not in my view permit the restriction of . . . political speech. And the same holds true for corporate electoral speech: A candidate should not be insulated from the most effective speech that the major participants in the economy and major incorporated interest groups can generate.

. . . The premise of the First Amendment is that the American people are neither sheep nor fools, and hence fully capable of considering both the substance of the speech presented to them and its proximate and ultimate source. If that premise is wrong, our democracy has a much greater problem to overcome than merely the influence of amassed wealth. Given the premises of democracy, there is no such thing as *too much* speech.

... [C]orporate (like noncorporate) allies will have greater access to the officeholder, and ... he will tend to favor the same causes as those who support him (which is usually *why* they supported him). That is the nature of politics— if not indeed human nature—and how this can properly be considered "corruption" (or "the appearance of corruption") with regard to corporate allies and not with regard to other allies is beyond me. ...

. . .

... This litigation is about preventing criticism of the government. ...Having abandoned that approach to a limited extent in *Buckley,* we abandon it much further today.

We will unquestionably be called upon to abandon it further still in the future. ...

. . .

... The federal election campaign laws ... can be expected to grow more voluminous, more detailed, and more complex in the years to come—and always, always, with the objective of reducing the excessive amount of speech.

Justice Thomas, concurring ... in part and dissenting in part with respect to BCRA Title II, and dissenting with respect to BCRA Titles I, V, and 311.

. . .

The joint opinion not only continues the errors of Buckley v. Valeo, by applying a low level of scrutiny to contribution ceilings, but also builds upon these errors by expanding the anticircumvention rationale beyond reason. ...

. . .

I must now address an issue on which I differ from all of my colleagues: the disclosure provisions ... The Court now [allows] the established right to anonymous speech to be stripped away based on the flimsiest of justifications.

. . .

I have long maintained that *Buckley* was incorrectly decided and should be overturned. ...

... The chilling endpoint of the Court's reasoning is not difficult to foresee: outright regulation of the press. None of the rationales offered by the defendants, and none of the reasoning employed by the Court, exempts the press. ...

. . .

SECTION 5. SPEECH AND ASSOCIATION RIGHTS OF GOVERNMENT EMPLOYEES

Connick v. Myers
461 U.S. 138, 103 S.Ct. 1684, 75 L.Ed.2d 708 (1983).

Justice White delivered the opinion of the Court.

In Pickering v. Board of Education, 391 U.S. 563 (1968), we stated that a public employee does not relinquish First Amendment rights to comment on matters of public interest by virtue of government employment. We also recognized that the State's interests as an employer in regulating the speech of its employees "differ significantly from those it possesses in connection with regulation of the speech of the citizenry in general." . . . The problem, we thought, was arriving "at a balance between the interests of the [employee], as a citizen, in commenting upon matters of public concern and the interest of the State, as an employer, in promoting the efficiency of the public services it performs through its employees." . . . We return to this problem today and consider whether the First and Fourteenth Amendments prevent the discharge of a state employee for circulating a questionnaire concerning internal office affairs.

I

The respondent, Sheila Myers, was employed as an Assistant District Attorney in New Orleans for five and a half years. She served at the pleasure of petitioner Harry Connick, the District Attorney for Orleans Parish. . . .

In the early part of October 1980, Myers was informed that she would be transferred to prosecute cases in a different section of the criminal court. Myers was strongly opposed to the proposed transfer and expressed her view to several of her supervisors, including Connick. Despite her objections, on October 6 Myers was notified that she was being transferred. Myers again spoke with Dennis Waldron, one of the First Assistant District Attorneys, expressing her reluctance to accept the transfer. A number of other office matters were discussed and Myers later testified that, in response to Waldron's suggestion that her concerns were not shared by others in the office, she informed him that she would do some research on the matter.

That night Myers prepared a questionnaire soliciting the views of her fellow staff members concerning office transfer policy, office morale, the need for a grievance committee, the level of confidence in supervisors, and whether employees felt pressured to work in political campaigns. Early the following morning, Myers typed and copied the questionnaire. She also met with Connick who urged her to accept the transfer. She said she would "consider" it. Connick then left the office. Myers then distributed the questionnaire to 15 Assistant District Attorneys. Shortly after noon, Dennis Waldron learned that Myers was distributing the survey. He immediately phoned Connick and informed him that Myers was creating a "mini-insurrection" within the office. Connick returned to the office and told Myers that she was being terminated because of her refusal to accept the transfer. She was also told that her distribution of the questionnaire was considered an act of insubordination. Connick particularly objected to the question which inquired whether employees "had confidence in and would rely on the word" of various superiors in the office, and to a question concerning pressure to work in political campaigns which he felt would be damaging if discovered by the press.

Myers filed suit under 42 U.S.C. § 1983, . . . contending that her employment was wrongfully terminated because she had exercised her constitutionally-protected right of free speech. The District Court agreed, ordered Myers reinstated, and awarded backpay, damages, and attorney's fees. . . .

. . . [T]he United States Court of Appeals for the Fifth Circuit . . . affirmed. . . .

II

For at least 15 years, it has been settled that a State cannot condition public employment on a basis that infringes the employee's constitutionally protected interest in freedom of expression. ... Our task, as we defined it in *Pickering,* is to seek "a balance between the interests of the [employee], as a citizen, in commenting upon matters of public concern and the interest of the State, as an employer, in promoting the efficiency of the public services it performs through its employees." ... The District Court, and thus the Court of Appeals as well, misapplied our decision in *Pickering* and consequently, in our view, erred in striking the balance for respondent.

A

... Connick contends at the outset that no balancing of interests is required in this case because Myers' questionnaire concerned only internal office matters and that such speech is not upon a matter of "public concern," as the term was used in *Pickering.* Although we do not agree that Myers' communication in this case was wholly without First Amendment protection, there is much force to Connick's submission. ... [G]overnment offices could not function if every employment decision became a constitutional matter.

For most of this century, the unchallenged dogma was that a public employee had no right to object to conditions placed upon the terms of employment—including those which restricted the exercise of constitutional rights. The classic formulation of this position was Justice Holmes, who, when sitting on the Supreme Judicial Court of Massachusetts, observed: "[A police-man] may have a constitutional right to talk politics, but he has no constitutional right to be a policeman." McAuliffe v. Mayor of New Bedford, 155 Mass. 216, 220, 29 N.E. 517, 517 (1892). For many years, Holmes' epigram expressed this Court's law. Adler v. Board of Education, 342 U.S. 485 (1952); Garner v. Los Angeles Bd. of Public Works, 341 U.S. 716 (1951); Public Workers v. Mitchell, 330 U.S. 75 (1947); United States v. Wurzbach, 280 U.S. 396 (1930); Ex parte Curtis, 106 U.S. 371 (1882).

The Court cast new light on the matter in a series of cases arising from the widespread efforts in the 1950s and early 1960s to require public employees, particularly teachers, to swear oaths of loyalty to the state and reveal the groups with which they associated. In Wieman v. Updegraff, 344 U.S. 183 (1952), the Court held that a State could not require its employees to establish their loyalty by extracting an oath denying past affiliation with Communists. In Cafeteria Workers v. McElroy, 367 U.S. 886 (1961), the Court recognized that the government could not deny employment because of previous membership in a particular party.... By the time Sherbert v. Verner, 374 U.S. 398 (1963), was decided, it was already "too late in the day to doubt that the liberties of religion and expression may be infringed by the denial of or placing of conditions upon a benefit or privilege." ... It was therefore no surprise when in Keyishian v. Board of Regents, [385 U.S. 589 (1967)], the Court invalidated New York statutes barring employment on the basis of membership in "subversive" organizations, observing that the theory that public employment which may be denied altogether may be subjected to any conditions, regardless of how unreasonable, had been uniformly rejected. ...

In all of these cases, the precedents in which *Pickering* is rooted, the invalidated statutes and actions sought to suppress the rights of public employees to participate in public affairs. The issue was whether government employees could be prevented or "chilled" by the fear of discharge from joining political parties and other associations that certain public officials might find "subversive." . . .

Pickering v. Board of Education, supra, followed from this understanding of the First Amendment. In *Pickering,* the Court held impermissible under the First Amendment the dismissal of a high school teacher for openly criticizing the Board of Education on its allocation of school funds between athletics and education and its methods of informing taxpayers about the need for additional revenue. Pickering's subject was "a matter of legitimate public concern" upon which "free and open debate is vital to informed decision-making by the electorate." . . .

Our cases following *Pickering* also involved safeguarding speech on matters of public concern. The controversy in Perry v. Sindermann, 408 U.S. 593 (1972), arose from the failure to rehire a teacher in the state college system who had testified before committees of the Texas Legislature and had become involved in public disagreement over whether the college should be elevated to 4-year status—a change opposed by the Regents. In Mt. Healthy City Board of Ed. v. Doyle, 429 U.S. 274 (1977), a public school teacher was not rehired because, allegedly, he had relayed to a radio station the substance of a memorandum relating to teacher dress and appearance that the school principal had circulated to various teachers. The memorandum was apparently prompted by the view of some in the administration that there was a relationship between teacher appearance and public support for bond issues, and indeed, the radio station promptly announced the adoption of the dress code as a news item. Most recently, in Givhan v. Western Line Consolidated School District, 439 U.S. 410 (1979), we held that First Amendment protection applies when a public employee arranges to communicate privately with his employer rather than to express his views publicly. Although the subject-matter of Mrs. Givhan's statements were not the issue before the Court, it is clear that her statements concerning the school district's allegedly racially discriminatory policies involved a matter of public concern.

Pickering, its antecedents and progeny, lead us to conclude that if Myer's questionnaire cannot be fairly characterized as constituting speech on a matter of public concern, it is unnecessary for us to scrutinize the reasons for her discharge. When employee expression cannot be fairly considered as relating to any matter of political, social, or other concern to the community, government officials should enjoy wide latitude in managing their offices, without intrusive oversight by the judiciary in the name of the First Amendment. Perhaps the government employer's dismissal of the worker may not be fair, but ordinary dismissals from government service which violate no fixed tenure or applicable statute or regulation are not subject to judicial review even if the reasons for the dismissal are alleged to be mistaken or unreasonable. . . .

We do not suggest, however, that Myers' speech, even if not touching upon a matter of public concern, is totally beyond the protection of the First Amendment. . . . For example, an employee's false criticism of his employer on grounds not of public concern may be cause for his discharge but would be entitled to the same protection in a libel action accorded an identical statement made by a man on the street. We hold only that when a public employee speaks not as a citizen upon matters of public concern, but instead as an employee upon matters only of personal interest, absent the most unusual circumstances, a federal court is not the appropriate forum in which to review the wisdom of a personnel decision taken by a public agency allegedly in reaction to the employee's behavior. . . . Our responsibility is to ensure that citizens are not deprived of fundamental rights by virtue of working for the government; this does not require a grant of immunity for employee grievances not afforded by the First Amendment to those who do not work for the State.

Whether an employee's speech addresses a matter of public concern must be determined by the content, form, and context of a given statement, as revealed by the whole record. In this case, with but one exception, the questions posed by Myers to her co-workers do not fall under the rubric of matters of "public concern." We view the questions pertaining to the confidence and trust that Myers' coworkers possess in various supervisors, the level of office morale, and the need for a grievance committee as mere extensions of Myers' dispute over her transfer to another section of the criminal court. Unlike the dissent, we do not believe these questions are of public import in evaluating the performance of the District Attorney as an elected official. Myers did not seek to inform the public that the District Attorney's Office was not discharging its governmental responsibilities in the investigation and prosecution of criminal cases. Nor did Myers seek to bring to light actual or potential wrongdoing or breach of public trust on the part of Connick and others. Indeed, the questionnaire, if released to the public, would convey no information at all other than the fact that a single employee is upset with the status quo. While discipline and morale in the workplace are related to an agency's efficient performance of its duties, the focus of Myers' questions is not to evaluate the performance of the office but rather to gather ammunition for another round of controversy with her superiors. These questions reflect one employee's dissatisfaction with a transfer and an attempt to turn that displeasure into a cause célèbre.[8]

To presume that all matters which transpire within a government office are of public concern would mean that virtually every remark—and certainly every criticism directed at a public official—would plant the seed of a constitutional case. While as a matter of good judgment, public officials should be receptive to constructive criticism offered by their employees, the First Amendment does not require a public office to be run as a roundtable for employee complaints over internal office affairs.

One question in Myers' questionnaire, however, does touch upon a matter of public concern. Question 11 inquires if assistant district attorneys "ever feel pressured to work in political campaigns on behalf of office supported candidates." . . . [T]he issue of whether assistant district attorneys are pressured to work in political campaigns is a matter of interest to the community upon which it is essential that public employees be able to speak out freely without fear of retaliatory dismissal.

B

Because one of the questions in Myers' survey touched upon a matter of public concern and contributed to her discharge, we must determine whether Connick was justified in discharging Myers. . . . [T]he State's burden in justifying a particular discharge varies depending upon the nature of the employee's expression. Although such particularized balancing is difficult, the courts must reach the most appropriate possible balance of the competing interests.

---

8. This is not a case like *Givhan,* supra, where an employee speaks out as a citizen on a matter of general concern, not tied to a personal employment dispute, but arranges to do so privately. Mrs. Givhan's right to protest racial discrimination—a matter inherently of public concern—is not forfeited by her choice of a private forum. . . . Here, however, a questionnaire not otherwise of public concern does not attain that status because its subject matter could, in different circumstances, have been the topic of a communication to the public that might be of general interest. . . .

C

The *Pickering* balance requires full consideration of the government's interest in the effective and efficient fulfillment of its responsibilities to the public. . . .

. . . Connick's judgment . . . was that Myers' questionnaire was an act of insubordination which interfered with working relationships. When close working relationships are essential to fulfilling public responsibilities, a wide degree of deference to the employer's judgment is appropriate. Furthermore, we do not see the necessity for an employer to allow events to unfold to the extent that the disruption of the office and the destruction of working relationships is manifest before taking action. We caution that a stronger showing may be necessary if the employee's speech more substantially involved matters of public concern.

. . .

Also relevant is the manner, time, and place in which the questionnaire was distributed. . . . Here the questionnaire was prepared and distributed at the office; the manner of distribution required not only Myers to leave her work but for others to do the same in order that the questionnaire be completed. Although some latitude in when official work is performed is to be allowed when professional employees are involved, and Myers did not violate announced office policy, the fact that Myers, unlike Pickering, exercised her rights to speech at the office supports Connick's fears that the functioning of his office was endangered.

Finally, the context in which the dispute arose is also significant. This is not a case where an employee, out of purely academic interest, circulated a questionnaire so as to obtain useful research. Myers acknowledges that it is no coincidence that the questionnaire followed upon the heels of the transfer notice. When employee speech concerning office policy arises from an employment dispute concerning the very application of that policy to the speaker, additional weight must be given to the supervisor's view that the employee has threatened the authority of the employer to run the office. . . .

III

Myers' questionnaire touched upon matters of public concern in only a most limited sense; her survey, in our view, is most accurately characterized as an employee grievance concerning internal office policy. The limited First Amendment interest involved here does not require that Connick tolerate action which he reasonably believed would disrupt the office, undermine his authority, and destroy close working relationships. Myers' discharge therefore did not offend the First Amendment. . . .

. . . Although today the balance is struck for the government, this is no defeat for the First Amendment. For it would indeed be a Pyrrhic victory for the great principles of free expression if the Amendment's safeguarding of a public employee's right, as a citizen, to participate in discussions concerning public affairs were confused with the attempt to constitutionalize the employee grievance that we see presented here. The judgment of the Court of Appeals is

Reversed.

Justice Brennan, with whom Justice Marshall, Justice Blackmun, and Justice Stevens join, dissenting.

. . . It is hornbook law . . . that speech about "the manner in which government is operated or should be operated" is an essential part of the communications necessary for self-governance the protection of which was a central purpose of the First Amendment. ... Because the questionnaire addressed such matters and its distribution did not adversely affect the operations of the District Attorney's Office or interfere with Myers' working relationship with her fellow employees, I dissent.

I

. . .

The Court's decision today is flawed in three respects. First, the Court distorts the balancing analysis required under *Pickering* by suggesting that one factor, the context in which a statement is made, is to be weighed *twice*—first in determining whether an employee's speech addresses a matter of public concern and then in deciding whether the statement adversely affected the government's interest as an employer. Second, in concluding that the effect of respondent's personnel policies on employee morale and the work performance of the District Attorney's Office is not a matter of public concern, the Court impermissibly narrows the class of subjects on which public employees may speak out without fear of retaliatory dismissal. Third, the Court misapplies the *Pickering* balancing test in holding that Myers could constitutionally be dismissed for circulating a questionnaire addressed to at least one subject that *was* "a matter of interest to the community," in the absence of evidence that her conduct disrupted the efficient functioning of the District Attorney's Office.

II

. . .

The Court seeks to distinguish *Givhan* on the ground that speech protesting racial discrimination is "inherently of public concern." Ante, n. 8. In so doing, it suggests that there are two classes of speech of public concern: statements "of public import" because of their content, form and context, and statements that, by virtue of their subject matter, are "inherently of public concern." In my view, however, whether a particular statement by a public employee is addressed to a subject of public concern does not depend on where it was said or why. The First Amendment affords special protection to speech that may inform public debate about how our society is to be governed— regardless of whether it actually becomes the subject of a public controversy.

. . .

IV

The Court's decision today inevitably will deter public employees from making critical statements about the manner in which government agencies are operated for fear that doing so will provoke their dismissal. As a result, the public will be deprived of valuable information with which to evaluate the performance of elected officials. Because protecting the dissemination of such information is an essential function of the First Amendment, I dissent.

RANKIN v. McPHERSON, 483 U.S. 378 (1987). McPherson was a clerical employee in a county constable's office. On hearing a radio report of the attempted assassination of President Reagan in March, 1981, she said to a fellow employee: "if they go for him again, I hope they get him." The court held that McPherson's discharge violated the first amendment. The statement was speech on a matter of public concern, and did not constitute a threat to kill the president. Asserted state interests did not outweigh McPherson's First Amendment rights. Her duties were clerical, and discharge was not based on an assessment that the remark demonstrated a character trait that made her unfit to perform that work. The remark did not disrupt the operation of the office, nor was there danger that it had discredited the office. Justice Marshall's opinion for the court concluded:

> "We cannot believe that every employee in Constable Rankin's office, whether computer operator, electrician, or file clerk, is equally required, on pain of discharge, to avoid any statement susceptible of being interpreted by the Constable as an indication that the employee may be unworthy of employment in his law enforcement agency. At some point, such concerns are so removed from the effective functioning of the public employer that they cannot prevail over the free speech rights of the public employee."

Justice Powell's concurrence remarked that in the case of private speech in the workplace on matters of public concern "it will be an unusual case" where discharge can be justified.

> "The risk that a single, offhand comment directed to only one other worker will lower morale, disrupt the work force, or otherwise undermine the mission of the office borders on the fanciful."

Justice Scalia, joined by Chief Justice Rehnquist and Justices White and O'Connor, dissented. The question was whether McPherson could "ride with the cops and cheer for the robbers." Although the First Amendment would prohibit criminal punishment for a statement expressing approval of a serious and violent crime, such a statement is not speech on a matter of public concern. Even if the statement was speech on a matter of public concern, the discharge was justified by interests in maintaining an esprit de corps and a proper public image for a law enforcement office.

United States Civil Service Commission v. National Association of Letter Carriers AFL–CIO

413 U.S. 548, 93 S.Ct. 2880, 37 L.Ed.2d 796 (1973).

Mr. Justice White delivered the opinion of the Court.

... [Section] 9(a) of the Hatch Act, now codified in 5 U.S.C. § 7324(a)(2), [prohibits] federal employees taking "an active part in political management or in political campaigns," ... A divided three-judge court sitting in the District of Columbia had held the section unconstitutional. We reverse the judgment of the District Court.

I

The case began when the National Association of Letter Carriers, six individual federal employees and certain local Democratic and Republican political committees filed a complaint, asserting on behalf of themselves and all federal employees that 5 U.S.C. § 7324(a)(2) was unconstitutional on its face and seeking an injunction against its enforcement.

. . . .

II

As the District Court recognized, the constitutionality of the Hatch Act's ban on taking an active part in political management or political campaigns has been here before. This very prohibition was attacked in [United Public Workers v. Mitchell, 330 U.S. 75 (1947)] . . .

. . .

We unhesitatingly reaffirm the *Mitchell* holding that Congress had, and has, the power to prevent Mr. Poole and others like him from holding a party office, working at the polls, and acting as party paymaster for other party workers. An Act of Congress going no farther would in our view unquestionably be valid. So would it be if, in plain and understandable language, the statute forbade activities such as organizing a political party or club; actively participating in fund-raising activities for a partisan candidate or political party; becoming a partisan candidate for, or campaigning for, an elective public office; actively managing the campaign of a partisan candidate for public office; initiating or circulating a partisan nominating petition or soliciting votes for a partisan candidate for public office; or serving as a delegate, alternate or proxy to a political party convention. Our judgment is that neither the First Amendment nor any other provision of the Constitution invalidates a law barring this kind of partisan political conduct by federal employees.

. . .

Until now, the judgment of Congress, the Executive, and the country appears to have been that partisan political activities by federal employees must be limited if the Government is to operate effectively and fairly, elections are to play their proper part in representative government, and employees themselves are to be sufficiently free from improper influences . . . The restrictions so far imposed on federal employees are not aimed at particular parties, groups, or points of view, but apply equally to all partisan activities of the type described. They discriminate against no racial, ethnic or religious minorities. Nor do they seek to control political opinions or beliefs, or to interfere with or influence anyone's vote at the polls.

. . . The problem in any case is to arrive at a balance between the interest of the [employee], as a citizen, in commenting upon matters of public concern and the interest of the [government], as an employer, in promoting the efficiency of the public services it performs through its employees. Although Congress is free to strike a different balance than it has, if it so chooses, we think the balance it has so far struck is sustainable by the obviously important interests sought to be served by the limitations on partisan political activities now contained in the Hatch Act.

. . .

. . . We agree with the basic holding of *Mitchell* that plainly identifiable acts of political management and political campaigning on the part of federal employees may constitutionally be prohibited. Until now this has been the judgment of the lower federal courts, and we do not understand the District Court in this case to have questioned the constitutionality of a law that was specifically limited to prohibiting the conduct in which Mr. Poole in the *Mitchell* case admittedly engaged.

III

But however constitutional the proscription of identifiable partisan conduct in understandable language may be, the District Court's judgment was that § 7324(a)(2) was both unconstitutionally vague and fatally overbroad. Appellees make the same contentions here, but we cannot agree that the section is unconstitutional on its face for either reason. . . .

. . . [J]udgment . . . reversed.

United States v. National Treasury Employees Union

513 U.S. 454, 115 S.Ct. 1003, 130 L.Ed.2d 964 (1995).

Justice Stevens delivered the opinion of the Court.

In 1989 Congress enacted a law that broadly prohibits federal employees from accepting any compensation for making speeches or writing articles. The prohibition applies even when neither the subject of the speech or article nor the person or group paying for it has any connection with the employee's official duties. We must decide whether that statutory prohibition comports with the Constitution's command that "Congress shall make no law . . . abridging the freedom of speech." We hold that it does not.

I

In 1967 Congress authorized the appointment every four years of a special Commission on Executive, Legislative, and Judicial Salaries, whose principal function would be to recommend appropriate levels of compensation for the top positions in all three branches of the Federal Government. Each of the first five quadrennial commissions recommended significant salary increases, but those recommendations went largely ignored. The Report of the 1989 Quadrennial Commission, however, was instrumental in leading to the enactment of the Ethics Reform Act of 1989, which contains the provision challenged in this case.

The 1989 Quadrennial Commission's report noted that inflation had decreased the salary levels for senior Government officials, measured in constant dollars, by approximately 35% since 1969. The report "also found that because their salaries are so inadequate, many members of Congress are supplementing their official compensation by accepting substantial amounts of 'honoraria' for meeting with interest groups which desire to influence their votes. Albeit to a less troubling extent, the practice of accepting honoraria also extends to top officials of the Executive and Judicial branches." . . . Accordingly, the Commission recommended that "salary levels for top officials be set at approximately the same amount in constant dollars" as those in effect in 1969 and further that "Congress enact legislation abolishing the practice of accepting honoraria in all three branches." . . .

The President's Commission on Federal Ethics Law Reform subsequently issued a report that endorsed the Quadrennial Commission's views. . . .

Although not adopted in their entirety, the two Commissions' recommendations echo prominently in the Ethics Reform Act of 1989. Section 703 of that Act provided a 25% pay increase to Members of Congress, federal judges, and Executive Branch employees above the salary grade GS–15. . . . Another section—the one at issue here—amended § 501(b) of the Ethics in Government Act of 1978 to create an "Honoraria Prohibition," which reads: "An individual may not receive any honorarium while that individual is a Member, officer or employee."

Section 505 of the Ethics Reform Act defined "officer or employee" to include nearly all employees of the Federal Government and "Member" to include any Representative, Delegate, or Resident Commissioner to Congress. The Congressional Operations Appropriations Act, 1992, extended both the salary increase and the prohibition against honoraria to the Senate. The 1989 Act defined "honorarium" to encompass any compensation paid to a Government employee for "an appearance, speech or article." The 1992 Appropriations Act amended that definition to exclude any series of appearances, speeches, or articles unrelated to the employee's official duties or status. The definition now reads as follows:

> "(3) The term 'honorarium' means a payment of money or any thing of value for an appearance, speech or article (including a series of appearances, speeches, or articles if the subject matter is directly related to the individual's official duties or the payment is made because of the individual's status with the Government) by a Member, officer or employee, excluding any actual and necessary travel expenses incurred by such individual...." ...

. . .

II

Two unions and several career civil servants employed full-time by various Executive departments and agencies filed suit in the United States District Court for the District of Columbia to challenge the constitutionality of the honoraria ban ...

. . .

The District Court granted respondents' motion for summary judgment ...

The Court of Appeals affirmed. ...

. . .

III

Federal employees who write for publication in their spare time have made significant contributions to the marketplace of ideas. They include literary giants like Nathaniel Hawthorne and Herman Melville, who were employed by the Customs Service; Walt Whitman, who worked for the Departments of Justice and Interior; and Bret Harte, an employee of the Mint. Respondents have yet to make comparable contributions to American culture, but they share with these great artists important characteristics that are relevant to the issue we confront.

... [R]espondents seek compensation for their expressive activities in their capacity as citizens, not as Government employees. They claim their employment status has no more bearing on the quality or market value of their literary output than it did on that of Hawthorne or Melville. With few exceptions, the content of respondents' messages has nothing to do with their jobs and does not even arguably have any adverse impact on the efficiency of the offices in which they work. They do not address audiences composed of co-workers or supervisors; instead, they write or speak for segments of the general public. Neither the character of the authors, the subject matter of their expression, the effect of the content of their expression on their official duties, nor the kind of audiences they address has any relevance to their employment.

. . .

... Respondents' expressive activities in this case fall within the protected category of citizen comment on matters of public concern rather than employee comment on matters related to personal status in the workplace. The speeches and articles for which they received compensation in the past were addressed to a public audience, were made outside the workplace, and involved content largely unrelated to their government employment.

The sweep of § 501(b) makes the Government's burden heavy. Unlike *Pickering* and its progeny, this case does not involve a post hoc analysis of one employee's speech and its impact on that employee's public responsibilities. . . . Rather, the Government asks us to apply *Pickering* to Congress' wholesale deterrent to a broad category of expression by a massive number of potential speakers. In Civil Service Comm'n v. Letter Carriers . . . we established that the Government must be able to satisfy a balancing test of the *Pickering* form to maintain a statutory restriction on employee speech. Because the discussion in that case essentially restated in balancing terms our approval of the Hatch Act in Public Workers v. Mitchell . . . we did not determine how the components of the *Pickering* balance should be analyzed in the context of a sweeping statutory impediment to speech.

We normally accord a stronger presumption of validity to a congressional judgment than to an individual executive's disciplinary action. . . . The widespread impact of the honoraria ban, however, gives rise to far more serious concerns than could any single supervisory decision. In addition, unlike an adverse action taken in response to actual speech, this ban chills potential speech before it happens. Cf. Near v. Minnesota ex rel. Olson, 283 U.S. 697 (1931). For these reasons, the Government's burden is greater with respect to this statutory restriction on expression than with respect to an isolated disciplinary action. The Government must show that the interests of both potential audiences and a vast group of present and future employees in a broad range of present and future expression are outweighed by that expression's "necessary impact on the actual operation" of the Government. . . .

Although § 501(b) neither prohibits any speech nor discriminates among speakers based on the content or viewpoint of their messages, its prohibition on compensation unquestionably imposes a significant burden on expressive activity. . . . Publishers compensate authors because compensation provides a significant incentive toward more expression. By denying respondents that incentive, the honoraria ban induces them to curtail their expression if they wish to continue working for the Government.

The ban imposes a far more significant burden on respondents than on the relatively small group of lawmakers whose past receipt of honoraria motivated its enactment. The absorbing and time-consuming responsibilities of legislators and policymaking executives leave them little opportunity for research or creative expression on subjects unrelated to their official responsibilities. Such officials often receive invitations to appear and talk about subjects related to their work because of their official identities. In contrast, invitations to rank-and-file employees usually depend only on the market value of their messages. The honoraria ban is unlikely to reduce significantly the number of appearances by high-ranking officials as long as travel expense reimbursement for the speaker and one relative is available as an alternative form of remuneration. In contrast, the denial of compensation for lower-paid, nonpolicymaking employees will inevitably diminish their expressive output.

The large-scale disincentive to Government employees' expression also imposes a significant burden on the public's right to read and hear what the employees would otherwise have written and said. . . . We have no way to measure the true cost of that burden, but we cannot ignore the risk that it might deprive us of the work of a future Melville or Hawthorne. The honoraria ban imposes the kind of burden that abridges speech under the First Amendment.

IV

Because the vast majority of the speech at issue in this case does not involve the subject matter of government employment and takes place outside the workplace, the Government is unable to justify § 501(b) on the grounds of immediate workplace disruption asserted in *Pickering* . . . Instead, the Government submits that the ban comports with the First Amendment because the prohibited honoraria were "reasonably deemed by Congress to interfere with the efficiency of the public service." . . .

. . . In Civil Service Commn. v. Letter Carriers . . . we noted that enactment of the Hatch Act in 1939 reflected "the conviction that the rapidly expanding Government work force should not be employed to build a powerful, invincible, and perhaps corrupt political machine." . . . An equally important concern was "to further serve the goal that employment and advancement in the Government service not depend on political performance, and at the same time to make sure that Government employees would be free from pressure and from express or tacit invitation to vote in a certain way or perform political chores in order to curry favor with their superiors rather than to act out their own beliefs." . . .

Thus, the Hatch Act aimed to protect employees' rights, notably their right to free expression, rather than to restrict those rights. Like the Hatch Act, the honoraria ban affects hundreds of thousands of federal employees. Unlike partisan political activity, however, honoraria hardly appear to threaten employees' morale or liberty. Moreover, Congress effectively designed the Hatch Act to combat demonstrated ill effects of Government employees' partisan political activities. In contrast, the Government has failed to show how it serves the interests it asserts by applying the honoraria ban to respondents.

The Government's underlying concern is that federal officers not misuse or appear to misuse power by accepting compensation for their unofficial and nonpolitical writing and speaking activities. This interest is undeniably powerful, but the Government cites no evidence of misconduct related to honoraria in the vast rank and file of federal employees below grade GS–16. . . . [T]he Government relies here on limited evidence of actual or apparent impropriety by legislators and high-level executives, together with the purported administrative costs of avoiding or detecting lower-level employees' violations of established policies.

. . . [T]he Government has based its defense of the ban on abuses of honoraria by Members of Congress. Congress reasonably could assume that payments of honoraria to judges or high-ranking officials in the Executive Branch might generate a similar appearance of improper influence. Congress could not, however, reasonably extend that assumption to all federal employees below Grade GS–16, an immense class of workers with negligible power to confer favors on those who might pay to hear them speak or to read their articles. A federal employee, such as a supervisor of mechanics at the Mint, might impair efficiency and morale by using political criteria to judge the performance of his or her staff. But one can envision scant harm, or appearance of harm, resulting from the same employee's accepting pay to lecture on the Quaker religion or to write dance reviews.

Although operational efficiency is undoubtedly a vital governmental interest, . . . several features of the honoraria ban's text cast serious doubt on the Government's submission that Congress perceived honoraria as so threatening to the efficiency of the entire federal service as to render the ban a reasonable response to the threat. . . . The first is the rather strange parenthetical reference to "a series of appearances, speeches, or articles" that the 1991 amendment inserted in the definition of the term "honorarium." The amended definition excludes such a series from the prohibited category unless "the subject matter is directly related to the individual's official duties or the payment is made because of the individual's status with the Government." In other words, accepting pay for a series of articles is prohibited if and only if a nexus exists between the author's employment and either the subject matter of the expression or the identity of the payor. For an individual article or speech, in contrast, pay is taboo even if neither the subject matter nor the payor bears any relationship at all to the author's duties.

Congress' decision to provide a total exemption for all unrelated series of speeches undermines application of the ban to individual speeches and articles with no nexus to Government employment. . . . The nexus limitation for series . . . unambiguously reflects a congressional judgment that agency ethics officials and the OGE can enforce the statute when it includes a nexus test. A blanket burden on the speech of nearly 1.7 million federal employees requires a much stronger justification than the Government's dubious claim of administrative convenience.

The definition's limitation of "honoraria" to expressive activities also undermines the Government's submission that the breadth of § 501 is reasonably necessary to protect the efficiency of the public service. . . . One might reasonably argue that expressive activities, because they occupy a favored position in the constitutional firmament, should be exempt from even a comprehensive ban on outside income. Imposing a greater burden on speech than on other off-duty activities assumed to pose the same threat to the efficiency of the federal service is, at best, anomalous.

The fact that § 501 singles out expressive activity for special regulation heightens the Government's burden of justification. . . . The Government has not persuaded us that § 501(b) is a reasonable response to the posited harms.

We also attach significance to the OGE regulations that limit the coverage of the statutory terms "appearance, speech or article." . . . The regulations exclude a wide variety of performances and writings that would normally appear to have no nexus with an employee's job, such as sermons, fictional writings, and athletic competitions . . . The exclusions, of course, make the task of the OGE and agency ethics officials somewhat easier, but they "diminish the credibility of the government's rationale" that paying lower-level employees for speech entirely unrelated to their work jeopardizes the efficiency of the entire federal service. . . .

These anomalies in the text of the statute and regulations underscore our conclusion: the speculative benefits the honoraria ban may provide the Government are not sufficient to justify this crudely crafted burden on respondents' freedom to engage in expressive activities. Section 501(b) violates the First Amendment.

V

After holding § 501(b) invalid because it was not as carefully tailored as it should have been, the Court of Appeals approved a remedy that is itself arguably overinclusive. The relief granted by the District Court and upheld by the Court of Appeals enjoined enforcement of the entire honoraria ban as applied to the entire Executive Branch of the Government. That injunction provides relief to senior executives who are not parties to this case. It also prohibits enforcement of the statute even when an obvious nexus exists between the employee's job and either the subject matter of his or her expression or the interest of the person paying for it. As an alternative to its request for outright reversal, the Government asks us to modify the judgment by upholding the statute as it applies, first, to employees not party to this action and, second, to situations in which a nexus is present.

. . . [W]e agree with the Government's first suggestion—that the relief should be limited to the parties before the Court. . . . [T]he Government conceivably might advance a different justification for an honoraria ban limited to more senior officials, thus presenting a different constitutional question than the one we decide today. . . .

Our obligation to avoid judicial legislation . . . persuades us to reject the Government's second suggestion—that we modify the remedy by crafting a nexus requirement for the honoraria ban. We cannot be sure that our attempt to redraft the statute to limit its coverage to cases involving an undesirable nexus between the speaker's official duties and either the subject matter of the speaker's expression or the identity of the payor would correctly identify the nexus Congress would have adopted in a more limited honoraria ban. . . . The process of drawing a proper nexus, even more than the defense of the statute's application to senior employees, would likely raise independent constitutional concerns whose adjudication is unnecessary to decide this case. We believe the Court of Appeals properly left to Congress the task of drafting a narrower statute.

Insofar as the judgment of the Court of Appeals affirms the injunction against enforcement of § 501(b) against respondents, it is affirmed; insofar as it grants relief to parties not before the Court, it is reversed. The case is remanded for further proceedings consistent with this opinion.

It is so ordered.

Justice O'Connor, concurring in the judgment in part and dissenting in part.

Although I agree that aspects of the honoraria ban run afoul of the First Amendment, I write separately for two reasons. First, I wish to emphasize my understanding of how our precedents . . . direct the Court's conclusion. Second, I write to express my disagreement with the Court's remedy, which in my view paints with too broad a brush.

I

. . .

. . . I agree with the Court that § 501 is unconstitutional to the extent that it bars this class of employees from receiving honoraria for expressive activities that bear no nexus to government employment.

II

. . . We do not decide the question—a far harder case for respondents, in my view—whether it is constitutional to apply the honoraria ban to speech by this class that bears a relationship to government employment. I believe that the Court overlooks this nuance when it enjoins all enforcement of § 501 against the class, any one of whose members may, in the future, receive honoraria for work-related activities. I would give respondents relief tailored to what they request: invalidation of the statute insofar as it applies to honoraria they receive for speech without nexus to government employment. . . .

. . .

Chief Justice Rehnquist, with whom Justice Scalia and Justice Thomas join, dissenting.

I believe that the Court's opinion is seriously flawed in two respects. First, its application of the First Amendment understates the weight which should be accorded to the governmental justifications for the honoraria ban and overstates the amount of speech which actually will be deterred. Second, its discussion of the impact of the statute which it strikes down is carefully limited to only a handful of the most appealing individual situations, but when it deals with the remedy it suddenly shifts gears and strikes down the statute as applied to the entire class of Executive Branch employees below grade GS–16. I therefore dissent.

I

. . .

. . . I cannot say that the balance that Congress has struck between its interests and the interests of its employees to receive compensation for their First Amendment expression is unreasonable. . . .

The Court largely ignores the Government's foremost interest—prevention of impropriety and the appearance of impropriety—by focusing solely on the burdens of the statute as applied to several carefully selected Executive Branch employees whose situations present the application of the statute where the Government's interests are at their lowest ebb . . .

. . .

. . . The theory underlying the Court's distinction—that federal employees below grade GS–16 have negligible power to confer favors on those who might pay to hear them speak or to read their articles—is seriously flawed. Tax examiners, bank examiners, enforcement officials, or any number of federal employees have substantial power to confer favors even though their compensation level is below Grade GS–16.

Furthermore, we rejected the same distinction in Public Workers v. Mitchell . . .

The Court dismisses the Hatch Act experience as irrelevant, because it aimed to protect employees' rights, notably their right to free expression, rather than to restrict those rights. This is, indeed, a strange characterization of § 9(a) of the Hatch Act. . . . [I]t can hardly be said that the Act protected the rights of workers who wished to engage in partisan political activity. . . .

The Government's related concern regarding the difficulties that would attach in administering a case-by-case analysis of the propriety of particular honoraria also supports the honoraria ban's validity. . . .

. . .

Unlike our prototypical application of *Pickering* which normally involves a response to the content of employee speech, the honoraria ban prohibits no speech and is unrelated to the message or the viewpoint expressed by the government employee. . . . Furthermore, the honoraria ban exempts from its prohibition travel and other expenses related to employee speech. . . . Because there is only a limited burden on respondents' First Amendment rights, Congress reasonably could have determined that its paramount interests in preventing impropriety and the appearance of impropriety in its work force justified the honoraria ban. . . .

. . .

II

. . . Even if I agreed that application of the honoraria ban to expressive activity unrelated to an employee's Government employment violated the First Amendment, I could not agree with the Court's remedy.

. . .

. . . I would affirm the Court of Appeals only insofar as its judgment affirmed the injunction against the enforcement of § 501(b) as applied to Executive Branch employees below grade GS–16 who seek honoraria that are unrelated to their Government employment.

Rutan v. Republican Party of Illinois

497 U.S. 62, 110 S.Ct. 2729, 111 L.Ed.2d 52 (1990).

Justice Brennan delivered the opinion of the Court.

To the victor belong only those spoils that may be constitutionally obtained. Elrod v. Burns, 427 U.S. 347 (1976), and Branti v. Finkel, 445 U.S. 507 (1980), decided that the First Amendment forbids government officials to discharge or threaten to discharge public employees solely for not being supporters of the political party in power, unless party affiliation is an appropriate requirement for the position involved. Today we are asked to decide the constitutionality of several related political patronage practices—whether promotion, transfer, recall, and hiring decisions involving low-level public employees may be constitutionally based on party affiliation and support. We hold that they may not.

I

The petition and cross-petition before us arise from a lawsuit protesting certain employment policies and practices instituted by Governor James Thompson of Illinois. On November 12, 1980, the Governor issued an executive order proclaiming a hiring freeze for every agency, bureau, board, or commission subject to his control. The order prohibits state officials from hiring any employee, filling any vacancy, creating any new position, or taking any similar action . . . without the Governor's "express permission after submission of appropriate requests to [his] office." . . .

Requests for the Governor's "express permission" have allegedly become routine. Permission has been granted or withheld through an agency expressly created for this purpose, the Governor's Office of Personnel (Governor's Office). . . .

By means of the freeze, according to petitioners, the Governor has been using the Governor's Office to operate a political patronage system to limit state employment and beneficial employment-related decisions to those who are supported by the Republican Party. In reviewing an agency's request that a particular applicant be approved for a particular position, the Governor's Office has looked at whether the applicant voted in Republican primaries in past election years, whether the applicant has provided financial or other support to the Republican Party and its candidates, whether the applicant has promised to join and work for the Republican Party in the future, and whether the applicant has the support of Republican Party officials at state or local levels.

Five people (including the three petitioners) brought suit against various Illinois and Republican Party officials in the United States District Court for the Central District of Illinois.... Cynthia B. Rutan has been working for the State since 1974 as a rehabilitation counselor. She claims that since 1981 she has been repeatedly denied promotions to supervisory positions for which she was qualified because she had not worked for or supported the Republican Party. Franklin Taylor, who operates road equipment for the Illinois Department of Transportation, claims that he was denied a promotion in 1983 because he did not have the support of the local Republican Party. Taylor also maintains that he was denied a transfer to an office nearer to his home because of opposition from the Republican Party chairmen in the counties in which he worked and to which he requested a transfer. James W. Moore claims that he has been repeatedly denied state employment as a prison guard because he did not have the support of Republican Party officials.

The two other plaintiffs, before the Court as cross-respondents, allege that they were not recalled after layoffs because they lacked Republican credentials. Ricky Standefer was a state garage worker who claims that he was not recalled, although his fellow employees were, because he had voted in a Democratic primary and did not have the support of the Republican Party. Dan O'Brien, formerly a dietary manager with the mental health department, contends that he was not recalled after a layoff because of his party affiliation and that he later obtained a lower paying position with the corrections department only after receiving support from the chairman of the local Republican Party.

The District Court dismissed the complaint ...

. . .

II

A

In *Elrod,* supra, we decided that a newly elected Democratic sheriff could not constitutionally engage in the patronage practice of replacing certain office staff with members of his own party "when the existing employees lack or fail to obtain requisite support from, or fail to affiliate with, that party." ... The plurality explained that conditioning public employment on the provision of support for the favored political party "unquestionably inhibits protected belief and association." ... It reasoned that conditioning employment on political activity pressures employees to pledge political allegiance to a party with which they prefer not to associate, to work for the election of political candidates they do not support, and to contribute money to be used to further policies with which they do not agree. The latter, the plurality noted, had been recognized by this Court as "tantamount to coerced belief." ... At the same time, employees are constrained from joining, working for or contributing to the political party and candidates of their own choice.... "[P]olitical belief and association constitute the core of those activities protected by the First Amendment," the plurality emphasized. Both the plurality and the concurrence drew support from Perry v. Sindermann, 408 U.S. 593 (1972), in which this Court held that the State's refusal to renew a teacher's contract because he had been publicly critical of its policies imposed an unconstitutional condition on the receipt of a public benefit....

The Court then decided that the government interests generally asserted in support of patronage fail to justify this burden on First Amendment rights because patronage dismissals are not the least restrictive means for fostering those interests.... The plurality acknowledged that a government has a significant interest in ensuring that it has effective and efficient employees. It expressed doubt, however, that "mere difference of political persuasion motivates poor performance" and concluded that, in any case, the government can ensure employee effectiveness and efficiency through the less drastic means of discharging staff members whose work is inadequate.... The plurality also found that a government can meet its need for politically loyal employees to implement its policies by the less intrusive measure of dismissing, on political grounds, only those employees in policymaking positions.... Finally, although the plurality recognized that preservation of the democratic process "may in some instances justify limitations on First Amendment freedoms," it concluded that the "process functions as well without the practice, perhaps even better." Patronage, it explained, "can result in the entrenchment of one or a few parties to the exclusion of others" and "is a very effective impediment to the associational and speech freedoms which are essential to a meaningful system of democratic government." ...

Four years later, in *Branti,* supra, we decided that the First Amendment prohibited a newly appointed public defender, who was a Democrat, from discharging assistant public defenders because they did not have the support of the Democratic Party. The Court rejected an attempt to distinguish the case from *Elrod,* deciding that it was immaterial whether the public defender had attempted to coerce employees to change political parties or had only dismissed them on the basis of their private political beliefs. We explained that conditioning continued public employment on an employee's having obtained support from a particular political party violates the First Amendment because of "the coercion of belief that necessarily flows from the knowledge that one must have a sponsor in the dominant party in order to retain one's job." ... "In sum," we said, "there is no requirement that dismissed employees prove that they, or other employees, have been coerced into changing, either actually or ostensibly, their political allegiance." ... To prevail, we concluded, public employees need show only that they were discharged because they were not affiliated with or sponsored by the Democratic Party....[5]

B

We first address the claims of the four current or former employees. Respondents urge us to view *Elrod* and *Branti* as inapplicable because the patronage dismissals at issue in those cases are different in kind from failure to promote, failure to transfer, and failure to recall after layoff. Respondents initially contend that the employee petitioners' First Amendment rights have not been infringed because they have no entitlement to promotion, transfer, or rehire. We rejected just such an argument in *Elrod* ... and *Branti....* In *Perry,* ... we held explicitly that the plaintiff teacher's lack of a contractual or tenure right to re-employment was immaterial to his First Amendment claim....

. . .

5. Branti v. Finkel ... also refined the exception created by Elrod v. Burns ... for certain employees. In *Elrod,* we suggested that policymaking and confidential employees probably could be dismissed on the basis of their political views.... In *Branti,* we said that a State demonstrates a compelling interest in infringing First Amendment rights only when it can show that "party affiliation is an appropriate requirement for the effective performance of the public office involved." ... The scope of this exception does not concern us here as respondents concede that the five employees who brought this suit are not within it.

Respondents next argue that the employment decisions at issue here do not violate the First Amendment because the decisions are not punitive, do not in any way adversely affect the terms of employment, and therefore do not chill the exercise of protected belief and association by public employees. This is not credible. Employees who find themselves in dead-end positions due to their political backgrounds are adversely affected. They will feel a significant obligation to support political positions held by their superiors, and to refrain from acting on the political views they actually hold, in order to progress up the career ladder. Employees denied transfers to workplaces reasonably close to their homes until they join and work for the Republican Party will feel a daily pressure from their long commutes to do so. And employees who have been laid off may well feel compelled to engage in whatever political activity is necessary to regain regular paychecks and positions corresponding to their skill and experience.

The same First Amendment concerns that underlay our decisions in *Elrod,* supra, and *Branti,* supra, are implicated here. Employees who do not compromise their beliefs stand to lose the considerable increases in pay and job satisfaction attendant to promotions, the hours and maintenance expenses that are consumed by long daily commutes, and even their jobs if they are not rehired after a "temporary" layoff. These are significant penalties and are imposed for the exercise of rights guaranteed by the First Amendment. Unless these patronage practices are narrowly tailored to further vital government interests, we must conclude that they impermissibly encroach on First Amendment freedoms. . . .

We find, however, that our conclusions in *Elrod,* supra, and *Branti,* supra, are equally applicable to the patronage practices at issue here. A government's interest in securing effective employees can be met by discharging, demoting or transferring staffmembers whose work is deficient. A government's interest in securing employees who will loyally implement its policies can be adequately served by choosing or dismissing certain high-level employees on the basis of their political views. . . . Likewise, the "preservation of the democratic process" is no more furthered by the patronage promotions, transfers, and rehires at issue here than it is by patronage dismissals. First, "political parties are nurtured by other, less intrusive and equally effective methods." . . . Political parties have already survived the substantial decline in patronage employment practices in this century. . . . Second, patronage decidedly impairs the elective process by discouraging free political expression by public employees. . . . Respondents, who include the Governor of Illinois and other state officials, do not suggest any other overriding government interest in favoring Republican Party supporters for promotion, transfer, and rehire.

We therefore determine that promotions, transfers, and recalls after layoffs based on political affiliation or support are an impermissible infringement on the First Amendment rights of public employees. In doing so, we reject the Seventh Circuit's view . . . that only those employment decisions that are the "substantial equivalent of a dismissal" violate a public employee's rights under the First Amendment. We find this test unduly restrictive because it fails to recognize that there are deprivations less harsh than dismissal that nevertheless press state employees and applicants to conform their beliefs and associations to some state-selected orthodoxy. . . . The First Amendment prevents the government, except in the most compelling circumstances, from wielding its power to interfere with its employees' freedom to believe and associate, or to not believe and not associate.

. . .

C

Petitioner James W. Moore presents the closely related question whether patronage hiring violates the First Amendment. Patronage hiring places burdens on free speech and association similar to those imposed by the patronage practices discussed above. A state job is valuable. Like most employment, it provides regular paychecks, health insurance, and other benefits. In addition, there may be openings with the State when business in the private sector is slow. There are also occupations for which the government is a major (or the only) source of employment, such as social workers, elementary school teachers, and prison guards. Thus, denial of a state job is a serious privation.

Nonetheless, respondents contend that the burden imposed is not of constitutional magnitude. . . .

. . . Under our sustained precedent, conditioning hiring decisions on political belief and association plainly constitutes an unconstitutional condition, unless the government has a vital interest in doing so. . . . We find no such government interest here, for the same reasons that we found the government lacks justification for patronage promotions, transfers or recalls.

The court below, having decided that the appropriate inquiry in patronage cases is whether the employment decision at issue is the substantial equivalent of a dismissal . . . reasoned that "rejecting an employment application does not impose a hardship upon an employee comparable to the loss of [a] job." Just as we reject the Seventh Circuit's proffered test, we [reject its distinction between hiring and dismissal.] . . .

. . . It is unnecessary here to consider whether not being hired is less burdensome than being discharged because the government is not pressed to do either on the basis of political affiliation. The question in the patronage context is not which penalty is more acute but whether the government, without sufficient justification, is pressuring employees to discontinue the free exercise of their First Amendment rights.

If Moore's employment application was set aside because he chose not to support the Republican Party, as he asserts, then Moore's First Amendment rights have been violated. Therefore, we find that Moore's complaint was improperly dismissed.

III

We hold that the rule of *Elrod* and *Branti* extends to promotion, transfer, recall, and hiring decisions based on party affiliation and support and that all of the petitioners and cross-respondents have stated claims upon which relief may be granted. . . .

. . .ᵃ

Justice Scalia, with whom the Chief Justice and Justice Kennedy join, and with whom Justice O'Connor joins as to Parts II and III, dissenting.

. . .

The merit principle for government employment is probably the most favored in modern America, having been widely adopted by civil-service legislation at both the state and federal levels. But there is another point of view, described in characteristically Jacksonian fashion by an eminent practitioner of the patronage system, George Washington Plunkitt of Tammany Hall:

a. A concurring opinion by Justice Stevens is omitted.

"I ain't up on sillygisms, but I can give you some arguments that nobody can answer.

"First, this great and glorious country was built up by political parties; second, parties can't hold together if their workers don't get offices when they win; third, if the parties go to pieces, the government they built up must go to pieces, too; fourth, then there'll be hell to pay." W. Riordon, Plunkitt of Tammany Hall 13 (1963).

It may well be that the Good Government Leagues of America were right, and that Plunkitt, James Michael Curley and their ilk were wrong; but that is not entirely certain. As the merit principle has been extended and its effects increasingly felt; as the Boss Tweeds, the Tammany Halls, the Pendergast Machines, the Byrd Machines and the Daley Machines have faded into history; we find that political leaders at all levels increasingly complain of the helplessness of elected government, unprotected by "party discipline," before the demands of small and cohesive interest-groups.

The choice between patronage and the merit principle—or, to be more realistic about it, the choice between the desirable mix of merit and patronage principles in widely varying federal, state, and local political contexts—is not so clear that I would be prepared, as an original matter, to chisel a single, inflexible prescription into the Constitution. Fourteen years ago, in Elrod v. Burns . . . the Court did that.

Elrod was limited however, as was the later decision of Branti v. Finkel, . . . to patronage firings, leaving it to state and federal legislatures to determine when and where political affiliation could be taken into account in hirings and promotions. Today the Court makes its constitutional civil-service reform absolute, extending to all decisions regarding government employment. Because the First Amendment has never been thought to require this disposition, which may well have disastrous consequences for our political system, I dissent.

I

. . .

Once it is acknowledged that the Constitution's prohibition against laws "abridging the freedom of speech" does not apply to laws enacted in the government's capacity as employer the same way it does to laws enacted in the government's capacity as regulator of private conduct, it may sometimes be difficult to assess what employment practices are permissible and what are not. That seems to me not a difficult question, however, in the present context. . . . [W]hen a practice not expressly prohibited by the text of the Bill of Rights bears the endorsement of a long tradition of open, widespread, and unchallenged use that dates back to the beginning of the Republic, we have no proper basis for striking it down. . . . When it appears that the latest "rule," or "three-part test," or "balancing test" devised by the Court has placed us on a collision course with such a landmark practice, it is the former that must be recalculated by us, and not the latter that must be abandoned by our citizens. I know of no other way to formulate a constitutional jurisprudence that reflects, as it should, the principles adhered to, over time, by the American people, rather than those favored by the personal (and necessarily shifting) philosophical dispositions of a majority of this Court.

. . . [P]atronage was, without any thought that it could be unconstitutional, a basis for government employment from the earliest days of the Republic until *Elrod*—and has continued unabated since *Elrod,* to the extent still permitted by that unfortunate decision. . . . Given that unbroken tradition regarding the application of an ambiguous constitutional text, there was in my view no basis for holding that patronage-based dismissals violated the First Amendment—much less for holding, as the Court does today, that even patronage hiring does so.

II

. . .

B

. . .

. . . [E]ven laying tradition entirely aside, it seems to me our balancing test is amply met. . . .

The whole point of my dissent is that the desirability of patronage is a policy question to be decided by the people's representatives; I do not mean, therefore, to endorse that system. But in order to demonstrate that a legislature could reasonably determine that its benefits outweigh its "coercive" effects, I must describe those benefits as the proponents of patronage see them: As Justice Powell discussed at length in his *Elrod* dissent, patronage stabilizes political parties and prevents excessive political fragmentation—both of which are results in which States have a strong governmental interest. Party strength requires the efforts of the rank-and-file, especially in "the dull periods between elections," to perform such tasks as organizing precincts, registering new voters, and providing constituent services. . . .

. . .

It is self-evident that eliminating patronage will significantly undermine party discipline; and that as party discipline wanes, so will the strength of the two-party system. . . .

The patronage system does not, of course, merely foster political parties in general; it fosters the two-party system in particular. When getting a job, as opposed to effectuating a particular substantive policy, is an available incentive for party-workers, those attracted by that incentive are likely to work for the party that has the best chance of displacing the "ins," rather than for some splinter group that has a more attractive political philosophy but little hope of success. . . .

Equally apparent is the relatively destabilizing nature of a system in which candidates cannot rely upon patronage-based party loyalty for their campaign support, but must attract workers and raise funds by appealing to various interest-groups. . . . There is little doubt that our decisions in *Elrod* and *Branti,* by contributing to the decline of party strength, have also contributed to the growth of interest-group politics in the last decade. . . .

Patronage, moreover, has been a powerful means of achieving the social and political integration of excluded groups. . . . By supporting and ultimately dominating a particular party "machine," racial and ethnic minorities have—on the basis of their politics rather than their race or ethnicity—acquired the patronage awards the machine had power to confer. . . . The abolition of patronage, however, prevents groups that have only recently obtained political power, especially blacks, from following this path to economic and social advancement.

. . .

While the patronage system has the benefits argued for above, it also has undoubted disadvantages. It facilitates financial corruption, such as salary kickbacks and partisan political activity on government-paid time. It reduces the efficiency of government, because it creates incentives to hire more and less-qualified workers and because highly qualified workers are reluctant to accept jobs that may only last until the next election. And, of course, it applies some greater or lesser inducement for individuals to join and work for the party in power.

... I do not deny that the patronage system influences or redirects, perhaps to a substantial degree, individual political expression and political association. But like the many generations of Americans that have preceded us, I do not consider that a significant impairment of free speech or free association.

... To oppose our *Elrod–Branti* jurisprudence, one need not believe that the patronage system is necessarily desirable; nor even that it is always and everywhere arguably desirable; but merely that it is a political arrangement that may sometimes be a reasonable choice, and should therefore be left to the judgment of the people's elected representatives....

C

... Even in the field of constitutional adjudication, where the pull of stare decisis is at its weakest ... one is reluctant to depart from precedent. But when that precedent is not only wrong, not only recent, not only contradicted by a long prior tradition, but also has proved unworkable in practice, then all reluctance ought to disappear. In my view that is the situation here....

. . .

III

Even were I not convinced that *Elrod* and *Branti* were wrongly decided, I would hold that they should not be extended beyond their facts, viz., actual discharge of employees for their political affiliation....

. . .

CHAPTER 16

FREEDOM OF THE PRESS

SECTION 1.   INTRODUCTION

A.   RELATIONSHIP BETWEEN THE SPEECH AND PRESS CLAUSES

The first amendment protects against "abridging the freedom of speech, or of the press." Does the latter phrase confer upon the press any freedom not otherwise conferred by the "freedom of speech" clause?

Justice Stewart argued in a speech that the free press clause does add to the protections accorded by the free speech clause. He said, in part:

"[T]he Free Press guarantee is, in essence, a *structural* provision of the Constitution. Most of the other provisions in the Bill of Rights protect specific liberties or specific rights of individuals: freedom of speech, freedom of worship, the right to counsel, the privilege against compulsory self-incrimination, to name a few. In contrast, the Free Press Clause extends protection to an institution. The publishing business is, in short, the only organized private business that is given explicit constitutional protection.

"This basic understanding is essential, I think, to avoid an elementary error of constitutional law. It is tempting to suggest that freedom of the press means only that newspaper publishers are guaranteed freedom of expression. They *are* guaranteed that freedom, to be sure, but so are we all, because of the Free Speech Clause. If the Free Press guarantee meant no more than freedom of expression, it would be a constitutional redundancy. Between 1776 and the drafting of our Constitution, many of the state constitutions contained clauses protecting freedom of the press while at the same time recognizing no general freedom of speech. By including both guarantees in the First Amendment, the Founders quite clearly recognized the distinction between the two.

"It is also a mistake to suppose that the only purpose of the constitutional guarantee of a free press is to insure that a newspaper will serve as a neutral forum for debate, a 'market place for ideas,' a kind of Hyde Park corner for the community. A related theory sees the press as a neutral conduit of information between the people and their elected leaders. These theories, in my view, again give insufficient weight to the institutional autonomy of the press that it was the purpose of the Constitution to guarantee."[1]

In a concurring opinion in a case concerned with other issues,[2] Chief Justice Burger expressed disagreement with Justice Stewart's position. He said:

"Those interpreting the Press Clause as extending protection only to, or creating a special role for, the 'institutional press' must either (a) assert such an intention on the part of the Framers for which no supporting evidence is available, . . . (b) argue that events after 1791 somehow operated to 'constitutionalize' this interpretation, see Benzanson, [The New Free Press Guarantee,

---

1.   *"Or of the Press,"* a speech given at Yale Law School, Nov. 2, 1974, as reprinted in 26 Hast.L.J. 631, 633–634 (1975).

2.   First Nat'l Bank of Boston v. Bellotti, 435 U.S. 765, 798–802 (1978).

63 Va.L.Rev. 731, 788 (1977)]; or (c) candidly acknowledging the absence of historical support, suggest that the intent of the Framers is not important today. See Nimmer, [Is Freedom of the Press a Redundancy: What Does It Add To Freedom of Speech?, 26 Hastings L.J. 639, 640–641 (1975)].

"To conclude that the Framers did not intend to limit the freedom of the press to one select group is not necessarily to suggest that the Press Clause is redundant. The Speech Clause standing alone may be viewed as a protection of the liberty to express ideas and beliefs, while the Press Clause focuses specifically on the liberty to disseminate expression broadly and 'comprehends every sort of publication which affords a vehicle of information and opinion.' ... Yet there is no fundamental distinction between expression and dissemination. The liberty encompassed by the Press Clause, although complementary to and a natural extension of Speech Clause liberty, merited special mention simply because it had been more often the object of official restraints....

"The second fundamental difficulty with interpreting the Press Clause as conferring special status on a limited group is one of definition.... The very task of including some entities within the 'institutional press' while excluding others, whether undertaken by legislature, court or administrative agency, is reminiscent of the abhorred licensing system of Tudor and Stuart England—a system the First Amendment was intended to ban from this country.... Further, the officials undertaking that task would be required to distinguish the protected from the unprotected on the basis of such variables as content of expression, frequency or fervor of expression, or ownership of the technological means of dissemination. Yet nothing in this Court's opinions supports such a confining approach to the scope of Press Clause protection....

"Because the First Amendment was meant to guarantee freedom to express and communicate ideas, I can see no difference between the right of those who seek to disseminate ideas by way of a newspaper and those who give lectures or speeches and seek to enlarge the audience by publication and wide dissemination."

B. REGULATION OF THE BUSINESS OF PUBLISHING

Minneapolis Star and Tribune Co. v. Minnesota Commissioner of Revenue

460 U.S. 575, 103 S.Ct. 1365, 75 L.Ed.2d 295 (1983).

Justice O'Connor delivered the opinion of the Court.

This case presents the question of a State's power to impose a special tax on the press and, by enacting exemptions, to limit its effect to only a few newspapers.

I

Since 1967, Minnesota has imposed a sales tax on most sales of goods for a price in excess of a nominal sum.... In general, the tax applies only to retail sales.... An exemption for industrial and agricultural users shields from the tax sales of components to be used in the production of goods that will themselves be sold at retail.... As part of this general system of taxation and in support of the sales tax,.... Minnesota also enacted a tax on the "privilege of using, storing or consuming in Minnesota tangible personal property." This use tax applies to any nonexempt tangible personal property unless the sales tax was paid on the sales price.... Like the classic use tax, this use tax protects the State's sales tax by eliminating the residents' incentive to travel to States with lower sales taxes to buy goods rather than buying them in Minnesota....

The appellant, Minneapolis Star and Tribune Company, "Star Tribune", is the publisher of a morning newspaper and an evening newspaper in Minneapolis. From 1967 until 1971, it enjoyed an exemption from the sales and use tax provided by Minnesota for periodic publications. ... In 1971, however, while leaving the exemption from the sales tax in place, the legislature amended the scheme to impose a "use tax" on the cost of paper and ink products consumed in the production of a publication. ... Ink and paper used in publications became the only items subject to the use tax that were components of goods to be sold at retail. In 1974, the legislature again amended the statute, this time to exempt the first $100,000 worth of ink and paper consumed by a publication in any calendar year, in effect giving each publication an annual tax credit of $4,000. ... Publications remained exempt from the sales tax ...

After the enactment of the $100,000 exemption, 11 publishers, producing 14 of the 388 paid circulation newspapers in the State, incurred a tax liability in 1974. Star Tribune was one of the 11, and, of the $893,355 collected, it paid $608,634, or roughly two-thirds of the total revenue raised by the tax. ... In 1975, 13 publishers, producing 16 out of 374 paid circulation papers, paid a tax. That year, Star Tribune again bore roughly two-thirds of the total receipts from the use tax on ink and paper. ...

Star Tribune instituted this action to seek a refund of the use taxes it paid from January 1, 1974 to May 31, 1975. It challenged the imposition of the use tax on ink and paper used in publications as a violation of the guarantees of freedom of the press and equal protection in the First and Fourteenth Amendments. The Minnesota Supreme Court upheld the tax against the federal constitutional challenge. ... We ... reverse.

II

Star Tribune argues that we must strike this tax on the authority of Grosjean v. American Press Co., Inc., 297 U.S. 233 (1936). Although there are similarities between the two cases, we agree with the State that *Grosjean* is not controlling.

In *Grosjean,* the State of Louisiana imposed a license tax of 2% of the gross receipts from the sale of advertising on all newspapers with a weekly circulation above 20,000. Out of at least 124 publishers in the State, only 13 were subject to the tax. After noting that the tax was "single in kind" and that keying the tax to circulation curtailed the flow of information, ... this Court held the tax invalid as an abridgment of the freedom of the press. Both the brief and the argument of the publishers in this Court emphasized the events leading up to the tax and the contemporary political climate in Louisiana. ... All but one of the large papers subject to the tax had "ganged up" on Senator Huey Long, and a circular distributed by Long and the governor to each member of the state legislature described "lying newspapers" as conducting "a vicious campaign" and the tax as "a tax on lying ..." ... Although the Court's opinion did not describe this history, it stated, "[The tax] is bad because, in the light of its history and of its present setting, it is seen to be a deliberate and calculated device in the guise of a tax to limit the circulation of information," ... an explanation that suggests that the motivation of the legislature may have been significant.

... We think that the result in *Grosjean* may have been attributable in part to the perception on the part of the Court that the state imposed the tax with an intent to penalize a selected group of newspapers. In the case currently before us, however, there is no legislative history and no indication, apart from the structure of the tax itself, of any impermissible or censorial motive on the part of the legislature. We cannot resolve the case by simple citation to *Grosjean*. Instead, we must analyze the problem anew under the general principles of the First Amendment.

III

Clearly, the First Amendment does not prohibit all regulation of the press. It is beyond dispute that the States and the Federal Government can subject newspapers to generally applicable economic regulations without creating constitutional problems. ... Minnesota, however, has not chosen to apply its general sales and use tax to newspapers. Instead, it has created a special tax that applies only to certain publications protected by the First Amendment. Although the State argues now that the tax on paper and ink is part of the general scheme of taxation, the use tax provision ... is facially discriminatory, singling out publications for treatment that is, to our knowledge, unique in Minnesota tax law.

Minnesota's treatment of publications differs from that of other enterprises in at least two important respects: it imposes a use tax that does not serve the function of protecting the sales tax, and it taxes an intermediate transaction rather than the ultimate retail sale. A use tax ordinarily serves to complement the sales tax by eliminating the incentive to make major purchases in States with lower sales taxes; it requires the resident who shops out-of-state to pay a use tax equal to the sales tax savings.... But the use tax on ink and paper serves no such complementary function; it applies to all uses, whether or not the taxpayer purchased the ink and paper in-state, and it applies to items exempt from the sales tax.

Further, the ordinary rule in Minnesota, as discussed above, is to tax only the ultimate, or retail, sale rather than the use of components like ink and paper.... Publishers, however, are taxed on their purchase of components, even though they will eventually sell their publications at retail.

By creating this special use tax, which, to our knowledge, is without parallel in the State's tax scheme, Minnesota has singled out the press for special treatment. We then must determine whether the First Amendment permits such special taxation.... The cases approving ... economic regulation, ... emphasized the general applicability of the challenged regulation to all businesses, ... suggesting that a regulation that singled out the press might place a heavier burden of justification on the State, and we now conclude that the special problems created by differential treatment do indeed impose such a burden.

. . . .

... A power to tax differentially, as opposed to a power to tax generally, gives a government a powerful weapon against the taxpayer selected. When the State imposes a generally applicable tax, there is little cause for concern. We need not fear that a government will destroy a selected group of taxpayers by burdensome taxation if it must impose the same burden on the rest of its constituency. See Railway Express Agency v. New York, 336 U.S. 106, 112–113 (1949) (Jackson, J., concurring). When the State singles out the press, though, the political constraints that prevent a legislature from passing crippling taxes of general applicability are weakened, and the threat of burdensome taxes becomes acute. That threat can operate as effectively as a censor to check critical comment by the press, undercutting the basic assumption of our political system that the press will often serve as an important restraint on government. . . .

. . .

IV

. . .

. . . Minnesota invites us to look beyond the form of the tax to its substance. The tax is, according to the State, merely a substitute for the sales tax, which, as a generally applicable tax, would be constitutional as applied to the press.[9] There are two fatal flaws in this reasoning. First, the State has offered no explanation of why it chose to use a substitute for the sales tax rather than the sales tax itself. . . . If the real goal of this tax is to duplicate the sales tax, it is difficult to see why the State did not achieve that goal by the obvious and effective expedient of applying the sales tax.

Further, even assuming that the legislature did have valid reasons for substituting another tax for the sales tax, we are not persuaded that this tax does serve as a substitute. The State asserts that this scheme actually *favors* the press over other businesses, because the same rate of tax is applied, but, for the press, the rate applies to the cost of components rather than to the sales price. We would be hesitant to fashion a rule that automatically allowed the State to single out the press for a different method of taxation as long as the effective burden was no different from that on other taxpayers or the burden on the press was lighter than that on other businesses. One reason for this reluctance is that the very selection of the press for special treatment threatens the press not only with the current *differential* treatment, but with the possibility of subsequent differentially *more burdensome* treatment. . . .

A second reason to avoid the proposed rule is that courts as institutions are poorly equipped to evaluate with precision the relative burdens of various methods of taxation. The complexities of factual economic proof always present a certain potential for error, and courts have little familiarity with the process of evaluating the relative economic burden of taxes. In sum, the possibility of error inherent in the proposed rule poses too great a threat to concerns at the heart of the First Amendment . . .

V

Minnesota's ink and paper tax violates the First Amendment not only because it singles out the press, but also because it targets a small group of newspapers. The effect of the $100,000 exemption enacted in 1974 is that only a handful of publishers pay any tax at all, and even fewer pay any significant amount of tax. . . . Even if we were willing to accept the premise that large businesses are more profitable and therefore better able to bear the burden of

---

9. Star Tribune insists that the premise of the State's argument—that a generally applicable sales tax would be constitutional—is incorrect . . . We think that Breard v. Alexandria, 341 U.S. 622 (1951) . . . rebuts Star Tribune's argument. There, we upheld an ordinance prohibiting door-to-door solicitation, even though it applied to prevent the door-to-door sale of subscriptions to maga- zines, an activity covered by the First Amendment. Although Martin v. Struthers, 319 U.S. 141 (1943), had struck down a similar ordinance as applied to the distribution of free religious literature, the *Breard* Court explained that case as emphasizing that the information distributed was religious in nature and that the distribution was noncommercial. . . .

the tax, the State's commitment to this "equity" is questionable, for the concern has not led the State to grant benefits to small businesses in general. And when the exemption selects such a narrowly defined group to bear the full burden of the tax, the tax begins to resemble more a penalty for a few of the largest newspapers than an attempt to favor struggling smaller enterprises.

VI

We need not and do not impugn the motives of the Minnesota legislature in passing the ink and paper tax. . . . Since Minnesota has offered no satisfactory justification for its tax on the use of ink and paper, the tax violates the First Amendment, and the judgment below is

Reversed.

Justice White, concurring in part and dissenting in part.

This case is not difficult. The exemption for the first $100,000 of paper and ink limits the burden of the Minnesota tax to only a few papers. This feature alone is sufficient reason to invalidate the Minnesota tax and . . . I subscribe to Part V of the Court's opinion and concur in the judgment.

. . .

There may be cases, I recognize, where the Court cannot confidently ascertain whether a differential method of taxation imposes a greater burden upon the press than a generally applicable tax. In these circumstances, I too may be unwilling to entrust freedom of the press to uncertain economic proof. But, as Justice Rehnquist clearly shows, this is not such a case. . . .

Justice Rehnquist, dissenting.

. . .

. . . We need no expert testimony from modern day Euclids or Einsteins to determine that the $1,224,747 paid in use taxes is significantly less burdensome than the $3,685,092 that could have been levied by a sales tax. *A fortiori,* the Minnesota taxing scheme which singles out newspapers for "differential treatment" has benefited, not burdened, the "freedom of speech, [and] of the press."

. . .

The Court finds in very summary fashion that the exemption newspapers receive for the first $100,000 of ink and paper used also violates the First Amendment because the result is that only a few of the newspapers actually pay a use tax. I cannot agree. As explained by the Minnesota Supreme Court, the exemption is in effect a $4,000 credit which benefits all newspapers. . . . *Minneapolis Star & Tribune* was benefited to the amount of $16,000 in the two years in question; $4,000 each year for its morning paper and $4,000 each year for its evening paper. . . . Absent any improper motive on the part of the Minnesota legislature in drawing the limits of this exemption, it cannot be construed as violating the First Amendment. . . .

. . .

SELECTIVE TAXATION AND REGULATION OF THE PRESS: CONTENT–BASED AND CONTENT–NEUTRAL SELECTIVITY

In Arkansas Writers' Project, Inc. v. Ragland, 481 U.S. 221 (1987), the Court invalidated a sales tax exemption for magazines that were "religious, professional, trade and sports journals," noting that selective taxation based on media content involved "a more disturbing use of selective taxation than

Minneapolis Star." The Court did not decide whether another provision of the challenged Arkansas statute—an exemption for all newspapers—was invalid. Differential taxation of different media was at issue in Leathers v. Medlock, 499 U.S. 439 (1991), where another Arkansas tax was upheld. Cable television operators complained of a law extending the general sales tax to cable television. The Court concluded that different taxation of different media was not constitutionally suspect if the tax did not single out the media, did not purposely interfere with First Amendment activities, and was not content-based.

The Court relied on this analysis in Simon & Schuster, Inc. v. Members of New York State Crime Victims Board, 502 U.S. 105 (1991), holding New York's "Son of Sam" law unconstitutional. If the work disclosed commission of a crime by the author, the law required the author's publisher to deposit funds payable to the author in an escrow account to compensate victims of that crime. The Court concluded that the statute was presumptively unconstitutional because it imposed a financial burden on speakers because of the content of their speech. The state's compelling interest in compensating victims from the fruits of crime could not justify a law that was limited to compensation from the proceeds of speech about that crime.

SECTION 2.   RESTRAINTS ON EDITORIAL JUDGMENT

Pittsburgh Press Co. v. Pittsburgh Commission on Human Relations

413 U.S. 376, 93 S.Ct. 2553, 37 L.Ed.2d 669 (1973).

Mr. Justice Powell delivered the opinion of the Court.

The Human Relations Ordinance of the City of Pittsburgh (the Ordinance) [forbids] newspapers to carry "help-wanted" advertisements in sex-designated columns except where the employer or advertiser is free to make hiring or employment referral decisions on the basis of sex. We are called upon to decide whether the Ordinance as so construed violates the freedoms of speech and of the press guaranteed by the First and Fourteenth Amendments....

. . .

Respondents rely principally on the argument that this regulation is permissible because the speech is commercial speech unprotected by the First Amendment. . . .

But Pittsburgh Press contends that . . . the focus in this case must be upon the exercise of editorial judgment by the newspaper as to where to place the advertisement rather than upon its commercial content....

. . .

. . . [W]e are not persuaded that either the decision to accept a commercial advertisement which the advertiser directs to be placed in a sex-designated column or the actual placement there lifts the newspaper's actions from the category of commercial speech. By implication at least, an advertiser whose want-ad appears in the "Jobs—Male Interest" column is likely to discriminate against women in his hiring decisions. Nothing in a sex-designated column heading sufficiently disassociates the designation from the want ads placed beneath it to make the placement severable for First Amendment purposes from the want-ads themselves. The combination, which conveys essentially the same message as an overtly discriminatory want ad, is in practical effect an integrated commercial statement.

Pittsburgh Press goes on to argue that if this package of advertisement and placement is commercial speech, then commercial speech should be accorded a higher level of protection ... Insisting that the exchange of information is as important in the commercial realm as in any other, the newspaper here would have us abrogate the distinction between commercial and other speech.

Whatever the merits of this contention may be in other contexts, it is unpersuasive in this case. Discrimination in employment is not only commercial activity, it is *illegal* commercial activity under the Ordinance. We have no doubt that a newspaper constitutionally could be forbidden to publish a want ad proposing a sale of narcotics or soliciting prostitutes. Nor would the result be different if the nature of the transaction were indicated by placement under columns captioned "Narcotics for Sale" and "Prostitutes Wanted" rather than stated within the four corners of the advertisement.

. . .

We emphasize that nothing in our holding allows government at any level to forbid *Pittsburgh Press* to publish and distribute advertisements commenting on the Ordinance, the enforcement practices of the Commission, or the propriety of sex preferences in employment. Nor, *a fortiori,* does our decision authorize any restriction whatever, whether of content or layout, on stories or commentary originated by Pittsburgh Press, its columnists, or its contributors. On the contrary, we reaffirm unequivocally the protection afforded to editorial judgment and to the free expression of views on these and other issues, however controversial. We hold only that the Commission's modified order, narrowly drawn to prohibit placement in sex-designated columns of advertisements for nonexempt job opportunities, does not infringe the First Amendment rights of Pittsburgh Press.

Affirmed.[a]

Miami Herald Publishing Co. v. Tornillo

418 U.S. 241, 94 S.Ct. 2831, 41 L.Ed.2d 730 (1974).

Mr. Chief Justice Burger delivered the opinion of the Court.

The issue in this case is whether a state statute granting a political candidate a right to equal space to reply to criticism and attacks on his record by a newspaper, violates the guarantees of a free press.

I

... [A]ppellee, Executive Director of the Classroom Teachers Association, apparently a teachers' collective-bargaining agent, was a candidate for the Florida House of Representatives. ... [A]ppellant printed editorials critical of appellee's candidacy. In response to these editorials appellee demanded that appellant print verbatim his replies, defending the role of the Classroom Teachers Association ... Appellant declined to print the appellee's replies, and

a. Dissenting opinions by Chief Justice Burger, Justice Douglas, Justice Stewart, and Justice Blackmun, are omitted.

appellee brought suit ... premised on Florida Statute § 104.38 (1973), a "right of reply" statute which provides that if a candidate for nomination or election is assailed regarding his personal character or official record by any newspaper, the candidate has the right to demand that the newspaper print, free of cost to the candidate, any reply the candidate may make to the newspaper's charges. The reply must appear in as conspicuous a place and in the same kind of type as the charges which prompted the reply, provided it does not take up more space than the charges. . . .

Appellant sought a declaration that § 104.38 was unconstitutional. . . .

... [T]he Florida Supreme Court [held] that § 104.38 did not violate constitutional guarantees. . . .

. . .

III

A

. . .

Appellant contends the statute is void on its face because it purports to regulate the content of a newspaper in violation of the First Amendment. Alternatively it is urged that the statute is void for vagueness since no editor could know exactly what words would call the statute into operation. It is also contended that the statute fails to distinguish between critical comment which is and which is not defamatory.

B

The appellee and supporting advocates of an enforceable right of access to the press vigorously argue that government has an obligation to ensure that a wide variety of views reach the public. The contentions of access proponents will be set out in some detail. It is urged that at the time the First Amendment to the Constitution was ratified in 1791 as part of our Bill of Rights the press was broadly representative of the people it was serving. While many of the newspapers were intensely partisan and narrow in their views, the press collectively presented a broad range of opinions to readers. Entry into publishing was inexpensive; pamphlets and books provided meaningful alternatives to the organized press for the expression of unpopular ideas and often treated events and expressed views not covered by conventional newspapers. A true marketplace of ideas existed in which there was relatively easy access to the channels of communication.

Access advocates submit that although newspapers of the present are superficially similar to those of 1791 the press of today is in reality very different from that known in the early years of our national existence. In the past half century a communications revolution has seen the introduction of radio and television into our lives, the promise of a global community through the use of communications satellites, and the specter of a "wired" nation by means of an expanding cable television network with two-way capabilities. The printed press, it is said, has not escaped the effects of this revolution. Newspapers have become big business and there are far fewer of them to serve a larger literate population. Chains of newspapers, national newspapers, national wire and news services, and one-newspaper towns, are the dominant features of a press that has become noncompetitive and enormously powerful and influential in its capacity to manipulate popular opinion and change the course of events. Major metropolitan newspapers have collaborated to establish news services national in scope. Such national news organizations provide syndicated "interpretive reporting" as well as syndicated features and commentary, all of which can serve as part of the new school of "advocacy journalism."

The elimination of competing newspapers in most of our large cities, and the concentration of control of media that results from the only newspaper's being owned by the same interests which own a television station and a radio station, are important components of this trend toward concentration of control of outlets to inform the public.

The result of these vast changes has been to place in a few hands the power to inform the American people and shape public opinion. Much of the editorial opinion and commentary that is printed is that of syndicated columnists distributed nationwide and, as a result, we are told, on national and world issues there tends to be a homogeneity of editorial opinion, commentary, and interpretative analysis. The abuses of bias and manipulative reportage are, likewise, said to be the result of the vast accumulations of unreviewable power in the modern media empires. In effect, it is claimed, the public has lost any ability to respond or to contribute in a meaningful way to the debate on issues. The monopoly of the means of communication allows for little or no critical analysis of the media except in professional journals of very limited readership. . . .

The obvious solution, which was available to dissidents at an earlier time when entry into publishing was relatively inexpensive, today would be to have additional newspapers. But the same economic factors which have caused the disappearance of vast numbers of metropolitan newspapers, have made entry into the marketplace of ideas served by the print media almost impossible. It is urged that the claim of newspapers to be "surrogates for the public" carries with it a concomitant fiduciary obligation to account for that stewardship. From this premise it is reasoned that the only effective way to insure fairness and accuracy and to provide for some accountability is for government to take affirmative action. The First Amendment interest of the public in being informed is said to be in peril because the "marketplace of ideas" is today a monopoly controlled by the owners of the market.

. . .

IV

However much validity may be found in these arguments, at each point the implementation of a remedy such as an enforceable right of access necessarily calls for some mechanism, either governmental or consensual. If it is governmental coercion, this at once brings about a confrontation with the express provisions of the First Amendment and the judicial gloss on that Amendment developed over the years.

. . .

Appellee's argument that the Florida statute does not amount to a restriction of appellant's right to speak because "the statute in question here has not prevented the *Miami Herald* from saying anything it wished" begs the core question. Compelling editors or publishers to publish that which " 'reason' tells them should not be published" is what is at issue in this case. The Florida statute operates as a command in the same sense as a statute or regulation forbidding appellant to publish specified matter. . . . The Florida statute exacts a penalty on the basis of the content of a newspaper. The first phase of the penalty resulting from the compelled printing of a reply is exacted in terms of the cost in printing and composing time and materials and in taking up space that could be devoted to other material the newspaper may have preferred to print. It is correct, as appellee contends, that a newspaper is not subject to the finite technological limitations of time that confront a broadcaster but it is not correct to say that, as an economic reality, a newspaper can proceed to infinite expansion of its column space to accommodate the replies that a government agency determines or a statute commands the readers should have available.

Faced with the penalties that would accrue to any newspaper that published news or commentary arguably within the reach of the right-of-access statute, editors might well conclude that the safe course is to avoid controversy. Therefore, under the operation of the Florida statute, political and electoral coverage would be blunted or reduced. . . .

Even if a newspaper would face no additional costs to comply with a compulsory access law and would not be forced to forgo publication of news or opinion by the inclusion of a reply, the Florida statute fails to clear the barriers of the First Amendment because of its intrusion into the function of editors. A newspaper is more than a passive receptacle or conduit for news, comment, and advertising. The choice of material to go into a newspaper, and the decisions made as to limitations on the size and content of the paper, and treatment of public issues and public officials—whether fair or unfair—constitute the exercise of editorial control and judgment. It has yet to be demonstrated how governmental regulation of this crucial process can be exercised consistent with First Amendment guarantees of a free press as they have evolved to this time. Accordingly, the judgment of the Supreme Court of Florida is reversed.

It is so ordered.[a]

Mr. Justice Brennan, with whom Mr. Justice Rehnquist joins, concurring.

I join the Court's opinion which, as I understand it, addresses only "right of reply" statutes and implies no view upon the constitutionality of "retraction" statutes affording plaintiffs able to prove defamatory falsehoods a statutory action to require publication of a retraction. . . .

SECTION 3.   PROHIBITION OF PUBLICATION OF GOVERNMENT INFORMATION

New York Times Co. v. United States [The Cases of the Pentagon Papers.]

403 U.S. 713, 91 S.Ct. 2140, 29 L.Ed.2d 822 (1971).

Per Curiam.

We granted certiorari in these cases in which the United States seeks to enjoin the *New York Times* and the *Washington Post* from publishing the contents of a classified study entitled "History of U.S. Decision–Making Process on Viet Nam Policy." [Commonly referred to as the "Pentagon Papers."]

"Any system of prior restraints of expression comes to this Court bearing a heavy presumption against its constitutional validity." . . . The Government "thus carries a heavy burden of showing justification for the imposition of such a restraint." . . . The District Court for the Southern District of New York in the *New York Times* case and the District Court for the District of Columbia

---

a. A concurring opinion by Justice White is omitted.

and the Court of Appeals for the District of Columbia Circuit in the *Washington Post* case held that the Government had not met that burden. We agree.

. . .

Mr. Justice Black, with whom Mr. Justice Douglas joins, concurring.

I adhere to the view that the Government's case against the Washington Post should have been dismissed and that the injunction against the New York Times should have been vacated without oral argument when the cases were first presented to this Court. I believe that every moment's continuance of the injunctions against these newspapers amounts to a flagrant, indefensible, and continuing violation of the First Amendment. . . . In my view it is unfortunate that some of my Brethren are apparently willing to hold that the publication of news may sometimes be enjoined. Such a holding would make a shambles of the First Amendment. . . .

. . .

. . . The Government argues in its brief that in spite of the First Amendment, "[t]he authority of the Executive Department to protect the nation against publication of information whose disclosure would endanger the national security stems from two interrelated sources: the constitutional power of the President over the conduct of foreign affairs and his authority as Commander-in-Chief."

. . . To find that the President has "inherent power" to halt the publication of news by resort to the courts would wipe out the First Amendment and destroy the fundamental liberty and security of the very people the Government hopes to make "secure." No one can read the history of the adoption of the First Amendment without being convinced beyond any doubt that it was injunctions like those sought here that Madison and his collaborators intended to outlaw in this Nation for all time.

. . .

Mr. Justice Douglas, with whom Mr. Justice Black joins, concurring.

. . .

. . . [T]he First Amendment provides that "Congress shall make no law . . . abridging the freedom of speech or of the press." That leaves, in my view, no room for governmental restraint on the press.

There is, moreover, no statute barring the publication by the press of the material which the Times and the Post seek to use. . . .

. . .

The stays in these cases that have been in effect for more than a week constitute a flouting of the principles of the First Amendment as interpreted in Near v. Minnesota.

Mr. Justice Brennan, concurring.

I

I write separately in these cases only to emphasize what should be apparent: that our judgments in the present cases may not be taken to indicate the propriety, in the future, of issuing temporary stays and restraining orders to block the publication of material sought to be suppressed by the Government. So far as I can determine, never before has the United States sought to enjoin a newspaper from publishing information in its possession. . . .

II

The error that has pervaded these cases from the outset was the granting of any injunctive relief whatsoever, interim or otherwise. The entire thrust of the Government's claim throughout these cases has been that publication of the material sought to be enjoined "could," or "might," or "may," prejudice the national interest in various ways. But the First Amendment tolerates absolutely no prior judicial restraints of the press predicated upon surmise or conjecture that untoward consequences may result. Our cases, it is true, have indicated that there is a single, extremely narrow class of cases in which the First Amendment's ban on prior judicial restraint may be overridden. Our cases have thus far indicated that such cases may arise only when the Nation "is at war," Schenck v. United States, 249 U.S. 47, 52 (1919), during which times "[n]o one would question but that a Government might prevent actual obstruction to its recruiting service or the publication of the sailing dates of transports or the number and location of troops." Near v. Minnesota, 283 U.S. 697, 716 (1931). . . . [I]n neither of these actions has the Government presented or even alleged that publication of . . . the material at issue would cause the happening of an event of that nature. . . . [O]nly governmental allegation and proof that publication must inevitably, directly and immediately cause the occurrence of an event kindred to imperiling the safety of a transport already at sea can support even the issuance of an interim restraining order. In no event may mere conclusions be sufficient . . . Unless and until the Government has clearly made out its case, the First Amendment commands that no injunction may issue.

Mr. Justice Stewart, with whom Mr. Justice White joins, concurring.

In the governmental structure created by our Constitution, the Executive is endowed with enormous power in the two related areas of national defense and international relations. . . .

In the absence of the governmental checks and balances present in other areas of our national life, the only effective restraint upon executive policy and power in the areas of national defense and international affairs may lie in an enlightened citizenry . . . [A] press that is alert, aware, and free most vitally serves the basic purpose of the First Amendment. For without an informed and free press there cannot be an enlightened people.

Yet it is elementary that the successful conduct of international diplomacy and the maintenance of an effective national defense require both confidentiality and secrecy. Other nations can hardly deal with this Nation in an atmosphere of mutual trust unless they can be assured that their confidences will be kept. And within our own executive departments, the development of considered and intelligent international policies would be impossible if those charged with their formulation could not communicate with each other freely, frankly, and in confidence. In the area of basic national defense the frequent need for absolute secrecy is, of course, self-evident.

I think there can be but one answer to this dilemma, if dilemma it be. The responsibility must be where the power is. . . . [I]t is the constitutional duty of the Executive . . . through the promulgation and enforcement of executive regulations, to protect the confidentiality necessary to carry out its responsibilities in the fields of international relations and national defense.

This is not to say that Congress and the courts have no role to play. Undoubtedly Congress has the power to enact specific and appropriate criminal laws to protect government property and preserve government secrets. Congress has passed such laws, and several of them are of very colorable relevance to the apparent circumstances of these cases. And if a criminal prosecution is instituted, it will be the responsibility of the courts to decide the applicability of the criminal law under which the charge is brought. Moreover, if Congress should pass a specific law authorizing civil proceedings in this field, the courts would likewise have the duty to decide the constitutionality of such a law as well as its applicability to the facts proved.

But in the cases before us we are asked neither to construe specific regulations nor to apply specific laws. We are asked, instead, to perform a function that the Constitution gave to the Executive, not the Judiciary. We are asked, quite simply, to prevent the publication by two newspapers of material that the Executive Branch insists should not, in the national interest, be published. I am convinced that the Executive is correct with respect to some of the documents involved. But I cannot say that disclosure of any of them will surely result in direct, immediate, and irreparable damage to our Nation or its people. That being so, there can under the First Amendment be but one judicial resolution of the issues before us. I join the judgments of the Court.

Mr. Justice White, with whom Mr. Justice Stewart joins, concurring.

I concur in today's judgments, but only because of the concededly extraordinary protection against prior restraints enjoyed by the press under our constitutional system. . . .

. . .

. . . [T]erminating the ban on publication of the relatively few sensitive documents the Government now seeks to suppress does not mean that the law either requires or invites newspapers or others to publish them or that they will be immune from criminal action if they do. . . .

. . .

. . . Congress has addressed itself to the problems of protecting the security of the country and the national defense from unauthorized disclosure of potentially damaging information. . . . It has not, however, authorized the injunctive remedy against threatened publication. . . .

Mr. Justice Marshall, concurring.

. . .

The problem here is whether in these particular cases the Executive Branch has authority to invoke the equity jurisdiction of the courts to protect what it believes to be the national interest. . . .

It would . . . be utterly inconsistent with the concept of separation of powers for this Court, to use its power of contempt to prevent behavior that Congress has specifically declined to prohibit.[a] . . .

Mr. Justice Harlan, with whom The Chief Justice and Mr. Justice Blackmun join, dissenting.

---

a. Dissenting opinions by Chief Justice Burger and Justice Blackmun are omitted.

... With all respect, I consider that the Court has been almost irresponsibly feverish in dealing with these cases.

. . .

Forced as I am to reach the merits of these cases, I dissent. ...

. . .

... It is plain to me that the scope of the judicial function in passing upon the activities of the Executive Branch of the Government in the field of foreign affairs is very narrowly restricted. This view is, I think, dictated by the concept of separation of powers upon which our constitutional system rests.

. . .

... I agree that, in performance of its duty to protect the values of the First Amendment against political pressures, the judiciary must review the initial Executive determination to the point of satisfying itself that the subject matter of the dispute does lie within the proper compass of the President's foreign relations power. ... Moreover, the judiciary may properly insist that the determination that disclosure of the subject matter would irreparably impair the national security be made by the head of the Executive Department concerned—here the Secretary of State or the Secretary of Defense—after actual personal consideration by that officer....

But in my judgment the judiciary may not properly go beyond these two inquiries and redetermine for itself the probable impact of disclosure on the national security....

Even if there is some room for the judiciary to override the executive determination, it is plain that the scope of review must be exceedingly narrow.
. . .

Pending further hearings in each case conducted under the appropriate ground rules, I would continue the restraints on publication. I cannot believe that the doctrine prohibiting prior restraints reaches to the point of preventing courts from maintaining the *status quo* long enough to act responsibly in matters of such national importance as those involved here.

PROTECTION OF THE COURTS AGAINST CRITICISM

The early history of the use of the contempt power to punish the press for criticism of judges and judicial action was recounted in section 1 of Chapter 13. In 1941 the Court reinterpreted the federal statute restricting the use of contempt as preventing the federal courts from punishing acts outside the geographical environs of the courthouse. Nye v. United States, 313 U.S. 33 (1941). Shortly thereafter the Court substantially eliminated the power of the state and federal courts to punish the press for publications alleged to interfere with judicial impartiality by holding that under the first amendment only publications that create an imminent and serious threat to the ability of the court fairly to decide issues before it can be punished. Bridges v. California, 314 U.S. 252 (1941); Pennekamp v. Florida, 328 U.S. 331 (1946); Craig v. Harney, 331 U.S. 367 (1947).

Nebraska Press Association v. Stuart

427 U.S. 539, 96 S.Ct. 2791, 49 L.Ed.2d 683 (1976).

Mr. Chief Justice Burger delivered the opinion of the Court.

The respondent State District Judge entered an order restraining the petitioners from publishing or broadcasting accounts of confessions or admissions made by the accused or facts "strongly implicative" of the accused in a widely reported murder of six persons. We granted certiorari to decide whether the entry of such an order on the showing made before the state court violated the constitutional guarantee of freedom of the press.

On the evening of October 18, 1975, local police found the six members of the Henry Kellie family murdered in their home in Sutherland, Neb., a town of about 850 people. Police released the description of a suspect, Erwin Charles Simants, to the reporters who had hastened to the scene of the crime. Simants was arrested and arraigned in Lincoln County Court the following morning, ending a tense night for this small rural community.

The crime immediately attracted widespread news coverage, by local, regional, and national newspapers, radio and television stations. Three days after the crime, the County Attorney and Simants' attorney joined in asking the County Court to enter a restrictive order relating to "matters that may or may not be publicly reported or disclosed to the public," because of the "mass coverage by news media" and the "reasonable likelihood of prejudicial news which would make difficult, if not impossible, the impaneling of an impartial jury and tend to prevent a fair trial." The County Court heard oral argument but took no evidence; no attorney for members of the press appeared at this stage. The County Court granted the prosecutor's motion for a restrictive order and entered it the next day, October 22. The order prohibited everyone in attendance from "releas[ing] or authoriz[ing] the release for public dissemination in any form or manner whatsoever any testimony given or evidence adduced"; ...

. . .

The Nebraska Supreme Court ... modified the District Court's order.... [to prohibit] reporting of only three matters: (a) the existence and nature of any confessions or admissions made by the defendant to law enforcement officers, (b) any confessions or admissions made to any third parties, except members of the press, and (c) other facts "strongly implicative" of the accused....

. . .

III

. . .

... The trial of Bruno Hauptmann in a small New Jersey community for the abduction and murder of the Charles Lindberghs' infant child, probably was the most widely covered trial up to that time, and the nature of the coverage produced widespread public reaction....

The excesses of press and radio and lack of responsibility of those in authority in the Hauptmann case and others of that era led to efforts to develop voluntary guidelines for courts, lawyers, press and broadcasters. ... The effort was renewed in 1965 when the American Bar Association embarked on a project to develop standards for all aspects of criminal justice, including guidelines to accommodate the right to a fair trial and the rights of a free press. ... The resulting standards, approved by the Association in 1968, received support from most of the legal profession. ...

In practice, of course, even the most ideal guidelines are subjected to powerful strains when a case such as Simants' arises, with reporters from many parts of the country on the scene. Reporters from distant places are unlikely to consider themselves bound by local standards. They report to editors outside the area covered by the guidelines, and their editors are likely to be guided only by their own standards. To contemplate how a state court can control acts of a newspaper or broadcaster outside its jurisdiction, even though the newspapers and broadcasts reach the very community from which jurors are to be selected, suggests something of the practical difficulties of managing such guidelines.

. . .

IV

. . .

In Sheppard v. Maxwell, 384 U.S. 333 (1966), the Court focused sharply on the impact of pretrial publicity and a trial court's duty to protect the defendant's constitutional right to a fair trial. . . . [T]he Court ordered a new trial for the petitioner, even though the first trial had occurred 12 years before. Beyond doubt the press had shown no responsible concern for the constitutional guarantee of a fair trial; the community from which the jury was drawn had been inundated by publicity hostile to the defendant. But the trial judge "did not fulfill his duty to protect [the defendant] from the inherently prejudicial publicity which saturated the community and to control disruptive influences in the courtroom." . . . The Court noted that "unfair and prejudicial news comment on pending trials has become increasingly prevalent," . . . and issued a strong warning:

"Due process requires that the accused receive a trial by an impartial jury free from outside influences. Given the pervasiveness of modern communications and the difficulty of effacing prejudicial publicity from the minds of the jurors, *the trial courts must take strong measures to ensure that the balance is never weighed against the accused . . . .* Of course, there is nothing that proscribes the press from reporting events that transpire in the courtroom. But where there is a reasonable likelihood that prejudicial news prior to trial will prevent a fair trial, the judge should *continue the case* until the threat abates, *or transfer it* to another county not so permeated with publicity. In addition, *sequestration of the jury* was something the judge should have raised sua sponte with counsel. If publicity during the proceedings threatens the fairness of the trial, a new trial should be ordered. But we must remember that reversals are but palliatives; the cure lies in those remedial measures that will prevent the prejudice at its inception. The courts must take such steps by rule and regulation that will protect their processes from prejudicial outside interferences. *Neither prosecutors, counsel for defense, the accused, witnesses, court staff nor enforcement officers coming under the jurisdiction of the court should be permitted to frustrate its function.* Collaboration between counsel and the press as to information affecting the fairness of a criminal trial is not only subject to regulation, but is highly censurable and worthy of disciplinary measures." . . .

Because the trial court had failed to use even minimal efforts to insulate the trial and the jurors from the "deluge of publicity," . . . the Court vacated the judgment of conviction and a new trial followed, in which the accused was acquitted.

Cases such as these are relatively rare, and we have held in other cases that trials have been fair in spite of widespread publicity. In Stroble v. California, 343 U.S. 181 (1952), for example, the Court affirmed a conviction and death sentence challenged on the ground that pretrial news accounts, including the prosecutor's release of the defendant's recorded confession, were allegedly so inflammatory as to amount to a denial of due process. The Court disapproved of the prosecutor's conduct, but noted that the publicity had receded some six weeks before trial, that the defendant had not moved for a change of venue, and that the confession had been found voluntary and admitted in evidence at trial. The Court also noted the thorough examination of jurors on *voir dire* and the careful review of the facts by the state courts, and held that petitioner had failed to demonstrate a denial of due process. . . .

Taken together, these cases demonstrate that pretrial publicity—even pervasive, adverse publicity—does not inevitably lead to an unfair trial. . . . [T]he measures a judge takes or fails to take to mitigate the effects of pretrial publicity—the measures described in *Sheppard*—may well determine whether the defendant receives a trial consistent with the requirements of due process. That this responsibility has not always been properly discharged is apparent from the decisions just reviewed.

. . .

V

. . . None of our decided cases on prior restraint involved restrictive orders entered to protect a defendant's right to a fair and impartial jury, but the opinions on prior restraint have a common thread relevant to this case.

. . .

A prior restraint, . . . has an immediate and irreversible sanction. If it can be said that a threat of criminal or civil sanctions after publication "chills" speech, prior restraint "freezes" it at least for the time.

. . .

VI

. . . [W]e must examine the evidence before the trial judge when the order was entered to determine (a) the nature and extent of pretrial news coverage; (b) whether other measures would be likely to mitigate the effects of unrestrained pretrial publicity; and (c) how effectively a restraining order would operate to prevent the threatened danger. The precise terms of the restraining order are also important. We must then consider whether the record supports the entry of a prior restraint on publication, one of the most extraordinary remedies known to our jurisprudence.

. . .

We have . . . examined this record to determine the probable efficacy of the measures short of prior restraint on the press and speech. There is no finding that alternative measures would not have protected Simants' rights, and the Nebraska Supreme Court did no more than imply that such measures might not be adequate. Moreover, the record is lacking in evidence to support such a finding.

. . .

To the extent that this order prohibited the reporting of evidence adduced at the open preliminary hearing, it plainly violated settled principles: . . .

The third prohibition of the order was defective in another respect as well. As part of a final order, entered after plenary review, this prohibition regarding "implicative" information is too vague and too broad to survive the scrutiny we have given to restraints on First Amendment rights....

. . .

Of necessity our holding is confined to the record before us. ... However difficult it may be, we need not rule out the possibility of showing the kind of threat to fair trial rights that would possess the requisite degree of certainty to justify restraint. This Court has frequently denied that First Amendment rights are absolute and has consistently rejected the proposition that a prior restraint can never be employed....

. . .

Mr. Justice Brennan, with whom Mr. Justice Stewart and Mr. Justice Marshall join, concurring in the judgment.

... The right to a fair trial by a jury of one's peers is unquestionably one of the most precious and sacred safeguards enshrined in the Bill of Rights. I would hold, however, that resort to prior restraints on the freedom of the press is a constitutionally impermissible method for enforcing that right; judges have at their disposal a broad spectrum of devices for ensuring that fundamental fairness is accorded the accused without necessitating so drastic an incursion on the equally fundamental and salutary constitutional mandate that discussion of public affairs in a free society cannot depend on the preliminary grace of judicial censors.

. . .

... [T]he necessary impact of reporting even confessions can never be so direct, immediate and irreparable that I would give credence to any notion that prior restraints may be imposed on that rationale. ... [A]t least in the context of prior restraints on publication, the decision of what, when, and how to publish is for editors, not judges.... Every restrictive order imposed on the press in this case was accordingly an unconstitutional prior restraint on the freedom of the press, and I would therefore reverse the judgment of the Nebraska Supreme Court and remand for further proceedings not inconsistent with this opinion.

Mr. Justice White, concurring.

Technically there is no need to go farther than the Court does to dispose of this case, and I join the Court's opinion. I should add, however, that ... there is grave doubt in my mind whether orders with respect to the press such as were entered in this case would ever be justifiable. It may be the better part of discretion, however, not to announce such a rule in the first case in which the issue has been squarely presented here. ... If the recurring result, however, in case after case is to be similar to our judgment today, we should at some point announce a more general rule and avoid the interminable litigation that our failure to do so would necessarily entail.

Mr. Justice Powell, concurring.

. . .

In my judgment a prior restraint properly may issue only when it is shown to be necessary to prevent the dissemination of prejudicial publicity that otherwise poses a high likelihood of preventing, directly and irreparably, the impaneling of a jury meeting the Sixth Amendment requirement of impartiality. ... Notwithstanding such a showing, a restraint may not issue unless it also is shown that previous publicity or publicity from unrestrained sources will not render the restraint inefficacious. . . .

. . .

Mr. Justice Stevens, concurring in the judgment.

For the reasons eloquently stated by Mr. Justice Brennan, I agree that the judiciary is capable of protecting the defendant's right to a fair trial without enjoining the press from publishing information in the public domain, and that it may not do so. Whether the same absolute protection would apply no matter how shabby or illegal the means by which the information is obtained, no matter how serious an intrusion on privacy might be involved, no matter how demonstrably false the information might be, no matter how prejudicial it might be to the interests of innocent persons, and no matter how perverse the motivation for publishing it, is a question I would not answer without further argument. . . .

The Florida Star v. B.J.F.

491 U.S. 524, 109 S.Ct. 2603, 105 L.Ed.2d 443 (1989).

[The report in this case appears, supra at p. 1335.]

SECTION 4.   GOVERNMENT DEMANDS FOR CONFIDENTIAL PRESS INFORMATION

Branzburg v. Hayes

408 U.S. 665, 92 S.Ct. 2646, 33 L.Ed.2d 626 (1972).

Opinion of the Court by Mr. Justice White, announced by The Chief Justice.

[Branzburg was a Louisville Courier–Journal reporter who observed two persons synthesizing hashish from marihuana. After making his observations the basis of a news article, he was called before a grand jury and refused to identify the persons involved. Pappas, a television-reporter-photographer, was sent to cover a Black Panther conference and gained entrance to Panther headquarters. He was called before a grand jury and refused to testify as to anything he heard while within the Panther headquarters. Caldwell was a New York Times reporter assigned to cover the Black Panthers and other militant groups. He was called to testify and bring his records before a federal grand jury. He refused to appear. All three cases raised the issue whether requiring reporters to appear and testify before state or federal grand juries was consistent with the First Amendment.]

Petitioners Branzburg and Pappas and respondent Caldwell press First Amendment claims that may be simply put: that to gather news it is often necessary to agree either not to identify the source of information published or to publish only part of the facts revealed, or both; that if the reporter is nevertheless forced to reveal these confidences to a grand jury, the source so identified and other confidential sources of other reporters will be measurably deterred from furnishing publishable information, all to the detriment of the free flow of information protected by the First Amendment. Although the newsmen in these cases do not claim an absolute privilege against official interrogation in all circumstances, they assert that the reporter should not be forced either to appear or to testify before a grand jury or at trial until and unless sufficient grounds are shown for believing that the reporter possesses information relevant to a crime the grand jury is investigating, that the information the reporter has is unavailable from other sources, and that the need for the information is sufficiently compelling to override the claimed invasion of First Amendment interests occasioned by the disclosure. . . .

. . . [W]ithout some protection for seeking out the news, freedom of the press could be eviscerated. But these cases involve no intrusions upon speech or assembly, no prior restraint or restriction on what the press may publish, and no express or implied command that the press publish what it prefers to withhold. . . .

The sole issue before us is the obligation of reporters to respond to grand jury subpoenas as other citizens do and to answer questions relevant to an investigation into the commission of crime. . . .

. . .

Despite the fact that news gathering may be hampered, the press is regularly excluded from grand jury proceedings, our own conferences, the meetings of other official bodies gathered in executive session, and the meetings of private organizations. Newsmen have no constitutional right of access to the scenes of crime or disaster when the general public is excluded, and they may be prohibited from attending or publishing information about trials if such restrictions are necessary to assure a defendant a fair trial before an impartial tribunal. . . .

It is thus not surprising that the great weight of authority is that newsmen are not exempt from the normal duty of appearing before a grand jury and answering questions relevant to a criminal investigation. At common law, courts consistently refused to recognize the existence of any privilege authorizing a newsman to refuse to reveal confidential information to a grand jury. . . .

. . .

A number of States have provided newsmen a statutory privilege of varying breadth, but the majority have not done so, and none has been provided by federal statute. Until now the only testimonial privilege for unofficial witnesses that is rooted in the Federal Constitution is the Fifth Amendment privilege against compelled self-incrimination. We are asked to create another by interpreting the First Amendment to grant newsmen a testimonial privilege that other citizens do not enjoy. This we decline to do. . . .

This conclusion itself involves no restraint on what newspapers may publish or on the type or quality of information reporters may seek to acquire, nor does it threaten the vast bulk of confidential relationships between reporters and their sources. . . . Only where news sources themselves are implicated in crime or possess information relevant to the grand jury's task need they or the reporter be concerned about grand jury subpoenas. Nothing before us indicates that a large number or percentage of *all* confidential news sources falls into either category and would in any way be deterred by our holding that the Constitution does not, as it never has, exempt the newsman from performing the citizen's normal duty of appearing and furnishing information relevant to the grand jury's task.

. . .

The argument that the flow of news will be diminished by compelling reporters to aid the grand jury in a criminal investigation is not irrational, nor are the records before us silent on the matter. But we remain unclear how often and to what extent informers are actually deterred from furnishing information when newsmen are forced to testify before a grand jury. . . .

Accepting the fact, however, that an undetermined number of informants not themselves implicated in crime will nevertheless, for whatever reason, refuse to talk to newsmen if they fear identification by a reporter in an official investigation, we cannot accept the argument that the public interest in possible future news about crime from undisclosed, unverified sources must take precedence over the public interest in pursuing and prosecuting those crimes reported to the press by informants and in thus deterring the commission of such crimes in the future.

. . .

The privilege claimed here is conditional, not absolute; given the suggested preliminary showings and compelling need, the reporter would be required to testify. Presumably, such a rule would reduce the instances in which reporters could be required to appear, but predicting in advance when and in what circumstances they could be compelled to do so would be difficult. . . .

We are unwilling to embark the judiciary on a long and difficult journey to such an uncertain destination. The administration of a constitutional newsman's privilege would present practical and conceptual difficulties of a high order. Sooner or later, it would be necessary to define those categories of newsmen who qualified for the privilege . . .

In each instance where a reporter is subpoenaed to testify, the courts would also be embroiled in preliminary factual and legal determinations with respect to whether the proper predicate had been laid for the reporters' appearance: Is there probable cause to believe a crime has been committed? Is it likely that the reporter has useful information gained in confidence? Could the grand jury obtain the information elsewhere? Is the official interest sufficient to outweigh the claimed privilege?

Thus, in the end, by considering whether enforcement of a particular law served a "compelling" governmental interest, the courts would be inextricably involved in distinguishing between the value of enforcing different criminal laws. By requiring testimony from a reporter in investigations involving some crimes but not in others, they would be making a value judgment that a legislature had declined to make . . .

At the federal level, Congress has freedom to determine whether a statutory newsman's privilege is necessary and desirable and to fashion standards and rules as narrow or broad as deemed necessary to deal with the evil discerned and, equally important, to refashion those rules as experience from time to time may dictate. There is also merit in leaving state legislatures free, within First Amendment limits, to fashion their own standards in light of the conditions and problems with respect to the relations between law enforcement officials and press in their own areas. It goes without saying, of course, that we are powerless to bar state courts responding in their own way and construing their own constitutions so as to recognize a newsman's privilege, either qualified or absolute.

. . .

Finally, as we have earlier indicated, news gathering is not without its First Amendment protections, and grand jury investigations if instituted or conducted other than in good faith, would pose wholly different issues for resolution under the First Amendment. Official harassment of the press undertaken not for purposes of law enforcement but to disrupt a reporter's relationship with his news sources would have no justification. Grand juries are subject to judicial control and subpoenas to motions to quash. We do not expect courts will forget that grand juries must operate within the limits of the First Amendment as well as the Fifth.

. . .

Mr. Justice Powell, concurring.

I add this brief statement to emphasize what seems to me to be the limited nature of the Court's holding. The Court does not hold that newsmen, subpoenaed to testify before a grand jury, are without constitutional rights with respect to the gathering of news or in safeguarding their sources. . . .

. . . [I]n the concluding portion of the opinion, the Court states that no harassment of newsmen will be tolerated. If a newsman believes that the grand jury investigation is not being conducted in good faith he is not without remedy. Indeed, if the newsman is called upon to give information bearing only a remote and tenuous relationship to the subject of the investigation, or if he has some other reason to believe that his testimony implicates confidential source relationships without a legitimate need of law enforcement, he will have access to the Court on a motion to quash and an appropriate protective order may be entered. The asserted claim to privilege should be judged on its facts by the striking of a proper balance between freedom of the press and the obligation of all citizens to give relevant testimony with respect to criminal conduct. The balance of these vital constitutional and societal interests on a case-by-case basis accords with the tried and traditional way of adjudicating such questions.

In short, the courts will be available to newsmen under circumstances where legitimate First Amendment interests require protection.

Mr. Justice Douglas, dissenting. . . .

. . .

It is my view that there is no "compelling need" that can be shown which qualifies the reporter's immunity from appearing or testifying before a grand jury, unless the reporter himself is implicated in a crime. His immunity in my view is therefore quite complete, for, absent his involvement in a crime, the First Amendment protects him against an appearance before a grand jury and if he is involved in a crime, the Fifth Amendment stands as a barrier. Since in my view there is no area of inquiry not protected by a privilege, the reporter need not appear for the futile purpose of invoking one to each question. And, since in my view a newsman has an absolute right not to appear before a grand jury it follows for me that a journalist who voluntarily appears before that body may invoke his First Amendment privilege to specific questions. . . .

. . .

Mr. Justice Stewart, with whom Mr. Justice Brennan and Mr. Justice Marshall join, dissenting.

. . . While Mr. Justice Powell's enigmatic concurring opinion gives some hope of a more flexible view in the future, the Court in these cases holds that a newsman has no First Amendment right to protect his sources when called before a grand jury . . . . . Not only will this decision impair performance of the press' constitutionally protected functions, but it will, I am convinced, in the long run, harm rather than help the administration of justice.

. . .

. . . [W]hen a reporter is asked to appear before a grand jury and reveal confidences, I would hold that the government must (1) show that there is probable cause to believe that the newsman has information that is clearly relevant to a specific probable violation of law; (2) demonstrate that the information sought cannot be obtained by alternative means less destructive of First Amendment rights; and (3) demonstrate a compelling and overriding interest in the information.

This is not to say that a grand jury could not issue a subpoena until such a showing were made, and it is not to say that a newsman would be in any way privileged to ignore any subpoena that was issued. Obviously, before the government's burden to make such a showing were triggered, the reporter would have to move to quash the subpoena, asserting the basis on which he considered the particular relationship a confidential one.

. . .

ZURCHER v. STANFORD DAILY, 436 U.S. 547 (1978). The court held that the First and Fourth Amendments did not preclude issuance of a search warrant for search of a newsroom. Justice White's opinion for the court concluded that the First Amendment did not immunize the media from search warrants issued on probable cause. Justice Powell, who supplied the controlling fifth vote, joined the court's opinion but also wrote a concurring opinion, in which he asserted that "a warrant which would be sufficient to support the search of an apartment or automobile would [not necessarily] be reasonable in supporting the search of a newspaper office." He concluded that, while there was no justification for a separate procedure for searches of the press, First Amendment values should be taken into account in making the "reasonableness" and "particularity" judgments under the Fourth Amendment.[1]

HERBERT v. LANDO, 441 U.S. 153 (1979). Herbert, a retired army officer, brought a diversity suit in federal court, claiming that a CBS television documentary on Vietnamese war atrocities defamed him. In pretrial deposition, the program's producer was asked questions about his opinions with respect to the material gathered by him and about his conversations with editorial colleagues. The court held that the First Amendment gave the producer no privilege to refuse to answer the questions. The libel plaintiff was a public figure who could not recover without proof of malice in the sense of knowing falsity or reckless disregard of the truth. Since that standard required plaintiff to prove the state of the defendant's mind, a First Amendment privilege against disclosure of the editorial process "would constitute a substantial interference with the ability of a defamation plaintiff to establish the ingredients of" his case. Justice White's opinion for the court did, however, indicate that editorial discussions may have some constitutional protection from "casual inquiry."

"There is no law that subjects the editorial process to private or official examination merely to satisfy curiosity or to serve some general end such as the public interest; and if there were, it would not survive constitutional scrutiny as the First Amendment is presently construed. No such problem exists here,

---

1. The Privacy Protection Act of 1980, 42 U.S.C. § 2000aa, requires state and federal law enforcement officers to use subpoena procedures to obtain documents from persons engaged in the communications industry. Search warrants are permitted in exceptional circumstances, such as when it is believed that the desired documents would be destroyed.

however, where there is a specific claim of injury arising from a publication that is alleged to have been knowingly or recklessly false."

SECTION 5.   PRESS ACCESS TO GOVERNMENT INFORMATION

PRESS ACCESS DECISIONS PRIOR TO 1980

No Supreme Court decision, prior to 1980, sustained a press claim that the First Amendment provided the press with a special right of access to information controlled by the government. The settled proposition, as explained by Justice Stewart for the Court in Pell v. Procunier, 417 U.S. 817 (1974), was that the "Constitution does not ... require government to accord the press special access to information not shared by members of the public generally." In *Pell,* the Court sustained a California policy placing limits on interviews with individual prisoners. In Houchins v. KQED, Inc., 438 U.S. 1 (1978), the Court sustained a county jail policy limiting reporters' access to jail facilities. Both decisions were by a closely divided Court, with the dissenters arguing that a First Amendment right of press access was necessary to allow the media to play its societal function in the discussion of public affairs.

In Gannett Co., Inc. v. DePasquale, 443 U.S. 368 (1979), the five-Justice majority rejected an alternative constitutional source of press access. In a murder case, pre-trial hearings to suppress evidence had been closed to the public and the press on motion of the criminal defendants. The Court held that the Sixth Amendment's guarantee of a public trial was only for the benefit of the accused, and did not give the public or the press any right of access to criminal trials. Significantly, one member of the majority, Justice Powell, wrote a concurrence arguing that there was a First Amendment right of press access to criminal proceedings distinct from the general public's right of access.

Richmond Newspapers, Inc. v. Virginia

448 U.S. 555, 100 S.Ct. 2814, 65 L.Ed.2d 973 (1980).

Mr. Chief Justice Burger announced the judgment of the Court and delivered an opinion, in which Mr. Justice White and Mr. Justice Stevens joined.

The narrow question presented in this case is whether the right of the public and press to attend criminal trials is guaranteed under the United States Constitution.

I

... Stevenson was convicted of second-degree murder in the Circuit Court of Hanover County, Va. The Virginia Supreme Court reversed the conviction ..., holding that a bloodstained shirt purportedly belonging to Stevenson had been improperly admitted into evidence....

Stevenson was retried in the same court. This second trial ended in a mistrial ... when a juror asked to be excused after trial had begun and no alternate was available.

A third trial ... also ended in a mistrial ... because a prospective juror had read about Stevenson's previous trials in a newspaper and had told other prospective jurors about the case before the retrial began.

Stevenson was tried in the same court for a fourth time ... Present in the courtroom when the case was called were appellants Wheeler and McCarthy, reporters for appellant Richmond Newspapers, Inc. Before the trial began, counsel for the defendant moved that it be closed to the public ...

The trial judge, who had presided over two of the three previous trials, asked if the prosecution had any objection to clearing the courtroom. The prosecutor stated he had no objection and would leave it to the discretion of the court. ... [The trial judge] ordered "that the Courtroom be kept clear of all parties except the witnesses when they testify." ...

Later that same day, ... appellants sought a hearing on a motion to vacate the closure order. The trial judge granted the request and scheduled a hearing to follow the close of the day's proceedings. When the hearing began, the court ruled that the hearing was to be treated as part of the trial; accordingly, he again ordered the reporters to leave the courtroom, and they complied.

. . .

... The court denied the motion to vacate and ordered the trial to continue the following morning "with the press and public excluded."

What transpired when the closed trial resumed the next day was disclosed in the following manner by an order of the court ...:

"[I]n the absence of the jury, the defendant by counsel made a Motion that a mis-trial be declared, which motion was taken under advisement. At the conclusion of the Commonwealth's evidence, the attorney for the defendant moved the Court to strike the Commonwealth's evidence on grounds stated to the record, which Motion was sustained by the Court. And the jury having been excused, the Court doth find the accused NOT GUILTY of Murder, as charged in the Indictment, and he was allowed to depart."

... Appellants then petitioned the Virginia Supreme Court for writs of mandamus and prohibition and filed an appeal from the trial court's closure order. ... [T]he Virginia Supreme Court dismissed the mandamus and prohibition petitions and, finding no reversible error, denied the petition for appeal.

. . .

II

We begin consideration of this case by noting that the precise issue presented here has not previously been before this Court for decision. In Gannett Co., Inc. v. DePasquale, ... the Court was not required to decide whether a right of access to *trials,* as distinguished from hearings on *pre*trial motions, was constitutionally guaranteed. The Court held that the Sixth Amendment's guarantee to the accused of a public trial gave neither the public nor the press an enforceable right of access to a *pre*trial suppression hearing. One concurring opinion specifically emphasized that "a hearing on a motion before trial to suppress evidence is not a *trial.* ..." ... Moreover, the Court did not decide whether the First and Fourteenth Amendments guarantee a right of the public to attend trials ...; nor did the dissenting opinion reach this issue. . . .

. . .

A

The ... modern criminal trial in Anglo–American justice ... has been open to all who cared to observe.

. . .

B

... [T]he historical evidence demonstrates conclusively that at the time when our organic laws were adopted, criminal trials both here and in England had long been presumptively open. This is no quirk of history; rather, it has long been recognized as an indispensable attribute of an Anglo–American trial. ...

. . .

People in an open society do not demand infallibility from their institutions, but it is difficult for them to accept what they are prohibited from observing. When a criminal trial is conducted in the open, there is at least an opportunity both for understanding the system in general and its workings in a particular case: ...

. . .

C

From this unbroken, uncontradicted history, supported by reasons as valid today as in centuries past, we are bound to conclude that a presumption of openness inheres in the very nature of a criminal trial under our system of justice....

... [T]he State presses [contends] that neither the Constitution nor the Bill of Rights contains any provision which by its terms guarantees to the public the right to attend criminal trials. Standing alone, this is correct, but there remains the question whether, absent an explicit provision, the Constitution affords protection against exclusion of the public from criminal trials.

III

A

... First Amendment ... freedoms share a common core purpose of assuring freedom of communication on matters relating to the functioning of government. Plainly it would be difficult to single out any aspect of government of higher concern and importance to the people than the manner in which criminal trials are conducted; as we have shown, recognition of this pervades the centuries-old history of open trials and the opinions of this Court.

... [T]he First Amendment guarantees of speech and press, standing alone, prohibit government from summarily closing courtroom doors which had long been open to the public at the time that Amendment was adopted....

... The explicit, guaranteed rights to speak and to publish concerning what takes place at a trial would lose much meaning if access to observe the trial could, as it was here, be foreclosed arbitrarily.

B

. . .

C

. . .

We hold that the right to attend criminal trials[17] is implicit in the guarantees of the First Amendment; ...

---

17. Whether the public has a right to attend trials of civil cases is a question not raised by this case, but we note that historically both civil and criminal trials have been presumptively open.

D

Having concluded there was a guaranteed right of the public under the First and Fourteenth Amendments to attend the trial of Stevenson's case, we return to the closure order challenged by appellants. ... Despite the fact that this was the fourth trial of the accused, the trial judge made no findings to support closure; no inquiry was made as to whether alternative solutions would have met the need to ensure fairness; there was no recognition of any right under the Constitution for the public or press to attend the trial. ... Absent an overriding interest articulated in findings, the trial of a criminal case must be open to the public. Accordingly, the judgment under review is

Reversed.

Mr. Justice Powell took no part in the consideration or decision of this case.

Mr. Justice White, concurring.

This case would have been unnecessary had Gannett Co. v. DePasquale, 443 U.S. 368 (1979), construed the Sixth Amendment to forbid excluding the public from criminal proceedings except in narrowly defined circumstances. But the Court there rejected the submission of four of us to this effect, thus requiring that the First Amendment issue involved here be addressed. On this issue, I concur in the opinion of The Chief Justice.

Mr. Justice Stevens, concurring.

This is a watershed case. Until today the Court has accorded virtually absolute protection to the dissemination of information or ideas, but never before has it squarely held that the acquisition of newsworthy matter is entitled to any constitutional protection whatsoever. An additional word of emphasis is therefore appropriate.

Twice before, the Court has implied that any governmental restriction on access to information, no matter how severe and no matter how unjustified, would be constitutionally acceptable so long as it did not single out the press for special disabilities not applicable to the public at large. ... Today, however, for the first time, the Court unequivocally holds that an arbitrary interference with access to important information is an abridgment of the freedoms of speech and of the press protected by the First Amendment.

It is somewhat ironic that the Court should find more reason to recognize a right of access today than it did in *Houchins*. For *Houchins* involved the plight of a segment of society least able to protect itself, an attack on a long-standing policy of concealment, and an absence of any legitimate justification for abridging public access to information about how government operates. In this case we are protecting the interests of the most powerful voices in the community, ... and it is likely that the closure order was motivated by the judge's desire to protect the individual defendant from the burden of a fourth criminal trial.

In any event, ... I agree that the First Amendment protects the public and the press from abridgment of their rights of access to information about the operation of their government, including the Judicial Branch; given the total absence of any record justification for the closure order entered in this case, that order violated the First Amendment.

Mr. Justice Brennan, with whom Mr. Justice Marshall joins, concurring in the judgment.

Gannett Co. v. DePasquale, . . . held that the Sixth Amendment right to a public trial was personal to the accused, conferring no right of access to pretrial proceedings that is separately enforceable by the public or the press . . . . . Because I believe that the First Amendment . . . secures such a public right of access, I agree with those of my Brethren who hold that, without more, agreement of the trial judge and the parties cannot constitutionally close a trial to the public.

I

. . . [T]he Court has not ruled out a public access component to the First Amendment in every circumstance. Read with care and in context, our decisions must therefore be understood as holding only that any privilege of access to governmental information is subject to a degree of restraint dictated by the nature of the information and countervailing interests in security or confidentiality. . . .

. . . [T]he First Amendment embodies more than a commitment to free expression and communicative interchange for their own sakes; it has a *structural* role to play in securing and fostering our republican system of self-government. . . . Implicit in this structural role is . . . the antecedent assumption that valuable public debate—as well as other civic behavior—must be informed. . . .

However, because "the stretch of this protection is theoretically endless," . . . it must be invoked with discrimination and temperance. . . . An assertion of the prerogative to gather information must . . . be assayed by considering the information sought and the opposing interests invaded.

. . . [A]t least two helpful principles may be sketched. First, the case for a right of access has special force when drawn from an enduring and vital tradition of public entree to particular proceedings or information. . . . Second, the value of access must be measured in specifics. . . . [W]hat is crucial in individual cases is whether access to a particular government process is important in terms of that very process.

. . .

II

. . .

Tradition, contemporaneous state practice, and this Court's own decisions manifest a common understanding that "[a] trial is a public event. What transpires in the court room is public property." . . .

III

. . .

Popular attendance at trials, in sum, substantially furthers the particular public purposes of that critical judicial proceeding. In that sense, public access is an indispensable element of the trial process itself. . . .

IV

. . . With regard to the case at hand, our ingrained tradition of public trials and the importance of public access to the broader purposes of the trial process, tip the balance strongly toward the rule that trials be open. What countervailing interests might be sufficiently compelling to reverse this presumption of openness need not concern us now,[24] . . .

Mr. Justice Stewart, concurring in the judgment.

. . .

. . . [T]he First Amendment right of members of the public and representatives of the press to attend civil and criminal trials is [not] absolute. Just as a legislature may impose reasonable time, place and manner restrictions upon the exercise of First Amendment freedoms, so may a trial judge impose reasonable limitations upon the unrestricted occupation of a courtroom by representatives of the press and members of the public. . . . [A] trial courtroom must be a quiet and orderly place. . . . Moreover, every courtroom has a finite physical capacity, and there may be occasions when not all who wish to attend a trial may do so.[3] And while there exist many alternative ways to satisfy the constitutional demands of a fair trial, those demands may also sometimes justify limitations upon the unrestricted presence of spectators in the courtroom.[5]

. . .

Mr. Justice Blackmun, concurring in the judgment.

My opinion and vote in partial dissent last Term in Gannett Co. v. DePasquale, 443 U.S. 368, 406 (1979), compels my vote to reverse the judgment of the Supreme Court of Virginia.

. . .

II

. . . I remain convinced that the right to a public trial is to be found where the Constitution explicitly placed it—in the Sixth Amendment.

The Court, however, has eschewed the Sixth Amendment route. . . .

. . . [W]ith the Sixth Amendment set to one side in this case, I am driven to conclude, as a secondary position, that the First Amendment must provide some measure of protection for public access to the trial. . . .

. . .

Mr. Justice Rehnquist, dissenting.

. . .

For the reasons stated in my separate concurrence in Gannett Co. v. DePasquale, . . . I do not believe that either the First or Sixth Amendment . . . require that a State's reasons for denying public access to a trial, where both the prosecuting attorney and the defendant have consented to an order of closure approved by the judge, are subject to any additional constitutional review at our hands. . . .

. . .

---

24. For example, national security concerns about confidentiality may sometimes warrant closures during sensitive portions of trial proceedings, such as testimony about state secrets. Cf. United States v. Nixon, 418 U.S. 683, 714–716 (1974).

3. In such situations, representatives of the press must be assured access. Houchins v. KQED, Inc., 438 U.S. 1, 16 (opinion concurring in the judgment).

5. This is not to say that only constitutional considerations can justify such restrictions. The preservation of trade secrets, for example, might justify the exclusion of the public from at least some segments of a civil trial. And the sensibilities of a youthful prosecution witness, for example, might justify similar exclusion in a criminal trial for rape, so long as the defendant's Sixth Amendment right to a public trial were not impaired. . . .

The issue here is not whether the "right" to freedom of the press conferred by the First Amendment to the Constitution overrides the defendant's "right" to a fair trial conferred by other Amendments to the Constitution; it is instead whether any provision in the Constitution may fairly be read to prohibit what the trial judge in the Virginia state court system did in this case. Being unable to find any such prohibition in the First, Sixth, Ninth, or any other Amendments to the United States Constitution, or in the Constitution itself, I dissent.

PRESS ACCESS DECISIONS SINCE RICHMOND NEWSPAPERS, INC. v. VIRGINIA

In Globe Newspaper Co. v. Superior Court, 457 U.S. 596 (1982), Justice Brennan's opinion for the Court read the *Richmond Newspapers* case simply as establishing a right of access to criminal trials embodied in the First Amendment. The Court held unconstitutional on its face a unique Massachusetts statute requiring exclusion of the press and public during testimony of the victim at trials for specified sexual offenses against persons under the age of 18. The Court conceded that the First Amendment might not preclude restrictions on public and press access in individual cases based on "particularized determinations."

In Press–Enterprise Co. v. Superior Court, 464 U.S. 501 (1984), the Court held that a state court's decision closing the six weeks of *voir dire* examination of jurors in a criminal trial violated the Constitution. Chief Justice Burger's opinion for the Court stated that the "presumption of openness" of criminal trials "may be overcome only by an overriding interest based on findings that closure is essential to preserve higher values and is narrowly tailored to serve that interest."

In Press–Enterprise Co. v. Superior Court (Press–Enterprise II), 478 U.S. 1 (1986), the Court held that a California statute, requiring that preliminary hearings in criminal cases be closed on a finding of "reasonable likelihood of substantial prejudice," violated the first amendment. Citing the preliminary hearing conducted by Chief Justice Marshall in 1807 in the trial of Aaron Burr, Chief Justice Burger's opinion for the Court concluded that "there has been a tradition of accessibility to preliminary hearings of the type conducted in California." California preliminary hearings were also "sufficiently like a trial" to justify the same right of access as to the trial. Thus, the preliminary hearing could only be closed to the public under the standards announced in *Richmond Newspapers* and *Press–Enterprise I*. Justice Stevens' dissent, joined by Justice Rehnquist, argued that a finding of "reasonable probability of prejudice" established interests in protecting a fair trial and the reputation of the accused that justified denying access to the preliminary hearing and its transcript "for at least the short time before trial."

SECTION 6.   SPECIAL PROBLEMS OF THE ELECTRONIC MEDIA

Columbia Broadcasting System, Inc. v. Democratic National Committee

412 U.S. 94, 93 S.Ct. 2080, 36 L.Ed.2d 772 (1973).

Mr. Chief Justice Burger delivered the opinion of the Court (Parts I, II, and IV) together with an opinion (Part III), in which Mr. Justice Stewart and Mr. Justice Rehnquist joined.

We granted the writs of certiorari in these cases to consider whether a broadcast licensee's general policy of not selling advertising time to individuals or groups wishing to speak out on issues they consider important violates the Federal Communications Act of 1934, 47 U.S.C. § 151 et seq., or the First Amendment.

. . .

The complainants in these actions are the Democratic National Committee (DNC) and the Business Executives' Move for Vietnam Peace (BEM), a national organization of businessmen opposed to United States involvement in the Vietnam conflict. In January 1970, BEM filed a complaint with the Commission charging that radio station WTOP in Washington, D.C., had refused to sell it time to broadcast a series of one-minute spot announcements expressing BEM views on Vietnam. WTOP, in common with many, but not all, broadcasters, followed a policy of refusing to sell time for spot announcements to individuals and groups who wished to expound their views on controversial issues. . . .

Four months later, in May 1970, DNC filed with the Commission a request for a declaratory ruling:

"That under the First Amendment to the Constitution and the Communications Act, a broadcaster may not, as a general policy, refuse to sell time to responsible entities, such as the DNC, for the solicitation of funds and for comment on public issues."

. . . DNC cited Red Lion Broadcasting Co. v. FCC, 395 U.S. 367 (1969), as establishing a limited constitutional right of access to the airwaves.

. . . [T]he Commission rejected respondents' claim that "responsible" individuals and groups have a right to purchase advertising time to comment on public issues without regard to whether the broadcaster has complied with the Fairness Doctrine. . . .

. . .

A majority of the Court of Appeals reversed the Commission, ...

. . .

I

Mr. Justice White's opinion for the Court in Red Lion Broadcasting Co. v. FCC . . . makes clear that the broadcast media pose unique and special problems not present in the traditional free speech case. Unlike other media, broadcasting is subject to an inherent physical limitation. Broadcast frequencies are a scarce resource; they must be portioned out among applicants. All who possess the financial resources and the desire to communicate by television or radio cannot be satisfactorily accommodated. The Court spoke to this reality when, in *Red Lion*, we said "it is idle to post an unabridgeable First Amendment right to broadcast comparable to the right of every individual to speak, write, or publish." . . .

Because the broadcast media utilize a valuable and limited public resource, there is also present an unusual order of First Amendment values. *Red Lion* discussed at length the application of the First Amendment to the broadcast media. In analyzing the broadcasters' claim that the Fairness Doctrine and two of its component rules violated their freedom of expression, we held that "[n]o one has a First Amendment right to a license or to monopolize a radio frequency; to deny a station license because 'the public interest' requires it 'is not a denial of free speech.' " . . . Although the broadcaster is not without protection under the First Amendment, . . . "[i]t is the right of the viewers and listeners, not the right of the broadcasters, which is paramount. . . . It is the right of the public to receive suitable access to social, political, esthetic, moral and other ideas and experiences which is crucial here. That right may not constitutionally be abridged either by Congress or by the FCC." *Red Lion,* [395 U.S.], at 390.

Balancing the various First Amendment interests involved in the broadcast media and determining what best serves the public's right to be informed is a task of a great delicacy and difficulty. . . . Congress and its chosen regulatory agency have established a delicately balanced system of regulation intended to serve the interests of all concerned. . . . Thus, before confronting the specific legal issues in these cases, we turn to an examination of the legislative and administrative development of our broadcast system over the last half century.

II

. . .

The legislative history of the Radio Act of 1927, the model for our present statutory scheme, . . . reveals that in the area of discussion of public issues Congress chose to leave broad journalistic discretion with the licensee. Congress specifically dealt with—and firmly rejected—the argument that the broadcast facilities should be open on a nonselective basis to all persons wishing to talk about public issues. . . .

. . . Congress after prolonged consideration adopted § 3(h), which specifically provides that "a person engaged in radio broadcasting shall not, insofar as such person is so engaged, be deemed a common carrier."

Other provisions of the 1934 Act also evince a legislative desire to preserve values of private journalism under a regulatory scheme which would insure fulfillment of certain public obligations. . . . [Section] 326 of the Act specifically provides that:

> "Nothing in this chapter shall be understood or construed to give the Commission the power of censorship over the radio communications or signals transmitted by any radio station, and no regulation or condition shall be promulgated or fixed by the Commission which shall interfere with the right of free speech by means of radio communication." . . .

From these provisions it seems clear that Congress intended to permit private broadcasting to develop with the widest journalistic freedom consistent with its public obligations. . . .

Subsequent developments in broadcast regulation illustrate how this regulatory scheme has evolved. Of particular importance, in light of Congress' flat refusal to impose a "common carrier" right of access for all persons wishing to speak out on public issues, is the Commission's "Fairness Doctrine," which evolved gradually over the years . . . Formulated under the Commission's power to issue regulations consistent with the "public interest," the doctrine imposes two affirmative responsibilities on the broadcaster: coverage of issues of public importance must be adequate and must fairly reflect differing viewpoints. . . . In fulfilling the Fairness Doctrine obligations, the broadcaster must provide free time for the presentation of opposing views if a paid sponsor is unavailable, . . . and it must initiate programming on public issues if no one else seeks to do so. . . .

. . .

With this background in mind, we next proceed to consider whether a broadcaster's refusal to accept editorial advertisements is governmental action violative of the First Amendment.

III

... The Court has not previously considered whether the action of a broadcast licensee such as that challenged here is "governmental action" for purposes of the First Amendment. The holding under review thus presents a novel question, and one with far-reaching implications. ...

The Court of Appeals held that broadcasters are instrumentalities of the Government for First Amendment purposes, relying on the thesis, familiar in other contexts, that broadcast licensees are granted use of part of the public domain and are regulated as "proxies" or " 'fiduciaries' of the people." These characterizations are not without validity for some purposes, but they do not resolve the sensitive constitutional issues inherent in deciding whether a particular licensee action is subject to First Amendment restraints.

In dealing with the broadcast media, as in other contexts, the line between private conduct and governmental action cannot be defined by reference to any general formula unrelated to particular exercises of governmental authority....

In deciding whether the First Amendment encompasses the conduct challenged here, it must be kept in mind that we are dealing with a vital part of our system of communication. ... To a large extent they share with the printed media the role of keeping people informed.

As we have seen, with the advent of radio a half century ago, ... Congress opted for a system of private broadcasters licensed and regulated by Government. The legislative history suggests that this choice was influenced not only by traditional attitudes toward private enterprise, but by a desire to maintain for licensees, so far as consistent with necessary regulation, a traditional journalistic role. The historic aversion to censorship led Congress to enact § 326 of the Act, which explicitly prohibits the Commission from interfering with the exercise of free speech over the broadcast frequencies. Congress pointedly refrained from divesting broadcasters of their control over the selection of voices; § 3(h) of the Act stands as a firm congressional statement that broadcast licensees are not to be treated as common carriers, obliged to accept whatever is tendered by members of the public. Both these provisions clearly manifest the intention of Congress to maintain a substantial measure of journalistic independence for the broadcast licensee.

... [V]ery early the licensee's role developed in terms of a "public trustee" charged with the duty of fairly and impartially informing the public audience. In this structure the Commission acts in essence as an "overseer," but the initial and primary responsibility for fairness, balance, and objectivity rests with the licensee. This role of the Government as an "overseer" and ultimate arbiter and guardian of the public interest and the role of the licensee as a journalistic "free agent" call for a delicate balancing of competing interests. The maintenance of this balance for more than 40 years has called on both the regulators and the licensees to walk a "tightrope" to preserve the First Amendment values written into the Radio Act and its successor, the Communications Act.

The tensions inherent in such a regulatory structure emerge more clearly when we compare a private newspaper with a broadcast licensee. The power of a privately owned newspaper to advance its own political, social, and economic views is bounded by only two factors: first, the acceptance of a sufficient number of readers—and hence advertisers—to assure financial success; and, second, the journalistic integrity of its editors and publishers. A broadcast licensee has a large measure of journalistic freedom but not as large as that exercised by a newspaper. A licensee must balance what it might prefer to do as a private entrepreneur with what it is required to do as a "public trustee." To perform its statutory duties, the Commission must oversee without censoring....

... The licensee's policy against accepting editorial advertising cannot be examined as an abstract proposition, but must be viewed in the context of its journalistic role. It does not help to press on us the idea that editorial ads are "like" commercial ads, for the licensee's policy against editorial spot ads is expressly based on a journalistic judgment that 10–to–60 second spot announcements are ill suited to intelligible and intelligent treatment of public issues; the broadcaster has chosen to provide a balanced treatment of controversial questions in a more comprehensive form. Obviously the licensee's evaluation is based on its own journalistic judgment of priorities and newsworthiness.

Moreover, the Commission has not fostered the licensee policy challenged here; it has simply declined to command particular action because it fell within the area of journalistic discretion. The Commission explicitly emphasized that "there is of course no Commission policy thwarting the sale of time to comment on public issues." ...

. . .

Were we to read the First Amendment to spell out governmental action in the circumstances presented here, few licensee decisions on the content of broadcasts or the processes of editorial evaluation would escape constitutional scrutiny. ... Congress, and the Commission as its agent, must remain in a posture of flexibility to chart a workable "middle course" in its quest to preserve a balance between the essential public accountability and the desired private control of the media.

More profoundly, it would be anomalous for us to hold, in the name of promoting the constitutional guarantees of free expression, that the day-to-day editorial decisions of broadcast licensees are subject to the kind of restraints urged by respondents. To do so in the name of the First Amendment would be a contradiction. Journalistic discretion would in many ways be lost to the rigid limitations that the First Amendment imposes on Government. Application of such standards to broadcast licensees would be antithetical to the very ideal of vigorous, challenging debate on issues of public interest. Every licensee is already held accountable for the totality of its performance of public interest obligations.

. . .

IV

There remains for consideration the question whether the "public interest" standard of the Communications Act requires broadcasters to accept editorial advertisements or, whether, assuming governmental action, broadcasters are required to do so by reason of the First Amendment.

. . .

The Commission was justified in concluding that the public interest in providing access to the marketplace of "ideas and experiences" would scarcely be served by a system so heavily weighted in favor of the financially affluent, or those with access to wealth. ... Even under a first-come-first-served system, proposed by the dissenting Commissioner in these cases, the views of the affluent could well prevail over those of others, since they would have it within their power to purchase time more frequently. Moreover, there is the substantial danger, as the Court of Appeals acknowledged, that the time allotted for editorial advertising could be monopolized by those of one political persuasion.

. . .

By minimizing the difficult problems involved in implementing ... a right of access, the Court of Appeals failed to come to grips with another problem of critical importance to broadcast regulation and the First Amendment—the risk of an enlargement of Government control over the content of broadcast discussion of public issues....

. . .

Reversed.[a]

Mr. Justice Stewart, concurring.

While I join [Parts I, II, and III of the Court's opinion], my views closely approach those expressed by Mr. Justice Douglas concurring in the judgment.

The First Amendment prohibits the Government from imposing controls upon the press. Private broadcasters are surely part of the press. ... Yet here the Court of Appeals held, and the dissenters today agree, that the First Amendment *requires* the Government to impose controls upon private broadcasters—in order to preserve First Amendment "values." The appellate court accomplished this strange convolution by the simple device of holding that private broadcasters *are* Government. This is a step along a path that could eventually lead to the proposition that private *newspapers* "are" Government. Freedom of the press would then be gone. In its place we would have such governmental controls upon the press as a majority of this Court at any particular moment might consider First Amendment "values" to require. It is a frightening specter.

I

. . .

The First Amendment protects the press *from* governmental interference; it confers no analogous protection *on* the Government. ... If, as the dissent today would have it, the proper analogy is to public forums—that is, if broadcasters are Government for First Amendment purposes—then broadcasters are inevitably drawn to the position of common carriers. For this is precisely the status of Government with respect to public forums—a status mandated by the First Amendment.

To hold that broadcaster action is governmental action would thus produce a result wholly inimical to the broadcasters' own First Amendment rights ...

. . .

Mr. Justice Douglas, concurring in the judgment.

While I join the Court in reversing the judgment below, I do so for quite different reasons.

a. A concurring opinion by Justice Blackmun, joined by Justice Powell, is omitted.

My conclusion is that the TV and radio stand in the same protected position under the First Amendment as do newspapers and magazines. ...

. . .

If a broadcast licensee is not engaged in governmental action for purposes of the First Amendment, I fail to see how constitutionally we can treat TV and radio differently than we treat newspapers....

. . .

... [T]he prospect of putting Government in a position of control over publishers is to me an appalling one, even to the extent of the Fairness Doctrine. ...

It is said, of course, that Government can control the broadcasters because their channels are in the public domain in the sense that they use the airspace that is the common heritage of all the people. But parks are also in the public domain. Yet people who speak there do not come under Government censorship. ... It is the tradition of Hyde Park, not the tradition of the censor, that is reflected in the First Amendment. TV and radio broadcasters are a vital part of the press; and since the First Amendment allows no Government control over it, I would leave this segment of the press to its devices.

Licenses are, of course, restricted in time and while, in my view, Congress has the power to make each license limited to a fixed term and nonreviewable, there is no power to deny renewals for editorial or ideological reasons. ...

. . .

Mr. Justice Brennan, with whom Mr. Justice Marshall concurs, dissenting.

. . .

[W]e have explicitly recognized that, in light of the unique nature of the electronic media, the public have strong First Amendment interests in the reception of a full spectrum of views—presented in a vigorous and uninhibited manner—on controversial issues of public importance. ... [T]he Court nevertheless upholds the absolute ban on editorial advertising because, in its view, the Commission's Fairness Doctrine, in and of itself, is sufficient to satisfy the First Amendment interests of the public. I cannot agree.

... [T]he Fairness Doctrine does not in any sense require broadcasters to allow "non-broadcaster" speakers to use the airwaves to express their own views on controversial issues of public importance. On the contrary, broadcasters may meet their fairness responsibilities through presentation of carefully edited news programs, panel discussions, interviews, and documentaries. As a result, broadcasters retain almost exclusive control over the selection of issues and viewpoints to be covered, the manner of presentation and, perhaps most important, who shall speak. Given this doctrinal framework, I can only conclude that the Fairness Doctrine, standing alone, is insufficient—in theory as well as in practice—to provide the kind of "uninhibited, robust, and wide-open" exchange of views to which the public is constitutionally entitled.

. . .

... [T]he *absolute* ban on editorial advertising seems particularly offensive because, although broadcasters refuse to sell any air time whatever to groups or individuals wishing to speak out on controversial issues of public importance, they make such air time readily available to those "commercial" advertisers who seek to peddle their goods and services to the public. Thus, as the system now operates, any person wishing to market a particular brand of beer, soap, toothpaste, or deodorant has direct, personal, and instantaneous access to the electronic media. He can present his own message, in his own words, in any format he selects and at a time of his own choosing. Yet a similar individual seeking to discuss war, peace, pollution, or the suffering of the poor is denied this right to speak. Instead, he is compelled to rely on the beneficence of a corporate "trustee" appointed by the Government to argue his case for him.

It has been long recognized ... that although access to public forums may be subjected to reasonable "time, place, and manner" regulations, "[s]elective exclusions from a public forum may not be based on *content* alone...." ... Here, of course, the differential treatment accorded "commercial" and "controversial" speech clearly violates that principle. ...

. . . .

CBS, INC. v. FEDERAL COMMUNICATIONS COMMISSION, 453 U.S. 367 (1981). The Carter–Mondale Presidential Committee requested each of the three major networks to sell time for a 30–minute program in connection with President Carter's formal announcement of his candidacy. Each of the networks declined, giving as a principal reason that it was too early to begin selling time for the 1980 presidential campaign. The committee filed a complaint with the Federal Communications Commission charging that the networks had violated their statutory obligation (under 47 U.S.C. § 312(a)(7)) "to allow reasonable access to or to permit purchase of reasonable amounts of time for the use of a broadcasting station by a legally qualified candidate for federal elective office on behalf of his candidacy." The Commission upheld the challenge. It held that under the statute it had the power to determine whether a campaign has begun and the statutory obligations have attached. It also held that the broadcasters must evaluate and respond to access requests on an individualized basis and offer reasons for denial which could be evaluated by the Commission. The Supreme Court, in an opinion by Chief Justice Burger, upheld the commission in its determination as to the meaning of the statute and its application in this case. Responding to the network's argument that, as so construed, the statute violated the First Amendment, the Court said:

"A licensed broadcaster is 'granted the free and exclusive use of a limited and valuable part of the public domain; when he accepts that franchise it is burdened by enforceable public obligations.' ...

"... Section 312(a)(7) ... makes a significant contribution to freedom of expression by enhancing the ability of candidates to present, and the public to receive, information necessary for the effective operation of the democratic process.

. . . .

"Section 312(a)(7) represents an effort by Congress to assure that an important resource—the airwaves—will be used in the public interest. We hold that the statutory right of access, as defined by the Commission and applied in these cases, properly balances the First Amendment rights of federal candidates, the public, and broadcasters."

Turner Broadcasting System v. Federal Communications Commission

520 U.S. 180, 117 S.Ct. 1174, 137 L.Ed.2d 369 (1997).

Justice Kennedy delivered the opinion of the Court, except as to a portion of Part II–A–1.

Sections 4 and 5 of the Cable Television Consumer Protection and Competition Act of 1992 require cable television systems to dedicate some of their channels to local broadcast television stations. ...

I

... Soon after Congress enacted the Cable Television ... [Act], appellants brought suit ... in the United States District Court for the District of Columbia, challenging the constitutionality of the must-carry provisions under the First Amendment. The three-judge District Court ... granted summary judgment for the Government and intervenor-defendants....

On appeal, we agreed with the District Court that must-carry does not "distinguish favored speech from disfavored speech on the basis of the ideas or views expressed," ... but is a content-neutral regulation designed "to prevent cable operators from exploiting their economic power to the detriment of broadcasters," and "to ensure that all Americans, especially those unable to subscribe to cable, have access to free television programming—whatever its content." ... We held that, under the intermediate level of scrutiny applicable to content-neutral regulations, must-carry would be sustained if it were shown to further an important or substantial governmental interest unrelated to the suppression of free speech, provided the incidental restrictions did not "burden substantially more speech than is necessary to further" those interests.... [A] four-Justice plurality concluded genuine issues of material fact remained regarding whether "the economic health of local broadcasting is in genuine jeopardy and need of the protections afforded by must-carry," and whether must-carry " 'burden[s] substantially more speech than is necessary to further the government's legitimate interests.' " ... [Turner Broadcasting System, Inc. v. FCC, 512 U.S. 622 (1994) (*Turner*).]

The District Court oversaw another 18 months of factual development on remand "yielding a record of tens of thousands of pages" of evidence.... Upon consideration of the expanded record, a divided panel of the District Court again granted summary judgment to appellees....

. . .

... [W]e now affirm.

II

We begin where the plurality ended in *Turner*, applying the standards for intermediate scrutiny enunciated in *O'Brien*.... As noted in *Turner*, must-carry was designed to serve "three interrelated interests: (1) preserving the benefits of free, over-the-air local broadcast television, (2) promoting the widespread dissemination of information from a multiplicity of sources, and (3) promoting fair competition in the market for television programming." ... We decided then, and now reaffirm, that each of those is an important governmental interest....

On remand, and again before this Court, both sides have advanced new interpretations of these interests in an attempt to recast them in forms "more readily proven." ... The Government downplays the importance of showing a risk to the broadcast industry as a whole and suggests the loss of even a few broadcast stations "is a matter of critical importance." Taking the opposite approach, appellants argue Congress' interest in preserving broadcasting is not implicated unless it is shown the industry as a whole would fail without must-carry, and suggest Congress' legitimate interest in "assuring that the public has access to a multiplicity of information sources" extends only as far as preserving "a minimum amount of television broadcast service."

These alternative formulations are inconsistent with Congress' stated interests in enacting must-carry. The congressional findings do not reflect concern that, absent must-carry, "a few voices, would be lost from the television marketplace." In explicit factual findings, Congress expressed clear concern that the "marked shift in market share from broadcast television to cable television services" . . . resulting from increasing market penetration by cable services, as well as the expanding horizontal concentration and vertical integration of cable operators, combined to give cable systems the incentive and ability to delete, reposition, or decline carriage to local broadcasters in an attempt to favor affiliated cable programmers. . . . Congress predicted that "absent the reimposition of [must-carry], additional local broadcast signals will be deleted, repositioned, or not carried," . . . with the end result that "the economic viability of free local broadcast television and its ability to originate quality local programming will be seriously jeopardized." . . .

At the same time, Congress was under no illusion that there would be a complete disappearance of broadcast television nationwide in the absence of must-carry. Congress recognized broadcast programming (and network programming in particular) "remains the most popular programming on cable systems," . . . . Indeed, reflecting the popularity and strength of some broadcasters, Congress included in the Cable Act a provision permitting broadcasters to charge cable systems for carriage of the broadcasters' signals. . . . Congress was concerned not that broadcast television would disappear in its entirety without must-carry, but that without it, "significant numbers of broadcast stations will be refused carriage on cable systems," and those "broadcast stations denied carriage will either deteriorate to a substantial degree or fail altogether." . . .

Nor do the congressional findings support appellants' suggestion that legitimate legislative goals would be satisfied by the preservation of a rump broadcasting industry providing a minimum of broadcast service to Americans without cable. . . . Congress enacted must-carry to "preserve the existing structure of the Nation's broadcast television medium while permitting the concomitant expansion and development of cable television." . . .

Although Congress set no definite number of broadcast stations sufficient for these purposes, the Cable Act's requirement that all cable operators with more than 12 channels set aside one-third of their channel capacity for local broadcasters . . . refutes the notion that Congress contemplated preserving only a bare minimum of stations. Congress' evident interest in "preserv[ing] the existing structure," . . . of the broadcast industry discloses a purpose to prevent any significant reduction in the multiplicity of broadcast programming sources available to noncable households. To the extent the appellants question the substantiality of the Government's interest in preserving something more than a minimum number of stations in each community, their position is meritless. It is for Congress to decide how much local broadcast television should be preserved for noncable households, and the validity of its determination " 'does not turn on a judge's agreement with the responsible decisionmaker concerning' . . . the degree to which [the Government's] interests should be promoted." . . .

The dissent proceeds on the assumption that must-carry is designed solely to be (and can only be justified as) a measure to protect broadcasters from cable operators' anticompetitive behavior. Federal policy, however, has long favored preserving a multiplicity of broadcast outlets regardless of whether the conduct that threatens it is motivated by anticompetitive animus or rises to the level of an antitrust violation. . . . Congress has an independent interest in preserving a multiplicity of broadcasters to ensure that all households have access to information and entertainment on an equal footing with those who subscribe to cable.

A

. . . The expanded record now permits us to consider whether the must-carry provisions were designed to address a real harm, and whether those provisions will alleviate it in a material way. . . . We turn first to the harm or risk which prompted Congress to act. The Government's assertion that "the economic health of local broadcasting is in genuine jeopardy and in need of the protections afforded by must-carry," rests on two component propositions: First, "significant numbers of broadcast stations will be refused carriage on cable systems" absent must-carry. Second, "the broadcast stations denied carriage will either deteriorate to a substantial degree or fail altogether."

In reviewing the constitutionality of a statute, "courts must accord substantial deference to the predictive judgments of Congress." . . . Even in the realm of First Amendment questions where Congress must base its conclusions upon substantial evidence, deference must be accorded to its findings as to the harm to be avoided and to the remedial measures adopted for that end, lest we infringe on traditional legislative authority to make predictive judgments when enacting nationwide regulatory policy.

1

We have no difficulty in finding a substantial basis to support Congress' conclusion that a real threat justified enactment of the must-carry provisions. We examine first the evidence before Congress and then the further evidence presented to the District Court on remand to supplement the congressional determination.

As to the evidence before Congress, there was specific support for its conclusion that cable operators had considerable and growing market power over local video programming markets. . . .

Evidence indicated the structure of the cable industry would give cable operators increasing ability and incentive to drop local broadcast stations from their systems, or reposition them to a less-viewed channel. . . .

. . .

The reasonableness of Congress' conclusion was borne out by the evidence on remand, which also reflected cable industry favoritism for integrated programmers. . . .

In addition, evidence before Congress, supplemented on remand, indicated that cable systems would have incentives to drop local broadcasters in favor of other programmers less likely to compete with them for audience and advertisers. . . . Empirical evidence also indicates that demand for premium cable services (such as pay-per-view) is reduced when a cable system carries more independent broadcasters. . . . Thus, operators stand to benefit by dropping broadcast stations.

. . . Congress could therefore reasonably conclude that cable systems would drop broadcasters in favor of programmers—even unaffiliated ones—less likely to compete with them for audience and advertisers. . . .

. . .

Substantial evidence demonstrated that absent must-carry the already "serious" ... problem of noncarriage would grow worse because "additional local broadcast signals will be deleted, repositioned, or not carried,"....

. . .

... The evidence on remand also indicated that the growth of cable systems' market power proceeded apace. The trend towards greater horizontal concentration continued ...

This is not a case in which we are called upon to give our best judgment as to the likely economic consequences of certain financial arrangements or business structures, or to assess competing economic theories and predictive judgments, as we would in a case arising, say, under the antitrust laws.... The issue before us is whether, given conflicting views of the probable development of the television industry, Congress had substantial evidence for making the judgment that it did. We need not put our imprimatur on Congress' economic theory in order to validate the reasonableness of its judgment.

2

The harm Congress feared was that stations dropped or denied carriage would be at a "serious risk of financial difficulty," and would "deteriorate to a substantial degree or fail altogether." Congress had before it substantial evidence to support its conclusion....

... We hold Congress could conclude from the substantial body of evidence before it that "absent legislative action, the free local off-air broadcast system is endangered." ...

. . .

Despite the considerable evidence before Congress and adduced on remand indicating that the significant numbers of broadcast stations are at risk, the dissent believes yet more is required before Congress could act. It demands more information.... The level of detail in factfinding required by the dissent would be an improper burden for courts to impose on the Legislative Branch. . . .

We think it apparent must-carry serves the Government's interests "in a direct and effective way." ... Must-carry ensures that a number of local broadcasters retain cable carriage, with the concomitant audience access and advertising revenues needed to support a multiplicity of stations. Appellants contend that even were this so, must-carry is broader than necessary to accomplish its goals. We turn to this question.

B

The second portion of the *O'Brien* inquiry concerns the fit between the asserted interests and the means chosen to advance them. Content-neutral regulations do not pose the same "inherent dangers to free expression" that content-based regulations do, and thus are subject to a less rigorous analysis, which affords the Government latitude in designing a regulatory solution.... Under intermediate scrutiny, the Government may employ the means of its choosing " 'so long as the ... regulation promotes a substantial governmental interest that would be achieved less effectively absent the regulation,' " and does not " 'burden substantially more speech than is necessary to further' " that interest....

The must-carry provisions have the potential to interfere with protected speech in two ways. First, the provisions restrain cable operators' editorial discretion in creating programming packages by "reduc[ing] the number of channels over which [they] exercise unfettered control." Second, the rules "render it more difficult for cable programmers to compete for carriage on the limited channels remaining."

Appellants say the burden of must-carry is great, but the evidence adduced on remand indicates the actual effects are modest. . . . Appellees contend the burdens of must-carry will soon diminish as cable channel capacity increases, as is occurring nationwide. . . .

. . . Appellants argue that the rate of growth in cable programming outstrips cable operators' creation of new channel space, that the rate of cable growth is lower than claimed, and that must-carry infringes First Amendment rights now irrespective of future growth. Finally, they say that regardless of the percentage of channels occupied, must-carry still represents "thousands of real and individual infringements of speech." . . .

. . .

Because the burden imposed by must-carry is congruent to the benefits it affords, we conclude must-carry is narrowly tailored to preserve a multiplicity of broadcast stations for the 40 percent of American households without cable. . . .

Appellants say the must-carry provisions are overbroad because they require carriage in some instances when the Government's interests are not implicated: the must-carry rules prohibit a cable system operator from dropping a broadcaster "even if the operator has no anticompetitive motives, and even if the broadcaster that would have to be dropped . . . would survive without cable access." . . . We are not persuaded that either possibility is so prevalent that must-carry is substantially overbroad. . . . Even on the doubtful assumption that a narrower but still practicable must-carry rule could be drafted to exclude all instances in which the Government's interests are not implicated, our cases establish that content-neutral regulations are not "invalid simply because there is some imaginable alternative that might be less burdensome on speech." . . .

. . .

. . . [A]fter careful examination of each of the alternatives suggested by appellants, we cannot conclude that any of them is an adequate alternative to must-carry for promoting the Government's legitimate interests. . . .

. . .

There is a final argument made by appellants that we do not reach. Appellant Time Warner Entertainment raises in its brief a separate First Amendment challenge to a subsection of the Cable Act . . . that requires carriage on unfilled must-carry channels of low power broadcast stations if the FCC determines that the station's programming "would address local news and informational needs which are not being adequately served by full power television broadcast stations because of the geographic distance of such full power stations from the low power station's community of license." . . . Because this question has received "only the most glancing" attention from the District Court and the parties, we have no more information about "the operation of, and justifications for, the low-power broadcast provisions" on which to base an informed determination than we did on the earlier appeal. . . . Even if the issue is "fairly included" in the broadly worded question presented, it is tangential to the main issue, and prudence dictates that we not decide this question based on such scant argumentation. . . .

III

Judgments about how competing economic interests are to be reconciled in the complex and fast-changing field of television are for Congress to make. ... Appellants' challenges to must-carry reflect little more than disagreement over the level of protection broadcast stations are to be afforded and how protection is to be attained. We cannot displace Congress' judgment respecting content-neutral regulations with our own, so long as its policy is grounded on reasonable factual findings supported by evidence that is substantial for a legislative determination. Those requirements were met in this case, and in these circumstances the First Amendment requires nothing more. The judgment of the District Court is affirmed.

It is so ordered.

Justice Stevens concurring.

... If this statute regulated the content of speech rather than the structure of the market, our task would be quite different.... Though I write to emphasize this important point, I fully concur in the Court's thorough opinion.

Justice Breyer concurring in part.

I join the opinion of the Court except insofar as Part II–A–1 relies on an anticompetitive rationale.... My conclusion rests, however, not upon the principal opinion's analysis of the statute's efforts to "promot[e] fair competition," but rather upon its discussion of the statute's other objectives....

. . .

In particular, I note (and agree) that a cable system, physically dependent upon the availability of space along city streets, at present (perhaps less in the future) typically faces little competition, that it therefore constitutes a kind of bottleneck that controls the range of viewer choice (whether or not it uses any consequent economic power for economically predatory purposes), and that some degree—at least a limited degree—of governmental intervention and control through regulation can prove appropriate when justified under *O'Brien* (at least when not "content based")....

. . .

Justice O'Connor with whom Justice Scalia, Justice Thomas and Justice Ginsburg join, dissenting.

... [T]he Court errs in two crucial respects. First, the Court disregards one of the principal defenses of the statute urged by appellees on remand: that it serves a substantial interest in preserving "diverse," "quality" programming that is "responsive" to the needs of the local community. The course of this litigation on remand and the proffered defense strongly reinforce my view that the Court adopted the wrong analytic framework in the prior phase of this case.... Second, the Court misapplies the "intermediate scrutiny" framework it adopts. Although we owe deference to Congress' predictive judgments and its evaluation of complex economic questions, we have an independent duty to identify with care the Government interests supporting the scheme, to inquire into the reasonableness of congressional findings regarding its necessity, and to examine the fit between its goals and its consequences.... The Court fails to discharge its duty here.

I

I did not join those portions of the principal opinion in *Turner* holding that the must-carry provisions of the Cable Act are content neutral and therefore subject to intermediate First Amendment scrutiny. ...

. . .

Much of the principal opinion treats the must-carry provisions as a species of antitrust regulation enacted by Congress in response to a perceived threat that cable system operators would otherwise engage in various forms of anticompetitive conduct . . .

I fully agree that promoting fair competition is a legitimate and substantial Government goal. But the Court nowhere examines whether the breadth of the must-carry provisions comports with a goal of preventing anticompetitive harms. Instead, in the course of its inquiry into whether the must-carry provisions are "narrowly tailored," the principal opinion simply assumes that most adverse carriage decisions are anticompetitively motivated, and that must-carry is therefore a measured response to a problem of anticompetitive behavior. . . .

. . . [T]he Court proceeds from the assumptions that adverse carriage decisions nationwide will affect broadcast markets in proportion to their size; and that all broadcast programming is watched by viewers. Neither assumption is logical or has any factual basis in the record.

. . .

II

The principal opinion goes to great lengths to avoid acknowledging that preferences for "quality," "diverse," and "responsive" local programming underlie the must-carry scheme, although the partial concurrence's reliance on such preferences is explicit. . . . I take the principal opinion at its word and evaluate the claim that the threat of anticompetitive behavior by cable operators supplies a content-neutral basis for sustaining the statute. It does not.

. . .

2

. . . When appellees are pressed to explain the Government's "substantial interest" in preserving noncable viewers' access to "vulnerable" or "marginal" stations with "relatively small" audiences, it becomes evident that the interest has nothing to do with anticompetitive behavior, but has everything to do with content-preserving "quality" local programming that is "responsive" to community needs. Indeed, Justice Breyer expressly declines to accept the anticompetitive rationale for the must-carry rules embraced by the principal opinion, and instead explicitly relies on a need to preserve a "rich mix" of "quality" programming.

3

I turn now to the evidence of harm to broadcasters denied carriage or repositioned. . . . The record on remand does not permit the conclusion, at the summary judgment stage, that Congress could reasonably have predicted serious harm to a significant number of stations in the absence of must-carry.

. . .

In sum, appellees are not entitled to summary judgment on whether Congress could conclude, based on reasonable inferences drawn from substantial evidence, that " 'absent legislative action, the free local off-air broadcast system is endangered.' " . . . A highly dubious economic theory has been advanced as the "substantial interest" supporting a First Amendment burden on cable operators and cable programmers. In finding that must-carry serves a substantial interest, the principal opinion necessarily accepts that theory. The partial concurrence does not, but neither does it articulate what threat to the availability of a "multiplicity" of broadcast stations would exist in a perfectly competitive market.

B

I turn now to the second portion of the *O'Brien* inquiry, which concerns the fit between the Government's asserted interests and the means chosen to advance them. The Court observes that "broadcast stations gained carriage on 5,880 channels as a result of must-carry," and recognizes that this forced carriage imposes a burden on cable system operators and cable programmers....

. . .

In my view, the statute is not narrowly tailored to serve a substantial interest in preventing anticompetitive conduct.... Congress has commandeered up to one third of each cable system's channel capacity for the benefit of local broadcasters, without any regard for whether doing so advances the statute's alleged goals....

Finally, I note my disagreement with the Court's suggestion that the availability of less-speech-restrictive alternatives is never relevant to *O'Brien*'s narrow tailoring inquiry....

. . .

. . . If Congress truly sought to address anticompetitive behavior by cable system operators, it passed the wrong law.... The availability of less restrictive alternatives—a leased-access regime and subsidies—reinforces my conclusion that the must-carry provisions are overbroad.

. . .

III

Finally, I note my disagreement with the Court's decision to sidestep a question reserved in *Turner* ...: whether the must-carry rules requiring carriage of low power stations ... survive constitutional scrutiny. A low power station qualifies for carriage only if the Federal Communications Commission determines that the station's programming "would address local news and informational needs which are not being adequately served by full power television broadcast stations because of the geographic distance of such full power stations from the low power station's community of license." ... As the *Turner* Court noted, "this aspect of § 4 appears to single out certain low-power broadcasters for special benefits on the basis of content." Because I believe that the must-carry provisions fail even intermediate scrutiny, it is clear that they would fail scrutiny under a stricter content-based standard.

. . .

In any event, the Court lets stand the District Court's seriously flawed legal reasoning on the point. The District Court concluded that the provisions "are very close to content-based legislation triggering strict scrutiny," but held that they do not "cross the line." That conclusion appears to have been based on the fact that the low power provisions are *viewpoint*-neutral. Whether a provision is viewpoint-neutral is irrelevant to the question whether it is also *content*-neutral....

. . .

Arkansas Educational Television Commission v. Forbes

523 U.S. 666, 118 S.Ct. 1633, 140 L.Ed.2d 875 (1998).

[The report in this case appears, supra page 1496.]

Greater New Orleans Broadcasting Association, Inc. v. United States

527 U.S. 173, 119 S.Ct. 1923, 144 L.Ed.2d 161 (1999).

[The report in this case appears, supra page 1440.]

United States v. Playboy Entertainment Group, Inc.

529 U.S. 803, 120 S.Ct. 1878, 146 L.Ed.2d 865 (2000).

[The report in this case appears, supra page 1369.]

Ashcroft v. ACLU

535 U.S. 564, 122 S.Ct. 1700, 152 L.Ed.2d 771 (2002)

[The report in this case appears, supra page 1375.]

CHAPTER 17

RELIGION AND THE CONSTITUTION

Introduction. This chapter deals with the first amendment's prohibitions of laws "respecting an establishment of religion" and of laws "prohibiting the free exercise thereof." As Justice Rutledge stated in his dissenting opinion in Everson v. Board of Educ., 330 U.S. 1, 40 (1947): " 'establishment' and 'free exercise' were correlative and coextensive ideas, representing only different facets of the single great and fundamental freedom." A single ideal of government neutrality in matters of religion forbids both government aid to and government burdens on religious groups, religious activities, and individual religious beliefs.

Despite their common purpose, there has been an uneasy tension between applications of the free exercise and establishment clauses, caused by potential conflict between the two constitutional commands. Consider a common example. Suppose a state university permits a wide range of speakers on political or social issues to use a particular university facility without charge. If speakers engaged in religious conversion, worship, or advocacy are singled out and denied permission to speak, does this constitute discrimination against religion in violation of the free exercise clause? If religious speakers are permitted, is the state subsidizing religious worship in violation of the establishment clause?

A question, then, that runs throughout this chapter is whether there is any single, reconciling interpretation of the establishment and free exercise clauses. A prominent attempt at reconciliation is Kurland, *Of Church and State and the Supreme Court*, 29 U.Chi.L.Rev. 1 (1961), *Selected Essays* 699 (1963). Professor Kurland's hypothesis is criticized in Pfeffer, *Religion—Blind Government*, 15 Stan.L.Rev. 389 (1963).

SECTION 1.   THE ESTABLISHMENT CLAUSE

A.   INTRODUCTION

Everson v. Board of Education

330 U.S. 1, 67 S.Ct. 504, 91 L.Ed. 711 (1947).

Mr. Justice Black delivered the opinion of the Court.

A New Jersey statute authorizes its local school districts to make rules and contracts for the transportation of children to and from schools. The appellee, a township board of education, acting pursuant to this statute authorized reimbursement to parents of money expended by them for the bus transportation of their children on regular busses operated by the public transportation system. Part of this money was for the payment of transportation of some children in the community to Catholic parochial schools. These church schools give their students, in addition to secular education, regular religious instruction con-

forming to the religious tenets and modes of worship of the Catholic Faith. The superintendent of these schools is a Catholic priest.

The appellant, in his capacity as a district taxpayer, filed suit in a state court challenging the right of the Board to reimburse parents of parochial school students. . . . The New Jersey Court of Errors and Appeals [held] that neither the statute nor the resolution passed pursuant to it was in conflict with the State constitution or the provisions of the Federal Constitution in issue. . . .

The only contention here is that the state statute and the resolution, in so far as they authorized reimbursement to parents of children attending parochial schools, violate the Federal Constitution in these two respects, which to some extent, overlap. *First.* They authorize the State to take by taxation the private property of some and bestow it upon others, to be used for their own private purposes. This, it is alleged, violates the due process clause of the Fourteenth Amendment. *Second.* The statute and the resolution forced inhabitants to pay taxes to help support and maintain schools which are dedicated to, and which regularly teach, the Catholic Faith. This is alleged to be a use of state power to support church schools contrary to the prohibition of the First Amendment which the Fourteenth Amendment made applicable to the states.

First. . . . It is much too late to argue that legislation intended to facilitate the opportunity of children to get a secular education serves no public purpose. . . . The same thing is no less true of legislation to reimburse needy parents, or all parents, for payment of the fares of their children so that they can ride in public busses to and from schools rather than run the risk of traffic and other hazards incident to walking or "hitchhiking." . . .

. . .

Second. The New Jersey statute is challenged as a "law respecting an establishment of religion." . . . .

A large proportion of the early settlers of this country came here from Europe to escape the bondage of laws which compelled them to support and attend government favored churches. . . .

These practices of the old world were transplanted to and began to thrive in the soil of the new America. The very charters granted by the English Crown to the individuals and companies designated to make the laws which would control the destinies of the colonials authorized these individuals and companies to erect religious establishments which all, whether believers or non-believers, would be required to support and attend. . . .

These practices became so commonplace as to shock the freedom-loving colonials into a feeling of abhorrence. The imposition of taxes to pay ministers' salaries and to build and maintain churches and church property aroused their indignation. It was these feelings which found expression in the First Amendment. No one locality and no one group throughout the Colonies can rightly be given entire credit for having aroused the sentiment that culminated in adoption of the Bill of Rights' provisions embracing religious liberty. But Virginia, where the established church had achieved a dominant influence in political affairs and where many excesses attracted wide public attention, provided a great stimulus and able leadership for the movement. The people there, as elsewhere, reached the conviction that individual religious liberty could be achieved best under a government which was stripped of all power to tax, to support, or otherwise to assist any or all religions, or to interfere with the beliefs of any religious individual or group.

The movement toward this end reached its dramatic climax in Virginia in 1785–86 when the Virginia legislative body was about to renew Virginia's tax levy for the support of the established church. Thomas Jefferson and James Madison led the fight against this tax. Madison wrote his great Memorial and Remonstrance against the law. In it, he eloquently argued that a true religion did not need the support of law; that no person, either believer or non-believer, should be taxed to support a religious institution of any kind; that the best interest of a society required that the minds of men always be wholly free; and that cruel persecutions were the inevitable result of government-established religions. Madison's Remonstrance received strong support throughout Virginia, and the Assembly postponed consideration of the proposed tax measure until its next session. When the proposal came up for consideration at that session, it not only died in committee, but the Assembly enacted the famous "Virginia Bill for Religious Liberty" originally written by Thomas Jefferson. The preamble to that Bill stated among other things that

> "Almighty God hath created the mind free; that all attempts to influence it by temporal punishments, or burthens, or by civil incapacitations, tend only to beget habits of hypocrisy and meanness, and are a departure from the plan of the Holy author of our religion who being Lord both of body and mind, yet chose not to propagate it by coercions on either ...; that to compel a man to furnish contributions of money for the propagation of opinions which he disbelieves, is sinful and tyrannical; that even the forcing him to support this or that teacher of his own religious persuasion, is depriving him of the comfortable liberty of giving his contributions to the particular pastor, whose morals he would make his pattern...."

And the statute itself enacted

> "That no man shall be compelled to frequent or support any religious worship, place, or ministry whatsoever, nor shall be enforced, restrained, molested, or burthened, in his body or goods, nor shall otherwise suffer on account of his religious opinions or belief...."

This Court has previously recognized that the provisions of the First Amendment, in the drafting and adoption of which Madison and Jefferson played such leading roles, had the same objective and were intended to provide the same protection against governmental intrusion on religious liberty as the Virginia statute.[a] ... Prior to the adoption of the Fourteenth Amendment, the First Amendment did not apply as a restraint against the states. Most of them did soon provide similar constitutional protections for religious liberty. But some states persisted for about half a century in imposing restraints upon the free exercise of religion and in discriminating against particular religious groups....

The meaning and scope of the First Amendment, preventing establishment of religion or prohibiting the free exercise thereof, in the light of its history and the evils it was designed forever to suppress, have been several times elaborated by the decisions of this Court prior to the application of the First Amendment to the states by the Fourteenth. The broad meaning given the Amendment by these earlier cases has been accepted by this Court in its decisions concerning an individual's religious freedom rendered since the Fourteenth

a. For a very different reading of the historical record, see Howe, *Religion and the Free Society: The Constitutional Question, Selected Essays* 780 (1963). Professor Howe, stressing that the Bill of Rights did not in its inception limit the states, argues that the prohibition on establishment was a "non-libertarian" limitation on national power. Compare Pfeffer, *Church, State, and Freedom* 134–143 (rev. ed. 1967).

Amendment was interpreted to make the prohibitions of the First applicable to state action abridging religious freedom. There is every reason to give the same application and broad interpretation to the "establishment of religion" clause. . . .

The "establishment of religion" clause of the First Amendment means at least this: Neither a state nor the Federal Government can set up a church. Neither can pass laws which aid one religion, aid all religions, or prefer one religion over another. Neither can force nor influence a person to go to or to remain away from church against his will or force him to profess a belief or disbelief in any religion. No person can be punished for entertaining or professing religious beliefs or disbeliefs, for church attendance or non-attendance. No tax in any amount, large or small, can be levied to support any religious activities or institutions, whatever they may be called, or whatever form they may adopt to teach or practice religion. Neither a state nor the Federal Government can, openly or secretly, participate in the affairs of any religious organizations or groups and vice versa. In the words of Jefferson, the clause against establishment of religion by law was intended to erect "a wall of separation between church and State." . . .

. . . New Jersey cannot consistently with the "establishment of religion" clause of the First Amendment contribute tax-raised funds to the support of an institution which teaches the tenets and faith of any church. On the other hand, other language of the amendment commands that New Jersey cannot hamper its citizens in the free exercise of their own religion. Consequently, it cannot exclude individual Catholics, Lutherans, Mohammedans, Baptists, Jews, Methodists, Non-believers, Presbyterians, or the members of any other faith, *because of their faith, or lack of it,* from receiving the benefits of public welfare legislation. While we do not mean to intimate that a state could not provide transportation only to children attending public schools, we must be careful, in protecting the citizens of New Jersey against state-established churches, to be sure that we do not inadvertently prohibit New Jersey from extending its general state law benefits to all its citizens without regard to their religious belief.

Measured by these standards, we cannot say that the First Amendment prohibits New Jersey from spending tax-raised funds to pay the bus fares of parochial school pupils as a part of a general program under which it pays the fares of pupils attending public and other schools. It is undoubtedly true that children are helped to get to church schools. There is even a possibility that some of the children might not be sent to the church schools if the parents were compelled to pay their children's bus fares out of their own pockets when transportation to a public school would have been paid for by the State. The same possibility exists where the state requires a local transit company to provide reduced fares to school children including those attending parochial schools, or where a municipally owned transportation system undertakes to carry all school children free of charge. Moreover, state-paid policemen, detailed to protect children going to and from church schools from the very real hazards of traffic, would serve much the same purpose and accomplish much the same result as state provisions intended to guarantee free transportation of a kind which the state deems to be best for the school children's welfare. And parents might refuse to risk their children to the serious danger of traffic accidents going to and from parochial schools, the approaches to which were not protected by policemen. Similarly, parents might be reluctant to permit their children to attend schools which the state had cut off from such general government services as ordinary police and fire protection, connections for sewage disposal, public highways and sidewalks. Of course, cutting off church schools from these services, so separate and so indisputably marked off from the religious function, would make it far more difficult for the schools to operate. But such is obviously not the purpose of the First Amendment. That Amendment requires the state to be a neutral in its relations with groups of religious believers and non-believers; it does not require the state to be their adversary. State power is no more to be used so as to handicap religions, than it is to favor them.

... [New Jersey's] legislation, as applied, does no more than provide a general program to help parents get their children, regardless of their religion, safely and expeditiously to and from accredited schools.

The First Amendment has erected a wall between church and state. That wall must be kept high and impregnable. We could not approve the slightest breach. New Jersey has not breached it here.

Affirmed.

Mr. Justice Jackson [with whom Mr. Justice Frankfurter joined], dissenting.

... The Court's opinion marshals every argument in favor of state aid and puts the case in its most favorable light, but much of its reasoning confirms my conclusions that there are no good grounds upon which to support the present legislation. In fact, the undertones of the opinion, advocating complete and uncompromising separation of Church from State, seem utterly discordant with its conclusion yielding support to their commingling in educational matters. The case which irresistibly comes to mind as the most fitting precedent is that of Julia who, according to Byron's reports, "whispering 'I will ne'er consent,'—consented."

. . .

Mr. Justice Rutledge, with whom Mr. Justice Frankfurter, Mr. Justice Jackson and Mr. Justice Burton agree, dissenting.

. . .

Two great drives are constantly in motion to abridge, in the name of education, the complete division of religion and civil authority which our forefathers made. One is to introduce religious education and observances into the public schools. The other, to obtain public funds for the aid and support of various private religious schools. ... In my opinion both avenues were closed by the Constitution. Neither should be opened by this Court. The matter is not one of quantity, to be measured by the amount of money expended. Now as in Madison's day it is one of principle, to keep separate the separate spheres as the First Amendment drew them; to prevent the first experiment upon our liberties; and to keep the question from becoming entangled in corrosive precedents. We should not be less strict to keep strong and untarnished the one side of the shield of religious freedom than we have been of the other.

The judgment should be reversed.

DENOMINATIONAL PREFERENCES

The Court was unanimous in *Everson* in the conclusion that the establishment clause forbids aid to all religions as well as aid to one religion. Still, in Larson v. Valente, 456 U.S. 228 (1982), the Court referred to the proposition that "one religious denomination cannot be officially preferred over another" as "the clearest command of the Establishment Clause." (The Court invalidated a charitable contribution statute that exempted from its requirements religious organizations that solicit less than 50 percent of their funds from nonmembers.)

THE "THREE–PART LEMON TEST"

In cases decided after 1971, it is common to begin opinions concerning the establishment clause by reciting standards summarized in Chief Justice Burger's opinion for the Court in Lemon v. Kurtzman, 403 U.S. 602, 612–613 (1971). To be valid against attack under the establishment clause:

> "First, the statute must have a secular legislative purpose; second, its principal or primary effect must be one that neither advances nor inhibits religion . . .; finally, the statute must not foster 'an excessive government entanglement with religion.' "

Despite their apparent simplicity, the three "*Lemon* standards"—which will be examined time and again in the cases to follow—have substantial ambiguities and remain controversial.

LAMB'S CHAPEL v. CENTER MORICHES UNION FREE SCHOOL DISTRICT, 508 U.S. 384 (1993). The school district permitted the use of school property for "social, civic and recreational meetings" but did not allow student bible clubs to meet on school property. The Court concluded that precluding use of school property by bible clubs was a violation of the free speech clause. The Court answered an argument, that allowing use of school property for bible study would be an establishment, by stating that "this would not have been an establishment of religion under the three-part test articulated in Lemon v. Kurtzman." In a concurrence, Justice Scalia objected to the court's use of the *Lemon* test, arguing that it was

> "[l]ike some ghoul in a late-night horror movie that repeatedly sits up in its grave and shuffles abroad, after being repeatedly killed and buried, *Lemon* stalks our Establishment Clause jurisprudence once again, frightening the little children and school attorneys of Center Moriches Union Free School District . . .
>
> " . . .
>
> " . . . It is there to scare us (and our audience) when we wish it to do so, but we can command it to return to the tomb at will. . . . When we wish to strike down a practice it forbids, we invoke it . . .; when we wish to uphold a practice it forbids, we ignore it entirely . . . Such a docile and useful monster is worth keeping around, at least in a somnolent state; one never knows when one might need him."

Justice White's opinion for the Court responded to Justice Scalia in a footnote.

> "While we are somewhat diverted by Justice Scalia's evening at the cinema, we return to the reality that there is a proper way to inter an established decision and *Lemon*, however frightening it might be to some, has not been overruled."

B. Government Religious Exercises, Ceremonies, Displays, and Practices

1. PUBLIC SCHOOLS

Zorach v. Clauson

343 U.S. 306, 72 S.Ct. 679, 96 L.Ed. 954 (1952).

Mr. Justice Douglas delivered the opinion of the Court.

New York City has a program which permits its public schools to release students during the school day so that they may leave the school buildings and school grounds and go to religious centers for religious instruction or devotional exercises. A student is released on written request of his parents. Those not released stay in the classrooms. The churches make weekly reports to the schools, sending a list of children who have been released from public school but who have not reported for religious instruction.

This "released time" program involves neither religious instruction in public school classrooms nor the expenditure of public funds. All costs, including the application blanks, are paid by the religious organizations. The case is therefore unlike McCollum v. Board of Education, 333 U.S. 203, which involved a "released time" program from Illinois. In that case the classrooms were turned over to religious instructors. We accordingly held that the program violated the First Amendment which (by reason of the Fourteenth Amendment) prohibits the states from establishing religion or prohibiting its free exercise.

Appellants, who are taxpayers and residents of New York City and whose children attend its public schools, challenge the present law, contending it is in essence not different from the one involved in the *McCollum* case. Their argument, stated elaborately in various ways, reduces itself to this: the weight and influence of the school is put behind a program for religious instruction; public school teachers police it, keeping tab on students who are released; the classroom activities come to a halt while the students who are released for religious instruction are on leave; the school is a crutch on which the churches are leaning for support in their religious training; without the cooperation of the schools this "released time" program, like the one in the *McCollum* case, would be futile and ineffective. The New York Court of Appeals sustained the law against this claim of unconstitutionality.

The briefs and arguments are replete with data bearing on the merits of this type of "released time" program.... Those matters are of no concern here, since our problem reduces itself to whether New York by this system has either prohibited the "free exercise" of religion or has made a law "respecting an establishment of religion" within the meaning of the First Amendment.

It takes obtuse reasoning to inject any issue of the "free exercise" of religion into the present case. No one is forced to go to the religious classroom and no religious exercise or instruction is brought to the classrooms of the public schools. A student need not take religious instruction. He is left to his own desires as to the manner or time of his religious devotions, if any.

There is a suggestion that the system involves the use of coercion to get public school students into religious classrooms. There is no evidence in the record before us that supports that conclusion.[6] The present record indeed tells us that the school authorities are neutral in this regard and do no more than release students whose parents so request. If in fact coercion were used, if it were established that any one or more teachers were using their office to persuade or force students to take the religious instruction, a wholly different case would be presented.[7] Hence we put aside that claim of coercion both as

6. Nor is there any indication that the public schools enforce attendance at religious schools by punishing absentees from the released time programs for truancy.

7. Appellants contend that they should have been allowed to prove that the system is in fact administered in a coercive manner. The New York Court of Appeals declined to grant a trial on this issue, noting, *inter alia,* that appellants had not properly raised their claim in the manner required by state practice. This independent state ground for decision precludes appellants from raising the issue of maladministration in this proceeding....

respects the "free exercise" of religion and "an establishment of religion" within the meaning of the First Amendment.

Moreover, apart from that claim of coercion, we do not see how New York by this type of "released time" program has made a law respecting an establishment of religion within the meaning of the First Amendment.... There cannot be the slightest doubt that the First Amendment reflects the philosophy that Church and State should be separated. And so far as interference with the "free exercise" of religion and an "establishment" of religion are concerned, the separation must be complete and unequivocal. The First Amendment within the scope of its coverage permits no exception; the prohibition is absolute. The First Amendment, however, does not say that in every and all respects there shall be a separation of Church and State. Rather, it studiously defines the manner, the specific ways, in which there shall be no concert or union or dependency one on the other. That is the common sense of the matter. Otherwise the state and religion would be aliens to each other—hostile, suspicious, and even unfriendly. Churches could not be required to pay even property taxes. Municipalities would not be permitted to render police or fire protection to religious groups. Policemen who helped parishioners into their places of worship would violate the Constitution. Prayers in our legislative halls; the appeals to the Almighty in the messages of the Chief Executive; the proclamations making Thanksgiving Day a holiday; "so help me God" in our courtroom oaths—these and all other references to the Almighty that run through our laws, our public rituals, our ceremonies would be flouting the First Amendment. A fastidious atheist or agnostic could even object to the supplication with which the Court opens each session: "God save the United States and this Honorable Court."

We would have to press the concept of separation of Church and State to these extremes to condemn the present law on constitutional grounds. The nullification of this law would have wide and profound effects. A Catholic student applies to his teacher for permission to leave the school during hours on a Holy Day of Obligation to attend a mass. A Jewish student asks his teacher for permission to be excused for Yom Kippur. A Protestant wants the afternoon off for a family baptismal ceremony. In each case the teacher requires parental consent in writing. In each case the teacher, in order to make sure the student is not a truant, goes further and requires a report from the priest, the rabbi, or the minister. The teacher in other words cooperates in a religious program to the extent of making it possible for her students to participate in it. Whether she does it occasionally for a few students, regularly for one, or pursuant to a systematized program designed to further the religious needs of all the students does not alter the character of the act.

We are a religious people whose institutions presuppose a Supreme Being. We guarantee the freedom to worship as one chooses. We make room for as wide a variety of beliefs and creeds as the spiritual needs of man deem necessary. We sponsor an attitude on the part of government that shows no partiality to any one group and that lets each flourish according to the zeal of its adherents and the appeal of its dogma. When the state encourages religious instruction or cooperates with religious authorities by adjusting the schedule of public events to sectarian needs, it follows the best of our traditions. For it then respects the religious nature of our people and accommodates the public service

---

The only allegation in the complaint that bears on the issue is that the operation of the program "has resulted and inevitably results in the exercise of pressure and coercion upon parents and children to secure attendance by the children for religious instruction." But this charge does not even implicate the school authorities. The New York Court of Appeals was therefore generous in labeling it a "conclusory" allegation....

to their spiritual needs. To hold that it may not would be to find in the Constitution a requirement that the government show a callous indifference to religious groups. That would be preferring those who believe in no religion over those who do believe. Government may not finance religious groups nor undertake religious instruction nor blend secular and sectarian education nor use secular institutions to force one or some religion on any person. But we find no constitutional requirement which makes it necessary for government to be hostile to religion and to throw its weight against efforts to widen the effective scope of religious influence. The government must be neutral when it comes to competition between sects. It may not thrust any sect on any person. It may not make a religious observance compulsory. It may not coerce anyone to attend church, to observe a religious holiday, or to take religious instruction. But it can close its doors or suspend its operations as to those who want to repair to their religious sanctuary for worship or instruction. No more than that is undertaken here.

. . .

In the *McCollum* case the classrooms were used for religious instruction and the force of the public school was used to promote that instruction. Here, as we have said, the public schools do no more than accommodate their schedules to a program of outside religious instruction. We follow the *McCollum* case. But we cannot expand it to cover the present released time program unless separation of Church and State means that public institutions can make no adjustments of their schedules to accommodate the religious needs of the people. We cannot read into the Bill of Rights such a philosophy of hostility to religion.

Affirmed.

Mr. Justice Black, dissenting.

. . .

. . . In considering whether a state has entered this forbidden field the question is not whether it has entered too far but whether it has entered at all. New York is manipulating its compulsory education laws to help religious sects get pupils. This is not separation but combination of Church and State. . . .

. . .[a]

Mr. Justice Jackson, dissenting.

. . .

A number of Justices just short of a majority of the majority that promulgates today's passionate dialectics joined in answering them in McCollum v. Board of Education . . . The distinction attempted between that case and this is trivial, almost to the point of cynicism, magnifying its nonessential details and disparaging compulsion which was the underlying reason for invalidity. A reading of the Court's opinion in that case along with its opinion in this case will show such difference of overtones and undertones as to make clear that the *McCollum* case has passed like a storm in a teacup. The wall which the Court was professing to erect between Church and State has become even more warped and twisted than I expected. Today's judgment will be more interesting

a. Justice Frankfurter's dissent, which emphasized his "agreement with Mr. Justice   Jackson's dissent," is omitted.

to students of psychology and of the judicial processes than to students of constitutional law.

Santa Fe Independent School District v. Doe

530 U.S. 290, 120 S.Ct. 2266, 147 L.Ed.2d 295 (2000).

Justice Stevens delivered the opinion of the Court.

Prior to 1995, the Santa Fe High School student who occupied the school's elective office of student council chaplain delivered a prayer over the public address system before each varsity football game for the entire season. This practice ... was challenged in District Court ... While these proceedings were pending in the District Court, the school district adopted a different policy that permits, but does not require, prayer initiated and led by a student at all home games. The District Court entered an order modifying that policy to permit only nonsectarian, nonproselytizing prayer. The Court of Appeals held that, even as modified by the District Court, the football prayer policy was invalid. . . .

I

. . .

Respondents commenced this action in April 1995 and moved for a temporary restraining order to prevent the District from violating the Establishment Clause at the imminent graduation exercises. In their complaint the Does alleged that the District had engaged in several proselytizing practices, such as promoting attendance at a Baptist revival meeting, encouraging membership in religious clubs, chastising children who held minority religious beliefs, and distributing Gideon Bibles on school premises. They also alleged that the District allowed students to read Christian invocations and benedictions from the stage at graduation ceremonies, and to deliver overtly Christian prayers over the public address system at home football games.

[T]he District Court entered an interim order ... With respect to the impending graduation, the order provided that "non-denominational prayer" consisting of " 'an invocation and/or benediction' " could be presented by a senior student or students selected by members of the graduating class. The text of the prayer was to be determined by the students, without scrutiny or preapproval by school officials. References to particular religious figures "such as Mohammed, Jesus, Buddha, or the like" would be permitted "as long as the general thrust of the prayer is non-proselytizing."

In response to that portion of the order, the District adopted a series of policies over several months dealing with prayer at school functions. The policies enacted in May and July for graduation ceremonies provided the format for the August and October policies for football games. The May policy provided:

> "The board has chosen to permit the graduating senior class, with the advice and counsel of the senior class principal or designee, to elect by secret ballot to choose whether an invocation and benediction shall be part of the graduation exercise. If so chosen the class shall elect by secret ballot, from a list of student volunteers, students to deliver nonsectarian, non-proselytizing invocations and benedictions for the purpose of solemnizing their graduation ceremonies."

[T]he senior class . . . voted, by secret ballot, to include prayer at the high school graduation. In a second vote the class elected two seniors to deliver the invocation and benediction.

In July, the District enacted another policy eliminating the requirement that invocations and benedictions be "nonsectarian and nonproselytising," but also providing that if the District were to be enjoined from enforcing that policy, the May policy would automatically become effective.

The August policy, which was titled "Prayer at Football Games," was similar to the July policy for graduations. . . . Like the July policy, it contained two parts, an initial statement that omitted any requirement that the content of the invocation be "nonsectarian and nonproselytising," and a fallback provision that automatically added that limitation if the preferred policy should be enjoined. . . . [T]he district's high school students voted to . . . to allow a student to say a prayer at football games. A week later, in a separate election, they selected a student "to deliver the prayer at varsity football games."

The final policy (October policy) is essentially the same as the August policy, though it omits the word "prayer" from its title, and refers to "messages" and "statements" as well as "invocations." It is the validity of that policy that is before us.

The District Court did enter an order precluding enforcement of the first, open-ended policy. Relying on our decision in Lee v. Weisman, 505 U.S. 577 (1992), it held that the school's "action must not 'coerce anyone to support or participate in' a religious exercise." Applying that test, it concluded that the graduation prayers appealed "to distinctively Christian beliefs," and that delivering a prayer "over the school's public address system prior to each football and baseball game coerces student participation in religious events." Both parties appealed, the District contending that the enjoined portion of the October policy was permissible and the Does contending that both alternatives violated the Establishment Clause. The Court of Appeals majority agreed with the Does.

. . .

We granted the District's petition for certiorari, limited to the following question: "Whether petitioner's policy permitting student-led, student-initiated prayer at football games violates the Establishment Clause." We conclude, as did the Court of Appeals, that it does.

II

. . . In Lee v. Weisman, 505 U.S. 577 (1992), we held that a prayer delivered by a rabbi at a middle school graduation ceremony violated that Clause. Although this case involves student prayer at a different type of school function, our analysis is properly guided by the principles that we endorsed in *Lee*.

As we held in that case:

> "The principle that government may accommodate the free exercise of religion does not supersede the fundamental limitations imposed by the Establishment Clause. It is beyond dispute that, at a minimum, the Constitution guarantees that government may not coerce anyone to support or participate in religion or its exercise, or otherwise act in a way which 'establishes a [state] religion or religious faith, or tends to do so.' "

. . .

In this case the District first argues that this principle is inapplicable to its October policy because the messages are private student speech, not public speech. It reminds us that "there is a crucial difference between government speech endorsing religion, which the Establishment Clause forbids, and private speech endorsing religion, which the Free Speech and Free Exercise Clauses protect." Board of Ed. of Westside Community Schools (Dist. 66) v. Mergens, 496 U.S. 226, 250 (1990) (opinion of O'Connor, J.). We certainly agree with that distinction, but we are not persuaded that the pregame invocations should be regarded as "private speech."

These invocations are authorized by a government policy and take place on government property at government-sponsored school-related events. Of course, not every message delivered under such circumstances is the government's own. We have held, for example, that an individual's contribution to a government-created forum was not government speech. See Rosenberger v. Rector and Visitors of Univ. of Va., 515 U.S. 819 (1995). Although the District relies heavily on *Rosenberger* and similar cases involving such forums, it is clear that the pregame ceremony is not the type of forum discussed in those cases. The Santa Fe school officials simply do not "evince either 'by policy or by practice,' any intent to open the [pregame ceremony] to 'indiscriminate use,' ... by the student body generally." ... Rather, the school allows only one student, the same student for the entire season, to give the invocation. The statement or invocation, moreover, is subject to particular regulations that confine the content and topic of the student's message. ...

Granting only one student access to the stage at a time does not, of course, necessarily preclude a finding that a school has created a limited public forum. Here, however, Santa Fe's student election system ensures that only those messages deemed "appropriate" under the District's policy may be delivered. That is, the majoritarian process implemented by the District guarantees, by definition, that minority candidates will never prevail and that their views will be effectively silenced.

Recently, in Board of Regents of Univ. of Wis. System v. Southworth, 529 U.S. 217 (2000), we explained why student elections that determine, by majority vote, which expressive activities shall receive or not receive school benefits are constitutionally problematic:

> "To the extent the referendum substitutes majority determinations for viewpoint neutrality it would undermine the constitutional protection the program requires. The whole theory of viewpoint neutrality is that minority views are treated with the same respect as are majority views. Access to a public forum, for instance, does not depend upon majoritarian consent. That principle is controlling here."

Like the student referendum for funding in *Southworth*, this student election does nothing to protect minority views but rather places the students who hold such views at the mercy of the majority....

In *Lee*, the school district made the related argument that its policy of endorsing only "civic or nonsectarian" prayer was acceptable because it minimized the intrusion on the audience as a whole. We rejected that claim by explaining that such a majoritarian policy "does not lessen the offense or isolation to the objectors. At best it narrows their number, at worst increases their sense of isolation and affront." Similarly, while Santa Fe's majoritarian election might ensure that most of the students are represented, it does nothing to protect the minority; indeed, it likely serves to intensify their offense.

Moreover, the District has failed to divorce itself from the religious content in the invocations. It has not succeeded in doing so, either by claiming that its policy is "one of neutrality rather than endorsement" or by characterizing the individual student as the "circuit-breaker" in the process. Contrary to the District's repeated assertions that it has adopted a "hands-off" approach to the pregame invocation, the realities of the situation plainly reveal that its policy involves both perceived and actual endorsement of religion. In this case, as we found in *Lee*, the "degree of school involvement" makes it clear that the pregame prayers bear "the imprint of the State and thus put school-age children who objected in an untenable position." ...

The District has attempted to disentangle itself from the religious messages by developing the two-step student election process. The text of the October policy, however, exposes the extent of the school's entanglement. The elections take place at all only because the school "board has chosen to permit students to deliver a brief invocation and/or message." The elections thus "shall" be conducted "by the high school student council" and "[u]pon advice and direction of the high school principal." The decision whether to deliver a message is first made by majority vote of the entire student body, followed by a choice of the speaker in a separate, similar majority election. Even though the particular words used by the speaker are not determined by those votes, the policy mandates that the "statement or invocation" be "consistent with the goals and purposes of this policy," which are "to solemnize the event, to promote good sportsmanship and student safety, and to establish the appropriate environment for the competition."

In addition to involving the school in the selection of the speaker, the policy, by its terms, invites and encourages religious messages. The policy itself states that the purpose of the message is "to solemnize the event." A religious message is the most obvious method of solemnizing an event. Moreover, the requirements that the message "promote good citizenship" and "establish the appropriate environment for competition" further narrow the types of message deemed appropriate, suggesting that a solemn, yet nonreligious, message, such as commentary on United States foreign policy, would be prohibited. Indeed, the only type of message that is expressly endorsed in the text is an "invocation"—a term that primarily describes an appeal for divine assistance. In fact, as used in the past at Santa Fe High School, an "invocation" has always entailed a focused religious message. ... [T]he students understood that the central question before them was whether prayer should be a part of the pregame ceremony. We recognize the important role that public worship plays in many communities, as well as the sincere desire to include public prayer as a part of various occasions so as to mark those occasions' significance. But such religious activity in public schools, as elsewhere, must comport with the First Amendment.

The actual or perceived endorsement of the message, moreover, is established by factors beyond just the text of the policy. Once the student speaker is selected and the message composed, the invocation is then delivered to a large audience assembled as part of a regularly scheduled, school-sponsored function conducted on school property. The message is broadcast over the school's public address system, which remains subject to the control of school officials. It is fair to assume that the pregame ceremony is clothed in the traditional indicia of school sporting events, which generally include not just the team, but also cheerleaders and band members dressed in uniforms sporting the school name and mascot. The school's name is likely written in large print across the field and on banners and flags. The crowd will certainly include many who display the school colors and insignia on their school T-shirts, jackets, or hats and who may also be waving signs displaying the school name. It is in a setting such as this that "[t]he board has chosen to permit" the elected student to rise and give the "statement or invocation."

In this context the members of the listening audience must perceive the pregame message as a public expression of the views of the majority of the student body delivered with the approval of the school administration. . . .

. . .

Most striking to us is the evolution of the current policy from the long-sanctioned office of "Student Chaplain" to the candidly titled "Prayer at Football Games" regulation. This history indicates that the District intended to preserve the practice of prayer before football games. The conclusion that the District viewed the October policy simply as a continuation of the previous policies is dramatically illustrated by the fact that the school did not conduct a new election, pursuant to the current policy, to replace the results of the previous election, which occurred under the former policy. Given these observations, and in light of the school's history of regular delivery of a student-led prayer at athletic events, it is reasonable to infer that the specific purpose of the policy was to preserve a popular "state-sponsored religious practice." . . .

School sponsorship of a religious message is impermissible because it sends the ancillary message to members of the audience who are nonadherents "that they are outsiders, not full members of the political community, and an accompanying message to adherents that they are insiders, favored members of the political community." . . . The delivery of such a message—over the school's public address system, by a speaker representing the student body, under the supervision of school faculty, and pursuant to a school policy that explicitly and implicitly encourages public prayer—is not properly characterized as "private" speech.

III

The District next argues that its football policy is distinguishable from the graduation prayer in *Lee* because it does not coerce students to participate in religious observances. Its argument has two parts: first, that there is no impermissible government coercion because the pregame messages are the product of student choices; and second, that there is really no coercion at all because attendance at an extracurricular event, unlike a graduation ceremony, is voluntary.

The reasons just discussed explaining why the alleged "circuit-breaker" mechanism of the dual elections and student speaker do not turn public speech into private speech also demonstrate why these mechanisms do not insulate the school from the coercive element of the final message. In fact, this aspect of the District's argument exposes anew the concerns that are created by the majoritarian election system. . . . [T]he issue resolved in the first election was "whether a student would deliver prayer at varsity football games," and the controversy in this case demonstrates that the views of the students are not unanimous on that issue.

One of the purposes served by the Establishment Clause is to remove debate over this kind of issue from governmental supervision or control. We explained in *Lee* that the "preservation and transmission of religious beliefs and worship is a responsibility and a choice committed to the private sphere." . . . The two student elections authorized by the policy, coupled with the debates that presumably must precede each, impermissibly invade that private sphere. The election mechanism, when considered in light of the history in which the policy in question evolved, reflects a device the District put in place that determines whether religious messages will be delivered at home football games. The mechanism encourages divisiveness along religious lines in a public school setting, a result at odds with the Establishment Clause. Although it is true that the ultimate choice of student speaker is "attributable to the students," the District's decision to hold the constitutionally problematic election is clearly "a choice attributable to the State,".…

The District further argues that attendance at the commencement ceremonies at issue in *Lee* "differs dramatically" from attendance at high school football games, which it contends "are of no more than passing interest to many students" and are "decidedly extracurricular," thus dissipating any coercion. Attendance at a high school football game, unlike showing up for class, is certainly not required in order to receive a diploma. Moreover, we may assume that the District is correct in arguing that the informal pressure to attend an athletic event is not as strong as a senior's desire to attend her own graduation ceremony.

There are some students, however, such as cheerleaders, members of the band, and, of course, the team members themselves, for whom seasonal commitments mandate their attendance, sometimes for class credit. The District also minimizes the importance to many students of attending and participating in extracurricular activities as part of a complete educational experience. As we noted in *Lee*, "[l]aw reaches past formalism." … To assert that high school students do not feel immense social pressure, or have a truly genuine desire, to be involved in the extracurricular event that is American high school football is "formalistic in the extreme." … We stressed in *Lee* the obvious observation that "adolescents are often susceptible to pressure from their peers towards conformity, and that the influence is strongest in matters of social convention." … High school home football games are traditional gatherings of a school community; they bring together students and faculty as well as friends and family from years present and past to root for a common cause. Undoubtedly, the games are not important to some students, and they voluntarily choose not to attend. For many others, however, the choice between whether to attend these games or to risk facing a personally offensive religious ritual is in no practical sense an easy one. The Constitution, moreover, demands that the school may not force this difficult choice upon these students for "[i]t is a tenet of the First Amendment that the State cannot require one of its citizens to forfeit his or her rights and benefits as the price of resisting conformance to state-sponsored religious practice." …

Even if we regard every high school student's decision to attend a home football game as purely voluntary, we are nevertheless persuaded that the delivery of a pregame prayer has the improper effect of coercing those present to participate in an act of religious worship. For "the government may no more use social pressure to enforce orthodoxy than it may use more direct means." As in *Lee*, "[w]hat to most believers may seem nothing more than a reasonable request that the nonbeliever respect their religious practices, in a school context may appear to the nonbeliever or dissenter to be an attempt to employ the machinery of the State to enforce a religious orthodoxy." … The constitutional command will not permit the District "to exact religious conformity from a student as the price" of joining her classmates at a varsity football game.

… [N]othing in the Constitution as interpreted by this Court prohibits any public school student from voluntarily praying at any time before, during, or after the schoolday. But the religious liberty protected by the Constitution is abridged when the State affirmatively sponsors the particular religious practice of prayer.

IV

Finally, the District argues repeatedly that the Does have made a premature facial challenge to the October policy that necessarily must fail. The District emphasizes, quite correctly, that until a student actually delivers a solemnizing message under the latest version of the policy, there can be no certainty that any of the statements or invocations will be religious. Thus, it concludes, the October policy necessarily survives a facial challenge.

This argument, however, assumes that we are concerned only with the serious constitutional injury that occurs when a student is forced to participate in an act of religious worship because she chooses to attend a school event. But the Constitution also requires that we keep in mind "the myriad, subtle ways in which Establishment Clause values can be eroded," . . . and that we guard against other different, yet equally important, constitutional injuries. One is the mere passage by the District of a policy that has the purpose and perception of government establishment of religion. Another is the implementation of a governmental electoral process that subjects the issue of prayer to a majoritarian vote.

The District argues that the facial challenge must fail because "Santa Fe's Football Policy cannot be invalidated on the basis of some 'possibility or even likelihood' of an unconstitutional application." Our Establishment Clause cases involving facial challenges, however, have not focused solely on the possible applications of the statute, but rather have considered whether the statute has an unconstitutional purpose. . . . Under the *Lemon* standard, a court must invalidate a statute if it lacks "a secular legislative purpose." . . . It is therefore proper, as part of this facial challenge, for us to examine the purpose of the October policy.

. . . [T]he text of the October policy alone reveals that it has an unconstitutional purpose. The plain language of the policy clearly spells out the extent of school involvement in both the election of the speaker and the content of the message. Additionally, the text of the October policy specifies only one, clearly preferred message—that of Santa Fe's traditional religious "invocation." Finally, the extremely selective access of the policy and other content restrictions confirm that it is not a content-neutral regulation that creates a limited public forum for the expression of student speech. Our examination, however, need not stop at an analysis of the text of the policy.

This case comes to us as the latest step in developing litigation brought as a challenge to institutional practices that unquestionably violated the Establishment Clause. One of those practices was the District's long-established tradition of sanctioning student-led prayer at varsity football games. The narrow question before us is whether implementation of the October policy insulates the continuation of such prayers from constitutional scrutiny. It does not. . . .

The District, nevertheless, asks us to pretend that we do not recognize what every Santa Fe High School student understands clearly—that this policy is about prayer. . . . We refuse to turn a blind eye to the context in which this policy arose, and that context quells any doubt that this policy was implemented with the purpose of endorsing school prayer.

Therefore, the simple enactment of this policy, with the purpose and perception of school endorsement of student prayer, was a constitutional violation. We need not wait for the inevitable to confirm and magnify the constitutional injury. In *Wallace* [v. Jaffree, 472 U.S. 38 (1985)] for example, we invalidated Alabama's as yet unimplemented and voluntary "moment of silence" statute based on our conclusion that it was enacted "for the sole purpose of expressing the State's endorsement of prayer activities for one minute at the beginning of each school day." . . . Therefore, even if no Santa Fe High School student were ever to offer a religious message, the October policy fails a facial challenge because the attempt by the District to encourage prayer is also at issue. Government efforts to endorse religion cannot evade constitutional reproach based solely on the remote possibility that those attempts may fail.

This policy . . . empowers the student body majority with the authority to subject students of minority views to constitutionally improper messages. The award of that power alone, regardless of the students' ultimate use of it, is not acceptable. Like the referendum in Board of Regents of Univ. of Wis. System v. Southworth, 529 U.S. 17 (2000), the election mechanism established by the District undermines the essential protection of minority viewpoints. . . . No further injury is required for the policy to fail a facial challenge.

. . .

The judgment of the Court of Appeals is, accordingly, affirmed.

It is so ordered.

Chief Justice Rehnquist, with whom Justice Scalia and Justice Thomas join, dissenting.

. . . [T]he tone of the Court's opinion . . . bristles with hostility to all things religious in public life. . . .

. . . [T]he fact that a policy might "operate unconstitutionally under some conceivable set of circumstances is insufficient to render it wholly invalid." . . . While there is an exception to this principle in the First Amendment overbreadth context because of our concern that people may refrain from speech out of fear of prosecution, . . . , there is no similar justification for Establishment Clause cases. No speech will be "chilled" by the existence of a government policy that might unconstitutionally endorse religion over nonreligion. Therefore, the question is not whether the district's policy may be applied in violation of the Establishment Clause, but whether it inevitably will be.

. . . The Court . . . applies the most rigid version of the oft-criticized test of Lemon v. Kurtzman, 403 U.S. 602 (1971).

Lemon has had a checkered career in the decisional law of this Court. . . .

Even if it were appropriate to apply the *Lemon* test here, the district's student-message policy should not be invalidated on its face. . . .

First, the Court misconstrues the nature of the "majoritarian election" permitted by the policy as being an election on "prayer" and "religion." To the contrary, the election permitted by the policy is a two-fold process whereby students vote first on whether to have a student speaker before football games at all, and second, if the students vote to have such a speaker, on who that speaker will be. It is conceivable that the election could become one in which student candidates campaign on platforms that focus on whether or not they will pray if elected. It is also conceivable that the election could lead to a Christian prayer before 90 percent of the football games. If, upon implementation, the policy operated in this fashion, we would have a record before us to review whether the policy, as applied, violated the Establishment Clause or unduly suppressed minority viewpoints. But it is possible that the students might vote not to have a pregame speaker, in which case there would be no threat of a constitutional violation. It is also possible that the election would not focus on prayer, but on public speaking ability or social popularity. And if student campaigning did begin to focus on prayer, the school might decide to implement reasonable campaign restrictions.

. . .

Second, with respect to the policy's purpose, the Court holds that "the simple enactment of this policy, with the purpose and perception of school endorsement of student prayer, was a constitutional violation." But the policy itself has plausible secular purposes: "[T]o solemnize the event, to promote good sportsmanship and student safety, and to establish the appropriate environment for the competition." . . . The Court grants no deference to—and appears openly hostile toward—the policy's stated purposes, and wastes no time in concluding that they are a sham.

. . . [I]it is easy to think of solemn messages that are not religious in nature, for example urging that a game be fought fairly. And sporting events often begin with a solemn rendition of our national anthem, with its concluding verse "And this be our motto: 'In God is our trust.' " Under the Court's logic, a public school that sponsors the singing of the national anthem before football games violates the Establishment Clause. Although the Court apparently believes that solemnizing football games is an illegitimate purpose, the voters in the school district seem to disagree. Nothing in the Establishment Clause prevents them from making this choice.

The Court bases its conclusion that the true purpose of the policy is to endorse student prayer on its view of the school district's history of Establishment Clause violations and the context in which the policy was written . . . But the context—attempted compliance with a District Court order—actually demonstrates that the school district was acting diligently to come within the governing constitutional law. . . .

The Court also relies on our decision in Lee v. Weisman . . . to support its conclusion. In *Lee*, we concluded that the content of the speech at issue, a graduation prayer given by a rabbi, was "directed and controlled" by a school official . . . In other words, at issue in *Lee* was government speech. Here, by contrast, the potential speech at issue, if the policy had been allowed to proceed, would be a message or invocation selected or created by a student. That is, if there were speech at issue here, it would be private speech. . . .

Had the policy been put into practice, the students may have chosen a speaker according to wholly secular criteria—like good public speaking skills or social popularity—and the student speaker may have chosen, on her own accord, to deliver a religious message. Such an application of the policy would likely pass constitutional muster. . . .

Finally, the Court seems to demand that a government policy be completely neutral as to content or be considered one that endorses religion. This is undoubtedly a new requirement, as our Establishment Clause jurisprudence simply does not mandate "content neutrality." That concept is found in our First Amendment speech cases and is used as a guide for determining when we apply strict scrutiny. . . .

But even our speech jurisprudence would not require that all public school actions with respect to student speech be content neutral. . . . Schools do not violate the First Amendment every time they restrict student speech to certain categories. But under the Court's view, a school policy under which the student body president is to solemnize the graduation ceremony by giving a favorable introduction to the guest speaker would be facially unconstitutional. Solemniza-tion "invites and encourages" prayer and the policy's content limitations prohibit the student body president from giving a solemn, yet non-religious, message like "commentary on United States foreign policy."

The policy at issue here may be applied in an unconstitutional manner, but it will be time enough to invalidate it if that is found to be the case. I would reverse the judgment of the Court of Appeals.

ELK GROVE UNIFIED SCHOOL DISTRICT v. NEWDOW, 124 S.Ct. 2301 (2004). In 1954, Congress amended the Flag Salute, adding the words "under God." Under state law, each public school must begin the school day with appropriate patriotic exercises. The Elk Grove School District implement-ed the law by requiring the flag salute, permitting students who object on religious grounds to abstain. Plaintiff, whose daughter attends school in the district, brought suit seeking a declaration that the addition of the words "under God" in 1954 violated the Establishment Clause. Four Justices joined Justice Stevens' opinion for the Court, which concluded that plaintiff did not have standing to bring the action. (He was not the custodial parent, and his daughter did not object to saying the Pledge of Allegiance.) Justice Stevens referred to the "deeply rooted commitment 'not to pass on questions of constitutionality' unless adjudication of the constitutional issue is necessary." Chief Justice Rehnquist, joined by Justices O'Connor and Thomas, objected to dismissal of the case. Justice O'Connor also wrote that she would sustain the Pledge on the ground that it did not "make a person's religious beliefs relevant to his or her standing in the political community by conveying a message that religion or a particular religious belief is favored or preferred." Justice Thomas also addressed the merits, indicating that he, too, would sustain the Flag Salute. He would substantially rethink the Establishment Clause, however, to permit state "establishment," subject to a requirement that Congress not interfere with state establishments. (Justice Scalia did not participate in the decision.)

Edwards v. Aguillard

482 U.S. 578, 107 S.Ct. 2573, 96 L.Ed.2d 510 (1987).

Justice Brennan delivered the opinion of the Court.

The question for decision is whether Louisiana's "Balanced Treatment for Creation—Science and Evolution—Science in Public School Instruction" Act (Creationism Act), La.Rev.Stat.Ann. §§ 17:286.1–17:286.7 (West 1982), is fa-cially invalid as violative of the Establishment Clause of the First Amendment.

I

The Creationism Act forbids the teaching of the theory of evolution in public schools unless accompanied by instruction in "creation science." ... No school is required to teach evolution or creation science. If either is taught, however, the other must also be taught. Ibid. The theories of evolution and creation science are statutorily defined as "the scientific evidences for [creation or evolution] and inferences from those scientific evidences." ...

Appellees, who include parents of children attending Louisiana public schools, Louisiana teachers, and religious leaders, challenged the constitutional-ity of the Act in District Court ... The District Court granted [appellees'] motion for summary judgment ...

The Court of Appeals affirmed.... We ... affirm.

II

The Establishment Clause forbids the enactment of any law "respecting an establishment of religion." The Court has applied a three-pronged test to determine whether legislation comports with the Establishment Clause. First, the legislature must have adopted the law with a secular purpose. Second, the statute's principal or primary effect must be one that neither advances nor inhibits religion. Third, the statute must not result in an excessive entanglement of government with religion. Lemon v. Kurtzman, . . .[4] State action violates the Establishment Clause if it fails to satisfy any of these prongs.

. . .

The Court has been particularly vigilant in monitoring compliance with the Establishment Clause in elementary and secondary schools. . . . Students in such institutions are impressionable and their attendance is involuntary. . . . The State exerts great authority and coercive power through mandatory attendance requirements, and because of the students' emulation of teachers as role models and the children's susceptibility to peer pressure.[5] . . .

. . .

III

Lemon's first prong focuses on the purpose that animated adoption of the Act. . . . If the law was enacted for the purpose of endorsing religion, "no consideration of the second or third criteria [of *Lemon*] is necessary." . . . In this case, appellants have identified no clear secular purpose for the Louisiana Act.

True, the Act's stated purpose is to protect academic freedom. . . . This phrase might, in common parlance, be understood as referring to enhancing the freedom of teachers to teach what they will. The Court of Appeals, however, correctly concluded that the Act was not designed to further that goal. . . . Even if "academic freedom" is read to mean "teaching all of the evidence" with respect to the origin of human beings, the Act does not further this purpose. The goal of providing a more comprehensive science curriculum is not furthered either by outlawing the teaching of evolution or by requiring the teaching of creation science.

A

While the Court is normally deferential to a State's articulation of a secular purpose, it is required that the statement of such purpose be sincere and not a sham. . . .

---

4. The *Lemon* test has been applied in all cases since its adoption in 1971, except in Marsh v. Chambers, 463 U.S. 783 (1983), where the Court held that the Nebraska Legislature's practice of opening a session with a prayer by a chaplain paid by the State did not violate the Establishment Clause. The Court based its conclusion in that case on the historical acceptance of the practice. Such a historical approach is not useful in determining the proper roles of church and state in public schools, since free public education was virtually nonexistent at the time the Constitution was adopted. . . .

5. The potential for undue influence is far less significant with regard to college students who voluntarily enroll in courses. "This distinction warrants a difference in constitutional results." Abington School Dist. v. Schempp, supra, at 253 (Brennan, J., concurring). Thus, for instance, the Court has not questioned the authority of state colleges and universities to offer courses on religion or theology. See Widmar v. Vincent, 454 U.S. 263, 271 (1981) (Powell, J.); id., at 281 (Stevens, J., concurring in judgment).

It is clear from the legislative history that the purpose of the legislative sponsor, Senator Bill Keith, was to narrow the science curriculum. During the legislative hearings, Senator Keith stated: "My preference would be that neither [creationism nor evolution] be taught." Such a ban on teaching does not promote—indeed, it undermines—the provision of a comprehensive scientific education.

It is equally clear that requiring schools to teach creation science with evolution does not advance academic freedom. The Act does not grant teachers a flexibility that they did not already possess to supplant the present science curriculum with the presentation of theories, besides evolution, about the origin of life. Indeed, the Court of Appeals found that no law prohibited Louisiana public school teachers from teaching any scientific theory. . . .

. . .

Furthermore, the goal of basic "fairness" is hardly furthered by the Act's discriminatory preference for the teaching of creation science and against the teaching of evolution. While requiring that curriculum guides be developed for creation science, the Act says nothing of comparable guides for evolution. . . . Similarly, research services are supplied for creation science but not for evolution. . . . Only "creation scientists" can serve on the panel that supplies the resource services. . . . The Act forbids school boards to discriminate against anyone who "chooses to be a creation-scientist" or to teach "creationism," but fails to protect those who choose to teach evolution or any other noncreation science theory, or who refuse to teach creation science. . . .

If the Louisiana Legislature's purpose was solely to maximize the comprehensiveness and effectiveness of science instruction, it would have encouraged the teaching of all scientific theories about the origins of humankind. But under the Act's requirements, teachers who were once free to teach any and all facets of this subject are now unable to do so. Moreover, the Act fails even to ensure that creation science will be taught, but instead requires the teaching of this theory only when the theory of evolution is taught. Thus we agree with the Court of Appeals' conclusion that the Act does not serve to protect academic freedom, but has the distinctly different purpose of discrediting "evolution by counterbalancing its teaching at every turn with the teaching of creationism. . . ."

B

. . .

. . . [W]e need not be blind in this case to the legislature's preeminent religious purpose in enacting this statute. There is a historic and contemporaneous link between the teachings of certain religious denominations and the teaching of evolution. It was this link that concerned the Court in Epperson v. Arkansas, 393 U.S. 97 (1968), which also involved a facial challenge to a statute regulating the teaching of evolution. In that case, the Court reviewed an Arkansas statute that made it unlawful for an instructor to teach evolution or to use a textbook that referred to this scientific theory. Although the Arkansas anti-evolution law did not explicitly state its predominate religious purpose, the Court could not ignore that "[t]he statute was a product of the upsurge of 'fundamentalist' religious fervor" that has long viewed this particular scientific theory as contradicting the literal interpretation of the Bible. . . . After reviewing the history of anti-evolution statutes, the Court determined that "there can be no doubt that the motivation for the [Arkansas] law was the same [as other anti-evolution statutes]: to suppress the teaching of a theory which, it was thought, 'denied' the divine creation of man." ... The Court found that there can be no legitimate state interest in protecting particular religions from scientific views "distasteful to them," ... and concluded "that the First Amendment does not permit the State to require that teaching and learning must be tailored to the principles or prohibitions of any religious sect or dogma," ...

These same historic and contemporaneous antagonisms between the teachings of certain religious denominations and the teaching of evolution are present in this case. The preeminent purpose of the Louisiana Legislature was clearly to advance the religious viewpoint that a supernatural being created humankind. The term "creation science" was defined as embracing this particular religious doctrine by those responsible for the passage of the Creationism Act. Senator Keith's leading expert on creation science, Edward Boudreaux, testified at the legislative hearings that the theory of creation science included belief in the existence of a supernatural creator. Senator Keith also cited testimony from other experts to support the creation-science view that "a creator [was] responsible for the universe and everything in it." The legislative history therefore reveals that the term "creation science," as contemplated by the legislature that adopted this Act, embodies the religious belief that a supernatural creator was responsible for the creation of humankind.

Furthermore, it is not happenstance that the legislature required the teaching of a theory that coincided with this religious view. The legislative history documents that the Act's primary purpose was to change the science curriculum of public schools in order to provide persuasive advantage to a particular religious doctrine that rejects the factual basis of evolution in its entirety. ...

In this case, the purpose of the Creationism Act was to restructure the science curriculum to conform with a particular religious viewpoint. Out of many possible science subjects taught in the public schools, the legislature chose to affect the teaching of the one scientific theory that historically has been opposed by certain religious sects. As in *Epperson,* the legislature passed the Act to give preference to those religious groups which have as one of their tenets the creation of humankind by a divine creator. The "overriding fact" that confronted the Court in *Epperson* was "that Arkansas' law selects from the body of knowledge a particular segment which it proscribes for the sole reason that it is deemed to conflict with ... a particular interpretation of the Book of Genesis by a particular religious group." ...

We do not imply that a legislature could never require that scientific critiques of prevailing scientific theories be taught. ... [T]eaching a variety of scientific theories about the origins of humankind to schoolchildren might be validly done with the clear secular intent of enhancing the effectiveness of science instruction. But because the primary purpose of the Creationism Act is to endorse a particular religious doctrine, the Act furthers religion in violation of the Establishment Clause.

. . .

V

The Louisiana Creationism Act advances a religious doctrine by requiring either the banishment of the theory of evolution from public school classrooms or the presentation of a religious viewpoint that rejects evolution in its entirety. The Act violates the Establishment Clause of the First Amendment because it seeks to employ the symbolic and financial support of government to achieve a religious purpose. The judgment of the Court of Appeals therefore is

Affirmed.

Justice Powell, with whom Justice O'Connor joins, concurring.

. . .

. . . The Establishment Clause is properly understood to prohibit the use of the Bible and other religious documents in public school education only when the purpose of the use is to advance a particular religious belief.

. . .

Justice White, concurring in the judgment.

As it comes to us, this is not a difficult case. . . .

. . .

Here, the District Judge, relying on the terms of the Act, discerned its purpose to be the furtherance of a religious belief, and a panel of the Court of Appeals agreed. Of those four judges, two are Louisianians. I would accept this view of the statute. Even if as an original matter I might have arrived at a different conclusion based on a reading of the statute and the record before us, I cannot say that the two courts below are so plainly wrong that they should be reversed. . . .

. . .

Justice Scalia, with whom The Chief Justice joins, dissenting.

Even if I agreed with the questionable premise that legislation can be invalidated under the Establishment Clause on the basis of its motivation alone, without regard to its effects, I would still find no justification for today's decision. . . . [T]he question of its constitutionality cannot rightly be disposed of on the gallop, by impugning the motives of its supporters.

I

. . . [T]he parties are sharply divided over what creation science consists of. Appellants insist that it is a collection of educationally valuable scientific data that has been censored from classrooms by an embarrassed scientific establishment. Appellees insist it is not science at all but thinly veiled religious doctrine. Both interpretations of the intended meaning of that phrase find considerable support in the legislative history.

. . .

II

. . .

B

. . .

In sum, even if one concedes, for the sake of argument, that a majority of the Louisiana Legislature voted for the Balanced Treatment Act partly in order to foster (rather than merely eliminate discrimination against) Christian fundamentalist beliefs, our cases establish that that alone would not suffice to invalidate the Act, so long as there was a genuine secular purpose as well. We have, moreover, no adequate basis for disbelieving the secular purpose set forth in the Act itself, or for concluding that it is a sham enacted to conceal the legislators' violation of their oaths of office. I am astonished by the Court's unprecedented readiness to reach such a conclusion, which I can only attribute to an intellectual predisposition created by the facts and the legend of Scopes v. State, 154 Tenn. 105, 289 S.W. 363 (1927)—an instinctive reaction that any governmentally imposed requirements bearing upon the teaching of evolution must be a manifestation of Christian fundamentalist repression. In this case, however, it seems to me the Court's position is the repressive one. The people of Louisiana, including those who are Christian fundamentalists, are quite entitled, as a secular matter, to have whatever scientific evidence there may be against evolution presented in their schools, just as Mr. Scopes was entitled to present whatever scientific evidence there was for it. . . .

. . .

Because I believe that the Balanced Treatment Act had a secular purpose, which is all the first component of the *Lemon* test requires, I would reverse the judgment of the Court of Appeals and remand for further consideration.

III

I have to this point assumed the validity of the *Lemon* "purpose" test. In fact, however, I think the pessimistic evaluation that The Chief Justice made of the totality of *Lemon* is particularly applicable to the "purpose" prong: it is "a constitutional theory [that] has no basis in the history of the amendment it seeks to interpret, is difficult to apply and yields unprincipled results. . . ." Wallace v. Jaffree, 472 U.S., at 112 (Rehnquist, J., dissenting).

. . .

Given the many hazards involved in assessing the subjective intent of governmental decisionmakers, the first prong of *Lemon* is defensible, I think, only if the text of the Establishment Clause demands it. That is surely not the case. . . . It is, in short, far from an inevitable reading of the Establishment Clause that it forbids all governmental action intended to advance religion; and if not inevitable, any reading with such untoward consequences must be wrong.

. . .

2.   RELIGIOUS SPEECH AND DISPLAYS ON PUBLIC PROPERTY

County of Allegheny v. American Civil Liberties Union

492 U.S. 573, 109 S.Ct. 3086, 106 L.Ed.2d 472 (1989).

Justice Blackmun announced the judgment of the Court and delivered the opinion of the Court with respect to Parts III–A, IV, and V, an opinion with respect to Parts I and II, in which Justice O'Connor and Justice Stevens join, an opinion with respect to Part III–B, in which Justice Stevens joins, and an opinion with respect to Part VI.

This litigation concerns the constitutionality of two recurring holiday displays located on public property in downtown Pittsburgh. The first is a creche placed on the Grand Staircase of the Allegheny County Courthouse. The second is a Chanukah menorah placed just outside the City–County Building, next to a Christmas tree and a sign saluting liberty. The Court of Appeals for the Third Circuit ruled that each display violates the Establishment Clause of the First Amendment because each has the impermissible effect of endorsing religion. . . . We agree that the creche display has that unconstitutional effect but reverse the Court of Appeals' judgment regarding the menorah display.

I

A

. . .

Since 1981, the county has permitted the Holy Name Society, a Roman Catholic group, to display a creche in the County Courthouse during the Christmas holiday season. . . .

. . . The . . . wooden representation of a manger, . . . has at its crest an angel bearing a banner that proclaims "Gloria in Excelsis Deo!"

During the 1986–1987 holiday season, the creche was on display on the Grand Staircase from November 26 to January 9. It had a wooden fence on three sides and bore a plaque stating: "This Display Donated by the Holy Name Society." . . . No figures of Santa Claus or other decorations appeared on the Grand Staircase. Cf. Lynch v. Donnelly, 465 U.S. 668, 671 (1984). . . .

. . .

B

The City–County Building is separate and a block removed from the County Courthouse . . .

For a number of years, the city has had a large Christmas tree under the middle arch outside the Grant Street entrance. Following this practice, city employees on November 17, 1986, erected a 45–foot tree under the middle arch and decorated it with lights and ornaments. A few days later, the city placed at the foot of the tree a sign bearing the Mayor's name and entitled "Salute to Liberty." Beneath the title, the sign stated:

> "During this holiday season, the City of Pittsburgh salutes liberty. Let these festive lights remind us that we are the keepers of the flame of liberty and our legacy of freedom."

At least since 1982, the city has expanded its Grant Street holiday display to include a symbolic representation of Chanukah, an 8–day Jewish holiday. . . .

. . .

Chanukah, like Christmas, is a cultural event as well as a religious holiday. . . .

. . .

On December 22 of the 1986 holiday season, the city placed at the Grant Street entrance to the City–County Building an 18–foot Chanukah menorah of an abstract tree-and-branch design. The menorah was placed next to the city's 45–foot Christmas tree, against one of the columns that supports the arch into which the tree was set. The menorah is owned by Chabad, a Jewish group, but is stored, erected, and removed each year by the city. The tree, the sign, and the menorah were all removed on January 13. . . .

II

This litigation began on December 10, 1986, when respondents, the Greater Pittsburgh Chapter of the American Civil Liberties Union and seven local residents, filed suit against the county and the city . . . Chabad was permitted to intervene to defend the display of its menorah.

. . . [T]he District Court denied respondent's request for a permanent injunction. . . .

. . . [T]he Court of Appeals reversed. . . .

. . .

III

A

. . .

. . . [T]his Court has come to understand the Establishment Clause to mean that government may not promote or affiliate itself with any religious doctrine or organization, may not discriminate among persons on the basis of their religious beliefs and practices, may not delegate a governmental power to a religious institution, and may not involve itself too deeply in such an institution's affairs. . . .

. . .

. . . [W]e have paid particularly close attention to whether the challenged governmental practice either has the purpose or effect of "endorsing" religion, a concern that has long had a place in our Establishment Clause jurisprudence. . . .

. . . [T]he prohibition against governmental endorsement of religion "preclude[s] government from conveying or attempting to convey a message that religion or a particular religious belief is *favored* or *preferred*." Wallace v. Jaffree, 472 U.S., at 70 (O'Connor, J., concurring in judgment) (emphasis added). . . .

. . . The Establishment Clause, at the very least, prohibits government from appearing to take a position on questions of religious belief or from "making adherence to a religion relevant in any way to a person's standing in the political community." Lynch v. Donnelly, 465 U.S., at 687 (O'Connor, J., concurring).

B

We have had occasion in the past to apply Establishment Clause principles to the government's display of objects with religious significance. In Stone v. Graham, 449 U.S. 39 (1980), we held that the display of a copy of the Ten Commandments on the walls of public classrooms violates the Establishment Clause. Closer to the facts of this litigation is Lynch v. Donnelly, supra, in which we considered whether the city of Pawtucket, R.I., had violated the Establishment Clause by including a creche in its annual Christmas display, located in a private park within the downtown shopping district. By a 5–4 decision in that difficult case, the Court upheld inclusion of the creche in the Pawtucket display, holding, inter alia, that the inclusion of the creche did not have the impermissible effect of advancing or promoting religion.

The rationale of the majority opinion in *Lynch* is none too clear: the opinion contains two strands, neither of which provides guidance for decision in subsequent cases. First, the opinion states that the inclusion of the creche in the display was "no more an advancement or endorsement of religion" than other "endorsements" this Court has approved in the past, 465 U.S., at 683— but the opinion offers no discernible measure for distinguishing between permissible and impermissible endorsements. Second, the opinion observes that any benefit the government's display of the creche gave to religion was no more than "indirect, remote, and incidental," ibid.—without saying how or why.

Although Justice O'Connor joined the majority opinion in *Lynch,* she wrote a concurrence that differs in significant respects from the majority opinion. The main difference is that the concurrence provides a sound analytical framework for evaluating governmental use of religious symbols.

First and foremost, the concurrence squarely rejects any notion that this Court will tolerate some government endorsement of religion. Rather, the concurrence recognizes any endorsement of religion as "invalid," . . . because it "sends a message to nonadherents that they are outsiders, not full members of the political community, and an accompanying message to adherents that they are insiders, favored members of the political community." . . .

Second, the concurrence articulates a method for determining whether the government's use of an object with religious meaning has the effect of endorsing religion. The effect of the display depends upon the message that the government's practice communicates: the question is "what viewers may fairly understand to be the purpose of the display." . . . That inquiry, of necessity, turns upon the context in which the contested object appears: "a typical museum setting, though not neutralizing the religious content of a religious painting, negates any message of endorsement of that content." Ibid. The concurrence thus emphasizes that the constitutionality of the creche in that case depended upon its "particular physical setting," ibid., and further observes: "Every government practice must be judged in its unique circumstances to determine whether it [endorses] religion." . . .

The concurrence applied this mode of analysis to the Pawtucket creche, seen in the context of that city's holiday celebration as a whole. In addition to the creche, the city's display contained: a Santa Claus House with a live Santa distributing candy; reindeer pulling Santa's sleigh; a live 40–foot Christmas tree strung with lights; statues of carolers in old-fashioned dress; candy-striped poles; a "talking" wishing well; a large banner proclaiming "SEASONS GREETINGS"; a miniature "Village" with several houses and a church; and various "cut-out" figures, including those of a clown, a dancing elephant, a robot, and a teddy bear. . . . The concurrence concluded that both because the creche is "a traditional symbol" of Christmas, a holiday with strong secular elements, and because the creche was "displayed along with purely secular symbols," the creche's setting "changes what viewers may fairly understand to be the purpose of the display" and "negates any message of endorsement" of "the Christian belief represented by the creche." . . .

The four *Lynch* dissenters agreed with the concurrence that the controlling question was "whether Pawtucket ha[d] run afoul of the Establishment Clause by endorsing religion through its display of the creche." . . . The dissenters also agreed with the general proposition that the context in which the government uses a religious symbol is relevant for determining the answer to that question. . . . They simply reached a different answer: the dissenters concluded that the other elements of the Pawtucket display did not negate the endorsement of Christian faith caused by the presence of the creche. . . .

Thus, despite divergence at the bottom line, the five Justices in concurrence and dissent in *Lynch* agreed upon the relevant constitutional principles: the government's use of religious symbolism is unconstitutional if it has the effect of endorsing religious belief, and the effect of the government's use of religious symbolism depends upon its context. . . . Accordingly, our present task is to determine whether the display of the creche and the menorah, in their respective "particular physical settings," has the effect of endorsing or disapproving religious beliefs. . . .

IV

. . .

Under the Court's holding in *Lynch,* the effect of a creche display turns on its setting. Here, unlike in *Lynch,* nothing in the context of the display detracts from the creche's religious message.... Here, in contrast, the creche stands alone: it is the single element of the display on the Grand Staircase.

. . .

... Thus, by permitting the "display of the creche in this particular physical setting," ... the county sends an unmistakable message that it supports and promotes the Christian praise to God that is the creche's religious message.

The fact that the creche bears a sign disclosing its ownership by a Roman Catholic organization does not alter this conclusion. On the contrary, the sign simply demonstrates that the government is endorsing the religious message of that organization, rather than communicating a message of its own. ...

Finally, the county argues that it is sufficient to validate the display of the creche on the Grand Staircase that the display celebrates Christmas, and Christmas is a national holiday. ... The government may acknowledge Christmas as a cultural phenomenon, but under the First Amendment it may not observe it as a Christian holy day by suggesting that people praise God for the birth of Jesus.

In sum, *Lynch* teaches that government may celebrate Christmas in some manner and form, but not in a way that endorses Christian doctrine. Here, Allegheny County has transgressed this line. ...

V

. . .

Justice Kennedy's reasons for permitting the creche on the Grand Staircase and his condemnation of the Court's reasons for deciding otherwise are so far-reaching in their implications that they require a response in some depth:

A

In *Marsh* [v. Chambers, 463 U.S. 783 (1983)], the Court relied specifically on the fact that Congress authorized legislative prayer at the same time that it produced the Bill of Rights. Justice Kennedy, however, argues that *Marsh* legitimates all "practices with no greater potential for an establishment of religion" than those "accepted traditions dating back to the Founding."

. . .

Justice Kennedy's reading of *Marsh* would gut the core of the Establishment Clause, as this Court understands it. The history of this Nation, it is perhaps sad to say, contains numerous examples of official acts that endorsed Christianity specifically.... Some of these examples date back to the Founding of the Republic, but this heritage of official discrimination against non-Christians has no place in the jurisprudence of the Establishment Clause. Whatever else the Establishment Clause may mean (and we have held it to mean no official preference even for religion over nonreligion ...), it certainly means at the very least that government may not demonstrate a preference for one particular sect or creed (including a preference for Christianity over other religions). ...

B

. . .

. . . In order to define precisely what government could and could not do under Justice Kennedy's "proselytization" test, the Court would have to decide a series of cases with particular fact patterns that fall along the spectrum of government references to religion (from the permanent display of a cross atop city hall to a passing reference to divine Providence in an official address). . . . Justice Kennedy's formulation of this essential Establishment Clause inquiry is no less fact-intensive than the "endorsement" formulation adopted by the Court. . . .

. . . [W]hen all is said and done, Justice Kennedy's effort to abandon the "endorsement" inquiry in favor of his "proselytization" test seems nothing more than an attempt to lower considerably the level of scrutiny in Establishment Clause cases. . . .

C

Of course, not all religious celebrations of Christmas located on government property violate the Establishment Clause. It obviously is not unconstitutional, for example, for a group of parishioners from a local church to go caroling through a city park on any Sunday in Advent or for a Christian club at a public university to sing carols during their Christmas meeting. . . . [A]ctivities of this nature do not demonstrate the government's allegiance to, or endorsement of, the Christian faith.

Equally obvious, however, is the proposition that not all proclamations of Christian faith located on government property are permitted by the Establishment Clause just because they occur during the Christmas holiday season, as the example of a Mass in the courthouse surely illustrates. . . .

VI

The display of the Chanukah menorah in front of the City–County Building may well present a closer constitutional question. The menorah, one must recognize, is a religious symbol: it serves to commemorate the miracle of the oil as described in the Talmud. But the menorah's message is not exclusively religious. The menorah is the primary visual symbol for a holiday that, like Christmas, has both religious and secular dimensions.

. . .

. . . If the city celebrates both Christmas and Chanukah as religious holidays, then it violates the Establishment Clause. The simultaneous endorsement of Judaism and Christianity is no less constitutionally infirm than the endorsement of Christianity alone.

Conversely, if the city celebrates both Christmas and Chanukah as secular holidays, then its conduct is beyond the reach of the Establishment Clause. . . .

. . .

. . . [T]he combination of the tree and the menorah communicates, not a simultaneous endorsement of both Christian and Jewish faith, but instead, a secular celebration of Christmas coupled with an acknowledgment of Chanukah as a contemporaneous alternative tradition.

. . .

The Mayor's sign further diminishes the possibility that the tree and the menorah will be interpreted as a dual endorsement of Christianity and Judaism.

. . .

The conclusion here that, in this particular context, the menorah's display does not have an effect of endorsing religious faith does not foreclose the possibility that the display of the menorah might violate either the "purpose" or "entanglement" prong of the *Lemon* analysis. These issues were not addressed by the Court of Appeals and may be considered by that court on remand.

VII

Lynch v. Donnelly confirms, and in no way repudiates, the long-standing constitutional principle that government may not engage in a practice that has the effect of promoting or endorsing religious beliefs. The display of the creche in the County Courthouse has this unconstitutional effect. The display of the menorah in front of the City–County Building, however, does not have this effect, given its "particular physical setting."

The judgment of the Court of Appeals is affirmed in part and reversed in part, and the cases are remanded for further proceedings.

. . .

Justice O'Connor, with whom Justice Brennan and Justice Stevens join as to Part II, concurring in part and concurring in the judgment.

I

. . .

The constitutionality of the two displays at issue in this case turns on how we interpret and apply the holding in Lynch v. Donnelly, 465 U.S. 668 (1984) . . .

. . .

I joined the majority opinion in *Lynch* because, as I read that opinion, it was consistent with the analysis set forth in my separate concurrence . . .

. . .

In *Lynch,* I concluded that the city's display of a creche in its larger holiday exhibit in a private park in the commercial district had neither the purpose nor the effect of conveying a message of government endorsement of Christianity or disapproval of other religions. . . . Nor, in my view, did Pawtucket's display of the creche along with secular symbols of the Christmas holiday objectively convey a message of endorsement of Christianity.

For the reasons stated in Part IV of the Court's opinion in this case, I agree that the creche displayed on the Grand Staircase of the Allegheny County Courthouse, the seat of county government, conveys a message to nonadherents of Christianity that they are not full members of the political community, and a corresponding message to Christians that they are favored members of the political community. . . .

II

. . .

Justice Kennedy submits that the endorsement test is inconsistent with our precedents and traditions because, in his words, if it were "applied without artificial exceptions for historical practice," it would invalidate many traditional practices recognizing the role of religion in our society. . . . [E]xamples of ceremonial deism do not survive Establishment Clause scrutiny simply by virtue of their historical longevity alone. Historical acceptance of a practice does not in itself validate that practice under the Establishment Clause if the practice violates the values protected by that Clause, just as historical acceptance of racial or gender based discrimination does not immunize such practices from scrutiny under the 14th Amendment.

Under the endorsement test, the "history and ubiquity" of a practice is relevant . . . because it provides part of the context in which a reasonable observer evaluates whether a challenged governmental practice conveys a message of endorsement of religion. It is the combination of the longstanding existence of practices such as opening legislative sessions with legislative prayers or opening Court sessions with "God save the United States and this honorable Court," as well as their nonsectarian nature, that lead me to the conclusion that those particular practices, despite their religious roots, do not convey a message of endorsement of particular religious beliefs. . . . The question under endorsement analysis, in short, is whether a reasonable observer would view such longstanding practices as a disapproval of their particular religious choices, in light of the fact that they serve a secular purpose rather than a sectarian one and have largely lost their religious significance over time. . . .

. . .

III

For reasons which differ somewhat from those set forth in Part VI of Justice Blackmun's opinion, I also conclude that the city of Pittsburgh's combined holiday display of a Chanukah menorah, a Christmas tree, and a sign saluting liberty does not have the effect of conveying an endorsement of religion. . . . Although Justice Blackmun's opinion acknowledges that a Christmas tree alone conveys no endorsement of Christian beliefs, it formulates the question posed by Pittsburgh's combined display of the tree and the menorah as whether the display "has the effect of endorsing *both* Christian and Jewish faiths, or rather simply recognizes that both Christmas and Chanukah are part of the same winter-holiday season, which has attained a secular status in our society." (emphasis added).

That formulation of the question disregards the fact that the Christmas tree is a predominantly secular symbol and, more significantly, obscures the religious nature of the menorah and the holiday of Chanukah. . . . In my view, the relevant question for Establishment Clause purposes is whether the city of Pittsburgh's display of the menorah, the religious symbol of a religious holiday, next to a Christmas tree and a sign saluting liberty sends a message of government endorsement of Judaism or whether it sends a message of pluralism and freedom to choose one's own beliefs.

. . . One need not characterize Chanukah as a "secular holiday" or strain to argue that the menorah has a "secular dimension," in order to conclude that the city of Pittsburgh's combined display does not convey a message of endorsement of Judaism or of religion in general.

. . .

In sum, I conclude that the city of Pittsburgh's combined holiday display had neither the purpose nor the effect of endorsing religion, but that Allegheny County's creche display had such an effect. Accordingly, I join Parts I, II, III–A, IV, V, and VII of the Court's opinion and concur in the judgment.

Justice Brennan, with whom Justice Marshall and Justice Stevens join, concurring in part and dissenting in part.

. . . I continue to believe that the display of an object that "retains a specifically Christian [or other] religious meaning," . . . is incompatible with the separation of church and state demanded by our Constitution. I therefore agree with the Court that Allegheny County's display of a creche at the county courthouse signals an endorsement of the Christian faith in violation of the Establishment Clause, and join Parts III–A, IV, and V of the Court's opinion. I cannot agree, however, that the city's display of a 45–foot Christmas tree and an 18–foot Chanukah menorah at the entrance to the building housing the Mayor's office shows no favoritism towards Christianity, Judaism, or both. Indeed, I should have thought that the answer as to the first display supplied the answer to the second.

. . .

Justice Stevens, with whom Justice Brennan and Justice Marshall join, concurring in part and dissenting in part.

. . .

In my opinion the Establishment Clause should be construed to create a strong presumption against the display of religious symbols on public property. There is always a risk that such symbols will offend nonmembers of the faith being advertised as well as adherents who consider the particular advertisement disrespectful. . . .

. . .

Justice Kennedy, with whom the Chief Justice, Justice White and Justice Scalia join, concurring in the judgment in part and dissenting in part.

The majority holds that the County of Allegheny violated the Establishment Clause by displaying a creche in the county courthouse, because the "principal or primary effect" of the display is to advance religion within the meaning of Lemon v. Kurtzman . . . This view of the Establishment Clause reflects an unjustified hostility toward religion, a hostility inconsistent with our history and our precedents, and I dissent from this holding. The creche display is constitutional, and, for the same reasons, the display of a menorah by the city of Pittsburgh is permissible as well. On this latter point, I concur in the result, but not the reasoning, of Part VI of Justice Blackmun's opinion.

I

In keeping with the usual fashion of recent years, the majority applies the *Lemon* test to judge the constitutionality of the holiday displays here in question. I am content for present purposes to remain within the *Lemon* framework, but do not wish to be seen as advocating, let alone adopting, that test as our primary guide in this difficult area. . . .

The only *Lemon* factor implicated in this case directs us to inquire whether the "principal or primary effect" of the challenged government practice is "one that neither advances nor inhibits religion." ... The requirement of neutrality inherent in that formulation has sometimes been stated in categorical terms. For example, in Everson v. Board of Education, 330 U.S. 1 (1947), the first case in our modern Establishment Clause jurisprudence, Justice Black wrote that the Clause forbids laws "which aid one religion, aid all religions, or prefer one religion over another." ...

These statements must not give the impression of a formalism that does not exist. Taken to its logical extreme, some of the language quoted above would require a relentless extirpation of all contact between government and religion. But that is not the history or the purpose of the Establishment Clause. Government policies of accommodation, acknowledgment, and support for religion are an accepted part of our political and cultural heritage....

Rather than requiring government to avoid any action that acknowledges or aids religion, the Establishment Clause permits government some latitude in recognizing and accommodating the central role religion plays in our society....

. . .

The ability of the organized community to recognize and accommodate religion in a society with a pervasive public sector requires diligent observance of the border between accommodation and establishment. Our cases disclose two limiting principles: government may not coerce anyone to support or participate in any religion or its exercise; and it may not, in the guise of avoiding hostility or callous indifference, give direct benefits to religion in such a degree that it in fact "establishes a [state] religion or religious faith, or tends to do so." ... These two principles, while distinct, are not unrelated, for it would be difficult indeed to establish a religion without some measure of more or less subtle coercion, be it in the form of taxation to supply the substantial benefits that would sustain a state-established faith, direct compulsion to observance, or governmental exhortation to religiosity that amounts in fact to proselytizing.

It is no surprise that without exception we have invalidated actions that further the interests of religion through the coercive power of government. Forbidden involvements include compelling or coercing participation or attendance at a religious activity, ... requiring religious oaths to obtain government office or benefits, Torcaso v. Watkins, 367 U.S. 488 (1961), or delegating government power to religious groups, Larkin v. Grendel's Den, Inc., 459 U.S. 116 (1982). The freedom to worship as one pleases without government interference or oppression is the great object of both the Establishment and the Free Exercise Clauses. Barring all attempts to aid religion through government coercion goes far toward attainment of this object....

As Justice Blackmun observes, some of our recent cases reject the view that coercion is the sole touchstone of an Establishment Clause violation. ... That may be true if by "coercion" is meant *direct* coercion in the classic sense of an establishment of religion that the Framers knew. But coercion need not be a direct tax in aid of religion or a test oath. Symbolic recognition or accommodation of religious faith may violate the Clause in an extreme case. I doubt not, for example, that the Clause forbids a city to permit the permanent erection of a large Latin cross on the roof of city hall. This is not because government speech about religion is per se suspect, as the majority would have it, but because such an obtrusive year-round religious display would place the government's weight behind an obvious effort to proselytize on behalf of a particular religion.

. . .

In determining whether there exists an establishment, or a tendency toward one, we refer to the other types of church-state contacts that have existed unchallenged throughout our history, or that have been found permissible in our caselaw. ... [I]n Marsh v. Chambers, we found that Nebraska's practice of employing a legislative chaplain did not violate the Establishment Clause, because "legislative prayer presents no more potential for establishment than the provision of school transportation, beneficial grants for higher education, or tax exemptions for religious organizations." ... Noncoercive government action within the realm of flexible accommodation or passive acknowledgment of existing symbols does not violate the Establishment Clause unless it benefits religion in a way more direct and more substantial than practices that are accepted in our national heritage.

II

These principles are not difficult to apply to the facts of the case before us. In permitting the displays on government property of the menorah and the creche, the city and county sought to do no more than "celebrate the season," and to acknowledge, along with many of their citizens, the historical background and the religious as well as secular nature of the Chanukah and Christmas holidays. This interest falls well within the tradition of government accommodation and acknowledgment of religion that has marked our history from the beginning. . . .

If government is to participate in its citizens' celebration of a holiday that contains both a secular and a religious component, enforced recognition of only the secular aspect would signify the callous indifference toward religious faith that our cases and traditions do not require ...

. . .

Our cases do not suggest, moreover, that the use of public property necessarily converts otherwise permissible government conduct into an Establishment Clause violation. To the contrary, in some circumstances the First Amendment may *require* that government property be available for use by religious groups ...

Nor can I comprehend why it should be that placement of a government-owned creche on private land is lawful while placement of a privately owned creche on public land is not. If anything, I should have thought government ownership of a religious symbol presented the more difficult question under the Establishment Clause, but as *Lynch* resolved that question to sustain the government action, the sponsorship here ought to be all the easier to sustain. In short, nothing about the religious displays here distinguishes them in any meaningful way from the creche we permitted in *Lynch*.

... On the same reasoning, I agree that the menorah display is constitutional.

III

The majority invalidates display of the creche, not because it disagrees with the interpretation of *Lynch* applied above, but because it chooses to discard the reasoning of the *Lynch* majority opinion in favor of Justice O'Connor's concurring opinion in that case. It has never been my understanding that a concurring opinion ... could take precedence over an opinion joined in its entirety by five Members of the Court. ...

. . .

A

. . .

... *Marsh* stands for the proposition, not that specific practices common in 1791 are an exception to the otherwise broad sweep of the Establishment Clause, but rather that the meaning of the Clause is to be determined by reference to historical practices and understandings. Whatever test we choose to apply must permit not only legitimate practices two centuries old but also any other practices with no greater potential for an establishment of religion....

If the endorsement test, applied without artificial exceptions for historical practice, reached results consistent with history, my objections to it would have less force. But, as I understand that test, the touchstone of an Establishment Clause violation is whether nonadherents would be made to feel like "outsiders" by government recognition or accommodation of religion. Few of our traditional practices recognizing the part religion plays in our society can withstand scrutiny under a faithful application of this formula.

B

. . .

... This test could provide workable guidance to the lower courts, if ever, only after this Court has decided a long series of holiday display cases, using little more than intuition and a tape measure. Deciding cases on the basis of such an unguided examination of marginalia is irreconcilable with the imperative of applying neutral principles in constitutional adjudication....

. . .

IV

. . .

A further contradiction arises from the majority's approach, for the Court also assumes the difficult and inappropriate task of saying what every religious symbol means.... This Court is ill equipped to sit as a national theology board, and I question both the wisdom and the constitutionality of its doing so. Indeed, were I required to choose between the approach taken by the majority and a strict separationist view, I would have to respect the consistency of the latter.

. . .

... I might have voted against installation of these particular displays were I a local legislative official. But we have no jurisdiction over matters of taste within the realm of constitutionally permissible discretion. Our role is enforcement of a written Constitution. In my view, the principles of the Establishment Clause and our Nation's historic traditions of diversity and pluralism allow communities to make reasonable judgments respecting the accommodation or acknowledgment of holidays with both cultural and religious aspects. No constitutional violation occurs when they do so by displaying a symbol of the holiday's religious origins.

I dissent.

EQUAL ACCESS FOR RELIGIOUS SPEECH ON PUBLIC PROPERTY

Religious speakers denied access to public property have sought to compel access on free speech grounds, while the government-owner of the property has sought to justify denial of access on establishment grounds. In Widmar v. Vincent, 454 U.S. 263 (1981), a student group was denied permission to conduct meetings on state university facilities because of a policy denying use of university facilities "for purposes of religious worship or religious teaching." (The group was an organization of evangelical Christian students whose on-campus meetings, open to the public, included prayer, hymns, Bible commentary, and religious discussion.) The exclusion was held to violate the First Amendment's Free Speech Clause. The "discriminatory exclusion" was "content-based," and could only be justified if "necessary to serve a compelling state interest and ... narrowly drawn to achieve that end." The exclusion was not necessary to serve the University's interest in maintaining separation of church and State because the religious group's benefit from access to the University's public forum was "incidental."

In Board of Education v. Mergens, 496 U.S. 226 (1990), students at a public secondary school were denied permission to form a Christian club "to read and discuss the Bible, to have fellowship, and to pray together" because school officials decided that a religious club at school would violate the Establishment Clause. The Court held that the school had violated a federal statute, the Equal Access Act, 20 U.S.C. §§ 4071–4074. The Act prohibits public secondary schools receiving federal funds, and maintaining a "limited public forum," from denying "equal access" to students on the basis of the content of their speech. By a vote of eight to one, but without a majority opinion, the Court held that the Equal Access Act did not violate the Establishment Clause. Justice O'Connor, joined by Chief Justice Rehnquist and Justices White and Blackmun, applied the three-part *Lemon* test. Granting equal access to secular and religious speech: was a secular purpose; did not have the primary effect of advancing religion because high school students will understand that the school does not endorse speech it merely permits; did not involve excessive entanglement because the Act prohibits faculty from regularly attending, directing or controlling activities of religious student groups. Justice Kennedy, joined by Justice Scalia, said there was no Establishment Clause violation because religious groups were not given benefits to a degree that established a state religion, and students were not coerced to participate in religious activity.

In Lamb's Chapel v. Center Moriches Union Free School District, 508 U.S. 384 (1993), exclusion of a non-student's religious speech from a public secondary school was held to violate the Free Speech Clause. An evangelical church and its pastor were denied permission to use school facilities to show a six-part film series containing lectures concerning "Christian family values." The Court relied on *Widmar* for its conclusion that the school district's "posited fears of an Establishment Clause violation are unfounded."

Capitol Square Review and Advisory Board v. Pinette

515 U.S. 753, 115 S.Ct. 2440, 132 L.Ed.2d 650 (1995).

Justice Scalia announced the judgment of the Court and delivered the opinion of the Court with respect to Parts I, II, and III, and an opinion with respect to Part IV, in which the Chief Justice, Justice Kennedy and Justice Thomas join.

... The question in this case is whether a State violates the Establishment Clause when, pursuant to a religiously neutral state policy, it permits a private party to display an unattended religious symbol in a traditional public forum located next to its seat of government.

I

Capitol Square is a 10–acre, state-owned plaza surrounding the Statehouse in Columbus, Ohio. For over a century the square has been used for public speeches, gatherings, and festivals advocating and celebrating a variety of causes, both secular and religious. ...

It has been the Board's policy "to allow a broad range of speakers and other gatherings of people to conduct events on the Capitol Square." ... The Board has also permitted a variety of unattended displays on Capitol Square: a State-sponsored lighted tree during the Christmas season, a privately-sponsored menorah during Chanukah, a display showing the progress of a United Way fundraising campaign, and booths and exhibits during an arts festival. ...

In November 1993, after reversing an initial decision to ban unattended holiday displays from the square during December 1993, the Board authorized the State to put up its annual Christmas tree. On November 29, 1993, the Board granted a rabbi's application to erect a menorah. That same day, the Board received an application from respondent Donnie Carr, an officer of the Ohio Ku Klux Klan, to place a cross on the square from December 8, 1993, to December 24, 1993. The Board denied that application on December 3, informing the Klan by letter that the decision to deny "was made upon the advice of counsel, in a good faith attempt to comply with the Ohio and United States Constitutions, as they have been interpreted in relevant decisions by the Federal and State Courts."

... [T]he Ohio Klan ... filed the present suit in the United States District Court for the Southern District of Ohio, seeking an injunction requiring the Board to issue the requested permit. The Board defended on the ground that the permit would violate the Establishment Clause. The District Court issued the injunction and ... the Board permitted the Klan to erect its cross. The Board then received, and granted, several additional applications to erect crosses on Capitol Square during December 1993 and January 1994.

On appeal by the Board, the United States Court of Appeals for the Sixth Circuit affirmed the District Court's judgment. ...

II

First, a preliminary matter: Respondents contend that we should treat this as a case in which freedom of speech (the Klan's right to present the message of the cross display) was denied because of the State's disagreement with that message's political content, rather than because of the State's desire to distance itself from sectarian religion. ... The record facts before us and the opinions below address only the Establishment Clause issue; that is the question upon which we granted certiorari; and that is the sole question before us to decide.

. . .

III

There is no doubt that compliance with the Establishment Clause is a state interest sufficiently compelling to justify content-based restrictions on speech.... Whether that interest is implicated here, however, is a different question. And we do not write on a blank slate in answering it. We have twice previously addressed the combination of private religious expression, a forum available for public use, content-based regulation, and a State's interest in complying with the Establishment Clause. Both times, we have struck down the restriction on religious content. . . .

In *Lamb's Chapel*, . . . the school district violated an applicant's free-speech rights by denying it use of the facilities solely because of the religious viewpoint of the program it wished to present. . . .

. . . [I[n Widmar . . . we examined a public university's exclusion of student religious groups from facilities available to other student groups. . . .

Quite obviously, the factors that we considered determinative in *Lamb's Chapel* and *Widmar* exist here as well. The State did not sponsor respondents' expression, the expression was made on government property that had been opened to the public for speech, and permission was requested through the same application process and on the same terms required of other private groups.

IV

Petitioners argue that one feature of the present case distinguishes it from *Lamb's Chapel* and *Widmar*: the forum's proximity to the seat of government, which, they contend, may produce the perception that the cross bears the State's approval. They urge us to apply the so-called "endorsement test," . . . and to find that, because an observer might mistake private expression for officially endorsed religious expression, the State's content-based restriction is constitutional.

We must note, to begin with, that it is not really an "endorsement test" of any sort, much less the "endorsement test" which appears in our more recent Establishment Clause jurisprudence, that petitioners urge upon us. "Endorsement" connotes an expression or demonstration of approval or support. . . . Our cases have accordingly equated "endorsement" with "promotion" or "favoritism." . . . We find it peculiar to say that government "promotes" or "favors" a religious display by giving it the same access to a public forum that all other displays enjoy. . . . Where we have tested for endorsement of religion, the subject of the test was either expression by the government itself, . . . or else government action alleged to discriminate in favor of private religious expression or activity . . . The test petitioners propose, which would attribute to a neutrally behaving government private religious expression, has no antecedent in our jurisprudence, and would better be called a "transferred endorsement" test.

Petitioners rely heavily on *Allegheny County* and *Lynch*, but each is easily distinguished. In *Allegheny County* we held that the display of a privately-sponsored creche on the "Grand Staircase" of the Allegheny County Courthouse violated the Establishment Clause. That staircase was not, however, open to all on an equal basis, so the County was favoring sectarian religious expression. . . . In *Lynch* we held that a city's display of a creche did not violate the Establishment Clause because, in context, the display did not endorse religion. . . . The opinion does assume, as petitioners contend, that the government's use of religious symbols is unconstitutional if it effectively endorses sectarian religious belief. But the case neither holds nor even remotely assumes that the government's neutral treatment of private religious expression can be unconstitutional.

Petitioners argue that absence of perceived endorsement was material in *Lamb's Chapel* and *Widmar*. We did state in *Lamb's Chapel* that there was "no realistic danger that the community would think that the District was endorsing religion or any particular creed,". ... But that conclusion was not the result of empirical investigation; it followed directly, we thought, from the fact that the forum was open and the religious activity privately sponsored. ... [W]e in effect said, given an open forum and private sponsorship, erroneous conclusions do not count. So also in *Widmar*. Once we determined that the benefit to religious groups from the public forum was incidental and shared by other groups, we categorically rejected the State's Establishment Clause defense. ...

What distinguishes *Allegheny County* and the dictum in *Lynch* from *Widmar* and *Lamb's Chapel* is the difference between government speech and private speech. ... Petitioners assert ... that the distinction disappears whenever private speech can be mistaken for government speech. That proposition cannot be accepted, at least where, as here, the government has not fostered or encouraged the mistake.

Of course, giving sectarian religious speech preferential access to a forum close to the seat of government (or anywhere else for that matter) would violate the Establishment Clause (as well as the Free Speech Clause, since it would involve content discrimination). And one can conceive of a case in which a governmental entity manipulates its administration of a public forum close to the seat of government (or within a government building) in such a manner that only certain religious groups take advantage of it, creating an impression of endorsement that is in fact accurate. But those situations, which involve governmental favoritism, do not exist here. ...

The contrary view, most strongly espoused by Justice Stevens, but endorsed by Justice Souter and Justice O'Connor as well, exiles private religious speech to a realm of less-protected expression heretofore inhabited only by sexually explicit displays and commercial speech. ... [I]t is outright perverse when one considers that private religious expression receives preferential treatment under the Free Exercise Clause. It is no answer to say that the Establishment Clause tempers religious speech. By its terms that Clause applies only to the words and acts of government. It was never meant, and has never been read by this Court, to serve as an impediment to purely private religious speech connected to the State only through its occurrence in a public forum.

Since petitioners' "transferred endorsement" principle cannot possibly be restricted to squares in front of state capitols, the Establishment Clause regime that it would usher in is most unappealing. ... Policy makers would find themselves in a vise between the Establishment Clause on one side and the Free Speech and Free Exercise Clauses on the other. Every proposed act of private, religious expression in a public forum would force officials to weigh a host of imponderables. How close to government is too close? What kind of building, and in what context, symbolizes state authority? If the State guessed wrong in one direction, it would be guilty of an Establishment Clause violation; if in the other, it would be liable for suppressing free exercise or free speech (a risk not run when the State restrains only its own expression).

... It has radical implications for our public policy to suggest that neutral laws are invalid whenever hypothetical observers may—even reasonably—confuse an incidental benefit to religion with state endorsement.

If Ohio is concerned about misperceptions, nothing prevents it from requiring all private displays in the Square to be identified as such. That would be a content-neutral "manner" restriction which is assuredly constitutional. ... But the State may not, on the claim of misperception of official endorsement, ban all private religious speech from the public square, or discriminate against it by requiring religious speech alone to disclaim public sponsorship.

* * *

Religious expression cannot violate the Establishment Clause where it (1) is purely private and (2) occurs in a traditional or designated public forum, publicly announced and open to all on equal terms. Those conditions are satisfied here, and therefore the State may not bar respondents' cross from Capitol Square.

The judgment of the Court of Appeals is

affirmed.[a]

Justice O'Connor, with whom Justice Souter and Justice Breyer join, concurring in part and concurring in the judgment.

I join Parts I, II, and III of the Court's opinion and concur in the judgment. ... I see no necessity to carve out, as the plurality opinion would today, an exception to the endorsement test for the public forum context.

For the reasons given by Justice Souter, whose opinion I also join, I conclude on the facts of this case that there is "no realistic danger that the community would think that the [State] was endorsing religion or any particular creed," ... I write separately, however, to emphasize that ... the endorsement test necessarily focuses upon the perception of a reasonable, informed observer.

I

. . .

While the plurality would limit application of the endorsement test ..., I believe that an impermissible message of endorsement can be sent in a variety of contexts, not all of which involve direct government speech or outright favoritism. It is true that neither *Allegheny* nor *Lynch*, our two prior religious display cases, involved the same combination of private religious speech and a public forum that we have before us today. Nonetheless, as Justice Souter aptly demonstrates, we have on several occasions employed an endorsement perspective in Establishment Clause cases where private religious conduct has intersected with a neutral governmental policy providing some benefit in a manner that parallels the instant case. Thus, while I join the discussion of *Lamb's Chapel* and Widmar v. Vincent, ... in Part III of the Court's opinion, I do so with full recognition that the factors the Court properly identifies ultimately led in each case to the conclusion that there was no endorsement of religion by the State. ...

. . .

None of this is to suggest that I would be likely to come to a different result from the plurality where truly private speech is allowed on equal terms in a vigorous public forum that the government has administered properly. ...

To the plurality's consideration of the open nature of the forum and the private ownership of the display, however, I would add the presence of a sign disclaiming government sponsorship or endorsement on the Klan cross, which would make the State's role clear to the community. ...

a. A concurring opinion by Justice Thomas is omitted.

... I part company with the plurality on a fundamental point: I disagree that "[i]t has radical implications for our public policy to suggest that neutral laws are invalid whenever hypothetical observers may—even reasonably—confuse an incidental benefit to religion with State endorsement." On the contrary, when the reasonable observer would view a government practice as endorsing religion, I believe that it is our duty to hold the practice invalid. ...

. . .

In the end, I would recognize that the Establishment Clause inquiry cannot be distilled into a fixed, per se rule. ...

II

Today, Justice Stevens reaches a different conclusion regarding whether the Board's decision to allow respondents' display on Capitol Square constituted an impermissible endorsement of the cross' religious message. Yet I believe it is important to note that we have not simply arrived at divergent results after conducting the same analysis. Our fundamental point of departure, it appears, concerns the knowledge that is properly attributed to the test's "reasonable observer [who] evaluates whether a challenged governmental practice conveys a message of endorsement of religion." In my view, proper application of the endorsement test requires that the reasonable observer be deemed more informed than the casual passerby postulated by the dissent.

. . .

I therefore disagree that the endorsement test should focus on the actual perception of individual observers, who naturally have differing degrees of knowledge. ... In my view, ... the endorsement test creates a more collective standard ... In this respect, the applicable observer is similar to the "reasonable person" in tort law ... A State has not made religion relevant to standing in the political community simply because a particular viewer of a display might feel uncomfortable.

. . .

The dissent's property-based argument fails to give sufficient weight to the fact that the cross at issue here was displayed in a forum traditionally open to the public. ... The reasonable observer would recognize the distinction between speech the government supports and speech that it merely allows in a place that traditionally has been open to a range of private speakers accompanied, if necessary, by an appropriate disclaimer.

In this case, I believe, the reasonable observer would view the Klan's cross display fully aware that Capitol Square is a public space in which a multiplicity of groups, both secular and religious, engage in expressive conduct. ... On the facts of this case, therefore, I conclude that the reasonable observer would not interpret the State's tolerance of the Klan's private religious display in Capitol Square as an endorsement of religion.

. . .

Justice Souter, with whom Justice O'Connor and Justice Breyer join, concurring in part and concurring in the judgment.

I concur in Parts I, II, and III of the Court's opinion. ...

... [M]y analysis of the Establishment Clause issue differs from Justice Scalia's, and I vote to affirm in large part because of the possibility of affixing a sign to the cross adequately disclaiming any government sponsorship or endorsement of it.

The plurality's opinion declines to apply the endorsement test to the Board's action, in favor of a per se rule ... This per se rule would be an exception to the endorsement test, not previously recognized and out of square with our precedents.

I

... [I]n some circumstances an intelligent observer may mistake private, unattended religious displays in a public forum for government speech endorsing religion. ...

... Given the domination of the square by the government's own displays, one would not be a dimwit as a matter of law to think that an unattended religious display there was endorsed by the government, even though the square has also been the site of three privately sponsored, unattended displays over the years ... When an individual speaks in a public forum, it is reasonable for an observer to attribute the speech, first and foremost, to the speaker, while an unattended display (and any message it conveys) can naturally be viewed as belonging to the owner of the land on which it stands.

In sum, I do not understand that I am at odds with the plurality when I assume that in some circumstances an intelligent observer would reasonably perceive private religious expression in a public forum to imply the government's endorsement of religion. My disagreement with the plurality is simply that I would attribute these perceptions of the intelligent observer to the reasonable observer of Establishment Clause analysis under our precedents, where I believe that such reasonable perceptions matter.

II

. . .

Allegheny County's endorsement test cannot be dismissed, as Justice Scalia suggests, as applying only to situations in which there is an allegation that the Establishment Clause has been violated through "expression by the government itself" or "government action ... discriminat[ing] in favor of private religious expression." ... Unless we are to retreat entirely to government intent and abandon consideration of effects, it makes no sense to recognize a public perception of endorsement as a harm only in that subclass of cases in which the government owns the display. ...

. . .

III

As for the specifics of this case, one must admit that a number of facts known to the Board, or reasonably anticipated, weighed in favor of upholding its denial of the permit. For example, the Latin cross the Klan sought to erect is the principal symbol of Christianity around the world, and display of the cross alone could not reasonably be taken to have any secular point. It was displayed immediately in front of the Ohio Statehouse, with the government's flags flying nearby, and the government's statues close at hand. For much of the time the cross was supposed to stand on the square, it would have been the only private display on the public plot (the menorah's permit expired several days before the cross actually went up). There was nothing else on the Statehouse lawn that would have suggested a forum open to any and all private, unattended religious displays.

Based on these and other factors, the Board was understandably concerned about a possible Establishment Clause violation if it had granted the permit. But a flat denial of the Klan's application was not the Board's only option to protect against an appearance of endorsement, and the Board was required to find its most "narrowly drawn" alternative. ... The Board, ... could have granted the application subject to the condition that the Klan attach a disclaimer ... In the alternative, the Board could have instituted a policy of restricting all private, unattended displays to one area of the square, with a permanent sign marking the area as a forum for private speech carrying no endorsement from the State.

With such alternatives available, the Board cannot claim that its flat denial was a narrowly tailored response to the Klan's permit application and thus cannot rely on that denial as necessary to ensure that the State did not "appea[r] to take a position on questions of religious belief." ... For these reasons, I concur in the judgment.

Justice Stevens, dissenting.

The Establishment Clause should be construed to create a strong presumption against the installation of unattended religious symbols on public property. Although the State of Ohio has allowed Capitol Square, the area around the seat of its government, to be used as a public forum, and although it has occasionally allowed private groups to erect other sectarian displays there, neither fact provides a sufficient basis for rebutting that presumption. On the contrary, the sequence of sectarian displays disclosed by the record in this case illustrates the importance of rebuilding the "wall of separation between church and State" that Jefferson envisioned.

. . .

II

. . .

In determining whether the State's maintenance of the Klan's cross in front of the Statehouse conveyed a forbidden message of endorsement, we should be mindful of the power of a symbol standing alone and unexplained. Even on private property, signs and symbols are generally understood to express the owner's views. The location of the sign is a significant component of the message it conveys.

. . .

III

. . .

... For a religious display to violate the Establishment Clause, I think it is enough that some reasonable observers would attribute a religious message to the State.

The plurality appears to rely on the history of this particular public forum—specifically, it emphasizes that Ohio has in the past allowed three other private unattended displays. Even if the State could not reasonably have been understood to endorse the prior displays, I would not find this argument convincing, because it assumes that all reasonable viewers know all about the history of Capitol Square-a highly unlikely supposition. But the plurality's argument fails on its own terms, because each of the three previous displays conveyed the same message of approval and endorsement that this one does.

. . .

Justice Ginsburg, dissenting.

We confront here . . . a large Latin cross that stood alone and unattended in close proximity to Ohio's Statehouse. . . . Near the stationary cross were the government's flags and the government's statues. No human speaker was present to disassociate the religious symbol from the State. No other private display was in sight. No plainly visible sign informed the public that the cross belonged to the Klan and that Ohio's government did not endorse the display's message.

If the aim of the Establishment Clause is genuinely to uncouple government from church, . . . a State may not permit, and a court may not order, a display of this character. . . . Justice Souter, in the final paragraphs of his opinion, suggests two arrangements that might have distanced the State . . .: a sufficiently large and clear disclaimer; or an area reserved for unattended displays carrying no endorsement from the State, a space plainly and permanently so marked. Neither arrangement is even arguably present in this case. The District Court's order did not mandate a disclaimer. And the disclaimer the Klan appended to the foot of the cross was unsturdy: it did not identify the Klan as sponsor; it failed to state unequivocally that Ohio did not endorse the display's message; and it was not shown to be legible from a distance. The relief ordered by the District Court thus violated the Establishment Clause.

Whether a court order allowing display of a cross, but demanding a sturdier disclaimer, could withstand Establishment Clause analysis is a question more difficult than the one this case poses. I would reserve that question for another day and case. But I would not let the prospect of what might have been permissible control today's decision on the constitutionality of the display the District Court's order in fact authorized.

Good News Club v. Milford Central School

533 U.S. 98, 121 S.Ct. 2093, 150 L.Ed.2d 151 (2001).

Justice Thomas delivered the opinion of the Court.

This case presents two questions. The first question is whether Milford Central School violated the free speech rights of the Good News Club when it excluded the Club from meeting after hours at the school. The second question is whether any such violation is justified by Milford's concern that permitting the Club's activities would violate the Establishment Clause. We conclude that Milford's restriction violates the Club's free speech rights and that no Establishment Clause concern justifies that violation.

I

. . . In 1992, respondent Milford Central School (Milford) enacted a community use policy adopting seven . . . purposes for which its building could be used after school. Two of the stated purposes are relevant here. First, district residents may use the school for "instruction in any branch of education, learning or the arts." Second, the school is available for "social, civic and recreational meetings and entertainment events, and other uses pertaining to the welfare of the community, provided that such uses shall be nonexclusive and shall be opened to the general public."

Stephen and Darleen Fournier reside within Milford's district and therefore are eligible to use the school's facilities as long as their proposed use is approved by the school. Together they are sponsors of the local Good News Club, a private Christian organization for children ages 6 to 12. Pursuant to Milford's policy, ... the Fourniers submitted a request to Dr. Robert McGruder, interim superintendent of the district, in which they sought permission to hold the Club's weekly afterschool meetings in the school cafeteria. ... McGruder formally denied the Fourniers' request on the ground that the proposed use—to have "a fun time of singing songs, hearing a Bible lesson and memorizing scripture," was "the equivalent of religious worship." According to McGruder, the community use policy, which prohibits use "by any individual or organization for religious purposes," foreclosed the Club's activities.

... Milford's attorney requested information to clarify the nature of the Club's activities. The Club sent a set of materials used or distributed at the meetings and the following description of its meeting:

> "The Club opens its session with Ms. Fournier taking attendance. As she calls a child's name, if the child recites a Bible verse the child receives a treat. After attendance, the Club sings songs. Next Club members engage in games that involve, inter alia, learning Bible verses. Ms. Fournier then relates a Bible story and explains how it applies to Club members' lives. The Club closes with prayer. Finally, Ms. Fournier distributes treats and the Bible verses for memorization."

McGruder and Milford's attorney reviewed the materials and concluded that "the kinds of activities proposed to be engaged in by the Good News Club were not a discussion of secular subjects such as child rearing, development of character and development of morals from a religious perspective, but were in fact the equivalent of religious instruction itself." ... [T]he Milford Board of Education adopted a resolution rejecting the Club's request to use Milford's facilities "for the purpose of conducting religious instruction and Bible study."

... [P]etitioners, the Good News Club, Ms. Fournier, and her daughter Andrea Fournier (collectively, the Club), filed an action under 42 U.S.C. § 1983 against Milford in the United States District Court for the Northern District of New York. ...

> ...

... [T]he District Court ... granted Milford's motion for summary judgment. ...

... [A] divided panel of the United States Court of Appeals for the Second Circuit affirmed. ...

There is a conflict among the Courts of Appeals on the question whether speech can be excluded from a limited public forum on the basis of the religious nature of the speech. ... We granted certiorari to resolve this conflict.

II

The standards that we apply to determine whether a State has unconstitutionally excluded a private speaker from use of a public forum depend on the nature of the forum.... We have previously declined to decide whether a school district's opening of its facilities ... creates a limited or a traditional public forum. ... Because the parties have agreed that Milford created a limited public forum when it opened its facilities in 1992, we need not resolve the issue here. Instead, we simply will assume that Milford operates a limited public forum.

When the State establishes a limited public forum, the State is not required to and does not allow persons to engage in every type of speech. The State may be justified "in reserving [its forum] for certain groups or for the discussion of certain topics." ... The State's power to restrict speech, however, is not without limits. The restriction must not discriminate against speech on the basis of viewpoint, ... and the restriction must be "reasonable in light of the purpose served by the forum," ...

III

Applying this test, we first address whether the exclusion constituted viewpoint discrimination. We are guided in our analysis by two of our prior opinions, *Lamb's Chapel* [v. Center Moriches Union Free School Dist., 508 U.S. 384 (1993)] and *Rosenberger* [v. Rector and Visitors of Univ. of Va., 515 U.S. 819 (1995)]. In *Lamb's Chapel*, we held that a school district violated the Free Speech Clause of the First Amendment when it excluded a private group from presenting films at the school based solely on the films' discussions of family values from a religious perspective. Likewise, in *Rosenberger*, we held that a university's refusal to fund a student publication because the publication addressed issues from a religious perspective violated the Free Speech Clause. Concluding that Milford's exclusion of the Good News Club based on its religious nature is indistinguishable from the exclusions in these cases, we hold that the exclusion constitutes viewpoint discrimination. Because the restriction is viewpoint discriminatory, we need not decide whether it is unreasonable in light of the purposes served by the forum.

Milford has opened its limited public forum to activities that serve a variety of purposes, including events "pertaining to the welfare of the community." ... In short, any group that "promote[s] the moral and character development of children" is eligible to use the school building.

Just as there is no question that teaching morals and character development to children is a permissible purpose under Milford's policy, it is clear that the Club teaches morals and character development to children. For example, no one disputes that the Club instructs children to overcome feelings of jealousy, to treat others well regardless of how they treat the children, and to be obedient, even if it does so in a nonsecular way. Nonetheless, because Milford found the Club's activities to be religious in nature—"the equivalent of religious instruction itself," it excluded the Club from use of its facilities.

Applying *Lamb's Chapel*, we find it quite clear that Milford engaged in viewpoint discrimination when it excluded the Club from the afterschool forum. In *Lamb's Chapel*, the local New York school district similarly had adopted ... "social, civic or recreational use" ... as a permitted use in its limited public forum. The district also prohibited use "by any group for religious purposes." ... Citing this prohibition, the school district excluded a church that wanted to present films teaching family values from a Christian perspective. We held that, because the films "no doubt dealt with a subject otherwise permissible" under the rule, the teaching of family values, the district's exclusion of the church was unconstitutional viewpoint discrimination. ...

Like the church in *Lamb's Chapel*, the Club seeks to address a subject otherwise permitted under the rule, the teaching of morals and character, from a religious standpoint. ... The only apparent difference between the activity of Lamb's Chapel and the activities of the Good News Club is that the Club chooses to teach moral lessons from a Christian perspective through live storytelling and prayer, whereas Lamb's Chapel taught lessons through films. This distinction is inconsequential. Both modes of speech use a religious viewpoint. Thus, the exclusion of the Good News Club's activities, like the exclusion of Lamb's Chapel's films, constitutes unconstitutional viewpoint discrimination.

Our opinion in *Rosenberger* also is dispositive. In *Rosenberger*, a student organization at the University of Virginia was denied funding for printing expenses because its publication, Wide Awake, offered a Christian viewpoint. Just as the Club emphasizes the role of Christianity in students' morals and character, Wide Awake "challenge[d] Christians to live, in word and deed, according to the faith they proclaim and . . . encourage[d] students to consider what a personal relationship with Jesus Christ means." . . . Because the university "select[ed] for disfavored treatment those student journalistic efforts with religious editorial viewpoints," we held that the denial of funding was unconstitutional. . . . Although in *Rosenberger* there was no prohibition on religion as a subject matter, our holding did not rely on this factor. Instead, we concluded simply that the university's denial of funding to print Wide Awake was viewpoint discrimination, just as the school district's refusal to allow Lamb's Chapel to show its films was viewpoint discrimination. Given the obvious religious content of Wide Awake, we cannot say that the Club's activities are any more "religious" or deserve any less First Amendment protection than did the publication of Wide Awake in *Rosenberger*.

Despite our holdings in *Lamb's Chapel* and *Rosenberger*, the Court of Appeals, like Milford, believed that its characterization of the Club's activities as religious in nature warranted treating the Club's activities as different in kind from the other activities permitted by the school. . . .

We disagree that something that is "quintessentially religious" or "decidedly religious in nature" cannot also be characterized properly as the teaching of morals and character development from a particular viewpoint. . . . What matters for purposes of the Free Speech Clause is that we can see no logical difference in kind between the invocation of Christianity by the Club and the invocation of teamwork, loyalty, or patriotism by other associations to provide a foundation for their lessons. . . . [W]e reaffirm our holdings in *Lamb's Chapel* and *Rosenberger* that speech discussing otherwise permissible subjects cannot be excluded from a limited public forum on the ground that the subject is discussed from a religious viewpoint. Thus, we conclude that Milford's exclusion of the Club from use of the school, pursuant to its community use policy, constitutes impermissible viewpoint discrimination.

IV

Milford argues that, even if its restriction constitutes viewpoint discrimination, its interest in not violating the Establishment Clause outweighs the Club's interest in gaining equal access to the school's facilities. . . . We disagree.

We have said that a state interest in avoiding an Establishment Clause violation "may be characterized as compelling," and therefore may justify content-based discrimination. . . . However, it is not clear whether a State's interest in avoiding an Establishment Clause violation would justify viewpoint discrimination. . . . We need not, however, confront the issue in this case, because we conclude that the school has no valid Establishment Clause interest.

We rejected Establishment Clause defenses similar to Milford's in . . . *Lamb's Chapel* . . . [W]e explained that "[t]he showing of th[e] film series would not have been during school hours, would not have been sponsored by the school, and would have been open to the public, not just to church members." . . .

. . .

Milford attempts to distinguish *Lamb's Chapel* . . . by emphasizing that Milford's policy involves elementary school children. According to Milford, children will perceive that the school is endorsing the Club and will feel coercive pressure to participate, because the Club's activities take place on school grounds, even though they occur during nonschool hours. This argument is unpersuasive.

First, we have held that "a significant factor in upholding governmental programs in the face of Establishment Clause attack is their neutrality towards religion." *Rosenberger*, . . . Milford's implication that granting access to the Club would do damage to the neutrality principle defies logic. For the "guarantee of neutrality is respected, not offended, when the government, following neutral criteria and evenhanded policies, extends benefits to recipients whose ideologies and viewpoints, including religious ones, are broad and diverse." *Rosenberger* . . . The Good News Club seeks nothing more than to be treated neutrally and given access to speak about the same topics as are other groups. Because allowing the Club to speak on school grounds would ensure neutrality, not threaten it, Milford faces an uphill battle in arguing that the Establishment Clause compels it to exclude the Good News Club.

Second, to the extent we consider whether the community would feel coercive pressure to engage in the Club's activities, . . . the relevant community would be the parents, not the elementary school children. It is the parents who choose whether their children will attend the Good News Club meetings. Because the children cannot attend without their parents' permission, they cannot be coerced into engaging in the Good News Club's religious activities. Milford does not suggest that the parents of elementary school children would be confused about whether the school was endorsing religion. Nor do we believe that such an argument could be reasonably advanced.

Third, whatever significance we may have assigned in the Establishment Clause context to the suggestion that elementary school children are more impressionable than adults, . . . we have never extended our Establishment Clause jurisprudence to foreclose private religious conduct during nonschool hours merely because it takes place on school premises where elementary school children may be present.

None of the cases discussed by Milford persuades us that our Establishment Clause jurisprudence has gone this far. For example, Milford cites Lee v. Weisman [505 U.S. 577 (1992)] for the proposition that "there are heightened concerns with protecting freedom of conscience from subtle coercive pressure in the elementary and secondary public schools," . . . In *Lee*, however, we concluded that attendance at the graduation exercise was obligatory. . . . We did not place independent significance on the fact that the graduation exercise might take place on school premises. . . . Here, where the school facilities are being used for a nonschool function and there is no government sponsorship of the Club's activities, *Lee* is inapposite.

Equally unsupportive is Edwards v. Aguillard, 482 U.S. 578 (1987), in which we held that a Louisiana law that proscribed the teaching of evolution as part of the public school curriculum, unless accompanied by a lesson on creationism, violated the Establishment Clause. In *Edwards*, we mentioned that students are susceptible to pressure in the classroom, particularly given their possible reliance on teachers as role models. But we did not discuss this concern in our application of the law to the facts. Moreover, we did note that mandatory attendance requirements meant that State advancement of religion in a school would be particularly harshly felt by impressionable students. But we did not suggest that, when the school was not actually advancing religion, the impressionability of students would be relevant to the Establishment Clause issue. Even if *Edwards* had articulated the principle Milford believes it did, the facts in *Edwards* are simply too remote from those here to give the principle any weight. *Edwards* involved the content of the curriculum taught by state teachers during the schoolday to children required to attend. Obviously, when individuals who are not schoolteachers are giving lessons after school to children permitted to attend only with parental consent, the concerns expressed in Edwards are not present.

Fourth, even if we were to consider the possible misperceptions by schoolchildren in deciding whether Milford's permitting the Club's activities would violate the Establishment Clause, the facts of this case simply do not support Milford's conclusion. There is no evidence that young children are permitted to loiter outside classrooms after the schoolday has ended. Surely even young children are aware of events for which their parents must sign permission forms. The meetings were held in a combined high school resource room and middle school special education room, not in an elementary school classroom. The instructors are not schoolteachers. And the children in the group are not all the same age as in the normal classroom setting; their ages range from 6 to 12. In sum, these circumstances simply do not support the theory that small children would perceive endorsement here.

Finally, even if we were to inquire into the minds of schoolchildren in this case, we cannot say the danger that children would misperceive the endorsement of religion is any greater than the danger that they would perceive a hostility toward the religious viewpoint if the Club were excluded from the public forum....

... We cannot operate ... under the assumption that any risk that small children would perceive endorsement should counsel in favor of excluding the Club's religious activity. We decline to employ Establishment Clause jurisprudence using a modified heckler's veto, in which a group's religious activity can be proscribed on the basis of what the youngest members of the audience might misperceive. ...

. . .

V

When Milford denied the Good News Club access to the school's limited public forum on the ground that the Club was religious in nature, it discriminated against the Club because of its religious viewpoint in violation of the Free Speech Clause of the First Amendment. Because Milford has not raised a valid Establishment Clause claim, we do not address the question whether such a claim could excuse Milford's viewpoint discrimination.

. . .

Justice Scalia, concurring.

I join the Court's opinion but write separately to explain further my views on two issues.

I

First, I join Part IV of the Court's opinion, regarding the Establishment Clause issue, with the understanding that its consideration of coercive pressure, and perceptions of endorsement, "to the extent" that the law makes such factors relevant, is consistent with the belief (which I hold) that in this case that extent is zero. ... Physical coercion is not at issue here; and so-called "peer pressure," if it can even been considered coercion, is, when it arises from private activities, one of the attendant consequences of a freedom of association that is constitutionally protected ... What is at play here is not coercion, but the compulsion of ideas—and the private right to exert and receive that compulsion (or to have one's children receive it) is protected by the Free Speech and Free Exercise Clauses, ... not banned by the Establishment Clause. A priest has as much liberty to proselytize as a patriot.

As to endorsement, I have previously written that "[r]eligious expression cannot violate the Establishment Clause where it (1) is purely private and (2) occurs in a traditional or designated public forum, publicly announced and open to all on equal terms." ...

II

Second, since we have rejected the only reason that respondent gave for excluding the Club's speech from a forum that clearly included it (the forum was opened to any "us[e] pertaining to the welfare of the community ...") I do not suppose it matters whether the exclusion is characterized as viewpoint or subject-matter discrimination. ...

As I understand it, the point of disagreement between the Court and the dissenters ... with regard to petitioner's Free Speech Clause claim is not whether the Good News Club must be permitted to present religious viewpoints on morals and character in respondent's forum....

The disagreement, rather, regards the portions of the Club's meetings that are not "purely" "discussions" of morality and character from a religious viewpoint. The Club, for example, urges children "who already believe in the Lord Jesus as their Savior" to "[s]top and ask God for the strength and the 'want' ... to obey Him,".... The dissenters ... say that the presence of such additional speech, because it is purely religious, transforms the Club's meetings into something different in kind from other, nonreligious activities that teach moral and character development.... I disagree.

. . .

From no other group does respondent require the sterility of speech that it demands of petitioners. ... The Club may not ... independently discuss the religious premise on which its views are based—that God exists and His assistance is necessary to morality. It may not defend the premise, and it absolutely must not seek to persuade the children that the premise is true. The children must, so to say, take it on faith. This is blatant viewpoint discrimination.

. . .

The dissenters emphasize that the religious speech used by the Club as the foundation for its views on morals and character is not just any type of religious speech.... In Justice Stevens' view, it is speech "aimed principally at proselytizing or inculcating belief in a particular religious faith." This does not ... distinguish the Club's activities from those of the other groups using respondent's forum—which have not, as Justice Stevens suggests, been restricted to roundtable "discussions" of moral issues. ...

Justice Souter, while agreeing that the Club's religious speech "may be characterized as proselytizing," thinks that it is even more clearly excludable from respondent's forum because it is essentially "an evangelical service of worship." But we have previously rejected the attempt to distinguish worship from other religious speech . . . If the distinction did have content, it would be beyond the courts' competence to administer. . . .

. . .

Justice Breyer, concurring in part.

I agree with the Court's conclusion and join its opinion to the extent that they are consistent with the following three observations. First, the government's "neutrality" in respect to religion is one, but only one, of the considerations relevant to deciding whether a public school's policy violates the Establishment Clause. . . .

Second, the critical Establishment Clause question here may well prove to be whether a child, participating in the Good News Club's activities, could reasonably perceive the school's permission for the club to use its facilities as an endorsement of religion. . . .

Third, the Court cannot fully answer the Establishment Clause question this case raises, given its procedural posture. . . .

To deny one party's motion for summary judgment . . . is not to grant summary judgment for the other side. There may be disputed "genuine issue[s]" of "material fact," . . . particularly about how a reasonable child participant would understand the school's role. . . . The Court's invocation of what is missing from the record and its assumptions about what is present in the record only confirm that both parties, if they so desire, should have a fair opportunity to fill the evidentiary gap in light of today's opinion. . . .

Justice Stevens, dissenting.

The Milford Central School has invited the public to use its facilities for educational and recreational purposes, but not for "religious purposes." Speech for "religious purposes" may reasonably be understood to encompass three different categories. First, there is religious speech that is simply speech about a particular topic from a religious point of view. . . . Second, there is religious speech that amounts to worship, or its equivalent. . . . Third, there is an intermediate category that is aimed principally at proselytizing or inculcating belief in a particular religious faith.

A public entity may not generally exclude even religious worship from an open public forum. . . . Similarly, a public entity that creates a limited public forum for the discussion of certain specified topics may not exclude a speaker simply because she approaches those topics from a religious point of view. . . .

. . . The novel question that this case presents concerns the constitutionality of a public school's attempt to limit the scope of a public forum it has created. More specifically, the question is whether a school can, consistently with the First Amendment, create a limited public forum that admits the first type of religious speech without allowing the other two.

. . . If a school decides to authorize after school discussions of current events in its classrooms, it may not exclude people from expressing their views simply because it dislikes their particular political opinions. But must it therefore allow organized political groups—for example, the Democratic Party, the Libertarian Party, or the Ku Klux Klan—to hold meetings, the principal purpose of which is not to discuss the current-events topic from their own unique point of view but rather to recruit others to join their respective groups? I think not. . . .

School officials may reasonably believe that evangelical meetings designed to convert children to a particular religious faith pose the same risk. And, just as a school may allow meetings to discuss current events from a political perspective without also allowing organized political recruitment, so too can a school allow discussion of topics such as moral development from a religious (or nonreligious) perspective without thereby opening its forum to religious prose-lytizing or worship. . . .

. . .

This case is undoubtedly close. Nonetheless, regardless of whether the Good News Club's activities amount to "worship," it does seem clear, based on the facts in the record, that the school district correctly classified those activities as falling within the third category of religious speech and therefore beyond the scope of the school's limited public forum. . . .

. . .

Justice Souter, with whom Justice Ginsburg joins, dissenting.

. . .

I

. . .

This case, like *Lamb's Chapel*, properly raises no issue about the reason-ableness of Milford's criteria for restricting the scope of its designated public forum. . . .

The sole question before the District Court was, therefore, whether, in refusing to allow Good News's intended use, Milford was misapplying its unchallenged restriction in a way that amounted to imposing a viewpoint-based restriction on what could be said or done by a group entitled to use the forum for an educational, civic, or other permitted purpose. . . .

. . .

. . . [T]he . . . undisputed facts in this case differ from those in *Lamb's Chapel*, as night from day. . . .

. . .

It is beyond question that Good News intends to use the public school premises not for the mere discussion of a subject from a particular, Christian point of view, but for an evangelical service of worship calling children to commit themselves in an act of Christian conversion. The majority avoids this reality only by resorting to the bland and general characterization of Good News's activity as "teaching of morals and character, from a religious stand-point." If the majority's statement ignores reality, as it surely does, then today's holding may be understood only in equally generic terms. Otherwise, indeed, this case would stand for the remarkable proposition that any public school opened for civic meetings must be opened for use as a church, syna-gogue, or mosque.

II

I also respectfully dissent from the majority's refusal to remand on all other issues, insisting instead on acting as a court of first instance in reviewing

Milford's claim that it would violate the Establishment Clause to grant Good News's application....

. . .

What we know about this case looks very little like ... *Lamb's Chapel*. The cohort addressed by Good News is not university students with relative maturity, or even high school pupils, but elementary school children as young as six. The Establishment Clause cases have consistently recognized the particular impressionability of schoolchildren, ... and the special protection required for those in the elementary grades in the school forum....

Nor is Milford's limited forum anything like the sites for wide-ranging intellectual exchange that were home to the challenged activities in ... *Lamb's Chapel*. See also *Rosenberger*....

The timing and format of Good News's gatherings ... may well affirmatively suggest the imprimatur of officialdom in the minds of the young children. The club is open solely to elementary students (not the entire community, as in Lamb's Chapel), only four outside groups have been identified as meeting in the school, and Good News is, seemingly, the only one whose instruction follows immediately on the conclusion of the official school day. ... In fact, the temporal and physical continuity of Good News's meetings with the regular school routine seems to be the whole point of using the school. When meetings were held in a community church, 8 or 10 children attended; after the school became the site, the number went up three-fold.

. . .

C. FINANCIAL AID TO CHURCH–RELATED SCHOOLS AND CHURCH–RELATED INSTRUCTION

1. ELEMENTARY AND SECONDARY SCHOOLS

AID TO PUPILS AND THEIR PARENTS

In *Everson* the Court upheld the provision of transportation of students to religious schools. In Board of Educ. v. Allen, 392 U.S. 236 (1968), the Court by a vote of 6 to 3 upheld a New York law providing for the loaning of text books free of charge to students in all private schools, including church schools. The Court decided that the state statute was valid because "no funds or books are furnished to parochial schools, and the financial benefit is to parents and children, not to schools. Perhaps free books make it more likely that some children choose to attend a sectarian school, but that was true of the state-paid bus fares in *Everson* and does not alone demonstrate an unconstitutional degree of support for a religious institution." Justice Black, who had written the *Everson* opinion, was one of the dissenters. He said: "[I]t is not difficult to distinguish books, which are the heart of any school, from bus fares, which provide a convenient and helpful general public transportation service."

PAYMENTS TO RELIGIOUS SCHOOLS

The *Allen* decision added fuel to the controversy whether direct government payments to religious elementary and secondary schools violated the establishment clause. In Lemon v. Kurtzman, 403 U.S. 602 (1971), however, the Court struck down a Pennsylvania statute authorizing reimbursement of nonpublic schools for part of the expenses of teachers' salaries, textbooks and instructional materials. A possible simple distinction between aid to religious schools and aid to parents and children, for expenses of attending religious schools, did not survive the next round of cases. In 1973, the Court concluded that direct grants to parents, to reimburse the costs of their children's attendance at nonpublic schools, were also invalid. Committee for Public Education and Religious Liberty v. Nyquist, 413 U.S. 756 (1973); Sloan v. Lemon, 413 U.S. 825 (1973).

TAX EXEMPTIONS, DEDUCTIONS AND CREDITS

In Walz v. Tax Commission of New York, 397 U.S. 664 (1970), the Court sustained the universal practice of exempting church property used for religious worship from the payment of real estate taxes. The Court concluded that the "unbroken practice" of according tax exemptions to churches had not led to an established church and had "operated affirmatively to help guarantee the free exercise of all forms of religious beliefs."

Two cases concerning tax treatment of parents' payments for the cost of religious education are in some tension. In Committee for Public Education & Religious Liberty v. Nyquist, 413 U.S. 756 (1973), the Court struck down a state law giving tax credits, whose amounts were determined by parental income, for each child attending a nonpublic school. The Court concluded that the tax credits were indistinguishable from direct tuition grants to parents—a practice also held invalid in *Nyquist*. In Mueller v. Allen, 463 U.S. 388 (1983), however, the Court sustained state income tax deductions for amounts spent on tuition, textbook, and transportation expenses of children attending elementary or secondary schools. The Court noted that the deduction was applicable to expenses for schooling of all children, including those attending public schools (although the most substantial benefit would flow to parents whose children attended schools charging tuition). Moreover, the tax benefit took the form of a deduction, rather than a fixed dollar credit.

The Court distinguished both Walz v. Tax Commission and Mueller v. Allen in Texas Monthly v. Bullock, 489 U.S. 1 (1989). The Court held that it was unconstitutional to exempt from a sales tax applicable to periodicals generally, sales of periodicals "published or distributed by a religious faith and that consist wholly of writings promulgating the teachings of the faith and books that consist wholly of writings sacred to a religious faith." Here, the exemption was equivalent to a subsidy amounting to state sponsorship of religious belief. In *Walz,* the tax exemption was within a broad class of charitable tax exemptions, and in *Mueller* the exemption was equally available to parents sending their children to nonsectarian schools.

Agostini v. Felton

521 U.S. 203, 117 S.Ct. 1997, 138 L.Ed.2d 391 (1997).

Justice O'Connor delivered the opinion of the Court.

In Aguilar v. Felton, 473 U.S. 402 (1985), this Court held that the Establishment Clause of the First Amendment barred the city of New York from sending public school teachers into parochial schools to provide remedial education to disadvantaged children pursuant to a congressionally mandated program. On remand, the District Court for the Eastern District of New York entered a permanent injunction reflecting our ruling. Twelve years later, petitioners—the parties bound by that injunction—seek relief from its operation. Petitioners maintain that *Aguilar* cannot be squared with our intervening Establishment Clause jurisprudence and ask that we explicitly recognize what our more recent cases already dictate: *Aguilar* is no longer good law. We agree with petitioners that *Aguilar* is not consistent with our subsequent Establishment Clause decisions and further conclude that, on the facts presented here, petitioners are entitled under Federal Rule of Civil Procedure 60(b)(5) to relief from the operation of the District Court's prospective injunction.

I

In 1965, Congress enacted Title I of the Elementary and Secondary Education Act of 1965, 79 Stat. 27, as modified, 20 U.S.C. § 6301 et seq., to "provid[e] full educational opportunity to every child regardless of economic background." ...

In 1978, six federal taxpayers—respondents here—sued the Board in the District Court for the Eastern District of New York. Respondents sought declaratory and injunctive relief, claiming that the Board's Title I program violated the Establishment Clause.... The District Court granted summary judgment for the Board, but the Court of Appeals for the Second Circuit reversed.... [T]his Court affirmed on the ground that the Board's Title I program necessitated an "excessive entanglement of church and state in the administration of [Title I] benefits." ... On remand, the District Court permanently enjoined the Board "from using public funds for any plan or program under [Title I] to the extent that it requires, authorizes or permits public school teachers and guidance counselors to provide teaching and counseling services on the premises of sectarian schools within New York City."

The Board, like other LEA's across the United States, modified its Title I program so it could continue serving those students who attended private religious schools. Rather than offer Title I instruction to parochial school students at their schools, the Board reverted to its prior practice of providing instruction at public school sites, at leased sites, and in mobile instructional units (essentially vans converted into classrooms) parked near the sectarian school. The Board also offered computer-aided instruction, which could be provided "on premises" because it did not require public employees to be physically present on the premises of a religious school.

It is not disputed that the additional costs of complying with *Aguilar*'s mandate are significant. Since the 1986–1987 school year, the Board has spent over $100 million providing computer-aided instruction, leasing sites and mobile instructional units, and transporting students to those sites.... These "*Aguilar* costs" ... reduce the amount of Title I money an LEA has available for remedial education, and LEA's have had to cut back on the number of students who receive Title I benefits....

In October and December of 1995, petitioners—the Board and a new group of parents of parochial school students entitled to Title I services—filed motions in the District Court seeking relief under Federal Rule of Civil Procedure 60(b) from the permanent injunction entered by the District Court on remand from our decision in Aguilar.... Specifically, petitioners pointed to the statements of five Justices in Board of Ed. of Kiryas Joel Village School Dist. v. Grumet, 512 U.S. 687 (1994), calling for the overruling of *Aguilar*. The District Court denied the motion.... The Court of Appeals for the Second Circuit [affirmed.] We ... reverse.

II

. . .

Petitioners point to three changes in the factual and legal landscape that they believe justify their claim for relief under Rule 60(b)(5). They first contend that the exorbitant costs of complying with the District Court's injunction constitute a significant factual development warranting modification of the injunction. Petitioners also argue that there have been two significant legal developments since *Aguilar* was decided: a majority of Justices have expressed their views that *Aguilar* should be reconsidered or overruled; and *Aguilar* has in any event been undermined by subsequent Establishment Clause decisions . . .

. . .

. . . [P]etitioners have failed to establish . . . significant change in factual conditions. . . .

. . . [T]he statements made by five Justices in *Kiryas Joel* do not, in themselves, furnish a basis for concluding that our Establishment Clause jurisprudence has changed. In *Kiryas Joel*, we considered the constitutionality of a New York law that carved out a public school district to coincide with the boundaries of the village of Kiryas Joel, which was an enclave of the Satmar Hasidic sect. Before the new district was created, Satmar children wishing to receive special educational services under the Individuals with Disabilities Education Act (IDEA), . . . could receive those services at public schools located outside the village. Because Satmar parents rarely permitted their children to attend those schools, New York created a new public school district within the boundaries of the village so that Satmar children could stay within the village but receive IDEA services on public school premises from publicly employed instructors. In the course of our opinion, we observed that New York had created the special school district in response to our decision in *Aguilar*, which had required New York to cease providing IDEA services to Satmar children on the premises of their private religious schools. . . . Five Justices joined opinions calling for reconsideration of *Aguilar*. [O'Connor, Kennedy, Scalia, Rehnquist and Thomas.] But the question of *Aguilar*'s propriety was not before us. The views of five Justices that the case should be reconsidered or overruled cannot be said to have effected a change in Establishment Clause law.

In light of these conclusions, petitioners' ability to satisfy the prerequisites of Rule 60(b)(5) hinges on whether our later Establishment Clause cases have so undermined *Aguilar* that it is no longer good law. We now turn to that inquiry.

III

A

In order to evaluate whether *Aguilar* has been eroded by our subsequent Establishment Clause cases, it is necessary to understand the rationale upon which *Aguilar*, as well as its companion case, School Dist. of Grand Rapids v. Ball, 473 U.S. 373 (1985), rested.

In *Ball*, the Court evaluated two programs implemented by the School District of Grand Rapids, Michigan. The district's Shared Time program, the one most analogous to Title I, provided remedial and "enrichment" classes, at public expense, to students attending nonpublic schools. The classes were taught during regular school hours by publicly employed teachers, using materials purchased with public funds, on the premises of nonpublic schools. The Shared Time courses were in subjects designed to supplement the "core curriculum" of the nonpublic schools. . . . Of the 41 nonpublic schools eligible for the program, 40 were " 'pervasively sectarian' " in character—that is, "the purpos[e] of [those] schools [was] to advance their particular religions." . . .

. . .

Distilled to essentials, the Court's conclusion that the Shared Time program in *Ball* had the impermissible effect of advancing religion rested on three assumptions: (i) any public employee who works on the premises of a religious school is presumed to inculcate religion in her work; (ii) the presence of public employees on private school premises creates a symbolic union between church and state; and (iii) any and all public aid that directly aids the educational function of religious schools impermissibly finances religious indoctrination, even if the aid reaches such schools as a consequence of private decisionmaking. Additionally, in *Aguilar* there was a fourth assumption: that New York City's Title I program necessitated an excessive government entanglement with religion because public employees who teach on the premises of religious schools must be closely monitored to ensure that they do not inculcate religion.

B

Our more recent cases have undermined the assumptions upon which *Ball* and *Aguilar* relied. . . .

1

. . . Our cases subsequent to *Aguilar* have . . . modified in two significant respects the approach we use to assess indoctrination. First, we have abandoned the presumption . . . that the placement of public employees on parochial school grounds inevitably results in the impermissible effect of state-sponsored indoctrination or constitutes a symbolic union between government and religion. In Zobrest v. Catalina Foothills School Dist., 509 U.S. 1 (1993), we examined whether the IDEA, 20 U.S.C. § 1400 et seq., was constitutional as applied to a deaf student who sought to bring his state-employed sign-language interpreter with him to his Roman Catholic high school. . . . Because the only *government* aid in *Zobrest* was the interpreter, who was herself not inculcating any religious messages, no *government* indoctrination took place and we were able to conclude that "the provision of such assistance [was] not barred by the Establishment Clause." . . . *Zobrest* therefore expressly rejected the notion—relied on in *Ball* and *Aguilar*—that, solely because of her presence on private school property, a public employee will be presumed to inculcate religion in the students. *Zobrest* also implicitly repudiated another assumption on which *Ball* and *Aguilar* turned: that the presence of a public employee on private school property creates an impermissible "symbolic link" between government and religion.

. . .

Second, we have departed from the rule relied on in *Ball* that all government aid that directly aids the educational function of religious schools is invalid. In Witters v. Washington Dept. of Servs. for Blind, 474 U.S. 481 (1986), we held that the Establishment Clause did not bar a State from issuing a vocational tuition grant to a blind person who wished to use the grant to attend a Christian college and become a pastor, missionary, or youth director. . . . In our view, this transaction was no different from a State's issuing a paycheck to one of its employees, knowing that the employee would donate part or all of the check to a religious institution. . . . Because the private school would not have provided an interpreter on its own, we also concluded that the aid in *Zobrest* did not indirectly finance religious education by "reliev[ing] the sectarian schoo[l] of costs [it] otherwise would have borne in educating [its] students."

Zobrest and *Witters* make clear that, under current law, the Shared Time program in *Ball* and New York City's Title I program in *Aguilar* will not, as a matter of law, be deemed to have the effect of advancing religion through indoctrination. Indeed, each of the premises upon which we relied in *Ball* to reach a contrary conclusion is no longer valid. . . .

. . .

What is most fatal to the argument that New York City's Title I program directly subsidizes religion is that it applies with equal force when those services are provided off-campus, and *Aguilar* implied that providing the services off-campus is entirely consistent with the Establishment Clause. . . .

. . .

3

We turn now to *Aguilar*'s conclusion that New York City's Title I program resulted in an excessive entanglement between church and state. . . . [T]he factors we use to assess whether an entanglement is "excessive" are similar to the factors we use to examine "effect." . . .

Not all entanglements, of course, have the effect of advancing or inhibiting religion. . . . Entanglement must be "excessive" before it runs afoul of the Establishment Clause. . . .

The pre-*Aguilar* Title I program does not result in an "excessive" entanglement that advances or inhibits religion. As discussed previously, the Court's finding of "excessive" entanglement in *Aguilar* rested on three grounds: (i) the program would require "pervasive monitoring by public authorities" to ensure that Title I employees did not inculcate religion; (ii) the program required "administrative cooperation" between the Board and parochial schools; and (iii) the program might increase the dangers of "political divisiveness." . . . Under our current understanding of the Establishment Clause, the last two considerations are insufficient by themselves to create an "excessive" entanglement. They are present no matter where Title I services are offered, and no court has held that Title I services cannot be offered off-campus. . . . Further, the assumption underlying the first consideration has been undermined. . . . [A]fter *Zobrest* we no longer presume that public employees will inculcate religion simply because they happen to be in a sectarian environment. . . .

. . . We . . . hold that a federally funded program providing supplemental, remedial instruction to disadvantaged children on a neutral basis is not invalid under the Establishment Clause when such instruction is given on the premises of sectarian schools by government employees pursuant to a program containing safeguards such as those present here. . . . Accordingly, we must acknowledge that *Aguilar*, as well as the portion of *Ball* addressing Grand Rapids' Shared Time program, are no longer good law.

C

The doctrine of *stare decisis* does not preclude us from recognizing the change in our law and overruling *Aguilar* and those portions of *Ball* inconsistent with our more recent decisions. . . . [It] is at its weakest when we interpret the Constitution because our interpretation can be altered only by constitutional amendment or by overruling our prior decisions. . . . As discussed above, our Establishment Clause jurisprudence has changed significantly since we decided

Ball and *Aguilar*, so our decision to overturn those cases rests on far more than "a present doctrinal disposition to come out differently ..." ...

. . .

For these reasons, we reverse the judgment of the Court of Appeals and remand to the District Court with instructions to vacate its September 26, 1985, order.

It is so ordered.

Justice Souter with whom Justice Stevens and Justice Ginsburg join, and with whom Justice Breyer joins as to Part II, dissenting.

In this novel proceeding, petitioners seek relief from an injunction the District Court entered 12 years ago to implement our decision in Aguilar v. Felton.... The result is to repudiate the very reasonable line drawn in *Aguilar* and *Ball*, and to authorize direct state aid to religious institutions on an unparalleled scale, in violation of the Establishment Clause's central prohibition against religious subsidies by the government.

I respectfully dissent.

I

. . .

... I believe *Aguilar* was a correct and sensible decision ...

. . .

In sum, if a line is to be drawn short of barring all state aid to religious schools for teaching standard subjects, the *Aguilar-Ball* line was a sensible one capable of principled adherence. It is no less sound, and no less necessary, today.

. . .

... In *Zobrest* and *Witters,* ... individual students were themselves applicants for individual benefits on a scale that could not amount to a systemic supplement. But under Title I, ... [t]he aid ... is not even formally aid to the individual students (and even formally individual aid must be seen as aid to a school system when so many individuals receive it that it becomes a significant feature of the system) ...

In sum, nothing since *Ball* and *Aguilar* and before this case has eroded the distinction between "direct and substantial" and "indirect and incidental." That principled line is being breached only here and now. ...[a]

Mitchell v. Helms

530 U.S. 793, 120 S.Ct. 2530, 147 L.Ed.2d 660 (2000).

Justice Thomas announced the judgment of the Court and delivered an opinion, in which the Chief Justice, Justice Scalia, and Justice Kennedy join.

As part of a longstanding school aid program known as Chapter 2, the Federal Government distributes funds to state and local governmental agencies,

a. A dissenting opinion by Justice Ginsburg, joined by Justices Stevens, Souter and Breyer, is omitted.

which in turn lend educational materials and equipment to public and private schools, with the enrollment of each participating school determining the amount of aid that it receives. The question is whether Chapter 2, as applied in Jefferson Parish, Louisiana, is a law respecting an establishment of religion, because many of the private schools receiving Chapter 2 aid in that parish are religiously affiliated. We hold that Chapter 2 is not such a law.

I

A

... Like the provision at issue in Agostini, Chapter 2 channels federal funds to local educational agencies (LEA's), which are usually public school districts, via state educational agencies (SEA's), to implement programs to assist children in elementary and secondary schools. Chapter 2 provides aid

> "for the acquisition and use of instructional and educational materials, including library services and materials (including media materials), assessments, reference materials, computer software and hardware for instructional use, and other curricular materials." ...

LEA's and SEA's must offer assistance to both public and private schools (although any private school must be nonprofit). ... Participating private schools receive Chapter 2 aid based on the number of children enrolled in each school, ... and allocations of Chapter 2 funds for those schools must generally be "equal (consistent with the number of children to be served) to expenditures for programs ... for children enrolled in the public schools of the [LEA]," ... LEA's must in all cases "assure equitable participation" of the children of private schools "in the purposes and benefits" of Chapter 2. ... LEA's and SEA's may not operate their programs "so as to supplant funds from non-Federal sources." ...

Several restrictions apply to aid to private schools. Most significantly, the "services, materials, and equipment" provided to private schools must be "secular, neutral, and nonideological." ... In addition, private schools may not acquire control of Chapter 2 funds or title to Chapter 2 materials, equipment, or property. ... A private school receives the materials and equipment ... by submitting to the LEA an application detailing which items the school seeks and how it will use them; the LEA, if it approves the application, purchases those items from the school's allocation of funds, and then lends them to that school.

In Jefferson Parish ... private schools have primarily used their allocations for nonrecurring expenses, usually materials and equipment. ... Among the materials and equipment provided have been library books, computers, and computer software, and also slide and movie projectors, overhead projectors, television sets, tape recorders, VCR's, projection screens, laboratory equipment, maps, globes, filmstrips, slides, and cassette recordings.

... [I]n an average year, about 30% of Chapter 2 funds spent in Jefferson Parish are allocated for private schools. For the 1985–1986 fiscal year, 41 private schools participated in Chapter 2. For the following year, 46 participated, and the participation level has remained relatively constant since then. Of these 46, 34 were Roman Catholic; 7 were otherwise religiously affiliated; and 5 were not religiously affiliated.

B

Respondents filed suit ... alleging, among other things, that Chapter 2, as applied in Jefferson Parish, violated the Establishment Clause of the First Amendment of the Federal Constitution. ...

. . .

[The United States District Court upheld Chapter 2.] The Fifth Circuit . . . held Chapter 2 unconstitutional. . . .

II

. . .

In this case, our inquiry under *Agostini*'s purpose and effect test is a narrow one. Because respondents do not challenge the District Court's holding that Chapter 2 has a secular purpose, . . . we will consider only Chapter 2's effect. . . . Considering Chapter 2 in light of our more recent case law, we conclude that it neither results in religious indoctrination by the government nor defines its recipients by reference to religion. We therefore hold that Chapter 2 is not a "law respecting an establishment of religion." . . .

A

As we indicated in *Agostini,* . . . the question whether governmental aid to religious schools results in governmental indoctrination is ultimately a question whether any religious indoctrination that occurs in those schools could reasonably be attributed to governmental action. . . . We have also indicated that the answer to the question of indoctrination will resolve the question whether a program of educational aid "subsidizes" religion, as our religion cases use that term. . . .

In distinguishing between indoctrination that is attributable to the State and indoctrination that is not, we have consistently turned to the principle of neutrality, upholding aid that is offered to a broad range of groups or persons without regard to their religion. If the religious, irreligious, and areligious are all alike eligible for governmental aid, no one would conclude that any indoctrination that any particular recipient conducts has been done at the behest of the government. For attribution of indoctrination is a relative question. If the government is offering assistance to recipients who provide, so to speak, a broad range of indoctrination, the government itself is not thought responsible for any particular indoctrination. To put the point differently, if the government, seeking to further some legitimate secular purpose, offers aid on the same terms, without regard to religion, to all who adequately further that purpose, . . . then it is fair to say that any aid going to a religious recipient only has the effect of furthering that secular purpose. The government, in crafting such an aid program, has had to conclude that a given level of aid is necessary to further that purpose among secular recipients and has provided no more than that same level to religious recipients.

As a way of assuring neutrality, we have repeatedly considered whether any governmental aid that goes to a religious institution does so "only as a result of the genuinely independent and private choices of individuals." . . . We have viewed as significant whether the "private choices of individual parents," as opposed to the "unmediated" will of government . . . determine what schools ultimately benefit from the governmental aid, and how much. For if numerous private choices, rather than the single choice of a government, determine the distribution of aid pursuant to neutral eligibility criteria, then a government cannot, or at least cannot easily, grant special favors that might lead to a religious establishment. Private choice also helps guarantee neutrality by mitigating the preference for pre-existing recipients that is arguably inherent in any governmental aid program . . . and that could lead to a program inadvertently favoring one religion or favoring religious private schools in general over nonreligious ones.

. . .

Agostini's second . . . criterion requires a court to consider whether an aid program "define[s] its recipients by reference to religion.". . . . [T]his second criterion looks to the same set of facts as does our focus, under the first criterion, on neutrality, . . . but the second criterion uses those facts to answer a somewhat different question—whether the criteria for allocating the aid "creat[e] a financial incentive to undertake religious indoctrination." . . .

[There is a] close relationship between this rule, incentives, and private choice. For to say that a program does not create an incentive to choose religious schools is to say that the private choice is truly "independent," . . . When such an incentive does exist, there is a greater risk that one could attribute to the government any indoctrination by the religious schools. . . .

. . . [S]imply because an aid program offers private schools, and thus religious schools, a benefit that they did not previously receive does not mean that the program, by reducing the cost of securing a religious education, creates, under *Agostini*'s second criterion, an "incentive" for parents to choose such an education for their children. For any aid will have some such effect. . . .

B

Respondents . . . argue first, and chiefly, that "direct, nonincidental" aid to the primary educational mission of religious schools is always impermissible. Second, they argue that provision to religious schools of aid that is divertible to religious use is similarly impermissible. Respondents' arguments are inconsistent with our more recent case law and we therefore reject them.

1

. . . [S]ome of our earlier cases . . . did emphasize the distinction between direct and indirect aid . . . [O]ur more recent cases address this purpose not through the direct/indirect distinction but rather through the principle of private choice . . . If aid to schools, even "direct aid," is neutrally available and, before reaching or benefiting any religious school, first passes through the hands (literally or figuratively) of numerous private citizens who are free to direct the aid elsewhere, the government has not provided any "support of religion,". . . . Although the presence of private choice is easier to see when aid literally passes through the hands of individuals . . . there is no reason why the Establishment Clause requires such a form.

. . .

. . . [R]espondents intend their direct/indirect distinction to require that any aid be literally placed in the hands of schoolchildren rather than given directly to the school for teaching those same children . . .

. . . [R]espondents' formalistic line breaks down in the application to real-world programs. In *Allen*, for example, although we did recognize that students themselves received and owned the textbooks, we also noted that the books provided were those that the private schools required for courses, that the schools could collect students' requests for books and submit them to the board of education, that the schools could store the textbooks, and that the textbooks were essential to the schools' teaching of secular subjects. . . . Whether one chooses to label this program "direct" or "indirect" is a rather arbitrary choice, one that does not further the constitutional analysis.

Of course, we have seen "special Establishment Clause dangers" . . . when money is given to religious schools or entities directly rather than . . . indirectly. . . . But direct payments of money are not at issue in this case, and we refuse to allow a "special" case to create a rule for all cases.

2

Respondents also contend that the Establishment Clause requires that aid to religious schools not be impermissibly religious in nature or be divertible to religious use. We agree with the first part of this argument but not the second. Respondents' "no divertibility" rule is inconsistent with our more recent case law and is unworkable. So long as the governmental aid is not itself "unsuitable for use in the public schools because of religious content," . . . and eligibility for aid is determined in a constitutionally permissible manner, any use of that aid to indoctrinate cannot be attributed to the government and is thus not of constitutional concern. And, of course, the use to which the aid is put does not affect the criteria governing the aid's allocation and thus does not create any impermissible incentive under *Agostini's* second criterion.

. . .

The issue is not divertibility of aid but rather whether the aid itself has an impermissible content. Where the aid would be suitable for use in a public school, it is also suitable for use in any private school. Similarly, the prohibition against the government providing impermissible content resolves the Establishment Clause concerns that exist if aid is actually diverted to religious uses. . . .

. . .

A concern for divertibility, as opposed to improper content, is misplaced not only because it fails to explain why the sort of aid that we have allowed is permissible, but also because it is boundless—enveloping all aid, no matter how trivial—and thus has only the most attenuated (if any) link to any realistic concern for preventing an "establishment of religion." Presumably, for example, government-provided lecterns, chalk, crayons, pens, paper, and paintbrushes would have to be excluded from religious schools under respondents' proposed rule. . . .

. . .

C

The dissent serves up a smorgasbord of 11 factors . . .

One of the dissent's factors deserves special mention: whether a school that receives aid (or whose students receive aid) is pervasively sectarian. The dissent is correct that there was a period when this factor mattered, particularly if the pervasively sectarian school was a primary or secondary school. . . . But that period is one that the Court should regret, and it is thankfully long past.

There are numerous reasons to formally dispense with this factor. First, its relevance in our precedents is in sharp decline. . . .

Second, the religious nature of a recipient should not matter to the constitutional analysis, so long as the recipient adequately furthers the government's secular purpose. . . . The pervasively sectarian recipient has not received any special favor, and it is most bizarre that the Court would . . . reserve special hostility for those who take their religion seriously, who think that their religion should affect the whole of their lives, or who make the mistake of being effective in transmitting their views to children.

Third, the inquiry into the recipient's religious views required by a focus on whether a school is pervasively sectarian is not only unnecessary but also offensive. It is well established, in numerous other contexts, that courts should refrain from trolling through a person's or institution's religious beliefs. . . . In addition, and related, the application of the "pervasively sectarian" factor collides with our decisions that have prohibited governments from discriminating in the distribution of public benefits based upon religious status or sincerity. . . .

Finally, hostility to aid to pervasively sectarian schools has a shameful pedigree that we do not hesitate to disavow. . . . Opposition to aid to "sectarian" schools acquired prominence in the 1870's with Congress's consideration (and near passage) of the Blaine Amendment, which would have amended the Constitution to bar any aid to sectarian institutions. Consideration of the amendment arose at a time of pervasive hostility to the Catholic Church and to Catholics in general, and it was an open secret that "sectarian" was code for "Catholic." . . . Notwithstanding its history, of course, "sectarian" could, on its face, describe the school of any religious sect, but the Court eliminated this possibility of confusion when, in Hunt v. McNair, 413 U.S., at 743, it coined the term "pervasively sectarian"—a term which, at that time, could be applied almost exclusively to Catholic parochial schools and which even today's dissent exemplifies chiefly by reference to such schools. . . .

. . . In short, nothing in the Establishment Clause requires the exclusion of pervasively sectarian schools from otherwise permissible aid programs, and other doctrines of this Court bar it. This doctrine, born of bigotry, should be buried now.

III

Applying the two relevant *Agostini* criteria, we see no basis for concluding that Jefferson Parish's Chapter 2 program "has the effect of advancing religion." . . . Chapter 2 does not result in governmental indoctrination, because it determines eligibility for aid neutrally, allocates that aid based on the private choices of the parents of schoolchildren, and does not provide aid that has an impermissible content. Nor does Chapter 2 define its recipients by reference to religion.

Taking the second criterion first, it is clear that Chapter 2 aid "is allocated on the basis of neutral, secular criteria that neither favor nor disfavor religion, and is made available to both religious and secular beneficiaries on a nondiscriminatory basis." . . .

Chapter 2 also satisfies the first *Agostini* criterion. The program makes a broad array of schools eligible for aid without regard to their religious affiliations or lack thereof. . . . Private decisionmaking controls . . . , and those decisions are independent because of the program's neutrality. . . . It is the students and their parents—not the government—who, through their choice of school, determine who receives Chapter 2 funds. The aid follows the child.

. . .

. . . Chapter 2 satisfies the first *Agostini* criterion because it does not provide to religious schools aid that has an impermissible content. . . . The chief aid at issue is computers, computer software, and library books. . . .

There is evidence that equipment has been, or at least easily could be, diverted for use in religious classes. . . . [M]onitoring by SEA and LEA officials is highly unlikely to prevent or catch diversion. [W]e agree with the dissent that there is evidence of actual diversion and that, were the safeguards anything other than anemic, there would almost certainly be more such evidence. ... In any event, ... the evidence of actual diversion and the weakness of the safeguards against actual diversion are not relevant to the constitutional inquiry, whatever relevance they may have under the statute and regulations.

. . .

IV

... Jefferson Parish need not exclude religious schools from its Chapter 2 program. ...

. . .

The judgment of the Fifth Circuit is reversed.

It is so ordered.

Justice O'Connor, with whom Justice Breyer joins, concurring in the judgment.

... I believe that *Agostini* ... controls the constitutional inquiry respecting Title II presented here, and requires the reversal ... I therefore concur in the judgment.

I

I write separately because, in my view, the plurality announces a rule of unprecedented breadth for the evaluation of Establishment Clause challenges to government school-aid programs. Reduced to its essentials, the plurality's rule states that government aid to religious schools does not have the effect of advancing religion so long as the aid is offered on a neutral basis and the aid is secular in content. The plurality also rejects the distinction between direct and indirect aid, and holds that the actual diversion of secular aid by a religious school to the advancement of its religious mission is permissible. Although the expansive scope of the plurality's rule is troubling, two specific aspects of the opinion compel me to write separately. First, the plurality's treatment of neutrality comes close to assigning that factor singular importance in the future adjudication of Establishment Clause challenges to government school-aid programs. Second, the plurality's approval of actual diversion of government aid to religious indoctrination is in tension with our precedents and, in any event, unnecessary to decide the instant case.

. . .

... I agree with Justice Souter's conclusion that our "most recent use of 'neutrality' to refer to generality or evenhandedness of distribution ... is relevant in judging whether a benefit scheme so characterized should be seen as aiding a sectarian school's religious mission, but this neutrality is not alone sufficient to qualify the aid as constitutional."

I also disagree with the plurality's conclusion that actual diversion of government aid to religious indoctrination is consistent with the Establishment Clause. ...

... [W]e decided *Witters* and *Zobrest* on the understanding that the aid was provided directly to the individual student who, in turn, made the choice of where to put that aid to use. ...

... I do not believe that we should treat a per-capita-aid program the same as the true private-choice programs ... First, when the government provides aid directly to the student beneficiary, that student can attend a religious school and yet retain control over whether the secular government aid will be applied toward the religious education. The fact that aid flows to the religious school and is used for the advancement of religion is therefore wholly dependent on the student's private decision. . . .

Second, I believe the distinction between a per-capita school-aid program and a true private-choice program is significant for purposes of endorsement. . . . In terms of public perception, a government program of direct aid to religious schools based on the number of students attending each school differs meaningfully from the government distributing aid directly to individual students who, in turn, decide to use the aid at the same religious schools. . . .

Finally, the distinction between a per-capita-aid program and a true private-choice program is important when considering aid that consists of direct monetary subsidies. . . . If, as the plurality contends, a per-capita-aid program is identical in relevant constitutional respects to a true private-choice program, then there is no reason that, under the plurality's reasoning, the government should be precluded from providing direct money payments to religious organizations (including churches) based on the number of persons belonging to each organization. And, because actual diversion is permissible under the plurality's holding, the participating religious organizations (including churches) could use that aid to support religious indoctrination. To be sure, the plurality does not actually hold that its theory extends to direct money payments. That omission, however, is of little comfort. In its logic—as well as its specific advisory language—the plurality opinion foreshadows the approval of direct monetary subsidies to religious organizations, even when they use the money to advance their religious objectives.

. . .

V

Respondents . . . contend that the evidence respecting the actual administration of Chapter 2 in Jefferson Parish demonstrates that the program violated the Establishment Clause. . . . [T]he plurality appears to contend that the Chapter 2 program can be upheld only if actual diversion of government aid to the advancement of religion is permissible under the Establishment Clause. . . . Justice Souter concludes that the Chapter 2 program, as applied in Jefferson Parish, violated the Establishment Clause. I disagree with both the plurality and Justice Souter. The limited evidence amassed by respondents . . . is at best de minimis and therefore insufficient to affect the constitutional inquiry.

. . .

. . . [R]espondents' Establishment Clause challenge must fail. As in *Agostini*, the Chapter 2 aid is allocated on the basis of neutral, secular criteria; the aid must be supplementary and cannot supplant non-Federal funds; no Chapter 2 funds ever reach the coffers of religious schools; the aid must be secular; any evidence of actual diversion is de minimis; and the program includes adequate safeguards. Regardless of whether these factors are constitutional requirements, they are surely sufficient to find that the program at issue here does not have the impermissible effect of advancing religion. . . .

Justice Souter, with whom Justice Stevens and Justice Ginsburg join, dissenting.

The First Amendment's Establishment Clause prohibits . . . not only the institution of an official church, but any government act favoring religion, a particular religion, or for that matter irreligion. Thus it bars the use of public funds for religious aid.

. . .

. . . The plurality position breaks fundamentally with Establishment Clause principle, and with the methodology painstakingly worked out in support of it. . . . From that new view of the law, and from a majority's mistaken application of the old, I respectfully dissent.

I

. . .

A

At least three concerns have been expressed since the founding and run throughout our First Amendment jurisprudence. First, compelling an individual to support religion violates the fundamental principle of freedom of conscience. . . .

Second, government aid corrupts religion. . . .

Third, government establishment of religion is inextricably linked with conflict. . . . In our own history, the turmoil thus produced has led to a rejection of the idea that government should subsidize religious education . . .

B

. . .

Today, the substantive principle of no aid to religious mission remains the governing understanding of the Establishment Clause as applied to public benefits inuring to religious schools. . . .

II

. . .

There is, of course, good reason for considering the generality of aid and the evenhandedness of its distribution in making close calls between benefits that in purpose or effect support a school's religious mission and those that do not. . . . Given the legitimacy of considering evenhandedness, then, there is no reason to avoid the term "neutrality" to refer to it. But one crucial point must be borne in mind.

. . . This kind of neutrality is relevant in judging whether a benefit scheme so characterized should be seen as aiding a sectarian school's religious mission, but this neutrality is not alone sufficient to qualify the aid as constitutional. It is to be considered only along with other characteristics of aid, its administration, its recipients, or its potential that have been emphasized over the years as indicators of just how religious the intent and effect of a given aid scheme really is.

. . .

At least three main lines of enquiry addressed particularly to school aid have emerged to complement evenhandedness neutrality. First, we have noted that two types of aid recipients heighten Establishment Clause concern: pervasively religious schools and primary and secondary religious schools. Second, we have identified two important characteristics of the method of distributing aid: directness or indirectness of distribution and distribution by genuinely independent choice. Third, we have found relevance in at least five characteristics of the aid itself: its religious content; its cash form; its divertibility or actually diversion to religious support; its supplantation of traditional items of religious school expense; and its substantiality.

. . .

. . . [W]e have consistently understood the Establishment Clause to impose a substantive prohibition against public aid to religion and, hence, to the religious mission of sectarian schools. Evenhandedness neutrality is one, non-dispositive pointer toward an intent and (to a lesser degree) probable effect on the permissible side of the line between forbidden aid and general public welfare benefit. Other pointers are facts about the religious mission and education level of benefited schools and their pupils, the pathway by which a benefit travels from public treasury to educational effect, the form and content of the aid, its adaptability to religious ends, and its effects on school budgets. The object of all enquiries into such matters is the same whatever the particular circumstances: is the benefit intended to aid in providing the religious element of the education and is it likely to do so?

. . . [O]ur predecessors were right in their prophecies that no simple test would emerge to allow easy application of the establishment principle.

The plurality, however, would reject that lesson. The majority misapplies it.

III

A

. . .

. . . [T]he plurality's new criterion is unequaled in the history of Establishment Clause interpretation. . . . [T]he plurality's proposal would replace the principle of no aid with a formula for generous religious support.

. . .

. . . [T]he plurality apparently assumes as a fact that equal amounts of aid to religious and nonreligious schools will have exclusively secular and equal effects, on both external perception and on incentives to attend different schools. But there is no reason to believe that this will be the case; the effects of same-terms aid may not be confined to the secular sphere at all. This is the reason that we have long recognized that unrestricted aid to religious schools will support religious teaching in addition to secular education, a fact that would be true no matter what the supposedly secular purpose of the law might be.

. . .

B

The plurality's conception of evenhandedness does not, however, control the case, whose disposition turns on the misapplication of accepted categories of school aid analysis. The facts most obviously relevant to the Chapter 2 scheme in Jefferson Parish are those showing divertibility and actual diversion in the circumstance of pervasively sectarian religious schools. . . .

. . . [T]he record here goes beyond risk, to instances of actual diversion. What one would expect from such paltry efforts at monitoring and enforcement naturally resulted, and the record strongly suggests that other, undocumented diversions probably occurred as well.

. . .

Indeed, the plurality readily recognizes that the aid in question here was divertible and that substantial evidence of actual diversion exists. . . .

IV

. . . [T]he plurality's notion of evenhandedness neutrality as a practical guarantee of the validity of aid to sectarian schools would be the end of the principle of no aid to the schools' religious mission. . . .

. . . To the plurality there is nothing wrong with aiding a school's religious mission; the only question is whether religious teaching obtains its tax support under a formally evenhanded criterion of distribution. The principle of no aid to religious teaching has no independent significance.

. . . [T]he plurality's choice to employ imputations of bigotry and irreligion as terms in the Court's debate makes one point clear: that in rejecting the principle of no aid to a school's religious mission the plurality is attacking the most fundamental assumption underlying the Establishment Clause, that government can in fact operate with neutrality in its relation to religion. I believe that it can, and so respectfully dissent.

. . .

Zelman v. Simmons–Harris

536 U.S. 639, 122 S.Ct. 2460, 153 L.Ed.2d 604 (2002).

Chief Justice Rehnquist delivered the opinion of the Court.

The State of Ohio has established a pilot program designed to provide educational choices to families with children who reside in the Cleveland City School District. The question presented is whether this program offends the Establishment Clause of the United States Constitution. We hold that it does not.

There are more than 75,000 children enrolled in the Cleveland City School District. The majority of these children are from low-income and minority families. Few of these families enjoy the means to send their children to any school other than an inner-city public school. For more than a generation, however, Cleveland's public schools have been among the worst performing public schools in the Nation. In 1995, a Federal District Court . . . placed the entire Cleveland school district under state control. . . . The district had failed to meet any of the 18 state standards for minimal acceptable performance. Only 1 in 10 ninth graders could pass a basic proficiency examination, and students at all levels performed at a dismal rate compared with students in other Ohio public schools. More than two-thirds of high school students either dropped or failed out before graduation. Of those students who managed to reach their senior year, one of every four still failed to graduate. Of those students who did graduate, few could read, write, or compute at levels comparable to their counterparts in other cities.

It is against this backdrop that Ohio enacted, among other initiatives, its Pilot Project Scholarship Program . . . The program provides financial assistance to families in any Ohio school district that is or has been "under federal court order requiring supervision and operational management of the district by the state superintendent."... Cleveland is the only Ohio school district to fall within that category.

The program provides two basic kinds of assistance to parents of children in a covered district. First, the program provides tuition aid for students in kindergarten through third grade, expanding each year through eighth grade, to attend a participating public or private school of their parent's choosing. ... Second, the program provides tutorial aid for students who choose to remain enrolled in public school. ...

The tuition aid portion of the program is designed to provide educational choices to parents who reside in a covered district. Any private school, whether religious or nonreligious, may participate in the program and accept program students so long as the school is located within the boundaries of a covered district and meets statewide educational standards. ... Participating private schools must agree not to discriminate on the basis of race, religion, or ethnic background, or to "advocate or foster unlawful behavior or teach hatred of any person or group on the basis of race, ethnicity, national origin, or religion." ... Any public school located in a school district adjacent to the covered district may also participate in the program. ... Adjacent public schools are eligible to receive a $2,250 tuition grant for each program student accepted in addition to the full amount of per-pupil state funding attributable to each additional student. ... All participating schools, whether public or private, are required to accept students in accordance with rules and procedures established by the state superintendent. ...

Tuition aid is distributed to parents according to financial need. Families with incomes below 200% of the poverty line are given priority and are eligible to receive 90% of private school tuition up to $2,250. ... For these lowest-income families, participating private schools may not charge a parental co-payment greater than $250. ... For all other families, the program pays 75% of tuition costs, up to $1,875, with no co-payment cap. ... These families receive tuition aid only if the number of available scholarships exceeds the number of low-income children who choose to participate. ... Where tuition aid is spent depends solely upon where parents who receive tuition aid choose to enroll their child. If parents choose a private school, checks are made payable to the parents who then endorse the checks over to the chosen school. ...

The tutorial aid portion of the program provides tutorial assistance through grants to any student in a covered district who chooses to remain in public school. Parents arrange for registered tutors to provide assistance to their children and then submit bills for those services to the State for payment. ... Students from low-income families receive 90% of the amount charged for such assistance up to $360. All other students receive 75% of that amount. ... The number of tutorial assistance grants offered to students in a covered district must equal the number of tuition aid scholarships provided to students enrolled at participating private or adjacent public schools. ...

The program has been in operation within the Cleveland City School District since the 1996–1997 school year. In the 1999–2000 school year, 56 private schools participated in the program, 46 (or 82%) of which had a religious affiliation. None of the public schools in districts adjacent to Cleveland have elected to participate. More than 3,700 students participated in the scholarship program, most of whom (96%) enrolled in religiously affiliated schools. Sixty percent of these students were from families at or below the poverty line. In the 1998–1999 school year, approximately 1,400 Cleveland public school students received tutorial aid. This number was expected to double during the 1999–2000 school year.

. . .

In July 1999, respondents filed this action in United States District Court, seeking to enjoin the reenacted program on the ground that it violated the Establishment Clause of the United States Constitution. . . . In December 1999, the District Court granted summary judgment for respondents. In December 2000, a divided panel of the Court of Appeals affirmed the judgment of the District Court . . . We . . . now reverse the Court of Appeals.

The Establishment Clause of the First Amendment, applied to the States through the Fourteenth Amendment, prevents a State from enacting laws that have the "purpose" or "effect" of advancing or inhibiting religion. *Agostini v. Felton,* 521 U. S. 203, 222–223 (1997) . . . There is no dispute that the program challenged here was enacted for the valid secular purpose of providing educational assistance to poor children in a demonstrably failing public school system. Thus, the question presented is whether the Ohio program nonetheless has the forbidden "effect" of advancing or inhibiting religion.

To answer that question, our decisions have drawn a consistent distinction between government programs that provide aid directly to religious schools . . . and programs of true private choice, in which government aid reaches religious schools only as a result of the genuine and independent choices of private individuals . . . While our jurisprudence with respect to the constitutionality of direct aid programs has "changed significantly" over the past two decades, . . . our jurisprudence with respect to true private choice programs has remained consistent and unbroken. Three times we have confronted Establishment Clause challenges to neutral government programs that provide aid directly to a broad class of individuals, who, in turn, direct the aid to religious schools or institutions of their own choosing. Three times we have rejected such challenges.

In Mueller [v. Allen, 463 U. S. 388 (1983)], we rejected an Establishment Clause challenge to a Minnesota program authorizing tax deductions for various educational expenses, including private school tuition costs, even though the great majority of the program's beneficiaries (96%) were parents of children in religious schools. . . . We . . . found it irrelevant to the constitutional inquiry that the vast majority of beneficiaries were parents of children in religious schools . . . That the program was one of true private choice, with no evidence that the State deliberately skewed incentives toward religious schools, was sufficient for the program to survive scrutiny under the Establishment Clause.

In Witters [v. Washington Dept. of Servs. for Blind, 474 U. S. 481 (1986)], we used identical reasoning to reject an Establishment Clause challenge to a vocational scholarship program that provided tuition aid to a student studying at a religious institution to become a pastor. . . .

Five Members of the Court, in separate opinions, emphasized the general rule from *Mueller* that the amount of government aid channeled to religious institutions by individual aid recipients was not relevant to the constitutional inquiry. . . . Our holding thus rested not on whether few or many recipients chose to expend government aid at a religious school but, rather, on whether recipients generally were empowered to direct the aid to schools or institutions of their own choosing.

Finally, in Zobrest [v. Catalina Foothills School Dist., 509 U. S. 1 (1993)], we applied *Mueller* and *Witters* to reject an Establishment Clause challenge to a federal program that permitted sign-language interpreters to assist deaf children enrolled in religious schools. Reviewing our earlier decisions, we stated that "government programs that neutrally provide benefits to a broad class of citizens defined without reference to religion are not readily subject to an Establishment Clause challenge." . . .

. . .

Mueller, *Witters*, and *Zobrest* thus make clear that where a government aid program is neutral with respect to religion, and provides assistance directly to a broad class of citizens who, in turn, direct government aid to religious schools wholly as a result of their own genuine and independent private choice, the program is not readily subject to challenge under the Establishment Clause. A program that shares these features permits government aid to reach religious institutions only by way of the deliberate choices of numerous individual recipients. The incidental advancement of a religious mission, or the perceived endorsement of a religious message, is reasonably attributable to the individual recipient, not to the government, whose role ends with the disbursement of benefits. . . . [W]e have never found a program of true private choice to offend the Establishment Clause.

We believe that the program challenged here is a program of true private choice, consistent with *Mueller*, *Witters*, and *Zobrest*, and thus constitutional. As was true in those cases, the Ohio program is neutral in all respects toward religion. It is part of a general and multifaceted undertaking by the State of Ohio to provide educational opportunities to the children of a failed school district. It confers educational assistance directly to a broad class of individuals defined without reference to religion, *i.e.*, any parent of a school-age child who resides in the Cleveland City School District. The program permits the participation of *all* schools within the district, religious or nonreligious. Adjacent public schools also may participate and have a financial incentive to do so. Program benefits are available to participating families on neutral terms, with no reference to religion. The only preference stated anywhere in the program is a preference for low-income families, who receive greater assistance and are given priority for admission at participating schools.

There are no "financial incentive[s]" that "ske[w]" the program toward religious schools. *Witters*, *supra*, at 487–488. Such incentives "[are] not present . . . where the aid is allocated on the basis of neutral, secular criteria that neither favor nor disfavor religion, and is made available to both religious and secular beneficiaries on a nondiscriminatory basis." *Agostini*, *supra*, at 231. . . .

Respondents suggest that even without a financial incentive for parents to choose a religious school, the program creates a "public perception that the State is endorsing religious practices and beliefs." . . . But we have repeatedly recognized that no reasonable observer would think a neutral program of private choice, where state aid reaches religious schools solely as a result of the numerous independent decisions of private individuals, carries with it the *imprimatur* of government endorsement. . . . The argument is particularly misplaced here since "the reasonable observer in the endorsement inquiry must be deemed aware" of the "history and context" underlying a challenged program. . . . Any objective observer familiar with the full history and context of the Ohio program would reasonably view it as one aspect of a broader undertaking to assist poor children in failed schools, not as an endorsement of religious schooling in general.

There also is no evidence that the program fails to provide genuine opportunities for Cleveland parents to select secular educational options for their school-age children. Cleveland schoolchildren enjoy a range of educational choices: They may remain in public school as before, remain in public school with publicly funded tutoring aid, obtain a scholarship and choose a religious school, obtain a scholarship and choose a nonreligious private school, enroll in a community school, or enroll in a magnet school. That 46 of the 56 private schools now participating in the program are religious schools does not condemn it as a violation of the Establishment Clause. The Establishment Clause question is whether Ohio is coercing parents into sending their children to religious schools, and that question must be answered by evaluating *all* options Ohio provides Cleveland schoolchildren, only one of which is to obtain a program scholarship and then choose a religious school.

... It is true that 82% of Cleveland's participating private schools are religious schools, but it is also true that 81% of private schools in Ohio are religious schools. To attribute constitutional significance to this figure, moreover, would lead to the absurd result that a neutral school-choice program might be permissible in some parts of Ohio, such as Columbus, where a lower percentage of private schools are religious schools, but not in inner-city Cleveland, where Ohio has deemed such programs most sorely needed, but where the preponderance of religious schools happens to be greater. Likewise, an identical private choice program might be constitutional in some States, such as Maine or Utah, where less than 45% of private schools are religious schools, but not in other States, such as Nebraska or Kansas, where over 90% of private schools are religious schools.

... The constitutionality of a neutral educational aid program simply does not turn on whether and why, in a particular area, at a particular time, most private schools are run by religious organizations, or most recipients choose to use the aid at a religious school. ...

. . .

Respondents finally claim that we should look to Committee for Public Ed. & Religious Liberty v. Nyquist, 413 U. S. 756 (1973), to decide these cases. We disagree for two reasons. First, the program in *Nyquist* was quite different from the program challenged here. *Nyquist* involved a New York program that gave a package of benefits exclusively to private schools and the parents of private school enrollees. Although the program was enacted for ostensibly secular purposes, ... we found that its "function" was "*unmistakably* to provide desired financial support for nonpublic, sectarian institutions,", ... Its genesis, we said, was that private religious schools faced "increasingly grave fiscal problems." ... The program thus provided direct money grants to religious schools. ... It provided tax benefits "unrelated to the amount of money actually expended by any parent on tuition," ensuring a windfall to parents of children in religious schools. ... It similarly provided tuition reimbursements designed explicitly to "offe[r] ... an incentive to parents to send their children to sectarian schools." ... Indeed, the program flatly prohibited the participation of any public school, or parent of any public school enrollee. ... Ohio's program shares none of these features.

Second, were there any doubt that the program challenged in *Nyquist* is far removed from the program challenged here, we expressly reserved judgment with respect to "a case involving some form of public assistance (*e.g.*, scholarships) made available generally without regard to the sectarian-nonsectarian, or public-nonpublic nature of the institution benefited." ... [W]e now hold that *Nyquist* does not govern neutral educational assistance programs that, like the program here, offer aid directly to a broad class of individual recipients defined without regard to religion.

In sum, the Ohio program is entirely neutral with respect to religion. It provides benefits directly to a wide spectrum of individuals, defined only by financial need and residence in a particular school district. It permits such individuals to exercise genuine choice among options public and private, secular and religious. The program is therefore a program of true private choice. In keeping with an unbroken line of decisions rejecting challenges to similar programs, we hold that the program does not offend the Establishment Clause.

. . .

Justice O'Connor, concurring.

... While I join the Court's opinion, I write separately for two reasons. First, although the Court takes an important step, I do not believe that today's decision, when considered in light of other longstanding government programs that impact religious organizations and our prior Establishment Clause jurisprudence, marks a dramatic break from the past. Second, given the emphasis the Court places on verifying that parents of voucher students in religious schools have exercised "true private choice," I think it is worth elaborating on the Court's conclusion that this inquiry should consider all reasonable educational alternatives to religious schools that are available to parents. To do otherwise is to ignore how the educational system in Cleveland actually functions.

I

These cases are different from prior indirect aid cases in part because a significant portion of the funds appropriated for the voucher program reach religious schools without restrictions on the use of these funds. The share of public resources that reach religious schools is not, however, as significant as respondents suggest. . . .

... Even if one assumes that all voucher students came from low-income families and that each voucher student used up the entire $2,250 voucher, at most $8.2 million of public funds flowed to religious schools under the voucher program in 1999–2000. . . .

Although $8.2 million is no small sum, it pales in comparison to the amount of funds that federal, state, and local governments already provide religious institutions. Religious organizations may qualify for exemptions from the federal corporate income tax, ... and property taxes in all 50 States, ... clergy qualify for a federal tax break on income used for housing expenses ... In addition, the Federal Government provides individuals, corporations, trusts, and estates a tax deduction for charitable contributions to qualified religious groups ... Finally, the Federal Government and certain state governments provide tax credits for educational expenses, many of which are spent on education at religious schools. . . .

. . .

... Federal dollars also reach religiously affiliated organizations through public health programs such as Medicare, ... and Medicaid, ..., through educational programs such as the Pell Grant program, ... and the G. I. Bill of Rights, ... and through child care programs such as the Child Care and Development Block Grant Program ...

. . .

Against this background, the support that the Cleveland voucher program provides religious institutions is neither substantial nor atypical of existing government programs. . . .

II

Nor does today's decision signal a major departure from this Court's prior Establishment Clause jurisprudence. A central tool in our analysis of cases in this area has been the *Lemon* test. . . .

The Court's opinion in these cases focuses on a narrow question related to the *Lemon* test: how to apply the primary effects prong in indirect aid cases? . . . Courts are instructed to consider two factors: first, whether the program administers aid in a neutral fashion, without differentiation based on the religious status of beneficiaries or providers of services; second, and more importantly, whether beneficiaries of indirect aid have a genuine choice among religious and nonreligious organizations when determining the organization to which they will direct that aid. If the answer to either query is "no," the program should be struck down under the Establishment Clause.

Justice Souter portrays this inquiry as a departure from *Everson*. A fair reading of the holding in that case suggests quite the opposite. . . . How else could the Court have upheld a state program to provide students transportation to public and religious schools alike? What the Court clarifies in these cases is that the Establishment Clause also requires that state aid flowing to religious organizations through the hands of beneficiaries must do so only at the direction of those beneficiaries. Such a refinement of the *Lemon* test surely does not betray *Everson*.

III

There is little question in my mind that the Cleveland voucher program is neutral as between religious schools and nonreligious schools. . . .

I do not agree that the nonreligious schools have failed to provide Cleveland parents reasonable alternatives to religious schools in the voucher program. . . .

. . .

In my view the more significant finding in these cases is that Cleveland parents who use vouchers to send their children to religious private schools do so as a result of true private choice. . . .

I find the Court's answer to the question whether parents of students eligible for vouchers have a genuine choice between religious and nonreligious schools persuasive. . . .

. . .

Based on the reasoning in the Court's opinion, which is consistent with the realities of the Cleveland educational system, I am persuaded that the Cleveland voucher program affords parents of eligible children genuine nonreligious options and is consistent with the Establishment Clause.

Justice Thomas, concurring.

. . .

. . . Today's decision properly upholds the program as constitutional, and I join it in full.

I

... I agree with the Court that Ohio's program easily passes muster under our stringent test, but, as a matter of first principles, I question whether this test should be applied to the States.

. . .

... When rights are incorporated against the States through the Fourteenth Amendment they should advance, not constrain, individual liberty.

... Thus, while the Federal Government may "make no law respecting an establishment of religion," the States may pass laws that include or touch on religious matters so long as these laws do not impede free exercise rights or any other individual religious liberty interest. By considering the particular religious liberty right alleged to be invaded by a State, federal courts can strike a proper balance between the demands of the Fourteenth Amendment on the one hand and the federalism prerogatives of States on the other.

... I can accept that the Fourteenth Amendment protects religious liberty rights. But I cannot accept its use to oppose neutral programs of school choice through the incorporation of the Establishment Clause. There would be a tragic irony in converting the Fourteenth Amendment's guarantee of individual liberty into a prohibition on the exercise of educational choice.

II

. . .

While the romanticized ideal of universal public education resonates with the cognoscenti who oppose vouchers, poor urban families just want the best education for their children, who will certainly need it to function in our high-tech and advanced society. ... If society cannot end racial discrimination, at least it can arm minorities with the education to defend themselves from some of discrimination's effects.

... [S]chool choice programs that involve religious schools appear unconstitutional only to those who would twist the Fourteenth Amendment against itself by expansively incorporating the Establishment Clause. Converting the Fourteenth Amendment from a guarantee of opportunity to an obstacle against education reform distorts our constitutional values and disserves those in the greatest need.

. . .

Justice Stevens, dissenting.

Is a law that authorizes the use of public funds to pay for the indoctrination of thousands of grammar school children in particular religious faiths a "law respecting an establishment of religion" within the meaning of the First Amendment? In answering that question, I think we should ignore three factual matters that are discussed at length by my colleagues.

First, the severe educational crisis that confronted the Cleveland City School District when Ohio enacted its voucher program is not a matter that should affect our appraisal of its constitutionality. ...

Second, the wide range of choices that have been made available to students *within the public school system* has no bearing on the question whether the State may pay the tuition for students who wish to reject public education entirely and attend private schools that will provide them with a sectarian education. ...

Third, the voluntary character of the private choice to prefer a parochial education over an education in the public school system seems to me quite irrelevant to the question whether the government's choice to pay for religious indoctrination is constitutionally permissible. Today, however, the Court seems to have decided that the mere fact that a family that cannot afford a private education wants its children educated in a parochial school is a sufficient justification for this use of public funds.

Justice Souter, with whom Justice Stevens, Justice Ginsburg, and Justice Breyer join, dissenting.

... If there were an excuse for giving short shrift to the Establishment Clause, it would probably apply here. But there is no excuse. Constitutional limitations are placed on government to preserve constitutional values in hard cases, like these. ... I therefore respectfully dissent.

The applicability of the Establishment Clause to public funding of benefits to religious schools was settled in *Everson ..., which inaugurated the modern era of establishment doctrine. The Court stated the principle in words from which there was no dissent:*

"No tax in any amount, large or small, can be levied to support any religious activities or institutions, whatever they may be called, or whatever form they may adopt to teach or practice religion." ...

The Court has never in so many words repudiated this statement, let alone, in so many words, overruled *Everson*.

Today, however, the majority holds that the Establishment Clause is not offended by Ohio's Pilot Project Scholarship Program. ... The money will thus pay for eligible students' instruction not only in secular subjects but in religion as well, in schools that can fairly be characterized as founded to teach religious doctrine and to imbue teaching in all subjects with a religious dimension ...

How can a Court consistently leave *Everson* on the books and approve the Ohio vouchers? The answer is that it cannot. It is only by ignoring *Everson* that the majority can claim to rest on traditional law in its invocation of neutral aid provisions and private choice to sanction the Ohio law. It is, moreover, only by ignoring the meaning of neutrality and private choice themselves that the majority can even pretend to rest today's decision on those criteria.

I

The majority's statements of Establishment Clause doctrine cannot be appreciated without some historical perspective on the Court's announced limitations on government aid to religious education, and its repeated repudiation of limits previously set. ... [D]octrinal bankruptcy has been reached today.

Viewed with the necessary generality, the cases can be categorized in three groups. In the period from 1947 to 1968, the basic principle of no aid to religion through school benefits was unquestioned. Thereafter for some 15 years, the Court termed its efforts as attempts to draw a line against aid that would be divertible to support the religious, as distinct from the secular, activity of an institutional beneficiary. Then, starting in 1983, concern with divertibility was gradually lost in favor of approving aid in amounts unlikely to afford substantial benefits to religious schools, when offered evenhandedly without regard to a recipient's religious character, and when channeled to a religious institution only by the genuinely free choice of some private individual. Now, the three stages are succeeded by a fourth, in which the substantial character of government aid is held to have no constitutional significance, and the espoused criteria of neutrality in offering aid, and private choice in directing it, are shown to be nothing but examples of verbal formalism.

. . . .

. . . [i]t was not until today that substantiality of aid has clearly been rejected as irrelevant by a majority of this Court, just as it has not been until today that a majority, not a plurality, has held purely formal criteria to suffice for scrutinizing aid that ends up in the coffers of religious schools. Today's cases are notable for their stark illustration of the inadequacy of the majority's chosen formal analysis.

II

Although it has taken half a century since *Everson* to reach the majority's twin standards of neutrality and free choice, the facts show that, in the majority's hands, even these criteria cannot convincingly legitimize the Ohio scheme.

A

Consider first the criterion of neutrality. . . . [I]n its limited significance, formal neutrality seemed to serve some purpose. Today, however, the majority employs the neutrality criterion in a way that renders it impossible to understand.

Neutrality in this sense refers, of course, to evenhandedness in setting eligibility as between potential religious and secular recipients of public money. . . . Thus, for example, the aid scheme in *Witters* provided an eligible recipient with a scholarship to be used at any institution within a practically unlimited universe of schools, . . . ; it did not tend to provide more or less aid depending on which one the scholarship recipient chose, and there was no indication that the maximum scholarship amount would be insufficient at secular schools. . . .

In order to apply the neutrality test, then, it makes sense to . . . ask whether the voucher provisions . . . were written in a way that skewed the scheme toward benefitting religious schools.

This, however, is not what the majority asks. The majority looks not to the provisions for tuition vouchers, . . . but to every provision for educational opportunity. . . .

The illogic is patent. If regular, public schools (which can get no voucher payments) "participate" in a voucher scheme with schools that can, and public expenditure is still predominantly on public schools, then the majority's reasoning would find neutrality in a scheme of vouchers available for private tuition in districts with no secular private schools at all. "Neutrality" as the majority employs the term is, literally, verbal and nothing more. . . .

Why the majority does not simply accept the fact that the challenge here is to the more generous voucher scheme and judge its neutrality in relation to religious use of voucher money seems very odd. It seems odd, that is, until one recognizes that comparable schools for applying the criterion of neutrality are also the comparable schools for applying the other majority criterion, whether the immediate recipients of voucher aid have a genuinely free choice of religious and secular schools to receive the voucher money. And in applying this second criterion, the consideration of "*all* schools" is ostensibly helpful to the majority position.

B

The majority addresses the issue of choice the same way it addresses neutrality, by asking whether recipients or potential recipients of voucher aid have a choice of public schools among secular alternatives to religious schools. Again, however, the majority asks the wrong question and misapplies the criterion. The majority has confused choice in spending scholarships with choice from the entire menu of possible educational placements, most of them open to anyone willing to attend a public school. . . . When the choice test is transformed from where to spend the money to where to go to school, it is cut loose from its very purpose.

Defining choice as choice in spending the money or channeling the aid is, moreover, necessary if the choice criterion is to function as a limiting principle at all. . . .

. . .

. . . [L]eaving the selection of alternatives for choice wide open, as the majority would, virtually guarantees the availability of a "choice" that will satisfy the criterion, limiting the choices to spending choices will not guarantee a negative result in every case. There may, after all, be cases in which a voucher recipient will have a real choice, with enough secular private school desks in relation to the number of religious ones, and a voucher amount high enough to meet secular private school tuition levels. . . .

It is not, of course, that I think even a genuine choice criterion is up to the task of the Establishment Clause when substantial state funds go to religious teaching; the discussion in Part III, *infra*, shows that it is not. The point is simply that if the majority wishes to claim that choice is a criterion, it must define choice in a way that can function as a criterion with a practical capacity to screen something out.

. . .

III

I do not dissent merely because the majority has misapplied its own law, for even if I assumed *arguendo* that the majority's formal criteria were satisfied on the facts, today's conclusion would be profoundly at odds with the Constitution. Proof of this is clear on two levels. The first is circumstantial, in the now discarded symptom of violation, the substantial dimension of the aid. The second is direct, in the defiance of every objective supposed to be served by the bar against establishment.

A

The scale of the aid to religious schools approved today is unprecedented, both in the number of dollars and in the proportion of systemic school expenditure supported. Each measure has received attention in previous cases. On one hand, the sheer quantity of aid, when delivered to a class of religious primary and secondary schools, was suspect on the theory that the greater the aid, the greater its proportion to a religious school's existing expenditures, and the greater the likelihood that public money was supporting religious as well as secular instruction. . . .

On the other hand, the Court has found the gross amount unhelpful for Establishment Clause analysis when the aid afforded a benefit solely to one individual, however substantial as to him, but only an incidental benefit to the religious school at which the individual chose to spend the State's money. . . .

The majority's reliance on the observations of five Members of the Court in *Witters* as to the irrelevance of substantiality of aid in that case is therefore beside the point in the matter before us, which involves considerable sums of public funds systematically distributed through thousands of students attending religious elementary and middle schools in the city of Cleveland.

. . .

B

It is virtually superfluous to point out that every objective underlying the prohibition of religious establishment is betrayed by this scheme, but something has to be said about the enormity of the violation. . . .

. . .

When government aid goes up, so does reliance on it; the only thing likely to go down is independence. If Justice Douglas in *Allen* was concerned with state agencies, influenced by powerful religious groups, choosing the textbooks that parochial schools would use, 392 U. S., at 265 (dissenting opinion), how much more is there reason to wonder when dependence will become great enough to give the State of Ohio an effective veto over basic decisions on the content of curriculums? A day will come when religious schools will learn what political leverage can do, just as Ohio's politicians are now getting a lesson in the leverage exercised by religion.

. . .

. . . *Everson*'s statement is still the touchstone of sound law, even though the reality is that in the matter of educational aid the Establishment Clause has largely been read away. True, the majority has not approved vouchers for religious schools alone, or aid earmarked for religious instruction. But no scheme so clumsy will ever get before us, and in the cases that we may see, like these, the Establishment Clause is largely silenced. I do not have the option to leave it silent, and I hope that a future Court will reconsider today's dramatic departure from basic Establishment Clause principle.

Justice Breyer, with whom Justice Stevens and Justice Souter join, dissenting.

I join Justice Souter's opinion, and I agree substantially with Justice Stevens. I write separately, however, to emphasize the risk that publicly financed voucher programs pose in terms of religiously based social conflict. I do so because I believe that the Establishment Clause concern for protecting the Nation's social fabric from religious conflict poses an overriding obstacle to the implementation of this well-intentioned school voucher program. And by explaining the nature of the concern, I hope to demonstrate why, in my view, "parental choice" cannot significantly alleviate the constitutional problem.

I

. . . The Clauses reflect the Framers' vision of an American Nation free of the religious strife that had long plagued the nations of Europe. . . .

In part for this reason, the Court's 20th century Establishment Clause cases—both those limiting the practice of religion in public schools and those limiting the public funding of private religious education—focused directly upon social conflict, potentially created when government becomes involved in religious education. . . .

. . .

The upshot is the development of constitutional doctrine that reads the Establishment Clause as avoiding religious strife, *not* by providing every religion with an *equal opportunity* (say, to secure state funding or to pray in the public schools), but by drawing fairly clear lines of *separation* between church and state—at least where the heartland of religious belief, such as primary religious education, is at issue.

II

. . .

Consider the voucher program here at issue. That program insists that the religious school accept students of all religions. Does that criterion treat fairly groups whose religion forbids them to do so? The program also insists that no participating school "advocate or foster unlawful behavior or teach hatred of any person or group on the basis of race, ethnicity, national origin, or religion." . . .

How are state officials to adjudicate claims that one religion or another is advocating, for example, civil disobedience in response to unjust laws, the use of illegal drugs in a religious ceremony, or resort to force to call attention to what it views as an immoral social practice? What kind of public hearing will there be in response to claims that one religion or another is continuing to teach a view of history that casts members of other religions in the worst possible light? How will the public react to government funding for schools that take controversial religious positions on topics that are of current popular interest— say, the conflict in the Middle East or the war on terrorism? . . .

. . .

III

. . . [V]oucher programs differ . . . in both *kind* and *degree* from aid programs upheld in the past. They differ in kind because they direct financing to a core function of the church: the teaching of religious truths to young children.

. . . History suggests, not that . . . private school teaching of religion is undesirable, but that *government funding* of this kind of religious endeavor is far more contentious than providing funding for secular textbooks, computers, vocational training, or even funding for adults who wish to obtain a college education at a religious university. . . .

Vouchers also differ in *degree*. The aid programs recently upheld by the Court involved limited amounts of aid to religion. But the majority's analysis here appears to permit a considerable shift of taxpayer dollars from public secular schools to private religious schools. . . . [T]he secular aid upheld in *Mitchell* differs dramatically from the present case. Although it was conceivable that minor amounts of money could have, contrary to the statute, found their way to the religious activities of the recipients, . . . that case is at worst the camel's nose, while the litigation before us is the camel itself.

IV

I do not believe that the "parental choice" aspect of the voucher program sufficiently offsets the concerns I have mentioned. Parental choice cannot help the taxpayer who does not want to finance the religious education of children. It will not always help the parent who may see little real choice between inadequate nonsectarian public education and adequate education at a school whose religious teachings are contrary to his own. It will not satisfy religious minorities unable to participate because they are too few in number to support the creation of their own private schools. It will not satisfy groups whose religious beliefs preclude them from participating in a government-sponsored program, and who may well feel ignored as government funds primarily support the education of children in the doctrines of the dominant religions. And it does little to ameliorate the entanglement problems or the related problems of social division ... Consequently, the fact that the parent may choose which school can cash the government's voucher check does not alleviate the Establishment Clause concerns associated with voucher programs.

V

The Court, in effect, turns the clock back. It adopts, under the name of "neutrality," an interpretation of the Establishment Clause that this Court rejected more than half a century ago. ... In a society composed of many different religious creeds, I fear that this present departure from the Court's earlier understanding risks creating a form of religiously based conflict potentially harmful to the Nation's social fabric. Because I believe the Establishment Clause was written in part to avoid this kind of conflict, ... I respectfully dissent.

2.   HIGHER EDUCATION

TILTON v. RICHARDSON, 403 U.S. 672 (1971). The higher education facilities act of 1963 provided for federal grants to institutions of higher education for the construction of academic facilities. The act provided that only facilities used for non–sectarian instruction would be financed and that the restriction to non–sectarian use would have to be observed for 20 years. The Court by a vote of 5 to 4, but without an opinion of the Court, sustained the application of the statute to grants made for buildings at four church–related colleges. The Court held invalid the portion of the Act that would have permitted religious uses of the buildings after 20 years.

HUNT v. MCNAIR, 413 U.S. 734 (1973). South Carolina established an Educational Facilities Authority to assist through the issuance of revenue bonds higher educational institutions in constructing and financing buildings, facilities and site preparation, but not including any facility for sectarian instruction or religious worship. The Act was challenged here as applied to the issuance of bonds to finance the construction of dining hall facilities at a Baptist College. The Court upheld the statute, relying on Tilton v. Richardson. It said: "aid normally may be thought to have a primary effect of advancing religion when it flows to an institution in which religion is so pervasive that a substantial portion of its functions are subsumed in the religious mission or when it funds a specifically religious activity in an otherwise substantially secular setting." In this case the court relied on the fact that the college had no religious test for faculty or student body and that the Baptist percentage of the student body (60%) was about the same as the percentage of Baptists in the surrounding community.

Roemer v. Board of Public Works

426 U.S. 736, 96 S.Ct. 2337, 49 L.Ed.2d 179 (1976).

Mr. Justice Blackmun announced the judgment of the Court and delivered an opinion in which The Chief Justice and Mr. Justice Powell joined.

We are asked once again to police the constitutional boundary between church and state. Maryland, this time, is the alleged trespasser. It has enacted a statute which, as amended, provides for annual noncategorical grants to private colleges, among them religiously affiliated institutions, subject only to the restrictions that the funds not be used for "sectarian purposes." A three-judge District Court, by a divided vote, refused to enjoin the operation of the statute, and a direct appeal has been taken to this Court. . . .

Plaintiffs in this suit, appellants here, are four individual Maryland citizens and taxpayers. Their complaint sought a declaration of the statute's invalidity, an order enjoining payments under it to church-affiliated institutions, and a declaration that the State was entitled to recover from such institutions any amounts already disbursed. In addition to the responsible state officials, plaintiff-appellants joined as defendants the . . . institutions they claimed were constitutionally ineligible for this form of aid: . . . College of Notre Dame, Mount Saint Mary's College, Saint Joseph College, and Loyola College. [All] four are affiliated with the Roman Catholic Church . . .

After carefully assessing the role that the Catholic Church plays in the lives of these institutions, a matter to which we return in greater detail below, and applying the three-part requirement of *Lemon I,* . . . that state aid such as this have a secular purpose, a primary effect other than the advancement of religion, and no tendency to entangle the State excessively in church affairs, the District Court ruled that the amended statute was constitutional . . .

II.

A system of government that makes itself felt as pervasively as ours could hardly be expected never to cross paths with the church. In fact, our State and Federal Governments impose certain burdens upon, and impart certain benefits to, virtually all our activities, and religious activity is not an exception. The Court has enforced a scrupulous neutrality by the State, as among religions, and also as between religious and other activities, but a hermetic separation of the two is an impossibility it has never required. It long has been established, for example, that the State may send a cleric, indeed even a clerical order, to perform a wholly secular task. In Bradfield v. Roberts, 175 U.S. 291 (1899), the Court upheld the extension of public aid to a corporation which, although composed entirely of members of a Roman Catholic sisterhood acting "under the auspices of said church," . . . was limited by its corporate charter to the secular purpose of operating a charitable hospital.

And religious institutions need not be quarantined from public benefits that are neutrally available to all. The Court has permitted the State to supply transportation for children to and from church-related as well as public schools. . . . It has done the same with respect to secular textbooks loaned by the State on equal terms to students attending both public and church-related elementary schools. . . . The Court has not been blind to the fact that in aiding a religious institution to perform a secular task, the State frees the institution's resources to be put to sectarian ends. If this were impermissible, however, a church could not be protected by the police and fire departments, or have its public sidewalk kept in repair. The Court never has held that religious activities must be discriminated against in this way.

Neutrality is what is required. The State must confine itself to secular objectives, and neither advance nor impede religious activity. Of course, that principle is more easily stated than applied. The Court has taken the view that a secular purpose and a facial neutrality may not be enough, if in fact the State is lending direct support to a religious activity. The State may not, for example, pay for what is actually a religious education, even though it purports to be paying for a secular one, and even though it makes its aid available to secular and religious institutions alike. The Court also has taken the view that the State's efforts to perform a secular task, and at the same time avoid aiding in the performance of a religious one, may not lead it into such an intimate relationship with religious authority that it appears either to be sponsoring or to be excessively interfering with that authority. . . .

. . .

III.

The first part of *Lemon I*'s three-part test is not in issue; appellants do not challenge the District Court's finding that the purpose of Maryland's aid program is the secular one of supporting private higher education generally, as an economic alternative to a wholly public system. The focus of the debate is on the second and third parts, those concerning the primary effect of advancing religion, and excessive church-state entanglement. We consider them in the same order.

A.

While entanglement is essentially a procedural problem, the primary effect question is the substantive one of what private educational activities, by whatever procedure, may be supported by state funds. *Hunt* requires (1) that no state aid at all go to institutions that are so "pervasively sectarian" that secular activities cannot be separated from sectarian ones, and (2) that if secular activities *can* be separated out, they alone may be funded.

(1) The District Court's finding in this case was that the appellee colleges are not "pervasively sectarian." This conclusion it supported with a number of subsidiary findings concerning the role of religion on these campuses:

. . .

We cannot say that the foregoing findings as to the role of religion in particular aspects of the colleges are clearly erroneous. . . . The general picture that the District Court has painted of the appellee institutions is similar in almost all respects to that of the church-affiliated colleges considered in *Tilton* and *Hunt*. We find no constitutionally significant distinction between them, at least for purposes of the "pervasive sectarianism" test.

(2) Having found that the appellee institutions are not "so permeated by religion that the secular side cannot be separated from the sectarian," the District Court proceeded to the next question posed by *Hunt*: whether aid in fact was extended only to "the secular side." This requirement the court regarded as satisfied by the statutory prohibition against sectarian use, and by the administrative enforcement of that prohibition through the Council for Higher Education. We agree. . . . We must assume that the colleges, and the Council, will exercise their delegated control over use of the funds in compliance with the statutory, and therefore the constitutional, mandate. It is to be expected that they will give a wide berth to "specifically religious activity," and thus minimize constitutional questions. Should such questions arise, the courts will consider them. . . .

B.

If the foregoing answer to the "primary effect" question seems easy, it serves to make the "excessive entanglement" problem more difficult. The statute itself clearly denies the use of public funds for "sectarian purposes." It seeks to avert such use, however, through a process of annual interchange—proposal and approval, expenditure and review—between the colleges and the Council. In answering the question whether this will be an "excessively entangling" relationship, we must consider the several relevant factors identified in prior decisions:

(1) First is the character of the aided institutions. . . . As the District Court found, the colleges perform "essentially secular educational functions," that are distinct and separable from religious activity. This finding, which is a prerequisite under the "pervasive sectarianism" test to any state aid at all, is also important for purposes of the entanglement test because it means that secular activities, for the most, can be taken at face value. There is no danger, or at least only a substantially reduced danger, that an ostensibly secular activity—the study of biology, the learning of a foreign language, an athletic event—will actually be infused with religious content or significance. The need for close surveillance of purportedly secular activities is correspondingly reduced. . . .

(2) As for the form of aid, we have already noted that no particular use of state funds is before us in this case. The *process* by which aid is disbursed, and a use for it chosen, are before us. We address this as a matter of the "resulting relationship" of secular and religious authority.

(3) As noted, the funding process is an annual one. . . .

We agree with the District Court that "excessive entanglement" does not necessarily result from the fact that the subsidy is an annual one. It is true that the Court favored the "one-time, single-purpose" construction grants in *Tilton* because they entailed "no continuing financial relationships or dependencies, no annual audits, and no government analysis of an institution's expenditures." . . . The present aid program cannot claim these aspects. But if the question is whether this case is more like *Lemon I* or more like *Tilton*—and surely that is the fundamental question before us—the answer must be that it is more like *Tilton.*

Tilton is distinguishable only by the form of aid. . . .

While the form-of-aid distinctions of *Tilton* are thus of questionable importance, the character-of-institution distinctions of *Lemon I* are most impressive. To reiterate a few of the relevant points: the elementary and secondary schooling in *Lemon* came at an impressionable age; the aided schools were "under the general supervision" of the Roman Catholic diocese; each had a local Catholic parish that assumed "ultimate financial responsibility" for it; the principals of the schools were usually appointed by church authorities; religion "pervade[d] the school system"; teachers were specifically instructed by the "Handbook of School Regulations" that "[r]eligious formation is not confined to formal courses; nor is it restricted to a single subject area." . . . These things made impossible what is crucial to a nonentangling aid program: the ability of the State to identify and subsidize separate secular functions carried out at the school, without on-the-site inspections being necessary to prevent diversion of the funds to sectarian purposes. The District Court gave primary importance to this consideration, and we cannot say it erred.

(4) As for political divisiveness, the District Court recognized that the annual nature of the subsidy, along with its promise of an increasing demand for state funds as the colleges' dependency grew, aggravated the danger of "[p]olitical fragmentation . . . on religious lines." . . . Nonetheless, the District Court found that the program "does not create a substantial danger of political entanglement." . . . Several reasons were given. As was stated in *Tilton,* the

danger of political divisiveness is "substantially less" when the aided institution is not an elementary or secondary school, but a college, "whose student constituency is not local but diverse and widely dispersed." ... Furthermore, political divisiveness is diminished by the fact that the aid is extended to private colleges generally, more than two thirds of which have no religious affiliation; this is in sharp contrast to *Nyquist,* for example, where 95% of the aided schools were Roman Catholic parochial schools. Finally, the substantial autonomy of the colleges was thought to mitigate political divisiveness, in that controversies surrounding the aid program are not likely to involve the Catholic Church itself, or even the religious character of the schools, but only their "fiscal responsibility and educational requirements." ...

The District Court's reasoning seems to us entirely sound. ...

. . .

The judgment of the District Court is affirmed.

It is so ordered.

Mr. Justice White, with whom Mr. Justice Rehnquist joins, concurring in the judgment.

While I join in the judgment of the Court, I am unable to concur in the plurality opinion ...

"It is enough for me that the [State is] financing a separable secular function of overriding importance in order to sustain the legislation here challenged." ... However, since 1970, the Court has added a third element to the inquiry: whether there is "an excessive government entanglement with religion." ... I have never understood the constitutional foundation for this added element ... Today's plurality opinion leaves the impression that the criterion really may not be "separate" at all. In affirming the District Court's conclusion that the legislation here does not create an "excessive entanglement" of church and state the plurality emphasizes with approval that "the District Court gave dominant importance to the character of the aided institutions and to its finding that they are capable of separating secular and religious functions." Yet these are the same factors upon which the plurality focus in concluding that the Maryland legislation satisfies the first part of the *Lemon I* test: that on the record the "appellee colleges are not 'pervasively sectarian,'" and that the aid at issue was capable of, and is in fact, extended only to "the secular side" of the appellee colleges' operations. It is unclear to me how the first and third parts of the *Lemon I* test are substantially different. ...

. . .

Mr. Justice Brennan, with whom Mr. Justice Marshall joins, dissenting.

I agree with Judge Bryan, dissenting from the judgment under review, that ... "[o]f telling decisiveness here is the payment of the grants directly to the colleges unmarked in purpose.... Presently the Act is simply a blunderbuss discharge of public funds to a church-affiliated or church-related college." In other words, the Act provides for payment of general subsidies to religious institutions from public funds and I have heretofore expressed my view that "[g]eneral subsidies of religious activities would, of course, constitute impermissible state involvement with religion." ...

The discrete interests of government and religion are mutually best served when each avoids too close a proximity to the other....

. . .

Mr. Justice Stewart, dissenting.

In my view, the decisive differences between this case and Tilton v. Richardson, 403 U.S. 672, lie in the nature of the theology courses that are a compulsory part of the curriculum at each of the appellee institutions and the type of governmental assistance provided to these church-affiliated colleges. In *Tilton* the Court emphasized that the theology courses were taught as academic subjects. . . .

. . . Here, by contrast, the District Court was unable to find that the compulsory religion courses were taught as an academic discipline. . . .

In the light of these findings, I cannot agree with the Court's assertion that there is "no constitutionally significant distinction" between the colleges in *Tilton* and those in the present case. . . .

For the reasons stated, and those expressed by Mr. Justice Brennan and Mr. Justice Stevens, I dissent from the judgment and opinion of the Court.

Mr. Justice Stevens, dissenting.

My views are substantially those expressed by Mr. Justice Brennan. However, I would add emphasis to the pernicious tendency of a state subsidy to tempt religious schools to compromise their religious mission without wholly abandoning it. The disease of entanglement may infect a law discouraging wholesome religious activity as well as a law encouraging the propagation of a given faith.

Rosenberger v. Rector and Visitors of the University of Virginia

515 U.S. 819, 115 S.Ct. 2510, 132 L.Ed.2d 700 (1995).

Justice Kennedy delivered the opinion of the Court.

The University of Virginia, [a state university] . . ., authorizes the payment of outside contractors for the printing costs of a variety of student publications. It withheld any authorization for payments on behalf of petitioners for the sole reason that their student paper "primarily promotes or manifests a particular belie[f] in or about a deity or an ultimate reality." That the paper did promote or manifest views within the defined exclusion seems plain enough. The challenge is to the University's regulation and its denial of authorization, the case raising issues under the Speech and Establishment Clauses of the First Amendment.

I

. . .

Before a student group is eligible to submit bills from its outside contractors for payment by the fund described below, it must become a "Contracted Independent Organization" (CIO). CIO status is available to any group the majority of whose members are students, whose managing officers are fulltime students, and that complies with certain procedural requirements. . . .

All CIOs may exist and operate at the University, but some are also entitled to apply for funds from the Student Activities Fund (SAF). . . . The SAF receives its money from a mandatory fee of $14 per semester assessed to each full-time student. . . .

Some, but not all, CIOs may submit disbursement requests to the SAF. . . . The Guidelines . . . specify . . . that the costs of certain activities of CIOs that are otherwise eligible for funding will not be reimbursed by the SAF. The student activities which are excluded from SAF support are religious activities, philanthropic contributions and activities, political activities, activities that would jeopardize the University's tax exempt status, those which involve payment of honoraria or similar fees, or social entertainment or related expenses. The prohibition on "political activities" is defined so that it is limited to electioneering and lobbying. The Guidelines provide that "[t]hese restrictions on funding political activities are not intended to preclude funding of any otherwise eligible student organization which . . . espouses particular positions or ideological viewpoints, including those that may be unpopular or are not generally accepted." A "religious activity," by contrast, is defined as any activity that "primarily promotes or manifests a particular belie[f] in or about a deity or an ultimate reality."

. . .

Petitioners' organization, Wide Awake Productions (WAP), qualified as a CIO. Formed by petitioner Ronald Rosenberger and other undergraduates in 1990, WAP was established "[t]o publish a magazine of philosophical and religious expression," "[t]o facilitate discussion which fosters an atmosphere of sensitivity to and tolerance of Christian viewpoints," and "[t]o provide a unifying focus for Christians of multicultural backgrounds." WAP publishes Wide Awake: A Christian Perspective at the University of Virginia. The paper's Christian viewpoint was evident from the first issue, in which its editors wrote that the journal "offers a Christian perspective on both personal and community issues, especially those relevant to college students at the University of Virginia." The editors committed the paper to a two-fold mission: "to challenge Christians to live, in word and deed, according to the faith they proclaim and to encourage students to consider what a personal relationship with Jesus Christ means." The first issue had articles about racism, crisis pregnancy, stress, prayer, C.S. Lewis' ideas about evil and free will, and reviews of religious music. In the next two issues, Wide Awake featured stories about homosexuality, Christian missionary work, and eating disorders, as well as music reviews and interviews with University professors. Each page of Wide Awake, and the end of each article or review, is marked by a cross. The advertisements carried in Wide Awake also reveal the Christian perspective of the journal. For the most part, the advertisers are churches, centers for Christian study, or Christian bookstores. By June 1992, WAP had distributed about 5,000 copies of Wide Awake to University students, free of charge.

WAP had acquired CIO status soon after it was organized. This is an important consideration in this case, for had it been a "religious organization," WAP would not have been accorded CIO status. As defined by the Guidelines, a "religious organization" is "an organization whose purpose is to practice a devotion to an acknowledged ultimate reality or deity." At no stage in this controversy has the University contended that WAP is such an organization.

A few months after being given CIO status, WAP requested the SAF to pay its printer $5,862 for the costs of printing its newspaper. The Appropriations Committee of the Student Council denied WAP's request on the ground that Wide Awake was a "religious activity" within the meaning of the Guidelines, i.e., that the newspaper "promote[d] or manifest[ed] a particular belie[f] in or about a deity or an ultimate reality." . . .

. . . WAP, Wide Awake, and three of its editors and members filed suit in the United States District Court for the Western District of Virginia . . . They alleged that refusal to authorize payment of the printing costs of the publication, solely on the basis of its religious editorial viewpoint, violated their rights to freedom of speech and press, to the free exercise of religion, and to equal protection of the law. ... The suit sought damages for the costs of printing the paper, injunctive and declaratory relief, and attorney's fees.

On cross-motions for summary judgment, the District Court ruled for the University ...

The United States Court of Appeals for the Fourth Circuit ... affirmed ..., concluding that the discrimination by the University was justified by the "compelling interest in maintaining strict separation of church and state."

II

It is axiomatic that the government may not regulate speech based on its substantive content or the message it conveys. ...

... [T]he State [is forbidden] from exercising viewpoint discrimination, even when the limited public forum is one of its own creation. In a case involving a school district's provision of school facilities for private uses, we declared that "[t]here is no question that the District, like the private owner of property, may legally preserve the property under its control for the use to which it is dedicated." Lamb's Chapel v. Center Moriches Union Free School Dist. 508 U.S. 384, 390 (1993). The necessities of confining a forum to the limited and legitimate purposes for which it was created may justify the State in reserving it for certain groups or for the discussion of certain topics. ... Once it has opened a limited forum, however, the State must respect the lawful boundaries it has itself set. ... Thus, in determining whether the State is acting to preserve the limits of the forum it has created so that the exclusion of a class of speech is legitimate, we have observed a distinction between, on the one hand, content discrimination, which may be permissible if it preserves the purposes of that limited forum, and, on the other hand, viewpoint discrimination, which is presumed impermissible when directed against speech otherwise within the forum's limitations. ...

The SAF is a forum more in a metaphysical than in a spatial or geographic sense, but the same principles are applicable. ... The most recent and most apposite case is our decision in *Lamb's Chapel* ... There, a school district had opened school facilities for use after school hours by community groups for a wide variety of social, civic, and recreational purposes. The district, however, had enacted a formal policy against opening facilities to groups for religious purposes. ... Our conclusion was unanimous: "[I]t discriminates on the basis of viewpoint to permit school property to be used for the presentation of all views about family issues and child-rearing except those dealing with the subject matter from a religious standpoint." ...

The University does acknowledge (as it must in light of our precedents) that "ideologically driven attempts to suppress a particular point of view are presumptively unconstitutional in funding, as in other contexts," but insists that this case does not present that issue because the Guidelines draw lines based on content, not viewpoint. As we have noted, discrimination against one set of views or ideas is but a subset or particular instance of the more general phenomenon of content discrimination. ... And, it must be acknowledged, the distinction is not a precise one. It is, in a sense, something of an understatement to speak of religious thought and discussion as just a viewpoint, as distinct from a comprehensive body of thought. The nature of our origins and destiny and their dependence upon the existence of a divine being have been subjects of philosophic inquiry throughout human history. We conclude, nonetheless, that here, as in *Lamb's Chapel*, viewpoint discrimination is the proper way to interpret the University's objections to Wide Awake. By the very terms of the SAF prohibition, the University does not exclude religion as a subject matter but selects for disfavored treatment those student journalistic efforts with religious editorial viewpoints. Religion may be a vast area of inquiry, but it also provides, as it did here, a specific premise, a perspective, a standpoint from which a variety of subjects may be discussed and considered. The prohibited perspective, not the general subject matter, resulted in the refusal to make third-party payments, for the subjects discussed were otherwise within the approved category of publications.

The dissent's assertion that no viewpoint discrimination occurs because the Guidelines discriminate against an entire class of viewpoints reflects an insupportable assumption that all debate is bipolar and that anti-religious speech is the only response to religious speech. Our understanding of the complex and multifaceted nature of public discourse has not embraced such a contrived description of the marketplace of ideas. If the topic of debate is, for example, racism, then exclusion of several views on that problem is just as offensive to the First Amendment as exclusion of only one. It is as objectionable to exclude both a theistic and an atheistic perspective on the debate as it is to exclude one, the other, or yet another political, economic, or social viewpoint. The dissent's declaration that debate is not skewed so long as multiple voices are silenced is simply wrong; the debate is skewed in multiple ways.

The University's denial of WAP's request for third-party payments in the present case is based upon viewpoint discrimination not unlike the discrimination the school district relied upon in *Lamb's Chapel* and that we found invalid. . . .

The University tries to escape the consequences of our holding in *Lamb's Chapel* by urging that this case involves the provision of funds rather than access to facilities. . . . Were the reasoning of Lamb's Chapel to apply to funding decisions as well as to those involving access to facilities, it is urged, its holding "would become a judicial juggernaut, constitutionalizing the ubiquitous content-based decisions that schools, colleges, and other government entities routinely make in the allocation of public funds."

To this end the University relies on our assurance in Widmar v. Vincent, [454 U.S. 263 (1981).] There, in the course of striking down a public university's exclusion of religious groups from use of school facilities made available to all other student groups, we stated: "Nor do we question the right of the University to make academic judgments as to how best to allocate scarce resources." . . . The quoted language in *Widmar* was but a proper recognition of the principle that when the State is the speaker, it may make content-based choices. When the University determines the content of the education it provides, it is the University speaking, and we have permitted the government to regulate the content of what is or is not expressed when it is the speaker or when it enlists private entities to convey its own message. . . . When the government disburses public funds to private entities to convey a governmental message, it may take legitimate and appropriate steps to ensure that its message is neither garbled nor distorted by the grantee. . . .

It does not follow, however, and we did not suggest in *Widmar*, that viewpoint-based restrictions are proper when the University does not itself speak or subsidize transmittal of a message it favors but instead expends funds to encourage a diversity of views from private speakers. A holding that the University may not discriminate based on the viewpoint of private persons whose speech it facilitates does not restrict the University's own speech, which is controlled by different principles. . . .

. . .

The University urges that, from a constitutional standpoint, funding of speech differs from provision of access to facilities because money is scarce and physical facilities are not. Beyond the fact that in any given case this proposition might not be true as an empirical matter, the underlying premise that the University could discriminate based on viewpoint if demand for space exceeded its availability is wrong as well. The government cannot justify viewpoint discrimination among private speakers on the economic fact of scarcity. Had the meeting rooms in *Lamb's Chapel* been scarce, had the demand been greater than the supply, our decision would have been no different. It would have been incumbent on the State, of course, to ration or allocate the scarce resources on some acceptable neutral principle; but nothing in our decision indicated that scarcity would give the State the right to exercise viewpoint discrimination that is otherwise impermissible.

. . .

III

Before its brief on the merits in this Court, the University had argued at all stages of the litigation that inclusion of WAP's contractors in SAF funding authorization would violate the Establishment Clause. Indeed, that is the ground on which the University prevailed in the Court of Appeals. We granted certiorari on this question: "Whether the Establishment Clause compels a state university to exclude an otherwise eligible student publication from participation in the student activities fund, solely on the basis of its religious viewpoint, where such exclusion would violate the Speech and Press Clauses if the viewpoint of the publication were nonreligious." The University now seems to have abandoned this position . . . That the University itself no longer presses the Establishment Clause claim is some indication that it lacks force; but as the Court of Appeals rested its judgment on the point and our dissenting colleagues would find it determinative, it must be addressed.

. . .

A central lesson of our decisions is that a significant factor in upholding governmental programs in the face of Establishment Clause attack is their neutrality towards religion. We have decided a series of cases addressing the receipt of government benefits where religion or religious views are implicated in some degree. . . . More than once have we rejected the position that the Establishment Clause even justifies, much less requires, a refusal to extend free speech rights to religious speakers who participate in broad-reaching government programs neutral in design. . . .

The governmental program here is neutral toward religion. There is no suggestion that the University created it to advance religion or adopted some ingenious device with the purpose of aiding a religious cause. The object of the SAF is to open a forum for speech and to support various student enterprises, including the publication of newspapers, in recognition of the diversity and creativity of student life. . . . WAP did not seek a subsidy because of its Christian editorial viewpoint; it sought funding as a student journal, which it was.

The neutrality of the program distinguishes the student fees from a tax levied for the direct support of a church or group of churches. A tax of that sort, of course, would run contrary to Establishment Clause concerns dating from the earliest days of the Republic. The apprehensions of our predecessors involved the levying of taxes upon the public for the sole and exclusive purpose of establishing and supporting specific sects. The exaction here, by contrast, is a student activity fee designed to reflect the reality that student life in its many dimensions includes the necessity of wide-ranging speech and inquiry and that student expression is an integral part of the University's educational mission. ... [T]he $14 paid each semester by the students is not a general tax designed to raise revenue for the University. ... The SAF cannot be used for unlimited purposes, much less the illegitimate purpose of supporting one religion. Much like the arrangement in *Widmar*, the money goes to a special fund from which any group of students with CIO status can draw for purposes consistent with the University's educational mission; and to the extent the student is interested in speech, withdrawal is permitted to cover the whole spectrum of speech, whether it manifests a religious view, an antireligious view, or neither. Our decision, then, cannot be read as addressing an expenditure from a general tax fund. Here, the disbursements from the fund go to private contractors for the cost of printing that which is protected under the Speech Clause of the First Amendment. This is a far cry from a general public assessment designed and effected to provide financial support for a church.

Government neutrality is apparent in the State's overall scheme in a further meaningful respect. The program respects the critical difference "between government speech endorsing religion, which the Establishment Clause forbids, and private speech endorsing religion, which the Free Speech and Free Exercise Clauses protect." ... The University has taken pains to disassociate itself from the private speech involved in this case. The Court of Appeals' apparent concern that Wide Awake's religious orientation would be attributed to the University is not a plausible fear, and there is no real likelihood that the speech in question is being either endorsed or coerced by the State ...

The Court of Appeals (and the dissent) are correct to extract from our decisions the principle that we have recognized special Establishment Clause dangers where the government makes direct money payments to sectarian institutions ... The error is not in identifying the principle but in believing that it controls this case. Even assuming that WAP is no different from a church and that its speech is the same as the religious exercises conducted in *Widmar* (two points much in doubt), the Court of Appeals decided a case that was, in essence, not before it, and the dissent would have us do the same. We do not confront a case where, even under a neutral program that includes nonsectarian recipients, the government is making direct money payments to an institution or group that is engaged in religious activity. Neither the Court of Appeals nor the dissent, we believe, takes sufficient cognizance of the undisputed fact that no public funds flow directly to WAP's coffers.

It does not violate the Establishment Clause for a public university to grant access to its facilities on a religion-neutral basis to a wide spectrum of student groups, including groups which use meeting rooms for sectarian activities, accompanied by some devotional exercises. ... This is so even where the upkeep, maintenance, and repair of the facilities attributed to those uses is paid from a student activities fund to which students are required to contribute. ... The government usually acts by spending money. Even the provision of a meeting room, as in ... *Widmar*, involved governmental expenditure, if only in the form of electricity and heating or cooling costs. The error made by the Court of Appeals, as well as by the dissent, lies in focusing on the money that is undoubtedly expended by the government, rather than on the nature of the benefit received by the recipient. ... If a religious student organization obtained access on that religion-neutral basis and used a computer to compose or a printer or copy machine to print speech with a religious content or viewpoint, the State's action in providing the group with access would no more violate the Establishment Clause than would giving those groups access to an assembly hall. ... Any benefit to religion is incidental to the government's provision of secular services for secular purposes on a religion-neutral basis. Printing is a routine, secular, and recurring attribute of student life.

By paying outside printers, the University in fact attains a further degree of separation from the student publication, for it avoids the duties of supervision, escapes the costs of upkeep, repair, and replacement attributable to student use, and has a clear record of costs. ...

Were the dissent's view to become law, it would require the University, in order to avoid a constitutional violation, to scrutinize the content of student speech, lest the expression in question-speech otherwise protected by the Constitution-contain too great a religious content. The dissent, in fact, anticipates such censorship as "crucial" in distinguishing between "works characterized by the evangelism of Wide Awake and writing that merely happens to express views that a given religion might approve." That eventuality raises the specter of governmental censorship, to ensure that all student writings and publications meet some baseline standard of secular orthodoxy. To impose that standard on student speech at a university is to imperil the very sources of free speech and expression. As we recognized in *Widmar*, official censorship would be far more inconsistent with the Establishment Clause's dictates than would governmental provision of secular printing services on a religion-blind basis. ... Merely to draw the distinction would require the university—and ultimately the courts—to inquire into the significance of words and practices to different religious faiths, and in varying circumstances by the same faith. Such inquiries would tend inevitably to entangle the State with religion in a manner forbidden by our cases. ...

* * *

... The viewpoint discrimination inherent in the University's regulation required public officials to scan and interpret student publications to discern their underlying philosophic assumptions respecting religious theory and belief. That course of action was a denial of the right of free speech and would risk fostering a pervasive bias or hostility to religion, which could undermine the very neutrality the Establishment Clause requires. There is no Establishment Clause violation in the University's honoring its duties under the Free Speech Clause.

The judgment of the Court of Appeals must be, and is, reversed. It is so ordered.

Justice O'Connor, concurring.

. . .

This case lies at the intersection of the principle of government neutrality and the prohibition on state funding of religious activities. ...

When two bedrock principles so conflict, understandably neither can provide the definitive answer. ...

. . .

So it is in this case. The nature of the dispute does not admit of categorical answers, nor should any be inferred from the Court's decision today. Instead, certain considerations specific to the program at issue lead me to conclude that by providing the same assistance to Wide Awake that it does to other publications, the University would not be endorsing the magazine's religious perspective.

First, the student organizations, at the University's insistence, remain strictly independent of the University. . . . Any reader of Wide Awake would be on notice of the publication's independence from the University. . . .

Second, financial assistance is distributed in a manner that ensures its use only for permissible purposes. A student organization seeking assistance must submit disbursement requests; if approved, the funds are paid directly to the third-party vendor and do not pass through the organization's coffers. This . . . ensures that the funds are used only to further the University's purpose in maintaining a free and robust marketplace of ideas, from whatever perspective. This feature also makes this case analogous to a school providing equal access to a generally available printing press (or other physical facilities), and unlike a block grant to religious organizations.

Third, assistance is provided to the religious publication in a context that makes improbable any perception of government endorsement of the religious message. . . .

Finally, . . . Unlike monies dispensed from state or federal treasuries, the Student Activities Fund is collected from students who themselves administer the fund and select qualifying recipients only from among those who originally paid the fee. The government neither pays into nor draws from this common pool . . . The Student Activities Fund, then, represents not government resources, whether derived from tax revenue, sales of assets, or otherwise, but a fund that simply belongs to the students.

The Court's decision today therefore neither trumpets the supremacy of the neutrality principle nor signals the demise of the funding prohibition in Establishment Clause jurisprudence. . . . [P]articular features of the University's program—such as the explicit disclaimer, the disbursement of funds directly to third-party vendors, the vigorous nature of the forum at issue, and the possibility for objecting students to opt out—convince me that providing such assistance in this case would not carry the danger of impermissible use of public funds to endorse Wide Awake's religious message.

Subject to these comments, I join the opinion of the Court.

Justice Thomas, concurring.

I agree with the Court's opinion and join it in full, but I write separately to express my disagreement with the historical analysis put forward by the dissent. . . .

. . .

Legal commentators have disagreed about the historical lesson to take from the Assessment Controversy. For some, the experience in Virginia is consistent with the view that the Framers saw the Establishment Clause simply as a prohibition on governmental preferences for some religious faiths over others. See R. Cord, Separation of Church and State: Historical Fact and Current Fiction 20–23 (1982); Smith, Getting Off on the Wrong Foot and Back on Again: A Reexamination of the History of the Framing of the Religion Clauses of the First Amendment and a Critique of the Reynolds and Everson Decisions, 20 Wake Forest L. Rev. 569, 590–591 (1984). Other commentators have rejected this view, concluding that the Establishment Clause forbids not only government preferences for some religious sects over others, but also government preferences for religion over irreligion. See, e.g., Laycock, "Non-preferential" Aid to Religion: A False Claim About Original Intent, 27 Wm. & Mary L. Rev. 875, 875 (1986).

I find much to commend the former view. . . .

But resolution of this debate is not necessary to decide this case. Under any understanding of the Assessment Controversy, the history cited by the dissent cannot support the conclusion that the Establishment Clause "categorically condemn[s] state programs directly aiding religious activity" when that aid is part of a neutral program available to a wide array of beneficiaries. . . Even if Madison believed that the principle of nonestablishment of religion precluded government financial support for religion per se (in the sense of government benefits specifically targeting religion), there is no indication that at the time of the framing he took the dissent's extreme view that the government must discriminate against religious adherents by excluding them from more generally available financial subsidies.

. . .

Justice Souter, with whom Justice Stevens, Justice Ginsburg, and Justice Breyer join, dissenting.

The Court today, for the first time, approves direct funding of core religious activities by an arm of the State. It does so, however, only after erroneous treatment of some familiar principles of law implementing the First Amendment's Establishment and Speech Clauses, and by viewing the very funds in question as beyond the reach of the Establishment Clause's funding restrictions as such. Because there is no warrant for distinguishing among public funding sources for purposes of applying the First Amendment's prohibition of religious establishment, I would hold that the University's refusal to support petitioners' religious activities is compelled by the Establishment Clause. I would therefore affirm.

I

. . .

A

. . .

Using public funds for the direct subsidization of preaching the word is categorically forbidden under the Establishment Clause, and if the Clause was meant to accomplish nothing else, it was meant to bar this use of public money. Evidence on the subject antedates even the Bill of Rights itself, as may be seen in the writings of Madison . . . Four years before the First Congress proposed the First Amendment, Madison gave his opinion on the legitimacy of using public funds for religious purposes, in the Memorial and Remonstrance Against Religious Assessments, which played the central role in ensuring the defeat of the Virginia tax assessment bill in 1786 and framed the debate upon which the Religion Clauses stand . . .

Madison wrote against a background in which nearly every Colony had exacted a tax for church support . . . Madison's Remonstrance captured the colonists' "conviction that individual religious liberty could be achieved best under a government which was stripped of all power to tax, to support, or otherwise to assist any or all religions, or to interfere with the beliefs of any religious individual or group." . . . Their sentiment as expressed by Madison in Virginia, led not only to the defeat of Virginia's tax assessment bill, but also directly to passage of the Virginia Bill for Establishing Religious Freedom, written by Thomas Jefferson. That bill's preamble declared that "to compel a man to furnish contributions of money for the propagation of opinions which he disbelieves, is sinful and tyrannical," ... and its text provided "[t]hat no man shall be compelled to frequent or support any religious worship, place, or ministry whatsoever ...," ....

The principle against direct funding with public money is patently violated by the contested use of today's student activity fee ... The University exercises the power of the State to compel a student to pay it, ... and the use of any part of it for the direct support of religious activity thus strikes at what we have repeatedly held to be the heart of the prohibition on establishment. ...

The Court, accordingly, has never before upheld direct state funding of the sort of proselytizing published in Wide Awake and, in fact, has categorically condemned state programs directly aiding religious activity ...

. . .

B

. . .

... In the doubtful cases (those not involving direct public funding), where there is initially room for argument about a law's effect, evenhandedness serves to weed out those laws that impermissibly advance religion by channeling aid to it exclusively. Evenhandedness is therefore a prerequisite to further enquiry into the constitutionality of a doubtful law, but evenhandedness goes no further. It does not guarantee success under Establishment Clause scrutiny.

. . .

C

. . .

... The common factual thread running through *Widmar* and *Lamb's Chapel*, is that a governmental institution created a limited forum for the use of students in a school or college, or for the public at large, but sought to exclude speakers with religious messages. ... [E]ach case drew ultimately on unexceptionable Speech Clause doctrine treating the evangelist, the Salvation Army, the millennialist or the Hare Krishna like any other speaker in a public forum. It was the preservation of free speech on the model of the street corner that supplied the justification going beyond the requirement of evenhandedness.

... The analogy breaks down entirely, however, if the cases are read more broadly than the Court wrote them, to cover more than forums for literal speaking. There is no traditional street corner printing provided by the government on equal terms to all comers, and the forum cases cannot be lifted to a higher plane of generalization without admitting that new economic benefits are being extended directly to religion in clear violation of the principle barring direct aid. The argument from economic equivalence thus breaks down on recognizing that the direct state aid it would support is not mitigated by the street corner analogy in the service of free speech. Absent that, the rule against direct aid stands as a bar to printing services as well as printers.

. . .

II

Given the dispositive effect of the Establishment Clause's bar to funding the magazine, there should be no need to decide whether in the absence of this bar the University would violate the Free Speech Clause by limiting funding as it has done. ... But the Court's speech analysis may have independent application, and its flaws should not pass unremarked.

. . .

... Other things being equal, viewpoint discrimination occurs when government allows one message while prohibiting the messages of those who can reasonably be expected to respond. ... It is precisely this element of taking sides in a public debate that identifies viewpoint discrimination and makes it the most pernicious of all distinctions based on content. Thus, if government assists those espousing one point of view, neutrality requires it to assist those espousing opposing points of view, as well.

There is no viewpoint discrimination in the University's application of its Guidelines to deny funding to Wide Awake. Under those Guidelines, a "religious activit[y]," which is not eligible for funding, is "an activity which primarily promotes or manifests a particular belief(s) in or about a deity or an ultimate reality." It is clear that this is the basis on which Wide Awake Productions was denied funding. ...

If the Guidelines were written or applied so as to limit only such Christian advocacy and no other evangelical efforts that might compete with it, the discrimination would be based on viewpoint. But that is not what the regulation authorizes; it applies to Muslim and Jewish and Buddhist advocacy as well as to Christian. And since it limits funding to activities promoting or manifesting a particular belief not only "in" but "about" a deity or ultimate reality, it applies to agnostics and atheists as well as it does to deists and theists ... The Guidelines, and their application to Wide Awake, thus do not skew debate by funding one position but not its competitors. As understood by their application to Wide Awake, they simply deny funding for hortatory speech that "primarily promotes or manifests" any view on the merits of religion; they deny funding for the entire subject matter of religious apologetics.

. . .

The Guidelines are thus substantially different from the access restriction considered in *Lamb's Chapel* . .

... [I]n *Lamb's Chapel* we unanimously determined that the access restriction, as applied to a speaker wishing to discuss family values from a Christian perspective, impermissibly distinguished between speakers on the basis of viewpoint. ... Equally obvious is the distinction between that case and this one, where the regulation is being applied, not to deny funding for those who discuss issues in general from a religious viewpoint, but to those engaged in promoting or opposing religious conversion and religious observances as such. If this amounts to viewpoint discrimination, the Court has all but eviscerated the line between viewpoint and content.

. . .

III

Since I cannot see the future I cannot tell whether today's decision portends much more than making a shambles out of student activity fees in public colleges. Still, my apprehension is whetted by Chief Justice Burger's warning in Lemon v. Kurtzman, 403 U.S. 602, 624 (1971): "in constitutional adjudication some steps, which when taken were thought to approach 'the verge,' have become the platform for yet further steps. A certain momentum develops in constitutional theory and it can be a 'downhill thrust' easily set in motion but difficult to retard or stop.''

I respectfully dissent.

SECTION 2.   THE FREE EXERCISE OF RELIGION

Sherbert v. Verner

374 U.S. 398, 83 S.Ct. 1790, 10 L.Ed.2d 965 (1963).

Mr. Justice Brennan delivered the opinion of the Court.

Appellant, a member of the Seventh-day Adventist Church was discharged by her South Carolina employer because she would not work on Saturday, the Sabbath Day of her faith. When she was unable to obtain other employment because from conscientious scruples she would not take Saturday work, she filed a claim for unemployment compensation benefits under the South Carolina Unemployment Compensation Act.... The appellee Employment Security Commission, in administrative proceedings under the statute, found that appellant's restriction upon her availability for Saturday work brought her within the provision disqualifying for benefits insured workers who fail, without good cause, to accept "suitable work when offered ... by the employment office or the employer...." The Commission's finding was sustained ... by the South Carolina Supreme Court,...[4] ....

II.

. . .

Significantly South Carolina expressly saves the Sunday worshiper from having to make the kind of choice which we were hold infringes the Sabbatarian's religious liberty. When in times of "national emergency" the textile plants are authorized by the State Commission of Labor to operate on Sunday, "no employee shall be required to work on Sunday ... who is conscientiously opposed to Sunday work...." The unconstitutionality of the disqualification of

---

4. It has been suggested that appellant is not within the class entitled to benefits under the South Carolina statute because her unemployment did not result from discharge or layoff due to lack of work. It is true that unavailability for work for some personal reasons not having to do with matters of conscience or religion has been held to be a basis of disqualification for benefits. But appellant claims that the Free Exercise Clause prevents the State from basing the denial of benefits upon the "personal reason" she gives for not working on Saturday. Where the consequence of disqualification so directly affects First Amendment rights, surely we should not conclude that every "personal reason" is a basis for disqualification in the absence of explicit language to that effect in the statute or decisions of the South Carolina Supreme Court. Nothing we have found in the statute or in the cited decisions, and certainly nothing in the South Carolina Court's opinion in this case so construes the statute. Indeed, the contrary seems to have been that court's basic assumption, for if the eligibility provisions were thus limited, it would have been unnecessary for the court to have decided appellant's constitutional challenge to the application of the statute under the Free Exercise Clause.

Likewise, the decision of the State Supreme Court does not rest upon a finding that appellant was disqualified for benefits because she had been "discharged for misconduct"—by reason of her Saturday absences—within the meaning of § 68–114(2). That ground was not adopted by the South Carolina Supreme Court, and the appellees do not urge in this Court that the disqualification rests upon that ground.

the Sabbatarian is thus compounded by the religious discrimination which South Carolina's general statutory scheme necessarily effects.

III.

We must next consider whether some compelling state interest enforced in the eligibility provisions of the South Carolina statute justifies the substantial infringement of appellant's First Amendment right. It is basic that no showing merely of a rational relationship to some colorable state interest would suffice; in this highly sensitive constitutional area, "[o]nly the gravest abuses, endangering paramount interests, give occasion for permissible limitation," ... No such abuse or danger has been advanced in the present case. The appellees suggest no more than a possibility that the filing of fraudulent claims by unscrupulous claimants feigning religious objections to Saturday work might not only dilute the unemployment compensation fund but also hinder the scheduling by employers of necessary Saturday work. But that possibility is not apposite here because no such objection appears to have been made before the South Carolina Supreme Court, and we are unwilling to assess the importance of an asserted state interest without the views of the state court. Nor, if the contention had been made below, would the record appear to sustain it; there is no proof whatever to warrant such fears of malingering or deceit as those which the respondents now advance. ... [E]ven if the possibility of spurious claims did threaten to dilute the fund and disrupt the scheduling of work, it would plainly be incumbent upon the appellees to demonstrate that no alternative forms of regulation would combat such abuses without infringing First Amendment rights.

In these respects, then, the state interest asserted in the present case is wholly dissimilar to the interests which were found to justify the less direct burden upon religious practices in Braunfeld v. Brown, [366 U.S. 599 (1961)]. The Court recognized that the Sunday closing law which that decision sustained undoubtedly served "to make the practice of [the Orthodox Jewish merchants'] ... religious beliefs more expensive," ... But the statute was nevertheless saved by a countervailing factor which finds no equivalent in the instant case—a strong state interest in providing one uniform day of rest for all workers. That secular objective could be achieved, the Court found, only by declaring Sunday to be that day of rest. Requiring exemptions for Sabbatarians, while theoretically possible, appeared to present an administrative problem of such magnitude, or to afford the exempted class so great a competitive advantage, that such a requirement would have rendered the entire statutory scheme unworkable. In the present case no such justifications underlie the determination of the state court that appellant's religion makes her ineligible to receive benefits.

IV.

... [We do not] declare the existence of a constitutional right to unemployment benefits on the part of all persons whose religious convictions are the cause of their unemployment. This is not a case in which an employee's religious convictions serve to make him a nonproductive member of society. Finally, nothing we say today constrains the States to adopt any particular form or scheme of unemployment compensation. Our holding today is only that South Carolina may not constitutionally apply the eligibility provisions so as to constrain a worker to abandon his religious convictions respecting the day of rest. ...

. . .

The judgment of the South Carolina Supreme Court is reversed and the case is remanded for further proceedings not inconsistent with this opinion.[a]

Mr. Justice Stewart, concurring in the result.

. . .

... I cannot agree that today's decision can stand consistently with Braunfeld v. Brown, supra. The Court says that there was a "less direct burden upon religious practices" in that case than in this. With all respect, I think the Court is mistaken, simply as a matter of fact. The *Braunfeld* case involved a state *criminal* statute. . . .

The impact upon the appellant's religious freedom in the present case is considerably less onerous. We deal here not with a criminal statute, but with the particularized administration of South Carolina's Unemployment Compensation Act. Even upon the unlikely assumption that the appellant could not find suitable non-Saturday employment, the appellant at the worst would be denied a maximum of 22 weeks of compensation payments. I agree with the Court that the possibility of that denial is enough to infringe upon the appellant's constitutional right to the free exercise of her religion. But it is clear to me that in order to reach this conclusion the Court must explicitly reject the reasoning of Braunfeld v. Brown. I think the *Braunfeld* case was wrongly decided and should be overruled, and accordingly I concur in the result reached by the Court in the case before us.

Mr. Justice Harlan, whom Mr. Justice White joins, dissenting.

. . .

South Carolina's Unemployment Compensation Law was enacted in 1936 in response to the grave social and economic problems that arose during the depression of that period. . . . Thus the purpose of the legislature was to tide people over, and to avoid social and economic chaos, during periods when *work was unavailable*. . . .

The South Carolina Supreme Court has uniformly applied this law in conformity with its clearly expressed purpose. It has consistently held that one is not "available for work" if his unemployment has resulted not from the inability of industry to provide a job but rather from personal circumstances, no matter how compelling. The reference to "involuntary unemployment" in the legislative statement of policy, whatever a sociologist, philosopher, or theologian might say, has been interpreted not to embrace such personal circumstances. . . . Thus in no proper sense can it be said that the State discriminated against the appellant on the basis of her religious beliefs or that she was denied benefits *because* she was a Seventh-day Adventist. She was denied benefits just as any other claimant would be denied benefits who was not "available for work" for personal reasons.[1]

---

a. A concurring opinion by Justice Douglas is omitted.

1. I am completely at a loss to understand note 4 of the Court's opinion. Certainly the Court is not basing today's decision on the unsupported supposition that *some* day, the South Carolina Supreme Court may conclude that there is *some personal* reason for unemployment that may not disqualify a claimant for relief. In any event, I submit it is perfectly clear that South Carolina would not compensate persons who became unem-

ployed for *any* personal reason, as distinguished from layoffs or lack of work, since the State Supreme Court's decisions make it plain that such persons would not be regarded as "available for work" within the manifest meaning of the eligibility requirements. Nor can I understand what this Court means when it says that "if the eligibility provisions were thus limited, it would have been unnecessary for the [South Carolina] court to have decided appellant's constitutional challenge. . . ."

... What the Court is holding is that if the State chooses to condition unemployment compensation on the applicant's availability for work, it is constitutionally compelled to *carve out an exception*—and to provide benefits— for those whose unavailability is due to their religious convictions.[2]

. . .

THOMAS v. REVIEW BOARD OF THE INDIANA EMPLOYMENT SECURITY DIVISION, 450 U.S. 707 (1981). Thomas, a Jehovah's Witness, quit his job because of religious opposition to participating in the production of armaments, when his employer transferred him to a department making turrets for military tanks. He was denied unemployment compensation. The Indiana Supreme Court upheld the denial, because the unemployment compensation statute denied compensation to employees "who quit work voluntarily for personal reasons" that were not objectively job–related. Relying on Sherbert v. Verner, the Supreme Court reversed.

The sole dissenter, Justice Rehnquist, contended that Sherbert v. Verner should be overruled. In a footnote, he argued that *Sherbert* was distinguishable from *Thomas* because the Indiana statute had been construed to make *every* personal subjective reason for refusing employment a basis for disqualification.

Wisconsin v. Yoder

406 U.S. 205, 92 S.Ct. 1526, 32 L.Ed.2d 15 (1972).

[Respondents Yoder, Yutzy and Miller were members of the Amish religious sect and residents of Wisconsin where it was required that children attend school until the age of 16. Because of their religion's tenets, they refused to send their children (ages 14 and 15) to school after completing the eighth grade. They believe that by sending their children to high school they would not only expose themselves to possible censure of their church community, but also endanger their own salvation and that of their children. It was agreed that respondents' religious beliefs were sincere. Those beliefs required members of the community to make their living by farming or closely related activities. High school, and higher education generally, was objected to because the values taught were in marked contrast with Amish values and way of life. Respondents were convicted of violating the Wisconsin compulsory attendance law; the Supreme Court of Wisconsin reversed the conviction, sustaining respondents' claim under the free exercise clause of the first amendment.]

Mr. Chief Justice Burger delivered the opinion of the Court.

. . .

The essence of all that has been said and written on the subject is that only those interests of the highest order and those not otherwise served can overbalance legitimate claims to the free exercise of religion. We can accept it as settled, therefore, that however strong the State's interest in universal

---

2. The Court does suggest, in a rather startling disclaimer, that its holding is limited in applicability to those whose religious convictions do not make them "nonproductive" members of society, noting that most of the Seventh-day Adventists in the Spartanburg area are employed. But surely this disclaimer cannot be taken seriously, for the Court cannot mean that the case would have come out differently if none of the Seventh-day Adventists in Spartanburg had been gainfully employed, or if the appellant's religion had prevented her from working on Tuesdays instead of Saturdays. Nor can the Court be suggesting that it will make a value judgment in each case as to whether a particular individual's religious convictions prevent him from being "productive." I can think of no more inappropriate function for this Court to perform.

compulsory education, it is by no means absolute to the exclusion or subordination of all other interests. . . .

. . .

So long as compulsory education laws were confined to eight grades of elementary basic education imparted in a nearby rural schoolhouse, with a large proportion of students of the Amish faith, the Old Order Amish had little basis to fear that school attendance would expose their children to the worldly influence they reject. But modern compulsory secondary education in rural areas is now largely carried on in a consolidated school, often remote from the student's home and alien to his daily home life. . . . The conclusion is inescapable that secondary schooling, by exposing Amish children to worldly influences in terms of attitudes, goals and values contrary to beliefs, and by substantially interfering with the religious development of the Amish child and his integration into the way of life of the Amish faith community at the crucial adolescent state of development, contravenes the basic religious tenets and practice of the Amish faith, both as to the parent and the child. . . .

In sum, the unchallenged testimony of acknowledged experts in education and religious history, almost 300 years of consistent practice, and strong evidence of a sustained faith pervading and regulating respondents' entire mode of life support the claim that enforcement of the State's requirement of compulsory formal education after the eighth grade would gravely endanger if not destroy the free exercise of respondents' religious beliefs.

. . .

The State advances two primary arguments in support of its system of compulsory education. It notes, as Thomas Jefferson pointed out early in our history, that some degree of education is necessary to prepare citizens to participate effectively and intelligently in our open political system if we are to preserve freedom and independence. Further, education prepares individuals to be self-reliant and self-sufficient participants in society. We accept these propositions.

However, the evidence adduced by the Amish in this case is persuasively to the effect that an additional one or two years of formal high school for Amish children in place of their long established program of informal vocational education would do little to serve those interests. Respondents' experts testified at trial, without challenge, that the value of all education must be assessed in terms of its capacity to prepare the child for life. It is one thing to say that compulsory education for a year or two beyond the eighth grade may be necessary when its goal is the preparation of the child for life in modern society as the majority live, but it is quite another if the goal of education be viewed as the preparation of the child for life in the separated agrarian community that is the keystone of the Amish faith. See Meyer v. Nebraska, 262 U.S., at 400. . . .

Whatever their idiosyncrasies as seen by the majority, this record strongly shows that the Amish community has been a highly successful social unit within our society even if apart from the conventional "mainstream." Its members are productive and very law-abiding members of society; they reject public welfare in any of its usual modern forms. The Congress itself recognized their self-sufficiency by authorizing exemption of such groups as the Amish from the obligation to pay social security taxes.

It is neither fair nor correct to suggest that the Amish are opposed to education beyond the eighth grade level. What this record shows is that they are opposed to conventional formal education of the type provided by a certified high school because it comes at the child's crucial adolescent period of religious development....

The State, however, supports its interest in providing an additional one or two years of compulsory high school education to Amish children because of the possibility that some such children will choose to leave the Amish community, and that if this occurs they will be ill-equipped for life. The State argues that if Amish children leave their church they should not be in the position of making their way in the world without the education available in the one or two additional years the State requires. However, on this record, that argument is highly speculative. There is no specific evidence of the loss of Amish adherents by attrition, nor is there any showing that upon leaving the Amish community Amish children, with their practical agricultural training and habits of industry and self-reliance would become burdens on society because of educational shortcomings....

In these terms, Wisconsin's interest in compelling the school attendance of Amish children to age 16 emerges as somewhat less substantial than requiring such attendance for children generally. For, while agricultural employment is not totally outside the legitimate concerns of the child labor laws, employment of children under parental guidance and on the family farm from age 14 to age 16 is an ancient tradition which lies at the periphery of the objectives of such laws. There is no intimation that the Amish employment of their children on family farms is in any way deleterious to their health or that Amish parents exploit children at tender years. Any such inference would be contrary to the record before us. Moreover, employment of Amish children on the family farm does not present the undesirable economic aspects of eliminating jobs which might otherwise be held by adults....

Contrary to the suggestion of the dissenting opinion of Mr. Justice Douglas, our holding today in no degree depends on the assertion of the religious interest of the child as contrasted with that of the parents. It is the parents who are subject to prosecution here for failing to cause their children to attend school, and it is their right of free exercise, not that of their children, that must determine Wisconsin's power to impose criminal penalties on the parent....

Our holding in no way determines the proper resolution of possible competing interests of parents, children, and the State in an appropriate state court proceeding in which the power of the State is asserted on the theory that Amish parents are preventing their minor children from attending high school despite their expressed desires to the contrary. Recognition of the claim of the State in such a proceeding would, of course, call into question traditional concepts of parental control over the religious upbringing and education of their minor children recognized in this Court's past decisions. It is clear that such an intrusion by a State into family decisions in the area of religious training would give rise to grave questions of religious freedom comparable to those raised here and those presented in Pierce v. Society of Sisters. On this record we neither reach nor decide those issues....

For the reasons stated we hold, with the Supreme Court of Wisconsin, that the First and Fourteenth Amendments prevent the State from compelling respondents to cause their children to attend formal high school to age 16. Our disposition of this case, however, in no way alters our recognition of the obvious fact that courts are not school boards or legislatures, and are ill-equipped to determine the "necessity" of discrete aspects of a State's program of compulsory education....

Nothing we hold is intended to undermine the general applicability of the State's compulsory school attendance statutes or to limit the power of the State to promulgate reasonable standards that, while not impairing the free exercise of religion, provide for continuing agricultural vocational education under parental and church guidance by the Old Order Amish or others similarly situated. The States have had a long history of amicable and effective relationships with church-sponsored schools, and there is no basis for assuming that, in this related context, reasonable standards cannot be established concerning the content of the continuing vocational education of Amish children under parental guidance, provided always that state regulations are not inconsistent with what we have said in this opinion.

Affirmed.

Mr. Justice Powell and Mr. Justice Rehnquist took no part in the consideration or decision of this case.

Mr. Justice Stewart, with whom Mr. Justice Brennan joins, concurring.

. . .

This case in no way involves any questions regarding the right of the children of Amish parents to attend public high schools, or any other institutions of learning, if they wish to do so. As the Court points out, there is no suggestion whatever in the record that the religious beliefs of the children here concerned differ in any way from those of their parents. . . .

Mr. Justice White, with whom Mr. Justice Brennan and Mr. Justice Stewart, join, concurring.

Cases such as this one inevitably call for a delicate balancing of important but conflicting interests. I join the opinion and judgment of the Court because I cannot say that the State's interest in requiring two more years of compulsory education in the ninth and tenth grades outweighs the importance of the concededly sincere Amish religious practice to the survival of that sect.

. . .

I join the Court because the sincerity of the Amish religious policy here is uncontested, because the potential adverse impact of the state requirement is great and because the State's valid interest in education has already been largely satisfied by the eight years the children have already spent in school.

Mr. Justice Douglas, dissenting in part.

I agree with the Court that the religious scruples of the Amish are opposed to the education of their children beyond the grade schools, yet I disagree with the Court's conclusion that the matter is within the dispensation of parents alone. The Court's analysis assumes that the only interests at stake in the case are those of the Amish parents on the one hand, and those of the State on the other. The difficulty with this approach is that, despite the Court's claim, the parents are seeking to vindicate not only their own free exercise claims, but also those of their high-school-age children.

. . .

. . . Frieda Yoder has in fact testified that her own religious views are opposed to high-school education. I therefore join the judgment of the Court as to respondent Jonas Yoder. But Frieda Yoder's views may not be those of Vernon Yutzy or Barbara Miller. I must dissent, therefore, as to respondents Adin Yutzy and Wallace Miller as their motion to dismiss also raised the question of their children's religious liberty.

This issue has never been squarely presented before today. Our opinions are full of talk about the power of the parents over the child's education. See Pierce v. Society of Sisters, 268 U.S. 510; Meyer v. Nebraska, 262 U.S. 390. And we have in the past analyzed similar conflicts between parent and State with little regard for the views of the child. See Prince v. Massachusetts, 321 U.S. 158. Recent cases, however, have clearly held that the children themselves have constitutionally protectible interests....

. . .

The views of the two children in question were not canvassed by the Wisconsin courts. The matter should be explicitly reserved so that new hearings can be held on remand of the case....

Employment Division, Department of Human Resources of Oregon v. Smith

494 U.S. 872, 110 S.Ct. 1595, 108 L.Ed.2d 876 (1990).

Justice Scalia delivered the opinion of the Court.

This case requires us to decide whether the Free Exercise Clause of the First Amendment permits the State of Oregon to include religiously inspired peyote use within the reach of its general criminal prohibition on use of that drug, and thus permits the State to deny unemployment benefits to persons dismissed from their jobs because of such religiously inspired use.

I

Oregon law prohibits the knowing or intentional possession of a "controlled substance" ... [including] the drug peyote, a hallucinogen derived from the plant Lophophpra williamsii Lemaire....

Respondents Alfred Smith and Galen Black were fired from their jobs with a private drug rehabilitation organization because they ingested peyote for sacramental purposes at a ceremony of the Native American Church, of which both are members. When respondents applied to petitioner Employment Division for unemployment compensation, they were determined to be ineligible for benefits because they had been discharged for work-related "misconduct"....

... The Oregon Supreme Court reasoned ... that the criminality of respondents' peyote use was irrelevant to resolution of their constitutional claim—since the purpose of the "misconduct" provision under which respondents had been disqualified was not to enforce the State's criminal laws but to preserve the financial integrity of the compensation fund, and since that purpose was inadequate to justify the burden that disqualification imposed on respondents' religious practice....

Before this Court in 1987, petitioner continued to maintain that the illegality of respondents' peyote consumption was relevant to their constitutional claim. We agreed, concluding that "if a State has prohibited through its criminal laws certain kinds of religiously motivated conduct without violating the First Amendment, it certainly follows that it may impose the lesser burden of denying unemployment compensation benefits to persons who engage in that conduct." Employment Div., Dept. of Human Resources of Oregon v. Smith, 485 U.S. 660, 670 (1988) (*Smith I*). We noted, however, that the Oregon Supreme Court had not decided whether respondents' sacramental use of peyote was in fact proscribed by Oregon's controlled substance law, and that this issue was a matter of dispute between the parties.... [W]e vacated the judgment of the Oregon Supreme Court and remanded for further proceedings. . . .

On remand, the Oregon Supreme Court held that respondents' religiously inspired use of peyote fell within the prohibition of the Oregon statute . . . It then considered whether that prohibition was valid under the Free Exercise Clause, and concluded that it was not. The court therefore reaffirmed its previous ruling that the State could not deny unemployment benefits to respondents for having engaged in that practice.

. . .

II

Respondents' claim for relief rests on our decisions in Sherbert v. Verner, supra, Thomas v. Review Board, Indiana Employment Security Div., supra, and Hobbie v. Unemployment Appeals Comm'n of Florida, 480 U.S. 136 (1987) . . . As we observed in *Smith I,* however, the conduct at issue in those cases was not prohibited by law. We held that distinction to be critical, for "if Oregon does prohibit the religious use of peyote, and if that prohibition is consistent with the Federal Constitution, there is no federal right to engage in that conduct in Oregon," and "the State is free to withhold unemployment compensation from respondents for engaging in work-related misconduct, despite its religious motivation." . . . Now that the Oregon Supreme Court has confirmed that Oregon does prohibit the religious use of peyote, we proceed to consider whether that prohibition is permissible under the Free Exercise Clause.

A

. . . The free exercise of religion means, first and foremost, the right to believe and profess whatever religious doctrine one desires. Thus, the First Amendment obviously excludes all "governmental regulation of religious *beliefs* as such." . . . The government may not compel affirmation of religious belief, see Torcaso v. Watkins, 367 U.S. 488 (1961), punish the expression of religious doctrines it believes to be false, United States v. Ballard, 322 U.S. 78, 86–88 (1944), impose special disabilities on the basis of religious views or religious status, see McDaniel v. Paty, 435 U.S. 618 (1978); . . . or lend its power to one or the other side in controversies over religious authority or dogma, see Presbyterian Church v. Hull Church, 393 U.S. 440, 445–452 (1969); Kedroff v. St. Nicholas Cathedral, 344 U.S. 94, 95–119 (1952); Serbian Eastern Orthodox Diocese v. Milivojevich, 426 U.S. 696, 708–725 (1976).

But the "exercise of religion" often involves not only belief and profession but the performance of (or abstention from) physical acts: assembling with others for a worship service, participating in sacramental use of bread and wine, proselytizing, abstaining from certain foods or certain modes of transportation. It would be true, we think (though no case of ours has involved the point), that a state would be "prohibiting the free exercise [of religion]" if it sought to ban such acts or abstentions only when they are engaged in for religious reasons, or only because of the religious belief that they display. It would doubtless be unconstitutional, for example, to ban the casting of "statutes that are to be used for worship purposes," or to prohibit bowing down before a golden calf.

Respondents in the present case, however, seek to carry the meaning of "prohibiting the free exercise [of religion]" one large step further. They contend that their religious motivation for using peyote places them beyond the reach of a criminal law that is not specifically directed at their religious practice, and that is concededly constitutional as applied to those who use the drug for other reasons. They assert, in other words, that "prohibiting the free exercise [of religion]" includes requiring any individual to observe a generally applicable law that requires (or forbids) the performance of an act that his religious belief forbids (or requires). As a textual matter, we do not think the words must be given that meaning. It is no more necessary to regard the collection of a general tax, for example, as "prohibiting the free exercise [of religion]" by those citizens who believe support of organized government to be sinful, than it is to regard the same tax as "abridging the freedom . . . of the press" of those publishing companies that must pay the tax as a condition of staying in business. . . .

. . . We have never held that an individual's religious beliefs excuse him from compliance with an otherwise valid law prohibiting conduct that the State is free to regulate. On the contrary, the record of more than a century of our free exercise jurisprudence contradicts that proposition. As described succinctly by Justice Frankfurter in Minersville School Dist. Bd. of Educ. v. Gobitis, 310 U.S. 586, 594–595 (1940):

> "Conscientious scruples have not, in the course of the long struggle for religious toleration, relieved the individual from obedience to a general law not aimed at the promotion or restriction of religious beliefs. The mere possession of religious convictions which contradict the relevant concerns of a political society does not relieve the citizen from the discharge of political responsibilities . . ."

We first had occasion to assert that principle in Reynolds v. United States, 98 U.S. 145 (1879), where we rejected the claim that criminal laws against polygamy could not be constitutionally applied to those whose religion commanded the practice. "Laws," we said, "are made for the government of actions, and while they cannot interfere with mere religious belief and opinions, they may with practices. . . . Can a man excuse his practices to the contrary because of his religious belief? To permit this would be to make the professed doctrines of religious belief superior to the law of the land, and in effect to permit every citizen to become a law unto himself." . . .

Subsequent decisions have consistently held that the right of free exercise does not relieve an individual of the obligation to comply with a "valid and neutral law of general applicability on the ground that the law proscribes (or prescribes) conduct that his religion prescribes (or proscribes)." United States v. Lee, 455 U.S. 252, 263, n. 3 (1982) (Stevens, J., concurring in judgment). . . . In Prince v. Massachusetts, 321 U.S. 158 (1944), we held that a mother could be prosecuted under the child labor laws for using her children to dispense literature in the streets, her religious motivation notwithstanding. We found no constitutional infirmity in "excluding [these children] from doing there what no other children may do." . . . In Braunfeld v. Brown, 366 U.S. 599 (1961) (plurality opinion), we upheld Sunday-closing laws against the claim that they burdened the religious practices of persons whose religions compelled them to refrain from work on other days. In Gillette v. United States, 401 U.S. 437, 461 (1971), we sustained the military selective service system against the claim that it violated free exercise by conscripting persons who opposed a particular war on religious grounds.

Our most recent decision involving a neutral, generally applicable regulatory law that compelled activity forbidden by an individual's religion was United States v. Lee . . . There, an Amish employer, on behalf of himself and his employees, sought exemption from collection and payment of Social Security taxes on the ground that the Amish faith prohibited participation in governmental support programs. We rejected the claim that an exemption was constitutionally required. There would be no way, we observed, to distinguish the Amish believer's objection to Social Security taxes from the religious objections that others might have to the collection or use of other taxes. "If, for example, a religious adherent believes war is a sin, and if a certain percentage of the federal budget can be identified as devoted to war-related activities, such individuals would have a similarly valid claim to be exempt from paying that percentage of the income tax. The tax system could not function if denominations were allowed to challenge the tax system because tax payments were spent in a manner that violates their religious belief." . . .

The only decisions in which we have held that the First Amendment bars application of a neutral, generally applicable law to religiously motivated action have involved not the Free Exercise Clause alone, but the Free Exercise Clause in conjunction with other constitutional protections, such as freedom of speech and of the press, see Cantwell v. Connecticut, 310 U.S. at 304–307 (invalidating a licensing system for religious and charitable solicitations under which the administrator had discretion to deny a license to any cause he deemed nonreligious); Murdock v. Pennsylvania, 319 U.S. 105 (1943) (invalidating a flat tax on solicitation as applied to the dissemination of religious ideas); Follett v. McCormick, 321 U.S. 573 (1944) (same), or the right of parents, acknowledged in Pierce v. Society of Sisters, 268 U.S. 510 (1925), to direct the education of their children, see Wisconsin v. Yoder, 406 U.S. 205 (1972) (invalidating compulsory school-attendance laws as applied to Amish parents who refused on religious grounds to send their children to school).[1] Some of our cases prohibiting compelled expression, decided exclusively upon free speech grounds, have also involved freedom of religion, cf. Wooley v. Maynard, 430 U.S. 705 (1977) (invalidating compelled display of a license plate slogan that offended individual religious beliefs); West Virginia Board of Education v. Barnette, 319 U.S. 624 (1943) (invalidating compulsory flag salute statute challenged by religious objectors). And it is easy to envision a case in which a challenge on freedom of association grounds would likewise be reinforced by Free Exercise Clause concerns. Cf. Roberts v. United States Jaycees, 468 U.S. 609, 622 (1984) ("An individual's freedom to speak, to worship, and to petition the government for the redress of grievances could not be vigorously protected from interference by the State [if] a correlative freedom to engage in group effort toward those ends were not also guaranteed.").

The present case does not present such a hybrid situation, but a free exercise claim unconnected with any communicative activity or parental right. Respondents urge us to hold, quite simply, that when otherwise prohibitable conduct is accompanied by religious convictions, not only the convictions but the conduct itself must be free from governmental regulation. We have never held that, and decline to do so now. There being no contention that Oregon's drug law represents an attempt to regulate religious beliefs, the communication of religious beliefs, or the raising of one's children in those beliefs, the rule to which we have adhered ever since *Reynolds* plainly controls. . . .

B

Respondents argue that even though exemption from generally applicable criminal laws need not automatically be extended to religiously motivated

---

1. Both lines of cases have specifically adverted to the non-free exercise principle involved. . . . *Yoder* said that "the Court's holding in *Pierce* stands as a charter of the rights of parents to direct the religious upbringing of their children. And, when the interests of parenthood are combined with a free exercise claim of the nature revealed by this record, more than merely a 'reasonable relation to some purpose within the competency of the State is required to sustain the validity of the State's requirement under the First Amendment.'" . . .

actors, at least the claim for a religious exemption must be evaluated under the balancing test set forth in Sherbert v. Verner ... We have never invalidated any governmental action on the basis of the *Sherbert* test except the denial of unemployment compensation. Although we have sometimes purported to apply the *Sherbert* test in contexts other than that, we have always found the test satisfied, see United States v. Lee, 455 U.S. 252 (1982); Gillette v. United States, 401 U.S. 437 (1971). In recent years we have abstained from applying the *Sherbert* test (outside the unemployment compensation field) at all. In Bowen v. Roy, 476 U.S. 693 (1986), we declined to apply *Sherbert* analysis to a federal statutory scheme that required benefit applicants and recipients to provide their Social Security numbers. The plaintiffs in that case asserted that it would violate their religious beliefs to obtain and provide a Social Security number for their daughter. We held the statute's application to the plaintiffs valid regardless of whether it was necessary to effectuate a compelling interest. ... In Lyng v. Northwest Indian Cemetery Protective Assn., 485 U.S. 439 (1988), we declined to apply *Sherbert* analysis to the Government's logging and road construction activities on lands used for religious purposes by several Native American Tribes, even though it was undisputed that the activities "could have devastating effects on traditional Indian religious practices," ... In Goldman v. Weinberger, 475 U.S. 503 (1986), we rejected application of the *Sherbert* test to military dress regulations that forbade the wearing of yarmulkes. In O'Lone v. Estate of Shabazz, 482 U.S. 342 (1987), we sustained, without mentioning the *Sherbert* test, a prison's refusal to excuse inmates from work requirements to attend worship services.

Even if we were inclined to breathe into *Sherbert* some life beyond the unemployment compensation field, we would not apply it to require exemptions from a generally applicable criminal law. The *Sherbert* test, it must be recalled, was developed in a context that lent itself to individualized governmental assessment of the reasons for the relevant conduct. As a plurality of the Court noted in *Roy,* a distinctive feature of unemployment compensation programs is that their eligibility criteria invite consideration of the particular circumstances behind an applicant's unemployment ... As the plurality pointed out in *Roy,* our decisions in the unemployment cases stand for the proposition that where the State has in place a system of individual exemptions, it may not refuse to extend that system to cases of "religious hardship" without compelling reason. ...

Whether or not the decisions are that limited, they at least have nothing to do with an across-the-board criminal prohibition on a particular form of conduct. Although, as noted earlier, we have sometimes used the *Sherbert* test to analyze free exercise challenges to such laws, ... we have never applied the test to invalidate one. We conclude today that the sounder approach, and the approach in accord with the vast majority of our precedents, is to hold the test inapplicable to such challenges. The government's ability to enforce generally applicable prohibitions of socially harmful conduct, like its ability to carry out other aspects of public policy, "cannot depend on measuring the effects of a governmental action on a religious objector's spiritual development." *Lyng,* supra, at 451. To make an individual's obligation to obey such a law contingent upon the law's coincidence with his religious beliefs, except where the State's interest is "compelling"—permitting him, by virtue of his beliefs, "to become a law unto himself," Reynolds v. United States, 98 U.S., at 167—contradicts both constitutional tradition and common sense.[2]

---

2. Justice O'Connor seeks to distinguish Lyng v. Northwest Indian Cemetery   Protective Assn., supra, and Bowen v. Roy, supra, on the ground that those cases in-

The "compelling government interest" requirement seems benign, because it is familiar from other fields. But using it as the standard that must be met before the government may accord different treatment on the basis of race, ... or before the government may regulate the content of speech, ... is not remotely comparable to using it for the purpose asserted here. What it produces in those other fields—equality of treatment, and an unrestricted flow of contending speech—are constitutional norms; what it would produce here—a private right to ignore generally applicable laws—is a constitutional anomaly.

Nor is it possible to limit the impact of respondents' proposal by requiring a "compelling state interest" only when the conduct prohibited is "central" to the individual's religion.... It is no more appropriate for judges to determine the "centrality" of religious beliefs before applying a "compelling interest" test in the free exercise field, than it would be for them to determine the "importance" of ideas before applying the "compelling interest" test in the free speech field.... Repeatedly and in many different contexts, we have warned that courts must not presume to determine the place of a particular belief in a religion or the plausibility of a religious claim....[4]

If the "compelling interest" test is to be applied at all, then, it must be applied across the board, to all actions thought to be religiously commanded. Moreover, if "compelling interest" really means what it says (and watering it down here would subvert its rigor in the other fields where it is applied), many laws will not meet the test. Any society adopting such a system would be courting anarchy, but that danger increases in direct proportion to the society's diversity of religious beliefs, and its determination to coerce or suppress none of them.... The rule respondents favor would open the prospect of constitutionally required religious exemptions from civic obligations of almost every conceivable kind—ranging from compulsory military service, see, e.g., Gillette v. United States, 401 U.S. 437 (1971), to the payment of taxes, see, e.g., United States v. Lee, supra; to health and safety regulation such as manslaughter and child neglect laws, see, e.g., Funkhouser v. State, 763 P.2d 695 (Okla.Crim.App. 1988), compulsory vaccination laws, see, e.g., Cude v. State, 237 Ark. 927, 377 S.W.2d 816 (1964), drug laws, see, e.g., Olsen v. Drug Enforcement Administration, 279 U.S.App.D.C. 1, 878 F.2d 1458 (1989), and traffic laws, see Cox v. New Hampshire, 312 U.S. 569 (1941); to social welfare legislation such as minimum wage laws, see Susan and Tony Alamo Foundation v. Secretary of Labor, 471 U.S. 290 (1985), child labor laws, see Prince v. Massachusetts, 321 U.S. 158 (1944), animal cruelty laws, see, e.g., Church of the Lukumi Babalu Aye Inc. v. City of Hialeah, 723 F.Supp. 1467 (S.D.Fla.1989), cf. State v. Massey, 229 N.C. 734, 51 S.E.2d 179, appeal dism'd, 336 U.S. 942 (1949), environmental protection laws, see United States v. Little, 638 F.Supp. 337 (D.Mont.1986), and laws providing for equality of opportunity for the races, see, e.g., Bob Jones Univer-

---

volved the government's conduct of "its own internal affairs," ... [I]t is hard to see any reason in principle or practicality why the government should have to tailor its health and safety laws to conform to the diversity of religious belief, but should not have to tailor its management of public lands, *Lyng, supra,* or its administration of welfare programs, *Roy, supra.*

4. ... Justice O'Connor ... agrees that "our determination ... cannot, and should not, turn on the centrality of the particular religious practice at issue." ... Earlier in her opinion, however, Justice O'Connor appears to contradict this, saying that the proper approach is "to determine whether the burden on the specific plaintiffs before us is constitutionally significant and whether the particular criminal interest asserted by the State before us is compelling." "Constitutionally significant burden" would seem to be "centrality" under another name.... There is no way out of the difficulty that, if general laws are to be subjected to a "religious practice" exception, *both* the importance of the law at issue *and* the centrality of the practice at issue must reasonably be considered....

sity v. United States, 461 U.S. 574, 603–604 (1983). The First Amendment's protection of religious liberty does not require this.

Values that are protected against government interference through enshrinement in the Bill of Rights are not thereby banished from the political process.... [A] society that believes in the negative protection accorded to religious belief can be expected to be solicitous of that value in its legislation.... It is therefore not surprising that a number of States have made an exception to their drug laws for sacramental peyote use. But to say that a nondiscriminatory religious-practice exemption is permitted, or even that it is desirable, is not to say that it is constitutionally required, and that the appropriate occasions for its creation can be discerned by the courts. It may fairly be said that leaving accommodation to the political process will place at a relative disadvantage those religious practices that are not widely engaged in; but that unavoidable consequence of democratic government must be preferred to a system in which each conscience is a law unto itself or in which judges weigh the social importance of all laws against the centrality of all religious beliefs.

Because respondents' ingestion of peyote was prohibited under Oregon law, and because that prohibition is constitutional, Oregon may, consistent with the Free Exercise Clause, deny respondents unemployment compensation when their dismissal results from use of the drug. The decision of the Oregon Supreme Court is accordingly reversed.

It is so ordered.

Justice O'Connor, with whom Justice Brennan, Justice Marshall, and Justice Blackmun join as to Parts I and II, concurring in the judgment.*

Although I agree with the result the Court reaches in this case, I cannot join its opinion. In my view, today's holding dramatically departs from well-settled First Amendment jurisprudence, appears unnecessary to resolve the question presented, and is incompatible with our Nation's fundamental commitment to individual religious liberty.

. . .

II

The Court today extracts from our long history of free exercise precedents the single categorical rule that "if prohibiting the exercise of religion ... is ... merely the incidental effect of a generally applicable and otherwise valid provision, the First Amendment has not been offended." Indeed, the Court holds that where the law is a generally applicable criminal prohibition, our usual free exercise jurisprudence does not even apply. To reach this sweeping result, however, the Court must not only give a strained reading of the First Amendment but must also disregard our consistent application of free exercise doctrine to cases involving generally applicable regulations that burden religious conduct.

A

... Because the First Amendment does not distinguish between religious belief and religious conduct, conduct motivated by sincere religious belief, like

---

* Although Justice Brennan, Justice Marshall, and Justice Blackmun join Parts I and II of the opinion, they do not concur in the judgment.

the belief itself, must therefore be at least presumptively protected by the Free Exercise Clause.

The Court today, however, interprets the Clause to permit the government to prohibit, without justification, conduct mandated by an individual's religious beliefs, so long as that prohibition is generally applicable. But a law that prohibits certain conduct—conduct that happens to be an act of worship for someone—manifestly does prohibit that person's free exercise of his religion. A person who is barred from engaging in religiously motivated conduct is barred from freely exercising his religion. Moreover, that person is barred from freely exercising his religion regardless of whether the law prohibits the conduct only when engaged in for religious reasons, only by members of that religion, or by all persons. It is difficult to deny that a law that prohibits religiously motivated conduct, even if the law is generally applicable, does not at least implicate First Amendment concerns.

. . .

To say that a person's right to free exercise has been burdened, of course, does not mean that he has an absolute right to engage in the conduct. . . . [W]e have respected both the First Amendment's express textual mandate and the governmental interest in regulation of conduct by requiring the Government to justify any substantial burden on religiously motivated conduct by a compelling state interest and by means narrowly tailored to achieve that interest. . . .

The Court attempts to support its narrow reading of the Clause by claiming that "[w]e have never held that an individual's religious beliefs excuse him from compliance with an otherwise valid law prohibiting conduct that the State is free to regulate." But as the Court later notes, as it must, in cases such as *Cantwell* and *Yoder* we have in fact interpreted the Free Exercise Clause to forbid application of a generally applicable prohibition to religiously motivated conduct. . . .

The Court endeavors to escape from our decisions in *Cantwell* and *Yoder* by labeling them "hybrid" decisions, but there is no denying that both cases expressly relied on the Free Exercise Clause, . . . and that we have consistently regarded those cases as part of the mainstream of our free exercise jurisprudence. Moreover, in each of the other cases cited by the Court to support its categorical rule, we rejected the particular constitutional claims before us only after carefully weighing the competing interests. . . . That we rejected the free exercise claims in those cases hardly calls into question the applicability of First Amendment doctrine in the first place. Indeed, it is surely unusual to judge the vitality of a constitutional doctrine by looking to the win-loss record of the plaintiffs who happen to come before us.

B

. . .

In my view, . . . the essence of a free exercise claim is relief from a burden imposed by government on religious practices or beliefs, whether the burden is imposed directly through laws that prohibit or compel specific religious practices, or indirectly through laws that, in effect, make abandonment of one's own religion or conformity to the religious beliefs of others the price of an equal place in the civil community. . . .

Indeed, we have never distinguished between cases in which a State conditions receipt of a benefit on conduct prohibited by religious beliefs and cases in which a State affirmatively prohibits such conduct. The *Sherbert* compelling interest test applies in both kinds of cases....

... Even if, as an empirical matter, a government's criminal laws might usually serve a compelling interest in health, safety, or public order, the First Amendment at least requires a case-by-case determination of the question, sensitive to the facts of each particular claim.... Given the range of conduct that a State might legitimately make criminal, we cannot assume, merely because a law carries criminal sanctions and is generally applicable, that the First Amendment never requires the State to grant a limited exemption for religiously motivated conduct.

. . .

Finally, the Court today suggests that the disfavoring of minority religions is an "unavoidable consequence" under our system of government and that accommodation of such religions must be left to the political process. In my view, however, the First Amendment was enacted precisely to protect the rights of those whose religious practices are not shared by the majority and may be viewed with hostility. The history of our free exercise doctrine amply demonstrates the harsh impact majoritarian rule has had on unpopular or emerging religious groups such as the Jehovah's Witnesses and the Amish....

III

The Court's holding today not only misreads settled First Amendment precedent; it appears to be unnecessary to this case. I would reach the same result applying our established free exercise jurisprudence.

. . .

... [T]he critical question in this case is whether exempting respondents from the State's general criminal prohibition "will unduly interfere with fulfillment of the governmental interest." ... Although the question is close, I would conclude that uniform application of Oregon's criminal prohibition is "essential to accomplish" its overriding interest in preventing the physical harm caused by the use of a ... controlled substance. Oregon's criminal prohibition represents that State's judgment that the possession and use of controlled substances, even by only one person, is inherently harmful and dangerous. Because the health effects caused by the use of controlled substances exist regardless of the motivation of the user, the use of such substances, even for religious purposes, violates the very purpose of the laws that prohibit them.... Moreover, in view of the societal interest in preventing trafficking in controlled substances, uniform application of the criminal prohibition at issue is essential to the effectiveness of Oregon's stated interest in preventing any possession of peyote....

For these reasons, I believe that granting a selective exemption in this case would seriously impair Oregon's compelling interest in prohibiting possession of peyote by its citizens. Under such circumstances, the Free Exercise Clause does not require the State to accommodate respondents' religiously motivated conduct....

Respondents contend that any incompatibility is belied by the fact that the Federal Government and several States provide exemptions for the religious use of peyote ... But other governments may surely choose to grant an exemption without Oregon, with its specific asserted interest in uniform application of its drug laws, being *required* to do so by the First Amendment. Respondents also note that the sacramental use of peyote is central to the tenets of the Native American Church, but I agree with the Court that . . . our determination of the constitutionality of Oregon's general criminal prohibition cannot, and should not, turn on the centrality of the particular religious practice at issue. This does not mean, of course, that courts may not make factual findings as to whether a claimant holds a sincerely held religious belief that conflicts with, and thus is burdened by, the challenged law. The distinction between questions of centrality and questions of sincerity and burden is admittedly fine, but it is one that is an established part of our free exercise doctrine. . . .

I would therefore adhere to our established free exercise jurisprudence and hold that the State in this case has a compelling interest in regulating peyote use by its citizens and that accommodating respondents' religiously motivated conduct "will unduly interfere with fulfillment of the governmental interest." *Lee,* 455 U.S., at 259. Accordingly, I concur in the judgment of the Court.

Justice Blackmun, with whom Justice Brennan and Justice Marshall join, dissenting.

This Court over the years painstakingly has developed a consistent and exacting standard to test the constitutionality of a state statute that burdens the free exercise of religion. Such a statute may stand only if the law in general, and the State's refusal to allow a religious exemption in particular, are justified by a compelling interest that cannot be served by less restrictive means.

Until today, I thought this was a settled and inviolate principle of this Court's First Amendment jurisprudence. . . .

. . .

. . . I agree with Justice O'Connor's analysis of the applicable free exercise doctrine, and I join parts I and II of her opinion. As she points out, "the critical question in this case is whether exempting respondents from the State's general criminal prohibition 'will unduly interfere with fulfillment of the governmental interest.'" I do disagree, however, with her specific answer to that question.

. . .

. . . The State's asserted interest . . . amounts only to the symbolic preservation of an unenforced prohibition. . . .

. . .

The State proclaims an interest in protecting the health and safety of its citizens from the dangers of unlawful drugs. It offers, however, no evidence that the religious use of peyote has ever harmed anyone. The factual findings of other courts cast doubt on the State's assumption that religious use of peyote is harmful. . . .

The carefully circumscribed ritual context in which respondents used peyote is far removed from the irresponsible and unrestricted recreational use of unlawful drugs. The Native American Church's internal restrictions on, and supervision of, its members' use of peyote substantially obviate the State's health and safety concerns. . . .

. . .

Finally, the State argues that granting an exception for religious peyote use would erode its interest in the uniform, fair, and certain enforcement of its drug laws. The State fears that, if it grants an exemption for religious peyote use, a flood of other claims to religious exemptions will follow. It would then be placed in a dilemma, it says, between allowing a patchwork of exemptions that would hinder its law enforcement efforts, and risking a violation of the Establishment Clause by arbitrarily limiting its religious exemptions. This argument, however, could be made in almost any free exercise case. . . .

The State's apprehension of a flood of other religious claims is purely speculative. Almost half the States, and the Federal Government, have maintained an exemption for religious peyote use for many years, and apparently have not found themselves overwhelmed by claims to other religious exemptions. . . .

Finally, although I agree with Justice O'Connor that courts should refrain from delving into questions of whether, as a matter of religious doctrine, a particular practice is "central" to the religion, I do not think this means that the courts must turn a blind eye to the severe impact of a State's restrictions on the adherents of a minority religion. . . .

Respondents believe, and their sincerity has never been at issue, that the peyote plant embodies their deity, and eating it is an act of worship and communion. Without peyote, they could not enact the essential ritual of their religion. . . .

If Oregon can constitutionally prosecute them for this act of worship, they, like the Amish, may be "forced to migrate to some other and more tolerant region." *Yoder,* 406 U.S., at 218. This potentially devastating impact must be viewed in light of the federal policy—reached in reaction to many years of religious persecution and intolerance—of protecting the religious freedom of Native Americans. See American Indian Religious Freedom Act, 92 Stat. 469, 42 U.S.C. § 1996 ("it shall be the policy of the United States to protect and preserve for American Indians their inherent right of freedom to believe, express, and exercise the traditional religions . . . , including but not limited to access to sites, use and possession of sacred objects, and the freedom to worship through ceremonials and traditional rites"). Congress recognized that certain substances, such as peyote, "have religious significance because they are sacred, they have power, they heal, they are necessary to the exercise of the rites of the religion, they are necessary to the cultural integrity of the tribe, and, therefore, religious survival." H.R.Rep. No. 95–1308, p. 2 (1978).

The American Indian Religious Freedom Act, in itself, may not create rights enforceable against government action restricting religious freedom, but this Court must scrupulously apply its free exercise analysis to the religious claims of Native Americans, however unorthodox they may be. Otherwise, both the First Amendment and the stated policy of Congress will offer to Native Americans merely an unfulfilled and hollow promise.

. . .

For these reasons, I conclude that Oregon's interest in enforcing its drug laws against religious use of peyote is not sufficiently compelling to outweigh respondents' right to the free exercise of their religion. Since the State could not constitutionally enforce its criminal prohibition against respondents, the interests underlying the State's drug laws cannot justify its denial of unemployment benefits. . . .

I dissent.

CHURCH OF THE LUKUMI BABALU AYE, INC. v. CITY OF HIALEAH, 508 U.S. 520 (1993). The church practices the Santeria religion, whose services include animal sacrifices. When the church proposed to build a house of worship in Hialeah, the city enacted ordinances that targeted the practice of animal sacrifice by the church. One ordinance provided that "[i]t shall be unlawful for any person, persons, corporations or associations to sacrifice any animal within the corporate limits of the city of Hialeah, Florida." "Sacrifice" was defined as "to unnecessarily kill, torment, torture, or mutilate an animal in a public or private ritual or ceremony not for the primary purpose of food consumption." The ordinance contained an exemption for slaughtering by "licensed establishment[s]" of animals "specifically raised for food purposes." The court held that the ordinances violated the free exercise clause since they were neither "neutral" nor "of general applicability." The ordinances were drafted so that "almost the only conduct subject to [them] is the religious exercise of Santeria church members." All of the asserted governmental purposes (protecting public health and preventing cruelty to animals) were only pursued in the context of Santeria religious practices. "A law that targets religious conduct for distinctive treatment or advances legitimate governmental interests only against conduct with a religious motivation will survive strict scrutiny only in rare cases."

Locke v. Davey

540 U.S. 712, 124 S.Ct. 1307, 158 L.Ed.2d 1 (2004).

Chief Justice Rehnquist delivered the opinion of the Court.

The State of Washington established the Promise Scholarship Program to assist academically gifted students with postsecondary education expenses. In accordance with the State Constitution, students may not use the scholarship at an institution where they are pursuing a degree in devotional theology. We hold that such an exclusion from an otherwise inclusive aid program does not violate the Free Exercise Clause of the First Amendment.

. . .

These two Clauses, the Establishment Clause and the Free Exercise Clause, are frequently in tension. . . . Yet we have long said that "there is room for play in the joints" between them. In other words, there are some state actions permitted by the Establishment Clause but not required by the Free Exercise Clause.

. . . [T]here is no doubt that the State could, consistent with the Federal Constitution, permit Promise Scholars to pursue a degree in devotional theology . . . and the State does not contend otherwise. The question before us, however, is whether Washington, pursuant to its own constitution, which has been authoritatively interpreted as prohibiting even indirectly funding religious instruction that will prepare students for the ministry, . . . can deny them such funding without violating the Free Exercise Clause.

Davey urges us to answer that question in the negative. He contends that under the rule we enunciated in *Church of Lukumi Babalu Aye, Inc. v. Hialeah,* . . . the program is presumptively unconstitutional because it is not facially neutral with respect to religion. We reject his claim of presumptive unconstitutionality, however; to do otherwise would extend the *Lukumi* line of cases well beyond not only their facts but their reasoning. In *Lukumi,* the city of Hialeah made it a crime to engage in certain kinds of animal slaughter. . . . In the present case, the State's disfavor of religion (if it can be called that) is of a far milder kind. It imposes neither criminal nor civil sanctions on any type of religious service or rite . . . [I]t does not require students to choose between their religious beliefs and receiving a government benefit. The State has merely chosen not to fund a distinct category of instruction.

... Because the Promise Scholarship Program funds training for all secular professions, Justice Scalia contends the State must also fund training for religious professions. But training for religious professions and training for secular professions are not fungible. Training someone to lead a congregation is an essentially religious endeavor. ... [T]he subject of religion is one in which both the United States and state constitutions embody distinct views—in favor of free exercise, but opposed to establishment—that find no counterpart with respect to other callings or professions. That a State would deal differently with religious education for the ministry than with education for other callings is a product of these views, not evidence of hostility toward religion.

Even though the differently worded Washington Constitution draws a more stringent line than that drawn by the United States Constitution, the interest it seeks to further is scarcely novel. In fact, we can think of few areas in which a State's antiestablishment interests come more into play. Since the founding of our country, there have been popular uprisings against procuring taxpayer funds to support church leaders, which was one of the hallmarks of an "established" religion. ...

Most States that sought to avoid an establishment of religion around the time of the founding placed in their constitutions formal prohibitions against using tax funds to support the ministry. ... The plain text of these constitutional provisions prohibited *any* tax dollars from supporting the clergy. We have found nothing to indicate ... that these provisions would not have applied so long as the State equally supported other professions or if the amount at stake was *de minimis*. That early state constitutions saw no problem in explicitly excluding *only* the ministry from receiving state dollars reinforces our conclusion that religious instruction is of a different ilk. ...

Far from evincing the hostility toward religion which was manifest in *Lukumi,* we believe that the entirety of the Promise Scholarship Program goes a long way toward including religion in its benefits. The program permits students to attend pervasively religious schools, so long as they are accredited. ... And under the Promise Scholarship Program's current guidelines, students are still eligible to take devotional theology courses. ...

In short, we find neither in the history or text of Article I, § 11 of the Washington Constitution, nor in the operation of the Promise Scholarship Program, anything that suggests animus towards religion. Given the historic and substantial state interest at issue, we therefore cannot conclude that the denial of funding for vocational religious instruction alone is inherently constitutionally suspect.

Without a presumption of unconstitutionality, Davey's claim must fail. The State's interest in not funding the pursuit of devotional degrees is substantial and the exclusion of such funding places a relatively minor burden on Promise Scholars. If any room exists between the two Religion Clauses, it must be here. We need not venture further into this difficult area in order to uphold the Promise Scholarship Program as currently operated by the State of Washington.

. . .

Justice Scalia, with whom Justice Thomas joins, dissenting.

. . .

The Court does not dispute that the Free Exercise Clause places some constraints on public benefits programs, but finds none here, based on a principle of " 'play in the joints.' " I use the term "principle" loosely, for that is not so much a legal principle as a refusal to apply *any* principle when faced with competing constitutional directives. There is nothing anomalous about constitutional commands that abut. A municipality hiring public contractors may not discriminate *against* blacks or *in favor of* them; it cannot discriminate a little bit each way and then plead "play in the joints" when haled into court. If the Religion Clauses demand neutrality, we must enforce them, in hard cases as well as easy ones.

Even if "play in the joints" were a valid legal principle, surely it would apply only when it was a close call whether complying with one of the Religion Clauses would violate the other. . . . The establishment question *would not even be close,* as is evident from the fact that this Court's decision in *Witters v. Washington Dept. of Servs. for Blind,* 474 U.S. 481, was unanimous. Perhaps some formally neutral public benefits programs are so gerrymandered and devoid of plausible secular purpose that they might raise specters of state aid to religion, but an evenhanded Promise Scholarship Program is not among them.

In any case, the State already has all the play in the joints it needs. There are any number of ways it could respect both its unusually sensitive concern for the conscience of its taxpayers *and* the Federal Free Exercise Clause. It could make the scholarships redeemable only at public universities (where it sets the curriculum), or only for select courses of study. Either option would replace a program that facially discriminates against religion with one that just happens not to subsidize it. The State could also simply abandon the scholarship program altogether. If that seems a dear price to pay for freedom of conscience, it is only because the State has defined that freedom so broadly that it would be offended by a program with such an incidental, indirect religious effect.

. . .

[T]he interest to which the Court defers is not fear of a conceivable Establishment Clause violation, budget constraints, avoidance of endorsement, or substantive neutrality—none of these. It is a pure philosophical preference: the State's opinion that it would violate taxpayers' freedom of conscience *not* to discriminate against candidates for the ministry. This sort of protection of "freedom of conscience" has no logical limit and can justify the singling out of religion for exclusion from public programs in virtually any context. . . .

II

The Court makes no serious attempt to defend the program's neutrality, and instead identifies two features thought to render its discrimination less offensive. The first is the lightness of Davey's burden. The Court offers no authority for approving facial discrimination against religion simply because its material consequences are not severe. I might understand such a test if we were still in the business of reviewing facially neutral laws that merely happen to burden some individual's religious exercise, but we are not. . . . The Court has not required proof of "substantial" concrete harm with other forms of discrimination, see, *e.g., Brown v. Board of Education,* . . . and it should not do so here.

The other reason the Court thinks this particular facial discrimination less offensive is that the scholarship program was not motivated by animus toward religion. The Court does not explain why the legislature's motive matters, and I fail to see why it should. . . .

The Court has not approached other forms of discrimination this way. When we declared racial segregation unconstitutional, we did not ask whether the State had originally adopted the regime, not out of "animus" against blacks, but because of a well-meaning but misguided belief that the races would be better off apart. . . . We do sometimes look to legislative intent to smoke out more subtle instances of discrimination, but we do so as a *supplement* to the core guarantee of facially equal treatment, not as a replacement for it. . . .

There is no need to rely on analogies, however, because we have rejected the Court's methodology in this very context. In *McDaniel v. Paty,* 435 U.S. 618 (1978), we considered a Tennessee statute that disqualified clergy from participation in the state constitutional convention. That statute, like the one here, was based upon a state constitutional provision—a clause in the 1796 Tennessee Constitution that disqualified clergy from sitting in the legislature. The State defended the statute as an attempt to be faithful to its constitutional separation of church and state, and we accepted that claimed benevolent purpose as bona fide. . . . Nonetheless, because it did not justify facial discrimination against religion, we invalidated the restriction. . . .

. . .

Today's holding is limited to training the clergy, but its logic is readily extendible, and there are plenty of directions to go. What next? Will we deny priests and nuns their prescription-drug benefits on the ground that taxpayers' freedom of conscience forbids medicating the clergy at public expense? This may seem fanciful, but recall that France has proposed banning religious attire from schools, invoking interests in secularism no less benign than those the Court embraces today. . . .

Justice Thomas, dissenting.

I write separately to note that, in my view, the study of theology does not necessarily implicate religious devotion or faith . . . . [T]he statute itself does not define "theology." And the usual definition of the term "theology" is not limited to devotional studies. "Theology" is defined as "[t]he study of the nature of God and religious truth" and the "rational inquiry into religious questions." American Heritage Dictionary 1794 (4th ed.2000). . . . These definitions include the study of theology from a secular perspective as well as from a religious one.

. . .

THE RELIGIOUS FREEDOM RESTORATION ACT

The Religious Freedom Restoration Act (PL 103–141; 42 U.S.C. § 2000bb), enacted in 1993, provides, in relevant part:

SEC. 2. CONGRESSIONAL FINDINGS AND DECLARATION OF PURPOSES.

(a) FINDINGS.—The Congress finds that?

(1) the framers of the Constitution, recognizing free exercise of religion as an unalienable right, secured its protection in the First Amendment to the Constitution;

(2) laws "neutral" toward religion may burden religious exercise as surely as laws intended to interfere with religious exercise;

(3) governments should not substantially burden religious exercise without compelling justification;

(4) in Employment Division v. Smith, 494 U.S. 872 (1990) the Supreme Court virtually eliminated the requirement that the govern-

ment justify burdens on religious exercise imposed by laws neutral toward religion; and

(5) the compelling interest test as set forth in prior Federal court rulings is a workable test for striking sensible balances between religious liberty and competing prior governmental interests.

(b) PURPOSES.—The purposes of this Act are?

(1) to restore the compelling interest test as set forth in Sherbert v. Verner, 374 U.S. 398 (1963) and Wisconsin v. Yoder, 406 U.S. 205 (1972) and to guarantee its application in all cases where free exercise of religion is substantially burdened; and

(2) to provide a claim or defense to persons whose religious exercise is substantially burdened by government.

SEC. 3.   FREE EXERCISE OF RELIGION PROTECTED.

(a) IN GENERAL.—Government shall not substantially burden a person's exercise of religion even if the burden results from a rule of general applicability, except as provided in subsection (b).

(b) EXCEPTION.—Government may substantially burden a person's exercise of religion only if it demonstrates that application of the burden to the person?

(1) is in furtherance of a compelling governmental interest; and

(2) is the least restrictive means of furthering that compelling governmental interest.

(c) JUDICIAL RELIEF.—A person whose religious exercise has been burdened in violation of this section may assert that violation as a claim or defense in a judicial proceeding and obtain appropriate relief against a government. Standing to assert a claim or defense under this section shall be governed by the general rules of standing under article III of the Constitution.

SEC. 5.   DEFINITIONS.

As used in this Act?

(1) the term "government" includes a branch, department, agency, instrumentality, and official (or other person acting under color of law) of the United States, a State, or a subdivision of a State;

(2) the term "State" includes the District of Columbia, the Commonwealth of Puerto Rico, and each territory and possession of the United States;

(3) the term "demonstrates" means meets the burdens of going forward with the evidence and of persuasion; and

(4) the term "exercise of religion" means the exercise of religion under the First Amendment to the Constitution.

SEC. 6.   APPLICABILITY.

(a) IN GENERAL.—This Act applies to all Federal and State law, and the implementation of that law, whether statutory or otherwise, and whether adopted before or after the enactment of this Act.

(b) RULE OF CONSTRUCTION.—Federal statutory law adopted after the date of the enactment of this Act is subject to this Act unless such law explicitly excludes such application by reference to this Act.

(c) RELIGIOUS BELIEF UNAFFECTED.—Nothing in this Act shall be construed to authorize any government to burden any religious belief.

City of Boerne v. Flores

521 U.S. 507, 117 S.Ct. 2157, 138 L.Ed.2d 624 (1997).

[The report in this case appears, supra page 1206.]

THE UNITED STATES SUPREME COURT

A Chart
1789–2005*

The following chart is designed to provide a means of identifying the composition of the Court at any specified date, and thereby to help the student follow the relationship between changes in the personnel and doctrines of the Court.

If the student is concerned with a decision bearing a date which approximates a change in the Court's personnel it will be necessary to consult the footnotes. These notes show, following the dates of birth and death, political affiliation, and home state at the time of appointment, each justice's dates of commission and termination of service. Of course, members do not always participate in decisions rendered during their term of service; the fact of participation must be independently verified. Large X's indicate vacancies.

* This chart was originally prepared by Paul Gay, and has been updated by the editors.

Washington 1789–1797	Adams 1797–1801	Jefferson 1801–1809	Madison 1809–1817

| Jay[1] 1789–   –1795 | 2 Ells-worth[10] 1796–1800 | Marshall[13] 1801– | |

| Rut-ledge 2 | John-son 7 | Paterson[8] 1793–   –1806 | Livingston[15] 1806– |

| Cushing[3] 1789–   –1810 | Story[17] 1811– |

| Wilson[4] 1789–   –1798 | Washington[11] 1798– |

| Blair[5] 1789–   –1796 | Chase[9] 1796–   –1811 | Duvall[18] 1811– |

| Iredell[6] 1790–   –1799 | Moore[12] 1799–   –1804 | Johnson[14] 1804– |

| Todd[16] 1807– |

1. John Jay, 1745–1829. Fed., N. Y. 9–26–1789 to 6–29–1795.

2. John Rutledge, 1739–1800. Fed., S. C. 9–26–1789 to 3–5–1791. Comm. C.J. 7–1–1795 (recess appoint.) pres. August term 1795, rejected by Senate 12–15–1795.

3. William Cushing, 1732–1810. Fed., Mass. 9–27–1789 to 9–13–1810.

4. James Wilson, 1742–1798. Fed., Pa. 9–29–1789 to 8–21–1798.

5. John Blair, 1732–1800. Fed., Va. 9–30–1789 to 1–27–1796.

6. James Iredell, 1751–1799. Fed., N. C. 2–10–1790 to 10–20–1799.

7. Thomas Johnson, 1732–1819. Fed., Md. 11–7–1791 to 2–1–1793.

8. William Paterson, 1745–1806. Fed., N. J. 3–4–1793 to 9–9–1806.

9. Samuel Chase, 1741–1811. Fed., Md. 1–27–1796 to 6–19–1811.

10. Oliver Ellsworth, 1745–1807. Fed., Conn. 3–4–1796 to 12–15–1800.

11. Bushrod Washington, 1762–1829. Fed., Va. 12–20–1798 to 11–26–1829.

12. Alfred Moore, 1755–1810. Fed., N. C. 12–10–1799 to 1–26–1804.

13. John Marshall, 1755–1835. Fed., Va. 1–31–1801 to 7–6–1835.

14. William Johnson, 1771–1834. Rep., S. C. 3–26–1804 to 8–4–1834.

15. [Henry] Brockholst Livingston, 1757–1823. Rep., N. Y. 11–10–1806 to 3–18–1823.

16. Thomas Todd, 1765–1826. Rep., Ky. 3–3–1807 to 2–7–1826. Post created by Congress by Act February 24, 1807.

17. Joseph Story, 1779–1845. Rep., Mass. 11–18–1811 to 9–10–1845.

18. Gabriel Duval[l], 1752–1844. Rep., Md. 11–18–1811 to 1–14–1835.

Monroe 1817–1825	J. Q. Adams 1825–1829	Jackson 1829–1837	Van Buren 1837–1841	Harrison 3/4–4/4 Tyler 1841–1845

Marshall —1835 | **Taney**[24] 1836–

Livingston –1823 | **Thompson**[19] 1823– —1843 | **N**[29]

Story

Washington –1829 | **Baldwin**[22] 1830– —1844

Duvall —1835 | **Barbour**[25] 1836– —1841 | **Daniel**[23] 1841–

Johnson —1834 | **Wayne**[23] 1835–

Todd –1826 | **Trimble**[20] '26–8 | **McLean**[21] 1829–

Catron[26] 1837–

McKinley[27] 1837–

19.   Smith Thompson, 1768–1843. Rep., N. Y. 12 9–1823 to 12–18–1843.

20.   Robert Trimble, 1777–1828. Rep., Ky. 5–9–1826 to 8–25–1828.

21.   John McLean, 1785–1861. Dem./Rep., Ohio 3–7–1829 to 4–4–1861.

22.   Henry Baldwin, 1780–1844. Dem., Pa. 1 6–1830 to 4–21–1844.

23.   James Moore Wayne, 1790–1867. Dem., Ga. 1–9–1835 to 7–5–1867.

24.   Roger Brooke Taney, 1777–1864. Dem., Md. 3–15–1836 to 10–12–1864.

25.   Philip Pendleton Barbour, 1783–1841. Dem., Va. 3–15–1836 to 2–25–1841.

26.   John Catron, ca. (1778–86) 1865. Dem., Tenn. 3–8–1837 to 5–30–1865. Post created by Congress by Act of March 3, 1837 and abolished by Congress by Act of July 23, 1866.

27.   John McKinley, 1780–1852. Dem., Ky./Ala. 9–25–1837 to 7–19–1852. Post created by Congress by Act of March 3, 1837.

28.   Peter Vivian Daniel, 1784–1860. Dem., Va. 3–3–1841 to 5–31–1860.

29.   Samuel Nelson, 1792–1873. Dem., N. Y. 2–13–1845 to 11–28–1872.

Polk 1845–1849	Taylor 1849–1850 Fillmore 1850–1853	Pierce 1853–1857	Buchanan 1857–1861	Lincoln 1861– 4/15/65	Johnson 1865–1869	Grant 1869–

Taney   Chase[39]
                              –1864 | 1864–   –1873

Nelson[29]
                                                                    –1872

| S | Woodbury[30] 1845– –1851 | Curtis[32] 1851– –1857 | Clifford[34] 1858– |

Grier[31] 1846–   –1870 | S[40] 1870–

Daniel   –1860 | Miller[36] 1862–

Wayne   –1867 | B[41] 1870–

McLean   –1861 | Swayne[35] 1862–

Catron   –1865*

McKinley –1852 | Campbell[33] 1853– –1861 | Davis[37] 1862–

Field[38] 1863–

30. Levi Woodbury, 1789–1851. Dem., N. H. 9–20–1845 to 9–4–1851.

31. Robert Cooper Grier, 1794–1870. Dem., Pa. 8–4–1846 to 1–31–1870.

32. Benjamin Robbins Curtis, 1809–1874. Whig, Mass. 12–20–1851 to 9–30–1857.

33. John Archibald Campbell, 1811–1889. Dem., Ala. 3–22–1853 to 4–30–1861.

34. Nathan Clifford, 1803–1881. Dem., Me. 1–12–1858 to 7–25–1881.

35. Noah Haynes Swayne, 1804–1884. Rep., Ohio 1–24–1862 to 1–24–1881.

36. Samuel Freeman Miller, 1816–1890. Rep., Iowa 7–16–1862 to 10–13–1890.

37. David Davis, 1815–1886. Rep./Dem., Ill. 12–8–1862 to 3–4–1877.

38. Stephen Johnson Field, 1816–1899. Dem., Cal. 3–10–1863 to 12–1–1897. Post created by Congress by Act of March 3, 1863.

39. Salmon Portland Chase, 1808–1873. Rep., Ohio 12–6–1864 to 5–7–1873.

40. William Strong, 1808–1895. Dem./Rep., Pa. 2–18–1870 to 12–14–1880.

41. Joseph P. Bradley, 1813–1892. Whig/Rep., N. J. 3–21–1870 to 1–22–1892.

* Post abolished by Congress by Act of July 23, 1866.

Grant −1877	Hayes 1877–1881	Garfield 3/4–9/19 Arthur 1881–1885	Cleveland 1885–1889	Harrison 1889–1893	Cleveland 1893–1897	McKinley 1897– 9/14/1901
Waite[43] 1874–			−1888	Fuller[50] 1888–		
Hunt[42] 1872–	−1882	Blatchford[48] 1882–		−1893	White[55] 1894–	
Clifford	−1881	Gray[47] 1881–				
Strong	−1880	Woods[45] 1880–	−1887	Lamar[49] 1888– −1893	Jackson[54] 1893–5	Peckham[56] 1895–
Miller			−1890	Brown[52] 1890–		
Bradley				−1892	Shiras[53] 1892–	
Swayne	−1881	Matthews[46] 1881–	−1889	Brewer[51] 1889–		
Davis −1877	Harlan[44] 1877–					
Field					−1897	McKenna[57] 1898–

42. Ward Hunt, 1810–1886. Rep., N. Y. 12–11–1872 to 1–27–1882.

43. Morrison Remick Waite, 1816–1888. Rep., Ohio 1–21–1874 to 3–23–1888.

44. John Marshall Harlan, 1833–1911. Rep., Ky. 11–29–1877 to 10–14–1911.

45. William Durnham Woods, 1824–1887. Rep., Ga. 12–21–1880 to 5–14–1887.

46. [Thomas] Stanley Matthews, 1824–1889. Rep., Ohio 5–12–1881 to 3–22–1889.

47. Horace Gray, 1828–1902. Rep., Mass. 12–20–1881 to 9–15–1902.

48. Samuel Blatchford, 1820–1893. Rep., N. Y. 3–22–1882 to 7–7–1893.

49. Lucius Quintus Cincinnatus Lamar, 1825–1893. Dem., Miss. 1–16–1888 to 1–23–1893.

50. Melville Weston Fuller, 1833–1910. Dem., Ill. 7–20–1888 to 7–4–1910.

51. David Josiah Brewer, 1837–1910. Rep., Kan. 12–18–1889 to 3–28–1910.

52. Henry Billings Brown, 1836–1913. Rep., Mich. 12–29–1890 to 5–28–1906.

53. George Shiras, 1832–1924. Rep., Pa. 7–26–1892 to 2–23–1903.

54. Howell Edmunds Jackson, 1832–1895. Whig/Dem., Tenn. 2–18–1893 to 8–8–1895.

55. Edward Douglass White, 1845–1921. Dem., La. Asso. Just. 2–19–1894 to 12–18–1910; C. J. 12–12–1910 to 5–19–1921.

56. Rufus Wheeler Peckham, 1838–1909. Dem., N. Y. 12–9–1895 to 10–24–1909.

57. Joseph McKenna, 1843–1926. Rep., Cal. 1–21–1898 to 1–5–1925.

T. Roosevelt 1901–1909	Taft 1909–1913	Wilson 1913–1921	Harding 1921– 8/2 /23	Coolidge 1923–1929

Fuller –1910	White[55] 1910–		–1921	Taft[69] 1921– –1930
White –1910	Van Devanter[63] 1910–			
Gray –1902	Holmes[58] 1902–			
Peckham –1909	Lurton[61] 1909– –1914	McReynolds[66] 1914–		
Brown –1906	Moody[60] 1906– –1910	Lamar[64] 1910– –1916	Brandeis[67] 1916–	
Shiras –1903	Day[59] 1903–		–1922	Butler[71] 1922–
Brewer –1910	Hughes[62] 1910– –1916	Clark[68] 1916– –1922	Sutherland[70] 1922–	
Harlan –1911	Pitney[65] 1912–		–1922	Sanford[72] 1923–
McKenna			–1925	Stone[73] 1925–

55. Edward Douglass White, 1845–1921. Dem., La. Asso. Just. 2–19–1894 to 12–18–1910; C. J. 12–12–1910 to 5–19–1921.

58. Oliver Wendell Holmes, 1841–1935. Rep., Mass. 12–4–1902 to 1–12–1932.

59. William Rufus Day, 1849–1923. Rep., Ohio 2–23–1903 to 11–13–1922.

60. William Henry Moody, 1853–1917. Rep., Mass. 12–12–1906 to 11–20–1910.

61. Horace Harmon Lurton, 1844–1914. Dem., Tenn. 12–20–1909 to 7–12–1914.

62. Charles Evans Hughes, 1862–1948. Rep., N. Y. Asso. Just. 5–2–1910 to 6–10–1916; C. J. 2–13–1930 to 6–30–1941.

63. Willis Van Devanter, 1859–1941. Rep., Wyo. 12–16–1910 to 6–2–1937.

64. Joseph Rucker Lamar, 1857–1916. Dem., Ga. 12–17–1910 to 1–2–1916.

65. Mahlon Pitney, 1858–1924. Rep., N. J. 3–13–1912 to 12–31–1922.

66. James Clark McReynolds, 1862–1946. Dem., Tenn. 8–29–1914 to 1–31–1941.

67. Louis Dembitz Brandeis, 1856–1941. Dem., Mass. 6–1–1916 to 2–13–1939.

68. John Hessin Clarke, 1857–1945. Dem., Ohio 7–24–1916 to 9–18–1922.

69. William Howard Taft, 1857–1930. Rep., Conn. 6–30–1921 to 2–3–1930.

70. George Sutherland, 1862–1942. Rep., Utah 9–5–1922 to 1–17–1938.

71. Pierce Butler, 1866–1939. Dem., Minn. 12–21–1922 to 11–16–1939.

72. Edward Terry Sanford, 1865–1930. Rep., Tenn. 1–29–1923 to 3–8–1930.

73.   Harlan Fiske Stone, 1872–1946. Rep., N. Y. Asso. Just. 2–5–1925 to 7–2–1941; C. J. 7–3–1941 to 4–22–1946.

Hoover 1929–1933	F. D. Roosevelt 1933–4/12/1945	Truman 1945–1953

T. '30	Hughes[62] 1930–	–1941	Stone[73] 1941–	–1946	Vinson[85] 1946–	–1953
	Van Devanter	–1937	Black[76] 1937–			
	Holmes –1932	Cardozo[75] 1932– –1938	Frankfurter[78] 1939–			
	McReynolds	–1941	B.[81] '41–2	Rutledge[83] 1943– –1949	Minton[87] 1949–	
	Brandeis	–1939	Douglas[79] 1939–			
	Butler	–1939	Murphy[80] 1940–	–1949	Clark[86] 1949–	
	Sutherland	–1938	Reed[77] 1938–			
S. '30	Roberts[74] 1930–		–1945	Burton[84] 1945–		
	Stone	(To C. J.) –1941	Jackson[82] 1941–			

62.   Charles Evans Hughes, 1862–1948. Rep., N. Y. Asso. Just. 5–2–1910 to 6–10–1916; C. J. 2–13–1930 to 6–30–1941.

73.   Harlan Fiske Stone, 1872–1946. Rep., N. Y. Asso. Just. 2–5–1925 to 7–2–1941; C. J. 7–3–1941 to 4–22–1946.

74.   Owen Josephus Roberts, 1875–1955. Rep., Pa. 5–20–1930 to 7–31–1945.

75.   Benjamin Nathan Cardozo, 1870–1938. Dem., N. Y. 3–2–1932 to 7–9–1938.

76.   Hugo Lafayette Black, 1886–1971. Dem., Ala. 8–18–1937 to 9–17–1971.

77.   Stanley Forman Reed, 1884–1980. Dem., Ky. 1–27–1938 to 2–25–1957.

78.   Felix Frankfurter, 1882–1965. Ind., Mass. 1–20–1939 to 8–28–1962.

79.   William Orville Douglas, 1898–1980. Dem., Conn. 4–15–1939 to 11–12–1975.

80.   Frank Murphy, 1890–1949. Dem., Mich. 1–18–1940 to 7–19–1949.

81.   James Francis Byrnes, 1879–1972. Dem., S. C. 6–25–1941 to 10–3–1942.

82.   Robert Hougwout Jackson, 1892–1954. Dem., N. Y. 7–11–1941 to 10–9–1954.

83.   Wiley Blount Rutledge, 1894–1949. Dem., Iowa 2–11–1943 to 9–10–1949.

84.   Harold Hitz Burton, 1888–1964. Rep., Ohio 9–22–1945 to 10–13–1958.

85.   Frederick Moore Vinson, 1890–1953. Dem., Ky. 6–21–1946 to 9–8–1953.

86.   Thomas Campbell Clark, 1899–1977. Dem., Texas 8–19–1949 to 6–12–1967.

87.   Sherman Minton, 1890–1965. Dem., Ind. 10–5–1949 to 10–15–1956.

Eisenhower 1953–1961	Kennedy 1961–1963	Johnson 1963–1969

Warren[88]
1953–

Black

Frankfurter		Goldberg[94]		Fortas[95]
	–1962	1962–	–1965	1965–

Minton	Brennan[90]
–1956	1956–

Douglas

Clark		Marshall[96]
	–1967	1967–

Reed		Whittaker[91]		White[93]
	–1957	1957–	–1962	1962–

Burton		Stewart[92]
	–1958	1958–

J '54	Harlan[89] 1954–

88. Earl Warren, 1891–1974, Rep., Cal. 10–2–1953 to 6–23–1969.

89. John Marshall Harlan, 1899–1971. Rep., N. Y. 3–17–1955 to 9–23–1971.

90. William Joseph Brennan, 1906–1997. Dem., N. J. 10–15–1956 to 7–20–1990.

91. Charles Evans Whittaker, 1901–1973. Rep., Mo. 3–19–1957 to 4–1–1962.

92. Potter Stewart, 1915–1985. Rep., Ohio 10–13–1958 to 7–7–1981.

93. Byron R. White, 1917–. Dem., Colo. 4–16–1962 to 6–28–1993.

94. Arthur Joseph Goldberg, 1908–1990. Dem., Ill. 10–1–1962 to 7–26–1965.

95. Abe Fortas, 1910–1982. Dem., Tenn. 10–4–1965 to 5–15–1969.

96. Thurgood Marshall, 1908–1993. Dem., N. Y. 10–2–1967 to 10–7–1991.

Nixon 1969–1974	Ford 1974–1977	Carter 1977–1981	Reagan 1981–1989
Warren −1969 / **Burger**[97] 1969–		−1986	**Rehnquist**[100] 1986–*
Black −1971 / **Powell**[99] 1971–		−1987	**Kennedy**[104] 1988–*
Fortas −1969 / **Blackmun**[98] 1970–			
Brennan			
Douglas −1975 / **Stevens**[101] 1975–*			
Marshall			
White			
Stewart −1981 / **O'Connor**[102] 1981–*			
Harlan −1971 / **Rehnquist**[100] 1971–		(To C. J.) −1986	**Scalia**[103] 1986–*

97. Warren Earl Burger, 1907–1995. Rep., Va. 6–23–1969 to 9–26–1986.

98. Harry Andrew Blackmun, 1908–1999. Rep., Minn. 5–14–1970 to 6–30–1994.

99. Lewis Franklin Powell, Jr., 1907–1998. Dem., Va. 12–19–1971 to 6–26–1987.

100. William Hubbs Rehnquist, 1924–. Rep., Ariz. Asso. Just. 12–15–1971 to 9–26–1986; C.J. 9–26–1986 to–.

101. John Paul Stevens, 1920–. Rep., Ill. 12–19–1975 to–.

102. Sandra Day O'Connor, 1930–. Rep., Ariz. 9–25–1981 to–.

103. Antonin Scalia, 1936–. Rep., Washington, D.C. 9–26–1986 to–.

104. Anthony M. Kennedy, 1936–. Rep., Cal. 2–18–1988 to–.

Bush 1989–1993	Clinton 1993–2001	G. W. Bush 2001–*

Rehnquist

Kennedy

Blackmun		Breyer[108]
	–1994	1994–*

Brennan	Souter[105]	
–1990	1990–*	

Stevens

Marshall	Thomas[106]	
	–1991	1991–*

White	Ginsburg[107]	
	–1993	1993–*

O'Connor

Scalia

---

105.   David H. Souter, 1939–. Rep., N.H. 10–19–1990 to–.

106.   Clarence Thomas, 1945–. Rep., Washington, D.C. 10–23–1991 to–.

107.   Ruth B. Ginsburg, 1933–. Dem., Washington, D.C. 8–10–1993 to–.

108.   Stephen G. Breyer, 1938–. Dem., Mass. 8–14–1994 to–.

* This table represents the composition of the Court to January 20, 2005.

INDEX

References are to pages

†